Kevin D. Ray

FAMILIAR QUOTATIONS

Familiar Quotations

by
JOHN BARTLETT

A COLLECTION OF PASSAGES,
PHRASES AND PROVERBS
TRACED TO THEIR SOURCES
IN ANCIENT AND MODERN
LITERATURE

Thirteenth and
CENTENNIAL EDITION
Completely Revised

Little, Brown and Company · Boston · Toronto

Thirteenth Edition Published November 1955

Fifteenth Printing

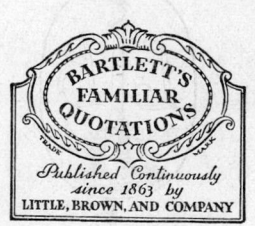

PREFACE TO THE THIRTEENTH AND CENTENNIAL EDITION

One hundred years ago there appeared the First Edition of FAMILIAR QUOTATIONS, a small, thin volume of 258 pages set in single column with an index which ran to a full 36 pages.

In his preface to the First Edition, John Bartlett wrote:

> The object of this work is to show, to some extent, the obligations our language owes to various authors for numerous phrases and familiar quotations which have become "household words."
>
> This Collection, originally made without any view of publication, has been considerably enlarged by additions from an English work on a similar plan, and is now sent forth with the hope that it may be found a convenient book of reference.
>
> Though perhaps imperfect in some respects, it is believed to possess the merit of accuracy, as the quotations have been taken from the original sources.
>
> Should this be favorably received, endeavors will be made to make it more worthy of the approbation of the public in a future edition.

Cambridge, May, 1855

The first nine editions of the book were under the editorship of John Bartlett, and the Ninth Edition, published in 1891, had grown to a volume of 1158 pages, 862 of text, 296 of index. In his preface to the Ninth Edition, Bartlett commented that it was the close of the volume's tentative life, a prophecy which was upset in 1914 with publication of the Tenth Edition under the editorship of Nathan Haskell Dole. Both the Eleventh Edition of 1937 and the Twelfth of 1948 continued to grow in size and stature under the joint editorship of Christopher Morley and Louella D. Everett.

The present Centennial Edition is, then, the thirteenth since the book first appeared. Our appreciation of the contributions of all those who have helped in the past is in no sense diminished by our belief that it is appropriate for this anniversary edition to be the responsibility of the firm's staff. We have borne in mind the original basis of selection which John Bartlett, a partner of Little, Brown, determined as "familiar or worthy of being familiar." We have learned to appreciate fully what John Bartlett said in his preface to the Fourth Edition: "It is not easy to determine in all cases the degree of familiarity that may belong to phrases and sentences which present themselves for admission; for what is familiar to one class of readers may be quite new to another."

In the laborious but stimulating task of revision the entire body of the text has been examined. Many quotations, because of the passage of time, seem to be no longer often repeated or likely to be remembered and have been dropped. Many well-known phrases which for one reason or another have never appeared in the book have been added.

The chronological sequence of authorship which has always made FAMILIAR QUOTATIONS of particular interest as a book to read as well as a book of reference has been preserved, and the debt of contemporary literature to that of other times and other tongues has been recognized by placing the ancient authors and those who wrote in foreign languages in chronological sequence. Only quotations from the Bible and those from unknown sources remain outside this pattern, which has been so useful in general reference and for showing the development of the language.

Because the body of our written and spoken expression has grown along so many avenues of knowledge, we have leaned heavily upon the advice and assistance of a large number of men and women of special scholarship and learning. Not only in this edition but through the years so many deep obligations to so many advisers have accrued that it is impossible here to make all the acknowledgments that should be made. It would be real negligence, however, not to mention the great contributions to the book made by Mr. Christopher Morley and Miss Louella D. Everett in preparation of the two preceding editions. In the Centennial Edition, which we hope will be as "favorably received" as was the First Edition, we must express our gratitude especially to Mrs. Emily Morison Beck, who has rendered highly competent and critical service in research and in processing the manuscript. Among other generous advisers, special thanks are due to Mr. Frank W. Cady, Professor Emeritus, of Middlebury College, Mr. Alston Hurd Chase of Phillips Academy at Andover, Mr. J. Frank

Dobie, Mr. Joseph Henry Jackson, Mr. W. Barton Leach of the Harvard Law School, Mr. David McCord and Mrs. Janet Payne Whitney. To the many unselfish individuals who write us almost daily with criticisms, suggestions and comments, we can only offer a blanket but appreciative word of thanks, for their interest does much toward perfecting BARTLETT.

Boston, Massachusetts
May 4, 1955

INDEX OF AUTHORS

Names preceded by the prepositional forms *d', de, de la, du, van,* and *von* which are not British or American names are listed in the order of the name, and not the order of the prepositional form. Where custom warrants both listings, the name is so given (as with Jean de la Fontaine, who is listed under both Fontaine and La Fontaine).

The asterisk (*) preceding a name indicates that quotations from that author included as Notes are so numerous that the editors consider it impracticable to give the numbers of all the pages where they occur.

ix

ANONYMOUS AND COLLECTIVE WORKS

FAMILIAR QUOTATIONS

ANCIENT EGYPT

To resist him that is set in authority is evil.

> The Instruction of Ptahhotep [1]
> [Circa 2675 B. C.]

There it o'ertook me that I fell down for thirst, I was parched, my throat burned, and I said: "This is the taste of death."

> The Story of Sinuke [1]
> [Circa 2000 B. C.]

There is none that hath turned his shaft, there is none that hath bent his bow.

> Ibid.

Then the ship perished, and of them that were in it not one survived. And I was cast on to an island by a wave of the sea.

> The Story of the Shipwrecked Sailor [1] [Circa 1700 B. C.?]

Everywhere he feels his Heart because its vessels run to all his limbs.

> The Beginning of the Secret Book of the Physician [2] [Circa 1550 B. C.]

Go not in and out in the court of justice, that thy name may not stink.

> The Wisdom of Anii [1]
> [Circa 900 B. C.]

HAMMURABI [3]
[Floruit 2100 B. C.]

I established law and justice in the land.

> Prologue

If a man owe a debt and Adad [4] inundate his field and carry away the

produce, or, through lack of water, grain have not grown in the field, in that year he shall not make any return of grain to the creditor, he shall alter his contract-tablet and he shall not pay the interest for that year.

> Sect. 48

If a man destroy the eye of another man, they shall destroy his eye.

> Sect. 196

HOMER [1]
[Circa 850 B. C.]

The wrath of Peleus' son, the direful spring
Of all the Grecian woes, O goddess, sing!

> Iliad.[1] Book I, Line 1

The distant Trojans never injur'd me.

> Ibid. Line 200

Words sweet as honey from his lips distill'd.

> Ibid. Line 332

Shakes his ambrosial curls, and gives the nod, —
The stamp of fate, and sanction of the god.

> Ibid. Line 684

And unextinguish'd laughter shakes the skies.[2]

> Ibid. Line 771

The man who acts the least, upbraids the most.

> Ibid. Book II, Line 311

Thick as autumnal leaves or driving sand.

> Ibid. Line 970

The glorious gifts of the gods may not be cast aside.

> Ibid.[3] Book III, Line 65

Chiefs, who no more in bloody fights engage,

---

[1] From ADOLF ERMAN [1854–1937]: The Literature of the Ancient Egyptians, translated [1927] by AYLWARD M. BLACKMAN.

[2] In The Papyrus Ebers, translated [1931] from the German version by CYRIL P. BRYAN.

[3] From ROBERT FRANCIS HARPER's The Code of Hammurabi King of Babylon, about 2100 B.C., second edition.

[4] The storm god.

---

[1] The translation is that of ALEXANDER POPE [1715] unless otherwise noted.

[2] The same line occurs in the translation of the Odyssey, Book VIII, L. 366.

[3] Translated [1950] by CHASE AND PERRY.

But, wise through time, and narrative
    with age,
In summer-days like grasshoppers re-
    joice,
A bloodless race, that send a feeble
    voice.
> *Iliad. Book III, Line 199*

She moves a goddess, and she looks a
    queen.
> *Ibid. Line 208*

But when he speaks, what elocution
    flows!
Soft as the fleeces of descending snows
The copious accents fall, with easy art;
Melting they fall, and sink into the
    heart.
> *Ibid. Line 283*

Ajax the great . . .
Himself a host.
> *Ibid. Line 293*

Wrapt in the cold embraces of the tomb.
> *Ibid. Line 312*

Plough the watery deep.
> *Ibid. Line 357*

And joyful nations join in leagues of
    peace.
> *Ibid. Line 401*

The day shall come, the great avenging
    day,
Which Troy's proud glories in the dust
    shall lay,
When Priam's powers and Priam's self
    shall fall,
And one prodigious ruin swallow all.
> *Ibid. Book IV, Line 196*

The first in banquets, but the last in
    fight.
> *Ibid. Line 401*

Gods! How the son degenerates from
    the sire!
> *Ibid. Line 451*

Not two strong men the enormous
    weight could raise, —
Such men as live in these degenerate
    days.[1]
> *Ibid. Book V, Line 371*

[1] A mass enormous! which in modern days
No two of earth's degenerate sons could
raise.
> *Book XX, L. 337*

Whose little body lodg'd a mighty
    mind.
> *Iliad. Book V, Line 999*

He held his seat; a friend to human
    race.
Fast by the road, his ever-open door
Obliged the wealthy, and reliev'd the
    poor.[1]
> *Ibid. Book VI, Line 18*

Like leaves on trees the race of man is
    found,
Now green in youth, now withering on
    the ground:
Another race the following spring sup-
    plies:
They fall successive, and successive
    rise.
> *Ibid. Line 181*

Inflaming wine, pernicious to man-
    kind.
> *Ibid. Line 330*

If yet, not lost to all the sense of shame.
> *Ibid. Line 350*

He, from whose lips divine persuasion
    flows.
> *Ibid. Book VII, Line 143*

Who dares think one thing, and another
    tell,
My heart detests him as the gates of
    Hell.[2]
> *Ibid. Book IX, Line 412*

Short is my date, but deathless my re-
    nown.
> *Ibid. Line 535*

Content to follow when we lead the
    way.
> *Ibid. Book X, Line 141*

He serves me most, who serves his
    country best.
> *Ibid. Line 201*

Praise from a friend, or censure from a
    foe,
Are lost on hearers that our merits
    know.
> *Ibid. Line 293*

The rest were vulgar deaths, unknown
    to fame.
> *Ibid. Book XI, Line 394*

Without a sign, his sword the brave
    man draws,

[1] See Sam Walter Foss, page 777b.
[2] See Pepys, page 284a.

And asks no omen but his country's cause.
>Iliad. Book XII, Line 283

A day to fire the brave, and warm the cold,
To gain new glories, or augment the old.
>Ibid. Line 321

And seem to walk on wings, and tread in air.
>Ibid. Book XIII, Line 106

Not vain the weakest, if their force unite.
>Ibid. Line 311

The best of things, beyond their measure, cloy.
>Ibid. Line 795

Heroes as great have died, and yet shall fall.
>Ibid. Book XV, Line 157

A noble mind disdains not to repent.
>Ibid. Line 227

And for our country 'tis a bliss to die.[1]
>Ibid. Line 583

Like strength is felt from hope, and from despair.
>Ibid. Line 852

Two friends, two bodies with one soul inspir'd.[2]
>Ibid. Book XVI, Line 267

Sleep and Death, two twins of winged race,
Of matchless swiftness, but of silent pace.
>Ibid. Line 831

How vain, without the merit, is the name!
>Ibid. Book XVII, Line 158

No season now for calm, familiar talk,
Like youths and maidens in an evening walk.
>Ibid. Book XXII, Line 169

Achilles absent was Achilles still.
>Ibid. Line 418

[1] See Horace, page 39a.
[2] A friend is one soul abiding in two bodies. — DIOGENES LAERTIUS [*circa* A.D. 200]: *On Aristotle*
>Two souls with but a single thought,
>Two hearts that beat as one.
>VON MÜNCH BELLINGHAUSEN [1806–1871]: *Ingomar the Barbarian, Act II*

Forever honour'd, and forever mourn'd.
>Iliad. Book XXII, Line 422

Unwept, unhonour'd, uninterr'd he lies! [1]
>Ibid. Line 484

It is not strength, but art, obtains the prize,
And to be swift is less than to be wise.
'Tis more by art, than force of num'rous strokes.
>Ibid. Book XXIII, Line 383

A green old age,[2] unconscious of decays.
>Ibid. Line 929

Two urns by Jove's high throne have ever stood,
The source of evil one, and one of good.
>Ibid. Book XXIV, Line 662

These things surely lie on the knees of the gods.
>Odyssey.[3] Book I, Line 267

Soon as the early, rosy-fingered dawn appeared.
>Ibid.[4] Book II, Line 1

Few sons are like their father, most are worse, few better than the father.
>Ibid.[4] Line 315

A favorable wind clear-eyed Athene sent, a brisk west wind that sang along the wine-dark sea.
>Ibid.[4] Line 420

An honest business never blush to tell.
>Ibid.[5] Book III, Line 20

Urge him with truth to frame his fair replies;
And sure he will: for Wisdom never lies.
>Ibid. Line 25

The lot of man; to suffer and to die.
>Ibid. Line 117

[1] See Scott, page 414a.
Unknelled, uncoffined, and unknown. — BYRON: *Childe Harold, Canto IV* [1818], *St. 179*
[2] See Dryden, page 276a.
[3] Translated [1879] by BUTCHER AND LANG.
[4] Translated [1884] by GEORGE H. PALMER.
[5] Translated [1725-1726] by ALEXANDER POPE. Pope engaged two friends, ELIJAH FENTON [1683–1730] and WILLIAM BROOME [1689–1745], to translate certain books of *The Odyssey* of Homer for him. The division of the work was: Pope — Books III, V, VII, IX, XIII, XIV, XVII, XXI, XXII, XXIV, and most of X and XV; Fenton — Books I, IV, XIX, and XX; Broome — Books II, VI, VIII, XI, XII, XVI, XVIII, XXIII.

A faultless body and a blameless mind.
Odyssey. Book III, Line 138

The long historian of my country's woes.
Ibid. Line 142

When now Aurora, daughter of the dawn,
With rosy lustre purpled o'er the lawn.
Ibid. Line 516

Wise to resolve, and patient to perform.
Ibid. Book IV (Fenton translation), Line 372

The leader, mingling with the vulgar host,
Is in the common mass of matter lost.
Ibid. Line 397

The people's parent, he protected all.
Ibid. Line 921

The big round tear stands trembling in her eye.
Ibid. Line 936

The windy satisfaction of the tongue.
Ibid. Line 1092

For a better and a higher gift than this there cannot be, when with accordant aims man and wife have a home. Great grief is it to foes and joy to friends; but they themselves best know its meaning.
Ibid.[1] Book VI, Line 182

No more was seen the human form divine.[2]
Ibid. Book X, Line 278

Ossa they strove to set upon Olympus, and upon Ossa leafy Pelion, that so the heavens might be scaled.
Ibid.[3] Book XI, Line 426

---

[1] Translated [1884] by GEORGE H. PALMER.
[2] See Milton, page 254b, and Blake, page 387b.
[3] Translated by GEORGE H. PALMER.
To pile Ossa on Pelion and roll leaf-crowned Olympus on Ossa. — VIRGIL [70-19 B. C.]: *Georgics, I, L. 28*
Then the omnipotent Father with his thunder made Olympus tremble, and from Ossa hurled Pelion. — OVID [43 B. C.-A. D. 17]: *Metamorphoses, I, L. 154*
Ossa they pressed down with Pelion's weight,
And on them both impos'd Olympus' hill.
FITZ-GEFFREY: *The Life and Death of Sir Francis Drake* [1596], *St. 99*
I would have you call to mind the strength

Oh woman, woman! when to ill thy mind
Is bent, all hell contains no fouler fiend.[1]
Odyssey. Book XI (Broome translation), Line 531

Rather I choose laboriously to bear
A weight of woes and breathe the vital air,
A slave to some poor hind that toils for bread,
Than reign the sceptred monarch of the dead.
Ibid. Line 597

And what so tedious as a twice-told tale.[2]
Ibid. Book XII (Broome translation), Line 538

He ceas'd; but left so pleasing on their ear
His voice, that list'ning still they seem'd to hear.
Ibid. Book XIII, Line 1

His native home deep imag'd in his soul.
Ibid. Line 38

The sex is ever to a soldier kind.
Ibid. Book XIV, Line 246

True friendship's laws are by this rule express'd,
Welcome the coming, speed the parting guest.[3]
Ibid. Book XV, Line 83

For too much rest itself becomes a pain.
Ibid. Line 429

Jove fix'd it certain that whatever day
Makes man a slave, takes half his worth away.
Ibid. Book XVII, Line 302

Unbless'd thy hand, if, in this low disguise,
Wander, perhaps, some inmate of the skies.[4]
Ibid. Line 576

---

of the ancient giants, that undertook to lay the high mountain Pelion on the top of Ossa, and set among those the shady Olympus. — RABELAIS: *Works, Book IV* [1548], *Chap. 38*
[1] See Otway, page 289b, and Congreve, page 298a.
[2] See Shakespeare, page 148a.
[3] See Pope, page 319b.
[4] See *Hebrews, XIII, 2*, on page 1063b.

Impatient straight to flesh his virgin
  sword.
> *Odyssey. Book XX (Fenton
>   translation), Line 461*

So ends the bloody business of the day.
> *Ibid. Book XXII, Line 516*

HESIOD [1]
[*Circa* 720 B. C. ?]

On the tongue of such an one they
shed a honeyed dew,[2] and from his lips
drop gentle words.
> *The Theogony. Line 82*

Night, having Sleep, the brother of
Death.[3]

From whose eyelids also as they
gazed dropped love.
> *Ibid. Line 910*

Both potter is jealous of potter and
craftsman of craftsman; and poor man
has a grudge against poor man, and
poet against poet.[4]
> *Works and Days. Line 25*

Fools! they know not how much half
exceeds the whole.[5]
> *Ibid. Line 40*

Oft hath even a whole city reaped
the evil fruit of a bad man.[6]
> *Ibid. Line 240*

For himself doth a man work evil in
working evils for another.
> *Ibid. Line 265*

Badness, look you, you may choose
easily in a heap: level is the path, and

[1] Translated by J. BANKS, with a few alterations.

[2] He on honey-dew hath fed. — COLERIDGE [1772–1834]: *Kubla Khan*

[3] See Daniel, page 122a.
Death and his brother Sleep. — SHELLEY: *Queen Mab* [1813], I
Sleep, Death's twin-brother. — TENNYSON: *In Memoriam* [1850], *Part LXVIII*

[4] In ev'ry age and clime we see
Two of a trade can never agree.
  GAY: *The Rat-catcher and Cats* [1727]
The potter envies the potter. — H. G. BOHN: *A Hand-Book of Proverbs* [1855]

[5] Pittacus said that half was more than the whole. — DIOGENES LAERTIUS [*circa* A. D. 200]: *Pittacus, II*

[6] One man's wickedness may easily become all men's curse. — PUBLILIUS SYRUS [*circa* 42 B. C.]: *Maxim 463*

right near it dwells. But before Virtue
the immortal gods have put the sweat
of man's brow; and long and steep is
the way to it, and rugged at the first.
> *Works and Days. Line 287*

Let it please thee to keep in order a
moderate-sized farm, that so thy gar-
ners may be full of fruits in their season.
> *Ibid. Line 304*

Invite the man that loves thee to a
feast, but let alone thine enemy.
> *Ibid. Line 342*

A bad neighbour is as great a misfortune as a good one is a great blessing.
> *Ibid. Line 346*

Gain not base gains; base gains are
the same as losses.
> *Ibid. Line 353*

If thou shouldst lay up even a little
upon a little, and shouldst do this often,
soon would even this become great.
> *Ibid. Line 360*

At the beginning of the cask and at
the end take thy fill, but be saving in
the middle; for at the bottom saving
comes too late. Let the price fixed with
a friend be sufficient, and even dealing
with a brother call in witnesses, but
laughingly.
> *Ibid. Line 366*

The morn, look you, furthers a man
on his road, and furthers him too in his
work.
> *Ibid. Line 579*

Observe moderation. In all, the fitting season is best.
> *Ibid. Line 694*

Neither make thy friend equal to a
brother; but if thou shalt have made
him so, be not the first to do him wrong.
> *Ibid. Line 707*

ARCHILOCHUS
[714?–676 B. C.]

The fox knows many things, but the
hedgehog knows one big thing.[1]
> *Fragment 103*

[1] The fox has many tricks, and the hedgehog only one, but that is the best of all. —
ERASMUS: *Adagia* [1500]

SOLON [1]
[638?–559 B. C.]

I grow old learning something new every day.

> VALERIUS MAXIMUS: *Book VIII, Chap. 7, Sect. 14*

MIMNERMUS
[*Floruit* 630–600 B. C.]

We are all clever enough at envying a famous man while he is yet alive, and at praising him when he is dead.

> *Fragment 1*

STESICHORUS [2]
[630–550 B. C.]

'Tis a vain and impotent thing to bewail the dead.

> STOBAEUS: *Anthology*

When a man dies, all his glory among men dies also.

> *Ibid.*

ALCAEUS [2]
[611–580 B. C.]

Not houses finely roofed or the stones of walls well-builded, nay nor canals and dockyards, make the city, but men able to use their opportunity.

> ARISTIDES: *Rhodian Oration*

Painting a lion from the claw.

> PLUTARCH: *On the Cessation of Oracles*

'Tis said that wrath is the last thing in a man to grow old.

> *Scholiast on Sophocles*

One that hath wine as a chain about his wits, such an one lives no life at all.

> DEMETRIUS: *On Poems* [3]

In fleeing the ashes he's fallen into the coals.

> APOSTOLIUS: *Proverbs*

[1] See also Diogenes Laertius' quotations from Solon, page 69b.
[2] Translated by J. M. EDMONDS.
[3] Papyrus of the first century B. C. found at Herculaneum.

SAPPHO OF LESBOS [1]
[*Circa* 610 B. C.]

Art thou the topmost apple
The gatherers could not reach,
Reddening on the bough?

> *To Atthis, paraphrase by*
> BLISS CARMAN

I loved thee, Atthis, once — long, long ago;
Long, long ago — the memory still is dear.
Stand face to face, friend, and unveil thine eyes,
Look deep in mine and keep the dead past clear
Of all regret.

> *To Atthis, paraphrase by*
> ANNE BUNNER

For to whomsoever I do good they harm me most.

> *Fragment 11* [2]

Evening, thou that bringest all, whatever the light-giving dawn scattered; thou bringest the sheep, thou bringest the goat, thou bringest the child to its mother.

> *Fragment 93* [2]

THEOGNIS
[570?–490? B. C.]

He who mistrusts most should be trusted least.

> *Sententiae. No. 223*

Be not too zealous; moderation is best in all things.

> *Ibid. No. 335*

Wine is wont to show the mind of man.[3]

> *Ibid. No. 500*

No one goes to Hades with all his immense wealth.[4]

> *Ibid. No. 725*

[1] Some say the Muses are nine but how carelessly! Look at the tenth, Sappho from Lesbos. — PLATO [427-347 B. C.] (Loeb Classical Library, *Greek Anthology, Vol. 3, P. 281*)
[2] Translated by MARY MILLS PATRICK.
[3] In wine there is truth. — PLINY [A. D. 23-79]: *Natural History, Book XIV, Sect. 141*
[4] For when he dieth he shall carry nothing away: his glory shall not descend after him. — *Psalm XLIX, 17*

ANACREON [1]
[563?–478 B. C.]

War spares not the brave but the cowardly.
> *The Greek Anthology. Book 7,*
> *Epigram 160*

Nor in those days did Persuasion shine all silver.
> *Scholiast on Pindar*

Doorkeepers that fight are a mischief.
> *Etymologicum Magnum*

Shining with desire and gleaming with unguents.
> PLUTARCH: *Amatorius*

SIMONIDES OF CEOS
[556–469 B. C.]

In silence also there's a worth that brings no risk.
> PLUTARCH: *Sayings of Emperors.*
> *Augustus Caesar*

There's no joy even in beautiful Wisdom, unless one have holy Health.
> SEXTUS EMPIRICUS: *Against the*
> *Mathematicians*

Whereas gold is the kindest of all hosts when it shines in the sky, it comes an evil guest unto those that receive it in their hand.
> PLUTARCH: *The Malignity of*
> *Herodotus*

He that would live completely happy must before all things belong to a country that is of fair report.
> AMMIANUS MARCELLINUS:
> *History*

The city is the teacher of the man.
> PLUTARCH: *Should Old Men*
> *Govern?*

Go tell the Spartans, thou that passeth by,
That here, obedient to their laws, we lie.
> *Thermopylae* [2]

---

[1] Translated by J. M. EDMONDS.
[2] Translated by WILLIAM LISLE BOWLES [1762–1850].
Ruskin said of this epitaph that it was the noblest group of words ever uttered by man. In Luderitzbucht Cemetery, South-West Africa, the lines, adapted to read:

AESOP
[*Floruit* 550 B. C.]

Any excuse will serve a tyrant.
> *The Wolf and the Lamb*

Beware lest you lose the substance by grasping at the shadow.
> *The Dog and the Shadow*

You may share the labours of the great, but you will not share the spoil.
> *The Lion's Share*

You have put your head inside a wolf's mouth and taken it out again in safety. That ought to be reward enough for you.
> *The Wolf and the Crane*

Better beans and bacon in peace than cakes and ale in fear.
> *The Town Mouse and the Country*
> *Mouse*

Only cowards insult dying majesty.
> *The Sick Lion*

Little friends may prove great friends.
> *The Lion and the Mouse*

Better no rule than cruel rule.
> *The Frogs Desiring a King*

A huge gap appeared in the side of the mountains. At last a tiny mouse poked its little head out of the gap.[1]
> *The Mountains in Labour*

Much outcry, little outcome.
> *Ibid.*

There is always someone worse off than yourself.
> *The Hares and the Frogs*

It is easy to be brave from a safe distance.
> *The Wolf and the Kid*

Tell England, ye who pass this monument,
That we who rest here, die content,
mark the grave of Rex and Wilfred Wilmslow, who fell in the battle of Stetting [November, 1914]. In Southport, England, the War Memorial bears another adaptation of the epitaph:
Tell Britain, ye who mark this monument,
Faithful to her we fell, and rest content.

[1] See Horace, page 41b.
A mountain was in labour, sending forth dreadful groans, and there was in the region the highest expectation. After all, it brought forth a mouse. — PHAEDRUS [*circa* A. D. 8]: *Book IV, Fable 22, 1*

You will only injure yourself if you take notice of despicable enemies.[1]

The Bald Man and the Fly

Outside show is a poor substitute for inner worth.

The Fox and the Mask

Borrowed plumes.

The Jay and the Peacock

It is not only fine feathers that make fine birds.

Ibid.

Self-conceit may lead to self-destruc-
tion.

The Frog and the Ox

Gratitude is the sign of noble souls.

Androcles

We often despise what is most useful to us.

The Hart and the Hunter

They found that even the Belly, in its dull quiet way, was doing necessary work for the Body, and that all must work together or the Body will go to pieces.

The Belly and the Members

I am sure the grapes are sour.[2]

The Fox and the Grapes

It is easy to despise what you cannot get.

Ibid.

Be content with your lot; one cannot be first in everything.

The Peacock and Juno

Familiarity breeds contempt.[3]

The Fox and the Lion

We can easily represent things as we wish them to be.

The Lion and the Statue

Then the Grasshopper knew it is best to prepare for the days of necessity.

The Ant and the Grasshopper

The little Reed, bending to the force of the wind, soon stood upright again when the storm had passed over.

The Tree and the Reed

Obscurity often brings safety.

Ibid.

The Lamb that belonged to the Sheep, whose skin the Wolf was wearing, began to follow the Wolf in the Sheep's clothing.

The Wolf in Sheep's Clothing

Appearances are deceptive.

Ibid.

The Dog barked at the Ox and attempted to bite it when it approached the manger in the hope of getting at the straw.

The Dog in the Manger [1]

People often grudge others what they cannot enjoy themselves.

Ibid

The boy called out "Wolf, Wolf!" and the villagers came out to help him. A few days afterward he tried the same trick, and again they came to his help. Shortly after this a Wolf actually came, but this time the villagers thought the boy was deceiving them again and nobody came to his help.

The Shepherd's Boy

A liar will not be believed, even when he speaks the truth.

Ibid.

Never soar aloft on an enemy's pinions.

The Tortoise and the Birds

Do but set the example yourself, and I will follow you. Example is the best precept.[2]

The Two Crabs

Never trust a friend who deserts you at a pinch.

The Two Fellows and the Bear

---

[1] A fly bit the bare pate of a bald man, who in endeavouring to crush it gave himself a hard slap. Then said the fly jeeringly, "You wanted to revenge the sting of a tiny insect with death; what will you do to yourself, who have added insult to injury?" — PHAE-DRUS [*circa* A.D. 8]: *Book V, Fable 3, 1*

[2] The fox, when he cannot reach the grapes, says they are not ripe. — GEORGE HERBERT: *Jacula Prudentum* [1640]

"They are too green," he said, "and only good for fools." — LA FONTAINE: *Book III* [1668], *Fable 11, The Fox and the Grapes*

[3] This is *Maxim 640* of Publilius Syrus. See Shakespeare, page 180a.

I find my familiarity with thee has bred

contempt.—CERVANTES: *Don Quixote, Part I* [1605], *Book III, Chap. 6*

[1] See Robert Burton, page 222a.

[2] Example is always more efficacious than precept. — SAMUEL JOHNSON: *Rasselas* [1759], *Chap. XXX*

United we stand, divided we fall.[1]
> *The Four Oxen and the Lion*

A little thing in hand is worth more than a great thing in prospect.[2]
> *The Fisher and the Little Fish*

Little by little does the trick.
> *The Crow and the Pitcher*

I will have nought to do with a man who can blow hot and cold with the same breath.
> *The Man and the Satyr*

Thinking to get at once all the gold the Goose could give, he killed it and opened it only to find, — nothing.
> *The Goose with the Golden Eggs*

Put your shoulder to the wheel.
> *Hercules and the Waggoner*

The gods help them that help themselves.
> *Ibid.*

Please all, and you will please none.
> *The Man, the Boy, and the Donkey*

Who is to bell the Cat? It is easy to propose impossible remedies.
> *Belling the Cat*

When the Hare awoke from his nap, he saw the Tortoise just near the winning post. Plodding wins the race.
> *The Hare and the Tortoise*

We would often be sorry if our wishes were gratified.[3]
> *The Old Man and Death*

[1] See George Pope Morris, page 499a.

[2] He is a fool who lets slip a bird in the hand for a bird in the bush. — PLUTARCH [A. D. 46–120]: *Of Garrulity*

A bird in hand is worth two in the bush. — CERVANTES: *Don Quixote, Part I* [1605], *Book IV, Chap. 4*

Better one byrde in hande than ten in the wood. — JOHN HEYWOOD: *Proverbes* [1546], *Part I, Chap. XI*

A feather in hand is better than a bird in the air. — GEORGE HERBERT: *Jacula Prudentum* [1640]

[3] Granting our wish one of Fate's saddest jokes is! — J. R. LOWELL [1819–1891]: *Two Scenes from the Life of Blondel, Sc. II, St. 2*

Beware, my lord! Beware lest stern Heaven hate you enough to hear your prayers! — ANATOLE FRANCE: *The Crime of Sylvestre Bonnard* [1881], *Part II, Chap. 4*

When the gods wish to punish us they answer our prayers. — WILDE: *An Ideal Husband* [1895], *Act II*

Union gives strength.
> *The Bundle of Sticks*

While I see many hoof-marks going in, I see none coming out. It is easier to get into the enemy's toils than out again.
> *The Lion, the Fox, and the Beasts*

The haft of the arrow had been feathered with one of the eagle's own plumes. We often give our enemies the means of our own destruction.[1]
> *The Eagle and the Arrow*

Nature will out.
> *The Cat-Maiden*

Do not count your chickens before they are hatched.[2]
> *The Milkmaid and Her Pail*

Men often applaud an imitation, and hiss the real thing.
> *The Buffoon and the Countryman*

Never trust the advice of a man in difficulties.
> *The Fox and the Goat*

[1] So in the Libyan fable it is told
That once an eagle, stricken with a dart,
Said, when he saw the fashion of the shaft,
"With our own feathers, not by others' hands,
Are we now smitten."
> AESCHYLUS [525–456 B. C.]. *Fragment 135* (Plumptre's translation)

That eagle's fate and mine are one,
 Which on the shaft that made him die
Espied a feather of his own,
 Wherewith he wont to soar so high.
> EDMUND WALLER [1605–1687]: *To a Lady Singing a Song of his Composing*

Like a young eagle, who has lent his plume
To fledge the shaft by which he meets his doom,
See their own feathers pluck'd to wing the dart
Which rank corruption destines for their heart.
> THOMAS MOORE [1780–1852]: *Corruption*

See Byron, page 452a.

[2] Many count their chickens before they are hatched. — CERVANTES: *Don Quixote, Part II* [1615], *Chap. 55*

To swallow gudgeons ere they're catch'd,
And count their chickens ere they're hatch'd.
> SAMUEL BUTLER: *Hudibras, Part II* [1664], *Canto III, L. 923*

Reckon not on your chickens before they are hatched. — JEFFERYS TAYLOR [1792–1853]: *The Milkmaid*

IBYCUS [1]
[*Floruit circa* 550 B.C.]

You cannot find a medicine for life when once a man is dead.

CHRYSIPPUS: *Negatives*

Every reef may be safely let out so long as the sail clears the top of the wave.

Scholiast on the Iliad

Contests allow no excuses, no more do friendships.

ZENOBIUS: *Proverbs*

The cranes of Ibycus.[2]

SIMPLICIUS
[*Floruit* 530 B.C.]

They [atoms] move in the void and catching each other up jostle together, and some recoil in any direction that may chance, and others become entangled with one another in various degrees according to the symmetry of their shapes and sizes and positions and order, and they remain together and thus the coming into being of composite things is effected.

De Caelo. 242, 15 [3]

HERACLITUS
[*Floruit* 513 B.C.]

Man's genius is a deity.

PLUTARCH: *Platonic Questions*

Character is Destiny.

MULLACH: *Fragments of Greek Philosophy*

There is nothing permanent except change.

ROGERS: *Student's History of Philosophy*

[1] Translated by J. M. EDMONDS.
[2] According to legend, Ibycus was murdered at sea, and his murderers were discovered through cranes that followed the ship. Hence, the "cranes of Ibycus" became a proverb for the agency of the gods in revealing crime.
[3] Quoted by CYRIL BAILEY: *The Greek Atomists and Epicurus.*

AESCHYLUS
[525–456 B.C.]

I would far rather be ignorant than wise in the foreboding of evil.[1]

Suppliants. Line 453

"Honour thy father and thy mother" stands written among the three laws of most revered righteousness.[2]

Ibid. Line 707

Myriad laughter of the ocean waves.

Prometheus Bound. Line 89

For somehow this is tyranny's disease, to trust no friends.

Ibid. Line 226

Words are the physicians of a mind diseased.[3]

Ibid. Line 378

Time as he grows old teaches many lessons.

Ibid. Line 981

God's mouth knows not to utter falsehood, but he will perform each word.[4]

Ibid. Line 1032

By suffering comes wisdom.

Agamemnon. Line 177

Too lightly opened are a woman's ears;
Her fence downtrod by many trespassers.

Ibid. Line 486

I think the slain
Care little if they sleep or rise again;
And we, the living, wherefore should we ache
With counting all our lost ones?

Ibid. Line 595

Sweet is a grief well ended.

Ibid. Line 805

[1] See Thomas Gray, page 347b.
[2] The reference is to three great laws ascribed to Triptolemus: namely, to honor parents; to worship the gods with the fruits of the earth; to hurt no living creature. The first two laws are also ascribed to the centaur Cheiron.
Honour thy father and thy mother. — *Exodus, XX, 12*
[3] Apt words have power to suage
The tumours of a troubl'd mind.
MILTON: *Samson Agonistes* [1671], *L. 184*
[4] God is not a man that he should lie; . . . hath he said, and shall he not do it? — *Numbers, XXIII, 19*

For not many men, the proverb saith,
Can love a friend whom fortune pros-
　　pereth
Unenvying.
Agamemnon. Line 832

I know how men in exile feed on
　dreams.
Ibid. Line 1668

Him who pitieth suffering men
Zeus pitieth, and his ways are sweet on
earth.
The Eumenides. Line 91

Fortune is a god and rules men's life.[1]
The Choëphoroe. Line 59

Destiny
Waiteth alike for them that men call
　free,
And them by others mastered.
Ibid. Line 101

It is for the doer to suffer.
Ibid. Line 313

Pleasantest
Of all ties is the tie of host and guest.
Ibid. Line 699

For he wishes not to seem, but to be,
the best.[2]
Seven Against Thebes. Line 592

God loves to help him who strives to
help himself.[3]
Fragment 223

O Death the Healer, scorn thou not, I
　pray,
To come to me: of cureless ills thou art

[1] Fortune commands men, and not men
fortune. — HERODOTUS [484–424 B. C.]: *Book
VII, Polymnia, Chap. 49*

[2] Meant, and taken by the audience, as a
reference to Aristides the Just.

[3] Heaven ne'er helps the men who will not
act. — SOPHOCLES [496–406 B. C.]: *Fragment
288* (Plumptre's translation)
Try first thyself, and after call in God;
For to the worker God himself lends aid.
EURIPIDES [484–406 B. C.]: *Hippoly-
tus, Fragment 435*
Help thyself, and God will help thee. —
GEORGE HERBERT: *Jacula Prudentum* [1640]
Help thyself, Heaven will help thee. — LA
FONTAINE: *Book VI* [1678–1679], *Fable 18*
God helps those who help themselves. —
ALGERNON SIDNEY: *Discourses on Govern-
ment* [1698], *Sect. XXIII.* FRANKLIN [1706–
1790]: *Poor Richard's Almanac*

The one physician. Pain lays not its
　touch
Upon a corpse.
Fragment 250 [1]

A prosperous fool is a grievous burden.
Fragment 383

Bronze is the mirror of the form;
wine, of the heart.
Fragment 384

It is not the oath that makes us believe the man, but the man the oath.
Fragment 385

PINDAR [2]
[522–442 B. C.]

The best of healers is good cheer.
Nemean Ode 4

Longer than deeds liveth the word.
Ibid.

It is the natal star that ruleth over
every deed.
Nemean Ode 5

For whatsoever one hath well said
goeth forth with a voice that never
dieth.
Isthmian Ode 4

Refrain from peering too far.
Olympian Ode 1

We are creatures of a day. What is
one, what is one not? Man is the dream
of a shadow.
Pythian Ode 8

The word that is overbearing is a
spur unto strife.
Fragment from Hymns

To foolish men belongeth a love for
things afar.
Paean 4

Every noble deed dieth, if sup-
pressed in silence.
*Eulogy on Alexander, Son of
Amyntas*

Whether the race of men on earth
mounteth a loftier tower by justice, or
by crooked wiles, my mind is divided
in telling clearly.
Fragment

[1] Translated by PLUMPTRE.
[2] Translated by SIR J. E. SANDYS.

SOPHOCLES
[496?–406 B. C.]

The ship of state — the gods once more,
After much rocking on a stormy surge,
Set her on even keel.

Antigone [1]

That pilot of the state
Who sets no hand to the best policy,
But remains tongue-tied through some
terror, seems
Vilest of men.

Ibid.

None love the messenger who brings
bad news.[2]

Ibid.

For money you would sell your soul.

Ibid.

A man of worth
In his own household will appear up-
right
In the state also.

Ibid.

There lives no greater fiend than Anarchy;
She ruins states, turns houses out of
doors,
Breaks up in rout the embattled sol-
diery.

Ibid.

Do not persist, then, to retain at heart
One sole idea, that the thing is right
Which your mouth utters, and nought
else beside.

Ibid.

Wonders are many, and none is more
wonderful than man.[3]

Ibid.

Though a man be wise
It is no shame for him to live and
learn.[4]

Ibid.

To err
From the right path is common to
mankind.[1]

Antigone

A day can prostrate and upraise again
All that is human.

Ajax [2]

To behold harms of our own hands'
doing,
Where none beside us wrought, causes
sharp ruing.

Ibid.

A woman should be seen, not heard.

Ibid.

I would not take the fellow at a gift
Who warms himself with unsubstantial
hopes;
But bravely to live on, or bravely end,[3]
Is due to gentle breeding.

Ibid.

In the ills of men
There is none sorer than Necessity.

Ibid.

Some mindfulness
A man should surely keep, of any thing
That pleased him once.

Ibid.

The happiest life consists in ignorance,
Before you learn to grieve and to rejoice.

Ibid.

Sleep, the universal vanquisher.

Ibid.

I for my own part, having learnt of
late
Those hateful to us we are not to hate
As though they might not soon be
friends again,
Intend to measure, now, the services
I render to my friend, as if not so
To abide for ever; for of mortals most
Find friendship an unstable anchorage.[4]

Ibid

---

[1] Translated by Sir George Young [1837–1930].

[2] See Shakespeare, page 152a.

[3] Translated by Jebb.

[4] It is good to live and learn. — Cervantes: *Don Quixote, Part II* [1615], *Chap. 32*
Live and learn,
Not first learn and then live.
Browning: *Parleyings with Certain People, With Christopher Smart* [1887], *IX*

[1] That men may err was never yet denied.
— Dryden: *The Hind and the Panther* [1687], *L. 61*
See Pope, page 311b.

[2] Translated by Sir George Young.

[3] Where life is more terrible than death, it is then the truest valour to dare to live. — Sir Thomas Browne: *Religio Medici* [1642] (Everyman ed.), *P. 49*

[4] Love him so, as if you were one day to hate

'Tis a long road knows no turning.
Ajax

Men of perverse opinion do not know
The excellence of what is in their hands,
Till some one dash it from them.
Ibid.

Death is not the worst; rather, in vain
To wish for death, and not to compass
it.
Electra [1]

The flower
Of our young manhood.[2]
Oedipus Tyrannus [1]

Towers and ships are nothingness,
Void of our fellow men to inhabit them.
Ibid.

This dim-seen track-mark of an ancient
crime.
Ibid.

The Sphinx
With her enigma.
Ibid.

I benefit myself in aiding him.
Ibid.

Now am I hail-fellow-well-met with
all.
Ibid.

Pride, when puffed up, vainly, with
many things
Unseasonable, unfitting, mounts the
wall,
Only to hurry to that fatal fall.[3]
Ibid.

That kindred only should behold and
hear
The griefs of kin, fits best with decency.
Ibid.

---

him and hate him so, as you were one day to
love him. — Attributed to CHILO [*fl.* 556 B. C.]
in MONTAIGNE's essay, *Of Friendship*

[1] Translated by SIR GEORGE YOUNG.
[2] The very flower of youth. — TERENCE
[185–159 B. C.]: *Eunuchus, Act II, Sc. 3, L. 27*
[3] See *Proverbs, XVI, 18,* on page 1039b.

Pryde goeth before, and shame cometh behynde. — *Treatise of a Gallant* [*circa* 1510]
    Pryde will have a fall;
For pryde goeth before and shame cometh
after.
    JOHN HEYWOOD: *Proverbes* [1546],
                Part I, Chap. X
Let pride go afore, shame will follow after.
—CHAPMAN, JONSON, AND MARSTON: *Eastward Ho* [1605], *Act IV, Sc. 1*

Of no mortal say
"That man is happy," till
Vexed by no grievous ill
He pass Life's goal.[1]
Oedipus Tyrannus. Closing lines

To know that all is well, even if late
We come to know it, is at least some
gain.
Trachiniae [2]

There is occasion for the vigilant
To fear for one who prospers, lest he
fall.
Ibid.

One must learn
By doing the thing; for though you
think you know it
You have no certainty, until you try.
Ibid.

If any
Count on two days, or any more, to
come,
He is a fool; for a man has no morrow,
Till with good luck he has got through
to-day.
Ibid.

War never slays a bad man in its course,
But the good always!
Philoctetes [2]

Winds are fair always, when you fly
from harm.
Ibid.

Who does not befriend himself
By doing good?
Oedipus Coloneus [2]

To the gods alone
Belongs it never to be old or die,
But all things else melt with all-power-
ful Time.
Ibid.

If a man to you
Refused a favour, when you begged
for it,

---

[1] See Herodotus, page 18b.
'Tis an old well-known proverb of mankind,
"You cannot tell men's fortunes till they die,
In any case, if they be good or bad."
                                Trachiniae
'Tis never seemly to felicitate
The fortunes of a man, as prosperous,
Before his life shall have been lived by him
Completely through.
            Tyndareus, Fragment 572
[2] Translated by SIR GEORGE YOUNG.

And would give nothing, and then
    afterwards,
When you were satisfied of your desire,
And all the grace was graceless, prof-
    fered it,
Would not the pleasure so received be
    vain? [1]

           Oedipus Coloneus

Never to have been born is much the
    best;
  And the next best, by far,
To return thence, by the way speediest,
  Where our beginnings are.

                Ibid.

This is our portion at the close of life,
Strengthless — companionless.

                Ibid.

It is the merit of a general
To impart good news, and to conceal
  the bad.

                Ibid.

The very hair on my head
Stands up for dread.[2]

                Ibid.

A remedy too strong for the disease.

       Tereus. Fragment 514 [3]

Truly, to tell lies is not honourable;
But when the truth entails tremendous
  ruin,
To speak dishonourably is pardonable.

       Creusa. Fragment 323

Sons are the anchors of a mother's life.

       Phaedra. Fragment 612

To him who is in fear everything
  rustles.

       Acrisius. Fragment 58

No falsehood lingers on into old age.

        Ibid. Fragment 59

Lady, cheer up; most of our ills, blowing loudly
In dreams by night, grow milder when
  'tis day.

        Ibid. Fragment 63

No man loves life like him that's growing old.

        Ibid. Fragment 64

War loves to prey upon the young.[1]

     Scyrian Women. Fragment 498

Heaven ne'er helps the men who will
  not act.[2]

    Unknown Dramas. Fragment 288

A wise gamester ought to take the dice
Even as they fall, and pay down quietly,
Rather than grumble at his luck.

        Ibid. Fragment 686

Truth ever has most strength of what
  men say.

        Ibid. Fragment 691

A woman's vows I write upon the wave.

        Ibid. Fragment 694

The friends of the unlucky are far
  away.

        Ibid. Fragment 773

If I am Sophocles, I am not mad;
and if I am mad, I am not Sophocles.

        Vita Anonyma [3]

EURIPIDES
[484–406 B. C.]

Old men's prayers for death are lying prayers, in which they abuse old
age and long extent of life. But when
death draws near, not one is willing to
die, and age no longer is a burden to
them.

        Alcestis.[4] *Line 669*

  I care for riches, to make gifts
To friends, or lead a sick man back to
  health
With ease and plenty. Else small aid
  is wealth
For daily gladness; once a man be done
With hunger, rich and poor are all as
  one.

        Electra.[5] *Line 539*

A hundred little things make likenesses
In brethren born, and show the father's
  blood.

        Ibid. Line 642

  [1] In peace, children inter their parents; war
violates the order of nature, and causes parents to inter their children. — HERODOTUS
[484–424 B. C.]: *Book I, Clio, Chap. 87*
  [2] See Euripides, page 17a.
  Help thyself, and God will help thee. —
GEORGE HERBERT: *Jacula Prudentum* [1640]
  See Franklin, page 330b.
  [3] Translated by PLUMPTRE.
  [4] Translated by MORRIS HICKEY MORGAN
  [5] Translated by SIR GILBERT MURRAY.

  [1] See Samuel Johnson, page 339a.
  [2] The hair of all stood up for fear. — Later
in same drama
  [3] The fragments are from the Everyman
Edition of *The Dramas of Sophocles.*

Danger gleams
Like sunshine to a brave man's eyes.
Iphigenia in Tauris.[1] *Line 115*
How oft the darkest hour of ill
Breaks brightest into dawn.[2]
Ibid. Line 723
I think that Fortune watcheth o'er our
lives,
Surer than we. But well said: he who
strives
Will find his gods strive for him
equally.[3]
Ibid. Line 910
The night
Is the safe time for robbers, as the light
For just men.
Ibid. Line 1024
Put not thy faith in any Greek.[4]
Ibid. Line 1205
The gifts of a bad man bring no good
with them.
Medea.[5] *Line 618*
Moderation, the noblest gift of
Heaven.
Ibid. Line 636
I know, indeed, the evil of that I pur-
pose; but my inclination gets the better
of my judgment.[6]
Ibid. Line 1078
To the fool, he who speaks wisdom
will sound foolish.
Bacchae. Line 480
Slowly but surely withal moveth the
might of the gods.[7]
Ibid. Line 882
Slight not what's near through aim-
ing at what's far.
Rhesus.[5] *Line 482*

[1] Translated by SIR GILBERT MURRAY.
[2] The darkest hour is that before the dawn.
— HAZLITT: *English Proverbs*
[3] See Sophocles, page 16b.
[4] See Virgil, page 37a.
[5] Translated by MORRIS HICKEY MORGAN.
[6] See Ovid, page 42b, and *Romans, VII, 19,*
on page 1060a.
I find my growing judgment daily instruct
me how to be better, but my untamed affections and confirmed vitiosity makes me daily
do worse. — SIR THOMAS BROWNE: *Religio
Medici* [1642] (Everyman ed.), *P. 47*
We naturally know what is good, but naturally pursue what is evil. — *Ibid., P. 61*
[7] See George Herbert, page 234b.

Thou didst bring me forth for all
the Greeks in common, not for thyself
alone.
Iphigenia in Aulis.[1] *Line 1386*
The company of just and righteous
men is better than wealth and a rich
estate.
Aegeus.[1] *Fragment 7*
A bad beginning makes a bad ending.
Aeolus.[1] *Fragment 32*
Time will explain it all. He is a talker,
and needs no questioning before he
speaks.
Ibid. Fragment 38
Waste not fresh tears over old griefs.
Alexander.[1] *Fragment 44*
The nobly born must nobly meet his
fate.[2]
Alcymene.[1] *Fragment 100*
Woman is woman's natural ally.
Alope.[1] *Fragment 109*
Man's best possession is a sympa-
thetic wife.
Antigone.[1] *Fragment 164*
Second thoughts are ever wiser.[3]
Hippolytus. Line 436
The tongue hath sworn, but the mind
is unsworn.[4]
Ibid. Line 612
Toil, says the proverb, is the sire of
fame.
Licymnius.[1] *Fragment 477*
Cowards do not count in battle; they
are there, but not in it.
Meleager.[1] *Fragment 523*
A woman should be good for every-

[1] Translated by MORRIS HICKEY MORGAN.
[2] If there be any good in nobility, I trow it
to be only this, that it imposeth a necessity
upon those which are noble, that they should
not suffer their nobility to degenerate from
the virtues of their ancestors. — BOETHIUS
[A. D. 470–525]: *De Consolatione Philosophiae, III, 6, 25*
Noblesse oblige (Nobility has its obligation). — BOHN: *Foreign Proverbs*
[3] Second thoughts, they say, are best. —
DRYDEN: *The Spanish Friar* [1681], *Act II,
Sc. 2*
Is it so true that second thoughts are best?
— TENNYSON: *Sea Dreams* [1864]
[4] This line was always quoted as an example of Sophist casuistry.

thing at home, but abroad good for nothing.

Meleager.[1] *Fragment 525*

Silver and gold are not the only coin; virtue too passes current all over the world.

Oedipus.[1] *Fragment 546*

Where two discourse, if the one's anger rise,
The man who lets the contest fall is wise.

Protesilaus.[1] *Fragment 656*

When good men die their goodness does not perish,
But lives though they are gone. As for the bad,
All that was theirs dies and is buried with them.[2]

Temenidae.[1] *Fragment 734*

Every man is like the company he is wont to keep.

Phoenix.[1] *Fragment 809*

Who knows but life be that which men call death,
And death what men call life?[3]

Phrixus.[1] *Fragment 830*

Whoso neglects learning in his youth, loses the past and is dead for the future.

Ibid. Fragment 927

The gods visit the sins of the fathers upon the children.[4]

Ibid. Fragment 970

In a case of dissension, never dare to judge till you've heard the other side.

Heracleidae.[1] (*Quoted by* ARISTOPHANES *in The Wasps*)

Leave no stone unturned.[5]

Ibid. 1002

---

[1] Translated by MORRIS HICKEY MORGAN.
[2] See Shakespeare, page 168a.
[3] See Aristophanes, page 23a.
[4] See *Exodus, XX, 5,* on page 1024b.
The sins of the father are to be laid upon the children. — SHAKESPEARE: *Merchant of Venice* [1596–1597], *Act III, Sc. 5, L. 1*
[5] This may be traced to a response of the Delphic oracle given to Polycrates, as the best means of finding a treasure buried by Xerxes' general, Mardonius, on the field of Plataea. The oracle replied, "Turn every stone." — LEUTSCH AND SCHNEIDEWIN: *Corpus Paraemiographorum Graecorum, Vol. I, P. 146*
I commend the old proverb, "For we must look about under every stone, lest an orator

Those whom God wishes to destroy, he first deprives of their senses.[1]

Fragment, Greek Iambic

These men won eight victories over the Syracusans when the favor of the gods was equal for both sides.

*Epitaph for the Athenians Slain
in Sicily*

HERODOTUS [2]
[484–424 B. C.]

A man trusts his ears less than his eyes.

Book I, Clio. Chap. 8

Call no man happy till you know the nature of his death; he is at best but fortunate.

Ibid. Chap. 32

They [the Persians] are accustomed to deliberate on matters of the highest moment when warm with wine; but whatever they in this situation may determine is again proposed to them on the morrow, in their cooler moments, by the person in whose house they had before assembled. If at this time also it meet their approbation, it is executed; otherwise it is rejected. Whatever also they discuss when sober, is always a second time examined after they have been drinking.[3]

Ibid. Chap. 133

---

bite us." — ARISTOPHANES [446–380 B.C.]: *The Trial of Euripides*
[1] Quos deus vult perdere, prius dementat.
In Boswell's *Life of Dr. Johnson* [1791] (Everyman ed.), *Vol. 2, Pp. 442–443,* this is quoted as a saying which everybody repeats, but nobody knows where to find.
Whom Fortune wishes to destroy she first makes mad. — PUBLILIUS SYRUS [*circa* 42 B.C.]: *Maxim 911*
When falls on man the anger of the gods,
First from his mind they banish understanding.
LYCURGUS [*fl.* 820 B.C.]
For those whom God to ruin has design'd,
He fits for fate, and first destroys their mind.
DRYDEN: *The Hind and the Panther* [1687], *Part III, L. 1093*
Whom the Gods would destroy they first make mad. — LONGFELLOW: *The Masque of Pandora* [1875], *VI*
[2] Translated by WILLIAM BELOE [1756–1817].
[3] The ancient Goths of Germany . . . had

They joined battle, and the Phocaeans won, yet it was but a Cadmean victory.[1]

Book I, Clio. Chap. 166

The art of medicine in Egypt is thus exercised: one physician is confined to the study and management of one disease; there are of course a great number who practice this art; some attend to the disorders of the eyes, others to those of the head, some take care of the teeth, others are conversant with all diseases of the bowels; whilst many attend to the cure of maladies which are less conspicuous.

Book II, Euterpe. Chap. 84

How much better it is to be envied than pitied.[2]

Book III, Thalia. Chap. 52

Envy is natural to man from the beginning.

Ibid. Chap. 80

They who mutually injure the state, mutually support each other.

Ibid. Chap. 82

You may have observed how the thunderbolt of Heaven chastises the insolence of the more enormous animals, whilst it passes over without injury the weak and insignificant: before these weapons of the gods you must have seen how the proudest palaces and the loftiest trees fall and perish.[3]

Book VII, Polymnia. Chap. 10

Every measure undertaken with temerity is liable to be perplexed with error, and punished by misfortune.

Book VII, Polymnia. Chap. 10

The Persian messengers travel with a velocity which nothing human can equal. . . . Neither snow, nor rain, nor heat, nor darkness, are permitted to obstruct their speed.[1]

Book VIII, Urania. Chap. 98

The king's arm is very long.

Ibid. Chap. 140

Nothing in human life is more to be lamented, than that a wise man should have so little influence.

Book IX, Calliope. Chap. 16

THUCYDIDES [2]
[471–401 B.C.]

Of the events of war, I have not ventured to speak from any chance information, nor according to any notion of my own; I have described nothing but what I saw myself, or learned from others of whom I made the most careful and particular inquiry. The task was a laborious one because eyewitnesses of the same occurrence gave different accounts of them as they remembered, or were interested in the actions of one side or the other. And very likely the strictly historical character of my narrative may be disappointing to the ear. But if he who desires to have before his eyes a true picture of the events which have happened, and of the like events which may be expected to happen hereafter in the order of human things, shall pronounce what I have written to be useful, then I shall be satisfied. My history is an everlasting possession, not

---

all of them a wise custom of debating every thing of importance to their state, twice; that is, — once drunk, and once sober: — Drunk — that their councils might not want vigour; and sober — that they might not want discretion. —STERNE: *Tristram Shandy* [1760–1767], *Book V, Chap. 17*
Appeal from Philip drunk to Philip sober. — VALERIUS MAXIMUS [1st century A.D.]: *Book VI, Chap. 2*
[1] A Cadmean (or a Pyrrhic) victory was one in which the victors suffered as much as their enemies. "One more such victory," said Pyrrhus, "and I am lost."
See Plutarch, page 59a.
[2] Pindar expresses the same sentiment in *Pythian Ode, I, 164.*
[3] It is the lofty pine that by the storm
   Is oftener tossed; towers fall with heavier
   crash

Which higher soar.
   HORACE [65–8 B.C.]: *Odes, Book II, X,*
   To Licinius, L. 9
The bigger they come, the harder they fall. — ROBERT FITZSIMMONS [1862–1917], pugilist, before his fight with James J. Jeffries, a heavier man, in San Francisco [July 25, 1902]
[1] Neither snow, nor rain, nor heat, nor gloom of night stays these couriers from the swift completion of their appointed rounds. — *Inscription on the Main Post Office, New York City, adapted from Herodotus*
[2] Translated by JOWETT.

a prize composition which is heard and forgotten.

Peloponnesian War. Book I, 22

Mankind is tolerant of the praises of others so long as each hearer thinks he can do as well or nearly as well himself, but, when the speaker rises above him, jealousy is aroused and he begins to be incredulous.

Ibid. Book II, 35, Funeral Speech of Pericles

We are called a democracy, for the administration is in the hands of the many and not of the few. But while the law secures equal justice to all alike in their private disputes, the claim of excellence is also recognised; and when a citizen is in any way distinguished, he is preferred to the public service, not as a matter of privilege, but as the reward of merit. Neither is poverty a bar, but a man may benefit his country whatever be the obscurity of his condition. There is no exclusiveness in our public life, and in our private intercourse we are not suspicious of one another, nor angry with our neighbour if he does what he likes; we do not put on sour looks at him which, though harmless, are not pleasant. While we are thus unconstrained in our private intercourse, a spirit of reverence pervades our public acts; we are prevented from doing wrong by respect for authority and for the laws, having an especial regard to those which are ordained for the protection of the injured as well as to those unwritten laws which bring upon the transgressor of them the reprobation of the general sentiment.

Ibid. 37

We cultivate the mind. We are lovers of the beautiful, yet simple in our tastes, without loss of manliness.

Ibid. 40

Day by day fix your eyes upon the greatness of Athens, until you become filled with the love of her; and when you are impressed by the spectacle of her glory, reflect that this empire has been acquired by men who knew their duty and had the courage to do it.

Peloponnesian War. Book II, 43, Funeral Speech of Pericles

The sacrifice which they collectively made was individually repaid to them; for they received again each one for himself a praise which grows not old, and the noblest of all sepulchres — I speak not of that in which their remains are laid, but of that in which their glory survives, and is proclaimed always and on every fitting occasion both in word and deed. For the whole earth is the sepulchre of famous men; not only are they commemorated by columns and inscriptions in their own country, but in foreign lands there dwells also an unwritten memorial of them, graven not on stone but in the hearts of men.

Ibid.

Men naturally despise those who court them, but respect those who do not give way to them.

Ibid. Book III, 39

SOCRATES [1]
[470–399 B. C.]

The life which is unexamined is not worth living.

Apology. 38

Either death is a state of nothingness and utter unconsciousness, or, as men say, there is a change and migration of the soul from this world to another.[2] . . . Now if death be of such a nature, I say that to die is to gain; for eternity is then only a single night.

Ibid. 40

No evil can happen to a good man, either in life or after death.

Ibid. 41

Man is a prisoner who has no right to open the door of his prison and run away. . . . A man should wait, and

[1] Translated by JOWETT.
[2] Either the soul is immortal and we shall not die, or it perishes with the flesh, and we shall not know that we are dead. Live, then, as if you were eternal. — ANDRÉ MAUROIS [1885-   ] (DURANT, *On the Meaning of Life, P. 53*)

not take his own life until God summons him.

Dialogues of PLATO. *Phaedo. 62*

Must not all things at the last be swallowed up in death?

Ibid. 72

Will you not allow that I have as much of the spirit of prophecy in me as the swans? For they, when they perceive that they must die, having sung all their life long, do then sing more lustily than ever, rejoicing in the thought that they are going to the god they serve.[1]

Ibid. 85

The partisan, when he is engaged in a dispute, cares nothing about the rights of the question, but is anxious only to convince his hearers of his own assertions.

Ibid. 91

False words are not only evil in themselves, but they infect the soul with evil.

Ibid.

The soul takes nothing with her to the other world but her education and culture; and these, it is said, are of the greatest service or of the greatest injury to the dead man, at the very beginning of his journey thither.

Ibid. 107

I think that I had better bathe before I drink the poison, and not give the women the trouble of washing my dead body.

Ibid. 115

I owe a cock to Asclepius; will you remember to pay the debt?

Ibid. 118 (The last words of Socrates)

---

[1] The jalous swan, ayens his deth that singeth. — CHAUCER: *The Parlement of Foules* [1372–1386], *L. 342*

Makes a swan-like end,
Fading in music.
SHAKESPEARE: *The Merchant of Venice* [1596-1597], *Act III, Sc. 2, L. 44*

I will play the swan and die in music. — *Othello* [1604–1605], *Act V, Sc. 2, L. 245*

See Shakespeare, page 148b.
See Byron, page 458b.

HIPPOCRATES [1]
[460–377 B. C.]

I swear by Apollo Physician, by Asclepius, by Health, by Panacea, and by all the gods and goddesses, making them my witnesses, that I will carry out, according to my ability and judgment, this oath and this indenture. To hold my teacher in this art equal to my own parents; to make him partner in my livelihood; when he is in need of money to share mine with him; to consider his family as my own brothers, and to teach them this art, if they want to learn it, without fee or indenture. I will use treatment to help the sick according to my ability and judgment, but never with a view to injury and wrongdoing. I will keep pure and holy both my life and my art. In whatsoever houses I enter, I will enter to help the sick, and I will abstain from all intentional wrongdoing and harm. And whatsoever I shall see or hear in the course of my profession in my intercourse with men, if it be what should not be published abroad, I will never divulge, holding such things to be holy secrets. Now if I carry out this oath, and break it not, may I gain forever reputation among all men for my life and for my art; but if I transgress it and forswear myself, may the opposite befall me.

The Physician's Oath

Healing is a matter of time, but it is sometimes also a matter of opportunity

Precepts. Chap. 1

Sometimes give your services for nothing, calling to mind a previous benefaction or present satisfaction. And if there be an opportunity of serving one who is a stranger in financial straits, give full assistance to all such. For where there is love of man, there is also love of the art. For some patients, though conscious that their condition is perilous, recover their health simply through their contentment with the

---

[1] Translated by WILLIAM HENRY RICH JONES [1817-1885].

goodness of the physician. And it is well to superintend the sick to make them well, to care for the healthy to keep them well, also to care for one's own self, so as to observe what is seemly.

Precepts. Chap. 6

In all abundance there is lack.

Ibid. Chap. 8

If for the sake of a crowded audience you do wish to hold a lecture, your ambition is no laudable one, and at least avoid all citations from the poets, for to quote them argues feeble industry.

Ibid. Chap. 12

Life is short and the art long.[1]

Aphorisms. Sect. I, 1

Extreme remedies are very appropriate for extreme diseases.[2]

Ibid. 6

ARISTOPHANES
[446–380 B. C.]

What heaps of things have bitten me
  to the heart!
A small few pleased me, very few, just
  four;
But those that vexed were sand-dune-
  hundredfold.

Acharnians [3]

If a word
Our orators let fall, save what pertains
To peace, I'll raise a storm of words,
  and rain
A very tempest of abuse upon them!

Ibid.[4]

He works and blows the coals

[1] Ars longa, vita brevis.
The lyf so short, the craft so long to lerne.
— CHAUCER: *The Parlement of Foules* [1372–1386], *Proem, L. 1*
Art's long, though time is short. — BROWNING: *The Ring and the Book* [1868–1869], *IX, Juris Doctor Johannes-Baptista Bottinius*
See Longfellow, page 521a.
[2] See Shakespeare, page 177b.
For a desperate disease a desperate cure. — MONTAIGNE: *Essays* [1580–1595], *Book II, Chap. 3*
Desperate cures must be to desperate ills applied. — DRYDEN: *The Hind and the Panther* [1687], *Part III, L. 1111*
[3] Translated by B. B. ROGERS.
[4] Translated by JOHN HOOKHAM FRERE [1769–1846].

And has plenty of other irons in the
  fire.[1]

Acharnians

Master, shall I begin with the usual
  jokes
That the audience always laugh at?

Frogs [2]

Lodgings, — free from bugs and fleas,
  if possible,
If you know any such.

Ibid.

Brekeke-kesh, koash, koash.[3]

Ibid.

The men that stood for office, noted for
  acknowledged worth,
And for manly deeds of honour, and
  for honourable birth;
Train'd in exercise and art, in sacred
  dances and in song,
All are ousted and supplanted by a base
  ignoble throng.

Ibid.

He collected audiences about him,
And flourish'd, and exhibited, and ha-
  rangued.

Ibid.

A vast expenditure of human voice.

Ibid.

Exalted ideas of fancy require
To be clothed in a suitable vesture of
  phrase.

Ibid.

I laugh'd till I cried.

Ibid.

If we withdraw the confidence we
  placed
In these our present statesmen, and
  transfer it
To those whom we mistrusted heretofore,
This seems I think our fairest chance
  for safety:
If with our present counsellors we fail,

[1]   It is always good
When a man has two irons in the fire.
FRANCIS BEAUMONT: *The Faithful Friends* [*circa* 1608], *Act I, Sc. 2*
[2] Translated by JOHN HOOKHAM FRERE [1769–1846].
[3] Adapted in college cheer: Brekeke-kex, koax, koax.

Then with their opposites we might succeed.

Frogs

Shame is the apprehension of a vision
Reflected from the surface of opinion —
The opinion of the public.

Ibid.

Perhaps death is life, and life is death,
And victuals and drink an illusion of
the senses;
For what is Death but an eternal sleep?
And does not Life consist in sleeping
and eating? [1]

Ibid.

Happy is the man possessing
The superior holy blessing
Of a judgment and a taste
Accurate, refined and chaste.

Ibid.

When shall I see those halcyon days? [2]

Clouds [3]

If you strike
Upon a thought that baffles you, break
off
From that entanglement and try another.
So shall your wits be fresh to start
again.

Ibid.

Old age is but a second childhood.

Ibid.

Throw fear to the wind.

Wasps [4]

Rais'd and swell'd with honours great
(such on bard yet never sate)
With meekness and modesty he bore
him;
And while his laurels grew, he kept ever
in his view
The heights yet unconquer'd before
him.

Ibid.

[1] See Euripides, page 18a.
[2] Expect Saint Martin's summer, halcyon
days. — SHAKESPEARE: *King Henry VI, Part
I* [1591], *Act I, Sc. 2, L. 131*
  The appellation of Halcyon-days, which
was applied to a rare and bloodless week of
repose. — GIBBON: *Decline and Fall of the
Roman Empire* [1776–1788], *Chap. 48*
[3] Translated by THOMAS MITCHELL [1783–
1845].
[4] Translated by RICHARD CUMBERLAND
[1732–1811].

O the days that are gone by, O the days
that are no more,
When my eye was bold and fearless,
and my hand was on the oar.

Wasps

Bitt'rest stroke of all we feel it, that an
idle brood be fed
At our cost, who never handled oar or
jav'lin, never bled,
Nor so much as rais'd a blister in their
suff'ring country's stead.

Ibid.

The wise may learn many things from
their foes.

Birds

DIONYSIUS THE ELDER
[430–367 B. C.]

Let thy speech be better than silence,
or be silent.

Fragment 6

XENOPHON
[*Circa* 430–355 B. C.]

Apollo said that every one's true
worship was that which he chanced to be.
use in the place where he chanced to be.

Recollections of Socrates. I, 3, 1

The sea! The sea! [1]

Anabasis. IV, vii, 24

I knew my son was mortal.[2]

DIOGENES LAERTIUS: *Xenophon.
Sect. 8*

PLATO [3]
[427–347 B. C.]

He who is of a calm and happy nature
will hardly feel the pressure of age, but
to him who is of an opposite disposition
youth and age are equally a burden.

The Republic. Book I, 329–D

No physician, in so far as he is a
physician, considers his own good in
what he prescribes, but the good of his
patient; for the true physician is also

[1] Thalatta! Thalatta!
  Hail to thee, O Sea, ageless and eternal!
  HEINRICH HEINE [1797–1856]: *Thalatta! Thalatta! St. 1*
[2] When his son was killed in battle.
[3] Translated by JOWETT.

a ruler having the human body as a subject, and is not a mere money-maker.

The Republic. Book I, 342–D

When there is an income-tax, the just man will pay more and the unjust less on the same amount of income.

Ibid. 343–D

Mankind censure injustice, fearing that they may be the victims of it and not because they shrink from committing it.

Ibid. 344–C

Necessity, who is the mother of invention.[1]

Ibid. Book II, 369–C

The beginning is the most important part of the work.

Ibid. 377–B

A fit of laughter which has been indulged to excess almost always produces a violent reaction.

Ibid. Book III, 388–E

Beauty of style and harmony and grace and good rhythm depend on simplicity.

Ibid. 400–D

Musical training is a more potent instrument than any other, because rhythm and harmony find their way into the inward places of the soul.

Ibid. 401–D

Gymnastic as well as music should begin in early years.

Ibid. 403–C

They do certainly give very strange and new-fangled names to diseases.

Ibid. 405–C

The judge should not be young; he should have learned to know evil, not from his own soul, but from late and long observation of the nature of evil

in others: knowledge should be his guide, not personal experience.

The Republic. Book III, 409–B

Everything that deceives may be said to enchant.

Ibid. 413–C

Under the influence either of poverty or of wealth, workmen and their work are equally liable to degenerate.

Ibid. Book IV, 421–E

Wealth is the parent of luxury and indolence, and poverty of meanness and viciousness, and both of discontent.

Ibid. 422

The direction in which education starts a man will determine his future life.

Ibid. 425–B

What is the prime of life? May it not be defined as a period of about twenty years in a woman's life, and thirty in a man's?

Ibid. Book V, 460–E

Let there be one man who has a city obedient to his will, and he might bring into existence the ideal polity about which the world is so incredulous.

Ibid. 502–B

Behold! human beings living in an underground den . . . Like ourselves . . . they see only their own shadows, or the shadows of one another, which the fire throws on the opposite wall of the cave.

Ibid. Book VII, 515–B

Astronomy compels the soul to look upwards and leads us from this world to another.

Ibid. 529

I have hardly ever known a mathematician who was capable of reasoning.

Ibid. 531–E

Solon was under a delusion when he said that a man when he grows old may learn many things — for he can no more learn much than he can run much; youth is the time for any extraordinary toil.

Ibid. 536–D

Bodily exercise, when compulsory, does no harm to the body; but knowl-

[1] Hunger is the teacher of the arts and the bestower of invention. — PERSIUS [A.D. 34–62]: *Prologue, L. 10*
Necessity, mother of invention. — WYCHERLEY: *Love in a Wood* [1671], *Act III, Sc. 3*
Art imitates Nature, and necessity is the mother of invention. — RICHARD FRANCK: *Northern Memoirs, edited by Scott* [written in 1658, published in 1694]
Sheer necessity, — the proper parent of an art so nearly allied to invention. — SHERIDAN: *The Critic* [1779], *Act I, Sc. 2*

edge which is acquired under compulsion obtains no hold on the mind.

The Republic. Book VII, 536–E

Let early education be a sort of amusement; you will then be better able to find out the natural bent.

Ibid. 537

Oligarchy: A government resting on a valuation of property, in which the rich have power and the poor man is deprived of it.

Ibid. Book VIII, 550–C

Democracy, which is a charming form of government, full of variety and disorder, and dispensing a sort of equality to equals and unequals alike.[1]

Ibid. 558–C

The people have always some champion whom they set over them and nurse into greatness. . . . This and no other is the root from which a tyrant springs; when he first appears he is a protector.

Ibid. 565–C

In the early days of his power, he is full of smiles, and he salutes every one whom he meets.

Ibid. 566–D

When the tyrant has disposed of foreign enemies by conquest or treaty, and there is nothing to fear from them, then he is always stirring up some war or other, in order that the people may require a leader.

Ibid. 566–E

Has he not also another object which is that they may be impoverished by payment of taxes, and thus compelled to devote themselves to their daily wants and therefore less likely to conspire against him?

Ibid. 567

What a poor appearance the tales of poets make when stripped of the colours which music puts upon them, and recited in simple prose.

Ibid. Book X, 601–B

[1] See Aristotle, page 26b.

There are three arts which are concerned with all things: one which uses, another which makes, a third which imitates them.

The Republic. Book X, 601–D

No human thing is of serious importance.

Ibid.

The soul of man is immortal and imperishable.

Ibid. 608–D

These are the Fates, daughters of Necessity . . . Lachesis singing of the past, Clotho of the present, Atropos of the future.

Ibid. 617–C

Beloved Pan, and all ye other gods who haunt this place, give me beauty in the inward soul; and may the outward and inward man be at one. May I reckon the wise to be the wealthy, and may I have such a quantity of gold as none but the temperate can carry.

Phaedrus. 279

The greatest penalty of evil-doing — namely, to grow into the likeness of bad men.

Laws. 728

Of all the animals, the boy is the most unmanageable.

Ibid. 808

You are young, my son, and, as the years go by, time will change and even reverse many of your present opinions. Refrain therefore awhile from setting yourself up as a judge of the highest matters.

Ibid. 888

And this which you deem of no moment is the very highest of all: that is whether you have a right idea of the gods, whereby you may live your life well or ill.

Ibid.

Not one of them who took up in his youth with this opinion that there are no gods, ever continued until old age faithful to his conviction.

Ibid.

ZEUXIS
[*Circa* 400 B. C.]

Criticism comes easier than craftsmanship.

Quoted by PLINY *in Natural History*

AESCHINES
[389–314 B. C.]

The sinews of affairs are cut.[1]

Ctesiphon. Chap. 53

ARISTOTLE
[384–322 B. C.]

Poverty is the parent of revolution and crime.

Politics.[2] *Book II*

Even when laws have been written down, they ought not always to remain unaltered.

Ibid.

The law has no power to command obedience except that of habit, which can only be given by time, so that a readiness to change from old to new laws enfeebles the power of the law.

Ibid.

That judges of important causes should hold office for life is not a good thing, for the mind grows old as well as the body.

Ibid.

Man is by nature a political animal.[3]

Ibid. Book III

It is plain that the state is not determined merely by community of place and by the exchange of mutual protec-

tion from harm and of good offices. These things must, indeed, exist, if there is to be a city, yet the existence of all of them does not at once constitute a state; there must be, both in households and families, a sharing of the good life, in a form at once complete and self-sufficient.

Politics. Book III

If liberty and equality, as is thought by some, are chiefly to be found in democracy, they will be best attained when all persons alike share in the government to the utmost.[1]

Ibid. Book IV

The best political community is formed by citizens of the middle class. Those States are likely to be well administered in which the middle class is large, and larger if possible than both the other classes, or at any rate than either singly; for the addition of the middle class turns the scale and prevents either of the extremes from being dominant.

Ibid.

Inferiors revolt in order that they may be equal, and equals that they may be superior. Such is the state of mind which creates revolutions.

Ibid. Book V

Revolutions break out when opposite parties, the rich and the poor, are equally balanced, and there is little or nothing between them; for, if either party were manifestly superior, the other would not risk an attack upon them.

Ibid.

Democracies are most commonly corrupted by the insolence of demagogues.

Ibid.

One swallow does not make a spring.[2]

Nicomachean Ethics. 1

---

[1] Ascribed to Demosthenes. DIOGENES LAERTIUS, in his *Life of Bion, Book IV, Chap. 7, Sect. 3,* represents Bion as saying, "Riches were the sinews of business," or, as the phrase may mean, "of the state." Referring perhaps to this maxim of the philosopher Bion, PLUTARCH says in his *Life of Cleomenes,* "He that first said that money was the sinews of affairs, seems especially in that saying to refer to war" (Modern Library Giant ed., P. *986*). Accordingly we find money called expressly "the sinews of war" in LIBANIUS, *Oration 46,* and by the scholiast on PINDAR, *Olymp., I, 4,* and in CICERO, *Philipp., V, 2,* "nervos belli, infinitam pecuniam."

[2] Translated by JOWETT.

[3] This phrase is used elsewhere by Aristotle.

[1] See Plato, page 25a.

[2] One swallow maketh not summer. — JOHN HEYWOOD: *Proverbes* [1546], *Part II, Chap. 5*
One swallowe prouveth not that summer is neare. — NORTHBROOKE: *Treatise against Dancing* [1577]
One swallow never makes a summer. —

Of evils we must choose the least.[1]
Nicomachean Ethics. II
All admit that in a certain sense the several kinds of character are bestowed by nature. Justice, a tendency to Temperance, Courage, and the other types of character are exhibited from the moment of birth.
Ibid. VI

Mothers are fonder of their children. For they have a more painful share in their production and they are more certain that they are their own.
Ibid. IX

In practical matters the end is not mere speculative knowledge of what is to be done, but rather the doing of it. It is not enough to know about Virtue, then, but we must endeavour to possess it, and to use it, or to take any other steps that may make us good.
Ibid. X

The generality of men are naturally apt to be swayed by fear rather than by reverence, and to refrain from evil rather because of the punishment that it brings, than because of its own foulness.
Ibid.

What makes men good is held by some to be nature, by others habit or training, by others instruction. As for the goodness that comes by nature, this is plainly not within our control, but is bestowed by some divine agency on certain people who truly deserve to be called fortunate.
Ibid.

Misfortune unites men, when the same thing is harmful to both.
Rhetoric. I
No one loves him whom he fears.
Ibid. II

CERVANTES: *Don Quixote, Part I* [1605], *Book II, Chap. 4*
[1] Of two evils, the least should be chosen. — CICERO [106–43 B.C.]: *De Officiis, III, 1*
Of harmes two, the lesse is for to chese. — CHAUCER: *Troilus and Criseyde* [1372–1386], *Book II, L. 470*
Of two evils the less is always to be chosen. — THOMAS A KEMPIS [1380–1471]: *Imitation of Christ, Book III, Chap. 12*

God is mightiest in power, fairest in beauty, immortal in existence, supreme in virtue; therefore, being invisible to every mortal nature, he is seen through his works themselves.
De Mundo. Chap 6

DEMOSTHENES
[384–322 B.C.]

I do not purchase regret at such a price.
Reply to Laïs
Though a man escape every other danger, he can never wholly escape those who do not want such a person as he is to exist.
De Falsa Legatione.[1] *228*
Every advantage in the past is judged in the light of the final issue.
First Olynthiac.[1] *11*
Like the diet prescribed by doctors, which neither restores the strength of the patient nor allows him to succumb, so these doles that you are now distributing neither suffice to ensure your safety nor allow you to renounce them and try something else.
Third Olynthiac.[1] *33*
To remind the man of the good turns you have done him is very much like a reproach.
De Corona.[1] *269*

MENANDER [2]
[343–292 B.C.]

You knew not how to live in clover.
The Girl from Samos. Act 2, Sc. 4
The man who first invented the art of supporting beggars made many wretched.
The Fishermen. Fragment
We live, not as we wish to, but as we can.
The Lady of Andros. Fragment
In many ways the saying "Know thyself" is not well said. It were more practical to say "Know other people." [3]
Thrasyleon. Fragment

---

[1] Translated by C. A. AND J. H. VINCE.
[2] Translated by FRANCIS G. ALLINSON.
[3] See Plutarch, page 60a.

No one gets rich quickly if he is honest.[1]

> *The Flatterer. Fragment*

Nor is it even possible for anyone to say while life lasts: "*That* is something that will not be my lot!"

> *The Drafting Officer. Fragment*

I call a fig a fig, a spade a spade.[2]

> *Unidentified minor fragment*

A woman is necessarily an evil, but he that gets the most tolerable one is lucky.

> *Ibid.*

Marriage, if one will face the truth, is an evil, but a necessary evil.[3]

> *Ibid.*

The land that gives poor nurture bears brave men.[4]

> *Ibid.*

Manner, not gold, is woman's best adornment.

> *Fragment. Quoted in The Spectator, January 3, 1712*

For our mind is God.

> PLUTARCH: *Platonic Questions*

BIDPAI OR PILPAY [5]
[*Circa* 326 B.C.?]

We ought to do our neighbour all the good we can. If you do good, good will be done to you; but if you do evil, the same will be measured back to you again.[1]

> *Chap. 1. Dabschelim and Pilpay*

It has been the providence of Nature to give this creature [the cat] nine lives instead of one.[2]

> *Ibid. Fable 3, The Greedy and Ambitious Cat*

There is no gathering the rose without being pricked by the thorns.[3]

> *Chap. 2. Fable 6, The Two Travellers*

Wise men say that there are three sorts of persons who are wholly deprived of judgment, — they who are ambitious of preferments in the courts of princes; they who make use of poison to show their skill in curing it; and they who intrust women with their secrets.

> *Ibid.*

Men are used as they use others.

> *Ibid. Fable 9, The King Who Became Just*

What is bred in the bone will never come out of the flesh.[4]

> *Ibid. Fable 14, The Two Fishermen*

Guilty consciences always make people cowards.[5]

> *Chap. 3. Fable 3, The Prince and His Minister*

Whoever . . . prefers the service of princes before his duty to his Creator, will be sure, early or late, to repent in vain.

> *Ibid.*

---

[1] No good man ever grew rich all at once. — PUBLILIUS SYRUS [*circa* 42 B.C.]: *Maxim 837*

[2] A similar saying is credited to Aristophanes by LUCIAN, *Quom. Hist. sit conscrib.*, 41
Brought up like a rude Macedon, and taught to call a spade a spade. — STEPHEN GOSSON: *Ephemerides of Phialo* [1579]
I think it good plain English, without fraud,
To call a spade a spade, a bawd a bawd.
JOHN TAYLOR, the "Water Poet" [1580–1653]

[3] Marriage is an evil that most men welcome. — *Fragment, Monost. 102*. Motto of *The Spectator*, December 29, 1711.

[4] This and the preceding quotation are translated by A. H. CHASE.

[5] Theodor Benfey [1809–1881], German Orientalist, in tracing the name Pilpay or Bidpai, found that it was an appellative applied to the chief pandit or court scholar of an Indian prince. The *Fables of Pilpay*, or *Kalilah and Dimnah*, are the Arabic translation of the Pahlavi translation of the Sanskrit original of the *Panchatantra*. The first English translation appeared in 1570.

[1] And with what measure ye mete, it shall be measured to you again. — *Matthew, VII, 2*

[2] A woman hath nine lives like a cat. — JOHN HEYWOOD: *Proverbes* [1546], *Part II, Chap. 4*

[3] Ne'er the rose without the thorn. — HERRICK: *The Rose* [1648]
Flowers of all hue, and without thorn the rose. — MILTON: *Paradise Lost* [1667], *Book IV, L. 256*

[4] It will not out of the flesh that is bred in the bone. — JOHN HEYWOOD: *Proverbes* [1546], *Part II, Chap. 8*

[5] A guilty conscience never feels secure. — PUBLILIUS SYRUS [*circa* 42 B.C.]: *Maxim 617*
See Shakespeare, page 174b.

There are some who bear a grudge even to those that do them good.
Chap. 3. Fable 6, A Religious Doctor

He that plants thorns must never expect to gather roses.[1]
Ibid. Fable 8, The Ignorant Physician

Honest men esteem and value nothing so much in this world as a real friend. Such a one is as it were another self, to whom we impart our most secret thoughts, who partakes of our joy, and comforts us in our affliction; add to this, that his company is an everlasting pleasure to us.
Chap. 4. Choice of Friends

That possession was the strongest tenure of the law.[2]
Chap. 5. Fable 4, The Cat and the Two Birds

Wild elephants are caught by tame;
With money it is just the same.
The Panchatantra.[3] Book I

EUCLID
[*Circa* 300 B. C.]

Pons asinorum (the bridge of asses).[4]
Elements. Book I, Proposition 5

There is no royal road to geometry.[5]
Quoted by PROCLUS: *Commentaria in Euclidem. Book 2, Chap. 4*

ARCHIMEDES
[287?–212 B. C.]

I have found it! [6]
VITRUVIUS POLLIO: *De Architectura. IX, 215*

---

[1] Whatsoever a man soweth, that shall he also reap. — *Galatians, VI, 7*
See Samuel Butler, page 239a.

[2] Possession is eleven points in the law. — COLLEY CIBBER: *Woman's Wit* [1697], *Act I*

[3] Translation adapted from ARTHUR W. RYDER.

[4] Too difficult for asses, or stupid boys, to get over.

[5] Ptolemy I, King of Egypt, wished to study geometry, without going over the thirteen parts of Euclid's *Elements.* He said that a short cut would be agreeable, whereupon Euclid answered that there was no royal road to geometry. Often misquoted as "no royal road to learning."

[6] Eureka! Said when he found the principle of specific gravity.

Give me where to stand, and I will move the earth.[1]
PAPPUS: *Collectio. Book VIII, Prop. 10, Sect. XI*

THEOCRITUS [2]
[THIRD CENTURY B. C.]

'Tis peace of mind, lad, we must find, and have a beldame nigh
To sit for us and spit for us and bid all ill go by.
The Harvest-Home. Line 126

O cricket is to cricket dear, and ant for ant doth long,
The hawk's the darling of his fere, and o' me the Muse and her song.
The Third Country Singing-Match. Line 31

O to be a frog, my lads, and live aloof from care.
The Reapers. Line 52

Thou 'lt cut thy finger, niggard, a splitting caraway.
Ibid. Line 55

A great love goes here with a little gift.
The Distaff. Line 24

CALLIMACHUS
[*Floruit* 260 B. C.]

A big book is a big nuisance.
Fragmenta Incerta, No. 359

This is the tomb of Callimachus that thou art passing.
He could sing well, and laugh well at the right time over the wine.
His Own Epitaph. Greek Anthology, Book VII, No. 415

PLAUTUS [3]
[254–184 B. C.]

What is yours is mine, and all mine is yours.[4]
Trinummus. Act II, Sc. 2, Line 48

Not by years but by disposition is wisdom acquired.
Ibid. Line 88

---

[1] Said with reference to the lever.

[2] Translated by J. M. EDMONDS.

[3] Translated by HENRY THOMAS RILEY [1816–1878].

[4] What's mine is yours, and what is yours is mine. — SHAKESPEARE: *Measure for Measure* [1604–1605], *Act V, Sc. 1, L. 529*

He whom the gods favour dies in youth.[1]

Bacchides. Act IV, Sc. 7, Line 18

You are seeking a knot in a bulrush.[2]

Menaechmi. Act II, Sc. 1, Line 22

In the one hand he is carrying a stone, while he shows the bread in the other.[3]

Aulularia. Act II, Sc. 2, Line 18

It was not for nothing that the raven was just now croaking on my left hand.[4]

Ibid. Act. IV, Sc. 3, Line 1

There are occasions when it is undoubtedly better to incur loss than to make gain.

Captivi. Act II, Sc. 2, Line 77

Patience is the best remedy for every trouble.[5]

Rudens. Act II, Sc. 5, Line 71

Consider the little mouse, how sagacious an animal it is which never entrusts its life to one hole only.[6]

Truculentus. Act. IV, Sc. 4, Line 15

---

[1] Those that God loves do not live long. — GEORGE HERBERT: *Jacula Prudentum* [2nd ed., 1651]
See Wordsworth, page 410b.
Heaven gives its favourites — early death. — BYRON: *Childe Harold, Canto IV* [1818], *St. 102*
"Whom the gods love die young," was said of yore. — BYRON: *Don Juan* [1819–1824], *Canto IV, St. 12*
[2] A proverbial expression implying a desire to create doubts and difficulties where there really are none. It occurs in TERENCE: *Andria, Act V, Sc. 4, L. 38;* also in ENNIUS: *Saturae, 46.*
[3] What man is there of you, whom if his son ask bread, will he give him a stone? — *Matthew, VII, 9*
[4] That raven on yon left-hand oak
(Curse on his ill-betiding croak!)
Bodes me no good.
JOHN GAY: *The Farmer's Wife and the Raven* [1727]
[5] Patience is a remedy for every sorrow. — PUBLILIUS SYRUS [*circa* 42 B.C.]: *Maxim 170*
[6] I holde a mouses herte nat worth a leek,
That hath but oon hole for to sterte to,
And if that faille, thanne is al y-do.
CHAUCER: *The Canterbury Tales* [*circa* 1387], *The Wife of Bath's Prologue, L. 572*
The mouse that hath but one hole is quickly taken. — GEORGE HERBERT: *Jacula Prudentum* [1640]
The mouse that always trusts to one poor hole

Nothing is there more friendly to a man than a friend in need.[1]

Epidicus. Act III, Sc. 3, Line 44

Things which you do not hope happen more frequently than things which you do hope.[2]

Mostellaria. Act I, Sc. 3, Line 40

To blow and swallow at the same moment is not easy.

Ibid. Act III, Sc. 2, Line 104

QUINTUS ENNIUS
[239–169 B.C.]

No sooner said than done — so acts your man of worth.

Annals. Book 9 (Quoted by PRISCIANUS)

I never indulge in poetics
Unless I am down with rheumatics.

Fragment of a Satire (Quoted by PRISCIANUS)

By delay he restored the state.[3]

Quoted by CICERO in De Senectute, IV

Let no one pay me honor with tears, nor celebrate my funeral with mourning.[4]

Quoted by CICERO, Ibid. XX

The ape, vilest of beasts, how like to us!

Quoted by CICERO in De Natura Deorum, Book I, Chap. 35

No one regards what is before his feet; we all gaze at the stars.

Iphigenia (Quoted by CICERO in De Divinatione, Book II, Chap. 13)

Can never be a mouse of any soul.
POPE: *Paraphrase of the Prologue* [1714], *L. 298*
[1] A friend in need is a friend indeed. — HAZLITT: *English Proverbs*
[2] The unexpected always happens. — *A common saying*
[3] This refers to Quintus Fabius Maximus, "Cunctator." Hence the "Fabian policy" of waiting.
[4] No funeral gloom, my dears, when I am gone,
Corpse-gazings, tears, black raiment, graveyard grimness.
WILLIAM ALLINGHAM [1828–1889]: *Diary*

The idle mind knows not what it is it wants.

> *Iphigenia. Chorus*

Whom they fear they hate.

> *Thyestes (Quoted by* CICERO *in De Officiis, II, 7)*

When Fortune's fickle, the faithful friend is found.[1]

> *Quoted by* CICERO *in De Amicitia, XVIII, 64*

MARCUS PORCIUS CATO
[234–149 B. C.]

Carthage must be destroyed.[2]

CAECILIUS STATIUS
[220–168 B. C.]

Let him draw out his old age to dotage drop by drop.

> *Hymnis (Quoted by* FESTUS)

The facts will promptly blunt his ardor.

> *The Changeling (Quoted by* CHARISIUS)

He plants trees to benefit another generation.

> *Synephebi (Quoted by* CICERO *in De Senectute, VII)*

POLYBIUS
[SECOND CENTURY B. C.]

For peace, with justice and honor, is the fairest and most profitable of possessions, but with disgrace and shameful cowardice it is the most infamous and harmful of all.

> *Histories. IV, 31*

Those who know how to win are much more numerous than those who know how to make proper use of their victories.

> *Ibid. X, 36*

There is no witness so dreadful, no accuser so terrible as the conscience that dwells in the heart of every man.

> *Ibid. XVIII, 43*

[1] In prosperity it is very easy to find a friend; but in adversity it is the most difficult of all things. — EPICTETUS [*circa* A. D. 60]: *Fragments, No. 127*

[2] Delenda est Carthago. Said to have been

TERENCE [1]
[185–159 B. C.]

Nothing in excess.[2]

> *Andria, Act. I, Sc. 1, Line 34*

Of surpassing beauty and in the bloom of youth.

> *Ibid. Line 45*

Hence these tears.

> *Ibid. Line 99*

That is a true proverb which is wont to be commonly quoted, that "all had rather it were well for themselves than for another."

> *Ibid. Act II, Sc. 5, Line 15*

The quarrels of lovers are the renewal of love.[3]

> *Ibid. Act III, Sc. 3, Line 23*

Look you, I am the most concerned in my own interests.[4]

> *Ibid. Act IV, Sc. 1, Line 12*

In fine, nothing is said now that has not been said before.[5]

> *Eunuchus. The Prologue, Line 41*

Immortal gods! how much does one man excel another! What a difference there is between a wise person and a fool!

> *Ibid. Act II, Sc. 2, Line 1*

I have everything, yet have nothing; and although I possess nothing, still of nothing am I in want.[6]

> *Ibid. Line 12*

There are vicissitudes in all things.

> *Ibid. Line 45*

---

the inevitable conclusion of all his speeches on any topic whatever.

[1] Translated by HENRY THOMAS RILEY [1816–1878].

[2] Ne quid nimis.

[3] The anger of lovers renews the strength of love. — PUBLILIUS SYRUS [*circa* 42 B. C.]: *Maxim 24*

The fallyng out of faithful frends renuyng is of love. — RICHARD EDWARDS: *The Paradise of Dainty Devices* [1576]

Let the falling out of friends be a renewing of affection. — LYLY: *Euphues* [1579]

The falling out of lovers is the renewing of love. — ROBERT BURTON: *Anatomy of Melancholy* [1621–1651], *Part III, Sect. 2*

[4] See Sir Thomas Browne, page 240b.

[5] See *Ecclesiastes, I, 10,* on page 1042a, and Robert Burton, page 221a.

[6] See *2 Corinthians, VI, 10,* on page 1062a, and Wotton, page 213a.

I did not care one straw.[1]
Eunuchus. Act III, Sc. 1, Line 21

Jupiter, now assuredly is the time when I could readily consent to be slain, lest life should sully this ecstasy with some disaster.[2]
Ibid. Sc. 5, Line 2

This and a great deal more like it I have had to put up with.
Ibid. Act IV, Sc. 6, Line 8

Take care and say this with presence of mind.[3]
Ibid. Line 31

It behooves a prudent person to make trial of everything before arms.
Ibid. Sc. 7, Line 19

I know the disposition of women: when you will, they won't; when you won't, they set their hearts upon you of their own inclination.
Ibid. Line 42

I took to my heels as fast as I could.
Ibid. Act V, Sc. 2, Line 5

Many a time, . . . from a bad beginning great friendships have sprung up.
Ibid. Line 34

I only wish I may see your head stroked down with a slipper.[4]
Ibid. Sc. 8, Line 1

I am a man, and nothing that concerns a man do I deem a matter of indifference to me.[5]
Heauton Timoroumenos. Act I, Sc. 1, Line 25

This is a wise maxim, "to take warning from others of what may be to your own advantage."
Ibid. Sc. 2, Line 36

That saying which I hear commonly repeated, — that time assuages sorrow.
Heauton Timoroumenos, Act III, Sc. 1, Line 12

Really, you have seen the old age of an eagle,[1] as the saying is.
Ibid. Sc. 2, Line 9

Many a time a man cannot be such as he would be, if circumstances do not admit of it.
Ibid. Act IV, Sc. 1, Line 53

Nothing is so difficult but that it may be found out by seeking.
Ibid. Sc. 2, Line 7

What now if the sky were to fall? [2]
Ibid. Line 41

Rigorous law is often rigorous injustice.[3]
Ibid. Sc. 4, Line 48

There is nothing so easy but that it becomes difficult when you do it with reluctance.
Ibid. Sc. 5, Line 1

Fortune helps the brave.[4]
Phormio. Act I, Sc. 4, Line 26

It is the duty of all persons, when affairs are the most prosperous, then in especial to reflect within themselves in what way they are to endure adversity.
Ibid. Act II, Sc. 1, Line 11

As many men, so many minds; [5] every one his own way.
Ibid. Sc. 4, Line 14

---

[1] Nor do they care a straw. — CERVANTES: *Don Quixote, Part I* [1605], *Book III, Chap. 9*

[2]   If it were now to die,
      'Twere now to be most happy.
SHAKESPEARE: *Othello* [1604–1605], *Act II, Sc. 1, L. 192*

[3] Literally, "with a present mind" — equivalent to CAESAR's *praesentia animi* (*De Bello Gallico, V, 43, 4*).

[4] According to LUCIAN, there was a story that Omphale used to beat Hercules with her slipper or sandal.

[5] Quoted by CICERO in *De Officiis, I, 30*. In the Latin, Homo sum: humani nihil a me alienum puto.

[1] This was a proverbial expression, signifying a hale and vigorous old age.

[2] Some ambassadors from the Celtae, being asked by Alexander what in the world they dreaded most, answered, that they feared lest the sky should fall upon them. — ARRIANUS [*circa* A.D. 100–170]: *Book I, 4*

[3] Extreme law, extreme injustice, is now become a stale proverb in discourse. — CICERO [106–43 B.C.]: *De Officiis, I, 33*

Extreme justice is often injustice. — RACINE: *La Thébaïde* [1664], *Act IV, Sc. 3*

Mais l'extrême justice est une extrême injure. — VOLTAIRE: *Oedipe* [1718], *Act III, Sc. 3*

[4] PLINY THE YOUNGER says (*Book 6, Letter 16*) that PLINY THE ELDER said this during the eruption of Vesuvius: "Fortune favours the brave."

[5] Quot homines, tot sententiae.
So many heads so many wits. — JOHN

As the saying is, I have got a wolf by the ears.[1]

Phormio. Act III, Sc. 2, Line 21

I bid him look into the lives of men as though into a mirror, and from others to take an example for himself.

Adelphoe. Act III, Sc. 3, Line 61

According as the man is, so must you humour him.

Ibid. Line 77

It is a maxim of old that among themselves all things are common to friends.[2]

Ibid. Act V, Sc. 3, Line 18

It is the common vice of all, in old age, to be too intent upon our interests.[3]

Ibid. Sc. 8, Line 30

MARCUS TULLIUS CICERO
[106–43 B. C.]

If you aspire to the highest place it is no disgrace to stop at the second, or even the third.

De Oratore. 1

The freer utterances of poetic license.[4]

Ibid. 38

For as lack of adornment is said to become some women, so this subtle oration, though without embellishment, gives delight.[5]

Ibid. 78

The mind of each man is the man himself.

De Republica. VI, 26

Thus in the beginning the world was so made that certain signs come before certain events.[6]

De Divinatione. I, 118

He was never less at leisure than when at leisure.[1]

De Officiis. III, 1, quoting
Scipio Africanus

What a time! What a civilization! [2]

Catiline. I, 1

For how many things, which for our own sake we should never do, do we perform for the sake of our friends.

De Amicitia.[3] XVI

When Fortune is fickle, the faithful friend is found.[4]

Ibid. XVII

Nothing can be more disgraceful than to be at war with him with whom you have lived on terms of friendship.

Ibid. XXI

He removes the greatest ornament of friendship, who takes away from it respect.

Ibid. XXII

There is no greater bane to friendship than adulation, fawning, and flattery.

Ibid. XXV

Laws are dumb in the midst of arms.[5]

Pro Milone. IV, 11

Who stood to gain? [6]

Ibid. XII, 32

The good of the people is the chief law.[7]

De Legibus. III, 3, 8

I am a Roman citizen.[8]

In Verrem. V, 57, 147

Heywood: *Proverbes* [1546], *Part I, Chap. 2*
So many men so many mindes. — Gascoigne: *Glass of Government* [1575]

[1] A proverbial expression, which, according to Suetonius, was frequently in the mouth of Tiberius Caesar.

[2] All things are in common among friends. — Diogenes Laertius [*circa* A.D. 200]: *Diogenes, VI*

[3] Cicero quotes this in *Tusculan Disputations, Book 3*. The maxim was a favorite one with the Stoic philosophers.

[4] Poetarum licentiae liberiora.

[5] See Milton, page 256a.

[6] See Thomas Campbell, page 432b.

[1] I was never less alone than when by myself. — Edward Gibbon: *Memoirs* [1796]
Never less alone than when alone. — Samuel Rogers: *Human Life* [1819]
In solitude, where we are least alone. — Byron: *Childe Harold's Pilgrimage, Canto III* [1816], *St. 90*

[2] O tempora! O mores!

[3] Translated by Cyrus R. Edmonds.

[4] In prosperity it is very easy to find a friend; but in adversity it is the most difficult of all things. — Epictetus [*circa* A.D. 60]: *Fragments, No. 127*
See Ovid, page 43a.

[5] Silent enim leges inter arma.
The clatter of arms drowns the voice of the law. — Montaigne: *Essays* [1580–1595], *Book III, Chap. 1*

[6] Cui bono fuerit.

[7] Salus populi suprema est lex.

[8] Civis Romanus sum.

Let them hate, provided that they fear.[1]

*Philippic. I, 14 (Quoted from
the tragedian Accius)*

Crimes are not to be measured by the issue of events, but from the bad intentions of men.

Paradox III

There is no place more delightful than home.

Epistolae. IV, 8

While the sick man has life there is hope.[2]

Ibid. IX, 10

I prefer to err with Plato.[3]

Tusculan Disputations. I, xvii, 39

For as I like a young man in whom there is something of the old, so I like an old man in whom there is something of the young; and he who follows this maxim, in body will possibly be an old man, but he will never be an old man in mind.

De Senectute.[4] XI

Old age is by nature rather talkative.

Ibid. XVI

Old age, especially an honored old age, has so great authority, that this is of more value than all the pleasures of youth.

Ibid. XVII

Intelligence, and reflection, and judgment, reside in old men, and if there had been none of them, no states could exist at all.

Ibid. XIX

The short period of life is long enough for living well and honourably.[5]

Ibid.

The harvest of old age is the recollection and abundance of blessings previously secured.

Ibid.

[1] Oderint, dum metuant.
[2] For the living there is hope, but for the dead there is none. — THEOCRITUS [THIRD CENTURY B. C.] *Idyl IV, 42*
See Gay, page 308a, and Goldsmith, page 353b.
[3] Errare malo cum Platone.
[4] Translated by CYRUS R. EDMONDS.
[5] Life is amply long for him who orders it properly. — SENECA [8 B. C.–A. D. 65]: *On the Shortness of Life, 1, 4*

Nor, in truth, would the honours of illustrious men continue after death, if their own spirits did not make us preserve a longer remembrance of them.

De Senectute. XXII

Old age is the consummation of life, just as of a play.

Ibid. XXIII

JULIUS CAESAR [1]
[102?–44 B. C.]

All Gaul is divided into three parts.[2]

De Bello Gallico, I, 1

LUCRETIUS
[95–55 B. C.]

To such evils could religion urge mankind.

De Rerum Natura. I, 101

Continual dropping wears away a stone.[3]

Ibid. 314

Pleasant it is, when winds disturb the surface of the vast sea, to watch from land another's mighty struggle.

Ibid. II, 1

The swift runners who hand over the lamp of life.

Ibid. 79

Why dost thou not withdraw from life like some sated banqueter and with calm spirit seek untroubled rest?

Ibid. III, 938

What is food to one man may be fierce poison to others.[4]

Ibid. IV, 637

[1] See also Plutarch, pages 56b and 59b.
[2] Gallia est omnis divisa in partes tres.
[3] For water continually dropping will wear hard rocks hollow. — PLUTARCH [A. D. 46–120]: *Of the Training of Children*
The soft droppes of rain perce the hard marble. — LYLY: *Euphues* [1579]
And drizling drops that often doe redound,
The firmest flint doth in continuance weare.
　　　EDMUND SPENSER: *Amoretti* [1595],
　　　　　　　　　　Sonnet 18
[4] What's one man's poison, signor,
　Is another's meat or drink.
　　　BEAUMONT AND FLETCHER: *Love's
　　　　　　Cure* [1647], *Act III, Sc. 2*

In the midst of the fountain of wit there arises something bitter, which stings in the very flowers.[1]

De Rerum Natura. IV, 1133

CATULLUS [2]
[87–54? B. C.]

Now he goes along the dark road, whence they say no one returns.

Odes. III

Let us live and love, my Lesbia, and value at a penny all the talk of crabbed old men.

Suns may set and rise again. For us, when once our brief day has set, there's the sleep of one everlasting night.[3]

Ibid. V

Over head and heels.[4]

Ibid. XX

Everybody has his own delusion assigned to him: but we do not see that part of the bag which hangs on our back.[5]

Ibid. XXII

Ah, what is more blessed than to put cares away, when the mind lays by its burden, and tired with labor of far travel we have come to our own home and rest on the couch we longed for? This it is which alone is worth all these toils.

Ibid. XXXI

For there is nothing more silly than a silly laugh.

Ibid. XXXIX

Oh, this age! how tasteless and ill-bred it is!

Ibid. XLIII

[1] See Byron, page 452b.
[2] Translated by F. W. CORNISH.
[3] Translated by E. M. BECK.
[4] Per caputque pedesque.
[5] Whosoever shall call me madman, shall hear as much from me, and shall learn to look back upon the bag that hangs behind him. — HORACE [65–8 B. C.]: *Satires, Book II, III*
Jupiter has loaded us with a couple of wallets: the one, filled with our own vices, he has placed at our backs; the other, heavy with those of others, he has hung before. — PHAEDRUS [*circa* A. D. 8]: *Book IV, Fable 10*
Not a soul is there who seeks to search into himself — not one! But the wallet of the person in front is kept carefully in view. PERSIUS [A. D. 34–62]: *Satires, IV*

Now spring brings back balmy warmth.

Odes. XLVI

Idleness ere now has ruined both kings and wealthy cities.

Ibid. LI [A Fragment]

What is it, Catullus? why do you not make haste to die?

Ibid. LII

Henceforth let no woman believe a man's oath, let none believe that a man's speeches can be trustworthy. They, while their mind desires something and longs eagerly to gain it, nothing fear to swear, nothing spare to promise; but as soon as the lust of their greedy mind is satisfied, they fear not then their words, they heed not their perjuries.[1]

Ibid. LXIV

It is not fit that men should be compared with gods.

Ibid. LXVIII

I hate and I love. Why I do so, perhaps you ask. I do not know, but I feel it and I am in torment.

Ibid. LXXXV

For ever, brother, hail and farewell.[2]

Ibid. CI

SALLUST
[86–34 B. C.]

The soul is the captain and ruler of the life of mortals.[3]

Jugurtha. Chap. 1

Experience has shown that to be true which Appius [4] says in his verses, that every man is the architect of his own fortune; [5] and this proverb is especially

[1] What a woman says to her ardent lover should be written in wind and running water. — *Odes, LXX*
[2] In perpetuum, frater, ave atque vale.
[3] For man is man and master of his fate. — TENNYSON: *Idylls of the King, Geraint and Enid* [1859], *I, L. 355*
I am the master of my fate:
I am the captain of my soul.
    W. E. HENLEY [1849–1903]: *To R. T. Hamilton Bruce (Invictus)*
Be the proud captain still of thine own fate. — J. B. KENYON [1858–1924]: *A Challenge*
[4] Appius Claudius Caecus, consul in 307 B. C.
[5] His own character is the arbiter of every

true of you, who have excelled others to such a degree that men are sooner wearied in singing the praises of your deeds than you in doing deeds worthy of praise.

> *Speech on the State, Addressed to Caesar in His Later Years. Chap. I, Sentence 2*

CORNELIUS NEPOS
[*Floruit* 75 B. C.]

More brawn than brain.

> *Epaminondas. Chap. V, Line 21*

VIRGIL
[70–19 B. C.]

Compare great things with small.[1]

> *Eclogues. I, Line 24*

A great order of the ages is born anew. Now the virgin, now the reign of Saturn, comes again; now a new progeny descends from heaven.[2]

> *Ibid. IV, Line 5*

We have now made you for a time out of marble.

> *Ibid. VII, Line 35*

Age carries all things, even the mind, away.

> *Ibid. IX, Line 51*

Love conquers all.[3]

> *Ibid. X, Line 69*

Farthest Thule.[4]

> *Georgics. I, Line 30*

Be favorable to bold beginnings.[1]

> *Georgics. I, Line 40*

Practice, by taking thought, might little by little hammer out divers arts.

> *Ibid. Line 133*

O but too happy the farmers, if they should know their own good fortune!

> *Ibid. Line 458*

Let the fields and the gliding streams in the valleys delight me. Inglorious, let me court the rivers and forests.

> *Ibid. II, Line 485*

Happy he who could learn the causes of things and who put beneath his feet all fears.[2]

> *Ibid. Line 490*

Happy also he who knows the country gods — Pan and old Sylvanus and the sisterhood of the Nymphs.

> *Ibid. Line 493*

Some trouble the dangerous seas with oars, others rush to arms.

> *Ibid. Line 503*

Arms and the man I sing.[3]

> *Aeneid. Book I, Line 1*

Fury ministers arms.[4]

> *Ibid. Line 150*

God will give an end to these things too.

> *Ibid. Line 199*

Perhaps some day it will be pleasant to remember these things.[5]

> *Ibid. Line 203*

The leader in the deed a woman.[6]

> *Ibid. Line 364*

She appeared a true goddess in her walk.

> *Ibid. Line 405*

Happy they whose walls already rise.

> *Ibid. Line 437*

---

one's fortune. — PUBLILIUS SYRUS [*circa* 42 B. C.]: *Maxim 283*
  Chiefly the mould of a man's fortune is in his own hands. — FRANCIS BACON: *Essays* [1597–1625], *Of Fortune*
  The brave man carves out his fortune, and every man is the son of his own works. — CERVANTES: *Don Quixote, Part I* [1605], *Chap. 4*
  [1] To compare
  Great things with small.
    MILTON: *Paradise Lost* [1667], *Book II, L. 921*
  [2] Magnus ab integro saeculorum nascitur ordo.
  Iam redit et Virgo, redeunt Saturnia regna;
  Iam nova progenies caelo demittitur alto.
  Interpreted by the Middle Ages as a prophecy of the birth of Christ. DANTE cites the lines in the *Purgatorio, Canto XXII, L. 70.*
  [3] Omnia amor vincit.
  [4] Ultima Thule.

[1] For the reverse side of the Great Seal of the United States (first used on the silver dollar certificates, series of 1935) this line of Virgil has been adapted, changed from the imperative mood, *Audacibus annue coeptis,* to the indicative mood, *Annuit coeptis,* He smiles on our beginnings.
[2] Virgil's tribute to Lucretius.
[3] Arma virumque cano.
[4] Furor arma ministrat.
[5] Forsan et haec olim meminisse iuvabit.
[6] Dux femina facti.

There are tears for misfortune.[1]
Aeneid. Book I, Line 462

A mind conscious of virtue may bring to thee suitable rewards.[2]
Ibid. Line 604

While rivers run into the sea, while on the mountains shadows move over the slopes, while heaven feeds the stars, ever shall thy honor, thy name, and thy praises endure.
Ibid. Line 607

Not unacquainted with sorrow, I have learned to aid the unfortunate.
Ibid. Line 630

I fear the Greeks, even when bringing gifts.[3]
Ibid. Book II, Line 49

I shudder at the word.[4]
Ibid. Line 204

The gods' thought was otherwise.[5]
Ibid. Line 428

O cursed lust for gold, to what dost thou not drive the hearts of men!
Ibid. Book III, Line 56

A fickle and changeful thing is woman ever.[6]
Ibid. Book IV, Line 569

Yield not to misfortunes but press forward the more boldly in their face.
Ibid. Book VI, Line 95

Easy is the descent to Hell; night and day the gates stand open; but to reclimb the slope, and escape to the outer air, this indeed is a task.
Ibid. Line 126

Faithful Achates.[7]
Ibid. Line 158 (and elsewhere)

[1] Sunt lacrimae rerum.
[2] The mind, conscious of rectitude, laughed to scorn the falsehood of report. — Ovid [43 B.C.–A.D. 18]: *Fasti, Book IV, L. 311*
[3] Timeo Danaos et dona ferentes. See Euripides, page 17a.
[4] Horresco referens.
[5] Dis aliter visum.
[6] Varium et mutabile semper femina. Woman often changes; foolish the man who trusts her. — FRANCIS I OF FRANCE [1494–1547], written by him with his ring on a window of the château of Chambord (BRANTÔME: *Oeuvres, VII, 395*)
 La donna è mobile. — PIAVE: *Libretto of* VERDI's *Rigoletto,* Duke's song
[7] Fidus Achates. Proverbial for a trusty

Fortunate isle, the abode of the blest.
Aeneid. Book VI, Line 639

Each of us suffers his own hell.
Ibid. Line 743

Others, I suppose, will more subtly mold the breathing bronze, draw forth the living features from the marble, plead causes better, mark with the rod the wanderings of the sky and foretell the rising stars: thou, Roman, be mindful to rule the peoples with imperial sway (these shall be thy arts) to impose the way of peace, to spare the conquered and put down the proud.
Ibid. Line 847

Implored the Genius of the place.
Ibid. Book VII, Line 136

Faith in the tale is old, but its fame is everlasting.
Ibid. Book IX, Line 79

It is enough to have perished once.
Ibid. Line 140

I could not bear a mother's tears.
Ibid. Line 289

Steep thyself in a bowl of summertime.
Minor Poems. Copa: Syrisca, a Dancing Girl,[1] *Line 29*

Here's Death, twitching my ear: "Live," says he, "for I'm coming." [2]
Ibid. Line 38

These lines made I, another steals my honors;
So you for others, oxen, bear the yoke;
So you for others, bees, store up your honey;
So you for others, sheep, put on your fleece;
So you for others, birds, construct your nests.[3]
Epigram (From CAIUS TIBERIUS DONATUS: *Life of Virgil)*

comrade; Achates was the faithful companion of Aeneas.
[1] Attributed to Virgil by CHARISIUS, the Grammarian, and by SUETONIUS, though modern scholars question the authenticity of all the minor poems.
[2] Quoted by Justice Oliver Wendell Holmes in a radio address on his ninetieth birthday [March 8, 1931].
[3] Virgil wrote a distich praising Caesar, and

HORACE
[65–8 B.C.]

But if you give me a place among the
bards of the lyre,
I shall lift my head till it strikes the
stars.
Odes. Book I, i, Line 35

For mortal daring nothing is too high.
In our blind folly we storm heaven it-
self.
Ibid. iii, Line 37

Pale Death, with impartial step,
knocks at the poor man's cottage and
at the palaces of kings.
Ibid. iv, Line 13

The brief span of life forbids us to
cherish a long hope.
Ibid. Line 15

There's no cause for despair! [1]
Ibid. vii, Line 27

Tomorrow we again embark upon the
boundless sea.
Ibid. Line 32

Melt me this cold, freely the firelogs
throwing
On hearth, my Thaliarchus! And
from crock
Two-eared, of Sabine make, unlock
Wine, with four years a-glowing! [2]
Ibid. ix, Line 5

What next morn's sun may bring, fore-
bear to ask;
But count each day that comes by gift
of chance
So much to the good.
Ibid. Line 13

Seize now and here the hour that is,
nor trust some later day! [1]
Odes. Book I, xi, Last line

Thrice happy they, and more, whom
an unbroken bond unites and whom
love, unsevered by bitter quarrels, shall
not release until the last day of all.
Ibid. xiii, Line 20

O fairer daughter of a fair mother.[2]
Ibid. xvi, Line 1

The pure in life and free from sin.[3]
Ibid. xxii, Line 1

What shame or measure can there be
to our grief for one so dear?
Ibid. xxiv, Line 1

What cannot be removed, becomes
lighter through patience.
Ibid. Line 19

One night waits all; Death's road we
all must go.
Ibid. xxviii, Line 16

Grant that in age I may not drift
Long years, my lyre forgot! [4]
Ibid. xxxi, Line 19

Now's the time for drinking! [5]
Ibid. xxxvii, Line 1

Cease your efforts to find where the
last rose lingers.
Ibid. xxxviii, Line 3

Remember when life's path is steep
to keep your mind even.
Ibid. Book II, iii, Line 1

Whoever cultivates the golden mean
avoids both the poverty of a hovel and
the envy of a palace.[6]
Ibid. x, Line 5

Bathyllus claimed the lines. To expose him,
Virgil wrote beneath the distich the following
incomplete verses, and Caesar asked Bathyl-
lus to finish the lines. He could not, and Virgil
then supplied the missing words (italicized be-
low):
Hos ego versiculos feci, tulit alter honores;
Sic vos non vobis, *fertis aratra boves;*
Sic vos non vobis, *mellificatis apes;*
Sic vos non vobis, *vellera fertis oves;*
Sic vos non vobis, *nidificatis aves.*

[1] Nil desperandum!
[2] Dissolve frigus, ligna super foco
Large reponens, atque benignius
Deprome quadrimum Sabina,
O Thaliarche, merum diota.
Inscription over the fireplace of the
Harvard Club of Boston

[1] Carpe diem, quam minimum credula pos-
tero.
[2] O matre pulchra filia pulchrior.
[3] Integer vitae, scelerisque purus.
[4] Not to be tuneless in old age! — DOBSON
[1840–1921]: *Henry Wadsworth Longfellow*
[5] Nunc est bibendum!
[6] Keep the golden mean. — PUBLILIUS SY-
RUS [*circa* 42 B.C.]: *Maxim 1072*
He that holds fast the golden mean,
And lives contentedly between
The little and the great,
Feels not the wants that pinch the poor,
Nor plagues that haunt the rich man's door.
WILLIAM COWPER [1731–1800]:
Translation of Horace, **Odes,**
Book II, x, St. 2
The proper mean. — VOLTAIRE: *Letter to*

Spring's flowers, howe'er they bloom, must fade again.

> *Odes. Book II, xi, Line 9*

Alas, Postumus, the fleeting years slip by.

> *Ibid. xiv, Line 1*

Death's boatman takes no bribe, nor brings
Ev'n skilled Prometheus back from Hades' shore.

> *Ibid. xviii, Line 35*

It is sweet and honourable to die for one's country.[1]

> *Ibid. Book III, ii, Line 13*

There is also a sure reward for faithful silence.

> *Ibid. Line 25*

The man who is just and firm of purpose can be shaken from his stern resolve neither by the rage of the people who urge him to crime nor by the countenance of the threatening tyrant.

> *Ibid. iii, Line 1*

Force without wisdom falls of its own weight.

> *Ibid. iv, Line 65*

Because you bear yourself as the gods' inferior, you rule.

> *Ibid. vi, Line 5*

Our sires' age was worse than our grandsires'. We their sons are more worthless than they: so in our turn we shall give the world a progeny yet more corrupt.[2]

> *Ibid. Line 46*

Skilled in the works of both languages.

> *Ibid. viii, Line 5*

With you I should love to live, with you be ready to die.

> *Ibid. ix, Line 24*

Gloriously false . . . a maid famous to all time.

> *Ibid. xi, Line 35*

I would not have borne this in my

flaming youth while Plancus was consul.[1]

> *Odes. Book III, xiv, Line 27*

As riches grow, care follows, and a thirst
For more and more.

> *Ibid. xvi, Line 17*

Learn calm to face what's pressing.

> *Ibid. xxix, Line 33*

He will through life be master of himself and a happy man who from day to day can have said, "I have lived": tomorrow the Father may fill the sky with black clouds or with cloudless sunshine.[2]

> *Ibid. Line 41*

I have built me a monument more lasting than bronze.

> *Ibid. xxx, Line 1*

I shall not wholly die. What's best of me
Shall 'scape the tomb.[3]

> *Ibid. Line 6*

Ev'n though the Golden Age upon the earth
Once more may live.[4]

> *Ibid. Book IV, ii, Line 39*

Summer treads
On heels of Spring.

> *Ibid. vii, Line 9*

---

[1] In my hot youth, when George the Third was king. — BYRON: *Don Juan* [1819–1824], *Canto 1, St. 212*

[2] Tomorrow let my sun his beams display,
Or in clouds hide them; I have lived my day.
COWLEY: *Discourse XI, Of Myself* [1661], *St. 11*
Happy the man, and happy he alone,
He who can call today his own;
He who, secure within, can say,
Tomorrow, do thy worst, for I have liv'd today.
DRYDEN: *Imitation of Horace. Book III, Ode xxix* [1685], *L. 65*
Serenely full, the epicure would say,
Fate cannot harm me; I have dined today.
SYDNEY SMITH [1771–1845]: *Recipe for Salad*

[3] I shall have more to say when I am dead.
EDWIN ARLINGTON ROBINSON [1869–1935]: *John Brown, last line*

[4] The golden age, which a blind tradition has hitherto placed in the past, is before us. — C. H. SAINT-SIMON [1760–1825], quoted by CARLYLE in *Sartor Resartus, Book 3, Chap. 5*

Count d'Argental [November 28, 1765]
[1] Dulce et decorum est pro patria mori. See Homer, page 5a.
[2] See Homer, page 4a.

We are dust and a shadow.
> *Odes. Book IV, vii, Line 16*

Brave men were living before Agamemnon; but all are overwhelmed in unending night, unwept, unknown, because they lacked a sacred bard.[1]
> *Ibid. ix, Line 25*

At the fit hour 'tis sweet to unbend.
> *Ibid. xii, Line 28*

The laugh will then be mine.
> *Epodes. xv, Line 24*

To bronze Jove changed Earth's golden time;
With bronze, then iron, stamped the age.
> *Ibid. xvi, Line 64*

Another yet the same.
> *Saecular Hymn.*[2] *Line 10*

Then, gods, to reverent youth grant purity,
Grant, gods, to quiet age a peaceful end.
> *Ibid. Line 45*

No one lives content with his condition, whether reason gave it him, or chance threw it in his way.
> *Satires.*[3] *Book I, i, Line 1*

We rarely find a man who can say he has lived happy, and content with his life can retire from the world like a satisfied guest.
> *Ibid. Line 117*

It is grievous to be caught.
> *Ibid. ii, Line 134*

This is a fault common to all singers, that among their friends they never are inclined to sing when they are asked, unasked they never desist.
> *Ibid. iii, Line 1*

The limbs of the mangled poet.
> *Ibid. iv, Line 62*

There are many who recite their writings in the middle of the forum; and who do it while bathing: the close-

ness of the place gives melody to the voice.
> *Satires. Book I, iv, Line 74*

Ridicule often decides matters of importance more effectually, and in a better manner, than severity.
> *Ibid. x, Line 14*

Carrying timber into a wood.[1]
> *Ibid. Line 34*

You that intend to write what is worthy to be read more than once, blot frequently: and take no pains to make the multitude admire you, content with a few judicious readers.
> *Ibid. Line 72*

Now learn what and how great benefits a temperate diet will bring along with it. In the first place you will enjoy good health.
> *Ibid. Book II, ii, Line 70*

In peace, as a wise man, he should make suitable preparation for war.[2]
> *Ibid. Line 110*

Live undaunted; and oppose gallant breasts against the strokes of adversity.[3]
> *Ibid. Line 135*

This was in my prayers.
> *Ibid. vi, Line 1*

O nights and banquets of the gods!
> *Ibid. Line 65*

At Rome, you long for the country; when you are in the country, fickle, you extol the absent city to the skies.
> *Ibid. vii, Line 28*

Get place and wealth, if possible with grace;

---

[1] How many, most famous while they lived, are utterly forgotten for want of writers! — BOETHIUS [A. D. 470?–525]: *De Consolatione Philosophiae, II, 7*

[2] Translated by DR. JOHN MARSHALL.

[3] Translated by CHRISTOPHER SMART [1722–1770].

[1] "Carrying coals to Newcastle." — JAMES MELVILLE: *Autobiography* [1583], *I, L. 163*
See Diogenes Laertius, page 71a.

[2] Who would desire peace should be prepared for war. — VEGETIUS [*circa* 375 B.C.]: *De Rei Militari, Book III, Prologue*
We should provide in peace what we need in war. — PUBLILIUS SYRUS [*circa* 42 B.C.]: *Maxim 709*
See Burton, page 223a, and Washington, page 367a.

[3] The company is Spartan; see how all their wounds are in front. — BASSUS: *The Greek Anthology, Book 9, Epigram 279*

If not, by any means get wealth and place.[1]

Epistles. Book I, i, Line 53

He has half the deed done, who has made a beginning.

Ibid. ii, Line 40

The covetous man is ever in want.

Ibid. Line 56

Sicilian tyrants never invented a greater torment than envy.

Ibid. Line 58

In the midst of hope and care, in the midst of fears and disquietudes, think every day that shines upon you is the last. Thus the hour, which shall not be expected, will come upon you an agreeable addition.

Ibid. iv, Line 12

When you have a mind to laugh, you shall see me, fat and sleek with good keeping, a hog of Epicurus' herd.

Ibid. Line 15

As soon as a man perceives how much the things he has discarded excel those which he pursues, let him return in time, and resume those which he relinquished.

Ibid. vii, Line 96

You may drive out nature with a fork, yet still she will return.

Ibid. x, Line 24

Whatever prosperous hour Providence bestows upon you, receive it with a thankful hand: and defer not the enjoyment of the comforts of life.

Ibid. xi, Line 22

They change their climate, not their disposition, who run beyond the sea.

Ibid. Line 27

That man is by no means poor, who has the use of everything he wants. If it is well with your belly, your back, and your feet, regal wealth can add nothing greater.

Ibid. xii, Line 4

Joys are not the property of the rich alone: nor has he lived ill, who at his birth and at his death has passed unnoticed.

Epistles. Book I, xvii, Line 9

To have been acceptable to the great is not the last of praises. It is not every man's lot to gain Corinth.[1]

Ibid. Line 35

The man who makes the experiment deservedly claims the honour and the reward.

Ibid. Line 42

A word, once sent abroad, flies irrevocably.[2]

Ibid. xviii, Line 70

And seek for truth in the groves of Academe.

Ibid. Book II, ii, Line 45

I have to submit to much in order to pacify the touchy tribe of poets.

Ibid. Line 102

Poets desire either to teach or to give pleasure.

Ibid. iii, Line 333

Men ever had, and ever will have, leave
To coin new words well suited to the age.
Words are like leaves, some wither ev'ry year,
And ev'ry year a younger race succeeds.

Ars Poetica.[3] Line 73

For Nature forms, and softens us within,
And writes our fortune's changes in our face.

Ibid. Line 130

The lab'ring mountain scarce brings forth a mouse.[4]

Ibid. Line 168

Old men are only walking hospitals.

Ibid. Line 202

---

[1] Translated by ALEXANDER POPE.
Get money; still get money, boy,
No matter by what means.
BEN JONSON: *Every Man in His Humour* [1598], Act II, Sc. 3

[1] 'Tis not every one who can afford to go to Corinth. — PLUTARCH [A.D. 46–120]: *Parallel Lives, Aristophanes*
There is but one road that leads to Corinth. —WALTER PATER: *Marius the Epicurean* [1885], Chap. 24
"There is but one way to Corinth," as of old. — ANDREW LANG: *Letters to Dead Authors* [1886], *To Lucian of Samosata*
[2] See *Ars Poetica, L. 438*, page 42a.
[3] Translated [1680] by the EARL OF ROSCOMMON.
[4] Parturient montes, nascetur ridiculus mus.

Five acts are the just measure of a play.
Ars Poetica. Line 226
And in one scene no more than three
should speak.
Ibid. Line 229
Whatever you teach, be brief, that
your readers' minds may readily com-
prehend and faithfully retain your
words. Everything superfluous slips
from the full heart.
Ibid. Line 335
He has carried every point who has
mingled profit with pleasure.
Ibid. Line 343
A string may jar in the best master's
hand,
And the most skilful archer miss his
aim.
Ibid. Line 387
Homer himself hath been observ'd to
nod.[1]
Ibid. Line 402
But words once spoke can never be re-
call'd.[2]
Ibid. Line 438
'Tis hard to find a man of great estate,
That can distinguish flatterers from
friends.
Ibid. Line 478
True friends appear less mov'd than
counterfeit;
As men that truly grieve at funerals
Are not so loud, as those that cry for
hire.
Ibid. Line 484

PROPERTIUS
[54 B. C.–A. D. 2]

Never change when love has found
its home.
Book I. Elegy 1, Line 36

[1] Indignor quandoque bonus dormitat
Homerus.
See Pope, page 310b.
[2] Thoughts unexpressed may sometimes fall
back dead;
But God himself can't kill them when
they're said.
WILL CARLETON [1845-1912]: *The
First Settler's Story*
Four things come not back: the spoken
word; the sped arrow; time past; the neg-

Let each man pass his days in that
wherein his skill is greatest.
Book II. Elegy 1, Line 46
Scandal has ever been the doom of
beauty.
Ibid. Elegy 32, Line 26

OVID
[43 B. C.–A. D. 18]

Every lover's a soldier and Cupid
has his camps.
Amores. I, ix, Line 1
They come to see; they come that
they themselves may be seen.[1]
The Art of Love. I, Line 99
It is expedient that there be gods,
and, as it's expedient, let us believe
there are.[2]
Ibid. Line 637
To be loved, be lovable.
Ibid. II, Line 107
Nothing is stronger than custom.
Ibid. Line 345
What you desire is not mortal.
Metamorphoses. II, Line 55
You will go most safely in the middle.
Ibid. Line 137
I see and approve better things, but
follow worse.[3]
Ibid. VII, Line 20
Poetry comes fine spun from a mind
at peace.
Tristia. Book I, Chap. 1, Line 39

lected opportunity. — OMAR IBN AL-HALIF:
Aphorism
[1] Spectatum veniunt, veniunt spectentur ut
ipsae.
And for to see, and eek for to be seye. —
CHAUCER: *The Canterbury Tales* [circa 1387],
The Wife of Bath's Prologue, L. 552
To see and to be seen. — BEN JONSON
[1573?-1637]: *Epithalamion, St. III, L. 4*
To see, be seen, to tell, and gather tales. —
POPE: *Paraphrases from Chaucer, The Wife
of Bath* [1714], *L. 282*
[2] See Voltaire, page 325b.
[3] Video meliora, proboque; deteriora se-
quor.
I know and love the good, yet, ah! the
worst pursue. — PETRARCH: *Sonnet CCXXV,
Canzone XXI, To Laura in Life* [circa 1327]
The better I see and approve, the worse I
follow. — SPINOZA'S translation in *Ethics*
[1677], *Part IV*
See Euripides, page 17a, and *Romans, VII,
19*, on page 1060a.

While fortune smiles you'll have a host
of friends,
But they'll desert you when the storm
descends.[1]
> *Tristia. Book I, Chap. 9, Line 5*

It is annoying to be honest to no
purpose.
> *Epistolae ex Ponto. Book II,*
> *Chap. 3, Line 14*

Note too that a faithful study of the
liberal arts humanizes character and
permits it not to be cruel.
> *Ibid. Chap. 9, Line 47*

Grateful must we be that the heart
may go whithersoever it will.
> *Ibid. Book III, Chap. 5, Line 48*

How little you know about the age
you live in if you fancy that honey is
sweeter than cash in hand.
> *Fasti. Book I, Line 191*

Janus. I bar the doors in time of
peace, lest peace depart.
> *Ibid. Line 279*

PUBLILIUS SYRUS [2]
[*Circa* 42 B.C.]

As men, we are all equal in the presence of death.
> *Maxim 1*

To do two things at once is to do
neither.
> *Maxim 7*

We are interested in others when they
are interested in us.[3]
> *Maxim 16*

Every one excels in something in
which another fails.
> *Maxim 17*

A god could hardly love and be wise.[4]
> *Maxim 25*

The loss which is unknown is no loss
at all.[5]
> *Maxim 38*

He sleeps well who knows not that
he sleeps ill.
> *Maxim 77*

A good reputation is more valuable
than money.[1]
> *Maxim 108*

It is well to moor your bark with two
anchors.
> *Maxim 119*

Learn to see in another's calamity the
ills which you should avoid.[2]
> *Maxim 120*

An agreeable companion on a journey
is as good as a carriage.
> *Maxim 143*

Society in shipwreck is a comfort to
all.[3]
> *Maxim 144*

Many receive advice, few profit by it.
> *Maxim 149*

While we stop to think, we often
miss our opportunity.
> *Maxim 185*

Whatever you can lose, you should
reckon of no account.
> *Maxim 191*

Even a single hair casts its shadow.
> *Maxim 228*

It is sometimes expedient to forget
who we are.
> *Maxim 233*

We may with advantage at times forget what we know.
> *Maxim 234*

Crime is honest for a good cause.[4]
> *Maxim 244*

You should hammer your iron when
it is glowing hot.[5]
> *Maxim 262*

---

[1] See Cicero, page 33b.

[2] Commonly called Publius, but spelled Publilius by PLINY in his *Natural History, 35,
Sect. 199.* Translated by DARIUS LYMAN. The
numbers are those of the translator.

[3] We always like those who admire us; we
do not always like those whom we admire. —
LA ROCHEFOUCAULD [1613–1680]: *Maxim 294*

[4] It is impossible to love and be wise. —
BACON: *Essays* [1597–1625], *Of Love*

[5] See Shakespeare, page 188b.

[1] See *Ecclesiastes, VII, 1*, on page 1042b, and
Bacon, page 120a.
A good name is better than riches. — CER-
VANTES: *Don Quixote, Part II* [1615], *Book
II, Chap. 33*

[2] The best plan is, as the common proverb
has it, to profit by the folly of others. —
PLINY [A.D. 23–79]: *Natural History, 18,
Sect. 31*

[3] See *Maxim 995*, page 46b.

[4] Honesta turpitudo est pro causa bona.
(The above is not Lyman's but a literal translation.)

[5] When the iron is hot, strike. — JOHN

What is left when honour is lost?
Maxim 265

A fair exterior is a silent recommendation.
Maxim 267

Fortune is not satisfied with inflicting one calamity.
Maxim 274

When Fortune is on our side, popular favour bears her company.
Maxim 275

When Fortune flatters, she does it to betray.[1]
Maxim 277

Fortune is like glass, — the brighter the glitter, the more easily broken.
Maxim 280

It is more easy to get a favour from Fortune than to keep it.
Maxim 282

An overtaxed patience gives way to fury.[2]
Maxim 289

There are some remedies worse than the disease.[3]
Maxim 301

Powerful indeed is the empire of habit.[4]
Maxim 305

Amid a multitude of projects, no plan is devised.[5]
Maxim 319

It is easy for men to talk one thing and think another.
Maxim 322

HEYWOOD: *Proverbes* [1546], *Part I, Chap. II*
Strike whilst the iron is hot. — RABELAIS: *Book II* [1534], *Chap. 31*
Nothing like striking while the iron is hot. — CERVANTES: *Don Quixote, Part II* [1615], *Book IV, Chap. 71*

[1] See Shakespeare, page 148a.

[2] See Dryden, page 277b.

[3] Marius said, "I see the cure is not worth the pain." — PLUTARCH [A.D. 46-120]: *Lives, Caius Marius*
The remedy is worse than the disease. — BACON: *Essays* [1597-1625], *Of Seditions*
I find the medicine worse than the malady. — BEAUMONT AND FLETCHER: *Love's Cure* [1647], *Act III, Sc. 2*

[4] See Plutarch, page 60a.

[5] He that hath many irons in the fire, some of them will cool. — HAZLITT: *English Proverbs*

When two do the same thing, it is not the same thing after all.
Maxim 338

A cock has great influence on his own dunghill.[1]
Maxim 357

Any one can hold the helm when the sea is calm.[2]
Maxim 358

No tears are shed when an enemy dies.
Maxim 376

The bow too tensely strung is easily broken.
Maxim 388

Treat your friend as if he might become an enemy.[3]
Maxim 402

No pleasure endures unseasoned by variety.[4]
Maxim 406

The judge is condemned when the criminal is absolved.[5]
Maxim 407

Practice is the best of all instructors.[6]
Maxim 439

He who is bent on doing evil can never want occasion.
Maxim 459

Never find your delight in another's misfortune.
Maxim 467

It is a bad plan that admits of no modification.
Maxim 469

It is better to have a little than nothing.
Maxim 484

----

[1] Every cocke is proud on his owne dunghill. — JOHN HEYWOOD: *Proverbes* [1546] *Part I, Chap. XI*

[2] See Shakespeare, page 181a.

[3] Treat your friend as if he will one day be your enemy, and your enemy as if he will one day be your friend. — LABERIUS [105-43 B.C.]: *Fragment*

[4] See Cowper, page 364a.

[5] Judex damnatur cum nocens absolvitur — the motto adopted for the *Edinburgh Review*.

[6] Practice makes perfect. — *Proverb*
The saying, "Practice is everything," is Periander's. — DIOGENES LAERTIUS [*circa* 200 A.D.]: *Periander, 6*

It is an unhappy lot which finds no enemies.

Maxim 499

The fear of death is more to be dreaded than death itself.[1]

Maxim 511

A rolling stone gathers no moss.[2]

Maxim 524

Never promise more than you can perform.

Maxim 528

A wise man never refuses anything to necessity.[3]

Maxim 540

No one should be judge in his own cause.[4]

Maxim 545

Necessity knows no law except to conquer.[5]

Maxim 553

Nothing can be done at once hastily and prudently.[6]

Maxim 557

We desire nothing so much as what we ought not to have.

Maxim 559

It is only the ignorant who despise education.

Maxim 571

Do not turn back when you are just at the goal.[7]

Maxim 580

It is not every question that deserves an answer.

Maxim 581

No man is happy who does not think himself so.[1]

Maxim 584

Never thrust your own sickle into another's corn.[2]

Maxim 593

You cannot put the same shoe on every foot.

Maxim 596

He bids fair to grow wise who has discovered that he is not so.

Maxim 598

Every day should be passed as if it were to be our last.[3]

Maxim 633

Money alone sets all the world in motion.

Maxim 656

He who has plenty of pepper will pepper his cabbage.

Maxim 673

You should go to a pear-tree for pears, not to an elm.[4]

Maxim 674

It is a very hard undertaking to seek to please everybody.

Maxim 675

Look for a tough wedge for a tough log.

Maxim 723

How happy the life unembarrassed by the cares of business!

Maxim 725

---

[1] See Shakespeare, page 184b.
[2] The rolling stone never gathereth mosse. — JOHN HEYWOOD: *Proverbes* [1546], *Part I, Chap. XI*
The stone that is rolling can gather no moss. — TUSSER: *Five Hundred Points of Good Husbandry* [1557]
[3] Yet do I hold that mortal foolish who strives against the stress of necessity. — EURIPIDES [480–406 B.C.]: *Mad Heracles, L. 281*
[4] It is not permitted to the most equitable of men to be a judge in his own cause. — PASCAL [1623–1662]: *Pensées, Chap. 4, 1*
[5]   And with necessity,
The tyrant's plea, excus'd his devilish deeds.
            MILTON: *Paradise Lost* [1667], *Book IV, L. 393*
Necessity is the argument of tyrants, it is the creed of slaves. — WILLIAM PITT: *Speech on the India Bill* [November, 1783]
[6] See Chaucer, page 82a, and Heywood, page 90b.
[7] When men are arrived at the goal, they

should not turn back. — PLUTARCH [A. D. 46–120]: *Of the Training of Children*
[1] No man can enjoy happiness without thinking that he enjoys it. — SAMUEL JOHNSON [1709–1784]: *The Rambler*
[2] Did thrust as now in others' corn his sickle. — DU BARTAS: *Divine Weekes and Workes* [1578], *Part II, Second Weeke*
Not presuming to put my sickle in another man's corn. — NICHOLAS YONGE: *Musica Transalpina, Epistle Dedicatory* [1588]
[3] Thou wilt find rest from vain fancies if thou doest every act in life as though it were thy last. — MARCUS AURELIUS [A. D. 121–180]: *Meditations, II, 5*
[4] You may as well expect pears from an elm. — CERVANTES: *Don Quixote, Part II* [1615], *Book IV, Chap. 40*

Pardon one offence, and you encourage the commission of many.
Maxim 750

They who plough the sea do not carry the winds in their hands.[1]
Maxim 759

He gets through too late who goes too fast.
Maxim 767

In every enterprise consider where you would come out.[2]
Maxim 777

It takes a long time to bring excellence to maturity.
Maxim 780

The highest condition takes rise in the lowest.
Maxim 781

It matters not what you are thought to be, but what you are.
Maxim 785

No one knows what he can do till he tries.
Maxim 786

The next day is never so good as the day before.
Maxim 815

Good health and good sense are two of life's greatest blessings.
Maxim 827

It matters not how long you live, but how well.
Maxim 829

It is vain to look for a defence against lightning.
Maxim 835

Everything is worth what its purchaser will pay for it.[3]
Maxim 847

It is better to learn late than never.[1]
Maxim 864

Better be ignorant of a matter than half know it.[2]
Maxim 865

Better use medicines at the outset than at the last moment.[3]
Maxim 866

Prosperity makes friends, adversity tries them.
Maxim 872

Let a fool hold his tongue and he will pass for a sage.
Maxim 914

He knows not when to be silent who knows not when to speak.
Maxim 930

You need not hang up the ivy-branch over the wine that will sell.[4]
Maxim 968

It is a consolation to the wretched to have companions in misery.[5]
Maxim 995

Unless degree is preserved, the first place is safe for no one.[6]
Maxim 1042

Confession of our faults is the next thing to innocency.
Maxim 1060

I have often regretted my speech, never my silence.[7]
Maxim 1070

---

[1] The pilot cannot mitigate the billows or calm the winds. — PLUTARCH [A.D. 46–120]: *Of the Tranquillity of the Mind*

[2] In every affair, consider what precedes and what follows, and then undertake it. — EPICTETUS [*circa* A.D. 60]: *That Everything Is to be Undertaken with Circumspection, Chap. 15*

[3]   What is worth in anything
    But so much money as 'twill bring?
    BUTLER: *Hudibras, Part I* [1663], *Canto I, L. 465*

[1] See Shakespeare, page 145b.

[2] See Pope, page 310b.

[3] A stitch in time saves nine. — *Old Proverb*

[4] Good wine needs no bush. — SHAKESPEARE: *As You Like It* [1598–1600], *Epilogue, L. 4*
Good wine needs neither bush nor preface
To make it welcome.
    SIR WALTER SCOTT: *Peveril of the Peak* [1822], *Chap. 4*

[5] See *Maxim 144,* page 43b.
'Tis the only comfort of the miserable to have partners in their woes. — CERVANTES: *Don Quixote, Part I* [1605], *Book III, Chap. 10*
It is a comfort to the unhappy to have companions in misery. — SPINOZA: *Ethics* [1677], *Part 4, Proposition 57, Note*

[6] See Shakespeare, page 181a.

[7] Simonides said that "he never repented that he held his tongue, but often that he had spoken." — PLUTARCH [A.D. 46–120]: *Rules for the Preservation of Health*

Speech is a mirror of the soul: as a man speaks, so is he.
Maxim 1073

SENECA [1]
[8 B. C.–A. D. 65]

What fools these mortals be.[2]
Epistles. 1, 3

It is not the man who has too little, but the man who craves more, that is poor.
Ibid. 2, 2

Love of bustle is not industry.
Ibid. 3, 5

Live among men as if God beheld you; speak to God as if men were listening.
Ibid. 10, 5

The best ideas are common property.
Ibid. 12, 11

Men do not care how nobly they live, but only how long, although it is within the reach of every man to live nobly, but within no man's power to live long.
Ibid. 22, 17

A great pilot can sail even when his canvas is rent.
Ibid. 30, 3

Man is a reasoning animal.
Ibid. 41, 8

That most knowing of persons, — gossip.
Ibid. 43, 1

It is quality rather than quantity that matters.
Ibid. 45, 1

You can tell the character of every man when you see how he receives praise.
Ibid. 52, 12

Nothing is so certain as that the evils of idleness can be shaken off by hard work.
Ibid. 56, 9

Not lost, but gone before.[3]
Ibid. 63, 16

[1] Translated by W. H. D. ROUSE.
[2] Tanta stultitia mortalium est.
See Shakespeare, page 142a.
[3] Non amittuntur, sed praemittuntur.
Not dead, but gone before. — SAMUEL ROGERS: *Human Life* [1819]

All art is but imitation of nature.
Epistles. 65, 3

It is a rough road that leads to the heights of greatness.
Ibid. 84, 13

The pilot . . . who has been able to say, "Neptune, you shall never sink this ship except on an even keel," has fulfilled the requirements of his art.[1]
Ibid. 85, 33

I was shipwrecked before I got aboard.
Ibid. 87, 1

It is better, of course, to know useless things than to know nothing.
Ibid. 88, 45

Do not ask for what you will wish you had not got.
Ibid. 95, 1

We are mad, not only individually, but nationally. We check manslaughter and isolated murders; but what of war and the much vaunted crime of slaughtering whole peoples?
Ibid. 95, 30

A great step towards independence is a good-humored stomach.
Ibid. 123, 3

Fire is the test of gold; adversity, of strong men.[2]
Moral Essays. On Providence, 5, 9

Whom they have injured they also hate.[3]
Ibid. On Anger, 2, 33

I do not distinguish by the eye, but

[1] The mariner of old said thus to Neptune in a great tempest, "O God! thou mayest save me if thou wilt, and if thou wilt, thou mayest destroy me; but whether or no, I will steer my rudder true." — MONTAIGNE: *Essays* [1580–1595], *Book II, Chap. 16*
[2] See Beaumont and Fletcher, page 228a.
[3] It belongs to human nature to hate those you have injured. — TACITUS [A. D. 54–119]: *Agricola, 42, 15*
Chi fa ingiuria non perdona mai (He never pardons those he injures). — *Italian Proverb*
The offender never pardons. — GEORGE HERBERT: *Jacula Prudentum* [1640]
Forgiveness to the injured does belong;
But they ne'er pardon who have done the wrong.
DRYDEN: *The Conquest of Granada* [1670], *Part II, Act I, Sc. 2*

by the mind, which is the proper judge of the man.
> *Moral Essays. On the Happy Life, 2, 2*

There is no great genius without some touch of madness.[1]
> *Ibid. On Tranquillity of the Mind, 17, 10*

A great fortune is a great slavery.
> *Ibid. To Polybius on Consolation, 6, 5*

Wherever the Roman conquers, there he dwells.
> *Ibid. To Helvia on Consolation, 7, 7*

He who receives a benefit with gratitude, repays the first instalment on his debt.
> *On Benefits. Book 2, 22, 1*

You roll my log, and I will roll yours.
> *Apocolocyntosis. Chap. 9*

Do you seek Alcides' equal? None is, except himself.[2]
> *Hercules Furens. 1, 1, 84*

Successful and fortunate crime is called virtue.[3]
> *Ibid. 255*

A good mind possesses a kingdom.[4]
> *Thyestes. 380*

---

[1] An ancient commonplace, which Seneca says he quotes from ARISTOTLE: No excellent soul is exempt from a mixture of madness. *Problemata, 30, 1.* It is also in PLATO: *Phaedrus, 245 A.*
Good sense travels on the well-worn paths; genius, never. And that is why the crowd, not altogether without reason, is so ready to treat great men as lunatics. — CESARE LOMBROSO [1836–1909]: *The Man of Genius, Preface*
See Dryden, page 276b.
[2] None but himself can be his parallel. — LEWIS THEOBALD [1688–1744]: *The Double Falsehood*
And but herself admits no parallel. — MASSINGER [1583–1640]: *Duke of Milan, Act IV, Sc. 3*
[3] Treason doth never prosper; what's the reason?
Why, if it prosper, none dare call it treason.
SIR JOHN HARINGTON [1561–1612]:
> *Epigrams, Of Treason*
[4] See Dyer, page 101b.

Light griefs are loquacious, but the great are dumb.[1]
> *Hippolytus. II, 3, 607*

PHAEDRUS [2]
[*Circa* A. D. 8]

Submit to the present evil, lest a greater one befall you.
> *Book I. Fable 2, 31*

He who covets what belongs to another deservedly loses his own.
> *Ibid. Fable 4, 1*

That it is unwise to be heedless ourselves while we are giving advice to others, I will show in a few lines.
> *Ibid. Fable 9, 1*

Whoever has even once become notorious by base fraud, even if he speaks the truth, gains no belief.
> *Ibid. Fable 10, 1*

By this story [The Fox and the Raven] it is shown how much ingenuity avails, and how wisdom is always an overmatch for strength.
> *Ibid. Fable 13, 13*

No one returns with good-will to the place which has done him a mischief.
> *Ibid. Fable 18, 1*

It has been related that dogs drink at the river Nile running along, that they may not be seized by the crocodiles.[3]
> *Ibid. Fable 25, 3*

Every one is bound to bear patiently the results of his own example.
> *Ibid. Fable 26, 12*

Come of it what may, as Sinon said.
> *Book III. The Prologue, 27*

Things are not always what they seem.[4]
> *Book IV. Fable 2, 5*

---

[1] See Montaigne, page 97b.
[2] Translated by HENRY THOMAS RILEY [1816–1878].
[3] PLINY, in his *Natural History, Book 8, Sect. 148*, and AELIAN, in his *Various Histories*, relate the same fact as to the dogs drinking from the Nile. "To treat a thing as the dogs do the Nile" was a common proverb with the ancients, signifying to do it superficially.
[4] Non semper ea sunt quae videntur.
See Longfellow, page 521a, and W. S. Gilbert, page 682b.

"1 knew that before you were born."
Let him who would instruct a wiser
man consider this as said to himself.
Book V. Fable 9, 4

PLINY THE ELDER [1]
[A. D. 23–79]

In comparing various authors with
one another, I have discovered that
some of the gravest and latest writers
have transcribed, word for word, from
former works, without making acknowledgment.
Natural History. Book I,
Dedication, Sect. 22

It is ridiculous to suppose that the
great head of things, whatever it be,
pays any regard to human affairs.
Ibid. Book II, Sect. 20

Everything is soothed by oil, and
this is the reason why divers send out
small quantities of it from their mouths,
because it smooths every part which is
rough.[2]
Ibid. Sect. 234

It is far from easy to determine
whether she [Nature] has proved to
him a kind parent or a merciless step-
mother.[3]
Ibid. Book VII, Sect. 1

[1] With some alterations, translated by JOHN
BOSTOCK [1773–1846] and HENRY THOMAS
RILEY [1816–1878].

[2] Why does pouring oil on the sea make it
clear and calm? Is it for that the winds, slip-
ping the smooth oil, have no force, nor cause
any waves? — PLUTARCH [A. D. 46–120]: *Natural Questions, IX*

Bishop Adain [A. D. 651] gave to a company
about to take a journey by sea "some holy oil,
saying, 'I know that when you go abroad you
will meet with a storm and contrary wind;
but do you remember to cast this oil I give
you into the sea, and the wind shall cease immediately.' " — BEDE [673–735]: *Ecclesiastical History, Book III, Chap. 14*

In JARED SPARKS's edition of BENJAMIN
FRANKLIN's *Works, Vol. VI, P. 354,* there are
letters between Franklin, Brownrigg, and Parish on the stilling of waves by means of oil.

[3] To man the earth seems altogether
No more a mother, but a step-dame
rather.
DU BARTAS [1544–1590]: *Divine
Weekes and Workes, First Weeke,
Third Day*

Man alone at the very moment of
his birth, cast naked upon the naked
earth, does she abandon to cries and
lamentations.[1]
Natural History. Book VII,
Sect. 2

To laugh, if but for an instant only,
has never been granted to man before
the fortieth day from his birth, and then
it is looked upon as a miracle of precocity.[2]
Ibid.

Man is the only one that knows nothing, that can learn nothing without being taught. He can neither speak nor
walk nor eat, and in short he can do
nothing at the prompting of nature
only, but weep.[3]
Ibid. Sect. 4

With man, most of his misfortunes
are occasioned by man.[4]
Ibid. Sect. 5

Indeed, what is there that does not
appear marvellous when it comes to our
knowledge for the first time? [5] How
many things, too, are looked upon as
quite impossible until they have been
actually effected?
Ibid. Sect. 6

The human features and countenance, although composed of but some
ten parts or little more, are so fashioned
that among so many thousands of men
there are no two in existence who can-

[1] He is born naked, and falls a-whining at
the first. — ROBERT BURTON: *Anatomy of
Melancholy* [1621–1651], *Part I, Sect. 2,
Memb. 3, Subsect. 10*

And when I was born, I drew in the common air, and fell upon the earth, which is of
like nature; and the first voice which I uttered was crying, as all others do. — *The Wisdom of Solomon, VII, 3*

It was the custom among the ancients to
place the newborn child upon the ground immediately after its birth.

[2] This term of forty days is mentioned by
ARISTOTLE in his *Natural History.*

[3] See Tennyson, page 552a.

[4] See Burns, page 390a.

[5] Omne ignotum pro magnifico (Everything that is unknown is taken to be grand).
— TACITUS [A.D. 54–119]: *Agricola, 30*

not be distinguished from one another.[1]
Natural History. Book VII,
Sect. 8

All men possess in their bodies a poison which acts upon serpents; and the human saliva, it is said, makes them take to flight, as though they had been touched with boiling water. The same substance, it is said, destroys them the moment it enters their throat.[2]

Ibid. Sect. 15

It has been observed that the height of a man from the crown of the head to the sole of the foot is equal to the distance between the tips of the middle fingers of the two hands when extended in a straight line.

Ibid. Sect. 77

When a building is about to fall down, all the mice desert it.[3]

Ibid. Book VIII, Sect. 103

Bears when first born are shapeless masses of white flesh a little larger than mice, their claws alone being prominent. The mother then licks them gradually into proper shape.[4]

Ibid. Sect. 126

Cincinnatus was ploughing his four

[1] It is the common wonder of all men, how among so many millions of faces there should be none alike. — SIR THOMAS BROWNE: *Religio Medici* [1642], *Part II, Sect. II*
Of a thousand shavers, two do not shave so much alike as not to be distinguished. — JOHNSON [1777]: *Boswell's Life, Vol. II, P. 120, Everyman ed.*
See Montaigne, page 99b.
[2] MADAME D'ABRANTES relates that when Bonaparte was in Cairo he sent for a serpent-detector (Psylli) to remove two serpents that had been seen in his house. He, having enticed one of them from his hiding place, caught it in one hand, just below the jaw-bone, in such a manner as to oblige the mouth to open, when, spitting into it, the effect was like magic: the reptile appeared struck with instant death. — *Memoirs, Vol. I, Chap. 59*
[3] This is alluded to by CICERO in his letters to Atticus, and is mentioned by AELIAN (*Animated Nature, Book VI, Chap. 41*). Compare the modern proverb, "Rats desert a sinking ship."
[4] Not unlike the bear which bringeth forth
In the end of thirty dayes a shapeless birth;
But after licking, it in shape she drawes,
And by degrees she fashions out the pawes,

jugera of land upon the Vaticanian Hill, — the same that are still known as the Quintian Meadows, — when the messenger brought him the dictatorship, finding him, the tradition says, stripped to the work.

Natural History. Book XVIII,
Sect. 20

The agricultural population, says Cato, produces the bravest men, the most valiant soldiers, and a class of citizens the least given of all to evil designs.

Ibid. Sect. 26

Why is it that we entertain the belief that for every purpose odd numbers are the most effectual?[1]

Ibid. Book XXVIII, Sect. 23

It was a custom with Apelles, to which he most tenaciously adhered, never to let any day pass, however busy he might be, without exercising himself by tracing some outline or other, — a practice which has now passed into a proverb.[2] It was also a practice with him, when he had completed a work, to exhibit it to the view of the passers-by in his studio, while he himself, concealed behind the picture, would listen to the criticisms. . . . Under these circumstances, they say that he was censured by a shoemaker for having represented the shoes with one latchet too few. The next day, the shoemaker, quite proud at seeing the former error corrected, thanks to his advice, began to

The head, and neck, and finally doth bring
To a perfect beast that first deformed thing.
DU BARTAS: *Divine Weekes and Workes* [1578], *First Weeke, First Day*
I had not time to lick it into form, as a bear doth her young ones. — ROBERT BURTON: *Anatomy of Melancholy* [1621-1651], *Democritus to the Reader*
See Montaigne, page 99a.
[1] The god delights in an odd number. — VIRGIL [70-19 B.C.]: *Eclogues, 8, 75*
See Shakespeare, page 180b, and Samuel Lover, page 485b.
[2] Nulla dies abeat, quin linea ducta supersit. --- ERASMUS [1465-1536]. Generally quoted, Nulla dies sine linea (No day without a line).

criticize the leg; upon which Apelles, full of indignation, popped his head out and reminded him that a shoemaker should give no opinion beyond the shoes,[1] — a piece of advice which has equally passed into a proverbial saying.

Natural History. Book XXXV, Sect. 84

LUCAN [2]
[A. D. 39–65]

The conqueror's cause found favor with the gods, the conquered's with Cato.

The Civil War. Book I, Line 128

He stands the shadow of a mighty name.

Ibid. Line 135

Poverty, the mother of manhood.

Ibid. Line 165

Delay is ever fatal to those who are prepared.

Ibid. Line 281

When the whole world is nodding to its fall, happy the man who has been able to learn already the lowly place appointed for him.

Ibid. Book IV, Line 393

Boldness is a mask for fear, however great.

Ibid. Line 702

Yonder trouble concerns the sky and sea, but not our bark; for Caesar treads the deck.[3]

Ibid. Book V, Line 584

PETRONIUS [ARBITER]
[Died *circa* A. D. 66]

Beware of the dog.[4]

Satyricon. Sect. 29

Without why or wherefore.

Ibid. Sect. 37

A man who is always ready to believe what is told him will never do well.

Ibid. Sect. 43

[1] Ne supra crepidam sutor judicaret (Let not a shoemaker judge above his shoe), or, Let the cobbler stick to his last.
[2] Translated by J. D. DUFF.
[3] See Plutarch, page 56b.
[4] Found with picture of a dog on a mosaic door in Pompeii.

One good turn deserves another.

Satyricon. Sect. 45

A man must have his faults.

Ibid.

Not worth his salt.

Ibid. Sect. 57

My heart was in my mouth.

Ibid. Sect. 62

Beauty and wisdom are rarely conjoined.

Ibid. Sect. 94

The careful felicity of Horace.

Ibid. Sect. 118

DIO CHRYSOSTOM [1]
[A. D. 40–120]

Diogenes: The man I know not, for I am not acquainted with his mind.

Fourth Discourse on Kingship. Chap. 17

Idleness and lack of occupation are the best things in the world to ruin the foolish.

Tenth Discourse, On Servants. Chap. 7

Like men with sore eyes: they find the light painful, while the darkness, which permits them to see nothing, is restful and agreeable.

Eleventh, or Trojan, Discourse. Chap. 2

Most men are so completely corrupted by opinion that they would rather be notorious for the greatest calamities than suffer no ill and be unknown.

Ibid. Chap. 6

Generally speaking, men are too cowardly to be willing to undergo severe suffering, since they fear death and pain, but they highly prize being mentioned as having suffered.

Ibid. Chap. 10

MARTIAL
[A. D. 40–102]

To yield to the stronger is valor's second prize.

On the Spectacles. Epigram 32

[1] Translated by J. W. COHOON.

I write long epigrams, you yourself write nothing. Yours are shorter.[1]

Epigrams. Book I, 110

Nothing is more confident than a bad poet.[2]

Ibid. Book II, 63

He does not write at all whose poems no man reads.

Ibid. Book III, 9

The flaw which is hidden is deemed greater than it is.

Ibid. 52

The bee enclosed and through the amber shown
Seems buried in the juice which was his own.[3]

Ibid. Book IV, 32

They pass and are charged against us.[4]

Ibid. Book V, 20

What is the use of brevity if it constitute a book?

Ibid. Book VIII, 29

The good man prolongs his life; to be able to enjoy one's past life is to live twice.[5]

Ibid. Book X, 23

---

[1] An epigram of two lines has every merit, and if you exceed three lines it is rhapsody. — CYRILLUS: *The Greek Anthology, Book 9, Epigram 369*

[2] Quoted by MONTAIGNE in *Of Presumption.*

[3] Whence we see spiders, flies, or ants entombed and preserved forever in amber, a more than royal tomb. — FRANCIS BACON: *Historia Vitae et Mortis* [1623], *Sylva Sylvarum, Cent. I, Exper. 100*

I saw a flie within a beade
Of amber cleanly buried.
HERRICK [1591–1674]: *On a Fly Buried in Amber*
See Pope, page 318b.

[4] Of the days and hours.

[5] Thus would I double my life's fading space;
For he that runs it well, runs twice his race.
COWLEY [1618–1667]: *Discourse XI, Of Myself, St. XI*
For he lives twice who can at once employ
The present well, and ev'n the past enjoy.
POPE [1688–1744]: *Imitation of Martial*

Neither fear, nor wish for, your last day.[1]

Epigrams. Book X, 47

There is no glory in outstripping donkeys.

Ibid. Book XII, 36

I can't live with you or without you.

Ibid. 47

The country in town.[2]

Ibid. 57

QUINTILIAN
[A. D. 42–118]

We give to necessity the praise of virtue.[3]

Institutiones Oratoriae. Book I, 8, 14

A liar should have a good memory.[4]

Ibid. Book IV, 2, 91

Vain hopes are often like the dreams of those who wake.

Ibid. Book VI, 2, 30

Those who wish to appear wise among fools, among the wise seem foolish.[5]

Ibid. Book X, 7, 21

---

[1] Nor love thy life, nor hate; but what thou liv'st
Live well; how long or short permit to Heaven.
MILTON: *Paradise Lost* [1667], *Book XI, L. 553*

[2] Rus in urbe.

[3] In the additions of Hadrianus Julius to the *Adages* of ERASMUS, he remarks, under the head of *Necessitatem edere*, that a very familiar proverb was current among his countrymen — "Necessitatem in virtutem commutare" (To make necessity a virtue).
Thus maketh vertue of necessitee. — CHAUCER: *Troilus and Criseyde* [1372–1386], *Book IV, L. 1586*
Others made a virtue of necessity. — RABELAIS: *Works, Book V* [1552], *Chap. 23*
Make a virtue of necessity. — ROBERT BURTON: *Anatomy of Melancholy* [1621–1651], *Part III, Sect. 3, Memb. 4, Subsect. I*

[4] He who has not a good memory should never take upon him the trade of lying. — MONTAIGNE: *Essays* [1580–1595], *Book I, Chap. IX, Of Liars*
Il faut bonne mémoire, après qu'on a menti. — CORNEILLE: *Le Menteur* [1642], *Act IV, Sc. 5*
Liars ought to have good memories. — ALGERNON SIDNEY: *Discourses on Government* [1698], *Chap. 2, Sect. XV*

[5] A wit with dunces, and a dunce with

PLUTARCH [1]
[A. D. 46–120]

As geographers, Sosius, crowd into the edges of their maps parts of the world which they do not know about, adding notes in the margin to the effect that beyond this lies nothing but sandy deserts full of wild beasts, and unapproachable bogs.[2]

Lives. Theseus, Page 3

From Theseus began the saying, "He is a second Hercules."

Ibid. Page 19

Caesar said he loved the treason, but hated the traitor.[3]

Ibid. Romulus, Page 36

The most perfect soul, says Heraclitus, is a dry light, which flies out of the body as lightning breaks from a cloud.

Ibid. Page 45

Anacharsis, coming to Athens, knocked at Solon's door, and told him that he, being a stranger, was come to be his guest, and contract a friendship with him; and Solon replying, "It is better to make friends at home," Ana-

---

wits. — POPE: *Dunciad* [1728], *Book IV, L. 90*
  A fool with judges, amongst fools a judge.
— COWPER: *Conversation* [1782], *L. 298*
  This man [Chesterfield], I thought, had been a lord among wits; but I find he is only a wit among lords. — SAMUEL JOHNSON: *Boswell's Life* [1791], *Vol. I, P. 159, Everyman ed.*
  [1] Modern Library Giant edition.
  [2] So geographers, in Afric maps,
  With savage pictures fill their gaps,
  And o'er unhabitable downs
  Place elephants for want of towns.
    SWIFT: *On Poetry, A Rhapsody* [1733]
  [3] Princes in this case do hate the traitor, though they love the treason. — SAMUEL DANIEL: *Tragedy of Cleopatra* [1594], *Act IV, Sc. 1*
  This principle is old, but true as fate, Kings may love treason, but the traitor hate.
    DEKKER: *The Honest Whore* [1604], *Part 1, Act IV, Sc. 4*
  Though I love the treason, I hate the traitor.
— PEPYS: *Diary* [March 7, 1667]
  T'abbor the makers, and their laws approve, Is to hate traitors and the treason love.
    DRYDEN: *The Hind and the Panther* [1687], *Part III, L. 706*

---

charsis replied, "Then you that are at home make friendship with me."

Lives. Solon, Page 99

Themistocles said that he certainly could not make use of any stringed instrument; could only, were a small and obscure city put into his hands, make it great and glorious.

Ibid. Themistocles, Page 134

Themistocles said to Antiphates, . . . "Time, young man, has taught us both a lesson."

Ibid. Page 145

Laughing at his own son, who got his mother, and, by his mother's means, his father also, to indulge him, he told him that he had the most power of any one in Greece: "For the Athenians command the rest of Greece, I command the Athenians, your mother commands me, and you command your mother." [1]

Ibid.

Of two who made love to his daughter, he preferred the man of worth to the one who was rich, saying he desired a man without riches, rather than riches without a man.

Ibid.

Themistocles replied that a man's discourse was like to a rich Persian carpet, the beautiful figures and patterns of which can be shown only by spreading and extending it out; when it is contracted and folded up, they are obscure and lost.[2]

Ibid. Page 152

Moderation is best, and to avoid all extremes.

Ibid. Camillus, Page 159

Caesar once, seeing some wealthy strangers at Rome, carrying up and down with them in their arms and bosoms young puppy-dogs and monkeys, embracing and making much of them, took occasion not unnaturally to ask

---

  [1] The same account appears in *Of the Training of Children* and in *Apophthegms of Kings and Great Commanders, Themistocles.*
  [2] Also found in *Apophthegms of Kings and Great Commanders, Themistocles.*

whether the women in their country were not used to bear children.

Lives. Pericles, Page 182

He who busies himself in mean occupations produces, in the very pains he takes about things of little or no use, an evidence against himself of his negligence and indisposition to what is really good.

Ibid. Page 183

So very difficult a matter is it to trace and find out the truth of anything by history.

Ibid. Page 194

Be ruled by time, the wisest counsellor of all.

Ibid. Page 198

Old women should not seek to be perfumed.

Ibid. Page 203

Trees, when they are lopped and cut, grow up again in a short time,[1] but men, being once lost, cannot easily be recovered.

Ibid. Page 207

To be turned from one's course by men's opinions, by blame, and by misrepresentation, shows a man unfit to hold an office.

Ibid. Fabius, Page 216

You know, Hannibal, how to gain a victory, but not how to use it.

Ibid. Page 224

One colour, indeed, they say the chameleon cannot assume; it cannot itself appear white; but Alcibiades, whether with good men or bad, could adapt himself to his company.

Ibid. Alcibiades, Page 249

Menenius Agrippa concluded, at length, with the celebrated fable: "It once happened that all the other members of a man mutinied against the stomach, which they accused as the only idle, uncontributing part in the whole body, while the rest were put to hardships and the expense of much

labour to supply and minister to its appetites." [1]

Lives. Coriolanus, Page 266

Men are usually more stung and galled by reproachful words than hostile actions.

Ibid. Timoleon, Page 316

A Roman divorced from his wife, being highly blamed by his friends, who demanded, "Was she not chaste? Was she not fair? Was she not fruitful?" holding out his shoe, asked them whether it was not new and well made. "Yet," added he, "none of you can tell where it pinches me." [2]

Ibid. Aemilius Paulus, Page 322

Petty repeated annoyances, arising from unpleasantness or incongruity of character, have been the occasion of such estrangement as to make it impossible for man and wife to live together with any content.

Ibid.

A man without one scar to show on his skin, that is smooth and sleek with ease and home-keeping habits, will undertake to define the office and duties of a general.

Ibid. Page 340

The saying of old Antigonus, who when he was to fight at Andros, and one told him, "The enemy's ships are more than ours," replied, "For how many then wilt thou reckon me?"

Ibid. Pelopidas, Page 348

Archimedes had stated, that given the force, any given weight might be moved; and even boasted . . . that if there were another earth, by going into it he could remove this.

Ibid. Marcellus, Page 367

Asking him if Aristides had ever done him any injury, "None at all," said he, "neither know I the man; but I am tired

---

[1] The lopped tree in time may grow again, Most naked plants renew both fruit and flower.
ROBERT SOUTHWELL [1561–1595]: *Times Go by Turns*

[1] See Aesop, page 10a.
[2] The wearer knows where the shoe wrings. — GEORGE HERBERT: *Jacula Prudentum* [1640]
I can tell where my own shoe pinches me. — CERVANTES: *Don Quixote, Part I* [1605], *Book IV, Chap. 5*

of hearing him everywhere called the Just."

Lives. Aristides, Page 396

Nor are we to use living creatures like old shoes or dishes and throw them away when they are worn out or broken with service.

Ibid. Marcus Cato, Page 415

It is a difficult task, O citizens, to make speeches to the belly, which has no ears.[1]

Ibid. Page 416

Cato used to assert that wise men profited more by fools, than fools by wise men; for that wise men avoided the faults of fools, but that fools would not imitate the good examples of wise men.

Ibid. Page 417

He said that in his whole life he most repented of three things: one was that he had trusted a secret to a woman; another, that he went by water when he might have gone by land; the third, that he had remained one whole day without doing any business of moment.

Ibid. Page 418

It was hard for him who had lived with one generation of men, to plead now before another.

Ibid. Page 422

Extraordinary rains pretty generally fall after great battles.

Ibid. Caius Marius, Page 507

Marius said that the law spoke too softly to be heard in such a noise of war.

Ibid. Page 511

Lycurgus . . . used to say that long hair made good-looking men more beautiful, and ill-looking men more terrible.

Ibid. Lysander, Page 525

Where the lion's skin will not reach, you must patch it out with the fox's.[2]

Ibid. Page 529

Moral habits, induced by public practices, are far quicker in making their way into men's private lives, than the failings and faults of individuals are in infecting the city at large.

Lives. Lysander, Page 535

As it is in the proverb, played Cretan against Cretan.[1]

Ibid. Page 537

Did you not know, then, that to-day Lucullus dines with Lucullus?

Ibid. Lucullus, Page 622

Economy, which in things inanimate is but money-making, when exercised over men becomes policy.

Ibid. Crassus, Page 651

Whoever tries for great objects must suffer something.

Ibid. Page 669

It is no great wonder if in long process of time, while fortune takes her course hither and thither, numerous coincidences should spontaneously occur. If the number and variety of subjects to be wrought upon be infinite, it is all the more easy for fortune, with such an abundance of material, to effect this similarity of results.[2]

Ibid. Sertorius, Page 678

Perseverance is more prevailing than violence; and many things which cannot be overcome when they are together, yield themselves up when taken little by little.

Ibid. Page 688

Good fortune will elevate even petty minds, and give them the appearance of a certain greatness and stateliness, as from their high place they look down upon the world; but the truly noble and resolved spirit raises itself, and becomes

---

[1] The belly has no ears, nor is it to be filled with fair words. — RABELAIS: *Book IV* [1548], *Chap. 67*

[2] The prince must be a lion, but he must also know how to play the fox. — NICOLÒ MACHIAVELLI: *The Prince* [1532]

[1] Cheat against cheat. The Cretans were notorious as liars.

[2] History repeats itself. — *Proverb*
What is this day supported by precedents will hereafter become a precedent. — THUCYDIDES [471–401 B.C.]: *Annals, XI, 24*
'Tis one and the same Nature that rolls on her course, and whoever has sufficiently considered the present state of things might certainly conclude as to both the future and the past. — MONTAIGNE: *Essays* [1580–1595], *Book II, Chap. 12, Apology for Raimond Sebond*

more conspicuous in times of disaster and ill fortune.

Lives. Eumenes, Page 703

Agesilaus being invited once to hear a man who admirably imitated the nightingale, he declined, saying he had heard the nightingale itself.

Ibid. Agesilaus, Page 726

If all the world were just, there would be no need of valour.

Ibid. Page 727

It is circumstance and proper measure that give an action its character, and make it either good or bad.

Ibid. Page 736

No man ever asked a favour with less offence, or conferred one with a better grace. When he gave, it was without assumption; when he received, it was with dignity and honour.

Ibid. Pompey, Page 740

Pompey bade Sylla recollect that more worshipped the rising than the setting sun.[1]

Ibid. Page 749

A dead man cannot bite.

Ibid. Page 795

Whenever Alexander heard Philip had taken any town of importance, or won any signal victory, instead of rejoicing at it altogether, he would tell his companions that his father would anticipate everything, and leave him and them no opportunities of performing great and illustrious actions.[2]

Ibid. Alexander, Page 804

When Alexander asked Diogenes whether he wanted anything, "Yes," said he, "I would have you stand from between me and the sun."

Ibid. Page 810

[1] See David Garrick, page 347a.
He [Tiberius] upbraided Macro in no obscure and indirect terms "with forsaking the setting sun and turning to the rising." — TACITUS [A.D. 54–119]: *Annals, Book IV, Chap. 47, 20*

[2] While Alexander was a boy, Philip had great success in his affairs, at which he did not rejoice, but told the children that were brought up with him, "My father will leave me nothing to do." — *Apophthegms of Kings and Great Commanders, Alexander*

Alexander finding himself unable to untie the Gordian knot, the ends of which were secretly twisted round and folded up within it, cut it asunder with his sword.

Lives. Alexander, Page 813

When asked why he parted with his wife, Caesar replied, "I wished my wife to be not so much as suspected."[1]

Ibid. Caesar, Page 860

For my part, I had rather be the first man among these fellows, than the second man in Rome.[2]

Ibid. Page 861

He who reflects on another man's want of breeding, shows he wants it as much himself.

Ibid. Page 865

Using the proverb frequently in their mouths who enter upon dangerous and bold attempts, "The die is cast," he took the river.[3]

Ibid. Page 874

"And this," said Caesar, "you know, young man, is more disagreeable for me to say than to do."

Ibid. Page 876

Go on, my friend, and fear nothing; you carry Caesar and his fortune in your boat.[4]

Ibid. Page 877

[Cleopatra] was at a loss how to get in undiscovered, till she thought of putting herself into the coverlet of a bed and lying at length, whilst Apollodorus tied up the bedding and carried it on his back through the gates to Caesar's apartment.

Ibid. Page 883

Caesar's barber, a busy listening fellow.

Ibid.

Caesar said to the soothsayer, "The ides of March are come"; who answered

[1] Caesar's wife ought to be above suspicion. — *Roman Apophthegms, Caesar*
[2] I had rather be the first in this town than second in Rome. — *Ibid.*
[3] Iacta alea est. The river is the Rubicon.
[4] See Lucan, page 51a.

him calmly, "Yes, they are come, but they are not past." [1]

Lives. Caesar, Page 890

Phocion's oratory, like small coin of great value, was to be estimated, not by its bulk, but its intrinsic worth.

Ibid. Phocion, Page 898

Even a nod from a person who is esteemed is of more force than a thousand arguments or studied sentences from others.

Ibid.

Demosthenes told Phocion, "The Athenians will kill you some day when they once are in a rage." "And you," said he, "if they once are in their senses."

Ibid. Page 901

Men, steered by popular applause, though they bear the name of governors, are in reality the mere underlings of the multitude. The man who is completely wise and virtuous has no need at all of glory, except so far as it disposes and eases his way of action by the greater trust that it procures him.

Ibid. Agis, Page 960

Pytheas once, scoffing at Demosthenes, said that his arguments smelt of the lamp.

Ibid. Demosthenes, Page 1026

Demosthenes overcame and rendered more distinct his inarticulate and stammering pronunciation by speaking with pebbles in his mouth.

Ibid. Page 1028

In his house he had a large looking-glass, before which he would stand and go through his exercises.

Ibid.

Cicero called Aristotle a river of flowing gold, and said of Plato's Dialogues, that if Jupiter were to speak, it would be in language like theirs.

Ibid. Cicero, Page 1054

No beast is more savage than man when possessed with power answerable to his rage.

Ibid. Page 1068

Authority and place demonstrate and try the tempers of men, by moving

[1] See Shakespeare, page 166a.

every passion and discovering every frailty.

Lives. Cicero, Page 1071

Medicine, to produce health, has to examine disease, and music, to create harmony, must investigate discord.

Ibid. Demetrius, Page 1073

Once Antigonus was told his son was ill, and went to see him. At the door he met some young beauty. Going in, he sat down by the bed and took his pulse. "The fever," said Demetrius, "has just left me." "Oh, yes," replied the father, "I met it going out at the door."

Ibid. Page 1083

"It is not," said Caesar, "these well-fed, long-haired men that I fear, but the pale and the hungry-looking"; meaning Brutus and Cassius, by whose conspiracy he afterwards fell. [1]

Ibid. Antony, Page 1111

There was no man of his time like Antony for addressing a multitude, or for carrying soldiers with him by the force of words.

Ibid. Page 1127

From PLUTARCH'S *Morals* [2]

It is a true proverb, that if you live with a lame man you will learn to halt.

Of the Training of Children

Eat not thy heart; which forbids to afflict our souls, and waste them with vexatious cares.

Ibid.

The very spring and root of honesty and virtue lie in the felicity of lighting on good education.

Ibid.

It is indeed a desirable thing to be well descended, but the glory belongs to our ancestors.

Ibid.

Nothing made the horse so fat as the king's eye.

Ibid.

Democritus said, words are but the shadow of actions.

Ibid.

[1] See Shakespeare, page 166b.
[2] By various translators, revised by WILLIAM WATSON GOODWIN [1831–1912].

It is a point of wisdom to be silent when occasion requires, and better than to speak, though never so well.[1]

Of the Training of Children

Abstain from beans; that is, keep out of public offices, for anciently the choice of the officers of state was made by beans.

Ibid.

The whole life of man is but a point of time; let us enjoy it, therefore, while it lasts, and not spend it to no purpose.

Ibid.

An old doting fool, with one foot already in the grave.

Ibid.

Xenophanes said, "I confess myself the greatest coward in the world, for I dare not do an ill thing."

Of Bashfulness

One made the observation of the people of Asia that they were all slaves to one man, merely because they could not pronounce that syllable No.[2]

Ibid.

Euripides was wont to say, "Silence is an answer to a wise man."

Ibid.

Zeno first started that doctrine that knavery is the best defence against a knave.[3]

Ibid.

Alexander wept when he heard from Anaxarchus that there was an infinite number of worlds; and his friends asking him if any accident had befallen him, he returns this answer: "Do you not think it a matter worthy of lamentation that when there is such a vast multitude of them, we have not yet conquered one?"

On the Tranquillity of the Mind

Like the man who threw a stone at a bitch, but hit his step-mother, on which he exclaimed, "Not so bad!"

Ibid.

Pittacus said, "Every one of you hath his particular plague, and my wife is mine; and he is very happy who hath this only."

On the Tranquillity of the Mind

He was a man, which, as Plato saith, is a very inconstant creature.[1]

Ibid.

All men whilst they are awake are in one common world; but each of them, when he is asleep, is in a world of his own.[2]

Of Superstition

I, for my own part, had much rather people should say of me that there neither is nor ever was such a man as Plutarch, than that they should say, "Plutarch is an unsteady, fickle, froward, vindictive, and touchy fellow."

Ibid.

Scilurus on his death-bed, being about to leave four-score sons surviving, offered a bundle of darts to each of them, and bade them break them. When all refused, drawing out one by one, he easily broke them, — thus teaching them that if they held together, they would continue strong; but if they fell out and were divided, they would become weak.[3]

Apophthegms of Kings and Great Commanders. Scilurus

Dionysius the Elder, being asked whether he was at leisure, he replied, "God forbid that it should ever befall me!"

Ibid. Dionysius

A prating barber asked Archelaus how he would be trimmed. He answered, "In silence."

Ibid. Archelaus

When Philip had news brought him of divers and eminent successes in one day, "O Fortune!" said he, "for all these so great kindnesses do me some small mischief."

Ibid. Philip

---

[1] Closed lips hurt no one, speaking may. — Cato the Censor [234–149 b.c.]: *Book I, Distich 12*

[2] See Coleridge, page 424b.

[3] Set a thief to catch a thief. — Bohn: *Handbook of Proverbs*

[1] See Montaigne, page 97b.

[2] A saying attributed to Heraclitus.

[3] Aesop's fable, *The Bundle of Sticks* has this theme.

See Franklin, page 331b.

a

Philip being arbitrator betwixt two wicked persons, he commanded one to fly out of Macedonia and the other to pursue him.

Apophthegms of Kings and Great Commanders. Philip

Being about to pitch his camp in a likely place, and hearing there was no hay to be had for the cattle, "What a life," said he, "is ours, since we must live according to the convenience of asses!"

Ibid.

He made one of Antipater's recommendation a judge; and perceiving afterwards that his hair and beard were dyed, he removed him, saying, "I could not think one that was faithless in his hair could be trusty in his deeds."

Ibid.

Being nimble and light-footed, his father encouraged him to run in the Olympic race. "Yes," said he, "if there were any kings there to run with me."

Ibid. Alexander

Pyrrhus said, "If I should overcome the Romans in another fight, I were undone." [1]

Ibid. Pyrrhus

Themistocles being asked whether he would rather be Achilles or Homer, said, "Which would you rather be, — a conqueror in the Olympic games, or the crier that proclaims who are conquerors?"

Ibid. Themistocles

Alcibiades had a very handsome dog, that cost him seven thousand drachmas; and he cut off his tail, "that," said he, "the Athenians may have this story to tell of me, and may concern themselves no further with me."

Ibid. Alcibiades

To Harmodius, descended from the ancient Harmodius, when he reviled Iphicrates [a shoemaker's son] for his mean birth, "My nobility," said he, "begins with me, but yours ends in you." [2]

Ibid. Iphicrates

[1] See Herodotus, page 19a.
[2] Curtius Rufus seems to me to be descended from himself (a saying of Tiberius). — TACI-

b

Once when Phocion had delivered an opinion which pleased the people, . . . he turned to his friend and said, "Have I not unawares spoken some mischievous thing or other?" [1]

Apophthegms of Kings and Great Commanders. Phocion

King Agis said, "The Lacedaemonians are not wont to ask how many, but where the enemy are."

Ibid. Agis

To one that promised to give him hardy cocks that would die fighting, "Prithee," said Cleomenes, "give me cocks that will kill fighting."

Ibid. Cleomenes

A soldier told Pelopidas, "We are fallen among the enemies." Said he, "How are we fallen among them more than they among us?"

Ibid. Pelopidas

Cato the Elder wondered how that city was preserved wherein a fish was sold for more than an ox.

Roman Apophthegms. Cato the Elder

Cato requested old men not to add the disgrace of wickedness to old age, which was accompanied with many other evils.

Ibid.

He said they that were serious in ridiculous matters would be ridiculous in serious affairs.

Ibid.

Cicero said loud-bawling orators were driven by their weakness to noise, as lame men to take horse.

Ibid. Cicero

After he routed Pharnaces Ponticus at the first assault, he wrote thus to his friends: "I came, I saw, I conquered." [2]

Ibid. Caesar

As Caesar was at supper the discourse was of death, — which sort was the

TUS [A. D. 54–119]: *Annals, Book XI, Chap. 21, 16*
I am my own ancestor. — JUNOT, DUC D'ABRANTES [1771–1813], when asked about his ancestry
[1] See Diogenes Laertius, page 71b.
[2] Veni, vidi, vici.
See Shakespeare, page 153b.

best. "That," said he, "which is unexpected."

Roman Apophthegms.
Caesar

As Athenodorus was taking his leave of Caesar, "Remember," said he, "Caesar, whenever you are angry, to say or do nothing before you have repeated the four-and-twenty letters to yourself."

Ibid. Caesar Augustus

"Young men," said Caesar, "hear an old man to whom old men hearkened when he was young."

Ibid.

Custom is almost a second nature.[1]

Rules for the Preservation of
Health. 18

Epaminondas is reported wittily to have said of a good man that died about the time of the battle of Leuctra, "How came he to have so much leisure as to die, when there was so much stirring?"

Ibid. 25

Socrates thought that if all our misfortunes were laid in one common heap, whence every one must take an equal portion, most persons would be contented to take their own and depart.[2]

Consolation to Apollonius

Diogenes the Cynic, when a little before his death he fell into a slumber, and his physician rousing him out of it asked him whether anything ailed him, wisely answered, "Nothing, sir; only one brother anticipates another, — Sleep before Death."

Ibid.

There are two sentences inscribed upon the Delphic oracle, hugely accommodated to the usages of man's life: "Know thyself,"[3] and "Nothing too

much"; and upon these all other precepts depend.

Consolation to Apollonius

Agesilaus was very fond of his children; and it is reported that once toying with them he got astride upon a reed as upon a horse, and rode about the room; and being seen by one of his friends, he desired him not to speak of it till he had children of his own.

Laconic Apophthegms. Of
Agesilaus the Great

Lysander, when Dionysius sent him two gowns, and bade him choose which he would carry to his daughter, said, "She can choose best," and so took both away with him.

Ibid. Of Lysander

And when the physician said, "Sir, you are an old man," "That happens," replied Pausanias, "because you never were my doctor."

Ibid. Of Pausanias

When one told Plistarchus that a notorious railer spoke well of him, "I'll lay my life," said he, "somebody hath told him I am dead, for he can speak well of no man living."

Ibid. Of Plistarchus

Said Periander, "Hesiod might as well have kept his breath to cool his pottage."[1]

The Banquet of the Seven
Wise Men. 14

Socrates said, "Bad men live that they may eat and drink, whereas good men eat and drink that they may live."[2]

How a Young Man Ought to
Hear Poems. 4

---

[1] Habit is a second nature. — MONTAIGNE: *Essays* [1580–1595], *Book III, Chap. 10*
See Shakespeare, page 132a.

[2] ADDISON's paper, *The Spectator, No. 558,* June 23, 1714, is on this theme.

[3] Plutarch ascribes this saying to Plato. It is also ascribed to Pythagoras, Chilo, Thales, Cleobulus, Bias, Solon, and Socrates; also to Phemonë, a mythical Greek poetess of the ante-Homeric period. JUVENAL (*Satire XI, 27*)

says that this precept descended from heaven.
Ful wys is he that can him-selven knowe.
— CHAUCER: *The Canterbury Tales* [*circa* 1387], *The Monk's Tale, Line 3329*
Make it thy business to know thyself, which is the most difficult lesson in the world. — CERVANTES: *Don Quixote, Part II* [1615], *Book IV, Chap. 42*
See Pope, page 316b.

[1] Spare your breath to cool your porridge. — RABELAIS: *Works, Book V* [1552], *Chap. 28*

[2] He used to say that other men lived to eat, but that he ate to live. — DIOGENES LAERTIUS [*circa* A. D. 200]: *Socrates, 14*
We should eat to live, not live to eat. —

That proverbial saying, "Ill news goes quick and far."

Of Inquisitiveness

Spintharus, speaking in commendation of Epaminondas, says he scarce ever met with any man who knew more and spoke less.

Of Hearing. 6

It is a thing of no great difficulty to raise objections against another man's oration, — nay, it is a very easy matter; but to produce a better in its place is a work extremely troublesome.

Ibid.

Antiphanes said merrily, that in a certain city the cold was so intense that words were congealed as soon as spoken, but that after some time they thawed and became audible; so that the words spoken in winter were articulated next summer.[1]

Of Man's Progress in Virtue

As those persons who despair of ever being rich make little account of small expenses, thinking that little added to a little will never make any great sum.

Ibid.

What is bigger than an elephant? But this also is become man's plaything, and a spectacle at public solemnities; and it learns to skip, dance, and kneel.

Of Fortune

No man ever wetted clay and then left it, as if there would be bricks by chance and fortune.

Ibid.

Alexander was wont to say, "Were I not Alexander, I would be Diogenes."

Of the Fortune or Virtue of Alexander the Great

When the candles are out all women are fair.[2]

Conjugal Precepts

MOLIÈRE: *L'Avare* [1668], *Act III, Sc. 5*
We must eat to live and live to eat. — FIELDING [1707–1754]: *The Miser, Act III, Sc. 3*
[1] Rabelais gives a somewhat similar account, referring to Antiphanes, in *Book IV, Chaps. 55* and *56.*
See Raspe (Baron Munchausen), page 369b.
[2] When all candles be out, all cats be gray. — JOHN HEYWOOD: *Proverbes* [1546], *Part I, Chap. 5*

Like watermen, who look astern while they row the boat ahead.[1]

Whether 'Twas Rightfully Said, Live Concealed

Socrates said he was not an Athenian or a Greek, but a citizen of the world.[2]

Of Banishment

The great god Pan is dead.[3]

Why the Oracles Cease to Give Answers

I am whatever was, or is, or will be; and my veil no mortal ever took up.[4]

Of Isis and Osiris

When Hermodotus in his poems described Antigonus as the son of Helios, "My valet-de-chambre," said he, "is not aware of this."[5]

Ibid.

---

[1] Like rowers, who advance backward. — MONTAIGNE: *Essays* [1580–1595], *Of Profit and Honour, Book III, Chap. I*
Like the watermen that row one way and look another. — ROBERT BURTON: *Anatomy of Melancholy* [1621-1651], *Democritus to the Reader*
[2] See Thomas Paine, page 371a, and William Lloyd Garrison, page 517a.
Diogenes, when asked from what country he came, replied, "I am a citizen of the world." — DIOGENES LAERTIUS [*circa* A.D. 200], *Diogenes, 6*
Citizen of the world, as I hold myself to be. — BOSWELL: *Life of Dr. Johnson* [1791], *Everyman Edition, Vol. I, P. 521*
[3] Great Pan is dead. — ELIZABETH BARRETT BROWNING [1806–1861]: *The Dead Pan, St. 26*
Plutarch relates (*Isis and Osiris*) that a ship well laden with passengers drove with the tide near the Isles of Paxi, when a loud voice was heard by most of the passengers calling unto one Thanus. The voice then said aloud to him, "When you are arrived at Palodes, take care to make it known that the great god Pan is dead."
[4] I am the things that are, and those that are to be, and those that have been. No one ever lifted my skirts; the fruit which I bore was the sun. — PROCLUS [A.D. 411?–485]: *On Plato's Timaeus* (Inscription in the temple of Neith at Sais, in Egypt)
[5] Few men have been admired by their domestics. — MONTAIGNE: *Essays* [1580–1595], *Book III, Chap. 2*
The phrase "No man is a hero to his valet" has often been attributed to Madame de Sévigné, but on the authority of MADAME AISSÉ (*Letters,* edited by Jules Ravenal, 1853) it belongs to Madame Cornuel [1614–1694].

We are more sensible of what is done against custom than against Nature.

Of Eating of Flesh. Tract 1

When Demosthenes was asked what was the first part of oratory, he answered, "Action"; and which was the second, he replied, "Action"; and which was the third, he still answered, "Action."

Lives of the Ten Orators

Xenophon says that there is no sound more pleasing than one's own praises.

Whether an Aged Man Ought to Meddle in State Affairs

Statesmen are not only liable to give an account of what they say or do in public, but there is a busy inquiry made into their very meals, beds, marriages, and every other sportive or serious action.

Political Precepts

Leo Byzantius said, "What would you do, if you saw my wife, who scarce reaches up to my knees? . . . Yet," went he on, "as little as we are, when we fall out with each other, the city of Byzantium is not big enough to hold us."

Ibid.

Cato said, "I had rather men should ask why my statue is not set up, than why it is."

Ibid.

It was the saying of Bion, that though the boys throw stones at frogs in sport, yet the frogs do not die in sport but in earnest.

Which Are the Most Crafty, Water or Land Animals? 7

For to err in opinion, though it be not the part of wise men, is at least human.[1]

Against Colotes

Simonides calls painting silent poetry, and poetry, speaking painting.

Whether the Athenians Were More Warlike or Learned. 3

Pythagoras, when he was asked what time was, answered that it was the soul of this world.

Platonic Questions

[1] See Pope, page 311b.

MANILIUS
[FIRST CENTURY A. D.]

As soon as we are born we begin to die, and the end depends upon the beginning.

Astronomica. IV, Line 16

JUVENAL
[A. D. 47–138]

Honesty is praised and starves.[1]

Satire I. Line 74

If nature refuses, indignation makes the verse.

Ibid. Line 79

Whatever men do — prayer, fear, anger, pleasure, joys, comings and goings — that is the stuff of which my little book is made.

Ibid. Line 85

He pardons the ravens and visits censure on the doves.

Satire II. Line 63

No man ever became extremely wicked all at once.[2]

Ibid. Line 83

Grammarian, orator, geometrician; painter, gymnastic teacher; fortune-teller, rope-dancer, physician, conjuror, — he knew everything.[3]

Satire III. Line 76

Unhappy poverty has no worse trait than that it makes men ridiculous.[4]

Ibid. Line 152

Not easily do they rise whose powers are hindered by straitened circumstances.

Ibid. Line 164

We all live in a state of ambitious poverty.

Ibid. Line 182

[1] A favorite quotation of Linnaeus, Swedish botanist and naturalist.
[2] Nemo repente fit turpissimus. See Beaumont and Fletcher, page 228b, and Racine, page 287b.
[3] See Dryden, page 277a.
[4] Nil habet infelix paupertas durius in se Quam quod ridiculos homines facit. See Samuel Johnson, page 335b.

A rare bird on earth and very like a black swan.[1]

Satire VI. Line 165

But who would guard the guards themselves? [2]

Ibid. Line 347

Nobility is the one only virtue.[3]

Satire VIII. Line 20

Hold it the greatest wrong to prefer life to honor and for life's sake to lose the reasons for living.

Ibid. Line 83

Two things only the people anxiously desire — bread and circuses.[4]

Satire X, Line 80

We should pray for a sane mind in a sound body.[5]

Ibid. Line 356

The greatest reverence is due a child! If you are contemplating a wicked act, despise not your child's tender years.

Satire XIV. Line 47

ONASANDER
[*Floruit* A. D. 49]

Vigor is found in the man who has not yet grown old, and discretion in the man who is not too young.

The General. Chap. 1, Sect. 10

Envy is a pain of mind that successful men cause their neighbours.

Ibid. Chap. 42, Paragraph 25

TACITUS
[A. D. 54–119]

The images of twenty of the most illustrious families — the Manlii, the Quinctii, and other names of equal splendour — were carried before it [the bier of Junia]. Those of Brutus and Cassius were not displayed; but for that very reason they shone with pre-eminent lustre.[6]

Annals. III, 76, 11

He had talents equal to business, and aspired no higher.

Annals. VI, 39, 17

Some might consider him as too fond of fame; for the desire of glory clings even to the best men longer than any other passion.[1]

History. IV, 6, 36

Whatever is unknown is magnified.

Agricola. Sect. 30

To plunder, to slaughter, to steal, these things they misname empire; and where they make a desert, they call it peace.[2]

Ibid.

It is characteristic of human nature to hate the man whom you have wronged.

Ibid. Sect. 42

EPICTETUS [3]
[*Circa* A. D. 60]

To a reasonable creature, that alone is insupportable which is unreasonable; but everything reasonable may be supported.

Discourses. Chap. 2

When you have shut your doors, and darkened your room, remember never to say that you are alone, for you are not alone; [4] but God is within, and your genius is within, — and what need have they of light to see what you are doing?

Ibid. Chap. 14

---

[1] Rara avis in terris nigroque simillima cygno.

[2] Sed quis custodiet ipsos custodes?

[3] See Chapman, page 117b.

[4] Duas tantum res anxius optat,
Panem et circenses.

[5] Orandum est ut sit mens sana in corpore sano.

[6] Lord John Russell, alluding to an expres-

sion used by him ("Conspicuous by his absence") in an address to the electors of the city of London, said, "It is not an original expression of mine, but is taken from one of the greatest historians of antiquity."

[1] Said of Helvidius Priscus.
See Milton, page 249a.

[2] Calgacus, addressing the Britons at the Battle of the Grampians, referring to the Romans.
Mark! where his carnage and his conquests cease!
He makes a solitude, and calls it — peace!
BYRON: *The Bride of Abydos* [1813],
Canto II, L. 428

[3] Translated [1865] by THOMAS WENTWORTH HIGGINSON.

[4] Though in a wilderness, a man is never alone. — SIR THOMAS BROWNE: *Religio Medici* [1642] (Everyman ed.), P. 82

No great thing is created suddenly, any more than a bunch of grapes or a fig. If you tell me that you desire a fig, I answer you that there must be time. Let it first blossom, then bear fruit, then ripen.

Discourses. Chap. 15

Any one thing in the creation is sufficient to demonstrate a Providence to an humble and grateful mind.

Ibid. Chap. 16

Were I a nightingale, I would act the part of a nightingale; were I a swan, the part of a swan.

Ibid.

Since it is Reason which shapes and regulates all other things, it ought not itself to be left in disorder.

Ibid. Chap. 17

Practise yourself, for heaven's sake, in little things; and thence proceed to greater.

Ibid. Chap. 18

Why, then, do you walk as if you had swallowed a ramrod?

Ibid. Chap. 21

Difficulties are things that show what men are.

Ibid. Chap. 24

The good or ill of man lies within his own will.

Ibid Chap. 25

In theory there is nothing to hinder our following what we are taught; but in life there are many things to draw us aside.

Ibid. Chap. 26

Appearances to the mind are of four kinds. Things either are what they appear to be; or they neither are, nor appear to be; or they are, and do not appear to be; or they are not, and yet appear to be. Rightly to aim in all these cases is the wise man's task.

Ibid. Chap. 27

The appearance of things to the mind is the standard of every action to man.

That We Ought Not to Be Angry with Mankind. 27

The materials of action are variable, but the use we make of them should be constant.

How Nobleness of Mind May Be Consistent with Prudence. 5

Shall I show you the muscular training of a philosopher? "What muscles are those?" — A will undisappointed; evils avoided; powers daily exercised; careful resolutions; unerring decisions.

Wherein Consists the Essence of Good. 8

What is the first business of one who studies philosophy? To part with self-conceit. For it is impossible for any one to begin to learn what he thinks that he already knows.

How to Apply General Principles to Particular Cases. 17

Every habit and faculty is preserved and increased by correspondent actions, — as the habit of walking, by walking; or running, by running.

How the Semblances of Things Are to Be Combated. 18

Whatever you would make habitual, practise it; and if you would not make a thing habitual, do not practise it, but habituate yourself to something else.

Ibid.

Reckon the days in which you have not been angry. I used to be angry every day; now every other day; then every third and fourth day; and if you miss it so long as thirty days, offer a sacrifice of thanksgiving to God.

Ibid.

Be not hurried away by excitement, but say, "Semblance, wait for me a little. Let me see what you are and what you represent. Let me try you."

Ibid.

There are some things which men confess with ease, and others with difficulty.

Of Inconsistency. 21

Who is there whom bright and agreeable children do not attract to play and creep and prattle with them?

Concerning a Person Whom He Treated with Disregard. 24

Two rules we should always have ready, — that there is nothing good or evil save in the will; and that we are not to lead events, but to follow them.

In What Manner We Ought to Bear Sickness. Book III, 10

First say to yourself what you would be; and then do what you have to do.

Concerning Such as Read and Dispute Ostentatiously. 23

Let not another's disobedience to Nature become an ill to you; for you were not born to be depressed and unhappy with others, but to be happy with them. And if any is unhappy, remember that he is so for himself; for God made all men to enjoy felicity and peace.

That We Ought Not to Be Affected by Things Not in Our Own Power. 24

Remember that you ought to behave in life as you would at a banquet. As something is being passed around it comes to you; stretch out your hand, take a portion of it politely. It passes on; do not detain it. Or it has not come to you yet; do not project your desire to meet it, but wait until it comes in front of you. So act toward children, so toward a wife, so toward office, so toward wealth.

The Encheiridion. 15

Everything has two handles, — one by which it may be borne; another by which it cannot.[1]

Ibid. 43

PLINY THE YOUNGER [2]
[A. D. 61–105]

Modestus said of Regulus that he was "the biggest rascal that walks upon two legs."

Letters.[3] Book I, Letter 5, 14

There is nothing to write about, you say. Well, then, write and let me know just this, — that there *is* nothing to

write about; or tell me in the good old style if you are well. That's right. I am quite well.[1]

Letters. Book I, Letter 11, 1

An object in possession seldom retains the same charm that it had in pursuit.[2]

Ibid. Book II, Letter 15, 1

He [Pliny the Elder] used to say that "no book was so bad but some good might be got out of it."[3]

Ibid. Book III, Letter 5, 10

This expression of ours, "Father of a family."[4]

Ibid. Book V, Letter 19, 2

That indolent but agreeable condition of doing nothing.[5]

Ibid. Book VIII, Letter 9, 3

Objects which are usually the motives of our travels by land and by sea are often overlooked and neglected if they lie under our eye. . . . We put off from time to time going and seeing what we know we have an opportunity of seeing when we please.

Ibid. Letter 20, 1

His only fault is that he has no fault.[6]

Ibid. Book IX, Letter 26, 1

EMPEROR HADRIAN
[A. D. 76–138]

Gentle little soul, hastening away, my body's guest and comrade, whither goest

---

[1] There is a right and wrong handle to everything. — RASPE: *Travels of Baron Munchausen* [1785], *Chap. 30*

[2] Translated [1746] by WILLIAM MELMOTH.

[3] Book VI, Letter 16, contains the description of the eruption of Vesuvius, A. D. 79, as witnessed by Pliny the Elder.

[1] This comes to inform you that I am in a perfect state of health, hoping you are in the same. Ay, that's the old beginning. — GEORGE COLMAN THE YOUNGER: *The Heir at Law* [1797], *Act III, Sc. 2*

[2] It has been a thousand times observed, and I must observe it once more, that the hours we pass with happy prospects in view, are more pleasing than those crowned with fruition. — GOLDSMITH: *The Vicar of Wakefield* [1766], *Chap. 10*

[3] "There is no book so bad," said the bachelor, "but something good may be found in it." — CERVANTES: *Don Quixote, Part II* [1615], *Chap. 3*

[4] Paterfamilias.

[5] Dolce far niente (Sweet doing-nothing). — *Italian proverb*

[6] The greatest of faults, I should say, is to be conscious of none. — CARLYLE: *Heroes and Hero-Worship* [1841], *The Hero as Prophet*

thou now, pale, fearful, pensive, not jesting, as of old? [1]

Morientis, Ad Animam Suam

I've no mind to be a Florus,
Strolling round among the drink-shops,
Skulking round among the cook-shops,
Victim of fat-gorged mosquitoes.

Retort to Florus [2]

MARCUS AURELIUS ANTONINUS [3]
[A. D. 121–180]

This Being of mine, whatever it really is, consists of a little flesh, a little breath, and the part which governs.

Meditations. II, 2

The ways of the gods are full of providence.

Ibid. 3

Thou wilt find rest from vain fancies if thou doest every act in life as though it were thy last.[4]

Ibid. 5

No state sorrier than that of the man who keeps up a continual round, and pries into "the secrets of the nether world," as saith the poet, and is curious in conjecture of what is in his neighbour's heart.

Ibid. 13

Though thou be destined to live three thousand years and as many myriads besides, yet remember that no man loseth other life than that which he liveth, nor liveth other than that which he loseth.

Ibid. 14

For a man can lose neither the past nor the future; for how can one take from him that which is not his? So remember these two points: first, that each thing is of like form from everlasting and comes round again in its cycle, and that it signifies not whether a man shall look upon the same things for a hundred years or two hundred, or for an infinity of time; second, that the longest lived and the shortest lived man, when they come to die, lose one and the same thing.

Meditations. II, 14

As for life, it is a battle and a sojourning in a strange land; but the fame that comes after is oblivion.

Ibid. 17

Waste not the remnant of thy life in those imaginations touching other folk, whereby thou contributest not to the common weal.

Ibid. III, 4

A man should *be* upright, not be *kept* upright.

Ibid. 5

Never esteem anything as of advantage to thee that shall make thee break thy word or lose thy self-respect.

Ibid. 7

By a tranquil mind I mean nothing else than a mind well ordered.

Ibid. IV, 3

Think on this doctrine, — that reasoning beings were created for one another's sake; that to be patient is a branch of justice, and that men sin without intending it.

Ibid.

The universe is change; our life is what our thoughts make it.

Ibid.

Nothing can come out of nothing,[1] any more than a thing can go back to nothing.

Ibid. 4

---

[1] Animula, vagula, blandula
   Hospes comesque corporis,
   Quae nunc abibis in loca,
   Pallidula, frigida, nudula,
   Nec, ut soles, dabis joca.
See Pope, page 312a.

[2] Florus, born in Africa [A. D. 74], Hadrian's friend, had addressed these lines to him (the third line has been lost):
   I've no mind to be a Caesar,
   Strolling round among the Britons
   .   .   .   .
   Victim of the Scythian hoar-frosts.

[3] Translated by MORRIS HICKEY MORGAN [1859–1910].

[4] See Publilius Syrus, *Maxim 633,* page 45b.

[1] De nihilo nihilum, in nihilum posse reverti. — PERSIUS [A. D. 34–62]: *Satires,* 3, L. 84

Nothing can be produced out of nothing. — DIOGENES LAERTIUS [*circa* A. D. 200]: *Diogenes of Apollonia, 2*

Death, like birth, is a secret of Nature.

Meditations. IV, 5

That which makes the man no worse than he was makes his life no worse: it has no power to harm, without or within.

Ibid. 8

Whatever happens at all happens as it should; thou wilt find this true, if thou shouldst watch narrowly.

Ibid. 10

How much time he gains who does not look to see what his neighbour says or does or thinks, but only at what he does himself, to make it just and holy.

Ibid. 18

Whatever is in any way beautiful hath its source of beauty in itself, and is complete in itself; praise forms no part of it. So it is none the worse nor the better for being praised.

Ibid. 20

All that is harmony for thee, O Universe, is in harmony with me as well. Nothing that comes at the right time for thee is too early or too late for me. Everything is fruit to me that thy seasons bring, O Nature. All things come of thee, have their being in thee, and return to thee.

Ibid. 23

"Let thine occupations be few," saith the sage,[1] "if thou wouldst lead a tranquil life."

Ibid. 24

Love the little trade which thou hast learned, and be content therewith.

Ibid. 31

Remember this, — that there is a proper dignity and proportion to be observed in the performance of every act of life.

Ibid. 32

All is ephemeral, — fame and the famous as well.

Ibid. 35

Observe always that everything is the result of a change, and get used to thinking that there is nothing Nature loves so well as to change existing forms and to make new ones like them.

Meditations. IV, 36

Search men's governing principles, and consider the wise, what they shun and what they cleave to.

Ibid. 38

Time is a sort of river of passing events, and strong is its current; no sooner is a thing brought to sight than it is swept by and another takes its place, and this too will be swept away.

Ibid. 43

All that happens is as usual and familiar as the rose in spring and the crop in summer.

Ibid. 44

Mark how fleeting and paltry is the estate of man, — yesterday in embryo, to-morrow a mummy or ashes. So for the hair's-breadth of time assigned to thee live rationally, and part with life cheerfully, as drops the ripe olive, extolling the season that bore it and the tree that matured it.

Ibid. 48

Deem not life a thing of consequence. For look at the yawning void of the future, and at that other limitless space, the past.

Ibid. 50

Always take the short cut; and that is the rational one. Therefore say and do everything according to soundest reason.

Ibid. 51

In the morning, when thou art sluggish at rousing thee, let this thought be present; "I am rising to a man's work."

Ibid. V, 1

A man makes no noise over a good deed, but passes on to another as a vine to bear grapes again in season.

Ibid. 6

Nothing happens to anybody which he is not fitted by nature to bear.

Ibid. 18

Live with the gods.

Ibid. 27

[1] DEMOCRITUS apud Senecam: *De Ira, III, 6; De Animi Tranquillitate, 13*

Look beneath the surface; let not the several quality of a thing nor its worth escape thee.

Meditations. VI, 3

The controlling Intelligence understands its own nature, and what it does, and whereon it works.

Ibid. 5

Do not think that what is hard for thee to master is impossible for man; but if a thing is possible and proper to man, deem it attainable by thee.

Ibid. 19

If any man can convince me and bring home to me that I do not think or act aright, gladly will I change; for I search after truth, by which man never yet was harmed.

Ibid. 21

What is not good for the swarm is not good for the bee.

Ibid. 54

How many, once lauded in song, are given over to the forgotten; and how many who sung their praises are clean gone long ago!

Ibid. VII, 6

One Universe made up of all that is; and one God in it all, and one principle of Being, and one Law, the Reason, shared by all thinking creatures, and one Truth.

Ibid. 9

The time is close when you shall forget all things and be by all forgotten.

Ibid. 21

It is man's peculiar duty to love even those who wrong him.

Ibid. 22

The art of living is more like wrestling than dancing, in so far as it stands ready against the accidental and the unforeseen, and is not apt to fall.

Ibid. 61

Remember this, — that very little is needed to make a happy life.

Ibid. 67

Remember that to change thy mind and to follow him that sets thee right, is to be none the less the free agent that thou wast before.

Ibid. VIII, 16

Look to the essence of a thing, whether it be a point of doctrine, of practice, or of interpretation.

Meditations. VIII, 22

Be not careless in deeds, nor confused in words, nor rambling in thought.

Ibid. 51

Think not disdainfully of death, but look on it with favour; for even death is one of the things that Nature wills.

Ibid. IX, 3

A wrong-doer is often a man that has left something undone, not always he that has done something.

Ibid. 5

Blot out vain pomp; check impulse; quench appetite; keep reason under its own control.

Ibid. 7

If you can, correct the evil by instruction; if not, remember that for this was patience given you. The gods, too, are patient with the like.

Ibid. 11

All things are the same, — familiar in enterprise, momentary in endurance, coarse in substance. All things now are as they were in the day of those whom we have buried.

Ibid. 14

Everything is in a state of metamorphosis. Thou thyself art in everlasting change and in corruption to correspond; so is the whole universe.

Ibid. 19

Forward, as occasion offers. Never look round to see whether any shall note it. . . . Be satisfied with success in even the smallest matter, and think that even such a result is no trifle.

Ibid. 29

Whatever may befall thee, it was preordained for thee from everlasting.

Ibid. X, 5

TERTULLIAN
[A. D. 160–240]

See how these Christians love one another.

Apologeticus. 39

Blood of the martyrs is the seed of the Church.
Apologeticus. 50

It is certain because it is impossible.[1]
De Carne Christi. 5

He who flees will fight again.[2]
De Fuga in Persecutione. 10

ATHENAEUS [3]
[*Circa* A. D. 200]

It was a saying of Demetrius Phalereus, that "Men having often abandoned what was visible for the sake of what was uncertain, have not got what

---

[1] Certum est, quia impossibile est. This is usually misquoted, "Credo quia impossibile" (I believe it because it is impossible). Also attributed to St. Augustine in the form "Credo quia absurdum."

[2] A corresponding Greek passage is ascribed to Menander.
> That same man that runnith awaie
> Maie again fight an other daie.
> ERASMUS: *Apothegms* [1542], translated by Udall
> Celuy qui fuit de bonne heure
> Peut combattre derechef.
> (He who flies in good time can fight again.)
> *Satyre Menippée* [1594]
> Qui fuit peut revenir aussi;
> Qui meurt, il n'en est pas ainsi.
> (He who flies can also return; it is not so with him who dies.)
> PAUL SCARRON [1610–1660]
> For those that fly may fight again,
> Which he can never do that's slain.
> SAMUEL BUTLER: *Hudibras, Part III* [1678], *Canto III, L. 243*
> He that fights and runs away
> May turn and fight another day;
> But he that is in battle slain
> Will never rise to fight again.
> JAMES RAY: *History of the Rebellion* [1752]
> For he who fights and runs away
> May live to fight another day;
> But he who is in battle slain
> Can never rise and fight again.
> GOLDSMITH: *The Art of Poetry on a New Plan* [1761]
> But since the man that runs away
> Lives to die another day,
> And cowards' funerals, when they come,
> Are not wept so well at home,
> Therefore, though the best is bad,
> Stand and do the best, my lad.
> A. E. HOUSMAN [1859–1936]: *The Day of Battle*

[3] Translated by CHARLES DUKE YONGE [1812–1891].

---

they expected, and have lost what they had, — being unfortunate by an enigmatical sort of calamity."
The Deipnosophists. VI, 23

Every investigation which is guided by principles of Nature fixes its ultimate aim entirely on gratifying the stomach.[1]
Ibid. VII, 11

Dorion, ridiculing the description of a tempest in the "Nautilus" of Timotheus, said that he had seen a more formidable storm in a boiling saucepan.[2]
Ibid. VIII, 19

On one occasion some one put a very little wine into a wine-cooler, and said that it was sixteen years old. "It is very small for its age," said Gnathaena.
Ibid. XIII, 47

DIOGENES LAERTIUS [3]
[*Circa* A. D. 200]

Writers differ with respect to the apophthegms of the Seven Sages, attributing the same one to various authors.
Thales. 14

Solon used to say that speech was the image of actions; . . . that laws were like cobwebs, — for that if any trifling or powerless thing fell into them, they held it fast; while if it were something weightier, it broke through them and was off.
Solon. 10

Solon gave the following advice: "Consider your honour, as a gentleman, of more weight than an oath."
Ibid. 12

As some say, Solon was the author of the apophthegm, "Nothing in excess."
Ibid. 16

---

[1] See Samuel Johnson, page 340a.
[2] A tempest in a teapot. — *Proverb*
[3] From *The Lives and Opinions of Eminent Philosophers*, translated by CHARLES DUKE YONGE [1812–1891].
> There is scarce any Philosopher but dies twice or thrice in Laertius; nor almost any life without two or three deaths in Plutarch. — SIR THOMAS BROWNE: *Urn Burial* [1658], *Chap. 3*

Chilo advised, "not to speak evil of the dead." [1]

Chilo. 2

Heraclitus says that Pittacus, when he had got Alcaeus into his power, released him, saying, "Forgiveness is better than revenge." [2]

Pittacus. 3

One of his sayings was, "Even the gods cannot strive against necessity." [3]

Ibid. 4

Another was, "Watch your opportunity." [4]

Ibid. 7

Bias used to say that men ought to calculate life both as if they were fated to live a long and a short time, and that they ought to love one another as if at a future time they would come to hate one another; for that most men were bad.

Bias. 5

Ignorance plays the chief part among men, and the multitude of words.[5]

Cleobulus. 4

Anarcharsis, on learning that the sides of a ship were four fingers thick, said that "the passengers were just that distance from death." [6]

Anarcharsis. 5

It was a common saying of Myson that men ought not to investigate things from words, but words from things; for that things are not made for the sake of words, but words for things.

Myson. 3

[1] De mortuis nil nisi bonum (Of the dead nothing but good).

[2] Forgiveness is better than punishment; for the one is proof of a gentle, the other of a savage nature. — Quoted by EPICTETUS [*circa* A. D. 60]: *Fragment 62*

[3] Necessity has no law. — RABELAIS: *Works, Book V* [1564], *Chap. 15*

See Shakespeare, page 169a.

[4] Observe the opportunity. — *Apocrypha: Ecclesiasticus, IV, 20*

[5] In the multitude of words there wanteth not sin. — *Proverbs, X, 19*

[6] "How thick do you judge the planks of our ship to be?" "Some two good inches and upward," returned the pilot. "It seems, then, we are within two fingers' breadth of damnation." — RABELAIS: *Works, Book IV* [1548], *Chap. 23*

Epimenides was sent by his father into the field to look for a sheep, turned out of the road at mid-day and lay down in a certain cave and fell asleep, and slept there fifty-seven years; and after that, when awake, he went on looking for the sheep, thinking that he had been taking a short nap.[1]

Epimenides. 2

Anaximander used to assert that the primary cause of all things was the Infinite, — not defining exactly whether he meant air or water or anything else.

Anaximander. 2

Anaxagoras said to a man who was grieving because he was dying in a foreign land, "The descent to Hades is the same from every place."

Anaxagoras. 6

Aristophanes turns Socrates into ridicule in his comedies, as making the worse appear the better reason.[2]

Socrates. 5

Often when he was looking on at auctions he would say, "How many things there are which I do not need!"

Ibid. 10

Socrates said, "Those who want fewest things are nearest to the gods."

Ibid. 11

He said that there was one only good, namely, knowledge; and one only evil, namely, ignorance.

Ibid. 14

He declared that he knew nothing, except the fact of his ignorance.

Ibid. 16

Being asked whether it was better to marry or not, he replied, "Whichever you do, you will repent it."

Ibid.

Aristippus being asked what were the most necessary things for well-born boys to learn, said, "Those things which they will put in practice when they become men."

Aristippus. 4

[1] The theme of IRVING's story of Rip Van Winkle.

[2] See Milton, page 253b.

Like sending owls to Athens, as the proverb goes.[1]

Plato. 32

Time is the image of eternity.

Ibid. 41

There is a written and an unwritten law. The one by which we regulate our constitutions in our cities is the written law; that which arises from custom is the unwritten law.

Ibid. 51

Plato was continually saying to Xenocrates, "Sacrifice to the Graces." [2]

Xenocrates. 3

Of a rich man who was niggardly he said, "That man does not own his estate, but his estate owns him."

Bion. 3

Very late in life, when he was studying geometry, some one said to Lacydes, "Is it then a time for you to be learning now?" "If it is not," he replied, "when will it be?"

Lacydes. 5

The question was put to him, what hope is; and his answer was, "The dream of a waking man."

Aristotle. 11

He used to say that personal beauty was a better introduction than any letter; but others say that it was Diogenes who gave this description of it, while Aristotle called beauty "the gift of God"; that Socrates called it "a short-lived tyranny"; Theophrastus, "a silent deceit"; Theocritus, "an ivory mischief."

Ibid.

On one occasion Aristotle was asked how much educated men were superior to those uneducated: "As much," said he, "as the living are to the dead." [3]

Ibid.

It was a saying of his that education

was an ornament in prosperity and a refuge in adversity.

Aristotle. 11

Asked what he gained from philosophy, he answered, "To do without being commanded what others do from fear of the laws."

Ibid.

The question was once put to him, how we ought to behave to our friends; and the answer he gave was, "As we should wish our friends to behave to us." [1]

Ibid.

He used to define justice as "a virtue of the soul distributing that which each person deserved."

Ibid.

Another of his sayings was, that education was the best viaticum of old age.

Ibid.

It was a favourite expression of Theophrastus that time was the most valuable thing that a man could spend.[2]

Theophrastus. 10

Antisthenes used to say that envious people were devoured by their own disposition, just as iron is by rust.

Antisthenes. 4

When he was praised by some wicked men, he said, "I am sadly afraid that I must have done some wicked thing." [3]

Ibid.

When asked what learning was the most necessary, he said, "Not to unlearn what you have learned."

Ibid.

Diogenes would frequently praise those who were about to marry, and yet did not marry.

Diogenes. 4

"Bury me on my face," said Diogenes; and when he was asked why, he

---

[1] See Horace, page 40b.

[2] Let us sacrifice to the Muses. — PLUTARCH [A.D. 46–120]: *The Banquet of the Seven Wise Men* (A saying of Solon)

[3] This used to be quoted "with great warmth" by Dr. Johnson, according to Boswell in his *Life* of Dr. Johnson [1791].

[1] Therefore all things whatsoever ye would that men should do to you, do ye even so to them. — *Matthew, VII, 12*

[2] Nothing is so dear and precious as time. — RABELAIS: *Works, Book V* [1564], *Chap. 5* Remember that time is money. — BENJAMIN FRANKLIN: *Advice to a Young Tradesman* [1748]

[3] See Plutarch, page 59b.

replied, "Because in a little while everything will be turned upside down."

Diogenes. 6

Plato having defined man to be a two-legged animal without feathers, Diogenes plucked a cock and brought it into the Academy, and said, "This is Plato's man." On which account this addition was made to the definition, — "With broad flat nails."

Ibid.

A man once asked Diogenes what was the proper time for supper, and he made answer, "If you are a rich man, whenever you please; and if you are a poor man, whenever you can." [1]

Ibid.

Diogenes lighted a candle in the daytime, and went round saying, "I am looking for a man." [2]

Ibid.

When asked what he would take to let a man give him a blow on the head, he said, "A helmet."

Ibid.

Once he saw a youth blushing, and addressed him, "Courage, my boy! that is the complexion of virtue." [3]

Ibid.

When asked what wine he liked to drink, he replied, "That which belongs to another."

Ibid.

When a man reproached him for going into unclean places, he said, "The sun too penetrates into privies, but is not polluted by them." [4]

Ibid.

[1] The rich when he is hungry, the poor when he has anything to eat. — RABELAIS: *Works, Book IV* [1548], *Chap. 64*

[2] Told also of Aesop.

[3] Blushing is the colour of virtue. — MATHEW HENRY [1662–1714]: *Commentaries, Jeremiah III*

[4] The spiritual virtue of a sacrament is like light: although it passes among the impure, it is not polluted. — ST. AUGUSTINE [A.D. 354–430]: *Tract on St. John, Chap. 5, 15*

The sun shineth upon the dunghill, and is not corrupted. — LYLY: *Euphues* [1579]

The sun, which passeth through pollutions and itself remains as pure as before. — BACON:

Diogenes said once to a person who was showing him a dial, "It is a very useful thing to save a man from being too late for supper."

Menedemus. 3

When Zeno was asked what a friend was, he replied, "Another I." [1]

Zeno. 19

They say that the first inclination which an animal has is to protect itself.

Ibid. 52

He calls drunkenness an expression identical with ruin. [2]

Pythagoras. 6

Among what he called his precepts were such as these: Do not stir the fire with a sword. Do not sit down on a bushel. Do not devour thy heart. [3]

Ibid. 17

In the time of Pythagoras that proverbial phrase "Ipse dixit" [4] was introduced into ordinary life.

Ibid. 25

It takes a wise man to discover a wise man.

Xenophanes. 3

Protagoras asserted that there were two sides to every question, exactly opposite to each other.

Protagoras. 3

Epicurus laid down the doctrine that pleasure was the chief good.

Epicurus. 6

LONGINUS
[*Circa* A.D. 210?–273]

Sublimity is the echo of a noble mind.

On the Sublime. Chap. IX

In the Odyssey one may liken Homer to the setting sun, of which the grandeur remains without the intensity.

Ibid.

Advancement of Learning [1605], *Book II*

Truth is as impossible to be soiled by any outward touch as the sunbeam. — MILTON: *The Doctrine and Discipline of Divorce* [1643]

[1] See Homer, page 5a.

[2] See Robert Hall, page 397b.

[3] See Plutarch, page 57b.

[4] He said it himself.

CONSTANTINE
[A. D. 288?–337]

In this sign shalt thou conquer.[1]
> EUSEBIUS: *Life of Constantine. I, 28*

ST. CHRYSOSTOM
[A. D. 327–407]

No one can harm the man who does himself no wrong.[2]
> *Letter to Olympia*

ST. JEROME [3]
[A. D. 345–420]

Avoid, as you would the plague, a clergyman who is also a man of business.
> *Letter 52, To Nepotian*

A fat paunch never breeds fine thoughts.
> *Ibid.*

The best almoner is he who keeps back nothing for himself.
> *Ibid.*

It is no fault of Christianity if a hypocrite falls into sin.
> *Letter 125, To Rusticus*

Preferring to store her money in the stomachs of the needy rather than hide it in a purse.
> *Letter 127, To Principia*

LONGUS
[FIFTH CENTURY]

There was never any yet that wholly could escape love, and never shall there be any, never so long as beauty shall be, never so long as eyes can see.
> *Daphnis and Chloe.*[4] *Proem, Chap. 2*

He is so poor that he could not keep a dog.
> *Ibid. Chap. 15*

[1] In hoc signo vinces. The words of Constantine's vision before his battle with Maxentius at Saxa Rubra, near Rome, A. D. 312.
[2] No one is injured save by himself. — ERASMUS [1465–1536]: *Adages*
[3] Translated by F. A. WRIGHT.
[4] The only known Greek prose romance (pastoral).

BOETHIUS
[A. D. 470?–525]

In every adversity of fortune, to have been happy is the most unhappy kind of misfortune.[1]
> *De Consolatione Philosophiae.
> Book II, 4, 4*

Who hath so entire happiness that he is not in some part offended with the condition of his estate?
> *Ibid. 41*

Nothing is miserable but what is thought so, and contrariwise, every estate is happy if he that bears it be content.
> *Ibid. 64*

From thee, great God, we spring, to thee we tend, —
Path, motive, guide, original and end.[2]
> *Ibid. Book III, 9, 27*

Who can give law to lovers? Love is a greater law to itself.
> *Ibid. 12, 47*

ST. BENEDICT [3]
[A. D. 480–543]

We are therefore about to establish a school of the Lord's service in which we hope to introduce nothing harsh or burdensome.
> *Rule of St. Benedict. Prologue*

ALI IBN-ABU-TALIB [4]
[602?–661]

He who has a thousand friends has not a
friend to spare,

[1] See Dante, page 75b, and Chaucer, page 78b.
> This is truth the poet sings,
> That a sorrow's crown of sorrow is remembering happier things.
> TENNYSON: *Locksley Hall* [1842],
> L. 75

> There is no greater sorrow
> Than to be mindful of the happy time
> In misery.
> LONGFELLOW: *Inferno* [1867],
> Canto V, L. 121
[2] Translated by SAMUEL JOHNSON, and used as motto to *The Rambler, No. 7* [1750].
[3] Founder of Western monasticism.
[4] Ali ibn-abu-Talib, son-in-law of Mohammed, and fourth caliph, who was for his courage called "The Lion of God," was mur-

And he who has one enemy will meet him everywhere.[1]

CAEDMON
[*Floruit* 670]

Light was first
Through the Lord's word
Named day:
Beauteous, bright creation!
Creation.[2] *The First Day*

The fiend with all his comrades
Fell then from heaven above,
Through as long as three nights and days,
The angels from heaven into hell;
And them all the Lord transformed to devils,
Because they his deed and word
Would not revere.
Ibid. The Fall of the Rebel Angels

ALCUIN
[735–804]

The voice of the people is the voice of God.[3]
Letter to Charlemagne
[A. D. *800*]

ABU MOHAMMED KASIM BEN ALI HARIRI
[1054–1122]

We praise Thee, O God,
For whatever perspicuity of language Thou hast taught us
And whatever eloquence Thou hast inspired us with.
Makamat. Prayer

Guard us from error in narration,
And keep us from folly even in pleasantry,
So that we may be safe from the censure of sarcastic tongues.
Ibid.

---

dered A. D. 661. He was the author of *A Hundred Sayings.*
[1] Translated by EMERSON.
[2] From the text of BENJAMIN THORPE [1782–1870].
[3] Vox populi, vox Dei.

ARCHIPOETA
[TWELFTH CENTURY]

I have a rendezvous with death within a tavern.[1]

MOSES BEN MAIMON (MAIMONIDES)
[1135–1204]

Anticipate charity by preventing poverty; assist the reduced fellowman, either by a considerable gift, or a sum of money, or by teaching him a trade, or by putting him in the way of business, so that he may earn an honest livelihood, and not be forced to the dreadful alternative of holding out his hand for charity. This is the highest step and the summit of charity's golden ladder.
Charity's Eight Degrees

WALTER DE MAP
[1140–1210]

Die I must, but let me die drinking in an inn!
Hold the wine-cup to my lips sparkling from the bin!
So, when angels flutter down to take me from my sin,
"Ah, God have mercy on this sot," the cherubs will begin.
Quoted by J. R. GREEN, *in A Short History of the English People, Chap. 3, Sect. 1* [2]

THOMAS OF ERCILDOUN
[1220–1297]

Whate'er betide,
Haig shall be Haig of Bemersyde.
Quoted by SIR WALTER SCOTT: *Thomas the Rhymer, Part 2, Minstrelsy of the Scottish Border*

ALFONSO THE WISE
[1221–1284]

Had I been present at the creation,

[1] See Alan Seeger, page 947b.
[2] There is also a translation by LEIGH HUNT: "The Jovial Priest's Confession."

I would have given some useful hints for the better ordering of the universe.[1]

ST. THOMAS AQUINAS
[*Circa* 1225–1274]

Three things are necessary for the salvation of man: to know what he ought to believe; to know what he ought to desire; and to know what he ought to do.

Two Precepts of Charity [*1273*]

DANTE ALIGHIERI
[1265–1321]

In the middle of the journey of our life I came to myself in a dark wood where the straight way was lost.[2]

Divine Comedy [3] [Circa *1300*].
Inferno, [4] *Canto I, Line 1*

And as he, who with panting breath has escaped from the deep sea to the shore, turns to the dangerous water and gazes.

Ibid. Line 22

Thou art my master and my author; [5] thou alone art he from whom I took the good style that hath done me honour.

Ibid. Line 85

Leave all hope, ye that enter.[6]

Ibid. Canto III, Line 9

Here must all distrust be left; all cowardice must here be dead.

Ibid. Line 14

The wretched souls of those who lived without infamy and without praise maintain this miserable mode.[7]

Ibid. Line 34

[1] CARLYLE says, in his *History of Frederick the Great, Book II, Chap.* 7, that this saying of Alfonso about Ptolemy's astronomy, "that it seemed a crank machine; that it was pity the Creator had not taken advice," is still remembered by mankind — this and no other of his many sayings.

[2] Nel mezzo del cammin di nostra vita
Mi ritrovai per una selva oscura,
Che la diritta via era smarrita.

[3] Text from *The Temple Classics,* J. M. Dent & Sons [1900].

[4] Translated by JOHN AITKEN CARLYLE, *The Temple Classics,* unless otherwise noted.

[5] Virgil.

[6] Lasciate ogni speranza, voi ch'entrate!

[7] Translated by CHARLES ELIOT NORTON [1902].

Let us not speak of them; but look, and pass on.

*Divine Comedy. Inferno,
Canto III, Line 51*

These unfortunates, who never were alive.

Ibid. Line 64

Into the eternal darkness, into fire and into ice.

Ibid. Line 87

I came into a place void of all light, which bellows like the sea in tempest, when it is combated by warring winds.

Ibid. Canto V, Line 28

Love, which quickly lays hold on gentle heart, seized this one for the fair person that was taken from me, and the mode still hurts me.[1]

Ibid. Line 100

Love, which absolves no loved one from loving, seized me for the pleasing of him so strongly that, as thou seest, it does not even now abandon me.[1]

Ibid. Line 103

What sweet thoughts, what longing led them to the woeful pass.

Ibid. Line 113

There is no greater pain than to recall a happy time in wretchedness.[2]

Ibid. Line 121

That day we read in it no farther.[3]

Ibid. Line 138

Pride, Envy, and Avarice are the three sparks that have set the hearts of all on fire.

Ibid. Canto VI, Line 74

But when thou shalt be in the sweet world, I pray thee recall me to the memory of man.

Ibid. Line 88

O ye who have sound understandings, regard the doctrine that is hidden under the veil of the strange verses! [1]

Ibid. Canto IX, Line 61

Already I had fixed my look on his;

[1] Translated by CHARLES ELIOT NORTON [1902].

[2]   Nessun maggior dolore
Che ricordarsi del tempo felice
Nella miseria.

See Boethius, page 73b, and Chaucer, page 78b.

[3] Quel giorno più non vi leggemmo avante.

and he rose upright with breast and countenance, as if he entertained great scorn of Hell.

Divine Comedy. Inferno,
Canto X, Line 34

"If thou follow thy star, thou canst not fail of glorious haven."

Ibid. Canto XV, Line 55

So conscience chide me not, I am prepared for Fortune as she wills.

Ibid. Line 91

He listens well who notes it.

Ibid. Line 99

A fit request should be followed with the work in silence.

Ibid. Canto XXIV, Line 77

Consider your origin; ye were not formed to live like brutes, but to follow virtue and knowledge.

Ibid. Canto XXVI, Line 119

And thence we issued out, again to see the stars.[1]

Ibid. Canto XXXIV, Line 139

To run over better waters the little vessel of my genius now hoists her sails, as she leaves behind her a sea so cruel.

Ibid. Purgatorio,[2] Canto I, Line 1

He goes seeking liberty, which is so dear, as he knows who for it renounces life.

Ibid. Line 71

O conscience, upright and stainless, how bitter a sting to thee is a little fault!

Ibid. Canto III, Line 8

For to lose time is most displeasing to him who knows most.

Ibid. Line 78

The Infinite Goodness has such wide arms that it takes whatever turns to it.

Ibid. Line 121

Unless, before then, the prayer assist me which rises from a heart that lives in grace: what avails the other, which is not heard in heaven?

Ibid. Canto IV, Line 133

Stand like a firm tower that never

shakes its top for blowing of the winds.

Divine Comedy. Purgatorio,
Canto V, Line 14

[Beatrice] who shall be a light between truth and intellect.

Ibid. Canto VI, Line 45

It was now the hour that turns back desire in those that sail the sea, and softens their hearts, the day when they have said to their sweet friends farewell, and which pierces the new pilgrim with love, if he hear from afar a bell that seems to deplore the dying day.

Ibid. Canto VIII, Line 1

Give us this day the daily manna, without which, in this rough desert, he backward goes, who toils most to go on.

Ibid. Canto XI, Line 13

Worldly renown is naught but a breath of wind, which now comes this way and now comes that, and changes name because it changes quarter.

Ibid. Line 100

O human race, born to fly upward, wherefore at a little wind dost thou so fall.

Ibid. Canto XII, Line 95

To a greater force, and to a better nature, ye, free, are subject, and that creates the mind in you, which the heavens have not in their charge. Therefore if the present world go astray, the cause is in you, in you it is to be sought.

Ibid. Canto XVI, Line 79

Every one confusedly conceives of a good in which the mind may be at rest, and desires it; wherefore every one strives to attain to it.

Ibid. Canto XVII, Line 127

Love kindled by virtue always kindles another, provided that its flame appear outwardly.

Ibid. Canto XXII, Line 10

Less than a drop of blood remains in me that does not tremble; I recognize the signals of the ancient flame.[1]

Ibid. Canto XXX, Line 46

But so much the more malign and wild does the ground become with bad

---

[1] E quindi uscimmo a riveder le stelle.
[2] Translated by CHARLES ELIOT NORTON [1902].

[1]   Men che dramma
Di sangue m'è rimaso, che no tremi;
Conosco i segni dell' antica fiamma.

seed and untilled, as it has the more of good earthly vigor.
> *Divine Comedy. Purgatorio,*
> *Canto XXX, Line 118*

Pure and disposed to mount unto the stars.[1]
> *Ibid. Canto XXXIII, Line 145*

The glory of Him who moves everything penetrates through the universe, and is resplendent in one part more and in another less.
> *Ibid. Paradiso,*[2] *Canto I, Line 1*

Great flame follows a tiny spark.
> *Ibid. Line 34*

And his will is our peace.[3]
> *Ibid. Canto III, Line 85*

The greatest gift which God in His bounty bestowed in creating, and the most conformed to His own goodness, and that which He prizes the most, was the freedom of the will, with which the creatures that have intelligence, they all and they alone, were and are endowed.
> *Ibid. Canto V, Line 19*

Thou shalt make proof how the bread of others savors of salt, and how hard a path is the descending and the mounting of another's stairs.
> *Ibid. Canto XVII, Line 58*

Vanquishing me with the light of a smile, she said to me: "Turn thee, and listen, for not only in my eyes is Paradise."
> *Ibid. Canto XVIII, Line 19*

The night which hides things from us.
> *Ibid. Canto XXIII, Line 3*

The Love which moves the sun and the other stars.[4]
> *Ibid. Canto XXXIII, Line 145*

WILLIAM OF WYKEHAM
[1324–1404]

Manners makyth man.
> *Motto of his two foundations,*
> *Winchester College and New*
> *College, Oxford*

[1] Puro e disposto a salire alle stelle.
[2] Translated by CHARLES ELIOT NORTON [1902].
[3] E la sua volontate è nostra pace.
[4] L'amor che move il sole e l'altre stelle.

GEOFFREY CHAUCER [1]
[?1343–1400]

Hard is the herte that loveth nought
In May.
> *The Romaunt of the Rose*
> *[Circa 1369]. Line 85*

The tyme, that may not sojourne,
But goth, and may never retourne,
As watir that doun renneth ay,
But never drope retourne may.
> *Ibid. Line 381*

As round as appil was his face.
> *Ibid. Line 819*

So that the more she yaf awey,
The more, ywis, she hadde alwey.
> *Ibid. Line 1159*

A ful gret fool is he, ywis,
That bothe riche and nygard is.
> *Ibid. Line 1171*

To rede, and drive the nyght away.
> *The Book of the Duchesse*
> *[1369]. Line 49*

Morpheus,
Thou knowest hym wel, the god of slep.
> *Ibid. Line 136*

I was waked
With smale foules a gret hepe,
That had affrayed me out of slepe.
> *Ibid. Line 294*

"Hyt is not al gold that glareth." [2]
> *The House of Fame [1374–*
> *1385]. Book I, Line 272*

[1] From the text of F. N. Robinson, *The Complete Works of Geoffrey Chaucer,* Houghton Mifflin Company [1933].
[2] Tyrwhitt says this is taken from the *Parabolae of* ALANUS DE INSULIS, who died in 1294: Non teneas aurum totum quod splendet ut aurum (Do not hold everything as gold which shines as gold).

But al thyng which that shineth as the gold
Nis nat gold, as that I have herd it told.
> *The Canterbury Tales [circa 1387],*
> *The Canon's Yeoman's Tale, L. 962*

All is not golde that outward shewith bright. — LYDGATE [1370?–1451?]: *On the Mutability of Human Affairs*

Gold all is not that doth golden seem. — SPENSER: *Faerie Queene, Book II* [1590], *Canto VIII, St. 14*

All that glisters is not gold, —
Often have you heard that told.
> SHAKESPEARE: *Merchant of Venice* [1596–1597], *Act II, Sc. 7, L. 65*

All is not gold that glisters. — CERVANTES:

Soun ys noght but eyr ybroken,
And every speche that ys spoken,
Lowd or pryvee, foul or fair,
In his substance ys but air.
> *The House of Fame. Book I,*
> *Line 765*

Venus clerk, Ovide,
That hath ysowen wonder wide
The grete god of Loves name.
> *Ibid. Book III, Line 1487*

The lyf so short, the craft so long to
lerne,[1]
Th'assay so hard, so sharp the con-
queryinge.
> *The Parliament of Fowls*
> *[1380–1386]. Line 1*

For out of olde feldes, as men seyth,
Cometh al this newe corn fro yer to
yere;
And out of olde bokes, in good feyth,
Cometh al this newe science that men
lere.
> *Ibid. Line 22*

Nature, the vicaire of the almyghty
lorde.
> *Ibid. Line 379*

"A fol can not be stille."
> *Ibid. Line 574*

Now welcome, somer, with thy sonne
softe,[2]
That hast this wintres weders over-
shake.
> *Ibid. Line 680*

A fool may ek a wys-man ofte gide.
> *Troilus and Criseyde* [Circa
> *1385]. Book I, Line 630*

Ek som tyme it is craft to seme fle
Fro thyng whych in effect men hunte
faste.
> *Ibid. Line 747*

Til crowes feet be growen under youre
yë.
> *Ibid. Book II, Line 403*

Don Quixote, Part II [1615], Book III, Chap.
33

All is not gold that glisteneth. — MIDDLE-
TON: *A Fair Quarrel* [1617], *Act V, Sc. 1*
All, as they say, that glitters is not gold. —
DRYDEN: *The Hind and the Panther* [1687],
L. 215

[1] See Hippocrates, page 22a.
[2] In a somer sesun, whan softe was the
sonne. — WILLIAM LANGLAND [1330?–1400?]:
The Vision of Piers Plowman, Prologue

Lord, this is an huge rayn!
This were a weder for to slepen inne!
> *Troilus and Criseyde. Book III,*
> *Line 656*

It is nought good a slepyng hound to
wake.[1]
> *Ibid. Line 764*

Right as an aspes leef she gan to quake.
> *Ibid. Line 1200*

For of fortunes sharpe adversitee
The worste kynde of infortune is this,
A man to han ben in prosperitee,
And it remembren, whan it passed is.[2]
> *Ibid. Line 1625*

Oon ere it herde, at tothir out it went.[3]
> *Ibid. Book IV, Line 434*

Ek wonder last but nyne nyght nevere
in towne.[4]
> *Ibid. Line 588*

But manly sette the world on six and
sevene;[5]
And if thow deye a martyr, go to
hevene!
> *Ibid. Line 622*

For tyme ylost may nought recovered
be.
> *Ibid. Line 1283*

I am right sory for youre hevynesse.
> *Ibid. Book V, Line 140*

For he that naught n'assaieth, naught
n'acheveth.
> *Ibid. Line 784*

Trewe as stiel.
> *Ibid. Line 831*

[1] See Dickens, page 579b.
[2] See Boethius, page 73b, and Dante, page
75b.
[3] Went in at the tone eare and out at
tother. — JOHN HEYWOOD: *Proverbes* [1546].
Part II, Chap. IX
[4] See Shakespeare, page 126b.
[5]   All is uneven,
    And everything is left at six and seven.
    SHAKESPEARE: *Richard II* [1595–1596],
        Act II, Sc. 2, L. 120
Let things go at sixes and sevens. — CER-
VANTES: *Don Quixote, Part I* [1605], *Book
IV, Chap. 3*
Things going on at sixes and sevens. —
GOLDSMITH: *The Good-Natured Man* [1768],
Act I
    Say, why is everything
    Either at sixes or at sevens?
    W. S. GILBERT: *H.M.S. Pinafore*
        [1878], *Act II, Fair Moon*

This sodeyn Diomede.
Troilus and Criseyde. Book V,
Line 1024
Ye, fare wel al the snow of ferne yere! [1]
Ibid. Line 1176
Ek gret effect men write in place lite;
Th' entente is al, and nat the lettres space.
Ibid. Line 1629
Go, litel bok, go, litel myn tragedye.
Ibid. Line 1786
And for ther is so gret diversite
In Englissh and in writyng of oure tonge,
So prey I God that non myswrite the,
Ne the mysmetre for defaute of tonge.
Ibid. Line 1793
O moral Gower, this book I directe
To the.
Ibid. Line 1856
Whan that the month of May
Is comen, and that I here the foules synge,
And that the floures gynnen for to spryngen,
Farewel my bok, and my devocioun!
The Legend of Good Women
[Circa 1386]. Line 36
That, of al the floures in the mede,
Thanne love I most thise floures white and rede,
Swiche as men callen daysyes in our toun.
Ibid. Line 41
Whan that Aprille with his shoures soote
The droghte of March hath perced to the roote.
The Canterbury Tales [Circa
1387]. Prologue, Line 1
And smale foweles maken melodye,
That slepen al the night with open yë,
(So priketh hem nature in hir corages);
Thanne longen folk to goon on pilgrimages.
Ibid. Line 9
He was a verray, parfit gentil knight.
Ibid. Line 72
He was as fressh as is the month of May.
Ibid. Line 92

[1] See Villon, page 83b.

He koude songes make, and wel endyte.
The Canterbury Tales. Prologue,
Line 95
Ful wel she soong the service dyvyne,
Entuned in hir nose ful semely;
And Frenssh she spak ful faire and fetisly,
After the scole of Stratford atte Bowe,
For Frenssh of Parys was to hir unknowe.
Ibid. Line 122
His palfrey was as broun as is a berye.
Ibid. Line 207
A Frere ther was, a wantowne and a mery.
Ibid. Line 208
Somwhat he lipsed, for his wantownesse,
To make his Englissh sweete upon his tonge.
Ibid. Line 264
A Clerk ther was of Oxenford also.
Ibid. Line 285
For hym was levere have at his beddes heed
Twenty bookes, clad in blak or reed,
Of Aristotle and his philosophie,
Than robes riche, or fithele, or gay sautrie,
But al be that he was a philosophre,
Yet hadde he but litel gold in cofre.
Ibid. Line 293
And gladly wolde he lerne, and gladly teche.
Ibid. Line 308
Nowher so bisy a man as he ther nas,
And yet he semed bisier than he was.
Ibid. Line 321
For he was Epicurus owene sone.
Ibid. Line 336
He was a good felawe.[1]
Ibid. Line 395
His studie was but litel on the Bible.
Ibid. Line 438
For gold in phisik is a cordial,
Therfore he lovede gold in special.
Ibid. Line 443

[1] If he be not fellow with the best king, thou shalt find him the best king of good fellows. — SHAKESPEARE: *King Henry V* [1598–1600], *Act V, Sc. 2, L. 259*

She was a worthy womman al hir lyve,
Housbondes at chirche dore she hadde fyve.
> *The Canterbury Tales. Prologue, Line 459*

This noble ensample to his sheep he yaf,
That first he wroghte, and afterward he taughte.
> *Ibid. Line 496*

If gold ruste, what shal iren do?
> *Ibid. Line 500*

But Cristes loore, and his apostles twelve,
He taughte, and first he folwed it hym-selve.
> *Ibid. Line 527*

And yet he hadde a thombe of gold.[1]
> *Ibid. Line 563*

That hadde a fyr-reed cherubynnes face.
> *Ibid. Line 624*

Wel loved he garleck, oynons, and eek lekes,
And for to drynken strong wyn, reed as blood.
> *Ibid. Line 634*

And whan that he wel dronken hadde the wyn,
Than wolde he speke no word but Latyn.
> *Ibid. Line 637*

Whoso shal telle a tale after a man,
He moot reherce as ny as evere he kan
Everich a word, if it be in his charge,
Al speke he never so rudeliche and large,
Or ellis he moot telle his tale untrewe,
Or feyne thing, or finde wordes new.
> *Ibid. Line 731*

For May wol have no slogardye a-night.
The sesoun priketh every gentil herte,
And maketh him out of his sleep to sterte.
> *Ibid. The Knight's Tale, Line 1042*

Ech man for hymself.
> *Ibid. Line 1182*

The bisy larke, messager of day.
> *Ibid. Line 1491*

[1] In allusion to the proverb, "Every honest miller has a golden thumb."

May, with alle thy floures and thy grene,
Welcome be thou, faire, fresshe May.
> *The Canterbury Tales. The Knight's Tale, Line 1510*

That "feeld hath eyen, and the wode hath eres".[1]
> *Ibid. Line 1522*

Now up, now doun, as boket in a welle.
> *Ibid. Line 1533*

For pitee renneth soone in gentil herte.
> *Ibid. Line 1761*

Cupido,
Upon his shuldres wynges hadde he two;
And blynd he was, as it is often seene;
A bowe he bar and arwes brighte and kene.
> *Ibid. Line 1963*

Up roos the sonne, and up roose Emelye.
> *Ibid. Line 2273*

Myn be the travaille, and thyn be the glorie!
> *Ibid. Line 2406*

And was al his chiere, as in his herte.
> *Ibid. Line 2683*

What is this world? what asketh men to have?
Now with his love, now in his colde grave
Allone, withouten any compaignye.
> *Ibid. Line 2777*

This world nys but a thurghfare ful of wo,
And we been pilgrymes, passing to and fro.
Deeth is an ende of every worldly soore.
> *Ibid. Line 2847*

Jhesu Crist, and seiynte Benedight,
Blesse this hous from every wikked wight.
> *Ibid. The Miller's Tale, Line 3483*

[1] Fieldes have eies and woodes have eares.
— John Heywood: *Proverbes* [1546], *Part II, Chap. V*
Wode has erys, felde has sigt. — *King Edward and the Shepherd, MS. [circa* 1300]
Walls have ears. — Cervantes: *Don Quixote, Part II* [1615], *Chap. 48*
> Woods have tongues
> As walls have ears.
> Tennyson: *Idylls of the King, Balin and Balan* [1885], *L. 522*

And broghte of myghty ale a large
quart.
*The Canterbury Tales. The
Miller's Tale, Line 3497*
Yet in our asshen olde is fyr yreke.[1]
*Ibid. The Reeve's Prologue,
Line 3882*
The gretteste clerkes been noght the
wisest men.[2]
Ibid. The Reeve's Tale, Line 4054
Thurgh thikke and thurgh thenne.[3]
Ibid. Line 4066
So was hir joly whistle wel ywet.
Ibid. Line 4155
At Cristemasse merie may ye daunce.
*Ibid. The Man of Law's Prologue,
Line 126*
She is mirour of alle curteisye.[4]
*Ibid. The Man of Law's Tale,
Line 166*
For in the sterres, clerer than is glas,
Is writen, God woot, whoso koude it
rede,
The deeth of every man.
Ibid. Line 194
Sathan, that evere us waiteth to bigile.
Ibid. Line 582
In his owene grece I made hym frye.[5]
*Ibid. The Wife of Bath's Prologue,
Line 487*
What thyng we may nat lightly have,
Therafter wol we crie alday and crave.
Ibid. Line 517
Greet prees at market maketh deere
ware,

[1] E'en in our ashes live their wonted fires.
— THOMAS GRAY: *Elegy in a Country
Churchyard* [1750], St. 23
[2] The greatest Clerkes be not the wisest
men. — JOHN HEYWOOD: *Proverbes* [1546],
Part II, Chap. V
[3] Through thicke and thin. — DU BARTAS:
Divine Weeks and Works [1578], Second
Week, Fourth Day
[4]   Call him bounteous Buckingham,
The mirror of all courtesy.
SHAKESPEARE: *Henry VIII* [1613],
Act II, Sc. 1, L. 53
[5] Frieth in her own grease. — JOHN HEY-
WOOD: *Proverbes* [1546], Part I, Chap. XI
The best way were to entertain him with
hope, till the wicked fire of lust have melted
him in his own grease. — SHAKESPEARE:
Merry Wives of Windsor [1601], Act II, Sc. 1,
L. 60

And to greet cheep is holde at litel prys.
*The Canterbury Tales. The Wife
of Bath's Prologue, Line 522*
But yet I hadde alwey a coltes tooth.
Gat-toothed I was, and that bicam
me weel.
Ibid. Line 601
"My lige lady, generally," quod he,
"Wommen desiren have sovereynetee
As well over hir housbond as hir love."
*Ibid. The Wife of Bath's Tale,
Line 1037*
Looke who that is moost vertuous al-
way,
Pryvee and apert, and most entendeth
ay
To do the gentil dedes that he kan;
Taak hym for the grettest gentil
man.
Ibid. Line 1113
That he is gentil that dooth gentil
dedis.[1]
Ibid. Line 1170
The lady of the hous ay stille sat.
*Ibid. The Summoner's Tale,
Line 2200*
For though we slepe or wake, or rome,
or ryde,
Ay fleeth the tyme, it nyl no man abyde.
Ibid. The Clerk's Tale, Line 118
Love is noght oold as whan that it is
newe.
Ibid. Line 857
This flour of wyfly pacience.
Ibid. Line 919
No wedded man so hardy be t'assaille
His wyves pacience, in trust to fynde
Grisildis, for in certein he shal faille!
Ibid. Line 1180
    It is no childes pley
To take a wyf withoute avysement.
*Ibid. The Merchant's Tale,
Line 1530*
Love is blynd.[2]
Ibid. Line 1598
My wit is thynne.
Ibid. Line 1682

[1] Handsome is that handsome does. —
GOLDSMITH: *The Vicar of Wakefield* [1766],
Chap. 1
[2] See Shakespeare, page 144b.

Ther nys no werkman, whatsoevere he
 be,
That may bothe werke wel and hastily; [1]
This wol be doon at leyser parfitly. [2]
> *The Canterbury Tales. The
> Merchant's Tale, Line 1832*

The Pegasee,
The hors that hadde winges for to flee.
> *Ibid. The Squire's Tale, Line 207*

Therfore bihoveth hire a ful long spoon
That shal ete with a feend. [3]
> *Ibid. Line 602*

Men loven of propre kynde new fangel-
 nesse.
> *Ibid. Line 610*

I am lorn with-outen remedye.
> *Ibid. Line 629*

Fy on possessioun
But-if a man be vertuous with-al.
> *Ibid. Line 686*

Pacience is an heigh vertu, certeyn.
> *Ibid. The Franklin's Tale,
> Line 773*

Servant in love, and lord in mariage.
> *Ibid. Line 793*

Taak this for fynal answere as of me.
> *Ibid. Line 987*

It is agayns the proces of nature.
> *Ibid. Line 1345*

Trouthe is the hyeste thyng that men
 may kepe.
> *Ibid. Line 1479*

For dronkenesse is verray sepulture
Of mannes wit and his discrecioun.
> *Ibid. The Pardoner's Tale,
> Line 558*

Mordre wol out, certeyn, it wol nat
 faille. [4]
> *Ibid. The Prioress's Tale, Line 1776*

[1] See John Heywood, page 90b, and Publilius Syrus, page 45a.
[2] Ease and speed in doing a thing do not
give the work lasting solidity or exactness of
beauty. — PLUTARCH [A.D. 46-120]: *Life of
Pericles*
[3] Hee must have a long spoon, shall eat
with the devill. — JOHN HEYWOOD: *Proverbes*
[1546], *Part II, Chap. V*
He must have a long spoon that must eat
with the devil. — SHAKESPEARE: *Comedy of
Errors* [1592-1593], *Act IV, Sc. 3, L. 64*
[4] Also in *The Nun's Priest's Tale, Lines
4242* and *4247*.

This may wel be rym dogerel.
> *The Canterbury Tales. Chaucer's
> Tale of Sir Thopas, Line 2115*

Ful wys is he that kan hymselven
 knowe! [1]
> *Ibid. The Monk's Tale, Line 3329*

He was of knyghthod and of fredom
 flour.
> *Ibid. Line 3832*

For whan a man hath over-greet a wit,
Ful oft hym happeth to mysusen it.
> *Ibid. The Canon Yeoman's Prologue,
> Line 648*

The firste vertu, sone, if thou wolt leere,
Is to restreyne and kepe wel thy tonge.
> *Ibid. The Manciple's Tale, Line 332*

Thing that is seyd, is seyd; and forth
 it gooth.
> *Ibid. Line 355*

For the proverbe seith that "manye
smale maken a greet." [2]
> *Ibid. The Parson's Tale, Line 361*

Reule wel thyself, that other folk canst
 rede.
> *Truth* [Circa *1390*]. *Line 6*

And trouthe thee shal delivere, it is no
 drede.
> *Ibid. Line 7*

The wrastling for this world axeth a fal.
> *Ibid. Line 16*

How easily murder is discovered! —
SHAKESPEARE: *Titus Andronicus* [1593-1594],
Act II, Sc. 3, L. 28
Truth will come to light; murder cannot be
hid long. — SHAKESPEARE: *Merchant of Venice*
[1596-1597], *Act II, Sc. 2, L. 86*
Murder, though it have no tongue, will speak
With most miraculous organ.
SHAKESPEARE: *Hamlet* [1600-1601],
Act II, Sc. 2, L. 630
Murder will out. — CERVANTES: *Don Quix-
ote, Part I* [1605], *Book III, Chap. 8*
Carcasses bleed at the sight of the mur-
derer. — ROBERT BURTON: *Anatomy of Mel-
ancholy* [1621-1651], *Part I, Sect. 1, Memb.
2, Subsect. 5*
Other sins only speak; murder shrieks out.
— JOHN WEBSTER: *Duchess of Malfi* [1623],
Act IV, Sc. 2
[1] See Plutarch, page 60a.
[2] Many small make a great. — JOHN HEY-
WOOD: *Proverbes* [1546], *Part I, Chap. XI*

JOHN WYCLIFFE
[? –1384]

I believe that in the end the truth will conquer.
> *To the Duke of Lancaster* [*1381*]
> (*Quoted by* J. R. GREEN: *A Short History of the English People. Chap. 5*)

THOMAS À KEMPIS
[1380–1471]

Be not angry that you cannot make others as you wish them to be, since you cannot make yourself as you wish to be.
> *Imitation of Christ* [Circa *1420*].
> *Book I, Chap. 16*

Man proposes, but God disposes.[1]
> *Ibid. Chap. 19*

What canst thou see elsewhere which thou canst not see here? Behold the heaven and the earth and all the elements; for of these are all things created.
> *Ibid. Chap. 20*

It is easier not to speak a word at all than to speak more words than we should.
> *Ibid.*

No man ruleth safely but he that is willingly ruled.
> *Ibid.*

And when he is out of sight, quickly also is he out of mind.[2]
> *Ibid. Chap. 23*

[1] This expression appears earlier in the *Chronicle of Battel Abbey, P. 27* (Lower's translation), and in *The Vision of Piers Plowman, L. 13994,* ed. *1550.*
Man appoints, and God disappoints. — CERVANTES: *Don Quixote, Part II* [1615], *Book IV, Chap. 55*
A man's heart deviseth his way; but the Lord directeth his steps. — *Proverbs, XVI, 9*
[2] Out of syght, out of mynd. — GOOGE: *Eglogs* [1563]
And out of mind as soon as out of sight. — FULKE GREVILLE [1554–1628]: *Sonnet LVI*
    Fer from eze, fer from herte,
    Quoth Hendyng.
      HENDYNG: *Proverbs, MS.* [*circa* 1320]
I do perceive that the old proverbis be not alwaies trew, for I do finde that the absence of my Nath. doth breede in me the more continuall remembrance of him. — LADY ANN BACON, *Letter to Lady Jane Cornwallis* [1613]

Love is swift, sincere, pious, pleasant, gentle, strong, patient, faithful, prudent, long-suffering, manly and never seeking her own; for wheresoever a man seeketh his own, there he falleth from love.
> *Imitation of Christ. Book III,*
> *Chap. 5*

JOHN FORTESCUE
[*Circa* 1395–1476]

Moche Crye and no Wull.[1]
> *De Laudibus Legum Angliae*
> [*1471*]. *Chap. 10*

Comparisons are odious.[2]
> *Ibid. Chap. 19*

HENRY VI
[1421–1471]

Kingdoms are but cares,
  State is devoid of stay;
Riches are ready snares,
  And hasten to decay.
> *From* SIR JOHN HARINGTON's
> *Nugae Antiquae* [*Published*
> *1769*]

FRANÇOIS VILLON
[1430–1484]

Where are the snows of yester-year?[3]
> *The Greater Testament.*[4] *Ballad*
> *of Old-Time Ladies*

All must come to the self-same bay;
Sons and servants, their days are told:
The wind carries their like away.
> *Ibid. Ballad of Old-Time Lords,*
> *No. 2*

[1] A great cry, but little wool. — CERVANTES: *Don Quixote, Part II* [1615], *Book III, Chap. 13*
All cry and no wool. — SAMUEL BUTLER: *Hudibras, Part I* [1663], *Canto I, L. 852*
[2] This was a well-known phrase in the 14th century, and has been repeated by many, including Lydgate, Shakespeare, and Swift.
[3] Où sont les neiges d'antan?
  Alas for lovers! Pair by pair
    The Wind has blown them all away;
  The young and yare, the fond and fair;
  Where are the Snows of Yesterday?
    JUSTIN H. McCARTHY [1861–1936]:
    A Ballad of Dead Ladies: After Villon, Envoy
[4] Translated by DANTE GABRIEL ROSSETTI [1828–1882].

Blonde or brunette, this rhyme applies,
Happy is he who knows them not.
> *The Greater Testament. Double
> Ballad to the Like Purport*

O Virgin clean,
To whom all sinners lift their hands on
high,
Made whole in faith through Thee their
go-between.
In this belief I will to live and die.
> *Ibid. Ballad of Homage to Our
> Lady*

There's no right speech out of Paris
town.
> *Ibid. Ballad of the Women of
> Paris*

If you have money, it doth not stay,
But this way and that it wastes amain:
What does it profit you, anyway?
Ill-gotten good is nobody's gain.
> *Ibid. Seemly Lesson to the Good-
> for-Noughts*

I know all save myself alone.
> *Ballad of Things Known and
> Unknown*

For he deserves not any fortune fair
Who would wish ill unto the realm of
France.
> *Ballad Against Those Who Missay
> of France*

These traitorous thieves, accursèd and
unfair,
The vintners that put water in our wine.
> *A Merry Ballad of Vintners*

In the amorous war
The wealthy gallant always gains the
day.
> *Ballad of Ladies' Love, No. 1*

ALDUS (MANUTIUS)
[1450–1515]

Talk of nothing but business, and
despatch that business quickly.
> *Placard on the door of the Aldine
> Press, Venice, established about
> 1490* [1]

[1] Quoted by THOMAS FROGNALL DIBDIN
[1776–1847] in *Introduction to the Knowledge of Rare and Valuable Editions of the
Greek and Latin Classics* [1802], *Vol. I, P. 436.*

LEONARDO DA VINCI
[1452–1519]

Whoever in discussion adduces authority uses not intellect but memory.
> *Note-Books* [1]

No counsel is more trustworthy than
that which is given upon ships that are
in peril.
> *Ibid.*

Intellectual passion drives out sensu-
ality.
> *Ibid.*

Let the street be as wide as the height
of the houses.
> *Ibid.*

No member needs so great a number
of muscles as the tongue; this exceeds
all the rest in the number of its movements.
> *Ibid.*

It is of no small benefit on finding
oneself in bed in the dark to go over
again in the imagination the main outlines of the forms previously studied, or
of other noteworthy things conceived
by ingenious speculation.
> *Ibid.*

As a well-spent day brings happy
sleep, so life well used brings happy
death.
> *Ibid.*

JOHN SKELTON
[Circa 1460–1529]

I saye, thou madde March hare.[2]
> *Replycation Against Certayne
> Yong Scolers*

There is nothynge that more dyspleaseth God,
Than from theyr children to spare the
rod.[3]
> *Magnyfycence. Line 1954
> [Circa 1525]*

[1] Translated by EDWARD MCCURDY.
[2] Mad as a March hare. — JOHN HEYWOOD:
Proverbes [1546], *Part II, Chap. V*
[3] He that spareth his rod hateth his son.—
Proverbs, XIII, 24
Spare the rod and spoil the child. — *English proverb, borrowed from the Latin and
traced to* circa A.D. *1000*
They spare the rod and spoyl the child. —

He ruleth all the roste.[1]
>*Why Come Ye Not to Courte.*
>>*Line 198*

By hoke ne by croke.[2]
>*Colyn Cloute* [Circa *1519*].
>>*Line 1240*

The wolfe from the dore.
>*Ibid. Line 1531*

Old proverbe says,
That byrd ys not honest
That fyleth hys owne nest.[3]
>*Poems against Garnesche*

Maide, wydowe, or wyffe.
>*Philip Sparrow*

DESIDERIUS ERASMUS
[1465–1536]

I know how busy you are in your library, which is your Paradise.[4]
>*Letter to Bishop Fisher* [*1524*]

NICOLÒ MACHIAVELLI [5]
[1469–1527]

There is nothing more difficult to take in hand, more perilous to conduct, or more uncertain in its success, than to

RALPH VENNING: *Mysteries and Revelations* [1649]
[1] Rule the rost. — JOHN HEYWOOD: *Proverbes* [1546], *Part I, Chap. V*
Her that ruled the rost. — THOMAS HEYWOOD: *History of Women* [ed. 1624]
Rules the roast. — JONSON, CHAPMAN, MARSTON: *Eastward Ho* [1605], *Act II, Sc. 1*
[2] By hooke or crooke. — JOHN HEYWOOD: *Proverbes* [1546], *Part I, Chap. XI*
The phrase has been said to derive from the custom of some manors where tenants were authorized to take firebote *by hook or by crook;* that is, so much of the underwood as may be cut with a crook, and so much of the loose timber as may be collected from the boughs by means of a hook. One of the earliest citations of this proverb occurs in John Wycliffe's *Controversial Tracts* [*circa* 1370].
[3] It is a foule byrd that fyleth his owne nest. — JOHN HEYWOOD: *Proverbes* [1546], *Part II, Chap. V*
[4] Nec me fugit quam assiduus sis in bibliotheca, quae tibi Paradisi loco est. — P. S. ALLEN: *Selections from Erasmus, P. 128*
[5] Every Country hath its Machiavel. — SIR THOMAS BROWNE: *Religio Medici* [1642] (Everyman ed.), *P. 24*

take the lead in the introduction of a new order of things.
>*The Prince.*[1] *Chap. 6*

The chief foundations of all states, new as well as old or composite, are good laws and good arms; and as there cannot be good laws where the state is not well armed, it follows that where they are well armed they have good laws.
>*Ibid. Chap. 12*

A prince should therefore have no other aim or thought, nor take up any other thing for his study, but war and its organisation and discipline, for that is the only art that is necessary to one who commands.
>*Ibid. Chap. 14*

Among other evils which being unarmed brings you, it causes you to be despised.
>*Ibid.*

When neither their property nor their honour is touched, the majority of men live content.
>*Ibid. Chap. 19*

There are three classes of intellects: one which comprehends by itself; another which appreciates what others comprehend; and a third which neither comprehends by itself nor by the showing of others; the first is the most excellent, the second is good, the third is useless.
>*Ibid. Chap. 22*

Where the willingness is great, the difficulties cannot be great.
>*Ibid. Chap. 26*

God is not willing to do everything, and thus take away our free will and that share of glory which belongs to us.
>*Ibid.*

MICHELANGELO
[1474–1564]

The more the marble wastes, the more the statue grows.
>*Sonnet*

If it be true that any beautiful thing

[1] Translated by W. K. MARRIOTT.

raises the pure and just desire of man from earth to God, the eternal fount of all, such I believe my love.

Sonnet

The power of one fair face makes my love sublime, for it has weaned my heart from low desires.

Sonnet

I live and love in God's peculiar light.

Ibid.

SIR THOMAS MORE [1]
[1478–1535]

They wonder much to hear that gold, which in itself is so useless a thing, should be everywhere so much esteemed, that even men for whom it was made, and by whom it has its value, should yet be thought of less value than it is.

Utopia [1516]. Of Jewels and Wealth

They have no lawyers among them, for they consider them as a sort of people whose profession it is to disguise matters.

Ibid. Of Law and Magistrates

Plato by a goodly similitude declareth, why wise men refrain to meddle in the commonwealth. For when they see the people swarm into the streets, and daily wet to the skin with rain, and yet can not persuade them to go out of the rain, they do keep themselves within their houses, seeing they cannot remedy the folly of the people.[2]

Ibid. Concerning the Best State of a Commonwealth

For men use, if they have an evil turn, to write it in marble: and whoso doth us a good turn we write it in dust.[3]

Richard III and his Miserable End [1543]

[1] Canonized by Pope Pius XI [1935].
[2] In the modern phrase, "not sense enough to come in out of the rain."
[3] Words writ in waters. — GEORGE CHAPMAN [1559?–1634?]: *Revenge for Honour, Act V, Sc. 2*
See Shakespeare, page 212a.
L'injure se grave en métal; et le bienfait

Assist me up, and in coming down I will shift for myself.

Said at the scaffold, on the way to execution

Wait till I put aside my beard, for that never committed treason.

To the headsman on the scaffold

MARTIN LUTHER
[1483–1546]

A mighty fortress is our God,
  A bulwark never failing;
Our helper He amid the flood
  Of mortal ills prevailing.[1]

Psalm, Ein' Feste Burg [2]

Tell your master that if there were as many devils at Worms as tiles on its roofs, I would enter.[3]

On approaching Worms

It is neither safe nor prudent to do aught against conscience. Here I stand —I cannot do otherwise. God help me. Amen.

Speech at the Diet of Worms

For where God built a church, there the Devil would also build a chapel.[4]

Table Talk. 67

s'escrit en l'onde. (An injury is engraved in metal, but a benefit is written in water.) — JEAN BERTAUT [*circa* 1611]
All your better deeds shall be in water writ, but this in marble. — BEAUMONT AND FLETCHER: *Philaster* [1620], *Act V, Sc. 3*
Here lies one whose name was writ in water. — *Keats's own Epitaph* [1821]
[1] Great God! there is no safety here below;
  Thou art my fortress, thou that seem'st my foe.
        FRANCIS QUARLES [1592–1644]: *Divine Poems*
[2] Translated by FREDERIC H. HEDGE.
[3] On the 16th of April, 1521, Luther entered the imperial city [of Worms]. . . . On his approach . . . the Elector's chancellor entreated him, in the name of his master, not to enter a town where his death was decided. The answer which Luther returned was simply this. — BARON VON BUNSEN [1791–1860]: *Life of Luther*
[4] Where God hath a temple, the Devil will have a chapel. — ROBERT BURTON: *Anatomy of Melancholy* [1621–1651], *Part III, Sect. 4, Memb. 1, Subsect. 1*
No sooner is a temple built to God but the Devil builds a chapel hard by. — GEORGE HERBERT: *Jacula Prudentum* [1640]

A faithful and good servant is a real godsend; but truly 'tis a rare bird in the land.
Table Talk. 156

It makes a difference whose ox is gored.[1]
Works [1854 edition]. Vol. 62, Page 449

HUGH LATIMER
[1485–1555]

Play the man, Master Ridley; we shall this day light such a candle, by God's grace, in England, as I trust shall never be put out.[2]
Addressed to Nicholas Ridley [1500–1555] as they were being burned alive at Oxford, for heresy, October 16, 1555.[3] (Quoted by J. R. GREEN: A Short History of the English People, Chap. 7)

SIR DAVID LYNDSAY
[1490–1555]

They gave me first ane thing they call *citandum;*
Within aucht days I gat but *libellandum;*
Within ane month I gat *ad opponendum;*
In ane half year I gat *inter loquendum;*
An syne I gat — how call ye it? — *ad replicandum;*
But, I could never ane word yet understand him.
The Exactions and Delay of the Law

But or they came half gate to *concludendum,*

[1] This is the moral of the fable of the lawyer, the farmer, and the farmer's ox, which was included in NOAH WEBSTER's *American Spelling Book* [1802], entitled *The Partial Judge.*
[2] I shall light a candle of understanding in thine heart, which shall not be put out. — *2 Esdras, XIV, 25*
[3] See Latimer and Ridley in the might
Of Faith stand coupled for a common flight!
WORDSWORTH [1770–1850]: *Ecclesiastical Sonnets, Part II, XXXIV, Latimer and Ridley*

The fient a plack was left for to defend him.
The Exactions and Delay of the Law

Thus they postponed me twa year, with their train,
Syne, *hodie ad octo,* bade me come again.
Ibid.

Of *pronunciandum* they made me wonder fain;
But I gat ne'er my gude grey meir again.
Ibid.

ST. IGNATIUS LOYOLA [1]
[1491–1556]

Teach us, good Lord, to serve Thee as Thou deservest:
To give and not to count the cost;
To fight and not to heed the wounds;
To toil and not to seek for rest;
To labour and not ask for any reward
Save that of knowing that we do Thy will.
Prayer for Generosity [1548]

FRANCIS I OF FRANCE
[1494–1547]

All is lost save honour.[2]
Letter to his Mother [1525]

FRANÇOIS RABELAIS
[1495–1553]

I am going to seek a great perhaps.[3]
PETER ANTHONY MOTTEUX: *Life of Rabelais*

Let down the curtain: the farce is done.
Ibid.

[1] Founder of the Society of Jesus.
[2] Tout est perdu fors l'honneur. The actual words written after his defeat at Pavia, 1525, were "De toutes choses ne m'est demeuré que l'honneur et la vie qui est saulvé." The letter is in DULAURE, *Histoire Civile, Physique et Morale de Paris* [1821–1825].
All gone but faith in God. — BISHOP JOHN McKIM [1852–1936]: Cabled message to tne New York headquarters of the Episcopal Church after the destruction of the mission by the Japanese earthquake [1923].
[3] Je m'en vay chercher un grand Peut-estre. This and the next utterance are attributed to Rabelais on his deathbed.

He left a paper sealed up, wherein were found three articles as his last will: "I owe much; I have nothing; I give the rest to the poor."

PETER ANTHONY MOTTEUX: *Life of Rabelais*

One inch of joy surmounts of grief a span,
Because to laugh is proper to the man.
Works. To the Readers

To return to our wethers.[1]
Ibid. Book I [*1532*], *Chap. 1*

One falls to the ground in trying to sit on two stools.[2]
Ibid. Chap. 2

I drink no more than a sponge.
Ibid. Chap. 5

Appetite comes with eating, says Angeston.[3]
Ibid. Chap. 5

Thought the moon was made of green cheese.[4]
Ibid. Chap. 11

He always looked a given horse in the mouth.[5]
Ibid.

[1] Revenons à nos moutons. — A proverb taken from the farce *L'Avocat Pierre Patelin*, by BLANCHET [1459–1519]
[2] Between two stools one sits on the ground. — *Les Proverbes del Vilain*, MS. Bodleian [*circa* 1303]
While betweene two stooles my taile goe to the ground. — JOHN HEYWOOD: *Proverbes* [1546] *Part I, Chap. II*
[3] My appetite comes to me while eating. — MONTAIGNE: *Essays* [1580–1595], *Book III, Chap. 9, Of Vanity*
[4] The moone is made of a greene cheese. — JOHN HEYWOOD: *Proverbes* [1546], *Part II, Chap. VII*
[5] No man ought to looke a given horse in the mouth. — JOHN HEYWOOD: *Proverbes* [1546], *Part I, Chap. 5*
A gift-horse should not be looked in the mouth. — CERVANTES: *Don Quixote, Part II* [1615], *Book IV, Chap. 62*
He ne'er consider'd it, as loth
To look a gift-horse in the mouth.
SAMUEL BUTLER: *Hudibras, Part I*, [1663], *Canto I, L. 489*
This proverb occurs in *Vulgaria Stambrigi* [*circa* 1510]. Archbishop Trench says the proverb is certainly as old as Jerome of the fourth century, who, when some found fault with certain writings of his, replied that they were free-will offerings, and that it did not behove to look a gift horse in the mouth.

By robbing Peter he paid Paul,[1]
. . . and hoped to catch larks if ever the heavens should fall.[2]
Works. Book I, Chap. 11

You do not speak gospel.[3]
Ibid. Chap. 13

He laid him squat as a flounder.
Ibid. Chap. 27

Send them home as merry as crickets.
Ibid. Chap. 29

War begun without good provision of money beforehand for going through with it is but as a breathing of strength and blast that will quickly pass away. Coin is the sinews of war.[4]
Ibid. Chap. 46

How shall I be able to rule over others, that have not full power and command of myself?[5]
Ibid. Chap. 52

Subject to a kind of disease, which at that time they called lack of money.[6]
Ibid. Book II [*1534*], *Chap. 16*

He did not care a button for it.
Ibid.

How well I feathered my nest.[7]
Ibid. Chap. 17

[1] To robbe Peter and pay Poule. — JOHN HEYWOOD: *Proverbes* [1546], *Part I, Chap. XI*
Rob Peter, and pay Paul. — ROBERT BURTON: *Anatomy of Melancholy* [1621–1651], *Democritus to the Reader*
Give not Saint Peter so much, to leave Saint Paul nothing. — GEORGE HERBERT: *Jacula Prudentum* [1640]
To rob Peter and pay Paul is said to have had its origin when, in the reign of Edward VI, the lands of St. Peter at Westminster were appropriated to raise money for the repair of St. Paul's in London. Also found in Wycliffe's *Works, Vol. III, P. 174.*
[2] When the skie falth we shall have Larkes. — JOHN HEYWOOD: *Proverbes* [1546], *Part I, Chap. IV*
[3] All is not Gospell that thou doest speake. — JOHN HEYWOOD: *Proverbes* [1546], *Part II, Chap. II*
[4] See Aeschines, page 26a.
[5] See Thomas à Kempis, page 83a.
[6] See Shakespeare, page 152b.
Or that eternal want of pence,
Which vexes public men.
TENNYSON: *Will Waterproof's Lyrical Monologue* [1842], *St. 6*
[7] Mr. Coventry had already feathered his nest. — PEPYS: *Diary*, June 7, 1662

So much is a man worth as he esteems himself.
Works. Book II, Chap. 29

A good crier of green sauce.
Ibid. Chap. 31

Then I began to think that it is very true which is commonly said, that the one half of the world knoweth not how the other half liveth.
Ibid. Chap. 32

This flea which I have in mine ear.
Ibid. Book III [1545], Chap. 31

You have there hit the nail on the head.[1]
Ibid. Chap. 34

Above the pitch, out of tune, and off the hinges.
Ibid. Book IV [1548], Chap. 19

I'll go his halves.
Ibid. Chap. 23

The Devil was sick, — the Devil a
monk would be;
The Devil was well, — the Devil a
monk was he.
Ibid. Chap. 24

Do not believe what I tell you here any more than if it were some tale of a tub.[2]
Ibid. Chap. 38

Which was performed to a T.[3]
Ibid. Chap. 41

He that has patience may compass anything.
Ibid. Chap. 48

We will take the good will for the deed.[4]
Ibid. Chap. 49

You are Christians of the best edition, all picked and culled.
Works. Book IV, Chap. 50

Would you damn your precious soul?
Ibid. Chap. 54

I perfectly feel even at my finger's end.
Ibid.

Let us fly and save our bacon.
Ibid. Chap. 55

Needs must when the Devil drives.[1]
Ibid. Chap. 57

Scampering as if the Devil drove them.
Ibid. Chap. 62

He freshly and cheerfully asked him how a man should kill time.
Ibid.

Whose cockloft is unfurnished.[2]
*Ibid. Book V [1552], Author's
Prologue*

Speak the truth and shame the Devil.[3]
Ibid.

---

[1] This hitteth the naile on the hed. — JOHN HEYWOOD: *Proverbes* [1546], *Part II, Chap. XI*

[2] The title of JONATHAN SWIFT's satire.

[3] We could manage this matter to a T. — STERNE: *Tristram Shandy, Book II* [1760], *Chap. 5*

You see they'd have fitted him to a T. — SAMUEL JOHNSON: *Boswell's Life* [1791]

You will find it shall echo my speech to a T. — THOMAS MOORE [1779–1852]: *Occasional Address for the Opening of the New Theatre of St. Stephen*

[4] The will for deed I doe accept. — DU BARTAS: *Divine Weeks and Works* [1578], *Second Week, Third Day, Part 2*

You must take the will for the deed. —

SWIFT: *Polite Conversation* [1738], *Dialogue II*

[1] He must needes goe whom the devill doth drive. — JOHN HEYWOOD: *Proverbes* [1546], *Part II, Chap. VII*

[2] Tall men are like houses of four stories, wherein commonly the uppermost room is worst furnished. — JAMES HOWELL (quoted): *Letter I, Book I, Sect. II* [1621]

Nature did never put her precious jewels into a garret four stories high, and therefore exceeding tall men had ever very empty heads. — FRANCIS BACON: *Apothegms* [1624], *No. 17*

Often the cockloft is empty in those whom Nature hath built many stories high. — THOMAS FULLER [1608–1661]: *Andronicus, Sect. VI, Par. 18, 1*

Such as take lodgings in a head
That's to be let unfurnished.
SAMUEL BUTLER: *Hudibras, Part I*
[1663], *Canto I, L. 161*

[3] While you live, tell truth and shame the devil! — SHAKESPEARE: *King Henry IV, Part I* [1597–1598], *Act III, Sc. 1, Line 58*

I'd tell the truth, and shame the devil. — SAMUEL JOHNSON: *Boswell's Life* [1791] (Everyman Edition), *Vol. I, P. 460*

Truth being truth,
Tell it and shame the devil.
BROWNING: *The Ring and
the Book* [1868–1869], *III,
The Other Half-Rome*

Plain as a nose in a man's face.[1]
Works. Book V, Author's Prologue
Like hearts of oak.[2]
Ibid.
You shall never want rope enough.
Ibid.
Looking as like . . . as one pea does like another.[3]
Ibid. Chap. 2
And thereby hangs a tale.
Ibid. Chap. 4
It is meat, drink, and cloth to us.
Ibid. Chap. 7
And so on to the end of the chapter.
Ibid. Chap. 10
What is got over the Devil's back is spent under the belly.[4]
Ibid. Chap. 11
We have here other fish to fry.[5]
Ibid. Chap. 12
What cannot be cured must be endured.
Ibid. Chap. 15
Thought I to myself, we shall never come off scot-free.
Ibid.
It is enough to fright you out of your seven senses.[6]
Ibid.

---

[1] See Shakespeare, page 132a.
As clear and as manifest as the nose in a man's face. — ROBERT BURTON: *Anatomy of Melancholy* [1621–1651], *Part III, Sect. 3, Memb. 4, Subsect. 1*
[2] See Garrick, page 347a.
[3] As lyke as one pease is to another. — LYLY: *Euphues* [1579]
         They say we are
         Almost as like as eggs.
     SHAKESPEARE: *The Winter's Tale* [1608–1611], *Act I, Sc. 2, L. 130*
As one egg is like another. — CERVANTES: *Don Quixote, Part II* [1615], *Book III, Chap. 14*
[4] Isocrates was in the right to insinuate that what is got over the Devil's back is spent under his belly. — LE SAGE: *Gil Blas* [1715–1735], *Book 8, Chap. 9*
[5] This is no time for me to mind niceties, and spelling of letters. I have other fish to fry. — CERVANTES: *Don Quixote, Part II* [1615], *Chap. 35*
[6] Huzza'd out of my seven senses. — ADDISON: *The Spectator,* November 5, 1714
Scared out of his seven senses. — SIR

Panurge had no sooner heard this, but he was upon the high-rope.
Works. Book V, Chap. 18
We saw a knot of others, about a baker's dozen.
Ibid. Chap. 23
I believe he would make three bites of a cherry.
Ibid.

JOHN HEYWOOD [1]
[1497–1580]

The loss of wealth is loss of dirt,
As sages in all times assert;
The happy man's without a shirt.[2]
Be Merry Friends

Let the world slide,[3] let the world go;
A fig for care, and a fig for woe!
If I can't pay, why I can owe,
And death makes equal the high and
    low.
Ibid.

Haste maketh waste.
Proverbes [1546]. Part I, Chap. II

Good to be merie and wise.
Ibid.

Beaten with his owne rod.
Ibid.

WALTER SCOTT: *Rob Roy* [1817], *Chap. 34*
[1] The *Proverbes* of JOHN HEYWOOD is the earliest collection of English colloquial sayings. It was first printed in 1546. The title of the edition of 1562 is *John Heywoodes Woorkes. A Dialogue conteyning the number in effect of all the proverbes in the English tounge, compact in a matter concernynge two maner of Maryages,* etc. The selection here given is from the edition of 1874 (a reprint of 1598), edited by JULIAN SHARMAN. See also the *Oxford Dictionary of English Proverbs* compiled by W. G. SMITH [1935].
[2] This line is the theme of many poems, e. g. SIR WALTER SCOTT: *The Search after Happiness; or, The Quest of Sultaun Solimaun.* JOHN HAY: *The Enchanted Shirt.* EDWIN MARKHAM: *The Shoes of Happiness.* EDGAR A. GUEST: *Envy*
[3] Let the world slide. — *Towneley Mysteries* [1420].
Let the world slip: we shall ne'er be younger. — SHAKESPEARE: *Taming of the Shrew* [1593–1594], *Induction, Sc. 2, L. 147*

Look ere ye leape.[1]

> *Proverbes. Part I, Chap. II*

He that will not when he may,
When he would he shall have nay.[2]

> *Ibid.*

The fat is in the fire.

> *Ibid.*

When the sunne shineth, make hay.

> *Ibid.*

The tide tarrieth no man.[3]

> *Ibid.*

Than catch and hold while I may,
fast binde, fast finde.[4]

> *Ibid.*

And while I at length debate and beate
the bush,
There shall steppe in other men and
catch the burdes.[5]

> *Ibid.*

Wedding is destiny,
And hanging likewise.[6]

> *Ibid.*

Happy man, happy dole.[7]

> *Ibid.*

[1] Thou shouldst have looked before thou
hadst leapt. — JONSON, CHAPMAN, MARSTON:
Eastward Ho [1605], *Act V, Sc. 1*
See Samuel Butler, page 239a.
[2] He that will not when he may,
When he will he shall have nay.
ROBERT BURTON: *Anatomy of Mel-
ancholy* [1621-1651], *Part III, Sect.
2, Memb. 5, Subsect. 5*
[3] See Chaucer, page 81b.
Time nor tide tarrieth no man. — ROBERT
GREENE: *Disputations* [1592]
Hoist up saile while gale doth last,
Tide and wind stay no man's pleasure.
ROBERT SOUTHWELL: *St. Peter's
Complaint* [1595]
Nae man can tether time or tide. — BURNS:
Tam O'Shanter [1787]
[4]   Fast bind, fast find;
A proverb never stale in thrifty mind.
SHAKESPEARE: *Merchant of Venice*
[1596-1597], *Act II, Sc. 5, L. 54*
[5] It is this proverb which Henry V is re-
ported to have uttered at the siege of Orleans:
"Shall I beat the bush and another take the
bird?"
[6] Hanging and wiving go by destiny. —
The Schole-hous for Women [1541]
See Shakespeare, page 145a.
Marriage and hanging go by destiny;
matches are made in heaven. — ROBERT BUR-
TON: *Anatomy of Melancholy* [1621-1651],
Part III, Sect. 2, Memb. 5, Subsect. 5
[7] Happy man be his dole. — SHAKESPEARE:

God never sends th' mouth but he
sendeth meat.[1]

> *Proverbes. Part I, Chap. IV*

Like will to like.

> *Ibid.*

A hard beginning maketh a good
ending.

> *Ibid.*

More frayd then hurt.

> *Ibid.*

Feare may force a man to cast beyond the moone.[2]

> *Ibid.*

Nothing is impossible to a willing
hart.

> *Ibid.*

The wise man sayth, store is no sore.

> *Ibid. Chap. V*

Let the world wagge, and take mine
ease in myne Inne.[3]

> *Ibid.*

Hold their noses to grinstone.[4]

> *Ibid.*

Better to give then to take.[5]

> *Ibid.*

A sleveless errand.[6]

> *Ibid. Chap. VII*

Merry Wives [1600-1601], *Act III, Sc. 4,
L. 68; Winter's Tale* [1609-1611], *Act I,
Sc. 2, L. 163*
[1] God sendeth and giveth both mouth and
the meat. — THOMAS TUSSER: *Five Hundred
Points of Good Husbandry* [1557]
God sends meat, and the Devil sends cooks.
— JOHN TAYLOR: *Works* [1630], *Vol. II, P. 85*
The holy prophet Zoroaster said,
The Lord who made thy teeth shall give
thee bread.
> *Persian couplet*
[2] To "cast beyond the moon" is a phrase in
frequent use by the old writers. LYLY: *Euphues* [1579]. THOMAS HEYWOOD: *A Woman
Killed with Kindness* [1607].
[3] Shall I not take mine ease in mine inn? —
SHAKESPEARE: *Henry IV* [1597-1598], *Part I,
Act III, Sc. 3, L. 91*
[4] And hold one another's noses to the
grindstone hard. — ROBERT BURTON: *Anatomy of Melancholy* [1621-1651], *Part III,
Sect. 1, Memb. 3*
[5] It is more blessed to give than to receive.
— *Acts, XX, 35*
[6] Sending every one of her children upon
some sleeveless errand, as she terms it. —
JOSEPH ADDISON: *The Spectator, No. 47*
[April 24, 1711] (referring to April Fool errands)

Reckeners without their host must recken twice.[1]
> *Proverbes. Part I, Chap. VIII*

Cut my cote after my cloth.[2]
> *Ibid.*

The neer to the church, the further from God.[3]
> *Ibid. Chap. IX*

Now for good lucke, cast an old shooe after me.
> *Ibid.*

Better is to bow then breake.[4]
> *Ibid.*

It hurteth not the toung to give faire words.[5]
> *Ibid.*

Two heads are better then one.
> *Ibid.*

A short horse is soone currid.
> *Ibid. Chap. X*

To tell tales out of schoole.
> *Ibid.*

To hold with the hare and run with the hound.
> *Ibid.*

She is nether fish nor flesh, nor good red herring.[6]
> *Ibid.*

All is well that endes well.[1]
> *Proverbes. Part I, Chap. X*

Of a good beginning cometh a good end.[2]
> *Ibid.*

Better late than never.[3]
> *Ibid.*

When the steede is stolne, shut the stable durre.[4]
> *Ibid.*

She looketh as butter would not melt in her mouth.
> *Ibid.*

The still sowe eats up all the draffe.
> *Ibid.*

Ill weede growth fast.[5]
> *Ibid.*

It is a deere collop
That is cut out of th' owne flesh.[6]
> *Ibid.*

Beggars should be no choosers.
> *Ibid.*

A man may well bring a horse to the water,
But he cannot make him drinke without he will.[7]
> *Ibid.*

---

[1] He reckoneth without his Hostesse. Love knoweth no lawes. — LYLY: *Euphues* [1579]

[2] A relic of the Sumptuary Laws. One of the earliest instances occurs, 1530, in the interlude of *Godly Queene Hester.*

[3] Qui est près de l'église est souvent loin de Dieu (He who is near the Church is often far from God). — *Les Proverbes Communs* [*circa* 1500]
> To Kerke the narre, from God more farre,
> Has bene an old sayd sawe.
> And he that strives to touch the starre,
> Oft stombles at a strawe.
> SPENSER: *The Shepheardes Calender* [1579], *July, L. 97*

[4] Rather to bowe than breke is profitable; Humylite is a thing commendable.
> *The Morale Proverbs of Cristyne,* translated from the French [1390] by Earl Rivers, and printed by Caxton in 1478

[5] Fair words never hurt the tongue. — JONSON, CHAPMAN, MARSTON: *Eastward Ho* [1605], *Act IV, Sc. 1*

[6] Meat so dressed and sauced and seasoned that you didn't know whether it was beef or mutton — flesh, fowl, or good red herring. — GEORGE DU MAURIER: *Trilby* [1894]

[1] Si finis bonus est, totum bonum erit (If the end is good, all will be good). — *Gesta Romanorum* [1472], *Tale LXVII*
> SHAKESPEARE: *All's Well That Ends Well* [1601–1603]

[2] Who that well his warke beginneth,
> The rather a good ende he winneth.
> GOWER: *Confessio Amantis* [*circa* 1386–1390]

[3] Potius sero quam nunquam. — LIVY [59 B.C.–A.D. 17]: *History, Book IV, Sect. 23*

[4] Quant le cheval est emblé dounke ferme fols l'estable (When the horse has been stolen, the fool shuts the stable). — *Les Proverbes del Vilain*

[5] Ewyl weed ys sone y-growe. — *MS. Harleian* [*circa* 1490]
> An ill weed grows apace. — GEORGE CHAPMAN: *An Humorous Day's Mirth* [1599]
> Great weeds do grow apace. — SHAKESPEARE: *Richard III* [1592–1593], *Act II, Sc. 4, L. 13*

[6] God knows thou art a collop of my flesh. — SHAKESPEARE: *Henry VI* [1591], *Part I, Act V, Sc. 4, L. 18*

[7] You may bring a horse to the river, but he will drink when and what he pleaseth. — GEORGE HERBERT: *Jacula Prudentum* [1640]

Men say, kinde will creepe where it may not goe.[1]

> *Proverbes. Part I, Chap. X*

The cat would eate fish, and would not wet her feete.[2]

> *Ibid.*

While the grasse groweth the horse starveth.[3]

> *Ibid.*

Rome was not built in one day.

> *Ibid. Chap. XI*

Yee have many strings to your bowe.[4]

> *Ibid.*

Children learne to creepe ere they can learne to goe.

> *Ibid.*

Better is halfe a lofe than no bread.

> *Ibid.*

Nought venter nought have.[5]

> *Ibid.*

Children and fooles cannot lye.[6]

> *Ibid.*

All is fish that comth to net.[7]

> *Ibid.*

Who is worse shod than the shoemaker's wife? [8]

> *Ibid.*

[1]   You know that love
Will creep in service when it cannot go.
   SHAKESPEARE: *Two Gentlemen of Verona* [1594–1595], *Act IV, Sc. 2, L. 19*
[2] Shakespeare alludes to this proverb in *Macbeth, Act I, Sc. 7, L. 44:*
Letting "I dare not" wait upon "I would,"
Like the poor cat i' the adage.
Cat lufat visch, ac he nele his feth wete. — *MS. Trinity College, Cambridge* [circa 1250]
[3] Whylst grass doth grow, oft sterves the seely steede. — WHETSTONE: *Promos and Cassandra* [1578]
   While the grass grows —
The proverb is something musty.
   SHAKESPEARE: *Hamlet* [1600–1601], *Act III, Sc. 2, L. 365*
[4] Two strings to his bow. — RICHARD HOOKER: *Laws of Ecclesiastical Polity, Book V* [1597], *Chap. LXXX*
[5] Nothing venture, nothing win. — W. S. GILBERT: *Iolanthe* [1882], *Act II*
[6] 'Tis an old saw, Children and fooles speake true. — LYLY: *Endymion* [1591]
[7] All's fish they get that cometh to net. — TUSSER: *Five Hundred Points of Good Husbandry* [1557], *February Abstract*
[8] Him that makes shoes go barefoot himself. — ROBERT BURTON: *Anatomy of Melancholy* [1621–1651], *Democritus to the Reader*

One good turne asketh another.

> *Proverbes. Part I, Chap. XI*

Who waite for dead men shall goe long barefoote.

> *Ibid.*

I pray thee let me and my fellow have A haire of the dog that bit us last night.[1]

> *Ibid.*

But in deede,
A friend is never knowne till a man have neede.

> *Ibid.*

New brome swepth cleene.

> *Ibid. Part II, Chap. I*

All thing is the woorse for the wearing.

> *Ibid.*

Burnt child fire dredth.[2]

> *Ibid. Chap. II*

Love me litle, love me long.[3]

> *Ibid.*

A fooles bolt is soone shot.[4]

> *Ibid. Chap. III*

A woman hath nine lives like a cat.[5]

> *Ibid. Chap. IV*

A peny for your thought.

> *Ibid.*

You stand in your owne light.

> *Ibid.*

Though chaunge be no robbry.

> *Ibid.*

Might have gone further and have fared worse.

> *Ibid.*

The grey mare is the better horse.

> *Ibid.*

Three may keepe counsayle, if two be away.[6]

> *Ibid. Chap. V*

[1] In old receipt books we find it invariably advised that an inebriate should drink sparingly in the morning some of the same liquor which he had drunk to excess overnight.
[2] Brend child fur dredth,
   Quoth Hendyng.
   Proverbs of Hendyng, MS [circa 1320]
[3] Pray love me little, so you love me long. — HERRICK: *Love Me Little, Love Me Long* [1648]
[4] Sottes bolt is sone shote. — *Proverbs of Hendyng, MS.* [circa 1320]
[5] See Bidpai, page 28b.
[6] Two may keep counsel when the third's

Small pitchers have wyde eares.[1]
> *Proverbes. Part II, Chap. V*

Many hands make light worke.
> *Ibid.*

Out of Gods blessing into the warme Sunne.[2]
> *Ibid.*

There is no fire without some smoke.[3]
> *Ibid.*

A cat may looke on a King.
> *Ibid.*

Have yee him on the hip.[4]
> *Ibid.*

It had need to bee
A wylie mouse that should breed in the cats eare.[5]
> *Ibid.*

Leape out of the frying pan into the fyre.
> *Ibid.*

Time trieth troth in every doubt.[6]
> *Ibid.*

Much water goeth by the mill That the miller knoweth not of.[7]
> *Ibid.*

_____

away. — SHAKESPEARE: *Titus Andronicus* [1593–1594], *Act IV, Sc. 2, L. 145*
Three can hold their peace if two be away. — GEORGE HERBERT: *Jacula Prudentum* [1640]

[1] Pitchers have ears. — SHAKESPEARE: *The Taming of the Shrew* [1593–1594], *Act IV, Sc. 4, L. 52; Richard III* [1592–1593], *Act II, Sc. 4, L. 37*
Little pitchers have wide ears. — GEORGE HERBERT: *Jacula Prudentum* [1640]

[2] Thou shalt come out of a warme sunne into Gods blessing. — LYLY: *Euphues* [1579]
Lest we leap out of the frying-pan into the fire; or, out of God's blessing into the warm sun. — CERVANTES: *Don Quixote, Part I* [1605], *Book III, Chap. 4*
Thou out of Heaven's benediction comest To the warm sun.
SHAKESPEARE: *King Lear* [1605–1606], *Act II, Sc. 2, L. 168*

[3] There can no great smoke arise, but there must be some fire. — LYLY: *Euphues* [1579]

[4] See Shakespeare, page 144a.

[5] A hardy mouse that is bold to breede In cattis eeris.
> *Order of Foles* [MS. *circa* 1450]

[6] Time tries the troth in everything. — TUSSER: *Five Hundred Points of Good Husbandry* [1557], *Author's Epistle, Chap. I*

[7] More water glideth by the mill Than wots the miller of.
SHAKESPEARE: *Titus Andronicus* [1593–1594], *Act II, Sc. 1, L. 85*

The moe the merrier.
> *Proverbes. Part II, Chap. VII*

To th' end of a shot and beginning of a fray.[1]
> *Ibid.*

It is better to be
An old man's derling than a yong man's werling.
> *Ibid.*

Be the day never so long,
Evermore at last they ring to evensong.[2]
> *Ibid.*

I know on which side my bread is buttred.
> *Ibid.*

Who is so deafe or so blinde as is hee That wilfully will neither heare nor see? [3]
> *Ibid. Chap. IX*

The wrong sow by th' eare.
> *Ibid.*

Love me, love my dog.[4]
> *Ibid.*

An ill winde that bloweth no man to good.[5]
> *Ibid.*

For when I gave you an inch, you tooke an ell.[6]
> *Ibid.*

_____

The miller sees not all the water that goes by his mill. — ROBERT BURTON: *Anatomy of Melancholy* [1621–1651], *Part III, Sect. 3, Memb. 4, Subsect. 1*

[1] See Shakespeare, page 151b.

[2] Be the day short or never so long, At length it ringeth to even song.
> *Quoted at the stake by George Tankerfield* [1555] (FOXE: *Book of Martyrs* [1563], *Chap. VII*)

[3] See Mathew Henry, page 292b.

[4] Qui me amat, amet et canem meum (Who loves me, let him love my dog also). — ST. BERNARD [*circa* 1150]: *Sermo Primus*

[5] See Tusser, page 96a.
Ill blows the wind that profits nobody. — SHAKESPEARE: *King Henry VI* [1591], *Part III, Act 2, Sc. 5, L. 55*
Falstaff. What wind blew you hither, Pistol?
Pistol. Not the ill wind which blows no man to good.
SHAKESPEARE: *Henry IV* [1597–1598], *Part II, Act V, Sc. 3, L. 87*

[6] Give an inch, he'll take an ell. — JOHN WEBSTER [1580–1625]: *Sir Thomas Wyatt*

Would yee both eat your cake and have your cake? [1]

Proverbes. Part II, Chap. IX

Every man for himselfe and God for us all.[2]

Ibid.

Though he love not to buy the pig in the poke.[3]

Ibid.

Enough is as good as a feast.

Ibid.

CHARLES V
[1500–1558]

To think that I attempted to force the reason and conscience of thousands of men into one mould and I cannot make two clocks agree! [4]

Quoted by HAVELOCK ELLIS: *The Task of Social Hygiene, Chap. 9*

Fortune hath somewhat the nature of a woman; if she be too much wooed, she is the farther off.

Quoted by FRANCIS BACON: *Advancement of Learning, Book II*

Myself and the lucky moment.

Quoted by PRESCOTT: *Philip II, Book I, Chap. 9*

Iron hand in a velvet glove.

Attributed to Charles V by CARLYLE: *Latter-Day Pamphlets, 11*

---

[1] Wouldst thou both eat thy cake and have it? — GEORGE HERBERT: *The Size* [1633]

[2] Every man for himself, his own ends, the Devil for all. — ROBERT BURTON: *Anatomy of Melancholy* [1621–1651], *Part III, Sect. I, Memb. III*

[3] For buying or selling of pig in a poke. — TUSSER· *Five Hundred Points of Good Husbandry* [1557], *September Abstract*

[4] "When Charles V retired in weariness from the greatest throne in the world to the solitude of the monastery at Yuste, he occupied his leisure for some weeks in trying to regulate two clocks. It proved very difficult. One day, it is recorded, he turned to his assistant and said [the sentence quoted above]." — HAVELOCK ELLIS

JOHN KNOX
[1505–1572]

A man with God is always in the majority.[1]

Inscription on Reformation Monument, Geneva, Switzerland

JOHN BRADFORD
[1510–1555]

The familiar story, that, on seeing evil-doers taken to the place of execution, he was wont to exclaim: "But for the grace of God there goes John Bradford," is a universal tradition, which has overcome the lapse of time.[2]

Biographical Notice, Parker Society edition, The Writings of John Bradford [1853], *Page xliii*

SIR THOMAS VAUX
[1510–1556]

Companion none is like
Unto the mind alone;
For many have been harmed by speech,
Through thinking, few or none.

Of a Contented Mind [1557]

RICHARD GRAFTON
[? –1572]

Thirty dayes hath Nouember,
Aprill, June, and September,
February hath xxviii alone,
And all the rest have xxxi.[3]

Chronicles of England [1562]

---

[1] Un homme avec Dieu est toujours dans la majorité.

[2] I never hear of such a case as this that I do not think of Baxter's words, and say, "There, but for the grace of God, goes Sherlock Holmes." — SIR ARTHUR CONAN DOYLE [1859–1930]: *The Boscombe Valley Mystery* (The reference is to RICHARD BAXTER [1615–1691], author of *The Saint's Everlasting Rest* and *The Call to the Unconverted*.)

[3] Junius, Aprilis, Septémq; Nouemq; tricenos,
    Vnum plus reliqui, Februs tenet octo vicenos,
    At si bissextus fuerit superadditur vnus.
        WILLIAM HARRISON: *Description of Britain, prefixed to* HOLINSHED'S *Chronicle* [1577]

Thirty days hath September,
April, June, and November,

GEORGIUS FABRICIUS
[1516–1571]

He doth raise his country's fame with
his own
And in the mouths of nations yet unborn
His praises shall be sung; Death comes
to all
But great achievements raise a monument
Which shall endure until the sun grows
cold.

*In Praise of Georgius Agricola
[1494–1555]. Quoted by* Herbert Clark Hoover *and* Lou
Henry Hoover *in their translation of* Agricola's *De Re Metal-
lica, Page xxiv*

THOMAS TUSSER
[1524–1580]

Except wind stands as never it stood,
It is an ill wind turns none to good.[1]

*A Description of the Properties
of Wind*

At Christmas play and make good
cheer,
For Christmas comes but once a year.

The Farmer's Daily Diet

February has twenty-eight alone,
All the rest have thirty-one;
Excepting leap year, — that's the time
When February's days are twenty-nine.

The Return from Parnassus [1606]

Thirty days hath September,
April, June, and November;
All the rest have thirty-one,
Excepting February alone,
Which hath but twenty-eight, in fine,
Till leap year gives it twenty-nine.

Common in the New England states

Fourth, eleventh, ninth, and sixth,
Thirty days to each affix;
Every other thirty-one
Except the second month alone.

*Common in Chester County, Pennsyl-
vania, among the Friends*

Compare the old Latin-class mnemonic:
In March, July, October, May,
The Ides are on the fifteenth day,
The Nones the seventh; all other months
besides
Have two days less for Nones and Ides.

[1] See Heywood, page 94b.

Such mistress, such Nan,
Such master, such man.[1]

*Five Hundred Points of Good Hus-
bandry [1557]. April's Abstract*

Who goeth a borrowing
Goeth a sorrowing.

Ibid. June's Abstract

'T is merry in hall
Where beards wag all.[2]

Ibid. August's Abstract

Dry sun, dry wind;
Safe bind, safe find.[3]

Washing

Hast thou a friend, as heart may wish at
will?
Then use him so, to have his friendship
still.
Wouldst have a friend, wouldst know
what friend is best?
Have God thy friend, who passeth all
the rest.

Posies for a Parlour

To Death we must stoop, be we high,
be we low,
But how, and how suddenly, few be
that know;
What carry we then but a sheet to the
grave,
To cover this carcass, of all that we
have?

Tenants of God's Farmstead

PIERRE DE RONSARD
[1524–1585]

When you are old, and in the candle
light
Sit spinning by the fire at close of day,
You'll sing my songs in praise of you,
and say:
"Thus Ronsard sang, whilst still my
eyes were bright." [4]

Sonnet XLIII.[5] To Helen [6]

[1] Tel maître, tel valet. Attributed to Chevalier Bayard by Cimber.

[2] Merry swithe it is in halle,
When the beards waveth alle.

Life of Alexander [1312]

[3] See Heywood, page 91a.

[4] "Ronsard me célébroit du temps que j'étois
belle."

Compare Yeats's adaptation: "When you
are old and gray and full of sleep," page 824a.

[5] Translated by William A. Drake.

[6] Madame de Surgères.

WILLIAM STEVENSON
[1530?-1575]

I cannot eat but little meat,
My stomach is not good;
But sure I think that I can drink
With him that wears a hood.
Gammer Gurton's Needle [*1575*].
Drinking Song, Act II

Back and side go bare, go bare,
Both foot and hand go cold;
But, belly, God send thee good ale
enough,
Whether it be new or old.
Ibid. Refrain

GABRIEL MEURIER
[1530-1601]

He who excuses himself accuses himself.[1]

Trésor des Sentences

ELIZABETH, QUEEN OF ENGLAND
[1533-1603]

The use of the sea and air is common
to all; neither can a title to the ocean
belong to any people or private persons,
forasmuch as neither nature nor public use and custom permit any possession thereof.
To the Spanish Ambassador [*1580*]

My care is like my shadow in the sun —
Follows me flying — flies when I pursue it.
On the Departure of Alençon
[*1582*]

I know I have the body of a weak
and feeble woman, but I have the heart
and stomach of a king, and of a king of
England too; and think foul scorn that
Parma or Spain, or any prince of Europe
should dare to invade the borders of
my realm.
*Speech to the Troops at Til-
bury on the Approach of the
Armada, 1588*

1 Qui s'excuse, s'accuse.
See Shakespeare, page 148b.

Though God hath raised me high,
yet this I count the glory of my crown:
that I have reigned with your loves.
The Golden Speech, 1601

Semper eadem (Ever the same).
Motto

I am no lover of pompous title, but
only desire that my name may be recorded in a line or two, which shall
briefly express my name, my virginity,
the years of my reign, the reformation
of religion under it, and my preservation of peace.
To her ladies, discussing her epitaph

'Twas God the word that spake it,
He took the Bread and brake it;
And what the word did make it,
That I believe, and take it.[1]
S. CLARKE, *Marrow of Ecclesi-
astical History* [*ed. 1675*].
Part II, Life of Queen Elizabeth

MICHEL DE MONTAIGNE [2]
[1533-1592]

Man in sooth is a marvellous vain,
fickle, and unstable subject.[3]
Essays.[4] Book I [*1580*], *Chap. 1,
That Men by Various Ways Ar-
rive at the Same End*

All passions that suffer themselves
to be relished and digested are but moderate.[5]
Ibid. Chap. 2, Of Sorrow

The thing of which I have most fear
is fear.[6]
Ibid. Chap. 17, Of Fear

He who should teach men to die

1 Answer on being asked her opinion of
Christ's presence in the Sacrament.
2 Translated by CHARLES COTTON [1630-
1687], revised by HAZLITT and WIGHT.
3 See Plutarch, page 58b.
4 This book of Montaigne the world has indorsed by translating it into all tongues. —
EMERSON: *Representative Men* [1850], *Montaigne*
5 See Seneca, page 48b, and Raleigh, page
111a.
6 C'est de quoy j'ay le plus de peur que la
peur.
See Thoreau, page 589a, and Roosevelt,
page 918b.

would at the same time teach them to live.[1]

> *Essays. Book I, Chap. 19, That to Study Philosophy Is to Learn to Die*

The laws of conscience, which we pretend to be derived from nature, proceed from custom.

> *Ibid. Chap. 22, Of Custom*

Accustom him to everything, that he may not be a Sir Paris, a carpet-knight,[2] but a sinewy, hardy, and vigorous young man.

> *Ibid. Chap. 25, On the Education of Children*

It can be of no importance to me of what religion my physician or my lawyer is; this consideration has nothing in common with the offices of friendship which they owe me.

> *Ibid. Chap. 27, Of Friendship*

There are some defeats more triumphant than victories.[3]

> *Ibid. Chap. 30, Of Cannibals*

---

[1] I have taught you, my dear flock, for above thirty years how to live, and I will show you in a very short time how to die. — SIR EDWIN SANDYS [1561–1629]: *Anglorum Speculum*

There taught us how to live; and (oh, too high
The price for knowledge!) taught us how to die.
> THOMAS TICKELL: *On the Death of Mr. Addison* [1719], *L. 81*

Teach him how to live,
And, oh still harder lesson! how to die.
> BEILBY PORTEUS [1731–1808]: *Death, L. 316*

In teaching me the way to live
It taught me how to die.
> GEORGE POPE MORRIS [1802–1864]: *My Mother's Bible, St. 4*

[2] One of those carpet-knights that abandon themselves to sleep and lazy ease. — CERVANTES: *Don Quixote, Part I* [1605], *Book III, Chap. 6*

See Robert Burton, page 222a.

Carpet knights are men who are by the prince's grace and favour made knights at home. . . . They are called carpet knights because they receive their honours in the court and upon carpets. — GERVASE MARKHAM: *Booke of Honour* [1625]

[3] See Plutarch, page 59a.

Nothing is so firmly believed as what we least know.

> *Essays. Book I, Chap. 31, Of Divine Ordinances*

A wise man never loses anything if he have himself.

> *Ibid. Chap. 38, Of Solitude*

Even opinion is of force enough to make itself to be espoused at the expense of life.

> *Ibid. Chap. 40, Of Good and Evil*

To which we may add this other Aristotelian consideration, that he who confers a benefit on any one loves him better than he is beloved by him again.[1]

> *Ibid. Book II [1580], Chap. 8, Of the Affection of Fathers*

The middle sort of historians (of which the most part are) spoil all; they will chew our meat for us.

> *Ibid. Chap. 10, Of Books*

The only good histories are those that have been written by the persons themselves who commanded in the affairs whereof they write.

> *Ibid.*

She [virtue] requires a rough and stormy passage; she will have either outward difficulties to wrestle with, or internal difficulties.[2]

> *Ibid. Chap. 11, Of Cruelty*

There is, nevertheless, a certain respect, and a general duty of humanity, that ties us, not only to beasts that have life and sense, but even to trees and plants.

> *Ibid.*

Some impose upon the world that they believe that which they do not; others, more in number, make themselves believe that they believe, not being able to penetrate into what it is to believe.

> *Ibid. Chap. 12, Apology for Raimond Sebond*[3]

---

[1] Benefactors appear to love in a greater degree those whom they benefit than those who are benefited love their benefactors. — ARISTOTLE [384–322 B.C.]: *Nicomachean Ethics, Book IX, Chap. 1*

[2] See Milton, page 250b–251a.

[3] Raimond Sebond, Spaniard, died in 1436,

When I play with my cat, who knows whether I do not make her more sport than she makes me?

Essays. Book II, Chap. 12, Apology for Raimond Sebond

The souls of emperors and cobblers are cast in the same mould. . . . The same reason that makes us wrangle with a neighbour causes a war betwixt princes.

Ibid.

Man is certainly stark mad; he cannot make a worm, and yet he will be making gods by dozens.

Ibid.

Why may not a goose say thus: "All the parts of the universe I have an interest in: the earth serves me to walk upon, the sun to light me; [1] the stars have their influence upon me; I have such an advantage by the winds and such by the waters, there is nothing that yon heavenly roof looks upon so favourably as me. I am the darling of Nature! Is it not man that keeps, lodges, and serves me?"

Ibid.

Arts and sciences are not cast in a mould, but are formed and perfected by degrees, by often handling and polishing, as bears leisurely lick their cubs into form.

Ibid.

He that I am reading seems always to have the most force.

Ibid.

How many worthy men have we known to survive their own reputation! [2]

Ibid. Chap. 16, Of Glory

There is another sort of glory, which is the having too good an opinion of our own worth.

Ibid. Chap. 17, Of Presumption

One may be humble out of pride.

Ibid.

Nature has presented us with a large faculty of entertaining ourselves alone;

and often calls us to it, to teach us that we owe ourselves partly to society, but chiefly and mostly to ourselves.

Essays. Book II, Chap. 18, On Giving the Lie

I find that the best virtue I have has in it some tincture of vice.

Ibid. Chap. 20, That We Taste Nothing Pure

Saying is one thing, and doing is another.

Ibid. Chap. 31, Of Anger

Is it not a noble farce, wherein kings, republics, and emperors have for so many ages played their parts, and to which the whole vast universe serves for a theatre? [1]

Ibid. Chap. 36, Of the Most Excellent Men

Nature forms us for ourselves, not for others; to be, not to seem.

Ibid. Chap. 37, Of the Resemblance of Children to Their Brothers

There never was in the world two opinions alike, no more than two hairs or two grains; the most universal quality is diversity. [2]

Ibid. Of the Resemblance of Children to Their Fathers

The public weal requires that men should betray, and lie, and massacre.

Ibid. Book III [1595], Chap. 1, Of Profit and Honesty

I will follow the right side even to the fire, but excluding the fire if I can.

Ibid.

Does not he to whom you betray another, to whom you were as welcome as to himself, know that you will at another time do as much for him?

Ibid.

I speak truth, not so much as I would, but as much as I dare; and I dare a little the more, as I grow older.

Ibid. Chap. 2, Of Repentance

Few men have been admired by their own domestics. [3]

Ibid.

---

at Toulouse, where he had lived as professor of medicine and theology.

[1] See Pope, page 316a.
[2] See Bentley, page 292b.

[1] See Shakespeare, page 161a.
[2] See Pliny, page 49b.
[3] See Plutarch, page 61b.

It [marriage] happens as with cages: the birds without despair to get in, and those within despair of getting out.[1]

Essays. Book III, Chap. 5, Upon Some Verses of Virgil

And to bring in a new word by the head and shoulders, they leave out the old one.

Ibid.

All the world knows me in my book, and my book in me.

Ibid.

'Tis so much to be a king, that he only is so by being so. The strange lustre that surrounds him conceals and shrouds him from us; our sight is there broken and dissipated, being stopped and filled by the prevailing light.[2]

Ibid. Chap. 7, Of the Inconvenience of Greatness

We are born to inquire after truth; it belongs to a greater power to possess it. It is not, as Democritus said, hid in the bottom of the deeps, but rather elevated to an infinite height in the divine knowledge.

Ibid. Chap. 8, Of the Art of Conversation

I moreover affirm that our wisdom itself, and wisest consultations, for the most part commit themselves to the conduct of chance.[3]

Ibid.

[1] I myself have loved a lady and pursued her with a great deal of under-age protestation, whom some three or four gallants that have enjoyed would with all their hearts have been glad to have been rid of. 'Tis just like a summer bird-cage in a garden: the birds that are without despair to get in, and the birds that are within despair and are in a consumption for fear they shall never get out. — JOHN WEBSTER: *The White Devil* [1612], *Act I, Sc. 2*

Wedlock, indeed, hath oft compared been
To public feasts, where meet a public rout, —
Where they that are without would fain go in,
And they that are within would fain go out.
SIR JOHN DAVIES [1569–1626]: *Contention Betwixt a Wife, etc.*

[2] See Tennyson, page 554a.
[3] Although men flatter themselves with their great actions, they are not so often the

What if he has borrowed the matter and spoiled the form, as it of. falls out?[1]

Essays. Book III, Chap. 8, Of the Art of Conversation

The oldest and best known evil was ever more supportable than one that was new and untried.

Ibid. Chap. 9, Of Vanity

Not because Socrates said so,[2] but because it is in truth my own disposition — and perchance to some excess — I look upon all men as my compatriots, and embrace a Pole as a Frenchman, making less account of the national than of the universal and common bond.

Ibid.

There is no man so good, who, were he to submit all his thoughts and actions to the laws, would not deserve hanging ten times in his life.

Ibid.

Saturninus said, "Comrades, you have lost a good captain to make him an ill general."

Ibid.

A little folly is desirable in him that will not be guilty of stupidity.[3]

Ibid.

We seek and offer ourselves to be gulled.

Ibid. Chap. 11, Of Cripples

I have never seen a greater monster or miracle in the world than myself.

Ibid.

Men are most apt to believe what they least understand.

Ibid.

I have here only made a nosegay of culled flowers, and have brought noth-

result of great design as of chance. — LA ROCHEFOUCAULD [1613–1680]: *Maxim 57*
[1] Defacing first, then claiming for his own. CHARLES CHURCHILL [1731–1764]: *The Apology, L. 233*
[2] See Plutarch, page 61b.
[3] Mix a little folly with your wisdom; a little nonsense is pleasant now and then. — HORACE [65–8 B.C.]: *Odes, IV*
See Horace Walpole, page 350a.

ing of my own but the thread that ties them together.[1]

Essays. Book III, Chap. 12,
Of Physiognomy

I am further of opinion that it would be better for us to have [no laws] at all than to have them in so prodigious numbers as we have.

Ibid. Chap. 13, Of Experience

There is more ado to interpret interpretations than to interpret the things, and more books upon books than upon all other subjects; we do nothing but comment upon one another.

Ibid.

What can we do with those people who will not believe anything unless it is in print? . . . I would as soon quote one of my friends as I would Aulus Gellius or Macrobius.

Ibid.

For truth itself has not the privilege to be spoken at all times and in all sorts.

Ibid.

Sits he on never so high a throne, a man still sits on his bottom.

Ibid.

The diversity of physical arguments and opinions embraces all sorts of methods.

Ibid.

Let us a little permit Nature to take her own way; she better understands her own affairs than we.

Ibid.

I have ever loved to repose myself, whether sitting or lying, with my heels as high or higher than my head.

Ibid.

I, who have so much and so universally adored this "excellent mediocrity" of ancient times, and who have concluded the most moderate measure the most perfect, shall I pretend to an unreasonable and prodigious old age?

Ibid.

Que scais-je (What do I know)?

Motto on his seal

---

[1] I am but a gatherer and disposer of other men's stuff, at my best value. — SIR HENRY WOTTON: *Preface to the Elements of Architecture* [1624]

I do not understand; I pause; I examine.

Inscription for his library

EDWARD DYER
[*Circa* 1540–1607]

My mind to me a kingdom is;
    Such present joys therein I find,
That it excels all other bliss
    That earth affords or grows by kind:
Though much I want which most would
        have,
Yet still my mind forbids to crave.

Rawlinson Poetry MS. 85, P. 17 [1]

Some have too much, yet still do crave;
    I little have, and seek no more:
They are but poor, though much they
        have,
    And I am rich with little store:
They poor, I rich; they beg, I give;
They lack, I have; they pine, I live.

Ibid.

JAN ZAMOYSKI
[1541–1605]

The king reigns, but does not govern.[2]

Speech in the Polish Parliament
[*1605*], *referring to King Sigismund III*

MARY STUART, QUEEN
OF SCOTS
[1542–1587]

In my end is my beginning.

Motto

---

[1] This poem became popular as a song, altered thus:
My mind to me a kingdom is;
    Such perfect joy therein I find,
As far exceeds all earthly bliss
    That God and Nature hath assigned.
Though much I want that most would have,
Yet still my mind forbids to crave.
        BYRD: *Psalmes, Sonnets, etc.* [1588]
My mind to me an empire is,
    While grace affordeth health.
        ROBERT SOUTHWELL [1561–1595]:
                Content and Rich
See Seneca, page 48a.

[2] Thiers adopted the epigram as the motto for his journal, the *Nationale*, which he established with Mignet and Carrel in 1830.

GUILLAUME DE SALLUSTE, SEIGNEUR DU BARTAS
[1544–1590]

The world's a stage,[1] where God's omnipotence,
His justice, knowledge, love, and providence
Do act the parts.
Divine Weekes and Workes [2]
[*1578*]. *First Week, First Day*

And reads, though running,[3] all these needful motions.
Ibid.

Mercy and justice, marching cheek by joule.
Ibid.

What is well done is done soon enough.
Ibid.

And swans seem whiter if swart crowes be by.
Ibid.

Night's black mantle covers all alike.[4]
Ibid.

Hot and cold, and moist and dry.[5]
Ibid. Second Day

Much like the French (or like ourselves, their apes),
Who with strange habit do disguise their shapes;
Who loving novels, full of affectation,
Receive the manners of each other nation.[6]
Ibid.

With tooth and nail.
Ibid.

From the foure corners of the worlde doe haste.[7]
Ibid.

[1] See Shakespeare, page 161a, and Du Bartas, page 103a.
[2] Translated [1606] by J. SYLVESTER [1563–1618].
[3] See *Habakkuk, II, 2*, on page 1049b, and Cowper, page 365b.
[4] Night . . . with thy black mantle. — SHAKESPEARE: *Romeo and Juliet* [1594–1595], *Act III, Sc. 2, L. 10 and 15*
[5] See Milton, page 254b.
[6] See Shakespeare, page 138b.
[7] See Shakespeare, page 149a and Donne, page 217b

Oft seen in forehead of the frowning skies.[1]
Divine Weekes and Workes.
First Week, Second Day

Bright-flaming, heat-full fire,
The source of motion.
Ibid.

For where's the state beneath the firmament
That doth excel the bees for government? [2]
Ibid. Fifth Day, Part 1

These lovely lamps, these windows of the soul.[3]
Ibid. Sixth Day

Or almost like a spider, who, confin'd
In her web's centre, shakt with every winde,
Moves in an instant if the buzzing flie
Stir but a string of her lawn canapie.[4]
Ibid.

Which serves for cynosure
To all that sail upon the sea obscure.
Ibid. Seventh Day

Living from hand to mouth.
Ibid. Second Week, First Day, Part 4

[1] See Milton, page 249b.
[2] So work the honey-bees,
Creatures that by a rule in Nature teach
The act of order to a peopled kingdom.
SHAKESPEARE: *King Henry V* [1598–1600], *Act I, Sc. 2, L. 187*
[3] The windows of mine eyes. — SHAKESPEARE: *King Richard III* [1592–1593], *Act V, Sc. 3, L. 117*
[4] Much like a subtle spider which doth sit
In middle of her web, which spreadeth wide;
If aught do touch the utmost thread of it
She feels it instantly on every side.
SIR JOHN DAVIES: *The Immortality of the Soul* [1599]
Our souls sit close and silently within,
And their own webs from their own entrails spin;
And when eyes meet far off, our sense is such
That, spider-like, we feel the tenderest touch.
DRYDEN: *Marriage à la Mode* [1673], *Act II, Sc. 1*
The spider's touch, how exquisitely fine!
Feels at each thread, and lives along the line.
POPE: *An Essay on Man* [1733–1734], *Epistle I, L. 217*

In the jaws of death.[1]
> *Divine Weekes and Workes. Second Week, First Day, Part 4*

Will change the pebbles of our puddly
    thought
To orient pearls.
> *Ibid. Third Day, Part 1*

Only that he may conform
To tyrant custom.
> *Ibid. Part 2*

Who breaks his faith, no faith is held
    with him.
> *Ibid. Fourth Day, Book 2*

Who well lives, long lives; for this age
    of ours
Should not be numbered by years, daies,
    and hours.
> *Ibid.*

My lovely living boy,
My hope, my hap, my love, my life, my
    joy.[2]
> *Ibid.*

Out of the book of Natur's learned
    brest.[3]
> *Ibid.*

Flesh of thy flesh, nor yet bone of thy
    bone.
> *Ibid.*

Weakened and wasted to skin and
    bone.
> *Ibid. Book 4*

I take the world to be but as a stage,
Where net-maskt men do play their
    personage.[4]
> *Dialogue Between Heraclitus and
Democritus*

Made no more bones.
> *The Maiden Blush*

[1] Out of the jaws of death. — SHAKESPEARE:
Twelfth Night [1598–1600], *Act III, Sc. 4,
L. 396*
See Tennyson, page 553b.
[2]   My fair son!
  My life, my joy, my food, my all the
world.
  SHAKESPEARE: *King John* [1596–
    1597], *Act III, Sc. 4, L. 103*
[3] The book of Nature is that which the
physician must read; and to do so he must
walk over the leaves. — PARACELSUS [1493–
1541]. Quoted in *Encyclopaedia Britannica*
(11th ed.), *Vol. 20, P. 749*
[4] See Shakespeare, page 161a, and Du
Bartas, page 102a.

MIGUEL DE CERVANTES
[1547–1616]

You are a King by your own Fireside, as much as any Monarch in his
Throne.
> *Don Quixote* [1] [1605–1615]. *The
Author's Preface, Page xix*

I was so free with him as not to mince
the matter.[2]
> *Ibid. Page xx*

They can expect nothing but their
labour for their pains.[3]
> *Ibid. Page xxiii*

Time out of mind.[4]
> *Ibid. Part I* [1605], *Book I,
Chap. 1, Page 4*

Which I have earned with the sweat
of my brows.
> *Ibid. Chap. 4, Page 22*

By a small sample we may judge of
the whole piece.
> *Ibid. Page 25*

Put you in this pickle.
> *Ibid. Chap. 5, Page 30*

Can we ever have too much of a good
thing?
> *Ibid. Chap. 6, Page 37*

Fortune may have yet a better success in reserve for you, and they who
lose to-day may win to-morrow.
> *Ibid. Chap. 7, Page 39*

The charging of his enemy was but
the work of a moment.
> *Ibid. Chap. 8, Page 50*

I don't know that ever I saw one in
my born days.
> *Ibid. Book II, Chap. 2, Page 57*

Those two fatal words, Mine and
Thine.[5]
> *Ibid. Chap. 3, Page 63*

[1] Translated in 1700–1703 by PETER AN-
THONY MOTTEUX [1660–1718]. The page
numbers are those of the Modern Library
Giant edition.
[2] See Shakespeare, page 187b.
You mince matters. — MOLIÈRE: *Tartuffe*
[1667], *Act I, Sc. 1*
[3] See Shakespeare, page 181a.
[4] Time out o' mind. — SHAKESPEARE: *Romeo and Juliet* [1594–1595], *Act I, Sc. 4,
L. 70*
[5] See Boileau, page 287a.

The eyes those silent tongues of Love.
Don Quixote. Part I, Book II,
Chap. 3, Page 65
As good-natured a soul as e'er trod on shoe of leather.
Ibid. Chap. 4, Page 69
And had a face like a blessing.[1]
Ibid.
He's a good man, I'll say that for him, and a true Christian every inch of him.
Ibid. Page 70
There's not the least thing can be said or done, but people will talk and find fault.[2]
Ibid.
Without a wink of sleep.[3]
Ibid. Page 72
Everything disturbs an absent lover.
Ibid. Page 84
It is a true saying, that a man must eat a peck of salt with his friend, before he knows him.
Ibid. Book III, Chap. 1, Page 92
Fortune leaves always some door open to come at a remedy.
Ibid. Page 94
Thank you for nothing.
Ibid.
Fair and softly goes far.
Ibid. Chap. 2, Page 97
May Old Nick [4] rock my cradle.
Ibid. Chap. 3, Page 103
No limits but the sky.[5]
Ibid. Page 110

[1] He had a face like a benediction. — JAR-VIS's translation
[2] See Samuel Dodge, page 557b.
Take wife, or cowl; ride you, or walk:
Doubt not but tongues will have their talk.
LA FONTAINE: *The Miller, His Son, and the Donkey* [1694]
Do you think you could keep people from talking? — MOLIÈRE: *Tartuffe* [1667], *Act I, Sc. 1*
[3] I have not slept one wink. — SHAKE-SPEARE: *Cymbeline* [1609–1610], *Act III, Sc. 4, L. 103*
[4] Nick Machiavel had ne'er a trick,
Though he gave his name to our Old Nick.
BUTLER: *Hudibras, Part III* [1678], *Canto 1, L. 1313*
[5] Modern saying: The sky's the limit.

To give the devil his due.
Don Quixote. Part I, Book III,
Chap. 3, Page 111
A peck of troubles.
Ibid. Chap. 4, Page 112
You're leaping over the hedge before you come to the stile.
Ibid. Page 117
Paid him in his own coin.
Ibid. Page 119
Bell, book, and candle.[1]
Ibid. Page 120
Every tooth in a man's head is more valuable than a diamond.
Ibid. Page 121
The famous Don Quixote de la Mancha, otherwise called The Knight of the Woeful Figure.[2]
Ibid. Chap. 5, Page 126
Let the worst come to the worst.
Ibid. Page 127
You are come off now with a whole skin.
Ibid.
Fear is sharp-sighted, and can see things under ground, and much more in the skies.
Ibid. Chap. 6, Page 131
A finger in every pie.[3]
Ibid. Page 133
No better than she should be.
Ibid.
Every dog has his day.
Ibid.
That's the nature of women, . . . not to love when we love them, and to love when we love them not.[4]
Ibid.
You may go whistle for the rest.
Ibid. Page 134
Ill-luck, you know, seldom comes alone.[5]
Ibid. Page 135

[1] See Shakespeare, page 148a.
[2] El Caballero de la Triste Figura. More accurately translated by Smollett as The Knight of the Sorrowful Countenance.
[3] No pie was baked at Castlewood but her little finger was in it. — THACKERAY: *The Virginians* [1857–1859], *Chap. 5*
[4] See Bernard Shaw, page 764b.
[5] See Shakespeare, page 178a.

Why do you lead me a wild-goose chase?

> *Don Quixote. Part I, Book III,*
> *Chap. 6, Page 136*

Experience, the universal Mother of Sciences.

> *Ibid. Chap. 7, Page 140*

I give up the ghost.

> *Ibid. Page 143*

Give me but that, and let the world rub, there I'll stick.

> *Ibid. Page 148*

Ne'er cringe nor creep, for what you by force may reap.

> *Ibid. Page 149*

'Tis an office of more trust to shave a man's beard than to saddle a horse.

> *Ibid. Page 151*

Sing away sorrow, cast away care.

> *Ibid. Chap. 8, Page 153*

After meat comes mustard; or, like money to a starving man at sea, when there are no victuals to be bought with it.

> *Ibid.*

Of good natural parts, and of a liberal education.

> *Ibid. Page 154*

A medley of kindred, that 'twould puzzle a convocation of casuists to resolve their degrees of consanguinity.

> *Ibid. Page 155*

Let every man mind his own business.

> *Ibid. Page 157*

Those who'll play with cats must expect to be scratched.

> *Ibid. Page 159*

Raise a hue and cry.

> *Ibid.*

Return to our flesh-pots of Egypt.

> *Ibid. Page 160*

'Tis the part of a wise man to keep himself to-day for to-morrow, and not venture all his eggs in one basket.

> *Ibid. Chap. 9, Page 162*

The ease of my burdens, the staff of my life.

> *Ibid. Page 163*

Within a stone's throw of it.

> *Ibid. Page 170*

The very remembrance of my former misfortune proves a new one to me.

> *Don Quixote. Part I, Book III,*
> *Chap. 10, Page 174*

Absence, that common cure of love.

> *Ibid. Page 177*

Lovers are commonly industrious to make themselves uneasy.

> *Ibid. Page 179*

From pro's and con's they fell to a warmer way of disputing.

> *Ibid. Page 181*

Naked came I into the world, and naked must I go out.

> *Ibid.*

Little said is soon amended.

> *Ibid. Page 184*

A close mouth catches no flies.

> *Ibid.*

She may guess what I should perform in the wet, if I do so much in the dry.[1]

> *Ibid. Chap. 11, Page 186*

Mere flim-flam stories, and nothing but shams and lies.

> *Ibid. Page 187*

Thou hast seen nothing yet.

> *Ibid. Page 190*

Between jest and earnest.

> *Ibid.*

Cutting the air as swift as a witch upon a broomstick.

> *Ibid. Page 191*

My love and hers have always been purely Platonic.

> *Ibid. Page 192*

There's no need to make an enquiry about a woman's pedigree, as there is of us men, when some badge of honour is bestowed on us.

> *Ibid. Page 194*

There are but two things that chiefly excite us to love a woman, an attractive beauty, and unspotted fame.

> *Ibid. Page 195*

'Tis ill talking of halters in the house of a man that was hanged.

> *Ibid.*

---

[1] An allusion to *Luke, XXIII, 31:* For if they do these things in a green tree, what shall be done in the dry?

My memory is so bad, that many times I forget my own name!

Don Quixote. Part I, Book III,
Chap. 11, Page 195

You're a devil at everything; and there's no kind of thing in the versal world but what you can turn your hand to.

Ibid. Page 196

'Twill grieve me so to the heart, that I shall cry my eyes out.

Ibid. Page 197

Ready to split his sides with laughing.

Ibid. Chap. 13, Page 208

As much a fool as he was, he loved money, and knew how to keep it when he had it, and was wise enough to keep his own counsel.

Ibid.

What man has assurance enough to pretend to know thoroughly the riddle of a woman's mind, and who could ever hope to fix her mutable nature? [1]

Ibid. Page 216

Demonstrations of love are never altogether displeasing to women, and the most disdainful, in spite of all their coyness, reserve a little complaisance in their hearts for their admirers.

Ibid. Book IV, Chap. 1, Page 226

My honour is dearer to me than my life.

Ibid. Page 228

On the word of a gentleman, and a Christian.

Ibid. Chap. 2, Page 236

Delay always breeds danger.[2]

Ibid. Page 240

Think before thou speakest.

Ibid. Chap. 3, Page 252

Let us forget and forgive injuries.

Ibid. Page 254

I must speak the truth, and nothing but the truth.

Ibid. Page 255

More knave than fool.

Ibid. Chap. 4, Page 261

A fig for your great captain.

Ibid. Chap. 5, Page 267

[1] See Virgil, page 37a.
[2] See Shakespeare, page 124b.

He that gives quickly gives twice.[1]

Don Quixote. Part I, Book IV,
Chap. 7, Page 291

Required in every good lover . . . the whole alphabet . . . Agreeable, Bountiful, Constant, Dutiful, Easy, Faithful, Gallant, Honourable, Ingenious, Kind, Loyal, Mild, Noble, Officious, Prudent, Quiet, Rich, Secret, True, Valiant, Wise . . . Young and Zealous.

Ibid. Page 292

Harp so on the same string.

Ibid. Chap. 8, Page 305

Virtue is the truest nobility.

Ibid. Chap. 9, Page 314

Here's the devil-and-all to pay.

Ibid. Chap. 10, Page 319

I begin to smell a rat.

Ibid.

I'll take my corporal oath on 't.

Ibid. Page 321

The proof of the pudding is in the eating.

Ibid. Page 322

Let none presume to tell me that the pen is preferable to the sword.[2]

Ibid. Page 325

It is past all controversy, that what costs dearest, is, and ought most to be valued.

Ibid. Chap. 11, Page 328

It seldom happens that any felicity comes so pure as not to be tempered and allayed by some mixture of sorrow.

Ibid. Chap. 14, Page 359

There's no striving against the stream; and the weakest still goes to the wall.

Ibid. Chap. 20, Page 404

The bow cannot always stand bent, nor can human frailty subsist without some lawful recreation.

Ibid. Chap. 21, Page 412

Faith without good works is dead.[3]

Ibid. Chap. 23, Page 423

[1] Bis dat qui cito dat. — *Latin proverb*
[2] See Edward Bulwer Lytton, page 510b.
Scholars' pens carry farther, and give a louder report than thunder. — SIR THOMAS BROWNE: *Religio Medici* [1642] (Everyman ed.), P. 70
[3] See James, page 1064a.

I would have nobody to control me, I would be absolute; and who but I? Now, he that is absolute can do what he likes; he that can do what he likes, can take his pleasure; he that can take his pleasure, can be content; and he that can be content, has no more to desire. So the matter's over; and come what will come, I am satisfied.

Don Quixote. Part I, Book IV,
Chap. 23, Page 423

Even a worm when trod upon, will turn again.

Ibid. Part II [*1615*]*, Book III,*
Author's Preface, Page 440

It is not the hand, but the understanding of a man, that may be said to write.[1]

Ibid. Page 441

How blind must he be that can't see through a sieve.

Ibid. Chap. 1, Page 450

When the head aches, all the members partake of the pains.[2]

Ibid. Chap. 2, Page 455

Youngsters read it, grown men understand it, and old people applaud it.

Ibid. Chap. 3, Page 464

The most artful part in a play is the fool's.

Ibid. Page 465

There are men that will make you books, and turn 'em loose into the world, with as much dispatch as they would do a dish of fritters.

Ibid.

He that publishes a book runs a very great hazard, since nothing can be more impossible than to compose one that may secure the approbation of every reader.

Ibid. Page 466

[1] Cervantes's left hand was maimed for life by gunshot wounds in the battle of Lepanto.
[2] For let our finger ache, and it indues
Our other healthful members even to that
　　sense
Of pain.
　　SHAKESPEARE: *Othello* [1604–1605],
　　　　　　Act III, Sc. 4, L. 145

Every man is as Heaven made him, and sometimes a great deal worse.

Don Quixote. Part II, Book III,
Chap. 4, Page 468

There's no sauce in the world like hunger.

Ibid. Chap. 5, Page 473

Birds of a feather flock together.

Ibid. Page 474

He casts a sheep's eye at the wench.

Ibid.

I ever loved to see everything upon the square.

Ibid. Page 475

Neither will I make myself anybody's laughing-stock.

Ibid.

Journey over all the universe in a map, without the expense and fatigue of travelling, without suffering the inconveniences of heat, cold, hunger, and thirst.

Ibid. Chap. 6, Page 479

Presume to put in her oar.

Ibid. Page 480

The fair sex.[1]

Ibid.

A little in one's own pocket is better than much in another man's purse. 'Tis good to keep a nest-egg. Every little makes a mickle.

Ibid. Chap. 7, Page 486

Remember the old saying, "Faint heart ne'er won fair lady."

Ibid. Chap. 10, Page 501

Fore-warned fore-armed.

Ibid. Page 502

As well look for a needle in a bottle of hay.

Ibid.

Are we to mark this day with a white or a black stone?

Ibid. Page 503

The very pink of courtesy.

Ibid. Chap. 13, Page 521

I'll turn over a new leaf.

Ibid. Page 524

[1] That sex which is therefore called fair. —
STEELE: *The Spectator, No. 302,* February 15, 1712

The pen is the tongue of the mind.
Don Quixote. Part II, Book III,
Chap. 16, Page 543

Modesty is a virtue not often found among poets, for almost every one of them thinks himself the greatest in the world.
Ibid. Chap. 18, Page 555

Marriage is a noose.
Ibid. Chap. 19, Page 564

There were but two families in the world, Have-much and Have-little.
Ibid. Chap. 20, Page 574

He preaches well that lives well, quoth Sancho, that's all the divinity I understand.
Ibid. Page 575

Love and War are the same thing, and stratagems and policy are as allowable in the one as in the other.
Ibid. Chap. 21, Page 580

A private sin is not so prejudicial in this world as a public indecency.
Ibid. Chap. 22, Page 582

There is no love lost, sir.[1]
Ibid.

Come back sound, wind and limb.
Ibid. Page 587

Patience, and shuffle the cards.[2]
Ibid. Chap. 23, Page 592

Tell me thy company, and I'll tell thee what thou art.[3]
Ibid. Page 594

---

[1] There is no hate lost between us. — MIDDLETON [1570–1627]: *The Witch, Act IV, Sc. 3*

[2] But patience, cousin, and shuffle the cards, till our hand is a stronger one. — SIR WALTER SCOTT: *Quentin Durward* [1823], *Chap. 8*

Cut the fiercest quarrels short
With "Patience, gentlemen, and shuffle."
W. M. PRAED [1802–1839].
Quince, St. 5

Men disappoint me so, I disappoint myself so, yet courage, patience, shuffle the cards. — MARGARET FULLER OSSOLI [1810–1850]: *Letter to the Reverend W. H. Channing*

[3] Tell me what you eat, and I will tell you what you are. — ANTHELME BRILLAT-SAVARIN [1755–1826]: *Physiologie du Goût, Aphorism 4*

Show me your garden and I shall tell you

To-morrow will be a new day.
Don Quixote. Part II, Book III,
Chap. 26, Page 618

You can see farther into a millstone than he.
Ibid. Chap. 28, Page 628

I can see with half an eye.
Ibid. Chap. 29, Page 632

Scum of the world.[1]
Ibid. Page 635

Old . . . that's an affront no woman can well bear.
Ibid. Chap. 31, Page 644

One of the most considerable advantages the great have over their inferiors, is to have servants as good as themselves.
Ibid. Page 645

Made 'em pay dear for their frolic.
Ibid. Chap. 32, Page 655

Great persons are able to do great kindnesses.
Ibid. Page 662

Honesty's the best policy.[2]
Ibid. Chap. 33, Page 666

An honest man's word is as good as his bond.
Ibid. Book IV, Chap. 34, Page 674

Heaven's help is better than early rising.
Ibid.

He would not budge an inch.
Ibid. Page 677

A blot in thy scutcheon to all futurity.
Ibid. Chap. 35, Page 681

There's a time for some things, and a time for all things; a time for great things, and a time for small things.[3]
Ibid. Page 682

With a grain of salt.
Ibid. Chap. 37, Page 690

---

what you are. — ALFRED AUSTIN: *The Garden That I Love* [1905]

[1] See R. H. Schauffler, page 904b.

[2] I hold the maxim no less applicable to public than to private affairs, that honesty is always the best policy. — GEORGE WASHINGTON: *Farewell Address* [1796]

[3] See *Ecclesiastes, III. 1,* on page 1042b.

There's a time for all things. — SHAKESPEARE: *The Comedy of Errors* [1592–1593], *Act II, Sc. 2, L. 67*

They had best not stir the rice, though it sticks to the pot.
Don Quixote. Part II, Book IV, Chap. 37, Page 691

They cover a dunghill with a piece of tapestry when a procession goes by.
Ibid.

Good wits jump; [1] a word to the wise is enough.
Ibid. Page 692

My understanding has forsook me, and is gone a wool-gathering.[2]
Ibid. Chap. 38, Page 692

Diligence is the mother of good fortune.
Ibid. Page 724

What a man has, so much he's sure of.
Ibid. Page 725

When a man says, "Get out of my house! what would you have with my wife?" there's no answer to be made.
Ibid. Page 726

The pot calls the kettle black.
Ibid. Page 727

Mum's the word.[3]
Ibid. Chap. 44, Page 729

When thou art at Rome, do as they do at Rome.[4]
Ibid. Chap. 54, Page 806

He that proclaims the kindnesses he has received, shows his disposition to repay 'em if he could.
Ibid. Chap. 58, Page 835

He that errs in so considerable a passage, may well be suspected to have committed many gross errors through the whole history.
Ibid. Chap. 59, Page 843

[1] Great wits jump. — STERNE: *Tristram Shandy, Vol. III* [1761–1762], *Chap. 9*

[2] My thoughts ran a wool-gathering; and I did like the countryman, who looked for his ass while he was mounted on his back. — *Don Quixote, P. 827*

Have you summoned your wits from woolgathering? — MIDDLETON: *The Family of Love* [1608], *Act V, Sc. 5*

[3] Cry "mum." — SHAKESPEARE: *The Merry Wives of Windsor* [1600–1601], *Act V, Sc. 2, L. 6*

[4] When they are at Rome, they do there as they see done. — ROBERT BURTON: *Anatomy of Melancholy* [1621–1651], *Memb. 2, Subsect. I*

I shall be as secret as the grave.
Don Quixote. Part II, Book IV, Chap. 62, Page 862

Now blessings light on him that first invented this same sleep! It covers a man all over, thoughts and all, like a cloak; 'tis meat for the hungry, drink for the thirsty, heat for the cold, and cold for the hot. 'Tis the current coin that purchases all the pleasures of the world cheap; and the balance that sets the king and the shepherd, the fool and the wise man even.
Ibid. Chap. 68, Page 898

The ass will carry his load, but not a double load; ride not a free horse to death.
Ibid. Chap. 71, Page 917

I thought it working for a dead horse, because I am paid beforehand.[1]
Ibid.

He . . . got the better of himself, and that's the best kind of victory one can wish for.
Ibid. Chap. 72, Page 924

Every man was not born with a silver spoon in his mouth.
Ibid. Chap. 73, Page 926

Die merely of the mulligrubs.
Ibid. Chap. 74, Page 932

Ne'er look for birds of this year in the nests of the last.[2]
Ibid. Page 933

There is a strange charm in the thoughts of a good legacy, or the hopes of an estate, which wondrously alleviates the sorrow that men would otherwise feel for the death of friends.
Ibid. Page 934

[1] It is a heart-rending delusion and a cruel snare to be paid for your work before you accomplish it. As soon as once your work is finished you ought to be promptly paid; but to receive your lucre one minute before it is due, is to tempt Providence to make a Micawber of you. — EDMUND GOSSE: *Gossip in a Library* [1891], *Beau Nash*

[2] For Time will teach thee soon the truth, There are no birds in last year's nest!
LONGFELLOW [1807–1882]: *It Is Not Always May, St. 6*

For if he like a madman lived,
At least he like a wise one died.
> *Don Quixote. Part II, Book IV,*
> *Chap. 74, Page 935 (Don*
> *Quixote's Epitaph)*

Don't put too fine a point to your wit
for fear it should get blunted.
> *The Little Gypsy (La Gitanilla)*

My heart is wax moulded as she
pleases, but enduring as marble to retain.[1]
> *Ibid.*

GILES FLETCHER
[1549?–1611]

He is a path, if any be misled;
He is a robe, if any naked be;
If any chance to hunger, he is bread;
If any be a bondman, he is free;
If any be but weak, how strong is he!
To dead men life is he, to sick men,
  health;
To blind men, sight, and to the needy,
  wealth;
A pleasure without loss, a treasure with-
out stealth.
> *Excellency of Christ*
> *[Circa 1593]*

A fool's paradise.[2]
> *The Sorcerer of Vain Delights*
> *[1593], Stanza 3*

SIR EDWARD COKE
[1552–1634]

The gladsome light of jurisprudence.
> *First Institute [1628]*

Reason is the life of the law; nay, the
common law itself is nothing else but

---

[1] Wax to receive, and marble to retain. —
BYRON: *Beppo* [1818], *St. 34*
[2] The earliest instance of this expression is
found in the *Paston Letters* [1462], *No. 457.*
The Paradise of Fools, to few unknown. —
MILTON: *Paradise Lost* [1667], *Book III,
L. 496*
Hence the fool's paradise. — ALEXANDER
POPE: *The Dunciad* [1728], *Book III, L. 9*
In this fool's paradise he drank delight. —
GEORGE DU MAURIER: *Peter Ibbetson* [1891]
XII, Players
What matter if it be a fool's paradise? Para-
dise is paradise, for whoever owns it! —
GEORGE DU MAURIER: *Peter Ibbetson* [1891]

reason. . . . The law, which is perfection of reason.[1]
> *First Institute*

For a man's house is his castle, *et
domus sua cuique tutissimum refu-
gium.*[2]
> *Third Institute [1644]*

The house of every one is to him as
his castle and fortress, as well for his
defence against injury and violence as
for his repose.
> *Semayne's Case. 5 Rep. 91*

They [corporations] cannot commit
treason, nor be outlawed nor excommu-
nicate, for they have no souls.
> *Case of Sutton's Hospital. 10 Rep. 32*

Magna Charta is such a fellow that
he will have no sovereign.
> *Debate in the Commons*
> *[May 17, 1628]*

Six hours in sleep, in law's grave study
  six,
Four spend in prayer, the rest on Nature fix.[3]
> *Translation of lines quoted by* COKE

SIR WALTER RALEIGH
[1552–1618]

If all the world and love were young,
And truth in every shepherd's tongue,
These pretty pleasures might me move
To live with thee, and be thy love.
> *The Nymph's Reply to the Pas-
> sionate Shepherd*[4] *(Printed in
> England's Helicon [1600]).
> Stanza 1*

---

[1] Let us consider the reason of the case. For
nothing is law that is not reason. — SIR JOHN
POWELL: *Coggs* vs. *Bernard, 2 Ld. Raym.
Rep. P. 911*
[2] One's home is the safest refuge to every-
one. — *Pandects* [6th Century A.D.], *Lib. II,
Tit. IV, De in Jus vocando*
I in mine own house am an emperor
And will defend what's mine.
MASSINGER: *The Roman Actor* [1629],
Act I, Sc. 2
[3] Seven hours to law, to soothing slumber
  seven;
Ten to the world allot, and all to heaven.
SIR WILLIAM JONES [1746–1794]
[4] An answer to MARLOWE's poem, *The Pas-
sionate Shepherd to His Love.* See page **123a.**

Fain would I climb, yet fear I to fall.
> *Written on a Windowpane* [1]

Fain would I, but I dare not; I dare,
and yet I may not;
I may, although I care not, for pleasure
when I play not.
> *Fain Would I*

Passions are likened best to floods and
streams:
The shallow murmur, but the deep are
dumb.[2]
> *The Silent Lover. Prelude*

Silence in love bewrays more woe
Than words, though ne'er so witty:
A beggar that is dumb, you know,
May challenge double pity.
> *Ibid. Stanza* 7

Go, Soul, the body's guest,
Upon a thankless arrant:
Fear not to touch the best,
The truth shall be thy warrant:
Go, since I needs must die,
And give the world the lie.
> *The Lie. Stanza* 1 [3] (*Printed in*
> FRANCIS DAVISON's *Poetical
> Rhapsody* [*1608*]; *manuscript
> copy traced to 1593*)

Give me my scallop-shell of quiet,
My staff of faith to walk upon,
My scrip of joy, immortal diet,
My bottle of salvation,
My gown of glory, hope's true gage,
And thus I'll take my pilgrimage.
> *His Pilgrimage* [*1604*]

---

[1] Under this Queen Elizabeth wrote, "If
thy heart fails thee, climb not at all." —
THOMAS FULLER: *Worthies of England*
[1662]

[2] Altissima quaeque flumina minimo sono
labi (The deepest rivers flow with the least
sound). — QUINTUS CURTIUS [1st Century
A. D.], *VII, 4, 13*
  Where the streame runneth smoothest, the
water is deepest. — LYLY: *Euphues and his
England* [1580]
  Smooth runs the water where the brook is
deep. — SHAKESPEARE: *Henry VI* [1591],
Part II, Act III, Sc. I, L. 53
  Take heed of still waters, the quick pass
away. — GEORGE HERBERT: *Jacula Prudentum* [1640]

[3] This poem was probably written by
Raleigh during his imprisonment in 1592. It
has also been attributed to Sir John Davies,

Methought I saw the grave where
Laura lay.
> *Verses to Edmund Spenser*

Shall I, like a hermit, dwell
On a rock or in a cell?
> *Poem*

If she undervalue me,
What care I how fair she be? [1]
> *Ibid.*

If she seem not chaste to me,
What care I how chaste she be?
> *Ibid.*

[History] hath triumphed over time,
which besides it nothing but eternity
hath triumphed over.
> *Historie of the World* [*1614*].
> *Preface*

O eloquent, just, and mightie Death!
whom none could advise, thou hast per-
swaded; what none hath dared, thou
hast done; and whom all the world
hath flattered, thou only hast cast out
of the world and despised. Thou hast
drawne together all the farre stretched
greatnesse, all the pride, crueltie, and
ambition of man, and covered it all
over with these two narrow words, *Hic
jacet!*
> *Ibid. Book V, Part I, Chap. 6,
> Conclusion*

Cowards [may] fear to die; but courage stout,
Rather than live in snuff, will be put
out.
> *Remains* [*ed. 1661*], *Page 258.
> On the snuff of a candle the
> night before he died*

Even such is time, that takes in trust
Our youth, our joys, our all we have,
And pays us but with age and dust;
Who in the dark and silent grave,
When we have wandered all our ways,
Shuts up the story of our days.
But from this earth, this grave, this
dust,

Joshua Sylvester, Lord Pembroke, and Richard Edwards.

[1] If she be not so to me,
  What care I how fair she be?
> GEORGE WITHER [1588–1667]:
> *The Shepherd's Resolution*

My God shall raise me up, I trust!
Written the night before his death; found in his Bible in the Gate-house at Westminster

RICHARD HOOKER
[1553–1600]

Of Law there can be no less acknowledged than that her seat is the bosom of God, her voice the harmony of the world. All things in heaven and earth do her homage, — the very least as feeling her care, and the greatest as not exempted from her power.
Laws of Ecclesiastical Polity [1594]. Book I

That to live by one man's will became the cause of all men's misery.
Ibid.

GEORGE KEITH, FIFTH EARL MARISCHAL
[1553–1623]

Thai half said. Quhat say thai? Let thame say.[1]
Family motto, Mitchell Tower, Marischal College, Aberdeen, Scotland, founded in 1593

JOHN LYLY
[Circa 1553–1606]

Be valyaunt, but not too venturous. Let thy attyre bee comely, but not costly.[2]
Euphues [1579] (Arber's reprint). Page 39

The finest edge is made with the blunt whetstone.
Ibid. Page 47

It seems to me (said she) that you are in some brown study.[3]
Ibid. Page 80

Many strokes overthrow the tallest oaks.[1]
Euphues. Page 81

Lette me stande to the maine chance.
Ibid. Page 104

It is a world to see.
Ibid. Page 116

A clere conscience is a sure carde.
Ibid. Page 207

Goe to bed with the Lambe, and rise with the Larke.[2]
Euphues and his England [1580]. Page 229

A comely olde man as busie as a bee.
Ibid. Page 252

Maydens, be they never so foolyshe, yet beeing fayre they are commonly fortunate.
Ibid. Page 279

Your eyes are so sharpe that you cannot onely looke through a Milstone, but cleane through the minde.
Ibid. Page 289

I am glad that my Adonis hath a sweete tooth in his head.
Ibid. Page 308

A Rose is sweeter in the budde than full blowne.[3]
Ibid. Page 314

Cupid and my Campaspe play'd
At cards for kisses: Cupid paid.
Alexander and Campaspe [1584]. Act III, Sc. 5

How at heaven's gates she claps her wings,
The morne not waking til she sings.[4]
Ibid. Act V, Sc. 1

---

[1] They say. What say they? Let them say. — *Motto over the fireplace in George Bernard Shaw's home*

[2] Costly thy habit as thy purse can buy,
But not express'd in fancy; rich, not gaudy.
SHAKESPEARE: *Hamlet* [1600–1601], *Act I, Sc. 3, L. 70*

[3] A brown study. — SWIFT: *Polite Conversation* [circa 1738]

[1] Many strokes, though with a little axe,
Hew down and fell the hardest-timber'd oak.
SHAKESPEARE: *Henry VI* [1591], *Part III, Act II, Sc. 1, L. 54*

[2] To rise with the lark and go to bed with the lamb. — BRETON: *Court and Country* [1618]
Rise with the lark, and with the lark to bed.
— JAMES HURDIS [1763–1801]: *The Village Curate*

[3] The rose is fairest when 'tis budding new.
— SCOTT: *Lady of the Lake* [1810], *Canto III, St. 1*

[4] See Shakespeare, page 204a.

EDMUND SPENSER
[1553?–1599]

But of all burdens, that a man can beare,
Moste is, a fooles talke to beare and to heare.
> *The Shepheardes Calender*
> [*1579*]. *Maye, Line 140*

Fierce warres and faithfull loves shall moralize my song.[1]
> *The Faerie Queene* [*1590*].
> *Introduction, Stanza 1*

A Gentle Knight was pricking on the plaine.
> *Ibid. Book I, Canto 1, Stanza 1*

A bold bad man.
> *Ibid. Stanza 37*

Her angels face
As the great eye of heaven shyned bright,
And made a sunshine in the shadie place.
> *Ibid. Canto 3, Stanza 4*

Ay me, how many perils doe enfold
The righteous man, to make him daily fall.[2]
> *Ibid. Canto 8, Stanza 1*

Is not short paine well borne, that brings long ease,
And layes the soule to sleepe in quiet grave?
Sleepe after toyle, port after stormie seas,
Ease after warre, death after life does greatly please.[3]
> *Ibid. Canto 9, Stanza 40*

All for love, and nothing for reward.
> *Ibid. Book II, Canto 8, Stanza 2*

Her berth was of the wombe of Morning dew,[4]

And her conception of the joyous Prime.
> *The Faerie Queene. Book III,*
> *Canto 6, Stanza 3*

Roses red and violets blew,
And all the sweetest flowres, that in the forrest grew.
> *Ibid. Stanza 6*

All that in this delightfull Gardin growes,
Should happie be, and have immortall blis.
> *Ibid. Stanza 41*

That Squire of Dames.
> *Ibid. Canto 8, Stanza 44*

How over that same dore was likewise writ,
Be bold, be bold, and every where *Be bold.*[1]
> *Ibid. Canto 11, Stanza 54*

Another yron dore, on which was writ,
Be not too bold.
> *Ibid.*

Dan Chaucer, well of English undefyled,
On Fames eternall beadroll worthie to be fyled.
> *Ibid. Book IV* [*1596*],
> *Canto 2, Stanza 32*

For all that nature by her mother wit
Could frame in earth.
> *Ibid. Canto 10, Stanza 21*

Me seemes the world is runne quite out of square,
From the first point of his appointed sourse,
And being once amisse growes daily wourse and wourse.
> *Ibid. Book V, Introduction,*
> *Stanza 1*

Ill can he rule the great, that cannot reach the small.
> *Ibid. Canto 2, Stanza 43*

---

[1] And moralized his song. — POPE: *Epistle to Dr. Arbuthnot* [*1735*], *L. 340*

[2] Ay me! what perils do environ
The man that meddles with cold iron!
> SAMUEL BUTLER: *Hudibras, Part I*
> [1663], *Canto III, L. 1*

[3] The last two lines are cut on Joseph Conrad's gravestone at Canterbury.

[4] The dew of thy birth is of the womb of the morning. — *Book of Common Prayer, Psalter, Psalm CX, 3*

[1] De l'audace, encore de l'audace, et toujours de l'audace (Boldness, again boldness, and always boldness). — DANTON: *Speech in the Legislative Assembly* [1792]
Write on your doors the saying wise and old.
"Be bold! be bold!" and everywhere — "Be bold;
Be not too bold!"
> LONGFELLOW: *Morituri Salutamus* [1875]

Who will not mercie unto others shew,
How can he mercy ever hope to have? [1]
> *The Faerie Queene. Book VI,*
> *Canto 1, Stanza 42*

The gentle minde by gentle deeds is
knowne.
For a man by nothing is so well bewrayed,
As by his manners.
> *Ibid. Canto 3, Stanza 1*

That here on earth is no sure happiness.
> *Ibid. Canto 11, Stanza 1*

The ever-whirling wheele
Of *Change,* the which all mortall things
doth sway.
> *Ibid. Book VII, Canto 6, Stanza 1*

Warres and allarums unto Nations
wide.
> *Ibid. Stanza 3*

But Times do change and move continually.
> *Ibid. Stanza 47*

For deeds doe die, how ever noblie
donne,
And thoughts of men do as themselves
decay,
But wise wordes taught in numbers for
to runne,
Recorded by the Muses, live for ay.
> *The Ruines of Time [1591].*
> *Line 400*

Full little knowest thou that hast not
tride,
What hell it is, in suing long to bide:
To loose good dayes, that might be
better spent;
To wast long nights in pensive discontent;
To speed to-day, to be put back tomorrow;
To feed on hope, to pine with feare and
sorrow.
> *Mother Hubberds Tale [1591].*
> *Line 895*

To fret thy soule with crosses and with
cares;
To eate thy heart through comfortlesse
dispaires; [2]

[1] Blessed are the merciful, for they shall obtain mercy. — *Matthew, V, 7*
[2] See Plutarch, page 57b.

To fawne, to crowche, to waite, to ride,
to ronne,
To spend, to give, to want, to be un-
donne.
Unhappie wight, born to desastrous
end,
That doth his life in so long tendance
spend.
> *Mother Hubberds Tale. Line 903*

What more felicitie can fall to creature,
Than to enjoy delight with libertie.
> *Muiopotmos: or The Fate of the*
> *Butterflie [1591]. Line 209*

I hate the day, because it lendeth light
To see all things, and not my love to
see.
> *Daphnaida [1591]. Line 407*

Death slue not him, but he made death
his ladder to the skies.
> *An Epitaph upon Sir Philip Sidney*
> *[1591]. Line 20*

A sweet attractive kinde of grace,
A full assurance given by lookes,
Continuall comfort in a face,
The lineaments of Gospell bookes,
I trowe that countenance cannot lie,
Whose thoughts are legible in the eie.
> *An Elegie, or Friends Passion,*
> *for his Astrophill* (SIR PHILIP
> SIDNEY). *Line 103* [1]

Was never eie, did see that face,
Was never eare, did heare that tong,
Was never minde, did minde his grace,
That ever thought the travell long,
But eies, and eares, and ev'ry
thought,
Were with his sweete perfections
caught.
> *Ibid. Line 109*

Though last not least.[2]
> *Colin Clouts Come Home Again*
> *[1595]. Line 144*

Tell her the joyous time wil not be
staid

[1] This elegy was printed anonymously in a
miscellany, *The Phoenix' Nest* [1593]. It has
been erroneously ascribed to Mathew Roydon
[1580–1622].
[2] See Shakespeare, page 167b and page 190b.
The last, not least in honour or applause.
— POPE: *The Dunciad* [1728], *Book IV, L.*
577

Unlesse she doe him by the forelock take.[1]
> *Amoretti* [*1595*]. *Sonnet 70*

The woods shall to me answer, and my Eccho ring.
> *Epithalamion* [*1595*]. *Line 18*

Behold whiles she before the altar stands
Hearing the holy priest that to her speakes
And blesseth her with his two happy hands.
> *Ibid. Line 223*

Ah! when will this long weary day have end,
And lende me leave to come unto my love?
> *Ibid. Line 278*

For of the soule the bodie forme doth take:
For soule is forme, and doth the bodie make.
> *An Hymne in Honour of Beautie* [*1596*]. *Line 132*

For all that faire is, is by nature good; [2]
That is a signe to know the gentle blood.
> *Ibid. Line 139*

Sweete Themmes! runne softly, till I end my Song.[3]
> *Prothalamion* [*1596*]. *Refrain*

I was promised on a time
To have reason for my rhyme;
From that time unto this season,
I received nor rhyme nor reason.
> *Lines on his Promised Pension* (*Quoted by* THOMAS FULLER *in Worthies of England* [*1662*])

HENRY IV OF FRANCE
[1553–1610]

If God grants me the usual length of life, I hope to make France so prosperous that every peasant will have a chicken in his pot on Sunday [1]
> *Said when he was crowned king,* *1589*

Paris is well worth a mass.[2]
> *Caquets de l'Accouchée* [*1622*]

SIR PHILIP SIDNEY
[1554–1586]

High-erected thoughts seated in the heart of courtesy.[3]
> *Arcadia* [*1590*]. *Book I*

They are never alone that are accompanied with noble thoughts.[4]
> *Ibid.*

Many-headed multitude.[5]
> *Ibid. Book II*

My dear, my better half.
> *Ibid. Book III*

"Fool!" said my muse to me, "look in thy heart, and write." [6]
> *Astrophel and Stella* [*1591*]

With how sad steps, O Moon, thou climb'st the skies!
> *Ibid.*

Have I caught my heav'nly jewel.[7]
> *Ibid. Second Song*

My true-love hath my heart, and I have his,
By just exchange one for the other given:

---

[1] See Alexander Smith, page 650b.

[2] Paris vaut bien une messe. — *Attributed either to* HENRY IV *or to his minister* SULLY *in conversation with the king*

[3] Great thoughts come from the heart. — VAUVENARGUES [1715–1747]: *Maxim CXXVII*

[4] He never is alone that is accompanied with noble thoughts. — BEAUMONT AND FLETCHER: *Love's Cure* [1647], *Act III, Sc. 3*

[5] This many-headed monster, Multitude. — DANIEL: *History of the Civil Wars* [1595], *Book II, St. 13*
See Shakespeare, page 202a.
This many-headed monster. — MASSINGER: *The Roman Actor* [1629], *Act III, Sc. 2*
There still remains, to mortify a wit,
The many-headed monster of the pit.
ALEXANDER POPE: *Epistle I, Book II* [1734], *L. 304*

[6] Look, then, into thine heart and write. — LONGFELLOW: *Voices of the Night* [1839], *Prelude*

[7] Quoted by SHAKESPEARE in *Merry Wives of Windsor, Act III, Sc. 3, L. 45*

Footnotes from left column:

[1] Take Time by the forelock. — THALES of Miletus [636–546 B.C.]

[2] See Shakespeare, page 185a.

[3] Sweet Thames, run softly till I end my song,
Sweet Thames, run softly, for I speak not loud or long.
> T. S. ELIOT: *The Waste Land* [1922], *Part III*

I hold his dear, and mine he cannot
  miss,
There never was a better bargain
  driven.
          The Bargain [1591]. Stanza 1

Sweet food of sweetly uttered knowledge.
          Defence of Poesy [1595]

He cometh unto you with a tale
which holdeth children from play, and
old men from the chimney-corner.
          Ibid.

I never heard the old song of Percy
and Douglas that I found not my heart
moved more than with a trumpet.
          Ibid.

THOMAS LODGE
[1558?–1625]

Love in my bosom like a bee
Doth suck his sweet.
          Rosalind [1590]

Her paps are centres of delight,
Her breasts are orbs of heavenly frame.
          Ibid.

GEORGE PEELE
[1558–1597]

His golden locks time hath to silver
  turned;
  O time too swift! O swiftness never
  ceasing!
His youth 'gainst time and age hath
  ever spurned,
  But spurned in vain; youth waneth
  by encreasing.
          *Polyhymnia [1590]. The Aged
          Man-at-Arms, Stanza 1*

His helmet now shall make a hive for
  bees,
  And lovers' songs be turned to holy
  psalms;
A man-at-arms must now serve on his
  knees,
  And feed on prayers, which are old
  age's alms.
          Ibid. Stanza 2

My merry, merry, merry roundelay
Concludes with Cupid's curse:

They that do change old love for new,
Pray gods, they change for worse!
          Cupid's Curse

GEORGE CHAPMAN
[1559–1634]

Promise is most given when the least
  is said.
          Hero and Leander [1598]

Black is a pearl in a woman's eye.[1]
          An Humorous Day's Mirth | 1599]

Exceeding fair she was not; and yet fair
In that she never studied to be fairer
Than Nature made her.
          All Fools [1605]. Act I, Sc. 1

I tell thee Love is Nature's second sun,
Causing a spring of virtues where he
  shines.
          Ibid.

Cornelia. What flowers are these?
Gazetta. The pansy this.
Cornelia. Oh, that's for lovers'
  thoughts.[2]
          Ibid. Act II, Sc. 1

Fortune, the great commandress of the
  world,
Hath divers ways to advance her followers:
To some she gives honour without deserving,
To other some, deserving without honour.
          Ibid. Act V, Sc. 1

Young men think old men are fools;
but old men know young men are fools.
          Ibid.

Keep thy shop, and thy shop will
keep thee. Light gains make heavy
purses.[3]
          Eastward Ho [4] *[1605]. Act I, Sc. 1*

Make ducks and drakes with shillings.
          Ibid.

Only a few industrious Scots perhaps,
who indeed are dispersed over the face
of the whole earth. But as for them,

---

[1] Black men are pearls in beauteous ladies'
eyes. — SHAKESPEARE: *Two Gentlemen of Verona* [1594–1595], *Act V, Sc. 2, L. 12*

[2] See Shakespeare, page 178a.

[3] See Franklin, page 331a.

[4] By Chapman, Jonson, and Marston.

there are no greater friends to English-men and England, when they are out on't, in the world, than they are. And for my own part, I would a hundred thousand of them were there [Virginia]; for we are all one countrymen now, ye know, and we should find ten times more comfort of them there than we do here.[1]

Eastward Ho. Act III, Sc. 2

I will neither yield to the song of the siren nor the voice of the hyena, the tears of the crocodile [2] nor the howling of the wolf.

Ibid. Act. V, Sc. 1

For one heat, all know, doth drive out another,
One passion doth expel another still.[3]

Monsieur D'Olive [1606].
Act V, Sc. 1

To put a girdle round about the world.[4]

Bussy D'Ambois [1607].
Act I, Sc. 1

So our lives
In acts exemplary, not only win
Ourselves good names, but doth to others give
Matter for virtuous deeds, by which we live.

Ibid.

Who to himself is law no law doth need,
Offends no law, and is a king indeed.

Ibid. Act II, Sc. 1

Give me a spirit that on this life's rough sea
Loves t' have his sails fill'd with a lusty wind,
Even till his sail-yards tremble, his masts crack,

And his rapt ship run on her side so low
That she drinks water, and her keel plows air.

Conspiracy of Charles, Duke of Byron [1608]. Act III, Sc. 1

They're only truly great who are truly good.[1]

Revenge for Honour [1654].
Act V, Sc. 2

ROBERT GREENE
[1560–1592]

Sweet are the thoughts that savour of content;
The quiet mind is richer than a crown. . . .
A mind content both crown and kingdom is.

Farewell to Folly

SIR JOHN HARINGTON
[1561–1612]

Fortune, men say, doth give too much to many,
But yet she never gave enough to any.

Epigrams. Of Fortune

The readers and the hearers like my books,
But yet some writers cannot them digest;
But what care I? for when I make a feast
I would my guests should praise it, not the cooks.

Ibid. Of Writers Who Carp at Other Men's Books

ROBERT SOUTHWELL
[1561–1595]

What thought can think, another thought can mend.

Look Home

Let this suffice, by this conceive the rest,

---

[1] This is the famous passage that gave offence to James I, and caused the imprisonment of the authors. The leaves containing it were cancelled and reprinted, and it only occurs in a few of the original copies. — RICHARD HERNE SHEPHERD

[2] These crocodile tears. — ROBERT BURTON: *Anatomy of Melancholy* [1621–1651], *Part III, Sect. 2, Memb. 2, Subsect. 4*
She's false, false as the tears of crocodiles. — SIR JOHN SUCKLING [1609–1642]: *The Sad One, Act IV, Sc. 5*

[3] See Shakespeare, page 134b.

[4] See Shakespeare, page 141b.

[1] See Juvenal, page 63a.
'Tis only noble to be good. — TENNYSON: *Lady Clara Vere de Vere* [1833], *St. 7*

He should, he could, he would, he did the best.
Look Home

Time goes by turns, and chances change by course,
From foul to fair, from better hap to worse.
Times Go by Turns

No joy so great but runneth to an end,
No hap so hard but may in time amend.
Ibid.

When sun is set the little stars will shine.
Scorn Not the Least

He that high growth on cedars did bestow,
Gave also lowly mushrumps leave to grow.
Ibid.

May never was the month of love,
For May is full of flowers;
But rather April, wet by kind,
For love is full of showers.
Love's Servile Lot

When Fortune smiles, I smile to think
How quickly she will frown.
I Envy Not Their Hap

As I in hoary winter night stood shivering in the snow,
Surprised was I with sudden heat which made my heart to glow;
And lifting up a fearful eye to view what fire was near
A pretty Babe all burning bright did in the air appear.
The Burning Babe. (A Christmas poem praised by BEN JONSON)

FRANCIS BACON
[1561–1626]

The monuments of wit survive the monuments of power.
Essex's Device [1595]

Knowledge is power. — Nam et ipsa **scientia** potestas est.[1]
Meditationes Sacrae [1597].
De Haeresibus

[1] A wise man is strong, yea, a man of knowledge increaseth strength. — *Proverbs, XXIV, 5.*
Knowledge is more than equivalent to

"Antiquitas saeculi juventus mundi."
These times are the ancient times, when the world is ancient, and not those which we account ancient *ordine retrogrado,* by a computation backward from ourselves.[1]
Advancement of Learning [1605].
Book I

For the glory of the Creator and the relief of man's estate.
Ibid.

It [Poesy] was ever thought to have some participation of divineness, because it doth raise and erect the mind by submitting the shews of things to the desires of the mind.
Ibid. Book II

Sacred and inspired divinity, the sabaoth and port of all men's labours and peregrinations.
Ibid.

Cleanness of body was ever deemed to proceed from a due reverence to God.[2]
Ibid.

---

force. — SAMUEL JOHNSON: *Rasselas* [1759], *Chap. XIII*

[1] As in the little, so in the great world, reason will tell you that old age or antiquity is to be accounted by the farther distance from the beginning and the nearer approach to the end, — the times wherein we now live being in propriety of speech the most ancient since the world's creation. — GEORGE HAKEWILL: *An Apologie or Declaration of the Power and Providence of God in the Government of the World* [1627]
For as old age is that period of life most remote from infancy, who does not see that old age in this universal man ought not to be sought in the times nearest his birth, but in those most remote from it? — PASCAL [1623–1662]: *Preface to the Treatise on Vacuum*
It is worthy of remark that a thought which is often quoted from Francis Bacon occurs in [Giordano] Bruno's "Cena di Cenere," published in 1584: I mean the notion that the later times are more aged than the earlier. — WHEWELL: *Philosophy of the Inductive Sciences* [1847], *Vol. II, P. 198*
We are Ancients of the earth,
And in the morning of the times.
TENNYSON: *The Day Dream* [1842], *L'Envoi*

[2] "Cleanliness is indeed next to godliness." — JOHN WESLEY [1703–1791] (quoted): *Sermon XCII, On Dress*
According to Rabbi A. S. Bettelheim,

States as great engines move slowly.
Advancement of Learning.
Book II

I do plainly and ingenuously confess that I am guilty of corruption, and do renounce all defense. I beseech your Lordships to be merciful to a broken reed.[1]

On being charged by Parliament with corruption in the exercise of his office [1621]

Like the strawberry wives, that laid two or three great strawberries at the mouth of their pot, and all the rest were little ones.

Apothegms [1624]. No. 54

Sir Henry Wotton used to say that critics are like brushers of noblemen's clothes.

Ibid. No. 64

Sir Amice Pawlet, when he saw too much haste made in any matter, was wont to say, "Stay a while, that we may make an end the sooner."

Ibid. No. 76

Alonso of Aragon was wont to say in commendation of age, that age appears to be best in four things, — old wood best to burn, old wine to drink, old friends to trust, and old authors to read.[2]

Ibid. No. 97

---

this is found in the Hebrew fathers. He cites Phinehas ben Yair, as follows: "The doctrines of religion are resolved into carefulness; carefulness into vigorousness; vigorousness into guiltlessness; guiltlessness into abstemiousness; abstemiousness into cleanliness; cleanliness into godliness" — literally, next to godliness.

[1] Thou trustest in the staff of this broken reed. — *Isaiah, XXXVI, 6*

[2] Is not old wine wholesomest, old pippins toothsomest, old wood burns brightest, old linen wash whitest? Old soldiers, sweetheart, are surest, and old lovers are soundest. — JOHN WEBSTER: *Westward Hoe* [1607], *Act II, Sc. 2*

Old friends are best. King James used to call for his old shoes; they were easiest for his feet. — SELDEN: *Table Talk* [1689], *Friends*

I love everything that's old, — old friends, old times, old manners, old books, old wine . . . and old friends are best! — GOLDSMITH: *She Stoops to Conquer* [1773], *Act I*

Old books, old wine, old Nankin blue. —

Cosmus, Duke of Florence, was wont to say of perfidious friends, that "We read that we ought to forgive our enemies; but we do not read that we ought to forgive our friends."

Apothegms. No. 206

Cato said the best way to keep good acts in memory was to refresh them with new.

Ibid. No. 247

Come home to men's business and bosoms.

Dedication to the Essays [Edition 1625]

No pleasure is comparable to the standing upon the vantage-ground of truth.

Of Truth

Men fear death as children fear to go in the dark; and as that natural fear in children is increased with tales, so is the other.

Of Death

Revenge is a kind of wild justice, which the more man's nature runs to, the more ought law to weed it out.

Of Revenge

It was a high speech of Seneca (after the manner of the Stoics), that "The good things which belong to prosperity are to be wished, but the good things that belong to adversity are to be admired."

Of Adversity

It is yet a higher speech of his than the other, "It is true greatness to have in one the frailty of a man and the security of a god."

Ibid.

Prosperity is the blessing of the Old Testament; adversity is the blessing of the New.

Ibid.

Prosperity is not without many fears and distastes; and adversity is not without comforts and hopes.

Ibid.

Virtue is like precious odours, —

AUSTIN DOBSON [1840–1921]: *Rondeau, To Richard Watson Gilder*

most fragrant when they are incensed or crushed.[1]

Of Adversity

He that hath wife and children hath given hostages to fortune; for they are impediments to great enterprises, either of virtue or mischief.

Of Marriage and Single Life

Wives are young men's mistresses, companions for middle age, and old men's nurses.

Ibid.

A good name is like a precious ointment; it filleth all around about, and will not easily away; for the odors of ointments are more durable than those of flowers.[2]

Of Praise

Men in great place are thrice servants, — servants of the sovereign or state, servants of fame, and servants of business.

Of Great Place

Mahomet made the people believe that he would call a hill to him, and from the top of it offer up his prayers for the observers of his law. The people assembled. Mahomet called the hill to come to him, again and again; and when the hill stood still he was never a whit abashed, but said, "If the hill will not come to Mahomet, Mahomet will go to the hill."

Of Boldness

The desire of power in excess caused the angels to fall; the desire of knowledge in excess caused man to fall.[3]

Of Goodness

I had rather believe all the fables in the legends and the Talmud and the Alcoran, than that this universal frame is without a mind.

Of Atheism

A little philosophy inclineth man's mind to atheism, but depth in philosophy bringeth men's minds about to religion.[1]

Ibid.

Travel, in the younger sort, is a part of education; in the elder, a part of experience. He that travelleth into a country before he hath some entrance into the language, goeth to school, and not to travel.

Of Travel

Princes are like to heavenly bodies, which cause good or evil times, and which have much veneration but no rest.[2]

Of Empire

Fortune is like the market, where many times, if you can stay a little, the price will fall.

Of Delays

In things that a man would not be seen in himself, it is a point of cunning to borrow the name of the world; as to say, "The world says," or "There is a speech abroad."

Of Cunning

There is a cunning which we in England call "the turning of the cat in the pan"; which is, when that which a man says to another, he lays it as if another had said it to him.

Ibid.

It is a good point of cunning for a man to shape the answer he would have in his own words and propositions, for it makes the other party stick the less.

Ibid

---

[1] As aromatic plants bestow
No spicy fragrance while they grow;
But crushed or trodden to the ground,
Diffuse their balmy sweets around.
GOLDSMITH: *The Captivity* [1764], *Act I*
The good are better made by ill,
As odours crushed are sweeter still.
SAMUEL ROGERS: *Jacqueline* [1814], *Stanza 3*

[2] See *Ecclesiastes, VII, 1*, on page 1042b, and Publilius Syrus, page 43b.

[3] Pride still is aiming at the blest abodes; Men would be angels, angels would be gods.

Aspiring to be gods if angels fell,
Aspiring to be angels men rebel.
ALEXANDER POPE: *Essay on Man, Epistle I* [1733], *L. 125*

[1] A little skill in antiquity inclines a man to Popery; but depth in that study brings him about again to our religion. — THOMAS FULLER: *The Holy State* [1642], *The True Church Antiquary*

[2] See Shelley, page 467a.

It hath been an opinion that the French are wiser than they seem, and the Spaniards seem wiser than they are; but howsoever it be between nations, certainly it is so between man and man.
Of Seeming Wise

There is a wisdom in this beyond the rules of physic. A man's own observation, what he finds good of and what he finds hurt of, is the best physic to preserve health.
Of Regimen of Health

Discretion of speech is more than eloquence; and to speak agreeably to him with whom we deal is more than to speak in good words or in good order.
Of Discourse

If a man look sharply and attentively, he shall see Fortune; for though she is blind, she is not invisible.[1]
Of Fortune

Young men are fitter to invent than to judge, fitter for execution than for counsel, and fitter for new projects than for settled business.
Of Youth and Age

Virtue is like a rich stone, — best plain set.
Of Beauty

There is no excellent beauty that hath not some strangeness in the proportion.
Ibid.

God Almighty first planted a garden.[2]
Of Gardens

---

[1] Fortune is painted blind, with a muffler afore her eyes, to signify to you that Fortune is blind. — SHAKESPEARE: *Henry V* [1598–1600], *Act III, Sc. 6, L. 31*

[2] See *Genesis, II, 8*, on page 1021b.
Divina natura dedit agros, ars humana aedificavit urbes (Divine Nature gave the fields, human art built the cities). — VARRO [116–27 B.C.]: *De Re Rustica, III, 1*
Gardens were before gardeners, and but some hours after the earth. — SIR THOMAS BROWNE: *The Garden of Cyrus* [1658], *Chap. I*
God the first garden made, and the first city Cain. — COWLEY: *The Garden* [1664], *Essay V*
God made the country, and man made the town. — COWPER: *The Task* [1785], *Book I, L. 749*
See Shakespeare, page 178a.

And because the breath of flowers is far sweeter in the air (where it comes and goes, like the warbling of music) than in the hand, therefore nothing is more fit for that delight than to know what be the flowers and plants that do best perfume the air.
Of Gardens

It is generally better to deal by speech than by letter.
Of Negotiating

Some books are to be tasted, others to be swallowed, and some few to be chewed and digested.
Of Studies

Reading maketh a full man, conference a ready man, and writing an exact man.
Ibid.

Histories make men wise; poets, witty; the mathematics, subtile; natural philosophy, deep; moral, grave; logic and rhetoric, able to contend.
Ibid.

The greatest vicissitude of things amongst men is the vicissitude of sects and religions.
Of Vicissitude of Things

I bequeath my soul to God. . . . My body to be buried obscurely. For my name and memory, I leave it to men's charitable speeches, and to foreign nations, and the next age.
From his Will [*1626*]

The world's a bubble, and the life of man
Less than a span.[1]
The World [*1629*]

Who then to frail mortality shall trust
But limns on water, or but writes in dust.
Ibid.

What then remains but that we still should cry

---

[1] Whose life is a bubble, and in length a span. — WILLIAM BROWNE: *Britannia's Pastorals* [1613], *Book I, Song*

See Sir John Davies, page 213b, and *The New England Primer*, page 1000b.

For being born, and, being born, to die? [1]
The World

I hold every man a debtor to his profession; from the which as men of course do seek to receive countenance and profit, so ought they of duty to endeavour themselves by way of amends to be a help and ornament thereunto.
Maxims of the Law [*1630*]. *Preface*

Books must follow sciences, and not sciences books.
Proposition touching Amendment of Laws

SAMUEL DANIEL
[1562–1619]

Care-charmer Sleep, son of the sable Night,
Brother to Death, in silent darkness born.[2]
Sonnet: To Delia [*1592*]

Make me to say when all my griefs are gone,
Happy the heart that sighed for such a one!
Sonnet: I Must Not Grieve [*1592*]

And for the few that only lend their ear,
That few is all the world.
Musophilus [*1599*]. *Stanza 97*

This is the thing that I was born to do.
Ibid. Stanza 100

Unless above himself he can
Erect himself, how poor a thing is man!
To the Countess of Cumberland
[*Circa 1600*]. *Stanza 12*

---

[1] This line frequently occurs in almost exactly the same shape among the minor poems of the time: "Not to be born, or, being born, to die." — WILLIAM DRUMMOND: *Poems* [1656]

[2] Care-charmer sleep, sweet ease in restless misery,
The captive's liberty, and his freedom's song,
Balm of the bruised heart, man's chief felicity,
Brother of quiet death, when life is too, too long!
BARTHOLOMEW GRIFFIN: *Fidessa More Chaste Than Kind* [1596]

See Hesiod, page 7a.

Love is a sickness full of woes,
All remedies refusing.
Hymen's Triumph [*1615*]

MICHAEL DRAYTON
[1563–1631]

Fair stood the wind for France.
The Ballad of Agincourt [*1605*]. *Stanza 1*

O, when shall Englishmen
With such acts fill a pen,
Or England breed again
Such a King Harry?
Ibid. Stanza 15

Since there's no help, come let us kiss and part.
Nay, I have done: you get no more of me,
And I am glad, yea glad with all my heart,
That thus so clearly, I myself can free.
Shake hands for ever, cancel all our vows,
And when we meet at any time again,
Be it not seen in either of our brows,
That we one jot of former love retain;
Now at the last gasp of love's latest breath,
When his pulse failing, passion speechless lies,
When faith is kneeling by his bed of death,
And innocence is closing up his eyes,
Now if thou wouldst, when all have given him over,
From death to life thou might'st him yet recover.
Sonnet [*1619*]

The coast was clear.
Nymphidia [*1627*]

Had in him those brave translunary things
That the first poets had.
(*Said of* MARLOWE) *To Henry Reynolds, of Poets and Poesy* [*1627*]

For that fine madness still he did retain
Which rightly should possess a poet's brain.
Ibid.

CHRISTOPHER MARLOWE
[1564–1593]

My men, like satyrs grazing on the
lawn,
Shall with their goat feet dance the
antic hay.
> *Edward II* [*1594*]. *Act 1, Sc. 1*

I'm armed with more than complete
steel, —
The justice of my quarrel.[1]
> *Lust's Dominion.*[2] *Act III, Sc. 4*

Who ever loved that loved not at first
sight?[3]
> *Hero and Leander* [*1598*]

Come live with me, and be my love;
And we will all the pleasures prove
That hills and valleys, dales and fields,
Woods or steepy mountain yields.[4]
> *The Passionate Shepherd to
> his Love* [*1599*]

By shallow rivers, to whose falls
Melodious birds sing madrigals.[5]
> *Ibid.*

And I will make thee beds of roses
And a thousand fragrant posies.[5]
> *Ibid.*

Hell hath no limits, nor is circumscribed
In one self-place; for where we are is
Hell,
And where Hell is, there must we ever
be.
> *Doctor Faustus* [*1604*]. *Sc. 5*

When all the world dissolves,
And every creature shall be purified,
All places shall be hell that are not
heaven.
> *Ibid.*

---

[1] See Shakespeare, page 125a.
[2] Attributed to Marlowe.
[3] Quoted in SHAKESPEARE'S *As You Like It*,
Act III, Sc. 5, L. 82
> None ever loved but at first sight they
> loved. — GEORGE CHAPMAN: *The Blind Beg-
> gar of Alexandria* [1598]
>
> I saw and loved. — GIBBON: *Memoirs*
> [1796]

[4] See Donne, page 216a.
[5] To shallow rivers, to whose falls
> Melodious birds sing madrigals;
> There will we make our peds of roses,
> And a thousand fragrant posies.
> > SHAKESPEARE: *Merry Wives of
> > Windsor* [1600–1601], *Act III,
> > Sc. 1, L. 17* (Sung by Evans)

Was this the face that launch'd a thousand ships,
And burnt the topless towers of Ilium?[1]
Sweet Helen, make me immortal with a
kiss!
Her lips suck forth my soul:[2] see,
where it flies!
> *Doctor Faustus. Sc. 14*

O, thou art fairer than the evening air
Clad in the beauty of a thousand stars.
> *Ibid.*

Now hast thou but one bare hour to
live,
And then thou must be damned perpetually;
Stand still, you ever moving spheres of
heaven,
That time may cease, and midnight
never come.
> *Ibid. Sc. 16*

O lente, lente currite noctis equi:[3]
The stars move still, time runs, the
clock will strike,
The devil will come, and Faustus must
be damn'd.
O I'll leap up to my God: who pulls
me down?
See see where Christ's blood streams in
the firmament.
One drop would save my soul, half a
drop, ah my Christ.
> *Ibid.*

Cut is the branch that might have
grown full straight,
And burnèd is Apollo's laurel bough,[4]
That sometime grew within this learnèd
man.
> *Ibid.*

I count religion but a childish toy,

---

[1] Was this fair face the cause, quoth she,
> Why the Grecians sacked Troy?
> > SHAKESPEARE: *All's Well that Ends
> > Well* [1601–1603], *Act I, Sc. 3, L. 75*

[2] Once he drew
> With one long kiss my whole soul through
> My lips.
> > TENNYSON: *Fatima* [1833] *St. 3*

[3] At si, quem malis, Cephalum complexa
> teneres,
> Clamares "lente currite noctis equi."
> > OVID [43 B.C.–A.D. 18]: *Amores, i., 13*

[4] See Shakespeare, page 201b.

And hold there is no sin but ignorance.[1]
The Jew of Malta [*Published
1633*]. *Act I*

Infinite riches in a little room.
Ibid.

Excess of wealth is cause of covetousness.
Ibid.

Now will I show myself to have more of the serpent than the dove; [2] that is, more knave than fool.
Ibid. Act II

WILLIAM SHAKESPEARE [3]
[1564–1616]

Hung be the heavens with black, yield day to night!
King Henry VI [*1591*]. *Part I,
Act I, Sc. 1, Line 1*

Fight till the last gasp.
Ibid. Sc. 2, Line 127

Expect Saint Martin's summer, halcyon days.
Ibid. Line 131

Glory is like a circle in the water,
Which never ceaseth to enlarge itself,
Till by broad spreading it disperse to nought.
Ibid. Line 133

The sun with one eye vieweth all the world.
Ibid. Sc. 4, Line 84

Unbidden guests
Are often welcomest when they are gone.
Ibid. Act II, Sc. 2, Line 55

Between two hawks, which flies the higher pitch;
Between two dogs, which hath the deeper mouth;
Between two blades, which bears the better temper;

Between two horses, which doth bear him best;
Between two girls, which hath the merriest eye;
I have, perhaps, some shallow spirit of judgment;
But in these nice sharp quillets of the law,
Good faith, I am no wiser than a daw.
*King Henry VI. Part I, Act II,
Sc. 4, Line 12*

I'll note you in my book of memory.
Ibid. Line 101

Just death, kind umpire of men's miseries.
Ibid. Sc. 5, Line 29

Fair be all thy hopes,
And prosperous be thy life in peace and war!
Ibid. Line 113

Chok'd with ambition of the meaner sort.
Ibid. Line 123

Friendly counsel cuts off many foes.
Ibid. Act III, Sc. 1, Line 184

Delays have dangerous ends.[1]
Ibid. Sc. 2, Line 33

Care is no cure, but rather corrosive,
For things that are not to be remedied.
Ibid. Sc. 3, Line 3

Of all base passions, fear is most accurs'd.
Ibid. Act V, Sc. 2, Line 18

She's beautiful and therefore to be wooed,
She is a woman, therefore to be won.[2]
Ibid. Sc. 3, Line 78

For what is wedlock forced, but a hell,
An age of discord and continual strife?
Whereas the contrary bringeth bliss,
And is a pattern of celestial peace.
Ibid. Sc. 5, Line 62

O Lord! that lends me life,
Lend me a heart replete with thankfulness!
Ibid. Part II, Act I, Sc. 1, Line 19

---

[1] There is no sin except stupidity. — OSCAR WILDE [1856–1900]: *The Critic as Artist, Part II*

[2] Be ye therefore wise as serpents, and harmless as doves. — *Matthew, X, 16*

[3] From the text of W. J. Craig, Oxford University Press. The dates and order, about which there is much conjecture, are those which Sir Edmund Chambers (*William Shakespeare* [1930]) thinks most probable.

---

[1] See Cervantes, page 106a.
All delays are dangerous in war. — DRYDEN: *Tyrannic Love* [1669], *Act I, Sc. 1*

[2] See *Titus Andronicus*, page 129b.

Whose large style
Agrees not with the leanness of his purse.
King Henry VI. Part II, Act I,
Sc. 1, Line 112

'Tis not my speeches that you do mislike,
But 'tis my presence that doth trouble ye.
Rancour will out.
Ibid. Line 141

Could I come near your beauty with my nails
I'd set my ten commandments in your face.
Ibid. Sc. 3, Line 144

Blessed are the peacemakers on earth.[1]
Ibid. Act II, Sc. 1, Line 34

God be prais'd, that to believing souls
Gives light in darkness, comfort in despair![2]
Ibid. Line 66

God defend the right!
Ibid. Sc. 3, Line 55

Sometimes hath the brightest day a cloud;
And after summer evermore succeeds
Barren winter, with his wrathful nipping cold:
So cares and joys abound, as seasons fleet.
Ibid. Sc. 4, Line 1

Now 'tis the spring, and weeds are shallow-rooted;
Suffer them now and they'll o'ergrow the garden.
Ibid. Act III, Sc. 1, Line 31

In thy face I see
The map of honour, truth, and loyalty.
Ibid. Line 202

What stronger breastplate than a heart untainted!
Thrice is he armed that hath his quarrel just,

And he but naked, though locked up in steel,
Whose conscience with injustice is corrupted.[1]
King Henry VI. Part II, Act III,
Sc. 2, Line 232

For wheresoe'er thou art in this world's globe,
I'll have an Iris that shall find thee out.
Ibid. Line 406

He dies, and makes no sign.
Ibid. Sc. 3, Line 29

Forbear to judge, for we are sinners all.[2]
Close up his eyes and draw the curtain close;
And let us all to meditation.
Ibid. Line 31

The gaudy, blabbing, and remorseful day
Is crept into the bosom of the sea.
Ibid. Act. IV, Sc. 1, Line 1

Small things make base men proud.
Ibid. Line 106

True nobility is exempt from fear.
Ibid. Line 129

I will make it felony to drink small beer.[3]
Ibid. Sc. 2, Line 75

The first thing we do, let's kill all the lawyers.
Ibid. Line 86

Is not this a lamentable thing, that of the skin of an innocent lamb should be made parchment? that parchment, being scribbled o'er, should undo a man?
Ibid. Line 88

Sir, he made a chimney in my father's house, and the bricks are alive at this day to testify it.
Ibid. Line 160

Thou hast most traitorously corrupted the youth of the realm in erect-

---

[1] Blessed are the peacemakers: for they shall be called the children of God. — *Matthew, V, 9*

[2] Though hopeless love finds comfort in despair,
It never can endure a rival's bliss!
RICHARD BRINSLEY SHERIDAN: *The Critic* [1779], *Act III, Sc. 1*

[1] See Marlowe, page 123a.

[2] Judge not, that ye be not judged. — *Matthew, VII, 1*

[3] Doth it not show vilely in me to desire small beer? — *King Henry IV* [1597–1598], *Part II, Act II, Sc. 2, L. 7*
See *Othello*, page 187a.
That questionable superfluity — small beer. — DOUGLAS JERROLD [1803–1857]: *The Tragedy of the Till*

ing a grammar-school; and whereas, before, our forefathers had no other books but the score and the tally, thou hast caused printing to be used; and, contrary to the king, his crown, and dignity, thou hast built a paper-mill.
> *King Henry VI. Part II, Act IV,*
> *Sc. 7, Line 35*

Beggars mounted run their horse to death.[1]
> *Ibid. Part III, Act I, Sc. 4, Line 127*

O tiger's heart wrapp'd in a woman's hide! [2]
> *Ibid. Line 137*

And many strokes, though with a little axe,
Hew down and fell the hardest-timbered oak.
> *Ibid. Act II, Sc. 1, Line 54*

To weep is to make less the depth of grief.
> *Ibid. Line 85*

Didst thou never hear
That things ill got had ever bad success?
And happy always was it for that son
Whose father for his hoarding went to hell?
> *Ibid. Sc. 2, Line 45*

Our hap is loss, our hope but sad despair.[3]
> *Ibid. Sc. 3, Line 9*

Thou setter up and plucker down of kings.[4]
> *Ibid. Line 37*

And what makes robbers bold but too much lenity?
> *Ibid. Sc. 6, Line 22*

[1] Set a beggar on horseback and he will ride a gal'op. — ROBERT BURTON: *Anatomy of Melancholy* [1621–1651], *Part II, Sect. 2, Memb. 2*
Set a beggar on horseback, and he'll outride the Devil. — BOHN: *Foreign Proverbs, German* [1855]
[2] ROBERT GREENE in *A Groats-Worth of Wit* [1592] burlesques this line: "Tyger's hart wrapt in a Player's hide."
[3] Thus repuls'd, our final hope
Is flat despair.
> MILTON: *Paradise Lost* [1667],
> *Book II, L. 142*
[4] Proud setter up and puller down of kings.
— *Act III, Sc. 3, L. 156*

My crown is in my heart, not on my head;
Not deck'd with diamonds and Indian stones,
Nor to be seen: my crown is call'd content;
A crown it is that seldom kings enjoy.
> *King Henry VI. Part III,*
> *Act III, Sc. 1. Line 62*

'Tis a happy thing
To be the father unto many sons.
> *Ibid. Sc. 2, Line 104*

Gloucester. That would be ten days' wonder at the least.
Clarence. That's a day longer than a wonder lasts.[1]
> *Ibid. Line 113*

Like one that stands upon a promontory,
And spies a far-off shore where he would tread,
Wishing his foot were equal with his eye.
> *Ibid. Line 135*

Yield not thy neck
To fortune's yoke, but let thy dauntless mind
Still ride in triumph over all mischance.
> *Ibid. Sc. 3, Line 16*

For how can tyrants safely govern home,
Unless abroad they purchase great alliance?
> *Ibid. Line 69*

Having nothing, nothing can he lose.
> *Ibid. Line 152*

Hasty marriage seldom proveth well.
> *Ibid. Act IV, Sc. 1, Line 18*

Let us be back'd with God and with the seas
Which he hath given for fence impregnable,
And with their helps only defend ourselves:
In them and in ourselves our safety lies.
> *Ibid. Line 43*

What fates impose, that men must needs abide;
It boots not to resist both wind and tide.
> *Ibid. Sc. 3, Line 57*

[1] See Chaucer, page 78b.

Now join your hands, and with your hands your hearts.
> *King Henry VI. Part III, Act IV, Sc. 6, Line 39*

For many men that stumble at the threshold
Are well foretold that danger lurks within.
> *Ibid. Sc. 7, Line 11*

A little fire is quickly trodden out;
Which, being suffered, rivers cannot quench.
> *Ibid. Sc. 8, Line 7*

When the lion fawns upon the lamb,
The lamb will never cease to follow him.
> *Ibid. Line 49*

What is pomp, rule, reign, but earth and dust?
And, live we how we can, yet die we must.
> *Ibid. Act V, Sc. 2, Line 27*

Every cloud engenders not a storm.
> *Ibid. Sc. 3, Line 13*

We are advertis'd by our loving friends.
> *Ibid. Sc. 3, Line 18*

What though the mast be now blown over-board,
The cable broke, the holding anchor lost,
And half our sailors swallow'd in the flood?
Yet lives our pilot still.
> *Ibid. Sc. 4, Line 3*

So part we sadly in this troublous world
To meet with joy in sweet Jerusalem.
> *Ibid. Sc. 5, Line 7*

Men ne'er spend their fury on a child.
> *Ibid. Line 57*

He's sudden if a thing comes in his head.
> *Ibid. Line 86*

Suspicion always haunts the guilty mind;
The thief doth fear each bush an officer.
> *Ibid. Sc. 6, Line 11*

This word "love," which greybeards call divine.
> *Ibid. Line 81*

Now is the winter of our discontent

Made glorious summer by this sun of York.
> *King Richard III* [*1592–1593*].
> *Act I, Sc. 1, Line 1*

Grim-visaged war hath smoothed his wrinkled front.
> *Ibid. Line 9*

To leave this keen encounter of our wits.
> *Ibid. Sc. 2, Line 116*

His better doth not breathe upon the earth.
> *Ibid. Line 141*

Look, how my ring encompasseth thy finger,
Even so thy breast encloseth my poor heart;
Wear both of them, for both of them are thine.
> *Ibid. Line 204*

Was ever woman in this humour wooed?
Was ever woman in this humour won?
> *Ibid. Line 229*

Framed in the prodigality of nature.
> *Ibid. Line 245*

The world is grown so bad,
That wrens make prey where eagles dare not perch.[1]
> *Ibid. Sc. 3, Line 70*

They that stand high have many blasts to shake them.
> *Ibid. Line 259*

And thus I clothe my naked villany
With odd old ends stol'n forth of holy writ,
And seem a saint when most I play the devil.
> *Ibid. Line 336*

Talkers are no good doers.
> *Ibid. Line 351*

O, I have passed a miserable night,
So full of ugly sights, of ghastly dreams,
That, as I am a Christian faithful man,
I would not spend another such a night,
Though 'twere to buy a world of happy days.
> *Ibid. Sc. 4, Line 2*

Lord, Lord! methought, what pain it was to drown:

---

[1] See Alexander Pope, page 312a.

What dreadful noise of waters in mine
ears!
What ugly sights of death within mine
eyes!

> *King Richard III. Act I,*
> *Sc. 4, Line 21*

I pass'd, methought, the melancholy
flood,
With that grim ferryman which poets
write of,
Unto the kingdom of perpetual night.

> *Ibid. Line 45*

Sorrow breaks seasons and reposing
hours,
Makes the night morning, and the noon-
tide night.

> *Ibid. Line 76*

Thou art a widow; yet thou art a
mother,
And hast the comfort of thy children
left thee.

> *Ibid. Act II, Sc. 2, Line 55*

A parlous boy.

> *Ibid. Sc. 4, Line 35*

So wise so young, they say, do never
live long.[1]

> *Ibid. Act III, Sc. 1, Line 79*

Off with his head!

> *Ibid. Sc. 4, Line 75*

Lives like a drunken sailor on a mast,
Ready with every nod to tumble down.

> *Ibid. Line 98*

Even in the afternoon of her best days.

> *Ibid. Sc. 7, Line 185*

Thou troublest me: I am not in the vein.

> *Ibid. Act IV, Sc. 2, Line 117*

The sons of Edward sleep in Abraham's
bosom.[2]

> *Ibid. Sc. 3, Line 38*

A grievous burthen was thy birth to me;
Tetchy and wayward was thy infancy.

> *Ibid. Sc. 4, Line 168*

An honest tale speeds best being plainly
told.

> *Ibid. Line 359*

Harp not on that string.

> *Ibid. Line 365*

[1] A little too wise, they say, do ne'er live
long. — MIDDLETON [1570–1627]: *The Phoenix, Act I, Sc. 1*

[2] The beggar died, and was carried by the
angels into Abraham's bosom. — *Luke, XVI,
22*

Thus far into the bowels of the land
Have we marched on without impedi-
ment.

> *King Richard III. Act V,*
> *Sc. 2, Line 3*

True hope is swift, and flies with swallow's wings;
Kings it makes gods, and meaner creatures kings.

> *Ibid. Line 23*

The king's name is a tower of strength.

> *Ibid. Sc. 3, Line 12*

Give me another horse! bind up my
wounds!

> *Ibid. Line 178*

O coward conscience, how dost thou
afflict me!

> *Ibid. Line 180*

My conscience hath a thousand several
tongues,
And every tongue brings in a several
tale,
And every tale condemns me for a villain.

> *Ibid. Line 194*

The early village cock
Hath twice done salutation to the morn.

> *Ibid. Line 210*

By the apostle Paul, shadows to-night
Have struck more terror to the soul of
Richard
Than can the substance of ten thousand
soldiers.

> *Ibid. Line 217*

Conscience is but a word that cowards
use,
Devis'd at first to keep the strong in
awe.

> *Ibid. Line 310*

A horse! a horse! my kingdom for a
horse!

> *Ibid. Sc. 4, Line 7*

I have set my life upon a cast,
And I will stand the hazard of the die:
I think there be six Richmonds in the
field.

> *Ibid. Line 9*

The pleasing punishment that women
bear.

> *The Comedy of Errors* [1592–
> 1593]. *Act I, Sc. 1, Line 46*

We may pity, though not pardon thee.
The Comedy of Errors.
Act I, Sc. 1, Line 97

To tell sad stories of my own mishaps.
Ibid. Line 120

Why, headstrong liberty is lash'd with woe.

There's nothing situate under heaven's eye

But hath his bound, in earth, in sea, in sky.
Ibid. Act. II, Sc. 1, Line 15

A wretched soul, bruised with adversity.
Ibid. Line 34

Every why hath a wherefore.[1]
Ibid. Sc. 2, Line 45

There's no time for a man to recover his hair that grows bald by nature.
Ibid. Line 74

What he hath scanted men in hair, he hath given them in wit.
Ibid. Line 83

Time himself is bald, and therefore to the world's end will have bald followers.
Ibid. Line 109

Small cheer and great welcome makes a merry feast.
Ibid. Act III, Sc. 1, Line 26

There is something in the wind.
Ibid. Line 69

We'll pluck a crow together.
Ibid. Line 83

For slander lives upon succession,
For ever housed where it gets possession.
Ibid. Line 105

Be not thy tongue thy own shame's orator
Ibid. Sc. 2, Line 10

Ill deeds are doubled with an evil word.
Ibid. Line 20

O! train me not, sweet mermaid, with thy note,
To drown me in thy sister flood of tears.
Ibid. Line 45

[1] See *King Henry V*, page 156b.
For every why he had a wherefore.—
SAMUEL BUTLER: *Hudibras, Part I* [1663], *Canto I, L. 132*

A back-friend, a shoulder-clapper.
The Comedy of Errors. Act IV, Sc. 2, Line 37

Give me your hand and let me feel your pulse.
Ibid. Sc. 4, Line 54

The venom clamours of a jealous woman
Poison more deadly than a mad dog's tooth.
Ibid. Act V, Sc. 1, Line 69

Unquiet meals make ill digestions.
Ibid. Line 74

One Pinch, a hungry lean-faced villain,
A mere anatomy.
Ibid. Line 238

A needy, hollow-eyed, sharp-looking wretch,
A living-dead man.
Ibid. Line 241

I hope I shall have leisure to make good.
Ibid. Line 378

Sleep in peace, slain in your country's wars!
Titus Andronicus [1593–1594].
Act I, Sc. 1, Line 91

Sweet mercy is nobility's true badge.
Ibid. Line 119

In peace and honour rest you here, my sons;
Rome's readiest champions, repose you here in rest,
Secure from worldly chances and mishaps!
Ibid. Line 150

These words are razors to my wounded heart.
Ibid. Line 314

He lives in fame that died in virtue's cause.
Ibid. Line 390

These dreary dumps.[1]
Ibid. Line 391

She is a woman, therefore may be woo'd;
She is a woman, therefore may be won.[2]
Ibid. Act II, Sc. 1, Line 82

What you cannot as you would achieve,

[1] And doleful dumps the mind oppress.—
Romeo and Juliet, Act IV, Sc. 5, L. 130
[2] See *King Henry VI*, page 124b.

You must perforce accomplish as you may.

> *Titus Andronicus. Act II,*
> *Sc. 1, Line 106*

Poor harmless fly.

> *Ibid. Act. III, Sc. 2, Line 63*

The eagle suffers little birds to sing.

> *Ibid. Act IV, Sc. 4, Line 82*

And if the boy have not a woman's gift
To rain a shower of commanded tears,
An onion will do well for such a shift.

> *The Taming of the Shrew* [1593–
> 1594]. *Induction, Sc. 1, Line 124*

No profit grows where is no pleasure ta'en;
In brief, sir, study what you most affect.

> *Ibid. Act I, Sc. 1, Line 39*

There's small choice in rotten apples.

> *Ibid. Line 137*

Whom should I knock?

> *Ibid. Sc. 2, Line 6*

To seek their fortunes further than at home,
Where small experience grows.

> *Ibid. Line 51*

As curst and shrewd
As Socrates' Xanthippe.

> *Ibid. Line 70*

Nothing comes amiss, so money comes withal.

> *Ibid. Line 82*

Tush, tush! fear boys with bugs.

> *Ibid. Line 214*

And do as adversaries do in law,
Strive mightily, but eat and drink as friends.

> *Ibid. Line 281*

I must dance barefoot on her wedding day,
And, for your love to her, lead apes in hell.

> *Ibid. Act II, Sc. 1, Line 32*

Old fashions please me best.

> *Ibid. Act III, Sc. 1, Line 81*

Who wooed in haste and means to wed at leisure.[1]

> *Ibid. Sc. 2, Line 11*

---

[1] Married in haste, we may repent at leisure. — CONGREVE: *The Old Bachelor* [1693?], *Act V, Sc. 1*

A little pot and soon hot.[1]

> *The Taming of the Shrew.*
> *Act IV, Sc. 1, Line 6*

It was the friar of orders grey,
As he forth walked on his way.[2]

> *Ibid. Line 148*

Sits as one new-risen from a dream.

> *Ibid. Line 189*

This is a way to kill a wife with kindness.

> *Ibid. Line 211*

Kindness in women, not their beauteous looks,
Shall win my love.

> *Ibid. Sc. 2, Line 41*

Our purses shall be proud, our garments poor:
For 'tis the mind that makes the body rich.

> *Ibid. Sc. 3, Line 173*

And as the sun breaks through the darkest clouds,
So honour peereth in the meanest habit.

> *Ibid. Line 175*

Forward, I pray, since we have come so far,
And be it moon, or sun, or what you please:
An if you please to call it a rush-candle,
Henceforth I vow it shall be so for me.

> *Ibid. Sc. 5, Line 12*

So bedazzled with the sun
That everything I look on seemeth green.

> *Ibid. Line 46*

My cake is dough.

> *Ibid. Act V, Sc. 1, Line 146*

He that is giddy thinks the world turns round.

> *Ibid. Sc. 2, Line 20*

A woman moved is like a fountain troubled,
Muddy, ill-seeming, thick, bereft of beauty.

> *Ibid. Line 143*

---

[1] He is a little chimney, and heated hot in a moment. — LONGFELLOW: *The Courtship of Miles Standish* [1858]

[2] THOMAS PERCY [1728–1811] composed *The Friar of Orders Grey* of various fragments of ancient ballads found in Shakespeare's plays. See page 1011b.

Such duty as the subject owes the prince,
Even such a woman oweth to her husband.

The Taming of the Shrew.
Act V, Sc. 2, Line 156

Bid me discourse, I will enchant thine ear.

Venus and Adonis [1593]. Line 145

Love is a spirit all compact of fire.

Ibid. Line 149

A red morn, that ever yet betoken'd
Wrack to the seaman, tempest to the field.

Ibid. Line 453

The owl, night's herald.

Ibid. Line 531

The path is smooth that leadeth on to danger.

Ibid. Line 788

Love comforteth like sunshine after rain.

Ibid. Line 799

The text is old, the orator too green.

Ibid. Line 806

Lo! here the gentle lark, weary of rest,
From his moist cabinet mounts up on high,
And wakes the morning.

Ibid. Line 853

For he being dead, with him is beauty slain,
And, beauty dead, black chaos comes again.[1]

Ibid. Line 1019

The grass stoops not, she treads on it so light.

Ibid. Line 1028

Beauty itself doth of itself persuade
The eyes of men without an orator.

The Rape of Lucrece [1594].
Line 29

Those that much covet are with gain so fond,
For what they have not, that which they possess
They scatter and unloose it from their bond,
And so, by hoping more, they have but less.

Ibid. Line 134

[1] See *Othello*, page 188a.

One for all, or all for one we gage.[1]

The Rape of Lucrece.
Line 144

Or sells eternity to get a toy.

Ibid. Line 214

Time's glory is to calm contending kings,
To unmask falsehood, and bring truth to light.

Ibid. Line 939

For greatest scandal waits on greatest state.

Ibid. Line 1006

For men have marble, women waxen minds.

Ibid. Line 1240

To see sad sights moves more than hear them told.

Ibid. Line 1324

Cloud-kissing Ilion.

Ibid. Line 1370

Lucrece swears he did her wrong.[2]

Ibid. Line 1462

Home-keeping youth have ever homely wits.

The Two Gentlemen of Verona
[1594–1595]. Act I, Sc. 1,
Line 2

I have no other but a woman's reason:
I think him so, because I think him so

Ibid. Sc. 2, Line 23

They do not love that do not show their love.

Ibid. Line 31

O! they love least that let men know their love.

Ibid. Line 32

Since maids, in modesty, say "No" to that
Which they would have the profferer construe "Ay."

Ibid. Line 53

What is't that you took up so gingerly?

Ibid. Line 68

O! how this spring of love resembleth
The uncertain glory of an April day!

Ibid. Sc. 3, Line 84

---

[1] All for one, one for all, that is our device. — ALEXANDRE DUMAS [1802–1870]: *The Three Musketeers, Chap. 9*
[2] Some villain hath done me wrong. — *King Lear* [1605–1606], *Act I, Sc. 2, L. 186*

O jest unseen, inscrutable, invisible,
As a nose on a man's face,[1] or a weath-
ercock on a steeple.
The Two Gentlemen of Verona.
Act II, Sc. 1, Line 145
He makes sweet music.
Ibid. Sc. 7, Line 28
That man that hath a tongue, I say, is
no man,
If with his tongue he cannot win a
woman.
Ibid. Act III, Sc. 1, Line 104
My thoughts do harbour with my
Sylvia nightly;
And slaves they are to me that send
them flying.
Ibid. Line 140
Who is Sylvia? what is she?
That all our swains commend her?
Holy, fair, and wise is she;
The heaven such grace did lend her.
Ibid. Act IV, Sc. 2, Line 40
Alas, how love can trifle with itself!
Ibid. Sc. 4, Line 185
How use doth breed a habit in a man![2]
Ibid. Act V, Sc. 4, Line 1
Make us heirs of all eternity.
Love's Labour's Lost [*1594–
1595*]. *Act I, Sc. 1, Line 7*
The huge army of the world's desires.
Ibid. Line 10
Or, having sworn too hard-a-keeping
oath,
Study to break it, and not break my
troth.
Ibid. Line 65
Why, all delights are vain; but that
most vain,
Which, with pain purchas'd, doth in-
herit pain.
Ibid. Line 72
Light seeking light doth light of light
beguile.
Ibid. Line 77
Study is like the heaven's glorious sun,
That will not be deep-search'd with
saucy looks;
Small have continual plodders ever
won,

[1] See Rabelais, page 90a.
[2] See Plutarch, page 60a.

Save base authority from others'
books.
These earthly godfathers of heaven's
lights
That give a name to every fixed star,
Have no more profit of their shining
nights
Than those that walk and wot not
what they are.
Love's Labour's Lost.
Act I, Sc. 1, Line 84
At Christmas I no more desire a rose
Than wish a snow in May's new-
fangled mirth;
But like of each thing that in season
grows.
Ibid. Line 105
A man in all the world's new fashion
planted,
That hath a mint of phrases in his brain.
Ibid. Line 163
And men sit down to that nourish-
ment which is called supper.
Ibid. Line 237
That unlettered small-knowing soul.
Ibid. Line 251
A child of our grandmother Eve, a
female; or, for thy more sweet under-
standing, a woman.
Ibid. Line 263
Affliction may one day smile again;
and till then, sit thee down, sorrow!
Ibid. Line 312
Devise, wit; write, pen; for I am for
whole volumes in folio.
Ibid. Sc. 2, Line 194
Beauty is bought by judgment of the
eye,
Not utter'd by base sale of chapmen's
tongues.
Ibid. Act II, Sc. 1, Line 15
A man of sovereign parts he is esteem'd;
Well fitted in arts, glorious in arms:
Nothing becomes him ill that he would
well.
Ibid. Line 44
A merrier man,
Within the limit of becoming mirth,
I never spent an hour's talk withal.
Ibid. Line 66
Delivers in such apt and gracious words
That aged ears play truant at his tales,

And younger hearings are quite ravished;
So sweet and voluble is his discourse.
Love's Labour's Lost.
Act II, Sc. 1, Line 73
Your wit's too hot, it speeds too fast, 'twill tire.
Ibid. Line 119
Warble, child; make passionate my sense of hearing.
Ibid. Act III, Sc. 1, Line 1
Remuneration! O! that's the Latin word for three farthings.
Ibid. Line 143
A very beadle to a humorous sigh.
Ibid. Line 185
This wimpled, whining, purblind, wayward boy,
This senior-junior, giant-dwarf, Dan Cupid;
Regent of love-rhymes, lord of folded arms,
The anointed sovereign of sighs and groans,
Liege of all loiterers and malcontents.
Ibid. Line 189
He hath not fed of the dainties that are bred in a book; he hath not eat paper, as it were; he hath not drunk ink.
Ibid. Act IV, Sc. 2, Line 25
Many can brook the weather that love not the wind.
Ibid. Line 34
You two are book-men.
Ibid. Line 35
These are begot in the ventricle of memory, nourished in the womb of pia mater, and delivered upon the mellowing of occasion.
Ibid. Line 70
By heaven, I do love, and it hath taught me to rhyme, and to be melancholy.
Ibid. Sc. 3, Line 13
The heavenly rhetoric of thine eye.
Ibid. Line 60
As upright as the cedar.
Ibid. Line 89
Sweet lords, sweet lovers, O! let us embrace.
As true we are as flesh and blood can be:

The sea will ebb and flow, heaven show his face;
Young blood doth not obey an old decree:
We cannot cross the cause why we were born.
Love's Labour's Lost.
Act IV, Sc. 3, Line 214
For where is any author in the world
Teaches such beauty as a woman's eye?
Learning is but an adjunct to ourself.
Ibid. Line 312
But love, first learned in a lady's eyes,
Lives not alone immured in the brain.
Ibid. Line 327
It adds a precious seeing to the eye.
Ibid. Line 333
As sweet and musical
As bright Apollo's lute, strung with his hair;
And when Love speaks, the voice of all the gods
Makes heaven drowsy with the harmony.
Ibid. Line 342
From women's eyes this doctrine I derive:
They sparkle still the right Promethean fire;
They are the books, the arts, the academes,
That show, contain, and nourish all the world.
Ibid. Line 350
He draweth out the thread of his verbosity finer than the staple of his argument.
Ibid. Act V, Sc. 1, Line 18
Moth. They have been at a great feast of languages, and stolen the scraps.
Costard. O! they have lived long on the alms-basket of words. I marvel thy master hath not eaten thee for a word; for thou art not so long by the head as *honorificabilitudinitatibus;* thou art easier swallowed than a flap-dragon.
Ibid. Line 39
In the posteriors of this day, which the rude multitude call the afternoon.
Ibid. Line 96

Let me take you a button-hole lower.
Love's Labour's Lost.
Act V, Sc. 2, Line 705

The naked truth of it is, I have no shirt.
Ibid. Line 715

A jest's prosperity lies in the ear
Of him that hears it, never in the tongue
Of him that makes it.
Ibid. Line 869

When daisies pied and violets blue,
  And lady-smocks all silver-white,
And cuckoo-buds of yellow hue
  Do paint the meadows with delight,
The cuckoo then, on every tree,
Mocks married men; for thus sings he,
      Cuckoo;
Cuckoo, cuckoo: O word of fear,
Unpleasing to a married ear.
Ibid. Line 902

When icicles hang by the wall,
  And Dick, the shepherd, blows his nail,
And Tom bears logs into the hall,
  And milk comes frozen home in pail,
When blood is nipp'd and ways be foul,
Then nightly sings the staring owl,
      Tu-who;
Tu-whit, tu-who — a merry note,
While greasy Joan doth keel the pot.
When all aloud the wind doth blow,
And coughing drowns the parson's saw;
And birds sit brooding in the snow,
And Marion's nose looks red and raw,
When roasted crabs hiss in the bowl.
Ibid. Line 920

The words of Mercury are harsh after the songs of Apollo.
Ibid. Line 938

A pair of star-cross'd lovers.
Romeo and Juliet [1594-1595].
Act I, Prologue, Line 6

An hour before the worshipp'd sun
Peered forth the golden window of the east.
Ibid. Sc. 1, Line 124

As is the bud bit with an envious worm,
Ere he can spread his sweet leaves to the air,
Or dedicate his beauty to the sun.
Ibid. Line 156

Alas! that love, so gentle in his view,
Should be so tyrannous and rough in proof.
Romeo and Juliet. Act I,
Sc. 1, Line 174

Saint-seducing gold.
Ibid. Line 220

He that is strucken blind cannot forget
The precious treasure of his eyesight lost.
Ibid. Line 238

One fire burns out another's burning,[1]
One pain is lessen'd by another's anguish.
Ibid. Sc. 2, Line 47

I will make thee think thy swan a crow.
Ibid. Line 92

One fairer than my love! the all-seeing sun
Ne'er saw her match since first the world begun.
Ibid. Line 97

That book in many eyes doth share the glory
That in gold clasps locks in the golden story.
Ibid. Sc. 3, Line 91

For I am proverb'd with a grandsire phrase.
Ibid. Sc. 4, Line 37

We burn daylight.
Ibid. Line 43

Benvolio. O! then, I see Queen Mab
  hath been with you! . . .
Mercutio. She is the fairies' midwife,
  and she comes
In shape no bigger than an agate-stone
On the fore-finger of an alderman,
Drawn with a team of little atomies
Athwart men's noses as they lie asleep.
Ibid. Line 53

True, I talk of dreams,
Which are the children of an idle brain,
Begot of nothing but vain fantasy.
Ibid. Line 97

Toes
Unplagu'd with corns.
Ibid. Sc. 5, Line 21

[1] See Chapman, page 117a.

For you and I are past our dancing
    days.[1]
> *Romeo and Juliet. Act I, Sc. 5,*
> *Line 35*

It seems she hangs upon the cheek of
    night
Like a rich jewel in an Ethiop's ear;
Beauty too rich for use, for earth too
    dear.
> *Ibid. Line 49*

My only love sprung from my only
    hate!
Too early seen unknown, and known
    too late!
> *Ibid. Line 142*

He jests at scars, that never felt a
    wound.
But, soft! what light through yonder
    window breaks?
It is the east, and Juliet is the sun.
> *Ibid. Act II, Sc. 2, Line 1*

She speaks, yet she says nothing.
> *Ibid. Line 12*

See, how she leans her cheek upon her
    hand.
O! that I were a glove upon that hand,
That I might touch that cheek.
> *Ibid. Line 23*

O Romeo, Romeo! wherefore art thou
    Romeo? [2]
Deny thy father, and refuse thy name;
Or, if thou wilt not, be but sworn my
    love,
And I'll no longer be a Capulet.
> *Ibid. Line 33*

What's in a name? That which we call
    a rose
By any other name would smell as
    sweet.
> *Ibid. Line 43*

For stony limits cannot hold love out.
> *Ibid. Line 67*

---

[1] My dancing days are done. — BEAUMONT
AND FLETCHER: *The Scornful Lady* [1616],
Act V, Sc. 3

[2] HENRY FIELDING burlesqued this in *Life
and Death of Tom Thumb the Great* [1730]
as follows:
Huncamunca. O Tom Thumb! Tom
Thumb! wherefore art thou Tom Thumb? —
Act II, Sc. 3

Alack! there lies more peril in thine eye
Than twenty of their swords.
> *Romeo and Juliet. Act II,*
> *Sc. 2, Line 71*

At lovers' perjuries,
They say, Jove laughs.[1]
> *Ibid. Line 92*

In truth, fair Montague, I am too fond.
> *Ibid. Line 98*

Romeo. Lady, by yonder blessed moon
    I swear,
That tips with silver all these fruit-tree
    tops, —
Juliet. O! swear not by the moon, the
    inconstant moon,
That monthly changes in her circled
    orb,
Lest that thy love prove likewise vari-
    able.
> *Ibid. Line 107*

Do not swear at all;
Or, if thou wilt, swear by thy gracious
    self,
Which is the god of my idolatry.
> *Ibid. Line 112*

Too like the lightning, which doth cease
    to be
Ere one can say it lightens.
> *Ibid. Line 119*

This bud of love, by summer's ripening
    breath,
May prove a beauteous flower when
    next we meet.
> *Ibid. Line 121*

A thousand times good-night!
> *Ibid. Line 154*

Love goes toward love, as schoolboys
    from their books;
But love from love, toward school with
    heavy looks.
> *Ibid. Line 156*

How silver-sweet sound lovers' tongues
    by night,
Like softest music to attending ears!
> *Ibid. Line 165*

---

[1] Perjuria ridet amantium Jupiter (Jupiter
laughs at the perjuries of lovers.) — TIBUL-
LUS [54?–18? B.C.]: *III, 6, 49*
  And Jove but laughs at lovers' perjury. —
DRYDEN: *Palamon and Arcite* [1680], *Book
II, L. 758*
  Dryden repeats this proverb in *Amphitryon*
[1690], *Act I, Sc. 2.*

Good night, good night! parting is such
sweet sorrow,
That I shall say good night till it be
morrow.
*Romeo and Juliet. Act II,
Sc. 2, Line 184*

O! mickle is the powerful grace that lies
In herbs, plants, stones, and their true
qualities:
For nought so vile that on the earth
doth live
But to the earth some special good doth
give,
Nor aught so good but strain'd from
that fair use
Revolts from true birth, stumbling on
abuse,
Virtue itself turns vice, being misap-
plied;
And vice sometime's by action dignified.
Ibid. Sc. 3, Line 15

Care keeps his watch in every old man's
eye,
And where care lodges, sleep will never
lie.
Ibid. Line 35

Wisely and slow; they stumble that run
fast.
Ibid. Line 94

Stabbed with a white wench's black eye.
Ibid. Sc. 4, Line 14

The courageous captain of compliments.
Ibid. Line 21

One, two, and the third in your bosom.
Ibid. Line 24

O flesh, flesh, how art thou fishified!
Ibid. Line 41

If thy wits run the wild-goose chase,
I have done.
Ibid. Line 77

A gentleman, nurse, that loves to
hear himself talk, and will speak more
in a minute than he will stand to in a
month.
Ibid. Line 155

Love's heralds should be thoughts,
Which ten times faster glide than the
sun's beams.
Ibid. Sc. 5, Line 4

I would thou hadst my bones, and I
thy news.
*Romeo and Juliet. Act II,
Sc. 5, Line 27*

The excuse that thou dost make in this
delay
Is longer than the tale thou dost excuse.
Ibid. Line 33

These violent delights have violent
ends.
Ibid. Sc. 6, Line 9

Therefore love moderately; long love
doth so;
Too swift arrives as tardy as too slow.
Ibid. Line 14

Here comes the lady: O! so light a foot
Will ne'er wear out the everlasting flint.
Ibid. Line 16

Thy head is as full of quarrels as an
egg is full of meat.[1]
Ibid. Act III, Sc. 1, Line 23

A word and a blow.[2]
Ibid. Line 44

A plague o' both your houses!
Ibid. Line 96

Romeo. Courage, man; the hurt cannot be much.
Mercutio. No, 'tis not so deep as a
well, nor so wide as a church-door; but
'tis enough, 'twill serve.
Ibid. Line 100

O! I am Fortune's fool.
Ibid. Line 142

Gallop apace, you fiery-footed steeds,
Towards Phoebus' lodging.
Ibid. Sc. 2, Line 1

When he shall die,
Take him and cut him out in little stars,
And he will make the face of heaven so
fine
That all the world will be in love with
night,
And pay no worship to the garish sun.
Ibid. Sc. 2, Line 21

Was ever book containing such vile
matter

[1] It's as full of good-nature as an egg's full
of meat. — RICHARD BRINSLEY SHERIDAN: *A
Trip to Scarborough* [1777], Act III, Sc. 4
[2] Word and a blow. — BUNYAN: *Pilgrim's
Progress* [1678], *Part I*

So fairly bound? O! that deceit should
dwell
In such a gorgeous palace.
Romeo and Juliet. Act III,
Sc. 2, Line 83

He was not born to shame:
Upon his brow shame is ashamed to sit.
Ibid. Line 91

Romeo, come forth; come forth, thou
fearful man:
Affliction is enamour'd of thy parts,
And thou art wedded to calamity.
Ibid. Sc. 3, Line 1

Adversity's sweet milk, philosophy.
Ibid. Line 54

Hang up philosophy!
Unless philosophy can make a Juliet.
Ibid. Line 56

The lark, the herald of the morn.
Ibid. Sc. 5, Line 6

Night's candles are burnt out, and joc-
und day
Stands tiptoe on the misty mountain-
tops.
Ibid. Line 9

I'll say yon grey is not the morning's
eye,
'Tis but the pale reflex of Cynthia's
brow;
Nor that is not the lark, whose notes
do beat
The vaulty heaven so high above our
heads:
I have more care to stay than will to go:
Come, death, and welcome: Juliet wills
it so.
How is't, my soul? let's talk; it is not
day.
Ibid. Line 19

Straining harsh discords and unpleasing
sharps.
Ibid. Line 28

All these woes shall serve
For sweet discourses in our time to
come.
Ibid. Line 52

Thank me no thankings, nor proud me
no prouds.
Ibid. Line 153

Is there no pity sitting in the clouds,
That sees into the bottom of my grief?
Ibid. Line 198

Past hope, past cure, past help!
Romeo and Juliet. Act IV,
Sc. 1, Line 45

Not stepping o'er the bounds of modesty.
Ibid. Sc. 2, Line 28

My dismal scene I needs must act alone.
Ibid. Sc. 3, Line 19

My bosom's lord sits lightly in his
throne.
Ibid. Act V, Sc. 1, Line 3

Ah me! how sweet is love itself possess'd,
When but love's shadows are so rich in
joy.
Ibid. Line 10

Well, Juliet, I will lie with thee tonight.
Ibid. Line 34

Meagre were his looks,
Sharp misery had worn him to the
bones.
Ibid. Line 40

A beggarly account of empty boxes.
Ibid. Line 45

Famine is in thy cheeks.
Ibid. Line 69

The world is not thy friend nor the
world's law.
Ibid. Line 72

Apothecary. My poverty, but not my
will, consents.
Romeo. I pay thy poverty, and not thy
will.
Ibid. Line 75

The strength
Of twenty men.
Ibid. Line 78

The time and my intents are savage-
wild,
More fierce and more inexorable far
Than empty tigers or the roaring sea.
Ibid. Sc. 3, Line 37

One writ with me in sour misfortune's
book.
Ibid. Line 82

Her beauty makes
This vault a feasting presence full of
light.
Ibid. Line 85

How oft when men are at the point of
death
Have they been merry!
*Romeo and Juliet. Act V,
Sc. 3, Line 88*
Beauty's ensign yet
Is crimson in thy lips and in thy cheeks,
And death's pale flag is not advanced
there.
Ibid. Line 94
Eyes, look your last!
Arms, take your last embrace!
Ibid. Line 112
O true apothecary!
Thy drugs are quick.
Ibid. Line 119
What's here? a cup, clos'd in my true
love's hand?
Ibid. Line 160
Pitiful sight! here lies the county slain,
And Juliet bleeding, warm, and newly
dead,
Who here hath lain these two days
buried.
Ibid. Line 174
The purest treasure mortal times afford
Is spotless reputation.
King Richard II [*1595–1596*].
Act I, Sc. 1, Line 177
Mine honour is my life; both grow in
one;
Take honour from me, and my life is
done.
Ibid. Line 182
The daintiest last, to make the end
most sweet.
Ibid. Sc. 3, Line 68
Truth hath a quiet breast.
Ibid. Line 96
How long a time lies in one little word!
Ibid. Line 213
Things sweet to taste prove in digestion
sour.
Ibid. Line 236
All places that the eye of heaven visits
Are to a wise man ports and happy
havens.
Ibid. Line 275
Suppose the singing birds musicians,
The grass whereon thou tread'st the
presence strew'd,

The flowers fair ladies, and thy steps
no more
Than a delightful measure or a dance;
For gnarling sorrow hath less power to
bite
The man that mocks at it and sets it
light.
*King Richard II. Act I,
Sc. 3, Line 288*
O, who can hold a fire in his hand
By thinking on the frosty Caucasus?
Or cloy the hungry edge of appetite
By bare imagination of a feast?
Or wallow naked in December snow
By thinking on fantastic summer's
heat?
O, no! the apprehension of the good
Gives but the greater feeling to the
worse.
Ibid. Line 294
Where'er I wander, boast of this I can,
Though banish'd, yet a true-born Eng-
lishman.[1]
Ibid. Line 308
The tongues of dying men
Enforce attention like deep harmony.
Ibid. Act II, Sc. 1, Line 5
The setting sun, and music at the close,
As the last taste of sweets, is sweetest
last,
Writ in remembrance, more than things
long past.
Ibid. Line 12
Report of fashions in proud Italy,
Whose manners still our tardy apish
nation
Limps after in base imitation.[2]
Ibid. Line 21
Small showers last long, but sudden
storms are short.
Ibid. Line 35
This royal throne of kings, this sceptred
isle,
This earth of majesty, this seat of Mars,
This other Eden, demi-paradise,
This fortress built by Nature for her-
self
Against infection and the hand of war,

[1] A stern, *a true-born Englishman.* — SAM-
UEL JOHNSON (BOSWELL: *Life* [1791])
[2] See Du Bartas, page 102a.

This happy breed of men, this little world,
This precious stone set in the silver sea,
Which serves it in the office of a wall
Or as a moat defensive to a house,
Against the envy of less happier lands,
This blessed plot, this earth, this realm, this England,
This nurse, this teeming womb of royal kings,
Fear'd by their breed and famous by their birth.
> *King Richard II. Act II, Sc. 1, Line 40*

England, bound in with the triumphant sea,
Whose rocky shore beats back the envious siege
Of watery Neptune.
> *Ibid. Line 61*

The ripest fruit first falls.
> *Ibid. Line 154*

Your fair discourse hath been as sugar,
Making the hard way sweet and delectable.
> *Ibid. Sc. 3, Line 6*

I count myself in nothing else so happy
As in a soul remembering my good friends.
> *Ibid. Line 46*

Evermore thanks, the exchequer of the poor.
> *Ibid. Line 65*

Grace me no grace, nor uncle me no uncle.
> *Ibid. Line 87*

The caterpillars of the commonwealth,
Which I have sworn to weed and pluck away.
> *Ibid. Line 166*

Things past redress are now with me past care.
> *Ibid. Line 171*

I see thy glory like a shooting star
Fall to the base earth from the firmament.
> *Ibid. Sc. 4, Line 19*

Eating the bitter bread of banishment.
> *Ibid. Act III, Sc. 1, Line 21*

Fires the proud tops of the eastern pines.
> *Ibid. Sc. 2, Line 42*

Not all the water in the rough rude sea
Can wash the balm off from an anointed king.
> *King Richard II. Act III, Sc. 2, Line 55*

O, call back yesterday, bid time return!
> *Ibid. Line 69*

The worst is death, and death will have his day.
> *Ibid. Line 103*

Let's talk of graves, of worms, and epitaphs.
> *Ibid. Line 145*

Let's choose executors and talk of wills.
> *Ibid. Line 148*

And nothing can we call our own but death;
And that small model of the barren earth,
Which serves as paste and cover to our bones.
For God's sake, let us sit upon the ground,
And tell sad stories of the death of kings:
How some have been deposed, some slain in war,
Some haunted by the ghosts they have depos'd,
Some poison'd by their wives, some sleeping kill'd;
All murder'd: for within the hollow crown
That rounds the mortal temples of a king
Keeps Death his court.
> *Ibid. Line 152*

Comes at the last, and with a little pin
Bores through his castle wall, and farewell king!
> *Ibid. Line 169*

Men judge by the complexion of the sky
The state and inclination of the day.
> *Ibid. Line 194*

He is come to open
The purple testament of bleeding war.
> *Ibid. Sc. 3, Line 93*

O! that I were as great
As is my grief, or lesser than my name,

Or that I could forget what I have been,
Or not remember what I must be now.
> *King Richard II. Act III, Sc. 3,*
> *Line 136*

And my large kingdom for a little grave,
A little little grave, an obscure grave.
> *Ibid. Line 153*

The noisome weeds, that without profit
suck
The soil's fertility from wholesome
flowers.
> *Ibid. Sc. 4, Line 38*

Superfluous branches
We lop away that bearing boughs may
live.
> *Ibid. Line 63*

Gave
His body to that pleasant country's
earth,
And his pure soul unto his captain
Christ,
Under whose colours he had fought so
long.
> *Ibid. Act IV, Sc. 1, Line 97*

So Judas did to Christ: but he, in
twelve,
Found truth in all but one; I, in twelve
thousand, none.
> *Ibid. Line 170*

Now is this golden crown like a deep
well
That owes two buckets filling one another;
The emptier ever dancing in the air,
The other down, unseen and full of
water:
That bucket down and full of tears
am I,
Drinking my griefs, whilst you mount
up on high.
> *Ibid. Line 184*

You may my glories and my state de-
pose,
But not my griefs; still am I king of
those.
> *Ibid. Line 192*

Some of you with Pilate wash your
hands
Showing an outward pity.[1]
> *Ibid. Line 239*

---

[1] Pilate . . . took water, and washed his
hands before the multitude, saying, I am in-

A mockery king of snow.
> *King Richard II. Act IV, Sc. 1,*
> *Line 260*

As in a theatre, the eyes of men,
After a well-graced actor leaves the
stage,
Are idly bent on him that enters next,
Thinking his prattle to be tedious.
> *Ibid. Act V, Sc. 2, Line 23*

No word like "pardon."
> *Ibid. Sc. 3, Line 118*

It is as hard to come as for a camel
To thread the postern of a small
needle's eye.[1]
> *Ibid. Sc. 5, Line 16*

How sour sweet music is
When time is broke and no proportion
kept!
So is it in the music of men's lives.
> *Ibid. Line 42*

I wasted time, and now doth time
waste me;
For now hath time made me his numbering clock;
My thoughts are minutes.
> *Ibid. Line 49*

The moon, like to a silver bow
New-bent in heaven.
> *A Midsummer-Night's Dream*
> *[1595–1596]. Act I, Sc. 1,*
> *Line 9*

To live a barren sister all your life,
Chanting faint hymns to the cold fruitless moon.
> *Ibid. Line 72*

But earthlier happy is the rose distill'd
Than that which withering on the virgin
thorn [2]
Grows, lives, and dies in single blessedness.
> *Ibid. Line 76*

For aught that I could ever read,
Could ever hear by tale or history,

---

nocent of the blood of this just person. —
Matthew, XXVII, 24
[1] It is easier for a camel to go through the
eye of a needle, than for a rich man to enter
into the kingdom of God. — *Matthew, XIX,
24*
[2] Maidens withering on the stalk. — Wordsworth: *Personal Talk* [1806], *St. 1*

The course of true love never did run smooth.
A Midsummer-Night's Dream.
Act I, Sc. 1, Line 132

Swift as a shadow, short as any dream,
Brief as the lightning in the collied night,
That, in a spleen, unfolds both heaven and earth,
And ere a man hath power to say, "Behold!"
The jaws of darkness do devour it up:
So quick bright things come to confusion.
Ibid. Line 144

Love looks not with the eyes, but with the mind,
And therefore is wing'd Cupid painted blind.[1]
Ibid. Line 234

Masters, spread yourselves.
Ibid. Sc. 2, Line 16

This is Ercles' vein.
Ibid. Line 43

I'll speak in a monstrous little voice.
Ibid. Line 55

I am slow of study.
Ibid. Line 70

That would hang us, every mother's son.
Ibid. Line 81

I will roar you as gently as any sucking dove; I will roar you, as 'twere any nightingale.
Ibid. Line 85

A proper man, as one shall see in a summer's day.
Ibid. Line 89

I must go seek some dew-drops here,
And hang a pearl in every cowslip's ear.
Ibid. Act II, Sc. 1, Line 14

I am that merry wanderer of the night.
I jest to Oberon, and make him smile
When I a fat and bean-fed horse beguile,
Neighing in likeness of a filly foal:

[1] See Chaucer, page 81b.
> I have heard of reasons manifold
> Why Love must needs be blind,
> But this the best of all I hold, —
> His eyes are in his mind.
>   COLERIDGE: *Reason for Love's Blindness* [1828]

And sometimes lurk I in a gossip's bowl,
In very likeness of a roasted crab.
A Midsummer-Night's Dream.
Act II, Sc. 1, Line 43

The human mortals.
Ibid. Line 101

The rude sea grew civil at her song,
And certain stars shot madly from their spheres
To hear the sea-maid's music.
Ibid. Line 152

And the imperial votaress passed on,
In maiden meditation, fancy-free.
Yet mark'd I where the bolt of Cupid fell:
It fell upon a little western flower,
Before milk-white, now purple with love's wound,
And maidens call it Love-in-idleness.
Ibid. Line 163

I'll put a girdle round about the earth
In forty minutes.[1]
Ibid. Line 175

It is not night when I do see your face.
Ibid. Line 221

For you in my respect are all the world:
Then how can it be said I am alone?
Ibid. Line 224

We cannot fight for love, as men may do;
We should be woo'd and were not made to woo.
Ibid. Line 241

I know a bank whereon the wild thyme blows,
Where oxlips and the nodding violet grows
Quite over-canopied with luscious woodbine,
With sweet musk-roses, and with eglantine.
Ibid. Line 249

Some to kill cankers in the musk-rose buds,
Some war with rere-mice for their leathern wings,
To make my small elves coats.
Ibid. Sc. 2, Line 3

The clamorous owl, that nightly hoots, and wonders

[1] See Chapman, page 117a.

At our quaint spirits.
A Midsummer-Night's Dream.
Act II, Sc. 2, Line 6
You spotted snakes with double tongue,
Thorny hedge-hogs, be not seen;
Newts, and blind-worms, do no wrong;
Come not near our fairy queen.
Ibid. Line 9
As a surfeit of the sweetest things
The deepest loathing to the stomach brings.[1]
Ibid. Line 137
A lion among ladies is a most dreadful thing.
Ibid. Act III, Sc. 1, Line 32
A calendar, a calendar! look in the almanack; find out moonshine.
Ibid. Line 55
Bless thee, Bottom! bless thee! thou art translated.
Ibid. Line 124
Lord, what fools these mortals be![2]
Ibid. Sc. 2, Line 115
So we grew together,
Like to a double cherry, seeming parted,
But yet an union in partition —
Two lovely berries moulded on one stem.
Ibid. Line 208
Though she be but little, she is fierce.
Ibid. Line 325
I have a reasonable good ear in music: let us have the tongs and the bones.
Ibid. Act IV, Sc. 1, Line 32
Truly, a peck of provender; I could munch your good dry oats. Methinks I have a great desire to a bottle of hay: good hay, sweet hay, hath no fellow.
Ibid. Line 36
I have an exposition of sleep come upon me.
Ibid. Line 44
My Oberon! what visions have I seen!
Methought I was enamour'd of an ass.
Ibid. Line 82
I never heard
So musical a discord, such sweet thunder.
Ibid. Line 118

[1] See *King Henry IV,* page 151a.
[2] See Seneca, page 47a.

I have had a dream, past the wit of man to say what dream it was.
A Midsummer-Night's Dream.
Act IV, Sc. 1, Line 211
The eye of man hath not heard, the ear of man hath not seen,[1] man's hand is not able to taste, his tongue to conceive, nor his heart to report, what my dream was.
Ibid. Line 218
A paramour is, God bless us! a thing of naught.
Ibid. Sc. 2, Line 14
Eat no onions nor garlic, for we are to utter sweet breath.
Ibid. Line 44
The lunatic, the lover, and the poet
Are of imagination all compact:
One sees more devils than vast hell can hold,
That is, the madman: the lover, all as frantic,
Sees Helen's beauty in a brow of Egypt:
The poet's eye, in a fine frenzy rolling,
Doth glance from heaven to earth, from earth to heaven;
And as imagination bodies forth
The forms of things unknown, the poet's pen
Turns them to shapes, and gives to airy nothing
A local habitation and a name.
Such tricks hath strong imagination,
That if it would but apprehend some joy,
It comprehends some bringer of that joy;
Or in the night, imagining some fear,
How easy is a bush supposed a bear!
Ibid. Act V, Sc. 1, Line 7
The true beginning of our end.[2]
Ibid. Line 111
The best in this kind are but shadows.
Ibid. Line 215
A very gentle beast, and of a good conscience.
Ibid. Line 232

[1] Eye hath not seen, nor ear heard. — *1 Corinthians, II, 9*
[2] I see the beginning of my end. — Massinger: *The Virgin Martyr* [1622], *Act III, Sc. 3*

This passion, and the death of a dear friend, would go near to make a man look sad.

A Midsummer-Night's Dream.
Act V, Sc. 1, Line 295

With the help of a surgeon, he might yet recover and prove an ass.

Ibid. Line 318

The iron tongue of midnight hath told twelve.

Ibid. Line 372

My ventures are not in one bottom trusted,
Nor to one place.

The Merchant of Venice [1596–1597]. Act I, Sc. 1, Line 42

Now, by two-headed Janus,
Nature hath framed strange fellows in her time.

Ibid. Line 50

You have too much respect upon the world:
They lose it that do buy it with much care.

Ibid. Line 74

I hold the world but as the world, Gratiano, —
A stage, where every man must play a part;
And mine a sad one.

Ibid. Line 77

Why should a man, whose blood is warm within,
Sit like his grandsire cut in alabaster?

Ibid. Line 83

There are a sort of men whose visages
Do cream and mantle like a standing pond.

Ibid. Line 88

I am Sir Oracle,
And when I ope my lips, let no dog bark!

Ibid. Line 93

I do know of these
That therefore only are reputed wise
For saying nothing.

Ibid. Line 95

Fish not, with this melancholy bait,
For this fool gudgeon, this opinion.

Ibid. Line 101

Gratiano speaks an infinite deal of nothing, more than any man in all Ven-

ice. His reasons are as two grains of wheat hid in two bushels of chaff: you shall seek all day ere you find them, and when you have them, they are not worth the search.

The Merchant of Venice.
Act I, Sc. 1, Line 114

In my school-days, when I had lost one shaft,
I shot his fellow of the selfsame flight
The selfsame way, with more advised watch,
To find the other forth; and by adventuring both,
I oft found both.

Ibid. Line 141

They are as sick that surfeit with too much, as they that starve with nothing.

Ibid. Sc. 2, Line 5

Superfluity comes sooner by white hairs, but competency lives longer.

Ibid. Line 9

If to do were as easy as to know what were good to do, chapels had been churches, and poor men's cottages princes' palaces.

Ibid. Line 13

The brain may devise laws for the blood, but a hot temper leaps o'er a cold decree.

Ibid. Line 19

He doth nothing but talk of his horse.

Ibid. Line 43

God made him, and therefore let him pass for a man.

Ibid. Line 59

When he is best, he is a little worse than a man; and when he is worst, he is little better than a beast.

Ibid. Line 93

I dote on his very absence.

Ibid. Line 118

My meaning in saying he is a good man, is to have you understand me that he is sufficient.

Ibid. Sc. 3, Line 15

Ships are but boards, sailors but men: there be land-rats and water-rats, water-thieves and land-thieves.

Ibid. Line 22

I will buy with you, sell with you, talk with you, walk with you, and so following; but I will not eat with you, drink with you, nor pray with you. What news on the Rialto?

The Merchant of Venice.
Act I, Sc. 3, Line 36

If I can catch him once upon the hip, I will feed fat the ancient grudge I bear him.

Ibid. Line 47

The devil can cite Scripture for his purpose.

Ibid. Line 99

A goodly apple rotten at the heart:
O, what a goodly outside falsehood hath!

Ibid. Line 102

For sufferance is the badge of all our tribe.

Ibid. Line 110

You call me misbeliever, cut-throat dog,
And spet upon my Jewish gaberdine.

Ibid. Line 111

Shall I bend low, and in a bondman's key,
With bated breath and whispering humbleness,
Say this?

Ibid. Line 124

O father Abram! what these Christians are,
Whose own hard dealings teaches them suspect
The thoughts of others!

Ibid. Line 161

I like not fair terms and a villain's mind.

Ibid. Line 180

Mislike me not for my complexion,
The shadow'd livery of the burnish'd sun.

Ibid. Act II, Sc. 1, Line 1

An honest, exceeding poor man.

Ibid. Sc. 2, Line 54

The young gentleman, according to Fates and Destinies and such odd sayings, the Sisters Three and such branches of learning, is indeed deceased; or, as you would say in plain terms, gone to heaven.

Ibid. Line 66

The very staff of my age, my very prop.

The Merchant of Venice.
Act II, Sc. 2, Line 71

It is a wise father that knows his own child.

Ibid. Line 83

Go to; here's a simple line of life; here's a small trifle of wives; alas! fifteen wives is nothing: eleven widows and nine maids is a simple coming-in for one man; and then to 'scape drowning thrice, and to be in peril of my life with the edge of a feather-bed, — here are simple 'scapes. Well, if Fortune be a woman, she's a good wench for this gear.

Ibid. Line 158

And the vile squealing of the wry-necked fife.

Ibid. Sc. 5, Line 30

Who riseth from a feast
With that keen appetite that he sits down?

Ibid. Sc. 6, Line 8

All things that are,
Are with more spirit chased than enjoy'd.

Ibid. Line 12

But love is blind, and lovers cannot see
The pretty follies that themselves commit.

Ibid. Line 36

Must I hold a candle to my shames?

Ibid. Line 41

A golden mind stoops not to show of dross.

Ibid. Sc. 7, Line 20

Young in limbs, in judgment old.

Ibid. Line 71

My daughter! O my ducats! O my daughter:
Fled with a Christian! O my Christian ducats!
Justice! the law! my ducats, and my daughter!
A sealed bag, two sealed bags of ducats,
Of double ducats, stol'n from me by my daughter!

Ibid. Sc. 8, Line 15

The fool multitude, that choose by show.

The Merchant of Venice.
Act II, Sc. 9, Line 26

Let none presume
To wear an undeserved dignity.
O! that estates, degrees, and offices
Were not deriv'd corruptly, and that clear honour
Were purchased by the merit of the wearer!

Ibid. Line 39

The ancient saying is no heresy:
"Hanging and wiving goes by destiny."[1]

Ibid. Line 83

Let him look to his bond.

Ibid. Act III, Sc. 1, Line 49

I am a Jew. Hath not a Jew eyes? Hath not a Jew hands, organs, dimensions, senses, affections, passions?

Ibid. Line 62

If you prick us, do we not bleed? if you tickle us, do we not laugh? if you poison us, do we not die? and if you wrong us, shall we not revenge?

Ibid. Line 65

The villany you teach me I will execute, and it shall go hard, but I will better the instruction.

Ibid. Line 76

I would not have given it for a wilderness of monkeys.

Ibid. Line 130

There's something tells me — but it is not love —
I would not lose you; and you know yourself,
Hate counsels not in such a quality.

Ibid. Sc. 2, Line 4

Makes a swan-like end,
Fading in music.[2]

Ibid. Line 44

Tell me where is fancy bred,
Or in the heart or in the head?
How begot, how nourished?
Reply, reply.

Ibid. Line 63

In law, what plea so tainted and corrupt
But being season'd with a gracious voice,

[1] See Heywood, page 91a.
[2] See Socrates, page 21a.

Obscures the show of evil?

The Merchant of Venice.
Act III, Sc. 2, Line 75

There is no vice so simple but assumes
Some mark of virtue on his outward parts.

Ibid. Line 81

Thus ornament is but the guiled shore
To a most dangerous sea.

Ibid. Line 97

The seeming truth which cunning times put on
To entrap the wisest.

Ibid. Line 100

How all the other passions fleet to air,
As doubtful thoughts, and rash-embrac'd despair
And shuddering fear, and green-ey'd jealousy.

O love! be moderate; allay thy ecstasy;
In measure rain thy joy; scant this excess;
I feel too much thy blessing: make it less,
For fear I surfeit!

Ibid. Line 109

An unlesson'd girl, unschool'd, unpractis'd;
Happy in this, she is not yet so old
But she may learn.

Ibid. Line 160

Here are a few of the unpleasant'st words
That ever blotted paper!

Ibid. Line 252

Thus when I shun Scylla, your father, I fall into Charybdis, your mother.[1]

Ibid. Sc. 5, Line 17

A harmless necessary cat.

Ibid. Act IV, Sc. 1, Line 55

What! wouldst thou have a serpent sting thee twice?

Ibid. Line 69

The weakest kind of fruit
Drops earliest to the ground.

Ibid. Line 115

[1] Incidis in Scyllam cupiens vitare Charybdim (You fall into Scylla in seeking to avoid Charybdis). — PHILIPPE GUALTIER: *Alexandreis* [*circa* 1200], *Book V, L. 301*

To hold opinion with Pythagoras
That souls of animals infuse themselves
Into the trunks of men.[1]
The Merchant of Venice.
Act IV, Sc. 1, Line 131

I never knew so young a body with
so old a head.[2]
Ibid. Line 163

The quality of mercy is not strain'd,
It droppeth as the gentle rain from
heaven
Upon the place beneath. It is twice
bless'd:
It blesseth him that gives and him that
takes.
'Tis mightiest in the mightiest: it be-
comes
The throned monarch better than his
crown;
His sceptre shows the force of temporal
power,
The attribute to awe and majesty,
Wherein doth sit the dread and fear of
kings;
But mercy is above this sceptred sway,
It is enthroned in the hearts of kings,
It is an attribute to God himself;
And earthly power doth then show lik-
est God's,
When mercy seasons justice. Therefore,
Jew,
Though justice be thy plea, consider
this,
That in the course of justice, none of us
Should see salvation: we do pray for
mercy;
And that same prayer doth teach us all
to render
The deeds of mercy.
Ibid. Line 184

To do a great right, do a little wrong.
Ibid. Line 216

---

[1] *Clown.* What is the opinion of Pythagoras
concerning wild fowl?
Malvolio. That the soul of our grandam
might haply inhabit a bird.
Twelfth-Night [1598–1600], *Act IV,
Sc. 2, L. 55*

[2] He is young, but, take it from me, a very
staid head. — THOMAS WENTWORTH, EARL OF
STRAFFORD [1593–1641]: Letter, commending
the Earl of Ormond to Charles I for appointment as Councillor

A Daniel come to judgment! yea, a
Daniel!
The Merchant of Venice.
Act IV, Sc. 1, Line 223

How much more elder art thou than thy
looks.
Ibid. Line 251

Is it so nominated in the bond?
Ibid. Line 260

'Tis not in the bond.
Ibid. Line 263

For herein Fortune shows herself more
kind
Than is her custom: it is still her use
To let the wretched man outlive his
wealth,
To view with hollow eye and wrinkled
brow
An age of poverty.
Ibid. Line 268

Speak me fair in death.
Ibid. Line 276

An upright judge, a learned judge!
Ibid. Line 324

A Daniel, still say I, a second Daniel! —
I thank thee, Jew, for teaching me that
word.
Ibid. Line 341

You take my house, when you do take
the prop
That doth sustain my house; you take
my life,
When you do take the means whereby
I live.
Ibid. Line 376

He is well paid that is well satisfied.
Ibid. Line 416

Lorenzo.   In such a night
Troilus methinks mounted the Troyan
walls,
And sigh'd his soul toward the Grecian
tents,
Where Cressid lay that night.
Jessica.   In such a night
Did Thisbe fearfully o'ertrip the dew,
And saw the lion's shadow ere himself,
And ran dismay'd away.
Lorenzo.   In such a night
Stood Dido with a willow in her hand

Upon the wild sea-banks, and waft her love
To come again to Carthage.

Jessica. In such a night
Medea gather'd the enchanted herbs
That did renew old Aeson.

The Merchant of Venice.
Act V, Sc. 1, Line 3

How sweet the moonlight sleeps upon this bank!
Here we will sit and let the sounds of music
Creep in our ears: soft stillness and the night
Become the touches of sweet harmony.
Sit, Jessica. Look how the floor of heaven
Is thick inlaid with patines of bright gold:
There's not the smallest orb which thou behold'st
But in his motion like an angel sings,
Still quiring to the young-eyed cherubins.
Such harmony is in immortal souls;
But whilst this muddy vesture of decay
Doth grossly close it in, we cannot hear it.

Ibid. Line 54

I am never merry when I hear sweet music.

Ibid. Line 69

The man that hath no music in himself,
Nor is not mov'd with concord of sweet sounds,
Is fit for treasons, stratagems, and spoils;
The motions of his spirit are dull as night,
And his affections dark as Erebus.
Let no such man be trusted.

Ibid. Line 83

How far that little candle throws his beams!
So shines a good deed in a naughty world.

Ibid. Line 90

How many things by season season'd are
To their right praise and true perfection!

Ibid. Line 107

This night, methinks, is but the daylight sick.

The Merchant of Venice.
Act V, Sc. 1, Line 124

A light wife doth make a heavy husband.

Ibid. Line 130

These blessed candles of the night.

Ibid. Line 220

And if his name be George, I'll call him Peter;
For new-made honour doth forget men's names.

King John [*1596–1597*]. *Act I,*
Sc. 1, Line 186

Sweet, sweet, sweet poison for the age's tooth.

Ibid. Line 213

Heaven lay not my transgression to my charge.

Ibid. Line 256

A hazard of new fortunes.

Ibid. Act II, Sc. 1, Line 71

For courage mounteth with occasion.

Ibid. Line 82

Saint George, that swing'd the dragon, and e'er since
Sits on his horse back at mine hostess' door.

Ibid. Line 288

He is the half part of a blessed man,
Left to be finished by such a she;
And she a fair divided excellence.
Whose fulness of perfection lies in him.

Ibid. Line 437

Talks as familiarly of roaring lions
As maids of thirteen do of puppy-dogs!

Ibid. Line 459

Zounds! I was never so bethump'd with words,
Since I first call'd my brother's father dad.[1]

Ibid. Line 466

I will instruct my sorrows to be proud;
For grief is proud, and makes his owner stoop.

Ibid. Act III, Sc. 1, Line 68

What hath this day deserv'd? what hath it done

---

[1] I was ne'er so thrummed since I was a gentleman. — THOMAS DEKKER: *The Honest Whore, Part I* [1604]. *Act IV, Sc. 2*

That it in golden letters should be set
Among the high tides in the calendar?
King John. Act III, Sc. 1, Line 84

Thou wear a lion's hide! doff it for shame,
And hang a calf's-skin on those recreant limbs.
Ibid. Line 128

Bell, book and candle shall not drive me back,
When gold and silver becks me to come on.[1]
Ibid. Sc. 3, Line 12

I had a thing to say,
But I will fit it with some better time.
Ibid. Line 25

O, amiable lovely death![2]
Ibid. Sc. 4, Line 25

Grief fills the room up of my absent child,
Lies in his bed, walks up and down with me,
Puts on his pretty looks, repeats his words,
Remembers me of all his gracious parts,
Stuffs out his vacant garments with his form.
Ibid. Line 93

Life is as tedious as a twice-told tale,
Vexing the dull ear of a drowsy man.
Ibid. Line 108

When Fortune means to men most good,
She looks upon them with a threatening eye.[3]
Ibid. Line 119

And he that stands upon a slippery place
Makes nice of no vile hold to stay him up.
Ibid. Line 137

To gild refined gold, to paint the lily,
To throw a perfume on the violet,
To smooth the ice, or add another hue
Unto the rainbow, or with taper-light
To seek the beauteous eye of heaven to garnish,
Is wasteful and ridiculous excess.
Ibid. Act IV, Sc. 2, Line 11

[1] See Cervantes, page 104b.
[2] See Walt Whitman, page 609b.
[3] See Publilius Syrus, page 44a.

And oftentimes excusing of a fault
Doth make the fault the worse by the excuse.[1]
King John. Act IV, Sc. 2, Line 30

We cannot hold mortality's strong hand.
Ibid. Line 82

There is no sure foundation set on blood,
No certain life achiev'd by others' death.
Ibid. Line 104

But if you be afeard to hear the worst,
Then let the worst unheard fall on your head.
Ibid. Line 134

Make haste; the better foot before.[2]
Ibid. Line 170

Another lean unwash'd artificer.
Ibid. Line 201

How oft the sight of means to do ill deeds
Makes ill deeds done!
Ibid. Line 219

Heaven take my soul, and England keep my bones.
Ibid. Sc. 3, Line 10

I am amaz'd, methinks, and lose my way
Among the thorns and dangers of this world.
Ibid. Line 140

Mocking the air with colours idly spread.
Ibid. Act V, Sc. 1, Line 72

The day shall not be up so soon as I,
To try the fair adventure of to-morrow.
Ibid. Sc. 5, Line 21

'Tis strange that death should sing.
I am the cygnet to this pale faint swan,
Who chants a doleful hymn to his own death,[3]
And from the organ-pipe of frailty sings
His soul and body to their lasting rest.
Ibid. Sc. 7, Line 20

Now my soul hath elbow-room.
Ibid. Line 28

[1] See Meurier, page 97a.
[2] Put forward your best foot! — BROWNING: *Respectability* [1855], St. 3
[3] See Socrates, page 21a.

This England never did, nor never shall,
Lie at the proud foot of a conqueror.
King John. Act V, Sc. 7, Line 112

Come the three corners of the world in
     arms,
And we shall shock them. Nought shall
     make us rue,
If England to itself do rest but true.
Ibid. Line 116

So shaken as we are, so wan with care.
King Henry IV [*1597–1598*].
     Part I, Act I, Sc. 1, Line 1

     In those holy fields
Over whose acres walk'd those blessed
     feet
Which fourteen hundred years ago were
     nail'd
For our advantage on the bitter cross.
Ibid. Line 24

Here is a dear and true industrious
     friend.
Ibid. Line 62

The blessed sun himself a fair hot
wench in flame-colour'd taffeta, — I see
no reason why thou shouldst be so superfluous to demand the time of the
day.
Ibid. Sc. 2, Line 10

Diana's foresters, gentlemen of the
shade, minions of the moon.
Ibid. Line 29

So far as my coin would stretch; and
where it would not, I have used my
credit.
Ibid. Line 61

Old father antic the law.
Ibid. Line 69

I would to God thou and I knew
where a commodity of good names were
to be bought.
Ibid. Line 92

Thou hast damnable iteration, and
art indeed able to corrupt a saint.
Ibid. Line 101

'Tis my vocation, Hal; 'tis no sin
for a man to labour in his vocation.
Ibid. Line 116

There's neither honesty, manhood,
nor good fellowship in thee.
Ibid. Line 154

If all the year were playing holidays,
To sport would be as tedious as to work.
*King Henry IV. Part I, Act I,
Sc. 2, Line 226*

You tread upon my patience.
Ibid. Sc. 3, Line 4

     That title of respect
Which the proud soul ne'er pays but to
     the proud.
Ibid. Line 8

Fresh as a bridegroom; and his chin
     new reap'd,
Showed like a stubble-land at harvest-
     home;
He was perfumed like a milliner,
And 'twixt his finger and his thumb he
     held
A pouncet-box, which ever and anon
He gave his nose and took 't away
     again.
Ibid. Line 34

And as the soldiers bore dead bodies
     by,
He call'd them untaught knaves, un-
     mannerly,
To bring a slovenly unhandsome corpse
Betwixt the wind and his nobility.
Ibid. Line 42

So pester'd with a popinjay.
Ibid. Line 50

God save the mark.
Ibid. Line 56

     And but for these vile guns,
He would himself have been a soldier.
Ibid. Line 63

     The blood more stirs
To rouse a lion than to start a hare!
Ibid. Line 197

By heaven, methinks it were an easy
     leap
To pluck bright honour from the pale-
     faced moon,
Or dive into the bottom of the deep,
Where fathom-line could never touch
     the ground,
And pluck up drowned honour by the
     locks.
Ibid. Line 201

Why, what a candy deal of courtesy
This fawning greyhound then did prof·
     fer me!
Ibid. Line 251

I know a trick worth two of that.
King Henry IV. Part I, Act II,
Sc. 1, Line 40
If the rascal have not given me medicines to make me love him, I'll be hanged.
Ibid. Sc. 2, Line 20
It would be argument for a week, laughter for a month, and a good jest for ever.
Ibid. Line 104
Falstaff sweats to death,
And lards the lean earth as he walks along.
Ibid. Line 119
Out of this nettle, danger, we pluck this flower, safety.
Ibid. Sc. 3, Line 11
I could brain him with his lady's fan.
Ibid. Line 26
Constant you are,
But yet a woman; and for secrecy,
No lady closer; for I well believe
Thou wilt not utter what thou dost not know;
And so far will I trust thee, gentle Kate.
Ibid. Line 113
A Corinthian, a lad of mettle, a good boy.
Ibid. Sc. 4, Line 13
A plague of all cowards, I say.
Ibid. Line 129
There live not three good men unhanged in England, and one of them is fat and grows old.
Ibid. Line 146
You care not who sees your back: call you that backing of your friends? A plague upon such backing!
Ibid. Line 168
I have peppered two of them. . . . I tell thee what, Hal, if I tell thee a lie, spit in my face; call me horse.
Ibid. Line 216
Give you a reason on compulsion! If reasons were as plentiful as blackberries, I would give no man a reason upon compulsion, I.
Ibid. Line 267
Mark now, how a plain tale shall put you down.
Ibid. Line 285

No more of that, Hal, an thou lovest me!
King Henry IV. Part I, Act II,
Sc. 4, Line 316
What doth gravity out of his bed at midnight?
Ibid. Line 328
A plague of sighing and grief! It blows a man up like a bladder.
Ibid. Line 370
You may buy land now as cheap as stinking mackerel.
Ibid. Line 399
That reverend vice, that grey iniquity, that father ruffian, that vanity in years.
Ibid. Line 505
If sack and sugar be a fault, God help the wicked! if to be old and merry be a sin, then many an old host that I know is damn'd: if to be fat be to be hated, then Pharaoh's lean kine are to be loved.
Ibid. Line 524
Banish plump Jack, and banish all the world.
Ibid. Line 534
Play out the play.
Ibid. Line 539
O, monstrous! but one half-pennyworth of bread to this intolerable deal of sack!
Ibid. Line 597
Diseased Nature oftentimes breaks forth
In strange eruptions.
Ibid. Act III, Sc. 1, Line 27
I am not in the roll of common men.
Ibid. Line 43
Glendower. I can call spirits from the vasty deep.
Hotspur. Why, so can I, or so can any man;
But will they come when you do call for them?
Ibid. Line 53
I had rather be a kitten and cry mew,
Than one of these same metre balladmongers.
Ibid. Line 128

But in the way of bargain, mark ye me,
I'll cavil on the ninth part of a hair.
King Henry IV. Part I, Act III,
Sc. 1, Line 138

A deal of skimble-skamble stuff.
Ibid. Line 153

Those musicians that shall play to you
Hang in the air a thousand leagues from
hence.
Ibid. Line 226

A good mouth-filling oath.
Ibid. Line 258

A fellow of no mark nor likelihood.
Ibid. Sc. 2, Line 45

And then I stole all courtesy from
heaven,
And drest myself in such humility
That I did pluck allegiance from men's
hearts.
Ibid. Line 52

To loathe the taste of sweetness,
whereof a little
More than a little is by much too much.[1]
Ibid. Line 72

The end of life cancels all bands.
Ibid. Line 157

An I have not forgotten what the inside of a church is made of, I am a
pepper-corn.
Ibid. Sc. 3, Line 8

Company, villanous company, hath
been the spoil of me.
Ibid. Line 10

Rob me the exchequer.
Ibid. Line 204

How has he the leisure to be sick
In such a justling time?
Ibid. Act IV, Sc. 1, Line 17

This sickness doth infect
The very life-blood of our enterprise.
Ibid. Line 28

That daffed the world aside,
And bid it pass.
Ibid. Line 96

Baited like eagles having lately
bathed. . . .
As full of spirit as the month of May,
And gorgeous as the sun at midsummer.
Ibid. Line 99

[1] See *A Midsummer Night's Dream*, page 142a.

The cankers of a calm world and a long
peace.
King Henry IV. Part I, Act IV,
Sc. 2, Line 32

Food for powder, food for powder;
they'll fill a pit as well as better.
Ibid. Line 72

To the latter end of a fray and the
beginning of a feast
Fits a dull fighter and a keen guest.[1]
Ibid. Line 86

I could be well content
To entertain the lag-end of my life
With quiet hours.
Ibid. Act V, Sc. 1, Line 23

I would 't were bedtime, Hal, and
all well.
Ibid. Line 126

Honour pricks me on. Yea, but how
if honour prick me off when I come on,
— how then? Can honour set to a leg?
no: or an arm? no: or take away the
grief of a wound? no. Honour hath no
skill in surgery, then? no. What is honour? a word. What is in that word honour; what is that honour? air. A trim
reckoning! Who hath it? he that died o'
Wednesday. Doth he feel it? no. Doth
he hear it? no. It is insensible, then?
yea, to the dead. But will it not live
with the living? no. Why? detraction
will not suffer it. Therefore I'll none of
it. Honour is a mere scutcheon. And so
ends my catechism.
Ibid. Line 131

Suspicion all our lives shall be stuck full
of eyes;
For treason is but trusted like the fox.
Ibid. Sc. 2, Line 8

Let me tell the world.[2]
Ibid. Line 65

The time of life is short;
To spend that shortness basely were too
long.
Ibid. Line 81

[1] See John Heywood, page 94b.
[2] I'll tell the world. — SHAKESPEARE: *Meas-ure for Measure* [1604–1605], Act II, Sc. 4, L. 154
Ay, tell the world! — BROWNING: *Para-celsus* [1835], Part II

Two stars keep not their motion in one sphere.
>*King Henry IV. Part I, Act V, Sc. 4, Line 65*

This earth, that bears thee dead,
Bears not alive so stout a gentleman.
>*Ibid. Line 92*

Thy ignominy sleep with thee in the grave,
But not remember'd in thy epitaph!
>*Ibid. Line 100*

I could have better spared a better man.
>*Ibid. Line 104*

The better part of valour is discretion.[1]
>*Ibid. Line 120*

Full bravely hast thou fleshed
Thy maiden sword.
>*Ibid. Line 132*

Lord, Lord, how this world is given to lying! I grant you I was down and out of breath; and so was he. But we rose both at an instant, and fought a long hour by Shrewsbury clock.
>*Ibid. Line 148*

I'll purge, and leave sack, and live cleanly.
>*Ibid. Line 168*

Rumour is a pipe
Blown by surmises, jealousies, conjectures,
And of so easy and so plain a stop
That the blunt monster with uncounted heads,
The still-discordant wavering multitude,[2]
Can play upon it.
>*Ibid. Part II, Induction, Line 15*

Even such a man, so faint, so spiritless,
So dull, so dead in look, so woe-begone,
Drew Priam's curtain in the dead of night,
And would have told him half his Troy was burnt.
>*Ibid. Act I, Sc. 1, Line 70*

Yet the first bringer of unwelcome news
Hath but a losing office, and his tongue
Sounds ever after as a sullen bell,

Remember'd knolling a departing friend.[1]
>*King Henry IV. Part II, Act I, Sc. 1, Line 100*

I am not only witty in myself, but the cause that wit is in other men.[2]
>*Ibid. Sc. 2, Line 10*

A rascally yea-forsooth knave.
>*Ibid. Line 40*

You lie in your throat if you say I am any other than an honest man.
>*Ibid. Line 97*

Some smack of age in you, some relish of the saltness of time.
>*Ibid. Line 112*

It is the disease of not listening, the malady of not marking, that I am troubled withal.
>*Ibid. Line 139*

We that are in the vaward of our youth.
>*Ibid. Line 201*

Have you not a moist eye, a dry hand, a yellow cheek, a white beard, a decreasing leg, an increasing belly?
>*Ibid. Line 206*

Every part about you blasted with antiquity.
>*Ibid. Line 210*

For my voice, I have lost it with hollaing and singing of anthems.
>*Ibid. Line 215*

Pray that our armies join not in a hot day; for, by the Lord, I take but two shirts out with me, and I mean not to sweat extraordinarily.
>*Ibid. Line 237*

It was always yet the trick of our English nation, if they have a good thing, to make it too common.
>*Ibid. Line 244*

I were better to be eaten to death with rust than to be scoured to nothing with perpetual motion.
>*Ibid. Line 249*

I can get no remedy against this consumption of the purse: borrowing only lingers and lingers it out, but the disease is incurable.
>*Ibid. Line 267*

---

[1] It show'd discretion the best part of valour. — BEAUMONT AND FLETCHER: *A King and No King* [1619], *Act II, Sc. 3*

[2] See Sir Philip Sidney, page 115b.

[1] See Sophocles, page 14a.

[2] See Samuel Johnson, page 343a.

Who lined himself with hope,
Eating the air on promise of supply.
King Henry IV. Part II, Act I,
Sc. 3, Line 27
When we mean to build,
We first survey the plot, then draw the
model;
And when we see the figure of the house,
Then must we rate the cost of the erec-
tion.[1]
Ibid. Line 41
A habitation giddy and unsure
Hath he that buildeth on the vulgar
heart.
Ibid. Line 89
Past and to come seem best; things
present worst.
Ibid. Line 108
A poor lone woman.
Ibid. Act II, Sc. 1, Line 37
I'll tickle your catastrophe.
Ibid. Line 68
He hath eaten me out of house and
home.
Ibid. Line 82
Let the end try the man.
Ibid. Sc. 2, Line 52
Thus we play the fools with the time,
and the spirits of the wise sit in the
clouds and mock us.
Ibid. Line 155
He was indeed the glass
Wherein the noble youth did dress
themselves.
Ibid. Sc. 3, Line 21
A good heart's worth gold.
Ibid. Sc. 4, Line 34
Aggravate your choler.
Ibid. Line 174
And let the welkin roar.
Ibid. Line 180
Is it not strange that desire should so
many years outlive performance?
Ibid. Line 283
Now comes in the sweetest morsel of
the night, and we must hence and leave
it unpicked.
Ibid. Line 401

[1] Which of you, intending to build a tower,
sitteth not down first, and counteth the cost,
whether he have sufficient to finish it? —
Luke, XIV, 28

O sleep, O gentle sleep,[1]
Nature's soft nurse! how have I
frighted thee,
That thou no more wilt weigh my eye-
lids down
And steep my senses in forgetfulness?
King Henry IV. Part II, Act III,
Sc. 1, Line 5
With all appliances and means to boot.
Ibid. Line 29
Uneasy lies the head that wears a
crown.
Ibid. Line 31
There is a history in all men's lives.
Ibid. Line 80
How many of mine old acquaintance
are dead!
Ibid. Sc. 2, Line 37
Death, as the Psalmist saith, is cer-
tain to all; all shall die.
Ibid. Line 41
Accommodated; that is, when a man
is, as they say, accommodated; or when
a man is, being, whereby a' may be
thought to be accommodated, — which
is an excellent thing.
Ibid. Line 86
Most forcible Feeble.
Ibid. Line 181
We have heard the chimes at mid-
night.
Ibid. Line 231
A man can die but once: we owe
God a death.
Ibid. Line 253
We ready are to try our fortunes
To the last man.
Ibid. Act IV, Sc. 2, Line 43
I may justly say, with the hook-nosed
fellow of Rome, "I came, saw, and over-
came." [2]
Ibid. Sc. 3, Line 44
If I had a thousand sons, the first
human principle I would teach them
should be, to forswear thin potations
and to addict themselves to sack.
Ibid. Line 133
Will Fortune never come with both
hands full

[1] Sleep, most gentle sleep. — OVID [43 B.C.–
A.D. 18]: *Metamorphoses, Book II, L. 624*
[2] See Plutarch, page 59b.

But write her fair words still in foulest letters?
> *King Henry IV. Part II, Act IV, Sc. 4, Line 103*

Golden care!
That keep'st the ports of slumber open wide
To many a watchful night!
> *Ibid. Sc. 5, Line 22*

Thy wish was father, Harry, to that thought.[1]
> *Ibid. Line 91*

Commit
The oldest sins the newest kind of ways.
> *Ibid. Line 124*

His cares are now all ended.
> *Ibid. Act. V, Sc. 2, Line 3*

I hope to see London once ere I die.
> *Ibid. Sc. 3, Line 61*

Falstaff. What! is the old king dead?
Pistol. As nail in door.[2]
> *Ibid. Line 123*

How ill white hairs become a fool and jester.
> *Ibid. Sc. 4, Line 53*

O! for a Muse of fire, that would ascend
The brightest heaven of invention!
> *King Henry V [1598–1600]. Prologue, Line 1*

Consideration like an angel came,
And whipped the offending Adam out of him.
> *Ibid. Act I, Sc. 1, Line 28*

Hear him debate of commonwealth affairs,
You would say it hath been all in all his study.
> *Ibid. Line 41*

Turn him to any cause of policy,
The Gordian knot of it he will unloose,
Familiar as his garter: that when he speaks,
The air, a chartered libertine, is still.
> *Ibid. Line 45*

[1] Men's thoughts are much according to their inclination, their discourse and speeches according to their learning and infused opinions. — FRANCIS BACON: *Essays* [1597–1625], *Of Custom and Education*
[2] As dead as a door nail. — WILLIAM LANGLAND: *The Vision of Piers Plowman* [?1360–1399], *Part 2, L. 183*

Therefore doth heaven divide
The state of man in divers functions,
Setting endeavour in continual motion;
To which is fixed, as an aim or butt,
Obedience; for so work the honey-bees,
Creatures that by a rule in nature teach
The act of order to a peopled kingdom.
> *King Henry V. Act I, Sc. 2, Line 183*

The singing masons building roofs of gold.
> *Ibid. Line 198*

Many things, having full reference
To one consent, may work contrariously;
As many arrows, loosed several ways,
Fly to one mark;
As many several ways meet in one town;
As many fresh streams meet in one salt sea;
As many lines close in the dial's centre;
So may a thousand actions, once afoot,
End in one purpose, and be all well borne
Without defeat.
> *Ibid. Line 205*

'Tis ever common
That men are merriest when they are from home.
> *Ibid. Line 271*

Now all the youth of England are on fire,
And silken dalliance in the wardrobe lies.
> *Ibid. Act II, Prologue, Line 1*

O England! model to thy inward greatness,
Like little body with a mighty heart,
What mightst thou do, that honour would thee do,
Were all thy children kind and natural!
> *Ibid. Line 16*

A' made a finer end and went away an it had been any christom child; a' parted even just between twelve and one, even at the turning o' the tide: for after I saw him fumble with the sheets and play with flowers and smile upon his fingers' ends, I knew there was but one way; for his nose was as sharp

as a pen, and a' babbled of green fields.
King Henry V. Act II, Sc. 3,
Line 11
As cold as any stone.
Ibid. Line 26
Self-love, my liege, is not so vile a sin
As self-neglecting.
Ibid. Sc. 4, Line 74
Once more unto the breach, dear
friends, once more;
Or close the wall up with our English
dead!
In peace there's nothing so becomes a
man
As modest stillness and humility;
But when the blast of war blows in our
ears,
Then imitate the action of the tiger:
Stiffen the sinews, summon up the
blood,
Disguise fair nature with hard-favour'd
rage;
Then lend the eye a terrible aspect.
Ibid. Act III, Sc. 1, Line 1
And sheathed their swords for lack of
argument.
Ibid. Line 21
I see you stand like greyhounds in the
slips,
Straining upon the start. The game's
afoot:
Follow your spirit; and, upon this
charge
Cry "God for Harry! England and
Saint George!"
Ibid. Line 31
I would give all my fame for a pot
of ale and safety.
Ibid. Sc. 2, Line 14
Men of few words are the best men.
Ibid. Line 40
He will maintain his argument as well
as any military man in the world.
Ibid. Line 89
I know the disciplines of wars.
Ibid. Line 156
What is it then to me if impious war,
Array'd in flames like to the prince of
fiends,
Do, with his smirch'd complexion, all
fell feats

Enlink'd to waste and desolation?
King Henry V. Act III, Sc. 3,
Line 15
A man that I love and honour with
my soul, and my heart, and my duty,
and my life, and my living, and my
uttermost power.
Ibid. Sc. 6, Line 7
Giddy Fortune's furious fickle wheel,
That goddess blind,
That stands upon the rolling restless
stone.
Ibid. Line 28
I thought upon one pair of English legs
Did march three Frenchmen.
Ibid. Line 161
We are in God's hand.
Ibid. Line 181
That island of England breeds very
valiant creatures: their mastiffs are of
unmatchable courage.
Ibid. Sc. 7, Line 155
You may as well say that's a valiant
flea that dare eat his breakfast on the
lip of a lion.
Ibid. Line 160
The hum of either army stilly sounds,
That the fixed sentinels almost receive
The secret whispers of each other's
watch;
Fire answers fire, and through their
paly flames
Each battle sees the other's umbered
face;
Steed threatens steed, in high and boast-
ful neighs
Piercing the night's dull ear; and from
the tents
The armourers, accomplishing the
knights,
With busy hammers closing rivets up,
Give dreadful note of preparation.
Ibid. Act IV, Prologue, Line 5
There is some soul of goodness in things
evil,
Would men observingly distil it out.
Ibid. Act IV, Sc. 1, Line 4
When blood is their argument.
Ibid. Line 151
Every subject's duty is the king's;
but every subject's soul is his own.
Ibid. Line 189

What infinite heart's ease
Must kings neglect that private men
enjoy!
And what have kings that privates have
not too,
Save ceremony, save general ceremony?
And what art thou, thou idol ceremony?
What kind of god art thou, that suffer'st
more
Of mortal griefs than do thy worship-
pers?
What are thy rents? what are thy
comings-in?
O ceremony! show me but thy worth.
King Henry V. Act IV,
Sc. 1, Line 256
'Tis not the balm, the sceptre and the
ball,
The sword, the mace, the crown impe-
rial,
The intertissued robe of gold and pearl,
The farced title running 'fore the king,
The throne he sits on, nor the tide of
pomp
That beats upon the high shore of this
world,
No, not all these, thrice-gorgeous cere-
mony,
Not all these, laid in bed majestical,
Can sleep so soundly as the wretched
slave,
Who with a body filled and vacant mind
Gets him to rest, crammed with distress-
ful bread.
Ibid. Line 280
Winding up days with toil and nights
with sleep.
Ibid. Line 299
O God of battles, steel my soldiers'
hearts;
Possess them not with fear; take from
them now
The sense of reckoning, if the opposed
numbers
Pluck their hearts from them.
Ibid. Line 309
He is as full of valour as of kindness;
Princely in both.
Ibid. Sc. 3, Line 15
But if it be a sin to covet honour,
I am the most offending soul alive.
Ibid. Line 28

This day is called the feast of Crispian:
He that outlives this day, and comes
safe home,
Will stand a tip-toe when this day is
named.
King Henry V. Act IV, Sc. 3, Line 40
We few, we happy few, we band of
brothers.
Ibid. Line 60
Those that leave their valiant bones in
France,
Dying like men, though buried in your
dunghills,
They shall be fam'd; for there the sun
shall greet them,
And draw their honours reeking up to
heaven.
Ibid. Line 98
The saying is true, "The empty ves-
sel makes the greatest sound."
Ibid. Sc. 4, Line 72
There is a river in Macedon, and
there is also moreover a river at Mon-
mouth; . . . and there is salmons in
both.
Ibid. Sc. 7, Line 28
There is occasions and causes why
and wherefore [1] in all things.
Ibid. Act V, Sc. 1, Line 3
By this leek, I will most horribly re-
venge. I eat and eat, I swear.
Ibid. Line 49
All hell shall stir for this.
Ibid. Line 72
A fellow of plain and uncoined con-
stancy.
Ibid. Sc. 2, Line 160
My comfort is, that old age, that ill
layer-up of beauty, can do no more
spoil upon my face.
Ibid. Line 246
O Kate! nice customs curtsy to great
kings. Dear Kate, you and I cannot be
confined within the weak list of a coun-
try's fashion.
Ibid. Line 271
He hath indeed better bettered ex-
pectation.
Much Ado about Nothing [1598–
1600]. Act I, Sc. 1, Line 15

[1] See *The Comedy of Errors,* page 129a.

How much better is it to weep at joy than to joy at weeping.
Much Ado about Nothing.
Act I, Sc. 1, Line 28

A very valiant trencher-man.
Ibid. Line 52

There's a skirmish of wit between them.
Ibid. Line 64

He wears his faith but as the fashion of his hat.
Ibid. Line 76

The gentleman is not in your books.
Ibid. Line 79

What! my dear Lady Disdain! are you yet living?
Ibid. Line 123

I would my horse had the speed of your tongue, and so good a continuer.
Ibid. Line 151

Shall I never see a bachelor of three-score again?
Ibid. Line 209

Benedick the married man.
Ibid. Line 278

He is of a very melancholy disposition.
Ibid. Act II, Sc. 1, Line 6

I could not endure a husband with a beard on his face: I had rather lie in the woollen.
Ibid. Line 31

He that hath a beard is more than a youth, and he that hath no beard is less than a man.
Ibid. Line 38

As merry as the day is long.
Ibid. Line 52

Would it not grieve a woman to be over-mastered with a piece of valiant dust? to make an account of her life to a clod of wayward marl?
Ibid. Line 62

I have a good eye, uncle; I can see a church by daylight.
Ibid. Line 86

Speak low, if you speak love.
Ibid. Line 104

Friendship is constant in all other things
Save in the office and affairs of love:
Therefore, all hearts in love use their
own tongues;

Let every eye negotiate for itself,
And trust no agent.
Much Ado about Nothing.
Act II, Sc. 1, Line 184

She speaks poniards, and every word stabs: if her breath were as terrible as her terminations, there were no living near her; she would infect to the north star.
Ibid. Line 257

Silence is the perfectest herald of joy: I were but little happy, if I could say how much.
Ibid. Line 319

It keeps on the windy side of care.[1]
Ibid. Line 328

There was a star danced, and under that was I born.
Ibid. Line 351

I will tell you my drift.[2]
Ibid. Line 406

He was wont to speak plain and to the purpose.
Ibid. Sc. 3, Line 19

Her hair shall be of what colour it please God.
Ibid. Line 36

Sigh no more, ladies, sigh no more,
  Men were deceivers ever;
One foot in sea and one on shore;
  To one thing constant never.
Ibid. Line 65

Sits the wind in that corner?
Ibid. Line 108

Bait the hook well: this fish will bite.
Ibid. Line 121

Happy are they that hear their detractions, and can put them to mending.
Ibid. Line 248

Shall quips and sentences and these paper bullets of the brain awe a man from the career of his humour? No; the world must be peopled. When I said I would die a bachelor, I did not think I should live till I were married.
Ibid. Line 260

The pleasant'st angling is to see the fish

[1] The windy side of the law. — *Twelfth-Night* [1598–1600], *Act III, Sc. 4, L. 183*
[2] We know your drift. — *Coriolanus* [1607–1608], *Act III, Sc. 3, L. 114*

Cut with her golden oars the silver stream,
And greedily devour the treacherous bait.

Much Ado about Nothing.
Act III, Sc. 1, Line 26

From the crown of his head to the sole of his foot, he is all mirth.

Ibid. Sc. 2, Line 9

He hath a heart as sound as a bell, and his tongue is the clapper; for what his heart thinks his tongue speaks.

Ibid. Line 12

Every one can master a grief but he that has it.

Ibid. Line 28

Are you good men and true?

Ibid. Sc. 3, Line 1

To be a well-favoured man is the gift of fortune; but to write and read comes by nature.

Ibid. Line 14

If they make you not then the better answer, you may say they are not the men you took them for.

Ibid. Line 49

They that touch pitch will be defiled.[1]

Ibid. Line 61

The fashion wears out more apparel than the man.

Ibid. Line 147

I thank God, I am as honest as any man living, that is an old man and no honester than I.

Ibid. Sc. 5, Line 15

A good old man, sir; he will be talking: as they say, When the age is in, the wit is out.

Ibid. Line 36

Well, God's a good man; an two men ride of a horse, one must ride behind.

Ibid. Line 39

O! what men dare do! what men may do! what men daily do, not knowing what they do!

Ibid. Act IV, Sc. 1, Line 19

---

[1] He that toucheth pitch shall be defiled therewith. — *Apocrypha: Ecclesiasticus, XIII, 1*

This pitch, as ancient writers do report, doth defile; so doth the company thou keepest. — *King Henry IV* [1597–1598], *Part I, Act II, Sc. 4, L. 460*

O! what authority and show of truth
Can cunning sin cover itself withal!

Much Ado about Nothing.
Act IV, Sc. 1, Line 35

I have mark'd
A thousand blushing apparitions
To start into her face; a thousand innocent shames
In angel whiteness beat away those blushes.

Ibid. Line 160

For it so falls out
That what we have we prize not to the worth
Whiles we enjoy it, but being lack'd and lost,
Why, then we rack the value; then we find
The virtue that possession would not show us
Whiles it was ours.

Ibid. Line 219

The idea of her life shall sweetly creep
Into his study of imagination,
And every lovely organ of her life
Shall come apparell'd in more precious habit,
More moving-delicate, and full of life
Into the eye and prospect of his soul.

Ibid. Line 226

Masters, it is proved already that you are little better than false knaves; and it will go near to be thought so shortly.

Ibid. Sc. 2, Line 23

Flat burglary as ever was committed.

Ibid. Line 54

Condemned into everlasting redemption.

Ibid. Line 60

O that he were here to write me down an ass!

Ibid. Line 80

A fellow that hath had losses, and one that hath two gowns, and every thing handsome about him.

Ibid. Line 90

Patch griefs with proverbs.

Ibid. Act V, Sc. 1, Line 17

Men
Can counsel and speak comfort to that grief

Which they themselves not feel.
> *Much Ado about Nothing.*
> *Act V, Sc. 1, Line 20*

Charm ache with air, and agony with words.
> *Ibid. Line 26*

'Tis all men's office to speak patience
To those that wring under the load of sorrow;
But no man's virtue nor sufficiency
To be so moral when he shall endure
The like himself.
> *Ibid. Line 27*

For there was never yet philosopher
That could endure the toothache patiently.
> *Ibid. Line 35*

Some of us will smart for it.
> *Ibid. Line 108*

What though care killed a cat,[1] thou hast mettle enough in thee to kill care.
> *Ibid. Line 135*

I was not born under a rhyming planet.
> *Ibid. Sc. 2, Line 40*

Done to death by slanderous tongues.
> *Ibid. Sc. 3, Line 3*

Fleet the time carelessly, as they did in the golden world.
> *As You Like It* [*1598–1600*].
> *Act I, Sc. 1, Line 126*

Always the dulness of the fool is the whetstone of the wits.
> *Ibid. Sc. 2, Line 59*

The little foolery that wise men have makes a great show.
> *Ibid. Line 97*

Well said: that was laid on with a trowel.
> *Ibid. Line 113*

In the world I fill up a place, which may be better supplied when I have made it empty.
> *Ibid. Line 206*

Your heart's desires be with you!
> *Ibid. Line 214*

---

[1] Let care kill a cat,
We'll laugh and grow fat.
> *Shirburn Ballads* [1585], *91*
Hang sorrow, care'll kill a cat. — JONSON:
Every Man in His Humour [1598], *Act I, Sc. 1*

One out of suits with fortune.
> *As You Like It. Act I, Sc. 2,*
> *Line 263*

My pride fell with my fortunes.
> *Ibid. Line 269*

Hereafter, in a better world than this,
I shall desire more love and knowledge of you.
> *Ibid. Line 301*

Celia. Not a word?
Rosalind. Not one to throw at a dog.
> *Ibid. Sc. 3, Line 2*

O, how full of briers is this working-day world!
> *Ibid. Line 12*

Beauty provoketh thieves sooner than gold.
> *Ibid. Line 113*

We'll have a swashing and a martial outside,
As many other mannish cowards have.
> *Ibid. Line 123*

Hath not old custom made this life more sweet
Than that of painted pomp? Are not these woods
More free from peril than the envious court?
> *Ibid. Act II, Sc. 1, Line 2*

Sweet are the uses of adversity;
Which, like the toad, ugly and venomous,
Wears yet a precious jewel in his head;
And this our life, exempt from public haunt,
Finds tongues in trees, books in the running brooks,
Sermons in stones, and good in every thing.
> *Ibid. Line 12*

The big round tears
Coursed one another down his innocent nose
In piteous chase.
> *Ibid. Line 38*

"Poor deer," quoth he, "thou mak'st a testament
As worldlings do, giving thy sum of more
To that which had too much."
> *Ibid. Line 47*

Sweep on, you fat and greasy citizens.
> *As You Like It. Act II, Sc. 1,*
> *Line 55*

And He that doth the ravens feed,
Yea, providently caters for the sparrow,
Be comfort to my age!
> *Ibid. Sc. 3, Line 43*

Though I look old, yet I am strong and
lusty;
For in my youth I never did apply
Hot and rebellious liquors in my blood.
> *Ibid. Line 47*

Therefore my age is as a lusty winter,
Frosty, but kindly.
> *Ibid. Line 52*

Thou art not for the fashion of these
times,
Where none will sweat but for promotion.
> *Ibid. Line 59*

Ay, now am I in Arden: the more
fool I. When I was at home I was in a
better place; but travellers must be content.
> *Ibid. Sc. 4, Line 16*

If you remember'st not the slightest
folly
That ever love did make thee run into,
Thou hast not lov'd.
> *Ibid. Line 34*

We that are true lovers run into
strange capers.
> *Ibid. Line 53*

Thou speakest wiser than thou art
ware of.
> *Ibid. Line 57*

I shall ne'er be 'ware of mine own
wit, till I break my shins against it.
> *Ibid. Line 59*

Under the greenwood tree
Who loves to lie with me,
And turn his merry note
Unto the sweet bird's throat,
Come hither, come hither, come hither:
  Here shall he see
  No enemy
But winter and rough weather.
> *Ibid. Sc. 5, Line 1*

I can suck melancholy out of a song
as a weasel sucks eggs.
> *Ibid. Line 12*

Who doth ambition shun
And loves to live i' the sun,

Seeking the food he eats,
And pleas'd with what he gets.
> *As You Like It. Act II, Sc. 5,*
> *Line 38*

Amiens. What's that "ducdame"?
Jaques. 'Tis a Greek invocation to
call fools into a circle.[1]
> *Ibid. Line 58*

I met a fool i' the forest,
A motley fool.
> *Ibid. Sc. 7, Line 12*

And rail'd on Lady Fortune in good
terms,
In good set terms.
> *Ibid. Line 16*

And then he drew a dial from his poke,
And looking on it with lack-lustre eye,
Says, very wisely, "It is ten o'clock:
Thus we may see," quoth he, "how the
world wags." [2]
> *Ibid. Line 20*

And so from hour to hour we ripe and
ripe,
And then from hour to hour we rot and
rot;
And thereby hangs a tale.[3]
> *Ibid. Line 26*

My lungs began to crow like chanti-
cleer,
That fools should be so deep-contem-
plative;
And I did laugh sans intermission
An hour by his dial.
> *Ibid. Line 30*

Motley's the only wear.
> *Ibid. Line 34*

If ladies be but young and fair,
They have the gift to know it.
> *Ibid. Line 37*

I must have liberty
Withal, as large a charter as the wind,
To blow on whom I please.
> *Ibid. Line 47*

The "why" is plain as way to parish
church.
> *Ibid. Line 52*

[1] Your name, even in life, was, alas! a kind
of *ducdame* to bring people of no very great
sense into your circle. — ANDREW LANG: *Letters to Dead Authors* [1886], *To Percy
Bysshe Shelley*
[2] So wags the world. — SIR WALTER SCOTT:
Ivanhoe [1819], *Chap. 37*
[3] See Rabelais, page 90a.

Under the shade of melancholy boughs,
Lose and neglect the creeping hours of
time;
If ever you have look'd on better days,
If ever been where bells have knoll'd to
church,
If ever sat at any good man's feast.
As You Like It. Act II,
Sc. 7, Line 111

True is it that we have seen better
days.
Ibid. Line 120

And wiped our eyes
Of drops that sacred pity hath engen-
der'd.
Ibid. Line 122

Oppress'd with two weak evils, age and
hunger.
Ibid. Line 132

The wide and universal theatre.
Ibid. Line 137

All the world 's a stage,
And all the men and women merely
players.[1]
They have their exits and their en-
trances;
And one man in his time plays many
parts,
His acts being seven ages. At first the
infant,
Mewling and puking in the nurse's
arms.
And then the whining school-boy, with
his satchel
And shining morning face, creeping like
snail
Unwillingly to school. And then the
lover,
Sighing like furnace, with a woful ballad
Made to his mistress' eyebrow. Then a
soldier,
Full of strange oaths, and bearded like
the pard;

[1] See Du Bartas, pages 102a and 103a, and
Montaigne, page 99b.
The world's a theatre, the earth a stage,
Which God and Nature do with actors fill.
THOMAS HEYWOOD: *Apology for Actors*
[1612]
The world's a stage on which all the parts
are played. — MIDDLETON: *A Game of Chess*
[1624], *Act V, Sc. 1*

Jealous in honour, sudden and quick in
quarrel,
Seeking the bubble reputation
Even in the cannon's mouth. And then
the justice,
In fair round belly with good capon
lined,
With eyes severe and beard of formal
cut,
Full of wise saws and modern in-
stances;
And so he plays his part. The sixth age
shifts
Into the lean and slipper'd pantaloon,
With spectacles on nose and pouch on
side;
His youthful hose, well saved, a world
too wide
For his shrunk shank; and his big
manly voice,
Turning again toward childish treble,
pipes
And whistles in his sound. Last scene of
all,
That ends this strange eventful his-
tory,
Is second childishness, and mere obliv-
ion,
Sans teeth, sans eyes, sans taste, sans
everything.
As You Like It. Act II,
Sc. 7, Line 139

Blow, blow, thou winter wind!
Thou art not so unkind
As man's ingratitude.
Ibid. Line 174

These trees shall be my books.
Ibid. Act III, Sc. 2, Line 5

The fair, the chaste, and unexpressive
she.
Ibid. Line 10

It goes much against my stomach.
Hast any philosophy in thee, shepherd?
Ibid. Line 21

He that wants money, means, and
content is without three good friends.
Ibid. Line 25

I am a true labourer: I earn that I
eat, get that I wear, owe no man hate,
envy no man's happiness, glad of other
men's good.
Ibid. Line 78

From the east to western Ind,
No jewel is like Rosalind.
As You Like It. Act III,
Sc. 2, Line 94
This is the very false gallop of verses.
Ibid. Line 120
Let us make an honourable retreat.
Ibid. Line 170
With bag and baggage.
Ibid. Line 171
O, wonderful, wonderful, and most wonderful wonderful! and yet again wonderful, and after that out of all whooping.
Ibid. Line 202
Answer me in one word.
Ibid. Line 238
It is as easy to count atomies as to resolve the propositions of a lover.
Ibid. Line 246
Do you not know I am a woman? when I think, I must speak.
Ibid. Line 265
I do desire we may be better strangers.
Ibid. Line 276
Jaques. What stature is she of?
Orlando. Just as high as my heart.
Ibid. Line 286
Time travels in divers paces with divers persons. I'll tell you who Time ambles withal, who Time trots withal, who Time gallops withal, and who he stands still withal.
Ibid. Line 328
Every one fault seeming monstrous till his fellow fault came to match it.
Ibid. Line 377
Everything about you demonstrating a careless desolation.
Ibid. Line 405
I would the gods had made thee poetical.
Ibid. Sc. 3, Line 16
The common executioner,
Whose heart the accustom'd sight of
death makes hard,
Falls not the axe upon the humbled
neck
But first begs pardon.
Ibid. Sc. 5, Line 3

The wounds invisible
That love's keen arrows make.
As You Like It. Act III,
Sc. 5, Line 30
Down on your knees,
And thank Heaven, fasting, for a good man's love.
Ibid. Line 57
I am falser than vows made in wine.
Ibid. Line 73
It is a melancholy of mine own, compounded of many simples, extracted from many objects, and indeed the sundry contemplation of my travels, which, by often rumination, wraps me in a most humorous sadness.
Ibid. Act IV, Sc. 1, Line 16
I had rather have a fool to make me merry than experience to make me sad.
Ibid. Line 28
Farewell, Monsieur Traveller: look you lisp and wear strange suits, disable all the benefits of your own country, be out of love with your nativity, and almost chide God for making you that countenance you are, or I will scarce think you have swam in a gondola.
Ibid. Line 35
I'll warrant him heart-whole.
Ibid. Line 51
Very good orators, when they are out, they will spit; and for lovers, lacking (God warn us!) matter, the cleanliest shift is to kiss.
Ibid. Line 77
Men have died from time to time, and worms have eaten them, but not for love.
Ibid. Line 110
For ever and a day.
Ibid. Line 151
Men are April when they woo, December when they wed: maids are May when they are maids, but the sky changes when they are wives.
Ibid. Line 153
My affection hath an unknown bottom, like the bay of Portugal.
Ibid. Line 219
The horn, the horn, the lusty horn
Is not a thing to laugh to scorn.
Ibid. Sc. 2, Line 17

Chewing the food of sweet and bitter fancy.

> *As You Like It. Act IV,*
> *Sc. 3, Line 103*

"So so" is good, very good, very excellent good; and yet it is not; it is but so so.

> *Ibid. Act V, Sc. 1, Line 30*

The fool doth think he is wise, but the wise man knows himself to be a fool.

> *Ibid. Line 35*

No sooner met but they looked; no sooner looked but they loved; no sooner loved but they sighed; no sooner sighed but they asked one another the reason; no sooner knew the reason but they sought the remedy.

> *Ibid. Sc. 2, Line 37*

How bitter a thing it is to look into happiness through another man's eyes!

> *Ibid. Line 48*

It was a lover and his lass,
    With a hey, and a ho, and hey nonino,
That o'er the green cornfield did pass,
    In the spring time, the only pretty ring time,
When birds do sing, hey ding a ding, ding;
Sweet lovers love the spring.

> *Ibid. Sc. 3, Line 18*

Here comes a pair of very strange beasts, which in all tongues are called fools.

> *Ibid. Sc. 4, Line 36*

An ill-favoured thing, sir, but mine own.[1]

> *Ibid. Line 60*

Rich honesty dwells like a miser, sir, in a poor house; as your pearl in your foul oyster.

> *Ibid. Line 62*

The Retort Courteous; . . . the Quip Modest; . . . the Reply Churlish; . . . the Reproof Valiant; . . . the Countercheck Quarrelsome; . . . the Lie Circumstantial; . . . the Lie Direct.

> *Ibid. Line 75*

[1] My glass is not large, but I drink out of my own. — ALFRED DE MUSSET [1810–1857]

Your "If" is the only peacemaker; much virtue in "If."

> *As You Like It. Act V, Sc. 4, Line 108*

What a case am I in.

> *Ibid. Epilogue, Line 7*

If music be the food of love,[1] play on;
Give me excess of it, that, surfeiting,
The appetite may sicken, and so die.
That strain again! it had a dying fall:
O! it came o'er my ear like the sweet sound
That breathes upon a bank of violets,
Stealing and giving odour!

> *Twelfth-Night* [*1598–1600*].
> *Act I, Sc. 1, Line 1*

O spirit of love! how quick and fresh art thou,
That notwithstanding thy capacity
Receiveth as the sea, nought enters there,
Of what validity and pitch soe'er,
But falls into abatement and low price,
Even in a minute: so full of shapes is fancy,
That it alone is high fantastical.

> *Ibid. Line 9*

When my tongue blabs, then let mine eyes not see.

> *Ibid. Sc. 2, Line 61*

I am sure care's an enemy to life.

> *Ibid. Sc. 3, Line 2*

Let them hang themselves in their own straps.

> *Ibid. Line 13*

I am a great eater of beef, and I believe that does harm to my wit.

> *Ibid. Line 92*

Wherefore are these things hid?

> *Ibid. Line 135*

Is it a world to hide virtues in?

> *Ibid. Line 142*

God give them wisdom that have it; and those that are fools, let them use their talents.

> *Ibid. Sc. 4, Line 14*

One draught above heat makes him a fool, the second mads him, and a third drowns him.

> *Ibid. Sc. 5, Line 139*

[1] Is not music the food of love? — RICHARD BRINSLEY SHERIDAN: *The Rivals* [1775], *Act II, Sc. 1*

We will draw the curtain and show you the picture.

Twelfth-Night. Act I, Sc. 5, Line 252

'Tis beauty truly blent, whose red and white
Nature's own sweet and cunning hand laid on:
Lady, you are the cruell'st she alive
If you will lead these graces to the grave
And leave the world no copy.

Ibid. Line 259

Make me a willow-cabin at your gate,
And call upon my soul within the house.

Ibid. Line 289

Holla your name to the reverberate hills,
And make the babbling gossip of the air
Cry out.

Ibid. Line 293

O mistress mine, where are you roaming?

Ibid. Act II, Sc. 3, Line 42

Journeys end in lovers meeting,
Every wise man's son doth know.

Ibid. Line 46

What is love? 'tis not hereafter;
Present mirth hath present laughter.

Ibid. Line 50

Then come kiss me, sweet and twenty,
Youth's a stuff will not endure.

Ibid. Line 54

He does it with a better grace, but I do it more natural.

Ibid. Line 91

Is there no respect of place, persons, nor time in you?

Ibid. Line 100

Sir Toby. Dost thou think, because thou art virtuous, there shall be no more cakes and ale?
Clown. Yes, by Saint Anne, and ginger shall be hot i' the mouth too.

Ibid. Line 124

My purpose is, indeed, a horse of that colour.

Ibid. Line 184

These most brisk and giddy-paced times.

Ibid. Sc. 4, Line 6

If ever thou shalt love,
In the sweet pangs of it remember me;
For such as I am all true lovers are,
Unstaid and skittish in all motions else,
Save in the constant image of the creature
That is beloved.

Twelfth-Night. Act II, Sc. 4, Line 15

Let still the woman take
An elder than herself: so wears she to him,
So sways she level in her husband's heart:
For, boy, however we do praise ourselves,
Our fancies are more giddy and unfirm,
More longing, wavering, sooner lost and worn,
Than women's are.

Ibid. Line 29

Then let thy love be younger than thyself,
Or thy affection cannot hold the bent.
For women are as roses, whose fair flower
Being once display'd, doth fall that very hour.

Ibid. Line 36

The spinsters and the knitters in the sun
And the free maids that weave their thread with bones,
Do use to chant it: it is silly sooth,
And dallies with the innocence of love,
Like the old age.

Ibid. Line 47

Duke. And what's her history?
Viola. A blank, my lord. She never told her love,
But let concealment, like a worm i' the bud,
Feed on her damask cheek: she pined in thought,
And with a green and yellow melancholy
She sat like patience on a monument,
Smiling at grief.

Ibid. Line 112

I am all the daughters of my father's house,
And all the brothers too.

Ibid. Line 122

Here comes the trout that must be caught with tickling.

    Twelfth-Night. Act II,
      Sc. 5, Line 25

I know my place, as I would they should do theirs.

    Ibid. Line 61

I may command where I adore.

    Ibid. Line 116

Some are born great, some achieve greatness, and some have greatness thrust upon them.

    Ibid. Line 159

He will come to her in yellow stockings, and 'tis a colour she abhors, and cross-garter'd a fashion she detests.

    Ibid. Line 220

Foolery, sir, does walk about the orb like the sun; it shines everywhere.

    Ibid. Act III, Sc. 1, Line 44

This fellow's wise enough to play the fool,
And to do that well craves a kind of wit.

    Ibid. Line 68

Music from the spheres.[1]

    Ibid. Line 122

How apt the poor are to be proud.

    Ibid. Line 141

Then westward-ho!

    Ibid. Line 148

Oh, what a deal of scorn looks beautiful
In the contempt and anger of his lip!

    Ibid. Line 159

Love sought is good, but given unsought, is better.

    Ibid. Line 170

You will hang like an icicle on a Dutchman's beard.

    Ibid. Sc. 2, Line 30

Let there be gall enough in thy ink.

    Ibid. Line 54

Laugh yourselves into stitches.

    Ibid. Line 75

I can no other answer make but thanks,
And thanks, and ever thanks.

    Ibid. Sc. 3, Line 14

Haply your eye shall light upon some toy

---

[1] The music of the spheres. — *Pericles* [1608–1609], *Act V, Sc. 1, L. 231*
See Sir Thomas Browne, page 240b.

You have desire to purchase.

    Twelfth-Night. Act III,
      Sc. 3, Line 44

This is very midsummer madness.

    Ibid. Sc. 4, Line 62

Put thyself into the trick of singularity.

    Ibid. Line 80

What, man! defy the Devil: consider, he's an enemy to mankind.

    Ibid. Line 109

If this were played upon a stage now, I could condemn it as an improbable fiction.

    Ibid. Line 142

More matter for a May morning.

    Ibid. Line 158

Still you keep o' the windy side of the law.[1]

    Ibid. Line 183

My remembrance is very free and clear from any image of offence done to any man.

    Ibid. Line 251

Hob, nob, is his word: give 't or take 't.

    Ibid. Line 265

I have heard of some kind of men that put quarrels purposely on others to taste their valour.

    Ibid. Line 269

He's a very devil.

    Ibid. Line 304

An I thought he had been valiant, and so cunning in fence, I'd have seen him damned ere I'd have challenged him.

    Ibid. Line 314

Out of my lean and low ability
I'll lend you something.

    Ibid. Line 380

I hate ingratitude more in a man
Than lying, vainness, babbling drunkenness,
Or any taint of vice whose strong corruption
Inhabits our frail blood.

    Ibid. Line 390

As the old hermit of Prague, that

---

[1] The windy side of care. — *Much Ado about Nothing* [1598–1600], *Act II, Sc. 1, L. 328*

never saw pen and ink, very wittily said to a niece of King Gorboduc, "That that is, is."

Twelfth-Night. Act IV, Sc. 2, Line 14

Thus the whirligig of time brings in his revenges.

Ibid. Act V, Sc. 1, Line 388

When that I was and a little tiny boy,
With hey, ho, the wind and the rain,
A foolish thing was but a toy,
For the rain it raineth every day.[1]

Ibid. Line 404

A surgeon to old shoes.

Julius Caesar [1598–1600].
Act I, Sc. 1, Line 26

As proper men as ever trod upon neat's leather.

Ibid. Line 27

Have you not made a universal shout,
That Tiber trembled underneath her banks,
To hear the replication of your sounds
Made in her concave shores?

Ibid. Line 48

Beware the ides of March.[2]

Ibid. Sc. 2, Line 18

Set honour in one eye and death i' the other,
And I will look on both indifferently.

Ibid. Line 86

Well, honour is the subject of my story.
I cannot tell what you and other men
Think of this life; but, for my single self,
I had as lief not be as live to be
In awe of such a thing as I myself.

Ibid. Line 92

Stemming it with hearts of controversy.

Ibid. Line 109

Why, man, he doth bestride the narrow world
Like a Colossus; and we petty men
Walk under his huge legs, and peep about
To find ourselves dishonourable graves.
Men at some time are masters of their fates:

[1] Parodied by the Fool in *King Lear;* see page 191b.
[2] See Plutarch, page 56b.

The fault, dear Brutus, is not in our stars,
But in ourselves, that we are underlings.

Julius Caesar. Act I, Sc. 2, Line 134

Upon what meat doth this our Caesar feed,
That he is grown so great? Age, thou art shamed!
Rome, thou hast lost the breed of noble bloods!

Ibid. Line 148

There was a Brutus once that would have brook'd
The eternal devil to keep his state in Rome
As easily as a king.

Ibid. Line 158

Let me have men about me that are fat;
Sleek-headed men, and such as sleep o' nights.
Yond Cassius has a lean and hungry look; [1]
He thinks too much: such men are dangerous.

Ibid. Line 191

He reads much;
He is a great observer, and he looks
Quite through the deeds of men.

Ibid. Line 200

Seldom he smiles, and smiles in such a sort
As if he mock'd himself, and scorn'd his spirit
That could be moved to smile at anything.

Ibid. Line 204

But, for my own part, it was Greek to me.

Ibid. Line 288

Yesterday the bird of night did sit,
Even at noon-day, upon the market-place,
Hooting and shrieking.

Ibid. Sc. 3, Line 26

O! he sits high in all the people's hearts:
And that which would appear offence in us,
His countenance, like richest alchemy,
Will change to virtue and to worthiness.

Ibid. Line 157

[1] See Plutarch, page 57b.

'Tis a common proof,
That lowliness is young ambition's lad-
    der,
Whereto the climber-upward turns his
    face;
But when he once attains the upmost
    round,
He then unto the ladder turns his back,
Looks in the clouds, scorning the base
    degrees
By which he did ascend.

Julius Caesar. Act II,
Sc. 1, Line 21

Therefore think him as a serpent's egg
Which, hatch'd, would, as his kind,
    grow mischievous,
And kill him in the shell.

Ibid. Line 32

Between the acting of a dreadful thing
And the first motion, all the interim is
Like a phantasma, or a hideous dream:
The Genius and the mortal instruments
Are then in council; and the state of
    man,
Like to a little kingdom, suffers then
The nature of an insurrection.

Ibid. Line 63

O conspiracy!
Sham'st thou to show thy dangerous
    brow by night,
When evils are most free?

Ibid. Line 77

Let's carve him as a dish fit for the
    gods.
Not hew him as a carcass fit for hounds.

Ibid. Line 173

But when I tell him he hates flatterers,
He says he does, being then most flat-
    tered.

Ibid. Line 207

Enjoy the honey-heavy dew of slumber.

Ibid. Line 230

You are my true and honourable wife,
As dear to me as are the ruddy drops
That visit my sad heart.[1]

Ibid. Line 288

Think you I am no stronger than my
    sex,

[1] Dear as the ruddy drops that warm my
heart. — THOMAS GRAY: *The Bard* [1757],
I, 3, L. 12

Being so father'd and so husbanded?

Julius Caesar. Act II, Sc. 1,
Line 296

When beggars die, there are no comets
    seen;
The heavens themselves blaze forth the
    death of princes.

Ibid. Sc. 2, Line 30

Cowards die many times before their
    deaths;
The valiant never taste of death but
    once.
Of all the wonders that I yet have
    heard,
It seems to me most strange that men
    should fear;
Seeing that death, a necessary end,
Will come when it will come.

Ibid. Line 32

See! Antony, that revels long o' nights,
Is notwithstanding up.

Ibid. Line 116

How hard it is for women to keep coun-
    sel.

Ibid. Sc. 4, Line 9

But I am constant as the northern star,
Of whose true-fix'd and resting quality
There is no fellow in the firmament.

Ibid. Act III, Sc. 1, Line 60

Et tu, Brute!

Ibid. Line 77

How many ages hence
Shall this our lofty scene be acted o'er,
In states unborn and accents yet un-
    known!

Ibid. Line 111

O mighty Caesar! dost thou lie so low?
Are all thy conquests, glories, triumphs,
    spoils,
Shrunk to this little measure?

Ibid. Line 148

The choice and master spirits of this
    age.

Ibid. Line 163

Though last, not least in love.[1]

Ibid. Line 189

O! pardon me, thou bleeding piece of
    earth,
That I am meek and gentle with these
    butchers!

[1] See Spenser, page 114b.

Thou art the ruins of the noblest man
That ever lived in the tide of times.
Julius Caesar. Act III,
Sc. 1, Line 254
Cry "Havoc!" and let slip the dogs of
war.
Ibid. Line 273
Romans, countrymen, and lovers!
hear me for my cause; and be silent,
that you may hear.
Ibid. Sc. 2, Line 13
Not that I loved Caesar less, but that
I loved Rome more.
Ibid. Line 22
As he was valiant I honour him: but,
as he was ambitious, I slew him.
Ibid. Line 27
If any, speak; for him have I of-
fended. I pause for a reply.
Ibid. Line 36
Friends, Romans, countrymen, lend me
your ears;
I come to bury Caesar, not to praise
him.
The evil that men do lives after them,
The good is oft interred with their
bones.[1]
Ibid. Line 79
For Brutus is an honourable man;
So are they all, all honourable men.
Ibid. Line 88
When that the poor have cried, Caesar
hath wept;
Ambition should be made of sterner
stuff.
Ibid. Line 97
O judgment! thou art fled to brutish
beasts,
And men have lost their reason.
Ibid. Line 110
But yesterday the word of Caesar might
Have stood against the world; now lies
he there,
And none so poor to do him reverence.
Ibid. Line 124
If you have tears, prepare to shed them
now.
Ibid. Line 174
See what a rent the envious Casca
made.
Ibid. Line 180

[1] See Euripides, page 18a.

This was the most unkindest cut of all.
Julius Caesar. Act III,
Sc. 2, Line 188
Great Caesar fell.
O! what a fall was there, my country-
men;
Then I, and you, and all of us fell down,
Whilst bloody treason flourish'd over
us.
Ibid. Line 194
What private griefs they have, alas! I
know not.
Ibid. Line 217
I come not, friends, to steal away your
hearts:
I am no orator, as Brutus is;
But, as you know me all, a plain blunt
man.
Ibid. Line 220
For I have neither wit, nor words, nor
worth,
Action, nor utterance, nor the power
of speech,
To stir men's blood: I only speak right
on.
Ibid. Line 225
Put a tongue
In every wound of Caesar, that should
move
The stones of Rome to rise and mutiny.
Ibid. Line 232
When love begins to sicken and decay,
It useth an enforced ceremony.
There are no tricks in plain and simple
faith.
Ibid. Act IV, Sc. 2, Line 20
You yourself
Are much condemn'd to have an itch-
ing palm.
Ibid. Sc. 3, Line 9
The foremost man of all this world.
Ibid. Line 22
I had rather be a dog, and bay the
moon,
Than such a Roman.
Ibid. Line 27
I'll use you for my mirth, yea, for my
laughter,
When you are waspish.
Ibid. Line 49
There is no terror, Cassius, in your
threats;

For I am arm'd so strong in honesty
That they pass by me as the idle wind,
Which I respect not.

> *Julius Caesar. Act IV,*
> *Sc. 3, Line 66*

A friend should bear his friend's infirmities,
But Brutus makes mine greater than they are.

> *Ibid. Line 85*

All his faults observed,
Set in a note-book, learn'd, and conn'd by rote.

> *Ibid. Line 96*

There is a tide in the affairs of men,
Which, taken at the flood, leads on to fortune;
Omitted, all the voyage of their life
Is bound in shallows and in miseries.

> *Ibid. Line 217*

We must take the current when it serves,
Or lose our ventures.

> *Ibid. Line 222*

The deep of night is crept upon our talk,
And nature must obey necessity.[1]

> *Ibid. Line 225*

But for your words, they rob the Hybla bees,
And leave them honeyless.

> *Ibid. Act V, Sc. 1, Line 34*

Forever, and forever, farewell, Cassius!
If we do meet again, why, we shall smile;
If not, why then, this parting was well made.

> *Ibid. Line 117*

O, that a man might know
The end of this day's business, ere it come.

> *Ibid. Line 123*

O Julius Caesar! thou art mighty yet!
Thy spirit walks abroad, and turns our swords
In our own proper entrails.

> *Ibid. Sc. 3, Line 94*

The last of all the Romans, fare thee well!

> *Ibid. Line 99*

---

[1] See Diogenes Laertius, page 70a.

This was the noblest Roman of them all.

> *Julius Caesar. Act V,*
> *Sc. 5, Line 68*

His life was gentle, and the elements
So mix'd in him that Nature might stand up
And say to all the world, "This was a man!"

> *Ibid. Line 73*

When my love swears that she is made of truth,
I do believe her, though I know she lies.

> *The Passionate Pilgrim* [*1599*].[1] *I*

Love's best habit is a soothing tongue.

> *Ibid.*

Bad in the best, though excellent in neither.

> *Ibid. VII*

Crabbed age and youth cannot live together.
Youth is full of pleasance, age is full of care.

> *Ibid. XII*

For this relief much thanks; 'tis bitter cold,
And I am sick at heart.

> *Hamlet* [*1600–1601*]. *Act I,*
> *Sc. 1, Line 8*

Not a mouse stirring.[2]

> *Ibid. Line 10*

But in the gross and scope of my opinion,
This bodes some strange eruption to our state.

> *Ibid. Line 68*

Whose sore task
Does not divide the Sunday from the week.

> *Ibid. Line 75*

This sweaty haste
Doth make the night joint-labourer with the day.

> *Ibid. Line 77*

In the most high and palmy state of Rome,
A little ere the mightiest Julius fell,
The graves stood tenantless and the sheeted dead

---

[1] The bulk of this volume is by others.
[2] See Clement Clarke Moore, page 437a.

Did squeak and gibber in the Roman streets.

Hamlet. Act I, Sc. 1, Line 113

And then it started like a guilty thing
Upon a fearful summons.

Ibid. Line 148

The cock, that is the trumpet of the morn.

Ibid. Line 150

Whether in sea or fire, in earth or air,
The extravagant and erring spirit hies
To his confine.

Ibid. Line 153

It faded on the crowing of the cock.
Some say that ever 'gainst that season comes
Wherein our Saviour's birth is cele-brated,
The bird of dawning singeth all night long:
And then, they say, no spirit can walk abroad;
The nights are wholesome; then no planets strike,
No fairy takes, nor witch hath power to charm,
So hallow'd and so gracious is the time.

Ibid. Line 157

So have I heard, and do in part believe it.
But, look, the morn in russet mantle clad,
Walks o'er the dew of yon high eastern hill.

Ibid. Line 165

The memory be green.[1]

Ibid. Sc. 2, Line 2

With one auspicious and one dropping eye,
With mirth in funeral and with dirge in marriage,
In equal scale weighing delight and dole.

Ibid. Line 11

A little more than kin, and less than kind.

Ibid. Line 65

Thou know'st 'tis common; all that live must die,

[1] See Thomas Moore, page 438a.

Passing through nature to eternity.

Hamlet. Act I, Sc. 2, Line 72

Seems, madam! Nay, it is; I know not "seems."
'Tis not alone my inky cloak, good mother,
Nor customary suits of solemn black.

Ibid. Line 76

But I have that within which passeth show;
These but the trappings and the suits of woe.

Ibid. Line 85

O! that this too too solid flesh would melt,
Thaw and resolve itself into a dew;
Or that the Everlasting had not fix'd
His canon 'gainst self-slaughter! O God! O God!
How weary, stale, flat, and unprofitable
Seem to me all the uses of this world.

Ibid. Line 129

Things rank and gross in nature
Possess it merely. That it should come to this!

Ibid. Line 136

Hyperion to a satyr; so loving to my mother
That he might not beteem the winds of heaven
Visit her face too roughly.

Ibid. Line 140

Why, she would hang on him,
As if increase of appetite had grown
By what it fed on.

Ibid. Line 143

Frailty, thy name is woman!

Ibid. Line 146

Like Niobe, all tears.

Ibid. Line 149

A beast, that wants discourse of reason.

Ibid. Line 150

It is not nor it cannot come to good.

Ibid. Line 158

A truant disposition.

Ibid. Line 169

Thrift, thrift, Horatio! the funeral baked meats
Did coldly furnish forth the marriage tables.

Would I had met my dearest foe[1] in heaven
Ere I had seen that day.
> *Hamlet. Act I, Sc.* **2,** *Line 180*

In my mind's eye, Horatio.
> *Ibid. Line 185*

He was a man, take him for all in all,
I shall not look upon his like again.
> *Ibid. Line 187*

Season your admiration for a while.
> *Ibid. Line 192*

In the dead vast and middle of the night.
> *Ibid. Line 198*

Arm'd at points exactly, cap-a-pe.
> *Ibid. Line 200*

Distill'd
Almost to jelly with the act of fear.
> *Ibid. Line 204*

A countenance more in sorrow than in anger.
> *Ibid. Line 231*

While one with moderate haste might tell a hundred.
> *Ibid. Line 237*

Hamlet. His beard was grizzled, no?
Horatio. It was, as I have seen it in his life,
A sable silver'd.
> *Ibid. Line 239*

Give it an understanding, but no tongue.
> *Ibid. Line 249*

All is not well;
I doubt some foul play.
> *Ibid. Line 254*

Foul deeds will rise,
Though all the earth o'erwhelm them, to men's eyes.
> *Ibid. Line 256*

The chariest maid is prodigal enough
If she unmask her beauty to the moon:
Virtue itself 'scapes not calumnious strokes;
The canker galls the infants of the spring
Too oft before their buttons be disclosed,

---

[1] And dearest enemy. — THOMAS MIDDLETON [1570?–1627]: *Anything for a Quiet Life, Act V, Sc. 1*

And in the morn and liquid dew of youth
Contagious blastments are most imminent.
> *Hamlet. Act I, Sc. 3, Line 36*

Do not, as some ungracious pastors do,
Show me the steep and thorny way to heaven,
Whiles, like a puff'd and reckless libertine,
Himself the primrose path of dalliance treads,[1]
And recks not his own rede.[2]
> *Ibid. Line 47*

Give thy thoughts no tongue.
> *Ibid. Line 59*

Be thou familiar, but by no means vulgar;
Those friends thou hast, and their adoption tried,
Grapple them to thy soul with hoops of steel.
> *Ibid. Line 61*

Beware
Of entrance to a quarrel, but, being in,
Bear 't that the opposed may beware of thee.
Give every man thy ear, but few thy voice;
Take each man's censure, but reserve thy judgment.
Costly thy habit as thy purse can buy,
But not express'd in fancy; rich, not gaudy;[3]
For the apparel oft proclaims the man.
> *Ibid. Line 65*

Neither a borrower, nor a lender be;
For loan oft loses both itself and friend,
And borrowing dulls the edge of husbandry.
This above all: to thine own self be true,

---

[1] See *Macbeth*, page 196b.
[2] Wel oghte a preest ensample for to yive,
By his clennesse, how that his sheep shold live.
> CHAUCER: *Canterbury Tales* [*circa* 1387], *Prologue, L. 504*

And may you better reck the rede,
Than ever did the adviser.
> ROBERT BURNS [1759–1796]: *Epistle to a Young Friend*

[3] Neat, not gaudy. — CHARLES LAMB: *Letter to Wordsworth* [1806]

And it must follow, as the night the day,
Thou canst not then be false to any
man.
Hamlet. Act I, Sc. 3, Line 75

Springes to catch woodcocks.
Ibid. Line 115

When the blood burns, how prodigal the
soul
Lends the tongue vows.
Ibid. Line 116

Be somewhat scanter of your maiden
presence.
Ibid. Line 121

The air bites shrewdly.
Ibid. Sc. 4, Line 1

But to my mind, though I am native
here
And to the manner born, — it is a custom
More honoured in the breach than the
observance.
Ibid. Line 14

Angels and ministers of grace defend
us!
Ibid. Line 39

Be thy intents wicked or charitable,
Thou comest in such a questionable
shape
That I will speak to thee.
Ibid. Line 42

What may this mean,
That thou, dead corse, again in com-
plete steel
Revisit'st thus the glimpses of the
moon,
Making night hideous,[1] and we fools of
nature
So horridly to shake our disposition
With thoughts beyond the reaches of
our souls?
Ibid. Line 51

I do not set my life at a pin's fee.
Ibid. Line 65

My fate cries out,
And makes each petty artery in this
body
As hardy as the Nemean lion's nerve.
Ibid. Line 81

[1] And makes night hideous. — ALEXANDER
POPE: *The Dunciad, Book III* [1728], L. 166

Unhand me, gentlemen,
By heaven! I'll make a ghost of him
that lets me!
Hamlet. Act I, Sc. 4, Line 84

Something is rotten in the state of Denmark.
Ibid. Line 90

I could a tale unfold whose lightest
word
Would harrow up thy soul, freeze thy
young blood,
Make thy two eyes, like stars, start
from their spheres,
Thy knotted and combined locks to
part,
And each particular hair to stand an
end,
Like quills upon the fretful porpentine.
Ibid. Sc. 5, Line 15

And duller shouldst thou be than the fat
weed
That rots itself in ease on Lethe wharf.
Ibid. Line 32

O my prophetic soul!
My uncle!
Ibid. Line 40

O Hamlet, what a falling-off was there!
Ibid. Line 47

But, soft! methinks I scent the morning
air;
Brief let me be. Sleeping within my
orchard,
My custom always of the afternoon.
Ibid. Line 58

In the porches of mine ears.
Ibid. Line 63

Cut off even in the blossoms of my sin,
Unhousel'd, disappointed, unaneled,
No reckoning made, but sent to my ac-
count
With all my imperfections on my head.
Ibid. Line 76

Leave her to heaven
And to those thorns that in her bosom
lodge,
To prick and sting her.
Ibid. Line 86

The glow-worm shows the matin to be
near,
And 'gins to pale his uneffectual fire.
Ibid. Line 89

While memory holds a seat
In this distracted globe. Remember
thee!
Yea, from the table of my memory
I'll wipe away all trivial fond records.
    Hamlet. Act I, Sc. 5, Line 96

Within the book and volume of my
brain.
    Ibid. Line 103

O villain, villain, smiling, damned villain!
My tables, — meet it is I set it down,
That one may smile, and smile, and be
a villain;
At least I'm sure it may be so in Denmark.
    Ibid. Line 106

There are more things in heaven and
earth, Horatio,
Than are dreamt of in your philosophy.
    Ibid. Line 166

To put an antic disposition on.
    Ibid. Line 172

Rest, rest, perturbed spirit!
    Ibid. Line 182

The time is out of joint; O cursed spite,
That ever I was born to set it right!
    Ibid. Line 188

Your bait of falsehood takes this carp
of truth:
And thus do we of wisdom and of reach,
With windlasses and with assays of
bias,
By indirections find directions out.
    Ibid. Act II, Sc. 1, Line 63

Ungarter'd, and down-gyved to his
ankle.
    Ibid. Line 80

This is the very ecstasy of love;
Whose violent property fordoes itself,
And leads the will to desperate under-
takings,
As oft as any passion under heaven
That does afflict our natures.
    Ibid. Line 102

Brevity is the soul of wit.
    Ibid. Sc. 2, Line 90

More matter, with less art.
    Ibid. Line 95

That he is mad, 'tis true; 'tis true 'tis
pity;
And pity 'tis 'tis true.
    Hamlet. Act II, Sc. 2, Line 97

Find out the cause of this effect,
Or rather say, the cause of this defect,
For this effect defective comes by cause.
    Ibid. Line 101

Doubt thou the stars are fire;
Doubt that the sun doth move;
Doubt truth to be a liar;
But never doubt I love.
    Ibid. Line 115

To be honest, as this world goes, is
to be one man picked out of ten thousand.
    Ibid. Line 179

Still harping on my daughter.
    Ibid. Line 190

Polonius. What do you read, my
lord?
Hamlet. Words, words, words.
    Ibid. Line 195

They have a plentiful lack of wit.
    Ibid. Line 204

Though this be madness, yet there is
method in 't.
    Ibid. Line 211

These tedious old fools!
    Ibid. Line 227

There is nothing either good or bad,
but thinking makes it so.
    Ibid. Line 259

O God! I could be bounded in a nutshell, and count myself a king of infinite space, were it not that I have bad
dreams.
    Ibid. Line 263

This goodly frame, the earth, seems
to me a sterile promontory; this most
excellent canopy, the air, look you, this
brave o'erhanging firmament, this majestical roof fretted with golden fire,
why, it appears no other thing to me
than a foul and pestilent congregation
of vapours. What a piece of work is a
man! how noble in reason! how infinite
in faculty! in form and moving how
express and admirable! in action how
like an angel! in apprehension how like
a god!
    Ibid. Line 317

Man delights not me; no, nor woman neither.
>   *Hamlet. Act II, Sc. 2, Line 330*

There is something in this more than natural, if philosophy could find it out.
>   *Ibid. Line 392*

I am but mad north-north-west; when the wind is southerly, I know a hawk from a handsaw.
>   *Ibid. Line 405*

They say an old man is twice a child.
>   *Ibid. Line 413*

O Jephthah, judge of Israel, what a treasure hadst thou!
>   *Ibid. Line 431*

One fair daughter and no more,
The which he loved passing well.
>   *Ibid. Line 435*

Come, give us a taste of your quality.
>   *Ibid. Line 460*

The play, I remember, pleased not the million; 'twas caviare to the general.
>   *Ibid. Line 465*

They are the abstracts and brief chronicles of the time: after your death you were better have a bad epitaph than their ill report while you live.
>   *Ibid. Line 555*

Use every man after his desert, and who should 'scape whipping?
>   *Ibid. Line 561*

O, what a rogue and peasant slave am I!
>   *Ibid. Line 584*

What's Hecuba to him or he to Hecuba,
That he should weep for her?
>   *Ibid. Line 593*

But I am pigeon-livered, and lack gall
To make oppression bitter.
>   *Ibid. Line 613*

The play's the thing
Wherein I'll catch the conscience of the king.
>   *Ibid. Line 641*

With devotion's visage
And pious action we do sugar o'er
The devil himself.
>   *Ibid. Act III, Sc. 1, Line 47*

To be, or not to be: that is the question:

Whether 'tis nobler in the mind to suffer
The slings and arrows of outrageous fortune,
Or to take arms against a sea of troubles,
And by opposing end them? To die: to sleep:
No more; and by a sleep to say we end
The heartache and the thousand natural shocks
That flesh is heir to, 'tis a consummation
Devoutly to be wish'd. To die, to sleep;
To sleep: perchance to dream: ay, there's the rub:
For in that sleep of death what dreams may come,
When we have shuffled off this mortal coil,
Must give us pause. There's the respect
That makes calamity of so long life;
For who would bear the whips and scorns of time,
The oppressor's wrong, the proud man's contumely,
The pangs of dispriz'd love, the law's delay,
The insolence of office and the spurns
That patient merit of the unworthy takes,
When he himself might his quietus make
With a bare bodkin? who would fardels bear,
To grunt and sweat under a weary life,
But that the dread of something after death,
The undiscover'd country from whose bourn
No traveller returns, puzzles the will
And makes us rather bear those ills we have
Than fly to others that we know not of?
Thus conscience does make cowards of us all; [1]
And thus the native hue of resolution
Is sicklied o'er with the pale cast of thought,

----

[1] See Bidpai, page 28b.

And enterprises of great pith and moment
With this regard their currents turn awry,
And lose the name of action.
Hamlet. Act III, Sc. 1, Line 56
Nymph, in thy orisons
Be all my sins remember'd.
Ibid. Line 89
For, to the noble mind
Rich gifts wax poor when givers prove unkind.
Ibid. Line 100
What should such fellows as I do crawling between earth and heaven? We are arrant knaves, all.
Ibid. Line 128
Be thou as chaste as ice, as pure as snow, thou shalt not escape calumny. Get thee to a nunnery, go.
Ibid. Line 142
I have heard of your paintings too, well enough; God has given you one face, and you make yourselves another.
Ibid. Line 150
O! what a noble mind is here o'erthrown:
The courtier's, soldier's, scholar's eye, tongue, sword.
Ibid. Line 159
The glass of fashion and the mould of form,
The observed of all observers!
Ibid. Line 162
Now see that noble and most sovereign reason,
Like sweet bells jangled, out of tune and harsh.
Ibid. Line 166
O, woe is me,
To have seen what I have seen, see what I see!
Ibid. Line 169
Speak the speech, I pray you, as I pronounced it to you, trippingly on the tongue; but if you mouth it, as many of your players do, I had as lief the town-crier spoke my lines. Nor do not saw the air too much with your hand, thus; but use all gently: for in the very torrent, tempest, and as I may say the whirlwind of passion, you must

acquire and beget a temperance, that may give it smoothness. Oh, it offends me to the soul to hear a robustious periwig-pated fellow tear a passion to tatters, to very rags, to split the ears of the groundlings, who for the most part are capable of nothing but inexplicable dumb-shows and noise. I would have such a fellow whipped for o'erdoing Termagant; it out-herods Herod.
Hamlet. Act III, Sc. 2, Line 1
Suit the action to the word, the word to the action; with this special observance, that you o'erstep not the modesty of nature.
Ibid. Line 20
To hold, as 'twere, the mirror up to nature; to show virtue her own feature, scorn her own image, and the very age and body of the time his form and pressure.
Ibid. Line 25
Though it make the unskilful laugh, cannot but make the judicious grieve.
Ibid. Line 29
Not to speak it profanely.
Ibid. Line 35
I have thought some of Nature's journeymen had made men and not made them well, they imitated humanity so abominably.
Ibid. Line 38
No; let the candied tongue lick absurd pomp,
And crook the pregnant hinges of the knee
Where thrift may follow fawning.
Ibid. Line 65
A man that fortune's buffets and rewards
Hast ta'en with equal thanks.
Ibid. Line 72
They are not a pipe for fortune's finger
To sound what stop she please. Give me that man
That is not passion's slave, and I will wear him
In my heart's core, ay, in my heart of heart,
As I do thee. Something too much of this.
Ibid. Line 75

And my imaginations are as foul
As Vulcan's stithy.

Hamlet. Act III, Sc. 2, Line 88

Nay, then, let the devil wear black,
for I'll have a suit of sables.

Ibid. Line 138

There's hope a great man's memory
may outlive his life half a year.

Ibid. Line 141

This is miching mallecho; it means
mischief.

Ibid. Line 149

Where love is great, the littlest doubts
are fear;
When little fears grow great, great love
grows there.

Ibid. Line 183

What to ourselves in passion we propose,
The passion ending, doth the purpose
lose.

Ibid. Line 206

The lady doth protest too much, methinks.

Ibid. Line 242

Let the galled jade wince, our withers
are unwrung.

Ibid. Line 256

Why, let the stricken deer go weep,[1]
The hart ungalled play;
For some must watch, while some must
sleep:
So runs the world away.

Ibid. Line 287

You would pluck out the heart of my
mystery.

Ibid. Line 389

Do you think I am easier to be played
on than a pipe?

Ibid. Line 393

Hamlet. Do you see yonder cloud
that's almost in shape of a camel?
Polonius. By the mass, and 'tis like
a camel, indeed.
Hamlet. Methinks it is like a weasel.
Polonius. It is backed like a weasel.
Hamlet. Or like a whale?
Polonius. Very like a whale.

Ibid. Line 400

[1] I was a stricken deer. — WILLIAM COW-
PER: *The Task* [1785], *Book III*

They fool me to the top of my bent.

Hamlet. Act III, Sc. 2, Line 408

By and by is easily said.

Ibid. Line 411

'Tis now the very witching time of
night,
When churchyards yawn and hell itself
breathes out
Contagion to this world.

Ibid. Line 413

I will speak daggers to her, but use
none.

Ibid. Line 421

O! my offence is rank, it smells to
heaven;
It hath the primal eldest curse upon 't,
A brother's murder.

Ibid. Sc. 3, Line 36

Now might I do it pat, now he is praying;
And now I'll do't: — and so he goes to
heaven;
And so I am revenged.

Ibid. Line 73

With all his crimes broad blown, as
flush as May.

Ibid. Line 81

My words fly up, my thoughts remain
below:
Words without thoughts never to
heaven go.

Ibid. Line 97

Dead, for a ducat, dead!

Ibid. Sc. 4, Line 23

And let me wring your heart; for so I
shall,
If it be made of penetrable stuff.

Ibid. Line 35

False as dicers' oaths.

Ibid. Line 45

A rhapsody of words.

Ibid. Line 48

See, what a grace was seated on this
brow;
Hyperion's curls; the front of Jove him-
self;
An eye like Mars, to threaten and com-
mand,
A station like the herald Mercury
New-lighted on a heaven-kissing hill,
A combination and a form indeed,

Where every god did seem to set his
seal,
To give the world assurance of a man.
Hamlet. Act III, Sc. 4, Line 55
At your age
The hey-day in the blood is tame, it's
humble.
Ibid. Line 68

O shame! where is thy blush? Rebel-
lious hell,
If thou canst mutine in a matron's
bones,
To flaming youth let virtue be as wax,
And melt in her own fire: proclaim no
shame
When the compulsive ardour gives the
charge,
Since frost itself as actively doth burn,
And reason panders will.
Ibid. Line 82

A king of shreds and patches.[1]
Ibid. Line 102

How is 't with you,
That you do bend your eye on vacancy?
Ibid. Line 115

Lay not that flattering unction to your
soul.
Ibid. Line 145

Confess yourself to heaven;
Repent what's past; avoid what is to
come.
Ibid. Line 149

For in the fatness of these pursy times
Virtue itself of vice must pardon beg.
Ibid. Line 153

Assume a virtue, if you have it not.
Ibid. Line 160

Refrain to-night,
And that shall lend a kind of easiness
To the next abstinence: the next more
easy;
For use almost can change the stamp
of nature.
Ibid. Line 165

I must be cruel, only to be kind.
Ibid. Line 178

[1] A wandering minstrel I —
A thing of shreds and patches.
W. S. GILBERT: *The Mikado*
[1885], *Act 1*

For 'tis the sport to have the enginer
Hoist with his own petar.
Hamlet. Act III, Sc. 4, Line 206
Diseases desperate grown
By desperate appliance are relieved,
Or not at all.[1]
Ibid. Act IV, Sc. 3, Line 9
A man may fish with the worm that
hath eat of a king, and eat of the fish
that hath fed of that worm.
Ibid. Line 29
We go to gain a little patch of ground,
That hath in it no profit but the name.
Ibid. Sc. 4, Line 18
How all occasions do inform against me,
And spur my dull revenge! What is a
man,
If his chief good and market of his
time
Be but to sleep and feed? a beast, no
more.[2]
Sure, he that made us with such large
discourse,
Looking before and after, gave us not
That capability and godlike reason
To fust in us unused.
Ibid. Line 32
Some craven scruple
Of thinking too precisely on th' event.
Ibid. Line 36
Rightly to be great
Is not to stir without great argument
But greatly to find quarrel in a straw
When honour's at the stake.
Ibid. Line 53
So full of artless jealousy is guilt,
It spills itself in fearing to be spilt.
Ibid. Sc. 5, Line 19
How should I your true love know
From another one?
By his cockle hat and staff,
And his sandal shoon.
Ibid. Line 23
He is dead and gone, lady,
He is dead and gone;
At his head a grass-green turf,
At his heels a stone.
Ibid. Line 29

[1] See Hippocrates, page 22a.
[2] The unmotived herd that only sleep and
feed. — JAMES RUSSELL LOWELL [1819–
1891]: *Under the Old Elm, Part VII, St. 3*

We know what we are, but know not what we may be.

Hamlet. Act IV, Sc. 5, Line 43

Come, my coach! Good night, sweet ladies; good night.

Ibid. Line 72

When sorrows come, they come not single spies,
But in battalions.

Ibid. Line 78

There's such divinity doth hedge a king,
That treason can but peep to what it would.

Ibid. Line 123

There's rosemary, that's for remembrance; . . . and there is pansies, that's for thoughts.[1]

Ibid. Line 174

You must wear your rue with a difference. There's a daisy; I would give you some violets, but they withered all when my father died.

Ibid. Line 181

A very riband in the cap of youth.

Ibid. Sc. 7, Line 77

One woe doth tread upon another's heel,
So fast they follow.[2]

Ibid. Line 164

Nature her custom holds,
Let shame say what it will.

Ibid. Line 188

There is no ancient gentlemen but gardeners, ditchers, and grave-makers; they hold up Adam's profession.[3]

Ibid. Act V, Sc. 1, Line 32

Cudgel thy brains no more about it.

Ibid. Line 61

---

[1] See Chapman, page 116b.
[2] Thus woe succeeds a woe, as wave a wave. — HERRICK: *Sorrows Succeed* [1648]
Woes cluster; rare are solitary woes;
They love a train, they tread each other's heel.
EDWARD YOUNG: *Night Thoughts* [1742–1745], *Night III, L. 63*
[3] See Francis Bacon, page 121a.
Oh, Adam was a gardener, and God who made him sees
That half a proper gardener's work is done upon his knees.
RUDYARD KIPLING [1865–1936]: *The Glory of the Garden, St. 8*

Has this fellow no feeling of his business, that he sings at grave-making?

Hamlet. Act V, Sc. 1, Line 71

Custom hath made it in him a property of easiness.

Ibid. Line 73

But age, with his stealing steps,
Hath claw'd me in his clutch.

Ibid. Line 77

A politician, . . . one that would circumvent God.

Ibid. Line 84

Why may not that be the skull of a lawyer? Where be his quiddities now, his quillets, his cases, his tenures, and his tricks?

Ibid. Line 104

One that was a woman, sir; but, rest her soul, she's dead.

Ibid. Line 145

How absolute the knave is! we must speak by the card, or equivocation will undo us.

Ibid. Line 147

The age is grown so picked that the toe of the peasant comes so near the heel of the courtier, he galls his kibe.

Ibid. Line 150

Alas, poor Yorick! I knew him, Horatio: a fellow of infinite jest, of most excellent fancy; he hath borne me on his back a thousand times; and now, how abhorred in my imagination it is! my gorge rises at it. Here hung those lips that I have kissed I know not how oft. Where be your gibes now? your gambols? your songs? your flashes of merriment, that were wont to set the table on a roar? Not one now, to mock your own grinning? quite chap-fallen? Now get you to my lady's chamber, and tell her, let her paint an inch thick, to this favour she must come; make her laugh at that.

Ibid. Line 201

To what base uses we may return, Horatio! Why may not imagination trace the noble dust of Alexander, till he find it stopping a bung-hole?

Ibid. Line 222

'Twere to consider too curiously, to consider so.
Hamlet. Act V, Sc. 1, Line 226
Imperious Caesar, dead and turn'd to clay,
Might stop a hole to keep the wind away.
Ibid. Line 235
Lay her i' the earth;
And from her fair and unpolluted flesh
May violets spring! [1]
Ibid. Line 260
A ministering angel shall my sister be. [2]
Ibid. Line 263
Sweets to the sweet: farewell!
Ibid. Line 265
I thought thy bride-bed to have deck'd, sweet maid,
And not have strew'd thy grave.
Ibid. Line 267
Though I am not splenetive and rash,
Yet have I in me something dangerous.
Ibid. Line 283
Forty thousand brothers
Could not, with all their quantity of love,
Make up my sum.
Ibid. Line 291
Nay, an thou'lt mouth,
I'll rant as well as thou.
Ibid. Line 305
Let Hercules himself do what he may,
The cat will mew and dog will have his day.
Ibid. Line 313
There's a divinity that shapes our ends,
Rough-hew them how we will.
Ibid. Sc. 2, Line 10
I once did hold it, as our statists do,
A baseness to write fair.
Ibid. Line 33
It did me yeoman's service.
Ibid. Line 36
Popp'd in between the election and my hopes.
Ibid. Line 65

[1] And from his ashes may be made
The violet of his native land.
TENNYSON: *In Memoriam* [1850], XVIII

See *Rubaiyat,* page 531b.
[2] See Sir Walter Scott, page 414b.

The bravery of his grief did put me
Into a towering passion.
Hamlet. Act V, Sc. 2, Line 79
'Tis the breathing time of day with me.
Ibid. Line 181
The most fond and winnowed opinions.
Ibid. Line 201
There's a special providence in the fall of a sparrow.[1] If it be now, 'tis not to come; if it be not to come, it will be now; if it be not now, yet it will come: the readiness is all. Since no man has aught of what he leaves, what is 't to leave betimes?
Ibid. Line 232
A hit, a very palpable hit.
Ibid. Line 295
This fell sergeant, death,
Is strict in his arrest.
Ibid. Line 350
Report me and my cause aright.
Ibid. Line 353
I am more an antique Roman than a Dane.
Ibid. Line 355
Horatio, what a wounded name,
Things standing thus unknown, shall live behind me.
If thou didst ever hold me in thy heart,
Absent thee from felicity awhile,
And in this harsh world draw thy breath in pain,
To tell my story.
Ibid. Line 358
The rest is silence.
Ibid. Line 372
Now cracks a noble heart. Good-night, sweet prince,
And flights of angels sing thee to thy rest!
Ibid. Line 373
O proud death! [2]
What feast is toward in thine eternal cell?
Ibid. Line 378

[1] See Alexander Pope, page 316a.
[2] See Donne, page 217b.

I will make a Star-chamber matter of it.

The Merry Wives of Windsor [*1600–1601*]. *Act I, Sc. 1, Line 2*

All his successors gone before him have done 't; and all his ancestors that come after him may.

Ibid. Line 14

Seven hundred pounds and possibilities is goot gifts.

Ibid. Line 65

I had rather than forty shillings I had my Book of Songs and Sonnets here.

Ibid. Line 205

If there be no great love in the beginning, yet heaven may decrease it upon better acquaintance, when we are married and have more occasion to know one another: I hope, upon familiarity will grow more contempt.[1]

Ibid. Line 255

"Convey," the wise it call. "Steal!" foh! a fico for the phrase!

Ibid. Sc. 3, Line 30

I am almost out at heels.

Ibid. Line 32

Thou art the Mars of malcontents.

Ibid. Line 111

Here will be an old abusing of God's patience and the king's English.

Ibid. Sc. 4, Line 5

Dispense with trifles.

Ibid. Act II, Sc. 1, Line 47

There's the humour of it.

Ibid. Line 139

Faith, thou hast some crotchets in thy head now.

Ibid. Line 158

Why, then the world's mine oyster, Which I with sword will open.

Ibid. Sc. 2, Line 2

This is the short and the long of it.

Ibid. Line 62

Unless experience be a jewel.

Ibid. Line 216

Like a fair house built on another man's ground.

Ibid. Line 229

[1] See Aesop, page 10a.

Better three hours too soon than a minute too late.

The Merry Wives of Windsor. Act II, Sc. 2, Line 332

We have some salt of our youth in us; we are the sons of women.

Ibid. Sc. 3, Line 50

I cannot tell what the dickens his name is.

Ibid. Act III, Sc. 2, Line 20

He capers, he dances, he has eyes of youth, he writes verses, he speaks holiday, he smells April and May.

Ibid. Line 71

O, what a world of vile ill-favour'd faults
Looks handsome in three hundred pounds a year!

Ibid. Sc. 4, Line 32

A woman would run through fire and water for such a kind heart.

Ibid. Line 106

If I be served such another trick, I'll have my brains ta'en out, and buttered, and give them to a dog for a new year's gift.

Ibid. Sc. 5, Line 7

I have a kind of alacrity in sinking.

Ibid. Line 13

As good luck would have it.[1]

Ibid. Line 86

The rankest compound of villanous smell that ever offended nostril.

Ibid. Line 95

A man of my kidney.

Ibid. Line 119

So curses all Eve's daughters, of what complexion soever.

Ibid. Act IV, Sc. 2, Line 24

Wives may be merry, and yet honest too.

Ibid. Line 110

This is the third time; I hope good luck lies in odd numbers. . . . There is divinity in odd numbers, either in nativity, chance, or death.[2]

Ibid. Act V, Sc. 1, Line 2

Life is a shuttle.

Ibid. Line 25

[1] As ill luck would have it. — CERVANTES: *Don Quixote, Part I* [1605], *Book I, Chap. II*
[2] See Pliny, page 50b.

Better a little chiding than a great deal of heartbreak.

> *The Merry Wives of Windsor.*
> *Act V, Sc. 3, Line 10*

I have had my labour for my travail.[1]

> *Troilus and Cressida* [*1601–1603*].
> *Act I, Sc. 1, Line 73*

Men prize the thing ungain'd more than it is.

> *Ibid. Sc. 2, Line 313*

The sea being smooth
How many shallow bauble boats dare sail
Upon her patient breast.[2]

> *Ibid. Sc. 3, Line 34*

The heavens themselves, the planets, and this centre,
Observe degree, priority, and place,
Insisture, course, proportion, season, form,
Office, and custom, in all line of order.

> *Ibid. Line 85*

O! when degree is shak'd,
Which is the ladder to all high designs,
The enterprise is sick.[3]

> *Ibid. Line 101*

Take but degree away, untune that string,
And, hark! what discord follows; each thing meets
In mere oppugnancy: the bounded waters
Should lift their bosoms higher than the shores
And make a sop of all this solid globe.

> *Ibid. Line 109*

Then everything includes itself in power,
Power into will, will into appetite;
And appetite, an universal wolf,
So doubly seconded with will and power,
Must make perforce a universal prey,
And last eat up himself.

> *Ibid. Line 119*

Like a strutting player, whose conceit
Lies in his hamstring, and doth think it rich
To hear the wooden dialogue and sound

'Twixt his stretch'd footing and the scaffoldage.

> *Troilus and Cressida. Act I, Sc. 3,*
> *Line 153*

And in such indexes, although small pricks
To their subsequent volumes, there is seen
The baby figure of the giant mass
Of things to come.

> *Ibid. Line 343*

Mongrel beef-witted lord.

> *Ibid. Act II, Sc. 1, Line 14*

Who wears his wit in his belly, and his guts in his head.

> *Ibid. Line 78*

Modest doubt is call'd
The beacon of the wise, the tent that searches
To the bottom of the worst.

> *Ibid. Sc. 2, Line 15*

'Tis mad idolatry
To make the service greater than the god.

> *Ibid. Line 56*

The remainder viands
We do not throw in unrespective sink
Because we now are full.

> *Ibid. Line 70*

The elephant hath joints, but none for courtesy: his legs are legs for necessity, not for flexure.

> *Ibid. Sc. 3, Line 114*

He that is proud eats up himself; pride is his own glass, his own trumpet, his own chronicle.

> *Ibid. Line 165*

Light boats sail swift, though greater hulks draw deep.

> *Ibid. Line 280*

I am giddy, expectation whirls me round.
The imaginary relish is so sweet
That it enchants my sense.

> *Ibid. Act III, Sc. 2, Line 17*

Words pay no debts.

> *Ibid. Line 56*

To fear the worst oft cures the worse.

> *Ibid. Line 77*

All lovers swear more performance than they are able, and yet reserve an ability that they never perform; vow-

---

[1] See Cervantes, page 103b.
[2] See Publilius Syrus, page 44b.
[3] See Publilius Syrus, page 46b.

ing more than the perfection of ten, and discharging less than the tenth part of one.

Troilus and Cressida. Act III, Sc. 2, Line 89

For to be wise, and love,
Exceeds man's might; that dwells with gods above.

Ibid. Line 163

Time hath, my lord, a wallet at his back,
Wherein he puts alms for oblivion.

Ibid. Sc. 3, Line 145

Perseverance, dear my lord,
Keeps honour bright: to have done, is to hang
Quite out of fashion, like a rusty mail
In monumental mockery.

Ibid. Line 150

For honour travels in a strait so narrow
Where one but goes abreast.

Ibid. Line 154

Time is like a fashionable host
That slightly shakes his parting guest by the hand,
And with his arms outstretch'd, as he would fly
Grasps in the comer: welcome ever smiles,
And farewell goes out sighing.

Ibid. Line 168

Beauty, wit,
High birth, vigour of bone, desert in service,
Love, friendship, charity, are subjects all
To envious and calumniating time.
One touch of nature makes the whole world kin.

Ibid. Line 171

And give to dust that is a little gilt
More laud than gilt o'er-dusted.

Ibid. Line 178

And, like a dew-drop from the lion's mane,
Be shook to air.

Ibid. Line 225

My mind is troubled, like a fountain stirr'd;
And I myself see not the bottom of it.

Ibid. Line 314

Be moderate, be moderate.

Troilus and Cressida. Act IV, Sc. 4, Line 1

As many farewells as be stars in heaven.

Ibid. Line 44

Sometimes we are devils to ourselves
When we will tempt the frailty of our powers,
Presuming on their changeful potency.

Ibid. Line 95

The kiss you take is better than you give.

Ibid. Sc. 5, Line 38

Fie, fie upon her!
There's language in her eye, her cheek, her lip,
Nay, her foot speaks; her wanton spirits look out
At every joint and motive of her body.

Ibid. Line 54

Daughters of the game.

Ibid. Line 63

What's past, and what's to come, is strew'd with husks
And formless ruin of oblivion.

Ibid. Line 165

The end crowns all,
And that old common arbitrator, Time,
Will one day end it.

Ibid. Line 223

He has not so much brain as ear-wax.

Ibid. Act V, Sc. 1, Line 58

Words, words, mere words, no matter from the heart.

Ibid. Sc. 3, Line 109

O world! world! world! thus is the poor agent despised.

Ibid. Sc. 10, Line 36

Love all, trust a few,
Do wrong to none: be able for thine enemy
Rather in power than use, and keep thy friend
Under thine own life's key: be check'd for silence,
But never tax'd for speech.

All's Well that Ends Well [1601–1603]. Act I, Sc. 1, Line 74

It were all one
That I should love a bright particular star

And think to wed it.
All's Well that Ends Well.
Act I, Sc. 1, Line 97

The hind that would be mated by the
lion
Must die for love.
Ibid. Line 103

Our remedies oft in ourselves do lie,
Which we ascribe to Heaven.
Ibid. Line 235

Service is no heritage.
Ibid. Sc. 3, Line 25

My friends were poor, but honest.
Ibid. Line 203

Great floods have flown
From simple sources.
Ibid. Act II, Sc. 1, Line 142

Oft expectation fails, and most oft
there
Where most it promises.
Ibid Line 145

I will show myself highly fed and
lowly taught.
Ibid. Sc. 2, Line 3

They say miracles are past.
Ibid. Sc. 3, Line 1

From lowest place when virtuous things
proceed,
The place is dignified by the doer's
deed.
Ibid. Line 132

A young man married is a man that's
marr'd.
Ibid. Line 315

Make the coming hour o'erflow with
joy,
And pleasure drown the brim.
Ibid. Sc. 4, Line 48

No legacy is so rich as honesty.
Ibid. Act III, Sc. 5, Line 13

The web of our life is of a mingled
yarn, good and ill together.
Ibid. Act IV, Sc. 3, Line 83

I am a man whom Fortune hath
cruelly scratched.
Ibid. Act V, Sc. 2, Line 28

Whose words all ears took captive.
Ibid. Sc. 3, Line 17

Praising what is lost
Makes the remembrance dear.
Ibid. Line 19

The inaudible and noiseless foot of
Time.[1]
All's Well that Ends Well.
Act V, Sc. 3, Line 41

Love that comes too late,
Like a remorseful pardon slowly carried.
Ibid. Line 57

All impediments in fancy's course
Are motives of more fancy.
Ibid. Line 216

The bitter past, more welcome is the
sweet.
Ibid. Line 339

Spirits are not finely touch'd
But to fine issues.
Measure for Measure [1604–
1605]. *Act I, Sc. 1, Line 35*

He was ever precise in promise-keep-
ing.
Ibid. Sc. 2, Line 80

Good counsellors lack no clients.
Ibid. Line 115

And liberty plucks justice by the nose.
Ibid. Sc. 3, Line 29

Who may, in the ambush of my name,
strike home.
Ibid. Line 41

I hold you as a thing ensky'd and
sainted.
Ibid. Sc. 4, Line 34

A man whose blood
Is very snow-broth; one who never feels
The wanton stings and motions of the
sense.
Ibid. Line 57

He arrests him on it;
And follows close the rigour of the
statute,
To make him an example.
Ibid. Line 66

Our doubts are traitors,
And make us lose the good we oft might
win
By fearing to attempt.
Ibid. Line 78

We must not make a scarecrow of the
law,
Setting it up to fear the birds of prey,

[1] How noiseless falls the foot of time! —
W. R. SPENCER [1769–1834]: *Lines to Lady
A. Hamilton*

And let it keep one shape, till custom
make it
Their perch, and not their terror.
Measure for Measure. Act II,
Sc. 1, Line 1

The jury, passing on the prisoner's life,
May in the sworn twelve have a thief
or two
Guiltier than him they try.
Ibid. Line 19

Some rise by sin, and some by virtue
fall.
Ibid. Line 38

Great with child, and longing for
stewed prunes.
Ibid. Line 94

They are not China dishes, but very
good dishes.
Ibid. Line 100

This will last out a night in Russia,
When nights are longest there.
Ibid. Line 144

His face is the worst thing about him.
Ibid. Line 167

Condemn the fault, and not the actor
of it?
Ibid. Sc. 2, Line 37

No ceremony that to great ones 'longs,
Not the king's crown, nor the deputed
sword,
The marshal's truncheon, nor the
judge's robe,
Become them with one half so good a
grace
As mercy does.[1]
Ibid. Line 59

Why, all the souls that were, were for-
feit once;
And He that might the vantage best
have took
Found out the remedy. How would you
be,
If He, which is the top of judgment,
should
But judge you as you are?
Ibid. Line 73

The law hath not been dead, though it
hath slept.
Ibid. Line 90

[1] See *Merchant of Venice*, page 146a.

O, it is excellent
To have a giant's strength; but it is
tyrannous
To use it like a giant.
Measure for Measure. Act II,
Sc. 2, Line 107

But man, proud man,
Drest in a little brief authority,
Most ignorant of what he's most as-
sured,
His glassy essence, like an angry ape,
Plays such fantastic tricks before high
heaven
As make the angels weep.
Ibid. Line 117

That in the captain's but a choleric
word
Which in the soldier is flat blasphemy.
Ibid. Line 130

It oft falls out,
To have what we would have, we speak
not what we mean.
Ibid. Sc. 4, Line 118

The miserable have no other medicine,
But only hope.
Ibid. Act III, Sc. 1, Line 2

A breath thou art,
Servile to all the skyey influences.
Ibid. Line 8

Thou hast nor youth nor age;
But, as it were, an after-dinner's sleep,
Dreaming on both; for all thy blessed
youth
Becomes as aged, and doth beg the alms
Of palsied eld; and when thou art old
and rich,
Thou hast neither heat, affection, limb,
nor beauty,
To make thy riches pleasant. What's
yet in this
That bears the name of life? Yet in this
life
Lie hid moe thousand deaths; yet
death we fear,
That makes these odds all even.
Ibid. Line 32

The sense of death is most in apprehension; [1]
And the poor beetle, that we tread upon,

[1] See Publilius Syrus, page 45a.

In corporal sufferance finds a pang as great
As when a giant dies.
Measure for Measure. Act III,
Sc. 1, Line 76

The cunning livery of hell.
Ibid. Line 93

Ay, but to die, and go we know not where;
To lie in cold obstruction and to rot;
This sensible warm motion to become
A kneaded clod; and the delighted spirit
To bathe in fiery floods, or to reside
In thrilling region of thick-ribbed ice;
To be imprison'd in the viewless winds,
And blown with restless violence round about
The pendent world.
Ibid. Line 116

The weariest and most loathed worldly life
That age, ache, penury, and imprisonment
Can lay on nature, is a paradise
To what we fear of death.
Ibid. Line 127

I have no superfluous leisure.
Ibid. Line 156

The hand that hath made you fair hath made you good.[1]
Ibid. Line 182

Virtue is bold, and goodness never fearful.
Ibid. Line 214

There, at the moated grange, resides this dejected Mariana.[2]
Ibid. Line 279

Pygmalion's images, newly made woman.
Ibid. Sc. 2, Line 48

This news is old enough, yet it is every day's news.
Ibid. Line 249

He who the sword of heaven will bear
Should be as holy as severe.
Ibid. Line 283

[1] See Spenser, page 115a.
[2] "Mariana in the moated grange." — The motto used by TENNYSON for the poem *Mariana* [1830].

O, what may man within him hide,
Though angel on the outward side!
Measure for Measure. Act III,
Sc. 2, Line 293

Take, O take those lips away,
That so sweetly were forsworn;
And those eyes, the break of day,
Lights that do mislead the morn:
But my kisses bring again, bring again;
Seals of love, but sealed in vain, sealed in vain.[1]
Ibid. Act IV, Sc. 1, Line 1

Every true man's apparel fits your thief.
Ibid. Sc. 2, Line 46

Death's a great disguiser.
Ibid. Line 185

We would, and we would not.
Ibid. Sc. 4, Line 37

A forted residence 'gainst the tooth of time
And razure of oblivion.
Ibid. Act V, Sc. 1, Line 12

Truth is truth
To the end of reckoning.
Ibid. Line 45

Neither maid, widow, nor wife.
Ibid. Line 173

They say best men are moulded out of faults,
And, for the most, become much more the better
For being a little bad.
Ibid. Line 440

What's mine is yours, and what is yours is mine.[2]
Ibid. Line 539

The bookish theoric.
Othello [1604–1605]. Act I,
Sc. 1, Line 24

We cannot all be masters.
Ibid. Line 43

[1] This song occurs in *Act V, Sc. 2* of FLETCHER's *Bloody Brother* [circa 1616], with the following additional stanza:
   Hide, O hide those hills of snow,
      Which thy frozen bosom bears,
   On whose tops the pinks that grow
      Are of those that April wears!
   But first set my poor heart free,
   Bound in those icy chains by thee.
[2] See Plautus, page 29b.

I will wear my heart upon my sleeve
For daws to peck at.
> *Othello. Act I, Sc. 1, Line 64*

Trust not your daughters' minds
By what you see them act.
> *Ibid. Line 171*

Keep up your bright swords, for the dew will rust them.
> *Ibid. Sc. 2, Line 58*

The wealthy curled darlings of our nation.
> *Ibid. Line 68*

Most potent, grave, and reverend signiors,
My very noble and approv'd good masters.
That I have ta'en away this old man's daughter,
It is most true; true, I have married her:
The very head and front of my offending
Hath this extent, no more. Rude am I in my speech,
And little bless'd with the soft phrase of peace.
> *Ibid. Sc. 3, Line 76*

Little shall I grace my cause
In speaking for myself. Yet, by your gracious patience,
I will a round unvarnish'd tale deliver
Of my whole course of love.
> *Ibid. Line 88*

A maiden never bold;
Of spirit so still and quiet, that her motion
Blush'd at herself.
> *Ibid. Line 94*

Still question'd me the story of my life
From year to year, the battles, sieges, fortunes
That I have passed.
> *Ibid. Line 129*

Wherein I spake of most disastrous chances,
Of moving accidents by flood and field,
Of hair-breadth 'scapes i' the imminent deadly breach.
> *Ibid. Line 134*

Hills whose heads touch heaven.
> *Ibid. Line 141*

And of the Cannibals that each other eat,
The Anthropophagi, and men whose heads
Do grow beneath their shoulders.
> *Othello. Act I, Sc. 3, Line 143*

My story being done,
She gave me for my pains a world of sighs:
She swore, in faith, 'twas strange, 'twas passing strange,
'Twas pitiful, 'twas wondrous pitiful:
She wish'd she had not heard it, yet she wish'd
That Heaven had made her such a man; she thank'd me,
And bade me, if I had a friend that loved her,
I should but teach him how to tell my story,
And that would woo her. Upon this hint I spake:
She loved me for the dangers I had pass'd,
And I loved her that she did pity them.
This only is the witchcraft I have used.
> *Ibid. Line 158*

I do perceive here a divided duty.
> *Ibid. Line 181*

To mourn a mischief that is past and gone
Is the next way to draw new mischief on.
> *Ibid. Line 204*

The robb'd that smiles, steals something from the thief.
> *Ibid. Line 208*

But words are words; I never yet did hear
That the bruis'd heart was pierced through the ear.
> *Ibid. Line 218*

Our bodies are our gardens, to the which our wills are gardeners; . . . either to have it sterile with idleness or manured with industry.
> *Ibid. Line 324*

Put money in thy purse.
> *Ibid. Line 345*

The food that to him now is as lus-

cious as locusts, shall be to him shortly
as bitter as coloquintida.
Othello. Act I, Sc. 3, Line 354
Framed to make women false.
Ibid. Line 404
One that excels the quirks of blazoning
pens.
Ibid. Act II, Sc. 1, Line 63
You are pictures out of doors,
Bells in your parlours, wild-cats in your
kitchens,
Saints in your injuries, devils being
offended,
Players in your housewifery, and house-
wives in your beds.
Ibid. Line 109
For I am nothing if not critical.
Ibid. Line 119
I am not merry; but I do beguile
The thing I am, by seeming otherwise.
Ibid. Line 122
She that was ever fair and never proud,
Had tongue at will and yet was never
loud.
Ibid. Line 148
Iago. She that could think and ne'er
disclose her mind,
See suitors following and not look be-
hind,
She was a wight, if ever such wight
were, —
Desdemona. To do what?
Iago. To suckle fools and chronicle
small beer.[1]
Desdemona. O most lame and impotent
conclusion!
Ibid. Line 158
You may relish him more in the
soldier than in the scholar.
Ibid. Line 165
If it were now to die,
'Twere now to be most happy.
Ibid. Line 192
Base men being in love have then a
nobility in their natures more than is
native to them.
Ibid. Line 218
Egregiously an ass.
Ibid. Line 321

[1] See *King Henry VI,* page 125b.

I have very poor and unhappy brains
for drinking.
Othello. Act II, Sc. 3, Line 34
Potations pottle-deep.
Ibid. Line 57
King Stephen was a worthy peer,
His breeches cost him but a crown;
He held them sixpence all too dear,
With that he called the tailor lown.[1]
Ibid. Line 93
'Tis pride that pulls the country down.
Ibid. Line 99
Well, God's above all; and there be
souls must be saved, and there be souls
must not be saved.
Ibid. Line 106
Silence that dreadful bell! it frights the
isle
From her propriety.
Ibid. Line 177
Your name is great
In mouths of wisest censure.
Ibid. Line 194
But men are men; the best sometimes
forget.
Ibid. Line 243
Thy honesty and love doth mince this
matter.[2]
Ibid. Line 249
Reputation, reputation, reputation!
Oh! I have lost my reputation. I have
lost the immortal part of myself, and
what remains is bestial.
Ibid. Line 264
Reputation is an idle and most false
imposition; oft got without merit, and
lost without deserving.
Ibid. Line 270
O thou invisible spirit of wine! if
thou hast no name to be known by, let
us call thee devil!
Ibid. Line 285
O God! that men should put an
enemy in their mouths to steal away
their brains; that we should with joy,

[1] These lines are from an old ballad, *Take
Thy Old Cloak About Thee.* See page ooo.
[2] Mince the matter. — CERVANTES: *Don
Quixote* [1605], *Author's Preface*
You mince matters. — MOLIÈRE: *Tartuffe*
[1664], *Act I, Sc. 1*

pleasance, revel, and applause, transform ourselves into beasts.

Othello. Act II, Sc. 3, Line 293

Good wine is a good familiar creature if it be well used.

Ibid. Line 315

How poor are they that have not patience!

Ibid. Line 379

Excellent wretch! Perdition catch my soul,
But I do love thee! and when I love thee not,
Chaos is come again.[1]

Ibid. Act III, Sc. 3, Line 90

Men should be what they seem.

Ibid. Line 126

Speak to me as to thy thinkings,
As thou dost ruminate, and give thy worst of thoughts
The worst of words.

Ibid. Line 131

Good name in man and woman, dear my lord,
Is the immediate jewel of their souls:
Who steals my purse steals trash; 'tis something, nothing;
'Twas mine, 'tis his, and has been slave to thousands;
But he that filches from me my good name
Robs me of that which not enriches him,
And makes me poor indeed.

Ibid. Line 155

O! beware, my lord, of jealousy;
It is the green-eyed monster which doth mock
The meat it feeds on: that cuckold lives in bliss
Who, certain of his fate, loves not his wronger;
But, O! what damned minutes tells he o'er
Who dotes, yet doubts; suspects, yet soundly loves!

Ibid. Line 165

Poor and content is rich, and rich enough.

Ibid. Line 172

[1] See *Venus and Adonis,* page 131a.

Think'st thou I'd make a life of jealousy,
To follow still the changes of the moon
With fresh suspicions? No; to be once in doubt
Is once to be resolved.

Othello. Act III, Sc. 3, Line 177

I humbly do beseech you of your pardon
For too much loving you.

Ibid. Line 212

If I do prove her haggard,
Though that her jesses were my dear heart-strings,
I'd whistle her off and let her down the wind,
To prey at fortune.

Ibid. Line 260

I am declined
Into the vale of years.

Ibid. Line 265

O curse of marriage!
That we can call these delicate creatures ours,
And not their appetites. I had rather be a toad,
And live upon the vapour of a dungeon,
Than keep a corner in the thing I love
For others' uses.

Ibid. Line 268

Trifles light as air
Are to the jealous confirmations strong
As proofs of holy writ.

Ibid. Line 323

Not poppy, nor mandragora,[1]
Nor all the drowsy syrups of the world,
Shall ever medicine thee to that sweet sleep
Which thou ow'dst yesterday.

Ibid. Line 331

I swear 'tis better to be much abused
Than but to know 't a little.

Ibid. Line 337

He that is robb'd, not wanting what is stolen,
Let him not know 't and he's not robb'd at all.[2]

Ibid. Line 343

O! now, for ever
Farewell the tranquil mind; farewell content!

[1] See *Antony and Cleopatra,* page 200a.
[2] See Publilius Syrus, page 43a.

Farewell the plumed troop and the big wars
That make ambition virtue! O, farewell!
Farewell the neighing steed, and the shrill trump,
The spirit-stirring drum, the ear-piercing fife,
The royal banner, and all quality,
Pride, pomp, and circumstance of glorious war!
And, O you mortal engines, whose rude throats
The immortal Jove's dread clamours counterfeit,
Farewell! Othello's occupation's gone!
Othello. Act III, Sc. 3, Line 348
Be sure of it; give me the ocular proof.
Ibid. Line 361
No hinge nor loop
To hang a doubt on.
Ibid. Line 366
On horror's head horrors accumulate.
Ibid. Line 371
Take note, take note, O world!
To be direct and honest is not safe.
Ibid. Line 378
But this denoted a foregone conclusion.
Ibid. Line 429
Swell, bosom, with thy fraught,
For 'tis of aspics' tongues!
Ibid. Line 450
Like to the Pontick sea,
Whose icy current and compulsive course
Ne'er feels retiring ebb, but keeps due on
To the Propontic and the Hellespont,
Even so my bloody thoughts, with violent pace,
Shall ne'er look back, ne'er ebb to humble love,
Till that a capable and wide revenge
Swallow them up.
Ibid. Line 454
Our new heraldry is hands, not hearts.
Ibid. Sc. 4, Line 48
'Tis the strumpet's plague
To beguile many, and be beguil'd by one.
Ibid. Act IV, Sc. 1, Line 97

They laugh that win.
Othello. Act IV, Sc. 1, Line 123
My heart is turn'd to stone; I strike it, and it hurts my hand. — O, the world hath not a sweeter creature: she might lie by an emperor's side, and command him tasks.
Ibid. Line 190
O, she will sing the savageness out of a bear!
Ibid. Line 198
But yet the pity of it, Iago! O! Iago, the pity of it, Iago!
Ibid. Line 205
Is this the nature
Whom passion could not shake? whose solid virtue
The shot of accident, nor dart of chance,
Could neither graze nor pierce?
Ibid. Line 277
I understand a fury in your words,
But not the words.
Ibid. Sc. 2, Line 31
Steep'd me in poverty to the very lips.
Ibid. Line 49
But, alas! to make me
A fixed figure for the time of scorn
To point his slow and moving finger at!
Ibid. Line 52
Patience, thou young and rose-lipp'd cherubin.
Ibid. Line 62
O thou weed!
Who art so lovely fair and smell'st so sweet
That the sense aches at thee, would thou hadst ne'er been born.
Ibid. Line 66
O Heaven! that such companions thou'dst unfold,
And put in every honest hand a whip
To lash the rascals naked through the world.
Ibid. Line 141
Unkindness may do much:
And his unkindness may defeat my life,
But never taint my love.
Ibid. Line 159
The poor soul sat sighing by a sycamore tree,
Sing all a green willow;

Her hand on her bosom, her head on her
    knee
Sing willow, willow, willow.
       Othello. Act IV, Sc. 3, Line 41
It makes us, or it mars us.
       Ibid. Act V, Sc. 1, Line 4
Every way makes my gain.
       Ibid. Line 14
He hath a daily beauty in his life.
       Ibid. Line 19
    This is the night
That either makes me or fordoes me
    quite.
       Ibid. Line 128
And smooth as monumental alabaster.
       Ibid. Sc. 2, Line 5
Put out the light, and then put out the
    light:
If I quench thee, thou flaming minister,
I can again thy former light restore
Should I repent me; but once put out
    thy light,
Thou cunning'st pattern of excelling
    nature,
I know not where is that Promethean
    heat
That can thy light relume.
       Ibid. Line 7
It is the very error of the moon;
She comes more near the earth than she
    was wont,
And makes men mad.
       Ibid. Line 107
Curse his better angel from his side,
And fall to reprobation.
       Ibid. Line 206
Here is my journey's end, here is my
    butt,
And very sea-mark of my utmost sail.
       Ibid. Line 268
An honourable murderer, if you will;
For naught I did in hate, but all in
    honour.
       Ibid. Line 295
I have done the state some service, and
    they know 't;
No more of that. I pray you, in your
    letters,
When you shall these unlucky deeds
    relate,
Speak of me as I am; nothing exten-
    uate,

Nor set down aught in malice: then,
    must you speak
Of one that loved not wisely but too
    well;
Of one not easily jealous, but, being
    wrought,
Perplex'd in the extreme; of one whose
    hand,
Like the base Indian, threw a pearl
    away
Richer than all his tribe; of one whose
    subdued eyes
Albeit unused to the melting mood,
Drop tears as fast as the Arabian trees
Their med'cinable gum.
       Othello. Act V, Sc. 2, Line 338
I took by the throat the circumcised
    dog,
And smote him thus.
       Ibid. Line 354
    My love's
More richer than my tongue.
       King Lear [1605–1606]. Act I,
       Sc. 1, Line 79
    Now, our joy,
Although our last, not least.
       Ibid. Line 84
Nothing will come of nothing.
       Ibid. Line 92
    Mend your speech a little,
Lest you may mar your fortunes.
       Ibid. Line 96
    I want that glib and oily art,
To speak and purpose not.
       Ibid. Line 227
A still-soliciting eye, and such a tongue
That I am glad I have not.
       Ibid. Line 234
Who in the lusty stealth of nature take
More composition and fierce quality
Than doth, within a dull, stale, tired
    bed,
Go to the creating a whole tribe of fops.
       Ibid. Sc. 2, Line 11
    We have seen the best of our time:
machinations, hollowness, treachery,
and all ruinous disorders, follow us
disquietly to our graves.
       Ibid. Line 125
    This is the excellent foppery of the
world, that, when we are sick in fortune, — often the surfeit of our own

behaviour, — we make guilty of our disasters the sun, the moon, and the stars: as if we were villains by necessity; fools by heavenly compulsion.

King Lear. Act I, Sc. 2, Line 129

That which ordinary men are fit for, I am qualified in; and the best of me is diligence.

Ibid. Sc. 4, Line 36

Truth's a dog must to kennel; he must be whipt out, when Lady the brach may stand by the fire and stink.

Ibid. Line 125

Have more than thou showest,
Speak less than thou knowest,
Lend less than thou owest.

Ibid. Line 133

Ingratitude, thou marble-hearted fiend!
More hideous, when thou show'st thee in a child,
Than the sea-monster.

Ibid. Line 283

How sharper than a serpent's tooth it is
To have a thankless child!

Ibid. Line 312

Striving to better, oft we mar what's well.

Ibid. Line 371

The son and heir of a mongrel bitch.

Ibid. Act II, Sc. 2, Line 23

I have seen better faces in my time
Than stands on any shoulder that I see
Before me at this instant.

Ibid. Line 99

A good man's fortune may grow out at heels.

Ibid. Line 158

Fortune, good night, smile once more; turn thy wheel.

Ibid. Line 180

Hysterica passio! down, thou climbing sorrow!
Thy element's below.

Ibid. Sc. 4, Line 57

That sir which serves and seeks for gain,
And follows but for form,
Will pack when it begins to rain,
And leave thee in the storm.

Ibid. Line 79

Nature in you stands on the very verge
Of her confine.

King Lear. Act II, Sc. 4, Line 149

Necessity's sharp pinch!

Ibid. Line 214

Our basest beggars
Are in the poorest thing superfluous:
Allow not nature more than nature needs,
Man's life is cheap as beast's.

Ibid. Line 276

Let not women's weapons, waterdrops,
Stain my man's cheeks!

Ibid. Line 280

I have full cause of weeping; but this heart
Shall break into a hundred thousand flaws,
Or e'er I'll weep. — O fool, I shall go mad!

Ibid. Line 287

Blow, winds, and crack your cheeks! rage! blow!

Ibid. Act III, Sc. 2, Line 1

I tax not you, you elements, with unkindness.

Ibid. Line 16

A poor, infirm, weak, and despised old man.

Ibid. Line 20

There was never yet fair woman but she made mouths in a glass.

Ibid. Line 35

I will be the pattern of all patience.

Ibid. Line 37

I am a man
More sinn'd against than sinning.

Ibid. Line 59

The art of our necessities is strange,
That can make vile things precious.

Ibid. Line 72

He that has and a little tiny wit, —
With hey, ho, the wind and the rain, —
Must make content with his fortunes fit,
Though the rain it raineth every day.[1]

Ibid. Line 76

Oh! that way madness lies; let me shun that.

Ibid. Sc. 4, Line 21

[1] See *Twelfth-Night*, page 166a.

Poor naked wretches, wheresoe'er you are,
That bide the pelting of this pitiless storm,
How shall your houseless heads and unfed sides,
Your looped and windowed raggedness, defend you
From seasons such as these?
King Lear. Act III, Sc. 4, Line 28
Take physic, pomp;
Expose thyself to feel what wretches feel,
That thou mayst shake the superflux to them,
And show the heavens more just.
Ibid. Line 33
Out-paramoured the Turk.
Ibid. Line 91
Is man no more than this? Consider him well. Thou owest the worm no silk, the beast no hide, the sheep no wool, the cat no perfume. — Ha! here's three on's are sophisticated! — Thou art the thing itself: unaccommodated man is no more but such a poor, bare forkt animal as thou art. — Off, off, you lendings! — Come, unbutton here.
Ibid. Line 105
'Tis a naughty night to swim in.
Ibid. Line 113
The green mantle of the standing pool.
Ibid. Line 137
But mice and rats and such small deer
Have been Tom's food for seven long year.
Ibid. Line 142
The prince of darkness is a gentleman.[1]
Ibid. Line 147
Poor Tom's a-cold.
Ibid. Line 151
Child Rowland to the dark tower came.[2]

[1] The Devil is a gentleman. — SHELLEY: *Peter Bell the Third* [1819], Part II, St. 2
[2] Child Roland to the dark tower came. — SIR WALTER SCOTT: *The Bridal of Triermain* [1813]
Dauntless the slug-horn to my lips I set,
And blew. "*Childe Roland to the Dark Tower came.*"
BROWNING: *Childe Roland to the Dark Tower Came* [1855], St. 34

His word was still, Fie, foh, and fum,
I smell the blood of a British man.
King Lear. Act III, Sc. 4, Line 185
He's mad that trusts in the tameness of a wolf, a horse's health, a boy's love, or a whore's oath.
Ibid. Sc. 6, Line 18
The little dogs and all,
Tray, Blanch, and Sweetheart, see, they bark at me.
Ibid. Line 65
Is there any cause in nature that makes these hard hearts?
Ibid. Line 80
I am tied to the stake, and I must stand the course.
Ibid. Sc. 7, Line 54
Out, vile jelly!
Ibid. Line 83
The lowest and most dejected thing of fortune.
Ibid. Act IV, Sc. 1, Line 3
The worst is not
So long as we can say, "This is the worst."
Ibid. Line 27
As flies to wanton boys, are we to the gods;
They kill us for their sport.
Ibid. Line 36
Sunshine and rain at once; her smiles and tears.
Ibid. Sc. 3, Line 20
It is the stars,
The stars above us, govern our conditions.
Ibid. Line 34
Our foster-nurse of nature is repose.
Ibid. Sc. 4, Line 12
In nothing am I chang'd
But in my garments.
Ibid. Sc. 6, Line 9
Come on, sir; here's the place: — stand still. —
How fearful
And dizzy 'tis to cast one's eyes so low!
The crows and choughs that wing the midway air
Show scarce so gross as beetles: half way down
Hangs one that gathers samphire, dreadful trade!

Methinks he seems no bigger than his head:
The fishermen that walk upon the beach
Appear like mice.
King Lear. Act IV, Sc. 6, Line 11
Nature's above art in that respect.
Ibid. Line 87
Ay, every inch a king.
Ibid. Line 110
The wren goes to't, and the small gilded fly
Does lecher in my sight.
Ibid. Line 115
Give me an ounce of civet, good apothecary, to sweeten my imagination.
Ibid. Line 133
A man may see how this world goes with no eyes. Look with thine ears: see how yond justice rails upon yon simple thief. Hark, in thine ear: change places; and, handy-dandy, which is the justice, which is the thief?
Ibid. Line 154
Through tatter'd clothes small vices do appear;
Robes and furr'd gowns hide all. Plate sin with gold,
And the strong lance of justice hurtless breaks;
Arm it in rags, a pigmy's straw does pierce it.
Ibid. Line 169
When we are born, we cry that we are come
To this great stage of fools. — This' a good block: —
It were a delicate stratagem to shoe
A troop of horse with felt: I'll put't in proof;
And when I have stol'n upon these sons-in-law,
Then, kill, kill, kill, kill, kill, kill!
Ibid. Line 187
Mine enemy's dog,
Though he had bit me, should have stood that night
Against my fire.
Ibid. Sc. 7, Line 36
I am a very foolish, fond old man,
Fourscore and upward, not an hour more or less;
And, to deal plainly,

I fear I am not in my perfect mind.
King Lear. Act IV, Sc. 7, Line 60
Pray you now, forget and forgive.
Ibid. Line 84
Men must endure
Their going hence, even as their coming hither.
Ripeness is all.
Ibid. Act V, Sc. 2, Line 9
Come, let's away to prison;
We two alone will sing like birds i' the cage:
When thou dost ask me blessing, I'll kneel down,
And ask of thee forgiveness: and we'll live,
And pray, and sing, and tell old tales and laugh
At gilded butterflies, and hear poor rogues
Talk of court news; and we'll talk with them too,
Who loses, and who wins; who's in, who's out;
And take upon's the mystery of things,
As if we were God's spies; and we'll wear out,
In a wall'd prison, packs and sets of great ones
That ebb and flow by the moon.
Ibid. Sc. 3, Line 8
Upon such sacrifices, my Cordelia,
The gods themselves throw incense.
Ibid. Line 20
The gods are just, and of our pleasant vices
Make instruments to plague us.
Ibid. Line 172
The wheel is come full circle.
Ibid. Line 176
His flaw'd heart, —
Alack! too weak the conflict to support;
'Twixt two extremes of passion, joy and grief,
Burst smilingly.
Ibid. Line 198
Her voice was ever soft,
Gentle, and low, an excellent thing in woman.
Ibid. Line 274
And my poor fool is hang'd! No, no, no life!

Why should a dog, a horse, a rat, have
    life,
And thou no breath at all? Thou'lt come
    no more,
Never, never, never, never, never!
Pray you, undo this button.
            King Lear. Act V, Sc. 3, Line 307
Vex not his ghost: O! let him pass! he
    hates him
That would upon the rack of this tough
    world
Stretch him out longer.
                        Ibid. Line 315
The weight of this sad time we must
    obey;
Speak what we feel, not what we ought
    to say.
The oldest hath borne most: we that
    are young
Shall never see so much, nor live so
    long.
                        Ibid. Line 325
First Witch. When shall we three meet
    again
In thunder, lightning, or in rain?
Second Witch. When the hurlyburly's
    done,
When the battle's lost and won.
        *Macbeth [1605–1606]. Act I,
                        Sc. 1, Line 1*
Fair is foul, and foul is fair:
Hover through the fog and filthy air.
                        Ibid. Line 12
Banners flout the sky.
                Ibid. Sc. 2, Line 50
A sailor's wife had chestnuts in her lap,
And munch'd, and munch'd, and
    munch'd: "Give me," quoth I:
"Aroint thee, witch!" the rump-fed
    ronyon cries.
                Ibid. Sc. 3, Line 4
Sleep shall neither night nor day
Hang upon his pent-house lid.
                        Ibid. Line 19
Dwindle, peak, and pine.
                        Ibid. Line 23
If you can look into the seeds of time,
And say which grain will grow and
    which will not.
                        Ibid. Line 58

Stands not within the prospect of be-
    lief.
        Macbeth. Act I, Sc. 3, Line 74
The earth hath bubbles, as the water
    has,
And these are of them.
                        Ibid. Line 79
    The insane root
That takes the reason prisoner.
                        Ibid. Line 84
And oftentimes, to win us to our harm,
The instruments of darkness tell us
    truths,
Win us with honest trifles, to betray 's
In deepest consequence.
                        Ibid. Line 123
    I am Thane of Cawdor:
If good, why do I yield to that sug-
    gestion
Whose horrid image doth unfix my hair
And make my seated heart knock at my
    ribs,
Against the use of nature? Present fears
Are less than horrible imaginings.
                        Ibid. Line 134
    Come what come may,
Time and the hour runs through the
    roughest day.
                        Ibid. Line 146
    Nothing in his life
Became him like the leaving it; he died
As one that had been studied in his
    death
To throw away the dearest thing he
    owed,
As 'twere a careless trifle.
                Ibid. Sc. 4, Line 7
    There's no art
To find the mind's construction in the
    face:
He was a gentleman on whom I built
An absolute trust.
                        Ibid. Line 11
More is thy due than more than all can
    pay.
                        Ibid. Line 21
Glamis thou art, and Cawdor; and shalt
    be
What thou art promis'd. Yet do I fear
    thy nature;

It is too full o' the milk of human kindness [1]
To catch the nearest way.
> *Macbeth. Act I, Sc. 5, Line 16*

The raven himself is hoarse
That croaks the fatal entrance of Dun-
can
Under my battlements. Come, you
spirits
That tend on mortal thoughts! unsex
me here,
And fill me from the crown to the toe
top full
Of direst cruelty; make thick my blood,
Stop up the access and passage to re-
morse,
That no compunctious visitings of na-
ture
Shake my fell purpose.
> *Ibid. Line 38*

Nor heaven peep through the blanket
of the dark,
To cry "Hold, hold!"
> *Ibid. Line 53*

Your face, my thane, is as a book where
men
May read strange matters. To beguile
the time,
Look like the time; bear welcome in
your eye,
Your hand, your tongue: look like the
innocent flower,
But be the serpent under 't.
> *Ibid. Line 63*

Duncan. This castle hath a pleasant
seat; the air
Nimbly and sweetly recommends itself
Unto our gentle senses.
Banquo.   This guest of summer,
The temple-haunting martlet, does ap-
prove
By his lov'd mansionry that the heav-
en's breath
Smells wooingly here: no jutty, frieze,
Buttress, nor coign of vantage, but this
bird
Hath made his pendent bed and procre-
ant cradle:

---

[1] The thunder of your words has soured
the milk of human kindness in my heart. —
RICHARD BRINSLEY SHERIDAN: *The Rivals*
[1775], *Act III, Sc. 4*

Where they most breed and haunt, I
have observed
The air is delicate.
> *Macbeth. Act I, Sc. 6, Line 1*

If it were done when 'tis done, then
'twere well
It were done quickly; if the assassina-
tion
Could trammel up the consequence,
and catch
With his surcease success; that but this
blow
Might be the be-all and the end-all here,
But here, upon this bank and shoal of
time,
We'd jump the life to come. But in
these cases
We still have judgment here; that we
but teach
Bloody instructions, which, being
taught, return
To plague the inventor; this even-
handed justice
Commends the ingredients of our poi-
son'd chalice
To our own lips.
> *Ibid. Sc. 7, Line 1*

Besides, this Duncan
Hath borne his faculties so meek, hath
been
So clear in his great office, that his vir-
tues
Will plead like angels, trumpet-tongued
against
The deep damnation of his taking-off;
And pity, like a naked new-born babe,
Striding the blast, or heaven's cheru-
bim, horsed
Upon the sightless couriers of the air,
Shall blow the horrid deed in every eye,
That tears shall drown the wind. I have
no spur
To prick the sides of my intent, but only
Vaulting ambition, which o'erleaps it-
self
And falls on the other.
> *Ibid. Line 16*

I have bought
Golden opinions from all sorts of people.
> *Ibid. Line 32*

Letting "I dare not" wait upon "I would,"
Like the poor cat i' the adage.[1]
>> *Macbeth. Act I, Sc. 7, Line 44*

I dare do all that may become a man;
Who dares do more is none.
>> *Ibid. Line 46*

Nor time nor place
Did then adhere.
>> *Ibid. Line 51*

Macbeth. If we should fail, —
Lady Macbeth.   We fail!
But screw your courage to the sticking-place,
And we'll not fail.
>> *Ibid. Line 59*

Memory, the warder of the brain.
>> *Ibid. Line 65*

There's husbandry in heaven;
Their candles are all out.
>> *Ibid. Act II, Sc. 1, Line 4*

Shut up
In measureless content.
>> *Ibid. Line 16*

Is this a dagger which I see before me,
The handle toward my hand? Come, let me clutch thee:
I have thee not, and yet I see thee still.
Art thou not, fatal vision, sensible
To feeling as to sight? or art thou but
A dagger of the mind, a false creation,
Proceeding from the heat-oppressed brain?
>> *Ibid. Line 33*

Now o'er the one half-world
Nature seems dead.
>> *Ibid. Line 49*

Thou sure and firm-set earth,
Hear not my steps, which way they walk, for fear
Thy very stones prate of my where-about.
>> *Ibid. Line 56*

The bell invites me.
Hear it not, Duncan; for it is a knell
That summons thee to heaven or to hell.
>> *Ibid. Line 62*

It was the owl that shriek'd, the fatal bellman,
Which gives the stern'st good-night.
>> *Ibid. Sc. 2, Line 4*

[1] See John Heywood, page 93a.

The attempt and not the deed
Confounds us.
>> *Macbeth. Act II, Sc. 2, Line 12*

Had he not resembled
My father as he slept I had done 't.
>> *Ibid. Line 14*

I had most need of blessing, and "Amen"
Stuck in my throat.
>> *Ibid. Line 33*

Methought I heard a voice cry, "Sleep no more!
Macbeth does murder sleep!" the innocent sleep,
Sleep that knits up the ravell'd sleave of care,
The death of each day's life, sore labour's bath,
Balm of hurt minds, great nature's second course,
Chief nourisher in life's feast.
>> *Ibid. Line 36*

"Glamis hath murder'd sleep, and therefore Cawdor
Shall sleep no more, Macbeth shall sleep no more!"
>> *Ibid. Line 43*

Infirm of purpose!
Give me the daggers. The sleeping and the dead
Are but as pictures; 'tis the eye of childhood
That fears a painted devil.
>> *Ibid. Line 52*

Will all great Neptune's ocean wash this blood
Clean from my hand? No, this my hand will rather
The multitudinous seas incarnadine,
Making the green one red.
>> *Ibid. Line 61*

Go the primrose way to the everlasting bonfire.
>> *Ibid. Sc. 3, Line 22*

It [drink] provokes the desire, but it takes away the performance.
>> *Ibid. Line 34*

The labour we delight in physics pain.
>> *Ibid. Line 56*

Tongue nor heart
Cannot conceive nor name thee!
>> *Ibid. Line 70*

Confusion now hath made his master-
piece!
Most sacrilegious murder hath broke
ope
The Lord's anointed temple, and stole
thence
The life o' the building!
      Macbeth. Act II, Sc. 3, Line 72
Downy sleep, death's counterfeit.
      Ibid. Line 83
Had I but died an hour before this
chance,
I had liv'd a blessed time; for, from
this instant,
There's nothing serious in mortality,
All is but toys; renown and grace is
dead.
The wine of life is drawn, and the mere
lees
Is left this vault to brag of.
      Ibid. Line 98
Who can be wise, amazed, temperate
and furious,
Loyal and neutral, in a moment?
      Ibid. Line 115
In the great hand of God I stand, and
thence
Against the undivulg'd pretence I fight
Of treasonous malice.
      Ibid. Line 137
To show an unfelt sorrow is an office
Which the false man does easy.
      Ibid. Line 143
A falcon, towering in her pride of place,
Was by a mousing owl hawk'd at and
kill'd.
      Ibid. Sc. 4, Line 12
I must become a borrower of the night
For a dark hour or twain.
      Ibid. Act III, Sc. 1, Line 27
Let every man be master of his time
Till seven at night.
      Ibid. Line 41
Murderer.   We are men, my liege.
Macbeth. Ay, in the catalogue ye go
for men.
      Ibid. Line 91
      I am one, my liege,
Whom the vile blows and buffets of the
world
Have so incensed that I am reckless
what

I do to spite the world.
      Macbeth. Act III, Sc. 1, Line 108
So weary with disasters, tugg'd with for-
tune,
That I would set my life on any chance,
To mend it or be rid on 't.
      Ibid. Line 112
      Things without all remedy
Should be without regard; what's done
is done.
      Ibid. Sc. 2, Line 11
We have scotch'd the snake, not kill'd
it.
      Ibid. Line 13
      Duncan is in his grave;
After life's fitful fever he sleeps well;
Treason has done his worst: nor steel,
nor poison,
Malice domestic, foreign levy, nothing
Can touch him further.
      Ibid. Line 22
      Come, seeling night,
Scarf up the tender eye of pitiful day,
And with thy bloody and invisible hand,
Cancel and tear to pieces that great
bond
Which keeps me pale! Light thickens,
and the crow
Makes wing to the rooky wood.
      Ibid. Line 45
Now spurs the lated traveller apace
To gain the timely inn.
      Ibid. Sc. 3, Line 6
But now I am cabin'd, cribb'd, confined,
bound in
To saucy doubts and fears.
      Ibid. Sc. 4, Line 24
Now, good digestion wait on appetite,
And health on both!
      Ibid. Line 38
Thou canst not say I did it; never shake
Thy gory locks at me.
      Ibid. Line 50
The air-drawn dagger.
      Ibid. Line 62
I drink to the general joy of the whole
table.
      Ibid. Line 89
Thou hast no speculation in those eyes
Which thou dost glare with!
      Ibid. Line 95

A thing of custom: 'tis no other;
Only it spoils the pleasure of the time.
　　Macbeth. Act III, Sc. 4, Line 97
　　What man dare, I dare:
Approach thou like the rugged Russian
　　bear,
The arm'd rhinoceros, or the Hyrcan
　　tiger,
Take any shape but that, and my firm
　　nerves
Shall never tremble.
　　　　　　Ibid. Line 99
　　Hence, horrible shadow!
Unreal mockery, hence!
　　　　　　Ibid. Line 106
Stand not upon the order of your going,
But go at once.
　　　　　　Ibid. Line 119
Macbeth.　　What is the night?
Lady Macbeth. Almost at odds with
　　morning, which is which.
　　　　　　Ibid. Line 126
　　I am in blood
Stepp'd in so far, that, should I wade
　　no more,
Returning were as tedious as go o'er.
　　　　　　Ibid. Line 136
　　My little spirit, see,
Sits in a foggy cloud, and stays for me.
　　　　　　Ibid. Sc. 5, Line 35
Double, double toil and trouble;
Fire burn and cauldron bubble.
　　　　Ibid. Act IV, Sc. 1, Line 10
Eye of newt, and toe of frog,
Wool of bat, and tongue of dog.
　　　　　　Ibid. Line 14
Finger of birth-strangled babe,
Ditch-deliver'd by a drab.
　　　　　　Ibid. Line 30
By the pricking of my thumbs,
Something wicked this way comes.
　　Open, locks,
　　Whoever knocks!
　　　　　　Ibid. Line 44
How now, you secret, black, and mid-
　　night hags!
　　　　　　Ibid. Line 48
A deed without a name.
　　　　　　Ibid. Line 49
Be bloody, bold, and resolute; laugh to
　scorn

The power of man, for none of woman
　born
Shall harm Macbeth.
　　　　Macbeth. Act IV, Sc. 1, Line 79
　　I'll make assurance double sure,
And take a bond of fate.
　　　　　　Ibid. Line 83
Macbeth shall never vanquish'd be un-
　til
Great Birnam wood to high Dunsinane
　hill
Shall come against him.[1]
　　　　　　Ibid. Line 92
Show his eyes, and grieve his heart;
Come like shadows, so depart!
　　　　　　Ibid. Line 110
What! will the line stretch out to the
　crack of doom?
　　　　　　Ibid. Line 117
The weird sisters.
　　　　　　Ibid. Line 136
　　When our actions do not,
Our fears do make us traitors.
　　　　　　Ibid. Sc. 2, Line 3
Things at the worst will cease, or else
　climb upward
To what they were before.
　　　　　　Ibid. Line 24
Angels are bright still, though the
　brightest fell.
　　　　　　Ibid. Sc. 3, Line 22
Pour the sweet milk of concord into
　hell,
Uproar the universal peace, confound
All unity on earth.
　　　　　　Ibid. Line 98
Give sorrow words; the grief that does
　not speak
Whispers the o'er-fraught heart and
　bids it break.
　　　　　　Ibid. Line 209
What! all my pretty chickens and their
　dam
At one fell swoop?
　　　　　　Ibid. Line 218
O! I could play the woman with mine
　eyes
And braggart with my tongue.
　　　　　　Ibid. Line 229

[1] Till Birnam wood remove to Dunsinane,
　I cannot taint with fear.
　　　　　　Act V, Sc. 3, L. 2

Out, damned spot! out, I say!
> *Macbeth. Act V, Sc. 1, Line 38*

Fie, my lord, fie! a soldier, and afeard?
> *Ibid. Line 40*

Yet who would have thought the old man to have had so much blood in him?
> *Ibid. Line 42*

The Thane of Fife had a wife: where is she now?
> *Ibid. Line 46*

All the perfumes of Arabia will not sweeten this little hand.
> *Ibid. Line 56*

Those he commands move only in command,
Nothing in love; now does he feel his title
Hang loose about him, like a giant's robe
Upon a dwarfish thief.
> *Ibid. Sc. 2, Line 19*

The devil damn thee black, thou cream-faced loon!
Where gott'st thou that goose look?
> *Ibid. Sc. 3, Line 11*

My way of life
Is fall'n into the sere, the yellow leaf;
And that which should accompany old age,
As honour, love, obedience, troops of friends,
I must not look to have; but in their stead,
Curses, not loud but deep; mouth-honour, breath,
Which the poor heart would fain deny, and dare not.
> *Ibid. Line 22*

Doctor. Not so sick, my lord,
As she is troubled with thick-coming fancies,
That keep her from her rest.
Macbeth. Cure her of that:
Canst thou not minister to a mind diseas'd,
Pluck from the memory a rooted sorrow,
Raze out the written troubles of the brain,
And with some sweet oblivious antidote

Cleanse the stuff'd bosom of that perilous stuff
Which weighs upon the heart?
Doctor.   Therein the patient
Must minister to himself.
Macbeth. Throw physic to the dogs: I'll none of it.
> *Macbeth. Act V, Sc. 3, Line 37*

I would applaud thee to the very echo,
That should applaud again.
> *Ibid. Line 53*

Hang out our banners on the outward walls;
The cry is still, "They come"; our castle's strength
Will laugh a siege to scorn.
> *Ibid. Sc. 5, Line 1*

My fell of hair
Would at a dismal treatise rouse and stir
As life were in 't. I have supp'd full with horrors.
> *Ibid. Line 11*

Tomorrow, and tomorrow, and tomorrow,
Creeps in this petty pace from day to day,
To the last syllable of recorded time;
And all our yesterdays have lighted fools
The way to dusty death. Out, out, brief candle!
Life's but a walking shadow, a poor player
That struts and frets his hour upon the stage
And then is heard no more: it is a tale
Told by an idiot, full of sound and fury,
Signifying nothing.
> *Ibid. Line 19*

I 'gin to be aweary of the sun.
> *Ibid. Line 49*

Blow, wind! come, wrack!
At least we'll die with harness on our back.
> *Ibid. Line 51*

I bear a charmed life.
> *Ibid. Sc. 7, Line 41*

And be these juggling fiends no more believ'd,
That palter with us in a double sense;

That keep the word of promise to our
 ear
And break it to our hope.
>> *Macbeth. Act V, Sc. 7, Line 48*

Live to be the show and gaze o' the time.
>> *Ibid. Line 53*

Lay on, Macduff,
And damn'd be him that first cries,
"Hold, enough!"
>> *Ibid. Line 62*

You shall see in him
The triple pillar of the world trans-
form'd
Into a strumpet's fool.
>> *Antony and Cleopatra* [*1606–*
>> *1607*]. *Act I, Sc. 1, Line 12*

There's beggary in the love that can
be reckon'd.
>> *Ibid. Line 15*

Let Rome in Tiber melt, and the wide
arch
Of the rang'd empire fall! Here is my
space.
>> *Ibid. Line 33*

In nature's infinite book of secrecy
A little I can read.
>> *Ibid. Sc. 2, Line 11*

On the sudden
A Roman thought hath struck him.
>> *Ibid. Line 90*

Eternity was in our lips and eyes,
Bliss in our brows bent.
>> *Ibid. Sc. 3, Line 35*

O! my oblivion is a very Antony,
And I am all forgotten.
>> *Ibid. Line 90*

Give me to drink mandragora.[1] . . .
That I might sleep out this great gap
of time
My Antony is away.
>> *Ibid. Sc. 5, Line 4*

The demi-Atlas of this earth, the arm
And burgonet of men.
>> *Ibid. Line 23*

"Where's my serpent of old Nile?"
>> *Ibid. Line 25*

A morsel for a monarch.
>> *Ibid. Line 31*

My salad days,
When I was green in judgment.
>> *Ibid. Line 73*

[1] See *Othello*, page 188b.

We, ignorant of ourselves,
Beg often our own harms, which the
 wise powers
Deny us for our good; so find we profit
By losing of our prayers.
>> *Antony and Cleopatra. Act II,*
>> *Sc. 1, Line 5*

Epicurean cooks
Sharpen with cloyless sauce his appetite.
>> *Ibid. Line 24*

You patch'd up your excuses.
>> *Ibid. Sc. 2, Line 60*

The barge she sat in, like a burnish'd
throne,
Burn'd on the water; the poop was
beaten gold,
Purple the sails, and so perfumed that
The winds were love-sick with them;
the oars were silver,
Which to the tune of flutes kept stroke,
and made
The water which they beat to follow
faster,
As amorous of their strokes. For her
own person,
It beggar'd all description.
>> *Ibid. Line 199*

Age cannot wither her, nor custom stale
Her infinite variety; other women cloy
The appetites they feed, but she makes
hungry
Where most she satisfies; for vilest
things
Become themselves in her, that the holy
priests
Bless her when she is riggish.
>> *Ibid. Line 243*

I have not kept my square; but that to
come
Shall all be done by the rule.
>> *Ibid. Sc. 3, Line 6*

'Twas merry when
You wager'd on your angling; when
your diver
Did hang a salt-fish on his hook, which
he
With fervency drew up.
>> *Ibid. Sc. 5, Line 15*

Though it be honest, it is never good
To bring bad news.
>> *Ibid. Line 85*

Come, thou monarch of the vine,
Plumpy Bacchus with pink eyne!
> *Antony and Cleopatra. Act II,*
> *Sc. 7, Line 120*

Who does i' the wars more than his
captain can
Becomes his captain's captain.
> *Ibid. Act III, Sc. 1, Line 21*

Celerity is never more admir'd
Than by the negligent.
> *Ibid. Sc. 7, Line 7*

We have kiss'd away
Kingdoms and provinces.
> *Ibid. Sc. 8, Line 7*

He wears the rose
Of youth upon him.
> *Ibid. Sc. 13, Line 20*

Men's judgments are
A parcel of their fortunes, and things
outward
Do draw the inward quality after them,
To suffer all alike.
> *Ibid. Line 31*

Let's have one other gaudy night.
> *Ibid. Line 182*

To business that we love we rise be-
time,
And go to 't with delight.
> *Ibid. Act IV, Sc. 4, Line 20*

This morning, like the spirit of a youth
That means to be of note, begins betimes.
> *Ibid. Line 26*

O infinite virtue! com'st thou smiling
from
The world's great snare uncaught?
> *Ibid. Sc. 8, Line 17*

The shirt of Nessus is upon me.
> *Ibid. Sc. 10, Line 56*

Sometimes we see a cloud that's drag-
onish;
A vapour sometime like a bear or lion,
A tower'd citadel, a pendant rock,
A forked mountain, or blue promontory
With trees upon 't.
> *Ibid. Sc. 12, Line 2*

That which is now a horse, even with
a thought
The rack dislimns, and makes it in-
distinct,
As water is in water.
> *Ibid. Line 9*

Unarm, Eros; the long day's task is
done,
And we must sleep.
> *Antony and Cleopatra. Act IV,*
> *Sc. 12, Line 35*

But I will be
A bridegroom in my death, and run
into 't
As to a lover's bed.
> *Ibid. Line 99*

I am dying, Egypt, dying; only
I here importune death awhile, until
Of many thousand kisses the poor last
I lay upon thy lips.
> *Ibid. Sc. 13, Line 18*

O! wither'd is the garland of the war,
The soldier's pole is fall'n; young boys
and girls
Are level now with men; the odds is
gone,
And there is nothing left remarkable
Beneath the visiting moon.
> *Ibid. Line 64*

Let's do it after the high Roman fashion.
> *Ibid. Line 87*

And it is great
To do that thing that ends all other
deeds,
Which shackles accidents, and bolts up
change.
> *Ibid. Act V, Sc. 2, Line 4*

For his bounty,
There was no winter in 't; an autumn
'twas
That grew the more by reaping.
> *Ibid. Line 86*

If there be, or ever were, one such,
It's past the size of dreaming.
> *Ibid. Line 96*

The bright day is done,
And we are for the dark.
> *Ibid. Line 192*

Mechanic slaves
With greasy aprons, rules, and hammers.
> *Ibid. Line 208*

A woman is a dish for the gods if the
devil dress her not.
> *Ibid. Line 274*

I have
Immortal longings in me.
> *Antony and Cleopatra. Act V,
> Sc. 2, Line 282*

If thou and nature can so gently part,
The stroke of death is as a lover's
pinch,
Which hurts, and is desir'd.
> *Ibid. Line 296*

Dost thou not see my baby at my
breast,
That sucks the nurse asleep?
> *Ibid. Line 311*

As she would catch another Antony
In her strong toil of grace.
> *Ibid. Line 348*

The gods sent not
Corn for the rich men only.
> *Coriolanus [1607–1608]. Act I,
> Sc. 1, Line 213*

Had I a dozen sons, each in my love
alike and none less dear than thine and
my good Marcius, I had rather eleven
die nobly for their country than one
voluptuously surfeit out of action.
> *Ibid. Sc. 3, Line 24*

All the yarn she spun in Ulysses' absence did but fill Ithaca full of moths.
> *Ibid. Line 93*

Nature teaches beasts to know their
friends.
> *Ibid. Act II, Sc. 1, Line 6*

A cup of hot wine with not a drop of
allaying Tiber in't.[1]
> *Ibid Line 52*

Bid them wash their faces,
And keep their teeth clean.
> *Ibid. Sc. 3, Line 65*

I thank you for your voices: thank you,
Your most sweet voices.
> *Ibid. Line 179*

The mutable, rank-scented many.
> *Ibid. Act III, Sc. 1, Line 65*

Hear you this Triton of the minnows?
Mark you
His absolute "shall"?
> *Ibid. Line 88*

---

[1] When flowing cups pass swiftly round
With no allaying Thames.
RICHARD LOVELACE: *To Althea from
Prison* [1649], *St. 2*

Enough, with over-measure.
> *Coriolanus. Act III, Sc. 1, Line 139*

What is the city but the people?
> *Ibid. Line 198*

His nature is too noble for the world:
He would not flatter Neptune for his
trident,
Or Jove for 's power to thunder. His
heart's his mouth:
What his breast forges, that his tongue
must vent;
And, being angry, does forget that ever
He heard the name of death.
> *Ibid. Line 254*

That it shall hold companionship in
peace
With honour, as in war.
> *Ibid. Sc. 2, Line 49*

I do love
My country's good with a respect more
tender,
More holy, more profound, than mine
own life.
> *Ibid. Sc. 3, Line 109*

Pride
Which out of daily fortune ever taints
The happy man.
> *Ibid. Act IV, Sc. 7, Line 37*

So our virtues
Lie in the interpretation of the time.
> *Ibid. Line 49*

You know the very road into his kindness,
And cannot lose your way.
> *Ibid. Act V, Sc. 1, Line 60*

Chaste as the icicle
That's curdied by the frost from purest
snow
And hangs on Dian's temple.
> *Ibid. Sc. 3, Line 65*

Is't possible that so short a time can
alter the condition of a man?
> *Ibid. Sc. 4, Line 10*

They'll give him death by inches.
> *Ibid. Line 43*

Splitting the air with noise.
> *Ibid. Sc. 5, Line 52*

If you have writ your annals true, 'tis
there
That, like an eagle in a dove-cote, **I**

Flutter'd your Volscians in Corioli:
Alone I did it.
> *Coriolanus. Act V, Sc. 5, Line 114*

Thou hast done a deed whereat valour
will weep.
> *Ibid. Line 135*

He shall have a noble memory.
> *Ibid. Line 155*

'Tis not enough to help the feeble up,
But to support him after.
> *Timon of Athens* [*1607–1608*].
> *Act I, Sc. 1, Line 108*

I call the gods to witness.
> *Ibid. Line 138*

Satiety of commendations.
> *Ibid. Line 167*

Ceremony was but devis'd at first
To set a gloss on faint deeds, hollow
welcomes,
Recanting goodness, sorry ere 'tis
shown;
But where there is true friendship, there
needs none.
> *Ibid. Sc. 2, Line 15*

Here's that which is too weak to be a
sinner,
Honest water, which ne'er left man i'
the mire.[1]
> *Ibid. Line 60*

Immortal gods, I crave no pelf;
I pray for no man but myself:
Grant I may never prove so fond,
To trust man on his oath or bond.
> *Ibid. Line 64*

Men shut their doors against a setting
sun.
> *Ibid. Line 152*

Every room
Hath blazed with lights and bray'd with
minstrelsy
> *Ibid. Act II, Sc. 2, Line 170*

Every man has his fault, and honesty
is his.
> *Ibid. Act III, Sc. 1, Line 30*

Policy sits above conscience.
> *Ibid. Sc. 2, Line 95*

Nothing emboldens sin so much as
mercy.
> *Ibid. Sc. 5, Line 3*

[1] Inscribed on the drinking fountain in the market-square of Stratford-on-Avon.

You fools of fortune, trencher-friends,
time's flies.
> *Timon of Athens. Act III, Sc. 6,*
> *Line 107*

We have seen better days.
> *Ibid. Act IV, Sc. 2, Line 27*

O! the fierce wretchedness that glory
brings us.
> *Ibid. Line 30*

I am Misanthropos, and hate mankind.
> *Ibid. Sc. 3, Line 53*

I'll example you with thievery:
The sun's a thief, and with his great
attraction
Robs the vast sea; the moon's an ar·
rant thief,
And her pale fire she snatches from the
sun;
The sea's a thief, whose liquid surge resolves
The moon into salt tears; the earth's a
thief,
That feeds and breeds by a composture
stolen
From general excrement: each thing's
a thief.
> *Ibid. Line 441*

Life's uncertain voyage.
> *Ibid. Act. V, Sc. 1, Line 207*

As an arrow shot
From a well-experienc'd archer hits the
mark
His eye doth level at.
> *Pericles* [*1608–1609*]. *Act I, Sc. 1,*
> *Line 163*

The sad companion, dull-eyed melancholy.
> *Ibid. Sc. 2, Line 2*

Third Fisherman. Master, I marvel
how the fishes live in the sea.
First Fisherman. Why, as men do
aland; the great ones eat up the little
ones.[1]
> *Ibid. Act II, Sc. 1, Line 29*

Lest the bargain should catch cold
and starve.
> *Cymbeline* [*1609–1610*]. *Act I,*
> *Sc. 4, Line 186*

[1] Men lived like fishes; the great ones devoured the small. — ALGERNON SIDNEY: *Discourses on Government* [1698], *Chap.* 2,
Sect. XVIII

Hath his bellyful of fighting.
Cymbeline. Act II, Sc. 1, Line 24
How bravely thou becomest thy bed!
Ibid. Sc. 2, Line 15
The most patient man in loss, the most coldest that ever turned up ace.
Ibid. Sc. 3, Line 1
Hark! hark! the lark at heaven's gate sings,
And Phoebus 'gins arise,[1]
His steeds to water at those springs
On chaliced flowers that lies;
And winking Mary-buds begin
To ope their golden eyes:
With everything that pretty is,
My lady sweet, arise.
Ibid. Line 22
As chaste as unsunn'd snow.
Ibid. Sc. 5, Line 13
Some griefs are med'cinable.
Ibid. Act III, Sc. 2, Line 33
Prouder than rustling in unpaid-for silk.
Ibid. Sc. 3, Line 24
So slippery that
The fear's as bad as falling.
Ibid. Line 48
The game is up.
Ibid. Line 107
Slander,
Whose edge is sharper than the sword, whose tongue
Outvenoms all the worms of Nile, whose breath
Rides on the posting winds and doth belie
All corners of the world.
Ibid. Sc. 4, Line 35
Against self-slaughter
There is a prohibition so divine
That cravens my weak hand.
Ibid. Line 78
It is no act of common passage, but
A strain of rareness.
Ibid. Line 94
Weariness
Can snore upon the flint when resty sloth
Finds the down pillow hard.
Ibid. Sc. 6, Line 33

[1] See Lyly, page 112b.

An angel! or, if not,
An earthly paragon!
Cymbeline. Act III, Sc. 6, Line 42
Society is no comfort
To one not sociable.
Ibid. Act IV, Sc. 2, Line 12
I wear not
My dagger in my mouth.
Ibid. Line 78
And put
My clouted brogues from off my feet.
Ibid. Line 213
Fear no more the heat o' the sun,
Nor the furious winter's rages;
Thou thy worldly task hast done,
Home art gone, and ta'en thy wages.
Golden lads and girls all must,
As chimney-sweepers, come to dust.
Ibid. Line 258
Fortune brings in some boats that are not steer'd.
Ibid. Sc. 3, Line 46
By medicine life may be prolong'd, yet death
Will seize the doctor too.
Ibid. Act V, Sc. 5, Line 29
To the onlie begetter.
Sonnets [Published 1609].
Dedication
When forty winters shall besiege my brow,
And dig deep trenches in thy beauty's field.
Sonnet 2
Thou art thy mother's glass, and she in thee
Calls back the lovely April of her prime.
Sonnet 3
Music to hear, why hear'st thou music sadly?
Sweets with sweet war not, joy delights in joy.
Sonnet 8
Shall I compare thee to a summer's day?
Thou art more lovely and more temperate:
Rough winds do shake the darling buds of May,
And summer's lease hath all too short a date.
Sonnet 18

But thy eternal summer shall not fade.
Sonnet 18

The painful warrior famoused for fight,
After a thousand victories, once foil'd,
Is from the books of honour razed quite,
And all the rest forgot for which he
toil'd.
Sonnet 25

When in disgrace with fortune and
men's eyes
I all alone beweep my outcast state.
And trouble deaf heaven with my boot-
less cries.
Sonnet 29

Desiring this man's art, and that man's
scope,
With what I most enjoy contented
least;
Yet in these thoughts myself almost
despising.
Ibid.

For thy sweet love remember'd such
wealth brings
That then I scorn to change my state
with kings.
Ibid.

When to the sessions of sweet silent
thought
I summon up remembrance of things
past,
I sigh the lack of many a thing I sought,
And with old woes new wail my dear
times' waste.
Sonnet 30

But if the while I think on thee, dear
friend,
All losses are restor'd and sorrows end.
Ibid.

Full many a glorious morning have I
seen.
Sonnet 33

Roses have thorns, and silver fountains
mud;
Clouds and eclipses stain both moon
and sun,
And loathsome canker lives in sweetest
bud.
All men make faults.
Sonnet 35

For nimble thought can jump both sea
and land.
Sonnet 44

Against that time when thou shalt
strangely pass,
And scarcely greet me with that sun,
thine eye,
When love, converted from the thing it
was,
Shall reasons find of settled gravity.
Sonnet 49

My grief lies onward, and my joy behind.
Sonnet 50

Like stones of worth they thinly placed
are,
Or captain jewels in the carcanet.
Sonnet 52

O! how much more doth beauty beauteous seem
By that sweet ornament which truth
doth give!
Sonnet 54

Not marble, nor the gilded monuments
Of princes, shall outlive this powerful
rhyme.
Sonnet 55

Like as the waves make towards the
pebbled shore,
So do our minutes hasten to their end.
Sonnet 60

Ruin hath taught me thus to ruminate, —
That Time will come and take my
love away.
Sonnet 64

Tir'd with all these, for restful death
I cry.
Sonnet 66

And art made tongue-tied by authority.
Ibid.

And simple truth miscall'd simplicity,
And captive good attending captain ill.
Ibid.

No longer mourn for me when I am
dead
Than you shall hear the surly sullen
bell
Give warning to the world that I am
fled
From this vile world, with vilest worms
to dwell.
Sonnet 71

That time of year thou may'st in me
behold

When yellow leaves, or none, or few, do hang
Upon those boughs which shake against the cold,
Bare ruin'd choirs, where late the sweet birds sang.
Sonnet 73

Clean starved for a look.
Sonnet 75

Your monument shall be my gentle verse,
Which eyes not yet created shall o'er-read;
And tongues to be your being shall re-hearse,
When all the breathers of this world are dead;
You still shall live — such virtue hath my pen —
Where breath most breathes, — even in the mouths of men.
Sonnet 81

Who is it that says most? which can say more
Than this rich praise, — that you alone are you?
Sonnet 84

Farewell! thou art too dear for my possessing,
And like enough thou know'st thy esti-mate.
Sonnet 87

Do not, when my heart hath 'scap'd this sorrow,
Come in the rearward of a conquer'd woe;
Give not a windy night a rainy morrow,
To linger out a purpos'd overthrow.
Sonnet 90

The summer's flower is to the summer sweet,
Though to itself it only live and die.
Sonnet 94

Lilies that fester smell far worse than weeds.
Ibid.

The hardest knife ill-used doth lose his edge.
Sonnet 95

From you I have been absent in the spring,

When proud-pied April, dress'd in all his trim,
Hath put a spirit of youth in everything.
Sonnet 98

Sweets grown common lose their dear delight.
Sonnet 102

To me, fair friend, you never can be old,
For as you were when first your eye I ey'd
Such seems your beauty still.
Sonnet 104

Still constant is a wondrous excellence.
Sonnet 105

When in the chronicle of wasted time
I see descriptions of the fairest wights,
And beauty making beautiful old rime
In praise of ladies dead and lovely knights,
Then, in the blazon of sweet beauty's best,
Of hand, of foot, of lip, of eye, of brow,
I see their antique pen would have ex-prest
Even such a beauty as you master now.
Sonnet 106

Not mine own fears, nor the prophetic soul
Of the wide world dreaming on things to come
Can yet the lease of my true love con-trol,
Suppos'd as forfeit to a confin'd doom.
The mortal moon hath her eclipse endur'd,
And the sad augurs mock their own presage.
Incertainties now crown themselves assured,
And peace proclaims olives of endless age.
Sonnet 107

That is my home of love; if I have ranged,
Like him that travels, I return again.
Sonnet 109

Alas, 'tis true I have gone here and there,
And made myself a motley to the view,
Gor'd mine own thoughts, sold cheap what is most dear,

Made old offences of affections new.
Sonnet 110

My nature is subdu'd
To what it works in, like the dyer's
hand.
Sonnet 111

Let me not to the marriage of true
minds
Admit impediments. Love is not love
Which alters when it alteration finds.
Sonnet 116

O, no! it is an ever-fixed mark,
That looks on tempests and is never
shaken;
It is the star to every wandering bark.
Ibid.

If this be error, and upon me prov'd,
I never writ, nor no man ever lov'd.
Ibid.

And ruin'd love, when it is built anew,
Grows fairer than at first, more strong,
far greater.
Sonnet 119

'Tis better to be vile than vile esteem'd,
When not to be receives reproach of be-
ing;
And the just pleasure lost, which is so
deem'd,
Not by our feeling, but by others' see-
ing.
Sonnet 121

No, I am that I am, and they that level
At my abuses reckon up their own.
Ibid.

To kiss the tender inward of thy hand.
Sonnet 128

The expense of spirit in a waste of
shame
Is lust in action; and till action, lust
Is perjur'd, murd'rous, bloody, full of
blame,
Savage, extreme, rude, cruel, not to
trust.
Enjoyed no sooner but despised
straight;
Past reason hunted; and no sooner had,
Past reason hated, as a swallow'd bait,
On purpose laid to make the taker mad:
Mad in pursuit, and in possession so;
Had, having, and in quest to have,
extreme;

A bliss in proof, — and prov'd, a very
woe;
Before, a joy propos'd; behind, a dream.
All this the world well knows; yet none
knows well
To shun the heaven that leads men to
this hell.
Sonnet 129

My mistress' eyes are nothing like the
sun;
Coral is far more red than her lips' red:
If snow be white, why then her breasts
are dun;
If hairs be wires, black wires grow on
her head.
Sonnet 130

That full star that ushers in the even.
Sonnet 132

When my love swears that she is made
of truth,
I do believe her, though I know she lies.
Sonnet 138

Two loves I have of comfort and despair,
Which like two spirits do suggest me
still.
Sonnet 144

For I have sworn thee fair, and thought
thee bright,
Who art as black as hell, as dark as
night.
Sonnet 147

You pay a great deal too dear for
what's given freely.
The Winter's Tale [*1610–1611*].
Act I, Sc. 1, Line 18

We were as twinn'd lambs that did frisk
i' the sun,
And bleat the one at the other: what
we changed
Was innocence for innocence.
Ibid. Sc. 2, Line 67

One good deed, dying tongueless,
Slaughters a thousand waiting upon
that.
Ibid. Line 92

Paddling palms and pinching fingers.
Ibid. Line 116

Affection! thy intention stabs the
centre:
Thou dost make possible things not so
held,

Communicatest with dreams.
The Winter's Tale. Act I, Sc. 2,
Line 139
He makes a July's day short as December.
Ibid. Line 169
Black brows, they say,
Become some women best, so that there be not
Too much hair there, but in a semi-circle,
Or a half-moon made with a pen.
Ibid. Act II, Sc. 1, Line 8
A sad tale's best for winter.
Ibid. Line 24
There's some ill planet reigns:
I must be patient till the heavens look
With an aspect more favourable.
Ibid. Line 104
The silence often of pure innocence
Persuades when speaking fails.
Ibid. Sc. 2, Line 41
It is a heretic that makes the fire,
Not she which burns in 't.
Ibid. Sc. 3, Line 116
I am a feather for each wind that blows.
Ibid. Line 153
What's gone and what's past help
Should be past grief.
Ibid. Act III, Sc. 2, Line 223
This is fairy gold.
Ibid. Sc. 3, Line 127
Then comes in the sweet o' the year.
Ibid. Act IV, Sc. 2, Line 3
A snapper-up of unconsidered trifles.
Ibid. Line 26
A merry heart goes all the day,
Your sad tires in a mile-a.
Ibid. Line 135
There's rosemary and rue; these keep
Seeming and savour all the winter long.
Ibid. Sc. 3, Line 74
Daffodils,
That come before the swallow dares, and take
The winds of March with beauty.
Ibid. Line 118
What you do
Still betters what is done.
Ibid. Line 135
When you do dance, I wish you

A wave o' the sea, that you might ever do
Nothing but that.
The Winter's Tale. Act IV, Sc. 3, Line 140
I love a ballad in print, a-life, for then we are sure they are true.
Ibid. Line 262
The self-same sun that shines upon his court
Hides not his visage from our cottage, but
Looks on alike.
Ibid. Line 457
To unpathed waters, undreamed shores.
Ibid. Line 580
Prosperity's the very bond of love,
Whose fresh complexion and whose heart together
Affliction alters.
Ibid. Line 586
Let me have no lying; it becomes none but tradesmen.
Ibid. Line 747
To purge melancholy.
Ibid. Line 792
Stars, stars!
And all eyes else dead coals.
Ibid. Act V, Sc. 1, Line 67
I was no gentleman born.
Ibid. Sc. 2, Line 146
What fine chisel
Could ever yet cut breath?
Ibid. Sc. 3, Line 78
There's time enough for that.
Ibid. Line 128
He hath no drowning mark upon him; his complexion is perfect gallows.
The Tempest [*1611–1612*].
Act I, Sc. 1, Line 33
Now would I give a thousand furlongs of sea for an acre of barren ground.
Ibid. Line 70
I would fain die a dry death.
Ibid. Line 73
What seest thou else
In the dark backward and abysm of time?
Ibid. Sc. 2, Line 49
I, thus neglecting worldly ends, all dedicated

To closeness and the bettering of my
mind.
The Tempest. Act I, Sc. 2, Line 89
By telling of it,
Made such a sinner of his memory,
To credit his own lie.
Ibid. Line 99
My library
Was dukedom large enough.
Ibid. Line 109
The very rats
Instinctively have quit it.
Ibid. Line 147
Knowing I lov'd my books, he furnish'd
me
From mine own library with volumes
that
I prize above my dukedom.
Ibid. Line 166
From the still-vexed Bermoothes.
Ibid. Line 229
I will be correspondent to command,
And do my spiriting gently.
Ibid. Line 297
Come unto these yellow sands,
And then take hands:
Curtsied when you have, and kiss'd
The wild waves whist.
Foot it featly here and there.
Ibid. Line 375
This music crept by me upon the waters,
Allaying both their fury, and my pas-
sion,
With its sweet air.
Ibid. Line 389
Full fathom five thy father lies;
Of his bones are coral made;
Those are pearls that were his eyes:
Nothing of him that doth fade
But doth suffer a sea-change
Into something rich and strange.[1]
Ibid. Line 394
The fringed curtains of thine eye ad-
vance.
Ibid. Line 405
Less too light winning
Make the prize light.
Ibid. Line 448
There's nothing ill can dwell in such a
temple:

[1] The last three lines are inscribed on Shelley's gravestone.

If the ill spirit have so fair a house,
Good things will strive to dwell with 't.
The Tempest. Act I, Sc. 2, Line 454
He receives comfort like cold por-
ridge.
Ibid. Act II, Sc. 1, Line 10
Gonzalo. Here is everything advanta-
geous to life.
Antonio. True; save means to live.
Ibid. Line 52
What is past is prologue.[1]
Ibid. Line 261
A very ancient and fish-like smell.
Ibid. Sc. 2, Line 27
Misery acquaints a man with strange
bedfellows.
Ibid. Line 42
I shall laugh myself to death.
Ibid. Line 167
'Ban, 'Ban, Ca-Caliban,
Has a new master — Get a new man.
Ibid. Line 197
Ferdinand. Here's my hand.
Miranda. And mine, with my heart in't.
Ibid. Act III, Sc. 1, Line 89
Moon-calf.
Ibid. Sc. 2, Line 25
Keep a good tongue in your head.
Ibid. Line 41
He that dies pays all debts.
Ibid. Line 143
The isle is full of noises,
Sounds and sweet airs, that give delight,
and hurt not.
Sometimes a thousand twangling in-
struments
Will hum about mine ears; and some-
times voices,
That, if I then had wak'd after long
sleep,
Will make me sleep again.
Ibid. Line 146
A kind
Of excellent dumb discourse.
Ibid. Sc. 3, Line 38
Do not give dalliance
Too much rein.
Ibid. Act IV, Sc. 1, Line 51

[1] Inscription on pedestal under "Female
Figure," East, National Archives Building,
Washington, D.C.

Our revels now are ended. These our
      actors,
As I foretold you, were all spirits, and
Are melted into air, into thin air;
And, like the baseless fabric of this
      vision,
The cloud-capp'd towers, the gorgeous
      palaces,
The solemn temples, the great globe
      itself,
Yea, all which it inherit, shall dissolve;
And, like this insubstantial pageant
      faded,
Leave not a rack behind. We are such
      stuff
As dreams are made on, and our little
      life
Is rounded with a sleep.
      The Tempest. Act IV, Sc. 1, Line 148
With foreheads villanous low.
                  Ibid. Line 252
      I'll break my staff,
Bury it certain fathoms in the earth,
And, deeper than did ever plummet
      sound
I'll drown my book.
            Ibid. Act V, Sc. 1, Line 54
Where the bee sucks, there suck I;
In a cowslip's bell I lie.
There I couch when owls do cry.
On the bat's back I do fly
After summer merrily:
Merrily, merrily shall I live now,
Under the blossom that hangs on the
      bough.
                  Ibid. Line 88

      O brave new world,
That has such people in't!
                  Ibid. Line 183
Let us not burden our remembrances
With a heaviness that's gone.
                  Ibid. Line 199
My ending is despair.
            Ibid. Epilogue, Line 15
Order gave each thing view.
      *King Henry VIII [1613]. Act I,
                  Sc. 1, Line 44*
      No man's pie is freed
From his ambitious finger.
                  Ibid. Line 52

The force of his own merit makes his
      way.
      *King Henry VIII. Act I, Sc. 1,
                  Line 64*
      Anger is like
A full-hot horse, who being allow'd his
      way,
Self-mettle tires him.
                  Ibid. Line 132
Heat not a furnace for your foe so hot
That it do singe yourself.
                  Ibid. Line 140
      New customs,
Though they be never so ridiculous,
Nay, let 'em be unmanly, yet are fol-
      low'd.
                  Ibid. Sc. 3, Line 2
The mirror of all courtesy.
            Ibid. Act II, Sc. 1, Line 53
Go with me, like good angels, to my end:
And, as the long divorce of steel falls on
      me,
Make of your prayers one sweet sacri-
      fice,
And lift my soul to heaven.
                  Ibid. Line 75
This bold bad man.
                  Ibid. Sc. 2, Line 44
      'Tis better to be lowly born,
And range with humble livers in con-
      tent,
Than to be perked up in a glistering
      grief
And wear a golden sorrow.
                  Ibid. Sc. 3, Line 19
      I would not be a queen
For all the world.
                  Ibid. Line 45
Orpheus with his lute made trees,
And the mountain-tops that freeze,
Bow themselves when he did sing.
            Ibid. Act III, Sc. 1, Line 3
Heaven is above all yet; there sits a
      judge
That no king can corrupt.
                  Ibid. Line 99
      'Tis well said again;
And 'tis a kind of good deed to say
      well:
And yet words are no deeds.
                  Ibid. Sc. 2, Line 153

And then to breakfast with
What appetite you have.
> *King Henry VIII. Act III,*
> *Sc. 2, Line 203*

I have touched the highest point of all
my greatness;
And from that full meridian of my
glory,
I haste now to my setting: I shall fall
Like a bright exhalation in the evening,
And no man see me more.
> *Ibid. Line 224*

Press not a falling man too far!
> *Ibid. Line 334*

Farewell! a long farewell, to all my
greatness!
This is the state of man: to-day he puts
forth
The tender leaves of hopes; to-morrow
blossoms,
And bears his blushing honours thick
upon him;
The third day comes a frost, a killing
frost;
And, when he thinks, good easy man,
full surely
His greatness is a-ripening, nips his
root,
And then he falls, as I do. I have ventured,
Like little wanton boys that swim on
bladders,
This many summers in a sea of glory,
But far beyond my depth: my high-
blown pride
At length broke under me, and now has
left me,
Weary and old with service, to the
mercy
Of a rude stream, that must forever
hide me.
Vain pomp and glory of this world, I
hate ye:
I feel my heart new opened. O! how
wretched
Is that poor man that hangs on princes'
favours!
There is, betwixt that smile we would
aspire to,
That sweet aspect of princes, and their
ruin,

More pangs and fears than wars or
women have —
And when he falls, he falls like Lucifer,
Never to hope again.
> *King Henry VIII. Act III,*
> *Sc. 2, Line 352*

A peace above all earthly dignities,
A still and quiet conscience.
> *Ibid. Line 380*

A load would sink a navy.
> *Ibid. Line 384*

And sleep in dull cold marble.
> *Ibid. Line 434*

I charge thee, fling away ambition:
By that sin fell the angels.
> *Ibid. Line 441*

Love thyself last: cherish those hearts
that hate thee;
Corruption wins not more than honesty.
Still in thy right hand carry gentle
peace,
To silence envious tongues: be just, and
fear not:
Let all the ends thou aim'st at be thy
country's,
Thy God's, and truth's; then if thou
fall'st, O Cromwell,
Thou fall'st a blessed martyr!
> *Ibid. Line 444*

Had I but served my God with half the
zeal [1]
I served my king, he would not in mine
age
Have left me naked to mine enemies.
> *Ibid. Line 456*

An old man, broken with the storms of
state,
Is come to lay his weary bones among
ye;
Give him a little earth for charity!
> *Ibid. Act IV, Sc. 2, Line 21*

He gave his honours to the world again,
His blessed part to heaven, and slept in
peace.
> *Ibid. Line 29*

---

[1] Had I served God as well in every part
As I did serve my king and master still,
My scope had not this season been so
short,
Nor would have had the power to do
me ill.
> THOMAS CHURCHYARD: *Death of*
> *Morton* [1593]

So may he rest; his faults lie gently on
him!
> *King Henry VIII. Act IV,*
> *Sc. 2, Line 31*

He was a man
Of an unbounded stomach.
> *Ibid. Line 33*

Men's evil manners live in brass; their
virtues
We write in water.[1]
> *Ibid. Line 45*

He was a scholar, and a ripe and good
one;
Exceeding wise, fair-spoken, and persuading;
Lofty and sour to them that loved him
not,
But to those men that sought him sweet
as summer.
> *Ibid. Line 51*

Yet in bestowing, madam,
He was most princely.
> *Ibid. Line 56*

After my death I wish no other herald,
No other speaker of my living actions,
To keep mine honour from corruption,
But such an honest chronicler as Grif-
fith.
> *Ibid. Line 69*

To dance attendance on their lordships'
pleasures.
> *Ibid. Act V, Sc. 2, Line 30*

'Tis a cruelty
To load a falling man.
> *Ibid. Sc. 3, Line 76*

You were ever good at sudden commendations.
> *Ibid. Line 122*

Those about her
From her shall read the perfect ways of
honour.
> *Ibid. Sc. 5, Line 37*

Nor shall this peace sleep with her;
but as when
The bird of wonder dies, the maiden
phoenix,
Her ashes new-create another heir
As great in admiration as herself.
> *Ibid. Line 40*

Wherever the bright sun of heaven shall
shine,

[1] See Sir Thomas More, page 86a.

His honour and the greatness of his
name
Shall be, and make new nations.
> *King Henry VIII. Act V, Sc. 5,*
> *Line 51*

A most unspotted lily shall she pass
To the ground, and all the world shall
mourn her.
> *Ibid. Line 62*

Some come to take their ease
And sleep an act or two.
> *Ibid. Epilogue, Line 2*

When as thine eye hath chose the
dame. . . .
Plainly say thou lov'st her well,
And set thy person forth to sell.
> *Sonnets to Sundry Notes of*
> *Music. IV*

The strongest castle, tower, and town,
The golden bullet beats it down.
> *Ibid.*

Have you not heard it said full oft,
A woman's nay doth stand for naught?
> *Ibid.*

Good friend, for Jesu's sake forbear
To dig the dust enclosed here.
Blest be the man that spares these
stones,
Cursed be he that moves my bones.
> *Shakespeare's Epitaph*

JOHN DAVIES
[1565?–1618]

Beauty's but skin deep.[1]
> *A Select Second Husband for*
> *Sir Thomas Overburie's Wife*
> *[1606]. VI*

THOMAS NASH
[1567–1601]

Spring, the sweet spring, is the year's
pleasant king;
Then blooms each thing, then maids
dance in a ring,

[1] All the beauty of the world, 'tis but skin
deep. — RALPH VENNING: *Orthodoxe Paradoxes* [3d ed., 1650], *The Triumph of Assurance, P. 41*
Many a dangerous temptation comes to us
in fine gay colours that are but skin-deep. —
MATHEW HENRY [1662–1714]: *Commentaries, Genesis, III*

Cold doth not sting, the pretty birds do
    sing.
Cuckoo, jug-jug, pu-we, to-witta-woo!
                  Spring

Brightness falls from the air;
Queens have died young and fair;
Dust hath closed Helen's eye.
        In Time of Pestilence

SIR HENRY WOTTON
[1568–1639]

Love lodged in a woman's breast
Is but a guest.
       A Woman's Heart [*1651*]

How happy is he born and taught,
    That serveth not another's will;
Whose armour is his honest thought,
    And simple truth his utmost skill!
    The Character of a Happy Life
        [*1651*]. *Stanza 1*

Who God doth late and early pray
    More of his grace than gifts to lend;
And entertains the harmless day
    With a religious book or friend.
        Ibid. Stanza 5

Lord of himself, though not of lands;
And having nothing, yet hath all.[1]
        Ibid. Stanza 6

You meaner beauties of the night,
    That poorly satisfy our eyes
More by your number than your light;
    You common people of the skies, —
What are you when the moon [2] shall
    rise?
      On his Mistress, the Queen of
        Bohemia.[3] *Stanza 1*

He first deceased; she for a little tried
To live without him, liked it not, and
    died.
    Upon the Death of Sir Albert
      Morton's Wife [*1651*]

[1] As having nothing, and yet possessing all
things. — 2 *Corinthians, VI, 10*
See Terence, page 31b.
[2] "Sun" in *Reliquiae Wottonianae* [eds.
1651, 1654, 1672, 1685]
[3] This was printed with music as early as
1624, in Est's "Sixth Set of Books," etc., and
is found in many MSS. — JOHN HANNAH:
The Courtly Poets [1870]

Hanging was the worst use a man
could be put to.
    The Disparity Between Buck-
      ingham and Essex [*1651*]

An ambassador is an honest man sent
to lie abroad for the commonwealth.[1]
    Reliquiae Wottonianae [*1651*]

The itch of disputing will prove the
scab of churches.[2]
    A Panegyric to King Charles [*1651*]

SIR JOHN DAVIES
[1569–1626]

What can we know? or what can we
    discern,
When error chokes the windows of the
    mind?
    The Vanity of Human Learning
        [*1596*]. *Stanza 15*

We that acquaint ourselves with ev'ry
    zone,
And pass both tropics, and behold each
    pole,
When we come home are to ourselves
    unknown,
And unacquainted still with our own
    soul.
        Ibid. Stanza 25

I know my soul hath power to know all
    things,
Yet is she blind and ignorant in all:
I know I'm one of Nature's little kings,
Yet to the least and vilest things am
    thrall.
        Ibid. Stanza 44

I know my life's a pain, and but a span;
I know my sense is mock'd in ev'ry
    thing:
And to conclude, I know myself a man.

[1] In a letter to Velserus [1612] Wotton
says that this "merry definition of an ambassador . . I had chanced to set down at my
friend's, Mr. Christopher Fleckamore, in his
Album."
[2] He directed the stone over his grave to be
inscribed:
Hic jacet hujus sententiae primus auctor:
DISPUTANDI PRURITUS ECCLESIARUM SCABIES.
      Nomen alias quaere
(Here lies the author of this phrase: "The
itch for disputing is the sore of churches."
Seek his name elsewhere.) (IZAAK WALTON:
Life of Wotton [1651])

Which is a proud, and yet a wretched thing.
> *The Vanity of Human Learning.*
> *Stanza 45*

MARTYN PARKER
[? –1656]

Ye gentlemen of England
> That live at home at ease,
Ah! little do you think upon
> The dangers of the seas.
> *Song*

When the stormy winds do blow.[1]
> *Ibid.*

THOMAS MIDDLETON
[1570–1627]

Better the day, better the deed.[2]
> *Michaelmas Term* [1607].
> *Act III, Sc. 1*

As true as I live.
> *The Family of Love* [1608].
> *Act V, Sc. 3*

That disease
Of which all old men sicken, — avarice.[3]
> *The Roaring Girl* [1611].
> *Act I, Sc. 1*

Beat all your feathers as flat down as pancakes.
> *Ibid.*

As the case stands.
> *The Old Law* [1656]. *Act II, Sc. 1*

On his last legs.
> *Ibid. Act V, Sc. 1*

As old Chaucer was wont to say, that broad famous English poet.
> *More Dissemblers besides Women*
> [1657]. *Act I, Sc. 4*

---

[1] When the battle rages loud and long,
And the stormy winds do blow.
     Thomas Campbell [1777–1844]:
         Ye Mariners of England

[2] The better the day, the worse deed. —
Mathew Henry [1662–1714]: *Commentaries, Genesis, III*
The better the day the better the deed. —
Dickens: *Edwin Drood* [1870], *Chap. 10*

[3] So for a good old-gentlemanly vice
I think I must take up with avarice.
     Byron: *Don Juan* [1819–1824],
         Canto I, St. 216

'Tis a stinger.[1]
> *More Dissemblers besides Women.*
> *Act III, Sc. 2*

How many honest words have suffered corruption since Chaucer's days!
> *No Wit, No Help, Like a Woman's*
> [1657]. *Act II, Sc. 1*

Anything for a Quiet Life.
> *Title of play* [1662]

This was a good week's labour.
> *Anything for a Quiet Life.*
> *Act V, Sc. 3*

Black spirits and white, red spirits and gray,
Mingle, mingle, mingle, you that mingle may.[2]
> *The Witch* [*published 1778*].
> *Act V, Sc. 2*

Though I say it that should not say it.
> *Wit at Several Weapons*
> (*probably in collaboration with William Rowley* [1585?–1642?]). *Act II, Sc. 2*

THOMAS DEKKER
[1570?–1641]

The reason why fond women love to buy
Adulterate complexion: here 'tis read, —
False colours last after the true be dead.
> *A Description of a Lady by Her Lover*

This age thinks better of a gilded fool
Than of a threadbare saint in wisdom's school.
> *Old Fortunatus* [1600]

Honest labour bears a lovely face.
> *Patient Grissell* [1603]. *Act I, Sc. 1*

Cast away care, he that loves sorrow
Lengthens not a day, nor can buy tomorrow;
Money is trash, and he that will spend it,
Let him drink merrily, fortune will send it.
> *The Sun's Darling* [1624] (*Revised by John Ford*)

---

[1] He 'as had a stinger. — Fletcher: *Wit without Money* [1639], *Act IV, Sc. 1*

[2] These lines are introduced into *Macbeth, Act IV, Sc. 1.* According to Steevens, "the song was, in all probability, a traditional one."

The best of men
That e'er wore earth about him was a
    sufferer;
A soft, meek, patient, humble, tranquil
    spirit,
The first true gentleman that ever
    breathed.
        The Honest Whore. Part I [*1604*],
                    Act I, Sc. 12

We are ne'er like angels till our passion
    dies.
        Ibid. Part II [*1630*], *Act I, Sc. 2*

JOHN DONNE [1]
[1573–1631]

I wonder by my troth, what thou, and I
Did, till we lov'd? were we not wean'd
    till then?
But suck'd on country pleasures, child-
    ishly?
Or snorted we in the seven sleepers'
    den?
        The Good Morrow. Stanza 1

And now good morrow to our waking
    souls,
Which watch not one another out of
    fear;
For love, all love of other sights con-
    trols,
And makes one little room, an every-
    where.
Let sea-discoverers to new worlds have
    gone,
Let maps to other, worlds on worlds
    have shown,
Let us possess one world, each hath one,
    and is one.
        Ibid. Stanza 2

My face in thine eye, thine in mine
    appears,
And true plain hearts do in the faces
    rest,
Where can we find two better hemi-
    spheres

[1] Except where otherwise stated, these
quotations are from the 1633 edition. The
"Songs and Sonnets" were written by Donne
before the turn of the century, according to
Ben Jonson "ere he was twenty-five years
old," but there is no evidence to show the
exact date of their composition.

Without sharp North, without declining
    West?
        The Good Morrow. Stanza 3

Go, and catch a falling star,
    Get with child a mandrake root,
Tell me, where all past years are,
    Or who cleft the Devil's foot.
        Song. Stanza 1

            And swear
            No where
Lives a woman true and fair.
        Ibid. Stanza 2

Though she were true, when you met
    her,
And last, till you write your letter,
            Yet she
            Will be
False, ere I come, to two, or three.
        Ibid. Stanza 3

I have done one braver thing
    Than all the Worthies did;
And yet a braver thence doth spring,
    Which is, to keep that hid.
        The Undertaking, Stanza 1

But he who loveliness within
    Hath found, all outward loathes,
For he who colour loves, and skin,
    Loves but their oldest clothes.
        Ibid. Stanza 4

And dare love that, and say so too,
And forget the He and She.
        Ibid. Stanza 5

    Busy old fool, unruly Sun,
        Why dost thou thus,
Through windows, and through cur-
    tains call on us?
Must to thy motions lovers' seasons
    run?
        The Sun Rising. Stanza 1

She is all states, and all princes, I,
Nothing else is.
        Ibid. Stanza 3

For God sake hold your tongue, and
    let me love.
        The Canonization. Stanza 1

I am two fools, I know,
For loving, and for saying so
    In whining poetry.
        The Triple Fool. Stanza 1

Who are a little wise, the best fools be.
        Ibid. Stanza 2

Sweetest love, I do not go,
  For weariness of thee,
Nor in hope the world can show
  A fitter love for me;
        But since that I
Must die at last, 'tis best,
To use my self in jest
  Thus by feign'd deaths to die.
              Song. Stanza 1

When I died last, and dear, I die
As often as from thee I go.
            The Legacy. Stanza 1

Oh do not die, for I shall hate
All women so, when thou art gone.
            The Fever. Stanza 1

Twice or thrice had I loved thee,
Before I knew thy face or name;
So in a voice, so in a shapeless flame,
Angels affect us oft, and worshipp'd be.
         Air and Angels. Stanza 1

    Just such disparity
As is 'twixt air and Angels' purity,
'Twixt women's love, and men's will
    ever be.
             Ibid. Stanza 2

All Kings, and all their favorites,
All glory of honours, beauties, wits,
The sun itself, which makes times, as
    they pass,
Is elder by a year, now, than it was
When thou and I first one another saw:
All other things, to their destruction
    draw,
  Only our love hath no decay;
This, no tomorrow hath, nor yesterday,
Running, it never runs from us away,
But truly keeps his first, last, everlast-
    ing day.
        The Anniversary. Stanza 1

    At their best
Sweetness and wit, they are but
    mummy, possess'd.
        Love's Alchemy. Stanza 2

Come live with me, and be my love,
And we will some new pleasures prove
Of golden sands, and crystal brooks,
With silken lines, and silver hooks.
        The Bait.[1] Stanza 1

Dull sublunary lovers' love
  (Whose soul is sense) cannot admit
Absence, because it doth remove
  Those things which elemented it.
    *A Valediction Forbidding Mourn-
           ing. Stanza 4*

Our two souls therefore, which are one,
  Though I must go, endure not yet
A breach, but an expansion,
  Like gold to airy thinness beat.
            Ibid. Stanza 6

If they be two, they are two so
  As stiff twin compasses are two,
Thy soul the fixt foot, makes no show
  To move, but doth, if the other do.
            Ibid. Stanza 7

Our eyes, upon one double string;
So to'entergraft our hands, as yet
Was all the means to make us one,
And pictures in our eyes to get
Was all our propagation.
          The Extasy. Line 8

Love's mysteries in souls do grow,
But yet the body is his book.
            Ibid. Line 71

I long to talk with some old lover's
    ghost,
Who died before the god of love was
    born.
        Love's Deity. Stanza 1

A bracelet of bright hair about the bone.
          The Relic. Stanza 1

So, so, break off this last lamenting kiss,
Which sucks two souls, and vapours
    both away.
        The Expiration. Stanza 1

    Ah cannot we
As well as cocks and lions jocund be,
After such pleasures?
        Farewell to Love [1635]

Love built on beauty, soon as beauty
    dies.
      Elegies. II, The Anagram

Nature's lay idiot, I taught thee to love.
            Ibid. VII

She, and comparisons are odious.[1]
    Ibid. VIII, The Comparison

---

[1] Included by Izaak Walton in *The Compleat Angler* [1653], *Chap. 9*, as "made by
Dr. Donne, and made to shew the world that

he could make soft verses, when he thought
them fit and worth his labour."
  See Marlowe, page 123a, and C. Day Lewis,
page 992b.
  [1] See Fortescue, page 83b.

No spring, nor summer beauty hath
such grace,
As I have seen in one autumnal face.
Elegies. IX, The Autumnal

O my America! my new-found land.
*Ibid. XIX, To His Mistress
Going to Bed [1669]*

Sir, more than kisses, letters mingle
souls;
For, thus friends absent speak.
*Verse Letter to Sir Henry Wotton.
Line 1*

Be thou thine own home, and in thy
self dwell.
Ibid. Line 47

And seeing the snail, which everywhere
doth roam,
Carrying his own house still, still is at
home,
Follow (for he is easy pac'd) this snail,
Be thine own palace, or the world's thy
jail.
Ibid. Line 49

And new Philosophy calls all in doubt,
The element of fire is quite put out;
The sun is lost, and the earth, and no
man's wit
Can well direct him where to look for it.
And freely men confess that this world's
spent,
When in the planets, and the firmament
They seek so many new; then see that
this
Is crumbled out again to his atomies.
'Tis all in pieces, all coherence gone;
All just supply, and all relation:
Prince, subject, Father, Son, are things
forgot.
*An Anatomie of the World. The
First Anniversary of the Death of
Mistress Elizabeth Drury [1611].
Line 205*

  Her pure, and eloquent blood
Spoke in her cheeks, and so distinctly
wrought,
That one might almost say, her body
thought.
*Of the Progress of the Soul. The
Second Anniversary of the
Death of Mistress Elizabeth
Drury [1612]. Line 244*

I am a little world made cunningly
Of elements, and an angelic sprite.
Holy Sonnets. V [1635]

At the round earth's imagin'd corners,[1]
blow
Your trumpets, angels, and arise, arise
From death, you numberless infinities
Of souls.
Ibid. VII

All whom war, dearth, age, agues, tyr-
annies,
Despair, law, chance, hath slain.
Ibid.

Death be not proud, though some have
called thee
Mighty and dreadful, for thou art not
so,
For those whom thou think'st thou dost
overthrow,
Die not, poor death, nor yet canst thou
kill me.
Ibid. X

One short sleep past, we wake eternally,
And death shall be no more; death,
thou shalt die.
Ibid.

Batter my heart, three-person'd God;
for you
As yet but knock, breath, shine, and
seek to mend.
Ibid. XIV

Since I am coming to that holy room,
Where, with thy quire of saints for
evermore,
I shall be made thy music; as I come
I tune the instrument here at the door,
And what I must do then, think here
before.
*Hymn to God my God, in My
Sickness [1635]. Stanza 1*

Whilst my physicians by their love are
grown
Cosmographers, and I their map, who
lie
Flat on this bed.
Ibid. Stanza 2

  I observe the physician with the same
diligence as he the disease.
Devotions [1624]. VI

[1] See Du Bartas, page 102a.

The flea, though he kill none, he does all the harm he can.
Devotions. XII

No man is an island, entire of itself; every man is a piece of the continent, a part of the main; if a clod be washed away by the sea, Europe is the less, as well as if a promontory were, as well as if a manor of thy friends or of thine own were; any man's death diminishes me, because I am involved in mankind; and therefore never send to know for whom the bell tolls; it tolls for thee.
Ibid. XVII

I throw myself down in my chamber, and I call in and invite God and his angels thither, and when they are there, I neglect God and his angels, for the noise of a fly, for the rattling of a coach, for the whining of a door.
Sermon LXXX, At the Funeral of Sir William Cokayne [1626]

BEN JONSON [1]
[1573?–1637]

It was a mighty while ago.
Every Man in his Humour [1598]. Act I, Sc. 3

As he brews, so shall he drink.
Ibid. Act II, Sc. 1

It must be done like lightning.
Ibid. Act IV, Sc. 5

True happiness
Consists not in the multitude of friends,
But in the worth and choice.
Cynthia's Revels [1600]. Act III, Sc. 2

Queen and huntress, chaste and fair,
Now the sun is laid to sleep,
Seated in thy silver chair,
State in wonted manner keep:
  Hesperus entreats thy light,
  Goddess, excellently bright.
Ibid. Act V, Sc. 3

That old bald cheater, Time.
The Poetaster [1601]. Act I, Sc. 1

[1] O rare Ben Jonson! — SIR JOHN YOUNG: *Epitaph.* (Which was done at the charge of Jack Young, who, walking there when the grave was covering, gave the fellow 18 pence to cut it. — JOHN AUBREY [1626–1697]: *Brief Lives)*

The world knows only two, — that's Rome and I.
Sejanus [1603]. Act V, Sc. 1

Calumnies are answered best with silence.
Volpone [1607]. Act II, Sc. 2

Come my Celia, let us prove,
While we can, the sports of love;
Time will not be ours forever,
He at length our good will sever.
Spend not then his gifts in vain;
Suns that set may rise again,
But if once we lose this light,
'Tis with us perpetual night.[1]
Song, To Celia [1607]

Still to be neat, still to be drest,
As you were going to a feast.
Epicene; Or, The Silent Woman [1609]. Act I, Sc. 1

Give me a look, give me a face,
That makes simplicity a grace;
Robes loosely flowing, hair as free,
Such sweet neglect more taketh me
Than all the adulteries of art:
They strike mine eyes, but not my heart.[2]
Ibid.

The dignity of truth is lost with much protesting.
Catiline's Conspiracy [1611]. Act III, Sc. 2

Truth is the trial of itself
  And needs no other touch,
And purer than the purest gold,
  Refine it ne'er so much.
On Truth [1616]. Stanza 1

Follow a shadow, it still flies you;
  Seem to fly it, it will pursue:
So court a mistress, she denies you;
  Let her alone, she will court you.
Follow a Shadow [1616]. Stanza 1

Preserving the sweetness of proportion and expressing itself beyond expression.
The Masque of Hymen [1616]

Underneath this stone doth lie
As much beauty as could die;
Which in life did harbour give
To more virtue than doth live.
Epitaph on Elizabeth, L. H. [1616]

[1] See Catullus, page 35a.
[2] See Herrick, page 230b.

Whilst that for which all virtue now is
 sold,
And almost every vice, — almighty
 gold.[1]
> *Epistle to Elizabeth, Countess of*
> *Rutland* [*1616*]

God wisheth none should wreck on a
 strange shelf:
To him man's dearer than to himself.
> *The Forest: To Sir Robert Wroth*
> [*1616*]

Drink to me only with thine eyes,
 And I will pledge with mine;
Or leave a kiss but in the cup
 And I'll not look for wine.[2]
The thirst that from the soul doth rise
 Doth ask a drink divine;
But might I of Jove's nectar sup,
 I would not change for thine.
> *Ibid. To Celia* [*1616*]. *Stanza 1*

I sent thee late a rosy wreath,
 Not so much honouring thee
As giving it a hope that there
 It could not wither'd be.
But thou thereon didst only breathe,
 And sent'st it back to me;
Since when it grows and smells, I swear,
 Not of itself, but thee.
> *Ibid. Stanza 2*

Reader, look,
Not at his picture, but his book.
> *On the Portrait of Shakespeare*
> *Prefixed to the First Folio* [*1623*]

Soul of the age!
The applause, delight, the wonder of
 our stage!
My Shakespeare, rise! I will not lodge
 thee by
Chaucer or Spenser, or bid Beaumont
 lie
A little further, to make thee a room:
Thou art a monument, without a tomb,
And art alive still, while thy book doth
 live,

And we have wits to read, and praise to
 give.
> *To the Memory of Shakespeare*
> [*1623*]

Marlowe's mighty line.
> *Ibid.*

Small Latin and less Greek.
> *Ibid.*

He was not of an age but for all time.
> *Ibid.*

Who casts to write a living line, must
 sweat.
> *Ibid.*

For a good poet's made, as well as born.
> *Ibid.*

Sweet Swan of Avon!
> *Ibid.*

Let those that merely talk and never
 think,
That live in the wild anarchy of drink.[1]
> *Underwoods* [*1640*]. *An Epistle,*
> *answering to One that asked to be*
> *sealed of the Tribe of Ben*

In small proportions we just beauties
 see,
And in short measures life may perfect
 be.
> *Ibid. To the Immortal Memory*
> *of Sir Lucius Cary and Sir*
> *Henry Morison*

The players have often mentioned it
as an honor to Shakespeare, that in his
writing, whatsoever he penned, he never
blotted out line. My answer hath been,
"Would he had blotted a thousand."
> *Timber, or Discoveries Made*
> *Upon Men and Matter* [*1640*]

I loved the man [Shakespeare] and
do honor his memory (on this side idol ·
atry) as much as any.
> *Ibid.*

Greatness of name in the father oft-
times overwhelms the son; they stand
too near one another. The shadow kills
the growth: so much, that we see the

---

[1] The flattering, mighty, nay, almighty
gold. — WOLCOT: *To Kien Long* [1782–1785],
Ode IV

See Irving, page 446b.

[2] Drink to me with your eyes alone. . . .
And if you will, take the cup to your lips
and fill it with kisses, and give it so to me. —
PHILOSTRATUS [*circa* A.D. 181–250]: *Letter*
XXIV

[1] Who think too little, and who talk too
much. — DRYDEN: *Absalom and Achitophel*
[1680], *Part I, L. 534*

They never taste who always drink;
They always talk who never think.
MATTHEW PRIOR [1664–1721]: *Upon*
a Passage in the Scaligerana

grandchild come more and oftener to be heir of the first.

Timber, or Discoveries Made Upon Men and Matter

Though the most be players, some must be spectators.

Ibid.

RICHARD BARNFIELD
[1574–1627]

The waters were his winding sheet, the sea was made for his tomb;
Yet for his fame the ocean sea, was not sufficient room.

Epitaph on Hawkins [1595]

As it fell upon a day
In the merry month of May,
Sitting in a pleasant shade
Which a grove of myrtles made.

Address to the Nightingale [1]

King Pandion he is dead,
All thy friends are lapp'd in lead.

Ibid.

Every one that flatters thee
Is no friend in misery.
Words are easy, like the wind;
Faithful friends are hard to find.
Every man will be thy friend
Whilst thou hast wherewith to spend:
But, if store of crowns be scant,
No man will supply thy want.

Ibid.

He that is thy friend indeed,
He will help thee in thy need.

Ibid.

JOSEPH HALL, BISHOP OF NORWICH
[1574–1656]

In bonds of love united, man and wife,
Long, yet too short, they spent a happy life.

Elegy on Sir Edward and Lady Lewkenor

So little in his purse, so much upon his back.

Portrait of a Poor Gallant

[1] This song, attributed to Shakespeare and included in his *Sonnets to Sundry Notes of Music,* is found in BARNFIELD's *Poems in Divers Humours,* published in 1598.

'Mongst all these stirs of discontented strife,
O, let me lead an academic life;
To know much, and to think for nothing, know
Nothing to have, yet think we have enow.

Discontent of Men with their Condition

Moderation is the silken string running through the pearl chain of all virtues.

Christian Moderation. Introduction

Death borders upon our birth, and our cradle stands in the grave.

Epistles. Decade III, Epistle 2

There is many a rich stone laid up in the bowels of the earth, many a fair pearl laid up in the bosom of the sea, that never was seen, nor never shall be.[1]

Contemplations. Book IV, The Veil of Moses

THOMAS CAMPION
[1575?–1620?]

Never love unless you can
Bear with all the faults of man:
Men will sometimes jealous be,
Though but little cause they see;
And hang the head, as discontent,
And speak what straight they will repent.

Never Love [Circa 1617]. Stanza 1

There is a garden in her face
Where roses and white lilies blow;
A heav'nly paradise is that place,
Wherein all pleasant fruits do grow;
There cherries grow that none may buy,
Till Cherry-ripe themselves do cry.

Cherry-Ripe [2] *[Circa 1617]. Stanza 1*

Those cherries fairly do enclose
Of orient pearl a double row,
Which when her lovely laughter shows,

[1] See Thomas Gray, page 348b.
[2] "Cherry-ripe" was a familiar st eet cry of the time.
See Herrick, page 230a.

They look like rosebuds fill'd with snow.
> *Cherry-Ripe. Stanza 2*

The summer hath his joys,
And winter his delights;
Though love and all his pleasures are but toys,
They shorten tedious nights.
> *Winter Nights* [Circa *1617*].
> *Stanza 2*

ROBERT BURTON
[1577–1640]

Naught so sweet as melancholy.[1]
> *Anatomy of Melancholy* [2] [*1621–1651*]. *The Author's Abstract*

I would help others, out of a fellow-feeling.[3]
> *Ibid. Democritus to the Reader*

They lard their lean books with the fat of others' works.[4]
> *Ibid.*

We can say nothing but what hath been said.[5] Our poets steal from Homer.

[1] There's naught in this life sweet,
If man were wise to see 't,
But only melancholy;
O sweetest Melancholy!
WILLIAM STRODE [1602–1645]:
A Song in Praise of Melancholy
JOHN FLETCHER introduced this song in his play, *The Nice Valour* [1647], *Act III, Sc. 3;* and it has also been attributed to him. See Fletcher, page 225b.
There's not a string attuned to mirth
But has its chord in melancholy.
HOOD [1799–1845]: *Ode to Melancholy*
[2] Burton's 'Anatomy of Melancholy,' he said, was the only book that ever took him out of bed two hours sooner than he wished to rise. — BOSWELL: *The Life of Dr. Johnson* [1791]
If the reader has patience to go through his volumes, he will be more improved for literary conversation than by the perusal of any twenty other works with which I am acquainted. — BYRON [1807], in MOORE's *Life*.
[3] A fellow-feeling makes one wondrous kind. — GARRICK: *Prologue on Quitting the Stage* [1776]
See Virgil, page 37a.
[4] See Shakespeare, page 150a.
[5] See Terence, page 31b.

. . . Our story-dressers do as much; he that comes last is commonly best.
> *Anatomy of Melancholy.*
> *Democritus to the Reader*

I say with Didacus Stella, a dwarf standing on the shoulders of a giant may see farther than a giant himself.[1]
> *Ibid.*

It is most true, *stylus virum arguit,* — our style bewrays us.[2]
> *Ibid.*

As that great captain, Ziska, would have a drum made of his skin when he was dead, because he thought the very noise of it would put his enemies to flight.
> *Ibid.*

Smile with an intent to do mischief, or cozen him whom he salutes.
> *Ibid.*

Penny wise, pound foolish.
> *Ibid.*

Women wear the breeches.
> *Ibid.*

Like Aesop's fox, when he had lost his tail, would have all his fellow foxes cut off theirs.[3]
> *Ibid.*

Hannibal, as he had mighty virtues, so had he many vices; he had two distinct persons in him.
> *Ibid.*

Every man hath a good and a bad angel attending on him in particular, all his life long.
> *Ibid. Part I, Sect. 2, Memb. 1,*
> *Subsect. 2*

That which Pythagoras said to his scholars of old, may be for ever applied to melancholy men, *A fabis abstinete,* eat no beans.
> *Ibid. Memb. 2, Subsect. 1*

[1] Pigmaei gigantum humeris impositi plusquam ipsi gigantes vident. — DIDACUS STELLA, in LUCAN [A. D. 39–65]: *De Bello Civili, 10, 11*
[2] Le style est l'homme même (The style is the man himself). — GEORGE LOUIS, COMTE DE BUFFON: *Discours sur le Style,* on admission to the French Academy [1753]
[3] AESOP [*floruit* 550 B. C.]: *Fables, Book V, Fable 5*

Cookery is become an art, a noble science; cooks are gentlemen.

Anatomy of Melancholy. Part I, Sect. 2, Memb. 2, Subsect. 2

As much valour is to be found in feasting as in fighting, and some of our city captains and carpet knights will make this good, and prove it.[1]

Ibid.

No rule is so general, which admits not some exception.

Ibid. Subsect. 3

Idleness is an appendix to nobility.

Ibid. Subsect. 6

Why doth one man's yawning make another yawn?

Ibid. Memb. 3, Subsect. 2

A nightingale dies for shame if another bird sings better.

Ibid. Subsect. 6

They do not live but linger.

Ibid. Subsect. 10

[Diseases] crucify the soul of man, attenuate our bodies, dry them, wither them, shrivel them up like old apples, make them so many anatomies.

Ibid.

[Desire] is a perpetual rack, or horsemill, according to Austin [St. Augustine], still going round as in a ring.

Ibid. Subsect. 11

[The rich] are indeed rather possessed by their money than possessors.

Ibid. Subsect. 12

Like a hog, or dog in the manger, he doth only keep it because it shall do nobody else good, hurting himself and others.[2]

Ibid.

Were it not that they are loath to lay out money on a rope, they would be hanged forthwith, and sometimes die to save charges.

Ibid.

A mere madness, to live like a wretch and die rich.

Ibid.

I may not here omit those two main plagues and common dotages of human

[1] See Montaigne, page 98a.
[2] See Aesop, page 10b.

kind, wine and women, which have infatuated and besotted myriads of people; they go commonly together.

Anatomy of Melancholy. Part I, Sect. 2, Memb. 3, Subsect. 13

All our geese are swans.[1]

Ibid. Subsect. 14

Though they [philosophers] write *contemptu gloriae,* yet as Hieron observes, they will put their names to their books.

Ibid.

They are proud in humility; proud in that they are not proud.[2]

Ibid.

We can make majors and officers every year, but not scholars.

Ibid. Subsect. 15

Hinc quam sic calamus saevior ense, patet. The pen worse than the sword.[3]

Ibid. Memb. 4, Subsect. 4

See one promontory (said Socrates of old), one mountain, one sea, one river, and see all.[4]

Ibid. Subsect. 7

Felix Plater notes of some young physicians, that study to cure diseases, catch them themselves, will be sick, and appropriate all symptoms they find related of others to their own persons.

Ibid. Sect. 3, Memb. 1, Subsect. 2

Aristotle said melancholy men of all others are most witty.

Ibid. Subsect. 3

[1] Every man thinks his own geese swans.
— DICKENS: *The Cricket on the Hearth* [1845], *Chirp the Second*
  Let the long contention cease!
  Geese are swans, and swans are geese.
      MATTHEW ARNOLD: *The Last Word* [1867], *St. 2*
[2] See Coleridge, page 422b.
[3] See Bulwer Lytton, page 510b.
Pyrrhus was used to say that Cineas had taken more towns with his words than he with his arms. — PLUTARCH [A.D. 46–120]: *Pyrrhus*
[4] All places, all airs, make unto me one country; I am in England everywhere, and under any meridian. — SIR THOMAS BROWNE: *Religio Medici* [1642], *Part II, Sect. 1*
A blade of grass is always a blade of grass, whether in one country or another. — SAMUEL JOHNSON, in MRS. PIOZZI's *Anecdotes of Johnson* [1786]

Like him in Aesop, he whipped his horses withal, and put his shoulder to the wheel.[1]

Anatomy of Melancholy. Part II, Sect. 1, Memb. 2

Seneca thinks the gods are well pleased when they see great men contending with adversity.

Ibid. Sect. 2, Memb. 1, Subsect. 1

Machiavel says virtue and riches seldom settle on one man.

Ibid. Memb. 2

Almost in every kingdom the most ancient families have been at first princes' bastards; their worthiest captains, best wits, greatest scholars, bravest spirits in all our annals, have been base [born].

Ibid.

As he said in Machiavel, *omnes eodem patre nati*, Adam's sons, conceived all and born in sin, etc. "We are by nature all as one, all alike, if you see us naked; let us wear theirs and they our clothes, and what is the difference?"

Ibid.

Who cannot give good counsel? 'Tis cheap, it costs them nothing.

Ibid. Memb. 3

Many things happen between the cup and the lip.[2]

Ibid.

Everything, said Epictetus, hath two handles, — the one to be held by, the other not.

Ibid.

All places are distant from heaven alike.

Ibid. Memb. 4

The commonwealth of Venice in their armoury have this inscription: "Happy

[1] AESOP [*floruit* 550 B.C.]: *Hercules and the Waggoner*
[2] There is many a slip 'twixt the cup and the lip. — PALLADAS [*floruit* A.D. 400]: *Greek Anthology, Book X, Epigram 32.* A very ancient proverb, sometimes attributed to Homer.
Though men determine, the gods do dispose; and oft times many things fall out between the cup and the lip. — ROBERT GREENE: *Perimedes the Blacke-Smith* [1588]

is that city which in time of peace thinks of war." [1]

Anatomy of Melancholy. Part II, Sect. 2, Memb. 6

Every man, as the saying is, can tame a shrew but he that hath her.

Ibid.

Divers have been relieved [of melancholy] by exonerating themselves to a faithful friend.

Ibid.

Tobacco, divine, rare, superexcellent tobacco, which goes far beyond all the panaceas, potable gold and philosopher's stones, a sovereign remedy to all diseases.

Ibid. Sect. 4, Memb. 2, Subsect. 2

"Let me not live," said Aretine's Antonia, "if I had not rather hear thy discourse than see a play."

Ibid. Part III, Sect. 1, Memb. 1, Subsect. 1

Birds of a feather will gather together.[2]

Ibid. Subsect. 2

No cord nor cable can so forcibly draw, or hold so fast, as love can do with a twined thread.[3]

Ibid. Sect. 2, Memb. 1, Subsect. 2

To enlarge or illustrate this power and effect of love is to set a candle in the sun.

Ibid.

He is only fantastical that is not in fashion.

Ibid. Memb. 2, Subsect. 3

[Quoting Seneca] Cornelia kept her in talk till her children came from

[1] See Horace, page 40b, and George Washington, page 367a.
[2] Beast knows beast; birds of a feather flock together. — ARISTOTLE [384–322 B.C.]: *Rhetoric, Book I, Chap. 11, Sect. 25*
[3] One hair of a woman can draw more than a hundred pair of oxen. — JAMES HOWELL: *Letters* [1621], *Book II, IV*
She knows her man, and when you rant and swear,
Can draw you to her with a single hair.
DRYDEN: *Persius* [1693], *Satire V, L. 246*
Beauty draws us with a single hair. — POPE: *The Rape of the Lock* [1712], *Canto II, L. 27*

school, "and these," said she, "are my jewels."

> *Anatomy of Melancholy. Part III,*
> *Sect. 2, Memb. 2, Subsect. 3*

Diogenes struck the father when the son swore.

> *Ibid. Subsect. 5*

Though it rain daggers with their points downward.

> *Ibid. Memb. 3*

Going as if he trod upon eggs.

> *Ibid.*

I light my candle from their torches.

> *Ibid. Memb. 5, Subsect. 1*

England is a paradise for women and hell for horses; Italy a paradise for horses, hell for women, as the diverb goes.[1]

> *Ibid. Sect. 3, Memb. 1, Subsect. 2*

If the world will be gulled, let it be gulled.

> *Ibid. Sect. 4, Memb. 1, Subsect. 2*

For "ignorance is the mother of devotion," as all the world knows.

> *Ibid.*

The fear of some divine and supreme powers keeps men in obedience.[2]

> *Ibid.*

Out of too much learning become mad.[3]

> *Ibid.*

The Devil himself, which is the author of confusion and lies.

> *Ibid. Subsect. 3*

Isocrates adviseth Demonicus, when he came to a strange city, to worship by all means the gods of the place.

> *Ibid. Subsect. 5*

When they are at Rome, they do there as they see done.

> *Ibid. Memb. 2, Subsect. 1*

One religion is as true as another.

> *Ibid.*

[1] England is the paradise of women, the purgatory of men, and the hell of horses. — JOHN FLORIO: *Second Frutes* [1591]

[2] The fear o' hell's a hangman's whip
To haud the wretch in order.
ROBERT BURNS [1759–1796]: *Epistle to a Young Friend*

[3] Much learning doth make thee mad. — *Acts, XXVI, 24*

They have cheveril consciences that will stretch.

> *Anatomy of Melancholy. Part III,*
> *Sect. 4, Memb. 2, Subsect. 3*

THOMAS WARD
[1577–1639]

Where to elect there is but one,
'Tis Hobson's choice, — take that or none.[1]

> *England's Reformation* [1630].
> *Chapter IV*

JOHN FLETCHER
[1579–1625]

Man is his own star; and the soul that can
Render an honest and a perfect man
Commands all light, all influence, all fate.
Nothing to him falls early, or too late.
Our acts our angels are, or good or ill,
Our fatal shadows that walk by us still.

> *The Honest Man's Fortune*
> *[1613]. (In collaboration with*
> *three other authors) Epilogue*

Man is his own star; and that soul that can
Be honest is the only perfect man.[2]

> *Ibid.*

Weep no more, nor sigh, nor groan,
Sorrow calls no time that's gone;

[1] Thomas Hobson [1544–1631], of whom Steele wrote in *The Spectator, No. 509* [October 14, 1712]:
Mr. Tobias Hobson, from whom we have the expression, . . . was a carrier, . . . the first in this Island who let out hackney-horses. He lived in Cambridge, and observing that the scholars rid hard, his manner was to keep a large stable of horses, with boots, bridles, and whips. . . . When a man came for an horse, he was led into the stable, where there was great choice, but he obliged him to take the horse which stood next to the stable-door; so that every customer was alike well served according to his chance, and every horse ridden with the same justice. From whence it became a proverb, when what ought to be your election was forced upon you, to say Hobson's Choice.

[2] An honest man's the noblest work of God. — POPE: *Essay on Man, Epistle IV* [1734], L. 248

Violets plucked, the sweetest rain
Makes not fresh nor grow again.[1]
> *The Queen of Corinth* [*1617*].
> (*In collaboration with Massinger and a third author*)
> *Act III, Sc. 2*

Drink today, and drown all sorrow;
You shall perhaps not do't tomorrow.
> *The Bloody Brother* [*1616*].
> (*In collaboration with Jonson and others*) *Act II, Sc. 2*

And he that will to bed go sober
Falls with the leaf in October.[2]
> *Ibid.*

Three merry boys, and three merry
boys,
And three merry boys are we,[3]
As ever did sing in a hempen string
Under the gallows-tree.
> *Ibid. Act III, Sc. 3*

Of all the paths lead to a woman's love
Pity's the straightest.[4]
> *The Knight of Malta* [*1618–1619*]. (*In collaboration with Massinger*) *Act I, Sc. 1*

Go to grass.
> *The Little French Lawyer* [*Circa 1619*]. (*In collaboration with Massinger*) *Act IV, Sc. 7*

There is no jesting with edge tools.
> *Ibid.*

Let's meet, and either do or die.[5]
> *The Island Princess* [*1621*].
> *Act II, Sc. 4*

---

[1] See *The Friar of Orders Gray*, page 1011b.
[2] The following well-known catch, or glee, is formed on this song:

He who goes to bed, and goes to bed sober,
Falls as the leaves do, and dies in October;
But he who goes to bed, and goes to bed mellow,
Lives as he ought to do, and dies an honest fellow.

[3] Three merry men be we. — PEELE: *Old Wives' Tale* [*1595*]
[4] Pity's akin to love. — THOMAS SOUTHERNE: *Oroonoko* [*1696*], Act II, Sc. 1
For pity melts the mind to love. — DRYDEN: *Alexander's Feast* [*1697*], L. 96
Pity swells the tide of love. — EDWARD YOUNG: *Night Thoughts* [*1742–1745*], *Night III, L. 107*
[5] Let us do or die! — ROBERT BURNS [*1759–1796*]: *Bannockburn*
This expression is a kind of common

Deeds, not words shall speak me.
> *The Lover's Progress* [*1623*].
> *Act III, Sc. 4*

Whistle, and she'll come to you.[1]
> *Wit Without Money* [*1639*].
> *Act IV, Sc. 4*

O woman, perfect woman! what distraction
Was meant to mankind when thou wast
made a devil!
> *Monsieur Thomas* [*1639*].
> *Act III, Sc. 1*

Hence, all you vain delights,
As short as are the nights
Wherein you spend your folly!
There's naught in this life sweet
But only melancholy.
> *Melancholy*[2] [*The Nice Valour, 1647*]

JOHN WEBSTER
[1580–1625]

I saw him now going the way of all
flesh.[3]
> *Westward Hoe* [*1607*]. (*In collaboration with Dekker*) *Act II, Sc. 2*

Call for the robin redbreast and the
wren,
Since o'er shady groves they hover,
And with leaves and flowers do cover
The friendless bodies of unburied men.
> *The White Devil* [*1612*].
> *Act V, Sc. 4*

But keep the wolf far thence, that's foe
to men,
For with his nails he'll dig them up
again.
> *Ibid.*

Prosperity doth bewitch men, seeming
clear;

---

property, being the motto, we believe, of a
Scottish family. — SIR WALTER SCOTT [*1771–1832*]: *Review of* THOMAS CAMPBELL's *Gertrude of Wyoming*
[1] Whistle, and I'll come to ye. — ROBERT BURNS [*1759–1796*]: *Whistle, etc.*
[2] See Robert Burton, page 221b, and Milton, page 245b.
[3] Title of the novel by Samuel Butler [*1903*].

But seas do laugh, show white, when
    rocks are near.
        The White Devil. Act V, Sc. 6

Glories, like glow-worms, afar off shine
    bright,
But look'd too near have neither heat
    nor light.
        Duchess of Malfi [*1623*].
                Act IV, Sc. 2

I know death hath ten thousand sev-
    eral doors
For men to take their exit.[1]
                    Ibid.

Heaven-gates are not so highly arch'd
As princes' palaces; they that enter
    there
Must go upon their knees.
                    Ibid.

Ferdinand. Cover her face; mine eyes
    dazzle; she died young.
Bosola. I think not so; her infelicity
Seem'd to have years too many.
                    Ibid.

Vain the ambition of kings
Who seek by trophies and dead things
To leave a living name behind,
And weave but nets to catch the wind.
    The Devil's Law Case [*1623*].
                    Song

SIR THOMAS OVERBURY
[1581–1613]

Give me, next good, an understanding
    wife,
By nature wise, not learnèd much by
    art;
Some knowledge on her part will, all
    her life,
More scope of conversation impart.
              A Wife [*1614*]

In part to blame is she,
Which hath without consent been only
    tried:

---

[1] Death hath a thousand doors to let out
life. — MASSINGER: *A Very Woman* [*1655*],
Act V, Sc. 4
Death hath so many doors to let out life.
— FLETCHER AND MASSINGER: *The Custom of
the Country* [*1647*], *Act II, Sc. 2*
The thousand doors that lead to death. —
SIR THOMAS BROWNE: *Religio Medici* [*1642*],
Part I, Sect. XLIV

He comes too near that comes to be de-
    nied.
                  A Wife

Books are a part of man's prerogative;
In formal ink they thoughts and voices
    hold,
That we to them our solitude may give,
And make time present travel that of
    old.
                    Ibid.

He disdains all things above his
reach, and preferreth all countries before his own.
    An Affectate Traveller [*1614*]

BISHOP RICHARD CORBET
[1582–1635]

Farewell rewards and fairies,[1]
Good housewives now may say.
    Farewell to the Fairies. Stanza 1

Nor too much wealth nor wit come to
    thee,
So much of either may undo thee.
        To His Son, Vincent Corbet

I wish thee all thy mother's graces,
Thy father's fortunes and his places.
                    Ibid.

PHILIP MASSINGER
[1583–1640]

Be wise;
Soar not too high to fall; but stoop to
    rise.
    Duke of Milan [*1623*]. *Act I, Sc. 2*

He that would govern others, first
    should be
Master of himself.
    The Bondman [*1624*]. *Act I, Sc. 3*

To be nobly born
Is now a crime.
        The Roman Actor [*1629*].
                    Act I, Sc. 1

Whose wealth
Arithmetic cannot number.
                  Ibid. Sc. 3

Grim death.[2]
                Ibid. Act IV, Sc. 2

---

[1] *Rewards and Fairies*, title of a book by
Kipling [1910].
[2] See Milton, page 254b.

A New Way to Pay Old Debts.
Title of Play [1632]

THOMAS HEYWOOD
[*Died* 1650?]

Pack clouds away, and welcome day,
With night we banish sorrow.
*Pack Clouds Away [1630].
Stanza 1*

I hold he loves me best that calls me
Tom.
*Hierarchie of the Blessed Angells
[1635]*

Seven cities warred for Homer being
dead,
Who living had no roof to shroud his
head.[1]
Ibid.

JOHN SELDEN
[1584–1654]

Equity is a roguish thing. For Law
we have a measure, know what to trust
to; Equity is according to the conscience of him that is Chancellor, and
as that is larger or narrower, so is
Equity. 'Tis all one as if they should
make the standard for the measure we
call a "foot" a Chancellor's foot; what
an uncertain measure would this be!
One Chancellor has a long foot, another a short foot, a third an indifferent
foot. 'Tis the same thing in the Chancellor's conscience.
Table Talk [1689]. Equity

Humility is a virtue all preach, none
practise; and yet everybody is content
to hear.
Ibid. Humility

'Tis not the drinking that is to be
blamed, but the excess.
Ibid.

[1] Seven cities strive for the learned root of
Homer:
Smyrna, Chios, Colophon, Ithaca, Pylos,
Argos, Athens.
UNKNOWN (*Greek Anthology,
Book VI, Epigram 298*)
Seven wealthy towns contend for Homer
dead,
Through which the living Homer begged
his bread.
THOMAS SEWARD [1708–
1790]: *On Homer*

Commonly we say a judgment falls
upon a man for something in him we
cannot abide.
Table Talk. Judgments

Ignorance of the law excuses no
man; not that all men know the law,
but because 'tis an excuse every man
will plead, and no man can tell how to
refute him.
Ibid. Law

No man is the wiser for his learning.
Ibid. Learning

Wit and wisdom are born with a man.
Ibid.

Few men make themselves masters
of the things they write or speak.
Ibid.

Take a straw and throw it up into
the air, — you may see by that which
way the wind is.
Ibid. Libels

Philosophy is nothing but discretion.
Ibid. Philosophy

Marriage is a desperate thing.
Ibid. Marriage

Thou little thinkest what a little
foolery governs the world.[1]
Ibid. Pope

They that govern the most make the
least noise.
Ibid. Power

Syllables govern the world.
Ibid.

Never king dropped out of the
clouds.
Ibid.

Never tell your resolution beforehand.
Ibid. Wisdom

Wise men say nothing in dangerous
times.
Ibid.

Pleasure is nothing else but the intermission of pain.
Ibid. Pleasure

Preachers say, Do as I say, not as I
do.
Ibid. Preaching

[1] Behold, my son, with how little wisdom
the world is governed. — AXEL OXENSTIERN
[1583–1654]

A King is a thing men have made for their own sakes, for quietness' sake. Just as in a Family one man is appointed to buy the meat.
Table Talk. Of a King

FRANCIS BEAUMONT
[1584–1616]

What things have we seen
Done at the Mermaid! heard words that have been
So nimble and so full of subtle flame
As if that everyone from whence they came
Had meant to put his whole wit in a jest,
And resolved to live a fool the rest
Of his dull life.
Letter to Ben Jonson [1640]

BEAUMONT AND FLETCHER [1]

Francis Beaumont [1584–1616] and John Fletcher [1579–1625]

No better than you should be.[2]
The Coxcomb [1610].
Act IV, Sc. 3
The devil take the hindmost!
Philaster [1610]. Act V
As cold as cucumbers.
Cupid's Revenge [1615].
Act I, Sc. 1
Calamity is man's true touchstone.[3]
Four Plays in One. The Triumph of Honour, Sc. 1
Kiss till the cow comes home.
Scornful Lady [1616].
Act III, Sc. 1
Beggars must be no choosers.
Ibid. Act V, Sc. 3

[1] Of whose partnership John Aubrey [1626–1697] said: "There was a wonderful consimility of fancy. They lived together not far from the playhouse, had one wench in the house between them, the same clothes and cloak, &c."
[2] She is no better than she should be. — Fielding: *The Temple Beau* [1730], Act IV, Sc. 3
[3] See Seneca, page 47b.

There is a method in man's wickedness, —
It grows up by degrees.[1]
A King and No King [1619].
Act V, Sc. 4
Upon my buried body lie lightly, gentle earth.
The Maid's Tragedy [1619].
Act I, Sc. 2

JOHN FORD
[1586–1639]

Diamond cut diamond.
The Lover's Melancholy [1629].
Act I, Sc. 1
'Tis Pity She's a Whore.
Title of Play [1633]

THOMAS RAINBOROUGH
[? –1648]

The poorest he that is in England hath a life to live as the greatest he.
In the Army debates at Putney
[October 29, 1647]

THOMAS HOBBES
[1588–1679]

Words are wise men's counters, — they do but reckon by them; but they are the money of fools.
Leviathan. Part I [1651],
Chap. IV

The privilege of absurdity; to which no living creature is subject but man only.
Ibid. Chap. V
Sudden glory is the passion which maketh those grimaces called laughter.
Ibid. Chap. VI

The secret thoughts of a man run over all things, holy, profane, clean, obscene, grave, and light, without shame or blame.
Ibid. Chap. VIII
During the time men live without a common power to keep them in awe, they are in that condition which is

[1] See Juvenal, page 62b, and Racine, page 287b.

called war; and such a war as is of every man against every man.
Leviathan. Part I, Chap. XIII

As the nature of foul weather lieth not in a shower or two of rain but in an inclination thereto of many days together, so the nature of war consisteth not in actual fighting but in the known disposition thereto during all the time there is no assurance to the contrary. All other time is peace.
Ibid.

[In a state of nature] No arts, no letters, no society, and, which is worst of all, continual fear and danger of violent death, and the life of man solitary, poor, nasty, brutish, and short.
Ibid.

The praise of ancient authors proceeds not from the reverence of the dead, but from the competition and mutual envy of the living.
Ibid. Review and Conclusion

Such truth as opposeth no man's profit nor pleasure is to all men welcome.
Ibid.

GEORGE WITHER
[1588–1667]

Shall I, wasting in despair,
Die because a woman's fair?
Or make pale my cheeks with care,
'Cause another's rosy are?
Be she fairer than the day,
Or the flowery meads in May,
If she be not so to me,
What care I how fair she be?
Sonnet 4 [1619]. Stanza 1

If she love me, this believe,
I will die, ere she shall grieve.
If she slight me when I woo,
I can scorn and let her go;
For if she be not for me,
What care I for whom she be?
Ibid. Stanza 5

'Twas I that beat the bush,
The bird to others flew.
*A Love Sonnet [1622].
Stanza 11*

Though I am young, I scorn to flit
On the wings of borrowed wit.
The Shepherd's Hunting [1622]

WILLIAM BRADFORD
[1590–1657]

They knew they were pilgrims.[1]
Of Plymouth Plantation [1620–1647]. Chap. 7

So they committed themselves to the will of God and resolved to proceed.
Ibid. Chap. 9

Being thus arrived in a good harbor, and brought safe to land, they fell upon their knees and blessed the God of Heaven who had brought them over the vast and furious ocean, and delivered them from all the perils and miseries thereof, again to set their feet on the firm and stable earth, their proper element.
Ibid.

Our fathers were Englishmen which came over this great ocean, and were ready to perish in this wilderness.
Ibid.

The loss of . . . honest and industrious men's lives cannot be valued at any price.
Ibid. Chap. 12

But it pleased God to visit us then with death daily, and with so general a disease that the living were scarce able to bury the dead.
Ibid.

Cold comfort to fill their hungry bellies.
Ibid. Chap. 13

Behold, now, another providence of God. A ship comes into the harbor.
Ibid.

Thus out of small beginnings greater things have been produced by His hand that made all things of nothing, and gives being to all things that are; and, as one small candle may light a thousand, so the light here kindled hath

[1] It was owing to this passage, first printed in 1669, that the *Mayflower's* company came eventually to be called the Pilgrim Fathers.

shone unto many, yea in some sort to our whole nation.

Of Plymouth Plantation. Chap. 21

WILLIAM BROWNE
[1591–1643]

Underneath this sable hearse
Lies the subject of all verse:
Sidney's sister, Pembroke's mother.
Death, ere thou hast slain another
Fair and learn'd and good as she,
Time shall throw a dart at thee.

*Epitaph on the Countess of
Pembroke [1621]*

There is no season such delight can bring,
As summer, autumn, winter, and the spring.

Variety

ROBERT HERRICK
[1591–1674]

I sing of brooks, of blossoms, birds, and bowers:
Of April, May, of June, and July-flowers.
I sing of May-poles, Hock-carts, wassails, wakes,
Of bride-grooms, brides, and of their bridal-cakes.

*Hesperides [1648]. Argument
of his Book*

What is a kiss? Why this, as some approve:
The sure, sweet cement, glue, and lime of love.

Ibid. A Kiss

Bid me to live, and I will live
  Thy Protestant to be,
Or bid me love, and I will give
  A loving heart to thee.

Ibid. To Anthea. Stanza 1

Cherry ripe, ripe, ripe, I cry,
Full and fair ones, — come and buy!
If so be you ask me where
They do grow, I answer, there,
Where my Julia's lips do smile, —
There's the land, or cherry-isle.

Ibid. Cherry Ripe [1]

[1] See Thomas Campion, page 220b.

Some asked how pearls did grow, and where?
  Then spoke I to my girl
To part her lips, and showed them there
  The quarelets of pearl.[1]

*Hesperides. The Rock of Rubies,
and the Quarrie of Pearls*

A sweet disorder in the dress
Kindles in clothes a wantonness.

Ibid. Delight in Disorder

A winning wave, deserving note,
In the tempestuous petticoat;
A careless shoe-string, in whose tie
I see a wild civility, —
Do more bewitch me than when art
Is too precise in every part.[2]

Ibid.

You say to me-wards your affection's strong;
Pray love me little, so you love me long.[3]

Ibid. Love me Little, Love me Long

Night makes no difference 'twixt the Priest and Clerk;
Joan as my Lady is as good i' the dark.

Ibid. No Difference i' th' Dark

Give me a kiss, and to that kiss a score;
Then to that twenty, add a hundred more:
A thousand to that hundred: so kiss on,
To make that thousand up a million.
Treble that million, and when that is done,
Let's kiss afresh, as when we first begun.

Ibid. To Anthea: Ah, My Anthea!

Gather ye rosebuds while ye may,
  Old Time is still a-flying,
And this same flower that smiles today
  Tomorrow will be dying.[4]

*Ibid. To the Virgins to make much
of Time*

Fair daffodils, we weep to see
You haste away so soon.

To Daffodils

[1] See Thomas Campion, page 220b.
[2] See Jonson, page 218b.
[3] See John Heywood, page 93b.
[4] Let us crown ourselves with rosebuds, before they be withered. — *Wisdom of Solomon, II, 8*
Gather the rose of love, whilest yet is time. — SPENSER: *The Faerie Queene, Book II* [1590], *Canto XII, St. 75*

Her pretty feet, like snails, did creep
  A little out, and then,[1]
As if they played at bo-peep,
  Did soon draw in again.
> *Hesperides. To Mistress*
> *Susanna Southwell*

Her eyes the glow-worm lend thee,
The shooting stars attend thee;
  And the elves also,
  Whose little eyes glow
Like the sparks of fire, befriend thee.
> *Ibid. The Night Piece to Julia*

Thus times do shift, — each thing his
  turn does hold;
New things succeed, as former things
  grow old.
> *Ibid. Ceremonies for*
> *Candlemas Eve*

Outdid the meat, outdid the frolic
  wine.
> *Ibid. Ode for Ben Jonson*

Attempt the end, and never stand to
  doubt;
Nothing's so hard but search will find
  it out.
> *Ibid. Seek and Find*

Here a little child I stand
Heaving up my either hand.
Cold as paddocks though they be,
Here I lift them up to Thee,
For a benison to fall
On our meat, and on us all.
> *Ibid. A Child's Grace*

Her legs were such Diana shows
When tuckt up she a-hunting goes
With buskins shortened to descry
The happy dawning of her thigh.
> *Ibid. The Vision*

Get up, sweet Slug-a-bed, and see
The dew bespangling herb and tree.
> *Ibid. Corinna's Going a-Maying*

Wash, dress, be brief in praying:
Few beads are best, when once we go
  a-Maying.
> *Ibid.*

Whenas in silks my Julia goes,
Then, then (methinks) how sweetly
  flows
That liquefaction of her clothes.
> *Ibid. Upon Julia's Clothes*

[1] See Suckling, page 261a.

HENRY KING, BISHOP
OF CHICHESTER
[1592–1669]

And that tame Lover who unlocks his
  heart
Unto his mistress, teaching her an art
To plague himself, shows her the secret
  way
How she may tyrannize another day!
> *The Steed that Comes to*
> *Understand* [1657]

Thou art the book, —
The library whereon I look.
> *Exequy on the Death of a*
> *Beloved Wife* [1657]

Then we shall rise
And view ourselves with clearer eyes
In that calm region where no night
Can hide us from each other's sight.
> *Ibid.*

Stay for me there; I will not fail
To meet thee in that hollow vale.
> *Ibid.*

FRANCIS QUARLES
[1592–1644]

Death aims with fouler spite
At fairer marks.[1]
> *Divine Fancies* [1632]

Sweet Phosphor, bring the day!
Light will repay
The wrongs of night.
> *Emblems* [1635]. *Book I,*
> *Emblem 14*

Be wisely worldly, be not worldly wise.
> *Ibid. Book II, Emblem 2*

This house is to be let for life or years;
Her rent is sorrow, and her income
  tears.
Cupid, 't has long stood void; her bills
  make known,
She must be dearly let, or let alone.
> *Ibid. Emblem 10, Epigram*

The slender debt to Nature's quickly
  paid,[2]
Discharged, perchance, with greater
  ease than made.
> *Ibid. Emblem 13*

[1] See Edward Young, page 306a.
[2] To die is a debt we must all of us discharge. — EURIPIDES: *Alcestis, L. 418*

The next way home's the farthest way about.[1]
Emblems. Book IV, Emblem 2, Epigram

It is the lot of man but once to die.
Ibid. Book V, Emblem 7

And what's a life? — a weary pilgrimage,
Whose glory in one day doth fill the stage
With childhood, manhood, and decrepit age.
What Is Life? Stanza 1

Let all thy joys be as the month of May,
And all thy days be as a marriage day:
Let sorrow, sickness, and a troubled mind
Be stranger to thee, let them never find
Thy heart at home.
To a Bride

The way to bliss lies not on beds of down,
And he that has no cross deserves no crown.
Esther

THOMAS RAVENSCROFT
[1592?–1635]

Nose, nose, nose, nose!
And who gave thee that jolly red nose?
Sinament and Ginger, Nutmegs and Cloves,
And that gave me my jolly red nose.
Deuteromelia [1609]. *Song No. 7* [2]

GEORGE HERBERT
[1593–1633]

Sweet day, so cool, so calm, so bright,
The bridal of the earth and sky.
The Temple [1633]. *Virtue, Stanza 1*

[1] The longest way round is the shortest way home. — BOHN: *Foreign Proverbs, Italian*
[2] Quoted by BEAUMONT AND FLETCHER, *The Knight of the Burning Pestle* [1613], *Act I, Sc. 3.* RAVENSCROFT'S *Deuteromelia* was a supplement to his *Pammelia*, which was the earliest collection of rounds, catches, and canons printed in England.

Sweet spring, full of sweet days and roses,
A box where sweets compacted lie.
The Temple. Virtue, Stanza 3

Only a sweet and virtuous soul,
Like seasoned timber, never gives.
Ibid. Stanza 4

Love bade me welcome; yet my soul drew back,
Guilty of dust and sin.
But quick-ey'd Love, observing me grow slack
From my first entrance in,
Drew nearer to me, sweetly questioning
If I lack'd anything.
Ibid. Love, Stanza 1

"You must sit down," says Love, "and taste my meat."
So I did sit and eat.
Ibid. Stanza 3

A verse may find him who a sermon flies.[1]
And turn delight into a sacrifice.
Ibid. The Church Porch, Stanza 1

Drink not the third glass, which thou canst not tame,
When once it is within thee.
Ibid. Stanza 5

Dare to be true: nothing can need a lie;
A fault which needs it most, grows two thereby.[2]
Ibid. Stanza 13

By all means use sometimes to be alone.
Ibid. Stanza 25

By no means run in debt: take thine own measure.
Who cannot live on twenty pound a year,
Cannot on forty.
Ibid. Stanza 30

Wit's an unruly engine, wildly striking

[1] That many people read a song
Who will not read a sermon.
WINTHROP MACKWORTH PRAED [1802–1839]:*The Chant of the Brazenhead, St. 1*
[2] And he that does one fault at first,
And lies to hide it, makes it two.
ISAAC WATTS [1674–1748]:
Song XV

Sometimes a friend, sometimes the engineer.

> *The Temple. The Church Porch, Stanza 41*

Be useful where thou livest.

> *Ibid. Stanza 55*

Sum up at night, what thou hast done by day.

> *Ibid. Stanza 76*

For thirty pence he did my death devise,[1]
Who at three hundred did the ointment prize.[2]

> *Ibid. The Sacrifice, Stanza 5*

Most things move th' under-jaw, the Crocodile not.[3]

Most things sleep lying, th' Elephant leans or stands.[4]

> *Ibid. Providence, Stanza 35*

Pulpits and Sundays, sorrow dogging sin,
Afflictions sorted, anguish of all sizes,
Fine nets and stratagems to catch us in,
Bibles laid open, millions of surprises.

> *Ibid. Sin, Stanza 2*

I struck the board, and cried, "No more;
    I will abroad."
What, shall I ever sigh and pine?
My lines and life are free; free as the road,
Loose as the wind, as large as store.
    Shall I be still in suit?
Have I no harvest but a thorn
To let me blood, and not restore
What I have lost with cordial fruit?
    Sure there was wine
Before my sighs did dry it; there was corn
Before my tears did drown it;

[1] See *King John and the Abbot of Canterbury*, page 1012a.

[2] Then saith one of his disciples, Judas Iscariot, Simon's son, which should betray him, Why was not this ointment sold for three hundred pence, and given to the poor? — *John, XII, 4-5*

[3] The crocodile does not move the lower jaw, but is the only animal that brings down its upper jaw to the under one. — HERODOTUS [484-424 B. C.], *Customs of the Egyptians*

[4] Leans the huge elephant. — JAMES THOMSON: *The Seasons, Summer* [1727], L. 725

Is the year only lost to me?
Have I no bays to crown it?

> *The Temple. The Collar*

But as I rav'd and grew more fierce and wild
    At every word,
Methought I heard one calling, "Child";
    And I replied, "My Lord."

> *Ibid.*

He would adore my gifts instead of Me,
And rest in Nature, not the God of Nature:
    So both should losers be.

> *Ibid. The Pulley, Stanza 3*

Let him be rich and weary, that at least,
If goodness lead him not, yet weariness
May toss him to my breast.

> *Ibid. Stanza 4*

Pleasing ware is half sold.

> *Jacula Prudentum [1640]*

Love, and a cough, cannot be hid.

> *Ibid.*

Deceive not thy physician, confessor, nor lawyer.

> *Ibid.*

Who would do ill ne'er wants occasion.

> *Ibid.*

A snow year, a rich year.

> *Ibid.*

Love your neighbour, yet pull not down your hedge.[1]

> *Ibid.*

The mill cannot grind with water that's past.

> *Ibid.*

Good words are worth much, and cost little.

> *Ibid.*

Hell is full of good meanings and wishings.[2]

> *Ibid.*

Whose house is of glass, must not throw stones at another.

> *Ibid.*

[1] See Robert Frost, page 879b.

[2] Sir, Hell is paved with good intentions. — SAMUEL JOHNSON [1775]: *Boswell's Life of Dr. Johnson, Everyman ed., Vol. I, P. 555* See William James, page 715a.

By suppers more have been killed than Galen ever cured.
Jacula Prudentum

The lion is not so fierce as they paint him.[1]
Ibid.

Go not for every grief to the physician, nor for every quarrel to the lawyer, nor for every thirst to the pot.
Ibid.

The best mirror is an old friend.
Ibid.

When you are an anvil, hold you still; when you are a hammer, strike your fill.[2]
Ibid.

He that lies with the dogs, riseth with fleas.
Ibid.

He that is not handsome at twenty, nor strong at thirty, nor rich at forty, nor wise at fifty, will never be handsome, strong, rich, or wise.
Ibid.

The buyer needs a hundred eyes, the seller not one.
Ibid.

My house, my house, though thou art small, thou art to me the Escurial.
Ibid.

Trust not one night's ice.
Ibid.

For want of a nail the shoe is lost, for want of a shoe the horse is lost, for want of a horse the rider is lost.[3]
Ibid.

Pension never enriched a young man.
Ibid.

One enemy is too much.[1]
Jacula Prudentum

Thursday come, and the week is gone.
Ibid.

Time is the rider that breaks youth.
Ibid.

Show me a liar, and I will show thee a thief.
Ibid.

One father is more than a hundred school-masters.
Ibid.

Reason lies between the spur and the bridle.
Ibid.

One sword keeps another in the sheath.
Ibid.

God's mill grinds slow, but sure.[2]
Ibid.

It is a poor sport that is not worth the candle.
Ibid.

He that lends, gives.
Ibid.

Poverty is no sin.
Ibid.

Words are women, deeds are men.[3]
Ibid.

To a close shorn sheep, God gives wind by measure.[4]
Ibid.

None knows the weight of another's burthen.
Ibid.

One hour's sleep before midnight is worth three after.
Ibid.

He hath no leisure who useth it not.
Ibid.

[1] The lion is not so fierce as painted. — THOMAS FULLER [1608–1661]: *Expecting Preferment*
[2] Stand like an anvil when it is beaten upon. — ST. IGNATIUS THEOPHORUS, Bishop of Antioch [A.D. 104]
When you are the anvil, bear —
When you are the hammer, strike.
EDWIN MARKHAM [1852–1940]: *Preparedness*
[3] A little neglect may breed mischief: for want of a nail, etc. — BENJAMIN FRANKLIN: *Maxim prefixed to Poor Richard's Almanac* [1757]

[1] See Ali Ibn-abu-Taleb, page 73b.
[2] See Euripides, page 17a.
Though the mills of God grind slowly, yet they grind exceeding small. — F. VON LOGAU [1604–1655]: *Retribution* (translated by LONGFELLOW)
[3] See Samuel Johnson, page 336b.
[4] Dieu mesure le froid à la brebis tondue (God regulates the cold to the shorn lamb). — HENRI ESTIENNE: *Prémices* [1594]
"God tempers the wind," said Maria, "to the shorn lamb." LAURENCE STERNE: *A Sentimental Journey* [1768]

Half the world knows not how the other half lives.

Jacula Prudentum

Life is half spent before we know what it is.

Ibid.

Every mile is two in winter.

Ibid.

The eye is bigger than the belly.

Ibid.

His bark is worse than his bite.

Ibid.

He that steals an egg will steal an ox.

Ibid. [*second edition, 1651*]

Of a pig's tail you can never make a good shaft.[1]

Ibid.

There is an hour wherein a man might be happy all his life could he find it.

Ibid.

Woe be to him who reads but one book.

Ibid.

IZAAK WALTON
[1593–1683]

But God, who is able to prevail, wrestled with him, as the angel did with Jacob, and marked him; marked him for his own.[2]

Life of Donne [*1640*]

Of which, if thou be a severe, sour-complexioned man, then I here disallow thee to be a competent judge.

The Compleat Angler [*1653–1655*]. *Author's Preface*

I have laid aside business, and gone a-fishing.

Ibid.

Angling may be said to be so like the

mathematics that it can never be fully learnt.

The Compleat Angler. Author's Preface

As no man is born an artist, so no man is born an angler.

Ibid.

I shall stay him no longer than to wish him a rainy evening to read this following discourse; and that if he be an honest angler, the east wind may never blow when he goes a fishing.

Ibid.

As the Italians say, Good company in a journey makes the way to seem the shorter.

Ibid. Part I, Chap. I

Doubt not but angling will prove to be so pleasant that it will prove to be, like virtue, a reward to itself.[1]

Ibid.

Sir Henry Wotton was a most dear lover and a frequent practiser of the Art of Angling; of which he would say, " 'Twas an employment for his idle time, which was then not idly spent, a rest to his mind, a cheerer of his spirits, a diverter of sadness, a calmer of unquiet thoughts, a moderator of passions, a procurer of contentedness"; and "that it begat habits of peace and patience in those that professed and practised it."

Ibid.

You will find angling to be like the virtue of humility, which has a calmness of spirit and a world of other blessings attending upon it.[2]

Ibid.

---

[1] You can't make a silk purse out of a sow's ear. — JONATHAN SWIFT: *Polite Conversation* [?1738], *Dialogue II*

As certainly as you can make a velvet cap out of a sow's ear. — STERNE: *Tristram Shandy* [1761–1768], *Book IV*

The proverb says you can't make a silk purse out of a sow's ear. — DICKENS: *David Copperfield* [1849–1850], *Chap. 30*

[2] See Thomas Gray, page 349a.

[1] Ipsa quidem virtus sibimet pulcherrima merces (Virtue herself is her own fairest reward). — SILIUS ITALICUS [A.D. 25?–99]: *Punica, Lib. XIII, L. 663*

Virtue was sufficient of herself for happiness. — DIOGENES LAERTIUS [*circa* A.D. 200]: *Plato, XLII*

That virtue is her own reward, is but a cold principle. — SIR THOMAS BROWNE: *Religio Medici* [1642], *Part I, Sect. XLVII*

Virtue is its own reward. — PRIOR [1664–1721]: *Imitations of Horace, Book III, Ode 2*

[2] There is certainly something in angling . . . that tends to produce a gentleness of

I remember that a wise friend of mine did usually say, "That which is everybody's business is nobody's business."
The Compleat Angler. Part I, Chap. II

An honest Ale-house where we shall find a cleanly room, Lavender in the Windows, and twenty Ballads stuck about the wall.
Ibid.

Good company and good discourse are the very sinews of virtue.
Ibid.

An excellent angler, and now with God.
Ibid. Chap. IV

Old-fashioned poetry, but choicely good.
Ibid.

I love such mirth as does not make friends ashamed to look upon one another next morning.
Ibid. Chap. V

No man can lose what he never had.
Ibid.

We may say of angling as Dr. Boteler [1] said of strawberries: "Doubtless God could have made a better berry, but doubtless God never did"; and so, if I might be judge, God never did make a more calm, quiet, innocent recreation than angling.
Ibid.

I in these flowery meads would be;
These crystal springs should solace me,
To whose harmonious bubbling noise,
I with my angle would rejoice.
Ibid. The Angler's Wish. Stanza 1

Thus use your frog: put your hook through his mouth and out at his gills, and then with a fine needle and silk sew the upper part of his leg with only one stitch to the arming wire of your hook, or tie the frog's leg above the upper joint to the armed wire; and in

so doing use him as though you loved him.
The Compleat Angler. Part I, Chap. VIII

This dish of meat is too good for any but anglers, or very honest men.
Ibid.

Look to your health; and if you have it, praise God, and value it next to a good conscience; for health is the second blessing that we mortals are capable of, — a blessing that money cannot buy.
Ibid. Chap. XXI

And upon all that are lovers of virtue, and dare trust in his Providence, and be quiet and go a-angling.
Ibid.

The great secretary of Nature and all learning, Sir Francis Bacon.[1]
Life of Herbert [1670]

THOMAS CAREW
[1595?–1639?]

Ask me no more where Jove bestows,
When June is past, the fading rose;
For in your beauty's orient deep
These flowers, as in their causes sleep.
To Celia [1640]. Stanza 1

Ask me no more whither doth haste
The nightingale when May is past;
For in your sweet dividing throat
She winters and keeps warm her note.
Ibid. Stanza 3

Ask me no more if East or West
The phoenix builds her spicy nest;
For unto you at last she flies,
And in your fragrant bosom dies.
Ibid. Stanza 5

Give me more love or more disdain;
The torrid or the frozen zone:
Bring equal ease unto my pain;
The temperate affords me none.
Mediocrity in Love Rejected [1640]

Thou shalt confess the vain pursuit
Of human glory yields no fruit
But an untimely grave.
On the Duke of Buckingham [1640]

spirit, and a pure serenity of mind. — WASHINGTON IRVING: *The Sketch-Book, The Angler*
[1] William Butler [1535–1618], styled by THOMAS FULLER in his *Worthies of England* the "Aesculapius of our age." This praise of the strawberry first appeared in the second edition of *The Angler*, 1655.

[1] Plato, Aristotle, and Socrates are secretaries of Nature. —JAMES HOWELL [1594–1666]: *Letters, Books II, Letter XI*

He that loves a rosy cheek,
　Or a coral lip admires,
Or from star-like eyes doth seek
　Fuel to maintain his fires; —
As old Time makes these decay,
So his flames must waste away,
　　Disdain Returned [*1640*]. *Stanza 1*
The firstling of the infant year.
　　　　　　　The Primrose [*1640*]
Then fly betimes, for only they
Conquer Love that run away.
　　　　Conquest by Flight [*1640*]
The magic of a face.
　　*Epitaph on the Lady S—— * [*1640*]

RENÉ DESCARTES
[1596–1650]

I think, therefore I am.[1]
　　Le Discours de la Méthode [*1637*]
Good sense is of all things in the
world the most equally distributed, for
everybody thinks himself so abundantly
provided with it, that even those most
difficult to please in all other matters
do not commonly desire more of it than
they already possess.
　　　　　　　　　　　　Ibid.
The greatest minds are capable of
the greatest vices as well as of the greatest virtues.
　　　　　　　　　　　　Ibid.

JAMES SHIRLEY
[1596–1666]

　　How little room
Do we take up in death, that, living
　　know
No bounds!
　　　　　　　　The Wedding [*1626*]
Only the actions of the just
Smell sweet and blossom in their dust.[2]
　　　　　　　　　　　　Ibid.
Death calls ye to the crowd of common
　　men.
　　　　Cupid and Death [*1653*]

[1] Cogito, ergo sum.
Je pense donc je suis.
[2] The sweet remembrance of the just
Shall flourish when he sleeps in dust.
　　NAHUM TATE AND NICHOLAS BRADY:
　　　　Psalm CXXXII [1696], *6*

The glories of our blood and state
　Are shadows, not substantial things;
There is no armour against fate;
　Death lays his icy hand on kings.
　　Contention of Ajax and Ulysses
　　　　　　　　　[*1659*]. *Sc. 3*
The garlands wither on your brow;
Then boast no more your mighty deeds.
　　　　　　　　　　　　Ibid.

OLIVER CROMWELL
[1599–1658]

The State, in choosing men to serve
it, takes no notice of their opinions. If
they be willing faithfully to serve it,
that satisfies.
　　Before the Battle of Marston
　　　　Moor [*July 2, 1644*]
A few honest men are better than
numbers. If you choose godly, honest
men to be captains of horse, honest men
will follow them.
　　Reorganization of the Army [*1645*]
I would have been glad to have lived
under my woodside, and to have kept
a flock of sheep, rather than to have
undertaken this government.
　　　　　To Parliament [*1658*]
Mr. Lely, I desire you would use all
your skill to paint my picture truly like
me, and not flatter me at all; but remark all these roughnesses, pimples,
warts, and everything as you see me,
otherwise I will never pay a farthing
for it.
　　HORACE WALPOLE: *Anecdotes of*
　　Painting in England [*1762–1771*]
I would be willing to live to be further serviceable to God and His people,
but my work is done! Yet God will be
with His people!
　　　　[*September 1, 1658, two days*
　　　　　　　　before his death]

SAMUEL BUTLER
[1600–1680]

When civil fury first grew high,
And men fell out they knew not why.
　　　　Hudibras. Part I [*1663*],
　　　　　　　　Canto I, Line 1

And pulpit, drum ecclesiastic,[1]
Was beat with fist instead of a stick.
> *Hudibras. Part I, Canto I,*
> *Line 11*

We grant, although he had much wit,
He was very shy of using it.
> *Ibid. Line 45*

Beside, 'tis known he could speak Greek
As naturally as pigs squeak; [2]
That Latin was no more difficile
Than to a blackbird 'tis to whistle.
> *Ibid. Line 51*

He could distinguish and divide
A hair 'twixt south and southwest side,
On either which he would dispute,
Confute, change hands, and still confute.
> *Ibid. Line 67*

He'd run in debt by disputation,
And pay with ratiocination.
> *Ibid. Line 77*

For rhetoric, he could not ope
His mouth, but out there flew a trope.
> *Ibid. Line 81*

For all a rhetorician's rules
Teach nothing but to name his tools.
> *Ibid. Line 89*

A Babylonish dialect
Which learned pedants much affect.
> *Ibid. Line 93*

For he by geometric scale
Could take the size of pots of ale.
> *Ibid. Line 121*

And wisely tell what hour o' the day
The clock does strike, by algebra.
> *Ibid. Line 125*

Where entity and quiddity,
The ghosts of defunct bodies, fly.
> *Ibid. Line 145*

'Twas Presbyterian true blue.
> *Ibid. Line 189*

[1] This is the first we hear of the "drum ecclesiastic" beating up for recruits in worldly warfare in our country. — WASHINGTON IRVING: *Knickerbocker's History of New York* [1809], *Book V, Chap. 7*

[2] He Greek and Latin speaks with greater ease
Than hogs eat acorns, and tame pigeons peas.
LIONEL CRANFIELD, EARL OF MIDDLESEX [1575-1645]: *Panegyric on Tom Coriate*

Such as do build their faith upon
The holy text of pike and gun.
> *Hudibras. Part I, Canto I,*
> *Line 193*

And prove their doctrine orthodox,
By apostolic blows and knocks.
> *Ibid. Line 199*

Compound for sins they are inclined to,
By damning those they have no mind to.
> *Ibid. Line 215*

The trenchant blade, Toledo trusty,
For want of fighting was grown rusty,
And ate into itself, for lack
Of somebody to hew and hack.
> *Ibid. Line 359*

For rhyme the rudder is of verses,
With which, like ships, they steer their courses.
> *Ibid. Line 463*

And force them, though it was in spite
Of Nature and their stars, to write.
> *Ibid. Line 647*

Great actions are not always true sons
Of great and mighty resolutions.
> *Ibid. Line 885*

I'll make the fur
Fly 'bout the ears of the old cur.
> *Ibid. Canto III, Line 277*

These reasons made his mouth to water.
> *Ibid. Line 379*

I am not now in fortune's power:
He that is down can fall no lower.[1]
> *Ibid. Line 871*

Cheer'd up himself with ends of verse
And sayings of philosophers.
> *Ibid. Line 1011*

Cleric before, and Lay behind;
A lawless linsey-woolsey brother,
Half of one order, half another.
> *Ibid. Line 1226*

But those that write in rhyme still make
The one verse for the other's sake;
For one for sense, and one for rhyme,
I think's sufficient at one time.
> *Ibid. Part II [1664], Canto I,*
> *Line 23*

Some have been beaten till they know
What wood a cudgel's of by th' blow;

[1] He that is down needs fear no fall. — BUNYAN: *Pilgrim's Progress* [1678], *Part II*

Some kick'd until they can feel whether
A shoe be Spanish or neat's leather.
Hudibras. Part II, Canto I,
Line 221

Such great achievements cannot fail,
To cast salt on a woman's tail.
Ibid. Line 277

Quoth she, I've heard old cunning stagers
Say fools for arguments use wagers.
Ibid. Line 297

For what is worth in anything
But so much money as 'twill bring?
Ibid. Line 465

She that with poetry is won
Is but a desk to write upon.
Ibid. Line 591

Love is a boy by poets styl'd;
Then spare the rod and spoil the child.[1]
Ibid. Line 843

The sun had long since in the lap
Of Thetis taken out his nap,
And, like a lobster boil'd the morn
From black to red began to turn.
Ibid. Canto II, Line 29

Oaths are but words, and words but wind.
Ibid. Line 107

For truth is precious and divine, —
Too rich a pearl for carnal swine.
Ibid. Line 257

He that imposes an oath makes it,
Not he that for convenience takes it;
Then how can any man be said
To break an oath he never made?
Ibid. Line 377

    As the ancients
Say wisely, have a care o' th' main chance,[2]
And look before you ere you leap; [3]
For as you sow, ye are like to reap.[4]
Ibid. Line 501

Doubtless the pleasure is as great
Of being cheated as to cheat.
Ibid. Canto III, Line 1

1 See Skelton, page 84b.
2 See Lyly, page 112b.
3 See Heywood, page 91a.
4 Whatsoever a man soweth, that shall he also reap. — *Galatians, VI, 7*

He made an instrument to know
If the moon shine at full or no.
Hudibras. Part II, Canto III,
Line 261

But Hudibras gave him a twitch
As quick as lightning in the breech,
Just in the place where honour's lodg'd,
As wise philosophers have judg'd;
Because a kick in that part more
Hurts honour than deep wounds before.
Ibid. Line 1065

As men of inward light are wont
To turn their optics in upon 't.
Ibid. Part III [*1678*], *Canto I,*
Line 481

What makes all doctrines plain and clear?
About two hundred pounds a year.
And that which was prov'd true before
Prove false again? Two hundred more.
Ibid. Line 1277

Nick Machiavel had ne'er a trick,
Though he gave his name to our Old Nick.[1]
Ibid. Line 1313

With crosses, relics, crucifixes,
Beads, pictures, rosaries, and pixes, —
The tools of working our salvation
By mere mechanic operation.
Ibid. Line 1495

The saints engage in fierce contests
About their carnal interests.
Ibid. Canto II, Introduction

True as the dial to the sun,[2]
Although it be not shin'd upon.
Ibid. Line 175

He that complies against his will
Is of his own opinion still.
Ibid. Canto III, Line 547

And poets by their sufferings grow,[3]
As if there were no more to do,

1 Out of his surname they have coined an epithet for a knave, and out of his Christian name a synonym for the Devil. — MACAULAY: *Machiavelli* [1827]
2 True as the needle to the pole,
  Or as the dial to the sun.
    BARTON BOOTH [1681–1733]: *Song*
3   Most wretched men
    Are cradled into poetry by wrong;
    They learn in suffering what they teach in song.
    SHELLEY: *Julian and Maddalo* [1818]

To make a poet excellent,
But only want and discontent.
Fragments

SIR KENELM DIGBY
[1603–1665]

The hot water is to remain upon it
[the tea] no longer than whiles you can
say the Miserere Psalm very leisurely.
The Closet Opened. Tea with Eggs

All Matter is indifferent to Form.
Of the Vegetation of Plants

SIR THOMAS BROWNE
[1605–1682]

I could never divide myself from
any man upon the difference of an opinion, or be angry with his judgment for
not agreeing with me in that from which
perhaps within a few days I should dissent myself.
Religio Medici [1642]. Part I,
Sect. VI

Many . . . have too rashly charged
the troops of error, and remain as
trophies unto the enemies of truth.
Ibid.

A man may be in as just possession of
truth as of a city, and yet be forced to
surrender.
Ibid.

I love to lose myself in a mystery, to
pursue my Reason to an *O altitudo!*
Ibid. Sect. IX

Rich with the spoils of Nature.[1]
Ibid. Sect. XIII

We carry with us the wonders, we
seek without us: there is all Africa and
her prodigies in us.
Ibid. Sect. XV

All things are artificial, for nature is
the art of God.[2]
Ibid. Sect. XVI

Obstinacy in a bad cause is but constancy in a good.
Ibid. Sect. XXV

---

[1] See Thomas Gray, page 348b.
[2] The course of Nature is the art of God. —
EDWARD YOUNG: *Night Thoughts* [1742–
1745], *Night IX, L. 1267*

Persecution is a bad and indirect way
to plant religion.
Religio Medici. Part I, Sect. XXV

This reasonable moderator, and equal
piece of justice, Death.
Ibid. Sect. XXXVIII

I am not so much afraid of death, as
ashamed thereof. 'Tis the very disgrace
and ignominy of our natures, that in a
moment can so disfigure us, that our
nearest friends, wife, and children,
stand afraid and start at us.
Ibid. Sect. XL

Whosoever enjoys not this life, I
count him but an apparition, though he
wear about him the sensible affections
of flesh. In these moral acceptions, the
way to be immortal is to die daily.
Ibid. Sect. XLV

How shall the dead arise, is no question of my Faith; to believe only possibilities, is not Faith, but mere philosophy.
Ibid. Sect. XLVIII

The heart of man is the place the
devils dwell in: I feel sometimes a hell
within myself.[1]
Ibid. Sect. LI

There is no road or ready way to
virtue.
Ibid. Sect. LV

They that endeavor to abolish vice,
destroy also virtue; for contraries,
though they destroy one another, are
yet the life of one another.
Ibid. Part II, Sect. IV

But how shall we expect charity towards others, when we are uncharitable
to our selves? *Charity begins at home,*
is the voice of the world; yet is every
man his greatest enemy, and, as it were,
his own executioner.
Ibid.

There is music even in the beauty,
and the silent note which Cupid strikes,
far sweeter than the sound of an instru-

---

[1] The mind is its own place, and in itself
Can make a heaven of hell, a hell of
heaven.
MILTON: *Paradise Lost* [1667],
Book I, L. 253
Which way I fly is Hell; myself am Hell.
— *Ibid., Book IV, L. 75*

ment; for there is a music wherever there is a harmony, order, or proportion; and thus far we may maintain the music of the spheres.

Religio Medici. Part II, Sect. IX

For the world, I count it not an inn, but an hospital; and a place not to live, but to die in.

Ibid. Sect. XI

There is surely a piece of divinity in us, something that was before the elements, and owes no homage unto the sun.

Ibid.

Ruat coelum, fiat voluntas tua.[1]

Ibid.

Sleep is a death; oh, make me try
By sleeping, what it is to die,
And as gently lay my head
On my grave, as now my bed!

Ibid. Sect. XII

When we desire to confine our words, we commonly say they are spoken under the rose.[2]

Vulgar Errors [1645]

An old and gray-headed error.

Ibid.

Times before you, when even living men were antiquities; when the living might exceed the dead, and to depart this world could not be properly said to go unto the greater number.[3]

Urn-Burial [1658]. Dedication

I look upon you as a gem of the old rock.[4]

Ibid.

Quietly rested under the drums and tramplings of three conquests.

Urn-Burial. Chapter 5

Time which antiquates antiquities, and hath an art to make dust of all things.

Ibid.

What song the Sirens sang, or what name Achilles assumed when he hid himself among women.

Ibid.

The iniquity of oblivion blindly scattereth her poppy.

Ibid.

Herostratus lives that burnt the temple of Diana; he is almost lost that built it.[1]

Ibid.

Oblivion is not to be hired: the greater part must be content to be as though they had not been, to be found in the register of God, not in the record of man.

Ibid.

The night of time far surpasseth the day, and who knows when was the equinox?

Ibid.

Man is a noble animal, splendid in ashes and pompous in the grave, solemnizing nativities and deaths with equal lustre, nor omitting ceremonies of bravery in the infamy of his nature.

Ibid.

To keep our eyes open longer were but to act our antipodes. The huntsmen are up in America, and they are already past their first sleep in Persia. But who can be drowsy at that hour which freed us from everlasting sleep? or have slumbering thoughts at that time, when sleep itself must end, and, as some conjecture, all shall awake again?

The Garden of Cyrus [1658]

---

[1] Though the sky fall, let Thy will be done. Fiat justitia et ruant coeli (Let justice be done though the heavens fall). — WILLIAM WATSON: *Ten Quodlibeticall Questions Concerning Religion and State* [1601]

[2] Sub rosa. This phrase, meaning secretly, is of unknown origin. With the ancients the rose was emblematic of secrecy, and when a host hung a rose above his tables, his guests understood that all words spoken under it were to remain secret. Later, roses were carved as decorations on the ceilings of council chambers and confessionals, with the same significance.

[3] 'Tis long since Death had the majority. — BLAIR: *The Grave* [1743], Part II, L. 449

[4] Adamas de rupe veteri praestantissimus (A most excellent diamond from the old rock).
See Burke, page 360b.

[1] The aspiring youth that fired the Ephesian dome
Outlives in fame the pious fool that raised it.
CIBBER [1671–1757]: *Richard III, Act III, Sc. 1*

EDMUND WALLER
[1605–1687]

Illustrious acts high raptures do infuse,
And every conqueror creates a muse.
> *Panegyric on Cromwell*

Under the tropic is our language spoke,
And part of Flanders hath receiv'd our yoke.
> *Upon the Death of the*
> *Lord Protector* [*1658*]

The yielding marble of her snowy breast.
> *On a Lady Passing through a*
> *Crowd of People* [*1664*]

To man, that was in th' evening made,
Stars gave the first delight;
Admiring, in the gloomy shade,
Those little drops of light.
> *An Apology for Having Loved*
> *Before* [*1664*]

That which her slender waist confin'd
Shall now my joyful temples bind;
No monarch but would give his crown
His arms might do what this has done.
> *On a Girdle* [*1664*]. *Stanza 1*

My joy, my grief, my hope, my love,
Did all within this circle move!
> *Ibid. Stanza 2*

A narrow compass! and yet there
Dwelt all that's good, and all that's fair;
Give me but what this riband bound,
Take all the rest the sun goes round!
> *Ibid. Stanza 3*

Go, lovely rose!
Tell her that wastes her time and me
That now she knows,
When I resemble her to thee,
How sweet and fair she seems to be.
> *Go, Lovely Rose* [*1664*]. *Stanza 1*

How small a part of time they share
That are so wondrous sweet and fair!
> *Ibid. Stanza 4*

For all we know
Of what the blessed do above
Is, that they sing, and that they love.
> *While I Listen to thy Voice*

Poets that lasting marble seek
Must come in Latin or in Greek.
> *Of English Verse* [*1668*]

And keeps the palace of the soul.[1]
> *Of Tea*

Poets lose half the praise they should have got,
Could it be known what they discreetly blot.
> *Upon Roscommon's Translation*
> *of Horace, De Arte Poetica*

The soul's dark cottage, batter'd and decay'd,
Lets in new light through chinks that Time has made.[2]
Stronger by weakness, wiser men become
As they draw near to their eternal home:
Leaving the old, both worlds at once they view
That stand upon the threshold of the new.
> *On the Divine Poems* [*1686*]

SIR WILLIAM DAVENANT
[1606–1668]

The lark now leaves his wat'ry nest
And, climbing, shakes his dewy wings.
> *Song* [*1637*]. *Stanza 1*

For angling-rod he took a sturdy oak;
For line, a cable that in storm ne'er broke;
His hook was such as heads the end of pole
To pluck down house ere fire consumes it whole;
The hook was baited with a dragon's tail, —
And then on rock he stood to bob for whale.
> *Britannia Triumphans* [*1637*]

The assembled souls of all that men held wise.
> *Gondibert* [*1651*]. *Book II,*
> *Canto V, Stanza 37*

I shall ask leave to desist, when I am

---

[1] The dome of thought, the palace of the soul. — BYRON: *Childe Harold, Canto II* [1812], *St. 6*

[2] To vanish in the chinks that Time has made. — SAMUEL ROGERS: *Italy* [1822], *Paestum*

interrupted by so great an experiment as dying.

> *His apology, in illness, for not having finished Gondibert*

How much pleasure they lose (and even the pleasures of heroic poesy are not unprofitable) who take away the liberty of a poet, and fetter his feet in the shackles of a historian.

> *Prefatory Letter to Thomas Hobbes (Quoted in Biographia Literaria [1817] by* S. T. COLERIDGE, *Chapter 22*

PIERRE CORNEILLE
[1606–1684]

Pierced to the depth of my heart by a blow unforeseen — and mortal.[1]

> *Le Cid [1636]. Act I, Sc. 6*

He who cares naught for death cares naught for threats.

> *Ibid. Act II, Sc. 1*

We triumph without glory when we conquer without danger.

> *Ibid. Sc. 2*

Brave men are brave from the very first.

> *Ibid. Sc. 3*

And the combat ceased for want of combatants.

> *Ibid. Act IV, Sc. 3*

Do your duty, and leave the rest to heaven.

> *Horace [1639]. Act II, Sc. 8*

All evils are equal when they are extreme.

> *Ibid. Act III, Sc. 4*

Who is all-powerful should fear everything.

> *Cinna [1639]. Act IV, Sc. 2*

By speaking of our misfortunes we often relieve them.

> *Polyeucte [1640]. Act I, Sc. 3*

The manner of giving is worth more than the gift.

> *Le Menteur [1642]. Act I, Sc. 1*

A liar is always lavish of oaths.

> *Ibid. Act III, Sc. 5*

A good memory is needed after one has lied.[1]

> *Le Menteur. Act IV, Sc. 5*

The fire which seems extinguished often slumbers beneath the ashes.

> *Rodogune [1644]. Act III, Sc. 4*

He who allows himself to be insulted deserves to be.

> *Héraclius [1664]. Act I, Sc. 2*

A service beyond all recompense Weighs so heavy that it almost gives offence.

> *Suréna [1674]. Act III, Sc. 1*

THOMAS FULLER
[1608–1661]

Drawing near her death, she sent most pious thoughts as harbingers to heaven; and her soul saw a glimpse of happiness through the chinks of her sickness-broken body.

> *Life of Monica [1642]*

He was one of a lean body and visage, as if his eager soul, biting for anger at the clog of his body, desired to fret a passage through it.[2]

> *Life of the Duke of Alva [1642]*

She commandeth her husband, in any equal matter, by constant obeying him.

> *Holy and Profane State [1642]. The Good Wife*

He knows little who will tell his wife all he knows.

> *Ibid. The Good Husband*

One that will not plead that cause wherein his tongue must be confuted by his conscience.

> *Ibid. The Good Advocate*

To smell to a turf of fresh earth is wholesome for the body; no less are thoughts of mortality cordial to the soul.

> *Ibid. The Virtuous Lady*

Their heads sometimes so little that there is no room for wit; sometimes so

---

[1] Percé jusques au fond du coeur
D'une atteinte imprévue aussi bien que mortelle.

[1] Liars ought to have good memories. — ALGERNON SIDNEY: *Discourses on Government* [1698], *Chap. 2, Sect. XV*
[2] See Dryden, page 276b.

long that there is no wit for so much room.

Holy and Profane State.
Of Natural Fools

Learning hath gained most by those books by which the printers have lost.

Ibid. Of Books

Deceive not thy self by overexpecting happiness in the married estate. Remember the nightingales which sing only some months in the spring, but commonly are silent when they have hatched their eggs.

Ibid. Of Marriage

They that marry ancient people, merely in expectation to bury them, hang themselves in hope that one will come and cut the halter.

Ibid.

Fame sometimes hath created something of nothing.

Ibid. Fame

Anger is one of the sinews of the soul; he that wants it hath a maimed mind.

Ibid. Of Anger

Light, God's eldest daughter, is a principal beauty in a building.

Ibid. Of Building

In Building, rather believe any man than an Artificer for matter of charges. Should they tell thee all the cost at the first, it would blast a young Builder in the budding.

Ibid.

JOHN MILTON
[1608–1674]

This is the month, and this the happy morn,
Wherein the Son of Heav'n's eternal King,
Of wedded maid and virgin mother born,
Our great redemption from above did bring;
For so the holy sages once did sing,
That He our deadly forfeit should release,

And with His Father work us a perpetual peace.

On the Morning of Christ's Nativity [*1629*]. *Stanza 1, Line 1*

It was the winter wild
While the Heav'n-born child
All meanly wrapt in the rude manger lies.

Ibid. Hymn, Stanza 1, Line 29

No war, or battle's sound
Was heard the world around.
The idle spear and shield were high up hung.

Ibid. Stanza 4, Line 53

Time will run back and fetch the Age of Gold.

Ibid. Stanza 14, Line 135

The Oracles are dumb;
No voice or hideous hum
Runs through the archèd roof in words deceiving.

Ibid. Stanza 19, Line 173

From haunted spring and dale
Edg'd with poplar pale
The parting genius is with sighing sent.

Ibid. Stanza 20, Line 184

Peor and Baalim
Forsake their temples dim.

Ibid. Stanza 22, Line 197

What needs my Shakespeare for his honour'd bones
The labour of an age in pilèd stones?
Or that his hallow'd relics should be hid
Under a star-ypointing pyramid?
Dear son of memory, great heir of fame,
What need'st thou such weak witness of thy name?

On Shakespeare [*1630*]

And so sepúlchred in such pomp dost lie,
That kings for such a tomb would wish to die.

Ibid.

How soon hath Time, the subtle thief of youth,
Stol'n on his wing my three-and-twentieth year.

On His Having Arrived at the Age of Twenty-three [*1631*]

As ever in my great Taskmaster's eye.

Ibid.

Such sweet compulsion doth in music
    lie.
            Arcades [*1630–1634*]. *Line 68*

Hence, loathèd Melancholy,
Of Cerberus and blackest Midnight
    born,
In Stygian cave forlorn,
'Mongst horrid shapes, and shrieks, and
    sights unholy.
            L'Allegro [*1632*]. *Line 1*

So buxom, blithe, and debonair.
            Ibid. Line 24

Haste thee, Nymph, and bring with
    thee
Jest, and youthful Jollity,
Quips and Cranks and wanton Wiles,
Nods and Becks and wreathèd Smiles.
            Ibid. Line 25

Sport, that wrinkled Care derides,
And Laughter, holding both his sides.
Come, and trip it, as you go,
On the light fantastic toe.
            Ibid. Line 31

The mountain nymph, sweet Liberty.
            Ibid. Line 36

Mirth, admit me of thy crew,
To live with her, and live with thee,
In unreprovèd pleasures free.
            Ibid. Line 38

While the cock with lively din
Scatters the rear of darkness thin,
And to the stack, or the barn door,
Stoutly struts his dames before,
Oft list'ning how the hounds and horn
Cheerly rouse the slumb'ring morn.
            Ibid. Line 49

And every shepherd tells his tale
Under the hawthorn in the dale.
            Ibid. Line 67

Meadows trim, with daisies pied,
Shallow brooks, and rivers wide;
Towers and battlements it sees
Bosom'd high in tufted trees,
Where perhaps some beauty lies,
The cynosure of neighboring eyes.
            Ibid. Line 75

And the jocund rebecks sound
To many a youth, and many a maid,
Dancing in the chequered shade.

And young and old come forth to play
On a sunshine holiday.
            L'Allegro. Line 94

Then to the spicy nut-brown ale.
            Ibid. Line 100

Then lies him down the lubber fiend,
And stretch'd out all the chimney's
    length,
Basks at the fire his hairy strength.
            Ibid. Line 110

Tower'd cities please us then,
And the busy hum of men.
            Ibid. Line 117

    Ladies, whose bright eyes
Rain influence, and judge the prize.
            Ibid. Line 121

And pomp, and feast, and revelry,
With mask, and antique pageantry,
Such sights as youthful poets dream
On summer eves by haunted stream.
Then to the well-trod stage anon,
If Jonson's learned sock be on,
Or sweetest Shakespeare, Fancy's child,
Warble his native wood-notes wild.
            Ibid. Line 127

And ever, against eating cares,
Lap me in soft Lydian airs,
Married to immortal verse,[1]
Such as the meeting soul may pierce,
In notes with many a winding bout
Of linkèd sweetness long drawn out.
            Ibid. Line 135

Untwisting all the chains that tie
The hidden soul of harmony.
            Ibid. Line 143

Such strains as would have won the ear
Of Pluto, to have quite set free
His half-regain'd Eurydice.
These delights, if thou canst give,
Mirth, with thee, I mean to live.
            Ibid. Line 148

Hence vain deluding Joys,
The brood of Folly without father
    bred!
            Il Penseroso [*1632*]. *Line 1*

The gay motes that people the sun-
    beams.
            Ibid. Line 8

---

[1] Wisdom married to immortal verse.—
WORDSWORTH: *The Excursion* [1814], *Book
VII*

Come pensive Nun, devout and pure,
Sober, steadfast, and demure.

> *Il Penseroso. Line 31*

And looks commercing with the skies,
Thy rapt soul sitting in thine eyes.

> *Ibid. Line 39*

Forget thyself to marble.

> *Ibid. Line 42*

And join with thee, calm Peace and
Quiet,
Spare Fast, that oft with gods doth
diet.

> *Ibid. Line 45*

And add to these retired Leisure,
That in trim gardens takes his pleasure.

> *Ibid. Line 49*

Sweet bird, that shunn'st the noise of
folly,
Most musical, most melancholy!

> *Ibid. Line 61*

I walk unseen
On the dry smooth-shaven green,
To behold the wandering moon,
Riding near her highest noon,
Like one that had been led astray
Through the heav'n's wide pathless
way,
And oft, as if her head she bow'd,
Stooping through a fleecy cloud.

> *Ibid. Line 65*

Oft, on a plat of rising ground,
I hear the far-off curfew sound
Over some wide-watered shore,
Swinging low with sullen roar.

> *Ibid. Line 73*

Where glowing embers through the
room
Teach light to counterfeit a gloom,
Far from all resort of mirth,
Save the cricket on the hearth.

> *Ibid. Line 79*

Sometime let gorgeous Tragedy
In sceptred pall come sweeping by,
Presenting Thebes, or Pelops' line,
Or the tale of Troy divine.

> *Ibid. Line 97*

Or bid the soul of Orpheus sing
Such notes as, warbled to the string,
Drew iron tears down Pluto's cheek.

> *Ibid. Line 105*

Or call up him that left half told
The story of Cambuscan bold.

> *Il Penseroso. Line 109*

Where more is meant than meets the
ear.

> *Ibid. Line 120*

When the gust hath blown his fill,
Ending on the rustling leaves,
With minute-drops from off the eaves.

> *Ibid. Line 128*

Hide me from day's garish eye,
While the bee with honied thigh,
That at her flowery work doth sing,
And the waters murmuring
With such consort as they keep,
Entice the dewy-feather'd sleep.

> *Ibid. Line 141*

And storied windows richly dight,
Casting a dim religious light.
There let the pealing organ blow,
To the full-voiced quire below,
In service high, and anthems clear
As may, with sweetness, through mine
ear
Dissolve me into ecstasies,
And bring all Heaven before mine eyes.

> *Ibid. Line 159*

Till old experience do attain
To something like prophetic strain.

> *Ibid. Line 173*

Before the starry threshold of Jove's
Court [1]
My mansion is.

> *Comus [1634]. Line 1*

Above the smoke and stir of this dim
spot
Which men call earth.

> *Ibid. Line 5*

Yet some there be that by due steps
aspire
To lay their just hands on that golden
key
That opes the palace of Eternity.

> *Ibid. Line 12*

An old, and haughty nation proud in
arms.

> *Ibid. Line 33*

What never yet was heard in tale or
song,

[1] See William Blake, page 386b.

From old or modern bard, in hall or
bower.

Comus. Line 44

Bacchus, that first from out the purple
grape
Crush'd the sweet poison of misusèd
wine.

Ibid. Line 46

These my sky-robes, spun out of Iris'
woof.

Ibid. Line 83

The star that bids the shepherd fold.

Ibid. Line 93

And the gilded car of day,
His glowing axle doth allay
In the steep Atlantic stream.

Ibid. Line 95

Midnight shout and revelry,
Tipsy dance and jollity.

Ibid. Line 103

What hath night to do with sleep?

Ibid. Line 122

Ere the blabbing eastern scout,
The nice morn, on th' Indian steep,
From her cabin'd loop-hole peep.

Ibid. Line 138

When the gray-hooded Even,
Like a sad votarist in palmer's weed,
Rose from the hindmost wheels of
Phoebus' wain.

Ibid. Line 188

A thousand fantasies
Begin to throng into my memory,
Of calling shapes, and beck'ning shad-
ows dire,
And airy tongues that syllable men's
names
On sands and shores and desert wilder-
nesses.

Ibid. Line 205

Was I deceiv'd, or did a sable cloud
Turn forth her silver lining on the
night?

Ibid. Line 221

Sweet Echo, sweetest nymph, that liv'st
unseen
Within thy airy shell
By slow Meander's margent green,
And in the violet-embroidered
vale.

Ibid. Line 230

How sweetly did they float upon the
wings
Of silence, through the empty-vaulted
night,
At every fall smoothing the raven down
Of darkness till it smil'd!

Comus. Line 249

Such sober certainty of waking bliss.

Ibid. Line 263

With thy long levell'd rule of streaming light.

Ibid. Line 340

Virtue could see to do what Virtue
would
By her own radiant light, though sun
and moon
Were in the flat sea sunk. And Wisdom's self
Oft seeks to sweet retired solitude,
Where, with her best nurse Contemplation,
She plumes her feathers, and lets grow
her wings.

Ibid. Line 373

The unsunn'd heaps
Of miser's treasure.

Ibid. Line 398

'Tis Chastity, my brother, Chastity:
She that has that, is clad in complete
steel.

Ibid. Line 420

Some say no evil thing that walks by
night,
In fog or fire, by lake or moorish fen,
Blue meagre hag, or stubborn unlaid
ghost,
That breaks his magic chains at curfew
time,
No goblin, or swart faery of the mine,
Hath hurtful power o'er true virginity.

Ibid. Line 432

How charming is divine philosophy!
Not harsh and crabbed, as dull fools
suppose,
But musical as is Apollo's lute,[1]
And a perpetual feast of nectar'd sweets
Where no crude surfeit reigns.

Ibid. Line 476

[1]   As sweet and musical
As bright Apollo's lute.
SHAKESPEARE: *Love's Labour's Lost*
[1594–1595], *Act IV, Sc. 3, L. 342*

Fill'd the air with barbarous dissonance.
> *Comus. Line 550*

I was all ear,
And took in strains that might create a soul
Under the ribs of Death.
> *Ibid. Line 560*

That power
Which erring men call Chance.
> *Ibid. Line 587*

Praising the lean and sallow abstinence.
> *Ibid. Line 709*

Beauty is Nature's coin, must not be hoarded,
But must be current, and the good thereof
Consists in mutual and partaken bliss.
> *Ibid. Line 739*

Beauty is Nature's brag, and must be shown
In courts, at feasts, and high solemnities,
Where most may wonder at the workmanship;
It is for homely features to keep home, —
They had their name thence; coarse complexions
And cheeks of sorry grain will serve to ply
The sampler, and to tease the huswife's wool.
What need a vermeil-tinctur'd lip for that,
Love-darting eyes, or tresses like the morn?
> *Ibid. Line 745*

Enjoy your dear wit, and gay rhetoric,
That hath so well been taught her dazzling fence.
> *Ibid. Line 790*

Sabrina fair,
  Listen where thou art sitting
Under the glassy, cool, translucent wave,
  In twisted braids of lilies knitting
The loose train of thy amber-dropping hair;
  Listen for dear honour's sake,

Goddess of the silver lake,
  Listen and save.
> *Comus. Line 859*

But now my task is smoothly done:
I can fly, or I can run.
> *Ibid. Line 1012*

Love Virtue, she alone is free,
She can teach ye how to climb
Higher than the sphery chime;
Or, if Virtue feeble were,
Heav'n itself would stoop to her.
> *Ibid. Line 1019*

I come to pluck your berries harsh and crude,
And with forc'd fingers rude
Shatter your leaves before the mellowing year.
> *Lycidas* [*1637*]. *Line 3*

He knew
Himself to sing, and build the lofty rhyme.
> *Ibid. Line 10*

Without the meed of some melodious tear.
> *Ibid. Line 14*

Hence with denial vain, and coy excuse.
> *Ibid. Line 18*

Under the opening eyelids of the morn,
We drove afield; and both together heard
What time the gray-fly winds her sultry horn,
Batt'ning our flocks with the fresh dews of night.
> *Ibid. Line 26*

But oh the heavy change, now thou art gone,
Now thou art gone and never must return!
> *Ibid. Line 37*

The gadding vine.
> *Ibid. Line 40*

As killing as the canker to the rose.
> *Ibid. Line 45*

Alas! what boots it with incessant care
To tend the homely slighted shepherd's trade,
And strictly meditate the thankless Muse?
Were it not better done as others use,

To sport with Amaryllis in the shade,
Or with the tangles of Neaera's hair?
Lycidas. Line 64

Fame is the spur that the clear spirit
  doth raise [1]
(That last infirmity of noble mind) [2]
To scorn delights, and live laborious
  days;
But the fair guerdon when we hope to
  find,
And think to burst out into sudden
  blaze,
Comes the blind Fury with th' abhorred
  shears
And slits the thin-spun life.
Ibid. Line 70

Fame is no plant that grows on mortal
  soil.
Ibid. Line 78

The strain I heard was of a higher mood.
Ibid. Line 87

It was that fatal and perfidious bark
Built in th' eclipse, and rigg'd with
  curses dark,
That sunk so low that sacred head of
  thine.
Ibid. Line 100

The Pilot of the Galilean lake;
Two massy keys he bore of metals
  twain
(The golden opes, the iron shuts
  amain).
Ibid. Line 109

Such as for their bellies' sake,
Creep and intrude, and climb into the
  fold.
Ibid. Line 114

The hungry sheep look up, and are not
  fed,
But, swoln with wind and the rank mist
  they draw,
Rot inwardly and foul contagion
  spread;
Besides what the grim wolf with privy
  paw

[1] See Tacitus, page 63b.
[2] That thirst (for applause), if the last infirmity of noble minds, is also the first infirmity of weak ones; and, on the whole, the strongest impulsive influence of average humanity. — RUSKIN: *Sesame and Lilies* [1865], *Of Kings' Treasuries,* 3

Daily devours apace, and nothing said.
Lycidas. Line 123

But that two-handed engine at the door
Stands ready to smite once, and smite
  no more.
Ibid. Line 130

Throw hither all your quaint enamell'd
  eyes,
That on the green turf suck the honied
  showers,
And purple all the ground with vernal
  flowers.
Ibid. Line 139

Whether beyond the stormy Hebrides,
Where thou perhaps under the whelm-
  ing tide
Visit'st the bottom of the monstrous
  world.
Ibid. Line 156

Look homeward, Angel, now, and melt
  with ruth.
Ibid. Line 163

For Lycidas your sorrow is not dead,
Sunk though he be beneath the watery
  floor;
So sinks the day-star in the ocean bed,
And yet anon repairs his drooping head,
And tricks his beams, and with new-
  spangled ore
Flames in the forehead of the morning
  sky.
Ibid. Line 166

He touch'd the tender stops of various
  quills,
With eager thought warbling his Doric
  lay.
Ibid. Line 188

At last he rose, and twitch'd his mantle
  blue:
Tomorrow to fresh woods and pastures
  new.
Ibid. Line 192

The lazy leaden-stepping Hours,
Whose speed is but the heavy plum-
  met's pace.
On Time [Circa *1637*]

All this earthy grossness quit,
Attired with stars we shall for ever sit,
Triumphing over Death, and Chance,
  and thee, O Time.
Ibid.

Thy liquid notes that close the eye of day.

Sonnet: To the Nightingale
[*Circa 1637*]

Where the bright seraphim in burning row
Their loud up-lifted angel trumpets blow.

At a Solemn Music [*Circa 1637*]

A poet soaring in the high reason of his fancies, with his garland and singing robes about him.

The Reason of Church Government [*1641*]. *Book II, Introduction*

By labour and intent study (which I take to be my portion in this life), joined with the strong propensity of nature, I might perhaps leave something so written to after times as they should not willingly let it die.

Ibid.

Beholding the bright countenance of truth in the quiet and still air of delightful studies.

Ibid.

He who would not be frustrate of his hope to write well hereafter in laudable things ought himself to be a true poem.

Apology for Smectymnuus [*1642*]

His words, like so many nimble and airy servitors, trip about him at command.

Ibid.

Litigious terms, fat contentions, and flowing fees.

Tractate of Education [*1644*]

Enflamed with the study of learning and the admiration of virtue; stirred up with high hopes of living to be brave men and worthy patriots, dear to God, and famous to all ages.

Ibid.

Ornate rhetorick taught out of the rule of Plato. . . . To which poetry would be made subsequent, or indeed rather precedent, as being less subtle and fine, but more simple, sensuous, and passionate.

Ibid.

In those vernal seasons of the year, when the air is calm and pleasant, it were an injury and sullenness against Nature not to go out and see her riches, and partake in her rejoicing with heaven and earth.

Tractate of Education

Books are not absolutely dead things, but do contain a potency of life in them to be as active as that soul was whose progeny they are; nay they do preserve as in a vial the purest efficacy and extraction of that living intellect that bred them.

Areopagitica [*1644*]

As good almost kill a man as kill a good book: who kills a man kills a reasonable creature, God's image; but he who destroys a good book kills reason itself.

Ibid.

A good book is the precious life-blood of a master-spirit, embalmed and treasured up on purpose to a life beyond life.

Ibid.

I cannot praise a fugitive and cloistered virtue, unexercised and unbreathed, that never sallies out and sees her adversary, but slinks out of the race where that immortal garland is to be run for, not without dust and heat.

Ibid.

Who shall silence all the airs and madrigals that whisper softness in chambers?

Ibid.

Where there is much desire to learn, there of necessity will be much arguing, much writing, many opinions; for opinion in good men is but knowledge in the making.

Ibid.

Methinks I see in my mind a noble and puissant nation rousing herself like a strong man after sleep, and shaking her invincible locks: methinks I see her as an eagle mewing her mighty youth, and kindling her undazzled eyes at the full midday beam.

Ibid.

Though all the winds of doctrine [1]

[1] *Winds of Doctrine,* used as title of a book by GEORGE SANTAYANA [1913].

were let loose to play upon the earth, so Truth be in the field, we do ingloriously, by licensing and prohibiting, to misdoubt her strength. Let her and Falsehood grapple: who ever knew Truth put to the worse in a free and open encounter? [1]

Areopagitica

Men of most renowned virtue have sometimes by transgressing most truly kept the law.

Tetrachordon [1644–1645]

That old man eloquent.

To the Lady Margaret Ley [1644?]

That would have made Quintilian stare and gasp.

On the Detraction which followed upon my writing certain Treatises [1645]

License they mean when they cry Liberty;
For who loves that must first be wise and good.

Ibid. II

In mirth that after no repenting draws.

Sonnet XI. To Cyriack Skinner [1646–1647?]

For other things mild Heav'n a time ordains,
And disapproves that care, though wise in show,
That with superfluous burden loads the day,
And, when God sends a cheerful hour, refrains.

Ibid.

For such kind of borrowing as this, if it be not bettered by the borrower, among good authors is accounted Plagiarè.

Iconoclastes [1649]. XXIII

Peace hath her victories
No less renown'd than war.

To the Lord General Cromwell [1652]

When I consider how my light is spent,

Ere half my days, in this dark world and wide,
And that one talent which is death to hide
Lodg'd with me useless.

Sonnet XV. On His Blindness [1652]

"Doth God exact day-labour, light denied?"

Ibid.

Who best
Bear his mild yoke, they serve him best; his state
Is kingly; thousands at his bidding speed,
And post o'er land and ocean without rest;
They also serve who only stand and wait.

Ibid.

Avenge, O Lord, thy slaughter'd saints, whose bones
Lie scatter'd on the Alpine mountains cold;
Ev'n them who kept thy truth so pure of old
When all our fathers worshipt stocks and stones.

On the Late Massacre in Piedmont [1655]

Yet I argue not
Against Heav'n's hand or will, nor bate one jot
Of heart or hope; but still bear up and steer
Right onward.

Sonnet XVII. To Cyriack Skinner, Upon his Blindness [1655?]

Methought I saw my late espoused saint,[1]
Brought to me like Alcestis from the grave.

On his Deceased Wife [1658?]

But oh! as to embrace me she inclin'd,
I wak'd, she fled, and day brought back my night.

Ibid.

Of Man's first disobedience, and the fruit
Of that forbidden tree whose mortal taste

---

[1] See Montaigne, page 98b.
Error of opinion may be tolerated where reason is left free to combat it. — JEFFERSON: *Inaugural Address* [March 4, 1801]

[1] See Sir Walter Raleigh, page 111b.

Brought death into the world, and all our woe.

Paradise Lost [*1667*]. *Book I, Line 1*

Things unattempted yet in prose or rhyme.

Ibid. Line 16

What in me is dark
Illumine, what is low raise and support;
That to the height of this great argument
I may assert eternal Providence,
And justify the ways of God to men.[1]

Ibid. Line 22

The infernal serpent; he it was, whose guile,
Stirr'd up with envy and revenge, deceived
The mother of mankind.

Ibid. Line 34

Him the Almighty Power
Hurled headlong flaming from th' eternal sky
With hideous ruin and combustion down
To bottomless perdition, there to dwell
In adamantine chains and penal fire
Who durst defy th' Omnipotent to arms.

Ibid. Line 44

As far as angels' ken.

Ibid. Line 59

Where peace
And rest can never dwell, hope never comes
That comes to all.

Ibid. Line 65

What though the field be lost?
All is not lost — th' unconquerable will,
And study of revenge, immortal hate,
And courage never to submit or yield.

Ibid. Line 105

Vaunting aloud, but racked with deep despair.

Ibid. Line 126

---

[1] See *Samson Agonistes*, page 26oa.
But vindicate the ways of God to man. —
POPE: *Essay on Man* [*1733–1734*], *Epistle I, L. 16*

To be weak is miserable,
Doing or suffering.

Paradise Lost. Book I, Line 157

And out of good still to find means of evil.

Ibid. Line 165

The seat of desolation, void of light.

Ibid. Line 181

A mind not to be chang'd by place or time.
The mind is its own place, and in itself
Can make a heaven of hell, a hell of heaven.[1]

Ibid. Line 253

Better to reign in hell than serve in heaven.

Ibid. Line 263

His spear, to equal which the tallest pine
Hewn on Norwegian hills to be the mast
Of some great ammiral, were but a wand
He walk'd with, to support uneasy steps
Over the burning marle.

Ibid. Line 292

Thick as autumnal leaves that strow the brooks
In Vallombrosa.

Ibid. Line 302

Awake, arise, or be forever fallen!

Ibid. Line 330

Spirits, when they please,
Can either sex assume, or both.

Ibid. Line 423

When night
Darkens the streets, then wander forth the sons
Of Belial, flown with insolence and wine.

Ibid. Line 500

Th' imperial ensign, which, full high advanc'd,
Shone like a meteor, streaming to the wind.[2]

Ibid. Line 536

Sonorous metal blowing martial sounds:
At which the universal host up sent

---

[1] See Sir Thomas Browne, page 24ob, and *Book IV, L. 73*, page 255a.
[2] Stream'd like a meteor to the troubled air. — THOMAS GRAY: *The Bard* [*1757*], *I, 2, L. 6*

A shout that tore hell's concave, and beyond
Frighted the reign of Chaos and old Night.

Paradise Lost. Book I, Line 540

Anon they move
In perfect phalanx, to the Dorian mood
Of flutes and soft recorders.

Ibid. Line 549

His form had yet not lost
All her original brightness, nor appear'd
Less than archangel ruin'd, and th' excess
Of glory obscur'd.

Ibid. Line 591

The sun . . .
In dim eclipse, disastrous twilight sheds
On half the nations, and with fear of change
Perplexes monarchs.

Ibid. Line 594

Thrice he assay'd, and thrice, in spite of scorn,
Tears, such as angels weep, burst forth.

Ibid. Line 619

Who overcomes
By force hath overcome but half his foe.

Ibid. Line 648

Mammon, the least erected spirit that fell
From heaven; for ev'n in heaven his looks and thoughts
Were always downward bent, admiring more
The riches of heaven's pavement, trodden gold,
Than aught divine or holy else enjoy'd
In vision beatific.

Ibid. Line 679

Let none admire
That riches grow in hell: that soil may best
Deserve the precious bane.

Ibid. Line 690

From morn
To noon he fell, from noon to dewy eve,
A summer's day; and with the setting sun

Dropp'd from the Zenith, like a falling star.

Paradise Lost. Book I, Line 742

High on a throne of royal state, which far
Outshone the wealth of Ormus and of Ind,
Or where the gorgeous East with richest hand
Showers on her kings barbaric pearl and gold,
Satan exalted sat, by merit rais'd
To that bad eminence.

Ibid. Book II, Line 1

The strongest and the fiercest spirit
That fought in heaven, now fiercer by despair.

Ibid. Line 44

Rather than be less,
Car'd not to be at all.

Ibid. Line 47

My sentence is for open war.

Ibid. Line 51

Which, if not victory, is yet revenge.

Ibid. Line 105

But all was false and hollow; though his tongue
Dropp'd manna, and could make the worse appear
The better reason,[1] to perplex and dash
Maturest counsels.

Ibid. Line 112

For who would lose,
Though full of pain, this intellectual being,
Those thoughts that wander through eternity,
To perish rather, swallow'd up and lost
In the wide womb of uncreated night,
Devoid of sense and motion?

Ibid. Line 146

His red right hand.[2]

Ibid. Line 174

Unrespited, unpitied, unrepriev'd.

Ibid. Line 185

The never-ending flight
Of future days.

Ibid. Line 221

---

[1] See Diogenes Laertius, page 70b.
[2] Rubente dextera. — HORACE [65–8 B.C.]: *Ode I, 2, 2, To Caesar Augustus*

Thus Belial with words clothed in reason's garb
Counselled ignoble ease, and peaceful sloth,
Not peace.
> *Paradise Lost. Book II, Line 226*
With grave
Aspect he rose, and in his rising seem'd
A pillar of state; deep on his front engraven
Deliberation sat, and public care;
And princely counsel in his face yet shone,
Majestic though in ruin.
> *Ibid. Line 300*
The palpable obscure.
> *Ibid. Line 406*
Long is the way
And hard, that out of hell leads up to light.
> *Ibid. Line 432*
Their rising all at once was as the sound
Of thunder heard remote.
> *Ibid. Line 476*
Others apart sat on a hill retir'd,
In thoughts more elevate, and reason'd high
Of providence, foreknowledge, will, and fate,
Fix'd fate, free-will, foreknowledge absolute;
And found no end, in wand'ring mazes lost.
> *Ibid. Line 557*
Arm th' obdur'd breast
With stubborn patience as with triple steel.
> *Ibid. Line 568*
Far off from these a slow and silent stream,
Lethe the River of Oblivion.
> *Ibid. Line 582*
At certain revolutions all the damn'd
Are brought: and feel by turns the bitter change
Of fierce extremes, — extremes by change more fierce;
From beds of raging fire to starve in ice
Their soft ethereal warmth, and there to pine

Immovable, infix'd, and frozen round,
Periods of time; thence hurried back to fire.
> *Paradise Lost. Book II, Line 596*
Whence and what art thou, execrable shape?
> *Ibid. Line 681*
Before mine eyes in opposition sits
Grim Death, my son and foe.
> *Ibid. Line 803*
Hot, cold, moist, and dry, four champions fierce,
Strive here for mast'ry.
> *Ibid. Line 898*
With ruin upon ruin, rout on rout,
Confusion worse confounded.
> *Ibid. Line 995*
And fast by, hanging in a golden chain,
This pendent world, in bigness as a star
Of smallest magnitude close by the moon.
> *Ibid. Line 1051*
Hail, holy light! offspring of heav'n first-born.
> *Ibid. Book III, Line 1*
Thus with the year
Seasons return; but not to me returns
Day, or the sweet approach of even or morn,
Or sight of vernal bloom or summer's rose,
Or flocks, or herds, or human face divine;
But cloud instead, and ever-during dark
Surrounds me; from the cheerful ways of men
Cut off, and for the book of knowledge fair
Presented with a universal blank
Of Nature's works, to me expung'd and raz'd,
And wisdom at one entrance quite shut out.
> *Ibid. Line 40*
See golden days, fruitful of golden deeds,
With joy and love triumphing.
> *Ibid. Line 337*
Dark with excessive bright.
> *Ibid. Line 380*

The hell within him.
Paradise Lost. Book IV, Line 20
Now conscience wakes despair
That slumber'd, — wakes the bitter memory
Of what he was, what is, and what must be
Worse.
Ibid. Line 23
At whose sight all the stars
Hide their diminish'd heads.[1]
Ibid. Line 34
A grateful mind
By owing owes not, but still pays, at once
Indebted and discharg'd.
Ibid. Line 55
Which way shall I fly
Infinite wrath and infinite despair?
Which way I fly is hell; myself am hell;[2]
And in the lowest deep a lower deep,
Still threat'ning to devour me, opens wide,
To which the hell I suffer seems a heaven.
Ibid. Line 73
So farewell hope, and, with hope, farewell fear,
Farewell remorse; all good to me is lost.
Evil, be thou my good.
Ibid. Line 108
And on the Tree of Life,
The middle tree and highest there that grew,
Sat like a cormorant.
Ibid. Line 194
A heaven on earth.
Ibid. Line 208
Flowers of all hue, and without thorn the rose.[3]
Ibid. Line 256
For contemplation he and valour form'd,
For softness she and sweet attractive grace;

[1] Ye little stars! hide your diminished rays. — POPE: *Moral Essays* [1731–1735], *Epistle III, L. 282*
[2] See Sir Thomas Browne, page 240b, and *Book I, L. 253*, page 252b.
[3] See Bidpai, page 28b.

He for God only, she for God in him.
Paradise Lost. Book IV, Line 297
Implied
Subjection, but requir'd with gentle sway,
And by her yielded, by him best receiv'd, —
Yielded with coy submission, modest pride,
And sweet, reluctant, amorous delay.
Ibid. Line 307
Adam the goodliest man of men since born
His sons, the fairest of her daughters Eve.
Ibid. Line 323
And with necessity,
The tyrant's plea,[1] excus'd his devilish deeds.
Ibid. Line 393
Imparadis'd in one another's arms.
Ibid. Line 506
Live while ye may,
Yet happy pair.
Ibid. Line 533
Now came still evening on, and twilight gray
Had in her sober livery all things clad.
Ibid. Line 598
The wakeful nightingale,
She all night long her amorous descant sung;
Silence was pleas'd: now glow'd the firmament
With living sapphires; Hesperus, that led
The starry host, rode brightest, till the moon,
Rising in clouded majesty, at length
Apparent queen, unveil'd her peerless light,
And o'er the dark her silver mantle threw.
Ibid. Line 602
The timely dew of sleep.
Ibid. Line 614
With thee conversing I forget all time,
All seasons, and their change; all please alike.

[1] Necessity is the argument of tyrants, it is the creed of slaves. — WILLIAM PITT: *Speech on the India Bill* [November, 1783]

Sweet is the breath of morn, her rising sweet,
With charm of earliest birds; pleasant the sun
When first on this delightful land he spreads
His orient beams on herb, tree, fruit, and flower,
Glist'ring with dew; fragrant the fertile earth
After soft showers; and sweet the coming on
Of grateful ev'ning mild, then silent night
With this her solemn bird, and this fair moon,
And these the gems of heaven, her starry train.

Paradise Lost. Book IV, Line 639

Millions of spiritual creatures walk the earth
Unseen, both when we wake, and when we sleep.

Ibid. Line 677

In naked beauty more adorn'd,
More lovely, than Pandora.[1]

Ibid. Line 713

Eas'd the putting off
These troublesome disguises which we wear.

Ibid. Line 739

Hail, wedded love, mysterious law, true source
Of human offspring.

Ibid. Line 750

Squat like a toad, close at the ear of Eve.

Ibid. Line 800

Abash'd the devil stood,
And felt how awful goodness is, and saw
Virtue in her shape how lovely.

Ibid. Line 846

All hell broke loose.

Ibid. Line 918

Like Teneriff or Atlas unremoved.

Ibid. Line 987

[1] See Cicero, page 33a.
When unadorned, adorned the most. —
THOMSON: *Autumn* [1730], L. 204

The starry cope
Of heaven.

Paradise Lost. Book IV, Line 992

His sleep
Was aery light, from pure digestion bred.

Ibid. Book V, Line 3

My latest found,
Heaven's last, best gift, my ever-new delight!

Ibid. Line 18

Good, the more
Communicated, more abundant grows.

Ibid. Line 71

These are thy glorious works, Parent of good!

Ibid. Line 153

A wilderness of sweets.

Ibid. Line 294

So saying, with despatchful looks in haste
She turns, on hospitable thoughts intent.

Ibid. Line 331

Nor jealousy
Was understood, the injur'd lover's hell.

Ibid. Line 449

The bright consummate flower.

Ibid. Line 481

Midnight brought on the dusky hour
Friendliest to sleep and silence.

Ibid. Line 667

Innumerable as the stars of night,
Or stars of morning, dewdrops which the sun
Impearls on every leaf and every flower.

Ibid. Line 745

Among the faithless, faithful only he.

Ibid. Line 897

Morn,
Wak'd by the circling hours, with rosy hand
Unbarr'd the gates of light.

Ibid. Book VI, Line 2

Servant of God, well done! Well hast thou fought
The better fight, who single hast maintained
Against revolted multitudes the cause

Of truth, in word mightier than they in
   arms.
      Paradise Lost. Book VI, Line 29
He onward came; far off his coming
   shone.
      Ibid. Line 768
   Let it profit thee to have heard,
By terrible example, the reward
Of disobedience.
      Ibid. Line 909
More safe I sing with mortal voice, un-
   chang'd
To hoarse or mute, though fall'n on
   evil days,
On evil days though fall'n, and evil
   tongues,
In darkness, and with dangers com-
   pass'd round,
And solitude.
      Ibid. Book VII, Line 24
   Still govern thou my song,
Urania, and fit audience find, though
   few.
      Ibid. Line 30
   Out of one man a race
Of men innumerable.
      Ibid. Line 155
   Heaven open'd wide
Her ever-during gates, harmonious
   sound,
On golden hinges moving.
      Ibid. Line 205
   God saw the Light was good;
And light from darkness by the hemi-
   sphere
Divided: Light the Day, and Darkness
   Night,
He named. Thus was the first Day even
   and morn.
      Ibid. Line 249
   There Leviathan
Hugest of living creatures, on the deep
Stretch'd like a promontory sleeps or
   swims,
And seems a moving land, and at his
   gills
Draws in, and at his trunk spouts out a
   sea.
      Ibid. Line 412
   Endued
With sanctity of reason.
      Ibid. Line 507

The Planets in their stations list'ning
   stood,
While the bright Pomp ascended jubi-
   lant.
Open, ye everlasting gates, they sung,
Open, ye heavens, your living doors;
   let in
The great Creator from his work re-
   turn'd
Magnificent, his six days' work, a world.
      Paradise Lost. Book VII, Line 563
A broad and ample road, whose dust
   is gold,
And pavement stars, as stars to thee ap-
   pear
Seen in the galaxy, that milky way
Which nightly as a circling zone thou
   seest
Powder'd with stars.
      Ibid. Line 577
The Angel ended, and in Adam's ear
So charming left his voice that he awhile
Thought him still speaking, still stood
   fix'd to hear.
      Ibid. Book VIII, Line 1
   To know
That which before us lies in daily life
Is the prime wisdom.
      Ibid. Line 192
Liquid lapse of murmuring streams.
      Ibid. Line 263
And feel that I am happier than I know.
      Ibid. Line 282
Among unequals what society
Can sort, what harmony or true de-
   light?
      Ibid. Line 383
Her virtue, and the conscience **of** her
   worth,
That would be woo'd, and not unsought
   be won.
      Ibid. Line 502
The sum of earthly bliss.
      Ibid. Line 522
Accuse not Nature! she hath done her
   part;
Do thou but thine!
      Ibid. Line 561
   Oft times nothing profits more
Than self-esteem, grounded on just and
   right

Well-manag'd.
Paradise Lost. Book VIII, Line 571
My unpremeditated verse.
Ibid. Book IX, Line 24
Pleas'd me, long choosing and begin-
ning late.
Ibid. Line 26
Unless an age too late, or cold
Climate, or years, damp my intended
wing.
Ibid. Line 44
Revenge, at first though sweet,[1]
Bitter ere long back on itself recoils.
Ibid. Line 171
For solitude sometimes is best society,
And short retirement urges sweet re-
turn.
Ibid. Line 249
At shut of evening flowers.
Ibid. Line 278
As one who long in populous city pent,[2]
Where houses thick and sewers annoy
the air.
Ibid. Line 445
God so commanded, and left that com-
mand
Sole daughter of his voice;[3] the rest,
we live
Law to ourselves, our reason is our law.
Ibid. Line 652
His words, replete with guile,
Into her heart too easy entrance won.
Ibid. Line 733
Her rash hand in evil hour
Forth reaching to the fruit, she pluck'd,
she eat:
Earth felt the wound, and Nature from
her seat,
Sighing through all her works, gave
signs of woe
That all was lost.
Ibid. Line 780
So dear I love him that with him all
deaths
I could endure, without him live no life.
Ibid. Line 832

[1] Sweet is revenge — especially to women.
— BYRON: *Don Juan* [1819–1824], *Canto 1,
St. 124*
[2] See Keats, page 477a.
[3] See Wordsworth, page 409b.

In her face excuse
Came prologue, and apology too
prompt.
Paradise Lost. Book IX, Line 853
O fairest of Creation, last and best
Of all God's works, creature in whom
excelled
Whatever can to sight or thought be
formed,
Holy, divine, good, amiable, or sweet!
How art thou lost, how on a sudden lost,
Defac'd, deflower'd, and now to Death
devote?
Ibid. Line 896
Yet I shall temper so
Justice with mercy, as may illustrate
most
Them fully satisfy'd, and thee appease.
Ibid. Book X, Line 77
She gave me of the tree, and I did eat.
Ibid. Line 143
Pandemonium, city and proud seat
Of Lucifer.
Ibid. Line 424
A dismal universal hiss, the sound
Of public scorn.
Ibid. Line 508
Death . . . on his pale horse.
Ibid. Line 588
How gladly would I meet
Mortality, my sentence, and be earth
Insensible! how glad would lay me
down
As in my mother's lap!
Ibid. Line 775
Demoniac frenzy, moping melancholy,
And moon-struck madness.
Ibid. Book XI, Line 485
And over them triumphant Death his
dart
Shook, but delay'd to strike, though oft
invok'd.
Ibid. Line 491
So may'st thou live, till, like ripe fruit,
thou drop
Into thy mother's lap, or be with ease
Gathered, not harshly plucked, for
death mature:
This is old age.
Ibid. Line 535
Nor love thy life, nor hate; but what
thou liv'st

Live well; how long or short permit to
Heaven.[1]
> *Paradise Lost. Book XI, Line 553*

A bevy of fair women.
> *Ibid. Line 582*

The evening star,
Love's harbinger.
> *Ibid. Line 588*

The brazen throat of war.
> *Ibid. Line 713*

An olive-leaf he brings, pacific sign.
> *Ibid. Line 860*

In me is no delay; with thee to go,
Is to stay here; without thee here to
stay,
Is to go hence unwilling; thou to me
Art all things under Heaven, all places
thou,
Who for my willful crime art banished
hence.
> *Ibid. Book XII, Line 615*

The world was all before them, where
to choose
Their place of rest, and Providence
their guide.
They hand in hand, with wand'ring
steps and slow,
Through Eden took their solitary way.
> *Ibid. Line 646*

Most men admire
Virtue who follow not her lore.
> *Paradise Regained [1671].*
> *Book I, Line 482*

Skill'd to retire, and in retiring draw
Hearts after them tangled in amorous
nets.
> *Ibid. Book II, Line 161*

Beauty stands
In the admiration only of weak minds
Led captive.
> *Ibid. Line 220*

Rocks whereon greatest men have oftest wreck'd.
> *Ibid. Line 228*

Of whom to be disprais'd were no small
praise.
> *Ibid. Book III, Line 56*

Elephants indorsed with towers.
> *Ibid. Line 329*

[1] See Martial, page 52b.

Dusk faces with white silken turbans
wreath'd.
> *Paradise Regained. Book IV,*
> *Line 76*

What honour that,
But tedious waste of time, to sit and
hear
So many hollow compliments and lies,
Outlandish flatteries?
> *Ibid. Line 122*

The childhood shows the man,
As morning shows the day.[1]
> *Ibid. Line 220*

Athens, the eye of Greece, mother of
arts
And eloquence.
> *Ibid. Line 240*

The olive grove of Academe,
Plato's retirement, where the Attic bird
Trills her thick-warbled notes the sum-
mer long.
> *Ibid. Line 244*

Socrates . . .
Whom, well inspir'd, the oracle pro-
nounc'd
Wisest of men.
> *Ibid. Line 274*

The first and wisest of them all professed
To know this only, that he nothing
knew.[2]
> *Ibid. Line 293*

Deep vers'd in books, and shallow in
himself.
> *Ibid. Line 327*

Till morning fair
Came forth with pilgrim steps, in amice
gray.
> *Ibid. Line 426*

Eyeless in Gaza, at the mill with slaves.
> *Samson Agonistes [1671]. Line 41*

O loss of sight, of thee I most complain!
> *Ibid. Line 68*

O dark, dark, dark, amid the blaze of
noon,
Irrecoverably dark, total eclipse
Without all hope of day!
> *Ibid. Line 80*

[1] See Wordsworth, page 406b.
[2] See Diogenes Laertius, page 70b.

The sun to me is dark
And silent as the moon,
When she deserts the night,
Hid in her vacant interlunar cave.
Samson Agonistes. Line 86

To live a life half dead, a living death
Ibid. Line 100

Ran on embattled armies clad in iron,
And, weaponless himself,
Made arms ridiculous.
Ibid. Line 129

Just are the ways of God,
And justifiable to men; [1]
Unless there be who think not God at
all.
Ibid. Line 293

A grain of manhood.
Ibid. Line 408

What boots it at one gate to make de-
fence,
And at another to let in the foe?
Ibid. Line 560

God of our fathers, what is man!
That thou towards him with hand so
various,
(Or might I say contrarious?)
Temper'st thy providence through his
short course.
Ibid. Line 667

But who is this, what thing of sea or
land, —
Female of sex it seems —
That so bedeck'd, ornate, and gay,
Comes this way sailing
Like a stately ship
Of Tarsus, bound for th' isles
Of Javan or Gadire,
With all her bravery on, and tackle
trim,
Sails fill'd, and streamers waving,
Courted by all the winds that hold them
play,
An amber scent of odorous perfume
Her harbinger?
Ibid. Line 710

Dalila. In argument with men a woman
ever
Goes by the worse, whatever be her
cause.

[1] See *Paradise Lost, Book I, L. 22,* page 252a.

Samson. For want of words, no doubt,
or lack of breath!
Samson Agonistes. Line 903

Fame, if not double-faced, is double-
mouthed,
And with contrary blast proclaims most
deeds;
On both his wings, one black, the other
white,
Bears greatest names in his wild aery
flight.
Ibid. Line 971

Yet beauty, though injurious, hath
strange power,
After offence returning, to regain
Love once possess'd.
Ibid. Line 1003

Love-quarrels oft in pleasing concord
end;
Not wedlock-treachery.
Ibid. Line 1008

Boast not of what thou would'st have
done, but do
What then thou would'st.
Ibid. Line 1104

He's gone, and who knows how he may
report
Thy words by adding fuel to the flame?
Ibid. Line 1350

For evil news rides post, while good
news baits.
Ibid. Line 1538

Suspense in news is torture.
Ibid. Line 1569

Nothing is here for tears, nothing to
wail
Or knock the breast; no weakness, no
contempt,
Dispraise, or blame; nothing but well
and fair,
And what may quiet us in a death so
noble.
Ibid. Line 1721

All is best, though we oft doubt
What the unsearchable dispose
Of Highest Wisdom brings about.
Ibid. Line 1745

Calm of mind, all passion spent.
Ibid. Line 1758

Such bickerings to recount, met often
in these our writers, what more worth
is it than to chronicle the wars of kites

or crows flocking and fighting in the air?

> *The History of England*
> *[1670]. Book IV*

SIR JOHN SUCKLING
[1609–1642]

Why so pale and wan, fond lover?
  Prithee, why so pale?
Will, when looking well can't move her,
  Looking ill prevail?
> *Song* [*1638*]. *Stanza 1*

Quit, quit, for shame, this will not move,
  This cannot take her.
If of herself she will not love,
  Nothing can make her.
  The devil take her!
> *Ibid. Stanza 3*

Death's no punishment: it is the sense,
The pains and fears afore, that makes
  a death.
> *Aglaura* [*1638*]. *Act V, Sc. 1*

But as when an authentic watch is
  shown,
Each man winds up and rectifies his
  own,
So in our very judgments.[1]
> *Ibid. Epilogue*

High characters (cries one), and he
  would see
Things that ne'er were, nor are, nor
  ne'er will be.[2]
> *The Goblins* [*1639*]. *Epilogue*

Her feet beneath her petticoat
Like little mice, stole in and out,[3]
  As if they feared the light;

[1] 'Tis with our judgments as our watches, none
Go just alike, yet each believes his own.
  POPE: *An Essay on Criticism*
  [*1711*], *Part I, L. 9*
[2] Whoever thinks a faultless piece to see,
Thinks what ne'er was, nor is, nor e'er
  shall be.
  POPE: *An Essay on Criticism*
  [*1711*], *Part II, L. 53*
There's no such thing in Nature, and
  you'll draw
A faultless monster which the world ne'er
  saw.
  JOHN SHEFFIELD, DUKE OF BUCK-
  INGHAMSHIRE [*1648–1721*]: *Essay
  on Poetry*
[3] See Herrick, page 231a.

But oh, she dances such a way!
No sun upon an Easter-day
  Is half so fine a sight.
> *A Ballad upon a Wedding* [*1641*].
> *Stanza 8*

Her lips were red, and one was thin,
Compared with that was next her chin,
Some bee had stung it newly.
> *Ibid. Stanza 11*

I prithee send me back my heart,
  Since I cannot have thine;
For if from yours you will not part,
  Why then shouldst thou have mine?
> *Fragmenta Aurea* [*1646*].
> *Song, Stanza 1*

'Tis not the meat, but 'tis the appetite
Makes eating a delight.
> *Ibid. Of Thee, Kind Boy,*
> *Stanza 3*

Spare diet is the cause love lasts,
For surfeits sooner kill than fasts.
> *Ibid. Against Absence*

Out upon it, I have loved
  Three whole days together;
And am like to love three more,
  If it prove fair weather.
> *Ibid. A Poem with the Answer,*
> *Stanza 1*

'Tis expectation makes a blessing dear,
Heaven were not heaven, if we knew
  what it were
> *Ibid. Against Fruition, Stanza 4*

Women are the baggage of life: they
  are
Troublesome, and hinder us in the great
  march,
And yet we cannot be without 'em.
> *The Tragedy of Brennoralt* [*1646*].
> *Act I, Sc. 1*

Success is a rare paint, hides all the
  ugliness.
> *Ibid.*

Sleep is as nice as woman,
The more I court it, the more it flies me.
> *Ibid. Act II, Sc. 1*

She is pretty to walk with,
And witty to talk with,
And pleasant, too, to think on.
> *Ibid.*

Her face is like the milky way i' the
  sky, —

A meeting of gentle lights without name.
> *The Tragedy of Brennoralt.*
> *Act III, Sc. 1*

SIR MATTHEW HALE [1]
[1609–1676]

Be not too rigid in matters purely conscientious, where all the harm is diversity of judgment.
> *Things Necessary to be Continually Had in Remembrance*

Be not biassed with compassion to the poor, or favour to the rich, in point of justice.
> *Ibid.*

Not to be solicitous what men will say or think.
> *Ibid.*

To abhor all private solicitations in matters depending.
> *Ibid.*

To be short, and sparing, at meals, that I may be the fitter for business.
> *Ibid.*

WILLIAM CARTWRIGHT
[1611–1643]

St. Francis and St. Benedight,
Bless this house from wicked wight,
From the nightmare and the Goblin
That is hight Good Fellow Robin.
Keep it from all evil spirits,
Fairies, weasels, bats, and ferrets
From curfew time to the next prime.
> *A House Blessing* [*1651*] [2]

Love makes those young whom age doth chill,
And whom he finds young, keeps young still.
> *To Chloe* [*1651*]

Tell me no more of minds embracing minds,
And hearts exchanged for hearts;
That spirits spirits meet, as winds do winds,
And mix their subtlest parts;

[1] Lord Chief Justice of England.
[2] Matthew, Mark, Luke, and John,
The bed be blest that I lye on.
> THOMAS ADY: *A Candle in the Dark* [1656]

That two unbodied essences may kiss,
And then like angels, twist and feel one bliss.
> *No Platonic Love* [*1651*]. *Stanza 1*

I was that silly thing that once was wrought
To practise this thin love;
I climbed from sex to soul, from soul to thought;
But thinking there to move,
Headlong I rolled from thought to soul, and then
From soul I lighted at the sex again.
> *Ibid. Stanza 2*

JAMES GRAHAM, FIRST MARQUESS OF MONTROSE
[1612–1650]

He either fears his fate too much,
  Or his deserts are small,
That dares not put it to the touch
  To gain or lose it all.[1]
> *My Dear and Only Love. Stanza 2*

I'll make thee glorious by my pen,
And famous by my sword.[2]
> *Ibid. Stanza 5*

THOMAS JORDAN
[1612–1685]

Let us drink and be merry, dance, joke, and rejoice,
With claret and sherry, theorbo and voice!
> *Coronemus Nos Rosis Antequam Marcescant.*[3] *Stanza 1*

Fish dinners will make a man spring like a flea.
> *Ibid. Stanza 2*

Though now she be pleasant and sweet to the sense,

[1] That puts it not unto the touch
  To win or lose it all.
    MARK NAPIER [1798–1879]: *Montrose and the Covenanters*
[2] I'll make thee famous by my pen,
  And glorious by my sword.
    SCOTT: *Legend of Montrose* [1819], *Chap. XV*
[3] One of the songs of Sir Henry Morgan's buccaneers was an adaptation of this poem.

Will be damnable mouldy a hundred
   years hence.
    Coronemus Nos Rosis Antequam
             Marcescant. Stanza 3
For health, wealth and beauty, wit,
   learning, and sense,
Must all come to nothing a hundred
   years hence.
             Ibid. Stanza 4

ISAAC DE BENSERADE
[1612–1691]

In bed we laugh, in bed we cry;
And, born in bed, in bed we die.
The near approach a bed may show
Of human bliss to human woe.
    A Son Lit (Translated by DR.
        SAMUEL JOHNSON)

RICHARD CRASHAW
[1613–1649]

The conscious water saw its God and
   blushed.[1]
    Epigrammata Sacra [1634].
       Aquae in Vinum Versae
Two went to pray? Oh, rather say
One went to brag, the other to pray;
One stands up close and treads on high
Where the other dares not send his eye;
One nearer to God's altar trod,
The other to the altar's God.
    Two Went Up to the Temple
          to Pray [1648]
Whoe'er she be,
That not impossible she,
That shall command my heart and me.
    Wishes to His Supposed
          Mistress [1648]
Where'er she lie,

[1] Nympha pudica Deum vidit et erubuit.—
Quoted by SAMUEL JOHNSON [1778], *Boswell's Life of Dr. Johnson, Vol. II, P. 218,
Everyman ed.* A footnote states that this line
has frequently been attributed to Dryden, but
appeared in Crashaw's *Epigrammata Sacra*
[1634].
   The bashful stream hath seen its God and
blushed. — AARON HILL [1685–1750]
    The water hears thy faintest word,
    And blushes into wine.
      JOHN SAMUEL BEWLEY MONSELL
      [1811–1875]: *Mysterious is Thy
      Presence, Lord, St. 1*

Locked up from mortal eye,
In shady leaves of destiny.
    Wishes to His Supposed Mistress
Days that need borrow
No part of their good morrow
From a fore-spent night of sorrow.
             Ibid.

Life that dares send
A challenge to his end,
And when it comes, say, Welcome,
   friend!
             Ibid.

Sydnaeian showers
Of sweet discourse, whose powers
Can crown old Winter's head with
   flowers.
             Ibid.

I would be married, but I'd have no
   wife,
I would be married to a single life.
       On Marriage [1648]
All is Caesar's; and what odds
So long as Caesar's self is God's?
        Mark XII [1648]
All those fair and flagrant things.
    The Flaming Heart Upon the
    Book of Saint Teresa [1652].
    Line 34
Love's passives are his activ'st part.
The wounded is the wounding heart.
         Ibid. Line 71
O thou undaunted daughter of desires!
         Ibid. Line 93
By all the eagle in thee, all the dove.
         Ibid. Line 95
Poor world, said I, what wilt thou do
   To entertain this starry stranger?
Is the best thou canst bestow,
   A cold and not too cleanly manger?
Contend, ye powers of heav'n and earth,
To fit a bed for this huge birth.
    Hymn of the Nativity [1652].
          Stanza 6
Proud world, said I, cease your contest,
   And let the mighty babe alone —
The phoenix builds the phoenix' nest,
   Love's architecture is his own;
The babe whose birth embraves this
   morn,
Made his own bed ere he was born.
        Ibid. Stanza 7

Welcome, all wonders in one sight!
Eternity shut in a span.
  Hymn of the Nativity. Full Chorus
A happy soul, that all the way
To heaven hath a summer's day.
  *In Praise of Lessius's Rule of
    Health*
The modest front of this small floor,
Believe me, reader, can say more
Than many a braver marble can, —
"Here lies a truly honest man!"
  Epitaph upon Mr. Ashton

JEREMY TAYLOR
[1613–1667]

When Abraham sat at his tent-door, according to his custom, waiting to entertain strangers, he espied an old man stooping and leaning on his staff, weary with age and travel, coming toward him, who was an hundred years of age; he received him kindly, washed his feet, provided supper, caused him to sit down; but observing that the old man ate and prayed not, nor begged for a blessing on his meat, asked him why he did not worship the God of heaven. The old man told him that he worshiped the fire only, and acknowledged no other God: at which answer Abraham grew so zealously angry, that he thrust the old man out of his tent, and exposed him to all the evils of the night and an unguarded condition. When the old man was gone, God called to him and asked him where the stranger was; he replied, "I thrust him away because he did not worship thee"; God answered him, "I have suffered him these hundred years, although he dishonored me, and couldst thou not endure him one night, when he gave thee no trouble?" Upon this, saith the story, Abraham fetched him back again, and gave him hospitable entertainment and wise instruction. Go thou and do likewise, and thy charity will be rewarded by the God of Abraham.
  The Liberty of Prophesying [*1646*]
Every man hath in his own life sins enough, in his own mind trouble enough: so that curiosity after the affairs of others cannot be without envy and an evil mind. What is it to me if my neighbour's grandfather were a Syrian, or his grandmother illegitimate, or that another is indebted five thousand pounds, or whether his wife be expensive?
  Holy Living [*1650–1651*]
He that is most knowing hath a capacity to become happy, which a less knowing prince or a rich person hath not.
  XXVIII Sermons [*1651*]
No man ever repented that he arose from the table sober, healthful, and with his wits about him.
  XXV Sermons [*1653*]

FRANÇOIS, DUC DE LA ROCHEFOUCAULD
[1613–1680]

Our virtues are most frequently but vices disguised.[1]
  *Reflections, or Sentences and
    Moral Maxims* [2]
We all have strength enough to endure the misfortunes of others.
  Maxim 19
Philosophy triumphs easily over past evils and future evils; but present evils triumph over it.[3]
  Maxim 22
We need greater virtues to sustain good fortune than bad.
  Maxim 25
Neither the sun nor death can be looked at steadily.
  Maxim 26
If we had no faults, we would not take so much pleasure in noticing them in others.
  Maxim 31

[1] This epigraph, which is the key to the system of La Rochefoucauld, is found in another form as No. 179 of the Maxims of the first edition, 1665; it is omitted from the second and third, and reappears for the first time in the fourth edition at the head of the Reflections. — AIMÉ MARTIN
[2] The fifth edition [1678] is the standard one.
[3] See Goldsmith, page 355a.

Jealousy feeds upon suspicion, and it turns into fury or it ends as soon as we pass from suspicion to certainty.

Maxim 32

Self-interest speaks all sorts of tongues, and plays all sorts of roles, even that of disinterestedness.

Maxim 39

We are never so happy nor so unhappy as we imagine.

Maxim 49

To succeed in the world, we do everything we can to appear successful.

Maxim 56

There is no disguise which can for long conceal love where it exists or simulate it where it does not.

Maxim 70

There are very few people who are not ashamed of having been in love when they no longer love each other.

Maxim 71

True love is like ghosts, which everybody talks about and few have seen.

Maxim 76

The love of justice is simply, in the majority of men, the fear of suffering injustice.

Maxim 78

Silence is the best tactic for him who distrusts himself.

Maxim 79

What men call friendship is only a reciprocal conciliation of interests, an exchange of good offices; it is in short simply a form of barter from which self-love always expects to gain something.

Maxim 83

It is more ignominious to mistrust our friends than to be deceived by them.

Maxim 84

Everyone complains of his memory, and no one complains of his judgment.

Maxim 89

Old people like to give good advice, as solace for no longer being able to provide bad examples.

Maxim 93

A man who is ungrateful is sometimes less to blame for it than his benefactor.

Maxim 96

The understanding is always the dupe of the heart.

Maxim 102

Nothing is given so profusely as advice.

Maxim 110

The true way to be deceived is to think oneself more clever than others.

Maxim 127

We would rather speak ill of ourselves than not talk about ourselves at all.

Maxim 138

Usually we praise only to be praised.

Maxim 146

Our repentance is not so much regret for the ill we have done as fear of the ill that may happen to us in consequence.

Maxim 180

Most people judge men only by their success or their good fortune.

Maxim 212

Hypocrisy is the homage that vice pays to virtue.

Maxim 218

Too great haste in paying off an obligation is a kind of ingratitude.

Maxim 226

There is great skill in knowing how to conceal one's skill.

Maxim 245

The pleasure of love is in loving. We are happier in the passion we feel than in that we arouse.[1]

Maxim 259

We always like those who admire us; we do not always like those whom we admire.

Maxim 294

The gratitude of most men is merely a secret desire to receive greater benefits.[2]

Maxim 298

[1] See Shelley, page 465b.
[2] Sir Robert Walpole's [1676–1745] definition of the gratitude of place-expectants, "That it is a lively sense of *future* favours." — WILLIAM HAZLITT: *English Comic Writers* [1819], *Wit and Humour*

Lovers never get tired of each other, because they are always talking about themselves.

Maxim 312

We pardon to the extent that we love.

Maxim 330

We rarely find that people have good sense unless they agree with us.[1]

Maxim 347

Jealousy is always born together with love, but it does not always die when love dies.

Maxim 361

Mediocre minds usually dismiss anything which reaches beyond their own understanding.

Maxim 375

The greatest fault of a penetrating wit is to go beyond the mark.

Maxim 377

We may give advice, but we do not inspire conduct.

Maxim 378

The veracity which increases with old age is not far from folly.

Maxim 416

Nothing prevents our being natural so much as the desire to appear so.

Maxim 431

In their first passion women love their lovers, in the others they love love.[2]

Maxim 471

Quarrels would not last long if the fault were only on one side.

Maxim 496

In the misfortune of our best friends we find something that is not exactly displeasing.[3]

Maxim 583

---

[1] "That was excellently observed," say I when I read a passage in another where his opinion agrees with mine. When we differ, then I pronounce him to be mistaken. — SWIFT [1667–1745]: *Thoughts on Various Subjects*

[2] See Byron, page 458a.

[3] In all distresses of our friends
We first consult our private ends;
While Nature, kindly bent to ease us,
Points out some circumstance to please us.
SWIFT [1667–1745]: *A Paraphrase of Rochefoucauld's Maxim*
Maxim 583 is one of the "Maximes sup-

To win that wonder of the world,
A smile from her bright eyes,
I fought my King, and would have hurled
The gods out of their skies.

To Madame de Longueville

RICHARD BAXTER
[1615–1691]

I preached as never sure to preach again,
And as a dying man to dying men.

Love Breathing Thanks and Praise

SIR JOHN DENHAM
[1615–1669]

Oh, could I flow like thee,[1] and make thy stream
My great example, as it is my theme!
Though deep, yet clear, though gentle yet not dull;
Strong without rage, without o'erflowing full.

Cooper's Hill [1642]. *Line 189*

I can no more believe old Homer blind,
Than those who say the sun hath never shined:
The age wherein he lived was dark, but he
Could not want sight who taught the world to see.

Progress of Learning [1668]

But whither am I strayed? I need not raise
Trophies to thee from other men's dispraise;
Nor is thy fame on lesser ruins built;
Nor needs thy juster title the foul guilt
Of Eastern kings, who, to secure their reign,
Must have their brothers, sons, and kindred slain.[2]

On Mr. John Fletcher's Works [1668]

---

primées" discarded before the 1678 edition.

[1] The River Thames.

[2] Poets are sultans, if they had their will;
For every author would his brother kill.
ROGER BOYLE, FIRST EARL OF ORRERY [1621–1679]

See Pope, page 318b.

SIR ROGER L'ESTRANGE
[1616–1704]

Though this may be play to you,
'Tis death to us.
> *Fables from Several Authors.*
> *Fable 398*

ABRAHAM COWLEY
[1618–1667]

What shall I do to be forever known,
And make the age to come my own?
> *The Motto*

This only grant me, that my means may
lie
Too low for envy, for contempt too
high.
> *The Vote* [*1636*]

Well then! I now do plainly see
This busy world and I shall ne'er agree;
The very honey of all earthly joy
Does of all meats the soonest cloy,
   And they, methinks, deserve my pity,
Who for it can endure the stings,
The crowd, and buzz and murmurings,
   Of this great hive, the city.
> *The Wish* [*1647*]

Ah yet, ere I descend to the grave
May I a small house and large garden
have;
And a few friends, and many books,
both true,
Both wise, and both delightful too!
> *Ibid.*

A mistress moderately fair.
> *Ibid.*

The world's a scene of changes, and to
be
Constant, in Nature were inconstancy.
> *Inconstancy* [*1647*]

Th' adorning thee with so much art
   Is but a barb'rous skill;
'Tis like the pois'ning of a dart,
   Too apt before to kill.
> *The Waiting Maid* [*1647*]

The thirsty earth soaks up the rain,
And drinks, and gapes for drink again.
The plants suck in the earth, and are
With constant drinking fresh and fair.
> *From Anacreon* [*1656*].
> *II, Drinking*

Fill all the glasses there, for why
Should every creature drink but I?
Why, man of morals, tell me why?
> *From Anacreon. II, Drinking*

A mighty pain to love it is,
And 'tis a pain that pain to miss;
But of all pains, the greatest pain
It is to love, but love in vain.
> *Ibid. VII, Gold*

His time is forever, everywhere his
   place.
> *Friendship in Absence*

Nothing is there to come, and nothing
   past,
But an eternal now does always last.[1]
> *Davideis* [*1656*]. *Book I,*
> *Line 25*

Ye fields of Cambridge, our dear Cam-
   bridge, say,
Have ye not seen us walking every day?
Was there not a tree about which did
   not know
   The love betwixt us two?
> *On the Death of Mr. William*
> *Harvey*

Life is an incurable disease.
> *To Dr. Scarborough* [*1656*]

Let but thy wicked men from out thee
go,
And all the fools that crowd thee so,
Even thou, who dost thy millions boast,
A village less than Islington wilt grow,
A solitude almost.
> *Of Solitude. VII*

The fairest garden in her looks,
And in her mind the wisest books.
> *The Garden. I*

Hence, ye profane! I hate ye all,
Both the great vulgar and the small.[2]
> *Horace. Book III, Ode 1*

Charm'd with the foolish whistling of a
   name.[3]
> *Virgil, Georgics. Book II, Line 72*

---

[1] One of our poets (which is it?) speaks of
an everlasting now. — ROBERT SOUTHEY: *The
Doctor* [1834–1847], *Chap. XXV*
[2] Odi profanum vulgus.
[3] Ravish'd with the whistling of a name. —
POPE: *Essay on Man* [1732–1734], *Epistle IV,*
L. 283

Words that weep and tears that speak.[1]
> _The Prophet_

Poet and Saint! to thee alone are given
The two most sacred names of earth
  and Heaven.
> _On the Death of Mr. Crashaw_
> _[1668]_

His _faith_, perhaps, in some nice tenets
  might
Be wrong; his _life_, I'm sure, was in the
  right.[2]
> _Ibid._

RICHARD LOVELACE
[1618–1658]

Oh, could you view the melody
  Of every grace
  And music of her face,[3]
You'd drop a tear;
  Seeing more harmony
  In her bright eye
Than now you hear.
> _Orpheus to Beasts [1649]_

Tell me not, sweet, I am unkind,
  That from the nunnery
Of thy chaste breast and quiet mind,
  To war and arms I fly.
> _To Lucasta: Going to the Wars_
> _[1649]. Stanza 1_

I could not love thee, dear, so much,
Lov'd I not honour more.
> _Ibid. Stanza 3_

When I lie tangled in her hair,
  And fettered to her eye,
The gods that wanton in the air
  Know no such liberty.
> _To Althea: From Prison_
> _[1649]. Stanza 1_

Fishes that tipple in the deep,
Know no such liberty.
> _Ibid. Stanza 2_

Stone walls do not a prison make,[4]
  Nor iron bars a cage;

Minds innocent and quiet take
  That for an hermitage;
If I have freedom in my love,
  And in my soul am free,
Angels alone that soar above
  Enjoy such liberty.[1]
> _To Althea: From Prison. Stanza 4_

If to be absent were to be
  Away from thee;
Or that when I am gone,
  You and I were alone;
Then, my Lucasta, might I crave
Pity from blust'ring wind, or swallow-
  ing wave.
> _To Lucasta: Going Beyond the_
> _Seas [1649]. Stanza 1_

ANDREW MARVELL
[1620–1678]

The inglorious arts of peace.
> _Upon Cromwell's return from_
> _Ireland [1650]_

He[2] nothing common did, or mean,
Upon that memorable scene,
But with his keener eye
The axe's edge did try.
> _Ibid._

But bowed his comely head
Down as upon a bed.
> _Ibid._

So much one man can do,
That does both act and know.
> _Ibid._

Had we but world enough, and time,
This coyness, lady, were no crime.
> _To His Coy Mistress_
> _[1650–1652]_

  I would
Love you ten years before the Flood:
And you should, if you please, refuse
Till the conversion of the Jews.
My vegetable love should grow
Vaster than empires, and more slow.
> _Ibid._

---

[1] Thoughts that breathe, and words that burn. — THOMAS GRAY: _Progress of Poesy_ [1754], III, 3, 4
[2] See Pope, page 317b.
[3] The mind, the music breathing from her face. — BYRON: _Bride of Abydos_ [1813], Canto I, St. 6
[4] Stone walls a prisoner make, but not a slave. — WORDSWORTH [1770–1850]: _Humanity_

[1] But though my wing is closely bound,
  My heart's at liberty;
  My prison walls cannot control
  The flight, the freedom of the soul.
    JEANNE GUYON [1648–1717]:
    A Prisoner's Song, Castle of
    Vincennes, France, St. 4
[2] King Charles I.

But at my back I always hear
Time's wingèd chariot hurrying near;
And yonder all before us lie
Deserts of vast eternity.
To His Coy Mistress

Then worms shall try
That long preserved virginity,
And your quaint honour turn to dust,
And into ashes all my lust.
The grave's a fine and private place,
But none, I think, do there embrace.
Ibid.

Though we cannot make our sun
Stand still, yet we will make him run.
Ibid.

Annihilating all that's made
To a green thought in a green shade.
The Garden [*1650–1652*]

Casting the body's vest aside,
My soul into the boughs does glide.
Ibid.

The world in all doth but two nations
bear, —
The good, the bad; and these mixed
everywhere.
The Loyal Scot [*1650–1652*]

My love is of a birth as rare
As 'tis for object strange and high;
It was begotten by despair
Upon impossibility.
The Definition of Love [*1650–
1652*]. *Stanza 1*

As lines, so loves oblique, may well
Themselves in every angle greet;
But ours, so truly parallel,
Though infinite, can never meet.
Ibid. Stanza 7

Where the remote Bermudas ride,
In th' ocean's bosom unespied.
Bermudas [*1657*]

Orange bright,
Like golden lamps in a green light.
Ibid.

And all the way, to guide their chime,
With falling oars they kept the time.[1]
Ibid.

---

[1] Faintly as tolls the evening chime
Our voices keep tune and our oars keep
time.
Thomas Moore [*1780–1852*]:
A Canadian Boat Song, St. 1

JEAN DE LA FONTAINE
[1621–1695]

We believe no evil till the evil's done.
Fables. Book I [*1668*], *Fable 8*

We heed no instincts but our own.
Ibid.

The opinion of the strongest is always the best.
Ibid. Fable 10

By the work one knows the workman.
Ibid. Fable 21

It is a double pleasure to deceive the deceiver.
Ibid. Book II [*1668*], *Fable 15*

It is impossible to please all the world and one's father.
Ibid. Book III [*1668*], *Fable 1*

In everything one must consider the end.[1]
Ibid. Fable 5

Beware, as long as you live, of judging people by appearances.
Ibid. Book VI [*1668*], *Fable 5*

The sign brings customers.
Ibid. Book VII [*1678–1679*],
Fable 15

Let ignorance talk as it will, learning has its value.
Ibid. Book VIII [*1678–1679*],
Fable 19

People who make no noise are dangerous.
Ibid. Fable 23

He knows the universe, and himself he does not know.
Ibid. Fable 26

No path of flowers leads to glory.
Ibid. Book X [*1678–1679*],
Fable 14

JEAN BAPTISTE MOLIÈRE
[1622–1673]

I always make the first verse well, but I have trouble making the others.
Les Précieuses Ridicules
[*1659*]. *Sc. 11*

---

[1] Whatsoever thou takest in hand, remember the end, and thou shalt never do amiss. —
Apocrypha, Ecclesiasticus, III, 36

The world, dear Agnes, is a strange affair.
L'École des Femmes [*1662*].
Act II, Sc. 6
There are fagots and fagots.
Le Médecin Malgré Lui
[*1666*]. *Act I, Sc. 6*
We have changed all that.
Ibid. Act II, Sc. 6
He's a wonderful talker, who has the art of telling you nothing in a great harangue.
Le Misanthrope [*1666*].
Act II, Sc. 5
He makes his cook his merit, and the world visits his dinners and not him.
Ibid.
You see him laboring to produce *bons mots.*
Ibid.
The more we love our friends, the less we flatter them; it is by excusing nothing that pure love shows itself.
Ibid.
Doubts are more cruel than the worst of truths.
Ibid. Act III, Sc. 7
Anyone may be an honourable man, and yet write verse badly.
Ibid. Act IV, Sc. 1
If everyone were clothed with integrity, if every heart were just, frank, kindly, the other virtues would be well-nigh useless, since their chief purpose is to make us bear with patience the injustice of our fellows.
Ibid. Act V, Sc. 1
It is a wonderful seasoning of all enjoyments to think of those we love.
Ibid. Sc. 4
There is no rampart that will hold out against malice.
Tartuffe [*1667*]. *Act I, Sc. 1*
Those whose conduct gives room for talk are always the first to attack their neighbours.
Ibid.
She is laughing up her sleeve at you.
Ibid. Sc. 6
A woman always has her revenge ready.
Ibid. Act II, Sc. 2

A heart that forgets us puts us on our mettle to forget just as quickly, and, if we don't succeed, at least we make believe we have succeeded.
Tartuffe. Act II, Sc. 4
Although I am a pious man, I am not the less a man.
Ibid. Act III, Sc. 3
I prefer an accommodating vice to an obstinate virtue.
Amphitryon [*1668*]. *Act I, Sc. 4*
One must eat to live, and not live to eat.
Ibid. Act III, Sc. 1
The true Amphitryon is the Amphitryon who gives dinners.[1]
Ibid. Sc. 5
You wanted it so, Georges Dandin, you wanted it so! [2] This suits you very nicely, and you are served right; you have precisely what you deserve.
Georges Dandin [*1668*].
Act I, Sc. 9
The beautiful eyes of my money-box! He speaks of it as a lover of his mistress!
L'Avare [*1668*]. *Act V, Sc. 3*
You are speaking before a man to whom all Naples is known.
Ibid. Sc. 5
Good Heavens! For more than forty years I have been speaking prose without knowing it.
Le Bourgeois Gentilhomme
[*1670*]. *Act II, Sc. 4*
All that is not prose is verse; and all that is not verse is prose.
Ibid.
My fair one, let us swear an eternal friendship.[3]
Ibid. Act IV, Sc. 1

[1] Le véritable Amphitryon est l'Amphitryon où l'on dine.
[2] Vous l'avez voulu, Georges Dandin, vous l'avez voulu.
[3] A sudden thought strikes me — let us swear an eternal friendship. — FRERE: *The Rovers* [1798]
Madam, I have been looking for a person who disliked gravy all my life; let us swear eternal friendship. — SYDNEY SMITH [1771-1845]: *Lady Holland's Memoir, Vol. I, Chap. 9*

I will maintain it before the whole world.
>   *Le Bourgeois Gentilhomme.*
>   *Act IV, Sc. 5*

What the devil was he doing in that galley? [1]
>   *Les Fourberies de Scapin*
>   [*1671*]. *Act II, Sc. 11*

Grammar, which knows how to control even kings. [2]
>   *Les Femmes Savantes* [*1672*].
>   *Act II, Sc. 6*

It is seasoned throughout with Attic salt.
>   *Ibid. Act III, Sc. 2*

Ah, there are no longer any children!
>   *Le Malade Imaginaire* [*1673*].
>   *Act II, Sc. 11*

Nearly all men die of their remedies, and not of their illnesses.
>   *Ibid. Act III, Sc. 3*

RICHARD RUMBOLD
[1622–1685]

I never could believe that Providence had sent a few men into the world, ready booted and spurred to ride, and millions ready saddled and bridled to be ridden.
>   *On the scaffold* [*1685*] (MA-
>   CAULAY'S *History of England,*
>   *Chap. 1*)

[1] Que diable allait-il faire dans cette galère?
What the deuce did he want on board a Turk's galley? — CYRANO DE BERGERAC: *Le Pédant Joué* [1654], *Act II, Sc. 4*
The saying of Molière came into his head: "But what the devil was he doing in that galley?" and he laughed at himself. — TOL-STOI: *War and Peace* [1865–1872], *Part IV, Chap. 6*
Often misquoted, "in that gallery," as in DICKENS'S *A Tale of Two Cities* [1859], *Book I, Chap. 5:* "What the devil do you do in that gallery there!"
[2] Sigismund [1361–1437], Emperor of the Holy Roman Empire, at the Council of Constance [1414], said to a prelate who had objected to his Majesty's grammar: "Ego sum rex Romanus, et supra grammaticam" (I am the Roman king, and am above grammar).

ALGERNON SIDNEY
[1622–1683]

This hand, unfriendly to tyrants,
Seeks with the sword placid repose
under liberty.[1]
>   *Life and Memoirs of Algernon*
>   *Sidney*

It is not necessary to light a candle in the sun.[2]
>   *Discourses on Government*
>   [*1698*]. *Sect. XXIII*

HENRY VAUGHAN
[1622–1695]

Dear Night! this world's defeat;
The stop to busy fools; care's check
  and curb;
The day of spirits; my soul's calm re-
  treat
Which none disturb!
Christ's progress, and His prayer-time;
The hours to which high Heaven doth
  chime.
>   *Silex Scintillans* [*1655*].
>   *The Night, Line 25*

My soul, there is a country
  Far beyond the stars
Where stands a wingèd sentry
  All skilful in the wars:
There, above noise and danger,
  Sweet Peace is crown'd with smiles,
And One born in a manger
  Commands the beauteous files.
>   *Ibid. Peace, Stanza 1*

I saw Eternity the other night
Like a great ring of pure and endless
  light.
All calm, as it was bright;
And round beneath it, Time in hours,
  days, years,

[1]　Manus haec, inimica tyrannis,
　　Ense petit placidam sub libertate quietem.
The second line is the motto of the Commonwealth of Massachusetts.
[2] Like his that lights a candle to the sun. — ANDREW FLETCHER [1655–1716]: *Letter to Sir Walter Aston*
And hold their farthing candle to the sun — EDWARD YOUNG: *Satire VII* [1725–1728], *L. 56*
And hold their glimmering tapers to the sun. — GEORGE CRABBE: *The Parish Register* [1807], *Part I, Introduction*

Driv'n by the spheres
Like a vast shadow mov'd; in which the
  world
And all her train were hurled.
  Silex Scintillans. The World

Happy those early days, when I
Shin'd in my angel-infancy.
Before I understood this place
Appointed for my second race.
  Ibid. The Retreat

But felt through all this fleshly dress
Bright shoots of everlastingness.
  Ibid.

They are all gone into the world of
  light,
And I alone sit lingering here;
Their very memory is fair and bright,
And my sad thoughts doth clear.
  Ibid. They Are All Gone,
  Stanza 1

I see them walking in an air of glory
  Whose light doth trample on my
  days, —
My days, which are at best but dull
  and hoary,
  Mere glimmering and decays.
  Ibid. Stanza 3

Dear, beauteous death, the jewel of the
  just!
Shining nowhere but in the dark;
What mysteries do lie beyond thy dust,
  Could man outlook that mark!
  Ibid. Stanza 5

BLAISE PASCAL
[1623–1662]

Things are always at their best in
their beginning.
  Lettres Provinciales [1656–
  1657]. No. 4

Too much and too little education
hinder the mind.
  Pensées [1670]. Sect. II, No. 72

I lay it down as a fact that, if all men
knew what others say of them, there
would not be four friends in the world.
  Ibid. No. 101

The state of man: inconstancy,
boredom, anxiety.[1]
  Pensées. Sect. II, No. 127

Cleopatra's nose, had it been shorter,
the whole aspect of the world would
have been changed.
  Ibid. No. 162

The eternal silence of these infinite
spaces terrifies me.
  Ibid. Sect. III, No. 206

We shall die alone.[2]
  Ibid. No. 211

Between us and hell or heaven there
is nothing but life, which of all things
is the frailest.
  Ibid. No. 213

The heart has its reasons which reason knows nothing of.[3]
  Ibid. Sect. IV, No. 277

We know the truth, not only by the
reason, but by the heart.
  Ibid. No. 282

Man is but a reed, the weakest in
nature, but he is a thinking reed.[4]
  Ibid. Sect. VI, No. 347

Man is neither angel nor brute; and
the misfortune is that he who would
act the angel acts the brute.[5]
  Ibid. No. 358

Evil is easy, and has infinite forms.
  Ibid. No. 408

To ridicule philosophy is really to
philosophize.[6]
  Ibid. Sect. VII, No. 430

What a chimera then is man! What a
novelty! What a monster, what a chaos,
what a contradiction, what a prodigy!
Judge of all things, feeble worm of the
earth, depository of truth, a sink of

[1] Condition de l'homme: inconstance, ennui, inquiétude.
[2] On mourra seul.
[3] Le coeur a ses raisons que la raison ne
connaît point.
[4] L'homme n'est qu'un roseau, le plus faible
de la nature, mais c'est un roseau pensant.
[5] L'homme n'est ni ange, ni bête; et le malheur veut que qui veut faire l'ange fait la
bête.
[6] Se moquer de la philosophie, c'est vrai-
ment philosopher.

uncertainty and error, the glory and the shame of the universe.[1]

Pensées. Sect. VII, No. 434

Self is hateful.[2]

Ibid. No. 455

Men never do evil so completely and cheerfully as when they do it from religious conviction.

Ibid. Sect. XIV, No. 894

WILLIAM WALKER
[1623–1684]

Learn to read slow: all other graces
Will follow in their proper places.[3]

The Art of Reading

GEORGE FOX [4]
[1624–1691]

The Lord showed me, so that I did see clearly, that he did not dwell in these temples which men had commanded and set up, but in people's hearts . . . his people were his temple, and he dwelt in them.

Journal [1694]

I used in my dealings the word *verily*, and it was a common saying among people that knew me, if George says *verily* there is no altering him.

Ibid.

The Lord opened unto me that being bred at Oxford or Cambridge was not enough to fit and qualify men to be ministers of Christ.

Ibid.

My relations were much troubled at me that I would not go with them to hear the priest; for I would get into the orchard or the fields with my Bible by myself.

Ibid.

I was glad that I was commanded to turn people to that inward light, spirit

and grace, by which all might know their salvation, and their way to God.

Journal

When the Lord sent me forth into the world, He forbade me to put off my hat to any, high or low.

Ibid.

Justice Bennet of Derby, was the first that called us Quakers, because I bid them tremble at the word of the Lord. This was in the year 1650.

Ibid.

He [Oliver Cromwell] said: "I see there is a people risen, that I cannot win either with gifts, honours, offices or places; but all other sects and people I can."

Ibid.

JOHN AUBREY
[1626–1697]

He [Hobbes] had read much, but his contemplation was much more than his reading. He was wont to say that if he had read as much as other men, he should have known no more than other men.

Brief Lives [Edition 1898]. I, 349

[William Oughtred, mathematician]
His wife was a penurious woman, and would not allow him to burne candle after supper, by which means many a good notion is lost.

Ibid. II, 110

Mr. William Shakespear was borne at Stratford upon Avon in the county of Warwick. His father was a butcher, and I have been told heretofore by some of the neighbours, that when he was a boy he exercised his father's trade, but when he killed a calfe he would doe it in a high style and make a speech.

Ben Johnson and he did gather humours of men dayly where ever they came.

Ibid. II, 225

JOHN BUNYAN
[1628–1688]

And so I penned
It down, until at last it came to be,

---

[1] See Pope, pages 316b–317a.
[2] Le moi est haïssable.
[3] Take time enough; all other graces
Will soon fill up their proper places.
JOHN BYROM [1692–1763]: *Advice to Preach Slow*
[4] The founder of the Society of Friends (Quakers).

For length and breadth, the bigness which you see.

Pilgrim's Progress [*1678*].
Apology for His Book

Some said, "John, print it"; others said, "Not so."
Some said, "It might do good"; others said, "No."

Ibid.

As I walk'd through the wilderness of this world.

Ibid. Part I

The name of the slough was Despond.

Ibid.

Every fat [vat] must stand upon his bottom.[1]

Ibid.

The name of the one was Obstinate and the name of the other was Pliable.

Ibid.

The gentleman's name was Mr. Worldly-Wise-Man.

Ibid.

He came to the house of the Interpreter.

Ibid.

The palace Beautiful.

Ibid.

The valley of Humiliation.

Ibid.

A foul Fiend coming over the field to meet him; his name is Apollyon.

Ibid.

The pilgrim they laid in a large upper chamber, whose window opened toward the sun-rising; the name of the chamber was Peace.

Ibid.

I will talk of things heavenly, or things earthly; things moral, or things evangelical; things sacred, or things profane; things past, or things to come; things foreign, or things at home; things more essential, or things circumstantial.

Ibid.

It beareth the name of Vanity Fair,

[1] Every tub must stand upon its bottom. — CHARLES MACKLIN: *The Man of the World* [*1781*], *Act I, Sc. 2*

because the town where 'tis kept is lighter than vanity.

Pilgrim's Progress. Part I

Hanging is too good for him, said Mr. Cruelty.

Ibid.

A castle called Doubting Castle, the owner whereof was Giant Despair.

Ibid.

They came to the Delectable Mountains.

Ibid.

A great horror and darkness fell upon Christian.

Ibid.

So I awoke, and behold it was a dream.

Ibid.

Some things are of that nature as to make
One's fancy chuckle, while his heart doth ache.

Ibid. The Author's Way of
Sending Forth His Second Part
of the Pilgrim

A man that could look no way but downwards with a muckrake in his hand.

Ibid. Part II

The first string that the musician usually touches is the bass, when he intends to put all in tune. God also plays upon this string first, when he sets the soul in tune for himself.

Ibid.

My sword I give to him that shall succeed me in my pilgrimage, and my courage and skill to him that can get it. My marks and scars I carry with me, to be a witness for me, that I have fought his battles who now will be my rewarder.

Ibid.

So he passed over, and all the trumpets sounded for him on the other side.

Ibid.

The captain of all these men of death that came against him to take him away, was the Consumption, for it was that that brought him down to the grave.

*The Life and Death of
Mr. Badman*

SIR WILLIAM TEMPLE
[1628–1699]

Books, like proverbs, receive their chief value from the stamp and esteem of ages through which they have passed.

*Miscellanea, Part II [1690].
Ancient and Modern Learning*

When all is done, human life is, at the greatest and the best, but like a froward child, that must be played with and humoured a little to keep it quiet till it falls asleep, and then the care is over.

Ibid. Of Poetry

No clap of thunder in a fair frosty day could more astonish the world than our declaration of war against Holland in 1672.

Memoirs [1692]. Vol. II

JOHN TILLOTSON
[1630–1694]

If God were not a necessary Being of Himself, He might almost seem to be made for the use and benefit of men.[1]

Sermon

They who are in highest places, and have the most power, have the least liberty, because they are most observed.

Reflections

WALTER POPE
[1630?–1714]

May I govern my passions with absolute sway,
And grow wiser and better, as strength wears away,
Without gout or stone, by a gentle decay.

The Old Man's Wish [1685]

[1] If God did not exist, it would be necessary to invent him. — VOLTAIRE [1694–1778]: *A l'Auteur du Livre des trois Imposteurs, Epître CXL*

JOHN DRYDEN
[1631–1700]

And threat'ning France, plac'd like a painted Jove,
Kept idle thunder in his lifted hand.

*Annus Mirabilis [1667].
Stanza 39*

I am resolved to grow fat, and look young till forty.[1]

*Secret Love, or The Maiden
Queen [1667]. Act III, Sc. 1*

He [Shakespeare] was the man who of all modern, and perhaps ancient poets, had the largest and most comprehensive soul.

Essay of Dramatic Poesy [1668]

He was naturally learn'd; he needed not the spectacles of books to read Nature; he looked inwards, and found her there.

Ibid.

Pains of love be sweeter far
Than all other pleasures are.

*Tyrannic Love [1669].
Act IV, Sc. 1*

I am as free as Nature first made man,
Ere the base laws of servitude began,
When wild in woods the noble savage ran.

*The Conquest of Granada [1669–
1670]. Part I, Act I, Sc. 1*

Fame then was cheap, and the first comer sped;
And they have kept it since by being dead.

Ibid. Epilogue

But Shakespeare's magic could not copied be;
Within that circle none durst walk but he.

The Tempest [1670]. Prologue

Death in itself is nothing; but we fear
To be we know not what, we know not where.

*Aureng-Zebe [1676].
Act IV, Sc. 1*

When I consider life, 'tis all a cheat.
Yet fool'd with hope, men favour the deceit;

[1] See Sir Walter Scott, page 417b.

Trust on, and think tomorrow will repay.
Tomorrow's falser than the former
day;
Lies worse, and while it says we shall be
blest
With some new joys, cuts off what we
possest.
Strange cozenage! None would live past
years again,
Yet all hope pleasure in what yet remain;
And from the dregs of life think to receive
What the first sprightly running could
not give.
> *Aureng-Zebe. Act IV, Sc. 1*

'Tis not for nothing that we life pursue;
It pays our hopes with something still
that's new.
> *Ibid.*

Errors, like straws, upon the surface
flow;
He who would search for pearls must
dive below.
> *All for Love* [*1678*]. *Prologue*

Men are but children of a larger growth.
> *Ibid. Act IV, Sc. 1*

With how much ease believe we what
we wish! [1]
Whatever is, is in its causes just.[2]
> *Oedipus* [*1679*] (*With* NA-
> THANIEL LEE). *Act III, Sc. 1*

His hair just grizzled,
As in a green old age.[3]
> *Ibid.*

Of no distemper, of no blast he died,
But fell like autumn fruit that mellow'd
long, —
Even wonder'd at, because he dropp'd
no sooner.
Fate seem'd to wind him up for four-
score years,
Yet freshly ran he on ten winters more;
Till like a clock worn out with eating
time,

[1] Men freely believe that which they desire.
—CAESAR [102?–44 B.C.]: *De Bello Gallico,
Book III, Sect. 18*
[2] See Pope, page 316b.
[3] See Homer, page 5b.

The wheels of weary life at last stood
still.
> *Oedipus* (*With* NATHANIEL LEE).
> *Act IV, Sc. 1*

Whate'er he did was done with so much
ease,
In him alone, 'twas natural to please.
> *Absalom and Achitophel.
> Part I* [*1680*], *Line 27*

Of these the false Achitophel was first,
A name to all succeeding ages curst.
For close designs and crooked counsels
fit,
Sagacious, bold, and turbulent of wit,
Restless, unfixed in principles and
place,
In power unpleas'd, impatient of dis-
grace;
A fiery soul, which, working out its
way,
Fretted the pygmy-body to decay:
And o'er-inform'd the tenement of
clay.[1]
A daring pilot in extremity;
Pleas'd with the danger, when the
waves went high
He sought the storms; but for a calm
unfit,
Would steer too nigh the sands to boast
his wit.
Great wits are sure to madness near
allied,
And thin partitions do their bounds
divide.[2]
> *Ibid. Line 150*

Bankrupt of life, yet prodigal of ease.
> *Ibid. Line 168*

And all to leave what with his toil he
won
To that unfeather'd two-legg'd thing,
a son.
> *Ibid. Line 169*

In friendship false, implacable in hate,
Resolv'd to ruin or to rule the state.
> *Ibid. Line 173*

[1] See Thomas Fuller, page 243b.
[2] Remembrance and reflection how allied!
What thin partitions sense from thought
divide!
> POPE: *Essay on Man* [*1733–1734*],
> *Epistle I, L. 225*
See Seneca, page 48a.

And heaven had wanted one immortal song.

> *Absalom and Achitophel.*
> *Part I, Line 197*

The people's prayer, the glad diviner's theme,
The young men's vision, and the old men's dream! [1]

> *Ibid. Line 238*

Behold him setting in his western skies,
The shadows lengthening as the vapours rise.

> *Ibid. Line 268*

Than a successive title long and dark,
Drawn from the mouldy rolls of Noah's ark.

> *Ibid. Line 301*

His courage foes, his friends his truth proclaim.

> *Ibid. Line 357*

Let him give on till he can give no more.

> *Ibid. Line 389*

All empire is no more than power in trust.

> *Ibid. Line 411*

Better one suffer, than a nation grieve.

> *Ibid. Line 416*

Who think too little, and who talk too much.[2]

> *Ibid. Line 534*

A man so various, that he seem'd to be
Not one, but all mankind's epitome;
Stiff in opinions, always in the wrong,
Was everything by starts, and nothing long;
But, in the course of one revolving moon
Was chymist, fiddler, statesman, and buffoon.[3]

> *Ibid. Line 545*

So over violent, or over civil,
That every man with him was God or Devil.

> *Ibid. Line 557*

His tribe were God Almighty's gentlemen.

> *Ibid. Line 645*

---

[1] Your old men shall dream dreams, your young men shall see visions. — *Joel, II, 28*
[2] See Jonson, page 219b.
[3] See Juvenal, page 62b.

Large was his wealth, but larger was his heart.

> *Absalom and Achitophel.*
> *Part I, Line 826*

Him of the western dome, whose weighty sense
Flows in fit words and heavenly eloquence.

> *Ibid. Line 868*

Of ancient race by birth, but nobler yet
In his own worth.

> *Ibid. Line 900*

Beware the fury of a patient man.[1]

> *Ibid. Line 1005*

Made still a blund'ring kind of melody;
Spurr'd boldly on, and dashed through thick and thin,
Through sense and nonsense, never out nor in.

> *Ibid. Part II [1682], Line 413*

For every inch that is not fool is rogue.

> *Ibid. Line 463*

There is a pleasure sure
In being mad which none but madmen know.[2]

> *The Spanish Friar [1681].*
> *Act II, Sc. 1*

And, dying, bless the hand that gave the blow.[3]

> *Ibid.*

He's a sure card.

> *Ibid.*

They say everything in the world is good for something.

> *Ibid. Act III, Sc. 2*

Or break the eternal Sabbath of his rest.

> *Ibid. Act V, Sc. 2*

All human things are subject to decay,
And, when fate summons, monarchs must obey.

> *Mac Flecknoe [1682]. Line 1*

The rest to some faint meaning make pretence,
But Shadwell never deviates into sense.
Some beams of wit on other souls may fall,

---

[1] See Publilius Syrus, page 44a.
[2] There is a pleasure in poetic pains
Which only poets know.
COWPER [1731–1800]: *The Timepiece, L. 285*
[3] Adore the hand that gives the blow. —
POMFRET [1667–1702]: *Verses to His Friend*

Strike through and make a lucid interval;
But Shadwell's genuine night admits no ray,
His rising fogs prevail upon the day.
Mac Flecknoe. Line 19

And torture one poor word ten thousand ways.
Ibid. Line 208

Wit will shine
Through the harsh cadence of a rugged line.
To the Memory of Mr. Oldham [1684]. Line 15

Happy the man, and happy he alone,
He who can call today his own;
He who, secure within, can say,
Tomorrow, do thy worst, for I have liv'd today.[1]
Imitation of Horace. Book III, Ode 29 [1685], Line 65

Not heaven itself upon the past has power;
But what has been, has been, and I have had my hour.
Ibid. Line 71

I can enjoy her [2] while she's kind;
But when she dances in the wind,
And shakes the wings and will not stay,
I puff the prostitute away.
Ibid. Line 81

And virtue, though in rags, will keep me warm.
Ibid. Line 87

Ill news is wing'd with fate, and flies apace.
Threnodia Augustalis [1685]. Line 49

Men met each other with erected look,
The steps were higher that they took;
Friends to congratulate their friends made haste,
And long inveterate foes saluted as they pass'd.
Ibid. Line 124

Since heaven's eternal year is thine.
To the Pious Memory of Mrs. Anne Killegrew [1686]. Line 15

---

[1] See Horace, page 39b.
[2] Fortune.

O gracious God! how far have we
Profan'd thy heavenly gift of poesy!
To the Pious Memory of Mrs. Anne Killegrew. Line 56

Her wit was more than man, her innocence a child.[1]
Ibid. Line 70

Art she had none, yet wanted none,
For nature did that want supply:
So rich in treasures of her own,
She might our boasted stores defy.
Ibid. Line 71

From harmony, from heavenly harmony,
This universal frame began:
From harmony to harmony
Through all the compass of the notes it ran,
The diapason closing full in Man.
A Song for St. Cecilia's Day [1687]. Stanza 1

What passion cannot Music raise and quell?
Ibid. Stanza 2

The trumpet's loud clangour
Excites us to arms,
With shrill notes of anger,
And mortal alarms.
The double double double beat
Of the thundering drum
Cries Hark! the foes come.
Ibid. Stanza 3

The soft complaining flute,
In dying notes, discovers
The woes of hopeless lovers.
Ibid. Stanza 4

The trumpet shall be heard on high
The dead shall live, the living die,
And Music shall untune the sky!
Ibid. Grand Chorus

She fear'd no danger, for she knew no sin.
The Hind and the Panther [1687]. Part I, Line 4

And doom'd to death, though fated not to die.
Ibid. Line 8

For truth has such a face and such a mien,

---

[1] Of manners gentle, of affections mild,
In wit a man; simplicity a child.
POPE: *Epitaph on Gay* [1730]

As to be lov'd needs only to be seen.[1]
The Hind and the Panther.
Part I, Line 33

Of all the tyrannies on human kind
The worst is that which persecutes
the mind.
Ibid. Line 239

And kind as kings upon their coronation
day.
Ibid. Line 271

Too black for heaven, and yet too white
for hell.
Ibid. Line 343

And leaves the private conscience for
the guide.
Ibid. Line 478

Eternal house, not built with mortal
hands!
Ibid. Line 494

Who can believe what varies every day,
Nor ever was, nor will be at a stay?
Ibid. Part II, Line 36

All have not the gift of martyrdom.
Ibid. Line 59

When the cause goes hard, the guilty
man
Excepts, and thins his jury all he can.
Ibid. Line 242

Reason to rule, mercy to forgive:
The first is law, the last prerogative.
Ibid. Line 261

War seldom enters but where wealth
allures.
Ibid. Line 706

Much malice mingled with a little wit.
Ibid. Part III, Line 1

Jealousy, the jaundice of the soul.
Ibid. Line 73

For present joys are more to flesh and
blood
Than a dull prospect of a distant good.
Ibid. Line 364

T'abhor the makers, and their laws ap-
prove,
Is to hate traitors and the treason love.[2]
Ibid. Line 706

Secret guilt by silence is betrayed.
Ibid. Line 763

---

[1] See Pope, page 317a.
[2] He loved treachery but hated a traitor. —
PLUTARCH [A. D. 46–120]: *Lives, Romulus,
Chap. 17, Sect. 3*

Possess your soul with patience.[1]
The Hind and the Panther.
Part III, Line 839

Our vows are heard betimes! and
Heaven takes care
To grant, before we can conclude the
prayer:
Preventing angels met it half the way,
And sent us back to praise, who came
to pray.[2]
Britannia Rediviva [1688]. Line 1

Three poets, in three distant ages born,
Greece, Italy, and England did adorn.
The first in loftiness of thought sur-
pass'd;
The next, in majesty; in both the last.
The force of Nature could no further
go.
To make a third, she join'd the former
two.
*Under Mr. Milton's Picture
[1688]*

This is the porcelain clay of human-
kind.[3]
Don Sebastian [1690]. Act I, Sc. 1

I have a soul that like an ample shield
Can take in all, and verge enough for
more.[4]
Ibid.

A knock-down argument: 'tis but a
word and a blow.
Amphitryon [1690]. Act I, Sc. 1

Whistling to keep myself from being
afraid.[5]
Ibid. Act III, Sc. 1

So softly death succeeded life in her,
She did but dream of heaven, and she
was there.
Eleonora [1692]. Line 315

Theirs was the giant race, before the
flood
Epistle to Congreve [1693]. Line 5

---

[1] In your patience possess ye your souls. —
Luke, XXI, 19
[2] See Goldsmith, page 356a.
[3] The precious porcelain of human clay. —
BYRON: *Don Juan* [1819–1824], *Canto IV,
St. 11*
[4] Give ample room and verge enough. —
THOMAS GRAY: *The Bard* [1757], *II, 1*
[5] Whistling aloud to bear his courage up. —
BLAIR: *The Grave* [1743], *L. 58*

Genius must be born, and never can be taught.
                    Epistle to Congreve. Line 60
Be kind to my remains; and oh defend,
Against your judgment, your departed friend!
                    Ibid. Line 72
Look round the habitable world: how few
Know their own good, or knowing it, pursue.
                    Juvenal. Satire X [1693]
None but the brave deserves the fair.
                    Alexander's Feast [1697]. Line 15
With ravish'd ears
The monarch hears;
Assumes the god,
Affects to nod,
And seems to shake the spheres.
                    Ibid. Line 37
Bacchus, ever fair and ever young.
                    Ibid. Line 54
    Rich the treasure,
    Sweet the pleasure, —
Sweet is pleasure after pain.
                    Ibid. Line 58
Sooth'd with the sound, the king grew vain;
Fought all his battles o'er again;
And thrice he routed all his foes, and thrice he slew the slain.
                    Ibid. Line 66
Fallen from his high estate,
    And welt'ring in his blood;
Deserted, at his utmost need,
By those his former bounty fed,
On the bare earth expos'd he lies,
With not a friend to close his eyes.
                    Ibid. Line 78
Softly sweet, in Lydian measures,
Soon he sooth'd his soul to pleasures.
War, he sung, is toil and trouble;
Honour but an empty bubble;
    Never ending, still beginning,
Fighting still, and still destroying.
If all the world be worth thy winning,
Think, oh think it worth enjoying:
    Lovely Thais sits beside thee,
    Take the good the gods provide thee.
                    Ibid. Line 97
Sigh'd and look'd, and sigh'd again.
                    Ibid. Line 120

And, like another Helen, fir'd another Troy.
                    Alexander's Feast. Line 154
Could swell the soul to rage, or kindle soft desire.
                    Ibid. Line 160
He rais'd a mortal to the skies,
She drew an angel down.
                    Ibid. Line 169
Words, once my stock, are wanting to commend
So great a poet and so good a friend.
                    Epistle to Peter Antony Motteux [1698]. Line 54
Better to hunt in fields, for health unbought,
Than fee the doctor for a nauseous draught.
The wise, for cure, on exercise depend;
God never made his work for man to mend.
                    Epistle to John Dryden of Chesterton [1700]. Line 92
A very merry, dancing, drinking,
Laughing, quaffing, and unthinking time.
                    The Secular Masque [1700]. Line 38
The sword within the scabbard keep,
And let mankind agree.
                    Ibid. Line 61
All, all of a piece throughout:
Thy chase had a beast in view;
Thy wars brought nothing about;
Thy lovers were all untrue.
'Tis well an old age is out,
And time to begin a new.
                    Ibid. Line 86
And new-laid eggs, which Baucis' busy care
Turn'd by a gentle fire and roasted rare.
                    Ovid, Metamorphoses [1700]. Book VIII, Baucis and Philemon, Line 97
Ill habits gather by unseen degrees, —
As brooks make rivers, rivers run to seas.
                    Ibid. Book XV, The Worship of Aesculapius, Line 155

Here is God's plenty. [Of Chaucer's *Canterbury Tales*]
Fables [*1700*]. *Preface*

For Art may err, but Nature cannot miss.
Ibid. The Cock and the Fox. Line 452

Old as I am, for ladies' love unfit,
The power of beauty I remember yet.
Ibid. Cymon and Iphigenia. Line 1

He trudg'd along unknowing what he sought,
And whistled as he went, for want of thought.
Ibid. Line 84

Love taught him shame; and shame, with love at strife,
Soon taught the sweet civilities of life.
Ibid. Line 133

She hugg'd the offender, and forgave the offence:
Sex to the last.[1]
Ibid. Line 367

And raw in fields the rude militia swarms,
Mouths without hands; maintain'd at vast expense,
In peace a charge, in war a weak defence.
Ibid. Line 400

Of seeming arms to make a short essay,
Then hasten to be drunk, — the business of the day.
Ibid. Line 407

He was exhal'd; his great Creator drew
His spirit, as the sun the morning dew.[2]
On the Death of a Very Young Gentleman [*1704*]

---

[1] And love the offender, yet detest the offence. — POPE: *Eloisa to Abelard* [1717], *L. 192*

[2] Early, bright, transient, chaste as morning dew,
She sparkl'd, was exhal'd, and went to heaven.
EDWARD YOUNG: *Night Thoughts* [1742-1745], *Night V, L. 600*

WILLIAM STOUGHTON
[1631-1701]

God sifted a whole nation that he might send choice grain over into this wilderness.[1]
Election Sermon at Boston [*April 29, 1669*]

BENEDICT (BARUCH) SPINOZA [2]
[1632-1677]

Nature abhors a vacuum.
Ethics [*1677*].[3] *Part I, Prop. XV, Note*

God and all the attributes of God are eternal.
Ibid. Prop. XIX

Nothing exists from whose nature some effect does not follow.
Ibid. Prop. XXXVI

He who would distinguish the true from the false must have an adequate idea of what is true and false.
Ibid. Part II, Prop. XLII, Proof

Will and Intellect are one and the same thing.
Ibid. Prop. XLIX, Corollary

He that can carp in the most eloquent or acute manner at the weakness of the human mind is held by his fellows as almost divine.
Ibid. Part III, Preface

Surely human affairs would be far happier if the power in men to be silent were the same as that to speak. But ex-

---

[1] God had sifted three kingdoms to find the wheat for this planting. — LONGFELLOW: *Courtship of Miles Standish* [1858], *IV*

[2] Ein Gottbetrunkener Mensch (A God-intoxicated man). — NOVALIS (FRIEDRICH VON HARDENBERG) [1772-1801]
The Lord blot out his name under heaven. The Lord set him apart for destruction from all the tribes of Israel, with all the curses of the firmament which are written in the Book of the Law. . . . There shall no man speak to him, no man write to him, no man show him any kindness, no man stay under the same roof with him, no man come nigh him. — Amsterdam Synagogue's curse on Spinoza [1656]

[3] Everyman edition, translated by ANDREW BOYLE.

perience more than sufficiently teaches that men govern nothing with more difficulty than their tongues.
Ethics. Part III, Prop. II, Note
Pride is therefore pleasure arising from a man's thinking too highly of himself.
Ibid. Prop. XXVI, Note
It may easily come to pass that a vain man may become proud and imagine himself pleasing to all when he is in reality a universal nuisance.
Ibid. Prop. XXX, Note
Sadness diminishes or hinders a man's power of action.
Ibid. Prop. XXXVII, Proof
Self-complacency is pleasure accompanied by the idea of oneself as cause.
Ibid. Prop. LI, Note
It therefore comes to pass that every one is fond of relating his own exploits and displaying the strength both of his body and his mind, and that men are on this account a nuisance one to the other.
Ibid. Prop. LIV, Note
I refer those actions which work out the good of the agent to courage, and those which work out the good of others to nobility. Therefore temperance, sobriety, and presence of mind in danger, etc., are species of courage; but modesty, clemency, etc., are species of nobility.
Ibid. Prop. LIX, Note
Fear cannot be without hope nor hope without fear.
Ibid. Definition XIII, Explanation
So long as a man imagines that he cannot do this or that, so long is he determined not to do it: and consequently, so long it is impossible to him that he should do it.
Ibid. Definition XXVIII, Explanation
Those who are believed to be most abject and humble are usually most ambitious and envious.
Ibid. Definition XXIX, Explanation
One and the same thing can at the same time be good, bad, and indifferent, e.g., music is good to the melancholy,

bad to those who mourn, and neither good nor bad to the deaf.
Ethics. Part IV, Preface
Man is a social animal.
Ibid. Prop. XXXV, Note
Men will find that they can prepare with mutual aid far more easily what they need, and avoid far more easily the perils which beset them on all sides, by united forces.
Ibid.
Avarice, ambition, lust, etc., are nothing but species of madness, although not enumerated among diseases.[1]
Ibid. Prop. XLIV, Note
It is the part of a wise man to feed himself with moderate pleasant food and drink, and to take pleasure with perfumes, with the beauty of growing plants, dress, music, sports, and theatres, and others places of this kind which man may use without any hurt to his fellows.
Ibid. Prop. XLV, Note 2
He whose honour depends on the opinion of the mob must day by day strive with the greatest anxiety, act and scheme in order to retain his reputation. For the mob is varied and inconstant, and therefore if a reputation is not carefully preserved it dies quickly.
Ibid. Prop. LVIII, Note
In refusing benefits caution must be used lest we seem to despise or to refuse them for fear of having to repay them in kind.
Ibid. Prop. LXX, Note
To give aid to every poor man is far beyond the reach and power of every man. . . . Care of the poor is incumbent on society as a whole.
Ibid. Appendix, XVII
None are more taken in by flattery than the proud, who wish to be the first and are not.
Ibid. XXI

[1] To me, avarice seems not so much a vice, as a deplorable piece of madness. — SIR THOMAS BROWNE: *Religio Medici* [1642]

Those are most desirous of honour and glory who cry out the loudest of its abuse and the vanity of the world.

Ethics. Part V, Prop. X, Note

We feel and know that we are eternal.

Ibid. Prop. XXIII, Note

All excellent things are as difficult as they are rare.

Ibid. Prop. XLII, Note

The things which . . . are esteemed as the greatest good of all, . . . can be reduced to these three headings: to wit, Riches, Fame, and Pleasure. With these three the mind is so engrossed that it cannot scarcely think of any other good.

Tractatus de Intellectus Emendatione [*1677*]. *I, 3*

Fame has also this great drawback, that if we pursue it we must direct our lives in such a way as to please the fancy of men, avoiding what they dislike and seeking what is pleasing to them.

Ibid. 5

The more intelligible a thing is, the more easily it is retained in the memory, and contrariwise, the less intelligible it is, the more easily we forget it.

Ibid. XI, 81

JOHN LOCKE
[1632–1704]

New opinions are always suspected, and usually opposed, without any other reason but because they are not already common.

Essay on Human Understanding [*1690*]. *Dedicatory Epistle*

No man's knowledge here can go beyond his experience.

Ibid. Book II, Chap. 1, Sect. 19

It is one thing to show a man that he is in error, and another to put him in possession of truth.

Ibid. Book IV, Chap. 7, Sect. 11

All men are liable to error; and most men are, in many points, by passion or interest, under temptation to it.

Ibid. Chap. 20, Sect. 17

A sound mind in a sound body,[1] is a short but full description of a happy state in this world.

Some Thoughts on Education [*1693*]. *Sect. 1*

Virtue is harder to be got than knowledge of the world; and, if lost in a young man, is seldom recovered.

Ibid. Sect. 64

He that will have his son have a respect for him and his orders, must himself have a great reverence for his son.

Ibid. Sect. 65

The only fence against the world is a thorough knowledge of it.

Ibid. Sect. 88

BISHOP RICHARD CUMBERLAND
[1632–1718]

It is better to wear out than to rust out.

Quoted by BISHOP GEORGE HORNE [*1730–1792*]: *Sermon on the Duty of Contending for the Truth*

WENTWORTH DILLON, EARL OF ROSCOMMON
[1633–1685]

Remember Milo's end,
Wedged in that timber which he strove to rend.

Essay on Translated Verse [*1684*]. *Line 87*

And choose an author as you choose a friend.

Ibid. Line 96

Immodest words admit of no defence,
For want of decency is want of sense.

Ibid. Line 113

The multitude is always in the wrong.

Ibid. Line 184

My God, my Father, and my Friend,
Do not forsake me in my end.

Translation of Dies Irae

---

[1] Mens sana in corpore sano. — JUVENAL [A. D. 40–125]: *Satire X, L. 356*

SAMUEL PEPYS
[1633–1703]

I pray God to keep me from being proud.

Diary. March 22, 1660

This morning came home my fine camlet cloak, with gold buttons, and a silk suit, which cost me much money, and I pray God to make me able to pay for it.

Ibid. July 1, 1660

And so to bed.

Ibid. July 22, 1660; December 7, 1660; May 19, 1662; etc.

I am unwilling to mix my fortune with him that is going down the wind.

Ibid. September 6, 1660

I did give ten shillings and no more, though I believe most of the rest did give more, and did believe that I did so too.

Ibid. November 5, 1660

One, by his own confession to me, that can put on two several faces, and look his enemies in the face with as much love as his friends. But, good God! what an age is this, and what a world is this! that a man cannot live without playing the knave and dissimulation.

Ibid. September 1, 1661

Though he be a fool, yet he keeps much company, and will tell all he sees or hears, so a man may understand what the common talk of the town is.

Ibid. September 2, 1661

Besides us and my uncle Fenner's family, there was none of any quality, but poor and rascally people.

Ibid. September 15, 1661

My wife, poor wretch.

Ibid. September 18, 1661; December 10, 1662; etc.

Thanks be to God, since my leaving drinking of wine, I do find myself much better, and do mind my business better, and do spend less money, and less time lost in idle company.

Ibid. January 26, 1662

As happy a man as any in the world, for the whole world seems to smile upon me.

Diary. October 31, 1662

Great talk among people how some of the Fanatiques do say that the end of the world is at hand, and that next Tuesday is to be the day. Against which, whenever it shall be, good God fit us all!

Ibid. November 25, 1662

Bought Hudibras again, it being certainly some ill humour to be so against that which all the world cries up to be the example of wit; for which I am resolved once more to read him, and see whether I can find it or no.[1]

Ibid. February 6, 1663

Got my father, brother Tom, and myself together, and I advised my father to good husbandry, and to be living within the compass of £50 a year, and all in such kind words, as not only made both them but myself to weep.

Ibid. May 1, 1663

Troubled to see my wife forced to sit in the back of the coach, though pleased to see her company none but women and one parson.

Ibid. June 15, 1663

Find myself £43 worse than I was the last month . . . chiefly arisen from my layings-out in clothes for myself and wife; viz., for her about £12, and for myself £55.

Ibid. October 31, 1663

Home, and dined, where I found an excellent mastiffe — his name Towser — sent me by a surgeon.

Ibid. February 17, 1664

To the Trinity House, where a very good dinner among the old soakers.

Ibid. February 15, 1665

I am at a loss to know whether it be my hare's foot which is my preservative, or my taking of a pill of turpentine every morning.

Ibid. March 26, 1665

[1] Pepys had bought *Hudibras*, December 26, 1662, but thought it "so silly an abuse of the Presbyter Knight going to the wars" that he sold it the same day.

Thus I ended this month with the greatest joy that ever I did any in my life, because I have spent the greatest part of it with abundance of joy, and honour, and pleasant journeys, and brave entertainments, and without cost of money.

Diary. July 31, 1665

But Lord! how everybody's looks, and discourse in the street, is of death, and nothing else; and few people going up and down, that the town is like a place distressed and forsaken.[1]

Ibid. August 30, 1665

Saw a wedding in the church; and strange to see what delight we married people have to see these poor fools decoyed into our condition.

Ibid. December 25, 1665

Musick and women I cannot but give way to, whatever my business is.

Ibid. March 9, 1666

The truth is, I do indulge myself a little the more in pleasure, knowing that this is the proper age of my life to do it; and, out of my observation that most men that do thrive in the world do forget to take pleasure during the time that they are getting their estate, but reserve that till they have got one, and then it is too late for them to enjoy it.

Ibid. March 10, 1666

Home, and, being washing-day, dined upon cold meat.

Ibid. April 4, 1666

Anon comes home my wife from Brampton, not looked for till Saturday, which will hinder me of a little pleasure, but I am glad of her coming.

Ibid. April 19, 1666

Musick is the thing of the world that I love most.

Ibid. July 30, 1666

Thus ends this year of publick wonder and mischief to this nation, and, therefore, generally wished by all people to have an end.

Ibid. December 31, 1666

Busy till night, pleasing myself mightily to see what a deal of business

[1] The time of the Great Plague.

goes off a man's hands when he stays by it.

Diary. January 14, 1667

Did satisfy myself mighty fair in the truth of the saying that the world do not grow old at all, but is in as good condition in all respects as ever it was.

Ibid. February 3, 1667

This day I am, by the blessing of God, 34 years old, in very good health and mind's content, and in condition of estate much beyond whatever my friends could expect of a child of their's, this day 34 years. The Lord's name be praised! and may I be thankful for it.

Ibid. February 23, 1667

To church; and with my mourning, very handsome, and new periwigg, make a great show.

Ibid. March 31, 1667

But to think of the clatter they make with his coach, and their own fine cloathes, and yet how meanly they live within doors, and nastily, and borrowing everything of neighbours.

Ibid. April 1, 1667

I have had it much in my thoughts lately that it is not too much for me now, in degree or cost, to keep a coach, but contrarily, that I am almost ashamed to be seen in a hackney.

Ibid. April 21, 1667

Whose red nose makes me ashamed to be seen with him.

Ibid. May 3, 1667

I staid talking below, while my wife dressed herself, which vexed me that she was so long about it.[1]

Ibid. July 14, 1667

Gives me some kind of content to remember how painful it is sometimes to keep money, as well as to get it.

Ibid. October 11, 1667

And there all my Fellow-Officers, and all the world that was within hearing, did congratulate me, and cry my speech as the best thing they ever heard.

Ibid. March 5, 1668

[1] In fairness to Mrs. Pepys, it should be added that they were rising at 4 A.M. that warm morning, for a picnic in the country.

Not to make any more speech, which, while my fame is good, I will avoid, for fear of losing it.

Diary. March 13, 1668

I find my wife hath something in her gizzard, that only waits an opportunity of being provoked to bring up; but I will not, for my content-sake, give it.

Ibid. June 17, 1668

I by little words find that she hath heard of my going to plays, and carrying people abroad every day, in her absence; and that I cannot but help the storm will break out in a little time.

Ibid. June 18, 1668

In appearance, at least, he being on all occasions glad to be at friendship with me, though we hate one another, and know it on both sides.

Ibid. September 22, 1668

I do hate to be unquiet at home.

Ibid. January 22, 1669

And so I betake myself to that course, which is almost as much as to see myself go into my grave; for which, and all the discomforts that will accompany my being blind, the good God prepare me!

Ibid. May 31, 1669 (final entry)

GEORGE SAVILE, MARQUESS OF HALIFAX
[1633–1695]

Children and fools want everything, because they want wit to distinguish; there is no stronger evidence of a crazy understanding than the making too large a catalogue of things necessary.

Advice to a Daughter [1688]

Popularity is a crime from the moment it is sought; it is only a virtue where men have it whether they will or no.

Moral Thoughts and Reflections [1750]

Misspending a man's time is a kind of self-homicide.

Ibid.

ROBERT SOUTH
[1634–1716]

Speech was given to the ordinary sort of men whereby to communicate their mind; but to wise men, whereby to conceal it.[1]

Sermon [1676]

NICHOLAS BOILEAU-DESPRÉAUX
[1636–1711]

Happy who in his verse can gently steer
From grave to light, from pleasant to severe.[2]

The Art of Poetry [1674].[3]
Canto I, Line 75

Whate'er is well-conceived is clearly said,
And the words to say it flow with ease.

Ibid. Line 153

Every age has its pleasures, its style of wit, and its own ways.

Ibid. Canto III, Line 374

The wisest man is he who does not fancy that he is so at all.

Satire 1. Line 46

He [Molière] pleases all the world, but cannot please himself.

Ibid. Line 94

In spite of every sage whom Greece can show,
Unerring wisdom never dwelt below;

---

[1] Speech was made to open man to man, and not to hide him; to promote commerce, and not betray it. — DAVID LLOYD [1635–1692]: *The Statesmen and Favourites of England since the Reformation* [1665, edited by Whitworth], *Vol. I, P. 503*
Men talk only to conceal the mind. — EDWARD YOUNG: *Love of Fame* [1725–1728], *Satire II, L. 208*
The true use of speech is not so much to express our wants as to conceal them. — GOLDSMITH: *The Bee, No. 3* [October 20, 1759]
Ils ne se servent de la pensée que pour autoriser leurs injustices, et n'emploient les paroles que pour déguiser leurs pensées (Men use thought only to justify their wrongdoings, and employ speech only to conceal their thoughts). — VOLTAIRE: *Dialogue XIV, Le Chapon et la Poularde* [1766]

[2] See Pope, page 318a.
[3] Translated by DRYDEN.

Folly in all of every age we see,
The only difference lies in the degree.
Satire 4. Line 37

Greatest fools are oft most satisfied.
Ibid. Line 128

If your descent is from heroic sires,
Show in your life a remnant of their
fires.
Satire 5. Line 43

Of all the creatures that creep, swim, or
fly,
Peopling the earth, the waters, and the
sky,
From Rome to Iceland, Paris to Japan,
I really think the greatest fool is man.
Satire 8. Line 1

Follows his wife like fringe upon her
gown.
Ibid. Line 47

A hero may be dragged in a romance
Through ten long volumes by the laws
of France.
Hence every year our books in torrents
run,
And Paris counts an author in each son.
Satire 9. Line 103

But satire, ever moral, ever new,
Delights the reader and instructs him,
too.
She, if good sense refine her sterling
page,
Oft shakes some rooted folly of the age.
Ibid. Line 257

Honor is like an island, rugged and
without a beach; once we have left it,
we can never return.
Satire 10. Line 167

Now two punctilious envoys, Thine and
Mine,
Embroil the earth about a fancied line;
And, dwelling much on right and much
on wrong,
Prove how the right is chiefly with the
strong.
Satire 11. Line 141

All Europe by conflicting Faiths was
rent,
And e'en the Orthodox on carnage
bent;
The blind avengers of Religion's cause

Forgot each precept of her peaceful
laws.
Satire 12. Line 169

The terrible burden of having nothing
to do.
Epistle XI

BISHOP THOMAS KEN
[1637–1711]

Teach me to live, that I may dread
The grave as little as my bed.
Morning and Evening Hymn.
Stanza 3

Praise God, from whom all blessings
flow!
Praise Him, all creatures here below!
Praise Him above, ye heavenly host!
Praise Father, Son, and Holy Ghost!
Ibid. Stanza 10

JEAN RACINE
[1639–1699]

It is no longer a passion hidden in
my veins: it is the goddess Venus herself fastened on her prey.[1]
Phèdre [1677]. Act I, Sc. 3

Innocence has nothing to dread.
Ibid. Act III, Sc. 6

Crime like virtue has its degrees; and
timid innocence was never known to
blossom suddenly into extreme license.[2]
Ibid. Act IV, Sc. 2

According to ancient, sacred custom.
Athalie [1691]. Act I, Sc. 1

To repair the irreparable ravages of
time.
Ibid. Act II, Sc. 5

SIR CHARLES SEDLEY
[1639?–1701]

When change itself can give no more,
'Tis easy to be true.
Reasons for Constancy. Stanza 4

Phyllis is my only joy,
Faithless as the winds or seas;

---

[1] Ce n'est plus une ardeur dans mes veines
cachée:
C'est Vénus toute entière à sa proie at-
tachée.
[2] See Juvenal, page 62b.

Sometimes coming, sometimes coy,
Yet she never fails to please.
Song [*1702*]. *Stanza 1*

SIR ISAAC NEWTON
[1642–1727]

I do not know what I may appear to the world; but to myself I seem to have been only like a boy playing on the seashore, and diverting myself in now and then finding a smoother pebble or a prettier shell than ordinary, whilst the great ocean of truth lay all undiscovered before me.
BREWSTER'S *Memoirs of Newton* [*1855*]. *Vol. II, Chap. XXVII*

O Diamond! Diamond! thou little knowest the mischief done!
Said to a pet dog who knocked over a candle and set fire to his papers

WILLIAM PENN
[1644–1718]

The receipts of cookery are swelled to a volume; but a good stomach excels them all.
Fruits of Solitude [1] [*1693*]

Truth often suffers more by the heat of its defenders, than from the arguments of its opposers.
Ibid.

Men are generally more careful of the breed of their horses and dogs than of their children.
Ibid.

It were endless to dispute upon everything that is disputable.
Ibid.

Have a care where there is more sail than ballast.
Ibid.

Passion is a sort of fever in the mind,

[1] A copy of this little book, wrote ROBERT LOUIS STEVENSON, "I carried in my pocket all about the San Francisco streets, read in streetcars and ferry-boats when I was sick unto death, and found in all times and places a peaceful and sweet companion."

which ever leaves us weaker than it found us.
Fruits of Solitude

The public must and will be served.
Ibid.

Much reading is an oppression of the mind, and extinguishes the natural candle, which is the reason of so many senseless scholars in the world.
Advice to His Children [*1699*]

JEAN DE LA BRUYÈRE
[1645–1696]

Liberality consists less in giving a great deal than in gifts well timed.
Les Caractères [*1688–1697*].
Du Coeur

To laugh at men of sense is the privilege of fools.
Ibid. De la Société

Most men make use of the first part of their life to render the other part wretched.
Ibid. De l'Homme

If women were by nature what they makes themselves by artifice, if their faces suddenly became as bright or as leaden as they make them with paint and powder, they would be inconsolable.
Ibid. Des Femmes

HENRY ALDRICH
[1647–1710]

If all be true that I do think,
There are five reasons we should drink:
Good wine — a friend — or being dry —
Or lest we should be by and by —
Or any other reason why.
Five Reasons for Drinking

JOHN WILMOT, EARL OF ROCHESTER
[1647–1680]

Here lies our sovereign lord the king,
Whose word no man relies on;

He never says a foolish thing,
  Nor ever does a wise one.
      *Written on the Bedchamber Door
          of Charles II* [1]

For pointed satire I would Buckhurst
  choose,
The best good man with the worst-
  natured muse.[2]
      *An Allusion to Horace. Satire X,
          Book I*

A merry monarch, scandalous and poor.
      A Satire on King Charles II

The world appears like a great family,
Whose lord, oppressed with pride and
  poverty,
(That to the few great bounty he may
  show)
Is fain to starve the numerous train
  below.
      Like a Great Family

There's not a thing on earth that I can
  name,
So foolish, and so false, as common
  fame.
      Did E'er This Saucy World

Reason, which fifty times to one does
  err,
Reason, an *ignis fatuus* of the mind.
      A Satire Against Mankind [1675].
          Line 11

Books bear him up a while, and make
  him try
To swim with bladders of philosophy.
      Ibid. Line 20

Then Old Age and Experience, hand in
  hand,
Lead him to death, and make him understand,
After a search so painful and so long,
That all his life he has been in the
  wrong.
      Ibid. Line 25

Dead, we become the lumber of the
  world.
      After Death

---

[1] Charles II's reply to Lord Rochester's
epigram was: "That is very true: for my
words are my own, and my actions are my
ministers'."

[2] Thou best-humour'd man with the worst-
humour'd muse! — GOLDSMITH: *Retaliation*
[1774], *Postscript*

JOHN SHEFFIELD, DUKE OF BUCKINGHAMSHIRE
[1648–1721]

Of all those arts in which the wise excel,
Nature's chief masterpiece is writing
  well.
      Essay on Poetry [1682]

Read Homer once, and you can read
  no more;
For all books else appear so mean, so
  poor,
Verse will seem prose; but still persist
  to read,
And Homer will be all the books you
  need.
      Ibid.

And when I feigned an angry look,
Alas! I loved you best.
      The Reconcilement [1701]

WILLIAM III, PRINCE OF ORANGE
[1650–1702]

There is one certain means by which
I can be sure never to see my country's
ruin: I will die in the last ditch.
      HUME: *History of England*
          [1754–1757]. *Chap. 65*

THOMAS OTWAY
[1651–1685]

What mighty ills have not been done by
  woman!
Who was 't betrayed the Capitol? — A
  woman!
Who lost Mark Antony the world? —
  A woman!
Who was the cause of a long ten years'
  war,
And laid at last old Troy in ashes? —
  Woman!
Destructive, damnable, deceitful
  woman!
      The Orphan [1680]. *Act III, Sc. 1*

Let us embrace, and from this very
moment vow an eternal misery together.
      Ibid. Act IV, Sc. 2

O woman! lovely woman! Nature
  made thee

To temper man: we had been brutes without you.
Venice Preserved [*1682*].
Act I, Sc. 1

FRANÇOIS DE SALIGNAC DE LA MOTHE FÉNELON
[1651–1715]

That weary listlessness, which renders life unsupportable to the voluptuous and the indolent, is unknown to those who can employ themselves by reading.
Télémaque [*1699*]. *Book II*

There were some who said that a man at the point of death was more free than all others, because death breaks every bond, and over the dead the united world has no power.
Ibid. Book V

Love is conquered only by flight. Against such an enemy, true courage consists in fear and retreat, in retreat without deliberation, and without looking back.
Ibid. Book VI

By labor Wisdom gives poignancy to pleasure, and by pleasure she restores vigor to labor.
Ibid. Book VII

Do not men die fast enough without being destroyed by each other? Can any man be insensible of the brevity of life? and can he who knows it, think life too long!
Ibid.

They that defy the tempest to gratify avarice and luxury, deserve shipwreck.
Ibid.

Courage is a virtue only in proportion as it is directed by prudence.
Ibid. Book X

No distinction so little excites envy as that which is derived from ancestors by a long descent.
Ibid.

To be always ready for war, said Mentor, is the surest way to avoid it.[1]
Ibid.

[1] See Horace, page 40b, and Washington, page 367a.

Some of the most dreadful mischiefs that afflict mankind proceed from wine; it is the cause of disease, quarrels, sedition, idleness, aversion to labour, and every species of domestic disorder.
Télémaque. Book X

The blood of a nation ought never to be shed except for its own preservation in the utmost extremity.
Ibid. Book XIII

Mankind, by the perverse depravity of their nature, esteem that which they have most desired as of no value the moment it is possessed, and torment themselves with fruitless wishes for that which is beyond their reach.
Ibid. Book XVIII

NAHUM TATE
[1652–1715]
AND
NICHOLAS BRADY
[1659–1726]

And though he promise to his loss,
He makes his promise good.
Psalms [*1696*]. *XV, 5*

The sweet remembrance of the just
Shall flourish when he sleeps in dust.
Ibid. CXII, 6

Permit the transports of a British Muse,
And pardon raptures that yourselves infuse.
Tate, *as Poet Laureate, to the Parliament* [*1701*]

THOMAS D'URFEY
[1653–1723]

O'er the hills and far away.[1]
Pills to Purge Melancholy

ANDREW FLETCHER OF SALTOUN
[1655–1716]

Give me the making of the songs of a nation, and I care not who makes its laws.
Conversation Concerning a Right Regulation of Government for the Common Good of Mankind [*1703*]

[1] See Gay, page 308b.

NATHANIEL LEE
[1655–1692]

Then he will talk — good gods! how he
will talk!
> *The Rival Queens, or, The*
> *Death of Alexander the Great*
> *[1677]. Act I, Sc. 3*

Vows with so much passion, swears with
so much grace,
That 'tis a kind of heaven to be de-
luded by him.
> *Ibid.*

When Greeks joined Greeks, then
was the tug of war.
> *Ibid. Act IV, Sc. 2*

'Tis beauty calls, and glory shows the
way.[1]
> *Ibid.*

Man, false man, smiling, destructive
man!
> *Theodosius [1680]. Act III, Sc. 2*

JOHN DENNIS
[1657–1734]

A man who could make so vile a pun
would not scruple to pick a pocket.
> *The Gentleman's Magazine.*
> *Vol. LI [1781], Page 324*

They will not let my play run; and
yet they steal my thunder.[2]

[1] "Leads the way" in the stage editions,
which contain various interpolations, among
them
   See the conquering hero comes!
   Sound the trumpet, beat the drums!
which was first used by Handel in *Joshua,*
and afterwards transferred to *Judas Mac-
cabaeus.* The text of both oratorios was written by Dr. Thomas Morell [1703–1784], a
clergyman.

[2] For his play *Appius and Virginia* [1709],
Dennis had invented a new species of thunder. "The tragedy however was coldly received, notwithstanding such assistance, and
was acted but a short time. Some nights after,
Mr. Dennis, being in the pit at the representation of *Macbeth,* heard his own thunder
made use of; upon which he rose in a violent
passion, and exclaimed, with an oath, that it
was his thunder. 'See,' said he, 'how the
rascals use me! They will not let my play
run, and yet they steal my thunder!'" —
Biographia Britannica, Vol. V, P. 103

JOHN NORRIS
[1657–1711]

How fading are the joys we dote upon!
Like apparitions seen and gone.
But those which soonest take their
flight
Are the most exquisite and strong, —
Like angels' visits, short and bright; [1]
Mortality's too weak to bear them long.
> *The Parting*

When after some delays, some dying
strife,
The soul stands shivering on the ridge
of life;
With what a dreadful curiosity
Does she launch out into the sea of vast
eternity.
> *The Meditation*

DANIEL DEFOE
[1661–1731]

Wherever God erects a house of prayer,
The Devil always builds a chapel
there; [2]
And 'twill be found, upon examination,
The latter has the largest congregation.
> *The True-Born Englishman*
> *[1701]. Part I, Line 1*

From this amphibious ill-born mob
began
That vain, ill-natur'd thing, an Englishman.
> *Ibid. Line 132*

Great families of yesterday we show,
And Lords whose parents were the Lord
knows who.
> *Ibid. Line 372*

In their religion they are so uneven,
That each man goes his own By-way to
heaven.
> *Ibid. Part II, Line 104*

And of all plagues with which mankind
are curst,
Ecclesiastic tyranny's the worst.
> *Ibid. Line 299*

[1] Like those of angels, short and far be-
tween. — ROBERT BLAIR: *The Grave* [1743],
L. 588
   Like angel visits, few and far between. —
THOMAS CAMPBELL: *Pleasures of Hope* [1799],
Part II, L. 378
[2] See Luther, page 86b.

When kings the sword of justice first
lay down,
They are no kings, though they possess
the crown.
Titles are shadows, crowns are empty
things,
The good of subjects is the end of
kings.
The True-Born Englishman.
Part II, Line 313
He bade me observe it, and I should
always find, that the calamities of life
were shared among the upper and lower
part of mankind; but that the middle
station had the fewest disasters.
Robinson Crusoe [1719]
One day, about noon, going towards
my boat, I was exceedingly surprised
with the print of a man's naked foot on
the shore, which was very plain to be
seen on the sand.
Ibid.
I let him know his name should be
Friday, which was the day I saved his
life.
Ibid.
I took my man Friday with me.
Ibid.

SIR SAMUEL GARTH
[1661-1719]

A barren superfluity of words.
The Dispensary [1] *[1699].*
Canto II, Line 95
To die is landing on some silent shore
Where billows never break, nor tem-
pests roar;
Ere well we feel the friendly stroke, 'tis
o'er.
Ibid. Canto III, Line 225
Hard was their lodging, homely was
their food;
For all their luxury was doing good.[2]
Claremont. Line 148

[1] Thou hast no faults, or I no faults can
spy;
Thou art all beauty, or all blindness I.
CHRISTOPHER CODRINGTON [1668-
1710]: *Lines Addressed to Garth
on His Dispensary*
[2] And learn the luxury of doing good. —
GOLDSMITH: *The Traveller* [1764], *L. 22*

RICHARD BENTLEY
[1662-1742]

It is a maxim with me that no man
was ever written out of reputation but
by himself.[1]
MONK'S *Life of Bentley*
The fortuitous or casual concourse of
atoms.
*Works [1692]. Vol. III, Sermon
VII, Page 147*

MATHEW HENRY
[1662-1714]

He rolls it under his tongue as a
sweet morsel.
*Commentaries [1708-1710].
Psalm XXXVI*
Our creature comforts.
Ibid. Psalm XXXVII
They that die by famine die by
inches.
Ibid. Psalm LIX
To fish in troubled waters.
Ibid. Psalm LX
Here is bread, which strengthens
man's heart, and therefore called the
staff of life.[2]
Ibid. Psalm CIV
Hearkners, we say, seldom hear good
of themselves.
Ibid. Ecclesiastes, VII
It was a common saying among the
Puritans, "Brown bread and the Gospel
is good fare."
Ibid. Isaiah, XXX
None so blind as those that will not
see.[3]
Ibid. Jeremiah, XX

[1] See Montaigne, page 99a.
[2] For, behold, the Lord, the Lord of hosts,
doth take away from Jerusalem and from
Judah the stay and the staff, the whole stay
of bread, and the whole stay of water.—
Isaiah, III, 1
Bread is the staff of life. — SWIFT: *Tale of
a Tub* [1704]
Corn, which is the staff of life. — EDWARD
WINSLOW: *Good News from New England*
[1624]
[3] O foolish people, and without understanding; which have eyes and see not; which have
ears, and hear not. — *Jeremiah, V, 21*

Judas had given them the slip.
> *Commentaries. Matthew, XXII*

After a storm comes a calm.
> *Ibid. Acts, IX*

It is good news, worthy of all acceptation! and yet not too good to be true.
> *Ibid. Timothy, I*

It is not fit the public trusts should be lodged in the hands of any, till they are first proved and found fit for the business they are to be entrusted with.[1]
> *Ibid. Timothy, III*

THOMAS (TOM) BROWN
[1663–1704]

I do not love thee, Doctor Fell.
The reason why I cannot tell;
But this alone I know full well,
I do not love thee, Doctor Fell.[2]
> *Written while a student at Christ Church, Oxford*

To treat a poor wretch with a bottle of Burgundy, and fill his snuff-box, is like giving a pair of laced ruffles to a man that has never a shirt on his back.[3]
> *Laconics* [1707]

WILLIAM WALSH
[1663–1708]

Of all the plagues a lover bears,
Sure rivals are the worst.
> *Song. Stanza 1*

I can endure my own despair,
But not another's hope.
> *Ibid. Stanza 2*

[1] See Burke, page 361b, Thomas Jefferson, page 375a, Clay, page 433b, Calhoun, page 442a, and Cleveland, page 689a.
The phrase, "public office is a public trust," has of late become common property. — CHARLES SUMNER [1872]

[2] Non amo te, Sabidi, nec possum dicere quare;

Hoc tantum possum dicere, non amo te.
(I do not love thee, Sabidius, nor can I say why; but this much I can say, I do not love thee). — MARTIAL [A.D. 40–102]: *Epigram I, 33*

Je ne vous aime pas, Hylas;
Je n'en saurois dire la cause,
Je sais seulement une chose;
C'est que je ne vous aime pas.
> COMTE DE BUSSY-RABUTIN
> [1618–1693]

[3] See Goldsmith, page 358a.

MATTHEW PRIOR
[1664–1721]

All jargon of the schools.[1]
> *I Am That I Am, An Ode* [1688]

Our hopes, like towering falcons, aim
At objects in an airy height;
The little pleasure of the game
Is from afar to view the flight.
> *To the Hon. Charles Montague*

Odds life! must one swear to the truth of a song?
> *A Better Answer*

Be to her virtues very kind;
Be to her faults a little blind.
Let all her ways be unconfin'd;
And clap your padlock — on her mind!
> *An English Padlock* [1707]

That if weak women went astray,
Their stars were more in fault than they.
> *Hans Carvel*

The end must justify the means.
> *Ibid.*

And thought the nation ne'er would thrive
Till all the whores were burnt alive.
> *Paulo Purganti*

And often took leave, but was loth to depart.[2]
> *The Thief and the Cordelier*

Nobles and heralds, by your leave,
Here lies what once was Matthew Prior;
The son of Adam and of Eve:
Can Bourbon or Nassau claim higher?[3]
> *Epitaph. Extempore*

[1] Noisy jargon of the schools. — POMFRET [1667–1702]: *Reason*
The sounding jargon of the schools. — COWPER: *Truth* [1782], L. 367
[2] As men that be lothe to departe do often take their leff [JOHN CLERK TO WOLSEY]. — HENRY ELLIS [1777–1869]: *Letters, Third Series, Vol. I, P. 262*
"A loth to depart" was the common term for a song, or a tune played, on taking leave of friends.
[3] The following epitaph was written long before the time of Prior:
> Johnnie Carnegie lais heer.
> Descendit of Adam and Eve.
> Gif ony con gang hieher,
> Ise willing give him leve.

Lays the rough paths of peevish Nature
even,
And opens in each heart a little heaven.
Charity

His noble negligences teach
What others' toils despair to reach.
Alma. Canto II, Line 7

Till their own dreams at length deceive
'em,
And oft repeating, they believe 'em.
Ibid. Canto III, Line 13

Abra was ready ere I called her name;
And though I called another, Abra
came.
*Solomon on the Vanity of the
World [1718]. Book II, Line 364*

Who breathes must suffer, and who
thinks must mourn;
And he alone is bless'd who ne'er was
born.
Ibid. Book III, Line 240

To John I ow'd great obligation;
But John, unhappily, thought fit
To publish it to all the nation:
Sure John and I are more than quit.
Epigram [1718]

In public employments industrious and
grave,
And alone with his friends, Lord! how
merry was he!
For My Own Monument

SIR JOHN VANBRUGH
[1664–1726]

No man worth having is true to his
wife, or can be true to his wife, or ever
was, or ever will be so.
*The Relapse [1697].
Act III, Sc. 2*

Belinda. Ay, but you know we must
return good for evil.
Lady Brute. That may be a mistake
in the translation.
*The Provoked Wife [1698].
Act I, Sc. 1*

Much of a muchness.
*The Provoked Husband [1728].
Act I, Sc. 1 (Completed by
Cibber).*

JOHN POMFRET
[1667–1702]

Heaven is not always angry when he
strikes,
But most chastises those whom most
he likes.[1]
*Verses to His Friend under
Affliction*

JONATHAN SWIFT
[1667–1745]

Seamen have a custom, when they
meet a whale, to fling him out an empty
tub by way of amusement, to divert him
from laying violent hands upon the
ship.
Tale of a Tub [1704]. Preface

Books, the children of the brain.
Ibid. Sect. I

As boys do sparrows, with flinging
salt upon their tails.
Ibid. Sect. VII

When a man's fancy gets astride on
his reason; when imagination is at cuffs
with the senses; and common understanding, as well as common sense, is
kicked out of doors; the first proselyte
he makes is himself.
Ibid. Sect. IX

This is the sublime and refined point
of felicity, called the possession of being
well-deceived: the serene, peaceful
state of being a fool among knaves.
Ibid.

Satire is a sort of glass, wherein beholders do generally discover everybody's face but their own.
Battle of the Books [1704]. Preface

The two noblest things, which are
sweetness and light.[2]
Ibid.

Laws are like cobwebs, which may
catch small flies, but let wasps and
hornets break through.
*A Tritical Essay upon the Facul-
ties of the Mind [1707]*

[1] Whom the Lord loveth he chasteneth. —
Hebrews, XII, 6
[2] See Matthew Arnold, page 623a.

There is nothing in this world constant, but inconstancy.

A Tritical Essay upon the Faculties of the Mind

'Tis very warm weather when one's in bed.

Journal to Stella. November 8, 1710

With my own fair hands.

Ibid. January 4, 1711

We are so fond of one another, because our ailments are the same.

Ibid. February 1, 1711

I love good creditable acquaintance; I love to be the worst of the company.

Ibid. May 17, 1711

We were to do more business after dinner; but after dinner is after dinner — an old saying and a true, "much drinking, little thinking."

Ibid. February 26, 1712

We have just enough religion to make us hate, but not enough to make us love one another.

Thoughts on Various Subjects [1711]

Censure is the tax a man pays to the public for being eminent.

Ibid.

Every man desires to live long, but no man would be old.

Ibid.

'Tis an old maxim in the schools,
That flattery's the food of fools;
Yet now and then your men of wit
Will condescend to take a bit.

Cadenus and Vanessa [1] *[1713]*

If Heaven had looked upon riches to be a valuable thing, it would not have given them to such a scoundrel.

Letter to Miss Vanhomrigh [August 12, 1720]

He [the Emperor] is taller by almost the breadth of my nail, than any of his court, which alone is enough to strike an awe into the beholders.

Gulliver's Travels [1727]. Part I, Chap. II, Voyage to Lilliput

Big-endians and small-endians.[1]

Ibid. Chap. IV

It is computed, that eleven thousand persons have, at several times, suffered death, rather than submit to break their eggs at the smaller end.

Ibid.

I cannot but conclude the bulk of your natives to be the most pernicious race of little vermin that nature ever suffered to crawl upon the surface of the earth.

Ibid. Part II, Chap. VII, Voyage to Brobdingnag

And he gave it for his opinion, that whoever could make two ears of corn, or two blades of grass, to grow upon a spot of ground where only one grew before, would deserve better of mankind, and do more essential service to his country, than the whole race of politicians put together.[2]

Ibid.

He had been eight years upon a project for extracting sunbeams out of cucumbers, which were to be put in phials hermetically sealed, and let out to warm the air in raw inclement summers.

Ibid. Part III, Chap. V, Voyage to Laputa

A set of phrases learn't by rote;
A passion for a scarlet coat;
When at a play to laugh, or cry,
Yet cannot tell the reason why:
Never to hold her tongue a minute;
While all she prates has nothing in it.

The Furniture of a Woman's Mind [1727]

---

[1] When the poem of "Cadenus and Vanessa" was the general topic of conversation, some one said, "Surely that Vanessa must be an extraordinary woman that could inspire the Dean to write so finely upon her." Mrs. Johnson smiled, and answered that "she thought that point not quite so clear; for it was well known the Dean could write finely upon a broomstick." — SAMUEL JOHNSON: *Lives of the Poets [1779–1781], Life of Swift*

[1] As the political parties of Whig and Tory are pointed out by the high and low heels of the Lilliputians (Framecksan and Hamecksan), those of Papist and Protestant are designated under the Big-endians and Small-endians.

[2] He who makes two blades of grass grow in place of one renders a service to the State. — VOLTAIRE: *Letter to M. Moreau [1765]*

For conversation well endu'd;
She calls it witty to be rude;
And, placing raillery in railing,
Will tell aloud your greatest failing.
*The Furniture of a Woman's
Mind*

In party, furious to her pow'r;
A bitter Whig, or Tory sour;
Her arguments directly tend
Against the side she would defend.
Ibid.

Not die here in a rage, like a poisoned
rat in a hole.
*Letter to Bolingbroke
[March 21, 1729]*

Yet malice never was his aim;
He lash'd the vice but spar'd the name.
No individual could resent,
Where thousands equally were meant.
His satire points at no defect
But what all mortals may correct;
For he abhorr'd that senseless tribe
Who call it humor when they gibe.
*Verses on the Death of Dean
Swift [1731]. Line 459*

Hobbes clearly proves that every crea-
ture
Lives in a state of war by nature.[1]
On Poetry, A Rhapsody [1733].

So, naturalists observe, a flea
Hath smaller fleas that on him prey;
And these have smaller still to bite
'em;
And so proceed *ad infinitum.*
Thus every poet, in his kind,
Is bit by him that comes behind.
Ibid.

Conversation is but carving!
Give no more to every guest
Than he's able to digest.
Give him always of the prime,
And but little at a time.
Carve to all but just enough,
Let them neither starve nor stuff,
And that you may have your due,
Let your neighbour carve for you.
Conversation

Under this window in stormy weather
I marry this man and woman together;

[1] See Hobbes, pages 228b–229a.

Let none but Him who rules the thun-
der
Put this man and woman asunder.
*Marriage Service from His
Chamber Window*

The sight of you is good for sore
eyes.[1]
*Polite Conversation [1738?].
Dialogue I*

'Tis as cheap sitting as standing.
Ibid.

I hate nobody: I am in charity with
the world.
Ibid.

I won't quarrel with my bread and
butter.
Ibid.

She's no chicken; she's on the wrong
side of thirty, if she be a day.
Ibid.

She wears her clothes as if they were
thrown on with a pitchfork.
Ibid.

He was a bold man that first eat an
oyster.
Ibid. Dialogue II

That is as well said as if I had said it
myself.
Ibid.

Fingers were made before forks, and
hands before knives.
Ibid.

She has more goodness in her little
finger than he has in his whole body.
Ibid.

Lord! I wonder what fool it was that
first invented kissing.
Ibid.

The best doctors in the world are
Doctor Diet, Doctor Quiet, and Doc-
tor Merryman.[2]
Ibid.

[1] What a sight for sore eyes that would be!
—WILLIAM HAZLITT [1778–1830]: *Of Per-
sons One Would Have Seen*
[2] Use three physicians
First, Dr. Quiet;
Next, Dr. Merryman,
And Dr. Dyet.
Regimen Sanitatis Salernitanum
[1607]

I'll give you leave to call me anything, if you don't call me "spade."
Polite Conversation. Dialogue II
May you live all the days of your life.
Ibid.

I always like to begin a journey on Sundays, because I shall have the prayers of the Church to preserve all that travel by land or by water.
Ibid.

I know Sir John will go, though he was sure it would rain cats and dogs.
Ibid.

I thought you and he were hand-in-glove.
Ibid.

She watches him as a cat would watch a mouse.
Ibid. Dialogue III
There was all the world and his wife.
Ibid.

Hail, fellow, well met,
All dirty and wet:
Find out if you can,
Who's master, who's man.
My Lady's Lamentation [*1765*].
Line 171
I shall be like that tree, — I shall die at the top.
Sir Walter Scott's *Life of Swift* [*1814*]

Ubi saeva indignatio ulterius cor lacerare nequit.[1]
Epitaph: Inscribed on Swift's grave, St. Patrick's, Dublin

SUSANNAH CENTLIVRE
[1667?–1723]

The real Simon Pure.
A Bold Stroke for a Wife [*1718*].
Act V, Sc. 1

ALAIN RENÉ LE SAGE
[1668–1747]

It may be said that his wit shines at the expense of his memory.[2]
Gil Blas [*1715–1735*].
Book III, Chap. 11

A flatterer can risk everything with great personages.
Gil Blas. Book IV, Chap. 7
Pride and conceit were the original sin of man.
Ibid. Book VII, Chap. 3
I wish you all sorts of prosperity with a little more taste.
Ibid. Chap. 4
The pleasure of talking is the inextinguishable passion of a woman, coeval with the act of breathing.
Ibid. Chap. 7
Glory is the true and honorable recompense of gallant actions.
Ibid. Chap. 12
Facts are stubborn things.[1]
Ibid. Book X, Chap. 1
Plain as a pike-staff.
Ibid. Book XII, Chap. 8

WILLIAM CONGREVE
[1670–1729]

Eternity was in that moment.
The Old Bachelor [*1693*].
Act IV, Sc. 7
It is the business of a comic poet to paint the vices and follies of human kind.
The Double Dealer [*1694*].
Epistle Dedicatory
Retired to their tea and scandal, according to their ancient custom.
Ibid. Act I, Sc. 1
Tho' marriage makes man and wife one flesh, it leaves 'em still two fools.
Ibid. Act II, Sc. 3
No mask like open truth to cover lies, As to go naked is the best disguise.
Ibid. Act V, Sc. 4
Thou liar of the first magnitude.
Love for Love [*1695*].
Act II, Sc. 2
I warrant you, if he danced till doomsday, he thought I was to pay the piper.
Ibid.

---

[1] Where savage indignation can no longer tear the heart.
[2] See Sheridan, page 382b.

[1] Facts are contrary 'z mules. — James Russell Lowell: *Biglow Papers, Series II* [1862], *No. 4*

Women are like tricks by sleight of
hand,
Which, to admire, we should not understand.
>*Love for Love. Act IV, Sc. 3*

Music hath charms to soothe the savage
breast,[1]
To soften rocks, or bend a knotted oak.
>*The Mourning Bride* [*1697*].
>*Act I, Sc. 1*

By magic numbers and persuasive
sound.
>*Ibid.*

Heaven has no rage like love to hatred
turned,
Nor hell a fury like a woman scorned.[2]
>*Ibid. Act III, Sc. 8*

Love's but a frailty of the mind,
When 'tis not with ambition joined:
A sickly flame, which, if not fed, ex-
pires,
And feeding, wastes in self-consuming
fires.
>*The Way of the World* [*1700*].
>*Act III, Sc. 12*

Thou art a retailer of phrases, and
dost deal in remnants of remnants.
>*Ibid. Act IV, Sc. 9*

If there's delight in love, 'tis when I
see
That heart which others bleed for, bleed
for me.
>*Ibid.*

Defer not till tomorrow to be wise,
Tomorrow's sun to thee may never
rise.[3]
>*Letter to Cobham*

RICHARD LEVERIDGE
[1670–1758]

When mighty roast beef was the Englishman's food,

---

[1] Music hath charms, we all may find,
Ingratiate deeply with the mind.
>Matthew Green [1696–1737]:
>*The Spleen, L. 141*

[2] We shall find no fiend in hell can match
the fury of a disappointed woman. — Colley
Cibber: *Love's Last Shift* [1696], *Act IV*

[3] Be wise today; 'tis madness to defer. —
Edward Young: *Night Thoughts* [1742–
1745], *Night I, L. 390*

It ennobled our hearts, and enriched
our blood,
Our soldiers were brave and our courtiers were good.
Oh! the roast beef of old England! [1]
>*The Roast Beef of Old England.*
>*Stanza 1*

COLLEY CIBBER
[1671–1757]

As good be out of the world as out of
the fashion.
>*Love's Last Shift* [*1696*]. *Act II*

Words are but empty thanks.
>*Woman's Wit* [*1697*]. *Act V*

Perish that thought!
>*Richard III* (*altered*) [*1700*].
>*Act V, Sc. 5*

This business will never hold water.
>*She Wou'd and She Wou'd Not*
>[*1703*]. *Act IV*

Old houses mended,
Cost little less than new before they're
ended.
>*The Double Gallant* [*1707*].
>*Prologue*

Oh, how many torments lie in the
small circle of a wedding-ring!
>*Ibid. Act I, Sc. 2*

Stolen sweets are best.
>*The Rival Fools* [*1709*]. *Act I*

JOSEPH ADDISON
[1672–1719]

For wheresoe'er I turn my ravish'd
eyes,
Gay gilded scenes and shining prospects
rise,
Poetic fields encompass me around,
And still I seem to tread on classic
ground.
>*A Letter from Italy* [*1703*]

And, pleased the Almighty's orders to
perform,

---

[1] Oh, the roast beef of England,
And old England's roast beef!
>Fielding [1707–1754]: *The Grub
Street Opera, Act III, Sc. 2*

Rides in the whirlwind and directs the
    storm.[1]
          The Campaign [*1704*]. *Line 91*
Reading is to the mind what exercise
is to the body.
          The Tatler [*1709–1711*].
                              No. 147
The spacious firmament on high,
With all the blue ethereal sky,
And spangled heavens, a shining frame,
Their great Original proclaim.
          Ode [*in The Spectator, No. 465,*
                    August 23, 1712]
Soon as the evening shades prevail,
The moon takes up the wondrous tale,
And nightly to the listening earth
Repeats the story of her birth;
While all the stars that round her burn,
And all the planets in their turn,
Confirm the tidings as they roll,
And spread the truth from pole to pole.
                              Ibid.
For ever singing as they shine,
"The hand that made us is divine."
                              Ibid.
Should the whole frame of Nature
    round him break,
In ruin and confusion hurled,
He, unconcerned, would hear the
    mighty crack,
And stand secure amidst a falling
    world.
          Horace. Ode III, Book III
Thy steady temper, Portius,
Can look on guilt, rebellion, fraud, and
    Caesar,
In the calm lights of mild philosophy.
          Cato [2] [*1713*]. *Act I, Sc. 1*
'Tis not in mortals to command success,
But we'll do more, Sempronius, — we'll
    deserve it.
                          Ibid. Sc. 2
Blesses his stars and thinks it luxury.
                          Ibid. Sc. 4

'Tis pride, rank pride, and haughtiness
    of soul;
I think the Romans call it stoicism.
                    Cato. Act I, Sc. 4
Were you with these, my prince, you'd
    soon forget
The pale, unripened beauties of the
    north.
                              Ibid.
Beauty soon grows familiar to the lover,
Fades in his eye, and palls upon the
    sense.
The virtuous Marcia towers above her
    sex.
                              Ibid.
    My voice is still for war.
Gods! can a Roman senate long debate
Which of the two to choose, slavery or
    death?
                    Ibid. Act II, Sc. 1
The woman that deliberates is lost.
                    Ibid. Act IV, Sc. 1
Curse on his virtues! they've undone
    his country.
                          Ibid. Sc. 4
    What pity is it
That we can die but once to save our
    country! [1]
                              Ibid.
When vice prevails, and impious men
    bear sway,
The post of honour is a private station.[2]
                              Ibid.
It must be so, — Plato, thou reasonest
    well!
Else whence this pleasing hope, this
    fond desire,
This longing after immortality?
Or whence this secret dread, and in-
    ward horror
Of falling into naught? Why shrinks
    the soul

[1] This line is frequently ascribed to Pope,
as it is repeated in his *Dunciad, Book III*
[1728], *L. 264.*
[2] The *Massachusetts Spy* used the following
lines from *Cato* as its motto from November
22, 1771 to April 6, 1775:

Do thou Great Liberty inspire our Souls —
And make our Lives in thy Possession happy —
Or, our Deaths glorious in thy just Defence.

[1] I only regret that I have but one life to
lose for my country. — NATHAN HALE [before
his execution, September 22, 1776]
[2] Give me, kind Heaven, a private station,
A mind serene for contemplation!
Title and profit I resign;
The post of honour shall be mine.
          GAY: *Fables, Part II* [1738], *The*
          Vulture, The Sparrow, and Other
          Birds

Back on herself, and startles at destruction?
'Tis the divinity that stirs within us;
'Tis Heaven itself that points out an hereafter,
And intimates eternity to man.
Eternity! thou pleasing, dreadful thought!
Cato. Act V, Sc. 1

Sweet are the slumbers of the virtuous man.
Ibid. Sc. 4

From hence, let fierce contending nations know
What dire effects from civil discord flow.
Ibid.

Round-heads and wooden-shoes are standing jokes.
The Drummer. Prologue, Line 8

If I can any way contribute to the diversion or improvement of the country in which I live, I shall leave it, when I am summoned out of it, with the secret satisfaction of thinking that I have not lived in vain.[1]
The Spectator. No. 1, March 1, 1711

I shall endeavour to enliven morality with wit, and to temper wit with morality.
Ibid. No. 10, March 11, 1711

True happiness is of a retired nature, and an enemy to pomp and noise; it arises, in the first place, from the enjoyment of one's self; and, in the next, from the friendship and conversation of a few select companions.
Ibid. No. 15, March 17, 1711

In all thy humours, whether grave or mellow,
Thou'rt such a touchy, testy, pleasant fellow;
Hast so much wit, and mirth, and spleen about thee,

There is no living with thee, nor without thee.[1]
The Spectator. No. 68, May 18, 1711

There is not a more unhappy being than a superannuated idol.
Ibid. No. 73, May 24, 1711

A man that has a taste of music, painting, or architecture, is like one that has another sense, when compared with such as have no relish of those arts.
Ibid. No. 93, June 16, 1711

There is not so variable thing in nature as a lady's head-dress.
Ibid. No. 98, June 21, 1711

There is no defence against reproach but obscurity.
Ibid. No. 101, June 26, 1711

Much may be said on both sides.
Ibid. No. 122, July 20, 1711

Authors have established it as a kind of rule, that a man ought to be dull sometimes; as the most severe reader makes allowances for many rests and nodding-places in a voluminous writer.
Ibid. No. 124, July 23, 1711

Books are the legacies that a great genius leaves to mankind, which are delivered down from generation to generation, as presents to the posterity of those who are yet unborn.
Ibid. No. 166, September 10, 1711

Good-nature is more agreeable in conversation than wit, and gives a certain air to the countenance which is more amiable than beauty.
Ibid. No. 169, September 13, 1711

Were I to prescribe a rule for drinking, it should be formed upon a saying quoted by Sir William Temple: the first glass for myself, the second for my friends, the third for good humour, and the fourth for mine enemies.
Ibid. No. 195, October 13, 1711

A true critic ought to dwell rather upon excellencies than imperfections, to discover the concealed beauties of a writer, and communicate to the world

---

[1] I shall pass through this world but once. If, therefore, there be any kindness I can show, or any good thing I can do, let me do it now; let me not defer it or neglect it, for I shall not pass this way again.— *Attributed to* ETIENNE DE GRELLET [1773–1855]

[1] A translation of MARTIAL [A. D. 40–102], XII, 47, who imitated OVID [43 B. C.–A. D. 18], *Amores, III, 11, 39.*

such things as are worth their observation.

> *The Spectator. No. 291,*
> *February 2, 1712*

Death only closes a man's reputation, and determines it as good or bad.

> *Ibid. No. 349, April 10, 1712*

Mirth is like a flash of lightning, that breaks through a gloom of clouds, and glitters for a moment; cheerfulness keeps up a kind of daylight in the mind, and fills it with a steady and perpetual serenity.

> *Ibid. No. 381, May 17, 1712*

Sir Roger made several reflections on the greatness of the British Nation; as, that one Englishman could beat three Frenchmen; that we could never be in danger of Popery so long as we took care of our fleet; that the Thames was the noblest river in Europe . . . with many other honest prejudices which naturally cleave to the heart of a true Englishman.

> *Ibid. No. 383, May 20, 1712*

The fraternity of the henpecked.[1]

> *Ibid. No. 482, September 12, 1712*

A man should always consider how much he has more than he wants, and how much more unhappy he might be than he really is.

> *Ibid. No. 574, July 30, 1714*

We are always doing something for Posterity, but I would fain see Posterity do something for us.

> *Ibid. No. 587, August 20, 1714*

See in what peace a Christian can die.

> *Dying words [1719], in* YOUNG,
> *Conjectures on Original Composition [1759]*

SIR RICHARD STEELE
[1672–1729]

I am come to a tavern alone to eat a steak, after which I shall return to the office.

> *Letters to His Wife.*
> *October 28, 1707*

I have partly succeeded in my business today, and enclose two guineas.

Dear Prue, I can't come home to dinner.

> *Letters to His Wife.*
> *January 3, 1708*

I was going home two hours ago, but was met by Mr. Griffith, who has kept me ever since. I will come within a pint of wine.

> *Ibid. Eleven at Night,*
> *January 5, 1708*

A little in drink, but at all times your faithful husband.

> *Ibid. September 27, 1708*

If you do not hear of me before three tomorrow afternoon, believe I am too fuddled to take care to observe your orders.

> *Ibid. October 25, 1708*

The finest woman in nature should not detain me an hour from you; but you must sometimes suffer the rivalship of the wisest men.

> *Ibid. September 17, 1712*

Though her mien carries much more invitation than command, to behold her is an immediate check to loose behaviour; to love her was a liberal education.[1]

> *Tatler [1709]. No. 49*

When you fall into a man's conversation, the first thing you should consider is, whether he has a greater inclination to hear you, or that you should hear him.

> *The Spectator. No. 49,*
> *April 26, 1711*

Of all the affections which attend human life, the love of glory is the most ardent.

> *Ibid. No. 139, August 9, 1711*

An old gentleman t'other day in discourse with a friend of his, (reflecting upon some adventures they had in youth together) cry'd out, Oh Jack, those were happy days!

> *Ibid. No. 153, August 25, 1711*

Age in a virtuous person, of either sex, carries in it an authority which makes it preferable to all the pleasures of youth.

> *Ibid. No. 153, August 25, 1711*

[1] See Byron, page 457a.

[1] Lady Elizabeth Hastings [1682–1739].

Among all the diseases of the mind there is not one more epidemical or more pernicious than the love of flattery.
The Spectator. No. 238, December 3, 1711
Will Honeycomb calls these over-offended ladies the outrageously virtuous.
Ibid. No. 266, January 4, 1712
A favour well bestowed is almost as great an honour to him who confers it as to him who receives it.
Ibid. No. 497, September 30, 1712

BENJAMIN SCHMOLKE
[1672–1737]

If wind and sky were always fair
The sailor would not watch the star,
And David's Psalms had ne'er been sung
If grief his heart had never wrung.
Bearing the Burden. Stanza 4

EDMOND HOYLE [1]
[1672–1769]

When in doubt, win the trick.
Twenty-four Rules for Learners. Rule 12

NICHOLAS ROWE
[1673–1718]

As if Misfortune made the throne her seat,
And none could be unhappy but the great.[2]
The Fair Penitent [1703]. Prologue
At length the morn and cold indifference came.
Ibid. Act I, Sc. 1
Is this that haughty gallant, gay Lothario?
Ibid. Act V, Sc. 1

[1] Hoyle published [1742] a *Short Treatise on Whist,* which in subsequent editions added rules for playing piquet, backgammon, chess, and other games. His *Laws* [1760] ruled whist playing until 1864, hence the saying, "according to Hoyle."
[2] None think the great unhappy, but the great. — EDWARD YOUNG: *The Love of Fame* [1725–1728], *Satire 1, L. 238*

ISAAC WATTS
[1674–1748]

Were I so tall to reach the pole,
Or grasp the ocean with my span,
I must be measured by my soul:
The mind's the standard of the man.
Horae Lyricae [1706]. Book II, False Greatness
Let dogs delight to bark and bite,
For God hath made them so;
Let bears and lions growl and fight,
For 'tis their nature too.
Divine Songs [1715]. XVI
But, children, you should never let
Such angry passions rise;
Your little hands were never made
To tear each other's eyes.
Ibid.
Birds in their little nests agree;
And 'tis a shameful sight
When children of one family
Fall out, and chide, and fight.
Ibid. XVII
How doth the little busy bee
Improve each shining hour,[1]
And gather honey all the day
From every opening flower!
Ibid. XX
For Satan finds some mischief still
For idle hands to do.
Ibid.
Hush, my dear, lie still and slumber!
Holy angels guard thy bed!
Heavenly blessings without number
Gently falling on thy head.
A Cradle Hymn
'Tis the voice of the sluggard; I heard him complain,
"You have wak'd me too soon, I must slumber again." [2]
The Sluggard. Stanza 1
Let me be dress'd fine as I will,
Flies, worms, and flowers, exceed me still.
Against Pride in Clothes. Stanza 4
Lord, in the morning thou shalt hear
My voice ascending high.
Psalm V [1719]

[1] See Lewis Carroll, page 656a.
[2] See Lewis Carroll, page 657b.

O God, our help in ages past,
Our hope for years to come,
Our shelter from the stormy blast,
And our eternal home.
    Psalm XC [*1719*]. *Stanza 1*
A thousand ages in Thy sight
Are like an evening gone;
Short as the watch that ends the night
Before the rising sun.
    Ibid. Stanza 4
Time, like an ever-rolling stream,
Bears all its sons away;
They fly forgotten, as a dream
Dies at the opening day.
    Ibid. Stanza 5
Joy to the world! the Lord is come;
Let earth receive her King.
Let ev'ry heart prepare Him room,
And heav'n and nature sing.
    Psalm XCVIII [*1719*]. *Stanza 1*
And while the lamp holds out to burn,
The vilest sinner may return.
    Hymns and Spiritual Songs.
    Book I, Hymn 88
Strange that a harp of thousand strings
Should keep in tune so long!
    Ibid. Book II, Hymn 19
Hark! from the tombs a doleful sound.
    Ibid. Hymn 63
The tall, the wise, the reverend head
Must lie as low as ours.
    Ibid.
When I can read my title clear
    To mansions in the skies,
I'll bid farewell to every fear,
    And wipe my weeping eyes.
    Ibid. Hymn 65
There is a land of pure delight,
    Where saints immortal reign;
Infinite day excludes the night,
    And pleasures banish pain.
    Ibid. Hymn 66

WILLIAM SOMERVILLE [1]
[1675–1742]

How humble, and how complaisant
Is the proud man reduced to want!

[1] Of whom DR. JOHNSON, in his *Lives of
the Poets,* made the famous remark, "He
writes very well for a gentleman."

With what a silly, hanging face
He bears his unforeseen disgrace!
    Ready Money [*1727*]
Let all the learned say what they can,
'Tis ready money makes the man.
    Ibid.
There is something in a face,
An air, and a peculiar grace,
Which boldest painters cannot trace.
    The Lucky Hit [*1727*]
So in each action 'tis success
That gives it all its comeliness.
    Ibid.
For what is virtue, courage, wit,
In all men, but a lucky hit?
    Ibid.
So, safe on shore the pensioned sailor
    lies,
And all the malice of the storm defies;
With ease of body blest and peace of
    mind
Pities the restless crew he left behind;
Whilst, in his cell, he meditates alone
On his great voyage to the world un-
    known.
    The Author, an Old Man, to
    His Arm-chair [*1750*]

SIR ROBERT WALPOLE
[1676–1745]

The balance of power.
    Speech [*1741*]
Flowery oratory he despised. He ascribed to the interested views of themselves or their relatives the declara-
tions of pretended patriots, of whom he
said, "All those men have their price."
    WILLIAM COXE: *Memoirs of Wal-*
    pole [*1798*], *Vol. IV, P. 369*
Anything but history, for history
must be false.
    Walpoliana. No. 141

HENRY ST. JOHN,
VISCOUNT BOLINGBROKE
[1678–1751]

Truth lies within a little and certain
compass, but error is immense.
    Reflections Upon Exile [*1716*]
I have read somewhere or other, —
in Dionysius of Halicarnassus, I think,

— that history is philosophy teaching by examples.[1]

> *On the Study and Use of History*
> *[1752]. Letter 2*

Nations, like men, have their infancy.
> *Ibid. Letter 4*

They [Thucydides and Xenophon] maintained the dignity of history.
> *Ibid. Letter 5*

It is the modest, not the presumptuous, inquirer who makes a real and safe progress in the discovery of divine truths. One follows Nature and Nature's God; that is, he follows God in his works and in his word.[2]
> *Letter to Mr. Pope*

GEORGE FARQUHAR
[1678–1707]

Like hungry guests, a sitting audience looks.
> *The Inconstant [1702].*
> *Prologue*

The prologue is the grace,
Each act, a course, each scene, a different dish.
> *Ibid.*

Cos. Pray now, what may be that same bed of honour?
Kite. Oh, a mighty large bed! bigger by half than the great bed at Ware: ten thousand people may lie in it together, and never feel one another.
> *The Recruiting Officer [1706].*
> *Act I, Sc. 1*

I believe they talked of me, for they laughed consumedly.
> *The Beaux' Stratagem [1707].*
> *Act III, Sc. 1*

[1] The contact with manners then is education; and this Thucydides appears to assert when he says history is philosophy learned from examples. — DIONYSIUS OF HALICARNASSUS [54?–7? B.C.]: *Ars Rhet. XI, 2*
[2] Slave to no sect, who takes no private road,
But looks through Nature up to Nature's God.
POPE: *Essay on Man [1732–1734], Epistle IV, L. 331*

'Twas for the good of my country that I should be abroad.[1]
> *The Beaux' Stratagem.*
> *Act III, Sc. 2*

THOMAS PARNELL
[1679–1718]

My days have been so wondrous free
  The little birds that fly
With careless ease from tree to tree,
  Were but as bless'd as I.
> *Song [2] [1714]. Stanza 1*

Still an angel appear to each lover beside,
But still be a woman to you.
> *When Thy Beauty Appears*
> *[1722]. Stanza 3*

We call it only pretty Fanny's way.
> *An Elegy to an Old Beauty*
> *[1722]. Stanza 4*

Let those love now who never loved before;
Let those who always loved, now love the more.
> *Translation of the Pervigilium*
> *Veneris [3]*

EDWARD YOUNG
[1683–1765]

The love of praise, howe'er conceal'd by art,

[1] Leaving his country for his country's sake. — CHARLES FITZ-GEFFREY: *The Life and Death of Sir Francis Drake* [1596], *St. 213*
True patriots all; for, be it understood,
We left our country for our country's good.
GEORGE BARRINGTON: *Prologue Written for the Opening of the Playhouse at New South Wales, January 16, 1796*
(According to the *Oxford Companion to English Literature*, "Barrington" was the adopted name of a notorious pickpocket who was transported to the penal settlement at Botany Bay.)
[2] Set to music by Francis Hopkinson; one of the earliest American songs.
[3] Written *circa* A.D. 350:
Cras amet qui nunquam amavit, quique amavit cras amet.
(Let him love tomorrow who never loved before; and he who has loved, let him love tomorrow.)

Reigns more or less, and glows in ev'ry heart.
Love of Fame [*1725–1728*].
Satire I, Line 51

Some for renown, on scraps of learning dote,
And think they grow immortal as they quote.
Ibid. Line 89

They that on glorious ancestors enlarge,
Produce their debt instead of their discharge.
Ibid. Line 147

Be wise with speed;
A fool at forty is a fool indeed.
Ibid. Satire II, Line 282

For her own breakfast she'll project a scheme,
Nor take her tea without a stratagem.
Ibid. Satire VI, Line 190

Think naught a trifle, though it small appear;
Small sands the mountain, moments make the year.
Ibid. Line 208

One to destroy is murder by the law,
And gibbets keep the lifted hand in awe;
To murder thousands takes a specious name,
War's glorious art, and gives immortal fame.[1]
Ibid. Satire VII, Line 55

The man that makes a character makes foes.
To Mr. Pope. Epistle I, Line 28

Their feet through faithless leather met the dirt,
And oftener chang'd their principles than shirt.
Ibid. Line 277

In records that defy the tooth of time.
The Statesman's Creed

Tired nature's sweet restorer, balmy sleep!
Night Thoughts [*1742–1745*].
Night I, Line 1

Night, sable goddess! from her ebon throne,

[1] See Porteus, page 366a–366b.

In rayless majesty, now stretches forth
Her leaden sceptre o'er a slumbering world.
Night Thoughts. Night I, Line 18

Creation sleeps! 'Tis as the general pulse
Of life stood still, and Nature made a pause, —
An awful pause! prophetic of her end.
Ibid. Line 23

Procrastination is the thief of time.
Ibid. Line 393

At thirty, man suspects himself a fool;
Knows it at forty, and reforms his plan;
At fifty chides his infamous delay,
Pushes his prudent purpose to resolve;
In all the magnanimity of thought
Resolves, and re-resolves; then dies the same.
Ibid. Line 417

All men think all men mortal but themselves.
Ibid. Line 424

Thy purpose firm is equal to the deed:
Who does the best his circumstance allows
Does well, acts nobly; angels could no more.
Ibid. Night II, Line 90

"I've lost a day!" — the prince who nobly cried,
Had been an emperor without his crown.[1]
Ibid. Line 99

Ah, how unjust to Nature and himself
Is thoughtless, thankless, inconsistent man!
Ibid. Line 112

Whose yesterdays look backwards with a smile.
Ibid. Line 334

[1] Once at supper, reflecting that he [Emperor Titus] had done nothing for any that day, he broke out into that memorable and justly admired saying, "My friends, I have lost a day!" — SUETONIUS [A.D. 70?–140?]: *Lives of the Twelve Caesars*
Think that day lost whose descending sun
Views from thy hand no noble action done.
J. BOBART: *Virtus sui Gloria* [*1697*]

Thoughts shut up want air,
And spoil, like bales unopen'd to the sun.

Night Thoughts. Night II,
Line 466

How blessings brighten as they take their flight!

Ibid. Line 602

Man wants but little, nor that little long.[1]

Ibid. Night IV, Line 118

A Christian is the highest style of man.

Ibid. Line 788

By night an atheist half believes a God.[2]

Ibid. Night V, Line 177

We see time's furrows on another's brow,
And death intrench'd, preparing his assault;
How few themselves in that just mirror see!

Ibid. Line 627

Like our shadows,
Our wishes lengthen as our sun declines.

Ibid. Line 661

Death loves a shining mark, a signal blow.[3]

Ibid. Line 1011

The man that blushes is not quite a brute.

Ibid. Night VII, Line 496

Too low they build, who build beneath the stars.[4]

Ibid. Night VIII, Line 215

Final Ruin fiercely drives
Her ploughshare o'er creation.[5]

Ibid. Night IX, Line 167

An undevout astronomer is mad.

Ibid. Line 771

SIR WILLIAM PULTENEY [6]
[1684–1764]

For twelve honest men have decided the cause,

Who are judges alike of the facts and the laws.

The Honest Jury

GEORGE BERKELEY, BISHOP OF CLOYNE
[1685–1753]

[Tar water] is of a nature so mild and benign and proportioned to the human constitution, as to warm without heating, to cheer but not inebriate.[1]

Siris [1744]. Paragraph 217

He who says there is no such thing as an honest man, you may be sure is himself a knave.

Maxims Concerning Patriotism

Ferments of the worst kind succeed to perfect inaction.

Ibid.

Westward the course of empire takes its way; [2]
The four first acts already past,
A fifth shall close the drama with the day:
Time's noblest offspring is the last.

On the Prospect of Planting Arts and Learning in America [1752]. Stanza 6

Our youth we can have but today,
We may always find time to grow old.

Can Love Be Controlled by Advice? [3]

JANE BRERETON
[1685–1740]

The picture placed the busts between
Adds to the thought much strength;
Wisdom and Wit are little seen,
But Folly's at full length.

On Beau Nash's Picture at Full Length between the Busts of Sir Isaac Newton and Mr. Pope [4]

being Stanhope and Walpole. Walpole said that he feared Pulteney's tongue more than another man's sword.

[1] See Cowper, page 364b.
[2] Westward the star of empire takes its way.
— JOHN QUINCY ADAMS: *Oration at Plymouth* [1802]
[3] In AIKEN: *Vocal Poetry* [1810]
[4] In ALEXANDER DYCE [1798–1869]: *Specimens of British Poetesses* (This epigram is generally ascribed to Chesterfield.)

[1] See Goldsmith, page 354b.
[2] See W. T. Cummings, page 991b.
[3] See Quarles, page 231b.
[4] Inscription on a wall of the Library of Congress, Washington, D.C.
[5] See Burns, page 391a.
[6] One of "the three grand allies," the others

AARON HILL
[1685–1750]

First, then, a woman will or won't, de-
  pend on 't;
If she will do 't she will; and there's
  an end on 't.
But if she won't, since safe and sound
  your trust is,
Fear is affront, and jealousy injustice.
Zara. Epilogue

Tender-handed stroke a nettle,
  And it stings you for your pains;
Grasp it like a man of mettle,
  And it soft as silk remains.[1]

'Tis the same with common natures:
  Use 'em kindly, they rebel;
But be rough as nutmeg-graters,
  And the rogues obey you well.
*Verses Written on a Window
in Scotland*

SAMUEL MADDEN
[1686–1765]

In an orchard there should be enough
to eat, enough to lay up, enough to be
stolen, and enough to rot upon the
ground.
Quoted by SAMUEL JOHNSON
[*1783*] (BOSWELL's *Life, Vol.
II, Page 457, Everyman edition*)

ALLAN RAMSAY
[1686–1758]

Farewell to Lochaber, farewell to my
  Jean,
Where heartsome wi' thee I hae mony
  days been;
For Lochaber no more, Lochaber no
  more,
We'll maybe return to Lochaber no
  more.
Lochaber No More [*1724*].
Stanza 1

My Peggy is a young thing,
Just entered in her teens.
Peggy [*1734?*]

[1] The world's a nettle; disturb it, it stings:
Grasp it firmly, it stings not.
  E. R. BULWER-LYTTON: *Lucile* [1860],
  Part I, Canto 3, II

THOMAS TICKELL
[1686–1740]

Just men, by whom impartial laws were
  given;
And saints who taught and led the way
  to heaven.
On the Death of Mr. Addison
[*1719*]. *Line 41*

The sweetest garland to the sweetest
maid.
*To a Lady with a Present of
Flowers* [*1729*]

HENRY CAREY
[1687?–1743]

Namby Pamby's little rhymes,
Little jingle, little chimes.
Namby Pamby [1]

Aldiborontiphoscophornio!
Where left you Chrononhotonthologos?
Chrononhotonthologos. Act I, Sc. 1

His cogitative faculties immersed
In cogibundity of cogitation.
Ibid.

Of all the girls that are so smart,
  There's none like pretty Sally.
She is the darling of my heart,
  And she lives in our alley.
Sally in Our Alley [*1729*]. *Stanza 1*

Of all the days that's in the week
  I dearly love but one day,
And that's the day that comes betwixt
  A Saturday and Monday.
Ibid. Stanza 4

God save our gracious king!
Long live our noble king!
  God save the king!
God Save the King [*1740?*]

JOHN GAY
[1688–1732]

'Twas when the sea was roaring
With hollow blasts of wind,

[1] Ambrose Phillips . . . who had the honour of bringing into fashion a species of composition which has been called, after his name,
Namby Pamby. — MACAULAY: *Review of
Aikin's Life of Addison* [1843]

A damsel lay deploring,
All on a rock reclin'd.
>   *The What d'ye Call It* [*1715*].
>   *Act II, Sc. 8*

All in the Downs the fleet was moor'd.
>   *Sweet William's Farewell to*
>   *Black-eyed Susan* [*1720*]

Adieu, she cried, and waved her lily
hand.
>   *Ibid.*

My lodging is on the cold ground,
And hard, very hard, is my fare,
But that which grieves me more
    Is the coldness of my dear.
>   *My Lodging is on the Cold*
>   *Ground* [*1720*]. *Stanza 1*

Remote from cities liv'd a swain,
Unvex'd with all the cares of gain;
His head was silver'd o'er with age,
And long experience made him sage.
>   *Fables, Part I* [*1727*]. *The*
>   *Shepherd and the Philosopher*

Whence is thy learning? Hath thy toil
O'er books consum'd the midnight oil?
>   *Ibid.*

Where yet was ever found a mother
Who'd give her booby for another?
>   *Ibid. The Mother, the Nurse,*
>   *and the Fairy*

When we risk no contradiction,
It prompts the tongue to deal in fiction.
>   *Ibid. The Elephant and the*
>   *Bookseller*

Lest men suspect your tale untrue,
Keep probability in view.
>   *Ibid. The Painter who Pleased*
>   *Nobody and Everybody*

Is there no hope? the sick man said;
The silent doctor shook his head.
>   *Ibid. The Sick Man and the Angel*

While there is life there's hope, he
cried.[1]
>   *Ibid.*

Those who in quarrels interpose
Must often wipe a bloody nose.
>   *Ibid. The Mastiffs*

I hate the man who builds his name
On ruins of another's fame.
>   *Ibid. The Poet and the Rose*

[1] See Cicero, page 34a.

The child whom many fathers share
Hath seldom known a father's care.
>   *Fables, Part I. The Hare*
>   *and Many Friends*

And when a lady's in the case,
You know all other things give place.
>   *Ibid.*

From wine what sudden friendship
    springs!
>   *Ibid. Part II* [*1738*]. *The*
>   *Squire and His Cur*

O Polly, you might have toy'd and
    kiss'd,
By keeping men off, you keep them on.
>   *The Beggar's Opera* [*1728*].
>   *Act I, Sc. 4, Air IX*

If with me you'd fondly stray.
Over the hills and far away.[1]
>   *Ibid. Sc. 13, Air XVI*

Fill ev'ry glass, for wine inspires us,
    And fires us
With courage, love and joy.
Women and wine should life employ.
Is there ought else on earth desirous?
>   *Ibid. Act II, Sc. 1, Air XIX*

If the heart of a man is depress'd with
    cares,
The mist is dispell'd when a woman ap-
    pears.
>   *Ibid. Sc. 3, Air XXI*

Youth's the season made for joys,
Love is then our duty.
>   *Ibid. Sc. 4, Air XXII*

Man may escape from rope and gun;
Nay, some have outliv'd the doctor's
    pill:
Who takes a woman must be undone,
That basilisk is sure to kill.
The fly that sips treacle is lost in the
    sweets,
So he that tastes woman, woman,
    woman,
He that tastes woman, ruin meets.
>   *Ibid. Sc. 8, Air XXVI*

How happy could I be with either,
Were t'other dear charmer away!
>   *Ibid. Sc. 13, Air XXXV*

The charge is prepar'd; the lawyers are
    met;

[1] See D'Urfey, page 290b.

The judges all ranged, — a terrible show!

> *The Beggar's Opera. Act III, Sc. 11, Air LVII*

Life is a jest, and all things show it;
I thought so once, but now I know it.[1]

> *My Own Epitaph*

ALEXANDER POPE [2]
[1688–1744]

Happy the man whose wish and care
A few paternal acres bound,
Content to breathe his native air
  In his own ground.

> *Ode on Solitude* [Circa *1700*].
> *Stanza 1*

Thus let me live, unseen, unknown,
Thus unlamented let me die;
Steal from the world, and not a stone
  Tell where I lie.

> *Ibid. Stanza 5*

Not chaos-like together crush'd and
  bruis'd,
But, as the world, harmoniously con-
  fus'd:
Where order in variety we see,
And where, though all things differ, all
  agree.

> *Windsor Forest* [*1704*]. *Line 13*

Oft, as in airy rings they skim the
  heath,
The clam'rous lapwings feel the leaden
  death;
Oft, as the mounting larks their notes
  prepare,
They fall, and leave their little lives
  in air.

> *Ibid. Line 131*

To dear-bought wisdom give the credit
due,

And think for once a woman tells you
  true.

> *Paraphrases from Chaucer. The Wife of Bath, Her Prologue* [Circa *1709*], *Line 3*

Curtain lectures made a restless night.

> *Ibid. Line 165*

Let all mankind this certain maxim
  hold;
Marry who will, our sex is to be sold.
With empty hands no tassels you can
  lure,
But fulsome love for gain we can en-
  dure;
For gold we love the impotent and old,
And heave, and pant, and kiss, and
  cling, for gold.
Yet with embraces curses oft I mixt,
Then kiss'd again, and chid, and rail'd
  betwixt.

> *Ibid. Line 170*

How quaint an appetite in women
  reigns!
Free gifts we scorn, and love what
  costs us pains.
Let men avoid us, and on them we leap;
A glutted market makes provision
  cheap.

> *Ibid. Line 259*

The wasting moth ne'er spoil'd my best
  array;
The cause was this, I wore it every day.

> *Ibid. Line 288*

  Whoe'er it be
That tells my faults, I hate him mortally!

> *Ibid. Line 351*

Love seldom haunts the breast where
  learning lies,
And Venus sets ere Mercury can rise.

> *Ibid. Line 369*

How vain that second life in others'
  breath,[1]
Th' estate which wits inherit after
  death!
Ease, health, and life for this they must
  resign,
(Unsure the tenure, but how vast the
  fine!)

---

[1] Life is an empty dream. — BROWNING: *Paracelsus, II* [1835]
  Life seems a jest of Fate's contriving. — J. R. LOWELL: *Harvard Commemoration Ode* [1865], *IV*
  [2] A thousand years may elapse before there shall appear another man with a power of versification equal to that of Pope. — DR. JOHNSON [1781]: BOSWELL'S *Life of Dr. Johnson*

[1] See *Essay on Man*, page 317b.

The great man's curse, without the gains, endure,
Be envied, wretched; and be flatter'd, poor;
All luckless wits their enemies profest,
And all successful, jealous friends at best.
Nor Fame I slight, nor for her favours call;
She comes unlook'd for, if she comes at all.
> *The Temple of Fame* [*1711*].
> *Line 505*

Unblemish'd let me live or die unknown;
Oh, grant an honest fame, or grant me none!
> *Ibid. Line 523*

How vast a memory has Love!
> *Sappho to Phaon* [*1712*]. *Line 52*

'Tis with our judgments as our watches, none
Go just alike, yet each believes his own.[1]
> *Essay on Criticism* [*1711*].
> *Part I, Line 9*

Let such teach others who themselves excel,
And censure freely who have written well.
> *Ibid. Line 15*

Some are bewilder'd in the maze of schools,
And some made coxcombs Nature meant but fools.
> *Ibid. Line 26*

One science only will one genius fit;
So vast is art, so narrow human wit.
> *Ibid. Line 60*

First follow Nature, and your judgment frame
By her just standard, which is still the same;
Unerring Nature, still divinely bright,
One clear, unchanged, and universal light,
Life, force, and beauty must to all impart,
At once the source, and end, and test of Art.
> *Ibid. Line 68*

[1] See Suckling, page 261a.

Music resembles poetry; in each
Are nameless graces which no methods teach,
And which a master-hand alone can reach.
> *Essay on Criticism. Part I,*
> *Line 143*

Those oft are stratagems which errors seem,
Nor is it Homer nods, but we that dream.[1]
> *Ibid. Line 177*

O may some spark of your celestial fire
The last, the meanest of your sons inspire,
(That on weak wings, from far, pursues your flights,
Glows while he reads, but trembles as he writes)
To teach vain Wits a science little known,
T'admire superior sense, and doubt their own.
> *Ibid. Line 195*

Of all the causes which conspire to blind
Man's erring judgment, and misguide the mind,
What the weak head with strongest bias rules,
Is pride, the never-failing vice of fools.
> *Ibid. Part II, Line 1*

A little learning is a dangerous thing;
Drink deep, or taste not the Pierian spring:
There shallow draughts intoxicate the brain,
And drinking largely sobers us again.
> *Ibid. Line 15*

Hills peep o'er hills, and Alps on Alps arise!
> *Ibid. Line 32*

'T is not a lip or eye we beauty call,
But the joint force and full result of all.
> *Ibid. Line 45*

Whoever thinks a faultless piece to see,
Thinks what ne'er was, nor is, nor e'er shall be.[2]
> *Ibid. Line 53*

True wit is Nature to advantage dress'd,

[1] See Horace, page 42a.
[2] See Suckling, page 261a.

What oft was thought, but ne'er so well
    express'd.
Essay on Criticism. Part II,
Line 97

Words are like leaves; and where they
    most abound,
Much fruit of sense beneath is rarely
    found.
Ibid. Line 109

Such labour'd nothings, in so strange
    a style,
Amaze th' unlearn'd, and make the
    learned smile.
Ibid. Line 126

In words, as fashions, the same rule will
    hold,
Alike fantastic if too new or old:
Be not the first by whom the new are
    tried,
Nor yet the last to lay the old aside.
Ibid. Line 133

    Some to church repair,
Not for the doctrine, but the music
    there.
These equal syllables alone require,
Though oft the ear the open vowels
    tire;
While expletives their feeble aid do
    join,
And ten low words oft creep in one dull
    line.
Ibid. Line 142

A needless Alexandrine ends the song,
That, like a wounded snake, drags its
    slow length along.
Ibid. Line 156

True ease in writing comes from art,
    not chance,
As those move easiest who have learn'd
    to dance.[1]
'Tis not enough no harshness gives of-
    fence;
The sound must seem an echo to the
    sense.
Ibid. Line 162

At ev'ry trifle scorn to take offence.
Ibid. Line 186

Yet let not each gay turn thy rapture
    move;

[1] Also in *Epistle II, Book II of Horace*
[1737], *L. 178.*

For fools admire, but men of sense ap-
    prove.
Essay on Criticism. Part II,
Line 190

Some judge of authors' names, not
    works, and then
Nor praise nor blame the writings, but
    the men.
Ibid. Line 212

What woeful stuff this madrigal would
    be
In some starv'd hackney sonneteer or
    me!
But let a lord once own the happy lines,
How the wit brightens! how the style
    refines!
Ibid. Line 218

Some praise at morning what they
    blame at night,
But always think the last opinion right.
Ibid. Line 230

Envy will merit as its shade pursue,
But like a shadow proves the substance
    true.
Ibid. Line 266

To err is human, to forgive divine.[1]
Ibid. Line 325

All seems infected that th' infected spy,
As all looks yellow to the jaundic'd eye.
Ibid. Line 358

Be silent always when you doubt your
    sense.
Ibid. Part III, Line 6

Men must be taught as if you taught
    them not,
And things unknown proposed as things
    forgot.
Ibid. Line 15

The bookful blockhead ignorantly read,
With loads of learned lumber in his
    head,
With his own tongue still edifies his
    ears,
And always list'ning to himself appears.

[1] See Sophocles, page 14b.
Then gently scan your brother man,
  Still gentler sister woman;
Though they may gang a kennin' wrang,
  To step aside is human.
ROBERT BURNS: *Address to the*
Unco Guid [1787]

All books he reads, and all he reads assails.
> *Essay on Criticism. Part III, Line 53*

For fools rush in where angels fear to tread.
> *Ibid. Line 66*

But where's the man who counsel can bestow,
Still pleas'd to teach, and yet not proud to know? [1]
> *Ibid. Line 72*

Careless of censure, nor too fond of fame,
Still pleas'd to praise, yet not afraid to blame,
Averse alike to flatter or offend,
Not free from faults, nor yet too vain to mend.
> *Ibid. Line 182*

Vital spark of heav'nly flame,
Quit, oh quit, this mortal frame!
Trembling, hoping, ling'ring, flying,
Oh, the pain, the bliss of dying! [2]
Cease, fond Nature, cease thy strife,
And let me languish into life!
> *The Dying Christian to His Soul [1712]. Stanza 1*

What dire offence from amorous causes springs!
What mighty contests rise from trivial things!
> *The Rape of the Lock [1712]. Canto I, Line 1*

On her white breast a sparkling cross she wore,
Which Jews might kiss, and infidels adore.
> *Ibid. Canto II, Line 7*

If to her share some female errors fall,
Look on her face, and you'll forget 'em all.
> *Ibid. Line 17*

Fair tresses man's imperial race ensnare,
And beauty draws us with a single hair.[3]
> *Ibid. Line 27*

[1] See Chaucer, page 79b.
[2] See Hadrian, page 65b.
[3] See Robert Burton, page 223b.

Here thou, great Anna! whom three realms obey,
Dost sometimes counsel take — and sometimes tea.
> *The Rape of the Lock. Canto III, Line 7*

At every word a reputation dies.
> *Ibid. Line 16*

The hungry judges soon the sentence sign,
And wretches hang that jurymen may dine.
> *Ibid. Line 21*

Coffee, which makes the politician wise.
> *Ibid. Line 117*

But when to mischief mortals bend their will,
How soon they find fit instruments of ill!
> *Ibid. Line 125*

The meeting points the sacred hair dissever
From the fair head, forever, and forever!
Then flash'd the living lightning from her eyes,
And screams of horror rend th' affrighted skies.
> *Ibid. Line 153*

Steel could the labour of the gods destroy,
And strike to dust th' imperial towers of Troy;
Steel could the works of mortal pride confound
And hew triumphal arches to the ground.
> *Ibid. Line 173*

Charms strike the sight, but merit wins the soul.
> *Ibid. Canto V, Line 34*

To wake the soul by tender strokes of art,
To raise the genius, and to mend the heart;
To make mankind, in conscious virtue bold,
Live o'er each scene, and be what they behold:

For this the Tragic Muse first trod the stage.
> *Prologue to Mr. Addison's Cato [1713]. Line 1*

A brave man struggling in the storms of fate,
And greatly falling with a falling state.
> *Ibid. Line 21*

Ignobly vain, and impotently great.
> *Ibid. Line 29*

Dear, damn'd, distracting town, farewell!
Thy fools no more I'll tease:
This year in peace, ye critics, dwell,
Ye harlots, sleep at ease!
> *A Farewell to London [1715].*
> *Stanza 1*

Luxurious lobster-nights, farewell,
For sober, studious days!
> *Ibid. Stanza 12*

Oh name for ever sad! for ever dear!
Still breath'd in sighs, still usher'd with a tear.
> *Eloisa to Abelard [1717]. Line 31*

Now warm in love, now with'ring in my bloom,
Lost in a convent's solitary gloom!
> *Ibid. Line 37*

Speed the soft intercourse from soul to soul,
And waft a sigh from Indus to the Pole.
> *Ibid. Line 57*

Curse on all laws but those which love has made!
Love, free as air at sight of human ties,
Spreads his light wings, and in a moment flies.
> *Ibid. Line 74*

No, make me mistress to the man I love;
If there be yet another name more free,
More fond than mistress, make me that to thee!
> *Ibid. Line 88*

And if I lose thy love, I lose my all.
> *Ibid. Line 118*

How happy is the blameless vestal's lot!
The world forgetting, by the world forgot.
> *Ibid. Line 207*

One thought of thee puts all the pomp to flight,
Priests, tapers, temples, swim before my sight.[1]
> *Eloisa to Abelard. Line 273*

He best can paint them who shall feel them most.
> *Ibid. Line 366*

What beck'ning ghost along the moonlight shade
Invites my steps, and points to yonder glade?
> *Elegy to the Memory of an Unfortunate Lady [1717].*
> *Line 1*

Is it, in Heav'n, a crime to love too well?
To bear too tender or too firm a heart,
To act a lover's or a Roman's part?
Is there no bright reversion in the sky
For those who greatly think, or bravely die?
> *Ibid. Line 6*

Ambition first sprung from your blest abodes,
The glorious fault of Angels and of Gods.
> *Ibid. Line 13*

By foreign hands thy dying eyes were clos'd,
By foreign hands thy decent limbs compos'd,
By foreign hands thy humble grave adorn'd,
By strangers honour'd, and by strangers mourn'd!
> *Ibid. Line 51*

How lov'd, how honour'd once, avails thee not,
To whom related, or by whom begot;
A heap of dust alone remains of thee:
'Tis all thou art, and all the proud shall be!
> *Ibid. Line 71*

It is certain no literal translation can be just to an excellent original in a superior language: but it is a great mistake to imagine (as many have done)

---

[1] Priests, altars, victims, swam before my sight. — EDMUND SMITH: *Phaedra and Hippolytus, adapted from Racine* [1707], *Act I, Sc. 1*

that a rash paraphrase can make amends for this general defect: which is no less in danger to lose the spirit of an ancient, by deviating into the modern manners of expression. If there be sometimes a darkness, there is often a light in antiquity, which nothing better preserves than a version almost literal.

Preface to the Iliad [*1717*]

Simplicity is the mean between ostentation and rusticity.

Ibid.

The fate of all extremes is such:
Men may be read, as well as books, too much.

Moral Essays [*1720–1735*].
Epistle I [*1733*], *Line 9*

To observations which ourselves we make,
We grow more partial for th' observer's sake.

Ibid. Line 11

Like following life through creatures you dissect,
You lose it in the moment you detect.

Ibid. Line 29

Not always actions show the man; we find
Who does a kindness is not therefore kind.

Ibid. Line 109

Who combats bravely is not therefore brave,
He dreads a death-bed like the meanest slave.
Who reasons wisely is not therefore wise;
His pride in reasoning, not in acting, lies.

Ibid. Line 115

'Tis education forms the common mind:
Just as the twig is bent the tree's inclined.

Ibid. Line 149

Manners with fortunes, humours turn with climes,
Tenets with books, and principles with times.

Ibid. Line 172

Give this cheek a little red.

Ibid. Line 251

And you, brave Cobham! to the latest breath
Shall feel your ruling passion strong in death.

Moral Essays. Epistle I, Line 262

Most women have no characters at all.

Ibid. Epistle II [*1735*], *Line 2*

Whether the charmer sinner it or saint it,
If folly grow romantic, I must paint it.

Ibid. Line 15

Choose a firm cloud before it fall, and in it
Catch, ere she change, the Cynthia of this minute.

Ibid. Line 19

Fine by defect, and delicately weak.

Ibid. Line 43

Chaste to her husband, frank to all beside,
A teeming mistress, but a barren bride.

Ibid. Line 71

Wise wretch! with pleasures too refin'd to please;
With too much spirit to be e'er at ease;
With too much quickness ever to be taught;
With too much thinking to have common thought.

Ibid. Line 95

"With ev'ry pleasing, ev'ry prudent part,
Say, what can Chloe want?" — She wants a heart,
She speaks, behaves, and acts just as she ought,
But never, never reach'd one gen'rous thought.

Ibid. Line 159

In men, we various ruling passions find;
In women, two almost divide the kind;
Those, only fixed, they first or last obey,
The love of pleasure, and the love of sway.

Ibid. Line 207

Men, some to business, some to pleasure take;
But every woman is at heart a rake.

Ibid. Line 215

She who ne'er answers till a husband cools,

Or if she rules him, never shows she
   rules;
Charms by accepting, by submitting,
   sways,
Yet has her humour most, when she
   obeys.
Moral Essays. Epistle II, Line 261

And mistress of herself though china
   fall.
               Ibid. Line 268

Woman's at best a contradiction still.
               Ibid. Line 270

Who shall decide when doctors disagree? [1]
   Ibid. Epistle III [1732], Line 1

Blest paper-credit! last and best supply!
That lends corruption lighter wings to
   fly!
               Ibid. Line 39

But thousands die without or this or
   that,
Die, and endow a college or a cat.
               Ibid. Line 95

The ruling passion, be it what it will,
The ruling passion conquers reason
   still.
               Ibid. Line 153

Who builds a church to God, and not
   to fame,
Will never mark the marble with his
   name.
               Ibid. Line 285

   Satan now is wiser than of yore,
And tempts by making rich, not making poor.
               Ibid. Line 351

Good sense, which only is the gift of
   Heaven,
And though no science, fairly worth the
   seven.
   Ibid. Epistle IV [1731], Line 43

Statesman, yet friend to truth; of soul
   sincere,
In action faithful, and in honour clear;
Who broke no promise, serv'd no private end,

[1] When doctors differ who decides amid
the milliard-headed throng? — SIR RICHARD
FRANCIS BURTON [1821–1890]: *The Kasidah
of Haji Abdu El-Yazdi, VIII, 29*

Who gain'd no title, and who lost no
   friend;
Ennobled by himself, by all approv'd
And prais'd, unenvied by the Muse he
   lov'd.
     *Moral Essays. Epistle V [1720],
                       Line 67*

   Blessed is he who expects nothing,
for he shall never be disappointed.[1]
   Letter to Gay [October 6, 1727]

You beat your pate, and fancy wit will
   come:
Knock as you please, there's nobody
   at home.[2]
   Epigram: An Empty House [1727]

Ye Gods! annihilate but space and
   time,
And make two lovers happy.
   *Martinus Scriblerus on the Art of
   Sinking in Poetry [1728]. Chap. XI*

Of manners gentle, of affections mild;
In wit a man, simplicity a child.
          Epitaph on Gay [1732]

Awake, my St. John! leave all meaner
   things
To low ambition and the pride of kings.
Let us, since life can little more supply
Than just to look about us, and to die,
Expatiate free o'er all this scene of
   man;
A mighty maze! but not without a
   plan.
      *Essay on Man [1733–1734].
               Epistle I, Line 1*

Eye Nature's walks, shoot folly as it
   flies,
And catch the manners living as they
   rise;
Laugh where we must, be candid where
   we can,
But vindicate the ways of God to man.[3]
               Ibid. Line 13

[1] Pope calls this the eighth beatitude (Ros-
coe's edition of Pope, *Vol. X, P. 184*).
   Blessed are those that nought expect,
   For they shall not be disappointed.
      JOHN WOLCOT ("Peter Pindar")
      [1738–1819]: *Ode to Pitt*
[2] His wit invites you by his looks to come,
But when you knock, it never is at home.
   COWPER: *Conversation* [1782],
                      L. 303
[3] See Milton, page 252a.

Say first, of God above or man below,
What can we reason but from what we
    know?
    Essay on Man. Epistle I, Line 17
Pleased to the last, he crops the flowery
    food,
And licks the hand just raised to shed
    his blood.
    Ibid. Line 83
Who sees with equal eye, as God of all,
A hero perish or a sparrow fall,
Atoms or systems into ruin hurl'd,
And now a bubble burst, and now a
    world.
    Ibid. Line 87
Hope springs eternal in the human
    breast:
Man never is, but always to be, blest.
    Ibid. Line 95
Lo, the poor Indian! whose untutor'd
    mind
Sees God in clouds, or hears him in the
    wind;
His soul proud Science never taught to
    stray
Far as the solar walk or milky way;
Yet simple nature to his hope has giv'n,
Behind the cloud-topped hill, an
    humbler heav'n.
    Ibid. Line 99
But thinks, admitted to that equal sky,
His faithful dog shall bear him com-
    pany.
    Ibid. Line 111
In pride, in reas'ning pride, our error
    lies;
All quit their sphere, and rush into the
    skies!
Pride still is aiming at the bless'd
    abodes,
Men would be Angels, Angels would be
    Gods.
Aspiring to be Gods if Angels fell,
Aspiring to be Angels men rebel.
    Ibid. Line 123
Seas roll to waft me, suns to light me
    rise;
My footstool earth, my canopy the
    skies.[1]
    Ibid. Line 139

[1] See Montaigne, page 99a.

All are but parts of one stupendous
    whole,
Whose body Nature is, and God the
    soul.
    Essay on Man. Epistle I, Line 267
As full, as perfect, in vile man that
    mourns
As the rapt seraph that adores and
    burns.
To Him no high, no low, no great, no
    small; [1]
He fills, he bounds, connects, and equals
    all!
    Ibid. Line 277
All nature is but art, unknown to thee;
All chance, direction, which thou canst
    not see;
All discord, harmony not understood;
All partial evil, universal good;
And spite of pride, in erring reason's
    spite,
One truth is clear, Whatever is, is
    right.[2]
    Ibid. Line 289
Know then thyself, presume not God
    to scan;
The proper study of mankind is man.[3]
Placed on this isthmus of a middle state,
A being darkly wise and rudely great:
With too much knowledge for the Scep-
    tic side,
With too much weakness for the Stoic's
    pride,
He hangs between, in doubt to act or
    rest;
In doubt to deem himself a God or
    Beast;
In doubt his mind or body to prefer;
Born but to die, and reas'ning but to
    err;

[1] There is no great and no small
   To the Soul that maketh all.
      EMERSON [1803–1882]: *Epigraph
               to History*
[2] See Dryden, page 276a.
[3] See Plutarch, page 60a.
   La vraie science et la vraie étude de
l'homme, c'est l'homme (The true science and
the true study of man is man). — PIERRE
CHARRON: *Traité de la Sagesse* [1601], *Book
I, Preface*
   Trees and fields tell me nothing: men are
my teachers. — PLATO [427–347 B.C.]: *Phaedrus*

Alike in ignorance, his reason such,
Whether he thinks too little or too
　　much;
Chaos of thought and passion, all con-
　　fused;
Still by himself abused or disabused;
Created half to rise, and half to fall;
Great lord of all things, yet a prey to
　　all;
Sole judge of truth, in endless error
　　hurled;
The glory, jest, and riddle of the world.
　　　　Essay on Man. Epistle II, Line 1
Fix'd like a plant on his peculiar spot,
To draw nutrition, propagate, and rot.
　　　　Ibid. Line 63
On life's vast ocean diversely we sail,
Reason the card, but passion is the gale.
　　　　Ibid. Line 107
And hence one master-passion in the
　　breast,
Like Aaron's serpent, swallows up the
　　rest.[1]
　　　　Ibid. Line 131
The young disease, that must subdue
　　at length,
Grows with his growth, and strength-
　　ens with his strength.
　　　　Ibid. Line 135
Vice is a monster of so frightful mien,
As to be hated needs but to be seen;
Yet seen too oft, familiar with her face,
We first endure, then pity, then em-
　　brace.
　　　　Ibid. Line 217
The learn'd is happy Nature to explore,
The fool is happy that he knows no
　　more;
The rich is happy in the plenty giv'n,
The poor contents him with the care of
　　Heav'n.
　　　　Ibid. Line 263
Behold the child, by Nature's kindly
　　law,
Pleased with a rattle, tickled with a
　　straw:
Some livelier plaything gives his youth
　　delight,

A little louder, but as empty quite:
Scarfs, garters, gold, amuse his riper
　　stage,
And beads and prayer-books are the
　　toys of age.
Pleased with this bauble still, as that
　　before,
Till tired he sleeps, and life's poor play
　　is o'er.
　　　　Essay on Man. Epistle II, Line 274
Learn of the little nautilus to sail,
Spread the thin oar, and catch the
　　driving gale.
　　　　Ibid. Epistle III, Line 177
For forms of government let fools con-
　　test;
Whate'er is best administer'd is best:
For modes of faith let graceless zealots
　　fight;
His can't be wrong whose life is in the
　　right.[1]
In faith and hope the world will dis-
　　agree,
But all mankind's concern is charity.
　　　　Ibid. Line 303
O happiness! our being's end and aim!
Good, pleasure, ease, content! whate'er
　　thy name:
That something still which prompts the
　　eternal sigh,
For which we bear to live, or dare to
　　die.
　　　　Ibid. Epistle IV, Line 1
Reason's whole pleasure, all the joys of
　　sense,
Lie in three words — health, peace, and
　　competence.
　　　　Ibid. Line 79
Worth makes the man, and want of it
　　the fellow;
The rest is all but leather or prunella.
　　　　Ibid. Line 203
What's Fame? a fancy'd life in others'
　　breath,
A thing beyond us, ev'n before our
　　death.
　　　　Ibid. Line 237
A wit's a feather, and a chief a rod;

---

[2] For they cast down every man his rod,
and they became serpents: but Aaron's rod
swallowed up their rods. — *Exodus, VII, 12*

[1] See Cowley, page 268a.

An honest man's the noblest work of God.[1]
Essay on Man. Epistle IV, Line 247
One self-approving hour whole years outweighs
Of stupid starers and of loud huzzas:
And more true joy Marcellus exil'd feels
Than Caesar with a senate at his heels.
Ibid. Line 255
If parts allure thee, think how Bacon shin'd,
The wisest, brightest, meanest of mankind!
Or ravish'd with the whistling of a name,[2]
See Cromwell, damn'd to everlasting fame!
Ibid. Line 281
Slave to no sect, who takes no private road,
But looks through Nature up to Nature's God.[3]
Ibid. Line 331
Form'd by thy converse, happily to steer
From grave to gay, from lively to severe.[4]
Ibid. Line 379
Say, shall my little bark attendant sail,
Pursue the triumph and partake the gale?
Ibid. Line 385
Thou wert my guide, philosopher, and friend.[5]
Ibid. Line 390
"Shut, shut the door, good John!" fatigued, I said;
"Tie up the knocker! say I'm sick, I'm dead."
Epistle to Dr. Arbuthnot [1735].
Prologue to the Satires, Line 1
Fire in each eye, and papers in each hand,
They rave, recite, and madden round the land.
Ibid. Line 5

Is there a parson much bemused in beer,
A maudlin poetess, a rhyming peer,
A clerk foredoom'd his father's soul to cross,
Who pens a stanza when he should engross?
Epistle to Dr. Arbuthnot. Prologue to the Satires, Line 15
Fired that the house[1] reject him, " 'Sdeath, I'll print it,
And shame the fools."
Ibid. Line 61
No creature smarts so little as a fool.
Ibid. Line 84
Destroy his fib, or sophistry — in vain!
The creature's at his dirty work again.
Ibid. Line 91
As yet a child, nor yet a fool to fame,
I lisp'd in numbers, for the numbers came.
Ibid. Line 127
This long disease, my life.
Ibid. Line 132
Pretty! in amber to observe the forms
Of hairs, or straws, or dirt, or grubs, or worms.[2]
The things, we know, are neither rich nor rare,
But wonder how the devil they got there.
Ibid. Line 169
Means not, but blunders round about a meaning;
And he whose fustian's so sublimely bad,
It is not poetry, but prose run mad.
Ibid. Line 186
Were there one whose fires
True Genius kindles, and fair Fame inspires,
Bless'd with each talent and each art to please,
And born to write, converse, and live with ease;
Should such a man, too fond to rule alone,
Bear, like the Turk, no brother near the throne;[3]

---

[1] See Burns, page 390b.
[2] See Cowley, page 267b.
[3] See Bolingbroke, page 304a.
[4] See Boileau, page 286b.
[5] Is this my guide, philosopher, and friend? — *Epistle I, Book I of Horace* [1733-1738], L. 177

[1] The theater.
[2] See Martial, page 52a.
[3] See Denham, page 266b.

View him with scornful, yet with jealous eyes,
And hate for arts that caus'd himself to rise;
Damn with faint praise, assent with civil leer,
And without sneering teach the rest to sneer;[1]
Willing to wound, and yet afraid to strike,
Just hint a fault, and hesitate dislike;
Alike reserv'd to blame or to commend,
A tim'rous foe, and a suspicious friend;
Dreading ev'n fools; by flatterers besieged,
And so obliging that he ne'er obliged;
Like Cato, give his little Senate laws,[2]
And sit attentive to his own applause.
Epistle to Dr. Arbuthnot. Prologue to the Satires, Line 193

Oh let me live my own, and die so too
(To live and die is all I have to do)!
Maintain a poet's dignity and ease,
And see what friends, and read what books I please.
Ibid. Line 261

Curst be the verse, how well soe'er it flow,
That tends to make one worthy man my foe.
Ibid. Line 283

Let Sporus tremble — What? that thing of silk,
Sporus, that mere white curd of ass's milk?
Satire or sense, alas! can Sporus feel?
Who breaks a butterfly upon a wheel?
Ibid. Line 305

Yet let me flap this bug with gilded wings,
This painted child of dirt, that stinks and stings;

[1] When needs he must, yet faintly then he praises;
Somewhat the deed, much more the means he raises:
So marreth what he makes, and praising most, dispraises.
PHINEAS FLETCHER: *The Purple Island* [1633], *Canto VII*
[2] While Cato gives his little senate laws. —
Prologue to Mr. Addison's Cato [1713], *L. 23*

Whose buzz the witty and the fair annoys,
Yet wit ne'er tastes, and beauty ne'er enjoys.
Epistle to Dr. Arbuthnot. Prologue to the Satires, Line 309

Eternal smiles his emptiness betray,
As shallow streams run dimpling all the way.
Ibid. Line 315

Wit that can creep, and pride that licks the dust.
Ibid. Line 333

Unlearn'd, he knew no schoolman's subtle art,
No language but the language of the heart.
Ibid. Line 398

Me, let the tender office long engage
To rock the cradle of reposing age;
With lenient arts extend a mother's breath,
Make languor smile, and smooth the bed of death;
Explore the thought, explain the asking eye,
And keep awhile one parent from the sky.
Ibid. Line 408

I cannot sleep a wink.
Satires, Epistles, and Odes of Horace [1733–1738]. *Satire I, Book II, Line 12*

Satire's my weapon, but I'm too discreet
To run amuck, and tilt at all I meet.
Ibid. Line 69

But touch me, and no minister so sore.
Ibid. Line 76

There St. John mingles with my friendly bowl,
The feast of reason and the flow of soul.
Ibid. Line 127

For I, who hold sage Homer's rule the best,
Welcome the coming, speed the going guest.[1]
Ibid. Satire II, Book II, Line 159

[1] This line is repeated in the translation of the *Odyssey, Book XV, L. 83,* with "parting" instead of "going." See Homer, page 6b.

I've often wish'd that I had clear,
For life, six hundred pounds a year;
A handsome house to lodge a friend,
A river at my garden's end,
A terrace walk, and half a rood
Of land set out to plant a wood.
> *Satires, Epistles, and Odes of Horace. Satire VI, Book II, Line 1*

Give me again my hollow tree,
A crust of bread, and liberty.
> *Ibid. Line 220*

A patriot is a fool in ev'ry age.
> *Epilogue to the Satires. Dialogue I, Line 41*

Laugh then at any but at fools or foes;
These you but anger, and you mend not those.
Laugh at your friends, and if your friends are sore,
So much the better, you may laugh the more.
> *Ibid. Line 53*

Let humble Allen, with an awkward shame,
Do good by stealth, and blush to find it fame.
Virtue may choose the high or low degree.
> *Ibid. Line 135*

Never gallop Pegasus to death.
> *Epistle I. Book I, Line 14*

When the brisk minor pants for twenty-one.
> *Ibid. Line 38*

Not to go back is somewhat to advance,
And men must walk, at least, before they dance.
> *Ibid. Line 53*

He's armed without that's innocent within.
> *Ibid. Line 94*

Get place and wealth, if possible with grace;
If not, by any means get wealth and place.
> *Ibid. Line 103*

Above all Greek, above all Roman fame.
> *Ibid. Book II, Line 26*

The mob of gentlemen who wrote with ease.
> *Epistle I. Book II, Line 108*

One simile that solitary shines
In the dry desert of a thousand lines.
> *Ibid. Line 111*

Then marble, soften'd into life, grew warm,
And yielding metal flow'd to human form.[1]
> *Ibid. Line 147*

Who says in verse what others say in prose.
> *Ibid. Line 202*

What will a child learn sooner than a song?
> *Ibid. Line 205*

Ev'n copious Dryden wanted, or forgot,
The last and greatest art — the art to blot.
> *Ibid. Line 280*

There still remains, to mortify a wit,
The many-headed monster of the pit.[2]
> *Ibid. Line 304*

We poets are (upon a poet's word)
Of all mankind the creatures most absurd:
The season when to come, and when to go,
To sing, or cease to sing, we never know.
> *Ibid. Line 358*

Call, if you will, bad rhyming a disease,
It gives men happiness, or leaves them ease.
> *Epistle II. Book II, Line 182*

The worst of madmen is a saint run mad.
> *Epistle VI. Book I, Line 27*

Vain was the chief's, the sage's pride!
They had no poet, and they died.
> *Odes. Book IV, Ode 9, Stanza 4*

Father of all! in every age,
In every clime adored,

---

[1] The canvas glow'd beyond ev'n Nature warm;
The pregnant quarry teem'd with human form.
> GOLDSMITH: *The Traveller* [1764], L. *137*

[2] See Sir Philip Sidney, page 115b.

By saint, by savage, and by sage,
  Jehovah, Jove, or Lord!
    The Universal Prayer [*1738*].
      Stanza 1

And binding Nature fast in fate,
Left free the human will.
    Ibid. Stanza 3

And deal damnation round the land.
    Ibid. Stanza 7

Teach me to feel another's woe,
  To hide the fault I see;
That mercy I to others show,
  That mercy show to me.[1]
    Ibid. Stanza 10

I am his Highness'[2] dog at Kew;
Pray tell me, sir, whose dog are you?
    On the Collar of a Dog

Nature and Nature's laws lay hid in
  night:
God said, Let Newton be! and all was
  light.
    *Epitaph Intended for Sir
      Isaac Newton*

Who dare to love their country, and
  be poor.
    *On His Grotto at Twickenham
      [1740]*

Party is the madness of many for the
gain of a few.
    *Thoughts on Various Subjects
      [1741]*

I never knew any man in my life
who could not bear another's misfortunes perfectly like a Christian.[3]
    Ibid.

A man should never be ashamed to
own he has been in the wrong, which is
but saying, in other words, that he is
wiser today than he was yesterday.
    Ibid.

It is with narrow-souled people as
with narrow-necked bottles; the less
they have in them the more noise they
make in pouring out.
    Ibid.

When men grow virtuous in their old

age, they only make a sacrifice to God
of the devil's leavings.[1]
    Thoughts on Various Subjects

True disputants are like true sports-
men, their whole delight is in the pursuit.
    Ibid.

There, take (says Justice), take ye each
  a shell:
We thrive at Westminster on fools like
  you;
'Twas a fat oyster — live in peace, —
  adieu.[2]
    Verbatim from Boileau

Whether thou choose Cervantes' serious air,
Or laugh and shake in Rabelais' easy
  chair.
    The Dunciad [*1743*].
      Book I, Line 21

Poetic Justice, with her lifted scale,
Where, in nice balance, truth with gold
  she weighs,
And solid pudding against empty
  praise.
    Ibid. Line 52

While pensive poets painful vigils keep,
Sleepless themselves to give their readers sleep.
    Ibid. Line 93

Next o'er his books his eyes begin to
  roll,
In pleasing memory of all he stole.
    Ibid. Line 127

Or where the pictures for the page
  atone,
And Quarles is sav'd by beauties not his
  own.
    Ibid. Line 139

How index-learning turns no student
  pale,
Yet holds the eel of science by the tail.
    Ibid. Line 279

---

[1] See Spenser, page 114a.
[2] Frederick, Prince of Wales.
[3] See La Rochefoucauld, page 264b.

[1] See La Rochefoucauld, page 265a.
[2] "Tenez voilà," dit-elle, "à chacun une
    écaille,
  Des sottises d'autrui nous vivons au
    Palais;
  Messieurs, l'huître étoit bonne. Adieu. Vi-
    vez en paix."
    BOILEAU [1636–1711]: *Epître II
    (à M. l'Abbé des Roches)*

And gentle Dullness ever loves a joke.
The Dunciad. Book II, Line 34

A brain of feathers, and a heart of lead.
Ibid. Line 44

Peel'd, patch'd, and piebald, linsey-woolsey brothers,
Grave mummers! sleeveless some and shirtless others.
That once was Britain.
Ibid. Book III, Line 115

And proud his mistress' order to perform,
Rides in the whirlwind and directs the storm.[1]
Ibid. Line 263

A wit with dunces, and a dunce with wits.[2]
Ibid. Book IV, Line 90

"The right divine of kings to govern wrong."
Ibid. Line 188

Stuff the head
With all such reading as was never read:
For thee explain a thing till all men doubt it,
And write about it, Goddess, and about it.
Ibid. Line 249

To happy convents, bosom'd deep in vines,
Where slumber abbots purple as their wines.
Ibid. Line 301

Led by my hand, he saunter'd Europe round,
And gather'd every vice on Christian ground.
Ibid. Line 311

Ev'n Palinurus nodded at the helm.
Ibid. Line 614

Religion, blushing, veils her sacred fires,
And unawares Morality expires.
Nor public flame nor private dares to shine;
Nor human spark is left, nor glimpse divine!
Lo! thy dread empire Chaos! is restor'd,
Light dies before thy uncreating word:

[1] See Addison, pages 298b–299a.
[2] See Quintilian, page 52b.

Thy hand, great Anarch! lets the curtain fall,
And universal darkness buries all.
The Dunciad. Book IV, Line 649

LADY MARY WORTLEY MONTAGU
[1689–1762]

And we meet with champagne and a chicken, at last.
The Lover [1748]

Be plain in dress, and sober in your diet;
In short, my deary, kiss me, and be quiet.
A Summary of Lord Lyttelton's Advice

Satire should, like a polished razor keen,
Wound with a touch that's scarcely felt or seen.
To the Imitator of the First Satire of Horace. Book II

This world consists of men, women, and Herveys.[1]
Letters [1763]. Vol. I

But the fruit that can fall without shaking
Indeed is too mellow for me.
Letters and Works [1837]. The Answer

JOHN BYROM
[1692–1763]

God bless the King, — I mean the faith's defender!
God bless — no harm in blessing — the Pretender!
But who pretender is, or who is king, —
God bless us all! — that's quite another thing.[2]
Miscellaneous Poems [1773]. To an Officer of the Army, extempore

[1] As the French say, there are three sexes, — men, women, and clergymen. — SYDNEY SMITH [1771–1845]: *Lady Holland's Memoir, Vol. I, Chap. 9*
[2] Quoted by SIR WALTER SCOTT in *Redgauntlet, Vol. II, Chap. 1*, Edinburgh edition [1832].

Some say, compar'd to Bononcini,
That Mynheer Handel's but a ninny;
Others aver that he to Handel
Is scarcely fit to hold a candle.
Strange all this difference should be
'Twixt Tweedledum and Tweedledee.
> *Miscellaneous Poems. On the Feuds between Handel and Bononcini*

As clear as a whistle.
> *Epistle to Lloyd*

PHILIP DORMER STANHOPE, EARL OF CHESTERFIELD
[1694–1773]

Measures not men.[1]
> *Letters. March 6, 1742*

Whatever is worth doing at all, is worth doing well.
> *Ibid. March 10, 1746*

The knowledge of the world is only to be acquired in the world, not in a closet.
> *Ibid. October 4, 1746*

An injury is much sooner forgotten than an insult.
> *Ibid. October 9, 1746*

Do as you would be done by, is the surest method of pleasing.
> *Ibid. October 9, 1747*

Take the tone of the company that you are in.
> *Ibid.*

I knew once a very covetous, sordid fellow,[2] who used to say, "Take care of the pence, for the pounds will take care of themselves."
> *Ibid. November 6, 1747*

Advice is seldom welcome; and those who want it most always like it least.
> *Ibid. January 29, 1748*

Speak of the moderns without contempt, and of the ancients without idolatry.
> *Ibid. February 22, 1748*

Wear your learning, like your watch, in a private pocket: and do not pull it

[1] See Goldsmith, page 355b, and Burke, page 359a.
[2] William Lowndes [1652–1724], Secretary of the Treasury in the reigns of William III, Queen Anne, and George I.

out and strike it, merely to show that you have one.
> *Letters. February 22, 1748*

Manners must adorn knowledge, and smooth its way through the world. Like a great rough diamond, it may do very well in a closet by way of curiosity, and also for its intrinsic value.
> *Ibid. July 1, 1748*

Women, then, are only children of a larger growth.
> *Ibid. September 5, 1748*

Women who are either indisputably beautiful, or indisputably ugly, are best flattered upon the score of their understandings; but those who are in a state of mediocrity, are best flattered upon their beauty, or at least their graces; for every woman who is not absolutely ugly thinks herself handsome.
> *Ibid.*

Without some dissimulation no business can be carried on at all.
> *Ibid. May 22, 1749*

Idleness is only the refuge of weak minds.
> *Ibid. July 20, 1749*

Style is the dress of thoughts.
> *Ibid. November 24, 1749*

Religion must still be allowed to be a collateral security, at least, to Virtue.
> *Ibid. January 8, 1750*

Despatch is the soul of business.
> *Ibid. February 5, 1750*

Knowledge may give weight, but accomplishments give lustre, and many more people see than weigh.
> *Ibid. May 8, 1750*

Let blockheads read what blockheads write.
> *Ibid. November 1, 1750*

Is it possible to love such a man?[1] No. The utmost I can do for him is to consider him as a respectable Hottentot.
> *Ibid. February 28, 1751*

It is commonly said, and more particularly by Lord Shaftesbury,[2] that ridicule is the best test of truth.
> *Ibid. February 6, 1752*

[1] Lord Lyttelton.
[2] Truth, 'tis supposed, may bear all lights; and one of those principal lights or natural

Every woman is infallibly to be gained by every sort of flattery, and every man by one sort or other.
Letters. March 16, 1752

Chapter of accidents.[1]
Ibid. February 16, 1753

Women, and young men, are very apt to tell what secrets they know, from the vanity of having been trusted.
Letters to His Son

I assisted at the birth of that most significant word "flirtation," which dropped from the most beautiful mouth in the world.
The World. No. 101

Unlike my subject now shall be my song;
It shall be witty, and it sha'n't be long.
Impromptu Lines

The dews of the evening most carefully shun, —
Those tears of the sky for the loss of the sun.
Advice to a Lady in Autumn

The nation looked upon him as a deserter, and he shrunk into insignificancy and an earldom.
Character of Pulteney

He adorned whatever subject he either spoke or wrote upon, by the most splendid eloquence.[2]
Character of Bolingbroke

FRANCIS HUTCHESON
[1694–1746]

That action is best which procures

the greatest happiness for the greatest numbers.[1]
Inquiry Concerning Moral Good and Evil [1720]. Sect. 3

VOLTAIRE
(FRANÇOIS MARIE AROUET)
[1694–1778]

Virtue debases itself in justifying itself.
Oedipe [1718]. Act I, Sc. 4

Crime has its heroes, error has its martyrs:
Of true zeal and false, what vain judges we are!
Henriade [1728]. Chant V, Line 200

He who is merely just is severe.
Letter to the King of Prussia [1740]

The first who was king was a fortunate soldier:
Who serves his country well has no need of ancestors.[2]
Mérope [1743]. Act I, Sc. 3

It is better to risk saving a guilty person than to condemn an innocent one.
Zadig [1747]. Chap. 6

The king [Frederick the Great] has sent me some of his dirty linen to wash; I will wash yours another time.[3]
Reply to General Manstein [1752]

This agglomeration which was called and which still calls itself the Holy Roman Empire is neither holy, nor Roman, nor an Empire.
Essai sur les Moeurs [1756]

All is for the best in the best of possible worlds.[4]
Candide [1759]. Chap. 1

---

mediums by which things are to be viewed in order to a thorough recognition is ridicule itself. — ANTHONY ASHLEY COOPER, LORD SHAFTESBURY: *Essay on the Freedom of Wit and Humour* [1709], *Part I, Sect. 1*

[1] The Chapter of Accidents is the longest chapter in the book. — Attributed to JOHN WILKES by SOUTHEY in *The Doctor* [1837], *Chap. 118*

[2] See Johnson, page 337b.
Il embellit tout ce qu'il touche (He adorns whatever he touches). — FÉNELON [1651–1715]: *Lettre sur les Occupations de l'Académie Française, Sect. IV*

[1] Priestley was the first (unless it was Beccaria) who taught my lips to pronounce this sacred truth, — that the greatest happiness of the greatest number is the foundation of morals and legislation. — JEREMY BENTHAM [1748–1832]: *Works, Vol. X, P. 142*

[2] What can they see in the longest kingly line in Europe, save that it runs back to a successful soldier? — SIR WALTER SCOTT: *Woodstock* [1826], *Chap. 37*

[3] See Napoleon, page 399b.

[4] Referring to the philosophy of Leibnitz and his followers.

If this is the best of possible worlds, what then are the others?
Candide. Chap. 6

Optimism, said Candide, is a mania for maintaining that all is well when things are going badly.
Ibid. Chap. 19

For what end, then, has this world been formed? . . . To plague us to death.
Ibid. Chap. 21

In this country [England] it is found good, from time to time, to kill one admiral to encourage the others.
Ibid. Chap. 23

This is the happiest of mortals, for he is above everything he possesses.
Ibid. Chap. 26

Labour preserves us from three great evils — weariness, vice, and want.
Ibid. Chap. 30

Let us work without disputing; it is the only way to render life tolerable.
Ibid.

We must cultivate our garden.[1]
Ibid.

In the case of news, we should always wait for the sacrament of confirmation.
Letter to Count d'Argental
[August 28, 1760]

The first among languages is that which possesses the largest number of excellent works.
Letter to Deodati de Tovazzi
[January 24, 1761]

There are truths which are not for all men, nor for all times.
Letter to Cardinal de Bernis
[April 23, 1761]

Whatever you do, crush the infamous thing [superstition], and love those who love you.[2]
Letter to d'Alembert
[November 28, 1762]

Common sense is not so common.
Dictionnaire Philosophique
[1764]. Self-love

In general, the art of government consists in taking as much money as possible from one class of citizens to give to the other.
Dictionnaire Philosophique. Money

The best is the enemy of the good.[1]
Ibid. Dramatic Art

Very learned women are to be found, in the same manner as female warriors; but they are seldom or never inventors.
Ibid. Women

The proper mean.[2]
Letter to Count d'Argental
[November 28, 1765]

Men use thought only to justify their wrongdoings, and speech only to conceal their thoughts.[3]
Dialogue 14. Le Chapon et la Poularde [1766]

I have never made but one prayer to God, a very short one: "O Lord, make my enemies ridiculous." And God granted it.
Letter to M. Damiliville
[May 16, 1767]

History is little else than a picture of human crimes and misfortunes.[4]
L'Ingénu [1767]. Chap. 10

It is said that God is always for the big battalions.[5]
Letter to M. le Riche
[February 6, 1770]

Thought depends absolutely on the stomach, but in spite of that, those who have the best stomachs are not the best thinkers.
Letter to d'Alembert
[August 20, 1770]

If God did not exist, it would be necessary to invent him.[6]
Épître à l'Auteur du Livre des Trois Imposteurs
[November 10, 1770]

Change everything, except your loves.
Sur l'Usage de la Vie

---

[1] Le mieux est l'ennemi du bien.
[2] Le juste milieu. See Horace, page 38b.
[3] See Robert South, page 286b.
[4] See Gibbon, page 369a.
[5] See Gibbon, page 369b.
Providence is always on the side of the last reserve. — *Attributed to* NAPOLEON
[6] See Ovid, page 42b, and Tillotson, page 275a.

---

[1] Il faut cultiver notre jardin.
[2] Quoi que vous fassiez, écrasez l'infâme, et aimez qui vous aime.

I am very fond of truth, but not at all of martyrdom.
Letter to d'Alembert
[February, 1776]

The secret of being a bore is to tell everything.
L'Enfant Prodigue. Preface

The embarrassment of riches.
Le Droit du Seigneur.
Act II, Sc. 6

He who thinks himself wise, O heavens! is a great fool.
Ibid. Act IV, Sc. 1

He who has not the spirit of his age,
Of his age has all the misery.[1]
Letter to Cideville

The superfluous, a very necessary thing.
Le Mondain. Line 21

Love truth, but pardon error.
Discours sur l'Homme. Discours 3

It seems clear to me that God designed us to live in society — just as He has given the bees the honey; and as our social system could not subsist without the sense of justice and injustice, He has given us the power to acquire that sense.
Letter to Frederick the Great [2]

I advise you to go on living solely to enrage those who are paying your annuities. It is the only pleasure I have left.
Letter to Madame du Deffand [2]

Liberty of thought is the life of the soul.
Essay on Epic Poetry
(written in English)

Whoe'er thou art, behold thy master,
He is, or was, or is to be.[3]
On a Statuette of Cupid in the
Cirey Gardens

I disapprove of what you say, but I will defend to the death your right to say it.
Attributed to Voltaire [4]

[1] Qui n'a pas l'esprit de son âge,
De son âge a tout le malheur.
[2] S. G. TALLENTYRE: *Voltaire in His Letters* [1919]
[3] Qui que tu sois, voici ton maître;
Il l'est — le fut — ou le doit être.
[4] This sentence is not Voltaire's, but was

FRANÇOIS QUESNAY
[1694–1774]

Laissez faire, laissez passer.[1]
Attributed to Quesnay

MATTHEW GREEN
[1696–1737]

Fling but a stone, the giant dies.
The Spleen [1737]. Line 93

Laugh and be well.
Ibid. Line 94

Happy the man, who, innocent,
Grieves not at ills he can't prevent;
His skiff does with the current glide,
Not puffing pulled against the tide.
Ibid. Line 365

By happy alchemy of mind
They turn to pleasure all they find.
Ibid. Line 610

Though pleased to see the dolphins play,
I mind my compass and my way.
Ibid. Line 826

WILLIAM OLDYS
[1696–1761]

Busy, curious, thirsty fly,
Drink with me, and drink as I.
On a Fly Drinking out of a Cup
of Ale. Stanza 1

Three-score summers, when they're gone,
Will appear as short as one.
Ibid. Stanza 2

---

first used in quoting a letter from Voltaire to Helvétius in *The Friends of Voltaire* [1906] by S. G. TALLENTYRE (E. Beatrice Hall). She claims it was a paraphrase of Voltaire's words in the *Essay on Tolerance,* "Think for yourselves and let others enjoy the privilege to do so too."

[1] Let it be, let it pass. The phrase is not readily translatable, and also appears as "Laissez faire, laissez aller." It has been attributed to PIERRE LE PESANT BOISGUILBERT [1676–1714] and JEAN CLAUDE GOURNAY [1712–1759], as well as to Quesnay. It was widely used by the Physiocrats in urging freedom from government interference, and was adopted by ADAM SMITH [1723–1790].

MADAME DU DEFFAND
[1697–1784]

He [Voltaire] has invented history.
FOURNIER: *L'Esprit dans l'Histoire*

The distance is nothing; it is only the first step which counts.[1]
Letter to d'Alembert
[*July 7, 1763*]

CHARLES MACKLIN
[?–1797]

The law is a sort of hocus-pocus science.[2]
Love à la Mode [*1759*]. *Act II, Sc. 1*

RICHARD SAVAGE
[1698–1743]

He lives to build, not boast, a generous race;
No tenth transmitter of a foolish face.
The Bastard [*1728*]. *Line 7*

May see thee now, though late, redeem thy name,
And glorify what else is damn'd to fame.
Character of Foster

WILLIAM WARBURTON, BISHOP OF GLOUCESTER
[1698–1779]

Orthodoxy is my doxy — heterodoxy is another man's doxy.[3]
Quoted by JOSEPH PRIESTLEY [*1733–1804*]: *Memoirs, Vol. I, Page 572*

---

[1] This remark refers to the legend that St. Denis, carrying his head in his hands, walked two leagues.
Voltaire wrote to Madame du Deffand [January, 1764] that one of her bon mots was quoted in the notes of *La Pucelle, Canto 1*: "Il n'y a que le premier pas qui coûte."

[2] Hocus was an old cunning attorney. — DR. JOHN ARBUTHNOT: *Law is a Bottomless Pit: or, History of John Bull* [1712], *Chap. 5*
The words of consecration, "*Hoc est corpus*," were travestied into a nickname for jugglery, as "Hocus-pocus." — JOHN RICHARD GREEN: *A Short History of the English People* [1874], *Chap. VII, Sect. 1*

[3] Priestley relates that, in a debate on the Test Laws, Lord Sandwich said: "I have heard frequent use of the words 'orthodoxy'

JOHN DYER
[1699–1758]

A little rule, a little sway,
A sunbeam in a winter's day,
Is all the proud and mighty have
Between the cradle and the grave.
Grongar Hill [*1726*]. *Line 89*

JAMES THOMSON
[1700–1748]

See, Winter comes to rule the varied year,[1]
Sullen and sad.
The Seasons. Winter [*1726*], *Line 1*

Welcome, kindred gloom!
Congenial horrors, hail!
Ibid. Line 5

Cruel as death, and hungry as the grave.
Ibid. Line 393

There studious let me sit,
And hold high converse with the mighty dead.
Ibid. Line 431

The kiss, snatch'd hasty from the sidelong maid.
Ibid. Line 625

The meek-ey'd Morn appears, mother of dews.
Ibid. Summer [*1727*], *Line 47*

Ships dim-discover'd dropping from the clouds.
Ibid. Line 946

Sigh'd and look'd unutterable things.
Ibid. Line 1188

Who stemm'd the torrent of a downward age.
Ibid. Line 1505

Come, gentle Spring! ethereal Mildness! come.
Ibid. Spring [*1728*], *Line 1*

But who can paint
Like Nature? Can imagination boast,
Amid its gay creation, hues like hers?
Ibid. Line 465

---

and 'heterodoxy' but I confess myself at a loss to know precisely what they mean." Bishop Warburton whispered his definition to him.

[1] O Winter, ruler of the inverted year. — COWPER: *The Task* [1784], *Book IV, Winter Evening, L. 34*

Delightful task! to rear the tender thought,
To teach the young idea how to shoot.
> *The Seasons. Spring, Line 1149*

An elegant sufficiency, content,
Retirement, rural quiet, friendship, books.
> *Ibid. Line 1158*

Crown'd with the sickle, and the wheaten sheaf,
While Autumn, nodding o'er the yellow plain,
Comes jovial on.
> *Ibid. Autumn [1730], Line 1*

For loveliness
Needs not the foreign aid of ornament,
But is when unadorn'd adorn'd the most.[1]
> *Ibid. Line 208*

He saw her charming, but he saw not half
The charms her downcast modesty conceal'd.
> *Ibid. Line 233*

For still the world prevail'd, and its dread laugh,
Which scarce the firm philosopher can scorn.
> *Ibid. Line 237*

Or where the Northern ocean, in vast whirls,
Boils round the naked melancholy isles
Of farthest Thulè, and th' Atlantic surge
Pours in among the stormy Hebrides.
> *Ibid. Line 871*

Shade, unperceiv'd, so softening into shade.
> *Hymn [1730]. Line 25*

From seeming evil still educing good.
> *Ibid. Line 114*

Come then, expressive silence, muse His praise.
> *Ibid. Line 118*

O Sophonisba! Sophonisba, O!
> *Sophonisba [1729]. Act III, Sc. 2*

As those we love decay, we die in part,
String after string is severed from the heart;
Till loosen'd life, at last but breathing clay,

[1] See Milton, page 256a.

Without one pang is glad to fall away.
> *On the Death of Mr. Aikman* [1]

Forever, Fortune, wilt thou prove
An unrelenting foe to love;
And when we meet a mutual heart,
Come in between and bid us part?
> *To Fortune*

When Britain first, at Heaven's command,
　Arose from out the azure main,
This was the charter of the land,
　And guardian angels sung this strain:
Rule, Britannia! Britannia, rule the waves!
Britons never will be slaves.
> *Alfred [1740]. Act II, Sc. 5*

A pleasing land of drowsy head it was,
Of dreams that wave before the half-shut eye;
And of gay castles in the clouds that pass,
Forever flushing round a summer sky:
There eke the soft delights that witchingly
Instill a wanton sweetness through the breast,
And the calm pleasures always hover'd nigh;
But whate'er smack'd of noyance or unrest
Was far, far off expell'd from this delicious nest.
> *The Castle of Indolence [1748].*
> *Canto I, Stanza 6*

O fair undress, best dress! it checks no vein,
But every flowing limb in pleasure drowns,
And heightens ease with grace.
> *Ibid. Stanza 26*

Plac'd far amid the melancholy main.
> *Ibid. Stanza 30*

"A penny saved is a penny got" —
Firm to this scoundrel maxim keepeth he.
> *Ibid. Stanza 50*

A bard here dwelt, more fat than bard beseems,
Who, void of envy, guile, and lust of gain,

[1] William Aikman [1682–1731], portrait painter.

On virtue still, and nature's pleasing
 themes,
Pour'd forth his unpremeditated strain.
The Castle of Indolence. Canto I,
Stanza 68
A little round, fat, oily man of God.
Ibid. Stanza 69
I care not, Fortune, what you me deny:
You cannot rob me of free Nature's
 grace,
You cannot shut the windows of the
 sky
Through which Aurora shows her
 brightening face.
Ibid. Canto II, Stanza 3
Health is the vital principle of bliss,
And exercise, of health.
Ibid. Stanza 55

PHILIP DODDRIDGE
[1702–1751]

Live while you live, the epicure would
 say,
And seize the pleasures of the present
 day;
Live while you live, the sacred preacher
 cries,
And give to God each moment as it flies.
Lord, in my views, let both united be:
I live in pleasure when I live to thee.
Epigram on His Family Arms [1]
Awake, my soul! stretch every nerve,
 And press with vigour on;
A heavenly race demands thy zeal,
 And an immortal crown.
Hymns [1755]. *Zeal and Vigour*
in the Christian Race, Stanza 1

ROBERT DODSLEY
[1703–1764]

One kind kiss before we part,
 Drop a tear and bid adieu;
Though we sever, my fond heart
 Till we meet shall pant for you.[2]
The Parting Kiss [1745]
No state of life but must to patience
 bow:

[1] The Latin proverb: Dum vivimus, viva-
mus (Let us live while we live).
[2] See Burns, page 392a.

The tradesman must have patience
 for his bill;
He must have patience who to law will
 go;
And should he lose his right, more
 patience still;
Yea, to prevent or heal full many a
 strife,
How oft, how long must man have
 patience with his wife.
To Patience [1745]

JONATHAN EDWARDS
[1703–1758]

Resolved, never to do anything which
I should be afraid to do if it were the
last hour of my life.
Seventy Resolutions
Intend to live in continual mortifica-
tion, and never to expect or desire any
worldly ease or pleasure.
Diary. 1723
A little, wretched, despicable crea-
ture; a worm, a mere nothing, and less
than nothing; a vile insect that has
risen up in contempt against the maj-
esty of Heaven and earth.
The Justice of God in the Damna-
tion of Sinners [1734]
I assert that nothing ever comes to
pass without a cause.
The Freedom of the Will [1754]
This dictate of common sense.
Ibid.

JOHN WESLEY
[1703–1791]

I look upon the world as my parish.
Journal. June 11, 1739
That execrable sum of all villanies,
commonly called the Slave Trade.
Ibid. February 12, 1772
Though I am always in haste, I am
never in a hurry.
Letters. December 10, 1777
Do all the good you can,
By all the means you can,
In all the ways you can,
In all the places you can,
At all the times you can,

To all the people you can,
As long as ever you can.
John Wesley's Rule

SOAME JENYNS
[1704–1787]

Let each fair maid, who fears to be disgraced,
Ever be sure to tie her garters fast,
Lest the loosed string, amidst the public hall,
A wished-for prize to some proud fop should fall.
The Art of Dancing [1752]

NATHANIEL COTTON
[1705–1788]

If solid happiness we prize,
Within our breasts this jewel lies,
  And they are fools who roam.
The world has nothing to bestow;
From our own selves our joys must flow,
  And that dear hut, our home.
The Fireside. Stanza 3

To be resign'd when ills betide,
Patient when favours are deni'd,
  And pleas'd with favours given, —
Dear Chloe, this is wisdom's part;
This is that incense of the heart [1]
Whose fragrance smells to heaven.
Ibid. Stanza 11

Yet still we hug the dear deceit.
Content. Vision IV

Hold the fleet angel fast until he bless thee.[2]
Tomorrow

BENJAMIN FRANKLIN [3]
[1706–1790]

We are a kind of posterity in respect to them.
Letter to William Strahan [1745]

---

[1] The incense of the heart may rise. — JOHN PIERPONT [1785–1866]: *Every Place a Temple*
[2] I will not let thee go, except thou bless me. — *Genesis, XXXII, 26*
  Like the patriarch's angel hold it fast
  Till it gives its blessing.
  WHITTIER [1807–1892]: *My Soul and I, St. 34*
[3] Eripuit coelo fulmen sceptrumque tyran-

8th and lastly. They are so grateful!!
Reasons for Preferring an Elderly Mistress [1745]

Remember that time is money.[1]
Advice to a Young Tradesman [1748]

God helps them that help themselves.[2]
Maxims prefixed to Poor Richard's Almanac [1757]

Dost thou love life? Then do not squander time, for that is the stuff life is made of.
Ibid.

Early to bed and early to rise,
Makes a man healthy, wealthy, and wise.[3]
Ibid.

Plough deep while sluggards sleep.
Ibid.

Never leave that till tomorrow which you can do today.
Ibid.

Three removes are as bad as a fire.
Ibid.

Little strokes fell great oaks.
Ibid.

A little neglect may breed mischief: for want of a nail the shoe was lost; for want of a shoe the horse was lost; and for want of a horse the rider was lost.[4]
Ibid.

He that goes a borrowing goes a sorrowing.
Ibid.

Vessels large may venture more,
But little boats should keep near shore.
Ibid.

---

nis (He snatched the lightning from heaven, and the scepter from tyrants) — a line attributed to Turgot, and inscribed on Houdon's bust of Franklin. Frederick von der Trenck [1726–1794] asserted at his trial [1794] that he was the author of this line.
[1] We reckon hours and minutes to be dollars and cents. — T. C. HALIBURTON [1796–1865]: *The Clockmaster*
[2] See Sophocles, page 16b.
[3] JOHN CLARKE: *Paraemiolgia* [1639]
My hour is eight o'clock, though it is an infallible rule, "Sanat, sanctificat, et ditat, surgere mane" (That he may be healthy, happy, and wise, let him rise early). — *A Health to the Gentle Profession of Servingmen* [1598]
[4] See Herbert, page 234a.

It is hard for an empty sack to stand upright.

> *Maxims prefixed to Poor
> Richard's Almanac*

Experience keeps a dear school, but fools will learn in no other.

> *Ibid.*

A word to the wise is enough, and many words won't fill a bushel.

> *Preface to Poor Richard Improved
> [1758]*

The used key is always bright.

> *Ibid.*

Lost time is never found again.

> *Ibid.*

He that riseth late, must trot all day.

> *Ibid.*

Keep thy shop, and thy shop will keep thee.[1]

> *Ibid.*

They that can give up essential liberty to obtain a little temporary safety deserve neither liberty nor safety.

> *Historical Review of Pennsylvania
> [1759]*

Idleness and pride tax with a heavier hand than kings and parliaments. If we can get rid of the former, we may easily bear the latter.

> *Letter on the Stamp Act
> [July 11, 1765]*

The grand leap of the whale up the Fall of Niagara is esteemed, by all who have seen it, as one of the finest spectacles in nature.

> *To the editor of a London newspaper [1765], intended to chaff the English for their ignorance of America*

Here Skugg lies snug
As a bug in a rug.

> *Letter to Miss Georgiana
> Shipley [September, 1772]*

There never was a good war or a bad peace.[2]

> *Letter to Josiah Quincy
> [September 11, 1773]*

You and I were long friends: you are now my enemy, and I am

> Yours,
> B. Franklin
> *Letter to William Strahan
> [July 5, 1775]*

We must all hang together, or assuredly we shall all hang separately.

> *At the signing of the Declaration of
> Independence [July 4, 1776]*

He has paid dear, very dear, for his whistle.

> *The Whistle [1779]*

Here you would know and enjoy what posterity will say of Washington. For a thousand leagues have nearly the same effect with a thousand years.

> *Letter to Washington
> [March 5, 1780]*

George Washington, Commander of the American armies, who, like Joshua of old, commanded the sun and the moon to stand still, and they obeyed him.

> *A Toast at a Dinner in Versailles* [1]

I wish the bald eagle had not been chosen as the representative of our country; he is a bird of bad moral character; like those among men who live by sharping and robbing, he is generally poor, and often very lousy.

The turkey is a much more respectable bird, and withal a true original native of America.

> *Letter to Sarah Bache
> [January 26, 1784]*

He [the sun] gives light as soon as he rises.

> *An Economical Project* [2] *[1784]*

Our Constitution is in actual operation; everything appears to promise

---

[1] See Chapman, page 116b.

[2] I cease not to advocate peace; even though unjust it is better than the most just war. — Cicero [106–43 B.C.]: *Epistolae ad Atticum, Book VII, Epistle 14*

It hath been said that an unjust peace is

to be preferred before a just war. — Samuel Butler: *Butler's Remains* [1759], *Speeches in the Rump Parliament*

[1] The British Minister had proposed a toast to George III, in which he likened him to the sun, and the French Minister had toasted Louis XVI, comparing him with the moon.

[2] A letter to the *Journal de Paris* advocating daylight saving.

that it will last; but in this world nothing is certain but death and taxes.
Letter to M. Leroy [*1789*]

The next thing most like living one's life over again seems to be a recollection of that life, and to make that recollection as durable as possible by putting it down in writing.
Autobiography [*1793–1868*].
Chap. I

Often I sat up in my room reading the greatest part of the night, when the book was borrowed in the evening and to be returned early in the morning, lest it should be missed or wanted.
Ibid.

Persons of good sense, I have since observed, seldom fall into disputation, except lawyers, university men, and men of all sorts that have been bred at Edinburgh.
Ibid.

Eat not to dullness; drink not to elevation.
Ibid. Chap. VI

An advantage itinerant preachers have over those who are stationary, the latter cannot well improve their delivery of a sermon by so many rehearsals.
Ibid. Chap. VII

I shall never ask, never refuse, nor ever resign an office.
Ibid. Chap. VIII

Human felicity is produced not so much by great pieces of good fortune that seldom happen, as by little advantages that occur every day.
Ibid. Chap. IX

When men are employed, they are best contented; for on the days they worked they were good-natured and cheerful, and, with the consciousness of having done a good day's work, they spent the evening jollily; but on our idle days they were mutinous and quarrelsome.
Ibid. Chap. X

HENRY FIELDING
[1707–1754]

All Nature wears one universal grin.
Tom Thumb the Great [*1730*].
Act I, Sc. 1

Today it is our pleasure to be drunk;
And this our queen shall be as drunk as we.
Ibid. Sc. 2

When I'm not thank'd at all, I'm thank'd enough;
I've done my duty, and I've done no more.
Ibid. Sc. 3

Lo, when two dogs are fighting in the streets,
With a third dog one of the two dogs meets;
With angry teeth he bites him to the bone,
And this dog smarts for what that dog has done.[1]
Ibid. Sc. 6

I am as sober as a judge.
Don Quixote in England [*1734*].
Act III, Sc. 14

This story will never go down.
Tumble-down Dick

The dusky night rides down the sky,
And ushers in the morn;
The hounds all join in glorious cry,
The huntsman winds his horn,
And a-hunting we will go.[2]
A-Hunting We Will Go [*1734*].
Stanza 1

---

[1] Thus when a barber and a collier fight,
The barber beats the luckless collier — white;
The dusty collier heaves his ponderous sack,
And big with vengeance beats the barber — black.
In comes the brick-dust man, with grime o'erspread,
And beats the collier and the barber — red:
Black, red, and white in various clouds are tost,
And in the dust they raise the combatants are lost.
CHRISTOPHER SMART [1722–1770]:
The Trip to Cambridge

[2] It's of three jovial huntsmen, and a-hunting they did go;

To whom nothing is given, of him can nothing be required.
>*Joseph Andrews* [*1742*].
>*Book II, Chap. 8*

I describe not men, but manners; not an individual, but a species.
>*Ibid. Book III, Chap. 1*

They are the affectation of affectation.
>*Ibid. Chap. 3*

Public schools are the nurseries of all vice and immorality.
>*Ibid. Chap. 5*

Some folks rail against other folks, because other folks have what some folks would be glad of.
>*Ibid. Book IV, Chap. 6*

Can any man have a higher notion of the rule of right and the eternal fitness of things?
>*The History of Tom Jones* [*1749*].
>*Book IV, Chap. 4*

Wisdom, whose lessons have been represented as so hard to learn by those who never were at her school, only teaches us to extend a simple maxim universally known. And this is, not to buy at too dear a price.
>*Ibid. Book VI, Chap. 3*

Distinction without a difference.
>*Ibid. Chap. 13*

The too inordinate fondness of a father . . . must be allowed the name of an amiable weakness.[1]
>*Ibid. Book X, Chap. 8*

Nothing more aggravates ill success than the near approach to good.
>*Ibid. Book XIII, Chap. 2*

Hairbreadth missings of happiness look like the insults of Fortune.
>*Ibid.*

The republic of letters.
>*Ibid. Book XIV, Chap. 1*

And they hunted, and they hollo'd, and they blew their horns also;
Look ye there!
>*The Three Jovial Huntsmen*
>(old English ballad), *St. 1*

[1] Amiable weaknesses of human nature. — GIBBON: *Decline and Fall of the Roman Empire* [1776-1788], *Chap. XIV*
It was an amiable weakness. — SHERIDAN: *The School for Scandal* [1777]

It hath been often said, that it is not death, but dying which is terrible.
>*Amelia* [*1751*]. *Book III, Chap. 4*

These are called the pious frauds of friendship.
>*Ibid. Book VI, Chap. 6*

When widows exclaim loudly against second marriages, I would always lay a wager that the man, if not the wedding-day, is absolutely fixed on.
>*Ibid. Chap. 8*

There is not in the universe a more ridiculous, nor a more contemptible animal, than a proud clergyman.
>*Ibid. Chap. 10*

One of my illustrious predecessors.[1]
>*Covent Garden Journal*
>[*January 11, 1752*]

Perhaps there is more of ostentation than of real utility in ships of this vast and unwieldy burthen.
>*Journal of a Voyage to Lisbon*
>[*1755*]

CARL LINNAEUS
[1707-1778]

To live by medicine is to live horribly.
>*Diaeta Naturalis. Introduction*

Nature does not proceed by leaps.[2]
>*Philosophia Botanica. Sect. 77*

Mingle your joys sometimes with your earnest occupation.
>*Quoted in biography of Linnaeus by* BENJAMIN DAYDON JONES, *Chap. 9*

A professor can never better distinguish himself in his work than by encouraging a clever pupil, for the true discoverers are among them, as comets amongst the stars.
>*Ibid.*

---

[1] Illustrious predecessor. — BURKE: *The Present Discontents* [1770]
I tread in the footsteps of illustrious men. . . . In receiving from the people the sacred trust twice confided to my illustrious predecessor [Andrew Jackson]. — MARTIN VAN BUREN: *Inaugural Address* [March 4, 1837]
[2] Natura non facit saltus.

Live innocently; God is here.
> *Quoted in biography of Linnaeus.*
> *Chap. 15 (Inscribed over the*
> *door of Linnaeus's bedchamber)*

If a tree dies, plant another in its place.
> *Ibid.*

GEORGES LOUIS LECLERC DE BUFFON
[1707–1788]

The style is the man himself.[1]
> *Discourse [On his admission to*
> *the French Academy, 1753]*

Genius is nothing but a great aptitude for patience.
> *Attributed* [2]

CHARLES WESLEY
[1707–1788]

"Christ, the Lord, is risen today,"
Sons of men and angels say,
Raise your joys and triumphs high,
Sing, ye heavens, and earth reply.
> *Hymns and Sacred Poems [1739].*
> *Christ, the Lord, is Risen Today*

Jesus, lover of my soul,
Let me to Thy bosom fly,
While the waters nearer roll,
While the tempest still is high;
Hide me, O my Saviour, hide,
Till the storm of life is past;
Safe into the haven glide,
O receive my soul at last.
> *Ibid. [1740]. Jesus, Lover of*
> *My Soul*

Gentle Jesus, meek and mild,
Look upon a little child;

---

[1] Le style est l'homme même.

[2] Le génie n'est autre chose qu'une grande aptitude à la patience.
This is quoted by MATTHEW ARNOLD in his *Essays in Criticism, A French Coleridge* [1865]. There is also a popular proverb: "Genius is patience." DISRAELI, *The Young Duke* [1831]: "Patience is a necessary ingredient of genius." LESLIE STEPHEN [1832–1904]: "Genius is a capacity for taking trouble." JAN WALAEUS also says: "Genius is an intuitive talent for labor." LORD SYDENHAM [1799–1841] defined genius as a consummate sense of proportion.
See Carlyle, page 476a.

Pity my simplicity,
Suffer me to come to thee.
> *Hymns and Sacred Poems [1742].*
> *Gentle Jesus, Meek and Mild*

Soldiers of Christ, arise,
And put your armour on.
> *Ibid. [1749] Soldiers of Christ,*
> *Arise*

Hark! the herald angels sing
Glory to the new-born King;
Peace on earth, and mercy mild,
God and sinners reconciled!
Joyful all ye nations rise,
Join the triumph of the skies;
With th' angelic host proclaim
Christ is born in Bethlehem.[1]
> *Ibid. [1753]. Christmas Hymn:*
> *Hark! the Herald Angels Sing*

WILLIAM PITT, EARL OF CHATHAM
[1708–1778]

The atrocious crime of being a young man, which the honorable gentleman [Walpole] has with such spirit and decency charged upon me, I shall neither attempt to palliate nor deny; but content myself with wishing that I may be one of those whose follies may cease with their youth, and not of that number who are ignorant in spite of experience.
> *Speech in the House of Commons* [2]
> *[March 6, 1741]*

I rejoice that America has resisted. Three millions of people, so dead to all the feelings of liberty, as voluntarily to submit to be slaves, would have been fit instruments to make slaves of the rest.
> *Ibid. [January 14, 1766]*

---

[1] George Whitefield altered lines 1 and 2, 7 and 8 from Wesley's original:
> Hark, how all the welkin rings,
> "Glory to the King of kings."

. . . . . .

> Universal nature say,
> "Christ the Lord is born today."

[2] This is the composition of Johnson founded on some note or statement of th actual speech. Johnson said, "That speech wrote in a garret, in Exeter Street." — BOS WELL: *Life of Dr. Johnson* [1791]

Confidence is a plant of slow growth in an aged bosom; youth is the season of credulity.
Speech in the House of Commons [January 14, 1766]

Unlimited power is apt to corrupt the minds of those who possess it.[1]
Case of Wilkes. Speech [January 9, 1770]

Where law ends, tyranny begins.
Ibid.

A long train of these practices has at length unwillingly convinced me that there is something behind the throne greater than the King himself.
Chatham Correspondence. Speech [March 2, 1770]

Reparation for our rights at home, and security against the like future violations.[2]
Letter to the Earl of Shelburne [September 29, 1770]

You cannot conquer America.
Speech [November 18, 1777]

If I were an American, as I am an Englishman, while a foreign troop was landed in my country I never would lay down my arms, — never! never! never!
Ibid.

I invoke the genius of the Constitution.
Ibid.

The poorest man may in his cottage bid defiance to all the force of the Crown. It may be frail; its roof may shake; the wind may blow through it; the storms may enter, the rain may enter, — but the King of England cannot enter; all his forces dare not cross the threshold of the ruined tenement!
Speech on the Excise Bill

[1] Power tends to corrupt; absolute power corrupts absolutely. — LORD ACTON: *Letter to Bishop Mandell Creighton* [1887]
[2] Indemnity for the past and security for the future. — LORD JOHN RUSSELL: *Life and Times of Charles James Fox* [1859–1860], *Vol. III, P. 345, Letter to the Hon. T. Maitland*

SAMUEL JOHNSON
[1709–1784]

Of all the griefs that harass the distrest,
Sure the most bitter is a scornful jest.[1]
London [1738]. Line 166

This mournful truth is ev'rywhere confess'd, —
Slow rises worth, by poverty depress'd.[2]
Ibid. Line 176

When learning's triumph o'er her barb'rous foes
First rear'd the stage, immortal Shakespeare rose;
Each change of many-colour'd life he drew,
Exhausted worlds, and then imagin'd new:
Existence saw him spurn her bounded reign,
And panting Time toil'd after him in vain.
Prologue at the Opening of Drury Lane Theatre [1747]

Cold approbation gave the ling'ring bays,
For those who durst not censure, scarce could praise.
Ibid.

Declamation roar'd, while Passion slept.
Ibid.

The wild vicissitudes of taste.
Ibid.

For we that live to please must please to live.
Ibid.

Studious to please, yet not ashamed to fail.
Prologue to the Tragedy of Irene [1749]

Let observation with extensive view
Survey mankind, from China to Peru.[3]
Vanity of Human Wishes [1749]. Line 1

[1] See Juvenal, page 62b.
[2] Three years later Johnson wrote, "Mere unassisted merit advances slowly, if — what is not very common — it advances at all."
[3] DE QUINCEY quotes with approval, but without naming him, the criticism of a writer who contends that this couplet amounts in effect to this: "Let observation with extensive

Deign on the passing world to turn
thine eyes,
And pause a while from learning to be
wise.
There mark what ills the scholar's life
assail, —
Toil, envy, want, the patron, and the
jail.
Vanity of Human Wishes. Line 157

A frame of adamant, a soul of fire,
No dangers fright him, and no labours
tire.
Ibid. Line 191

He left the name at which the world
grew pale,
To point a moral, or adorn a tale.
Ibid. Line 221

Enlarge my life with multitude of days,
In health, in sickness, thus the sup-
pliant prays;
Hides from himself his state, and shuns
to know
That life protracted is protracted woe.
Ibid. Line 255

Superfluous lags the veteran on the
stage.
Ibid. Line 308

Must helpless man, in ignorance sedate,
Roll darkling down the torrent of his
fate?
Ibid. Line 345

Secure, whate'er he gives, he gives the
best.
Ibid. Line 356

With these celestial Wisdom calms the
mind,
And makes the happiness she does not
find.
Ibid. Line 367

From thee, great God, we spring, to
thee we tend, —
Path, motive, guide, original and end.[1]
Motto to The Rambler, No. 7
[1750]

Curiosity is one of the permanent
and certain characteristics of a vigorous
mind.
The Rambler [March 12, 1751]

No place affords a more striking conviction of the vanity of human hopes,
than a public library.
The Rambler [March 23, 1751]

Parnassus has its flowers of transient
fragrance, as well as its oaks of towering height, and its laurels of eternal
verdure.
Ibid.

Life is surely given us for higher
purposes than to gather what our ancestors have wisely thrown away.
Ibid. [May 14, 1751]

It is one of the maxims of the civil
law, that definitions are hazardous.
Ibid. [May 28, 1751]

Praise like gold and diamonds owes
its value only to its scarcity.
Ibid. [June 6, 1751]

Almost all absurdity of conduct
arises from the imitation of those whom
we can not resemble.
Ibid. [July 2, 1751]

I am not so lost in lexicography as
to forget that *words are the daughters
of earth, and that things are the sons
of heaven.*[1]
Preface to His Dictionary [1755]

I dismiss it with frigid tranquillity,
having little to fear or hope from censure or from praise.
Ibid.

CLUB — An assembly of good fellows, meeting under certain conditions.
Definition in the Dictionary

ESSAY — A loose sally of the mind;
an irregular indigested piece; not a
regular and orderly composition.
Ibid.

EXCISE — A hateful tax levied upon
commodities, and adjudged not by
the common judges of property, but
wretches hired by those to whom excise
is paid.
Ibid.

GRUBSTREET — The name of a street
near Moorsfield, London, much inhab-
ited by writers of small histories, dictionaries, and temporary poems.
Ibid.

---

observation observe mankind extensively." —
Rhetoric [1828]
[1] A translation of Boethius's *De Consolatione Philosophiae, III, 9, 27.*

[1] See Herbert, page 234b.

OATS — A grain which in England is generally given to horses, but in Scotland supports the people.[1]

Definition in the Dictionary

He is no wise man that will quit a certainty for an uncertainty.

The Idler [1758–1760]. No. 57

What is read twice is commonly better remembered than what is transcribed.

Ibid. No. 74

Ye who listen with credulity to the whispers of fancy, and pursue with eagerness the phantoms of hope; who expect that age will perform the promises of youth, and that the deficiencies of the present day will be supplied by the morrow, — attend to the history of Rasselas, Prince of Abyssinia.

Rasselas [1759]. Chap. I

"I fly from pleasure," said the prince, "because pleasure has ceased to please; I am lonely because I am miserable, and am unwilling to cloud with my presence the happiness of others."

Ibid. Chap. III

A man used to vicissitudes is not easily dejected.

Ibid. Chap. XII

Few things are impossible to diligence and skill.

Ibid.

I live in the crowd of jollity, not so much to enjoy company as to shun myself.

Ibid. Chap. XVI

Many things difficult to design prove easy to performance.

Ibid.

The first years of man must make provision for the last.

Ibid. Chap. XVII

The endearing elegance of female friendship.

Ibid. Chap. XLVI

---

[1] It was pleasant to me to find, that "oats," the "food of horses," were so much used as the food of the people in Dr. Johnson's own town. — BOSWELL: *Life of Dr. Johnson* [1791], *Everyman ed., Vol. I, P. 628*
I own that by my definition of *oats* I meant to vex them [the Scotch]. — *Ibid., Vol. II, P. 434*

How small of all that human hearts endure,
That part which laws or kings can cause or cure!
Still to ourselves in every place consigned,
Our own felicity we make or find.

Lines Added to GOLDSMITH'S *Traveller [1763–1764]*

That man is little to be envied whose patriotism would not gain force upon the plain of Marathon, or whose piety would not grow warmer among the ruins of Iona.

Journey to the Western Islands [1775]. Inch Kenneth

"To Oliver Goldsmith, Poet, Naturalist, Historian, who left scarcely any style of writing untouched, and touched nothing that he did not adorn." [1]

Epitaph on Goldsmith [June 22, 1776]

Whoever wishes to attain an English style, familiar but not coarse, and elegant but not ostentatious, must give his days and nights to the volumes of Addison.

Lives of the Poets [1779–1781]. Life of Addison

To be of no church is dangerous. Religion, of which the rewards are distant, and which is animated only by faith and hope, will glide by degrees out of the mind unless it be invigorated and reimpressed by external ordinances, by stated calls to worship, and the salutary influence of example.

Ibid. Life of Milton

His [Garrick's] death eclipsed the gayety of nations, and impoverished the public stock of harmless pleasure.[2]

Ibid. Life of Edmund Smith

Officious, innocent, sincere,
Of every friendless name the friend.

Verses on the Death of Mr. Robert Levet [1783]. Stanza 2

---

[1] Olivarii Goldsmith, Poetae, Physici, Historici, Qui nullum fere scribendi genus non tetigit, Nullum quod tetigit non ornavit.
[2] Quoted by BOSWELL, *Life of Dr. Johnson, Everyman ed., Vol. I, P. 39*, and *Vol. II, P. 275.*

In misery's darkest cavern known,
  His useful care was ever nigh.
Where hopeless anguish pour'd his
    groan,
  And lonely want retir'd to die.
        Verses on the Death of Mr.
        Robert Levet. Stanza 5
His virtues walk'd their narrow round,
Nor made a pause, nor left a void.
        Ibid. Stanza 7
Then, with no throbs of fiery pain,[1]
  No cold gradations of decay,
Death broke at once the vital chain,
  And freed his soul the nearest way.
        Ibid. Stanza 9
Tomorrow I purpose to regulate my
room.
      Prayers and Meditations [*Pub-*
      lished 1785]. *1764*
Preserve me from unseasonable and
immoderate sleep.
        Ibid. 1767
Every man naturally persuades him-
self that he can keep his resolutions,
nor is he convinced of his imbecility but
by length of time and frequency of experiment.
        Ibid. 1770
This world, where much is to be done
and little to be known.
      Ibid. Against Inquisitive and
      Perplexing Thoughts
Gratitude is a fruit of great cultivation; you do not find it among gross
people.
      BOSWELL's *Tour to the Hebrides*
      [*Published 1785*]. [*September*
      20, 1773]
A fellow that makes no figure in company, and has a mind as narrow as the
neck of a vinegar-cruet.
        Ibid. [*September 30, 1773*]
Here closed in death th' attentive eyes
That saw the manners in the face.
        Epitaph on Hogarth [*1786*]
The hoary Sage replied,
Come, my lad, and drink some beer.
    MRS. PIOZZI: *Anecdotes of Samuel*
        Johnson [*1786*]
If the man who turnips cries

  [1] Variant: Then with no throbbing fiery
pain.

Cry not when his father dies,
'Tis a proof that he had rather
Have a turnip than his father.[1]
    MRS. PIOZZI: *Anecdotes of*
        Samuel Johnson
He was a very good hater.
        Ibid.
The law is the last result of human
wisdom acting upon human experience
for the benefit of the public.
        Ibid.
The use of travelling is to regulate
imagination by reality, and instead of
thinking how things may be, to see them
as they are.
        Ibid.
Dictionaries are like watches; the
worst is better than none, and the best
cannot be expected to go quite true.
        Ibid.
Books that you may carry to the fire
and hold readily in your hand, are the
most useful after all.
    Apophthegms from HAWKINS's
        Life of Johnson [*1787*]
Round numbers are always false.
        Ibid.
As with my hat [2] upon my head
  I walk'd along the Strand,
I there did meet another man
  With his hat in his hand.[3]
    Ibid. Anecdotes of Johnson by
      GEORGE STEEVENS
Abstinence is as easy to me as tem-
perance would be difficult.
    Anecdotes of Johnson by
      HANNAH MORE
Boswell. That, Sir, was great forti-
tude of mind.
Johnson. No, Sir; stark insensibility.
    BOSWELL's *Life of Dr. Johnson* [4]
    [*1791*]. *Vol. I, Page 28*

  [1] Burlesque of Lope de Vega's lines,
"Se acquier los leones vence," etc.
  [2] Elsewhere found, "I put my hat."
  [3] A parody on the ballad, *The Hermit of
Warkworth.*
  [4] Everyman edition, 2 volumes.
  The Life of Johnson is assuredly a great, a
very great work. Homer is not more decidedly
the first of heroic poets, Shakespeare is not
more decidedly the first of dramatists, Demosthenes is not more decidedly the first of
orators, than Boswell is the first of biogra-

On clean-shirt-day he went abroad, and paid visits.

BOSWELL's *Life of Dr. Johnson.*
Vol. I, Page 56

Tom Birch is as brisk as a bee in conversation; but no sooner does he take a pen in his hand, than it becomes a torpedo to him, and benumbs all his faculties.

Ibid. Page 92

I'll come no more behind your scenes, David; for the silk stockings and white bosoms of your actresses excite my amorous propensities.[1]

Ibid. Page 117

Wretched un-idea'd girls.

Ibid. Page 148

Is not a patron, my lord, one who looks with unconcern on a man struggling for life in the water, and when he has reached ground encumbers him with help? The notice which you have been pleased to take of my labours, had it been early, had been kind; but it has been delayed till I am indifferent, and cannot enjoy it; till I am solitary, and cannot impart it; till I am known, and do not want it.[2]

Ibid. Page 156

Sir, he [Bolingbroke] was a scoundrel and a coward; a scoundrel for charging a blunderbuss against religion and morality; a coward, because he had not resolution to fire it off himself, but left half a crown to a beggarly Scotchman to draw the trigger at his death.

Ibid. Page 160

If a man does not make new acquaintances as he advances through life, he will soon find himself left alone. A man,

---

ohers. He has no second. — MACAULAY: *Samuel Johnson* [1831]

[1] To David Garrick [1749].
[2] Letter to Lord Chesterfield [February 7, 1755].

What is a Patron? Johnson knew,
And well that lifelike portrait drew.
He is a Patron who looks down
With careless eye on men who drown;
But if they chance to reach the land,
Encumbers them with helping hand.
AUSTIN DOBSON [1840–1921]: *The Noble Patron*

See Sophocles, pages 15b–16a.

sir, should keep his friendship in a constant repair.

BOSWELL's *Life of Dr. Johnson.*
Vol. I, Page 182

Towering in the confidence of twenty-one.[1]

Ibid. Page 197

Being in a ship is being in a jail, with the chance of being drowned.

Ibid. Page 215

Nothing is little to him that feels it with great sensibility.[2]

Ibid. Page 230

Bounty always receives part of its value from the manner in which it is bestowed.[3]

Ibid. Page 233

Every man's affairs, however little, are important to himself.[4]

Ibid. Page 235

A man of genius has been seldom ruined but by himself.[5]

Ibid. Page 236

Sir, I think all Christians, whether Papists or Protestants, agree in the essential articles, and that their differences are trivial, and rather political than religious.[6]

Ibid. Page 251

The noblest prospect which a Scotchman ever sees, is the high-road that leads him to England.

Ibid. Page 264

A man ought to read just as inclina-

---

[1] Letter to Bennet Langton [January 9, 1758].
[2] Letter to Joseph Baretti [July 20, 1762].
[3] Letter to the Earl of Bute [July 20, 1762].
[4] To the same [November 3, 1762].
[5] Letter to Joseph Baretti [December 21, 1762].
[6] All denominations of Christians have really little difference in point of doctrine, though they may differ widely in external forms. — *Vol. I, P. 411* [1772]

I do not find that the age or country makes the least difference; no, nor the language the actor spoke, nor the religion which they professed, — whether Arab in the desert, or Frenchman in the Academy. I see that sensible men and conscientious men all over the world were of one religion of well-doing and daring. — EMERSON: *Lectures and Biographical Sketches* [1884], *The Preacher*

See Disraeli, page 513b.

tion leads him; for what he reads as a task will do him little good.[1] A young man should read five hours in a day, and so may acquire a great deal of knowledge.

BOSWELL's *Life of Dr. Johnson.*
Vol. 1, Page 266

If he does really think that there is no distinction between virtue and vice, why, sir, when he leaves our houses let us count our spoons.

Ibid. Page 268

If I accustom a servant to tell a lie for *me*, have I not reason to apprehend that he will tell many lies for *himself?*
Ibid. Page 270

Sir, your levellers wish to level *down* as far as themselves; but they cannot bear levelling *up* to themselves.
Ibid. Page 277

Sherry[2] is dull, naturally dull; but it must have taken him a great deal of pains to become what we now see him. Such an excess of stupidity, sir, is not in Nature.
Ibid. Page 280

Sir, a woman preaching is like a dog's walking on his hind legs. It is not done well; but you are surprised to find it done at all.
Ibid. Page 287

I look upon it, that he who does not mind his belly will hardly mind anything else.[3]
Ibid. Page 290

This was a good dinner enough, to be sure, but it was not a dinner to *ask* a man to.
Ibid. Page 291

The gloomy calm of idle vacancy.[4]
Ibid. Page 294

---

[1] The book which you read from a sense of duty, or because for any reason you must, does not commonly make friends with you. — WILLIAM DEAN HOWELLS: *My Literary Passions* [1895], *Chap.* 7
[2] Thomas Sheridan [1719–1788], actor, lecturer, and author.
[3] See Athenaeus, page 69b.
[4] Letter to Boswell [December 8, 1763].
See Cowper, page 365a.

[Of Sir John Hawkins] A very unclubable man.

BOSWELL's *Life of Dr. Johnson.*
Vol. I, Page 298

He[1] is one of the many who have made themselves *public*, without making themselves *known*.

Ibid. Page 310

I cannot see that lectures can do so much good as reading the books from which the lectures are taken.

Ibid. Page 315

Were he not to marry again, it might be concluded that his first wife had given him a disgust to marriage; but by taking a second wife he pays the highest compliment to the first, by showing that she made him so happy as a married man, that he wishes to be so a second time.

Ibid. Page 360

It matters not how a man dies, but how he lives.

Ibid. Page 37

That fellow seems to me to possess but one idea, and that is a wrong one.
Ibid. Page 39

A gentleman who had been very unhappy in marriage, married immediately after his wife died: Johnson said it was the triumph of hope over experience.

Ibid. Page 39

A decent provision for the poor is the true test of civilization.

Ibid. Page 39

Whatever philosophy may determine of material nature, it is certainly true of intellectual nature, that it abhors a vacuum.

Ibid. Page 40

Nobody can write the life of a man but those who have eat and drunk and lived in social intercourse with him.
Ibid. Page 42

---

[1] William Kenrick [1725–1779], a writer who attacked Goldsmith, Garrick, Fielding, Johnson, and Colman.
[2] See Disraeli, page 512a.
[3] They only who live with a man can write his life with any genuine exactness and discrimination; and few people who have lived

The way to make sure of power and influence is by lending money confidentially to your neighbours at a small interest, or perhaps no interest at all, and having their bonds in your possession.

BOSWELL'S *Life of Dr. Johnson.*
Vol. I, Page 422

I am a great friend to public amusements; for they keep people from vice.
Ibid. Page 424

A cow is a very good animal in the field; but we turn her out of a garden.
Ibid. Page 436

Much may be made of a Scotchman if he be caught young.
Ibid. Page 440

The way to spread a work is to sell it at a low price. No man will send to buy a thing that costs even sixpence, without an intention to read it.
Ibid. Page 465

An old tutor of a college said to one of his pupils: Read over your compositions, and wherever you meet with a passage which you think is particularly fine, strike it out.[1]
Ibid. Page 470

You are the most unscottified of your countrymen.
Ibid. Page 473

Was ever poet so trusted before?[2]
Ibid. Page 502

Attack is the reaction. I never think I have hit hard unless it rebounds.
Ibid. Page 540

A man will turn over half a library to make one book.
Ibid. Page 545

Patriotism is the last refuge of a scoundrel.
Ibid. Page 547

Knowledge is of two kinds: we know a subject ourselves, or we know where we can find information upon it.
Ibid. Page 558

In lapidary inscriptions a man is not upon oath.
BOSWELL'S *Life of Dr. Johnson.*
Vol. I, Page 589

There is now less flogging in our great schools than formerly, but then less is learned there; so that what the boys get at one end they lose at the other.
Ibid.

There is nothing which has yet been contrived by man by which so much happiness is produced as by a good tavern or inn.[1]
Ibid. Page 620

A man is very apt to complain of the ingratitude of those who have risen far above him.
Ibid. Vol. II, Page 5

If a man could say nothing against a character but what he can prove, history could not be written.
Ibid. Page 13

No man but a blockhead ever wrote except for money.
Ibid. Page 16

While grief is fresh, every attempt to divert only irritates.
Ibid. Page 21

Life is a progress from want to want, not from enjoyment to enjoyment.
Ibid. Page 36

Life admits not of delays; when pleasure can be had, it is fit to catch it. Every hour takes away part of the things that please us, and perhaps part of our disposition to be pleased.[2]
Ibid. Page 98

In every volume of poems something good may be found.
Ibid. Page 117

---

[1] Whoe'er has travell'd life's dull round,
    Where'er his stages may have been,
    May sigh to think he still has found
    His warmest welcome at an inn.
WILLIAM SHENSTONE [1714–1763]:
Written on a Window of an Inn at Henley
ROBERT LEIGHTON [1611–1684], Archbishop of Glasgow, often said that if he were to choose a place to die in, it should be an inn. — *Works, Vol. I, P. 76*
[2] Letter to Boswell [September 1, 1777].

---

with a man know what to remark about him.
Vol. I, P. 617
[1] See Sydney Smith, page 419b.
[2] Of Oliver Goldsmith, in a letter to Boswell [July 4, 1774].

When a man is tired of London, he is tired of life; for there is in London all that life can afford.

Boswell's *Life of Dr. Johnson.*
Vol. II, Page 131

Everything that enlarges the sphere of human powers, that shows man he can do what he thought he could not do, is valuable.

Ibid. Page 168

It is a man's own fault, it is from want of use, if his mind grows torpid in old age.

Ibid. Page 183

Johnson had said that he could repeat a complete chapter of "The Natural History of Iceland," from the Danish of Horrebow, the whole of which was exactly (Ch. LXXII. *Concerning snakes*) thus: "There are no snakes to be met with throughout the whole island."[1]

Ibid. Page 201

As the Spanish proverb says, "He, who would bring home the wealth of the Indies, must carry the wealth of the Indies with him," so it is in travelling, a man must carry knowledge with him if he would bring home knowledge.

Ibid. Page 216

It is better to live rich, than to die rich.

Ibid. Page 218

I would rather be attacked than unnoticed. For the worst thing you can do to an author is to be silent as to his works.

Ibid. Page 257

I remember a passage in Goldsmith's "Vicar of Wakefield," which he was afterwards fool enough to expunge: "I do not love a man who is zealous for nothing."

Ibid. Page 267

Claret is the liquor for boys, port for men; but he who aspires to be a hero must drink brandy.

Ibid. Page 271

[1] Chapter XLII is still shorter: "There are no owls of any kind in the whole island."

Worth seeing? yes; but not worth going to see.

Boswell's *Life of Dr. Johnson.*
Vol. II, Page 291

A Frenchman must be always talking, whether he knows anything of the matter or not; an Englishman is content to say nothing, when he has nothing to say.

Ibid. Page 326

Of Dr. Goldsmith he said, "No man was more foolish when he had not a pen in his hand, or more wise when he had."

Ibid. Page 336

The applause of a single human being is of great consequence.

Ibid. Page 338

Come to me, my dear Bozzy, and let us be as happy as we can.[1]

Ibid. Page 366

The potentiality of growing rich beyond the dreams of avarice.[2]

Ibid. Page 376

Classical quotation is the *parole* of literary men all over the world.

Ibid. Page 386

My friend was of opinion that when a man of rank appeared in that character [as an author], he deserved to have his merits handsomely allowed.

Ibid. Page 39.

A jest breaks no bones.

Ibid. Page 40.

To let friendship die away by negligence and silence, is certainly not wise. It is voluntarily to throw away one of the greatest comforts of this weary pilgrimage.

Ibid. Page 41

Whatever you have, spend less.[4]

Ibid. Page 42.

[1] Letter to Boswell [March 14, 1781].
[2] I am rich beyond the dreams of avarice — Edward Moore: *The Gamester* [1753] *Act II, Sc. 2*
[3] Usually quoted as "When a nobleman writes a book, he ought to be encouraged."
[4] Letter to Boswell [December 7, 1782

I never have sought the world; the world was not to seek me.[1]

> BOSWELL's *Life of Dr. Johnson.*
> *Vol. II, Page 436*

He is not only dull himself, but the cause of dullness in others.[2]

> *Ibid. Page 441*

Clear your mind of cant.

> *Ibid. Page 469*

Who drives fat oxen should himself be fat.[3]

> *Ibid. Page 535*

I have found you an argument; I am not obliged to find you an understanding.

> *Ibid. Page 536*

Blown about with every wind of criticism.[4]

> *Ibid. Page 539*

Don't *attitudenize.*

> *Ibid. Page 541*

I look upon every day to be lost, in which I do not make a new acquaintance.

> *Ibid. Page 579*

Life is very short, and very uncertain; let us spend it as well as we can.

> *Ibid. Page 583*

God bless you, my dear.

> *Ibid. Page 609 (His last words)*

GEORGE, LORD LYTTELTON
[1709–1773]

Women, like princes, find few real friends.

> *Advice to a Lady*

What is your sex's earliest, latest care,
Your heart's supreme ambition? To be fair.

> *Ibid.*

The lover in the husband may be lost.

> *Ibid.*

---

[1] I have not loved the world, nor the world me. — BYRON: *Childe Harold, Canto III* [1816], *St. 113*
See Emerson, pages 502b–503a.
[2] See Shakespeare, page 152b.
[3] A parody on "Who rules o'er freemen should himself be free," from BROOKE's *Gustavus Vasa* [1739].
[4] Carried about with every wind of doctrine. — *Ephesians, IV, 14*

Where none admire, 'tis useless to excel;
Where none are beaux, 'tis vain to be a belle.

> *Soliloquy on a Beauty in the Country*

ALICIA[1] RUTHERFORD COCKBURN
[1712–1794]

I've seen the smiling
Of Fortune beguiling,
I've felt all her favours and found her decay;
Sweet was her blessing,
Kind her caressing:
But now they are fled, are fled far away.

> *The Flowers of the Forest.*
> *Stanza 1*

GEORGE GRENVILLE
[1712–1770]

A wise government knows how to enforce with temper or to conciliate with dignity.

> *Speech against the Expulsion of John Wilkes, House of Parliament* [*1769*]

EDWARD MOORE
[1712–1757]

Can't I another's face commend,
And to her virtues be a friend,
But instantly your forehead lowers,
As if *her* merit lessen'd *yours?*

> *The Farmer, the Spaniel, and the Cat* [*1756*]

The maid who modestly conceals
Her beauties, while she hides, reveals;
Give but a glimpse, and fancy draws
Whate'er the Grecian Venus was.

> *The Spider and the Bee* [*1756*]

Time still, as he flies, brings increase to her truth,
And gives to her mind what he steals from her youth.

> *The Happy Marriage* [*1756*]

---

[1] Sometimes given as Alison.

JEAN JACQUES ROUSSEAU
[1712-1778]

Never exceed your rights, and they will soon become unlimited.

A Discourse on Political Economy [1758]

Money is the seed of money, and the first guinea is sometimes more difficult to acquire than the second million.

Ibid.

Man is born free, and everywhere he is in chains.[1]

Contrat Social [1762]. *Book I, Chap. 1*

The strongest is never strong enough to be always the master, unless he transforms strength into right, and obedience into duty.

Ibid. Chap. 3

The right of conquest has no foundation other than the right of the strongest.

Ibid. Chap. 4

The body politic, like the human body, begins to die from its birth, and bears in itself the causes of its destruction.

Ibid. Book III, Chap. 11

As soon as public service ceases to be the chief business of the citizens, and they would rather serve with their money than with their persons, the State is not far from its fall.

Ibid. Chap. 15

Good laws lead to the making of better ones; bad ones bring about worse. As soon as any man says of the affairs of the State, "What does it matter to me?" the State may be given up for lost.

Ibid.

God makes all things good; man meddles with them and they become evil.

Émile, ou De l'Éducation [1762]. *Book I*

I shall always maintain that whoso says in his heart, "There is no God,"

---

[1] L'homme est né libre, et partout il est dans les fers.

while he takes the name of God upon his lips, is either a liar or a madman.

Émile, ou De l'Éducation. Book I

People who know little are usually great talkers, while men who know much say little.

Ibid.

What wisdom can you find that is greater than kindness?

Ibid. Book II

The happiest is he who suffers least; the most miserable is he who enjoys least. Ever more sorrow than joy, — this is the lot of all of us.

Ibid.

Nature never deceives us; it is always we who deceive ourselves.

Ibid. Book III

There exists one book, which, to my taste, furnishes the happiest treatise of natural education. What then is this marvelous book? Is it Aristotle? Is it Pliny, is it Buffon? No, — it is *Robinson Crusoe*.

Ibid.

Self-love makes more libertines than love.

Ibid. Book IV

Provided a man is not mad, he can be cured of every folly but vanity.

Ibid.

A man says what he knows, a woman says what will please.

Ibid. Book V

Where is the man who owes nothing to the land in which he lives? Whatever that land may be, he owes to it the most precious thing possessed by man, the morality of his actions and the love of virtue.

Ibid.

I have entered on a performance which is without precedent, and will have no imitator. I propose to show my fellow-mortals a man in all the integrity of nature; and this man shall be myself.

Confessions [1782]. *Book I*

Remorse goes to sleep during a prosperous period and wakes up in adversity.

Ibid.

It is too difficult to think nobly when one only thinks to get a living.

Confessions. Book II

Hatred, as well as love, renders its votaries credulous.

Ibid. Book V

At length I recollected the thoughtless saying of a great princess, who, on being informed that the country people had no bread, replied, "Let them eat cake." [1]

Ibid. Book VI

The thirst after happiness is never extinguished in the heart of man.

Ibid. Book IX

He thinks like a philosopher, and acts like a king.

Ibid. Book XII

JOSIAH TUCKER, DEAN OF GLOUCESTER
[1712–1799]

What is true of a shopkeeper is true of a shopkeeping nation.[2]

Tract Against Going to War for the Sake of Trade [1763]

LAURENCE STERNE
[1713–1768]

Only the brave know how to forgive. . . . A coward never forgave; it is not in his nature.

Sermons. Vol. I [1760], *No. 12*

"Pray, my dear," quoth my mother, "have you not forgot to wind up the clock?" — "Good G—!" cried my father, making an exclamation, but taking care to moderate his voice at the same time, — "Did ever woman, since the creation of the world, interrupt a man with such a silly question?" [1]

Tristram Shandy. Book I [1760], *Chap. 1*

So long as a man rides his hobby-horse peaceably and quietly along the King's highway, and neither compels you or me to get up behind him, — pray, Sir, what have either you or I to do with it?

Ibid. Chap. 7

For every ten jokes, thou hast got an hundred enemies.

Ibid. Chap. 12

He was within a few hours of giving his enemies the slip for ever.

Ibid.

Whistled up to London, upon a Tom Fool's errand.

Ibid. Chap. 16

'Tis known by the name of perseverance in a good cause, — and of obstinacy in a bad one.

Ibid. Chap. 17

Persuasion hung upon his lips.

Ibid. Chap. 19

Digressions, incontestably, are the sunshine; — they are the life, the soul of reading; — take them out of this book for instance, — you might as well take the book along with them.

Ibid. Chap. 22

The history of a soldier's wound beguiles the pain of it.

Ibid. Chap. 25

The desire of knowledge, like the thirst of riches, increases ever with the acquisition of it.

Ibid. Book II [1760], *Chap. 3*

Writing, when properly managed (as you may be sure I think mine is) is but a different name for conversation.

Ibid. Chap. 11

Go, poor devil, get thee gone! Why should I hurt thee? This world surely

---

[1] "Qu'ils mangent de la brioche."
This remark is usually attributed to Marie Antoinette, after her arrival in France in 1770, but the sixth book of the *Confessions* was written two or three years before that date.

[2] See Adam Smith, page 352b.
Let Pitt then boast of his victory to his nation of shopkeepers. — BERTRAND BARÈRE: *Speech* [June 11, 1794]
But it may be said as a rule, that every Englishman in the Duke of Wellington's army paid his way. The remembrance of such a fact surely becomes a nation of shopkeepers. — THACKERAY: *Vanity Fair* [1847–1848], *Vol. I, Chap. 28*

[1] I wish either my father or my mother, or indeed both of them, as they were in duty both equally bound to it, had minded what they were about when they begot me. — *Ibid.*

is wide enough to hold both thee and me.[1]

> *Tristram Shandy. Book II,*
> *Chap. 12*

That's another story,[2] replied my father.

> *Ibid. Chap. 17*

Trust that man in nothing who has not a Conscience in everything.

> *Ibid. Chap. 17*

Good — bad — indifferent.

> *Ibid. Book III* [*1761–1762*],
> *Chap. 2*

"Our armies swore terribly in Flanders," cried my uncle Toby, — "but nothing to this."

> *Ibid. Chap. 11*

Of all the cants which are canted in this canting world, though the cant of hypocrites may be the worst, the cant of criticism is the most tormenting!

> *Ibid. Chap. 12*

When Ernulphus [3] cursed — no part escaped him.

> *Ibid.*

'Twould be as much as my life was worth.

> *Ibid. Chap. 20*

Before an affliction is digested, consolation ever comes too soon; and after it is digested, it comes too late.

> *Ibid. Chap. 29*

The sweat of a man's brows, and the exudations of a man's brains, are as much a man's own property as the breeches upon his backside.

> *Ibid. Chap. 34*

One of the two horns of my dilemma.

> *Ibid. Book IV* [*1761–1762*],
> *Chap. 26*

The feather put into his cap of having been abroad.

> *Ibid. Chap. 31*

---

[1] Uncle Toby to the fly.
[2] But that is another story. — KIPLING: *Plain Tales from the Hills* [1888], *Three and — an Extra*
[3] Ernulph or Arnulph [1040–1124], French Benedictine and Bishop of Rochester.

Now or never was the time.

> *Tristram Shandy. Book IV,*
> *Chap. 31*

Sciences may be learned by rote, but wisdom not.

> *Ibid. Book V* [*1761–1762*],
> *Chap. 32*

O blessed health! . . . thou art above all gold and treasure . . . He that has thee, has little more to wish for; — and he that is so wretched as to want thee, — wants everything with thee.

> *Ibid. Chap. 33*

The Accusing Spirit, which flew up to heaven's chancery with the oath, blushed as he gave it in; and the Recording Angel, as he wrote it down, dropped a tear upon the word and blotted it out forever.[1]

> *Ibid. Book VI* [*1761–1762*],
> *Chap. 8*

A man should know something of his own country, too, before he goes abroad.

> *Ibid. Book VII* [*1765*], *Chap. 2*

I am sick as a horse.

> *Ibid.*

Ho! 'tis the time of salads.

> *Ibid. Chap. 17*

"They order," said I, "this matter better in France."

> *A Sentimental Journey* [*1768*].
> *Line 1*

I pity the man who can travel from Dan to Beersheba and cry, " 'Tis all barren!"

> *Ibid. In the Street, Calais*

Tant pis and *tant mieux*, being two of the great hinges in French conversation, a stranger would do well to set himself right in the use of them before he gets to Paris.

> *Ibid. Montreuil*

Hail, ye small, sweet courtesies of life! for smooth do ye make the road of it.

> *Ibid. The Pulse, Paris*

---

[1] But sad as angels for the good man's sin,
Weep to record, and blush to give it in.
CAMPBELL: *Pleasures of Hope* [1799],
Part II, L. 357

"Disguise thyself as thou wilt, still, Slavery," said I, "still thou art a bitter draught."

A Sentimental Journey. The Passport, The Hotel at Paris

"God tempers the wind," said Maria, "to the shorn lamb." [1]

Ibid. Maria

WILLIAM SHENSTONE
[1714–1763]

Her cap, far whiter than the driven snow,
Emblems right meet of decency does yield.

*The Schoolmistress [1737].
Stanza 6*

WILLIAM WHITEHEAD
[1715–1785]

With indignation I survey
Such skill and judgment thrown away;
The time profusely squandered there
On vulgar arts beneath thy care,
If well employed at less expense
Had taught thee honour, virtue, sense.

*The Youth and the Philosopher
[1774]*

DAVID GARRICK
[1716–1779]

Let others hail the rising sun:
I bow to that whose course is run.

On the Death of Mr. Pelham

Heart of oak are our ships,
Heart of oak are our men,
 We always are ready,
 Steady, boys, steady,
We'll fight, and we'll conquer again and again.

Heart of Oak [Circa 1770]

Here lies Nolly Goldsmith, for shortness called Noll,
Who wrote like an angel, and talk'd like poor Poll.

Impromptu Epitaph on Goldsmith

[1] See Herbert, page 234b.

THOMAS GRAY
[1716–1771]

Ye distant spires, ye antique towers,
That crown the wat'ry glade.

*On a Distant Prospect of Eton
College [1742]. Stanza 1*

Still as they run they look behind,
They hear a voice in every wind,
And snatch a fearful joy.

Ibid. Stanza 4

Alas! regardless of their doom,
The little victims play;
No sense have they of ills to come,
Nor care beyond today.

Ibid. Stanza 6

Grim-visag'd comfortless Despair.

Ibid. Stanza 7

To each his suff'rings; all are men,
Condemn'd alike to groan, —
The tender for another's pain,
Th' unfeeling for his own.

Yet ah! why should they know their fate,
Since sorrow never comes too late,
And happiness too swiftly flies?
Thought would destroy their paradise.
No more; where ignorance is bliss,
'Tis folly to be wise. [1]

Ibid. Stanza 10

Daughter of Jove, relentless power,
Thou tamer of the human breast,
Whose iron scourge and torturing hour
The bad affright, afflict the best!

*Hymn to Adversity [1742].
Stanza 1*

What sorrow was, thou bad'st her know,
And from her own she learn'd to melt at others' woe.

Ibid. Stanza 2

What female heart can gold despise?
What cat's averse to fish?

*On the Death of a Favourite Cat
[1747]. Stanza 4*

A fav'rite has no friend!

Ibid. Stanza 6

As sickly plants betray a niggard earth,

[1] He that increaseth knowledge increaseth sorrow. — *Ecclesiastes, I, 18*

Whose barren bosom starves her gen'rous birth.
> *The Alliance of Education and Government* [Circa *1748*]

The social smile, the sympathetic tear.
> *Ibid.*

When love could teach a monarch to be wise,
And gospel-light first dawn'd from Bullen's eyes.[1]
> *Ibid.*

The curfew tolls the knell of parting day,
The lowing herd wind slowly o'er the lea,
The ploughman homeward plods his weary way,
And leaves the world to darkness and to me.
> *Elegy in a Country Churchyard* [*1750*]. *Stanza 1*

Now fades the glimmering landscape on the sight,
And all the air a solemn stillness holds,
Save where the beetle wheels his droning flight,
And drowsy tinklings lull the distant folds.
> *Ibid. Stanza 2*

Save that from yonder ivy-mantled tow'r
The moping owl does to the moon complain.
> *Ibid. Stanza 3*

Each in his narrow cell forever laid,
The rude forefathers of the hamlet sleep.
> *Ibid. Stanza 4*

Nor grandeur hear with a disdainful smile
The short and simple annals of the poor.
> *Ibid. Stanza 8*

The boast of heraldry, the pomp of pow'r,
And all that beauty, all that wealth e'er gave,
Awaits alike the inevitable hour:

The paths of glory lead but to the grave.
> *Elegy in a Country Churchyard.*
> *Stanza 9*

Where thro' the long-drawn aisle and fretted vault
The pealing anthem swells the note of praise.
> *Ibid. Stanza 10*

Can storied urn, or animated bust
Back to its mansion call the fleeting breath?
Can honour's voice provoke the silent dust,
Or flatt'ry soothe the dull cold ear of death?
> *Ibid. Stanza 11*

Hands, that the rod of empire might have sway'd,
Or waked to ecstasy the living lyre.
> *Ibid. Stanza 12*

But Knowledge to their eyes her ample page
Rich with the spoils of time did ne'er unroll; [1]
Chill penury repress'd their noble rage
And froze the genial current of the soul.
> *Ibid. Stanza 13*

Full many a gem of purest ray serene.[2]
The dark unfathom'd caves of ocean bear:
Full many a flower is born to blush unseen,
And waste its sweetness on the desert air.
> *Ibid. Stanza 14*

Some village Hampden, that with dauntless breast
The little tyrant of his fields withstood,
Some mute inglorious Milton here may rest,
Some Cromwell guiltless of his country's blood.
> *Ibid. Stanza 1*

---

[1] The monarch is Henry VIII; Anne Boleyn's name is here spelled (as it is in Shakespeare's *Henry VIII*) as it is pronounced.

[1] See Sir Thomas Browne, page 240a.
[2] Every single phrase is a string of perfect gems, of purest ray serene, strung together on a loose golden thread. — GEORGE DU MAURIER *Trilby, Part VI* [1894]

Forbade to wade through slaughter to
a throne,
And shut the gates of mercy on man-
kind.
Elegy in a Country Churchyard.
Stanza 17

Far from the madding crowd's ignoble
strife
Their sober wishes never learn'd to
stray;
Along the cool sequester'd vale of life
They kept the noiseless tenor of their
way.[1]
Ibid. Stanza 19

Implores the passing tribute of a sigh.
Ibid. Stanza 20

For who, to dumb forgetfulness a prey,
This pleasing anxious being e'er re-
sign'd,
Left the warm precincts of the cheer-
ful day,
Nor cast one longing ling'ring look
behind?
Ibid. Stanza 22

E'en from the tomb the voice of nature
cries,
E'en in our ashes live their wonted
fires.[2]
Ibid. Stanza 23

Mindful of th' unhonour'd dead.
Ibid. Stanza 24

Here rests his head upon the lap of
earth,
A youth to fortune and to fame unknown.
Fair Science frown'd not on his humble birth,
And Melancholy mark'd him for her
own.[3]
Ibid. The Epitaph, Stanza 1

Large was his bounty, and his soul sincere,
Heaven did a recompense as largely
send:
He gave to mis'ry (all he had) a tear,

He gained from Heav'n ('twas all he
wish'd) a friend.
Elegy in a Country Churchyard.
The Epitaph, Stanza 2

No farther seek his merits to disclose,
Or draw his frailties from their dread
abode,
(There they alike in trembling hope
repose),
The bosom of his Father and his God.
Ibid. Stanza 3

The meanest floweret of the vale,
The simplest note that swells the gale,
The common sun, the air, the skies,
To him are opening paradise.
Ode on the Pleasure Arising from
Vicissitude [1754]. Line 53

O'er her warm cheek and rising bosom
move
The bloom of young Desire and purple
light of Love.
The Progress of Poesy [1754].
I, 3, Line 16

Far from the sun and summer-gale,
In thy green lap was Nature's Darling[1]
laid.
Ibid. III, 1, Line 1

Or ope the sacred source of sympathetic tears.
Ibid. III, 1, Line 12

He[2] pass'd the flaming bounds of
place and time:
The living throne, the sapphire-blaze,
Where angels tremble while they gaze,
He saw; but, blasted with excess of
light,
Closed his eyes in endless night.
Ibid. 2, Line 4

Ruin seize thee, ruthless king,
Confusion on thy banners wait;
Though fann'd by Conquest's crimson
wing,
They mock the air with idle state.
The Bard [1759]. I, 1, Line 1

Weave the warp, and weave the woof,
The winding-sheet of Edward's race.
Give ample room and verge enough,
The characters of hell to trace.
Ibid. II, 1, Line 1

---

[1]   In sober state,
Through the sequestered vale of rural life,
The venerable patriarch guileless held
The tenor of his way.
     PORTEUS [1731–1808]: *Death, L. 108*
[2] See Chaucer, page 81a.
[3] See Walton, page 235a.

[1] Shakespeare.
[2] Milton.

Fair laughs the morn, and soft the
zephyr blows,
While proudly riding o'er the azure
realm,
In gallant trim the gilded vessel goes,
Youth on the prow, and Pleasure at
the helm;
Regardless of the sweeping whirlwind's
sway,
That, hush'd in grim repose, expects
his evening prey.
The Bard. II, 2, Line 9

Visions of glory, spare my aching
sight;
Ye unborn ages, crowd not on my soul!
Ibid. III, 1, Line 11

And truth severe, by fairy fiction drest.
Ibid. 3, Line 3

Now my weary lips I close;
Leave me, leave me to repose!
Descent of Odin [1761]. Line 71

Iron sleet of arrowy shower
Hurtles in the darken'd air.
The Fatal Sisters [1761]

Too poor for a bribe, and too proud to
importune;
He had not the method of making a
fortune.
On His Own Character [1761]

Sweet is the breath of vernal shower,
The bee's collected treasures sweet,
Sweet music's melting fall, but sweeter
yet
The still small voice of gratitude.
Ode for Music [1769]

HORACE WALPOLE
[1717–1797]

Harry Vane, Pulteney's toad-eater.
Letter to Sir Horace Mann [1742]
The world is a comedy to those that
think, a tragedy to those that feel.
Ibid. [1769]
A careless song, with a little non-
sense in it now and then, does not mis-
become a monarch.[1]
Ibid. [1774]

[1] A little nonsense now and then
Is relished by the wisest men.
ANONYMOUS

The whole [Scotch] nation hitherto
has been void of wit and humour, and
even incapable of relishing it.
Letter to Sir Horace Mann [1778]
Prognostics do not always prove
prophecies, — at least the wisest prophets make sure of the event first.
Letter to Thomas Walpole [1785]

SAMUEL FOOTE
[1720–1777]

Born in a cellar, and living in a garret.[1]
The Author. Act II

Matt Minikin won't set fire to the
Thames though he lives near the
Bridge.
Trip to Calais [1776]

So she went into the garden to cut
a cabbage leaf to make an apple pie;
and at the same time a great she-bear,
coming up the street, pops its head into
the shop. "What! no soap?" So he died,
and she very imprudently married the
barber; and there were present the
Picninnies, and the Joblillies, and the
Garyulies, and the Grand Panjandrum
himself, with the little round button at
top, and they all fell to playing the
game of catch as catch can, till the
gunpowder ran out at the heels of their
boots.
*Nonsense written to test the
boasted memory of Charles
Macklin, The Quarterly Review [1854], Credited to Foote
by MARIA EDGEWORTH in Harry
and Lucy, Concluded, Volume
II*

THOMAS GIBBONS
[1720–1785]

That man may last, but never lives,
Who much receives, but nothing gives;
Whom none can love, whom none can
thank, —
Creation's blot, creation's blank.
When Jesus Dwelt

[1] Born in the garret, in the kitchen bred. —
BYRON: *A Sketch* [1816]

DENNIS O'KELLY
[1720–1787]

It will be Eclipse first, the rest no-where.

Declaration at Epsom [May 3, 1769] when the great race horse, Eclipse, was to run his first race. Annals of Sporting, Volume II, Page 271

JOHN WOOLMAN
[1720–1772]

Though the change from day to night is by a motion so gradual as scarcely to be perceived, yet when night is come we behold it very different from the day; and thus as people become wise in their own eyes, and prudent in their own sight, customs rise up from the spirit of this world, and spread by little, and little, till a departure from the simplicity that there is in Christ becomes as distinguishable as light from darkness, to such who are crucified to the world.

Considerations on the True Harmony of Mankind

GILBERT WHITE
[1720–1793]

The tortoise, like other reptiles, has an arbitrary stomach as well as lungs; and can refrain from eating as well as breathing for a great part of the year.
Natural History of Selborne. April 12, 1772

WILLIAM COLLINS
[1721–1759]

Well may your hearts believe the truths I tell:
'Tis virtue makes the bliss, where'er we dwell.
Persian Eclogues [1742]. I, Selim, or The Shepherd's Moral, Line 5

Curst be the gold and silver which persuade

Weak men to follow far-fatiguing trade.
Persian Eclogues. II, Hassan, or The Camel Driver, Line 31

How sleep the brave, who sink to rest
By all their country's wishes bless'd!
Ode Written in the Year 1746. Stanza 1

By fairy hands their knell is rung;
By forms unseen their dirge is sung.
There Honour comes, a pilgrim grey,
To bless the turf that wraps their clay,
And Freedom shall awhile repair,
To dwell a weeping hermit there!
Ibid. Stanza 2

In numbers warmly pure and sweetly strong.
Ode to Simplicity [1747]. Stanza 1

Now air is hush'd, save where the weak-eyed bat,
With short shrill shriek, flits by on leathern wing,
Or where the beetle winds
His small but sullen horn.
Ode to Evening [1747]. Stanza 3

'Twas sad by fits, by starts 'twas wild.
The Passions [1747]. Line 28

With eyes up-rais'd, as one inspir'd,
Pale Melancholy sate retir'd;
And, from her wild, sequester'd seat,
In notes by distance made more sweet,
Pour'd thro' the mellow horn her pensive soul.
Ibid. Line 57

In hollow murmurs died away.
Ibid. Line 68

O Music, sphere-descended maid,
Friend of Pleasure, Wisdom's aid!
Ibid. Line 95

JEANNE, MARQUISE DE POMPADOUR
[1721–1764]

After us the deluge.[1]
Reputed reply to Louis XV [November 5, 1757] after the defeat of the French and Austrian armies by Frederick the Great in the battle of Rossbach

[1] Après nous le déluge.
The attribution to Mme. de Pompadour is

TOBIAS SMOLLETT
[1721–1771]

He was formed for the ruin of our sex.
Roderick Random [1748]. Chap. 22

Thy fatal shafts unerring move,
I bow before thine altar, Love!
Ibid. Chap. 40

CHRISTOPHER SMART
[1722–1770]

O servant of God's holiest charge,
The minister of praise at large.
A Song to David. Stanza 3

SIR WILLIAM BLACKSTONE
[1723–1780]

The royal navy of England hath ever been its greatest defence and ornament; it is its ancient and natural strength, — the floating bulwark of our island.
Commentaries [1765–1769].
Vol. I, Book I, Chap. XIII

Time whereof the memory of man runneth not to the contrary.[1]
Ibid. Chap. XVIII

ADAM SMITH
[1723–1790]

The real price of everything, what everything really costs to the man who wants to acquire it, is the toil and trouble of acquiring it.
Wealth of Nations [1776]

To found a great empire for the sole purpose of raising up a people of customers may at first sight appear a project fit only for a nation of shopkeepers. It is, however, a project altogether unfit for a nation of shopkeepers; but extremely fit for a nation whose

made by Després in *Mémoires de Madame de Hausset,* also by Sainte-Beuve and La Tour, but Larousse in *Fleurs Historiques* attributes the saying to the King. It was original with neither, for it is an old French proverb.

[1] The favorite phrase of their law is "a custom whereof the memory of man runneth not back to the contrary." — Emerson: *English Traits* [1856]

Government is influenced by shopkeepers.[1]
Wealth of Nations

JOHN HOME
[1724–1808]

In the first days
Of my distracting grief, I found myself
As women wish to be who love their lords.
Douglas [1756]. Act I, Sc. 1

I'll woo her as the lion woos his brides.
Ibid.

My name is Norval; on the Grampian hills
My father feeds his flocks; a frugal swain,
Whose constant cares were to increase his store,
And keep his only son, myself, at home.
Ibid. Act III, Sc. 1

Like Douglas conquer, or like Douglas die.
Ibid. Act V, Sc. 1

RICHARD GIFFORD
[1725–1807]

Verse sweetens toil, however rude the sound;
She feels no biting pang the while she sings;
Nor, as she turns the giddy wheel around,
Revolves the sad vicissitudes of things.[2]
Contemplation

LOGAN, MINGO CHIEF
[1725–1780]

I appeal to any white man to say if he ever entered Logan's cabin hungry and he gave him not meat; if ever he came cold and naked and he clothed him not?
Message to Lord Dunmore, Governor of Virginia [November 11, 1774], in Notes on Virginia, by Thomas Jefferson

[1] See Josiah Tucker, page 345a.
[2] See Bacon, page 121b.

JAMES OTIS
[1725–1783]

An act against the constitution is void.

Argument Against the Writs of Assistance [1] [1761]

Taxation without representation is tyranny.[2]

Attributed [1763]

WILLIAM PRESCOTT
[1726–1795]

Don't fire until you see the whites of their eyes.[3]

At Bunker Hill, June 17, 1775

OLIVER GOLDSMITH
[1728–1774]

One writer, for instance, excels at a plan or a title-page, another works away the body of the book, and a third is a dab at an index.

The Bee. No. 1, October 6, 1759

What cities, as great as this, have . . . promised themselves immortality! Posterity can hardly trace the situation of some. The sorrowful traveller wanders over the awful ruins of others. . . . Here stood their citadel, but now grown over with weeds; there their senate-house, but now the haunt of every noxious reptile; temples and theatres stood here, now only an undistinguished heap of ruins.

Ibid. No. 4, October 27, 1759

Good people all, with one accord,
Lament for Madam Blaize,

---

[1] In John Adams, *Works* [1850–1856], *Vol. II, P. 522.*

[2] This maxim was the guide and watchword of all the friends of liberty. Otis actually said: "No parts of His Majesty's dominions can be taxed without their consent." *Rights of the Colonies* [1764], *P. 64.*

[3] Silent till you see the whites of their eyes. — Prince Charles of Prussia, at Jagerndorf, May 23, 1745

By push of bayonets; no firing till you see the whites of their eyes. — Frederick the Great, at Prague, May 6, 1757

Who never wanted a good word —
From those who spoke her praise.

Elegy on Mrs. Mary Blaize
[1759]. Stanza 1

A night-cap deck'd his brows instead of bay,
A cap by night, a stocking all the day.

Description of an Author's Bed-chamber [1760]

That strain once more; it bids remembrance rise.

The Captivity, An Oratorio
[1764]. Act I

O Memory! thou fond deceiver.

Ibid.

To the last moment of his breath,
On hope the wretch relies;
And even the pang preceding death
Bids expectation rise.[1]

Ibid. Act II

Hope, like the gleaming taper's light,
Adorns and cheers our way;
And still, as darker grows the night,
Emits a brighter ray.

Ibid.

Remote, unfriended, melancholy, slow,
Or by the lazy Scheldt, or wandering Po.

The Traveller [1764]. *Line 1*

Where'er I roam, whatever realms to see,
My heart untravell'd fondly turns to thee;
Still to my brother turns, with ceaseless pain,
And drags at each remove a lengthening chain.

Ibid. Line 7

Such is the patriot's boast, where'er we roam,
His first, best country ever is, at home.

Ibid. Line 73

Where wealth and freedom reign contentment fails,
And honour sinks where commerce long prevails.

Ibid. Line 91

Man seems the only growth that dwindles here.[2]

Ibid. Line 126

---

[1] See Cicero, page 34a.
[2] Italy.

By sports like these are all their cares
   beguil'd,
The sports of children satisfy the child.
      The Traveller. Line 153

But winter ling'ring chills the lap of
   May.
      Ibid. Line 172

Cheerful at morn, he [1] wakes from short
   repose,
Breasts the keen air, and carols as he
   goes.
      Ibid. Line 185

So the loud torrent, and the whirlwind's roar,
But bind him to his native mountains
   more.
      Ibid. Line 217

They please, are pleas'd, they give to
   get esteem,
Till, seeming blest, they grow to what
   they seem.[2]
      Ibid. Line 266

To men of other minds my fancy flies,
Embosom'd in the deep where Holland
   lies.
Methinks her patient sons before me
   stand,
Where the broad ocean leans against
   the land.
      Ibid. Line 281

Pride in their port, defiance in their
   eye,
I see the lords of humankind [3] pass by.
      Ibid. Line 327

The land of scholars, and the nurse of
   arms.[4]
      Ibid. Line 356

For just experience tells, in every soil,
That those that think must govern
   those that toil.
      Ibid. Line 372

Laws grind the poor, and rich men rule
   the law.
      Ibid. Line 386

Vain, very vain, my weary search to
   find

---

[1] The Swiss peasant.
[2] The character of the French.
[3] The British.
[4] England.

That bliss which only centres in the
   mind.
      The Traveller. Line 423

I . . . chose my wife, as she did her
wedding-gown, not for a fine glossy
surface, but such qualities as would
wear well.
      The Vicar of Wakefield [1766].
          Chap. 1

We sometimes had those little rubs
which Providence sends to enhance the
value of its favours.
      Ibid.

Handsome is that handsome does.[1]
      Ibid.

That virtue which requires to be
ever guarded is scarce worth the sen-
tinel.
      Ibid. Chap. 5

I find you want me to furnish you
with argument and intellects too.
      Ibid. Chap. 7

Man wants but little here below,
Nor wants that little long.[2]
      *Ibid. Chap. 8, The Hermit (Edwin
        and Angelina), Stanza 8*

She was all of a muck of sweat.
      Ibid. Chap. 9

They would talk of nothing but high
life, and high-lived company, with
other fashionable topics, such as pictures, taste, Shakespeare, and the musical glasses.[3]
      Ibid.

Conscience is a coward, and those
faults it has not strength enough to prevent it seldom has justice enough to
accuse.
      Ibid. Chap. 13

A kind and gentle heart he had,
To comfort friends and foes;
The naked every day he clad
When he put on his clothes.
      *Ibid. Chap. 17, An Elegy on the
        Death of a Mad Dog, Stanza 3*

---

[1] See Chaucer, page 81b.
[2] See Edward Young, page 306a, and
Oliver Wendell Holmes, page 536a.
[3] "Shall we talk about Shakespeare?" he
asked sarcastically. "Or the musical glasses?"
— ALDOUS HUXLEY: *Point Counter Point*
[1928], *Chap. 21*

And in that town a dog was found,
As many dogs there be,
Both mongrel, puppy, whelp, and
  hound,
And curs of low degree.

> *The Vicar of Wakefield. Chap.
> 17, An Elegy on the Death of a
> Mad Dog, Stanza 4*

The dog, to gain some private ends,
Went mad, and bit the man.

> *Ibid. Stanza 5*

The man recovered of the bite —
The dog it was that died.

> *Ibid. Stanza 8*

When lovely woman stoops to folly,
And finds too late that men betray,
What charm can soothe her melan-
  choly?
What art can wash her guilt away? [1]

> *Ibid. Chap. 24, Song, Stanza 1*

The only art her guilt to cover,
To hide her shame from every eye,
To give repentance to her lover,
And wring his bosom, is — to die.

> *Ibid. Stanza 2*

To what a fortuitous concurrence do
we not owe every pleasure and convenience of our lives.

> *Ibid. Chap. 31*

This same philosophy is a good horse
in the stable, but an arrant jade on a
journey. [2]

> *The Good-Natur'd Man [1768].*
> *Act I*

He calls his extravagance, generosity; and his trusting everybody, universal benevolence.

> *Ibid.*

All his faults are such that one loves
him still the better for them.

> *Ibid.*

Friendship is a disinterested commerce between equals; love, an abject
intercourse between tyrants and slaves.

> *Ibid.*

Silence gives consent.

> *Ibid. Act II*

Measures, not men, have always been
my mark. [1]

> *The Good-Natur'd Man. Act II*

Sweet Auburn! loveliest village of the
plain.

> *The Deserted Village [1770].*
> *Line 1*

The hawthorn bush, with seats beneath
  the shade,
For talking age and whispering lovers
  made.

> *Ibid. Line 13*

The bashful virgin's sidelong looks of
love.

> *Ibid. Line 29*

Ill fares the land, to hastening ills a
  prey,
Where wealth accumulates, and men
  decay;
Princes and lords may flourish or may
  fade;
A breath can make them, as a breath
  has made;
But a bold peasantry, their country's
  pride,
When once destroy'd, can never be supplied.

> *Ibid. Line 51*

His best companions, innocence and
  health;
And his best riches, ignorance of
  wealth.

> *Ibid. Line 61*

How happy he who crowns in shades
  like these,
A youth of labour with an age of ease!

> *Ibid. Line 99*

Bends to the grave with unperceived
  decay,
While resignation gently slopes the
  way,
And all his prospects brightening to
  the last,
His heaven commences ere the world
  be past.

> *Ibid. Line 109*

The watch-dog's voice that bay'd the
  whispering wind,

---

[1] See T. S. Eliot, page 944a.
[2] See La Rochefoucauld, page 264b.

[1] See Chesterfield, page 323a, and Burke,
page 359a.

And the loud laugh that spoke the vacant mind.[1]

> *The Deserted Village. Line 121*

A man he was to all the country dear,
And passing rich with forty pounds a year.

> *Ibid. Line 141*

Careless their merits or their faults to scan,
His pity gave ere charity began.
Thus to relieve the wretched was his pride,
And even his failings lean'd to Virtue's side.

> *Ibid. Line 161*

And, as a bird each fond endearment tries
To tempt its new-fledg'd offspring to the skies,
He tried each art, reprov'd each dull delay,
Allur'd to brighter worlds, and led the way.

> *Ibid. Line 167*

Truth from his lips prevail'd with double sway,
And fools, who came to scoff, remain'd to pray.[2]

> *Ibid. Line 179*

Even children follow'd with endearing wile,
And pluck'd his gown, to share the good man's smile.

> *Ibid. Line 183*

A man severe he was, and stern to view;
I knew him well, and every truant knew;
Well had the boding tremblers learn'd to trace
The day's disasters in his morning face;
Full well they laugh'd, with counter-feited glee,
At all his jokes, for many a joke had he;

Full well the busy whisper, circling round,
Convey'd the dismal tidings when he frown'd.
Yet was he kind; or if severe in aught,
The love he bore to learning was in fault;
The village all declar'd how much he knew;
'Twas certain he could write, and cipher too.

> *The Deserted Village. Line 197*

In arguing too, the parson own'd his skill,
For e'en though vanquished, he could argue still;
While words of learned length and thundering sound
Amaz'd the gazing rustics rang'd around,
And still they gaz'd, and still the wonder grew,
That one small head could carry all he knew.

> *Ibid. Line 209*

Where village statesmen talk'd with looks profound,
And news much older than their ale went round.

> *Ibid. Line 223*

The whitewash'd wall, the nicely sanded floor,
The varnish'd clock that click'd behind the door;
The chest contriv'd a double debt to pay, —
A bed by night, a chest of drawers by day.[1]

> *Ibid. Line 227*

The twelve good rules, the royal game of goose.[2]

> *Ibid. Line 232*

---

[1] Frequent and loud laughter is the characteristic of folly and ill manners: it is the manner in which the mob express their silly joy at silly things, and they call it being merry. In my mind there is nothing so illiberal and so ill-bred as audible laughter. — LORD CHESTERFIELD: *Letters* [March 9, 1748]

[2] See Dryden, page 279b.

[1] A cap by night, a stocking all the day. — *Description of an Author's Bed-chamber.* See page 353b.

[2] The twelve good rules were ascribed to Charles I: (1) urge no healths; (2) profane no divine ordinances; (3) touch no state matters; (4) reveal no secrets; (5) pick no quarrels; (6) make no comparisons; (7) maintain no ill opinions; (8) keep no bad company; (9) encourage no vice; (10) make no long

To me more dear, congenial to my
heart,
One native charm, than all the gloss
of art.
> *The Deserted Village. Line 253*

And, ev'n while fashion's brightest arts
decoy,
The heart distrusting asks, if this be
joy.
> *Ibid. Line 263*

Her modest looks the cottage might
adorn,
Sweet as the primrose peeps beneath
the thorn.
> *Ibid. Line 329*

In all the silent manliness of grief.
> *Ibid. Line 384*

O Luxury! thou curst by Heaven's decree!
> *Ibid. Line 385*

Thou source of all my bliss and all my
woe,
That found'st me poor at first, and
keep'st me so.
> *Ibid. Line 413*

The very pink of perfection.
> *She Stoops to Conquer* [*1773*].
> *Act I*

Let schoolmasters puzzle their brain,
With grammar, and nonsense, and
learning;
Good liquor, I stoutly maintain,
Gives genius a better discerning.
> *Ibid.*

The genteel thing is the genteel thing
at any time. If so be that a gentleman
bees in a concatenation accordingly.
> *Ibid.*

I'll be with you in the squeezing of a
lemon.
> *Ibid.*

A modest woman, dressed out in all
her finery, is the most tremendous object of the whole creation.
> *Ibid. Act II*

This is Liberty Hall.
> *She Stoops to Conquer. Act II*

They liked the book the better the
more it made them cry.
> *Ibid.*

Ask me no questions, and I'll tell you
no fibs.[1]
> *Ibid. Act III*

The very pink of courtesy and circumspection.
> *Ibid. Act IV*

Our Garrick's a salad; for in him we
see
Oil, vinegar, sugar, and saltness agree!
> *Retaliation* [*1774*]. *Line 11*

Here lies our good Edmund,[2] whose
genius was such,
We scarcely can praise it, or blame it
too much;
Who, born for the universe, narrow'd
his mind,
And to party gave up what was meant
for mankind . . .
Who, too deep for his hearers, still went
on refining,
And thought of convincing, while they
thought of dining:
Though equal to all things, for all
things unfit;
Too nice for a statesman, too proud for
a wit.
> *Ibid. Line 29*

His conduct still right, with his argument wrong.
> *Ibid. Line 46*

A flattering painter,[3] who made it his
care
To draw men as they ought to be, not
as they are.
> *Ibid. Line 63*

Here lies David Garrick, describe me,
who can,
An abridgment of all that was pleasant
in man.
> *Ibid. Line 93*

---

meals; (11) repeat no grievances; (12) lay
no wagers.
Goose: A game played with counters on a
board divided into compartments, in some of
which a goose was depicted. — *Oxford English Dictionary*

[1] Them that asks no questions isn't told a
lie. — KIPLING [1865–1936]: *A Smuggler's
Song, St. 6*
[2] Edmund Burke.
[3] Richard Cumberland [1732–1811], author of such sentimental comedies as *The
West Indian* and *The Brothers.*

As a wit, if not first, in the very first line.
Retaliation. Line 96

On the stage he was natural, simple, affecting;
'Twas only that when he was off he was acting.
Ibid. Line 101

He cast off his friends, as a huntsman his pack,
For he knew when he pleas'd he could whistle them back.
Ibid. Line 107

Who pepper'd the highest was surest to please.
Ibid. Line 112

When they talk'd of their Raphaels, Correggios, and stuff,
He shifted his trumpet and only took snuff.[1]
Ibid. Line 145

Such dainties to them, their health it might hurt;
It's like sending them ruffles, when wanting a shirt.[2]
The Haunch of Venison [1776]

[To Dr. Johnson] If you were to make little fishes talk, they would talk like whales.
Boswell's *Life of Dr. Johnson* [*1791*]. *Vol. I, Page 466, Everyman Edition*

I consider an author's literary reputation to be alive only while his name will insure a good price for his copy from the bookseller's.
Ibid. Page 468

There is no arguing with Johnson: for if his pistol misses fire, he knocks you down with the butt end of it.
Ibid. Vol. II, Page 509

THOMAS WARTON
[1728–1790]

All-powerful Ale! whose sorrow-soothing sweets

[1] Sir Joshua Reynolds, who was exceedingly deaf.
[2] See Tom Brown, page 293a.

Oft I repeat in vacant afternoon.
A Panegyric on Oxford Ale [1]

With British ale improving British worth.
Ibid.

Thus too, the matchless bard, whose lay resounds
The Splendid Shilling's praise, in nightly gloom
Of lonesome garret, pined for cheerful ale.[2]
Ibid.

Nor rough, nor barren, are the winding ways
Of hoar antiquity, but strewn with flowers.
Written on a Blank Leaf of
Dugdale's *Monasticon* [*1777*]

JOHN STARK
[1728–1822]

There, my boys, are your enemies, redcoats and Tories. You must beat them — or Molly Stark is a widow tonight.
At the Battle of Bennington,
August 16, 1777

JOHN PARKER
[1729–1775]

Stand your ground. Don't fire unless fired upon; but if they mean to have a war, let it begin here!
To his Minute Men at Lexington,
April 19, 1775

EDMUND BURKE
[1729–1797]

The writers against religion, whilst they oppose every system, are wisely

[1] From *The Oxford Sausage* [1764], a famous miscellany of Oxford rhymes and satires, reprinted in several subsequent editions.
[2] Happy the man who, void of care and strife,
In silken or in leathern purse retains
A splendid shilling. He nor hears with pain
New oysters cried, nor sighs for cheerful ale.
John Philips: *The Splendid Shilling* [1701]

careful never to set up any of their own.

A Vindication of Natural Society [*1756*]

I am convinced that we have a degree of delight, and that no small one, in the real misfortunes and pains of others.[1]

On the Sublime and Beautiful [*1756*]. *Sect. XIV*

Custom reconciles us to everything.
Ibid. Sect. XVIII

There is, however, a limit at which forbearance ceases to be a virtue.

Observations on a Late Publication on the Present State of the Nation [*1769*]

The wisdom of our ancestors.[2]
Ibid.

When bad men combine, the good must associate; else they will fall one by one, an unpitied sacrifice in a contemptible struggle.

Thoughts on the Cause of the Present Discontents [*April 23, 1770*]

Of this stamp is the cant of, Not men, but measures;[3] a sort of charm by which many people get loose from every honourable engagement.
Ibid.

So to be patriots as not to forget we are gentlemen.
Ibid.

Public life is a situation of power and energy; he trespasses against his duty who sleeps upon his watch, as well as he that goes over to the enemy.
Ibid.

Reflect how you are to govern a people who think they ought to be free, and think they are not. Your scheme yields no revenue; it yields nothing but discontent, disorder, disobedience; and such is the state of America, that after wading up to your eyes in blood, you could only end just where you begun; that is, to tax where no revenue is to be

found, to — my voice fails me; my inclination indeed carries me no farther — all is confusion beyond it.

First Speech on Conciliation with America. American Taxation [*April 19, 1774*]

It ought to be the happiness and glory of a representative to live in the strictest union, the closest correspondence, and the most unreserved communication with his constituents. Their wishes ought to have great weight with him; their opinion high respect; their business unremitted attention. It is his duty to sacrifice his repose, his pleasures, his satisfaction, to theirs; and above all, ever, and in all cases, to prefer their interests to his own.

Speech to the Electors of Bristol [*November 3, 1774*]

Your representative owes you, not his industry only, but his judgment; and he betrays instead of serving you if he sacrifices it to your opinion.
Ibid.

The concessions of the weak are the concessions of fear.

Second Speech on Conciliation with America. The Thirteen Resolutions [*March 22, 1775*]

There is America, which at this day serves for little more than to amuse you with stories of savage men and uncouth manners, yet shall, before you taste of death, show itself equal to the whole of that commerce which now attracts the envy of the world.
Ibid.

When we speak of the commerce with our colonies, fiction lags after truth, invention is unfruitful, and imagination cold and barren.
Ibid.

A people who are still, as it were, but in the gristle, and not yet hardened into the bone of manhood.
Ibid.

Through a wise and salutary neglect [of the colonies], a generous nature has been suffered to take her own way to perfection; when I reflect upon these effects, when I see how profitable they

---

[1] See La Rochefoucauld, page 266a.
[2] Also in the *Discussion on the Traitorous Correspondence Bill* [1793].
[3] See Goldsmith, page 355b.

have been to us, I feel all the pride of power sink and all presumption in the wisdom of human contrivances melt and die away within me. My rigour relents. I pardon something to the spirit of liberty.

Second Speech on Conciliation with America. The Thirteen Resolutions

The use of force alone is but *temporary*. It may subdue for a moment; but it does not remove the necessity of subduing again: and a nation is not governed, which is perpetually to be conquered.

Ibid.

Abstract liberty, like other mere abstractions, is not to be found.

Ibid.

The religion most prevalent in our northern colonies is a refinement on the principles of resistance: it is the dissidence of dissent, and the protestantism of the Protestant religion.

Ibid.

In no country [America] perhaps in the world is law so general a study. . . . This study renders men acute, inquisitive, dexterous, prompt in attack, ready in defence, full of resources. . . . They augur misgovernment at a distance, and snuff the approach of tyranny in every tainted breeze.

Ibid.

I do not know the method of drawing up an indictment against an whole people.

Ibid.

It is not, what a lawyer tells me I *may* do; but what humanity, reason, and justice, tell me I ought to do.

Ibid.

The march of the human mind is slow.

Ibid.

Freedom and not servitude is the cure of anarchy; as religion, and not atheism, is the true remedy for superstition.

Ibid.

All government — indeed, every human benefit and enjoyment, every vir-

tue and every prudent act — is founded on compromise and barter.

Second Speech on Conciliation with America. The Thirteen Resolutions

Instead of a standing revenue, you will have therefore a perpetual quarrel.

Ibid.

Slavery they can have anywhere. It is a weed that grows in every soil.

Ibid.

Deny them this participation of freedom, and you break that sole bond, which originally made, and must still preserve the unity of the empire.

Ibid.

It is the love of the British people; it is their attachment to their government, from the sense of the deep stake they have in such a glorious institution, which gives you both your army and your navy, and infuses into both that liberal obedience, without which your army would be a base rabble, and your navy nothing but rotten timber.

Ibid.

Magnanimity in politics is not seldom the truest wisdom; and a great empire and little minds go ill together.

Ibid.

By adverting to the dignity of this high calling, our ancestors have turned a savage wilderness into a glorious empire: and have made the most extensive, and the only honourable conquests, not by destroying, but by promoting the wealth, the number, the happiness of the human race.

Ibid.

He was not merely a chip of the old block, but the old block itself.

On Pitt's First Speech [February 26, 1781]. From WRAX-ALL'S *Memoirs, First Series, Vol. I, Page 342*

The people never give up their liberties but under some delusion.

Speech at County Meeting of Buckinghamshire [1784]

There never was a bad man that had ability for good service.

Speech in Opening the Impeachment of Warren Hastings [*1788*]

They made and recorded a sort of institute and digest of anarchy, called the Rights of Man.

On the Army Estimates [*1790*]

People will not look forward to posterity who never look backward to their ancestors.[1]

Reflections on the Revolution in France [*1790*]

You had that action and counteraction which, in the natural and in the political world, from the reciprocal struggle of discordant powers draws out the harmony of the universe.

Ibid.

The unbought grace of life, the cheap defence of nations, the nurse of manly sentiment and heroic enterprise is gone.

Ibid.

That chastity of honour which felt a stain like a wound.

Ibid.

Vice itself lost half its evil by losing all its grossness.

Ibid.

Kings will be tyrants from policy, when subjects are rebels from principle.

Ibid.

Learning will be cast into the mire and trodden down under the hoofs of a swinish multitude.

Ibid.

Because half-a-dozen grasshoppers under a fern make the field ring with their importunate chink, whilst thousands of great cattle, reposed beneath the shadow of the British oak, chew the cud and are silent, pray do not imagine that those who make the noise are the only inhabitants of the field; that of course they are many in number; or that, after all, they are other than the little shrivelled, meagre, hopping, though loud and troublesome insects of the hour.

Reflections on the Revolution in France

In their nomination to office they will not appoint to the exercise of authority as to a pitiful job, but as to a holy function.

Ibid.

He that wrestles with us strengthens our nerves and sharpens our skill. Our antagonist is our helper.

Ibid.

To execute laws is a royal office; to execute orders is not to be a king. However, a political executive magistracy, though merely such, is a great trust.[1]

Ibid.

You can never plan the future by the past.[2]

Letter to a Member of the National Assembly [*1791*]

The cold neutrality of an impartial judge.

Preface to Brissot's Address [*1794*]

All men that are ruined, are ruined on the side of their natural propensities.

On a Regicide Peace [*1796*]

Example is the school of mankind, and they will learn at no other.

Ibid.

Mere parsimony is not economy. . . . Expense, and great expense, may be an essential part of true economy.

Letter to a Noble Lord [*1796*]

Economy is a distributive virtue, and consists not in saving but in selection. Parsimony requires no providence, no sagacity, no powers of combination, no comparison, no judgment.

Ibid.

I would rather sleep in the southern corner of a little country churchyard than in the tomb of the Capulets.

Letter to Matthew Smith

And having looked to Government

---

[1] The Democratic Party is like a mule — without pride of ancestry or hope of posterity. — IGNATIUS DONNELLY [1831–1901]: *Speech in the Minnesota Legislature*

[1] See Mathew Henry, page 293a, Jefferson, page 375a, Clay, page 433b, and Calhoun, page 442a.

[2] See Patrick Henry, page 368b.

for bread, on the very first scarcity they will turn and bite the hand that fed them.

Thoughts and Details on Scarcity [*1800*]

JOHN SCOTT
[1730–1783]

I hate that drum's discordant sound,
Parading round, and round, and round:
To me it talks of ravaged plains,
And burning towns, and ruined swains,
And mangled limbs, and dying groans,
And widows' tears, and orphans' moans;
And all that Misery's hand bestows
To fill the catalogue of human woes.

I Hate That Drum's Discordant Sound. Stanza 2

JOSIAH WEDGWOOD
[1730–1795]

Am I not a man and brother?
On a Medallion [1] [*1787*]

CHARLES CHURCHILL
[1731–1764]

He mouths a sentence as curs mouth a bone.

The Rosciad [*1761*]. *Line 322*

But, spite of all the criticising elves,
Those who would make us feel — must feel themselves.[2]

Ibid. Line 961

Apt alliteration's artful aid.

The Prophecy of Famine [*1763*]. *Line 86*

There webs were spread of more than common size,
And half-starved spiders prey'd on half-starved flies.

Ibid. Line 327

[1] Representing a Negro in chains, with one knee on the ground and both hands lifted up to heaven. This was adopted as a seal by the Anti-Slavery Society of London.

[2]   Si vis me flere, dolendum est
    Primum ipsi tibi
(If you wish me to weep, you yourself must first feel grief).
        HORACE [65–8 B.C.]: *Ars Poetica, L. 102*

With curious art the brain, too finely wrought,
Preys on herself, and is destroyed by thought.

Epistle to William Hogarth [*1763*]. *Line 645*

Men the most infamous are fond of fame,
And those who fear not guilt yet start at shame.

The Author [*1763*]. *Line 233*

Be England what she will,
With all her faults she is my country still.[1]

The Farewell. Line 27

WILLIAM COWPER
[1731–1800]

What peaceful hours I once enjoy'd!
How sweet their memory still!
But they have left an aching void
The world can never fill.

Olney Hymns [*1779*]. *Walking with God*

God moves in a mysterious way
His wonders to perform;
He plants his footsteps in the sea
And rides upon the storm.

Ibid. Light Shining out of Darkness

Behind a frowning providence
He hides a shining face.

Ibid.

Happiness depends, as Nature shows,
Less on exterior things than most suppose.

Table Talk [*1782*]. *Line 246*

Freedom has a thousand charms to show,

[1] England, with all thy faults I love thee still,
    My country!
        COWPER: *The Task* [1784], *Book II, The Timepiece, L. 206*
Our country! In her intercourse with foreign nations may she always be in the right; but our country, right or wrong. — STEPHEN DECATUR: *Toast given at Norfolk* [April, 1816]
I hope to find my country in the right: however, I will stand by her, right or wrong. — JOHN JORDAN CRITTENDEN [1787–1863]: *On the Mexican War*

That slaves, howe'er contented, never
know.
Table Talk. Line 260
Manner is all in all, whate'er is writ,
The substitute for genius, sense, and
wit.
Ibid. Line 542
Low ambition and the thirst of praise.[1]
Ibid. Line 591
Made poetry a mere mechanic art.
Ibid. Line 654
Lights of the world, and stars of human
race.
The Progress of Error [*1782*].
Line 97
How much a dunce that has been sent
to roam
Excels a dunce that has been kept at
home!
Ibid. Line 415
A fool must now and then be right by
chance.
Conversation [*1782*]. *Line 96*
He would not, with a peremptory tone,
Assert the nose upon his face his own.
Ibid. Line 121
A moral, sensible, and well-bred man
Will not affront me, — and no other
can.
Ibid. Line 193
Pernicious weed! [2] whose scent the fair
annoys,
Unfriendly to society's chief joys:
Thy worst effect is banishing for hours
The sex whose presence civilizes ours.
Ibid. Line 251
I cannot talk with civet in the room,
A fine puss-gentleman that's all per-
fume.
Ibid. Line 283
Our wasted oil unprofitably burns,
Like hidden lamps in old sepulchral
urns.
Ibid. Line 357
A business with an income at its heels
Furnishes always oil for its own wheels.
Retirement [*1782*]. *Line 615*
Absence of occupation is not rest,[3]

A mind quite vacant is a mind dis-
tress'd.
Retirement. Line 623
An idler is a watch that wants both
hands,
As useless if it goes as if it stands.
Ibid. Line 681
Built God a church, and laugh'd His
word to scorn.[1]
Ibid. Line 688
Philologists, who chase
A panting syllable through time and
space,
Start it at home, and hunt it in the
dark
To Gaul, to Greece, and into Noah's
ark.
Ibid. Line 691
I praise the Frenchman,[2] his remark
was shrewd, —
How sweet, how passing sweet, is soli-
tude!
But grant me still a friend in my retreat,
Whom I may whisper, Solitude is sweet.
Ibid. Line 739
I am monarch of all I survey,
My right there is none to dispute.
*Verses Supposed to be Written
by Alexander Selkirk* [*1782*].
Stanza 1
O Solitude! where are the charms
That sages have seen in thy face?
Ibid.
How fleet is a glance of the mind!
Compared with the speed of its flight
The tempest itself lags behind,
And the swift-winged arrows of light.
Ibid. Stanza 6
There goes the parson, O illustrious
spark!
And there, scarce less illustrious, goes
the clerk.
*On Observing Some Names of
Little Note* [*1782*]
That though on pleasure she was bent,
She had a frugal mind.
History of John Gilpin [*1785*].
Stanza 8

[1] See Pope, page 315b.
[2] Tobacco.
[3] See John Sullivan Dwight, page 583a.

[1] Voltaire, who built a church at Ferney
[1760–1761], with the inscription "Deo erexit
Voltaire."
[2] La Bruyère.

A hat not much the worse for wear.
History of John Gilpin. Stanza 46

Now let us sing, Long live the king,
And Gilpin, Long live he;
And when he next doth ride abroad,
May I be there to see!
Ibid. Stanza 63

God made the country, and man made
the town.[1]
The Task [1785]. *Book I,*
The Sofa, Line 749

Oh for a lodge in some vast wilderness,[2]
Some boundless contiguity of shade,
Where rumour of oppression and de-
ceit,
Of unsuccessful or successful war,
Might never reach me more.
Ibid. Book II, The Timepiece,
Line 1

Mountains interposed
Make enemies of nations, who had else
Like kindred drops been mingled into
one.
Ibid. Line 17

Slaves cannot breathe in England; if
their lungs
Receive our air, that moment they are
free!
They touch our country, and their
shackles fall.
Ibid. Line 40

Presume to lay their hand upon the
ark [3]
Of her magnificent and awful cause.
Ibid. Line 231

Transforms old print
To zigzag manuscript, and cheats the
eyes
Of gallery critics by a thousand arts.
Ibid. Line 363

Variety's the very spice of life.[4]
Ibid. Line 606

----

[1] See Bacon, page 121a.
[2] Oh that I had in the wilderness a lodging-
place of wayfaring men! — *Jeremiah, IX, 2*
See Byron, page 454b.
[3] Uzzah put forth his hand to the ark of
God, and took hold of it . . . and the anger
of the Lord was kindled against Uzzah. —
2 Samuel, VI, 6–7
[4] See Publilius Syrus, page 44b.

His head,
Not yet by time completely silver'd
o'er,
Bespoke him past the bounds of freak-
ish youth,
But strong for service still, and un-
impair'd.
The Task. Book II, The
Timepiece, Line 702

Guilty splendour.
Ibid. Book III, The Garden,
Line 70

I was a stricken deer [1] that left the herd
Long since.
Ibid. Line 108

Great contest follows, and much
learned dust.
Ibid. Line 161

From reveries so airy, from the toil
Of dropping buckets into empty wells,
And growing old in drawing nothing
up.[2]
Ibid. Line 188

Riches have wings,[3] and grandeur is a
dream.
Ibid. Line 265

Who loves a garden loves a greenhouse
too.
Ibid. Line 566

Now stir the fire, and close the shutters
fast,
Let fall the curtains, wheel the sofa
round,
And while the bubbling and loud-hiss-
ing urn
Throws up a steamy column, and the
cups
That cheer but not inebriate wait on
each,
So let us welcome peaceful evening in.
Ibid. Book IV, The Winter
Evening, Line 36

'Tis pleasant, through the loopholes of
retreat,
To peep at such a world, to see the stir
Of the great Babel; and not feel the
crowd.
Ibid. Line 88

----

[1] See Shakespeare, page 176a.
[2] See Sydney Smith, page 419a.
[3] Riches certainly make themselves wings.
— *Proverbs, XXIII, 5*

O Winter, ruler of the inverted year! [1]
*The Task. Book IV, The Winter
Evening, Line 120*

With spots quadrangular of diamond
form,
Ensanguined hearts, clubs typical of
strife,
And spades, the emblems of untimely
graves.
Ibid. Line 217

In indolent vacuity of thought.[2]
Ibid. Line 297

It seems the part of wisdom.
Ibid. Line 336

All learned, and all drunk!
Ibid. Line 478

Gloriously drunk, obey the important
call.
Ibid. Line 510

Silently as a dream the fabric rose;
No sound of hammer or of saw was
there.[3]
*Ibid. Book V, The Winter
Morning Walk, Line 144*

But war's a game, which, were their
subjects wise,
Kings would not play at.
Ibid. Line 187

There is in souls a sympathy with
sounds;
And as the mind is pitch'd the ear is
pleased
With melting airs or martial, brisk or
grave;
Some chord in unison with what we
hear
Is touch'd within us, and the heart
replies.
How soft the music of those village
bells

1 See Thomson, page 327b.
2 See Samuel Johnson, page 340a.
3 So that there was neither hammer nor axe,
nor any tool of iron heard in the house while
it was in building. — *1 Kings, VI, 7*
No hammers fell, no ponderous axes rung,
Like some tall palm the mystic fabric sprung,
Majestic silence!
REGINALD HEBER [1783–1826]:
Palestine

Falling at intervals upon the ear
In cadence sweet!
*The Task. Book VI, Winter Walk
at Noon, Line 1*

Here the heart
May give a useful lesson to the head,
And Learning wiser grow without his
books.
Ibid. Line 85

Knowledge is proud that he has learn'd
so much;
Wisdom is humble that he knows no
more.
Ibid. Line 96

An honest man, close-button'd to the
chin,
Broadcloth without, and a warm heart
within.
Epistle to Joseph Hill [1785]

Shine by the side of every path we
tread
With such a lustre, he that runs may
read.[1]
Tirocinium [1785]. *Line 79*

Toll for the brave!
The brave that are no more,
All sunk beneath the wave,
Fast by their native shore!
On the Loss of the Royal George [2]
[1791]. *Stanza 1*

And still to love, though prest with ill,
In wintry age to feel no chill,
With me is to be lovely still,
My Mary!
To Mary [1791]. *Stanza 11*

Beware of desp'rate steps! The dark-
est day
(Live till tomorrow) will have pass'd
away.
The Needless Alarm [1794].
Moral

1 Write the vision, and make it plain, upon
tables, that he may run that readeth it. —
Habakkuk, II, 2
2 The *Royal George* was an English man-
of-war of 108 guns, which suddenly heeled
over, under the strain caused by the shifting
of her guns, while being refitted at Spithead,
August 29, 1782. The commander, Admiral
Kempenfeldt, and eight hundred of the sailors, marines, and visitors on board, were
drowned.

I shall not ask Jean Jacques Rousseau
If birds confabulate or no.

Pairing Time Anticipated
[*Circa 1794*]

Misses! the tale that I relate
This lesson seems to carry, —
Choose not alone a proper mate,
But proper time to marry.

Ibid. Moral

Oh that those lips had language! Life
has pass'd
With me but roughly since I heard thee
last.

*On the Receipt of My Mother's
Picture* [*1798*]

ERASMUS DARWIN
[1731–1802]

No radiant pearl which crested For-
tune wears,
No gem that twinkling hangs from
Beauty's ears,
Not the bright stars which Night's
blue arch adorn,
Nor rising suns that gild the vernal
morn,
Shine with such lustre as the tear that
flows
Down Virtue's manly cheek for others'
woes.

The Botanic Garden. Part II
[*1789*], *Canto III, Line 459*

CHARLES LEE
[1731–1782]

Beware that your Northern laurels
do not change to Southern willows.[1]

*To General Horatio Gates after
surrender of Burgoyne at Sara-
toga* [*October 17, 1777*]

BEILBY PORTEUS
[1731–1808]

One murder made a villain,
Millions, a hero. Princes were privileged

[1] Gates was later defeated by Cornwallis at
Camden, South Carolina [August 16, 1780],
and was relieved of his command.

To kill, and numbers sanctified the
crime.[1]

Death. Line 154

War its thousands slays, Peace, its ten
thousands.

Ibid. Line 178

Love is something so divine,
Description would but make it less;
'Tis what I feel, but can't define,
'Tis what I know, but can't express.

On Love

GEORGE WASHINGTON
[1732–1799]

Labour to keep alive in your breast
that little spark of celestial fire, —
conscience.

*Rule from the copybook of
Washington when a schoolboy.*
JARED SPARKS's *Life of Washington* [*1839*], *Vol. II, Page
109*

When is the time for brave men to
exert themselves in the cause of liberty
and their country, if this is not? Should
any difficulties that they may have to
encounter at this important crisis, deter
them? God knows, there is not a difficulty, that you both [Schuyler and
General Montgomery] very justly complain of, which I have not in an eminent
degree experienced, that I am not every
day experiencing; but we must bear up
against them, and make the best of
mankind as they are, since we cannot
have them as we wish.

To Major General Philip Schuyler
[*December 24, 1775*]

It follows then as certain as that
night succeeds the day, that without a
decisive Naval force we can do nothing
definitive. And with it, every thing
honourable and glorious.

To Lafayette [*November 15,
1781*]

If men are to be precluded from offering their sentiments on a matter,
which may involve the most serious and
alarming consequences that can invite
the consideration of mankind, reason is

[1] See Young, page 305a.

of no use to us; the freedom of speech may be taken away, and dumb and silent we may be led, like sheep to the slaughter.
Address to Officers of the Army [March 15, 1783]

Almighty God, we make our earnest prayer that Thou wilt keep the United States in Thy holy protection; that Thou wilt incline the hearts of the citizens to cultivate a spirit of subordination and obedience to government; to entertain a brotherly affection and love for one another and for their fellow-citizens of the United States at large.
Prayer after Inauguration [1789]

To be prepared for war is one of the most effectual means of preserving peace.[1]
First Annual Address, to both Houses of Congress [January 8, 1790]

The basis of our political system is the right of the people to make and to alter their constitutions of government.
Farewell Address [September 17, 1796]

Let me now . . . warn you in the most solemn manner against the baneful effects of the spirit of party.
Ibid.

Observe good faith and justice toward all nations. Cultivate peace and harmony with all. . . . The nation which indulges toward another an habitual hatred or an habitual fondness is in some degree a slave. It is a slave to its animosity or to its affection, either of which is sufficient to lead it astray from its duty and its interest.
Ibid.

It is our true policy to steer clear of permanent alliances with any portion of the foreign world.
Ibid.

There can be no greater error than to expect or calculate upon real favors from nation to nation.
Ibid.

[1] See Horace, page 40b, and Burton, page 223a.

PIERRE DE BEAUMARCHAIS
[1732-1799]

I quickly laugh at everything, for fear of having to cry.[1]
*Le Barbier de Séville [1775].
Act I, Sc. 2*

If you assure me that your intentions are honourable.
Ibid. Act IV, Sc. 6

JOHN ADAMS
[1735-1826]

All great changes are irksome to the human mind, especially those which are attended with great dangers and uncertain effects.
Letter to James Warren [April 22, 1776]

Yesterday the greatest question was decided which ever was debated in America; and a greater perhaps never was, nor will be, decided among men. A resolution was passed without one dissenting colony, that these United Colonies are, and of right ought to be, free and independent States.
Letter to Abigail Adams [July 3, 1776]

The second day of July, 1776,[2] will be the most memorable epocha in the history of America. I am apt to believe that it will be celebrated by succeeding generations as the great anniversary festival. It ought to be commemorated as the day of deliverance, by solemn acts of devotion to God Almighty. It ought to be solemnized with pomp and parade, with shows, games, sports, guns, bells, bonfires, and illuminations, from one end of this continent to the other, from this time forward for evermore.
Ibid.

[1] Je me presse de rire de tout, de peur d'être obligé d'en pleurer.
See Byron, page 458b, and Lincoln, page 540a.
[2] On July 2, 1776, the resolution for independence, drafted by Richard Henry Lee of Virginia, was adopted by a committee including John Adams. On July 4 the Declaration of Independence was agreed to, en-

The happiness of society is the end of government.
> *Thoughts on Government* [*1776*]

Fear is the foundation of most governments.
> *Ibid.*

Where annual elections end, there slavery begins.
> *Ibid.*

The judicial power ought to be distinct from both the legislative and executive, and independent upon both, that so it may be a check upon both.
> *Ibid.*

A government of laws, and not of men.
> *Original Draft of Massachusetts Constitution* [*1779*]

JAMES BEATTIE
[1735–1803]

He thought as a sage, though he felt as a man.
> *The Hermit*

ISAAC BICKERSTAFF
[1735–1812?]

There was a jolly miller once lived on the River Dee;
He worked and sang from morn till night; no lark more blithe than he.
> *Love in a Village* [*1762*]. *Act I, Sc. 2*

And this the burthen of his song, for ever used to be,
"I care for nobody, not I, if no one cares for me." [1]
> *Ibid.*

JOHN LANGHORNE
[1735–1779]

The child of misery, baptized in tears.
> *The Country Justice. Part I*

---

grossed, signed by John Hancock, and sent to the legislatures of the States.

[1] Naebody cares for me,
  I care for naebody.
    ROBERT BURNS [1759–1796]: *I Hae a Wife o' My Ain, St. 4*
  I envy none, no, no, not I,
  And no one envies me.
    CHARLES MACKAY [1814–1889]: *The King and the Miller*

WILLIAM JULIUS MICKLE
[1735–1788]

The dews of summer nights did fall,
  The moon (sweet regent of the sky) [1]
Silvered the walls of Cumnor Hall
  And many an oak that grew thereby.
> *Cumnor Hall* [*1784*]. *Stanza 1*

For there's nae luck about the house,
  There's nae luck at a';
There's little pleasure in the house
  When our gudeman's awa.
> *The Mariner's Wife. Stanza 1*

CHARLES JOSEPH, PRINCE DE LIGNE
[1735–1814]

The Congress doesn't run — it waltzes. [2]
> *Comment to La Garde–Chambonacs* [*1814*]

PATRICK HENRY
[1736–1799]

Caesar had his Brutus; Charles the First his Cromwell; and George the Third ["Treason!" cried the Speaker] — *may profit by their example. If this* be treason, make the most of it.
> *Speech on the Stamp Act, House of Burgesses, Williamsburg, Virginia* [*May 29, 1765*]

I am not a Virginian, but an American.
> *Speech in First Continental Congress, Philadelphia* [*October 14, 1774*]

I have but one lamp by which my feet are guided, and that is the lamp of experience. I know no way of judging of the future but by the past. [3]
> *Speech in Virginia Convention, St. John's Episcopal Church, Richmond, Virginia* [*March 23, 1775*]

We are not weak if we make a proper

---

[1] Now Cynthia, named fair regent of the night. — GAY: *Trivia* [1716], *Book III*
[2] Le Congrès ne marche pas, il danse. Said of the Congress of Vienna.
[3] See Burke, page 361b.

use of those means which the God of Nature has placed in our power. . . . The battle, sir, is not to the strong alone; [1] it is to the vigilant, the active, the brave.

> *Speech in Virginia Convention, St. John's Episcopal Church, Richmond, Virginia*

Is life so dear, or peace so sweet, as to be purchased at the price of chains and slavery? Forbid it, Almighty God! I know not what course others may take, but as for me, give me liberty, or give me death!

> *Ibid.*

EDWARD GIBBON
[1737–1794]

The various modes of worship, which prevailed in the Roman world, were all considered by the people as equally true; by the philosopher, as equally false; and by the magistrate, as equally useful.

> *Decline and Fall of the Roman Empire [1776–1788]. Chap. 2*

The reign of Antoninus is marked by the rare advantage of furnishing very few materials for history; which is indeed little more than the register of the crimes, follies, and misfortunes of mankind.[2]

> *Ibid. Chap. 3*

It has been calculated by the ablest politicians that no State, without being soon exhausted, can maintain above the hundredth part of its members in arms and idleness.

> *Ibid. Chap. 5*

In every deed of mischief he [Adronicus] had a heart to resolve, a head to contrive, and a hand to execute.[3]

> *Ibid. Chap. 48*

[1] The race is not to the swift, nor the battle to the strong. — *Ecclesiastes, IX, 11*

[2] See Voltaire, page 325b.

[3] He [Hampden] had a head to contrive, a tongue to persuade, and a hand to execute any mischief. — EDWARD HYDE, EARL OF CLARENDON [1608–1674]: *History of the Rebellion* [1702–1704], *Vol. III, Book 7, Sect. 84* See Junius, page 1002a.

Our sympathy is cold to the relation of distant misery.

> *Decline and Fall of the Roman Empire. Chap. 49*

The winds and waves are always on the side of the ablest navigators.[1]

> *Ibid. Chap. 68*

Vicissitudes of fortune, which spares neither man nor the proudest of his works, which buries empires and cities in a common grave.

> *Ibid. Chap. 71*

All that is human must retrograde if it do not advance.

> *Ibid.*

I saw and loved.

> *Memoirs*

On the approach of spring I withdrew without reluctance from the noisy and extensive scene of crowds without company, and dissipation without pleasure.

> *Ibid.*

RUDOLF ERICH RASPE
[1737–1794]

What in the dark I had taken to be a stump of a little tree appearing above the snow, to which I had tied my horse, proved to have been the weathercock of the church steeple.

> *Travels of Baron Munchausen [1785]. Chap. 2*

We all did our duty, which, in the patriot's, soldier's, and gentleman's language, is a very comprehensive word, of great honour, meaning, and import.

> *Ibid. Chap. 5*

The sprigs took root in my horse's body, grew up, and formed a bower over me.

> *Ibid.*

His tunes were frozen up in the horn, and came out now by thawing.[2]

> *Ibid. Chap. 6*

If any of the company entertain a doubt of my veracity, I shall only say to such, I pity their want of faith.

> *Ibid.*

[1] See Voltaire, page 325b.

[2] See Plutarch, page 61a.

I had the very sling in my pocket which assisted David in slaying Goliath.
Travels of Baron Munchausen.
Chap. 10

Upon this island of cheese grows great plenty of corn, the ears of which produce loaves of bread, ready made.
Ibid. Chap. 20

I have ever confined myself to facts.
Ibid.

A traveller has a right to relate and embellish his adventures as he pleases, and it is very unpolite to refuse that deference and applause they deserve.
Ibid. Chap. 21

There is a right and wrong handle to everything.[1]

Ibid. Chap. 30

THOMAS PAINE
[1737–1809]

From the east to the west blow the
trumpet to arms!
Through the land let the sound of it
flee;
Let the far and the near all unite, with
a cheer,
In defence of our Liberty Tree.
The Liberty Tree [*July, 1775*].
Stanza 4

Society in every state is a blessing, but government, even in its best state, is but a necessary evil; in its worst state, an intolerable one.
Common Sense [*1776*]

Suspicion is the companion of mean souls, and the bane of all good society.
Ibid.

When we are planning for posterity, we ought to remember that virtue is not hereditary.

Ibid.

These are the times that try men's souls. The summer soldier and the sunshine patriot will, in this crisis, shrink from the service of his country; but he that stands it *now,* deserves the love and thanks of man and woman. Tyranny, like hell, is not easily conquered; yet we have this consolation with us,

[1] See Epictetus, page 65a.

that the harder the conflict, the more glorious the triumph. What we obtain too cheap, we esteem too lightly; 'tis dearness only that gives everything its value. Heaven knows how to put a proper price upon its goods; and it would be strange indeed, if so celestial an article as *Freedom* should not be highly rated.
The American Crisis. No. I
[*December 23, 1776*]

Panics, in some cases, have their uses; they produce as much good as hurt. Their duration is always short; the mind soon grows through them and acquires a firmer habit than before. But their peculiar advantage is, that they are the touchstone of sincerity and hypocrisy, and bring things and men to light, which might otherwise have lain forever undiscovered.

Ibid.

Not a place upon earth might be so happy as America. Her situation is remote from all the wrangling world, and she has nothing to do but to trade with them.

Ibid.

A bad cause will ever be supported by bad means and bad men.
Ibid. No. II [*January 13, 1777*]

Those who expect to reap the blessings of freedom must, like men, undergo the fatigue of supporting it.
Ibid. No. IV [*September 12, 1777*]

It is not a field of a few acres of ground, but a cause, that we are defending, and whether we defeat the enemy in one battle, or by degrees, the consequences will be the same.

Ibid

We fight not to enslave, but to set a country free, and to make room upon the earth for honest men to live in.
Ibid.

It is the object only of war that makes it honourable. And if there was ever a *just* war since the world began, it is this in which America is now engaged.
Ibid. No. V [*March 21, 1778*]

Character is much easier kept than recovered.
The American Crisis. No. XIII [April 19, 1783]

War involves in its progress such a train of unforeseen and unsupposed circumstances that no human wisdom can calculate the end. It has but one thing certain, and that is to increase taxes.
Prospects on the Rubicon [1787]

[Burke] is not affected by the reality of distress touching his heart, but by the showy resemblance of it striking his imagination. He pities the plumage, but forgets the dying bird.
Rights of Man. Part I [1791]

My country is the world, and my religion is to do good.[1]
Ibid. Part II [1792], Chap. 5

And the final event to himself [Burke] has been, that, as he rose like a rocket, he fell like a stick.
Letter to the Addressers

I believe in one God and no more, and I hope for happiness beyond this life. I believe in the equality of man; and I believe that religious duties consist in doing justice, loving mercy, and endeavoring to make our fellow-creatures happy.
The Age of Reason [1793]. Part I

It is with a pious fraud as with a bad action; it begets a calamitous necessity of going on.
Ibid.

When authors and critics talk of the sublime, they see not how nearly it borders on the ridiculous.[2]
Ibid. Part II, Note

JACQUES DELILLE
[1738–1813]

Fate makes our relatives, choice makes our friends.
La Pitié [1803]. Canto I

[1] See W. L. Garrison, page 517a.
[2] See Napoleon, page 399b.

JOHN WOLCOT
("PETER PINDAR")
[1738–1819]

What rage for fame attends both great and small!
Better be damned than mentioned not at all.
To the Royal Academicians

Care to our coffin adds a nail, no doubt,
And every grin so merry draws one out.
Expostulatory Odes. XV

HESTER LYNCH THRALE
(PIOZZI)
[1739–1821]

The tree of deepest root is found
Least willing still to quit the ground:
'Twas therefore said by ancient sages,
    That love of life increased with years
So much, that in our latter stages,
When pain grows sharp and sickness rages,
    The greatest love of life appears.
Three Warnings

Johnson's conversation was by much too strong for a person accustomed to obsequiousness and flattery; it was mustard in a young child's mouth.
Quoted in BOSWELL'S *Life of Dr. Johnson [1791], Vol. II, Page 396, Everyman Edition*

DANIEL BLISS
[1740–1806]

God wills us free, man wills us slaves,
I will as God wills, God's will be done.
Epitaph on gravestone of John Jack, "A Native of Africa, who died March 1773, aged about 60 years. Tho' born in a land of slavery he was born free."

JAMES BOSWELL
[1740–1795]
See also under SAMUEL JOHNSON

That favourite subject, Myself.
Letter to Temple [July 26, 1763]

We cannot tell the precise moment when friendship is formed. As in filling a vessel drop by drop, there is at last a drop which makes it run over; so in a series of kindnesses there is at last one which makes the heart run over.

Life of Dr. Johnson [1791],
Everyman Edition, Vol. II,
Page 122

I think no innocent species of wit or pleasantry should be suppressed; and that a good pun may be admitted among the smaller excellencies of lively conversation.

Ibid. Page 537

AUGUSTUS MONTAGUE TOPLADY
[1740–1778]

Rock of Ages, cleft for me,
Let me hide myself in thee.

Rock of Ages [1775]. Stanza 1

LOUIS SÉBASTIEN MERCIER
[1740–1814]

Extremes meet.

Tableaux de Paris [1782].
Vol. IV, Chap. 348, Title

SÉBASTIEN R. N. CHAMFORT
[1741–1794]

The most wasted day of all is that on which we have not laughed.

Maxims and Thoughts. 1

Chance is a nickname for Providence.

Ibid. 62

JOHANN KASPAR LAVATER
[1741–1801]

Say not you know another entirely, till you have divided an inheritance with him.

Aphorisms on Man [1] *[Circa*
1788]. No. 157

He who, when called upon to speak a disagreeable truth, tells it boldly and has done is both bolder and milder than

---

[1] These Aphorisms were much admired and privately annotated by WILLIAM BLAKE. See the one-volume edition of BLAKE's *Poetry and Prose*, edited by GEOFFREY KEYNES.

---

he who nibbles in a low voice and never ceases nibbling.[1]

Aphorisms on Man. No. 302

Trust not him with your secrets, who, when left alone in your room, turns over your papers.

Ibid. No. 449

The public seldom forgive twice.

Ibid. No. 606

Venerate four characters: the sanguine, who has checked volatility and the rage for pleasure; the choleric who has subdued passion and pride; the phlegmatic emerged from indolence; and the melancholy who has dismissed avarice, suspicion and asperity.

Ibid. No. 609

If you mean to know yourself, interline such of these aphorisms as affect you agreeably in reading, and set a mark to such as left a sense of uneasiness with you; and then shew your copy to whom you please.

Ibid. No. 643

WILLIAM PALEY
[1743–1805]

Who can refute a sneer?

Moral Philosophy [1785]. Vol. II,
Book V, Chap. 9

ANNA LETITIA (AIKIN) BARBAULD
[1743–1825]

Life! we've been long together
Through pleasant and through cloudy
  weather;
'Tis hard to part when friends are
  dear,—
Perhaps 'twill cost a sigh, a tear;
Then steal away, give little warning,
  Choose thine own time;
Say not "Good night," but in some
  brighter clime
Bid me "Good morning."

Life. Stanza 3

This dead of midnight is the noon of thought.

A Summer's Evening Meditation

---

[1] Blake's marginal comment on this was "Damn such!"

THOMAS JEFFERSON
[1743–1826]

A lively and lasting sense of filial duty is more effectually impressed on the mind of a son or daughter by reading King Lear, than by all the dry volumes of ethics, and divinity, that ever were written.

Letter to Robert Skipwith [August 3, 1771]

The God who gave us life, gave us liberty at the same time.

Summary View of the Rights of British America [1774]

When, in the course of human events, it becomes necessary for one people to dissolve the political bands which have connected them with another, and to assume among the powers of the earth the separate and equal station to which the laws of nature and of nature's God[1] entitle them, a decent respect to the opinions of mankind requires that they should declare the causes which impel them to the separation. We hold these truths to be self-evident; that all men are created equal; that they are endowed by their creator with certain unalienable rights;[2] that among these are life, liberty, and the pursuit of happiness; that to secure these rights, governments are instituted among men, deriving their just powers from the consent of the governed; that whenever any form of government becomes destructive to these ends, it is the right of the people to alter or to abolish it, and to institute new government, laying its foundation on such principles, and organizing its powers in such form, as to them shall seem most likely to effect their safety and happiness.

Declaration of Independence [July 4, 1776]

[1] See Bolingbroke, page 304a.
[2] The phrase is frequently misquoted "inalienable."
All men are born free and equal, and have certain natural, essential and unalienable rights. — *Constitution of Massachusetts* [1778]

We must therefore . . . hold them [the British] as we hold the rest of mankind, enemies in war, in peace friends.

Declaration of Independence

And for the support of this declaration, with a firm reliance on the protection of divine providence, we mutually pledge to each other our lives, our fortunes, and our sacred honor.

Ibid.

Ignorance is preferable to error; and he is less remote from the truth who believes nothing, than he who believes what is wrong.

Notes on the State of Virginia [1781–1785]. Query VI

A single zealot may commence persecutor, and better men be his victims.

Ibid. Query XVII

Indeed, I tremble for my country when I reflect that God is just.

Ibid. Query XVIII

Those who labor in the earth are the chosen people of God, if ever he had a chosen people, whose breasts He has made His peculiar deposit for substantial and genuine virtue.

Ibid. Query XIX

He who permits himself to tell a lie once, finds it much easier to do it a second and third time, till at length it becomes habitual; he tells lies without attending to it, and truths without the world's believing him. This falsehood of the tongue leads to that of the heart, and in time depraves all its good dispositions.

Letter to Peter Carr [August 19, 1785]

The basis of our government being the opinion of the people, the very first object should be to keep that right; and were it left to me to decide whether we should have a government without newspapers, or newspapers without a government, I should not hesitate a moment to prefer the latter.

Letter to Colonel Edward Carrington [January 16, 1787]

Experience declares that man is the only animal which devours his own kind; for I can apply no milder term to the governments of Europe, and to the general prey of the rich on the poor.

Letter to Colonel Edward Carrington [January 16, 1787]

I hold it, that a little rebellion, now and then, is a good thing, and as necessary in the political world as storms in the physical.

Letter to James Madison [January 30, 1787]

What country before ever existed a century and a half without a rebellion? . . . The tree of liberty must be refreshed from time to time with the blood of patriots and tyrants. It is its natural manure.

Letter to William Stevens Smith [November 13, 1787]

The republican is the only form of government which is not eternally at open or secret war with the rights of mankind.

Letter to William Hunter [March 11, 1790]

We are not to expect to be translated from despotism to liberty in a featherbed.

Letter to Lafayette [April 2, 1790]

Let what will be said or done, preserve your *sang froid* immovably, and to every obstacle, oppose patience, perseverance, and soothing language.

Letter to William Short [March 18, 1792]

Delay is preferable to error.

Letter to George Washington [May 16, 1792]

Offices are as acceptable here as elsewhere, and whenever a man has cast a longing eye on them, a rottenness begins in his conduct.

Letter to Tench Coxe [May 21, 1799]

I have sworn upon the altar of God, eternal hostility against every form of tyranny over the mind of man.

Letter to Dr. Benjamin Rush [September 23, 1800]

If there be any among us who would wish to dissolve this Union or to change its republican form, let them stand undisturbed as monuments of the safety with which error of opinion may be tolerated where reason is left free to combat it.

First Inaugural Address [March 4, 1801]

But would the honest patriot, in the full tide of successful experiment, abandon a government which has so far kept us free and firm, on the theoretic and visionary fear that this government, the world's best hope, may by possibility want energy to preserve itself?

Ibid.

Sometimes it is said that man cannot be trusted with the government of himself. Can he, then, be trusted with the government of others? Or have we found angels in the forms of kings to govern him? Let history answer this question.

Ibid.

Still one thing more, fellow citizens — a wise and frugal government, which shall restrain men from injuring one another, which shall leave them otherwise free to regulate their own pursuits of industry and improvement, and shall not take from the mouth of labor the bread it has earned. This is the sum of good government, and this is necessary to close the circle of our felicities.

Ibid.

Equal and exact justice to all men, of whatever state or persuasion, religious or political; peace, commerce, and honest friendship with all nations — entangling alliances with none; . . . freedom of religion; freedom of the press; freedom of person under the protection of the *habeas corpus;* and trial by juries impartially selected — these principles form the bright constellation which has gone before us, and guided our steps through an age of revolution and reformation. The wisdom of our sages and the blood of our heroes have been devoted to their attainment. They should be the creed of our political faith

— the text of civil instruction — the touchstone by which to try the services of those we trust; and should we wander from them in moments of error or alarm, let us hasten to retrace our steps and to regain the road which alone leads to peace, liberty, and safety.

First Inaugural Address

Of the various executive abilities, no one excited more anxious concern than that of placing the interests of our fellow-citizens in the hands of honest men, with understanding sufficient for their stations.

Letter to Elias Shipman and Others of New Haven [July 12, 1801]

If a due participation of office is a matter of right, how are vacancies to be obtained? Those by death are few; by resignation, none.

Ibid.

Whensoever hostile aggressions . . . require a resort to war, we must meet our duty and convince the world that we are just friends and brave enemies.

Letter to Andrew Jackson [December 3, 1806]

When a man assumes a public trust, he should consider himself as public property.[1]

Remark to Baron von Humboldt [1807]

If, in my retirement to the humble station of a private citizen, I am accompanied with the esteem and approbation of my fellow citizens, trophies obtained by the blood-stained steel, or the tattered flags of the tented field, will never be envied. The care of human life and happiness, and not their destruction, is the first and only legitimate object of good government.

To the Republican Citizens of Washington County, Maryland [March 31, 1809]

Politics, like religion, hold up the torches of martyrdom to the reformers of error.

Letter to James Ogilvie [August 4, 1811]

[1] See Mathew Henry, page 293a, Burke, page 361b, and Calhoun, page 442a.

The earth belongs to the living, not to the dead.

Letter to John W. Eppes [June 24, 1813]

I agree with you that there is a natural aristocracy among men. The grounds of this are virtue and talents.

Letter to John Adams [October 28, 1813]

Merchants have no country. The mere spot they stand on does not constitute so strong an attachment as that from which they draw their gains.

Letter to Horatio G. Spafford [March 17, 1814]

If a nation expects to be ignorant and free, in a state of civilization, it expects what never was and never will be.

Letter to Colonel Charles Yancey [January 6, 1816]

Enlighten the people generally, and tyranny and oppressions of body and mind will vanish like evil spirits at the dawn of day.

Letter to Du Pont de Nemours [April 24, 1816]

I have the consolation to reflect that during the period of my administration not a drop of the blood of a single fellow citizen was shed by the sword of war or of the law.

Letter to Count Dugnani, Papal Nuncio [February 14, 1818]

I know no safe depository of the ultimate powers of the society but the people themselves; and if we think them not enlightened enough to exercise their control with a wholesome discretion, the remedy is not to take it from them, but to inform their discretion.

Letter to William Charles Jarvis [September 28, 1820]

Amplification is the vice of modern oratory. It is an insult to an assembly of reasonable men, disgusting and revolting instead of persuading. Speeches measured by the hour, die by the hour.

Letter to David Harding, President of the Jefferson Debating Society of Hingham [April 20, 1824]

Men by their constitutions are naturally divided into two parties: 1. Those who fear and distrust the people, and wish to draw all powers from them into the hands of the higher classes. 2. Those who identify themselves with the people, have confidence in them, cherish and consider them as the most honest and safe, although not the most wise depository of the public interests. In every country these two parties exist; and in every one where they are free to think, speak, and write, they will declare themselves.

Letter to Henry Lee
[August 10, 1824]

Never buy what you do not want, because it is cheap; it will be dear to you.

A Decalogue of Canons for Observation in Practical Life
[February 21, 1825]

When angry, count ten before you speak; if very angry, an hundred.

Ibid.

The good old Dominion, the blessed mother of us all.

Thoughts on Lotteries [1826]

CONSTITUTION OF THE UNITED STATES
[1787]

We the People of the United States, in Order to form a more perfect Union, establish Justice, insure domestic Tranquillity, provide for the common defense, promote the general Welfare, and secure the Blessings of Liberty to ourselves and our Posterity, do ordain and establish this Constitution for the United States of America.

Preamble

Treason against the United States, shall consist only in levying War against them, or in adhering to their Enemies, giving them aid and comfort. No person shall be convicted of Treason unless on the Testimony of two witnesses to the same overt act, or on confession in open court.

Article III, Section 3

Congress shall make no law respecting an establishment of religion, or prohibiting the free exercise thereof; or abridging the freedom of speech, or of the press; or the right of the people peaceably to assemble, and to petition the government for a redress of grievances.

First Amendment [1791]

JOSIAH QUINCY
[1744–1775]

Blandishments will not fascinate us, nor will threats of a "halter" intimidate. For, under God, we are determined that wheresoever, whensoever, or howsoever we shall be called to make our exit, we will die free men.

Observations on the Boston Port Bill [1774]

ROWLAND HILL
[1744–1833]

Why should the Devil have all the good tunes?

Sermons. Quoted in Broome, *Life, Page 93*

HANNAH MORE
[1745–1833]

Since trifles make the sum of human things,
And half our misery from our foibles springs.

Sensibility

In men this blunder still you find,—
All think their little set mankind.

Florio and His Friend

Small habits well pursued betimes
May reach the dignity of crimes.

Ibid.

Some phrase that with the public took
Was all he read of any book.

Ibid.

WILLIAM SCOTT, LORD STOWELL
[1745–1836]

A dinner lubricates business.
> *Quoted in* BOSWELL'S *Life of Dr. Johnson, London edition* [*1835*], *Vol. VIII, Page* 67

The elegant simplicity of the three per cents.[1]
> *Quoted in* CAMPBELL'S *Lives of the Lord Chancellors* [*1857*], *Vol. X, Chap.* 212

CHARLES DIBDIN
[1745–1814]

Did you ever hear of Captain Wattle?
He was all for love, and a little for the bottle.
> *Captain Wattle and Miss Roe*

Here, a sheer hulk, lies poor Tom Bowling,
The darling of our crew;
No more he'll hear the tempest howling,
For death has broach'd him to.
> *Tom Bowling*

Faithful below he did his duty,
But now he's gone aloft.
> *Ibid.*

Spanking Jack was so comely, so pleasant, so jolly,
Though winds blew great guns, still he'd whistle and sing;
Jack loved his friend, and was true to his Molly,
And if honour gives greatness, was great as a king.
> *The Sailor's Consolation*

WILLIAM PITT
[? –1840]

One night came on a hurricane,
The sea was mountains rolling,
When Barney Buntline turned his quid,
And said to Billy Bowling:
"A strong nor-wester's blowing, Bill;
Hark! don't ye hear it roar, now?
Lord help 'em, how I pities all
Unhappy folks on shore now!"
> *The Sailor's Consolation. Stanza* 1

[1] The sweet simplicity of the three per cents.
— DISRAELI: *Endymion* [1880], *Chap. 96*

JAMES HOOK
[1746–1827]

A little farm well tilled,
A little barn well filled,
A little wife well willed,
Give me, give me.
> *The Soldier's Return. Stanza* 1

I like the farm well tilled,
And I like the house well filled,
But no wife at all
Give me, give me.
> *Ibid. Stanza* 3

SIR WILLIAM JONES
[1746–1794]

On parent knees, a naked new-born child,
Weeping thou sat'st while all around thee smiled;
So live, that sinking in thy last long sleep,
Calm thou mayst smile, while all around thee weep.
> *From the Persian* [*1786*]

CHARLES COTESWORTH PINCKNEY
[1746–1825]

Millions for defence, but not one cent for tribute.[1]
> *When Minister to the French Republic* [*1797*]

JOHN PAUL JONES
[1747–1792]

I have not yet begun to fight.
> *Aboard the Bonhomme Richard,*[2]
> *September 23, 1779*

JOHN O'KEEFFE
[1747–1833]

A glass is good, and a lass is good,
And a pipe to smoke in cold weather;

[1] Inscribed on the cenotaph in his memory in St. Michael's Church, Charleston, South Carolina. What Pinckney really said was more forcible — "not *a damned penny* for tribute."
[2] Engaged with the British frigate *Serapis*, off Flamborough Head, England.

The world is good, and the people are
good,
And we're all good fellows together.
Sprigs of Laurel. Act II, Sc. 1
And why I'm so plump the reason I
tell, —
Who leads a good life is sure to live
well.
*Merry Sherwood. A Friar of
Orders Gray, Stanza 1*

SAMUEL PARR [1]
[1747–1825]

Now that the old lion is dead, every
ass thinks he may kick at him.
*While dining with Sir Joshua
Reynolds, after the death of Dr.
Johnson. Quoted in* BOSWELL'S
*Life of Dr. Johnson [1791],
Vol. II, Page 612, Everyman
Edition*

JOHN LOGAN
[1748–1788]

Thou hast no sorrow in thy song,
No winter in thy year.
To the Cuckoo
Oh could I fly, I'd fly with thee!
We'd make with joyful wing
Our annual visit o'er the globe,
Companions of the spring.
Ibid.

JOHN EDWIN
[1749–1790]

A man's ingress into the world is naked
and bare,
His progress through the world is
trouble and care;
And lastly, his egress out of the world,
is nobody knows where.
If we do well here, we shall do well
there:
I can tell you no more if I preach a
whole year.
*The Eccentricities of John Ed-
win [second edition, London,
1791], Vol. I, Page 74*

[1] Dr. Parr composed the Latin epitaph for
the monument to Dr. Johnson, placed in St.
Paul's Cathedral, London, February, 1790.

JOHANN WOLFGANG
VON GOETHE
[1749–1832]

If you inquire what the people are
like here, I must answer, "The same as
everywhere!"
*The Sorrows of Werther
[1774–1787]. May 17th*
The history of science is science it-
self; the history of the individual, the
individual.
Mineralogy and Geology
Who never ate his bread in sorrow,
Who never spent the darksome hours
Weeping, and watching for the mor-
row, —
He knows you not, ye heavenly
Powers.
*Wilhelm Meister's Apprenticeship
[1786–1830]. Book II, Chap. 13*
Who longs in solitude to live,
Ah! soon his wish will gain:
Men hope and love, men get and give,
And leave him to his pain.
Ibid. Book III, Chap. 1
Know'st thou the land where the lemon-
trees bloom,
Where the gold orange glows in the deep
thicket's gloom,
Where a wind ever soft from the blue
heaven blows,
And the groves are of laurel and myrtle
and rose? [1]
Ibid.
One ought, every day at least, to hear
a little song, read a good poem, see a
fine picture, and, if it were possible, to
speak a few reasonable words.[2]
Ibid. Book V, Chap. 1
To know of some one here and there
whom we accord with, who is living on
with us, even in silence, — this makes
our earthly ball a peopled garden.
Ibid. Book VII, Chap. 5
Art is long, life short; [3] judgment
difficult, opportunity transient.
Ibid. Chap. 9

[1] See Byron, page 455b.
[2] See Charles Eliot Norton, page 637b
[3] See Hippocrates, page 22a.

Three things are to be looked to in a building: that it stand on the right spot; that it be securely founded; that it be successfully executed.

Elective Affinities [1] *[1808].*
Book I, Chap. 9

The sum which two married people owe to one another defies calculation. It is an infinite debt, which can only be discharged through all eternity.

Ibid.

A pretty foot is a great gift of nature.

Ibid. Chap. 11

One is never satisfied with a portrait of a person that one knows.

Ibid. Book II, Chap. 2

The fate of the architect is the strangest of all. How often he expends his whole soul, his whole heart and passion, to produce buildings into which he himself may never enter.

Ibid. Chap. 3

Let us live in as small a circle as we will, we are either debtors or creditors before we have had time to look round.

Ibid. Chap. 4

Mediocrity has no greater consolation than in the thought that genius is not immortal.

Ibid. Chap. 5

A teacher who can arouse a feeling for one single good action, for one single good poem, accomplishes more than he who fills our memory with rows on rows of natural objects, classified with name and form.

Ibid. Chap. 7

No one feels himself easy in a garden which does not look like the open country.

Ibid. Chap. 8

We lay aside letters never to read them again, and at last we destroy them out of discretion, and so disappears the most beautiful, the most immediate breath of life, irrecoverably for ourselves and for others.

Ibid. Chap. 9

[1] Translated by JAMES ANTHONY FROUDE [1818–1894].

Know'st thou yesterday, its aim and reason?
Work'st thou well today for worthier things?
Then calmly wait the morrow's hidden season,
And fear thou not what hap soe'er it brings.

Zahme Xenien. Book IV
[1821]

If I work incessantly to the last, nature owes me another form of existence when the present one collapses.

Letter to Eckermann
[February 4, 1829]

The artist may be well advised to keep his work to himself till it is completed, because no one can readily help him or advise him with it . . . but the scientist is wiser not to withhold a single finding or a single conjecture from publicity.

Essay on Experimentation

Man errs, while his struggle lasts. [1]
Faust [1808–1832], Part I
[1808]. Prologue in Heaven

Two souls dwell, alas! in my breast. [2]
Ibid. Before the Gate

I am the spirit that always denies. [3]
Ibid. Study

My peace is gone,
My heart is heavy. [4]
Ibid. Gretchen at the Spinning
Wheel

Who strives always to the utmost, him can we save. [5]
Ibid. Part II [1832]

He only earns his freedom and existence who daily conquers them anew. [6]
Ibid.

[1] Es irrt der Mensch, so lang er strebt.
[2] Zwei Seelen wohnen, ach! in meiner Brust.
[3] Ich bin der Geist der stets verneint.
[4] Meine Ruh' ist hin,
    Mein Herz ist schwer.
[5] Wer immer strebens sich bemüht,
    Den können wir erlösen.
[6] Nur der verdient sich Freiheit wie das
    Leben
    Der täglich sic erobern muss.

I was fair, too, and that was my undoing! [1]

Faust. Part II

The Eternal Feminine draws us on. [2]

Ibid. Last line

Without haste, but without rest. [3]

Motto

More light! [4]

Last words

EDWARD JENNER
[1749–1823]

The hollow winds begin to blow;
The clouds look black, the glass is low;
The soot falls down, the spaniels sleep,
And spiders from their cobwebs peep.
'Twill surely rain; I see with sorrow
Our jaunt must be put off tomorrow.

Forty Signs of Rain

LADY ANNE BARNARD
[1750–1825]

When the sheep are in the fauld, and
the kye's come hame,
And a' the weary warld to rest are gone,
The waes o' my heart fall in showers
frae my ee,
Unkenn'd by my gudeman, who sleeps
sound by me.

Auld Robin Gray [1771]. Stanza 1

So I will do my best a gude wife to be,
For Auld Robin Gray he is kind to me.

Ibid. Stanza 9

JOHN PHILPOT CURRAN
[1750–1817]

It is the common fate of the indolent
to see their rights become a prey to the
active. The condition upon which God
hath given liberty to man is eternal
vigilance; [5] which condition if he break,

[1] Schön war ich auch, und das war mein
Verderben.
[2] Das Ewig-Weibliche zieht uns hinan.
[3] Ohne Hast, aber ohne Rast.
[4] Mehr Licht!
[5] Commonly quoted: Eternal vigilance is
the price of liberty.
There is one safeguard known generally to
the wise, which is an advantage and security

servitude is at once the consequence of
his crime and the punishment of his
guilt.

Speech upon the Right of
Election [1790]

JOHN TRUMBULL
[1750–1831]

But optics sharp it needs, I ween,
To see what is not to be seen.

McFingal [1782]. Canto I, Line 67

But as some muskets so contrive it
As oft to miss the mark they drive at,
And though well aimed at duck or
plover,
Bear wide, and kick their owners over.

Ibid. Line 93

As though there were a tie
And obligation to posterity.
We get them, bear them, breed, and
nurse:
What has posterity done for us?

Ibid. Canto II, Line 121

No man e'er felt the halter draw,
With good opinion of the law.

Ibid. Canto III, Line 489

RICHARD BRINSLEY
SHERIDAN
[1751–1816]

Mrs. Malaprop. Illiterate him, I say,
quite from your memory.

The Rivals [1775]. Act I, Sc. 2

'Tis safest in matrimony to begin
with a little aversion.

Ibid.

A circulating library in a town is as
an evergreen tree of diabolical knowledge.

Ibid.

A progeny of learning.

Ibid.

Don't let your simplicity be imposed
on.

Ibid.

Never say more than is necessary.

Ibid. Act II, Sc. 1

to all, but especially to democracies as against
despots. What is it? Distrust. — DEMOSTHENES [*circa* 385–322 B. C.]: *Philippic 2, Sect. 24*

I know you are laughing in your sleeve.
The Rivals. Act II, Sc. 1

He is the very pine-apple of politeness!
Ibid. Act III, Sc. 3

If I reprehend anything in this world, it is the use of my oracular tongue, and a nice derangement of epitaphs!
Ibid.

As headstrong as an allegory on the banks of the Nile.
Ibid.

Too civil by half.
Ibid. Sc. 4

Our ancestors are very good kind of folks; but they are the last people I should choose to have a visiting acquaintance with.
Ibid. Act IV, Sc. 1

No caparisons, miss, if you please. Caparisons don't become a young woman.
Ibid. Sc. 2

We will not anticipate the past; so mind, young people, — our retrospection will be all to the future.
Ibid.

You are not like Cerberus, three gentlemen at once, are you?
Ibid.

The quarrel is a very pretty quarrel as it stands; we should only spoil it by trying to explain it.
Ibid. Sc. 3

You're our envoy; lead the way, and we'll precede.
Ibid. Act V, Sc. 1

There's nothing like being used to a thing.
Ibid. Sc. 3

My valour is certainly going! it is sneaking off! I feel it oozing out, as it were, at the palm of my hands!
Ibid.

I own the soft impeachment.
Ibid.

Thro' all the drama — whether damned or not —
Love gilds the scene, and women guide the plot.
Ibid. Epilogue

An apothecary should never be out of spirits.
St. Patrick's Day [*1775*].
Act I, Sc. 1

A fluent tongue is the only thing a mother don't like her daughter to resemble her in.
Ibid. Sc. 2

Death's a debt; his mandamus binds all alike — no bail, no demurrer.
Ibid. Act II, Sc. 4

I had rather follow you to your grave than see you owe your life to any but a regular-bred physician.
Ibid.

I ne'er could any lustre see
In eyes that would not look on me;
I ne'er saw nectar on a lip
But where my own did hope to sip.
The Duenna [*1775*]. *Act I, Sc. 2*

I loved him for himself alone.
Ibid. Sc. 3

I was struck all of a heap.
Ibid. Act II, Sc. 2

A bumper of good liquor
Will end a contest quicker
Than justice, judge, or vicar.[1]
Ibid. Sc. 3

Conscience has no more to do with gallantry than it has with politics.
Ibid. Sc. 4

Tale-bearers are as bad as the talemakers.
The School for Scandal [*1777*].
Act I, Sc. 1

You shall see them on a beautiful quarto page, where a neat rivulet of text shall meander through a meadow of margin.
Ibid.

You had no taste when you married me.
Ibid. Sc. 2

Here's to the maiden of bashful fifteen;
Here's to the widow of fifty;
Here's to the flaunting, extravagant quean,

[1] The government of a nation is often decided over a cup of coffee, or the fate of empires changed by an extra bottle of Johannisberg. — G. P. R. JAMES: *Richelieu* [1829], *Chap. 16*

And here's to the housewife that's
thrifty!
  Let the toast pass;
  Drink to the lass;
I'll warrant she'll prove an excuse for
the glass.
The School for Scandal.
Act III, Sc. 3

An unforgiving eye, and a damned
disinheriting countenance.
Ibid. Act IV, Sc. 1

Be just before you're generous.
Ibid.

There is not a passion so strongly
rooted in the human heart as envy.
The Critic [*1779*]. *Act I, Sc. 1*

The newspapers! Sir, they are the
most villainous, licentious, abominable,
infernal — Not that I ever read them!
No, I make it a rule never to look into
a newspaper.
Ibid.

Egad, I think the interpreter is the
hardest to be understood of the two!
Ibid. Sc. 2

A practitioner in panegyric, or, to
speak more plainly, a professor of the
art of puffing.
Ibid.

The number of those who undergo
the fatigue of judging for themselves
is very small indeed.[1]
Ibid.

Certainly nothing is unnatural that
is not physically impossible.
Ibid. Act II, Sc. 1

Though hopeless love finds comfort in
despair,
It never can endure a rival's bliss! [2]
Ibid. Act III, Sc. 1

An oyster may be crossed in love.[2]
Ibid.

[1] See J. R. Lowell, page 603b, and Bryce,
page 698a.
We must view with profound respect the
infinite capacity of the human mind to resist the introduction of useful knowledge. —
THOMAS RAYNESFORD LOUNSBURY [1838-
1915]: Quoted in *The Freshman and His
College* [1913], by FRANCIS CUMMINS LOCK-
WOOD, *P. 44*
[2] From the interpolated tragedy, *The Spanish Armada.*

The Right Honorable gentleman is
indebted to his memory for his jests,
and to his imagination for his facts.
Sheridaniana. Speech in Reply to
Mr. Dundas

You write with ease to show your
breeding,
But easy writing's curst hard reading.
Clio's Protest. In THOMAS
MOORE's *Life of Sheridan*
[*1825*], *Vol. I, Page 155*

JAMES MADISON
[1751–1836]

To secure the public good, and private rights, against the danger of . . .
faction, and at the same time to preserve
the spirit and form of popular government, is then the great object to which
our inquiries are directed.
The Federalist [*1787–1788*].
No. 10

I believe there are more instances of
the abridgment of the freedom of the
people by gradual and silent encroachments of those in power than by violent
and sudden usurpations.
Speech in the Virginia Convention
[*June 16, 1788*]

JOHANN HEINRICH VOSS
[1751–1826]

Who does not love wine, women, and
song
Remains a fool his whole life long.[1]
Couplet

PHILIP FRENEAU
[1752–1832]

From Susquehanna's utmost springs
Where savage tribes pursue their
game,
His blanket tied with yellow strings,
A shepherd of the forest came.
The Indian Student. Stanza 1

[1] Wer nicht liebt Wein, Weib und Gesang,
Der bleibt ein Narr sein Leben lang.
The couplet has also been attributed to
Luther, apparently on no better authority
than an eighteenth-century jingle in which
"Luther" is needed to rhyme with "Futter."
It is REDLICH who ascribes it to Voss.

In spite of all the learned have said,
I still my old opinion keep;
The posture that we give the dead
Points out the soul's eternal sleep.
*The Indian Burying-Ground.
Stanza 1*

Then rushed to meet the insulting foe;
They took the spear, but left the
shield.[1]
To the Memory of the Americans who Fell at Eutaw [September 8, 1781]

LEONARD McNALLY
[1752–1820]

On Richmond Hill there lived a lass
More bright than May-day morn;
Whose smiles all other maids' surpass,
A rose without a thorn.
*The Lass of Richmond Hill.
Stanza 1*

ROBERT HAWKER
[1753–1827]

Lord, dismiss us with thy blessing,
Hope, and comfort from above;
Let us each, thy peace possessing,
Triumph in redeeming love.
Benediction

MADAME ROLAND
[1754–1793]

O Liberty! Liberty! what crimes are
committed in thy name!
LAMARTINE: *Histoire des
Girondins [1847]*

JOEL BARLOW
[1754–1813]

The laws of husking every wight can
tell —
And sure no laws he ever keeps so
well:
For each red ear a general kiss he gains.
Hasty-Pudding

[1] When Prussia hurried to the field,
And snatched the spear, but left the shield.
SCOTT: *Marmion* [1808], *Introduction
to Canto III*

WILLIAM DRENNAN
[1754–1820]

Nor one feeling of vengeance presume
to defile
The cause, or the men, of the Emerald
Isle.[1]
Erin [1795]. Stanza 3

GEORGE CRABBE
[1754–1832]

Books cannot always please, however
good;
Minds are not ever craving for their
food.
*The Borough [1810]. Letter
XXIV, Schools*

In idle wishes fools supinely stay;
Be there a will, and wisdom finds a way.
The Birth of Flattery

Cut and come again.
*Tales [1812]. VII, The Widow's
Tale*

But 'twas a maxim he had often tried,
That right was right, and there he
would abide.
*Ibid. XV, The Squire and
the Priest*

And took for truth the test of ridicule.[2]
*Tales of the Hall [1819].
Book VIII, The Sisters*

Time has touched me gently in his race,
And left no odious furrows in my face.
Ibid. Book XVII, The Widow

[1] The first known use of this appellation
for Ireland.

[2] How comes it to pass, then, that we appear such cowards in reasoning, and are so
afraid to stand the test of ridicule? — AN-
THONY COOPER, EARL OF SHAFTESBURY [1671–
1713]: *Characteristics, A Letter Concerning
Enthusiasm, Sect. 2*
Truth, 'tis supposed, may bear all lights;
and one of these principal lights or natural
mediums by which things are to be viewed in
order to a thorough recognition is ridicule
itself. — SHAFTESBURY: *Essay on the Freedom
of Wit and Humour, Sect. 1*
'Twas the saying of an ancient sage (Gor-
gias Leontinus, *apud* Aristotle's "Rhetoric,"
lib. iii. c. 18), that humour was the only test
of gravity, and gravity of humour. For a subject which would not bear raillery was suspicious; and a jest which would not bear a
serious examination was certainly false wit. —
Ibid., Sect. 5

The ring, so worn as you behold,
So thin, so pale, is yet of gold.
A Marriage Ring

CHARLES MAURICE DE TALLEYRAND-PÉRIGORD
[1754–1838]

Black as the devil,
Hot as hell,
Pure as an angel,
Sweet as love.[1]
Recipe for Coffee
They have learned nothing, and forgotten nothing.[2]
Attributed to Talleyrand by the Chevalier de Panat in a letter to Mallet du Pan [January, 1796]
It is the beginning of the end.[3]
Quoted in EDOUARD FOURNIER: *L'Esprit dans l'Histoire [1857]*

BERTRAND BARÈRE
[1755–1841]

The tree of liberty only grows when watered by the blood of tyrants.
Speech in the National Convention [1792]
It is only the dead who do not return.
Speech [1794]

HENRY LEE
[1756–1818]

To the memory of the Man, first in war, first in peace, and first in the hearts of his countrymen.
Resolutions Presented to the House of Representatives on the Death of Washington [December, 1799]

[1] Noir comme le diable,
Chaud comme l'enfer,
Pur comme un ange,
Doux comme l'amour.
This appears as an inscription on many old coffeepots.
[2] Ils n'ont rien appris, ni rien oublié. Said of the Bourbons.
[3] "C'est le commencement de la fin." Reported to have been Talleyrand's comment on receiving the news of the battle of Borodino in 1812.

JAMES GILLRAY
[1757–1815]

The Old Lady of Threadneedle Street.[1]
Title of cartoon [1797]

WILLIAM BLAKE
[1757–1827]

How sweet I roam'd from field to field,
And tasted all the summer's pride,
Till I the prince of love beheld
Who in the sunny beams did glide.
*Poetical Sketches [1783].
Song, Stanza 1*

He loves to sit and hear me sing,
Then, laughing, sports and plays with me;
Then stretches out my golden wing,
And mocks my loss of liberty.
Ibid. Stanza 4

My silks and fine array,
My smiles and languish'd air,
By love are driv'n away;
And mournful lean despair
Brings me yew to deck my grave:
Such end true lovers have.
Ibid. Song, Stanza 1

Like a fiend in a cloud,
With howling woe,
After night I do crowd,
And with night will go;
I turn my back to the east,
From whence comforts have increas'd;
For light doth seize my brain
With frantic pain.
Ibid. Mad Song, Stanza 3

How have you left the ancient love
That bards of old enjoy'd in you!
The languid strings do scarcely move!
The sound is forc'd, the notes are few!
Ibid. To the Muses, Stanza 4

Does the eagle know what is in the pit?
Or wilt thou go ask the mole?
Can Wisdom be put in a silver rod?
Or Love in a golden bowl?
*The Book of Thel [1789].
Thel's Motto*

[1] The Bank of England.

Piping down the valleys wild,
Piping songs of pleasant glee,
On a cloud I saw a child.
Songs of Innocence [*1789*].
Introduction, Stanza 1

And I made a rural pen,
And I stain'd the water clear,
And I wrote my happy songs
Every child may joy to hear.
Ibid. Stanza 5

Little Lamb, who made thee?
Dost thou know who made thee?
Gave thee life, and bid thee feed
By the stream and o'er the mead;
Gave thee clothing of delight,
Softest clothing, woolly, bright.
Ibid. The Lamb, Stanza 1

My mother bore me in the southern
wild,
And I am black, but O! my soul is
white;
White as an angel is the English child,
But I am black, as if bereav'd of light.
Ibid. The Little Black Boy,
Stanza 1

"And we are put on earth a little space,
That we may learn to bear the beams
of love;
And these black bodies and this sun-
burnt face
Is but a cloud, and like a shady grove."
Ibid. Stanza 4

I'll shade him from the heat, till he can
bear
To lean in joy upon our father's knee;
And then I'll stand and stroke his silver
hair,
And be like him, and he will then love
me.
Ibid. Stanza 7

When my mother died I was very
young,
And my father sold me while yet my
tongue
Could scarcely cry " 'weep! 'weep!
'weep!"
So your chimneys I sweep, and in soot
I sleep.
Ibid. The Chimney Sweeper,
Stanza 1

To Mercy, Pity, Peace, and **Love**
All pray in their distress;
And to these virtues of delight
Return their thankfulness.
Songs of Innocence. The Divine
Image, Stanza 1

The moon like a flower
In heaven's high bower,
With silent delight
Sits and smiles on the night.
Ibid. Night, Stanza 1

And there the lion's ruddy eyes
Shall flow with tears of gold,
And pitying the tender cries,
And walking round the fold,
Saying "Wrath, by his meekness,
And by his health, sickness,
Is driven away
From our immortal day."
Ibid. Stanza 5

"For, wash'd in life's river,
My bright mane for ever
Shall shine like the gold
As I guard o'er the fold."
Ibid. Stanza 6

When the voices of children are heard
on the green
And laughing is heard on the hill,
My heart is at rest within my breast
And everything else is still.
Ibid. Nurse's Song, Stanza 1

Can I see another's woe,
And not be in sorrow too?
Can I see another's grief,
And not seek for kind relief?
Ibid. On Another's Sorrow,
Stanza 1

Rintrah roars and shakes his fires in
the burden'd air;
Hungry clouds swag on the deep.
The Marriage of Heaven and
Hell [*Circa 1793*]. *The Argu-*
ment

The busy bee has no time for sorrow.
Ibid. Proverbs of Hell

No bird soars too high, if he soars
with his own wings.
Ibid.

The pride of the peacock is the glory
of God.

The lust of the goat is the bounty of
God.

The wrath of the lion is the wisdom of God.

The nakedness of woman is the work of God.
The Marriage of Heaven and Hell.
Proverbs of Hell

Think in the morning. Act in the noon. Eat in the evening. Sleep in the night.
Ibid.

The weak in courage is strong in cunning.
Ibid.

Improvement makes straight roads; but the crooked roads without improvement are roads of genius.
Ibid.

Never seek to tell thy love
Love that never told can be;
For the gentle wind does move
Silently, invisibly.

I told my love, I told my love,
I told her all my heart,
Trembling, cold, in ghastly fears —
Ah, she doth depart.

Soon as she was gone from me
A traveller came by
Silently, invisibly —
O, was no deny.
Poems from MSS. [Circa *1793*].
Untitled Poem

I asked a thief to steal me a peach:
He turned up his eyes.
I ask'd a lithe lady to lie her down:
Holy and meek she cries.

As soon as I went an angel came:
He wink'd at the thief
And smil'd at the dame,
And without one word spoke
Had a peach from the tree,
And 'twixt earnest and joke
Enjoy'd the Lady.
Ibid. Untitled Poem

Sleep, Sleep, beauty bright
Dreaming o'er the joys of night.
Sleep, Sleep: in thy sleep
Little sorrows sit and weep.
Ibid. A Cradle Song, Stanza 1

Love to faults is always blind,
Always is to joy inclin'd,
Lawless, wing'd, and unconfin'd,
And breaks all chains from every mind.
Poems from MSS. Untitled Poem

The sword sung on the barren heath,
The sickle in the fruitful field:
The sword he sung a song of death,
But could not make the sickle yield.
Ibid. Untitled Poem

Abstinence sows sand all over
The ruddy limbs and flaming hair,
But desire gratified
Plants fruits of life and beauty there.
Ibid. Untitled Poem

If you trap the moment before it's ripe,
The tears of repentance you'll certainly wipe;
But if once you let the ripe moment go
You can never wipe off the tears of woe.
Ibid. Untitled Poem

He who binds to himself a joy
Does the winged life destroy;
But he who kisses the joy as it flies
Lives in eternity's sun rise.
Ibid. Eternity

What is it men in women do require?
The lineaments of Gratified Desire.
What is it women do in men require?
The lineaments of Gratified Desire.
Ibid. The Question Answer'd

The look of love alarms
Because 'tis fill'd with fire;
But the look of soft deceit
Shall win the lover's hire.
Ibid. Untitled Poem

Hear the voice of the Bard!
Who Present, Past, and Future, sees;
Whose ears have heard
The Holy Word
That walk'd among the ancient trees.
Songs of Experience [*1794*].
Introduction, Stanza 1

"Turn away no more;
Why wilt thou turn away?
The starry floor,
The wat'ry shore,
Is giv'n thee till the break of day." [1]
Ibid. Stanza 4

"Love seeketh not itself to please,
Nor for itself hath any care,

[1] See Milton, page 246b.

But for another gives its ease,
And builds a Heaven in Hell's despair."
*Songs of Experience. The Clod
and the Pebble, Stanza 1*

"Love seeketh only self to please,
To bind another to its delight,
Joys in another's loss of ease,
And builds a Hell in Heaven's despite."
Ibid. Stanza 3

O Rose, thou art sick!
The invisible worm
That flied in the night,
In the howling storm,

Has found out thy bed
Of crimson joy,
And his dark secret love
Does thy life destroy.
Ibid. The Sick Rose.

Little Fly,
Thy summer's play
My thoughtless hand
Has brush'd away.
Ibid. The Fly, Stanza 1

Am not I
A fly like thee?
Or art not thou
A man like me?
Ibid. Stanza 2

For I dance,
And drink, and sing,
Till some blind hand
Shall brush my wing.
Ibid. Stanza 3

Tiger! Tiger! burning bright
In the forests of the night,
What immortal hand or eye
Could frame thy fearful symmetry?
Ibid. The Tiger, Stanza 1

In what distant deeps or skies
Burnt the fire of thine eyes?
On what wings dare he aspire?
What the hand dare seize the fire?
Ibid. Stanza 2

What the hammer? what the chain?
In what furnace was thy brain?
What the anvil? what dread grasp
Dare its deadly terrors clasp?
Ibid. Stanza 4

When the stars threw down their spears,
And water'd heaven with their tears,
Did he smile his work to see?
Did he who made the Lamb make thee?
*Songs of Experience. The
Tiger, Stanza 5*

In every cry of every man,
In every infant's cry of fear,
In every voice, in every ban,
The mind-forg'd manacles I hear.
Ibid. London, Stanza 2

But most thro' midnight streets I hear
How the youthful harlot's curse
Blasts the new born infant's tear,
And blights with plagues the marriage
hearse.
Ibid. Stanza 4

My mother groan'd! my father wept.
Into the dangerous world I leapt:
Helpless, naked, piping loud:
Like a fiend hid in a cloud.
Ibid. Infant Sorrow, Stanza 1

I was angry with my friend:
I told my wrath, my wrath did end.
I was angry with my foe:
I told it not, my wrath did grow.
Ibid. A Poison Tree, Stanza 1

Cruelty has a human heart,
And jealousy a human face;
Terror the human form divine,
And secrecy the human dress.
Ibid. A Divine Image, Stanza 1

My spectre around me night and day
Like a wild beast guards my way.
My emanation far within
Weeps incessantly for my sin.
*Poems From MSS. [Circa
1800–1803]. Untitled Poem,
Stanza 1*

And throughout all eternity
I forgive you, you forgive me.
Ibid. Stanza 14

Mock on, mock on, Voltaire, Rousseau;
Mock on, mock on: 'tis all in vain!
You throw the sand against the wind,
And the wind blows it back again.
Ibid. Untitled Poem, Stanza 1

Terror in the house does roar,
But Pity stands before the door.
Ibid. Fragment

There is a smile of love,
And there is a smile of deceit,

And there is a smile of smiles
In which these two smiles meet.
        Poems [*Circa 1803*]. *The Smile,*
                        Stanza 1
And there is a frown of hate,
And there is a frown of disdain,
And there is a frown of frowns
Which you strive to forget in vain.
                Ibid. Stanza 2
For it sticks in the heart's deep core
And it sticks in the deep back bone;
And no smile that ever was smil'd,
But only one smile alone.
                Ibid. Stanza 3
To see a world in a grain of sand
And a heaven in a wild flower,
Hold infinity in the palm of your hand
And eternity in an hour.
        Ibid. Auguries of Innocence,
                        Line 1
A robin redbreast in a cage
Puts all Heaven in a rage.
                Ibid. Line 5
A dog starv'd at his master's gate
Predicts the ruin of the state.
                Ibid. Line 9
He who shall hurt the little wren
Shall never be belov'd by men.
                Ibid. Line 29
A truth that's told with bad intent
Beats all the lies you can invent.
                Ibid. Line 53
Every tear from every eye
Becomes a babe in eternity.
                Ibid. Line 67
He who shall teach the child to doubt
The rotting grave shall ne'er get out.
                Ibid. Line 77
He who doubts from what he sees
Will ne'er believe, do what you please.
If the sun and moon should doubt,
They'd immediately go out.
                Ibid. Line 97
The harlot's cry from street to street
Shall weave old England's winding
        sheet.
                Ibid. Line 105
Every night and every morn
Some to misery are born.
Every morn and every night
Some are born to sweet delight.
                Ibid. Line 109

And did those feet in ancient time
Walk upon England's mountains green?
And was the holy Lamb of God
On England's pleasant pastures seen?
        Milton [*1804–1808*]. *Stanza 1*
And did the countenance divine
Shine forth upon our clouded hills?
And was Jerusalem builded here
Among those dark Satanic mills?
                Ibid. Stanza 2
Bring me my bow of burning gold:
Bring me my arrows of desire:
Bring me my spear: O clouds unfold!
Bring me my chariot of fire.
                Ibid. Stanza 3
I will not cease from mental fight,
Nor shall my sword sleep in my hand
Till we have built Jerusalem
In England's green and pleasant land.
                Ibid. Stanza 4
The Angel that presided at my birth
Said: "Little creature, formed of joy
        and mirth,
Go, love without the help of any thing
        on earth."
                Fragment [*Circa 1810*]
The vision of Christ that thou dost see
Is my vision's greatest enemy:
Thine has a great hook nose like thine,
Mine has a snub nose like to mine.
                The Everlasting Gospel
                        [*Circa 1818*]
Both read the Bible day and night,
But thou read'st black where I read
        white.
                        Ibid.
This life's dim windows of the soul
Distorts the heavens from pole to pole
And leads you to believe a lie
When you see with, not thro', the eye
That was born in a night to perish in a
        night.
                        Ibid.
    Poetry fettered fetters the human
race. Nations are destroyed or flourish
in proportion as their poetry, painting,
and music are destroyed or flourish.
                Jerusalem [*1804–1820*].
                        Chap. I, Preface
For a tear is an intellectual thing,
And a sigh is the sword of an angel king,

And the bitter groan of a martyr's woe
Is an arrow from the Almighty's bow.
> *Jerusalem. Chap. II, Sect. 52*

England! awake! awake! awake!
Jerusalem thy sister calls!
Why wilt thou sleep the sleep of death
And close her from thy ancient walls?
> *Ibid. Chap. III, Sect. 77,
> Stanza 1*

And now the time returns again:
Our souls exult, and London's towers
Receive the Lamb of God to dwell
In England's green and pleasant
bowers.
> *Ibid. Stanza 3*

JOHN PHILIP KEMBLE
[1757–1823]

Perhaps it was right to dissemble your
love,
But — why did you kick me down
stairs?
> *The Panel. Act I, Sc. 1*

ROYALL TYLER [1]
[1757–1826]

Why should our thoughts to distant
countries roam,
When each refinement may be found
at home?
> *The Contrast* [1787]. *Prologue*

This outlandish lingo.
> *Ibid. Act II, Sc. 2*

By the living jingo, you look so top-
ping, I took you for one of the agents
to Congress.
> *Ibid.*

Since General Shays has sneaked off
and given us the bag to hold.
> *Ibid.*

I am at the end of my tether.
> *Ibid. Act III, Sc. 1*

---

[1] Tyler was born in Boston, was graduated
from Harvard, practiced law, and helped to
suppress Shays's Rebellion. Three weeks after
seeing *The School for Scandal* in New York,
he wrote *The Contrast*, the second play to
be written by an American. He also wrote a
novel, *The Algerine Captive* [1797], and was
Chief Justice of the State Supreme Court in
Vermont from 1807 to 1813.

JAMES MONROE
[1758–1831]

National honor is national property
of the highest value.
> *First Inaugural Address
> [March 4, 1817]*

The American continents . . . are
henceforth not to be considered as subjects for future colonization by any European powers.
> *Annual Message to Congress
> [December, 1823] (The Mon-
> roe Doctrine)*

We owe it, therefore, to candor, and
to the amicable relations existing between the United States and those powers to declare that we should consider
any attempt on their part to extend
their system to any portion of this
hemisphere as dangerous to our peace
and safety. With the existing colonies
or dependencies of any European power
we . . . shall not interfere. But with
the governments . . . whose independence we have . . . acknowledged, we
could not view any interposition for
the purpose of oppressing them, or controlling, in any other manner, their
destiny, by any European power, in any
other light than as a manifestation of
an unfriendly disposition towards the
United States.
> *Ibid.*

HORATIO NELSON
[1758–1805]

In the battle off Cape St. Vincent,
Nelson gave orders for boarding the
San Josef, exclaiming "Westminster
Abbey, or victory!"
> SOUTHEY's *Life of Nelson*
> [1813]. *Vol. I*

England expects every man will do
his duty.[1]
> *Ibid. Vol. II [Battle of
> Trafalgar]*

---

[1] This famous sentence is thus first reported: "Say to the fleet, England confides
that every man will do his duty." Captain
Pasco, Nelson's flag lieutenant, suggested sub-
stituting "expects" for "confides," which was

Kiss me, Hardy.
> SOUTHEY's *Life of Nelson. Vol. II*
> *[Battle of Trafalgar]*

May the great God, whom I worship,
grant to my country and for the benefit
of Europe in general, a great and glorious victory, and may no misconduct
in anyone tarnish it, and may humanity after the victory be the predominant
feature in the British fleet.
> *Prayer written in his diary*
> *[October 21, 1805]*

ROBERT BURNS
[1759–1796]

Wee, sleekit, cowrin, tim'rous beastie,
O, what a panic's in thy breastie!
Thou need na start awa sae hasty
> Wi' bickering brattle!
> *To a Mouse [1785]. Stanza 1*

I'm truly sorry man's dominion
Has broken Nature's social union.
> *Ibid. Stanza 2*

The best laid schemes o' mice and men
> Gang aft a-gley;
An' lea'e us nought but grief and pain,
> For promis'd joy.
> *Ibid. Stanza 7*

When chill November's surly blast
Made fields and forests bare.
> *Man Was Made to Mourn*
> *[1786]. Stanza 1*

Man's inhumanity to man
Makes countless thousands mourn.
> *Ibid. Stanza 7*

Beneath the milk-white thorn that
> scents the evening gale.
> *The Cotter's Saturday Night*
> *[1786]. Stanza 9*

He wales a portion with judicious care;
And "Let us worship God," he says,
> with solemn air.
> *Ibid. Stanza 12*

From scenes like these, old Scotia's
> grandeur springs,
That makes her loved at home, re-
> vered abroad:

---

adopted. Captain Blackwood, who commanded the *Euryalus,* says that the correction
suggested was from "Nelson expects" to "England expects."

Princes and lords are but the breath
> of kings,[1]
"An honest man's the noblest work of
God." [2]
> *The Cotter's Saturday Night.*
> *Stanza 19*

Gie me ae spark o' Nature's fire,
That's a' the learning I desire.
> *First Epistle to J. Lapraik*
> *[1786]. Stanza 13*

Gif ye want ae friend that's true,
I'm on your list.
> *Ibid. Stanza 15*

I winna blaw about mysel,
As ill I like my fauts to tell.
> *Ibid. Stanza 16*

My worthy friend, ne'er grudge an'
> carp,
Tho' Fortune use you hard an' sharp.
> *Second Epistle to J. Lapraik*
> *[1786]. Stanza 8*

The social, friendly, honest man,
> Whate'er he be,
'Tis he fulfills great Nature's plan,
> And none but he.
> *Ibid. Stanza 15*

Morality, thou deadly bane,
Thy tens o' thousands thou hast slain!
> *A Dedication to Gavin Hamilton*
> *[1786]*

It's hardly in a body's pow'r,
To keep, at times, frae being sour.
> *Epistle to Davie [1786].*
> *Stanza 2*

O Life! how pleasant, in thy morning,
Young Fancy's rays the hills adorn-
> ing!
Cold-pausing Caution's lesson scorn-
> ing,
> We frisk away,
Like schoolboys, at th' expected warn-
> ing,
> To joy an' play.
> *Epistle to James Smith*
> *[1786]. Stanza 15*

Misled by fancy's meteor ray,
> By passion driven;
But yet the light that led astray
> Was light from heaven.
> *The Vision [1786]. II, Stanza 18*

[1] See Goldsmith, page 355b.
[2] See Pope, pages 317b–318a.

And, like a passing thought, she fled
    In light away.
          The Vision. II, Stanza 24

His lockèd, lettered, braw brass collar
Showed him the gentleman an' scholar.
          The Twa Dogs [*1786*]. *Stanza 3*

An' there began a lang digression
About the lords o' the creation.
          Ibid. Stanza 6

Oh wad some power the giftie gie us
To see oursels as others see us!
It wad frae monie a blunder free us,
    An' foolish notion.
          To a Louse [*1786*]. *Stanza 8*

Wee, modest, crimson-tippèd flow'r,
Thou's met me in an evil hour;
For I maun crush amang the stoure
    Thy slender stem:
To spare thee now is past my pow'r,
    Thou bonie gem.
          To a Mountain Daisy
             [*1786*]. *Stanza 1*

Stern Ruin's ploughshare drives elate,
    Full on thy bloom.[1]
          Ibid. Stanza 9

O life! thou art a galling load,
Along a rough, a weary road,
    To wretches such as I!
      Despondency [*1786*]. *Stanza 1*

Perhaps it may turn out a sang,
Perhaps turn out a sermon.
      Epistle to a Young Friend
            [*1786*]. *Stanza 1*

A man may tak a neebor's part,
Yet hae nae cash to spare him.
          Ibid. Stanza 4

I waive the quantum o' the sin,
The hazard of concealing;
But, och! it hardens a' within,
And petrifies the feeling!
          Ibid. Stanza 6

To catch Dame Fortune's golden smile,
Assiduous wait upon her;
And gather gear by ev'ry wile
That's justified by honor:
Not for to hide it in a hedge,
Nor for a train-attendant;
But for the glorious privilege
Of being independent.
          Ibid. Stanza 7

[1] See Edward Young, page 306a.

An atheist's laugh's a poor exchange
For Deity offended!
      Epistle to a Young Friend. Stanza 9

There's nought but care on ev'ry han',
In every hour that passes, O:
What signifies the life o' man,
An' 't were nae for the lasses, O.
      Green Grow the Rashes, O
            [*1787*]. *Stanza 1*

Auld Nature swears, the lovely dears
Her noblest work she classes, O:
Her prentice han' she try'd on man,
An' then she made the lasses, O.
          Ibid. Stanza 5

Green grow the rashes, O;
Green grow the rashes, O;
The sweetest hours that e'er I spend,
Are spent among the lasses, O.
          Ibid. Chorus

Some books are lies frae end to end.
      Death and Dr. Hornbook
            [*1787*]. *Stanza 1*

John Barleycorn got up again,
And sore surpris'd them all.
      John Barleycorn [*1787*]. *Stanza 3*

Affliction's sons are brothers in distress;
A brother to relieve, — how exquisite
    the bliss!
      A Winter Night [*1787*]. *Stanza 8*

A dear-lov'd lad, convenience snug,
A treach'rous inclination —
But, let me whisper i' your lug,
Ye're aiblins nae temptation.
      Address to the Unco Guid
            [*1787*]. *Stanza 6*

Then gently scan your brother man,
Still gentler sister woman;
Tho' they may gang a kennin wrang,
To step aside is human:
One point must still be greatly dark,
The moving *why* they do it;
And just as lamely can ye mark
How far perhaps they rue it.
          Ibid. Stanza 7

O, my luve is like a red, red rose,
That's newly sprung in June.
O, my luve is like the melodie,
That's sweetly play'd in tune.
      Johnson's Musical Museum
      [*1787–1796*]. *A Red, Red
      Rose, Stanza 1*

Contented wi' little, and cantie wi' mair.
Johnson's Musical Museum. Contented wi' Little, Stanza 1

Ye banks and braes o' bonie Doon,
How can ye bloom sae fresh and fair?
How can ye chant, ye little birds,
And I sae weary fu' o' care!
Thou'll break my heart, thou warbling
bird,
That wantons thro' the flowering thorn!
Thou minds me o' departed joys,
Departed never to return.
*Ibid. The Banks o' Doon,
Stanza 1*

Chords that vibrate sweetest pleasure
Thrill the deepest notes of woe.
*Ibid. Sensibility How Charming,
Stanza 4*

Ae fond kiss, and then we sever!
Ae farewell, and then forever!
Ibid. Ae Fond Kiss, Stanza 1

But to see her was to love her,
Love but her, and love for ever.[1]
Had we never lov'd sae kindly,
Had we never lov'd sae blindly,
Never met — or never parted —
We had ne'er been broken-hearted.
Ibid. Stanza 2

It was a' for our rightfu' King
We left fair Scotland's strand.
*Ibid. It Was A' For Our Rightfu'
King, Stanza 1*

Now a' is done that men can do,
And a' is done in vain.
Ibid. Stanza 2

He turn'd him right and round about
Upon the Irish shore,
And gae his bridle reins a shake,
With adieu for evermore,
My dear —
And adieu for evermore!
Ibid. Stanza 3

John Anderson my jo, John,
When we were first acquent,
Your locks were like the raven,
Your bonie brow was brent;
But now your brow is beld, John,
Your locks are like the snaw,

[1] See Samuel Rogers, page 396b, and Halleck, page 462b.

But blessings on your frosty pow,
John Anderson my jo!
*Johnson's Musical Museum. John
Anderson My Jo, Stanza 1*

John Anderson my jo, John,
We clamb the hill thegither,
And monie a cantie day, John,
We've had wi' ane anither;
Now we maun totter down, John,
And hand in hand we'll go,
And sleep thegither at the foot,
John Anderson my jo!
Ibid. Stanza 2

Farewell to the Highlands, farewell to
the North,
The birthplace of valour, the country
of worth!
Wherever I wander, wherever I rove,
The hills of the Highlands for ever I
love.
*Ibid. My Heart's in the
Highlands, Stanza 1*

My heart's in the Highlands, my heart
is not here,
My heart's in the Highlands a-chasing
the deer.
Ibid. Chorus

Should auld acquaintance be forgot,
And never brought to mind?
Should auld acquaintance be forgot,
And auld lang syne!
*Auld Lang Syne [1788].
Stanza 1*

For auld lang syne, my dear,
For auld lang syne,
We'll tak a cup o' kindness yet
For auld lang syne!
Ibid. Chorus

Flow gently, sweet Afton, among thy
green braes!
Flow gently, I'll sing thee a song in thy
praise!
My Mary's asleep by thy murmuring
stream —
Flow gently, sweet Afton, disturb not
her dream!
Sweet Afton [1789]. Stanza 1

Thou stock dove whose echo resounds
thro' the glen,
Ye wild whistling blackbirds in yon
thorny den,

Thou green-crested lapwing, thy
screaming forbear —
I charge you, disturb not my slumbering fair!
Sweet Afton. Stanza 2

To make a happy fireside clime
To weans and wife,
That's the true pathos and sublime
Of human life.
Epistle to Dr. Blacklock
[1789]. Stanza 9

This day Time winds th' exhausted
chain,
To run the twelvemonth's length again.
New Year's Day, 1791. Stanza 1

The voice of Nature loudly cries,
And many a message from the skies,
That something in us never dies.
Ibid. Stanza 3

When Nature her great masterpiece
design'd,
And fram'd her last, best work, the hu-
man mind,
Her eye intent on all the wondrous
plan,
She form'd of various stuff the various
Man.
To Robert Graham [1791].
Stanza 1

She is a winsome wee thing,
She is a handsome wee thing,
She is a lo'esome wee thing,
This sweet wee wife o' mine.
My Wife's a Winsome Wee Thing
[1792]. Chorus

The golden hours on angel wings
Flew o'er me and my dearie;
For dear to me as light and life
Was my sweet Highland Mary.
Highland Mary [1792]. Stanza 2

But, oh! fell death's untimely frost,
That nipt my flower sae early.
Ibid. Stanza 3

If there's a hole in a' your coats,
I rede you tent it;
A chiel's amang you takin' notes,
And faith he'll prent it.
On the Late Captain Grose's
Peregrinations thro' Scotland
[1793]. Stanza 1

Some hae meat and canna eat,
And some wad eat that want it;
But we hae meat, and we can eat,
And sae the Lord be thankit.
The Selkirk Grace [1793]

O Mary, at thy window be!
It is the wish'd, the trysted hour.
Mary Morison [1793]. Stanza 1

The lovely Mary Morison!
Ibid.

Whare sits our sulky, sullen dame,
Gathering her brows like gathering
storm,
Nursing her wrath to keep it warm.
Tam o' Shanter [1793]. Stanza 1

Ah, gentle dames! it gars me greet
To think how monie counsels sweet,
How monie lengthened, sage advices,
The husband frae the wife despises.
Ibid. Stanza 4

His ancient, trusty, drouthy cronie;
Tam lo'ed him like a vera brither, —
They had been fou for weeks thegither.
Ibid. Stanza 5

The landlady and Tam grew gracious
Wi' secret favours, sweet and precious.
Ibid.

The landlord's laugh was ready chorus.
Ibid.

Kings may be blest, but Tam was
glorious,
O'er a' the ills o' life victorious.
Ibid. Stanza 6

But pleasures are like poppies spread,
You seize the flower, its bloom is shed;
Or like the snow falls in the river,
A moment white, then melts forever.
Ibid. Stanza 7

That hour, o' night's black arch the
keystane.
Ibid.

Inspiring bold John Barleycorn,
What dangers thou canst make us
scorn!
Ibid. Stanza 11

As Tammie glow'red, amazed, and curious,
The mirth and fun grew fast and furious.
Ibid. Stanza 13

Her cutty sark,[1] o' Paisley harn,
That while a lassie she had worn,
In longitude tho' sorely scanty,
It was her best, and she was vauntie,
> *Tam o' Shanter. Stanza 16*

Life is but a day at most,
Sprung from night, — in darkness lost:
Hope not sunshine ev'ry hour,
Fear not clouds will always lour.
> *Written in Friars Carse Hermitage* [*1793*]. *Stanza 2*

Scots, wha hae wi' Wallace bled,
Scots, wham Bruce has aften led,
Welcome to your gory bed
   Or to victorie!
> *Scots, Wha Hae* [*1794*]. *Stanza 1*

Now's the day, and now's the hour:
See the front o' battle lour,
See approach proud Edward's power —
   Chains and slaverie!
> *Ibid. Stanza 2*

Lay the proud usurpers low!
Tyrants fall in every foe!
Liberty's in every blow!
   Let us do, or die!
> *Ibid. Stanza 6*

The rank is but the guinea's stamp,
The man's the gowd for a' that.
> *Is There for Honest Poverty* [*1795*]. *Stanza 1*

A prince can mak a belted knight,
A marquis, duke, and a' that;
But an honest man's aboon his might,
Guid faith, he mauna fa' that.
> *Ibid. Stanza 4*

For a' that, and a' that,
An' twice as muckle 's a' that,
I've lost but ane, I've twa behin',
I've wife eneugh for a' that.
> *Posthumous Pieces. The Jolly Beggars, Chorus*

God knows, I'm no the thing I should be,
Nor am I even the thing I could be.
> *Ibid. To the Reverend John M'Math, Stanza 8*

If there's another world, he lives in bliss;
If there is none, he made the best of this.
> *Posthumous Pieces. Epitaph on William Muir*

In durance vile here must I wake and weep,
And all my frowsy couch in sorrow steep.
> *Ibid. Epistle from Esopus to Maria*

It's guid to be merry and wise,
It's guid to be honest and true,
It's guid to support Caledonia's cause
And bide by the buff and the blue.
> *Ibid. Here's a Health to Them That's Awa', Stanza 1*

JOHANN CHRISTOPH FRIEDRICH VON SCHILLER
[1759–1805]

There are three lessons I would write,
Three words as with a burning pen,
In tracings of eternal light,
Upon the hearts of men.
> *Hope, Faith, and Love. Stanza 1*

Thus grave these lessons on thy soul, —
Hope, faith, and love; and thou shalt find
Strength when life's surges rudest roll,
Light when thou else wert blind!
> *Ibid. Stanza 5*

The richest monarch in the Christian world;
The sun in my own dominions never sets.[1]
> *Don Carlos* [*1787*]. *Act I, Sc. 6*

When the wine goes in, strange things come out.
> *The Piccolomini* [*1799*]. *Act II, Sc. 12*

Against stupidity the very gods
Themselves contend in vain.[2]
> *The Maid of Orleans* [*1801*]. *Act III, Sc. 6*

---

[1] The famous tea clipper, *Cutty Sark*, designed by Hercules Linton and built in 1869, had the story of Tam o' Shanter carved upon her bow and counter. Nannie with flying locks and scanty shift was the figurehead.

[1] See Scott, page 417b, and Daniel Webster, page 444a.

[2] Against boredom even the gods themselves struggle in vain. — NIETZSCHE [1844–1900]: *The Antichrist, 48*

This feat of Tell, the archer, will be told
While yonder mountains stand upon
their base.
By Heaven! the apple's cleft right
through the core.
William Tell [*1804*]. *Act III, Sc. 3*

MASON LOCKE WEEMS
[1759–1825]

"George," said his father, "do you
know who killed that beautiful little
cherry tree yonder in the garden?" . . .
Looking at his father with the sweet
face of youth brightened with the
inexpressible charm of all-conquering
truth, he bravely cried out, "I can't tell
a lie. I did cut it with my hatchet."
The Life of George Washing-
ton: With Curious Anecdotes,
Equally Honorable to Himself
and Exemplary to His Young
Countrymen [*1800*]

JOSEPH ROUGET DE LISLE
[1760–1836]

Ye sons of France, awake to glory!
Hark! hark! what myriads bid you rise!

. . . . .

To arms! to arms! ye brave!
The avenging sword unsheathe!
March on! march on! all hearts re-
solved
On victory or death!
The Marseillaise [1] [*1792*]

AUGUST FRIEDRICH
FERDINAND VON KOTZEBUE
[1761–1819]

There is another and a better world.
The Stranger [*1798*]. *Act I, Sc. 1*

[1] Allons, enfants de la patrie,
Le jour de gloire est arrivé!

Aux armes, citoyens!
Formez vos bataillons!
Marchons! Marchons! Qu'un sang impur
Abreuve nos sillons!
Composed in the garrison at Strasbourg
and originally called *Chant de guerre de l'ar-*
mée du Rhin, the *Marseillaise* took its name
from the patriots of Marseilles who first made

JOANNA BAILLIE
[1762–1851]

Oh, swiftly glides the bonnie boat,
Just parted from the shore,
And to the fisher's chorus-note
Soft moves the dipping oar.[1]
Oh, Swiftly Glides the Bonnie
Boat
The wild-fire dances on the fen,
The red star sheds its ray;
Uprouse ye then, my merry men!
It is our op'ning day.
The Outlaw's Song. Stanza 1
Oh, who shall lightly say that fame
Is nothing but an empty name,
When but for those, our mighty dead,
All ages past a blank would be.
The Worth of Fame. Stanza 2
Good-morrow to thy sable beak
And glossy plumage dark and sleek,
Thy crimson moon and azure eye,
Cock of the heath, so wildly shy.
The Heath-Cock. Stanza 1

ANDREW CHERRY
[1762–1812]

Loud roared the dreadful thunder,
The rain a deluge showers.
The Bay of Biscay
As she lay, on that day,
In the bay of Biscay, O!
Ibid.

GEORGE COLMAN, THE
YOUNGER
[1762–1836]

Tell 'em Queen Anne's dead.[2]
The Heir-at-Law [*1797*]
On their own merits modest men are
dumb.
Ibid. Epilogue
And what's impossible can't be,
And never, never comes to pass.
The Maid of the Moor

it known in Paris. The English version in the
text is that usually found in the songbooks.
[1] See Marvell, page 269a.
[2] The phrase became proverbial for telling
what everybody knows.

But when ill indeed,
E'en dismissing the doctor don't always
succeed.
Lodgings for Single Gentlemen
When taken,
To be well shaken.
The Newcastle Apothecary
O Miss Bailey!
Unfortunate Miss Bailey!
Love Laughs at Locksmiths.
Act II, Song
'Tis a very fine thing to be father-in-law
To a very magnificent three-tailed Bashaw!
Blue Beard. Act II, Sc. 5
I had a soul above buttons.
Sylvester Daggerwood, or New
Hay at the Old Market. Sc. 1
Mynheer Vandunck, though he never
was drunk,
Sipped brandy and water gayly.
Mynheer Vandunck

JOSEPH FOUCHÉ
[1763–1820]

"It is more than a crime; it is a
blunder," [1] — words which I record,
because they have been repeated and
attributed to others.
Memoirs

Death is an eternal sleep.
Inscription placed by his orders
on the gates of the cemeteries
[1794]

SAMUEL ROGERS
[1763–1855]

Sweet Memory! wafted by thy gentle
gale,
Oft up the stream of Time I turn my
sail.
The Pleasures of Memory
[1792]. Part II, I

She was good as she was fair,
None — none on earth above her!
As pure in thought as angels are:
To know her was to love her. [1]
Jacqueline [2] [1814]. *Stanza 1*
A guardian angel o'er his life presiding,
Doubling his pleasures, and his cares
dividing.
Human Life
To fireside happiness, to hours of ease
Blest with that charm, the certainty to
please.
Ibid.
The soul of music slumbers in the shell
Till waked and kindled by the master's
spell;
And feeling hearts, touch them but
rightly, pour
A thousand melodies unheard before!
Ibid.
Mine be a cot beside the hill;
A beehive's hum shall soothe my ear;
A willowy brook that turns a mill,
With many a fall shall linger near. [3]
A Wish. Stanza 1
That very law which moulds a tear
And bids it trickle from its source, —
That law preserves the earth a sphere,
And guides the planets in their course.
On a Tear. Stanza 6
Go! you may call it madness, folly;
You shall not chase my gloom away!
There's such a charm in melancholy
I would not if I could be gay.
To ——. Stanza 1
Ward has no heart, they say, but I
deny it:
He has a heart, and gets his speeches
by it.
Epigram

ROBERT HALL
[1764–1831]

His [Burke's] imperial fancy has
laid all Nature under tribute, and has

[1] "C'est plus qu'un crime, c'est une faute," reputedly Fouché's comment on the murder of the Duc d'Enghien [1804]. Fouché's family denied the authenticity of the *Memoirs*, and the remark has also been commonly attributed to Talleyrand. Sainte-Beuve ascribes it to Boulay de la Meurthe.

[1] See Burns, page 392a, and Halleck, page 462b.
[2] First published in the same volume with Byron's *Lara*, neither author appending his name to his work.
[3] See Yeats, page 824b.

collected riches from every scene of the creation and every walk of art.

Apology for the Freedom of the Press

Call things by their right names. . . . Glass of brandy and water! That is the current but not the appropriate name: ask for a glass of liquid fire and distilled damnation.

GREGORY's *Life of Hall*

THOMAS MORTON
[1764–1838]

Push on, — keep moving.

A Cure for the Heartache [1797]. Act II, Sc. 1

Approbation from Sir Hubert Stanley is praise indeed.

Ibid. Act V, Sc. 2

What will Mrs. Grundy say? What will Mrs. Grundy think? [1]

Speed the Plough [1798]. Act I, Sc. 1

ANN RADCLIFFE
[1764–1823]

Fate sits on these dark battlements and frowns,
And as the portal opens to receive me,
A voice in hollow murmurs through the courts
Tells of a nameless deed.[2]

Motto of her novel The Mysteries of Udolpho [1794]

HELEN D'ARCY CRANSTOUN (MRS. DUGALD STEWART)
[1765–1838]

I weep not for the silent dead,
Their pains are past, their sorrows o'er.[3]

The Song of Genius

CATHERINE MARIA FANSHAWE
[1765–1834]

'Twas whisper'd in heaven, 'twas mutter'd in hell,
And echo caught faintly the sound as it fell;
On the confines of earth 'twas permitted to rest,
And the depths of the ocean its presence confess'd.

Enigma: The Letter H

MARY LAMB
[1765–1847]

Thou straggler into loving arms,
Young climber-up of knees.

A Child. Stanza 3

SIR JAMES MACKINTOSH
[1765–1832]

Diffused knowledge immortalizes itself.

Vindiciae Gallicae [1791]

The Commons, faithful to their system, remained in a wise and masterly inactivity.

Ibid.

The frivolous work of polished idleness.

Dissertation on Ethical Philosophy [1830]. Remarks on Thomas Brown

Disciplined inaction.

History of the Revolution in England in 1688 [1834]. Chap. VII

MADAME DE STAËL
[1766–1817]

The sight of such a monument is like a continuous and stationary music.[1]

Corinne [1807]. Book IV, Chap. 3

---

[1] See Herbert Spencer, page 614b.
[2] See Shakespeare, page 198a.
[3] Quoted by SIR WALTER SCOTT in *The Talisman [1825] Chap. 26.*

[1] Since it [architecture] is music in space, as it were a frozen music. . . . If architecture in general is frozen music. — FRIEDRICH VON SCHELLING [1775–1854]: *Philosophie der Kunst, Pp. 576, 593*

To understand all makes us very indulgent.[1]

Corinne. Book XVIII, Chap. 5

ERNST F. MÜNSTER [2]
[1766–1839]

Absolutism tempered by assassination.

Description of the Russian Constitution

ISAAC D'ISRAELI
[1766–1848]

Whatever is felicitously expressed risks being worse expressed: it is a wretched taste to be gratified with mediocrity when the excellent lies before us.

Curiosities of Literature [1834].
On Quotation

They [the early writers] looked with alarm upon the halo of immortality that encircled the printing-press.

Amenities of Literature [1841].
Vol. II, Page 278

CAROLINA OLIPHANT, LADY NAIRNE
[1766–1845]

Sweet's the laverock's note and lang,
  Lilting wildly up the glen;
But aye to me he sings ae sang,
  Will ye no come back again?

Will Ye No Come Back Again?
[1846]. Stanza 5

Would you be young again?
  So would not I —
One tear to memory given,
  Onward I'd hie.

Would You Be Young Again?
[Looking Backward]. Stanza 1

[1] To all the gossip that I hear
  I'll give no faith; to what I see
  But only half, for it is clear
  All that led up is dark to me.
  Learn we the larger life to live,
  To comprehend is to forgive.
    HENRIETTA A. HUXLEY [1825–1914]:
    "Tout Comprendre, C'est Tout Pardonner"
[2] Hanoverian envoy at St. Petersburg.

Gude nicht, and joy be wi' you a'.

Gude Nicht [1846]

A penniless lass wi' a lang pedigree.

The Laird o' Cockpen [1846].
Stanza 2

NANCY DENNIS SPROAT
[1766–1826]

How pleasant is Saturday night,
  When I've tried all the week to be good,
And not spoke a word that was bad,
  And obliged every one that I could.

Lullabies for Children [1818].
Saturday Night, Stanza 1

HENRI BENJAMIN CONSTANT
[1767–1830]

I am not the rose, but I have lived with her.[1]

Attributed

JOHN QUINCY ADAMS
[1767–1848]

Think of your forefathers! Think of your posterity! [2]

Speech at Plymouth
[December 22, 1802]

In charity to all mankind, bearing no malice or ill-will to any human being, and even compassionating those who hold in bondage their fellow-men, not knowing what they do.[3]

Letter to A. Bronson
[July 30, 1838]

My wants are many, and, if told,
Would muster many a score;
And were each wish a mint of gold,
I still should long for more.

The Wants of Man [1841].
Stanza 1

This is the last of earth! I am content.

Last Words [February 21, 1848]

[1] Je ne suis pas la rose, mais j'ai vécu avec elle. — Attributed to CONSTANT by ABRAHAM HAYWARD in his introduction to the *Autobiography and Letters* [1861] of MRS. PIOZZI
[2] Et majores vestros et posteros cogitate. — TACITUS [*circa* A.D. 55–117]: *Agricola, 32, 26*
[3] See Abraham Lincoln, page 542a.

398

ANDREW JACKSON
[1767–1845]

Our Federal Union: it must be preserved.

Toast given on the Jefferson Birthday Celebration [1830]

It is to be regretted that the rich and powerful too often bend the acts of government to their selfish purposes. . . . Every man is equally entitled to protection by law; but when the laws undertake to add . . . artificial distinctions, to grant titles, gratuities, and exclusive privileges, to make the rich richer and the potent more powerful, the humble members of society — the farmers, mechanics, and laborers — who have neither the time nor the means of securing like favors to themselves, have a right to complain of the injustice of their government.

Message Vetoing the Bank Bill [July 10, 1832]

There are no necessary evils in government. Its evils exist only in its abuses. If it would confine itself to equal protection, and, as Heaven does its rains, shower its favors alike on the high and the low, the rich and the poor, it would be an unqualified blessing.

Ibid.

You are uneasy; you never sailed with *me* before, I see.[1]

PARTON'S *Life of Jackson. Vol. III, Page 493*

NAPOLEON BONAPARTE
[1769–1821]

Soldiers, from the summit of yonder pyramids forty centuries look down upon you.

In Egypt [July 21, 1798]

Go, sir, gallop, and don't forget that the world was made in six days. You can ask me for anything you like, except time.

To one of his aides [1803]. Quoted in R. M. JOHNSTON, The Corsican

From the sublime to the ridiculous is but a step.[1]

To the Abbé du Pradt, on the return from Russia [1812], referring to the retreat from Moscow

What is the throne? — a bit of wood gilded and covered with velvet. I am the state [2] — I alone am here the representative of the people. Even if I had done wrong you should not have reproached me in public — people wash their dirty linen at home. France has more need of me than I of France.

To the Senate [1814]

France is invaded; I go to put myself at the head of my troops, and, with God's help and their valour, I hope soon to drive the enemy beyond the frontier.

At Paris [January 23, 1814]

The bullet that will kill me is not yet cast.

At Montereau [February 17, 1814]

The Allied Powers having proclaimed that the Emperor Napoleon is the sole obstacle to the re-establishment of peace in Europe, he, faithful to his oath, declares that he is ready to descend from the throne, to quit France, and even to relinquish life, for the good of his country.

Act of Abdication [April 4, 1814]

Unite for the public safety, if you would remain an independent nation.

Proclamation to the French People [June 22, 1815]

---

[1] A remark made to an elderly gentleman who was sailing with Jackson down Chesapeake Bay in an old steamboat.

[1] Du sublime au ridicule il n'y a qu'un pas. The saying has been attributed also to Talleyrand.
See Paine, page 371a.

[2] The expression "L'état c'est moi" ("I am the state"), commonly attributed to Louis XIV, was apparently first ascribed to him by DULAURE in his *Histoire de Paris* [1863], and can claim no historical authenticity. Even if a pure fabrication of Dulaure's, however, it has a usefulness of its own in providing a concise symbol of the attitude of Louis XIV toward absolute monarchy.

Wherever wood can swim, there I am sure to find this flag of England.
At Rochefort [July, 1815]

Whatever shall we do in that remote spot? Well, we will write our Memoirs. Work is the scythe of time.
On board H. M. S. Bellerophon
[August, 1815]

I generally had to give in [speaking of his relations with the Empress Josephine].
On St. Helena [May 19, 1816]

My maxim was, *la carrière est ouverte aux talents*, without distinction of birth or fortune.
On St. Helena [March 3, 1817]

Our hour is marked, and no one can claim a moment of life beyond what fate has predestined.
To Dr. Arnott [April, 1821]

I am neither an atheist nor a rationalist; I believe in God, and am of the religion of my father. I was born a Catholic, and will fulfill all the duties of that church, and receive the assistance which she administers.
On St. Helena [April 18, 1821]

I could not unbend the bow; and France has been deprived of the liberal institutions I intended to give her.
Bourrienne: *Memoirs, Vol. X, Page 425 [May 3, 1821]*

All was not lost until the moment when all had succeeded.
Ibid. On anniversary of Battle of Waterloo, Page 39

Madame Montholon having inquired what troops he considered the best, "Those which are victorious, Madame," replied the Emperor.
Ibid. Page 399

Tête d'armée (Head of the army).
Last words [May 5, 1821]

Two o'clock in the morning courage.
Quoted in Las Cases, *Napoleon at St. Helena [1823]*

An army marches on its stomach.
Attributed to Napoleon

Every French soldier carries a marshal's baton in his knapsack.[1]
Attributed to Napoleon

JOHN HOOKHAM FRERE
[1769–1846]

And don't confound the language of the nation
With long-tailed words in *osity* and *ation*.
The Monks and the Giants.
Canto I, Line 6

Despair in vain sits brooding over the putrid eggs of hope.
The Rovers. Act I, Sc. 2

ARTHUR WELLESLEY, DUKE OF WELLINGTON
[1769–1852]

Nothing except a battle lost can be half so melancholy as a battle won.
Dispatch [1815]

There is no mistake; there has been no mistake; and there shall be no mistake.
Letter to Mr. Huskisson

I care not one twopenny damn.[2]
Quoted in George Otto Trevelyan: *Life and Letters of Lord Macaulay [1876], Vol. II, Page 221*

It is very true that I have said that I considered Napoleon's presence in the field equal to forty thousand men in the balance. This is a very loose way of talking; but the idea is a very different one from that of his presence at a battle being equal to a reinforcement of forty thousand men.
Stanhope, *Conversations with Wellington [1888], Page 81*

The battle of Waterloo was won on the playing fields of Eton.
Quoted in Fraser, *Words on Wellington [1889]*

---

[1] Tout soldat français porte dans sa giberne le bâton de maréchal de France.

[2] Quoted, as the Duke's oath, in a letter from Macaulay to T. F. Ellis, March 6, 1849.

DAVID EVERETT
[1770–1813]

You'd scarce expect one of my age
To speak in public on the stage;
And if I chance to fall below
Demosthenes or Cicero,
Don't view me with a critic's eye,
But pass my imperfections by.
Large streams from little fountains
flow,
Tall oaks from little acorns grow.[1]
> *Lines written for a school dec-*
> *lamation for Ephraim H. Far-*
> *rar, aged seven, New Ipswich,*
> *New Hampshire [1791]*

These thoughts inspire my youthful
mind
To be the greatest of mankind;
Great, not like Caesar, stained with
blood,
But only great as I am good.
> *Lines written for a school dec-*
> *lamation [1791]*

GEORGE CANNING
[1770–1827]

When our perils are past, shall our
gratitude sleep?
No, — here's to the pilot that weathered
the storm.
> *Song for the Inauguration of the*
> *Pitt Club [May 25, 1802]*

I give thee sixpence! I will see thee
damned first.
> *The Friend of Humanity and the*
> *Knife-Grinder. Stanza 9*

A steady patriot of the world alone,
The friend of every country but his
own.[2]
> *New Morality. Line 113*

And finds, with keen, discriminating
sight,
Black's not so black, — nor white so
very white.
> *Ibid. Line 199*

Give me the avowed, the erect, the
manly foe,
Bold I can meet, — perhaps may turn
his blow!
But of all plagues, good Heaven, thy
wrath can send,
Save, save, oh save me from the *candid*
friend! [1]
> *New Morality. Line 207*

I think of those companions true
Who studied with me at the U-
-niversity of Göttingen.
> *Song sung by Rogero in the bur-*
> *lesque play, The Rovers. Stanza 1*

Here rests, and let no saucy knave
Presume to sneer and laugh,
To learn that mouldering in the grave
Is laid a British Calf.
> *Epitaph on the Tombstone*
> *Erected over the Marquis of*
> *Anglesea's Leg, Lost at the*
> *Battle of Waterloo. Stanza 1*

She saw two legs were lost on him
Who never meant to run.
> *Ibid. Stanza 9*

In matters of commerce the fault of
the Dutch
Is offering too little and asking too
much.
> *Dispatch to Sir Charles Bagot,*
> *British Minister at The Hague*
> *[January 31, 1826]*

I called the New World into existence
to redress the balance of the Old.
> *The King's Message [December*
> *12, 1826]*

GEORG WILHELM FRIEDRICH HEGEL
[1770–1831]

Peoples and governments never have
learned anything from history, or acted
on principles deduced from it.
> *Philosophy of History [1832].*[2]
> *Introduction*

---

[1] The lofty oak from a small acorn grows.
— LEWIS DUNCOMBE [1711–1730]: *De Mini-*
mis Maxima (translation)
   Parvis e glandibus quercus. — *Latin motto*
[2] This refers to the Jacobin.
See Overbury, page 226b.

[1] Defend me from my friends; I can defend myself from my enemies. — *Remark at-*
tributed to Maréchal Villars when taking
leave of Louis XIV
[2] Translated by J. SIBREE.

Amid the pressure of great events, a general principle gives no help.

Philosophy of History.
Introduction

To him who looks upon the world rationally, the world in its turn presents a rational aspect. The relation is mutual.

Ibid.

The history of the world is none other than the progress of the consciousness of freedom.

Ibid.

We may affirm absolutely that nothing great in the world has been accomplished without passion.

Ibid.

It is easier to discover a deficiency in individuals, in states, and in Providence, than to see their real import and value.

Ibid.

Life has a value only when it has something valuable as its object.

Ibid.

Serious occupation is labor that has reference to some want.

Ibid. Part I, Sect. 2, Chap. 1

It is a matter of perfect indifference where a thing originated; the only question is: "Is it true in and for itself?"

Ibid. Part III, Sect. 3, Chap. 2

When liberty is mentioned, we must always be careful to observe whether it is not really the assertion of private interests which is thereby designated.

Ibid. Part IV, Sect. 3, Chap. 2

The Few assume to be the *deputies*, but they are often only the *despoilers* of the Many.

Ibid. Chap. 3

JAMES HOGG [1]
[1770–1835]

She left this world of sorrow and pain,
And returned to the Land of Thought again.

Kilmeny

[1] The "Ettrick Shepherd"

Charlie is my darling,
The young Chevalier.

Charlie Is My Darling. Refrain

Love is like a dizziness,
It winna let a poor body
Gang about his bizziness.

Love Is Like a Dizziness. Stanza 1

PIERRE JACQUES ÉTIENNE, COUNT CAMBRONNE
[1770–1842]

The Guard dies, but never surrenders.[1]

Inscribed upon the monument
erected to him at Nantes

JOSEPH HOPKINSON
[1770–1842]

Hail, Columbia! happy land!
Hail, ye heroes! heaven-born band!
Who fought and bled in Freedom's
cause,
Who fought and bled in Freedom's
cause,
And when the storm of war was gone,
Enjoyed the peace your valor won.
Let independence be our boast,
Ever mindful what it cost;
Ever grateful for the prize,
Let its altar reach the skies!

Hail, Columbia.[2] Stanza 1

WILLIAM ROBERT SPENCER
[1770–1834]

When the black-lettered list to the gods
was presented,

[1] This phrase, attributed to Cambronne, who was made prisoner at Waterloo, was vehemently denied by him. It was invented by Rougemont, a prolific author of *mots*, two days after the battle, in the "Indépendant." — FOURNIER: *L'Esprit dans l'Histoire*

[2] The musical setting of *Hail, Columbia*, generally attributed to Philip Phile, was originally *The President's March*, written in 1789 as an inaugural march for George Washington. In 1798, Joseph Hopkinson was asked by Mr. Fox, a young actor-singer, to write verses to the music of the march, to introduce at a benefit performance. The song was repeated eight times, and when sung the ninth time, the audience stood and joined in the chorus.

(The list of what Fate for each mortal intends,)
At the long string of ills a kind goddess relented,
And slipped in three blessings — wife, children, and friends.
Wife, Children, and Friends.
Stanza 1

Oh! where does faithful Gêlert roam,
The flow'r of all his race?
So true, so brave; a lamb at home,
A lion in the chase!
Beth-Gêlert. Stanza 4

JOHN TOBIN
[1770–1804]

The man that lays his hand upon a woman,
Save in the way of kindness, is a wretch
Whom 'twere gross flattery to name a coward.
The Honeymoon [1805]. Act II,
Sc. 1

She's adorned
Amply that in her husband's eye looks lovely, —
The truest mirror that an honest wife
Can see her beauty in.
Ibid. Act III, Sc. 4

WILLIAM WORDSWORTH [1]
[1770–1850]

And homeless near a thousand homes I stood,
And near a thousand tables pined and wanted food.
Guilt and Sorrow [Written 1791–
1794]. Part II, Stanza 41

A simple child,
That lightly draws its breath,
And feels its life in every limb,
What should it know of death?
We Are Seven [1798]. Stanza 1

O Reader! had you in your mind
Such stores as silent thought can bring,

O gentle Reader! you would find
A tale in everything.
Simon Lee [1798]. Stanza 9

In that sweet mood when pleasant thoughts
Bring sad thoughts to the mind.
Lines Written in Early Spring
[1798]. Stanza 1

And 'tis my faith, that every flower
Enjoys the air it breathes.
Ibid. Stanza 3

Nor less I deem that there are Powers
Which of themselves our minds impress;
That we can feed this mind of ours
In a wise passiveness.
Expostulation and Reply [1798].
Stanza 6

Up! up! my friend, and quit your books;
Or surely you'll grow double:
Up! up! my friend, and clear your looks;
Why all this toil and trouble?
The Tables Turned [1798].
Stanza 1

Come forth into the light of things,
Let Nature be your teacher.
Ibid. Stanza 4

One impulse from a vernal wood
May teach you more of man,
Of moral evil and of good,
Than all the sages can.
Ibid. Stanza 6

Sensations sweet,
Felt in the blood, and felt along the heart.
Lines Composed a Few Miles
Above Tintern Abbey [1798]

That best portion of a good man's life, —
His little, nameless, unremembered, acts
Of kindness and of love.
Ibid.

That blessed mood,
In which the burthen of the mystery,
In which the heavy and the weary weight
Of all this unintelligible world,
Is lightened.
Ibid.

[1] Coleridge said to Wordsworth, "Since Milton, I know of no poet with so many *felicities* and unforgettable lines and stanzas as you." — HENRY NELSON COLERIDGE: *Memoir* [1847]

The sounding cataract
Haunted me like a passion; the tall rock,
The mountain, and the deep and gloomy wood,
Their colours and their forms, were then to me
An appetite; a feeling and a love,
That had no need of a remoter charm,
By thoughts supplied, nor any interest
Unborrowed from the eye.
*Lines Composed a Few Miles
Above Tintern Abbey*
But hearing oftentimes
The still, sad music of humanity.
Ibid.

A sense sublime
Of something far more deeply inter-fused,
Whose dwelling is the light of setting suns,
And the round ocean and the living air,
And the blue sky, and in the mind of man;
A motion and a spirit, that impels
All thinking things, all objects of all thought,
And rolls through all things.
Ibid.
Knowing that Nature never did betray
The heart that loved her.
Ibid.
Men who can hear the Decalogue and feel
No self-reproach.
*The Old Cumberland Beggar
[Written 1798]*
As in the eye of Nature he has lived,
So in the eye of Nature let him die!
Ibid.
Full twenty times was Peter feared,
For once that Peter was respected.
*Peter Bell [Written 1798].
Part I, Stanza 3*
A primrose by a river's brim
A yellow primrose was to him,
And it was nothing more.
Ibid. Stanza 12
The soft blue sky did never melt
Into his heart; he never felt
The witchery of the soft blue sky!
Ibid. Stanza 15

On a fair prospect some have looked,
And felt, as I have heard them say,
As if the moving time had been
A thing as steadfast as the scene
On which they gazed themselves away.
Peter Bell. Part 1, Stanza 16
As if the man had fixed his face,
In many a solitary place,
Against the wind and open sky!
Ibid. Stanza 26 [1]
Many are our joys
In youth, but oh! what happiness to live
When every hour brings palpable access
Of knowledge, when all knowledge is delight,
And sorrow is not there!
*The Prelude [Written 1799–
1805]. Book II*
Where the statue stood
Of Newton with his prism and silent face,
The marble index of a mind forever
Voyaging through strange seas of thought, alone.
Ibid. Book III
There's not a man
That lives who hath not known his god-like hours.
Ibid.
When from our better selves we have too long
Been parted by the hurrying world, and droop,
Sick of its business, of its pleasures tired,
How gracious, how benign, is Solitude.
Ibid. Book IV
'Tis told by one whom stormy waters threw,
With fellow-sufferers by the shipwreck spared,

---

[1] The original edition [1819] had the following as the fourth stanza from the end of Part I, which was omitted in all subsequent editions:
Is it a party in a parlour?
Crammed just as they on earth were crammed, —
Some sipping punch, some sipping tea,
But, as you by their faces see,
All silent and all damned.

Upon a desert coast, that having brought
  To land a single volume, saved by chance,
A treatise on Geometry.
                    The Prelude. Book VI
                  Multitudes of hours
Pilfered away, by what the Bard who sang
Of the Enchanter Indolence [1] hath called
"Good-natured lounging," and behold a map
Of my collegiate life.
                              Ibid.
              How men lived
Even next-door neighbours, as we say, yet still
Strangers, not knowing each the other's name.
                    Ibid. Book VII
Bliss was it in that dawn to be alive,
But to be young was very heaven!
                    Ibid. Book XI
One of those heavenly days that cannot die.
                    Nutting [*1799*]
What fond and wayward thoughts will slide
  Into a lover's head!
"O mercy!" to myself I cried,
  "If Lucy should be dead!"
          *Strange Fits of Passion Have I
              Known* [*1799*]. *Stanza 7*
She dwelt among the untrodden ways
  Beside the springs of Dove,
A maid whom there were none to praise
  And very few to love.[2]
      *Lucy: She Dwelt Among the Un-
        trodden Ways* [*1799*]. *Stanza 1*
A violet by a mossy stone
  Half hidden from the eye! —

[1] THOMSON'S *Castle of Indolence* [1748].
[2] He lived amidst th' untrodden ways
    To Rydal Lake that lead;
  A bard whom there were none to praise,
    And very few to read.
  Unread his works — his "Milk White Doe"
    With dust is dark and dim;
  It's still in Longmans' shop, and oh!
    The difference to him!
        — *Parody by* HARTLEY COLERIDGE
                    [1796–1849]

Fair as a star, when only one
  Is shining in the sky.
      *Lucy: She Dwelt Among the Un-
          trodden Ways. Stanza 2*
She lived unknown, and few could know
  When Lucy ceased to be;
But she is in her grave, and, oh,
  The difference to me!
                    Ibid. Stanza 3
Three years she grew in sun and shower,
Then Nature said, "A lovelier flower
On earth was never sown;
This Child I to myself will take;
She shall be mine, and I will make
A Lady of my own."
        *Lucy: Three Years She Grew in
          Sun and Shower* [*1799*]. *Stanza 1*
"The stars of midnight shall be dear
To her; and she shall lean her ear
In many a secret place
Where rivulets dance their wayward round,
And beauty born of murmuring sound
Shall pass into her face."
                    Ibid. Stanza 5
A slumber did my spirit seal;
  I had no human fears:
She seemed a thing that could not feel
  The touch of earthly years.

No motion has she now, no force;
  She neither hears nor sees;
Rolled round in earth's diurnal course,
  With rocks, and stones, and trees.
        A Slumber Did My Spirit Seal
                              [*1799*]
One that would peep and botanize
Upon his mother's grave.
      A Poet's Epitaph [*1799*]. *Stanza 5*
And you must love him, ere to you
He will seem worthy of your love.
                    Ibid. Stanza 11
The harvest of a quiet eye.
                    Ibid. Stanza 13
Yet sometimes, when the secret cup
Of still and serious thought went round,
It seemed as if he drank it up —
He felt with spirit so profound.
          Matthew [*1799*]. *Stanza 7*

The sweetest thing that ever grew
Beside a human door.
> *Lucy Gray* [*1799*]. *Stanza 2*

A youth to whom was given
So much of earth — so much of heaven.
> *Ruth* [*1799*]. *Stanza 21*

Poetry is the breath and finer spirit
of all knowledge; it is the impassioned
expression which is in the countenance
of all Science.
> *Lyrical Ballads, Second Edition*
> [*1800*]. *Preface*

In spite of difference of soil and climate, of language and manners, of laws
and customs, — in spite of things silently gone out of mind, and things
violently destroyed, the Poet binds together by passion and knowledge the
vast empire of human society, as it is
spread over the whole earth, and over
all time.
> *Ibid.*

I have said that poetry is the spontaneous overflow of powerful feelings:
it takes its origin from emotion recollected in tranquillity.
> *Ibid.*

All men feel an habitual gratitude,
and something of an honourable bigotry, for the objects which have long
continued to please them.
> *Ibid.*

Something between a hindrance and a
help.
> *Michael* [*1800*]

Drink, pretty creature, drink!
> *The Pet Lamb* [*1800*]

May no rude hand deface it,
And its forlorn *hic jacet!*
> *Ellen Irwin* [*1800*]. *Stanza 7*

She gave me eyes, she gave me ears;
And humble cares, and delicate fears;
A heart, the fountain of sweet tears;
And love, and thought, and joy.
> *The Sparrows' Nest* [*1801*].
> *Stanza 2*

My heart leaps up when I behold
A rainbow in the sky:
So was it when my life began;
So is it now I am a man.
> *My Heart Leaps Up When I*
> *Behold* [*1802*]

The Child is father of the Man; [1]
And I could wish my days to be
Bound each to each by natural piety.
> *My Heart Leaps Up When I Behold*

Sweet childish days, that were as long
As twenty days are now.
> *To a Butterfly* [*1802*]. *Part II,*
> *I've Watched You Now a Full*
> *Half-hour, Stanza 2*

Often have I sighed to measure
By myself a lonely pleasure,
Sighed to think, I read a book
Only read, perhaps, by me.
> *To the Small Celandine* [*1802*].
> *Part II, Stanza 4*

I thought of Chatterton, the marvellous boy,
The sleepless soul that perished in his
pride;
Of him who walked in glory and in
joy
Following his plough, along the mountain-side:
By our own spirits are we deified:
We Poets in our youth begin in gladness;
But thereof come in the end despondency and madness.
> *Resolution and Independence*
> [*1802*]. *Stanza 7*

That heareth not the loud winds when
they call,
And moveth all together, if it moves at
all.
> *Ibid. Stanza 11*

Choice word and measured phrase,
above the reach
Of ordinary men.
> *Ibid. Stanza 14*

And mighty poets in their misery dead.
> *Ibid. Stanza 17*

Earth has not anything to show more
fair:
Dull would he be of soul who could
pass by
A sight so touching in its majesty.
> *Composed Upon Westminster*
> *Bridge* [*September 3, 1802*]

Ne'er saw I, never felt, a calm so deep!
The river glideth at his own sweet will;

[1] See Milton, page 259b.

Dear God! the very houses seem
asleep;
And all that mighty heart is lying still!
*Composed Upon Westminster
Bridge*

It is a beauteous evening, calm and
free,
The holy time is quiet as a nun
Breathless with adoration.
It Is a Beauteous Evening [*1802*]

Thou liest in Abraham's bosom all the
year;
And worship'st at the Temple's inner
shrine,
God being with thee when we know it
not.
Ibid.

Once did She hold the gorgeous east in
fee:
And was the safeguard of the west.
*On the Extinction of the Venetian
Republic* [*1802*]

Men are we, and must grieve when
even the shade
Of that which once was great, is passed
away.
Ibid.

And, when she took unto herself a Mate,
She must espouse the everlasting Sea.
Ibid.

Thou hast left behind
Powers that will work for thee; air,
earth, and skies;
There's not a breathing of the common
wind
That will forget thee; thou hast great
allies;
Thy friends are exultations, agonies,
And love, and man's unconquerable
mind.
To Toussaint L'Ouverture

Plain living and high thinking are no
more:
The homely beauty of the good old
cause
Is gone; our peace, our fearful inno-
cence,
And pure religion breathing household
laws.
*O Friend! I Know Not Which
Way I Must Look* [*1802*]

Milton! thou should'st be living at this
hour:
England hath need of thee; she is a
fen
Of stagnant waters.
London, 1802

Thy soul was like a star, and dwelt
apart:
Thou hadst a voice whose sound was
like the sea:
Pure as the naked heavens, majestic,
free,
So didst thou travel on life's common
way,
In cheerful godliness.
Ibid.

We must be free or die, who speak the
tongue
That Shakespeare spake; the faith and
morals hold
Which Milton held.
It Is Not To Be Thought Of [*1802*]

We meet thee, like a pleasant thought,
When such are wanted.
To the Daisy [*1802*]. *Stanza 3*

The poet's darling
Ibid. Stanza 4

Thou unassuming commonplace
Of Nature.
To the Same Flower [*1802*].
Stanza 1

Oft on the dappled turf at ease
I sit, and play with similes,
Loose type of things through all de-
grees.
Ibid. Stanza 2

And stepping westward seemed to be
A kind of heavenly destiny.
Stepping Westward [*1803*].
Stanza 2

For old, unhappy, far-off things,
And battles long ago.
The Solitary Reaper [*1803*].
Stanza 3

Some natural sorrow, loss, or pain,
That has been, and may be again.
Ibid.

The music in my heart I bore
Long after it was heard no more.
Ibid. Stanza 4

Because the good old rule
Sufficeth them, the simple plan,

That they should take, who have the power,
And they should keep who can.
Rob Roy's Grave [*1803*]. *Stanza 9*
Yon foaming flood seems motionless as ice;
Its dizzy turbulence eludes the eye,
Frozen by distance.
Address to Kilchurn Castle [*1803*]
A brotherhood of venerable trees.
Sonnet Composed at —— Castle [*1803*]
A remnant of uneasy light.
The Matron of Jedborough [*1803*]
Oh for a single hour of that Dundee
Who on that day the word of onset gave!
Sonnet, in the Pass of Killicranky [*1803*]
There was a time when meadow, grove, and stream,
The earth, and every common sight,
To me did seem
Apparelled in celestial light,
The glory and the freshness of a dream.
It is not now as it hath been of yore; —
Turn wheresoe'er I may,
By night or day,
The things which I have seen I now can see no more.
Ode. Intimations of Immortality [1]
[*1803–1806*]. *Stanza 1*
The Rainbow comes and goes,
And lovely is the Rose.
Ibid. Stanza 2
The sunshine is a glorious birth;
But yet I know, where'er I go,
That there hath passed away a glory from the earth.
Ibid.
Where is it now, the glory and the dream?
Ibid. Stanza 4
Our birth is but a sleep and a forgetting:
The soul that rises with us, our life's star,
Hath had elsewhere its setting,

[1] The Ode on Immortality is the high water mark which the intellect has reached in this age. — EMERSON: *English Traits* [1856]

And cometh from afar:
Not in entire forgetfulness,
And not in utter nakedness,
But trailing clouds of glory do we come
From God, who is our home:
Heaven lies about us in our infancy! [1]
Shades of the prison-house begin **to** close
Upon the growing boy.
Ode. Intimations of Immortality. *Stanza 5*
At length the man perceives it die away,
And fade into the light of common day.
Ibid.
As if his whole vocation
Were endless imitation.
Ibid. Stanza 7
High instincts before which our mortal nature
Did tremble like a guilty thing surprised.
Ibid. Stanza 9
Truths that wake,
To perish never.
Ibid.
Though inland far we be,
Our souls have sight of that immortal sea
Which brought us hither.
Ibid.
Though nothing can bring back the hour
Of splendour in the grass, of glory in the flower.
Ibid. Stanza 10
In years that bring the philosophic mind.
Ibid.
The clouds that gather round the setting sun
Do take a sober colouring from an eye
That hath kept watch o'er man's mortality.
Ibid. Stanza 11

[1] Not only around our infancy
Doth heaven with all its splendors lie;
Daily, with souls that cringe and plot,
We Sinais climb and know it not.
    JAMES RUSSELL LOWELL: *The Vision of Sir Launfal* [1848], *Part I, Prelude, St. 2*

To me the meanest flower that blows can give
Thoughts that do often lie too deep for tears.
> *Ode. Intimations of Immortality.*
> *Stanza 11*

O blithe New-comer! I have heard,
I hear thee and rejoice.
O Cuckoo! shall I call thee bird,
Or but a wandering voice?
> *To the Cuckoo* [*1804*]. *Stanza 1*

She was a phantom of delight
When first she gleamed upon my sight;
A lovely apparition, sent
To be a moment's ornament;
Her eyes as stars of twilight fair,
Like twilight's, too, her dusky hair,
But all things else about her drawn
From May-time and the cheerful dawn.
> *She Was a Phantom of Delight*
> [*1804*]. *Stanza 1*

A creature not too bright or good
For human nature's daily food;
For transient sorrows, simple wiles,
Praise, blame, love, kisses, tears, and smiles.
> *Ibid. Stanza 2*

And now I see with eye serene
The very pulse of the machine.
> *Ibid. Stanza 3*

The reason firm, the temperate will,
Endurance, foresight, strength, and skill;
A perfect woman, nobly planned,
To warn, to comfort, and command.
> *Ibid.*

I wandered lonely as a cloud
That floats on high o'er vales and hills,
When all at once I saw a crowd,
A host, of golden daffodils;
Beside the lake, beneath the trees;
Fluttering and dancing in the breeze.
> *I Wandered Lonely as a Cloud*
> [*1804*]. *Stanza 1*

Ten thousand saw I at a glance,
Tossing their heads in sprightly dance.
> *Ibid. Stanza 2*

A poet could not but be gay,
In such a jocund company:
I gazed — and gazed — but little thought

What wealth to me the show had brought.
> *I Wandered Lonely as a Cloud.*
> *Stanza 3*

That inward eye
Which is the bliss of solitude.
> *Ibid. Stanza 4*

Stern Daughter of the Voice of God! [1]
> *Ode to Duty* [*1805*]. *Stanza 1*

A light to guide, a rod
To check the erring, and reprove.
> *Ibid.*

Thou dost preserve the stars from wrong;
And the most ancient heavens, through Thee, are fresh and strong.
> *Ibid. Stanza 6*

The light that never was, on sea or land;
The consecration, and the Poet's dream.
> *Suggested by a Picture of Peele*
> *Castle in a Storm* [*1805*]. *Stanza 4*

Shalt show us how divine a thing
A woman may be made.
> *To a Young Lady* [*1805*]. *Dear*
> *Child of Nature, Stanza 2*

But an old age serene and bright,
And lovely as a Lapland night,
Shall lead thee to thy grave.
> *Ibid. Stanza 3*

Who is the happy Warrior? Who is he
That every man in arms would wish to be?
> *Character of the Happy Warrior*
> [*1806*]

But who, if he be called upon to face
Some awful moment to which Heaven has joined
Great issues, good or bad for human-kind,
Is happy as a lover.
> *Ibid.*

And, through the heat of conflict, keeps the law
In calmness made, and sees what he foresaw.
> *Ibid.*

Whom neither shape of danger can dismay,

[1] See Milton, page 258a.

Nor thought of tender happiness betray.
> *Character of the Happy Warrior*

Like, — but oh how different!
> *Yes, It Was the Mountain Echo*
> *[1806]*

The world is too much with us; late
and soon,
Getting and spending, we lay waste our
powers:
Little we see in Nature that is ours.
> *The World Is Too Much With*
> *Us [1806]*

    Great God! I'd rather be
A Pagan suckled in a creed outworn; [1]
So might I, standing on this pleasant
lea,
Have glimpses that would make me
less forlorn;
Have sight of Proteus rising from the
sea;
Or hear old Triton blow his wreathed
horn.
> *Ibid.*

Where lies the land to which yon Ship
must go? [2]
Fresh as a lark mounting at break of
day,
Festively she puts forth in trim array.
> *Where Lies the Land [1806]*

Blessed barrier between day and day.
> *To Sleep [1806]. II, A Flock*
> *of Sheep*

Maidens withering on the stalk. [3]
> *Personal Talk [1806].*
> *Sonnet 1*

Dreams, books, are each a world; and
books, we know,
Are a substantial world, both pure and
good.

[1]   Good Lord! I'd rather be
Quite unacquainted with the A.B.C.
Than write such hopeless rubbish as thy
    worst.
        JAMES KENNETH STEPHEN: *Sonnet,*
                Wordsworth [1891]
[2] Where lies the land to which the ship
    would go?
Far, far ahead, is all her seamen know.
      ARTHUR HUGH CLOUGH [1819–1861]:
                Songs of Absence
[3] Withering on the virgin thorn. — SHAKE-
SPEARE: *A Midsummer-Night's Dream* [1595–
1596], Act I, Sc. 1, L. 77

Round these, with tendrils strong as
flesh and blood,
Our pastime and our happiness will
grow.
> *Personal Talk. Sonnet 3*

A power is passing from the earth.
> *Lines on the Expected Dissolution*
> *of Mr. Fox [1806]. Stanza 5*

Two voices are there: one is of the
sea, [1]
One of the mountains; each a mighty
voice.
> *Thought of a Briton on the Sub-*
> *jugation of Switzerland [1807]*

The silence that is in the starry sky,
The sleep that is among the lonely
hills.
> *Song at the Feast of Brougham*
> *Castle [1807]*

A few strong instincts, and a few plain
rules.
> *Alas! What Boots the Long*
> *Laborious Quest? [1809]*

    Strongest minds
Are often those of whom the noisy
world
Hears least.
> *The Excursion* [2] *[Published*
> *1814]. Book I*

The imperfect offices of prayer and
praise.
> *Ibid.*

    The good die first, [3]
And they whose hearts are dry as sum-
mer dust
Burn to the socket.
> *Ibid.*

Wrongs unredressed, or insults unavenged.
> *Ibid. Book III*

Society became my glittering bride.
> *Ibid.*

[1] Two voices are there: one is of the deep.
And one is of an old half-witted sheep
Which bleats articulate monotony,
And indicates that two and one are three.
      JAMES KENNETH STEPHEN: *Sonnet,*
                Wordsworth [1891]
[2] This will never do. — FRANCIS JEFFREY:
Opening sentence, review of WORDSWORTH'S
Excursion, Edinburgh Review [1814]
[3] See Plautus, page 30a.

There is a luxury in self-dispraise;
And inward self-disparagement affords
To meditative spleen a grateful feast.
The Excursion. Book IV

I have seen
A curious child, who dwelt upon a tract
Of inland ground, applying to his ear
The convolutions of a smooth-lipped shell,
To which, in silence hushed, his very soul
Listened intensely; and his countenance soon
Brightened with joy, for from within were heard
Murmurings, whereby the monitor expressed
Mysterious union with its native sea.[1]
Ibid.

One in whom persuasion and belief
Had ripened into faith, and faith become
A passionate intuition.
Ibid.

Spires whose "silent finger points to heaven."[2]
Ibid. Book VI

Wisdom married to immortal verse.
Ibid. Book VII

A man he seems of cheerful yesterdays
And confident tomorrows.
Ibid.

[1] But I have sinuous shells of pearly hue ...
Shake one, and it awakens; then apply
Its polisht lips to your attentive ear,
And it remembers its august abodes,
And murmurs as the ocean murmurs there.
WALTER SAVAGE LANDOR: *Gebir,
Book I* [1798]
Upon a mountain height, far from the sea,
I found a shell,
And to my listening ear the lonely thing
Ever a song of ocean seemed to sing,
Ever a tale of ocean seemed to tell.
EUGENE FIELD [1850–1895]:
The Wanderer, St. 1
[2] An instinctive taste teaches men to build
their churches in flat countries with spire
steeples, which, as they cannot be referred to
any other object, point as with silent finger to
the sky and stars. — COLERIDGE: *The Friend*
[1809], *No. 14*

Her bosom heaves and spreads, her stature grows;
And she expects the issue in repose.
Laodamia [*1814*]. *Stanza 2*
The gods approve
The depth, and not the tumult, of the soul.
Ibid. Stanza 13
An ampler ether, a diviner air.
Ibid. Stanza 18
But thou that didst appear so fair
To fond imagination,
Dost rival in the light of day
Her delicate creation.
Yarrow Visited [*1814*]. *Stanza 6*
And beauty, for confiding youth,
Those shocks of passion can prepare
That kill the bloom before its time;
And blanch, without the owner's crime,
The most resplendent hair.
Lament of Mary Queen of Scots
[*1817*]. *Stanza 6*
Enough if something from our hands have power
To live, and act, and serve the future hour.
*The River Duddon, Sonnet:
Afterthought* [*1820*]
We feel that we are greater than we know.
Ibid.
The feather, whence the pen
Was shaped that traced the lives of these good men,
Dropped from an angel's wing.[1]
*Ecclesiastical Sonnets. Part III, V,
Walton's Book of Lives* [*1821*]
Give all thou canst; high Heaven rejects the lore
Of nicely-calculated less or more.
Ibid. XLIII, Inside of King's College Chapel, Cambridge [*1821*]
But hushed be every thought that springs
From out the bitterness of things.
*Elegiac Stanzas, Addressed to
Sir G. H. B.* [*1824*]. *Stanza 7*

[1] The pen wherewith thou dost so heavenly sing
Made of a quill from an angel's wing.
HENRY CONSTABLE [1562–
1613]: *Sonnet*

Ethereal minstrel! pilgrim of the sky!
　　　To a Skylark [*1825*]. *Stanza 1*

Type of the wise who soar, but never
　　roam,
True to the kindred points of heaven
　　and home.
　　　　　Ibid. Stanza 2

Scorn not the sonnet. Critic, you have
　　frowned,
Mindless of its just honours; with this
　　key
Shakespeare unlocked his heart.[1]
　　　Scorn Not the Sonnet [*1827*]

Look for the stars, you'll say that there
　　are none;
Look up a second time, and, one by
　　one,
You mark them twinkling out with sil-
　　very light,
And wonder how they could elude the
　　sight!
　　　Calm Is the Fragrant Air [*1832*]

Small service is true service while it
　　lasts.
Of humblest friends, bright creature!
　　scorn not one:
The daisy, by the shadow that it casts,
Protects the lingering dewdrop from
　　the sun.
　　　To a Child, Written in her Album
　　　　　　　　　[*1834*]

How does the meadow-flower its bloom
　　unfold?
Because the lovely little flower is free
Down to its root, and, in that freedom,
　　bold.
　　　*A Poet! He Hath Put His
　　　Heart to School* [*1842*]

Minds that have nothing to confer
Find little to perceive.
　　　Yes, Thou art Fair [*1845*].
　　　　　　　　Stanza 2

[1] "With this same key
　　Shakespeare unlocked his heart" once
　　more!
　　Did Shakespeare? If so, the less Shake-
　　speare he!
　　　ROBERT BROWNING: *House*
　　　　　[*1876*], *St. 10*

THOMAS DIBDIN
[*1771–1841*]

Oh, it's a snug little island!
A right little, tight little island.
　　　　　The Snug Little Island

JAMES MONTGOMERY
[*1771–1854*]

Tomorrow — oh, 'twill never be,
If we should live a thousand years!
Our time is all today, today.
　　　　　　　　　Today

Give me the hand that is honest and
　　hearty,
Free as the breeze and unshackled by
　　party.
　　　Give Me Thy Hand. Stanza 2

The rose has but a summer reign,
The daisy never dies.
　　　　The Daisy. Stanza 10

"The Press! — What is the Press?" I
　　cried;
When thus a wondrous voice replied:
"In me all human knowledge dwells;
The oracle of oracles,
Past, present, future, I reveal,
Or in oblivion's silence seal;
What I preserve can perish never,
What I forego is lost forever."
　　　　　The Press. Stanza 1

All that philosophers have sought,
Science discovered, genius wrought;
All that reflective memory stores,
Or rich imagination pours;
All that the wit of man conceives,
All that he wishes, hopes, believes;
All that he loves, or fears, or hates,
All that to heaven and earth relates,
— These are the lessons that I teach
In speaking silence, silent speech.
　　　　　　Ibid. Stanza 4

Counts his sure gains, and hurries back
　　for more.
　　　The West Indies. Part III

Hope against hope, and ask till ye re-
　　ceive.
　　　*The World before the Flood.
　　　　Canto V, Stanza 10*

Joys too exquisite to last,
And yet *more* exquisite when past.
　　　The Little Cloud. Stanza 9

Bliss in possession will not last;
Remembered joys are never past;
At once the fountain, stream, and sea,
They were, they are, they yet shall be.
The Little Cloud. Stanza 10

Friend after friend departs;
  Who hath not lost a friend?
There is no union here of hearts
  That finds not here an end.
Friends. Stanza 1

'Tis not the whole of life to live,
Nor all of death to die.
The Issues of Life and Death.
Stanza 2

Who, that hath ever been,
  Could bear to be no more?
Yet who would tread again the scene
  He trod through life before?
The Falling Leaf. Stanza 7

Here in the body pent,
  Absent from Him I roam,
Yet nightly pitch my moving tent
  A day's march nearer home.
At Home in Heaven

Prayer is the soul's sincere desire,
  Uttered or unexpressed;
The motion of a hidden fire
  That trembles in the breast.
What is Prayer? Stanza 1

Prayer is the burden of a sigh,
  The falling of a tear;
The upward glancing of an eye,
  When none but God is near.
Ibid. Stanza 2

SIR WALTER SCOTT
[1771–1832]

The way was long, the wind was cold,
The Minstrel was infirm and old;
His withered cheek, and tresses gray,
Seem'd to have known a better day.
The Lay of the Last Minstrel
[1805]. Introduction

Such is the custom of Branksome Hall.
Ibid. Canto I, Stanza 7

What shall be the maiden's fate?
Who shall be the maiden's mate?
Ibid. Stanza 16

If thou would'st view fair Melrose
aright,

Go visit it by the pale moonlight.
The Lay of the Last Minstrel.
Canto II, Stanza 1

I cannot tell how the truth may be;
I say the tale as 'twas said to me.
Ibid. Stanza 22

In peace, Love tunes the shepherd's
  reed;
In war, he mounts the warrior's steed;
In halls, in gay attire is seen;
In hamlets, dances on the green.
Love rules the court, the camp, the
  grove,
And men below, and saints above;
For love is heaven, and heaven is love.
Ibid. Canto III, Stanza 2

Her blue eyes sought the west afar,
For lovers love the western star.
Ibid. Stanza 24

    Ne'er
Was flattery lost on poet's ear;
A simple race! they waste their toil
For the vain tribute of a smile.
Ibid. Canto IV, Interlude
after Stanza 35

Call it not vain: they do not err
Who say, that when the poet dies,
Mute Nature mourns her worshipper,
And celebrates his obsequies.
Ibid. Canto V, Stanza 1

True love's the gift which God has
  given
To man alone beneath the heaven:
It is not fantasy's hot fire,
  Whose wishes, soon as granted, fly;
It liveth not in fierce desire,
  With dead desire it doth not die;
It is the secret sympathy,
The silver link, the silken tie,
Which heart to heart and mind to mind
In body and in soul can bind.
Ibid. Stanza 13

Breathes there the man, with soul so
  dead,
Who never to himself hath said,
  This is my own, my native land!
Whose heart hath ne'er within him
  burn'd [1]
As home his footsteps he hath turn'd,

[1] Did not our heart burn within us while
he talked with us by the way? — *Luke,*
XXIV, 32

From wandering on a foreign strand?
If such there breathe, go, mark him
   well;
For him no minstrel raptures swell;
High though his titles, proud his name,
Boundless his wealth as wish can
   claim, —
Despite those titles, power, and pelf,
The wretch, concentred all in self,
Living, shall forfeit fair renown,
And, doubly dying, shall go down
To the vile dust, from whence he
   sprung,
Unwept, unhonour'd, and unsung.[1]
                 The Lay of the Last Minstrel.
                         Canto VI, Stanza 1

O Caledonia! stern and wild,
Meet nurse for a poetic child!
Land of brown heath and shaggy wood;
Land of the mountain and the flood!
                         Ibid. Stanza 2

November's sky is chill and drear,
November's leaf is red and sear.
       Marmion [*1808*]. *Introduction*
                 to Canto I, Stanza 1

Stood for his country's glory fast,
And nail'd her colors to the mast!
                         Ibid. Stanza 10

Just at the age 'twixt boy and youth,
When thought is speech, and speech is
   truth.
       Ibid. Introduction to Canto II,
                         Stanza 4

When, musing on companions gone,
We doubly feel ourselves alone.
                         Ibid. Stanza 5

To bring my tribute to his grave: —
'Tis little — but 'tis all I have.
       Ibid. Introduction to Canto IV,
                         Stanza 5

Where's the coward that would not
   dare
To fight for such a land?
                 Ibid. Canto IV, Stanza 30

Lightly from fair to fair he flew,
And loved to plead, lament, and sue;
Suit lightly won, and short-lived pain,
For monarchs seldom sigh in vain.
                 Ibid. Canto V, Stanza 9

[1] See Homer, page 5b.

Oh, young Lochinvar is come out of the
   West,
Through all the wide Border his steed
   was the best.
       Marmion. Canto V, Stanza 12
                 [*Lochinvar, Stanza 1*]
So faithful in love, and so dauntless in
   war,
There never was knight like the young
   Lochinvar.
                         Ibid.
For a laggard in love, and a dastard in
   war,
Was to wed the fair Ellen of brave
   Lochinvar.
                 Ibid. [*Lochinvar, Stanza 2*]
With a smile on her lips, and a tear in
   her eye.
                 Ibid. [*Lochinvar, Stanza 5*]
Heap on more wood! — the wind is
   chill;
But let it whistle as it will,
We'll keep our Christmas merry still.
       Ibid. Introduction to Canto VI,
                         Stanza 1
England was merry England, when
Old Christmas brought his sports again.
'Twas Christmas broach'd the mightiest
   ale;
'Twas Christmas told the merriest tale;
A Christmas gambol oft could cheer
The poor man's heart through half the
   year.
Still linger, in our northern clime,
Some remnants of the good old time.
                         Ibid. Stanza 4
       And dar'st thou, then,
To beard the lion in his den,
The Douglas in his hall?
                 Ibid. Canto VI, Stanza 14
Oh, what a tangled web we weave,
When first we practise to deceive!
                         Ibid. Stanza 17
O woman! in our hours of ease,
Uncertain, coy, and hard to please,
And variable as the shade
By the light quivering aspen made;
When pain and anguish wring the
   brow,
A ministering angel thou! [1]
                         Ibid. Stanza 30

[1] See Shakespeare, page 179a.

"Charge, Chester, charge! on, Stanley, on!"
Were the last words of Marmion.
Marmion. Canto VI,
Stanza 32

To all, to each, a fair good-night,
And pleasing dreams, and slumbers light.
Ibid. L'Envoy, To the Reader

The stag at eve had drunk his fill,
Where danced the moon on Monan's rill,
And deep his midnight lair had made
In lone Glenartney's hazel shade.
The Lady of the Lake [1810].
Canto I, Stanza 1

In listening mood she seemed to stand,
The guardian Naiad of the strand.
Ibid. Stanza 17

And ne'er did Grecian chisel trace
A Nymph, a Naiad, or a Grace
Of finer form, or lovelier face.
Ibid. Stanza 18

A foot more light, a step more true,
Ne'er from the heath-flower dash'd the dew.
Ibid.

On his bold visage middle age
Had slightly press'd its signet sage,
Yet had not quench'd the open truth
And fiery vehemence of youth:
Forward and frolic glee was there,
The will to do, the soul to dare.
Ibid. Stanza 21

Soldier, rest! thy warfare o'er,
Sleep the sleep that knows not breaking,
Dream of battled fields no more,
Days of danger, nights of waking.
Ibid. Stanza 31

Hail to the Chief who in triumph advances! [1]
Ibid. Canto II, Stanza 19

Some feelings are to mortals given,
With less of earth in them than heaven.
Ibid. Stanza 22

Like the dew on the mountain,
Like the foam on the river,

Like the bubble on the fountain,
Thou art gone, and forever!
The Lady of the Lake. Canto III,
Stanza 16 [Coronach, Stanza 3]

Come one, come all! this rock shall fly
From its firm base as soon as I.
Ibid. Canto V, Stanza 10

And the stern joy which warriors feel
In foemen worthy of their steel.
Ibid.

Who o'er the herd would wish to reign,
Fantastic, fickle, fierce, and vain!
Vain as the leaf upon the stream,
And fickle as a changeful dream;
Fantastic as a woman's mood,
And fierce as Frenzy's fever'd blood.
Thou many-headed monster [1] thing,
Oh who would wish to be thy king!
Stanza 30

Where, where was Roderick then!
One blast upon his bugle horn
Were worth a thousand men!
Ibid. Canto VI, Stanza 18

Where lives the man that has not tried
How mirth can into folly glide,
And folly into sin!
The Bridal of Triermain [1813].
Canto I, Stanza 21

Long loved, long woo'd, and lately won,
My life's best hope, and now mine own.
Ibid. Introduction to Canto II,
Stanza 1

Two sisters by the goal are set,
Cold Disappointment and Regret;
One disenchants the winner's eyes,
And strips of all its worth the prize,
While one augments its gaudy show,
More to enhance the loser's woe.
Rokeby [1813]. Canto I,
Stanza 31

Still are the thoughts to memory dear.
Ibid. Stanza 33

A mother's pride, a father's joy.
Ibid. Canto III, Stanza 15

Oh, Brignall banks are wild and fair,
And Greta woods are green,
And you may gather garlands there
Would grace a summer's queen.
Ibid. Stanza 16

The tear down childhood's cheek that flows

[1] These verses were set to music by JAMES SANDERSON [1769–1841?], and this march has become traditionally attached to the President of the United States.

[1] See Sir Philip Sidney, page 115b.

Is like the dewdrop on the rose;
When next the summer breeze comes by,
And waves the bush, the flower is dry.
Rokeby. Canto IV, Stanza 1

Thus aged men, full loth and slow,
The vanities of life forego,
And count their youthful follies o'er,
Till Memory lends her light no more.
Ibid. Canto V, Stanza 1

Oh, many a shaft at random sent
Finds mark the archer little meant!
And many a word, at random spoken,
May soothe or wound a heart that's
broken!
The Lord of the Isles [1815].
Canto V, Stanza 18

Randolph, thy wreath has lost a rose.[1]
Ibid. Canto VI, Stanza 18

There was — and O! how many sor-
rows crowd
Into these two brief words!
Ibid. Conclusion

Then strip, lads, and to it, though
sharp be the weather,
And if, by mischance, you should
happen to fall,
There are worse things in life than a
tumble on heather,
And life is itself but a game at football.
Song [2] [1815]. Stanza 5

A lawyer without history or literature is a mechanic, a mere working
mason; if he possesses some knowledge
of these, he may venture to call himself
an architect.
Guy Mannering [1815]. Chap. 37

Bluid is thicker than water.[3]
Ibid. Chap. 38

It's no fish ye're buying, it's men's
lives.[4]
The Antiquary [1816]. Chap. 11

[1] Robert Bruce's censure of Randolph for
permitting a body of English cavalry to pass
his flank on the day before the battle of Bannockburn [June 24, 1314].
A rose hath fallen from thy chaplet. —
Halidon Hall [1822], Act II, Sc. 2
[2] On the lifting of the banner of the House
of Buccleuch at a great football match on
Carterhaugh.
[3] This proverb is found as early as the
seventeenth century.
[4] See Thomas Hood, page 489a.

Come as the winds come, when
Forests are rended;
Come as the waves come, when
Navies are stranded.
Pibroch of Donald Dhu [1816].
Stanza 4

Sound, sound the clarion, fill the fife!
To all the sensual world proclaim,
One crowded hour of glorious life
Is worth an age without a name.[1]
Old Mortality [1816]. Chap. 34

Time will rust the sharpest sword,
Time will consume the strongest cord;
That which moulders hemp and steel,
Mortal arm and nerve must feel.
Harold the Dauntless [1817].
Canto I, Stanza 4

Cursed war and racking tax
Have left us scarcely raiment to our
backs.
The Search after Happiness [2]
[1817]. Stanza 16

Paddy had not — a shirt to his back!
Ibid. Stanza 22

Sea of upturned faces.
Rob Roy [1817]. Chap. 20

Lochow and the adjacent districts
formed the original seat of the Campbells. The expression of "a far cry to
Lochow" was proverbial.
Ibid. Chap. 29, Note

There's a gude time coming.
Ibid. Chap. 32

My foot is on my native heath, and
my name is MacGregor.
Ibid. Chap. 34

Jock, when ye hae naething else to
do, ye may be aye sticking in a tree; it
will be growing, Jock, when ye're sleeping.[3]
The Heart of Midlothian
[1818]. Chap. 8

Vacant heart, and hand, and eye,
Easy live and quiet die.
The Bride of Lammermoor
[1819]. Chap. 3, Lucy Ashton's
Song

[1] See *Count Robert of Paris*, page 418a.
[2] See John Heywood, page 90b.
[3] The dying words of a Highland laird to
his son.

The happy combination of fortuitous circumstances.[1]

> *The Monastery* [*1820*]. *Answer of the Author of Waverley to the Letter of Captain Clutterbuck*

Within that awful volume [2] lies
The mystery of mysteries!

> *Ibid. Chap. 12*

And better had they ne'er been born,
Who read to doubt, or read to scorn.

> *Ibid.*

When we are handfasted, as we term it, we are man and wife for a year and day; that space gone by, each may choose another mate, or, at their pleasure, may call the priest to marry them for life; and this we call handfasting.[3]

> *Ibid. Chap. 25*

Spur not an unbroken horse; put not your ploughshare too deep into new land.

> *Ibid.*

Meat eaten without either mirth or music is ill of digestion.

> *Ibid.*

When I hae a saxpence under my
> thumb,
Then I get credit in ilka town;
But when I am poor, they bid me gae
> by,
O, poverty parts good company.

> *The Abbot* [*1820*]. *Chap. 7*

The jolly old landlord said, "nothing's to pay."

> *The Pirate* [*1821*]. *Chap. 23*

Ah, County Guy, the hour is nigh,
The sun has left the lea.
The orange flower perfumes the bower,
The breeze is on the sea.

> *Quentin Durward* [*1823*]. *Chap. 4*

[1] See Daniel Webster, page 444a.
Fortuitous combination of circumstances. — DICKENS: *Our Mutual Friend* [1864–1865], Vol. II, *Chap. 7*
[2] The Bible.
[3] This custom of handfasting actually prevailed in the upland days. It arose partly from the want of priests. While the convents subsisted, monks were detached on regular circuits through the wilder districts, to marry those who had lived in this species of connexion. — ANDREW LANG: *Note in his edition of The Monastery.*

Fat, fair, and forty.[1]

> *St. Ronan's Well* [*1823*]. *Chap. 7*

Tell that to the marines — the sailors won't believe it.[2]

> *Redgauntlet* [*1824*]. *Vol. II, Chap. 7*

Too much rest is rust.[3]

> *The Betrothed* [*1825*]. *Chap. 13*

The playbill, which is said to have announced the tragedy of Hamlet, the character of the Prince of Denmark being left out.

> *The Talisman* [*1825*]. *Introduction*

Rouse the lion from his lair.

> *Ibid. Heading, Chap. 6*

Recollect that the Almighty, who gave the dog to be companion of our pleasures and our toils, hath invested him with a nature noble and incapable of deceit.

> *Ibid. Chap. 24*

If you keep a thing seven years, you are sure to find a use for it.

> *Woodstock* [*1826*]. *Chap. 28*

The sun never sets on the immense empire of Charles V.[4]

> *Life of Napoleon* [*1827*]

Come fill up my cup, come fill up my
> can,
Come saddle your horses, and call up
> your men;

[1] See Dryden, page 275b.
Lord —— is going to marry Lady ——, a fat, fair, and fifty card-playing resident of the Crescent. — MRS. MELESINA TRENCH [1768–1827], in a letter [February 18, 1816]
[2] "Right," quoth Ben, "that will do for the marines." — BYRON: *The Island* [1823], *Canto II, last line*
"That will do for the marines, but the sailors won't believe it" is an old saying.
[3] German proverb: Rast ich, so rost ich (When I rest, I rust).
[4] See Daniel Webster, page 444a.
Why should the brave Spanish soldier brag the sun never sets in the Spanish dominions, but ever shineth on one part or other we have conquered for our king? — CAPTAIN JOHN SMITH: *Advertisements for the Unexperienced, &c.* [1631]
It may be said of them [the Hollanders] as of the Spaniards, that the sun never sets on their dominions. — GAGE: *New Survey of the West Indies* [1648], *Epistle Dedicatory*

Come open the West Port, and let me
gang free,
And it's room for the bonnets of Bonny
Dundee!
The Doom of Devorgoil [*1830*].
Bonny Dundee, Chorus
One hour of life, crowded to the full
with glorious action, and filled with
noble risks, is worth whole years of
those mean observances of paltry de-
corum.[1]
Count Robert of Paris [*1832*].
Chap. 25
Heaven knows its time; the bullet
has its billet.
Ibid.

SYDNEY SMITH
[1771–1845]

The schoolboy whips his taxed top;
the beardless youth manages his taxed
horse with a taxed bridle on a taxed
road; and the dying Englishman, pouring his medicine, which has paid seven
per cent, into a spoon that has paid
fifteen per cent, flings himself back
upon his chintz bed which has paid
twenty-two per cent, and expires in the
arms of an apothecary who has paid a
license of a hundred pounds for the
privilege of putting him to death.
Review of SEYBERT's *Annals of
the United States* [*1820*]
In the four quarters of the globe,
who reads an American book, or goes
to an American play, or looks at an
American picture or statue?
Ibid.
Correspondences are like small-
clothes before the invention of suspenders; it is impossible to keep them up.
Letter to Mrs. Crowe
[*January 31, 1841*]
If you choose to represent the various parts in life by holes upon a table,
of different shapes, — some circular,
some triangular, some square, some oblong, — and the persons acting these
parts by bits of wood of similar shapes,
we shall generally find that the trian-

[1] See *Old Mortality*, page 416b.

gular person has got into the square
hole, the oblong into the triangular,
and a square person has squeezed himself into the round hole. The officer
and the office, the doer and the thing
done, seldom fit so exactly that we can
say they were almost made for each
other.[1]
Sketches of Moral Philosophy
[*1850*]
That knuckle-end of England,—
that land of Calvin, oat-cakes, and
sulphur.
LADY HOLLAND's *Memoir*
[*1855*]. *Vol. I, Chap. 2*
No one minds what Jeffrey says:
. . . it is not more than a week ago
that I heard him speak disrespectfully
of the equator.
Ibid.
Preaching has become a by-word for
long and dull conversation of any
kind; and whoever wishes to imply, in
any piece of writing, the absence of
everything agreeable and inviting,
calls it a sermon.
Ibid. Chap. 3
It is always right that a man should
be able to render a reason for the faith
that is within him.
Ibid.
Avoid shame, but do not seek glory,
— nothing so expensive as glory.
Ibid. Chap. 4
It is no part of the duty of a clergyman to preach upon subjects purely
political, but it is not therefore his
duty to avoid religious subjects which
have been distorted into political subjects.
Ibid.
Take short views, hope for the best,
and trust in God.
Ibid. Chap. 6
Hope is the belief, more or less
strong, that joy will come; desire is
the wish it may come. There is no
word to designate the remembrance of
joys past.
Ibid.

[1] Generally accepted as the origin of the
phrase "A square peg in a round hole."

Looked as if she had walked straight out of the ark.

Lady Holland's Memoir.
Vol. I, Chap. 7

Great men hallow a whole people, and lift up all who live in their time.

Ibid.

Not body enough to cover his mind decently with; his intellect is improperly exposed.

Ibid. Chap. 9

He has spent all his life in letting down empty buckets into empty wells; and he is frittering away his age in trying to draw them up again.[1]

Ibid.

Ah, you flavour everything; you are the vanilla of society.

Ibid.

My living in Yorkshire was so far out of the way, that it was actually twelve miles from a lemon.

Ibid.

As the French say, there are three sexes, — men, women, and clergymen.[2]

Ibid.

Daniel Webster struck me much like a steam-engine in trousers.

Ibid.

"Heat, ma'am!" I said; "it was so dreadful here, that I found there was nothing left for it but to take off my flesh and sit in my bones."

Ibid.

I have gout, asthma, and seven other maladies, but am otherwise very well.

Ibid. Chap. 10

When you rise in the morning, form a resolution to make the day a happy one to a fellow-creature.

Ibid.

Live always in the best company when you read.

Ibid.

Never give way to melancholy; resist it steadily, for the habit will encroach.

Ibid.

He was a one-book man. Some men

have only one book in them; others, a library.

Lady Holland's Memoir.
Vol. I, Chap. 11

Marriage resembles a pair of shears, so joined that they can not be separated; often moving in opposite directions, yet always punishing anyone who comes between them.[1]

Ibid.

Macaulay is like a book in breeches. . . . He has occasional flashes of silence, that make his conversation perfectly delightful.

Ibid.

Let onion atoms lurk within the bowl And, half suspected, animate the whole.

Ibid. Recipe for Salad

Don't tell me of facts, I never believe facts; you know Canning said nothing was so fallacious as facts, except figures.

Ibid.

What you don't know would make a great book.

Ibid.

In composing, as a general rule, run your pen through every other word you have written; you have no idea what vigor it will give your style.[2]

Ibid.

Thank God for tea! What would the world do without tea? — how did it exist? I am glad I was not born before tea.

Ibid.

That sign of old age, extolling the past at the expense of the present.

Ibid.

We know nothing of tomorrow; our business is to be good and happy today.

Ibid. Chap. 12

WILLIAM BARNES RHODES
[1772–1826]

Bombastes. So have I heard on Afric's burning shore

---

[1] See Cowper, page 364b.
[2] See Lady Mary Wortley Montagu, page 322b.

[1] We are the two halves of a pair of scissors, when apart, Pecksniff, but together we are something. — DICKENS: *Martin Chuzzlewit* [1843–1844], *Chap. 11*
[2] See Samuel Johnson, page 341a.

A hungry lion give a grievous roar;
The grievous roar echoed along the
   shore.
Artaxaminous. So have I heard on
   Afric's burning shore
Another lion give a grievous roar;
And the first lion thought the last a
   bore.
                 Bombastes Furioso [*1810*].
                               Act I, Sc. 4

FRANÇOIS HORACE BASTIEN SÉBASTIANI
[1772–1851]

Order reigns in Warsaw.[1]
          Announcement of the fall of
                               Warsaw

JOSIAH QUINCY, JR.
[1772–1864]

If this bill [for the admission of Orleans Territory as a State] passes, I am
compelled to declare it as my deliberate
opinion that the bonds of this Union
are virtually dissolved; that the States
which compose it are free from their
moral obligations; and that, as it will
be the right of all, so it will be the duty
of some, to prepare definitely for a
separation — amicably if they can;
violently if they must.[2]
          Speech in the U. S. House of
          Representatives, January 14,
          1811

SAMUEL TAYLOR COLERIDGE
[1772–1834]

Poor little Foal of an oppressed race!
I love the languid patience of thy face.
                 To a Young Ass [*1794*]

[1] Des lettres que je reçois de Pologne m'an-
noncent que la tranquillité règne à Varsovie.
— DUMAS [1802–1870]: *Mémoires, Second
Series, Vol. IV, Chap. 3*
[2] The gentleman [Quincy] cannot have forgotten his own sentiment, uttered even on the
floor of this House, "Peaceably if we can,
forcibly if we must." — HENRY CLAY: *Speech*
[January 8, 1813]

Ere sin could blight or sorrow fade,
   Death came with friendly care;
The opening bud to heaven conveyed,
   And bade it blossom there.
               Epitaph on an Infant [*1794*]
Blest hour! it was a luxury — to be
   left!
          Reflections on Having Left a
               Place of Retirement [*1795*]
This Lime-tree Bower My Prison.
                 Title of Poem [*1797*]
In Xanadu did Kubla Khan
A stately pleasure-dome decree:
Where Alph, the sacred river, ran
Through caverns measureless to man
Down to a sunless sea.
So twice five miles of fertile ground
With walls and towers were girdled
   round.
                      Kubla Khan [*1797*]
A savage place! as holy and enchanted
As e'er beneath a waning moon was
   haunted
By woman wailing for her demon-lover.
                                     Ibid.
Ancestral voices prophesying war!
                                     Ibid.
A damsel with a dulcimer
In a vision once I saw:
It was an Abyssinian maid,
And on her dulcimer she played,
Singing of Mount Abora.
                                     Ibid.
That sunny dome! those caves of ice!
And all who heard should see them
   there,
And all should cry, Beware! Beware!
His flashing eyes, his floating hair!
Weave a circle round him thrice,
And close your eyes with holy dread,
For he on honey-dew hath fed,[1]
And drunk the milk of Paradise.
                                     Ibid.
And the spring comes slowly up this
   way.
                 Christabel. Part I [*1797*]
Her gentle limbs did she undress,
And lay down in her loveliness.
                                     Ibid.
A sight to dream of, not to tell!
                                     Ibid.

[1] See Hesiod, page **7a**.

a

And constancy lives in realms above;
And life is thorny; and youth is vain;
And to be wroth with one we love
Doth work like madness in the brain.
Christabel. Part II [1800]

It is an ancient Mariner,
And he stoppeth one of three.
"By thy long grey beard and glittering
eye,
Now wherefore stopp'st thou me?"
*The Ancient Mariner [1798–
1834]. Part I, Stanza 1*

The guests are met, the feast is set:
May'st hear the merry din.
Ibid. Stanza 2

He holds him with his glittering eye —
The Wedding-Guest stood still,
And listens like a three years' child:
The Mariner hath his will.
Ibid. Stanza 4

The ship was cheered, the harbour
cleared,
Merrily did we drop
Below the kirk, below the hill,
Below the lighthouse top.
Ibid. Stanza 6

The Wedding-Guest here beat his
breast,
For he heard the loud bassoon.
Ibid. Stanza 8

The bride hath paced into the hall,
Red as a rose is she.
Ibid. Stanza 9

And now there came both mist and
snow,
And it grew wondrous cold:
And ice, mast-high, came floating by,
As green as emerald.
Ibid. Stanza 13

The ice was here, the ice was there,
The ice was all around:
It cracked and growled, and roared and
howled,
Like noises in a swound!
Ibid. Stanza 15

"God save thee, ancient Mariner!
From fiends, that plague thee thus! —
Why look'st thou so?" — "With my
cross-bow
I shot the Albatross."
Ibid. Stanza 20

b

The fair breeze blew, the white foam
flew,
The furrows followed free;
We were the first that ever burst
Into that silent sea.
*The Ancient Mariner.
Part II, Stanza 5*

As idle as a painted ship
Upon a painted ocean.
Ibid. Stanza 8

Water, water, every where,
Nor any drop to drink.
Ibid. Stanza 9

The very deep did rot: O Christ!
That ever this should be!
Yea, slimy things did crawl with legs
Upon the slimy sea.
Ibid. Stanza 10

About, about, in reel and rout
The death-fires danced at night.
Ibid. Stanza 11

I bit my arm, I sucked the blood,
And cried, A sail! a sail!
Ibid. Part III, Stanza 4

Without a breeze, without a tide,
She steadies with upright keel!
Ibid. Stanza 6

Her lips were red, her looks were free,
Her locks were yellow as gold:
Her skin was white as leprosy,
The nightmare Life-in-Death was she,
Who thicks man's blood with cold.
Ibid. Stanza 11

The sun's rim dips, the stars rush out:
At one stride comes the dark;
With far-heard whisper o'er the sea
Off shot the spectre-bark.
Ibid. Stanza 13

We listened and looked sideways up!
Fear at my heart, as at a cup,
My life-blood seemed to sip.
Ibid. Stanza 14

The hornèd Moon, with one bright star
Within the nether tip.
Ibid.

Each turned his face with a ghastly
pang,
And cursed me with his eye.
Ibid. Stanza 15

And thou art long, and lank, and
　brown,
As is the ribbed sea-sand.[1]
The Ancient Mariner.
Part IV, Stanza 1

Alone, alone, all, all alone;
Alone on a wide, wide sea.
Ibid. Stanza 3

The moving moon went up the sky,
And nowhere did abide;
Softly she was going up,
And a star or two beside.
Ibid. Stanza 10

Her beams bemocked the sultry main,
Like April hoar-frost spread;
But where the ship's huge shadow lay,
The charmèd water burnt alway
A still and awful red.
Ibid. Stanza 11

A spring of love gushed from my heart,
And I blessed them unaware.
Ibid. Stanza 14

Oh sleep! it is a gentle thing,
Beloved from pole to pole.
Ibid. Part V, Stanza 1

A noise like of a hidden brook
In the leafy month of June,
That to the sleeping woods all night
Singeth a quiet tune.
Ibid. Stanza 17

"The man hath penance done,
And penance more will do."
Ibid. Stanza 25

Like one that on a lonesome road
Doth walk in fear and dread,
And having once turned round, walks
　on,
And turns no more his head;
Because he knows a frightful fiend
Doth close behind him tread.
Ibid. Part VI, Stanza 10

Is this the hill? is this the kirk?
Is this mine own countree?
Ibid. Stanza 14

O Wedding-Guest! This soul hath been
Alone on a wide wide sea:
So lonely 'twas, that God himself
Scarce seemèd there to be.
Ibid. Part VII, Stanza 19

He prayeth well who loveth well
Both man and bird and beast.
The Ancient Mariner.
Part VII, Stanza 22

He prayeth best who loveth best
All things both great and small;
For the dear God who loveth us,
He made and loveth all.
Ibid. Stanza 23

A sadder and a wiser man
He rose the morrow morn.
Ibid. Stanza 25

Yes, while I stood and gazed, my tem-
　ples bare,
And shot my being through earth, sea,
　and air,
Possessing all things with intensest
　love,
O Liberty! my spirit felt thee there.
France: An Ode [1798]. V

Forth from his dark and lonely hiding-
　place
(Portentous sight!) the owlet Atheism,
Sailing on obscene wings athwart the
　noon,
Drops his blue-fringèd lids, and holds
　them close,
And hooting at the glorious sun in
　heaven
Cries out, "Where is it?"
Fears in Solitude [1798]

And the Devil did grin, for his darling
　sin
Is pride that apes humility.[1]
The Devil's Thoughts [2] *[1799].*
Stanza 6

Strongly it bears us along in swelling
　and limitless billows;
Nothing before and nothing behind but
　the sky and the ocean.
*The Homeric Hexameter (trans-
lated from Schiller) [1799?]*

In the hexameter rises the fountain's
　silvery column,
In the pentameter aye falling in melody
　back.
*The Ovidian Elegiac Metre
(from Schiller) [1799]*

---

[1] A note by Coleridge in *Sibylline Leaves*
[1817] says: "For [these] lines I am indebted
to Mr. Wordsworth."

[1] See Robert Burton, page 222b.
[2] This poem was written in collaboration

All thoughts, all passions, all delights,
Whatever stirs this mortal frame,
All are but ministers of Love,
　And feed his sacred flame.
　　　　　Love [*1799*]. *Stanza 1*

Saved from outrage worse than death.
　　　　　Ibid. Stanza 14

Tranquillity! thou better name
Than all the family of Fame.
　　　Ode to Tranquillity [*1801*].
　　　　　　　　Stanza 1

Aloof with hermit-eye I scan
The present work of present man —
A wild and dream-like trade of blood
　and guile,
Too foolish for a tear, too wicked for a
　smile.
　　　　　Ibid. Stanza 4

Hast thou a charm to stay the morning
　star
In his steep course?
　　Hymn in the Vale of Chamouni
　　　　　　　　[*1802*]

Risest from forth thy silent sea of
　pines.
　　　　　　　　Ibid.

Motionless torrents! silent cataracts!
　　　　　　　　Ibid.

Ye living flowers that skirt the eternal
　frost.
　　　　　　　　Ibid.

Earth, with her thousand voices, praises
　God.
　　　　　　　　Ibid.

What is an Epigram? A dwarfish
　whole,
Its body brevity, and wit its soul.[1]
　　　　　An Epigram [*1802*]

I see, not feel, how beautiful they are.
　　Dejection: An Ode [*1802*].
　　　　　　　　Stanza 2

O Lady! we receive but what we give
And in our life alone does Nature live.
　　　　　Ibid. Stanza 4

Joy is the sweet voice, Joy the luminous
　cloud —
　We in ourselves rejoice!

And thence flows all that charms or ear
　or sight,
　All melodies the echoes of that voice,
All colours a suffusion of that light.
　　　Dejection: An Ode. Stanza 5

How seldom, friend! a good great man
　inherits
Honor or wealth, with all his worth and
　pains!
It sounds like stories from the land of
　spirits
If any man obtains that which he mer-
　its,
Or any merit that which he obtains.

　　·　　·　　·　　·　　·

Greatness and goodness are not means,
　but ends!
Hath he not always treasures, always
　friends,
The good great man? Three treasures,
　— love, and light,
And calm thoughts, regular as infant's
　breath; —
And three firm friends, more sure than
　day and night, —
Himself, his Maker, and the Angel
　Death.
　　　The Good Great Man [*1802*]

Trochee trips from long to short;
From long to long in solemn sort
Slow Spondee stalks.
　　　　　Metrical Feet [*1806*]

What outward form and feature are
　He guesseth but in part;
But what within is good and fair
　He seeth with the heart.
　　　Reason For Love's Blindness
　　　　　　　　[*1811?*]

Poetry is not the proper antithesis to
prose, but to science. Poetry is opposed
to science, and prose to metre. The
proper and immediate object of science
is the acquirement, or communication,
of truth; the proper and immediate object of poetry is the communication of
immediate pleasure.
　　　Definitions of Poetry [*1811*]

Reviewers are usually people who
would have been poets, historians, biographers, if they could; they have tried

with Southey, who also imitated it in *The
Devil's Walk,* quoted on page 427a.
[1] See Shakespeare, page 173a.

their talents at one or the other, and have failed; therefore they turn critics.[1]

Lectures on Shakespeare and Milton [1811–1812]

Iago's soliloquy, the motive-hunting of a motiveless malignity — how awful it is!

Ibid.

I wish our clever young poets would remember my homely definitions of prose and poetry; that is, prose, — words in their best order; poetry, — the best words in their best order.

Ibid.

That passage is what I call the sublime dashed to pieces by cutting too close with the fiery four-in-hand round the corner of nonsense.

Ibid.

Not the poem which we have *read*, but that to which we *return*, with the greatest pleasure, possesses the genuine power, and claims the name of *essential poetry*.

Biographia Literaria [1817].
Chap. 1

Every reform, however necessary, will by weak minds be carried to an excess, that itself will need reforming.

Ibid.

Experience informs us that the first defence of weak minds is to recriminate.

Ibid. Chap. 2

Through all the works of Chaucer, there reigns a cheerfulness, a manly hilarity, which makes it almost impossible to doubt a correspondent habit of feeling in the author himself.

Ibid.

Men whose dearest wishes are fixed on objects wholly out of their own power, become in all cases more or less impatient and prone to anger.

Ibid.

[1] Reviewers, with some rare exceptions, are a most stupid and malignant race. As a bankrupt thief turns thief-taker in despair, so an unsuccessful author turns critic. — SHELLEY: *Fragments of Adonais* [1821]
See Disraeli, page 513a.

Veracity does not consist in *saying*, but in the intention of *communicating* truth.

Biographia Literaria. Chap. 9

The lamentable difficulty I have always experienced in saying "No."

Ibid. Chap. 10

To have lived in vain must be a painful thought to any man, and especially so to him who has made literature his profession.

Ibid.

Never pursue literature as a trade.

Ibid. Chap. 11

The first range of hills that encircles the scanty vale of human life is the horizon for the majority of its inhabitants. On *its* ridges the common sun is born and departs. From *them* the stars rise, and touching *them*, they vanish.

Ibid. Chap. 12

It was agreed that my endeavors [in the plan of the *Lyrical Ballads*] should be directed to persons and characters supernatural, or at least romantic; yet so as to transfer from our inward nature a human interest and a semblance of truth sufficient to procure for these shadows of imagination that willing suspension of disbelief for the moment, which constitutes poetic faith.

Ibid. Chap. 14

Good sense is the body of poetic genius, fancy its drapery, motion its life, and imagination the soul.

Ibid.

Our myriad-minded Shakespeare.[1]

Ibid. Chap. 15

The sense of musical delight, with the power of producing it, is a gift of imagination; and this together with the power of reducing multitude into unity of effect, and modifying a series of thoughts by some one predominant thought or feeling, may be cultivated and improved, but can never be learned. It is in these that *poeta nascitur non fit*.

Ibid.

[1] "A phrase," says Coleridge, "which I have borrowed from a Greek monk, who applies it to a patriarch of Constantinople."

Polysyllabic (or what the common people call, *dictionary*) words.
Biographia Literaria. Chap. 20

The infallible test of a blameless style: namely, its untranslatableness in words of the same language, without injury to the meaning.
Ibid. Chap. 22

A poem is not necessarily obscure, because it does not aim to be popular. It is enough if a work be perspicuous to those for whom it is written.
Ibid.

Talk of the devil, and his horns appear, says the proverb.
Ibid. Chap. 23

The knight's bones are dust,
And his good sword rust;
His soul is with the saints, I trust.
The Knight's Tomb [*1817?*]

The Eighth Commandment was not made for bards.
The Reproof and Reply [*1823*]

Nought cared this body for wind or weather,
When youth and I lived in 't together.
Youth and Age [*1823–1832*].
Stanza 1

Flowers are lovely; love is flower-like;
Friendship is a sheltering tree;
Oh the joys that came down shower-like,
Of friendship, love, and liberty,
Ere I was old!
Ibid. Stanza 2

In many ways doth the full heart reveal
The presence of the love it would conceal.
Motto to Poems Written in Later Life [*1826*]

I counted two-and-seventy stenches,
All well defined, and several stinks.
Cologne [*1828*]

The river Rhine, it is well known,
Doth wash your city of Cologne;
But tell me, nymphs! what power divine
Shall henceforth wash the river Rhine?
Ibid.

The happiness of life is made up of minute fractions — the little soon forgotten charities of a kiss or smile, a kind look, a heartfelt compliment, and the countless infinitesimals of pleasurable and genial feeling.
The Friend. The Improvisatore
[*1828*]

Beneath this sod
A poet lies, or that which once seemed he —
Oh, lift a thought in prayer for S.T.C.!
That he, who many a year, with toil of breath,
Found death in life, may here find life in death.
Epitaph written for himself
[*1833*]

JOHN RANDOLPH
[1773–1833]

The surest way to prevent war is not to fear it.
Speech, U. S. House of Representatives [*March 5, 1806*]

He is a man of splendid abilities, but utterly corrupt. He shines and stinks like rotten mackerel by moonlight.[1]
Of Edward Livingston

WILLIAM HENRY HARRISON
[1773–1841]

We admit of no government by divine right . . . the only legitimate right to govern is an express grant of power from the governed.
Inaugural Address [*March 4, 1841*]

Never with my consent shall an officer of the people, compensated for his services out of their pockets, become the pliant instrument of the Executive will.
Ibid.

[1] Quoted in W. CABELL BRUCE: *John Randolph of Roanoke* [1923], *Vol. II, P. 197.*
'Tis vain for present fame to wish.
Our persons first must be forgotten;
For poets are like stinking fish,
They never shine until they're rotten.
MACDONALD CLARKE [1798–1842]: *Epigram*

A decent and manly examination of the acts of Government should be not only tolerated, but encouraged.
Inaugural Address

ROBERT SOUTHEY
[1774–1843]

"You are old, Father William," the young man cried,
"The few locks which are left you are gray;
You are hale, Father William, a hearty old man, —
Now tell me the reason I pray."
The Old Man's Comforts, and How He Gained Them.[1] *Stanza 1*

"In the days of my youth," Father William replied,
"I remembered that youth could not last;
I thought of the future, whatever I did,
That I never might grieve for the past."
Ibid. Stanza 4

Bishop Hatto fearfully hastened away,
And he crossed the Rhine without delay,
And reached his tower, and barred with care
All the windows, and doors, and loopholes there.
God's Judgment on a Wicked Bishop.[2] *Stanza 12*

[1] Of several parodies of this poem, the one by Lewis Carroll is probably better known than the original. See page 656a.
"You are old, Father William, and though one would think
All the veins in your body were dry,
Yet the end of your nose is red as a pink;
I beg your indulgence, but why?"
LEE O. HARRIS AND JAMES WHITCOMB RILEY: *Father William, St. 1*

[2] Hatto, in the time of the great famine of 914, when he saw the poor exceedingly oppressed by famine, assembled a great company of them together into a barn at Kaub and burnt them . . . because he thought the famine would sooner cease if those poor folks were despatched out of the world. . . . But God . . . sent against him a plague of mice . . . and the prelate retreated to a tower in the Rhine . . . but the mice chased him con-

It was a summer's evening;
Old Kaspar's work was done,
And he before his cottage door
Was sitting in the sun;
And by him sported on the green
His little grandchild Wilhelmine.
The Battle of Blenheim [*1798*].
Stanza 1

He came to ask what he had found,
That was so large, and smooth, and round.
Ibid. Stanza 2

" 'Tis some poor fellow's skull," said he,
"Who fell in the great victory."
Ibid. Stanza 3

But what they fought each other for,
I could not well make out.
Ibid. Stanza 6

"And every body praised the Duke,
Who this great fight did win."
"But what good came of it at last?"
Quoth little Peterkin.
"Why, that I cannot tell," said he;
"But 'twas a famous victory."
Ibid. Stanza 11

One dreadful sound could the Rover hear,
A sound as if with the Inchcape Bell
The Devil below was ringing his knell.
The Inchcape Rock.[1] *Stanza 17*

Where Washington hath left
His awful memory
A light for after times!
Ode Written during the War with America [*1814*]

My days among the dead are past;
Around me I behold,
Where'er these casual eyes are cast,
The mighty minds of old;
My never-failing friends are they,
With whom I converse night and day.
My Days Among the Dead Are Past [*1818*]. *Stanza 1*

tinually . . . and at last he was most miserably devoured. — THOMAS CORYAT: *Crudities* [1611]

[1] A rock in the North Sea, off the Firth of Tay, Scotland, dangerous to navigators because it is covered with every tide. There is a tradition that a warning bell was fixed on the rock by the Abbot of Aberbrothok, which was stolen by a sea pirate, who perished on the rock a year later. Southey's ballad deals with this tradition.

Yet leaving here a name, I trust,
That will not perish in the dust.
> *My Days Among the Dead*
> *Are Past. Stanza 4*

The laws are with us, and God on our side.
> *On the Rise and Progress of*
> *Popular Disaffection* [1817]

Agreed to differ.
> *Life of Wesley* [1820]

The Satanic school.
> *Vision of Judgment* [1821].
> *Original Preface*

So I told them in rhyme,
For of rhymes I had store.
> *The Cataract of Lodore*

And so never ending, but always descending.
> *Ibid.*

"And wherefore do the poor complain?"
The rich man asked of me —
"Come walk abroad with me," I said,
"And I will answer thee."
> *The Complaints of the Poor.*
> *Stanza 1*

From his brimstone bed, at break of day,
A-walking the Devil is gone,
To look at his little snug farm of the World,
And see how his stock went on.
> *The Devil's Walk. Stanza 1*

How then was the Devil dressed?
O, he was in his Sunday's best;
His coat was red, and his breeches were blue,
And there was a hole where his tail came through.
> *Ibid. Stanza 3*

He passed a cottage with a double coach-house, —
A cottage of gentility;
And he owned with a grin,
That his favourite sin
Is pride that apes humility.[1]
> *Ibid. Stanza 8*

He was always found
Among your ten and twenty pound subscribers,

Your benefactors in the newspapers.
His alms were money put to interest
In the other world.
> *The Alderman's Funeral*

As frozen as charity.[1]
> *The Soldier's Wife. Stanza 4*

Blue, darkly, deeply, beautifully blue.[2]
> *Madoc in Wales. Part I, 5*

What will not woman, gentle woman dare,
When strong affection stirs her spirit up?
> *Ibid. Part II, 2*

And last of all an Admiral came,
A terrible man with a terrible name, —
A name which you all know by sight very well,
But which no one can speak, and no one can spell.
> *The March to Moscow. Stanza 8*

They sin who tell us love can die;
With life all other passions fly,
All others are but vanity. . . .
Love is indestructible,
Its holy flame forever burneth;
From heaven it came, to heaven returneth. . . .
It soweth here with toil and care,
But the harvest-time of love is there.
> *The Curse of Kehama. Canto X,*
> *Stanza 10*

Thou hast been called, O sleep! the friend of woe;
But 'tis the happy that have called thee so.
> *Ibid. Canto XV, Stanza 11*

JANE AUSTEN
[1775–1817]

What dreadful hot weather we have! It keeps me in a continual state of inelegance.
> *Letter to her sister Cassandra.*
> *September 18, 1796*

[1] See Coleridge, page 422b.

[1] See Hood, page 489b, and O'Reilly, page 729b.
[2] "Darkly, deeply, beautifully blue,"
As some one somewhere sings about the sky.
> BYRON: *Don Juan* [1819–1824],
> *Canto IV, St. 110*

Miss Blachford is agreeable enough. I do not want people to be very agreeable, as it saves me the trouble of liking them a great deal.
Letter to her sister Cassandra.
December 24, 1798

She was highly rouged, and looked rather quietly and contentedly silly than anything else.
Ibid. May 12, 1801

It is a truth universally acknowledged, that a single man in possession of a good fortune, must be in want of a wife.

However little known the feelings or views of such a man may be on his first entering a neighbourhood, this truth is so well fixed in the minds of the surrounding families, that he is considered as the rightful property of some one or other of their daughters.
Pride and Prejudice [1813].
Chap. 1

Mr. Collins had only to change from Jane to Elizabeth — and it was soon done — done while Mrs. Bennet was stirring the fire.
Ibid. Chap. 15

My dear, I have two small favours to request. First, that you will allow me the free use of my understanding on the present occasion; and secondly, of my room. I shall be glad to have the library to myself as soon as may be.
Ibid. Chap. 20

Those who do not complain are never pitied.
Ibid.

Mrs. Bennet was restored to her usual querulous serenity.
Ibid. Chap. 42

You ought certainly to forgive them, as a Christian, but never to admit them in your sight, or allow their names to be mentioned in your hearing.
Ibid. Chap. 57

For what do we live, but to make sport for our neighbours, and laugh at them in our turn?
Ibid.

I have been a selfish being all my life, in practice, though not in principle.
Pride and Prejudice. Chap. 58

The little bit (two inches wide) of ivory on which I work with so fine a brush as produces little effect after much labour.[1]
Letter to J. Edward Austen.
December 16, 1816

"Only a novel" . . . in short, only some work in which the greatest powers of the mind are displayed, in which the most thorough knowledge of human nature, the happiest delineation of its varieties, the liveliest effusions of wit and humour are conveyed to the world in the best chosen language.
Northanger Abbey [1818].
Chap. 5

You [men] have difficulties, and privations, and dangers enough to struggle with. You are always labouring and toiling, exposed to every risk and hardship. Your home, country, friends, all quitted. Neither time, nor health, nor life, to be called your own. It would be too hard, indeed . . . if woman's feelings were to be added to all this.
Persuasion [1818]. Chap. 23

CHARLES LAMB
[1775–1834]

I have had playmates, I have had companions,
In my days of childhood, in my joyful school-days.
All, all are gone, the old familiar faces.
Old Familiar Faces [1796]

I have something more to do than feel.
Letter to Coleridge after the death of Lamb's mother [1796]

[1] [Miss Austen] had a talent for describing the involvements and feelings and characters of ordinary life which is to me the most wonderful I ever met with. The Big Bow-Wow strain I can do myself like any now going; but the exquisite touch, which renders ordinary commonplace things and characters interesting, from the truth of the description and the sentiment, is denied to me. — SCOTT: *Journal* [March 14, 1826]

The not unpeaceful evening of a day
Made black by morning storms.

    Poem-letter to Coleridge [*1797*]

For God's sake (I never was more serious) don't make me ridiculous any more by terming me gentle-hearted in print [1] . . . substitute drunken dog, ragged head, seld-shaven, odd-eyed, stuttering, or any other epithet which truly and properly belongs to the gentleman in question.

    Letter to Coleridge [*August, 1800*]

Separate from the pleasure of your company, I don't much care if I never see a mountain in my life. I have passed all my days in London, until I have formed as many and intense local attachments, as any of you mountaineers can have done with dead nature. The lighted shops of the Strand and Fleet Street, the innumerable trades, tradesmen and customers, coaches, waggons, playhouses, all the bustle and wickedness round about Covent Garden, the very women of the town, the watchmen, drunken scenes, rattles. . . . I often shed tears in the motley Strand from fullness of joy at so much life.

    Letter to Wordsworth [*1801*]

I have confessed to you my utter inability to remember in any comprehensive way what I read. I can vehemently applaud, or perversely stickle, at *parts;* but I cannot grasp at a whole.

    Letter to Godwin [*1803*]

Gone before
To that unknown and silent shore.

    Hester [*1803*]. *Stanza 7*

A good-natured woman, which is as much as you can expect from a friend's wife, whom you got acquainted with a bachelor.

    Letter to Hazlitt [*1805*]

Neat, not gaudy.

    Letter to Wordsworth [*1806*]

This very night I am going to leave off tobacco! Surely there must be some

---

[1] For thee, my gentle-hearted Charles, to whom
No sound is dissonant which tells of life.
    COLERIDGE: *This Lime-tree Bower My Prison* [*1797*]

other world in which this unconquerable purpose shall be realized.

    Letter to Thomas Manning [*1815*]

Anything awful makes me laugh. I misbehaved once at a funeral.

    Letter to Southey [*1815*]

An archangel a little damaged.
    Lamb's Description of Coleridge.
    Letter to Wordsworth [*1816*]

Fanny Kelly's divine plain face.

    Letter to Mrs. Wordsworth
    [*1818*]

The red-letter days, now become, to all intents and purposes, dead-letter days.

    Essays of Elia [*1823*]. *Oxford*
    in the Vacation [1]

The human species, according to the best theory I can form of it, is composed of two distinct races, the men who borrow, and the men who lend.

    Ibid. The Two Races of Men

Borrowers of books — those mutilators of collections, spoilers of the symmetry of shelves, and creators of odd volumes.

    Ibid.

Of all sound of all bells — (bells, the music nighest bordering upon heaven) — most solemn and touching is the peal which rings out the Old Year.

    Ibid. New Year's Eve

A clear fire, a clean hearth, and the rigour of the game.

    Ibid. Mrs. Battle's Opinions on
    Whist

Sentimentally I am disposed to harmony; but organically I am incapable of a tune.

    Ibid. A Chapter on Ears

Credulity is the man's weakness, but the child's strength.

    Ibid. Witches, and Other Night
    Fears

Parents do not know what they do when they leave tender babes alone to go to sleep in the dark.

    Ibid.

---

[1] Which, it has been pointed out, was actually written at Cambridge. See E. V. LUCAS: *Lamb and the Universities.*

Not many sounds in life, and I include all urban and all rural sounds, exceed in interest a knock at the door.[1]
Essays of Elia. Valentine's Day

A God-send, as our familiarly pious ancestors termed a benefit received where the benefactor was unknown.
Ibid.

The custom of saying grace at meals had, probably, its origin in the early times of the world, and the hunter-state of man, when dinners were precarious things, and a full meal was something more than a common blessing.
Ibid. Grace Before Meat

A fair sepulchre in the grateful stomach of the judicious epicure.
Ibid. A Dissertation upon Roast Pig

Presents, I often say, endear absents.
Ibid.

It argues an insensibility.
Ibid.

Nothing is to me more distasteful than that entire complacency and satisfaction which beam in the countenances of a new-married couple.
Ibid. The Behaviour of Married People

I came home for ever!
Letter to Bernard Barton [1825], on leaving his "33 years' desk" at the East India House

Who first invented work, and bound the free
And holiday-rejoicing spirit down . . .
To that dry drudgery at the desk's dead wood?
Work

The economy of Heaven is dark
And wisest clerks have missed the mark.
On an Infant Dying as Soon as Born [1827]

[1] Doorbells are like a magic game,
  Or the grab-bag at a fair —
You never know when you hear one ring
  Who may be waiting there.
  RACHEL FIELD [1894–1942]:
  Doorbells

Martin, if dirt was trumps, what hands you would hold!
Lamb's Suppers, in LEIGH HUNT: *Lord Byron and His Contemporaries [1828]*

Some cry up Haydn, some Mozart,
Just as the whim bites. For my part,
I do not care a farthing candle
For either of them, nor for Handel.
Letter to Mrs. William Hazlitt [1830]

A bird appears a thoughtless thing . . .
No doubt he has his little cares,
And very hard he often fares,
The which so patiently he bears.
Crumbs to the Birds

Reputation said: "If once we sever,
Our chance of future meeting is but vain:
Who parts from me, must look to part for ever,
For Reputation lost comes not again."
Love, Death, and Reputation. Stanza 4

For thy sake, tobacco, I
Would do anything but die.
A Farewell to Tobacco

He has left off reading altogether, to the great improvement of his originality.
Last Essays of Elia [1833]. Detached Thoughts on Books and Reading

Books think for me.
Ibid.

Books which are no books.
Ibid.

To be strong-backed and neat-bound is the desideratum of a volume. Magnificence comes after.
Ibid.

Newspapers always excite curiosity. No one ever lays one down without a feeling of disappointment.
Ibid.

If there be a regal solitude, it is a sick bed.
Ibid. The Convalescent

How sickness enlarges the dimensions of a man's self to himself.
Ibid.

Let me caution persons grown old in active business, not lightly, nor without weighing their own resources, to forego their customary employment all at once, for there may be danger in it.
Last Essays of Elia. The Superannuated Man

Your absence of mind we have borne, till your presence of body came to be called in question by it.
Ibid. Amicus Redivivus

A pun is a pistol let off at the ear; not a feather to tickle the intellect.
Ibid. Popular Fallacies: IX, That the Worst Puns are the Best

A presentation copy . . . is a copy of a book which does not sell, sent you by the author, with his foolish autograph at the beginning of it; for which, if a stranger, he only demands your friendship; if a brother author, he expects from you a book of yours, which does not sell, in return.
Ibid. XI, That We Must Not Look a Gift-Horse in the Mouth

The growing infirmities of age manifest themselves in nothing more strongly, than in an inveterate dislike of interruption.
Ibid. XII, That Home is Home Though it is Never so Homely

The good things of life are not to be had singly, but come to us with a mixture.
Ibid. XIII, That You Must Love Me and Love My Dog

It has happened not seldom that one work of some author has so transcendently surpassed in execution the rest of his compositions, that the world has agreed to pass a sentence of dismissal upon the latter, and to consign them to total neglect and oblivion.
Eliana. Estimate of Defoe's Secondary Novels

Cannot the heart in the midst of crowds feel frightfully alone?
Ibid.

The greatest pleasure I know is to do a good action by stealth, and to have it found out by accident.
Table Talk. In the Athenaeum [*1834*]

WALTER SAVAGE LANDOR
[1775–1864]

Rose Aylmer, whom these wakeful eyes
May weep, but never see,
A night of memories and of sighs
I consecrate to thee.
Rose Aylmer [*1806*]

There are no fields of amaranth on this side of the grave; there are no voices, O Rhodopè, that are not soon mute, however tuneful; there is no name, with whatever emphasis of passionate love repeated, of which the echo is not faint at last.
Imaginary Conversations [*1824–1829*]. *Aesop and Rhodopè, I*

Elegance in prose composition is mainly this: a just admission of topics and of words; neither too many nor too few of either; enough of sweetness in the sound to induce us to enter and sit still; enough of illustration and reflection to change the posture of our minds when they would tire; and enough of sound matter in the complex to repay us for our attendance.
Ibid. Chesterfield and Chatham

Of all failures, to fail in a witticism is the worst, and the mishap is the more calamitous in a drawn out and detailed one.
Ibid.

'Tis verse that gives
Immortal youth to mortal maids.
Verse

Around the child bend all the three
Sweet Graces — Faith, Hope, Charity.
Around the man bend other faces —
Pride, Envy, Malice, are his Graces.
Around the Child

Children are what the mothers are.
No fondest father's fondest care
Can fashion so the infant heart.
Children

When we play the fool, how wide
The theatre expands! beside,
How long the audience sits before us!
How many prompters! what a chorus!
Plays [*1846*]. *Stanza 2*

There is delight in singing, tho' none
hear
Beside the singer.
To Robert Browning [*1846*]

I strove with none, for none was worth
my strife;
Nature I loved; and next to Nature,
Art.

I warm'd both hands before the fire of
life;
It sinks, and I am ready to depart.
*Dying Speech of an Old
Philosopher* [*1853*]

THOMAS CAMPBELL
[1777–1844]

'Tis distance lends enchantment to the
view,
And robes the mountain in its azure
hue.[1]
Pleasures of Hope [*1799*].
Part I, Line 7

Hope, for a season, bade the world farewell,
And Freedom shriek'd as Kosciusko
fell!
Ibid. Line 381

Who hath not own'd, with rapture-
smitten frame,
The power of grace, the magic of a
name?
Ibid. Part II, Line 5

And muse on Nature with a poet's eye.
Ibid. Line 98

That gems the starry girdle of the year.
Ibid. Line 194

Cease, every joy, to glimmer on my
mind,
But leave, oh leave the light of Hope
behind!

[1] The mountains too, at a distance, appear
airy masses and smooth, but seen near at hand
they are rough. — DIOGENES LAERTIUS [*circa*
A. D. 200]: *Pyrrho, IX*

What though my wingèd hours of bliss
have been
Like angel visits, few and far between.[1]
Pleasures of Hope. Part II, Line 375

On the green banks of Shannon, when
Sheelah was nigh,
No blithe Irish lad was so happy as I;
No harp like my own could so cheerily
play,
And wherever I went was my poor dog
Tray.
The Harper [*1799*]. *Stanza 1*

Ye mariners of England,
That guard our native seas;
Whose flag has braved, a thousand
years,
The battle and the breeze!
Ye Mariners of England [*1800*].
Stanza 1

Britannia needs no bulwarks,
No towers along the steep;
Her march is o'er the mountain waves,
Her home is on the deep.
Ibid. Stanza 3

The meteor flag of England
Shall yet terrific burn,
Till danger's troubled night depart,
And the star of peace return.
Ibid. Stanza 4

Oh! once the harp of Innisfail
Was strung full high to notes of glad-
ness;
But yet it often told a tale
Of more prevailing sadness.
O'Connor's Child. Stanza 1

'Tis the sunset of life gives me mystical
lore,
And coming events cast their shadows
before.[2]
Lochiel's Warning [*1802*]

The combat deepens. On, ye brave,
Who rush to glory or the grave!

[1] See John Norris, page 291b.
[2] See Cicero, page 33a.
Often do the spirits
Of great events stride on before the events,
And in today already walks tomorrow.
COLERIDGE: *Wallenstein* [1799–
1800], *Part II, Act V, Sc. 1*
Poets are the hierophants of an unappre-
hended inspiration; the mirrors of the gigantic
shadows which futurity casts upon the present.
— SHELLEY: *A Defence of Poetry* [*1821*]

Wave, Munich! all thy banners wave,
And charge with all thy chivalry!
　　　Hohenlinden [*1802*]. *Stanza 7*
Few, few shall part where many meet!
The snow shall be their winding-sheet
And every turf beneath their feet
Shall be a soldier's sepulchre.
　　　　　　　Ibid. Stanza 8
There was silence deep as death,
And the boldest held his breath,
For a time.
　　　Battle of the Baltic [*1805*].
　　　　　　　　　　Stanza 2
For his country he sigh'd, when at twilight repairing
To wander alone by the wind-beaten hill.
　　　The Exile of Erin. Stanza 1
Star that bringest home the bee,
And sett'st the weary labourer free!
　　Song to the Evening Star. Stanza 1
Oh, how hard it is to find
The one just suited to our mind!
　　　　　　Song. Stanza 1
To live in hearts we leave behind
Is not to die.[1]
　　　Hallowed Ground. Stanza 6
Oh leave this barren spot to me!
Spare, woodman, spare the beechen
　　tree! [2]
　　The Beech-Tree's Petition. Stanza 1
Drink ye to her that each loves best!
　　And if you nurse a flame
That's told but to her mutual breast,
　　We will not ask her name.
　　　Drink Ye to Her. Stanza 1
A stoic of the woods, — a man without
　　a tear.
　　Gertrude of Wyoming [*1809*].
　　　　　　　Part I, Stanza 23
Triumphal arch, that fill'st the sky
　　When storms prepare to part,
I ask not proud Philosophy
　　To teach me what thou art.
　　　To the Rainbow [*1819*].
　　　　　　　　　　Stanza 1

[1] They are not dead who live
　　In hearts they leave behind.
　　　HUGH ROBERT ORR [1887-　]:
　　　　　They Softly Walk, St. 1
[2] See George Pope Morris, page 498b.

HENRY CLAY
[1777-1852]

If you wish to avoid foreign collision,
you had better abandon the ocean.
　　Speech, U. S. House of Repre-
　　　sentatives [*January 22, 1812*]
It would not be thought very just or
wise to arraign the honorable professions of law and physic because the one
produces the pettifogger and the other
the quack.
　　Speech, U. S. House of Repre-
　　　sentatives [*April 26, 1820*]
Government is a trust, and the officers of the government are trustees; and
both the trust and the trustees are created for the benefit of the people.[1]
　　Speech at Ashland, Kentucky
　　　　　　　　[*March, 1829*]
The arts of power and its minions
are the same in all countries and in all
ages. It marks its victim; denounces it;
and excites the public odium and the
public hatred, to conceal its own abuses
and encroachments.
　　Speech, U. S. Senate [*March 14,
　　　　　　　　　　　1834*]
Precedents deliberately established
by wise men are entitled to great
weight. They are evidence of truth, but
only evidence. . . . But a solitary
precedent . . . which has never been
re-examined, can not be conclusive.
　　Speech, U. S. Senate [*February
　　　　　　　　　　18, 1835*]
I have heard something said about
allegiance to the South. I know no
South, no North, no East, no West, to
which I owe any allegiance.
　　　　　　　Speech [*1848*]
Sir, I would rather be right than be
President.
　　　　　　　Speech [*1850*]
General Alexander Smyth, a tedious
speaker in Congress, observed: "You,
sir, speak for the present generation;
but I speak for posterity."
"Yes," said Mr. Clay, "and you seem

[1] See Burke, page 361b, Jefferson, page
375a, and Calhoun, page 442a.

resolved to speak until the arrival of your audience."

Quoted by EPES SARGENT *in*
Life of Henry Clay

COLONEL VALENTINE BLACKER
[1778–1823]

Put your trust in God, my boys, and keep your powder dry!

Oliver Cromwell's Advice [*1834*]

WILLIAM HAZLITT
[1778–1830]

One of the pleasantest things in the world is going a journey; but I like to go by myself.

On Going a Journey

The soul of a journey is liberty, perfect liberty, to think, feel, do just as one pleases.

Ibid.

Oh! it is great to shake off the trammels of the world and of public opinion — to lose our importunate, tormenting, everlasting personal identity and become the creature of the moment, clear of all ties . . . to be known by no other title than *the Gentleman in the parlour!*

Ibid.

What I mean by living to one's self is living in the world, as in it, not of it. . . . It is to be a silent spectator of the mighty scene of things; . . . to take a thoughtful, anxious interest or curiosity in what is passing in the world, but not to feel the slightest inclination to make or meddle with it.

On Living to One's Self

Even in the common affairs of life, in love, friendship, and marriage, how little security have we when we trust our happiness in the hands of others!

Ibid.

There is not a more mean, stupid, dastardly, pitiful, selfish, spiteful, envious, ungrateful animal than the Public.

It is the greatest of cowards, for it is afraid of itself.

On Living to One's Self

When a man is dead, they put money in his coffin, erect monuments to his memory, and celebrate the anniversary of his birthday in set speeches. Would they take any notice of him if he were living? No!

Ibid.

Horas non numero nisi serenas [1] — is the motto of a sun-dial near Venice. There is a softness and a harmony in the words and in the thought unparalleled.

On a Sun-Dial

If our hours were all serene, we might probably take almost as little note of them, as the dial does of those that are clouded.

Ibid.

No young man believes he shall ever die.

The Feeling of Immortality in Youth

There is a feeling of Eternity in youth, which makes us amends for everything. To be young is to be as one of the Immortal Gods.

Ibid.

The young are prodigal of life from a superabundance of it; the old are tenacious on the same score, because they have little left, and cannot enjoy even what remains of it.

Ibid.

As we advance in life, we acquire a keener sense of the value of time. Nothing else, indeed, seems of any consequence; and we become misers in this respect.

Ibid.

The only true retirement is that of the heart; the only true leisure is the repose of the passions. To such persons it makes little difference whether they are young or old; and they die as they have lived, with graceful resignation.

Ibid.

If I have not read a book before, it

[1] I count only the sunny hours.

is, to all intents and purposes, new to me, whether it was printed yesterday or three hundred years ago.

On Reading New Books

When I take up a work that I have read before (the oftener the better) I know what I have to expect. The satisfaction is not lessened by being anticipated.

On Reading Old Books

Persons without education certainly do not want either acuteness or strength of mind in what concerns themselves, or in things immediately within their observation; but they have no power of abstraction, no general standard of taste, or scale of opinion. They see their objects always near, and never in the horizon. Hence arises that egotism which has been remarked as the characteristic of self-taught men.

The Round Table. I, 26

It is better to be able neither to read nor write than to be able to do nothing else.

On the Ignorance of the Learned

Men of genius do not excel in any profession because they labour in it, but they labour in it, because they excel.

Characteristics

We are not hypocrites in our sleep.

On Dreams

"The English," says Froissart, "amused themselves sadly after the fashion of their country." They have indeed a way of their own. Their mirth is a relaxation from gravity, a challenge to dull care to be gone; and one is not always clear at first, whether the appeal is successful.

Merry England

When a person dies who does any one thing better than any one else in the world, it leaves a gap in society.

Table Talk [1821-1822] (On the death of John Cavanagh, famous player of fives, a kind of handball)

HENRY PETER, LORD BROUGHAM
[1778–1868]

Let the soldier be abroad if he will, he can do nothing in this age. There is another personage, — a personage less imposing in the eyes of some, perhaps insignificant. The schoolmaster is abroad,[1] and I trust to him, armed with his primer, against the soldier in full military array.

Speech, Opening of Parliament [January 29, 1828]

In my mind, he was guilty of no error, he was chargeable with no exaggeration, he was betrayed by his fancy into no metaphor, who once said that all we see about us, kings, lords, and Commons, the whole machinery of the State, all the apparatus of the system, and its varied workings, end in simply bringing twelve good men into a box.

Present State of the Law [February 7, 1828]

Pursuit of Knowledge under Difficulties.

Title of Book [1830]

Death was now armed with a new terror.

Attributed to Brougham [2]

JOHN GALT
[1779–1839]

From the lone sheiling of the misty island

[1] At the first meeting of the London Mechanics' Institution, 1825, John Reynolds, head of a school in Clerkenwell, acted as secretary of the meeting. Lord Brougham, who spoke at this meeting, said in the course of his remarks, "Look out, gentlemen, the schoolmaster is abroad." The phrase attracted little attention at that time, but when used in a speech three years later, it at once became popular.

[2] Brougham delivered a very warm panegyric upon the ex-Chancellor, and expressed a hope that he would make a good end, although to an expiring Chancellor death was now armed with a new terror. — LORD JOHN CAMPBELL: *Lives of the Chancellors* [1849], *Vol. VII, P. 163*

Lord St. Leonards attributes this phrase to

Mountains divide us, and the waste of seas —
Yet still the blood is strong, the heart is Highland,
And we in dreams behold the Hebrides.[1]
Canadian Boat Song. Stanza 2

FRANCIS SCOTT KEY
[1779–1843]

Oh, say can you see by the dawn's early light,
What so proudly we hailed at the twilight's last gleaming?
Whose broad stripes and bright stars, thro' the perilous fight,
O'er the ramparts we watched were so gallantly streaming?
And the rockets' red glare, the bombs bursting in air,
Gave proof thro' the night that our flag was still there.
Oh, say does that star-spangled banner yet wave
O'er the land of the free and the home of the brave?
The Star-Spangled Banner [September 14, 1814]. Stanza 1

Then conquer we must, for our cause it is just, —
And this be our motto, — "In God is our trust!"
Ibid. Stanza 4

JOSEPH STORY
[1779–1845]

Whene'er you speak, remember every cause

Sir Charles Wetherell, who used it on the occasion referred to by Lord Campbell.

[1] This poem appeared in *Noctes Ambrosianae*, No. 46, in *Blackwood's Magazine*, September, 1829. It is generally credited to John Galt, but JOHN WILSON ("Christopher North") has also been suggested as the author. JOHN GIBSON LOCKHART noted, on a copy of the poem in his own handwriting, that the song had been sent to him by a friend in Upper Canada. Galt, author of *Annals of the Parish*, was in Canada in 1824 and 1826. The poem was likewise found in the handwriting of Hugh Montgomerie, twelfth Earl of Eglinton [1739–1819], ascribed to a Gaelic origin.

Stands not on eloquence, but stands on laws;
Pregnant in matter, in expression brief,
Let every sentence stand with bold relief;
On trifling points not time nor talents waste,
A sad offence to learning and to taste;
Nor deal with pompous phrase, nor e'er suppose
Poetic flights belong to reasoning prose.
Advice to Young Lawyers. Stanza 1

Here shall the Press the People's right maintain,
Unaw'd by influence and unbrib'd by gain;
Here patriot Truth her glorious precepts draw,
Pledg'd to Religion, Liberty, and Law.
Motto of the Salem Register (In W. W. STORY, Life and Letters of Joseph Story [1851])

HORACE SMITH
[1779–1849]

Thinking is but an idle waste of thought,
And nought is everything, and everything is nought.
Rejected Addresses. Cui Bono? Stanza 8

In the name of the Prophet — figs.
Johnson's Ghost

Although corruption may our frame consume,
The immortal spirit in the skies may bloom.
Address to the Mummy at Belzoni's Exhibition. Stanza 13

WILLIAM LAMB, VISCOUNT MELBOURNE
[1779–1848]

I wish I was as cocksure of anything as Tom Macaulay is of everything.
In COWPER, Melbourne's Papers [1889]. Preface

THOMAS, LORD DENMAN
[1779–1854]

A delusion, a mockery, and a snare.
O'Connell v. The Queen (in 11 Clark and Finnelly Reports)

The mere repetition of the *Cantilena* of lawyers cannot make it law, unless it can be traced to some competent authority; and if it be irreconcilable, to some clear legal principle.
Ibid.

CLEMENT CLARKE MOORE
[1779–1863]

'Twas the night before Christmas, when all through the house
Not a creature was stirring, — not even a mouse; [1]
The stockings were hung by the chimney with care,
In hopes that St. Nicholas soon would be there.
A Visit from St. Nicholas [December, 1823]

"Happy Christmas to all, and to all a good-night!"
Ibid.

CHARLES CALEB COLTON
[1780–1832]

Imitation is the sincerest of flattery.
The Lacon

WILLIAM ELLERY CHANNING
[1780–1842]

I call that mind free which jealously guards its intellectual rights and powers, which calls no man master, which does not content itself with a passive or hereditary faith, which opens itself to light whencesoever it may come, which receives new truth as an angel from Heaven.
Spiritual Freedom

[1] See Shakespeare, page 169b.

The office of government is not to confer happiness, but to give men opportunity to work out happiness for themselves.
The Life and Character of Napoleon Bonaparte

CHARLES MINER
[1780–1865]

When I see a merchant over-polite to his customers, begging them to taste a little brandy and throwing half his goods on the counter, — thinks I, that man has an axe to grind.
Who'll Turn Grindstones [1]

THOMAS MOORE
[1780–1852]

Weep on! and, as thy sorrows flow,
I'll taste the luxury of woe.
Juvenile Poems. Anacreontic, Press the Grape, Stanza 2

How shall we rank thee upon glory's page?
Thou more than soldier and just less than sage!
Poems Relating to America. To Thomas Hume, Stanza 6

I knew by the smoke, that so gracefully curl'd
Above the green elms, that a cottage was near;
And I said, "If there's peace to be found in the world,
A heart that was humble might hope for it here!"
Ibid. Ballad Stanzas, 1

They made her a grave, too cold and damp
For a soul so warm and true;
And she's gone to the Lake of the Dismal Swamp,
Where, all night long, by a firefly lamp,
She paddles her white canoe.
Ibid. The Lake of the Dismal Swamp, Stanza 1

[1] From *Essays from the Desk of Poor Robert the Scribe* [1815].

Faintly as tolls the evening chime,
Our voices keep tune and our oars keep
   time.[1]
> *Poems Relating to America. A*
> *Canadian Boat-Song, Stanza 1*

Row, brothers, row, the stream runs
   fast,
The rapids are near, and the daylight's
   past.
> *Ibid.*

Go where glory waits thee!
But while fame elates thee,
  Oh, still remember me!
> *Irish Melodies* [*1807–1834*].
> *Go Where Glory Waits Thee,*
> *Stanza 1*

Oh, breathe not his name! let it sleep
   in the shade,
Where cold and unhonour'd his relics
   are laid.
> *Ibid. Oh Breathe Not His Name,*
> *Stanza 1*

And the tear that we shed, though in
   secret it rolls,
Shall long keep his memory green in our
   souls.[2]
> *Ibid. Stanza 2*

The harp that once through Tara's halls
  The soul of music shed,
Now hangs as mute on Tara's walls
  As if that soul were fled.
So sleeps the pride of former days,
  So glory's thrill is o'er;
And hearts that once beat high for
   praise
  Now feel that pulse no more.
> *Ibid. The Harp That Once*
> *Through Tara's Halls, Stanza 1*

And the heart that is soonest awake to
   the flowers
Is always the first to be touch'd by the
   thorns.
> *Ibid. Oh, Think Not My Spirits*
> *Are Always as Light, Stanza 1*

Rich and rare were the gems she wore,
And a bright gold ring on her wand
   she bore.
> *Ibid. Rich and Rare Were the*
> *Gems She Wore, Stanza 1*

[1] See Marvell, page 269a.
[2] See Shakespeare, page 170a.

There is not in the wide world a valley
   so sweet
As that vale in whose bosom the bright
   waters meet.[1]
> *Irish Melodies. The Meeting of*
> *the Waters, Stanza 1*

Come, send round the wine, and leave
   points of belief
To simpleton sages, and reasoning fools.
> *Ibid. Come, Send Round the*
> *Wine, Stanza 1*

Shall I ask the brave soldier, who fights
   by my side
In the cause of mankind, if our creeds
   agree?
Shall I give up the friend I have valued
   and tried,
If he kneel not before the same altar
   with me? [2]
> *Ibid. Stanza 2*

Ah! little they think who delight in her
   strains,
How the heart of the Minstrel is breaking.
> *Ibid. She is Far from the Land,*
> *Stanza 2*

Believe me, if all those endearing young
   charms
Which I gaze on so fondly today,
Were to change by tomorrow and fleet
   in my arms,
Like fairy gifts fading away,
Thou would'st still be adored as this
   moment thou art,
Let thy loveliness fade as it will,
And around the dear ruin each wish of
   my heart
Would entwine itself verdantly still.
> *Ibid. Believe Me, If All Those*
> *Endearing Young Charms,*
> *Stanza 1*

[1] The vale of Avoca, County Wicklow, Ire-
land, where the Avonmore and Avonbeg meet
to form the river Avoca.
[2] I do not question school nor creed
  Of Christian, Protestant, or Priest;
  I only know that creeds to me
  Are but new names for mystery,
  That good is good from east to east,
  And more I do not know nor need
  To know, to love my neighbor well.
> JOAQUIN MILLER [1841–1913]: *The*
> *Tale of the Tall Alcalde*

No, the heart that has truly lov'd never
forgets,
But as truly loves on to the close;
As the sunflower turns on her god, when
he sets,
The same look which she turn'd when
he rose.
> *Irish Melodies. Believe Me, If
> All Those Endearing Young
> Charms, Stanza 2*

And when once the young heart of a
maiden is stolen,
The maiden herself will steal after it
soon.
> *Ibid. Ill Omens, Stanza 1*

'Tis sweet to think, that, where'er we
rove,
We are sure to find something blissful and dear;
And that when we're far from the lips
we love,
We've but to make love to the lips
we are near.
> *Ibid. 'Tis Sweet to Think,
> Stanza 1*

But there's nothing half so sweet in life
As love's young dream.
> *Ibid. Love's Young Dream,
> Stanza 1*

To live with them is far less sweet,
Than to remember thee.
> *Ibid. I Saw Thy Form, Stanza 3*

Eyes of unholy blue.
> *Ibid. By That Lake Whose
> Gloomy Shore, Stanza 2*

'Tis the last rose of summer,
Left blooming alone;
All her lovely companions
Are faded and gone;
No flower of her kindred,
No rosebud is nigh,
To reflect back her blushes,
Or give sigh for sigh.
> *Ibid. The Last Rose of Summer,
> Stanza 1*

When true hearts lie wither'd
And fond ones are flown,
Oh, who would inhabit
This bleak world alone?
> *Ibid. Stanza 3*

And the best of all ways
To lengthen our days

Is to steal a few hours from the night,
my dear.
> *Irish Melodies. The Young May
> Moon, Stanza 1*

You may break, you may shatter the
vase if you will,
But the scent of the roses will hang
round it still.
> *Ibid. Farewell! But Whenever*

No eye to watch, and no tongue to
wound us,
All earth forgot, and all heaven around
us.
> *Ibid. Come O'er the Sea,
> Stanza 2*

The light that lies [1]
In woman's eyes.
> *Ibid. The Time I've Lost in
> Wooing, Stanza 1*

My only books
Were woman's looks,
And folly's all they've taught me.
> *Ibid.*

I know not, I ask not, if guilt's in that
heart,
I but know that I love thee, whatever
thou art.
> *Ibid. Come, Rest in This Bosom,
> Stanza 2*

A Persian's heaven is easily made:
'Tis but black eyes and lemonade.
> *Intercepted Letters, or The Two-
> Penny Post Bag [1813]. VI*

Oft in the stilly night,
Ere slumber's chain has bound me,
Fond memory brings the light
Of other days around me;
The smiles, the tears,
Of boyhood's years,
The words of love then spoken;
The eyes that shone
Now dimmed and gone,
The cheerful hearts now broken.
> *National Airs [1815]. Oft in the
> Stilly Night, Stanza 1*

---

[1]   O dreamy eyes,
They tell sweet lies of Paradise;
And in those eyes the love-light lies
And lies — and lies — and lies!
      ANITA OWEN: *Dreamy Eyes
                [circa 1894]*

I feel like one,
Who treads alone
Some banquet-hall deserted,
Whose lights are fled,
Whose garlands dead,
And all but he departed.
> *National Airs. Oft in the Stilly*
> *Night, Stanza 2*

Came but for Friendship and took away
Love.
> *Ibid. A Temple to Friendship,*
> *Stanza 2*

As half in shade and half in sun
This world along its path advances,
May that side the sun's upon
Be all that e'er shall meet thy glances!
> *Ibid. Peace Be Around Thee,*
> *Stanza 2*

If I speak to thee in friendship's name,
Thou think'st I speak too coldly;
If I mention love's devoted flame,
Thou say'st I speak too boldly.
> *Ibid. How Shall I Woo? Stanza 1*

A friendship that like love is warm;
A love like friendship steady.
> *Ibid. Stanza 3*

Young Love may go,
For aught I care,
To Jericho!
> *Ibid. When Love Is Kind, Stanza 6*

So Life's year begins and closes;
Days though shortening still can
shine;
What though youth gave love and roses,
Age still leaves us friends and wine.
> *Ibid. Spring and Autumn,*
> *Stanza 1*

Give smiles to those who love you less,
But keep your tears for me.
> *When Midst the Gay I Meet.*
> *Stanza 1*

This world is all a fleeting show,
For man's illusion given;
The smiles of joy, the tears of woe,
Deceitful shine, deceitful flow, —
There's nothing true but Heaven.
> *Sacred Songs. This World is All*
> *a Fleeting Show, Stanza 1*

Sound the loud timbrel o'er Egypt's
dark sea!

Jehovah has triumph'd, — his people
are free.
> *Sacred Songs. Sound the*
> *Loud Timbrel*

As down in the sunless retreats of the
ocean
Sweet flowers are springing no mortal
can see,
So, deep in my soul the still prayer of
devotion,
Unheard by the world, rises silent to
Thee.
> *Ibid. As Down in the Sunless*
> *Retreats, Stanza 1*

Ask a woman's advice, and, whate'er
she advise,
Do the very reverse and you're sure to
be wise.
> *Satirical and Humorous Poems.*
> *How to Make a Good Politician,*
> *Stanza 1*

There was a little man, and he had a
little soul;
And he said, Little Soul, let us try, try,
try!
> *Ibid. Little Man and Little Soul,*
> *Stanza 1*

Oh, call it by some better name,
For friendship sounds too cold.
> *Ballads and Songs. Oh, Call It*
> *by Some Better Name, Stanza 1*

To sigh, yet feel no pain;
To weep, yet scarce know why;
To sport an hour with Beauty's chain,
Then throw it idly by.
> *Miscellaneous Poems. The Blue*
> *Stocking, VI*

And from the lips of Truth one mighty
breath
Shall like a whirlwind scatter in its
breeze
The whole dark pile of human mockeries: —
Then shall the reign of mind commence
on earth,
And starting fresh as from a second
birth,
Man in the sunshine of the world's new
spring

Shall walk transparent like some holy thing!
> *Lalla Rookh [1817]. Part I, The Veiled Prophet of Khorassan*

The heaven of each is but what each desires.
> *Ibid.*

There's a bower of roses by Bendemeer's stream,
And the nightingale sings round it all the day long.[1]
> *Ibid. Part II*

But Faith, fanatic Faith, once wedded fast
To some dear falsehood, hugs it to the last.
> *Ibid. Part III*

One morn a Peri at the gate
Of Eden stood disconsolate.
> *Ibid. Part IV, Paradise and the Peri*

Take all the pleasures of all the spheres
And multiply each through endless years, —
One minute of heaven is worth them all.
> *Ibid.*

But the trail of the serpent is over them all.
> *Ibid.*

Oh! ever thus, from childhood's hour,
  I've seen my fondest hope decay;
I never loved a tree or flower,
  But 'twas the first to fade away.
I never nurs'd a dear gazelle
  To glad me with its soft black eye,
But when it came to know me well
  And love me it was sure to die.[2]
> *Ibid. Part V, The Fire-Worshippers*

Paradise itself were dim
And joyless, if not shared with him!
> *Ibid. Part VI*

---

[1] As I recall them the roses bloom again, and the nightingales sing by the calm Bendemeer. — THACKERAY: *The Newcomes* [1853–1855], Chap. 1

[2] I never had a piece of toast
  Particularly long and wide
  But fell upon the sanded floor,
  And always on the buttered side.
> JAMES PAYN: *Poem* [1884]

Alas! how light a cause may move
Dissension between hearts that love!
> *Lalla Rookh. Part VIII, The Light of the Haram*

Like that celestial bird whose nest
Is found beneath far Eastern skies,
Whose wings though radiant when at rest
Lose all their glory when he flies.
> *Ibid.*

Fly to the desert, fly with me,
Our Arab tents are rude for thee.
> *Ibid.*

Humility, that low, sweet root
From which all heavenly virtues shoot.
> *The Loves of the Angels [1823].
Third Angel's Story*

COMMANDER JAMES LAWRENCE, U.S.N.
[1781–1813]

Tell the men to fire faster and not to give up the ship; fight her till she sinks.
> *On Board the Chesapeake
> [June 1, 1813]*

EBENEZER ELLIOTT
[1781–1849]

When wilt Thou save the people?
O God of mercy, when?
Not kings and lords, but nations!
Not thrones and crowns, but men!
Flowers of Thy heart, O God, are they;
Let them not pass, like weeds, away —
God save the people!
> *Corn Law Rhymes [1828]. When Wilt Thou Save the People? Stanza 1*

What is a communist? One who hath yearnings
For equal division of unequal earnings.
> *Poetical Works [1846]. Epigram*

THOMAS HART BENTON
[1782–1858]

This new page opened in the book of our public expenditures, and this new departure taken, which leads into the bottomless gulf of civil pensions and family gratuities.

> *Speech, U. S. Senate, Against a Grant to President Harrison's Widow [April, 1841]*

JOHN C. CALHOUN
[1782–1850]

Protection and patriotism are reciprocal.

> *Speech, U. S. House of Representatives [December 12, 1811]*

The very essence of a free government consists in considering offices as public trusts,[1] bestowed for the good of the country, and not for the benefit of an individual or a party.

> *Speech [February 13, 1835]*

A power has risen up in the government greater than the people themselves, consisting of many and various and powerful interests, combined into one mass, and held together by the cohesive power of the vast surplus in the banks.[2]

> *Speech [May 27, 1836]*

The surrender of life is nothing to sinking down into acknowledgment of inferiority.

> *Speech, U. S. Senate [February 19, 1847]*

ANN TAYLOR
[1782–1866]
JANE TAYLOR
[1783–1824]

Who ran to help me when I fell,
And would some pretty story tell,
Or kiss the place to make it well?
My mother.

> *Original Poems for Infant Minds [1804]. My Mother [By* ANN TAYLOR*], Stanza 6*

One honest John Tompkins, a hedger and ditcher,
Although he was poor, did not want to be richer;

---

[1] See Burke, page 361b, Jefferson, page 375a, and Clay, page 433b.
[2] From this speech comes the phrase, "Cohesive power of public plunder."

For all such vain wishes in him were prevented
By a fortunate habit of being contented.

> *Original Poems for Infant Minds. Contented John [By* JANE TAYLOR*], Stanza 1*

Twinkle, twinkle, little star,
How I wonder what you are,
Up above the world so high,
Like a diamond in the sky.[1]

> *Rhymes for the Nursery [1806]. The Star, Stanza 1*

I thank the goodness and the grace
  Which on my birth have smiled,
And made me, in these Christian days,
  A happy Christian child.

> *Hymns for Infant Minds [1810]. A Child's Hymn of Praise, Stanza 1*

Oh, that it were my chief delight
  To do the things I ought!
Then let me try with all my might
  To mind what I am taught.

> *Ibid. For a Very Little Child*

There's hardly anything so small,
  So trifling or so mean,
That we may never want at all,
  For service unforeseen;
And wilful waste, depend upon 't,
Brings, almost always, woeful want!

> *Ibid. The Pin [By* ANN TAYLOR*], Stanza 6*

'Twas fancied by some, who but slightly had seen them,
There was not a pin to be chosen between them.

> *Ibid. Jane and Eliza [By* ANN TAYLOR*], Stanza 2*

DANIEL WEBSTER
[1782–1852]

Whatever makes men good Christians, makes them good citizens.

> *Speech at Plymouth, Massachusetts [2] [December 22, 1820]*

---

[1] Twinkle, twinkle, little bat!
How I wonder what you're at!
Up above the world you fly,
Like a tea-tray in the sky.
> LEWIS CARROLL: *Alice's Adventures in Wonderland [1865]*

[2] This oration will be read five hundred

Labor in this country is independent and proud. It has not to ask the patronage of capital, but capital solicits the aid of labor.[1]

Speech [April 2, 1824]

We wish that this column, rising towards heaven among the pointed spires of so many temples dedicated to God, may contribute also to produce in all minds a pious feeling of dependence and gratitude. We wish, finally, that the last object to the sight of him who leaves his native shore, and the first to gladden his who revisits it, may be something which shall remind him of the liberty and the glory of his country.

Address on Laying the Corner-Stone of the Bunker Hill Monument [June 17, 1825]

Mind is the great lever of all things; human thought is the process by which human ends are ultimately answered.

Ibid.

Knowledge, in truth, is the great sun in the firmament. Life and power are scattered with all its beams.

Ibid.

Let our object be our country, our whole country, and nothing but our country.

Ibid.

Sink or swim, live or die, survive or perish, I give my hand and my heart to this vote.[2]

Discourse in Commemoration of Adams and Jefferson, Faneuil Hall, Boston [August 2, 1826]

It is my living sentiment, and by the blessing of God it shall be my dying sentiment, — Independence now and Independence forever.[1]

Discourse in Commemoration of Adams and Jefferson, Faneuil Hall, Boston

Washington is in the clear upper sky.

Ibid.

The gentleman has not seen how to reply to this, otherwise than by supposing me to have advanced the doctrine that a national debt is a national blessing.[2]

Second Speech on Foote's Resolution [January 26, 1830]

I shall enter on no encomium upon Massachusetts; she needs none. There she is.[3] Behold her, and judge for yourselves. There is her history; the world knows it by heart. The past, at least, is secure. There is Boston and Concord and Lexington and Bunker Hill; and there they will remain forever.

Ibid.

The people's government, made for the people, made by the people, and answerable to the people.[4]

Ibid.

When my eyes shall be turned to behold for the last time the sun in heaven, may I not see him shining on the broken and dishonored fragments of a once glorious Union; on States dissevered, discordant, belligerent; on a land rent with civil feuds, or drenched, it may be, in fraternal blood.

Ibid.

years hence with as much rapture as it was heard. It ought to be read at the end of every century, and indeed at the end of every year, forever and ever. — JOHN ADAMS: *Letter to Webster* [December 23, 1821]

[1] See Lincoln, page 539b.

[2] Mr. Adams, describing a conversation with Jonathan Sewall in 1774, says: "I answered that the die was now cast; I had passed the Rubicon. Swim or sink, live or die, survive or perish with my country was my unalterable determination." — JOHN ADAMS: *Works* [1850-1856], *Vol. IV, P. 8*

Live or die, sink or swim. — GEORGE PEELE: *Edward I* [1584?]

Both Adams and Jefferson died on July 4, 1826.

[1] Mr. Webster says of Mr. Adams: "On the day of his death, hearing the noise of bells and cannon, he asked the occasion. On being reminded that it was 'Independent Day,' he replied, 'Independence forever.'" — *Webster's Works* [1903], *Vol. I, P. 150*

[2] A national debt, if it is not excessive, will be to us a national blessing. — ALEXANDER HAMILTON: *Letter to Robert Morris* [April 30, 1781]

[3] This is generally misquoted as "Massachusetts, there she stands."

[4] Our sovereign, the people. — CHARLES JAMES FOX: Toast [1798], for which his name was erased from the Privy Council.

See Lincoln, page 541a, and Theodore Parker, page 560a.

Liberty and Union, now and forever, one and inseparable.

Second Speech on Foote's Resolution

There is no refuge from confession but suicide; and suicide is confession.

Argument on the Murder of Captain White [April 6, 1830]

There is nothing so powerful as truth, — and often nothing so strange.[1]

Ibid.

Fearful concatenation of circumstances.[2]

Ibid.

A sense of duty pursues us ever. It is omnipresent, like the Deity. If we take to ourselves the wings of the morning, and dwell in the uttermost parts of the sea, duty performed or duty violated is still with us, for our happiness or our misery. If we say the darkness shall cover us, in the darkness as in the light our obligations are yet with us.

Ibid.

He smote the rock of the national resources, and abundant streams of revenue gushed forth. He touched the dead corpse of Public Credit, and it sprung upon its feet.[3]

Speech on Hamilton [March 10, 1831]

God grants liberty only to those who love it, and are always ready to guard and defend it.

Speech [June 3, 1834]

On this question of principle, while actual suffering was yet afar off, they [the Colonies] raised their flag against a power to which, for purposes of foreign conquest and subjugation, Rome in the height of her glory is not to be compared, — a power which has dotted over the surface of the whole globe with her possessions and military posts,

whose morning drum-beat, following the sun,[1] and keeping company with the hours, circles the earth with one continuous and unbroken strain of the martial airs of England.

Speech [May 7, 1834]

One country, one constitution, one destiny.

Speech [March 15, 1837]

There are persons who constantly clamor. They complain of oppression, speculation, and pernicious influence of wealth. They cry out loudly against all banks and corporations, and a means by which small capitalists become united in order to produce important and beneficial results. They carry on mad hostility against all established institutions. They would choke the fountain of industry and dry all streams.

Speech, U. S. Senate [March 12, 1838]

When tillage begins, other arts follow. The farmers therefore are the founders of human civilization.

Remarks on Agriculture [January 13, 1840]

America has furnished to the world the character of Washington. And if our American institutions had done nothing else, that alone would have entitled them to the respect of mankind.

Completion of Bunker Hill Monument [June 17, 1843]

Thank God! I — I also — am an American!

Ibid.

Justice, sir, is the great interest of man on earth.

On Mr. Justice Story [September 12, 1845]

Inconsistencies of opinion, arising from changes of circumstances, are often justifiable.[2]

Speech [July 25 and 27, 1846]

---

[1] See Byron, page 460a.

[2] See Scott, page 417a.

[3] He it was that first gave to the law the air of a science. He found it a skeleton, and clothed it with life, colour, and complexion; he embraced the cold statue, and by his touch it grew into youth, health, and beauty. — BARRY YELVERTON, LORD AVONMORE [1736–1805]: *On Blackstone*

[1] See Scott, page 417b.

[2] L'homme absurde est celui qui ne change jamais (The absurd man is he who never changes). — AUGUSTE MARSEILLE BARTHÉLEMY: *Ma Justification* [1832]

Liberty exists in proportion to wholesome restraint.
> *Speech at the Charleston Bar Dinner [May 10, 1847]*

The law: It has honored us; may we honor it.
> *Ibid.*

I have read their platform, and though I think there are some unsound places in it, I can stand upon it pretty well. But I see nothing in it both new and valuable. "What is valuable is not new, and what is new is not valuable."
> *Speech at Marshfield, Massachusetts [September 1, 1848]*

I was born an American; I will live an American; I shall die an American.[1]
> *Speech [July 17, 1850]*

Faneuil Hall, the cradle of American liberty.
> *Letter [April, 1851]*

Men hang out their signs indicative of their respective trades: shoemakers hang out a gigantic shoe; jewelers, a monster watch; and the dentist hangs out a gold tooth; but up in the mountains of New Hampshire, God Almighty has hung out a sign to show that there He makes men.
> *The Old Man of the Mountain [2]*

I still live.
> *Last words [October 24, 1852]*

REGINALD HEBER
[1783–1826]

Failed the bright promise of your early day.
> *Palestine*

Brightest and best of the sons of the morning,
Dawn on our darkness, and lend us thine aid.
> *Hymns. Epiphany, Stanza 1*

By cool Siloam's shady rill
How sweet the lily grows!
> *Ibid. First Sunday after Epiphany, No. II*

[1] See Patrick Henry, page 368b.
[2] A natural rock formation in the shape of a human profile, in the Presidential Range of the White Mountains. It gave Hawthorne the theme of his story *The Great Stone Face*.

The Son of God goes forth to war,
A kingly crown to gain;
His blood-red banner streams afar;
Who follows in His train?
> *Hymns. The Son of God Goes Forth to War, Stanza 1*

From Greenland's icy mountains,
From India's coral strand,
Where Afric's sunny fountains
Roll down their golden sand.
> *Ibid. Missionary Hymn, Stanza 1*

Though every prospect pleases,
And only man is vile:
In vain with lavish kindness
The gifts of God are strown;
The heathen in his blindness
Bows down to wood and stone.
> *Ibid. Stanza 2*

Holy, Holy, Holy! Lord God Almighty!
Early in the morning our song shall rise to Thee:
Holy, Holy, Holy! Merciful and Mighty!
God in Three Persons, Blessed Trinity.
> *Ibid. Holy, Holy, Holy!*

Holy, Holy, Holy! all the Saints adore Thee,
Casting down their golden crowns around the glassy sea.
> *Ibid.*

WASHINGTON IRVING
[1783–1859]

How convenient it would be to many of our great men and great families of doubtful origin, could they have the privilege of the heroes of yore, who, whenever their origin was involved in obscurity, modestly announced themselves descended from a god.
> *Knickerbocker's History of New York [1809]. Book II, Chap. 3*

Who ever hears of fat men heading a riot, or herding together in turbulent mobs? — no — no, 'tis your lean, hungry men who are continually worrying society, and setting the whole community by the ears.[1]
> *Ibid. Book III, Chap. 2*

[1] See Shakespeare, page 166b.

Your true dull minds are generally preferred for public employ, and especially promoted to city honors; your keen intellects, like razors, being considered too sharp for common service.

Knickerbocker's History of New York. Book III, Chap. 2

His wife "ruled the roast," and in governing the governor, governed the province, which might thus be said to be under petticoat government.

Ibid. Book IV, Chap. 4

The most glorious hero that ever desolated nations might have mouldered into oblivion among the rubbish of his own monument, did not some historian take him into favor, and benevolently transmit his name to posterity.

Ibid. Book V, Chap. 1

There is in every true woman's heart a spark of heavenly fire, which lies dormant in the broad daylight of prosperity; but which kindles up, and beams and blazes in the dark hour of adversity.

The Sketch-Book [1819–1820].
The Wife

Those men are most apt to be obsequious and conciliating abroad, who are under the discipline of shrews at home.

Ibid. Rip Van Winkle

A curtain lecture is worth all the sermons in the world for teaching the virtues of patience and long-suffering.

Ibid.

A sharp tongue is the only edge tool that grows keener with constant use.

Ibid.

That happy age when a man can be idle with impunity.

Ibid.

A woman's whole life is a history of the affections.

Ibid. The Broken Heart

Language gradually varies, and with it fade away the writings of authors who have flourished their allotted time.

Ibid. The Mutabilities of Literature

There rise authors now and then, who seem proof against the mutability of

language, because they have rooted themselves in the unchanging principles of human nature.

The Sketch-Book. The Mutabilities of Literature

His [the author's] renown has been purchased, not by deeds of violence and blood, but by the diligent dispensation of pleasure.

Ibid. Westminster Abbey [The Poets' Corner]

The sorrow for the dead is the only sorrow from which we refuse to be divorced. Every other wound we seek to heal, every other affliction to forget; but this wound we consider it a duty to keep open; this affliction we cherish and brood over in solitude.

Ibid. Rural Funerals

Whenever a man's friends begin to compliment him about looking young, he may be sure that they think he is growing old.

Bracebridge Hall [1822].
Bachelors

The land of literature is a fairy land to those who view it at a distance, but, like all other landscapes, the charm fades on a nearer approach, and the thorns and briars become visible. The republic of letters is the most factious and discordant of all republics, ancient or modern.

Tales of a Traveller [1824].
Notoriety

The almighty dollar,[1] that great object of universal devotion throughout our land, seems to have no genuine devotees in these peculiar villages.

Wolfert's Roost [1855]. The Creole Village

Those calm, sunny seasons in the commercial world, which are known by the name of "times of unexampled prosperity."

Ibid. "A Time of Unexampled Prosperity"

[Captain Delaplace[2]] gazed at [Ethan] Allen in bewildered astonish-

[1] See Jonson, page 219a.
[2] Commandant at Fort Ticonderoga, New York, May 10, 1775.

446

ment. "By whose authority do you act?" exclaimed he. "In the name of the great Jehovah, and the Continental Congress!" replied Allen.
Life of Washington [1855–1859].
Vol. I, Chap. 38

HENRI BEYLE
(STENDHAL)
[1783–1842]

One can acquire everything in solitude — except character.
Fragments. I
Prudery is a kind of avarice, the worst of all.
Ibid. V
In matters of sentiment, the public has very crude ideas; and the most shocking fault of women is that they make the public the supreme judge of their lives.
Ibid. IX
A wise woman never yields by appointment. It should always be an unforeseen happiness.
De l'Amour [1822]. Chap. 60
The Baron could not produce epigrams; he required at least four sentences of six lines each to be brilliant.
The Red and the Black [1831].
Chap. 34
I see but one rule: *to be clear*. If I am not clear, all *my world* crumbles to nothing.
Reply to Balzac. October 30,
1840 [1]
Wit lasts no more than two centuries.
Ibid.
It is the nobility of their style which will make our writers of 1840 unreadable forty years from now.
Manuscript Note [1840]

ALLAN CUNNINGHAM
[1784–1842]

A wet sheet and a flowing sea,
A wind that follows fast,

[1] In reference to *The Charterhouse of Parma* [1839].

And fills the white and rustling sail,
And bends the gallant mast.
The Songs of Scotland [1825].
A Wet Sheet and a Flowing Sea,
Stanza 1
While the hollow oak our palace is,
Our heritage the sea.
Ibid. Stanza 3
When looks were fond and words were few.
Ibid. Poet's Bridal-day Song,
Stanza 2
John Grumlie swore by the light o' the moon,
And the green leaves on the tree,
That he could do more work in a day
Than his wife could do in three.
Ibid. John Grumlie,[1] *Stanza 1*
But henceforth I maun mind the plow,
And ye maun bide at hame.
Ibid. Stanza 6
It's hame and it's hame, hame fain wad I be,
O, hame, hame, hame to my ain countree!
Ibid. It's Hame and It's Hame

LEIGH HUNT
[1784–1859]

This Adonis in loveliness was a corpulent man of fifty.[2]
The Examiner [March 22, 1812]
Where the light woods go seaward from the town.
The Story of Rimini [1816].
Canto I, Line 18
But most he loved a happy human face.
Ibid. Canto III, Line 110

[1] Adapted from the old ballad *The Wife of Auchtermuchty.* Another adaptation is *Darby and Joan,* by St. John Honeywood [1763–1798]:
When Darby saw the setting sun,
He swung his scythe and home he run,
Sat down, drank off his quart, and said:
"My work is done, I'll go to bed."
[2] For this reference to the Prince Regent. Hunt was imprisoned. But he was allowed to redecorate the walls of his prison with a trellis of roses, had his family with him, and visitors were freely admitted — Byron, indeed, gave a dinner party in his honor at the jail.

With spots of sunny openings, and with
nooks
To lie and read in, sloping into brooks.
> *The Story of Rimini. Canto III,*
> *Line 418*

The world was all forgot, the struggle
o'er,
Desperate the joy. — That day they
read no more.[1]
> *Ibid. Line 607*

Green little vaulter in the sunny grass.
> *To the Grasshopper and the*
> *Cricket* [*1817*]

Abou Ben Adhem (may his tribe increase!)
Awoke one night from a deep dream
of peace.
> *Abou Ben Adhem* [*1838*]

An angel writing in a book of gold.
> *Ibid.*

Write me as one who loves his fellow-
men.
> *Ibid.*

And show'd the names whom love of
God had bless'd,
And lo! Ben Adhem's name led all the
rest.
> *Ibid.*

Jenny kissed me when we met,
Jumping from the chair she sat in;
Time, you thief, who love to get
Sweets into your list, put that in:
Say I'm weary, say I'm sad,
Say that health and wealth have
missed me,
Say I'm growing old, but add,
Jenny kissed me.[2]
> *Rondeau* [*1838*]

Stolen sweets are always sweeter,
Stolen kisses much completer,
Stolen looks are nice in chapels,
Stolen, stolen, be your apples.
> *Song of Fairies Robbing an*
> *Orchard*

Oh for a seat in some poetic nook,

Just hid with trees and sparkling with
a brook!
> *Politics and Poetics. Line 72*

"No love," quoth he, "but vanity, sets
love a task like that."
> *The Glove and the Lions.*[1]
> *Stanza 4*

Learn the right
Of coining words in the quick mint of
joy.
> *A Rustic Walk and Dinner.*
> *Line 33*

Some people say it is a very easy
thing to get up of a cold morning. You
have only, they tell you, to take the
resolution; and the thing is done.
> *Getting Up on Cold Mornings*

She thinks the young women of the
present day too forward, and the men
not respectful enough; but hopes her
grandchildren will be better; though
she differs with her daughter in several
points respecting their management.
> *The Old Lady*

Those who have lost an infant are
never, as it were, without an infant
child. They are the only persons who,
in one sense, retain it always.
> *Deaths of Little Children*

A fireside is a great opiate.
> *A Few Thoughts on Sleep*

It has been said of ladies when they
write letters, that they put their minds
in their postscripts — let out the real
objects of their writing, as if it were
a second thought, or a thing comparatively indifferent.
> *Anacreon*

The only place a new hat can be carried into with safety is a church, for
there is plenty of room there.
> *A Chapter on Hats*

The maid-servant, the sailor, and
the schoolboy, are the three beings that
enjoy a holiday beyond all the rest of
the world.
> *The Maid-Servant*

---

[1] See Dante, page 75b.
[2] The "Jenny" was Jane Welsh Carlyle, who
kissed Hunt when he brought Carlyle good
news.

[1] SCHILLER wrote a poem on the same
theme, and BROWNING'S *The Glove* [1845] is
a later version of the familiar legend.

JAMES SHERIDAN KNOWLES
[1784–1862]

A sound so fine, there's nothing lives
'Twixt it and silence.
Virginius [*1820*]. *Act V, Sc. 2*

LADY CAROLINE LAMB
[1785–1828]

Mad, bad, and dangerous to know.
Of Byron, in her Journal

THOMAS DE QUINCEY
[1785–1859]

It is notorious that the memory strengthens as you lay burdens upon it, and becomes trustworthy as you trust it.
Confessions of an English Opium-Eater [1] [*1822–1856*]. *Page 30*
Call for the grandest of all earthly spectacles, what is that? It is the sun going to his rest. Call for the grandest of all human sentiments, what is that? It is that man should forget his anger before he lies down to sleep. [2]
Ibid. Page 86
The reception one meets with from the women of a family generally determines the tenor of one's whole entertainment.
Ibid. Page 132
Mails from the North — the East — the West — the South — whence, according to some curious etymologists, comes the magical word NEWS.
Ibid. Page 145
Oxford Street, stony-hearted stepmother, thou that listenest to the sighs of orphans, and drinkest the tears of children.
Ibid. Page 174
Dyspepsy is the ruin of most things: empires, expeditions, and everything else.
Letter to Hessey [*1823*]
If once a man indulges himself in murder, very soon he comes to think little of robbing; and from robbing he

[1] Everyman edition.
[2] See *Ephesians, IV, 26*, at page 1062b.

next comes to drinking and Sabbath-breaking, and from that to incivility and procrastination.
Murder Considered as One of the Fine Arts [*1827*]
Worlds of fine thinking lie buried in that vast abyss [newspapers], never to be disentombed or restored to human admiration.
Reminiscences of the English Lake Poets. Coleridge

THOMAS LOVE PEACOCK
[1785–1866]

How troublesome is day!
It calls us from our sleep away;
It bids us from our pleasant dreams
    awake,
And sends us forth to keep or break
Our promises to pay.
How Troublesome Is Day
None better knew the feast to sway,
    Or keep mirth's boat in better trim;
For Nature had but little clay
    Like that of which she moulded him.
Headlong Hall [*1816*]. *Chap. 5,
In His Last Binn Sir Peter Lies,
Stanza 2*
A heeltap! a heeltap! I never could
    bear it!
So fill me a bumper, a bumper of
    claret!
Ibid. Song.
Not drunk is he who from the floor
Can rise alone and still drink more;
But drunk is he, who prostrate lies,
Without the power to drink or rise.
The Misfortunes of Elphin
[*1829*]. *Heading, Chap. 3,
translated from the Welsh*
The mountain sheep are sweeter,
But the valley sheep are fatter;
We therefore deemed it meeter
To carry off the latter.
Ibid. Chap. 11
Ancient sculpture is the true school of modesty. But where the Greeks had modesty, we have cant; where they had poetry, we have cant; where they had patriotism, we have cant; where they had anything that exalts, delights, or

adorns humanity, we have nothing but cant, cant, cant.

> *Crotchet Castle* [*1831*]. *Chap. 7*

He remembered too late, on his thorny green bed,
Much that well may be thought cannot wisely be said.

> *Ibid. The Priest and the Mulberry Tree, Stanza 5*

OLIVER HAZARD PERRY
[1785–1820]

We have met the enemy, and they are ours.

> *Letter to General Harrison* [*dated "United States Brig Niagara. Off the Western Sisters. Sept. 10, 1813, 4 P. M."*]

JOHN PIERPONT
[1785–1866]

The Yankee boy, before he's sent to school,
Well knows the mystery of that magic tool,
The pocket-knife.

> *Whittling, A Yankee Portrait. Stanza 1*

SAMUEL WOODWORTH
[1785–1842]

How dear to this heart are the scenes of my childhood,
When fond recollection presents them to view.

> *The Old Oaken Bucket*

Then soon with the emblem of truth overflowing,
And dripping with coolness, it rose from the well.

> *Ibid.*

The old oaken bucket, the iron-bound bucket,
The moss-covered bucket, which hung in the well.

> *Ibid.*

Pickaxe, shovel, spade, crowbar, hoe, and barrow,

Better not invade, Yankees have the marrow.

> *The Patriotic Diggers* [*1814*]. *Stanza 1*

We'll show him that Kentucky boys
Are Alligator-horses.

> *The Hunters of Kentucky.*[1] *Stanza 2*

So Pakenham he made his brags
If he in fight was lucky,
He'd have their gals and cotton bags,
In spite of old Kentucky.

> *Ibid. Stanza 4*

DAVID CROCKETT
[1786–1836]

I leave this rule for others when I'm dead,
Be always sure you're right — then go ahead.[2]

> *Autobiography* [*1834*]

Don't shoot, colonel, I'll come down: I know I'm a gone coon.[3]

> *Story told by Crockett of a treed raccoon*

WILLIAM LEARNED MARCY
[1786–1857]

They see nothing wrong in the rule that to the victor belong the spoils of the enemy.

> *Speech, U. S. Senate* [*January, 1832*]

WINFIELD SCOTT
[1786–1866]

Say to the seceded States, "Wayward sisters, depart in peace."

> *Letter to W. H. Seward* [*March 3, 1861*]

[1] This ballad, having the subtitle *Half Horse and Half Alligator,* celebrates the participation of the Kentuckians, under the command of General John Coffee, in the Battle of New Orleans, January 8, 1815. It was published as a broadside in Boston, and, in 1826, collected in a volume, *Melodies, Duets, Trios, Songs, and Ballads,* by JAMES M. CAMPBELL.
[2] Crockett's motto in the War of 1812.
[3] The expression "gone coon" was current during the Revolutionary War, originating in the plea of a spy, dressed in raccoon skins, to his discoverer, an English rifleman. — *Century Cyclopedia of Names*

RICHARD HENRY DANA
[1787–1879]

A voice within us speaks the startling word,
"Man, thou shalt never die!"
Immortality

BRYAN WALLER PROCTER ("BARRY CORNWALL")
[1787–1874]

The sea! the sea! the open sea!
The blue, the fresh, the ever free!
The Sea. Stanza 1

Touch us gently, Time! [1]
Let us glide adown thy stream
Gently, — as we sometimes glide
Through a quiet dream.
A Petition to Time. Stanza 1

Humble voyagers are we,
O'er life's dim, unsounded sea.
Ibid. Stanza 2

EMMA WILLARD
[1787–1870]

Rocked in the cradle of the deep,
I lay me down in peace to sleep.
The Cradle of the Deep [1831]

RICHARD HARRIS BARHAM
[1788–1845]

The Lady Jane was tall and slim,
The Lady Jane was fair.
Ingoldsby Legends [1840]. *The Knight and the Lady*

The Devil must be in that little Jackdaw!
Ibid. The Jackdaw of Rheims

The Cardinal rose with a dignified look,
He call'd for his candle, his bell, and his book!
In holy anger, and pious grief,
He solemnly cursed that rascally thief!
He cursed him at board, he cursed him in bed;
From the sole of his foot to the crown of his head;
He cursed him in sleeping, that every night

[1] See Crabbe, page 383b.

He should dream of the devil, and wake in a fright;
He cursed him in living, he cursed him in drinking,
He cursed him in coughing, in sneezing, in winking;
He cursed him in sitting, in standing, in lying;
He cursed him in walking, in riding, in flying,
He cursed him living, he cursed him dying! —
Never was heard such a terrible curse!
But what gave rise to no little surprise,
Nobody seem'd one penny the worse!
Ingoldsby Legends. The Jackdaw of Rheims

Heedless of grammar, they all cried,
That's him!
Ibid.

GEORGE NOEL GORDON, LORD BYRON
[1788–1824]

Friendship is Love without his wings.
L'Amitié est l'Amour sans Ailes [1806]

I only know we loved in vain;
I only feel — farewell! farewell!
Farewell! If Ever Fondest Prayer [1808]. *Stanza 2*

When we two parted
In silence and tears,
Half broken-hearted,
To sever for years.
When We Two Parted [1808]. *Stanza 1*

Near this spot are deposited the remains of one who possessed Beauty without Vanity, Strength without Insolence, Courage without Ferocity, and all the Virtues of Man, without his Vices. This Praise, which would be unmeaning Flattery if inscribed over human ashes, is but a just tribute to the Memory of Boatswain, a Dog.
Inscription on the Monument of a Newfoundland Dog [1808]

The poor dog, in life the firmest friend,

The first to welcome, foremost to defend.

Inscription on the Monument of a Newfoundland Dog

I'll publish right or wrong:
Fools are my theme, let satire be my song.

English Bards and Scotch Reviewers [*1809*]. *Line 5*

'Tis pleasant, sure, to see one's name in print;
A book's a book, although there's nothing in 't.

Ibid. Line 51

A man must serve his time to every trade
Save censure — critics are all ready made.

Ibid. Line 63

With just enough of learning to misquote.

Ibid. Line 66

As soon
Seek roses in December, ice in June;
Hope constancy in wind, or corn in chaff;
Believe a woman or an epitaph,
Or any other thing that's false, before
You trust in critics.

Ibid. Line 75

Better to err with Pope, than shine with Pye.

Ibid. Line 102

'Twas thine own genius gave the final blow,
And help'd to plant the wound that laid thee low:
So the struck eagle, stretch'd upon the plain,
No more through rolling clouds to soar again,
View'd his own feather on the fatal dart,
And wing'd the shaft that quiver'd in his heart.[1]

Ibid. Line 826

Though Nature's sternest painter, yet the best.[2]

Ibid. Line 839

[1] See Aesop, page 11b.
[2] Crabbe.

Maid of Athens, ere we part,
Give, oh give me back my heart!

Maid of Athens [*1810*]. *Stanza 1*

Vex'd with mirth the drowsy ear of night.

Childe Harold's Pilgrimage.
Canto I [*1812*], *Stanza 2*

Had sigh'd to many, though he loved but one.

Ibid. Stanza 5

Maidens, like moths, are ever caught by glare,
And Mammon wins his way where seraphs might despair.

Ibid. Stanza 9

Might shake the saintship of an anchorite.

Ibid. Stanza 11

Adieu! adieu! my native shore
Fades o'er the waters blue.

Ibid. Stanza 13

My native land, good night!

Ibid.

Still from the fount of joy's delicious springs
Some bitter o'er the flowers its bubbling venom flings.[1]

Ibid. Stanza 82

War, war is still the cry, — "war even to the knife!"[2]

Ibid. Stanza 86

The dome of thought, the palace of the soul.[3]

Ibid. Canto II [*1812*],
Stanza 6

Once more upon the waters, yet once more!
And the waves bound beneath me as a steed
That knows his rider!

Ibid. Canto III [*1816*], *Stanza 2*

There was a sound of revelry by night,
And Belgium's capital had gather'd then
Her beauty and her chivalry, and bright
The lamps shone o'er fair women and brave men.

[1] See Lucretius, page 35a.
[2] "War even to the knife" was the reply of Palafox, the governor of Saragossa, when summoned to surrender by the French, who besieged that city in 1808.
[3] See Waller, page 242b.

A thousand hearts beat happily; and when
Music arose with its voluptuous swell,
Soft eyes look'd love to eyes which spake again,
And all went merry as a marriage bell.
But hush! hark! a deep sound strikes like a rising knell!
Childe Harold's Pilgrimage. Canto III, Stanza 21

Did ye not hear it? — No! 'twas but the wind,
Or the car rattling o'er the stony street.
On with the dance! let joy be unconfined;
No sleep till morn, when Youth and Pleasure meet
To chase the glowing hours with flying feet.
Ibid. Stanza 22

And there was mounting in hot haste.
Ibid. Stanza 25

Or whispering, with white lips, "The foe! They come! they come!"
Ibid.

Like to the apples on the Dead Sea's shore,
All ashes to the taste.
Ibid. Stanza 34

He who ascends to mountain-tops, shall find
The loftiest peaks most wrapt in clouds and snow;
He who surpasses or subdues mankind
Must look down on the hate of those below.
Ibid. Stanza 45

All tenantless, save to the crannying wind.
Ibid. Stanza 47

History's purchased page to call them great.
Ibid. Stanza 48

The castled crag of Drachenfels
Frowns o'er the wide and winding Rhine.
Ibid. Stanza 55

To fly from, need not be to hate, mankind.
Ibid. Stanza 69

By the blue rushing of the arrowy Rhone.
Childe Harold's Pilgrimage Canto III, Stanza 71

I live not in myself, but I become
Portion of that around me: [1] and to me
High mountains are a feeling, but the hum
Of human cities torture.
Ibid. Stanza 72

The sky is changed, — and such a change! O night
And storm, and darkness! ye are wondrous strong,
Yet lovely in your strength, as is the light
Of a dark eye in woman!
Ibid. Stanza 92

Exhausting thought,
And hiving wisdom with each studious year.
Ibid. Stanza 107

Sapping a solemn creed with solemn sneer.
Ibid.

Fame is the thirst of youth.
Ibid. Stanza 112

I have not loved the world, nor the world me; [2]
I have not flatter'd its rank breath, nor bow'd
To its idolatries a patient knee.
Ibid. Stanza 113

I stood
Among them, but not of them; in a shroud
Of thoughts which were not their thoughts.
Ibid.

I stood in Venice on the Bridge of Sighs,
A palace and a prison on each hand.
Ibid. Canto IV [1818], Stanza 1

Where Venice sate in state, throned on her hundred isles.
Ibid.

The thorns which I have reap'd are of the tree

[1] I am a part of all that I have met. — TENNYSON: *Ulysses* [1842]
[2] See Johnson, page 343a, and Emerson, pages 502b–503a.

planted; they have torn me, and I bleed.
I should have known what fruit would spring from such a seed.
Childe Harold's Pilgrimage.
Canto IV, Stanza 10

Parting day
Dies like the dolphin, whom each pang imbues
With a new colour as it gasps away,
The last still loveliest, till — 'tis gone, and all is gray.
Ibid. Stanza 29

Italia! O Italia! thou who hast
The fatal gift of beauty.[1]
Ibid. Stanza 42

Let these describe the undescribable.
Ibid. Stanza 53

The starry Galileo, with his woes.
Ibid. Stanza 54

Ungrateful Florence! Dante sleeps afar,
Like Scipio, buried by the upbraiding shore.
Ibid. Stanza 57

The poetry of speech.
Ibid. Stanza 58

Then farewell Horace, whom I hated so,
Not for thy faults, but mine.
Ibid. Stanza 77

O Rome! my country! city of the soul!
Ibid. Stanza 78

The Niobe of nations! there she stands,
Childless and crownless, in her voiceless woe.
Ibid. Stanza 79

I speak not of men's creeds — they rest between
Man and his Maker.
Ibid. Stanza 95

Yet, Freedom! yet thy banner, torn, but flying,
Streams like the thunder-storm against the wind.
Ibid. Stanza 98

'Tis but the same rehearsal of the past . . .

[1] Based on the famous sonnet of VINCENZO DA FILICAJA [1642–1707]:
Italia, Italia! O tu cui feo la sorte.

And History, with all her volumes vast,
Hath but one page.
Childe Harold's Pilgrimage.
Canto IV, Stanza 108

Egeria! sweet creation of some heart
Which found no mortal resting-place so fair
As thine ideal breast.
Ibid. Stanza 115

Death, the sable smoke where vanishes the flame.
Ibid. Stanza 124

Butcher'd to make a Roman holiday!
Ibid. Stanza 141

"While stands the Coliseum, Rome shall stand;
When falls the Coliseum, Rome shall fall;
And when Rome falls — the world." ·
Ibid. Stanza 145

Oh! that the desert were my dwelling-place,[2]
With one fair spirit for my minister,
That I might all forget the human race,
And, hating no one, love but only her!
Ibid. Stanza 177

There is a pleasure in the pathless woods,
There is a rapture on the lonely shore,
There is society, where none intrudes,
By the deep sea, and music in its roar:
I love not man the less, but Nature more.
Ibid. Stanza 178

Roll on, thou deep and dark blue ocean, roll!
Ten thousand fleets sweep over thee in vain;
Man marks the earth with ruin, — his control
Stops with the shore.
Ibid. Stanza 179

Time writes no wrinkle on thine azure brow —

[1] The saying of the ancient pilgrims, quoted from BEDE by GIBBON, *The Decline and Fall of the Roman Empire* [1781], *Chap. LXXI.*
[2] Oh that I had in the wilderness a lodging-place of wayfaring men! — *Jeremiah, IX,* 2
See Cowper, page 364a.

Such as creation's dawn beheld, thou rollest now.[1]
> *Childe Harold's Pilgrimage.*
> *Canto IV, Stanza 182*

Thou glorious mirror, where the Almighty's form
Glasses itself in tempests.
> *Ibid. Stanza 183*

And I have loved thee, Ocean! and my joy
Of youthful sports was on thy breast to be
Borne, like thy bubbles, onward; from a boy
I wantoned with thy breakers, . . .
And trusted to thy billows far and near,
And laid my hand upon thy mane,[2] — as I do here.
> *Ibid. Stanza 184*

I awoke one morning and found myself famous.
> *Entry in Memoranda after publication of first two cantos of Childe Harold's Pilgrimage.* Quoted by THOMAS MOORE, *Life of Byron* [1830], *Chap. 14*

Such is the aspect of this shore;
'Tis Greece, but living Greece no more!
So coldly sweet, so deadly fair,
We start, for soul is wanting there.
> *The Giaour* [1813]. *Line 90*

Shrine of the mighty! can it be
That this is all remains of thee?
> *Ibid. Line 106*

And lovelier things have mercy shown
To every failing but their own;
And every woe a tear can claim,
Except an erring sister's shame.
> *Ibid. Line 418*

The keenest pangs the wretched find
Are rapture to the dreary void,
The leafless desert of the mind,
The waste of feelings unemployed.
> *Ibid. Line 957*

[1] And thou vast ocean, on whose awful face
Time's iron feet can print no ruin-trace.
ROBERT MONTGOMERY: *The Omnipresence of the Deity* [1830]
[2] He laid his hand upon "the Ocean's mane,"
And played familiar with his hoary locks.
ROBERT POLLOK [1798–1827]: *The Course of Time, Book IV, L. 689*

Better to sink beneath the shock
Than moulder piecemeal on the rock.
> *The Giaour. Line 969*

The cold in clime are cold in blood,
Their love can scarce deserve the name.
> *Ibid. Line 1099*

I die, — but first I have possess'd,
And come what may, I *have been* bless'd.
> *Ibid. Line 1114*

She was a form of life and light
That, seen, became a part of sight,
And rose, where'er I turn'd mine eye,
The morning-star of memory!
> *Ibid. Line 1127*

Know ye the land where the cypress and myrtle
Are emblems of deeds that are done in their clime;
Where the rage of the vulture, the love of the turtle,
Now melt into sorrow, now madden to crime?[1]
> *The Bride of Abydos* [1813].
> *Canto I, Stanza 1*

Where the virgins are soft as the roses they twine,
And all save the spirit of man is divine?
> *Ibid.*

The fatal facility of the octosyllabic verse.
> *The Corsair* [1814]. *Dedication*

He left a corsair's name to other times,
Link'd with one virtue, and a thousand crimes.
> *Ibid. Canto III, Stanza 24*

The Cincinnatus of the West,
Whom envy dared not hate,
Bequeathed the name of Washington
To make man blush there was but one![2]
> *Ode to Napoleon Bonaparte* [1814]. *II*

Lord of himself, — that heritage of woe!
> *Lara* [1814]. *Canto I, Stanza 2*

[1] See Goethe, page 378b.
[2] See *Don Juan,* page 459a, and *The Age of Bronze,* page 460b.

The hand that kindles cannot quench
the flame.
          Lara. Canto II, Stanza 11

She walks in beauty, like the night
Of cloudless climes and starry skies;
And all that's best of dark and bright
Meet in her aspect and her eyes;
Thus mellow'd to that tender light
Which Heaven to gaudy day denies.
          Hebrew Melodies [1815]. She
          Walks in Beauty, Stanza 1

The Assyrian came down like the wolf
on the fold,
And his cohorts were gleaming in purple and gold;
And the sheen of their spears was like
stars on the sea,
When the blue wave rolls nightly on
deep Galilee.
          Ibid. The Destruction of Sen-
          nacherib,[1] *Stanza 1*

For the Angel of Death spread his wings
on the blast.
          Ibid. Stanza 3

And the might of the Gentile, unsmote
by the sword,
Hath melted like snow in the glance
of the Lord!
          Ibid. Stanza 6

Fare thee well! and if forever,
Still forever, fare thee well.
          Fare Thee Well [1816]. Stanza 1

Sighing that Nature form'd but one
such man,
And broke the die, in moulding Sheridan.[2]
          Monody on the Death of Sheridan
          [1816]. Line 117

My hair is gray, but not with years,
Nor grew it white
In a single night,

---

[1] And it came to pass that night, that the
angel of the Lord went out, and smote in the
camp of the Assyrians an hundred fourscore
and five thousand: and when they arose early
in the morning, behold, they were all dead
corpses. — *2 Kings, XIX, 35*
[2] Natura il fece, e poi ruppe la stampa
(Nature made him, and then broke the
mould). — ARIOSTO: *Orlando Furioso* [1532],
Canto X, St. 84

As men's have grown from sudden fears.
          The Prisoner of Chillon [1816].
          Stanza 1

O God! it is a fearful thing
To see the human soul take wing
In any shape, in any mood.
          Ibid. Stanza 8

A light broke in upon my brain, —
It was the carol of a bird;
It ceased, and then it came again,
The sweetest song ear ever heard.
          Ibid. Stanza 10

I had a dream which was not all a
dream.
          Darkness [1816]

Though the day of my destiny's over,
And the star of my fate hath declined.
          Stanzas to Augusta [1816].
          Stanza 1

My boat is on the shore,
And my bark is on the sea;
But, before I go, Tom Moore,
Here's a double health to thee!
          To Thomas Moore [1817].
          Stanza 1

Here's a sigh to those who love me,
And a smile to those who hate;
And, whatever sky's above me,
Here's a heart for every fate.[1]
          Ibid. Stanza 2

So we'll go no more a-roving
So late into the night.
          Letter to Thomas Moore
          [February 26, 1817]

Mont Blanc is the monarch of moun-
tains;
They crowned him long ago
On a throne of rocks, in a robe of
clouds,
With a diadem of snow.
          Manfred [1817]. Act I, Sc. 1

She was not old, nor young, nor at the
years
Which certain people call a "certain
age,"
Which yet the most uncertain age appears.
          Beppo [1818]. Stanza 22

For most men (till by losing rendered
sager)

---

[1] See Longfellow, page 521a.

Will back their own opinions by a wager.
Beppo. Stanza 27

Besides, they always smell of bread and butter.
Ibid. Stanza 39

That soft bastard Latin,
Which melts like kisses from a female mouth.
Ibid. Stanza 44

One hates an author that's all author.
Ibid. Stanza 75

O Mirth and Innocence! O milk and water!
Ye happy mixtures of more happy days.
Ibid. Stanza 80

And if we do but watch the hour,
There never yet was human power
Which could evade, if unforgiven,
The patient search and vigil long
Of him who treasures up a wrong.
Mazeppa [1819]. Stanza 10

In virtues nothing earthly could surpass her,
Save thine "incomparable oil," Macassar!
Don Juan. Canto I [1819], Stanza 17

But, oh! ye lords of ladies intellectual,
Inform us truly, — have they not henpeck'd you all? [1]
Ibid. Stanza 22

The languages, especially the dead,
The sciences, and most of all the abstruse,
The arts, at least all such as could be said
To be the most remote from common use.
Ibid. Stanza 40

Her maids were old, and if she took a new one,
You might be sure she was a perfect fright.
Ibid. Stanza 48

Her stature tall, — I hate a dumpy woman.
Ibid. Stanza 61

[1] See Addison, page 301a.

What men call gallantry, and gods adultery,
Is much more common where the climate's sultry.
Don Juan. Canto I, Stanza 63

Christians have burnt each other, quite persuaded
That all the Apostles would have done as they did.
Ibid. Stanza 83

A little still she strove, and much repented,
And whispering, "I will ne'er consent," — consented.
Ibid. Stanza 117

'Tis sweet to hear the watch-dog's honest bark
Bay deep-mouth'd welcome as we draw near home;
'Tis sweet to know there is an eye will mark
Our coming, and look brighter when we come.
Ibid. Stanza 123

Sweet is revenge — especially to women.[1]
Ibid. Stanza 124

Man's love is of man's life a thing apart;
'Tis woman's whole existence.
Ibid. Stanza 194

There's nought, no doubt, so much the spirit calms
As rum and true religion.
Ibid. Canto II [1819], Stanza 34

A solitary shriek, the bubbling cry
Of some strong swimmer in his agony.
Ibid. Stanza 53

'Tis very certain the desire of life
Prolongs it.
Ibid. Stanza 64

'Tis said that persons living on annuities
Are longer lived than others.
Ibid. Stanza 65

All who joy would win
Must share it, — happiness was born a twin.
Ibid. Stanza 172

[1] See Milton, page 258a.

Let us have wine and women, mirth and
  laughter,
Sermons and soda-water the day after.[1]
  Don Juan. Canto II, Stanza 178
In her first passion woman loves her
  lover,
In all the others, all she loves is love.[2]
  Ibid. Canto III [1821], Stanza 3
Think you, if Laura had been Petrarch's
  wife,
He would have written sonnets all his
  life?
  Ibid. Stanza 7
All tragedies are finished by a death,
All comedies are ended by a marriage.
  Ibid. Stanza 9
  He was the mildest manner'd man
That ever scuttled ship or cut a throat.
  Ibid. Stanza 41
Even good men like to make the pub-
  lic stare.
  Ibid. Stanza 81
The isles of Greece, the isles of Greece!
Where burning Sappho loved and
  sung. . . .
Eternal summer gilds them yet,
But all, except their sun, is set.
  Ibid. Stanza 86, 1
The mountains look on Marathon,
And Marathon looks on the sea;
And musing there an hour alone,
I dreamed that Greece might still be
  free.
  Ibid. 3
And where are they? and where art
  thou,
My country? On thy voiceless shore
The heroic lay is tuneless now —
The heroic bosom beats no more!
And must thy lyre, so long divine,
Degenerate into hands like mine?
  Ibid. 5
Earth! render back from out thy breast
A remnant of our Spartan dead!
Of the three hundred grant but three,
To make a new Thermopylae.
  Ibid. 7
You have the Pyrrhic dance as yet,
Where is the Pyrrhic phalanx gone?

[1] See Dickens, page 577a, and George Ade,
page 829a.
[2] See La Rochefoucauld, page 266a.

Of two such lessons, why forget
The nobler and the manlier one?
You have the letters Cadmus gave —
Think ye he meant them for a slave?
  Don Juan. Canto III, Stanza 86, 10
Fill high the bowl with Samian wine!
  Ibid. 11
Place me on Sunium's marble steep,
Where nothing save the waves and I
May hear our mutual murmurs sweep;
There, swan-like, let me sing and die.[1]
A land of slaves shall ne'er be mine —
Dash down yon cup of Samian wine!
  Ibid. 16
But words are things, and a small drop
  of ink,
Falling like dew upon a thought, pro-
  duces
That which makes thousands, perhaps
  millions, think.
  Ibid. Stanza 88
And glory long has made the sages
  smile,
'Tis something, nothing, words, illusion,
  wind —
Depending more upon the historian's
  style
Than on the name a person leaves
  behind.
  Ibid. Stanza 90
Ah, surely nothing dies but something
  mourns.
  Ibid. Stanza 108
And if I laugh at any mortal thing,
'Tis that I may not weep.[2]
  Ibid. Canto IV [1821], Stanza 4
  And her face so fair
Stirr'd with her dream, as rose-leaves
  with the air.[3]
  Ibid. Stanza 29
  These two hated with a hate
Found only on the stage.
  Ibid. Stanza 93

[1] See Socrates, page 21a.
[2] See Beaumarchais, page 367b, and Lincoln, page 540a.
[3]   All her innocent thoughts
  Like rose-leaves scatter'd.
    JOHN WILSON ("CHRISTOPHER
    NORTH"): *On the Death of a
    Child* [1812]

"Arcades ambo," — *id est*, blackguards both.
Don Juan. Canto IV, Stanza 93

I've stood upon Achilles' tomb,
And heard Troy doubted: time will doubt of Rome.
Ibid. Stanza 101

There's not a sea the passenger e'er pukes in,
Turns up more dangerous breakers than the Euxine.
Ibid. Canto V [1821], Stanza 5

And put himself upon his good behaviour.
Ibid. Stanza 47

That all-softening, overpowering knell,
The tocsin of the soul — the dinner bell.
Ibid. Stanza 49

The women pardon'd all except her face.
Ibid. Stanza 113

Polygamy may well be held in dread,
Not only as a sin, but as a bore.
Ibid. Canto VI [1823], Stanza 12

The drying up a single tear has more
Of honest fame than shedding seas of gore.
Ibid. Canto VIII [1823], Stanza 3

Not so Leonidas and Washington,
Whose every battle-field is holy ground,
Which breathes of nations saved, not worlds undone.[1]
Ibid. Stanza 5

Half-pay for life makes mankind worth destroying.
Ibid. Stanza 14

George Washington had thanks and nought beside,
Except the all-cloudless glory (which few men's is)
To free his country.[1]
Ibid. Canto IX [1823], Stanza 8

"Gentlemen farmers" — a race worn out quite.
Ibid. Stanza 32

[1] See *Ode to Napoleon*, page 455b, and *The Age of Bronze*, page 460b.

When Bishop Berkeley said "there was no matter,"
And proved it, — 'twas no matter what he said.
Don Juan. Canto XI [1823], Stanza 1

And, after all, what is a lie? 'Tis but
The truth in masquerade; and I defy
Historians, heroes, lawyers, priests, to put
A fact without some leaven of a lie.
Ibid. Stanza 37

'Tis strange the mind, that very fiery particle,
Should let itself be snuff'd out by an article.
Ibid. Stanza 60

Ready money is Aladdin's lamp.
Ibid. Canto XII [1823], Stanza 12

Cervantes smil'd Spain's chivalry away.
Ibid. Canto XIII [1823], Stanza 11

Society is now one polish'd horde,
Formed of two mighty tribes, the *Bores* and *Bored*.
Ibid. Stanza 95

All human history attests
That happiness for man, — the hungry sinner! —
Since Eve ate apples, much depends on dinner.[1]
Ibid. Stanza 99

Death, so called, is a thing which makes men weep,
And yet a third of life is passed in sleep.
Ibid. Canto XIV [1823], Stanza 3

Of all the horrid, hideous notes of woe,
Sadder than owl-songs or the midnight blast,
Is that portentous phrase, "I told you so."
Ibid. Stanza 50

[1] For a man seldom thinks with more earnestness of anything than he does of his dinner. — PIOZZI: *Anecdotes of Samuel Johnson* [1786]

'Tis strange, but true; for truth is always strange, —
Stranger than fiction.[1]
Don Juan. Canto XIV,
Stanza 101

The Devil hath not, in all his quiver's choice,
An arrow for the heart like a sweet voice.
Ibid. Canto XV [1824],
Stanza 13

A lovely being, scarcely formed or moulded,
A rose with all its sweetest leaves yet folded.
Ibid. Stanza 43

The antique Persians taught three useful things, —
To draw the bow, to ride, and speak the truth.
Ibid. Canto XVI [1824],
Stanza 1

All farewells should be sudden.
Sardanapalus [1821]. Act V

The best of prophets of the future is the past.
Journal [January 28, 1821]

The world is a bundle of hay,
Mankind are the asses that pull,
Each tugs in a different way, —
And the greatest of all is John Bull!
Letter to Thomas Moore
[June 22, 1821]

He seems
To have seen better days, as who has not
Who has seen yesterday?
Werner [1822]. Act I, Sc. 1

The "good old times" — all times when old are good.
The Age of Bronze [1823].
Stanza 1

Whose [2] game was empires and whose stakes were thrones,

Whose table earth, whose dice were human bones.
The Age of Bronze. Stanza 3

While Franklin's quiet memory climbs to heaven,
Calming the lightning which he thence had riven,
Or drawing from the no less kindled earth
Freedom and peace to that which boasts his birth;
While Washington's a watchword, such as ne'er
Shall sink while there's an echo left to air.[1]
Ibid. Stanza 5

How often we forget all time, when lone,
Admiring Nature's universal throne,
Her woods, her wilds, her waters, the intense
Reply of hers to our intelligence.
The Island [1823]. Canto II,
Stanza 16

Sublime tobacco! which from east to west
Cheers the tar's labour or the Turkman's rest.[2]
Ibid. Stanza 19

Divine in hookas, glorious in a pipe
When tipp'd with amber, mellow, rich, and ripe;
Like other charmers, wooing the caress
More dazzlingly when daring in full dress;
Yet thy true lovers more admire by far
Thy naked beauties — give me a cigar!
Ibid.

What's drinking?
A mere pause from thinking!
The Deformed Transformed
[1824]. Act III, Sc. 1

My days are in the yellow leaf; [3]

---

[1] See *Ode to Napoleon*, page 455b, and *Don Juan*, page 459a.

[2] Whatever Aristotle, and his worthy cabal, may say of it,
Tobacco is divine, there is nothing to equal it.
PIERRE CORNEILLE: *Le Festin de Pierre* [1673], *Act I, Sc. 1*

[3] See Shakespeare, pages 199a and 205b–206a.

---

[1] Le vrai peut quelquefois n'être pas vraisemblable (Truth may sometimes be improbable). — BOILEAU [1636–1711]: *L'Art Poétique, III, L. 48*
See Daniel Webster, page 444a.
Truth is stranger than fiction, but not so popular. — AUTHOR UNKNOWN
[2] Napoleon.

The flowers and fruits of love are
gone;
The worm, the canker, and the grief
Are mine alone!
On My Thirty-sixth Year [*1824*].
Stanza 2

Seek out — less often sought than
found —
A soldier's grave, for thee the best;
Then look around, and choose thy
ground,
And take thy rest.
Ibid. Stanza 10

ARTHUR SCHOPENHAUER
[1788–1860]

Hatred comes from the heart; contempt from the head; and neither feeling is quite within our control.
Studies in Pessimism.[1]
Psychological Observations

If a man sets out to hate all the miserable creatures he meets, he will not
have much energy left for anything
else; whereas he can despise them, one
and all, with the greatest ease.
Ibid.

Every man takes the limits of his own
field of vision for the limits of the
world.
Ibid.

Not to go to the theatre is like making one's toilet without a mirror.
Ibid.

Every parting gives a foretaste of
death;[2] every coming together again a
foretaste of the resurrection.
Ibid.

There is no absurdity so palpable but
that it may be firmly planted in the human head if you only begin to inculcate
it before the age of five, by constantly
repeating it with an air of great solemnity.
Ibid.

It is a curious fact that in bad days
we can very vividly recall the good time

that is now no more; but that in good
days we have only a very cold and imperfect memory of the bad.
*Studies in Pessimism. Psycho-
logical Observations*

The fundamental fault of the female
character is that it has no sense of justice.
Ibid. On Women

Dissimulation is innate in woman,
and almost as much a quality of the
stupid as of the clever.
Ibid.

Noise is the most impertinent of all
forms of interruption. It is not only an
interruption, but also a disruption of
thought.
Ibid. On Noise

The most general survey shows us
that the two foes of human happiness
are pain and boredom.
*Essays. Personality, or What a
Man Is*

A man who has no mental needs, because his intellect is of the narrow and
normal amount, is, in the strict sense of
the word, what is called a *philistine*.[1]
Ibid.

Pride is an established conviction of
one's own paramount worth in some
particular respect; while vanity is the
desire of rousing such a conviction in
others. Pride works from within; it is
the direct appreciation of oneself. Vanity is the desire to arrive at this appreciation indirectly, from without.
Ibid. Pride

Ignorance is degrading only when
found in company with riches.
Ibid. On Books and Reading

Intellect is invisible to the man who
has none.[2]
*Ibid. Our Relation to Others,
Sect. 23*

There is no more mistaken path to
happiness than worldliness, revelry,
high life.
*Ibid. Our Relation to Ourselves,
Sect. 24*

To be alone is the fate of all great

---

[1] Translated by T. BAILEY SAUNDERS, Modern Library edition.
[2] Partir c'est mourir un peu. — *French
proverb*

[1] See Matthew Arnold, page 621b.
[2] See La Rochefoucauld, page 266a.

minds — a fate deplored at times, but still always chosen as the less grievous of two evils.
Essays. Our Relation to Ourselves, Sect. 24

Do not shorten the morning by getting up late; look upon it as the quintessence of life, as to a certain extent sacred.
Counsels and Maxims. Chap. 2

Speak without emphasizing your words. Leave other people to discover what it is that you have said; and as their minds are slow, you can make your escape in time.
Ibid. Chap. 3

HANNAH FLAGG GOULD
[1789–1865]

Alone I walked the ocean strand;
A pearly shell was in my hand;
I stooped and wrote upon the sand
My name — the year — the day.
A Name on the Sand. Stanza 1

A wave came rolling high and fast,
And washed my lines away.
Ibid.

WILLIAM KNOX
[1789–1825]

Oh why should the spirit of mortal be proud?
Like a fast-flitting meteor, a fast-flying cloud,
A flash of the lightning, a break of the wave,
He passes from life to his rest in the grave.
Songs of Israel [1824]. Mortality,[1] Stanza 1

'Tis the wink of an eye, 'tis the draught of a breath,
From the blossom of health to the paleness of death.
Ibid. Stanza 14

CHARLES PHILLIPS
[1789–1859]

Grand, gloomy, and peculiar, he sat upon the throne a sceptred hermit,

[1] This poem was a favorite of Abraham Lincoln.

wrapped in the solitude of his own originality.
The Character of Napoleon

SARAH JOSEPHA HALE
[1790–1879]

Mary had a little lamb,
Its fleece was white as snow,
And everywhere that Mary went
The lamb was sure to go;
He followed her to school one day,
That was against the rule;
It made the children laugh and play
To see a lamb in school.
Mary's Lamb. In the Juvenile Miscellany [September, 1830]

FITZ-GREENE HALLECK
[1790–1867]

Strike — till the last armed foe expires;
Strike — for your altars and your fires;
Strike — for the green graves of your sires;
God — and your native land!
Marco Bozzaris.[1] Stanza 3

But to the hero, when his sword
Has won the battle for the free,
Thy voice sounds like a prophet's word,
And in its hollow tones are heard
The thanks of millions yet to be.
Ibid. Stanza 6

One of the few, the immortal names
That were not born to die.
Ibid. Stanza 7

Green be the turf above thee,
Friend of my better days!
None knew thee but to love thee,[2]
Nor named thee but to praise.
On the Death of Joseph Rodman Drake

They love their land because it is their own,
And scorn to give aught other reason why;
Would shake hands with a king upon his throne,

[1] A Greek patriot, born about 1788, killed in a night attack against the Turks, near Missolonghi, Greece, August 20, 1823.
[2] See Burns, page 392a, and Rogers, page 396b.

And think it kindness to his Majesty.
Connecticut
This bank-note world.
Alnwick Castle. Stanza 7

ALPHONSE DE LAMARTINE
[1790–1869]

"O time, arrest your flight! and you, propitious hours, arrest your course! Let us savor the fleeting delights of our most beautiful days!" [1]
The Lake [1820]. Stanza 6

I say to this night: "Pass more slowly"; and the dawn will come to dispel the night. [2]
Ibid. Stanza 8

Limited in his nature, infinite in his desires, man is a fallen god who remembers the heavens.
Méditations Poétiques [1820]. Sermon 2

What is our life but a succession of preludes to that unknown song whose first solemn note is sounded by Death? [3]
Ibid. Second Series, Sermon 15

Man, it seems, is not able to bear the languid rest on Nature's bosom, and when the trumpet sounds the signal of danger, he hastens to join his comrades, no matter what the cause that calls him to arms. He rushes into the thickest of the fight and amid the uproar of the battle regains confidence in himself and his powers.
Ibid.

Experience is the only prophecy of wise men.
Speech, at Mâcon [1847]

To love for the sake of being loved is human, but to love for the sake of loving is angelic.
Graziella [1849]. Part IV, Chap. 5

[1] "O temps, suspends ton vol! et vous, heures propices,
Suspendez votre cours!
Laissez-nous savourer les rapides délices
Des plus beaux de nos jours!"
[2] Je dis à cette nuit: "Sois plus lente"; et l'aurore
Va dissiper la nuit.
[3] This passage was used by Liszt as a heading for his tone poem *Les Préludes*.

The more I see of the representatives of the people, the more I admire my dogs.
From COUNT D'ORSAY: *Letter to John Forster [1850]*

SAMUEL GILMAN
[1791–1858]

Fair Harvard! Thy sons to thy Jubilee throng,
And with blessings surrender thee o'er,
By these festival rites, from the age that is past,
To the age that is waiting before.
Ode, Bicentennial, Harvard University [September 8, 1836]. Stanza 1

First flower of their wilderness, star of their night,
Calm rising through change and through storm.
Ibid.

HENRY HART MILMAN
[1791–1868]

And the cold marble leapt to life a god.
The Belvedere Apollo

Too fair to worship, too divine to love.
Ibid.

LYDIA HUNTLEY SIGOURNEY
[1791–1865]

Ye say that all have passed away —
That noble race and brave . . .
But their name is on your waters [1] —
Ye may not wash it out.
Indian Names. Stanza 1

Your mountains build their monument,
Though ye destroy their dust.
Ibid. Stanza 5

Through the open window's space
Behold, a camel thrust his face.

[1] We will give the names of our fearless race
To each bright river whose course we trace.
FELICIA D. HEMANS [1793–1835]:
Song of Emigration

"My nose is cold," he meekly cried,
"Oh, let me warm it by thy side."
    The Camel's Nose. Stanza 1

To evil habit's earliest wile
Lend neither ear, nor glance, nor
  smile —
Choke the dark fountain ere it flows,
Nor e'en admit the camel's nose.
    Ibid. Stanza 4

CHARLES SPRAGUE
[1791–1875]

 Here lived and loved another race
of beings. Beneath the same sun that
rolls over your heads the Indian hunter
pursued the panting deer. . . . The
Indian of falcon glance and lion bearing, the theme of the touching ballad,
the hero of the pathetic tale, is gone.
    The American Indian

CHARLES WOLFE
[1791–1823]

Not a drum was heard, not a funeral
  note,
As his corse to the rampart we hurried.
  The Burial of Sir John Moore
   at Corunna [1817]. *Stanza 1*

But he lay like a warrior taking his
  rest
With his martial cloak around him.
    Ibid. Stanza 3

We carved not a line, and we raised
  not a stone,
But we left him alone with his glory.
    Ibid. Stanza 8

JOHN KEBLE
[1792–1866]

The trivial round, the common task,
Would furnish all we ought to ask.
   The Christian Year [1827].
    Morning, Stanza 10

Abide with me from morn till eve,
For without Thee I cannot live;
Abide with me when night is nigh,
For without Thee I dare not die.
   Ibid. Evening, Stanza 4

JOHN HOWARD PAYNE
[1792–1852]

'Mid pleasures and palaces though we
  may roam,
Be it ever so humble, there's no place
  like home; [1]
A charm from the skies seems to hal-
  low us there,
Which sought through the world is
  ne'er met with elsewhere.
  Home, Sweet Home (From the opera
   Clari, the Maid of Milan [1823])

PERCY BYSSHE SHELLEY
[1792–1822]

Once, early in the morning,
  Beelzebub arose,
With care his sweet person adorning,
  He put on his Sunday clothes. [2]
   The Devil's Walk, A Ballad
    [1812]. *Stanza 1*

How wonderful is Death,
Death and his brother Sleep. [3]
    Queen Mab [1813]. *I*

Power, like a desolating pestilence,
Pollutes whate'er it touches; and obe-
  dience,
Bane of all genius, virtue, freedom,
  truth,
Makes slaves of men, and, of the hu-
  man frame,
A mechanized automaton.
    Ibid. III

  Heaven's ebon vault,
Studded with stars unutterably bright,
Through which the moon's unclouded
  grandeur rolls,
Seems like a canopy which love had
  spread
To curtain her sleeping world.
    Ibid. IV

The awful shadow of some unseen
  Power
Floats though unseen among us,
  — visiting

[1] Home is home, be it never so homely. —
English Proverb [*circa* 1300]
[2] See Southey, page 427a.
[3] See Hesiod, page 7a, and Daniel, page
122a.

This various world with as inconstant wing
As summer winds that creep from flower to flower.
Hymn to Intellectual Beauty [1816]. Stanza 1

Spirit of Beauty, that dost consecrate
With thine own hues all thou dost shine upon
Of human thought or form.
Ibid. Stanza 2

Some say that gleams of a remoter world
Visit the soul in sleep, — that death is slumber,
And that its shapes the busy thoughts outnumber
Of those who wake and live.
Mont Blanc [1816]. Stanza 3

I met a traveller from an antique land
Who said: "Two vast and trunkless legs of stone
Stand in the desert. Near them, on the sand,
Half sunk, a shattered visage lies, whose frown,
And wrinkled lip, and sneer of cold command,
Tell that its sculptor well those passions read."
Ozymandias [1817]

"My name is Ozymandias, king of kings:
Look on my works, ye Mighty, and despair!"
Nothing beside remains. Round the decay
Of that colossal wreck, boundless and bare
The lone and level sands stretch far away.
Ibid.

With hue like that when some great painter dips
His pencil in the gloom of earthquake and eclipse.
The Revolt of Islam [1817]. Canto V, Stanza 23

I could lie down like a tired child,
And weep away the life of care

Which I have borne and yet must bear.
Stanzas Written in Dejection near Naples [1818]. Stanza 4

Forms more real than living man,
Nurslings of immortality!
Prometheus Unbound [1818–1819]. Act I

Like stars half quencht in mists of silver dew.
Ibid. Act II, Sc. 1

All love is sweet,
Given or returned. Common as light is love,
And its familiar voice wearies not ever. . . .
They who inspire it most are fortunate,
As I am now; but those who feel it most
Are happier still.[1]
Ibid. Sc. 5

Death is the veil which those who live call life;
They sleep, and it is lifted.
Ibid. Act III, Sc. 3

Good, great and joyous, beautiful and free;
This is alone Life, Joy, Empire, and Victory.
Ibid. Act IV, closing lines

I love all waste
And solitary places; where we taste
The pleasure of believing what we see
Is boundless, as we wish our souls to be.
Julian and Maddalo [1819]. Line 14

Thou Paradise of exiles, Italy!
Ibid. Line 57

It is our will
That thus enchains us to permitted ill —
We might be otherwise — we might be all
We dream of happy, high, majestical.
Where is the love, beauty and truth we seek,
But in our mind?
Ibid. Line 170

Me — who am as a nerve o'er which do creep

[1] See La Rochefoucauld, page 265b.

The else unfelt oppressions of this earth.
Julian and Maddalo. Line 449

Most wretched men
Are cradled into poetry by wrong;
They learn in suffering what they teach in song.[1]
Ibid. Line 543

Chameleons feed on light and air:
Poets' food is love and fame.
An Exhortation [1819]. Stanza 1

O wild West Wind, thou breath of Autumn's being,
Thou, from whose unseen presence the leaves dead
Are driven, like ghosts from an enchanter fleeing,
Yellow, and black, and pale, and hectic red,
Pestilence-stricken multitudes.
Ode to the West Wind [1819].
Stanza 1

Wild Spirit, which art moving everywhere;
Destroyer and preserver; hear, oh, hear!
Ibid.

Make me thy lyre, even as the forest is:
What if my leaves are falling like its own!
The tumult of thy mighty harmonies
Will take from both a deep, autumnal tone,
Sweet though in sadness. Be thou, Spirit fierce,
My spirit! Be thou me, impetuous one!
Ibid. Stanza 5

O Wind,
If Winter comes, can Spring be far behind?
Ibid.

The seed ye sow, another reaps;
The wealth ye find, another keeps;
The robes ye weave, another wears;
The arms ye forge, another bears.
Song to the Men of England
[1819]. Stanza 5

Nothing in the world is single,
All things by a law divine

[1] See Butler, page 239b.

In one spirit meet and mingle.
Love's Philosophy [1819].
Stanza 1

I arise from dreams of thee
In the first sweet sleep of night,
When the winds are breathing low,
And the stars are shining bright.
The Indian Serenade [1819].
Stanza 1

The Champak odours fail,
Like sweet thoughts in a dream.
Ibid. Stanza 2

Hell is a city much like London —
A populous and smoky city.
Peter Bell the Third [1819].
Part III, Stanza 1

Teas,
Where small talk dies in agonies.
Ibid. Stanza 12

He had as much imagination
As a pint-pot.
Ibid. Part IV, Stanza 8

A lovely lady, garmented in light
From her own beauty.
The Witch of Atlas [1820].
Stanza 5

A Sensitive Plant in a garden grew,
And the young winds fed it with silver dew.
The Sensitive Plant [1820].
I, Stanza 1

For love and beauty and delight,
There is no death nor change.
Ibid. Conclusion, Stanza 6

I bring fresh showers for the thirsting flowers,
From the seas and the streams.
The Cloud [1820].
Stanza 1

That orbèd maiden with white fire laden,
Whom mortals call the moon.
Ibid. Stanza 4

I am the daughter of Earth and Water,
And the nursling of the Sky;
I pass through the pores of the ocean and shores,
I change, but I cannot die.
Ibid. Stanza 6

Hail to thee, blithe spirit!
Bird thou never wert.

That from Heaven, or near it,
  Pourest thy full heart
In profuse strains of unpremeditated
  art.
      To a Skylark [*1821*]. *Stanza 1*
And singing still dost soar, and soar-
  ing ever singest.
      Ibid. Stanza 2
Thou art unseen, — but yet I hear thy
  shrill delight.
      Ibid. Stanza 4
We look before and after,
  And pine for what is not;
Our sincerest laughter
  With some pain is fraught;
Our sweetest songs are those that tell
  of saddest thought.
      Ibid. Stanza 18
Teach me half the gladness
  That thy brain must know,
Such harmonious madness
  From my lips would flow,
The world should listen then, as I am
  listening now.
      Ibid. Stanza 21
Kings are like stars — they rise and
  set, they have
The worship of the world, but no re-
  pose.[1]
      Hellas [*1821*]. *Line 195*
The world's great age begins anew,
  The golden years return,
The earth doth like a snake renew
  Her winter weeds outworn.
      Ibid. Line 1060
The world is weary of the past,
Oh, might it die or rest at last!
      Ibid. Final Chorus
What! alive, and so bold, O earth?
      *Written on Hearing the News of
      the Death of Napoleon* [*1821*].
      Stanza 1
I weep for Adonais — he is dead!
Oh, weep for Adonais! though our tears
Thaw not the frost which binds so dear
  a head!
      Adonais [*1821*]. *I*
Till the Future dares
Forget the Past, his fate and fame shall
  be

1 See Bacon, page 120b.

An echo and a light unto eternity!
      Adonais. I
Most musical of mourners, weep again!
      Ibid. IV
But now, thy youngest, dearest one has
  perished,
The nursling of thy widowhood.
      Ibid. VI
To that high Capital, where kingly
  Death
Keeps his pale court in beauty and
  decay,
He came.
      Ibid. VII
Lost Angel of a ruined Paradise!
She knew not 't was her own; as with
  no stain
She faded, like a cloud which had out-
  wept the rain.
      Ibid. X
  Desires and Adorations,
Winged Persuasions and veiled Desti-
  nies,
Splendours, and Glooms, and glimmer-
  ing Incarnations
Of hopes and fears, and twilight Fan-
  tasies;
And Sorrow, with her family of Sighs,
And Pleasure, blind with tears, led by
  the gleam
Of her own dying smile instead of eyes,
Came in slow pomp.
      Ibid. XIII
Ah woe is me! Winter is come and gone,
But grief returns with the revolving
  year.
      Ibid. XVIII
Alas! that all we loved of him should
  be,
But for our grief, as if it had not been,
And grief itself be mortal!
      Ibid. XXI
As long as skies are blue, and fields
  are green,
Evening must usher night, night urge
  the morrow,
Month follow month with woe, and
  year wake year to sorrow.
      Ibid.
Why didst thou leave the trodden paths
  of men

Too soon, and with weak hands though mighty heart
Dare the unpastured dragon in his den?
Defenceless as thou wert, oh, where was then
Wisdom the mirrored shield, or scorn the spear?
Adonais. XXVII

The Pilgrim of Eternity,[1] whose fame
Over his living head like heaven is bent,
An early but enduring monument,
Came, veiling all the lightnings of his song
In sorrow.
Ibid. XXX

A pard-like spirit, beautiful and swift.
Ibid. XXXII

In mockery of monumental stone.
Ibid. XXXV

Peace, peace! he is not dead, he doth not sleep —
He hath awakened from the dream of life.
Ibid. XXXIX

He has outsoared the shadow of our night;
Envy and calumny and hate and pain,
And that unrest which men miscall delight
Can touch him not and torture not again;
From the contagion of the world's slow stain
He is secure, and now can never mourn
A heart grown cold, a head grown gray in vain.
Ibid. XL

He lives, he wakes — 'tis Death is dead, not he.
Ibid. XLI

He is made one with Nature: there is heard
His voice in all her music, from the moan
Of thunder to the song of night's sweet bird.
Ibid. XLII

He is a portion of the loveliness
Which once he made more lovely.
Ibid. XLIII

[1] Byron.

And many more, whose names on Earth are dark,
But whose transmitted effluence can not die
So long as fire outlives the parent spark,
Rose, robed in dazzling immortality.
Adonais. XLVI

The One remains, the many change and pass;
Heaven's light forever shines, Earth's shadows fly;
Life, like a dome of many-coloured glass,
Stains the white radiance of Eternity,
Until Death tramples it to fragments.
Ibid. LII

The soul of Adonais, like a star,
Beacons from the abode where the Eternal are.
Ibid. LV

Music, when soft voices die,
Vibrates in the memory;
Odours, when sweet violets sicken,
Live within the sense they quicken.

Rose leaves, when the rose is dead,
Are heaped for the beloved's bed;
And so thy thoughts, when thou art gone,
Love itself shall slumber on.
To —— : Music, When Soft Voices Die [*1821*]

The desire of the moth for the star,
Of the night for the morrow,
The devotion to something afar
From the sphere of our sorrow.
To —— : One Word Is Too Often Profaned [*1821*]. *Stanza 2*

Rarely, rarely, comest thou,
Spirit of Delight!
Song: Rarely, Rarely, Comest Thou [*1821*]. *Stanza 1*

I love tranquil solitude
And such society
As is quiet, wise, and good.
Ibid. Stanza 7

Poets are the hierophants of an unapprehended inspiration; the mirrors of the gigantic shadows which futurity casts upon the present.[1]

A Defence of Poetry [*1821*]

Poetry is the record of the best and happiest moments of the happiest and best minds.

Ibid.

Poets are the unacknowledged legislators of the world.

Ibid.

We rest. A dream has power to poison sleep;
We rise. One wandering thought pollutes the day.

Mutability [*1821*]. *I, Stanza* **3**

Man's yesterday may ne'er be like his morrow;
Naught may endure but Mutability.

Ibid. Stanza **4**

The flower that smiles today
  Tomorrow dies;
All that we wish to stay
  Tempts and then flies.
What is this world's delight?
Lightning that mocks the night,
  Brief even as bright.

Ibid. II, Stanza **1**

There is no sport in hate when all the rage
Is on one side.

Lines to a Reviewer [*1821*]

When the lamp is shattered
The light in the dust lies dead: —
When the cloud is scattered
The rainbow's glory is shed.

When the Lamp is Shattered [*1822*].
Stanza **1**

Best and brightest, come away!
Fairer far than this fair day.

To Jane. An Invitation [*1822*]

Sing again, with your dear voice revealing
  A tone
Of some world far from ours,
Where music and moonlight and feeling
  Are one.

To Jane: The Keen Stars Were Twinkling [*1822*]. *Stanza* **4**

[1] See Campbell, page 432b.

FREDERICK MARRYAT
[1792–1848]

I haven't the gift of the gab, my sons —
because I'm bred to the sea.

The Old Navy. Stanza **1**

JOHN CLARE
[1793–1864]

I am! yet what I am who cares, or knows?
My friends forsake me like a memory lost.

*Written in Northampton
County Asylum*

The world was on thy page
Of victories but a comma.

To Napoleon

The wind and clouds, now here, now there,
  Hold no such strange dominion
As woman's cold, perverted will,
  And soon estranged opinion.

When Lovers Part

If life had a second edition, how I would correct the proofs.[1]

*In a letter to a friend.
Quoted in Foreword to*
J. W. AND ANNE TIBBLE'S
John Clare: A Life [*1932*]

FELICIA DOROTHEA
HEMANS
[1793–1835]

The stately homes of England!
  How beautiful they stand,
Amidst their tall ancestral trees,
  O'er all the pleasant land! [2]

The Homes of England. Stanza **1**

[1] Compare the epitaph written for himself (at the age of twenty-two) by BENJAMIN FRANKLIN: "Benjamin Franklin, Printer . . . Will Appear Once More, In a New and More Elegant Edition, Revised and Corrected by the Author."

[2] Those comfortably padded lunatic asylums, which are known, euphemistically, as the stately homes of England. — VIRGINIA

The breaking waves dashed high
  On a stern and rock-bound coast,
And the woods, against a stormy sky,
  Their giant branches tossed.
        *The Landing of the Pilgrim
              Fathers. Stanza 1*

A band of exiles moored their bark
On a wild New England shore.
        Ibid. Stanza 2

Ay, call it holy ground,
  The soil where first they trod!
They have left unstained what there
    they found —
Freedom to worship God.
        Ibid. Stanza 10

The boy [1] stood on the burning deck,
  Whence all but he had fled;
The flame that lit the battle's wreck
  Shone round him o'er the dead.
        Casabianca. Stanza 1

There came a burst of thunder sound;
The boy, — oh! where was he?
        Ibid. Stanza 9

In the busy haunts of men.
        *Tale of the Secret Tribunal.
              Part I*

Oh, call my brother back to me!
  I cannot play alone:
The summer comes with flower and
    bee, —
  Where is my brother gone?
        The Child's First Grief. Stanza 1

Wave may not foam nor wild wind
    sweep
Where rest not England's Dead.
        England's Dead

Woolf [1882-1941]: *The Common Reader:
Lady Dorothy Nevill*
    The stately homes of England,
      How beautiful they stood
    Before their recent owners
      Relinquished them for good.
        E. V. Knox [1881-   ]: *The
              Stately Homes*
[1] Giacomo Casabianca, whose father, Louis,
at the battle of the Nile, 1798, commanded
the flagship *Orient*. It took fire and blew up,
the commander was mortally wounded, and
when most of the crew fled, Giacomo remained aboard, in an effort to help his gallant
father.

WILLIAM CULLEN BRYANT
[1794-1878]

To him who in the love of Nature holds
Communion with her visible forms,
    she speaks
A various language.
        Thanatopsis [*1817-1821*]

Go forth, under the open sky, and list
To Nature's teachings.
        Ibid.

    The hills,
Rock-ribbed, and ancient as the sun.
        Ibid.

Old ocean's gray and melancholy
    waste.
        Ibid.

    All that tread
The globe are but a handful to the
    tribes
That slumber in its bosom.
        Ibid.

So live, that when thy summons comes
    to join
The innumerable caravan which
    moves
To that mysterious realm, where each
    shall take
His chamber in the silent halls of
    death,
Thou go not, like the quarry-slave at
    night,
Scourged to his dungeon, but, sustained
    and soothed
By an unfaltering trust, approach thy
    grave,
Like one that wraps the drapery of his
    couch
About him, and lies down to pleasant
    dreams.
        Ibid.

He who, from zone to zone,
Guides through the boundless sky thy
    certain flight,
In the long way that I must tread alone,
  Will lead my steps aright.
        To a Waterfowl [*1818*]. *Stanza 8*

Here the free spirit of mankind, at
    length,
Throws its last fetters off; and who
    shall place

A limit to the giant's unchained
strength,
Or curb his swiftness in the forward
race?
The Ages [1821]. Stanza 33

The stormy March has come at last,
With wind, and cloud, and changing
skies;
I hear the rushing of the blast,
That through the snowy valley flies.
March. Stanza 1

The groves were God's first temples.
A Forest Hymn

Rogue's Island once — but when the
rogues were dead,
Rhode Island was the name it took
instead.
*A Meditation on Rhode Island
Coal. Stanza 1*

The melancholy days are come, the
saddest of the year,
Of wailing winds, and naked woods,
and meadows brown and sere.
*The Death of the Flowers [1832].
Stanza 1*

Chained in the market-place he stood,
A man of giant frame,
Amid the gathering multitude
That shrunk to hear his name.
The African Chief. Stanza 1

Loveliest of lovely things are they,
On earth, that soonest pass away.
The rose that lives its little hour
Is prized beyond the sculptured flower.
*A Scene on the Banks of the
Hudson. Stanza 3*

Thou blossom bright with autumn dew,
And colored with the heaven's own
blue,
That openest when the quiet light
Succeeds the keen and frosty night.
*To the Fringed Gentian [1832].
Stanza 1*

These are the gardens of the Desert,
these
The unshorn fields, boundless and
beautiful,
For which the speech of England has
no name —
The Prairies.
The Prairies

The praise of those who sleep in earth,
The pleasant memory of their worth,
The hope to meet when life is past,
Shall heal the tortured mind at last.
The Living Lost. Stanza 3

Truth, crushed to earth, shall rise
again;
The eternal years of God are hers;
But Error, wounded, writhes in pain,
And dies among his worshippers.
The Battle-Field. Stanza 9

The fiercest agonies have shortest reign.
Mutation

Oh mother of a mighty race,
Yet lovely in thy youthful grace!
*Oh Mother of a Mighty Race.
Stanza 1*

Man foretells afar
The courses of the stars; the very hour
He knows when they shall darken or
grow bright;
Yet doth the eclipse of Sorrow and of
Death
Come unforewarned.
An Evening Revery

Oh, slow to smite and swift to spare,
Gentle and merciful and just!
Who, in the fear of God, didst bear
The sword of power, a nation's
trust!
The Death of Lincoln. Stanza 1

EDWARD EVERETT
[1794–1865]

As a work of art, I know few things
more pleasing to the eye, or more capable of affording scope and gratifica-
tion to a taste for the beautiful, than
a well-situated, well-cultivated farm.
*Address at Buffalo, New York
[October 9, 1857]*

I am no aristocrat. I do not own a
quadruped larger than a cat, and she
an indifferent mouser; nor any kind of
vehicle, with the exception, possibly, of
a wheelbarrow.
Mount Vernon Papers. No 7

The days of palmy prosperity are
not those most favorable to the display
of public virtue or the influence of wise
and good men. In hard, doubtful, un-

prosperous, and dangerous times, the disinterested and patriotic find their way, by a species of public instinct, unopposed, joyfully welcomed, to the control of affairs.
Mount Vernon Papers. No. 14
When I contemplate the extent to which the moral sentiments, the intelligence, the affections of so many millions of people, — sealed up by a sacred charm within the cover of a letter, — daily circulate through a country, I am compelled to regard the Post-office, next to Christianity, as the right arm of our modern civilization.
Ibid. No. 27

WILLIAM WHEWELL
[1794–1866]

And so no force, however great, can stretch a cord, however fine, into a horizontal line which shall be absolutely straight.[1]
Elementary Treatise on Mechanics [1819]. The Equilibrium of Forces on a Point

JOHN GARDINER CALKINS BRAINARD
[1795–1828]

Death has shaken out the sands of thy glass.
Lament for Long Tom

NARCISSE ACHILLE, COMTE DE SALVANDY
[1795–1856]

We are dancing on a volcano.
At a fête given by the Duc d'Orléans to the King of Naples [1830]

JOHN WOODCOCK GRAVES
[1795–1886]

D' ye ken John Peel with his coat so gay?
D' ye ken John Peel at the break of day?

[1] Reputed to be an example of unconscious but perfect rhyme.

D' ye ken John Peel when he's far far away
With his hounds and his horn in the morning?
'Twas the sound of his horn brought me from my bed,
And the cry of his hounds, which he oft-times led,
For Peel's view-hallo would waken the dead,
Or the fox from his lair in the morning.
John Peel [1832]

THOMAS CARLYLE
[1795–1881]

He who would write heroic poems should make his whole life a heroic poem.
Life of Schiller [1823–1824]
The only thing connected with him [Richter], we think, that has reached this country is his saying, — imported by Madame de Staël, and thankfully pocketed by most newspaper critics, — "Providence has given to the French the empire of the land; to the English that of the sea; to the Germans that of — the air!"
Richter [1827]
True humour springs not more from the head than from the heart; it is not contempt, its essence is love; it issues not in laughter, but in still smiles, which lie far deeper.
Ibid.
The great law of culture is: Let each become all that he was created capable of being.
Ibid.
Literary men are . . . a perpetual priesthood.
State of German Literature [1827]. Fichte
In every man's writings, the character of the writer must lie recorded.
Goethe [1828]
We are firm believers in the maxim that, for all right judgment of any man or thing, it is useful, nay essential,

to see his good qualities before pronouncing on his bad.

Goethe

How does the poet speak to men, with power, but by being still more a man than they?

Burns [1828]

A poet without love were a physical and metaphysical impossibility.

Ibid.

Aesop's Fly, sitting on the axle of the chariot, has been much laughed at for exclaiming: What a dust I do raise!

On Boswell's Life of Johnson [1832]

Whoso belongs only to his own age, and reverences only its gilt Popinjays or soot-smeared Mumbojumbos, must needs die with it.

Ibid.

The stupendous Fourth Estate, whose wide world-embracing influences what eye can take in? [1]

Ibid.

Of all outward evils Obscurity is perhaps in itself the least.

Ibid.

Loud clamor is always more or less insane.

Ibid.

All work is as seed sown; it grows and spreads, and sows itself anew.

Ibid.

Love is ever the beginning of Knowledge, as fire is of light.

Essays. Death of Goethe [1832]

Music is well said to be the speech of angels.

Ibid. The Opera

[1] The gallery in which the reporters sit has become a fourth estate of the realm. — MACAULAY: *On Hallam's Constitutional History* [1828]

Burke said there were Three Estates in Parliament; but, in the Reporters' Gallery yonder, there sat a Fourth Estate more important far than they all. It is not a figure of speech, or witty saying; it is a literal fact, — very momentous to us in these times. — *Heroes and Hero-Worship* [1841], *The Hero as Man of Letters*

A mystic bond of brotherhood makes all men one.

Essays. Goethe's Works [1832]

Everywhere the human soul stands between a hemisphere of light and another of darkness on the confines of two everlasting hostile empires, — Necessity and Free Will.

Ibid.

Man makes the circumstances, and spiritually as well as economically is the artificer of his own fortune. . . . Man's circumstances are the element he is appointed to live and work in; . . . so that in another no less genuine sense, it can be said circumstances make the man.[1]

Diderot [1833]

No man who has once heartily and wholly laughed can be altogether irreclaimably bad.

Sartor Resartus [1833–1834]. Book I, Chap. 4

The man who cannot laugh is not only fit for treasons, stratagems and spoils; but his whole life is already a treason and a stratagem.

Ibid.

He who first shortened the labor of Copyists by device of *Movable Types* was disbanding hired Armies, and cashiering most Kings and Senates, and creating a whole new Democratic world: he had invented the Art of printing.

Ibid. Chap. 5

Be not the slave of Words.

Ibid. Chap. 8

Wonder is the basis of Worship.

Ibid. Chap. 10

Biography is by nature the most universally profitable, universally pleasant of all things: especially biography of distinguished individuals.

Ibid. Chap. 11

What you see, yet can not see over, is as good as infinite.

Ibid. Book II, Chap. 1

Sarcasm I now see to be, in general, the language of the Devil; for which

[1] See Disraeli, page 511.

reason I have, long since, as good as renounced it.

Sartor Resartus. Book II, Chap. 4

To consume your own choler, as some chimneys consume their own smoke;[1] to keep a whole Satanic School spouting, if it must spout, inaudibly, is a negative yet no slight virtue, nor one of the commonest in these times.

Ibid. Chap. 6

Alas! the fearful Unbelief is unbelief in yourself.

Ibid. Chap. 7

Produce! Were it but the pitifulest infinitesimal fraction of a product, produce it in God's name.

Ibid. Chap. 9

As the Swiss inscription says: *Sprechen ist silbern, Schweigen ist golden,* — "Speech is silvern, Silence is golden"; or, as I might rather express it, Speech is of Time, Silence is of Eternity.[2]

Ibid. Book III, Chap. 3

Wouldst thou plant for Eternity, then plant into the deep infinite faculties of man.

Ibid.

Two men I honour, and no third. First, the toilworn craftsman that with earth-made implement laboriously conquers the earth, and makes her man's. . . . A second man I honour, and still more highly: Him who is seen toiling for the spiritually indispensable; not daily bread, but the bread of life.

Ibid. Chap. 4

That there should one man die ignorant who had capacity for knowledge, this I call a tragedy.

Ibid.

[1] See *Heroes and Hero-Worship,* page 475b. Consume your own smoke. — BROWNING: *Pacchiarotto* [1876], *XXV*
Would that he consumed his own smoke. — MELVILLE: *Moby Dick* [1851], *Chap. XCVI*
See Osler, page 743b.
[2] Silence is deep as Eternity; speech is shallow as Time. — CARLYLE: *Sir Walter Scott* [1838]

Trust not the heart of that man for whom old clothes are not venerable.

Sartor Resartus. Book III, Chap. 6

The Public is an old woman. Let her maunder and mumble.

Journal [*1835*]

It is now almost my sole rule of life to clear myself of cants and formulas, as of poisonous Nessus shirts.

Letter to His Wife [*1835*]

No lie you can speak or act but it will come, after longer or shorter circulation, like a bill drawn on Nature's Reality, and be presented there for payment, — with the answer, No effects.

The French Revolution [*1837*].
Vol. I, Book III, Chap. 1

To a shower of gold most things are penetrable.

Ibid. Chap. 7

"The people may eat grass":[1] hasty words, which fly abroad irrevocable, — and will send back tidings.

Ibid. Chap. 9

O poor mortals, how ye make this earth bitter for each other.

Ibid. Book V, Chap. 5

Battles, in these ages, are transacted by mechanism; with the slightest possible development of human individuality or spontaneity; men now even die, and kill one another, in an artificial manner.

Ibid. Book VII, Chap. 4

There were certain runaways whom Fritz the Great bullied back into the battle with a: "*R* —, *wollt ihr ewig leben,* Unprintable Offscouring of Scoundrels, would ye live forever!"[2]

Ibid. Vol. II, Book I, Chap. 4

There is no heroic poem in the world but is at bottom a biography, the life of a man; also, it may be said, there is no life of a man, faithfully recorded,

[1] The remark of Foullon, when his finance scheme raised the question: What will the people do?
[2] A similar phrase was current during both World Wars. See Sandburg, page 898b.

but is a heroic poem of its sort, rhymed or unrhymed.
> *Sir Walter Scott* [*1838*]

There is a great discovery still to be made in Literature, that of paying literary men by the quantity they do not write.
> *Ibid.*

No man lives without jostling and being jostled; in all ways he has to elbow himself through the world, giving and receiving offence.
> *Ibid.*

All greatness is unconscious, or it is little and naught.
> *Ibid.*

The uttered part of a man's life, let us always repeat, bears to the unuttered, unconscious part a small unknown proportion. He himself never knows it, much less do others.
> *Ibid.*

It can be said of him, when he departed he took a Man's life along with him. No sounder piece of British manhood was put together in that eighteenth century of Time.
> *Ibid.*

The Christian religion of late ages has been continually dissipating itself into Metaphysics; and threatens now to disappear, as some rivers do, in deserts of barren sand.
> *Ibid.*

Nothing that was worthy in the past departs; no truth or goodness realized by man ever dies, or can die.
> *Ibid.*

The barrenest of all mortals is the sentimentalist.
> *Ibid.*

Democracy is, by the nature of it, a self-cancelling business; and gives in the long run a net result of zero.
> *Chartism* [*1839*]. *Chap. 6, Laissez-Faire*

No sadder proof can be given by a man of his own littleness than disbelief in great men.
> *Heroes and Hero-Worship* [*1841*]. *The Hero as Divinity*

The history of the world is but the biography of great men.[1]
> *Heroes and Hero-Worship. The Hero as Divinity*

We must get rid of Fear.
> *Ibid.*

A vein of poetry exists in the hearts of all men.
> *Ibid. The Hero as Poet*

The Age of Miracles is forever here!
> *Ibid. The Hero as Priest*

In books lies the soul of the whole Past Time: the articulate audible voice of the Past, when the body and material substance of it has altogether vanished like a dream.
> *Ibid. The Hero as Man of Letters*

All that mankind has done, thought, gained or been: it is lying as in magic preservation in the pages of books.
> *Ibid.*

The true University of these days is a Collection of Books.
> *Ibid.*

The suffering man ought really to consume his own smoke; there is no good in emitting smoke till you have made it into fire.[2]
> *Ibid.*

Adversity is sometimes hard upon a man; but for one man who can stand prosperity, there are a hundred that will stand adversity.
> *Ibid.*

"A fair day's-wages for a fair day's-work": it is as just a demand as governed men ever made of governing. It is the everlasting right of man.
> *Past and Present* [*1843*]. *Book I, Chap. 3*

Fire is the best of servants; but what a master![3]
> *Ibid. Book II, Chap. 9*

All work, even cotton-spinning, is noble; work is alone noble. . . . A

---

[1] History is the essence of innumerable biographies. — *On History* [1830]
See Emerson, page 501b.
[2] See *Sartor Resartus,* page 474a.
[3] Mammon is like fire: the usefulest of all servants, if the frightfulest of all masters! — *Book IV, Chap. 7*

life of ease is not for any man, nor for any god.

> *Past and Present. Book III,*
> *Chap. 4*

Every noble crown is, and on earth will forever be, a crown of thorns.

> *Ibid. Chap. 7*

Even in the meanest sorts of Labor, the whole soul of a man is composed into a kind of real harmony the instant he sets himself to work.

> *Ibid. Chap. 11*

Blessed is he who has found his work; let him ask no other blessedness.

> *Ibid.*

There is endless merit in a man's knowing when to have done.

> *Francia [1845]*

He that works and *does* some Poem, not he that merely *says* one, is worthy of the name of Poet.

> *Introduction to Cromwell's*
> *Letters and Speeches [1845]*

Respectable Professors of the Dismal Science.[1]

> *Latter Day Pamphlets. No. 1 [1850]*

A Parliament speaking through reporters to Buncombe and the twenty-seven millions, mostly fools.

> *Ibid. No. 6*

The fine arts once divorcing themselves from *truth* are quite certain to fall mad, if they do not die.

> *Ibid. No. 8*

A healthy hatred of scoundrels.

> *Ibid. No. 12*

Genius . . . which is the transcendent capacity for taking trouble first of all.[2]

> *Life of Frederick the Great [1858–*
> *1865]. Book IV, Chap. III*

[1] Referring to political economy and social science, Carlyle also in his *Occasional Discourse on the Negro Question* [1849] speaks of "What we might call, by way of Eminence, the Dismal Science."

[2] The more widely current version is "an infinite capacity for taking pains." See Buffon, page 334a.

Happy the people whose annals are blank in history-books.[1]

> *Life of Frederick the Great.*
> *Book XVI, Chap. I*

So here hath been dawning
Another blue day:
Think, wilt thou let it
Slip useless away?

> *Today*

What is Man? A foolish baby,
Vainly strives, and fights, and frets.
Demanding all, deserving nothing,
One small grave is what he gets.

> *Cui Bono. Stanza 3*

My whinstone house my castle is;
I have my own four walls.

> *My Own Four Walls*

Lord Bacon could as easily have created the planets as he could have written Hamlet.

> *Remark in discussion*

JOSEPH RODMAN DRAKE
[1795–1820]

When Freedom from her mountain-height
Unfurled her standard to the air,
She tore the azure robe of night,
And set the stars of glory there.
She mingled with its gorgeous dyes
The milky baldric of the skies,
And striped its pure, celestial white
With streakings of the morning light.

> *The American Flag [1819]. Stanza 1*

Forever float that standard sheet!
Where breathes the foe but falls before us,
With Freedom's soil beneath our feet,
And Freedom's banner streaming o'er us?

> *Ibid. Stanza 5*

JOHN KEATS
[1795–1821]

I stood tip-toe upon a little hill,
The air was cooling, and so very still.

> *Poems [1817]. I Stood Tip-toe,*
> *Line 1*

[1] Carlyle identifies this as "Montesquieu's aphorism."

And then there crept
A little noiseless noise among the leaves,
Born of the very sigh that silence
   heaves.
   Poems. I Stood Tip-toe, Line 10

Open afresh your round of starry folds,
Ye ardent marigolds!
    Ibid. Line 47

Where swarms of minnows show their
   little heads,
Staying their wavy bodies 'gainst the
   streams.
    Ibid. Line 72

Sometimes goldfinches one by one will
   drop
From low hung branches; little space
   they stop;
But sip, and twitter, and their feathers
   sleek;
Then off at once, as in a wanton freak:
Or perhaps, to show their black, and
   golden wings,
Pausing upon their yellow flutterings.
    Ibid. Line 87

Woman! when I behold thee flippant,
   vain,
Inconstant, childish, proud, and full of
   fancies.
   *Ibid. Woman! When I Behold
    Thee Flippant, Vain*

To one who has been long in city pent,
'Tis very sweet to look into the fair
And open face of heaven.
   *Ibid. Sonnet, To One Who Has
    Been Long in City Pent*

E'en like the passage of an angel's tear
That falls through the clear ether silently.
    Ibid.

Much have I travell'd in the realms of
   gold,
And many goodly states and kingdoms
   seen;
Round many western islands have I
   been
Which bards in fealty to Apollo hold.
   *Ibid. Sonnet, On First Looking
    into Chapman's Homer*

Then felt I like some watcher of the
   skies
When a new planet swims into his ken;

Or like stout Cortez when with eagle
   eyes
He star'd at the Pacific — and all his
   men
Look'd at each other with a wild sur-
   mise —
Silent, upon a peak in Darien.
   *Poems. Sonnet, On First Looking
    into Chapman's Homer*

Hear ye not the hum
Of mighty workings? —
Listen awhile ye nations, and be dumb.
   *Ibid. Sonnet, Addressed to
    Haydon*

The poetry of earth is never dead.
   *Ibid. On the Grasshopper and
    the Cricket*

Life is but a day;
A fragile dew-drop on its perilous way
From a tree's summit.
   Ibid. Sleep and Poetry, Line 85

O for ten years, that I may overwhelm
Myself in poesy.
    Ibid. Line 96

A drainless shower
Of light is poesy; 'tis the supreme of
   power;
'Tis might half slumb'ring on its own
   right arm.
    Ibid. Line 235

But strength alone though of the Muses
   born
Is like a fallen angel: trees uptorn,
Darkness, and worms, and shrouds, and
   sepulchres
Delight it; for it feeds upon the burrs,
And thorns of life; forgetting the great
   end
Of poesy, that it should be a friend
To soothe the cares, and lift the
   thoughts of man.
    Ibid. Line 241

My spirit is too weak — mortality
Weighs heavily on me like unwilling
   sleep,
And each imagin'd pinnacle and steep
Of godlike hardship, tells me I must die
Like a sick Eagle looking at the sky.
   *Sonnet, On Seeing the Elgin
    Marbles [Written 1817]*

It keeps eternal whisperings around
Desolate shores, and with its mighty swell
Gluts twice ten thousand Caverns.
Sonnet, On the Sea [*Written 1817*]

In a drear-nighted December
Too happy, happy tree
Thy branches ne'er remember
Their green felicity.
Stanzas [*Written 1817*]

I am certain of nothing but the holiness of the heart's affections and the truth of imagination — what the imagination seizes as beauty must be truth — whether it existed before or not.
Letter to Benjamin Bailey [*November 22, 1817*]

O for a life of Sensations rather than of Thoughts!
Ibid.

At once it struck me what quality went to form a Man of Achievement, especially in Literature, and which Shakespeare possessed so enormously — I mean *Negative Capability,* that is, when a man is capable of being in uncertainties, mysteries, doubts, without any irritable reaching after fact and reason.
Letter to George and Thomas Keats [*December 22, 1817*]

We hate poetry that has a palpable design upon us — and if we do not agree, seems to put its hand in its breeches pocket. Poetry should be great and unobtrusive, a thing which enters into one's soul, and does not startle or amaze with itself, but with its subject.
Letter to John Hamilton Reynolds [*February 3, 1818*]

Poetry should surprise by a fine excess, and not by singularity. It should strike the reader as a wording of his own highest thoughts, and appear almost as a remembrance.
Letter to John Taylor [*February 27, 1818*]

If poetry comes not as naturally as leaves to a tree it had better not come at all.
Ibid.

Axioms in philosophy are not axioms until they are proved upon our pulses: we read fine things but never feel them to the full until we have gone the same steps as the author.[1]
Letter to John Hamilton Reynolds [*May 3, 1818*]

Shed no tear — O shed no tear!
The flower will bloom another year.
Weep no more — O weep no more!
Young buds sleep in the root's white core.
Faery Songs. I [*Written 1818*]

Blue! Gentle cousin of the forest-green,
Married to green in all the sweetest flowers, —
Forget-me-not, — the blue bell, — and, that Queen
Of secrecy, the violet.
Sonnet, Blue [*Written 1818*]

There is not a fiercer hell than the failure in a great object.
Endymion [*1818*]. *Preface*

The imagination of a boy is healthy, and the mature imagination of a man is healthy; but there is a space of life between, in which the soul is in a ferment, the character undecided, the way of life uncertain, the ambition thick-sighted: thence proceeds mawkishness, and the thousand bitters which those men I speak of must necessarily taste in going over the following pages.
Ibid.

A thing of beauty is a joy for ever:
Its loveliness increases; it will never
Pass into nothingness; but still will keep
A bower quiet for us, and a sleep
Full of sweet dreams, and health, and quiet breathing.
Ibid. Book I, Line 1

The grandeur of the dooms
We have imagined for the mighty dead.
Ibid. Line 20

O magic sleep! O comfortable bird,

[1] Nothing ever becomes real till it is experienced — even a proverb is no proverb to you till your life has illustrated it. — *Letter to George and Georgiana Keats* [February 14-May 3, 1819]

That broodest o'er the troubled sea of
the mind
Till it is hush'd and smooth!
Endymion. Book I, Line 453

Time, that aged nurse,
Rock'd me to patience.
Ibid. Line 705

Wherein lies happiness? In that which
becks
Our ready minds to fellowship divine,
A fellowship with essence; till we
shine,
Full alchemiz'd, and free of space. Be-
hold
The clear religion of heaven!
Ibid. Line 777

The crown of these
Is made of love and friendship, and sits
high
Upon the forehead of humanity.
Ibid. Line 800

A hope beyond the shadow of a dream.
Ibid. Line 857

Pleasure is oft a visitant; but pain
Clings cruelly to us.
Ibid. Line 906

'Tis the pest
Of love, that fairest joys give most un-
rest.
Ibid. Book II, Line 365

To sorrow,
I bade good-morrow,
And thought to leave her far away
behind;
But cheerly, cheerly,
She loves me dearly;
She is so constant to me, and so kind.
Ibid. Book IV, Line 173

There is an awful warmth about my
heart like a load of immortality.
*Letter to John Hamilton Reynolds
[September 22, 1818]*

I begin to get a little acquainted
with my own strength and weakness.
Praise or blame has but a momentary
effect on the man whose love of beauty
in the abstract makes him a severe
critic on his own works.
*Letter to James Hessey
[October 9, 1818]*

In *Endymion,* I leaped headlong into
the sea, and thereby have become better acquainted with the soundings, the
quicksands, and the rocks, than if I
had stayed upon the green shore, and
piped a silly pipe, and took tea and
comfortable advice.
*Letter to James Hessey
[October 9, 1818]*

I would sooner fail than not be
among the greatest.
Ibid.

When I have fears that I may cease to
be
Before my pen has glean'd my teeming
brain.
*Sonnet, When I Have Fears
[Written 1818]*

When I behold, upon the night's starr'd
face,
Huge cloudy symbols of a high romance.
Ibid.

Then on the shore
Of the wide world I stand alone, and
think
Till love and fame to nothingness do
sink.
Ibid.

Bright star, would I were stedfast as
thou art —
Not in lone splendour hung aloft the
night
And watching, with eternal lids apart,
Like nature's patient, sleepless Eremite,
The moving waters at their priestlike
task
Of pure ablution round earth's human
shores.
*Sonnet, Bright Star [Written
1819]*

Pillow'd upon my fair love's ripening
breast,
To feel for ever its soft fall and swell,
Awake for ever in a sweet unrest,
Still, still to hear her tender-taken
breath,
And so live ever — or else swoon to
death.
Ibid.

The day is gone, and all its sweets are
gone!

Sweet voice, sweet lips, soft hand, and
softer breast.
Sonnet, The Day Is Gone
[Written 1819]

O what can ail thee, knight at arms,
Alone and palely loitering?
The sedge has withered from the lake,
And no birds sing!
La Belle Dame Sans Merci
[Written 1819]. Stanza 1

I met a lady in the meads
Full beautiful, a faery's child;
Her hair was long, her foot was light,
And her eyes were wild.
Ibid. Stanza 4

She looked at me as she did love,
And made sweet moan.
Ibid. Stanza 5

"La belle dame sans merci
Thee hath in thrall!"
Ibid. Stanza 10

A man's life of any worth is a continual Allegory — and very few eyes
can see the mystery of his life — a life
like the Scriptures, figurative. . . .
Lord Byron cuts a figure, but he is not
figurative. Shakespeare led a life of
allegory: his works are the comments
on it.
*Letter to George and Georgiana
Keats [February 14–May 3,
1819]*

This living hand, now warm and ca-
pable
Of earnest grasping, would, if it were
cold
And in the icy silence of the tomb,
So haunt thy days and chill thy dream-
ing nights
That thou would wish thine own heart
dry of blood
So in my veins red life might stream
again,
And thou be conscience-calm'd — see
here it is —
I hold it towards you.
*Lines Supposed to Have Been
Addressed to Fanny Brawne
[Written 1819]*

Love in a hut, with water and a crust,
Is — Love, forgive us! — cinders,
ashes, dust.
*Poems [1820]. Lamia, Part II,
Line 1*

There was an awful rainbow once in
heaven:
We know her woof, her texture; she is
given
In the dull catalogue of common
things.
Philosophy will clip an angel's wings.
Ibid. Line 231

Too many tears for lovers have been
shed,
Too many sighs give we to them in fee,
Too much of pity after they are dead,
Too many doleful stories do we see,
Whose matter in bright gold were best
be read.
*Ibid. Isabella (The Pot of
Basil), Stanza 12*

St. Agnes' Eve — Ah, bitter chill it
was!
The owl, for all his feathers, was a-cold.
The hare limp'd trembling through the
frozen grass,
And silent was the flock in woolly fold.
Ibid. The Eve of St. Agnes, Stanza 1

The silver, snarling trumpets 'gan to
chide.
Ibid. Stanza 4

She sigh'd for Agnes' dreams, the sweetest of the year.
Ibid. Stanza 7

Asleep in lap of legends old.
Ibid. Stanza 15

Sudden a thought came like a full-
blown rose,
Flushing his brow, and in his pained
heart
Made purple riot.
Ibid. Stanza 16

A poor, weak, palsy-stricken, churchyard thing.
Ibid. Stanza 18

As though a tongueless nightingale
should swell
Her throat in vain, and die, heart-
stifled in her dell.
Ibid. Stanza 23

Full on this casement shone the wintry moon,
And threw warm gules on Madeline's fair breast.
>   *Poems. The Eve of St. Agnes,*
>   *Stanza 25*

Unclasps her warmed jewels one by one;
Loosens her fragrant bodice; by degrees
Her rich attire creeps rustling to her knees.
>   *Ibid. Stanza 26*

And still she slept an azure-lidded sleep.
>   *Ibid. Stanza 30*

And the long carpets rose along the gusty floor.
>   *Ibid. Stanza 40*

And they are gone: aye, ages long ago
These lovers fled away into the storm.
>   *Ibid. Stanza 42*

My heart aches, and a drowsy numbness pains
  My sense, as though of hemlock I had drunk,
Or emptied some dull opiate to the drains
  One minute past, and Lethe-wards had sunk.
>   *Ibid. Ode to a Nightingale,*
>   *Stanza 1*

Thou, light-winged Dryad of the trees,
  In some melodious plot
Of beechen green, and shadows numberless,
  Singest of summer in full-throated ease.
>   *Ibid.*

O, for a draught of vintage! that hath been
  Cool'd a long age in the deep-delved earth,
Tasting of Flora and the country green,
  Dance, and Provençal song, and sunburnt mirth!
O, for a beaker full of the warm South,
  Full of the true, the blushful Hippocrene,

With beaded bubbles winking at the brim,
  And purple-stained mouth.
>   *Poems. Ode to a Nightingale,*
>   *Stanza 2*

Fade far away, dissolve, and quite forget
What thou among the leaves hast never known,
The weariness, the fever, and the fret
  Here, where men sit and hear each other groan.
>   *Ibid. Stanza 3*

Where youth grows pale, and spectre-thin, and dies;
Where but to think is to be full of sorrow
  And leaden-eyed despairs.
>   *Ibid.*

Already with thee! tender is the night.
>   *Ibid. Stanza 4*

I cannot see what flowers are at my feet,
  Nor what soft incense hangs upon the boughs,
But, in embalmed darkness, guess each sweet.
>   *Ibid. Stanza 5*

The murmurous haunt of flies on summer eves.
>   *Ibid.*

Darkling I listen; and, for many a time
  I have been half in love with easeful Death,
Call'd him soft names in many a mused rhyme,
  To take into the air my quiet breath;
Now more than ever seems it rich to die,
  To cease upon the midnight with no pain,
  While thou art pouring forth thy soul abroad
    In such an ecstasy!
Still wouldst thou sing, and I have ears in vain —
  To thy high requiem become a sod.
>   *Ibid. Stanza 6*

Thou wast not born for death, immortal Bird!
No hungry generations tread thee down;
The voice I hear this passing night was heard

In ancient days by emperor and clown:
Perhaps the self-same song that found a path
 Through the sad heart of Ruth, when, sick for home,
She stood in tears amid the alien corn;
 The same that oft-times hath
Charm'd magic casements, opening on the foam
Of perilous seas, in faery lands forlorn.
 Poems. Ode to a Nightingale,
 Stanza 7

Forlorn! the very word is like a bell
To toll me back from thee to my sole self!
 Ibid. Stanza 8

Was it a vision, or a waking dream?
Fled is that music: — Do I wake or sleep?
 Ibid.

Thou still unravish'd bride of quietness,
 Thou foster-child of silence and slow time,
Sylvan historian, who canst thus express
A flowery tale more sweetly than our rhyme:
What leaf-fring'd legend haunts about thy shape?
 Ibid. Ode on a Grecian Urn,
 Stanza 1

What men or gods are these? What maidens loth?
What mad pursuit? What struggle to escape?
 What pipes and timbrels? What wild ecstasy?
 Ibid.

Heard melodies are sweet, but those unheard
Are sweeter.
 Ibid. Stanza 2

For ever wilt thou love, and she be fair!
 Ibid.

Who are these coming to the sacrifice?
 To what green altar, O mysterious priest,

Lead'st thou that heifer lowing at the skies,
 And all her silken flanks with garlands drest?
 Poems. Ode on a Grecian Urn,
 Stanza 4

O Attic shape! Fair attitude!
 Ibid. Stanza 5

"Beauty is truth, truth beauty," — that is all
Ye know on earth, and all ye need to know.
 Ibid.

 To make delicious moan
Upon the midnight hours.
 Ibid. Ode to Psyche, Stanza 3

A bright torch, and a casement ope at night,
To let the warm Love in!
 Ibid. Stanza 5

Ever let the fancy roam,
Pleasure never is at home.
 Ibid. Fancy, Line 1

Bards of Passion and of Mirth,
Ye have left your souls on earth!
Have ye souls in heaven too?
 Ibid. Ode Written on the Blank
 Page before Beaumont and
 Fletcher's Fair Maid of the Inn

Souls of Poets dead and gone,
What Elysium have ye known,
Happy field or mossy cavern,
Choicer than the Mermaid Tavern?
Have ye tippled drink more fine
Than mine host's Canary wine?
 Ibid. Lines on the Mermaid
 Tavern

Season of mists and mellow fruitfulness,
Close bosom-friend of the maturing sun.
 Ibid. To Autumn, Stanza 1

Who hath not seen thee oft amid thy store?
 Sometimes whoever seeks abroad may find
Thee sitting careless on a granary floor,
 Thy hair soft-lifted by the winnowing wind;
Or on a half-reap'd furrow sound asleep,
 Drows'd with the fume of poppies, while thy hook

Spares the next swath and all its twined
    flowers.
        Poems. To Autumn, Stanza 2

Then in a wailful choir the small gnats
    mourn
Among the river sallows.
           Ibid. Stanza 3

No, no, go not to Lethe, neither twist
Wolf's-bane, tight-rooted, for its poi-
    sonous wine.
        Ibid. Ode on Melancholy,
                  Stanza 1

Nor let the beetle, nor the death-moth
    be
Your mournful Psyche.
               Ibid.

Then glut thy sorrow on a morning rose.
           Ibid. Stanza 2

She dwells with Beauty — Beauty that
    must die.
           Ibid. Stanza 3

His soul shall taste the sadness of her
    might,
And be among her cloudy trophies hung.
               Ibid.

Deep in the shady sadness of a vale
Far sunken from the healthy breath of
    morn,
Far from the fiery noon, and eve's one
    star,
Sat gray-hair'd Saturn, quiet as a stone.
    Ibid. Hyperion, Book I, Line 1

That large utterance of the early Gods!
             Ibid. Line 51

For to bear all naked truths,
And to envisage circumstance, all calm,
That is the top of sovereignty.
      Ibid. Book II, Line 203

    Here lies one whose name was writ
in water.[1]
    Epitaph for himself [1821]

---

[1] Among the many things he has requested
of me to-night, this is the principal, — that on
his gravestone shall be this inscription. — *Letter from Severn, in* RICHARD MONCKTON
MILNES: *Life, Letters, and Literary Remains
of John Keats* [1848]
    See Sir Thomas More, page 86a.

SIR THOMAS NOON TALFOURD
[1795–1854]

    'Tis a little thing
To give a cup of water; yet its draught
Of cool refreshment, drained by fev-
    ered lips,
May give a shock of pleasure to the
    frame
More exquisite than when nectarean
    juice
Renews the life of joy in happiest
    hours.
      Ion [1835]. Act I, Sc. 2

ALFRED BUNN
[1796–1860]

I dreamt that I dwelt in marble halls,
With vassals and serfs at my side.
      The Bohemian Girl [1843].
               Act II, Song

But — I also dreamt, which pleas'd me
    most,
That you loved me still the same.
               Ibid.

HARTLEY COLERIDGE
[1796–1849]

The soul of man is larger than the sky,
Deeper than ocean, or the abysmal dark
Of the unfathomed center.
          To Shakespeare

She is not fair to outward view
    As many maidens be;
Her loveliness I never knew
    Until she smiled on me:
Oh! then I saw her eye was bright,
A well of love, a spring of light.
      Song, She Is Not Fair

Her very frowns are fairer far
Than smiles of other maidens are.
               Ibid.

THOMAS CHANDLER HALI-BURTON ("SAM SLICK")
[1796–1865]

I want you to see Peel, Stanley, Graham, Shiel, Russell, Macauley, Old Joe,

and so on. These men are all upper-crust here.[1]

Sam Slick in England.[2] Chap. XXIV

Circumstances alter cases.

The Old Judge. Chap. XV

We can do without any article of luxury we have never had; but when once obtained, it is not in human natur' to surrender it voluntarily.

The Clockmaker

HORACE MANN
[1796–1859]

Lost, yesterday, somewhere between sunrise and sunset, two golden hours, each set with sixty diamond minutes. No reward is offered, for they are gone forever.

Aphorism

Be ashamed to die until you have won some victory for humanity.

Commencement Address, Antioch College [1859]

JAMES ROBINSON PLANCHÉ
[1796–1880]

Gentle Zitella, whither away?
Love's ritornella list, while I play.

The Brigand. Love's Ritornella

WILLIAM HICKLING PRESCOTT
[1796–1859]

The surest test of the civilization of a people — at least, as sure as any — afforded by mechanical art is to be found in their architecture, which presents so noble a field for the display of the grand and the beautiful, and which, at the same time, is so intimately connected with the essential comforts of life.

The Conquest of Peru [1847]. Book I, Chap. 5

Where there is no free agency, there can be no morality. Where there is no

[1] Those families, you know, are our upper-crust, — not upper ten thousand. — JAMES FENIMORE COOPER: *The Ways of the Hour* [1850], *Chap. VI*

[2] The "Sam Slick" papers first appeared in a weekly paper in Nova Scotia in 1836.

temptation, there can be little claim to virtue.[1] Where the routine is rigorously proscribed by law, the law, and not the man, must have the credit of the conduct.

The Conquest of Peru. Book I, Chap. 5

Drawing his sword he [Pizarro] traced a line with it on the sand from East to West. Then, turning towards the South, "Friends and comrades!" he said, "on that side are toil, hunger, nakedness, the drenching storm, desertion, and death; on this side ease and pleasure. There lies Peru with its riches; here, Panama and its poverty. Choose, each man, what best becomes a brave Castilian. For my part, I go to the South." So saying, he stepped across the line.

Ibid. Book II, Chap. 4

RICHARD RYAN
[1796–1849]

O, saw ye the lass wi' the bonnie blue een?
Her smile is the sweetest that ever was seen,
Her cheek like the rose is, but fresher, I ween,
She's the loveliest lassie that trips on the green.

O, Saw Ye the Lass

JOSEPH AUGUSTINE WADE
[1796–1845]

Meet Me by Moonlight Alone.

Title of Poem

THOMAS HAYNES BAYLY
[1797–1839]

Those who have wealth must be watchful and wary,
Power, alas! naught but misery brings!

I'd Be a Butterfly. Stanza 2

[1] There's many a life of sweet content Whose virtue is environment.
WALTER LEARNED [1847–1915]: *On the Fly-Leaf of Manon Lescaut*

Oh no! we never mention her, —
  Her name is never heard;
My lips are now forbid to speak
  That once familiar word.
        Oh No! We Never Mention Her

Why don't the men propose, Mamma?
Why don't the men propose?
        Why Don't the Men Propose?

She wore a wreath of roses
The first night that we met.
        She Wore a Wreath

Friends depart, and memory takes them
To her caverns, pure and deep.
        Teach Me to Forget

Tell me the tales that to me were so
  dear,
Long, long ago, long, long ago.
        Long, Long Ago [1]

Oh pilot, 'tis a fearful night!
There's danger on the deep.
        The Pilot

Absence makes the heart grow fonder: [2]
Isle of Beauty, fare thee well!
        Isle of Beauty

My fond affection thou hast seen,
  Then judge of my regret
To think more happy thou hadst been
  If we had never met.
        To My Wife

I'm saddest when I sing.
        You Think I Have a Merry Heart

SAMUEL LOVER
[1797–1868]

Reproof on her lip, but a smile in her
  eye.
        Rory O'More [*1836*]. *Stanza 1*

For dhrames always go by contrairies,
  my dear.
        Ibid. Stanza 2

[1] A popular temperance song, *Where Are the Friends That to Me Were So Dear?* was set to the tune of *Long, Long Ago.*
[2] I find that absence still increases love. — CHARLES HOPKINS: *To C. C.* [1694]
  Distance sometimes endears friendship, and absence sweeteneth it. — JAMES HOWELL: *Familiar Letters* [1650], *Book I, Sect. 1, No. 6*

"That's eight times today that you've
  kissed me before."
"Then here goes another," says he, "to
  make sure,
For there's luck in odd numbers," says
  Rory O'More.[1]
        Rory O'More. Stanza 3

As she sat in the low-backed car
The man at the turn-pike bar
Never asked for the toll
But just rubbed his old poll
And looked after the low-backed car.
        The Low-Backed Car. Stanza 1

And with my advice, faith I wish you'd
  take me.
        Widow Machree [*1839*]

Sure the shovel and tongs
To each other belongs.
        Ibid.

HEINRICH HEINE [2]
[1797–1856]

"Oh, 'tis Love that makes us grateful,
Oh, 'tis Love that makes us rich!"
So sings man, and every fateful
Echo bears his amorous speech.
        O, die Liebe macht uns selig.
        Stanza 1

Toward France there journeyed two
  grenadiers
Who had been captured in Russia;
And they hung their heads and their
  eyes had tears
As they came to the border of Prussia.
        Nach Frankreich zogen zwei
        Grenadier'. Stanza 1

A pine tree stands so lonely
In the North where the high winds
  blow,
He sleeps; and the whitest blanket
Wraps him in ice and snow.
        Ein Fichtenbaum steht einsam.
        Stanza 1

[1] See Pliny, page 50b.
[2] Translated by LOUIS UNTERMEYER.
  Therefore a secret unrest
  Tortured thee, brilliant and bold.
        MATTHEW ARNOLD: *Heine's Grave*
        [1867]

From grief too great to banish
Come songs, my lyric minions.[1]
    Aus meinen grossen Schmerzen.
                Stanza 1

When two who love are parted,
  They talk, as friend to friend,
Clasp hands and weep a little,
  And sigh without an end.
    Wenn zwei von einander scheiden.
                Stanza 1

I do not know why this confronts me,
  This sadness, this echo of pain;
A curious legend still haunts me,
  Still haunts and obsesses my brain.[2]
    Ich weiss nicht, was soll es be-
    deuten (The Lorelei). Stanza 1

The years keep coming and going,
  Men will arise and depart;
Only one thing is immortal:
  The love that is in my heart.
    Die Jahre kommen und gehen.
                Stanza 1

Child, you are like a flower,
So sweet and pure and fair.[3]
    Du bist wie eine Blume. Stanza 1

He who, for the first time, loves,
  Even vainly, is a God.
But the man who loves again,
  And still vainly, is a fool.
    Wer zum erstenmale liebt.
                Stanza 1

Oh what lies there are in kisses!
    In den Küssen, welche Lüge.
                Stanza 1

The sea has its pearls,
  The heaven its stars, —
But my heart, my heart,
  My heart has its love.
    Das Meer hat seine Perlen.
                Stanza 1

The deep, blue eyes of Springtime
  Peer from the grass beneath;

[1] Out of my own great woe
    I make my little songs.
      Translated by ELIZABETH BARRETT
                    BROWNING
See Butler, page 239b.
[2] Ich weiss nicht, was soll es bedeuten,
    Dass ich so traurig bin;
    Ein Märchen aus alten Zeiten,
    Das kommt mir nicht aus dem Sinn.
[3] Du bist wie eine Blume,
    So hold und schön und rein.

They are the tender violets
  That I will twine in a wreath.
    Die blauen Frühlingsaugen.
                Stanza 1

Your eyes' blue depths are lifted,
  With love and friendship stirred.
They smile; and, lost in dreaming,
  I cannot speak a word.[1]
    Mit deinen blauen Augen.
                Stanza 1

Good-Fortune is a giddy maid,
  Fickle and restless as a fawn;
She smooths your hair; and then the
    jade
Kisses you quickly, and is gone.[2]
    Das Glück ist eine leichte Dirne.
                Stanza 1

But Madam Sorrow scorns all this,
  She shows no eagerness for flitting;
But with a long and fervent kiss
  Sits by your bed — and brings her
    knitting.
            Ibid. Stanza 2

This is America!
This is the new world!
Not the present European
Wasted and withering sphere.
    Vitzliputzli. Prelude, Dieses ist
           Amerika! Stanza 1

For Sleep is good, but Death is better
    still —
The best is never to be born at all.[3]
    Gross ist die Ähnlichkeit der
            beiden schönen

  If one has no heart, one cannot write
for the masses.
        Letter to Julius Campe
           [March 18, 1840]

[1] Mit deinen blauen Augen
    Siehst du mich lieblich an,
    Da wird mir so träumend zu Sinne,
    Dass ich nicht sprechen kann.
[2] See Dryden, page 278a.
Good Luck is the gayest of all gay girls,
  Long in one place she will not stay,
Back from your brow she strokes the curls,
  Kisses you quick and flies away.
But Madame Bad Luck soberly comes . . .
  And sits by your bed, and brings her knit-
    ting.
      JOHN HAY [1838–1905]: *Good and*
             Bad Luck (After Heine)
[3] See Sophocles, page 16a.

Ordinarily he is insane, but he has lucid moments when he is only stupid.

> *Of Savoye, appointed ambassador to Frankfurt by Lamartine [1848]*

To publish even one line of an author which he himself has not intended for the public at large — especially letters which are addressed to private persons — is to commit a despicable act of felony.

> *Quoted by* Swinburne *as heading for In Sepulcretis*

WILLIAM MOTHERWELL
[1797–1835]

I've wandered east, I've wandered west,
   Through mony a weary way;
But never, never can forget
   The luve o' life's young day!

> *Jeannie Morrison. Stanza 1*

MARY WOLLSTONECRAFT SHELLEY
[1797–1851]

I beheld the wretch — the miserable monster whom I had created.

> *Frankenstein [1818]. Chap. 5*

MACDONALD CLARKE
[1798–1842]

Whilst twilight's curtain spreading far,
Was pinned with a single star.

> *Death in Disguise. Line 227*

Ha! see where the wild-blazing Grogshop appears,
As the red waves of wretchedness swell;
How it burns on the edge of tempestuous years —
The horrible Light-house of Hell!

> *The Rum-hole*

JOHN ADAMS DIX
[1798–1879]

If any one attempts to haul down the American flag, shoot him on the spot.

> *Official Dispatch to Treasury Officer in New Orleans [January 29, 1861]*

ROBERT GILFILLAN
[1798–1850]

There's a hope for every woe,
   And a balm for every pain,
But the first joys of our heart
   Come never back again!

> *The Exile's Song. Stanza 4*

THOMAS HOOD
[1798–1845]

Ben Battle was a soldier bold,
   And used to war's alarms;
But a cannon-ball took off his legs,
   So he laid down his arms!

> *Faithless Nellie Gray [1826]. Stanza 1*

His death, which happened in his berth,
   At forty-odd befell:
They went and told the sexton, and
   The sexton tolled the bell.

> *Faithless Sally Brown [1826]. Stanza 17*

There is a silence where hath been no sound,
There is a silence where no sound may be,
In the cold grave — under the deep, deep sea,
Or in wide desert where no life is found.

> *Sonnet, Silence [1827]*

We watched her breathing through the night,
   Her breathing soft and low,
As in her breast the wave of life
   Kept heaving to and fro.

> *The Death-Bed [1827]. Stanza 1*

Our very hopes belied our fears,
   Our fears our hopes belied; —
We thought her dying when she slept,
   And sleeping when she died.

> *Ibid. Stanza 3*

I remember, I remember
The house where I was born,
The little window where the sun
Came peeping in at morn;
He never came a wink too soon
Nor brought too long a day.

> *I Remember, I Remember [1827]. Stanza 1*

I remember, I remember
The fir-trees dark and high;
I used to think their slender tops
Were close against the sky:
It was a childish ignorance,
But now 'tis little joy
To know I'm farther off from heaven
Than when I was a boy.
> *I Remember, I Remember. Stanza 4*

She stood breast-high amid the corn,[1]
Clasped by the golden light of morn,
Like the sweetheart of the sun,
Who many a glowing kiss had won.
> *Ruth* [*1827*]. *Stanza 1*

Thus she stood amid the stooks,
Praising God with sweetest looks.
> *Ibid. Stanza 4*

And there is even a happiness
That makes the heart afraid.
> *Ode to Melancholy* [*1827*]

There's not a string attuned to mirth
But has its chord in melancholy.
> *Ibid.*

But evil is wrought by want of thought,
As well as want of heart.
> *The Lady's Dream* [*1827*].
> *Stanza 16*

I saw old Autumn in the misty morn
Stand shadowless like silence, listening
To silence.
> *Ode, Autumn* [*1827*]. *Stanza 1*

Peace and rest at length have come,
All the day's long toil is past,
And each heart is whispering, "Home,
Home at last."
> *Home at Last* [*1827*]

Straight down the Crooked Lane,
And all round the Square.
> *A Plain Direction. Stanza 1*

Two stern-faced men set out from Lynn
Through the cold and heavy mist,
And Eugene Aram walked between,
With gyves upon his wrist.
> *The Dream of Eugene Aram*
> [*1829*]. *Stanza 36*

Never go to France
Unless you know the lingo,
If you do, like me,
You will repent, by jingo.
> *French and English* [*1839*].
> *Stanza 1*

[1] See Keats, page 482a.

No warmth, no cheerfulness, no healthful ease,
No comfortable feel in any member —
No shade, no shine, no butterflies, no bees,
No fruits, no flowers, no leaves, no birds,
    November!
> *No*

Seem'd washing his hands with invisible soap
In imperceptible water.
> *Miss Kilmansegg and Her Precious Leg* [*1841–1843*]. *Her Christening, Stanza 10*

O bed! O bed! delicious bed!
That heaven upon earth to the weary head!
> *Ibid. Her Dream, Stanza 7*

He lies like a hedgehog rolled up the wrong way,
Tormenting himself with his prickles.
> *Ibid. Stanza 14*

There's a double beauty whenever a swan
Swims on a lake, with her double thereon.[1]
> *Ibid. Her Honeymoon, Stanza 9*

Home-made dishes that drive one from home.
> *Ibid. Her Misery, Stanza 1*

Gold! Gold! Gold! Gold!
Bright and yellow, hard and cold.
> *Ibid. Her Moral*

Spurned by the young, but hugged by the old
To the very verge of the churchyard mould.
> *Ibid.*

How widely its agencies vary, —
To save — to ruin — to curse — to bless, —
As even its minted coins express,
Now stamped with the image of Good Queen Bess,
And now of a Bloody Mary.
> *Ibid.*

[1] The swan on still St. Mary's lake
Float double, swan and shadow!
Wordsworth: *Yarrow Unvisited*
[*1803*], *St. 6*

Another tumble! — that's his precious
  nose!
    Parental Ode to My Infant Son.
                              Stanza 3

Boughs are daily rifled
  By the gusty thieves,
And the book of Nature
  Getteth short of leaves.
          The Season. Stanza 2

With fingers weary and worn,
  With eyelids heavy and red,
A woman sat in unwomanly rags
  Plying her needle and thread —
    Stitch! stitch! stitch!
    The Song of the Shirt [*1843*].
                   Stanza 1

O men, with sisters dear!
  O men, with mothers and wives!
It is not linen you're wearing out,
  But human creatures' lives! [1]
           Ibid. Stanza 4

Sewing at once with a double thread,
A shroud as well as a shirt.
                    Ibid.

O God! that bread should be so dear,
And flesh and blood so cheap!
           Ibid. Stanza 5

No blessed leisure for love or hope,
But only time for grief.
          Ibid. Stanza 10

My tears must stop, for every drop
Hinders needle and thread.
                    Ibid.

A wife who preaches in her gown,
And lectures in her night-dress.
    The Surplice Question. Stanza 2

One more unfortunate,
  Weary of breath,
Rashly importunate,
  Gone to her death!
    The Bridge of Sighs [*1844*].
                   Stanza 1

Take her up tenderly,
  Lift her with care;
Fashioned so slenderly,
  Young, and so fair!
          Ibid. Stanza 2

[1] See Scott, page 416a.

Alas for the rarity
Of Christian charity
  Under the sun! [1]
    The Bridge of Sighs. Stanza 9

O'er the earth there comes a bloom;
Sunny light for sullen gloom;
Warm perfume for vapour cold —
I smell the rose above the mould!
    Farewell, Life [*1845*]. *Stanza 2*

GEORGE LINLEY
[1798–1865]

Among our ancient mountains,
And from our lovely vales,
Oh, let the prayer re-echo:
"God bless the Prince of Wales!"
    God Bless the Prince of Wales.
                   Stanza 1

Tho' lost to sight, to memory dear
  Thou ever wilt remain;
One only hope my heart can cheer, —
  The hope to meet again.
                 Song [2]

ROBERT POLLOK
[1798–1827]

Sorrows remembered sweeten present
  joy.
  The Course of Time. Book I, Line 464

HENRY SCOTT RIDDELL
[1798–1870]

Then Scotland's dales and Scotland's
  vales,
  And Scotland's hills for me;
I'll drink a cup to Scotland yet,
  Wi' a' the honours three.
      Scotland Yet. Stanza 2

[1] See Southey, page 427b, and O'Reilly,
page 729b.
[2] This song was written and composed,
probably about 1830, by Linley for the well-
known tenor Augustus Braham, and sung by
him.
  Absent or dead, still let a friend be dear. —
ALEXANDER POPE: *Epistle to Robert, Earl of
Oxford and Mortimer* [1721]

AMOS BRONSON ALCOTT
[1799–1888]

Greater is he who is above temptation than he who being tempted overcomes.
Orphic Sayings [1840]. No. 12

The true teacher defends his pupils against his own personal influence. He inspires self-trust. He guides their eyes from himself to the spirit that quickens him. He will have no disciple.
Ibid. The Teacher

Who loves a garden still his Eden keeps,
Perennial pleasures plants, and wholesome harvests reaps.
Tablets [1868]

Nature is thought immersed in matter.
Ibid.

I press thee to my heart as Duty's faithful child.
Sonnet to Louisa May Alcott [1882]

RUFUS CHOATE
[1799–1859]

The courage of New England was the "courage of Conscience." It did not rise to that insane and awful passion, the love of war for itself.
Address at Ipswich Centennial [1834]

The final end of Government is not to exert restraint but to do good.
Speech, U. S. Senate [July 2, 1841]

There was a state without king or nobles; there was a church without a bishop; [1] there was a people governed by grave magistrates which it had

[1] See Junius, page 1002a.

It [Calvinism] established a religion without a prelate, a government without a king. — GEORGE BANCROFT: *History of the United States* [1834–1876], *Vol. III, Chap. VI*

Compare the anonymous poem, *The Puritans' Mistake,* published by Oliver Ditson in 1844:
Oh, we are weary pilgrims; to this wilderness we bring
A Church without a bishop, a State without a King.

selected, and by equal laws which it had framed.
Speech before the New England Society [December 22, 1843]

We join ourselves to no party that does not carry the flag and keep step to the music of the Union.
Letter to the Whig Convention, Worcester [October 1, 1855]

Its constitution the glittering and sounding generalities [1] of natural right which make up the Declaration of Independence.
Letter to the Maine Whig Committee [1856]

HONORÉ DE BALZAC
[1799–1850]

I believe in the incomprehensibility of God.
Letter to Madame de Hanska [1837]

Those sweetly smiling angels with pensive looks, innocent faces, and cash-boxes for hearts.
Cousin Bette [1846]. Chap. 15

Love and hate are emotions that feed on themselves; but of the two hate is the more enduring. Love is limited by our limited strength — it draws its power from living and giving; but hate is like death and avarice — it is a sort of active abstraction, apart from people and things.
Ibid. Chap. 16

MARY HOWITT
[1799–1888]

Old England is our home, and Englishmen are we;

[1] Six years earlier, Choate gave a lecture in Providence, a review of which, by FRANKLIN J. DICKMAN, appeared in the *Journal* of December 14, 1849. Dickman wrote: "We fear that the glittering generalities of the speaker have left an impression more delightful than permanent." It would seem that Dickman must have the credit of inventing the phrase "glittering generalities," unless his report was merely echoing words used by Choate in the lecture.

Our tongue is known in every clime,
  our flag in every sea.
                    Old England Is Our Home

"Will you walk into my parlour?" said
  the spider to the fly;
" 'Tis the prettiest little parlour that
  ever you did spy."
                    The Spider and the Fly

Buttercups and daisies,
Oh, the pretty flowers;
Coming ere the Springtime,
To tell of sunny hours.
                    Buttercups and Daisies

GEORGE PAYNE RAINSFORD JAMES
[1799–1860]

Thou'rt an ass, Robin, thou'rt an ass,
  To think that great men be
More gay than I that lie on the grass
  Under the greenwood tree.
I tell thee no, I tell thee no,
The Great are slaves to their gilded
  show.
          Richelieu [*1829*]. *Chap. 3,*
            Robber's Song, Stanza 1

Turning over a page or two in the
book of Nature, I found that the most
brilliant actions and the greatest events
were generally brought about from the
meanest motives and most petty
causes.
                    Ibid. Chap. 5

A single word has sometimes lost or
won an empire — even less than a
single word, if we may believe the history of Darius's horse, who proclaimed
his master emperor without speaking.[1]
                    Ibid. Chap. 6

Age is the most terrible misfortune
that can happen to any man; other
evils will mend, this is every day getting worse.
                    Ibid. Chap. 14

[1] The seven candidates for the throne of
Persia agreed that he should be king whose
horse neighed first. The horse of Darius was
the first.

THOMAS NOEL
[1799–1861]

Rattle his bones over the stones!
He's only a pauper, whom nobody
  owns!
                The Pauper's Drive. Stanza 1
Let him push at the door, — in the
  chimney roar,
And rattle the window-pane;
Let him in at us spy with his icicle eye,
But he shall not entrance gain.
                Old Winter. Stanza 5

JULIA CRAWFORD
[1800–1885]

Kathleen mavourneen! the grey dawn
  is breaking,
The horn of the hunter is heard on the
  hill.
          Kathleen Mavourneen [*1835*].
                          Stanza 1
Hast thou forgotten how soon we must
  sever?
Oh! hast thou forgotten this day we
  must part?
It may be for years, and it may be
  forever;
Then why art thou silent, thou voice
  of my heart?
                          Ibid.

THOMAS BABINGTON, LORD MACAULAY
[1800–1859]

That is the best government which
desires to make the people happy, and
knows how to make them happy.
          On Mitford's History of
                  Greece [*1824*]
Free trade, one of the greatest blessings which a government can confer on
a people, is in almost every country unpopular.
                          Ibid.
Press where ye see my white plume
  shine, amidst the ranks of war,
And be your oriflamme today the helmet of Navarre.
                Ivry [*1824*]. *Line 29*

Nobles by the right of an earlier creation, and priests by the imposition of a mightier hand.

On Milton [*1825*]

The dust and silence of the upper shelf.

Ibid.

Perhaps no person can be a poet, or even can enjoy poetry, without a certain unsoundness of mind.

Ibid.

Nothing is so useless as a general maxim.

On Niccolo de Machiavelli [*1827*]

The English Bible, — a book which if everything else in our language should perish, would alone suffice to show the whole extent of its beauty and power.

On John Dryden [*1828*]

His imagination resembled the wings of an ostrich. It enabled him to run, though not to soar.

Ibid.

Ye diners-out from whom we guard our spoons.[1]

Political Georgics

Men are never so likely to settle a question rightly as when they discuss it freely.

Southey's Colloquies [*1830*]

Nothing is so galling to a people, not broken in from the birth, as a paternal or, in other words, a meddling government, a government which tells them what to read and say and eat and drink and wear.

Ibid.

He had a head which statuaries loved to copy, and a foot the deformity of which the beggars in the streets mimicked.

On Moore's Life of Lord Byron
[*1831*]

- We know no spectacle so ridiculous as the British public in one of its periodical fits of morality.

Ibid.

From the poetry of Lord Byron they drew a system of ethics compounded of misanthropy and voluptuousness, — a system in which the two great commandments were to hate your neighbour and to love your neighbour's wife.

On Moore's Life of Lord Byron

What a singular destiny has been that of this remarkable man! — To be regarded in his own age as a classic, and in ours as a companion! To receive from his contemporaries that full homage which men of genius have in general received only from posterity; to be more intimately known to posterity than other men are known to their contemporaries!

On Boswell's Life of Johnson
[*1831*]

That wonderful book, while it obtains admiration from the most fastidious critics, is loved by those who are too simple to admire it.

On Bunyan's Pilgrim's Progress
[*1831*]

The conformation of his mind was such that whatever was little seemed to him great, and whatever was great seemed to him little.

On Horace Walpole [*1833*]

Such night in England ne'er had been, nor ne'er again shall be.

The Armada [*1833*]. *Line 34*

An acre in Middlesex is better than a principality in Utopia.[1]

On Lord Bacon [*1837*]

Every schoolboy knows who imprisoned Montezuma, and who strangled Atahualpa.

On Lord Clive [*1840*]

She [the Roman Catholic Church] may still exist in undiminished vigour when some traveller from New Zealand shall, in the midst of a vast solitude, take his stand on a broken arch of London Bridge to sketch the ruins of St. Paul's.[2]

*On Ranke's History of the
Popes* [*1840*]

[1] The louder he talked of his honor, the faster we counted our spoons. — EMERSON: *Conduct of Life* [1860], *Worship*

[1] See Tennyson, page 549a.
[2] Macaulay used a similar image in 1824 in the concluding paragraph of a review of MIT-

She [the Catholic Church] thoroughly understands what no other Church has ever understood, how to deal with enthusiasts.

On Ranke's History of the Popes

The Chief Justice was rich, quiet, and infamous.

On Warren Hastings [1841]

I shall not be satisfied unless I produce something which shall for a few days supersede the last fashionable novel on the tables of young ladies.

*Letter to Macvey Napier
[November 5, 1841]*

In order that he might rob a neighbour whom he had promised to defend, black men fought on the coast of Coromandel and red men scalped each other by the great lakes of North America.

On Frederic the Great [1842]

We hardly know an instance of the strength and weakness of human nature

---

FORD's *Greece* and in his review of MILL's *Essay on Government* in 1829.

Who knows but that hereafter some traveller like myself will sit down upon the banks of the Seine, the Thames, or the Zuyder Zee, where now, in the tumult of enjoyment, the heart and the eyes are too slow to take in the multitude of sensations? Who knows but he will sit down solitary amid silent ruins, and weep a people inurned and their greatness changed into an empty name? — CONSTANTIN DE VOLNEY [1757–1820]: *Ruins, Chap. II*

The next Augustan age will dawn on the other side of the Atlantic. There will, perhaps, be a Thucydides at Boston, a Xenophon at New York, in time a Virgil at Mexico, and a Newton at Peru. At last some curious traveller from Lima will visit England, and give a description of the ruins of St. Paul's, like the editions of Balbec and Palmyra. — HORACE WALPOLE: *Letter to Sir Horace Mann* [November 24, 1774]

In the firm expectation that when London shall be a habitation of bitterns, when St. Paul and Westminster Abbey shall stand shapeless and nameless ruins in the midst of an unpeopled marsh, when the piers of Waterloo Bridge shall become the nuclei of islets of reeds and osiers, and cast the jagged shadows of their broken arches on the solitary stream, some Transatlantic commentator will be weighing in the scales of some new and now unimagined system of criticism the respective merits of the Bells and the Fudges and their historians. — SHELLEY: *Dedication to Peter Bell the Third* [1819]

---

so striking and so grotesque as the character of this haughty, vigilant, resolute, sagacious blue-stocking, half Mithridates and half Trissotin, bearing up against a world in arms, with an ounce of poison in one pocket and a quire of bad verses in the other.

On Frederic the Great

Lars Porsena of Clusium
  By the Nine Gods he swore
That the great house of Tarquin
  Should suffer wrong no more.
By the Nine Gods he swore it,
  And named a trysting day,
And bade his messengers ride forth
East and west and south and north,
  To summon his array.

*Lays of Ancient Rome [1842].
Horatius, Stanza 1*

To every man upon this earth
  Death cometh soon or late;
And how can man die better
  Than facing fearful odds
For the ashes of his fathers,
  And the temples of his gods?

Ibid. Stanza 27

Those behind cried "Forward!"
And those before cried "Back!"

Ibid. Stanza 50

Oh, Tiber! father Tiber!
  To whom the Romans pray,
A Roman's life, a Roman's arms,
  Take thou in charge this day.

Ibid. Stanza 59

A man who has never looked on Niagara has but a faint idea of a cataract; and he who has not read Barère's Memoirs may be said not to know what it is to lie.

*Mémoires de Bertrand Barère
[1843]*

The highest proof of virtue is to possess boundless power without abusing it.

*Review of Aikin's Life of
Addison [1843]*

There you sit,[1] doing penance for the disingenuousness of years.

*Speech, House of Commons
[April 14, 1845]*

---

[1] Sir Robert Peel.

Forget all feuds, and shed one English
tear
O'er English dust. A broken heart lies
here.
    Epitaph on a Jacobite [*1845*]

Those who compare the age in which
their lot has fallen with a golden age
which exists only in imagination, may
talk of degeneracy and decay; but no
man who is correctly informed as to the
past, will be disposed to take a morose
or desponding view of the present.
    History of England [*1849–1861*].
    Vol. I, Chap. 1

I shall cheerfully bear the reproach
of having descended below the dignity
of history if I can succeed in placing
before the English of the nineteenth
century a true picture of the life of
their ancestors.
    Ibid.

The Puritan hated bear-baiting, not
because it gave pain to the bear, but
because it gave pleasure to the spectators.[1]
    Ibid. Chap. 2

There were gentlemen and there
were seamen in the navy of Charles II.
But the seamen were not gentlemen, and
the gentlemen were not seamen.
    Ibid. Chap. 3

The ambassador [of Russia] and
the grandees who accompanied him
were so gorgeous that all London
crowded to stare at them, and so filthy
that nobody dared to touch them. They
came to the court balls dropping pearls
and vermin.
    Ibid. Vol. V, Chap. 23

Your Constitution is all sail and no
anchor.
    Letter to H. S. Randall, author
    of a Life of Thomas Jefferson
    [*May 23, 1857*]

I met Sir Bulwer Lytton, or Lytton
Bulwer. He is anxious about some
scheme for some association of literary
men. I detest all such associations. I

[1] Even bear-baiting was esteemed heathenish and unchristian: the sport of it, not the
inhumanity, gave offence. — HUME: *History
of England* [*1754–1757*], *Vol. I, Chap. LXII*

hate the notion of gregarious authors.
The less we have to do with each other,
the better.
    Quoted in GEORGE OTTO TRE-
    VELYAN: *Life and Letters of*
    Lord Macaulay [*1877*]. *Vol. II,*
    Page 245

Soon fades the spell, soon comes the
night;
Say will it not be then the same,
Whether we played the black or white,
Whether we lost or won the game?
    Sermon in a Churchyard. Stanza 8

Who never forgot that the end of
Government is the happiness of the
governed.
    Inscription for the Statue of
    Lord William Bentinck

SIR HENRY TAYLOR
[1800–1886]

His food
Was glory, which was poison to his
mind
And peril to his body.
    Philip Van Artevelde [*1834*].
    Part I, Act I, Sc. 5

The world knows nothing of its greatest men.
    Ibid.

He that lacks time to mourn, lacks
time to mend.
Eternity mourns that.
    Ibid.

We figure to ourselves
The thing we like; and then we build
it up,
As chance will have it, on the rock or
sand, —
For thought is tired of wandering o'er
the world,
And homebound Fancy runs her bark
ashore.
    Ibid.

Such souls,
Whose sudden visitations daze the
world,
Vanish like lightning, but they leave
behind
A voice that in the distance far away
Wakens the slumbering ages.
    Ibid.

RICHARD BETHELL, LORD WESTBURY
[1800–1873]

Take a note of that; his Lordship says he will turn it over in what he is pleased to call his mind.[1]

NASH: *Life of Lord Westbury* [*1888*]. *Vol. I, Page 158*

JANE WELSH CARLYLE
[1801–1866]

Medical men all over the world having merely entered into a tacit agreement to call all sorts of maladies people are liable to, in cold weather, by one name; so that one sort of treatment may serve for all, and their practice be thereby greatly simplified.

Letter to John Welsh [*March 4, 1837*]

Some new neighbours, that came a month or two ago, brought with them an accumulation of all the things to be guarded against in a London neighbourhood, viz., a pianoforte, a lap-dog, and a parrot.

Letter to Mrs. Carlyle [*May 6, 1839*]

Never does one feel oneself so utterly helpless as in trying to speak comfort for great bereavement. I will not try it. Time is the only comforter for the loss of a mother.

Letter to Thomas Carlyle [*December 27, 1853*]

If peace and quietness be not in one's own power, one can always give oneself at least bodily fatigue — no such bad succedaneum after all.

Journal. October 23, 1855

When one has been threatened with a great injustice, one accepts a smaller as a favour.

Ibid. November 21, 1855

1 Reported to have been spoken in an audible whisper, from the barristers' table, in reference to a presiding judge. According to Nash, Lord Westbury always disclaimed invention of the mot.

DAVID GLASGOW FARRAGUT
[1801–1870]

Damn the torpedoes! Captain Drayton, go ahead! Jouett, full speed!

At Mobile Bay [*August 5, 1864*]

JOHN HENRY, CARDINAL NEWMAN
[1801–1890]

Time hath a taming hand.

Persecution [*1832*]. *Stanza 3*

Lead, kindly Light, amid the encircling gloom;
Lead thou me on!
The night is dark, and I am far from home;
Lead thou me on!
Keep thou my feet: I do not ask to see
The distant scene; one step enough for me.

The Pillar of the Cloud [*1833*]. *Stanza 1*

And with the morn, those angel faces smile
Which I have loved long since, and lost awhile.

Ibid. Stanza 3

Growth is the only evidence of life.

Apologia pro Vita Sua [*1864*]

It is thy very energy of thought
Which keeps thee from thy God.

Dream of Gerontius [*1866*]. *Part III*

Who lets his feelings run
In soft luxurious flow,
Shrinks when hard service must be done,
And faints at every woe.

Flowers Without Fruit [*1868*]

Living Nature, not dull Art
Shall plan my ways and rule my heart.

Nature and Art [*1868*]. *Stanza 12*

Weep not for me:
Be blithe as wont, nor tinge with gloom
The stream of love that circles home,
Light hearts and free!

Joy in the gifts Heaven's bounty lends,
Nor miss my face, dear friends!
   I still am near.
A Voice from Afar [Knowledge]
[1868]. Stanza 1

It is almost a definition of a gentleman to say he is one who never inflicts pain.
Idea of a University [1873]. The
Man of the World

If he be an unbeliever, he will be too profound and large-minded to ridicule religion or to act against it; he is too wise to be a dogmatist or fanatic in his infidelity. He respects piety and devotion; he even supports institutions as venerable, beautiful, or useful, to which he does not assent; he honours the ministers of religion, and it contents him to decline its mysteries without assailing or denouncing them.
Ibid.

A great memory does not make a philosopher, any more than a dictionary can be called a grammar.
Ibid. Knowledge in Relation to
Learning

Ex Umbris et Imaginibus in Veritatem! (From shadows and symbols into the truth.)
Epitaph at Edgbaston, composed
by himself

BRIGHAM YOUNG
[1801–1877]

This is the place!
On first seeing the valley of the
Great Salt Lake, July 24, 1847 [1]

ALLEN C. SPOONER
[*Floruit* 1846]

I mused upon the Pilgrim flock
Whose luck it was to land

---

[1] Brigham Young and 142 men, three women and two children were the vanguard of Mormon pioneers who explored westward from Nebraska to find a new home for their Church. Mahonri M. Young, noted sculptor and grandson of Brigham Young, designed the "This is The Place Monument," which was dedicated on the spot on the centennial, July 24, 1947.

Upon almost the only rock
Among the Plymouth sand.
Old Times and New. Stanza 2
(Written for the New England
Society Festival, New York,
December 22, 1846)

ALEXANDRE DUMAS
THE ELDER
[1802–1870]

There are virtues which become crimes by exaggeration.
The Count of Monte Cristo
[1841–1845]. Chap. 90

Great is truth. Fire cannot burn, nor water drown it.
Ibid. Chap. 113

All human wisdom is summed up in two words, — wait and hope.
Ibid. Chap. 117

All for one, one for all, that is our device.[1]
The Three Musketeers [1844].
Chap. 9

Nothing succeeds like success.[2]
Ange Pitou [1854]. Vol. I, Page 72

Let us look for the woman.[3]
The Mohicans of Paris
[1854–1855]. Vol. III,
Chaps. 10 and 11

VICTOR HUGO
[1802–1885]

Let us, while waiting for new monuments, preserve the ancient monuments.
Note added to the Definitive
Edition of Notre Dame de Paris
[1832]

Popularity? It is glory's small change.
Ruy Blas [1838]. Act III, Sc. 5

The three problems of the age — the degradation of man by poverty, the ruin of woman by starvation, and the

---

[1] See Shakespeare, page 131b.
[2] Rien ne réussit comme le succès. — *French proverb*
[3] Cherchons la femme. "Cherchez la femme" is attributed to Joseph Fouché [1759–1820].

dwarfing of childhood by physical and spiritual night.
                    Les Misérables [1] [*1862*].
                                        Preface

The supreme happiness of life is the conviction that we are loved.
            Ibid. Fantine, Book V, Chap. 4

For prying into any human affairs, none are equal to those whom it does not concern.
                        Ibid. Chap. 8

The malicious have a dark happiness.
                        Ibid. Chap. 9

Great grief is a divine and terrible radiance which transfigures the wretched.
                        Ibid. Chap. 13

Napoleon . . . mighty somnambulist of a vanished dream.
            Ibid. Cosette, Book I, Chap. 13

Thank heaven, nations are great aside from the dismal chances of the sword.
                        Ibid. Chap. 16

Waterloo is a battle of the first rank won by a captain of the second.
                                        Ibid.

Would you realize what Revolution is, call it Progress; and would you realize what Progress is, call it Tomorrow.
                        Ibid. Chap. 17

What is that to the Infinite?
                        Ibid. Chap. 18

Great blunders are often made, like large ropes, of a multitude of fibres.
            Ibid. Book V, Chap. 10

Upon the first goblet he read this inscription: Monkey wine; upon the second: lion wine; upon the third: sheep wine; upon the fourth: swine wine. These four inscriptions expressed the four descending degrees of drunkenness: the first, that which enlivens; the second, that which irritates; the third, that which stupefies; finally the last, that which brutalizes.
                Ibid. Book VI, Chap. 9

[1] Translated by CHARLES E. WILBOUR, Modern Library Giant.

A man is not idle because he is absorbed in thought. There is a visible labour and there is an invisible labour.
                *Les Misérables. Cosette,
                        Book VII, Chap. 8*

To be buried in Père Lachaise is like having mahogany furniture.
            Ibid. Book VIII, Chap. 5

No one ever keeps a secret so well as a child.
                        Ibid. Chap. 8

The peculiarity of prudery is to multiply sentinels, in proportion as the fortress is less threatened.[1]
            Ibid. Marius, Book II, Chap. 8

Nothing will mix and amalgamate more easily than an old priest and an old soldier. In reality, they are the same kind of man. One has devoted himself to his country upon earth, the other to his country in heaven; there is no other difference.
            Ibid. Book III, Chap. 2

He had the appearance of a caryatid in vacation; he was supporting nothing but his reverie.
            Ibid. Book IV, Chap. 2

Life, misfortunes, isolation, abandonment, poverty, are battlefields which have their heroes; obscure heroes, sometimes greater than the illustrious heroes.
            Ibid. Book V, Chap. 1

A creditor is worse than a master; for a master owns only your person, a creditor owns your dignity, and can belabour that.
                        Ibid. Chap. 2

Social prosperity means man happy, the citizen free, the nation great.
        Ibid. Saint Denis, Book I, Chap. 4

Nothing is more dangerous than discontinued labour; it is habit lost. A habit easy to abandon, difficult to resume.
            Ibid. Book II, Chap. 1

[1] That is the refuge of all old coquettes; it is hard for them to be deserted by the gallants, and from such a desertion, in their spite, they take refuge in the trade of a prude. — MOLIÈRE: *Tartuffe* [1667], *Act I, Sc. 1*

Thought is the labour of the intellect, reverie is its pleasure.

> *Les Misérables. Saint Denis, Book II, Chap. 1*

Where the telescope ends, the microscope begins. Which of the two has the grander view?

> *Ibid. Book III, Chap. 3*

A compliment is something like a kiss through a veil.

> *Ibid. Book VIII, Chap. 1*

Great perils have this beauty, that they bring to light the fraternity of strangers.

> *Ibid. Book XII, Chap. 4*

Philosophy is the microscope of thought.

> *Ibid. Jean Valjean, Book II, Chap. 2*

When grace is joined with wrinkles, it is adorable. There is an unspeakable dawn in happy old age.

> *Ibid. Book V, Chap. 2*

Nothing is more gentle than smoke, nothing more frightful. . . . Smoke rising through the trees may signify the most charming thing in the world, the hearth; or the most terrible, a conflagration.

> *Ninety-Three [1879]. Part I, Book IV, Chap. 7*

The sublimest song to be heard on earth is the lisping of the human soul on the lips of children.

> *Ibid. Part III, Book III, Chap. 1*

Nothing is so like a soul as a bee. It goes from flower to flower as a soul from star to star, and it gathers honey as a soul gathers light.

> *Ibid. Chap. 3*

To rise at six, to dine at ten,
To sup at six, to sleep at ten,
Makes a man live for ten times ten.

> *Inscription over the door of Hugo's study*

I represent a party which does not yet exist: the party of revolution, civilization.

This party will make the twentieth century.

There will issue from it first the United States of Europe, then the United States of the World.

> *Prophecy in autograph on the wall of the room in which Hugo died, Place des Vosges, Paris*

LYDIA MARIA CHILD
[1802–1880]

Genius hath electric power
  Which earth can never tame,
Bright suns may scorch and dark
    clouds lower,
  Its flash is still the same.

> *Marius Amid the Ruins of Carthage*

Over the river and through the wood,
To grandfather's house we'll go;
  The horse knows the way
  To carry the sleigh,
Through the white and drifted snow.

> *Thanksgiving Day. Stanza 1*

ALBERT GORTON GREENE
[1802–1868]

Old Grimes is dead, that good old man
  We never shall see more;
He used to wear a long black coat
  All buttoned down before.

> *Old Grimes. Stanza 1*

He had no malice in his mind,
No ruffles on his shirt.

> *Ibid. Stanza 8*

His knowledge hid from public gaze,
  He did not bring to view,
Nor made a noise town-meeting days,
  As many people do.

> *Ibid. Stanza 10*

LETITIA ELIZABETH LANDON
[1802–1838]

Few, save the poor, feel for the poor.

> *The Poor*

Were it not better to forget
Than but remember and regret?

> *Despondency*

GEORGE POPE MORRIS
[1802–1864]

Woodman, spare that tree!
  Touch not a single bough! [1]

[1] See Campbell, page 433a.

In youth it sheltered me,
And I'll protect it now.
> *Woodman, Spare That Tree*
> *[1830]. Stanza 1*

The iron-armed soldier, the true-
hearted soldier,
The gallant old soldier of Tippecanoe.[1]
> *Campaign Song for William*
> *Henry Harrison [1840]*

A song for our banner! The watchword
recall
Which gave the Republic her station:
"United we stand, divided we fall!"[2]
It made and preserves us a nation![3]
> *The Flag of Our Union.*

'Tis ever thus, when in life's storm
Hope's star to man grows dim,
An angel kneels, in woman's form,
And breathes a prayer for him.
> *Pocahontas. Stanza 3*

EDWARD COOTE PINKNEY
[1802–1828]

I fill this cup to one made up
Of loveliness alone,
A woman, of her gentle sex
The seeming paragon;
To whom the better elements
And kindly stars have given
A form so fair, that, like the air,
'Tis less of earth than heaven.
> *A Health [1825]. Stanza 1*

Her every tone is music's own,
Like those of morning birds,
And something more than melody
Dwells ever in her words.
> *Ibid. Stanza 2*

---

[1] Morris's words, sung to the tune of "The Old Oaken Bucket," were immensely popular. For the first time in our land the power of song was invoked to aid a Presidential candidate. — BEN PERLEY POORE: *Reminiscences* [1886]

[2] See Aesop, page 11a.
Then join hand in hand, brave Americans all! By uniting we stand, by dividing we fall.
JOHN DICKINSON: *The Liberty Song* [1768]

[3] Bless'd with victory and peace,
  may our Heaven-rescued land
Praise the Power that hath made
  and preserved us a nation.
FRANCIS SCOTT KEY: *The Star-Spangled Banner* [1814], St. 4

Look out upon the stars, my love,
And shame them with thine eyes.
> *A Serenade [1825]*

WINTHROP MACKWORTH PRAED
[1802–1839]

And oh! I shall find how, day by day,
All thoughts and things look older;
How the laugh of pleasure grows less
gay,
And the heart of friendship colder.
> *Twenty-eight and Twenty-nine*

She was our queen, our rose, our star;
And then she danced — O Heaven, her
dancing!
> *The Belle of the Ball*

His talk was like a stream which runs
With rapid change from rocks to roses,
It slipped from politics to puns;
It passed from Mahomet to Moses.
> *The Vicar. Stanza 5*

Events are writ by History's pen:
Though causes are too much to care
for:—
Fame talks about the where and when,
While folly asks the why and where-
fore.
> *Epitaph on the Late King of*
> *the Sandwich Islands. Stanza 4*

Dame Fortune is a fickle gipsy,
And always blind, and often tipsy;
Sometimes for years and years together,
She'll bless you with the sunniest
weather,
Bestowing honour, pudding, pence,
You can't imagine why or whence; —
Then in a moment — Presto, pass! —
Your joys are withered like the grass.
> *The Haunted Tree*

DAVID CHRISTY
[1802– ?]

Cotton is King; or, The Economical
Relations of Slavery.
> *Title of Book [1855]* [1]

---

[1] Take away *time is money,* and what is left of England? take away *cotton is king,* and what is left of America? — VICTOR HUGO: *Les Misérables* [1862], **Marius, Book IV,** *Chap. 4*

THOMAS LOVELL BEDDOES
[1803–1849]

The anchor heaves, the ship swings
    free,
The sails swell full. To sea, to sea!
Sailor's Song. Stanza 2

If there were dreams to sell,
    What would you buy?
Some cost a passing-bell;
    Some a light sigh.
Dream-Pedlary

That divinest hope, which none can
    know of
Who have not laid their dearest in the
    grave.
Death's Jest Book [1850]

If thou wilt ease thine heart
Of love and all its smart,
Then sleep, dear, sleep.

But wilt thou cure thy heart
Of love and all its smart,
Then die, dear, die.
Ibid.

WILLIAM ALLEN
[1803–1879]

Fifty-four forty, or fight! [1]
Speech, U. S. Senate [1844]

GEORGE BORROW
[1803–1881]

O England! long, long may it be ere
the sun of thy glory sink beneath the
wave of darkness! Though gloomy and
portentous clouds are now gathering
rapidly around thee, still, still may it
please the Almighty to disperse them,
and to grant thee a futurity longer in
duration and still brighter in renown
than thy past! Or, if thy doom be at
hand, may that doom be a noble one,
and worthy of her who has been styled
the Old Queen of the waters!
The Bible in Spain [1842]

O ye gifted ones, follow your calling,
for, however various your talents may
be, ye can have but one calling capable
of leading ye to eminence and renown;
follow resolutely the one straight path
before you, it is that of your good
angel, let neither obstacles nor temptations induce ye to leave it; bound along
if you can; if not, on hands and knees
follow in it, perish in it, if needful; but
ye need not fear that; no one ever yet
died in the true path of his calling before he had attained the pinnacle.
Lavengro [1851]. Chap. 21

Trust not a man's words if you
please, or you may come to very erroneous conclusions; but at all times
place implicit confidence in a man's
countenance in which there is no deceit;
and of necessity there can be none. If
people would but look each other more
in the face, we should have less cause
to complain of the deception of the
world; [1] nothing so easy as physiognomy nor so useful.
Ibid. Chap. 22

Translation is at best an echo.
Ibid. Chap. 25

There's night and day, brother, both
sweet things; sun, moon, and stars,
brother, all sweet things; there's likewise a wind on the heath. Life is very
sweet, brother; who would wish to
die?
Ibid.

I learnt . . . to fear God, and to
take my own part.
Ibid. Chap. 86

Youth is the only season for enjoyment, and the first twenty-five years
of one's life are worth all the rest of
the longest life of man, even though
those five-and-twenty be spent in penury and contempt, and the rest in the
possession of wealth, honours, respectability.
The Romany Rye [1857]. Chap. 30

---

[1] This phrase was adopted as the slogan of
the war party, in the presidential election
of 1844. At the time, war with England regarding the Oregon question seemed imminent.
The Democratic convention of 1844 had demanded the reoccupation of the whole of
Oregon up to 54° 40′, but the new president,
James K. Polk, compromised with Great
Britain on the forty-ninth parallel.

[1] See Dickens, page 580a.

WILLIAM DRIVER
[1803–1886]

I name thee Old Glory.
Words on Hoisting the Flag *

RALPH WALDO EMERSON
[1803–1882]

Four snakes gliding up and down a hollow for no purpose that I could see — not to eat, not for love, but only gliding.
Journal. April 11, 1834
Give me health and a day, and I will make the pomp of emperors ridiculous.
Nature [1836]. Chap. 3, Beauty
He who has mastered any law in his private thoughts, is master to that extent of all men whose language he speaks, and of all into whose language his own can be translated.
The American Scholar [1837]
Wherever Macdonald sits, there is the head of the table.[2]
Ibid.
If the single man plant himself indomitably on his instincts, and there abide, the huge world will come round to him.[3]
Ibid.
Men grind and grind in the mill of a truism, and nothing comes out but what was put in. But the moment they desert the tradition for a spontaneous thought, then poetry, wit, hope, virtue, learning, anecdote, all flock to their aid.
Literary Ethics [1838]

[1] On August 10, 1831, a large American flag was presented to Captain William Driver of the brig *Charles Doggett* by a band of women, in recognition of his humane service in bringing back the British mutineers of the ship *Bounty* from Tahiti to their former home, Pitcairn Island. As the flag was hoisted to the masthead, Captain Driver proclaimed, "I name thee Old Glory." The flag is now in the Smithsonian Institution, Washington, D. C.
[2] Emerson's sentence is usually quoted with the substitution of "Macgregor" for "Macdonald."
[3] See Disraeli, page 512a.
All things come round to him who will but wait. — LONGFELLOW: *Tales of a Wayside Inn, The Student's Tale* [1863]

I wish to write such rhymes as shall not suggest a restraint, but contrariwise the wildest freedom.
Journal. June 27, 1839
Time dissipates to shining ether the solid angularity of facts.
Essays: First Series [1841]. History
There is properly no History; only Biography.[1]
Ibid.
Nature is a mutable cloud, which is always and never the same.
Ibid.
A man is a bundle of relations, a knot of roots, whose flower and fruitage is the world.
Ibid.
The virtue in most request is conformity. Self-reliance is its aversion. It loves not realities and creators, but names and customs.
Ibid. Self-Reliance
Whoso would be a man must be a non-conformist.
Ibid.
A foolish consistency is the hobgoblin of little minds, adored by little statesmen and philosophers and divines.
Ibid.
To be great is to be misunderstood.
Ibid.
An institution is the lengthened shadow of one man.
Ibid.
Nothing can bring you peace but yourself.
Ibid.
Every sweet has its sour; every evil its good.
Ibid. Compensation
For every thing you have missed, you have gained something else; and for every thing you gain. you lose something.
Ibid.
Everything in Nature contains all the powers of Nature. Everything is made of one hidden stuff.
Ibid.

[1] See Carlyle, page 475b.

It is as impossible for a man to be cheated by any one but himself, as for a thing to be, and not to be, at the same time.

Essays: First Series. Compensation

There is no luck in literary reputation. They who make up the final verdict upon every book are not the partial and noisy readers of the hour when it appears; but a court as of angels, a public not to be bribed, not to be entreated, and not to be overawed, decides upon every man's title to fame.

Ibid. Spiritual Laws

All mankind love a lover.

Ibid. Love

No man ever forgot the visitations of that power to his heart and brain, which created all things new; which was the dawn in him of music, poetry, and art.

Ibid.

Thou art to me a delicious torment.

Ibid. Friendship

Happy is the house that shelters a friend.

Ibid.

A friend is a person with whom I may be sincere. Before him, I may think aloud.

Ibid.

A friend may well be reckoned the masterpiece of Nature.

Ibid.

Two may talk and one may hear, but three cannot take part in a conversation of the most sincere and searching sort.

Ibid.

The only reward of virtue is virtue; the only way to have a friend is to be one.

Ibid.

I do then with my friends as I do with my books. I would have them where I can find them, but I seldom use them.

Ibid.

Do what we can, summer will have its flies. If we walk in the woods, we must feed mosquitoes

Ibid. Prudence

In skating over thin ice our safety is in our speed.

Essays: First Series. Prudence

Heroism feels and never reasons and therefore is always right.

Ibid. Heroism

Nothing great was ever achieved without enthusiasm.

Ibid. Circles

Nothing astonishes men so much as common sense and plain dealing.

Ibid. Art

There is always a certain meanness in the argument of conservatism, joined with a certain superiority in its fact.

The Conservative [*1842*]

Nature and Books belong to the eyes that see them.

Essays: Second Series [*1844*].
Experience

No house, though it were the Tuileries, or the Escurial, is good for anything without a master.

Ibid. Manners

The only gift is a portion of thyself.[1]

Ibid. Gifts

The less government we have, the better — the fewer laws, and the less confided power.

Ibid. Politics

Money, which represents the prose of life, and which is hardly spoken of in parlors without an apology, is, in its effects and laws, as beautiful as roses.

Ibid. Nominalist and Realist

Every man is wanted, and no man is wanted much.

Ibid.

And with Caesar to take in his hand the army, the empire, and Cleopatra, and say, "All these will I relinquish if you will show me the fountains of the Nile."

Ibid. New England Reformers

The reward of a thing well done, is to have done it.

Ibid.

Good-bye, proud world! I'm going home;

[1] See J. R. LOWELL, page 600a, and Whitman, page 608a–608b.

Thou art not my friend and I'm not thine.[1]

Poems [*1847*]. *Good-bye, Stanza 1*

Oh, when I am safe in my sylvan home,
I tread on the pride of Greece and Rome;
And when I am stretched beneath the pines
Where the evening star so holy shines,
I laugh at the lore and the pride of man,
At the sophist schools, and the learned clan;
For what are they all in their high conceit,
When man in the bush with God may meet?

Ibid. Stanza 4

Nor knowest thou what argument
Thy life to thy neighbor's creed has lent.
All are needed by each one;
Nothing is fair or good alone.

Ibid. Each and All, Stanza 1

I wiped away the weeds and foam,
I fetched my sea-born treasures home;
But the poor, unsightly, noisome things
Had left their beauty on the shore,
With the sun and the sand and the wild uproar.

Ibid. Stanza 3

I like a church; I like a cowl;
I love a prophet of the soul;
And on my heart monastic aisles
Fall like sweet strains or pensive smiles;
Yet not for all his faith can see
Would I that cowlèd churchman be.

Ibid. The Problem, Stanza 1

Not from a vain or shallow thought
His awful Jove young Phidias brought.

Ibid. Stanza 2

The hand that rounded Peter's dome,
And groined the aisles of Christian Rome,
Wrought in a sad sincerity;
Himself from God he could not free;
He builded better than he knew; —
The conscious stone to beauty grew.

Ibid.

[1] See Johnson, page 343a.

Earth proudly wears the Parthenon
As the best gem upon her zone.

Poems. The Problem, Stanza 3

The passive Master lent his hand
To the vast soul that o'er him planned.[1]

Ibid.

Enclosed
In a tumultuous privacy of storm.

Ibid. The Snow-Storm

To mimic in slow structures, stone by stone,
Built in an age, the mad wind's night-work,
The frolic architecture of the snow.

Ibid.

Life is too short to waste
In critic peep or cynic bark,
Quarrel or reprimand:
'Twill soon be dark;
Up! mind thine own aim, and
God speed the mark!

Ibid. To J. W.

There's no rood has not a star above it.

Ibid. Musketaquid

All sorts of things and weather
Must be taken in together,
To make up a year
And a Sphere.

Ibid. Fable, The Mountain and the Squirrel

If eyes were made for seeing,
Then Beauty is its own excuse for being.[2]

Ibid. The Rhodora

Things are in the saddle,
And ride mankind.

Ibid. Ode Inscribed to W. H. Channing

There are two laws discrete,
Not reconciled, —
Law for man, and law for thing.

Ibid.

Olympian bards who sung
Divine ideas below,
Which always find us young,
And always keep us so.

Ibid. Ode to Beauty

[1] This couplet is inscribed on the boulder marking Emerson's grave in Sleepy Hollow Cemetery, Concord, Massachusetts.
[2] See Elizabeth Barrett Browning, page 519b, and Whittier, page 526b.

Heartily know,
When half-gods go,
The gods arrive.
> *Poems. Give All to Love, Stanza 4*

Love not the flower they pluck, and
know it not,
And all their botany is Latin names.
> *Ibid. Blight*

By the rude bridge that arched the
flood,
Their flag to April's breeze unfurled,
Here once the embattled farmers stood,
And fired the shot heard round the
world.
> *Ibid. Hymn Sung at the Completion of the Battle Monument, Concord [July 4, 1837], Stanza 1*

Hast thou named all the birds without
a gun? [1]
Loved the wood-rose, and left it on its
stalk?
> *Ibid. Forbearance*

I hate quotations. Tell me what you
know.
> *Journal. May, 1849*

He is great who is what he is from
Nature, and who never reminds us of
others.
> *Representative Men [1850].*
> *Uses of Great Men*

When nature removes a great man,
people explore the horizon for a successor; but none comes, and none will.
His class is extinguished with him. In
some other and quite different field, the
next man will appear.
> *Ibid.*

Every hero becomes a bore at last.
> *Ibid.*

Great geniuses have the shortest biographies.
> *Ibid. Plato, or, The Philosopher*

Keep cool: it will be all one a hundred years hence. [2]
> *Ibid. Montaigne, or, The Skeptic*

[1] See S. W. Foss, page 777b.
[2] What matters what anybody thinks? "It
will be all the same a hundred years hence."

Is not marriage an open question,
when it is alleged, from the beginning
of the world, that such as are in the institution wish to get out, and such as
are out wish to get in? [1]
> *Representative Men. Montaigne,*
> *or, The Skeptic*

Thought is the property of him who
can entertain it, and of him who can
adequately place it.
> *Ibid. Shakespeare, or, The Poet*

"There shall be no Alps," he said.
> *Ibid. Napoleon, or, The Man of*
> *the World*

[Napoleon] directed Bourrienne to
leave all his letters unopened for three
weeks, and then observed with satisfaction how large a part of the correspondence had thus disposed of itself,
and no longer required an answer.
> *Ibid.*

The word *liberty* in the mouth of Mr.
Webster sounds like the word *love* in
the mouth of a courtezan.
> *Journal. February 12 (?), 1851*

I trust a good deal to common fame,
as we all must. If a man has good corn,
or wood, or boards, or pigs, to sell, or
can make better chairs or knives, crucibles or church organs, than anybody
else, you will find a broad hard-beaten
road to his house, though it be in the
woods. [2]
> *Ibid. February, 1855*

That is the most sensible proverb ever invented. — GEORGE DU MAURIER: *Peter Ibbetson* [1891]

[1] See Montaigne, page 100a.

[2] The editors, E. W. EMERSON and W. E.
FORBES, appended a footnote: "There has
been much inquiry in the newspapers recently
as to whether Mr. Emerson wrote a sentence
very like the above which has been attributed
to him in print. The Editors do not find the
latter in his works, but there can be little
doubt that it was a memory quotation by
some hearer, or, quite probably, correctly
reported from one of his lectures, the same
image in differing words."

If a man can write a better book, preach a
better sermon, or make a better mouse-trap
than his neighbor, though he builds his
house in the woods the world will make a
beaten path to his door. — SARAH S. B. YULE
AND MARY S. KEENE: *Borrowings* [1889], *re-*

Classics which at home are drowsily read have a strange charm in a country inn, or in the transom of a merchant brig.

English Traits [1856]

I find the Englishman to be him of all men who stands firmest in his shoes.

Ibid. Manners

A creative economy is the fuel of magnificence.

Ibid. Aristocracy

Coal is a portable climate.

Conduct of Life [1860]. Wealth

The world is his, who has money to go over it.

Ibid.

The farmer is covetous of his dollar, and with reason. . . . He knows how many strokes of labor it represents. His bones ache with the day's work that earned it.

Ibid.

Art is a jealous mistress,[1] and, if a man have a genius for painting, poetry, music, architecture, or philosophy, he makes a bad husband, and an ill-provider.

Ibid.

One of the benefits of a college education is to show the boy its little avail.

Ibid. Culture

All educated Americans, first or last, go to Europe.

Ibid.

Solitude, the safeguard of mediocrity, is to genius the stern friend.

Ibid.

A man known to us only as a celebrity in politics or in trade, gains largely in our esteem if we discover that he has some intellectual taste or skill.

Ibid.

There is always a best way of doing everything, if it be to boil an egg. Manners are the happy ways of doing things.

Ibid. Behavior

Your manners are always under examination, and by committees little suspected, — a police in citizens' clothes, — but are awarding or denying you very high prizes when you least think of it.

Conduct of Life. Behavior

The alleged power to charm down insanity, or ferocity in beasts, is a power behind the eye.

Ibid.

Fine manners need the support of fine manners in others.

Ibid.

The highest compact we can make with our fellow is, — "Let there be truth between us two forevermore."

Ibid.

It is sublime to feel and say of another, I need never meet, or speak, or write to him: we need not reinforce ourselves, or send tokens of remembrance: I rely on him as on myself: if he did thus or thus, I know it was right.

Ibid.

There is no beautifier of complexion, or form, or behavior, like the wish to scatter joy and not pain around us.

Ibid.

We must be as courteous to a man as we are to a picture, which we are willing to give the advantage of a good light.

Ibid.

There is one topic peremptorily forbidden to all well-bred, to all rational mortals, namely, their distempers. If you have not slept, or if you have slept, or if you have headache, or sciatica, or leprosy, or thunder-stroke, I beseech you, by all angels, to hold your peace.

Ibid.

Shallow men believe in luck.[1]

Ibid. Worship

'Tis a Dutch proverb, that "paint costs nothing," such are its preserving qualities in damp climates.

Ibid. Considerations by the Way

Our chief want in life is somebody who shall make us do what we can.

Ibid.

---

ported by Mrs. Yule as having been used by Emerson in an address

[1] See Sharswood, page 560b.

[1] Luck is infatuated with the efficient. —*Persian proverb*

Make yourself necessary to some-body.
Conduct of Life. Considerations by the Way

Beauty without grace is the hook without the bait.
Ibid. Beauty

Never read any book that is not a year old.
Ibid. In Praise of Books

I should as soon think of swimming across Charles River, when I wish to go to Boston, as of reading all my books in originals, when I have them rendered for me in my mother tongue.
Ibid.

Great men are they who see that spiritual is stronger than any material force; that thoughts rule the world.
Progress of Culture, Phi Beta Kappa Address [July 18, 1867]

And striving to be man, the worm
Mounts through all the spires of form.
May-Day and Other Pieces [1867]. May-Day

God said, I am tired of kings,
I suffer them no more.
Ibid. Boston Hymn [Read January 1, 1863], Stanza 2

Oh, tenderly the haughty day
Fills his blue urn with fire.
Ibid. Ode [Sung July 4, 1857], Stanza 1

Go put your creed into your deed,
Nor speak with double tongue.
Ibid. Stanza 5

I think no virtue goes with size.
Ibid. The Titmouse

For well the soul, if stout within,
Can arm impregnably the skin.
Ibid.

So nigh is grandeur to our dust,
So near is God to man,
When Duty whispers low, *Thou must,*
The youth replies, *I can.*
Ibid. Voluntaries, III

Nor sequent centuries could hit
Orbit and sum of Shakespeare's wit.
Ibid. Solution

Born for success he seemed,
With grace to win, with heart to hold,

With shining gifts that took all eyes.
May-Day and Other Pieces. In Memoriam E. B. E.

Nor mourn the unalterable Days
That Genius goes and Folly stays.
Ibid.

Fear not, then, thou child infirm,
There's no god dare wrong a worm.
Ibid. Compensation, I

He thought it happier to be dead,
To die for Beauty, than live for bread.
Ibid. Beauty

Wilt thou seal up the avenues of ill?
Pay every debt, as if God wrote the bill.
Ibid. "Suum Cuique"

Too busied with the crowded hour to fear to live or die.
Ibid. Nature

Daughters of Time, the hypocritic Days,
Muffled and dumb like barefoot der-vishes,
And marching single in an endless file,
Bring diadems and fagots in their hands.
Ibid. Days

I, too late,
Under her solemn fillet saw the scorn.
Ibid.

It is time to be old,
To take in sail.
Ibid. Terminus

Obey the voice at eve obeyed at prime.
Ibid.

Though love repine, and reason chafe,
There came a voice without reply, —
" 'Tis man's perdition to be safe,
When for the truth he ought to die."
Ibid. Sacrifice

For what avail the plough or sail,
Or land or life, if freedom fail?
Ibid. Boston, Stanza 5

What care though rival cities soar
Along the stormy coast,
Penn's town, New York, and Baltimore,
If Boston knew the most!
Ibid. Stanza 9

If the red slayer think he slays,
Or if the slain think he is slain,
They know not well the subtle ways
I keep, and pass, and turn again.
Ibid. Brahma

They reckon ill who leave me out;
  When me they fly, I am the wings;
I am the doubter and the doubt,
  And I the hymn the Brahmin sings.
May-Day and Other Pieces.
Brahma

Draw, if thou canst, the mystic line,
Severing rightly his from thine,
Which is human, which divine.
Ibid. Worship

That book is good
Which puts me in a working mood.
Unless to Thought is added Will,
Apollo is an imbecile.
Ibid. Fragments on the Poetic Gift

In the vaunted works of Art
The master-stroke is Nature's part.[1]
Ibid. Art

I am the owner of the sphere,
Of the seven stars and the solar year,
Of Caesar's hand, and Plato's brain,
Of Lord Christ's heart, and Shake-
  speare's strain.
Ibid. History

Ever from one who comes tomorrow
Men wait their good and truth to bor-
  row.
Ibid. Merlin's Song

The music that can deepest reach,
And cure all ill, is cordial speech.
Ibid.

A day for toil, an hour for sport,
But for a friend is life too short.
Ibid.

Some of your hurts you have cured,
And the sharpest you still have sur-
  vived,
But what torments of grief you en-
  dured
From evils which never arrived! [2]
Ibid. Borrowing [From the French]

A ruddy drop of manly blood
  The surging sea outweighs,

The world uncertain comes and goes,
  The lover rooted stays.
May-Day and Other Pieces.
Friendship

Me too thy nobleness has taught
  To master my despair;
The fountains of my hidden life
  Are through thy friendship fair.
Ibid.

God may forgive sins, he said, but
awkwardness has no forgiveness in
heaven or earth.
Society and Solitude [1870]

The most advanced nations are always those who navigate the most.
Ibid. Civilization

Hitch your wagon to a star.
Ibid.

The true test of civilization is, not
the census, nor the size of cities, nor
the crops — no, but the kind of man
the country turns out.
Ibid.

Raphael paints wisdom; Handel sings
it, Phidias carves it, Shakespeare writes
it, Wren builds it, Columbus sails it,
Luther preaches it, Washington arms
it, Watt mechanizes it.
Ibid. Art

Every genuine work of art has as
much reason for being as the earth and
the sun.
Ibid.

We boil at different degrees.
Ibid. Eloquence

The ornament of a house is the
friends who frequent it.
Ibid. Domestic Life

We have the newspaper, which does
its best to make every square acre of
land and sea give an account of itself
at your breakfast-table.
Ibid. Works and Days

Can anybody remember when the
times were not hard and money not
scarce?
Ibid.

A man builds a fine house; and now
he has a master, and a task for life; he
is to furnish, watch, show it, and keep
it in repair the rest of his days.
Ibid.

---

[1] Nature paints the best part of a picture,
carves the best part of the statue, builds the
best part of the house, and speaks the best
part of the oration. — *Society and Solitude*
[1870], *Art*

[2] Let us be of good cheer, however, remembering that the misfortunes hardest to
bear are those which never come. — JAMES
RUSSELL LOWELL: *Democracy and Addresses*
[1884]

'Tis the good reader that makes the good book.
Society and Solitude. Success

We do not count a man's years until he has nothing else to count.
Ibid. Old Age

Poetry teaches the enormous force of a few words, and, in proportion to the inspiration, checks loquacity.
Parnassus [1874]. Preface

There are two classes of poets, — the poets by education and practice, these we respect; and poets by nature, these we love.
Ibid.

No lover of poetry can spare Chaucer, or should grudge the short study required to command the archaisms of his English, and the skill to read the melody of his verse.
Ibid.

Life is not so short but that there is always time enough for courtesy.
*Letters and Social Aims [1876].
Social Aims*

I have heard with admiring submission the experience of the lady who declared that the sense of being perfectly well-dressed gives a feeling of inward tranquillity which religion is powerless to bestow.
Ibid.

Do not say things. What you are stands over you the while, and thunders so that I cannot hear what you say to the contrary.
Ibid.

Abraham Lincoln . . . who was at home and welcome with the humblest, and with a spirit and a practical vein in the times of terror that commanded the admiration of the wisest. His heart was as great as the world, but there was no room in it to hold the memory of a wrong.
Ibid. Greatness

Next to the originator of a good sentence is the first quoter of it.[1]
Ibid. Quotation and Originality

[1] There is not less wit nor less invention in applying rightly a thought one finds in a book, than in being the first author of that

When Shakespeare is charged with debts to his authors, Landor replies, "Yet he was more original than his originals. He breathed upon dead bodies and brought them into life."
*Letters and Social Aims. Quotation
and Originality*

In fact, it is as difficult to appropriate the thoughts of others as it is to invent.
Ibid.

By necessity, by proclivity, and by delight, we all quote.
Ibid.

Every good poem that I know I recall by its rhythm also. Rhyme is a pretty good measure of the latitude and opulence of a writer. If unskilled, he is at once detected by the poverty of his chimes.
Ibid. Poetry and Imagination

Wit makes its own welcome, and levels all distinctions.
Ibid. The Comic

The perception of the comic is a tie of sympathy with other men.
Ibid.

What is a weed? A plant whose virtues have not yet been discovered.[1]
Fortune of the Republic [1878]

All thoughts of a turtle are turtles, and of a rabbit, rabbits.
*The Natural History of
Intellect [1893]*

When you strike at a king, you must kill him.
Recollected by OLIVER WENDELL
HOLMES, JR. *Quoted in* MAX
LERNER: *The Mind and Faith of
Justice Holmes [1943]*

thought. — BAYLE: *Dictionnaire Historique et Critique* [1697–1702]
Though old the thought and oft exprest,
'Tis his at last who says it best.
    JAMES RUSSELL LOWELL: *For an
        Autograph* [1868]
[1] A weed is no more than a flower in disguise. — JAMES RUSSELL LOWELL: *A Fable for Critics* [1848]
A weed is but an unloved flower! — ELLA WHEELER WILCOX [1850–1919]: *The Weed, St. 1*

ROBERT STEPHEN HAWKER
[1803–1875]

And shall Trelawny die?
Here's twenty thousand Cornish men
Will know the reason why.
> *The Song of the Western Men.*[1]
> *Stanza 1*

RICHARD HENRY HENGIST HORNE
[1803–1884]

'Tis always morning somewhere in the world.
> *Orion* [*1843*]. *Book III,*
> *Canto II*

A sweet content
Passing all wisdom or its fairest flower.
> *Ibid.*

The wisdom of mankind creeps slowly on,
Subject to every doubt that can retard
Or fling it back upon an earlier time.
> *Ibid.*

DOUGLAS JERROLD
[1803–1857]

He is one of those wise philanthropists who in a time of famine would vote for nothing but a supply of toothpicks.
> *Wit and Opinions of Douglas*
> *Jerrold* [*1859*]

Dogmatism is puppyism come to its full growth.
> *Ibid.*

The surest way to hit a woman's heart is to take aim kneeling.
> *Ibid.*

That fellow would vulgarize the day of judgment.
> *Ibid. A Comic Author*

[1] This ballad commemorates the commitment to the Tower of London of Sir Jonathan Trelawny [1650–1721], with six other prelates, in 1688, for refusing to recognize the Declaration of Indulgence issued by James II. "And shall Trelawny die?" has been a popular phrase throughout Cornwall since the imprisonment of the seven bishops. Hawker wrote the ballad in 1825.

The best thing I know between France and England is the sea.
> *Wit and Opinions of Douglas Jer-*
> *rold. The Anglo-French Alliance*

Some people are so fond of ill-luck that they run half-way to meet it.
> *Ibid. Meeting Troubles Half-Way*

Earth is here [Australia] so kind, that just tickle her with a hoe and she laughs with a harvest.
> *Ibid. A Land of Plenty*

The ugliest of trades have their moments of pleasure. Now, if I were a grave-digger, or even a hangman, there are some people I could work for with a great deal of enjoyment.
> *Ibid. Ugly Trades*

He was so good he would pour rose-water on a toad.
> *Ibid. A Charitable Man*

As for the brandy, "nothing extenuate"; and the water, put nought in in malice.
> *Ibid. Shakespeare Grog*

Talk to him of Jacob's ladder, and he would ask the number of the steps.
> *Ibid. A Matter-of-fact Man*

CHARLES SWAIN
[1803–1874]

Let tomorrow take care of tomorrow, —
Leave things of the future to fate;
What's the use to anticipate sorrow? —
Life's troubles come never too late!
> *Imaginary Evils. Stanza 1*

SARAH HELEN POWER WHITMAN
[1803–1878]

Star of resplendent front! Thy glorious eye
Shines on me still from out yon clouded sky.
> *Arcturus* (*To Edgar Allan Poe*)

The summer skies are darkly blue,
The days are still and bright,
And Evening trails her robes of gold
Through the dim halls of Night.[1]
> *Summer's Call*

[1] See Longfellow, page 520b.

ROBERT SMITH SURTEES
[1803-1864]

Full o' beans and benevolence.
Handley Cross [*1843*]. *Chap. 27*

Three things I never lends — my 'oss, my wife, and my name.
Hillingdon Hall [*1845*]. *Chap. 33*

More people are flattered into virtue than bullied out of vice.
The Analysis of the Hunting Field
[*1846*]. *Chap. 1*

Better be killed than frightened to death.
Mr. Facey Romford's Hounds
[*1865*]. *Chap. 32*

EDWARD BULWER LYTTON
[1803-1873]

A good heart is better than all the heads in the world.
The Disowned [*1828*]. *Chap. 33*

The easiest person to deceive is one's own self.
Ibid. Chap. 42

The magic of the tongue is the most dangerous of all spells.
Eugene Aram [*1832*]. *Book I,*
Chap. 7

When stars are in the quiet skies,
Then most I pine for thee;
Bend on me then thy tender eyes,
As stars look on the sea.
Ernest Maltravers [*1837*].
Book III, Chap. 1

Rank is a great beautifier.
The Lady of Lyons [*1838*].
Act II, Sc. 1

Love, like Death,
Levels all ranks, and lays the shepherd's crook
Beside the sceptre.
Ibid. Act III, Sc. 2

You speak
As one who fed on poetry.
Richelieu [*1839*]. *Act I, Sc. 1*

The mate for beauty
Should be a man, and not a money-chest.
Ibid. Sc. 2

Great men gain doubly when they make foes their friends.
Richelieu. Act I, Sc. 2

Beneath the rule of men entirely great,
The pen is mightier than the sword.[1]
Ibid. Act II, Sc. 2

In the lexicon of youth, which fate reserves
For a bright manhood, there is no such word
As "fail."
Ibid.

To what a reed
We bind our destinies, when man we love.[2]
The Duchess de la Vallière.
Act III, Sc. 3

What's affection, but the power we give another to torment us?
Darnley. Act II, Sc. 1

A good cigar is as great a comfort to a man as a good cry to a woman.
Ibid. Act III, Sc. 2

He who has little silver in his pouch must have the more silk on his tongue.
The Last of the Barons [*1843*].
Book I, Chap. 3

Out-babying Wordsworth and out-glittering Keats.[3]
The New Timon [*1846*]. *Part I*

Alone! — that worn-out word,
So idly spoken, and so coldly heard;
Yet all that poets sing and grief hath known
Of hopes laid waste, knells in that word
ALONE!
Ibid. Part II

That should be a warning to you never again to fall into the error of the would-be scholar — namely, quote second-hand.
My Novel [*1853*]. *Chap. 19*

The worst part of an eminent man's conversation is, nine times out of ten,

---

[1] See Burton, page 222b.
Eloquence a hundred times has turned the scale of war and peace at will. — EMERSON: *Progress of Culture* [1867]
[2] See Pascal, page 272b.
[3] Tennyson.

to be found in that part which he means to be clever.

Caxtonia. Differences Between the Urban and Rural Temperament

In science, read, by preference, the newest works; in literature, the oldest. The classic literature is always modern.

Ibid. Hints on Mental Culture

In science, address the few, in literature the many. In science, the few must dictate opinion to the many; in literature, the many, sooner or later, force their judgment on the few.

Ibid. Readers and Writers

BENJAMIN DISRAELI, EARL OF BEACONSFIELD
[1804-1881]

The microcosm of a public school.
Vivian Grey [1826]. Book I, Chap. II

I hate definitions.
Ibid. Book II, Chap. VI

Experience is the child of Thought, and Thought is the child of Action. We can not learn men from books.
Ibid. Book V, Chap I

Variety is the mother of Enjoyment.
Ibid. Chap. IV

There is moderation even in excess.
Ibid. Book VI, Chap. I

I repeat . . . that all power is a trust; that we are accountable for its exercise; that from the people and for the people all springs, and all must exist.[1]
Ibid. Chap. VII

Man is not the creature of circumstances. Circumstances are the creatures of men.[2]
Ibid.

The disappointment of manhood succeeds to the delusion of youth: let us hope that the heritage of old age is not despair.
Ibid. Book VIII, Chap. IV

A dark horse which had never been thought of, and which the careless St.

[1] See Webster, page 443b, Lincoln, page 541a, and Parker, page 560a.
[2] See Carlyle, page 473b.

James had never even observed in the list, rushed past the grand stand in sweeping triumph.
The Young Duke [1831]. Book I, Chap. V

Yes, I am a Jew, and when the ancestors of the right honourable gentleman were brutal savages in an unknown island, mine were priests in the temple of Solomon.[1]
Reply to a taunt by Daniel O'Connell [2]

What we anticipate seldom occurs; [3] what we least expected generally happens.
Henrietta Temple [1837]. Book II, Chap. IV

Nature has given us two ears but only one mouth.
Ibid. Book VI, Chap. XXIV

Though I sit down now, the time will come when you will hear me.[4]
Maiden Speech in the House of Commons [1837]

[1] In his *Reminiscences of Sixty Years in the National Metropolis* [1886], BEN PERLEY POORE quotes this reply of Senator Judah P. Benjamin [1811-1884] to a Senator of German extraction who taunted him with being a Jew: "The gentleman will please remember that when his half-civilized ancestors were hunting the wild boar in the forests of Silesia, mine were the Princes of the earth."

[2] Disraeli's name shows he is by descent a Jew. His father became a convert. He is the better for that in this world, and I hope he will be the better for it in the next. I have the happiness of being acquainted with some Jewish families in London, and among them more accomplished ladies, or more humane, cordial, high-minded, or better-educated gentlemen I have never met. It will not be supposed, therefore, that when I speak of Disraeli as the descendant of a Jew, that I mean to tarnish him on that account. They were once the chosen people of God. There were miscreants among them, however, also, and it must certainly have been from one of these that Disraeli descended. He possesses just the qualities of the impenitent thief who died upon the Cross, whose name, I verily believe, must have been Disraeli. — DANIEL O'CONNELL: *Speech,* at trades union meeting in Dublin [1835]

[3] See Emerson, page 507a.
[4] See William Lloyd Garrison, page 517a.

Free trade is not a principle, it is an expedient.[1]

On Import Duties [April 25, 1843]

The noble lord [2] is the Rupert of debate.

Speech [April, 1844]

Youth is a blunder; manhood a struggle; old age a regret.

Coningsby [1844]. Book III, Chap. I

Property has its duties as well as its rights.[3]

Sybil [1845]. Book II, Chap. XI

Little things affect little minds.

Ibid. Book III, Chap. II

We all of us live too much in a circle.[4]

Ibid. Chap. VII

Mr. Kremlin was distinguished for ignorance; for he had only one idea, and that was wrong.[5]

Ibid. Book IV, Chap. V

The right honorable gentleman [6] caught the Whigs bathing and walked away with their clothes.

Speech, House of Commons [February 28, 1845]

A conservative government is an organized hypocrisy.

Speech on Agricultural Interests [March 17, 1845]

He was fresh and full of faith that "something would turn up." [7]

Tancred [1847]. Book III, Chap. VI

Everything comes if a man will only wait.[8]

Ibid. Book IV, Chap. VIII

---

[1] It is a condition which confronts us, not a theory. — GROVER CLEVELAND: *Annual Message* [1887], referring to the tariff
[2] Lord Stanley.
[3] Property has its duties as well as its rights. — CAPTAIN THOMAS DRUMMOND (inventor of the Drummond l'ght): *Letter to the Landlords of Tipperary* [May 22, 1838]
[4] The life of man is a self-evolving circle. — EMERSON: *Essays, First Series* [1841], *Circles*
[5] See Johnson, page 340b.
[6] Sir Robert Peel.
[7] See Dickens, page 579a.
[8] See Emerson, page 501a.

A precedent embalms a principle.

Speech on the Expenditures of the Country [February 22, 1848]

Justice is truth in action.

Speech [February 11, 1851]

This shows how much easier it is to be critical than to be correct.

Speech [January 24, 1860]

Posterity is a most limited assembly. Those gentlemen who reach posterity are not much more numerous than the planets.

Speech [June 3, 1862]

The characteristic of the present age is craving credulity.

Speech at Oxford Diocesan Conference [November 25, 1864]

Is man an ape or an angel? [1] I, my lord, I am on the side of the angels. I repudiate with indignation and abhorrence those new fangled theories.

Ibid.

In the character of the victim [Lincoln], and even in the accessories of his last moments, there is something so homely and innocent that it takes the question, as it were, out of all the pomp of history and the ceremonial of diplomacy — it touches the heart of nations and appeals to the domestic sentiment of mankind.

Address, House of Commons [May 1, 1865]

Ignorance never settles a question.

Ibid. [May 14, 1866]

Individualities may form communities, but it is institutions alone that can create a nation.

Speech at Manchester [1866]

However gradual may be the growth of confidence, that of credit requires still more time to arrive at maturity.

Speech [November 9, 1867]

The secret of success is constancy to purpose.

Speech [June 24, 1870]

When a man fell into his anecdotage, it was a sign for him to retire.

Lothair [1870]. Chap. XXVIII

[1] See Charles Darwin, page 530b.

Every woman should marry — and no man.
Lothair. Chap. XXX

You know who the critics are? The men who have failed in literature and art.[1]
Ibid. Chap. XXXV

"My idea of an agreeable person," said Hugo Bohun, "is a person who agrees with me."
Ibid.

Increased means and increased leisure are the two civilizers of man.
Speech to the Conservatives of Manchester [April 3, 1872]

A university should be a place of light, of liberty, and of learning.
Speech, House of Commons [March 11, 1873]

The author who speaks about his own books is almost as bad as a mother who talks about her own children.
Speech [November 19, 1873]

The health of the people is really the foundation upon which all their happiness and all their powers as a State depend.
Speech [July 24, 1877]

A sophistical rhetorician [Gladstone], inebriated with the exuberance of his own verbosity, and gifted with an egotistical imagination that can at all times command an interminable and inconsistent series of arguments to malign an opponent and to glorify himself.
Speech at Riding School, London [July 27, 1878]

A series of congratulatory regrets.
Lord Hartington's Resolution on the Berlin Treaty [July 27, 1878]

The hare-brained chatter of irresponsible frivolity.
Speech, Guildhall, London [November 9, 1878]

His Christianity was muscular.
Endymion [1880]. Chap. XIV

The Athanasian Creed is the most splendid ecclesiastical lyric ever poured forth by the genius of man.
Ibid. Chap. LII

[1] See Coleridge, page 423b.

The world is a wheel, and it will all come round right.
Endymion. Chap. LXX

"As for that," said Waldershare, "sensible men are all of the same religion." "And pray, what is that?" inquired the prince. "Sensible men never tell."
Ibid. Chap. LXXXI

NATHANIEL HAWTHORNE
[1804–1864]

Sleeping or waking, we hear not the airy footsteps of the strange things that almost happen.
Twice-Told Tales [1837]. David Swan

The sky, now gloomy as an author's prospects.
Ibid. Sights from a Steeple

Our Creator would never have made such lovely days, and have given us the deep hearts to enjoy them, above and beyond all thought, unless we were meant to be immortal.
Mosses from an Old Manse [1846]. The Old Manse

That lack of energy that distinguishes the occupants of almshouses, and all other human beings who depend for subsistence on charity, on monopolized labor, or anything else, but their own independent exertions.
The Scarlet Letter [1850]. The Custom-House

Human nature will not flourish, any more than a potato, if it be planted and replanted, for too long a series of generations, in the same worn-out soil.
Ibid.

Neither the front nor the back entrance of the Custom-House opens on the road to Paradise.
Ibid.

It is a good lesson — though it may often be a hard one — for a man who has dreamed of literary fame . . . to step aside out of the narrow circle in which his claims are recognized, and to find how utterly devoid of significance, beyond that circle, is all that he achieves, and all he aims at.

The Scarlet Letter. The Custom-House

The black flower of civilized society, a prison.

Ibid. Chap. 1

On the breast of her gown, in red cloth, surrounded with an elaborate embroidery and fantastic flourishes of gold-thread, appeared the letter A.

Ibid. Chap. 2

It is to the credit of human nature, that, except where its selfishness is brought into play, it loves more readily than it hates.

Ibid. Chap. 13

Let men tremble to win the hand of woman, unless they win along with it the utmost passion of her heart.

Ibid. Chap. 15

No man, for any considerable period, can wear one face to himself, and another to the multitude, without finally getting bewildered as to which may be the true.

Ibid. Chap. 20

Life is made up of marble and mud.

The House of the Seven Gables [1851]. Chap. 2

Providence seldom vouchsafes to mortals any more than just that degree of encouragement which suffices to keep them at a reasonably full exertion of their powers.

Ibid. Chap. 3

A stale article, if you dip it in a good, warm, sunny smile, will go off better than a fresh one that you've scowled upon.

Ibid. Chap. 4

Life, within doors, has few pleasanter prospects than a neatly arranged and well-provisioned breakfast-table.

Ibid. Chap. 7

What other dungeon is so dark as one's own heart! What jailer so inexorable as one's self!

Ibid. Chap. 11

There is no greater bugbear than a strong-willed relative, in the circle of his own connections.

The House of the Seven Gables. Chap. 11

Once in every half-century, at longest, a family should be merged into the great, obscure mass of humanity, and forget all about its ancestors.

Ibid. Chap. 12

The world owes all its onward impulses to men ill at ease. The happy man inevitably confines himself within ancient limits.

Ibid. Chap. 20

Of all the events which constitute a person's biography, there is scarcely one . . . to which the world so easily reconciles itself as to his death.

Ibid. Chap. 21

A revolution, or anything that interrupts social order, may afford opportunities for the individual display of eminent virtues; but its effects are pernicious to general morality.

The Snow Image [1851]. Old News, Chap. 3

It is a token of healthy and gentle characteristics, when women of high thoughts and accomplishments love to sew; especially as they are never more at home with their own hearts than while so occupied.

The Marble Faun [1860]. Chap. 5

Every young sculptor seems to think that he must give the world some specimen of indecorous womanhood, and call it Eve, Venus, a Nymph, or any name that may apologize for a lack of decent clothing.

Ibid. Chap. 14

This greatest mortal consolation, which we derive from the transitoriness of all things — from the right of saying, in every conjuncture, — "This, too, will pass away." [1]

Ibid. Chap. 16

At no time are people so sedulously careful to keep their trifling appoint-

[1] See Lincoln, page 538b.

ments, attend to their ordinary occupations, and thus put a commonplace aspect on life, as when conscious of some secret that if suspected would make them look monstrous in the general eye.
The Marble Faun. Chap. 20

Nobody, I think, ought to read poetry, or look at pictures or statues, who cannot find a great deal more in them than the poet or artist has actually expressed.[1]
Ibid. Chap. 41

Caskets! — a vile modern phrase, which compels a person of sense and good taste to shrink more disgustfully than ever before from the idea of being buried at all.
Our Old Home [1863].
About Warwick

That odd state of mind wherein we fitfully and teasingly remember some previous scene or incident, of which the one now passing appears to be but the echo and reduplication.
Ibid. Near Oxford

Old soldiers, I know not why, seem to be more accostable than old sailors.
Ibid. Up the Thames

It is not the statesman, the warrior, or the monarch that survives, but the despised poet, whom they may have fed with their crumbs, and to whom they owe all that they now are or have — a name.
Ibid.

Mountains are earth's undecaying monuments.
Sketches from Memory [1868]. The Notch of the White Mountains

THOMAS KIBBLE HERVEY
[1804–1859]

Like ships, that sailed for sunny isles,
But never came to shore.
The Devil's Progress

[1] Every book is written with a constant secret reference to the few intelligent persons whom the writer believes to exist in the million. . . . The artist has always the masters in his eye. — EMERSON: *Progress of Culture* [1867]

SARAH FLOWER ADAMS
[1805–1848]

Though like the wanderer,
  The sun gone down,
Darkness be over me,
  My rest a stone;
Yet in my dreams I'd be
Nearer, my God, to Thee,
  Nearer to Thee.
Nearer, My God, to Thee. Stanza 2

He sendeth sun, he sendeth shower,
Alike they're needful to the flower;
And joys and tears alike are sent
To give the soul fit nourishment.
As comes to me or cloud or sun,
Father! thy will, not mine, be done.
He Sendeth Sun, He Sendeth Shower

Once have a priest for enemy, good bye
To peace.
Vivia Perpetua. Act III, Sc. 2

WILLIAM HARRISON AINSWORTH
[1805–1884]

She must be seen to be appreciated.
Old Saint Paul's [1841].
Book I, Chap. 3

ALEXIS DE TOCQUEVILLE
[1805–1859]

I know of no country, indeed, where the love of money has taken stronger hold on the affections of men and where a profounder contempt is expressed for the theory of the permanent equality of property.
Democracy in America.[1] Part I
[1835], Chap. 3

Within these limits the power vested in the American courts of justice of pronouncing a statute to be unconstitutional forms one of the most powerful barriers that have ever been devised against the tyranny of political assemblies.
Ibid. Chap. 6

I have never been more struck by the

[1] The Henry Reeve text, as revised by Francis Bowen, corrected and edited by Phillips Bradley [1945].

good sense and the practical judgment of the Americans than in the manner in which they elude the numberless difficulties resulting from their Federal Constitution.

Democracy in America. Part I,
Chap. 8

In this question, therefore, there is no medium between servitude and license; in order to enjoy the inestimable benefits that the liberty of the press ensures, it is necessary to submit to the inevitable evils that it creates.

Ibid. Chap. 9

An American cannot converse, but he can discuss, and his talk falls into a dissertation. He speaks to you as if he was addressing a meeting; and if he should chance to become warm in the discussion, he will say "Gentlemen" to the person with whom he is conversing.

Ibid. Chap. 14

I cannot believe that a republic could hope to exist at the present time if the influence of lawyers in public business did not increase in proportion to the power of the people.

Ibid. Chap. 16

They [the Americans] have all a lively faith in the perfectibility of man, they judge that the diffusion of knowledge must necessarily be advantageous, and the consequences of ignorance fatal; they all consider society as a body in a state of improvement, humanity as a changing scene, in which nothing is, or ought to be, permanent: and they admit that what appears to them today to be good, may be superseded by something better tomorrow.

Ibid. Chap. 18

America is a land of wonders, in which everything is in constant motion and every change seems an improvement. The idea of novelty is there indissolubly connected with the idea of amelioration. No natural boundary seems to be set to the efforts of man; and in his eyes what is not yet done is only what he has not yet attempted to do.

Ibid.

Democratic nations care but little for what has been, but they are haunted by visions of what will be; in this direction their unbounded imagination grows and dilates beyond all measure. . . . Democracy, which shuts the past against the poet, opens the future before him.

Democracy in America. Part II
[1840], First Book, Chap. 17

Thus not only does democracy make every man forget his ancestors, but it hides his descendants and separates his contemporaries from him; it throws him back forever upon himself alone and threatens in the end to confine him entirely within the solitude of his own heart.

Ibid. Second Book, Chap. 2

It is strange to see with what feverish ardor the Americans pursue their own welfare, and to watch the vague dread that constantly torments them lest they should not have chosen the shortest path which may lead to it.

Ibid. Chap. 13

If I were asked . . . to what the singular prosperity and growing strength of that people [the Americans] ought mainly to be attributed, I should reply: To the superiority of their women.

Ibid. Third Book, Chap. 12

The love of wealth is therefore to be traced, as either a principal or accessory motive, at the bottom of all that the Americans do; this gives to all their passions a sort of family likeness. . . . It may be said that it is the vehemence of their desires that makes the Americans so methodical; it perturbs their minds, but it disciplines their lives.

Ibid. Chap. 17

SAMUEL WILBERFORCE [1]
[1805–1873]

If I were a cassowary
  On the plains of Timbuctoo,

---

[1] Bishop of Oxford, and later of Winchester — nicknamed "Soapy Sam."

I would eat a missionary,
Coat and bands and hymn-book, too.[1]
Impromptu

WILLIAM LLOYD GARRISON
[1805–1879]

My country is the world; my countrymen are mankind.[2]
Prospectus of The Public Liberator
[1830]

I am in earnest. I will not equivocate; I will not excuse; I will not retreat a single inch; and I will be heard! [3]
Salutatory of The Liberator
[*January 1, 1831*]

I will be as harsh as truth and as uncompromising as justice.
The Liberator. Vol. I, No. 1
[1831]

The compact which exists between the North and the South is a covenant with death and an agreement with hell.[4]
Resolution adopted by the Anti-Slavery Society [*January 27, 1843*]

With reasonable men, I will reason; with humane men I will plead; but to tyrants I will give no quarter, nor waste arguments where they will certainly be lost.
W. P. AND F. J. T. GARRISON: *William Lloyd Garrison* [*1885–1889*]. *Vol. I, Page 188*

Since the creation of the world there has been no tyrant like Intemperance, and no slaves so cruelly treated as his.
Ibid. Page 268

We may be personally defeated, but our principles never.
Ibid. Page 402

Wherever there is a human being, I see God-given rights inherent in that being, whatever may be the sex or complexion.
Ibid. Vol. III, Page 390

[1] Variant: Skin and bones and hymn-book, too.
[2] See Plutarch, page 61b, and Paine, page 371a.
[3] See Disraeli, page 511b.
[4] We have made a covenant with death, and with hell are we at agreement. — *Isaiah, XXVIII. 15*

The success of any great moral enterprise does not depend upon numbers.
W. P. AND F. J. T. GARRISON: *William Lloyd Garrison. Vol. III, Page 473*

You can not possibly have a broader basis for any government than that which includes all the people, with all their rights in their hands, and with an equal power to maintain their rights.[1]
Ibid. Vol. IV, Page 224

WILLIAM PITT PALMER
[1805–1884]

I couldn't stand it, sir, at all,
But up and kissed her on the spot!
I know — boo-hoo — I ought to not,
But, somehow, from her looks — boo-hoo —
I thought she kind o' wished me to!
The Smack in School

COLONEL SIDNEY SHERMAN
[1805–1873]

Remember the Alamo!
Battle Cry, San Jacinto [*April 21, 1836*]

JOHN STUART MILL
[1806–1873]

The sole end for which mankind are warranted, individually or collectively, in interfering with the liberty of action of any of their number is self-protection.
Liberty [1859]. *Introduction*

If all mankind minus one, were of one opinion, and only one person were of the contrary opinion, mankind would be no more justified in silencing that one person, than he, if he had the power, would be justified in silencing mankind.
Ibid. Chap. 2

We can never be sure that the opinion we are endeavoring to stifle is a false opinion; and if we were sure, stifling it would be an evil still.
Ibid.

[1] See Webster, page 443b, Lincoln, page 541a, and Parker, page 560a.

To question all things; — never to turn away from any difficulty; to accept no doctrine either from ourselves or from other people without a rigid scrutiny by negative criticism; letting no fallacy, or incoherence, or confusion of thought, step by unperceived; above all, to insist upon having the meaning of a word clearly understood before using it, and the meaning of a proposition before assenting to it; — these are the lessons we learn from ancient dialecticians.

Inaugural Address as Rector,
University of St. Andrews
[February 1, 1867]

ELIZABETH BARRETT BROWNING
[1806–1861]

Of all the thoughts of God that are
Borne inward into souls afar,
Along the Psalmist's music deep,
Now tell me if that any is,
For gift or grace, surpassing this:
"He giveth his beloved — sleep." [1]
The Sleep [1838]. *Stanza 1*

Thou large-brained woman and large-hearted man.
To George Sand, A Desire [1844]

Or from Browning some "Pomegranate," which, if cut deep down the middle,
Shows a heart within blood-tinctured of a veined humanity.
Lady Geraldine's Courtship
[1844]. *Stanza 41*

Poets ever fail in reading their own verses to their worth.
Ibid. Stanza 42

There Shakespeare, on whose forehead climb
The crowns o' the world; O eyes sublime
With tears and laughters for all time!
A Vision of Poets [1844].
Line 298

[1] *Psalm CXXVII, 2*

Life treads on life, and heart on heart:
We press too close in church and mart
To keep a dream or grave apart.
A Vision of Poets. Conclusion,
Line 820

Knowledge by suffering entereth,
And life is perfected by death.
Ibid. Line 929

And I smiled to think God's greatness flowed around our incompleteness, —
Round our restlessness, His rest.
Rhyme of the Duchess May
[1844]. *Conclusion, Stanza 11*

Do ye hear the children weeping, O my brothers,
Ere the sorrow comes with years?
The Cry of the Children
[1844]. *Stanza 1*

The child's sob in the silence curses deeper
Than the strong man in his wrath.
Ibid. Stanza 13

I tell you hopeless grief is passionless.
Grief [1844]

Therefore to this dog will I,
Tenderly not scornfully,
Render praise and favor:
With my hand upon his head,
Is my benediction said
Therefore and for ever.
To Flush, My Dog [1844].
Stanza 14

And lips say "God be pitiful,"
Who ne'er said "God be praised."
The Cry of the Human [1844].
Stanza 1

But since he had
The genius to be loved, why let him have
The justice to be honoured in his grave.
Crowned and Buried [1844].
Stanza 27

"Yes," I answered you last night;
"No," this morning, sir, I say:
Colors seen by candle-light
Will not look the same by day.[1]
The Lady's "Yes" [1844].
Stanza 1

[1] To say why gals acts so or so,
Or don't, 'ould be presumin';

By thunders of white silence, over-
thrown.
> *Hiram Powers's Greek Slave*
> [*1850*]

Unless you can muse in a crowd all day
On the absent face that fixed you;
Unless you can love, as the angels may,
With the breadth of heaven betwixt
you;
Unless you can dream that his faith is
fast,
Through behoving and unbehoving;
Unless you can die when the dream is
past —
Oh, never call it loving!
> *A Woman's Shortcomings*
> [*1850*]. *Stanza 5*

"Guess now who holds thee?" —
"Death," I said. But there
The silver answer rang, — "Not Death,
but Love."
> *Sonnets from the Portuguese*
> [*1850*]. *I*

Go from me. Yet I feel that I shall stand
Henceforward in thy shadow.
> *Ibid. VI*

> The widest land
Doom takes to part us, leaves thy hand
in mine
With pulses that beat double. What I do
And what I dream include thee, as the
wine
Must taste of its own grapes.
> *Ibid.*

If thou must love me, let it be for
nought
Except for love's sake only.
> *Ibid. XIV*

Mebby to mean *yes* an' say *no*
Comes nateral to women.
> JAMES RUSSELL LOWELL: *The Biglow*
> *Papers, Series II* [1867], *St. 18*

You gave me the key to your heart, my
love;
Then why do you make me knock?
"Oh, that was yesterday; Saints above,
Last night I changed the lock!"
> JOHN BOYLE O'REILLY [1844–
> 1890]: *Constancy*

And if I loved you Wednesday,
Well, what is that to you?
I do not love you Thursday —
So much is true.
> EDNA ST. VINCENT MILLAY [1892–
> 1950]: *Thursday*

When our two souls stand up erect and
strong,
Face to face, silent, drawing nigh and
nigher.
> *Sonnets from the Portuguese. XXII*

To drop some golden orb of perfect song
Into our deep, dear silence.
> *Ibid.*

God only, who made us rich, can make
us poor.
> *Ibid. XXIV*

How do I love thee? Let me count the
ways.
> *Ibid. XLIII*

I shall but love thee better after death.
> *Ibid.*

> Women know
The way to rear up children (to be
just),
They know a simple, merry, tender
knack
Of tying sashes, fitting baby-shoes,
And stringing pretty words that make
no sense.
> *Aurora Leigh* [1] [*1857*]. *Book I,*
> *Line 47*

Life, struck sharp on death,
Makes awful lightning.
> *Ibid. Line 210*

> The beautiful seems right
By force of Beauty, and the feeble
wrong
Because of weakness.
> *Ibid. Line 753*

As sings the lark when sucked up out
of sight
In vortices of glory and blue air.
> *Ibid. Line 1055*

> Men do not think
Of sons and daughters, when they fall
in love.
> *Ibid. Book II, Line 608*

I should not dare to call my soul my
own.
> *Ibid. Line 786*

God answers sharp and sudden on some
prayers,
And thrusts the thing we have prayed
for in our face,
A gauntlet with a gift in 't.
> *Ibid. Line 952*

[1] See Edward Fitzgerald, page 533b.

Every wish
Is like a prayer, with God.[1]
Aurora Leigh. Book II, Line 954

Is the blue in eyes
As awful as in stockings?
Ibid. Book III, Line 379

How many desolate creatures on the
earth
Have learnt the simple dues of fellow-
ship
And social comfort, in a hospital.
Ibid. Line 1122

A little sunburnt by the glare of life.
Ibid. Book IV, Line 1140

Let no one till his death
Be called unhappy. Measure not the
work
Until the day's out and the labor done.
Ibid. Book V, Line 76

Men get opinions as boys learn to spell,
By reiteration chiefly.
Ibid. Book VI, Line 6

Since when was genius found respectable?
Ibid. Line 275

Earth's crammed with heaven,
And every common bush afire with
God;
But only he who sees takes off his
shoes —
The rest sit round it and pluck black-
berries.
Ibid. Book VII, Line 820

We walked too straight for fortune's
end,
We loved too true to keep a friend;
At last we're tired, my heart and I.
My Heart and I [1862]. Stanza 2

Grief may be joy misunderstood;
Only the Good discerns the good.
De Profundis [1862]. Stanza 21

CHARLES FENNO HOFFMAN
[1806–1884]

We were not many — we who stood
Before the iron sleet that day;
Yet many a gallant spirit would

[1] See James Montgomery, page 413a.

Give half his years, if he but could
Have been with us at Monterey.
Monterey. Stanza 1

NATHANIEL PARKER WILLIS
[1806–1867]

The shadows lay along Broadway,
'Twas near the twilight tide.
Unseen Spirits. Stanza 1

The sin forgiven by Christ in Heaven
By man is cursed alway.
Ibid. Stanza 5

CHARLES FRANCIS ADAMS
[1807–1886]

It would be superfluous in me to point
out to your Lordship that this is war.
*Dispatch to Earl Russell
[September 5, 1863]*

CHARLES JEFFERYS
[1807–1865]

Oh! if I were Queen of France, or still
better, Pope of Rome,
I'd have no fighting men abroad, no
weeping maids at home;
All should be at peace; or, if kings must
show their might,
Why, let them who make the quarrel be
the only men to fight.
Jeannette and Jeannot. Stanza 4

Were only kings themselves to fight,
there'd be an end of war.
Jeannot's Answer. Stanza 4

HENRY WADSWORTH LONGFELLOW
[1807–1882]

Music is the universal language of
mankind, — poetry their universal
pastime and delight.
Outre-Mer [1833–1834]

I heard the trailing garments of the
Night [1]
Sweep through her marble halls.
Hymn to Night [1839]. Stanza 1

Tell me not, in mournful numbers,
Life is but an empty dream!

[1] See Sarah Whitman, page 509b.

For the soul is dead that slumbers,
And things are not what they seem.[1]
A Psalm of Life [*1839*]. *Stanza 1*
Life is real! Life is earnest!
And the grave is not its goal;
Dust thou art, to dust returnest,
Was not spoken of the soul.
Ibid. Stanza 2
Art is long, and Time is fleeting,[2]
And our hearts, though stout and
brave,
Still, like muffled drums, are beating
Funeral marches to the grave.[3]
Ibid. Stanza 4
Trust no Future, howe'er pleasant!
Let the dead Past bury its dead!
Act, act in the living present!
Heart within, and God o'erhead!
Ibid. Stanza 6
Lives of great men all remind us
We can make our lives sublime,
And, departing, leave behind us
Footprints on the sands of time.
Ibid. Stanza 7
Let us, then, be up and doing,
With a heart for any fate; [4]
Still achieving, still pursuing,
Learn to labour and to wait.
Ibid. Stanza 9
There is a Reaper whose name is
Death,
And, with his sickle keen,
He reaps the bearded grain at a breath,
And the flowers that grow between.
The Reaper and the Flowers
[*1839*]. *Stanza 1*
The hooded clouds, like friars,
Tell their beads in drops of rain.
Midnight Mass for the Dying
Year [*1839*]. *Stanza 4*
Who ne'er his bread in sorrow ate,
Who ne'er the mournful midnight hours
Weeping upon his bed has sate,
He knows you not, ye Heavenly
Powers.[5]
Hyperion [*1839*]. *Book I, Motto*

---

[1] See Phaedrus, page 48b.
[2] See Hippocrates, page 22a.
[3] Our lives are but our marches to the
grave. — BEAUMONT AND FLETCHER: *The Hu-*
morous Lieutenant [1619], Act III, Sc. 5
[4] See Byron, page 456b.
[5] Wer nie sein Brod mit Thränen ass,

Look not mournfully into the Past.
It comes not back again. Wisely im-
prove the Present. It is thine. Go forth
to meet the shadowy Future, without
fear, and with a manly heart.[1]
Hyperion. Book IV, Chap. 8
It was the schooner Hesperus,
That sailed the wintry sea;
And the skipper had taken his little
daughter,
To bear him company.
The Wreck of the Hesperus
[*1842*]. *Stanza 1*
Blue were her eyes as the fairy-flax.
Ibid. Stanza 2
Christ save us all from a death like this,
On the reef of Norman's Woe!
Ibid. Stanza 22
Under the spreading chestnut-tree
The village smithy stands;
The smith a mighty man is he
With large and sinewy hands.
The Village Blacksmith [*1842*].
Stanza 1
His brow is wet with honest sweat,
He earns whate'er he can,
And looks the whole world in the face,
For he owes not any man.
Ibid. Stanza 2
Something attempted, something done,
Has earned a night's repose.
Ibid. Stanza 7
No one is so accursed by fate,
No one so utterly desolate,
But some heart, though unknown,
Responds unto his own.
Endymion [*1842*]. *Stanza 8*

Wer nicht die kummervollen Nächte
Auf seinem Bette weinend sass,
Der kennt euch nicht, ihr himmlischen
Mächte.
GOETHE: *Wilhelm Meister's Ap-*
prenticeship [1786–1830], *Book*
II, Chap. 13
[1] Blicke nicht trauernd in die Vergangen-
heit,
Sie kommt nicht wieder, nutze weise die
Gegenwart,
Sie ist dein, der düsteren Zukunft geh
ohne
Furcht mit männliche Sinne entgegen.
Inscription on Chapel of St. Gilgen,
near Salzburg

Into each life some rain must fall,
Some days must be dark and dreary.
> *The Rainy Day* [*1842*]. *Stanza 3*

I like that ancient Saxon phrase, which calls
The burial-ground God's-Acre!
> *God's-Acre* [*1842*]. *Stanza 1*

Standing with reluctant feet,
Where the brook and river meet,
Womanhood and childhood fleet!
> *Maidenhood* [*1842*]. *Stanza 3*

A banner with the strange device,
Excelsior!
> *Excelsior* [*1842*]. *Stanza 1*

Stars of the summer night!
Far in yon azure deeps,
Hide, hide your golden light!
She sleeps.
> *The Spanish Student* [*1842*].
> *Act I, Sc. 3, Serenade*

She floats upon the river of his thoughts.
> *Ibid. Act II, Sc. 3*

Were half the power, that fills the world with terror,
Were half the wealth, bestowed on camps and courts,
Given to redeem the human mind from error,
There were no need of arsenals or forts.
> *The Arsenal at Springfield*
> [*1845*]. *Stanza 9*

The day is done, and the darkness
Falls from the wings of Night,
As a feather is wafted downward
From an eagle in his flight.
> *The Day Is Done* [*1845*].
> *Stanza 1*

A feeling of sadness and longing
That is not akin to pain,
And resembles sorrow only
As the mist resembles the rain.
> *Ibid. Stanza 3*

Some simple and heartfelt lay.
> *Ibid. Stanza 4*

The bards sublime,
Whose distant footsteps echo
Through the corridors of Time.
> *Ibid. Stanza 5*

And the night shall be filled with music,
And the cares, that infest the day,

Shall fold their tents, like the Arabs,
And as silently steal away.
> *The Day Is Done. Stanza 11*

The horologe of Eternity
Sayeth this incessantly, —
"Forever — never!
Never — forever!"
> *The Old Clock on the Stairs*
> [*1845*]. *Stanza 9*

I shot an arrow into the air,
It fell to earth, I knew not where.
> *The Arrow and the Song*
> [*1845*]. *Stanza 1*

Though the mills of God grind slowly,
yet they grind exceeding small; [1]
Though with patience He stands waiting, with exactness grinds He all.
> *Retribution*

This is the forest primeval. The murmuring pines and the hemlocks.
> *Evangeline* [*1847*]. *Prelude*

Alike were they free from
Fear, that reigns with the tyrant, and envy, the vice of republics.
> *Ibid. Part I, 1*

When she had passed, it seemed like the ceasing of exquisite music.
> *Ibid.*

Silently one by one, in the infinite meadows of heaven
Blossomed the lovely stars, the forget-me-nots of the angels.
> *Ibid. 3*

Talk not of wasted affection! affection never was wasted;
If it enrich not the heart of another, its waters, returning
Back to their springs, like the rain, shall fill them full of refreshment:
That which the fountain sends forth returns again to the fountain.
> *Ibid. Part II, 1*

Give what you have. To some one, it may be better than you dare to think.
> *Kavanagh* [*1849*]

Sail on, O Ship of State!
Sail on, O Union, strong and great!
Humanity with all its fears,
With all the hopes of future years,
Is hanging breathless on thy fate!
> *The Building of the Ship* [*1849*]

[1] See George Herbert, page 234b.

Our hearts, our hopes, are all with thee,
Our hearts, our hopes, our prayers, our
tears,
Our faith triumphant o'er our fears,
Are all with thee, — are all with thee!
The Building of the Ship
There is no flock, however watched and
tended,
But one dead lamb is there!
There is no fireside, howsoe'er de-
fended,
But has one vacant chair!
Resignation [*1849*]. *Stanza 1*
There is no Death! What seems so is
transition;
This life of mortal breath
Is but a suburb of the life elysian,
Whose portal we call Death.
Ibid. Stanza 5
Nothing useless is, or low;
Each thing in its place is best;
And what seems but idle show
Strengthens and supports the rest.
The Builders [*1849*]. *Stanza 2*
God sent his Singers upon earth
With songs of sadness and of mirth.
The Singers [*1849*]. *Stanza 1*
But the great Master said, "I see
No best in kind, but in degree;
I gave a various gift to each,
To charm, to strengthen, and to teach."
Ibid. Stanza 6
All your strength is in your union.
All your danger is in discord;
Therefore be at peace henceforward,
And as brothers live together.
The Song of Hiawatha
[*1855*]. *Part I*
By the shore of Gitche Gumee,
By the shining Big-Sea-Water,
Stood the wigwam of Nokomis,
Daughter of the Moon, Nokomis.
Ibid. Part III
From the waterfall he named her,
Minnehaha, Laughing Water.
Ibid. Part IV
As unto the bow the cord is,
So unto the man is woman,
Though she bends him, she obeys him,
Though she draws him, yet she follows,
Useless each without the other!
Ibid. Part X

If we could read the secret history
of our enemies, we should find in each
man's life sorrow and suffering enough
to disarm all hostility.
Driftwood [*1857*]
If I am not worth the wooing, I
surely am not worth the winning.
The Courtship of Miles Standish
[*1858*]. *Part III*
"Why don't you speak for yourself,
John?"
Ibid.
God had sifted three kingdoms to find
the wheat for this planting.
Ibid. Part IV
Saint Augustine! well hast thou said,
That of our vices we can frame
A ladder, if we will but tread
Beneath our feet each deed of shame.[1]
The Ladder of Saint Augustine
[*1858*]. *Stanza 1*
The heights by great men reached and
kept
Were not attained by sudden flight,
But they, while their companions slept,
Were toiling upward in the night.
Ibid. Stanza 10
All houses wherein men have lived and
died
Are haunted houses.
Haunted Houses [*1858*]. *Stanza 1*
The long mysterious Exodus of death.
The Jewish Cemetery at Newport
[*1858*]. *Stanza 1*
Pride and humiliation hand in hand
Walked with them through the world
where'er they went;
Trampled and beaten were they as the
sand,
And yet unshaken as the continent.
Ibid. Stanza 12
A boy's will is the wind's will,
And the thoughts of youth are long,
long thoughts.
My Lost Youth [*1858*]. *Stanza 1*
Spanish sailors with bearded lips,
And the beauty and mystery of the
ships,
And the magic of the sea.
Ibid. Stanza 3

[1] See Tennyson, page 551b.

A Lady with a Lamp [1] shall stand
In the great history of the land,
A noble type of good,
Heroic womanhood.
>*Santa Filomena* [*1858*]. *Stanza 10*

Ye are better than all the ballads
That ever were sung or said;
For ye are living poems,
And all the rest are dead.
>*Children* [*1858*]. *Stanza 9*

Between the dark and the daylight,
When the night is beginning to lower,
Comes a pause in the day's occupations,
That is known as the Children's
Hour.
>*The Children's Hour* [*1860*].
>*Stanza 1*

I hear in the chamber above me
The patter of little feet.
>*Ibid. Stanza 2*

Grave Alice, and laughing Allegra,
And Edith with golden hair.
>*Ibid. Stanza 3*

Listen, my children, and you shall hear,
Of the midnight ride of Paul Revere,
On the eighteenth of April, in Seventy-
five;
Hardly a man is now alive
Who remembers that famous day and
year.
>*Tales of a Wayside Inn* [*1863–*
>*1874*]. *Paul Revere's Ride,*
>*Stanza 1*

One if by land, and two if by sea;
And I on the opposite shore will be,
Ready to ride and spread the alarm
Through every Middlesex village and
farm.
>*Ibid. Stanza 2*

The fate of a nation was riding that
night.
>*Ibid. Stanza 8*

A voice in the darkness, a knock at the
door,
And a word that shall echo forevermore!
>*Ibid. Stanza 14*

A town that boasts inhabitants like me
Can have no lack of good society.
>*Ibid. The Birds of Killingworth,*
>*Stanza 6*

[1] Florence Nightingale [1820–1910].

His form was ponderous, and his step
was slow;
There never was so wise a man before;
He seemed the incarnate "Well, I told
you so!"
>*Tales of a Wayside Inn. The Birds*
>*of Killingworth, Stanza 9*

How can I tell the signals and the signs
By which one heart another heart di-
vines?
How can I tell the many thousand ways
By which it keeps the secret it betrays?
>*Ibid. Emma and Eginhard, Stanza 8*

Ships that pass in the night, and speak
each other in passing,
Only a signal shown and a distant voice
in the darkness;
So on the ocean of life we pass and
speak one another,[1]
Only a look and a voice; then darkness
again and a silence.
>*Ibid. Elizabeth, IV*

Time has laid his hand
Upon my heart, gently, not smiting it,
But as a harper lays his open palm
Upon his harp to deaden its vibrations.
>*The Golden Legend* [*1872*].
>*IV, The Cloisters*

The grave itself is but a covered bridge
Leading from light to light, through a
brief darkness.[2]
>*Ibid. V, A Covered Bridge at*
>*Lucerne*

Don't cross the bridge till you come
to it,
Is a proverb old, and of excellent wit.
>*Ibid. VI, The School of Salerno*

[1] And soon, too soon, we part with pain,
To sail o'er silent seas again.
THOMAS MOORE [1779–1852]: *Meeting of the Ships*
Two lives that once part are as ships that divide. — EDWARD BULWER LYTTON [1805–1873]: *A Lament*
As vessels starting from ports thousands of miles apart pass close to each other in the naked breadths of the ocean, nay, sometimes even touch in the dark. — HOLMES: *Professor at the Breakfast Table* [1860]
[2] Death seems but a covered way
Which opens into light.
WHITTIER [1807–1892]: *My Psalm, St. 14*

"O Caesar, we who are about to die
Salute you!" was the gladiators' cry
In the arena, standing face to face
With death and with the Roman popu-
    lace.
            Morituri Salutamus [*1875*].
                                Stanza 1

Let him not boast who puts his armor on
As he who puts it off, the battle done.
                        Ibid. Stanza 9

Better like Hector in the field to die,
Than like a perfumed Paris turn and
    fly.
                        Ibid. Stanza 10

Ye, against whose familiar names not
    yet
The fatal asterisk of death is set.
                        Ibid. Stanza 11

The love of learning, the sequestered
    nooks,
And all the sweet serenity of books.
                        Ibid. Stanza 21

        Ah, nothing is too late,
Till the tired heart shall cease to palpi-
    tate.
Cato learned Greek at eighty; Sopho-
    cles
Wrote his grand Oedipus, and Simoni-
    des
Bore off the prize of verse from his
    compeers,
When each had numbered more than
    fourscore years.
                        Ibid. Stanza 22

For age is opportunity no less
Than youth itself, though in another
    dress,
And as the evening twilight fades away
The sky is filled with stars, invisible
    by day.
                        Ibid. Stanza 24

So when a great man dies,
For years beyond our ken,
The light he leaves behind him lies
Upon the paths of men.
            From Collections [*1875–1882*].
                Charles Sumner, Stanza 9

Sweet the memory is to me
Of a land beyond the sea,
Where the waves and mountains meet,

Where, amid her mulberry-trees
Sits Amalfi in the heat.
            From Collections. Amalfi, Stanza 1

The birds, God's poor who cannot wait.
            Ibid. The Sermon of St. Francis,
                                Stanza 3

She knew the life-long martyrdom,
    The weariness, the endless pain
Of waiting for some one to come
    Who nevermore would come again.
            Ibid. Vittoria Colonna, Stanza 6

Stay, stay at home, my heart, and rest;
Home-keeping hearts are happiest.
                Ibid. Song, Stanza 1

So Nature deals with us, and takes
    away
Our playthings one by one, and by the
    hand
Leads us to rest.
                        Ibid. Nature

Not in the clamor of the crowded street,
Not in the shouts and plaudits of the
    throng,
But in ourselves, are triumph and de-
    feat.
                        Ibid. The Poets

Nothing that is can pause or stay;
The moon will wax, the moon will wane,
The mist and cloud will turn to rain,
The rain to mist and cloud again,
    Tomorrow be today.
                        Kéramos [*1878*]

Turn, turn, my wheel! 'Tis nature's
    plan
The child should grow into the man.
                                Ibid.

The willow pattern, that we knew
In childhood, with its bridge of blue.
                                Ibid.

Three Silences there are: the first of
    speech,
The second of desire, the third of
    thought;
This is the lore a Spanish monk, dis-
    traught
With dreams and visions, was the first
    to teach.
            The Three Silences of Molinos [1]

[1] Miguel Molinos [1640–1696], Spanish
mystic, one of the early Quietists.

In the long, sleepless watches of the
night.
The Cross of Snow [1879]
The holiest of all holidays are those
Kept by ourselves in silence and apart;
The secret anniversaries of the heart.
Holidays

Your silent tents of green [1]
  We deck with fragrant flowers;
Yours has the suffering been,
  The memory shall be ours.
Decoration Day. Stanza 6

Great is the art of beginning, but greater
  the art is of ending;
Many a poem is marred by a superfluous verse.
Elegiac Verse. Stanza 14

Out of the shadows of night
The world rolls into light;
It is daybreak everywhere.
The Bells of San Blas.[2] Stanza 11

There was a little girl
  Who had a little curl
Right in the middle of her forehead;
  And when she was good
  She was very, very good,
But when she was bad she was horrid.
There Was a Little Girl [3]

ROBERT MONTGOMERY
[1807–1855]

The soul aspiring pants its source to
  mount,
As streams meander level with their
  fount.[4]
The Omnipresence of the Deity
[1828]. Part I

---

1   The low green tent
  Whose curtain never outward swings.
      WHITTIER: *Snow-Bound* [1866]
  [2] The last poem written by Longfellow,
dated March 15, 1882. He died March 24.
  [3] BLANCHE ROOSEVELT TUCKER, in *The
Home Life of Henry W. Longfellow* [1882],
states that these lines were written by the poet
for his children on a day when Edith did not
want to have her hair curled.
  [4] We take this to be, on the whole, the
worst similitude in the world. In the first
place, no stream meanders or can possibly
meander level with the fount. In the next
place, if streams did meander level with their
founts, no two motions can be less like each
other than that of meandering level and that

RICHARD CHENEVIX
TRENCH
[1807–1886]

True servant's title he may wear,
  He only who has not
For his lord's gifts, how rich soe'er,
  His lord himself forgot.
The Spilt Pearls. Stanza 8

Lord, what a change within us one
  short hour
Spent in Thy presence will prevail to
  make!
Prayer

We kneel, how weak! we rise, how full
  of power!
Ibid.

Make channels for the stream of love
Where they may broadly run,
And love has overflowing streams
To fill them every one.
The Law of Love

JOHN GREENLEAF
WHITTIER
[1807–1892]

The Present, the Present is all thou hast
  For thy sure possessing;
Like the patriarch's angel hold it fast
  Till it gives its blessing.[1]
My Soul and I. Stanza 34

The Night is mother of the Day,
  The Winter of the Spring,
And ever upon old Decay
  The greenest mosses cling.
A Dream of Summer. Stanza 4

Art's perfect forms no moral need,
  And beauty is its own excuse;[2]
But for the dull and flowerless weed
Some healing virtue still must plead.
Songs of Labor [1850].
Dedication, Stanza 5

Heap high the farmer's wintry hoard!
  Heap high the golden corn!

---

of mounting upwards. — MACAULAY: *Review
of Montgomery's Poems* [1830]
  These lines were omitted in the subsequent
edition of the poem.
  [1] See Cotton, page 330a.
  [2] In a footnote, Whittier acknowledges his
indebtedness for this line to EMERSON'S *The
Rhodora.* See Emerson, page 503b.

No richer gift has Autumn poured
  From out her lavish horn!
The Corn-Song. Stanza 1

What calls back the past, like the rich
  pumpkin pie?
The Pumpkin. Stanza 3

The tissue of the Life to be
  We weave with colors all our own,
And in the field of Destiny
  We reap as we have sown.
Raphael. Stanza 16

So fallen! so lost! the light withdrawn
  Which once he wore!
The glory from his gray hairs gone
  Forevermore!
Ichabod [1] [*1850*]. *Stanza 1*

From those great eyes
  The soul has fled:
When faith is lost, when honor dies,
  The man is dead!
Ibid. Stanza 8

Yet sometimes glimpses on my sight,
Through present wrong the eternal
  right;
And, step by step, since time began,
I see the steady gain of man.
The Chapel of the Hermits
[*1853*]. *Stanza 11*

Search thine own heart. What paineth
  thee
In others in thyself may be.
Ibid. Stanza 85

Blessings on thee, little man,
Barefoot boy, with cheek of tan!
The Barefoot Boy [*1856*].
Stanza 1

Health that mocks the doctor's rules,
Knowledge never learned of schools.
Ibid. Stanza 2

The age is dull and mean. Men creep,
Not walk.
Lines Inscribed to Friends under
Arrest for Treason Against the
Slave Power [*1856*]. *Stanza 1*

God's ways seem dark, but, soon or
  late,
They touch the shining hills of day.
Lines Inscribed to Friends under
Arrest for Treason Against the
Slave Power. Stanza 5

Nature speaks in symbols and in signs.
To Charles Sumner

Tradition wears a snowy beard, romance is always young.
Mary Garvin. Stanza 4

Better heresy of doctrine, than heresy
  of heart.
Ibid. Stanza 22

For of all sad words of tongue or pen,
The saddest are these: "It might have
  been!"
Maud Muller [*1856*]. *Stanza 53*

Old Floyd Ireson, for his hard heart,
Tarred and feathered and carried in a
  cart
  By the women of Marblehead.
Skipper Ireson's Ride
[*1860*]. *Stanza 1*

Round the silver domes of Lucknow,
  Moslem mosque and Pagan shrine,
Breathed the air to Britons dearest,
  The air of Auld Lang Syne.[1]
The Pipes at Lucknow. Stanza 9

The windows of my soul I throw
Wide open to the sun.
My Psalm. Stanza 2

No longer forward nor behind
  I look in hope or fear;
But, grateful, take the good I find,
  The best of now and here.
Ibid. Stanza 3

Perish with him the folly that seeks
  through evil good.
Brown of Ossawatomie. Stanza 6

"Shoot, if you must, this old gray head,
But spare your country's flag," she said.
Barbara Frietchie [*1864*].
Stanza 18

A shade of sadness, a blush of shame,
Over the face of the leader came.
Ibid. Stanza 19

---

[1] This poem was the outcome of the surprise and grief and forecast of evil consequences which I felt on reading the seventh
of March speech of Daniel Webster in support
of the "compromise," and the Fugitive Slave
Law. — WHITTIER'S *Note*

[1] It was the pipes of the Highlanders,
And now they played "Auld Lang Syne."
ROBERT TRAILL SPENCE LOWELL
[1816-1891]: *The Relief of Lucknow, September 25, 1857*

"Who touches a hair of yon gray head
Dies like a dog! March on!" he said.
Barbara Frietchie. Stanza 21
Shut in from all the world without,
We sat the clean-winged hearth about.
Snow-Bound [*1866*]
Melt not in an acid sect
The Christian pearl of charity.
Ibid.
Angel of the backward look.
Ibid.
Life is ever lord of Death
And Love can never lose its own.
Ibid.
To eat the lotus of the Nile
And drink the poppies of Cathay.
The Tent on the Beach
[*1867*]. *Stanza 4*
And so beside the Silent Sea
I wait the muffled oar.
The Eternal Goodness
[*1867*]. *Stanza 19*
I know not where His islands lift
Their fronded palms in air;
I only know I cannot drift
Beyond His love and care.
Ibid. Stanza 20
Flowers spring to blossom where she
walks
The careful ways of duty;
Our hard, stiff lines of life with her
Are flowing curves of beauty.[1]
Among the Hills [*1869*].
Stanza 52
If woman lost us Eden, such
As she alone restore it.
Ibid. Stanza 60
Sweeter than any sung
My songs that found no tongue;
Nobler than any fact
My wish that failed of act.
My Triumph. Stanza 9
Others shall sing the song,
Others shall right the wrong, —
Finish what I begin,
And all I fail of win.
Ibid. Stanza 10

[1] Straight is the line of Duty,
Curved is the line of Beauty,
Follow the straight line, thou shalt see
The curved line ever follow thee.
WILLIAM MACCALL [1812–1888]: *Duty*

Dear Lord and Father of mankind,
Forgive our foolish ways!
Reclothe us in our rightful mind,
In purer lives Thy service find,
In deeper reverence, praise.
The Brewing of Soma [*1872*]
God is and all is well.[1]
My Birthday. Stanza 2
He brings cool dew in his little bill,
And lets it fall on the souls of sin:
You can see the mark on his red breast
still
Of fires that scorch as he drops it in.[2]
The Robin. Stanza 4

SALMON PORTLAND CHASE
[1808–1873]

The Constitution, in all its provisions, looks to an indestructible Union composed of indestructible States.
Decision in Texas v. White,
7 Wallace 725 [*1868*]

The only way to resumption is to resume.
Letter to Horace Greeley
[*March 17, 1866*]

[1] See Browning, page 567a.
[2] Far, far away, is a land of woe and darkness, spirits of evil and fire. Day after day a little bird flies there, bearing in his bill a drop of water to quench the flame. So near the burning stream does he fly that his feathers are scorched by it, and hence he is named "Bron-rhuddyn" — breast-burned. — *Carmarthenshire Legend of the Robin*
Sweet Robin, I have heard them say
That thou wert there upon the day
That Christ was crowned in cruel scorn,
And bore away one bleeding thorn;
That so the blush upon thy breast
In shameful sorrow was imprest,
And thence thy genial sympathy
With our redeemed humanity.
WILLIAM CROSWELL DOANE [1832–
1913]: *Robin Redbreast*
When Christ was taken from the rood,
One thorn upon the ground,
Still moistened with the Precious Blood,
An early robin found,
And wove it crosswise in his nest,
Where, lo, it reddened all his breast!
JOHN BANISTER TABB [1845–1909]:
Robin Redbreast

GAGE—SMITH

FRANCES DANA GAGE
[1808–1884]

The home we first knew on this beautiful earth,
The friends of our childhood, the place of our birth,
In the heart's inner chamber sung always will be,
As the shell ever sings of its home in the sea! [1]

Home

MAURICE DE MACMAHON
[1808–1893]

Here I am, and here I stay.[2]

At Sevastopol [September, 1855]

ANDREW JOHNSON
[1808–1875]

We are swinging round the circle.

On the Presidential Reconstruction Tour [August, 1866]

THOMAS MILLER
[1808–1874]

What though upon his hoary head
Have fallen many a winter's snow?
His wreath is still as green and red
As 'twas a thousand years ago.
For what has he to do with care!
His wassail-bowl and old arm-chair
Are ever standing ready there,
For Christmas comes but once a year.

Christmas Comes but Once a Year

[1] As a sea-shell of the sea
Ever shall I sing of thee.
GEORGE MEREDITH [1828–1909]:
Love Within the Lover's Breast
Gather a shell from the strown beach
And listen at its lips: they sigh
The same desire and mystery,
The echo of the whole sea's speech.
DANTE GABRIEL ROSSETTI [1828–1882]: *The Sea Limits, St. 4*
See Wordsworth, page 411a.

[2] J'y suis, j'y reste. Reply to the Commander-in-Chief, from the trenches before Malakoff, in the siege of Sevastopol, when warned to beware of an explosion which might follow the retreat of the Russians.

CAROLINE ELIZABETH SHERIDAN NORTON, LADY MAXWELL
[1808–1877]

Love not! love not! ye hapless sons of clay;
Hope's gayest wreaths are made of earthly flowers —
Things that are made to fade and fall away,
Ere they have blossomed for a few short hours.

Love Not

A soldier of the Legion lay dying in Algiers;
There was lack of woman's nursing, there was dearth of woman's tears.

Bingen on the Rhine. Stanza 1

GEORGE WASHINGTON PATTEN
[1808–1882]

Keep honor, like your sabre, bright,
Shame coward fear — and then,
If we must perish in the fight,
Oh! let us die like men.

Oh! Let Us Die Like Men. Stanza 4

Joys that we've tasted
May sometimes return,
But the torch when once wasted,
Ah! how can it burn?

Joys That We've Tasted. Stanza 1

SAMUEL FRANCIS SMITH
[1808–1895]

My country, 'tis of thee,
Sweet land of liberty,
Of thee I sing:
Land where my fathers died,
Land of the pilgrims' pride,
From every mountain-side
Let freedom ring.

America [1831]

Our fathers' God, to thee,
Author of liberty,
To thee I sing;
Long may our land be bright
With freedom's holy light;

529

Protect us by thy might,
Great God, our King!

America

CHARLES ROBERT DARWIN
[1809–1882]

I have called this principle, by which each slight variation, if useful, is preserved, by the term Natural Selection.
The Origin of Species
[1859]. Chap. 3

The expression often used by Mr. Herbert Spencer, of the Survival of the Fittest, is more accurate, and is sometimes equally convenient.[1]
Ibid.

We will now discuss in a little more detail the Struggle for Existence.[2]
Ibid.

Even when we are quite alone, how often do we think with pleasure or pain of what others think of us — of their imagined approbation or disapprobation.
The Descent of Man
[1871]. Chap. 4

The highest possible stage in moral culture is when we recognize that we ought to control our thoughts.
Ibid.

The presence of a body of well-instructed men, who have not to labor for their daily bread, is important to a degree which cannot be overestimated; as all high intellectual work is carried on by them, and on such work material progress of all kinds mainly depends, not to mention other and higher advantages.
Ibid. Chap. 5

Progress has been much more general than retrogression.
Ibid.

[1] This survival of the fittest which I have here sought to express in mechanical terms, is that which Mr. Darwin has called "natural selection, or the preservation of favoured races in the struggle for life." — HERBERT SPENCER: *Principles of Biology* [1864–1867], *Indirect Equilibration*

[2] The perpetual struggle for room and food. — MALTHUS: *On Population* [1798], *Chap. III*

The Simiadae then branched off into two great stems, the New World and Old World monkeys; and from the latter at a remote period, Man, the wonder and the glory of the universe, proceeded.[1]
The Descent of Man. Chap. 6

False facts are highly injurious to the progress of science, for they often endure long; but false views, if supported by some evidence, do little harm, for every one takes a salutary pleasure in proving their falseness.
Ibid. Chap. 21

Physiological experiment on animals is justifiable for real investigation, but not for mere damnable and detestable curiosity.[2]
Letter to E. Ray Lankester

I love fools' experiments. I am always making them.
Remark cited in Life of Darwin

As for a future life, every man must judge for himself between conflicting vague probabilities.
Life and Letters, Edited by
FRANCIS DARWIN *[1887]*

Believing as I do that man in the distant future will be a far more perfect creature than he now is, it is an intolerable thought that he and all other sentient beings are doomed to

[1] I confess freely to you, I could never look long upon a monkey, without very mortifying reflections. — CONGREVE: *Letter to Dennis* [1695]

Pouter, tumbler and fantail are from the same source;
The racer and hack may be traced to one horse;
So men were developed from monkeys, of course,
Which nobody can deny.
LORD CHARLES NEAVES [1800–1876]:
The Origin of Species
See Benjamin Disraeli, page 512b.

[2] The main cause of this unparalleled progress in physiology, pathology, medicine and surgery has been the fruitful application of the experimental method of research, just the same method which has been the great lever of all scientific advance in modern times. — DR. WILLIAM H. WELCH [1850–1934]: *Argument against Antivivisection Bill* (Senate No. 34), Fifty-sixth Congress, First Session [February 21, 1900]

complete annihilation after such long-continued slow progress. To those who fully admit the immortality of the human soul, the destruction of our world will not appear so dreadful.

Life and Letters, Edited by
FRANCIS DARWIN

EDWARD FITZGERALD
[1809–1883]

Wake! For the Sun who scatter'd into flight
The Stars before him from the Field of night,
  Drives Night along with them from Heav'n and strikes
The Sultan's Turret with a Shaft of Light.
The Rubáiyát of Omar Khayyám.[1] *Stanza 1*

Awake! for Morning in the Bowl of Night
Has flung the Stone that puts the Stars to flight:
  And Lo! the Hunter of the East has caught
The Sultan's Turret in a Noose of Light.
Ibid. Stanza 1, First Edition

Now the New Year reviving old Desires,
The thoughtful Soul to Solitude retires.
Ibid. Stanza 4

Iram indeed is gone with all his Rose.
Ibid. Stanza 5

Come, fill the Cup, and in the fire of Spring
Your Winter-garment of Repentance fling:
  The Bird of Time has but a little way
To flutter — and the Bird is on the Wing.
Ibid. Stanza 7

The Leaves of Life keep falling one by one.
Ibid. Stanza 8

Each Morn a thousand Roses brings, you say:

[1] Translated in four editions, 1859, 1868, 1872, and 1879. The fourth edition is used here, unless otherwise stated.

Yes, but where leaves the Rose of Yesterday?
The Rubáiyát of Omar Khayyám.
Stanza 9

A Book of Verses underneath the Bough,
A Jug of Wine, a Loaf of Bread — and Thou
Beside me singing in the Wilderness —
Oh, Wilderness were Paradise enow!
Ibid. Stanza 12

Ah, take the Cash, and let the Credit go,
Nor heed the rumble of a distant Drum!
Ibid. Stanza 13

The Worldly Hope men set their Hearts upon
Turns Ashes — or it prospers; and anon,
  Like Snow upon the Desert's dusty Face,
Lighting a little hour or two — is gone.
Ibid. Stanza 16

Think, in this batter'd Caravanserai
Whose Portals are alternate Night and Day,
  How Sultan after Sultan with his Pomp
Abode his destin'd Hour, and went his way.
Ibid. Stanza 17

They say the Lion and the Lizard keep
The Courts where Jamshyd gloried and drank deep:
  And Bahram, that great Hunter — the Wild Ass
Stamps o'er his Head, but cannot break his sleep.
Ibid. Stanza 18

I sometimes think that never blows so red
The Rose as where some buried Caesar bled;
  That every Hyacinth the Garden wears
Dropt in her Lap from some once lovely Head.[1]
Ibid. Stanza 19

Ah, my Belovèd, fill the Cup that clears

[1] See Shakespeare, page 179a, and Tennyson, page 551b.

TODAY of past Regrets and future Fears:

Tomorrow! — Why, Tomorrow I may be

Myself with Yesterday's Sev'n thousand Years.

The Rubáiyát of Omar Khayyám.
Stanza 21

For some we loved, the loveliest and the best

That from his Vintage rolling Time hath prest.

Ibid. Stanza 22

Ah, make the most of what we yet may spend,

Before we too into the Dust descend;

Dust into Dust, and under Dust, to lie,

Sans Wine, sans Song, sans Singer, and — sans End!

Ibid. Stanza 24

Myself when young did eagerly frequent

Doctor and Saint, and heard great argument

About it and about: but evermore

Came out by the same door where in I went.

Ibid. Stanza 27

And this was all the Harvest that I reap'd —

"I came like Water, and like Wind I go."

Ibid. Stanza 28

There was the Door to which I found no Key;

There was the Veil through which I might not see.

Some little talk awhile of ME and THEE

There was — and then no more of THEE and ME.

Ibid. Stanza 32

"While you live,

Drink! — for, once dead, you never shali return."

Ibid. Stanza 35

Tomorrow's tangle to the winds resign.

Ibid. Stanza 41

So when that Angel of the darker Drink

At last shall find you by the river-brink,

And, offering his Cup, invite your Soul

Forth to your Lips to quaff — you shall not shrink.

The Rubáiyát of Omar Khayyám.
Stanza 43

And fear not lest Existence closing your

Account, and mine, should know the like no more;

The Eternal Sákí from that Bowl has pour'd

Millions of Bubbles like us, and will pour.[1]

Ibid. Stanza 46

A Hair perhaps divides the False and True.

Ibid. Stanza 49

Waste not your Hour, nor in the vain pursuit

Of This and That endeavour and dispute.

Ibid. Stanza 54

Striking from the Calendar

Unborn Tomorrow and dead Yesterday.

Ibid. Stanza 57

The Grape that can with Logic absolute

The Two-and-Seventy jarring Sects confute.

Ibid. Stanza 59

The Flower that once has blown for ever dies.

Ibid. Stanza 63

Strange, is it not? that of the myriads who

Before us pass'd the door of Darkness through,

Not one returns to tell us of the Road,

Which to discover we must travel too.

Ibid. Stanza 64

I sent my Soul through the Invisible,

Some letter of that After-life to spell:

And by and by my Soul return'd to me,

And answer'd "I Myself am Heav'n and Hell." [2]

Ibid. Stanza 66

[1] See Tennyson, page 546b.
[2] See Milton, page 252b.

Heav'n but the Vision of fulfill'd Desire,
And Hell the Shadow from a Soul on fire.
*The Rubáiyát of Omar Khayyám.
Stanza 67*

We are no other than a moving row
Of Magic Shadow-shapes that come and go.
Ibid. Stanza 68

This Chequer-board of Nights and Days.
Ibid. Stanza 69

The Moving Finger writes; and, having writ,
Moves on: nor all your Piety nor Wit
Shall lure it back to cancel half a Line,
Nor all your Tears wash out a Word of it.
Ibid. Stanza 71

That inverted Bowl they call the Sky,
Whereunder crawling coop'd we live and die.
Ibid. Stanza 72

And this I know: whether the one True Light
Kindle to Love, or Wrath-consume me quite,
One Flash of It within the Tavern caught
Better than in the Temple lost outright.
Ibid. Stanza 77

"And He that with his hand the Vessel made
Will surely not in after Wrath destroy."
Ibid. Stanza 85

Indeed the Idols I have loved so long
Have done my credit in this World much wrong:
Have drown'd my Glory in a shallow Cup,
And sold my Reputation for a Song.
Ibid. Stanza 93

I wonder often what the Vintners buy
One half so precious as the stuff they sell.
Ibid. Stanza 95

Yet Ah, that Spring should vanish with the Rose!

That Youth's sweet-scented manuscript should close!
*The Rubáiyát of Omar Khayyám.
Stanza 96*

Ah Love! could you and I with Him conspire
To grasp this Sorry Scheme of Things entire,
Would not we shatter it to bits — and then
Remould it nearer to the Heart's Desire!
Ibid. Stanza 99

Yon rising Moon that looks for us again —
How oft hereafter will she wax and wane;
How oft hereafter rising look for us
Through this same Garden — and for *one* in vain!
Ibid. Stanza 100

And when like her, O Sákí, you shall pass
Among the Guests Star-scatter'd on the Grass,
And in your joyous errand reach the spot
Where I made One — turn down an empty Glass!
Ibid. Stanza 101

The King in a carriage may ride,
And the Beggar may crawl at his side;
But in the general race,
They are traveling all the same pace.
Chronomoros

Mrs. Browning's death was rather a relief to me, I must say; no more Aurora Leighs, thank God!
Letter [*July 15, 1861*] [1]

Taste is the feminine of genius.
Letter to James Russell Lowell
[*October, 1877*]

[1] Aye, dead! and were yourself alive, good Fitz,
How to return your thanks would pass my wits.
Kicking you seems the common lot of curs,
While more appropriate greeting lends you grace.
Surely to spit there glorifies your face,
Spitting with lips once sanctified by hers.
ROBERT BROWNING in *The Athenaeum* [July 13, 1889]

WILLIAM EWART GLADSTONE
[1809–1898]

To be engaged in opposing wrong affords. under the conditions of our mental constitution, but a slender guarantee for being right.
Time and Place of Homer [1858]. Introduction

Decision by majorities is as much an expedient as lighting by gas.
Speech, House of Commons [1858]

The disease of an evil conscience is beyond the practice of all the physicians of all the countries in the world.
Speech, Plumstead [1878]

National injustice is the surest road to national downfall.
Ibid.

All the world over, I will back the masses against the classes.
Speech, Liverpool [June 28, 1886]

I have always regarded that Constitution as the most remarkable work known to me in modern times to have been produced by the human intellect, at a single stroke (so to speak), in its application to political affairs.[1]
Letter to the committee in charge of the celebration of the Centennial Anniversary of the American Constitution [July 20, 1887]

Selfishness is the greatest curse of the human race.
Speech, Hawarden [May 28, 1890]

OLIVER WENDELL HOLMES [2]
[1809–1894]

Ay, tear her tattered ensign down!
Long has it waved on high,

And many an eye has danced to see
That banner in the sky.
Old Ironsides [1830]. Stanza 1

Nail to the mast her holy flag,
Set every threadbare sail,
And give her to the god of storms,
The lightning and the gale!
Ibid. Stanza 3

Thou say'st an undisputed thing
In such a solemn way.
To an Insect. Stanza 7

One sad, ungathered rose
On my ancestral tree.
My Aunt. Stanza 6

You think they are crusaders, sent
From some infernal clime,
To pluck the eyes of Sentiment
And dock the tail of Rhyme,
To crack the voice of Melody
And break the legs of Time.
The Music Grinders. Stanza 9

And silence, like a poultice, comes
To heal the blows of sound.
Ibid. Stanza 10

And since, I never dare to write
As funny as I can.
The Height of the Ridiculous. Stanza 8

When the last reader reads no more.
The Last Reader

Age, like distance, lends a double charm.[1]
A Rhymed Lesson. Urania

And when you stick on conversation's burs,
Don't strew your pathway with those dreadful *urs*.
Ibid.

Be sure your tailor is a man of sense.
Ibid.

Wear seemly gloves; not black, nor yet too light,
And least of all the pair that once was white.
Ibid.

Have a good hat; the secret of your looks

---

[1] As the British Constitution is the most subtle organism which has proceeded from progressive history, so the American Constitution is the most wonderful work ever struck off at a given time by the brain and purpose of man. — *Kin Beyond the Sea* [*North American Review*, September, 1878]

[2] The most successful combination the world has ever seen, of physician and man of

letters. — SIR WILLIAM OSLER, quoted in HARVEY CUSHING: *Life of Sir William Osler* [1925], *Vol. I, Chap. 15*

[1] See Campbell, page 432a.

Lives with the beaver in Canadian
brooks;
Virtue may flourish in an old cravat,
But man and nature scorn the shocking hat.[1]
> *A Rhymed Lesson. Urania*

Learn the sweet magic of a cheerful
face;
Not always smiling, but at least serene.
> *The Morning Visit*

Wake in our breast the living fires,
The holy faith that warmed our sires;
Thy hand hath made our Nation free;
To die for her is serving Thee.
> *Army Hymn. Stanza 2*

The lusty days of long ago,
When you were Bill and I was Joe.
> *Bill and Joe. Stanza 1*

Where are the Marys, and Anns, and
Elizas,
Loving and lovely of yore?
> *Questions and Answers. Stanza 3*

Oh for one hour of youthful joy!
Give back my twentieth spring!
> *The Old Man Dreams. Stanza 1*

Old Time is a liar! We're twenty tonight!
> *The Boys. Stanza 1*

Where the snow-flakes fall thickest
there's nothing can freeze!
> *Ibid. Stanza 2*

One flag, one land, one heart, one hand,
One Nation, evermore!
> *Voyage of the Good Ship Union.*
> *Stanza 12*

Good to the heels the well-worn slipper
feels
  When the tired player shuffles off the
  buskin;
A page of Hood may do a fellow good
  After a scolding from Carlyle or
  Ruskin.
> *How Not to Settle It. Stanza 3*

When lawyers take what they would
give
And doctors give what they would take.
> *Latter-day Warnings. Stanza 4*

  Learn to give
Money to colleges while you live.
Don't be silly and think you'll try

To bother the colleges, when you die,
With codicil this, and codicil that,
That Knowledge may starve while Law
grows fat;
For there never was pitcher that
wouldn't spill,
And there's always a flaw in a donkey's
will.
> *Parson Turell's Legacy*

  Where we love is home,
Home that our feet may leave, but not
our hearts.
> *Homesick in Heaven. Stanza 5*

There is no time like the old time, when
you and I were young.[1]
> *No Time Like the Old Time.*
> *Stanza 1*

'Tis like stirring living embers when,
at eighty, one remembers
All the achings and the quakings of "the
times that tried men's souls." [2]
> *Grandmother's Story of Bunker*
> *Hill Battle. Stanza 1*

The style's the man, so books avow;
The style's the woman, anyhow.
> *How the Old Horse Won the Bet.*
> *Stanza 2*

I read it in the story-book, that, for to
kiss his dear,
Leander swam the Hellespont, — and
I will swim this here.
> *The Ballad of the Oysterman.*
> *Stanza 3*

Lean, hungry, savage, anti-everythings.
> *A Modest Request. The Speech.*

This body in which we journey
across the isthmus between the two
oceans is not a private carriage, but an
omnibus.
> *The Guardian Angel. Chap. 3*

A thought is often original, though
you have uttered it a hundred times.
> *The Autocrat of the Break-*
> *fast-Table [1858]. I*

---

[1] See *The Autocrat of the Breakfast-Table*,
page 536a.

[1] The good old times, the grand old times,
the great old times! — DICKENS: *The Chimes*
[1844], *First Quarter*
  There are no days like the good old days,
  The days when we were youthful!
    EUGENE FIELD [1850–1895]: *Old*
     Times, Old Friends, Old Love
[2] See Thomas Paine, page 370a.

Everybody likes and respects self-made men. It is a great deal better to be made in that way than not to be made at all.
The Autocrat of the Breakfast-Table. I

Insanity is often the logic of an accurate mind overtaxed.
Ibid.

Put not your trust in money, but put your money in trust.
Ibid. II

Sin has many tools, but a lie is the handle which fits them all.
Ibid. VI

There is that glorious epicurean paradox uttered by my friend the historian,[1] in one of his flashing moments: "Give us the luxuries of life, and we will dispense with its necessaries."[2]
Ibid.

Boston State-house is the hub of the solar system. You couldn't pry that out of a Boston man, if you had the tire of all creation straightened out for a crowbar.
Ibid.

The axis of the earth sticks out visibly through the centre of each and every town or city.
Ibid.

The world's great men have not commonly been great scholars, nor its great scholars great men.
Ibid.

Knowledge and timber shouldn't be much used till they are seasoned.
Ibid.

The hat is the *ultimum moriens* of respectability.[3]
Ibid. XIII

Little I ask; my wants are few,
I only wish a hut of stone,

[1] John Lothrop Motley [1814–1877].
[2] Said Scopas of Thessaly, "We rich men count our felicity and happiness to lie in these superfluities, and not in those necessary things." — PLUTARCH [A.D. 46–120]: *On the Love of Wealth*
[3] See *A Rhymed Lesson*, pages 534b–535a.

(A *very plain* brown stone will do,)
That I may call my own.[1]
Contentment [*1858*]. *Stanza 1*
Build thee more stately mansions, O my soul,
As the swift seasons roll!
Leave thy low-vaulted past!
Let each new temple, nobler than the last,
Shut thee from heaven with a dome more vast,
Till thou at length art free,
Leaving thine outgrown shell by life's unresting sea!
The Chambered Nautilus [*1858*]. *Stanza 5*
Have you heard of the wonderful one-hoss shay,
That was built in such a logical way
It ran a hundred years to a day?
The Deacon's Masterpiece [*1858*]. *Stanza 1*
A general flavor of mild decay.
Ibid. Stanza 10
It went to pieces all at once, —
All at once, and nothing first,
Just as bubbles do when they burst.
Ibid. Stanza 11
I firmly believe that if the whole *materia medica* as now used could be sunk to the bottom of the sea, it would be all the better for mankind — and all the worse for the fishes.[2]
Address, Massachusetts Medical Society [*May 30, 1860*]
He comes of the Brahmin caste of New England. This is the harmless, inoffensive, untitled aristocracy.
The Brahmin Caste of New England [*1860*]
It makes men imperious to sit a horse.
Elsie Venner [*1861*]

[1] See Goldsmith, page 354b.
[2] Stir the mixture well
     Lest it prove inferior,
   Then put half a drop
     Into Lake Superior.
   Every other day
     Take a drop in water,
   You'll be better soon
     Or at least you oughter.
     BISHOP WILLIAM CROSWELL DOANE [1832–1913]: *Lines on Homoeopathy*

To be seventy years young is sometimes far more cheerful and hopeful than to be forty years old.

> *On the Seventieth Birthday of Julia Ward Howe* [*May 27, 1889*]

ABRAHAM LINCOLN
[1809–1865]

If the good people, in their wisdom, shall see fit to keep me in the background, I have been too familiar with disappointments to be very much chagrined.

> *Address, New Salem, Illinois* [*March 9, 1832*]

I go for all sharing the privileges of the government who assist in bearing its burdens.

> *Letter to Editor of the Sangamon Journal, New Salem, Illinois* [*June 13, 1836*]

If destruction be our lot we must ourselves be its author and finisher. As a nation of freemen we must live through all time, or die by suicide.

> *Address, Young Men's Lyceum, Springfield, Illinois* [*January 27, 1838*]

There is no grievance that is a fit object of redress by mob law.

> *Ibid.*

Towering genius disdains a beaten path. It seeks regions hitherto unexplored.

> *Ibid.*

I am not a Know-Nothing; that is certain. How could I be? How can any one who abhors the oppression of Negroes be in favor of degrading classes of white people? Our progress in degeneracy appears to me to be pretty rapid. As a nation we began by declaring that "all men are created equal." We now practically read it "all men are created equal, except Negroes." When the Know-Nothings get control, it will read "all men are created equal, except Negroes and foreigners and Catholics." When it comes to this, I shall prefer emigrating to some country where they make no pretense of loving liberty — to

Russia, for instance, where despotism can be taken pure, and without the base alloy of hypocrisy.

> *Letter to Joshua F. Speed* [*August 24, 1855*]

"A house divided against itself cannot stand." [1] I believe this government cannot endure permanently half slave and half free. I do not expect the Union to be dissolved — I do not expect the house to fall — but I do expect it will cease to be divided. It will become all one thing, or all the other. Either the opponents of slavery will arrest the further spread of it, and place it where the public mind shall rest in the belief that it is in the course of ultimate extinction; or its advocates will push it forward till it shall become alike lawful in all the States, old as well as new, North as well as South.

> *Speech, Republican State Convention, Springfield, Illinois* [*June 16, 1858*]

Nobody has ever expected me to be President. In my poor, lean, lank face nobody has ever seen that any cabbages were sprouting out.

> *Second Campaign Speech against Douglas,*[2] *Springfield, Illinois* [*July 17, 1858*]

As I would not be a *slave,* so I would not be a *master.* This expresses my idea of democracy. Whatever differs from this, to the extent of the difference, is no democracy.[3]

> *Fragment* [*August 1, 1858?*], *in* ROY P. BASLER: *The Collected Works of Abraham Lincoln* [*1953*]. *Vol. II, Page 532*

When . . . you have succeeded in dehumanizing the Negro; when you

---

[1] If a house be divided against itself, that house cannot stand. — *Mark, III, 25*

[2] They have seen in his [Douglas's] round, jolly, fruitful face, post-offices, land-offices, marshalships and cabinet appointments, chargéships and foreign missions, bursting and sprouting out in wonderful exuberance, ready to be laid hold of by their greedy hands. — *Ibid.*

[3] See *Address to Indiana Regiment,* page 542a–542b.

have put him down and made it impossible for him to be but as the beasts of the field; when you have extinguished his soul in this world and placed him where the ray of hope is blown out as in the darkness of the damned, are you quite sure that the demon you have roused will not turn and rend you? What constitutes the bulwark of our own liberty and independence? It is not our frowning battlements, our bristling sea coasts, our army and our navy. These are not our reliance against tyranny. All of those may be turned against us without making us weaker for the struggle. Our reliance is in the love of liberty which God has planted in us. Our defence is in the spirit which prized liberty as the heritage of all men, in all lands everywhere. Destroy this spirit and you have planted the seeds of despotism at your own doors. Familiarize yourselves with the chains of bondage and you prepare your own limbs to wear them. Accustomed to trample on the rights of others, you have lost the genius of your own independence and become the fit subjects of the first cunning tyrant who rises among you.

Speech, Edwardsville, Illinois [September 11, 1858]

That is the issue that will continue in this country when these poor tongues of Judge Douglas and myself shall be silent. It is the eternal struggle between these two principles — right and wrong — throughout the world. They are the two principles that have stood face to face from the beginning of time; and will ever continue to struggle. The one is the common right of humanity, and the other the divine right of kings. It is the same principle in whatever shape it develops itself. It is the same spirit that says, "You toil and work and earn bread, and I'll eat it." No matter in what shape it comes, whether from the mouth of a king who seeks to bestride the people of his own nation and live by the fruit of their labor, or from one race of men as an apology for enslaving another race, it is the same tyrannical principle.

Reply, Seventh and Last Joint Debate, Alton, Illinois [October 15, 1858]

This is a world of compensation; and he who would be no slave must consent to have no slave. Those who deny freedom to others deserve it not for themselves, and, under a just God, cannot long retain it.

Letter to H. L. Pierce and Others [April 6, 1859]

It is said an Eastern monarch once charged his wise men to invent him a sentence to be ever in view, and which should be true and appropriate in all times and situations. They presented him the words: "And this, too, shall pass away." [1] How much it expresses! How chastening in the hour of pride! How consoling in the depths of affliction! . . . And yet, let us hope, it is not quite true. Let us hope, rather, that by the best cultivation of the physical world beneath and around us, and the best intellectual and moral world within us, we shall secure an individual, social, and political prosperity and happiness, whose course shall be onward and upward, and which, while the earth endures, shall not pass away.

Address, Wisconsin State Agricultural Society, Milwaukee [September 30, 1859]

Let us have faith that right makes might, and in that faith let us to the end dare to do our duty as we understand it.

Address, Cooper Union, New York [February 27, 1860]

No one, not in my situation, can appreciate my feeling of sadness at this parting. To this place, and the kindness of these people, I owe everything. Here I have lived a quarter of a century, and have passed from a young to an old man. Here my children have been born, and one is buried. I now leave, not knowing when or whether ever I may return, with a task before

[1] See Hawthorne, page 514b.

me greater than that which rested upon Washington. Without the assistance of that Divine Being who ever attended him, I cannot succeed. With that assistance I cannot fail. Trusting in Him who can go with me, and remain with you, and be everywhere for good, let us confidently hope that all will yet be well.

Farewell Address, Springfield, Illinois [February 11, 1861]

If we do not make common cause to save the good old ship of the Union on this voyage, nobody will have a chance to pilot her on another voyage.

Address, Cleveland, Ohio [February 15, 1861]

I have never had a feeling, politically, that did not spring from the sentiments embodied in the Declaration of Independence. . . . I have often inquired of myself what great principle or idea it was that kept this Confederacy so long together. . . . It was that which gave promise that in due time the weights would be lifted from the shoulders of all men, and that all should have an equal chance.

Speech in Independence Hall, Philadelphia [February 22, 1861]

It is safe to assert that no government proper ever had a provision in its organic law for its own termination.

First Inaugural Address [March 4, 1861]

This country, with its institutions, belongs to the people who inhabit it. Whenever they shall grow weary of the existing government, they can exercise their constitutional right of amending it, or their revolutionary right to dismember or overthrow it.

Ibid.

Why should there not be a patient confidence in the ultimate justice of the people? Is there any better or equal hope in the world?

Ibid.

While the people retain their virtue and vigilance, no administration, by any extreme of wickedness or folly, can

very seriously injure the government in the short space of four years.

First Inaugural Address

We are not enemies, but friends. We must not be enemies. Though passion may have strained, it must not break our bonds of affection. The mystic chords of memory, stretching from every battlefield and patriot grave to every living heart and hearth-stone all over this broad land, will yet swell the chorus of the Union when again touched, as surely they will be, by the better angels of our nature.

Ibid.

I think the necessity of being *ready* increases. — Look to it.

Letter (this is the whole message) to Governor Andrew G. Curtin of Pennsylvania [April 8, 1861]

Labor is prior to, and independent of, capital. Capital is only the fruit of labor, and could never have existed if labor had not first existed. Labor is the superior of capital, and deserves much the higher consideration. Capital has its rights, which are as worthy of protection as any other rights.

First Annual Message to Congress [December 3, 1861]

It is difficult to make a man miserable while he feels he is worthy of himself and claims kindred to the great God who made him.

Address on Colonization to a Negro Deputation at Washington [August 14, 1862]

My paramount object in this struggle is to save the Union, and is not either to save or to destroy slavery. If I could save the Union without freeing any slave, I would do it; and if I could do it by freeing all the slaves, I would do it; and if I could save it by freeing some and leaving others alone, I would also do that.

Letter to Horace Greeley [August 22, 1862]

I shall try to correct errors when shown to be errors, and I shall adopt new views so fast as they shall appear to be true views. . . . and I intend no modification of my oft-expressed personal wish that all men everywhere could be free.

Letter to Horace Greeley
[August 22, 1862]

The President takes the result of the New York elections philosophically, and will, doubtless, profit by the lesson. When Colonel Forney inquired of him how he felt about New York, he replied: "Somewhat like the boy in Kentucky, who stubbed his toe while running to see his sweetheart. The boy said he was too big to cry, and far too badly hurt to laugh." [1]

Frank Leslie's Illustrated Weekly
[November 22, 1862]

A nation may be said to consist of its territory, its people, and its laws. The territory is the only part which is of certain durability.

Second Annual Message to Congress
[December 1, 1862]

If there ever could be a proper time for mere catch arguments, that time surely is not now. In times like the present, men should utter nothing for which they would not willingly be responsible through time and in eternity.

Ibid.

Fellow-citizens, we cannot escape history. We of this Congress and this administration will be remembered in spite of ourselves. No personal significance or insignificance can spare one or another of us. The fiery trial through which we pass will light us down, in honor or dishonor, to the last generation. We say we are for the Union. The world will not forget that we say this. We know how to save the Union. The world knows we do

know how to save it. We — even we here — hold the power and bear the responsibility. In giving freedom to the slave, we assure freedom to the free — honorable alike in what we give and what we preserve. We shall nobly save or meanly lose the last, best hope of earth. Other means may succeed; this could not fail. The way is plain, peaceful, generous, just — a way which, if followed, the world will forever applaud, and God must forever bless.

Second Annual Message
to Congress

Beware of rashness, but with energy and sleepless vigilance go forward and give us victories.

Letter to Major-General Joseph
Hooker [January 26, 1863]

The Father of Waters [1] again goes unvexed to the sea.

Letter to James C. Conkling
[August 26, 1863]

Among freemen there can be no successful appeal from the ballot to the bullet, and . . . they who take such appeal are sure to lose their case and pay the cost.

Ibid.

I have endured a great deal of ridicule without much malice; and have received a great deal of kindness, not quite free from ridicule. I am used to it.

Letter to James H. Hackett
[November 2, 1863]

Fourscore and seven years ago our fathers brought forth on this continent a new nation, conceived in liberty, and dedicated to the proposition that all men are created equal.

Now we are engaged in a great civil war, testing whether that nation, or any nation so conceived and so dedicated, can long endure. We are met on a great battlefield of that war. We have come to dedicate a portion of that field as a final resting-place for those who here gave their lives that that nation might live. It is altogether fitting and proper that we should do this.

But, in a larger sense, we cannot

[1] The election referred to resulted in a victory for Horatio Seymour, Democratic candidate for governor of New York. Moreover, throughout the North the Democrats picked up a number of congressional seats and won a number of state elections.

Adlai E. Stevenson, Democratic candidate for the presidency in 1952, quoted this remark of Lincoln's in a television speech after losing the election.

[1] See Stephen Vincent Benét, page 979b.

dedicate — we cannot consecrate — we cannot hallow — this ground. The brave men, living and dead, who struggled here, have consecrated it far above our poor power to add or detract. The world will little note nor long remember what we say here, but it can never forget what they did here. It is for us, the living, rather to be dedicated here to the unfinished work which they who fought here have thus far so nobly advanced. It is rather for us to be here dedicated to the great task remaining before us — that from these honored dead we take increased devotion to that cause for which they gave the last full measure of devotion; that we here highly resolve that these dead shall not have died in vain; that this nation, under God, shall have a new birth of freedom; and that government of the people, by the people, for the people, shall not perish from the earth.[1]

> *Address at Gettysburg*
> *[November 19, 1863]*

I claim not to have controlled events, but confess plainly that events have controlled me.

> *Letter to A. G. Hodges*
> *[April 4, 1864]*

The world has never had a good definition of the word liberty, and the American people, just now, are much in want of one.

> *Address, Sanitary Fair, Baltimore*
> *[April 18, 1864]*

It is no fault in others that the Methodist Church sends more soldiers to the field, more nurses to the hospital, and more prayers to heaven than any. God bless the Methodist Church. Bless all the churches, and blessed be God, who, in this our great trial, giveth us the churches.

> *To a Methodist Delegation*
> *[May 14, 1864]*

I do not allow myself to suppose that either the convention or the League have concluded to decide that I am either the greatest or best man in America, but rather they have concluded that it is not best to swap horses while crossing the river, and have further concluded that I am not so poor a horse that they might not make a botch of it in trying to swap.

> *Reply to the National Union*
> *League [June 9, 1864]*

Truth is generally the best vindication against slander.

> *Letter to Secretary Stanton, refusing to dismiss Postmaster-General Montgomery Blair*
> *[July 18, 1864]*

It has long been a grave question whether any government, not too strong for the liberties of its people, can be strong enough to maintain its existence in great emergencies.

> *Response to a Serenade*
> *[November 10, 1864]*

Human nature will not change. In any future great national trial, compared with the men of this, we shall have as weak and as strong, as silly and as wise, as bad and as good.

> *Ibid.*

Dear Madam: I have been shown in the files of the War Department a statement of the Adjutant-General of Massachusetts that you are the mother of five sons who have died gloriously on the field of battle. I feel how weak and fruitless must be any words of mine which should attempt to beguile you from the grief of a loss so overwhelming. But I cannot refrain from tendering to you the consolation that may be found in the thanks of the Republic they died to save. I pray that our heavenly Father may assuage the anguish of your bereavement, and leave you only the cherished memory of the loved and lost, and the solemn pride that must be yours to have laid so costly a sacrifice upon the altar of freedom.

> *Letter to Mrs. Bixby, whose five sons were reported killed in battle* [1] *[November 21, 1864]*

---

[1] See Webster, page 443b, Garrison, page 517b, and Theodore Parker, page 560a.

[1] In reality, only two of Mrs. Bixby's sons had died in action, but Lincoln was unaware of this when he wrote the letter.

It may seem strange that any men should dare to ask a just God's assistance in wringing their bread from the sweat of other men's faces; but let us judge not, that we be not judged.

Second Inaugural Address
[March 4, 1865]

The Almighty has His own purposes.
Ibid.

Fondly do we hope — fervently do we pray — that this mighty scourge of war may speedily pass away. Yet, if God wills that it continue until all the wealth piled by the bondsman's two hundred and fifty years of unrequited toil shall be sunk, and until every drop of blood drawn with the lash shall be paid by another drawn with the sword, as was said three thousand years ago, so still it must be said, "The judgments of the Lord are true and righteous altogether."
Ibid.

With malice toward none; with charity for all; with firmness in the right, as God gives us to see the right,[1] let us strive on to finish the work we are in; to bind up the nation's wounds; to care for him who shall have borne the battle, and for his widow, and his orphan — to do all which may achieve and cherish a just and lasting peace among ourselves, and with all nations.
Ibid.

Men are not flattered by being shown that there has been a difference of purpose between the Almighty and them. To deny it, however, in this case, is to deny that there is a God governing the world. It is a truth which I thought needed to be told, and, as whatever of humiliation there is in it falls most directly on myself, I thought others might afford for me to tell it.

Letter to Thurlow Weed
[March 15, 1865]

I have always thought that all men should be free; but if any should be slaves, it should be first those who desire it for themselves, and secondly

those who desire it for others. Whenever I hear any one arguing for slavery, I feel a strong impulse to see it tried on him personally.[1]

Address to an Indiana Regiment
[March 17, 1865]

Important principles may and must be inflexible.

Last public address, Washington
[April 11, 1865]

If you once forfeit the confidence of your fellow citizens, you can never regain their respect and esteem. It is true that you may fool all the people some of the time; you can even fool some of the people all the time; but you can't fool all of the people all the time.

To a caller at the White House.
In ALEXANDER K. McCLURE: *Lincoln's Yarns and Stories* *[1904], Page 124*

One night he dreamed that he was in a crowd, when someone recognized him as the President, and exclaimed in surprise, "He is a very common-looking man." Whereupon he answered, "Friend, the Lord prefers common-looking people. That is the reason he makes so many of them."

JAMES MORGAN: *Our Presidents* *[1924], Chap. 6*

If I were to try to read, much less answer, all the attacks made on me, this shop might as well be closed for any other business. I do the very best I know how — the very best I can; and I mean to keep doing so until the end. If the end brings me out all right, what is said against me won't amount to anything. If the end brings me out wrong, ten angels swearing I was right would make no difference.

Conversation at the White House, reported by FRANCIS B. CARPENTER: *Six Months at the White House with Abraham Lincoln* *[1866]*

If you call a tail a leg, how many legs has a dog? Five? No, calling a tail a leg don't *make* it a leg.

Traditionally attributed to Lincoln

[1] See John Quincy Adams, page 398b.

[1] See *Fragment*, page 537b.

RICHARD MONCKTON MILNES (BARON HOUGHTON)
[1809–1885]

I wandered by the brookside,
 I wandered by the mill;
I could not hear the brook flow,
 The noisy wheel was still.
The Brookside. Stanza 1

The beating of my own heart
Was all the sound I heard.
Ibid.

The hills of manhood wear a noble face
 When seen from far;
The mist of light from which they take
 their grace
 Hides what they are.
Carpe Diem

Mohammed's truth lay in a holy Book,
Christ's in a sacred Life
Mohammedanism

A fair little girl sat under a tree,
Sewing as long as her eyes could see;
Then smoothed her work, and folded it
 right,
And said, "Dear work, good-night,
 good-night."
Good-Night and Good-Morning.
Stanza 1

They who have steeped their souls in
 prayer
Can every anguish calmly bear.
The Sayings of Rabia. IV

Lady Moon, Lady Moon, where are
 you roving?
 Over the sea.
Lady Moon, Lady Moon, whom are
 you loving?
 All that love me!
A Child's Song

The sense of humour is the just balance of all the faculties of man, the best security against the pride of knowledge and the conceits of the imagination, the strongest inducement to submit with a wise and pious patience to the vicissitudes of human existence.
Memoir of Thomas Hood

EDGAR ALLAN POE
[1809–1849]

O, human love! thou spirit given,
On Earth, of all we hope in Heaven!
Which fall'st into the soul like rain
Upon the Siroc-wither'd plain.
Tamerlane [1827]

All that we see or seem
Is but a dream within a dream.
A Dream Within a Dream [1827]

Sound loves to revel in a summer night.
Al Aaraaf [1829]. Part II

It is with literature as with law or empire — an established name is an estate in tenure, or a throne in possession.
Poems [1831]. Preface, Letter
to Mr. B——

Helen, thy beauty is to me
 Like those Nicean barks of yore,
That gently, o'er a perfumed sea,
 The weary, wayworn wanderer bore
 To his own native shore.
To Helen [1831]. Stanza 1

On desperate seas long wont to roam,
 Thy hyacinth hair, thy classic face,
Thy Naiad airs have brought me home
To the glory that was Greece,
And the grandeur that was Rome.
Ibid. Stanza 2

In Heaven a spirit doth dwell
 "Whose heart-strings are a lute"; [1]
None sing so wildly well
As the angel Israfel.
Israfel [1831]. Stanza 1

If I could dwell
Where Israfel
 Hath dwelt, and he where I,
He might not sing so wildly well
 A mortal melody,
While a bolder note than this might
 swell
From my lyre within the sky.
Ibid. Stanza 8

Whose wreathed friezes intertwine
The viol, the violet, and the vine.
The City in the Sea [1831].
Stanza 2

---

[1] And the angel Israfel, whose heartstrings are a lute, and who has the sweetest voice of all God's creatures. — *The Koran*

While from a proud tower in the town
Death looks gigantically down.
> *The City in the Sea. Stanza 3*

Ah, broken is the golden bowl! [1] — the
spirit flown forever!
Let the bell toll! — a saintly soul floats
on the Stygian river;
And, Guy De Vere, hast *thou* no tear?
— weep now or never more!
> *Lenore* [*1831*]. *Stanza 1*

A dirge for her the doubly dead in that
she died so young.
> *Ibid.*

Vastness! and Age! and Memories of
Eld!
Silence! and Desolation! and dim
Night!
> *The Coliseum* [*1833*]. *Stanza 1*

Thou wast that all to me, love,
For which my soul did pine —
A green isle in the sea, love,
A fountain and a shrine,
All wreathed with fairy fruits and
flowers,
And all the flowers were mine.
> *To One in Paradise* [*1834*].
> *Stanza 1*

And all my days are trances,
And all my nightly dreams
Are where thy grey eye glances,
And where thy footstep gleams —
In what ethereal dances,
By what eternal streams.
> *Ibid. Stanza 4*

Those who dream by day are cog-
nizant of many things which escape
those who dream only by night.
> *Eleonora* [*1841*]

There are chords in the hearts of the
most reckless which can not be touched
without emotion. Even with the utterly lost, to whom life and death are
equally jests, there are matters of which
no jest can be made.
> *The Masque of the Red
> Death* [*1842*]

And much of Madness, and more of Sin,
And Horror the soul of the plot.
> *The Conqueror Worm* [*1843*].
> *Stanza 3*

[1] See *Ecclesiastes, XII, 6,* on page 1043b.

While the angels, all pallid and wan,
Uprising, unveiling, affirm
That the play is the tragedy, "Man,"
And its hero, the Conqueror Worm.
> *The Conqueror Worm. Stanza 5*

There is something in the unselfish
and self-sacrificing love of a brute,
which goes directly to the heart of him
who has had frequent occasion to test
the paltry friendship and gossamer
fidelity of mere Man.
> *The Black Cat* [*1843*]

Perverseness is one of the primitive
impulses of the human heart.
> *Ibid.*

The boundaries which divide Life
from Death are at best shadowy and
vague. Who shall say where the one
ends, and where the other begins?
> *The Premature Burial* [*1844*]

With me poetry has been not a purpose, but a passion; and the passions
should be held in reverence: they must
not — they cannot at will be excited,
with an eye to the paltry compensations, or the more paltry commendations, of mankind.
> *The Raven and Other Poems*
> [*1845*]. *Preface*

Once upon a midnight dreary, while I
pondered, weak and weary,
Over many a quaint and curious volume
of forgotten lore —
While I nodded, nearly napping, suddenly there came a tapping,
As of some one gently rapping, rapping
at my chamber door.
> *The Raven* [*1845*].
> *Stanza 1*

Ah, distinctly I remember it was in the
bleak December;
And each separate dying ember wrought
its ghost upon the floor.
Eagerly I wished the morrow; — vainly
I had sought to borrow
From my books surcease of sorrow —
sorrow for the lost Lenore —
For the rare and radiant maiden whom
the angels name Lenore —
Nameless *here* for evermore.
> *Ibid. Stanza 2*

And the silken sad uncertain rustling of each purple curtain
Thrilled me — filled me with fantastic terrors never felt before.
The Raven. Stanza 3

Deep into that darkness peering, long I stood there, wondering, fearing,
Doubting, dreaming dreams no mortal ever dared to dream before.
Ibid. Stanza 5

Perched upon a bust of Pallas just above my chamber door —
Perched, and sat, and nothing more.
Ibid. Stanza 7

"Ghastly grim and ancient Raven wandering from the Nightly shore —
Tell me what thy lordly name is on the Night's Plutonian shore!"
Quoth the Raven, "Nevermore."
Ibid. Stanza 8

Whom unmerciful Disaster
Followed fast and followed faster.
Ibid. Stanza 11

"Prophet!" said I, "thing of evil! — prophet still, if bird or devil!
By that Heaven that bends above us — by that God we both adore —
Tell this soul with sorrow laden."
Ibid. Stanza 16

"Take thy beak from out my heart, and take thy form from off my door!"
Quoth the Raven, "Nevermore."
Ibid. Stanza 17

And the Raven, never flitting, still is sitting, *still* is sitting
On the pallid bust of Pallas just above my chamber door;
And his eyes have all the seeming of a demon's that is dreaming,
And the lamp-light o'er him streaming throws his shadow on the floor;
And my soul from out that shadow that lies floating on the floor
Shall be lifted — nevermore!
Ibid. Stanza 18

The Imp of the Perverse.
Title of Story [1845]

The object Truth, or the satisfaction of the intellect, and the object Passion, or the excitement of the heart, are, although attainable, to a certain extent, in poetry, far more readily attainable in prose.
The Philosophy of Composition .*[1846]*

The skies they were ashen and sober;
The leaves they were crispèd and sere —
The leaves they were withering and sere;
It was night in the lonesome October
Of my most immemorial year.
Ulalume [1847]. Stanza 1

It was down by the dank tarn of Auber,
In the ghoul-haunted woodland of Weir.
Ibid.

Here once, through an alley Titanic,
Of cypress, I roamed with my soul —
Of cypress, with Psyche, my soul.
Ibid. Stanza 2

And now, as the night was senescent
And star-dials pointed to morn —
As the star-dials hinted of morn —
At the end of our path a liquescent
And nebulous lustre was born.
Ibid. Stanza 4

Thus I pacified Psyche and kissed her,
And tempted her out of her gloom.
Ibid. Stanza 8

Can it be fancied that Deity ever vindictively
Made in his image a mannikin merely to madden it? [1]
The Rationale of Verse [1848]

A Quixotic sense of the honorable — of the chivalrous.
Letter to Mrs. Whitman [October 18, 1848]

And o'er his heart a shadow
Fell as he found
No spot of ground
That looked like Eldorado.
Eldorado [1849]

And the fever called "Living"
Is conquered at last.
For Annie [1849]

---

[1] What! out of senseless Nothing to provoke
A conscious Something to resent the yoke.
FITZGERALD: *The Rubáiyát of Omar Khayyám* [1859–1879], *St. 78*

And this maiden she lived with no
  other thought
Than to love and be loved by me.
        Annabel Lee [*1849*]. *Stanza 1*

She was a child and *I* was a child,
  In this kingdom by the sea,
But we loved with a love that was more
  than love —
I and my Annabel Lee —
With a love that the wingèd seraphs
  of Heaven
  Coveted her and me.
              Ibid. Stanza 2

And neither the angels in Heaven above
  Nor the demons down under the sea,
Can ever dissever my soul from the
  soul
  Of the beautiful Annabel Lee.
              Ibid. Stanza 5

In her sepulchre there by the sea —
In her tomb by the side of the sea.
              Ibid. Stanza 6

  Keeping time, time, time,
    In a sort of Runic rhyme,
To the tintinnabulation that so musi-
  cally wells
From the bells, bells, bells, bells,
  Bells, bells, bells.
          The Bells [*1849*]. *Stanza 1*

Hear the loud alarum bells —
    Brazen bells!
What a tale of terror, now, their
  turbulency tells!
              Ibid. Stanza 3

  I would define, in brief, the Poetry
of words as the Rhythmical Creation of
Beauty. Its sole arbiter is Taste.
        The Poetic Principle [*1850*]

ALFRED, LORD TENNYSON
[*1809–1892*]

Dowered with the hate of hate, the
  scorn of scorn,
The love of love.
        The Poet [*1830*]. *Stanza 1*
For it was in the golden prime
Of good Haroun Alraschid.
        Recollections of the Arabian
            Nights [*1830*]. *Stanza 2*

She said, "I am aweary, aweary,
I would that I were dead!"
          Mariana [*1830*]. *Refrain*
A still small voice spake unto me,
"Thou art so full of misery,
Were it not better not to be?"
        The Two Voices [*1833*]. *Stanza 1*
This truth within thy mind rehearse,
That in a boundless universe
Is boundless better, boundless worse.
              Ibid. Stanza 9
Tho' thou wert scattered to the wind,
Yet is there plenty of the kind.[1]
              Ibid. Stanza 11
I know that age to age succeeds,
Blowing a noise of tongues and deeds,
A dust of systems and of creeds.
              Ibid. Stanza 69
Like glimpses of forgotten dreams.
              Ibid. Stanza 127
No life that breathes with human
  breath
Has ever truly longed for death.
              Ibid. Stanza 132
    In after-dinner talk,
Across the walnuts and the wine.
        The Miller's Daughter [*1833*].
                  Stanza 4
O mother Ida, many-fountained Ida,
Dear mother Ida, hearken ere I die.
        Oenone [*1833*]. *Line 22*
Self-reverence, self-knowledge, self-
  control,
These three alone lead life to sovereign
  power.
              Ibid. Line 142
I built my soul a lordly pleasure-house,
Wherein at ease for aye to dwell.
        The Palace of Art [*1833*].
                  Stanza 1
At me you smiled, but unbeguiled
I saw the snare, and I retired:
The daughter of a hundred Earls,
You are not one to be desired.
        Lady Clara Vere de Vere [*1833*].
                  Stanza 1
A simple maiden in her flower
Is worth a hundred coats-of-arms.
              Ibid. Stanza 2

[1] See Fitzgerald, page 532b.

The lion on your old stone gates
Is not more cold to you than I.
Lady Clara Vere de Vere. Stanza 3
Her manners had not that repose
Which stamps the caste of Vere de
Vere.
Ibid. Stanza 5
From yon blue heavens above us bent,
The gardener Adam and his wife
Smile at the claims of long descent.
Ibid. Stanza 7
Kind hearts are more than coronets,
And simple faith than Norman blood.
Ibid.

If time be heavy on your hands,
Are there no beggars at your gate,
Nor any poor about your lands?
Oh! teach the orphan-boy to read,
Or teach the orphan-girl to sew.
Ibid. Stanza 9
You must wake and call me early, call
me early, mother dear;
Tomorrow 'ill be the happiest time of
all the glad New Year, —
Of all the glad New Year, mother, the
maddest, merriest day;
For I'm to be Queen o' the May, mother,
I'm to be Queen o' the May.
The May Queen [1833].
Stanza 1
There is sweet music here that softer
falls
Than petals from blown roses on the
grass.
The Lotos-Eaters [1833]. Choric
Song, Stanza 1
Music that gentlier on the spirit lies,
Than tir'd eyelids upon tir'd eyes;
Music that brings sweet sleep down
from the blissful skies.
Ibid.
Ah, why
Should life all labour be?
Ibid. Stanza 4
Let us alone. Time driveth onward fast,
And in a little while our lips are dumb.
Let us alone. What is it that will last?
All things are taken from us, and become
Portions and parcels of the dreadful
Past.
Ibid.

Give us long rest or death, dark death
or dreamful ease.
The Lotos-Eaters. Choric Song.
Stanza 4
A daughter of the gods, divinely tall,
And most divinely fair.
A Dream of Fair Women [1833].
Stanza 22
God gives us love. Something to love
He lends us; but when love is grown
To ripeness, that on which it throve
Falls off, and love is left alone.
To J. S. [1833]. Stanza 4
Sleep sweetly, tender heart, in peace;
Sleep, holy spirit, blessed soul,
While the stars burn, the moons increase,
And the great ages onward roll.
Ibid. Stanza 18
Willows whiten, aspens quiver,
Little breezes dusk and shiver.
The Lady of Shalott [1833].
Part I, Stanza 1
But who hath seen her wave her hand?
Or at the casement seen her stand?
Or is she known in all the land,
The Lady of Shalott?
Ibid. Stanza 3
All in the blue unclouded weather.
Ibid. Part III, Stanza 3
"Tirra lirra," by the river
Sang Sir Lancelot.
Ibid. Stanza 4
She left the web, she left the loom,
She made three paces thro' the room,
She saw the water-lily bloom,
She saw the helmet and the plume,
She looked down to Camelot.
Ibid. Stanza 5
But Lancelot mused a little space;
He said, "She has a lovely face;
God in his mercy lend her grace,
The Lady of Shalott."
Ibid. Part IV, Stanza 6
The old order changeth, yielding place
to new;
And God fulfills himself in many ways,
Lest one good custom should corrupt
the world.
Morte d'Arthur [1842].
Line 408

More things are wrought by prayer
Than this world dreams of. Wherefore,
   let thy voice
Rise like a fountain for me night and
   day.
               Morte d'Arthur. Line 415

More black than ashbuds in the front
   of March.
        The Gardener s Daughter [1842]

The long mechanic pacings to and fro,
The set gray life, and apathetic end.
            Love and Duty [1842]

     Ah! when shall all men's good
Be each man's rule, and universal peace
Lie like a shaft of light across the land?
       The Golden Year [1842]. *Line 47*

Thro' all the circle of the golden year.
                 Ibid. Line 50

It little profits that an idle king,
By this still hearth, among these
   barren crags,
Match'd with an aged wife, I mete and
   dole
Unequal laws unto a savage race.
           Ulysses [1842]. *Line 1*

Much have I seen and known; cities of
   men
And manners, climates, councils, gov-
   ernments,
Myself not least, but honour'd of them
   all;
And drunk delight of battle with my
   peers,
Far on the ringing plains of windy
   Troy.
                Ibid. Line 13

How dull it is to pause, to make an end,
To rust unburnished, not to shine in
   use,
As tho' to breathe were life!
                Ibid. Line 22

     This gray spirit yearning in desire
To follow knowledge like a sinking star,
Beyond the utmost bound of human
   thought.
                Ibid. Line 30

This is my son, mine own Telemachus.
                Ibid. Line 33

     The deep
Moans round with many voices. Come,
   my friends,

'Tis not too late to seek a newer world.
              Ulysses. Line 55

It may be we shall touch the Happy
   Isles,
And see the great Achilles, whom we
   knew.
                Ibid. Line 63

To strive, to seek, to find, and not to
   yield.[1]
                Ibid. Line 70

Comrades, leave me here a little, while
   as yet 'tis early morn:
Leave me here, and when you want me,
   sound upon your bugle horn.
        Locksley Hall [1842]. *Line 1*

In the spring a livelier iris changes on
   the burnished dove;
In the spring a young man's fancy
   lightly turns to thoughts of love.
                Ibid. Line 19

He will hold thee, when his passion
   shall have spent its novel force,
Something better than his dog, a little
   dearer than his horse.
                Ibid. Line 49

The many-winter'd crow that leads the
   clanging rookery home.
                Ibid. Line 68

Like a dog, he hunts in dreams.
                Ibid. Line 79

With a little hoard of maxims preaching down a daughter's heart.
                Ibid. Line 94

But the jingling of the guinea helps the
   hurt that Honour feels.
                Ibid. Line 105

For I dipt into the future, far as human
   eye could see,
Saw the Vision of the world, and all
   the wonder that would be;
Saw the heavens fill with commerce,
   argosies of magic sails,
Pilots of the purple twilight, dropping
   down with costly bales;
Heard the heavens fill with shouting,
   and there rain'd a ghastly dew

---

[1] Inscribed on the memorial cross erected to the memory of Captain Robert Falcon Scott and his men at Hut Point in the Antarctic.

From the nations' airy navies grappling
in the central blue.
Locksley Hall. Line 119

Till the war drum throbbed no longer
and the battle flags were furled
In the Parliament of Man, the Federation of the world.
Ibid. Line 127

Yet I doubt not through the ages one
increasing purpose runs,
And the thoughts of men are widened
with the process of the suns.
Ibid. Line 137

Knowledge comes, but wisdom lingers.
Ibid. Line 141

Woman is the lesser man, and all thy
passions, match'd with mine,
Are as moonlight unto sunlight, and as
water unto wine.
Ibid. Line 151

I will take some savage woman, she
shall rear my dusky race.
Ibid. Line 168

I the heir of all the ages, in the foremost files of time.
Ibid. Line 178

Let the great world spin forever down
the ringing grooves of change.
Ibid. Line 182

Better fifty years of Europe than a
cycle of Cathay.
Ibid. Line 184

And on her lover's arm she leant,
And round her waist she felt it fold,
And far across the hills they went
In that new world which is the old.
*The Day-Dream [1842]. The
Departure, Stanza 1*

And o'er the hills, and far away
Beyond their utmost purple rim,
Beyond the night, across the day,
Thro' all the world she followed him.
Ibid. Stanza 4

My strength is as the strength of ten,
Because my heart is pure.
Sir Galahad [1842]. Stanza 1

Others' follies teach us not,
Nor much their wisdom teaches;
And most, of sterling worth, is what
Our own experience preaches.
Will Waterproof's Lyrical Monologue [1842]. Stanza 22

And wheresoe'r thou move, good luck
Shall fling her old shoe after.
Will Waterproof's Lyrical Monologue. Stanza 27

As she fled fast through sun and shade
The happy winds upon her played,
Blowing the ringlet from the braid.
Sir Launcelot and Queen Guinevere [1842]. Stanza 5

Cophetua sware a royal oath;
"This beggar maid shall be my
queen!"[1]
*The Beggar Maid [1842].
Stanza 2*

For now the poet can not die,
Nor leave his music as of old,
But round him ere he scarce be cold
Begins the scandal and the cry.
*To ——, after Reading a Life and
Letters [1842]. Stanza 4*

He gave the people of his best:
His worst he kept, his best he gave.
Ibid. Stanza 7

Break, break, break,
On thy cold gray stones, O Sea!
And I would that my tongue could utter
The thoughts that arise in me.
*Break, Break, Break [1842].
Stanza 1*

O well for the fisherman's boy,
That he shouts with his sister at
play!
O well for the sailor lad,
That he sings in his boat on the bay!
Ibid. Stanza 2

And the stately ships go on
To their haven under the hill;
But O for the touch of a vanish'd hand,
And the sound of a voice that is still!
Ibid. Stanza 3

But the tender grace of a day that is
dead
Will never come back to me.
Ibid. Stanza 4

Veneer'd with sanctimonious theory.
*The Princess [1847]. Prologue,
Line 117*

With prudes for proctors, dowagers for
deans,

[1] See *Ballads*, page 1011b.

And sweet girl-graduates in their golden hair.
> *The Princess. Prologue, Line 141*

A rosebud set with little willful thorns,
And sweet as English air could make her, she.
> *Ibid. Line 153*

A little street half garden and half house.
> *Ibid. Part I, Line 211*

When we fall out with those we love
And kiss again with tears!
> *Ibid. Part II, Song*

And quoted odes, and jewels five-words-long
That on the stretched forefinger of all Time
Sparkle forever.
> *Ibid. Line 355*

Sweet and low, sweet and low,
  Wind of the western sea,
Low, low, breathe and blow,
  Wind of the western sea!
Over the rolling waters go,
Come from the dying moon, and blow,
  Blow him again to me;
While my little one, while my pretty one, sleeps.
> *Ibid. Part III, Song*

The splendour falls on castle walls
And snowy summits old in story.
The long light shakes across the lakes,
And the wild cataract leaps in glory.
Blow, bugle, blow, set the wild echoes flying,
Blow, bugle; answer, echoes, dying, dying, dying.
> *Ibid. Part IV, Song, Stanza 1*

The horns of Elfland faintly blowing.
> *Ibid. Stanza 2*

O Love, they die in yon rich sky,
  They faint on hill or field or river:
Our echoes roll from soul to soul,
  And grow forever and forever.
> *Ibid. Stanza 3*

There sinks the nebulous star we call the sun.
> *Ibid. Line 1*

Tears, idle tears, I know not what they mean,
Tears from the depth of some divine despair

Rise in the heart, and gather to the eyes,
In looking on the happy autumn-fields,
And thinking of the days that are no more.
> *The Princess. Part IV, Song, Stanza 1*

Dear as remembered kisses after death,
And sweet as those by hopeless fancy feign'd
On lips that are for others; deep as love,
Deep as first love, and wild with all regret;
O Death in Life, the days that are no more.
> *Ibid. Stanza 4*

O Swallow, Swallow, flying, flying South,
Fly to her, and fall upon her gilded eaves,
And tell her, tell her, what I tell to thee.
> *Ibid. Song, Stanza 1*

Man is the hunter; woman is his game.
> *Ibid. Part V, Line 147*

Man for the field and woman for the hearth:
Man for the sword and for the needle she:
Man with the head and woman with the heart:
Man to command and woman to obey;
All else confusion.
> *Ibid. Line 427*

Home they brought her warrior dead.
She nor swoon'd, nor utter'd cry:
All her maidens, watching, said,
"She must weep or she will die."
> *Ibid. Part VI, Song, Stanza 1*

The woman is so hard
Upon the woman.
> *Ibid. Line 205*

Ask me no more: thy fate and mine are seal'd:
I strove against the stream and all in vain:
Let the great river take me to the main:
No more, dear love, for at a touch I yield;
  Ask me no more.
> *Ibid. Part VII, Song, Stanza 3*

Now sleeps the crimson petal, now the
  white;
Nor waves the cypress in the palace
  walk;
Nor winks the gold fin in the porphyry
  font:
The fire-fly wakens: waken thou with
  me.
          The Princess. Part VII, Song,
                      Stanza 1
Now lies the Earth all Danaë to the
  stars,
And all thy heart lies open unto me.
          Ibid. Stanza 3
      Sweet is every sound,
Sweeter thy voice, but every sound is
  sweet;
Myriads of rivulets hurrying thro' the
  lawn,
The moan of doves in immemorial elms,
And murmuring of innumerable bees.
          Ibid. Line 203
      Happy he
With such a mother! faith in woman-
  kind
Beats with his blood, and trust in all
  things high
Comes easy to him; and tho' he trip
  and fall,
He shall not blind his soul with clay.
          Ibid. Line 308
Some sense of duty, something of a
  faith,
Some reverence for the laws ourselves
  have made,
Some patient force to change them
  when we will,
Some civic manhood firm against the
  crowd.
          Ibid. Conclusion, Line 54
Strong Son of God, immortal Love,
  Whom we, that have not seen thy
    face,
  By faith, and faith alone, embrace,
Believing where we cannot prove.
      In Memoriam [*1850*]. *Prologue,*
                      Stanza 1
Our little systems have their day.
          Ibid. Stanza 5
Let knowledge grow from more to more,
  But more of reverence in us dwell;

That mind and soul, according well,
May make one music as before.
      In Memoriam. Prologue, Stanza 7
I held it truth, with him who sings
  To one clear harp in divers tones,
  That men may rise on stepping-stones
Of their dead selves to higher things.
          Ibid. Part I, Stanza 1
I sometimes hold it half a sin
  To put in words the grief I feel;
  For words, like Nature, half reveal
And half conceal the Soul within.
          Ibid. Part V, Stanza 1
But, for the unquiet heart and brain
  A use in measured language lies;
  The sad mechanic exercise,
Like dull narcotics numbing pain.
          Ibid. Stanza 2
      Never morning wore
To evening, but some heart did break.
          Ibid. Part VI, Stanza 2
And topples round the dreary west
A looming bastion fringed with fire.
          Ibid. Part XV, Stanza 5
And from his ashes may be made
The violet of his native land.[1]
          Ibid. Part XVIII, Stanza 1
I do but sing because I must,
And pipe but as the linnets sing.[2]
          Ibid. Part XXI, Stanza 6
The shadow cloaked from head to foot.
          Ibid. Part XXIII, Stanza 1
Who keeps the keys of all the creeds.
          Ibid. Stanza 2
And Thought leapt out to wed with
  Thought
Ere Thought could wed itself with
  Speech.
          Ibid. Stanza 4
And round us all the thicket rang
To many a flute of Arcady.
          Ibid. Stanza 6
'Tis better to have loved and lost
Than never to have loved at all.[3]
          Ibid. Part XXVII, Stanza 4

[1] See Shakespeare, page 179a, and Fitzgerald, page 531b.
[2] Ich singe, wie der Vogel singt
    Der in den Zweigen wohnet.
    GOETHE: *Wilhelm Meister's Apprentice-
    ship* [*1786–1830*], *Book II, Chap. 11*
[3] Say what you will, 'tis better to be left

Her eyes are homes of silent prayer.
In Memoriam. Part XXXII,
Stanza 1

Thrice blest whose lives are faithful
prayers,
  Whose loves in higher love endure;
  What souls possess themselves so
pure,
Or is there blessedness like theirs?
Ibid. Stanza 4

Whose faith has centre everywhere,
Nor cares to fix itself to form.
Ibid. Part XXXIII, Stanza 1

How fares it with the happy dead?
Ibid. Part XLIV, Stanza 1

Short swallow-flights of song, that dip
Their wings in tears, and skim away.
Ibid. Part XLVIII, Stanza 4

Be near me when my light is low.
Ibid. Part L, Stanza 1

And Time, a maniac scattering dust,
And Life, a Fury slinging flame.
Ibid. Stanza 2

Do we indeed desire the dead
Should still be near us at our side?
Ibid. Part LI, Stanza 1

Hold thou the good; define it well;
  For fear divine Philosophy
  Should push beyond her mark, and
be
Procuress to the Lords of Hell.
Ibid. Part LIII, Stanza 4

Oh yet we trust that somehow good
Will be the final goal of ill.
Ibid. Part LIV, Stanza 1

But what am I?
An infant crying in the night:
An infant crying for the light:
And with no language but a cry.[1]
Ibid. Stanza 5

than never to have been loved. — CONGREVE:
The Way of the World [1700], *Act II, Sc. 6*
  Better to love amiss than nothing to have
loved. — CRABBE: *Tales* [1812], *XIV, The
Struggles of Conscience*
What voice did on my spirit fall,
  Peschiera, when thy bridge I crost?
'Tis better to have fought and lost
Than never to have fought at all.
  ARTHUR HUGH CLOUGH [1819–1861]:
Peschiera
  [1] See Pliny, page 49b.

So careful of the type she seems,
So careless of the single life.
In Memoriam. Part LV,
Stanza 2

The great world's altar-stairs,
That slope through darkness up to God.
Ibid. Stanza 4

And faintly trust the larger hope.
Ibid. Stanza 5

Nature, red in tooth and claw.
Ibid. Part LVI, Stanza 4

Who battled for the True, the Just.
Ibid. Stanza 5

The sweetest soul
That ever look'd with human eyes.
Ibid. Part LVII, Stanza 3

Who breaks his birth's invidious bar,
And grasps the skirts of happy chance,
And breasts the blows of circumstance.
Ibid. Part LXIV, Stanza 2

And lives to clutch the golden keys,
  To mould a mighty state's decrees,
And shape the whisper of the throne.
Ibid. Stanza 3

So many worlds, so much to do,
So little done, such things to be.[1]
Ibid. Part LXXIII, Stanza 1

O last regret, regret can die!
Ibid. Part LXXVIII, Stanza 5

The little speedwell's darling blue.
Ibid. Part LXXXIII, Stanza 2

God's finger touch'd him, and he slept.
Ibid. Part LXXXV, Stanza 5

There lives more faith in honest doubt,[2]
Believe me, than in half the creeds.
Ibid. Part XCVI, Stanza 3

He seems so near, and yet so far.
Ibid. Part XCVII, Stanza 6

Ring out, wild bells, to the wild sky!
Ibid. Part CVI, Stanza 1

Ring out the old, ring in the new,
Ring, happy bells, across the snow!
Ibid. Stanza 2

[1] How little I have gained,
  How vast the unattained.
    WHITTIER [1807–1892]: *My Triumph,*
St. 7
  [2] Who never doubted never half believed.
  Where doubt there truth is — 'tis her
  shadow.
    P. J. BAILEY [1816–1902]: *Festus:*
A Country Town

Ring in the nobler modes of life
With sweeter manners, purer laws.
In Memoriam. Part CVI,
Stanza 4

Ring out old shapes of foul disease,
  Ring out the narrowing lust of gold;
  Ring out the thousand wars of old,
Ring in the thousand years of peace!
Ibid. Stanza 7

Ring in the valiant man and free,
  The larger heart, the kindlier hand!
  Ring out the darkness of the land,
Ring in the Christ that is to be!
Ibid. Stanza 8

The blind hysterics of the Celt.
Ibid. Part CIX, Stanza 4

And thus he bore without abuse
  The grand old name of gentleman,
  Defamed by every charlatan,
And soiled with all ignoble use.
Ibid. Part CXI, Stanza 6

Wearing all that weight
Of learning lightly like a flower.
Ibid. Conclusion, Stanza 10

One God, one law, one element,
  And one far-off divine event,
To which the whole creation moves.
Ibid. Stanza 36

He clasps the crag with crooked hands;
Close to the sun in lonely lands,
Ring'd with the azure world he stands.

The wrinkled sea beneath him crawls;
He watches from his mountain walls,
And like a thunderbolt he falls.
The Eagle [*1851*]

This laurel greener from the brows
Of him that utter'd nothing base.[1]
To the Queen [*1851*]. *Stanza 2*

Broad-based upon her people's will,
And compass'd by the inviolate sea.
Ibid. Stanza 9

Rich in saving common-sense,
And, as the greatest only are,
In his simplicity sublime.
Oh good gray head which all men knew!
Ode on the Death of the Duke of
Wellington [*1852*]. *Stanza 4*

[1] Wordsworth, Tennyson's predecessor as poet laureate.

O iron nerve to true occasion true,
O fall'n at length, that tower of
  strength
Which stood four-square to all the
  winds that blew.
Ode on the Death of the Duke
of Wellington. Stanza 4

Not once or twice in our rough island
  story
The path of duty was the way to glory.[1]
Ibid. Stanza 8

We are not cotton-spinners all.
The Third of February, 1852.
Stanza 8

Half a league, half a league,
  Half a league onward,
All in the valley of death
  Rode the six hundred.
The Charge of the Light Brigade
[*1854*]. *Stanza 1*

Some one had blundered:
Theirs not to make reply,
Theirs not to reason why,
Theirs but to do and die.
Ibid. Stanza 2

Cannon to right of them,
Cannon to left of them,
Cannon in front of them
  Volley'd and thunder'd. . . .
Into the jaws of death,
Into the mouth of hell
  Rode the six hundred.
Ibid. Stanza 3

For men may come and men may go,
But I go on forever.
Song from The Brook [*1855*].
Stanza 6

Faultily faultless, icily regular, splen-
  didly null.
Maud [*1855*]. *Part I, II*

That jewelled mass of millinery,
That oiled and curled Assyrian Bull.
Ibid. VI, Stanza 6

One still strong man in a blatant land.
Ibid. X, Stanza 5

Gorgonized me from head to foot,
With a stony British stare.
Ibid. XIII, Stanza 2

Come into the garden, Maud,
  For the black bat, night, has flown,

[1] See Thomas Gray, page 348a–348b.

Come into the garden, Maud,
  I am here at the gate alone.
      Maud. Part I, XXII, Stanza 1
All night have the roses heard
  The flute, violin, bassoon;
All night has the casement jessamine
  stirr'd
To the dancers dancing in tune;
Till a silence fell with the waking bird,
  And a hush with the setting moon.
            Ibid. Stanza 3
Queen rose of the rosebud garden of
  girls.
            Ibid. Stanza 9
She is coming, my own, my sweet;
  Were it ever so airy a tread,
My heart would hear her and beat,
  Were it earth in an earthy bed;
My dust would hear her and beat,
  Had I lain for a century dead;
Would start and tremble under her feet,
  And blossom in purple and red.
           Ibid. Stanza 11
Ah Christ, that it were possible
  For one short hour to see
The souls we loved, that they might
  tell us
What and where they be.
      Ibid. Part II, IV, Stanza 3
And after many a summer dies the
  swan.
        Tithonus [1860]. Line 4
Here at the quiet limit of the world.
             Ibid. Line 7
Wearing the white flower of a blame-
  less life,
Before a thousand peering littlenesses,
In that fierce light which beats upon a
  throne,
And blackens every blot.
    Idylls of the King [1859–1885].
         Dedication, Line 24
Man's word is God in man.
      Ibid. The Coming of Arthur,
                Line 132
Large divine and comfortable words.[1]
            Ibid. Line 267
Live pure, speak true, right wrong, fol-
  low the King —

[1] Hear what comfortable words our Saviour
Christ saith unto all who truly turn to him. —
Book of Common Prayer, Holy Communion

Else, wherefore born?
    Idylls of the King. Gareth and
           Lynette, Line 117
A damsel of high lineage, and a brow
May-blossom, and a cheek of apple-
  blossom,
Hawk-eyes; and lightly was her slen-
  der nose
Tip-tilted like the petal of a flower.
           Ibid. Line 574
Our hoard is little, but our hearts are
  great.
    Ibid. The Marriage of Geraint,
               Line 352
For man is man and master of his fate.[1]
           Ibid. Line 355
The useful trouble of the rain.
   Ibid. Geraint and Enid, Line 770
The world will not believe a man re-
  pents;
And this wise world of ours is mainly
  right.
           Ibid. Line 899
The whole wood-world is one full peal
  of praise.
   Ibid. Balin and Balan, Line 444
Mere white truth in simple nakedness.
           Ibid. Line 509
As love, if love be perfect, casts out
  fear,
So hate, if hate be perfect, casts out
  fear.
    Ibid. Merlin and Vivien, Line 41
Faith and unfaith can ne'er be equal
  powers:
Unfaith in aught is want of faith in all.
           Ibid. Line 384
It is the little rift within the lute,
That by and by will make the music
  mute,
And ever widening slowly silence all.
           Ibid. Line 386
    Blind and naked Ignorance
Delivers brawling judgments, un-
  ashamed,
On all things all day long.
           Ibid. Line 662
For men at most differ as heaven and
  earth,

[1] See Sallust, page 35b.

But women, worst and best, as heaven
and hell.
*Idylls of the King. Merlin and
Vivien, Line 812*
Elaine the fair, Elaine the loveable,
Elaine, the lily maid of Astolat.
Ibid. Lancelot and Elaine. Line 1
But, friend, to me
He is all fault who hath no fault at all.
For who loves me must have a touch
of earth.
Ibid. Line 131
In me there dwells
No greatness, save it be some far-off
touch
Of greatness to know well I am not
great.
Ibid. Line 447
The shackles of an old love straitened
him,
His honour rooted in dishonour stood,
And faith unfaithful kept him falsely
true.
Ibid. Line 870
Sweet is true love tho' given in vain,
in vain;
And sweet is death who puts an end
to pain.
Ibid. Line 1000
He makes no friend who never made
a foe.
Ibid. Line 1082
Figs out of thistles.
*Ibid. The Last Tournament,
Line 356*
The greater man the greater courtesy.
Ibid. Line 628
The vow that binds too strictly snaps
itself.
Ibid. Line 652
For courtesy wins woman all as well
As valor may.
Ibid. Line 702
For manners are not idle, but the fruit
Of loyal nature and of noble mind.
Ibid. Guinevere, Line 333
To love one maiden only, cleave to her,
And worship her by years of golden
deeds.
Ibid. Line 472
No more subtle master under heaven
Than is the maiden passion for a maid,

Not only to keep down the base in man,
But teach high thought, and amiable
words
And courtliness, and the desire of fame,
And love of truth, and all that makes
a man.
*Idylls of the King. Guinevere,
Line 475*
To where beyond these voices there is
peace.
Ibid. Line 692
I found Him in the shining of the stars,
I mark'd Him in the flowering of His
fields,
But in His ways with men I find Him
not.
*Ibid. The Passing of Arthur,
Line 9*
For why is all around us here
As if some lesser god had made the
world,
But had not force to shape it as he
would?
Ibid. Line 13
Clothed in white samite, mystic, won-
derful.
Ibid. Line 199
Cast all your cares on God; that an-
chor holds.
Enoch Arden [1864]
Insipid as the queen upon a card.
Aylmer's Field [1864]
Marriages are made in Heaven.[1]
Ibid.
He that wrongs his friend
Wrongs himself more, and ever bears
about
A silent court of justice in his breast,
Himself the judge and jury, and him-
self
The prisoner at the bar, ever con-
demn'd.
Ibid.
The worst is yet to come.[2]
Ibid.

[1] Marriage is Destiny, made in heaven.
— Lyly: *Mother Bombie* [1594]
  If marriages
Are made in Heaven, they should be happier.
  Southerne: *The Fatal Marriage* [1694]
  See Heywood, page 91a.
[2] See Browning, page 572a, and Philander
Johnson, page 830a.

That a lie which is half a truth is ever
the blackest of lies,
That a lie which is all a lie may be met
and fought with outright,
But a lie which is part a truth is a
harder matter to fight.
The Grandmother [*1864*].
Stanza 8

Doänt thou marry for munny, but goä
wheer munny is!
Northern Farmer: New Style
[*1869*]. *Stanza 5*

Speak to Him thou for He hears, and
Spirit with Spirit can meet —
Closer is He than breathing, and nearer
than hands and feet.
The Higher Pantheism [*1869*].
Stanza 6

Flower in the crannied wall,
I pluck you out of the crannies,
I hold you here, root and all, in my
hand,
Little flower — but *if* I could under-
stand
What you are, root and all, and all in
all,
I should know what God and man is.
Flower in the Crannied Wall
[*1869*]

At Flores in the Azores Sir Richard
Grenville lay,
And a pinnace, like a flutter'd bird,
came flying from far away;
"Spanish ships of war at sea! we have
sighted fifty-three!"
The Revenge [*1878*]. *Stanza 1*

Then sware Lord Thomas Howard:
" 'Fore God I am no coward."
Ibid.

"I should count myself the coward if I
left them, my Lord Howard,
To these Inquisition dogs and the devil-
doms of Spain."
Ibid. Stanza 2

All the charm of all the Muses often
flowering in a lonely word.
To Virgil [*1882*]

Old men must die, or the world would
grow mouldy, would only breed
the past again.
Becket [*1884*]. *Prologue*

Cleave ever to the sunnier side **of**
doubt,
And cling to Faith beyond the forms
of Faith.
The Ancient Sage [*1885*]

The shell must break before the bird
can fly.
Ibid.

Slav, Teuton, Kelt, I count them all
My friends and brother souls,
With all the peoples, great and small,
That wheel between the poles.
The Charge of the Heavy
Brigade. Epilogue [*1885*]

The song that nerves a nation's heart
Is in itself a deed.
Ibid.

That man's the best Cosmopolite
Who loves his native country best.
Hands All Round [*1885*]

Love your enemy, bless your haters,
said the Greatest of the great;
Christian love among the Churches
looked the twin of heathen hate.
Locksley Hall Sixty Years
After [*1886*]. *Line 85*

Charm us, orator, till the lion look no
larger than the cat.
Ibid. Line 112

Authors — essayist, atheist, novelist,
realist, rhymester, play your part,
Paint the mortal shame of nature with
the living hues of art.
Ibid. Line 139

Not of the sunlight,
Not of the moonlight,
Not of the starlight!
O young Mariner,
Down to the haven,
Call your companions,
Launch your vessel
And crowd your canvas,
And, ere it vanishes
Over the margin,
After it, follow it,
Follow the Gleam.[1]
Merlin and the Gleam [*1889*].
Stanza 10

[1] The Gleam . . . signifies in my poem
the higher poetic imagination. — *In* HALLAM
TENNYSON: *Alfred, Lord Tennyson, A
Memoir* [*1897*], *Vol. II, P. 366*

Sunset and evening star,
    And one clear call for me!
And may there be no moaning of the
    bar,
    When I put out to sea.
        Crossing the Bar [*1889*].
                Stanza 1
But such a tide as moving seems asleep,
    Too full for sound and foam,
When that which drew from out the
    boundless deep
Turns again home.
        Ibid. Stanza 2
Twilight and evening bell,
And after that the dark.
        Ibid. Stanza 3
I hope to see my Pilot face to face
When I have crossed the bar.
        Ibid. Stanza 4

ROBERT CHARLES WINTHROP
[1809–1894]

Our Country, — whether bounded
by the St. John's and the Sabine, or
however otherwise bounded [1] or described, and be the measurements more
or less, — still our Country, to be
cherished in all our hearts, to be defended by all our hands.
        Toast at Faneuil Hall [*Fourth
            of July, 1845*]
A star for every State, and a State
for every star.
    Address on Boston Common [*1862*]
Slavery is but half abolished, eman-
cipation is but half completed, while
millions of freemen with votes in their
hands are left without education. Justice to them, the welfare of the States
in which they live, the safety of the
whole Republic, the dignity of the elective franchise, — all alike demand that
the still remaining bonds of ignorance
shall be unloosed and broken, and the

[1] The United States — bounded on the
north by the Aurora Borealis, on the south by
the precession of the equinoxes, on the east
by the primeval chaos, and on the west by the
Day of Judgment. — JOHN FISKE [1842–
1901]: *Bounding the United States*

minds as well as the bodies of the eman-
cipated go free.
        Yorktown Oration [*1881*]

SAMUEL DODGE
[*Floruit* 1868]

You may go through this world, but
    'twill be very slow
If you listen to all that is said as you
    go;
You'll be worried and fretted and kept
    in a stew,
For meddlesome tongues must have
    something to do,
For people will talk, you know.
        People Will Talk. Stanza 1

PHINEAS TAYLOR BARNUM
[1810–1891]

There's a sucker born every minute.
                Attributed

WILLIAM HENRY CHANNING
[1810–1884]

To live content with small means; to
seek elegance rather than luxury, and
refinement rather than fashion; to be
worthy, not respectable, and wealthy,
not rich; to study hard, think quietly,
talk gently, act frankly; to listen to
stars and birds, to babes and sages,
with open heart; to bear all cheerfully,
do all bravely, await occasions, hurry
never. In a word, to let the spiritual,
unbidden and unconscious, grow up
through the common. This is to be my
symphony.

        My Symphony

DANIEL CLEMENT COLESWORTHY
[1810–1893]

A little word in kindness spoken,
    A motion or a tear,

Has often healed the heart that's
  broken,
And made a friend sincere.
A Little Word. Stanza 1

Then deem it not an idle thing
  A pleasant word to speak;
The face you wear — the thoughts you
  bring —
  The heart may heal or break.
Ibid. Stanza 3

SIR FRANCIS HASTINGS DOYLE
[1810–1888]

Last night, among his fellow roughs,
  He jested, quaffed, and swore;
A drunken private of the Buffs,
  Who never looked before.
Today, beneath the foeman's frown,
  He stands in Elgin's place,
Ambassador from Britain's crown,
  And type of all her race.
The Private of the Buffs. Stanza 1

ELIZABETH CLEGHORN GASKELL
[1810–1865]

A man is *so* in the way in the house.
Cranford [1851–1853]. Chap. 1

Correspondence, which bears much
the same relation to personal intercourse that the books of dried plants
I sometimes see ("Hortus Siccus," I
think they call the thing) do to the
living and fresh flowers in the lanes
and meadows.
Ibid. Chap. 3

One gives people in grief their own
way.
Ibid. Chap. 6

A little credulity helps one on
through life very smoothly.
Ibid. Chap. 11

I'll not listen to reason. . . . Reason always means what some one else
has got to say.
Ibid. Chap. 14

GENERAL PIERRE BOSQUET
[1810–1861]

It is magnificent, but it is not war.[1]
*Said of the charge of the Light
Brigade at the battle of Bala-
klava [October 25, 1854]*

ALFRED DE MUSSET
[1810–1857]

How glorious it is — and also how
painful — to be an exception.
Le Merle Blanc. I

Things they don't understand always
cause a sensation among the English.
Ibid. VIII

Never were there so many sleepless
nights as in the time of this man [Na-
poleon]. Never did one see so many
anguished mothers gaze from the ramparts of the towns. Never was there
such silence when one spoke of death.
And yet there was never so much joy,
life, warlike music, in all hearts. There
was never such pure sunshine as that
which dried all this blood. People said
that God made it for this man; they
called it Austerlitz weather. But he
made it himself with his incessant gun-
fire, and the only clouds were on the
morrow of his battles.
*Confession d'un Enfant du
Siècle [1836]. Chap. 2*

POPE LEO XIII (GIACCHINO PECCI)
[1810–1903]

Every man has by nature the right to
possess property as his own.
*Encyclical Letter on the Condi-
tion of Labor [May 15, 1891]*

It is impossible to reduce human society to one level.
Ibid.

It is one thing to have a right to the
possession of money, and another to
have a right to use money as one
pleases.
Ibid.

[1] C'est magnifique, mais **ce n'est pas la**
guerre.
See Tennyson, page 553b.

When a society is perishing, the true advice to give to those who would restore it is to recall it to the principles from which it sprung.

Encyclical Letter on the
Condition of Labor

Among the purposes of a society should be to try to arrange for a continuous supply of work at all times and seasons.

Ibid.

JAMES SLOANE GIBBONS
[1810–1892]

We are coming, Father Abraham, three
hundred thousand more,
From Mississippi's winding stream and
from New England's shore;
We leave our ploughs and workshops,
our wives and children dear,
With hearts too full for utterance, with
but a silent tear.

Three Hundred Thousand More.[1]
Stanza 1

WILLIAM MILLER
[1810–1872]

Wee Willie Winkie rins through the
toun,
Upstairs and dounstairs, in his nicht-
goun,
Tirlin' at the window, cryin' at the
lock,
"Are the weans in their bed? for it's
nou ten o'clock."

Willie Winkie

MARGARET FULLER
(OSSOLI)
[1810–1850]

I myself am more divine than any I
see.

Letter to Emerson
[March 1, 1838]

The golden-rod is one of the fairy, magical flowers; it grows not up to seek human love amid the light of day, but

[1] First printed in the *New York Evening Post*, July 16, 1862.

to mark to the discerning what wealth lies hid in the secret caves of earth.

Journal [September, 1840]

Beware of over-great pleasure in being popular or even beloved. As far as an amiable disposition and powers of entertainment make you so, it is happiness, but if there is one grain of plausibility, it is a poison.

Letter to her brother Arthur
[December 20, 1840]

What I mean by the Muse is that unimpeded clearness of the intuitive powers, which a perfectly truthful adherence to every admonition of the higher instincts would bring to a finely organized human being. . . . Should these faculties have free play, I believe they will open new, deeper and purer sources of joyous inspiration than have yet refreshed the earth.

Woman in the Nineteenth
Century [1845]

It does not follow because many books are written by persons born in America that there exists an American literature. Books which imitate or represent the thoughts and life of Europe do not constitute an American literature. Before such can exist, an original idea must animate this nation and fresh currents of life must call into life fresh thoughts along its shores.

In the New York Tribune [1846]

Truth is the nursing mother of genius. No man can be absolutely true to himself, eschewing cant, compromise, servile imitation, and complaisance, without becoming original for there is in every creature a fountain of life which, if not choked back by stones and other dead rubbish, will create a fresh atmosphere, and bring to life fresh beauty.

Ibid.

When an immortal poet was secure only of a few copyists to circulate his works, there were princes and nobles to patronize literature and the arts. Here is only the public, and the public must learn how to cherish the nobler and rarer plants, and to plant the aloe, able

to wait a hundred years for its bloom, or its garden will contain, presently, nothing but potatoes and pot-herbs.
> *In the New York Tribune*

This was one of the rye-bread days, all dull and damp without.
> *Diary. Quoted by* THOMAS WENTWORTH HIGGINSON: *Life of Margaret Fuller Ossoli [1884], Chap. 7*

For precocity some great price is always demanded sooner or later in life.
> *Ibid. Chap. 18*

Genius will live and thrive without training, but it does not the less reward the watering-pot and pruning-knife.
> *Ibid.*

I accept the universe.[1]
> *Attributed*

THEODORE PARKER
[1810–1860]

Truth never yet fell dead in the streets; it has such affinity with the soul of man, the seed however broadcast will catch somewhere and produce its hundredfold.
> *A Discourse of Matters Pertaining to Religion [1842]*

Truth stood on one side and Ease on the other; it has often been so.
> *Ibid.*

Man never falls so low that he can see nothing higher than himself.
> *Essay, A Lesson for the Day*

All men desire to be immortal.
> *A Sermon on the Immortal Life [September 20, 1846]*

A democracy, — that is a government of all the people, by all the people, for all the people;[2] of course, a government of the principles of eternal justice, the unchanging law of God; for shortness' sake I will call it the idea of Freedom.
> *The American Idea* [1] *[1850]*

We look to Thee; Thy truth is still the Light
Which guides the nations, groping on their way,
Stumbling and falling in disastrous night,
Yet hoping ever for the perfect day.
> *The Way, the Truth, and the Life. Stanza 2*

EDMUND HAMILTON SEARS
[1810–1876]

Calm on the listening ear of night
Come Heaven's melodious strains,
Where wild Judea stretches far
Her silver-mantled plains.
> *Christmas Song [1834]*

It came upon the midnight clear,
That glorious song of old,
From Angels bending near the earth
To touch their harps of gold;
"Peace on the earth, good will to men,
From Heaven's all gracious King."
The world in solemn stillness lay
To hear the angels sing.
> *The Angels' Song [1850]*

When Peace shall over all the earth
Its ancient splendors fling
And the whole world send back the song
Which now the angels sing.
> *Ibid.*

GEORGE SHARSWOOD
[1810–1883]

It is not uncommon to hear the expression, "The law is a jealous mistress." It is true that this profession, like all others, demands of those who

---

[1] By God! she'd better. — CARLYLE'S *reported comment*

[2] See Daniel Webster, page 443b, William Lloyd Garrison, page 517b, and Lincoln, page 541a.
Parker used the same phrase in a speech delivered in Boston [May 31, 1854] and in a sermon in Music Hall, Boston [July 4, 1858]. WILLIAM H. HERNDON visited Boston and on his return to Springfield, Illinois, took with him some of Parker's sermons and addresses. In his *Abraham Lincoln, Vol. II, P. 65,* Herndon says that Lincoln marked with pencil the portion of the Music Hall address, "Democracy is direct self-government, over all the people, by all the people, for all the people."

[1] Speech at the New England Anti-Slavery Convention, Boston [May 29, 1850].

would succeed in it an earnest and entire devotion.[1]

Memoir of William Blackstone,
Blackstone's Commentaries
[1860]

MARTIN FARQUHAR TUPPER
[1810–1889]

A babe in a house is a well-spring of pleasure.

Proverbial Philosophy [1838–
1842]. Of Education

Analogy is milk for babes, but abstract truths are strong meat.

Ibid.

God, from a beautiful necessity, is Love.

Ibid. Of Immortality

Error is a hardy plant: it flourisheth in every soil.

Ibid. Of Truth in Things False

Wait, thou child of hope, for Time shall teach thee all things.

Ibid. Of Good in Things Evil

Clamorous pauperism feasteth
While honest Labor, pining, hideth his sharp ribs.

Ibid. Of Discretion

Well-timed silence hath more eloquence than speech.

Ibid.

It is well to lie fallow for a while.

Ibid. Of Recreation

A good book is the best of friends, the same today and for ever.

Ibid. Of Reading

Who can wrestle against Sleep? —
Yet is that giant very gentleness.

Ibid. Of Beauty

Nature's own Nobleman, friendly and frank,
Is a man with his heart in his hand!

Nature's Nobleman [1844].
Stanza 1

---

1 I will not say with Lord Hale, that "The Law will admit of no rival," . . . but I will say that it is a jealous mistress, and requires a long and constant courtship. It is not to be won by trifling favors, but by lavish homage. — JOSEPH STORY: *The Value and Importance of Legal Studies* [1829]

See Emerson, page 505a.

Hope and be happy that all's for the best!

All's for the Best [1844].
Stanza 3

Never go gloomily, man with a mind!
Hope is a better companion than fear.

Cheer Up [1844]. Stanza 1

JOHN BRIGHT
[1811–1889]

And even if I were alone, if mine were a solitary voice, raised amid the din of arms and the clamours of a venal press, I should have the consolation I have tonight — and which I trust will be mine to the last moment of my existence — the priceless consolation that no word of mine has tended to the squandering of my country's treasure or the spilling of one single drop of my country's blood.[1]

Speech on the Crimean War,
House of Commons [December
22, 1854]

The Angel of Death has been abroad throughout the land; you may almost hear the beating of his wings.

Speech, House of Commons
[February 23, 1855]

Force is no remedy.

On the Irish Troubles [1880]

My opinion is that the Northern States will manage somehow to muddle through.

Said during the American Civil
War. Quoted in JUSTIN MC-
CARTHY: *Reminiscences [1899]*

THÉOPHILE GAUTIER
[1811–1872]

Everything passes. Robust art alone is eternal. The bust outlasts the citadel.[2]

L'Art

---

1 See Jefferson, page 375b.
2 Tout passe. L'art robuste
    Seul a l'éternité;
    Le buste
    Survit à la cité.

HORACE GREELEY
[1811–1872]

A widow of doubtful age will marry almost any sort of a white man.
> *Letter to Dr. Rufus Wilmot Griswold*

If, on a full and final review, my life and practice shall be found unworthy of my principles, let due infamy be heaped on my memory; but let none be thereby led to distrust the principles to which I proved recreant, nor yet the ability of some to adorn them by a suitable life and conversation. To unerring time be all this committed.
> *Statement [1846], quoted in* JAMES PARTON: *Life of Horace Greeley [1855]*

The best business you can go into you will find on your father's farm or in his workshop. If you have no family or friends to aid you, and no prospect opened to you there, turn your face to the great West,[1] and there build up a home and fortune.
> *To Aspiring Young Men. Ibid. Page 414*

The illusion that times that were are better than those that are, has probably pervaded all ages.
> *The American Conflict [1864–1866]*

Wisdom is never dear, provided the article be genuine.
> *Address on Agriculture, Houston, Texas [May 23, 1871]*

FRANCES SARGENT OSGOOD
[1811–1850]

Work — for some good, be it ever so slowly;
Cherish some flower, be it ever so lowly;
Labor! — all labor is noble and holy!
Let thy great deeds be thy prayer to thy God!
> *Laborare est Orare.*[2] *Stanza 6*

[1] See J. B. L. Soule, page 585a.
[2] To labor is to pray. — Motto of BENEDICT [480–543], *founder of the Benedictine Order*

WENDELL PHILLIPS
[1811–1884]

Take the whole range of imaginative literature, and we are all wholesale borrowers. In every matter that relates to invention, to use, or beauty or form, we are borrowers.
> *Lecture, The Lost Arts [1838]*

We live under a government of men — and morning newspapers.
> *Speech [January 28, 1852]*

Revolutions are not made; they come. A revolution is as natural a growth as an oak. It comes out of the past. Its foundations are laid far back.
> *Ibid.*

The best use of laws is to teach men to trample bad laws under their feet.
> *Speech [April 12, 1852]*

What the Puritans gave the world was not thought, but action.
> *Speech [December 21, 1855]*

One on God's side is a majority.
> *Speech [November 1, 1859]*

Every man meets his Waterloo at last.
> *Ibid.*

Truth is one forever absolute, but opinion is truth filtered through the moods, the blood, the disposition of the spectator.
> *Idols [October 4, 1859]*

Difference of religion breeds more quarrels than difference of politics.
> *Speech [November 7, 1860]*

Governments exist to protect the rights of minorities. The loved and the rich need no protection, — they have many friends and few enemies.
> *Speech [December 21, 1860]*

Revolutions never go backward.[1]
> *Speech [February 17, 1861]*

Some doubt the courage of the Negro. Go to Haiti and stand on those fifty thousand graves of the best sol-

[1] I know, and all the world knows, that revolutions never go backward. — WILLIAM HENRY SEWARD: *Speech at Rochester on the Irrepressible Conflict* [October, 1858]

diers France ever had, and ask them what they think of the Negro's sword.
Address on Toussaint L'Ouverture [*1861*]

Aristocracy is always cruel.
Ibid.

HARRIET BEECHER STOWE [1]
[1811–1896]

Eliza made her desperate retreat across the river just in the dusk of twilight. The grey mist of evening, rising slowly from the river, enveloped her as she disappeared up the bank, and the swollen current and floundering masses of ice presented a hopeless barrier between her and her pursuer.
Uncle Tom's Cabin [*1852*]. *Chap. 8*

I 'spect I growed. Don't think nobody never made me.
Ibid. Chap. 20

I's wicked — I is. I's mighty wicked, anyhow. I can't help it.
Ibid.

Whipping and abuse are like laudanum: you have to double the dose as the sensibilities decline.
Ibid.

It lies around us like a cloud,
  A world we do not see;
Yet the sweet closing of an eye
  May bring us there to be.
The Other World [*1867*]. *Stanza 1*

CHARLES SUMNER
[1811–1874]

There is the National flag. He must be cold, indeed, who can look upon its folds rippling in the breeze without pride of country. If in a foreign land,

---

[1] We have seen an American woman write a novel of which a million copies were sold in all languages, and which had one merit, of speaking to the universal heart, and was read with equal interest to three audiences, namely, in the parlor, in the kitchen, and in the nursery of every house. — EMERSON: *Society and Solitude* [1870], *Success*

the flag is companionship, and country itself, with all its endearments.
Are We a Nation? [*November 19, 1867*]

White is for purity; red, for valor; blue for justice. And altogether, bunting, stripes, stars, and colors, blazing in the sky, make the flag of our country, to be cherished by all our hearts, to be upheld by all our hands.
Ibid.

WILLIAM MAKEPEACE THACKERAY
[1811–1863]

Although I enter not,
Yet round about the spot
  Ofttimes I hover;
And near the sacred gate,
With longing eyes I wait,
  Expectant of her.
At the Church Gate [1]

The play is done; the curtain drops,
  Slow falling to the prompter's bell:
A moment yet the actor stops,
  And looks around, to say farewell.
It is an irksome word and task;
  And when he's laughed and said his say,
He shows, as he removes the mask,
  A face that's anything but gay.
Doctor Birch and His Young Friends. Epilogue, The End of the Play, Stanza 1

Christmas is here:
Winds whistle shrill,
Icy and chill.
Little care we;
Little we fear
Weather without,
Sheltered about
The Mahogany Tree.
The Mahogany Tree. Stanza 1

Though more than half the world was his,
He [2] died without a rood his own;

---

[1] In *Pendennis* [1848–1850], *Vol. I, Chap. 31,* the third and fourth lines read:
  Sometimes I hover,
  And at the sacred gate.
[2] Napoleon Bonaparte; the ballad was written in Paris at the time of the second funeral of Napoleon [1840].

And borrow'd from his enemies
Six foot of ground to lie upon.
      The Chronicle of the Drum. Part II

Werther had a love for Charlotte
   Such as words could never utter;
Would you know how first he met her?
   She was cutting bread and butter.[1]
      Sorrows of Werther. Stanza 1

Charlotte was a married lady,
   And a moral man was Werther,
And for all the wealth of Indies,
   Would do nothing for to hurt her.
      Ibid. Stanza 2

So he sighed and pined and ogled,
   And his passion boiled and bubbled,
Till he blew his silly brains out
   And no more was by it troubled.
      Ibid. Stanza 3

Charlotte, having seen his body
   Borne before her on a shutter,
Like a well-conducted person,
   Went on cutting bread and butter.
      Ibid. Stanza 4

Away from the world and its toils and
   its cares,
I've a snug little kingdom up four pairs
   of stairs.
      The Cane-Bottom'd Chair. Stanza 1

A man — I let the truth out —
Who's had almost every tooth out,
Cannot sing as once he sung,
When he was young as you are young,
When he was young and lutes were
   strung,
And love-lamps in the casement hung.
   Mrs. Katherine's Lantern. Stanza 6

The rose upon my balcony the morning
   air perfuming,
Was leafless all the winter time and
   pining for the spring.
      The Rose Upon My Balcony.
         Stanza 1

There lived a sage in days of yore,
And he a handsome pigtail wore;

But wondered much and sorrowed more
Because it hung behind him.
      A Tragic Story (from von
         Chamisso). Stanza 1

In the brave days when I was twenty-
   one.
      The Garret. Refrain

There were three sailors of Bristol City
Who took a boat and went to sea.
But first with beef and captain's bis-
   cuits
And pickled pork they loaded she.
There was gorging Jack and guzzling
   Jimmy,
And the youngest he was little Billee.
Now when they got as far as the
   Equator
They'd nothing left but one split pea.
      Little Billee

Says gorging Jim to guzzling Jacky,
We have no wittles, so we must eat *we.*
      Ibid.

There's little Bill as is young and
   tender,
We're old and tough — so let's eat *he.*
      Ibid.

This I set down as a positive truth.
A woman with fair opportunities, and
without a positive hump, may marry
whom she likes.[1]
      Vanity Fair [*1847–1848*].
         Vol. I, Chap. 4

Them's my sentiments.
      Ibid. Chap. 21

Everybody in Vanity Fair must have
remarked how well those live who are
comfortably and thoroughly in debt;
how they deny themselves nothing;
how jolly and easy they are in their
minds.
      Ibid. Chap. 22

When we say of a gentleman that he
lives elegantly on nothing a year, we
use the word "nothing" to signify some-

---

[1] Charlotte held a brown loaf in her hand,
and was cutting slices for the little ones
all round in proportion to their age and appetite. — GOETHE: *The Sorrows of Werther*
[1774]

[1] I should like to see any kind of a man,
distinguishable from a gorilla, that some good
and even pretty woman could not shape a
husband out of. — OLIVER WENDELL HOLMES:
The Professor at the Breakfast-Table [1860]
   The whole world is strewn with snares,
traps, gins and pitfalls for the capture of men
by women. — BERNARD SHAW: *Man and Superman* [1903], *Epistle Dedicatory*

thing unknown; meaning, simply, that we don't know how the gentleman in question defrays the expenses of his establishment.
Vanity Fair. Vol. I, Chap. 35

How to Live Well on Nothing a Year.
Ibid. Title of Chap. 36

Mother is the name for God in the lips and hearts of little children.[1]
Ibid. Chap. 37

I think I could be a good woman if I had five thousand a year.[2]
Ibid. Vol. II, Chap. 1

A comfortable career of prosperity, if it does not make people honest, at least keeps them so.
Ibid.

By economy and good management, — by a sparing use of ready money and by paying scarcely anybody, — people can manage, for a time at least, to make a great show with very little means.
Ibid. Chap. 11

Ah! *Vanitas Vanitatum!* Which of us is happy in this world? Which of us has his desire? or, having it, is satisfied? — Come, children, let us shut up the box and the puppets, for our play is played out.
Ibid. Chap. 27

He who meanly admires mean things is a Snob.
The Book of Snobs [*1848*].
Chap. 2

Rake's Progress.[3]
Pendennis [*1848–1850*]. *Title of Chap. 19*

Yes, I am a fatal man, Madame Fribsbi. To inspire hopeless passion is my destiny.
Ibid. Chap. 23

[1] The mother's face and voice are the first conscious objects as the infant soul unfolds, and she soon comes to stand in the very place of God to her child. — GRANVILLE STANLEY HALL: *Article in Pedagogical Seminary* [June, 1891]

[2] See Huxley, page 633b.

[3] *The Rake's Progress* is the title of one of the famous series of paintings and engravings by William Hogarth [1697–1764].

Remember, it's as easy to marry a rich woman as a poor woman.
Pendennis. Chap. 28

Of the Corporation of the Goose-quill — of the Press, . . . of the fourth estate.[1] . . . There she is — the great engine — she never sleeps. She has her ambassadors in every quarter of the world — her courtiers upon every road. Her officers march along with armies, and her envoys walk into statesmen's cabinets. They are ubiquitous.
Ibid. Chap. 30

The best way is to make your letters safe. I never wrote a letter in all my life that would commit me, and demmy, sir, I have had some experience of women.
Ibid. Chap. 64

How hard it is to make an Englishman acknowledge that he is happy!
Ibid. Chap. 69

This Bouillabaisse a noble dish is — A sort of soup, or broth, or brew.
The Ballad of Bouillabaisse [*1849*].
Stanza 2

Ho, pretty page, with the dimpled chin, That never has known the barber's shear,
All your wish is woman to win, This is the way that boys begin, — Wait till you come to Forty Year.
Rebecca and Rowena [*1850*]. *The Age of Wisdom, Stanza 1*

'Tis not the dying for a faith that's so hard, Master Harry — every man of every nation has done that — 'tis the living up to it that's difficult.[2]
Henry Esmond [*1852*]. *Book I, Chap. 6*

'Tis strange what a man may do, and a woman yet think him an angel.
Ibid. Chap. 7

Fiction carries a greater amount of truth in solution than the volume which purports to be all true.
The English Humorists [*1853*].
Steele

Harlequin without his mask is known to present a very sober countenance,

[1] See Carlyle, page 473a.

[2] See Adlai E. Stevenson, page 986b.

and was himself, the story goes, the melancholy patient whom the Doctor advised to go and see Harlequin.[1]

The English Humorists. Swift

The true pleasure of life is to live with your inferiors.

The Newcomes [*1853–1855*].
Chap. 9

The wicked are wicked, no doubt, and they go astray and they fall, and they come by their deserts; but who can tell the mischief which the very virtuous do?

Ibid. Chap. 20

Just as the last bell struck, a peculiar sweet smile shone over his face, and he lifted up his head a little, and quickly said "Adsum!" and fell back. It was the word we used at school, when names were called; and lo, he, whose heart was as that of a little child, had answered to his name, and stood in the presence of The Master.

Ibid. Chap. 80

A pedigree reaching as far back as the Deluge.

The Rose and the Ring [*1855*].
Chap. 2

The book of female logic is blotted all over with tears, and Justice in their courts is forever in a passion.

The Virginians [*1857–1859*].
Chap. 4

Heaven does not choose its elect from among the great and wealthy.

Ibid. Chap. 5

Women like not only to conquer, but to be conquered.

Ibid.

Next to the very young, I suppose the very old are the most selfish.

Ibid. Chap. 61

'Tis hard with respect to Beauty, that its possessor should not have even

---

[1] A patient one day presented himself to Abernethy; after careful examination the celebrated practitioner said, "You need amusement; go and hear Grimaldi; he will make you laugh, and that will be better for you than any drugs." "My God," exclaimed the invalid, "but I *am* Grimaldi!" — CESARE LOMBROSO [1836–1909]: *The Man of Genius, Part I, Chap. 2*

a life-enjoyment of it, but be compelled to resign it after, at the most, some forty years' lease.

The Virginians. Chap. 73

For a steady self-esteem and indomitable confidence in our own courage, greatness, magnanimity, who can compare with Britons, except their children across the Atlantic?

Ibid. Chap. 89

Through all the doubt and darkness, the danger and long tempest of the war, I think it was only the American leader's [1] indomitable soul that remained entirely steady.

Ibid. Chap. 90

To endure is greater than to dare; to tire out hostile fortune; to be daunted by no difficulty; to keep heart when all have lost it; to go through intrigue spotless; to forego even ambition when the end is gained — who can say this is not greatness?

Ibid. Chap. 92

Bravery never goes out of fashion.

The Four Georges [*1860*].
George II

As we go on the downhill journey, the milestones are gravestones, and on each more and more names are written; unless haply you live beyond man's common age, when friends have dropped off, and, tottering, and feeble, and unpitied, you reach the terminus alone.

The Roundabout Papers [*1861–1862*]. *On Letts' Diary*

ROBERT BROWNING
[1812–1889]

Sun-treader,[2] life and light be thine forever!

Pauline [*1833*]

I go to prove my soul!

I see my way as birds their trackless way.

I shall arrive! what time, what circuit first,

I ask not; but unless God send his hail

---

[1] George Washington.
[2] Shelley.

Or blinding fire-balls, sleet or stifling
  snow,
In some time, his good time, I shall
  arrive:
He guides me and the bird. In his good
  time!
        Paracelsus [*1835*]. *Part I*
Measure your mind's height by the
  shade it casts!
        Ibid. Part III

    Every joy is gain
And gain is gain, however small.
        Ibid. Part IV
Over the sea our galleys went.
        Ibid.

The sad rhyme of the men who proudly
  clung
To their first fault, and withered in
  their pride.
        Ibid.

I give the fight up: let there be an end,
A privacy, an obscure nook for me.
I want to be forgotten even by God.
        Ibid. Part V
Would you have your songs endure?
Build on the human heart.
        Sordello [*1840*]. *II*

    Thoughts may be
Over-poetical for poetry.
        Ibid. III

    'Twere too absurd to slight
For the hereafter the today's delight!
        Ibid. VI

    Any nose
May ravage with impunity a rose.
        Ibid.

Day!
Faster and more fast,
O'er night's brim, day boils at last.
    Pippa Passes [*1841*]. *Introduction*
The year's at the spring
And day's at the morn;
Morning's at seven;
The hillside's dew-pearled;
The lark's on the wing;
The snail's on the thorn:
God's in his heaven —
All's right with the world.[1]
        Ibid. Part I

[1] See Voltaire, page 324b, and Whittier,
page 528b.

One may do whate'er one likes
In Art: the only thing is, to make sure
That one does like it.
        Pippa Passes. Part II
Some unsuspected isle in far-off seas.
        Ibid.
In the morning of the world,
When earth was nigher heaven than
  now.
        Ibid. Part III
All service ranks the same with God:
With God, whose puppets, best and
  worst,
Are we; there is no last nor first.
        Ibid. Part IV
Marching along, fifty-score strong,
Great-hearted gentlemen, singing this
  song.
        Bells and Pomegranates [*1841–
        1846*]. *Cavalier Tunes, I,
        Marching Along*
Boot, saddle, to horse, and away!
        Ibid. III, Boot and Saddle
Just for a handful of silver he left us,
Just for a riband to stick in his coat.
        Ibid. The Lost Leader [1]
We that had loved him so, followed
  him, honoured him,
    Lived in his mild and magnificent
    eye,
Learned his great language, caught his
  clear accents,
    Made him our pattern to live and to
    die!
        Ibid.
Shakespeare was of us, Milton was for
  us,
Burns, Shelley, were with us — they
  watch from their graves!
        Ibid.
One more devils'-triumph and sorrow
  for angels,
One more wrong to man, one more insult
  to God!
        Ibid.
We shall march prospering, — not thro'
  his presence;
    Songs may inspirit us, — not from
    his lyre;
Deeds will be done, — while he boasts
  his quiescence,

[1] Often taken as reference to Wordsworth.

Still bidding crouch whom the rest
bade aspire.
> *Bells and Pomegranates.*
> *The Lost Leader*

Never glad confident morning again!
> *Ibid.*

I sprang to the stirrup, and Joris, and
he;
I galloped, Dirck galloped, we galloped
all three.
> *Ibid. How They Brought the*
> *Good News from Ghent to Aix,*
> *Stanza 1*

And into the midnight we galloped
abreast.
> *Ibid.*

Round the cape of a sudden came the
sea,
And the sun looked over the mountain's rim:
And straight was a path of gold for
him,
And the need of a world of men for
me.
> *Ibid. Parting at Morning*

Let's contend no more, Love,
Strive nor weep:
All be as before, Love,
— Only sleep!
> *Ibid. A Woman's Last Word,*
> *Stanza 1*

Where the apple reddens
Never pry —
Lest we lose our Edens,
Eve and I.
> *Ibid. Stanza 5*

Teach me, only teach, Love!
As I ought
I will speak thy speech, Love,
Think thy thought.
> *Ibid. Stanza 7*

That shall be tomorrow
Not tonight:
I must bury sorrow
Out of sight.
> *Ibid. Stanza 9*

Beautiful Evelyn Hope is dead!
> *Ibid. Evelyn Hope, Stanza 1*

You will wake, and remember, and
understand.
> *Ibid. Stanza 7*

Where the quiet-coloured end of evening smiles.
> *Bells and Pomegranates. Love*
> *Among the Ruins, Stanza 1*

Earth's returns
For whole centuries of folly, noise and
sin!
> *Ibid. Stanza 7*

This world, and the wrong it does.
> *Ibid. Old Pictures in Florence,*
> *Stanza 7*

What a man's work comes to! So he
plans it,
Performs it, perfects it, makes amends
For the toiling and moiling, and then,
sic transit!
> *Ibid. Stanza 10*

What's come to perfection perishes.
Things learned on earth, we shall practise in heaven:
Works done least rapidly, Art most
cherishes.
> *Ibid. Stanza 17*

Your ghost will walk, you lover of trees,
(If our loves remain)
In an English lane.
> *Ibid. De Gustibus*

Italy! my Italy!
Queen Mary's saying serves for me —
(When fortune's malice
Lost her — Calais):
Open my heart, and you will see
Graved inside of it, "Italy."
> *Ibid.*

Oh, to be in England,
Now that April's there,
And whoever wakes in England
Sees, some morning, unaware,
That the lowest boughs and the brush-
wood sheaf
Round the elm-tree bole are in tiny
leaf,
While the chaffinch sings on the orchard
bough
In England — now!
> *Ibid. Home-Thoughts, from*
> *Abroad, Stanza 1*

That's the wise thrush; he sings each
song twice over,

Lest you should think he never could
    recapture
The first fine careless rapture!

> *Bells and Pomegranates. Home-*
> *Thoughts, from Abroad, Stanza 2*

Nobly, nobly Cape St. Vincent to the
    North-west died away;
Sunset ran, one glorious blood-red,
    reeking into Cadiz Bay.

> *Ibid. Home-thoughts, from the Sea*

How well I know what I mean to do
When the long dark autumn evenings
    come.

> *Ibid. By the Fireside, Stanza 1*

O woman-country! [1] wooed not wed.

> *Ibid. Stanza 6*

Oh, the little more, and how much it is!
And the little less, and what worlds
    away!

> *Ibid. Stanza 39*

If two lives join, there is oft a scar.
They are one and one, with a shadowy
    third;
One near one is too far.

> *Ibid. Stanza 46*

Only I discern
Infinite passion, and the pain
Of finite hearts that yearn.

> *Ibid. Two in the Campagna,*
> *Stanza 12*

This is a spray the Bird clung to,
Making it blossom with pleasure.

> *Ibid. Misconceptions, Stanza 1*

Room after room,
I hunt the house through
We inhabit together.

> *Ibid. Love in a Life, Stanza 1*

Escape me?
Never —
Beloved!
While I am I, and you are you.

> *Ibid. Life in a Love, Stanza 1*

To dry one's eyes and laugh at a fall,
And baffled, get up and begin again.

> *Ibid. Stanza 2*

Ah, did you once see Shelley plain,
    And did he stop and speak to you,
And did you speak to him again?
    How strange it seems and new! [2]

> *Ibid. Memorabilia, I*

[1] Italy.
[2] And did you once find Browning plain?

There's a woman like a dewdrop, she's
    so purer than the purest.

> *Bells and Pomegranates. A Blot*
> *in the 'Scutcheon, Act I, Sc. 3*

When is man strong until he feels
    alone? [1]

> *Ibid. Colombe's Birthday, Act III*

You know, we French stormed Ratis-
    bon.

> *Ibid. Incident of the French Camp,*
> *Stanza 1*

"You're wounded!" "Nay," the soldier's
    pride
Touched to the quick, he said:
"I'm killed, Sire!" And his chief beside,
    Smiling the boy fell dead.

> *Ibid. Stanza 5*

That's my last Duchess painted on the
    wall.

> *Ibid. My Last Duchess*

She had
A heart — how shall I say? — too soon
    made glad.

> *Ibid.*

The lie was dead,
And damned, and truth stood up in-
    stead.

> *Ibid. Count Gismond, Stanza 13*

Morning, evening, noon and night,
"Praise God!" sang Theocrite.

> *Ibid. The Boy and the Angel*

Just my vengeance complete,
    The man sprang to his feet,
Stood erect, caught at God's skirts, and
    prayed!
—So, *I* was afraid!

> *Ibid. Instans Tyrannus,*
> *Stanza 7*

When a man's busy, why, leisure
Strikes him as wonderful pleasure:
'Faith, and at leisure once is he?
Straightway he wants to be busy.

> *Ibid. The Glove, Stanza 1*

And did he really seem quite clear?
And did you read the book again?
How strange it seems and queer.
CHARLES WILLIAM STUBBS [1845–1912]:
    Parody
[1] The strongest man on earth is he who
stands most alone. — IBSEN: *An Enemy of*
the People [1882], *Act V*

Who knows but the world may end
tonight?
> *Bells and Pomegranates. The Last
> Ride Together, Stanza 2*

Fail I alone, in words and deeds?
Why, all men strive, and who succeeds?
> *Ibid. Stanza 5*

All labor, yet no less
Bear up beneath their unsuccess.
Look at the end of the work, contrast
The petty done, the undone vast,
This present of theirs with the hopeful
past!
> *Ibid.*

What hand and brain went ever paired?
What heart alike conceived and dared?
What act proved all its thought had
been?
> *Ibid. Stanza 6*

Sing, riding's a joy! For me I ride.
> *Ibid. Stanza 7*

Earth being so good, would heaven
seem best?
> *Ibid. Stanza 9*

Hamelin Town's in Brunswick,
By famous Hanover city.
> *Ibid. The Pied Piper of Hamelin,
> Stanza 1*

Rats!
They fought the dogs and killed the
cats,
And bit the babies in the cradles,
And ate the cheeses out of the vats,
And licked the soup from the cooks'
own ladles.
> *Ibid. Stanza 2*

With shrieking and squeaking
In fifty different sharps and flats.
> *Ibid.*

When the liquor's out, why clink the
cannikin?
> *Ibid. The Flight of the
> Duchess, XVI*

It's a long lane that knows no turnings.
> *Ibid. XVII*

That low man seeks a little thing to do,
Sees it and does it;
This high man, with a great thing to
pursue,
Dies ere he knows it.

That low man goes on adding one to
one,
His hundred's soon hit;
This high man, aiming at a million,
Misses an unit.
That has the world here — should he
need the next,
Let the world mind him!
This throws himself on God, and un-
perplexed
Seeking shall find Him.
> *Bells and Pomegranates. A
> Grammarian's Funeral*

And inasmuch as feeling, the East's
gift,
Is quick and transient, — comes, and
lo, is gone —
While Northern thought is slow and
durable.
> *Ibid. Luria, Act V*

Ah, but a man's reach should exceed
his grasp,
Or what's a heaven for?
> *Men and Women* [*1855*].
> *Andrea del Sarto* [1]

How I shall lie through centuries,
And hear the blessed mutter of the
mass,
And see God made and eaten all day
long,
And feel the steady candle-flame, and
taste
Good strong thick stupefying incense
smoke!
> *Ibid. The Bishop Orders His Tomb
> at Saint Praxed's Church*

Truth that peeps
Over the glass's edge when dinner's
done,
And body gets its sop and holds its
noise
And leaves soul free a little.
> *Ibid. Bishop Blougram's Apology*

The common problem, yours, mine,
every one's,
Is — not to fancy what were fair in life
Provided it could be, — but, finding
first

---

[1] The poem is based on the account of the
artist given in VASARI'S *Lives of the Painters*.

What may be, then find how to make it fair
Up to our means.
Men and Women. Bishop Blougram's Apology

Just when we are safest, there's a sunset-touch,
A fancy from a flower-bell, some one's death,
A chorus-ending from Euripides.
Ibid.

One wise man's verdict outweighs all the fools'.
Ibid.

Our interest's on the dangerous edge of things.
The honest thief, the tender murderer,
The superstitious atheist, demirep
That loves and saves her soul in new French books.
Ibid.

You call for faith:
I show you doubt, to prove that faith exists.
The more of doubt, the stronger faith, I say,
If faith o'ercomes doubt.
Ibid.

When the fight begins within himself,
A man's worth something.
Ibid.

Dear dead women, with such hair, too
— what's become of all the gold
Used to hang and brush their bosoms?
I feel chilly and grown old.
Ibid. A Toccata of Galuppi's, Stanza 15

The sin I impute to each frustrate ghost
Is — the unlit lamp and the ungirt loin.
Ibid. The Statue and the Bust, Stanza 83

God made all the creatures, and gave them our love and our fear,
To give sign, we and they are his children, one family here.
Ibid. Saul, VI

How good is man's life, the mere living! how fit to employ
All the heart and the soul and the senses forever in joy!
Ibid. IX

I have lived, seen God's hand through a lifetime, and all was for best.
Men and Women. Saul, IX

God is seen God
In the star, in the stone, in the flesh, in the soul and the clod.
Ibid. XVII

'Tis not what man Does which exalts him, but what man Would do!
Ibid. XVIII

The sprinkled isles,
Lily on lily, that o'erlace the sea.
Ibid. Cleon

And I have written three books on the soul,
Proving absurd all written hitherto,
And putting us to ignorance again.
Ibid.

Rafael made a century of sonnets.
Ibid. One Word More, II

Does he paint? he fain would write a poem, —
Does he write? he fain would paint a picture.
Ibid. VIII

Where my heart lies, let my brain lie also.
Ibid. XIV

God be thanked, the meanest of his creatures
Boasts two soul-sides, one to face the world with,
One to show a woman when he loves her!
Ibid. XVII

Oh, their Rafael of the dear Madonnas,
Oh, their Dante of the dread Inferno,
Wrote one song — and in my brain I sing it,
Drew one angel — borne, see, on my bosom!
Ibid. XIX

Was there naught better than to enjoy?
No feat which, done, would make time break,
And let us pent-up creatures through
Into eternity, our due?
No forcing earth teach heaven's employ?
Dramatis Personae [1864]. Dis Aliter Visum, Stanza 24

That out of three sounds he frame, not
   a fourth sound, but a star.
   Dramatis Personae. Abt Vogler,[1]
   Stanza 7
What was good shall be good, with for
   evil so much good more;
On the earth the broken arcs; in the
   heaven, a perfect round.
   Ibid. Stanza 9
The high that proved too high, the
   heroic for earth too hard,
The passion that left the ground to lose
   itself in the sky.
   Ibid. Stanza 10
Sorrow is hard to bear, and doubt is
   slow to clear,
Each sufferer says his say, his scheme
   of the weal and woe:
But God has a few of us whom he
   whispers in the ear;
The rest may reason and welcome:
   'tis we musicians know.
   Ibid. Stanza 12
Grow old along with me!
The best is yet to be,
The last of life, for which the first was
   made.
Our times are in his hand.
   Ibid. Rabbi Ben Ezra, Stanza 1
Irks care the crop-full bird? Frets
   doubt the maw-crammed beast?
   Ibid. Stanza 4
   Then welcome each rebuff
   That turns earth's smoothness rough,
Each sting that bids nor sit nor stand,
   but go!
   Be our joys three-parts pain!
   Strive, and hold cheap the strain;
Learn, nor account the pang; dare,
   never grudge the throe!
   Ibid. Stanza 6
What I aspired to be,
And was not, comforts me.
   Ibid. Stanza 7
Therefore I summon age
To grant youth's heritage.
   Ibid. Stanza 13
Thou waitedst age: wait death nor be
   afraid!
   Ibid. Stanza 19

[1] The Abt or Abbé George Joseph Vogler

Look not thou down but up!
   *Dramatis Personae. Rabbi
   Ben Ezra, Stanza 30*
Stung by the splendour of a sudden
   thought.
   Ibid. A Death in the Desert
Progress, man's distinctive mark alone,
Not God's, and not the beasts': God is,
   they are;
Man partly is, and wholly hopes to be.
   Ibid.
Letting the rank tongue blossom into
   speech.
   Ibid. Caliban upon Setebos
How sad and bad and mad it was — [1]
But then, how it was sweet!
   Ibid. Confessions, Stanza 9
Fear death? — to feel the fog in my
   throat,
The mist in my face.
   Ibid. Prospice
No! let me taste the whole of it, fare
   like my peers,
   The heroes of old,
Bear the brunt, in a minute pay glad
   life's arrears
   Of pain, darkness, and cold.
   Ibid.
Hold me but safe again within the bond
Of one immortal look.
   Ibid. Eurydice to Orpheus
This could but have happened once, —
And we missed it, lost it forever.
   Ibid. Youth and Art, Stanza 17
All that I own is a print,
An etching, a mezzotint.
   Ibid. A Likeness
He never saw, never before today,
What was able to take his breath away.
A face to lose youth for, to occupy age
With the dream of, meet death with.[2]
   Ibid.
We find great things are made of little
   things,
And little things go lessening till at last

[1749–1824] was a composer, professor,
Kapellmeister, and writer on music.
[1] See Swinburne, page 695a.
[2] A face that a man might die for. — SIR
ARTHUR CONAN DOYLE: *The Adventures of
Sherlock Holmes: A Scandal in Bohemia*
[1892]

Comes God behind them.
> *Dramatis Personae. Mr. Sludge,*
> *"The Medium"*

I'm — now the President, now Jenny
  Lind,
Now Emerson, now the Benicia Boy.[1]
> *Ibid.*

Boston's a hole, the herring-pond is
  wide,
V-notes are something, liberty still
  more.
Beside, is he the only fool in the world?
> *Ibid.*

It's wiser being good than bad;
  It's safer being meek than fierce;
It's fitter being sane than mad.
  My own hope is, a sun will pierce
The thickest cloud earth ever stretched;
  That, after Last, returns the First,
Though a wide compass round be
  fetched;
  That what began best can't end
    worst,
  Nor what God blessed once, prove
accurst.
> *Ibid. Apparent Failure, Stanza 7*

O Lyric Love, half angel and half bird,
And all a wonder and a wild desire.
> *The Ring and the Book*
> *[1868–1869]. I*

Call in law when a neighbor breaks
  your fence,
Cribs from your field, tampers with
  rent or lease,
Touches the purse or pocket, — but
  woos your wife?
No: take the old way trod when men
  were men!
> *Ibid. II, Half-Rome*

There is but one way to browbeat this
  world,
Dumb-founder doubt, and repay scorn
  in kind, —
To go on trusting, namely, till faith
  move
Mountains.
> *Ibid. III, The Other Half-Rome*

"The serpent tempted me and I did
  eat."
So much of paradisal nature, Eve's!

[1] The Benicia Boy was John C. Heenan, a
prizefighter of Benicia, California.

Her daughters ever since prefer to urge
"Adam so starved me I was fain accept
The apple any serpent pushed my
  way."
> *The Ring and the Book. IV,*
> *Tertium Quid*

The truth was felt by instinct here,
— Process which serves a world of
  trouble and time.
> *Ibid.*

'Twas a thief said the last kind word
  to Christ:
Christ took the kindness and forgave
  the theft.
> *Ibid. VI, Giuseppe Caponsacchi*

All poetry is difficult to read,
— The sense of it is, anyhow.
> *Ibid. VII, Pompilia*

No work begun shall ever pause for
  death!
> *Ibid.*

So, let him wait God's instant men call
  years;
Meantime hold hard by truth and his
  great soul,
Do out the duty! Through such souls
  alone
God stooping shows sufficient of his
  light
For us i' the dark to rise by.
> *Ibid.*

Faultless to a fault.
> *Ibid. IX, Juris Doctor Johannes-*
> *Baptista Bottinius*

The curious crime, the fine
Felicity and flower of wickedness.
> *Ibid. X, The Pope*

What I call God,
And fools call Nature.[1]
> *Ibid.*

Why comes temptation, but for man to
  meet
And master and make crouch beneath
  his foot,
And so be pedestaled in triumph?
> *Ibid.*

[1] Some call it Evolution,
And others call it God.

. . . .

Some of us call it Autumn,
And others call it God.
> W. H. CARRUTH [1859–1924]: *Each in*
> *His Own Tongue*

White shall not neutralize the black,
    nor good
Compensate bad in man, absolve him
    so:
Life's business being just the terrible
    choice.
> *The Ring and the Book. X,*
> *The Pope*

You never know what life means till
    you die:
Even throughout life, 'tis death that
    makes life live,
Gives it whatever the significance.
> *Ibid. XI, Guido*

Save the squadron, honor France, love
    thy wife the Belle Aurore!
> *Hervé Riel [1871]. Stanza 11*

A man in armor is his armor's slave.
> *Herakles [1871]*

Life's a little thing!
Such as it is, then, pass life pleasantly
From day to night, nor once grieve all
    the while.
> *Ibid.*

In God's good time,
Which does not always fall on Satur-
    day
When the world looks for wages.[1]
> *Ibid.*

The great mind knows the power of
    gentleness,
Only tries force, because persuasion
    fails.
> *Ibid.*

'Twas not for every Gawain to gaze
    upon the Grail!
> *Fifine at the Fair [1872]. IV*

No creature's made so mean
But that, some way, it boasts, could we
    investigate,
Its supreme worth.
> *Ibid. XXIX*

So absolutely good is truth, truth never
    hurts
The teller.
> *Ibid. XXXII*

---

[1] The old Tuscan proverb, *"Iddio non paga sabato"; "God does not pay Saturdays." — Life in Letters of William Dean Howells, Vol. II, P. 169, Letter to Mrs. James T. Fields* [February 23, 1903]

Death reads the title clear —
What each soul for itself conquered
    from out things here.
> *Fifine at the Fair. LV*

Clash forth life's common chord,
    whence, list how there ascend
Harmonics far and faint, till our per-
    ception end.
> *Ibid. LXII*

That far land we dream about,
Where every man is his own architect.
> *Red Cotton Night-Cap*
> *Country [1873]. II*

A secret's safe
'Twixt you, me, and the gate-post!
> *The Inn Album [1875]. II*

Ignorance is not innocence but sin.
> *Ibid. V*

No ear! or if ear, so tough-gristled —
He thought that he sung while he
    whistled.
> *Pacchiarotto [1876]. XXVI*

Have you found your life distasteful?
    My life did and does smack sweet.
Was your youth of pleasure wasteful?
    Mine I saved and hold complete.
Do your joys with age diminish?
    When mine fail me, I'll complain.
Must in death your daylight finish?
    My sun sets to rise again.
> *At the "Mermaid" [1876]. Stanza 10*

I find earth not gray but rosy,
    Heaven not grim but fair of hue.
Do I stoop? I pluck a posy.
    Do I stand and stare? [1] All's blue.
> *Ibid. Stanza 12*

"With this same key
Shakespeare unlocked his heart" [2] once
    more!
Did Shakespeare? If so, the less Shake-
    speare he!
> *House [1876]. Stanza 10*

Because a man has shop to mind
    In time and place, since flesh must
    live,
Needs spirit lack all life behind,

---

[1] What is this life if, full of care,
    We have no time to stand and stare?
WILLIAM HENRY DAVIES [1871–1940]:
> *Leisure*

[2] See Wordsworth, page 412a.

All stray thoughts, fancies fugitive,
All loves except what trade can give?
>   *Shop* [*1876*]. *Stanza 20*

Good, to forgive;
  Best, to forget!
Living, we fret;
  Dying, we live.
>   *La Saisiaz* [*1877*]. *Introduction,*
>   *Stanza 1*

Can we love but on condition that the
  thing we love must die?
>   *Ibid.*

Such a starved bank of moss
  Till, that May-morn,
Blue ran the flash across:
  Violets were born!
>   *The Two Poets of Croisic* [*1878*].
>   *Introduction, Stanza 1*

Sky — what a scowl of cloud
  Till, near and far,
Ray on ray split the shroud:
  Splendid, a star!
>   *Ibid. Stanza 2*

    As if true pride
Were not also humble!
>   *Lines Written in an Album* [*1882*]

Wanting is — what?
  Summer redundant,
  Blueness abundant,
  — Where is the blot?
>   *Wanting is — What?* [1] [*1883*]

Out of the wreck I rise.
>   *Ixion* [*1883*]

    Climb the rounds
Of life's long ladder, one by slippery
  one.
>   *Jochanan Hakkadosh* [*1883*].
>   *Stanza 27*

What Youth deemed crystal, Age finds
  out was dew
Morn set a-sparkle, but which noon
  quick dried.
>   *Ibid. Stanza 101*

Never the time and the place
And the loved one all together!
>   *Never the Time and the*
>   *Place* [*1883*]

---

[1] Browning is — what?
  Riddle redundant,
  Baldness abundant,
  Sense, who can spot?
  ANONYMOUS, in *Punch* [April 21, 1883]

Help me with knowledge — for Life's
  Old — Death's New!
>   *Epitaph on Levi Lincoln*
>   *Thaxter, 1824–1884*

What if the rose-streak of morning
Pale and depart in a passion of tears?
Once to have hoped is no matter for
  scorning!
Love once — e'en love's disappoint-
  ment endears!
A minute's success pays the failure of
  years.
>   *Apollo and the Fates* [*1886*].
>   *Stanza 42*

Oh, fancies that might be, oh, facts
  that are!
>   *Asolando* [*1889*].
>   *Inapprehensiveness*

Songs, Spring thought perfection,
  Summer criticizes:
What in May escaped detection,
  August, past surprises,
Notes, and names each blunder.
>   *Ibid. Flute-Music, with an*
>   *Accompaniment, Stanza 11*

One who never turned his back but
  marched breast forward,
Never doubted clouds would break,
Never dreamed, though right were
  worsted, wrong would triumph,
Held we fall to rise, are baffled to fight
  better,
Sleep to wake.
>   *Ibid. Epilogue, Stanza 3*

No, at noonday in the bustle of man's
  work-time
Greet the unseen with a cheer!
>   *Ibid. Stanza 4*

SAMUEL DICKINSON
BURCHARD
[1812–1891]

We are Republicans, and don't propose to leave our party and identify
ourselves with the party whose ante-
cedents have been Rum, Romanism,
and Rebellion.
>   *Speaking for a deputation of*
>   *clergymen calling upon James*
>   *G. Blaine, the Republican*
>   *Presidential candidate, New*
>   *York* [*October 29, 1884*]

CHARLES DICKENS
[1812–1870]

I hold my inventive faculty on the stern condition that it must master my whole life, often have complete possession of me, make its own demands upon me, and sometimes for months together put everything else away from me.

> *Letters* [*1833–1870*] (*Edited by* MAMIE DICKENS AND GEORGINA HOGARTH

He had used the word in its Pickwickian sense.

> *Pickwick Papers* [*1836–1837*]. *Chap. 1*

Did it ever strike you on such a morning as this that drowning would be happiness and peace?

> *Ibid. Chap. 5*

"It wasn't the wine," murmured Mr. Snodgrass, in a broken voice. "It was the salmon."

> *Ibid. Chap. 8*

I wants to make your flesh creep.

> *Ibid.*

"Can I unmoved see thee dying
On a log
Expiring frog!"

> *Ibid. Chap. 15*

Tongue; well that's a wery good thing when it an't a woman's.

> *Ibid. Chap. 19*

Be wery careful o' vidders all your life.

> *Ibid. Chap. 20*

The wictim o' connubiality, as Blue Beard's domestic chaplain said, with a tear of pity, ven he buried him.

> *Ibid.*

Despair seldom comes with the first severe shock of misfortune. A man has confidence in untried friends, he remembers the many offers of service so freely made by his boon companions when he wanted them not; he has hope — the hope of happy inexperience.

> *Ibid. Chap. 21*

I have heerd how many ord'nary women one vidder's equal to, in pint o' comin' over you. I think it's five-and-twenty, but I don't rightly know vether it a'n't more.

> *Pickwick Papers. Chap. 23*

Bold Turpin vunce, on Hounslow Heath,
His bold mare Bess bestrode.

> *Ibid. Chap. 43, Romance*

Please, sir, I want some more.

> *Oliver Twist* [*1837–1838*]. *Chap. 2*

There are books of which the backs and covers are by far the best parts.

> *Ibid. Chap. 14*

I'll eat my head.

> *Ibid.*

I only know two sorts of boys. Mealy boys, and beef-faced boys.

> *Ibid.*

There is something about a roused woman, especially if she add to all her other strong passions, the fierce impulses of recklessness and despair, which few men like to provoke.

> *Ibid. Chap. 16*

There's light enough for wot I've got to do.

> *Ibid. Chap. 47*

"If the law supposes that," said Mr. Bumble, . . . "the law is a ass, a idiot."

> *Ibid. Chap. 51*

He had but one eye, and the popular prejudice runs in favour of two.

> *Nicholas Nickleby* [*1838–1839*]. *Chap. 4*

Subdue your appetites, my dears, and you've conquered human natur.

> *Ibid. Chap. 5*

There are only two styles of portrait painting; the serious and the smirk.

> *Ibid. Chap. 10*

Oh! they're too beautiful to live, much too beautiful!

> *Ibid. Chap. 14*

I pity his ignorance and despise him.

> *Ibid. Chap. 15*

The two countesses had no outlines at all, and the dowager's was a demd outline.

> *Ibid. Chap. 34*

A demd, damp, moist, unpleasant body!

> *Ibid.*

Bring in the bottled lightning, a clean tumbler, and a corkscrew.

> *Nicholas Nickleby. Chap. 49*

All is gas and gaiters.

> *Ibid.*

My life is one demd horrid grind.

> *Ibid. Chap. 64*

He has gone to the demnition bow-wows.

> *Ibid.*

What is the odds so long as the fire of soul is kindled at the taper of conwiviality, and the wing of friendship never moults a feather . . . and the present moment is the least happiest of our existence.

> *The Old Curiosity Shop* [*1841*]. *Chap. 2*

She's the ornament of her sex.

> *Ibid. Chap. 5*

In love of home, the love of country has its rise.

> *Ibid. Chap. 38*

That vague kind of penitence which holidays awaken next morning.

> *Ibid. Chap. 40*

The memory of those who lie below passes away so soon. At first they tend them, morning, noon, and night; they soon begin to come less frequently; from once a day, to once a week; from once a week to once a month; then at long and uncertain intervals; then, not at all.

> *Ibid. Chap. 54*

"Did you ever taste beer?" "I had a sip of it once," said the small servant. "Here's a state of things!" cried Mr. Swiveller. . . . "She *never* tasted it — it can't be tasted in a sip!"

> *Ibid. Chap. 57*

It was a maxim with Foxey — our revered father, gentlemen — "Always suspect everybody."

> *Ibid. Chap. 66*

When Death strikes down the innocent and young, for every fragile form from which he lets the panting spirit free, a hundred virtues rise, in shapes of mercy, charity, and love, to walk the world, and bless it.

> *Ibid. Chap. 72*

Oh gracious, why wasn't I born old and ugly?

> *Barnaby Rudge* [*1841*]. *Chap. 70*

Any man may be in good spirits and good temper when he's well dressed. There an't much credit in that.

> *Martin Chuzzlewit* [*1843–1844*]. *Chap. 5*

With affection beaming in one eye, and calculation shining out of the other.

> *Ibid. Chap. 8*

Regrets are the natural property of gray hairs.

> *Ibid. Chap. 10*

Keep up appearances whatever you do.

> *Ibid. Chap. 11*

"Do other men for they would do you." That's the true business precept.

> *Ibid.*

Buy an annuity cheap, and make your life interesting to yourself and everybody else that watches the speculation.

> *Ibid. Chap. 18*

Leave the bottle on the chimley-piece, and don't ask me to take none, but let me put my lips to it when I am so dispoged.

> *Ibid. Chap. 19*

"She's the sort of woman now," said Mould, . . . "one would almost feel disposed to bury for nothing: and do it neatly, too!"

> *Ibid. Chap. 25*

He'd make a lovely corpse.

> *Ibid.*

What we've got to do, is to keep up our spirits, and be neighbourly. We shall come all right in the end, never fear.

> *Ibid. Chap. 33*

A man ain't got no right to be a public man, unless he meets the public views.

> *Ibid. Chap. 34*

Here are all kinds of employers wanting all sorts of servants, and all sorts of servants wanting all kinds of

employers, and they never seem to come together.
Martin Chuzzlewit. Chap. 36
Oh Sairey, Sairey, little do we know wot lays afore us!
Ibid. Chap. 40
I don't believe there's no sich a person!
Ibid. Chap. 49
Old Marley was as dead as a doornail. . . . The wisdom of our ancestors is in the simile.
A Christmas Carol [1843].
Stave One
Secret, and self-contained, and solitary as an oyster.
Ibid.
I wear the chain I forged in life.
Ibid.
In came a fiddler — and tuned like fifty stomach-aches. In came Mrs. Fezziwig, one vast substantial smile.
Ibid. Stave Two
Let's have the shutters up . . . before a man can say Jack Robinson.[1]
Ibid.
As good as gold.
Ibid. Stave Three
"God bless us every one!" said Tiny Tim, the last of all.
Ibid.
It *was* a turkey! He could never have stood upon his legs, that bird! He would have snapped 'em off short in a minute, like sticks of sealing-wax.
Ibid. Stave Five
It was always said of him, that he knew how to keep Christmas well if any man alive possessed the knowledge.
Ibid. Stave Five
Facts and Figures! Put 'em down!
The Chimes [1844]. First Quarter
The New Year, like an Infant Heir to the whole world, was waited for, with welcomes, presents, and rejoicings.
Ibid. Second Quarter

O let us love our occupations,
Bless the squire and his relations,
Live upon our daily rations,
And always know our proper stations.
The Chimes. Second Quarter
Oh the nerves, the nerves; the mysteries of this machine called Man! Oh the little that unhinges it: poor creatures that we are!
Ibid. Third Quarter
Give us, in mercy, better homes when we're a-lying in our cradles; give us better food when we're a-working for our lives; give us kinder laws to bring us back when we're a-going wrong; and don't set Jail, Jail, Jail afore us, everywhere we turn.
Ibid.
He's tough, ma'am, tough, is J. B. Tough and devilish sly.
Dombey and Son [1848]. Chap. 7
I want to know what it says. . . . The sea, Floy, what it is that it keeps on saying.[1]
Ibid. Chap. 8
"Wal'r, my boy," replied the Captain, "in the Proverbs of Solomon you will find the following words, 'May we never want a friend in need, nor a bottle to give him!' When found, make a note of."
Ibid. Chap. 15
Cows are my passion.
Ibid. Chap. 21
A mind equal to any undertaking that he puts it alongside of.
Ibid. Chap. 23
The bearings of this observation lays in the application on it.
Ibid.
You'll find us rough, Sir, but you'll find us ready.
David Copperfield [1849–1850].
Chap. 3
I am a lone lorn creetur . . . and everythink goes contrairy with me.
Ibid.
I'd better go into the house, and die and be a riddance!
Ibid.

---

[1] I'd do it as soon as say Jack Robinson. — FANNY BURNEY: *Evelina* [1778], *Letter 82*
I'd get her off before you could say Jack Robinson. — MARIA EDGEWORTH: *The Absentee* [1812], *Chap. 2*

[1] See Joseph Edwards Carpenter, page 582b.

Barkis is willin'.
David Copperfield. Chap. 5

That he may be ready — in case of anything turning up.[1]
Ibid. Chap. 12

I never will desert Mr. Micawber.
Ibid.

Annual income twenty pounds, annual expenditure nineteen nineteen six, result happiness. Annual income twenty pounds, annual expenditure twenty pounds ought and six, result misery.
Ibid.

It's a mad world. Mad as Bedlam.
Ibid. Chap. 14

I'm a very umble person.[2]
Ibid. Chap. 16

The winds you are going to tempt, have wafted thousands upon thousands to fortune, and brought thousands upon thousands happily back.
Ibid.

The mistake was made of putting some of the trouble out of King Charles's head into my head.[3]
Ibid. Chap. 17

I only ask for information.
Ibid. Chap. 20

It was as true . . . as turnips is. It was as true . . . as taxes is. And nothing's truer than them.
Ibid. Chap. 21

What a world of gammon and spinnach it is, though, ain't it!
Ibid. Chap. 22

Nobody's enemy but his own.
Ibid. Chap. 25

Accidents will occur in the best-regulated families.
Ibid. Chap. 28

Ride on! Rough-shod if need be, smooth-shod if that will do, but ride on! Ride on over all obstacles, and win the race!
David Copperfield. Chap. 28

A long pull, and a strong pull, and a pull all together.
Ibid. Chap. 30

People can't die, along the coast . . . except when the tide's pretty nigh out. They can't be born, unless it's pretty nigh in — not properly born, till flood. He's a going out with the tide.[1]
Ibid.

There wasn't room to swing a cat there.
Ibid. Chap. 35

I ate umble pie with an appetite.
Ibid. Chap. 39

Let sleeping dogs lie — who wants to rouse 'em?
Ibid.

Skewered through and through with office-pens, and bound hand and foot with red tape.
Ibid. Chap. 43

It's only my child-wife.
Ibid. Chap. 44

A man must take the fat with the lean.
Ibid. Chap. 51

Trifles make the sum of life.
Ibid. Chap. 53

The seamen said it blew great guns.
Ibid. Chap. 55

This is a London particular. . . . A fog, miss.
Bleak House [*1852–1853*]. *Chap. 3*

Not to put too fine a point upon it.
Ibid. Chap. 32

One always begins to forgive a place as soon as it's left behind.
Little Dorrit [*1857–1858*]. *Book I, Chap. 2*

Whatever was required to be done, the Circumlocution Office was beforehand with all the public departments in the art of perceiving — HOW NOT TO DO IT.
Ibid. Chap. 10

---

[1] See Disraeli, page 512a.

[2] Not only humble but umble, which I look upon to be the comparative, or, indeed, superlative degree. — ANTHONY TROLLOPE: *Doctor Thorne* [1858], *Chap. 4*

[3] "King Charles's Head" has passed into common use in the English language as a phrase meaning some whimsical obsession. — G. B. STERN [1890-   ]: *Monogram*

[1] See Sir James Frazer, page 759a.

A person who can't pay, gets another person who can't pay, to guarantee that he can pay.

> *Little Dorrit. Book I, Chap. 23*

Papa, potatoes, poultry, prunes, and prism, are all very good words for the lips: especially prunes and prism.

> *Ibid. Book II, Chap. 5*

It is at least as difficult to stay a moral infection as a physical one.

> *Ibid. Chap. 13*

It was the best of times, it was the worst of times, it was the age of wisdom, it was the age of foolishness, it was the epoch of belief, it was the epoch of incredulity, it was the season of Light, it was the season of Darkness, it was the spring of hope, it was the winter of despair.

> *A Tale of Two Cities [1859].*
> *Book I, Chap. 1*

A wonderful fact to reflect upon, that every human creature is constituted to be that profound secret and mystery to every other.

> *Ibid. Chap. 3*

The calm that must follow all storms — emblem to humanity of the rest and silence into which the storm called Life must hush at last.

> *Ibid. Chap. 6*

Detestation of the high is the involuntary homage of the low.

> *Ibid. Book II, Chap. 9*

It is a far, far better thing that I do, than I have ever done; it is a far, far better rest that I go to, than I have ever known.

> *Ibid. Book III, Chap. 15*

I have known a vast quantity of nonsense talked about bad men not looking you in the face. Don't trust that conventional idea. Dishonesty will stare honesty out of countenance, any day in the week, if there is anything to be got by it.

> *Hunted Down [1859]. Chap. 2*

In the little world in which children have their existence, whosoever brings them up, there is nothing so finely perceived and so finely felt, as injustice.

> *Great Expectations [1860–1861].*
> *Chap. 9*

Probably every new and eagerly expected garment ever put on since clothes came in, fell a trifle short of the wearer's expectation.

> *Ibid. Chap. 19*

Throughout life, our worst weaknesses and meannesses are usually committed for the sake of the people whom we most despise.

> *Ibid. Chap. 27*

My best of wishes for your merry Christmases and your happy New Years, your long lives and your true prosperities. Worth twenty pound good if they are delivered as I send them. Remember? Here's a final prescription added, "To be taken for life."

> *Doctor Marigold's Prescriptions*
> *[1865]. Chap. 1*

EDWARD LEAR
[1812–1888]

There was an Old Man with a beard,
Who said: "It is just as I feared!
Two Owls and a Hen,
Four Larks and a Wren
Have all built their nests in my beard."

> *Book of Nonsense [1846]. Limerick*

How pleasant to know Mr. Lear!
Who has written such volumes of stuff!
Some think him ill-tempered and queer,
But a few think him pleasant enough.

> *Nonsense Songs [1871].*
> *Preface, Stanza 1*

His body is perfectly spherical,
He weareth a runcible hat.

> *Ibid. Stanza 5*

The Owl and the Pussy-cat went to sea
In a beautiful pea-green boat,
They took some honey, and plenty of money,
Wrapped up in a five-pound note.
The Owl looked up to the stars above,
And sang to a small guitar,
"O lovely Pussy! O Pussy, my love,

What a beautiful Pussy you are,
    You are,
    You are!
What a beautiful Pussy you are!"
    *Nonsense Songs. The Owl and
        the Pussy-cat, Stanza 1*
Pussy said to the Owl, "You elegant
    fowl!
How charmingly sweet you sing!
O let us be married! too long we have
    tarried:
But what shall we do for a ring?"
They sailed away, for a year and a day,
    To the land where the Bong-tree
      grows
And there in a wood a Piggy-wig stood
    With a ring at the end of his nose.
        Ibid. Stanza 2
"Dear Pig, are you willing to sell for
    one shilling
Your ring?" Said the Piggy, "I will."
        Ibid. Stanza 3
They dined on mince, and slices of
    quince,
    Which they ate with a runcible
      spoon;
And hand in hand, on the edge of the
    sand,
    They danced by the light of the
      moon.
        Ibid.
They went to sea in a Sieve, they did,
    In a Sieve they went to sea:
In spite of all their friends could say.
    Ibid. The Jumblies, Stanza 1
But we don't care a button! we don't
    care a fig!
In a Sieve we'll go to sea!
Far and few, far and few,
    Are the lands where the Jumblies
      live;
Their heads are green, and their hands
    are blue,
And they went to sea in a Sieve.
        Ibid.

Calico Pie,
    The little Birds fly
Down to the calico tree,
    Their wings were blue,
    And they sang "Tilly-loo!"
Till away they flew, —
And they never came back to me!

They never came back!
    They never came back!
They never came back to me!
    *Nonsense Songs. Calico Pie,
        Stanza 1*

Calico Jam,
    The little Fish swam,
Over the syllabub sea.
        Ibid. Stanza 2

Who, or why, or which, or what,
Is the Akond of Swat?
    The Akond of Swat [1] *[1873]*

She sate upon her Dobie,
    To watch the Evening Star,
And all the Punkahs as they passed,
    Cried, "My! how fair you are!"
      The Cummerbund [1874].
        Stanza 1

On the top of the Crumpetty Tree
    The Quangle Wangle sat,
But his face you could not see,
    On account of his Beaver Hat.
    Nonsense Songs [1877]. *The
    Quangle Wangle's Hat, Stanza 1*

On the coast of Coromandel
    Where the early pumpkins blow,
    In the middle of the woods
Lived the Yonghy-Bonghy-Bò.
Two old chairs, and half a candle,
One old jug without a handle, —
    These were all his worldly goods.
    *Ibid. The Courtship of the
    Yonghy-Bonghy-Bò, Stanza 1*

[1] What, what, what,
    What's the news from Swat?
      Sad news,
      Bad news,
    Comes by cable led
    Through the Indian Ocean's bed,
    Through the Persian Gulf, the Red
    Sea and the Med-
    Iterranean — he's dead;
    The Ahkoond is dead!
      GEORGE THOMAS LANIGAN: *A
        Threnody* [1878], *St. 1*
Now the Ahkoond of Swat is a vague sort of
    man
Who lives in a country far over the sea;
Pray tell me, good reader, if tell me you can,
What's the Ahkoond of Swat to you folks
    or to me?
    EUGENE FIELD: *The Ahkoond of Swat*
        [1884]

There he heard a Lady talking,
To some milk-white Hens of Dork-
   ing, —
'Tis the Lady Jingly Jones!
   Nonsense Songs. The Courtship of
     the Yonghy-Bonghy-Bò, Stanza 2
"I would be your wife most gladly!"
(Here she twirled her fingers madly,)
"But in England I've a mate!"
                Ibid. Stanza 5
When awful darkness and silence reign
Over the great Gromboolian plain,
  Through the long, long wintry nights.
       Ibid. The Dong with the
         Luminous Nose, Stanza 1
The Pobble who has no toes
Had once as many as we;
When they said, "Some day you may
   lose them all;" —
He replied, — "Fish fiddle de-dee!"
    Ibid. The Pobble Who Has No
             Toes, Stanza 1
Ploffskin, Pluffskin, Pelican jee!
We think no Birds so happy as we!
Plumpskin, Ploshkin, Pelican jill!
We think so then, and we thought so
   still.
       Ibid. The Pelican Chorus

WILLIAM JAMES LINTON
[1812–1898]

He boasts nor wealth nor high descent,
   yet he may claim to be
A gentleman to match the best of any
   pedigree:
His blood hath run in peasant veins
   through many a noteless year;
Yet, search in every prince's court,
   you'll rarely find his peer.
For he's one of Nature's Gentlemen,
   the best of every time.
     Nature's Gentleman.[1] Stanza 1

NORMAN MACLEOD
[1812–1872]

Courage, brother! do not stumble,
  Though thy path be dark as night;
There's a star to guide the humble,
  Trust in God and do the Right.
     Trust in God [1857]. Stanza 1

[1] See Eliza Cook, page 591a.

WILLIAM EDMONDSTOUNE AYTOUN
[1813–1865]

News of battle! — news of battle!
  Hark! 'tis ringing down the street;
And the archways and the pavement
  Bear the clang of hurrying feet.
     Edinburgh after Flodden
           [1849]. Stanza 1
Nowhere beats the heart so kindly
As beneath the tartan plaid!
   Charles Edward at Versailles
   on the Anniversary of Culloden
   [1849]. Line 219
They bore within their breasts the grief
  That fame can never heal —
The deep, unutterable woe
  Which none save exiles feel.
    The Island of the Scots
       [1849]. Stanza 12

HENRY WARD BEECHER
[1813–1887]

A thoughtful mind, when it sees a
Nation's flag, sees not the flag only,
but the Nation itself; and whatever
may be its symbols, its insignia, he
reads chiefly in the flag the Government, the principles, the truths, the
history which belongs to the Nation
that sets it forth.
        The American Flag
Where is human nature so weak as
in the book-store!
   Star Papers. Subtleties of Book
                Buyers
You cannot forget if you would,
those golden kisses all over the cheeks
of the meadow, queerly called dandelions.
   Ibid. A Discourse on Flowers

JOSEPH EDWARDS CARPENTER
[1813–1885]

What are the wild waves saying,[1]
  Sister, the whole day long,

[1] See Dickens, page 578b.

That ever amid our playing
  I hear but their low, lone song?
                What Are the Wild Waves
                  Saying? Stanza 1

Yes! but there's something greater
  That speaks to the heart alone:
'Tis the voice of the great Creator
  Dwells in that mighty tone.
                Ibid. Refrain

CHRISTOPHER PEARSE CRANCH
[1813–1892]

Thought is deeper than all speech,
  Feeling deeper than all thought;
Souls to souls can never teach
  What unto themselves was taught.
                Thought [Gnosis]. Stanza 1

We are spirits clad in veils;
  Man by man was never seen;
All our deep communing fails
  To remove the shadowy screen.
                Ibid. Stanza 2

O Light divine! we need no fuller test
  That all is ordered well;
We know enough to trust that all is
    best
  Where Love and Wisdom dwell.
                Oh, Love Supreme

JOHN SULLIVAN DWIGHT
[1813–1893]

Is not true leisure
One with true toil? [1]
                Rest. Stanza 1

Rest is not quitting
  The busy career,
Rest is the fitting
  Of self to its sphere.
                Ibid. Stanza 4

'Tis the brook's motion,
  Clear without strife,
Fleeing to ocean
  After its life.
                Ibid. Stanza 5

Work, and thou wilt bless the day
  Ere the toil be done;
They that work not, can not pray,
  Can not feel the sun.
God is living, working still,

[1] See Cowper, page 363a.

All things work and move;
Work, or lose the power to will,
  Lose the power to love.
                Working

JOSEPH HOOKER
[1813–1879]

Well, General, we have not had many
dead cavalrymen lying about lately.
                Remark to General William
                Woods Averell, of the Cavalry
                [November, 1862]

ELIJAH KELLOGG
[1813–1901]

If ye are men, follow me! Strike
down your guard, gain the mountain
passes, and then do bloody work, as
did your sires at old Thermopylae! Is
Sparta dead? Is the old Grecian spirit
frozen in your brains, that you do
cower like a belabored hound beneath
his master's lash? O comrades, warriors, Thracians! If we must fight, let
us fight for ourselves. If we must
slaughter, let it be under the clear sky,
by the bright waters, in noble, honorable battle!
                Spartacus to the Gladiators
                  [1846]

EPES SARGENT
[1813–1880]

A life on the ocean wave,
  A home on the rolling deep;
Where the scattered waters rave,
  And the winds their revels keep!
Like an eagle caged I pine
  On this dull, unchanging shore:
Oh, give me the flashing brine,
  The spray and the tempest's roar!
                A Life on the Ocean Wave
                  [1847]. Stanza 1

HENRY STEVENSON WASHBURN
[1813–1903]

We shall meet, but we shall miss him,
  There will be one vacant chair;

We shall linger to caress him
When we breathe our evening prayer.[1]
The Vacant Chair. Stanza 1

THOMAS OSBORNE DAVIS
[1814–1845]

Come in the evening, or come in the
morning,
Come when you're looked for, or come
without warning.
The Welcome. Stanza 1

FREDERICK WILLIAM FABER
[1814–1863]

The sea, unmated creature, tired and
lone,
Makes on its desolate sands eternal
moan.
The Sorrowful World

Hark! Hark! my soul, angelic songs
are swelling
O'er earth's green fields, and ocean's
wave-beat shore;
How sweet the truth those blessed
strains are telling
Of that new life when sin shall be no
more!
Pilgrims of the Night

O Paradise! O Paradise!
Who doth not crave for rest?
Who would not seek the happy land
Where they that love are blest?
Paradise

CHARLES MACKAY
[1814–1889]

But the sunshine aye shall light the
sky,
As round and round we run;
And the truth shall ever come upper-
most,
And justice shall be done.
Eternal Justice. Stanza 4

Cannon-balls may aid the truth,
But thought's a weapon stronger;
We'll win our battles by its aid; —
Wait a little longer.
The Good Time Coming. Stanza 1

[1] See Longfellow, page 523a.

The smallest effort is not lost,
Each wavelet on the ocean tost
Aids in the ebb-tide or the flow;
Each rain-drop makes some floweret
blow;
Each struggle lessens human woe.
The Old and the New

There is no such thing as death.
In Nature nothing dies.
From each sad remnant of decay
Some forms of life arise.
There Is No Such Thing as Death

Old Tubal Cain was a man of might,
In the days when earth was young.
Tubal Cain. Stanza 1

Not alone for the blade was the bright
steel made,
And he fashioned the first plowshare.[1]
Ibid. Stanza 4

To the West! to the West! to the land
of the free,
Where the mighty Missouri rolls down
to the sea.
To the West. Stanza 1

Where the prairies, like seas where the
billows have rolled,
Are broad as the kingdoms and empires of old.
Ibid. Stanza 2

Make my coffee strong!
The Quarrel

If happy I and wretched he,
Perhaps the king would change with
me.
Differences

MICHAEL WENTWORTH BECK
[1815–1843]

This world is not so bad a world
As some would like to make it;
Though whether good, or whether bad,
Depends on how we take it.
The World As It Is. Stanza 1

[1] Tubal fashioned the hand-flung spears
And showed his neighbours peace.
KIPLING [1865–1936]: *Jubal and Tubal Cain, St. 3*

RICHARD HENRY DANA
[1815–1882]

Six days shalt thou labor and do all
thou art able,
And on the seventh — holystone the
decks and scrape the cable.
> *Two Years Before the Mast*
> *[1840]. Chap. 3, Philadelphia*
> *Catechism*

Like a true ship, committed to her
element once for all at her Launching,
she perished at sea.
> *Ibid. Twenty-Four Years After*
> *[1869]*

DANIEL DECATUR EMMETT
[1815–1904]

I wish I was in de land ob cotton,
Old times dar am not forgotten.
Look away, look away,
Look away, Dixie Land.
> *Dixie [1859]*

In Dixie's land, we'll took our stand,
To lib an' die in Dixie!
Away, away,
Away down South in Dixie.
> *Ibid.*

JOHN BABSONE LANE SOULE
[1815–1891]

Go west, young man.[1]
> *Article in the Terre Haute,*
> *Indiana, Express [1851]*

ANTHONY TROLLOPE
[1815–1882]

He argued that the principal duty
which a parent owed to a child was to
make him happy.
> *Doctor Thorne [1858]. Chap. 3*

---

[1] Horace Greeley [1811–1872] used the
expression in an editorial in *The New York
Tribune* (see Greeley, page 562a). As the
saying, "Go west, young man, and grow up
with the country," gained popularity, Greeley
printed Soule's article, to show the source of
his inspiration.

Many men have stated that the advice was
given to them by Greeley, among them William S. Verity [1837–1930], who said Greeley
had given it to him in 1859.

In these days a man is nobody unless his biography is kept so far posted
up that it may be ready for the national
breakfast-table on the morning after
his demise.
> *Doctor Thorne. Chap. 25*

How I do hate those words, "an excellent marriage." In them is contained
more of wicked worldliness than any
other words one ever hears spoken.
> *The Small House at Allington*
> *[1864]. Chap. 39*

Those who offend us are generally
punished for the offence they give; but
we so frequently miss the satisfaction
of knowing that we are avenged!
> *Ibid. Chap. 50*

She understood how much louder a
cock can crow in its own farmyard than
elsewhere.
> *The Last Chronicle of Barset*
> *[1867]. Vol. I, Chap. 17*

Always remember that when you go
into an attorney's office door, you will
have to pay for it, first or last.
> *Ibid. Chap. 20*

It is a comfortable feeling to know
that you stand on your own ground.
Land is about the only thing that can't
fly away.
> *Ibid. Vol. II, Chap. 58*

It's dogged as does it.
> *Ibid. Chap. 61*

Nothing reopens the springs of love
so fully as absence, and no absence so
thoroughly as that which must needs
be endless.
> *Ibid. Chap. 67*

PHILIP JAMES BAILEY
[1816–1902]

Let each man think himself an act of
God,
His mind a thought, his life a breath of
God;
And let each try, by great thoughts and
good deeds,
To show the most of Heaven he hath
in him.
> *Festus [1839]. Proem*

Evil and good are God's right hand and left.
> *Festus. Proem*

Art is man's nature; nature is God's art.
> *Ibid.*

It matters not how long we live, but how.
> *Ibid. Wood and Water*

The world must have great minds, even as great spheres
Or suns, to govern lesser restless minds.
> *Ibid. Water and Wood*

Men might be better if we better deemed
Of them. The worst way to improve the world
Is to condemn it.[1]
> *Ibid. A Mountain, Sunrise*

It is much less what we do
Than what we think, which fits us for the future.
> *Ibid. Alcove and Garden*

The first and worst of all frauds is to cheat
Oneself.
> *Ibid. Anywhere*

We live in deeds, not years; in thoughts, not breaths;
In feelings, not in figures on a dial.
We should count time by heart-throbs.
He most lives
Who thinks most — feels the noblest
— acts the best.
> *Ibid. A Country Town*

Envy's a coal comes hissing hot from hell.
> *Ibid.*

The sole equality on earth is death.
> *Ibid.*

America, thou, half-brother of the world;
With something good and bad of every land.
> *Ibid. The Surface*

Who can mistake great thoughts?
They seize upon the mind — arrest, and search,

[1] The surest plan to make a Man
Is, think him so.
JAMES RUSSELL LOWELL: *The Biglow Papers* [1848], *Jonathan to John, St. 9*

And shake it.
> *Festus. A Village Feast*

The worst men often give the best advice.
> *Ibid.*

Man is a military animal,
Glories in gunpowder, and loves parade.
> *Ibid. A Metropolis*

There is no disappointment we endure
One half so great as that we are to ourselves.[1]
> *Ibid. The Sun*

CHARLOTTE BRONTË
[1816–1855]

Life, believe, is not a dream
So dark as sages say;
Oft a little morning rain
Foretells a pleasant day.
> *Life* [*1846*]. *Stanza 1*

The human heart has hidden treasures,
In secret kept, in silence sealed; —
The thoughts, the hopes, the dreams, the pleasures,
Whose charms were broken if revealed.
> *Evening Solace* [*1846*]. *Stanza 1*

Reader, I married him.
> *Jane Eyre* [*1847*]. *Chap. 38*

An abundant shower of curates has fallen upon the north of England.
> *Shirley* [*1849*]. *Chap. 1*

FRANCES BROWN
[1816–1864]

Oh! those blessed times of old! with their chivalry and state;
I love to read their chronicles, which such brave deeds relate;
I love to sing their ancient rhymes, to hear their legends told —
But, Heaven be thanked! I live not in those blessed times of old!
> *Oh! the Pleasant Days of Old.*
> *Stanza 7*

[1] Every really able man, if you talk sincerely with him, considers his work, however much admired, as far short of what it should be. — EMERSON: *Immortality* [1875]

JAMES THOMAS FIELDS
[1816–1881]

How sweet and gracious, even in common speech,
Is that fine sense which men call Courtesy!
                              Courtesy

It transmutes aliens into trusting
  friends,
And gives its owner passport round the
  globe.
                                  Ibid.

Just then, with a wink and a sly normal
  lurch,
The owl, very gravely, got down from
  his perch,
Walked round, and regarded his fault-
  finding critic
(Who thought he was stuffed) with a
  glance analytic.
                          The Owl-Critic

"I'm an owl; you're another. Sir Critic,
  good day!"
And the barber kept on shaving.
                                  Ibid.

The skipper stormed, and tore his hair,
  Hauled on his boots and roared to
    Marden,
"Nantucket's sunk, and here we are
  Right over old Marm Hackett's gar-
    den!"
    The Nantucket Skipper. Stanza 10

'Tis a fearful thing in winter
  To be shattered in the blast,
And to hear the rattling trumpet
  Thunder, "Cut away the mast!"
      Ballad of the Tempest. Stanza 2

Is not God upon the ocean,
Just the same as on the land? [1]
                        Ibid. Stanza 5

---

[1] Sir Humphrey Gilbert [1539?–1583], on
embarking on his ill-fated voyage homeward,
— "We are as near to Heaven by sea as by
land." — J. R. GREEN: *A Short History of
the English People* [1874], *Chap.* 8
    "Do not fear! Heaven is as near,"
    He said, "by water as by land!"
        LONGFELLOW: *Sir Humphrey Gilbert*
                          [1849], *St.* 6

ELLEN STURGIS HOOPER
[1816–1841]

I slept and dreamed that life was
  beauty.
I woke — and found that life was
  duty;
Was my dream, then, a shadowy lie?
Toil on, sad heart, courageously,
And thou shalt find thy dream shall be
A noonday light and truth to thee.
                        Beauty and Duty

JOHN GODFREY SAXE
[1816–1887]

There's a castle in Spain, very charm-
  ing to see,
  Though built without money or toil;
Of this handsome estate I am owner in
  fee,
  And paramount lord of the soil.
            My Castle in Spain. Stanza 1

Though we may think we are specially
  blest,
We are certain to pay for the favors we
  get!
          The Gifts of the Gods. Stanza 1

I wish that practising was not
So different from preaching.
                      Wishing. Stanza 4

I'm growing fonder of my staff;
  I'm growing dimmer in the eyes;
I'm growing fainter in my laugh;
  I'm growing deeper in my sighs;
I'm growing careless of my dress;
  I'm growing frugal of my gold;
I'm growing wise; I'm growing —
  yes, —
  I'm growing old!
            I'm Growing Old. Stanza 3

He takes the strangest liberties, —
But never takes his leave!
                My Familiar. Stanza 2

A frown is no extinguisher —
It does not put him out!
                        Ibid. Stanza 6

In battle or business, whatever the
  game,
In law or in love, it is ever the same;
In the struggle for power, or the scramble for pelf,

Let this be your motto, — Rely on
   yourself!
For, whether the prize be a ribbon or
   throne,
The victor is he who can go it alone! [1]
       The Game of Life. Stanza 7

It was six men of Indostan
  To learning much inclined,
Who went to see the Elephant
  (Though all of them were blind),
That each by observation
  Might satisfy his mind.
    The Blind Men and the Elephant.
       Stanza 1

'Tis wise to learn; 'tis God-like to
  create.
       The Library

I asked of Echo, 't other day
(Whose words are few and often
  funny),
What to a novice she could say
Of courtship, love, and matrimony?
  Quoth Echo, plainly: — "Matter-o'-
  money."
       Echo. Stanza 1

MICHAEL JOSEPH BARRY
[1817–1889]

But whether on the scaffold high
  Or in the battle's van,
The fittest place where man can die
Is where he dies for man!
    The Place Where Men Should Die. [2]
       Stanza 5

JOHN BARTHOLOMEW
GOUGH
[1817–1886]

What is a minority? The chosen heroes of this earth have been in a minority. There is not a social, political, or
religious privilege that you enjoy today that was not bought for you by the
blood and tears and patient suffering
of the minority. It is the minority that
have stood in the van of every moral

conflict, and achieved all that is noble
in the history of the world.
       What Is a Minority?

TOM TAYLOR
[1817–1880]

You lay a wreath on murdered Lincoln's bier,
You, who, with mocking pencil, wont
  to trace,
Broad for the self-complacent British
  sneer,
His length of shambling limb, his fur-
  rowed face.
    Abraham Lincoln Foully
    Assassinated. [1] *Stanza 1*

HENRY DAVID THOREAU
[1817–1862]

I am a parcel of vain strivings tied
By a chance bond together.
       Sic Vita [1841]. Stanza 1

Great God, I ask thee for no meaner
  pelf
Than that I may not disappoint myself,
That in my action I may soar as high
As I can now discern with this clear
  eye.
       A Prayer [1842]. Stanza 1

Any man more right than his neighbors constitutes a majority of one.
       Civil Disobedience [1849]

My life is like a stroll upon the beach,
As near the ocean's edge as I can go.
    My Life Is Like a Stroll upon
    the Beach [1849]. Stanza 1

It takes two to speak the truth, —
one to speak, and another to hear.
    A Week on the Concord and
    Merrimack Rivers [1849].
    Wednesday

I saw a delicate flower had grown up
two feet high between the horses' feet
and the wheel track. An inch more to
right or left had sealed its fate, or an
inch higher. Yet it lived to flourish, and

---

[1] He travels the fastest who travels alone.
— KIPLING [1865–1936]: *The Winners*
  [2] Printed in *The Dublin Nation,* September
28, 1844.

[1] Printed in *Punch,* London, May 6, 1865.
(Taylor became editor of *Punch* in 1874.) It
was at a performance of Taylor's play, *Our
American Cousin,* that Lincoln was shot.

never knew the danger it incurred. It did not borrow trouble, nor invite an evil fate by apprehending it.
Journal. September, 1850
Nothing is so much to be feared as fear.[1]
Ibid. September 7, 1851
The blue-bird carries the sky on his back.
Ibid. April 3, 1852
The perception of beauty is a moral test.
Ibid. June 21, 1852
The youth gets together his materials to build a bridge to the moon, or, perchance, a palace or temple on the earth, and, at length, the middle-aged man concludes to build a woodshed with them.[2]
Ibid. July 14, 1852
Fire is the most tolerable third party.
Ibid. January 2, 1853
Some circumstantial evidence is very strong, as when you find a trout in the milk.
Ibid. November 11, 1854
That man is the richest whose pleasures are the cheapest.
Ibid. March 11, 1856
When the playful breeze drops in the pool, it springs to right and left, quick as a kitten playing with dead leaves.
Ibid. April 9, 1859
The savage in man is never quite eradicated.
Ibid. September 26, 1859
The fate of the country . . . does not depend on what kind of paper you drop into the ballot-box once a year, but on what kind of man you drop from your chamber into the street every morning.
Slavery in Massachusetts [1854]
I have travelled a good deal in Concord.
Walden [1854]. I, Economy

[1] See F. D. Roosevelt, page 918b.
[2] At noon he bounded out for food, and nothing less than roast lion would content him. But by suppertime milk toast would do. — Quoted without provenance in *We Accept With Pleasure*, by BERNARD DE VOTO [1897–]

Public opinion is a weak tyrant compared with our own private opinion. What a man thinks of himself, that it is which determines, or rather indicates, his fate.
Walden. I, Economy
The mass of men lead lives of quiet desperation.
Ibid.
It is a characteristic of wisdom not to do desperate things.
Ibid.
As if you could kill time without injuring eternity.
Ibid.
Most of the luxuries, and many of the so-called comforts, of life are not only not indispensable, but positive hindrances to the elevation of mankind.
Ibid.
It is true, I never assisted the sun materially in his rising; but, doubt not, it was of the last importance only to be present at it.
Ibid.
For many years I was self-appointed inspector of snow-storms and rain-storms, and did my duty faithfully.
Ibid.
Beware of all enterprises that require new clothes.
Ibid.
The swiftest traveller is he that goes afoot.
Ibid.
It is not necessary that a man should earn his living by the sweat of his brow, unless he sweats easier than I do.
Ibid.
The man who goes alone can start today; but he who travels with another must wait till that other is ready.
Ibid.
There is no odor so bad as that which arises from goodness tainted.
Ibid.
There are a thousand hacking at the branches of evil to one who is striking at the root.
Ibid.

Philanthropy is almost the only virtue which is sufficiently appreciated by mankind.

Walden. I, Economy

To him whose elastic and vigorous thought keeps pace with the sun, the day is a perpetual morning.

Ibid. II, Where I Lived, and What I Lived For

To be awake is to be alive.

Ibid.

I went to the woods because I wished to live deliberately, to front only the essential facts of life, and see if I could not learn what it had to teach, and not, when I came to die, discover that I had not lived.

Ibid.

Our life is frittered away by detail. . . . Simplify, simplify.

Ibid.

Time is but the stream I go a-fishing in.

Ibid.

Books must be read as deliberately and reservedly as they were written.

Ibid. III, Reading

What is called eloquence in the forum is commonly found to be rhetoric in the study.

Ibid.

The works of the great poets have never yet been read by mankind, for only great poets can read them.

Ibid.

How many a man has dated a new era in his life from the reading of a book.

Ibid.

I love a broad margin to my life.

Ibid. IV, Sounds

Our horizon is never quite at our elbows.

Ibid. V, Solitude

I never found the companion that was so companionable as solitude. We are for the most part more lonely when we go abroad among men than when we stay in our chambers. A man thinking or working is always alone, let him be where he will.

Ibid.

I had three chairs in my house: one for solitude, two for friendship, three for society.

Walden. VI, Visitors

Ministers who spoke of God as if they enjoyed a monopoly of the subject.

Ibid.

I was determined to know beans.

Ibid. VII, The Beanfield

There is never an instant's truce between virtue and vice. Goodness is the only investment that never fails.

Ibid. XI, Higher Laws

While men believe in the infinite, some ponds will be thought to be bottomless.

Ibid. XVI, The Pond in Winter

Through our own recovered innocence we discern the innocence of our neighbors.

Ibid. XVII, Spring

If one advances confidently in the direction of his dreams, and endeavors to live the life which he has imagined, he will meet with a success unexpected in common hours.

Ibid. XVIII, Conclusion

If a man does not keep pace with his companions, perhaps it is because he hears a different drummer. Let him step to the music which he hears, however measured or far away.

Ibid.

Love your life, poor as it is. You may perhaps have some pleasant, thrilling, glorious hours, even in a poorhouse. The setting sun is reflected from the windows of the almshouse as brightly as from the rich man's abode.

Ibid. Conclusion

It is life near the bone where it is sweetest.

Ibid.

Rather than love, than money, than fame, give me truth.

Ibid.

Men will lie on their backs, talking about the fall of man, and never make an effort to get up.

Life Without Principle [*1863*]

Whate'er we leave to God. God does
    And blesses us.
            Inspiration [*1894*]. *Proem*
I hear beyond the range of sound,
    I see beyond the range of sight,
New earths and skies and seas around,
    And in my day the sun doth pale his
        light.
                    Ibid. Stanza 7
She with one breath attunes the spheres,
And also my poor human heart.
                    Ibid. Stanza 15

ELIZA COOK
[1818–1889]

Whom do we dub as Gentlemen? The
    knave, the fool, the brute —
If they but own full tithe of gold, and
    wear a courtly suit.
            Nature's Gentleman. Stanza 1
They hold the rank no king can give,
    no station can disgrace;
Nature puts forth her Gentleman, and
    monarchs must give place.[1]
                    Ibid. Stanza 6
I love it, I love it; and who shall dare
To chide me for loving that old arm-
    chair?
            The Old Arm-Chair
How cruelly sweet are the echoes that
    start
When memory plays an old tune on the
    heart!
                Old Dobbin. Stanza 16
Better build schoolrooms for "the boy"
Than cells and gibbets for "the man." [2]
            A Song for the Ragged Schools.
                        Stanza 12
How busy we are on Tom Tiddler's
    ground
Looking for gold and silver.[3]
            Tom Tiddler's Ground. Stanza 1
Whenever you find your heart despair
    Of doing some goodly thing,

[1] See Linton, page 582a.
[2] Give them a chance — if you stint them
now, tomorrow you'll have to pay
A larger bill for a darker ill.
    DENIS A. McCARTHY [1870–1931]:
        Give Them a Place to Play, St. 4
[3] Here we are on Tom Tiddler's ground,
picking up gold and silver. — *A children's
game*

Con over this strain, try bravely again,
    And remember the Spider and King.[1]
                Try Again. Stanza 16

CECIL FRANCES
ALEXANDER
[1818–1895]

All things bright and beautiful,
    All creatures great and small,
All things wise and wonderful,
    The Lord God made them all.
        All Things Bright and Beautiful
                    [*1848*]. *Stanza 1*
The rich man in his castle,
    The poor man at his gate,
God made them, high or lowly,
    And ordered their estate.
                    Ibid. Stanza 3
There is a green hill far away,
    Without a city wall,
Where the dear Lord was crucified,
    Who died to save us all.
        There Is a Green Hill [*1848*].
                        Stanza 1
Once in royal David's city
    Stood a lowly cattle shed,
Where a Mother laid her Baby
    In a manger for his bed:
Mary was that Mother mild,
Jesus Christ her little Child.
        Once in Royal David's City
                    [*1848*]. *Stanza 1*

EMILY BRONTË
[1818–1848]

Sleep not, dream not; this bright day
Will not, cannot last for aye;
Bliss like thine is bought by years
Dark with torment and with tears.
            Sleep Not [*1846*]. *Stanza 1*
The Bluebell is the sweetest flower
    That waves in summer air:
Its blossoms have the mightiest power
    To soothe my spirit's care.
            The Bluebell [*1846*]. *Stanza 1*
Love is like the wild rose-briar;
    Friendship like the holly-tree.

[1] Robert Bruce, liberator and king [1306–
1329] of Scotland.

591

The holly is dark when the rose-briar
  blooms,
  But which will bloom most con-
    stantly?
                Love and Friendship [*1846*].
                        Stanza 1
I'll walk where my own nature would
  be leading —
It vexes me to choose another guide —
Where the grey flocks in ferny glens are
  feeding,
Where the wild wind blows on the
  mountain-side.
        Often Rebuked [*1846*]. *Stanza 4*
Cold in the earth — and fifteen wild
  Decembers
From those brown hills have melted
  into spring:
Faithful, indeed, is the spirit that re-
  members
After such years of change and suffer-
  ing!
                Remembrance [*1846*]
No coward soul is mine,
  No trembler in the world's storm-
    troubled sphere:
I see Heaven's glories shine,
  And faith shines equal, arming me
    from fear.
        Last Lines [*1846*]. *Stanza 1*
There is not room for Death.[1]
                Ibid. Stanza 7
I lingered round them, under that
benign sky: watched the moths fluttering among the heath and hare-bells;
listened to the soft wind breathing
through the grass; and wondered how
any one could ever imagine unquiet
slumbers for the sleepers in that quiet
earth.
        Wuthering Heights [*1847*].
                Last Words

WILLIAM ELLERY CHANNING
[1818–1901]

Habitant of castle gray,
Creeping thing in sober way,

[1] See Dylan Thomas, page 996b.

Visible sage mechanician,
Skillfulest arithmetician.
                The Spider
Most joyful let the Poet be;
It is through him that all men see.
        *The Poet of the Old and
                New Times*
A wail in the wind is all I hear;
A voice of woe for a lover's loss.
                Lament for Thoreau
The hills are reared, the seas are
  scooped in vain
If learning's altar vanish from the
  plain.
        Inscription for the Alcott House [1]

GEORGE DUFFIELD
[1818–1888]

Stand up! — stand up for Jesus!
                Hymn

WILLIAM MAXWELL EVARTS
[1818–1901]

The pious ones of Plymouth, who,
reaching the Rock, first fell upon their
own knees and then upon the aborig-
ines.[2]
        Quoted by Henry Watterson
        *in The Louisville Courier-
        Journal* [*July 4, 1913*]

JOHN JAMES ROBERT
MANNERS, DUKE
OF RUTLAND
[1818–1906]

Let wealth and commerce, laws and
  learning die,
But leave us still our old nobility.
        England's Trust. Part III, Line 231

JOHN MASON NEALE
[1818–1866]

Good King Wenceslas look'd out,
  On the Feast of Stephen;

[1] This couplet is painted over the mantel
in Alcott House, Concord, Massachusetts.
[2] This pun has also been attributed to Oliver
Wendell Holmes, Bill Nye, and George Fris-
bie Hoar.

When the snow lay round about,
　Deep and crisp and even.
　　　　Good King Wenceslas. Stanza 1
"Bring me flesh and bring me wine,
Bring me pine-logs hither."
　　　　　　　　Ibid. Stanza 3
Page and monarch, forth they went,
　Forth they went together,
Through the rude winds' wild lament
　And the bitter weather.
　　　　　　　　　　　　Ibid.

In his master's steps he trod,
　Where the snow lay dinted;
Heat was in the very sod
　Which the Saint had printed.
Wherefore, Christian men, be sure,
　Wealth or rank possessing,
Ye who now do bless the poor
　Shall yourselves find blessing.
　　　　　　　　Ibid. Stanza 5
O come, O come, Emmanuel,
And ransom captive Israel.
　　　O Come, O Come, Emmanuel
　　　(*translated from the Latin,*
　　　Veni, Veni, Emmanuel)
Jerusalem the golden, with milk and
　honey blest,
Beneath thy contemplation sink heart
　and voice oppressed.
　　　Hymn (translated from the
　　　　Latin, Urbs Syon Aurea)
Brief life is here our portion.
　　　　　　　　　　　　Hymn

KARL MARX
[1818–1883]

Religion . . . is the opium of the
people.
　　　Critique of the Hegelian Phi-
　　　losophy of Right [*1844*]. *In-*
　　　troduction
The history of all hitherto existing
society is the history of class struggles.
　　　Manifesto of the Communist
　　　　　　Party [1] [*1848*]. *I*
Of all the classes that stand face to
face with the bourgeoisie today the
proletariat alone is a really revolutionary class. The other classes decay and

[1] Written in collaboration with Friedrich
Engels. Translated by Samuel Moore.

finally disappear in the race of modern
industry; the proletariat is its special
and essential product.[1]
　　　Manifesto of the Communist
　　　　　　　　Party. I
Pauperism develops more rapidly
than population and wealth.
　　　　　　　　　　　　Ibid.

In proportion as the antagonism between classes within the nation vanishes, the hostility of one nation to another will come to an end.
　　　　　　　　　　　Ibid. II

The ruling ideas of each age have
ever been the ideas of its ruling class.
　　　　　　　　　　　　Ibid.

Christian Socialism is but the holy
water with which the priest consecrates
the heartburnings of the aristocrat.
　　　　　　　　　　　Ibid. III

The proletarians have nothing to lose
but their chains. They have a world to
win. Workers of the world, unite!
　　　　　　　　　　　Ibid. IV

Nothing can have value without being an object of utility. If it be useless, the labor contained in it is useless,
cannot be reckoned as labor, and cannot therefore create value.
　　　Capital [2] [*1867–1883*]. *Part II,*
　　　　　　Chap. 3, Page 33
The capitalist himself is a practical
man, who, it is true, does not always
reflect on what he says outside his office,
but who always knows what he does
inside the latter.
　　　　　Ibid. Chap. 5, Page 43
Constant labor of one uniform kind
destroys the intensity and flow of a
man's animal spirits, which find recrea-

[1] By bourgeoisie is meant the class of modern capitalists, owners of the means of social
production and employers of wage-labor. By
proletariat, the class of modern wage-laborers
who, having no means of production of their
own, are reduced to selling their labor-power
in order to live. — Friedrich Engels [1820–
1895]: *Footnote to Manifesto of the Communist Party*
[2] Abridged edition prepared by Julian
Borchardt, translated by Stephen L. Trask,
Modern Library edition.

tion and delight in mere change of activity.

Capital. Part II, Chap. 9,
Page 74

The intellectual desolation, artificially produced by converting immature human beings into mere machines.

Ibid. Chap. 10, Page 102

The battle of competition is fought by cheapening of commodities.

Ibid. Chap. 13, Page 168

The only part of the so-called national wealth that actually enters into the collective possessions of modern peoples is their national debt.

Ibid. Chap. 14, Page 199

Capitalist production begets, with the inexorability of a law of nature, its own negation.

Ibid. Chap. 15, Page 204

When commercial capital occupies a position of unquestioned ascendancy, it everywhere constitutes a system of plunder.

Ibid. Chap. 21, Page 262

From each according to his abilities, to each according to his needs.

Critique of the Gotha Program [1]
[1875]

IVAN SERGEYEVICH TURGENIEV
[1818–1883]

That air of superiority to the rest of the world which usually disappears when once the twenties have been passed.

Fathers and Sons [2] *[1862].*
Chap. 4

That awkwardness which overtakes a young man when, just ceased to be a boy, he returns to the spot where hitherto he has ranked as a mere child.

Ibid.

That dim, murky period when regrets come to resemble hopes, and hopes are beginning to resemble regrets.

Ibid. Chap. 7

[1] Modern Library edition.
[2] Translated by C. J. Hogarth.

I agree with no man's opinions. I have some of my own.

Fathers and Sons. Chap. 13

The temerity to believe in nothing.

Ibid. Chap. 14

A picture may instantly present what a book could set forth only in a hundred pages.

Ibid. Chap. 16

The sensuous joy of magnanimity.

Ibid. Chap. 17

Whatever a man prays for, he prays for a miracle. Every prayer reduces itself to this: "Great God, grant that twice two be not four."

Prayer

Don't forget me, but do not call me to mind either, in the midst of daily cares, pleasures and needs. . . . I do not want to disturb your life, I do not want to impede its quiet course.

Literary Remains [published in 1930]. When I Shall Be No More

HENRY WHEELER SHAW ("JOSH BILLINGS")
[1818–1885]

A sekret ceases tew be a sekret if it iz once confided — it iz like a dollar bill, once broken, it iz never a dollar agin.

Affurisms [1] *[1865]*

Love iz like the meazles; we kant have it bad but onst, and the later in life we have it the tuffer it goes with us.

Ibid.

Put an Englishman into the garden of Eden, and he would find fault with the whole blarsted consarn; — put a Yankee in, and he would see where he could alter it to advantage; — put an Irishman in, and he would want tew boss the thing; — put a Dutchman in, and he would proceed tew plant it.

Ibid.

Better make a weak man your enemy than your friend.

Ibid.

[1] From *Josh Billings: His Sayings.*

I never knu a man trubbled with melankolly, who had plenty to dew, and did it.

Affurisms

Poverty iz the step-mother ov genius.

Ibid.

Manifest destiny iz the science ov going tew bust, or enny other place before yu git thare.

Manifest Destiny

Thare iz such a thing az manifest destiny, but when it occurs it iz like the number ov rings on the rakoon's tale, ov no great consequense only for ornament.

Ibid.

The wheel that squeaks the loudest Is the one that gets the grease.

The Kicker

It is better to know nothing than to know what ain't so.[1]

Proverb [1874]

MAX SCHNECKENBURGER
[1819–1849]

So long as blood shall warm our veins, While for the sword one hand remains, One arm to bear a gun, — no more Shall foot of foeman tread thy shore! Dear Fatherland, no fear be thine, Firm stands thy guard along the Rhine.

The Watch on the Rhine.[2]
Stanza 4

ARTHUR HUGH CLOUGH
[1819–1861]

Grace is given of God, but knowledge is bought in the market.

The Bothie of Tober-na-Vuolich
[1848]. Part IV

A world where nothing is had for nothing.

Ibid. Part VIII

As ships, becalmed at eve, that lay
  With canvas drooping, side by side,
Two towers of sail, at dawn of day

---

[1] Better know nothing than half-know many things. — NIETZSCHE: *Thus Spake Zarathustra* [1883–1891], Part IV, 64

[2] Translated by JOHN R. THOMPSON [1823–1873].

Are scarce long leagues apart descried.

Qua Cursum Ventus [1849].
Stanza 1

It fortifies my soul to know
That, though I perish, Truth is so:
That, howsoe'er I stray and range,
Whate'er I do, Thou dost not change.
I steadier step when I recall
That, if I slip, Thou dost not fall.

"With Whom Is No Variableness" [1]
[1862]

Because we can't do all we would, Does it follow, to do nothing's good?

Dipsychus [1862]. Part I, Sc. 4

And almost every one when age,
  Disease, or sorrows strike him,
Inclines to think there is a God,
  Or something very like Him.

Ibid. Sc. 5

This world is very odd we see,
  We do not comprehend it;
But in one fact we all agree,
  God won't, and we can't, mend it.

Ibid. Part II, Sc. 2

How pleasant it is to have money!

Ibid.

Haunt not the fringy edges of the fight But the pell-mell of men.

Ibid. Sc. 4

That out of sight is out of mind [2]
Is true of most we leave behind;
It is not sure, nor can be true,
My own and only love, of you.

Songs of Absence [1862]

Say not, the struggle naught availeth,
  The labour and the wounds are vain,
The enemy faints not, nor faileth,
  And as things have been they remain.

Say Not the Struggle Naught
Availeth [1862]. Stanza 1

For while the tired waves, vainly breaking,
Seem here no painful inch to gain,
Far back, through creeks and inlets making,
  Comes silent, flooding in, the main.

Ibid. Stanza 3

---

[1] *James, I, 17.*

[2] See Thomas à Kempis, page 83a.

And not by eastern windows only,
  When daylight comes, comes in the
    light;
In front, the sun climbs slow, how
    slowly,
  But westward, look, the land is
    bright.
           Say Not the Struggle Naught
                   Availeth. Stanza 4

GEORGE ELIOT
(MARIAN EVANS CROSS)
[1819–1880]

'Tis God gives skill,
But not without men's hands: He could
    not make
Antonio Stradivari's violins
Without Antonio.
                        Stradivarius

O may I join the choir invisible
Of those immortal dead who live again
In minds made better by their presence.
     O May I Join the Choir Invisible

May I reach
That purest heaven, be to other souls
The cup of strength in some great
    agony.
                              Ibid.

Life is too precious to be spent in
this weaving and unweaving of false
impressions, and it is better to live
quietly under some degree of misrepresentation than to attempt to remove
it by the uncertain process of letter-
writing.
        Letter to Mrs. Peter Taylor
                    [June 8, 1856]

Boots and shoes are the greatest
trouble of my life. Everything else one
can turn and turn about, and make old
look like new; but there's no coaxing
boots and shoes to look better than
they are.
        Amos Barton [*1857*]. *Chap. 2*

It's no trifle at her time of life to
part with a doctor who knows her constitution.
        Janet's Repentance [*1857*].
                             Chap. 3

Any coward can fight a battle when
he's sure of winning; but give me the
man who has pluck to fight when he's
sure of losing. That's my way, sir; and
there are many victories worse than a
defeat.
        Janet's Repentance. Chap. 6

Opposition may become sweet to a
man when he has christened it persecution.
                        Ibid. Chap. 8

It's but little good you'll do a-water-
ing the last year's crops.
        Adam Bede [*1859*]. *Chap. 18*

He was like a cock who thought the
sun had risen to hear him crow.
                        Ibid. Chap. 33

I've never any pity for conceited
people, because I think they carry their
comfort about with them.[1]
        The Mill on the Floss [*1860*].
                      Book V, Chap. 4

Below their names it was written:
"In their death they were not divided." [2]
                Ibid. Last line of book

The years seem to rush by now, and
I think of death as a fast approaching
end of a journey — double and treble
reason for loving as well as working
while it is day.
        Letter to Miss Sara Hennell
                [November 22, 1861]

It seems to me much better to read
a man's own writing than to read what
others say about him, especially when
the man is first-rate and the "others"
are third-rate.
        Letter to Miss Hennell
                [October 28, 1865]

I have the conviction that excessive
literary production is a social offence.
        Letter to Alexander Main
                [September 11, 1871]

I like not only to be loved, but also
to be told that I am loved. I am not sure
that you are of the same kind. But
the realm of silence is large enough
beyond the grave. This is the world of

---

[1] There is not enough of love and goodness in the world to throw any of it away
on conceited people. — NIETZSCHE [1844–
1900]: *Human, All Too Human, 129*
[2] *2 Samuel, I, 23*

light and speech, and I shall take leave to tell you that you are very dear.

Letter to Mrs. Burne-Jones
[May 11, 1875]

All biography diminishes in interest when the subject has won celebrity — or some reputation that hardly comes up to a celebrity. But autobiography at least saves a man or woman that the world is curious about from the publication of a string of mistakes called "Memoirs."

Letter to Miss Sara Hennell
[November 22, 1876]

Blessed is the man who, having nothing to say, abstains from giving in words evidence of the fact.

Impressions of Theophrastus
Such [1879]

THOMAS DUNN ENGLISH
[1819–1902]

Oh! don't you remember sweet Alice, Ben Bolt?
Sweet Alice, whose hair was so brown,
Who wept with delight when you gave her a smile,
And trembled with fear at your frown?
Ben Bolt [1]
Though little dangers they may fear,
When greater dangers men environ
Then women show a front of iron;
And, gentle in their manner, they
Do bold things in a quiet way.
Betty Zane. [2] *Stanza 1*

JOSIAH GILBERT HOLLAND
[1819–1881]

Heaven is not reached at a single bound;

[1] First published in *The New York Mirror*, September 2, 1843. It was set to music, an adaptation of an old German melody, by NELSON KNEASS, and sung in the play *The Battle of Buena Vista*. In 1894 GEORGE DU MAURIER used the song in his novel *Trilby* and it at once became popular.

[2] Fort Henry (now Wheeling, West Virginia) was attacked by Simon Girty and a band of Wyandot Indians, September 27–28, 1777. Betty Zane ran from the blockhouse to the log hut on the hill, and returned with a cask of gunpowder wrapped in her apron.

But we build the ladder by which we rise
From the lowly earth to the vaulted skies,
And we mount to its summit round by round. [1]
Gradatim. Stanza 1

He could see naught but vanity in beauty,
And naught but weakness in a fond caress,
And pitied men whose views of Christian duty
Allowed indulgence in such foolishness.
Daniel Gray. Stanza 9

God give us men! A time like this demands
Strong minds, great hearts, true faith, and ready hands;
Men whom the lust of office does not kill;
Men whom the spoils of office cannot buy;
Men who possess opinions and a will;
Men who have honor; men who will not lie.
The Day's Demand

JULIA WARD HOWE
[1819–1910]

Mine eyes have seen the glory of the coming of the Lord;
He is trampling out the vintage where the grapes of wrath are stored;
He hath loosed the fateful lightning of His terrible, swift sword;
His truth is marching on.
Battle Hymn of the Republic
[1862]. Stanza 1

In the beauty of the lilies Christ was born across the sea,
With a glory in His bosom that transfigures you and me;
As He died to make men holy, let us die to make men free.
Ibid. Stanza 5

Weave no more silks, ye Lyons looms,
To deck our girls for gay delights!

[1] Step after step the ladder is ascended. — GEORGE HERBERT: *Jacula Prudentum* [1640]

The crimson flower of battle blooms,
And solemn marches fill the nights.
Our Orders

CHARLES KINGSLEY
[1819–1875]

Oh! that we two were Maying.
The Saint's Tragedy [*1848*].
Act II, Sc. 9

"O Mary, go and call the cattle home,
And call the cattle home,
And call the cattle home,
Across the sands of Dee;"
The western wind was wild and dank
with foam,
And all alone went she.
The Sands of Dee. Stanza 1

The cruel crawling foam.
Ibid. Stanza 4

For men must work, and women must
weep,
And there's little to earn and many to
keep,
Though the harbor bar be moaning.
The Three Fishers. Stanza 1

For men must work, and women must
weep,
And the sooner it's over, the sooner to
sleep;
And good-bye to the bar and its
moaning.
Ibid. Stanza 3

Be good, sweet maid, and let who will
be clever;
Do noble things, not dream them, all
day long;
And so make Life, Death, and that vast
Forever
One grand sweet song.
A Farewell. Stanza 3

The world goes up and the world goes
down,
And the sunshine follows the rain;
And yesterday's sneer and yesterday's
frown
Can never come over again.
Dolcino to Margaret

Oh England is a pleasant place for
them that's rich and high,

But England is a cruel place for such
poor folks as I.
The Last Buccaneer. Stanza 1

In the light of fuller day,
Of purer science, holier laws.[1]
On the Death of a Certain Journal [2]
[*1848–1849*]. *Stanza 5*

A lone man's companion, a bachelor's
friend, a hungry man's food, a sad man's
cordial, a wakeful man's sleep, and a
chilly man's fire . . . there's no herb
like unto it [tobacco] under the canopy
of heaven.
Westward Ho [*1855*]. *Chap. 7*

More ways of killing a cat than chok-
ing her with cream.
Ibid. Chap. 20

Thank God every morning when you
get up that you have something to do
that day which must be done, whether
you like it or not. Being forced to work,
and forced to do your best, will breed
in you temperance and self-control,
diligence and strength of will, cheerfulness and content, and a hundred virtues which the idle never know.
Town and Country Sermons [*1861*]

Clear and cool, clear and cool,
By laughing shallow, and dreaming
pool;
Cool and clear, cool and clear,
By shining shingle, and foaming wear;
Under the crag where the ouzel sings,
And the ivied wall where the church-bell
rings;
Undefiled, for the undefiled;
Play by me, bathe in me, mother and
child.
Water Babies [*1863*]. *Song I,*
Stanza 1

When all the world is young, lad,
And all the trees are green;
And every goose a swan, lad,
And every lass a queen;
Then hey for boot and horse, lad,
And round the world away:
Young blood must have its course, lad,
And every dog his day.[3]
Ibid. Song II, Stanza 1

[1] See Tennyson, page 553a.
[2] *The Christian Socialist.*
[3] See Shakespeare, page 179a.

When all the world is old, lad,
And all the trees are brown;
And all the sport is stale, lad,
And all the wheels run down.
Water Babies. Song II, Stanza 2

God grant you find one face there
You loved when all was young!
Ibid.

I once had a sweet little doll, dears,
The prettiest doll in the world;
Her cheeks were so red and so white,
    dears,
And her hair was so charmingly curled.
Ibid. Song IV, Stanza 1

We were crawling slowly along, looking out for Virgin Garda; the first of those numberless isles which Columbus, so goes the tale, discovered on St. Ursula's day, and named them after the saint and her eleven thousand mythical virgins. Unfortunately, English buccaneers have since given to most of them less poetic names. The Dutchman's Cap, Broken Jerusalem, The Dead Man's Chest,[1] Rum Island, and so forth, mark a time and race more prosaic.
At Last [1870]. Chap. 1

To be discontented with the divine discontent, and to be ashamed with the noble shame, is the very germ and first upgrowth of all virtue.
Health and Education [1874].
The Science of Health

Some say that the age of chivalry is past, that the spirit of romance is dead. The age of chivalry is never past, so long as there is a wrong left unredressed on earth.
Life [1879]. Vol. II, Chap. 28

JAMES RUSSELL LOWELL
[1819–1891]

She doeth little kindnesses
Which most leave undone, or despise.
My Love [1840]. Stanza 4

Be noble! and the nobleness that lies
In other men, sleeping, but never dead,
Will rise in majesty to meet thine own.
Sonnet IV [1840]

[1] See R. L. Stevenson, pages 749b–750a.

Great Truths are portions of the soul
    of man;
Great souls are portions of Eternity.
Sonnet VI [1841]

His words were simple words enough,
    And yet he used them so,
That what in other mouths was rough
In his seemed musical and low.
The Shepherd of King Admetus
[1842]. Stanza 5

All thoughts that mould the age begin
Deep down within the primitive soul.
An Incident in a Railroad Car
[1842]. Stanza 13

Who speaks the truth stabs Falsehood
    to the heart.
L'Envoi [1843]

No man is born into the world whose
    work
Is not born with him; there is always
    work,
And tools to work withal, for those who
    will;
And blessèd are the horny hands of toil.
A Glance Behind the Curtain
[1843]

They are slaves who fear to speak
For the fallen and the weak. . . .
They are slaves who dare not be
In the right with two or three.
Stanzas on Freedom [1843]. IV

The nurse of full-grown souls is solitude.
Columbus [1844]

Once to every man and nation comes
    the moment to decide,
In the strife of Truth with Falsehood,
    for the good or evil side.
The Present Crisis [1844].
Stanza 5

Truth forever on the scaffold, Wrong
    forever on the throne.[1]
Ibid. Stanza 8

Then it is the brave man chooses, while
    the coward stands aside,

[1] Worth on foot, and rascals in the coach.
— DRYDEN: *Art of Poetry* [1685], L. 376
Wrong rules the land, and waiting Justice sleeps. — J. G. HOLLAND [1819–1881]: *The Day's Demand*

Doubting in his abject spirit, till his Lord is crucified.

The Present Crisis. Stanza 11

They must upward still, and onward, who would keep abreast of Truth.

Ibid. Stanza 18

Dear common flower, that grow'st beside the way,
Fringing the dusty road with harmless gold.

To the Dandelion [*1845*].
Stanza 1

The birch, most shy and ladylike of trees.

An Indian-Summer Reverie [*1846*].
Stanza 8

Not only around our infancy
Doth heaven with all its splendors lie;
Daily, with souls that cringe and plot,
We Sinais climb and know it not.

The Vision of Sir Launfal [*1848*].
Part I, Prelude, Stanza 2

'Tis heaven alone that is given away;
'Tis only God may be had for the asking.

Ibid. Stanza 4

And what is so rare as a day in June?
Then, if ever, come perfect days;
Then Heaven tries the earth if it be in tune,
And over it softly her warm ear lays.

Ibid. Stanza 5

He gives only the worthless gold
Who gives from a sense of duty.

Ibid. Part I, Stanza 6

The gift without the giver is bare; [1]
Who gives himself with his alms feeds three, —
Himself, his hungering neighbor, and me.

Ibid. Part II, Stanza 8

Got the ill name of augurs, because they were bores.

A Fable for Critics [*1848*]

There comes Emerson first, whose rich words, every one,
Are like gold nails in temples to hang trophies on;
Whose prose is grand verse, while his verse, the Lord knows,

[1] See Emerson, page 502b.

Is some of it pr— No, 'tis not even prose.[1]

A Fable for Critics

And I honoi the man who is willing to sink
Half his present repute for the freedom to think,
And, when he has thought, be his cause strong or weak,
Will risk t' other half for the freedom to speak.

Ibid.

There comes Poe, with his raven, like Barnaby Rudge,
Three fifths of him genius and two fifths sheer fudge.

Ibid.

Nature fits all her children with something to do,
He who would write and can't write, can surely review.[2]

Ibid.

Ez fer war, I call it murder, —
There you hev it plain an' flat;
I don't want to go no furder
Than my Testyment fer that. . . .
An' you've gut to git up airly
Ef you want to take in God.

The Biglow Papers. Series I
[*1848*], *No. 1, Stanza 5*

Laborin' man an' laborin' woman
Hev one glory an' one shame;
Ev'y thin' thet's done inhuman
Injers all on 'em the same.

Ibid. Stanza 10

This goin' ware glory waits ye haint one agreeable feetur.

Ibid. No. 2, Stanza 6

But John P.
Robinson, he
Sez they didn't know everythin' down in Judee.

Ibid. No. 3, Stanza 8

A marciful Providunce fashioned us holler
O' purpose thet we might our principles swaller.

Ibid. No. 4, Stanza 2

[1] Meredith is a prose Browning, and **so** is Browning — OSCAR WILDE [1854–1900]: *The Critic as Artist*
[2] See Disraeli, page 513a.

I should like to shoot
The holl gang, by the gret horn spoon!
The Biglow Papers. Series I,
No. 5, Stanza 2

I du believe with all my soul
In the gret Press's freedom,
To pint the people to the goal
An' in the traces lead 'em.
Ibid. No. 6, Stanza 7

I *don't* believe in princerple,
But oh I *du* in interest.
Ibid. Stanza 9

It ain't by princerples nor men
My preudunt course is steadied, —
I scent wich pays the best, an' then
Go into it baldheaded.
Ibid. Stanza 10

Of my merit
On thet pint you yourself may jedge;
All is, I never drink no sperit,
Nor I haint never signed no pledge.
Ibid. No. 7, Stanza 9

Ez to my princerples, I glory
In hevin' nothin' o' the sort.
Ibid. Stanza 10

God makes sech nights, all white an'
still,
Fur'z you can look or listen.
*Ibid. Series II [1866], The
Courtin', Stanza 1*

His heart kep' goin' pity-pat,
But hern went pity-Zekle.
Ibid. Stanza 15

All kin' o' smily round the lips,
An' teary round the lashes.
Ibid. Stanza 21

My gran'ther's rule was safer 'n 'tis
to crow:
Don't never prophesy — onless ye
know.
Ibid. No. 2

It's 'most enough to make a deacon
swear.
Ibid.

Folks never understand the folks they
hate.
Ibid.

Ef you want peace, the thing you've
gut tu du
Is jes' to show you're up to fightin', tu.[1]
Ibid.

[1] See Washington, page 367a.

Bad work follers ye ez long's ye live.
*The Biglow Papers. Series II,
No. 2*

Our papers don't purtend to print on'y
wut Guv'ment choose,
An' thet insures us all to git the very
best o' noose.
Ibid. No. 3

No, never say nothin' without you're
compelled tu,
An' then don't say nothin' thet you can
be held tu.
Ibid. No. 5

Wut's words to them whose faith an'
truth
On War's red techstone rang true
metal,
Who ventered life an' love an' youth
For the gret prize o' death in battle?
Ibid. No. 10, Stanza 17

They came three thousand miles, and
died,
To keep the Past upon its throne;
Unheard, beyond the ocean tide,
Their English mother made her moan.[1]
*Graves of Two English Sol-
diers on Concord Battle-
ground [1849]. Stanza 3*

Slowly the Bible of the race is writ,
And not on paper leaves nor leaves of
stone;
Each age, each kindred, adds a verse
to it,
Texts of despair or hope, of joy or
moan.
Bibliolatres [1849]. Stanza 6

There is nothing so desperately monotonous as the sea, and I no longer
wonder at the cruelty of pirates.
Fireside Travels [1864]. At Sea

It is by presence of mind in untried
emergencies that the native metal of a
man is tested.
Abraham Lincoln [1864]

What men call treasure and the Gods
call dross.
*Ode Recited at the Harvard
Commemoration [1865]. IV*

[1] Inscribed on the memorial to the two
British soldiers, Concord, Massachusetts.

Each year to ancient friendships adds
   a ring,
As to an oak.
      Under the Willows [*1868*]

The shell disdained a soul had gained,
The lyre had been discovered.
    The Finding of the Lyre [*1868*].
             Stanza 4

Not failure, but low aim, is crime.
  For an Autograph [*1868*]. *Stanza 5*

When I was a beggarly boy,
  And lived in a cellar damp,
I had not a friend nor a toy,
  But I had Aladdin's lamp.
     Aladdin [*1868*]. *Stanza 1*

Safe in the hallowed quiets of the past.
   The Cathedral[1] [*1869*]. *Stanza 9*

The one thing finished in this hasty
  world.
                Ibid.

The wisest man could ask no more of
  Fate
Than to be simple, modest, manly, true,
Safe from the Many, honored by the
  Few;
To count as naught in World, or
  Church, or State;
But inwardly in secret to be great.
    Sonnet, Jeffries Wyman [*1874*]

For me Fate gave, whate'er she else
  denied,
A nature sloping to the southern side;
I thank her for it, though when clouds
  arise
Such Natures double-darken gloomy
  skies.
   Epistle to George William Curtis
        [*1874*]. *Postscript*

Like him who, in the desert's awful
  frame,
Notches his cockney initials on the
  Sphinx.
   *Sonnet on Being Asked for an
    Autograph in Venice* [*1875*]

The Maple puts her corals on in May.
       The Maple [*1875*]

In vain we call old notions fudge,
And bend our conscience to our dealing;

[1] Chartres.

The Ten Commandments will not
  budge,
And stealing will continue stealing.[1]
    International Copyright
      [*November 20, 1885*]

These pearls of thought in Persian gulfs
  were bred,
Each softly lucent as a rounded moon;
The diver Omar plucked them from
  their bed,
Fitzgerald strung them on an English
  thread.
   In a Copy of Omar Khayyám
      [*1888*]. *Stanza 1*

   As brief
As a dragon-fly's repose.
    Scherzo [*1888*]. *Stanza 3*

In life's small things be resolute and
  great
To keep thy muscle trained: know'st
  thou when Fate
Thy measure takes, or when she'll say
  to thee,
"I find thee worthy; do this deed for
  me"?
        Sayings [*1888*]. *I*

As life runs on, the road grows strange
With faces new, and near the end
The milestones into headstones change,
'Neath every one a friend.
   Sixty-Eighth Birthday [*1889*]

Solitude is as needful to the imagination as society is wholesome for the
character.
              Dryden

A wise scepticism is the first attribute
of a good critic.
    Shakespeare Once More

Truly there is a tide in the affairs of
men, but there is no gulf-stream setting forever in one direction.
  New England Two Centuries Ago

There is no better ballast for keeping
the mind steady on its keel, and saving
it from all risk of crankiness, than business.
                Ibid.

Puritanism, believing itself quick
with the seed of religious liberty, laid,

[1] Motto of the American Copyright League.

without knowing it, the egg of democracy.

New England Two Centuries Ago

It was in making education not only common to all, but in some sense compulsory on all, that the destiny of the free republics of America was practically settled.

Ibid.

Talent is that which is in a man's power; genius is that in whose power a man is.

Rousseau and the Sentimentalists

Every man feels instinctively that all the beautiful sentiments in the world weigh less than a single lovely action.

Ibid.

It is singular how impatient men are with over-praise of others, how patient with over-praise of themselves; and yet the one does them no injury, while the other may be their ruin.

Literary Remains of the Reverend Homer Wilbur

Things always seem fairer when we look back at them, and it is out of that inaccessible tower of the past that Longing leans and beckons.

A Few Bits of Roman Mosaic

An umbrella is of no avail against a Scotch Mist.

On a Certain Condescension in Foreigners

The soil out of which such men as he are made is good to be born on, good to live on, good to die for and to be buried in.

Garfield

Mishaps are like knives, that either serve us or cut us, as we grasp them by the blade or the handle.

Cambridge Thirty Years Ago

No man, I suspect, ever lived long in the country without being bitten by these meteorological ambitions. He likes to be hotter and colder, to have been more deeply snowed up, to have more trees and larger blown down than his neighbors.

My Garden Acquaintance

As if old age were never kindly as well as frosty; as if it had no reverend

graces of its own as good in their way as the noisy impertinence of childhood, the elbowing self-conceit of youth, or the pompous mediocrity of middle life!

A Good Word for Winter

What a sense of security in an old book which Time has criticised for us!

A Library of Old Authors

There is no good in arguing with the inevitable. The only argument available with an east wind is to put on your overcoat.

Democracy and Addresses

It is curious how tyrannical the habit of reading is, and what shifts we make to escape thinking.[1] There is no bore we dread being left alone with so much as our own minds.

A Moosehead Journal

There are few brains that would not be better for living on their own fat a little while.

Ibid.

HERMAN MELVILLE
[1819–1891]

Sailor or landsman, there is some sort of Cape Horn for all. Boys! beware of it; prepare for it in time. Greybeards! thank God it is passed.

White-Jacket [1850]. Chap. 26

Call me Ishmael.

Moby Dick [1851]. Chap. 1

But oh! shipmates! on the starboard hand of every woe, there is a sure delight; and higher the top of that delight, than the bottom of the woe is deep. Is not the main-truck higher than the kelson is low? Delight is to him — a far, far upward, and inward delight — who against the proud gods and commodores of this earth, ever stands forth his own inexorable self.

Ibid. Chap. 9

And eternal delight and deliciousness will be his, who coming to lay him down, can say with his final breath — O Father! — chiefly known to me by Thy rod — mortal or immortal, here I

[1] See Sheridan, page 382a, and Bryce, page 698a.

die. I have striven to be Thine, more than to be this world's, or mine own. Yet this is nothing; I leave eternity to Thee; for what is man that he should live out the lifetime of his God?

Moby Dick. Chap. 9

The Nantucketer, out of sight of land, furls his sails and lays him to his rest, while under his very pillow rush herds of walruses and whales.

Ibid. Chap. 14

A whale ship was my Yale College and my Harvard.

Ibid. Chap. 24

Thou great democratic God! who didst not refuse to the swart convict, Bunyan, the pale poetic pearl; Thou who didst clothe with doubly hammered leaves of finest gold, the stumped and paupered arm of old Cervantes; Thou who didst pick up Andrew Jackson from the pebbles; who didst hurl him upon a warhorse; who didst thunder him higher than a throne!

Ibid. Chap. 26

The starred and stately nights seemed haughty dames in jewelled velvets, nursing at home in lonely pride the memory of their absent conquering Earls, the golden helmeted suns!

Ibid. Chap. 29

This it is, that for ever keeps God's true princes of the Empire from the world's hustings; and leaves the highest honors that this air can give, to those men who become famous more through their infinite inferiority to the choice hidden handful of the Divine Inert, than through their undoubted superiority over the dead level of the mass.

Ibid. Chap. 33

For as this appalling ocean surrounds the verdant land, so in the soul of man there lies one insular Tahiti, full of peace and joy, but encompassed by all the horrors of the half known life.

Ibid. Chap. 58

Give me a condor's quill! Give me Vesuvius' crater for an inkstand! . . . To produce a mighty book, you must choose a mighty theme.

Ibid. Chap. 104

And meet it is, that over these sea-pastures, wide-rolling watery prairies and Potters' Fields of all four continents, the waves should rise and fall, and ebb and flow unceasingly; for here, millions of mixed shades and shadows, drowned dreams, somnambulisms, reveries; all that we call lives and souls, lie dreaming, dreaming, still; tossing like slumberers in their beds; the ever-rolling waves but made so by their restlessness.

Moby Dick. Chap. 111

Where lies the final harbor, whence we unmoor no more?

Ibid. Chap. 114

But if the great sun move not of himself; but is as an errand-boy in heaven; nor one single star can revolve, but by some invisible power; how then can this one small heart beat; this one small brain think thoughts; unless God does that beating, does that thinking, does that living, and not I. By heaven, man, we are turned round and round in this world, like yonder windlass, and Fate is the handspike.

Ibid. Chap. 132

Thinking is, or ought to be, a coolness and a calmness; and our poor hearts throb, and our poor brains beat too much for that.

Ibid. Chap. 135

An old, old sight, and yet somehow so young; aye, and not changed a wink since I first saw it, a boy, from the sandhills of Nantucket! The same! — the same! — the same to Noah as to me. There's a soft shower to leeward. Such lovely leewardings! They must lead somewhere — to something else than common land, more palmy than the palms.

Ibid.

Now small fowls flew screaming over the yet yawning gulf; a sullen white surf beat against its steep sides; then all collapsed, and the great shroud of the sea rolled on as it rolled five thousand years ago.

Ibid.

There is no faith, and no stoicism, and no philosophy, that a mortal man can possibly evoke, which will stand the final test in a real impassioned onset of Life and Passion upon him. Faith and philosophy are air, but events are brass.

Pierre [1852]

All dies! and not alone
The aspiring trees and men and grass;
The poets' forms of beauty pass,
And noblest deeds they are undone,
Even truth itself decays, and lo,
From truth's sad ashes pain and false-
    hood grow.

The Lake

THOMAS WILLIAM PARSONS
[1819–1892]

Sorrow and the scarlet leaf,
  Sad thoughts and sunny weather:
Ah me, this glory and this grief
  Agree not well together!

A Song for September

JOHN RUSKIN
[1819–1900]

He is the greatest artist who has embodied, in the sum of his works, the
greatest number of the greatest ideas.

*Modern Painters. Vol. I [1843],
Part I, Chap. 2, Sect. 9*

The greatest thing a human soul ever does in this world is to *see* something, and tell what it *saw* in a plain way. Hundreds of people can talk for one who can think, but thousands can think for one who can see. To see clearly is poetry, prophecy, and religion, all in one.

*Ibid. Vol. III [1856], Part IV,
Chap. 16, Sect. 28*

In order that people may be happy in their work, these three things are needed: They must be fit for it: They must not do too much of it: And they must have a sense of success in it.

Pre-Raphaelitism [1851]

Remember that the most beautiful things in the world are the most useless; peacocks and lilies for instance.

*The Stones of Venice [1851–1853].
Vol. I, Chap. 2*

It is chiefly by private, not by public, effort that your city must be adorned.

*Lectures on Architecture and
Painting [1853]. I*

Blue colour is everlastingly appointed by the Deity to be a source of
delight.

Ibid.

There is no Wealth but Life.

Unto This Last [1862]. Sect. 77

That country is the richest which nourishes the greatest number of noble and happy human beings; that man is richest who, having perfected the functions of his own life to the utmost, has also the widest helpful influence, both personal, and by means of his possessions, over the lives of others.

Ibid.

Life being very short, and the quiet hours of it few, we ought to waste none of them in reading valueless books.[1]

Sesame and Lilies [1865]. Preface

The greatest efforts of the race have always been traceable to the love of praise, as its greatest catastrophes to the love of pleasure.

Ibid. Of Kings' Treasuries, Sect. 3

All books are divisible into two classes: the books of the hour, and the books of all time.

Ibid. Sect. 8

There are masked words abroad, I say, which nobody understands, but which everybody uses, and most people will also fight for, live for, or even die for, fancying they mean this, or that, or the other, of things dear to them.

Ibid. Sect. 16

The very cheapness of literature is making even wise people forget that if a book is worth reading, it is worth buying. No book is worth anything which is not worth *much;* nor is it

[1] Life is too short for reading inferior books. — JAMES BRYCE: *Address at Rutgers College* [November 10, 1911]

serviceable, until it has been read, and re-read, and loved, and loved again; and marked, so that you can refer to the passages you want in it.

Sesame and Lilies. Of Kings'
Treasuries, Sect. 32

When men are rightly occupied, their amusement grows out of their work, as the colour-petals out of a fruitful flower.

Ibid. Sect. 39

He only is advancing in life, whose heart is getting softer, whose blood warmer, whose brain quicker, whose spirit is entering into living peace. And the men who have this life in them are the true lords or kings of the earth — they, and they only.

Ibid. Sect. 42

This is the true nature of home — it is the place of Peace; the shelter, not only from all injury, but from all terror, doubt, and division.

Ibid. Of Queens' Gardens,
Sect. 68

Borrowers are nearly always ill-spenders, and it is with lent money that all evil is mainly done, and all unjust war protracted.

The Crown of Wild Olive [1866].
Work, Sect. 34

Give a little love to a child, and you get a great deal back.

Ibid. Sect. 49

There's no music in a "rest," Katie, that I know of: but there's the making of music in it. And people are always missing that part of the life-melody.

Ethics of the Dust [1866].
Lecture 4, The Crystal Orders

Life without industry is guilt, industry without art is brutality.

Lectures on Art [1870]. III, The
Relation of Art to Morals

Engraving, then, is, in brief terms, the Art of Scratch.

Ariadne Florentina [1873–1876].
Lecture I

Trust thou thy Love: if she be proud, is she not sweet?

Trust thou thy Love: if she be mute, is she not pure?

Lay thou thy soul full in her hands, low at her feet;

Fail, Sun and Breath! — yet, for thy peace, she shall endure.

Trust Thou Thy Love

WILLIAM WETMORE STORY
[1819–1895]

Give me the old enthusiasms back,

Give me the ardent longings that I lack, —

The glorious dreams that fooled me in my youth,

The sweet mirage that lured me on its track, —

And take away the bitter, barren truth.

Ah, yes! Success, I fear, has come too late!

Girolamo, Detto Il Fiorentino

Mosquito critics with a poisonous sting.

Ibid.

Of every noble work the silent part is best,

Of all expression that which can not be expressed.

The Unexpressed

We live as much in all that we have lost

As what we own.

Sonnet, After Long Days of
Dull Perpetual Rain

QUEEN VICTORIA
[1819–1901]

We are not amused.

Comment, upon seeing an imitation of herself by the Honorable Alexander Grantham Yorke, Groom-in-Waiting to the Queen

WILLIAM ROSS WALLACE
[1819–1881]

The hand that rocks the cradle is the hand that rules the world.

The Hand That Rules the World.
Stanza 1

WALT WHITMAN
[1819–1892]

The United States themselves are essentially the greatest poem. . . . Here at last is something in the doings of man that corresponds with the broadcast doings of the day and night.

Preface to Leaves of Grass [*1855*],
First Edition

The proof of a poet is that his country absorbs him as affectionately as he has absorbed it.

Ibid.

Once fully enslaved, no nation, state, city of this earth, ever afterward resumes its liberty.

Leaves of Grass [*1855–1892*].[1]
To the States

I hear America singing, the varied carols I hear.

Ibid. I Hear America Singing

Shut not your doors to me proud libraries.

Ibid. Shut Not Your Doors

I will write the evangel-poem of comrades and of love.

Ibid. Starting from Paumanok, 6

I say the whole earth and all the stars in the sky are for religion's sake.

Ibid. 7

None has begun to think how divine he himself is, and how certain the future is.

Ibid.

I say the real and permanent grandeur of these States must be their religion.

Ibid.

[1] The first edition of *Leaves of Grass* consisted of 94 quarto pages and included the preface which set forth Whitman's faith and his poetic theory. Enlarged and revised editions followed. The tenth edition (from which the text used here is taken) was the last edition supervised by Whitman himself, literally from his deathbed, and hence it is sometimes called the "Deathbed Edition." Whitman wrote of it, "as there are now several editions of *Leaves of Grass,* different texts and dates, I wish to say that I prefer and recommend this present one."

Nothing can happen more beautiful than death.[1]

Leaves of Grass. Starting from Paumanok, 12

I celebrate myself and sing myself,
And what I assume you shall assume.

Ibid. Song of Myself, 1

I loafe and invite my soul.

Ibid.

Creeds and schools in abeyance.

Ibid.

Urge and urge and urge,
Always the procreant urge of the world.

Ibid. 3

I have no mockings or arguments; I witness and wait.

Ibid. 4

A kelson of the creation is love.

Ibid. 5

A child said *What is grass?* fetching it to one with full hands.

Ibid. 6

Or I guess it is the handkerchief of the Lord.

Ibid.

And now it seems to me the beautiful uncut hair of graves.

Ibid.

All goes onward and outward, nothing collapses,
And to die is different from what any one supposed, and luckier.

Ibid.

I find no sweeter fat than sticks to my own bones.

Ibid. 20

Whether I come to my own [2] today or in ten thousand or ten million years,

[1] Why fear death? Death is only a beautiful adventure. — CHARLES FROHMAN [1860–1915]: Last words to a group of friends as the *Lusitania* was sinking [May 7, 1915]

Why should I fear Death's call? Can there e'er be
In life more beautiful adventure than
To re-embark upon that unknown sea?
JAMES TERRY WHITE [1845–1920]:
Why Fear? St. 1

[2] Nor time, nor space, nor deep, nor high,
Can keep my own away from me.
JOHN BURROUGHS [1837–1931]:
Waiting, St. 6

I can cheerfully take it now, or with equal cheerfulness I can wait.
> *Leaves of Grass. Song of Myself, 20*

I am he that walks with the tender and growing night,
I call to the earth and sea half-held by the night.
Press close bare-bosom'd night — press close magnetic nourishing night!
Night of south winds — night of the large few stars!
Still nodding night — mad naked summer night.
> *Ibid. 21*

I dote on myself, there is that lot of me and all so luscious.
> *Ibid. 24*

I hear the violoncello, ('tis the young man's heart's complaint).
> *Ibid. 26*

I believe a leaf of grass is no less than the journey-work of the stars.
> *Ibid. 31*

And the tree-toad is a chef-d'oeuvre for the highest. . . .
And a mouse is miracle enough to stagger sextillions of infidels.
> *Ibid.*

I think I could turn and live with animals, they are so placid and self-contain'd,
I stand and look at them long and long.
They do not sweat and whine about their condition,
They do not lie awake in the dark and weep for their sins,
They do not make me sick discussing their duty to God,
Not one is dissatisfied, not one is demented with the mania of owning things,
Not one kneels to another, nor to his kind that lived thousands of years ago,
Not one is respectable or unhappy over the whole earth.
> *Ibid. 32*

Behold, I do not give lectures or a little charity,

When I give I give myself.[1]
> *Leaves of Grass. Song of Myself, 40*

And when you rise in the morning you will find what I tell you is so.
> *Ibid.*

I have said that the soul is not more than the body,
And I have said that the body is not more than the soul,
And nothing, not God, is greater to one than one's self is.
> *Ibid. 48*

In the faces of men and women I see God.
> *Ibid.*

Do I contradict myself?
Very well then I contradict myself,
(I am large, I contain multitudes.)
> *Ibid. 51*

I sound my barbaric yawp over the roofs of the world.
> *Ibid. 52*

If any thing is sacred the human body is sacred.
> *Ibid. Children of Adam, I Sing the Body Electric, 8*

I hear it was charged against me that I sought to destroy institutions,
But really I am neither for nor against institutions.
> *Ibid. I Hear It Was Charged Against Me*

When I peruse the conquer'd fame of heroes and the victories of mighty generals, I do not envy the generals.
> *Ibid. When I Peruse the Conquer'd Fame*

Afoot and light-hearted I take to the open road,
Healthy, free, the world before me,
The long brown path before me leading wherever I choose.
> *Ibid. Song of the Open Road, 1*

Henceforth I ask not good-fortune, I myself am good-fortune,
Henceforth I whimper no more, postpone no more, need nothing,
Done with indoor complaints, libraries, querulous criticisms,

[1] See Emerson, page 502b.

Strong and content I travel the open road.
> *Leaves of Grass. Song of the Open Road, 1*

The earth, that is sufficient,
I do not want the constellations any nearer,
I know they are very well where they are,
I know they suffice for those who belong to them.
> *Ibid.*

A great city is that which has the greatest men and women.
> *Ibid. Song of the Broad-Axe, 4*

In this broad earth of ours,
Amid the measureless grossness and the slag,
Enclosed and safe within its central heart,
Nestles the seed perfection.
> *Ibid. Song of the Universal, 1*

Through the battle, through defeat, moving yet and never stopping,
Pioneers! O pioneers!
> *Ibid. Pioneers! O Pioneers! 13*

Youth, large, lusty, loving — Youth, full of grace, force, fascination,
Do you know that Old Age may come after you, with equal grace, force, fascination?
> *Ibid. Youth, Day, Old Age and Night, 1*

Out of the cradle endlessly rocking,
Out of the mocking-bird's throat, the musical shuttle.
> *Ibid. Out of the Cradle Endlessly Rocking*

Soothe! soothe! soothe!
Close on its wave soothes the wave behind,
And again another behind embracing and lapping every one close,
But my love soothes not me, not me.
> *Ibid.*

O darkness! O in vain!
O I am very sick and sorrowful.
> *Ibid.*

Whereto answering, the sea,
Delaying not, hurrying not,
Whisper'd me through the night, and very plainly before daybreak,

Lisp'd to me the low and delicious word death.
> *Leaves of Grass. Out of the Cradle Endlessly Rocking*

Roaming in thought over the Universe, I saw the little that is Good steadily hastening towards immortality,
And the vast that is Evil I saw hastening to merge itself and become lost and dead.[1]
> *Ibid. Roaming in Thought After Reading Hegel*

Over all the sky — the sky! far, far out of reach, studded, breaking out, the eternal stars.
> *Ibid. Bivouac on a Mountain Side*

Give me the splendid silent sun, with all his beams full-dazzling!
> *Ibid. Give Me the Splendid Silent Sun, 1*

Beautiful that war and all its deeds of carnage must in time be utterly lost,
That the hands of the sisters Death and Night incessantly softly wash again and ever again, this soiled world;
For my enemy is dead, a man divine as myself is dead.
> *Ibid. Reconciliation*

When lilacs last in the door-yard bloom'd,
And the great star early droop'd in the western sky in the night,
I mourn'd, and yet shall mourn with ever-returning spring.
> *Ibid. When Lilacs Last in the Door-yard Bloom'd, 1*

O sane and sacred death.
> *Ibid. 7*

Come lovely and soothing death,[2]
Undulate round the world, serenely arriving, arriving,
In the day, in the night, to all, to each,
Sooner or later, delicate death.
> *Ibid. 14*

Prais'd be the fathomless universe,

---

[1] Evil perpetually tends to disappear. — HERBERT SPENCER [1820–1903]: *The Evanescence of Evil*

[2] See Shakespeare, page 148a.

For life and joy, and for objects and
knowledge curious,
And for love, sweet love — But praise!
praise! praise!
For the sure-enwinding arms of cool-
enfolding Death.
*Leaves of Grass. When Lilacs Last
in the Door-yard Bloom'd, 14*

O Captain! my Captain! our fearful
trip is done!
The ship has weather'd every rack,
the prize we sought is won,
The port is near, the bells I hear, the
people all exulting.
Ibid. O Captain! My Captain! 1

The ship is anchor'd safe and sound, its
voyage closed and done,
From fearful trip the victor ship comes
in with object won.
Ibid. 3

Exult O shores, and ring O bells!
But I with mournful tread,
Walk the deck my Captain lies,
Fallen cold and dead.
Ibid.

This dust was once the man,
Gentle, plain, just and resolute, under
whose cautious hand,
Against the foulest crime in history
known in any land or age,
Was saved the Union of these States.
Ibid. This Dust Was Once the Man

The whole theory of the universe is
directed unerringly to one single
individual — namely to You.
Ibid. By Blue Ontario's Shore, 15

Not till the sun excludes you do I ex-
clude you.
Ibid. To a Common Prostitute

Liberty is to be subserved whatever
occurs.
*Ibid. To a Foil'd European
Revolutionaire, 1*

O we can wait no longer,
We too take ship O soul,
Joyous we too launch out on trackless
seas,
Fearless for unknown shores.
Ibid. Passage to India, 8

What do you suppose will satisfy the

soul, except to walk free and own
no superior?
*Leaves of Grass. Laws for
Creations, 3*

To me every hour of the light and dark
is a miracle,
Every cubic inch of space is a miracle.
Ibid. Miracles, 2

Sail, sail thy best, ship of Democracy.
Of value is thy freight, 'tis not the
Present only,
The Past is also stored in thee.
*Ibid. Thou Mother with Thy
Equal Brood, 4*

Society waits unform'd, and is for a
while between things ended and
things begun.
Ibid. Thoughts, 1

Our life is closed, our life begins,
The long, long anchorage we leave,
The ship is clear at last, she leaps!
She swiftly courses from the shore,
Joy, shipmate, joy.
Ibid. Joy, Shipmate, Joy!

Camerado, this is no book,
Who touches this touches a man.
Ibid. So Long!

The world, the race, the soul — in
space and time the universes,
All bound as is befitting each — all
surely going somewhere.
Ibid. Going Somewhere

I am the Poem of Earth, said the voice
of the rain,
Eternal I rise impalpable out of the
land and the bottomless sea.
Ibid. The Voice of the Rain

Soon to be lost for aye in the darkness
— loth, O so loth to depart!
Garrulous to the very last.
Ibid. After the Supper and Talk

None of the artists or pictures has
caught the deep, though subtle and indirect expression of this man's face.
There is something else there. One of
the great portrait painters of two or
three centuries ago is needed.
*Specimen Days. Of Lincoln,
August 12, 1863*

I never see that man [Lincoln] without feeling that he is one to become personally attach'd to, for his combination

of purest, heartiest tenderness, and native western form of manliness.
Specimen Days. The Inauguration,
March 4, 1865

He leaves for America's history and biography, so far, not only its most dramatic reminiscence — he leaves, in my opinion, the greatest, best, most characteristic, artistic, moral personality.
Ibid. Death of President
Lincoln, April 16, 1865

The real war will never get in the books.
Ibid. The Real War, etc.

Tone your wants and tastes down low enough, and make much of negatives, and of mere daylight and the skies.
Ibid. An Interregnum Paragraph

After you have exhausted what there is in business, politics, conviviality, and so on — have found that none of these finally satisfy, or permanently wear — what remains? Nature remains.
Ibid. New Themes Entered Upon

In the civilization of to-day it is undeniable that, over all the arts, literature dominates, serves beyond all.
Democratic Vistas [1871]

The main social, political spine-character of the States will probably run along the Ohio, Missouri and Mississippi rivers, and west and north of them, including Canada.
Ibid.

Political democracy, as it exists and practically works in America, with all its threatening evils, supplies a training-school for making first-class men. It is life's gymnasium, not of good only, but of all.
Ibid.

It is native personality, and that alone, that endows a man to stand before presidents or generals, or in any distinguish'd collection, with *aplomb* — and *not* culture, or any knowledge or intellect whatever.
Ibid.

To have great poets, there must be great audiences, too.
Notes Left Over. Ventures, on
an Old Theme

Hast Thou, pellucid, in Thy azure depths, medicine for case like mine?
Specimen Days. The Sky,
October 20, 1876

One is never entirely without the instinct of looking around.
Ibid. One of the Human Kinks

You must not know too much, or be too precise or scientific about birds and trees and flowers and water-craft; a certain free margin, and even vagueness — perhaps ignorance, credulity — helps your enjoyment of these things.
Ibid. Birds, May 14, 1881

No really great song can ever attain full purport till long after the death of its singer — till it has accrued and incorporated the many passions, many joys and sorrows, it has itself aroused.
November Boughs [1888].
The Bible as Poetry

No one will ever get at my verses who insists upon viewing them as a literary performance.
Goodbye, My Fancy [1891]. A
Backward Glance O'er Travel'd
Roads

There is no week nor day nor hour, when tyranny may not enter upon this country, if the people lose their roughness and spirit of defiance — Tyranny may always enter — there is no charm, no bar against it — the only bar against it is a large resolute breed of men.
Notes for Lecturers on Democracy and "Adhesiveness." C. J.
FURNESS: *Walt Whitman's*
Workshop [1928]

URANIA LOCKE STOUGHTON BAILEY ("JULIA GILL")
[1820–1882]

I want to be an angel,
　And with the angels stand,
A crown upon my forehead,
　A harp within my hand.
I Want to Be an Angel. Stanza 1

WILLIAM COX BENNETT
[1820–1895]

"God wills but ill," the doubter said,
  "Lo, time doth evil only bear;
Give me a sign His love to prove,
  His vaunted goodness to declare!"
The poet pointed where a flower,
  A simple daisy, starred the sod,
And answered, "Proof of love and power
  Behold, behold a smile of God!"
                   A Thought

Oh! come you from the Indies, and,
  soldier, can you tell
Aught of the gallant Ninetieth, and
  who are safe and well?
O soldier, say my son is safe — for
  nothing else I care,
And you shall have a mother's thanks
  — shall have a widow's prayer.
            From India. Stanza 1

HENRY HOWARD
BROWNELL
[1820–1872]

As vonce I valked by a dismal svamp,
There sot an Old Cove in the dark and
  damp,
And at everybody as passed that road
A stick or a stone this Old Cove
  throwed.
And venever he flung his stick or his
  stone,
He'd set up a song of "Let me alone." [1]
               Let Us Alone

ALICE CARY
[1820–1871]

Work, and your house shall be duly fed:
Work, and rest shall be won;
I hold that a man had better be dead
Than alive when his work is done.
                   Work

Kiss me, though you make believe;
Kiss me, though I almost know
You are kissing to deceive.
             Make Believe

---

[1] All we ask is to be let alone. — JEFFERSON DAVIS: *First Message to the Confederate Congress* [March, 1861]

Three little bugs in a basket,
And hardly room for two.
            Three Bugs

JEAN INGELOW
[1820–1897]

But two are walking apart forever,
And wave their hands for a mute
  farewell.
            Divided. VI, 5

A sweeter woman ne'er drew breath
Than my sonne's wife, Elizabeth.
     High Tide on the Coast of
     Lincolnshire, 1571. Stanza 11

Man dwells apart, though not alone,
  He walks among his peers unread;
The best of thoughts which he hath
  known
  For lack of listeners are not said.
         Afterthought. Stanza 1

It is a comely fashion to be glad, —
Joy is the grace we say to God.
              Dominion

Like coral insects multitudinous
The minutes are whereof our life is
  made.
                  Work

    Blondel, when his lay
Pierced the strong tower, and Richard
  answered it.[1]
               Wishing

I marked my love by candle-light
Sewing her long white seam.
     The Long White Seam. Stanza 1

A land where all the men are stones,
Or all the stones are men.
         A Land That Living
            Warmth Disowns

THEODORE O'HARA
[1820–1867]

On Fame's eternal camping-ground
  Their silent tents are spread,

---

[1] There is a tradition that Blondel, a French troubadour, attendant and friend of Richard Coeur de Lion, discovered Richard, imprisoned in the castle of Dürrenstein, by singing beneath the tower window a song which they had composed and to which the king responded.

And Glory guards, with solemn round,
　The bivouac of the dead.
　　　　　The Bivouac of the Dead.[1]
　　　　　　　　　Stanza 1
Sons of the Dark and Bloody ground,[2]
　Ye must not slumber there,
Where stranger steps and tongues re-
　sound
　Along the heedless air.
　　　　　　Ibid. Stanza 9

GEORGE FREDERICK ROOT
[1820–1895]

Tramp! Tramp! Tramp! the boys are
　marching,
Cheer up, comrades, they will come,
And beneath the starry flag
We shall breathe the air again
Of the free land in our own beloved
　home.
　　　　Tramp! Tramp! Tramp! [1862]
Yes, we'll rally round the flag, boys,
　we'll rally once again,
Shouting the battle-cry of Freedom,
We will rally from the hill-side, we'll
　gather from the plain,
Shouting the battle-cry of Freedom.
　　The Battle-Cry of Freedom [1863]

SIR WILLIAM HOWARD
RUSSELL
[1820–1907]

The Russians dashed on towards
that thin red-line streak tipped with a
line of steel.[3]
　　　*Correspondence to the London
　　　Times from the Crimea, describ-
　　　ing the British infantry at
　　　Balaklava* [October 25, 1854]

[1] Written in August, 1847, to commemorate
the Americans slain in the battle of Buena
Vista, February 22–23, 1847.
[2] Translation of the Indian name Kentucky.
[3] Soon the men of the column began to
see that though the scarlet line was slender,
it was very rigid and exact. — A. W. KING-
LAKE [1809–1891]: *Invasion of the Crimea,
Vol. III, P. 455*
It's "Thin red line of 'eroes" when the
drums begin to roll. — KIPLING [1865–1936]:
Tommy, St. 3

WILLIAM TECUMSEH
SHERMAN
[1820–1891]

War is cruel and you cannot refine it.
　　　　*Reply to the protest of the
　　　　Atlanta, Georgia, city govern-
　　　　ment on invasion* [1864]
Hold the fort! I am coming!
　　　　*Signaled to General Corse in
　　　　Allatoona from the top of Ken-
　　　　esaw* [October 5, 1864]
I am tired and sick of war. Its glory
is all moonshine. It is only those who
have neither fired a shot nor heard the
shrieks and groans of the wounded who
cry aloud for blood, more vengeance,
more desolation. War is hell.
　　　　*Attributed to an address before
　　　　the graduating class, Michigan
　　　　Military Academy* [June 19,
　　　　1879], *in a letter published in
　　　　The National Tribune, Wash-
　　　　ington, D. C., November 26,
　　　　1914*

JOHN TYNDALL
[1820–1893]

Heat Considered as a Mode of Motion.
　　　　Title of Treatise [1863]
It is not my habit of mind to think
otherwise than solemnly of the feeling
which prompts prayer. It is a power
which I should like to see guided, not
extinguished — devoted to practicable
objects instead of wasted upon air.
　　　　*Fragments of Science. Vol. II,
　　　　Prayer as a Form of Physical
　　　　Energy*
Life is a wave, which in no two consecutive moments of its existence is
composed of the same particles.
　　　　　　Ibid. Vitality
We are truly heirs of all the ages;
but as honest men it behooves us to
learn the extent of our inheritance, and
as brave ones not to whimper if it should
prove less than we had supposed.
　　　　　Ibid. Matter and Force
The mind of man may be compared
to a musical instrument with a certain

range of notes, beyond which in both directions we have an infinitude of silence.

> *Fragments of Science. Vol. II,*
> *Matter and Force*

The brightest flashes in the world of thought are incomplete until they have been proved to have their counterparts in the world of fact.

> *Ibid. Scientific Materialism*

Believing, as I do, in the continuity of nature, I cannot stop abruptly where our microscopes cease to be of use. Here the vision of the mind authoritatively supplements the vision of the eye. By a necessity engendered and justified by science I cross the boundary of the experimental evidence, and discern in that Matter which we, in our ignorance of its latent powers, and notwithstanding our professed reverence for its Creator, have hitherto covered with opprobrium, the promise and potency of all terrestrial Life.

> *Ibid. Address at Belfast*
> *[August 19, 1874]*

It is as fatal as it is cowardly to blink facts because they are not to our taste.

> *Ibid. Science and Man*

Charles Darwin, the Abraham of scientific men — a searcher as obedient to the command of truth as was the patriarch to the command of God.

> *Ibid.*

Superstition may be defined as constructive religion which has grown incongruous with intelligence.

> *Ibid.*

Religious feeling is as much a verity as any other part of human consciousness; and against it, on the subjective side, the waves of science beat in vain.

> *Ibid. Professor Virchow and*
> *Evolution*

HERBERT SPENCER
[1820–1903]

Progress, therefore, is not an accident, but a necessity. . . . It is a part of nature.

> *Social Statics* [*1851*]. *Part I,*
> *Chap. 2*

Education has for its object the formation of character.

> *Social Statics. Part II, Chap. 17*

Opinion is ultimately determined by the feelings, and not by the intellect.

> *Ibid. Part IV, Chap. 30*

Morality knows nothing of geographical boundaries or distinctions of race.

> *Ibid.*

No one can be perfectly free till all are free; no one can be perfectly moral till all are moral; no one can be perfectly happy till all are happy.

> *Ibid.*

Architecture, sculpture, painting, music, and poetry, may truly be called the efflorescence of civilized life.

> *Essays on Education* [*1861*].
> *Education: What Knowledge Is*
> *of Most Worth?*

Every cause produces more than one effect.

> *Ibid. On Progress: Its Law*
> *and Cause*

The tyranny of Mrs. Grundy [1] is worse than any other tyranny we suffer under.

> *Ibid. On Manners and Fashion*

Old forms of government finally grow so oppressive that they must be thrown off even at the risk of reigns of terror.

> *Ibid.*

Music must take rank as the highest of the fine arts — as the one which, more than any other, ministers to human welfare.

> *Ibid. On the Origin and Function*
> *of Music*

We too often forget that not only is there "a soul of goodness in things evil," [2] but very generally a soul of truth in things erroneous.

> *First Principles* [*1861*]

The fact disclosed by a survey of the past that majorities have been wrong must not blind us to the complemen-

---

[1] See Thomas Morton, page 397a.
[2] There is some soul of goodness in things evil
Would men observingly distill it out.
     SHAKESPEARE: *King Henry V* [*1598–1600*], *Act IV, Sc. 1, L. 4*

tary fact that majorities have usually not been entirely wrong.
First Principles

Volumes might be written upon the impiety of the pious.
Ibid.

We have unmistakable proof that throughout all past time, there has been a ceaseless devouring of the weak by the strong.
Ibid.

This survival of the fittest.
Principles of Biology [1864–1867].
Part III, Chap. 12

The Republican form of government is the highest form of government: but because of this it requires the highest type of human nature — a type nowhere at present existing.
Essays [1891]. The Americans

The ultimate result of shielding men from the effects of folly is to fill the world with fools.
Ibid. State Tamperings with Money Banks

GUSTAVE NADAUD
[1820–1893]

I'm growing old, I've sixty years;
I've labored all my life in vain.
In all that time of hopes and fears,
I've failed my dearest wish to gain.
I see full well that here below
Bliss unalloyed there is for none,
My prayer would else fulfillment
know —
Never have I seen Carcassonne! [1]
Carcassonne.[2] Stanza 1

They tell me every day is there
Not more nor less than Sunday gay;
In shining robes and garments fair
The people walk upon their way.
Ibid. Stanza 3

[1] I can scarce believe the tale
Borne to me on every gale!
You have been to Carcassonne?
Looked its stately towers upon?
JULIA CAROLINE RIPLEY DORR [1825–1913]: *To One Who Went to Carcassonne, St. 1*
[2] Translated by JOHN R. THOMPSON [1823–1873].

SIR RICHARD FRANCIS BURTON
[1821–1890]

Why meet we on the bridge of Time to
'change one greeting and to part?
The Kasidah of Haji Abdu El-Yazdi. I, 11

Why must we meet, why must we part,
why must we bear this yoke of
MUST,
Without our leave or asked or given,
by tyrant Fate on victim thrust?
Ibid. 13

Hardly we learn to wield the blade before the wrist grows stiff and old;
Hardly we learn to ply the pen ere
Thought and Fancy faint with
cold.
Ibid. III, 32

Life, atom of that Infinite Space
that stretcheth, 'twixt the Here
and There.
Ibid. 36

Indeed he knows not how to know who
knows not also how to un-know.
Ibid. VI, 18

Mankind a future life must have to
balance life's unequal lot.
Ibid. VIII, 9

Do what thy manhood bids thee do,
from none but self expect applause;
He noblest lives and noblest dies who
makes and keeps his self-made
laws.
Ibid. 37

JOSEPH WARREN FABENS
[1821–1875]

I've seen the land of all I love
Fade in the distance dim;
I've watched above the blighted heart,
Where once proud hope had been;
But I've never known a sorrow
That could with that compare,
When off the blue Canaries
I smoked my last cigar.
My Last Cigar. Stanza 4

FREDERICK LOCKER–LAMPSON
[1821–1895]

"Vanitas vanitatum" has rung in the ears
Of gentle and simple for thousands of years;
The wail still is heard, yet its notes never scare
Either simple or gentle from Vanity Fair.
Vanity Fair

What an arm — what a waist
For an arm!
To My Grandmother

The world's as ugly, ay, as Sin, —
And almost as delightful.
The Jester's Plea

And many are afraid of God —
And more of Mrs. Grundy.[1]
Ibid.

WILLIAM H. VANDERBILT
[1821–1885]

The public be damned.[2]
Reply to a newspaper reporter
[circa 1883]

GEORGE JOHN WHYTE–MELVILLE
[1821–1878]

When you sleep in your cloak there's no lodging to pay.
Boots and Saddles

For everything created
In the bounds of earth and sky
Has such longing to be mated,
It must couple or must die.
Like to Like

In the choice of a horse and a wife, a man must please himself, ignoring the opinion and advice of friends.
Riding Recollections [1878]

Education should be as gradual as the moonrise, perceptible not in progress but in result.
Ibid.

[1] See Thomas Morton, page 397a.
[2] There are various versions of the occasion of this remark. See letters in *New York Times,* August 25, 1918, and *New York Herald,* October 1, 1918.

Pluck takes us into a difficulty; nerve brings us out of it. Both are comprised in the noble quality we call valor.
Riding Recollections

MARY BAKER EDDY
[1821–1910]

The prayer that reforms the sinner and heals the sick is an absolute faith that all things are possible to God, — a spiritual understanding of Him, an unselfed love.
Science and Health with Key to the Scriptures [1875]. Page 1

In the year 1866, I discovered the Christ Science or divine laws of Life, Truth, and Love, and named my discovery Christian Science.[1]
Ibid. Page 107

Jesus of Nazareth was the most scientific man that ever trod the globe. He plunged beneath the material surface of things, and found the spiritual cause.
Ibid. Page 313

The basis of all health, sinlessness, and immortality is the great fact that God is the only Mind; and this Mind must be not merely believed, but it must be understood.
Ibid. Page 339

Spirit is the real and eternal; matter is the unreal and temporal.
Ibid. Page 468

Sickness, sin and death, being inharmonious, do not originate with God, nor belong to His government.
Ibid. Page 472

Being is holiness, harmony, immortality. It is already proved that a knowledge of this, even in small degree, will uplift the physical and moral standard of mortals, will increase longevity, will purify and elevate character. Thus

[1] The words "Christian Science" were not original with Mary Baker Eddy, but she was the first to give them wide circulation. In 1840, Abraham Coles used the words in verse, as also did Sara Josepha Hale, in 1848. In 1850, William Adams published a series of addresses on Moral Philosophy and called his work *Christian Science.* — NORMAN BEASLEY: *The Cross and the Crown* [1952], *P. 13n*

progress will finally destroy all error, and bring immortality to light.

Science and Health with Key to the Scriptures. Page 492

Divine Love always has met and always will meet every human need.

Ibid. Page 494

How would you define Christian Science?

As the law of God, the law of good, interpreting and demonstrating the divine Principle and rule of universal harmony.

Rudimental Divine Science [1891].
Page 1

To live and let live, without clamor for distinction or recognition; to wait on divine Love; to write truth first on the tablet of one's own heart, — this is the sanity and perfection of living, and my human ideal.

Message to the Mother Church for 1902. Page 2

To live so as to keep human consciousness in constant relation with the divine, the spiritual, and the eternal, is to individualize infinite power; and this is Christian Science.

The First Church of Christ, Scientist, and Miscellany [1906]. Page 160

It matters not what be thy lot,
So Love doth guide;
For storm or shine, pure peace is thine,
Whate'er betide.

Satisfied. Stanza 1

Blest Christmas morn, though murky clouds
Pursue thy way,
Thy light was born where storm enshrouds
Nor dawn nor day!

Christmas Morn. Stanza 1

O'er waiting harp-strings of the mind
There sweeps a strain,
Low, sad, and sweet, whose measures bind
The pow'r of pain.

O'er Waiting Harp-strings of the Mind. Stanza 1

My prayer, some daily good to do
To Thine, for Thee —

An off'ring pure of Love, whereto
God leadeth me.

O'er Waiting Harp-strings of the Mind. Stanza 7

HENRI-FRÉDÉRIC AMIEL
[1821–1881]

Truth is the secret of eloquence and of virtue, the basis of moral authority; it is the highest summit of art and of life.

Journal [1883]

Doing easily what others find difficult is talent; doing what is impossible for talent is genius.

Ibid.

A man without passion is only a latent force, only a possibility, like a stone waiting for the blow from the iron to give forth sparks.

Ibid.

If ignorance and passion are the foes of popular morality, it must be confessed that moral indifference is the malady of the cultivated classes.

Ibid.

Pure truth cannot be assimilated by the crowd; it must be communicated by contagion.

Ibid.

FYODOR DOSTOYEVSKY
[1821–1881]

Man is a pliable animal, a being who gets accustomed to everything!

The House of the Dead (Prison Life in Siberia) [1] [1861–1862]. Part I, Chap. 2

With ready-made opinions one cannot judge of crime. Its philosophy is a little more complicated than people think. It is acknowledged that neither convict prisons, nor the hulks, nor any system of hard labour ever cured a criminal.

Ibid.

Humane treatment may raise up one in whom the divine image has long been

[1] Everyman edition.

obscured. It is with the unfortunate, above all, that humane conduct is necessary.

> *The House of the Dead (Prison Life in Siberia). Part I, Chap. 9*

Tyranny is a habit capable of being developed, and at last becomes a disease. . . . The man and the citizen disappear for ever in the tyrant.

> *Ibid. Part II, Chap. 3*

Even those who have renounced Christianity and attack it, in their inmost being still follow the Christian ideal, for hitherto neither their subtlety nor the ardour of their hearts has been able to create a higher ideal of man and of virtue than the ideal given by Christ of old. When it has been attempted, the result has been only grotesque.

> *The Brothers Karamazov* [1] *[1880]. Part II, Book IV, Chap. 1*

Until you have become really, in actual fact, a brother to every one, brotherhood will not come to pass. No sort of scientific teaching, no kind of common interest, will ever teach men to share property and privileges with equal consideration for all. Every one will think his share too small and they will be always envying, complaining and attacking one another.

> *Ibid. Book VI, Chap. 2*

The true security is to be found in social solidarity rather than in isolated individual effort.

> *Ibid.*

Be not forgetful of prayer. Every time you pray, if your prayer is sincere, there will be new feeling and new meaning in it, which will give you fresh courage, and you will understand that prayer is an education.

> *Ibid. Chap. 3*

Love all God's creation, the whole and every grain of sand in it. Love every leaf, every ray of God's light. Love the animals, love the plants, love

everything. If you love everything, you will perceive the divine mystery in things. Once you perceive it, you will begin to comprehend it better every day. And you will come at last to love the whole world with an all-embracing love.

> *The Brothers Karamazov. Part II, Book VI, Chap. 3*

Men reject their prophets and slay them, but they love their martyrs and honour those whom they have slain.

> *Ibid.*

CHARLES BAUDELAIRE
[1821–1867]

The poet is like the prince of the clouds who haunts the tempest and laughs at the man with the bow; exiled on the ground amid the hue and cry, his giant's wings prevent him from walking.[1]

> *Fleurs du Mal* [1861]. *L'Albatros, Stanza 4*

Mother of memories, mistress of mistresses.[2]

> *Ibid. Le Balcon, Stanza 1*

My child, my sister, think of the sweetness of going away there to live together![3]

> *Ibid. L'Invitation au Voyage, Stanza 1*

There, all is order and beauty, luxury, calm, and voluptuousness.[4]

> *Ibid. Refrain*

I have more memories than if I were a thousand years old.[5]

> *Ibid. Spleen, Line 1*

---

[1] Le Poète est semblable au prince des nuées
Qui hante la tempête et se rit de l'archer;
Exilé sur le sol au milieu des huées,
Ses ailes de géant l'empêchent de marcher.
[2] Mère des souvenirs, maîtresse des maîtresses.
[3]   Mon enfant, ma soeur,
        Songe à la douceur
D'aller là-bas vivre ensemble!
[4] Là, tout n'est qu'ordre et beauté,
Luxe, calme et volupté.
[5] J'ai plus de souvenirs que si j'avais mille ans.

---

[1] Translated by CONSTANCE GARNETT. Modern Library edition.

To the best, to the most beautiful who is my joy and my well-being.[1]
> *Les Epaves* [*1866*]. *Hymne,*
> *Stanza 5*

What do I care that you are good? Be beautiful! and be sad! [2]
> *Nouvelles Fleurs du Mal* [*1866–*
> *1868*]. *Madrigal Triste, Stanza 1*

There can be no progress (real, that is, moral) except in the individual and by the individual himself.
> *Mon Coeur Mis à Nu* [*1887*]. *XV*

There are in every man, at every hour, two simultaneous postulations, one towards God, the other towards Satan.
> *Ibid. XIX*

There exist only three beings worthy of respect: the priest, the soldier, the poet. To know, to kill, to create.
> *Ibid. XXII*

To be a great man and a saint for oneself, that is the one important thing.
> *Ibid. LII*

MATTHEW ARNOLD
[1822–1888]

One lesson, Nature, let me learn of thee.
> *Sonnet 1, Quiet Work* [*1849*]

Be his
My special thanks, whose even-balanced soul,
From first youth tested up to extreme old age,
Business could not make dull, nor passion wild:
Who saw life steadily and saw it whole.[3]
> *Sonnet 2, To a Friend* [*1849*]

Others abide our question. Thou art free.
We ask and ask: Thou smilest and art still,
Out-topping knowledge.
> *Sonnet 3, Shakespeare* [*1849*]

The will is free:
Strong is the Soul, and wise, and beautiful:

[1] A la très-bonne, à la très-belle
Qui fait ma joie et ma santé.
[2] Que m'importe que tu sois sage?
Sois belle ! et sois triste !
[3] Sophocles.

The seeds of godlike power are in us still:
Gods are we, Bards, Saints, Heroes, if we will.
> *Sonnet 4, Written in Emerson's*
> *Essays* [*1849*]

France, famed in all great arts, in none supreme.
> *Sonnet 10, To a Republican*
> *Friend, 1848* [*1849*]

To its own impulse every creature stirs:
Live by thy light, and Earth will live by hers.
> *Sonnet 11, Religious Isolation*
> [*1849*]

Come, dear children, let us away;
Down and away below.
Now my brothers call from the bay;
Now the great winds shorewards blow;
Now the salt tides seawards flow;
Now the wild white horses play,
Champ and chafe and toss in the spray.
> *The Forsaken Merman*
> [*1849*]. *Stanza 1*

One last look at the white-wall'd town,
And the little grey church on the windy shore.
> *Ibid. Stanza 3*

Sand-strewn caverns, cool and deep,
Where the winds are all asleep;
Where the spent lights quiver and gleam;
Where the salt weed sways in the stream;
Where the sea-beasts rang'd all round
Feed in the ooze of their pasture-ground.
> *Ibid. Stanza 4*

Children dear, were we long alone?
The sea grows stormy, the little ones moan.
> *Ibid. Stanza 6*

She will start from her slumber
When gusts shake the door;
She will hear the winds howling,
Will hear the waves roar.
> *Ibid. Stanza 8*

Here came a mortal,
But faithless was she.
And alone dwell for ever
The kings of the sea.
> *Ibid.*

From grief that is but passion;
From mirth that is but feigning;
From tears that bring no healing;
From wild and weak complaining;
　Thine old strength revealing;
　Save, oh, save.
Stagirius [*1849*]
Fate gave, what Chance shall not control,
His sad lucidity of soul.
Resignation [*1849*]
Yet they, believe me, who await
No gifts from Chance, have conquered Fate.
Ibid.
Resolve to be thyself: and know, that he
Who finds himself, loses his misery.
Self-Dependence [*1852*].
Stanza 8
We cannot kindle when we will
The fire that in the heart resides.
Morality [*1852*]. *Stanza 1*
But tasks in hours of insight will'd
Can be through hours of gloom fulfill'd.
Ibid.
With aching hands and bleeding feet
　We dig and heap, lay stone on stone;
We bear the burden and the heat
　Of the long day, and wish 'twere done.
Not till the hours of light return
All we have built do we discern.
Ibid. Stanza 2
Calm Soul of all things! make it mine
　To feel, amid the city's jar,
That there abides a peace of thine,
　Man did not make, and can not mar.
Lines Written in Kensington Gardens [*1852*]. *Stanza 10*
Physician of the Iron Age,
Goethe has done his pilgrimage.
He took the suffering human race,
He read each wound, each weakness clear —
And struck his finger on the place
And said — Thou ailest here, and here.
Memorial Verses [*1852*].
Stanza 3
Time may restore us in his course
Goethe's sage mind and Byron's force;

But where will Europe's latter hour
Again　find　Wordsworth's　healing power?
Memorial Verses. Stanza 5
Children of men! not that your age excel
In pride of life the ages of your sires;
But that ye think clear, feel deep, bear fruit well,
The Friend of man desires.
Progress [*1852*]
Still bent to make some port he knows not where,
Still standing for some false impossible shore.
A Summer Night [*1852*]
Be neither saint nor sophist-led, but be a man.
Empedocles on Etna [*1852*].
Act I, Sc. 2, Line 136
We do not what we ought;
　What we ought not, we do;
And lean upon the thought
　That Chance will bring us through.
Ibid. Line 237
Nature, with equal mind,
Sees all her sons at play,
Sees man control the wind,
The wind sweep man away.
Ibid. Line 257
Is it so small a thing
To have enjoyed the sun,
To have lived light in the spring,
To have loved, to have thought, to have done;
To have advanced true friends, and beat down baffling foes?
Ibid. Act II, Line 397
The day in its hotness,
The strife with the palm;
The night in its silence,
The stars in their calm.
Ibid. Line 465
The same heart beats in every human breast.
The Buried Life [*1852*]. *Stanza 2*
But often in the world's most crowded streets,
But often, in the din of strife,
There rises an unspeakable desire
After the knowledge of our buried life.
Ibid. Stanza 6

A man becomes aware of his life's flow.
The Buried Life. Stanza 7

And then he thinks he knows
The Hills where his life rose,
And the Sea where it goes.
Ibid. Stanza 8

Go, for they call you, Shepherd, from
the hill.
The Scholar Gypsy [1853].
Stanza 1

Crossing the stripling Thames at Bab-
lock-hithe,
Trailing in the cool stream thy fingers
wet,
As the slow punt swings round.
Ibid. Stanza 8

Thou waitest for the spark from
heaven! and we,
Light half-believers in our casual
creeds . . .
Who hesitate and falter life away,
And lose tomorrow the ground won
today.
Ibid. Stanza 18

This strange disease of modern life.
Ibid. Stanza 21

Still nursing the unconquerable hope,
Still clutching the inviolable shade.
Ibid. Stanza 22

Strew on her roses, roses,
And never a spray of yew!
In quiet she reposes;
Ah, would that I did too!
Requiescat [1853]. Stanza 1

Her cabin'd, ample spirit,
It flutter'd and fail'd for breath.
Tonight it doth inherit
The vasty hall of death.
Ibid. Stanza 4

Hark! ah, the nightingale —
The tawny-throated!
Hark, from that moonlit cedar what a
burst!
What triumph! hark! — what pain!
Philomela [1853]. Stanza 1

Eternal passion!
Eternal pain!
Ibid. Stanza 3

What shelter to grow ripe is ours?
What leisure to grow wise?
Stanzas in Memory of the
Author of "Obermann" [1] *[1853].*
Stanza 18

We, in some unknown Power's employ,
Move on a rigorous line;
Can neither, when we will, enjoy;
Nor, when we will, resign.
Ibid. Stanza 34

Truth sits upon the lips of dying men.
Sohrab and Rustum [1853].
Line 656

Wandering between two worlds, one
dead,
The other powerless to be born.
Stanzas from the Grande Char-
treuse [1855]. Stanza 15

Peace, peace is what I seek, and public
calm;
Endless extinction of unhappy hates.
Merope [1858]

With women the heart argues, not the
mind.
Ibid.

Whispering from her towers the last
enchantments of the Middle Age [Ox-
ford]. . . . Home of lost causes, and
forsaken beliefs, and unpopular names,
and impossible loyalties!
Essays in Criticism, First Series
[1865]. Preface

I am bound by my own definition of
criticism: a disinterested endeavor to
learn and propagate the best that is
known and thought in the world.
Ibid. Function of Criticism at
the Present Time

Poetry is simply the most beautiful,
impressive and widely effective mode
of saying things, and hence its importance.
Ibid. Heinrich Heine

Philistine must have originally
meant, in the mind of those who invented the nickname, a strong, dogged,
unenlightened opponent of the children
of the light.
Ibid.

---

[1] Étienne Pivert de Sénancour [1770–1846],
French author. His most notable work, *Ober-*
mann, was published in 1804.

On the breast of that huge Mississippi of falsehood called history, a
foam-bell more or less is of no consequence.[1]

Essays in Criticism, First Series.
Literary Influence of Academies

The great apostle of the Philistines,
Lord Macaulay.

Ibid. Joubert

The sea is calm tonight,
The tide is full, the moon lies fair
Upon the Straits.

Dover Beach [1867]. Stanza 1

Begin, and cease, and then again begin,
With tremulous cadence slow, and bring
The eternal note of sadness in.

Ibid.

The sea of faith
Was once, too, at the full, and round
earth's shore
Lay like the folds of a bright girdle
furl'd;
But now I only hear
Its melancholy, long, withdrawing roar,
Retreating to the breath
Of the night-wind down the vast edges
drear
And naked shingles of the world.

Ibid. Stanza 3

Ah, love, let us be true
To one another! for the world, which
seems
To lie before us like a land of dreams,
So various, so beautiful, so new,
Hath really neither joy, nor love, nor
light,
Nor certitude, nor peace, nor help for
pain;
And we are here as on a darkling plain

[1] History never embraces more than a small
part of reality. — LA ROCHEFOUCAULD [1613-
1680]: *Paul Sabatier*
     How oft we sigh
When histories charm to think that histories
     lie!
                     THOMAS MOORE [1780-1852]:
                                  The Skeptic
History is nothing more than the belief
in the senses, the belief in falsehood. —
NIETZSCHE [1844-1900]: *The Twilight of the
Idols, "Reason" in Philosophy, I*
History is bunk. — HENRY FORD [1863-
1947]

Swept with confused alarms of struggle
and flight,
Where ignorant armies clash by night.

Dover Beach. Stanza 4

It is — last stage of all —
When we are frozen up within, and
quite
The phantom of ourselves,
To hear the world applaud the hollow
ghost
Which blamed the living man.

Growing Old [1867]. Stanza 7

Hear it, O Thyrsis, still our Tree is
there!
Ah, vain! These English fields, this up-
land dim,
These brambles pale with mist engar-
landed,
That lone, sky-pointing tree, are not
for him.
To a boon southern country he is fled,
And now in happier air,
Wandering with the great Mother's
train divine . . .
Within a folding of the Apennine.

Thyrsis [1867]. Stanza 18

Creep into thy narrow bed,
Creep, and let no more be said!
Vain thy onset! all stands fast;
Thou thyself must break at last.

The Last Word [1867]. Stanza 1

Let the long contention cease!
Geese are swans, and swans are geese.[1]

Ibid. Stanza 2

Charge once more, then, and be dumb!
Let the victors, when they come,
When the forts of folly fall,
Find thy body by the wall.

Ibid. Stanza 4

Was Christ a man like us? — Ah! let
us try
If we then, too, can be such men as he!

The Better Part [1867]

Spare me the whispering, crowded
room,
The friends who come and gape and go,
The ceremonious air of gloom —
All, which makes death a hideous show.

A Wish [1867]. Stanza 4

[1] See Burton, page 222b.

Cruel, but composed and bland,
Dumb, inscrutable and grand,
So Tiberius might have sat,
Had Tiberius been a cat.
Poor Matthias [*1867*]
Coldly, sadly descends
The autumn evening. The Field
Strewn with its dank yellow drifts
Of withered leaves, and the elms,
Fade into dimness apace.
Rugby Chapel [*1867*]. *Stanza 1*
Most men eddy about
Here and there — eat and drink,
Chatter and love and hate,
Gather and squander, are raised
Aloft, are hurl'd in the dust,
Striving blindly, achieving
Nothing; and then they die.
Ibid. Stanza 6
Friends who set forth at our side
Falter, are lost in the storm!
We, we only, are left!
Ibid. Stanza 8
Then, in such hour of need
Of your fainting, dispirited race,
Ye, like angels, appear,
Beacons of Hope ye appear!
Languor is not in your heart,
Weakness is not in your word,
Weariness not on your brow.
Ibid. Stanza 13
Our society distributes itself into
Barbarians, Philistines, and Populace;
and America is just ourselves, with the
Barbarians quite left out, and the
Populace nearly.
Culture and Anarchy [*1869*].
Preface
The pursuit of perfection, then, is the
pursuit of sweetness and light.[1] . . .
He who works for sweetness and light
united, works to make reason and the
will of God prevail.
Ibid.
One has often wondered whether
upon the whole earth there is anything
so unintelligent, so unapt to perceive
how the world is really going, as an
ordinary young Englishman of our
upper class.
Ibid.

[1] See Swift, page 294b.

Below the surface stream, shallow and
light,
Of what we say and feel — below the
stream,
As light, of what we think we feel, there
flows
With noiseless current, strong, obscure
and deep,
The central stream of what we feel in-
deed.
St. Paul and Protestantism [1]
[*1870*]
Culture, the acquainting ourselves
with the best that has been known and
said in the world.
Literature and Dogma [*1873*].
Preface
Conduct is three-fourths of our life
and its largest concern.
Ibid. Chap. 1
A beautiful and ineffectual angel,
beating in the void his luminous wings
in vain.
*Essays in Criticism, Second
Series* [*1888*]. *Shelley*

ULYSSES S. GRANT
[1822–1885]

No terms except an unconditional
and immediate surrender can be ac-
cepted. I propose to move immediately
upon your works.
*To General S. B. Buckner, Fort
Donelson* [*February 16, 1862*]
I propose to fight it out on this line,
if it takes all summer.
*Dispatch to Washington, Be-
fore Spottsylvania Court House*
[*May 11, 1864*]
Let us have peace.
*Accepting a Nomination for the
Presidency* [*May 29, 1868*]
I know no method to secure the re-
peal of bad or obnoxious laws so effec-
tive as their stringent execution.
Inaugural Address
[*March 4, 1869*]
Let no guilty man escape, if it can
be avoided. No personal considerations

[1] For an acknowledgment of Arnold's authorship of this interpolated verse, see his
Letters, Vol. II, P. 32, February 21, 1870.

should stand in the way of performing a public duty.

> *Indorsement of a Letter relating to the Whiskey Ring [July 29, 1875]*

Leave the matter of religion to the family altar, the church, and the private school, supported entirely by private contributions. Keep the church and the State for ever separate.

> *Speech at Des Moines, Iowa [1875]*

Labor disgraces no man; unfortunately you occasionally find men disgrace labor.

> *Speech at Midland International Arbitration Union, Birmingham, England [1877]*

They [the Pilgrim Fathers] fell upon an ungenial climate, where there were nine months of winter and three months of cold weather and that called out the best energies of the men, and of the women too, to get a mere subsistence out of the soil, with such a climate. In their efforts to do that they cultivated industry and frugality at the same time — which is the real foundation of the greatness of the Pilgrims.

> *Speech at New England Society Dinner [December 22, 1880]*

EDWARD EVERETT HALE
[1822–1909]

I am only one,
But still I am one.
I cannot do everything,
But still I can do something;
And because I cannot do everything
I will not refuse to do the something
  that I can do.

> *For the Lend-a-Hand Society*

Its pink and white are everywhere,
A ray of sun — and all the slope
Laughs with its white and red.
"It is the Mayflower of our hope;
The spring is come."

> *The Finding of the First Mayflower. Stanza 3*

Behind all these men you have to do with, behind officers, and government, and people even, there is the Country Herself, your Country, and . . . you belong to Her as you belong to your own mother. Stand by Her, boy, as you would stand by your mother.

> *The Man Without a Country [1865]*

He loved his country as no other man has loved her, but no man deserved less at her hands.

> *Ibid. Epitaph of Philip Nolan*

I taught him four speeches. . . .
1. "Very well, thank you. And you?" This for an answer to casual salutations.
2. "I am very glad you liked it."
3. "There has been so much said, and, on the whole, so well said, that I will not occupy the time."
4. "I agree, in general, with my friend the other side of the room."

> *My Double and How He Undid Me [1868]*

It is not necessary to finish your sentences in a crowd, but by a sort of mumble, omitting sibilants and dentals. This, indeed, if your words fail you, answers even in public extempore speech, but better where other talking is going on.

> *Ibid.*

To look up and not down,
To look forward and not back,
To look out and not in, and
To lend a hand.[1]

> *Ten Times One Is Ten [1870]*

Let the scroll
Fill as it may as years unroll;
But when again she calls her youth
To serve her in the ranks of Truth,
May she find all one heart, one soul —
At home or on some distant shore —
"All present, or accounted for!"

> *Alma Mater's Roll [For a Harvard dinner, 1875]*

[1] Rule of the Harry Wadsworth Club.

THOMAS HUGHES
[1822–1896]

Life isn't all beer and skittles; [1] but beer and skittles, or something better of the same sort, must form a good part of every Englishman's education.
Tom Brown's School days
[1857]. Part I, Chap. 2

He never wants anything but what's right and fair; only when you come to settle what's right and fair, it's everything that he wants and nothing that you want. And that's his idea of a compromise. Give me the Brown compromise when I'm on his side.
Ibid. Part II, Chap. 2

GEORGE LIPPARD
[1822–1854]

There was tumult in the city,
  In the quaint old Quaker town,
And the streets were rife with people
  Pacing restless up and down.
Independence Bell. Stanza 1

When a nation's life's at hazard,
We've no time to think of men!
Ibid. Stanza 3

"IK. MARVEL" (DONALD GRANT MITCHELL)
[1822–1908]

Ashes follow blaze inevitably as death follows life. Misery treads on the heels of joy; anguish rides swift after pleasure.
Reveries of a Bachelor [1850].
First Reverie, Part III

Blessed be letters — they are the monitors, they are also the comforters, and they are the only true heart-talkers.
Ibid. Second Reverie

JOHN TYLER PETTEE
[1822–1907]

Pray for peace and grace and spiritual food,

For wisdom and guidance, for all these are good,
But don't forget the potatoes.
Prayer and Potatoes

EDWARD JOHN PHELPS
[1822–1900]

Waiting for that delusive train
That, always coming, never comes,
Till weary and worn, cold and forlorn,
And paralyzed in every function,
  I hope in hell
  Their souls may dwell
Who first invented Essex Junction.
Essex Junction. Stanza 1

THOMAS BUCHANAN READ
[1822–1872]

The old, old sea, as one in tears,
Comes murmuring with its foamy lips,
And knocking at the vacant piers,
Calls for its long-lost multitude of ships.
Come, Gentle Trembler. Stanza 5

I stood by the open casement
  And looked upon the night,
And saw the westward-going stars
  Pass slowly out of sight.
The Celestial Army. Stanza 1

Boone, the pioneer,
Whose statue, in the eternal niche of fame,
Leans on his gleaming rifle; and whose name
Is carved so deep in the Kentuckian rocks,
It may not be effaced.
The New Pastoral. Book XXVII

The terrible grumble, and rumble, and roar,
Telling the battle was on once more,
And Sheridan twenty miles away.
Sheridan's Ride. Stanza 1

I hate the sin, but I love the sinner.
What a Word May Do. Stanza 1

---

[1] It's a regular holiday to them — all porter **and** skittles. . . . Down-hearted fellers as can't svig away at the beer, nor play at skittles neither. — DICKENS: *Pickwick Papers* [1836–1837], *Chap. 41*

BERNARD ELLIOTT BEE
[1823–1861]

See, there is Jackson, standing like
a stone-wall.
> *Of General T. J. Jackson, at the
> Battle of Bull Run* [1] *[July 21,
> 1861]*

GEORGE HENRY BOKER
[1823–1890]

"Freedom!" their battle-cry, —
"Freedom! or leave to die!"
> *The Black Regiment. Stanza 5*

Lay him low, lay him low,
In the clover or the snow!
What cares he? he cannot know.
> *Dirge for a Soldier.* [2] *Stanza 1*

"Give me but two brigades," said
Hooker, frowning at fortified
Lookout.
> *Battle of Lookout Mountain.* [3]
> *Stanza 1*

All through the long, long polar day,
The vessels westward sped;
And wherever the sail of Sir John was
blown,
The ice gave way and fled.
> *The Ballad of Sir John Franklin.* [4]
> *Stanza 7*

And there, while thread shall hang to
thread,
Oh, let that ensign fly!
The noblest constellation set
Against the Northern sky.
> *The Cumberland.* [5] *Stanza 37*

I am that blessing which men fly from
— Death.
> *Countess Laura. Stanza 13*

Love is that orbit of the restless soul
Whose circle grazes the confines of
space,

Bounding within the limits of its race
Utmost extremes.
> *Sonnet, Love*

WILLIAM BRIGHTY RANDS ("MATTHEW BROWNE")
[1823–1882]

Never do today what you can
Put off till tomorrow. [1]
> *Lilliput Levee*

Great wide, beautiful, wonderful world,
With the wonderful waters round you
curled,
And the wonderful grass upon your
breast,
World, you are beautifully drest.
> *The Child's World. Stanza 1*

You are more than the earth, though
you are such a dot;
You can love and think, and the earth
cannot!
> *Ibid. Stanza 5*

JULIA A. FLETCHER CARNEY
[1823–1908]

Little drops of water, little grains of
sand,
Make the mighty ocean and the pleasant land.
So the little moments, humble though
they be,
Make the mighty ages of eternity.
> *Little Things [1845]*

Little deeds of kindness, little words of
love,
Help to make earth happy like the
heaven above.
> *Ibid.*

WILLIAM JOHNSON CORY
[1823–1892]

All beauteous things for which we live
By laws of time and space decay.

---

[1] Bee was killed in this battle.
[2] General Philip Kearny, killed near Chan-
tilly, Virginia, September 1, 1862.
[3] Chattanooga, Tennessee, November 24,
1863.
[4] Arctic explorer [1786–1847].
[5] Sunk by the *Merrimac,* off Hampton
Roads, Virginia [March 8, 1862]. Commanded
by Lieutenant George U. Morris, she went
down with all on board and colors flying.
Most of the crew were lost.

[1] No idleness, no laziness, no procrastination; never put off till tomorrow what you
can do today. — LORD CHESTERFIELD: *Letters,*
December 26, 1749

But oh, the very reason why
I clasp them, is because they die.
>> *Mimnermus in Church. Stanza 4*

Somewhere beneath the sun,
These quivering heart-strings prove it,
Somewhere there must be one
Made for this soul, to move it.
>> *Amaturus*

For waste of scheme and toil we grieve,
For snowflakes on the wave we sigh,
For writings on the sand that leave
Naught for tomorrow's passer-by.
>> *On Livermead Sands. Stanza 1*

They told me, Heraclitus, they told me
     you were dead;
They brought me bitter news to hear
     and bitter tears to shed.
I wept, as I remembered, how often you
     and I
Had tired the sun with talking and sent
     him down the sky.
And now that thou art lying, my dear
     old Carian guest,
A handful of grey ashes, long long ago
     at rest,
Still are thy pleasant voices, thy
     Nightingales,[1] awake,
For Death, he taketh all away, but
     them he cannot take.
>> *Heraclitus,[2] Paraphrase from*
>> *Callimachus* [3]

BARTHOLOMEW DOWLING
[1823–1863]

We meet 'neath the sounding rafter,
     And the walls around are bare;

[1] *The Nightingales* was the title of the poems left by HERACLITUS [*floruit* 500 B. C.].
[2] They tell me, Heraclitus, thou art dead,
And many are the tears for thee I shed,
With memories of those summer nights
     opprest
When we together talked the sun to rest.
Alas! my guest, my friend! no more art
     thou;
Long, long ago wert ashes, and yet now
Thy Nightingales live on, I hear them
     sing,
E'en death spares them, who spares not
     anything.
     LILLA CABOT PERRY [1848–1933]: translated from CALLIMACHUS, *Greek Anthology, Book VII, Epigram 80*
[3] *Floruit* 260 B. C.

As they shout back our peals of laugh-
     ter
It seems that the dead are there.
Then stand to your glasses steady!
     We drink in our comrades' eyes:
One cup to the dead already —
     Hurrah for the next that dies!
>> *The Revel.*[1] *Stanza 1*

THOMAS WENTWORTH HIGGINSON
[1823–1911]

The test of an author is not to be found merely in the number of his phrases that pass current in the corner of newspapers . . . but in the number of passages that have really taken root in younger minds.
>> *Margaret Fuller Ossoli* [*1884*].
>> *Chap. 18*

When a thought takes one's breath away, a lesson on grammar seems an impertinence.
>> *Preface to* EMILY DICKINSON'S
>> *Poems, First Series* [*1890*]

An easy thing, O Power Divine,
To thank Thee for these gifts of Thine,
For summer's sunshine, winter's snow,
For hearts that kindle, thoughts that
     glow;
But when shall I attain to this —
To thank Thee for the things I miss?
>> *The Things I Miss*

Age, I make light of it,
     Fear not the sight of it,
Time's but our playmate, whose toys
     are divine.
>> *Sixty and Six: A Fountain*
>> *of Youth*

JOHN KELLS INGRAM
[1823–1907]

Who fears to speak of Ninety-eight?
     Who blushes at the name?
When cowards mock the patriot's fate,
     Who hangs his head for shame?
>> *The Memory of the Dead.*[2]
>> *Stanza 1*

[1] Commemorating those who died in a great cholera epidemic in India.
[2] First published anonymously in *The Dublin Nation*, April 1, 1843.

GEORGE MARTIN LANE
[1823–1897]

The waiter he to him doth call,
And gently whispers — "One Fishball."
The waiter roars it through the hall,
The guests they start at "One Fish-
ball!"
The guest then says, quite ill at ease,
"A piece of bread, sir, if you please."
The waiter roars it through the hall:
"We don't give bread with one Fish-
ball!"

> *One Fish-ball,*[1] *Couplets 7–10*
> [*Harper's Monthly, July, 1855*]

FRANCIS PARKMAN
[1823–1893]

The growth of New England was a
result of the aggregate efforts of a busy
multitude, each in his narrow circle toiling for himself, to gather competence or
wealth. The expansion of New France
was the achievement of a gigantic ambition striving to grasp a continent. It
was a vain attempt.

> *Pioneers of France in the New
> World* [*1865*]. *Introduction*

A boundless vision grows upon us; an
untamed continent; vast wastes of forest verdure; mountains silent in primeval sleep; river, lake, and glimmering
pool; wilderness oceans mingling with
the sky. Such was the domain which
France conquered for Civilization.
Plumed helmets gleamed in the shade of
its forests, priestly vestments in its dens
and fastnesses of ancient barbarism.
Men steeped in antique learning, pale
with the close breath of the cloister,
here spent the noon and evening of
their lives, ruled savage hordes with a
mild, parental sway, and stood serene
before the direst shapes of death. Men
of courtly nurture, heirs to the polish of
a far-reaching ancestry, here, with their

[1] The author was Professor of Latin at
Harvard; PROFESSOR MORGAN's memoir of him
says that the embarrassment of the "lone
fish-ball" was an actual experience.

dauntless hardihood, put to shame the
boldest sons of toil.

> *Pioneers of France in the
> New World. Introduction*

Faithfulness to the truth of history
involves far more than a research, however patient and scrupulous, into special facts. Such facts may be detailed
with the most minute exactness, and
yet the narrative, taken as a whole,
may be unmeaning or untrue. The nar-
rator must seek to imbue himself with
the life and spirit of the time. He must
study events in their bearings near and
remote; in the character, habits, and
manners of those who took part in
them. He must himself be, as it were, a
sharer or a spectator of the action he
describes.

> *Ibid.*

If any pale student, glued to his desk,
here seek an apology for a way of life
whose natural fruit is that pallid and
emasculate scholarship of which New
England has had too many examples, it
will be far better that this sketch had
not been written. For the student there
is, in its season, no better place than the
saddle, and no better companion than
the rifle or the oar.

> *Autobiography* [*1868*] (*Proceed-
> ings of the Massachusetts His-
> torical Society, Vol. VIII, Page
> 353*)

The most momentous and far-reaching question ever brought to issue on
this continent was: Shall France remain here or shall she not?

> *Montcalm and Wolfe* [*1884*].
> *Introduction*

The French Revolution began at the
top — in the world of fashion, birth,
and intellect — and propagated itself
downwards.

> *Ibid.*

Versailles was a gulf into which the
labor of France poured its earnings, and
it was never full.

> *Ibid. Page 11*

France built its best colony on a prin-

head in gentle spite,
...ite,
...no spies thee waving here,
...in beauty can compare
...th night.   *To a Lily*

...thy lake dost see
...: so she
...s her image in her eyes
...ted. Thus did Venus rise
...out the sea.   *Ibid.*

CAROLINE ATHERTON BRIGGS MASON
[1823–1890]

Do they miss me at home — do they
      miss me?
'Twould be an assurance most dear,
To know that this moment some loved
      one
Were saying, "I wish he were here."
      Do They Miss Me at Home?   Stanza 1

His grave a nation's heart shall be,
His monument a people free!
      President Lincoln's Grave

EDWARD HAZEN PARKER
[1823–1896]

Life's race well run,
Life's work well done,
Life's victory won,
Now cometh rest.
      Funeral Ode on James A. Garfield   Stanza 1

COVENTRY PATMORE
[1823–1896]

Life is not life at all without...ight.
                    Vi...the haprest
None thrives for long...
      dream.
      Tired Memory

Ah, wasteful woma...
On her sweet self set he...
Knowing man cannot choose bu...
How has she cheapened Paradise!
How given for nought her priceless gift,
How spoiled the bread and spilled the
      wine,
Which, spent with due respective thrift,
Had made brutes men and men divine!
      Ibid. Canto 3, Prelude 3, Unthrift

Love wakes men, once a lifetime each;
They lift their heavy lids, and look;
And, lo, what one sweet page can teach
They read with joy, then shut the book.
      Ibid. Canto 8, Prelude 2,
      The Re...ution

Why, having won her, do I w...?
Because her spirit's vesta...race
Provokes me always to ...brace.
But, spirit-like, eludes...to 12, Prelude 1,
      Ibid. Book II, ...he Married Lover

For want of me... world's course will
      not fail...
When all its ...ork is done, t... lie shall
      rot; ...s great, and s...ll prevail,
The tr... ...e cares whether ...prevail or
When...
      ...e Unknown Eros [77]. Book I,
      Canto 12, M...na est Veritas ...sometimes say

...f I were dead, you... *...If I Were D...*
"Poor Child!"...
      Ibid. Canto ... land,

A Woman is a for...e he settle...g,
Of which, thoug...ite unders...
A man will ne...s, and to...man
...he customs, ...   that
      ...   not co...e, do,
Some... ...proved ...pen to
Christian...ld that ...a race,
neverthe...er the ...
questio...

has been much affected by it, and whether the external and visible evil and good which have come of it do not pretty nearly balance one another.

Christianity and Progress

Atheism in art, as well as in life, has only to be pressed to its last consequences in order to become ridiculous.

Emotional Art

The poet, as a rule, should avoid religion altogether as a direct subject.

Bad Morality Is Bad Art

It is a great consolation to reflect that, among all the bewildering changes to which the world is subject, the character of woman cannot be altered.

Ibid.

EDWARD POLLOCK
[1823–1858]

There's something in the parting hour
  Will chill the warmest heart,
Yet kindred, comrades, lovers, friends,
  Are fated all to part.

The Parting Hour

The one who goes is happier
Than those he leaves behind.

Ibid.

THEODORE DE BANVILLE
[1823–1891]

We'll to the wood no more, the
laurel-trees are cut.[1]

Nous n'irons plus aux bois

PHOEBE CARY
[1824–1874]

I think true love is never blind,
  But rather brings an added light,
An inner vision quick to find
  The beauties hid from common sight.

plenty of what *Love. Stanza 1*
I'll listen to pity's even to you,
think the little
the much you give is great

Legend of the hall.
Holland. I, Stanza 8

[1] Nous n'irons plus aux bois
sont coupés. From an old nursery riers

Sometimes, I think, the things we see
Are shadows of the things to be;
  That what we plan we build;
That every hope that hath been crossed,
And every dream we thought was lost,
  In heaven shall be fulfilled.

Dreams and Realities. Stanza 7

And though hard be the task,
"Keep a stiff upper lip."

Keep a Stiff Upper Lip

One sweetly solemn thought
  Comes to me o'er and o'er;
I am nearer home today
  Than I ever have been before.

Nearer Home. Stanza 1

For of all the hard things to bear and
  grin,
The hardest is being taken in.

Kate Ketcham (Parody on
WHITTIER'S *Maud Muller)*

LUCY LARCOM
[1824–1893]

Oh, her heart's adrift, with one
On an endless voyage gone!
  Night and morning
Hannah's at the window binding shoes.

Hannah Binding Shoes. Stanza 2

I do not own an inch of land,
But all I see is mine.

A Strip of Blue

If the world seems cold to you,
Kindle fires to warm it!

Three Old Saws

If the world's a wilderness,
Go, build houses in it!

Ibid.

If the world's a vale of tears,
Smile, till rainbows span it!

Ibid.

There is light in shadow and shadow in
  light,
And black in the blue of the sky.

Black in Blue Sky. Stanza 2

GEORGE WILLIAM CURTIS
[1824–1892]

While we read history we make history.

Call of Freedom

Every great crisis of human history is a pass of Thermopylae, and there is always a Leonidas and his three hundred to die in it, if they can not conquer.
The Call of Freedom

Imagination is as good as many voyages — and how much cheaper.
Prue and I [*1856*]. *Preface*

Happiness is speechless.
Ibid. Chap. 4

The pride of ancestry increases in the ratio of distance.
Ibid. Chap. 6

It is a great pity that men and women forget that they have been children. Parents are apt to be foreigners to their sons and daughters. Maturity is the gate of Paradise which shuts behind us; and our memories are gradually weaned from the glories in which our nativity was cradled.
Ibid. Chap. 7

Love is the coldest of critics.
Ibid.

Gentlemen, this is the convention of free speech, and I have been given the floor. I have only a few words to say to you, but I shall say them if I stand here until tomorrow morning.
At the Republican National Convention [*1860*]

CHARLES GODFREY LELAND
[*1824–1903*]

Hans Breitmann gife a barty —
Where ish dat barty now?
Hans Breitmann's Barty [*1857*]

If all the world must see the world
As the world the world hath seen,
Then it were better for the world
That the world had never been.
The World and the World

"A New Year's gift to the world," said the Frost,
"Rich lace curtains which nothing cost."
Frost Pictures. Stanza 4

They saw a Dream of Loveliness descending from the train.
The Masher

The brave deserve the lovely — every woman may be won.
The Masher

ALEXANDRE DUMAS THE YOUNGER
[*1824–1895*]

Business? It's quite simple. It's other people's money.
La Question d'Argent [*1857*].
Act II, Sc. 7

GEORGE MACDONALD
[*1824–1905*]

Alas! how easily things go wrong!
A sigh too much or a kiss too long,
And there follows a mist and a weeping rain,
And life is never the same again.
Phantastes. Song

Where did you come from, baby dear?
Out of the everywhere into the here.
At the Back of the North Wind.
Baby, Stanza 1

Where did you get those eyes so blue?
Out of the sky as I came through.
Ibid. Stanza 2

They were all looking for a king
To slay their foes and lift them high;
Thou cam'st, a little baby thing
That made a woman cry.
That Holy Thing. Stanza 1

Said the Wind to the Moon, "I will blow you out!"
The Wind and the Moon.
Stanza 1

WALTER CHALMERS SMITH
[*1824–1908*]

And all through life I see a cross —
Where sons of God yield up their breath;
There is no gain except by loss;
There is no life except by death;
There is no vision but by faith.
Olrig Grange. Book 6

JOHN WHITTAKER WATSON
[1824–1890]

O the snow, the beautiful snow,
Filling the sky and the earth below.
Over the house-tops, over the street,
Over the heads of the people you meet,
Dancing,
Flirting,
Skimming along,
Beautiful snow, it can do nothing
    wrong.
Beautiful Snow [1869]. *Stanza 1*

HENRY DE LAFAYETTE WEBSTER
[1824–1896]

The years creep slowly by, Lorena,
The snow is on the grass again.
Lorena.[1] *Stanza 1*

ADELINE DUTTON TRAIN WHITNEY
[1824–1906]

The sun of life has crossed the line;
The summer-shine of lengthened light
Faded and failed — till, where I stand,
'Tis equal day and equal night.
Equinoctial. Stanza 1
I bow me to the threatening gale:
I know when that is overpast,
Among the peaceful harvest days
An Indian Summer comes at last.
Ibid. Stanza 6

EDWARD HENRY BICKERSTETH, BISHOP OF EXETER
[1825–1906]

Give us men!
Men from every rank,
Fresh and free and frank;
Men of thought and reading,
Men of light and leading,
Men of loyal breeding,
The nation's welfare speeding.
Give Us Men. Stanza 1

[1] One of the most popular songs of the Civil War period.

RICHARD DODDRIDGE BLACKMORE
[1825–1900]

Women, who are, beyond all doubt,
the mothers of all mischief, also nurse
that babe to sleep when he is too noisy.
Lorna Doone [1869]. *Chap. 57*

WILLIAM ALLEN BUTLER
[1825–1902]

Dresses for breakfasts, and dinners,
    and balls;
Dresses to sit in, and stand in, and
    walk in;
Dresses to dance in, and flirt in, and
    talk in;
Dresses in which to do nothing at all;
Dresses for Winter, Spring, Summer,
    and Fall.
Nothing to Wear [1]
This same Miss McFlimsey of Madison
    Square,
The last time we met was in utter de-
    spair,
Because she had nothing whatever to
    wear!
Ibid.

JULIA CAROLINE RIPLEY DORR
[1825–1913]

Under thy hooded mantle I can see
Thy wavelets of soft hair, like those
    that lie
On a girl's forehead; and thy unlined
    brow,
Pregnant with thought inbreathed, be-
    trayeth not
One of thy secrets saving this alone, —
That thou hast loved and suffered.[2]
In Rock Creek Cemetery

[1] *Harper's Weekly*, February 7, 1857.
[2] The sculpture by Augustus Saint-Gaudens for the grave of Mrs. Henry Adams, Rock Creek Cemetery, Washington, D. C.
    This is not death, nor sorrow, nor sad Hope;
    Nor rest that follows strife, but oh, more dread!
    'Tis Life, for all its agony, serene,
    Immortal, and unmournful and content.
    RICHARD WATSON GILDER [1844–1909]:
        The Saint-Gaudens Memorial

HENRIETTA A. HEATHORN (MRS. THOMAS H. HUXLEY)
[1825–1914]

Be not afraid, ye waiting hearts that
weep,
For God still giveth His belovèd sleep,[1]
And if an endless sleep He wills — so
best.[2]
Browning's Funeral, December 31,
1889

To all the gossip that I hear
I'll give no faith; to what I see
But only half, for it is clear
All that led up is dark to me.
 Learn we the larger life to live,
 To comprehend is to forgive.
 "Tout Comprendre, C'est Tout
 Pardonner"

THOMAS HENRY HUXLEY
[1825–1895]

I cannot but think that he who finds
a certain proportion of pain and evil
inseparably woven up in the life of the
very worms, will bear his own share
with more courage and submission.
 On the Educational Value of
 the Natural History Sciences
 [1854]

To a person uninstructed in natural
history, his country or seaside stroll is
a walk through a gallery filled with
wonderful works of art, nine-tenths of
which have their faces turned to the
wall.
 Ibid.

Education is the instruction of the
intellect in the laws of Nature, under
which name I include not merely things
and their forces, but men and their
ways; and the fashioning of the affections and of the will into an earnest and
loving desire to move in harmony with
those laws.
 A Liberal Education [1868]

For every man the world is as fresh
as it was at the first day, and as full of

[1] He giveth his beloved sleep. — *Psalm*
CXXVII, 2
[2] These lines were carved on Huxley's tomb
by his own request.

untold novelties for him who has the
eyes to see them.
 A Liberal Education

The chess-board is the world, the
pieces are the phenomena of the universe, the rules of the game are what
we call the laws of Nature. The player
on the other side is hidden from us.
We know that his play is always fair,
just, and patient. But also we know, to
our cost, that he never overlooks a mistake, or makes the smallest allowance
for ignorance.
 Ibid.

If some great Power would agree to
make me always think what is true
and do what is right, on condition of
being turned into a sort of clock and
wound up every morning before I got
out of bed, I should instantly close with
the offer.
 On Descartes' Discourse on Method
 [1870]. Method and Results

There is the greatest practical benefit
in making a few failures early in life.
 On Medical Education [1870]

That mysterious independent variable of political calculation, Public
Opinion.
 Universities, Actual and Ideal
 [1874]

Veracity is the heart of morality.
 Ibid.

Becky Sharp's acute remark that it
is not difficult to be virtuous on ten
thousand a year [1] has its application to
nations; and it is futile to expect a
hungry and squalid population to be
anything but violent and gross.
 Joseph Priestley [1874]

Logical consequences are the scarecrows of fools and the beacons of wise
men.
 Animal Automatism [1874]

Size is not grandeur, and territory
does not make a nation.
 On University Education [1876]

Perhaps the most valuable result of
all education is the ability to make
yourself do the thing you have to do,

[1] See Thackeray, page 565a.

when it ought to be done, whether you like it or not; it is the first lesson that ought to be learned; and however early a man's training begins, it is probably the last lesson that he learns thoroughly.
Technical Education [*1877*]

The great end of life is not knowledge but action.
Ibid.

If a little knowledge is dangerous, where is the man who has so much as to be out of danger?
On Elemental Instruction in Physiology [*1877*]

Irrationally held truths may be more harmful than reasoned errors.
The Coming of Age of "The Origin of Species" [*1880*]

It is the customary fate of new truths to begin as heresies and to end as superstitions.
Ibid.

FRANCIS TURNER PALGRAVE
[1825–1897]

Time's corrosive dewdrop eats
The giant warrior to a crust
Of earth in earth and rust in rust.
A Danish Barrow

ADELAIDE ANNE PROCTER
[1825–1864]

One by one the sands are flowing,
  One by one the moments fall;
Some are coming, some are going;
  Do not strive to grasp them all.
One by One. Stanza 1

Seated one day at the organ,
  I was weary and ill at ease,
And my fingers wandered idly
  Over the noisy keys.
A Lost Chord. Stanza 1

But I struck one chord of music
Like the sound of a great Amen.
Ibid. Stanza 2

It seemed the harmonious echo
From our discordant life.
Ibid. Stanza 4

RICHARD HENRY STODDARD
[1825–1903]

Pale in her fading bowers the Summer
  stands,
Like a new Niobe with claspèd hands,
Silent above the flowers, her children
  lost,
Slain by the arrows of the early Frost.
Ode

Joy may be a miser,
But Sorrow's purse is free.
Persian Song

BAYARD TAYLOR
[1825–1878]

Till the sun grows cold,
  And the stars are old,
And the leaves of the Judgment Book
  unfold.
Bedouin Song

They sang of love, and not of fame;
  Forgot was Britain's glory;
Each heart recalled a different name,
  But all sang "Annie Laurie."
The Song of the Camp. Stanza 5

The bravest are the tenderest, —
The loving are the daring.
Ibid. Stanza 11

The violet loves a sunny bank,
  The cowslip loves the lea;
The scarlet creeper loves the elm,
  But I love — thee.
Proposal. Stanza 1

Learn to live, and live to learn,
Ignorance like a fire doth burn,
Little tasks make large return.
To My Daughter. Stanza 1

WILLIAM WHITING
[1825–1878]

Eternal Father! strong to save,
Whose arm hath bound the restless
  wave,
Who bidd'st the mighty ocean deep
Its own appointed limits keep:
  O, hear us when we cry to Thee
  For those in peril on the sea!
*Eternal Father, Strong to Save.
Stanza 1*

G. W. HUNT
[*Floruit* 1878]

We don't want to fight, but, by jingo,
  if we do,
We've got the ships, we've got the men,
  we've got the money, too.
We've fought the Bear before, and
  while Britons shall be true,
The Russians shall not have Constantinople.
                          Song [1] [*1878*]

FREDERICK TEMPLE
HAMILTON BLACKWOOD,
LORD DUFFERIN
[1826–1902]

In the market-place lay a dead dog.
Of the group gathered around it, one
said: "This carcass is disgusting." Another said, "The sight of it is torment."
Every man spoke in this strain. But
Jesus drew near and said, "Pearls are
not equal in whiteness to his teeth.
Look not on the failures of others and
the merits of thyself; cast thine eye on
thine own fault."
        *Installation Address as Lord
        Rector of St. Andrew's Univer-
        sity* [*1891*]

GEORGE W. BUNGAY
[1826–1892]

In rituals and faith excel!
Chimed out the Episcopalian bell.
      The Creeds of the Bells. Stanza 2
All is well! is well! is well!
Pealed out the good old Dutch church
  bell.
                          Ibid. Stanza 3
O swell! ye rising waters, swell!
Pealed out the clear-toned Baptist bell.
                          Ibid. Stanza 4
    Do well!
Rang out the Unitarian bell.
                          Ibid. Stanza 5

[1] Sung by Gilbert Hastings Macdermott
(Farrell) [1845–1901], "the great Macdermott." The song gave the terms "jingo" and
"jingoism" to the political vocabulary, though
the phrase "by jingo" had been used earlier
by Goldsmith and Thomas Hood.

Salvation's free, we tell! we tell!
Shouted the Methodistic bell.
      The Creeds of the Bells. Stanza 6
    No hell!
Rang out the Universalist bell.
                          Ibid. Stanza 7
All hail, ye saints, the chorus swell!
Chimed in the Roman Catholic bell.
                          Ibid. Stanza 10
Drink from the well!
In rapture rang the Temperance bell.
                          Ibid. Stanza 11

DINAH MARIA MULOCK
CRAIK
[1826–1887]

Two hands upon the breast,
  And labour's done; [1]
Two pale feet crossed in rest,
  The race is won.
                      Now and Afterwards
Love that asketh love again
Finds the barter nought but pain;
Love that giveth in full store
Aye receives as much, and more.
        Love that Asketh Love Again
God rest ye, merry gentlemen! let
  nothing you dismay,
For Jesus Christ, our Saviour, was
  born on Christmas day.
            A Christmas Carol. Stanza 1
Douglas, Douglas, tender and true!
        Douglas, Tender and True. [2]
                                Stanza 1
Oh, my son's my son till he gets him a
  wife,
But my daughter's my daughter all her
  life.
                          Young and Old

STEPHEN COLLINS FOSTER
[1826–1864]

The day goes by like a shadow o'er the
  heart,
With sorrow where all was delight;

[1] Two hands upon the breast, and labor is
past. — *Russian proverb*
[2] O Douglas, O Douglas!
    Tendir and trewe.
    SIR RICHARD HOLLAND: *The Buke of
      the Howlat* [*circa* 1450], *St. 31*

The time has come when the darkies
have to part:
Then my old Kentucky Home, good
night!
*My Old Kentucky Home.
Stanza 2*

Weep no more, my lady,
Oh! weep no more today!
We will sing one song for the old Ken-
tucky Home,
For the old Kentucky Home far away.
Ibid. Chorus

Way down upon the Swanee River,
Far, far away,
There's where my heart is turning ever;
There's where the old folks stay.
All up and down the whole creation,
Sadly I roam,
Still longing for the old plantation,
And for the old folks at home.
The Old Folks at Home. Stanza 1

All the world is sad and dreary
Ev'rywhere I roam,
Oh! darkies, how my heart grows
weary,
Far from the old folks at home.
Ibid. Chorus

I'm coming, I'm coming, for my head is
bending low;
I hear those gentle voices calling, "Old
Black Joe."
Old Black Joe. Stanza 3

O, Susanna! O, don't you cry for me,
I've come from Alabama, wid my banjo
on my knee.
O, Susanna. Chorus

I come down dah wid my hat caved in,
Doodah! doodah!
I go back home wid a pocket full of tin,
Oh! doodah day!
Gwine to run all night!
Gwine to run all day!
I'll bet my money on de bobtail nag —
Somebody bet on de bay.
Camptown Races

I dream of Jeanie with the light brown
hair,
Borne like a vapor on the summer air;
I see her tripping where the bright
streams play,

Happy as the daisies that dance on her
way.
*Jeanie with the Light Brown
Hair. Stanza 1*

Beautiful dreamer, wake unto me,
Starlight and dewdrop are waiting for
thee;
Sounds of the rude world heard in the
day,
Lulled by the moonlight have all
passed away.
Beautiful Dreamer. Stanza 1

COATES KINNEY
[1826–1904]

What a bliss to press the pillow
Of a cottage-chamber bed
And to listen to the patter
Of the soft rain overhead!
Rain on the Roof. Stanza 1

That subdued, subduing strain
Which is played upon the shingles
By the patter of the rain.
Ibid. Stanza 6

ETHEL LYNN BEERS
[1827–1879]

All quiet along the Potomac tonight,
No sound save the rush of the river,
While soft falls the dew on the face of
the dead, —
The picket's off duty forever.
*The Picket Guard [1861].
Stanza 6*

EDWARD STUYVESANT
BRAGG
[1827–1912]

They love him most for the enemies
he has made.[1]
*Speech seconding the nomina-
tion of Grover Cleveland for
the Presidency, Democratic
National Convention, Chicago
[July 9, 1884]*

[1] An adaptation of Governor Bragg's expression became a Cleveland campaign slogan:
"We love him for the enemies he has made."

MORTIMER COLLINS
[1827–1876]

There was an Ape in the days that were
   earlier;
Centuries passed, and his hair became
   curlier;
Centuries more gave a thumb to his
   wrist —
Then he was Man — and a Positivist.
                           The Positivists
A man is as old as he's feeling,
A woman as old as she looks.
                     How Old Are You?

ROSE TERRY COOKE
[1827–1892]

Yet courage, soul! nor hold thy
   strength in vain,
In hope o'ercome the steeps God set
   for thee;
For past the Alpine summits of great
   pain,
Lieth thine Italy.[1]
                      Beyond. Stanza 4

CHARLES B. FAIRBANKS
("AGUECHEEK")
[1827–1859]

Cleanliness is a great virtue; but
when it is carried to such an extent that
you cannot find your books and papers
which you left carefully arranged on
your table — when it gets to be a mon-
omania with man or woman — it becomes a bore.
     *My Unknown Chum. Antwerp
                        and Brussels*
Slander, like Death, loves a shining
mark.[2]
     Ibid. Napoleon the Third
Foreign travel ought to soften prejudices, religious or political, and liberalize a man's mind; but how many there
are who seem to have travelled for the
purpose of getting up their rancour

[1] Hannibal, encouraging his men: Quarum
alterum latus Italiae sit. — LIVY [59 B.C.–
A.D. 17]: *Ab Urbe Condita Libri, XXI, 30, 5*
[2] See Edward Young, page 306a.

against all that is opposed to their notions.
     *My Unknown Chum. The Philos-
        ophy of Foreign Travel*

FRANCIS MILES FINCH
[1827–1907]

These in the robings of glory,
   Those in the gloom of defeat,
All with the battle-blood gory,
   In the dusk of eternity meet:
Under the sod and the dew,
   Waiting the judgment-day;
Under the laurel, the Blue,
   Under the willow, the Gray.
     The Blue and the Gray. Stanza 2

CHARLES ELIOT NORTON
[1827–1908]

I think that a knowledge of Greek
thought and life, and of the arts in
which the Greeks expressed their
thought and sentiment, essential to
high culture. A man may know everything else, but without this knowledge
he remains ignorant of the best intellectual and moral achievements of his
own race.
     Letter to F. A. Tupper [*1885*]
Whatever your occupation may be
and however crowded your hours with
affairs, do not fail to secure at least a
few minutes every day for refreshment
of your inner life with a bit of poetry.
     *Used by a Boston newspaper as
      a heading for a column of re-
      printed poems*

JOHN TOWNSEND
TROWBRIDGE
[1827–1916]

Men are polished, through act and
   speech,
   Each by each,
As pebbles are smoothed on the rolling
   beach.
                       A Home Idyl

With years a richer life begins,
  The spirit mellows:
Ripe age gives tone to violins,
  Wine, and good fellows.
                    Three Worlds

WILLIAM ALLINGHAM
[1828–1889]

Up the airy mountain,
  Down the rushy glen,
We daren't go a-hunting
  For fear of little men.
              The Fairies. Stanza 1

ROBERT BARNABAS BROUGH
[1828–1860]

My Lord Tomnoddy is thirty-four;
The Earl can last but a few years more.
My Lord in the Peers will take his
    place:
Her Majesty's councils his words will
    grace.
Office he'll hold and patronage sway;
Fortunes and lives he will vote away;
And what are his qualifications? —
    ONE!
He's the Earl of Fitzdotterel's eldest
    son.
                 My Lord Tomnoddy

ELIZABETH RUNDLE CHARLES
[1828–1896]

To know how to say what other people only think, is what makes men poets and sages; and to dare to say what others only dare to think, makes men martyrs or reformers.
       *Chronicles of the Schönberg-
            Cotta Family, XIV*

GERALD MASSEY
[1828–1907]

Where our vanguard camps Today
Our rear shall march Tomorrow.
           Today and Tomorrow

GEORGE MEREDITH
[1828–1913]

I expect that Woman will be the last thing civilized by Man.
       *The Ordeal of Richard Feverel
            [1859]. Chap. 1*

Who rises from prayer a better man, his prayer is answered.
              Ibid. Chap. 12

The sun is coming down to earth, and the fields and the waters shout to him golden shouts.
              Ibid. Chap. 19

Kissing don't last: cookery do!
              Ibid. Chap. 28

See ye not, Courtesy
Is the true Alchemy,
Turning to gold all it touches and tries?
    The Song of Courtesy [1859]. IV

The old hound wags his shaggy tail,
  And I know what he would say:
It's over the hills we'll bound, old
    hound,
  Over the hills, and away.
           Over the Hills [1859]

I've studied men from my topsy-turvy
  Close, and, I reckon, rather true.
Some are fine fellows: some, right
    scurvy:
  Most, a dash between the two.
         Juggling Jerry [1859]. VII

Two of a trade, lass, never agree.
                      Ibid. IX

Life is but the pebble sunk;
Deeds, the circle growing!
       *The Head of Bran the Blest
           [1860]. IV, Stanza 4*

Not till the fire is dying in the grate,
Look we for any kinship with the stars.
Oh, wisdom never comes when it is gold,
And the great price we pay for it full
    worth;
We have it only when we are half earth.
              Modern Love [1862]. IV

And if I drink oblivion of a day,
So shorten I the stature of my soul.
                      Ibid. XII

The actors are, it seems, the usual
    three:
Husband, and wife, and lover.
                      Ibid. XXV

That rarest gift
To Beauty, Common Sense.
                    Modern Love. XXXII
How many a thing which we cast to
    the ground,
When others pick it up becomes a
    gem!
                    Ibid. XLI

In tragic life, God wot,
No villain need be! Passions spin the
    plot:
We are betrayed by what is false
    within.
                    Ibid. XLIII
Their sense is with their senses all
    mixed in,
Destroyed by subtleties these women
    are!
                    Ibid. XLVIII
Ah, what a dusty answer gets the soul
When hot for certainties in this our
    life!
                    Ibid. L
Into the breast that gives the rose
Shall I with shuddering fall?
        The Spirit of Earth in Autumn
                    [1862]. Stanza 1
Earth knows no desolation.
She smells regeneration
In the moist breath of decay.
                    Ibid. Stanza 14
Cynicism is intellectual dandyism.
        The Egoist [*1879*]. *Chap.* **7**
In . . . the book of Egoism, it is
written, Possession without obligation
to the object possessed approaches
felicity.
                Ibid. Chap. 14
On a starred night Prince Lucifer up-
rose.
Tired of his dark dominion swung the
    fiend . . .
He reached a middle height, and at the
    stars,
Which are the brain of heaven, he
    looked, and sank.
Around the ancient track marched, rank
    on rank,
The army of unalterable law.
        Lucifer in Starlight [*1883*]

Enter these enchanted woods,
    You who dare.
        The Woods of Westermain
                    [*1883*]. *Stanza 1*
She whom I love is hard to catch and
    conquer,
Hard, but O the glory of the winning
    were she won!
        Love in the Valley [*1883*].
                    Stanza 2
Darker grows the valley, more and
    more forgetting:
So were it with me if forgetting could
    be willed.
Tell the grassy hollow that holds the
    bubbling well-spring,
Tell it to forget the source that keeps
    it filled.
                    Ibid. Stanza 5
Love that so desires would fain keep
    her changeless;
Fain would fling the net, and fain have
    her free.
                    Ibid. Stanza 6
    Thence had he the laugh . . .
Broad as ten thousand beeves
At pasture.
        The Spirit of Shakespeare [*1883*]
    Civil limitation daunts
His utterance never; the nymphs blush,
    not he.
        An Orson of the Muse [*Walt
                    Whitman*] [*1883*]
    A witty woman is a treasure; a witty
beauty is a power.
        Diana of the Crossways
                    [*1885*]. *Chap. 1*
    The well of true wit is truth itself.
                    Ibid.
    Ireland gives England her soldiers,
her generals too.
                    Ibid. Chap. 2
With patient inattention hear him
    prate.
        Bellerophon [*1887*]. *Stanza 4*
Full lasting is the song, though he,
The singer, passes.
        The Thrush in February
                    [*1888*]. *Stanza 17*
Cannon his name,
Cannon his voice, he came.
        Napoleon [*1891*]. *1*

For Order's cause he laboured, as inclined
A soldier's training and his Euclid
mind. . . .
That creature, woman, was the sofa
soft,
When warriors their dusty armour
doffed,
And read their manuals for the making truce
With rosy frailties framed to reproduce.
        Napoleon. IX
    Evermore shall tyrant Force
Beget the greater for its overthrow.
        Ibid. XIII
For iron Winter held her firm;
Across her sky he laid his hand;
And bird he starved, he stiffened worm;
A sightless heaven, a shaven land.
        Tardy Spring [*1891*]
Now the North wind ceases,
The warm South-west awakes,
The heavens are out in fleeces,
And earth's green banner shakes.
        Ibid.
Sword of Common Sense! . . .
Bright, nimble of the marrow-nerve
To wield thy double edge. retort
Or hold the deadlier reserve.
    Ode to the Comic Spirit [*1892*]

FITZ-JAMES O'BRIEN
[1828–1862]

The enchanted circle of the Upper
Ten.[1]
        The Diamond Lens [*1858*].
        Chap. 2
    It was of a famous vintage, that of
1848, a year when war and wine throve
together.
        Ibid. Chap. 4

DANTE GABRIEL ROSSETTI
[1828–1882]

The blessed damozel leaned out
    From the gold bar of Heaven:
Her eyes were deeper than the depth
    Of waters stilled at even;

[1] See Haliburton, page 483b.

She had three lilies in her hand,
    And the stars in her hair were seven
        The Blessed Damozel [*1850*].
        Stanza 1
And the souls mounting up to God
Went by her like thin flames.
        Ibid. Stanza 7
I have been here before,
    But when or how I can not tell;
I know the grass beyond the door,
    The sweet keen smell,
The sighing sound, the lights around
    the shore.
        Sudden Light [*1881*]. *Stanza 1*
Still we say as we go, —
    "Strange to think by the way,
Whatever there is to know,
    That shall we know one day."
        The Cloud Confines [*1881*].
        Stanza 1
Was it a friend or foe that spread these
    lies?
Nay, who but infants question in such
    wise,
'Twas one of my most intimate enemies.
        Fragment [*1881*]
A Sonnet is a moment's monument, —
Memorial from the Soul's eternity
To one dead deathless hour.
        The House of Life [*1881*].
        Proem
And though thy soul sail leagues and
    leagues beyond, —
Still, leagues beyond those leagues,
    there is more sea.
        Ibid. 73, The Choice, III
Look in my face: my name is Might-
    have-been;
I am also called No-more, Too-late,
    Farewell.
        Ibid. 97, A Superscription

GEORGE WALTER
THORNBURY
[1828–1876]

The fool that eats till he is sick must
    fast till he is well,
The wooer who can flatter most will
    bear away the belle.
        The Jester's Sermon

HENRIK IBSEN
[1828–1906]

A lie, turned topsy-turvy, can be prinked and tinseled out, decked in plumage new and fine, till none knows its lean old carcass.
Peer Gynt [*1867*]. *Act I*

For fortune such as I've enjoyed I have to thank America. My amply furnished library I owe to Germany's later schools. From France, again, I get my waistcoats, my manners, and my spice of wit — from England an industrious hand, and keen sense for my own advantage. The Jew has taught me how to wait. Some taste for *dolce far niente* I have received from Italy — and one time, in a perilous pass, to eke the measure of my days, I had recourse to Swedish steel.
Ibid. Act IV

Marriage is a thing you've got to give your whole mind to.
The League of Youth [*1869*].
Act IV

These heroes of finance are like beads on a string — when one slips off, all the rest follow.
Ibid.

He has the luck to be unhampered by either character, or conviction, or social position; so that Liberalism is the easiest thing in the world for him.
Ibid. Act V

Look into any man's heart you please, and you will always find, in every one, at least one black spot which he has to keep concealed.
Pillars of Society [*1877*].
Act III

The spirit of truth and the spirit of freedom — they are the pillars of society.
Ibid. Act IV

There can be no freedom or beauty about a home life that depends on borrowing and debt.
A Doll's House [*1879*]. *Act I*

A barrister's profession is such an uncertain thing, especially if he won't undertake unsavory cases.
A Doll's House. Act I

There are some people one loves best, and others whom one would almost always rather have as companions.
Ibid. Act II

To crave for happiness in this world is simply to be possessed by a spirit of revolt. What right have we to happiness?
Ghosts [*1881*]. *Act I*

It is not only what we have inherited from our fathers that exists again in us, but all sorts of old dead ideas and all kinds of old dead beliefs and things of that kind. They are not actually alive in us; but there they are dormant, all the same, and we can never be rid of them. Whenever I take up a newspaper and read it, I fancy I see ghosts creeping between the lines. There must be ghosts all over the world.
Ibid. Act II

I hold that man is in the right who is most closely in league with the future.
Letter to Georg Brandes
[*January 3, 1882*]

A community is like a ship; every one ought to be prepared to take the helm.
An Enemy of the People
[*1882*]. *Act I*

The most crying need in the humbler ranks of life is that they should be allowed some part in the direction of public affairs. That is what will develop their faculties and intelligence and self-respect.
Ibid. Act II

The public doesn't require any new ideas. The public is best served by the good, old-fashioned ideas it already has.
Ibid.

An editor cannot always act as he would prefer. He is often obliged to bow to the wishes of the public in unimportant matters. Politics are the most important thing in life — for a newspaper.
Ibid. Act III

The most dangerous enemy to truth

and freedom among us is the compact majority.

> *An Enemy of the People. Act. IV*

You should never wear your best trousers when you go out to fight for freedom and truth.

> *Ibid. Act V*

Rob the average man of his life-illusion, and you rob him of his happiness at the same stroke.

> *The Wild Duck [1884]. Act V*

Vine-leaves in his hair.

> *Hedda Gabler [1890]. Act II*

COUNT LYOF NIKOLAYE-VITCH TOLSTOI
[1828–1910]

The Frenchman is conceited from supposing himself mentally and physically to be inordinately fascinating both to men and to women. An Englishman is conceited on the ground of being a citizen of the best-constituted state in the world, and also because he as an Englishman always knows what is the correct thing to do, and knows that everything that he, as an Englishman, does do is indisputably the correct thing. An Italian is conceited from being excitable and easily forgetting himself and other people. A Russian is conceited precisely because he knows nothing and cares to know nothing, since he does not believe it possible to know anything fully. A conceited German is the worst of them all, and the most hardened of all, and the most repulsive of all; for he imagines that he possesses the truth in a science of his own invention, which is to him absolute truth.

> *War and Peace [1865–1872].*[1]
> *Part IX, Chap. 10*

The subject of history is the life of peoples and of humanity. To catch and pin down in words — that is, to describe directly the life, not only of humanity, but even of a single people, appears to be impossible.[2]

> *Ibid. Epilogue, Part II, Chap. 1*

[1] Translated by CONSTANCE GARNETT. Modern Library Giant.
[2] See Francis Parkman, page 628b.

If the will of every man were free, that is, if every man could act as he chose, the whole of history would be a tissue of disconnected accidents.

> *War and Peace. Epilogue, Part II, Chap. 8*

The most powerful weapon of ignorance — the diffusion of printed matter.

> *Ibid.*

Time is infinite movement without one moment of rest.

> *Ibid. Chap. 10*

All happy families resemble one another; every unhappy family is unhappy in its own fashion.

> *Anna Karenina [1875–1876].*[1]
> *Part I, Chap. 1*

War on the one hand is such a terrible, such an atrocious, thing, that no man, especially no Christian man, has the right to assume the responsibility of beginning it.

> *Ibid. Part VIII, Chap. 15*

Error is the force that welds men together; truth is communicated to men only by deeds of truth.

> *My Religion [1884]. Chap. 12*

The happiness of men consists in life. And life is in labor.

> *What Shall We Do Then? [1886]. Chap. 38*

The vocation of every man and woman is to serve other people.

> *Ibid. Chap. 40, Note*

The whole trade in the luxuries of life is brought into existence and supported by the requirements of women.

> *The Kreutzer Sonata [1890]. Chap. 9*

His face was of that insipidly pleasing kind which women call "not bad-looking."

> *Ibid. Chap. 19*

The more is given the less the people will work for themselves, and the less

[1] Translated by NATHAN HASKELL DOLE [1852–1935].

they work the more their poverty will increase.[1]

Help for the Starving. Part III
[January, 1892]

The only significance of life consists in helping to establish the kingdom of God; and this can be done only by means of the acknowledgment and profession of the truth by each one of us.

The Kingdom of God [1893].
Chap. 12

Art is a human activity having for its purpose the transmission to others of the highest and best feelings to which men have risen.

What Is Art? [1898]. Chap. 8

GEORGE WILLIAM CHILDS
[1829–1894]

Do not keep the alabaster boxes of your love and tenderness sealed up until your friends are dead. Fill their lives with sweetness. Speak approving, cheering words while their ears can hear them, and while their hearts can be thrilled and made happier by them.

A Creed

ROSCOE CONKLING
[1829–1888]

He will hew to the line of right, let the chips fall where they may.

Speech nominating General Grant for a third term, National Republican Convention, Chicago [June 5, 1880]

CHARLES GRAHAM HALPINE ("MILES O'REILLY")
[1829–1868]

And if asked what state he hails from,
This our sole reply shall be,
"From near Appomattox Court-house,
With its famous apple-tree."[2]

A Bumper to Grant. Stanza 8

[1] If you stop supporting that crowd, it will support itself. — SENECA [8 B.C.–A.D. 65]: *Epistle 20, 7*

[2] Quoted by Roscoe Conkling in his speech nominating Grant for the Presidency, Republican Convention [June, 1880].

There's never a bond, old friend, like this, —
We have drunk from the same canteen!

The Canteen. Stanza 1

The constellation of O'Ryan, ignorantly and falsely spelled Orion.

Subtitle of poem, Irish Astronomy

JOSEPH JEFFERSON
[1829–1905]

God bless the little church around the corner.[1]

In GEORGE MACADAM: *The Little Church Around the Corner [1925]*

SILAS WEIR MITCHELL
[1829–1914]

Death's but one more tomorrow.

Of One Who Seemed to Have Failed

Show me his friends and I the man shall know;
This wiser turn a larger wisdom lends:
Show me the books he loves and I shall know
The man far better than through mortal friends.

Books and the Man. Stanza 1

The first thing to be done by a biographer in estimating character is to examine the stubs of the victim's chequebooks.

Quoted in CUSHING: *Life of Sir William Osler [1925]. Vol. I, Chap. 21, Page 583*

JOSHUA DAVENPORT ROBINSON
[1829–1866]

I shall see his toys and his empty chair,
And the horse he used to ride,

[1] Said after the death of George Holland, a well-loved old actor, in December, 1870. A certain New York rector declined to hold the funeral in his church and recommended Jefferson to "a little church around the corner." This was the Church of the Transfiguration, East 29th Street, popularly known ever since by that term of affection.

And they will speak with a silent speech
Of the little boy that died.
The Little Boy That Died.
Stanza 3

CARL SCHURZ
[1829–1906]

Ideals are like stars; you will not succeed in touching them with your hands. But like the seafaring man on the desert of waters, you choose them as your guides, and following them you will reach your destiny.[1]
Address, Faneuil Hall, Boston
[April 18, 1859]

You are underrating the President [Lincoln]. I grant that he lacks higher education and his manners are not in accord with European conceptions of the dignity of a chief magistrate. He is a well-developed child of nature and is not skilled in polite phrases and poses. But he is a man of profound feeling, correct and firm principles and incorruptible honesty. His motives are unquestionable, and he possesses to a remarkable degree the characteristic, God-given trait of this people, sound common sense.
Letter to Theodore Petrasch
[October, 1864]

Our country, right or wrong.[2] When right, to be kept right; when wrong, to be put right.
Address, Anti-Imperialistic Conference, Chicago [October 17, 1899]

HENRY TIMROD
[1829–1867]

Spring, with that nameless pathos in
the air
Which dwells with all things fair,
Spring, with her golden suns and silver
rain,
Is with us once again.
Spring. Stanza 1

[1] See Emerson, page 507b.
[2] See Charles Churchill, page 362b.

There is no holier spot of ground
Than where defeated valor lies,
By mourning beauty crowned!
Ode, Decorating the Graves of the Confederate Dead, Magnolia Cemetery, Charleston, South Carolina [1867]. Stanza 5

CHARLES DUDLEY WARNER
[1829–1900]

To own a bit of ground, to scratch it with a hoe, to plant seeds, and watch the renewal of life, — this is the commonest delight of the race, the most satisfactory thing a man can do.
My Summer in a Garden [1870].
Preliminary

Broad acres are a patent of nobility; and no man but feels more of a man in the world if he have a bit of ground that he can call his own. However small it is on the surface, it is four thousand miles deep; and that is a very handsome property.
Ibid.

What a man needs in gardening is a cast-iron back, with a hinge in it.
Ibid. Third Week

If you wish to save men from any particular vice, set up a tremendous cry of warning about some other, and they will all give their special efforts to the one to which attention is called.[1]
Ibid. Tenth Week

If you do things by the job, you are perpetually driven: the hours are scourges. If you work by the hour, you gently sail on the stream of Time, which is always bearing you on to the haven of Pay, whether you make any effort, or not.
Ibid. Eleventh Week

The toad, without which no garden would be complete.
Ibid. Thirteenth Week

[1] When classes are exasperated against each other, the peace of the world is always kept by striking a new note. Instantly the units part, and form in a new order, and those who were opposed are now side by side. — EMERSON: *Progress of Culture* [1883]

True it is that politics makes strange bedfellows.
> *My Summer in a Garden.*
> *Fifteenth Week*

What small potatoes we all are, compared with what we might be!
> *Ibid.*

Public opinion is stronger than the legislature, and nearly as strong as the ten commandments.
> *Ibid. Sixteenth Week*

The thing generally raised on city land is taxes.
> *Ibid.*

CHARLES HAMILTON AÏDÉ
[1830–1906]

I sit beside my lonely fire
And pray for wisdom yet:
For calmness to remember
Or courage to forget.
> *Remember or Forget*

CHARLOTTE ALINGTON BARNARD ("CLARIBEL")
[1830–1869]

I cannot sing the old songs I sang long years ago,
For heart and voice would fail me, and foolish tears would flow.
> *I Cannot Sing the Old Songs* [1]

Take back the heart that thou gavest,
What is my anguish to thee?
Take back the freedom thou cravest,
Leaving the fetters to me.
> *Take Back the Heart*

NOAH BROOKS
[1830–1903]

Conductor, when you receive a fare,
Punch in the presence of the passenjare.
A blue trip slip for an eight cent fare,
A buff trip slip for a six cent fare,
A pink trip slip for a five cent fare,
Punch in the presence of the passenjare.

[1] I can not sing the old songs now!
It is not that I deem them low;
'Tis that I can't remember how
They go.
C. S. CALVERLEY [1831–1884]: *Changed*

Punch, brothers, punch with care,
Punch in the presence of the passenjare.
> *Inspired by a notice to conductors, posted in New York horse-cars* [1]

THOMAS EDWARD BROWN
[1830–1897]

A Garden is a lovesome thing, God wot!
Rose plot,
Fringed pool,
Ferned grot —
The veriest school
Of Peace; and yet the fool
Contends that God is not —
Not God! in Gardens! when the eve is cool?
Nay, but I have a sign:
'Tis very sure God walks in mine.
> *My Garden*

EMILY DICKINSON [2]
[1830–1886]

This is my letter to the world,
That never wrote to me, —
The simple news that Nature told,
With simple majesty.
> *Part I, Life. Fly-leaf, Stanza 1*

Success is counted sweetest
By those who ne'er succeed.
> *Ibid. I, Stanza 1*

Our share of night to bear,
Our share of morning.
> *Ibid. II, Stanza 1*

Here a star, and there a star,
Some lose their way.
Here a mist, and there a mist,
Afterwards — day!
> *Ibid. Stanza 2*

If I can stop one heart from breaking,
I shall not live in vain;
If I can ease one life the aching,
Or cool one pain,
Or help one fainting robin

[1] The jingle attained celebrity following its publication in MARK TWAIN's *Literary Nightmare (Punch, Brothers, Punch)* [1876]. An account of its origin is given in A. B. PAINE's *Mark Twain* [1912], *Vol. I, P. 555.*

[2] *The Poems of Emily Dickinson,* edited by BIANCHI AND HAMPSON [1937].

Unto his nest again,
I shall not live in vain.
                    Part I, Life. VI

Much madness is divinest sense
To a discerning eye;
Much sense the starkest madness.
'Tis the majority
In this, as all, prevails.
Assent, and you are sane;
Demur, — you're straightway danger-
ous,
And handled with a chain.
                    Ibid. XI

The soul selects her own society,
Then shuts the door.
                    Ibid. XIII, Stanza 1

To fight aloud is very brave,
But gallanter, I know,
Who charge within the bosom,
The cavalry of woe.
                    Ibid. XVI, Stanza 1

I taste a liquor never brewed,
From tankards scooped in pearl.
                    Ibid. XX, Stanza 1

Inebriate of air am I,
And debauchee of dew,
Reeling, through endless summer days,
From inns of molten blue.
                    Ibid. Stanza 2

Till seraphs swing their snowy hats,
And saints to windows run,
To see the little tippler
Leaning against the sun!
                    Ibid. Stanza 4

He ate and drank the precious words,
His spirit grew robust;
He knew no more that he was poor,
Nor that his frame was dust.
He danced along the dingy days,
And this bequest of wings
Was but a book. What liberty
A loosened spirit brings.
                    Ibid. XXI

I'm nobody! Who are you?
Are you nobody, too?
Then there's a pair of us — don't tell!
They'd banish us, you know.
                    Ibid. XXVII, Stanza 1

How dreary to be somebody!
How public, like a frog

To tell your name the livelong day
To an admiring bog!
                    Part I, Life. XXVII, Stanza 2

Hope is the thing with feathers
That perches in the soul,
And sings the tune without the words,
And never stops at all.
                    Ibid. XXXII, Stanza 1

For each ecstatic instant
We must an anguish pay
In keen and quivering ratio
To the ecstasy.
                    Ibid. XXXVII, Stanza 1

The thought beneath so slight a film
Is more distinctly seen, —
As laces just reveal the surge,
Or mists the Apennine.
                    Ibid. XL

The soul unto itself
Is an imperial friend, —
Or the most agonizing spy
An enemy could send.
                    Ibid. XLI, Stanza 1

God gave a loaf to every bird,
But just a crumb to me.
                    Ibid. LIII, Stanza 1

Just lost when I was saved!
Just felt the world go by!
Just girt me for the onset with eternity,
When breath blew back,
And on the other side
I heard recede the disappointed tide!
                    Ibid. LXXXIII, Stanza 1

A word is dead
When it is said,
    Some say.
I say it just
Begins to live
    That day.
                    Ibid. LXXXIX

My life closed twice before its close;
It yet remains to see
If Immortality unveil
A third event to me.

So huge, so hopeless to conceive,
As these that twice befell.
Parting is all we know of heaven,
And all we need of hell.
                    Ibid. XCVI

We never know how high we are
Till we are called to rise;
And then, if we are true to plan,
Our statures touch the skies.
    Part I, Life. XCVII, Stanza 1

There is no frigate like a book
To take us lands away,
Nor any coursers like a page
Of prancing poetry.

This traverse may the poorest take
Without oppress of toll;
How frugal is the chariot
That bears a human soul!
    Ibid. XCIX

A bird came down the walk:
He did not know I saw;
He bit an angle-worm in halves
And ate the fellow, raw.
    Part II, Nature. XXIII, Stanza 1

God made a little gentian;
It tried to be a rose
And failed, and all the summer laughed.
    Ibid. XLVIII

Besides the autumn poets sing,
A few prosaic days
A little this side of the snow
And that side of the haze.
    Ibid. XLIX, Stanza 1

The pedigree of honey
Does not concern the bee;
A clover, any time, to him
Is aristocracy.
    Ibid. LVI

Some keep the Sabbath going to church;
I keep it staying at home,
With a bobolink for a chorister,
And an orchard for a dome.
    Ibid. LVII, Stanza 1

I'll tell you how the sun rose, —
A ribbon at a time.
The steeples swam in amethyst,
The news like squirrels ran.
    Ibid. LXXIII, Stanza 1

These are the days when birds come
    back,
A very few, a bird or two,
To take a backward look.
    Ibid. LXXVIII, Stanza 1

These are the days when skies put on
The old, old sophistries of June, —
A blue and gold mistake.
    Part II, Nature. LXXVIII,
        Stanza 2

The morns are meeker than they were,
The nuts are getting brown;
The berry's cheek is plumper,
The rose is out of town.
    Ibid. LXXIX, Stanza 1

The sky is low, the clouds are mean,
A travelling flake of snow
Across a barn or through a rut
Debates if it will go.

A narrow wind complains all day
How some one treated him;
Nature, like us, is sometimes caught
Without her diadem.
    Ibid. LXXX

There's a certain slant of light,
On winter afternoons,
That oppresses, like the weight
Of cathedral tunes.
    Ibid. LXXXII, Stanza 1

Alter? When the hills do.
Falter? When the sun
Question if his glory
Be the perfect one.
    Part III, Love. III, Stanza 1

Elysium is as far as to
The very nearest room,
If in that room a friend await
Felicity or doom.
    Ibid. IV, Stanza 1

"Going to him! Happy letter! Tell
    him —
Tell him the page I didn't write;
Tell him I only said the syntax,
And left the verb and pronoun out."
    Ibid. XXIII, Stanza 1

Love is anterior to life,
Posterior to death,
Initial of creation, and
The exponent of breath.
    Ibid. XXXVII

Heart, we will forget him!
    You and I, to-night!
You may forget the warmth he gave,
    I will forget the light.
    XLVII, Stanza 1

That short, potential stir
That each can make but once,
That bustle so illustrious
'Tis almost consequence,

Is the *éclat* of death.
Oh, thou unknown renown
That not a beggar would accept,
Had he the power to spurn!
Part IV, Time and Eternity. XIII

I never saw a moor,
I never saw the sea;
Yet know I how the heather looks,
And what a wave must be.

I never spoke with God,
Nor visited in heaven;
Yet certain am I of the spot
As if the chart were given.
Ibid. XVII

The sweeping up the heart,
And putting love away
We shall not want to use again
Until eternity.
Ibid. XXII, Stanza 2

Afraid? Of whom am I afraid?
Not death; for who is he?
The porter of my father's lodge
As much abasheth me.
Ibid. XXIV, Stanza 1

Because I could not stop for Death,
He kindly stopped for me;
The carriage held but just ourselves
And Immortality.
Ibid. XXVII, Stanza 1

If I shouldn't be alive
When the robins come,
Give the one in red cravat
A memorial crumb.
Ibid. XXXVII, Stanza 1

Adventure most unto itself
The Soul condemned to be;
Attended by a Single Hound —
Its own Identity.
Part V, The Single Hound. I

Glory is that bright tragic thing,
That for an instant
Means Dominion,
Warms some poor name
That never felt the sun,

Gently replacing
In oblivion.
Part V, The Single Hound. XX

This quiet Dust was Gentlemen and
Ladies,
And Lads and Girls;
Was laughter and ability and sighing,
And frocks and curls.
Ibid. LXXIV

Eden is that old-fashioned House
We dwell in every day,
Without suspecting our abode
Until we drive away.
Ibid. CVIII

Of course I prayed —
And did God care?
He cared as much
As on the air
A bird had stamped her foot
And cried "Give me!"
Part VI, Further Poems. 2,
XXXVIII, Stanza 1

A bayonet's contrition
Is nothing to the Dead!
Part VII, Additional Poems. 1, I,
Stanza 4

I thought that nature was enough
Till human nature came,
But that the other did absorb
As firmament a flame.
New Poems.[1] 149, Stanza 1

I tasted careless then.
I did not know the wine
Came once a world, did you?
Oh, had you told me so,
This thirst would blister easier now!
Ibid. 292, Stanza 3

The dying is a trifle, past,
But living — this include
The dying multifold without
The respite to be dead.
Ibid. 305, Stanza 2

But blossom were I,
I would rather be
Thy moment
Than a bee's eternity.
Ibid. 311, Stanza 2

The poets light but lamps,
Themselves go out;

[1] *Bolts of Melody* [1945] edited by MABEL
LOOMIS TODD AND MILLICENT TODD BINGHAM.

The wicks they stimulate,
If vital light

Inhere as do the suns,
Each age a lens
Disseminating their
Circumference.
New Poems. 432

If I read a book and it makes my whole body so cold no fire can ever warm me, I know that is poetry. If I feel physically as if the top of my head were taken off, I know that is poetry. These are the only ways I know it. Is there any other way?
Quoted in Life and Letters of Emily Dickinson [*1924*], *by* MARTHA GILBERT DICKINSON BIANCHI

PAUL HAMILTON HAYNE
[1830–1886]

I see the cloud-born squadrons of the gale,
Their lines of rain like glittering spears deprest.
A Storm in the Distance. Stanza 1

JAMES PROCTOR KNOTT
[1830–1911]

Duluth! The word fell upon my ear with a peculiar and indescribable charm, like the gentle murmur of a low fountain stealing forth in the midst of roses, or the soft sweet accent of an angel's whisper in the bright, joyous dream of sleeping innocence. 'Twas the name for which my soul had panted for years, as the hart panteth for the water-brooks.[1]
Speech on the St. Croix & Bayfield Railroad Bill, U. S. House of Representatives [*January 27, 1871*]

[1] Congressman Knott's ironic eulogy of Duluth — then a mere wilderness village — helped to defeat the railroad bill and, paradoxically, furnished Duluth its title of "zenith city of the unsalted seas."

CHRISTINA GEORGINA ROSSETTI
[1830–1894]

Hope is like a harebell trembling from its birth,
Love is like a rose the joy of all the earth,
Faith is like a lily lifted high and white,
Love is like a lovely rose the world's delight.
Harebells and sweet lilies show a thornless growth,
But the rose with all its thorns excels them both.
Hope Is Like a Harebell

Does the road wind up-hill all the way?
Yes, to the very end.
Up-Hill [*1861*]. *Stanza 1*

My heart is like a singing bird.
A Birthday [*1861*]. *Stanza 1*

When I am dead, my dearest,
Sing no sad songs for me;
Plant thou no roses at my head,
Nor shady cypress tree.
Song [*1862*]. *Stanza 1*

I shall not see the shadows,
I shall not feel the rain.
Ibid. Stanza 2

Remember me when I am gone away,
Gone far away into the silent land.
Remember [*1862*]

Better by far you should forget and smile
Than that you should remember and be sad.
Ibid.

All earth's full rivers can not fill
The sea, that drinking thirsteth still.
By the Sea

One day in the country
Is worth a month in town.
Summer

O Earth, lie heavily upon her eyes;
Seal her sweet eyes weary of watching, Earth.
Rest [*1862*]

Silence more musical than any song.
Ibid.

In the bleak mid-winter
Frosty wind made moan,
Earth stood hard as iron,

Water like a stone;
Snow had fallen, snow on snow,
  Snow on snow,
In the bleak mid-winter,
Long ago.
                              Mid-Winter

ALEXANDER SMITH
[1830–1867]

Some books are drenchèd sands
On which a great soul's wealth lies all
  in heaps,
Like a wrecked argosy.
          A Life Drama [*1853*]. *Sc. 2*
Like a pale martyr in his shirt of fire.
                                   Ibid.
In winter, when the dismal rain
  Came down in slanting lines,
And Wind, that grand old harper, smote
  His thunder-harp of pines.
                                   Ibid.
A poem round and perfect as a star.
                                   Ibid.
The saddest thing that can befall a soul
Is when it loses faith in God and
  woman.
                            Ibid. Sc. 12
The soul of man is like the rolling
  world,
One half in day, the other dipt in night;
The one has music and the flying cloud,
The other, silence and the wakeful
  stars.
                                Horton
Each time we love,
We turn a nearer and a broader mark
To that keen archer, Sorrow, and he
  strikes.
                           A Boy's Dream
Time has fallen asleep in the afternoon sunshine.
        Dreamthorp [*1863*]. *First Essay*
It is not of so much consequence
what you say, as how you say it. Memorable sentences are memorable on account of some single irradiating word.
      Ibid. On the Writing of Essays
The world is not so much in need
of new thoughts as that when thought
grows old and worn with usage it
should, like current coin, be called in,

and, from the mint of genius, reissued
fresh and new.
              Dreamthorp. On the
                 Writing of Essays
Death is the ugly fact which Nature
has to hide, and she hides it well.
        Ibid. Of Death and the
               Fear of Dying
Everything is sweetened by risk.
                                   Ibid.
In life there is nothing more unexpected and surprising than the arrivals
and departures of pleasure. If we find
it in one place today, it is vain to seek
it there tomorrow. You can not lay a
trap for it.
                                   Ibid.
A man's real possession is his memory. In nothing else is he rich, in nothing else is he poor.
                                   Ibid.
Scotland had invaded England more
than once, but the blue bonnets never
went over the border [1] so triumphantly
as when they did so in the shape of
songs and ballads.
             Ibid. William Dunbar
Just consider what a world this would
be if ruled by the best thoughts of men
of letters! Ignorance would die at once,
war would cease, taxation would be
lightened, not only every Frenchman,
but every man in the world, would have
his hen in the pot.[2]
                Ibid. Men of Letters
To be occasionally quoted is the only
fame I care for.
                                   Ibid.
A man gazing on the stars is proverbially at the mercy of the puddles
on the road.
                                   Ibid.
Trifles make up the happiness or the
misery of mortal life. The majority of
men slip into their graves without having encountered on their way thither

[1] When the Blue Bonnets came over the
Border. — SCOTT: *The Monastery* [1820],
Chap. 25, Border Ballad
[2] See Henry IV, page 115a–115b.
A chicken in every pot. — *Republican cam-
paign slogan* [1932]

any signal catastrophe or exaltation of fortune or feeling.

Dreamthorp. Men of Letters

The skin of the man of letters is peculiarly sensitive to the bite of the critical mosquito; and he lives in a climate in which such mosquitoes swarm. He is seldom stabbed to the heart — he is often killed by pin-pricks.

Ibid.

Every man's road in life is marked by the graves of his personal likings.

Ibid. On the Importance of a Man to Himself

In the wide arena of the world, failure and success are not accidents as we so frequently suppose, but the strictest justice. If you do your fair day's work, you are certain to get your fair day's wage — in praise or pudding, whichever happens to suit your taste.

Ibid.

The great man is the man who does a thing for the first time.

Ibid.

How deeply seated in the human heart is the liking for gardens and gardening.[1]

Ibid. Books and Gardens

A man does not plant a tree for himself, he plants it for posterity.

Ibid.

A good portrait is a kind of biography, and neither painter nor biographer can carry out his task satisfactorily unless he be admitted behind the scenes.

Ibid. On Vagabonds

CHARLES STUART CALVERLEY
[1831–1884]

I have a liking old
For thee, though manifold
Stories, I know, are told,
    Not to thy credit!

Ode to Tobacco. Stanza 2

I sit alone at present, dreaming darkly of a Dun.

In the Gloaming

[1] See Charles Dudley Warner, page 644b.

The farmer's daughter hath soft brown hair
(*Butter and eggs and a pound of cheese*)
And I met with a ballad, I can't say where,
That wholly consisted of lines like these.

Ballad, after William Morris [The Auld Wife]. Part I, Stanza 6

And this song is considered a perfect gem,
And as to the meaning, it's what you please.

Ibid. Part II, Stanza 4

Mine was a joke for the ages;
Full of intricate meaning and pith;
A feast for your scholars and sages —
How it would have rejoiced Sydney Smith!
'Tis such thoughts that ennoble a mortal;
And, singling him out from the herd,
Fling wide immortality's portal —
— But what was the word?

Flight. Stanza 9

As the flight of a bird in the air
Is the flight of a joke.

Ibid. Stanza 10

Forever; 'tis a single word!
    Our rude forefathers deemed it two:
Can you imagine so absurd
    A view?

Forever

When the forest-nymphs are beading
    Fern and flower with silvery dew
My infallible proceeding
    Is to wake, and think of you.

The 14th of February

MARY MAPES DODGE
[1831–1905]

Whimpy, little Whimpy,
    Cried so much one day,
His grandma couldn't stand it,
    And his mother ran away.

Little Whimpy. Stanza 1

Whenever a snowflake leaves the sky,
It turns and turns to say "Good-by!
Good-by, dear clouds, so cool and gray!"

Then lightly travels on its way.
> *Snowflakes*

Life is a mystery as deep as ever death
can be;
Yet oh, how sweet it is to us, this life
we live and see!
> *The Two Mysteries. Stanza 3*

But I believe that God is overhead;
And as life is to the living, so death is to
the dead.
> *Ibid. Stanza 5*

JAMES ABRAM GARFIELD
[1831–1881]

Fellow-citizens! God reigns, and the
Government at Washington still lives!
> *Speech on Assassination of Lincoln, New York [April 15, 1865]*

For mere vengeance I would do nothing. This nation is too great to look for
mere revenge. But for the security of
the future I would do everything.
> *Ibid.*

I am not willing that this discussion
should close without mention of the
value of a true teacher. Give me a log
hut, with only a simple bench, Mark
Hopkins [1] on one end and I on the
other, and you may have all the buildings, apparatus and libraries without
him.
> *Address to Williams College Alumni, New York [December 28, 1871][2]*

HELEN HUNT JACKSON
[1831–1885]

O suns and skies and clouds of June,
And flowers of June together,

[1] Mark Hopkins [1802–1887], president of
Williams College [1836–1872], and president
of the American Board of Commissioners for
Foreign Missions [1857–1881].
For Education is, Making Men;
So is it now, so was it when
Mark Hopkins sat on one end of a log
And James Garfield sat on the other.
ARTHUR GUITERMAN [1871–1943]:
Education
[2] In BURKE A. HINSDALE: *President Garfield and Education* [1882], P. 43.

Ye cannot rival for one hour
October's bright blue weather.
> *October's Bright Blue Weather. Stanza 1*

Find me the men on earth who care
Enough for faith or creed today
To seek a barren wilderness
For simple liberty to pray.
> *The Pilgrim Forefathers. Stanza 5*

On the king's gate the moss grew gray;
The king came not. They called him
dead
And made his eldest son one day
Slave in his father's stead.
> *Coronation. Stanza 10*

Oh, write of me, not "Died in bitter
pains,"
But "Emigrated to another star!"
> *Emigravit*

Father, I scarcely dare to pray,
So clear I see, now it is done,
How I have wasted half my day,
And left my work but just begun.
> *A Last Prayer. Stanza 1*

My body, eh. Friend Death, how now?
Why all this tedious pomp of writ?
Thou hast reclaimed it sure and slow
For half a century, bit by bit.
> *Habeas Corpus.[1] Stanza 1*

There is nothing so skilful in its own
defence as imperious pride.
> *Ramona [1884]. Chap. 13*

Wounded vanity knows when it is
mortally hurt; and limps off the field,
piteous, all disguises thrown away. But
pride carries its banner to the last.
> *Ibid.*

There cannot be found in the animal
kingdom a bat, or any other creature, so
blind in its own range of circumstance
and connection, as the greater majority
of human beings are in the bosoms of
their families.
> *Ibid.*

That indescribable expression peculiar to people who hope they have not
been asleep, but know they have.
> *Ibid. Chap. 14*

[1] Her last poem, left unfinished.

EDWARD ROBERT BULWER LYTTON, EARL OF LYTTON ("OWEN MEREDITH") [1]
[1831–1891]

Love thou the rose, yet leave it on its stem.[2]
> *The Wanderer* [1857]. *Prologue, Part I, 19*

But I am sick of all the din
That's made in praising Verdi,
Who only know a violin
Is not a hurdy-gurdy.
> *The Wanderer in France.*
> *"Prensus in Aegaeo"*

My life is a torn book. But at the end
A little page, quite fair, is saved, my friend,
Where thou didst write thy name.
> *The Wanderer in Holland.*
> *Jacqueline*

The heart of a man's like that delicate weed
Which requires to be trampled on, boldly indeed,
Ere it gives forth the fragrance you wish to extract.
> *Lucile* [1860]. *Part I, Canto 1, IV*

Whene'er I hear French spoken as I approve,
I feel myself quietly falling in love.
> *Ibid. Canto 2, XII*

We may live without poetry, music and art;
We may live without conscience and live without heart;
We may live without friends; we may live without books;
But civilized man can not live without cooks.
> *Ibid. XIX*

He may live without books, — what is knowledge but grieving?
He may live without hope, — what is hope but deceiving?
He may live without love, — what is passion but pining?

[1] Lord Lytton, the Viceroy, who still lives in the literary hall of fame as the author of Lucile — a vast, stale Victorian piece of poetry. — WILLIAM E. WOODWARD: *Meet General Grant* [1928], *Part 4, Chap. 30*
[2] See Emerson, page 504a.

But where is the man that can live without dining?
> *Lucile. Part I, Canto 2, XXIV*

The face the most fair to our vision allowed
Is the face we encounter and lose in the crowd.
The thought that most thrills our existence is one
Which, before we can frame it in language, is gone.
> *Ibid. Canto 5, I*

Ay, there are some good things in life, that fall not away with the rest.
And, of all best things upon earth, I hold that a faithful friend is the best.
> *Last Words of a Sensitive Second-Rate Poet*

Talk not of genius baffled. Genius is master of man.
Genius does what it must, and talent does what it can.
> *Ibid.*

PHILIP HENRY SHERIDAN
[1831–1888]

The only good Indians I ever saw were dead.[1]
> *Remark at Fort Cobb, Indian Territory* [*January, 1869*]

ROWLAND HOWARD
[*Floruit* 1876]

Waste not, want not, is a maxim I would teach.
Let your watchword be dispatch, and practise what you preach;
Do not let your chances like sunbeams pass you by,
For you never miss the water till the well runs dry.
> *You Never Miss the Water* [2]

[1] Edward Sylvester Ellis [1840–1916] reported that after Custer's fight with Black Kettle's band of Cheyenne Indians, the Comanche Chief Toch-a-way (Turtle Dove) was presented to General Sheridan. The Indian said: "Me Toch-a-way, me good Indian." The General's reply, as reported by Ellis, is given in the text; the phrase is more often heard in the version "The only good Indian is a dead Indian."
[2] In *Peterson's Magazine*, 1876.

LOUISA MAY ALCOTT
[1832–1888]

Christmas won't be Christmas without any presents.
> *Little Women* [*1868*]. *Chap. 1*

A little kingdom I possess,
Where thoughts and feelings dwell;
And very hard the task I find
Of governing it well.
> Quoted in EDNAH D. CHENEY:
> *Louisa May Alcott, Her Life,
> Letters, and Journals* [*1889*].
> *Chap. 3, My Kingdom,*[1] *Stanza 1*

I do not ask for any crown
But that which all may win;
Nor try to conquer any world
Except the one within.
> *Ibid. Stanza 4*

I had a pleasant time with my mind,
for it was happy.
> *Ibid.*

Resolved to take Fate by the throat
and shake a living out of her.
> *Ibid.*

For such as he there is no death; —
His life the eternal life commands;
Above man's aims his nature rose.
The wisdom of a just content
Made one small spot a continent,
And tuned to poetry Life's prose.[2]
> *Ibid. Chap. 7, Thoreau's Flute,*[3]
> *Stanza 2*

My definition [of a philosopher] is
of a man up in a balloon, with his family and friends holding the ropes which
confine him to earth and trying to haul
him down.
> *Ibid. Chap. 10*

Now I am beginning to live a little,
and feel less like a sick oyster at low
tide.
> *Ibid. Chap. 11*

Philosophers sit in their sylvan hall
And talk of the duties of man,
Of Chaos and Cosmos, Hegel and Kant,
With the Oversoul well in the van;
All on their hobbies they amble away

[1] Written at the age of thirteen.
[2] The word "tuned" is frequently misprinted as "turned."
[3] In *The Atlantic Monthly*, September,
1863.

And a terrible dust they make;
Disciples devout both gaze and adore,
As daily they listen and bake.
> *Philosophers* [1]

ELIZABETH AKERS ALLEN
[1832–1911]

Backward, turn backward, O Time, in
your flight,
Make me a child again just for tonight!
> *Rock Me to Sleep* [*1860*].
> *Stanza 1*

Behold, we live through all things —
famine, thirst,
Bereavement, pain; all grief and
misery,
All woe and sorrow; life inflicts its
worst
On soul and body — but we can not die,
Though we be sick, and tired, and faint,
and worn, —
Lo, all things can be borne!
> *Endurance. Stanza 5*

Unremembered and afar
I watched you as I watched a star,
Through darkness struggling into view,
And loved you better than you knew.
> *Left Behind. Stanza 5*

Let all unselfish spirits heed
The story of Johnny Appleseed.
He had another and prouder name
In far New England, whence he came,
But by this title, and this alone,
Was the kindly wanderer loved and
known.
> *Johnny Appleseed.*[2] *Stanza 1*

Carve not upon a stone when I am dead
The praises which remorseful mourners
give

[1] Quoted in FLORENCE WHITING BROWN:
Alcott and the Concord School of Philosophy
[1926], *P. 46.*
[2] John Chapman [1774–1847].
Remember Johnny Appleseed,
All ye who love the apple;
He served his kind by Word and Deed,
In God's grand greenwood chapel.
  WILLIAM HENRY VENABLE [1836–1918]:
> *Johnny Appleseed, St. 25*
See Vachel Lindsay, page 903b.

To women's graves — a tardy recom-
pense —
But speak them while I live.¹
Till Death. Stanza 6

SIR EDWIN ARNOLD
[1832–1904]

Shall any gazer see with mortal eyes,
Or any searcher know by mortal mind?
Veil after veil will lift — but there must
be
Veil upon veil behind.
The Light of Asia [1879].
Book VIII

Weep awhile, if ye are fain, —
Sunshine still must follow rain;
Only not at death, for death,
Now I know, is that first breath
Which our souls draw when we enter
Life, which is of all life centre.
After Death In Arabia

Nor ever once ashamed
So we be named
Press-men; Slaves of the Lamp; Serv-
ants of Light.
The Tenth Muse. Stanza 18

Not an eye, however dull,
But seems — somewhere — beautiful.
Facies Non Omnibus Una

We are they who will not take
From palace, priest, or code,
A meaner Law than "Brotherhood" —
A lower Lord than God.
*Armageddon: A War Song of
the Future. Stanza 4*

¹ I fancy when I go to rest some one will
bring to light
Some kindly word or goodly act long buried
out of sight;
But, if it's all the same to you, just give to
me, instead,
The bouquets while I'm living and the knock-
ing when I'm dead.
Louis Edwin Thayer [1878–]:
Of Post-Mortem Praises, St. 1
If with pleasure you are viewing any work a
man is doing,
If you like him or you love him, tell him now.
. . . .
Do not wait till life is over and he's under-
neath the clover,
For he cannot read his tombstone when he's
dead!
Berton Braley [1882–]: *Do It
Now, St. 1 and 2*

Somewhere there waiteth in this world
of ours
For one lone soul, another lonely soul —
Each chasing each through all the
weary hours,
And meeting strangely at one sudden
goal;
Then blend they — like green leaves
with golden flowers,
Into one beautiful and perfect whole —
And life's long night is ended, and the
way
Lies open onward to eternal day.¹
Destiny

We are the voices of the wandering
wind,
Which moan for rest and rest can never
find;
Lo! as the wind is, so is mortal life,
A moan, a sigh, a sob, a storm, a strife.
The Deva's Song

WILLIAM CROSWELL DOANE
[1832–1913]

Their Lent is over, and their Easter
won.
Death

I am quite sure he thinks that I am
God —
Since he is God on whom each one de-
pends
For life and all things that His bounty
sends —
My dear old dog, most constant of all
friends.
Cluny

LEWIS CARROLL
(CHARLES LUTWIDGE
DODGSON)
[1832–1898]

All in the golden afternoon
Full leisurely we glide
For both our oars, with little skill
By little arms are plied

¹ A sublime hope cheers ever the faithful
heart, that elsewhere, in other regions of the
universal powers, souls are now acting, enduring and daring, which can love us, and which
we can love. — Emerson: *Friendship* [1841]

While little hands make vain pretence
Our wanderings to guide.
> *Alice's Adventures in Wonderland* [*1865*]. *Introduction, Stanza 1*

"What is the use of a book," thought Alice, "without pictures or conversations?"
> *Ibid. Chap. 1*

Do cats eat bats? . . . Do bats eat cats?
> *Ibid.*

Curiouser and curiouser!
> *Ibid. Chap. 2*

How doth the little crocodile
Improve his shining tail,
And pour the waters of the Nile
On every golden scale! [1]

How cheerfully he seems to grin,
How neatly spreads his claws,
And welcomes little fishes in
With gently smiling jaws!
> *Ibid.*

"I'll be judge, I'll be jury," said cunning old Fury; "I'll try the whole cause, and condemn you to death."
> *Ibid. Chap. 3*

Oh my fur and whiskers!
> *Ibid. Chap. 4*

"I can't explain *myself*, I'm afraid, sir," said Alice, "because I'm not myself, you see."

"I don't see," said the Caterpillar.
> *Ibid. Chap. 5*

"You are old, Father William," the young man said,
"And your hair has become very white;
And yet you incessantly stand on your head —
Do you think, at your age, it is right?" [2]
> *Ibid. Stanza 1*

"In my youth," said his father, "I took to the law,
And argued each case with my wife;
And the muscular strength, which it gave to my jaw,
Has lasted the rest of my life."
> *Ibid. Stanza 6*

"I have answered three questions, and that is enough,"

[1] See Isaac Watts, page 302b.
[2] See Southey, page 426a.

Said his father. "Don't give yourself airs!
Do you think I can listen all day to such stuff?
Be off, or I'll kick you down-stairs!"
> *Alice's Adventures in Wonderland. Chap. 5, Stanza 8*

"I shall sit here," he said, "on and off, for days and days."
> *Ibid. Chap. 6*

"If everybody minded their own business," said the Duchess in a hoarse growl, "the world would go round a deal faster than it does."
> *Ibid.*

"Talking of axes," said the Duchess, "chop off her head!"
> *Ibid.*

Speak roughly to your little boy,
And beat him when he sneezes:
He only does it to annoy,
Because he knows it teases.
> *Ibid.*

"All right," said the Cat; and this time it vanished quite slowly, beginning with the end of the tail, and ending with the grin, which remained some time after the rest of it had gone.
> *Ibid.*

"Then you should say what you mean," the March Hare went on.

"I do," Alice hastily replied; "at least — at least I mean what I say — that's the same thing, you know."

"Not the same thing a bit!" said the Hatter. "Why, you might just as well say that 'I see what I eat' is the same thing as 'I eat what I see'!"
> *Ibid. Chap. 7*

"It was the *best* butter," the March Hare meekly replied.
> *Ibid.*

Twinkle, twinkle, little bat!
How I wonder what you're at!
Up above the world you fly,
Like a tea-tray in the sky.
> *Ibid.*

"Take some more tea," the March Hare said to Alice, very earnestly.

"I've had nothing yet," Alice replied in an offended tone: "so I can't take more."

"You mean you can't take *less*," said the Hatter: "it's very easy to take *more* than nothing."
Alice's Adventures in Wonderland.
Chap. 7

They drew all manner of things — everything that begins with an M . . . , such as mouse-traps, and the moon, and memory, and muchness — you know you say things are "much of a muchness."
Ibid.

The Queen turned crimson with fury, and after glaring at her for a moment like a wild beast, began screaming, "Off with her head! Off with —"
Ibid. Chap. 8

"Tut, tut, child," said the Duchess. "Everything's got a moral if only you can find it."
Ibid. Chap. 9

And the moral of that is — "Oh, 'tis love, 'tis love, that makes the world go round!"
Ibid.

Take care of the sense and the sounds will take care of themselves.
Ibid.

"We called him Tortoise because he taught us," said the Mock Turtle angrily. "Really you are very dull!"
Ibid.

"Reeling and Writhing, of course, to begin with," the Mock Turtle replied, "and the different branches of Arithmetic — Ambition, Distraction, Uglification, and Derision."
Ibid.

"Will you walk a little faster?" said a whiting to a snail,
"There's a porpoise close behind us, and he's treading on my tail."
Ibid. Chap. 10

"Will you, won't you, will you, won't you, will you join the dance?"
Ibid.

"The further off from England the nearer is to France —
Then turn not pale, beloved snail, but come and join the dance."
Ibid. Stanza 3

'Tis the voice of the Lobster: I heard him declare
"You have baked me too brown, I must sugar my hair." [1]
Alice's Adventures in Wonderland.
Chap. 10, Stanza 3

Soup of the evening, beautiful soup!
Ibid.

Sentence first — verdict afterwards.
Ibid. Chap. 12

Child of the pure, unclouded brow
And dreaming eyes of wonder!
Though time be fleet and I and thou
Are half a life asunder,
Thy loving smile will surely hail
The love-gift of a fairy-tale.
Alice Through the Looking-Glass [*1872*]. *Introduction, Stanza 1*

"The horror of that moment," the King went on, "I shall never, *never* forget!"
"You will, though," the Queen said, "if you don't make a memorandum of it."
Ibid. Chap. 1

'Twas brillig, and the slithy toves
Did gyre and gimble in the wabe;
All mimsy were the borogoves,
And the mome raths outgrabe.
Ibid. Jabberwocky, Stanza 1

"Beware the Jabberwock, my son!
The jaws that bite, the claws that catch!
Beware the Jubjub bird, and shun
The frumious Bandersnatch!"
Ibid. Stanza 2

And, as in uffish thought he stood,
The Jabberwock, with eyes of flame,
Came whiffling through the tulgey wood,
And burbled as it came!
Ibid. Stanza 4

One, two! One, two! And through and through
The vorpal blade went snicker-snack!
He left it dead, and with its head
He went galumphing back.
Ibid. Stanza 5

"And hast thou slain the Jabberwock?
Come to my arms, my beamish boy!

[1] See Isaac Watts, page 302b.

O frabjous day! Callooh! Callay!"
He chortled in his joy.
Alice Through the Looking-Glass.
Chap. 1, Jabberwocky, Stanza 6

Curtsey while you're thinking what
to say. It saves time.
Ibid. Chap. 2

"Now! Now!" cried the Queen.
"Faster! Faster!"
Ibid.

"A slow sort of country!" said the
Queen. "Now, *here,* you see, it takes all
the running you can do, to keep in the
same place. If you want to get somewhere else, you must run at least twice
as fast as that!"
Ibid.

Speak in French when you can't
think of the English for a thing — turn
out your toes when you walk — and remember who you are!
Ibid.

"If you think we're wax-works," he
said, "you ought to pay, you know.
Wax-works weren't made to be looked
at for nothing. Nohow!"
Ibid. Chap. 4

"Contrariwise," continued Tweedledee, "if it was so, it might be; and if it
were so, it would be; but as it isn't, it
ain't. That's logic."
Ibid.

The sun was shining on the sea,
Shining with all his might:
He did his very best to make
The billows smooth and bright —
And this was odd, because it was
The middle of the night.
Ibid. The Walrus and the
Carpenter, Stanza 1

The Walrus and the Carpenter
Were walking close at hand:
They wept like anything to see
Such quantities of sand:
"If this were only cleared away,"
They said, "it would be grand!"
Ibid. Stanza 4

"If seven maids with seven mops
Swept it for half a year,
Do you suppose," the Walrus said,
"That they could get it clear?"

"I doubt it," said the Carpenter.
And shed a bitter tear.
Alice Through the Looking-
Glass. Chap. 4, The Walrus and
the Carpenter, Stanza 5

"O Oysters, come and walk with us!"
The Walrus did beseech.
"A pleasant walk, a pleasant talk,
Along the briny beach."
Ibid. Stanza 6

And thick and fast they came at last,
And more, and more, and more —
All hopping through the frothy waves,
And scrambling to the shore.
Ibid. Stanza 9

"The time has come," the Walrus said,
"To talk of many things:
Of shoes — and ships — and sealing-
wax —
Of cabbages — and kings —
And why the sea is boiling hot —
And whether pigs have wings."
Ibid. Stanza 11

"But wait a bit," the Oysters cried,
"Before we have our chat;
For some of us are out of breath,
And all of us are fat!"
Ibid. Stanza 12

The Carpenter said nothing but
"The butter's spread too thick!"
Ibid. Stanza 16

"I weep for you," the Walrus said:
"I deeply sympathize."
With sobs and tears he sorted out
Those of the largest size,
Holding his pocket-handkerchief
Before his streaming eyes.
Ibid. Stanza 17

But answer came there none —
And this was scarcely odd, because
They'd eaten every one.
Ibid. Stanza 18

Twopence a week, and jam every
other day.
Ibid. Chap. 5

"The rule is, jam to-morrow, and
jam yesterday — but never jam today."

"It must come sometimes to 'jam today,' " Alice objected.

"No, it can't," said the Queen. "It's

jam every other day: to-day isn't any other day, you know."
Alice Through the Looking-Glass. Chap. 5
"It's a poor sort of memory that only works backwards," the Queen remarked.
Ibid.
Consider anything, only don't cry!
Ibid.
"There's no use trying," she said: "one *can't* believe impossible things."
"I daresay you haven't had much practice," said the Queen. "When I was your age, I always did it for half-an-hour a day. Why, sometimes I've believed as many as six impossible things before breakfast."
Ibid.
They gave it me — for an unbirthday present.
Ibid. Chap. 6
"But 'glory' doesn't mean 'a nice knock-down argument,'" Alice objected.
"When *I* use a word," Humpty Dumpty said, in rather a scornful tone, "it means just what I choose it to mean — neither more nor less."
"The question is," said Alice, "whether you *can* make words mean so many different things."
"The question is," said Humpty Dumpty, "which is to be master — that's all."
Ibid.
It's as large as life and twice as natural.
Ibid. Chap. 7
His answer trickled through my head, Like water through a sieve.
Ibid. Chap. 8
What's the French for fiddle-de-dee?
Ibid. Chap. 9
It isn't etiquette to cut any one you've been introduced to. Remove the joint!
Ibid.
He would answer to "Hi!" or to any loud cry
Such as "Fry me!" or "Fritter my wig!"
To "What-you-may-call-um!" or

"What-was-his-name!"
But especially "Thing-um-a-jig!"
The Hunting of the Snark [1876].
Fit I, Stanza 9
"What's the good of Mercator's North Poles and Equators,
Tropics, Zones and Meridian Lines?"
So the Bellman would cry: and the crew would reply
"They are merely conventional signs!"
Ibid. Fit II, Stanza 3
It frequently breakfasts at five-o'clock tea,
And dines on the following day.
Ibid. Stanza 17
There was silence supreme! Not a shriek, not a scream,
Scarcely even a howl or a groan,
As the man they called "Ho!" told his story of woe
In an antediluvian tone.
Ibid. Fit III, Stanza 3
It is this, it is this that oppresses my soul.
Ibid. Stanza 11
And my heart is like nothing so much as a bowl
Brimming over with quivering curds.
Ibid.
You may charge me with murder — or want of sense —
(We are all of us weak at times):
But the slightest approach to a false pretence
Was never among my crimes!
Ibid. Fit IV, Stanza 4
They sought it with thimbles, they sought it with care;
They pursued it with forks and hope;
They threatened its life with a railway-share;
They charmed it with smiles and soap.
Ibid. Fit V, Stanza 1
For the Snark *was* a Boojum, you see.
Ibid. Fit VIII, Stanza 9
He thought he saw an Elephant,
That practised on a fife:
He looked again, and found it was
A letter from his wife.
"At length I realize," he said,
"The bitterness of Life!"
Sylvie and Bruno [1889]. *Chap. 5*

He thought he saw a Buffalo
  Upon the chimney-piece:
He looked again, and found it was
  His sister's husband's niece.
        Sylvie and Bruno. Chap. 6
He thought he saw an Albatross
  That fluttered round the lamp:
He looked again, and found it was
  A penny-postage-stamp.
"You'd best be getting home," he said,
  "The nights are very damp."
        Ibid. Chap. 12

BENJAMIN H. HILL
[1832–1882]

He was a foe without hate, a friend without treachery, a soldier without cruelty, and a victim without murmuring. He was a public officer without vices, a private citizen without wrong, a neighbor without reproach, a Christian without hypocrisy, and a man without guilt. He was Caesar without his ambition, Frederick without his tyranny, Napoleon without his selfishness, and Washington without his reward.
        Tribute to Robert E. Lee [1]

NORA PERRY
[1832–1896]

Tying her bonnet under her chin,
She tied her raven ringlets in;
But not alone in the silken snare
Did she catch her lovely floating hair,
For, tying her bonnet under her chin,
She tied a young man's heart within.
        The Love-Knot. Stanza 1
What silences we keep, year after year,
With those who are most near to us,
  and dear!
        Too Late. Stanza 1
Some day of days, threading the street
  With idle, heedless pace,
  Unlooking for such grace,
I shall behold your face!
        Some Day of Days. Stanza 1
Who knows the thoughts of a child?
        Who Knows? Stanza 1

[1] Quoted in *Robert E. Lee* [1911], by THOMAS NELSON PAGE.

They sat and combed their beautiful
  hair,
Their long, bright tresses, one by one,
As they laughed and talked in the
  chamber there,
After the revel was done.
        After the Ball. Stanza 1

HENRY CLAY WORK
[1832–1884]

Father, dear father, come home with
  me now,
  The clock in the belfry strikes one;
You said you were coming right home
  from the shop
  As soon as your day's work was done.
        Come Home, Father [1864].
        Stanza 1
Bring the good old bugle, boys, we'll
  sing another song;
Sing it with a spirit that will start the
  world along,
Sing it as we used to sing it — fifty
  thousand strong,
  As we were marching through
  Georgia.
        Marching Through Georgia
        [1865]. *Stanza 1*
"Hurrah! hurrah! we bring the Jubilee!
Hurrah! Hurrah! the flag that makes
  you free!"
So we sang the chorus from Atlanta to
  the sea,
  As we were marching through
  Georgia.
        Ibid. Chorus

WILHELM BUSCH [1]
[1832–1908]

Youth should heed the older-witted
  When they say, don't go too far —
Now their sins are all committed,
  Lord, how virtuous they are!
        Pious Helen (Die fromme
        Helene)

[1] Famous artist and cartoonist, author of the German classic for children, *Max and Moritz* [1865].

ISAAC HILL BROMLEY
[1833–1898]

Listen! John A. Logan is the Head Center, the Hub, the King Pin, the Main Spring, Mogul and Mugwump [1] of the final plot by which partisanship was installed in the Commission.
Editorial in New York Tribune
[February 16, 1877]

Bring me honey of Hymettus, bring me stores of Attic salt;
I am weary of the commonplace, to dulness call a halt!
These dinner speeches tire me, they are tedious, flat, and stale:
From a hundred thousand banquet tables comes a melancholy wail,
As a hundred thousand banqueters sit up in evening dress
And salute each mouldy chestnut with a signal of distress.
Our Chauncey.[2] *Stanza 2*

MARY ABIGAIL DODGE
("GAIL HAMILTON")
[1833–1896]

Whatever an author puts between the two covers of his book is public property; whatever of himself he does not put there is his private property, as much as if he had never written a word.
Country Living and Country Thinking [1862]. Preface

The moment an audacious head is lifted one inch above the general level, pop! goes the unerring rifle of some biographical sharpshooter, and it is all over with the unhappy owner.
Skirmishes and Sketches. The New School of Biography

What's virtue in man can't be vice in a cat.
Both Sides

[1] A mugwump is a person educated beyond his intellect. — HORACE PORTER [1837–1921] in the Cleveland-Blaine campaign [1884]
[2] In praise of Chauncey M. Depew, read at the annual dinner of the New York Yale Alumni Association [January 23, 1891].

ADAM LINDSAY GORDON
[1833–1870]

Question not, but live and labour
Till yon goal be won,
Helping every feeble neighbour,
Seeking help from none;
Life is mostly froth and bubble,[1]
Two things stand like stone —
Kindness in another's trouble,
Courage in our own.
Ye Wearie Wayfarer. Finis Exoptatus, Stanza 8

For good undone and gifts misspent and resolutions vain,
'Tis somewhat late to trouble. This I know —
I should live the same life over, if I had to live again;
And the chances are I go where most men go.
The Sick Stockrider

A little season of love and laughter,
Of light and life, and pleasure and pain,
And a horror of outer darkness after,
And dust returneth to dust again.
The Swimmer

In a thousand years we shall all forget
The things that trouble us now.
After the Quarrel

On earth there's little worth a sigh,
And nothing worth a tear!
To My Sister. Stanza 8

Lay me low, my work is done,
I am weary. Lay me low.
Valedictory

JOHN JAMES INGALLS
[1833–1900]

Every man is the center of a circle, whose fatal circumference he can not pass.
Eulogy on Benjamin Hill, U. S. Senate [January 23, 1882]

The purification of politics is an iridescent dream.
Article in New York World [1890]

Next in profusion to the divine profusion of water, light and air, those three physical facts which render exist-

[1] See Gay, page 209a.

ence possible, may be reckoned the universal beneficence of grass.

Blue Grass

I knock unbidden once at every gate!
If sleeping, wake; if feasting, rise before
I turn away. It is the hour of fate.

Opportunity [1891]

ROBERT GREEN INGERSOLL
[1833–1899]

Like an armed warrior, like a plumed knight, James G. Blaine marched down the halls of the American Congress and threw his shining lance full and fair against the brazen forehead of every traitor to his country and every maligner of his fair reputation.

Speech, nominating Blaine for President, at the National Republican Convention, Cincinnati [June 15, 1876]

Though Scotland boasts a thousand names,
Of patriot, king and peer,
The noblest, grandest of them all
Was loved and cradled here.

The Birthplace of Burns, Ayr [1]
[August 19, 1878]

These heroes are dead. They died for liberty — they died for us. They are at rest. They sleep in the land they made free, under the flag they rendered stainless, under the solemn pines, the sad hemlocks, the tearful willows, the embracing vines. They sleep beneath the shadows of the clouds, careless alike of sunshine or storm, each in the windowless palace of rest. Earth may run red with other wars — they are at peace. In the midst of battles, in the roar of conflict, they found the serenity of death.

Vision of War [Speech at Indianapolis, September 21, 1876]

I am the inferior of any man whose rights I trample under foot. Men are not superior by reason of the accidents

[1] This poem hangs in Burns's birthplace, Ayr.

of race or color. They are superior who have the best heart — the best brain.

Liberty

The superior man is the providence of the inferior. He is eyes for the blind, strength for the weak, and a shield for the defenseless. He stands erect by bending above the fallen. He rises by lifting others.

Ibid.

Every cradle asks us, "Whence?" and every coffin, "Whither?" The poor barbarian, weeping above his dead, can answer these questions as intelligently as the robed priest of the most authentic creed.

Address at a Little Boy's Grave

We, too, have our religion, and it is this: Help for the living, hope for the dead.

Ibid.

Few rich men own their own property. The property owns them.

Address to the McKinley League, New York [October 29, 1896]

An honest God is the noblest work of man.

The Gods

In nature there are neither rewards nor punishments — there are consequences.

Some Reasons Why

Justice is the only worship.
Love is the only priest.
Ignorance is the only slavery.
Happiness is the only good.
The time to be happy is now,
The place to be happy is here,
The way to be happy is to make others so.

Creed

DAVID ROSS LOCKE
("PETROLEUM V. NASBY")
[1833–1888]

The contract 'twixt Hannah, God and me,
Was not for one or twenty years, but for eternity.

Hannah Jane [1871]. Stanza 29

SIR LEWIS MORRIS
[1833–1907]

The wind that sighs before the dawn
Chases the gloom of night,
The curtains of the East are drawn,
And suddenly — 'tis light.
Le Vent de l'Esprit. Stanza 1

Call no faith false which e'er hath
brought
Relief to any laden life,
Cessation from the pain of thought,
Refreshment 'mid the dust of strife.
Tolerance. Stanza 1

EDMUND CLARENCE
STEDMAN
[1833–1908]

Prison-mate and dock-yard fellow,
Blades to Meg and Molly dear,
Off to capture Porto Bello
Sailed with Morgan the Buccaneer!
Morgan.[1] Stanza 1

Crops failed; wealth took a flight;
house, treasure, land,
Slipped from my hold — thus plenty
comes and goes.
One friend I had, but he too loosed his
hand
(Or was it I?) the year I met with Rose.
The World Well Lost. Stanza 2

"Oh, anywhere! Forward! 'Tis all the
same, Colonel:
You'll find lovely fighting along the
whole line!"
Kearny[2] at Seven Pines. Stanza 3

Look on this cast, and know the hand
That bore a nation in its hold:
From this mute witness understand
What Lincoln was, — how large of
mould.
The Hand of Lincoln. Stanza 1

Give us a man of God's own mould,
Born to marshal his fellow-men;
One whose fame is not bought and sold
At the stroke of a politician's pen.
Wanted — A Man. Stanza 2

[1] The old bold mate of Henry Morgan. —
JOHN MASEFIELD [1878–   ]: *Captain Stratton's Fancy*
[2] General Philip Kearny [1815–1862].

Not thou, not thou — 'tis we
Are deaf, are dumb, are blind!
Helen Keller. Stanza 4

JULIA LOUISE MATILDA
WOODRUFF
[1833–1909]

Out of the strain of the Doing,
Into the peace of the Done.
Harvest Home [*1910*]

JOHN EMERICH EDWARD
DALBERG, LORD ACTON
[1834–1902]

Power tends to corrupt; absolute
power corrupts absolutely.
*Letter to Bishop Mandell
Creighton, 1887*

HORATIO ALGER
[1834–1899]

'Twas on Lake Erie's broad expanse,
One bright midsummer day,
The gallant steamer Ocean Queen
Swept proudly on her way.
John Maynard.[1] Stanza 1

Three hundred grateful voices rise
In praise to God that He
Hath saved them from the fearful fire,
And from the engulfing sea.
Ibid. Stanza 11

GEORGE ARNOLD
[1834–1865]

"Learn while you're young," he often
said,
"There is much to enjoy down here be-
low;
Life for the living, and rest for the
dead!"
Said the jolly old pedagogue, long ago.
The Jolly Old Pedagogue. Stanza 2

[1] John Maynard was a pilot on a steamboat
plying between Detroit and Buffalo. The
steamer did not carry boats, and one summer
afternoon, when proceeding with large quantities of resin and tar on board, it caught fire,
seven miles from Buffalo. Passengers and crew
crowded the forward part of the ship. John
Maynard stayed at the helm and beached **the**

"The living need charity more than the dead."

The Jolly Old Pedagogue. Stanza 3

I,
Being dry,
Sit, idly sipping here
My Beer.

Beer

SIR JOHN LUBBOCK, LORD AVEBURY
[1834–1913]

The world would be better and brighter if our teachers would dwell on the Duty of Happiness as well as on the Happiness of Duty, for we ought to be as cheerful as we can, if only because to be happy ourselves is a most effectual contribution to the happiness of others.

The Pleasures of Life
[1887–1889]

The idle man does not know what it is to enjoy rest. Hard work, moreover, not only tends to give us rest for the body, but, what is even more important, peace to the mind.

Ibid.

SABINE BARING-GOULD
[1834–1924]

Onward, Christian soldiers,
    Marching as to war,
With the Cross of Jesus
    Going on before.

Onward, Christian Soldiers

Through the night of doubt and sorrow
Onward goes the pilgrim band,
Singing songs of expectation,
Marching to the Promised Land.

*Through the Night of Doubt
and Sorrow: Translated from
the Danish of B. S. INGEMANN*

Now the day is over,
    Night is drawing nigh;
Shadows of the evening
    Steal across the sky.

Now the Day Is Over. Stanza 1

Comfort every sufferer
Watching late in pain;
Those who plan some evil,
    From their sin restrain.

Now the Day Is Over. Stanza 5

CHARLES FARRAR BROWNE ("ARTEMUS WARD")
[1834–1867]

The Puritans nobly fled from a land of despotism to a land of freedim, where they could not only enjoy their own religion, but could prevent everybody else from enjoyin *his.*

The London Punch Letters.[1]
No. V [1866]

My pollertics, like my religion, being of an exceedin' accommodatin' character.

The Crisis

The fack can't be no longer disgised that a Krysis is onto us.

Ibid.

I am not a politician, and my other habits are good.

Fourth of July Oration

The prevailin' weakness of most public men is to Slop over. G. Washington never slopt over.

Ibid.

I can't sing. As a singist I am not a success. I am saddest when I sing. So are those who hear me. They are sadder even than I am.

Artemus Ward's Lecture

N. B. This is rote Sarcastikul.

A Visit to Brigham Young

Did you ever have the measels, and if so, how many?

The Census

I have alreddy given Two cousins to the war, & I stand reddy to sacrifiss my wife's brother ruther 'n not see the rebelyin krusht. And if wuss comes to wuss, I'll shed ev'ry drop of blud my able-bodid relations has got.

To the Prince of Wales

---

ship, all lives being saved except his own. —
JOHN B. GOUGH [1817–1886]: *Sermon*

[1] The Puritan's idea of Hell is a place where everybody has to mind his own business. —
Attributed to WENDELL PHILLIPS [1811–1884]

Why is this thus? What is the reason of this thusness?

Moses, the Sassy

He is dreadfully married. "He's the most married man I ever saw in my life."

Ibid.

Let us all be happy and live within our means, even if we have to borrow the money to do it with.

Natural History

The sun has a right to "set" where it wants to, and so, I may add, has a hen.

A Morman Romance. IV

They cherish his mem'ry, and them as sell picturs of his birth-place, etc., make it prof'tible cherishin' it.

At the Tomb of Shakespeare

GEORGE LOUIS PALMELLA BUSSON DU MAURIER
[1834–1896]

That aristocratic flavor, so grateful and comforting to scholar and ignoramus alike, which the costly British public-school system (and the British accent) alone can impart to a dead language.

Peter Ibbetson [1891]. Page 49

The wretcheder one is, the more one smokes; and the more one smokes, the wretcheder one gets — a vicious circle!

Ibid. Page 135

Songs without words are best.

Ibid. Page 162

Happiness is like time and space — we make and measure it ourselves; it is a fancy — as big, as little, as you please; just a thing of contrasts and comparisons.

Ibid. Page 399

All will be well for us all, and of such a kind that all who do not sigh for the moon will be well content.

Ibid. Page 415

He had never heard such music as this, never dreamt such music was possible. He was conscious, while it lasted, that he saw deeper into the beauty, the sadness of things, the very heart of

them, and their pathetic evanescence, as with a new inner eye — even into eternity itself, beyond the veil.

Trilby.[1] Part 1

Lovely female shapes are terrible complicators of the difficulties and dangers of this earthly life, especially for their owner.

Ibid.

A wave of religious emotion rolled over Little Billee and submerged him; swept him off his little legs, swept him out of his little self, drowned him in a great seething surge of love — love of his kind, love of love, love of life, love of death, love of all that is and ever was and ever will be.

Ibid. Part III

That is the worst of those dear people who have charm; they are so terrible to do without, when once you have got accustomed to them and all their ways.

Ibid. Part V

She was one of those rarely gifted beings who cannot look or speak or even stir without waking up (and satisfying) some vague longing that lies dormant in the hearts of most of us.

Ibid. Part VII

There can be prayers without words just as well as songs, I suppose.

Ibid. Part VIII

Grief tires more than anything, and brings a deeper slumber.

Ibid.

A little work, a little play,
To keep us going — and so, good-day!

A little warmth, a little light,
Of love's bestowing — and so, good-night! [2]

[1] *Trilby* was published serially in *Harper's Monthly,* beginning with the January, 1894, issue.
[2]   La vie est vaine:
       Un peu d'amour,
       Un peu de haine . . .
       Et puis — Bonjour!

    La vie est brève:
       Un peu d'espoir,
       Un peu de rêve

A little fun, to match the sorrow
Of each day's growing — and so, good-
morrow!

A little trust that when we die
We reap our sowing! and so — good-
by!
Trilby. Part VIII

CHARLES WILLIAM ELIOT
[1834–1926]

In the modern world the intelligence
of public opinion is the one indispensable condition of social progress.
Inaugural Address [1869]
Enter to grow in wisdom.
*Inscription on the Outside of the
1890 Gate to Harvard Yard*
Depart better to serve thy country
and mankind.
*Inscription on the Inside of the
1890 Gate to Harvard Yard*
To the Fifty-fourth Regiment of
Massachusetts Infantry:
The white officers, taking life and
honor in their hands, cast in their lot
with men of a despised race unproved
in war, and risked death as inciters of
servile insurrection if taken prisoners,
besides encountering all the common
perils of camp march and battle.
The black rank and file volunteered
when disaster clouded the Union cause,
served without pay for eighteen months
till given that of white troops, faced
threatened enslavement if captured,
were brave in action, patient under
heavy and dangerous labors, and cheerful amid hardships and privations.
Together they gave to the nation and
the world undying proof that Americans
of African descent possess the pride,
courage, and devotion of the patriot
soldier. One hundred and eighty thousand such Americans enlisted under the
Union flag in 1863–1865.
*Inscription on Robert Gould
Shaw Monument, Boston Common [1897]*

Et puis — Bon soir!
LEON MONTENAEKEN [1859–?]:
Peu de Chose

Carrier of news and knowledge
Instrument of trade and commerce
Promoter of mutal acquaintance
Among men and nations and hence
Of peace and good will.

Carrier of love and sympathy
Messenger of friendship
Consoler of the lonely
Servant of the scattered family
Enlarger of the public life.
*Inscriptions for the East and
West Pavilions, Post Office,
Washington, D. C.*[1]

WALTER KITTREDGE
[1834–1905]

We're tenting tonight on the old camp-
ground,
Give us a song to cheer
Our weary hearts, a song of home
And friends we love so dear.
*Tenting on the Old Camp-ground.
Stanza 1*

WILLIAM MORRIS
[1834–1896]

I know a little garden-close,
Set thick with lily and red rose,
Where I would wander if I might
From dewy morn to dewy night.
*The Life and Death of Jason
[1867]. A Garden by the Sea,
Stanza 1*
The idle singer of an empty day.
*The Earthly Paradise [1868–
1870]. An Apology, Stanza 1*
Dreamer of dreams, born out of my
due time,

[1] These inscriptions were edited by WOOD-
ROW WILSON, to read:
Carrier of news and knowledge
Instrument of trade and
Promoter of mutual acquaintance
Of peace and good will
Among men and nations.

Messenger of sympathy and love
Servant of parted friends
Consoler of the lonely
Bond of the scattered family
Enlarger of the common life.

Why should I strive to set the crooked
straight?
The Earthly Paradise. An
Apology, Stanza 4

Forget six counties overhung with
smoke,
Forget the snorting steam and piston
stroke,
Forget the spreading of the hideous
town;
Think rather of the pack-horse on the
down,
And dream of London, small, and white,
and clean.
Ibid. Prologue

Love is enough, though the world be
a-waning.
Love Is Enough

RODEN BERKELEY WRIOTHESLEY NOEL
[1834–1894]

After battle sleep is best,
After noise, tranquillity.
The Old

The bass eternal of the sea.
Beatrice

RICHARD REALF
[1834–1878]

Back of the canvas that throbs, the
painter is hinted and hidden;
Into the statue that breathes, the soul
of the sculptor is bidden.
Indirection. Stanza 3

Back of the sound broods the silence,
back of the gift stands the giving;
Back of the hand that receives thrill
the sensitive nerves of receiving.
Ibid. Stanza 4

ABRAM JOSEPH RYAN
[1834–1886]

But far on the deep there are billows
That never shall break on the beach;
And I have heard songs in the Silence
That never shall float into speech.
Song of the Mystic. Stanza 9

Hearts that are great are always lone,
They never will manifest their best;
Their greatest greatness is unknown —
Earth knows a little — God, the rest.
A Thought. Stanza 3

A land without ruins is a land without memories — a land without memories is a land without history.
A Land Without Ruins.
Foreword

Crowns of roses fade — crowns of
thorns endure. Calvaries and crucifix-
ions take deepest hold of humanity —
the triumphs of might are transient —
they pass and are forgotten — the sufferings of right are graven deepest on
the chronicle of nations.
Ibid.

FRANK RICHARD STOCKTON
[1834–1902]

He could open either door he pleased.
. . . If he opened the one, there came
out of it a hungry tiger, the fiercest and
most cruel that could be procured,
which immediately sprang upon him,
and tore him to pieces, as a punishment
for his guilt. . . . But if the accused
person opened the other door, there
came forth from it a lady, the most
suitable to his years and station that
his Majesty could select among his fair
subjects. . . . So I leave it with all of
you: Which came out of the opened
door — the lady or the tiger?
The Lady or the Tiger? [1884]

JAMES THOMSON
[1834–1882]

Give a man a horse he can ride,
Give a man a boat he can sail;
And his rank and wealth, his strength
and health
On sea nor shore shall fail.
Sunday Up the River [1869].
XV, Stanza 1

Give a man a pipe he can smoke,
Give a man a book he can read:
And his home is bright with a calm de-
light,

Though the room be poor indeed.
                Sunday Up the River. XV,
                                Stanza 2
The City is of Night; perchance of
    Death,
But certainly of Night.
                The City of Dreadful Night
                [1874]. Proem
Dateless oblivion and divine repose.
                                Ibid. XIII
The wine of Love is music,
    And the feast of Love is song:
And when Love sits down to the ban-
    quet,
Love sits long.
                        The Vine. Stanza 1

CHARLES HENRY WEBB ("JOHN PAUL")
[1834–1905]

Turn out more ale, turn up the light;
I will not go to bed tonight.
Of all the foes that man should dread
The first and worst one is a bed.
                Dum Vivimus Vigilamus.
                                Stanza 1
Friends I have had both old and young,
And ale we drank and songs we sung:
Enough you know when this is said,
That, one and all, — they died in bed.
In bed they died and I'll not go
Where all my friends have perished so.
                                Ibid.
That 'tis well to be off with the old love
Before one is on with the new
Has somehow passed into a proverb,[1]
But who follows its teaching may rue.
                Proverbum Sap. Stanza 1
Were the proverb not wiser if mended,
And the fickle and wavering told
To be sure that they're on with the new
    love
Before being off with the old?
                        Ibid. Stanza 3

[1] It's gude to be merry and wise,
    It's gude to be honest and true;
    It's gude to be off with the old love,
    Before you are on with the new.
        ANONYMOUS [1816]: Quoted by AN-
    THONY TROLLOPE in *Barchester Tow-
    ers* [1857], *Chap. 46.*
    See Bernard Shaw, page 764a.

Of Christian souls more have been
    wrecked on shore
Than ever were lost at sea.
                With a Nantucket Shell. Stanza 3

JAMES McNEILL WHISTLER
[1834–1903]

Two and two continue to make four,
in spite of the whine of the amateur for
three, or the cry of the critic for five.
                Whistler v. *Ruskin* [1] *[1878]*
Nature sings her exquisite song to the
artist alone, her son and her master —
her son in that he loves her, her master
in that he knows her.
                        Ten O'Clock [1888]
The rare Few, who, early in Life,
have rid Themselves of the Friendship
of the Many.
                The Gentle Art of Making Enemies
                        [1890]. Dedication
To say of a picture, as is often said
in its praise, that it shows great and
earnest labour, is to say that it is incomplete and unfit for view.
                Ibid. Propositions, 2
Industry in Art is a necessity — not
a virtue — and any evidence of the
same, in the production, is a blemish,
not a quality; a proof, not of achievement, but of absolutely insufficient
work, for work alone will efface the
footsteps of work.[2]
                                Ibid.
The masterpiece should appear as
the flower to the painter — perfect in
its bud as in its bloom — with no reason
to explain its presence — no mission to
fulfill — a joy to the artist, a delusion
to the philanthropist — a puzzle to the
botanist — an accident of sentiment
and alliteration to the literary man.
                                Ibid.

[1] In Whistler's lawsuit for libel. Ruskin had
written of Whistler's *Nocturne in Black and
Gold,* "I have seen, and heard, much of
Cockney impudence before now; but never
expected to hear a coxcomb ask two hundred
guineas for flinging a pot of paint in the
public's face." — *Fors Clavigera, Letter 79*
[1877]
[2] Ars est celare artem (Art lies in concealing
art). — *Latin proverb*

Art should be independent of all clap-trap — should stand alone, and appeal to the artistic sense of eye and ear, without confounding this with emotions entirely foreign to it, as devotion, pity, love, patriotism, and the like. All these have no kind of concern with it.

The Gentle Art of Making Enemies.
Propositions, 2

The imitator is a poor kind of creature. If the man who paints only the tree, or flower, or other surface he sees before him were an artist, the king of artists would be the photographer. It is for the artist to do something beyond this: in portrait painting to put on canvas something more than the face the model wears for that one day; to paint the man, in short, as well as his features.

Ibid.

One cannot continually disappoint a Continent.[1]

Ibid.

Wilde. I wish I'd said that.
Whistler. You will, Oscar, you will.
Quoted in L. C. INGLEBY: *Oscar Wilde* [*1907*]

I am not arguing with you — I am telling you.

Quoted by JOSEPH AND ELIZABETH ROBINS PENNELL *in Life of Whistler* [*1908*]

"I only know of two painters in the world," said a newly introduced feminine enthusiast to Whistler, "yourself and Velasquez." "Why," answered Whistler in dulcet tones, "why drag in Velasquez?"

D. C. SEITZ: *Whistler Stories*
[*1913*]

ALFRED AUSTIN
[1835–1913]

So long as Faith with Freedom reigns,
And loyal Hope survives,
And gracious Charity remains
To leaven lowly lives;

[1] Referring to a contemplated visit to the United States.

While there is one untrodden tract
For intellect or will,
And men are free to think and act,
Life is worth living still.

Is Life Worth Living? [1]

Why should we lodge in marble or in bronze
Spirits more vast than earth, or sea, or sky?
Wiser the silent worshiper who cons
Their page for Wisdom that will never die.

On the Proposal to Erect a Statue to Shakespeare in London

Gods for themselves are monuments enough.

Ibid.

An earl by right, by courtesy a man.
The Season

THOMAS BRIGHAM BISHOP
[1835–1905]

John Brown's body lies a-mouldering in the grave,
His soul goes marching on.
John Brown's Body

Shoo, fly! don't bodder me! I belong to Company G,
I feel like a morning star.
Shoo, Fly. Refrain

PHILLIPS BROOKS
[1835–1893]

O little town of Bethlehem!
How still we see thee lie;
Above thy deep and dreamless sleep
The silent stars go by;
Yet in thy dark streets shineth
The everlasting Light;
The hopes and fears of all the years
Are met in thee tonight.

O Little Town of Bethlehem.
Stanza 1

While mortals sleep, the angels keep
Their watch of wond'ring love.
O morning stars together

[1] See William James, page 715b.

Proclaim the holy birth,
And praises sing to God the King
And peace to men on earth.
O Little Town of Bethlehem.
Stanza 2

Life comes before literature, as the material always comes before the work. The hills are full of marble before the world blooms with statues.
Literature and Life

Do not pray for easy lives. Pray to be stronger men! Do not pray for tasks equal to your powers. Pray for powers equal to your tasks.
Sermons. Going up to Jerusalem

Greatness, after all, in spite of its name, appears to be not so much a certain size as a certain quality in human lives. It may be present in lives whose range is very small.
Ibid. Purpose and Use of Comfort

May I try to tell you again where your only comfort lies? It is not in forgetting the happy past. People bring us well-meant but miserable consolation when they tell what time will do to help our grief. We do not want to lose our grief, because our grief is bound up with our love and we could not cease to mourn without being robbed of our affections.
Letter to a friend on the death of his mother [*November 19, 1891*]

SAMUEL BUTLER
[1835–1902]

The man who lets himself be bored is even more contemptible than the bore.
The Fair Haven [*1873*]. *Memoir, Chap. 3*

Stowed away in a Montreal lumber room
The Discobolus standeth and turneth his face to the wall;
Dusty, cobweb-covered, maimed and set at naught,

Beauty crieth in an attic and no man regardeth.
O God! O Montreal!
A Psalm of Montreal.[1] *Stanza 1*
The Discobolus is put here because he is vulgar —
He has neither vest nor pants with which to cover his limbs;
I, Sir, am a person of most respectable connections. —
My brother-in-law is haberdasher to Mr. Spurgeon.
O God! O Montreal!
Ibid. Stanza 5
A hen is only an egg's way of making another egg.
Life and Habit [*1877*]. *Chap. 8*
It is far safer to know too little than too much. People will condemn the one, though they will resent being called upon to exert themselves to follow the other.
The Way of All Flesh[2] [*1903*]. *Chap. 5*
Adversity, if a man is set down to it by degrees, is more supportable with equanimity by most people than any great prosperity arrived at in a single lifetime.[3]
Ibid.
It is our less conscious thoughts and our less conscious actions which mainly mould our lives and the lives of those who spring from us.
Ibid.
To me it seems that youth is like spring, an over-praised season — delightful if it happen to be a favoured one, but in practice very rarely favoured and more remarkable, as a general rule, for biting east winds than genial breezes.
Ibid. Chap. 6
In old age we live under the shadow of Death, which, like a sword of Dam-

[1] This satirical presentation of the conflict between Greek art and modern gospels was evoked by the discovery of a plaster cast of the Discobolus in a Montreal storeroom. The poem was written in Canada in 1875, and published in 1884.
[2] See John Webster, page 225b.
[3] See Carlyle, page 475b.

ocles, may descend at any moment, but we have so long found life to be an affair of being rather frightened than hurt that we have become like the people who live under Vesuvius, and chance it without much misgiving.

The Way of All Flesh. Chap. 6

A pair of lovers are like sunset and sunrise: there are such things every day but we very seldom see them.

Ibid. Chap. 11

Taking numbers into account, I should think more mental suffering had been undergone in the streets leading from St. George's, Hanover Square, than in the condemned cells of Newgate.

Ibid. Chap. 13

Every man's work, whether it be literature or music or pictures or architecture or anything else, is always a portrait of himself, and the more he tries to conceal himself the more clearly will his character appear in spite of him.

Ibid. Chap. 14

A virtue, to be serviceable, must, like gold, be alloyed with some commoner but more durable metal.

Ibid. Chap. 19

One great reason why clergymen's households are generally unhappy is because the clergyman is so much at home and close about the house.

Ibid. Chap. 24

The advantage of doing one's praising for oneself is that one can lay it on so thick and exactly in the right places.

Ibid. Chap. 34

The best liar is he who makes the smallest amount of lying go the longest way — who husbands it too carefully to waste it where it can be dispensed with.

Ibid. Chap. 39

If people would dare to speak to one another unreservedly, there would be a good deal less sorrow in the world a hundred years hence.

Ibid. Chap. 44

Everyone has a mass of bad work in him which he will have to work off and get rid of before he can do better — and indeed, the more lasting a man's ultimate good work, the more sure he is to pass through a time, and perhaps a very long one, in which there seems very little hope for him at all. We must all sow our spiritual wild oats.

The Way of All Flesh. Chap. 51

It is in the uncompromisingness with which dogma is held and not in the dogma or want of dogma that the danger lies.

Ibid. Chap. 68

When people get it into their heads that they are being specially favoured by the Almighty, they had better as a general rule mind their p's and q's.

Ibid. Chap. 71

An empty house is like a stray dog or a body from which life has departed.[1]

Ibid. Chap. 72

A man's friendships are, like his will, invalidated by marriage — but they are also no less invalidated by the marriage of his friends.

Ibid. Chap. 75

I reckon being ill as one of the great pleasures of life, provided one is not too ill and is not obliged to work till one is better.

Ibid. Chap. 80

Life is the art of drawing sufficient conclusions from insufficient premises.

Note-Books [*1912*]. *Lord, What Is Man?*

All progress is based upon a universal innate desire on the part of every organism to live beyond its income.

Ibid.

Though analogy is often misleading, it is the least misleading thing we have.

Ibid. Music, Pictures, and Books

I have gone in for posthumous fame. . . . Posterity will give a man a fair

[1] I suppose I've passed it a hundred times, but I always stop for a minute
And look at the house, the tragic house, the house with nobody in it.
JOYCE KILMER [1886–1918]: *The House With Nobody In It*

hearing; his own times will not do so if he is attacking vested interests, and I have attacked two powerful sets of vested interests at once — the Church and Science.

Note-Books. Homo Unius Libri

Ideas and opinions, like living organisms, have a normal rate of growth which cannot be either checked or forced beyond a certain point. The more unpopular an opinion is, the more necessary is it that the holder should be somewhat punctilious in his observance of conventionalities generally.

Ibid. The Art of Propagating Opinion

I do not think America is a good place in which to be a genius. A genius can never expect to have a good time anywhere, but America is about the last place in which life will be endurable at all for an inspired writer.

Ibid. Cash and Credit

Genius . . . has been defined as a supreme capacity for taking trouble. . . . It might be more fitly described as a supreme capacity for getting its possessors into trouble of all kinds and keeping them therein so long as the genius remains.

Ibid. Genius

An apology for the Devil: It must be remembered that we have only heard one side of the case. God has written all the books.

Ibid. Higgledy-Piggledy: An Apology for the Devil

God is Love, I dare say. But what a mischievous devil Love is.

Ibid. God Is Love

To live is like love, all reason is against it, and all healthy instinct for it.

Ibid. Life and Love

The Ancient Mariner would not have taken so well if it had been called *The Old Sailor.*

Ibid. Titles and Subjects

The public buys its opinions as it buys its meat, or takes in its milk, on the principle that it is cheaper to do this than to keep a cow. So it is, but the milk is more likely to be watered.

Note-Books. Sequel to "Alps and Sanctuaries"

I do not mind lying, but I hate inaccuracy.

Ibid. Truth and Convenience: Falsehood

How holy people look when they are sea-sick!

Ibid. The Channel Passage

O Critics, Cultured Critics!
Who will praise me after I am dead,
Who will see in me both more and less
    than I intended,
But who will swear that whatever it was
    it was all perfectly right;
You will think you are better than the
    people who, when I was alive,
    swore that whatever I did was
    wrong,
And damned my books for me as fast as
    I could write them;
But you will not be better, you will be
    just the same, neither better nor
    worse,
And you will go for some future Butler
    as your fathers have gone for me;
Oh, how I should have hated you!

To Critics and Others

RICHARD GARNETT
[1835–1906]

Man and Woman may only enter Paradise hand in hand. Together, the myth tells us, they left it and together must they return.

*De Flagello Myrteo [1905].
Preface, XII*

Evergreens are said to be associated with Death as emblems of immortality, and this is true. But there is another and perhaps a deeper symbol: that all seasons are alike to him, as to them.

Ibid. Preface, XXXI

The three eldest children of Necessity: God, the World, and Love.

Ibid. I

Love is God's essence; Power but

his attribute; therefore is his love greater than his power.

De Flagello Myrteo. IV

To become Love, Friendship needs what Morality needs to become Religion — the fire of emotion.

Ibid. LV

Perfect Love casts out Prudery together with Fear.

Ibid. LIX

Joy to forgive and joy to be forgiven
Hang level in the balances of Love.

Ibid. LXII

When Silence speaks for Love she has much to say.

Ibid. XCIX

Is life worth living? This if thou inquire,
'Tis probable that thou hast never lived,
And palpable that thou hast never loved.[1]

Ibid. CCVII

Sweet are the words of Love, sweeter his thoughts:
Sweetest of all what Love nor says nor thinks.

Ibid. CCL

Ascend above the restrictions and conventions of the World, but not so high as to lose sight of them.

Ibid. CCCXXXIII

"Let the man that woos to win
Woo with an unhairy chin."
Thus she said, and as she bid
Each devoted Vizier did.

The Fair Circassian. Stanza 3

SIR ALFRED COMYN LYALL
[1835–1911]

"I think till I'm weary of thinking,"
Said the sad-eyed Hindu King,
"And I see but shadows around me,
Illusion in everything."

The Hindu King's Reply to the Missionary

[1] See Alfred Austin, page 669a–669b, and William James, page 715b.

JOHN LUCKEY McCREERY
[1835–1906]

There is no death! The stars go down
To rise upon some other shore,
And bright in heaven's jeweled crown
They shine for evermore.

*There Is No Death [1863].
Stanza 1*

ADAH ISAACS MENKEN
[1835–1868]

Where is the promise of my years,
Once written on my brow?
Ere errors, agonies, and fears
Brought with them all that speaks in tears,
Ere I had sunk beneath my peers; —
Where sleeps that promise now?

El Suspiro (Infelix) [1868]

I stand a wreck on Error's shore,
A spectre not within the door,
A houseless shadow evermore,
An exile lingering here.

Ibid.

LOUISE CHANDLER MOULTON
[1835–1908]

Bend low, O dusky Night,
And give my spirit rest,
Hold me to your deep breast,
And put old cares to flight.
Give back the lost delight
That once my soul possest,
When Love was loveliest.

Tonight

I hied me off to Arcady —
The month it was the month of May,
And all along the pleasant way,
The morning birds were mad with glee,
And all the flowers sprang up to see,
As I went on to Arcady.

The Secret of Arcady

BISHOP HENRY CODMAN POTTER
[1835–1908]

We have exchanged the Washingtonian dignity for the Jeffersonian simplicity, which was in truth only another name for the Jacksonian vulgarity.

Address at the Washington Centennial Service in St. Paul's Chapel, New York [April 30, 1889]

HARRIET PRESCOTT SPOFFORD
[1835–1921]

The awful phantom of the hungry poor.
Sonnet, A Winter's Night

CELIA LAIGHTON THAXTER
[1835–1894]

Sad soul, take comfort, nor forget
That sunrise never failed us yet.
The Sunrise Never Failed Us Yet. Stanza 4

Across the narrow beach we flit,
One little sand-piper and I;
And fast I gather, bit by bit,
The scattered drift-wood, bleached and dry.
The wild waves reach their hands for it,
The wild wind raves, the tide runs high,
As up and down the beach we flit,
One little sand-piper and I.
The Sand-Piper

MARK TWAIN [1]
(SAMUEL LANGHORNE CLEMENS)
[1835–1910]

I'll resk forty dollars that he can out-jump any frog in Calaveras county.
The Celebrated Jumping Frog [1865]

[1] I was a fresh, new journalist, and needed a *nom de guerre;* so I confiscated the ancient mariner's discarded one ["Mark Twain"], and have done my best to make it remain what it was in his hands — a sign and symbol and warrant that whatever is found in its company may be gambled on as being the petrified truth. — *Life on the Mississippi* [1883], *Chap. 50* (The earlier use of the pen name was by Captain Isaiah Sellers, in *The New Orleans Picayune*.)
The phrase "mark twain," meaning "two

I don't see no p'ints about that frog that's any better'n any other frog.
The Celebrated Jumping Frog

Soap and education are not as sudden as a massacre, but they are more deadly in the long run.
The Facts Concerning the Recent Resignation [1867]

Tomorrow night I appear for the first time before a Boston audience — 4000 critics.
Letter to Pamela Clemens Moffet [November 9, 1869]

They spell it Vinci and pronounce it Vinchy; foreigners always spell better than they pronounce.
The Innocents Abroad [1869]. Chap. 19

I do not want Michael Angelo for breakfast — for luncheon — for dinner — for tea — for supper — for between meals.
Ibid. Chap. 27

Lump the whole thing! say that the Creator made Italy from designs by Michael Angelo!
Ibid.

Guides cannot master the subtleties of the American joke.
Ibid.

There's millions in it!
The Gilded Age [1] [1873]

Barring that natural expression of villainy which we all have, the man looked honest enough.
A Mysterious Visit [1875]

This poor little one-horse town.
The Undertaker's Chat [1875]

Tom appeared on the sidewalk with a bucket of whitewash and a long-handled brush. He surveyed the fence, and all gladness left him and a deep

fathoms deep," was employed in making soundings on the Mississippi river boats.
By American literature in the proper sense we ought to mean literature written in an American way, with an American turn of language and an American cast of thought. The test is that it couldn't have been written anywhere else. — STEPHEN LEACOCK [1869-1944]: *Mark Twain as a National Asset*
[1] Written in collaboration with CHARLES DUDLEY WARNER.

melancholy settled down upon his spirit. Thirty yards of board fence nine feet high. Life to him seemed hollow, and existence but a burden.

> *The Adventures of Tom Sawyer* [*1876*]. *Chap. 2*

Work consists of whatever a body is *obliged* to do . . . Play consists of whatever a body is not obliged to do.

> *Ibid.*

The minister gave out his text and droned along monotonously through an argument that was so prosy that many a head by and by began to nod — and yet it was an argument that dealt in limitless fire and brimstone and thinned the predestined elect down to a company so small as to be hardly worth the saving.

> *Ibid. Chap. 5*

There was no getting around the stubborn fact that taking sweetmeats was only "hooking," while taking bacon and hams and such valuables was plain simple *stealing* — and there was a command against that in the Bible. So they inwardly resolved that so long as they remained in the business, their piracies should not again be sullied with the crime of stealing.

> *Ibid. Chap. 13*

To promise not to do a thing is the surest way in the world to make a body want to go and do that very thing.

> *Ibid. Chap. 22*

She makes me wash, they comb me all to thunder . . . The widder eats by a bell; she goes to bed by a bell; she gits up by a bell — everything's so awful reg'lar a body can't stand it.

> *Ibid. Chap. 35*

A baby is an inestimable blessing and bother.

> *Letter to Annie Webster* [*September 1, 1876*]

There is a sumptuous variety about the New England weather that compels the stranger's admiration — and regret. The weather is always doing something there; always attending strictly to business; always getting up new designs and trying them on people to see how they will go. But it gets through more business in Spring than in any other season. In the Spring I have counted one hundred and thirty-six different kinds of weather inside of twenty-four hours.

> *New England Weather, Speech at dinner of New England Society, New York* [*December 22, 1876*]

Probable nor'-east to sou'-west winds, varying to the southard and westard and eastard and points between; high and low barometer, sweeping round from place to place; probable areas of rain, snow, hail, and drought, succeeded or preceded by earthquakes with thunder and lightning.

> *Ibid.*

We haven't all had the good fortune to be ladies; we haven't all been generals, or poets, or statesmen; but when the toast works down to the babies, we stand on common ground.

> *Answering a Toast to the Babies, Banquet in Honor of General U. S. Grant, Palmer House, Chicago* [*November 14, 1879*]

Among the three or four million cradles now rocking in the land are some which this nation would preserve for ages as sacred things, if we could know which ones they are.

> *Ibid.*

It is the longest river in the world — four thousand three hundred miles. . . . It is also the crookedest river in the world, since in one part of its journey it uses up one thousand three hundred miles to cover the same ground that the crow would fly over in six hundred and seventy-five.

> *Life on the Mississippi* [*1883*]. *Chap. 1*

The world and the books are so accustomed to use, and over-use, the word "new" in connection with our country, that we early get and permanently retain the impression that there is nothing old about it.

> *Ibid.*

Sired by a hurricane, dam'd by an earthquake.

Life on the Mississippi. Chap. 3

When I'm playful I use the meridians of longitude and parallels of latitude for a seine, and drag the Atlantic Ocean for whales. I scratch my head with the lightning and purr myself to sleep with the thunder.

Ibid.

The Child of Calamity.

Ibid.

I was gratified to be able to answer promptly, and I did. I said I didn't know.

Ibid. Chap. 6

Your true pilot cares nothing about anything on earth but the river, and his pride in his occupation surpasses the pride of kings.

Ibid. Chap. 7

By the Shadow of Death, but he's a lightning pilot!

Ibid.

A limb of Satan.[1]

Ibid. Chap. 8

I'll learn him or kill him.

Ibid.

Give an Irishman lager for a month, and he's a dead man. An Irishman is lined with copper, and the beer corrodes it. But whiskey polishes the copper and is the saving of him.

Ibid. Chap. 23

Spread open on the rack, where the plaintive singer had left it, *Ro*-holl on, silver *moo*-hoon, guide the *trav*-el-lerr his *way*.

Ibid. Chap. 38

All the modern inconveniences.

Ibid. Chap. 43

The educated Southerner has no use for an *r*, except at the beginning of a word.

Ibid. Chap. 44

The Northern word "guess" — imported from England, where it used to be common, and now regarded by satirical Englishmen as a Yankee original —

[1] Also in *The Prince and the Pauper, Chap. 13.*

is but little used among Southerners. They say "reckon."

Life on the Mississippi. Chap. 44

In the South the war is what A. D. is elsewhere; they date from it.

Ibid. Chap. 45

War talk by men who have been in a war is always interesting; whereas moon talk by a poet who has not been in the moon is likely to be dull.

Ibid.

Sir Walter [Scott] had so large a hand in making Southern character as it existed before the war that he is in great measure responsible for the war.

Ibid. Chap. 46

It was without a compeer among swindles. It was perfect, it was rounded, symmetrical, complete, colossal.

Ibid. Chap. 52

When I retired from the rebel army in '61 I retired upon Louisiana in good order; at least in good enough order for a person who had not yet learned how to retreat according to the rules of war, and had to trust to native genius.

Ibid. Chap. 53

Persons attempting to find a motive in this narrative will be prosecuted; persons attempting to find a moral in it will be banished; persons attempting to find a plot in it will be shot.

By Order of the Author.

Adventures of Huckleberry Finn [*1884*]. *Notice*

You don't know about me without you have read a book by the name of *The Adventures of Tom Sawyer;* but that ain't no matter. That book was made by Mr. Mark Twain, and he told the truth, mainly. There was things which he stretched, but mainly he told the truth.

Ibid. Chap. 1

Jim was most ruined for a servant, because he got stuck up on account of having seen the devil and been rode by witches.

Ibid. Chap. 2

We catched fish and talked, and we took a swim now and then to keep off sleepiness. It was kind of solemn, drift-

ing down the big, still river, laying on our backs looking up at the stars, and we didn't ever feel like talking loud, and it warn't often that we laughed — only a little kind of a low chuckle. We had mighty good weather as a general thing, and nothing ever happened to us at all.
Adventures of Huckleberry Finn.
Chap. 12

It most froze me to hear such talk. . . . Thinks I, this is what comes of my not thinking. Here was this nigger, which I had as good as helped to run away, coming right out flat-footed and saying he would steal his children — children that belonged to a man I didn't even know, a man that hadn't ever done me no harm.
Ibid. Chap. 16

Pilgrim's Progress, about a man that left his family, it didn't say why. I read considerable in it now and then. The statements was interesting but tough.
Ibid. Chap. 17

There warn't anybody at the church, except maybe a hog or two, for there warn't any lock on the door, and hogs likes a puncheon floor in summer-time because it's cool. If you notice, most folks don't go to church only when they've got to; but a hog is different.
Ibid. Chap. 18

We said there warn't no home like a raft, after all. Other places do seem so cramped up and smothery, but a raft don't. You feel mighty free and easy and comfortable on a raft.
Ibid.

A monstrous big river.
Ibid. Chap. 19

I was trying to make my mouth say I would do the right thing and the clean thing, and go and write to that nigger's owner and tell where he was; but deep down in me I knowed it was a lie, and He knowed it. You can't pray a lie — I found that out.
Ibid. Chap. 21

I was a-trembling because I'd got to decide forever betwixt two things, and I knowed it. I studied for a minute, sort

of holding my breath, and then says to myself, "All right, then, I'll *go* to hell."
Adventures of Huckleberry Finn.
Chap. 21

Hain't we got all the fools in town on our side? And ain't that a big enough majority in any town? [1]
Ibid. Chap. 26

An experienced, industrious, ambitious, and often quite picturesque liar.
The Private History of a Campaign That Failed [1885]

He is now fast rising from affluence to poverty.
Henry Ward Beecher's Farm [1885]

He [George Washington Cable] has taught me to abhor and detest the Sabbath-day and hunt up new and troublesome ways to dishonor it.
Letter to William Dean Howells [February 27, 1885]

Whenever the literary German dives into a sentence, that is the last you are going to see of him till he emerges on the other side of his Atlantic with his verb in his mouth.
A Connecticut Yankee at King Arthur's Court [1889]. Chap. 22

Weather is a literary speciality, and no untrained hand can turn out a good article on it.
The American Claimant [1892]. Foreword

Tell the truth or trump — but get the trick.
Pudd'nhead Wilson [1894]. Pudd'nhead Wilson's Calendar, Chap. 1

Adam was but human — this explains it all. He did not want the apple for the apple's sake, he wanted it only because it was forbidden.
Ibid. Chap. 2

Whoever has lived long enough to find out what life is, knows how deep a debt of gratitude we owe to Adam, the

[1] See *Pudd'nhead Wilson's New Calendar,* page 679a.

first great benefactor of our race. He brought death into the world.

> *Pudd'nhead Wilson. Pudd'nhead Wilson's Calendar, Chap. 3*

Training is everything. The peach was once a bitter almond; cauliflower is nothing but cabbage with a college education.

> *Ibid. Chap. 5*

Habit is habit, and not to be flung out of the window by any man, but coaxed down-stairs a step at a time.

> *Ibid. Chap. 6*

One of the most striking differences between a cat and a lie is that a cat has only nine lives.

> *Ibid. Chap. 7*

The holy passion of Friendship is of so sweet and steady and loyal and enduring a nature that it will last through a whole lifetime, if not asked to lend money.

> *Ibid. Chap. 8*

Why is it that we rejoice at a birth and grieve at a funeral? It is because we are not the person involved.

> *Ibid. Chap. 9*

All say, "How hard it is that we have to die" — a strange complaint to come from the mouths of people who have had to live.

> *Ibid. Chap. 10*

When angry, count four; when very angry, swear.[1]

> *Ibid.*

Courage is resistance to fear, mastery of fear — not absence of fear.

> *Ibid. Chap. 12*

Nothing so needs reforming as other people's habits.

> *Ibid. Chap. 15*

Put all your eggs in the one basket and — WATCH THAT BASKET.

> *Ibid.*

If you pick up a starving dog and make him prosperous, he will not bite you. This is the principal difference between a dog and a man.

> *Ibid. Chap. 16*

[1] See Jefferson, page 376a.

Few things are harder to put up with than the annoyance of a good example.

> *Pudd'nhead Wilson. Pudd'nhead Wilson's Calendar, Chap. 19*

It were not best that we should all think alike; it is difference of opinion that makes horse-races.

> *Ibid.*

Be good and you will be lonesome.

> *Following the Equator [1897]. Caption for Author's Photograph on Shipboard, Frontispiece of First Edition*

When in doubt tell the truth.

> *Ibid. Vol. I, Pudd'nhead Wilson's New Calendar, Chap. 2*

Truth is the most valuable thing we have. Let us economize it.

> *Ibid. Chap. 7*

It could probably be shown by facts and figures that there is no distinctly native American criminal class except Congress.

> *Ibid. Chap. 8*

Everything human is pathetic. The secret source of Humor itself is not joy but sorrow. There is no humor in heaven.

> *Ibid. Chap. 10*

We should be careful to get out of an experience only the wisdom that is in it — and stop there; lest we be like the cat that sits down on a hot stove-lid. She will never sit down on a hot stove-lid again — and that is well; but also she will never sit down on a cold one anymore.

> *Ibid. Chap. 11*

We can secure other people's approval, if we do right and try hard; but our own is worth a hundred of it, and no way has been found out of securing that.

> *Ibid. Chap. 14*

It is easier to stay out than get out.

> *Ibid. Chap. 18*

Pity is for the living, envy is for the dead.

> *Ibid. Chap. 19*

It is by the goodness of God that in our country we have those three unspeakably precious things: freedom of speech, freedom of conscience, and the prudence never to practise either of them.

> *Following the Equator. Vol. I, Pudd'nhead Wilson's New Calendar, Chap. 20*

"*Classic.*" A book which people praise and don't read.

> *Ibid. Chap. 25*

Man is the Only Animal that blushes. Or needs to.

> *Ibid. Chap. 27*

Let us be thankful for the fools. But for them the rest of us could not succeed.[1]

> *Ibid. Chap. 28*

There are several good protections against temptations, but the surest is cowardice.

> *Ibid. Chap. 36*

There is an old time toast which is golden for its beauty. "When you ascend the hill of prosperity may you not meet a friend."

> *Ibid. Vol. II, Chap. 5*

Each person is born to one possession which outvalues all his others — his last breath.

> *Ibid. Chap. 6*

It takes your enemy and your friend, working together, to hurt you to the heart; the one to slander you and the other to get the news to you.

> *Ibid. Chap. 9*

Grief can take care of itself, but to get the full value of a joy you must have somebody to divide it with.

> *Ibid. Chap. 12*

In statesmanship get the formalities right, never mind about the moralities.

> *Ibid. Chap. 29*

Everyone is a moon, and has a dark side which he never shows to anybody.

> *Ibid. Chap. 30*

The reports of my death are greatly exaggerated.

> *Cable from London to the Associated Press [1897]*

A round man cannot be expected to

[1] See *Huckleberry Finn*, page 677b.

fit in a square hole right away. He must have time to modify his shape.

> *More Tramps Abroad [1897]*

In Boston they ask, How much does he know? In New York, How much is he worth? In Philadelphia, Who were his parents?

> *What Paul Bourget Thinks of Us [1899]*

The silent colossal National Lie that is the support and confederate of all the tyrannies and shams and inequalities and unfairnesses that afflict the peoples — that is the one to throw bricks and sermons at.

> *My First Lie, and How I Got Out of It [1900]*

Always do right. This will gratify some people, and astonish the rest.[1]

> *To the Young People's Society, Greenpoint Presbyterian Church, Brooklyn [February 16, 1901]*

A powerful agent is the right word. Whenever we come upon one of those intensely right words in a book or a newspaper the resulting effect is physical as well as spiritual, and electrically prompt.

> *Essay on William Dean Howells [1906]*

It may be called the Master Passion, the hunger for self-approval.

> *What Is Man? [1906]. Chap. 6*

The fact that man knows right from wrong proves his *intellectual* superiority to the other creatures; but the fact that he can *do* wrong proves his *moral* inferiority to any creature that *cannot*.

> *Ibid.*

Thunder is good, thunder is impressive; but it is lightning that does the work.

> *Letter to an Unidentified Person [1908]*

As out of place as a Presbyterian in Hell.

> *Quoted in* ALBERT BIGELOW PAINE: *Mark Twain [1912]*

[1] President Truman kept this saying on his desk in the White House.

"You tell me whar a man gits his corn pone, en I'll tell you what his 'pinions is."

Europe and Elsewhere [*1925*].
Corn Pone Opinions

Its name is Public Opinion. It is held in reverence. It settles everything. Some think it is the voice of God.

Ibid.

Biographies are but the clothes and buttons of the man — the biography of the man himself cannot be written.

Autobiography [*1924*]. *Vol. I,*
Page 2

Of all the creatures that were made he [man] is the most detestable. Of the entire brood he is the only one — the solitary one — that possesses malice. That is the basest of all instincts, passions, vices — the most hateful. . . . He is the only creature that inflicts pain for sport, knowing it to *be* pain. . . . Also — in all the list he is the only creature that has a nasty mind.

Ibid. Vol. II, Page 7

The trade of critic, in literature, music, and the drama, is the most degraded of all trades.

Ibid. Page 69

I believe that our Heavenly Father invented man because he was disappointed in the monkey.

Quoted in BERNARD DE VOTO: *Mark Twain in Eruption* [*1940*]

Familiarity breeds contempt — and children.

Notebooks

Good breeding consists in concealing how much we think of ourselves and how little we think of the other person.

Ibid.

Death, the only immortal who treats us all alike, whose pity and whose peace and whose refuge are for all — the soiled and the pure, the rich and the poor, the loved and the unloved.

Ibid. Memorandum written on
his deathbed

Loyalty to petrified opinion never yet broke a chain or freed a human soul.

Inscription beneath his bust in
the Hall of Fame

The calm confidence of a Christian with four aces.

Attributed

THOMAS BAILEY ALDRICH
[1836–1907]

Somewhere — in desolate wind-swept space —
In   Twilight-land — in   No-man's land —
Two hurrying Shapes met face to face,
And bade each other stand.

Identity. Stanza 1

So precious life is! Even to the old
The hours are as a miser's coins!

Broken Music. Stanza 4

A man should live in a garret aloof,
And have few friends, and go poorly clad,
With an old hat stopping a chink in the roof,
To keep the Goddess constant and glad.

The Flight of the Goddess.
Stanza 1

We knew it would rain, for the poplars showed
The white of their leaves.

Before the Rain. Stanza 3

You do poets and their song
A grievous wrong,
If your own soul does not bring
To their high imagining
As much beauty as they sing.

Appreciation. Stanza 2

It has become almost an honor
Not to be crowned.

Popularity

Some weep because they part,
And languish broken-hearted,
And others — O my heart! —
Because they never parted.

The Difference

Sweet courtesy has done its most
If you have made each guest forget
That he himself is not the host.

Hospitality

My mind lets go a thousand things,
Like dates of wars and deaths of kings.

Memory

I vex me not with brooding on the years

That were ere I drew breath: why
  should I then
Distrust the darkness that may fall
  again
When life is done?

> *I Vex Me Not*

What is more cheerful, now, in the
fall of the year, than an open-wood-
fire? Do you hear those little chirps
and twitters coming out of that piece
of apple-wood? Those are the ghosts of
the robins and blue-birds that sang
upon the bough when it was in blossom last Spring. In Summer whole
flocks of them come fluttering about
the fruit-trees under the window: so I
have singing birds all the year round.

> *Miss Mehitabel's Son*

It was very pleasant to me to get a
letter from you the other day. Perhaps
I should have found it pleasanter if I
had been able to decipher it. I don't
think that I mastered anything beyond
the date (which I knew) and the signature (which I guessed at). There's
a singular and a perpetual charm in a
letter of yours; it never grows old, it
never loses its novelty. . . . Other
letters are read and thrown away and
forgotten, but yours are kept forever
— unread. One of them will last a
reasonable man a lifetime.

> *Letter to Professor Edward*
> *Sylvester Morse*

EDWARD ERNEST BOWEN
[1836–1901]

Forty years on, when afar and asunder
Parted are those who are singing today.

> *Forty Years On, Harrow Foot-*
> *ball Song* [1872]

JOSEPH CHAMBERLAIN
[1836–1914]

I never like being hit without striking
back.

> *Speech on Tariff Reform,*
> *Greenock, Scotland* [*October 7,*
> *1903*]

Provided that the City of London remains as it is at present, the clearing-
house of the world.

> *Speech, Guildhall, London*
> [*January 19, 1904*]

The day of small nations has long
passed away. The day of Empires has
come.

> *Speech, Birmingham*
> [*May 12, 1904*]

JOHN CLIFFORD
[1836–1923]

And so, I thought, the anvil of God's
  Word
For ages skeptic blows have beat upon;
Yet, though the noise of falling blows
  was heard,
The anvil is unharmed — the hammers
  gone.

> *Hammer and Anvil. Stanza 3*

WILLIAM SCHWENCK GILBERT [1]
[1836–1911]

Of all the ships upon the blue,
No ship contain'd a better crew
Than that of worthy Captain Reece,
Commanding of The Mantelpiece.

> *The "Bab" Ballads* [*1866–*
> *1871*]. *Captain Reece, Stanza 1*

The Times and Saturday Review
Beguiled the leisure of the crew.

> *Ibid. Stanza 7*

I write the pretty mottoes which you
  find inside the crackers.

> *Ibid. Ferdinando and Elvira*

And down in fathoms many went the
  captain and the crew;
Down went the owners — greedy men
  whom hope of gain allured:
Oh, dry the starting tear, for they were
  heavily insured.

> *Ibid. Etiquette, Stanza 1*

Oh, I am a cook and a captain bold
  And the mate of the *Nancy* brig,

[1] His foe was folly and his weapon wit. —
ANTHONY HOPE HAWKINS, *Inscription on Gil-*
bert Memorial, Victoria Embankment, Lon-
don

And a bo'sun tight, and a midshipmite,
And the crew of the captain's gig.
*The "Bab" Ballads. The Yarn of
the "Nancy Bell," Stanza 3*

As innocent as a new-laid egg.
Engaged [*1877*]. *Act I*

I'm called Little Buttercup — dear
little Buttercup,
Though I could never tell why.
H. M. S. Pinafore [*1878*]. *Act I*

I am the Captain of the *Pinafore;*
And a right good captain too!
Ibid.

And I'm never, never sick at sea!
What, never?
No, never!
What, *never?*
Hardly ever!
He's hardly ever sick at sea!
Then give three cheers, and one cheer
more
For the hardy Captain of the *Pinafore!*
Ibid.

Bad language or abuse,
I never, never use,
Whatever the emergency;
Though "Bother it" I may
Occasionally say,
I never never use a big, big D.
Ibid.

And so do his sisters, and his cousins,
and his aunts!
His sisters and his cousins,
Whom he reckons up by dozens,
And his aunts!
Ibid.

When I was a lad I served a term
As office boy to an Attorney's firm.
I cleaned the windows and I swept the
floor
And I polished up the handle of the big
front door.
I polished up that handle so care-
fullee
That now I am the Ruler of the
Queen's Navee!
Ibid.

Now landsmen all, whoever you may be,
If you want to rise to the top of the tree
If your soul isn't fettered to an office
stool,

Be careful to be guided by this golden
rule —
Stick close to your desks and *never go
to sea,*
And you all may be Rulers of the
Queen's Navee!
H. M. S. Pinafore. Act I

Things are seldom what they seem,
Skim milk masquerades as cream.[1]
Ibid. Act II

He is an Englishman!
For he himself has said it,
And it's greatly to his credit,
That he is an Englishman!
Ibid.

For he might have been a Roosian,
A French or Turk or Proosian,
Or perhaps Itali-an.
But in spite of all temptations
To belong to other nations,
He remains an Englishman.
Ibid.

It is, it is a glorious thing
To be a Pirate King.
Pirates of Penzance [*1879*].
Act I

I am the very model of a modern
Major-General.
Ibid.

I know the Kings of England, and I
quote the fights historical,
From Marathon to Waterloo, in order
categorical.
Ibid.

When the foeman bares his steel,
Tarantara, tarantara!
We uncomfortable feel,
Tarantara.
Ibid. Act II

When constabulary duty's to be done,
The policeman's lot is not a happy one!
Ibid.

Come, friends, who plough the sea,
Truce to navigation,
Take another station;
Let's vary piracee
With a little burglaree.[2]
Ibid.

[1] See Phaedrus, page 48b, and Longfellow,
page 521a.
[2] The roistering chorus "Hail, hail, the

Twenty love-sick maidens we,
Love-sick all against our will.
            Patience [*1881*]. *Act I*
You must lie upon the daisies and dis-
    course in novel phrases of your
    complicated state of mind,
The meaning doesn't matter if it's only
    idle chatter of a transcendental
    kind.
  And everyone will say,
  As you walk your mystic way,
"If this young man expresses himself in
    terms too deep for *me*,
Why, what a very singularly deep
    young man this deep young man
    must be!"
            Ibid.
Then a sentimental passion of a veg-
    etable fashion must excite your
    languid spleen,
An attachment à la Plato for a bashful
    young potato, or a not too French
    French bean!
Though the Philistines may jostle, you
    will rank as an apostle in the high
    aesthetic band,
If you walk down Piccadilly with a
    poppy or a lily in your medieval
    hand.
  And everyone will say,
  As you walk your flowery way,
"If he's content with a vegetable love
    which would certainly not suit *me*,
Why, what a most particularly pure
    young man this pure young man
    must be!"
            Ibid.
Prithee, pretty maiden, will you marry
    me?
(Hey, but I'm hopeful, willow, willow,
    waly!)
            Ibid.
While this magnetic,
Peripatetic
Lover, he lived to learn,
By no endeavor,
Can magnet ever
Attract a Silver Churn!
            Ibid. Act II

gang's all here" is sung to Sir Arthur Sullivan's music for these lines.

Sing "Hey to you — good day to
    you" —
Sing "Bah to you — ha! ha! to you" —
Sing "Booh to you — pooh, pooh, to
    you."
            Patience. Act II
"High diddle diddle"
Will rank as an idyll,
If I pronounce it chaste!
            Ibid.
Francesca di Rimini, miminy, piminy,
Je-ne-sais-quoi young man!
            Ibid.
A greenery-yallery, Grosvenor Gallery,
Foot-in-the-grave young man!
            Ibid.
I see no objection to stoutness, in
    moderation.
            Iolanthe [*1882*]. *Act I*
None shall part us from each other,
  One in life and death are we:
All in all to one another —
  I to thee and thou to me!
Thou the tree and I the flower —
  Thou the idol; I the throng —
Thou the day and I the hour —
  Thou the singer; I the song!
            Ibid.
Bow, bow, ye lower middle classes!
Bow, bow, ye tradesmen, bow, ye
    masses.
            Ibid.
The Law is the true embodiment
Of everything that's excellent.
It has no kind of fault or flaw,
And I, my Lords, embody the Law.
            Ibid.
Pretty young wards in Chancery.
            Ibid.
A pleasant occupation for
A rather susceptible Chancellor!
            Ibid.
For I'm not so old, and not so plain,
And I'm quite prepared to marry again.
            Ibid.
Spurn not the nobly-born
With love affected,
Nor treat with virtuous scorn
The well-connected.
            Ibid.
Hearts just as pure and fair
May beat in Belgrave Square

As in the lowly air
Of Seven Dials.
Iolanthe. Act I

Here's a pretty kettle of fish!
Ibid. Act II

When I went to the Bar as a very young
man,
(Said I to myself, said I).
Ibid.

I am an intellectual chap,
And think of things that would astonish
you.
I often think it's comical
How nature always does contrive
That every boy and every gal,
That's born into the world alive,
Is either a little Liberal,
Or else a little Conservative!
Ibid.

The House of Peers, throughout the
war,
Did nothing in particular,
And did it very well.
Ibid.

Oh, Captain Shaw!
Type of true love kept under!
Could thy Brigade
With cold cascade
Quench my great love, I wonder!
Ibid.

When you're lying awake with a dismal
headache, and repose is taboo'd by
anxiety,
I conceive you may use any language
you choose to indulge in, without
impropriety.
Ibid.

For you dream you are crossing the
Channel, and tossing about in a
steamer from Harwich —
Which is something between a large
bathing machine and a very small
second class carriage.
Ibid.

Faint heart never won fair lady!
Nothing venture, nothing win —
Blood is thick, but water's thin —
In for a penny, in for a pound —
It's Love that makes the world go
round!
Ibid.

Politics we bar,
They are not our bent:
On the whole we are
Not intelligent.
Princess Ida [*1884*]. *Act I*

I love my fellow-creatures — I do all
the good I can —
Yet everybody says I'm such a disagree-
able man!
And I can't think why!
Ibid.

Darwinian Man, though well-behaved,
At best is only a monkey shaved!
Ibid. Act II

A wandering minstrel I —
A thing of shreds and patches,
Of ballads, songs and snatches,
And dreamy lullaby!
The Mikado [*1885*]. *Act I*

I can't help it. I was born sneering.
Ibid.

As some day it may happen that a victim must be found,
I've got a little list — I've got a little
list.
Of society offenders who might well be
under ground,
And who never would be missed —
who never would be missed.
Ibid.

The idiot who praises, with enthusiastic
tone,
All centuries but this, and every country but his own.[1]
Ibid.

Three little maids from school are we,
Pert as a schoolgirl well can be,
Filled to the brim with girlish glee.
Ibid.

Ah, pray make no mistake,
We are not shy;
We're very wide awake,
The moon and I!
Ibid.

Here's a pretty state of things!
Here's a pretty how-de-do.
Ibid.

[1] See Overbury, page 226b, and Canning,
page 401a.

My object all sublime
I shall achieve in time —
To make the punishment fit the crime.
                    The Mikado. Act II

A source of innocent merriment!
Of innocent merriment.
                                        Ibid.

On a cloth untrue
With a twisted cue
And elliptical billiard balls.
                                        Ibid.

I drew my snickersnee!
                                        Ibid.

The flowers that bloom in the spring,
    Tra la,
Have nothing to do with the case.
                                        Ibid.

On a tree by a river a little tom-tit
Sang "Willow, titwillow, titwillow!"
And I said to him, "Dicky-bird, why do
    you sit
Singing 'Willow, titwillow, titwillow!' "
                                        Ibid.

"Is it weakness of intellect, birdie?" I
    cried,
"Or a rather tough worm in your little
    inside?"
With a shake of his poor little head he
    replied,
"Oh, Willow, titwillow, titwillow!"
                                        Ibid.

There's a fascination frantic
    In a ruin that's romantic;
Do you think you are sufficiently de-
    cayed?
                                        Ibid.

Hail the Bridegroom — hail the Bride!
When the nuptial knot is tied.
                    Ruddigore [1887]. Act I

I have a song to sing O!
Sing me your song, O!
                    The Yeomen of the Guard
                    [1888]. Act I

It's a song of a merryman, moping
    mum,
Whose soul was sad, and whose glance
    was glum,
Who sipped no sup, and who craved no
    crumb,
    As he sighed for the love of a ladye.
                                        Ibid.

He led his regiment from behind —
He found it less exciting.
                    The Gondoliers [1889]. Act I

That celebrated,
Cultivated,
Underrated
    Nobleman,
The Duke of Plaza Toro!
                                        Ibid.

No soldier in that gallant band
    Hid half as well as he did.
He lay concealed throughout the war,
    And this preserved his gore, O!
                                        Ibid.

Of that there is no manner of doubt —
No probable, possible shadow of
    doubt —
No possible doubt whatever.
                                        Ibid.

Life's a pudding full of plums;
Care's a canker that benumbs,
Wherefore waste our elocution
On impossible solution?
Life's a pleasant institution,
Let us take it as it comes!
                                        Ibid.

Life's perhaps the only riddle
That we shrink from giving up.
                                        Ibid.

The gratifying feeling that our duty has
    been done.
                                        Ibid.

Take a pair of sparkling eyes.
                                        Ibid.

The world has joked incessantly for
    over fifty centuries,
And every joke that's possible has long
    ago been made.
                    His Excellency: The Played-
                    Out Humorist [1894]

Humour is a drug which it's the fashion
    to abuse.
                                        Ibid.

WASHINGTON GLADDEN
[1836–1918]

In the darkest night of the year,
    When the stars have all gone out,
That courage is better than fear,
    That faith is truer than doubt.
                    Ultima Veritas. Stanza 4

BRET HARTE (FRANCIS BRETT HARTE)
[1836–1902]

The patient stars
Lean from their lattices, content to wait.
All is illusion till the morning bars
Slip from the levels of the Eastern gate.
Night is too young, O friend! day is too
    near;
Wait for the day that maketh all things
    clear.
  Not yet, O friend, not yet!
     Cadet Grey. Song, Not Yet

All is not true,
All is not ever as it seemeth now.
          Ibid.

What lieth dark, O love, bright day will
    fill;
Wait for thy morning, be it good or ill.
          Ibid.

Fades the light,
  And afar
Goeth day, cometh night;
  And a star
Leadeth all,
Speedeth all
  To their rest.[1]
     Ibid. Bugle Song

Love, good-night!
  Must thou go
  When the day
And the light
  Need thee so?
          Ibid.

Until points of gravest import yielded
    slowly one by one,
And by Love was consummated what
    Diplomacy begun.
     Concepcion de Arguello

Never a tear bedims the eye
That time and patience will not dry;
Never a lip is curved with pain
That can't be kissed into smiles again.
     The Lost Galleon [1867]

  [1] Fading light
    Dims the sight,
      And the stars gem the sky,
    Gleaming bright,
      From afar drawing nigh,
    Falls the night.
    JOSEPH BERG ESENWEIN [1867–1946]:
          Taps, St. 1

Which I wish to remark,
  And my language is plain,
That for ways that are dark
  And for tricks that are vain,
The heathen Chinee is peculiar.
   Plain Language from Truthful
     James [1870]. *Stanza 1*

Ah Sin was his name.
         Ibid. Stanza 2

With the smile that was childlike and
    bland.
         Ibid. Stanza 4

We are ruined by Chinese cheap labor.
         Ibid. Stanza 7

And ever since then, when the clock
    strikes two,
She walks unbidden from room to
    room,
And the air is filled that she passes
    through
  With a subtle, sad perfume.
    A Newport Romance. Stanza 6

And on that grave where English oak
    and holly
  And laurel wreaths entwine,
Deem it not all a too presumptuous
    folly,
  This spray of Western pine!
    Dickens in Camp. Stanza 10

These things are managed so well in
    France.[1]
     The Tale of a Pony

Brief words, when actions wait, are
    well:
The prompter's hand is on his bell;
The coming heroes, lovers, kings,
Are idly lounging in the wings;
Behind the curtain's mystic fold
The glowing future lies unrolled.
   Address at opening of the Cali-
    fornia Theatre, San Francisco
    [*January 19, 1870*]

What was it the Engines said,
Pilots touching, — head to head
Facing on the single track,
Half a world behind each back?
   What the Engines Said (Open-
    ing of the Pacific Railroad)[2]

  [1] See Sterne, page 346b.
  [2] Drill, ye tarriers, drill,
    And it's work all day
    Without sugar in your tay,

I reside at Table Mountain, and my
   name is Truthful James;
I am not up to small deceit, or any sinful games.
       The Society upon the Stanislaus

He smiled a kind of sickly smile, and
   curled up on the floor,
And the subsequent proceedings interested him no more.
       Ibid.

For there be women, fair as she,
Whose verbs and nouns do more agree.
       Mrs. Judge Jenkins

Oh, yer's yer good old whiskey,
Drink it down.
       Two Men of Sandy Bar [*1876*].
       Act IV

One big vice in a man is apt to keep
out a great many smaller ones.
       Ibid.

Give me a man that is capable of a
devotion to anything, rather than a
cold, calculating average of all the virtues!
       Ibid.

I'm acquainted with affliction,
Chiefly in the form of fiction,
As 'tis offered up by strangers
   At the consul's open door.
       At the Consul's Open Door [1]

I think I know all fancy
Styles of active mendicancy.
       Ibid.

I know the worthy tourist,
Who by accident the purest,
Lost his letters, watch and wallet,
From the cold deck coming o'er.
       Ibid.

When you're working for the U.P. Railway.
     *Laborers' song during the construc-
     tion of the Union Pacific Railway*
[1] Written while Harte was United States
consul at Glasgow [1880–1885], after receiving a note of warning from Bristol, England, that an impostor pretending to be a
destitute American had been procuring money
from United States consuls.

FRANCES RIDLEY
HAVERGAL
[1836–1879]

Silence is no certain token
   That no secret grief is there;
Sorrow which is never spoken
   Is the heaviest load to bear.
       Misunderstood. Stanza **15**

FITZHUGH LUDLOW
[1836–1870]

While we wait for the napkin, the soup
   gets cold,
While the bonnet is trimming, the face
   grows old,
When we've matched our buttons, the
   pattern is sold,
And everything comes too late — too
   late.
       Too Late. Stanza **2**

SARAH MORGAN BRYANT
PIATT
[1836–1919]

Other suns will shine as golden,
   Other skies be just as blue;
Other south winds blow as softly,
   Gently drinking up the dew.
       Today. Stanza **1**

WILLIAM JEFFREY PROWSE
[1836–1870]

Though the latitude's rather uncertain,
And the longitude likewise is vague,
Still the people I pity who know not the
   City,
The beautiful City of Prague.
       The City of Prague. Stanza **5**

MARY ASHLEY TOWNSEND
[1836–1901]

I believe if I should die
And you should kiss my eyelids when I
   lie
Cold, dead, and dumb to all the world
   contains,

The folded orbs would open at thy
breath,
And, from its exile in the isles of death,
Life would come gladly back along my
veins.
Creed. Stanza 1

WILLIAM WINTER
[1836–1917]

Who cares for nothing alone is free, —
Sit down, good fellow, and drink with
me!
Orgia

His love was like the liberal air, —
Embracing all, to cheer and bless;
And every grief that mortals share
Found pity in his tenderness.
I. H. Bromley

Fierce for the right, he bore his part
In strife with many a valiant foe;
But Laughter winged his polished dart,
And kindness tempered every blow.
Ibid.

Cold the stars are, cold the earth is,
Everything is grim and cold!
Strange and drear the sound of mirth is
— Life and I are old.
Age

CESARE LOMBROSO
[1836–1909]

Klopstock was questioned regarding
the meaning of a passage in his poem.
He replied, "God and I both knew what
it meant once; now God alone knows." [1]
*The Man of Genius. Part I,
Chap. 2*

The appearance of a single great
genius is more than equivalent to the
birth of a hundred mediocrities.
Ibid. Part II, Chap. 2

"Lawsuit mania" . . . a continual
craving to go to law against others,
while considering themselves the injured party.
Ibid. Part III, Chap. 3

The ignorant man always adores
what he cannot understand.
Ibid.

[1] Also attributed to Browning, apropos of
his *Sordello.*

Men in general, but more particularly the insane, love to speak of themselves, and on this theme they even
become eloquent.
*The Man of Genius.
Part IV, Chap. 1*

MARY GARDINER BRAINARD
[1837–1905]

I see not a step before me as I tread on
another year;
But I've left the Past in God's keeping,
— the Future His mercy shall
clear;
And what looks dark in the distance,
may brighten as I draw near.
Not Knowing. Stanza 2

JOHN BURROUGHS
[1837–1921]

In sorrow he learned this truth —
One may return to the place of his
birth,
He cannot go back to his youth.
The Return. Stanza 3

Serene, I fold my hands and wait,
Nor care for wind, nor tide, nor sea;
I rave no more 'gainst time or fate,
For lo! my own shall come to me.
Waiting. Stanza 1

I was born with a chronic anxiety
about the weather.
Is It Going to Rain?

Literature is an investment of genius
which pays dividends to all subsequent
times.
Literary Fame

It is always easier to believe than to
deny. Our minds are naturally affirma-
tive.
*The Light of Day. The Modern
Skeptic*

Time does not become sacred to us
until we have lived it.
The Spell of the Past

Nature teaches more than she
preaches. There are no sermons in

stones. It is easier to get a spark out of a stone than a moral.
> *Time and Change. The Gospel of Nature*

I go to books and to nature as a bee goes to the flower, for a nectar that I can make into my own honey.
> *The Summit of the Years*

Life is a struggle, but not a warfare.
> *Ibid.*

GROVER CLEVELAND
[1837–1908]

Public officers are the servants and agents of the people, to execute the laws which the people have made.
> *Letter accepting the nomination for Governor of New York* [*October, 1882*]

Your every voter, as surely as your chief magistrate, exercises a public trust.[1]
> *Inaugural Address* [*March 4, 1885*]

However plenty silver dollars may become, they will not be distributed as gifts among the people.
> *First Annual Message* [*December 8, 1885*]

The so-called debtor class . . . are not dishonest because they are in debt.
> *Ibid.*

After an existence of nearly twenty years of almost innocuous desuetude these laws are brought forth.
> *Message* [*March 1, 1886*]

When more of the people's sustenance is exacted through the form of taxation than is necessary to meet the just obligations of Government and expenses of its economical administration, such exaction becomes ruthless extor-

tion and a violation of the fundamental principles of a free Government.
> *Second Annual Message* [*December, 1886*]

It is a condition which confronts us — not a theory.[1]
> *Third Annual Message* [*December 6, 1887*]

The lessons of paternalism ought to be unlearned and the better lesson taught that while the people should patriotically and cheerfully support their Government, its functions do not include the support of the people.
> *Inaugural Address* [*March 4, 1893*]

I have tried so hard to do the right.
> *Last Words*

ADMIRAL GEORGE DEWEY
[1837–1917]

You may fire when you are ready, Gridley.
> *Addressed to the Captain of Dewey's Flagship, at the Battle of Manila Bay, May 1, 1898*

WILLIAM DEAN HOWELLS
[1837–1920]

We live, but a world has passed away
With the years that perished to make us men.
> *The Mulberries*

Lord, for the erring thought
Not into evil wrought:
Lord, for the wicked will
Betrayed and baffled still:
For the heart from itself kept,
Our thanksgiving accept.
> *Thanksgiving*

Though I move with leaden feet,
Light itself is not so fleet;
And before you know me gone
Eternity and I are one.
> *Time*

I know his name, I know his note,
  That so with rapture takes my soul;
Like flame the gold beneath his throat,
  His glossy cope is black as coal.
> *The Song the Oriole Sings*

[1] The familiar saying "Public office is a public trust" seems to have been paraphrased from various campaign speeches by Cleveland in 1884.
See Mathew Henry, page 293a, Burke, page 361b, Jefferson, page 375a, Clay, page 433b, and Calhoun, page 442a.

[1] See Disraeli, page 512a.

He who sleeps in continual noise is wakened by silence.
Pordenone. IV

See how today's achievement is only tomorrow's confusion;
See how possession always cheapens the thing that was precious.
Ibid.

Yes, death is at the bottom of the cup,
And every one that lives must drink it up;
And yet between the sparkle at the top
And the black lees where lurks that bitter drop,
There swims enough good liquor, Heaven knows,
To ease our hearts of all their other woes.
If

The first night, when at night I went about
Locking the doors and windows everywhere,
After she died, I seemed to lock her out
In the starred silence and the homeless air.
Experience

Tossing his mane of snows in wildest eddies and tangles,
Lion-like March cometh in, hoarse, with tempestuous breath.
Earliest Spring. Stanza 1

They were Americans, and they knew how to worship a woman.
The Lady of the Aroostook [1879]

The Bostonian who leaves Boston ought to be condemned to perpetual exile.
The Rise of Silas Lapham [1885]. Chap. 5

The man of letters must make up his mind that in the United States the fate of a book is in the hands of the women.
Literature and Life [1902]

Does it afflict you to find your books wearing out? I mean literally. . . . The mortality of all inanimate things is terrible to me, but that of books most of all.
Letter to Charles Eliot Norton [April 6, 1903]

I am not sorry for having wrought in common, crude material so much; that is the right American stuff; and perhaps hereafter, when my din is done, if any one is curious to know what that noise was, it will be found to have proceeded from a small insect which was scraping about on the surface of our life and trying to get into its meaning for the sake of the other insects larger or smaller. That is, such has been my unconscious work; consciously, I was always, as I still am, trying to fashion a piece of literature out of the life next at hand.
Letter to Charles Eliot Norton [April 26, 1903]

Last night, after I got back from my Balfour tailor, I expressed my surprise that B. should go to such a simple shop. "Well, I don't think, sir, Mr. Balfour cares much for his clothes, sir. Them distinguished men can't, sir. Their thoughts soars to 'igher things, sir."
Letter to Mrs. Howells [April 12, 1904], quoting his London landlord

Spain, where most of my boyhood was passed while I was working at case in my father's printing-office in Northern Ohio.
Letter to Brander Matthews [July 22, 1911], referring to his love for Don Quixote

HENRY SAMBROOKE LEIGH
[1837–1883]

In form and feature, face and limb,
I grew so like my brother,
That folks got taking me for him
And each for one another.
The Twins. Stanza 1

And when I died the neighbors came
And buried brother John.
Ibid. Stanza 5

My love she is a kitten,
And my heart's a ball of string.
My Love and My Heart. Stanza 1

JOHN L. PARKER
[1837–1917]

The little brown button,
The sacred bronze button,
The Grand Army button
He wears on his coat.
The Little Bronze Button

INNES RANDOLPH
[1837–1887]

I am a good old rebel —
  Yes; that's just what I am —
And for this land of freedom
  I do not give a dam'.
I'm glad I fit agin 'em,
  And I only wish we'd won;
And I don't ax no pardon
  For anything I've done.
A Good Old Rebel (Unreconstructed). Stanza 1

ALGERNON CHARLES SWINBURNE
[1837–1909]

Maiden and mistress of the months and
  stars
Now folded in the flowerless fields of
  heaven.
Atalanta in Calydon [*1865*].
Line 1

When the hounds of spring are on
  winter's traces,
The mother of months in meadow or
  plain
Fills the shadows and windy places
With lisp of leaves and ripple of rain;
And the brown bright nightingale
  amorous
Is half assuaged for Itylus,
For the Thracian ships and the foreign
  faces,
The tongueless vigil, and all the pain.
Ibid. Chorus, Stanza 1

Come with bows bent and with empty-
  ing of quivers,
Maiden most perfect, lady of light,
With a noise of winds and many rivers,
With a clamour of waters, and with
  might;
Bind on thy sandals, O thou most fleet,

Over the splendour and speed of thy
  feet,
For the faint east quickens, the wan
  west shivers,
Round the feet of the day and the feet
  of the night.
*Atalanta in Calydon. Chorus,
Stanza 2*

For winter's rains and ruins are over,
And all the season of snows and sins;
The days dividing lover and lover,
The light that loses, the night that wins;
And time remembered is grief forgotten,
And frosts are slain and flowers begotten,
And in green underwood and cover
Blossom by blossom the spring begins.
Ibid. Stanza 4

Before the beginning of years
There came to the making of man
Time, with a gift of tears;
Grief, with a glass that ran;
Pleasure, with pain for leaven;
Summer, with flowers that fell;
Remembrance fallen from heaven,
And madness risen from hell;
Strength without hands to smite;
Love that endures for a breath;
Night, the shadow of light,
And life, the shadow of death.
Ibid. Chorus, Stanza 1

Eyesight and speech they wrought
For the veils of the soul therein,
A time for labour and thought,
A time to serve and to sin; [1]
They gave him light in his ways,
And love, and a space for delight,
And beauty and length of days,
And night, and sleep in the night.
His speech is a burning fire;
With his lips he travaileth;
In his heart is a blind desire,
In his eyes foreknowledge of death;
He weaves, and is clothed with derision;
Sows, and he shall not reap;
His life is a watch or a vision
Between a sleep and a sleep.
Ibid. Stanza 3

We have seen thee, O Love, thou art
  fair; thou art goodly, O Love.
Ibid. Chorus

[1] See *Ecclesiastes*, *III*, *2*, on page 1042b.

For words divide and rend;
But silence is most noble till the end.
      Atalanta in Calydon. Chorus

O wise among women, and wisest,
    Our Lady of Pain.
      Dolores [1866]. Stanza 5

    Change in a trice
The lilies and languors of virtue
For the raptures and roses of vice.
      Ibid. Stanza 9

O splendid and sterile Dolores,
    Our Lady of Pain.
      Ibid.

Ah beautiful passionate body
That never has ached with a heart!
      Ibid. Stanza 11

The delight that consumes the desire,
The desire that outruns the delight.
      Ibid. Stanza 14

Despair the twin-born of devotion.
      Ibid.

I have passed from the outermost portal
To the shrine where a sin is a prayer.
      Ibid. Stanza 17

For the crown of our life as it closes
Is darkness, the fruit thereof dust;
No thorns go as deep as a rose's,
And love is more cruel than lust.
Time turns the old days to derision,
Our loves into corpses or wives;
And marriage and death and division
Make barren our lives.
      Ibid. Stanza 20

What ailed us, O gods, to desert you
For creeds that refuse and restrain?
Come down and redeem us from virtue,
    Our Lady of Pain.
      Ibid. Stanza 35

Then love was the pearl of his oyster,
And Venus rose red out of wine.
      Ibid. Stanza 39

Lo, this is she that was the world's de-
    light.
      Laus Veneris [1866]. Stanza 3

Ah yet would God this flesh of mine
    might be
Where air might wash and long leaves
    cover me,
Where tides of grass break into foam of
    flowers,

Or where the wind's feet shine along the
    sea.
      Laus Veneris. Stanza 14

O sad kissed mouth, how sorrowful it
    is!
      Ibid. Stanza 79

To have known love, how bitter a thing
    it is.
      Ibid. Stanza 103

There will no man do for your sake, I
    think,
What I would have done for the least
    word said.
I had wrung life dry for your lips to
    drink,
Broken it up for your daily bread.
      The Triumph of Time [1866].
      Stanza 12

I wish we were dead together today,
Lost sight of, hidden away out of sight,
Clasped and clothed in the cloven clay,
Out of the world's way, out of the light.
      Ibid. Stanza 15

At the door of life, by the gate of breath,
There are worse things waiting for men
    than death.
      Ibid. Stanza 20

I will go back to the great sweet mother,
Mother and lover of men, the sea.
      Ibid. Stanza 33

There lived a singer in France of old,
By the tideless dolorous midland sea.
In a land of sand and ruin and gold
There shone one woman, and none but
    she.
      Ibid. Stanza 41

O brother, the gods were good to you.
Sleep, and be glad while the world en-
    dures.
Be well content as the years wear
    through;
Give thanks for life, and the loves and
    lures.
      Ibid. Stanza 43

I shall never be friends again with
    roses;
I shall loathe sweet tunes.
      Ibid. Stanza 45

Marvellous mercies and infinite love.
      Les Noyades [1866].
      Stanza 1

I am sick of singing; the bays burn deep
    and chafe: I am fain
To rest a little from praise and grievous
    pleasure and pain.
        Hymn to Proserpine: After the
        Proclamation in Rome of the
        Christian Faith [1866]
Thou hast conquered, O pale Galilean;
    the world has grown grey from thy
    breath;
We have drunken of things Lethean,
    and fed on the fullness of death.
Laurel is green for a season, and love is
    sweet for a day;
But love grows bitter with treason, and
    laurel outlives not May.
Sleep, shall we sleep after all? for the
    world is not sweet in the end;
For the old faiths loosen and fall, the
    new years ruin and rend.
                        Ibid.
I shall die as my fathers died, and sleep
    as they sleep; even so.
For the glass of the years is brittle
    wherein we gaze for a span.
                        Ibid.
For there is no God found stronger than
    death; and death is a sleep.
                        Ibid.
If you loved me ever so little,
    I could bear the bonds that gall,
    I could dream the bonds were brittle;
        You do not love me at all.
    Satia Te Sanguine [1866]. *Stanza 1*
While he lives let a man be glad,
For none hath joy of his death.
        A Lamentation [1866]. *I, 4*
If love were what the rose is,
    And I were like the leaf,
Our lives would grow together
In sad or singing weather.
        A Match [1866]. *Stanza 1*
If you were April's lady,
    And I were lord in May.
                Ibid. Stanza 5
If you were queen of pleasure,
    And I were king of pain,
We'd hunt down love together,
Pluck out his flying feather,
And teach his feet a measure,
    And find his mouth a rein.
                Ibid. Stanza 6

For in the time we know not of
    Did fate begin
Weaving the web of days that wove
    Your doom, Faustine.
        Faustine [1866]. *Stanza 24*
A love machine
With clockwork joints of supple gold —
No more, Faustine.
                Ibid. Stanza 36
Take hand and part with laughter;
    Touch lips and part with tears;
Once more and no more after,
    Whatever comes with years.
        Rococo [1866]. *Stanza 1*
Forget that I remember,
And dream that I forget.
                Ibid. Stanza 2
The burden of long living. Thou shalt
    fear
Waking, and sleeping mourn upon thy
    bed;
And say at night "Would God the day
    were here,"
And say at dawn "Would God the day
    were dead." [1]
        A Ballad of Burdens [1866].
                        Stanza 4
For life is sweet, but after life is death.
This is the end of every man's desire.
                Ibid. L'Envoy
O love, O lover, loose or hold me fast,
I had thee first, whoever have thee last.
                Erotion [1866]
I shall remember while the light lives
    yet
And in the night-time I shall not forget.
Though (as thou wilt) thou leave me
    ere life leave,
I will not, for thy love I will not, grieve.
                        Ibid.
Here, where the world is quiet;
    Here, where all trouble seems
Dead winds' and spent waves' riot
    In doubtful dreams of dreams.
        The Garden of Proserpine [1866].
                        Stanza 1

[1] In the morning thou shalt say, Would God
it were even! and at even thou shalt say,
Would God it were morning! for the fear of
thine heart wherewith thou shalt fear, and for
the sight of thine eyes which thou shalt see. —
Deuteronomy, XXVIII, 67

I am tired of tears and laughter,
  And men that laugh and weep;
Of what may come hereafter
  For men that sow and reap:
I am weary of days and hours,
Blown buds of barren flowers,
Desires and dreams and powers
  And everything but sleep.
            The Garden of Proserpine.
                        Stanza 2

We are not sure of sorrow,
  And joy was never sure.
Today will die tomorrow;
  Time stoops to no man's lure;
And love, grown faint and fretful,
With lips but half regretful
Sighs, and with eyes forgetful
  Weeps that no loves endure.
            Ibid. Stanza 10

From too much love of living,
  From hope and fear set free,
We thank with brief thanksgiving
  Whatever gods may be
That no life lives forever;
That dead men rise up never;
That even the weariest river
  Winds somewhere safe to sea.[1]
            Ibid. Stanza 11

Ah that such sweet things should be fleet,
Such fleet things sweet!
            Félise [1866]. Stanza 22

Those eyes the greenest of things blue,
The bluest of things grey.
            Ibid. Stanza 24

Eyes colored like a water-flower,
And deeper than the green sea's glass;
Eyes that remember one sweet hour —
In vain we swore it should not pass.
            Ibid. Stanza 36

Live and let live, as I will do,
Love and let love, and so will I.
But, sweet, for me no more with you:
Not while I live, not though I die.
        Good-night, good-bye.
            Ibid. Stanza 59

I remember the way we parted,
  The day and the way we met;
You hoped we were both broken-
  hearted

---

[1] No matter how long the river, the river will reach the sea. — EUGENE FITCH WARE ("IRONQUILL") [1841–1911]: *The Blizzard*

And knew we should both forget.
            An Interlude [1866]. Stanza 11

And the best and the worst of this is
  That neither is most to blame,
If you have forgotten my kisses
  And I have forgotten your name.
            Ibid. Stanza 14

And through the trumpet of a child of
  Rome
Rang the pure music of the flutes of
  Greece.
        *Song for the Centenary of
        Walter Savage Landor [1866].
        Stanza 17*

I am that which began;
  Out of me the years roll;
Out of me God and man;
  I am equal and whole;
God changes, and man, and the form of
  them bodily; I am the soul.
            Hertha [1871]. Stanza 1

Before ever land was,
  Before ever the sea,
Or soft hair of the grass,
  Or fair limbs of the tree,
Or the flesh-coloured fruit of my
  branches,
I was, and thy soul was in me.
            Ibid. Stanza 2

A creed is a rod,
  And a crown is of night;
But this thing is God,
  To be man with thy might,
To grow straight in the strength of thy
  spirit, and to live out thy life as the
  light.
            Ibid. Stanza 15

In the grey beginning of years, in the
  twilight of things that began,
The word of the earth in the ears of
  the world, was it God? was it man?
            Hymn of Man [1871]

Ask nothing more of me, sweet,
All I can give you I give;
Heart of my heart, were it more,
More would be laid at your feet:
Love that should help you to live,
Song that should spur you to soar.
            The Oblation [1871]. Stanza 1

It is long since Mr. Carlyle expressed his opinion that if any poet or other literary creature could really be "killed off by one critique" or many, the sooner he was so despatched the better; a sentiment in which I for one humbly but heartily concur.

> *Under the Microscope* [*1872*]

A blatant Bassarid of Boston, a rampant Maenad of Massachusetts.[1]

> *Ibid.*

To wipe off the froth of falsehood from the foaming lips of inebriated virtue, when fresh from the sexless orgies of morality and reeling from the delirious riot of religion, may doubtless be a charitable office.

> *Ibid.*

The more congenial page of some tenth-rate poeticule worn out with failure after failure and now squat in his hole like the tailless fox, he is curled up to snarl and whimper beneath the inaccessible vine of song.

> *Ibid.*

The tadpole poet will never grow into anything bigger than a frog; not though in that stage of development he should puff and blow himself till he bursts with windy adulation at the heels of the laureled ox.

> *Ibid.*

Many loves of many a mood and many a kind
Fill the life of man, and mould the secret mind.

> *Erechtheus* [*1876*]

Poor splendid wings so frayed and soiled and torn!

> *A Ballad of François Villon*
> [*1878*]. *Stanza 3*

Villon, our sad bad glad mad brother's name.[2]

> *Ibid. Refrain*

In a coign of the cliff between lowland and highland,
At the sea-down's edge between windward and lee,

Walled round with rocks as an inland island,
The ghost of a garden fronts the sea.[1]

> *A Forsaken Garden* [*1878*].
> *Stanza 1*

There is no help for these things; none to mend,
And none to mar; not all our songs, O friend,
Will make death clear or make life durable.

> *Ave atque Vale: In Memory*
> *of Charles Baudelaire* [*1878*].
> *Stanza 16*

Sleep; and if life was bitter to thee, pardon,
If sweet, give thanks; thou hast no more to live;
And to give thanks is good, and to forgive.

> *Ibid. Stanza 17*

Body and spirit are twins: God only knows which is which.

> *The Higher Pantheism in a*
> *Nutshell* [*1880*]. *Stanza 7*

God, whom we see not, is: and God, who is not, we see:
Fiddle, we know, is diddle: and diddle, we take it, is dee.

> *Ibid. Stanza 12*

A little soul scarce fledged for earth
Takes wing with heaven again for goal
Even while we hailed as fresh from birth
A little soul.

> *A Baby's Death* [*1883*]. *I, 1*

Who knows but on their sleep may rise
Such light as never heaven let through
To lighten earth from Paradise?

> *Ibid. IV, 2*

All our past acclaims our future: Shakespeare's voice and Nelson's hand,
Milton's faith and Wordsworth's trust in this our chosen and chainless land,

---

[1] The reference is to Harriet Beecher Stowe, whose accusations against Byron in her article, "The True Story of Lady Byron's Life" [*Atlantic Monthly*, September, 1869], and in her book, *Lady Byron Vindicated* [1870], aroused strong protests in England.

[2] See Browning, page 572b.

[1] On the grass of the cliff, at the edge of the steep,
God planted a garden, a garden of sleep.
CLEMENT W. SCOTT [1841–1904]: *The Garden of Sleep*

Bear as witness: come the world against her, England yet shall stand.
England, An Ode [*1884*]. *II, 5*

Faith in faith established evermore
Stands a sea-mark in the tides of time.
A Sea-Mark [*1884*]. *Stanza 5*

Not with dreams, but with blood and with iron,[1]
Shall a nation be moulded to last.
A Word for the Country [*1884*].
Stanza 13

Is not Precedent indeed a King of men?
A Word from the Psalmist [*1884*].
Stanza 4

HENRY BROOKS ADAMS
[1838–1918]

Accident counts for much in companionship as in marriage.
The Education of Henry Adams
[*1907*]. *Chap. 4*

Women have, commonly, a very positive moral sense; that which they will, is right; that which they reject, is wrong; and their will, in most cases, ends by settling the moral.
Ibid. Chap. 6

All experience is an arch, to build upon.[2]
Ibid.

Only on the edge of the grave can man conclude anything.
Ibid.

Although the Senate is much given to admiring in its members a superiority less obvious or quite invisible to outsiders, one Senator seldom proclaims his own inferiority to another, and still more seldom likes to be told of it.
Ibid. Chap. 7

Friends are born, not made.
Ibid.

[1] Not by speechifying and counting majorities are the great questions of the time to be solved . . . but by iron and blood [Eisen und Blut]. — BISMARCK: *Speech, Prussian Diet* [September 30, 1862]
[2] Yet all experience is an arch wherethrough Gleams that untraveled world.
TENNYSON: *Ulysses* [1842]

A friend in power is a friend lost.[1]
The Education of Henry Adams.
Chap. 7

The effect of power and publicity on all men is the aggravation of self, a sort of tumor that ends by killing the victim's sympathies.
Ibid. Chap. 10

Young men have a passion for regarding their elders as senile.
Ibid. Chap. 11

Knowledge of human nature is the beginning and end of political education.
Ibid. Chap. 12

These questions of taste, of feeling, of inheritance, need no settlement. Everyone carries his own inch-rule of taste, and amuses himself by applying it, triumphantly, wherever he travels.
Ibid.

Intimates are predestined.
Ibid. Chap. 13

His first struggle with a sleeping-car made him doubt the value — to him — of a Pullman civilization.
Ibid. Chap. 16

Chaos often breeds life, when order breeds habit.
Ibid.

At best, the renewal of broken relations is a nervous matter.
Ibid.

Sumner's [2] mind had reached the calm of water which receives and reflects images without absorbing them; it contained nothing but itself.
Ibid.

The difference is slight, to the influence of an author, whether he is read by five hundred readers, or by five hundred thousand; if he can select the five hundred, he reaches the five hundred thousand.
Ibid. Chap. 17

The newspaper-man is, more than most men, a double personality; and his person feels best satisfied in its double

[1] See *Chap. 28*, page 697b.
[2] Charles Sumner [1811–1874].

instincts when writing in one sense and thinking in another.
    The Education of Henry Adams.
    Chap. 17

A teacher affects eternity; he can never tell where his influence stops.
    Ibid. Chap. 20

One friend in a lifetime is much; two are many; three are hardly possible. Friendship needs a certain parallelism of life, a community of thought, a rivalry of aim.
    Ibid.

What one knows is, in youth, of little moment; they know enough who know how to learn.
    Ibid. Chap. 21

He had often noticed that six months' oblivion amounts to newspaper-death, and that resurrection is rare. Nothing is easier, if a man wants it, than rest, profound as the grave.
    Ibid. Chap. 22

Morality is a private and costly luxury.
    Ibid.

Nothing is more tiresome than a superannuated pedagogue.
    Ibid. Chap. 23

The study of history is useful to the historian by teaching him his ignorance of women. . . . The woman who is known only through a man is known wrong.
    Ibid.

He too serves a certain purpose who only stands and cheers.[1]
    Ibid. Chap. 24

Practical politics consists in ignoring facts.
    Ibid.

Nothing in education is so astonishing as the amount of ignorance it accumulates in the form of inert facts.
    Ibid. Chap. 25

[1] And if I should lose, let me stand by the road
  And cheer as the winners go by !
    BERTON BRALEY [1882–   ]: *Prayer of a Sportsman*

Power when wielded by abnormal energy is the most serious of facts.
    The Education of Henry Adams.
    Chap. 28

Those who seek education in the paths of duty are always deceived by the illusion that power in the hands of friends is an advantage to them.[1]
    Ibid.

Power is poison. Its effect on Presidents had been always tragic, chiefly as an almost insane excitement at first, and a worse reaction afterwards; but also because no mind is so well balanced as to bear the strain of seizing unlimited force without habit or knowledge of it; and finding it disputed with him by hungry packs of wolves and hounds whose lives depend on snatching the carrion.
    Ibid.

A certain chronic irritability — a sort of Bostonitis — which, in its primitive Puritan forms, seemed due to knowing too much of his neighbors and thinking too much of himself.
    Ibid.

Modern politics is, at bottom, a struggle not of men but of forces.
    Ibid.

We combat obstacles in order to get repose, and, when got, the repose is insupportable.
    Ibid. Chap. 29

Simplicity is the most deceitful mistress that ever betrayed man.
    Ibid. Chap. 30

No one means all he says, and yet very few say all they mean, for words are slippery and thought is viscous.
    Ibid. Chap. 31

The movement from unity into multiplicity, between 1200 and 1900, was unbroken in sequence, and rapid in acceleration. Prolonged one generation longer, it would require a new social mind.
    Ibid. Chap. 34

Even in America, the Indian Summer of life should be a little sunny and a little sad, like the season, and infinite

[1] See *Chap. 7*, page 696b.

in wealth and depth of tone — but never hustled.

The Education of Henry Adams. Chap. 35

Perhaps some day — say 1938, their centenary — they [1] might be allowed to return together for a holiday, to see the mistakes of their own lives made clear in the light of the mistakes of their successors; and perhaps then, for the first time since man began his education among the carnivores, they would find a world that sensitive and timid natures could regard without a shudder.

Ibid. Closing words

JAMES BRYCE [2]
[1838–1922]

Law will never be strong or respected unless it has the sentiment of the people behind it. If the people of a State make bad laws, they will suffer for it. They will be the first to suffer. Suffering, and nothing else, will implant that sentiment of responsibility which is the first step to reform.

The American Commonwealth [1888]. Vol. I, Page 352

To the vast majority of mankind nothing is more agreeable than to escape the need for mental exertion. . . . To most people nothing is more troublesome than the effort of thinking.[3]

Studies in History and Jurisprudence [1901]. Obedience

The greatest liberty that man has taken with Nature.[4]

South America [1912]

What you want [in Washington] is to have a city which every one who comes from Maine, Texas, Florida, Arkansas, or Oregon can admire as being something finer and more beautiful than he had ever dreamed of before;

---

[1] Adams and his two friends John Hay [1838–1905] and Clarence King [1842–1901].
[2] Ambassador from Great Britain to the United States, 1906–1913.
[3] See R. B. Sheridan, page 382a.
[4] The Panama Canal.

something which makes him even more proud to be an American.

The Nation's Capital [1]

You have never sufficiently foreseen how enormously rich and populous a nation you are going to be.

Ibid.

Medicine, the only profession that labours incessantly to destroy the reason for its own existence.

Address at dinner for General W. C. Gorgas [March 23, 1914]

GEORGE COOPER
[1838–1927]

Sweet Genevieve,
The days may come, the days may go,
But still the hands of mem'ry weave
The blissful dreams of long ago.

Sweet Genevieve [Circa 1877]

JOHN HAY
[1838–1905]

A keerless man in his talk was Jim,
    And an awkward hand in a row,
He never flunked, and he never lied, —
    I reckon he never knowed how.

Jim Bludso

"I'll hold her nozzle agin the bank
Till the last galoot's ashore."

Ibid.

And they all had trust in his cussedness,
And knowed he would keep his word.

Ibid.

He weren't no saint — but at jedgment
    I'd run my chance with Jim,
'Longside of some pious gentlemen
    That wouldn't shook hands with him.
He seen his duty, a dead-sure thing, —
    And went for it thar and then;
And Christ ain't a-going to be too hard
    On a man that died for men.

Ibid.

I don't go much on religion,
    I never ain't had no show;
But I've got a middlin' tight grip, sir,
    On the handful o' things I know.
I don't pan out on the prophets

---

[1] In *The National Geographic Magazine,* 1913.

And free-will, and that sort of
thing, —
But I b'lieve in God and the angels
Ever sence one night last spring.
Little Breeches

And I think that saving a little child,
And fotching him to his own,
Is a derned sight better business
Than loafing around The Throne.
Ibid.

The night comes down, the lights burn
blue;
And at my door the Pale Horse stands,[1]
To bear me forth to unknown lands.
The Stirrup Cup

Bring me tonight a lotus tied
With thread from a house where none
has died.[2]
The Law of Death

There are three species of creatures who
when they seem coming are going,
When they seem going they come:
Diplomats, women, and crabs.
Distichs. II

When you break up housekeeping, you
learn the extent of your treasures.
Ibid. IX

Who would succeed in the world should
be wise in the use of his pronouns.
Utter the You twenty times, where you
once utter the I.
Ibid. XIII

True luck consists not in holding the
best of the cards at the table:
Luckiest he who knows just when to
rise and go home.
Ibid. XV

Try not to beat back the current, yet be
not drowned in its waters;
Speak with the speech of the world,
think with the thoughts of the few.
Ibid. XVII

---

[1] A pale horse: and his name that sat on him
was Death. — *Revelation, VI, 8*
[2] "A grain of mustard-seed," the sage replied,
"Found where none old or young has ever
died,
Will cure the pain you carry in your
side."
JOHN WHITE CHADWICK [1840–1904]:
Buddha's Lesson

GEORGE WASHINGTON JOHNSON
[1838–1917]

I wandered today to the hill, Maggie,
To watch the scene below,
The creek and the old rusty mill,
Maggie,
As we used to, long ago.
When You and I Were Young,
Maggie [1866]. Stanza 1

To me you're as fair as you were, Mag-
gie,
When you and I were young.
Ibid. Stanza 3

And now we are aged and gray, Maggie,
The trials of life nearly done,
Let us sing of the days that are gone,
Maggie,
When you and I were young.
Refrain

WILLIAM EDWARD HARTPOLE LECKY
[1838–1903]

Offspring of an idle hour,
Whence has come thy lasting power?
On an Old Song

The stately ship is seen no more,
The fragile skiff attains the shore;
And while the great and wise decay,
And all their trophies pass away,
Some sudden thought, some careless
rhyme,
Still floats above the wrecks of Time.
Ibid.

JOHN, VISCOUNT MORLEY
[1838–1923]

No man can climb out beyond the
limitations of his own character.
Critical Miscellanies [1871].
Robespierre

A great interpreter of life ought not
himself to need interpretation.
Emerson

The most frightful idea that has
ever corroded human nature — the
idea of eternal punishment.
Vauvenargues

Where it is a duty to worship the sun it is pretty sure to be a crime to examine the laws of heat.

Voltaire [*1872*]

A man will already be in no mean Paradise if at the hour of sunset a ray of good hope may fall upon him like harmonies of music.

Ibid.

Those who would treat politics and morality apart will never understand the one or the other.

Rousseau [*1873*]

You can not demonstrate an emotion or prove an aspiration.

Ibid.

Evolution is not a force but a process; not a cause but a law.

On Compromise [*1874*]

It is not enough to do good; one must do it the right way.

Ibid.

You have not converted a man because you have silenced him.

Ibid.

Literature — the most seductive, the most deceiving, the most dangerous of professions.

Burke [*1879*]

Great economic and social forces flow with a tidal sweep over communities that are only half conscious of that which is befalling them. Wise statesmen are those who foresee what time is thus bringing, and endeavor to shape institutions and to mold men's thought and purpose in accordance with the change that is silently surrounding them.

Life of Richard Cobden [*1881*]

The great business of life is to be, to do, to do without, and to depart.

Address on Aphorisms [*1887*]

The gravity and concision of Thucydides are of specially wholesome example in these days of over-coloured and over-voluminous narrative.

Ibid.

Simplicity of character is no hindrance to subtlety of intellect.

Life of Gladstone [*1903*]

Every man of us has all the centuries in him.

Ibid.

There are some books which cannot be adequately reviewed for twenty or thirty years after they come out.

Recollections [*1917*]. *Vol. I, Book 2, Chap. 8*

The proper memory for a politician is one that knows what to remember and what to forget.

Ibid. Vol. II, Book 4, Chap. 2

In my creed, waste of public money is like the sin against the Holy Ghost.

Ibid. Book 5, Chap. 3

Success depends on three things: who says it, what he says, how he says it; and of these three things, what he says is the least important.

Ibid. Chap. 4

Excess of severity is not the path to order. On the contrary, it is the path to the bomb.

Ibid.

MARGARET ELIZABETH SANGSTER
[1838–1912]

I know — yet my arms are empty,
That fondly folded seven,
And the mother heart within me
Is almost starved for heaven.

Are the Children at Home?

Never yet was a springtime,
Late though lingered the snow,
That the sap stirred not at the whisper
Of the southwind, sweet and low;
Never yet was a springtime
When the buds forgot to blow.

Awakening

GEORGE LEYBOURNE
[? –1884]

He flies through the air with the greatest of ease,
This daring young man on the flying trapeze;

His figure is handsome, all girls he can
please,
And my love he purloined her away!
The Man on the Flying Trapeze
[*1860*]

JOSEPH MALINES [1]
[*Floruit* 1895]

Better put a strong fence 'round the
top of the cliff,
Than an ambulance down in the valley.
A Fence or an Ambulance.
Stanza 7

HEZEKIAH BUTTERWORTH
[1839–1905]

The bird with the broken pinion
Never soared as high again.
The Bird with a Broken Wing
One taper lights a thousand,
Yet shines as it has shone;
And the humblest light may kindle
A brighter than its own.
The Taper. Stanza 10

FRANCIS PHARCELLUS
CHURCH
[1839–1906]

Virginia, your little friends are wrong.
They have been affected by the skepticism of a skeptical age. They do not believe except they see. They think that
nothing can be which is not compre-
hensible by their little minds. All minds,
Virginia, whether they be men's or children's, are little. In this great universe
of ours man is a mere insect, an ant,
in his intellect, as compared with the
boundless world about him, as measured by the intelligence capable of
grasping the whole of truth and knowledge.
Editorial: Is There a Santa
Claus? [2]
Not believe in Santa Claus? You
might as well not believe in fairies.
. . . No Santa Claus! Thank God, he

[1] Editor of *The Reciter*, an English publication.
[2] First published in *The New York Sun*,
September 21, 1897, in reply to an inquiry
from Virginia O'Hanlon.

lives, and he lives forever. A thousand
years from now, Virginia, nay, ten
times ten thousand years from now, he
will continue to make glad the heart of
childhood.
Editorial: Is There a Santa Claus?

WALTER PATER
[1839–1894]

Every intellectual product must be
judged from the point of view of the
age and the people in which it was produced.
The Renaissance [*1873*].
Mirandola
Its generous belief that nothing which
had ever interested the human mind
could wholly lose its vitality.
Ibid.
That sweet look of devotion which
men have never been able altogether to
love, and which still makes the born
saint an object almost of suspicion to
his earthly brethren.
Ibid. Botticelli
The sunless pleasures of weary people, whose care for external things is
slackening.
Ibid. Michelangelo
Hers is the head upon which all "the
ends of the world are come," and the
eyelids are a little weary. It is a beauty
wrought out from within upon the flesh,
the deposit, little cell by cell, of strange
thoughts and fantastic reveries and exquisite passions. Set it for a moment
beside one of those white Greek goddesses or beautiful women of antiquity,
and how would they be troubled by this
beauty, into which the soul with all its
maladies has passed?
Ibid. Leonardo da Vinci
[*Mona Lisa*]
She is older than the rocks among
which she sits; like the vampire, she
has been dead many times, and learned
the secrets of the grave; and has been
a diver in deep seas, and keeps their
fallen day about her; and trafficked for
strange webs with Eastern merchants:
and as Leda, was the mother of Helen

of Troy, and, as Saint Anne, the mother of Mary; and all this has been to her but as the sound of lyres and flutes, and lives only in the delicacy with which it has moulded the changing lineaments, and tinged the eyelids and the hands.
The Renaissance. Leonardo da Vinci [Mona Lisa]
All art constantly aspires towards the condition of music.
Ibid. The School of Giorgione
They [1] form a circle which in an age of great troubles, losses, anxieties, can amuse itself with art, poetry, intrigue.
Ibid. Du Bellay
Religions, as they grow by natural laws out of man's life, are modified by whatever modifies his life.
Ibid. Winckelmann
Let us understand by poetry all literary production which attains the power of giving pleasure by its form, as distinct from its matter.
Ibid.
To burn always with this hard, gemlike flame, to maintain this ecstasy, is success in life.
Ibid. Conclusion
What we have to do is to be for ever curiously testing new opinions and courting new impressions.
Ibid.
Art comes to you proposing frankly to give nothing but the highest quality to your moments as they pass.
Ibid.
A book, like a person, has its fortunes with one; is lucky or unlucky in the precise moment of its falling in our way, and often by some happy accident counts with us for something more than its independent value.
Marius the Epicurean [1885]. Chap. 6
To know when one's self is interested, is the first condition of interesting other people.
Ibid.
Given the hardest terms, supposing our days are indeed but a shadow, even

[1] The poets of the *Pléiade*.

so, we may well adorn and beautify, in scrupulous self-respect, our souls, and whatever our souls touch upon.
Marius the Epicurean. Chap. 8
By the attainment of a true philosophy to attain happiness; or, having missed both, to perish, as one of the vulgar herd.
Ibid. Chap. 24
I hardly know wherein philosophy and wine are alike unless it be in this, that the philosophers exchange their ware for money, like the winemerchants; some of them with a mixture of water or worse, or giving short measure.
Ibid.
We need some imaginative stimulus, some not impossible ideal such as may shape vague hope, and transform it into effective desire, to carry us year after year, without disgust, through the routine-work which is so large a part of life.
Ibid. Chap. 25
The aim of a true philosophy must lie, not in futile efforts towards the complete accommodation of man to the circumstances in which he chances to find himself, but in the maintenance of a kind of candid discontent, in the face of the very highest achievement.
Ibid.
Through the survival of their children, happy parents are able to think calmly, and with a very practical affection, of a world in which they are to have no direct share.
Ibid.

JAMES RYDER RANDALL
[1839–1908]

Hark to an exiled son's appeal,
  Maryland, my Maryland!
My Mother State, to thee I kneel.
Maryland, My Maryland [1861].
Stanza 2
From hill to hill, from creek to creek,
Potomac calls to Chesapeake,
  Maryland, my Maryland.
Ibid. Stanza 7

SAMUEL JOHN STONE
[1839–1900]

Where did I come from, then? Ah,
  where indeed?
This is a riddle monstrous hard to read.
I have it! Why, of course,
All things are moulded by some plastic
  force
Out of some atoms somewhere up in
  space,
Fortuitously concurrent anyhow —
There, now!
That's plain as is the beak upon my
  face.
*Soliloquy of a Rationalistic
    Chicken* [1]

What I can't see, I never will believe in!
Ibid.

WILFRID SCAWEN BLUNT
[1840–1922]

He who has once been happy is for aye
Out of destruction's reach.
Sonnet, With Esther

Nor has the world a better thing,
  Though one should search it round,
Than thus to live one's own sole king,
  Upon one's own sole ground.
The Old Squire. Stanza 14

Ay, this is the famed rock, which Her-
  cules
And Goth and Moor bequeathed us. At
  this door
England stands sentry.
Sonnet, Gibraltar

HENRY BURTON
[1840–1930]

Have you had a kindness shown?
  Pass it on.
Pass It On. [2] *Stanza 1*

Hold thy lighted lamp on high,
Be a star in someone's sky.
Ibid. Stanza 4

[1] In *Harper's Monthly,* September, 1875.
[2] Official poem of the International Sunshine Society.

TIMOTHY J. CAMPBELL
[1840–1904]

What's the Constitution between
friends? [1]
Attributed [Circa *1885*]

JOHN WHITE CHADWICK
[1840–1904]

If good men were only better,
Would the wicked be so bad?
A Timely Question. Stanza 1

It singeth low in every heart,
  We hear it each and all, —
A song of those who answer not,
  However we may call.
Auld Lang Syne. Stanza 1

HENRY AUSTIN DOBSON
[1840–1921]

Once at the Angelus
  (Ere I was dead),
Angels all glorious
  Came to my bed.
"Good-Night, Babette!"

Time goes, you say? Ah no!
Alas, Time stays, *we* go.
The Paradox of Time. Stanza 1

The ladies of St. James's!
  They're painted to the eyes;
Their white it stays for ever,
  Their red it never dies:
But Phyllida, my Phyllida!
  Her color comes and goes;
It trembles to a lily, —
  It wavers to a rose.
The Ladies of St. James's. Stanza 4

Far better, in some nook unknown,
  To sleep for once — and soundly —
Than still survive in wistful stone,
  Forgotten more profoundly.
*To an Unknown Bust in the
    British Museum. Stanza 6*

Yet would today when Courtesy grows
  chill,
And life's fine loyalties are turned to
  jest,

[1] Campbell's reported comment to President Cleveland, who refused to support a
bill urged by Campbell on the grounds that
it was unconstitutional. Campbell was a Tam-
many representative from New York.

Some fire of thine might burn within us
    still!
Ah, would but one might lay his lance
    in rest,
And charge in earnest — were it but
    a mill!
                 Don Quixote

Form is the Cage and Sense the Bird.
The Poet twirls them in his Mind,
And wins the Trick with both combined.
                 The Toyman

He praised the Thing he understood;
'Twere well if every Critic would.
       The 'Squire at Vauxhall. Moral 2

I intended an Ode,
   And it turned to a Sonnet.
It began *à la mode*,
I intended an Ode;
But Rose crossed the road
In her latest new bonnet;
I intended an Ode;
And it turned to a Sonnet.
                 Urceus Exit

Love comes back to his vacant dwell-
    ing, —
The old, old Love that we knew of
    yore!
          The Wanderer. Stanza 1

In the work-a-day world, — for its
    needs and woes,
There is place and enough for the pains
    of prose;
But whenever the May-bells clash and
    chime,
Then hey! — for the ripple of laughing
    rhyme!
       The Ballad of Prose and Rhyme.
                       Envoy

Fame is a food that dead men eat, —
I have no stomach for such meat.
    Fame Is a Food that Dead Men
                Eat. Stanza 1

The Press is too much with us: small
    and great;
We are undone of chatter and *on dit*,
Report, retort, rejoinder, repartee,
Mole-hill and mare's nest, fiction up-to-
    date.
    A Pleasant Invective Against
                  Printing

WILLIAM CHANNING GANNETT
[1840–1923]

The poem hangs on the berry bush
    When comes the poet's eye;
The street begins to masquerade
    When Shakespeare passes by.
The Christ sees white in Judas's heart
    And loves His traitor well;
The God, to angel His new heaven,
    Explores His lowest hell.
             We See as We Are

THOMAS HARDY
[1840–1928]

When I set out for Lyonnesse,
    A hundred miles away,
    The rime was on the spray,
And starlight lit my lonesomeness.
    When I Set Out for Lyonnesse
                     [1870]

Good, but not religious-good.
    Under the Greenwood Tree
             [1872]. Chap. 2

The kingly brilliance of Sirius pierced
the eye with a steely glitter, the star
called Capella was yellow, Aldebaran
and Betelgueux shone with a fiery red.
To persons standing alone on a hill
during a clear midnight such as this, the
roll of the world eastward is almost a
palpable movement.
    Far From the Madding Crowd
            [1874]. Chap. 2

In fact, precisely at this transitional
point of its nightly roll into darkness
the great and particular glory of the
Egdon waste began, and nobody could
be said to understand the heath who
had not been there at such a time. It
could best be felt when it could not
clearly be seen.
    The Return of the Native [1878].
                      Chap. 1

The place became full of a watchful
intentness now; for when other things
sank brooding to sleep the heath appeared slowly to awake and listen.
                     Ibid.

The great inviolate place had an ancient permanence which the sea cannot

claim. Who can say of a particular sea that it is old? Distilled by the sun, kneaded by the moon, it is renewed in a year, in a day, or in an hour. The sea changed, the fields changed, the rivers, the villages, and the people changed, yet Egdon remained.

The Return of the Native. Chap. 1

Like the British Constitution, she owes her success in practice to her inconsistencies in principle.

The Hand of Ethelberta [*1876*]

A lover without indiscretion is no lover at all.

Ibid.

That cold accretion called the world, which, so terrible in the mass, is so unformidable, even pitiable, in its units.

Tess of the D'Urbervilles [*1891*]. *Chap. 13*

That shabby corner of God's allotment where He lets the nettles grow, and where all unbaptized infants, notorious drunkards, suicides, and others of the conjecturally damned are laid.

Ibid. Chap. 14

The chronic melancholy which is taking hold of the civilized races with the decline of belief in a beneficent power.

Ibid. Chap. 18

The debatable land between predilection and love.

Ibid. Chap. 20

Patience, that blending of moral courage with physical timidity.

Ibid. Chap. 43

"Justice" was done, and the President of the Immortals (in Aeschylean phrase) had ended his sport with Tess.

Ibid. Chap. 59

William Dewy, Tranter Reuben, Farmer Ledlow late at plough, Robert's kin, and John's and Ned's, And the Squire, and Lady Susan, lie in Mellstock churchyard now!

Friends Beyond [*1898*]. *Stanza 1*

We have triumphed: this achievement turns the bane to antidote, Unsuccesses to success,

Many thought-worn eves and morrows to a morrow free of thought.

Friends Beyond. Stanza 4

No more need we corn and clothing, feel of old terrestrial stress; Chill detraction stirs no sigh; Fear of death has even bygone us: death gave all that we possess.

Ibid. Stanza 5

That faiths by which my comrades stand Seem fantasies to me, And mirage-mists their Shining Land, Is a strange destiny.

The Impercipient [*1898*]. *Stanza 1*

He who breathes All's-Well to these Breathes no All's-Well to me.

Ibid. Stanza 3

I leant upon a coppice gate When Frost was spectre-gray, And Winter's dregs made desolate The weakening eye of day.

The Darkling Thrush [*1900*]. *Stanza 1*

An aged thrush, frail, gaunt, and small, In blast-beruffled plume.

Ibid. Stanza 3

So little cause for carollings Of such ecstatic sound Was written on terrestrial things Afar or nigh around, That I could think there trembled through His happy good-night air Some blessed Hope, whereof he knew And I was unaware.

Ibid. Stanza 4

What of the Immanent Will and its designs? The Will has woven with an absent heed Since life first was; and ever so will weave.

The Dynasts [*1904–1908*]. *Part I, Fore-Scene*

A local cult called Christianity.

Ibid. Spirit of the Years, Sc. 6

Aggressive Fancy working spells Upon a mind o'erwrought.

Ibid. Sc. 6, Napoleon

Ere systemed suns were globed and lit
The slaughters of the race were writ.
> *The Dynasts. Part II, Sc. 5,*
> *Semi-chorus*

My argument is that War makes rattling good history; but Peace is poor reading.
> *Ibid. Spirit Sinister*

To see stand weeping by
A woman once embraced, will try
The tension of a man the most austere.
> *The Contretemps. Stanza 6*

One pairing is as good as another
Where all is venture!
> *Ibid. Stanza 10*

You have not known
Men's lives, deaths, toils, and teens;
You are but a heap of stick and stone:
A new house has no sense of the have-
beens.[1]
> *The Two Houses. Stanza 5*

"Yes; quaint and curious war is!
You shoot a fellow down
You'd treat if met where any bar **is**,
Or help to half-a-crown."
> *The Man He Killed. Stanza 5*

We have lost somewhat, afar and near,
Gentlemen,
The thinning of our ranks each year
Affords a hint we are nigh undone,
That we shall not be ever again
The marked of many, loved of one.
> *An Ancient to Ancients. Stanza 3*

Much is there waits you we have
missed;
Much lore we leave you worth the
knowing;
Much, much has lain outside our ken.
Nay, rush not: time serves; we are
going.
> *Ibid. Stanza 10*

A star looks down at me,
And says: "Here I and you

---

[1] There's nothing mournful about it; it cannot be sad and lone
For the lack of something within it that
it has never known.
JOYCE KILMER [1886–1918]: *The House*
with Nobody in It, St. 5

Stand, each in our degree:
What do you mean to do?"
> *Waiting Both. Stanza* **1**

We two kept house, the Past and I,
The Past and I;
I tended while it hovered nigh,
Leaving me never alone.
> *The Ghost of the Past. Stanza 1*

Woman much missed, how you call to
me, call to me,
Saying that now you are not as you were
When you had changed from the one
who was all to me,
But as at first, when our day was fair.
> *The Voice* [*1912*]

What of the faith and fire within us
Men who march away
Ere the barn-cocks say
Night is growing gray?
> *Men Who March Away* [*1914*]

Only a man harrowing clods
In a slow silent walk
With an old horse that stumbles and
nods
Half asleep as they stalk.

Only thin smoke without flame
From the heaps of couch grass;
Yet this will go onward the same
Though Dynasties pass.

Yonder a maid and her wight
Come whispering by;
War's annals will cloud into night
Ere their story die.
> *In Time of "The Breaking of*
> *Nations"* [*1915*]

Yes, yes; I am old. In me appears
The history of a hundred years.
Empires', kings', captives' births and
deaths;
Strange faiths and fleeting shibboleths;
Tragedy, comedy, through my pages
Beyond all mummed on any stages;
Cold hearts beat hot, hot hearts beat
cold,
And I beat on.
> *The Newspaper Soliloquizes:*
> *London Observer, March 14,*
> *1926*

ROSSITER JOHNSON
[1840–1931]

O for a lodge in a garden of cucum-
  bers! [1]
O for an iceberg or two at control!
O for a vale which at mid-day the dew
  cumbers!
O for a pleasure trip up to the Pole!
  Ninety-nine in the Shade. Stanza 1

WILLIAM HENRY HARRISON ("ADIRONDACK") MURRAY
[1840–1904]

Ah, friends, dear friends, as years go on
  and heads get gray, how fast the
  guests do go!
Touch hands, touch hands, with those
  that stay.
Strong hands to weak, old hands to
  young, around the Christmas
  board, touch hands.
The false forget, the foe forgive, for
  every guest will go and every fire
  burn low and cabin empty stand.
Forget, forgive, for who may say that
  Christmas day may ever come to
  host or guest again.
Touch hands!
  John Norton's Vagabond

ROSSITER WORTHINGTON RAYMOND
[1840–1918]

Life is eternal; and love is immortal;
and death is only a horizon; and a
horizon is nothing save the limit of our
sight.
  A Commendatory Prayer

WILLIAM GRAHAM SUMNER
[1840–1910]

The Forgotten Man [2] . . . delving
away in patient industry, supporting
his family, paying his taxes, casting his
vote, supporting the church and the
school . . . but he is the only one for
whom there is no provision in the great

scramble and the big divide. Such is
the Forgotten Man. He works, he votes,
generally he prays — but his chief business in life is to pay. . . . Who and
where is the Forgotten Man in this case,
who will have to pay for it all?
  Speech, The Forgotten Man [1883]

JOHN ADDINGTON SYMONDS
[1840–1893]

No seed shall perish which the soul hath
  sown.
  Sonnet: Versöhnung, A Belief

Gods fade; but God abides and in
  man's heart
Speaks with the clear unconquerable
  cry
Of energies and hopes that can not
  die.
  Sonnet, On the Sacro Monte

She smiled, and the shadows departed;
  She shone, and the snows were rain;
And he who was frozen-hearted
  Bloomed up into love again.
  Eyebright

These things shall be, — a loftier race
Than e'er the world hath known shall
  rise
With flame of freedom in their souls,
And light of knowledge in their eyes.
  The Days That Are to Be

KATHARINE KENT CHILD WALKER
[1840–1916]

However divinity schools may refuse
to "skip" in unison, and may butt and
butter each other about the doctrine
and origin of human depravity, all will
join devoutly in the credo, I believe
in the total depravity of inanimate
things.
  *The Total Depravity of Inanimate
  Things [1864]*

The elusiveness of soap, the knotti-
ness of strings, the transitory nature of
buttons, the inclination of suspenders
to twist and of hooks to forsake their

---

[1] As a lodge in a garden of cucumbers. —
Isaiah, I, 8
[2] See Franklin D. Roosevelt, page 918b.

lawful eyes, and cleave only unto the hairs of their hapless owner's head.

The Total Depravity of Inanimate Things

HENRY WATTERSON
[1840–1921]

Things have come to a helluva pass
When a man can't cudgel his own jack-ass.

Reply when rebuked for criticizing the Governor of Kentucky

ELIZABETH WORDSWORTH
[1840–1932]

If all the good people were clever,
And all clever people were good,
The world would be nicer than ever
We thought that it possibly could.

But somehow, 'tis seldom or never
The two hit it off as they should;
The good are so harsh to the clever,
The clever so rude to the good!

The Clever and the Good [1890]

ÉMILE ZOLA
[1840–1902]

Truth is on the march and nothing can stop it.

J'Accuse [1898]

JOHN WILSON [1]
[? –1889]

Oh for a book and a shady nook,
either in door or out;
With the green leaves whisp'ring over-head, or the street cries all about.
Where I may read all at my ease,
both of the new and old;
For a jolly good book whereon to look is better to me than gold.

For a Catalogue of Secondhand Books

ROBERT BUCHANAN
[1841–1901]

The Fleshly School of Poetry.

Title of Article [1871]

[1] A London bookseller, friend of Austin Dobson.

The sweet post-prandial cigar.

De Berny

Alone at nights,
I read my Bible more and Euclid less.

An Old Dominie's Story

Beauty and Truth, tho' never found,
are worthy to be sought.

To David in Heaven

I saw the starry Tree
Eternity
Put forth the blossom Time.

Proteus

Full of a sweet indifference.

Charmian

I say, the world is lovely,
And that loveliness is enough.

Artist and Model

A race that binds
Its body in chains and calls them Lib-erty,
And calls each fresh link Progress.

Political Mystics. Titan and Avatar

JUSTICE OLIVER WENDELL HOLMES, JR.
[1841–1935]

The life of the law has not been logic: it has been experience.

The Common Law [1881]

I think that, as life is action and passion, it is required of a man that he should share the passion and action of his time at peril of being judged not to have lived.

Memorial Day Address [1884]

Through our great good fortune, in our youth our hearts were touched with fire.

Ibid.

The Law, wherein, as in a magic mirror, we see reflected not only our own lives, but the lives of all men that have been! When I think on this majestic theme, my eyes dazzle.[1]

To the Suffolk Bar Association [1885]

[1] See John Webster, page 226a.

I say to you in all sadness of conviction, that to think great thoughts you must be heroes as well as idealists.

The Profession of the Law [*1886*]

Thus only can you gain the secret isolated joy of the thinker, who knows that, a hundred years after he is dead and forgotten, men who never heard of him will be moving to the measure of his thought, — the subtle rapture of a postponed power, which the world knows not because it has no external trappings, but which to his prophetic vision is more real than that which commands an army.

Ibid.

The prophecies of what the courts will do in fact, and nothing more pretentious, are what I mean by the law.

The Path of the Law [*1897*]

Certainty generally is illusion, and repose is not the destiny of man.

Ibid.

The remoter and more general aspects of the law are those which give it universal interest. It is through them that you not only become a great master in your calling, but connect your subject with the universe and catch an echo of the infinite, a glimpse of its unfathomable process, a hint of the universal law.

Ibid.

The rule of joy and the law of duty seem to me all one.

Speech at Bar Association Dinner,
Boston [*1900*]

Life is an end in itself, and the only question as to whether it is worth living is whether you have enough of it.

Ibid.

A great man represents a great ganglion in the nerves of society, or, to vary the figure, a strategic point in the campaign of history, and part of his greatness consists in his being *there*.

John Marshall [*1901*]

Taxes are what we pay for civilized society.

Compañia de Tabacos v. *Collector,*
275 U. S. 87, 100 [*1904*]

Great cases like hard cases make bad law.

Northern Securities Co. v. *United States, 193 U. S. 197, 400* [*1904*]

The Fourteenth Amendment does not enact Mr. Herbert Spencer's *Social Statics.*

Lochner v. *New York, 198 U. S.*
45, 75 [*1905*]

General propositions do not decide concrete cases. The decision will depend on a judgment or intuition more subtle than any articulate major premise.

Ibid. Page 78

Life is painting a picture, not doing a sum.

The Class of '61 [*Speeches, 1913*]

I learned in the regiment and in the class the conclusion, at least, of what I think the best service that we can do for our country and for ourselves: To see so far as one may, and to feel the great forces that are behind every detail . . . ; to hammer out as compact and solid a piece of work as one can, to try to make it first rate, and to leave it unadvertised.

Ibid.

The only prize much cared for by the powerful is power. The prize of the general is not a bigger tent, but command.

Law and the Court [*1913*]

Judges are apt to be naif, simpleminded men, and they need something of Mephistopheles. We too need education in the obvious — to learn to transcend our own convictions and to leave room for much that we hold dear to be done away with short of revolution by the orderly change of law.

Ibid.

I recognize without hesitation that judges do and must legislate, but they can do so only interstitially; they are confined from molar to molecular motions.

Southern Pacific Co. v. *Jensen,*
244 U. S. 205, 221 [*1917*]

The common law is not a brooding omnipresence in the sky but the articu-

late voice of some sovereign or quasi-sovereign that can be identified.
Southern Pacific Co. v. *Jensen,
244 U. S. 205, 221. Page 222*

Certitude is not the test of certainty.
Natural Law [*1918*]

When men have realized that time has upset many fighting faiths, they may come to believe even more than they believe the very foundations of their own conduct that the ultimate good desired is better reached by free trade in ideas — that the best test of truth is the power of the thought to get itself accepted in the competition of the market, and that truth is the only ground upon which their wishes safely can be carried out. That at any rate is the theory of our Constitution. It is an experiment, as all life is an experiment.
Abrams v. *United States, 250 U. S.
616, 630* [*1919*]

Upon this point a page of history is worth a volume of logic.
New York Trust Co. v. *Eisner,
256 U. S. 345, 349* [*1921*]

It is said that this manifesto is more than a theory, that it was an incitement. Every idea is an incitement.
Gitlow v. *New York, 268 U. S.
652, 673* [*1925*]

Three generations of imbeciles are enough.
Buck v. *Bell, 274 U. S.
200, 207* [*1927*]

For my part I think it a less evil that some criminals should escape than that the government should play an ignoble part. . . . If the existing code does not permit district attorneys to have a hand in such dirty business, it does not permit the judge to allow such iniquities to succeed.
Olmstead v. *United States, 277 U. S.
438, 470* [*1928*]

If there is any principle of the Constitution that more imperatively calls for attachment than any other it is the principle of free thought — not free thought for those who agree with us

but freedom for the thought that we hate.
United States v. *Schwimmer,
279 U. S. 644, 653* [*1928*]

The riders in a race do not stop short when they reach the goal. There is a little finishing canter before coming to a standstill. There is time to hear the kind voice of friends and to say to one's self: "The work is done." But just as one says that, the answer comes: "The race is over, but the work never is done while the power to work remains." The canter that brings you to a standstill need not be only coming to rest. It cannot be, while you still live. For to live is to function. That is all there is in living.
*Radio address on his ninetieth
birthday* [*March 8, 1931*]

Life seems to me like a Japanese picture which our imagination does not allow to end with the margin. We aim at the infinite and when our arrow falls to earth it is in flames.
*Message to the Federal Bar Asso-
ciation* [*February 29, 1932*]

WILLIAM HENRY HUDSON
[1841–1922]

When I meet with a falsehood, I care not who the great persons who proclaim it may be, I do not try to like it or believe it or mimic the fashionable prattle of the world about it.
The Purple Land [*1885*]. *Chap. 28*

You cannot fly like an eagle with the wings of a wren.
Afoot in England [*1909*]. *Chap. 6*

When I hear people say they have not found the world and life so agreeable or interesting as to be in love with it, or that they look with equanimity to its end, I am apt to think they have never been properly alive nor seen with clear vision the world they think so meanly of, or anything in it — not a blade of grass. Only I know that mine is an exceptional case, that the visible world is to me more beautiful and interesting than to most persons, that the delight I experienced in my communings with Nature did not pass away, leaving nothing but a recollection of vanished happiness to intensify a present pain. The happiness was never lost, . . . so that in my worst times, when I was compelled to exist shut out from Nature in London for long periods, sick and poor and friendless, I could yet always feel that it was infinitely better to be than not to be.

> *Far Away and Long Ago* [*1918*].
> *Chap. 24*

SIR RICHARD CLAVER-HOUSE JEBB
[1841–1905]

At the middle point of the [Greek] stage, some steps — known as "Charon's staircase," because the ghost sometimes comes up by them — lead down into what we should call the pit.

> *Greek Literature* [*1877*]

MARY ARTEMISIA LATHBURY [1]
[1841–1913]

Day is dying in the west;
Heaven is touching earth with rest.
> *Day Is Dying in the West*
> [*1877*]. *Stanza 1*

Children of yesterday,
  Heirs of tomorrow,
What are you weaving?
  Labor and sorrow?
Look to your looms again,
  Faster and faster
Fly the great shuttles
  Prepared by the Master.
Life's in the loom,
Room for it — room!
> *Song of Hope. Stanza 1*

[1] Miss Lathbury was known as the Chautauqua Laureate.

JOAQUIN [1] MILLER
(CINCINNATUS HEINE MILLER)
[1841?–1913]

That man who lives for self alone
Lives for the meanest mortal known.
> *Walker in Nicaragua. Chant I,*
> *Stanza 1*

In men whom men condemn as ill
I find so much of goodness still,[2]
In men whom men pronounce divine
I find so much of sin and blot,
I do not dare to draw a line
Between the two, where God has not.[3]
> *Byron*

The bravest battle that ever was fought;
Shall I tell you where and when?
On the maps of the world you will find
  it not;
It was fought by the mothers of men.
> *The Bravest Battle. Stanza 1*

The soul that feeds on books alone —
I count that soul exceeding small
That lives alone by book and creed, —
A soul that has not learned to read.
> *The Larger College. Stanza 10*

Honor and glory forever more
  To this good man gone to rest;
Peace on the dim Plutonian shore; [4]
  Rest in the land of the blest.
> *Peter Cooper, April, 1883.*
> *Stanza 1*

[1] In a paper, *How I Came to be a Writer of Books* [*Lippincott's Magazine*, 1886], quoted in STUART P. SHERMAN's introduction to *The Poetical Works of Joaquin Miller* [1923], Miller explains the origin of his pen name. His first writing was a public letter in defense of Joaquin Murietta, the outlaw. A Sacramento newspaper banteringly identified him with the outlaw, and friends continued the banter. The name "Joaquin" clung to him, so Miller accepted it and used it in the title of his first book and thereafter.

[2] See Shakespeare, page 155b.

[3] There is so much good in the worst of us,
And so much bad in the best of us,
That it hardly behooves any of us
To talk about the rest of us.
  First printed in *The Marion* (Kansas) *Record*, owned by Governor Edward Wallis Hoch [1849–1925], and assumed to have been written by him

[4] See Poe, page 545a.

The biggest dog has been a pup.
> *William Brown of Oregon.*
> *Stanza 5*

Behind him lay the gray Azores,
  Behind the Gates of Hercules;
Before him not the ghost of shores,
  Before him only shoreless seas.
> *Columbus. Stanza 1*

He gained a world; he gave that world
Its grandest lesson: "On! sail on!"
> *Ibid. Stanza 5*

The Lightning reached a fiery rod,
And on Death's fearful forehead wrote
The autograph of God.
> *With Love to You and Yours.*
> *Part I, Canto III*

PIERRE AUGUSTE RENOIR
[1841–1919]

I have a predilection for painting
that lends joyousness to a wall.
> AMBROISE VOLLARD: *Renoir*
> [*1919*]

MINOT JUDSON SAVAGE
[1841–1918]

There comes an hour of sadness
  With the setting of the sun,
Not for the sins committed,
  But the things I have not done.
> *Things Not Done*

A man's truest monument must be a
man.
> *The Song of a Man (Phillips*
> *Brooks). Stanza 8*

CLEMENT WILLIAM SCOTT
[1841–1904]

Oh, promise me that some day you and I
Will take our love together to some sky
Where we can be alone and faith renew,
And find the hollows where those flowers
grew.
> *Oh, Promise Me* [*1888*]

EDWARD ROWLAND SILL
[1841–1887]

At the punch-bowl's brink
Let the thirsty think
  What they say in Japan:

"First the man takes a drink,
Then the drink takes a drink,
  Then the drink takes the man!"
> *An Adage from the Orient*

No pity, Lord, could change the heart
From red with wrong to white as wool;
The rod must heal the sin: but Lord,
Be merciful to me, a fool!
> *The Fool's Prayer*

'Tis by our follies that so long
We hold the earth from heaven away.
> *Ibid.*

The ill-timed truth we might have
  kept —
Who knows how sharp it pierced and
  stung?
The word we had not sense to say —
Who knows how grandly it had rung?
> *Ibid.*

Earth bears no balsam for mistakes;
Men crown the knave, and scourge the
  tool
That did his will.[1]
> *Ibid.*

What may we take into the vast For-
  ever?
  That marble door
Admits no fruit of all our long endeavor,
  No fame-wreathed crown we wore,
  No garnered lore.
> *The Future*

SIR HENRY MORTON STANLEY
[1841–1904]

Doctor Livingstone, I presume?
> *On meeting Livingstone in Ujiji,*
> *Central Africa* [*November 10,*
> *1871*]

EUGENE FITCH WARE
("IRONQUILL")
[1841–1911]

Human hopes and human creeds
Have their root in human needs.
> *The Rhymes of Ironquill.*
> *Preface*

---

[1] The law locks up both man and woman
Who steals the goose from off the common,

Man builds no structure which outlives
a book.
The Book

O Dewey was the morning
  Upon the first of May,
And Dewey was the Admiral
  Down in Manila Bay;
And Dewey were the Regent's eyes,
  "Them" orbs of royal blue!
And Dewey feel discouraged?
  I Dew not think we Dew.
*In the Topeka (Kansas) Daily
  Capital, May 3, 1898*

Work brings its own relief;
He who most idle is
Has most of grief.
Today

No evil deed live oN.
The Palindrome

I'm ignorant of music, but still, in spite
  of that,
I always drop a quarter in an organ-
  grinder's hat.
The Organ-Grinder

The ballads of the people are the bulwarks of the State.
Ibid.

The highest of renown
Are the surest stricken down;
But the stupid and the clown
They remain.
Paresis

The Turks,
Becoming somewhat sad,
Surrendered every
Consonant they had.
The Siege of Djklxprwbz

Oft the statesman and the saint
Think they're doing good, but ain't.
Aesop's Fables. No. 17

The days of long-haired poets now are
  o'er;
The short-haired poet seems to have the
  floor.
The Short-Haired Poet. Stanza 3

But lets the greater felon loose
Who steals the common from the goose.
ANONYMOUS. *Quoted by* EDWARD POTTS
CHEYNEY: *Social and Industrial His-
tory of England* [1901], *Introduction*

The farmer works the soil,
The agriculturist works the farmer.
The Kansas Bandit

CHARLES FOLLEN ADAMS
[1842–1918]

I haf von funny leedle poy
  Vot gomes schust to mine knee;
Der queerest schap, der createst rogue,
  As efer you dit see.
He runs, und schumps, und schmashes
  dings
  In all barts off der house:
But vot off dot? He vas mine son,
  Mine leedle Yawcob Strauss.
Yawcob Strauss. Stanza 1

I vants to gondradict dot shap
  Dot made dis leedle shoke:
"A voman vas der glinging vine,
  Und man der shturdy oak."
Der Oak und der Vine. Stanza 1

AMBROSE BIERCE
[1842–1914 ?]

Mark how my fame rings out from zone
  to zone:
A thousand critics shouting: "He's unknown!"
Couplet

Cynic, perforce, from study of mankind
In the false volume of his single mind,
He damned his fellows for his own un-
  worth,
And, bad himself, thought nothing good
  on earth.
He yearned to squander what he lived
  to save
And did not, for he could not, cheat the
  grave.
An Epitaph

To men a man is but a mind. Who cares
What face he carries or what form he
  wears?
But woman's body is the woman. O
Stay thou, my sweetheart, and do never
  go.
The Devil's Dictionary [1] *[1906]*

[1] First published as *The Cynic's Word
Book*, retitled in 1911.

Advice: the smallest current coin.
The Devil's Dictionary

Bore: a person who talks when you wish him to listen.
Ibid.

Edible: good to eat, and wholesome to digest, as a worm to a toad, a snake to a pig, a pig to a man, and a man to a worm.
Ibid.

Garter: an elastic band intended to keep a woman from coming out of her stockings and desolating the country.
Ibid.

Labor: one of the processes by which A acquires property for B.
Ibid.

Marriage: a community consisting of a master, a mistress, and two slaves, making in all, two.
Ibid.

Piracy: commerce without its folly-swaddles, just as God made it.
Ibid.

Prejudice: a vagrant opinion without visible means of support.
Ibid.

Saint: a dead sinner revised and edited.
Ibid.

Woman would be more charming if one could fall into her arms without falling into her hands.
Epigrams

You are not permitted to kill a woman who has injured you, but nothing forbids you to reflect that she is growing older every minute. You are avenged 1440 times a day.
Ibid.

Self-denial is indulgence of a propensity to forego.
Ibid.

CHARLES EDWARD CARRYL
[1842–1920]

The night was thick and hazy
When the *Piccadilly Daisy*

Carried down the crew and Captain in the sea;
And I think the water drowned 'em,
For they never, never found 'em,
And I know they didn't come ashore with me.
Robinson Crusoe. Stanza 1

I had that fellow Friday
Just to keep the tavern tidy.
Ibid. Stanza 3

Canary birds feed on sugar and seed,
Parrots have crackers to crunch;
And as for the poodles, they tell me the noodles
Have chicken and cream for their lunch.
But there's never a question
About my digestion —
Anything does for me!
The Plaint of the Camel.
Stanza 1

A capital ship for an ocean trip
Was the "Walloping Window-blind."
No gale that blew dismayed her crew
Or troubled the Captain's mind.
The man at the wheel was taught to feel
Contempt for the wildest blow,
And it often appeared, when the weather had cleared,
That he'd been in his bunk below.
Davy and the Goblin, A Nautical
Ballad. Stanza 1

INA DONNA COOLBRITH
[1842–1928]

He walks with God upon the hills!
And sees, each morn, the world arise
New-bathed in light of paradise.
The Poet

CHARLES MONROE DICKINSON
[1842–1924]

When the lessons and tasks are all ended,
And the school for the day is dismissed,
And the little ones gather around me
To bid me "good-night" and be kissed.
The Children. Stanza 1

WILLIAM JAMES
[1842–1910]

Habit is thus the enormous fly-wheel of society, its most precious conservative agent. It alone is what keeps us all within the bounds of ordinance.

The Principles of Psychology
[1890]. Chap. 10

It is well for the world that in most of us, by the age of thirty, the character has set like plaster, and will never soften again.

Ibid.

There is no more miserable human being than one in whom nothing is habitual but indecision.

Ibid.

No matter how full a reservoir of *maxims* one may possess, and no matter how good one's *sentiments* may be, if one have not taken advantage of every concrete opportunity to *act,* one's character may remain entirely unaffected for the better. With mere good intentions, hell is proverbially paved.[1]

Ibid.

Keep the faculty of effort alive in you by a little gratuitous exercise every day. That is, be systematically ascetic or heroic in little unnecessary points, do every day or two something for no other reason than that you would rather not do it, so that when the hour of dire need draws nigh, it may find you not unnerved and untrained to stand the test.

Ibid.

The hell to be endured hereafter, of which theology tells, is no worse than the hell we make for ourselves in this world by habitually fashioning our characters in the wrong way.

Ibid.

No state [of mind] once gone can recur and be identical with what it was before.

Ibid. Chap. 11

[1] Hell is paved with good intentions. — JOHN RAY: *English Proverbs* [1670]
See George Herbert, page 233b.
Hell is paved with good intentions, not with bad ones. — BERNARD SHAW [1856–1950]: *Maxims for Revolutionists*

We are not only gregarious animals, liking to be in sight of our fellows, but we have an innate propensity to get ourselves noticed, and noticed favorably, by our kind. No more fiendish punishment could be devised, were such a thing physically possible, than that one should be turned loose in society and remain absolutely unnoticed by all the members thereof.

The Principles of Psychology.
Chap. 12

In the practical as in the theoretic life, the man whose acquisitions *stick* is the man who is always achieving and advancing, whilst his neighbors, spending most of their time in relearning what they once knew but have forgotten, simply hold their own.

Ibid. Chap. 18

Genius, in truth, means little more than the faculty of perceiving in an unhabitual way.

Ibid. Chap. 20

The great source of terror to infancy is solitude.

Ibid. Chap. 25

A thing is important if any one *think* it important.

Ibid. Chap. 28

If this life be not a real fight, in which something is eternally gained for the universe by success, it is no better than a game of private theatricals from which one may withdraw at will. But it *feels* like a real fight.

The Will to Believe [1897]

The deepest thing in our nature is . . . this dumb region of the heart in which we dwell alone with our willingnesses and unwillingnesses, our faiths and fears.

Ibid.

Be not afraid of life. Believe that life *is* worth living, and your belief will help create the fact.[1]

Ibid.

The whole drift of my education goes to persuade me that the world of our present consciousness is only one out of

[1] See Alfred Austin, page 669a–669b.

many worlds of consciousness that exist.

The Varieties of Religious Experience [*1902*]. *Lecture XX*

Man, biologically considered, and whatever else he may be in the bargain, is simply the most formidable of all the beasts of prey, and, indeed, the only one that preys systematically on its own species.

Remarks at the Peace Banquet [*October 7, 1904*]

Man lives *by* habits, indeed, but what he lives *for* is thrills and excitements.

Ibid.

JOHN ALEXANDER JOYCE
[1842–1915]

You must leave your many millions
And the gay and festive crowd;
Though you roll in royal billions,
There's no pocket in a shroud.[1]
There's No Pocket in a Shroud.
Stanza 1

I shall love you in December
With the love I gave in May! [2]
Question and Answer. Stanza 8

SIDNEY LANIER
[1842–1881]

The sun is a-wait at the ponderous gate
of the West.
The Marshes of Glynn
[*1877*]. *IV, 3*

Ye marshes, how candid and simple and
nothing-withholding and free
Ye publish yourselves to the sky and
offer yourselves to the sea!
Tolerant plains, that suffer the sea and
the rains and the sun,
Ye spread and span like the catholic
man who hath mightily won
God out of knowledge and good out of
infinite pain

[1] You Can't Take It With You. — *Title of Comedy by* MOSS HART AND GEORGE KAUFMAN [*1937*]
[2] Will you love me in December as you do in May? — JAMES J. WALKER, *set to music by* ERNEST R. BALL [*1905*]

And sight out of blindness and purity
out of a stain.
The Marshes of Glynn. IV, 6

As the marsh-hen secretly builds on the
watery sod,
Behold I will build me a nest on the
greatness of God:
I will fly in the greatness of God as the
marsh-hen flies
In the freedom that fills all the space
'twixt the marsh and the skies:
By so many roots as the marsh-grass
sends in the sod
I will heartily lay me a-hold on the
greatness of God:
Oh, like to the greatness of God is the
greatness within
The range of the marshes, the liberal
marshes of Glynn.
Ibid. 7

Out of the hills of Habersham,
Down the valleys of Hall.
Song of the Chattahoochee
[*1877*]. *Stanza 1*

Downward the voices of Duty call —
Downward, to toil and be mixed with
the main,
The dry fields burn, and the mills are to
turn.
Ibid. Stanza 5

The incalculable Up-and-Down of
Time.
Clover [*1877*]

Life! thou sea-fugue, writ from east to
west,
Love, Love alone can pore
On thy dissolving score
Of harsh half-phrasings,
Blotted ere writ,
And double erasings
Of chords most fit.
The Symphony [*1877*]

Music is Love in search of a word.
Ibid.

Into the woods my Master went,
Clean forspent, forspent.
Into the woods my Master came,
Forspent with love and shame.
A Ballad of Trees and the Master
[*1877*]. *Stanza 1*

'Twas on a tree they slew Him — last
When out of the woods He came.
A Ballad of Trees and the Master.
Stanza 2

Now in the sea's red vintage melts the
　　sun,
As Egypt's pearl dissolved in rosy
　　wine,
And Cleopatra night drinks all.
Evening Song. Stanza 2

My soul is sailing through the sea,
But the Past is heavy and hindereth me.
Barnacles [*1877*]. *Stanza 1*

DAVID LAW PROUDFIT
("PELEG ARKWRIGHT")
[*1842–1897*]

A man sat on a rock and sought
　　Refreshment from his thumb;
A dinotherium wandered by
　　And scared him some.

His name was Smith. The kind of rock
　　He sat upon was shale.
One feature quite distinguished him —
　　He had a tail.
Prehistoric Smith

Nature abhors imperfect work
　　And on it lays her ban;
And all creation must despise
　　A tailless man.
Ibid.

MAY RILEY SMITH
[*1842–1927*]

Strange we never prize the music
Till the sweet-voiced bird has flown,
Strange that we should slight the violets
Till the lovely flowers are gone.
If We Knew [*1867*]

HUGH ANTOINE D'ARCY
[*1843–1925*]

"Say, boys! if you give me just another
　　whiskey I'll be glad,
And I'll draw right here a picture of the
　　face that drove me mad.
Give me that piece of chalk with which
　　you mark the baseball score,

You shall see the lovely Madeleine
　　upon the bar-room floor."
The Face upon the Floor [*1887*] [1]
With chalk in hand the vagabond be-
　　gan
To sketch a face that well might buy
　　the soul of any man.
Then as he placed another lock upon
　　the shapely head,
With a fearful shriek he leaped and fell
　　across the picture — dead!
Ibid.

SARAH DOUDNEY
[*1843–1926*]

Oh, the wasted hours of life
　　That have drifted by!
Oh, the good that might have been,
　　Lost without a sigh!
The Lesson of the Water-Mill
[*1864*]

ANNA E. HAMILTON
[*1843–1876*]

This learned I from the shadow of a
　　tree,
That to and fro did sway against a wall,
Our shadow selves, our influence, may
　　fall
Where we ourselves can never be.
Influence

HENRY JAMES
[*1843–1916*]

The face of nature and civilization
in this our country is to a certain point a
very sufficient literary field. But it will
yield its secrets only to a really *grasping*
imagination. . . . To write well and
worthily of American things one need
even more than elsewhere to be a
master.
Letter to Charles Eliot Norton
[*January 16, 1871*]
It's a complex fate, being an American, and one of the responsibilities it

---

[1] Often given as "The Face on the Barroom Floor."

entails is fighting against a superstitious valuation of Europe.

> *Letter* [*1872*]. *Quoted in* PERCY LUBBOCK, *Letters of Henry James* [*1920*], *Vol. I, Page 13*

If the picturesque were banished from the face of the earth, I think the idea would survive in some typical American breast.

> *Transatlantic Sketches* [*1875*]

It takes a great deal of history to produce a little literature.

> *Hawthorne* [*1879*]. *Chap. 1*

Whatever question there may be of his [Thoreau's] talent, there can be none, I think, of his genius. It was a slim and crooked one, but it was eminently personal. He was unperfect, unfinished, inartistic; he was worse than provincial — he was parochial.

> *Ibid. Chap. 4*

Cats and monkeys, monkeys and cats — all human life is there.

> *The Madonna of the Future* [*1879*]

There are few hours in life more agreeable than the hour dedicated to the ceremony known as afternoon tea.

> *The Portrait of a Lady* [*1881*]

At moments she discovered she was grotesquely wrong, and then she treated herself to a week of passionate humility.

> *Ibid.*

The real offence, as she ultimately perceived, was her having a mind of her own at all. Her mind was to be his — attached to his own like a small garden-plot to a deer-park.

> *Ibid.*

The only reason for the existence of a novel is that it does attempt to represent life.

> *The Art of Fiction* [*1888*]

The only obligation to which in advance we may hold a novel, without incurring the accusation of being arbitrary, is that it be interesting.

> *Ibid.*

The advantage, the luxury, as well as the torment and responsibility of the novelist, is that there is no limit to what he may attempt as an executant — no limit to his possible experiments, efforts, discoveries, successes.

> *The Art of Fiction*

The power to guess the unseen from the seen, to trace the implications of things, to judge the whole piece by the pattern, the condition of feeling life in general so completely that you are well on your way to knowing any particular corner of it — this cluster of gifts may almost be said to constitute experience. . . . If experience consists of impressions, it may be said that impressions *are* experience. . . . Therefore, if I should certainly say to a novice, "Write from experience and experience only," I should feel that this was rather a tantalizing monition if I were not careful immediately to add, "Try to be one of the people on whom nothing is lost."

> *Ibid.*

We must grant the artist his subject, his idea, his *donnée:* our criticism is applied only to what he makes of it. . . . If we pretend to respect the artist at all, we must allow him his freedom of choice, in the face, in particular cases, of innumerable presumptions that the choice will not fructify. Art derives a considerable part of its beneficial exercise from flying in the face of presumptions.

> *Ibid.*

There are few things more exciting to me . . . than a psychological reason.

> *Ibid.*

The practice of "reviewing" . . . in general has nothing in common with the art of criticism.

> *Criticism* [*1893*]

The critical sense is so far from frequent that it is absolutely rare, and the possession of the cluster of qualities that minister to it is one of the highest distinctions. . . . In this light one sees the critic as the real helper of the artist, a torch-bearing outrider, the interpreter, the brother. . . . Just in proportion as he is sentient and restless, just in proportion as he reacts and reciprocates and penetrates, is the critic a valuable instrument.

Criticism

However incumbent it may be on most of us to do our duty, there is, in spite of a thousand narrow dogmatisms, nothing in the world that any one is under the least obligation to *like* — not even (one braces one's self to risk the declaration) a particular kind of writing.

Flaubert [1893]

The time-honored bread-sauce of the happy ending.

Theatricals: Second Series [1895]

"Live all you can; it's a mistake not to. It doesn't so much matter what you do in particular, so long as you have had your life. If you haven't had that what *have* you had? . . . What one loses one loses; make no mistake about that. . . . The right time is *any* time that one is still so lucky as to have. . . . Live!"

The Ambassadors [1903]. Book Fifth, Chap. 2

Really, universally, relations stop nowhere, and the exquisite problem of the artist is eternally but to draw, by a geometry of his own, the circle within which they shall happily *appear* to do so.

Prefaces [1907–1909]. Roderick Hudson

There is, I think, no more nutritive or suggestive truth . . . than that of the perfect dependence of the "moral" sense of a work of art on the amount of felt life concerned in producing it. The question comes back thus, obviously, to the kind and the degree of the artist's prime sensibility, which is the soil out of which his subject springs.

Ibid. The Portrait of a Lady

To see deep difficulty braved is at any time, for the really addicted artist, to feel almost even as a pang the beautiful incentive, and to feel it verily in such sort as to wish the danger intensified. The difficulty most worth tackling

can only be for him, in these conditions, the greatest the case permits of.

Prefaces. The Portrait of a Lady

Life being all inclusion and confusion, and art being all discrimination and selection, the latter, in search of the hard latent *value* with which it alone is concerned, sniffs round the mass as instinctively and unerringly as a dog suspicious of some buried bone.

Ibid. The Spoils of Poynton

The fatal futility of Fact.

Ibid.

No themes are so human as those that reflect for us, out of the confusion of life, the close connexion of bliss and bale, of the things that help with the things that hurt, so dangling before us for ever that bright hard medal, of so strange an alloy, one face of which is somebody's right and ease and the other somebody's pain and wrong.

Ibid. What Maisie Knew

The effort really to see and really to represent is no idle business in face of the *constant* force that makes for muddlement. The great thing is indeed that the muddled state too is one of the very sharpest of the realities, that it also has colour and form and character, has often in fact a broad and rich comicality.

Ibid.

To criticise is to appreciate, to appropriate, to take intellectual possession, to establish in fine a relation with the criticised thing and to make it one's own.

Ibid.

The historian, essentially, wants more documents than he can really use; the dramatist only wants more liberties than he can really take.

Ibid. The Aspern Papers

The ever-importunate murmur, "Dramatise it, dramatise it!"

Ibid. The Altar of the Dead

In art economy is always beauty.

Ibid.

The terrible *fluidity* of self-revelation.

Ibid. The Ambassadors

The anomalous fact is that the theatre, so called, can flourish in barbarism, but that any *drama* worth speaking of can develop but in the air of civilization.
Letter to C. E. Wheeler
[April 9, 1911]

I'm glad you like adverbs — I adore them; they are the only qualifications I really much respect.
Letter to Miss M. Betham Edwards [January 5, 1912]

We must know, as much as possible, in our beautiful art, . . . what we are talking about — and the only way to know is to have lived and loved and cursed and floundered and enjoyed and suffered. I think I don't regret a single "excess" of my responsive youth — I only regret, in my chilled age, certain occasions and possibilities I didn't embrace.
Letter to Hugh Walpole
[August 21, 1913]

I still, in presence of life . . . have reactions — as many as possible. . . . It's, I suppose, because I am that queer monster, the artist, an obstinate finality, an inexhaustible sensibility. Hence the reactions — appearances, memories, many things, go on playing upon it with consequences that I note and "enjoy" (grim word!) noting. It all takes doing — and I *do*. I believe I shall do yet again — it is still an act of life.
Letter to Henry Adams
[March 21, 1914]

The effect, if not the prime office, of criticism is to make our absorption and our enjoyment of the things that feed the mind as aware of itself as possible, since that awareness quickens the mental demand, which thus in turn wanders further and further for pasture. This action on the part of the mind practically amounts to a reaching out for the reasons of its interest, as only by its ascertaining them can the interest grow more various. This is the very education of our imaginative life.
The New Novel [1914]

It is art that *makes* life, makes interest, makes importance, for our consideration and application of these things, and I know of no substitute whatever for the force and beauty of its process.
Letter to H. G. Wells
[July 10, 1915]

The full, the monstrous demonstration that Tennyson was not Tennysonian.
The Middle Years [1917].
Chap. 6

To take what there *is,* and use it, without waiting forever in vain for the preconceived — to dig deep into the actual and get something out of *that* — this doubtless is the right way to live.
Notebooks [1948]

FREDERIC WILLIAM HENRY MYERS
[1843–1901]

Look when the clouds are blowing
And all the winds are free:
In fury of their going
They fall upon the sea.
But though the blast is frantic,
And though the tempest raves,
The deep immense Atlantic
Is still beneath the waves.
Wind, Moon, and Tides

Coldly sublime, intolerably just.
Saint Paul

In no single act or passion can salvation stand; far hence, beyond Orion and Andromeda, the cosmic process works and shall work forever through unbegotten souls.
Human Personality. Chap. X

JOSEPHINE POLLARD
[1843–1892]

Though he has Eden to live in,
Man cannot be happy alone.
We Cannot Be Happy Alone.
Stanza 5

GEORGE BIRDSEYE
[1844–1919]

The longest day is in June, they say;
   The shortest in December.
They did not come to me that way:
   The shortest I remember
You came a day with me to stay,
   And filled my heart with laughter;
The longest day — you were away —
   The very next day after.
Shortest and Longest [*1889*]

ROBERT BRIDGES [1]
[1844–1930]

Beneath the crisp and wintry carpet hid
A million buds but stay their blossom-
   ing;
And trustful birds have built their nests
   amid
The shuddering boughs, and only wait
   to sing
Till one soft shower from the south shall
   bid,
And hither tempt the pilgrim steps of
   Spring.
The Growth of Love [*1876*].
Sonnet 6

Beauty being the best of all we know
Sums up the unsearchable and secret
   aims
Of nature.
Ibid. Sonnet 8

I live on hope and that I think do all
Who come into this world.
Ibid. Sonnet 63

Behind the western bars
The shrouded day retreats,
And unperceived the stars
Steal to their sovran seats.
The Clouds Have Left the Sky.
Stanza 3

And whiter grows the foam,
The small moon lightens more;
And as I turn me home,
My shadow walks before.
Ibid. Stanza 4

Whither, O splendid ship, thy white
   sails crowding,

Leaning across the bosom of the urgent
   West,
That fearest nor sea rising, nor sky
   clouding,
Whither away, fair rover, and what thy
   quest?
A Passer-By. Stanza 1

I have loved flowers that fade,
   Within whose magic tents
Rich hues have marriage made
   With sweet unmemoried scents.
I Have Loved Flowers That Fade.
Stanza 1

Ah! little at best can all our hopes avail
   us
To lift this sorrow, or cheer us, when in
   the dark,
   Unwilling, alone we embark,
And the things we have seen and have
   known and have heard of, fail us.
On a Dead Child. Stanza 7

Gird on thy sword, O man, thy strength
   endue,
In fair desire thine earth-born joy renew.
Live thou thy life beneath the making
   sun
Till Beauty, Truth, and Love in thee
   are one.
A Hymn of Nature. VII, Stanza 1

When first we met we did not guess
That Love would prove so hard a mas-
   ter.
Of more than common friendliness
When first we met we did not guess.
Triolet

So sweet love seemed that April morn,
When first we kissed beside the thorn,
So strangely sweet, it was not strange
We thought that love could never
   change.
Shorter Poems. Book V, 5

My delight and thy delight
Walking, like two angels white,
In the gardens of the night.
New Poems. Number 9

Love, from whom the world begun,
Hath the secret of the sun.
Love can tell, and love alone,
Whence the million stars were strewn,
Why each atom knows its own.
Ibid.

---

[1] Poet laureate from 1913 until his death. He was succeeded by John Masefield.

Wisdom will repudiate thee, if thou
　　think to enquire
WHY things are as they are or whence
　　they came: thy task
is first to learn WHAT IS, and in pur-
　　suant knowledge
pure intellect will find pure pleasure
　　and the only ground
for a philosophy conformable to truth.
　　　　　　The Testament of Beauty
　　　　　　　　　　　　[1929]

Our hope is ever livelier than despair,
　　our joy
livelier and more abiding than our sor-
　　rows are.
　　　　　　　　　　　　　　Ibid.

For what were pleasure if never con-
　　templation gave
a spiritual significance to objects of
　　sense,
nor in thought's atmosphere poet vision
　　arose?
　　　　　　　　　　　　　　Ibid.

Man, in the unsearchable darkness,
　　knoweth one thing
that as he is, so was he made: and if
　　the Essence
and characteristic faculty of humanity
is our conscient Reason and our desire
　　of knowledge,
that was Nature's Purpose in the mak-
　　ing of man.
　　　　　　　　　　　　　　Ibid.

ROBERT JONES BURDETTE
[1844–1914]

I love the man who knows it all,
From east to west, from north to south,
Who knows all things, both great and
　　small,
And tells it with his tiresome mouth.
　　　　　　　He Knows It All. Stanza 1

There are two days in the week about
which and upon which I never worry.
Two carefree days, kept sacredly free
from fear and apprehension. One of
these days is Yesterday. . . . And the
other day I do not worry about is Tomorrow.
　　　　　　　　　　The Golden Day

It isn't the experience of today that
drives men mad. It is the remorse for
something that happened yesterday,
and the dread of what tomorrow may
disclose.
　　　　　　　　　　The Golden Day

GEORGE WASHINGTON CABLE
[1844–1925]

There came to port last Sunday night
　　The queerest little craft,
Without an inch of rigging on;
　　I looked and looked — and laughed!
　　　　　　The New Arrival. Stanza 1
She has no manifest but this,
　　No flag floats o'er the water;
She's too new for the British Lloyd's —
　　My daughter! O my daughter!
　　　　　　　　　Ibid. Stanza 2

EDWARD CARPENTER
[1844–1929]

There is nothing that is evil except
because a man has not mastery over it;
and there is no good thing that is not
evil if it have a mastery over a man.
　　　*Towards Democracy. The Secret
　　　　　　　　　of Time and Satan*
Every new movement or manifestation of human activity, when unfamil-
iar to people's minds, is sure to be mis-
represented and misunderstood.
　　　*The Drama of Love and Death.
　　　　　　　　　　Chap. 8, Note*
The first condition of social happiness and prosperity must be the sense
of the Common Life.
　　　*Pagan and Christian Creeds.
　　　　　　　　　　　　Chap. 17*

EDWARD A. CHURCH
[1844–1929]

Of all the words the Evangelists record,
To comfort souls perplexèd and dis-
　　tressed,
This ever seems to me divinest, best —
The thought that Peter spoke — "Thou
　　knowest, Lord."
　　　　　　Sonnet, Thou Knowest

MARY AINGE DE VERE ("MADELINE BRIDGES")
[1844–1920]

There are loyal hearts, there are spirits
   brave,
There are souls that are pure and true;
Then give to the world the best you
   have,
And the best will come back to you.
Life's Mirror. Stanza 1

ANATOLE FRANCE
[1844–1924]

I do not know any reading more
easy, more fascinating, more delightful
than a catalogue.
*The Crime of Sylvestre Bon-
nard* [1] *[1881]. The Log, December 24, 1849*
All the historical books which contain no lies are extremely tedious.
Ibid.
Lovers who love truly do not write
down their happiness.
Ibid. November 30, 1859
To know is nothing at all; to imagine
is everything.
Ibid. Part II, Chap. 2
He flattered himself on being a man
without any prejudices; and this pretension itself is a very great prejudice.
Ibid. Chap. 4
Those who have given themselves the
most concern about the happiness of
peoples have made their neighbours
very miserable.
Ibid.
Man is so made that he can only find
relaxation from one kind of labor by
taking up another.[2]
Ibid.
People who have no weaknesses are
terrible; there is no way of taking advantage of them.
Ibid.
The whole art of teaching is only the
art of awakening the natural curiosity

[1] Translated by LAFCADIO HEARN. Modern
Library edition.
[2] See Karl Marx, pages 593b–594a.

of young minds for the purpose of satis-
fying it afterwards.
*The Crime of Sylvestre Bonnard.
Part II, Chap. 4*
The faculty of doubting is rare
among men. A few choice spirits carry
the germ of it in them, but these do not
develop without training.
*Penguin Island [1908].
Book VI, Chap. 2*
A tale without love is like beef with-
out mustard: an insipid dish.
*The Revolt of the Angels
[1914]. Chap. 8*
We have medicines to make women
speak; we have none to make them keep
silence.
*The Man Who Married a Dumb
Wife.[1] Act II, Sc. 4*
The good critic is he who narrates the
adventures of his soul among master-
pieces.
La Vie Littéraire. Preface
We reproach people for talking about
themselves; but it is the subject they
treat best.
Ibid. Journal des Goncourt

RICHARD WATSON GILDER
[1844–1909]

Through love to light! Oh wonderful
   the way
That leads from darkness to the per-
   fect day!
After-song
How to the singer comes the song?
How to the summer fields
Come flowers? How yields
Darkness to happy morn? How doth
   the night
Bring stars?
*How to the Singer Comes the
Song? Stanza 4*
What is a sonnet? 'Tis a pearly shell
That murmurs of the far-off murmur-
   ing sea;
A precious jewel carved most curi-
   ously;
It is a little picture painted well.
The Sonnet

[1] Translated by CURTIS HIDDEN PAGE.

I count my time by times that I meet
thee;
These are my yesterdays, my morrows,
noons
And nights; these my old moons and
my new moons.

The New Day. Book IV, 6

GERARD MANLEY HOPKINS [1]
[1844-1889]

The world is charged with the grandeur
of God. . . .
There lives the dearest freshness deep
down things.

God's Grandeur [2]

Glory be to God for dappled things —
For skies of couple-colour as a brindled
cow;
For rose-moles all in stipple upon trout
that swim.

Pied Beauty

All things counter, original, spare,
strange;
Whatever is fickle, freckled (who
knows how?)
With swift, slow; sweet, sour; adazzle,
dim;
He fathers-forth whose beauty is past
change:
Praise him.

Ibid.

I caught this morning morning's minion,
kingdom of daylight's dauphin,
dapple-dawn-drawn Falcon, in his
riding
Of the rolling level underneath him
steady air, and striding
High there, how he rung upon the rein
of a wimpling wing
In his ecstasy!

The Windhover

[1] He has left us only 90 poems — but so
essential that they will colour and convert the
development of English poetry for many decades to come. — HERBERT READ [1893-   ]
in *The Criterion*, April, 1931
[2] Hopkins's poems were published posthumously, first in a small selection by Robert
Bridges, then in a nearly complete edition in
1918, reissued with some additions in 1930.

Brute beauty and valour and act, oh,
air, pride, plume, here
Buckle!

The Windhover

As kingfishers catch fire, dragonflies
draw flame.

Sonnet

Each mortal thing does one thing and
the same:
Deals out that being indoors each one
dwells.

Ibid.

Nor worst, there is none. Pitched past
pitch of grief.

Sonnet

O the mind, mind has mountains;
cliffs of fall
Frightful, sheer, no-man-fathomed.

Sonnet

Elected Silence, sing to me
And beat upon my whorlèd ear,
Pipe me to pastures still and be
The music that I care to hear.

The Habit of Perfection

I say that we are wound
With mercy round and round
As if with air.

Mary Mother of Divine Grace

World-mothering air, air wild,
Wound with thee, in thee isled,
Fold home, fast fold thy child.

Ibid.

Summer ends now; now, barbarous in
beauty, the stooks rise
Around; up above, what wind-walks!
what lovely behaviour
Of silk-sack clouds! Has wilder, will-
ful-wavier
Meal-drift moulded ever and melted
across skies?

Hurrahing in Harvest

I have asked to be
Where no storms come,
Where the green swell is in the havens
dumb
And out of the swing of the sea.

Heaven-Haven

I kiss my hand
To the stars, lovely-asunder
Starlight, wafting him out of it; and
Glow, glory in thunder. . . .

Since tho' he is under the world's splendour and wonder,
His mystery must be instressed, stressed;
For I greet him the days I meet him, and bless when I understand.
The Wreck of the Deutschland.
Stanza 5

That night, that year
Of now done darkness I wretch lay wrestling with (my God!) my God.
Carrion Comfort

To lift up the hands in prayer gives God glory, but a man with a dungfork in his hand, a woman with a slop-pail, give him glory too. He is so great that all things give him glory if you mean they should. So then, my brethren, live.
An Address on St. Ignatius

ANDREW LANG
[1844-1912]

You can cover a great deal of country in books.
To the Gentle Reader. Stanza 5

Here stand my books, line upon line
They reach the roof, and row by row,
They speak of faded tastes of mine,
And things I did, but do not, know.
Ballade of His Books. Stanza 1

Why, why are rhymes so rare to *love?*
Ballade of Difficult Rhymes

There's a joy without canker or cark,
There's a pleasure eternally new,
'Tis to gloat on the glaze and the mark
Of china that's ancient and blue.
Ballade of Blue China. Stanza 1

Here's a pot with a cot in a park,
In a park where the peach-blossoms blew;
Where the lovers eloped in the dark,
Lived, died, and were changed into two
Bright birds that eternally flew
Through the boughs of the may, as they sang;
'Tis a tale was undoubtedly true
In the reign of the Emperor Hwang.
Ibid. Stanza 3

So gladly, from the songs of modern speech

Men turn, and see the stars, and feel the free
Shrill wind beyond the close of heavy flowers;
And, through the music of the languid hours,
They hear like ocean on a western beach
The surge and thunder of the Odyssey.
Sonnet, The Odyssey

Why ladies read what they *do* read
Is a thing that no man may explain.
A Remonstrance with the Fair.
Stanza 1

Who wins his love shall lose her,
Who loses her shall gain.
Lost Love. Stanza 1

In dreams she grows not older
The lands of dream among;
Though all the world wax colder,
Though all the songs be sung,
In dreams doth he behold her
Still fair and kind and young.
Ibid. Stanza 4

And, if one Rag of Character they spare,
Comes the Biographer, and strips it bare!
Letters to Dead Authors [1886].
Epistle to Mr. Alexander Pope

Contemporary spites do not harm true genius.
Ibid. To M. Chapelain

The dusty and stony ways of contemporary criticism.
Ibid. To Edgar Allan Poe

The eye of each man sees but what it has the power of seeing.
Ibid. To Homer

My mind is gay but my soul is melancholy.
Quoted by Mrs. Lang *in Preface, The Poetical Works of Andrew Lang* [1923]

JAMES HILARY MULLIGAN
[1844-1916]

The moonlight is the softest, in Kentucky,

Summer days come oftest, in Kentucky,
  Friendship is the strongest,
  Love's fires glow the longest,
  Yet a wrong is always wrongest,
    In Kentucky.
        In Kentucky. Stanza 1

Songbirds are sweetest, in Kentucky,
Thoroughbreds the fleetest, in Kentucky;
  The mountains tower proudest,
  Thunder peals the loudest,
  The landscape is the grandest,
  And politics the damnedest,
    In Kentucky.
        Ibid. Stanza 7

FRIEDRICH WILHELM NIETZSCHE
[1844–1900]

Our destiny exercises its influence over us even when, as yet, we have not learned its nature: it is our future that lays down the law of our today.
    Human, All Too Human [1]
        [1878]. 7

One must have a good memory to be able to keep the promises one makes.
    Ibid. 59

One will rarely err if extreme actions be ascribed to vanity, ordinary actions to habit, and mean actions to fear.
    Ibid. 74

How poor the human mind would be without vanity! It resembles a well stocked and ever renewed ware-emporium that attracts buyers of every class: they can find almost everything, have almost everything, provided they bring with them the right kind of money — admiration.
    Ibid.

Every tradition grows ever more venerable — the more remote is its origin, the more confused that origin is. The reverence due to it increases from generation to generation. The tradition finally becomes holy and inspires awe.
    Ibid. 96

[1] Translated by ALEXANDER HARVEY.

I teach you the Superman. Man is something that is to be surpassed.
    Thus Spake Zarathustra [1] *[1883–1891]. Prologue, Chap. 3*

Man is a rope stretched between the animal and the Superman — a rope over an abyss.
    Ibid. Chap. 4

I want to teach men the sense of their existence, which is the Superman, the lightning out of the dark cloud man.
    Ibid. Chap. 7

No small art is it to sleep: it is necessary for that purpose to keep awake all day.
    Ibid. Part I, Chap. 2

This is the hardest of all: to close the open hand out of love, and keep modest as a giver.
    Ibid. Part II, Chap. 23

Beggars, however, one should entirely do away with! Verily, it annoyeth one to give unto them, and it annoyeth one not to give unto them.[2]
    Ibid. Chap. 25

Distrust all in whom the impulse to punish is powerful.
    Ibid. Chap. 29

Thoughts that come with doves' footsteps guide the world.
    Ibid. Chap. 44

We ought to learn from the kine one thing: ruminating.
    Ibid. Part IV, Chap. 68

Then learnedst thou how much harder it is to give properly than to take properly, and that bestowing well is an art — the last, subtlest master-art of kindness.
    Ibid.

If ye would go up high, then use your own legs! Do not get yourselves *carried* aloft; do not seat yourselves on other people's backs and heads!
    Ibid. Chap. 73

[1] Translated by THOMAS COMMON.
[2] There is surely a Physiognomy, which those experienced and Master Mendicants observe, whereby they instantly discover a merciful aspect, and will single out a face wherein they spy the signatures and marks of Mercy. — SIR THOMAS BROWNE: *Religio Medici* [1642] (Everyman ed.), *P. 66*

From people who merely pray we must become people who bless.
Notes on Thus Spake Zarathustra. 82

It is certainly not the least charm of a theory that it is refutable.
Beyond Good and Evil [1] [*1885–1886*]. *I, 18*

No one is such a liar as the indignant man.
Ibid. II, 26

It is not the strength but the duration of great sentiments that makes great men.
Ibid. IV, 72

Woman learns how to hate in proportion as she forgets how to charm.
Ibid. 84

Where there is neither love nor hatred in the game, woman's play is mediocre.
Ibid. 115

In revenge and in love woman is more barbarous than man.
Ibid. 139

The thought of suicide is a great consolation: [2] by means of it one gets successfully through many a bad night.
Ibid. 157

There are few pains so grievous as to have seen, divined, or experienced how an exceptional man has missed his way and deteriorated.
Ibid. V, 203

Blessed are the forgetful: for they get the better even of their blunders.
Ibid. VII, 217

Is not life a hundred times too short for us to bore ourselves?
Ibid. 227

One does not know — cannot know — the best that is in one.
Ibid. VIII, 249

The melancholia of everything completed!
Ibid. IX, 277

The "masters" have been done away with; the morality of the vulgar man has triumphed.
Genealogy of Morals [1] [*1887*].
First Essay, Aphorism 9

The broad effects which can be obtained by punishment in man and beast, are the increase of fear, the sharpening of the sense of cunning, the mastery of the desires; so it is that punishment tames man, but does not make him "better."
Ibid. Second Essay, Aphorism 15

A married philosopher belongs to comedy.
Ibid. Third Essay, Aphorism 7

Every tiny step forward in the world was formerly made at the cost of mental and physical torture.
Ibid. Aphorism 9

The sick are the greatest danger for the healthy; it is not from the strongest that harm comes to the strong, but from the weakest.
Ibid. Aphorism 14

A strong and well-constituted man digests his experiences (deeds and misdeeds all included) just as he digests his meats, even when he has some tough morsels to swallow.
Ibid. Aphorism 16

Nothing ever succeeds which exuberant spirits have not helped to produce.
The Twilight of the Idols [2] [*1888*].
Preface

Contentment preserves one even from catching cold. Has a woman who knew that she was well dressed ever caught cold? — No, not even when she had scarcely a rag to her back.
Ibid. Maxims and Missiles, 25

Without music life would be a mistake.
Ibid. 33

He who laughs best today, will also laugh last. [3]
Ibid. 43

---

[1] Translated by HELEN ZIMMERN.
[2] We are in the power of no calamity while death is in our own. — SIR THOMAS BROWNE: *Religio Medici* [1642] (Everyman ed.), *P. 50*

[1] Translated by HORACE B. SAMUEL.
[2] Translated by ANTHONY M. LUDOVICI.
[3] Better the last smile than the first laughter. — JOHN RAY: *English Proverbs* [1670]. This is a variant of the familiar saying, "He laughs

That which needs to be proved cannot be worth much.

The Twilight of the Idols. The Problem of Socrates, 5

Unconscious gratitude for a good digestion (sometimes called "brotherly love").

Ibid. Morality as the Enemy of Nature, 3

Two great European narcotics, alcohol and Christianity.

Ibid. Things the Germans Lack, 2

Dancing in all its forms cannot be excluded from the curriculum of all noble education: dancing with the feet, with ideas, with words, and, need I add that one must also be able to dance with the pen?

Ibid. 7

In the architectural structure, man's pride, man's triumph over gravitation, man's will to power, assume a visible form. Architecture is a sort of oratory of power by means of forms.

Ibid. Skirmishes in a War with the Age, 11

If a man have a strong faith he can indulge in the luxury of scepticism.

Ibid. 12

The sick man is a parasite of society. In certain cases it is indecent to go on living. To continue to vegetate in a state of cowardly dependence upon doctors and special treatments, once the meaning of life, the right to life, has been lost, ought to be regarded with the greatest contempt by society.

Ibid. 36

Liberal institutions straightway cease from being liberal the moment they are soundly established: once this is attained no more grievous and more thorough enemies of freedom exist than liberal institutions.

Ibid. 38

It is my ambition to say in ten sentences what everyone else says in a whole book, — what everyone else does *not* say in a whole book.

Ibid. 51

Love is the state in which man sees things most widely different from what they are. The force of illusion reaches its zenith here, as likewise the sweetening and transfiguring power. When a man is in love he endures more than at other times; he submits to everything.

The Antichrist [1] [*1888*].

Aphorism 23

Our statesmen — a body of men who are otherwise so unembarrassed, and such thorough anti-Christians in deed — still declare themselves Christians and still flock to communion.[2]

Ibid. Aphorism 39

God created woman. And boredom did indeed cease from that moment — but many other things ceased as well! Woman was God's *second* mistake.

Ibid. Aphorism 48

Life always gets harder toward the summit — the cold increases, responsibility increases.

Ibid. Aphorism 57

I call Christianity the one great curse, the one enormous and innermost perversion, the one great instinct of revenge, for which no means are too venomous, too underhand, too underground and too petty, — I call it the one immortal blemish of mankind.

Ibid. Aphorism 62

My doctrine is: Live that thou mayest desire to live again, — that is thy duty, — for in any case thou wilt live again!

Eternal Recurrence.[1] *27*

Even a thought, even a possibility, can shatter us and transform us.

Ibid. 30

Nothing on earth consumes a man more quickly than the passion of resentment.

Ecce Homo [1] [*1888*]

I believe only in French culture, and regard everything else in Europe which calls itself "culture" as a misunderstanding. I do not even take the German kind into consideration.

Ibid.

---

best who laughs last," known in many languages.

[1] Translated by ANTHONY M. LUDOVICI.
[2] The reference is probably to Bismarck.

Wherever Germany extends her sway, she ruins culture.
Ecce Homo

As an artist, a man has no home in Europe save in Paris.
Ibid.

Simply by being compelled to keep constantly on his guard, a man may grow so weak as to be unable any longer to defend himself.
Ibid.

My time has not yet come either; some are born posthumously.
Ibid.

No one can draw more out of things, books included, than he already knows. A man has no ears for that to which experience has given him no access.
Ibid.

The Germans are like women, you can scarcely ever fathom their depths — they haven't any.[1]
Ibid.

After coming in contact with a religious man, I always feel that I must wash my hands.
Ibid.

All prejudices may be traced back to the intestines. A sedentary life is the real sin against the Holy Ghost.[2]
Ibid.

One must separate from anything that forces one to repeat No again and again.
Ibid.

JOHN BOYLE O'REILLY
[1844–1890]

They who see the Flying Dutchman never, never reach the shore.
The Flying Dutchman

Doubt is brother-devil to Despair.
Prometheus

The world is large when weary leagues two loving hearts divide

[1] Man thinks woman profound — why? Because he can never fathom her depths. Woman is not even shallow. — *The Twilight of the Idols, Maxims and Missiles,* 27
[2] Translated by CLIFTON P. FADIMAN. Modern Library edition.

But the world is small when your enemy is loose on the other side.
Distance

The red rose whispers of passion
And the white rose breathes of love;
O, the red rose is a falcon,
And the white rose is a dove.
A White Rose. Stanza 1

You may grind their souls in the self-same mill,
You may bind them, heart and brow;
But the poet will follow the rainbow still,
And his brother will follow the plow.
The Rainbow's Treasure.
Stanza 5

The wealth of mankind is the wisdom they leave.
Rules of the Road

Be silent and safe — silence never betrays you.
Ibid.

"I had" is a heartache, "I have" is a fountain,
You're worth what you saved, not the million you made.
Ibid.

This truth keep in sight, — every man on the planet
Has just as much right as yourself to the road.
Ibid.

The organized charity, scrimped and iced,
In the name of a cautious, statistical Christ.[1]
In Bohemia. Stanza 5

Oh, I long for the glow of a kindly heart and the grasp of a friendly hand!
And I'd rather live in Bohemia than in any other land.
Ibid. Stanza 6

Well blest is he who has a dear one dead;
A friend he has whose face will never change —

[1] See Southey, page 427b, and Hood, page 489b.

A dear communion that will not grow
    strange;
The anchor of a love is death.
                    Forever. Stanza 3

ARTHUR WILLIAM EDGAR O'SHAUGHNESSY
[1844–1881]

We are the music-makers,
    And we are the dreamers of dreams,
Wandering by lone sea-breakers,
    And sitting by desolate streams;
World-losers and world-forsakers,
    On whom the pale moon gleams:
Yet we are the movers and shakers
    Of the world for ever, it seems.
                    Ode. Stanza 1
One man with a dream, at pleasure,
    Shall go forth and conquer a crown;
And three with a new song's measure
    Can trample an empire down.
                    Ibid. Stanza 2
For each age is a dream that is dying,
    Or one that is coming to birth.
                    Ibid. Stanza 3

WILLIAM ARCHIBALD SPOONER [1]
[1844–1930]

Kinquering Congs their titles take.
    Announcing the hymn in college
                        chapel
You have deliberately tasted two
worms and you can leave Oxford by the
town drain.
                    Dismissing a student
This audience of beery wenches.
                    At a woman's college
I remember your name perfectly, but
I just can't think of your face.
                    A greeting

MAURICE THOMPSON
[1844–1901]

A soft Kentucky strain was in his voice,
And the Ohio's deeper boom was there,

---

[1] Canon Spooner, for many years warden
of New College, Oxford, was famous for un-
intentional transpositions of word and
thought. This form of metathesis became
known as a "spoonerism."

With some wild accents of old Wabash
    days,
    And winds of Illinois;
And when he spoke he took us unaware,
With his high courage and unselfish
    ways.
                    At Lincoln's Grave

MRS. EDWARD CRASTER

The centipede was happy quite
    Until a toad in fun
Said, "Pray, which leg goes after
    which?"
That worked her mind to such a pitch,
She lay distracted in a ditch,
    Considering how to run.
        Credited, in Cassell's Weekly,
            to Pinafore Poems [1871]

DR. BREWSTER HIGLEY

Oh, give me a home where the buffalo
    roam,
Where the deer and the antelope play,
Where seldom is heard a discouraging
    word
And the skies are not cloudy all day.
        Home on the Range [1873]

JARRETT AND PALMER
[*Floruerunt* 1866]

Legs are staple articles and will never
go out of fashion while the world lasts.
        Of the original production
        [1866] of their Grand Magical
        Spectacular Drama, The Black
        Crook, by Charles M. Barras
        [1826–1873]

R. L. SHARPE
[*Floruit* 1890]

Each is given a bag of tools,
    A shapeless mass,
    A book of rules;
And each must make,
    Ere life is flown,
A stumbling-block
    Or a stepping-stone.
        Stumbling-Block or Stepping-
                Stone. Stanza 2

JOHN B. BOGART [1]
[1845–1921]

When a dog bites a man, that is not news, because it happens so often. But if a man bites a dog, that is news.

Quoted by Frank M. O'Brien
in The Story of The Sun [*1918*]

JOHN HENRY BONER
[1845–1903]

Ah, we fondly cherish
  Faded things
That had better perish.
  Memory clings
To each leaf it saves.

Gather Leaves and Grasses

Here lived the soul enchanted
  By melody of song;
Here dwelt the spirit haunted
  By a demoniac throng.

Poe's Cottage at Fordham

WILL CARLETON
[1845–1912]

Worm or beetle — drought or tempest — on a farmer's land may fall,
Each is loaded full o' ruin, but a mortgage beats 'em all.

The Tramp's Story

I've watched my duty, straight an' true,
  An' tried to do it well;
Part of the time kept heaven in view,
  An' part steered clear of hell.

*The New Church Doctrine.
Stanza 2*

Not a log in this buildin' but its memories has got,
And not a nail in this old floor but touches a tender spot.

*Out of the Old House, Nancy.
Stanza 17*

He has seen old views and patients disappearing, one by one,
He has learned that Death is master both of Science and of Art.

The Country Doctor. Stanza 3

[1] City editor of *The Sun*, New York, 1873–1890.

Things at home are crossways, and Betsey and I are out.

Betsey and I Are Out. Stanza 1

I have talked with Betsey, and Betsey has talked with me,
And so we've agreed together that we can't never agree.

Ibid. Stanza 3

Betsey, like all good women, had a temper of her own.

Ibid. Stanza 4

The more we arg'ed the question the more we didn't agree.

Ibid. Stanza 5

You see, when we came to division, there was things that wouldn't divide.

*Betsey Destroys the Paper.
Stanza 6*

I'm going away today with a handsomer man than you.

*Gone with a Handsomer Man.
Stanza 4*

  To appreciate heaven well
'Tis good for a man to have some fifteen minutes of hell.

Ibid. Stanza 20

Over the hill to the poor-house I'm trudgin' my weary way.

*Over the Hill to the Poor-House.
Stanza 1*

She had an edication, an' that was good for her;
But when she twitted me on mine, 'twas carryin' things too fur.

Ibid. Stanza 14

WILLIAM ULICK O'CONNOR CUFFE (LORD DESART)
[1845–1898]

Mother Hubbard, you see, was old: there being no mention of others, we may presume she was alone; a widow — a friendless, old, solitary widow. Yet did she despair? Did she sit down and weep, or read a novel, or wring her hands? No! She went to the cupboard.

*Mock Sermon: Old Mother
Hubbard* [*1877*]

CHARLES FLETCHER DOLE
[1845–1927]

Good Will is the mightiest practical force in the universe.
Cleveland Address

The Golden Rule works like gravitation.
Ibid.

Democracy is on trial in the world, on a more colossal scale than ever before.
The Spirit of Democracy

EDWARD HARRIGAN
[1845–1911]

The drums and fifes, how sweetly they did play,
As we march'd, march'd, march'd in the Mulligan Guard.
The Mulligan Guard [1873]

DANIEL WEBSTER HOYT
[1845–1936]

If you have a friend worth loving,
Love him. Yes, and let him know
That you love him, ere life's evening
Tinge his brow with sunset glow.
Why should good words ne'er be said
Of a friend till he is dead? [1]
A Sermon in Rhyme [1878].
Stanza 1

If you hear a song that thrills you,
Sung by any child of song,
Praise it. Do not let the singer
Wait deservèd praises long.
Why should one who thrills your heart
Lack the joy you may impart?
Ibid. Stanza 2

MARGARET THOMSON JANVIER ("MARGARET VANDEGRIFT")
[1845–1913]

You needn't be trying to comfort me —
I tell you my dolly is dead!
There's no use in saying she isn't, with a crack like that in her head.
The Dead Doll. Stanza 1

[1] See Elizabeth Akers Allen, pages 654b–655a.

GEORGE KENNAN
[1845–1924]

Heroism, the Caucasian mountaineers say, is endurance for one moment more.
Letter to Henry Munroe Rogers
[July 25, 1921]

EUGENE LEE-HAMILTON
[1845–1907]

Things bygone are the only things that last:
The present is mere grass, quick-mown away;
The past is stone, and stands for ever fast.
Roman Baths

HAMILTON WRIGHT MABIE
[1845–1916]

The peculiarity of the New England hermit has not been his desire to get near to God, but his anxiety to get away from man.
Backgrounds of Literature.
Emerson and Concord

GEORGE SAINTSBURY
[1845–1933]

It must be remembered that the point of honour which decrees that a man must not under any circumstances accept money from a woman with whom he is on certain terms, is of very modern growth, and is still tempered by the proviso that he may take as much as he likes or can get from his wife.
Preface to FIELDING'S *Tom Jones*

One of the commonest but most uncritical faults of criticism — the refusal to consider what it is that the author intended to give us.
Ibid.

Men will try to persuade themselves, or at least others, that they read poetry because it is a criticism of life, because it expresses the doubts and fears and thoughts and hopes of the time, because it is a substitution for religion, because it is a relief from serious work, because and because and because. As a matter of fact, they (that is to say, those of them who like it generally) read it because they like it, because it communicates an experience of half-sensual, half-intellectual pleasure to them.

Corrected Impressions [*1895*].
Tennyson

Criticism is the endeavor to find, to know, to love, to recommend, not only the best, but all the good, that has been known and thought and written in the world.

A History of Criticism [*1900–1904*]

It is the first duty of the novelist to let himself be read — anything else that he gives you is a bonus, a trimming, a dessert.

History of the English Novel
[*1913*]

I have never tried to be in the fashion for the sake of being in it, and seldom, I think, to be out of it for the sake of being out of it. Logic and history have been the only external guides I have accepted in temporal things, except where pure taste has reigned alone.

Notes on a Cellar Book [*1920*].
Preface

When they [wines] were good they pleased my sense, cheered my spirits, improved my moral and intellectual powers, besides enabling me to confer the same benefits on other people.

Ibid.

ARABELLA EUGENIA SMITH
[1845–1916]

If I should die tonight,
My friends would look upon my quiet
    face,
Before they laid it in its resting place,
And deem that death had left it almost
    fair.

If I Should Die Tonight.[1]
Stanza 1

[1] The parody by BEN KING [1857–1894] has become better known than the original:
If I should die tonight
And you should come in deepest grief and
woe —

CHARLES WILLIAM STUBBS
[1845–1912]

I sat alone with my conscience
    In a place where time had ceased,
And we talked of my former living
    In the land where the years increased.
Conscience and Future
Judgment [*1876*]

To sit alone with my conscience
Will be judgment enough for me.[1]
Ibid.

JOHN BANISTER TABB
[1845–1909]

The ghost am I
Of winds that die
Alike on land or sea.
The Fog. Stanza 1

How many an acorn falls to die
    For one that makes a tree!
How many a heart must pass me by
    For one that cleaves to me!
Compensation. Stanza 1

Out of the dusk a shadow,
    Then a spark;
Out of the cloud a silence,
    Then a lark;
Out of the heart a rapture,
    Then a pain;
Out of the dead, cold ashes,
    Life again.
Evolution

Back to the primal gloom
Where life began.
Going Blind

And in the School of Darkness learn
    What mean
"The things unseen."
Ibid.

JAMES TERRY WHITE
[1845–1920]

If thou of fortune be bereft
And in thy store there be but left

And say: "Here's that ten dollars that I owe,"
I might arise in my large white cravat
And say, "What's that?"
[1] There's just ae thing I cannae bear,
An' that's my conscience.
    R. L. STEVENSON [1850–1894]: *In Scots,*
    XIV. My Conscience

Two loaves, sell one and with the dole
Buy hyacinths to feed thy soul.
Not by Bread Alone: After
Hippocrates [*1907*]

SARAH CHAUNCEY WOOLSEY ("SUSAN COOLIDGE") [1845–1905]

Men die, but sorrow never dies.
The "Cradle Tomb" at Westminster
These are weighty secrets, and we must
whisper them.
Secrets
"A commonplace life," we say, and we
sigh;
But why should we sigh as we say?
The commonplace sun in the common-
place sky
Makes up the commonplace day.
Commonplace
And God, who studies each common-
place soul,
Out of commonplace things makes His
beautiful whole.
Commonplace

CHARLES DUPEE BLAKE [1846–1903]

Rock-a-bye-baby on the tree top,
When the wind blows the cradle will
rock,
When the bough breaks the cradle will
fall,
And down will come baby, cradle and
all.
Attributed

"MICHAEL FIELD" (KATHARINE BRADLEY) [1846–1914] (EDITH COOPER) [1862–1913]

The enchanting miracles of change.
Renewal
Come, mete out my loneliness, O wind,
For I would know
How far the living who must stay be-
hind
Are from the dead who go.
Mete Out My Loneliness

Among the hills I trace the path that I
must wend;
I watch, not bidding him farewell, the
sun descend.
Sweet and of their nature vacant are
the days I spend —
Quiet as a plough laid by at the furrow's end.
Old Age

JOSEPH IGNATIUS CONSTANTINE CLARKE [1846–1925]

"Wherever there's Kellys there's trou-
ble," said Burke.
"Wherever fighting's the game,
Or a spice of danger in grown man's
work,"
Said Kelly, "you'll find my name."
The Fighting Race. Stanza 2
"Oh, the fighting races don't die out,
If they seldom die in bed."
Ibid. Stanza 5

RICHARD LEWIS NETTLESHIP [1846–1892]

The only strength for me is to be
found in the sense of a personal presence everywhere, it scarcely matters
whether it be called human or divine; a
presence which only makes itself felt at
first in this and that particular form
and feature.
Lectures and Memories. I, 72

ALEXANDER MacGREGOR ROSE [1846–1898]

Der Kaiser auf der Vaterland
Und Gott on high, all dings gommand,
Ve two, ach, don'd you understandt?
Meinself — und Gott.
Hoch! Der Kaiser (Kaiser &
Co.) [1] [*1897*]. *Stanza 1*

[1] These verses created a stir when recited
by Captain (later Rear Admiral) Joseph Bul-
lock Coghlan [1844–1908] at a dinner given
in his honor at the Union League Club, New
York, April 21, 1899.

734

Gott pulls mit me, und I mit him.
Hoch! Der Kaiser (Kaiser & Co.).
Stanza 16

HENRYK SIENKIEWICZ
[1846–1916]

The greater philosopher a man is, the more difficult it is for him to answer the foolish questions of common people.
Quo Vadis.[1] *Chap. 19*

EDWARD NOYES WESTCOTT
[1846–1898]

Yes, an' no, an' mebbe, an' mebbe not.
David Harum [1898]. Chap. 1
Do unto the other feller the way he'd like to do unto you an' do it fust.
Ibid. Chap. 20
They say a reasonable number of fleas is good fer a dog — keeps him from broodin' over bein' a dog.
Ibid. Chap. 32
The' ain't nothin' truer in the Bible 'n that sayin' thet them that has gits.
Ibid Chap. 35
I've often had to notice that a man'll sometimes do the foolishest thing or meanest thing in his hull life after he's dead.
Ibid.

JOHN PETER ALTGELD [2]
[1847–1902]

In writing "Progress and Poverty," he dipped his pen into the tears of the human race, and with celestial clearness wrote down what he conceived to be eternal truths.
Memorial Address on Henry George [1897]
When he died, there was nowhere a soul that cried out: "There is one iron hand less to grind us, one wolf less to

tear our flesh," but everywhere a feeling that a friend of the race had gone.
Memorial Address on Henry George

HENRY AUGUSTIN BEERS
[1847–1926]

He sang one song and died — no more but that;
A single song and carelessly complete.
The Singer of One Song [1]
So through the poets' orchestra, which weaves
One music from a thousand stops and strings,
Pierces the note of that immortal song:
"High over all the lonely bugle grieves." [2]
Ibid.

ALEXANDER GRAHAM BELL
[1847–1922]

Mr. Watson, come here, I want you.
To his assistant [March 10, 1876]; the first intelligible words transmitted by telephone

THOMAS ALVA EDISON
[1847–1931]

There is no substitute for hard work.
Life [1932]. Chap. 24
Genius is one per cent inspiration and ninety-nine per cent perspiration.
Ibid.

EDGAR FAWCETT
[1847–1904]

She remembers so many graves
That no one else will remember.
The Grass. Stanza 3
In some blithe moment, was it Nature's choice
To dower a scrap of sunset with a voice?
To an Oriole

---

[1] Translated by JEREMIAH CURTIN [1838–1906].
[2] VACHEL LINDSAY's poem on Altgeld, *The Eagle That Is Forgotten*, is cited on page 902b.

[1] Grenville Mellen [1799–1841].
[2] And high above the fight the lonely bugle grieves! — GRENVILLE MELLEN: *Ode on the Celebration of the Battle of Bunker Hill, June 17, 1825*

WALTER LEARNED
[1847–1915]

A lure more strong, a wish more faint,
Makes one a monster, one a saint.
> *On the Flyleaf of "Manon Lescaut"*

O carping world! If there's an age
Where youth and manhood keep
An equal poise, alas! I must
  Have passed it in my sleep.
> *To Critics. Stanza 3*

Her lips were so near
That — what else could I do?
> *An Explanation*

This world is a difficult world, indeed,
  And people are hard to suit,
And the man who plays on the violin
  Is a bore to the man with the flute.
> *Consolation. Stanza 4*

JOHN LOCKE
[1847–1889]

O Ireland, isn't it grand you look —
  Like a bride in her rich adornin'?
And with all the pent-up love of my heart
  I bid you the top o' the mornin'!
> *The Exile's Return (Dawn on the Irish Coast). Stanza 1*

ALICE MEYNELL
[1847–1922]

My heart shall be thy garden. Come, my own,
Into thy garden; thine be happy hours
Among my fairest thoughts, my tallest flowers,
From root to crowning petal thine alone.
> *Sonnet, The Garden*

She walks — the lady of my delight —
  A shepherdess of sheep.
Her flocks are thoughts. She keeps them white;
  She guards them from the steep.
> *The Shepherdess. Stanza 1*

She holds her little thoughts in sight,
  Though gay they run and leap.
She is so circumspect and right;
  She has her soul to keep.
> *Ibid. Stanza 2*

I must not think of thee; and, tired yet strong,
I shun the thought that lurks in all delight —
The thought of thee — and in the blue heaven's height
And in the sweetest passage of a song.
> *Sonnet, Renouncement*

With the first dream that comes with the first sleep
I run, I run, I am gathered to thy heart.
> *Ibid.*

O heavenly colour, London town
  Has blurred it from her skies;
And, hooded in an earthly brown,
  Unheaven'd the city lies.
> *November Blue. Stanza 1*

It is principally for the sake of the leg that a change in the dress of man is so much to be desired. . . . The leg is the best part of the figure . . . and the best leg is the man's. Man should no longer disguise the long lines, the strong forms, in those lengths of piping or tubing that are of all garments the most stupid.
> *Essays. Unstable Equilibrium*

LLOYD MIFFLIN
[1847–1921]

Inscrutable, colossal, and alone.
> *Sesostris*

JULIA A. MOORE [1]
[1847–1920]

Dear Friends, I write for money,
  With a kind heart and hand,
I wish to make no Enemies
  Throughout my native land.
Kind friends, now I close my rhyme,
  And lay my pen aside,
Between me and my critics
  I leave you to decide.
> *To My Friends and Critics. Stanza 6*

[1] "The Sweet Singer of Michigan," of whom Mark Twain wrote: "The one and unfailing great quality which distinguishes her poetry from Shakespeare's and makes it precious to us is its stern and simple irrelevancy." — *Following the Equator* [1897], *Vol. II, Chap. 8*

Leave off the agony, leave off style,
Unless you've got money by you all the
    while.
If you look about you you'll often have
    to smile
To see so many poor people putting on
    style.
Leave Off the Agony in Style

MILTON NOBLES
[1847–1924]

The villain still pursued her.
The Phoenix [1875]. Act I, Sc. 3

WILLIAM EDWARD NORRIS
[1847–1925]

If your lips would keep from slips,
    Five things observe with care:
To whom you speak; of whom you
    speak;
And how, and when, and where.
Nursery Rhyme, Quoted in
Thirlby Hall

JAMES JEFFREY ROCHE
[1847–1908]

A brave endeavor
To do thy duty, whate'er its worth,
Is better than life with love forever,
And love is the sweetest thing on earth.
Sir Hugo's Choice

What gain is it to the people that a God
    laid down His life,
If twenty centuries after, His world be
    a world of strife?
For the People. Stanza 4

Yea, the gateway shall be free
Unto all, from sea to sea;
And no fratricidal slaughter
Shall defile its sacred water;
But — the hand that ope'd the gate
    shall forever hold the key!
Panama

I'd rather be handsome than homely;
    I'd rather be youthful than old;
If I can't have a bushel of silver
    I'll do with a barrel of gold.
Contentment

All loved Art in a seemly way
With an earnest soul and a capital A.
The V-A-S-E

ARCHIBALD PHILIP PRIMROSE, EARL OF ROSEBERY
[1847–1929]

Few speeches which have produced
an electrical effect on an audience can
bear the colourless photography of a
printed record.
Life of Pitt [1891]

It is beginning to be hinted that we
are a nation of amateurs.
Rectorial Address, Glasgow
[November 16, 1900]

GEORGE ROBERT SIMS
[1847–1922]

Lor', but women's rum cattle to deal
    with, the first man found that to
    his cost,
And I reckon it's just through a woman
    the last man on earth'll be lost.
Moll Jarvis o' Morley

O gleaming lamps of London,
That gem of the city's crown,
What fortunes be within you,
O Lights of London Town?
The Lights of London Town.
Stanza 1

You come here to see how paupers the
    season of Christmas spend;
You come here to watch us feeding, as
    they watch the captured beast.
Christmas Day in the
Workhouse. Stanza 8

ARTHUR JAMES BALFOUR
[1848–1930]

The energies of our system will decay, the glory of the sun will be dimmed,
and the earth, tideless and inert, will no
longer tolerate the race which has for a
moment disturbed its solitude. Man will
go down into the pit, and all his
thoughts will perish.
The Foundations of Belief [1895]

Biography should be written by an acute enemy.

> *Quoted by* S. K. RATCLIFFE *in The London Observer, January 30, 1927*

JOHN VANCE CHENEY
[1848–1922]

Who drives the horses of the sun
  Shall lord it but a day;
Better the lowly deed were done,
  And kept the humble way.
> *The Happiest Heart. Stanza 1*

The happiest heart that ever beat
Was in some quiet breast
That found the common daylight sweet,
And left to Heaven the rest.
> *Ibid. Stanza 3*

JOHN CHURTON COLLINS
[1848–1908]

Truth is the object of philosophy, but not always of philosophers.
> *Aphorisms quoted by* LOGAN PEARSALL SMITH: *A Treasury of English Aphorisms*

Mistrust a subordinate who never finds fault with his superior.
> *Ibid.*

The secret of success in life is known only to those who have not succeeded.
> *Ibid.*

If men were as unselfish as women, women would very soon become more selfish than men.
> *Ibid.*

DIGBY MACKWORTH DOLBEN
[1848–1867]

The world is young today:
  Forget the gods are old,
  Forget the years of gold
When all the months were May.
> *A Song*

SAMUEL MILLER HAGEMAN
[1848–1905]

Every sound shall end in silence, but the silence never dies.
> *Silence [1876]. Stanza 10*

Earth is but the frozen echo of the silent voice of God.
> *Silence. Stanza 19*

JOEL CHANDLER HARRIS
[1848–1908]

How many po' sinners'll be kotched out late
En fin' no latch ter de golden gate?
No use fer ter wait twell ter-morrer,
De sun mus'n't set on yo' sorrer,
Sin's ez sharp ez a bamboo-brier, —
O Lord! fetch de mo'ners up higher!
> *Uncle Remus: His Songs and His Sayings [1881]*

Hit look lak sparrer-grass, hit feel lak sparrer-grass, hit tas'e lak sparrer-grass, en I bless ef 'taint sparrer-grass.
> *Nights with Uncle Remus [1883]. Chap. 27*

No 'pollygy aint gwine ter make h'ar come back whar de b'iling water hit.
> *Ibid. Chap. 45*

Tar-baby ain't sayin' nuthin', en Brer Fox, he lay low.
> *Uncle Remus: Legends of the Old Plantation*

Ez soshubble ez a baskit er kittens.
> *Ibid.*

Bred en bawn in a brier-patch, Brer Fox.
> *Ibid.*

You do de pullin', Sis Cow, en I'll do de gruntin'.
> *Ibid.*

He diggy, diggy, diggy, but no meat dar!
> *Ibid.*

W'en ole man Rabbit say "scoot," dey scooted, en w'en old Miss Rabbit say "scat," dey scatted.
> *Ibid.*

Lazy fokes' stummucks don't git tired.
> *Uncle Remus: Plantation Proverbs*

Jay-bird don't rob his own nes'.
> *Ibid.*

Licker talks mighty loud w'en it gits loose fum de jug.
> *Ibid.*

Hongry rooster don't cackle w'en he fine a wum.
Uncle Remus: Plantation Proverbs

Youk'n hide de fier, but w'at you gwine do wid de smoke?
Ibid.

Dogs don't bite at de front gate.
Ibid.

Watch out w'en youer gittin' all you want. Fattenin' hogs ain't in luck.
Ibid.

Hop light, ladies,
  Oh, Miss Loo!
Oh, swing dat yaller gal!
  Do, boys, do!
Plantation Play Song

When you've got a thing to say,
Say it! Don't take half a day.
When your tale's got little in it,
Crowd the whole thing in a minute!
Life is short — a fleeting vapor —
Don't you fill the whole blamed paper
With a tale which, at a pinch,
Could be cornered in an inch!
Boil her down until she simmers,
Polish her until she glimmers.
Advice to Writers for the Daily Press

JORIS KARL HUYSMANS
[1848–1907]

The pleasure of travel, which only exists as a matter of fact in retrospect and seldom in the present, at the instant when it is being experienced.
Against the Grain [1] *[1884]. Chap. 3*

One could revel, for instance, in long explorations while near one's own fireside, stimulating the restive or sluggish mind, if need be, by reading some narrative of travel in distant lands.
Ibid.

Is there a woman, whose form is more dazzling, more splendid than the two locomotives that pass over the Northern Railroad lines?
Ibid.

[1] Translated by JOHN HOWARD.

The diamond has become notoriously common since every tradesman has taken to wearing it on his little finger.
Against the Grain. Chap. 5

The loveliest tune imaginable becomes vulgar and insupportable as soon as the public begins to hum it and the hurdy-gurdies make it their own.
Ibid. Chap. 9

Perfumes, in fact, rarely come from the flowers whose names they bear . . . with the exception of the inimitable jasmine, which it is impossible to counterfeit.
Ibid. Chap. 10

Art is the only clean thing on earth, except holiness.
Les Foules de Lourdes [1906]

RICHARD JEFFERIES
[1848–1887]

Give me fullness of life like to the sea and the sun; give me fullness of physical life, mind equal and beyond their fullness; give me a greatness and perfection of soul higher than all things; give me my inexpressible desire.
The Story of My Heart [1883]. *Chap. VI*

No thought which I have ever had has satisfied my soul.
Ibid.

The most extraordinary spectacle is the vast expenditure of labor and time wasted in obtaining mere subsistence.
Ibid. Chap. X

The world works only for today, as the world worked twelve thousand years ago, and our children's children will still have to toil and slave for the bare necessities of life.
Ibid.

I hope succeeding generations will be able to be idle. I hope that nine-tenths of their time will be leisure time; that they may enjoy their days, and the earth, and the beauty of this beautiful world; that they may rest by the sea and dream; that they may dance and sing, and eat and drink.
Ibid. Chap. XI

Let me exhort everyone to do their utmost to think outside and beyond our present circle of ideas. For every idea gained is a hundred years of slavery remitted.

The Story of My Heart. Chap. XI

VILFREDO PARETO
[1848–1923]

Give me a fruitful error any time, full of seeds, bursting with its own corrections. You can keep your sterile truth for yourself.

Comment on Kepler

CHARLOTTE AUGUSTA ("CARLOTTA") PERRY
[1848-1914]

The sails we see on the ocean
  Are as white as white can be;
But never one in the harbor
  As white as the sails at sea.
Distance, the Enchantress.
Stanza 1

It was only a glad "Good morning,"
  As she passed along the way,
But it spread the morning's glory
  Over the livelong day.
Good Morning

EBEN EUGENE REXFORD
[1848–1916]

Darling, I am growing old,
Silver threads among the gold
Shine upon my brow today;
Life is fading fast away.
Silver Threads Among
the Gold [1873]

BARONESS BERTHA VON SUTTNER
[1848–1914]

After the verb "To Love," "To Help" is the most beautiful verb in the world!
Epigram

WILL HENRY THOMPSON
[1848–1918]

Then at the brief command of Lee
Moved out that matchless infantry,

With Pickett leading grandly down,
To rush against the roaring crown
Of those dread heights of destiny.[1]
The High Tide at Gettysburg
[1888]. Stanza 2

The voice that rang through Shiloh's woods
And Chickamauga's solitudes,
The fierce South cheering on her sons!
Ibid. Stanza 3

FREDERIC EDWARD WEATHERLY
[1848–1929]

Playing all my heart remembers,
  Old, old songs from far away;
Golden Junes and bleak Decembers
  Rise around me as I play.
Fiddle and I. Stanza 2

Always the same, Darby, my own,
Always the same to your old wife Joan.
Darby and Joan. Stanza 1

The sailor's wife the sailor's star shall be.
Nancy Lee

ROLLIN JOHN WELLS
[1848–1923]

A little more tired at close of day,
A little less anxious to have our way;
A little less ready to scold and blame,
A little more care of a brother's name;
And so we are nearing our journey's end,
Where time and eternity meet and blend.
Growing Old. Stanza 1

JAMES LANE ALLEN
[1849–1925]

The birds are moulting. If man could only moult also — his mind once a year its errors, his heart once a year its useless passions.
A Kentucky Cardinal [1894]

By degrees the comforting light of what you may actually do and be in an imperfect world will shine close to you and all around you, more and more. It

[1] See Cone, page 781b.

is this that will lead you never to perfection, but always toward it.
The Choir Invisible [*1897*].
Chap. 20

JOSEPH GREEN FRANCIS
[1849–1930]

A Tam o' Shanter Dog
And a plaintive piping Frog,
With a Cat whose one extravagance
was clothes,
Went to see a Bounding Bug
Dance a jig upon a rug,
While a Beetle balanced bottles on his
nose.
The Book of Cheerful Cats

EDMUND GOSSE
[1849-1928]

The girls nowadays display a shocking freedom; but they were partly led into it by the relative laxity of their mothers, who, in their turn, gave great anxiety to a still earlier generation.
The Whole Duty of Woman
There never, we suppose, from the beginning of the world, was a man-preacher who did not warn the women of his congregation against the vanity of fair raiment.
Ibid.
The wizard silence of the hours of dew.
The White Throat
The Past is like a funeral gone by,
The Future comes like an unwelcome
guest.
May-Day
I do not hunger for a well-stored mind,
I only wish to live my life, and find
My heart in unison with all mankind.
Lying in the Grass

WILLIAM ERNEST HENLEY
[1849-1903]

The Hospital, grey, quiet, old,
Where Life and Death like friendly
chafferers meet.
In Hospital [*1888*]. *Enter Patient*
Far in the stillness a cat
Languishes loudly.
Ibid. Vigil

A well-bred silence always at command.
In Hospital. Lady-Probationer
From the winter's grey despair,
From the summer's golden languor,
Death, the lover of Life,
Frees us for ever.
Ibid. Ave, Caesar
Bland as a Jesuit, sober as a hymn.
Ibid. House-Surgeon
Valiant in velvet, light in ragged luck,
Most vain, most generous, sternly critical,
Buffoon and poet, lover and sensualist:
A deal of Ariel, just a streak of Puck,
Much Antony, of Hamlet most of all,
And something of the Shorter-Catechist
Ibid. Apparition [*Robert
Louis Stevenson*]
As dust that drives, as straws that blow,
Into the night go one and all.
Ballade of Dead Actors
The ways of Death are soothing and
serene,
And all the words of Death are grave
and sweet.
In Memoriam R. G. C. B. [*1888*]
What is to come we know not. But we
know
That what has been was good.
What Is to Come [*1888*]
Out of the night that covers me,
Black as the Pit from pole to pole,
I thank whatever gods may be
For my unconquerable soul.
Echoes. IV [*1888*], *In Memoriam R. T. Hamilton Bruce*
[*"Invictus"*], *Stanza 1*
In the fell clutch of circumstance,
I have not winced nor cried aloud:
Under the bludgeonings of chance
My head is bloody, but unbowed.
Ibid. Stanza 2
It matters not how strait the gate,
How charged with punishments the
scroll,
I am the master of my fate;
I am the captain of my soul.[1]
Ibid. Stanza 4
The nightingale has a lyre of gold,
The lark's is a clarion call,

[1] See Sallust, page 35b.

And the blackbird plays but a boxwood
flute,
But I love him best of all.
Echoes. XVIII [1888],
To A. D.

A late lark twitters from the quiet skies.
Ibid. XXXV [1888], In Memoriam
Margaritae Sorori

Night with her train of stars
And her great gift of sleep.
Ibid.

So be my passing!
My task accomplished and the long day
done,
My wages taken, and in my heart
Some late lark singing.
Ibid.

Or ever the knightly years were gone
  With the old world to the grave,
I was a King in Babylon
  And you were a Christian Slave.
Ibid. XXXVII [1888], To W. A.

The Spirit of Wine
Sang in my glass, and I listened
With love to his odorous music,
His flushed and magnificent song.
Ibid. XLI, To R. A. M. S.

    These poor Might-Have-Beens,
These fatuous, ineffectual Yesterdays!
To James McNeill Whistler

For Death and Time bring on the prime
Of God's own chosen weather,
And we lie in the peace of the Great
Release
As once in the grass together.
In Memoriam R. L. S.

What have I done for you,
England, my England?
Rhymes and Rhythms. XXV

In the street of By-and-By
Stands the hostelry of Never,
Dream from deed he must dissever
Who his fortune here would try.
In the Street of By-and-By

SARAH ORNE JEWETT
[1849–1909]

A harbor, even if it is a little harbor,
is a good thing, since adventurers come
into it as well as go out, and the life in
it grows strong, because it takes something from the world and has something
to give in return.
Country By-Ways. River
Driftwood

We were standing where there was a
fine view of the harbor and its long
stretches of shore all covered by the
great army of the pointed firs, darkly
cloaked and standing as if they waited
to embark. As we looked far seaward
among the outer islands, the trees
seemed to march seaward still, going
steadily over the heights and down to
the water's edge.
The Country of the Pointed Firs
[1896]

God bless them all who die at sea!
If they must sleep in restless waves,
God make them dream they are ashore,
With grass above their graves.
The Gloucester Mother [1908].
Stanza 3

The thing that teases the mind over
and over for years, and at last gets
itself put down rightly on paper —
whether little or great, it belongs to
Literature.
Letter to Willa Cather. Quoted
in Preface to The Country of
the Pointed Firs and Other
Stories [1925]

EMMA LAZARUS
[1849–1887]

Give me your tired, your poor,
Your huddled masses yearning to
  breathe free,
The wretched refuse of your teeming
  shore,
Send these, the homeless, tempest-
  tossed, to me:
I lift my lamp beside the golden door.
The New Colossus: Inscription
for the Statue of Liberty, New
York Harbor

SIR WILLIAM OSLER
[1849-1919]

The greater the ignorance the greater the dogmatism.
> *In Montreal Medical Journal* [*1902*]

The philosophies of one age have become the absurdities of the next, and the foolishness of yesterday has become the wisdom of tomorrow.
> *Ibid.*

The natural man has only two primal passions, to get and to beget.
> *Science and Immortality* [*1904*]. *Chap. 2*

We forget that the measure of the value of a nation to the world is neither the bushel nor the barrel, but mind; and that wheat and pork, though useful and necessary, are but dross in comparison with those intellectual products which alone are imperishable.
> *Aequanimitas and Other Addresses* [*1904*]. *Teacher and Student*

When schemes are laid in advance, it is surprising how often the circumstances fit in with them.
> *Ibid. Internal Medicine as a Vocation*

A well trained sensible family doctor is one of the most valuable assets in a community, worth today, as in Homer's time, many another man. . . . Few men live lives of more devoted self-sacrifice.
> *Ibid. Chauvinism in Medicine*

Amid an eternal heritage of sorrow and suffering our work is laid.
> *Ibid. The Student Life*

Tact is the saving virtue without which no woman can be a success.
> *Commencement Address to Nurses, Johns Hopkins University* [*May 7, 1913*]

Speck in cornea, 50¢.
> *Entry in his account-book, first fee as a practicing physician. From Life of Sir William Osler by* HARVEY CUSHING [*1925*], *Vol. I, Chap. 6*

After all, there is no such literature as a Dictionary.
> *Life of Sir William Osler. Vol. I, Chap. 11*

The desire to take medicine is perhaps the greatest feature which distinguishes man from animals.
> *Ibid. Chap. 14*

This is yet the childhood of the world, and a supine credulity is still the most charming characteristic of man.
> *Ibid.*

We are here to add what we can *to*, not to get what we can *from*, Life.[1]
> *Ibid.*

Humanity has but three great enemies; fever, famine and war; of these by far the greatest, by far the most terrible, is fever.
> *Ibid.*

Though a little one, the master-word [Work] looms large in meaning. It is the open sesame to every portal, the great equalizer in the world, the true philosopher's stone which transmutes all the base metal of humanity into gold.[2]
> *Ibid. Chap. 22*

Things cannot always go your way. Learn to accept in silence the minor aggravations, cultivate the gift of taciturnity and consume your own smoke [3] with an extra draught of hard work, so that those about you may not be annoyed with the dust and soot of your complaints.
> *Ibid.*

Take the sum of human achievement in action, in science, in art, in literature — subtract the work of the men above forty, and while we should miss great treasures, even priceless treasures, we would practically be where we are

[1] Also in *Doctor and Nurse,* in *Aequanimitas and Other Addresses* [1904].
[2] Lecture, *The Master-Word in Medicine,* Toronto, October 1, 1903, also in *Aequanimitas.*
[3] See Carlyle, page 474a.

to-day. . . . The effective, moving, vitalizing work of the world is done between the ages of twenty-five and forty.[1]

> *Life of Sir William Osler. Vol. I, Chap. 24 (The Fixed Period)*

My second fixed idea is the uselessness of men above sixty years of age, and the incalculable benefit it would be in commercial, political, and in professional life, if as a matter of course, men stopped work at this age.[2]

> *Ibid.*

In that charming novel, "The Fixed Period," [by] Anthony Trollope, . . . the plot hinges upon the admirable scheme of a college into which at sixty men retired for a year of contemplation before a peaceful departure by chloroform. That incalculable benefits might follow such a scheme is apparent to anyone who, like myself, is nearing the limit, and who has made a careful study of the calamities which may befall men during the seventh and eighth decades.[2]

> *Ibid.*

Nothing will sustain you more potently than the power to recognize in your humdrum routine, as perhaps it may be thought, the true poetry of life — the poetry of the commonplace, of the ordinary man, of the plain, toil-worn woman, with their loves and their joys, their sorrows and their griefs.

> *Ibid. (The Student Life)*

Lift up one hand to heaven and thank your stars if they have given you the proper sense to enable you to appreciate the inconceivably droll situations in which we catch our fellow creatures.

> *Ibid.*

---

[1] Address at Johns Hopkins University, Baltimore, February 22, 1905.

[2] This valedictory address caused much discussion and misquotation. It was headlined in the press "OSLER RECOMMENDS CHLOROFORM AT SIXTY," and occasioned many columns of letters, caustic cartoons, and the like, until to "Oslerize" became a byword.

I have three personal ideals. One, to do the day's work well and not to bother about to-morrow. . . . The second ideal has been to act the Golden Rule, as far as in me lay, toward my professional brethren and toward the patients committed to my care. And the third has been to cultivate such a measure of equanimity as would enable me to bear success with humility, the affection of my friends without pride, and to be ready when the day of sorrow and grief came to meet it with the courage befitting a man.

> *Life of Sir William Osler. Vol. I, Chap. 24 (Farewell Dinner [May 2, 1905])*

Throw all the beer and spirits into the Irish Channel, the English Channel, and the North Sea for a year, and people in England would be infinitely better. It would certainly solve all the problems with which the philanthropists, the physicians, and the politicians have to deal.[1]

> *Ibid. Vol. II, Chap. 26*

No man is really happy or safe without a hobby, and it makes precious little difference what the outside interest may be — botany, beetles or butterflies, roses, tulips or irises; fishing, mountaineering or antiquities — anything will do so long as he straddles a hobby and rides it hard.[2]

> *Ibid. Chap. 29*

Nothing in life is more wonderful than faith — the one great moving force which we can neither weigh in the balance nor test in the crucible.

> *Ibid. Chap. 30*

In the life of a young man the most essential thing for happiness is the gift of friendship.

> *Ibid. Chap. 31*

---

[1] Address at Working Men's College, Camden Town, November 17, 1906.

[2] Address, Medical Library Association, Belfast, July 28, 1909.

No bubble is so iridescent or floats longer than that blown by the successful teacher.
Life of Sir William Osler. Vol. II, Chap. 31

The nation's Valhalla [Westminster Abbey].
Ibid. Chap. 32

It is one of the greatest blessings that so many women are so full of tact. The calamity happens when a woman who has all the other riches of life just lacks that one thing.[1]
Ibid. Chap. 33

The quest for righteousness is Oriental, the quest for knowledge, Occidental.[2]
Ibid. Chap. 34

In science the credit goes to the man who convinces the world, not to the man to whom the idea first occurs.[3]
Ibid. Chap. 38

JAMES WHITCOMB RILEY
[1849–1916]

O'er folded blooms
    On swirls of musk,
The beetle booms adown the glooms
    And bumps along the dusk.
The Beetle. Stanza 7

The ripest peach is highest on the tree.
The Ripest Peach. Stanza 1

An' the Gobble-uns'll git you
Ef you don't watch out.
Little Orphant Annie. Stanza 1

His Mammy heered him holler, an' his Daddy heered him bawl,
An' when they turn't the kivvers down, he wasn't there at all!
Ibid. Stanza 2

It hain't no use to grumble and complain,
    It's jest as easy to rejoice;

[1] Commencement Address, Johns Hopkins Hospital School of Nursing, May 7, 1913.
[2] Address, Jewish Historical Society of England, April 27, 1914.
[3] Address, Royal Society of Medicine, Historical Section, May 15, 1918.

When God sorts out the weather and sends rain,
    Why rain's my choice.
Wet-Weather Talk

Heaven holds all for which you sigh —
There! littfe girl; don't cry!
A Life-Lesson. Stanza 3

I can see the pink sunbonnet and the little checkered dress
She wore when first I kissed her and she answered the caress
With the written declaration that, "as surely as the vine
Grew 'round the stump," she loved me — that old sweetheart of mine.
An Old Sweetheart of Mine. Stanza 12

When over the fair fame of friend or foe
The shadow of disgrace shall fall, instead
Of words of blame, or proof of thus and so,
Let something good be said.
Let Something Good Be Said. Stanza 1

Fer the world is full of roses, and the roses full of dew,
And the dew is full of heavenly love that drips fer me and you.
Thoughts fer the Discuraged Farmer. Stanza 5

Tell you what I like the best —
'Long about knee-deep in June,
Bout the time strawberries melts
On the vine, — some afternoon
Like to jes' git out and rest,
And not work at nothin' else.
Knee-deep in June. Stanza 1

Oh! the old swimmin'-hole! When I last saw the place,
The scene was all changed, like the change in my face.
The Old Swimmin'-Hole. Stanza 5

Work is the least o' my idees
When the green, you know, gits back in the trees!
When the Green Gits Back in the Trees. Stanza 1

O, the Raggedy Man he works fer Pa,
An' he's the goodest man ever you saw!
The Raggedy Man. Stanza 1

There's a boil on his ear and a corn on
his chin, —
He calls it a dimple — but dimples
stick in.
    The Man in the Moon. Stanza 3

A pictur' that no painter has the col-
orin' to mock —
When the frost is on the punkin and the
fodder's in the shock.
    When the Frost Is on the Punkin.
        Stanza 2

Le's go a-visitin' back to Griggsby's
Station —
Back where we ust to be so happy and
so pore!
    Griggsby's Station. Stanza 1

EDWARD BELLAMY [1]
[1850–1898]

If we could have devised an arrangement for providing everybody with
music in their homes, perfect in quality,
unlimited in quantity, suited to every
mood, and beginning and ceasing at
will, we should have considered the
limit of human felicity already attained.
    Looking Backward [1887]

Your system was liable to periodical
convulsions, overwhelming alike the
wise and unwise, the successful cut-
throat as well as his victim. I refer to
the business crises at intervals of five to
ten years, which wrecked the industries
of the nation.
    Ibid.

AUGUSTINE BIRRELL
[1850–1933]

Libraries are not made; they grow.
    Obiter Dicta. Book-Buying

Good as it is to inherit a library, it is
better to collect one.
    Ibid.

[1] There is at least a fair chance that another fifty years will confirm Edward Bellamy's position as one of the most authentic
prophets of our age. — HEYWOOD BROUN
[1931]

FLORENCE EARLE COATES
[1850–1927]

The messenger of sure and swift relief,
Welcomed with wailings and reproachful grief;
The friend of those that have no friend
but me,
I break all chains, and set all captives
free.
    Death. Stanza 2

There is always room for beauty: mem-
ory
A myriad lovely blossoms may enclose,
But, whatsoe'er hath been, there still
must be
Room for another rose.
    The Poetry of Earth. Stanza 1

EUGENE FIELD
[1850–1895]

I feel a sort of yearnin' 'nd a chokin' in
my throat
When I think of Red Hoss Mountain
'nd of Casey's tabble dote!
    Casey's Table d'Hôte. Stanza 1

He could whip his weight in wildcats.
    Modjesky as Cameel. Stanza 10

Let my temptation be a book,
Which I shall purchase, hold, and keep.
    The Bibliomaniac's Prayer.
        Stanza 2

No matter what conditions
  Dyspeptic come to feaze,
The best of all physicians
  Is Apple-pie and cheese!
    Apple-Pie and Cheese. Stanza 5

I like the Anglo-Saxon speech
  With its direct revealings;
It takes a hold, and seems to reach
  'Way down into your feelings.
    "Good-by — God Bless You!"
        Stanza 1

I'm sure no human heart goes wrong
That's told "Good-by — God bless
you!"
    Ibid. Stanza 2

I never lost a little fish — yes, I am free
to say
It always was the biggest fish I caught
that got away.
    Our Biggest Fish. Stanza 2

How gracious those dews of solace that
over my senses fall
At the clink of the ice in the pitcher the
boy brings up the hall!
The Clink of the Ice. Stanza 1

When one's all right, he's prone to spite
The doctor's peaceful mission;
But when he's sick, it's loud and quick
He bawls for a physician.[1]
Doctors. Stanza 2

When I demanded of my friend what
viands he preferred,
He quoth: "A large cold bottle, and a
small hot bird!"
The Bottle and the Bird. Stanza 1

Have you ever heard of the Sugar-Plum
Tree?
'Tis a marvel of great renown!
It blooms on the shore of the Lollipop
sea
In the garden of Shut-Eye Town.
The Sugar-Plum Tree. Stanza 1

Wynken, Blynken, and Nod one night
Sailed off in a wooden shoe —
Sailed on a river of crystal light
Into a sea of dew.
Wynken, Blynken, and Nod.
Stanza 1

The little toy dog is covered with dust,
But sturdy and stanch he stands;
And the little toy soldier is red with
rust,
And his musket moulds in his hands;
Time was when the little toy dog was
new,
And the soldier was passing fair;
And that was the time when our Little
Boy Blue
Kissed them and put them there.
Little Boy Blue. Stanza 1

The Rock-a-By Lady from Hushaby
street
Comes stealing; comes creeping.
The Rock-a-By Lady. Stanza 1

Have you ever heard the wind go
"Yooooo"?

'Tis a pitiful sound to hear!
It seems to chill you through and
through
With a strange and speechless fear.
The Night Wind. Stanza 1

The Dinkey-Bird goes singing
In the amfalula tree!
The Dinkey-Bird. Stanza 1

The gingham dog went "Bow-wow-
wow!"
And the calico cat replied "Mee-ow!"
The air was littered, an hour or so,
With bits of gingham and calico.
The Duel. Stanza 2

Father calls me William, sister calls me
Will,
Mother calls me Willie, but the fellers
call me Bill!
Jest 'Fore Christmas. Stanza 1

'Most all the time, the whole year
round, there ain't no flies on me,
But jest 'fore Christmas I'm as good
as I kin be!
Ibid.

Shuffle-Shoon and Amber-Locks
Sit together, building blocks;
Shuffle-Shoon is old and gray,
Amber-Locks a little child,
But together at their play
Age and Youth are reconciled.
Shuffle-Shoon and Amber-Locks.
Stanza 1

Mother tells me "Happy dreams!" and
takes away the light,
An' leaves me lyin' all alone an' seein'
things at night.
Seein' Things. Stanza 1

Strive not to hew your path through
life — it really doesn't pay;
Be sure the salve of flattery soaps all
you do and say;
Herein the only royal road to fame and
fortune lies:
Put not your trust in vinegar — mo-
lasses catches flies!
Uncle Eph. Stanza 4

---

[1] Three faces wears the doctor: when first
sought
An Angel's; and a god's the cure half-
wrought;

But when, the cure complete, he seeks his
fee,
The Devil looks less terrible than he.
ANONYMOUS

FRED GILBERT
[1850–1903]

The Man Who Broke the Bank at Monte Carlo.

Title of song [*1892*]

JOHN CHEEVER GOODWIN
[1850–1912]

For that elephant ate all night,
And that elephant ate all day;
Do what he could to furnish him food,
The cry was still *more hay.*

Wang: The Man with an Elephant on His Hands [*1891*]

LAFCADIO HEARN
[1850–1904]

My friends are much more dangerous than my enemies. . . . These latter help me so much by their unconscious aid that I almost love them. They help me to maintain the isolation indispensable to quiet regularity of work.

Letter to Ernest Fenollosa, 1899. Quoted by VERA MCWILLIAMS: *Lafcadio Hearn* [*1946*]

HENRY CABOT LODGE
[1850–1924]

New England has a harsh climate, a barren soil, a rough and stormy coast, and yet we love it, even with a love passing that of dwellers in more favored regions.

Address, New England Society of New York [*December 22, 1884*]

Of "Americanism" of the right sort we cannot have too much. Mere vaporing and boasting become a nation as little as a man. But honest, outspoken pride and faith in our country are infinitely better and more to be respected than the cultivated reserve which sets it down as ill-bred and in bad taste ever to refer to our country except by way of deprecation, criticism, or general negation.

Ibid.

Let every man honor and love the land of his birth and the race from which he springs and keep their memory green. It is a pious and honorable duty. But let us have done with British-Americans and Irish-Americans and German-Americans, and so on, and all be Americans. . . . If a man is going to be an American at all let him be so without any qualifying adjectives; and if he is going to be something else, let him drop the word American from his personal description.[1]

The Day We Celebrate (Forefathers' Day), Address, New England Society of Brooklyn [*December 21, 1888*]

It is the flag just as much of the man who was naturalized yesterday, as of the man whose people have been here many generations.

Address [*1915*]

He was a great patriot, a great man; above all, a great American. His country was the ruling, mastering passion of his life from the beginning even unto the end.

Theodore Roosevelt: Address Before Congress [*February 9, 1919*]

PHILIP BOURKE MARSTON
[1850–1887]

A little time for laughter,
A little time to sing,
A little time to kiss and cling,
And no more kissing after.[2]

After. Stanza 1

LAURA ELIZABETH RICHARDS
[1850–1943]

Sure, honor's name will aye be richer
For the bright name of Molly Pitcher.

Molly Pitcher

Great is truth and shall prevail,[3]
Therefore must we weep and wail.

The Mameluke and the Hospodar

[1] See Theodore Roosevelt, page 780a.
[2] See Du Maurier, pages 665b–666a.
[3] See *1 Esdras, IV, 41,* on page 1065a.
For (magna est veritas & praevalebit) great

Every little wave had its nightcap on.
A Song for Hal

Ponsonby Perks,
He fought with Turks,
Performing many wonderful works.
Nonsense Verses. Stanza 2

ROBERT RICHARDSON
[1850–1901]

Warm summer sun, shine friendly here;
Warm western wind, blow kindly here;
Green sod above, rest light, rest light —
Good-night, Annette! Sweetheart, good-night.[1]

To Annette

ROBERT LOUIS STEVENSON
[1850–1894]

Mankind was never so happily inspired as when it made a cathedral.
An Inland Voyage [1878]. Noyon

Every man is his own doctor of divinity, in the last resort.
Ibid.

For my part, I travel not to go anywhere, but to go. I travel for travel's sake. The great affair is to move.
Travels with a Donkey [1878]

Marriage is like life in this — that it is a field of battle, and not a bed of roses.
Virginibus Puerisque [1881].
I, Chap. 1

Times are changed with him who marries; there are no more by-path meadows, where you may innocently linger, but the road lies long and straight and dusty to the grave.
Ibid. Chap. 2

---

is truth, & shall prevail. — THOMAS BROOKS: *The Crown and Glory of Christianity* [1662]

[1] Mark Twain adapted this verse, by the Australian poet Richardson, for the stone marking the grave of his daughter, Olivia Susan Clemens, who died August 18, 1896, aged twenty-four:
Warm summer sun, shine kindly here;
Warm southern wind, blow softly here;
Green sod above, lie light, lie light —
Good-night, dear heart, good-night, good-night.

Man is a creature who lives not upon bread alone but principally by catchwords.
Virginibus Puerisque. I, Chap. 2

The cruellest lies are often told in silence.
Ibid. Chap. 4, Truth of Intercourse

Old and young, we are all on our last cruise.
Ibid. II, Crabbed Age and Youth

It is better to be a fool than to be dead.
Ibid.

Give me the young man who has brains enough to make a fool of himself.
Ibid.

Books are good enough in their own way, but they are a mighty bloodless substitute for life.
Ibid. III, An Apology for Idlers

Perpetual devotion to what a man calls his business, is only to be sustained by perpetual neglect of many other things.
Ibid.

There is no duty we so much underrate as the duty of being happy.
Ibid.

To travel hopefully is a better thing than to arrive.
Ibid. VI, El Dorado

To be what we are, and to become what we are capable of becoming, is the only end of life.
Familiar Studies of Men and Books [1882]

I am in the habit of looking not so much to the nature of a gift as to the spirit in which it is offered.
New Arabian Nights [1882].
The Suicide Club

Fifteen men on the Dead Man's Chest — [1]
Yo-ho-ho, and a bottle of rum!

[1] Treasure Island came out of Kingsley's "At Last," where I got the Dead Man's Chest — and that was the seed. — R. L. STEVENSON, *Letter to Sidney Colvin*
See Charles Kingsley, page 599a.

Drink and the devil had done for the rest —
Yo-ho-ho, and a bottle of rum!
> *Treasure Island* [*1883*]

Doctors is all swabs.
> *Ibid. Chap. 3* [*Billy Bones*]

Many's the long night I've dreamed of cheese — toasted, mostly.
> *Ibid. Chap. 15* [*Ben Gunn*]

There's no music like a little river's. It plays the same tune (and that's the favourite) over and over again, and yet does not weary of it like men fiddlers. It takes the mind out of doors; and though we should be grateful for good houses, there is, after all, no house like God's out-of-doors.
> *Prince Otto* [*1885*]. *Chap. 2*

For all the story-books you read:
For all the pains you comforted:
For all you pitied, all you bore,
In sad and happy days of yore . . .
Take, nurse, the little book you hold!
> *A Child's Garden of Verses* [*1885*]. *To Alison Cunningham from Her Boy*

In winter I get up at night
And dress by yellow candle-light.
In summer, quite the other way,
I have to go to bed by day.
> *Ibid. Bed in Summer, Stanza 1*

I have to go to bed and see
The birds still hopping on the tree,
Or hear the grown-up people's feet
Still going past me on the street.
> *Ibid. Stanza 2*

A child should always say what's true
And speak when he is spoken to,
And behave mannerly at table;
At least as far as he is able.
> *Ibid. Whole Duty of Children*

Whenever the moon and stars are set,
Whenever the wind is high,
All night long in the dark and wet,
A man goes riding by.
Late in the night when the fires are out,
Why does he gallop and gallop about?
> *Ibid. Windy Nights, Stanza 1*

Dark brown is the river,
    Golden is the sand,

It flows along for ever,
    With trees on either hand.
> *A Child's Garden of Verses. Where Go the Boats, Stanza 1*

The pleasant land of counterpane.
> *Ibid. The Land of Counterpane, Stanza 4*

I have a little shadow that goes in and out with me,
And what can be the use of him is more than I can see.
He is very, very like me from the heels up to the head;
And I see him jump before me, when I jump into my bed.
> *Ibid. My Shadow, Stanza 1*

The friendly cow all red and white,
    I love with all my heart:
She gives me cream with all her might,
    To eat with apple-tart.
> *Ibid. The Cow, Stanza 1*

The world is so full of a number of things,
I'm sure we should all be as happy as kings.
> *Ibid. Happy Thought*

The eternal dawn, beyond a doubt,
    Shall break on hill and plain,
And put all stars and candles out
    Ere we be young again.
> *To Minnie*

Little Indian, Sioux or Crow,
Little frosty Eskimo,
Little Turk or Japanee,
O! don't you wish that you were me?
> *Ibid. Foreign Children*

I feel very strongly about putting questions; it partakes too much of the style of the day of judgment. You start a question, and it's like starting a stone. You sit quietly on the top of a hill; and away the stone goes, starting others.
> *The Strange Case of Dr. Jekyll and Mr. Hyde* [*1886*]

Am I no a bonny fighter?
> *Kidnapped* [*1886*]. *Chap. 10* [*Alan Breck*]

Of all my verse, like not a single line;
But like my title, for it is not mine.
That title from a better man [1] I stole:

[1] Ben Jonson.

Ah how much better, had I stol'n the whole!
Underwoods [*1887*]. *Foreword*

There are men and classes of men that stand above the common herd: the soldier, the sailor, and the shepherd not unfrequently; the artist rarely; rarelier still, the clergyman; the physician almost as a rule. He is the flower (such as it is) of our civilization.
Ibid. Dedication

Generosity he has, such as is possible to those who practise an art, never to those who drive a trade; discretion, tested by a hundred secrets; tact, tried in a thousand embarrassments; and what are more important, Heraclean cheerfulness and courage.
Ibid.

Gratitude is but a lame sentiment; thanks, when they are expressed, are often more embarrassing than welcome.
Ibid.

Go, little book, and wish to all
Flowers in the garden, meat in the hall,
A bin of wine, a spice of wit,
A house with lawns enclosing it,
A living river by the door,
A nightingale in the sycamore!
Ibid. Envoy

Youth now flees on feathered foot.
Ibid. To Will H. Low [1]

Life is over, life was gay:
We have come the primrose way.
Ibid.

Dear Andrew, with the brindled hair.[2]
Ibid. To Andrew Lang

Under the wide and starry sky,
Dig the grave and let me lie.
Glad did I live and gladly die,
And I laid me down with a will.
Ibid. Requiem, Stanza 1

[1] American painter [1853–1932], whose wife translated Stevenson's *Strange Case of Dr. Jekyll and Mr. Hyde* into French.
[2] Dear Louis of the awful cheek!
Who told you it was right to speak,
Where all the world might hear and stare,
Of other fellows' "brindled hair"?
ANDREW LANG [1844–1912]: *To R. L. S.*

This be the verse you grave for me:
Here he lies where he longed to be;
Home is the sailor, home from sea,
And the hunter home from the hill.
Underwoods. Requiem, Stanza 2

If I have faltered more or less
In my great task of happiness.
Ibid. The Celestial Surgeon

If beams from happy human eyes
Have moved me not; if morning skies,
Books, and my food, and summer rain
Knocked on my sullen heart in vain: —
Lord, thy most pointed pleasure take
And stab my spirit broad awake.
Ibid.

Yet, O stricken heart, remember, O remember
How of human days he lived the better part.
April came to bloom and never dim December
Breathed its killing chills upon the head or heart.
Ibid. In Memoriam F. A. Stilwell [1] [*1881*]

Let first the onion flourish there,
Rose among roots, the maiden-fair
Wine-scented and poetic soul
Of the capacious salad bowl.
Ibid. To a Gardener

My body, which my dungeon is,
And yet my parks and palaces.
Ibid. XXXVII

There are kind hearts still, for friends to fill
And fools to take and break them;
But the nearest friends are the auldest friends
And the grave's the place to seek them.
Ibid. In Scots, XVI, Stanza 3

I have thus played the sedulous ape to Hazlitt, to Lamb, to Wordsworth, to Sir Thomas Browne, to Defoe, to Hawthorne, to Montaigne, to Baudelaire and to Obermann.
Memories and Portraits [*1887*].
A College Magazine

[1] Lady Colvin's son by her first marriage; he died at the age of eighteen.

"A Penny Plain and Twopence Coloured."

> *Memories and Portraits. Essay about Skelt's Juvenile Drama*

Wealth I ask not, hope nor love,
  Nor a friend to know me;
All I ask, the heaven above
  And the road below me.

> *Songs of Travel. The Vagabond, Stanza 4*

I will make you brooches and toys for
  your delight
Of bird-song at morning and star-shine
  at night.

> *Ibid. Romance, Stanza 1*

And this shall be for music when no
  one else is near,
The fine song for singing, the rare song
  to hear!

> *Ibid. Stanza 3*

God, if this were enough,
That I see things bare to the buff.

> *Ibid. If This Were Faith*

Bright is the ring of words
When the right man rings them.

> *Ibid. XIV*

In the highlands, in the country places,
Where the old plain men have rosy
  faces,
And the young fair maidens
  Quiet eyes.

> *Ibid. XV*

I have trod the upward and the downward slope;
I have endured and done in days before;
I have longed for all, and bid farewell
  to hope;
And I have lived and loved and closed
  the door.

> *Ibid. XXII*

Trusty, dusky, vivid, true,
With eyes of gold and bramble-dew,
Steel-true and blade-straight
The great artificer
Made my mate.

> *Ibid. XXV, To My Wife, Stanza 1*

Be it granted me to behold you again
  in dying,
Hills of home!

> *Ibid. XLIII, To S. R. Crockett*

Let any man speak long enough, he
will get believers.

> *The Master of Ballantrae* [*1889*].
> *Summary of Events*

Not every man is so great a coward
as he thinks he is — nor yet so good a
Christian.

> *Ibid. Mr. Mackellar's Journey*

Do you know what the Governor of
South Carolina said to the Governor
of North Carolina? It's a long time
between drinks, observed that powerful
thinker.[1]

> *The Wrong Box* [*1889*].
> *Chap. 8*

If I have at all learned the trade of
using words to convey truth and to
arouse emotion, you have at last furnished me with a subject.

> *An Open Letter on Father
> Damien*

Still obscurely fighting the lost fight
of virtue, still clinging, in the brothel
or on the scaffold, to some rag of honour, the poor jewel of their souls!

> *Across the Plains* [*1892*].
> *Pulvis et Umbra*

So long as we love we serve; so long
as we are loved by others, I would almost say that we are indispensable; and
no man is useless while he has a friend.

> *Ibid. Lay Morals*

To be honest, to be kind — to earn
a little and spend a little less, to make
upon the whole a family happier for his
presence, to renounce when that shall
be necessary and not to be embittered,
to keep a few friends, but these without
capitulation — above all, on the same
grim condition, to keep friends with

---

[1] Of the several traditions relating to the
origin of this remark, the most reasonable one
traces it to John Motley Morehead [1796–
1866], who was Governor of North Carolina
1841–1845. He was visited by James H. Hammond [1807–1864], who was Governor of
South Carolina 1842–1844. They engaged in
discussion and argument, and when the latter
waxed hot, Governor Morehead was reported
by a servant to have exclaimed: "It's a long
time between drinks." — Personal letter from
John Motley Morehead, November 21, 1934

himself — here is a task for all that a man has of fortitude and delicacy.
A Christmas Sermon

If your morals make you dreary, depend upon it, they are wrong. I do not say give them up, for they may be all you have, but conceal them like a vice lest they should spoil the lives of better and simpler people.
Ibid.

Here lies one who meant well, tried a little, failed much: — surely that may be his epitaph of which he need not be ashamed.
Ibid.

Chiefs! Our road is not built to last a thousand years, yet in a sense it is. When a road is once built, it is a strange thing how it collects traffic, how every year as it goes on, more and more people are found to walk thereon, and others are raised up to repair and perpetuate it, and keep it alive.[1]
Vailima Letters [1895]. Address to the Chiefs on the Opening of the Road of Gratitude, October, 1894

You cannot run away from a weakness; you must some time fight it out or perish; and if that be so, why not now, and where you stand?
The Amateur Emigrant [1896]

To be a gentleman is to be one all the world over, and in every relation and grade of society.
Ibid.

Culture is not measured by the greatness of the field which is covered by our knowledge, but by the nicety with which we can perceive relations in that field, whether great or small.
Ibid.

---

[1] Robert Louis Stevenson was a roadmender. . . . Ay, and with more than his pen. . . . I wonder was he ever so truly great, so entirely the man we know and love, as when he inspired the chiefs to make a highway in the wilderness. Surely no more fitting monument could exist to his memory than the Road of Gratitude, cut, laid, and kept by the pure-blood tribe kings of Samoa. — MICHAEL FAIRLESS (MARGARET FAIRLESS BARBER) [1869–1901]: *The Roadmender, Chap. 5*

Ice and iron cannot be welded
Weir of Hermiston [1896]

Give us grace and strength to forbear and to persevere. Give us courage and gaiety and the quiet mind, spare to us our friends, soften to us our enemies.
Prayer[1]

Youth is wholly experimental.
Letter to a Young Gentleman

ROSE HARTWICK THORPE
[1850–1939]

She breathed the husky whisper:—
"Curfew must not ring tonight."
Curfew Must Not Ring Tonight. Stanza 2

Long, long years I've rung the curfew from that gloomy, shadowed tower;
Every evening, just at sunset, it has told the twilight hour;
I have done my duty ever, tried to do it just and right,
Now I'm old I will not falter, — Curfew it must ring tonight.
Ibid. Stanza 3

Out she swung — far out; the city seemed a speck of light below,
There 'twixt heaven and earth suspended as the bell swung to and fro.
Ibid. Stanza 7

ELLA WHEELER WILCOX
[1850–1919]

Talk happiness. The world is sad enough
Without your woe. No path is wholly rough.
Speech. Stanza 1

Talk faith. The world is better off without
Your uttered ignorance and morbid doubt.
Ibid. Stanza 2

Talk health. The dreary, never-ending tale
Of mortal maladies is more than stale;

---

[1] On the bronze memorial to Stevenson in St. Giles Cathedral, Edinburgh, Scotland.

You cannot charm or interest or please
By harping on that minor chord, dis-
ease.
Say you are well, or all is well with you,
And God shall hear your words and
make them true.
Speech. Stanza 3

The two kinds of people on earth that
I mean
Are the people who lift and the people
who lean.
To Lift or to Lean

It ever has been since time began,
And ever will be, till time lose breath,
That love is a mood — no more — to
man,
And love to woman is life or death.
Blind. Stanza 1

Laugh, and the world laughs with you;
Weep, and you weep alone;
For the sad old earth must borrow its
mirth,
But has trouble enough of its own.
Solitude. Stanza 1

Feast, and your halls are crowded;
Fast, and the world goes by.
Ibid. Stanza 3

So many gods, so many creeds,
So many paths that wind and wind,
When just the art of being kind
Is all this sad world needs.
The World's Need

No question is ever settled
Until it is settled right.
Settle the Question Right

We flatter those we scarcely know,
We please the fleeting guest,
And deal full many a thoughtless blow
To those who love us best.
Life's Scars. Stanza 3

ROSE HENNIKER HEATON

She answered by return of post
The invitation of her host.
She caught the train she said she would,
And changed at junctions as she should.
She brought a light and smallish box
And keys belonging to the locks.
The Perfect Guest

She left no little things behind
Excepting loving thoughts and kind.
Ibid.

SAMUEL VALENTINE COLE
[1851–1925]

"Hammer away, ye hostile hands,
Your hammers break, God's anvil
stands."
The Unthwarted Plan

Where'er men go, in heaven, or earth,
or hell,
They find themselves, and that is all
they find.
The Difference

The man who knows and knows he
knows,[1]
To him your homage bring;
He wields the power that waits and
wins,
And he is rightful king.
An Old Saw Reset. Stanza 1

FERDINAND FOCH
[1851–1929]

A guest at a dinner given in honor of
Marshal Foch in Denver, Colorado,
said that there was nothing but wind
in French politeness. Marshal Foch re-
torted: "Neither is there anything but
wind in a pneumatic tire, yet it eases
wonderfully the jolts along life's highway."
Attributed

My center is giving way, my right is
pushed back, situation excellent, I am
attacking.[2]
*Said at the Second Battle of
the Marne, 1918*

EDWARD SMITH UFFORD
[1851–1929]

Throw out the life-line across the dark
wave,

[1] He who knows not, and knows not that
he knows not, is a fool. Shun him.
He who knows not, and knows that he
knows not, is simple. Teach him.
He who knows, and knows not that he
knows, is asleep. Waken him.
He who knows, and knows that he knows,
is wise. Follow him.
Arabic apothegm
[2] Mon centre cède, ma droite recule, situation excellente, j'attaque. — *Quoted by* B. H.
LIDDELL HART, *Reputations Ten Years After*
[1928]

There is a brother whom someone
   should save,
Throw out the life-line, throw out the
   life-line,
   Someone is sinking today.
     Throw Out the Life-line
     (revivalist hymn) [*1884*]

FRANCIS WILLIAM
BOURDILLON
[1852–1921]

The night has a thousand eyes,
   And the day but one;
Yet the light of the bright world dies,
   With the dying sun.
     Light. Stanza 1
The mind has a thousand eyes,
   And the heart but one;
Yet the light of a whole life dies,
   When love is done.
     Ibid. Stanza 2

Upon the valley's lap
   The dewy morning throws
A thousand pearly drops
   To wash a single rose.
So, often in the course
   Of life's few fleeting years,
A single pleasure costs
   The soul a thousand tears.
     Upon the Valley's Lap

ROBERT BONTINE
CUNNINGHAME-GRAHAM
[1852–1936]

Success, which touches nothing that
it does not vulgarize, should be its own
reward . . . the odium of success is
hard enough to bear, without the added
ignominy of popular applause.
     Success [*1902*]
The ancient seat of pedantry [Ox-
ford], where they manufacture prigs as
fast as butchers in Chicago handle
hogs.
     With the North-West Wind
God forbid that I should go to any
heaven in which there are no horses.
     Letter to Theodore Roosevelt
            [*1917*]
Handsomely, as he who lay in it
might well have said, they lowered the

coffin down. The priest had left his
Latin and said a prayer or two in English, and I was glad of it, for English
surely was the speech the Master Mariner most loved, and honoured in the
loving with new graces of his own.
     Harboured [*The burial of*
     Joseph Conrad, 1924]

NATHAN HASKELL DOLE [1]
[1852–1935]

What other State compares with Maine
   In glorious coasts, where ocean tides
Have for long ages beat in vain
   To storm the coves where safety
     hides;
Where pillared cliffs like sentries stand
To guard the entries to the land,
     From Kittery to Calais!
     The State of Maine. Stanza 1

EDWIN MARKHAM
[1852–1940]

Why build these cities glorious
   If man unbuilded goes?
In vain we build the world, unless
   The builder also grows.
     Man-Making
Bowed by the weight of centuries he
   leans
Upon his hoe and gazes on the ground,
The emptiness of ages in his face,
And on his back the burden of the
   world.
     The Man with the Hoe [2] [*1899*].
          Stanza 1
O masters, lords and rulers in all lands,
Is this the handiwork you give to God?
     Ibid. Stanza 3
Here was a man to hold against the
   world,
A man to match the mountains [3] and
   the sea.
     Lincoln, the Man of the People
        [*1901*]. *Stanza 1*

[1] Editor of the tenth edition of *Bartlett's
Familiar Quotations* [1914].
[2] Millet's painting.
[3] A man to match his mountains, **not to**
   creep

The color of the ground was in him, the red earth,
The smack and tang of elemental things.
Lincoln, the Man of the People.
Stanza 2
So came the Captain with the mighty heart;
And when the judgment thunders split the house,
Wrenching the rafters from their ancient rest,
He held the ridgepole up, and spiked again
The rafters of the Home.
Ibid. Stanza 4
And when he fell in whirlwind, he went down
As when a lordly cedar, green with boughs,
Goes down with a great shout upon the hills,
And leaves a lonesome place against the sky.
Ibid.
Three times I came to your friendly door;
Three times my shadow was on your floor.
I was the beggar with bruisèd feet;
I was the woman you gave to eat;
I was the child on the homeless street.
How the Great Guest Came
He drew a circle that shut me out —
Heretic, rebel, a thing to flout.
But Love and I had the wit to win:
We drew a circle that took him in.
Outwitted

GEORGE MOORE
[1852–1933]

After all there is but one race — humanity.
The Bending of the Bough. Act III
The difficulty in life is the choice.
Act IV

Dwarfed and abased below them.
WHITTIER: *Among the Hills* [1869],
Prelude
Bring me men to match my mountains. —
SAM WALTER FOSS [1858–1911]: *The Coming American*

The wrong way always seems the more reasonable.
The Bending of the Bough. Act IV
A quotation, a chance word heard in an unexpected quarter, puts me on the trail of the book destined to achieve some intellectual advancement in me.
Confessions of a Young Man
[1888]. XII
English, Scotchmen, Jews, do well in Ireland — Irishmen never; even the patriot has to leave Ireland to get a hearing.
Ave [1911]. Overture
My one claim to originality among Irishmen is that I have never made a speech.
Ibid. Chap. 4
As the moon is more interested in the earth than in any other thing, there is always some woman more interested in a man's mind than in anything else, who is willing to follow it sentence by sentence.
Ibid. Chap. 10
A man travels the world over in search of what he needs and returns home to find it.
The Brook Kerith [1916].
Chap. 11
My definition of pure poetry, something that the poet creates outside of his own personality.
Anthology of Pure Poetry.
Introduction

HENRY VAN DYKE
[1852–1933]

If all the skies were sunshine,
Our faces would be fain
To feel once more upon them
The cooling plash of rain.
If All the Skies. Stanza 1
Men have dulled their eyes with sin,
And dimmed the light of heaven with doubt,
And built their temple-walls to shut thee in,
And framed their iron creeds to shut thee out.
God of the Open Air. Stanza 3

"Raise the stone, and thou shalt find
me; cleave the wood and there
am I." [1]
> *The Toiling of Felix. Part I,*
> *Prelude*

This is the gospel of labour, ring it, ye
bells of the kirk!
The Lord of Love came down from
above, to live with the men who
work;
This is the rose that He planted, here
in the thorn-curst soil:
Heaven is blest with perfect rest, but
the blessing of Earth is toil.
> *Ibid. Envoy, Stanza 5*

So it's home again, and home again,
America for me.
My heart is turning home again, and
there I long to be.
> *"America for Me." Stanza 2*

Oh, London is a man's town, there's
power in the air;
And Paris is a woman's town, with
flowers in her hair.
> *Ibid. Stanza 3*

I want a ship that's westward bound to
plough the rolling sea,
To the blessèd Land of Room Enough
beyond the ocean bars,
Where the air is full of sunlight and the
flag is full of stars.
> *Ibid. Stanza 6*

This is my work; my blessing, not my
doom;
Of all who live, I am the one by whom
This work can best be done in the right
way.
> *The Three Best Things. I, Work*

Not to the swift, the race:
Not to the strong, the fight: [2]
Not to the righteous, perfect grace:
Not to the wise, the light.
> *Reliance. Stanza 1*

[1] *Oxyrhynchus Logia Agrapha, The Un-written Sayings of Jesus, Fifth Logion.*
[2] See *Ecclesiastes, IX, 11,* on page 1043a.
> In anguish we uplift
> A new unhallowed song:
> The race is to the swift;
> The battle to the strong.
>> JOHN DAVIDSON [1857–1909]:
>> *War-Song, St. 1*

Oh, was I born too soon, my dear, or
were you born too late,
That I am going out the door while you
come in the gate?
> *Rencontre. Stanza 1*

The lintel low enough to keep out pomp
and pride:
The threshold high enough to turn de-ceit aside.
> *For the Friends at Hurstmont.*
> *The Door*

Self is the only prison that can ever
bind the soul.
> *The Prison and the Angel*

Individuality is the salt of common
life. You may have to live in a crowd,
but you do not have to live like it, nor
subsist on its food.
> *The School of Life*

It is with rivers as it is with people:
the greatest are not always the most
agreeable nor the best to live with.
> *Little Rivers. Chap. 2*

The first day of spring is one thing,
and the first spring day is another. The
difference between them is sometimes as
great as a month.
> *Fisherman's Luck. Chap. 5*

YOUNG EWING ALLISON
[1853–1932]

The very texture of every enduring
work of art must imbed the glowing life
of its own times and the embers of the
past. If it does not cover space as his-tory it must plumb the depths of emo-tion in an individual to reach the uni-versal perception.
> *"My Old Kentucky Home"*

HALL CAINE
[1853–1931]

I reject the monstrous theory that
while a man may redeem the past a
woman never can.
> *The Eternal City. Part VI,*
> *Chap. 18*

A great outrage on the spirit of Jus-tice breaks down all barriers of race
and nationality.
> *Ibid. Part VII, Chap. 5*

EDGAR WATSON HOWE
[1853-1937]

A really busy person never knows how much he weighs.
Country Town Sayings [*1911*]

What people say behind your back is your standing in the community.
Ibid.

There is nothing so well known as that we should not expect something for nothing — but we all do and call it Hope.
Ibid.

ROBERT UNDERWOOD JOHNSON
[1853-1937]

For lover or nightingale who can wait?
Whenever he cometh he cometh late.
Spring at the Villa Conti

Song's but solace for a day;
Wine's a traitor not to trust;
Love's a kiss and then away;
Time's a peddler deals in dust.
Hearth-Song. Stanza 2

CECIL JOHN RHODES
[1853-1902]

I desire to encourage and foster an appreciation of the advantages which will result from the union of the English-speaking peoples throughout the world, and to encourage in the students from the United States of America an attachment to the country from which they have sprung without I hope withdrawing them or their sympathies from the land of their adoption or birth.
Will, establishing the Rhodes Scholarships

Educational relations make the strongest tie.
Ibid.

So little done — so much to do.
Last words

IRWIN RUSSELL [1]
[1853-1879]

De man what keeps pullin' de grapevine shakes down a few bunches at leas'.
Precepts at Parting [*1888*].
Stanza 3

You mus' reason with a mule.
Nebuchadnezzar [*1888*].
Stanza 3

You bless us, please sah, eben ef we's doin' wrong tonight,
Kase den we'll need de blessin' more'n ef we's doin' right;
An' let de blessin' stay wid us untel we comes to die
An' goes to keep our Christmas wid dem sheriffs in de sky.
Christmas Night in the Quarters [*1917*]. *Blessing the Dance*

JAMES A. BLAND
[1854-1911]

Carry me back to old Virginny,
There's where the cotton and the corn and taters grow;
There's where the birds warble sweet in the springtime,
There's where this old darky's heart am long'd to go.
Carry Me Back to Old Virginny [*1875*]

WILLIAM HENRY DRUMMOND
[1854-1907]

De win' can blow lak hurricane
An' s'pose she blow some more,
You can't get drown on Lac St. Pierre
So long you stay on shore.
The Wreck of the "Julie Plante."
Stanza 6

Do w'at you lak wit' your old gran-'pere

[1] Among the first — if not the very first — of Southern writers to appreciate the literary possibilities of the Negro character. — JOEL CHANDLER HARRIS [1848-1908]

For w'en you're beeg feller he won't be
　　dere —
　　Leetle Bateese!
　　　　　　Little Bateese. Stanza 7
To the hut of the peasant, or lordly
　　hall,
To the heart of the king, or humblest
　　thrall,
Sooner or late, love comes to all.
　　　　The Grand Seigneur. Stanza 1

SIR JAMES GEORGE FRAZER
[1854–1941]

Dwellers by the sea cannot fail to be
impressed by the sight of its ceaseless
ebb and flow, and are apt, on the principles of that rude philosophy of sympathy and resemblance . . . to trace a
subtle relation, a secret harmony, between its tides and the life of man. . . .
The belief that most deaths happen at
ebb tide is said to be held along the
east coast of England from Northumberland to Kent.[1]
　　　　The Golden Bough.[2] Chap. 3
　The heaviest calamity in English
history, the breach with America,
might never have occurred if George
the Third had not been an honest dullard.
　　　　　　　　　　　Ibid.
　By religion, then, I understand a
propitiation or conciliation of powers
superior to man which are believed to
direct and control the course of nature
and of human life.
　　　　　　　Ibid. Chap. 4
It is a common rule with primitive
people not to waken a sleeper, because
his soul is away and might not have
time to get back.
　　　　　　　Ibid. Chap. 18
　The awe and dread with which the
untutored savage contemplates his

[1] Just between twelve and one, even at the
turning o' the tide. — SHAKESPEARE: *King
Henry V* [1598–1600], *Act II, Sc. 3* (Falstaff's
death)
　See Dickens, page 579b.
[2] Abridged one-volume edition [1922]. The
original appeared in twelve volumes from
1890 to 1915.

mother-in-law are amongst the most
familiar facts of anthropology.
　　　　The Golden Bough. Chap. 18
The world cannot live at the level of
its great men.
　　　　　　Ibid. Chap. 37

THOMAS RILEY MARSHALL
[1854–1925]

What this country needs is a good
five-cent cigar.[1]
　　　Remark to John Crockett, Chief
　　Clerk of the United States Senate

CHARLES LEONARD MOORE
[1854–1923]

Thine the great grave where dark De
　　Soto sleeps —
A new Columbus of the forest deeps.
　　　　　　To America [1896]
And now for what comes next
Thou waitest in thine invulnerable
　　West,
Blazoning more large thy living-lettered
　　text,
"Chance and the tools to those who use
　　them best."
　　　　　　　　　　　Ibid.

EVA MARCH TAPPAN
[1854–1930]

We drove the Indians out of the land,
But a dire revenge these redmen
　　planned,
For they fastened a name to every
　　nook,
And every boy with a spelling-book
Will have to toil till his hair turns gray
Before he can spell them the proper
　　way.[2]
　　　　　On the Cape. Stanza 1

EDITH MATILDA THOMAS
[1854–1925]

The god of music dwelleth out of doors.
　　　　　　　　　　　Music

[1] What this country needs is a good five-
cent nickel. — FRANKLIN P. ADAMS [1932]
[2] See Lydia Sigourney, page 463b.

The love of my life came not
As love unto others is cast;
For mine was a secret wound —
But the wound grew a pearl, at last.
The Deep-Sea Pearl. Stanza 1

WILLARD DUNCAN VANDIVER
[1854–1932]

I come from a State that raises corn
and cotton and cockleburs and Democrats, and frothy eloquence neither
convinces nor satisfies me. I am from
Missouri. You have got to show me.
*Speech at a naval banquet in
Philadelphia, while a Representative in Congress from Missouri, and a member of the
House Committee on Naval Affairs [1899]*

MARY DOW BRINE
[*Floruit* 1878]

She's somebody's mother, boys, you
know,
For all she's aged and poor and slow.
Somebody's Mother [1878]

GERALD BRENNAN
[*Floruit* 1899]

Th' mem'ry comes like a banshee me-
self an' me wealth between,
An' I long for a mornin's mornin' in
Shanahan's ould shebeen.
*Shanahan's Ould Shebeen
[1899]. Stanza 4*
If you couldn't afford good whiskey,
he'd take you on trust for beer.
Ibid. Stanza 5

WILLIAM COWPER BRANN [1]
[1855–1898]

Boston runs to brains as well as to
beans and brown bread. But she is
cursed with an army of cranks whom

[1] Known as "The Iconoclast," from the
name of his paper, first published in Austin,
Texas, and later in Waco.

nothing short of a strait-jacket or a
swamp-elm club will ever control.
*From The Iconoclast. Beans
and Blood*
No man can be a patriot on an empty
stomach.
Ibid. Old Glory [July 4, 1893]
It has the subtle flavor of an old
pair of sox.
Ibid. Godey's Magazine
The Lydian notes of Andrew Carnegie as he warbles a riant roundelay in
praise of poverty, or laments in pathetic
spondees the woes of the man with
spondulix.
Ibid. Our American Czars
Every few years our industrial system gets the jim-jams. Capital flies to
cover, factories close and labor goes
tramping across the country seeking
honest employment and receiving a
warm welcome — from militia com-
panies with shotted guns. . . . We are
slowly emerging from the crash of '93,
and the cuckoos are cock-sure that a
country fairly bursting with wealth was
saved from the demnition bowwows by
the blessed expedient of going into debt.
*Speech, Slave or Sovereign
[August 10, 1895]*

HENRY CUYLER BUNNER
[1855–1896]

Love must kiss that mortal's eyes
Who hopes to see fair Arcady.
The Way to Arcady
That pitcher of mignonette
Is a garden in heaven set
To the little sick child in the basement.
A Pitcher of Mignonette
Off with your hat as the flag goes by!
And let the heart have its say;
You're man enough for a tear in your
eye
That you will not wipe away.
The Old Flag. Stanza 1
It was an old, old, old, old lady,
And a boy that was half-past three;
And the way that they played together
Was beautiful to see.
"One, Two, Three." Stanza 1

I have a bookcase, which is what
Many much better men have not.
There are no books inside, for books,
I am afraid, might spoil its looks.
But I've three busts, all second-hand,
Upon the top. You understand
I could not put them underneath —
Shake, Mulleary and Go-ethe.
Shake, Mulleary and Go-ethe.
Stanza 1

EUGENE VICTOR DEBS
[1855–1926]

While there is a lower class I am in
it, while there is a criminal element I
am of it; while there is a soul in prison,
I am not free.
Labor and Freedom

FRANK FRANKFORT MOORE
[1855–1931]

He knew that to offer a man friendship when love is in his heart is like
giving a loaf of bread to one who is
dying of thirst.
The Jessamy Bride. Chap. 9

To strike at a serpent that hisses may
only cause it to spring.
Ibid. Chap. 19

Destiny has more resources than the
most imaginative composer of fiction.
Ibid. Chap. 22

WALTER HINES PAGE
[1855–1918]

Every letter of declination ought to
be written by a skilful man — a diplomatist who can write an unpleasant
truth without offence.
A Publisher's Confession [*1905*]

There is one thing better than good
government, and that is government in
which all the people have a part.
Life and Letters [*1922–1925*].
Vol. III, Page 31

SIR ARTHUR WING PINERO
[1855–1934]

You may dive into many waters, but
there is *one* social Dead Sea.
The Second Mrs. Tanqueray
[*1893*]. *Act I*

From forty till fifty a man is at heart
either a stoic or a satyr.
Ibid.

There are two sorts of affection —
the love for a woman you respect, and
the love for the woman you — love.
Ibid. Act II

It is only one step from toleration to
forgiveness.
Ibid.

I believe the future is only the past
again, entered through another gate.
Ibid. Act IV

How many "coming men" has one
known! Where on earth do they all
go to?
The Notorious Mrs. Ebbsmith
[*1895*]. *Act I*

There's only one hour in a woman's
life. . . . One supreme hour. Her poor
life is like the arch of a crescent; so
many years lead up to that hour, so
many weary years decline from it.
Ibid. Act III

Vanity is the cause of a great deal of
virtue in men; the vainest are those who
like to be thought respectable.
Ibid. Act IV

OLIVE SCHREINER
("RALPH IRON")
[1855–1920]

It came to pass that after a time the
artist was forgotten, but the work lived.
Dreams. The Artist's Secret

If you are an artist, may no love of
wealth or fame or admiration and no
fear of blame or misunderstanding
make you ever paint, with pen or brush,
an ideal or a picture of external life
otherwise than as you see it.
Ibid. Chap. 7

WILLIAM SHARP
("FIONA MACLEOD")
[1855–1905]

My heart is a lonely hunter that hunts
on a lonely hill.
The Lonely Hunter. Stanza 6

I hear the little children of the wind
Crying solitary in lonely places.
Little Children of the Wind

CY WARMAN
[1855–1914]

Every daisy in the dell knows my se-
cret, knows it well,
And yet I dare not tell, sweet Marie.
Sweet Marie [1893]. Stanza 1

GEORGE EDWARD
WOODBERRY
[1855–1930]

O, inexpressible as sweet,
  Love takes my voice away;
I cannot tell thee when we meet
  What most I long to say.
Song

Where are the friends that I knew in my
  Maying,
In the days of my youth, in the first of
  my roaming?
We were dear; we were leal; oh, far we
  went straying,
Now never a heart to my heart comes
  homing!
Comrades. Stanza 1

JOSEPH TABRAR
[Floruit 1892]

Daddy wouldn't buy me a bow-wow!
  bow-wow!
Daddy wouldn't buy me a bow-wow!
  bow-wow!
I've got a little cat,
And I'm very fond of that,
But I'd rather have a bow-wow, wow.
Daddy Wouldn't Buy Me a
Bow-Wow [1892]

SUSAN HART DYER
[Floruit 1912]

Zamboanga! Zamboanga! [1]
With the starlight on the sea,
And the blue hills of Basilan
Looming off mysteriously.
Zamboanga [1912]. Stanza 2

FRANCIS BELLAMY
[1856–1931]

I pledge allegiance to the flag of the
United States and to the republic for
which it stands, one nation, indivisible,
with liberty and justice for all. [2]
The Pledge of Allegiance to the
Flag [1892]

KENYON COX
[1856–1919]

Work thou for pleasure — paint, or
  sing, or carve
The thing thou lovest, though the body
  starve —
Who works for glory misses oft the
  goal;
Who works for money coins his very
  soul.
Work for the work's sake, then, and it
  may be
That these things shall be added unto
  thee.
Work [1895]

[1] Oh, the monkeys have no tails in Zam-
  boanga,
  They were chewed off by the whales. . . .
    Zamboanga, Mindanao.
  From the transport you look damn well,
  But before I'd serve again in Zambo-
    anga,
  I'd rather serve a hitch in hell.
  U. S. Infantry song of the Philippines
[2] In 1888 James B. Upham [1845–1905]
wrote a rough draft of the pledge which
Bellamy, as chairman of a committee for a
national school program to celebrate the four-
hundredth anniversary of the discovery of
America, helped to put into its final form.
The pledge was officially emended to read
"one nation under God" by a joint resolution
of Congress approved by the President,
June 14, 1954.

ELBERT HUBBARD
[1856–1915]

It is not book learning young men need, nor instruction about this and that, but a stiffening of the vertebrae which will cause them to be loyal to a trust, to act promptly, concentrate their energies, do a thing — "carry a message to Garcia." [1]

A Message to Garcia [*1900*]

The man who is anybody and who does anything is surely going to be criticized, vilified, and misunderstood. This is a part of the penalty for greatness, and every great man understands it; and understands, too, that it is no proof of greatness. The final proof of greatness lies in being able to endure contumely without resentment.

Get Out or Get in Line

If you work for a man, in heaven's name work for him! If he pays you wages that supply you your bread and butter, work for him — speak well of him, think well of him, stand by him and stand by the institution he represents.

Ibid.

ABBOTT LAWRENCE LOWELL
[1856–1943]

While a bright future beckoned, they freely gave their lives and fondest hopes for us and our allies, that we might learn from them courage in peace to spend our lives making a better world for others.

Inscription, Memorial Church, Harvard College, above the names of Harvard men who died in the First World War

[1] After the declaration of the Spanish-American War. Andrew Summers Rowan, then Lieutenant, United States Bureau of Military Intelligence, was sent to communicate with General Calixto Garcia. He landed in an open boat near Turquino Peak, April 24, 1898, executed the mission, and brought back information regarding the insurgent army.

EDWARD SANDFORD MARTIN
[1856–1939]

A Little Brother of the Rich.

Title of poem

Succor the Poor, my sisters, I,
While heaven shall still vouchsafe me health,
Will strive to share and mollify
The trials of abounding wealth.

A Little Brother of the Rich.
Stanza 5

Within my earthly temple there's a crowd.
There's one of us that's humble; one that's proud.
There's one that's broken-hearted for his sins,
And one who, unrepentant, sits and grins.
There's one who loves his neighbor as himself,
And one who cares for naught but fame and pelf.
From much corroding care would I be free
If once I could determine which is Me.

Mixed

ROBERT EDWIN PEARY
[1856–1920]

We returned from the Pole to Cape Columbia in only sixteen days . . . the exhilaration of success lent wings to our sorely battered feet. But Ootah, the Eskimo, had his own explanation. Said he: "The devil is asleep or having trouble with his wife, or we should never have come back so easily."

The North Pole [*1910*]

HENRI PHILIPPE PÉTAIN
[1856–1951]

They shall not pass.[1]

Verdun, February 26, 1916

[1] Ils ne passeront pas. The inscription on the Verdun medal is: "On ne passe pas."

LIZETTE WOODWORTH REESE
[1856–1935]

When I consider Life and its few
    years —
A wisp of fog betwixt us and the sun;
A call to battle, and the battle done
Ere the last echo dies within our ears.
Tears

The burst of music down an unlistening
    street.
Ibid.

How each hath back what once he
    stayed to weep;
Homer his sight, David his little lad!
Ibid.

Creeds grow so thick along the way,
Their boughs hide God.
Doubt

Glad that I live am I;
That the sky is blue;
Glad for the country lanes,
And the fall of dew.
A Little Song of Life. Stanza 1

GEORGE BERNARD SHAW
[1856–1950]

My method is to take the utmost
trouble to find the right thing to say,
and then to say it with the utmost levity.
Answers to Nine Questions

A prosperous man of business, who
probably never read anything but a
newspaper since he left school.
Cashel Byron's Profession
[1886]. Chap. 5

All this struggling and striving to
make the world better is a great mistake; not because it isn't a good thing
to improve the world if you know how
to do it, but because striving and struggling is the worst way you could set
about doing anything.
Ibid. Chap. 6

It's well to be off with the Old
Woman before you're on with the
New.[1]
The Philanderer [1893]. Act II

[1] See C. H. Webb, page 668a.

The fickleness of the women I love is
only equalled by the infernal constancy
of the women who love me.
The Philanderer. Act II

The test of a man or woman's breeding is how they behave in a quarrel.
Ibid. Act IV

People are always blaming their circumstances for what they are. I don't
believe in circumstances. The people
who get on in this world are the people
who get up and look for the circumstances they want, and, if they can't
find them, make them.
Mrs. Warren's Profession
[1893]. Act II

There are no secrets better kept than
the secrets that everybody guesses.
Ibid. Act III

A great devotee of the Gospel of Getting On.
Ibid. Act IV

We have no more right to consume
happiness without producing it than to
consume wealth without producing it.
Candida [1898]. Act I

I'm only a beer teetotaller, not a
champagne teetotaller.
Ibid. Act III

We don't bother much about dress
and manners in England, because, as a
nation we don't dress well and we've no
manners.
You Never Can Tell
[1898]. Act I

A family enjoying the unspeakable
peace and freedom of being orphans.
Ibid. Act II

The great advantage of a hotel is that
it's a refuge from home life.
Ibid.

There is only one religion, though
there are a hundred versions of it.
Plays Pleasant and Unpleasant
[1898]. Vol. II, Preface

You're not a man, you're a machine.
Arms and the Man [1898].
Act III

The worst sin towards our fellow
creatures is not to hate them, but to be

indifferent to them: that's the essence of inhumanity.
The Devil's Disciple [*1901*].
Act II

This is the true joy in life, the being used for a purpose recognized by yourself as a mighty one; the being thoroughly worn out before you are thrown on the scrap heap; the being a force of Nature instead of a feverish selfish little clod of ailments and grievances complaining that the world will not devote itself to making you happy.
Man and Superman [*1903*].
Epistle Dedicatory

A lifetime of happiness! No man alive could bear it: it would be hell on earth.
Ibid. Act I

The more things a man is ashamed of, the more respectable he is.
Ibid.

You think that you are Ann's suitor; that you are the pursuer and she the pursued; that it is your part to woo, to persuade, to prevail, to overcome. Fool: it is you who are the pursued, the marked-down quarry, the destined prey.
Ibid. Act II

Marry Ann; and at the end of a week you'll find no more inspiration in her than in a plate of muffins.
Ibid.

An Englishman thinks he is moral when he is only uncomfortable.
Ibid. Act III

He who can, does. He who cannot, teaches.
Ibid. Maxims for Revolutionists, Page 230

Marriage is popular because it combines the maximum of temptation with the maximum of opportunity.
Ibid. Page 231

If you strike a child, take care that you strike it in anger, even at the risk of maiming it for life. A blow in cold blood neither can nor should be forgiven.
Ibid. Page 234

The greatest of evils and the worst of crimes is poverty.
Major Barbara [*1907*]. *Preface*

I can't talk religion to a man with bodily hunger in his eyes.
Ibid. Act II

Home life as we understand it is no more natural to us than a cage is natural to a cockatoo.
Getting Married [*1911*].
Preface

In the extreme instances of reaction against convention, female murderers get sheaves of offers of marriage.
Ibid.

When two people are under the influence of the most violent, most insane, most delusive, and most transient of passions, they are required to swear that they will remain in that excited, abnormal, and exhausting condition continuously until death do them part.
Ibid.

A man is like a phonograph with half-a-dozen records. You soon get tired of them all; and yet you have to sit at table whilst he reels them off to every new visitor.
Ibid. (The Play)

In England we always let an institution strain itself until it breaks.
Ibid.

The whole strength of England lies in the fact that the enormous majority of the English people are snobs.
Ibid.

You don't learn to hold your own in the world by standing on guard, but by attacking, and getting well hammered yourself.
Ibid.

Religion is a great force — the only real motive force in the world; but what you fellows don't understand is that you must get at a man through his own religion and not through yours.
Ibid.

The modest cough of a minor poet.
The Dark Lady of the Sonnets
[*1914*]

This writing of plays is a great matter, forming as it does the minds and

affections of men in such sort that whatsoever they see done in show on the
stage, they will presently be doing in
earnest in the world, which is but a
larger stage.
The Dark Lady of the Sonnets

I like a bit of a mongrel myself,
whether it's a man or a dog; they're
the best for every day.
Misalliance [*1914*]. *Episode I*

If parents would only realize how
they bore their children!
Ibid.

He's a gentleman: look at his boots.
Pygmalion [*1916*]. *Act I*

Women upset everything. When you
let them into your life, you find that the
woman is driving at one thing and
you're driving at another.
Ibid. Act II

I have to live for others and not for
myself; that's middle class morality.
Ibid. Act V

The great secret, Eliza, is not having
bad manners or good manners or any
other particular sort of manners, but
having the same manner for all human
souls: in short, behaving as if you were
in Heaven, where there are no third-
class carriages, and one soul is as good
as another.
Ibid.

Independence? That's middle class
blasphemy. We are all dependent on
one another, every soul of us on earth.
Ibid.

All great truths begin as blasphemies.
Annajanska. [*1919*]

The nauseous sham goodfellowship
our democratic public men get up for
shop use.
Back to Methuselah [*1921*].
*Gospel of the Brothers Barna-
bas*

Life is a disease; and the only difference between one man and another is
the stage of the disease at which he
lives.
Ibid.

I enjoy convalescence. It is the part
that makes the illness worth while.
*Back to Methuselah. Gospel of
the Brothers Barnabas*

A nap, my friend, is a brief period of
sleep which overtakes superannuated
persons when they endeavor to entertain unwelcome visitors or to listen to
scientific lectures.
*Ibid. Tragedy of an Elderly
Gentleman*

Everything happens to everybody
sooner or later if there is time enough.
*Ibid. As Far As Thought Can
Reach*

Silence is the most perfect expression
of scorn.
Ibid.

The worst cliques are those which
consist of one man.
Ibid.

Assassination is the extreme form of
censorship.
The Rejected Statement. Part 1

The Jews generally give value. They
make you pay; but they deliver the
goods. In my experience the men who
want something for nothing are invariably Christians.
Saint Joan [*1924*]. *Scene IV*

One man that has a mind and knows
it, can always beat ten men who haven't
and don't.
The Apple Cart [*1930*]. *Act I*

Every person who owes his life to
civilized society and who has enjoyed
since his childhood its very costly protections and advantages should appear
at reasonable intervals before a properly qualified jury to justify his existence, which should be summarily and
painlessly terminated if he fails to justify it and it develops that he is a
positive nuisance and more trouble than
he is worth. Nothing less will really
make people responsible citizens.
*Radio address from London to
America* [*October 11, 1931*]

You put up in New York Harbor a

monstrous idol which you called "Liberty." [1]

> *Speech, Metropolitan Opera House,*[2] *New York* [*April 11, 1933*]

You in America should trust to that volcanic political instinct which I have divined in you.

> *Ibid.*

BOOKER TALIAFERRO WASHINGTON
[1856–1915]

No race can prosper till it learns that there is as much dignity in tilling a field as in writing a poem.

> *Up From Slavery* [*1901*]

KATE DOUGLAS WIGGIN
[1856–1923]

My heart is open wide tonight
For stranger, kith or kin.
I would not bar a single door
Where Love might enter in.

> *The Romance of a Christmas Card*

OSCAR FINGAL O'FLAHERTIE WILLS WILDE
[1856–1900]

Tread lightly, she is near
  Under the snow,
Speak gently, she can hear
  The daisies grow.

> *Requiescat. Stanza 1*

Think of all
The suns that go to make one speedwell blue!

> *Quia Multum Amavi. Stanza 4*

These are the letters which Endymion wrote
To one he loved in secret, and apart.

[1] "I see," said he, speaking to some American friends, "that you too put up monuments to your great dead!" — Story of a distinguished Frenchman on a visit to the United States during Prohibition, in RALPH NEVILL: *Paris of Today* [1924]

[2] A radio broadcast, made before the Academy of Political Science.

And now the brawlers of the auction mart
Bargain and bid for each poor blotted note.

> *On the Sale by Auction of Keats's Love Letters*

And yet, and yet,
These Christs that die upon the barricades,
God knows it I am with them, in some ways.

> *Sonnet to Liberty: Not That I Love Thy Children*

Down the long and silent street,
The dawn, with silver-sandaled feet,
Crept like a frightened girl.

> *The Harlot's House*

A poet can survive everything but a misprint.

> *The Children of the Poets*

As for borrowing Mr. Whistler's ideas about art, the only thoroughly original ideas I have ever heard him express have had reference to his own superiority as a painter over painters greater than himself.

> *Reply to an attack by James McNeill Whistler, Truth* [*January 9, 1890*]

Meredith is a prose Browning, and so is Browning. He used poetry as a medium for writing in prose.

> *The Critic as Artist* [*1891*]. *Part I*

An age that has no criticism is either an age in which art is immobile, hieratic, and confined to the reproduction of formal types, or an age that possesses no art at all.

> *Ibid.*

It is through Art, and through Art only, that we can realize our perfection; through Art and Art only that we can shield ourselves from the sordid perils of actual existence.

> *Ibid. Part II*

As long as war is regarded as wicked, it will always have its fascination. When it is looked upon as vulgar, it will cease to be popular.

> *Ibid.*

There is no sin except stupidity.[1]
The Critic as Artist. Part II

There is no such thing as a moral or an immoral book. Books are well written, or badly written. That is all.
The Picture of Dorian Gray
[1891]. Preface

All art is quite useless.
Ibid.

There is only one thing in the world worse than being talked about, and that is not being talked about.
Ibid. Chap. 1

Conscience and cowardice are really the same things.
Ibid.

Laughter is not at all a bad beginning for a friendship, and it is far the best ending for one.
Ibid.

The only way to get rid of a temptation is to yield to it.
Ibid. Chap. 2

He knew the precise psychological moment [2] when to say nothing.
Ibid.

The only difference between a caprice and a lifelong passion is that the caprice lasts a little longer.
Ibid.

Children begin by loving their parents; as they grow older they judge them; sometimes they forgive them.
Ibid. Chap. 5

Conscience makes egotists of us all.
Ibid. Chap. 8

When a woman marries again it is because she detested her first husband. When a man marries again, it is because

he adored his first wife.[1] Women try their luck; men risk theirs.
The Picture of Dorian Gray.
Chap. 15

Over the piano was printed a notice: Please do not shoot the pianist. He is doing his best.
Impressions of America. Leadville

Now-a-days we are all of us so hard up, that the only pleasant things to pay are compliments. They're the only things we *can* pay.
Lady Windermere's Fan
[1892]. Act I

I can resist everything except temptation.
Ibid.

We are all in the gutter, but some of us are looking at the stars.
Ibid. Act III

In this world there are only two tragedies. One is not getting what one wants, and the other is getting it.
Ibid.

What is a cynic? A man who knows the price of everything, and the value of nothing.
Ibid.

Experience is the name everyone gives to their mistakes.
Ibid.

I have never admitted that I am more than twenty-nine, or thirty at the most. Twenty-nine when there are pink shades, thirty when there are not.[2]
Ibid. Act IV

Mrs. Allonby. They say, Lady Hunstanton, that when good Americans die they go to Paris.[3]
Lady Hunstanton. Indeed? And when bad Americans die, where do they go to?

---

[1] See Marlowe, page 124a.
[2] In all considerations the psychological momentum or factor must be allowed to play a prominent part, for without its co-operation there is little to be hoped from the work of the artillery. — *Neue Preussische Kreuzzeitung*, December 16, 1870, commenting upon the siege of Paris.
An error in translation gave us "psychological moment" (i.e. the critical moment). The Parisians ridiculed the phrase as an example of German pedantry, but it speedily became universal.

[1] See Samuel Johnson, page 340b.
[2] When you come to write my epitaph, Charles, let it be in these delicious words, "She had a long twenty-nine."—JAMES M. BARRIE [1860–1937]: *Rosalind*
[3] Good Americans, when they die, go to Paris. — THOMAS GOLD APPLETON [1812–1884], *quoted by* OLIVER WENDELL HOLMES in *Autocrat of the Breakfast Table* [1858]

Lord Illingworth. Oh, they go to America.

A Woman of No Importance
[1893]. Act I

The youth of America is their oldest tradition. It has been going on now for three hundred years.

Ibid.

Nothing spoils a romance so much as a sense of humour in the woman.

Ibid.

Men always want to be a woman's first love. That is their clumsy vanity. We women have a more subtle instinct about things. What we like is to be a man's last romance.

Ibid. Act II

I suppose society is wonderfully delightful. To be in it is merely a bore. But to be out of it simply a tragedy.

Ibid. Act III

Talk to every woman as if you loved her, and to every man as if he bored you, and at the end of your first season you will have the reputation of possessing the most perfect social tact.

Ibid.

I delight in men over seventy. They always offer one the devotion of a lifetime.

Ibid. Act IV

Really, if the lower orders don't set us a good example, what on earth is the use of them?

The Importance of Being Earnest [1895]. Act I

I have invented an invaluable permanent invalid called Bunbury, in order that I may be able to go down into the country whenever I choose.

Ibid.

Memory is the diary that we all carry about with us.

Ibid. Act II

I never travel without my diary. One should always have something sensational to read in the train.

Ibid.

No woman should ever be quite accurate about her age. It looks so calculating.

Ibid. Act III

An acquaintance that begins with a compliment is sure to develop into a real friendship.

An Ideal Husband [1895]. Act I

Nothing produces such an effect as a good platitude.

Ibid.

Private information is practically the source of every large modern fortune.

Ibid. Act II

To love oneself is the beginning of a lifelong romance.

Ibid. Act III

I never saw a man who looked
　With such a wistful eye
Upon that little tent of blue
　Which prisoners call the sky,
And at every wandering cloud that
　trailed
　Its ravelled fleeces by.

The Ballad of Reading Gaol
[1898]. Part I, Stanza 3

When a voice behind me whispered low,
"That fellow's got to swing."

Ibid. Stanza 4

Yet each man kills the thing he loves,
　By each let this be heard,
Some do it with a bitter look,
　Some with a flattering word.
The coward does it with a kiss,
　The brave man with a sword!

Ibid. Stanza 7

It is sweet to dance to violins
　When Love and Life are fair:
To dance to flutes, to dance to lutes
　Is delicate and rare:
But it is not sweet with nimble feet
　To dance upon the air!

Ibid. Part II, Stanza 9

Like two doomed ships that pass in
　storm
We had crossed each other's way:
But we made no sign, we said no word,
　We had no word to say.

Ibid. Stanza 12

Something was dead in each of us,
And what was dead was Hope.

Ibid. Stanza 31

And the wild regrets, and the bloody
　sweats,
　None knew so well as I:

For he who lives more lives than one
More deaths than one must die.
                The Ballad of Reading Gaol.
                        Part II, Stanza 37

I know not whether Laws be right,
  Or whether Laws be wrong;
All that we know who lie in gaol
  Is that the wall is strong;
And that each day is like a year,
  A year whose days are long.
                Ibid. Part V, Stanza 1

The vilest deeds like poison-weeds
  Bloom well in prison-air:
It is only what is good in Man
  That wastes and withers there:
Pale Anguish keeps the heavy gate
  And the Warder is Despair.
                        Ibid. Stanza 5

How else but through a broken heart
May Lord Christ enter in?
                        Ibid. Stanza 14

Where there is sorrow there is holy
ground.
                        De Profundis [*1905*]

WOODROW WILSON
[1856–1924]

The United States must be neutral in
fact as well as in name. . . . We must
be impartial in thought as well as in
action.
                Message to the U. S. Senate
                        [*August 19, 1914*]

You deal in the raw material of
opinion, and, if my convictions have
any validity, opinion ultimately governs
the world.
                Address to the Associated Press
                        [*April 20, 1915*]

There is such a thing as a man being
too proud to fight.
                Address to Foreign-Born Citizens
                        [*May 10, 1915*]

The things that the flag stands for
were created by the experiences of a
great people. Everything that it stands
for was written by their lives. The flag
is the embodiment, not of sentiment,
but of history. It represents the experiences made by men and women, the ex-

periences of those who do and live under that flag.
                Address [*June 14, 1915*]

We have stood apart, studiously
neutral.
                Message to Congress
                        [*December 7, 1915*]

There must be, not a balance of
power, but a community of power; not
organized rivalries, but an organized
common peace.
                Address to the U. S. Senate
                        [*January 22, 1917*]

It must be a peace without victory.
. . . Victory would mean peace forced
upon the loser, a victor's terms imposed
upon the vanquished. It would be accepted in humiliation, under duress, at
an intolerable sacrifice, and would leave
a sting, a resentment, a bitter memory
upon which terms of peace would rest,
not permanently, but only as upon
quicksand. Only a peace between equals
can last.
                        Ibid.

I am seeking only to face realities and
to face them without soft concealments.
                        Ibid.

A little group of willful men reflecting no opinion but their own have rendered the great Government of the
United States helpless and contemptible.
                Statement made in reference to
                certain members of the Senate [1]
                        [*March 4, 1917*]

Armed neutrality is ineffectual
enough at best.
                *Address to Congress, asking for
                a declaration of war* [*April 2,
                1917*]

The world must be made safe for
democracy.
                        Ibid.

It is a fearful thing to lead this great
peaceful people into war . . . we shall
fight for the things which we have al-

[1] Eleven Senators had conducted a filibuster
against a bill authorizing the arming of American merchant vessels.

ways carried nearest our hearts, — for democracy, for the right of those who submit to authority to have a voice in their own Governments, for the rights and liberties of small nations, for a universal dominion of right by such a concert of free peoples as shall bring peace and safety to all nations and make the world itself at last free. To such a task we can dedicate our lives and our fortunes, everything that we are and everything that we have, with the pride of those who know that the day has come when America is privileged to spend her blood and her might for the principles that gave her birth and happiness and the peace which she has treasured. God helping her, she can do no other.

Address to Congress, asking for a declaration of war [April 2, 1917]

1. Open covenants of peace, openly arrived at.
2. Absolute freedom of navigation upon the seas.
5. A free, open-minded, and absolutely impartial adjustment of all colonial claims.
8. The wrong done to France by Prussia in 1871 in the matter of Alsace-Lorraine . . . should be righted.
10. The peoples of Austria-Hungary . . . should be accorded the freest opportunity of autonomous development.
13. An independent Polish state should be erected . . . which should be assured a free and secure access to the sea.
14. A general association of nations must be formed . . . for the purpose of affording mutual guarantees of political independence and territorial integrity to great and small states alike.

Address to Congress (The Fourteen Points) [January 8, 1918]

Sometimes people call me an idealist. Well, that is the way I know I am an American. America is the only idealistic nation in the world.

Address at Sioux Falls [September 8, 1919]

The highest and best form of efficiency is the spontaneous cooperation of a free people.

Quoted by BERNARD BARUCH, *in American Industry at War: A Report of the War Industries Board [March, 1921]*

I cannot refrain from saying it: I am not one of those who have the least anxiety about the triumph of the principles I have stood for. I have seen fools resist Providence before and I have seen their destruction, as will come upon these again — utter destruction and contempt. That we shall prevail is as sure as that God reigns.

Last public words, to a group of people gathered outside his house on Armistice Day, 1923

GERTRUDE FRANKLIN ATHERTON
[1857–1948]

Women love the lie that saves their pride, but never an unflattering truth.

The Conqueror [1902]. Book III, Chap. 6

To put a tempting face aside when duty demands every faculty . . . is a lesson which takes most men longest to learn.

Ibid.

The perfect friendship of two men is the deepest and highest sentiment of which the finite mind is capable; women miss the best in life.

Ibid. Chap. 12

No matter how hard a man may labor, some woman is always in the background of his mind. She is the one reward of virtue.

Ibid. Book IV, Chap. 3

ALICE BROWN
[1857–1948]

Praise not the critic, lest he think
You crave the shelter of his ink;
But pray his halo, when he dies,
May tip the steelyards of the skies.

The Critic

Yet thou, O banqueter on worms,
Who wilt not let corruption pass! —
Dost search out mildew, mould and
    stain,
Beneath a magnifying-glass.
The Slanderer

JOSEPH CONRAD
[1857–1924]

A work that aspires, however humbly, to the condition of art should carry
its justification in every line.
The Nigger of the Narcissus
[1898]. Preface

But the artist appeals to that part of
our being which is not dependent on
wisdom; to that in us which is a gift
and not an acquisition — and, therefore, more permanently enduring. He
speaks to our capacity for delight and
wonder, to the sense of mystery surrounding our lives: to our sense of pity,
and beauty, and pain.
Ibid.

The ship, a fragment detached from
the earth, went on lonely and swift like
a small planet.
Ibid. Chap. 2

Goodbye, brothers! You were a good
crowd. As good a crowd as ever fisted
with wild cries the beating canvas of a
heavy foresail; or tossing aloft, invisible in the night, gave back yell for yell
to a westerly gale.
Ibid. Chap. 5

I am a great foe of favouritism in
public life, in private life, and even in
the delicate relationship of an author to
his works.
Lord Jim [1900]. Author's Note

There is a weird power in a spoken
word. . . . And a word carries far —
very far — deals destruction through
time as the bullets go flying through
space.
Ibid. Chap. 15

That faculty of beholding at a hint
the face of his desire and the shape of
his dream, without which the earth
would know no lover and no adventurer.
Ibid. Chap. 16

Felicity, felicity — how shall I say
it? — is quaffed out of a golden cup in
every latitude: the flavour is with you
— with you alone, and you can make it
as intoxicating as you please.
Lord Jim. Chap. 16

It is when we try to grapple with another man's intimate need that we perceive how incomprehensible, wavering,
and misty are the beings that share with
us the sight of the stars and the warmth
of the sun.
Ibid.

You shall judge of a man by his foes
as well as by his friends.
Ibid. Chap. 34

Vanity plays lurid tricks with our
memory.
Ibid. Chap. 41

Some great men owe most of their
greatness to the ability of detecting in
those they destine for their tools the
exact quality of strength that matters
for their work.
Ibid. Chap. 42

Only a moment; a moment of
strength, of romance, of glamour — of
youth! . . . A flick of sunshine upon a
strange shore, the time to remember,
the time for a sigh, and — goodbye! —
Night — Goodbye . . . !
Youth [1902]

She strode like a grenadier, was
strong and upright like an obelisk, had
a beautiful face, a candid brow, pure
eyes, and not a thought of her own in
her head.
Tales of Unrest [1902].
The Return

What greatness had not floated on
the ebb of that river [the Thames]
into the mystery of an unknown earth!
. . . The dreams of men, the seed of
commonwealths, the germs of empires.
Heart of Darkness [1902]

Running all over the sea trying to
get behind the weather.
Typhoon [1902]. Chap. 2

The sea never changes and its works,
for all the talk of men, are wrapped in
mystery.
Ibid.

I have known the sea too long to believe in its respect for decency.
Typhoon. Chap. 2

An elemental force is ruthlessly frank.
Ibid.

The air of the New World seems favorable to the art of declamation.
Nostromo [1904]. Chap. 6

Efficiency of a practically flawless kind may be reached naturally in the struggle for bread. But there is something beyond — a higher point, a subtle and unmistakable touch of love and pride beyond mere skill; almost an inspiration which gives to all work that finish which is almost art — which *is* art.
The Mirror of the Sea [1906].
The Fine Art

The East Wind, an interloper in the dominions of Westerly Weather, is an impassive-faced tyrant with a sharp poniard held behind his back for a treacherous stab.
Ibid. Rulers of East and West

The autocratic sway of the West Wind, whether forty north or forty south of the equator, is characterized by an open, generous, frank, barbarous recklessness. For he is a great autocrat, and to be a great autocrat you must be a great barbarian.
Ibid.

What all men are really after is some form, or perhaps only some formula, of peace.
Under Western Eyes [1911].
Part I

A man's real life is that accorded to him in the thoughts of other men by reason of respect or natural love.
Ibid. 1

Let a fool be made serviceable according to his folly.
Ibid. 3

The belief in a supernatural source of evil is not necessary; men alone are quite capable of every wickedness.
Ibid. Part II, 4

Why should a man certain of immortality think of his life at all?
Under Western Eyes. Part II, 4

No woman is an absolute fool. . . . No woman is ever completely deceived.
Ibid. 5

That strange impulse of indiscretion, common to men who lead secret lives, and accounting for the invariable existence of "compromising documents" in all the plots and conspiracies of history.
Ibid. Part III, 1

You can't ignore the importance of a good digestion. The joy of life . . . depends on a sound stomach, whereas a bad digestion inclines one to skepticism, incredulity, breeds black fancies and thoughts of death.
Ibid. 3

All ambitions are lawful except those which climb upward on the miseries or credulities of mankind.
A Personal Record [1912].
Preface

The sight of human affairs deserves admiration and pity. And he is not insensible who pays them the undemonstrative tribute of a sigh which is not a sob, and of a smile which is not a grin.
Ibid.

Only in men's imagination does every truth find an effective and undeniable existence. Imagination, not invention, is the supreme master of art as of life.
Ibid. Chap. 1

For Englishmen especially, of all the races of the earth, a task, any task, undertaken in an adventurous spirit acquires the merit of romance.
Ibid. Chap. 5

There are on earth no actors too humble and obscure not to have a gallery; that gallery which envenoms the play by stealthy jeers, counsels of anger, amused comments, or words of perfidious compassion.
Chance [1914]. Part II, Chap. 4

There is no rest for a messenger till the message is delivered.
The Rescue [1920]. Part VI, 8

In plucking the fruit of memory one runs the risk of spoiling its bloom.
The Arrow of Gold [*1919*].
Author's Note

Historian of fine consciences.
Notes on Life and Letters [*1921*]. *Henry James, An Appreciation*

Most of us, if you will pardon me for betraying the universal secret, have, at some time or other, discovered in ourselves a readiness to stray far, ever so far, on the wrong road.
Ibid. A Happy Wanderer

What humanity needs is not the promise of scientific immortality, but compassionate pity in this life and infinite mercy on the Day of Judgment.
Ibid. The Life Beyond

JOHN DAVIDSON
[1857–1909]

My feet are heavy now but on I go,
My head erect beneath the tragic years.
I Felt the World A-spinning

Fame is the breath of power:
What valid work was ever for itself
Wrought solely, be it war, art, statesmanship?
Smith

Dance and sing, we are eternal;
Let us still be mad with drinking:
'Tis a madness less infernal
Than the madness caused by thinking.
*Song of Bacchantes and Satyrs.
Stanza 1*

The lowliest men would sooner face
A thousand dreadful deaths, than come
Before their loved ones in disgrace.
A Ballad of a Coward. Stanza 12

Some diplomat no doubt
Will launch a heedless word,
And lurking war leap out.
War-Song

And blood in torrents pour
In vain — always in vain,
For war breeds war again.
Ibid.

Do I believe in Heaven and Hell? I do;
We have them here; the world is nothing else.
*Dedication to the Generation
Knocking at the Door*

Men should no longer degrade themselves under such appellations as Christian, Mohammedan, Agnostic, Monist, etc. Men are the Universe become conscious: the simplest man should consider himself too great to be called after any name.
Fleet Street and Other Poems
[*1909*]. *Foreword*

HENRY BLAKE FULLER
[1857–1929]

The martyrdom involved in a fortnight's entertainment of anybody whomsoever.[1]
*The Chevalier of Pensieri-Vani.
Chap. 10*

GEORGE GISSING
[1857–1903]

In the days to come, as through all time that is past, man will lord it over his fellow, and earth will be stained red from veins of young and old. That sweet and sounding name of *patria* becomes an illusion and a curse.
By the Ionian Sea [*1901*]. *XVIII*

It is because nations tend to stupidity and baseness that mankind moves so slowly; it is because individuals have a capacity for better things that it moves at all.
*The Private Papers of Henry
Ryecroft* [*1903*]. *I, 16*

The mind which renounces, once and for ever, a futile hope, has its compensation in ever-growing calm.
Ibid. 20

Education is a thing of which only the few are capable; teach as you will

---

[1] No one can be so welcome a guest that he will not annoy his host after three days. —
PLAUTUS: *Miles Gloriosus* [205 B.C.]
Fish and guests in three days are stale. —
JOHN LYLY: *Euphues* [1579]

only a small percentage will profit by your most zealous energy.

The Private Papers of Henry Ryecroft. I, 22

For the man sound in body and serene of mind there is no such thing as bad weather; every sky has its beauty, and storms which whip the blood do but make it pulse more vigorously.

Ibid. IV, 1

BENJAMIN FRANKLIN KING, JR.
[1857–1894]

Old friends are most too home-like now.
They know your age, and when
You got expelled from school, and lots
Of other things.

Like the New Friends Best

Nothing to do but work,
Nothing to eat but food,
Nothing to wear but clothes
To keep one from going nude.

*The Pessimist (The Sum of Life).
Stanza 1*

Nothing to breathe but air,
Quick as a flash 'tis gone;
Nowhere to fall but off,
Nowhere to stand but on.

Ibid. Stanza 2

Nowhere to go but out,
Nowhere to come but back.

Ibid. Stanza 4

Her folks an' hiz'n
An' hiz'n an' her'n
Never speak to each other
From what I can learn.

Her Folks an' Hiz'n

SIR RONALD ROSS [1]
[1857–1932]

I know this little thing
A myriad men will save.
O Death, where is thy sting?
Thy victory, O grave?

*Referring to the discovery that
malaria is carried by mosquitoes*

[1] Ross received a Nobel prize in 1902 for his researches in malaria control.

EDGAR SMITH
[1857–1938]

You may tempt the upper classes
With your villainous demi-tasses,
But Heaven will protect the Working
Girl.

*Heaven Will Protect the
Working Girl [1]*

FRANK LEBBY STANTON
[1857–1927]

Jest a-wearyin' fer you —
All the time a-feelin' blue;
Wishin' fer you — wonderin' when
You'll be comin' home again.

Wearyin' for You. Stanza 1

Sweetes' li'l' feller —
Everybody knows;
Dunno what ter call 'im,
But he's mighty lak' a rose!

Mighty Lak' a Rose. Stanza 1

THORSTEIN VEBLEN
[1857–1929]

Conspicuous consumption of valuable goods is a means of reputability to the gentleman of leisure.

*The Theory of the Leisure Class
[1899]. Chap. 4*

With the exception of the instinct of self-preservation, the propensity for emulation is probably the strongest and most alert and persistent of the economic motives proper.

Ibid. Chap. 5

The requirement of conspicuous wastefulness is not commonly present, consciously, in our canons of taste, but it is none the less present as a constraining norm selectively shaping and sustaining our sense of what is beautiful, and guiding our discrimination with respect to what may legitimately be approved as beautiful and what may not.

Ibid. Chap. 6

The dog . . . commends himself to our favour by affording play to our pro-

[1] Sung by Marie Dressler [1873–1934] in *Tillie's Nightmare.*

pensity for mastery, and as he is also an item of expense, and commonly serves no industrial purpose, he holds a well-assured place in men's regard as a thing of good repute.

The Theory of the Leisure Class.
Chap. 6

The visible imperfections of the hand-wrought goods, being honorific, are accounted marks of superiority in point of beauty, or serviceability, or both. Hence has arisen that exaltation of the defective, of which John Ruskin and William Morris were such eager spokesmen in their time. . . . The Kelmscott Press reduced the matter to an absurdity by issuing books for modern use, edited with the obsolete spelling, printed in black-letter, and bound in limp vellum fitted with thongs.

Ibid.

Priestly vestments show, in accentuated form, all the features that have been shown to be evidence of a servile status and a vicarious life.

Ibid. Chap. 7

The walking-stick serves the purpose of an advertisement that the bearer's hands are employed otherwise than in useful effort, and it therefore has utility as an evidence of leisure.

Ibid. Chap. 10

The sporting man's sense of luck and chance is an inarticulate or inchoate animism . . . it implies the possibility of propitiating, or of deceiving and cajoling, or otherwise disturbing the unfolding of propensities resident in the objects which constitute the apparatus and accessories of any game of skill or chance. There are few sporting men who are not in the habit of wearing charms or talismans.

Ibid. Chap. 11

The adoption of the cap and gown is one of the striking atavistic features of modern college life.

Ibid. Chap. 14

The classics have scarcely lost in absolute value as a voucher of scholastic respectability, since for this purpose it is only necessary that the scholar should be able to put in evidence some learning which is conventionally recognized as evidence of wasted time.

The Theory of the Leisure Class.
Chap. 14

As felicitous an instance of futile classicism as can well be found is the conventional spelling of the English language. English orthography satisfies all the requirements of the canons of reputability under the law of conspicuous waste. It is archaic, cumbrous, and ineffective; its acquisition consumes much time and effort; failure to acquire it is easy of detection.

Ibid.

HENRY WILLARD AUSTIN
[1858-1912]

Genius, that power which dazzles mortal eyes,
Is oft but perseverance in disguise.

Perseverance Conquers All

JOHN BURNS
[1858-1943]

The St. Lawrence is water, and the Mississippi is muddy water; but that, sir, is liquid history.

Said on the terrace of the House of Commons, to transatlantic visitors who belittled the size of the Thames

WILLISTON FISH
[1858-1939]

I, Charles Lounsbury, being of sound and disposing mind and memory [he lingered on the word memory], do now make and publish this my last will and testament, in order, as justly as I may, to distribute my interests in the world among succeeding men.

A Last Will [1]

I leave to children exclusively, but only for the life of their childhood, all and every the dandelions of the fields

[1] In *Harper's Weekly*, September 3, 1898, reprinted by request of many readers in the issue of December 12, 1908.

and the daisies thereof, with the right to play among them freely.

A Last Will

And I devise to children the yellow shores of creeks and the golden sands beneath the waters thereof, with the dragon-flies that skim the surface of said waters.

Ibid.

To lovers I devise their imaginary world, with whatever they may need, as the stars of the sky, the red, red roses by the wall, the snow of the hawthorn, the sweet strains of music, or aught else they may desire to figure to each other the lastingness and beauty of their love.

Ibid.

To those who are no longer children, or youths, or lovers, I leave, too, the knowledge of what a rare, rare world it is.

Ibid.

SAM WALTER FOSS
[1858–1911]

The plain man is the basic clod
From which we grow the demigod;
And in the average man is curled
The hero stuff that rules the world.

In Memoriam. Stanza 2

Seek not for fresher founts afar,
Just drop your bucket where you are.

Opportunity

No financial throe volcanic
Ever yet was known to scare it;
Never yet was any panic
Scared the firm of Grin and Barrett.

The Firm of Grin and Barrett. Stanza 1

A hundred thousand men were led
By one calf near three centuries dead.
They followed still his crooked way,
And lost one hundred years a day;
For thus such reverence is lent
To well-established precedent.

The Calf-Path

A rodless Walton of the brooks,
A bloodless sportsman, I. [1]

The Bloodless Sportsman

The woods are made for the hunters of dreams,
The brooks for the fishers of song;
To the hunters who hunt for the gunless game
The streams and the woods belong.

Ibid.

Let me live in my house by the side of the road
Where the race of men go by;
They are good, they are bad, they are weak, they are strong,
Wise, foolish — so am I.
Then why should I sit in the scorner's seat,
Or hurl the cynic's ban?
Let me live in my house by the side of the road
And be a friend of man.

The House by the Side of the Road.[2] Stanza 5

On the thirty-second day of the thirteenth month of the eighth day of the week,
On the twenty-fifth hour and the sixty-first minute, we'll find all things that we seek.

The Eighth Day of the Week

I say the very things that make the greatest Stir
An' the most interestin' things, are things that didn't occur.[3]

Things That Didn't Occur

He had a startling genius, but somehow it didn't emerge;
Always on the evolution of things that wouldn't evolve;
Always verging toward some climax, but he never reached the verge;

[1] See Emerson, page 504a.
[2] See Homer, page 4b.
And greatly was he loved, for courteously
He welcomed to his house beside the way
All comers.
　　HOMER [*circa* 850 B.C.]: *Iliad, Book VI,* translated by WILLIAM CULLEN BRYANT
[3] See Emerson, page 507a, and James Russell Lowell, page 507a, footnote 2.

Always nearing the solution of some theme he could not solve.
The Inventor [1]

REMY DE GOURMONT
[1858–1915]

Aesthetic emotion puts man in a state favorable to the reception of erotic emotion. Art is the accomplice of love. Take love away and there is no longer art.
Decadence [2]

I do not believe it useful to generalize opinions, to teach admirations. It is for each man to procure himself the emotion he needs, and the morality which suits him.
Ibid.

It is because peoples do not know each other that they hate each other so little.
Ibid.

There are too few obscure writers in French. We accustom ourselves like cowards to love only writing that is easy and that will soon be elementary.
Ibid.

JOHN TROTWOOD MOORE
[1858–1929]

Only the game fish swims up stream. [3]
The Unafraid

EDITH NESBIT
[1858–1924]

The chestnut's proud, and the lilac's pretty,
The poplar's gentle and tall,

But the plane tree's kind to the poor dull city —
I love him best of all!
Child's Song in Spring

ADOLPH S. OCHS
[1858–1935]

All the news that's fit to print.
Motto of The New York Times [1]

AGNES REPPLIER
[1858–1950]

That little band of authors who, unknown to the wide careless world, remain from generation to generation the friends of a few fortunate readers.
Preface to James Howell

THEODORE ROOSEVELT
[1858–1919]

I wish to preach, not the doctrine of ignoble ease, [2] but the doctrine of the strenuous life.
Speech before the Hamilton Club, Chicago [April 10, 1899]

Far better it is to dare mighty things, to win glorious triumphs, even though checkered by failure, than to take rank with those poor spirits who neither enjoy much nor suffer much, because they live in the gray twilight that knows not victory nor defeat.
Ibid.

We must remember not to judge any public servant by any one act, and especially should we beware of attacking the men who are merely the occasions and not the causes of disaster.
Ibid.

---

[1] Ef you want to be sick of your life,
Jest come and change places with me a
   spell — for I'm an inventor's wife.
Mrs. E. T. Corbett: *The Inventor's Wife* [1883]

[2] Translated by W. A. Bradley.

[3] Quoted by Grantland Rice [1880–1954] in *The Ballade of the Gamefish* and *Expanding the Theme.*
   Only the gamefish swims upstream,
   But the sensible fish swims down.
Ogden Nash [1902–]: *When You Say That, Smile*

[1] When Adolph Ochs bought *The New York Times* in 1896 he adopted this motto, which has been printed in every issue since.
"It is hard to think of any group of seven words that have aroused more newspaper controversy." — Gerald W. Johnson: *An Honorable Titan* (biography of Ochs) [1946]

[2]   Me . . . dulcis alebat
Parthenope, studiis florentem ignobilis otii (Sweet Parthenope [Naples] nourished me flourishing in studies of ignoble ease).
Virgil [70–19 b.c.]: *Georgics, Book 4, L. 563*

Death is always and under all circumstances a tragedy, for if it is not, then it means that life itself has become one.

> *Letter to Cecil Spring-Rice*
> *[March 12, 1900]*

I am as strong as a bull moose and you can use me to the limit.

> *Letter to Mark Hanna*
> *[June 27, 1900]*

No man is justified in doing evil on the ground of expediency.

> *The Strenuous Life [1900]*

If we seek merely swollen, slothful ease and ignoble peace, if we shrink from the hard contests where men must win at the hazard of their lives and at the risk of all they hold dear, then bolder and stronger peoples will pass us by, and will win for themselves the domination of the world.

> *Ibid.*

The first requisite of a good citizen in this Republic of ours is that he shall be able and willing to pull his weight.

> *Speech, New York [November 11, 1902]*

There is a homely adage which runs, "Speak softly and carry a big stick; you will go far." If the American nation will speak softly and yet build and keep at a pitch of the highest training a thoroughly efficient navy, the Monroe Doctrine will go far.

> *Speech at Minnesota State Fair*
> *[September 2, 1901]*

A man who is good enough to shed his blood for his country is good enough to be given a square deal afterwards. More than that no man is entitled to, and less than that no man shall have.

> *Speech at Springfield, Illinois*
> *[July 4, 1903]*

Chronic wrongdoing, or an impotence which results in a general loosening of the ties of civilized society, may in America . . . ultimately require intervention by some civilized nation, and in the Western Hemisphere the adherence of the United States to the Monroe Doctrine may force the United States, however reluctantly, in flagrant cases of such wrongdoing or impotence, to the exercise of an international police power.

> *Annual Message to Congress*
> *(Corollary to the Monroe Doctrine) [December 6, 1904]*

Men with the muck-rake are often indispensable to the well-being of society, but only if they know when to stop raking the muck.

> *Address, Laying of the Cornerstone, Office Building of House of Representatives, Washington [April 14, 1906]*

Malefactors of great wealth.

> *Speech at Provincetown, Massachusetts [August 20, 1907]*

Nature-faker.

> *Everybody's Magazine*
> *[September, 1907]*

To waste, to destroy, our natural resources, to skin and exhaust the land instead of using it so as to increase its usefulness, will result in undermining in the days of our children the very prosperity which we ought by right to hand down to them amplified and developed.

> *Message to Congress [December 3, 1907]*

The object of government is the welfare of the people. The material progress and prosperity of a nation are desirable chiefly so far as they lead to the moral and material welfare of all good citizens.

> *The New Nationalism [1910]*

Every man holds his property subject to the general right of the community to regulate its use to whatever degree the public welfare may require it.

> *Speech, Osawatomie*
> *[August 31, 1910]*

The lunatic fringe in all reform movements.

> *Autobiography [1913]*

We demand that big business give the people a square deal; in return we must insist that when any one engaged in big business honestly endeavors to do right he shall himself be given a square deal.

> *Ibid.*

We stand equally against government by a plutocracy and government by a mob. There is something to be said for government by a great aristocracy which has furnished leaders to the nation in peace and war for generations; even a democrat like myself must admit this. But there is absolutely nothing to be said for government by a plutocracy, for government by men very powerful in certain lines and gifted with "the money touch," but with ideals which in their essence are merely those of so many glorified pawn-brokers.

Letter to Sir Edward Grey [November 15, 1913]

There is no room in this country for hyphenated Americanism. . . . The one absolutely certain way of bringing this nation to ruin, of preventing all possibility of its continuing to be a nation at all, would be to permit it to become a tangle of squabbling nationalities.

Speech before the Knights of Columbus, New York [October 12, 1915]

We have room for but one language here, and that is the English language, for we intend to see that the crucible turns our people out as Americans, and not as dwellers in a polyglot boarding house.[1]

Letter read at the All-American Festival, New York [January 5, 1919]

LANGDON SMITH
[1858-1908]

When you were a tadpole and I was a fish,
In the Paleozoic time.
Evolution [1895]. Stanza 1

CLARENCE URMY
[1858-1923]

Old songs are best — how sweet to hear
The strains to home and memory dear!

[1] See Henry Cabot Lodge, page 748b.

Old books are best — how tale and rhyme
Float with us down the stream of time!
Old Songs Are Best
Not what we have, but what we use;
Not what we see, but what we choose —
These are the things that mar or bless
The sum of human happiness.
The Things that Count. Stanza 1

SIR WILLIAM WATSON
[1858-1935]

April, April,
Laugh thy girlish laughter;
Then, the moment after,
Weep thy girlish tears.
Song
What is so sweet and dear
As a prosperous morn in May,
The confident prime of the day,
And the dauntless youth of the year,
When nothing that asks for bliss,
Asking aright, is denied,
And half of the world a bridegroom is,
And half of the world a bride.
Ode in May. Stanza 2
The Poet gathers fruit from every tree,
Yea, grapes from thorns, and figs from thistles, he.
Epigram
Say what thou wilt, the young are happy never.
Give me bless'd Age, beyond the fire and fever, —
Past the delight that shatters, hope that stings,
And eager flutt'ring of life's ignorant wings.
Epigram
Strange the world about me lies,
Never yet familiar grown —
Still disturbs me with surprise,
Haunts me like a face half known.
World-Strangeness. Stanza 1
Five-and-thirty black slaves,
Half-a-hundred white,
All their duty but to sing
For their Queen's delight.
The Key-board. Stanza 1
For still the ancient riddles mar
Our joy in man, in leaf, in star.

The Whence and Whither give no rest,
The Wherefore is a hopeless quest.
　　　　An Epistle to N. A. Stanza 4
To dress, to call, to dine, to break
No canon of the social code,
The little laws that lacqueys make,
The futile decalogue of Mode, —
How many a soul for these things lives,
With pious passion, grave intent!
While Nature careless-handed gives
The things that are more excellent.
　　　　　The Things That Are More
　　　　　Excellent. Stanza 6
The sense of greatness keeps a nation
great.
　　　　　　　Our Eastern Treasure
Lo, with the ancient
Roots of man's nature,
Twines the eternal
　Passion of song.
　　　　　England My Mother. Part II,
　　　　　Stanza 1
Ever Love fans it,
Ever Life feeds it,
Time cannot age it,
　Death cannot slay.
　　　　　　　　Ibid. Stanza 2
Trees in their blooming,
Tides in their flowing,
Stars in their circling,
　Tremble with song.
　　　　　　　　Ibid. Stanza 5
She is not old, she is not young,
The woman with the serpent's tongue.
　　　　　The Woman With the Serpent's
　　　　　Tongue [1]
Who half makes love to you today,
Tomorrow gives her guest away.
　　　　　　　　　　Ibid.

KATHARINE LEE BATES
[1859–1929]

O beautiful for spacious skies,
　For amber waves of grain,
For purple mountain majesties
　Above the fruited plain!
America! America!

[1] Was he a "guest" — who dares to wrong
His hostess in so foul a song?
O poet with the coward's tongue!
　RICHARD LE GALLIENNE [1866–1947]:
　The Poet with a Coward's Tongue

God shed his grace on thee
And crown thy good with brotherhood
From sea to shining sea!
　　　　　America the Beautiful [1893].
　　　　　Stanza 1
O beautiful for patriot dream
　That sees beyond the years
Thine alabaster cities gleam
　Undimmed by human tears!
　　　　　　　Ibid. Stanza 4

HAROLD EDWIN BOULTON
[1859–1935]

Speed, bonnie boat, like a bird on the
　wing;
　Onward, the sailors cry:
Carry the lad that's born to be King
　Over the sea to Skye.
　　　　　Skye Boat Song. Stanza 1

HELEN GRAY CONE
[1859–1934]

Pickett's Virginians were passing
　through;
Supple as steel and brown as leather,
Rusty and dusty of hat and shoe,
Wonted to hunger and war and
　weather;
Peerless, fearless, an army's flower!
Sterner soldiers the world saw never,
Marching lightly, that summer hour,
To death and failure and fame forever.[1]
　　　　　Greencastle Jenny. Stanza 4

SIR ARTHUR CONAN DOYLE
[1859–1930]

London, that great cesspool into
which all the loungers of the Empire are
irresistibly drained.
　　　　　A Study in Scarlet [1887]
When you have eliminated the impossible, whatever remains, however improbable, must be the truth.
　　　　　The Sign of Four [1890]. *Chap. 6*
It is my belief, Watson, founded
upon my experience, that the lowest
and vilest alleys of London do not
present a more dreadful record of sin

[1] See Will Henry Thompson, page 740a–740b.

than does the smiling and beautiful countryside.

The Adventures of Sherlock Holmes [1891]. Copper Beeches

To Sherlock Holmes she is always *the* woman.

Ibid. A Scandal in Bohemia

You know my methods, Watson.

The Memoirs of Sherlock Holmes [1894]. The Crooked Man

"Excellent!" I [Watson] cried. "Elementary," said he [Holmes].

Ibid.

Art in the blood is liable to take the strangest forms.

Ibid. The Greek Interpreter

They were the footprints of a gigantic hound!

The Hound of the Baskervilles [1902]. Chap. 2

Come, Watson, come! The game is afoot.

The Return of Sherlock Holmes [1904]. The Adventure of the Abbey Grange

The fair sex is your department.

Ibid. (To Dr. Watson) The Second Stain

It is a great thing to start life with a small number of really good books which are your very own.

Through the Magic Door [1908]

No British autobiography has ever been frank, and consequently no British autobiography has ever been good. Of all forms of literature it is the one least adapted to the national genius. You could not imagine a British Rousseau, still less a British Benvenuto Cellini.

Ibid.

Several incidents in my life have convinced me of spiritual interposition — of the promptings of some beneficent force outside ourselves, which tries to help us where it can.

Ibid.

The bow was made in England,
Of true wood, of yew wood,
The wood of English bows.

The Song of the Bow. Stanza 1

One favor we entreat,
We were called a little early, and our toilet's not complete.
We've no quarrel with the shirt,
But the breeches wouldn't hurt,
For the evening air is chilly in Cremona.[1]

Cremona. Stanza 20

ARTHUR WENTWORTH HAMILTON EATON
[1859–1937]

O give me a place in the garden of song,
I would linger and labor there all summer long,
There are corners to care for, stray beds to make bloom,
I ask not for wages, I only seek room
In the garden of song.

The Garden of Song. Stanza 1

HAVELOCK ELLIS
[1859–1939]

To be a leader of men one must turn one's back on men.

Introduction to HUYSMANS' *Against the Grain*

The text of the Bible is but a feeble symbol of the Revelation held in the text of Men and Women.

Impressions and Comments

God is an Unutterable Sigh in the Human Heart, said the old German mystic.

Ibid.

Without an element of the obscene there can be no true and deep aesthetic or moral conception of life. . . . It is only the great men who are truly obscene. If they had not dared to be obscene they could never have dared to be great.

Ibid.

The omnipresent process of sex, as it is woven into the whole texture of

[1] In the surprise attack on Cremona, February 1, 1702, the Irish Brigade rushed out to resist the invaders, without waiting to dress.

our man's or woman's body, is the pattern of all the process of our life.

The New Spirit

If men and women are to understand each other, to enter into each other's nature with mutual sympathy, and to become capable of genuine comradeship, the foundation must be laid in youth.

The Task of Social Hygiene.
Chap. 1

The larger our great cities grow, the more irresistible becomes the attraction which they exert on the children of the country, who are fascinated by them, as the birds are fascinated by the lighthouse or the moths by the candle.

Ibid. Chap. 5

There are few among us who have not suffered from too early familiarity with the Bible and the conceptions of religion.

Ibid. Chap. 7

The German feels nothing of that sensitive jealousy with which the French seek to guard private life and the rights of the individual.

Ibid. Chap. 9

The Englishman's reverence for the individual's rights goes beyond the Frenchman's, for in France there is a tendency to subordinate the individual to the family, and in England the interests of the individual predominate.

Ibid.

So far as business and money are concerned, a country gains nothing by a successful war, even though that war involves the acquisition of immense new provinces.

Ibid. Chap. 10

Conquest brings self-conceit and intolerance, the reckless inflation and dissipation of energies. Defeat brings prudence and concentration; it ennobles and fortifies.

Ibid.

There has never been any country at every moment so virtuous and so wise

that it has not sometimes needed to be saved from itself.

The Task of Social Hygiene.
Chap. 10

Those persons who are burning to display heroism may rest assured that the course of social evolution will offer them every opportunity.

Ibid.

The family only represents one aspect, however important an aspect, of a human being's functions and activities. . . . A life is beautiful and ideal, or the reverse, only when we have taken into our consideration the social as well as the family relationship.

Little Essays of Love and Virtue.
Chap. 1

One can know nothing of giving aught that is worthy to give unless one also knows how to take.

Ibid.

That indeed were a world fit to perish, wherein the moralist had set up the ignoble maxim: Safety first.

Ibid. Chap. 2

The by-product is sometimes more valuable than the product.

Ibid. Chap. 3

All civilization has from time to time become a thin crust over a volcano of revolution.

Ibid. Chap. 7

The greatest task before civilization at present is to make machines what they ought to be, the slaves, instead of the masters of men.

Ibid.

The art of dancing stands at the source of all the arts that express themselves first in the human person. The art of building, or architecture, is the beginning of all the arts that lie outside the person; and in the end they unite.

The Dance of Life. Chap. 2

Dancing is the loftiest, the most moving, the most beautiful of the arts, because it is no mere translation or abstraction from life; it is life itself.

Ibid.

783

The place where optimism most flourishes is the lunatic asylum.
The Dance of Life. Chap. 3
Thinking in its lower grades is comparable to paper money, and in its higher forms it is a kind of poetry.
Ibid.
In philosophy, it is not the attainment of the goal that matters, it is the things that are met with by the way.
Ibid.
Every man of genius sees the world at a different angle from his fellows, and there is his tragedy.
Ibid.
The mathematician has reached the highest rung on the ladder of human thought.
Ibid.
A man must not swallow more beliefs than he can digest.
Ibid. Chap. 5
The Promised Land always lies on the other side of a wilderness.
Ibid.
What we call "morals" is simply blind obedience to words of command.
Ibid. Chap. 6
The world's greatest thinkers have often been amateurs; for high thinking is the outcome of fine and independent living, and for that a professional chair offers no special opportunities.
Ibid.
For the artist life is always a discipline, and no discipline can be without pain. That is so even of dancing, which of all the arts is most associated in the popular mind with pleasure. To learn to dance is the most austere of disciplines.
Ibid.
The prevalence of suicide, without doubt, is a test of height in civilization; it means that the population is winding up its nervous and intellectual system to the utmost point of tension and that sometimes it snaps.[1]
Ibid. Chap. 7
The sun and the moon and the stars would have disappeared long ago — as

[1] See Nietzsche, page 727a.

even their infinitely more numerous analogues on the earth beneath are likely to disappear — had they happened to be within the reach of predatory human hands.
The Dance of Life. Chap. 7
Had there been a Lunatic Asylum in the suburbs of Jerusalem, Jesus Christ would infallibly have been shut up in it at the outset of his public career. That interview with Satan on a pinnacle of the Temple would alone have damned him, and everything that happened after could but have confirmed the diagnosis.
Impressions and Comments.
Series III

H. W. FOWLER
[1859–1933]
AND
F. G. FOWLER
[1871–1918]

Prefer geniality to grammar.
The King's English [1906].
Chap. 2
The obvious is better than obvious avoidance of it.
Modern English Usage [1] *[1926]*

KENNETH GRAHAME
[1859–1932]

As a rule, indeed, grown-up people are fairly correct on matters of fact; it is in the higher gift of imagination that they are so sadly to seek.
The Golden Age [1895]. The Finding of the Princess
A man can stand very much in the cause of love: poverty, aunts, rivals, barriers of every sort, — all these only serve to fan the flame. But personal ridicule is a shaft that reaches the very vitals.
Ibid. "Young Adam Cupid"
The year was in its yellowing time, and the face of Nature a study in old gold.
Ibid. A Harvesting

[1] Written by H. W. Fowler.

Those who painfully and with bleeding feet have scaled the crags of mastery over musical instruments have yet their loss in this, — that the wild joy of strumming has become a vanished sense.

The Golden Age. A Harvesting

I began to like this man. He answered your questions briefly and to the point, and never tried to be funny. I felt I could be confidential with him.

Ibid. The Roman Road

Monkeys, who very sensibly refrain from speech, lest they should be set to earn their livings.

Ibid. "Lusisti Satis"

Grown-up people really ought to be more careful. Among themselves it may seem but a small thing to give their word and take back their word.

The Magic Ring

There is nothing — absolutely nothing — half so much worth doing as simply messing about in boats . . . or with boats. . . . In or out of 'em, it doesn't matter.

The Wind in the Willows [*1908*]. *Chap. 1*

ALFRED EDWARD HOUSMAN [1] [1859–1936]

Loveliest of trees, the cherry now
Is hung with bloom along the bough.
A Shropshire Lad [*1896*]. *II*

[1] I was brought up in the Church of England and in the High Church party, which is much the best religion I have ever come across. But Lemprière's "Classical Dictionary," read when I was eight, made me prefer paganism to Christianity; I abandoned Christianity at thirteen, and became an atheist at twenty-one. . . .

I am not a pessimist but a pejorist (as George Eliot said she was not an optimist but a meliorist); and that philosophy is founded on my observation of the world, not on anything so trivial and irrelevant as personal history. Secondly, I did not begin to write poetry in earnest until the really emotional part of my life was over; and my poetry, so far as I could make out, sprang chiefly from physical causes, such as a relaxed

Now, of my threescore years and ten,
Twenty will not come again,
And take from seventy springs a score,
It only leaves me fifty more.
A Shropshire Lad. II
And since to look at things in bloom
Fifty springs are little room,
About the woodlands I will go
To see the cherry hung with snow.
Ibid.
Clay lies still, but blood's a rover;
  Breath's a ware that will not keep.
Up, lad: when the journey's over
  There'll be time enough to sleep.
Ibid. IV, Reveille
If the heats of hate and lust
  In the house of flesh are strong,
Let me mind the house of dust
  Where my sojourn shall be long.
Ibid. XII
When I was one-and-twenty
  I heard a wise man say,
"Give crowns and pounds and guineas
  But not your heart away;
Give pearls away and rubies
  But keep your fancy free."
But I was one-and-twenty,
  No use to talk to me.
Ibid. XIII
"The heart out of the bosom
  Was never given in vain;
'Tis paid with sighs a-plenty
  And sold for endless rue."
And I am two-and-twenty,
  And Oh, 'tis true, 'tis true.
Ibid.
His folly has not fellow
  Beneath the blue of day
That gives to man or woman
  His heart and soul away.
Ibid. XIV
Oh, when I was in love with you,
  Then I was clean and brave,
And miles around the wonder grew
  How well I did behave.
Ibid. XVIII
And now the fancy passes by,
  And nothing will remain,

sore throat during my most prolific period, the first five months of 1895.
Autobiographical note written for a French translation of his poems

And miles around they'll say that I
   Am quite myself again.
                  A Shropshire Lad. XVIII

Today, the roads all runners come,
Shoulder-high, we bring you home,
And set you at your threshold down,
Townsman of a stiller town.
              *Ibid. XIX, To an Athlete
                      Dying Young*

And silence sounds no worse than
   cheers
After earth has stopped the ears.
                              Ibid.

In summertime on Bredon
   The bells they sound so clear;
Round both the shires they ring them
   In steeples far and near,
   A happy noise to hear.
                        Ibid. XXI

Here of a Sunday morning
   My love and I would lie,
And see the colored counties,
   And hear the larks so high
   About us in the sky.
                              Ibid.

They tolled the one bell only,
   Groom there was none to see,
The mourners followed after,
   And so to church went she,
   And would not wait for me.
                              Ibid.

The bells they sound on Bredon,
   And still the steeples hum.
"Come all to church, good people," —
   Oh, noisy bells, be dumb;
   I hear you, I will come.
                              Ibid.

That is the land of lost content,
   I see it shining plain,
The happy highways where I went
   And cannot come again.
                        Ibid. XL

Oh, 'tis jesting, dancing, drinking
   Spins the heavy world around.
If young hearts were not so clever,
Oh, they would be young for ever:
Think no more; 'tis only thinking
   Lays lads underground.
                        Ibid. XLIX

With rue my heart is laden
   For golden friends I had,

For many a rose-lipt maiden
   And many a lightfoot lad.
                        A Shropshire Lad. LIV
By brooks too broad for leaping
The lightfoot boys are laid.
                              Ibid.
And cowards' funerals, when they
   come,
Are not wept so well at home,
Therefore, though the best is bad,
Stand and do the best, my lad.
              Ibid. LVI, The Day of Battle
Why, if 'tis dancing you would be,
There's brisker pipes than poetry.
                        Ibid. LXII
Oh many a peer of England brews
Livelier liquor than the Muse,
And malt does more than Milton can
To justify God's ways to man.[1]
Ale, man, ale's the stuff to drink
For fellows whom it hurts to think.
                              Ibid.

Oh, I have been to Ludlow fair
And left my necktie God knows where,
And carried half way home, or near,
Pints and quarts of Ludlow beer.
                              Ibid.

Luck's a chance, but trouble's sure,
I'd face it as a wise man would,
And train for ill and not for good.
                              Ibid.

Mithridates, he died old.[2]
                              Ibid.

We'll to the woods no more,
The laurels all are cut,[3]
The bowers are bare of bay
That once the Muses wore.
              Last Poems [1922]. Foreword
The troubles of our proud and angry
   dust
Are from eternity, and shall not fail.
Bear them we can, and if we can we
   must.

---

[1] See Milton, page 252a.
[2] Housman's passage is based on the belief
of the ancients that Mithridates the Great
[*circa* 135–63 B.C.] had so saturated his body
with poisons that none could injure him.
When captured by the Romans he tried in
vain to poison himself, then ordered a Gallic
mercenary to kill him.
[3] See Théodore de Banville, page 630a.

Shoulder the sky, my lad, and drink your ale.
Last Poems. IX

Pass me the can, lad; there's an end of May.
Ibid.

Could man be drunk for ever
With liquor, love, or fights,
Lief should I rouse at morning
And lief lie down of nights.
Ibid. X

But men at whiles are sober
And think by fits and starts.
And if they think, they fasten
Their hands upon their hearts.
Ibid.

The laws of God, the laws of man,
He may keep that will and can;
Not I: let God and man decree
Laws for themselves and not for me.
Ibid. XII

And how am I to face the odds
Of man's bedevilment and God's?
I, a stranger and afraid
In a world I never made.
Ibid.

These, in the day when heaven was falling,
The hour when earth's foundations fled,
Followed their mercenary calling
And took their wages and are dead.
Ibid. XXXVII, Epitaph on an Army of Mercenaries [1]

They say my verse is sad: no wonder;
Its narrow measure spans
Tears of eternity, and sorrow,
Not mine, but man's.
More Poems [*1936*]

The thoughts of others
Were light and fleeting,
Of lovers' meeting
Or luck or fame;
Mine were of trouble
And mine were steady,
So I was ready
When trouble came.
Ibid. VI

The rainy Pleiads wester,
Orion plunges prone,

And midnight strikes and hastens,
And I lie down alone.
More Poems. XI

Oh, the pearl seas are yonder,
The gold and amber shore;
Shires where the girls are fonder,
Towns where the pots hold more.
Ibid. XXXIII

Silent hills indenting
The orange band of eve.
Ibid.

We now to peace and darkness
And earth and thee restore
Thy creature that thou madest
And wilt cast forth no more.
Ibid. XLVII, For My Funeral

Good night. Ensured release,
Imperishable peace,
Have these for yours.[1]
While sky and sea and land
And earth's foundations stand
And heaven endures.
Ibid. XLVIII, Alta Quies

Good literature continually read for pleasure must, let us hope, do some good to the reader: must quicken his perception though dull, and sharpen his discrimination though blunt, and mellow the rawness of his personal opinions.
The Name and Nature of Poetry [2]

Poems very seldom consist of poetry and nothing else; and pleasure can be derived also from their other ingredients.
Ibid.

Good religious poetry, whether in Keble or Dante or Job, is likely to be most justly appreciated and most discriminatingly relished by the undevout.
Ibid.

Even when poetry has a meaning, as it usually has, it may be inadvisable to draw it out. . . . Perfect understanding will sometimes almost extinguish pleasure.
Ibid.

[1] These three lines are on the tablet over Housman's grave in the parish church at Ludlow, Shropshire.

[2] The Leslie Stephen Lecture, delivered at Cambridge University, May 9, 1933.

[1] The British regulars who made the retreat from Mons, beginning August 24, 1914.

Experience has taught me, when I am shaving of a morning, to keep watch over my thoughts, because, if a line of poetry strays into my memory, my skin bristles so that the razor ceases to act. . . . The seat of this sensation is the pit of the stomach.

The Name and Nature of Poetry

I have seldom written poetry unless I was rather out of health, and the experience, though pleasurable, was generally agitating and exhausting.

Ibid.

JEROME KLAPKA JEROME
[1859–1927]

Let your boat of life be light, packed with only what you need — a homely home and simple pleasures, one or two friends, worth the name, some one to love and some one to love you,[1] a cat, a dog, and a pipe or two, enough to eat and enough to wear, and a little more than enough to drink; for thirst is a dangerous thing.

Three Men in a Boat [*1889*].
Chap. 3

Fox-terriers are born with about four times as much original sin in them as other dogs.

Ibid. Chap. 13

They [bagpipes] appear to be a trying instrument to perform upon. You have to get enough breath for the whole tune before you start.

Ibid. Chap. 14

It is in the circumstantial detail, the embellishing touches of probability, the general air of scrupulous — almost of pedantic — veracity, that the experienced angler is seen.

Ibid. Chap. 17

"Nothing, so it seems to me," said the stranger, "is more beautiful than the love that has weathered the storms of life. . . . The love of the young for the young, that is the beginning of life.

[1] Find someone to love . . . and, oh, some-one to love you. — SACHA GUITRY: *Deburau* [*1918*]

But the love of the old for the old, that is the beginning of — of things longer."

The Passing of the Third Floor Back [*1908*]

There is a certain satisfaction in feeling you are bearing with heroic resignation the irritating folly of others.

Ibid.

Leave-takings are but wasted sadness. Let me pass out quietly.

Ibid.

WILLIAM JAMES LAMPTON
[1859–1917]

Same old slippers,
  Same old rice,
Same old glimpse of
  Paradise.

June Weddings. Stanza 10

Where the corn is full of kernels
And the colonels full of corn.

Kentucky

CHARLES FLETCHER LUMMIS
[1859–1928]

I am bigger than anything that can happen to me. All these things, sorrow, misfortune, and suffering, are outside my door. I am in the house and I have the key.

Epigram

NORA ARCHIBALD SMITH
[1859–1934]

They'd knock on a tree and would timidly say
To the Spirit who might be within there that day:
"Fairy fair, Fairy fair, wish thou me well;
'Gainst evil witcheries weave me a spell!"

Knocking on Wood. Stanza 3

SIR CECIL ARTHUR SPRING-RICE
[1859–1918]

I vow to thee, my country — all earthly things above —

Entire and whole and perfect, the service of my love,
The love that asks no questions: the love that stands the test,
That lays upon the altar the dearest and the best:
The love that never falters, the love that pays the price,
The love that makes undaunted the final sacrifice.
        I Vow to Thee, My Country [1]

CHARLES E. STANTON [2]
[1859–1933]

Lafayette, we are here.[3]
        Address at the Tomb of Lafayette, Picpus Cemetery, Paris [*July 4, 1917*]

JAMES KENNETH STEPHEN
[1859–1892]

When the Rudyards cease from kipling
And the Haggards ride no more.
        Lapsus Calami. To R. K.
If all the harm that women have done
Were put in a bundle and rolled into one,
Earth would not hold it,
The sky could not enfold it,
It could not be lighted nor warmed by the sun.
        Ibid. A Thought, Stanza 1

[1] Written January 12, 1918, on his last night as British Ambassador in Washington.
[2] Nephew of Edwin M. Stanton, Secretary of War in Lincoln's Cabinet. He was chief disbursing officer of the American Expeditionary Forces in France, and was deputed by General Pershing to speak on behalf of the A. E. F. on this occasion.
[3] The remark has also been attributed to General Pershing, who in *My Experiences in the World War* [1931] says he cannot remember having said "anything so splendid." However, one of the uniformed American correspondents present upon the July 4, 1917, occasion, Naboth Hedin, states that he heard Pershing pronounce the phrase three weeks earlier on June 14, his second day in Paris. "Pershing stepped up to it [Lafayette's grave] and saluted in his best manner and then said in a loud voice, 'Lafayette, we are here.' I was about twenty feet away." (*Letter from Naboth Hedin to Samuel Eliot Morison* [June

Of sentences that stir my bile,
    Of phrases I detest,
There's one beyond all others vile:
    "He did it for the best."
        Lapsus Calami. The Malefactor's Plea, Stanza 1
Once there was a famous nation
    With a long and glorious past:
Very splendid was its station,
    And its territory vast.
        A Political Allegory
To the nation now occurred an
    Opportunity of saying
What they thought about the burden
    Which the government was laying
On their shoulders: and they said it
    In uncompromising terms.
        Ibid.
But the nation — mark the moral,
    For its value is untold —
During each successive quarrel
    Grew and prospered as of old.
        Ibid.

FRANCIS THOMPSON
[1859–1907]

The fairest things have fleetest end,
    Their scent survives their close:
But the rose's scent is bitterness
    To him that loved the rose.
        Daisy. Stanza 10
She went her unremembering way,
    She went and left in me
The pang of all the partings gone,
    And partings yet to be.
        Ibid. Stanza 12
Nothing begins, and nothing ends,
    That is not paid with moan;
For we are born in other's pain,
    And perish in our own.
        Ibid. Stanza 15
Look for me in the nurseries of Heaven.[1]
        To My Godchild
The innocent moon, which nothing does but shine,
Moves all the labouring surges of the world.
        Sister Songs. Part II

21, 1954].) Stanton used the phrase again on July 14.
[1] This line is inscribed on Thompson's tombstone in Kensal Green.

I fear to love thee, Sweet, because
Love's the ambassador of loss.
To Olivia

I fled Him, down the nights and down
the days;
I fled Him, down the arches of the
years;
I fled Him, down the labyrinthine ways
Of my own mind; and in the mist
of tears
I hid from Him, and under running
laughter.
The Hound of Heaven [*1893*].
Stanza 1

Across the margent of the world I fled,
And troubled the gold gateways of
the stars.
Ibid. Stanza 2

Still with unhurrying chase,
And unperturbèd pace,
Deliberate speed, majestic instancy,
Came on the following Feet,
And a Voice above their beat —
"Naught shelters thee, who wilt not
shelter Me."
Ibid.

I stand amid the dust o' the mounded
years —
My mangled youth lies dead beneath
the heap.
My days have crackled and gone up in
smoke.
Ibid. Stanza 4

Ever and anon a trumpet sounds
From the hid battlements of Eternity.
Ibid.

All which I took from thee I did but
take,
Not for thy harms,
But just that thou might'st seek it
in My arms.
All which thy child's mistake
Fancies as lost, I have stored for thee
at home.
Ibid. Stanza 5

There is no expeditious road
To pack and label men for God,
And save them by the barrel-load.
A Judgment in Heaven. Epilogue

Thou canst not stir a flower
Without troubling of a star.
The Mistress of Vision

From stones and poets you may know,
Nothing so active is, as that which least
seems so.
Contemplation

Happiness is the shadow of things past,
Which fools still take for that which is
to be!
From the Night of Forebeing

O world invisible, we view thee,
O world intangible, we touch thee,
O world unknowable, we know thee.
*The Kingdom of God ("In No
Strange Land"). Stanza 1*

The drift of pinions, would we hearken,
Beats at our own clay-shuttered doors.
Ibid. Stanza 3

The angels keep their ancient places; —
Turn but a stone, and start a wing!
'Tis ye, 'tis your estrangèd faces,
That miss the many-splendoured thing.
Ibid. Stanza 4

Upon thy so sore loss
Shall shine the traffic of Jacob's ladder
Pitched betwixt Heaven and Charing
Cross.
Ibid. Stanza 5

Short arm needs man to reach to
Heaven
So ready is Heaven to stoop to him.
Grace of the Way. Stanza 6

Know you what it is to be a child?
It is to be something very different
from the man of to-day. It is to have
a spirit yet streaming from the waters
of baptism; it is to believe in love, to
believe in loveliness, to believe in belief; it is to be so little that the elves
can reach to whisper in your ear; it is to
turn pumpkins into coaches, and mice
into horses, lowness into loftiness, and
nothing into everything, for each child
has its fairy godmother in its soul.
Shelley [1]

Children's griefs are little, certainly;
but so is the child, so is its endurance,
so is its field of vision, while its nervous
impressionability is keener than ours.
Grief is a matter of relativity; the sorrow should be estimated by its propor-

[1] In *The Dublin Review*. July, 1908.

tion to the sorrower; a gash is as painful to one as an amputation to another.
Shelley

Few poets were so mated before, and no poet was so mated afterwards, until Browning stooped and picked up a fair-coined soul that lay rusting in a pool of tears.
Ibid.

The designs of his bright imagination were never etched by the sharp fumes of necessity.
Ibid.

A poet must to some extent be a chameleon, and feed on air. But it need not be the musty breath of the multitude.
Ibid.

NIXON WATERMAN
[1859–1944]

We shall do so much in the years to come,
But what have we done today?
We shall give our gold in a princely sum,
But what did we give today?
What Have We Done Today?
No man can feel himself alone
The while he bravely stands
Between the best friends ever known —
His two good, honest hands.
Interludes

SIDNEY WEBB
(BARON PASSFIELD)
[1859–1947]
AND
BEATRICE WEBB
[1858–1943]

The inevitability of gradualness.
Presidential address, British Labour Party Congress [1923]

JANE ADDAMS
[1860–1935]

Private beneficence is totally inadequate to deal with the vast numbers of the city's disinherited.
Twenty Years at Hull House [1910]

The common stock of intellectual enjoyment should not be difficult of access because of the economic position of him who would approach it.
Twenty Years at Hull House

JAMES MATTHEW BARRIE
[1860–1937]

The humourist's like a man firin' at a target — he doesna ken whether he hits or no till them at the target tells 'im.
A Window in Thrums [1889]. Chap. 5

Those who bring sunshine to the lives of others cannot keep it from themselves.
Ibid. Chap. 18

The life of every man is a diary in which he means to write one story, and writes another; and his humblest hour is when he compares the volume as it is with what he vowed to make it.
The Little Minister [1891]. Chap. 1

The most gladsome thing in the world is that few of us fall very low; the saddest that, with such capabilities, we seldom rise high.
Ibid. Chap. 3

It's a weary warld, and nobody bides in't.
Ibid. Chap. 4

Has it ever struck you that the trouts bite best on the Sabbath? God's critters tempting decent men.
Ibid. Chap. 8

You canna expect to be baith grand and comfortable.
Ibid. Chap. 10

A house is never still in darkness to those who listen intently; there is a whispering in distant chambers, an unearthly hand presses the snib of the window, the latch rises. Ghosts were created when the first man woke in the night.
Ibid. Chap. 22

Let no one who loves be called altogether unhappy. Even love unreturned has its rainbow.

> *The Little Minister. Chap. 24*

Them that has china plates themsels is the maist careful no to break the china plates of others.

> *Ibid. Chap. 26*

Though it was really one laugh with a tear in the middle I counted it as two.

> *Margaret Ogilvy [1896]. Chap. 1*

We never understand how little we need in this world until we know the loss of it.

> *Ibid. Chap. 8*

In dinner talk it is perhaps allowable to fling on any faggot rather than let the fire go out.

> *Tommy and Grizel [1900].*
> *Chap. 3*

Shall we make a new rule of life from tonight: always to try to be a little kinder than is necessary?

> *The Little White Bird [1902].*
> *Chap. 4*

Poets are people who despise money except what you need for today.

> *Ibid. Chap. 15*

When the first baby laughed for the first time, the laugh broke into a thousand pieces and they all went skipping about, and that was the beginning of fairies.

> *Peter Pan [1904]. Act I*

Every time a child says "I don't believe in fairies" there is a little fairy somewhere that falls down dead.

> *Ibid.*

Do you believe in fairies? . . . If you believe, clap your hands!

> *Ibid. Act IV*

Alick. What *is* charm, exactly, Maggie?

Maggie. Oh, it's — it's a sort of bloom on a woman. If you have it, you don't need to have anything else; and if you don't have it, it doesn't much matter what else you have. Some women, the few, have charm for all;

and most have charm for one. But some have charm for none.[1]

> *What Every Woman Knows [1908].*
> *Act I*

The tragedy of a man who has found himself out.

> *Ibid. Act IV*

Every man who is high up loves to think that he has done it all himself; and the wife smiles, and lets it go at that.

> *Ibid.*

One's religion is whatever he is most interested in, and yours is Success.

> *The Twelve-Pound Look [1910]*

The greatest glory that has ever come to me was to be swallowed up in London, not knowing a soul, with no means of subsistence, and the fun of working till the stars went out. To have known any one would have spoilt it. I did not even quite know the language.

> *Courage: Rectorial Address at St.*
> *Andrew's [May 3, 1922]*

Mighty are the Universities of Scotland, and they will prevail. But even in your highest exultations never forget that they are not four, but five. The greatest of them is the poor, proud homes you come out of, which said so long ago: "There shall be education in this land."

> *Ibid.*

For several days after my first book was published I carried it about in my pocket, and took surreptitious peeps at

---

[1] What is charm? It is what the violet has and the camellia has not. — MARION CRAWFORD [1854–1909]: *Children of the King, Chap. 5*

"Charm" — which means the power to effect work without employing brute force — is indispensable to women. Charm is a woman's strength just as strength is a man's charm. — HAVELOCK ELLIS [1859–1939]: *The Task of Social Hygiene, Chap. 3*

Charm is the measure of attraction's power
To chain the fleeting fancy of the hour,
And rival all the spell of Beauty's dower.
> LOUISA CARROLL THOMAS [1865–   ]:
> *What Is Charm? St. 1*

it to make sure that the ink had not faded.

Speech at the Critics' Circle, London [1922]

JOHN COLLINS BOSSIDY
[1860–1928]

And this is good old Boston,
  The home of the bean and the cod,
Where the Lowells talk to the Cabots
  And the Cabots talk only to God.[1]
Toast, Midwinter Dinner, Holy Cross Alumni [1910]

WILLIAM JENNINGS BRYAN
[1860–1925]

The humblest citizen of all the land, when clad in the armor of a righteous cause, is stronger than all the hosts of Error.

Speech at the National Democratic Convention, Chicago [1896]

You shall not press down upon the brow of labor this crown of thorns. You shall not crucify mankind upon a cross of gold.

Ibid.

If the Father deigns to touch with divine power the cold and pulseless heart of the buried acorn and to make it burst forth from its prison walls, will He leave neglected in the earth the soul of man made in the image of his Creator?

The Prince of Peace

If matter mute and inanimate, though changed by the forces of Nature into a multitude of forms, can never die, will the spirit of man suffer annihilation when it has paid a brief visit, like a royal guest, to this tenement of clay?

Ibid.

[1] Patterned on the toast given at the twenty-fifth anniversary dinner of the Harvard Class of 1880, by a Westerner.
  Here's to old Massachusetts,
    The home of the sacred cod,
  Where the Adamses vote for Douglas,
    And the Cabots walk with God.

CHARLES TOWNSEND COPELAND
[1860–1952]

For the common man, the best memorial is some beneficent thing or function that shall bear his name.
Tribute to Nathaniel Southgate Shaler [1906]. Copeland Reader

A man is always better than a book.
Ibid.

To blame him were absurd; to pity were profane.
Not "Poor Charles Lamb." Copeland Reader Introduction

Whenever we encounter the typical essayist, he is found to be a tatler, a spectator, a rambler, a lounger, and, in the best sense, a citizen of the world.
Ibid.

HARRY MICAJAH DAUGHERTY
[1860–1941]

In a smoke-filled room in some hotel.[1]
Republican National Convention, Chicago, June, 1920

HAMLIN GARLAND
[1860–1940]

Do you fear the force of the wind,
  The slash of the rain?
Go face them and fight them,
  Be savage again.
Do You Fear the Wind?

The palms of your hands will thicken,
  The skin of your cheek will tan,
You'll go ragged and weary and swarthy,
  But you'll walk like a man!
Ibid.

[1] Daugherty, manager for Senator Warren G. Harding, predicted that the convention would be deadlocked and would be decided by a group of men who "will sit down about two o'clock in the morning around a table in a smoke-filled room." The room was in the suite occupied by George Harvey, rooms 804–805 in the Blackstone Hotel.

CHARLOTTE PERKINS STETSON GILMAN
[1860–1935]

Cried all, "Before such things can come,
You idiotic child,
You must alter Human Nature!"
And they all sat back and smiled.
Similar Cases

Said I, in scorn all burning hot,
  In rage and anger high,
"You ignominious idiot!
  Those wings are made to fly!"
A Conservative. Stanza 5

"I do not want to be a fly!
I want to be a worm!"
Ibid. Stanza 6

I ran against a Prejudice
That quite cut off the view.
An Obstacle. Stanza 1

There's a whining at the threshold —
  There's a scratching at the floor —
To work! To work! In Heaven's name!
  The wolf is at the door!
The Wolf at the Door. Stanza 6

The people people have for friends
  Your common sense appal,
But the people people marry
  Are the queerest folk of all.
Queer People

Human life consists in mutual service. No grief, pain, misfortune, or "broken heart," is excuse for cutting off one's life while any power of service remains. But when all usefulness is over, when one is assured of an unavoidable and imminent death, it is the simplest of human rights to choose a quick and easy death in place of a slow and horrible one.
Note written before her suicide
[August 17, 1935]

WILLIAM RALPH INGE
[1860–1954]

Literature flourishes best when it is half a trade and half an art.
The Victorian Age [1922]

JUSTIN HUNTLY M'CARTHY
[1860–1936]

On level lines of woodwork stand
My books obedient to my hand.
My Books
The playwrights mouth, the preachers jangle,
  The critics challenge and defend,
And Fiction turns the Muses' mangle —
  Of making books there is no end.[1]
A Ballade of Book-Making.
Stanza 2

JAMES BALL NAYLOR
[1860–1945]

King David and King Solomon
  Led merry, merry lives,
With many, many lady friends
  And many, many wives;
But when old age crept over them —
  With many, many qualms,
King Solomon wrote the Proverbs
  And King David wrote the Psalms.
Ancient Authors

BLISS PERRY
[1860–1953]

The fact is, we are not a book-reading people. The vast majority of our ninety-odd millions of population have no literary appetites which cannot be supplied by the newspapers, the magazines, and an occasional "best-seller" novel.
The Praise of Folly. Criticism in
American Periodicals

FRANK DEMPSTER SHERMAN
[1860–1916]

Of all the threads of rhyme
  Which I have spun,
I shall be glad if Time
  Save only one.
His Desire

Out of the scabbard of the night,
  By God's hand drawn,

[1] See *Ecclesiastes, XII, 12,* on page 1044a.

Flashes his shining sword of light,
And lo, — the dawn!

Dawn

Hark to the noisy caravans of brown,
Intrepid Sparrows, — Arabs of the air!

City Sparrows

OWEN WISTER
[1860–1938]

When you call me that, *smile!*

The Virginian [*1902*]. *Chap. 2*

RICHARD BURTON
[1861–1940]

From their folded mates they wander
   far,
Their ways seem harsh and wild;
They follow the beck of a baleful star,
Their paths are dream-beguiled.

Black Sheep

BLISS CARMAN
[1861–1929]

An open hand, an easy shoe,
And a hope to make the day go through.

The Joys of the Road

No fidget and no reformer, just
A calm observer of ought and must.

Ibid.

Make me over, mother April,
When the sap begins to stir!

Spring Song. Stanza 1

Make me over in the morning
From the rag-bag of the world!
Scraps of dream and duds of daring,
Home-brought stuff from far sea-faring.

Ibid. Stanza 12

The scarlet of the maples can shake me
   like a cry
Of bugles going by.

A Vagabond Song. Stanza 2

There is something in October sets the
   gypsy blood astir.

Ibid. Stanza 3

Here we came when love was young.
Now that love is old,

Shall we leave the floor unswept
And the hearth acold?

The Homestead. Stanza 1

I took a day to search for God,
And found Him not. But as I trod
By rocky ledge, through woods un-
   tamed,
Just where one scarlet lily flamed,
I saw His footprint in the sod.

Vestigia. Stanza 1

I often wish that I could rid the
world of the tyranny of facts. What
are facts but compromises? A fact
merely marks the point where we have
agreed to let investigation cease.

In The Atlantic Monthly,
May, 1906

LOUISE IMOGEN GUINEY
[1861–1920]

He has done with roofs and men,
Open, Time, and let him pass.

Ballad of Kenelm

A short life in the saddle, Lord!
Not long life by the fire.

The Knight Errant. Stanza 2

Cowley said it engagingly: *Bene qui*
latuit, bene vixit: he lives well, that has
lain well hidden. The pleasantest condition of life is in incognito.

Patrins. On the Delights of an
Incognito

A passing salute to this world and her
   pitiful beauty.

The Wild Ride. Stanza 5

A certain sesquipedalianism is natural to Americans: witness our press
editorials, our Fourth of July orations,
and the public messages of all our Presidents since Lincoln.

In Scribner's Magazine,
January, 1911

Quotations (such as have point and
lack triteness) from the great old authors are an act of filial reverence on
the part of the quoter, and a blessing
to a public grown superficial and external.

Ibid.

JOHN LUTHER LONG
[1861–1927]

To die with honour when one can no longer live with honour.[1]
Madame Butterfly [1897] (*inscription on Samurai blade*)

EDWARD MacDOWELL
[1861–1908]

A house of Dreams untold
That looks out over the whispering tree-tops
And faces the setting sun.
House of Dreams [2]

BYRON RUFUS NEWTON
[1861–1938]

Vulgar of manner, overfed,
Overdressed and underbred;
Heartless, Godless, hell's delight,
Rude by day and lewd by night.
Owed to New York [1906]
Purple-robed and pauper-clad,
Raving, rotting, money-mad;
A squirming herd in Mammon's mesh,
A wilderness of human flesh;
Crazed with avarice, lust, and rum,
New York, thy name's Delirium.
Ibid.

"JOHN OXENHAM" (WILLIAM ARTHUR DUNKERLEY)
[1861–1941]

Art thou lonely, O my brother?
Share thy little with another!
Stretch a hand to one unfriended,
And thy loneliness is ended.
Lonely Brother
But see how high!—
It reaches up
To God's blue sky!
The Philosopher's Garden

[1] One should die proudly when it is no longer possible to live proudly. — NIETZSCHE [1844–1900]: *The Twilight of the Idols, Skirmishes in a War with the Age, 36*
[2] Preface to his composition, *From a Log Cabin,* and inscribed on the memorial tablet near his grave.

Kneel always when you light a fire!
The Sacrament of Fire
Thank God for sleep!
And, when you cannot sleep,
Still thank Him that you live
To lie awake.
The Sacrament of Sleep
To every man there openeth
A Way, and Ways, and a Way,
The High Soul climbs the High Way,
The Low Soul gropes the Low,
And in between, on the misty flats,
The rest drift to and fro.
The Ways
And every man decideth
The Way his soul shall go.
Ibid.
Only through Me can come the great awakening;
Wrong cannot right the wrongs that Wrong hath done;
Only through Me, all other gods forsaking,
Can ye attain the heights that must be won.
Dies Irae — Dies Pacis

SIR WALTER RALEIGH [1]
[1861–1922]

I wish I loved the Human Race;
I wish I loved its silly face;
I wish I liked the way it walks;
I wish I liked the way it talks;
And when I'm introduced to one
I wish I thought *What Jolly Fun!*
Wishes of an Elderly Man (Wished at a Garden-Party, June, 1914)

WENDELL PHILLIPS STAFFORD
[1861–   ]

My heart is where the hills fling up
Green garlands to the day.
'Tis where the blue lake brims her cup,
The sparkling rivers play.
My heart is on the mountain still,
Where'er my steps may be,

[1] Professor of English literature at Oxford from 1904, and author of critical works on Milton, Wordsworth, Shakespeare, and others.

Vermont, O maiden of the hills,
My heart is there with thee!
Vermont: A Song. Stanza 1

RABINDRANATH TAGORE
[1861–1941]

When one knows thee, then alien there is none, then no door is shut. Oh, grant me my prayer that I may never lose the touch of the one in the play of the many.
Gitanjali [1913]

Come out of thyself,
Stand in the open;
Within thy heart wilt thou hear
The response of all the world.
Sheaves. The Invitation

When I bring you coloured toys, my child, I understand why there is such a play of colours on clouds, on water, and why flowers are painted in tints.
*The Crescent Moon [1913].
When and Why*

I do not love him because he is good, but because he is my little child.
Ibid. The Judge

I alone have a right to blame and punish, for he only may chastise who loves.[1]
Ibid.

Years mature into fruit
So that some small seeds of moments
May outlive them.
*On Visiting Yale University
[1932]*

ALFRED NORTH
WHITEHEAD
[1861–1947]

The human body is an instrument for the production of art in the life of the human soul.
*Adventures of Ideas [1933].
Chap. 18*

A general definition of civilization: a civilized society is exhibiting the five qualities of Truth, Beauty, Adventure, Art, Peace.
Ibid. Chap. 19

[1] See Pomfret, page 294b.

The deliberate aim at Peace very easily passes into its bastard substitute, Anaesthesia.
Adventures of Ideas. Chap. 20

Youth is life as yet untouched by tragedy. . . . When youth has once grasped where Beauty dwells — with a real knowledge and not as a mere matter of literary phraseology — its self-surrender is absolute.
Ibid.

There are no whole truths; all truths are half-truths. It is trying to treat them as whole truths that plays the devil.
*Dialogues of Alfred North
Whitehead [1953].[1] Page 16*

The vitality of thought is in adventure. *Ideas won't keep.* Something must be done about them. When the idea is new, its custodians have fervour, live for it, and, if need be, die for it.
Ibid. Page 100

Intelligence is quickness to apprehend as distinct from ability, which is capacity to act wisely on the thing apprehended.
Ibid. Page 135

Our minds are finite, and yet even in these circumstances of finitude we are surrounded by possibilities that are infinite, and the purpose of human life is to grasp as much as we can out of that infinitude.
Ibid. Page 163

A culture is in its finest flower before it begins to analyze itself.
Ibid. Page 169

The ideas of Freud were popularized by people who only imperfectly understood them, who were incapable of the great effort required to grasp them in their relationship to larger truths, and who therefore assigned to them a prominence out of all proportion to their true importance.
Ibid. Page 211

Art is the imposing of a pattern on experience, and our esthetic enjoyment in recognition of the pattern.
Ibid. Page 228

[1] As recorded by Lucien Price.

A philosopher of imposing stature doesn't think in a vacuum. Even his most abstract ideas are, to some extent, conditioned by what is or is not known in the time when he lives.

Dialogues of Alfred North Whitehead. Page 229

With the sense of sight, the idea communicates the emotion, whereas, with sound, the emotion communicates the idea, which is more direct and therefore more powerful.

Ibid. Page 231

Intellect is to emotion as our clothes are to our bodies: we could not very well have civilized life without clothes, but we would be in a poor way if we had only clothes without bodies.

Ibid. Page 232

No period of history has ever been great or ever can be that does not act on some sort of high, idealistic motives, and idealism in our time has been shoved aside, and we are paying the penalty for it.

Ibid. Page 276

The English never abolish anything. They put it in cold storage.

Ibid. Page 309

Shakespeare wrote better poetry for not knowing too much; Milton, I think, knew too much finally for the good of his poetry.

Ibid. Page 369

JOHN KENDRICK BANGS
[1862–1922]

Shakespeare was not accounted great
When good Queen Bess ruled England's
  state,
So why should I today repine
Because the laurel is not mine?
Consolation. Stanza 1

I think mankind by thee would be less
  bored
If only thou wert not thine own reward.
A Hint to Virtue

To dig and delve in nice clean dirt
Can do a mortal little hurt.
Gardening

"I'm just as big for me," said he,
"As you are big for you!"
The Little Elfman. Stanza 2

ARTHUR CHRISTOPHER BENSON
[1862–1925]

Land of Hope and Glory, Mother of
  the Free,
How shall we extol thee, who are born
  of thee?
Wider still and wider shall thy bounds
  be set;
God, who made thee mighty, make thee
  mightier yet.
Land of Hope and Glory. Chorus

Edward Fitzgerald said that he wished we had more lives of obscure persons; one wants to know what other people are thinking and feeling about it all. . . . If the dullest person in the world would only put down sincerely what he or she thought about his or her life, about work and love, religion and emotion, it would be a fascinating document.

From a College Window

ALBERT JEREMIAH BEVERIDGE
[1862–1927]

This party comes from the grass roots. It has grown from the soil of the people's hard necessities.

Address as Temporary Chairman of the Bull Moose Convention, Chicago [August 5, 1912]

JAMES W. BLAKE
[1862–1935]

East Side, West Side, all around the
  town,
The tots sang "Ring-a-rosie," "London
  Bridge is falling down";
Boys and girls together, me and Mamie
  O'Rourke,

Tripped the light fantastic on the sidewalks of New York.
The Sidewalks of New York [1]
[*1894*]

CARRIE JACOBS BOND
[*1862–1946*]

When you come to the end of a perfect day.
A Perfect Day. Stanza 1
For mem'ry has painted this perfect day
With colors that never fade,
And we find at the end of a perfect day
The soul of a friend we've made.
Ibid. Stanza 2

NICHOLAS MURRAY BUTLER
[*1862–1947*]

An expert is one who knows more and more about less and less.
Commencement Address,
Columbia University

GOLDSWORTHY LOWES DICKINSON
[*1862–1932*]

A fundamental, and as many believe, the most essential part of Christianity, is its doctrine of reward and punishment in the world beyond; and a religion which had nothing at all to say about this great enigma we should hardly feel to be a religion at all.
The Greek View of Life [*1898*].
Chap. 1, Sect. 11
Dissatisfaction with the world in which we live and determination to realize one that shall be better, are the prevailing characteristics of the modern spirit.
Ibid. Chap. 5
Chinese poetry is of all poetry I know the most human and the least symbolic or romantic. It contemplates life just as it presents itself, without any veil of ideas, any rhetoric or sentiment; it simply clears away the obstruction

[1] The music of the song was composed by Charles B. Lawlor [1852–1925].

which habit has built up between us and the beauty of things.
An Essay on the Civilizations of
India, China, and Japan [*1914*].
Page 47
The United States of America — the greatest potential force, material, moral, and spiritual, in the world.
The Choice Before Us [*1917*].
Chap. 1

To the man who has the religion of peace, the supreme value is love. To the man who has the religion of war, the supreme value is strife.
Ibid. Chap. 3

Government is everywhere to a great extent controlled by powerful minorities, with an interest distinct from that of the mass of the people.
Ibid. Chap. 4

The true way for one civilization to "conquer" another is for it to be so obviously superior in this or that point that others desire to imitate it.
Ibid. Chap. 5

War is not "inevitable," but proceeds from definite and removable causes.
Ibid. Chap. 9

Nations are quite capable of starving every other side of life — education, sanitation, housing, public health, everything that contributes to life, physical, intellectual, moral, and spiritual, in order to maintain their armaments.
Ibid. Chap. 11

ANNIE JOHNSON FLINT
[*1862–1932*]

The thrones are rocking to their fall —
It is the twilight of the Kings!
The Twilight of the Kings

Have you come to the Red Sea place in your life,
Where, in spite of all you can do,
There is no way out, there is no way back,
There is no other way but through?
At the Place of the Sea. Stanza 1

NORMAN GALE
[1862–1942]

Here in the country's heart
　Where the grass is green,
Life is the same sweet life
　As it e'er hath been.
The Country Faith. Stanza 1

Write: — He had made a finer man
　And left increased renown behind,
If he had only shut his books
　To read the chapters of mankind!
Last Words. Stanza 10

EDWARD, VISCOUNT GREY OF FALLODON
[1862–1933]

The lamps are going out all over Europe; we shall not see them lit again in our lifetime.
Comment, August 4, 1914, standing at the windows of his room in the Foreign Office, London, as the lamplighters were turning off the lights in St. James's Park

O. HENRY
(WILLIAM SYDNEY PORTER)
[1862–1910]

No calamity so touches the common heart of humanity as does the straying of a little child. Their feet are so uncertain and feeble; the ways are so steep and strange.
The Four Million [1906].
Between Rounds

If men knew how women pass the time when they are alone, they'd never marry.
Ibid. Memoirs of a Yellow Dog

What a woman wants is what you're out of. She wants more of a thing when it's scarce.
Heart of the West [1907].
Cupid à la Carte

Love and business and family and religion and art and patriotism are nothing but shadows of words when a man's starving.
Ibid.

Esau, that swapped his copyright for a partridge.
Heart of the West.
Cupid à la Carte

There is one day that is ours. There is one day when all we Americans who are not self-made go back to the old home to eat saleratus biscuits and marvel how much nearer to the porch the old pump looks than it used to. . . . Thanksgiving Day . . . is the one day that is purely American.
The Trimmed Lamp [1907].
Two Thanksgiving Day Gentlemen

One day the christeners of apartment houses and the cognominators of sleeping-cars will meet, and there will be some jealous and sanguinary knifing.
Ibid. The Country of Elusion

Perhaps there is no happiness in life so perfect as the martyr's.
Ibid.

Bohemia is nothing more than the little country in which you do not live.
Ibid.

Lost, your Excellency. Lost associations and societies. Lost right reverends and wrong reverends of every order. Lost reformers and lawmakers, born with heavenly compassion in your hearts, but with the reverence of money in your souls. And lost thus around us every day.[1]
Ibid. Elsie in New York

When a poor man finds a long-hidden quarter-dollar that has slipped through a rip in his vest lining, he sounds the pleasure of life with a deeper plummet than any millionaire can hope to cast.
The Voice of the City [1908].
The Complete Life of John Hopkins

You're the goods.
Ibid. From Each According to His Ability

It was beautiful and simple as all truly great swindles are.
The Gentle Grafter [1908].
The Octopus Marooned

[1] A paraphrase of the closing lines of Chapter 47 of Dickens's *Bleak House.*

There are two times when you can never tell what is going to happen. One is when a man takes his first drink; and the other is when a woman takes her latest.

The Gentle Grafter. The Octopus Marooned

He was outwardly decent and managed to preserve his aquarium, but inside he was impromptu and full of unexpectedness.

Ibid.

It brings up happy old days when I was only a farmer and not an agriculturist.

Ibid. Modern Rural Sports

Living as high as prize fighters out of training.

Ibid. A Tempered Wind

Busy as a one-armed man with the nettle-rash pasting on wall-paper.

Ibid. The Ethics of Pig

Bagdad-on-the-Subway.[1]

Roads of Destiny [*1909*]. *The Discounters of Money*

History is bright and fiction dull with homely men who have charmed women.

Ibid. "Next to Reading Matter"

You can't appreciate home till you've left it, money till it's spent, your wife till she's joined a woman's club, nor Old Glory till you see it hanging on a broomstick on the shanty of a consul in a foreign town.

Ibid. The Fourth in Salvador

Men to whom life had appeared as a reversible coat — seamy on both sides.

Options [*1909*]. *The Hiding of Black Bill*

A man asleep is certainly a sight to make angels weep. Now, a woman asleep you regard as different. No matter how she looks, you know it's better for all hands for her to be that way.

Ibid.

The big city is like a mother's knee to many who have strayed far and found the roads rough beneath their uncertain feet. At dusk they come home and sit upon the door-step.

Options. Supply and Demand

Better fifty years of Europe than a cyclone in the bay.[1]

Ibid. He Also Serves

She would have made a splendid wife, for crying only made her eyes more bright.

Ibid. No Story

A kind of mixture of fools and angels — they rush in and fear to tread at the same time.[2]

Ibid. The Moment of Victory

A story with a moral appended is like the bill of a mosquito. It bores you, and then injects a stinging drop to irritate your conscience.

Strictly Business [*1910*]. *The Gold That Glittered*

Except in street cars one should never be unnecessarily rude to a lady.

Ibid.

She plucked from my lapel the invisible strand of lint (the universal act of woman to proclaim ownership).

Ibid. A Ramble in Aphasia

Californians are a race of people; they are not merely inhabitants of a State.

Ibid. A Municipal Report

Take of London fog 30 parts; malaria 10 parts; gas leaks 20 parts; dewdrops gathered in a brick-yard at sunrise 25 parts; odor of honeysuckle 15 parts. Mix. The mixture will give you an approximate conception of a Nashville drizzle.

Ibid.

Most wonderful of all are words, and how they make friends one with another, being oft associated, until not even obituary notices them do part.

Whirligigs [*1910*]. *Calloway's Code*

It couldn't have happened anywhere but in little old New York.[3]

Ibid. A Little Local Color

---

[1] Also in *A Madison Square Arabian Night, A Night in New Arabia,* and "*What You Want.*"

[1] See Tennyson, page 549a.
[2] See Pope, page 312a.
[3] Also in *A Midsummer Knight's Dream,*

There was too much scenery and fresh air. What I need is a steam-heated flat with no ventilation or exercise.
Letter [April 15, 1910]

I was made by a Dago and presented to the American people on behalf of the French Government for the purpose of welcomin' Irish immigrants into the Dutch city of New York.
Sixes and Sevens [1911]. The Lady Higher Up [1]

May his liver turn to water, and the bones of him crack in the cold of his heart. May dog fennel grow upon his ancestors' graves, and the grandsons of his children be born without eyes. May whiskey turn to clabber in his mouth, and every time he sneezes may he blister the soles of his feet. And the smoke of his pipe — may it make his eyes water, and the drops fall on the grass that his cows eat and poison the butter that he spreads on his bread.[2]
Ibid. Transformation of Martin Burney

A straw vote only shows which way the hot air blows.
Rolling Stones [1913]. A Ruler of Men

We may achieve climate, but weather is thrust upon us.
Ibid. A Fog in Santone

Take it from me — he's got the goods.
The Unprofitable Servant

"You can tell your paper," the great man said,
"I refused an interview.
I have nothing to say on the question, sir;
Nothing to say to you."
And then he talked till the sun went down
And the chickens went to roost.
Poems. Nothing to Say

Past One at Rooney's, and *The Rubber Plant's Story.*
[1] The Statue of Liberty.
[2] See Synge, pages 856b–857a.

Turn up the lights; I don't want to go home in the dark.
Last words (quoted in the biography by C. ALPHONSO SMITH)

ELLA HIGGINSON
[1862–1940]

Oh, every year hath its winter,
And every year hath its rain —
But a day is always coming
When the birds go north again.
When the Birds Go North Again. Stanza 1

One leaf is for hope, and one is for faith,
And one is for love, you know,
And God put another in for luck.
Four-Leaf Clover. Stanza 2

Forgive you? — Oh, of course, dear,
A dozen times a week!
We women were created
Forgiveness but to speak.
Wearing Out Love. Stanza 1

MAURICE MAETERLINCK
[1862–1949]

The future is a world limited by ourselves; in it we discover only what concerns us and, sometimes, by chance, what interests those whom we love the most.
Joyzelle. Act I

Men's weaknesses are often necessary to the purposes of life.
Ibid. Act II

I have never for one instant seen clearly within myself; how then would you have me judge the deeds of others? [1]
Pelleas and Melisande [1892]. Act I, Sc. 3

Each young and beautiful being shapes around it events that are themselves young, beautiful, and happy.
Ibid. Act IV, Sc. 2

---

[1] No man can justly censure or condemn another, because indeed no man truly knows another. . . . Further, no man can judge another, because no man knows himself. — SIR THOMAS BROWNE: *Religio Medici* [1642]

Old men have need to touch sometimes with their lips the brow of a woman or the cheek of a child, that they may believe again in the freshness of life.

Pelleas and Melisande.
Act IV, Sc. 2

There are no dead.

The Blue Bird [1909].
Act IV, Sc. 2

WALT MASON
[1862–1939]

The little green tents where the soldiers sleep and the sunbeams play and the women weep, are covered with flowers today.

The Little Green Tents

The statesman throws his shoulders back, and straightens out his tie, And says, "My friends, unless it rains, the weather will be dry." And when this thought into our brains has percolated through, We common people nod our heads and loudly cry, "How true!"

The Statesman

There's a man in the world who is never turned down, wherever he chances to stray; he gets the glad hand in the populous town, out where the farmers make hay; he's greeted with pleasure on deserts of sand, and deep in the aisles of the woods; wherever he goes there's the welcoming hand — he's the Man Who Delivers the Goods.

The Man Who Delivers the Goods

Little drops of water poured into the milk, give the milkman's daughter lovely gowns of silk. Little grains of sugar mingled with the sand, make the grocer's assets swell to beat the band.

Little Things

SIR HENRY NEWBOLT
[1862–1938]

To set the cause above renown,
To love the game beyond the prize,
To honor, while you strike him down,
The foe that comes with fearless eyes;

To count the life of battle good
And dear the land that gave you birth,
And dearer yet the brotherhood
That binds the brave of all the earth.

The Island Race. Clifton Chapel,
Stanza 2

Qui procul hinc, the legend's writ, —
The frontier-grave is far away —
Qui ante diem periit:
Sed miles, sed pro patria.[1]

Ibid. Stanza 4

Drake he was a Devon man, an' ruled the Devon seas.

Ibid. Drake's Drum, Stanza 2

"Take my drum to England, hang et by the shore,
Strike et when your powder's runnin' low;
If the Dons sight Devon, I'll quit the port o' Heaven,
An' drum them up the Channel as we drummed them long ago."

Ibid.

When the strong command
Obedience is best.

A Ballad of John Nicholson

And now he saw with lifted eyes
The East like a great chancel rise,
And deep through all his senses drawn,
Received the sacred wine of dawn.

The Last Word

Now the sunset breezes shiver,
And she's fading down the river,
But in England's song for ever
She's the Fighting Téméraire.

The Fighting Téméraire

"Play up! play up! and play the game!"

Vitai Lampada

England! where the sacred flame
Burns before the inmost shrine,
Where the lips that love thy name
Consecrate their hopes and thine,
Where the banners of thy dead
Weave their shadows overhead,
Watch beside thine arms tonight,
Pray that God defend the Right.

The Vigil. Stanza 1

[1] Who died far away, before his time: but as a soldier, for his country.

EDEN PHILLPOTTS
[1862–1960]

A sudden wakin', a sudden weepin',
A li'l suckin', a li'l sleepin';
A cheel's full joys an' a cheel's short
    sorrows,
Wi' a power o' faith in gert to-morrows.
        Man's Days. Stanza 1

His father's sister had bats in the
belfry and was put away.
        Peacock House

ROBERT CAMERON ROGERS
[1862–1912]

The hours I spent with thee, dear heart,
  Are as a string of pearls to me;
I count them over, every one apart,
  My rosary, my rosary.
        My Rosary

Visions I no longer see,
And smoke is only smoke to me,
  Now I am old.
        The Old Smoker

EDITH WHARTON
[1862–1937]

There are two ways of spreading light:
    to be
The candle or the mirror that reflects
    it.
        Vesalius in Zante

Mrs. Ballinger is one of the ladies
who pursue Culture in bands, as though
it were dangerous to meet it alone.
        Xingu [1916]

I was never allowed to read the popular American children's books of my
day because, as my mother said, the
children spoke bad English *without the
author's knowing it.*
    A Backward Glance [1934].
        Chap. 3

To [Henry] James's intimates, however, these elaborate hesitancies, far
from being an obstacle, were like a cob-
web bridge flung from his mind to
theirs, an invisible passage over which
one knew that silver-footed ironies,
veiled jokes, tiptoe malices, were stealing to explode a huge laugh at one's
feet.
    A Backward Glance. Chap. 8

"Summer afternoon — summer afternoon; to me those have always been the
two most beautiful words in the English
language."
    (*Said by* HENRY JAMES *to* MRS.
    WHARTON) *Ibid. Chap. 10*

THE REVEREND E. J. HARDY
[*Floruit* 1910]

How To Be Happy Though Married.
    Title of book [1910]

HENRY HOLCOMB BENNETT
[1863–1924]

Hats off!
Along the street there comes
A blare of bugles, a ruffle of drums,
A flash of color beneath the sky:
    Hats off!
The flag is passing by.
    The Flag Goes By. Stanza 1

GAMALIEL BRADFORD
[1863–1932]

I sometimes wish that God were back
  In this dark world and wide;
For though some virtues he might lack,
  He had his pleasant side.
        Exit God

That odd, fantastic ass, Rousseau,
  Declared himself unique.
How men persist in doing so,
  Puzzles me more than Greek.
        Rousseau

The sins that tarnish whore and thief
  Beset me every day.
My most ethereal belief
  Inhabits common clay.
        Ibid.

OLIVER HERFORD
[1863–1935]

God made Man
  Frail as a bubble;
God made Love,
  Love made Trouble.

God made the Vine,
  Was it a sin
That Man made Wine
  To drown Trouble in?
A Plea

The Gargoyle often makes his perch
On a cathedral or a church,
Where, mid ecclesiastic style,
He smiles an early-Gothic smile.
The Gargoyle

Children, behold the Chimpanzee:
He sits on the ancestral tree
From which we sprang in ages gone.
The Chimpanzee

Ermined and minked and Persian-
  lambed,
Be-puffed (be-painted, too, alas!)
Be-decked, be-diamonded —
  be-damned!
The women of the better class.
The Women of the Better Class.
Stanza 4

RUFUS M. JONES
[1863–1948]

A little five-year-old boy, who had
been bombed out of his home and
evacuated to the country, said: "Now
I am nobody's nothing."
American Friends Service
Committee, Annual Report
[1943]. Foreword

JAMES MICHAEL KIERAN [1]
[1863–1936]

The Brain Trust.
Description of the professorial
advisers chosen by Franklin D.
Roosevelt in his first Presiden-
tial campaign [1932]

JOSEPH P. MacCARTHY
[1863–1934]

You must select the Puritans for
your ancestors. You must have a sheltered youth and be a graduate of Harvard. . . . Eat beans on Saturday
night and fish-balls on Sunday morn-

[1] Dr. Kieran was president of Hunter College, New York City.

ing. . . . You must be a D.A.R., a
Colonial Dame, an S.A.R. or belong
to the Mayflower Society. . . . You
must read the Atlantic Monthly. . . .
You must make sure in advance that
your obituary appears in the Boston
Transcript. There is nothing else.
To be Happy in New England,
Letter to the Editor of The
Christian Register

ARTHUR MACHEN
[1863–1947]

It was better, he thought, to fail in
attempting exquisite things than to
succeed in the department of the utterly contemptible.
The Hill of Dreams [1907].
Chap. 5

A. EDWARD NEWTON
[1863–1940]

Young man, get a hobby; preferably
get two, one for indoors and one for
out; get a pair of hobby-horses that
can safely be ridden in opposite directions.
Amenities of Book-Collecting
[1918]. Chap. 1

Possession is the grave of bliss. No
sooner do we own some great book than
we want another.
Ibid. Chap. 3

Only when a man is safely ensconced
under six feet of earth, with several
tons of enlauding granite upon his
chest, is he in a position to give advice
with any certainty, and then he is silent.
Ibid. Chap. 4

From contemplation one may become wise, but knowledge comes only
from study.
A Magnificent Farce [1921].
Chap. 8

I wish that some one would give a
course in how to live. It can't be taught
in the colleges: that's perfectly obvi-

ous, for college professors don't know any better than the rest of us.
This Book-Collecting Game [*1928*]. *Chap. 10*

Gilbert White discovered the formula for complete happiness, but he died before making the announcement, leaving it for me to do so. It is to be very busy with the unimportant.
Ibid.

CLARENCE OUSLEY
[1863–1948]

When the mint is in the liquor and its fragrance on the glass,
It breathes a recollection that can never, never pass.
When the Mint Is in the Liquor. *Stanza 1*

SIR ARTHUR THOMAS QUILLER-COUCH
[1863–1944]

Literature is not an abstract science, to which exact definitions can be applied. It is an art, the success of which depends on personal persuasiveness, on the author's skill to give as on ours to receive.
Inaugural Lecture at Cambridge University [*1913*]

JAMES HARVEY ROBINSON
[1863–1935]

Political campaigns are designedly made into emotional orgies which endeavor to distract attention from the real issues involved, and they actually paralyze what slight powers of cerebration man can normally muster.
The Human Comedy [*1937*]. *Chap. 9*

With supreme irony, the war to "make the world safe for democracy" [1] ended by leaving democracy more unsafe in the world than at any time since the collapse of the revolutions of 1848.
Ibid.

[1] See Woodrow Wilson, page 770b.

GEORGE SANTAYANA
[1863–1952]

O World, thou choosest not the better part!
It is not wisdom to be only wise,
And on the inward vision close the eyes,
But it is wisdom to believe the heart.
O World, Thou Choosest Not [*1894*]

Columbus found a world, and had no chart,
Save one that faith deciphered in the skies;
To trust the soul's invincible surmise
Was all his science and his only art.
Ibid.

Heaven is to be at peace with things;
Come chaos now, and in a whirlwind's rings
Engulf the planets. I have seen the best.
Sonnet 49 [*1894*]

Beauty is pleasure regarded as the quality of a thing.
The Sense of Beauty [*1896*]. *The Nature of Beauty*

The infinity which moves us is the sense of multiplicity in uniformity. Accordingly, things which have enough multiplicity, as the lights of a city seen across water, have an effect similar to that of the stars, if less intense; whereas a star, if alone, because the multiplicity is lacking, makes a wholly different impression.
Ibid. Form

Beauty as we feel it is something indescribable: what it is or what it means can never be said.
Ibid. Expression

Beauty is a pledge of the possible conformity between the soul and nature, and consequently a ground of faith in the supremacy of the good.
Ibid.

Fanaticism consists in redoubling your efforts when you have forgotten your aim.
The Life of Reason [*1905–1906*]. *Vol. I*

The human race, in its intellectual life, is organized like the bees: the masculine soul is a worker, sexually atrophied, and essentially dedicated to impersonal and universal arts; the feminine is a queen, infinitely fertile, omnipresent in its brooding industry, but passive and abounding in intuitions without method and passions without justice.

The Life of Reason. Vol. II

Let a man once overcome his selfish terror at his own finitude, and his finitude is, in one sense, overcome.

Introduction to The Ethics of
Spinoza [1910]

Perhaps the only true dignity of man is his capacity to despise himself.

Ibid.

Miracles are propitious accidents, the natural causes of which are too complicated to be readily understood.

Ibid.

The Bible is literature, not dogma.

Ibid.

American life is a powerful solvent. It seems to neutralise every intellectual element, however tough and alien it may be, and to fuse it in the native good-will, complacency, thoughtlessness, and optimism.

Character and Opinion in the
United States [1920]

All his life he [the American] jumps into the train after it has started and jumps out before it has stopped; and he never once gets left behind, or breaks a leg.

Ibid.

He carries his English weather in his heart wherever he goes, and it becomes a cool spot in the desert, and a steady and sane oracle amongst all the delirium of mankind.

Soliloquies in England [1922].
The British Character

England is the paradise of individuality, eccentricity, heresy, anomalies, hobbies, and humours.

Ibid.

The world is a perpetual caricature of itself; at every moment it is the mockery and the contradiction of what it is pretending to be.

Ibid. Dickens

There is no cure for birth and death save to enjoy the interval.

Soliloquies in England. War Shrines

I like to walk about amidst the beautiful things that adorn the world; but private wealth I should decline, or any sort of personal possessions, because they would take away my liberty.

Ibid. The Irony of Liberalism

My atheism, like that of Spinoza, is true piety towards the universe and denies only gods fashioned by men in their own image, to be servants of their human interests.

Ibid. On My Friendly Critics

The young man who has not wept is a savage, and the old man who will not laugh is a fool.

Dialogues in Limbo [1925]. III

There is nothing impossible in the existence of the supernatural: its existence seems to me decidedly probable.

The Genteel Tradition at Bay
[1931]

ERNEST LAWRENCE THAYER
[1863–1940]

The outlook wasn't brilliant for the Mudville nine that day.

Casey at the Bat.[1] *Stanza 1*

There was ease in Casey's manner as he stepped into his place,
There was pride in Casey's bearing, and a smile on Casey's face,
And when, responding to the cheers, he lightly doffed his hat,
No stranger in the crowd could doubt 'twas Casey at the bat.

Ibid. Stanza 6

"Strike one," the umpire said.

Ibid. Stanza 8

---

[1] First printed in *The San Francisco Examiner,* June 3, 1888.

> Yet I'd take my chance with fame,
> Calmly let it go at that,
> With the right to sign my name
> Under "Casey at the Bat."

GRANTLAND RICE [1880–1954]: *The Masterpiece*

From the benches black with people
    there went up a muffled roar,
Like the beating of the storm-waves on
    a stern and distant shore.
        Casey at the Bat. Stanza 9
With a smile of Christian charity great
    Casey's visage shone;
He stilled the rising tumult; he bade
    the game go on.
        Ibid. Stanza 10
Oh! somewhere in this favored land the
    sun is shining bright;
The band is playing somewhere, and
    somewhere hearts are light;
And somewhere men are laughing and
    somewhere children shout,
But there is no joy in Mudville —
    mighty Casey has struck out.
        Ibid. Stanza 13

HARRY BRAISTED
[*Floruit* 1896]

You're Not the Only Pebble on the
Beach.

        Title of song [1896]

JOSEPH HAYDEN
[*Floruit* 1896]

There'll be a hot time in the old town
tonight.
    A Hot Time in the Old Town [1]
        [1896]

OSCAR W. FIRKINS
[1864–1932]

I should have enjoyed the country
[Switzerland] more thoroughly if the
poets and romancers had not corrupted
my mind with their pestiferous superlatives.

        Letter [August 3, 1913] [2]

[1] Theodore August Metz [1848–1936]
composed a march, *A Hot Time in the Old
Town Tonight,* in 1886 for the McIntyre
and Heath minstrel show. In 1896 Joseph
Hayden wrote words for the music, and the
song was published. It became the favorite
rallying song of Theodore Roosevelt's Rough
Riders in Cuba, and later was Roosevelt's
campaign song.
[2] These quotations are from *Memoirs and
Letters of O. W. Firkins,* 1934.

My state is contentment *within* despair.
        Letter [December 29, 1922]
The great art includes much that the
small art excludes: humor, pain, and
evil. Much that is repulsive when alone
becomes beautiful in its relation. To
find the ennobling relation is the task
of life and of art.
        Lecture Notes
A classic is produced by the cooperation of the public with the author. A
classic is a work which is fit to enter
into permanent relations with a large
section of mankind.[1]
        Ibid.

RICHARD HOVEY
[1864–1900]

Whose furthest footstep never strayed
Beyond the village of his birth
Is but a lodger for the night
In this old wayside inn of earth.
    More Songs from Vagabondia
        [1896]. Envoy, Stanza 1
For it's always fair weather
When good fellows get together
With a stein on the table and a good
    song ringing clear.
    A Stein Song [1898]. Stanza 1
I do not know beneath what sky
    Nor on what seas shall be thy fate:
I only know it shall be high,
    I only know it shall be great.
        Unmanifest Destiny [1898].
        Stanza 7
There are worser ills to face
    Than foeman in the fray;
And many a man has fought because —
    He feared to run away.
    The Marriage of Guenevere.
        Act IV, Sc. 3
I have need of the sky,
I have business with the grass.
        I Have Need of the Sky
Eleazar Wheelock was a very pious
    man;
He went into the wilderness to teach
    the Indian,

[1] See Mark Twain, page 679a.

With a *Gradus ad Parnassum,* a Bible,
and a drum,
And five hundred gallons of New England rum. . . .
Eleazar was the faculty, and the whole
curriculum
Was five hundred gallons of New England rum.
Dartmouth College song

MARK ANTONY DE WOLFE HOWE
[1864–1960]

The village sleeps, a name unknown, till
men
With life-blood stain its soil, and pay
the due
That lifts it to eternal fame, — for then
'Tis grown a Gettysburg or Waterloo.
Distinction

Not for the star-crowned heroes, the
men that conquer and slay,
But a song for those that bore them, the
mothers braver than they!
With never a blare of trumpets, with
never a surge of cheers,
They march to the unseen hazard —
pale, patient volunteers.
The Valiant

Now, thieving Time, take what you
must —
Quickness to hear, to move, to see;
When dust is drawing near to dust
Such diminutions needs must be.
Yet leave, O leave exempt from plunder
My curiosity, my wonder!
*Thieving Time (Aged eighty-
seven)*

ROBERT LOVEMAN
[1864–1923]

It is not raining rain to me,
It's raining daffodils;
In every dimpled drop I see
Wild flowers on the hills.
April Rain [1901]. Stanza 1

A health unto the happy!
A fig for him who frets! —
It is not raining rain to me,
It's raining violets.
Ibid. Stanza 4

PAUL ELMER MORE [1]
[1864–1937]

As our private memory is not a
merely passive retention of sensations,
so in literature the critical spirit is at
work as a conscious energy of selection. The function of criticism is far
removed from the surrender to luxurious revery.
*Shelburne Essays [1904–1935].
Criticism*

Great music is a psychical storm,
agitating to fathomless depths the mystery of the past within us. Or we might
say that it is a prodigious incantation.
There are tones that call up all ghosts
of youth and joy and tenderness; —
there are tones that evoke all phantom
pains of perished passion; — there are
tones that revive all dead sensations of
majesty and might and glory, — all expired exultations, — all forgotten mag-
nanimities. Well may the influence of
music seem inexplicable to the man
who idly dreams that his life began
less than a hundred years ago! He who
has been initiated into the truth knows
that to every ripple of melody, to every billow of harmony, there answers
within him, out of the Sea of Death
and Birth, some eddying immeasurable
of ancient pleasure and pain.
Ibid. Lafcadio Hearn

ANDREW BARTON ("BANJO") PATERSON
[1864–1941]

Once a jolly swagman camped by a
billy-bong,
Under the shade of a kulibar tree,
And he sang as he sat and waited for
his billy-boil,

[1] To read him is to enter an austere and
elevated realm of ideas and to know a man
who, in the guise of a critic, is authentically
concerned with the first and last things of
human experience. — WALTER LIPPMANN, in
The Saturday Review of Literature, March
15, 1930

"You'll come a-waltzing, Matilda, with
me." [1]
> *Waltzing Matilda. Australian*
> *Soldiers' Marching Song*

STEPHEN PHILLIPS
[1864–1915]

Thy face remembered is from other
worlds,
It has been died for, though I know not
when,
It has been sung of, though I know not
where.
> *Marpessa*

The half of music, I have heard men
say,
Is to have grieved.
> *Ibid.*

Out of our sadness have we made this
world
So beautiful.
> *Ibid.*

The constable with lifted hand
Conducting the orchestral Strand.
> *The Wife*

JOSEPH BERT SMILEY
[1864–1903]

Thirty years with that tongue so sharp?
Ho! Angel Gabriel! Give him a Harp!
> *St. Peter at the Gate* (*Thirty*
> *Years with a Shrew*). *Stanza 13*

See that on finest ambrosia he feeds,
He's had about all the Hades he needs;
It isn't just hardly the thing to do
To roast him on earth and the future,
too.
> *Ibid. Stanza 14*

ISRAEL ZANGWILL
[1864–1926]

Scratch the Christian and you find
the pagan — spoiled.
> *Children of the Ghetto* [*1892*]

America is God's Crucible, the great
Melting-Pot where all the races of
Europe are melting and re-forming!
> *The Melting Pot* [*1908*]. *Act I*

[1] Swagman = highwayman; billy-bong =
brook; kulibar = gum tree; billy-boil = coffee.

In how many lives does Love really
play a dominant part? The average tax-
payer is no more capable of a "grand
passion" than of a grand opera.
> *Romeo and Juliet and Other*
> *Love Stories*

JOHN BENNETT
[1865–   ]

If Life's a lie, and Love's a cheat,
  As I have heard men say,
Then here's a health to fond deceit —
  God bless you, dear, today!
> *God Bless You, Dear, Today.*
> *Stanza 3*

A hundred years from now, dear heart,
  We shall not care at all.
It will not matter then a whit,
  The honey or the gall.
> *In a Rose Garden* [*1895*]. *Stanza 1*

We are all but fellow-travellers
  Along Life's weary way;
If any man can play the pipes,
  In God's name, let him play.
> *Year Book, Poetry Society of*
> *South Carolina* [*1921*]

MADISON JULIUS CAWEIN
[1865–1914]

Some reckon time by stars,
  And some by hours;
Some measure days by dreams,
  And some by flowers;
My heart alone records
  My days and hours.
> *Some Reckon Time by Stars.*
> *Stanza 1*

Here is the place where Loveliness
  keeps house,
Between the river and the wooded hills.
> *Here Is the Place*

An old Spanish saying is that "a kiss
without a moustache is like an egg
without salt."
> *Nature-Notes*

ROBERT WILLIAM
CHAMBERS
[1865–1933]

Sez Corporal Madden to Private Mc-
Fadden:

"Yer figger wants padd'n —
Sure, man, ye've no shape!
Behind ye yer shoulders
Stick out like two bowlders;
Yer shins are as thin
As a pair of pen-holders!"
The Recruit. Stanza 3

FRANK MOORE COLBY
[1865–1925]

True satire is not the sneering substance that we know, but satire that includes the satirist.
The Colby Essays [1926]. Vol. I

Men will confess to treason, murder, arson, false teeth, or a wig. How many of them will own up to a lack of humor?
Ibid.

Nobody can describe a fool to the life, without much patient self-inspection.
Ibid.

Every man ought to be inquisitive through every hour of his great adventure down to the day when he shall no longer cast a shadow in the sun. For if he dies without a question in his heart, what excuse is there for his continuance? [1]
Ibid.

In spite of the large population of this planet, men and women remain to-day the most inaccessible things on it.
Ibid. Vol. II

A new movement is not a stampede to some new object, but a stampede away from some old person.
Ibid.

The attempt to turn a complex problem of the head into a simple moral question for the heart to answer, is of course a necessary part of all political discussions.
Ibid.

I have found some of the best reasons I ever had for remaining at the bottom simply by looking at the men at the top.
Ibid.

[1] See M. A. De Wolfe Howe, page 809a.

A "new thinker," when studied closely, is merely a man who does not know what other people have thought.
The Margin of Hesitation

Were it not for the presence of the unwashed and the half-educated, the formless, queer and incomplete, the unreasonable and absurd, the infinite shapes of the delightful human tadpole, the horizon would not wear so wide a grin.
Imaginary Obligations

In public we say the race is to the strongest; in private we know that a lopsided man runs the fastest along the little side-hills of success.
Constrained Attitudes

Journalists have always been our most old-fashioned class, being too busy with the news of the day to lay aside the mental habits of fifty years before.
Ibid.

HOLMAN FRANCIS DAY
[1865–1935]

He pasted a sheet of postage stamps
    from snout clear down to tail,
Put on a quick delivery stamp, and
    sent the cod by mail.
Cure for Homesickness

The purest affection the heart can hold
Is the honest love of a nine-year-old.
That May-basket for Mabel Fry

If ye only knew the backaches in an
    old stun' wall!
An Old Stun' Wall

H. A. L. FISHER [1]
[1865–1940]

All political decisions are taken under great pressure, and if a treaty serves its turn for ten or twenty years, the

[1] Fisher was Warden of New College, Oxford, and one of the eminent historians of Trevelyan's era. He wrote a life of Napoleon and *The History of the Napoleonic Tradition*.

wisdom of its framers is sufficiently confirmed.[1]

Political Prophecies [*1918*]

It is easier for eight or nine elderly men to feel their way towards unanimity, if they are not compelled to conduct their converging manoeuvres under the microscopes and telescopes of the Press, but are permitted to shuffle about a little in slippers.

An International Experiment[2] [*1921*]

Purity of race does not exist. Europe is a continent of energetic mongrels.

A History of Europe [*1934*]. *Chap.* 1

Politics is the art of human happiness.

Ibid. Chap. 31

Taine pointed out that history was made by men, that men had bodies, that bodies were now healthy, now disordered, and that the state of the body inevitably affected the action of the mind. The study of the human body was part of the historian's duty. The accidents of health had more to do with the march of great events than was ordinarily suspected.

Paris at High Noon [*1941*]

KING GEORGE V
[1865–1936]

If I may be regarded as in some true sense the head of this great and widespread family, sharing its life and sustained by its affection, this will be a full reward for the long and sometimes anxious labours of my reign.

Radio greeting to the British Empire [*Christmas Day, 1934*]

FREDERIC WILLIAM GOUDY
[1865–1947]

I am the voice of today, the herald of tomorrow. . . . I coin for you the

---

[1] Thirty years is the life of most great treaties. — R. B. MOWAT: *A History of Great Britain* [1922]
[2] The League of Nations.

enchanting tale, the philosopher's moralizing, and the poet's visions. . . . I am the leaden army that conquers the world — I am TYPE.

The Type Speaks

"LAURENCE HOPE" (ADELA FLORENCE CORY NICOLSON) [1865–1904]

Less than the dust, beneath thy chariot wheel,
Less than the weed, that grows beside thy door,
Less than the rust, that never stained thy sword,
Less than the need thou hast in life of me,
Even less am I.

Less Than the Dust. Stanza 1

For this is Wisdom; to love, to live,
To take what Fate, or the Gods, may give.

The Teak Forest

To have, — to hold, — and, — in time, — let go!

Ibid.

Pale hands I loved beside the Shalimar,
Where are you now? Who lies beneath your spell?
Whom do you lead on Rapture's roadway, far,
Before you agonize them in farewell?

Kashmiri Song. Stanza 1

Yet I, this little while ere I go hence,
Love very lightly now, in self-defence.

Verse by Taj Mahomed

Men should be judged, not by their tint of skin,
The Gods they serve, the Vintage that they drink,
Nor by the way they fight, or love, or sin,
But by the quality of thought they think.

Men Should Be Judged

Often devotion to virtue arises from sated desire.

I Arise and Go Down to the River. Stanza 6

LAURENCE HOUSMAN
[1865–]

Minority is no disproof:
Wisdom is not so strong and fleet
As never to have known defeat.
Advocatus Diaboli

RUDYARD KIPLING
[1865–1936]

I have eaten your bread and salt.
I have drunk your water and wine.
The deaths ye died I have watched
beside
And the lives ye led were mine.
*Departmental Ditties [1886].
Prelude, Stanza 1*

Little Tin Gods on Wheels.
Public Waste. Stanza 4

Trust me, Today's Most Indispensables,
Five hundred men can take your place
or mine.
The Last Department. Stanza 8

The blush that flies at seventeen
Is fixed at forty-nine.
My Rival. Stanza 2

The toad beneath the harrow knows
Exactly where each tooth-point goes;
The butterfly upon the road
Preaches contentment to that toad.
Pagett, M. P.

Cross that rules the Southern Sky!
Stars that sweep, and turn, and fly,
Hear the Lovers' Litany: —
"Love like ours can never die!"
The Lovers' Litany. Stanza 2

And a woman is only a woman, but a
good cigar is a Smoke.
The Betrothed. Stanza 25

The temper of chums, the love of your
wife,[1] and a new piano's tune —
Which of the three will you trust at the
end of an Indian June?
Certain Maxims of Hafiz. IV

[1] It is as foolish to make experiments upon
the constancy of a friend, as upon the chastity
of a wife. — SAMUEL JOHNSON: *Letter to
James Boswell* [September 9, 1779]

You'll never plumb the Oriental mind,
And if you did, it isn't worth the toil.
One Viceroy Resigns

It takes a great deal of Christianity
to wipe out uncivilized Eastern instincts, such as falling in love at first
sight.
*Plain Tales from the Hills [1888].
Lispeth*

Ride with an idle whip, ride with an
unused heel,
But, once in a way, there will come a
day
When the colt must be taught to feel
The lash that falls, and the curb that
galls, and the sting of the rowelled steel.
*Ibid. The Conversion of
Aurelian McGoggin*

Never praise a sister to a sister, in
the hope of your compliments reaching
the proper ears.
Ibid. False Dawn

If you hit a pony over the nose at
the outset of your acquaintance, he may
not love you, but he will take a deep
interest in your movements ever afterwards.
Ibid.

Meddling with another man's folly is
always thankless work.
Ibid. The Rescue of Pluffles

Many religious people are deeply
suspicious. They seem — for purely religious purposes, of course — to know
more about iniquity than the Unregenerate.
Ibid. Watches of the Night

She was as immutable as the Hills.
But not quite so green.
Ibid. Venus Annodomini

Youth had been a habit of hers for
so long, that she could not part with it.
Ibid.

Every one is more or less mad on one
point.[1]
*Ibid. On the Strength of a
Likeness*

[1] Semel insanivimus omnes (We have all
once been mad).—JOHANNES BAPTISTA
MANTUANUS [1448–1516]: *Eclogues, No. 1*

After marriage arrives a reaction, sometimes a big, sometimes a little, one; but it comes sooner or later, and must be tided over by both parties if they desire the rest of their lives to go with the current.

Plain Tales from the Hills.
Three and — an Extra

This is worth remembering. Speaking to, or crying over, a husband never did any good yet.

Ibid.

A woman's guess is much more accurate than a man's certainty.

Ibid.

The silliest woman can manage a clever man; but it needs a very clever woman to manage a fool!

Ibid.

Lo, I have wrought in common clay
Rude figures of a rough-hewn race.

Soldiers Three [1888]. Dedication, Stanza 2

Oh, East is East, and West is West, and never the twain shall meet,
Till Earth and Sky stand presently at God's great Judgment Seat.
But there is neither East nor West, Border, nor Breed, nor Birth,
When two strong men stand face to face, though they come from the ends of the earth!

The Ballad of East and West [1889]

The first proof a man gives of his interest in a woman is by talking to her about his own sweet self. If the woman listens without yawning, he begins to like her. If she flatters the animal's vanity, he ends by adoring her.

Under the Deodars [1889].
The Education of Otis Yeere

More men are killed by overwork than the importance of the world justifies.

The Phantom 'Rickshaw [1889]

There aren't twelve hundred people in the world who understand pictures. The others pretend and don't care.

The Light That Failed [1890].
Chap. 7

Overloaded, undermanned, meant to founder, we
Euchred God Almighty's storm, bluffed the Eternal Sea!

The Ballad of the "Bolivar"
[1890]. Stanza 12

Man that is born of woman is small potatoes and few in a hill.

Life's Handicap [1891]. The
Head of the District

The end of the fight is a tombstone white with the name of the late deceased,
And the epitaph drear: "A Fool lies here who tried to hustle the East."

The Naulahka [1892]. Chap. 5

When Earth's last picture is painted, and the tubes are twisted and dried,
When the oldest colours have faded, and the youngest critic has died,
We shall rest, and, faith, we shall need it — lie down for an aeon or two,
Till the Master of All Good Workmen shall put us to work anew.

When Earth's Last Picture Is
Painted [1892]. Stanza 1

I am sick of endless sunshine, sick of blossom-burdened bough.
Give me back the leafless woodlands where the winds of Springtime range —
Give me back one day in England, for it's Spring in England now! [1]

In Springtime. Stanza 1

They rise to their feet as He passes by, gentlemen unafraid.

Barrack Room Ballads [1892].
Dedication, Stanza 5

The Liner she's a lady, and if a war should come,
The Man-o'-War's 'er 'usband, and 'e'd bid 'er stay at home;
But, oh, the little cargo-boats that fill with every tide!
'E'd 'ave to up an' fight for them for they are England's pride.

The Liner She's a Lady. Stanza 5

And what should they know of England who only England know?

The English Flag

[1] See Browning, page 568b.

There be triple ways to take, of the
  eagle or the snake,
Or the way of a man with a maid; [1]
But the sweetest way to me is a ship's
  upon the sea
In the heel of the North-East Trade.
      The Long Trail. Stanza 4

We have fed our sea for a thousand
  years
And she calls us, still unfed,
Though there's never a wave of all her
  waves
But marks our English dead.
      *A Song of the English [1893]. The
      Song of the Dead, II, Stanza 1*

If blood be the price of admiralty,
Lord God, we ha' paid in full!
                            Ibid.

Deeper than speech our love, stronger
  than life our tether,
But we do not fall on the neck or kiss
  when we come together.
      Ibid. England's Answer

Go to your work and be strong, halting
  not in your ways,
Baulking the end half-won for an instant dole of praise.
Stand to your work and be wise — certain of sword and pen,
Who are neither children nor Gods, but
  men in a world of men!
                            Ibid.

He wrapped himself in quotations [2]
— as a beggar would enfold himself in
the purple of Emperors.
      *Many Inventions [1893]. The
      Finest Story in the World*

Ever the wide world over, lass,
  Ever the trail held true,
Over the world and under the world,
  And back at the last to you.
      The Gipsy Trail. Stanza 2

The wild hawk to the wind-swept sky,
  The deer to the wholesome wold

[1] See *Proverbs, XXX, 19*, on page 1041b.
[2] In literature quotation is good only when
the writer whom I follow goes my way, and,
being better mounted than I, gives me a cast.
— EMERSON: *Quotation and Originality*
[1876]

And the heart of a man to the heart of
  a maid,
  As it was in the days of old.
      The Gipsy Trail. Stanza 11

They change their skies above them,
But not their hearts that roam.
      The Native-born. Stanza 2

There's a Legion that never was 'listed,
That carries no colours or crest.
      The Lost Legion. Stanza 1

To go and find out and be damned
(Dear boys!).
                            Ibid.

I can rip your very heartstrings out
  with those.
      *The Song of the Banjo [1894].
      Stanza 6*

"Something hidden. Go and find it. Go
  and look behind the Ranges —
Something lost behind the Ranges.
  Lost and waiting for you. Go!" [1]
      The Explorer. Stanza 2

Who hath desired the Sea? — the sight
  of salt water unbounded —
The heave and the halt and the hurl
  and the crash of the comber wind-
  hounded?
      The Sea and the Hills. Stanza 1

So and no otherwise — hillmen desire
  their Hills!
                            Ibid.

Absolute, unvarying rigidity, rigidity!
      The Ship that Found Herself

They copied all they could follow, but
  they couldn't copy my mind.
      The "Mary Gloster" [1894]

When Pack meets with Pack in the
  Jungle, and neither will go from
  the trail,
Lie down till the leaders have spoken
  — it may be fair words shall prevail.
      *The Second Jungle Book [1895].
      The Law of the Jungle, Stanza 6*

Now these are the Laws of the Jungle,
  and many and mighty are they;
But the head and the hoof of the Law

[1] "Because it is there." — *Said by* GEORGE
LEIGH MALLORY [1886–1924] *when asked
why he wanted to climb Mt. Everest*

and the haunch and the hump is
— Obey!
*The Second Jungle Book. The Law
of the Jungle, Refrain*
He who rebukes the world is rebuked
by the world.
Ibid. The Undertakers
He had been, as the old law recom-
mends, twenty years a youth, twenty
years a fighter, though he had never
carried a weapon in his life, and twenty
years head of a household.
Ibid. Miracle of Purun Bhagat
Cock the gun that is not loaded, cook
the frozen dynamite —
But oh, beware my Country, when my
Country grows polite!
Et Dona Ferentes [*1896*].
Stanza 11
Daughter am I in my mother's house;
But mistress in my own.
Our Lady of the Snows [1] [*1897*].
Stanza 1
God of our fathers, known of old,
Lord of our far-flung battle-line,
Beneath whose awful Hand we hold
Dominion over palm and pine —
Lord God of Hosts, be with us yet,
Lest we forget — lest we forget!
Recessional [*1897*]. *Stanza 1*
The tumult and the shouting dies;
The Captains and the Kings depart:
Still stands Thine ancient sacrifice,
An humble and a contrite heart.
Ibid. Stanza 2
Lo, all our pomp of yesterday
Is one with Nineveh and Tyre!
Ibid. Stanza 3
If, drunk with sight of power, we loose
Wild tongues that have not Thee in
awe,
Such boastings as the Gentiles use,
Or lesser breeds without the Law.
Ibid. Stanza 4
And he wrote for them wonderful verses
that swept the land like flame,
Till the fatted souls of the English were
scourged with the thing called
Shame.
*The Last of the Light Brigade.
Stanza 8*

[1] The Dominion of Canada.

God gives all men all earth to love,
But since man's heart is small,
Ordains for each one spot shall prove
Belovèd over all.
Sussex. Stanza 12
A fool there was and he made his prayer
(Even as you and I!)
To a rag and a bone and a hank of hair
(We called her the woman who did not
care)
But the fool he called her his lady
fair —
(Even as you and I!)
The Vampire [*1897*]. *Stanza 1*
Oh, the years we waste and the tears
we waste
And the work of our head and hand
Belong to the woman who did not
know . . .
And did not understand.
Ibid. Stanza 2
Make ye no truce with Adam-zad —
the Bear that walks like a Man! [1]
The Truce of the Bear. Stanza 2
The Goth and the shameless Hun!
The Rowers. Stanza 11
All we have of freedom, all we use or
know —
This our fathers bought for us long and
long ago.
The Old Issue. Stanza 5
Ancient Right unnoticed as the breath
we draw —
Leave to live by no man's leave, under-
neath the law.
Ibid. Stanza 6
Little Friend of All the World.
Kim [*1901*]. *Chap. 1*
We have had a jolly good lesson, and it
serves us jolly well right!
The Lesson [*1902*]. *Stanza 2*
We have forty million reasons for fail-
ure, but not a single excuse.
Ibid. Stanza 8
With the flannelled fools at the wicket
or the muddied oafs at the goals.
The Islanders [*1902*]
No doubt but ye are the People — ab-
solute, strong, and wise;
Whatever your heart has desired ye
have not withheld from your eyes.

[1] Russia.

On your own heads, in your own hands,
the sin and the saving lies!
The Islanders

Creation's cry goes up on high
From age to cheated age:
"Send us the men who do the work
For which they draw the wage!"
The Wage-Slaves. Stanza 3

This is our lot if we live so long and
labour unto the end —
That we outlive the impatient years
and the much too patient friend:
And because we know we have breath
in our mouth and think we have
thoughts in our head,
We shall assume that we are alive,
whereas we are really dead.
The Old Men. Stanza 1

Take up the White Man's burden.
*The White Man's Burden.
Stanza 1*

Your new-caught, sullen peoples,
Half-devil and half-child.
Ibid.

But, spite all modern notions, I've
found her first and best —
The only certain packet for the Islands
of the Blest.
The Three-Decker. Stanza 1

The Devil whispered behind the leaves,
"It's pretty, but is it Art?"
The Conundrum of the Workshops

Ah! what avails the classic bent
And what the cultured word,
Against the undoctored incident
That actually occurred?
The Benefactors. Stanza 1

It is not learning, grace nor gear,
Nor easy meat and drink,
But bitter pinch of pain and fear
That makes creation think.
Ibid. Stanza 3

There are nine and sixty ways of con-
structing tribal lays,
And–every–single–one–of–them–is–
right.
In the Neolithic Age. Stanza 5

You must hack through much deposit
Ere you know for sure who was it
Came to burial with such honour in the
Files

(Only seven seasons back beneath the
Files).
"Very great our loss and grievous —
So our best and brightest leave us,
And it ends the Age of Giants," say
the Files.
The Files

When your Imp of Blind Desire
Bids you set the Thames afire,
You'll remember men have done so —
in the Files.
Ibid.

And the naked soul of Tomlinson grew
white as a rain-washed bone.
Tomlinson

The sin they do by two and two they
must pay for one by one.
Ibid.

Those who have passed to the further
shore
May be hailed — at a price — on the
road to En-dor.[1]
En-Dor. Stanza 2

The female of the species is more
deadly than the male.
*The Female of the Species.
Stanza 1*

"Confound Romance!" . . . And all
unseen
Romance brought up the nine-fifteen.
The King

My son was killed while laughing at
some jest. I would I knew
What it was, and it might serve me in
a time when jests are few.
Epitaphs of the War. A Son

"What are the bugles blowin' for?" said
Files-on-Parade.
To turn you out, to turn you out," the
Colour-Sergeant said.
Danny Deever. Stanza 1

They've taken of his buttons off an' cut
his stripes away,
An' they're hangin' Danny Deever in
the mornin'.
Ibid.

We aren't no thin red 'eroes.[2]
Tommy. Stanza 4

[1] Behold there is a woman that hath
a familiar spirit at En-dor. — *1 Samuel,
XXVIII, 7*
[2] See Sir W. H. Russell, page 613a.

Single men in barricks don't grow into plaster saints.
Tommy. Stanza 4

It's Tommy this, an' Tommy that, an' "Chuck 'im out, the brute!"
But it's "Saviour of 'is country," when the guns begin to shoot.
Ibid. Stanza 5

So 'ere's *to* you, Fuzzy-Wuzzy, at your 'ome in the Soudan;
You're a pore benighted 'eathen but a first-class fightin' man.
"Fuzzy-Wuzzy." Stanza 1

'E's all 'ot sand an' ginger when alive,
An' 'e's generally shammin' when 'e's dead.
Ibid. Stanza 4

The uniform 'e wore
Was nothin' much before,
An' rather less than 'arf o' that be'ind.
Gunga Din. Stanza 2

An' for all 'is dirty 'ide
'E was white, clear white, inside
When 'e went to tend the wounded under fire!
Ibid. Stanza 3

Though I've belted you an' flayed you,
By the livin' Gawd that made you,
You're a better man than I am, Gunga Din!
Ibid. Stanza 5

'Ave you 'eard o' the Widow at Windsor
With a hairy gold crown on 'er 'ead?
The Widow at Windsor. Stanza 1

Walk wide o' the Widow at Windsor,
For 'alf o' Creation she owns:
We 'ave bought 'er the same with the sword an' the flame,
An' we've salted it down with our bones!
Ibid. Stanza 2

By the old Moulmein Pagoda, lookin' lazy at the sea,
There's a Burma girl a-settin', and I know she thinks o' me;
For the wind is in the palm-trees, and the temple-bells they say:
"Come you back, you British soldier; come you back to Mandalay!"
Come you back to Mandalay,
Where the old Flotilla lay;

Can't you 'ear their paddles chunkin' from Rangoon to Mandalay?
On the road to Mandalay,
Where the flyin'-fishes play,
An' the dawn comes up like thunder outer China 'crost the Bay!
Mandalay. Stanza 1

I've a neater, sweeter maiden in a cleaner, greener land.
Ibid. Stanza 5

Ship me somewheres east of Suez, where the best is like the worst,
Where there aren't no Ten Commandments an' a man can raise a thirst.
Ibid. Stanza 6

Back to the Army again, sergeant,
Back to the Army again.
Out o' the cold an' the rain.
"Back to the Army Again."
Refrain

For there isn't a job on the top of the earth the beggar don't know, nor do.
"Soldier an' Sailor Too." Stanza 2

'E's a sort of a bloomin' cosmopolouse — soldier an' sailor too.
Ibid.

To stand an' be still to the *Birken'ead* drill [1] is a damn' tough bullet to chew.
Ibid. Stanza 5

I've taken my fun where I've found it.
The Ladies. Stanza 1

An' I learned about women from 'er.
Ibid. Refrain

For the Colonel's Lady an' Judy O'Grady
Are sisters under their skins!
Ibid. Stanza 8

We met upon the level an' we parted on the Square,
An' I was Junior Deacon in my Mother-Lodge out there.
The Mother-Lodge. Refrain

To the legion of the lost ones, to the cohort of the damned.
Gentlemen-Rankers. Stanza 1

We're poor little lambs who've lost our way,
Baa! Baa! Baa!

See Anonymous, page 1003b.

We're little black sheep who've gone
   astray,
  Baa-aa-aa!
Gentlemen-rankers out on the spree,
Damned from here to Eternity,
God ha' mercy on such as we,
  Baa! Yah! Baa!
     Gentlemen-Rankers. Refrain

We have done with Hope and Honour,
  we are lost to Love and Truth,
We are dropping down the ladder rung
  by rung;
And the measure of our torment is the
  measure of our youth.
God help us, for we knew the worst too
  young!
     Ibid. Stanza 4

The backbone of the Army is the Non-
  commissioned Man!
    The 'Eathen. Stanza 18

For to admire an' for to see,
For to be'old this world so wide —
It never done no good to me
But I can't drop it if I tried!
    "For to Admire." Refrain

He's an absent-minded beggar, but he
  heard his country's call,
And his reg'ment didn't need to send
  to find him!
    The Absent-minded Beggar.
        Stanza 3

Boots — boots — boots — boots —
  movin' up and down again!
There's no discharge in the war! [1]
    Boots. Stanza 1

The bachelor may risk 'is 'ide
  To 'elp you when you're downed;
But the married man will wait beside
  Till the ambulance comes round.
    The Married Man. Stanza 5

The married man must sink or swim
An' — 'e can't afford to sink!
    Ibid. Stanza 7

If England was what England seems,
An' not the England of our dreams,
But only putty, brass, an' paint,
'Ow quick we'd drop 'er! But she ain't.
    The Return. Refrain

[1] There is no discharge in that war. — *Ecclesiastes, VIII, 8*

One man in a thousand, Solomon says,
Will stick more close than a brother.[1]
    The Thousandth Man. Stanza 1
But the Thousandth Man will stand by
  your side
To the gallows-foot — and after!
    Ibid. Stanza 4
Down to Gehenna or up to the Throne,
He travels the fastest who travels
  alone.[2]
    The Winners. Stanza 1
When the body that lived at your single
  will,
With its whimper of welcome, is stilled
  (how still!)
When the spirit that answered your
  every mood
Is gone — wherever it goes — for good,
You will discover how much you care,
And will give your heart to a dog to
  tear.
    The Power of the Dog. Stanza 4
The arrows of our anguish
Fly farther than we guess.
    The Rabbi's Song. Stanza 3
I keep six honest serving-men
  (They taught me all I knew);
Their names are What and Why and
  When
And How and Where and Who.
    Just-So Stories [1902]. *The
    Elephant's Child*
The great grey-green, greasy Lim-
popo River, all set about with fever-
trees.
    Ibid.
Yes, weekly from Southampton,
Great steamers, white and gold,
Go rolling down to Rio
(Roll down — roll down to Rio!).
And I'd like to roll to Rio
Some day before I'm old!
    *Ibid. The Beginning of the
    Armadilloes, Stanza 4*
When the ship goes *wop* (with a wiggle
  between)
And the steward falls into the soup-
  tureen . . .

[1] See *Ecclesiastes, VII, 28*, on page 1043a.
[2] He may well win the race that runs by
himself. — BENJAMIN FRANKLIN: *Poor Richard's Almanac* [1757]

Why, then you will know (if you
  haven't guessed)
You're "Fifty North and Forty West!"
  Just-So Stories. How the Whale
  Got His Throat

The Camel's hump is an ugly lump
Which well you may see at the Zoo;
But uglier yet is the Hump we get
From having too little to do.
  Ibid. How the Camel Got
  His Hump

We get the Hump —
Cameelious Hump —
The Hump that is black and blue!
  Ibid.

The cure for this ill is not to sit still,
Or frowst with a book by the fire;
But to take a large hoe and a shovel
  also,
And dig till you gently perspire.
  Ibid.

  The Cat. He walked by himself, and
all places were alike to him.
  Ibid. The Cat That Walked
  By Himself

He went through the Wet Wild
Woods, waving his wild tail, and walking by his wild lone. But he never told
anybody.
  Ibid.

We must go back with Policeman
  Day —
Back from the City of Sleep!
  The City of Sleep. Stanza 1

If I were damned of body and soul,
I know whose prayers would make me
  whole,
Mother o' mine, O mother o' mine.
  Mother o' Mine

'Tisn't beauty, so to speak, nor good
talk necessarily. It's just It. Some
women'll stay in a man's memory if
they once walked down a street.
  Traffics and Discoveries [1904].
  Mrs. Bathurst

Anything green that grew out of the
  mould
Was an excellent herb to our fathers of
  Old.
  "Our Fathers of Old." Stanza 1

Wonderful little our fathers knew,
Half their remedies cured you dead —
Most of their teaching was quite un-
  true.
  "Our Fathers of Old." Stanza 3

Of all the trees that grow so fair,
  Old England to adorn,
Greater are none beneath the Sun,
  Than Oak, and Ash, and Thorn.[1]
  Puck of Pook's Hill [1906].
  A Tree Song, Stanza 1

Land of our Birth, we pledge to thee
Our love and toil in the years to be.
  Ibid. The Children's Song, Stanza 1

Teach us Delight in simple things,
And Mirth that has no bitter springs.
  Ibid. Stanza 7

Take of English earth as much
As either hand may rightly clutch.
In the taking of it breathe
Prayer for all who lie beneath.
  Rewards and Fairies [1910].
  A Charm, Stanza 1

If you can meet with Triumph and
  Disaster
And treat those two impostors just the
  same.
  Ibid. If, Stanza 2

If you can talk with crowds and keep
  your virtue,
Or walk with Kings — nor lose the
  common touch.
  Ibid. Stanza 4

Yours is the Earth and everything
  that's in it,
And — which is more — you'll be a
  Man, my son!
  Ibid.

And thrones on Shrieking Circumstance
The Sacredly Absurd.
  The Necessitarian. Stanza 3

If once you have paid him the Dane-
  geld
You never get rid of the Dane.
  Danegeld. Stanza 4

Say "we," "us" and "ours" when you're
  talking instead of "you fellows"
  and "I."
  Norman and Saxon. Stanza 6

[1] See *Glasgerion*, page 1012a.

At Runnymede, at Runnymede,
What say the reeds at Runnymede?
The Reeds of Runnymede.
Stanza 1
When Crew and Captain understand
each other to the core,
It takes a gale and more than a gale to
put their ship ashore.
Together. Stanza 2
The snow lies thick on Valley Forge,
The ice on the Delaware,
But the poor dead soldiers of King
George
They neither know nor care.
The American Rebellion. II,
After, Stanza 1
When 'Omer smote 'is bloomin' lyre,
He'd 'eard men sing by land an' sea;
An' what he thought 'e might require,
'E went an' took — the same as me!
When 'Omer Smote 'is Bloomin'
Lyre. Stanza 1
Our England is a garden, and such gar-
dens are not made
By singing: — "Oh, how beautiful!"
and sitting in the shade.
The Glory of the Garden.
Stanza 5
As I pass through my incarnations in
every age and race,
I make my proper prostrations to the
gods of the Market Place;
Peering through reverent fingers, I
watch them flourish and fall,
And the Gods of the Copybook Max-
ims, I notice, outlast them all.
The Gods of the Copybook
Maxims. Stanza 1
For all we take we must pay, but the
price is cruel high.
The Courting of Dinah Shadd.
Chap. 1
Never show a woman that ye care
the snap av a finger for her, an' begad
she'll come bleatin' to your boot heels.
Ibid. Chap. 2
As the day wears and the impetus of
the morning dies away, there will come
upon you an overwhelming sense of the
uselessness of your toil. This must be
striven against.
The Judgment of Dungara

Hot and bothered.
Independence [1]
If you have not your own rations you
must feed out of your Tribe's hands —
with all that that implies.
Ibid.
A man may be festooned with the
whole haberdashery of success, and go
to his grave a castaway.
Ibid.
Enough work to do, and strength
enough to do the work.
A Doctor's Work [2]
That packet of assorted miseries
which we call a Ship.
The First Sailor
Never again will I spend another
winter in this accursed bucket-shop of
a refrigerator called England.
Letter to Sidney Colvin [3]
For all we have and are,
For all our children's fate,
Stand up and take the war.
The Hun is at the gate!
"For All We Have and Are"
[1914]. Stanza 1
There is but one task for all —
One life for each to give.
What stands if Freedom fall?
Who dies if England live?
Ibid. Stanza 4
He became an officer *and* a gentle-
man, which is an enviable thing.
Only a Subaltern
Tea fights. [4]
Ibid.
An imperfectly denatured animal in-
termittently subject to the unpredicta-
ble reactions of an unlocated spiritual
area.
Surgeons and the Soul [1923]
(Definition of man)
I taught Turkey all he ever knew of
French, and he tried to make Stalky

[1] Rectorial Address, St. Andrew's, October
10, 1923.
[2] Address, October, 1908, at Middlesex Hospital (where Kipling died in 1936).
[3] Quoted by E. V. Lucas: *The Colvins and
Their Friends* [1928], *P. 294.*
[4] Giggle, gabble, gobble, git. — OLIVER
WENDELL HOLMES [1809–1894], *description
of a tea party*

and me comprehend a little Latin. There is much to be said for this system, if you want a boy to learn anything, because he will remember what he gets from an equal where his master's words are forgotten.

> *Something of Myself for My Friends Known and Unknown* [*1937*]. *Chap. 2.*

When your Daemon is in charge, do not try to think consciously. Drift, wait, and obey.

> *Ibid. Chap. 8*

If I have given you delight
By aught that I have done,
Let me lie quiet in that night
Which shall be yours anon.

> *The Appeal.*[1] *Stanza 1*

ERICH FRIEDRICH WILHELM LUDENDORFF
[1865–1937]

I decline Christianity because it is Jewish, because it is international and because, in cowardly fashion, it preaches Peace on Earth.

> *Deutsche Gottesglaube*

MORGAN SHEPARD ("JOHN MARTIN")
[1865–1947]

Perhaps I ain't relijus,
But when I say a prayer,
I sort er feel inside er me
That God is always there.

> *Relijus. Stanza 1*

LOGAN PEARSALL SMITH [2]
[1865–1946]

What a bore it is, waking up in the morning always the same person. I wish

[1] Final poem in the Definitive Edition of *Rudyard Kipling's Verse* [1940].

[2] Two weeks before his death, a friend asked him half jokingly if he had discovered any meaning in life. "Yes," he replied, "there is a meaning; at least, for me, there is one thing that matters — to set a chime of words tinkling in the minds of a few fastidious people." — CYRIL CONNOLLY [1903–   ]: *A Tribute to Logan Pearsall Smith*, in *The New Statesman and Nation*

I were unflinching and emphatic, and had big, bushy eyebrows and a Message for the Age. I wish I were a deep Thinker, or a great Ventriloquist.

> *Trivia* [*1902*]. *Green Ivory*

But when in modern books, reviews, and thoughtful magazines I read about the Needs of the Age, its Complex Questions, its Dismays, Doubts, and Spiritual Agonies, I feel an impulse to go out and comfort that bewildered Epoch, to wipe away its tears, still its cries, and speak edifying words of Consolation to it.

> *Ibid. My Mission*

The minds of all of us are haunted by thoughts which have not yet found expression, and it is often the happy fortune of the aphorist to drag from its obscurity some such dim intuition, or confused bit of experience; to clothe it in words and bring it into daylight for our delighted recognition.

> *A Treasury of English Aphorisms* [*1928*]. *Introduction*

There are two things to aim at in life: first, to get what you want; and, after that, to enjoy it. Only the wisest of mankind achieve the second.

> *Afterthoughts* [*1931*]

Happiness is a wine of the rarest vintage, and seems insipid to a vulgar taste.

> *Ibid.*

How awful to reflect that what people say of us is true!

> *Ibid.*

Solvency is entirely a matter of temperament and not of income.

> *Ibid.*

That we should practise what we preach is generally admitted; but anyone who preaches what he and his hearers practise must incur the gravest moral disapprobation.

> *Ibid.*

It is almost always worth while to be cheated; people's little frauds have an interest which more than repays what they cost us.

> *Ibid.*

Why are happy people not afraid of Death, while the insatiable and the unhappy so abhor that grim feature?
Afterthoughts

When they come downstairs from their Ivory Towers, Idealists are apt to walk straight into the gutter.
Ibid.

The indefatigable pursuit of an unattainable Perfection, even though it consist in nothing more than in the pounding of an old piano, is what alone gives a meaning to our life on this unavailing star.
Ibid.

Eat with the Rich, but go to the play with the Poor, who are capable of Joy.
Ibid.

We need new friends; some of us are cannibals who have eaten their old friends up: others must have ever-renewed audiences before whom to re-enact an ideal version of their lives.
Ibid.

A best-seller is the gilded tomb of a mediocre talent.
Ibid.

What I like in a good author is not what he says, but what he whispers.
Ibid.

People say that life is the thing, but I prefer reading.
Ibid.

Most of all I envy the octogenarian poet [1] who joined three words —
"Go, lovely Rose" —
so happily together, that he left his name to float down through Time on the wings of a phrase and a flower.
Ibid.

Thank heavens, the sun has gone in, and I don't have to go out and enjoy it.
Ibid.

What with its crude awakenings can youth know of the rich returns of awareness to elderly people from their afternoon naps; of their ironic thoughts and long retrospections, and the sweetness they taste of not being dead?
Ibid.

[1] Edmund Waller [1606–1687]. See page 242a.

How I should like to distil my disesteem of my contemporaries into prose so perfect that all of them would have to read it!
Afterthoughts

ARTHUR SYMONS
[1865–1945]

And I would have, now love is over,
An end to all, an end:
I cannot, having been your lover,
Stoop to become your friend!
After Love. Stanza 3

Life is a dream in the night, a fear among fears,
A naked runner lost in a storm of spears.
In the Wood of Finvara. Stanza 1

I broider the world upon a loom,
I broider with dreams my tapestry;
Here in a little lonely room
I am master of earth and sea,
And the planets come to me.
The Loom of Dreams. Stanza 1

He knew that the whole mystery of beauty can never be comprehended by the crowd, and that while clearness is a virtue of style, perfect explicitness is not a necessary virtue.
The Symbolist Movement in Literature [1899]. Gérard de Nerval

Without charm there can be no fine literature, as there can be no perfect flower without fragrance.
Ibid. Stéphane Mallarmé

The mystic too full of God to speak intelligibly to the world.
Ibid. Arthur Rimbaud

Many excellent writers, very many painters, and most musicians are so tedious on any subject but their own.
Ibid.

Criticism is properly the rod of divination: a hazel-switch for the discovery of buried treasure, not a birch-twig for the castigation of offenders.
An Introduction to the Study of Browning [1906]. Preface

The great things in poetry are song at the core, but externally mere speech.
Dramatis Personae [*1923*].
Sir William Watson

HERBERT TRENCH
[1865–1923]

A circumnavigator of the soul.
Shakespeare. Stanza 4

WILLIAM BUTLER YEATS
[1865–1939]

Down by the salley gardens my love
and I did meet;
She passed the salley gardens with little
snow-white feet.
She bid me take love easy, as the leaves
grow on the tree;
But I, being young and foolish, with
her would not agree.
Down by the Salley Gardens [*1889*]
She bid me take life easy, as the grass
grows on the weirs;
But I was young and foolish, and now
am full of tears.
Ibid.
The years like great black oxen tread
the world
And God, the herdsman, goads them on
behind.
The Countess Cathleen [*1892*]
Red Rose, proud Rose, sad Rose of all
my days!
Come near me, while I sing the ancient
ways.
To the Rose Upon the Rood of
Time [*1893*]. *Stanza 1*
I find under the boughs of love and
hate,
In all poor foolish things that live a day,
Eternal beauty wandering on her way.
Ibid.
When you are old and grey and full of
sleep,
And nodding by the fire, take down this
book.[1]
When You Are Old [*1893*]
How many loved your moments of glad
grace,

[1] See Ronsard, page 96b.

And loved your beauty, with love false
or true,
But one man loved the pilgrim soul in
you,
And loved the sorrows of your chang-
ing face.
When You Are Old
I will arise and go now, and go to In-
nisfree,
And a small cabin build there, of clay
and wattles made:
Nine bean-rows will I have there, a hive
for the honeybee,
And live alone in the bee-loud glade.
The Lake Isle of Innisfree [1] [*1893*].
Stanza 1
And I shall have some peace there, for
peace comes dropping slow,
Dropping from the veils of the morning
to where the cricket sings;
There midnight's all a glimmer, and
noon a purple glow,
And evening full of the linnet's wings.
Ibid. Stanza 2
I hear it in the deep heart's core.
Ibid. Stanza 3
A pity beyond all telling
Is hid in the heart of love.
The Pity of Love [*1893*]
The brawling of a sparrow in the eaves,
The brilliant moon and all the milky
sky,
And all that famous harmony of leaves,
Had blotted out man's image and his
cry.
A girl arose that had red mournful lips
And seemed the greatness of the world
in tears,
Doomed like Odysseus and the labour-
ing ships
And proud as Priam murdered with his
peers;

[1] I had still the ambition, formed in Sligo in my teens, of living in imitation of Thoreau on Innisfree, a little island in Lough Gill, and when walking through Fleet Street very homesick I heard a little tinkle of water and saw a fountain in a shop-window which balanced a little ball upon its jet, and began to remember lake water. From the sudden remembrance came my poem Innisfree. — *The Trembling of the Veil* (autobiography) [*1926*]
See Samuel Rogers, page 396b.

Arose, and on the instant clamorous eaves,
A climbing moon upon an empty sky,
And all that lamentation of the leaves,
Could but compose man's image and his cry.
　　　　The Sorrow of Love [*1893*]
The land of faery,
Where nobody gets old and godly and grave,
Where nobody gets old and crafty and wise,
Where nobody gets old and bitter of tongue.
　　The Land of Heart's Desire [*1894*]
When we are young
We long to tread a way none trod before,
But find the excellent old way through love
And through the care of children to the hour
For bidding Fate and Time and Change good-bye.
　　　　　　　　　　　　Ibid.
I would mould a world of fire and dew
With no one bitter, grave, or over wise,
And nothing marred or old to do you wrong.
　　　　　　　　　　　　Ibid.
　　Land of Heart's Desire,
Where beauty has no ebb, decay no flood,
But joy is wisdom, Time an endless song.
　　　　　　　　　　　　Ibid.
Though I am old with wandering
Through hollow lands and hilly lands,
I will find out where she has gone,
And kiss her lips and take her hands;
And walk among long dappled grass,
And pluck till time and times are done
The silver apples of the moon,
The golden apples of the sun.
　　The Song of Wandering Aengus
　　　　　　　[*1899*]. *Stanza 3*
All things uncomely and broken, all things worn out and old,
The cry of a child by the roadway, the creak of a lumbering cart,
The heavy steps of the ploughman, splashing the wintry mould,

Are wronging your image that blossoms a rose in the deeps of my heart.
　　*The Lover Tells of the Rose in
　　　　His Heart* [*1899*]. *Stanza 1*
The wrong of unshapely things is a wrong too great to be told.
　　　　　　　Ibid. Stanza 2
Had I the heavens' embroidered cloths,
Enwrought with gold and silver light.
　　*He Wishes for the Cloths of
　　　　　　　Heaven* [*1899*]
But I, being poor, have only my dreams;
I have spread my dreams under your feet;
Tread softly because you tread on my dreams.
　　　　　　　　　　　　Ibid.
When I play on my fiddle in Dooney,
Folk dance like a wave of the sea.
　　The Fiddler of Dooney [*1899*].
　　　　　　　　　　　Stanza 1
For the good are always the merry,
Save by an evil chance,
And the merry love the fiddle,
And the merry love to dance.
　　　　　　　Ibid. Stanza 4
O heart! O heart! if she'd but turn her head,
You'd know the folly of being comforted.
　　The Folly of Being Comforted
　　　　　　　　　　　[*1904*]
Never give all the heart, for love
Will hardly seem worth thinking of
To passionate women if it seem
Certain, and they never dream
That it fades out from kiss to kiss.
　　Never Give All the Heart [*1904*]
I heard the old, old men say,
"All that's beautiful drifts away
Like the waters."
　　*The Old Men Admiring Them-
　　　selves in the Water* [*1904*]
Why, what could she have done, being what she is?
Was there another Troy for her to burn?
　　　　No Second Troy [*1910*]
The fascination of what's difficult
Has dried the sap out of my veins, and rent

Spontaneous joy and natural content
Out of my heart.
            The Fascination of What's
                    Difficult [1910]
Wine comes in at the mouth
And love comes in at the eye;
That's all we shall know for truth
Before we grow old and die.
            A Drinking Song [1910]
Though leaves are many, the root is
    one;
Through all the lying days of my youth
I swayed my leaves and flowers in the
    sun;
Now I may wither into the truth.
    The Coming of Wisdom with Time
                    [1910]
Be secret and exult,
Because of all things known
That is most difficult.
        To a Friend Whose Work Has
            Come to Nothing [1914]
I made my song a coat
Covered with embroideries
Out of old mythologies
From heel to throat;
But the fools caught it,
Wore it in the world's eyes
As though they'd wrought it.
Song, let them take it,
For there's more enterprise
In walking naked.
                    A Coat [1914]
I know that I shall meet my fate
Somewhere among the clouds above;
Those that I fight I do not hate,
Those that I guard I do not love;
My country is Kiltartan Cross,
My countrymen Kiltartan's poor.
        An Irish Airman Foresees His
                    Death [1919]
Nor law, nor duty bade me fight,
Nor public men, nor cheering crowds,
A lonely impulse of delight
Drove to this tumult in the clouds;
I balanced all, brought all to mind,
The years to come seemed waste of
    breath,
A waste of breath the years behind
In balance with this life, this death.
                    Ibid.

All the wild witches, those most noble
    ladies,
For all their broom-sticks and their
    tears,
Their angry tears, are gone.
    Lines Written in Dejection [1919]
I mourn for that most lonely thing; and
    yet God's will be done:
I knew a phoenix in my youth, so let
    them have their day.
        His Phoenix [1919]. *Stanza 4*
We have lit upon the gentle, sensitive
    mind
And lost the old nonchalance of the
    hand;
Whether we have chosen chisel, pen or
    brush,
We are but critics, or but half create.
        Ego Dominus Tuus [1919]
All changed, changed utterly:
A terrible beauty is born.
            Easter 1916 [1921]
Nothing that we love over-much
Is ponderable to our touch.
        Towards Break of Day [1921].
                    Stanza 3
The blood-dimmed tide is loosed, and
    everywhere
The ceremony of innocence is drowned;
The best lack all conviction, while the
    worst
Are full of passionate intensity.
        The Second Coming [1921]
And what rough beast, its hour come
    round at last,
Slouches towards Bethlehem to be
    born?
                    Ibid.
    For such,
Being made beautiful overmuch,
Consider beauty a sufficient end,
Lose natural kindness and maybe
The heart-revealing intimacy
That chooses right, and never find a
    friend.
        A Prayer for My Daughter
                    [1921]. *Stanza 3*
If there's no hatred in a mind
Assault and battery of the wind
Can never tear the linnet from the leaf.
            Ibid. Stanza 7

An intellectual hatred is the worst,
So let her think opinions are accursed.
   A Prayer for My Daughter. Stanza 8

A musician who would give me pleasure should not repeat a line, or put more than one note to a syllable. I am a poet not a musician, and dislike to have my words distorted or their animation destroyed, even though the musician claims to have expressed their meaning in a different medium.
   A Note on the Setting of These Poems to Music [*1922*]

An aged man is but a paltry thing,
A tattered coat upon a stick, unless
Soul clap its hands and sing.
   Sailing to Byzantium [*1928*].
   Stanza 2

Consume my heart away; sick with desire
And fastened to a dying animal
It knows not what it is; and gather me
Into the artifice of eternity.
   Ibid. Stanza 3

Once out of nature I shall never take
My bodily form from any natural thing,
But such a form as Grecian goldsmiths make
Of hammered gold and gold enamelling
To keep a drowsy Emperor awake;
Or set upon a golden bough to sing
To lords and ladies of Byzantium
Of what is past, or passing, or to come.[1]
   Ibid. Stanza 4

Does the imagination dwell the most
Upon a woman won or a woman lost?
   The Tower [*1928*]. *II, Stanza 13*

Much did I rage when young,
Being by the world oppressed,
But now with flattering tongue
It speeds the parting guest.
   Youth and Age [*1928*]

Everything that man esteems
Endures a moment or a day.
Love's pleasure drives his love away,

---

[1] I have read somewhere that in the Emperor's palace at Byzantium was a tree made of gold and silver, and artificial birds that sang. — YEATS'S *Note*

The painter's brush consumes his dreams.
   Two Songs From a Play [*1928*].
   II, Stanza 2

But what is Whiggery?
A levelling, rancorous, rational sort of mind
That never looked out of the eye of a saint
Or out of a drunkard's eye.
   The Seven Sages [*1933*]

No man has ever lived that had enough
Of children's gratitude or woman's love.
   Vacillation [*1933*]. *Stanza 3*

What were all the world's alarms
To mighty Paris when he found
Sleep upon a golden bed
That first dawn in Helen's arms?
   Words for Music Perhaps [*1933*].
   Lullaby, Stanza 1

Speech after long silence; it is right,
All other lovers being estranged or dead,

.   .   .   .   .

That we descant and yet again descant
Upon the supreme theme of Art and Song:
Bodily decrepitude is wisdom; young
We loved each other and were ignorant.
   Ibid. After Long Silence

I carry the sun in a golden cup,
The moon in a silver bag.
   Ibid. Those Dancing Days Are Gone, Refrain

I gave what other women gave
That stepped out of their clothes,
But when this soul, its body off,
Naked to naked goes,
He it has found shall find therein
What none other knows.
   A Woman Young and Old [*1933*].
   A Last Confession, Stanza 3

He that sings a lasting song
Thinks in a marrow-bone.
   A Prayer for Old Age [*1935*].
   Stanza 1

I pray — for fashion's word is out
And prayer comes round again —
That I may seem, though I die old,
A foolish, passionate man.
   Ibid. Stanza 3

Irish poets, learn your trade,
Sing whatever is well made.
Last Poems [*1936-1939*].
Under Ben Bulben, V
On limestone quarried near the spot
By his command these words are cut:
Cast a cold eye
On life, on death.
Horseman, pass by! [1]
Ibid. VI

HARRY DACRE
[*Floruit* 1892]

Daisy, Daisy, give me your answer, do!
I'm half crazy, all for the love of you!
  It won't be a stylish marriage,
  I can't afford a carriage,
But you'll look sweet upon the seat
Of a bicycle built for two!
Daisy Bell [*1892*]

HENRY J. SAYERS
[? –1932]

Ta-ra-ra-boom-de-ay!
Title of minstrel show number
[*1891*], *made famous by Lottie*
Collins in 1892 [2]
A sweet Tuxedo girl you see,
Queen of swell society,
Fond of fun as fond can be
When it's on the strict Q. T.
I'm not too young, I'm not too old,
Not too timid, not too bold,
Just the kind you'd like to hold —
Just the kind for sport I'm told —
Ta-ra-ra-boom-de-ay.
Ibid. Stanza 1 of original version

GEORGE W. YOUNG
[*Floruit* 1900]

The word must be spoken that bids you
  depart —
Though the effort to speak it should
  shatter my heart —

Though in silence, with blighted affec-
  tion, I pine,
Yet the lips that touch liquor must
  never touch mine!
The Lips That Touch Liquor.
Stanza 5

GEORGE ADE [1]
[1866–1944]

A good folly is worth what you pay
for it.
Fables in Slang [*1899*]. *A Lot*
for Three Dollars
In uplifting, get underneath.
Ibid. The Good Fairy
He had been kicked in the Head by
a Mule when young and believed every-
thing he read in the Sunday Papers.
Ibid. The Slim Girl
Only the more rugged mortals should
attempt to keep up with current liter-
ature.
Ibid. Didn't Care for Story-books
Never put off until Tomorrow what
should have been Done early in the
Seventies.
Forty Modern Fables [*1901*].
The Third and Last Call
To insure Peace of Mind ignore the
Rules and Regulations.
Ibid. The Crustacean
If it were not for the Presents, an
Elopement would be Preferable.
Ibid. The General Manager of
the Love Affair
Stay with the Procession or you will
Never Catch up.
Ibid. The Old-Time Pedagogue
The Time to enjoy a European trip
is about Three Weeks after Unpacking.
Ibid. The Hungry Man
Draw your Salary before Spending it.
Ibid. The People's Choice

---

[1] These lines are now inscribed on Yeats's
grave.
[2] Douglas Gilbert, in *Lost Chords* [1942],
quotes the *New York Herald:* "London has
gone stark mad over the refrain" [February
28, 1892].

[1] Somehow I always like to think
Of *Georgeade* as a Summer Drink,
Sparkling and cool, with just a Tang
Of Pleasant Effervescent Slang.
OLIVER HERFORD [1863–1935]:
Celebrities I Have Never Met

The Man was a Pinhead in a good many Respects, but he was Wise as a Serpent.
>*Forty Modern Fables. The Wise Piker*

For Parlor Use the Vague Generality is a Life-Saver.
>*Ibid.*

Last night at twelve I felt immense, But now I feel like thirty cents.
>*The Sultan of Sulu* [*1902*]. *Remorse*

But, R – e – m – o – r – s – e!
The water-wagon is the place for me;
It is no time for mirth and laughter,
The cold, gray dawn of the morning after! [1]
>*Ibid.*

MARTHA GILBERT DICKINSON BIANCHI [2]
[1866–1943]

Deeper than chords that search the soul and die,
Mocking to ashes color's hot array, —
Closer than touch, — within our hearts they lie —
The words we do not say.
>*The Words We Do Not Say*

HENRY BLOSSOM
[1866–1919]

I Want What I Want When I Want It.
>*Mlle. Modiste* [*1905*]. *Title of song*

GELETT BURGESS
[1866–1951]

I'd rather have Fingers than Toes,
I'd rather have Eyes than a Nose;
And as for my Hair
I'm glad it's all there,
I'll be awfully sad when it goes.
>*Nonsense Verses*

Leave the lady, Willy, let the racket rip,
She is going to fool you, you have lost your grip,

[1] See Byron, page 458a, and Dickens, page 577a.
[2] Niece of Emily Dickinson.

Your brain is in a muddle, and your heart is in a whirl,
Come along with me, Willy, never mind the girl!
>*Willy and the Lady. Stanza 1*

I never saw a Purple Cow,
I never hope to see one;
But I can tell you, anyhow,
I'd rather see than be one.
>*The Purple Cow* [*1895*]

Ah, yes, I wrote the "Purple Cow" —
I'm sorry, now, I wrote it!
But I can tell you, anyhow,
I'll kill you if you quote it.
>*Cinq Ans Après*

Not the quarry, but the chase,
Not the laurel, but the race,
Not the hazard, but the play,
Make me, Lord, enjoy alway.
>*A Prayer*

EDMUND VANCE COOKE
[1866–1932]

The Woman tempted me — and tempts me still!
Lord God, I pray You that she ever will!
>*Adam*

'Tis not the weight of jewel or plate,
Or the fondle of silk and fur;
'Tis the spirit in which the gift is rich,
As the gifts of the wise ones were;
And we are not told whose gift was gold
Or whose was the gift of myrrh.
>*The Spirit of the Gift*

Oh, a trouble's a ton, or a trouble's an ounce,
Or a trouble is what you make it,
And it isn't the fact that you're hurt that counts,
But only how did you take it.
>*How Did You Die? Stanza 1*

My pa held me up to the moo-cow-moo,
So clost I could almost touch,
En' I fed him a couple of times or two,
En' I wasn't a fraid-cat — much.
>*The Moo-Cow-Moo. Stanza 1*

PHILANDER JOHNSON
[1866–1939]

Sometimes the new friends
Leave the heart aglow,
But it's when they're like the men
We cherished long ago.
Old Friends. Stanza 2

Cheer up, the worst is yet to come.[1]
Shooting Stars

RICHARD LE GALLIENNE
[1866–1947]

There's too much beauty upon this
earth
For lonely men to bear.
*A Ballad of Too Much Beauty.
Stanza 1*

One asked of Regret,
And I made reply:
To have held the bird,
And let it fly.
Regret

Shadow and sun — so too our lives are
made —
Here learn how great the sun, how
small the shade!
For Sundials

May is building her house. With apple
blooms
She is roofing over the glimmering
rooms.
*May Is Building Her House.
Stanza 1*

Behind the times I know I am,
But what is a tired man to do?
I light my pipe, and read Charles Lamb.
*Ballade of the Noisiness of the
Times. Stanza 1*

Ah London! London! our delight,
Great flower that opens but at night.
A Ballad of London

Yet all the while my Lord I meet
In every London lane and street.
The Second Crucifixion

"Name your favorite writer" should
be one of the first questions in the Engagement Catechism.
*The Quest of the Golden Girl
[1896]. Book II, Chap. 6*

[1] See Tennyson, page 555b.

Wild oats will get sown some time,
and one of the arts of life is to sow them
at the right time.
*The Quest of the Golden Girl.
Book III, Chap. 9*

WALTER MALONE
[1866–1915]

They do me wrong who say I come no
more
When once I knock and fail to find you
in;
For every day I stand outside your
door,
And bid you wake, and rise to fight and
win.
Opportunity. Stanza 1

And if a lowly singer dries one tear,
Or soothes one humble human heart
in pain,
Be sure his homely verse to God is dear,
And not one stanza has been sung in
vain.
The Humbler Poets. Stanza 3

THOMAS L. MASSON
[1866–1934]

Obey That Impulse.
*Subscription slogan for "Life," of
which he was editor, 1893–1922*

A Safe and Sane Fourth.
Slogan

GEORGE BARR McCUTCHEON
[1866–1928]

"You brute!" hissed the Countess.
Graustark [1901]. Chap. 16

GILBERT MURRAY
[1866–1957]

Romantic plays with happy endings
are almost of necessity inferior in artistic value to true tragedies. Not, one
would hope, simply because they end
happily; happiness in itself is certainly
not less beautiful than grief; but because a tragedy in its great moments
can generally afford to be sincere, while

romantic plays live in an atmosphere of ingenuity and make-believe.
*Preface to the Iphigenia in
Tauris of Euripides*

The life and liberty and property and happiness of the common man throughout the world are at the absolute mercy of a few persons whom he has never seen, involved in complicated quarrels that he has never heard of.
*The League of Nations and the
Democratic Idea* [*1921*]

JOHN JEROME ROONEY
[1866–1934]

The steel decks rock with the lightning
    shock, and shake with the great
    recoil,
And the sea grows red with the blood
    of the dead and reaches for his
    spoil —
But not till the foe has gone below or
    turns his prow and runs,
Shall the voice of peace bring sweet
    release to the men behind the guns!
*The Men Behind the Guns.
Stanza 4*

LINCOLN STEFFENS
[1866–1936]

"So you've been over into Russia?" said Bernard Baruch, and I answered very literally, "I have been over into the future, and it works." [1]
Autobiography [*1931*]. *Chap. 18*

BERT LESTON TAYLOR
[1866–1921]

When quacks with pills political would
    dope us,
When politics absorbs the livelong day,
I like to think about the star Canopus,
So far, so far away!
Canopus. Stanza 1

These scoffers, these obstructionists,
    These fossils — who are they?

[1] On Steffens's return from the Bullitt mission, 1919.

The glad young, mad young futurists
    Who prance around today.
So Shall It Be. Stanza 6

Everywhere I look I see —
    Fact or fiction, life or play,
Still the little game of Three:
    B and C in love with A.
Old Stuff. Stanza 3

And when the fragrant day is done,
    Night — and a shoal of stars.
The Road to Anywhere. Stanza 5

HERBERT GEORGE WELLS
[1866–1946]

The past is but the beginning of a beginning, and all that is and has been is but the twilight of the dawn. . . . A day will come when beings who are now latent in our thoughts and hidden in our loins shall stand upon this earth as one stands upon a footstool, and shall laugh and reach out their hands amid the stars.
The Discovery of the Future
[*1901*]

Nothing could have been more obvious to the people of the early twentieth century than the rapidity with which war was becoming impossible. And as certainly they did not see it. They did not see it until the atomic bombs burst in their fumbling hands.
The World Set Free [*1914*]

The catastrophe of the atomic bombs which shook men out of cities and businesses and economic relations, shook them also out of their old-established habits of thought, and out of the lightly held beliefs and prejudices that came down to them from the past.
Ibid.

Human history becomes more and more a race between education and catastrophe.
The Outline of History [*1920*].
Chap. 15

The professional military mind is by necessity an inferior and unimaginative mind; no man of high intellectual quality would willingly imprison his gifts in such a calling.

> *The Outline of History. Chap. 40*

The Great War and the Petty Peace.

> *Ibid.*

Human history is in essence a history of ideas.

> *Ibid.*

Every one of these hundreds of millions of human beings is in some form seeking happiness. . . . Not one is altogether noble nor altogether trustworthy nor altogether consistent; and not one is altogether vile. Not a single one but has at some time wept.

> *Ibid.*

A federation of all humanity, together with a sufficient measure of social justice to ensure health, education, and a rough equality of opportunity, would mean such a release and increase of human energy as to open a new phase in human history.

> *Ibid. Chap. 41*

Our true nationality is mankind.

> *Ibid.*

An artist who theorizes about his work is no longer artist but critic.

> *The Temptation of Harringay*

While the poor little affairs of obscure, industrious men of letters are made the subject of intensive research, the far more romantic, thrilling and illuminating documents about the seekers and makers of great fortunes, are neither gathered nor cherished.

> *The Work, Wealth and Happiness of Mankind* [*1931*]. *Chap. 10*

In England we have come to rely upon a comfortable time-lag of fifty years or a century intervening between the perception that something ought to be done and a serious attempt to do it.

> *Ibid. Chap. 11*

The Shape of Things to Come.[1]

> *Title of Book* [*1933*]

The crazy combative patriotism that plainly threatens to destroy civilization

---

[1] The baby figure of the giant mass
Of things to come.
 SHAKESPEARE: *Troilus and Cressida*
 [1601–1603], *Act I, Sc. 3, L. 345*

is very largely begotten by the schoolmaster and the schoolmistress in their history lessons. They take the growing mind at a naturally barbaric phase and they inflame and fix its barbarism.

> *The Informative Content of Education* [*1937*]

STANLEY BALDWIN
[1867–1947]

When you think about the defence of England you no longer think of the chalk cliffs of Dover. You think of the Rhine. That is where our frontier lies today.

> *Speech in the House of Commons* [*July 30, 1934*]

ENOCH ARNOLD BENNETT
[1867–1931]

The Old Wives' Tale.[1]

> *Title of novel* [*1908*]

Being a husband is a whole-time job.

> *The Title* [*1918*]. *Act I*

Pessimism, when you get used to it, is just as agreeable as optimism.

> *Things That Have Interested Me* [*1918*]

The price of justice is eternal publicity.

> *Ibid. Second Series* [*1923*]

ROSCOE CONKLING ENSIGN BROWN
[1867–1946]

With equal care weigh well the record of the wisdom and the folly of mankind.

> *Inscription for the wall of the Central Library, Brooklyn*

Farther than the arrow, higher than wings, fly poet's song and prophet's word.

> *Inscription for a door of the Library*

---

[1] A fool he is to believe the tales of an old wife. — ALEXANDER BARCLAY: *The Ship of Fools* [1508]
 Old wives' foolish tales of Robin Hood. — NICHOLAS UDALL [1542]

WILLIAM CECIL DAMPIER-WHETHAM
[1867–1952]

Beyond the bright searchlights of science,
Out of sight of the windows of sense,
Old riddles still bid us defiance,
Old questions of Why and of Whence.
*The Recent Development of
Physical Science* [1904]

ERNEST DOWSON
[1867–1900]

They are not long, the weeping and the laughter,
Love and desire and hate:
I think they have no portion in us after
We pass the gate.
Vitae Summa Brevis [1896].
Stanza 1

I have been faithful to thee, Cynara! in my fashion.
*Non Sum Qualis Eram Bonae Sub
Regno Cynarae* [1] [1896]. *Refrain*

I have forgot much, Cynara! gone with the wind,
Flung roses, roses, riotously with the throng.
Ibid. Stanza 3

I cried for madder music and for stronger wine.
Ibid. Stanza 4

You would have understood me, had you waited;
I could have loved you, dear! as well as he:
Had we not been impatient, dear! and fated
Always to disagree.
*You Would Have Understood
Me* [1896]. *Stanza 1*

What is the use of speech? Silence were fitter:
Lest we should still be wishing things unsaid.
Ibid. Stanza 2

[1] I am not the man I was under the reign of the good Cynara. — HORACE [65–8 B. C.]
Book IV, Ode 1, Ad Venerem

From troublous sights and sounds set free;
In such a twilight hour of breath,
Shall one retrace his life, or see,
Through shadows, the true face of death?
Extreme Unction. Stanza 3

FINLEY PETER DUNNE
("MR. DOOLEY")
[1867–1936]

An Anglo-Saxon, Hinnissy, is a German that's forgot who was his parents.
. . . I'm wan iv th' hottest Anglo-Saxons that iver come out iv Anglo-Saxony.
*Mr. Dooley in Peace and in War
[1898]. On the Anglo-Saxon*

Life'd not be worth livin' if we didn't keep our inimies.
Ibid. On New Year's Resolutions

Whin th' case is all over, the jury'll pitch th' tistimony out iv the window, an' consider three questions: "Did Lootgert look as though he'd kill his wife? Did his wife look as though she ought to be kilt? Isn't it time we wint to supper?"
Ibid. On Expert Testimony

Th' dead ar-re always pop'lar. I knowed a society wanst to vote a monyment to a man an' refuse to help his fam'ly, all in wan night.
Ibid. On Charity

"Th' American nation in th' Sixth Ward is a fine people," he says. "They love th' eagle," he says, "on th' back iv a dollar."
Ibid. On Oratory in Politics

'Tis . . . "Hands acrost th' sea an' into some wan's pocket," an' "Take up th' white man's burden an' hand it to th' coons," an' "An open back dure an' a closed fr-ront dure."
*Mr. Dooley in the Hearts of His
Countrymen* [1899]. *The De-
cline of National Feeling*

"I think," said Mr. Dooley, "that if th' Christyan Scientists had some science an' th' doctors more Christianity, it wudden't make anny diff'rence which ye called in — if ye had a good nurse."

Mr. Dooley's Opinions [*1900*].
Christian Science

No matther whether th' constitution follows th' flag or not, th' supreme coort follows th' iliction returns.

Ibid. The Supreme Court's Decisions

In me younger days 't was not considhered rayspictable f'r to be an athlete. An athlete was always a man that was not sthrong enough f'r wurruk. Fractions dhruv him fr'm school an' th' vagrancy laws dhruv him to baseball.

Ibid. On Athletics

I think a lie with a purpose is wan iv th' worst kind an' th' mos' profitable.

Ibid. On Lying

Th' dimmycratic party ain't on speakin' terms with itsilf.

Ibid. Mr. Dooley Discusses Party Politics

Th' raypublican party broke ye, but now that ye're down we'll not turn a cold shoulder to ye. Come in an' we'll keep ye — broke.

Ibid.

Hogan's r-right whin he says: "Justice is blind." Blind she is, an' deef an' dumb an' has a wooden leg.

Ibid. Cross-Examinations

No wan cares to hear what Hogan calls: "Th' short an' simple scandals iv th' poor."

Ibid.

'Twas founded be th' Puritans to give thanks f'r bein' presarved fr'm th' Indyans, an' . . . we keep it to give thanks we are presarved fr'm th' Puritans.

Ibid. Thanksgiving

Vice . . . is a creature of such heejous mien . . . that th' more ye see it th' betther ye like it.

Ibid. The Crusade Against Vice

Glory be, whin business gets above sellin' tinpinny nails in a brown paper cornucopy, 't is hard to tell it fr'm murther.

Ibid. On Wall Street

Degrees is good things because they livils all ranks.

Mr. Dooley's Opinions.
Colleges and Degrees

"D' ye think th' colledges has much to do with th' progress iv th' wurruld?" asked Mr. Hennessy.

"D'ye think," said Mr. Dooley, " 'tis th' mill that makes th' wather run?"

Ibid.

'Tis "Th' Biography iv a Hero be Wan who Knows." [1] 'Tis "Th' Darin' Exploits iv a Brave Man be an Actual Eye Witness." 'Tis "Th' Account iv th' Desthruction iv Spanish Power in th' Ant Hills," as it fell fr'm th' lips iv Tiddy Rosenfelt an' was took down be his own hands. . . . But if I was him I'd call th' book "Alone in Cubia."

Mr. Dooley's Philosophy [*1900*].
A Book Review

A war expert . . . is a man ye niver heerd iv befure. If ye can think iv annywan whose face is onfamilyar to ye an' ye don't raymimber his name, an' he's got a job on a pa-aper ye didn't know was published, he's a war expert.

Ibid. The War Expert

Th' enthusyasm iv this counthry, Hinnissy, always makes me think iv a bonfire on an ice-floe. It burns bright so long as ye feed it, an' it looks good, but it don't take hold, somehow, on th' ice.

Ibid. The Boer Mission

" 'Twill civilize th' Chinnymen," said Mr. Hennessy.

" 'Twill civilize thim stiff," said Mr. Dooley.

Ibid. The Future of China (*On German intervention in China*)

"Me dear boy, what special branch iv larnin' wud ye like to have studied f'r ye be our compitint profissors?"

Ibid. The Education of the Young
(*A college president to a prospective student*)

If ye live enough befure thirty ye won't care to live at all afther fifty.

Ibid. Casual Observations

[1] Theodore Roosevelt's *The Rough Riders* [1899].

Among men, Hinnissy, wet eye manes dhry heart.

Mr. Dooley's Philosophy.
Casual Observations

A fanatic is a man that does what he thinks th' Lord wud do if He knew th' facts iv th' case.

Ibid.

A vote on th' tallysheet is worth two in the box.

Ibid.

I care not who makes th' laws iv a nation if I can get out an injunction.

Ibid.

'Tis as hard f'r a rich man to enther th' kingdom iv Hiven as it is f'r a poor man to get out iv Purgatory.

Ibid.

Thrust ivrybody — but cut th' ca-ards.

Ibid.

A man that'd expict to thrain lobsters to fly in a year is called a loonytic; but a man that thinks men can be tu-rrned into angels be an iliction is called a rayformer an' remains at large.

Ibid.

Miracles are laughed at be a nation that r-reads thirty millyon newspapers a day an' supports Wall sthreet.

Ibid.

Th' higher up a coort is, the less [the judges] see iv each other. Their office hours are fr'm a quarther to wan leap years. Ye take a lively lawyer that's wurruked twinty hours a day suin' sthreet railrood comp'nies an' boost him onto a high coort an' he can't think out iv a hammock. Th' more exalted . . . th' joodicyal station, th' more it's like a dormitory.

Observations by Mr. Dooley
[1902]. The Law's Delays

Unforchunitly diplomacy on'y goes as far as the dure. It is onable to give protection to th' customer, so whin he laves th' shop th' sthrong arm men iv th' Sinit knocks him down an' takes fr'm him ivrything he got inside an' more too. Di-plomacy has become a philanthropic pursoot like shop-keepin',

but politics, me lords, is still th' same ol' spoort iv highway robb'ry.

Observations by Mr. Dooley.
International Amenities

Ye see, a prince is a gr-reat man in th' ol' counthry, but he niver is as gr-reat over there as he is here. Whin he's at home he's something th' people can't help an' they don't mind him. He's like an iron lamp post, station'ry, ornymintal, an' useful to let people know where they are. But whin he comes to this home iv raypublican simplicity, he's all that th' wurrud prince wud imply, an' it implies more to us thin to annywan else.

Ibid. Prince Henry's Reception

Spain was our frind till th' war was over. Thin she rounded on us an' sold us th' Ph'lippines.

Ibid. European Intervention

Th' flag [1] floats free an' well guarded over th' govermint offices, an' th' cheery people go an' come on their errands — go out alone an' come back with th' throops. Iverywhere happiness, contint, love iv th' shtep-mother counthry, ex-cipt in places where there ar-re people.

Ibid. The Philippine Peace

A rayformer thinks he was ilicted because he was a rayformer, whin th' thruth iv th' matther is he was ilicted because no wan knew him. Ye can al-ways ilict a man in this counthry on that platform. If I was runnin' f'r office, I'd change me name, an' have printed on me cards: "Give him a chanst; he can't be worse."

Ibid. Reform Administration

A reg'lar pollytician can't give away an' alley without blushin', but a busi-ness man who is in pollytics jus' to see that th' civil sarvice law gets thurly enfoorced, will give Lincoln Park an' th' public libr'y to th' beef thrust, charge an admission price to th' lake front an' make it a felony f'r annywan to buy stove polish outside iv his store, an' have it all put down to public im-

---

[1] The American flag in the Philippines.

provemints with a pitcher iv him in th'
corner stone.

Observations by Mr. Dooley.
Reform Administration
"I don't like a rayformer," said Mr.
Hennessy.

"Or anny other raypublican," said
Mr. Dooley.

Ibid.

If a man is wise, he gets rich an' if
he gets rich, he gets foolish, or his wife
does. That's what keeps the money
movin' around.

Ibid. Newport

"Oh, well," said Mr. Hennessy, "we
are as th' Lord made us."

"No," said Mr. Dooley, "lave us be
fair. Lave us take some iv th' blame
oursilves."

Ibid.

"What d'ye think iv th' man down
in Pinnsylvanya [1] who says th' Lord
an' him is partners in a coal mine?"
asked Mr. Hennessy. . . .

"Has he divided th' profits?" asked
Mr. Dooley.

Ibid. Machinery

But th' best thing about a little judicyous swearin' is that it keeps th' temper. 'Twas intinded as a compromise
between runnin' away an' fightin'. Befure it was invinted they was on'y th'
two ways out iv an argymint.

Ibid. Swearing

It must be a good thing to be good or
ivrybody wudden't be pretendin' he
was. But I don't think they'se anny
such thing as hypocrisy in th' wurruld.
They can't be. If ye'd turn on th' gas
in th' darkest heart ye'd find it had a
good raison for th' worst things it done,
a good varchous raison, like needin' th'
money or punishin' th' wicked or tachin'
people a lesson to be more careful, or
protectin' th' liberties iv mankind, or
needin' th' money.

Ibid. Hypocrisy

I don't think we injye other people's
sufferin', Hinnissy. It isn't acshally in-
jyement. But we feel betther f'r it.

Ibid. Enjoyment

[1] George Baer.

Whin a woman discovers she has a
soul, Hinnissy, 'tis time she was sint
to a rest-cure. It niver comes till late
in life, an' ye can't tell what she'll do
about it.

Dissertations by Mr. Dooley
[1906]. Royal Doings
Why shud a woman want to be
thin onless she is thin? Th' idee iv
female beauty that all gr-reat men,
fr'm Julius Caesar to mesilf, has held,
is much more like a bar'l thin a clothes-
pole.

Ibid. Banting

"Ye know a lot about [raising chil-
dren]," said Mr. Hennessy.

"I do," said Mr. Dooley. "Not bein'
an author, I'm a gr-reat critic."

Ibid. The Bringing Up of Children

Th' old story iv th' ant an' th' grasshopper — th' ant that ye can step on
an' th' grasshopper ye can't catch.

Ibid. The Labor Troubles

It's too bad that th' goolden days
has passed, Hinnissy. Capital still pats
labor on th' back, but on'y with an axe.
Labor rayfuses to be threated as a
frind. It wants to be threated as an
inimy. It thinks it gets more that way.
They ar-re still a happy fam'ly, but it's
more like an English fam'ly. They don't
speak.

Ibid.

"Annyhow, I bet no wan iver took
Binjamin Franklin f'r a waiter."

"I wondher why?" asked Mr. Hennessy.

"I don't know," said Mr. Dooley,
"onless it was that even in th' prisnce
iv a king Binjamin Franklin niver felt
like a waiter."

Ibid. Diplomatic Uniforms

"If ye had a boy wud ye sind him to
colledge?" asked Mr. Hennessy.

"Well," said Mr. Dooley, "at th' age
whin a boy is fit to be in colledge I
wudden't have him around th' house."

Ibid. The Intellectual Life

Th' prisidincy is th' highest office in
th' gift iv th' people. Th' vice-prisidincy
is th' next highest an' th' lowest. It
isn't a crime exactly. Ye can't be sint

to jail f'r it, but it's a kind iv a disgrace. It's like writin' anonymous letters.

Dissertations by Mr. Dooley.
The Vice-President

Some vice-prisidints have been so anxious f'r th' prisidint's safety that they've had to be warned off th' White House grounds.

Ibid.

It is his jooty to rigorously enforce th' rules iv th' Sinit. There ar-re none. Th' Sinit is ruled be courtesy, like th' longshoreman's union.

Ibid.

Prisidint Eliot . . . has communicated th' sad fact to th' clargy. Nawthin' th' clargy likes so much as a sad fact.

Ibid. The American Family

Libries niver encouraged lithrachoor anny more thin tombstones encourage livin'. No wan iver wrote annythin' because he was tol' that a hundherd years fr'm now his books might be taken down fr'm a shelf in a granite sepulcher an' some wan wud write "Good" or "This man is crazy" in th' margin. What lithrachoor needs is fillin' food.

Ibid. The Carnegie Libraries

Slug-ye'er-spouse is an internaytional spoort that has niver become pop'lar on our side iv th' wather. An American lady is not th' person that anny man but a thrained athlete wud care to raise his hand again' save be way iv smoothin' her hair.

Ibid. Corporal Punishment

Won't [public flogging] be fine? Th' govermint gives us too little amusemint nowadays. Th' fav'rite pastime iv civilized man is croolty to other civilized man.

Ibid.

"Spare th' rod an' spile th' child," said Mr. Hennessy.

"Yes," said Mr. Dooley, "but don't spare th' rod an' ye spile th' rod, th' child, an' th' child's father."

Ibid.

This home iv opporchunity where

ivry man is th' equal iv ivry other man befure th' law if he isn't careful.

Dissertations by Mr. Dooley.
The Food We Eat

"Ye ra-aly do think dhrink is a nicissry evil?" said Mr. Hennessy.

"Well," said Mr. Dooley, "if it's an evil to a man, it's not nicissry, an' if it's nicissry it's an evil."

Ibid. The Bar

"He made [money]," said Mr. Dooley, "because he honestly loved it with an innocint affiction. He was thrue to it. Th' reason ye have no money is because ye don't love it f'r itsilf alone. Money won't iver surrinder to such a flirt."

Mr. Dooley on Making a Will
and Other Evil Necessities
[1919]. On Making a Will

"Is th' President [1] a good goluf player, d'ye know, at all?" asked Mr. Hennessy . . .

"As a goluf player he cud give Lincoln a sthroke a hole," said Mr. Dooley.

Ibid. On Golf

JOHN GALSWORTHY
[1867–1933]

Justice is a machine that, when some one has once given it the starting push, rolls on of itself.

Justice [1910]. Act II

Public opinion's always in advance of the Law.

Windows [1922]. Act I

The value of a sentiment is the amount of sacrifice you are prepared to make for it.

Ibid. Act II

By the cigars they smoke, and the composers they love, ye shall know the texture of men's souls.

Indian Summer of a Forsyte
[1920]. Chap. 1

He ordered himself a dozen oysters; but, suddenly remembering that the

[1] President Wilson.

month contained no "r," changed them to a fried sole.[1]

> *The White Monkey* [*1924*].
> *Part III, Chap. 7*

It has often been remarked that the breakfast-tables of people who avow themselves indifferent to what the Press may say of them are garnished by all the newspapers on the morning when there is anything to say.

> *The Silver Spoon* [*1926*].
> *Part II, Chap. 2*

If you do not think about the future, you cannot have one.

> *Swan Song* [*1928*].
> *Part II, Chap. 6*

A man of action, forced into a state of thought, is unhappy until he can get out of it.

> *Maid in Waiting* [*1931*].
> *Chap. 3*

Politicians are marvels of energy and principle when they're out of office, but when they get in, they simply run behind the machine.

> *Ibid. Chap. 5*

There's just one rule for politicians all over the world: Don't say in Power what you say in Opposition; if you do, you only have to carry out what the other fellows have found impossible.

> *Ibid. Chap. 7*

One's eyes are what one is, one's mouth what one becomes.

> *Flowering Wilderness* [*1932*].
> *Chap. 2*

The beginnings and endings of all human undertakings are untidy, the building of a house, the writing of a novel, the demolition of a bridge, and, eminently, the finish of a voyage.

> *Over the River* [*1933*]. *Chap. 1*

How to save the old that's worth sav-

---

[1] It is unseasonable and unwholesome in all months that have not an *R* in their name to eat an oyster. — WILLIAM BUTLER: *Dyet's Dry Dinner* [1599]

Let's sing a song of glory to Themistocles O'Shea,

Who ate a dozen oysters on the second day of May.

STODDARD KING [1889–1933]: *The Man Who Dared*

ing, whether in landscape, houses, manners, institutions, or human types, is one of our greatest problems, and the one that we bother least about.

> *Over the River. Chap. 39*

LLOYD McKIM GARRISON
[1867–1900]

Like misers, our usurious memories bring

Their coins each day of greedy reckoning —

Grieved, if they miss one as they count their store,

Or find one brass, long loved as gold before.

> *Souvenirs*

"JOHN OLIVER HOBBES"
(MRS. P. M. T. CRAIGIE)
[1867–1906]

A false success made by the good humor of outside influences is always peaceful; a real success made by the qualities of the thing itself is always a declaration of war.

> *The Dream and the Business*
> [*1906*]

LIONEL JOHNSON
[1867–1902]

The splendid silence clings
Around me: and around
The saddest of all kings
Crown'd, and again discrown'd.

> *By the Statue of King Charles*
> *at Charing Cross. Stanza 2*

Vanquished in life, his death
By beauty made amends.

> *Ibid. Stanza 8*

I know you: solitary griefs,
Desolate passions, aching hours!
I know you: tremulous beliefs,
Agonized hopes, and ashen flowers!

> *The Precept of Silence. Stanza 1*

Some players upon plaintive strings
Publish their wistfulness abroad;
I have not spoken of these things,
Save to one man, and unto God.

> *Ibid. Stanza 3*

ERNEST FENWICK JOHNSTONE
[1867–1938]

I dreamed that I went to the City of
　Gold,
To Heaven resplendent and fair,
And after I entered that beautiful fold
By one in authority there I was told
　That not a Vermonter was there.
No Vermonters in Heaven.
Stanza 1

We give them the best the Kingdom
　provides;
They have everything here that they
　want,
But not a Vermonter in Heaven abides;
A very brief period here he resides,
　Then hikes his way back to Vermont.
Ibid. Stanza 6

CHARLES EDWARD MONTAGUE
[1867–1928]

A gifted small girl has explained that
pins are a great means of saving life,
"by not swallowing them."
Dramatic Values [*1911*]

"The freedom of Europe," "The war
to end war," "The overthrow of milita-
rism," "The cause of civilization" —
most people believe so little now in anything or anyone that they would find it
hard to understand the simplicity and
intensity of faith with which these
phrases were once taken among our
troops, or the certitude felt by hundreds
of thousands of men who are now dead
that if they were killed their monument
would be a new Europe not soured or
soiled with the hates and greeds of the
old.
Disenchantment [*1922*]. *Chap. 13*

A lie will easily get you out of a
scrape, and yet, strangely and beautifully, rapture possesses you when you
have taken the scrape and left out the
lie.
Ibid. Chap. 15

War hath no fury like a non-combatant.
Ibid.

"I was born below par to th' extent
of two whiskies."
Fiery Particles [*1923*]

Burgundy was the winiest wine, the
central, essential, and typical wine, the
soul and greatest common measure of
all the kindly wines of the earth.
Judith

GEORGE W. RUSSELL ("AE")
[1867–1935]

Our hearts were drunk with a beauty
Our eyes could never see.
The Unknown God

Twilight, a timid fawn, went glimmer-
　ing by,
And Night, the dark-blue hunter, fol-
　lowed fast.
Refuge

With these heaven-assailing spires
　All that was in clay or stone
Fabled of rich Babylon
　By these children is outdone.
New York. Stanza 1

HENRY LEWIS STIMSON [1]
[1867–1950]

The only way to make a man trustworthy is to trust him; and the surest
way to make him untrustworthy is to
distrust him and show your distrust.
The Bomb and the Opportunity
[*Harper's Magazine, March,*
1946]

The only deadly sin I know is cyni-
cism.
On Active Service in Peace and
War [*1948*]. *Introduction*

HARRY LEON WILSON
[1867–1939]

I can be pushed just so far.
Ruggles of Red Gap [*1915*]

MARY HUNTER AUSTIN
[1868–1934]

Whisper of the wind along the sage,
Only wait till I can get the word —

[1] Secretary of War, 1911–1913 and 1940–
1945; Secretary of State, 1929–1933.

Never was it printed in a page,
Never was it spoken, never heard.
Whisper of the Wind

What need has he of clocks who knows
When highest peaks are gilt and rose
Day has begun?
Clocks and Calendars. Stanza 1

THOMAS WILLIAM HODGSON CROSLAND
[1868–1924]

The Unspeakable Scot.
Title of satiric essay

NORMAN DOUGLAS
[1868–1952]

You can tell the ideals of a nation by its advertisements.
South Wind [*1917*]. *Chap. 7*

Men have lost sight of distant horizons. Nobody writes for humanity, for civilization; they write for their country, their sect; to amuse their friends or annoy their enemies.
Ibid. Chap. 8

No one can expect a majority to be stirred by motives other than ignoble.
Ibid. Chap. 10

A love-match is generally a failure and a money-match is always a mistake. The heroes, the saints and sages — they are those who face the world alone.
Ibid. Chap. 11

No great man is ever born too soon or too late. When we say that the time is not ripe for this or that celebrity, we confess by implication that this very man, and no other, is required.
Ibid. Chap. 13

For three consecutive months they could barely afford the most unnecessary luxuries of life.
Ibid. Chap. 20

Many a man who thinks to found a home discovers that he has merely opened a tavern for his friends.
Ibid. Chap. 24

WILLIAM EDWARD BURGHARDT DuBOIS
[1868–1963]

Herein lies the tragedy of the age: not that men are poor — all men know something of poverty; not that men are wicked — who is good? Not that men are ignorant — what is truth? Nay, but that men know so little of men.
The Souls of Black Folk [*1903*]

MAXIM GORKY
[1868–1936]

It is quiet here and restful and the air is delicious. There are gardens everywhere, nightingales sing in the gardens and police spies lie in the bushes. There are nightingales in every garden, but police spies only in mine, I think. They sit under my windows in the darkness of the night and try to get a glimpse of how I spread sedition in Russia.
Letter to Chekhov

Lies — there you have the religion of slaves and taskmasters.[1]
The Lower Depths [*1903*]

The double-headed eagle of the autocracy was not merely the coat of arms of the Empire, but an exceedingly live and actively pernicious bird.
Talks on Craftsmanship

RONALD ARTHUR HOPWOOD
[1868–1949]

The strength of the ship is the Service,
And the strength of the Service, the ship.
The Laws of the Navy. Stanza 2

On the strength of one link in the cable
Dependeth the might of the chain:
Who knows when thou mayest be tested?
So live that thou bearest the strain.
Ibid. Stanza 5

They prosper who burn in the morning
The letters they wrote over night.
Ibid. Stanza 17

[1] The censor forbade this line to be spoken on the stage.

FRANK McKINNEY ("KIN") HUBBARD ("ABE MARTIN")
[1868–1930]

Miss Fawn Lippincut says she wouldn' marry th' best man on earth, but we supposed she wuz much younger.
Abe Martin's Sayings and Sketches [*1915*]

Miss Tawney Apple is confined t' her home by a swollen dresser drawer.
Ibid.

Mr. and Mrs. Lettie Plum, married in June, couldn' git ther car out o' garage last evenin', so they had to go to bed hungry.
Ibid.

It's no disgrace t' be poor, but it might as well be.
Ibid.

He was a power politically fer years, but he never got prominent enough t' have his speeches garbled.
Ibid.

When a fellow says it hain't the money but the principle o' the thing, it's th' money.
Hoss Sense and Nonsense [*1926*]

Nobuddy ever fergits where he buried a hatchet.
Abe Martin's Broadcast [*1930*]

GRENVILLE KLEISER
[1868–1953]

She gleans how long you wish to stay;
She lets you go without delay.
The Ideal Hostess

She is not difficult to please;
She can be silent as the trees.
She shuns all ostentatious show;
She knows exactly when to go.[1]
The Ideal Guest

HERMAN W. KNICKERBOCKER
[1868–1934]

If I had the power today by the simple turning of my hand to endow myself

[1] See Rose Henniker Heaton, page 754a.

with personal immortality, in my infinite ignorance I would refuse to turn my hand. God knows best.
Eulogy at the funeral of Riley Grannan, Rawhide, Nevada [*April 3, 1908*]

AGNES LEE
[1868–1939]

Bed is the boon for me!
It's well to bake and sweep,
But hear the word of old Lizette:
It's better than all to sleep.
Old Lizette on Sleep. Stanza 1

There's nothing, nothing, nothing, I say,
That's worth the lying awake!
Ibid. Stanza 3

EDWARD VERRALL LUCAS
[1868–1938]

The French never allow a distinguished son of France to lack a statue.
Wanderings and Diversions [*1926*].
Zigzags in France

Americans are people who prefer the Continent to their own country, but refuse to learn its languages.
Ibid. The Continental Dictionary

Ticket Collector. — The man who never wants to see your ticket unless you are asleep.
Ibid.

He says one of the two things that men who have lasted for a hundred years always say — either that they have drunk whisky and smoked all their lives, or that neither tobacco nor spirits ever made the faintest appeal to them.
Ibid. Secrets

People in hotels strike no roots. The French phrase for chronic hotel guests even says so: they are called dwellers *sur la branche*.
Ibid. To Be Let or Sold

A genius is a man who does unique things of which nobody would expect him to be capable.
Reading, Writing and Remembering [*1932*]

There can be no defence like elaborate courtesy.

Reading, Writing and Remembering

Has any reader ever found perfect accuracy in the newspaper account of any event of which he himself had inside knowledge?

Of Accuracy

The art of life is to keep down acquaintances. One's friends one can manage, but one's acquaintances can be the devil.

Over Bremerton's

WILLIAM TYLER PAGE
[1868–1942]

I believe in the United States of America as a Government of the people, by the people, for the people; whose just powers are derived from the consent of the governed; a democracy in a republic, a sovereign Nation of many sovereign States; a perfect Union one and inseparable; established upon those principles of freedom, equality, justice and humanity for which American patriots sacrificed their lives and fortunes. I therefore believe it is my duty to my country to love it, to support its Constitution, to obey its laws, to respect its flag, and to defend it against all enemies.

The American's Creed[1]

EDMOND ROSTAND
[1868–1918]

A great nose indicates a great man —
Genial, courteous, intellectual,
Virile, courageous.

Cyrano de Bergerac[2] [*1897*].
Act I

Free fighters, free lovers, free spenders —
The Cadets of Gascoyne — the defenders
Of old homes, old names, and old splendors.

Ibid. Act II

[1] Adopted by the House of Representatives, April 3, 1918.
[2] Translated by BRIAN HOOKER.

A Bear. How do you know I am a diplomat?
Chinese Woman. Why, by the skilful way you hide your claws.

L'Aiglon[1] [*1900*]. *Act IV*
(*A Masquerade*)

I fall back dazzled at beholding myself all rosy red,
At having, I myself, caused the sun to rise.

Chantecler [*1907*]. *Act II, Sc. 3*

And sounding in advance its victory,
My song jets forth so clear, so proud, so peremptory,
That the horizon, seized with a rosy trembling,
Obeys me.

Ibid.

ROBERT FALCON SCOTT
[1868–1912]

Make the boy interested in natural history if you can; it is better than games; they encourage it at some schools.

Last Message to His Wife

He [Oates][2] said: "I am just going outside, and may be some time." He went out into the blizzard, and we have not seen him since. . . . We knew that poor Oates was walking to his death, but though we tried to dissuade him, we knew that it was the act of a brave man and an English gentleman. We all hope to meet the end with a similar spirit, and assuredly the end is not far.

Diary. March 16, 1912

Had we lived, I should have had a tale to tell of the hardihood, endurance, and courage of my companions which would have stirred the heart of every Englishman. These rough notes and our dead bodies must tell the tale.

Journal. Message to the Public[3]

[1] Translated by LOUIS N. PARKER.
[2] Lawrence Edward Grace Oates [1880–1912], of the Inniskilling Dragoons, a member of Scott's last Antarctic expedition.
[3] Inscribed on the memorial to Captain Scott and his companions, Waterloo Place, London.

WILLIAM ALLEN WHITE
[1868–1944]

And thus the King of Boyville first set his light little foot upon the soil of an unknown country.
> *The King of Boyville* [*1896*]

What's the Matter with Kansas?
> *Editorial in Emporia Gazette.*
> *August 15, 1896*

Tin horn politicians.
> *Emporia Gazette. October 25, 1901*

"Company" merges into the family when clean towels are not kept in the bathroom every morning. A man is no longer company when they change sheets on his bed only once in two weeks. . . . When sons-in-law come home to visit for years at a time, the question will be seen to have considerable importance.
> *Ibid. June 4, 1906*

The fresh-water college is doing a great work.
> *Ibid. June 10, 1907*

All dressed up, with nowhere to go.
> *Of the Progressive Party in 1916, after Theodore Roosevelt retired from Presidential competition*

Put fear out of your heart. This Nation will survive, this State will prosper, the orderly business of life will go forward if only men can speak in whatever way given them to utter what their hearts hold — by voice, by posted card, by letter or by press. Reason never has failed men. Only force and oppression have made the wrecks in the world.
> *Emporia Gazette. 1922*

Consistency is a paste jewel that only cheap men cherish.[1]
> *Ibid. November 17, 1923*

The talent of a meat packer, the morals of a money changer and the manners of an undertaker.
> *Obituary of Frank A. Munsey.*
> *December, 1925*

[1] Commenting on an item in the Topeka *Capital:* "The *Emporia Gazette* is the best loved paper in Kansas because its editor never looks in yesterday's files to see if what he proposes to write today is consistent."

LAURENCE BINYON
[1869–1943]

For Mercy, Courage, Kindness, Mirth,
There is no measure upon earth.
Nay, they wither, root and stem,
If an end be set to them.
> *A Song*

They shall grow not old, as we that are
left grow old:
Age shall not weary them, nor the years
condemn.
At the going down of the sun and in the
morning
We will remember them.
> *For the Fallen. Stanza 4*

ELLIS PARKER BUTLER
[1869–1937]

Pigs is Pigs.
> *Title of story* [*1906*]

It is other folks' dogs and children that make most of the bad feelin's between neighbors.
> *The Confessions of a Daddy*
> [*1907*]. *Chap. 1*

NEVILLE CHAMBERLAIN
[1869–1940]

For the second time in our history, a British Prime Minister has returned from Germany bringing peace with honor. I believe it is peace for our time. . . . Go home and get a nice quiet sleep.[1]
> *Address from 10 Downing Street,*
> *September 30, 1938, upon return*
> *to London after the Munich con-*
> *ference with Hitler, Daladier,*
> *and Mussolini*

[1] As reported in the *New York Times*, October 1, 1938.
While we endeavor to maintain peace, I certainly should be the last to forget that, if peace cannot be maintained with honour, it is no longer peace. — LORD JOHN RUSSELL: *Speech at Greenock, Scotland* [September 19, 1853]
Lord Salisbury and myself have brought you back peace — but a peace, I hope, with honour, which may satisfy our sovereign, and tend to the welfare of the country. — BENJAMIN DISRAELI: *Report on the Berlin Congress* [July 16, 1878]

Hitler has missed the bus.
Speech in the House of Commons,
April 4, 1940

"MICHAEL FAIRLESS"
(MARGARET FAIRLESS
BARBER)
[1869–1901]

The people who make no roads are ruled out from intelligent participation in the world's brotherhood.
The Roadmender. I, 5
Necessity can set me helpless on my back, but she cannot keep me there; nor can four walls limit my vision.
Ibid. II, 6
Revelation is always measured by capacity.
Ibid. III, 3

ANDRÉ GIDE
[1869-1951]

What another would have done as well as you, do not do it. What another would have said as well as you, do not say it; written as well, do not write it. Be faithful to that which exists nowhere but in yourself — and thus make yourself indispensable.
Les Nourritures Terrestres. Envoi
A unanimous chorus of praise is not an assurance of survival; authors who please everyone at once are quickly exhausted. I would prefer to think that a hundred years hence people will say we did not properly understand him [Anatole France].
Pretexts

STRICKLAND GILLILAN
[1869–1954]

Make 'em brief, Finnigin!
Finnigin to Flannigan. Stanza 3
Bilin' down 's repoort, wuz Finnigin!
An' he writed this here: "*Musther Flannigan —*
Off agin, on agin,
Gone agin. — FINNIGIN."
Ibid. Stanza 6

Just stand aside and watch yourself go by;
Think of yourself as "he" instead of "I."
Watch Yourself Go By. Stanza 1

FREDERIC LAWRENCE
KNOWLES
[1869–1905]

Each little lyrical
Grave or satirical
Musical miracle!
On a Flyleaf of Burns's Songs
Helen's lips are drifting dust; [1]
Ilion is consumed with rust.
Love Triumphant
This body is my house — it is not I:
Triumphant in this faith I live and die.
The Tenant
Joy is a partnership,
Grief weeps alone;
Many guests had Cana,
Gethsemane had one.
Grief and Joy

STEPHEN LEACOCK
[1869–1944]

If I were founding a university I would found first a smoking room; then when I had a little more money in hand I would found a dormitory; then after that, or more probably with it, a decent reading room and a library. After that, if I still had more money that I couldn't use, I would hire a professor and get some textbooks.
Oxford As I See It
He flung himself from the room, flung himself upon his horse and rode madly off in all directions.
Gertrude the Governess
Golf may be played on Sunday, not being a game within the view of the law, but being a form of moral effort.
Other Fancies [1923]. Why
I Refuse to Play Golf
The average man goes to church six times a year and has attended Sunday

[1] See Thomas Nash, page 213a.

School for two afternoons and can sing
half a hymn.
Winnowed Wisdom [*1926*].
Preface
The general idea, of course, in any
first class laundry, is to see that no
shirt or collar ever comes back twice.
Ibid. Chap. 6

EDGAR LEE MASTERS
[1869–1950]

All, all, are sleeping on the hill.
Spoon River Anthology [*1915*].
The Hill, Refrain
Out of me unworthy and unknown
The vibrations of deathless music;
"With malice toward none, with charity
for all."
Ibid. Anne Rutledge
I am Anne Rutledge who sleep beneath
these weeds,
Beloved in life of Abraham Lincoln,
Wedded to him, not through union,
But through separation.
Ibid.
To this generation I would say:
Memorize some bit of verse of truth or
beauty.
Ibid. Mrs. George Reece
Hats may make divorces.
Ibid. Mrs. Williams
And there is the silence of age,
Too full of wisdom for the tongue to
utter it
In words intelligible to those who have
not lived
The great range of life.
Silence

WILLIAM VAUGHN MOODY
[1869–1910]

Jill-o'er-the-ground is purple blue,
Blue is the quaker-maid,
The wild geranium holds its dew
Long in the boulder's shade.
Gloucester Moors [*1901*]. *Stanza 2*
This earth is not the steadfast place
We landsmen build upon;
From deep to deep she varies pace,
And while she comes is gone.
Ibid. Stanza 4

But on, but on does the old earth steer
As if her port she knew.
Gloucester Moors. Stanza 5
Then not to kneel, almost
Seemed like a vulgar boast.
Good Friday [*1901*]. *Stanza 9*
Gigantic, wilful, young,
Chicago sitteth at the northwest gates,
With restless violent hands and casual
tongue
Moulding her mighty fates.
An Ode in Time of Hesitation
[*1901*]. *Stanza 3*
Our fluent men of place and conse-
quence
Fumble and fill their mouths with hol-
low phrase,
Or for the end-all of deep arguments
Intone their dull commercial liturgies.
Ibid. Stanza 7
Blindness we may forgive, but baseness
we will smite.
Ibid. Stanza 9
Shrill and high, newsboys cry
The worst of the city's infamy.
In New York [*1901*]. *Stanza 4*
The roaring street is hung for miles
With fierce electric fire.
Ibid. Stanza 9

JESSIE BELLE RITTENHOUSE
[1869–1948]

My debt to you, Belovèd,
Is one I cannot pay
In any coin of any realm
On any reckoning day.
Debt

I worked for a menial's hire,
Only to learn, dismayed,
That any wage I had asked of Life,
Life would have paid.
My Wage

EDWIN ARLINGTON
ROBINSON
[1869–1935]

We cannot know how much we learn
From those who never will return,
Until a flash of unforeseen
Remembrance falls on what has been.
Flammonde

To shake the tree
Of life itself and bring down fruit unheard-of.
*Ben Jonson Entertains a Man
from Stratford*

I would have rid the earth of him
Once, in my pride. . . .
I never knew the worth of him
Until he died.
An Old Story

Life is the game that must be played:
This truth at least, good friends, we
know;
So live and laugh, nor be dismayed
As one by one the phantoms go.
Ballade by the Fire. Envoy

The songs of one who strove to play
The broken flutes of Arcady.
Ballade of Broken Flutes

There be two men of all mankind
That I'm forever thinking on:
They chase me everywhere I go, —
Melchizedek, Ucalegon.
Two Men

Like dead, remembered footsteps on old
floors.
The Pity of the Leaves

And thus we die,
Still searching, like poor old astrono-
mers
Who totter off to bed and go to sleep
To dream of untriangulated stars.
Octaves. XI

The saddest among kings of earth,
Bowed with a galling crown, this man
Met rancor with a cryptic mirth,
Laconic — and Olympian.
The Master: Lincoln

Wearing upon his forehead, with no
fear,
The laurel of approved iniquity.
Uncle Ananias

Miniver Cheevy, child of scorn,
Grew lean while he assailed the
seasons;
He wept that he was ever born,
And he had reasons.
Miniver Cheevy [*1910*]. *Stanza 1*

Miniver loved the Medici,
Albeit he had never seen one;

He would have sinned incessantly
Could he have been one.
Miniver Cheevy. Stanza 5

Miniver Cheevy, born too late,
Scratched his head and kept on
thinking;
Miniver coughed and called it fate,
And kept on drinking.
Ibid. Stanza 8

Who of us, being what he is,
May scoff at others' ecstasies?
However we may shine today,
More-shining ones are on the way.
Atherton's Gambit

I shall have more to say when I am
dead.
John Brown

Like a physician who can do no good,
But knows how soon another would
have his fee
Were he to tell the truth.
Avon's Harvest

Art's long hazard, where no man may
choose
Whether he play to win, or toil to lose.
Caput Mortuum

Love that's wise
Will not say all it means.
Tristram [*1927*]. *Part VII*

For when a woman is left too much
alone,
Sooner or later she begins to think;
And no man knows what then she may
discover.
Ibid.

There is a little watchman in my heart
Who is always telling me what time
it is.
Ibid. Part VIII

Love must have wings to fly away from
love,
And to fly back again.
Ibid.

I like rivers
Better than oceans, for we see both
sides.
An ocean is forever asking questions
And writing them aloud along the
shore.
Roman Bartholow. Part III

Once in a life, they tell us, and once
  only,
So great a thing as a great love may
  come —
To crown us, or to mark us with a scar
No craft or custom shall obliterate.
              Roman Bartholow. Part IV

  Of all small things
That have the most infernal power to
  grow,
Few may be larger than a few small
  words
That may not say themselves and be
  forgotten.
              Genevieve and Alexandra

Here where the wind is always north-
  north-east
And children learn to walk on frozen
  toes.
              New England

GEORGE STERLING
[1869–1926]

Thou art the star for which all evening
waits.
              Aldebaran at Dusk

BOOTH TARKINGTON
[1869–1946]

  Penrod was doing something very un-
usual and rare, something almost never
accomplished except by colored people or by a boy in school on a spring
day: he was doing really nothing at all.
He was merely a state of being.
              Penrod [1914]. Chap. 8

  There are two things that will be believed of any man whatsoever, and one
of them is that he has taken to drink.
              Ibid. Chap. 10

  They were upon their great theme:
"When I get to be a man!" Being human, though boys, they considered
their present estate too commonplace to
be dwelt upon. So, when the old men
gather, they say: "When I was a boy!"
It really is the land of nowadays that
we never discover.
              Ibid. Chap. 26

CAROLYN WELLS
[1869–1942]

Youth is a silly, vapid state;
Old age with fears and ills is rife;
This simple boon I beg of Fate —
A thousand years of Middle Life!
              My Boon

"A noble theme!" the tyro cried,
And straightway scribbled off a sonnet.
"A noble theme," the poet sighed,
"I am not fit to write upon it."
              Humility

I love the Christmas-tide, and yet,
  I notice this, each year I live;
I always like the gifts I get,
  But how I love the gifts I give!
              A Thought

The books we think we ought to read
  are poky, dull and dry;
The books that we would like to read
  we are ashamed to buy;
The books that people talk about we
  never can recall;
And the books that people give us, Oh,
  they're the worst of all.
              On Books

The Smile That Won't Come Off.
          Winning slogan in a contest

FRANK LLOYD WRIGHT
[1869–1959]

  No house should ever be *on* any hill
or on anything. It should be *of* the
hill, belonging to it, so hill and house
could live together each the happier for
the other.
          An Autobiography [1932]

BERNARD MANNES BARUCH
[1870–1965]

  America has never forgotten — and
will never forget — the nobler things
that brought her into being and that
light her path — the path that was entered upon only one hundred and fifty
years ago. . . . How young she is! It
will be centuries before she will adopt
that maturity of custom — the cloth-

ing of the grave — that some people believe she is already fitted for.
> *Address on accepting The Churchman Award, New York* [*May 23, 1944*]

Oh, oh — someone's taken the office.
> *On finding the park bench, where he usually held conference, occupied by others* [TIME, *April 22, 1946*]

HILAIRE BELLOC
[1870–1953]

Child! do not throw this book about;
Refrain from the unholy pleasure
Of cutting all the pictures out!
Preserve it as your chiefest treasure.
> *A Bad Child's Book of Beasts.*
> *Dedication*

When people call this beast to mind,
They marvel more and more
At such a little tail behind,
So large a trunk before.
> *Ibid. The Elephant*

I shoot the Hippopotamus
With bullets made of platinum,
Because if I use leaden ones
His hide is sure to flatten 'em.
> *Ibid. The Hippopotamus*

The Whale that wanders round the Pole
Is not a table fish.
You cannot bake or boil him whole
Nor serve him in a dish.
> *Ibid. The Whale*

Balliol made me, Balliol fed me,
Whatever I had she gave me again:
And the best of Balliol loved and led me.
God be with you, Balliol men.
> *To the Balliol Men Still in Africa*
> [*1900*]

Here richly, with ridiculous display,
The Politician's corpse was laid away.
While all of his acquaintance sneered and slanged,
I wept; for I had longed to see him hanged.
> *Epitaph on the Politician Himself*

Oh, he didn't believe in Adam and Eve —
He put no faith therein;

His doubts began with the fall of man,
And he laughed at original sin.
> *Song of the Pelagian Heresy*

The Tipple's aboard and the night is young,
The door's ajar and the Barrel is sprung,
I am singing the best song ever was sung
And it has a rousing chorus.
> *West Sussex Drinking Song.*
> *Chorus*

How slow the Shadow creeps: but when 'tis past
How fast the Shadows fall. How fast! How fast!
> *For a Sundial*

Loss and Possession, Death and Life are one,
There falls no shadow where there shines no sun.
> *Ibid.*

The moon on the one hand, the dawn on the other:
The moon is my sister, the dawn is my brother.
The moon on my left and the dawn on my right.
My brother, good morning: my sister, good night.
> *The Early Morning*

The great hills of the South Country
They stand along the sea;
And it's there walking in the high woods
That I could wish to be,
And the men that were boys when I was a boy
Walking along with me.
> *The South Country. Stanza 2*

If I ever become a rich man,
Or if ever I grow to be old,
I will build a house with deep thatch
To shelter me from the cold,
And there shall the Sussex songs be sung
And the story of Sussex told.
> *Ibid. Stanza 9*

And the men that were boys when I was a boy
Shall sit and drink with me.
> *Ibid. Stanza 10*

From quiet homes and first beginning,
  Out to the undiscovered ends,
There's nothing worth the wear of win-
    ning
  But laughter and the love of friends.
                        Dedicatory Ode

Of Courtesy, it is much less
Than Courage of Heart or Holiness,
Yet in my walks it seems to me
That the Grace of God is in Courtesy.
                        Courtesy

Do you remember an Inn,
Miranda?
Do you remember an Inn?
And the tedding and the spreading
Of the straw for a bedding,
And the fleas that tease in the High
    Pyrenees,
And the wine that tasted of the tar?
                        Tarantella

I said to Heart, "How goes it?" Heart
    replied:
"Right as a Ribstone Pippin!" But it
    lied.
                        The False Heart

Now just imagine how it feels
When first your toes and then your
    heels,
And then by gradual degrees,
Your shins and ankles, calves and
    knees,
Are slowly eaten, bit by bit.
No wonder Jim detested it!
                        Cautionary Tales. Jim

The Chief Defect of Henry King
Was chewing little bits of String.
                        Ibid. Henry King

Physicians of the Utmost Fame
Were called at once; but when they
    came
They answered, as they took their Fees,
"There is no Cure for this Disease."
                        Ibid.

"Oh, my Friends, be warned by me,
That Breakfast, Dinner, Lunch and
    Tea
Are all the Human Frame re-
    quires . . ."
With that the Wretched Child expires.
                        Ibid.

Matilda told such Dreadful Lies,

It made one Gasp and Stretch one's
    Eyes;
Her Aunt, who, from her Earliest
    Youth,
Had kept a Strict Regard for Truth,
Attempted to Believe Matilda:
The effort very nearly killed her.
                        Cautionary Tales. Matilda

It happened that a few Weeks later
Her Aunt was off to the Theatre
To see that Interesting Play
The Second Mrs. Tanqueray.
                        Ibid.

For every time She shouted "Fire!"
They only answered "Little Liar!"
And therefore when her Aunt returned,
Matilda, and the House, were burned.
                        Ibid.

The nicest child I ever knew
Was Charles Augustus Fortescue.
        Ibid. Charles Augustus Fortescue

When I am dead, I hope it may be said:
"His sins were scarlet, but his books
    were read."
                        On His Books

BENJAMIN NATHAN CARDOZO
[1870–1938]

A trustee is held to something stricter
than the morals of the market place.
Not honesty alone, but the punctilio
of an honor the most sensitive, is then
the standard of behavior.
        Meinhard v. *Salmon, 249 N.Y.*
                        458, 464 [1928]

JOHN IRVING DILLON
[1870–1938]

I lift my glass in a grateful toast
To those glorious days of the used-to-
    be —
Days that live on in memory,
Bathed in a shimmering golden haze —
Our still-remembered "olden days"!
            Those Olden Days. Stanza 11

LORD ALFRED DOUGLAS
[1870–1945]

I have been profligate of happiness
And reckless of the world's hostility,

The blessèd part has not been given to me
Gladly to suffer fools.[1]
To Olive

MRS. J. BORDEN HARRIMAN
[1870–   ]

Next to entertaining or impressive talk, a thoroughgoing silence manages to intrigue most people.
*From Pinafores to Politics [1923].
Chap. 4*

ARTHUR J. LAMB
[1870–1928]

Her beauty was sold for an old man's gold,
She's a bird in a gilded cage.
A Bird in a Gilded Cage [1900]
"He don't know Nellie like I do,"
Said the saucy little bird on Nellie's hat.
The Bird on Nellie's Hat [1906]

SIR HARRY LAUDER
[1870–1950]

Oh, it's nice to get up in the mornin',
But it's nicer to lie in bed.
Song

Just a wee doch-an'-dorris
Before we gang awa' . . .
If y' can say
It's a braw brecht moonlecht necht,
Yer a' recht, that's a'.
Song

Roamin' in the gloamin'
By the bonny banks of Clyde.
Song

I Love a Lassie.
Title of Song

NIKOLAI LENIN
[1870–1924]

Political institutions are a superstructure resting on an economic foundation.
*The Three Sources and Three Constituent Parts of Marxism [2]
[1913]*

[1] For ye suffer fools gladly, seeing ye yourselves are wise. — *2 Corinthians, XI, 19*
[2] Translated by MAX EASTMAN.

Capital, created by the labour of the worker, oppresses the worker by undermining the small proprietor and creating an army of the unemployed.
The Three Sources and Three Constituent Parts of Marxism

Capital has conquered throughout the world, but its victory is only an earnest of the victory of labour over capital.
Ibid.

People always have been and they always will be stupid victims of deceit and self-deception in politics, until they learn behind every kind of moral, religious, political, social phrase, declaration and promise to seek out the interests of this or that class or classes.
Ibid.

Uneven economic and political development is an absolute law of capitalism. Hence, the victory of socialism is possible, first in a few or even one single capitalist country taken separately.
*Collected Works. Vol. XVIII,
Page 272*

International imperialism disposing of the might of capital cannot coexist with the Soviet Republic. Conflict is unavoidable, and here is the greatest difficulty of the Russian Revolution, its greatest historical task, that of provoking the International Revolution.
Ibid. Vol. XXII, Page 37

It is true that liberty is precious — so precious that it must be rationed.
Attributed. Quoted by SIDNEY AND BEATRICE WEBB *in Soviet Communism: A New Civilization? [1936]. Page 1036*

The most important thing in illness is never to lose heart.
To his mother. Quoted by HEWLETT JOHNSON *in The Secret of Soviet Strength [1943]*

DENIS ALOYSIUS McCARTHY
[1870–1931]

This is the land where hate should die,
No feuds of faith, no spleen of race,

No darkly-brooding fear should try
Beneath our flag to find a place.
*This Is the Land Where Hate
Should Die. Stanza 1*

HECTOR HUGH MUNRO ("SAKI")
[1870–1916]

She took to telling the truth about
her age; she said she was forty-two and
five months. . . . It may have been
pleasing to the angels, but her elder
sister was not gratified.
*Reginald [1904]. Reginald on
Besetting Sins*
The cook was a good cook, as cooks
go; and as cooks go she went.
Ibid.
Women and elephants never forget
an injury.
Ibid.
I might have been a gold-fish in a
glass bowl for all the privacy I got.
Ibid. The Innocence of Reginald
The Western custom of one wife and
hardly any mistresses.
*Reginald in Russia [1910]. A
Young Turkish Catastrophe*
Hating anything in the way of ill-
natured gossip ourselves, we are always
grateful to those who do it for us and
do it well.
Ibid. The Soul of Laploshka
Poverty keeps together more homes
than it breaks up.
*The Chronicles of Clovis [1911].
Esmé*
His socks compelled one's attention
without losing one's respect.
Ibid. "Ministers of Grace"
"It was their Silver Wedding; such
lots of silver presents, quite a show."
"We must not grudge them their
show of presents after twenty-five years
of married life; it is the silver lining to
their cloud."
The Unbearable Bassington [1912]
Sherard Blaw, the dramatist who had
discovered himself, and who had given
so ungrudgingly of his discovery to the
world.
Ibid.

The sacrifices of friendship were
beautiful in her eyes as long as she was
not asked to make them.
*Beasts and Super-Beasts [1914].
Fur*
"The man is a common murderer."
"A common murderer, possibly, but
a very uncommon cook."
Ibid. The Blind Spot
Waldo is one of those people who
would be enormously improved by
death.
Ibid. The Feast of Nemesis
Children with Hyacinth's tempera-
ment don't know better as they grow
older; they merely know more.
*The Toys of Peace [1919].
Hyacinth*
In baiting a mouse-trap with cheese,
always leave room for the mouse.
*The Square Egg [1924]. The
Infernal Parliament*
Confront a child, a puppy, and a kit-
ten with a sudden danger; the child will
turn instinctively for assistance, the
puppy will grovel in abject submission,
the kitten will brace its tiny body for a
frantic resistance.
Ibid. The Achievement of the Cat
A little inaccuracy sometimes saves
tons of explanation.
Ibid. The Comments of Moung Ka

FRANK NORRIS
[1870–1902]

He's the kind of man that gets up a
reputation for being clever and artistic
by running down the very one particular thing that every one likes, and
cracking up some book or picture or
play that no one has ever heard of.
The Pit [1903]. Chap. 2

ROSCOE POUND
[1870–1964]

The law must be stable, but it must
not stand still.
*Introduction to the Philosophy
of Law [1922]*

EDDIE NEWTON AND
T. LAURENCE SEIBERG
[*Floruerunt* 1900]

Casey Jones! Orders in his hand.
Casey Jones! Mounted to the cabin,
Took his farewell journey to that prom-
ised land.
> *Casey Jones* [*1900*] (*Adapted
> from verses and melody by*
> WALLACE SAUNDERS) [1]

HAROLD BEGBIE
[1871–1929]

"The Christian ideal," it is said, "has
not been tried and found wanting; it
has been found difficult, and left untried."
> *Life of William Booth*

JOHN JOY BELL
[1871–1934]

I've never traveled for more 'n a day,
I never was one to roam,
But I likes to sit on the busy quay,
Watchin' the ships that says to me —
"Always somebody goin' away,
Somebody gettin' home."
> *On the Quay. Stanza 1*

RALPH BERGENGREN
[1871–1947]

Christmas itself may be called into
question
If carried so far it creates indigestion.[2]
> *The Unwise Christmas*

[1] Of the many versions of this traditional
ballad, the most familiar is printed in CARL
SANDBURG's *The American Songbag* [1927].
It begins:
  Come all you rounders, for I want you to
    hear
  The story of a brave engineer.
  Casey Jones was the rounder's name,
  On a big eight-wheeler of a mighty fame.
[2] Ye Tables groan before ye Feaste,
  Ye Feasters groan thereafter.
    ARTHUR GUITERMAN [1871–1943]:
    A True Bill Agaynst Christmasse

STEPHEN CRANE
[1871–1900]

He had fought like a pagan who defends his religion.
> *The Red Badge of Courage* [*1895*].
> *Chap. 17*

Within him, as he hurled himself forward, was born a love, a despairing
fondness for this flag which was near
him. It was a creation of beauty and
invulnerability.
> *Ibid. Chap. 19*

None of them knew the color of the
sky.
> *The Open Boat* [*1898*]

A man said to the universe:
"Sir, I exist!"
"However," replied the universe,
"The fact has not created in me
A sense of obligation."
> *War Is Kind* [*1899*]. *Fragment*

THOMAS AUGUSTINE DALY
[1871–1948]

I gotta love for Angela,
I love Carlotta, too.
I no can marry both o' dem,
So w'at I gona do?
> *Between Two Loves. Stanza 1*

Da spreeng ees com'; but oh, da joy
  Eet ees too late!
He was so cold, my leetla boy,
  He no could wait.
> *Da Leetla Boy. Stanza 1*

Flo was fond of Ebenezer —
"Eb," for short, she called her beau.
Talk of tides of love, great Caesar!
  You should see them — Eb and Flo.
> *The Tides of Love*

Sing clear, O! throstle,
  Thou golden-tongued apostle
And little brown-frocked brother
  Of the loved Assisian!
> *To a Thrush*

W'at good eesa wife eef she don'ta be
fat?
> *Da Styleesha Wife*

"Eat hearty, and give the old ship a
good name!"
> *Grace for the Ship*

The Man, the One and Only One —
First Gentleman on Earth —
Said: "How about a little fun?
Come! let us have some mirth!"
The First New Year's Eve.
Stanza 1

"Fifteen-two and a pair" —
Look at them! Granny and Gramp',
Playing so peacefully there —
And what of the wild young scamp [1]
Who fashioned this quiet game
For numberless Darbies and Joans?
Gone with the wind like a flame;
Peace to his mouldering bones!
The Game of Cribbage

WILLIAM HENRY DAVIES
[1871–1940]

What glorious sunsets have their birth
In Cities fouled by smoke!
This tree — whose roots are in a
drain —
Becomes the greenest Oak!
Love's Rivals

Fools have their second childhood, but
the Great
Still keep their first, and have no second
state.
Men That Think

I am as certain of my song,
When first it warms the brain,
As woman of her unborn child,
Or wind that carries rain.
The Birth of Song

I had Ambition, by which sin
The angels fell;
I climbed and, step by step, O Lord,
Ascended into Hell.
Ambition

I'll make my Joy a secret thing,
My face shall wear a mask of care;
And those who hunt a Joy to death,
Shall never know what sport is there!
Hunting Joy. Stanza 3

[1] Cribbage was invented by Sir John
Suckling [1609–1642], according to the account in the *Brief Lives* of JOHN AUBREY
[1626–1697].

LADY PAMELA WYNDHAM
GLENCONNER
[1871–1928]

Bitter are the tears of a child:
Sweeten them.
Deep are the thoughts of a child:
Quiet them.
Sharp is the grief of a child:
Take it from him.
Soft is the heart of a child:
Do not harden it.
A Child

Giving presents is a talent; to know
what a person wants, to know when and
how to get it, to give it lovingly, and
well. Unless a character possesses this
talent there is no moment more annihilating to ease than that in which a present is received and given.
Edward Wyndham Tennant:
A Memoir. Chap. 5

ARTHUR GUITERMAN
[1871–1943]

The Antiseptic Baby and the Prophy-
lactic Pup
Were playing in the garden when the
Bunny gamboled up;
They looked upon the Creature with a
loathing undisguised; —
It wasn't Disinfected and it wasn't
Sterilized.
Strictly Germ-Proof. Stanza 1

The Cat on your hearthstone to this
day presages,
By solemnly sneezing, the coming of
rain! [1]
The First Cat. Stanza 7

Oh, the saddest of sights in a world of
sin
Is a little lost pup with his tail tucked
in!
Little Lost Pup. Stanza 1

[1] While rain depends, the pensive cat gives
o'er
Her frolics, and pursues her tail no more.
JONATHAN SWIFT: *Description of a*
City Shower [1710]

The finest thing in London is the
   Bobby; [1]
Benignant information is his hobby.
         The Lyric Baedeker. London

Amoebas at the start
   Were not complex;
They tore themselves apart
   And started Sex.
         Sex. Stanza 1

The three-toed tree-toad
Sings his sweet ode
   To the moon.
         Nocturne

Of all cold words of tongue or pen
The worst are these: "I knew him
   when — " [2]
    Prophets in Their Own Country

Oh, the Brown Missouri Mule has a
   copper-plated throat
And the welkin splits apart when he
   hits an upper note.
      Mule Song. Stanza 1

BURTON J. HENDRICK
[1871–1949]

The dissenting opinions of one generation become the prevailing interpretation of the next.
    Bulwark of the Republic [*1937*]

RALPH HODGSON
[1871–1962]

'Twould ring the bells of Heaven
The wildest peal for years,
If Parson lost his senses
And people came to theirs,
And he and they together
Knelt down with angry prayers
For tamed and shabby tigers
And dancing dogs and bears,
And wretched, blind pit ponies,
And little hunted hares.
      The Bells of Heaven

But oh, the den of wild things in
The darkness of her eyes!
        The Gypsy Girl

[1] The constable with lifted hand
  Conducting the orchestral Strand.
    STEPHEN PHILLIPS [1864–1915]:
              The Wife

[2] See Whittier, page 527b.

God loves an idle rainbow
No less than labouring seas.
         A Wood Song

Time, you old gypsy man,
   Will you not stay,
Put up your caravan
   Just for one day?
    Time, You Old Gypsy Man.
            Stanza 1

Pity him, this dupe of dream,
Leader of the herd again
Only in his daft old brain,
Once again the bull supreme.
         The Bull

Oh, had our simple Eve
Seen through the make-believe!
        Eve. Stanza 5

I climbed the hill as light fell short,
And rooks came home in scramble sort.
      The Song of Honor

I stared into the sky,
As wondering men have always done
Since beauty and the stars were one,
Though none so hard as I.
         Ibid.

Reason has moons, but moons not hers
   Lie mirrored on her sea,
Confounding her astronomers,
   But O! delighting me.
         Reason

JAMES WELDON JOHNSON
[1871–1938]

O black and unknown bards of long
   ago,
How came your lips to touch the sacred
   fire?
How, in your darkness, did you come to
   know
The power and beauty of the minstrel's
   lyre?
    O Black and Unknown Bards.
            Stanza 1

And God stepped out on space,
And He looked around and said,
"*I'm lonely —*
I'll make me a world."
    The Creation: A Negro Sermon.
            Stanza 1

CHARLES RANN KENNEDY
[1871–1950]

A peculiar kind of fear they call courage.

The Terrible Meek [1912]
The meek, the terrible meek, the fierce agonizing meek, are about to enter into their inheritance.

Ibid.

WILBUR DICK NESBIT
[1871–1927]

Who waits upon the when and how
Remains forever in the rear.
A Plea for the Friendless Present.
Stanza 4
Each page of them Quotations that this
    Bartlett man got out
Is sure to have old Ibid's prose or
    poems strung about.
"Old Ibid." Stanza 2
I'm gettin' so, when I read things particularly fine,
I know that Ibid's name will be below
    the endin' line.

Ibid.

HERBERT GEORGE PONTING
[1871–1935]

On the outside grows the furside, on the
    inside grows the skinside;
So the furside is the outside, and the
    skinside is the inside.

The Sleeping Bag [1]

MARCEL PROUST
[1871–1922]

When from a long-distant past nothing subsists, after the people are dead, after the things are broken and scattered, still, alone, more fragile, but with more vitality, more unsubstantial, more persistent, more faithful, the smell and taste of things remain poised a long

[1] For *The South Polar Times*, Midwinter Day, June 22, 1911, prepared by the men of Captain Robert Falcon Scott's last Antarctic expedition. Ponting was the photographer for the Scott expedition.

time, like souls, ready to remind us, waiting and hoping for their moment, amid the ruins of all the rest; and bear unfaltering, in the tiny and almost impalpable drop of their essence, the vast structure of recollection.

Remembrance of Things Past [1]
[1913–1926]. *Swann's Way*

In his younger days a man dreams of possessing the heart of the woman whom he loves; later, the feeling that he possesses the heart of a woman may be enough to make him fall in love with her.

Ibid.

What artists call posterity is the posterity of the work of art.

Ibid. Within a Budding Grove,
Part I

The time which we have at our disposal every day is elastic; the passions that we feel expand it, those that we inspire contract it; and habit fills up what remains.

Ibid.

Untruthfulness and dishonesty were with me, as with most people, called into being in so immediate, so contingent a fashion, and in self-defence, by some particular interest, that my mind, fixed on some lofty ideal, allowed my character, in the darkness below, to set about those urgent, sordid tasks, and did not look down to observe them.

Ibid. The Guermantes Way, Part I

Like everybody who is not in love, he imagined that one chose the person whom one loved after endless deliberations and on the strength of various qualities and advantages.

Ibid. Cities of the Plain, Part I

We passionately long that there may be another life in which we shall be similar to what we are here below. But we do not pause to reflect that, even without waiting for that other life, in this life, after a few years we are un-

[1] *A la Recherche du Temps Perdu*, translated by C. K. Scott Moncrieff, except the last section, *The Past Recaptured*, which was translated by Frederick A. Blossom.

faithful to what we have been, to what we wished to remain immortally.

Remembrance of Things Past. Cities of the Plain, Part II

It is often simply from want of the creative spirit that we do not go to the full extent of suffering. And the most terrible reality brings us, with our suffering, the joy of a great discovery, because it merely gives a new and clear form to what we have long been ruminating without suspecting it.

Ibid.

The bonds that unite another person to ourself exist only in our mind. Memory as it grows fainter relaxes them, and notwithstanding the illusion by which we would fain be cheated and with which, out of love, friendship, politeness, deference, duty, we cheat other people, we exist alone. Man is the creature that cannot emerge from himself, that knows his fellows only in himself; when he asserts the contrary, he is lying.

Ibid. The Sweet Cheat Gone

We do not succeed in changing things according to our desire, but gradually our desire changes. The situation that we hoped to change because it was intolerable becomes unimportant. We have not managed to surmount the obstacle, as we were absolutely determined to do, but life has taken us round it, led us past it, and then if we turn round to gaze at the remote past, we can barely catch sight of it, so imperceptible has it become.

Ibid.

There is not a woman in the world the possession of whom is as precious as that of the truths which she reveals to us by causing us to suffer.

Ibid.

We are healed of a suffering only by experiencing it to the full.

Ibid.

Happiness is beneficial for the body but it is grief that develops the powers of the mind.

Ibid. The Past Recaptured

As for happiness, it has hardly more than one useful quality, namely to make unhappiness possible. In our happiness, we should form very sweet bonds, full of confidence and attachment, in order that the sundering of them may cause us that priceless rending of the heart which is called unhappiness.

Remembrance of Things Past. The Past Recaptured

JOHN MILLINGTON SYNGE
[1871–1909]

It's in a lonesome place you do have to be talking with someone, and looking for someone, in the evening of the day.

In the Shadow of the Glen [*1903*]

What is the price of a thousand horses against a son where there is one son only?

Riders to the Sea [*1904*]

Bartley will have a fine coffin out of the white boards, and a deep grave surely. What more can we want than that? No man at all can be living for ever, and we must be satisfied.

Ibid.

When I was writing "The Shadow of the Glen" I got more aid than any learning could have given me from a chink in the floor of the old Wicklow house where I was staying, that let me hear what was being said by the servant girls in the kitchen.

The Playboy of the Western World [*1907*]. *Preface*

Drink a health to the wonders of the western world, the pirates, preachers, poteen-makers, with the jobbing jockies; parching peelers, and the juries fill their stomachs selling judgments of the English law.

Ibid. Act II

May I meet him with one tooth and it aching, and one eye to be seeing seven and seventy divils in the twists of the road, and one old timber leg on him to limp into the scalding grave. There he is now crossing the strands, and that the

Lord God would send a high wave to wash him from the world.[1]

> *The Playboy of the Western World. Act II*

Aid me for to win her, and I'll be asking God to stretch a hand to you in the hour of death, and lead you short cuts through the Meadows of Ease, and up the floor of Heaven to the Footstool of the Virgin's Son.

> *Ibid.*

A man who is not afraid of the sea will soon be drowned, he said, for he will be going out on a day he shouldn't. But we do be afraid of the sea, and we do only be drownded now and again.

> *The Aran Islands* [*1907*]

There is no language like the Irish for soothing and quieting.

> *Ibid.*

A translation is no translation, he said, unless it will give you the music of a poem along with the words of it.

> *Ibid.*

PAUL VALÉRY
[1871–1945]

The folly of mistaking a paradox for a discovery, a metaphor for a proof, a torrent of verbiage for a spring of capital truths, and oneself for an oracle, is inborn in us.

> *Introduction to the Method of Leonardo da Vinci*[2]

Collect all the facts that can be collected about the life of Racine and you will never learn from them the art of his verse. All criticism is dominated by the outworn theory that the man is the cause of the work as in the eyes of the law the criminal is the cause of the

[1] May the grass grow at your door and the fox build his nest on your hearthstone. May the light fade from your eyes, so you never see what you love. May your own blood rise against you, and the sweetest drink you take be the bitterest cup of sorrow. May you die without benefit of clergy; may there be none to shed a tear at your grave, and may the hearthstone of hell be your best bed forever. — *Traditional Wexford curse*

See O. Henry, page 802a.

[2] Translated by THOMAS McGREEVY.

crime. Far rather are they both the effects.

> *Introduction to the Method of Leonardo da Vinci*

ALBERT EDWARD WIGGAM
[1871–1957]

Intelligence appears to be the thing that enables a man to get along without education. Education appears to be the thing that enables a man to get along without the use of his intelligence.

> *The New Decalogue of Science* [*1923*]

Statesmanship should quickly learn the lesson of biology, as stated by Conklin, that "Wooden legs are not inherited, but wooden heads are."

> *Ibid.*

EVERARD JACK APPLETON
[1872–1931]

Somewhere she waits to make you win,
  Your soul in her firm white hands;
Somewhere the gods have made for you
  The woman who understands.

> *The Woman Who Understands*

SIR MAX BEERBOHM
[1872–1956]

Most women are not so young as they are painted.

> *A Defence of Cosmetics*

Zuleika, on a desert island, would have spent most of her time in looking for a man's foot-print.

> *Zuleika Dobson* [*1911*]. *Chap. 2*

She was hardly more affable than a cameo.

> *Ibid. Chap. 3*

The dullard's envy of brilliant men is always assuaged by the suspicion that they will come to a bad end.

> *Ibid. Chap. 4*

Ordinary saints grow faint to posterity; whilst quite ordinary sinners pass vividly down the ages.

> *Ibid. Chap. 6*

She was one of the people who say "I don't know anything about music really, but I know what I like." [1]
Zuleika Dobson. Chap. 9

The Oxford spirit — that gentlest spirit, so lingering and searching, so dear to them who as youths were brought into ken of it, so exasperating to them who were not.
Ibid. Chap. 12

Of all the objects of hatred, a woman once loved is the most hateful.
Ibid. Chap. 13

I have known no man of genius who had not to pay, in some affliction or defect either physical or spiritual, for what the gods had given him.
No. 2, The Pines

It seems to be a law of nature that no man ever is loth to sit for his portrait. A man may be old, he may be ugly, he may be burdened with grave responsibilities to the nation, and that nation be at a crisis of its history; but none of these considerations, nor all of them together, will deter him from sitting for his portrait.
Quia Imperfectum

To say that a man is vain means merely that he is pleased with the effect he produces on other people. A conceited man is satisfied with the effect he produces on himself.
Ibid.

Strange, when you come to think of it, that of all the countless folk who have lived before our time on this planet not one is known in history or in legend as having died of laughter.
Laughter

LÉON BLUM
[1872–1950]

Life does not give itself to one who tries to keep all its advantages at once.

I have often thought morality may perhaps consist solely in the courage of making a choice.
Quoted in The Practical Cogitator. [1]
Page 97

No government can remain stable in an unstable society and an unstable world.
A l'Échelle Humaine [1945].
Page 54

JAMES BONE
[1872–1962]

"London!" It has the sound of distant thunder.
The London Perambulator [1925]

The mighty fleet of Wren, with their topgallants and mainsails of stone.
Ibid.

It was in London that Whistler discovered the nocturne.
Ibid.

The City of Dreadful Height.
Description of New York [2]

To make a cliché is to make a classic. [3]
Farewell speech on Fleet Street, December 29, 1945

He made righteousness readable.
Of C. P. Scott [1846–1932], *editor of the Manchester Guardian*

PATRICK REGINALD CHALMERS
[1872–1942]

Oh, bright as a berry,
  They're red and they're rare,
The setters from Kerry,
  And Cork and Kildare!
The Red Dogs

"I find," said 'e, "things very much as 'ow I've always found,

---

[1] Bromide No. 1. — GELETT BURGESS: *Are You a Bromide?* [1906]
In art I pull no high-brow stuff,
I know what I like, and that's enough.
WILLIAM W. WOOLLCOTT [1877–1949]:
I Am a One Hundred Percent American, St. 3

[1] Selected and arranged by CHARLES P. CURTIS, JR., and FERRIS GREENSLET [1945].
[2] In *The Manchester Guardian.*
[3] Apropos the phrase "ocean greyhound," first said by his father, David Drummond Bone, Glasgow journalist, referring to the *Alaska* [1881], first ship to cross the Atlantic in less than a week.

For mostly they goes up and down or
  else goes round and round."
            Roundabouts and Swings.
                 Stanza 2
What's lost upon the roundabouts we
  pulls up on the swings!
                   Ibid.
A little dog
  Walked out that day with These,
Round eyes agog
  For butterflies and bees,
Wet nose for smells that please.
     A Chosen Saint.[1] *Stanza 3*

CALVIN COOLIDGE
[1872–1933]

There is no right to strike against the
public safety by anybody, anywhere,
any time.
    *Telegram to Samuel Gompers,
    President of the American Fed-
    eration of Labor, on the occa-
    sion of the Boston police strike
    [September 14, 1919]*
Inflation is repudiation.
  Speech, Chicago [January 11, 1922]
The business of America is business.
    *Speech before the Society of
    American Newspaper Editors
    [January 17, 1925]*
They hired the money, didn't they?
    *Referring to the European war
              debts [1925]*
I do not choose to run for President
in 1928.
    *Statement to reporters, Rapid
    City, South Dakota [August 2,
    1927]*
I love Vermont because of her hills
and valleys, her scenery and invigor-
ating climate, but most of all because
of her indomitable people.
    *Address from train platform,
    Bennington, Vermont [Septem-
    ber 21, 1928]*

[1] Go thou with this man, and God, which
dwelleth in heaven, prosper your journey,
and the angel of God keep you company. So
they went forth both, and the young man's
dog with them. — *The Apocrypha: Tobit,
V, 16*

JAMES B. DOLLARD
[1872–   ]

I'm sick o' New York City an' the
  roarin' o' the thrains
That rowl above the blessèd roofs an'
  undernaith the dhrains;
Wid dust an' smoke an' divilmint I'm
  moidhered head an' brains,
  An' I'm thinkin' o' the skies of ould
    Kilkinny!
                Ould Kilkinny!

PAUL LAURENCE DUNBAR
[1872–1906]

Folks ain't got no right to censuah otha
  folks about dey habits;
Him dat giv' de squir'ls de bushtails
  made de bobtails fu' de rabbits.
              Accountability
You cain't sta't no notes a-flyin'
  Lak de ones dat rants and rings
From de kitchen to de big woods
  When Malindy sings.
          When Malindy Sings
There is a heaven, for ever, day by day,
The upward longing of my soul doth
  tell me so.
There is a hell, I'm quite as sure; for
  pray,
If there were not, where would my
  neighbors go?
                 Theology
Speak up, Ike, an' 'spress yo'se'f.
             Encouragement
Sweetah den de music of a lovesick
  mockin'-bird,
Comin' f'om de gal you loves better den
  yo' kin,
"Howdy, honey, howdy, won't you step
  right in?"
      "Howdy, Honey, Howdy!"
Heish yo' mouf, I's only tu'nin' of de
  chillun in de bed.
      *The Turning of the Babies
                 in the Bed*
It's easy 'nough to titter w'en de stew
  is smokin' hot,
But hit's mighty ha'd to giggle w'en
  dey's nuffin' in de pot.
              Philosophy

Poor was the loan at best —
God! but the interest!
The Debt. Stanza 3

LEARNED HAND
[1872–1961]

Justice, I think, is the tolerable accommodation of the conflicting interests of society, and I don't believe there is any royal road to attain such accommodations concretely.
Quoted by PHILIP HAMBURGER: *The Great Judge* [LIFE, *November 4, 1946*]

I had rather take my chance that some traitors will escape detection than spread abroad a spirit of general suspicion and distrust, which accepts rumor and gossip in place of undismayed and unintimidated inquiry.
Speech, Convocation of the Board of Regents, University of the State of New York [*October 24, 1952*]

That community is already in the process of dissolution where each man begins to eye his neighbor as a possible enemy, where nonconformity with the accepted creed, political as well as religious, is a mark of disaffection; where denunciation, without specification or backing, takes the place of evidence; where orthodoxy chokes freedom of dissent; where faith in the eventual supremacy of reason has become so timid that we dare not enter our convictions in the open lists, to win or lose.
Ibid.

The mutual confidence on which all else depends can be maintained only by an open mind and a brave reliance upon free discussion.
Ibid.

MILDRED HOWELLS
[1872–   ]

And so it criticized each flower,
This supercilious seed;
Until it woke one summer hour,
And found itself a weed.
The Difficult Seed. Stanza 5

Oh, tell me how my garden grows,
Where I no more may take delight,
And if some dream of me it knows,
Who dream of it by day and night.
Oh, Tell Me How My Garden Grows. Stanza 5

RUPERT HUGHES
[1872–1948]

Dear little child, this little book
Is less a primer than a key
To sunder gates where wonder waits
Your "Open Sesame!"
With a First Reader

JOHN McCRAE
[1872–1918]

In Flanders fields the poppies blow
Between the crosses, row on row.
In Flanders Fields.[1] *Stanza 1*

Take up our quarrel with the foe:
To you from failing hands we throw
The torch; be yours to hold it high.
If ye break faith with us who die
We shall not sleep, though poppies grow
In Flanders fields.
Ibid. Stanza 3

PATRICK F. O'KEEFE
[1872–1934]

Say It with Flowers.[2]
Slogan for the Society of American Florists [*1917*]

CALE YOUNG RICE
[1872–1943]

Spring has come up from the South again,
With soft mists in her hair,
And a warm wind in her mouth again,
And budding everywhere.
The Immortal. Stanza 1

You who are old,
And have fought the fight,
And have won or lost or left the fight,

[1] In *Punch*, December 8, 1915.
[2] Say It with Music. — *Title of song by* IRVING BERLIN [*1921*]

Weight us not down
With fears of the world, as we run!
The Young to the Old

BERTRAND RUSSELL
[1872–   ]

It is preoccupation with possession, more than anything else, that prevents men from living freely and nobly.
*Principles of Social Recon-
struction* [*1916*]

Mathematics possesses not only truth, but supreme beauty — a beauty cold and austere, like that of sculpture, without appeal to any part of our weaker nature, sublimely pure, and capable of a stern perfection such as only the greatest art can show.
The Study of Mathematics

Mathematics takes us into the region of absolute necessity, to which not only the actual world, but every possible world, must conform.
Ibid.

The psychology of adultery has been falsified by conventional morals, which assume, in monogamous countries, that attraction to one person cannot coexist with a serious affection for another. Everybody knows that this is untrue.
Marriage and Morals [*1929*]. *XVI*

A good society is a means to a good life for those who compose it; not something having a kind of excellence on its own account.
Authority and the Individual
[*1949*]

ELLERY SEDGWICK
[1872–   ]

Autobiographies ought to begin with Chapter Two.
The Happy Profession [*1946*].
Chap. 1

Maternal testimony notwithstanding, babies are like as biscuits in a pan.
Ibid.

In America, getting on in the world means getting out of the world we have known before.
Ibid.

Democracy's real test lies in its respect for minority opinion.
The Happy Profession. Chap. 5

Against the misuse of words every editorial prejudice should be fixed in concrete.
Ibid. Chap. 18

ALBERT PAYSON TERHUNE
[1872–1942]

Win without boasting. Lose without excuse.
More About Dog Shows

ERNEST VINCENT WRIGHT
[1872–1939]

Then all of us prepare to rise
And hold our bibs before our eyes,
And be prepared for some surprise
When father carves the duck.
When Father Carves the Duck
[*1891*]. *Stanza 1*

CARL LOTUS BECKER
[1873–1945]

Economic distress will teach men, if anything can, that realities are less dangerous than fancies, that fact-finding is more effective than fault-finding.
Progress and Power [*1935*]

The significance of man is that he is that part of the universe that asks the question, What is the significance of Man? He alone can stand apart imaginatively and, regarding himself and the universe in their eternal aspects, pronounce a judgment: The significance of man is that he is insignificant and is aware of it.
Ibid.

Those of us who think that we are a nation of starry-eyed idealists [1] who have been twice tricked by the British into a European war in order to pull their chestnuts out of the fire have read the history of this country to little purpose. . . . The truth is rather that the existence and friendliness of the British

[1] See Henry Agard Wallace, page 948b.

861

Empire and the power of the British Fleet have for more than a century enabled us to roast our own chestnuts at leisure and eat them in security.
Progress and Power

HENRY NOEL BRAILSFORD
[1874–1958]

Music is neither secular nor religious. It can at best suggest the beating of the pulse, the rhythm of the blood that accompanies a given order of ideas.
On Handel's Largo

The musician who tries to rival the painter by describing external things, is a magician who has thrown aside his wand to wield a quarter-staff.
The Sea in Music

GUY WETMORE CARRYL
[1873–1904]

You call it a waste of time, this taste
　For popular tunes, and yet
Good-bye to care when you whistle the
　air
Of the song that you can't forget.
The Organ Man. Stanza 3

And in his dim, uncertain sight
Whatever wasn't must be right,
From which it follows he had strong
Convictions that what was, was wrong.
*The Iconoclastic Rustic and the
Apropos Acorn. Stanza 2*

In every new and smart disease,
From housemaid's knee to heart disease,
She recognized the symptoms as her
　own!
*How Jack Found That Beans May
Go Back on a Chap. Stanza 2*

The people wait at the haven's gate to
　greet the men who win!
Thank God for peace! Thank God for
　peace, when the great gray ships
　come in!
*When the Great Gray Ships
Come In. Stanza 4*

ARTHUR CHAPMAN
[1873–1935]

Out where the handclasp's a little
　stronger,
Out where the smile dwells a little
　longer,
That's where the West begins.
*Out Where the West Begins.
Stanza 1*

Out where the skies are a trifle bluer,
Out where friendship's a little truer.
Ibid. Stanza 2

Where there's more of singing and less
　of sighing,
Where there's more of giving and less of
　buying,
And a man makes friends without half
　trying.
Ibid. Stanza 3

WALTER DE LA MARE
[1873–1956]

Slowly, silently, now the moon
Walks the night in her silver shoon.
Silver

"World of divine delight," heart whispereth,
Though all its all lie but 'twixt birth
　and death.
Divine Delight

Here lies a most beautiful lady,
Light of step and heart was she.
An Epitaph

"Is there anybody there?" said the
　Traveller,
Knocking on the moonlit door;
And his horse in the silence champed
　the grasses
Of the forest's ferny floor.
The Listeners

"Tell them that I came, and no one
　answered,
That I kept my word," he said.
Ibid.

If I were Lord of Tartary,
　Myself and me alone,
My bed should be of ivory,
　Of beaten gold my throne.
Tartary. Stanza 1

'Tis the immortal thought
  Whose passion still
Makes of the unchanging
  The unchangeable.
        When the Rose Is Faded.
          Stanza 3

No lovelier hills than thine have laid
  My tired thoughts to rest:
No peace of lovelier valleys made
  Like peace within my breast.
        England. Stanza 1

Hi! handsome hunting man,
Fire your little gun.
Bang! Now the animal
Is dead and dumb and done.
Nevermore to peep again, creep again,
  leap again,
Eat or sleep or drink again, oh, what
  fun!
        Hi!

Memory — that strange deceiver!
Who can trust her? How believe her —
While she hoards with equal care
The poor and trivial, rich and rare;
Yet flings away, as wantonly,
Grave fact and loveliest fantasy?
        Memory

Poor Jim Jay
Got stuck fast
In Yesterday.
        Jim Jay

It's a very odd thing —
As odd as can be —
That whatever Miss T. eats
Turns into Miss T.
        Miss T.

Three jolly gentlemen,
In coats of red,
Rode their horses
Up to bed.
        The Huntsmen

Not the briefest moment — yours or
  mine —
Can ever come again.
        Not One. Stanza 2

Be not too wildly amorous of the far,
Nor lure thy fantasy to its utmost scope.
        The Imagination's Pride

I met at eve the Prince of Sleep,
  His was a still and lovely face,

He wandered through a valley steep,
  Lovely in a lonely place.
        I Met at Eve

MARK FENDERSON
[1873–1944]

What's the use? Yesterday an egg,
tomorrow a feather duster.
        Caption of Cartoon, The
          Dejected Rooster

FORD MADOX (HUEFFER) FORD
[1873–1939]

Sometimes wind and sometimes rain,
Then the sun comes back again;
Sometimes rain and sometimes snow,
Goodness, how we'd like to know
Why the weather alters so.
        Children's Song. Stanza 1

Only two classes of books are of universal appeal: the very best and the very worst.
        Joseph Conrad [*1924*]

PERCY HAMMOND
[1873–1936]

The female knee is a joint and not an entertainment.
        Dramatic Review

DANIEL GREGORY MASON
[1873–   ]

The ideal of Independence requires resistance to the herd spirit now so widespread, to our worship of quantity and indifference to quality, to our unthinking devotion to organization, standardization, propaganda, and advertising.
        Artistic Ideals [*1927*]

Art of any profundity can be appreciated only slowly, gradually, in leisurely contemplation.
        Ibid.

JAMES JACKSON MONTAGUE
[1873–1941]

My beagle bit a Kleagle
Of the Ku Klux Klan.
> *Doomed. Stanza 1*

But no one ever is allowed in Sleepy-
town, unless
He goes to bed in time to take the
Sleepytown Express!
> *The Sleepytown Express. Stanza 1*

ELIZABETH CUTTER
(MRS. DWIGHT WHITNEY)
MORROW
[1873–1955]

My friend and I have built a wall
Between us thick and wide:
The stones of it are laid in scorn
And plastered high with pride.
> *Wall. Stanza 1*

There is no lover like an island shore
For lingering embrace;
No tryst so faithful as the turning tide
At its accustomed place.
> *Islands. Stanza 1*

ALBERT JAY NOCK
[1873–1945]

All Souls College, Oxford, planned
better than it knew when it limited the
number of its undergraduates to four;
four is exactly the right number for any
college which is really intent on getting
results.
> *Memoirs of a Superfluous Man*
> *[1943]. III, Chap. 3*

Money does not pay for anything,
never has, never will. It is an economic
axiom as old as the hills that goods and
services can be paid for only with goods
and services.
> *Ibid. Chap. 13*

As sheer casual reading-matter, I still
find the English dictionary the most
interesting book in our language.
> *Ibid. IV, Chap. 1*

SIME SILVERMAN [1]
[1873–1933]

Wall Street Lays An Egg.
> *Headline announcing the stock*
> *market crash of October, 1929*

Sticks Nix Hicks Pix.
> *Headline, meaning that the*
> *rural audiences do not care for*
> *moving pictures dealing with*
> *country themes*

ALFRED EMANUEL SMITH [2]
[1873–1944]

The kiss of death.
> *Alluding to Hearst's support of*
> *Ogden Mills, Smith's unsuccess-*
> *ful opponent in the 1926 cam-*
> *paign for Governor of New*
> *York State*

Let's look at the record.
> *Campaign Speeches [1928]*

The Governor of New York State
does not have to be an acrobat.
> *Speech in behalf of Franklin*
> *D. Roosevelt [1928]*

Nobody shoots at Santa Claus.
> *Campaign Speeches [1936]*

No matter how thin you slice it, it's
still boloney.
> *Ibid.*

H. M. TOMLINSON
[1873–   ]

The sea is at its best at London, near
midnight, when you are within the
arms of a capacious chair, before a
glowing fire, selecting phases of the
voyages you will never make.
> *The Sea and the Jungle [1912]*

[1] Silverman, who founded and edited the
famous theatrical trade paper *Variety* [1905],
had perhaps more influence on American
slang than any man of his time.

[2] He is the Happy Warrior of the political
battlefield. — FRANKLIN D. ROOSEVELT: *Nominating Speech, Democratic National Convention* [June 26, 1924] (See Wordsworth,
pages 409b–410a.)
Al Smith knew as much as any living man
of the art of democratic government. — EL-
LERY SEDGWICK: *The Happy Profession*
[1946], *Chap. 17*

How many grave speeches, which have surprised, shocked, and directed the nation, have been made by Great Men too soon after a noble dinner, words winged by the Press without an accompanying and explanatory wine list.
Waiting for Daylight [*1922*]
The reader who is illuminated is, in a real sense, the poem.
Between the Lines [*1930*]
Bad and indifferent criticism of books is just as serious as a city's careless drainage.
Ibid.
What was created in Concord, though in so airy a fashion, may be standing to America's credit when her vast engine shops are homes for spiders.
The Road to Concord [*1931*]

LENA GUILBERT FORD
[*Floruit* 1915]

Keep the home fires burning,
While your hearts are yearning,
Though your lads are far away
They dream of home.
There's a silver lining
Through the dark cloud shining,
Turn the dark cloud inside out,
Till the boys come home.
Keep the Home Fires Burning [*1915*]

SIR NORMAN ANGELL
[1874–   ]

The Great Illusion.
Title of book [*1910*] *on the futility of war*
The power of words is such that they have prevented our learning some of the most important events in the world's history.
Let the People Know [*1943*]. *Chap. 7: Words That Are Assassins*

MAURICE BARING
[1874–1945]

All theories of what a good play is, or how a good play should be written, are futile. A good play is a play which when acted upon the boards makes an audience interested and pleased. A play that fails in this is a bad play.
Have You Anything to Declare?

CHARLES AUSTIN BEARD
[1874–1948]
AND
MARY RITTER BEARD
[1876–   ]

At no time, at no place, in solemn convention assembled, through no chosen agents, had the American people officially proclaimed the United States to be a democracy. The Constitution did not contain the word or any word lending countenance to it, except possibly the mention of "We, the people," in the preamble . . . when the Constitution was framed no respectable person called himself or herself a democrat.
America in Midpassage [*1939*]. *Chap. 17*

SIR DAVID WILLIAM BONE
[1874–   ]

We sailors are jealous for our vessels. Abuse us if you will, but have a care for what you may say of our ships. We alone are entitled to call them bitches, wet brutes, stubborn craft, but we will stand for no such liberties from the beach.
Merchantmen-at-Arms

GORDON BOTTOMLEY
[1874–1948]

Many deaths have place in men
Before they come to die;
Joys must be used and spent, and then
Abandoned and passed by.
New Year's Eve, 1913
When you destroy a blade of grass
You poison England at her roots.
To Ironfounders and Others

Your worship is your furnaces,
Which, like old idols, lost obscenes,
Have molten bowels; your vision is
Machines for making more machines.
To Ironfounders and Others

ANNA HEMPSTEAD BRANCH
[1874–1937]

Order is a lovely thing;
On disarray it lays its wing,
Teaching simplicity to sing.
The Monk in the Kitchen
His screaming stallions maned with
whistling wind.
Nimrod Wars with the Angels
God wove a web of loveliness,
Of clouds and stars and birds,
But made not anything at all
So beautiful as words.
*Songs for My Mother: Her
Words. Stanza 5*
Oh, grieve not, ladies, if at night
Ye wake to feel your beauty going.
It was a web of frail delight,
Inconstant as an April snowing.
Grieve Not, Ladies. Stanza 1

ARTHUR HENRY REGINALD BULLER
[1874–1944]

There was a young lady named Bright,
Whose speed was far faster than light;
She set out one day
In a relative way,
And returned home the previous night.
Limerick [1]

GILBERT KEITH CHESTERTON
[1874–1936]

Nothing sublimely artistic has ever
arisen out of mere art, any more than
anything essentially reasonable has
ever arisen out of the pure reason.
There must always be a rich moral soil
for any great aesthetic growth.
A Defence of Nonsense

[1] *Punch,* December 19, 1923.

Every great literature has always
been allegorical — allegorical of some
view of the whole universe.
A Defence of Nonsense
The whole difference between construction and creation is exactly this:
that a thing constructed can only be
loved after it is constructed; but a
thing created is loved before it exists.
Preface to DICKENS'S
Pickwick Papers
A man knows what style of book he
wants to write when he knows nothing
else about it.
Ibid.
A good joke is the one ultimate and
sacred thing which cannot be criticized.
Our relations with a good joke are di-
rect and even divine relations.
Ibid.
The world will never starve for won-
ders; but only for want of wonder.
*Inscription on General Motors
Building, Century of Progress
Exposition, Chicago*
But they that fought for England,
Following a fallen star,
Alas, alas for England
They have their graves afar.
Elegy in a Country Churchyard
Thieves respect property. They
merely wish the property to become
their property that they may more per-
fectly respect it.
Ibid.
Mr. Max Beerbohm attempted to
analyze the jokes at which the mob
laughs. He divided them into three sec-
tions: jokes about bodily humiliation,
jokes about things alien, such as foreigners, and jokes about bad cheese.
Cockneys and Their Jokes
Art is limitation; the essence of
every picture is the frame.
Orthodoxy. Chap. 3
You can free things from alien or accidental laws, but not from the laws of
their own nature. . . . Do not go
about as a demagogue, encouraging triangles to break out of the prison of
their three sides. If a triangle breaks

out of its three sides, its life comes to a lamentable end.
Orthodoxy. Chap. 3

Heights were made to be looked at, not to be looked from.
The Innocence of Father Brown
(The Hammer of God)

The English poor, broken in every revolt, bullied by every fashion, long despoiled of property, and now being despoiled of liberty, entered history with a noise of trumpets, and turned themselves in two years into one of the iron armies of the world.
A Short History of England [*1917*]

The cold queen of England is looking
   in the glass;
The shadow of the Valois is yawning at
   the Mass.
Lepanto

Don John of Austria is going to the
   war.
Ibid.

The hidden room in man's house where
   God sits all the year,
The secret window whence the world
   looks small and very dear.
Ibid.

Cervantes on his galley sets the sword
   back in the sheath
(Don John of Austria rides homeward
   with a wreath).
And he sees across a weary land a
   straggling road in Spain,
Up which a lean and foolish knight forever rides in vain.
Ibid.

To an open house in the evening
Home shall men come,
To an older place than Eden
And a taller town than Rome.
The House of Christmas

Burn from my brain and from my
   breast
Sloth, and the cowardice that clings,
And stiffness and the soul's arrest:
And feed my brain with better things.
A Ballade of a Book-Reviewer

The strangest whim has seized me . . .
   After all
I think I will not hang myself today.
A Ballade of Suicide

St. George he was for England,
And before he killed the dragon
He drank a pint of English ale
Out of an English flagon.
The Englishman

Step softly, under snow or rain,
To find the place where men can pray;
The way is all so very plain
That we may lose the way.
The Wise Men

And Noah he often said to his wife
   when he sat down to dine,
"I don't care where the water goes if
   it doesn't get into the wine."
Wine and Water

Before the Roman came to Rye or out
   to Severn strode,
The rolling English drunkard made the
   rolling English road.
The Rolling English Road

Tea is like the East he grows in,
A great yellow Mandarin
With urbanity of manner
And unconsciousness of sin.
The Song of Right and Wrong

Cocoa is a cad and coward.
Ibid.

For the great Gaels of Ireland
   Are the men that God made mad,
For all their wars are merry,
   And all their songs are sad.[1]
The Ballad of the White Horse.
Book II

And if ever ye ride in Ireland,
   The jest may yet be said,
There is the land of broken hearts,
   And the land of broken heads.
Ibid. Book V

I also had my hour;
One far fierce hour and sweet:
There was a shout about my ears,
And palms before my feet.
The Donkey

The Yankee is a dab at electricity and
   crime,
He tells you how he hustles and it takes
   him quite a time,

[1] For the Young Gaels of Ireland
   Are the lads that drive me mad;
For half their words need footnotes,
   And half their rhymes are bad.
ARTHUR GUITERMAN [1871-1943]:
The Young Celtic Poets, St. 1

I like his hospitality that's cordial and
frank,
I do not mind his money but I do not
like his swank.
A Song of Self-Esteem

The face of Father Brown . . .
could shine with ignorance as well as
with knowledge.[1]
The Wisdom of Father Brown

SIR WINSTON SPENCER CHURCHILL [2]
[1874–1965]

I pass with relief from the tossing
sea of Cause and Theory to the firm
ground of Result and Fact.
The Malakand Field Force [1898]

It is better to be making the news
than taking it; to be an actor rather
than a critic.
Ibid.

Nothing in life is so exhilarating as
to be shot at without result.
Ibid.

There are men in the world who derive as stern an exaltation from the
proximity of disaster and ruin, as others
from success.
Ibid.

Terminological inexactitude.
*Speech, House of Commons,
February 22, 1906*

The maxim of the British people is
"Business as usual."
*Speech, Guildhall, November 9,
1914*

By being so long in the lowest form
[at Harrow] I gained an immense advantage over the cleverer boys. . . .
I got into my bones the essential structure of the ordinary British sentence —
which is a noble thing. Naturally I am

biassed in favor of boys learning English; and then I would let the clever
ones learn Latin as an honor, and Greek
as a treat.
*Roving Commission: My Early
Life [1930]*

Decided only to be undecided, resolved to be irresolute, adamant for
drift, solid for fluidity, all-powerful to
be impotent.[1]
While England Slept [1936]

Dictators ride to and fro upon tigers
which they dare not dismount. And the
tigers are getting hungry.
Ibid.

I have watched this famous island
descending incontinently, fecklessly,
the stairway which leads to a dark gulf.
It is a fine broad stairway at the beginning, but after a bit the carpet ends.
A little farther on there are only flag-
stones, and a little farther on still these
break beneath your feet.
Ibid.

The German dictator, instead of
snatching the victuals from the table,
has been content to have them served
to him course by course.
*Speech on the Munich Agree-
ment, House of Commons,
October 5, 1938*

That long [Canadian] frontier from
the Atlantic to the Pacific Oceans,
guarded only by neighborly respect
and honorable obligations, is an example to every country and a pattern
for the future of the world.
*Speech in honor of R. B.
Bennett, Canada Club, London,
April 20, 1939*

I cannot forecast to you the action
of Russia. It is a riddle wrapped in a
mystery inside an enigma.
Broadcast, October 1, 1939

For each and for all, as for the
Royal Navy, the watchword should be,
"Carry on, and dread nought."
*Speech on Traffic at Sea, House
of Commons, December 6, 1939*

---

[1] My father, a good man, told me "Never
lose your ignorance; you cannot replace it."
— ERICH MARIA REMARQUE, interviewed in
The New York Times, January 27, 1946

[2] See also Roosevelt and Churchill, page
922a.

[1] Of Stanley Baldwin's policies.

I have nothing to offer but blood, toil, tears and sweat.[1]

> *First Statement as Prime Minister, House of Commons, May 13, 1940*

Victory at all costs, victory in spite of all terror, victory however long and hard the road may be; for without victory there is no survival.

> *Ibid.*

We shall not flag or fail. We shall fight in France, we shall fight on the seas and oceans, we shall fight with growing confidence and growing strength in the air, we shall defend our island, whatever the cost may be, we shall fight on the beaches, we shall fight on the landing grounds, we shall fight in the fields and in the streets, we shall fight in the hills; we shall never surrender.

> *Speech on Dunkirk, House of Commons, June 4, 1940*

If we open a quarrel between the past and the present, we shall find that we have lost the future.

> *Speech, House of Commons (later broadcast), June 18, 1940*

Let us therefore brace ourselves to our duties, and so bear ourselves that, if the British Empire and its Common-

---

[1] Mollifie it with thy teares, or sweat, or blood. — JOHN DONNE: *An Anatomy of the World* [1611], *I, 430–431*

Year after year they voted cent per cent,
Blood, sweat, and tear-wrung millions —
why? for rent!
BYRON: *The Age of Bronze* [1823], *XIV*

A similar phrase was also used by GIUSEPPE GARIBALDI [1807–1882] in his *Address to the Thousand.*

It [poetry] is forged slowly and patiently, link by link, with sweat and blood and tears. — LORD ALFRED DOUGLAS: *Collected Poems* [1919]

Their sweat, their tears, their blood bedewed the endless plain. — WINSTON S. CHURCHILL: *The Unknown War* [1931], referring to the armies of the Czar before the Russian Revolution

Churchill referred to his promise of blood, toil, tears and sweat in subsequent speeches on October 8, 1940, May 7 and December 2, 1941, and January 27 and November 10, 1942.

---

wealth last for a thousand years, men will still say: "This was their finest hour."

> *Speech, House of Commons, June 18, 1940*

We shall defend every village, every town and every city. The vast mass of London itself, fought street by street, could easily devour an entire hostile army; and we would rather see London laid in ruins and ashes than that it should be tamely and abjectly enslaved.

> *Radio Broadcast, July 14, 1940*

Never in the field of human conflict was so much owed by so many to so few.

> *Tribute to the Royal Air Force, House of Commons, August 20, 1940*

The British Empire and the United States will have to be somewhat mixed up together in some of their affairs for mutual and general advantage. For my own part, looking out upon the future, I do not view the process with any misgivings. I could not stop it if I wished; no one can stop it. Like the Mississippi, it just keeps rolling along.[1] Let it roll. Let it roll on full flood, inexorable, irresistible, benignant, to broader lands and better days.

> *Ibid.*

This wicked man Hitler, the repository and embodiment of many forms of soul-destroying hatred, this monstrous product of former wrongs and shame.

> *Radio Broadcast, September 11, 1940*

Death and sorrow will be the companions of our journey; hardship our garment; constancy and valor our only shield. We must be united, we must be undaunted, we must be inflexible.

> *Report on the War Situation, House of Commons, October 8, 1940*

---

[1] Ol' Man River [Mississippi] . . . he keeps on rollin' along. — OSCAR HAMMERSTEIN 2ND [1927], *music by* JEROME KERN

We are waiting for the long-promised invasion. So are the fishes.

> *Radio Broadcast to the French People, October 21, 1940*

The only guide to a man is his conscience; the only shield to his memory is the rectitude and sincerity of his actions.

> *Tribute to Neville Chamberlain, House of Commons, November 12, 1940*

To die at the height of a man's career, the highest moment of his effort here in this world, universally honored and admired, to die while great issues are still commanding the whole of his interest, to be taken from us at a moment when he could already see ultimate success in view — is not the most unenviable of fates.[1]

> *Report on the War Situation, House of Commons, December 19, 1940*

I do not resent criticism, even when, for the sake of emphasis, it parts for the time with reality.

> *Speech, House of Commons, January 22, 1941*

Here is the answer which I will give to President Roosevelt. . . . Give us the tools, and we will finish the job.

> *Radio Broadcast, February 9, 1941*

This is one of those cases in which the imagination is baffled by the facts.

> *Remark in the House of Commons, May 13, 1941 [following the parachute descent in Scotland by Rudolf Hess]*

The British nation is unique in this respect. They are the only people who like to be told how bad things are, who like to be told the worst.

> *Report on the War Situation, House of Commons, June 10, 1941*

A vile race of quislings[2] — to use the new word which will carry the scorn of mankind down the centuries.

> *Speech at St. James's Palace, London, June 12, 1941*

The destiny of mankind is not decided by material computation. When great causes are on the move in the world . . . we learn that we are spirits, not animals, and that something is going on in space and time, and beyond space and time, which, whether we like it or not, spells duty.

> *Radio Broadcast to America on receiving the Honorary Degree of Doctor of Laws from the University of Rochester, New York, June 16, 1941*

We will have no truce or parley with you [Hitler], or the grisly gang who work your wicked will. You do your worst — and we will do our best.

> *Speech, London County Council, July 14, 1941*

The V sign is the symbol of the unconquerable will of the occupied territories, and a portent of the fate awaiting the Nazi tyranny.

> *A Message to the People of Europe on the Launching of the "V for Victory" Propaganda Campaign, July 20, 1941*

Nothing is more dangerous in wartime than to live in the temperamental atmosphere of a Gallup Poll,[1] always feeling one's pulse and taking one's temperature.

> *Report on the War Situation, House of Commons, September 30, 1941*

Do not let us speak of darker days; let us speak rather of sterner days. These are not dark days: these are great days — the greatest days our country has ever lived; and we must all thank God that we have been allowed, each of us according to our stations, to

[1] Lord Lothian, British Ambassador to the United States, died in Washington, December 12, 1940.

[2] Vidkun Quisling, head of the Nasjonal Samling party in Norway, who co-operated and collaborated with the Nazis when Germany invaded Norway, April 9, 1940. Quisling was executed October 23, 1945.

[1] Dr. George H. Gallup founded the British Institute of Public Opinion in 1936.

play a part in making these days memorable in the history of our race.
> *Address to the Boys of Harrow School, October 29, 1941*

In the past we have had a light which flickered, in the present we have a light which flames, and in the future there will be a light which shines over all the land and sea.
> *Speech on War with Japan, House of Commons, December 8, 1941, and later broadcast*

What kind of people do they [the Japanese] think we are?
> *Speech to United States Congress, December 24, 1941*

We have not journeyed all this way across the centuries, across the oceans, across the mountains, across the prairies, because we are made of sugar candy.
> *Speech to the Canadian Senate and House of Commons, Ottawa, broadcast, December 30, 1941*

When I warned [the French] that Britain would fight on alone whatever they did, their generals told their Prime Minister and his divided Cabinet, "In three weeks England will have her neck wrung like a chicken." Some chicken; some neck.
> *Ibid.*

The late M. Venizelos [1] observed that in all her wars England — he should have said Britain, of course — always wins one battle — the last.
> *Speech at the Lord Mayor's Day Luncheon, London, November 10, 1942*

Now this is not the end. It is not even the beginning of the end.[2] But it is, perhaps, the end of the beginning.
> *Ibid.*

I have not become the King's First Minister in order to preside over the liquidation of the British Empire.
> *Ibid.*

[1] Eleutherios Venizelos [1864–1936], Greek statesman.
[2] See Talleyrand, page 384a.

The soft under-belly of the Axis.
> *Report on the War Situation, House of Commons, November 11, 1942*

There is no finer investment for any community than putting milk into babies.
> *Radio Broadcast: A Four Years' Plan, March 21, 1943*

The proud German Army has once again proved the truth of the saying, "The Hun is always either at your throat or at your feet."
> *Speech to United States Congress, May 19, 1943*

I quote the words of your great general, Nathan Bedford Forrest, the eminently successful Confederate leader. Asked the secret of his victories, Forrest said, "I git thar fustest with the mostest men." [1]
> *A Talk to the American Press in Washington, May 25, 1943*

The House of Commons thrives on criticism, it is perfectly impervious to newspaper abuse or taunts from any quarter, and it is capable of digesting almost anything or almost any body of gentlemen, whatever be the views with which they arrive.
> *Speech on Rebuilding the House of Commons, October 28, 1943*

There was a man who sold a hyena skin while the beast still lived and who was killed in hunting it.
> *Speech on Allied War Gains, House of Commons, August 2, 1944*

"Not in vain" may be the pride of those who survived and the epitaph of those who fell.[2]
> *Speech, House of Commons, September 28, 1944*

[1] General Nathan Bedford Forrest [1821–1877], Confederate cavalry leader. Historians deny that the General said it in such rustic terms, but the saying has become classic in this version.
[2] The eight thousand paratroopers of the First British Airborne Division who landed ïŧ Arnhem, Holland, behind the German lines, in September, 1944, and held the area for nine days and nights, with a loss of six thou-

The United States is a land of free speech. Nowhere is speech freer — not even here where we sedulously cultivate it even in its most repulsive form.
Speech, House of Commons, September 28, 1944

He died in harness, and we may well say in battle harness, like his soldiers, sailors and airmen who died side by side with ours and carrying out their tasks to the end all over the world. What an enviable death was his.
Tribute to President Franklin D. Roosevelt in the House of Commons, April 17, 1945

In Franklin Roosevelt there died the greatest American friend we have ever known — and the greatest champion of freedom who has ever brought help and comfort from the new world to the old.
Ibid.

I think "No comment" is a splendid expression. I am using it again and again. I got it from Sumner Welles.
To reporters at Washington airport, after conferring with President Truman at the White House, February 12, 1946

An iron curtain [1] has descended across the Continent.
Address at Westminster College, Fulton, Missouri, March 5, 1946

This address to which I have given the title, "The Sinews of Peace."
Ibid.

In War: Resolution. In Defeat: Defiance. In Victory: Magnanimity. In Peace: Good Will.
The Second World War: Moral of the Work. Vol. I, The Gathering Storm [1948]

No one can guarantee success in war, but only deserve it.
The Second World War: Moral of the Work. Vol. II, Their Finest Hour [1949]

When you have to kill a man it costs nothing to be polite.
Ibid. Vol. III, The Grand Alliance [1950]

This is the sort of impertinence up with which I will not put.[1]
Attributed

ISABEL FISKE CONANT
[1874–   ]

He who loves an old house
Never loves in vain,
How can an old house
Used to sun and rain,
To lilac and larkspur,
And an elm above,
Ever fail to answer
The heart that gives it love?
Old House. Stanza 1

CLARENCE DAY
[1874–1935]

When eras die, their legacies
Are left to strange police.
Professors in New England guard
The glory that was Greece.
Thoughts Without Words

The parting injunctions
Of mothers and wives
Are one of those functions
That poison their lives.
Scenes from the Mesozoic

It is possible that our race may be an accident, in a meaningless universe, living its brief life uncared-for, on this dark, cooling star: but even so — and all the more — what marvelous creatures we are! What fairy story, what tale from the Arabian Nights of the jinns, is a hundredth part as wonderful

---

sand men. Major General R. E. Urquhart, the Division commander, sent the radio message to Field Marshal Montgomery: "All will be ordered to break out rather than surrender."

[1] According to the London *Times*, the expression "iron curtain" was coined by Ludwig Schwerin von Krosigk, Hitler's Minister of Finance, and was used by Goebbels in his propaganda material for some years before Churchill adopted it.

[1] Reportedly a press worker had "corrected," on the printer's proof of Churchill's memoirs, a sentence which had ended idiomatically with a preposition; Churchill restored the original order, with the marginal comment quoted above.

as this true fairy story of simians! It is so much more heartening, too, than the tales we invent. A universe capable of giving birth to many such accidents is — blind or not — a good world to live in, a promising universe.
This Simian World [*1920*]. *XIX*

Father declared he was going to buy a new plot in the cemetery, a plot all for himself. "And I'll buy one on a corner," he added triumphantly, "where I can get out!"

Mother looked at him, startled but admiring, and whispered to me, "I almost believe he could do it."
Life with Father [*1935*]

THEODOSIA GARRISON
[1874–1944]

I never crossed your threshold with a grief
But that I went without it.
The Closed Door. Stanza 1

The kindliest thing God ever made,
His hand of very healing laid
Upon a fevered world, is shade.
Shade. Stanza 1

ELLEN GLASGOW
[1874–1945]

I have observed with wonder so many intellectual and literary fashions that I have come at last to rely positively upon one conviction alone. No idea is so antiquated that it was not once modern. No idea is so modern that it will not some day be antiquated. . . . To seize the flying thought before it escapes us is our only touch with reality.
Address to the Modern Language Association [*1936*]

Preserve, within a wild sanctuary, an inaccessible valley of reveries.
A Certain Measure [*1943*]

Tilling the fertile soil of man's vanity.
Ibid.

HARRY GRAHAM
[1874–1936]

Billy, in one of his nice new sashes,
Fell in the fire and was burnt to ashes;
Now, although the room grows chilly,
I haven't the heart to poke poor Billy.
Ruthless Rhymes for Heart-less Homes [*1899*]. *Tender-Heartedness*

Auntie, did you feel no pain
Falling from that apple tree?
Would you do it, please, again?
'Cos my friend here didn't see.
Ibid. Appreciation

HERBERT CLARK HOOVER
[1874–1964]

A great social and economic experiment [Prohibition], noble in motive and far-reaching in purpose.
Letter to Senator William E. Borah, February 28, 1928

The American system of rugged individualism.
Campaign speech, New York [*October 22, 1928*]

While I can make no claim for having introduced the term "rugged individualism," I should be proud to have invented it. It has been used by American leaders for over a half-century in eulogy of those God-fearing men and women of honesty whose stamina and character and fearless assertion of rights led them to make their own way in life.
The Challenge to Liberty [*1934*]. *Chap. 5*

A good many things go around in the dark besides Santa Claus.
Address, John Marshall Republican Club, St. Louis, Missouri [*December 16, 1935*]

Older men declare war. But it is youth that must fight and die. And it is youth who must inherit the tribulation, the sorrow, and the triumphs that are the aftermath of war.[1]

> *Speech, Republican National Convention, Chicago, June 27, 1944*

HAROLD L. ICKES
[1874–1952]

I am against government by crony.

> *On resigning as Secretary of the Interior, February, 1946*

ALVIN SAUNDERS JOHNSON
[1874–   ]

As in the bosom of the earth vestiges of all earlier life may still be found, so in the bosom of public opinion are to be found vestiges of the early dinosaurs of thought.

> *On German Pacification* [*1944*]

HEWLETT JOHNSON [2]
[1874–   ]

Not so easily does a people liberate itself from its social past. Many ideas, customs, intolerances, and tolerances, too, cling on unperceived by those who think that they live in days where all things are new.

> *The Soviet Power: The Socialist Sixth of the World* [*1940*]. *Book II, 2*

Nothing is better calculated to drive men to desperation than when, in attempting to carry out beneficial reform, they find the whole world aligned against them. The more especially so if amongst those so aligned they discover men who had preached the same ideal, but now dreaded its concrete realization.

> *Ibid. 3*

W. L. MACKENZIE KING
[1874–1950]

Labor can do nothing without capital, capital nothing without labor, and

[1] See Grantland Rice, page 910a.
[2] Dean of Canterbury.

neither labor or capital can do anything without the guiding genius of management; and management, however wise its genius may be, can do nothing without the privileges which the community affords.

> *Canadian Club Speech, Montreal* [*March 17, 1919*]

Government, in the last analysis, is organized opinion. Where there is little or no public opinion, there is likely to be bad government, which sooner or later becomes autocratic government.

> *Message of the Carillon* [*1927*]. *Page 139*

HENRY HERBERT KNIBBS
[1874–1945]

When he is hidden from the sun,
   And grasses grow where he is laid,
Men mark the good a man has done,
   And glorify the name he made.
> *The Journey*

Adventure was his coronal,
And all his wealth was wandering.
> *Ibid.*

After the coffee things ain't so bad.
> *That Inside Song*

You haven't whipped religion; just a man.
> *The Fighting Parson*

AMY LOWELL
[1874–1925]

Hung all over with mouse-traps of metres, and cages
Of bright-plumaged rhythms, with pages and pages
Of colors slit up into streaming confetti.
> *A Critical Fable* [*1922*] (*passage describing herself*)

I walk down the garden paths,
And all the daffodils
Are blowing, and the bright blue squills.
> *Patterns*

A pattern called a war.
Christ! What are patterns for?
> *Ibid.*

All about us peal the loud, sweet **Te**
Deums of the Canterbury bells.
  Madonna of the Evening Flowers
Heart-leaves of lilac all over New England,[1]
Roots of lilac under all the soil of New
England,
Lilac in me because I am New England.
                          Lilacs
The sight of a white church above thin
trees in a city square
Amazes my eyes as though it were the
Parthenon.
                Meeting-House Hill

WILLIAM SOMERSET MAUGHAM
[1874–1965]

There are two good things in life,
freedom of thought and freedom of
action.
  Of Human Bondage [*1915*].
                      Chap. 23
Like all weak men he laid an exaggerated stress on not changing one's
mind.
                Ibid. Chap. 39
People ask you for criticism, but
they only want praise.
                Ibid. Chap. 50
There is nothing so degrading as the
constant anxiety about one's means of
livelihood. . . . Money is like a sixth
sense without which you cannot make
a complete use of the other five.
                Ibid. Chap. 51
The mystic sees the ineffable, and
the psycho-pathologist the unspeakable.
  The Moon and Sixpence [*1919*].
                        Chap. 1
I forget who it was that recommended men for their soul's good to do
each day two things they disliked: [2]
. . . it is a precept that I have fol-

---

[1] Stands the lilac-bush tall-growing with
heart-shaped leaves of rich green. — WALT
WHITMAN: *When Lilacs Last in the Dooryard Bloom'd* [1865–1866]
[2] See William James, page 715a, and T. H.
Huxley, pages 633b–634a.

lowed scrupulously; for every day **I**
have got up and I have gone to bed.
  The Moon and Sixpence. Chap. 2
Impropriety is the soul of wit.[1]
                Ibid. Chap. 4
Conscience is the guardian in the individual of the rules which the community has evolved for its own preservation.
                Ibid. Chap. 14
It is not true that suffering ennobles
the character; happiness does that
sometimes, but suffering, for the most
part, makes men petty and vindictive.
                Ibid. Chap. 17
A woman can forgive a man for the
harm he does her, but she can never
forgive him for the sacrifices he makes
on her account.
                Ibid. Chap. 41
He made one laugh sometimes by
speaking the truth, but this is a form of
humour which gains its force only by
it unusualness.
                Ibid. Chap. 44
Do you know that conversation is
one of the greatest pleasures in life?
But it wants leisure.
  The Trembling of a Leaf
            [*1921*]. *Chap. 3*
The tragedy of love is indifference.
                Ibid. Chap. 4
I would sooner read a time-table or
a catalogue than nothing at all. They
are much more entertaining than half
the novels that are written.
        The Summing Up [*1938*]
Life is too short to do anything for
oneself that one can pay others to do
for one.
                      Ibid.
You must not pursue a success, but
fly from it.
                      Ibid.
If a nation values anything more
than freedom, it will lose its freedom;
and the irony of it is that if it is comfort or money that it values more, it
will lose that too.
  Strictly Personal [*1941*].
                      Chap. 31

---

[1] See Shakespeare, page 173a.

As deserted as a playwright after the first night of an unsuccessful play.
The Razor's Edge [*1944*].
Chap. 3
As mean as cat's meat.
Quoted in THOMAS F. BRADY: *The Eighty Years of Mr. Maugham, New York Times Magazine* [*January 24, 1954*]
I am an agnostic with sympathies.
Ibid.

ALICE DUER MILLER
[*1874–1942*]

When a woman like that whom I've seen so much
All of a sudden drops out of touch,
Is always busy and never can
Spare you a moment, it means a Man.
Forsaking All Others [*1931*]
I have loved England, dearly and deeply,
Since that first morning, shining and pure,
The white cliffs of Dover, I saw rising steeply
Out of the sea that once made her secure.
The White Cliffs [*1940*]
I am American bred,
I have seen much to hate here — much to forgive,
But in a world where England is finished and dead,
I do not wish to live.
Ibid.

ROSELLE MERCIER MONTGOMERY
[*1874–1933*]

Companioned years have made them comprehend
The comradeship that lies beyond a kiss.
The young ask much of life — they ask but this,
To fare the road together to its end.
For a Wedding Anniversary
Oh, there are many things that women know,

That no one tells them, no one needs to tell;
And that they know, their dearest never guess! [1]
Ulysses Returns: Penelope Speaks
Never a ship sails out of the bay
But carries my heart as a stowaway.
The Stowaway

PAUL RICHARD
[*1874–*]

The vagabond, when rich, is called a tourist.
The Scourge of Christ [*1929*]. *Page 40*
When the rich assemble to concern themselves with the business of the poor it is called charity. When the poor assemble to concern themselves with the business of the rich it is called anarchy.
Ibid. Page 63
Hunting — the least honourable form of war on the weak.
Ibid. Page 142

EDWARD HERSEY RICHARDS
[*1874–*]

A wise old owl sat on an oak,
The more he saw the less he spoke;
The less he spoke the more he heard;
Why aren't we like that wise old bird?
A Wise Old Owl

JOHN DAVISON ROCKEFELLER, JR.
[*1874–1964*]

I believe that every right implies a responsibility; every opportunity, an obligation; every possession, a duty.
Ten Principles: Address in behalf of United Service Organizations, New York [*July 8, 1941*]

[1] Never believe her love is blind,
All his faults are locked securely
In a closet of her mind.
SARA TEASDALE [*1884–1933*]: *Appraisal*

ROBERT WILLIAM SERVICE
[1874-1958]

This is the Law of the Yukon, that only
  the Strong shall thrive;
That surely the Weak shall perish, and
  only the Fit survive.[1]
Dissolute, damned and despairful, crip-
  pled and palsied and slain,
This is the Will of the Yukon, — Lo,
  how she makes it plain!
The Law of the Yukon

Master, I've done Thy bidding, and the
  light is low in the west,
And the long, long shift is over . . .
  Master, I've earned it — Rest.
The Song of the Wage-Slave

Back of the bar, in a solo game, sat
  Dangerous Dan McGrew,
And watching his luck was his light-o'-
  love, the lady that's known as
  Lou.
The Shooting of Dan McGrew.
Stanza 1

The Northern Lights have seen queer
  sights,
But the queerest they ever did see
Was that night on the marge of Lake
  Lebarge
I cremated Sam McGee.
The Cremation of Sam McGee.
Stanza 1

A promise made is a debt unpaid.
Ibid. Stanza 8

There's a race of men that don't fit in,
  A race that can't stay still;
So they break the hearts of kith and
  kin,
And they roam the world at will.
The Men That Don't Fit In.
Stanza 1

Fate has written a tragedy; its name is
  "The Human Heart."
The Theatre is the House of Life,
  Woman the mummer's part;

[1] Now this is the Law of the Jungle — as
  old and as true as the sky;
And the Wolf that shall keep it may
  prosper, but the Wolf that shall
  break it must die.
KIPLING: *The Law of the Jungle* [1895]

The Devil enters the prompter's box
  and the play is ready to start.
The Harpy. Stanza 12

God made a heart of gold, of gold,
  Shining and sweet and true;
Gave it a home of fairest mould,
  Blest it, and called it — You.
Sunshine. VI

I just think that dreams are best,
  Just to sit and fancy things;
Give your gold no acid test,
  Try not how your silver rings.
Dreams Are Best. Stanza 1

The man who can fight to Heaven's
  own height
Is the man who can fight when he's
  losing.
Carry On

Ah! the clock is always slow;
It is later than you think.
It Is Later than You Think

That classic that the world has lost,
The Little Book I Never Wrote.
My Masterpiece. Stanza 2

When we, the Workers, all demand:
  "What are we fighting for?" . . .
Then, then we'll end that stupid crime,
  that devil's madness — War.
Michael

GERTRUDE STEIN
[1874-1946]

Rose is a rose is a rose is a rose.
Sacred Emily

The Autobiography of Alice B.
Toklas.
Title of book [1933]

Pigeons in the grass alas.
Four Saints in Three Acts [1934]

Before the Flowers of Friendship
Faded Friendship Faded.
Title

In the United States there is more
space where nobody is than where anybody is.
This is what makes America what
it is.
The Geographical History
of America [1936]

ARTHUR STRINGER
[1874–1950]

Beauty is not immortal. In a day
Blossom and June and rapture pass
away.
A Fragile Thing Is Beauty.
Stanza 2

Our bitterest wine is always drained
from crushed ideals.
The Devastator

HARRY WILLIAMS
[1874–1924]
AND JACK JUDGE
[1878–1938]

It's a long way to Tipperary, it's a long
way to go;
It's a long way to Tipperary, to the
sweetest girl I know!
Good-bye, Piccadilly, farewell, Leicester Square,
It's a long, long way to Tipperary, but
my heart's right there!
Tipperary [*1908*]

In the Shade of the Old Apple Tree.
Title of Song

WILLIAM E. WOODWARD
[1874–1950]

The turning points of lives are not
the great moments. The real crises are
often concealed in occurrences so trivial
in appearance that they pass unob-
served.
George Washington [*1926*].
Chap. 3, Part 2

Vanity as an impulse has without
doubt been of far more benefit to civilization than modesty has ever been.
Ibid. Chap. 5, Part 1

Here is another bead on the string of
confusions.
Meet General Grant [*1929*].
Chap. 27, Part 5

EDMUND CLERIHEW
BENTLEY
[1875–   ]

Sir Christopher Wren
Said "I am going to dine with some
men.
If anybody calls
Say I am designing St. Paul's."
Biography for Beginners

John Stuart Mill
By a mighty effort of will
Overcame his natural bonhomie
And wrote "Principles of Political
Economy."
Ibid.

George the Third
Ought never to have occurred.
One can only wonder
At so grotesque a blunder.[1]
Ibid.

ABBIE FARWELL BROWN
[1875–1927]

They named their rocky farmlands,
Their hamlets by the sea,
For the mother-towns that bred them
In racial loyalty.
Names. Stanza 7

No matter what my birth may be,
No matter where my lot is cast,
I am the heir in equity
Of all the precious Past.
The Heritage. Stanza 1

JOHN BUCHAN,
LORD TWEEDSMUIR
[1875–1940]

We can only pay our debt to the past
by putting the future in debt to ourselves.
*Address to the People of Can-
ada, on the Coronation of
George VI, May 12, 1937*

---

[1] George the First was always reckoned
Vile, but viler George the Second;
And what mortal ever heard
Any good of George the Third?
When from earth the Fourth descended
God be praised, the Georges ended!
WALTER SAVAGE LANDOR: *Epigram,
after hearing* THACKERAY's *lectures
on the Four Georges* [*1855*]

LOUISE DRISCOLL
[1875–   ]

There you will find what
  Every man needs,
Wild religion
  Without any creeds.
Spring Market. Stanza 5

Villon among the birds is he,
A bold, bright rover, bad and free;
Yet not without such loveliness
As makes the curse upon him less.
The Blue Jay. Stanza 1

GILBERT EMERY
[1875–1945]

They're a poor lot, the men, all of
'em, and dirty, too — but the thing is,
darlin', to get one that cleans easy.
Tarnish [1923]. Act III

ELLEN THORNEYCROFT FOWLER
[1875–1929]

The inner half of every cloud
  Is bright and shining;
I therefore turn my clouds about,
And always wear them inside out
  To show the lining.
The Wisdom of Folly. Stanza 3

ROBERT FROST
[1875–1963]

I'm going out to clean the pasture
  spring;
I'll only stop to rake the leaves away
(And wait to watch the water clear, I
  may):
I shan't be gone long. — You come too.
The Pasture

Ah, when to the heart of man
  Was it ever less than a treason
To go with the drift of things,
  To yield with a grace to reason,
And bow and accept the end
  Of a love or a season?
Reluctance [1913]. Stanza 4

Something there is that doesn't love a
wall.
Mending Wall [1914]

My apple trees will never get across
And eat the cones under his pines, I
  tell him.
He only says, "Good fences make good
  neighbors."
Mending Wall

The nearest friends can go
With anyone to death, comes so far
  short
They might as well not try to go at all.
Home Burial [1914]

Nothing to look backward to with
  pride,
And nothing to look forward to with
  hope.
*The Death of the Hired Man
  [1914]*

"Home is the place where, when you
  have to go there,
They have to take you in." "I should
  have called it
Something you somehow haven't to deserve."
Ibid.

As a child misses the unsaid Good-
  night,
And falls asleep with heartache.
The Black Cottage [1914]

Most of the change we think we see in
  life
Is due to truths being in and out of
  favor.
Ibid.

The blue's but a mist from the breath
  of the wind,
A tarnish that goes at a touch of the
  hand.
Blueberries [1914]

The best way out is always through.
A Servant to Servants [1914]

Pressed into service means pressed out
  of shape.
The Self-Seeker [1914]

Two roads diverged in a wood, and I —
I took the one less traveled by,
And that has made all the difference.
The Road Not Taken [1916]

I'd like to get away from earth awhile
And then come back to it and begin
  over.

May no fate willfully misunderstand
  me

And half grant what I wish and snatch
me away
Not to return. Earth's the right place
for love:
I don't know where it's likely to go
better.
Birches [*1916*]
I wonder about the trees:
Why do we wish to bear
Forever the noise of these
More than another noise
So close to our dwelling place?
The Sound of the Trees [*1916*]
The Hyla breed
That shouted in the mist a month ago,
Like ghost of sleigh-bells in a ghost of
snow.
Hyla Brook [*1916*]
I met a Californian who would
Talk California — a state so blessed,
He said, in climate, none had ever died
there
A natural death.
New Hampshire [*1923*].
Stanza 3
Do you know,
Considering the market, there are more
Poems produced than any other thing?
No wonder poets sometimes have to
seem
So much more business-like than busi-
ness men.
Their wares are so much harder to get
rid of.
Ibid. Stanza 17
She's one of the two best states in the
Union.
Vermont's the other.
Ibid. Stanza 18
Anything I can say about New Hamp-
shire
Will serve almost as well about Ver-
mont,
Excepting that they differ in their
mountains.
The Vermont mountains stretch ex-
tended straight;
New Hampshire mountains curl up in a
coil.
Ibid. Stanza 19
Why make so much of fragmentary
blue

In here and there a bird, or butterfly,
Or flower, or wearing-stone, or open
eye,
When heaven presents in sheets the
solid hue?
Fragmentary Blue [*1923*].
Stanza 1
Keep cold, young orchard. Good-bye
and keep cold.
Dread fifty above more than fifty be-
low.
Good-bye and Keep Cold [*1923*]
Whose woods these are I think I know.
His house is in the village though;
He will not see me stopping here
To watch his woods fill up with snow.
*Stopping by Woods on a Snowy
Evening* [*1923*]. *Stanza 1*
My little horse must think it queer
To stop without a farmhouse near.
Ibid. Stanza 2
He gives his harness bells a shake
To ask if there is some mistake.
Ibid. Stanza 3
The woods are lovely, dark and deep.
But I have promises to keep,
And miles to go before I sleep.
Ibid. Stanza 4
Some say the world will end in fire,
Some say in ice.
From what I've tasted of desire
I hold with those who favor fire.
But if it had to perish twice,
I think I know enough of hate
To say that for destruction ice
Is also great
And would suffice.
Fire and Ice [*1923*]
We heard the miniature thunder where
he fled.
The Runaway [*1923*]
Love at the lips was touch
As sweet as I could bear;
And once that seemed too much;
I lived on air.
To Earthward [*1923*]. *Stanza 1*
Now no joy but lacks salt
That is not dashed with pain
And weariness and fault;
I crave the stain

Of tears, the aftermark
Of almost too much love,
The sweet of bitter bark
And burning clove.
Ibid. Stanzas 5 and 6
Tree at my window, window tree,
My sash is lowered when night comes
on;
But let there never be curtain drawn
Between you and me.
Tree at My Window [1928].
Stanza 1
That day she put our heads together,
Fate had her imagination about her,
Your head so much concerned with
outer,
Mine with inner, weather.
Ibid. Stanza 4
I have been one acquainted with the
night.
Acquainted with the Night
[1928]
If, as they say, some dust thrown in my
eyes
Will keep my talk from getting over-
wise,
I'm not the one for putting off the
proof.
Let it be overwhelming.
Dust in the Eyes [1928]
Don't join too many gangs. Join few if
any.
Join the United States and join the
family —
But not much in between unless a col-
lege.
Build Soil [1932]
Never ask of money spent
Where the spender thinks it went.
Nobody was ever meant
To remember or invent
What he did with every cent.
The Hardship of Accounting
[1936]
I never dared be radical when young
For fear it would make me conservative
when old.
Precaution [1936]
And were an epitaph to be my story
I'd have a short one ready for my own.
I would have written of me on my
stone:

I had a lover's quarrel with the world.
The Lesson for Today [1942]
Happiness Makes Up in Height for
What It Lacks in Length.
Title of poem [1942]
Any eye is an evil eye
That looks in on to a mood apart.
A Mood Apart [1947]

ZANE GREY
[1875–1939]

We'll use a signal I have tried and
found far-reaching and easy to yell.
Waa-hoo!
The Last of the Plainsmen.
Chap. 4

MINNIE LOUISE HASKINS
[1875–   ]

And I said to the man who stood at
the gate of the year: "Give me a light
that I may tread safely into the unknown." And he replied: "Go out into
the darkness and put your hand into
the hand of God. That shall be to you
better than light and safer than a
known way." [1] So I went forth, and
finding the Hand of God, trod gladly
into the night. And He led me towards
the hills and the breaking of day in
the lone East.
God Knows [1908]. Proem

FREDERICK PALMER
LATIMER
[1875–1940]

I wish I were a little rock,
 A-sitting on a hill,
A-doing nothing, all day long,
 But just a-sitting still;
I wouldn't eat, I wouldn't sleep,
 I wouldn't even wash —
I'd sit and sit a thousand years,
 And rest myself, b'Gosh!
The Weary Wisher

[1] Quoted by George VI in a radio broadcast to the Empire, December 25, 1939.

PERCY MACKAYE
[1875–1956]

Because he[1] never wore his sentient
   heart
For crows and jays to peck, ofttimes to
   such
He seemed a silent fellow, who o'er-
   much
Held from the general gossip-ground
   apart,
Or tersely-spoke, and tart.
                    Uriel. Stanza 11
Inward, not outward, throbs the eternal
   war
Where each is his own Norman Conqueror.
         Sonnet, Norman Conquest
                              [1944]

THOMAS MANN
[1875–1955]

We are most likely to get angry and
excited in our opposition to some idea
when we ourselves are not quite certain
of our own position, and are inwardly
tempted to take the other side.
         Buddenbrooks [*1903*]. *Part*
                   VIII, Chap. 2
Grandfather used to say about a
dish that had no particular taste or
consistency: it tastes as if you were
hanging your tongue out of the window!
            Ibid. Part X, Chap. 1
Beauty can pierce one like a pain.
            Ibid. Part XI, Chap. 2
Space, like time, engenders forgetfulness; but it does so by setting us bodily
free from our surroundings and giving
us back our primitive, unattached state.
. . . Time, we say, is Lethe; but
change of air is a similar draught, and,
if it works less thoroughly, does so more
quickly.
      The Magic Mountain [*1924*].[2]
                        Chap. 1
A man lives not only his personal
life, as an individual, but also, con-

[1] William Vaughn Moody.
[2] Translated by H. T. Lowe-Porter.

sciously or unconsciously, the life of
his epoch and his contemporaries.
      The Magic Mountain. Chap. 2
The solemn, discreet, almost overawed bearing which the young German's respect for authority leads him
to assume in the presence of pens, ink,
and paper, or anything else which bears
to his mind an official stamp.
                    Ibid. Chap. 4
I have the feeling that once I am at
home again I shall need to sleep three
weeks on end to get rested from the
rest I've had!
                           Ibid.
The only religious way to think of
death is as part and parcel of life; to
regard it, with the understanding and
the emotions, as the inviolable condition of life.
                    Ibid. Chap. 5
Time has no divisions to mark its
passage, there is never a thunder-storm
or blare of trumpets to announce the
beginning of a new month or year.
Even when a new century begins it is
only we mortals who ring bells and fire
off pistols.
                           Ibid.
Order and simplification are the first
steps toward the mastery of a subject
— the actual enemy is the unknown.
                           Ibid.
The proud embarrassment of the
artist, tasting the enjoyment of looking
on his own works with the eyes of
strangers.
                           Ibid.
Human reason needs only to will
more strongly than fate, and she *is*
fate.
                    Ibid. Chap. 6
Opinions cannot survive if one has
no chance to fight for them.
                           Ibid.
Chop-fallen funeral processions, with
their dignity curtailed by present-day
traffic conditions.
                           Ibid.
One quickly gets readiness in an art
where strong desire comes in play.
                           Ibid.

All interest in disease and death is only another expression of interest in life.
The Magic Mountain. Chap. 6

What perplexes the world is the disparity between the swiftness of the spirit, and the immense unwieldiness, sluggishness, inertia, permanence of matter.
Ibid.

The invention of printing and the Reformation are and remain the two outstanding services of central Europe to the cause of humanity.
Ibid.

Speech is civilization itself. The word, even the most contradictory word, preserves contact — it is silence which isolates.
Ibid.

A man's dying is more the survivors' affair than his own.
Ibid.

What we call mourning for our dead is perhaps not so much grief at not being able to call them back as it is grief at not being able to want to do so.
Ibid. Chap. 7

Time cools, time clarifies; no mood can be maintained quite unaltered through the course of hours.
Ibid.

Seven is a good handy figure in its way, picturesque, with a savour of the mythical; one might say that it is more filling to the spirit than a dull academic half-dozen.
Ibid.

In the Word is involved the unity of humanity, the wholeness of the human problem, which permits nobody to separate the intellectual and artistic from the political and social, and to isolate himself within the ivory tower of the "cultural" proper.
An Exchange of Letters [1]
[January, 1937]

[1] Reply, written from Zurich, to the Dean of the Philosophical Faculty at Bonn University. The latter had written to Thomas Mann, who had left Germany in 1933, that his name had been struck off the list of Honorary Doctors.

God help our darkened and desecrated country and teach it to make its peace with the world and with itself.
An Exchange of Letters

Hold fast the time! Guard it, watch over it, every hour, every minute! Unregarded it slips away, like a lizard, smooth, slippery, faithless, a pixy-wife. Hold every moment sacred. Give each clarity and meaning, each the weight of thine awareness, each its true and due fulfilment.
The Beloved Returns [1939]

HUGHES MEARNS
[1875–   ]

As I was going up the stair
I met a man who wasn't there.
He wasn't there again today.
I wish, I wish he'd stay away.
The Psychoed

FRANK WARD O'MALLEY
[1875–1932]

Life is just one damned thing after another. [1]
Quoted in The Literary Digest,
November 5, 1932

VILDA SAUVAGE OWENS
[1875–1950]

If I ever have time for things that matter,
If ever I have the smallest chance,
I'm going to live in
Little Broom Gardens,
Moat-by-the-Castle,
Nettlecombe, Hants.
If I Ever Have Time for the Things That Matter. Stanza 1

[1] Also attributed to Elbert Hubbard; the phrase probably precedes them both.
ODTAA, title of book by John Masefield [1926]; and Tom Treanor, war correspondent, entitled his book *One Damn Thing After Another* [1944].

RAINER MARIA RILKE
[1875–1926]

Her smile was not meant to be seen by anyone and served its whole purpose in being smiled.
The Journal of My Other Self [1]

He was a poet and hated the approximate.
Ibid.

Love consists in this, that two solitudes protect and touch and greet each other.
Letters to a Young Poet [2]

The future enters into us, in order to transform itself in us, long before it happens.
Ibid.

We're never single-minded, unperplexed, like migratory birds.
The Duino Elegies. Fourth Elegy

The most visible joy can only reveal itself to us when we've transformed it, within.
Ibid. Seventh Elegy

Death is the side of life which is turned away from us.
Letter to his Polish Translator, W. von Hulewicz

A good marriage is that in which each appoints the other guardian of his solitude.
Letters [3]

Once the realization is accepted that even between the *closest* human beings infinite distances continue to exist, a wonderful living side by side can grow up, if they succeed in loving the distance between them which makes it possible for each to see the other whole against the sky.
Ibid.

In the difficult are the friendly forces, the hands that work on us.
Ibid.

Works of art are indeed always products of having-been-in-danger, of

[1] Translated by JOHN LINTON [1930].
[2] Translated by M. D. HERTER NORTON [1934].
[3] Translated by JANE BARNARD GREENE and M. D. HERTER NORTON.

having-gone-to-the-very-end in an experience, to where man can go no further.
Letters

RAFAEL SABATINI
[1875–1950]

Born with the gift of laughter and the sense that the world was mad,[1] and that was his only patrimony.
Scaramouche. Chap. 1

RIDGELY TORRENCE
[1875–1950]

God gave them Youth, God gave them Love, and even God can give no more.
The House of a Hundred Lights. The Young Lovers

Of all the languages of earth in which the human kind confer
The Master Speaker is the Tear: it is the Great Interpreter.
Ibid. The Conclusion of the Whole Matter

I was weak as a rained-on bee.
Eye-Witness. The Tramp Sings

EVELYN UNDERHILL
[1875–1941]

I saw the race fulfil
The spiral of its steep ascent, predestined of the Will.
Yet not unled, but shepherded by one they may not see —
The one who walked with starry feet the western road by me!
Uxbridge Road. Stanza 5

[1] Inscribed over a door in the Hall of Graduate Studies, Yale University. The architect, John Donald Tuttle, explained in a letter in *The New Yorker* [December 8, 1934] his recoiling from collegiate Gothic, "a type of architecture that had been designed expressly . . . to enable yeomen to pour molten lead through slots on their enemies below. As a propitiatory gift to my gods . . . and to make them forget by appealing to their senses of humor, I carved the inscription over the door."

THOMAS WALSH
[1875–1928]

A little world — we truly say
While days are young and careless-
hearted;
From clime to clime we speed today,
Earth's paths are cleared and ocean's
charted;
But ah, how large a world we stray
When thou and I are parted!
Zither Song

MOIRA O'NEILL
[*Floruit* 1900]

Youth's for an hour,
Beauty's a flower,
But love is the jewel that wins the
world.
*Songs of the Glens of Antrim
[1900]. Beauty's a Flower*
"If she was tall?" Like a king's own
daughter.
"If she was fair?" Like a mornin' o'
May.
A Broken Song. Stanza 2
The memory's fairly spoilt on me
Wid mindin' to forget.
Forgettin'. Stanza 5

SHERWOOD ANDERSON
[1876–1941]

Everyone in the world is Christ and
they are all crucified.
*Winesburg, Ohio [1919]. The
Philosopher*
I am a lover and have not found my
thing to love.
Ibid. Tandy

WILLA SIBERT CATHER
[1876–1947]

Oh, this is the joy of the rose:
That it blows,
And goes.
In Rose-Time
Where are the loves that we have loved
before
When once we are alone, and shut the
door?
L'Envoi

Fireflies gleam in the damp and
mould, —
All that is left of the Caesars' gold.
The Palatine. Stanza 3
No one can build his security upon
the nobleness of another person.
*Alexander's Bridge [1912].
Chap. 8*
There are only two or three human
stories, and they go on repeating them-
selves as fiercely as if they had never
happened before.
*O Pioneers! [1913]. Part II,
Chap. 4*
I like trees because they seem more
resigned to the way they have to live
than other things do.
Ibid. Chap. 8
We all like people who do things,
even if we only see their faces on a
cigar-box lid.
*The Song of the Lark [1915].
Part I, Chap. 18*
Artistic growth is, more than it is
anything else, a refining of the sense
of truthfulness. The stupid believe
that to be truthful is easy; only the
artist, the great artist, knows how
difficult it is.
Ibid. Part VI, Chap. 11
Winter lies too long in country
towns; hangs on until it is stale and
shabby, old and sullen.
*My Ántonia [1918]. Book II,
Chap. 7*
Old men are like that, you know. It
makes them feel important to think
they're in love with somebody.
Ibid. Book III, Chap. 4
Art, it seems to me, should simplify.
That, indeed, is very nearly the whole
of the higher artistic process; finding
what conventions of form and what detail one can do without and yet preserve the spirit of the whole — so that
all that one has suppressed and cut
away is there to the reader's consciousness as much as if it were in type
on the page.
On the Art of Fiction [1920]

That irregular and intimate quality of things made entirely by the human hand.
Death Comes for the Archbishop [*1927*]. *Book I, Chap. 3*

The Miracles of the Church seem to me to rest not so much upon faces or voices or healing power coming suddenly near to us from afar off, but upon our perceptions being made finer, so that for a moment our eyes can see and our ears can hear what is there about us always.
Ibid. Chap. 4

The universal human yearning for something permanent, enduring, without shadow of change.
Ibid. Book III, Chap. 3

Only solitary men know the full joys of friendship. Others have their family; but to a solitary and an exile his friends are everything.
Shadows on the Rock [*1931*]. *Book III, Chap. 5*

There are all those early memories; one cannot get another set; one has only those.
Ibid. Book IV, Chap. 2

These coppers, big and little, these brooms and clouts and brushes, were tools; and with them one made, not shoes or cabinet-work, but life itself. One made a climate within a climate; one made the days, — the complexion, the special flavor, the special happiness of each day as it passed; one made life.
Ibid. Chap. 3

Sometimes a neighbor whom we have disliked a lifetime for his arrogance and conceit lets fall a single commonplace remark that shows us another side, another man, really; a man uncertain, and puzzled, and in the dark like ourselves.
Ibid. Epilogue

SARAH NORCLIFFE CLEGHORN
[1876–1959]

The golf links lie so near the mill
That almost every day

The laboring children can look out
And watch the men at play.
Quatrain [*1915*]

IRVIN SHREWSBURY COBB
[1876–1944]

It smells like gangrene starting in a mildewed silo, it tastes like the wrath to come, and when you absorb a deep swig of it you have all the sensations of having swallowed a lighted kerosene lamp. A sudden, violent jolt of it has been known to stop the victim's watch, snap his suspenders and crack his glass eye right across.
Definition of "Corn Licker" given to the Distillers' Code Authority, N. R. A.

Echoes, stealing upward, from those beneath the sod;
"No creed or dogma has produced a satisfying God."
Schedule for Plan for Going Elsewhere

I charge my family . . . that they shall put on none of the bogus habiliments of so-called mourning. Folds of black crepe never ministered to the memory of the departed.
Letter of Instructions to be opened after his death

Lay my ashes at the roots of a dogwood tree in Paducah at the proper planting season. Should the tree live, that will be monument enough for me.
Ibid.

CLARENCE JAMES DENNIS
[1876–1938]

Me name is Mud.
The Sentimental Bloke [*1916*]. *A Spring Song, Stanza 2*

A suddin notion stops me wiv a jar —
Wot if Doreen, I thinks, should grow to be
A fat ole weepin' willer like 'er Mar!
Ibid. Mar, Stanza 24

RICHARD BUTLER GLAENZER
[1876–1937]

Indian only in this:
Your sudden way
Of stealing on us — but to kiss
With peace, not slay!
Indian Summer. Stanza 1

WALLACE IRWIN
[1876–   ]

It's happy goes as lucky goes
To Romany in June.
From Romany to Rome. Stanza 1

Of all the fish that swim or swish
In ocean's deep autocracy,
There's none possess such haughtiness
As the codfish aristocracy.
Codfish Aristocracy. Stanza 1

I ask to know.
Letters of a Japanese Schoolboy

"Sayin' nothin'," says the goldsmith,
"is a woman's rarest skill."
"Birds should sing," remarked the Doctor, "but a woman should be still."
The Chamber of Tranquillity.
Stanza 10

CHARLES FRANCIS KETTERING
[1876–1958]

A man must have a certain amount of intelligent ignorance to get anywhere.
On his seventieth birthday,
August 29, 1946

We should all be concerned about the future because we will have to spend the rest of our lives there.
Seed for Thought [1949]

MAXIM MAXIMOVICH LITVINOV
[1876–1951]

To strengthen the League of Nations is to abide by the principle of collective security . . . to abide by the principle that peace is indivisible.[1]
Speech at League of Nations,
Geneva, condemning Italian aggression in Ethiopia [July 1,
1936]

GRACE FALLOW NORTON
[1876–   ]

I have loved many, the more and the few —
I have loved many, that I might love you.
Song of the Sum of All

POPE PIUS XII (EUGENIO PACELLI)
[1876–1958]

Whoever dared raise a hand against Rome would be guilty of matricide in the eyes of the civilized world and in the eternal judgments of God.
Address to the College of Cardinals,
Rome [June 2, 1944]

Private property is a natural fruit of labor, a product of intense activity of man, acquired through his energetic determination to ensure and develop with his own strength his own existence and that of his family, and to create for himself and his own an existence of just freedom, not only economic, but also political, cultural and religious.
Radio broadcast [September 1,
1944]

If a worker is deprived of hope to acquire some personal property, what other natural stimulus can be offered him that will inspire him to hard work, labor, saving and sobriety today, when so many nations and men have lost everything and all they have left is their capacity for work?
Ibid.

[1] In an earlier speech at the League, on September 5, 1935, during the Italian preparations for the invasion, Litvinov used a similar phrase: "The thesis of the indivisibility of peace. . . . It has now become clear to the whole world that each war is the creation of a preceding war and the generator of new present or future wars."

The church contradicts and condemns State Absolutism based on the false principle that the authority of the state is unlimited and controls the entire field of public and private life, invading even the realm of ideas, beliefs and conscience.
Wisdom — Not Weapons of War [1]
The American people have a genius for splendid and unselfish action, and into the hands of America God has placed the destinies of afflicted humanity.
Ibid.

A. S. W. ROSENBACH
[1876–1952]

After love, book collecting is the most exhilarating sport of all.
A Book Hunter's Holiday [*1936*]
Brooklyn has the proud distinction of having had more distinguished bibliophiles than any other city of its size in the world.
Ibid.

GEORGE MACAULAY TREVELYAN
[1876–1962]

A man and what he loves and builds have but a day and then disappear; nature cares not — and renews the annual round untired. It is the old law, sad but not bitter. Only when man destroys the life and beauty of nature, there is the outrage.
Grey of Fallodon [*1937*].
Book I, Chap. 3
Serbia . . . that little land of ferocious heroes.
Ibid. Book II, Chap. 8
Disinterested intellectual curiosity is the life blood of real civilisation.
English Social History [*1942*].
Preface
Education . . . has produced a vast population able to read but unable to distinguish what is worth reading.
Ibid. Chap. 18

[1] In *Collier's*, January 5, 1946.

BERTHA ADAMS BACKUS
[*Floruit* 1911]

Build for yourself a strong-box,
Fashion each part with care;
When it's strong as your hand can
make it,
Put all your troubles there.
Then Laugh [*1911*]. *Stanza 1*

TED OLSON
[*Floruit* 1912]

Honor and truth and manhood —
These are the things that stand,
Though the sneer and jibe of the cynic
tribe
Are loud through the width of the
land.
Things That Endure. Stanza 1
But a lie, whatever the guise it wears,
Is a lie as it was of yore,
And a truth that has lasted a million
years
Is good for a million more.
Ibid. Stanza 3

THOMAS CURTIS CLARK
[1877–   ]

Let us no more be true to boasted race
or clan,
But to our highest dream, the brotherhood of man.
The New Loyalty

GRACE NOLL (MRS. NORMAN H.) CROWELL
[1877–   ]

God wrote His loveliest poem on the
day
He made the first tall silver poplar tree,
And set it high upon a pale-gold hill
For all the new enchanted earth to see.
Silver Poplars. Stanza 1

ANTHONY EUWER
[1877–   ]

As a beauty I'm not a great star.
Others are handsomer far;

But my face — I don't mind it
Because I'm behind it;
It's the folks out in front that I jar.
Limerick [1]

WILHELM FRICK
[1877–1946]

Right is for National Socialists that
which serves the German people.
Address to Lawyers,
October 3, 1933

ROSE FYLEMAN
[1877–   ]

The Fairies have never a penny to
spend,
They haven't a thing put by,
But theirs is the dower of bird and of
flower,
And theirs are the earth and the sky.
The Fairies Have Never a Penny
to Spend. Stanza 1

There are fairies at the bottom of our
garden!
The Fairies. Stanza 1

The Queen — now can you guess who
that could be
(She's a little girl by day, but at night
she steals away)?
Well — it's me!
Ibid. Stanza 3

SIR JAMES HOPWOOD JEANS
[1877–1946]

Taking a very gloomy view of the
future of the human race, let us suppose that it can only expect to survive
for two thousand million years longer,
a period about equal to the past age of
the earth. Then, regarded as a being
destined to live for threescore years and
ten, humanity, although it has been
born in a house seventy years old, is
itself only three days old.
The Wider Aspects of
Cosmogony [1928]

[1] Often quoted by Woodrow Wilson.

RICHARD R. KIRK
[1877–   ]

Thrice blessed are our friends: they
come, they stay,
And presently they go away.
Thrice Blessed

A book's an Inn whose patrons' praise
Depends on seasons and on days,
On dispositions, and — in fine —
Not wholly on the landlord's wine.
A Book's an Inn

DOUGLAS MALLOCH
[1877–1938]

Here's the secret of the riddle for successes everywhere —
There's some little second fiddle that
is carrying the air.
The Plain Member. Stanza 3

The river belongs to the Nation,
The levee, they say, to the State;
The Government runs navigation,
The Commonwealth, though, pays the
freight.
Now, here is the problem that's
heavy —
Please, which is the right or the
wrong —
When the water runs over the levee,
To whom does the river belong?
Uncle Sam's River. Stanza 1

If it's your Mississippi in dry time,
If it's yours, Uncle Sam, when it's wet,
If it's your Mississippi in fly time,
In flood time it's your Mississippi yet.
Ibid. Stanza 6

Courage is to feel
The daily daggers of relentless steel
And keep on living.
Courage. Stanza 2

You have to believe in happiness,
Or happiness never comes. . . .
Ah, that's the reason a bird can sing —
On his darkest day he believes in
Spring.
You Have to Believe

He who makes a garden
Works hand-in-hand with God.
Who Makes a Garden

ANGELO PATRI
[1877–1965]

In one sense there is no death. The life of a soul on earth lasts beyond his departure. You will always feel that life touching yours, that voice speaking to you, that spirit looking out of other eyes, talking to you in the familiar things he touched, worked with, loved as familiar friends. He lives on in your life and in the lives of all others that knew him.[1]
Keep Children from Funerals
[November 30, 1938]

LEONARD H. ROBBINS
[1877–1947]

Be true while there yet is time.
For this is the cry of a thousand souls
that down to the Pit have trod —
Who keeps the Truth from the people
stands in the way of God!
The Truth and John Billington.
Stanza 8

THEODORE GOODRIDGE
ROBERTS
[1877–1953]

The wide seas and the mountains called
to him
And gray dawn saw his campfires in
the rain.
A Vagrant's Epitaph. Stanza 1

LAURA SIMMONS
[1877–1949]

What though you hide it in your
trunk —
Ere sailing hour has set?
Jammed down beneath your old blue
serge?
Don't think you can forget!

[1] Even the death of friends will inspire us as much as their lives. . . . Their memories will be incrusted over with sublime and pleasing thoughts, as their monuments are overgrown with moss. — THOREAU: *A Week on the Concord and Merrimack Rivers* [1849], *Concord River*

The face within that passport book
Will rise to haunt you yet.
Your Passport Picture

CHARLES HANSON TOWNE
[1877–1949]

Youth, there are countless stories
spread
By gentlemen whose hair is gray.
Believe them not, but me instead —
The Nineties were not really gay.
Ballade of Gentle Denial

I need not shout my faith. Thrice eloquent
Are quiet trees and the green listening
sod.
Hushed are the stars, whose power is
never spent;
The hills are mute — yet how they
speak of God!
Silence

How softly runs the afternoon
Beneath the billowy clouds of June!
How Softly Runs the Afternoon

ARTHUR UPSON
[1877–1908]

My days are phantom days, each one
The shadow of a hope;
My real life never was begun
Nor any of my real deeds done.
Phantom Life

Wine that was spilt in haste
Arising in fumes more precious;
Garlands that fell forgot
Rooting to wondrous bloom.
After a Dolmetsch Concert.
Stanza 2

WILLIAM W. WOOLLCOTT
[1877–1949]

I am a One Hundred Percent American;
I am a super patriot.
I Am a One Hundred Percent
American. Stanza 1

I am an anti-Darwin intellectual.
The man that says that any nice young
boy or gal

Is a descendant of the ape
Shall never from Hell's fire escape.
    I Am a One Hundred Percent
    American. Stanza 2

McLANDBURGH WILSON
[*Floruit* 1915]

Our hero is a man of peace,
Preparedness he implores;
His sword within its scabbard sleeps,
But mercy, how it snores!
    Theodore Roosevelt
'Twixt the optimist and pessimist
The difference is droll:
The optimist sees the doughnut
But the pessimist sees the hole.
    Optimist and Pessimist

LOUIS KAUFMAN ANSPACHER
[1878–1947]

Marriage is that relation between
man and woman in which the independence is equal, the dependence mutual,
and the obligation reciprocal.
    Address, Boston [*December 30,*
    1934]

KARLE WILSON (MRS. THOMAS ELLIS) BAKER
[1878–]

Brother, the creed would stifle me
That shelters you.[1]
    Creeds. Stanza 2
Let me grow lovely, growing old —
  So many fine things do:
Laces, and ivory, and gold,
  And silks need not be new.
    Old Lace: Let Me Grow Lovely
Today I have grown taller from walk-
ing with the trees.
    Good Company

[1] My creed may have no lift of hope for
    you,
  And yours might drive me down the
    slopes of hell.
    LEWIS WORTHINGTON SMITH
    [1866–]: *Creeds*

I love the friendly faces of old sorrows;
I have no secrets that they do not
  know.
    I Love the Friendly Faces.
    Stanza 1

AMELIA JOSEPHINE BURR
[1878–]

As one who looks on a face through a
  window, through life I have looked
  on God.
Because I have loved life, I shall have
  no sorrow to die.
    A Song of Living. Stanza 3

HENRY SEIDEL CANBY
[1878–1961]

We can put our children on wheels to
see the world, but we cannot give them
the kind of home that any town provided in the nineties, not at any price.
    The Age of Confidence. Chap. 14
Arrogance, pedantry, and dogmatism
are the occupational diseases of those
who spend their lives directing the intellects of the young.
    Alma Mater
[Walt Whitman] remembered things
impossible for us, impossible but intelligible, and which will become unintelligible at our peril.
    Classic Americans. Walt Whitman
Skunk cabbages! a thousand sonnets
died in that misnomer.
    Meditations in the Woods

PIERRE CARTIER
[1878–]

While in France we consider it takes
three generations to go from shirtsleeves to wealth,[1] here, in America,
where accelerated speed is an important
element of success, it takes but one generation to complete the same process.
    Address, French Chamber of
    Commerce of the United States,
    New York, September 27, 1940

[1] There's no' but three generations atween
clog and clog. — *Lancashire Proverb*
  Three generations from shirtsleeves to
shirtsleeves. — *Attributed to* ANDREW CAR-
NEGIE [1835–1919]

GEORGE MICHAEL COHAN
[1878–1942]

No matter what may happen, whatever
  may befall,
I only know I'm mighty glad I'm living,
  that is all.
I'm Mighty Glad I'm Living

You won't do any business, if you
  haven't got a band:
The folks expect a street parade and
  uniforms so grand.
You Won't Do Any Business

Always Leave Them Laughing When
You Say Good-bye.
Title of song

Give my regards to Broadway,
  Remember me to Herald Square,
Tell all the gang at Forty-second Street
  That I will soon be there.
Give My Regards to Broadway
[1904]

Hurried and worried until we're buried,
  and there's no curtain call,
Life's a very funny proposition, after
  all.
Life's a Funny Proposition [1907]

    The Yanks are coming,
The drums rum-tumming everywhere.
Over There [1917]

And we won't come back till it's over
  over there.
Ibid.

What's all the shootin' for?
The Tavern [1920]

GRACE HAZARD CONKLING
[1878–1958]

I have an understanding with the hills
At evening when the slanted radiance
  fills
Their hollows, and the great winds let
  them be,
And they are quiet and look down at
  me.
After Sunset

Invisible beauty has a word so brief
A flower can say it or a shaken leaf,
But few may ever snare it in a song.
Ibid.

To build the trout a crystal stair.
The Whole Duty of
Berkshire Brooks

He who gives a passion-flower
Always asks it back.
Tampico

ALFRED EDGAR COPPARD
[1878–1957]

Truth is truth and love is love,
Give us grace to taste thereof;
But if truth offend my sweet,
Then I will have none of it.
Mendacity. Stanza 1

Ere this trick of truth undo me,
Little love, my love, come to me.
Ibid. Stanza 3

ADELAIDE CRAPSEY
[1878–1914]

These be
Three silent things:
The falling snow . . . the hour
Before the dawn . . . the mouth of
  one
Just dead.
Cinquain: Triad

EDWARD JOHN MORETON
DRAX PLUNKETT,
LORD DUNSANY
[1878–1957]

A new thing came and they could not
  see,
A new wind blew and they would not
  feel it.
In His Own Country. Stanza 1

May you go safe, my friend, across that
  dizzy way
No wider than a hair, by which your
  people go
From Earth to Paradise; may you go
  safe today
With stars and space above, and time
  and stars below.
May You Go Safe: On the
Death of a Muhammedan
Friend. Stanza 1

When we break up under the heavy years and go down into eternity our thoughts like small lost rafts float on awhile upon Oblivion's sea. They will not carry much over those tides, our names and a phrase or two and little else.

Fifty-One Tales. The Raft Builders

HARRY EMERSON FOSDICK
[1878–　　]

The Sea of Galilee and the Dead Sea are made of the same water. It flows down, clear and cool, from the heights of Hermon and the roots of the cedars of Lebanon. The Sea of Galilee makes beauty of it, for the Sea of Galilee has an outlet. It gets to give. It gathers in its riches that it may pour them out again to fertilize the Jordan plain. But the Dead Sea with the same water makes horror. For the Dead Sea has no outlet. It gets to keep.

The Meaning of Service [*1920*]

WILFRID WILSON GIBSON
[1878–　　]

One song leads on to another,
One friend to another friend,
So I'll travel along
With a friend and a song.
　　　The Empty Purse. Stanza 1
All life moving to one measure —
Daily bread.
　　All Life Moving to One Measure
Just what it meant to smile and smile
And let my son go cheerily —
My son . . . and wondering all the while
What stranger would come back to me.
　　　The Return. Stanza 2

OLIVER ST. JOHN GOGARTY
[1878–1957]

Only the Lion and the Cock,
As Galen says, withstand Love's shock.
So, Dearest, do not think me rude
If I yield now to lassitude,

But sympathize with me. I know
You would not have me roar, or crow.
　　　　　After Galen
I give more praise to Troy's redoubt
For Love kept in, than War kept out.
　　　　　On Troy
And up the back-garden
The sound comes to me
Of the lapsing, unsoilable,
Whispering sea.
　　　　　Ringsend
What should we know,
For better or worse,
Of the Long Ago,
Were it not for Verse?
　　　　　Verse
A vitalized symbol
Of earth and of storm,
Of Chaos contracted
To intricate form.
　　　　The Crab Tree
If but the will be firmly bent,
No stuff resists the mind's intent.
　　　The Image-Maker

DONALD ROBERT PERRY MARQUIS
[1878–1937]

The saddest ones are those that wear
The jester's motley garb.
　　　The Tavern of Despair
The world hath just one tale to tell, and
　　it is very old,
A little tale — a simple tale — a tale
　　that's easy told:
"There was a youth in Babylon who
　　greatly loved a maid!"
　　　News from Babylon
No doubt the cherubs earn their wage
Who wind each ticking star.
　　　　The Rebel
Noah an' Jonah an' Cap'n John Smith,
Mariners, travelers, magazines of myth,
Settin' up in Heaven, chewin' and a-
　　chawin'
Eatin' their terbaccy, talkin' and a-
　　jawin'.
　　Noah an' Jonah an' Cap'n
　　　John Smith [*1921*]

For I want to hire out as the Skipper
(Who dodges life's stress and its
    strains)
Of the Trolley, the Toonerville Trolley,
The Trolley that Meets all the Trains.
                The Toonerville Trolley:
                        To Fontaine Fox
    A dollar a line,
The Uplifting stuff brings a dollar a
    line!
                Yes, Song Is Coming into Its
                        Own Again
And similar goddamned phrases.
                Ballade of Goddamned Phrases [1]
I pray Thee make my column read,
And give me thus my daily bread.
Endow me, if Thou grant me wit,
Likewise with sense to mellow it.
                                Prayer
Comet, shake out your locks and let
    them flare
Across the startled heaven of my soul!
Pluck out the hairpins, Sue, and let her
    roll!
Don't be so stingy with your blooming
    hair.
                Sonnets to a Red-Haired Lady
                        [1922]. I
I love you as New Englanders love pie!
                                Ibid. XII
One boob may die, but deathless is
    The royal race of hicks —
When Ahab went to Ascalon
    They sold him gilded bricks.
                                Boob Ballad
    Oh, what the hell, it's Spring!
And just for the sake of argyment, I'll
    show 'em who is king.
                David and Bathsheba (As Inter-
                        preted by the Old Soak)
    There will be no beans in the Almost
Perfect State.[2]
                The Almost Perfect State [1927]
    For a territory the size of the United
States five millions of people would be
about right. . . . The human popula-
tion of the entire world should be kept

well under a hundred millions. . . . If
the world were not so full of people,
and most of them did not have to work
so hard, there would be more time for
them to get out and lie on the grass,
and there would be more grass for
them to lie on.
                The Almost Perfect State
    Of middle age the best that can be
said is that a middle-aged person has
likely learned how to have a little fun
in spite of his troubles.
                                Ibid.
oh i should worry and fret
death and i will coquette
there s a dance in the old dame yet
toujours gai toujours gai
                archy [1] *and mehitabel [1927].*
                        the song of mehitabel
procrastination is the
art of keeping
up with yesterday
                ibid. certain maxims of archy
an optimist is a guy that has never
    had much experience
                                ibid.
    what in hell
have i done to deserve all these kittens
                ibid. mehitabel and her kittens
dance mehitabel dance
caper and shake a leg
what little blood is left
will fizz like wine in a keg
                ibid. mehitabel dances with boreas
    i have noticed that when chickens
quit quarreling over their food they
often find that there is enough for all
of them i wonder if it might not be the
same way with the human race
                archy's life of mehitabel [1933].
                        random thoughts by archy
    so unlucky
that he runs into accidents
which started out to happen
to somebody else
                        ibid. archy says
theres life in the old dame yet
                ibid. the retreat from hollywood

---

[1] Inspired by a protest from General Ian
Hamilton, Commander of the Mediterranean
Expeditionary Force [1915], against turning
his cables into hackneyed phrases.
[2] See Robert Burton, page 221b.

[1] archy, a cockroach, is unable to use the
shift key on the typewriter and therefore
cannot print capital letters.

Dreadful things are Just as apt to happen when stupid people control a situation as when definitely ill-natured people are in charge.
Chapters for the Orthodox [1934]. Chap. 8

All religion, all life, all art, all expression come down to this: to the effort of the human soul to break through its barrier of loneliness, of intolerable loneliness, and make some contact with another seeking soul, or with what all souls seek, which is (by any name) God.
Ibid. Chap. 11

it is a cheering thought to think
that god is on the side of the best digestion [1]
archy does his part [1935]. the big bad wolf

there is bound to be a certain amount of
trouble running any country
if you are president the trouble happens to you
but if you are a tyrant you can arrange things so
that most of the trouble happens to other people
ibid. archy's newest deal

there is always
a comforting thought
in time of trouble when
it is not our trouble
ibid. comforting thoughts

too many creatures
both insects and humans
estimate their own value
by the amount of minor irritation
they are able to cause
to greater personalities than themselves
ibid. pride

the females of all species are most
dangerous when they appear to retreat
ibid. a farewell

To stroke a platitude until it purrs like an epigram.
The Sun Dial

[1] Give me a good digestion, Lord,
And also something to digest.
ANONYMOUS: *A Pilgrim's Grace, St. 1*

Publishing a volume of verse is like dropping a rose-petal down the Grand Canyon and waiting for the echo.
The Sun Dial

Poetry is what Milton saw when he went blind.
Ibid.

If you make people think they're thinking, they'll love you. If you really make them think they'll hate you.
Ibid.

An Idea isn't responsible for the people who believe in it.
Ibid.

A man has jest naturally got to have something to cuss around and boss, so's to keep himself from finding out he don't amount to nothing.
Danny's Own Story

JOHN MASEFIELD [1]
[1878–   ]

Theirs be the music, the colour, the glory, the gold;
Mine be a handful of ashes, a mouthful of mould.
Of the maimed, of the halt and the blind in the rain and the cold —
Of these shall my songs be fashioned, my tales be told.
A Consecration. Stanza 7

I must down to the seas again, to the lonely sea and the sky,
And all I ask is a tall ship and a star to steer her by,
And the wheel's kick and the wind's song and the white sail's shaking,
And a grey mist on the sea's face and a grey dawn breaking.
Sea-Fever [1902]. Stanza 1

I must down to the seas again, for the call of the running tide
Is a wild call and a clear call that may not be denied.
Ibid. Stanza 2

I must down to the seas again, to the vagrant gypsy life,
To the gull's way and the whale's way where the wind's like a whetted knife;

[1] Appointed Poet Laureate, 1930.

And all I ask is a merry yarn from a
  laughing fellow-rover,
And quiet sleep and a sweet dream
  when the long trick's over.
           Sea-Fever. Stanza 3

Dunno about Life — it's jest a tramp
  alone
From wakin'-time to doss.
Dunno about Death — it's jest a quiet
  stone
All over-grey wi' moss.
           Vagabond

It's a warm wind, the west wind, full of
  birds' cries.
           The West Wind

One road leads to London,
  One road runs to Wales,
My road leads me seawards
  To the white dipping sails.
           Roadways

My road calls me, lures me
  West, east, south, and north;
Most roads lead men homewards,
  My road leads me forth.
           Ibid.

In quest of that one beauty
God put me here to find.
           Ibid.

The schooners and the merry crews are
  laid away to rest,
A little south the sunset in the Islands
  of the Blest.
      A Ballad of John Silver

Commonplace people dislike tragedy,
because they dare not suffer and cannot
exult. The truth and rapture of man are
holy things, not lightly to be scorned.
A carelessness of life and beauty marks
the glutton, the idler, and the fool in
their deadly path across history.
    The Tragedy of Nan [*1909*].
           Preface

And he who gives a child a treat
Makes joy-bells ring in Heaven's street,
And he who gives a child a home
Builds palaces in Kingdom come.
    The Everlasting Mercy [*1911*]

To get the whole world out of bed
And washed, and dressed, and warmed,
  and fed,

To work, and back to bed again,
Believe me, Saul, costs worlds of pain.
     The Everlasting Mercy

O Christ who holds the open gate,
O Christ who drives the furrow
  straight,
O Christ, the plough, O Christ, the
  laughter
Of holy white birds flying after.
           Ibid.

The rain that makes things new,
The earth that hides things old.
           Ibid.

The days that make us happy make us
  wise.
           Biography

In the dark womb where I began
My mother's life made me a man.
Through all the months of human birth
Her beauty fed my common earth.
I cannot see, nor breathe, nor stir,
But through the death of some of her.
       C. L. M. Stanza 1

Quinquireme of Nineveh from distant
  Ophir,
Rowing home to haven in sunny Pales-
  tine,
With a cargo of ivory,
And apes and peacocks,[1]
Sandalwood, cedarwood, and sweet
  white wine.
      Cargoes. Stanza 1

Dirty British coaster with a salt-caked
  smoke stack,
Butting through the Channel in the
  mad March days,
With a cargo of Tyne coal,
Road-rail, pig-lead,
Firewood, iron-ware, and cheap tin
  trays.
        Ibid. Stanza 3

So I'm for drinking honestly, and dying
  in my boots.
   Captain Stratton's Fancy. Stanza 7

Oh London Town's a fine town, and
  London sights are rare,

   [1] Once in three years came the navy of
Tharshish, bringing gold, and silver, ivory,
and apes, and peacocks — *1 Kings, X, 22*

And London ale is right ale, and brisk's
the London air.
London Town. Stanza 1

All the great things of life are swiftly
done,
Creation, death, and love the double
gate.
However much we dawdle in the sun
We have to hurry at the touch of Fate;
When Life knocks at the door no one
can wait,
When Death makes his arrest we have
to go.
The Widow in the Bye Street
[1912]. Part 2

Love is a flame to burn out human
wills,
Love is a flame to set the will on fire,
Love is a flame to cheat men into mire.
One of the three, we make Love what
we choose.
Ibid.

What good can painting do to anyone?
I don't say never do it; far from
that —
No harm in sometimes painting just
for fun.
Keep it for fun, and stick to what
you're at.
Dauber [1913]. Part 2

Spit brown, my son, and get a hairy
breast.
Ibid.

What am I, Life? A thing of watery
salt
Held in cohesion by unresting cells,
Which work they know not why, which
never halt,
Myself unwitting where their Master
dwells?
Sonnets. 14

O beautiful is love and to be free
Is beautiful, and beautiful are friends.
Love, freedom, comrades, surely make
amends
For all these thorns through which we
walk to death.
Enslaved

Bitter it is, indeed, in human Fate
When Life's supreme temptation comes
too late.
The Woman Speaks

Go forth to seek: the quarry never
found
Is still a fever to the questing hound,
The skyline is a promise, not a bound.
The Wanderer of Liverpool

I touch my country's mind, I come to
grips
With half her purpose, thinking of
these ships,
That art untouched by softness, all
that line
Drawn ringing hard to stand the test
of brine.
Ships

Then the black-bright, smooth-running,
clicking clean
Brushed, oiled and dainty typewriting
machine,
With tins of ribbons waiting for the
blows
Which soon will hammer them to verse
and prose.
Shopping in Oxford

Man consists of body, mind, and imagination. His body is faulty, his mind
untrustworthy, but his imagination
has made him remarkable. In some
centuries, his imagination has made life
on this planet an intense practice of all
the lovelier energies.
Shakespeare and Spiritual Life
[1924]

There is another way to truth: by
the minute examination of facts. That
is the way of the scientist: a hard and
noble and thankless way. It is not the
way of the great poet, the rare unreasonable who comes once in ten generations. He apprehends truth by power:
the truth which he apprehends cannot
be defined, save by greater power, and
there is no greater power.
Ibid.

One ought to see everything that one
has a chance of seeing; because in life
not many have one chance and none
has two.
Sard Harker [1924]

When Custom presses on the souls
apart,
Who seek a God not worshipped by the
herd,

Forth, to the wilderness, the chosen
  start
Content with ruin, having but the
  Word.
> *Lines on the Tercentenary of*
> *Harvard College* [*1936*]

CARL SANDBURG
[1878–   ]

I am the people — the mob — the
  crowd — the mass.
Do you know that all the great work
  of the world is done through me?
> *I Am the People, the Mob*
> [*1916*]

I know a Jew fish crier down on Max-
  well Street with a voice like a
  north wind blowing over corn
  stubble in January. . . .
His face is that of a man terribly glad
  to be selling fish.
> *Fish Crier* [*1916*]

Hog Butcher for the World,
Tool Maker, Stacker of Wheat,
Player with Railroads and the Nation's
  Freight Handler;
Stormy, husky, brawling,
City of the Big Shoulders.
> *Chicago* [*1916*]

I won't take my religion from any man
  who never works except with his
  mouth and never cherishes any
  memory except the face of the
  woman on the American silver dollar.
> *To a Contemporary Bunk-*
> *shooter* [*1916*]

The fog comes on little cat feet.
> *Fog* [*1916*]

Pile the bodies high at Austerlitz and
  Waterloo.
Shovel them under and let me work —
I am the grass; I cover all.
> *Grass* [*1918*]

And pile them high at Gettysburg
And pile them high at Ypres and Ver-
  dun.
Shovel them under and let me work.
Two years, ten years, and passengers
  ask the conductor:

What place is this?
Where are we now?
> *Grass*

O prairie mother, I am one of your
  boys.
I have loved the prairie as a man with
  a heart shot full of pain over love.
> *Prairie*

I tell you the past is a bucket of ashes.
> *Ibid.*

The peace of great churches be for you,
Where the players of lofty pipe organs
Practice old lovely fragments, alone.
> *For You*

The peace of great books be for you,
Stains of pressed clover leaves on pages,
Bleach of the light of years held in
  leather.
> *Ibid.*

For the gladness here where the sun is
  shining at evening on the weeds of
  the river,
Our prayer of thanks.
> *Our Prayer of Thanks*

For the laughter of children who tumble barefooted and bareheaded in
  the summer grass.
> *Ibid.*

The republic is a dream.
Nothing happens unless first a dream.
> *Washington Monument by Night*

When Abraham Lincoln was shoveled
  into the tombs, he forgot the copperheads and the assassin . . . in
  the dust, in the cool tombs.
> *Cool Tombs* [*1918*]

That sergeant at Belleau Woods,
Walking into the drumfires, calling his
  men,
"Come on, you . . . Do you want to
  live forever?" [1]
> *Losers* [*1921*]

Always he kept on asking: "Where did
  that blood come from?"
> *Ossawatomie* [*1921*]

The French who found the Ohio River
  named it
La Belle Rivière, meaning a woman
  easy to look at.
> *Whiffs of the Ohio River at*
> *Cincinnati*

[1] See Thomas Carlyle, page 474b.

The marvelous rebellion of man at all signs reading "Keep Off." [1]

Who Am I?

Take any streetful of people buying clothes and groceries, cheering a hero or throwing confetti and blowing tin horns . . . tell me if the lovers are losers . . . tell me if any get more than the lovers . . . in the dust . . . in the cool tombs.

Ibid.

Lay me on an anvil, O God.
Beat me and hammer me into a crowbar.
Let me pry loose old walls.
Let me lift and loosen old foundations.

Prayers of Steel

Look out how you use proud words.
When you let proud words go, it is not easy to call them back.
They wear long boots, hard boots.

Primer Lesson

Time is a sandpile we run our fingers in.

Hotel Girl

Man is a long time coming.
Man will yet win.
Brother may yet line up with brother:
This old anvil laughs at many broken hammers.
There are men who can't be bought.

The People Will Live On
[1936]

Time is a great teacher.
Who can live without hope?
In the darkness with a great bundle of grief the people march.

Ibid.

LOUIS EDWIN THAYER
[1878–   ]

Here is a toast that I want to give
   To a fellow I'll never know;
To the fellow who's going to take my place

[1] It was marked, in large black letters, "Office of the Manager — Keep Out." So Jurgen opened this door. — JAMES BRANCH CABELL: *Jurgen* [1919], *Chap.* 44

When it's time for me to go.

To My Successor [1909].
Stanza 1

EDWARD THOMAS
[1878–1917]

Out of the night, two cocks together crow,
Cleaving the darkness with a silver blow.

Cock-Crow

HANS ZINSSER
[1878–1940]

Now death is merciful. He calls me hence
Gently, with friendly soothing of my fears
Of ugly age and feeble impotence
And cruel disintegration of slow years.

Sonnets

How sweet the Summer! And the Autumn shone
Like warmth within our hearts as in the sky,
Ripening rich harvests that our love had sown.
How good that ere the Winter comes, I die!
Then, ageless in your heart, I'll come to rest
Serene and proud, as when you loved me best.

Ibid.

ETHEL BARRYMORE
[1879–1959]

That's all there is: there isn't any more.

Added, with permission of the author [Thomas Raceward], as the curtain line of "Sunday" [1904]

SIR WILLIAM BEVERIDGE
[1879–1963]

Simple effluxion of time. [1]

Social Insurance [1942]

[1] The *Oxford English Dictionary* traces the phrase "effluxion of time" back to JOHN MOLLE: *The Living Librarie* [1621].

The object of government in peace and in war is not the glory of rulers or of races, but the happiness of the common man.

Social Insurance

JAMES BRANCH CABELL
[1879–1958]

Why is the King of Hearts the only one that hasn't a moustache?

The Rivet in Grandfather's Neck [1915]

Divers queens who die with Antony But live a great while first with Julius.

Retractions. V

"Men's hands are by ordinary soiled in climbing," quoth the Centaur.

Jurgen [1919]. *Chap. 5*

Now I am wiser: for I know there is not any memory with less satisfaction in it than the memory of some temptation we resisted.

Ibid. Chap. 7

I am willing to taste any drink once.

Ibid. Chap. 16

I shall marry in haste, and repeat at leisure.

Ibid. Chap. 38

There is no faith stronger than that of a bad-tempered woman in her own infallibility.

Ibid. Chap. 39

Poetry is man's rebellion against being what he is.

Ibid. Chap. 44

The optimist proclaims that we live in the best of all possible worlds; and the pessimist fears this is true.

The Silver Stallion [1926]. *Chap. 26*

LEE WILSON DODD
[1879–1933]

Much that I sought, I could not find;
Much that I found, I could not bind;
Much that I bound, I could not free;
Much that I freed returned to me.

Ronde Macabre

ALBERT EINSTEIN
[1879–1955]

The most beautiful thing we can experience is the mysterious. It is the source of all true art and science.

"What I Believe," Forum [*October, 1930*]

As long as there are sovereign nations possessing great power, war is inevitable.

Einstein on the Atomic Bomb. Atlantic Monthly, November, 1945

I do not believe that civilization will be wiped out in a war fought with the atomic bomb. Perhaps two thirds of the people of the earth might be killed, but enough men capable of thinking, and enough books, would be left to start again, and civilization could be restored.

Ibid.

Since I do not foresee that atomic energy is to be a great boon for a long time, I have to say that for the present it is a menace. Perhaps it is well that it should be. It may intimidate the human race into bringing order into its international affairs, which, without the pressure of fear, it would not do.

Ibid.

Every intellectual who is called before one of the committees ought to refuse to testify, i. e., he must be prepared . . . for the sacrifice of his personal welfare in the interest of the cultural welfare of his country. . . . This kind of inquisition violates the spirit of the Constitution.

If enough people are ready to take this grave step they will be successful. If not, then the intellectuals of this country deserve nothing better than the slavery which is intended for them.

Letter to William Frauenglass,[1] *May 16, 1953*

[1] Einstein's letter was published in the *New York Times*, June 12, 1953; Mr. Frauenglass had been subpoenaed to testify before the Senate Internal Security Subcommittee, then under the chairmanship of Senator Jenner of Indiana.

JOHN ERSKINE
[1879–1951]

The Moral Obligation to Be Intelligent.

Title of book [1915]

The body travels more easily than the mind, and until we have limbered up our imagination we continue to think as though we had stayed home. We have not really budged a step until we take up residence in someone else's point of view.

The Complete Life [1943].
Chap. 8, Foreigners

W. C. FIELDS
[1879–1946]

It ain't a fit night out for man or beast.

The Fatal Glass of Beer

DOROTHY CANFIELD FISHER
[1879–1958]

A mother is not a person to lean on but a person to make leaning unnecessary.

Her Son's Wife [1926]

The skull of life suddenly showed through its smile.

Bonfire [1933]

EDWARD MORGAN FORSTER
[1879–   ]

Railway termini . . . are our gates to the glorious and the unknown. Through them we pass out into adventure and sunshine, to them, alas! we return. In Paddington all Cornwall is latent and the remoter west; down the inclines of Liverpool Street lie fenlands and the illimitable Broads; Scotland is through the pylons of Euston; Wessex behind the poised chaos of Waterloo.

Howards End [1910]. *Chap. 2*

It will be generally admitted that Beethoven's Fifth Symphony is the most sublime noise that has ever penetrated into the ear of man.

Howards End. Chap. 5

It is thus, if there is any rule, that we ought to die — neither as victim nor as fanatic, but as the seafarer who can greet with an equal eye the deep that he is entering, and the shore that he must leave.

Ibid. Chap. 12

Only connect! That was the whole of her sermon. Only connect the prose and the passion, and both will be exalted, and human love will be seen at its height. Live in fragments no longer. Only connect, and the beast and the monk, robbed of the isolation that is life to either, will die.

Ibid. Chap. 22

The historian must have some conception of how men who are not historians behave.

Abinger Harvest [1936].
Captain Edward Gibbon

It is not that the Englishman can't feel — it is that he is afraid to feel. He has been taught at his public school that feeling is bad form. He must not express great joy or sorrow, or even open his mouth too wide when he talks — his pipe might fall out if he did.

Ibid. Notes on English Character

English literature is a flying fish. It is a sample of the life that goes on day after day beneath the surface; it is a proof that beauty and emotion exist in the salt, inhospitable sea.

Ibid.

How rare, how precious is frivolity! How few writers can prostitute all their powers! They are always implying "I am capable of higher things."

Ibid. Ronald Firbank

EDMUND L. GRUBER
[1879–1941]

Over hill, over dale, we have hit the
    dusty trail
And those caissons go rolling along.
Countermarch! Right about! hear
    those wagon soldiers shout

While those caissons go rolling along.
Oh, it's hi-hi-yee! for the field artil-
leree,
Shout out your numbers loud and
strong,
And where'er we go, you will always
know
That those caissons are rolling along.
The Caisson Song [1]

JOHN HAYNES HOLMES
[1879–1964]

If Christians were Christians, there
would be no anti-Semitism. Jesus was
a Jew. There is nothing that the ordinary Christian so dislikes to remember as this awkward historical fact. But
it happens, none the less, to be true.
*The Sensible Man's View of
Religion* [1933]

Priests are no more necessary to religion than politicians to patriotism.
Ibid.

The universe is not hostile, nor yet
is it friendly. It is simply indifferent.
Ibid.

The life of humanity upon this
planet may yet come to an end, and a
very terrible end. But I would have
you notice that this end is threatened
in our time not by anything that the
universe may do to us, but only by
what man may do to himself.
Ibid.

VACHEL LINDSAY
[1879–1931]

Record it for the grandson of your
son —
A city is not builded in a day:

Our little town cannot complete her
soul
Till countless generations pass away.
*On the Building of Springfield
[1912]. Stanza 2*

Booth died blind and still by faith he
trod,
Eyes still dazzled by the ways of God.
*General William Booth Enters
into Heaven [1913]*

Sleep softly . . . eagle forgotten . . .
under the stone,
Time has its way with you there and
the clay has its own.
Sleep on, O brave-hearted, O wise man,
that kindled the flame —
To live in mankind is far more than to
live in a name.
The Eagle That Is Forgotten [1]
[1913]. Stanza 5

Factory windows are always broken.
Somebody's always throwing bricks,
Somebody's always heaving cinders,
Playing ugly Yahoo tricks.
Factory Windows. Stanza 1

See how the generations pass
Like sand through Heaven's blue hour-
glass.
Shantung

I want live things in their pride to re-
main.
I will not kill one grasshopper vain
Though he eats a hole in my shirt like
a door.
I let him out, give him one chance
more.
Perhaps, while he gnaws my hat in his
whim,
Grasshopper lyrics occur to him.
The Santa Fé Trail [1914]

Fat black bucks in a wine-barrel room,
Barrel-house kings; with feet unstable,
Sagged and reeled and pounded on the
table,
Pounded on the table,

---

[1] Major Gruber wrote this song when he
was a lieutenant in the 5th Field Artillery in
the Philippines. In April, 1908, the 1st Battalion came from the United States to relieve
the 2nd Battalion, and Lieutenant Gruber
was asked to write a song that would sym-
bolize the spirit of the reunited regiment.
There are many variant wordings.

[1] John Peter Altgeld [1847–1902], Governor of Illinois, 1893–1897, widely criticized
for pardoning, in June, 1893, the anarchists
who had been serving life terms in prison
since the Haymarket riot in Chicago, May 4,
1886. Altgeld, in pardoning them, declared
that "the judge conducted the trial with
malicious ferocity."

Beat an empty barrel with the handle
of a broom.
The Congo [*1914*]. *Part I*

Then I saw the Congo, creeping
through the black,
Cutting through the forest with **a**
golden track.
Ibid.

Be careful what you do,
Or Mumbo-Jumbo, God of the Congo,
And all of the other
Gods of the Congo,
Mumbo-Jumbo will hoo-doo you.
Ibid.

A bronzed, lank man! His suit of an-
cient black,
A famous high top-hat and plain worn
shawl
Make him the quaint great figure that
men love,
The prairie-lawyer, master of us all.
*Abraham Lincoln Walks at
Midnight* [*1914*]. *Stanza 3*

They spoke, I think, of perils past.
They spoke, I think, of peace at last.
One thing I remember:
Spring came on forever,
Spring came on forever,
Said the Chinese nightingale.
The Chinese Nightingale [*1917*]

Then you died on the prairie, and
scorned all disgraces,
O broncho that would not be broken of
dancing.
*The Broncho That Would Not
Be Broken* [*1917*]. *Stanza 5*

Highly establish
In the name of God,
The United States of Europe, Asia, and
the World.
Sew the Flags Together [*1918*]

The flower-fed buffaloes of the spring
In the days of long ago,
Ranged where the locomotives sing
And the prairie flowers lie low.
The Flower-Fed Buffaloes

God make our blunders wise.
Litany of the Heroes. Stanza 16

Come let us forget our ivory-towers,[1]
brothers,
Come let us be bold with our songs.
*Every Soul Is a Circus. Part IV,
The Pontoon Bridge Miracle*

Planting the trees that would march
and train
On, in his name to the great Pacific,
Like Birnam Wood to Dunsinane,[2]
Johnny Appleseed swept on.[3]
In Praise of Johnny Appleseed

I find strange thoughts in me, on war
and peace. . . . This is not the last
chance good men all over the world
will have to fight.
*Letter to Eleanor Dougherty,
October 12, 1918*[4]

The more probable chance for me
will come in some little row where
strikers are being shot down. . . .
I would be with the fool strikers, right
or wrong.
Ibid.

[1] Charles-Augustin Sainte-Beuve [1804–
1869] is the first writer known to have likened
a poet's retreat to an ivory tower. In his
Pensées d'Août, To M. Villemain, St. 3, dated
October, 1837, he wrote:
Hugo, dur partisan
. . . combattit sous l'armure,
Et tint haut sa bannière au milieu du mur-
mure:
Il la maintient encore; et Vigny, plus secret,
Comme en sa tour d'ivoire, avant midi, ren-
trait
(Hugo, stern partisan
. . . fought under armor,
And held his banner high in the midst of the
tumult:
He holds it still; and Vigny, more secret,
As if in his tower of ivory, retired before
noon).
The poet, retired in his Tower of Ivory, isolated, according to his desire, from the world
of man, resembles, whether he so wishes or
not, another solitary figure, the watcher enclosed for months at a time in a lighthouse
at the head of a cliff. — JULES DE GAULTIER
[1858–?]: *La Guerre et les Destinées de
l'Art*
The Ivory Tower is the title of an unfinished novel [1917] by Henry James.
[2] See Shakespeare, page 198b.
[3] See E. A. Allen, page 654b.
[4] Published by his sister, Olive Lindsay
Wakefield, in the *Saturday Review of Literature,* October 20, 1945.

ST. JOHN LUCAS
[1879–1934]

The curate thinks you have no soul;
I know that he has none.[1]

My Dog

GEORGE WASHINGTON LYON
[1879–　　]

Worry, the interest paid by those who borrow trouble.

Epigram, in Judge,
March 1, 1924

DIXON LANIER MERRITT
[1879–　　]

A wonderful bird is the pelican,
His bill will hold more than his belican.
He can take in his beak
Food enough for a week,
But I'm damned if I see how the helican.

The Pelican [1910]

HAROLD MONRO
[1879–1932]

How lonely we shall be!
What shall we do,
You without me,
I without you?

Midnight Lamentation

FELIX RIESENBERG
[1879–1939]

The sea has always been a seducer, a careless lying fellow, not feminine, as many writers imagine, but strongly masculine in its allurement. The king of the sea, with his whiskers of weed and his trident and dolphins, truly represents the main and gives it character. The sea, like a great sultan, supports thousands of ships, his lawful wives. These he caresses and chastises as the case may be. This explains the feminine gender of all proper vessels.

Vignettes of the Sea

[1] There are things that even the youngest curate cannot explain. — LEONARD MERRICK: *One Man's View* [1897]

WILL ROGERS
[1879–1935]

All I know is just what I read in the papers.

Prefatory remark

I tell you Folks, all Politics is Apple Sauce.

The Illiterate Digest [1924].
Page 30

Everything is funny as long as it is happening to somebody else.

Ibid. Page 131

More men have been elected between Sundown and Sunup, than ever were elected between Sunup and Sundown.

Ibid. Page 152

I never met a man I didn't like.

Address, Boston [June, 1930]

A comedian can only last till he either takes himself serious or his audience takes him serious.

Syndicated newspaper article,
June 28, 1931

I not only "don't choose to run"[1] [for President] but I don't even want to leave a loophole in case I am drafted, so I won't "choose." I will say "won't run" no matter how bad the country will need a comedian by that time.

Ibid.

Politics has got so expensive that it takes lots of money to even get beat with.

Ibid.

ROBERT HAVEN SCHAUFFLER
[1879–　　]

At the gate of the West I stand,
On the isle where the nations throng,
We call them "scum o' the earth."[2]

Scum o' the Earth

JOSEPH STALIN
[1879–1953]

The Soviet regime possesses all the requisites for the upbuilding of a fully

[1] See Calvin Coolidge, page 859a.
[2] See Cervantes, page 108b.

socialized society, provided it can overcome its internal difficulties. We are witnessing a temporary stabilization of capitalism and the stabilization of the Soviet regime. A temporary equilibrium has been established between the two stabilizations. This compromise is the basic feature of the present situation.[1]

Speech to Party Officials,
May 9, 1925

In the U.S.S.R. work is the duty of every able-bodied citizen, according to the principle: "He who does not work, neither shall he eat."

In the U.S.S.R. the principle of socialism is realised: "From each according to his ability, to each according to his work." [2]

Constitution of the Union
of Soviet Socialist Republics
[1936]. Article 12

Citizens of the U.S.S.R. have the right to work.

Ibid. Article 118

Citizens of the U.S.S.R. have the right to rest.

Ibid. Article 119

Citizens of the U.S.S.R. have the right to maintenance in old age.

Ibid. Article 120

Citizens of the U.S.S.R. have the right to education

Ibid. Article 121

The victory of socialism in Russia is not complete because the danger of intervention from capitalist countries continues. The problem can be solved only by uniting the serious efforts of the international proletariat with the still more serious efforts of the entire Soviet people.

Letter to Comrade Ivanov,
February 14, 1938

Socialism can succeed only on the basis of a high productivity of labor, higher than under capitalism, on the basis of an abundance of products and

of articles of consumption of all kinds, on the basis of a prosperous and cultured life for all members of society.

Quoted by HEWLETT JOHNSON *in The Soviet Power: The Socialist Sixth of the World [1940], Book III, 8*

History shows that there are no invincible armies.

Address broadcast, Declaration of War, July 3, 1941 (Germany invaded Russia June 22, 1941)

In case of a forced retreat of Red Army units, all rolling stock must be evacuated; to the enemy must not be left a single engine, a single railway car, not a single pound of grain or a gallon of fuel. . . . In occupied regions conditions must be made unbearable for the enemy and all his accomplices. They must be hounded and annihilated at every step and all their measures frustrated.

Ibid. [The "scorched earth" edict]

All working people must be roused to defend our freedom, our honor, our country. . . . All the forces of the people for the demolition of the enemy.

Ibid.

The Hitlerite blackguards have covered Europe with gallows and concentration camps. . . . They have turned Europe into a prison of nations, and this they call the new order in Europe.

Address to the Moscow Soviet,
November 6, 1942

BESSIE ANDERSON (MRS. ARTHUR J.) STANLEY
[1879–   ]

He has achieved success who has lived well, laughed often and loved much.

Success (prize-winning definition in a contest conducted by the Brown Book Magazine, 1904)

---

[1] This statement was popularized as "socialism in one country" and used in arguing against the position of Leon Trotsky.
[2] See Karl Marx, page 594a.

WALLACE STEVENS
[1879–1955]

Complacencies of the peignoir, and late
Coffee and oranges in a sunny chair.
Sunday Morning [1923]. Stanza 1

In the isolation of the sky,
At evening, casual flocks of pigeons
  make
Ambiguous undulations as they sink,
Downward to darkness, on extended
  wings.
Ibid. Stanza 8

Just as my fingers on these keys
Make music, so the self-same sounds
On my spirit make a music, too.
Peter Quince at the Clavier [1923].
Stanza 1

Beauty is momentary in the mind —
The fitful tracing of a portal;
But in the flesh it is immortal.
The body dies; the body's beauty lives.
Ibid. Stanza 4

The essential gaudiness of poetry.
Stevens's note to The Emperor
of Ice-Cream

The essential thing in form is to be
free in whatever form is used. A free
form does not assure freedom. As a
form, it is just one more form. So that
it comes to this, I suppose, that I believe in freedom regardless of form.
A Note on Poetry [1937]

ROSE PASTOR STOKES
[1879–1933]

Some pray to marry the man they love,
  My prayer will somewhat vary:
I humbly pray to Heaven above
  That I love the man I marry.
My Prayer

SIMEON STRUNSKY
[1879–1948]

Statistics are the heart of democracy.
Topics of the Times,
November 30, 1944

No colonization without misrepresentation.
No Mean City [1] *[1944]. Chap. 1*

People who want to understand
democracy should spend less time in
the library with Aristotle and more
time on the buses and in the subway.
Ibid. Chap. 2

To renew ties with the past need not
always be daydreaming; it may be tapping old sources of strength for new
tasks.
Ibid. Chap. 20

Nearly a century ago the foreigners
were saying that the national American
motto was "Hurry up!" They were the
first words which the immigrant heard
at Castle Garden, probably from his
own kinsmen who had preceded him to
America by a few years and were now
hustling him home from the dock.
Ibid. Chap. 30

Famous remarks are very seldom
quoted correctly.
Ibid. Chap. 38

GEORGE ASAF
(GEORGE H. POWELL)
[1880–1951]

What's the use of worrying?
  It never was worth while,
So, pack up your troubles in your old
  kit-bag,
  And smile, smile, smile.
Pack Up Your Troubles in
Your Old Kit-Bag [1915]

HENRY HOWARTH
BASHFORD
[1880–   ]

As I came down the Highgate Hill
  I met the sun's bravado,
And saw below me, fold on fold,
Grey to pearl and pearl to gold,
This London like a land of old,
  The land of Eldorado.
Romances. Stanza 1

[1] A citizen of no mean city. — *Acts, XXI,*
39

JOSEPH CLARK GREW
[1880–1965]

This [sartorial convention] is a real problem with which I shall have to wrestle during the next few days, for of such stuff is diplomacy made.[1]
> *Ten Years in Japan [1944].*
> *July 20, 1932*

We have a phrase in English "straight from the horse's mouth." I never knew why the particular animal chosen was a horse, especially as most horses are generally not very communicative. But the meaning is clear enough. What I shall say in Japan in the ensuing months comes "straight from the horse's mouth."[2]
> *Ibid. October 19, 1939*

ROBERT BROWNING HAMILTON
[1880–   ]

I walked a mile with Pleasure.
  She chattered all the way,
But left me none the wiser
  For all she had to say.
> *Along the Road. Stanza 1*

I walked a mile with Sorrow,
  And ne'er a word said she;
But, oh, the things I learned from her
  When Sorrow walked with me!
> *Ibid. Stanza 2*

BRIAN HOOKER
[1880–1946]

O youth foregone, foregoing!
O dream unseen, unsought!
God give you joy of knowing
What life your death has bought.[3]
> *A. D. 1919. Stanza 5*

[1] In a diplomat's soul you may find iron ore, but it is usually oil — and in a whale of a diplomat you'll find the whole equipment — the blubber of charity, the whalebone of flexibility, the oil of commodity. A great diplomat is a regular Moby Dick. — FRANCIS HACKETT: *Review of* ROGER B. MERRIMAN, *Suleiman the Magnificent, The New York Times* [January 4, 1945]

[2] Address before the America-Japan Society.

[3] Inscription on a tablet at Yale University

HELEN KELLER
[1880–   ]

Literature is my Utopia. Here I am not disfranchised. No barrier of the senses shuts me out from the sweet, gracious discourse of my book-friends. They talk to me without embarrassment or awkwardness.
> *The Story of My Life [1902]*

DOUGLAS MacARTHUR
[1880–1964]

I shall return.
> *Message on leaving Corregidor*
> *for Australia, March 11, 1942*

The President of the United States has ordered me to break through the Japanese lines and proceed from Corregidor to Australia for the purpose, as I understand it, of organizing the American offensive against Japan. A primary purpose of this is relief of the Philippines. I came through and I shall return.
> *Statement on arrival from Philippines in Adelaide, Australia[1]*
> *[March 20, 1942]*

This is the Voice of Freedom, General MacArthur speaking. People of the Philippines: I have returned.
> *Upon landing at Leyte Island*
> *[October 20, 1944]*

I see that the old flagpole still stands. Have your troops hoist the colors to its peak, and let no enemy ever haul them down.
> *To Colonel George M. Jones and 503rd Regimental Combat Team, who recaptured Corregidor [March 2, 1945]*

It is fatal to enter any war without the will to win it.
> *Speech, Republican National Convention [July 7, 1952]*

commemorating the Yale men who died in the First World War.

[1] On assuming Supreme Command in the Southwest Pacific.

GEORGE
CATLETT MARSHALL
[1880–1959]

The refusal of the British and Russian peoples to accept what appeared to be inevitable defeat was the great factor in the salvage of our civilization.
Biennial Report of the Chief of Staff of the U. S. Army, September 1, 1945

If man does find the solution for world peace it will be the most revolutionary reversal of his record we have ever known.
Ibid.

HENRY LOUIS MENCKEN
[1880–1956]

The virulence of the national appetite for bogus revelation.
A Book of Prefaces [*1917*].
Chap. 1, Sect. 2

To the man with an ear for verbal delicacies — the man who searches painfully for the perfect word, and puts the way of saying a thing above the thing said — there is in writing the constant joy of sudden discovery, of happy accident.
Ibid. Chap. 2, Sect. 2

Poverty is a soft pedal upon all branches of human activity, not excepting the spiritual.
Ibid. Chap. 4, Sect. 3

Formalism is the hall-mark of the national culture.
Ibid. Sect. 6

Time is a great legalizer, even in the field of morals.
Ibid.

The prophesying business is like writing fugues; it is fatal to every one save the man of absolute genius.
Prejudices, First Series [*1919*].
Chap. 2

The public . . . demands certainties; it must be told definitely and a bit raucously that this is true and that is false. But there *are* no certainties.
Ibid. Chap. 3

All successful newspapers are ceaselessly querulous and bellicose. They never defend anyone or anything if they can help it; if the job is forced upon them, they tackle it by denouncing someone or something else.
Prejudices, First Series. Chap. 13

The great artists of the world are never Puritans, and seldom even ordinarily respectable.
Ibid. Chap. 16

To be in love is merely to be in a state of perceptual anaesthesia — to mistake an ordinary young man for a Greek god or an ordinary young woman for a goddess.
Ibid.

All the more pretentious American authors try to write chastely and elegantly; the typical literary product of the country is still a refined essay in the *Atlantic Monthly*, perhaps gently jocose but never rough — by Emerson, so to speak, out of Charles Lamb.
The American Language [*1919*]

Philadelphia is the most pecksniffian of American cities, and thus probably leads the world.
Ibid.

It is the dull man who is always sure, and the sure man who is always dull.
Prejudices, Second Series [*1920*].
Chap. 1

There are no mute, inglorious Miltons,[1] save in the hallucinations of poets. The one sound test of a Milton is that he functions as a Milton.
Ibid. Third Series [*1922*], *Chap. 3*

Nine times out of ten, in the arts as in life, there is actually no truth to be discovered; there is only error to be exposed.
Ibid.

Injustice is relatively easy to bear; what stings is justice.
Ibid.

Poetry is a comforting piece of fiction set to more or less lascivious music.
Ibid. Chap. 7

[1] See Gray, page 348b.

Faith may be defined briefly as an illogical belief in the occurrence of the improbable.

> *Prejudices, Third Series. Chap. 14*

To be happy one must be (*a*) well fed, unhounded by sordid cares, at ease in Zion, (*b*) full of a comfortable feeling of superiority to the masses of one's fellow men, and (*c*) delicately and unceasingly amused according to one's taste. It is my contention that, if this definition be accepted, there is no country in the world wherein a man constituted as I am — a man of my peculiar weakness, vanities, appetites, and aversions — can be so happy as he can be in the United States. Going further, I lay down the doctrine that it is a sheer physical impossibility for such a man to live in the United States and *not* be happy.

> *On Being an American* [*1922*]

The difference between a moral man and a man of honor is that the latter regrets a discreditable act, even when it has worked and he has not been caught.

> *Prejudices, Fourth Series* [*1924*].
> *Chap. 11*

Nothing can come out of an artist that is not in the man.

> *Ibid. Fifth Series* [*1926*].
> *Chap. 5*

Christian endeavor is notoriously hard on female pulchritude.

> *The Aesthetic Recoil*

The learned are seldom pretty fellows, and in many cases their appearance tends to discourage a love of study in the young.

> *The New Webster International Dictionary* [*1934*]

The Gaseous Vertebrata who own, operate and afflict the universe have treated me with excessive politeness.

> *Happy Days* [*1940*]. *Preface*

When A annoys or injures B on the pretense of improving B, A is a scoundrel.

> *Newspaper Days: 1899–1906*
> [*1941*]

I've made it a rule never to drink by daylight and never to refuse a drink after dark.

> *Quoted in New York Post,*
> *September 18, 1945*

ALFRED NOYES
[1880–1958]

There's a magic in the distance, where the sea-line meets the sky.

> *Forty Singing Seamen. Stanza 9*

Go down to Kew in lilac-time (it isn't far from London!)
And you shall wander hand in hand with love in summer's wonderland.

> *Barrel-Organ. Stanza 5*

The wind was a torrent of darkness among the gusty trees,
The moon was a ghostly galleon tossed upon cloudy seas,
The road was a ribbon of moonlight over the purple moor,
And the highwayman came riding —
Riding — riding —
The highwayman came riding, up to the old inn-door.

> *The Highwayman*

The landlord's black-eyed daughter,
Bess, the landlord's daughter,
Plaiting a dark red love-knot into her long black hair.

> *Ibid.*

I'll come to thee by moonlight, though hell should bar the way.

> *Ibid.*

Calling as he used to call, faint and far away,
In Sherwood, in Sherwood, about the break of day.

> *Sherwood*

The cymbals crash,
And the dancers walk,
With long silk stockings
And arms of chalk.

> *A Victory Dance.*[1] *Stanza 1*

God how the dead men
Grin by the wall,

[1] The symphonic poem *Victory Ball*, composed by Ernest Schelling [1876–1939], was inspired by this poem.

Watching the fun
Of the Victory Ball.
A Victory Dance. Stanza 9

EDMUND LESTER PEARSON
[1880–1937]

No agreement about books can make us look upon another man with so friendly an eye as the discovery that he belonged to our period, and shared our special enthusiasms about reading, in the years that stretched between the sixth birthday and the sixteenth.
Books in Black or Red [*1923*]

GRANTLAND RICE
[1880–1954]

Where the puddle is shallow, the weak-
fish stay
To drift along with the current's flow;
To take the tide as it moves each day
With the idle ripples that come and go.
Ballade of the Gamefish
When the One Great Scorer comes to
write against your name —
He marks — not that you won or lost
— but how you played the game.[1]
Alumnus Football
All wars are planned by old men
In council rooms apart,
Who plan for greater armament
And map the battle chart.[2]
Two Sides of War. Stanza 1
I've noticed nearly all the dead
Were hardly more than boys.
Ibid. Stanza 4

LYTTON STRACHEY
[1880–1932]

Bertie[3] seemed to display a deep-seated repugnance to every form of mental exertion.
Queen Victoria [*1921*]. *Chap. 6*
In women's hearts he[4] had always

[1] But just this line ye grave for me:
"He played the game."
ROBERT WILLIAM SERVICE [1874–   ]:
The Lost Master
[2] See Herbert Hoover, pages 873b–874a.
[3] Edward VII as a child.
[4] Disraeli.

read as in an open book. . . . He real-ised everything — the interacting complexities of circumstance and character, the pride of place mingled so inextricably with personal arrogance, the super-abundant emotionalism, the ingenuousness of outlook, the solid, the laborious respectability, shot through so incongruously by temperamental cravings for the coloured and the strange, the singular intellectual limitations, and the mysteriously essential female elements impregnating every particle of the whole. A smile hovered over his impassive features, and he dubbed Victoria "the Faery."
Queen Victoria. Chap. 8
Perhaps of all the creations of man language is the most astonishing.
Words and Poetry

RICHARD HENRY TAWNEY
[1880–1962]

The burden of our civilization is . . . that industry itself has come to hold a position of exclusive predominance among human interests, which no single interest, and least of all the provision of the material means of existence, is fit to occupy.
The Acquisitive Society
Industrialized communities neglect the very objects for which it is worth while to acquire riches in their feverish preoccupation with the means by which riches can be acquired.
Ibid.

NANCY BYRD TURNER
[1880–   ]

When I go up to London
'Twill be in April weather.
I'll have a riband on my rein
And flaunt a scarlet feather.
Going Up to London
Death is only an old door
Set in a garden wall.
Death a Quiet Door

MARGARET WIDDEMER
[1880–   ]

I have shut my little sister in from life
    and light
(For a rose, for a ribbon, for a wreath
    across my hair),
I have made her restless feet still until
    the night,
Locked from sweets of summer and
    from wild spring air.
            The Factories. Stanza 1

The old road to Paradise
Easy it is missed!
        The Old Road to Paradise.
                    Stanza 2

Carnations and my first love! And he
    was seventeen,
And I was only twelve years — a
    stately gulf between.
            Carnations. Stanza 1

Well, if the thing is over, better it is
    for me,
The lad was ever a rover, loving and
    laughing and free.
        Mary, Helper of Heartbreak.
                    Stanza 1

Mary, helper of heartbreak, send him
    to me tonight!
            Ibid. Stanza 3

THOMAS RUSSELL YBARRA
[1880–   ]

A Christian is a man who feels
  Repentance on a Sunday
For what he did on Saturday
  And is going to do on Monday.
            The Christian

ALBERT JAY COOK
[*Floruit* 1917]

It's Heaven, Hell or Hoboken [1] before
    next Christmas Day.
        Heaven, Hell or Hoboken [2]

[1] Hoboken was a port of embarkation and
return for the American Expeditionary Forces
during the First World War.
[2] Published in *The Stars and Stripes*.

LASCELLES ABERCROMBIE
[1881–1938]

Crumble, crumble,
Voiceless things;
No faith can last
That never sings.
        The Stream's Song. Stanza 6

For the last hour
To joy belongs;
The steadfast perish,
But not the songs.
           Ibid. Stanza 7

FRANKLIN PIERCE ADAMS
("F.P.A.")
[1881–1960]

Christmas is over and Business is
Business.
        For the Other 364 Days

"Up, to the office, . . . and so to bed."
    A Ballade of Mr. Samuel Pepys.
                    Refrain

  If vigilance yet above you
Hover, count the times I love you;
And if slumber still repel you,
Count the times I do not tell you.
                Lullaby

Ruthlessly pricking our gonfalon bub-
    ble,
Making a Giant hit into a double,
Words that are weighty with nothing
    but trouble:
    "Tinker to Evers to Chance."
        Baseball's Sad Lexicon

The rich man has his motor car,
  His country and his town estate.
He smokes a fifty-cent cigar
  And jeers at Fate.
        The Rich Man. Stanza 1

Yet though my lamp burn low and dim,
  Though I must slave for liveli-
    hood —
Think you that I would change with
    him?
  You bet I would!
            Ibid. Stanza 3

The best you get is an even break.
    Ballade of Schopenhauer's
                  Philosophy

I shot a poem into the air,
It was reprinted everywhere
From Bangor to the Rocky Range
And always credited to
    — Exchange.
      Frequently

O bards of rhyme and metre free,
My gratitude goes out to ye
For all your deathless lines — ahem!
Let's see now . . . What *is* one of
them?
    To a Vers Librist

Of making many books there is no
end —
So Sancho Panza said, and so say I.
Thou wert my guide, philosopher and
friend
When only one is shining in the sky.
    Lines on and from "Bartlett's
      Familiar Quotations"

Go, lovely Rose that lives its little
hour!
Go, little booke! and let who will be
clever!
Roll on! From yonder ivy-mantled
tower
The moon and I could keep this up
forever.
       Ibid.

Prints, approaches the well-known
date;
Time to wallop and stigmatize;
Time for the wearisome old debate;
Why did it win the Pulitzer Prize?
    Ballade of the Annual Query.
       L'Envoi

MARY ANTIN
[1881–1949]

So at last I was going to America!
Really, really going, at last! The
boundaries burst. The arch of heaven
soared. A million suns shone out for
every star. The winds rushed in from
outer space, roaring in my ears, "America! America!"
    The Promised Land [*1912*]

WITTER BYNNER
[1881–]

Name me no names for my disease,
  With uninforming breath;
I tell you I am none of these,
  But homesick unto death.
    The Patient to the Doctors.
       Stanza 1

Give her such beauty of body and mind
  As the leaves of an aspen tree
When they vary from silver to green in
  the wind,
  And who shall be lovely as she?
     A Prayer for Beauty

You must keep your goal in sight,
Labor toward it day and night,
Then at last arriving there —
You shall be too old to care.
       Wisdom

What's the use of a new-born
  child? [1] . . .
To raise the dead heart? — to set wild
The fettered hope?
      Poor Richard

A leader is best
When people barely know that he
  exists.
    The Way of Life According to
       Laotzu

The biggest problem in the world
Could have been solved when it was
small.
       Ibid.

JOSEPH CAMPBELL
[1881–1944]

As a white candle
In a holy place,
So is the beauty
Of an aged face.
    The Old Woman. Stanza 1

Her thoughts as still
As the waters
Under a ruined mill.
     Ibid. Stanza 3

[1] "What is the use of this new invention?"
some one asked Franklin. "What is the use
of a new-born child?" was his reply. —
JAMES PARTON: *The Life and Times of
Benjamin Franklin* [1864], *Vol. II, P. 514.*
(A footnote states that the anecdote is taken
from the memoirs of Baron de Grimm.)

FRANCIS CARLIN (J. F. C. MacDONNELL)
[1881–1945]

That which is in disorder
Has neither rule nor rhyme,
Like the stars at Heaven's border
And the troubled laughter of Time.
The Raveled Edge. Stanza 3

ROBERT WILLIAM CHAPMAN
[1881–   ]

A house is infinitely communicative, and tells many things besides the figure of its master's income. There are houses that confess intellectual penury, and houses that reek of enlightenment.
The Portrait of a Scholar
[1920]

A quotation, like a pun, should come unsought, and then be welcomed only for some propriety or felicity justifying the intrusion.
Ibid. The Art of Quotation

A collector should not be too careful to be sure of what he buys, or the sporting spirit will atrophy; and he who collects that he may have the best collection, or a better than his friend's, is little more than a miser.
Ibid. Silver Spoons

PADRAIC COLUM
[1881–   ]

Oh, to have a little house!
To own the hearth and stool and all!
An Old Woman of the Roads.
Stanza 1

And I am praying God on high,
And I am praying Him night and day,
For a little house — a house of my own —
Out of the wind's and the rain's way.
Ibid. Stanza 6

JOHN FREEMAN
[1881–1929]

Who may regret what was, since it has made

Himself himself? All that I was I am,
And the old childish joy now lives in me
At sight of a green field or a green tree.
All That I Was I Am

EDGAR ALBERT GUEST
[1881–1959]

Somebody said that it couldn't be done,
But he with a chuckle replied
That "maybe it couldn't," but he would be one
Who wouldn't say so till he'd tried.
It Couldn't Be Done [1]

The things that haven't been done before,
Those are the things to try;
Columbus dreamed of an unknown shore
At the rim of the far-flung sky.
*The Things That Haven't Been
Done Before*

It takes a heap o' livin' in a house
t' make it home,
A heap o' sun an' shadder, an' ye sometimes have t' roam
Afore ye really 'preciate the things ye lef' behind,
An' hunger fer 'em somehow, with 'em allus on yer mind.
Home

Let me be a little kinder,
Let me be a little blinder
To the faults of those around me,
Let me praise a little more.
A Creed

I'd rather see a sermon than hear one any day;
I'd rather one should walk with me than merely tell the way.
Sermons We See

In this bright little package, now isn't it odd?
You've a dime's worth of something known only to God!
The Package of Seeds

[1] The world would sleep if things were run
By men who say, "It can't be done!"
PHILANDER JOHNSON [1866–1939]:
"It Can't Be Done"

Here is one of God's miracles soon to
unfold,
Thus for ten cents an ounce is Divinity
sold!

The Package of Seeds

JOHN EDWARD HAZZARD
[1881–1935]

It worries me to beat the band
To hear folks say our lives is grand;
Wish they'd try some one-night stand.
Ain't it awful, Mabel!

Ain't It Awful, Mabel!

WILLIAM McFEE
[1881–   ]

A trouble is a trouble, and the general idea, in the country, is to treat it
as such.

*Casuals of the Sea [1916].
Book I, 4*

The world belongs to the enthusiast
who keeps cool.

Ibid. 14

The nobility of soul which is libel-
lously miscalled "proper pride."

Ibid. 17

If fate means you to lose, give him
a good fight anyhow.

Ibid. Book II, 2

Doing what's right is no guarantee
against misfortune.

Ibid. 6

It's the people who're comfortable
who have time to worry over little
trivial things.

Ibid.

Responsibility's like a string we can
only see the middle of. Both ends are
out of sight.

Ibid.

The alluring yet ineluctable problem
of human folly.

Aliens [1917]. Preface

A certain incomprehensible reticence
of soul which is peculiar to the English.

Command [1922]. Chap. 6

The bourgeois artist who retains his
integrity is the only really happy man
in the modern world. He is unable to

envy anybody because nobody has anything he can use which is not his already.

*More Harbours of Memory
[1934]. Introduction*

JOHN GNEISENAU
NEIHARDT
[1881–   ]

Give me high noon — and let it then
be night!

Let Me Live Out My Years

And grant me, when I face the grisly
Thing,
One haughty cry to pierce the gray
Perhaps!
O let me be a tune-swept fiddlestring
That feels the Master Melody — *and
snaps!*

Ibid.

STUART PRATT SHERMAN
[1881–1926]

The delectable form which intelligence takes in its moments of surplus
power — the form of wit.

*Introduction [1923] to Ameri-
can Prose Masters by* W. C.
BROWNELL

WILLIAM TEMPLE
(ARCHBISHOP OF CANTER-
BURY)
[1881–1944]

There is no structural organization
of society which can bring about the
coming of the Kingdom of God on
earth, since all systems can be perverted by the selfishness of man.

The Malvern Manifesto [1]

Human status ought not to depend
upon the changing demands of the economic process.

Ibid.

The existing industrial order tends
to recklessness and sacrilege in the

[1] Drawn up by a Conference of the Province of York, January 10, 1941; signed for
the Conference by Temple, then Archbishop
of York.

treatment of natural resources . . . it is largely responsible for the problem of the "mass man" who easily develops the herd psychology.

The Malvern Manifesto

MARY WEBB
[1881–1927]

The past is only the present become invisible and mute; and because it is invisible and mute, its memoried glances and its murmurs are infinitely precious. We are tomorrow's past.

Precious Bane [*1924*].[1]
Foreword

It made me gladsome to be getting some education, it being like a big window opening.

Ibid. Book I, Chap. 5

Saddle your dreams afore you ride 'em.

Ibid. Chap. 6

If you stop to be kind, you must swerve often from your path.

Ibid. Book II, Chap. 3

It's the folk that depend on us for this and for the other that we most do miss. So the mother is more let and hindered lacking the little creatures clinging to her skirt than she is when they be there, for she has no heart for her work.

Ibid. Book IV, Chap. 4

PELHAM GRENVILLE WODEHOUSE
[1881–　　]

He spoke with a certain what-is-it in his voice, and I could see that, if not actually disgruntled, he was far from being gruntled.

The Code of the Woosters

[1] That soil may best
Deserve the precious bane.
MILTON: *Paradise Lost* [1667],
Book I, L. 689

BERTON BRALEY
[1882–　　]

The grammar has a rule absurd
Which I would call an outworn myth:
"A preposition is a word
You mustn't end a sentence with!"[1]

*No Rule to Be Afraid Of.
Stanza 1*

And so they sailed away, these three,
Mencken,
Nathan
And God.[2]

Three Minus One. Stanza 1

With doubt and dismay you are smitten,
You think there's no chance for you, son?
Why, the best books haven't been written,
The best race hasn't been run.

Opportunity. Stanza 1

Back of the beating hammer
By which the steel is wrought,
Back of the workshop's clamor
The seeker may find the Thought.

The Thinker. Stanza 1

Back of the Job — the Dreamer
Who's making the dream come true!

Ibid. Stanza 4

JOHN DRINKWATER
[1882–1937]

This be my pilgrimage and goal,
Daily to march and find
The secret phrases of the soul,
The evangels of the mind.

Vocation

And not a girl goes walking
Along the Cotswold lanes
But knows men's eyes in April
Are quicker than their brains.

Cotswold Love

Grant us the will to fashion as we feel,
Grant us the strength to labor as we know,

[1] See Churchill, page 872b.
[2] See Eugene Field, page 747a.

Grant us the purpose, ribbed and edged
  with steel,
To strike the blow.
> *A Prayer. Stanza 9*

SIR ARTHUR STANLEY EDDINGTON
[1882–1944]

It is one thing for the human mind to extract from the phenomena of nature the laws which it has itself put into them; it may be a far harder thing to extract laws over which it has no control. It is even possible that laws which have not their origin in the mind may be irrational, and we can never succeed in formulating them.
> *Space, Time, and Gravitation*
> *[1920]*

SAMUEL GOLDWYN
[1882–   ]

For years I have been known for saying "include me out," but today I am giving it up forever. From now on let me say: "Oxford and Balliol, include me in."
> *Address to the Students of Balliol College, Oxford [March 1, 1945]*

In two words: im-possible.
> *Quoted by* ALVA JOHNSON:
> *The Great Goldwyn*

HERMANN HAGEDORN
[1882–1964]

Down the fair-chambered corridor of
  years,
The quiet shutting, one by one, of
  doors.
> *Doors*

WILLIAM FREDERICK HALSEY, JR.
[1882–   ]

Strike repeat Strike.
> *Reply to division commanders in South Pacific, when asked for his instructions, October 24, 1942*

Hit hard, hit fast, hit often.
> *Formula for waging war*

Send them our latitude and longitude.
> *Retort to the enemy's question, "Where is the American Fleet?" October, 1944*

Our ships have been salvaged and are retiring at high speed toward the Japanese fleet.
> *Radio message, October, 1944, after Japanese claims that most of the U. S. Third Fleet had either been sunk or had retired*

HUGH S. JOHNSON
[1882–1942]

There was never a war at arms that was not merely the extension of a preceding war of commerce grown fiercer until the weapons of commerce seemed no longer sufficiently deadly.[1]
> *Radio broadcast for "World Peaceways" [1935]*

JAMES JOYCE
[1882–1941]

When thou hast heard his name upon
  The bugles of the cherubim,
Begin thou softly to unzone
Thy girlish bosom unto him
And softly to undo the snood
That is the sign of maidenhood.
> *Chamber Music [1907].*
> *XI, Stanza 2*

Pity is the feeling which arrests the mind in the presence of whatsoever is grave and constant in human sufferings and unites it with the human sufferer.
> *A Portrait of the Artist as a Young Man [1916]. Chap. 5*

Welcome, O life! I go to encounter for the millionth time the reality of experience and to forge in the smithy of my soul the uncreated conscience of my

---

[1] War is not merely a political act, but also a political instrument, a continuation of political relations, a carrying out of the same by other means. — KARL VON CLAUSEWITZ: *On War* [1832]

race. Old father, old artificer, stand me now and ever in good stead.
> *A Portrait of the Artist as a*
> *Young Man. Concluding words*
> *of Stephen Dedalus*

A man of genius makes no mistakes. His errors are volitional and are the portals of discovery.
> *Ulysses* [1] *[1922]. II*

Around us fear, descending
Darkness of fear above
And in my heart how deep unending
Ache of love!
> *Pomes Penyeach [1927]. On the*
> *Beach at Fontana*

Why, why, why! Weh, O weh!
I'se so silly to be flowing but I no canna stay!
> *Finnegans Wake [1939].*
> *Song of The River*

FIORELLO H. LaGUARDIA
[1882–1948]

Ticker tape ain't spaghetti.
> *Speech to the United Nations*
> *Relief and Rehabilitation Ad-*
> *ministration, March 29, 1946*

WINIFRED MARY LETTS
[1882–   ]

I saw the spires of Oxford
  As I was passing by,
The gray spires of Oxford
  Against a pearl-gray sky.
> *The Spires of Oxford. Stanza 1*

That God once loved a garden
We learn in Holy writ.
And seeing gardens in the Spring
I well can credit it.
> *Stephen's Green. Stanza 1*

[1] In respect of the recurrent emergence of the theme of sex in the minds of his characters, it must always be remembered that his locale was Celtic and his season Spring . . . whilst in many places the effect of "Ulysses" on the reader undoubtedly is somewhat emetic, nowhere does it tend to be an aphrodisiac. "Ulysses" may, therefore, be admitted into the United States. — JUDGE JOHN M. WOOLSEY: *Decision of U. S. District Court* [December 6, 1933]

PHILIP HENRY KERR, MARQUESS OF LOTHIAN [1]
[1882–1940]

A limitation of armaments by political appeasement.[2]
> *Letter to The Times (London),*
> *May, 1934*

JACQUES MARITAIN
[1882–   ]

In the modern social order, the *person* is sacrificed to the *individual*. The individual is given universal suffrage, equality of rights, freedom of opinion; while the person, isolated, naked, with no social armor to sustain and protect him, is left to the mercy of all the devouring forces which threaten the life of the soul, exposed to relentless actions and reactions of conflicting interests and appetites. . . . It is a homicidal civilization.
> *Three Reformers [1925]*

ALAN ALEXANDER MILNE
[1882–1956]

Hush! Hush! Whisper who dares!
Christopher Robin is saying his prayers.
> *When We Were Very Young.*
> *Vespers*

They're changing guard at Buckingham Palace —
Christopher Robin went down with Alice.
> *Ibid. Buckingham Palace*

The King asked
The Queen, and
The Queen asked
The Dairymaid:
"Could we have some butter for
The Royal slice of bread?"
> *Ibid. The King's Breakfast*

"Nobody, my darling,
Could call me
A fussy man —
  BUT

[1] See Winston Churchill, page 870a.
[2] One of the most portentous slogans of the period was coined here. — KONRAD HEIDEN: *Der Führer* [1944], P. 714

I do like a little bit of butter to my
  bread!"
> *When We Were Very Young.*
> *The King's Breakfast*

It isn't really
Anywhere!
It's somewhere else
Instead!
> *Ibid. Halfway Down, Stanza 2*

What shall I call my dear little dor-
  mouse?
His eyes are small, but his tail is e-nor-
  mouse.
> *Ibid. The Christening*

Christopher Robin goes
Hoppity, hoppity,
Hoppity, hoppity, hop.
Whenever I tell him
Politely to stop it, he
Says he can't possibly stop.
> *Ibid. Hoppity*

James James
Morrison Morrison
Weatherby George Dupree
Took great
Care of his Mother
Though he was only three.
James James
Said to his Mother,
"Mother," he said, said he:
"You must never go down to the end of
  the town, if you don't go down
  with me."
> *Ibid. Disobedience*

Christopher Robin
Had wheezles
And sneezles.
> *Now We Are Six. Sneezles*

If I were a bear,
  And a big bear, too,
I shouldn't much care
  If it froze or snew.
> *Ibid. Furry Bear*

I am a Bear of Very Little Brain,
and long words Bother me.
> *Winnie-the-Pooh. Chap. 4*

Time for a little something.
> *Ibid. Chap. 6*

FRANKLIN DELANO
ROOSEVELT
[1882–1945]

There is nothing I love as much as a
good fight.
> *Interview, New York Times*
> *[January 22, 1911]*

These unhappy times call for the
building of plans . . . that build from
the bottom up and not from the top
down, that put their faith once more in
the forgotten man [1] at the bottom of
the economic pyramid.
> *Radio address [April 7, 1932]*

The country needs and, unless I mistake its temper, the country demands
bold, persistent experimentation. It is
common sense to take a method and
try it: If it fails, admit it frankly and
try another. But above all, try something.
> *Address at Oglethorpe University*
> *[May 22, 1932]*

I pledge you, I pledge myself,
to a new deal for the American people.
> *Speech accepting the nomina-*
> *tion for the Presidency, Demo-*
> *cratic National Convention,*
> *Chicago [July 2, 1932]*

This campaign marks the beginning
of a new deal in American politics, and
in the conduct of the American government.
> *Campaign speech at Indianapolis*
> *[October 20, 1932]*

There is no indispensable man.
> *Campaign speech at New York*
> *[November 3, 1932]*

The only thing we have to fear is
fear itself.[2]
> *First Inaugural Address*
> *[March 4, 1933]*

---

[1] See William Graham Summer, page 707a–
707b.
All honor to the one that in this hour
Cries to the world as from a lighted tower —
Cries for the Man Forgotten.
> EDWIN MARKHAM [1852–1940]: *The*
> *Forgotten Man*

[2] See Thoreau, page 589a.

The money changers have fled from their high seats in the temple of our civilization.

First Inaugural Address

In the field of world policy I would dedicate this nation to the policy of the good neighbor.[1]

Ibid.

If I were asked to state the great objective which Church and State are both demanding for the sake of every man and woman and child in this country, I would say that that great objective is "a more abundant life."

Address before Federal Council of Churches of Christ [*December 6, 1933*]

I am not for a return to that definition of liberty under which for many years a free people were being gradually regimented into the service of the privileged few. I prefer and I am sure you prefer that broader definition of liberty under which we are moving forward to greater freedom, to greater security for the average man than he has ever known before in the history of America.

Fireside Chat [*September 30, 1934*]

We have earned the hatred of entrenched greed.

Message to Congress [*January 3, 1936*]

The truth is found when men are free to pursue it.

Address at Temple University [*February 22, 1936*]

Out of this modern civilization economic royalists carved new dynasties. . . . The royalists of the economic order have conceded that political freedom was the business of the Government, but they have maintained that economic slavery was nobody's business.

Speech accepting renomination [*June 27, 1936*]

[1] I am as desirous of being a good neighbor as I am of being a bad subject. — THOREAU: *Civil Disobedience* [1849]

This generation of Americans has a rendezvous with destiny.

Speech accepting renomination

I have seen war. . . . I hate war.

Address at Chautauqua [*August 14, 1936*]

I have not sought, I do not seek, I repudiate the support of any advocate of Communism or of any other alien "ism" which would by fair means or foul change our American democracy.

Address at Syracuse [*September 29, 1936*]

I should like to have it said of my first Administration that in it the forces of selfishness and of lust for power met their match. I should like to have it said of my second Administration that in it these forces met their master.

Speech, Madison Square Garden [*October 31, 1936*]

Men with a passion for anonymity.

Report of President's Committee on Administrative Management [*January 12, 1937*]

We have always known that heedless self-interest was bad morals; we know now that it is bad economics.

Second Inaugural Address [*January 20, 1937*]

I see one-third of a nation ill-housed, ill-clad, ill-nourished.

Ibid.

The test of our progress is not whether we add more to the abundance of those who have much; it is whether we provide enough for those who have too little.

Ibid.

The epidemic of world lawlessness is spreading. When an epidemic of physical disease starts to spread, the community approves and joins in a quarantine of the patients in order to protect the health of the community against the spread of the disease. . . . The will for peace on the part of peace-loving nations must express itself to the end that nations that may be tempted to violate their agreements and the rights of others will desist from such a course. There must be positive endeavors to preserve peace.

> *Speech at Chicago* [1] [*October 5, 1937*]

War is a contagion.

> *Ibid.*

History proves that dictatorships do not grow out of strong and successful governments, but out of weak and helpless ones. If by democratic methods people get a government strong enough to protect them from fear and starvation, their democracy succeeds; but if they do not, they grow impatient. Therefore, the only sure bulwark of continuing liberty is a government strong enough to protect the interests of the people, and a people strong enough and well enough informed to maintain its sovereign control over its government.

> *Fireside Chat* [*April 14, 1938*]

Remember, remember always that all of us, and you and I especially, are descended from immigrants and revolutionists. [2]

> *Address to Daughters of the American Revolution* [*April 21, 1938*]

A program whose basic thesis is not that the system of free private enterprise for profit has failed in this generation, but that it has not yet been tried.

> *Message on Concentration of Economic Power* [*April 29, 1938*]

The Democratic Party will live and continue to receive the support of the majority of Americans just so long as it remains a liberal party.

> *Address, Denton, Maryland* [*September 5, 1938*]

The Soviet Union, as everybody who has the courage to face the fact knows, is run by a dictatorship as absolute as any other dictatorship in the world.

> *Address to American Youth Congress* [*February 10, 1940*]

On this tenth day of June, 1940, the

[1] The "Quarantine the Aggressors" speech.
[2] See *Campaign Speech, Boston*, page 921b.

hand that held the dagger has struck it into the back of its neighbor. [1]

> *Address to the Graduating Class, University of Virginia, Charlottesville* [*June 10, 1940*]

Eternal truths will be neither true nor eternal unless they have fresh meaning for every new social situation.

> *Address, University of Pennsylvania* [*September 20, 1940*]

And while I am talking to you mothers and fathers, I give you one more assurance. I have said this before, but I shall say it again and again and again: Your boys are not going to be sent into any foreign wars.

> *Campaign speech in Boston* [*October 30, 1940*]

That great historic trio . . . Martin, Barton and Fish. [2]

> *Ibid.*

It is an unfortunate human failing that a full pocketbook often groans more loudly than an empty stomach.

> *Speech in Brooklyn* [*November 1, 1940*]

We must be the great arsenal of democracy.

> *Fireside Chat* [*December 29, 1940*]

In the future days, which we seek to make secure, we look forward to a world founded upon four essential human freedoms. The first is freedom of speech and expression — everywhere in the world. The second is freedom of every person to worship God in his own way — everywhere in the world. The third is freedom from want . . . everywhere in the world. The fourth is freedom from fear . . . anywhere in the world.

> *Message to Congress* [*January 6, 1941*]

One great difference which has characterized this division [between liberal

[1] A few hours before President Roosevelt's address, Count Ciano, Italy's Foreign Minister, had notified the French Ambassador that Italy considered herself at war with France beginning June 11.
[2] Joseph Martin, Bruce Barton, and Hamilton Fish.

and conservative parties] has been that the liberal party — no matter what its particular name was at the time — believed in the wisdom and efficacy of the will of the great majority of the people, as distinguished from the judgment of a small minority. . . . The other great difference between the two parties has been this: The liberal party is a party which believes that, as new conditions and problems arise beyond the power of men and women to meet as individuals, it becomes the duty of the Government itself to find new remedies with which to meet them. The liberal party insists that the Government has the definite duty to use all its power and resources to meet new social problems with new social controls — to insure to the average person the right to his own economic and political life, liberty, and the pursuit of happiness.

Introduction to Public Papers and Addresses, 1938 Volume [*1941*]

We, too, born to freedom, and believing in freedom, are willing to fight to maintain freedom. We, and all others who believe as deeply as we do, would rather die on our feet than live on our knees.[1]

Response on receiving the degree of Doctor of Civil Law conferred by Oxford University, at a special convocation, Harvard University [2] [*June 19, 1941*]

When you see a rattlesnake poised to strike, you do not wait until he has struck before you crush him.

Fireside Chat [*September 11, 1941*]

Yesterday, December 7, 1941 — a date which will live in infamy — the United States of America was suddenly and deliberately attacked by naval and air forces of the Empire of Japan.

War Message to Congress [*December 8, 1941*]

[1] The phrase was a watchword with the Republican forces in the Spanish Civil War, 1936–1939, and is usually attributed to the celebrated woman leader, La Pasionaria.

[2] Read by Major General Edwin M. Watson, serving as proxy for President Roosevelt.

Never before have we had so little time in which to do so much.[1]

Fireside Chat [*February 23, 1942*]

We all know that books burn — yet we have the greater knowledge that books cannot be killed by fire. People die, but books never die. No man and no force can abolish memory. . . . In this war, we know, books are weapons.

Message to the American Booksellers Association [*April 23, 1942*]

It is not a tax bill but a tax relief bill providing relief not for the needy but for the greedy.

Message to the House vetoing the tax bill [*February 22, 1944*]

These Republican leaders have not been content with attacks on me, or my wife, or on my sons. No, not content with that, they now include my little dog, Fala. Well, of course, I don't resent attacks, . . . but Fala *does* resent them. . . . I think I have a right to resent, to object to libelous statements about my dog.[2]

Speech, Teamsters' Dinner, Washington [*September 23, 1944*]

All of our people all over the country — except the pure-blooded Indians — are immigrants or descendants of immigrants, including even those who came over here on the Mayflower.[3]

Campaign Speech, Boston [*November 4, 1944*]

The American people are quite competent to judge a political party that works both sides of a street.

Ibid.

[1] See Churchill, page 869b.

[2] This was Roosevelt's rejoinder to the charge that the President, at a cost of several million dollars to the taxpayers, had sent a destroyer back to the Aleutian Islands to fetch his Scottie, Fala, allegedly stranded there. When Fala heard these baseless stories of government extravagance on his account, "his Scotch soul was furious. He has not been the same dog since."

[3] See *Address to D. A. R.*, page 920a.

Perfectionism, no less than isolationism or imperialism or power politics, may obstruct the paths to international peace.
State of the Union Message [January 6, 1945]

We have learned that we cannot live alone, at peace; that our own well-being is dependent on the well-being of other nations, far away. We have learned that we must live as men, and not as ostriches, nor as dogs in the manger. We have learned to be citizens of the world, members of the human community.
Fourth Term Inaugural Address [January 20, 1945]

More than an end to war, we want an end to the beginnings of all wars.
Address written for Jefferson Day Dinners broadcast, April 13, 1945 [1]

The only limit to our realization of tomorrow will be our doubts of today. Let us move forward with strong and active faith.
Ibid.

FRANKLIN D. ROOSEVELT
AND
WINSTON CHURCHILL

FIRST, their countries seek no aggrandizement, territorial or other.

SECOND, they desire to see no territorial changes that do not accord with the freely expressed wishes of the peoples concerned. . . .
The Atlantic Charter, drawn up aboard U.S.S. Augusta, off the coast of Maine, issued August 14, 1941

SIXTH, after the final destruction of the Nazi tyranny, they hope to see established a peace which will afford to all nations the means of dwelling in safety within their own boundaries, and which will afford assurance that all

[1] President Roosevelt died April 12, at Warm Springs, Georgia.

the men in all the lands may live out their lives in freedom from fear and want. . . .
The Atlantic Charter

EIGHTH, they believe that all of the nations of the world, for realistic as well as spiritual reasons, must come to the abandonment of the use of force. Since no future peace can be maintained if land, sea or air armaments continue to be employed by nations which threaten, or may threaten, aggression outside of their frontiers, they believe, pending the establishment of a wider and permanent system of general security, that the disarmament of such nations is essential.
Ibid.

JAMES STEPHENS
[1882–1950]

I hear a sudden cry of pain!
There is a rabbit in a snare.
The Snare

Forgive us all our trespasses,
Little creatures, everywhere!
Little Things. Stanza 5

In cloud and clod to sing
Of everything and anything.
The Pit of Bliss

I heard a bird at dawn
Singing sweetly on a tree,
That the dew was on the lawn,
And the wind was on the lea;
But I didn't listen to him,
For he didn't sing to me.
The Rivals. Stanza 1

I was singing all the time,
Just as prettily as he.
Ibid. Stanza 3

Women are wiser than men because they know less and understand more.
The Crock of Gold [1930]. Chap. 2

Virtue is the performance of pleasant actions.
Ibid. Chap. 10

Women and birds are able to see without turning their heads, and that is

indeed a necessary provision, for they are both surrounded by enemies.
The Demi-Gods. Chap. 2

If a person desires to be a humorist it is necessary that the people around him shall be at least as wise as he is, otherwise his humor will not be comprehended.
Ibid. Chap. 27

Something depressing comes on the mind when it has been too extensively occupied with the female sex.
In the Land of Youth. Chap. 28

The Bad poet is super-abundant in all anthologies of verse.
Preface to A Trophy of Arms [1936], by RUTH PITTER

VIRGINIA WOOLF [1]
[1882–1941]

Those comfortably padded lunatic asylums which are known, euphemistically, as the stately homes of England.[2]
The Common Reader [1925].
Lady Dorothy Nevill

Trivial personalities decomposing in the eternity of print.
Ibid. The Modern Essay

There is no room for the impurities of literature in an essay.
Ibid.

That complete statement which is literature.
Ibid. How It Strikes a Contemporary

The word-coining genius, as if thought plunged into a sea of words and came up dripping.
Ibid. An Elizabethan Play

[1] Virginia Woolf is the best living example of that sort of mind which had its innings in letters in the eighteenth century — a mind partly critical, partly philosophical, highly imaginative, incapable of the vaster emotions but so subtle in its emotionalized intellectuality, so polished, that it makes most other contemporary writers appear to be parvenus of the intellect. — MARY M. COLUM in *The New York Herald-Tribune,* May 8, 1927

The talent of this generation which is most certain of survival. — REBECCA WEST: *Ending in Earnest* [1931]

[2] See Felicia D. Hemans, page 469b.

The beauty of the world has two edges, one of laughter, one of anguish, cutting the heart asunder.
A Room of One's Own [1929]

Women have served all these centuries as looking-glasses possessing the magic and delicious power of reflecting the figure of man at twice its natural size.
Ibid.

Surely it was time someone invented a new plot, or that the author came out from the bushes.
Between the Acts [1941]

SIR ANDREW BROWNE CUNNINGHAM
[1883-   ]

We are so outnumbered there's only one thing to do. We must attack.[1]
Before attacking the Italian fleet at Taranto, November, 1940

MAX EASTMAN
[1883–   ]

I don't know why it is we are in such a hurry to get up when we fall down. You might think we would lie there and rest a while.
The Enjoyment of Laughter [1936]. Part III, Chap. 4

Modernity is a poor thing to feel priggish about; it only makes you a more obvious mark for the prigs of a new modernity to sneer back at. No man can keep up with the times for more than seventy years, and after that his frantic efforts to do so look silly forever.
Ibid. Part V, Chap. 4

ARTHUR DAVISON FICKE
[1883–1945]

No man of elder years than fifty Should be empowered with lands and gold.

[1] Quoted in *British Commanders,* published by British Information Services [1945].

It turns them shrewd and over-thrifty,
It makes them cruel and blind and cold.
Youth and Age. Stanza 1

Old men in impotence can beget
New wars to kill the lusty young.
Young men can sing: old men forget
That any song was ever sung.
Ibid. Stanza 3

KAHLIL GIBRAN
[1883–1931]

Let there be spaces in your togetherness.[1]

The Prophet [1923]. On Marriage

You may give them your love but not your thoughts,
For they have their own thoughts.
You may house their bodies but not their souls,
For their souls dwell in the house of tomorrow, which you cannot visit, not even in your dreams.
You may strive to be like them, but seek not to make them like you.
For life goes not backward nor tarries with yesterday.
You are the bows from which your children as living arrows are sent forth.
Ibid. On Children

You give but little when you give of your possessions. It is when you give of yourself that you truly give.[2]
Ibid. On Giving

Work is love made visible. And if you cannot work with love but only with distaste, it is better that you should leave your work and sit at the gate of the temple and take alms of those who work with joy.
Ibid. On Work

The lust for comfort, that stealthy thing that enters the house a guest, and then becomes a host, and then a master.
Ibid. On Houses

When one of you falls down he falls for those behind him, a caution against the stumbling stone. Ay, and he falls for those ahead of him, who though

[1] See Rilke, page 884a.
[2] See James Russell Lowell, page 600a.

faster and surer of foot, yet removed not the stumbling stone.
The Prophet. On Crime and Punishment

You pray in your distress and in your need; would that you might pray also in the fullness of your joy and in your days of abundance.
Ibid. On Prayer

He who wears his morality but as his best garment were better naked.
Ibid. On Religion

I have learned silence from the talkative, toleration from the intolerant, and kindness from the unkind; yet strange, I am ungrateful to those teachers.
Sand and Foam [1926]

We shall never understand one another until we reduce the language to seven words.
Ibid.

JOHN CEREDIGION JONES
[1883–1947]

All's well, for over there among his peers
A happy warrior sleeps.[1]
The Returning Man. Stanza 4

HARRY KEMP
[1883–1960]

I pitied him in his blindness;
But can I boast, "I see"?
Perhaps there walks a spirit
Close by, who pities me.
Blind. Stanza 2

JOHN MAYNARD KEYNES
(LORD KEYNES)
[1883–1946]

He [Clemenceau] had one illusion — France; and one disillusion — mankind, including Frenchmen.
Economic Consequences of the Peace [1919]. Chap. 3

Watching the company, with six or

[1] These lines are inscribed over the archway of the Memorial Chamber in the Peace Tower, Parliament Buildings, Ottawa.
See Wordsworth, pages 409b–410a.

seven senses not available to ordinary men, judging character, motive, and subconscious impulse, perceiving what each was thinking and even what each was going to say next, and compounding with telepathic instinct the argument or appeal best suited to the vanity, weakness, or self interest of his immediate auditor.[1]

Economic Consequences of the Peace. Chap. 3

He [Woodrow Wilson] could write Notes from Sinai or Olympus; he could remain unapproachable in the White House or even in the Council of Ten and be safe. But if he once stepped down to the intimate quality of the Four, the game was evidently up.

Ibid.

To make the defeated Central Empires into good neighbors.

Ibid. Chap. 6

We have been moved already beyond endurance, and need rest.

Ibid. Chap. 7

Marxian Socialism must always remain a portent to the historians of Opinion — how a doctrine so illogical and so dull can have exercised so powerful and enduring an influence over the minds of men, and, through them, the events of history.

The End of Laissez-Faire [*1925*]. *Chap. 3*

Thrift may be the handmaid and nurse of Enterprise. But equally she may not. . . . For the engine which drives Enterprise is not Thrift, but Profit.

A Treatise on Money [*1930*]

The love of money as a possession — as distinguished from the love of money as a means to the enjoyments and realities of life — will be recognised for what it is, a somewhat disgusting morbidity, one of those semi-criminal, semi-pathological propensities which one hands over with a shudder to the specialists in mental disease.

Essays in Persuasion [*1931*]. *Part V*

[1] Lloyd George.

In the United States, it is almost inconceivable what rubbish a public man has to utter today if he is to keep respectable.

In the Atlantic Monthly [*May, 1932*]

Words ought to be a little wild for they are the assault of thoughts on the unthinking.

In the New Statesman and Nation [*July 15, 1933*]

His [Newton's] peculiar gift was the power of holding continuously in his mind a purely mental problem until he had seen through it. . . . Anyone who has ever attempted a pure scientific or philosophical thought knows how one can hold a problem momentarily in one's mind and apply all one's power of concentration to piercing through it, and how it will dissolve and escape and you find that what you are surveying is blank.

Essays in Biography [*1933*]

There is no harm in being sometimes wrong — especially if one is promptly found out.

Ibid.

Practical men, who believe themselves to be quite exempt from any intellectual influences, are usually the slaves of some defunct economist. . . . It is ideas, not vested interests, which are dangerous for good or evil.

The General Theory of Employment, Interest and Money [*1936*]

BENITO MUSSOLINI
[1883–1945]

War alone brings up to its highest tension all human energy and puts the stamp of nobility upon the peoples who have the courage to face it.

Written for The Italian Encyclopedia [1]

Fortunately the Italian people is not yet accustomed to eating several times per day.

Speech [*December, 1930*] [1]

[1] Quoted in GEORGE SELDES: *Sawdust Caesar* [1935].

We have buried the putrid corpse of liberty.
> *Speech* [1]

The Italian race is a race of sheep. Eighteen years are not enough to change them. It takes a hundred and eighty, and maybe a hundred and eighty centuries.
> *Quoted in The Ciano Diaries*
> *[January 29, 1940]*

It is humiliating to remain with our hands folded while others write history. It matters little who wins. To make a people great it is necessary to send them to battle even if you have to kick them in the pants. This is what I shall do.
> *Ibid. [April 11, 1940]*

GEOFFREY ANKETELL STUDDERT-KENNEDY ("WOODBINE WILLIE" [2])
[1883–1929]

When Jesus came to Birmingham, they
> simply passed Him by,
They never hurt a hair of Him, they
> only let Him die.
> *Indifference*

HOWARD ARNOLD WALTER
[1883–1918]

I would be true, for there are those who
> trust me;
I would be pure, for there are those
> who care;
I would be strong, for there is much to
> suffer;
I would be brave, for there is much to
> dare.
> *My Creed*

ANGELA MORGAN
[*Floruit* 1920]

Work!
Thank God for the swing of it,

---

[1] Quoted in MAURICE PARMELEE: *Bolshevism, Fascism and the Liberal-Democratic State* [1934].
[2] The affectionate nickname given him by the soldiers to whom, while chaplain, he distributed cigarettes in the trenches.

For the clamoring, hammering ring
> of it,
Passion of labor daily hurled
On the mighty anvils of the world.
> *Work: A Song of Triumph*

LAURA BENÉT
[1884–   ]

Lost in the spiral of his conscience, he
Detachedly takes rest.
> *The Snail*

ERNEST BEVIN
[1884–1951]

There has never been a war yet which, if the facts had been put calmly before the ordinary folk, could not have been prevented. The common man is the greatest protection against war.
> *Speech, House of Commons*
> *[November, 1945]*

WILL CUPPY
[1884–1949]

The Dodo never had a chance. He seems to have been invented for the sole purpose of becoming extinct and that was all he was good for.
> *How to Become Extinct [1941]*

EDOUARD DALADIER
[1884–   ]

If French and German blood is now to be spilled, as it was twenty-five years ago . . . then each of the two peoples will fight confident of its own victory. But surely Destruction and Barbarism will be the real victors.
> *Letter to Adolf Hitler,*
> *August 26, 1939*

The weakness of democracies is that once a general has been built up in public opinion it becomes impossible to remove him.
> *Quoted by* PERTINAX [1] *in Grave*
> *Diggers of France [1944].*
> *Page 87*

[1] André Géraud.

A phrase has spread from civilians to soldiers and back again: "This is a phony war." [1]

> *Quoted by* PERTINAX *in Grave Diggers of France. Page 139 [Speech to the Deputies, December 22, 1939]*

JAMES ELROY FLECKER
[1884–1915]

Oh shall I never be home again?
Meadows of England shining in the rain
Spread wide your daisied lawns.
> *Brumana*

I am Don Juan, curst from age to age
By priestly tract and sentimental stage:
Branded a villain or believed a fool,
Battered by hatred, seared by ridicule.
> *Don Juan Declaims*

My brother and good friend, the Sun.
> *A Western Voyage*

West of these out to seas colder than the Hebrides
I must go
Where the fleet of stars is anchored and the young
Star-captains glow.
> *The Dying Patriot*

We who with songs beguile your pilgrimage
And swear that Beauty lives though lilies die,
We Poets of the proud old lineage
Who sing to find your hearts, we know not why.
> *The Golden Journey to Samarkand [1913]. Prologue*

When even lovers find their peace at last,
And Earth is but a star, that once had shone.
> *Ibid.*

What would ye, ladies? It was ever thus;
Men are unwise and curiously planned.
> *Ibid. Epilogue*

I have seen old ships sail like swans asleep.
> *The Old Ships [1915]*

[1] The French was "une drôle de guerre."

A ship, an isle, a sickle moon —
With few but with how splendid stars. [1]
> *A Ship, An Isle, A Sickle Moon*

TEXAS GUINAN
[1884–1933]

Hello, sucker!
> *Greeting to night club patrons*

A big butter-and-egg man. [2]
> *Describing a lavish spender or theatrical "angel"*

FRANZ KAFKA
[1884–1924]

The true way goes over a rope which is not stretched at any great height but just above the ground. It seems more designed to make people stumble than to be walked upon.
> *The Great Wall of China. Reflections*

You do not need to leave your room. Remain sitting at your table and listen. Do not even listen, simply wait. Do not even wait, be quite still and solitary. The world will freely offer itself to you to be unmasked, it has no choice, it will roll in ecstasy at your feet.
> *Ibid.*

Only our concept of Time makes it possible for us to speak of the Day of Judgment by that name; in reality it is a summary court in perpetual session.
> *Letters* [3]

All human error is impatience, a premature renunciation of method, a delusive pinning down of a delusion.
> *Ibid.*

There are two cardinal sins from which all the others spring; impatience and laziness.
> *Ibid.*

FANNY HEASLIP LEA
[1884–1955]

It's odd to think we might have been
Sun, moon and stars unto each other —

[1] See Whitman, page 608a.
[2] Title of play by George S. Kaufman, 1925.
[3] Quoted in *Franz Kafka* by MAX BROD.

Only, I turned down one little street
As you went up another.
Fate. Stanza 5

SEAN O'CASEY
[1884–1964]

The whole world is in a state of chassis.
Juno and the Paycock

CHARLES LEO O'DONNELL
[1884–1934]

I have never been able to school my
eyes
Against young April's blue surprise.
Wonder

KEITH PRESTON
[1884–1927]

Imperial Caesar dead and turned to
clay
Estopped a hole to keep the wind
away;
The great god Ra whose shrine once
covered acres
Is filler now for cross-word puzzle
makers.
The Destiny That Shapes Our Ends

Love, lay thy phobias to rest,
Inhibit thy taboo!
We twain shall share, forever blest,
A complex built for two.
Love Song, Freudian

Among our literary scenes,
Saddest this sight to me,
The graves of little magazines
That died to make verse free.
The Liberators

He must not laugh at his own wheeze:
A snuff box has no right to sneeze.
The Humorist

I am the captain of my soul; [1]
I rule it with stern joy;
And yet I think I had more fun
When I was a cabin boy.
An Awful Responsibility

[1] See W. E. Henley, page 741b.

ODELL SHEPARD
[1884–   ]

October in New England,
And I not there to see
The glamour of the goldenrod,
The flame of the maple tree!
Home Thoughts. Stanza 1

SARA TEASDALE
[1884–1933]

When I am dead and over me bright
April
Shakes out her rain-drenched hair,
Though you should lean above me
broken-hearted,
I shall not care.
I Shall Not Care. Stanza 1

When I can look Life in the eyes,
Grown calm and very coldly wise,
Life will have given me the Truth,
And taken in exchange — my youth.
Wisdom

How many million Aprils came
Before I ever knew
How white a cherry bough could be,
A bed of squills, how blue!
Blue Squills. Stanza 1

Strephon's kiss was lost in jest,
Robin's lost in play,
But the kiss in Colin's eyes
Haunts me night and day.
The Look. Stanza 2

Let it be forgotten, as a flower is for-
gotten,
Forgotten as a fire that once was sing-
ing gold,
Let it be forgotten for ever and ever,
Time is a kind friend, he will make
us old.
Let It Be Forgotten. Stanza 1

I make the most of all that comes,
And the least of all that goes.
The Philosopher. Stanza 4

For better than the minting
Of a gold crowned king
Is the safe memory
Of a lovely thing.
The Coin

Spend all you have for loveliness,
Buy it, and never count the cost;

For one white singing hour of peace
Count many a year of strife well lost.
                                    Barter
Forget me for a month, a year,
But, oh, beloved, think of me
When unexpected beauty burns
Like sudden sunlight on the sea.
        Vignettes Overseas: Off Algiers

HARRY S. TRUMAN
[1884–   ]

When they told me yesterday what
had happened, I felt like the moon, the
stars and all the planets had fallen on
me.
        *Statement to reporters, April 13,
        1945, the day after his accession
        to the Presidency*
The responsibility of the great states
is to serve and not to dominate the
world.
        *First Message to Congress,
        April 16, 1945*
When Kansas and Colorado have a
quarrel over the water in the Arkansas
River they don't call out the National
Guard in each State and go to war over
it. They bring a suit in the Supreme
Court of the United States and abide
by the decision. There isn't a reason in
the world why we cannot do that inter-
nationally.
        Speech in Kansas City, April, 1945
Sixteen hours ago an American airplane dropped one bomb on Hiroshima.
. . . It is a harnessing of the basic
power of the universe. The force from
which the sun draws its power has been
loosed against those who brought war
to the Far East.
        *First announcement of the
        atomic bomb, August 6, 1945*
The release of atomic energy constitutes a new force too revolutionary to
consider in the framework of old ideas.[1]
        *Message to Congress on atomic
        energy, October 3, 1945*

[1] At Magny's dinner. They said that Berthe-
lot had predicted that in a hundred years
of physical and chemical science man would
learn to know the atom, and that with this
knowledge he would be able, at his will, to

Means of destruction hitherto unknown, against which there can be no
adequate military defense, and in the
employment of which no single nation
can in fact have a monopoly.
        *Declaration on Atomic Energy
        by President Truman and Prime
        Ministers Clement Attlee and
        W. L. Mackenzie King at the
        White House, Washington, No-
        vember 15, 1945*
Effective, reciprocal, and enforceable
safeguards acceptable to all nations.
                                    Ibid.

We must embark on a bold new program for making the benefits of our
scientific advances and industrial progress available for the improvement and
growth of under-developed areas. More
than half the people of the world are living in conditions approaching misery.
Their food is inadequate. They are the
victims of disease. Their economic life is
primitive and stagnant. Their poverty
is a handicap and a threat both to them
and to more prosperous areas.
        *Inaugural Address (Point Four
        Program) [January 20, 1949]*

SOPHIE TUCKER
[1884–1966]

From birth to age eighteen, a girl
needs good parents. From eighteen
to thirty-five, she needs good looks.
From thirty-five to fifty-five, she needs

dim, extinguish or relight the sun like a
Carcel lamp. Claude Bernard, for his part, is
said to have announced that with a hundred
years more of physiological knowledge we
would be able to make the organic law ourselves — to manufacture human life, in competition with the Creator.
    For our part we did not raise any objection
to all this talk, but we do believe that at that
particular stage of scientific development, the
good Lord, with a flowing white beard, will
arrive on Earth with his chain of keys and
will say to humanity, just as they do at
the Art Gallery at five o'clock, "Gentlemen,
it's closing time." (*"Messieurs, on ferme."*)
— EDMOND DE GONCOURT AND JULES DE GON-
COURT: *Journals*, April 7, 1869

a good personality. From fifty-five on, she needs good cash.

Said at sixty-nine

HUGH WALPOLE
[1884-1941]

We are so largely the playthings of Fate in our fears. To one, fear of the dark, to another of physical pain, to a third of public ridicule, to a fourth of poverty, to a fifth of loneliness — for all of us our own particular creature lurks in ambush. Nor is it our choice of place or creature.

The Old Ladies [*1924*]

ANNA WICKHAM
(MRS. PATRICK HEPBURN)
[1884–   ]

The true male never yet walked
Who liked to listen when his mate
    talked.

The Affinity

Because of the body's hunger are we
    born,
And by contriving hunger are we fed;
Because of hunger is our work well
    done,
And so our songs well sung, and things
    well said.

Sehnsucht

ARTHUR WALLACE
CALHOUN
[1885–   ]

Gentlemen of the old régime in the South would say, "A woman's name should appear in print but twice — when she marries and when she dies."

Social History of the American Family [*1918*], *Vol. II, Page 326, citing* MYRTA LOCKETT AVARY: *Dixie After the War* [*1906*], *Page 23*

ISAK DINESEN
[1885-1962]

What is man, when you come to think upon him, but a minutely set, ingenious machine for turning, with in-

finite artfulness, the red wine of Shiraz into urine?

Seven Gothic Tales

WILL DURANT
[1885–   ]

A statesman cannot afford to be a moralist.

What Is Civilization?

The finger that turns the dial rules the air.

Ibid.

Civilization exists by geological consent, subject to change without notice.

Ibid.

The health of nations is more important than the wealth of nations.

Ibid.

Conscience is the deposit of a Mississippi of prohibitions.

Ibid.

DuBOSE HEYWARD
[1885-1940]

It is cruel for a woman with her man
    gone,
An' the younguns allus hungry, an'
    winter comin' on.

Black Christmas

Here lies a spendthrift who believed
    That only those who spend may
    keep;
Who scattered seeds, yet never grieved
Because a stranger came to reap.

Epitaph for a Poet

KAREN HORNEY, M.D.
[1885–   ]

Fortunately [psycho-]analysis is not the only way to resolve inner conflicts. Life itself still remains a very effective therapist.

Our Inner Conflicts [*1945*]

RING LARDNER
[1885-1933]

A good many young writers make the mistake of enclosing a stamped, self-addressed envelope, big enough for the manuscript to come back in. This is too much of a temptation to the editor.

How to Write Short Stories [*1924*]

Mother set facing the front of the train, as it makes her giddy to ride backwards. I set facing her, which does not affect me.

The Golden Honeymoon [*1924*]

D. H. LAWRENCE
[1885–1930]

I never saw a wild thing
Sorry for itself.

Self-Pity

When I wish I was rich, then I know I
am ill.

Riches

When I read Shakespeare I am struck
with wonder
That such trivial people should muse
and thunder
In such lovely language.

*When I Read Shakespeare.
Stanza 1*

And Hamlet, how boring, how boring to
live with,
So mean and self-conscious, blowing
and snoring
His wonderful speeches, full of other
folks' whoring!

Ibid. Stanza 3

My mother was a superior soul
A superior soul was she,
Cut out to play a superior role
In the god-damn bourgeoisie.

Red-Herring. Stanza 2

One realm we have never conquered
— the pure present. One great mystery
of time is terra incognita to us — the
instant. The most superb mystery we
have hardly recognized — the immediate, instant self. The quick of all time
is the instant. The quick of all
the universe, of all creation, is the incarnate, carnal self.

New Poems [*1918*]. *Preface*

Men are free when they are in a living homeland, not when they are straying and breaking away. . . . The most
unfree souls go west, and shout of freedom. Men are freest when they are
most unconscious of freedom. The
shout is a rattling of chains.

*Studies in Classic American
Literature* [*1923*]. *Chap. 1*

Necessary, for ever necessary, to
burn out false shames and smelt the
heaviest ore of the body into purity.

Lady Chatterley's Lover [*1928*]

SINCLAIR LEWIS
[1885–1951]

Not only Gopher Prairie, but ten
thousand towns from Albany to San
Diego . . . not a dozen buildings
which suggested that, in the fifty years
of Gopher Prairie's existence, the citizens had realized that it was either
desirable or possible to make this, their
common home, amusing or attractive.

Main Street [*1920*]. *Chap. 4*

His name was George F. Babbitt,
and . . . he was nimble in the calling
of selling houses for more than people
could afford to pay.

Babbitt [*1922*]. *Chap. 1*

A sensational event was changing
from the brown suit to the gray the
contents of his pockets. He was earnest
about these objects. They were of eternal importance, like baseball or the Republican Party.

Ibid.

Pastoral visiting:
No partiality.
Don't neglect hired girls, be cordial.
Guard conversation, pleasing man-
ner and laugh and maybe one funny
story but no scandal or crit. of others.
Stay only 15–30 minutes.
Ask if like to pray with, not insist.
Rem gt opportunities during sick-
ness, sorrow, marriage.
Ask jokingly why husband not of-
tener to church.

Elmer Gantry [*1927*]. *Chap. 8,
notes on Practical Theology
lectures*

Every compulsion is put upon writers
to become safe, polite, obedient, and
sterile. In protest, I declined election

to the National Institute of Arts and Letters some years ago, and now I must decline the Pulitzer Prize.[1]

> *Letter declining the Pulitzer Prize for his novel, Arrowsmith* [*1926*]

To a true-blue professor of literature in an American university, literature is not something that a plain human being, living today, painfully sits down to produce. No; it is something dead.

> *The American Fear of Literature, address given at Stockholm, on receiving the Nobel Prize for Literature* [*December 12, 1930*]

Our American professors like their literature clear and cold and pure and very dead.

> *Ibid.*

It Can't Happen Here.

> *Title of Book* [*1935*]

A "lady" is a woman so incompetent as to have to take refuge in a secluded class, like kings and idiots, who have to be treated with special kindness because they can't take it.

> *Debate with Lewis Browne: Has the Modern Woman Made Good? Town Hall, New York* [*November 19, 1941*]

ANDRÉ MAUROIS
[1885–   ]

The minds of different generations are as impenetrable one by the other as are the monads of Leibniz.

> *Ariel*[2] [*1924*]. *Chap. 12*

If in the eyes of an Irishman there is any one being more ridiculous than an Englishman, it is an Englishman who loves Ireland.

> *Ibid. Chap. 13*

Learning is nothing without cultivated manners, but when the two are combined in a woman you have one of the most exquisite products of civilization.

> *Ibid. Chap. 16*

[1] Lewis became a member of the National Institute in 1935.
[2] Translated by ELLA D'ARCY.

Modesty and unselfishness — these are virtues which men praise — and pass by.

> *Ariel. Chap. 24*

That mixture of Christian sorrow and mundane relish which the virtuous employ in talking of the vicious.

> *Ibid. Chap. 26*

There are certain persons for whom pure Truth is a poison.

> *Ibid. Chap. 29*

Housekeeping in common is for women the acid test.

> *Ibid. Chap. 35*

CHESTER WILLIAM NIMITZ
[1885–   ]

A ship is always referred to as "she" because it costs so much to keep one in paint and powder.

> *Talk before the Society of Sponsors of the United States Navy* [*February 13, 1940*]

WILLIAM ALEXANDER PERCY
[1885–1942]

I heard a bird at break of day
Sing from the autumn trees
A song so mystical and calm,
So full of certainties.

> *Overtones*

EZRA POUND
[1885–   ]

Sing we for love and idleness,
Naught else is worth the having.

> *An Immortality*

And I would rather have my sweet,
Though rose-leaves die of grieving,
Than do high deeds in Hungary
To pass all men's believing.

> *Ibid.*

The apparition of these faces in the crowd;
Petals on a wet, black bough.

> *In a Station of the Metro* [*1916*]

That age is gone;
Pierre de Maensac is gone.

I have walked over these roads;
I have thought of them living.
> *Provincia Deserta* [*1916*]

Some other mouth
May be as fair as hers,
Might, in new ages, gain her wor-
shippers,
When our two dusts with Waller's shall
be laid,
Siftings on siftings in oblivion,
Till change hath broken down
All things save Beauty alone.
> *Hugh Selwyn Mauberley*
> [*1920*]. *Envoi*

I was
And I no more exist;
Here drifted
An hedonist.
> *Ibid. The Age Demanded*

They will come no more,
The old men with beautiful manners.
> *I Vecchii*

Poetry ought to be as well written as prose.
> *Quoted by T. S. Eliot: The Use*
> *of Poetry* [*1933*], *Chap. 4*

Real education must ultimately be limited to men who insist on know-ing, the rest is mere sheep-herding.
> *A, B, C of Reading* [*1934*].
> *Page 70*

It is only after long experience that most men are able to define a thing in terms of its own genus, painting as painting, writing as writing. You can spot the bad critic when he starts by discussing the poet and not the poem.
> *Ibid. Page 71*

There is no reason why the same man should like the same book at 18 and at 48.
> *Ibid. Page 72*

Any one who is too lazy to master the comparatively small glossary neces-sary to understand Chaucer deserves to be shut out from the reading of good books forever.
> *Ibid. Page 87*

Men do not understand books until they have had a certain amount of life, or at any rate no man understands a deep book, until he has seen and lived at least part of its contents.
> *A, B, C of Reading. Page 88*

KENNETH ROBERTS
[1885–1957]

On every side of us are men who hunt perpetually for their personal Northwest Passage, too often sacri-ficing health, strength, and life it-self to the search; and who shall say they are not happier in their vain but hopeful quest than wiser, duller folks who sit at home, venturing nothing and, with sour laughs, deriding the seekers for that fabled thoroughfare?
> *Northwest Passage* [*1937*].
> *Foreword*

GEOFFREY SCOTT
[1885–1929]

In my garden goes a fiend
Dark and wild, whose name is Wind.
> *Wind*

LOUIS UNTERMEYER
[1885–   ]

And though these shattering walls are thin,
May they be strong to keep hate out
And hold love in.
> *Prayer for a New House.*
> *Stanza 4*

God, if You wish for our love,
Fling us a handful of stars!
> *Caliban in the Coal Mines.*
> *Stanza 4*

God, though this life is but a wraith,
Although we know not what we use,
Although we grope with little faith,
Give me the heart to fight — and lose.
> *Prayer. Stanza 1*

From compromise and things half done,
Keep me with stern and stubborn pride;
And when at last the fight is won,
God, keep me still unsatisfied.
> *Ibid. Stanza 5*

CARL VAN DOREN
[1885–1950]

The first writers are first and the rest, in the long run, nowhere but in anthologies.
> *What Is American Literature?*

I give him back, in his grand dimensions, to his nation and the world.
> *Benjamin Franklin* [*1938*]

HAROLD TUCKER WEBSTER
[1885–1952]

Caspar Milquetoast: The Timid Soul.
> *Character in Series of Cartoons*

The Thrill that Comes Once in a Lifetime.
> *Title of Series of Cartoons*

HUMBERT WOLFE
[1885–1940]

Who thought of the lilac?
"I," dew said,
"I made up the lilac
out of my head."
> *The Lilac. Stanza 1*

Like a small grey
coffee-pot
sits the squirrel.
> *The Grey Squirrel. Stanza 1*

Listen! the wind is rising,
  and the air is wild with leaves,
We have had our summer evenings,
  now for October eves!
> *Autumn (Resignation). Stanza 2*

ELINOR HOYT WYLIE
[1885–1928]

We shall walk in velvet shoes:
  Wherever we go
Silence will fall like dews
  On white silence below.
> *Velvet Shoes* [*1921*]. *Stanza 4*

Avoid the reeking herd,
  Shun the polluted flock,
Live like that stoic bird
  The eagle of the rock.
> *The Eagle and the Mole* [*1921*].
> *Stanza 1*

If you would keep your soul
  From spotted sight or sound,
Live like the velvet mole;
  Go burrow underground.
> *The Eagle and the Mole. Stanza 5*

Say not of Beauty she is good,
Or aught but beautiful.
> *Beauty* [*1921*]

Enshrine her and she dies, who had
The hard heart of a child.
> *Ibid.*

Down to the Puritan marrow of my
    bones
There's something in this richness that
    I hate.
I love the look, austere, immaculate,
Of landscapes drawn in pearly mono-
    tones.
> *Wild Peaches* [*1921*]. *Stanza 4*

I was, being human, born alone;
I am, being woman, hard beset;
I live by squeezing from a stone
The little nourishment I get.
> *Let No Charitable Hope* [*1923*].
> *Stanza 2*

My soul, be not disturbed
By planetary war;
Remain securely orbed
In this contracted star.
> *Address to My Soul* [*1928*].
> *Stanza 1*

A subtle spirit has my path attended,
In likeness not a lion but a pard;
And when the arrows flew like hail,
    and hard,
He licked my wounds, and all my
    wounds were mended.
> *One Person* [*1928*]. *Sonnet IX*

My lord, adjudge my strength, and set
    me where
I bear a little more than I can bear.
> *Ibid. Sonnet XVI*

My late discovered earth and early sky.
> *Ibid. Sonnet XVII*

If any have a stone to throw
It is not I, ever or now.
> *The Pebble*

Pity the prickly star that frightens
The Christ Child with its shattered
    spear;

Pity the midnight when it lightens;
  Pity me, my dear.
                    Pity Me. Stanza 3
The worst and best are both inclined
To snap like vixens at the truth;
But, O, beware the middle mind
That purrs and never shows a tooth!
              Nonsense Rhyme. Stanza 2
Honied words like bees,
Gilded and sticky, with a little sting.
                       Pretty Words
Hail, element of earth, receive thy
  own,
And cherish, at thy charitable breast,
This man, this mongrel beast:
He plows the sand, and, at his hardest
  need,
He sows himself for seed.
       Hymn to Earth [*1929*]. *Stanza 6*
Receive him as thy lover for an hour
Who will not weary, by a longer stay,
The kind embrace of clay.
                     Ibid. Stanza 7

ZOË AKINS
[1886–1958]

The Greeks Had a Word For It.
            Title of play [*1930*]
So much do I love wandering,
  So much I love the sea and sky,
That it will be a piteous thing
  In one small grave to lie.
          The Wanderer. Stanza 2

WILLIAM ROSE BENÉT
[1886–1950]

I flung my soul to the air like a falcon
  flying. . . .
  I shall start a heron soon
  In the marsh beneath the moon —
A strange white heron rising with silver
  on its wings.
       The Falconer of God [*1914*].
                        Stanza 1
  I beat forever
The fens and the sedges.
The pledge is still the same — for all
  disastrous pledges,
  All hopes resigned!

My soul still flies above me for the
  quarry it shall find.
        The Falconer of God. Stanza 4
Rain, with a silver flail;
  Sun, with a golden ball;
Ocean, wherein the whale
  Swims minnow-small.
                 Whale. Stanza 1
Monarch is night
Of all eldest things,
Pain and affright,
Rapturous wings.
                 Night. Stanza 3
O Love, a thousand, thousand voices,
From night to dawn, from dawn to
  night,
Have cried the passion of their choices
To orb your name and keep it bright.
       The Name of Love. Stanza 1
In vast infant sagacity brooding.
                       Mad Blake
Jesse James was a two-gun man
  (*Roll on, Missouri!*)
        Jesse James: American Myth
In seven states he cut up dadoes.
He's gone with the buffler an' the des-
  peradoes.
                          Ibid.
What did your body say to mine
deep in velvet night's delight?
*On heaven's wall a golden vine clambers
  bright.*
        The Dust Which Is God [*1941*].
                That Rin Sae Deep

VAN WYCK BROOKS
[1886–1963]

His wife not only edited his works
but edited him.
       The Ordeal of Mark Twain [*1920*].
                        Chap. 5
Even the Concord ice had bubbles
in it. As wood and grass were its only
staples, Emerson advised his fellow
townsmen to manufacture schoolteachers and make them the best in the
world.
       The Flowering of New England
                [*1936*]. *Chap. 13*

FRANCES CORNFORD
[1886–   ]

O why do you walk through the fields
    in gloves,
    Missing so much and so much?
O fat white woman whom nobody loves,
Why do you walk through the fields in
    gloves
When the grass is as soft as the breast
    of doves
And shivering-sweet to the touch?
    To a Fat Lady Seen from the Train

ROY HELTON
[1886–   ]

Oaks are the true conservatives;
They hold old leaves till summer gives
A green exchange
    Come Back to Earth. XLIX
What is a common man?
    Where is a common tree?
I'll pick one common buttercup
    But challenge two or three,
For every one bears instant proof
    Of its identity.
    Ibid. LIII, Stanza 1

AL JOLSON
[1886–1950]

You ain't heard nothin' yet, folks.
    *Ad lib remark introduced in the
    first talking motion picture,
    "The Jazz Singer," July, 1927*

JOYCE KILMER
[1886–1918]

Because the road was steep and long
    And through a dark and lonely land,
God set upon my lips a song
    And put a lantern in my hand.
    Love's Lantern
They say that life is a highway and its
    milestones are the years.
    Roofs
I think that I shall never see
A poem lovely as a tree.
A tree whose hungry mouth is prest

Against the earth's sweet flowing
    breast.
    Trees [1]
Poems are made by fools like me,
But only God can make a tree.
    Ibid.
The pleasantest sort of poet
Is the poet who's old and wise.
    Old Poets
Her lips' remark was: "Oh, you kid!"
Her soul spoke thus (I know it did):
"O king of realms of endless joy,
My own, my golden grocer's boy."
    Servant Girl and Grocer's Boy
A house that has echoed a baby's laugh
    and held up his stumbling feet,
Is the saddest sight, when it's left alone,
    that ever your eyes could meet.
    The House with Nobody in It
In a wood they call the Rouge Bouquet
There is a new-made grave today,
Built by never a spade nor pick
Yet covered with earth ten metres
    thick.
    Rouge Bouquet

ARTHUR KROCK
[1886–   ]

The President [Franklin D. Roosevelt] told the chairman to "clear everything with Sidney" (Hillman),[2] which gave to the C. I. O. organization that dominated the proceedings the veto power it later exercised.
    New York Times, July 25, 1944
The words ["clear everything with Sidney"] applied only to the Vice Presidential nomination of the Democrats at Chicago.
    Ibid. October 24, 1944

DAVID MORTON
[1886–1957]

Who walks with Beauty has no need of
    fear;

[1] First published in *Poetry: A Magazine of Verse,* Chicago, August, 1913.
See Heywood Broun, page B-952, and Ogden Nash, page B-121.
[2] Sidney Hillman [1887–1946], Chairman of the Political Action Committee of the C. I. O., and president of the Amalgamated Clothing Workers.

The sun and moon and stars keep pace
with him;
Invisible hands restore the ruined year,
And time, itself, grows beautifully dim.
Who Walks with Beauty
My faith is all a doubtful thing,
  Wove on a doubtful loom, —
Until there comes, each showery spring,
  A cherry-tree in bloom.
Symbol

SHAEMAS O'SHEEL
[1886–1954]

They went forth to battle, but they
  always fell; [1]
Their eyes were fixed above the sullen
  shields;
Nobly they fought and bravely, but not
  well,
And sank heart-wounded by a subtle
  spell.
They Went Forth to Battle.
Stanza 1
He whom a dream hath possessed
  knoweth no more of doubting.
He Whom a Dream Hath
Possessed. Stanza 1

SIEGFRIED SASSOON
[1886–   ]

Soldiers are citizens of death's grey
  land.
Dreamers
Soldiers are dreamers; when the guns
  begin
They think of firelit homes, clean beds,
  and wives.
Ibid.
And when the war is done and youth
  stone dead
I'd toddle safely home and die — in
  bed.
Base Details
Who will remember, passing through
  this Gate,
The unheroic Dead who fed the guns?

[1] They came forth to battle, but they
always fell. — JAMES MACPHERSON [1736–
1796]: *Poems of Ossian, Cath-Loda, Duan
Second*

Who shall absolve the foulness of their
  fate, —
Those doomed, conscripted, unvictori-
  ous ones?
On Passing the New Menin Gate

VINCENT STARRETT
[1886–   ]

The day before yesterday always has
been a glamor day. The present is sordid and prosaic. Time colors history as
it does a meerschaum pipe.
Buried Caesars. Robert Neilson
Stephens and The Costume
Novel

CARROLL A. WILSON
[1886–1947]

"Familiar quotations" . . . are more
than familiar; they are something part
of us. . . . These echoes from the past
have two marked characteristics — a
simple idea, and an accurate rhythmic
beat.
Preface to First Appearance in
Print of Some 400 Familiar
Quotations [1935]

ED WYNN
[1886–   ]

Every radish I ever pulled up seemed
to have a mortgage attached to it.
Explaining Why He Sold His Farm

LEONARD BACON
[1887–1954]

Technique! The very word is like the
  shriek
Of outraged Art. It is the idiot name
Given to effort by those who are too
  weak,
Too weary, or too dull to play the
  game.
The mighty have no theory of tech-
  nique.
Ph.D's. Sophia Trenton
Those who dwell upon ivory towers [1]
Have heads of the same material.
Tower of Ivory

[1] See Vachel Lindsay, page 903b.

BRUCE BAIRNSFATHER
[1887–1959]

Well, if you knows of a better 'ole,
go to it.
Fragments from France [1915].
Caption of cartoon

RUPERT BROOKE
[1887–1915]

Somewhere, behind Space and Time,
Is wetter water, slimier slime!
Heaven

And in that Heaven of all their wish,
There shall be no more land, say fish.
Ibid.

The hawthorn hedge puts forth its
buds,
And my heart puts forth its pain.
All Suddenly the Spring Comes Soft

Unkempt about those hedges blows
An English unofficial rose.
The Old Vicarage, Grantchester

Curates, long dust, will come and go
On lissom, clerical, printless toe.
Ibid.

England's the one land, I know,
Where men with Splendid Hearts may
go;
And Cambridgeshire, of all England,
The shire for Men who Understand.
Ibid.

For Cambridge people rarely smile,
Being urban, squat, and packed with
guile.
Ibid.

Stands the Church clock at ten to three?
And is there honey still for tea?
Ibid.

Breathless, we flung us on the windy
hill,
Laughed in the sun, and kissed the
lovely grass.
The Hill

And then you suddenly cried, and
turned away.
Ibid.

For what they'd never told me of,
And what I never knew,

It was that all the time, my love,
Love would be merely you.
Song

But there's wisdom in women, of more
than they have known,
And thoughts go blowing through them,
are wiser than their own.
There's Wisdom in Women

These I have loved:
White plates and cups, clean-gleam-
ing . . .
The cool kindliness of sheets, that soon
Smooth away trouble; and the rough
male kiss
Of blankets; grainy wood; live hair
that is
Shining and free; blue-massing clouds;
the keen
Unpassioned beauty of a great ma-
chine;
The benison of hot water; furs to touch,
The good smell of old clothes.
The Great Lover

If I should die, think only this of me:
That there's some corner of a foreign
field
That is for ever England.
The Soldier

This heart, all evil shed away,
A pulse in the eternal mind, no less
Gives somewhere back the thoughts by
England given.
Ibid.

Now, God be thanked, Who has
matched us with His hour,
And caught our youth, and wakened us
from sleeping.
Peace

The worst friend and enemy is but
Death.
Ibid.

Blow out, you bugles, over the rich
dead!
There's none of these so lonely and
poor of old,
But, dying, has made us rarer gifts
than gold.
The Dead. 1

Honour has come back, as a king, to
earth,
And paid his subjects with a royal
wage;

And Nobleness walks in our ways
  again;
And we have come into our heritage.
The Dead. I

ISAAC GOLDBERG
[1887–1938]

Diplomacy is to do and say
The nastiest thing in the nicest way.
The Reflex

JAMES NORMAN HALL
[1887–1951]

The thing that numbs the heart is this:
  That men cannot devise
Some scheme of life to banish fear
  That lurks in most men's eyes.
Fear

SIDNEY HILLMAN [1]
[1887–1946]

Politics is the science of how who
gets what, when and why.
Political Primer for All Americans
[*1944*]

EARNEST A. HOOTON
[1887–1954]

Up from the Ape.
Title of Book [*1931*]
Why Men Behave Like Apes, and
Vice Versa.
Title of Book [*1940*]

ROBINSON JEFFERS
[1887–1962]

The gulls, the cloud-calligraphers of
  windy spirals before a storm.
The Cycle
While this America settles in the mould
  of its vulgarity, heavily thicken-
  ing to empire,
And protest, only a bubble in the
  molten mass, pops and sighs out,
  and the mass hardens.
Shine, Perishing Republic
[*1924*]. *Stanza 1*

[1] See Arthur Krock, page 936b.

All these tidal gatherings, growth and
  decay,
Shining and darkening, are forever
Renewed; and the whole cycle impeni-
  tently
Revolves, and all the past is fu-
  ture.
Practical People
All the arts lose virtue
Against the essential reality
Of creatures going about their business
  among the equally
Earnest elements of nature.
Boats in a Fog [*1924*]
Lend me the stone strength of the past
  and I will lend you
The wings of the future, for I have
  them.
To the Rock That Will Be a
Cornerstone
Divinely superfluous beauty
Rules the games, presides over des-
  tinies, makes trees grow
And hills tower, waves fall.
The incredible beauty of joy.
Divinely Superfluous Beauty
The beauty of things was born before
  eyes and sufficient to itself; the
  heart-breaking beauty
Will remain when there is no heart to
  break for it.
Credo
The deep dark-shining
Pacific leans on the land,
Feeling his cold strength
To the outmost margins.
Night [*1925*]
Humanity is the mold to break away
  from, the crust to break through,
  the coal to break into fire,
The atom to be split.
Roan Stallion [*1925*]

SIR BERNARD MONTGOMERY (VISCOUNT MONTGOMERY OF ALAMEIN)
[1887–   ]

To us is given the honor of striking
a blow for freedom which will live in
history, and in the better days that lie

ahead men will speak with pride of our doings.

> *Message to his troops, June 5, 1944, on the eve of the Allied invasion of Europe*

I am not a bit anxious about my battles. If I am anxious I don't fight them. I wait until I am ready.

> *Quoted in "British Commanders," published [1945] by British Information Services*

MARIANNE MOORE
[1887–   ]

The monkeys
winked too much and were afraid of
    snakes. The zebras, supreme in
their abnormality; the elephants, with
    their fog-colored skin
and strictly practical appendages
    were there.

> *The Monkeys [1921]*

Denunciations do not affect
    the culprit; nor blows, but it
is torture to him to not be spoken to.

> *Spenser's Ireland [1941]. Stanza 1*

The Irish say your trouble is their
trouble and your
    joy their joy? I wish
I could believe it;
I am troubled, I'm dissat-
    isfied, I'm Irish.

> *Ibid. Stanza 6*

They're fighting that I
may yet recover from the disease, *my
self;* some have it lightly, some will
    die.[1]

> *In Distrust of Merits [1944].
> Stanza 3*

There never was a war that was
    not inward; I must
fight till I have conquered in myself
    what
causes war, but I would not believe it.
    I inwardly did nothing.
    O Iscariotlike crime!
    Beauty is everlasting
And dust is for a time.

> *Ibid. Stanza 8*

[1] See Pascal, page 273a.

SAMUEL ELIOT MORISON
[1887–   ]

A tough but nervous, tenacious but restless race [the Yankees]; materially ambitious, yet prone to introspection, and subject to waves of religious emotion. . . . A race whose typical member is eternally torn between a passion for righteousness and a desire to get on in the world.

> *Maritime History of Massachusetts [1921]. Chap. 2*

Never, in these United States, has the brain of man conceived, or the hand of man fashioned, so perfect a thing as the clipper ship. . . . The *Flying Cloud* was our Rheims, the *Sovereign of the Seas* our Parthenon, the *Lightning* our Amiens; but they were monuments carved from snow. For a brief moment of time they flashed their splendor around the world, then disappeared with the sudden completeness of the wild pigeon.

> *Ibid. Chap. 23*

He [Columbus] enjoyed long stretches of pure delight such as only a seaman may know, and moments of high, proud exultation that only a discoverer can experience.

> *Admiral of the Ocean Sea [1942].
> Chap. 49*

FAIRFIELD OSBORN
[1887–   ]

We do not live to extenuate the miseries of the past nor to accept as incurable those of the present.

> *The Limits of the Earth.
> Chap. 10*

H. I. PHILLIPS
[1887–1965]

Horse-sense in an atmosphere of
Pomp and glory,
Self-effacement in a generation
Of self-salesmanship,
A Vermont Yankee in
King Ballyhoo's Court!

> *Calvin Coolidge*

EDITH SITWELL
[1887–1964]

Every hundred years or so it becomes necessary for a change to take place in the body of poetry . . . a fresh movement appears and produces a few great men, and once more the force and vigour die from the results of age; the movement is carried on by weak and worthless imitators, and a change becomes necessary again.
Poetry and Criticism [1926]

Still falls the Rain —
Dark as the world of man, black as our
loss —
Blind as the nineteen hundred and
forty nails
Upon the Cross.
Still Falls the Rain [1940]

ALEXANDER WOOLLCOTT
[1887–1943]

The two oldest professions in the world — ruined by amateurs.[1]
The Knock at the Stage-Door
[*The Actor and the Street-walker*]

"Ladies, just a little more virginity, if you don't mind."
Capsule Criticism [*Beerbohm Tree to the Extras*]

There is less in this than meets the eye.
A companion's comment at a Maeterlinck play [*attributed to Tallulah Bankhead*]

I must get out of these wet clothes and into a dry Martini.
Quoted in Reader's Digest

Babies in silk hats playing with dynamite.
Of diplomats. Quoted by Samuel Hopkins Adams: *A. Woollcott* [1945]

[1] The most ancient profession in the world.
— Kipling: *Soldiers Three* [1888], *On the City Wall*

Germany was the cause of Hitler just as much as Chicago is responsible for the Chicago *Tribune*.
Last words before the microphone [*January 23, 1943*], "*People's Platform*" *program*

ROLAND YOUNG
[1887–1953]

And here's the happy bounding flea —
You cannot tell the he from she.
The sexes look alike, you see;
But she can tell, and so can he.
The Flea

OWEN HALL
(JAMES DAVIS)
[? –1907]

O tell me, pretty maiden, are there any more at home like you?
Floradora [1900]. *Act II*

IRVING BERLIN
[1888–   ]

Come on and hear, come on and hear,
Alexander's Ragtime Band.
Alexander's Ragtime Band [1911]

You've got to get up, you've got to get up,
You've got to get up this morning!
Oh! How I Hate to Get Up in the Morning [1917]

God bless America,
Land that I love;
Stand beside her and guide her
Through the night with a light from above.
God Bless America [1]

HENRY BESTON
[1888–   ]

The neon glow of the age of comfort and violence.
Review of John Burroughs's America, in The Freeman [*February 11, 1952*]

[1] The song was written in 1917, and first sung by Kate Smith, Armistice Day, 1938. (Copyright, 1939.)

HEYWOOD BROUN
[1888–1939]

In the march up to the heights of fame there comes a spot close to the summit in which man reads "nothing but detective stories."
G.K.C. [*1922*]

"Trees" (if I have the name right) is one of the most annoying pieces of verse within my knowledge. The other one is Kipling's "If," with third place reserved for Henley's "Invictus." "Trees" maddens me, because it contains the most insincere line ever written by mortal man. Surely the Kilmer tongue must have been not far from the Kilmer cheek when he wrote, "Poems are made by fools like me."
It Seems to Me [*1935*]. *"Trees," "If," and "Invictus"*

Life is a copycat and can be bullied into following the master artist who bids it come to heel.
Ibid. Nature the Copycat

I have known people to stop and buy an apple on the corner and then walk away as if they had solved the whole unemployment problem.
Ibid. Chummy Charlie

The Irish are the cry-babies of the Western world. Even the mildest quip will set them off into resolutions and protests.
Ibid. The Piece That Got Me Fired

The swaggering underemphasis of New England.
Heywood Broun: Collected Edition [*1941*]

DANA BURNET
[1888–   ]

I'd rather have an inch of dog than miles of pedigree.
The Road to Vagabondia. Stanza 3

DALE CARNEGIE
[1888–1955]

How to Win Friends and Influence People.
Title of book [*1938*]

J. FRANK DOBIE
[1888–1964]

The average Ph.D. thesis is nothing but a transference of bones from one graveyard to another.
A Texan in England [*1945*]. *Chap. 1*

Conform and be dull.
The Voice of the Coyote [*1949*]. *Introduction*

Putting on the spectacles of science in expectation of finding the answer to everything looked at signifies inner blindness.
Ibid.

Reading great books whets but never slacks the thirst for greatness.
Tom Lea: A Portfolio of Six Paintings [*1953*]. *Introduction*

THOMAS STEARNS ELIOT
[1888–1965]

Let us go then, you and I,
When the evening is spread out against the sky
Like a patient etherised upon a table.
The Love Song of J. Alfred Prufrock [*1917*]

In the room the women come and go Talking of Michelangelo.
Ibid.

I have measured out my life with coffee spoons.
Ibid.

I should have been a pair of ragged claws
Scuttling across the floors of silent seas.
Ibid.

Should I, after tea and cakes and ices,
Have the strength to force the moment
to its crisis?
*The Love Song of J. Alfred
Prufrock*

I have seen the moment of my greatness
flicker,
And I have seen the eternal Footman
hold my coat, and snicker,
And in short, I was afraid.
Ibid.

I grow old . . . I grow old . . .
I shall wear the bottoms of my trousers
rolled.
Ibid.

Do I dare to eat a peach?
I shall wear white flannel trousers, and
walk upon the beach.
I have heard the mermaids singing,
each to each.
I do not think that they will sing to me.
Ibid.

The readers of the *Boston Evening
Transcript*
Sway in the wind like a field of ripe
corn.
The Boston Evening Transcript
[1917]

Upon the glazen shelves kept watch
Matthew and Waldo, guardians of the
faith,
The army of unalterable law.[1]
Cousin Nancy

We have been, let us say, to hear the
latest Pole
Transmit the Preludes, through his hair
and finger-tips.
Portrait of a Lady [1917]. I

My smile falls heavily among the bric-
à-brac.
Ibid. III

I am aware of the damp souls of house-
maids
Sprouting despondently at area gates.
Morning at the Window [1917]

Stand on the highest pavement of the
stair —
Lean on a garden urn —
Weave, weave the sunlight in your hair.
La Figlia Che Piange [1917]

[1] See Meredith, page 639a.

Simple and faithless as a smile and
shake of the hand.
La Figlia Che Piange

It [tradition] cannot be inherited,
and if you want it you must obtain it
by great labour.
*Tradition and the Individual
Talent [1919]*

There is a great deal, in the writing
of poetry, which must be conscious and
deliberate. In fact, the bad poet is usually unconscious where he ought to be
conscious, and conscious where he
ought to be unconscious.
Ibid.

Poetry is not a turning loose of emotion, but an escape from emotion; it is
not the expression of personality, but
an escape from personality. But, of
course, only those who have personality and emotions know what it means
to want to escape from these things.
Ibid

The broad-backed hippopotamus
Rests on his belly in the mud;
Although he seems so firm to us
He is merely flesh and blood.
The Hippopotamus [1920]

Webster was much possessed by death
And saw the skull beneath the skin.
Whispers of Immortality [1920]

Uncorseted, her friendly bust
Gives promise of pneumatic bliss.
Ibid.

Reorganized upon the floor
She yawns and draws a stocking up.
*Sweeney Among the Nightingales
[1920]*

After such knowledge, what forgive-
ness? Think now
History has many cunning passages,
contrived corridors
And issues, deceives with whispering
ambitions,
Guides us by vanities.
Gerontion [1920]

April is the cruellest month, breeding
Lilacs out of the dead land, mixing
Memory and desire, stirring
Dull roots with spring rain.
*The Waste Land [1922]. I, The
Burial of the Dead*

And I will show you something different
from either
Your shadow at morning striding be-
hind you
Or your shadow at evening rising to
meet you;
I will show you fear in a handful of
dust.
*The Waste Land. I, The
Burial of the Dead*

Hurry up please its time.
Ibid. II, A Game of Chess

But at my back from time to time I
hear
The sound of horns and motors, which
shall bring
Sweeney to Mrs. Porter in the spring.
O the moon shone bright on Mrs. Porter
And on her daughter
They wash their feet in soda water.
Ibid. III, The Fire Sermon

When lovely woman stoops to folly and
Paces about her room again, alone,
She smoothes her hair with automatic
hand,
And puts a record on the gramophone.
Ibid.

Between the idea
And the reality
Between the motion
And the act
Falls the Shadow.
The Hollow Men [1925]. V

This is the way the world ends
Not with a bang but a whimper.
Ibid.

Humility is the most difficult of all
virtues to achieve; nothing dies harder
than the desire to think well of oneself.
*Shakespeare and the Stoicism of
Seneca [1927]*

We know too much, and are convinced of too little. Our literature is a
substitute for religion, and so is our
religion.
*A Dialogue on Dramatic Poetry
[1928]*

Because I do not hope to turn again
Because I do not hope
Because I do not hope to turn.
Ash-Wednesday [1930]. I

Lady, three white leopards sat under
a juniper-tree.
Ash-Wednesday. II

Blown hair is sweet, brown hair over
the mouth blown.
Ibid.

The white sails still fly seaward, sea-
ward flying
Unbroken wings.
Ibid. VI

And the lost heart stiffens and rejoices
In the lost lilac and the lost sea voices
And the weak spirit quickens to rebel
For the bent golden-rod and the lost
sea smell.
Ibid.

Teach us to care and not to care
Teach us to sit still
Even among these rocks,
Our peace in His will.[1]
Ibid.

What seas what shores what grey rocks
and what islands
What water lapping the bow
And scent of pine and the woodthrush
singing through the fog
What images return
O my daughter.
Marina [1930]

Yet we have gone on living,
Living and partly living.
*Murder in the Cathedral [1935].
Part I*

The last temptation is the greatest
treason:
To do the right deed for the wrong
reason.
Ibid.

Human kind cannot bear very much
reality.
Ibid. Part II

Footfalls echo in the memory
Down the passage which we did not
take
Towards the door we never opened
Into the rose-garden.
*Four Quartets [1943].
Burnt Norton*

Garlic and sapphires in the mud
Clot the bedded axle-tree.
Ibid.

[1] See Dante, page 77*a*.

In my beginning is my end.
> *Four Quartets. East Coker*

Each venture
Is a new beginning, a raid on the inarticulate
With shabby equipment always deteriorating
In the general mess of imprecision of feeling.
> *Ibid.*

In my end is my beginning.[1]
> *Ibid.*

I do not know much about gods; but
I think that the river
Is a strong brown god — sullen, untamed and intractable.
> *Ibid. The Dry Salvages*

The backward look behind the assurance
Of recorded history, the backward halflook
Over the shoulder, towards the primitive terror.
> *Ibid.*

Music heard so deeply
That it is not heard at all, but you
are the music
While the music lasts.
> *Ibid.*

Only undefeated
Because we have gone on trying;
We, content at the last
If our temporal reversion nourish
(Not too far from the yew-tree)
The life of significant soil.
> *Ibid.*

What the dead had no speech for, when living,
They can tell you, being dead: the communication
Of the dead is tongued with fire beyond the language of the living.
> *Ibid. Little Gidding*

ALINE (MRS. JOYCE) KILMER
[1888–1941]

I shall not be afraid any more,
Either by night or day;

[1] See Mary, Queen of Scots, page 101b.

What would it profit me to be afraid
With you away?
> *I Shall Not Be Afraid. Stanza 1*

I'm sorry you are wiser,
I'm sorry you are taller;
I liked you better foolish,
And I liked you better smaller.
> *For the Birthday of a Middle-
> Aged Child. Stanza 1*

Things have a terrible permanence
When people die.
> *Things. Stanza 6*

WILLIAM L. LAURENCE
[1888–   ]

The Atomic Age began at exactly 5:30 Mountain War Time on the morning of July 16, 1945, on a stretch of semi-desert land about fifty airline miles from Alamogordo, New Mexico.

At that great moment in history, ranking with the moment in the long ago when man first put fire to work for him and started on his march to civilization, the vast energy locked within the hearts of the atoms of matter was released for the first time in a burst of flame such as had never before been seen on this planet.[1]
> *In the New York Times,
> September 26, 1945*

A great ball of fire about a mile in diameter, changing colors as it kept shooting upward, from deep purple to orange, expanding, growing bigger, rising as it was expanding, an elemental force freed from its bonds after being chained for billions of years.
> *Ibid.*

At first it was a giant column that soon took the shape of a supramundane mushroom. For a fleeting instant it took the form of the Statue of Liberty magnified many times.
> *Ibid.*

[1] As if the earth, water, gases, lightning and caloric had not a million energies, the discovery of any one of which could change the art of war again, and put an end to war by the exterminating forces man can apply. — EMERSON: *The Fortune of the Republic* [1878]

T. E. LAWRENCE [1]
[1888–1935]

I loved you, so I drew these tides of men into my hands and wrote my will across the sky in stars.
Seven Pillars of Wisdom [1926].
Dedication

Arabs could be swung on an idea as on a cord; for the unpledged allegiance of their minds made them obedient servants. None of them would escape the bond till success had come, and with it responsibility and duty and engagements. Then the idea was gone and the work ended — in ruins.
Ibid. Chap. 3

There could be no honour in a sure success, but much might be wrested from a sure defeat.
Revolt in the Desert [1927].
Chap. 19

It came upon me freshly how the secret of uniform was to make a crowd solid, dignified, impersonal: to give it the singleness and tautness of an upstanding man. This death's livery which walled its bearers from ordinary life, was sign that they had sold their wills and bodies to the State: and contracted themselves into a service not the less abject for that its beginning was voluntary.
Ibid. Chap. 35

EUGENE O'NEILL
[1888–1953]

Dat ole davil, sea.
Anna Christie [1922]. *Act I*

We's all poor nuts and things happen, and we yust get mixed in wrong, that's all.
Ibid. Act IV

[1] Changed his name to T. E. Shaw, 1927. Appearing first in the war news from Arabia as a personage rather more incredible than Prester John, and presently emerging into clear definition as the author of one of the great histories of the world, recording his own conquests at an age at which young company officers are hardly allowed to speak at the mess table. — BERNARD SHAW, in *The New York Evening Post*, April 16, 1927

For de little stealin' dey gits you in jail soon or late. For de big stealin' dey makes you emperor and puts you in de Hall o' Fame when you croaks. If dey's one thing I learns in ten years on de Pullman cars listenin' to de white quality talk, it's dat same fact.
The Emperor Jones [1920]. *Sc. 1*

Yank. Sure! Lock me up! Put me in a cage! Dat's de on'y answer yuh know. G'wan, lock me up!
Policeman. What you been doin'?
Yank. Enough to gimme life for! I was born, see? Sure, dat's de charge. Write it in de blotter. I was born, get me!
The Hairy Ape [1922]

He couldn't design a cathedral without it looking like the First Supernatural Bank!
The Great God Brown [1926]

Our lives are merely strange dark interludes in the electrical display of God the Father!
Strange Interlude [1928]

JOHN CROWE RANSOM
[1888–   ]

Two evils, monstrous either one apart,
Possessed me, and were long and loath at going:
A cry of Absence, Absence, in the heart,
And in the wood the furious winter blowing.
Winter Remembered

Hands hold much of heat in little storage.
They Hail the Sunrise

The lazy geese, like a snow cloud
Dripping their snow on the green grass,
Tricking and stopping, sleepy and proud,
Who cried in goose, Alas.
Bells for John Whiteside's Daughter

Here lies a lady of beauty and high degree.
Of chills and fever she died, of fever and chills,
The delight of her husband, her aunts, an infant of three,

And of medicos marvelling sweetly on her ills.
Here Lies a Lady

Long, long before men die I sometimes read
Their stoic backs as plain as graveyard stones.
The Resurrection

And kept their blue eyes blue to any weather.
Men

Mouth he remembered: the quaint orifice
From which came heat that flamed upon the kiss.
The Equilibrists

In Heaven you have heard no marriage is,
No white flesh tinder to your lecheries,
Your male and female tissue sweetly shaped
Sublimed away, and furious blood escaped.
Ibid.

Equilibrists lie here; stranger, tread light;
Close, but untouching in each other's sight;
Mouldered the lips and ashy the tall skull,
Let them lie perilous and beautiful.
Ibid.

He rose and was himself again.
Simply another morning, and simply Jane.
Morning

God have mercy on the sinner
Who must write with no dinner,
No gravy and no grub,
No pewter and no pub,
No belly and no bowels,
Only consonants and vowels.
Survey of Literature

Athens, a fragile kingdom by the foam,
Assumed the stranger's yoke; but then behold how meek
Those unbred Caesars grew, who spent their fruits of Rome
Forever after, trying to be Greek.
Triumph

ROBERT EMMONS ROGERS
[1888–1941]

Marry the boss's daughter.
Advice to the Class of 1929, Massachusetts Institute of Technology

LEW SARETT
[1888–1954]

God, let me flower as I will!
For I am weary of the chill
Companionship of waxen vines
And hothouse-nurtured columbines.
Let Me Flower as I Will

In yonder room he lies
With pennies on his eyes.
Requiem for a Croesus

ALAN SEEGER
[1888–1916]

Whether I am on the winning or losing side is not the point with me: it is being on the side where my sympathies lie that matters, and I am ready to see it through to the end. Success in life means doing that thing than which nothing else conceivable seems more noble or satisfying or remunerative, and this enviable state I can truly say that I enjoy, for had I the choice I would be nowhere else in the world than where I am.[1]
Letter to his mother [July 3, 1915]

I have a rendezvous with Death[2]
At some disputed barricade,
When Spring comes back with rustling shade
And apple-blossoms fill the air.
I Have a Rendezvous with Death

When Spring trips north again this year,

[1] I think he would not wish himself any where but where he is. — SHAKESPEARE: *King Henry V* [1598–1600], Act IV, Sc. 1, L. 125
[2] See Archipoeta, page 74b.
I have a rendezvous with Life,
When Spring's first heralds hum.
COUNTEE CULLEN [1903–1946]: *I Have a Rendezvous with Life*

And I to my pledged word am true,
I shall not fail that rendezvous.
I Have a Rendezvous with Death

SAMUEL SHELLABARGER
[1888–1954]

Frequent indifference to external fact, though regrettable, is still relatively unimportant, for portraiture is not photography.
*The Chevalier Bayard [1928].
Chap. 1*
A man, a nation, a millennium, grows and is strong, or declines and perishes, in proportion to the spiritual content of each. But when nothing spiritual remains, what is left to man but the worship of vanity? Lord Vanity rules our present world.
Lord Vanity [1953]. Chap. 14
When it has leveled everything, fire burns itself out, and so does a lie.
Ibid.

BARTOLOMEO VANZETTI
[1888–1927]

I found myself compelled to fight back from my eyes the tears, and quanch my heart trobling to my throat to not weep before him. But Sacco's name will live in the hearts of the people when your name, your laws, institutions and your false god are but a dim rememoring of a cursed past in which man was wolf to the man.
Last Speech to the Court [1]

HENRY AGARD WALLACE
[1888–1965]

The object of this war is to make sure that everybody in the world has the privilege of drinking a quart of milk a day.[2]
*Address: The Price of Free
World Victory [May 8, 1942]*

[1] Vanzetti and Nicolo Sacco, Italian anarchists, were executed August 23, 1927, by the Commonwealth of Massachusetts on charges, never conclusively proved, of murder and robbery.
[2] This statement became twisted into the

The century on which we are entering can be and must be the century of the common man.
*Address: The Price of Free
World Victory*
The hair goes with the hide.
Answer when questioned by reporters why he had not mentioned the Democratic Vice-Presidential candidate, Harry S. Truman, in his campaign speech in Madison Square Garden, New York, September 21, 1944
The people who are fighting against me know that they are not fighting a starry-eyed liberal or mystic. If they really thought that, they wouldn't be worried.[1]
*Speech at Testimonial Dinner,
New York, January 29, 1945*

CONRAD AIKEN
[1889–   ]

Music I heard with you was more than music,
And bread I broke with you was more than bread.
Music I Heard with You [1914]
Stars in the purple dusk above the rooftops
Pale in a saffron mist and seem to die,
And I myself on a swiftly tilting planet
Stand before a glass and tie my tie.
Senlin. Morning Song
One by one in the moonlight there,
Neighing far off on the haunted air,
The unicorns come down to the sea.
Ibid. Evening Song
Rock meeting rock can know love better
Than eyes that stare or lips that touch.
All that we know in love is bitter,
And it is not much.
Annihilation. Stanza 8
All lovely things will have an ending,
All lovely things will fade and die,

purported slogan "Milk for Hottentots," which was disclaimed by Mr. Wallace.
[1] See C. L. Becker, page 861b.

And youth, that's now so bravely
  spending,
Will beg a penny by and by.
   *All Lovely Things Will Have an
                         Ending*
O Altitudo in the bloodstream swims.[1]
   And in the Human Heart [*1940*].
                         Sonnet VI
Ice is the silent language of the peak;
and fire the silent language of the star.
         Ibid. Sonnet X
Shadow to you, the subtle — light to
  me,
the nimble — and the twilight soul
  between,
in which, embracing, we may learn to
  be,
and having learned to be, may learn to
  mean.
         Ibid. Sonnet X
For brief as water falling will be death,
and brief as flower falling, or a leaf,
brief as the taking, and the giving,
  breath;
thus natural, thus brief, my love, is
  grief.
         Ibid. Sonnet XVIII
Shape has no shape, nor will your thinking shape it;
space has no confines; and no borders
  time.
And yet, to think the abyss is to escape
  it.
         Ibid. Sonnet XXVI
Nor will that morning come which is
  not strange,
who have, each day, such wonders to
  exchange.
         Ibid. Sonnet XXXVIII

HERVEY ALLEN
[1889–1949]

Mornings, the flower-women hawk their
  wares —
Bronze caryatids of a genial race,
Bearing the bloom-heaped baskets on
  their heads.
                         Palmetto Town
Grow up as soon as you can. It pays.
The only time you really live fully is

[1] See Sir Thomas Browne, page 240a.

from thirty to sixty. . . . The young
are slaves to dreams; the old servants
of regrets. Only the middle-aged have
all their five senses in the keeping of
their wits.
   Anthony Adverse [*1933*]. *Chap. 31*
What is even a wise book but a blast
from the lungs made visible to the
eyes?
                         Ibid.
Practise what I call a decent mammalian philosophy.
                         Ibid.

ROBERT CHARLES
BENCHLEY
[1889–1945]

I haven't been abroad in so long that
I almost speak English without an accent.
         The Old Sea Rover Speaks
Can anyone help me out by furnishing the last three words to the following stanza which I learned in school
and of which I have forgotten the last
three words, thereby driving myself
crazy! —
"I'm sorry that I spelt the word,
  I hate to go above you,
Because — the brown eyes lower fell,
  Because, you see, — —— ——."
                 Inside Benchley [*1921*]
An Austrian scientist has come out
with the announcement that there is no
such thing as a hundred per cent male
or a hundred per cent female. If this is
true, it is really a big step forward.
   *Ibid. A Talk to Young Men:
   Graduation Address on "The
   Decline of Sex"*

CHRISTOPHER DAWSON
[1889–   ]

As soon as men decide that all means
are permitted to fight an evil, then their
good becomes indistinguishable from
the evil that they set out to destroy.
   *The Judgment of the Nations
                         [1942]*
Religion has withdrawn into isolated
strongholds, where it remains on the

defensive, surveying the land through the narrow loopholes in the fortifications.

The Judgment of the Nations

CHARLES DIVINE
[1889–1950]

Where hearts were high and fortunes low, and onions in the stew.

At the Lavender Lantern. Stanza 3

A crooked street goes past my door, entwining love of every land;
It wanders, singing, round the world, to Askelon and Samarkand.

The Crooked Street of Dreams.
Stanza 1

PHILIP GUEDALLA
[1889–1944]

Biography, like big game hunting, is one of the recognized forms of sport, and it is as unfair as only sport can be.

Supers and Supermen [1920]

No picture of life in Calais was too ludicrous to be believed in Dover; that is one of the advantages of being an Island Race.[1]

Ibid.

There is no Gibbon but Gibbon, and Gibbon is his prophet.[2] The solemn march of his cadences, the majestic impropriety of his innuendo are without rivals in the respective annals of British eloquence and British indelicacy.

Ibid.

The work of Henry James has always seemed divisible by a simple dynastic arrangement into three reigns: James I, James II, and the Old Pretender.

Ibid.

An Englishman is a man who lives on an island in the North Sea governed by Scotsmen.

Ibid.

[1] There are several versions of a supposed London newspaper headline, the best known perhaps being "THICK FOG OVER CHANNEL: CONTINENT ISOLATED."
[2] There is no God but God, and Mohammed is his prophet. — *Moslem creed* (the first phrase is from *The Koran, Chap. 3*)

The cheerful clatter of Sir James Barrie's cans as he went round with the milk of human kindness.

Some Critics

Strange that pre-eminence in Germany has more than once been indicated by an eccentric pattern in the hair upon the upper lip.

The Hundred Years [1936]

The true history of the United States is the history of transportation . . . in which the names of railroad presidents are more significant than those of Presidents of the United States.

Ibid.

There is no plant in the whole world of more cautious growth than Anglo-American negotiation.

Mr. Churchill [1942] (apropos the wedding of Mr. Churchill's parents)

The little ships, the unforgotten un-Homeric catalogue of *Mary Jane* and *Peggy IV*, of *Folkestone Belle*, *Boy Billy*, and *Ethel Maud*, of *Lady Haig* and *Skylark* . . . the little ships of England brought the army home.

Ibid. (Evacuation of Dunkirk)

ADOLF HITLER
[1889–1945]

During the next thousand years no revolution will take place in Germany.

Address at Party Rally,
September, 1934

The Sudetenland is the last territorial claim I have to make in Europe.

Address at Sports Palast,
September 26, 1938

I know that one is able to win people far more by the spoken than by the written word, and that every great movement on this globe owes its rise to the great speakers and not to the great writers.

Mein Kampf.[1] Preface

The one means that wins the easiest victory over reason: terror and force.

Ibid. Vol. I, Chap. 2, Page 53

[1] Complete and Unabridged Edition [1940].

A majority can never replace the man. . . . Just as a hundred fools do not make one wise man, an heroic decision is not likely to come from a hundred cowards.

Mein Kampf. Vol. I, Chap. 3,
Page 105

There is only one real "statesman" once in a blue moon in one nation, and not a hundred or more at a time.

Ibid. Page 113

For if a man is not ready or able to fight for his existence, righteous Providence has already decreed his doom. The world is not intended for cowardly nations.

Ibid. Page 123

Every movement with great aims has anxiously to watch that it does not lose connection with the great masses.

Ibid. Page 137

I consider the foundation or the destruction of a religion essentially more important than the foundation or destruction of a State, let alone a party.

Ibid. Page 148

The efficiency of the truly national leader consists primarily in preventing the division of the attention of a people, and always in concentrating it on a single enemy.

Ibid. Page 152

Mankind has grown strong in eternal struggles and it will only perish through eternal peace.

Ibid. Chap. 4, Page 175

The greater the amount of room a people has at its disposal, the greater is also its natural protection; because military victories over nations crowded in small territories have always been reached more quickly and more easily.

Ibid. Page 177

Strength lies not in defense but in attack.

Ibid. Page 191

All propaganda has to be popular and has to adapt its spiritual level to the perception of the least intelligent of those towards whom it intends to direct itself.

Ibid. Chap. 6, Page 232

As soon as by one's own propaganda even a glimpse of right on the other side is admitted, the cause for doubting one's own right is laid.

Mein Kampf. Vol. I, Chap. 6,
Page 237

In the size of the lie there is always contained a certain factor of credibility, since the great masses of the people . . . will more easily fall victims to a great lie than to a small one.

Ibid. Chap. 10, Page 313

If an idea is right in itself, and if thus armed it embarks on the struggle in this world, it is invincible and every persecution will lead to its inner strengthening.

Ibid. Chap. 12, Page 487

Germany will be either a world power or will not be at all.

Ibid. Vol. II, Chap. 14, Page 950

Never tolerate the establishment of two continental powers in Europe.

Ibid. Page 963

An intelligent victor will, whenever possible, present his demands to the vanquished in installments.

Ibid. Chap. 15, Page 968

The more extortions thus cheerfully accepted, the more unjustified does it seem to people finally to set about defending themselves.

Ibid.

After fifteen years of work I have achieved, as a common German soldier and merely with my fanatical will power, the unity of the German nation, and have freed it from the death sentence of Versailles.[1]

Proclamation to the Troops on taking over the leadership of the German armed forces [December 21, 1941]

[1] The Allied and Associated Governments affirm and Germany accepts the responsibility of Germany and her Allies for causing all the loss and damage to which the Allied and Associated Governments and their nationals have been subjected as a consequence of the war imposed upon them by the aggression of Germany and her Allies. — *Treaty of Versailles, Article 231 (the "War Guilt Clause")* [June 28, 1919]

This war no longer bears the characteristics of former inter-European conflicts. It is one of those elemental conflicts which usher in a new millennium and which shake the world once in a thousand years.

Speech before the Reichstag
[April 26, 1942]

Whomsoever England allies herself with, she will see her allies stronger than she is herself at the end of this war.

Ibid.

If the German people despair, they will deserve no better than they get. If they despair, I will not be sorry for them if God lets them down.

Speech at Munich on the Twentieth Anniversary of the Munich Beer Hall Putsch, broadcast November 8, 1943

EDWIN POWELL HUBBLE
[1889-   ]

On the grand scale, the Observable Region [of space] is very much the same everywhere and in all directions — in other words, it is homogeneous.

The Exploration of Space [1945]

STODDARD KING
[1889-1933]

A writer owned an Asterisk,
  And kept it in his den,
Where he wrote tales (which had large
    sales)
  Of frail and erring men;
And always, when he reached the point
  Where carping censors lurk,
He called upon the Asterisk
  To do his dirty work.

The Writer and the Asterisk.
Stanza 1

There's a long, long trail a-winding
  Into the land of my dreams,
Where the nightingales are singing
  And a white moon beams:
There's a long, long night of waiting
  Until my dreams all come true,

Till the day when I'll be going down
  That long, long trail with you.

The Long, Long Trail [1913]

WALTER LIPPMANN
[1889-   ]

Copeland of Harvard once remarked when he was asked whether he had enjoyed a tea party, "if I had not been there I should have been very much bored." [1]

William Bolitho — A Memoir

In foreign relations, as in all other relations, a policy has been formed only when commitments and power have been brought into balance.

U. S. Foreign Policy [1943]

The final test of a leader is that he leaves behind him in other men the conviction and the will to carry on. . . . The genius of a good leader is to leave behind him a situation which common sense, without the grace of genius, can deal with successfully.

Roosevelt Has Gone
[April 14, 1945]

KATHERINE MANSFIELD
[1889-1923]

Whenever I prepare for a journey I prepare as though for death. Should I never return, all is in order. This is what life has taught me.

Journal, 1922

I want, by understanding myself, to understand others. I want to be all that I am capable of becoming. . . . This all sounds very strenuous and serious. But now that I have wrestled with it, it's no longer so. I feel happy — deep down. *All is well.*

Ibid. (end of her journal)

[1] I quite agree with Alexandre Dumas who, when asked how he had enjoyed a fearfully dull party, said, "I should not have enjoyed it if *I* had not been there." How delightful one is to oneself. — LAURA TENNANT: *Letter to Sidney Colvin*, December, 1884 (*Quoted in* E. V. LUCAS: *The Colvins and Their Friends, P. 188*)

FRANCIS JOSEPH, CARDINAL SPELLMAN
[1889–   ]

Somewhere — the place it matters not
— somewhere
I saw a child, hungry and thin of
face —
Eyes in whose pools life's joys no
longer stirred,
Lips that were dead to laughter's eager
kiss,
Yet parted fiercely to a crust of bread.
Prayer for Children [1944]

W. J. TURNER
[1889–1946]

If love means affection, I
Love old trees, hats, coats and
things,[1]
Anything that's been with me
In my daily sufferings.
Epithalamium. Stanza 3
How often does a man need to see a
woman?
Once!
Once is enough, but a second time will
confirm it.
The Word Made Flesh?

ELMER FRANK ANDREWS
[1890–   ]

If a man has an office with a desk on
which there is a buzzer, and if he can
press that buzzer and have somebody
come dashing in response — then he's
an executive.
*Address before the Trade Asso-
ciation Executives' Forum of
Chicago* [December 9, 1938]

WILLIAM BOLITHO
[1890–1930]

The adventurer is within us, and he
contests for our favour with the social
man we are obliged to be. These two
sorts of life are incompatibles; one we
hanker after, the other we are obliged

[1] See Bacon, page 119a.

to. There is no other conflict so deep
and bitter as this.
Twelve Against the Gods [1929].
Introduction
We, like the eagles, were born to be
free. Yet we are obliged, in order to live
at all, to make a cage of laws for ourselves and to stand on the perch. We
are born as wasteful and unremorseful
as tigers; we are obliged to be thrifty,
or starve, or freeze. We are born to
wander, and cursed to stay and dig.
Ibid.
His real glory is that of all adventurers: to have been the tremendous
outsider.
Ibid. Christopher Columbus
The world will never learn to beware
of these stately gentlemen with the
fixed calm look straight in your eyes,
who never joke, and never waver, profuse in cautious hints and allusions,
but practised in rightly placed silences
— which is why the confidence trick is
still running.
Ibid.
The most dangerous enterprise in
the world, the foundation of a religion.
Ibid. Mahomet
That great bourn of all common
sense: compromise.
Ibid.
You need more tact in the dangerous
art of giving presents than in any other
social action.[1]
Ibid. Lola Montez
Contrary to male sentimentality and
psychology, the confrontation of a hostile crowd, to a woman, is like a tonic.
Ibid.
An adventure differs from a mere
feat in that it is tied to the eternally
unattainable. Only one end of the rope
is in the hand, the other is not visible,
and neither prayers, nor daring, nor
reason can shake it free.
Ibid. Napoleon III
Freeing oppressed nationalities is
perhaps the most dangerous of all
philanthropic enterprises.
Ibid.

[1] See Lady Glenconner, page 853b.

The voice of the people needs **a** whole art of harmonic transcription to be understood.
Twelve Against the Gods.
Woodrow Wilson

VANNEVAR BUSH
[1890–]

The scene changes but the aspirations of men of good will persist.
Modern Arms and Free Men [*1949*]. *Foreword*
If democracy loses its touch, then no great war will be needed to overwhelm it. If it keeps and enhances its strength, no great war need come again.
Ibid. Page 263
Fear can not be banished, but it can be calm and without panic; and it can be mitigated by reason and evaluation.
Ibid.

KAREL ČAPEK
[1890–1938]

Rossum's Universal Robots.[1]
R. U. R. [*1920*]
O Lord, grant that in some way it may rain every day, say from about midnight until three o'clock in the morning . . . gentle and warm so that it can soak in . . . that there may be plenty of dew and little wind, enough worms, no plant-lice and snails, no mildew, and that once a week thin liquid manure and guano may fall from heaven.
The Gardener's Year [*1931*].
The Gardener's Prayer

MARCUS COOK CONNELLY
[1890–]

Gangway for de Lawd God Jehovah!
The Green Pastures [2]
God. I'll jest r'ar back an' pass a miracle.
Ibid.

[1] The term "robot" came into English through Čapek's play.
[2] First produced in 1930. Suggested by Roark Bradford's stories, *Ol' Man Adam an' His Chillun.*

Gabriel. How about cleanin' up de whole mess of 'em and sta'tin all over ag'in wid some new kind of animal?
God. An' admit I'm licked?
The Green Pastures
Even bein' Gawd ain't a bed of roses.
Ibid.

ELMER DAVIS
[1890–1958]

Atomic warfare is bad enough; biological warfare would be worse; but there is something that is worse than either. The French can tell you what it is; or the Czechs, or the Greeks, or the Norwegians, or the Filipinos; it is subjection to an alien oppressor.
No World, If Necessary [1]
One world or none, say the atomic scientists. Has it occurred to them that if their one world turned out to be totalitarian and obscurantist, we might better have no world at all?
Ibid.

CHARLES ANDRÉ JOSEPH MARIE DE GAULLE
[1890–]

France has lost a battle. But France has not lost the war.
Broadcast from London to the French people after the fall of France, June 18, 1940

DWIGHT DAVID EISENHOWER
[1890–]

Humility must always be the portion of any man who receives acclaim earned in the blood of his followers and the sacrifices of his friends.
Address at Guildhall on receiving the Freedom of the City of London, July 12, 1945
Since this century's beginning a time of tempest has seemed to come upon the continents of the earth.
Inaugural Address [*January 20, 1953*]

[1] In the *Saturday Review of Literature,* March 30, 1946.

In the final choice a soldier's pack is not so heavy a burden as a prisoner's chains.

Inaugural Address

As it is an ancient truth that freedom cannot be legislated into existence, so it is no less obvious that freedom cannot be censored into existence.

President's Letter to American Library Association Convention [June, 1953]

SIR ALAN PATRICK HERBERT
[1890–   ]

When laughing Ann trips down the
    street
The sun comes out as well,
The town is at her twinkling feet,
    The crier rings his bell,
The young men leap like little fish,
    Policemen stand and purr,
While husbands look behind and wish
    That they had married her.

Laughing Ann. Stanza 1

I'm not a jealous woman, but I *can't*
    see what he sees in her,
I can't see *what* he sees in her, I can't
    see what he *sees* in her!

I Can't Think What He Sees in Her

Holy Deadlock.

Title of novel [1934] satirizing the paradoxes of British divorce law [1]

The Common Law of England has been laboriously built upon a mythical figure — the figure of "The Reasonable Man."

Uncommon Law [1935]. Page 1

The critical period in matrimony is breakfast-time.

Ibid. Page 98

An Act of God was defined as *something which no reasonable man could have expected.*

Ibid. Page 316

[1] Herbert's book and his campaign in the House of Commons were of major importance in bringing about the reform embodied in the Matrimonial Causes Bill of 1937.

I regard the pub as a valuable institution.

Letter to the Electors of Oxford University [1935] [1]

They tell us that capitalism is doomed: Karl Marx, I believe, made the same announcement 80 years ago. He may still be right: but the old clock ticks on.

Ibid.

We shall not produce equality by turning everything upside-down.

Ibid.

SAMUEL HOFFENSTEIN
[1890–1947]

I play with the bulls and the bears;
I'm the Bartlett of market quotations.

Songs for an Old-Fashioned Lute. VI

The stars, like measles, fade at last.

The Mimic Muse. V

Babies haven't any hair;
Old men's heads are just as bare; —
Between the cradle and the grave
Lies a haircut and a shave.

Songs of Faith in the Year after Next. VIII

Little by little we subtract
Faith and Fallacy from Fact,
The Illusory from the True,
And starve upon the residue.

Rag-Bag, II. Observation, Stanza 1

    The heart's dead
Are never buried.

Summer Day

GERALD WHITE JOHNSON
[1890–   ]

A man who has tried to play Mozart, and failed, through that vain effort comes into position better to understand the man who tried to paint the Sistine Madonna, and did.

A Little Night-Music [1937]

England has proved that the heroes are not all dead. England has shown

[1] Herbert was elected to the House of Commons, November, 1935, as one of the two representatives of Oxford University.

that there are also brave men after Agamemnon.[1] England has taught us that even our generation can produce glory and honor and undying fame. England restores our belief that faith and loyalty are still able to lift common men to greatness.

Editorial, In Praise of England.
The Baltimore Sun [September,
1940]

Nothing changes more constantly than the past; for the past that influences our lives does not consist of what actually happened, but of what men believe happened.

American Heroes and Hero-
Worship [1943]. Chap. 1

Heroes are created by popular demand, sometimes out of the scantiest materials . . . such as the apple that William Tell never shot, the ride that Paul Revere never finished, the flag that Barbara Frietchie never waved.

Ibid.

ROBERT LEY
[1890–1945]

Strength through Joy.[2]
Instruction for the German Labor
Front, December 2, 1933

CHRISTOPHER MORLEY
[1890–1957]

And of all man's felicities
The very subtlest one, say I,
Is when for the first time he sees
His hearthfire smoke against the sky.
A Hallowe'en Memory. Stanza 5

Heaven is not built of country seats,
But little queer suburban streets.
To the Little House. Stanza 4

The man who never in his life
Has washed the dishes with his wife
Or polished up the silver plate —
He still is largely celibate.
Washing the Dishes. Stanza 4

Now fades the glossy, cherished anthracite;

[1] See Horace, page 40a.
[2] Kraft durch Freude.

The radiators lose their temperature:
How ill avail, on such a frosty night,
The short and simple flannels of the poor.[1]
Elegy Written in a Country
Coal-Bin

Unhappy lovers always should be Frenchmen,
So sweet a tongue for any kind of pain!
Toulemonde. III

Women all
Raiment themselves most brightly for the dark
Which is, on information and belief,
Their true dominion.
Ibid. VI

I bid you, mock not Eros;
He knows not doubt or shame,
And, unaware of proverbs,
The burnt child craves the flame.
Of a Child That Had Fever

When you sell a man a book you don't sell him just twelve ounces of paper and ink and glue — you sell him a whole new life.
Parnassus on Wheels [1917].
Chap. 4

"Dear me," cried Mrs. Spaniel, "what will the neighbors think?"

"They won't," said Gissing, "I don't doubt they'll talk, but they won't think. Thinking is very rare."
Where the Blue Begins [1922]

He is too experienced a parent ever to make positive promises.
Thunder on the Left [1925].
Chap. 5

If you have to keep reminding yourself of a thing, perhaps it isn't so.
Ibid. Chap. 9

April prepares her green traffic light and the world thinks Go.
John Mistletoe [1931]. 8

[1] Daily she came from Bromley to the City,
Pink underclothes of crêpe de Chine she
wore,
So that in each backyard she viewed with pity
The short and simple flannels of the poor.
OLIVER HERFORD(?), *quoted by*
A. EDWARD NEWTON, *Derby Day*

A human being: an ingenious assembly of portable plumbing.
Human Being [*1932*]. *Chap. 11*
How great a bonfire the savages of New York kindle for their evening meal!
Ibid. Chap. 33
That faint but sensitive enteric expectancy which suggests the desirability of a cocktail. . . . A drink has been arranged and will shortly take place.
Swiss Family Manhattan [*1932*]. *Chap. 9*
The enemies of the Future are always the very nicest people.
Kitty Foyle [*1939*]. *Chap. 5*
Dancing is wonderful training for girls, it's the first way you learn to guess what a man is going to do before he does it.
Ibid. Chap. 11
The evening papers print what they do and get away with it because by afternoon the human mind is ruined anyhow.
Ibid. Chap. 25
New York, the nation's thyroid gland.
Shore Leave [*1939*]
Town that made thinking feel, and feeling think;
She has a motto to recall when needed:
I may make heavy weather, but not sink.
"Fluctuat nec Mergitur" [1] [*1940*]
There was so much handwriting on the wall
That even the wall fell down.
Around the Clock [*1943*]
Since men learned print, no night is wholly black.
The Watchman's Sonnet
All joys I bless, but I confess
There is one greatest thrill:
What the dentist does when he stops the buzz
And puts away the drill.
Song in a Dentist's Chair. Stanza 1
Man must learn, or his name is mud,
To relish the ebb as well as the flood.
Toulemonde: Intermezzo [*1944*]

[1] The motto of Paris.

Global citizens began it
When Men-about-town became Men-about-planet.
Toulemonde: Intermezzo
When ego, fantailed like a peacock
Can find the needle in the haycock
And hold the needle's eye and thread it —
Is that millennium? You said it!
Ibid.
Chattering voltage like a broken wire
The wild cicada cried, Six weeks to frost!
End of August
Why do they put the Gideon Bibles only in the bedrooms, where it's usually too late, and not in the barroom downstairs?
Contribution to a Contribution

ALLAN NEVINS
[1890–   ]

The former allies had blundered in the past by offering Germany too little, and offering even that too late,[1] until finally Nazi Germany had become a menace to all mankind.
Germany Disturbs the Peace, in Current History, May, 1935

GEORGE SELDES
[1890–   ]

Sawdust Caesar.[2]
Title of book [*1932*]

FRED M. VINSON
[1890–1953]

Wars are not "acts of God." They are caused by man, by man-made insti-

[1] It is the old trouble — too late. Too late with Czechoslovakia, too late with Poland, certainly too late with Finland. It is always too late, or too little, or both. — DAVID LLOYD GEORGE: *Speech, House of Commons,* March 13, 1940, *the day after the fall of Finland*
"Too Late," caption of famous cartoon by SIR JOHN TENNIEL in *Punch* [February, 1885], when the relief expedition to Khartoum reached there two days after the death of Gordon.
[2] Mussolini.

tutions, by the way in which man has organized his society. What man has made, man can change.

Speech at Arlington National Cemetery, Memorial Day, 1945

AGATHA CHRISTIE

It is completely unimportant. That is why it is so interesting.

The Murder of Roger Ackroyd [*1926*]

"RED" ROWLEY
[*Floruit* 1915]

Mademoiselle from Armenteers,
Hasn't been kissed in forty years,
Hinky dinky, parley-voo.
Mademoiselle from Armentières[1]
Mademoiselle from St. Nazaire,
She never heard of underwear.

Ibid.

ELY CULBERTSON[2]
[1891–1955]

The bizarre world of cards . . . a world of pure power politics where rewards and punishments were meted out immediately. A deck of cards was built like the purest of hierarchies, with every card a master to those below it, a lackey to those above it. And there were "masses" — long suits — which always asserted themselves in the end, triumphing over the kings and aces.

Total Peace [*1943*]. *Chap. 1*

Power politics is the diplomatic name for the law of the jungle.

Must We Fight Russia? [*1946*]. *Chap. 2*

We must conquer war, or war will conquer us.

Ibid.

[1] Soldier song of World War I, with innumerable versions. The tune and verse structure were based on a song long known in the British Army, composed by Alfred James Walden ("Harry Wincott") [1867–1947].

[2] I became a kind of one-man Peace Foundation, endowed not by Carnegie or Rockefeller but by the bridge players. — ELY CULBERTSON, in *The Commonweal*

God and the politicians willing, the United States can declare peace upon the world, and win it.

Must We Fight Russia? Chap. 5

DAVID LOW
[1891–1963]

I have never met anybody who wasn't against War. Even Hitler and Mussolini were, according to themselves.

In the New York Times, February 10, 1946

ELLIOT PAUL
[1891–1958]

She had a complete ignorance of everything a woman does not need to know.

The Life and Death of a Spanish Town [*1942*]. *Chap. 1*

Patience makes women beautiful in middle age.

Ibid. Chap. 2

There was Madrid, and I carry it like a photograph in the inside-pocket of my mind and each day it wears, is soiled, gets thinner, cracks, wrinkles — still it is Madrid.

Ibid. Chap. 7

Government forms which had been printed in such a way that there was never enough space in which to provide answers to ambiguous questions.

The Last Time I Saw Paris[1] [*1942*]. *Part I, 3*

The last time I see Paris will be on the day I die. The city was inexhaustible, and so is its memory.

Ibid. Part II, 23

[1] The last time I saw Paris, her heart was warm and gay,
I heard the laughter of her heart in every street café.
OSCAR HAMMERSTEIN 2ND [1895–   ]:
The Last Time I Saw Paris

HAROLD WILLIAM THOMPSON
[1891–   ]

Body, Boots and Britches.[1]
Title of a volume of New York folklore [1940]

HERBERT V. WILEY
[1891–1954]

Stand by to crash.
Last command to the crew of the falling U. S. Navy dirigible Akron [April 4, 1933]

STELLA BENSON
[1892–1933]

Call no man foe, but never love a stranger.
Build up no plan, nor any star pursue.
Go forth with crowds; in loneliness is danger.
To the Unborn. Stanza 3
Family jokes, though rightly cursed by strangers, are the bond that keeps most families alive.
Pipers and a Dancer. Chap. 9

JOHN PEALE BISHOP
[1892–1944]

Things I have hated: A certain shade of brown
Which elder ladies love; wet roofs that drip
Their huge drops on your neck; short sheets that slip
And leave your ankles freezing; fires that smoke;
Carved, heavy furniture of varnished oak.
The Great Hater

PEARL S. BUCK
[1892–   ]

Be born anywhere, little embryo novelist, but do not be born under the shadow of a great creed, not under the burden of original sin, not under the

[1] A New York State phrase to express completeness, as "lock, stock and barrel."

doom of salvation. Go out and be born among gypsies or thieves or among happy workaday people who live in the sun and do not think about their souls.
Advice to Unborn Novelists

RAYMOND CLAPPER
[1892–1945]

It's a wise crack that knows its own father.
Quoted in Washington Tapestry by OLIVE EWING CLAPPER [1946]

ROBERT PETER TRISTRAM COFFIN
[1892–1955]

If men could still be holy anywhere,
  It would be in towers such as these
That line the coasts with lamps and warn the ships —
  The holy towers of the silences.
Towers of Silence
A man should choose with careful eye
The things to be remembered by.
The Weather Vane
Life and death upon one tether
And running beautiful together.
Crystal Moment

J. B. S. HALDANE
[1892–1964]

Science is vastly more stimulating to the imagination than are the classics.
Daedalus

ROBERT H. JACKSON
[1892–1954]

The first trial in history for crimes against the peace of the world imposes a grave responsibility. The wrongs which we seek to condemn and punish have been so calculated, so malignant and so devastating that civilization cannot tolerate their being ignored because it cannot survive their being repeated.
Opening Address before the International Military Tribunal [1945]

959

The day that this country ceases to be free for irreligion, it will cease to be free for religion.
> *Dissenting opinion, Zorach* v. *Clausor, 343 U.S. 306, 325* [*1952*]

HOWARD MUMFORD JONES
[1892–   ]

They say the forties are the dangerous ages.
> *The Forties* [*1937*]

Therefore we are leaders, we who are dull
But eminent. Our shining names are told,
Our notable acts, our virtues are enrolled
In Who's Who in America for you to cull.
> *Ibid. V*

A few unrepentant old sinners wonder if Marx
Also explains the unsocialized pairs in the parks.
> *Ibid. XXXII*

Persecution is the first law of society because it is always easier to suppress criticism than to meet it.
> *Primer of Intellectual Freedom* [*1949*]. *Introduction*

JOHN KIERAN
[1892–   ]

Who harbors in memory a wealth of valued verse has laid up unto himself treasures that moths will not corrupt nor thieves break in and steal. This is the conviction of one who . . . as a soldier in World War I, trudged the desolate sector of the Somme and the ruined region of Arras with little limp volumes of Shakespeare in his pockets and miniature collections of Burns, Browning, Swinburne, and Tennyson wedged in his pack between the top of the blanket roll and the strapped-down flap that held his mess kit.
> *Poems I Remember* [*1942*]. *Foreword*

ARCHIBALD MacLEISH
[1892–   ]

Sometimes within the brain's old ghostly house,
I hear, far off, at some forgotten door,
A music and an eerie faint carouse,
And stir of echoes down the creaking floor.
> *Chambers of Imagery. Stanza 1*

Beauty is that Medusa's head
Which men go armed to seek and sever.
It is most deadly when most dead,
And dead will stare and sting forever.
> *Beauty*

The trumpet of
Time in our ears and the brazen and
Breaking shout of our days!
> *Panic: Chorus*

A poem should not mean
But be.
> *Ars Poetica* [*1926*]

There with vast wings across the canceled skies,
There in the sudden blackness the black pall
Of nothing, nothing, nothing — nothing at all.
> *The End of the World* [*1926*]

The world was always yours: you would not take it.
> *Speech to a Crowd*

And here face downward in the sun
To feel how swift how secretly
The shadow of the night comes on . . .
> *You, Andrew Marvell* [*1930*]

Christ but this earth goes over to the squall of time!
Hi but she heels to it — rail down: ribs down: rolling
Dakotas under her hull! And the night climbing
Sucking the green from the ferns by these Berkshire boulders!
> *The Sunset Piece*

She lies on her left side her flank golden:
Her hair is burned black with the strong sun:
The scent of her hair is of rain in the dust on her shoulders:

She has brown breasts and the mouth
of no other country.
>*Frescoes for Mr. Rockefeller's
City* [*1933*]. *Landscape as a
Nude*

The one man who should never attempt an explanation of a poem is its author. If the poem can be improved by its author's explanations it never should have been published, and if the poem cannot be improved by its author's explanations the explanations are scarcely worth reading.
>*Poems* [*1938*]. *Author's Note*

America was promises . . .
It was Man who had been promised.
>*America Was Promises* [*1939*]

The perversion of the mind is only possible when those who should be heard in its defense are silent.
>*The Irresponsibles* [*1940*]

The scholar digs his ivory cellar in the ruins of the past and lets the present sicken as it will.
>*Ibid.*

Races didn't bother the Americans. They were something a lot better than any race. They were a People. They were the first self-constituted, self-declared, self-created People in the history of the world. And their manners were their own business. And so were their politics. And so, but ten times so, were their souls.
>*A Time to Act* [*1943*]

EARL MARLATT
[1892–]

Fancy the rapture
Of being there
When the world was made!
>*May Morning.*[1] *Stanza 1*

EDWARD POWYS MATHERS
[1892–]

A love-sick heart dies when the heart is whole,

---

[1] It must have been May Morning when the world was made. — *Old Provençal chanson*

For all the heart's health is to be sick
with love.
>*Fard. Translation from the
Hindustani of Miyan Jagnu,
Eighteenth Century*

Before you love,
Learn to run through snow
Leaving no footprint.
>*Translation of a Turkish Proverb*

EDNA ST. VINCENT MILLAY
[1892–1950]

And what are you that, missing you,
I should be kept awake
As many nights as there are days
With weeping for your sake?
>*The Philosopher*

Death devours all lovely things:
Lesbia with her sparrow
Shares the darkness, — presently
Every bed is narrow.
>*Passer Mortuus Est. Stanza 1*

All I could see from where I stood
Was three long mountains and a wood.
>*Renascence* [*1917*]

I would I were alive again
To kiss the fingers of the rain,
To drink into my eyes the shine
Of every slanting silver line,
To catch the freshened, fragrant breeze
From drenched and dripping apple-
>trees.
>>*Ibid.*

I know not how such things can be,
I only know there came to me
A fragrance such as never clings
To aught save happy living things.
>*Ibid.*

The world stands out on either side
No wider than the heart is wide;
Above the world is stretched the sky, —
No higher than the soul is high.[1]
The heart can push the sea and land
Farther away on either hand;
The soul can split the sky in two,
And let the face of God shine through.
>*Ibid.*

---

[1] See Hartley Coleridge, page 483b.

The fabric of my faithful love
No power shall dim or ravel
Whilst I stay here, — but oh, my dear,
If I should ever travel!
To the Not Impossible Him.
Stanza 3

I know I am but summer to your heart,
And not the full four seasons of the
year.
Two Seasons. Sonnet 1

I drank at every vine.
The last was like the first.
I came upon no wine
So wonderful as thirst.
Feast. Stanza 1

I only know that summer sang in me
A little while, that in me sings no more.
What Lips My Lips Have Kissed

Euclid alone
Has looked on Beauty bare.[1] Fortunate
they
Who, though once only and then but
far away,
Have heard her massive sandal set on
stone.
The Harp-Weaver [1923].
Sonnet 22

Pity me that the heart is slow to learn
What the swift mind beholds at every
turn.
Sonnet: Pity Me Not Because
the Light of Day

My candle burns at both ends;
It will not last the night;
But, ah, my foes, and, oh, my friends —
It gives a lovely light.[2]
Figs from Thistles. First Fig

Oh, come again to Astolat!
I will not ask you to be kind;

[1] Mathematics possesses not only truth, but supreme beauty — a beauty cold and austere, like that of sculpture, without appeal to any part of our weaker nature, yet sublimely pure, and capable of a stern perfection such as only the greatest art can show. — BERTRAND RUSSELL: *The Principles of Mathematics* [1903]
[2] I burned my candle at both ends,
And now have neither foes nor friends.
SAMUEL HOFFENSTEIN [1890-1947]:
Songs of Fairly Utter Despair, VIII

And you may go when you will go,
And I will stay behind.
Elaine. Stanza 1

Music my rampart, and my only one.
On Hearing a Symphony of
Beethoven

Read me, do not let me die!
Search the fading letters, finding
Steadfast in the broken binding
All that once was I!
The Poet and His Book. Stanza 6

Who builds her a house with love for
timber,
Builds her a house of foam;
And I'd rather be bride to a lad gone
down
Than widow to one safe home.
Keen. Stanza 5

If ever I said, in grief or pride,
I tired of honest things, I lied.
The Goose Girl

I will be the gladdest thing under the
sun!
I will touch a hundred flowers and not
pick one.
Afternoon on a Hill

Life goes on forever like the gnawing of
a mouse.
Ashes of Life. Stanza 3

Thanks be to God, the world is wide,
And I am going far from home!
And I forgot in Camelot
The man I loved in Rome.
Fugitive. Stanza 1

My heart is warm with the friends I
make,
And better friends I'll not be knowing;
Yet there isn't a train I wouldn't take,
No matter where it's going.
Travel. Stanza 3

I am not resigned to the shutting away
of loving hearts in the hard
ground.
So it is, and so it will be, for so it has
been, time out of mind:
Into the darkness they go, the wise and
the lovely. Crowned
With lilies and with laurel they go;
but I am not resigned.
Dirge Without Music. Stanza 1

I had a little Sorrow,
Born of a little Sin.
The Penitent. Stanza 1

Whether or not we find what we are
seeking
Is idle, biologically speaking.
*Sonnet: I Shall Forget You
Presently*

Love is not all: it is not meat nor
drink
Nor slumber nor a roof against the
rain;
Nor yet a floating spar to men that
sink.
Fatal Interview. XXX

See how these masses mill and swarm
And troop and muster and assail:
God! we could keep this planet warm
By friction, if the sun should fail.
*Three Sonnets in Tetrameter
[1938]. I*

This little life, from here to there —
Who lives it safely anywhere? . . .
(The tidal wave devours the shore:
There *are* no islands any more.)
There Are No Islands, Any More [1]
[June 14, 1940]

HENRY VOLLAM MORTON
[1892–]

One drink of wine, and you act like
a monkey; two drinks, and you strut
like a peacock; three drinks, and you
roar like a lion; and four drinks — you
behave like a pig.[2]
*In the Steps of St. Paul [1936].
Chap. 1*

The perfect place for a writer is in
the hideous roar of a city, with men
making a new road under his window
in competition with a barrel organ, and
on the mat a man waiting for the rent.
Ibid. Chap. 4

[1] Great Britain no longer is an island. The
strategic implication will be clear very soon.
England is an island in so far as she is lonely,
cut off from the world. Hunger is staring her
in the face. — HITLER: *Radio speech,* July 1,
1940
We cannot be an island. — FRANKLIN D.
ROOSEVELT: *Radio address,* March 8, 1941
[2] Moral of an Arabian story about Adam
and the fruit of a vine.

St. Nicholas, in addition to protect-
ing sailors, children, travellers, and
merchants, is also the patron saint of
pawnbrokers. The story goes that a
nobleman of the saint's native town,
Parara in Asia Minor, had lost all his
money, and did not know how he could
endow his three beautiful daughters. St.
Nicholas, hearing of his trouble, went
by night and flung through the window
three bags of gold with which the nobleman was able to provide handsome
dowries. These three bags are shown in
all early ikons as three gold apples, and
the gold apples of St. Nicholas are the
origin of the pawnbroker's sign.[1]
In the Steps of St. Paul. Chap. 7

REINHOLD NIEBUHR
[1892–]

Goodness, armed with power, is corrupted; and pure love without power is
destroyed.
Beyond Tragedy [1938]

Man's capacity for justice makes
democracy possible, but man's inclination to injustice makes democracy necessary.
*The Children of Light and the
Children of Darkness [1944]*

BASIL O'CONNOR
[1892–]

The world cannot continue to wage
war like physical giants and to seek
peace like intellectual pygmies.
*Address at National Conference of
Christians and Jews [1945]*

LEVERETT SALTONSTALL
[1892–]

The real New England Yankee is a
person who takes the midnight train
home from New York.
Press conference [May 4, 1939]

[1] *Webster's New International Dictionary*
says that the pawnbroker's three gilt balls
are "from the coat of arms of Lombardy.
The first moneylenders in London were
Lombards."

SIR OSBERT SITWELL
[1892–　]

Nothing exists which the British bour-
　geoisie
Does not understand;
Therefore there is no death
— And, of course, no life.
At the House of Mrs. Kinfoot

WENDELL LEWIS WILLKIE
[1892–1944]

There are no distant points in the
world any longer. . . . Our thinking
in the future must be world-wide
　Radio Address [October 26, 1942]
　and One World [1943]. Chap. 1

I believe the moral losses of expediency always far outweigh the temporary
gains. And I believe that every drop of
blood saved through expediency will
be paid for by twenty drawn by the
sword.[1]
　One World. Chap. 4

There exists in the world today a
gigantic reservoir of good will toward
us, the American people.
　Ibid. Chap. 10

Freedom is an indivisible word.[2] If
we want to enjoy it, and fight for it, we
must be prepared to extend it to everyone, whether they are rich or poor,
whether they agree with us or not, no
matter what their race or the color of
their skin.
　Ibid. Chap. 13

From the battlefields of Italy to the
gold-star homes here in America, Negroes have learned that there is nothing
more democratic than a bullet or a
splinter of steel.
　An American Program [1944].
　Chap. 2

The Constitution does not provide
for first and second class citizens.
　Ibid.

Our sovereignty is not something to
be hoarded, but something to be used.
　Ibid. Chap. 7

[1] See Lincoln, page 542a.
[2] See Litvinov, page 887a–887b.

FAITH BALDWIN
[1893–　]

I think that Life has spared those mor-
　tals much —
And cheated them of more — who have
　not kept
A breathless vigil by the little bed
Of some beloved child.
　Vigil

MORRIS BISHOP
[1893–　]

After the day is over
　And the passers-by are rare
The lights burn low in the barber-shop
　And the shades are drawn with care
To hide the haughty barbers
　Cutting each other's hair.
　The Tales the Barbers Tell

There I stood, and humbly scanned
　The miracle that sense appals,
And I watched the tourists stand
　Spitting in Niagara Falls.
　Public Aid for Niagara Falls.
　Stanza 4

OMAR BRADLEY
[1893–　]

But it [Pearl Harbor], and the subsequent lessons we learned, day by day,
until September 1945, should have
taught all military men that our military forces are one team — in the game
to win regardless of who carries the
ball. This is no time for "fancy dans"
who won't hit the line with all they
have on every play, unless they can
call the signals. Each player on this
team — whether he shines in the spot-
light of the backfield or eats dirt in
the line — must be an all-American.
　Testimony, Hearings Before the
　Committee on Armed Services,
　House of Representatives [Oc-
　tober 19, 1949]

Red China is not the powerful nation
seeking to dominate the world. Frankly,
in the opinion of the Joint Chiefs of
Staff, this strategy would involve us in
the wrong war, at the wrong place, at

the wrong time, and with the wrong enemy.

> *Testimony, Hearings Before the Committee on Armed Services and the Committee on Foreign Affairs, U. S. Senate* [*May 15, 1951*]

ELIZABETH COATSWORTH
[1893–   ]

To a life that seizes
  Upon content,
Locality seems
  But accident.
> *To Daughters, Growing Up.*
> *Stanza 7*

JAMES BRYANT CONANT
[1893–   ]

Behavior which appears superficially correct but is intrinsically corrupt always irritates those who see below the surface.
> *Baccalaureate Address, Harvard College* [*June 17, 1934*]

Slogans are both exciting and comforting, but they are also powerful opiates for the conscience. . . . Some of mankind's most terrible misdeeds have been committed under the spell of certain magic words or phrases.
> *Ibid.*

He who enters a university walks on hallowed ground.
> *Notes on the Harvard Tercentenary* [*1936*]

Each honest calling, each walk of life, has its own elite, its own aristocracy based on excellence of performance.
> *Our Fighting Faith. "In This Country There Are No Classes"* [1]

Liberty like charity must begin at home.
> *Ibid. Our Unique Heritage* [2]

[1] Baccalaureate Sermon, June 16, 1940. The title is taken from a statement in an address by JAMES A. GARFIELD [1831–1881]: *The Future of the Republic: Its Dangers and its Hopes* [1873].

[2] Address, opening of the first wartime

The primary concern of American education today is not the development of the appreciation of the "good life" in young gentlemen born to the purple. . . . Our purpose is to cultivate in the largest possible number of our future citizens an appreciation of both the responsibilities and the benefits which come to them because they are Americans and are free.
> *Annual Report to the Board of Overseers, Harvard University* [1]
> [*January 11, 1943*]

HANS FALLADA (RUDOLF DITZEN)
[1893–1947]

Little Man, What Now?
> *Title of novel* [*1932*]

HERMANN GOERING
[1893–1946]

Shoot first and inquire afterwards, and if you make mistakes, I will protect you.
> *Instruction for the Prussian Police, 1933*

HAROLD JOSEPH LASKI
[1893–1950]

It would be madness to let the purposes or the methods of private enterprise set the habits of the age of atomic energy.
> *Plan or Perish* [*1945*]

ANITA LOOS
[1893–   ]

Gentlemen always seem to remember blondes.
> *Gentlemen Prefer Blondes* [*1925*].
> *Chap. 1*

---

summer term, Harvard College, June 30, 1942.

[1] Describing his purpose, as President of Harvard University, in appointing a University Committee on the Objectives of a General Education in a Free Society. The committee's report was published [1945] under the title *General Education in a Free Society*.

She always believed in the old adage, "Leave them while you're looking good."
Gentlemen Prefer Blondes. Chap. 1
A girl never really looks as well as she does on board a steamship, or even a yacht.
Ibid.

JOHN PHILLIPS MARQUAND
[1893–1960]

It is worth while for anyone to have behind him a few generations of honest, hard-working ancestry.
The Late George Apley [*1937*]. *Chap. 3*
His father watched him across the gulf of years and pathos which always must divide a father from his son.
Ibid. Chap. 10
Marriage . . . is a damnably serious business, particularly around Boston.
Ibid. Chap. 11
There is a certain phase in the life of the aged when the warmth of the heart seems to increase in direct proportion with the years. This is a time of life when a solicitous family does well to watch affectionately over the vagaries of its unattached relatives, particularly of those who are comfortably off.
Ibid. Chap. 23

WILFRED OWEN
[1893–1918]

What passing-bells for these who died as cattle?
Only the monstrous anger of the guns.
Only the stuttering rifles' rapid rattle
Can patter out their hasty orisons.
The Anthem for Doomed Youth

DOROTHY PARKER
[1893–   ]

Where's the man could ease a heart
Like a satin gown?
The Satin Dress. Stanza 1

Yet this the need of woman, this her curse:
To range her little gifts, and give, and give,
Because the throb of giving's sweet to bear.
I Know I Have Been Happiest
Four be the things I am wiser to know:
Idleness, sorrow, a friend, and a foe.
Inventory
Four be the things I'd been better without:
Love, curiosity, freckles, and doubt.
Ibid.
And this is the sum of a lasting lore:
Scratch a lover, and find a foe.
Ballade of a Great Weariness. Stanza 1
Men seldom make passes
At girls who wear glasses.
News Item
Accursed from their birth they be
Who seek to find monogamy,
Pursuing it from bed to bed —
I think they would be better dead.
Reuben's Children
You are brief and frail and blue —
Little sisters, I am, too.
You are heaven's masterpieces —
Little loves, the likeness ceases.
Sweet Violets
Guns aren't lawful;
Nooses give;
Gas smells awful;
You might as well live.
Résumé
Why is it no one ever sent me yet
One perfect limousine, do you suppose?
Ah no, it's always just my luck to get
One perfect rose.
One Perfect Rose. Stanza 3
Then if my friendships break and bend,
There's little need to cry
The while I know that every foe
Is faithful till I die.
The Leal. Stanza 2
He lies below, correct in cypress wood,
And entertains the most exclusive worms.
Epitaph for a Very Rich Man
The man she had was kind and clean
And well enough for every day,

But, oh, dear friends, you should have
  seen
The one that got away!
> *The Fisherwoman*

There was nothing more fun than a
man!
> *The Little Old Lady in
> Lavender Silk*

The affair between Margot Asquith
and Margot Asquith will live as one of
the prettiest love stories in all literature.
> *Review in the New Yorker of
> the Autobiography of Margot
> Asquith*

SIR HERBERT READ
[1893–]

The only literature which is at the
same time vital and popular is the literature of the music-hall.
> *Phases of English Poetry [1928]*

Poetry can never again become a
popular art until the poet gives himself
wholly to "the cadence of consenting
feet."[1]
> *Ibid.*

The no-man's-years between the
wars. [1919–1939]
> *Annals of Innocence and
> Experience [1940]*

JOACHIM VON
RIBBENTROP
[1893–1945]

The Führer is always right.
> *Königsberg address,
> August 24, 1939*

ROBERT LEROY RIPLEY
[1893–1949]

Believe It or Not.
> *Title of syndicated
> newspaper feature*

[1] The quotation is from FRANCIS BARTON
GUMMERE: *The Beginnings of Poetry* [1901].

DOROTHY LEIGH SAYERS
[1893–1957]

Death seems to provide the minds of
the Anglo-Saxon race with a greater
fund of innocent amusement than any
other single subject . . . the tale must
be about dead bodies or very wicked
people, preferably both, before the
Tired Business Man can feel really
happy.
> *The Third Omnibus of Crime
> [1935]. Introduction*

Do you promise that your Detectives
shall well and truly detect the Crimes
presented to them, using those Wits
which it shall please you to bestow
upon them and not placing reliance
upon, nor making use of, Divine Revelation, Feminine Intuition, Mumbo-
Jumbo, Jiggery-Pokery, Coincidence or
the Act of God?
> *The Mind of the Maker [1941].
> Chap. XI (Membership oath of
> the Detection Club, London,
> quoted by Miss Sayers)*

HAROLD CLAYTON UREY [1]
[1893–]

We need first of all to be thoroughly
frightened.
> *Speech on the Atomic Bomb,
> December 3, 1945*

The most dangerous situation that
humanity has ever faced in all history.
> *One World or None [1946].
> Chap. 2*

JOHN VAN ALSTYN WEAVER
[1893–1938]

Don't you ever try to go there —
It's to dream of, not to find.
Lovely things like that is always
  Mostly in your mind.
> *Legend. Stanza 7*

Sure enough, the towers and castles
  Went like lightnin' out of sight —
Nothin' there but filthy Jersey
  On a drizzly night.
> *Ibid. Stanza 9*

[1] Winner of Nobel Prize for Physics, 1934.

WINIFRED WELLES
[1893–1939]

My squirrel with his tail curved up
Like half a silver lyre.
> *Silver for Midas. Stanza 4*

Oh all you safe and smooth of heart
  Listen to song from me,
Whose wooden throat was once a part
  Of the north side of a tree! [1]
> *The Violin. Stanza 4*

MAE WEST
[1893–   ]

Come up and see me sometime.
> *Diamond Lil* [2] *[1932]*

Beulah, peel me a grape.
> *She Done Him Wrong* [1933]

DON BLANDING
[1894–   ]

It's more than just an easy word for
  casual good-bye;
It's gayer than a greeting, and it's sadder than a sigh.
> *Aloha Oe: Its Meaning*

It's said a hundred different ways, in
  sadness and in joy,
Aloha means "I love you." So I say
  "Aloha Oe."
> *Ibid.*

EDWARD ESTLIN CUMMINGS [3]
[1894–1962]

All in green went my love riding
on a great horse of gold
into the silver dawn.
> *All in green went my love riding*
> *[1923]*

[1] Arbor viva, tacui; mortua, cano. (When I was part of a living tree, I was silent; now dead, I sing.) — *Inscription found on an old violin*

[2] The play was later made into a movie, *She Done Him Wrong*.

[3] The terror of typesetters, an enigma to book reviewers, and the special target of all the world's literary philistines. — *Publisher's note, Modern Library edition of The Enormous Room*

Softer be they than slippered sleep
the lean lithe deer
the fleet flown deer.
> *All in green went my love riding*

four lean hounds crouched low and
  smiling
my heart fell dead before.
> *Ibid.*

turning from the tremendous lie of
  sleep
i watch the roses of the day grow deep.
> *it is at moments after i have*
> *dreamed [1923]*

Humanity i love you because
when you're hard up you pawn your
intelligence to buy a drink.
> *Humanity i love you [1925]*

this is the garden: colours come and go,
frail azures fluttering from night's outer
  wing
strong silent greens serenely lingering,
absolute lights like baths of golden
  snow.
> *this is the garden [1925]*

    among
the slow deep trees perpetual of sleep
some silver-fingered fountain steals the
  world.
> *Ibid*

for life's not a paragraph
And death i think is no parenthesis.
> *Since feeling is first [1926]*

along the brittle treacherous bright
  streets
of memory comes my heart, singing like
an idiot, whispering like a drunken man

who(at a certain corner, suddenly)
  meets
the tall policeman of my mind.
> *along the brittle treacherous*
> *bright streets [1926]*

nobody, not even the rain, has such
  small hands
> *somewhere i have never*
> *travelled [1931]*

Always the beautiful answer who
asks a more beautiful question.
> *Collected Poems [1938].*
> *Introduction*

lady through whose profound and fragile lips

the sweet small clumsy feet of April
   came
into the ragged meadow of my soul.
Collected Poems. 189
King Christ, this world is all aleak;
and lifepreservers there are none:
and waves which only He may walk
Who dares to call Himself a man.
Ibid. 258
open your thighs to fate and (if you can
withholding nothing) World, conceive
   a man.
Ibid. 293
he sang his didn't he danced his did.
50 Poems. 29

RACHEL FIELD
[1894–1942]

You won't know why, and you can't
   say now
Such a change upon you came,
But — once you have slept on an
   island
You'll never be quite the same!
*If Once You Have Slept On An
Island [1926]*

ESTHER FORBES
[1894 ? –   ]

Women have almost a genius for
anti-climaxes.
O Genteel Lady! [1926]
Most American heroes of the Revolutionary period are by now two men,
the actual man and the romantic image.
Some are even three men — the actual
man, the image, and the debunked remains.
Paul Revere [1942]

AGNES KENDRICK GRAY
[1894–   ]

Sure, 'tis God's ways is very quare,
   An' far beyont my ken,
How o' the selfsame clay he makes
   Poets an' useful men.
The Shepherd to the Poet. Stanza 4

ALDOUS LEONARD HUXLEY
[1894–1963]

It is far easier to write ten passably
effective Sonnets, good enough to take
in the not too inquiring critic, than one
effective advertisement that will take in
a few thousand of the uncritical buying
public.
On the Margin [1923]
There are not enough *bon mots* in
existence to provide any industrious
conversationalist with a new stock for
every social occasion.
*Point Counter Point [1928].
Chap. 7*
A bad book is as much of a labour to
write as a good one; it comes as sin-
cerely from the author's soul.
Ibid. Chap. 13
There is no substitute for talent. In-
dustry and all the virtues are of no
avail.
Ibid.
Parodies and caricatures are the most
penetrating of criticisms.
Ibid. Chap. 28
There's only one corner of the uni-
verse you can be certain of improving,
and that's your own self.
Time Must Have a Stop [1944]
Blood of the world, time stanchless
   flows;
The wound is mortal and is mine.
Seasons
Over her the swan shook slowly free
The folded glory of his wings, and made
A white-walled tent of soft and lumi-
   nous shade.
Leda
A poor degenerate from the ape,
Whose hands are four, whose tail's a
   limb,
I contemplate my flaccid shape
And know I may not rival him
Save with my mind.
First Philosopher's Song
But when the wearied Band
Swoons to a waltz, I take her hand,
And there we sit in peaceful calm
Quietly sweating palm to palm.
Frascati's

JOSEPH HENRY JACKSON
[1894–1955]

Did you ever hear anyone say "That work had better be banned because I might read it and it might be very damaging to me"?

In the San Francisco Chronicle
[*1953*]

CHARLES LANGBRIDGE
MORGAN
[1894–   ]

The art of living does not consist in preserving and clinging to a particular mood of happiness, but in allowing happiness to change its form without being disappointed by the change; for happiness, like a child, must be allowed to grow up.

An English Retrospect [1]

Freedom from interruption may be counted by artists as not the least of the five freedoms.

A Fifth Freedom [2]

ROBERT NATHAN
[1894–   ]

Because my grief seems quiet and
    apart,
Think not for such a reason it is less.
True sorrow makes a silence in the
    heart,
Joy has its friends, but grief its lone-
    liness.

A Cedar Box [*1929*]. *Sonnet VII*

Toward men and toward God, she maintained a respectful attitude, lightened by the belief that in a crisis she could deal adequately with either of them.

The Road of Ages [*1935*].
Chap. 2

Bells in the country,
    They sing the heart to rest
When night is on the high road
    And day is in the west.

Bells in the Country

[1] *Menander's Mirror, Times Literary Supplement,* London, May 20, 1944.
[2] *Menander's Mirror,* April 28, 1945.

It is but just that there should rise,
At peace beneath our Western skies,
From out the hearts of free-born men,
This little town again.[1]

Lidice. Stanza 2

WESTBROOK PEGLER
[1894–   ]

The Era of Wonderful Nonsense.[2]

Mr. Gump Himself

For the fifth year in succession I have pored over the catalogue of dogs in the show at Madison Square Garden without finding a dog named Rover, Towser, Sport, Spot or Fido.

Who is the man who can call from his back door at night: "Here, Champion Alexander of Clane o' Wind-Holme! Here, Champion Alexander of Clane o' Wind-Holme"?

Here, Rover!

I am a member of the rabble in good standing.

The Lynching Story

After a quiet study of the rules and tools of civilized table warfare your correspondent has decided that the French combine the greatest simplicity with the best results.

France in One Easy Lesson

PHELPS PUTNAM
[1894–1948]

We have insulted you as Lady Luck.

Hymn to Chance

Hard-boiled, unbroken egg, what can
    you care
For the enfolded passion of the Rose?

Hasbrouck and the Rose

[1] On July 12, 1942, a group of Americans, predominantly of Czech origin, renamed their town of Stern Park Garden, Illinois, in memory of Lidice, the village destroyed by Hitler. The inscription on a granite shaft reads: "In memory of the people of Lidice, Czechoslovakia, destroyed by barbarism but living forever in the hearts of all those who love freedom, this monument is erected by the free people of America at Lidice, Illinois."
[2] The period of spending and speculation during the "Coolidge Prosperity."

KENNETH CLAIBORNE
ROYALL [1]
[1894–   ]

A "brass hat" is an officer of at least one rank higher than you whom you don't like and who doesn't like you.[2]
Speech, Chamber of Commerce, Wilson, North Carolina, February 15, 1946

BEARDSLEY RUML
[1894–   ]

It takes only a period of about a dozen years to implant a basic culture in the mind of man — the period between the age of two and the age of fourteen. In a psycho-biological sense, history, tradition and custom are only about twelve years old.
World Trade and Peace: Address, National Foreign Trade Convention, November 14, 1945

MARGARET E. SANGSTER
[1894–   ]

Oh, cakes and friends we should choose
    with care,
Not always the fanciest cake that's
    there
Is the best to eat! And the plainest
    friend
Is sometimes the finest one in the end!
French Pastry. Stanza 3

GENEVIEVE TAGGARD
[1894–1948]

Try tropic for your balm,
Try storm,
And after storm, calm.
Try snow of heaven, heavy, soft, and
    slow,
Brilliant and warm.
Nothing will help, and nothing do much
    harm.
Of the Properties of Nature for Healing an Illness. Stanza 1

[1] Brigadier-General in World War II.
[2] Some big brass hat from the War Office.
— JAMES HILTON: *Good-bye, Mr. Chips* [1934], *Chap. 14*

Terror touches me when I
Dream I am touching a butterfly.
The Enamel Girl

Defiant even now, it tugs and moans
To be untangled from these mother's
    bones.
With Child. Stanza 3

JAMES THURBER
[1894–1961]

Well, if I called the wrong number, why did you answer the 'phone?
Caption for cartoon

The War Between Men and Women.
Series of cartoons

Humor is emotional chaos remembered in tranquillity.[1]
Quoted by MAX EASTMAN *in The Enjoyment of Laughter* [1936]

Is Sex Necessary?
Title of Book [1929] *written with* E. B. WHITE

Let Your Mind Alone.
Title of Book [1937]

Early to rise and early to bed makes a male healthy and wealthy and dead.
Fables for Our Time [1940].
The Shrike and the Chipmunks

You might as well fall flat on your face as lean over too far backward.
Ibid. The Bear Who Let It Alone

MARK VAN DOREN
[1894–   ]

Wit is the only wall
Between us and the dark.
Wit. Stanza 1

He talked, and as he talked
    Wallpaper came alive;
Suddenly ghosts walked
    And four doors were five.
The Story Teller. Stanza 1

Grass nibbling inward
Like green fire.
Former Barn Lot. Stanza 3

The sun
Drew semicircles smooth and high.

[1] See Wordsworth, page 406a.

A week was seven domes across a desert,
And any afternoon took long to die.
The Difference. Stanza 1

DUKE OF WINDSOR (KING EDWARD VIII)
[1894–   ]

I have found it impossible to carry the heavy burden of responsibility and to discharge my duties as King as I would wish to do without the help and support of the woman I love.
Farewell broadcast after abdication [December 11, 1936]

RICHARD BUCKMINSTER FULLER
[1895–   ]

We must think of our whole economics in terms of a preventive pathology instead of a curative pathology.
Don't oppose forces; use them.
God is a verb,
Not a noun.
No More Secondhand God

KING GEORGE VI
[1895–1952]

The highest of distinctions is service to others.
Broadcast greeting to the empire after his coronation, May 12, 1937
We shall prevail.
Broadcast on declaration of war, September 3, 1939

ROBERT GRAVES
[1895–   ]

As you are woman, so be lovely:
As you are lovely, so be various,
Merciful as constant, constant as various,
So be mine, as I yours for ever.
Pygmalion to Galatea

With a fork drive Nature out,
She will ever yet return.[1]
Marigolds
Hate is a fear, and fear is rot
That cankers root and fruit alike:
Fight cleanly then, hate not, fear not
Strike with no madness when you strike.
Hate Not, Fear Not
"How is your trade, Aquarius,
This frosty night?"
"Complaints is many and various,
And my feet are cold," says Aquarius.
Star Talk. Stanza 5
I do not love the Sabbath,
The soapsuds and the starch,
The troops of solemn people
Who to Salvation march.
The Boy Out of Church
Resolved that church and Sabbath
Were never made for man.[2]
Ibid.
A well-chosen anthology is a complete dispensary of medicine for the more common mental disorders, and may be used as much for prevention as cure.
On English Poetry. XXIX
"Blonde or dark, sir?" says enough
Whether of women, drink, or snuff.
Blonde or Dark?
Truth-loving Persians do not dwell upon
The trivial skirmish fought near Marathon.
The Persian Version

ROBERT HILLYER
[1895–1961]

Men lied to them, and so they went to die.
Thermopylae and Golgotha [1919]
We whom life changes with its every whim
Remember now his steadfastness. In him
Was a perfection, an unconscious grace,

[1] Naturam expelles furca, tamen usque recurret. — HORACE [65–8 B.C.]: *Epistles, I, 10, 24*
[2] See *Mark, II, 27,* on page 1055b.

Life could not mar, and death can not
efface.
  A Parting in April. In Memoriam: Le Baron Russell Briggs
  [*1934*]
Each finger nail a crimson petal, seen
Through a pale garnishing of nicotine.
  A Letter to the Editor [*1936*]
Silence! the Columnist is on the
  sill! . . .
She enters with triumphant condescension
Exuding promises of Sunday mention.
Impishly coy, grandiloquent with
  power,
She bids await the inevitable hour
When printer's ink shall scatter her
  largesse
On writers who have won their own
  success.
  Ibid.

ROBERT KEITH LEAVITT
[1895–   ]

People don't ask for facts in making
up their minds. They would rather have
one good, soul-satisfying emotion than
a dozen facts.
  Voyages and Discoveries [*1939*]
You do not have to shout. But if you
whisper . . . the whisper had better
be good.
  Ibid. [*1940*]

LEWIS MUMFORD
[1895–   ]

People have hesitated to call Whitman's poems poetry; it is useless to
deny that they belong to sacred literature.
  The Golden Day [*1926*]. *V*
The jolly and comfortable bourgeois
tradition of the Victorian age, a state
of mind composed of felt slippers and
warm bellywash.
  Ibid. VIII
In Whitman and Melville letters

again became as racy as the jabber of
a waterside saloon.
  The Golden Day. VIII

EDWARD E. PARAMORE, JR.
[1895–   ]

Oh, the North Countree is a hard
  countree
That mothers a bloody brood;
And its icy arms hold hidden charms
  For the greedy, the sinful and lewd.
And strong men rust, from the gold
  and the lust
That sears the Northland soul.
  The Ballad of Yukon Jake [*1921*]
Oh, tough as a steak was Yukon
  Jake —
Hard-boiled as a picnic egg.
  Ibid.

FULTON JOHN SHEEN
[1895–   ]

Baloney is flattery so thick it cannot
be true, and blarney is flattery so thin
we like it.
  *Address before the Ancient
  Order of Hibernians, Boston*
  [*December 3, 1938*]

PIERRE VAN PAASSEN
[1895–   ]

That detached and baronial air of
superiority the Briton habitually affects when circumstances beyond his
control bring him into the presence of
creatures of a lesser breed.
  That Day Alone [*1941*]. *Sect. I*
Recklessness — that appearance of
courage, which is not true courage.
  Ibid. Sect. IV, 8
Half of our misery and weakness derives from the fact that we have broken
with the soil and that we have allowed
the roots that bound us to the earth to
rot. We have become detached from
the earth, we have abandoned her. And
a man who abandons nature has begun
to abandon himself.
  Ibid. Sect. VI

LEON SAMSON
[*Floruit* 1930]

Money is the power of impotence.
The New Humanism [*1930*].
Page 206

The Diplomat sits in silence, watching the world with his ears.
Ibid. Page 291

Property is the pivot of civilization.
Ibid. Page 316

War is a transfer of property from nation to nation.
Ibid.

Revolution is a transfer of property from class to class.
Ibid.

JOHN RODERIGO DOS PASSOS
[1896–   ]

The chilly December day
two shivering bicycle mechanics from Dayton, Ohio,[1]
first felt their homemade contraption whittled out of hickory sticks,
gummed together with Arnstein's bicycle cement,
stretched with muslin they'd sewn on their sister's sewingmachine in their own backyard on Hawthorn Street in Dayton, Ohio,
soar into the air
above the dunes and the wide beach at Kitty Hawk.[2]
The Big Money [*1936*]. (*The Campers at Kitty Hawk*)

IRA C. EAKER [3]
[1896–   ]

I do not intend to do any talking until we have done more fighting, but this I can say now. I hope when we have gone you will all be glad we came.
Speech before Mayor, the Town Council and servicemen welcoming the American Eighth Air Force at High Wycombe, England, July, 1942

[1] The Wright brothers, Wilbur and Orville.
[2] December 17, 1903.
[3] Lieutenant General, United States Air Force.

IRWIN EDMAN
[1896–1954]

Whene'er with wild elation
Tremblingly I smite the lyre,
Comes the swift and kind damnation:
"He's a clever versifier."
The Curse of Faint Praise

The gift of gaiety may itself be the greatest good fortune, and the most serious step toward maturity.
In The Bookman [*May, 1926*]

F. SCOTT FITZGERALD
[1896–1940]

The victor belongs to the spoils.
The Beautiful and Damned [*1921*]

The test of a first-rate intelligence is the ability to hold two opposed ideas in the mind at the same time, and still retain the ability to function.
The Crack-up [*1936*]

In a real dark night of the soul it is always three o'clock in the morning.[1]
Ibid.

It was about then [1920] that I wrote a line which certain people will not let me forget: "She was a faded but still lovely woman of twenty-seven."
Early Success [*1937*]

Egyptian Proverb: The worst things:
To be in bed and sleep not,
To want for one who comes not,
To try to please and please not.
Note-Books [2]

The rhythm of the weekend, with its birth, its planned gaieties, and its announced end, followed the rhythm of life and was a substitute for it.
Ibid.

Show me a hero and I will write you a tragedy.
Ibid.

Fitzgerald. The rich are different from us.

[1] See Napoleon, page 400a.
[2] In *The Crack-up*, edited by Edmund Wilson [1945].

Hemingway. Yes, they have more money.
Note-Books [1]

It grows harder to write, because there is much less weather than when I was a boy and practically no men and women at all.
Ibid.

"I had to sink my yacht to make the guests go home."
Ibid.

Draw your chair up close to the edge of the precipice and I'll tell you a story.
Ibid.

It is in the thirties that we want friends. In the forties we know they won't save us any more than love did.
Ibid.

The easiest way to get a reputation is to go outside the fold, shout around for a few years as a violent atheist or a dangerous radical, and then crawl back to the shelter.
Ibid.

The hangover became a part of the day as well allowed-for as the Spanish siesta.
My Lost City [2]

HAROLD N. GILBERT
[1896–   ]

Keep 'em flying.
Slogan of the Air Forces, poster caption, World War II

LOUIS GINSBERG
[1896–   ]

Love that is hoarded moulds at last
Until we know some day
The only thing we ever have
Is what we give away.
Song. Stanza 1

GRAHAM LEE HEMMINGER
[1896–1949]

Tobacco is a dirty weed. I like it.
It satisfies no normal need. I like it.

It makes you thin, it makes you lean,
It takes the hair right off your bean.
It's the worst darn stuff I've ever seen.
I like it. [1]
Tobacco

JOE JACOBS
[1896–1940]

We was robbed!
After the fight between Max Schmeling and Jack Sharkey, June 21, 1932, when Sharkey had been awarded the decision and the heavyweight title, Jacobs, Schmeling's manager, shouted into the radio microphone this protest which was heard from coast to coast

I should of stood in bed.
Jacobs left a sick-bed to go to Detroit in October, 1935, to attend the World's Series. He bet on Chicago, which lost to Detroit. When he returned to New York he made this comment to the sports writers who came to interview him.

ERIC A. JOHNSTON
[1896–   ]

America and defeat cannot be made to rhyme.
America Unlimited [1944]

DODIE SMITH
[1896–   ]

I have found that sitting in a place where you have never sat before can be inspiring.
I Capture the Castle

DIXIE WILLSON
[1896–   ]

He may look just the same to you,
And he may be just as fine,
But the next-door dog is the next-door dog,
And mine — is — mine!
Next-Door Dog

[1] Quoted in a footnote by Edmund Wilson.
[2] In *The Crack-up,* edited by Edmund Wilson [1945].

[1] First published in *Penn State Froth,* November, 1915.

LUTHER W. YOUNGDAHL
[1896–   ]

When public excitement runs high as to alien ideologies, is the time when we must be particularly alert not to impair the ancient landmarks set up in the Bill of Rights.
> *United States* v. *Lattimore, 112 F.*
> *Supp. 507, 518, May 2, 1953*

JOSEPH AUSLANDER
[1897–   ]

Spring had come
Like the silver needle-note of a fife,
Like a white plume and a green lance
    and a glittering knife
And a jubilant drum.
> *Steel*

ELIZABETH ASQUITH BIBESCO
[1897–1945]

I have made a great discovery.
What I love belongs to me. Not the chairs and tables in my house, but the masterpieces of the world.
It is only a question of loving them enough.
> *Balloons* [1923]

Being in a hurry is one of the tributes he pays to life.
> *Ibid.*

It is sometimes the man who opens the door who is the last to enter the room.
> *The Fir and the Palm* [1924].
> *Chap. 13*

You are such a wonderful Baedeker to life. All the stars are in the right places.
> *Ibid.*

It is never any good dwelling on good-byes. It is not the being together that it prolongs, it is the parting.
> *Ibid. Chap. 15*

BERNARD DE VOTO
[1897–1955]

New England is a finished place. Its destiny is that of Florence or Venice, not Milan, while the American empire careens onward toward its unpredicted end. . . . It is the first American section to be finished, to achieve stability in the conditions of its life. It is the first old civilization, the first permanent civilization in America.
> *New England: There She Stands.*
> *Harper's Magazine, March, 1932*

The West begins where the average annual rainfall drops below twenty inches. When you reach the line which marks that drop — for convenience, the one hundredth meridian — you have reached the West.
> *The Plundered Province. Harper's*
> *Magazine, August, 1934*

Pessimism is only the name that men of weak nerves give to wisdom.
> *Mark Twain: The Ink of History.*
> *Address, University of Missouri,*
> *December, 1935*

Art is the terms of an armistice signed with fate.
> *Mark Twain at Work* [1942]

The achieved West had given the United States something that no people had ever had before, an internal, domestic empire.
> *The Year of Decision* [1943]

Between the amateur and the professional, . . . there is a difference not only in degree but in kind. The skillful man is, within the function of his skill, a different integration, a different nervous and muscular and psychological organization. . . . A tennis player or a watchmaker or an airplane pilot is an automatism but he is also criticism and wisdom.
> *Across the Wide Missouri* [1947]

Novelists, whatever else they may be besides, are also children talking to children — in the dark.
> *The World of Fiction* [1950]

You can no more keep a martini in the refrigerator than you can keep a kiss there. The proper union of gin and vermouth is a great and sudden glory; it is one of the happiest marriages on earth and one of the shortest-lived.
> *The Hour* [1951]

The water of life was given to us to

make us see for a while that we are more nearly men and women, more nearly kind and gentle and generous, pleasanter and stronger, than without its vision there is any evidence we are.
The Hour [*1951*]

One of the facts which define the United States is that its national and its imperial boundaries are the same. Another is that it is a political unit which occupies a remarkably coherent geographical unit of continental extent.
The Course of Empire [*1952*]

History abhors determinism but cannot tolerate chance.
Ibid.

The dawn of knowledge is usually the false dawn.
Ibid.

SIR ANTHONY EDEN
[1897–   ]

Every succeeding scientific discovery makes greater nonsense of old-time conceptions of sovereignty.
Speech, House of Commons, November 22, 1945

WILLIAM FAULKNER
[1897–1962]

He [the writer] must teach himself that the basest of all things is to be afraid; and, teaching himself that, forget it forever, leaving no room in his workshop for anything but the old verities and truths of the heart, the old universal truths lacking which any story is ephemeral and doomed — love and honor and pity and pride and compassion and sacrifice.
Speech upon receiving the Nobel Prize, Stockholm, December 10, 1950

I decline to accept the end of man.
Ibid.

I believe that man will not merely endure: he will prevail.
Ibid.

PAUL JOSEPH GOEBBELS
[1897–1945]

We can do without butter, but, despite all our love of peace, not without arms. One cannot shoot with butter but with guns.[1]
Address in Berlin, January 17, 1936

DAVID McCORD
[1897–   ]

A handful of sand is an anthology of the universe.
Once and for All [*1929*]. *Introduction*

Call home the child, whose credulous first hours
Burn at the heart of living, and surprise
The better reason with unbidden truth.
A Bucket of Bees [*1934*]

March is outside the door
Flaming some old desire
As man turns uneasily from his fire.
The Crows [*1934*]

The cricket's gone, we only hear machines;
In erg and atom they exact their pay.
And life is largely lived on silver screens,
And chemistry anneals the common clay.
Ballade of Time and Space [*1935*]

By and by
God caught his eye.
Epitaphs: The Waiter

Still for us where Cottons mather
In the spring the Willas cather
As of yore.
And What's More: On Stopping at a New Hampshire Inn [*1941*]

I recommend for plain dis-ease
A good post-operative sneeze;
You might as well be on the rack
When every stitch takes up its slack.
Ibid. Convalescence: The Sneeze

[1] Probably the origin of the slogan, "Guns or butter," popularly attributed to Hermann Goering, who in a radio broadcast later in the year said: "Guns will make us powerful; butter will only make us fat."

The sun lies supple on the bricks;
I walk the fluent street.
    Yellow Chartreuse [*1941*]

I want to know not his earning power
but his yearning power.[1]
    Epigram

RUTH PITTER
[1897–   ]

Though our world burn, the small dim
    words
Stand here in steadfast grace,
And sing, like the indifferent birds
About a ruined place.
    On an Old Poem. Stanza 2

I go about, but cannot find
The blood-relations of the mind.
    The Lost Tribe. Stanza 1

ERICH MARIA REMARQUE
[1897–   ]

The army report confined itself to
the single sentence: All quiet on the
Western Front.
    *All Quiet on the Western
    Front* [2] [*1929*]

ANDERSON M. SCRUGGS
[1897–   ]

Yet after brick and steel and stone are
    gone,
And flesh and blood are dust, the dream
    lives on.
    Sonnet. Only the Dream is Real

THORNTON NIVEN WILDER
[1897–   ]

The whole purport of literature,
which is the notation of the heart. Style
is but the faintly contemptible vessel
in which the bitter liquid is recommended to the world.
    The Bridge of San Luis Rey
    [*1927*]. *II*

[1] There are three ingredients in the good
life: learning, earning, and yearning. —
CHRISTOPHER MORLEY: *Parnassus on Wheels*
[1917], *Chap. 10*
[2] Im Westen Nichts Neues.

For what human ill does not dawn
seem to be an alleviation?
    The Bridge of San Luis Rey. III

We come from a world where we
have known incredible standards of excellence, and we dimly remember beauties which we have not seized again.
    Ibid. IV

A man looks pretty small at a wedding, George. All those good women
standing shoulder to shoulder, making
sure that the knot's tied in a mighty
public way.
    Our Town [*1938*]

The dead don't stay interested in us
living people for very long. Gradually,
gradually, they let go hold of the earth
. . . and the ambitions they had . . .
and the pleasures they had . . . and
the things they suffered . . . and the
people they loved. They get weaned
away from earth — that's the way I
put it, weaned away.
    Ibid.

That's what it was to be alive. To
move about in a cloud of ignorance; to
go up and down trampling on the feelings of those about you. To spend and
waste time as though you had a million years. To be always at the mercy
of one self-centered passion, or another. Now you know — that's the
happy existence you wanted to go back
to.
    Ibid.

STEPHEN VINCENT BENÉT
[1898–1943]

I died in my boots like a pioneer
With the whole wide sky above me.
    The Ballad of William Sycamore

He could fiddle all the bugs off a sweet-
    potato-vine.
    The Mountain Whippoorwill
    [*1923*]. *Stanza 22*

Oh, Georgia booze is mighty fine booze,
The best yuh ever poured yuh,
But it eats the soles right offen yore
    shoes,
For Hell's broke loose in Georgia.
    Ibid. Stanza 48

He cleansed and anointed, took fresh
apparel,
And worshiped the Lord in a tuneful
carol.
> *King David* [*1923*]. *Part VI,*
> *Stanza 5*

Down where the taproots of New England trees
Suck bare existence from the broken
stones.
> *The Golden Corpse* [*1925*].
> *Sonnet 4*

The years have hardier tasks
Than listening to a whisper or a sigh.
They creep among us with a bag of
masks
And fit them to our brows obsequiously.
> *Ibid. Sonnet 5*

I have fallen in love with American
names,
The sharp names that never get fat,
The snakeskin-titles of mining-claims,
The plumed war-bonnet of Medicine
Hat,
Tucson and Deadwood and Lost Mule
Flat.
> *American Names* [*1927*]. *Stanza 1*

American Muse, whose strong and
diverse heart
So many men have tried to understand
But only made it smaller with their
art,
Because you are as various as your
land.
> *John Brown's Body* [*1928*].
> *Invocation*

Thames and all the rivers of the kings
Ran into Mississippi and were drowned.
> *Ibid.*

Honesty rare as a man without self-
pity,
Kindness as large and plain as a prairie
wind.
> *Ibid.*

The small, dim noises, thousand-fold,
That all old houses and forests hold.
> *Ibid. Book 2*

Make war on the men — the ladies
have too-long memories.
> *Ibid. Book 4*

Broad-streeted Richmond . . .
The trees in the streets are old trees
used to living with people,
Family-trees that remember your
grandfather's name.
> *John Brown's Body. Book 4*

Stonewall Jackson, wrapped in his
beard and his silence.
> *Ibid.*

Such horses are
The jewels of the horseman's hands
and thighs,
They go by the word and hardly need
the rein.
> *Ibid.*

A great victor, in defeat as great,
No more, no less, always himself in
both.
> *Ibid.*

The ant finds kingdoms in a foot of
ground.
> *Ibid.*

But all of them are sure they know
God's will.
I am the only man who does not know
it.
> *Ibid. Book 5*

"Let us cross the river," he said, "and
rest under the shade of the trees." [1]
> *Ibid. Book 6*

Sherman's buzzin' along to de sea,
Like Moses ridin' on a bumblebee.
> *Ibid. Book 8*

Rolling, rolling from Arkansas, Kansas,
Iowa,
Rolling from Ohio, Wisconsin, Illinois,
Rolling and shouting:
Till, at last, it is Mississippi,
The Father of Waters. [2]
> *Ode to Walt Whitman* [*1935*]. *I*

This is the man they ate at the green
table
Pulling their gloves on ere they touched
the meat.
This is the fruit of war, the fruit of
peace,

[1] Stonewall Jackson's last words actually
were, "Let us cross the river and rest in the
shade." [May 10, 1863]
[2] See Lincoln, page 540b.

The ripeness of invention, the new lamb.
> *Litany for Dictatorships* [*1936*]

We thought we were done with these things but we were wrong.
We thought, because we had power, we had wisdom.
> *Ibid.*

Our fathers and ourselves sowed dragon's teeth.
Our children know and suffer the armed men.
> *Ibid.*

If two New Hampshiremen aren't a match for the devil, we might as well give the country back to the Indians.
> *The Devil and Daniel Webster* [*1936*]

Even the damned may salute the eloquence of Mr. Webster.
> *Ibid.*

The fall with his sachem colors, the summer wind by the shore,
The spring like an Indian runner, beautiful, stripped, and swift,
They knew these things in their season
— and yet there was something more
And they thought not only of harvest, when they thanked their God for His gift.
> *Ode for the Tercentenary of the Founding of New Haven, Connecticut, June 6, 1938*

Our earth is but a small star in the great universe. Yet of it we can make, if we choose, a planet unvexed by war, untroubled by hunger or fear, undivided by senseless distinctions of race, color or theory.
> *Prayer, written for and read by President Franklin D. Roosevelt to the United Nations on Flag Day, June 14, 1942*

They were half of the first families in Virginia.
Well, where do you start, when you start counting F.F.V.s?
> *Western Star* [*1943*]. *Book I, Page 81*

That queer sense of relief and shame
Which comes to those who make sensible decisions.
> *Western Star. Book I, Page 128*

There were human beings aboard the Mayflower,
Not merely ancestors.
> *Ibid. Page 133*

Remember that when you say
"I will have none of this exile and this stranger
For his face is not like my face and his speech is strange,"
You have denied America with that word.
> *Ibid. Page 180*

HORACE GREGORY
[1898–   ]

My boyhood saw
Greek islands floating over Harvard Square.[1]
> *Chorus for Survival. XIV*

CECILY R. HALLACK
[1898–1938]

Lord of the pots and pipkins, since I have no time to be
A saint by doing lovely things and vigilling with Thee,
By watching in the twilight dawn, and storming Heaven's gates,
Make me a saint by getting meals and washing up the plates!
> *The Divine Office of the Kitchen. Stanza 1*

CLIVE STAPLES LEWIS
[1898–1963]

The safest road to Hell is the gradual one — the gentle slope, soft underfoot, without sudden turnings, without milestones, without signposts.
> *The Screwtape Letters* [*1941*]. *XII*

The Future is something which everyone reaches at the rate of sixty minutes an hour, whatever he does, whoever he is.
> *Ibid. XXV*

[1] The speaker in the poem is Emerson.

The long, dull, monotonous years of middle-aged prosperity or middle-aged adversity are excellent campaigning weather [for the Devil].

The Screwtape Letters. XXVIII

ANTHONY CLEMENT McAULIFFE
[1898–]

Nuts!

Reply [December 23, 1944] to German major and captain who brought an ultimatum from their commander, demanding the surrender of the men of the 101st Airborne Division who had been trapped for seven days at Bastogne

DONALD CULROSS PEATTIE
[1898–]

It is natural that women should like the birds whose domestic affairs can be observed under the eaves; they love the sweetest singers, the brightest plumage, the species not too shy to be seen at close range. For them the waders and swimmers, the awkward of leg, the harsh of cry, the wild of soul, have seldom the same appeal. But that which flees from men, that will men have. Women of all people ought to understand this, but they do not, quite.

An Almanac for Moderns [1935].
November 9

In Thomas Henry Huxley Darwinism had a champion in invincible armor. For sheer glitter his mind has seldom had an equal in any land or age and he laid waste about him with the weapon of truth. "The cradle of every science," he chuckled, "is surrounded by dead theologians as that of Hercules was with strangled serpents."

Ibid. February 13

The beauty of a butterfly's wing, the beauty of all things, is not a slave to purpose, a drudge sold to futurity. It is excrescence, superabundance, random ebullience, and sheer delightful waste to be enjoyed in its own high right.

An Almanac for Moderns.
March 13

The time to hear bird music is between four and six in the morning. Seven o'clock is not too late, but by eight the fine rapture is over, due, I suspect, to the contentment of the inner man that comes with breakfast; a poet should always be hungry or have a lost love.

Ibid. April 22

AMELIA EARHART PUTNAM
[1898–1937]

Courage is the price that life exacts for granting peace.
The soul that knows it not, knows no release
From little things.

Courage

DOROTHY E. REID

A goosegirl ermined is a goosegirl still
And geese will gabble everywhere she goes.

Not in Andersen

LOUIS ADAMIC
[1899–1951]

There is a certain blend of courage, integrity, character and principle which has no satisfactory dictionary name but has been called different things at different times in different countries. Our American name for it is "guts."

A Study in Courage [1] [1944]

NOEL COWARD
[1899–]

Mad dogs and Englishmen go out in the mid-day sun;
The Japanese don't care to, the Chinese wouldn't dare to;
Hindus and Argentines sleep firmly from twelve to one,
But Englishmen detest a siesta.

Mad Dogs and Englishmen

[1] An essay on Marshal Tito of Yugoslavia.

In Rangoon the heat of noon is just
what the natives shun . . .
In Bangkok at twelve o'clock they foam
at the mouth and run . . .
In Bengal to move at all is seldom if
ever done.
Mad Dogs and Englishmen

HART CRANE
[1899–1932]

Adagios of islands, O my Prodigal.
Voyages [1926]. *II*
Damp tonnage and alluvial march of
days . . .
Tortured with history, its one will —
flow.
The Bridge [1930]. *The River*
(*Mississippi*)
Bunched in mutual glee
The bearings glint, — O murmurless
and shined
In oilrinsed circles of blind ecstasy!
Ibid. The Power House
O, early following thee, I searched the
hill
Blue-writ and odor-firm with violets.
To Walt Whitman
Why do I often meet your visage here,[1]
Your eyes like agate lanterns — on and
on
Below the toothpaste and the dandruff
ads?
The Tunnel (*New York Subway*)

ERNEST HAYCOX
[1899–1950]

No sensible man watches his feet
hit ground. He looks ahead to see what
kind of ground they'll hit next.
Pioneer Loves. Call This
Land Home

ERNEST HEMINGWAY [2]
[1899–1961]

The real thing, the sequence of motion and fact which made the emotion
and which would be as valid in a year

[1] Edgar Allan Poe.
[2] Awarded the Nobel Prize in 1954 for
The Old Man and the Sea [1952].

or in ten years or, with luck and if you
stated it purely enough, always, was
beyond me and I was working very
hard to try to get it.
Death in the Afternoon [1932].
Chap. 1
So far, about morals, I know only
that what is moral is what you feel
good after and what is immoral is what
you feel bad after.
Ibid.
All our words from loose using have
lost their edge.
Ibid. Chap. 7
Bullfighting is the only art in which
the artist is in danger of death and in
which the degree of brilliance in the
performance is left to the fighter's
honor.
Ibid. Chap. 9
When writing a novel a writer should
create living people; people not characters. A *character* is a caricature.
Ibid. Chap. 16
Prose is architecture, not interior
decoration, and the Baroque is over.
Ibid.
There are some things which cannot
be learned quickly, and time, which is
all we have, must be paid heavily for
their acquiring. They are the very simplest things and because it takes a
man's life to know them the little new
that each man gets from life is very
costly and the only heritage he has to
leave.
Ibid.
Every novel which is truly written
contributes to the total of knowledge
which is there at the disposal of the
next writer who comes, but the next
writer must pay, always, a certain
nominal percentage in experience to
be able to understand and assimilate
what is available as his birthright and
what he must, in turn, take his departure from.
Ibid.
A serious writer is not to be confused with a solemn writer. A serious

writer may be a hawk or a buzzard or even a popinjay, but a solemn writer is always a bloody owl.
Death in the Afternoon. Chap. 16

A growing ecstasy of ordered, formal, passionate, increasing disregard for death. . . . It is impossible to believe the emotional and spiritual intensity and pure, classic beauty that can be produced by a man, an animal and a piece of scarlet serge draped over a stick.
Ibid. Chap. 18

All modern American literature comes from one book by Mark Twain called *Huckleberry Finn.* If you read it you must stop where the Nigger Jim is stolen from the boys. That is the real end. The rest is just cheating. But it's the best book we've had. All American writing comes from that. There was nothing before. There has been nothing as good since.
The Green Hills of Africa [*1935*]. *Chap. 1*

Not this August, nor this September; you have this year to do in what you like. Not next August, nor next September; that is still too soon; they are still too prosperous from the way things pick up when armament factories start at near capacity; they never fight as long as money can still be made without. . . . But the year after that or the year after that they fight.
Notes on the Next War [1]

The Fifth Column.[2]
Title of play [*1938*]

The world is a fine place and worth fighting for.
For Whom the Bell Tolls [*1940*]

And he felt the earth move out and away from under them.
Ibid.

[1] In *Esquire,* September, 1935.
[2] The phrase originated in a radio address by one of Franco's generals, Emilio Mola, during the Spanish Civil War [1936–1939]. He was leading four columns of troops against Madrid, and boasted that he had a "fifth column" of sympathizers within Madrid who would support him.

Cowardice, as distinguished from panic, is almost always simply a lack of ability to suspend the functioning of the imagination. Learning to suspend your imagination and live completely in the very second of the present with no before and no after is the greatest gift a soldier can acquire.
Men at War [*1942*]. *Introduction*

Easy writing makes hard reading.
Quoted in SAMUEL PUTNAM, *Paris Was Our Mistress* [*1947*]

The first and most important thing of all, at least for writers today, is to strip language clean, to lay it bare down to the bone.
Ibid.

All good books are alike in that they are truer than if they had really happened and after you are finished reading one you will feel that all that happened to you and afterwards it all belongs to you; the good and the bad, the ecstasy, the remorse and sorrow, the people and the places and how the weather was. If you can get so that you can give that to people, then you are a writer.
Quoted in CARLOS BAKER, *Hemingway: The Writer as Artist* [*1952*], *Chap. 3*

ROBERT MAYNARD HUTCHINS
[1899–   ]

The most distressing aspect of the world into which you are going is its indifference to the basic issues, which now, as always, are moral issues.
Convocation Address, University of Chicago, June, 1945

We call Japanese soldiers fanatics when they die rather than surrender, whereas American soldiers who do the same thing are heroes.
Ibid.

A world community means common understanding, a common tradition, common ideas, and common ideals.

. . . The task is overwhelming, and the chance of success is slight. We must take the chance or die.

The Atomic Bomb versus Civilization, December, 1945

We do not know what education could do for us, because we have never tried it.

Ibid.

The policy of repression of ideas cannot work and never has worked.

Testimony before the Boyles Committee [1949]

ERIC LINKLATER
[1899–]

Scratch my back with a garden rake.

The Pirates in the Deep Green Sea [1949]. Chap. 2

ALAN PORTER
[1899–1942]

Every countenance
That warms and lights the heart of the beholder
Shews, clear and true, the signature of pain.

The Signature of Pain

Let him that beds a princess fear
To show himself too free,
And ceremoniously draw near:
There should between true lovers be
An excellent immodesty.

A Plea That Shame Be Forgotten

I am not one that would be thinned
Into an immaterial wind:
I have no longing to be seen
A part of April's fledge of green,
Or burn where summer suns have been.

Death. Stanza 2

Were death forgotten, days were white
Circles of unimpaired delight.

Ibid. Stanza 4

LELAND STOWE
[1899–]

An American will tinker with anything he can put his hands on. But how rarely can he be persuaded to tinker with an abstract idea.

They Shall Not Sleep [1944]

E. B. WHITE
[1899–]

The critic leaves at curtain fall
To find, in starting to review it,
He scarcely saw the play at all
For watching his reaction to it.

Critic

All poets who, when reading from their own works, experience a choked feeling, are major. For that matter, all poets who read from their own works are major, whether they choke or not.

How to Tell a Major Poet from a Minor Poet

"It's broccoli, dear."
"I say it's spinach, and I say the hell with it."

Caption for cartoon by Carl Rose in The New Yorker

Commuter — one who spends his life
In riding to and from his wife;
A man who shaves and takes a train
And then rides back to shave again.

Commuter

It is easier for a man to be loyal to his club than to his planet; the by-laws are shorter, and he is personally acquainted with the other members.

One Man's Meat

Democracy is the recurrent suspicion that more than half of the people are right more than half of the time.

World Government and Peace [1]

His words leap across rivers and mountains, but his thoughts are still only six inches long.

Ibid.

Everybody likes to hear about a man laying down his life for his country, but nobody wants to hear about a country giving her shirt for her planet.

Ibid.

[1] Reprinted from *The New Yorker*, 1943–1945.

OSCAR WILLIAMS
[1900–   ]

The prodigious exuberance of the miniature human beings
Tests the chutes of gravitation, seventeen trees from the zoo.
The Children's Playground
Get up and out, my man, the day is bursting with moments . . .
Rise, my good man, from your bed of straws in the wind.
The Answer

DENIS WILLIAM BROGAN
[1900–   ]

The Englishman is interested in contemporary America. It evokes no response to tell him that Boston is like an English town. He has seen quite enough English towns and would rather hear about New York or Chicago, which are not like English towns.
The English People [1943]
American social fences have to be continually repaired; in England they are like wild hedges; they grow if left alone.
Ibid.
A people that has licked a more formidable enemy than Germany or Japan, primitive North America . . . a country whose national motto has been "root, hog, or die."
The American Character [1944]
Any well-established village in New England or the northern Middle West could afford a town drunkard, a town atheist, and a few Democrats.
Ibid.

JOHN MASON BROWN
[1900–   ]

Brutus seemed no more than a resounding set of vocal cords wrapped up in a toga.
Two on the Aisle [1938]
To many people dramatic criticism must seem like an attempt to tattoo soap bubbles.
Broadway in Review [1940]

Death re-creates an individual out of someone who has fallen singly from the ranks. In his loneliness by a foreign roadside, this man or that ceases to be Government Issue, a mass commodity produced by a mass response out of a mass need and hope. He once again becomes man's issue, and woman's, too.
Many a Watchful Night [1944]

ELIZABETH, QUEEN MOTHER OF ENGLAND
[1900–   ]

The children will not leave unless I do. I shall not leave unless their father does, and the King will not leave the country in any circumstances whatever.
Reported answer to press query regarding the Princesses' leaving England after the bombing of Buckingham Palace in 1940

JAMES HILTON
[1900–1954]

Anno domini — that's the most fatal complaint of all in the end.
Good-bye, Mr. Chips [1934]. *Chap. 1*
The austere serenity of Shangri-La. Its forsaken courts and pale pavilions shimmered in repose from which all the fret of existence had ebbed away, leaving a hush as if moments hardly dared to pass.
Lost Horizon [1933]. *Chap. 5*
When the High Lama asked him whether Shangri-La was not unique in his experience, and if the Western world could offer anything in the least like it, he answered with a smile: "Well, yes — to be quite frank it reminds me very slightly of Oxford."
Ibid. Chap. 9
Perhaps the exhaustion of the passions is the beginning of wisdom, if you care to alter the proverb. That also, my son, is the doctrine of Shangri-La.
Ibid. Chap. 10
Memory put a red star in the corner like pictures in a gallery that get sold.
Time and Time Again [1953]

If you forgive people enough you belong to them, and they to you, whether either person likes it or not — squatter's rights of the heart.
Time and Time Again

RICHARD HUGHES
[1900–   ]

Puddings should be
Full of currants, for me:
Boiled in a pail,
Tied in the tail
Of an old bleached shirt:
So hot that they hurt.
Poets, Painters, Puddings

MARTHA OSTENSO
[1900–   ]

Pity the Unicorn,
Pity the Hippogriff,
Souls that were never born
Out of the land of If!
The Unicorn and the Hippogriff.
Stanza 1

ERNIE PYLE
[1900–1945]

I write from the worm's-eye point of view.
Here Is Your War [*1943*]

If you go long enough without a bath even the fleas will let you alone.
Ibid.

Then darkness enveloped the whole American armada. Not a pinpoint of light showed from those hundreds of ships as they surged on through the night toward their destiny, carrying across the ageless and indifferent sea tens of thousands of young men, fighting for . . . for . . . well, at least for each other.[1]
Brave Men [*1944*]

ADLAI STEVENSON
[1900–1965]

More important than winning the election, is governing the nation. That

[1] Description of the Normandy beachhead, June, 1944.

is the test of a political party — the acid, final test.
Speech accepting nomination, Democratic National Convention, Chicago, July 26, 1952

Let's talk sense to the American people. Let's tell them the truth, that there are no gains without pains.
Ibid.

What do we mean by patriotism in the context of our times? . . . A patriotism that puts country ahead of self; a patriotism which is not short, frenzied outbursts of emotion, but the tranquil and steady dedication of a lifetime. There are words that are easy to utter, but this is a mighty assignment. For it is often easier to fight for principles than to live up to them.[1]
Speech, New York City, August 27, 1952

When an American says that he loves his country, he means not only that he loves the New England hills, the prairies glistening in the sun, the wide and rising plains, the great mountains, and the sea. He means that he loves an inner air, an inner light in which freedom lives and in which a man can draw the breath of self-respect.
Ibid.

This is the first time I have ever heard of a party going into battle under the slogan, "Throw the rascals in."
Speech, Phoenix, Arizona, September 12, 1952

A hungry man is not a free man.
Speech, Kasson, Minnesota, September 6, 1952

A wise man does not try to hurry history.
Speech, San Francisco, September 9, 1952

The time to stop a revolution is at the beginning, not the end.
Ibid.

Your public servants serve you right.
Speech, Los Angeles, September 11, 1952

[1] See Thackeray, page 565b.

Those who corrupt the public mind are just as evil as those who steal from the public purse.
Speech, Albuquerque, New Mexico, September 12, 1952

Nature is neutral. Man has wrested from nature the power to make the world a desert or to make the deserts bloom. There is no evil in the atom; only in men's souls.[1]
Speech, Hartford, Connecticut, September 18, 1952

Government [in a democracy] cannot be stronger or more tough-minded than its people. It cannot be more inflexibly committed to the task than they. It cannot be wiser than the people.
Speech, Chicago, September 29, 1952

As citizens of this democracy, you are the rulers and the ruled, the law-givers and the law-abiding, the beginning and the end.
Ibid.

VIOLET ALLEYN STOREY
[1900–]

I have a small-town soul.
It makes me want to know
Wee, unimportant things
About the folks that go
Past on swift journeyings.
Ironical

WILLIAM LINDSAY WHITE
[1900–]

They Were Expendable.
Title of book [1942]

THOMAS WOLFE
[1900–1938]

Which of us has known his brother? Which of us has looked into his father's heart? Which of us has not remained forever prison-pent? Which of us is not forever a stranger and alone?
Look Homeward, Angel! [2] [1929].
Foreword

[1] See J. Robert Oppenheimer, page 992b.
[2] See Milton, page 249b.

Most of the time we think we're sick, it's all in the mind.
Look Homeward, Angel! Part I, 1

Making the world safe for hypocrisy.
Ibid. Part III, 36

It is Europeans, for the most part, who have constructed these great ships, but without America they have no meaning. These ships are alive with the supreme ecstasy of the modern world, which is the voyage to America.
Of Time and the River [1935].
Book VIII

The young men of this land are not, as they are often called, a "lost" race — they are a race that never yet has been discovered. And the whole secret, power, and knowledge of their own discovery is locked within them — they know it, feel it, have the whole thing in them — and they cannot utter it.
The Web and the Rock [1939].
Chap. 13

There is no spectacle on earth more appealing than that of a beautiful woman in the act of cooking dinner for someone she loves.
Ibid. Chap. 28

If a man has a talent and cannot use it, he has failed. If he has a talent and uses only half of it, he has partly failed. If he has a talent and learns somehow to use the whole of it, he has gloriously succeeded, and won a satisfaction and a triumph few men ever know.
Ibid. Chap. 30

EMPEROR HIROHITO OF JAPAN
[1901–]

The ties between us and our people have always stood upon mutual trust and affection. They do not depend upon mere legends and myths. They are not predicated on the false conception that the Emperor is divine and that the Japanese people are superior to other races and fated to rule the world.
New Year Rescript [1946]

CORNELIA OTIS SKINNER
[1901–   ]

Woman's virtue is man's greatest invention.
Paris '90

CORNELIA OTIS SKINNER
[1901–   ]
AND
EMILY KIMBROUGH
[1899–   ]

We were young enough still to harbor the glad illusion that organized forms of get-together were commendable.
Our Hearts Were Young and Gay

JAN STRUTHER
[1901–1952]

She saw every personal relationship as a pair of intersecting circles. . . . Probably perfection is reached when the area of the two outer crescents, added together, is exactly equal to that of the leaf-shaped piece in the middle. On paper there must be some neat mathematical formula for arriving at this; in life, none.
Mrs. Miniver [*1940*]

It took me forty years on earth
To reach this sure conclusion:
There is no Heaven but clarity,
No Hell except confusion.
All Clear

CHARLES A. WAGNER
[1901–   ]

When I loved you and you loved me,
You were the sky, the sea, the tree.
Now skies are skies, and seas are seas,
And trees are brown and they are trees.
When I Loved You

ROY CAMPBELL
[1902–   ]

You praise the firm restraint with
    which they write —
I'm with you there, of course:

They use the snaffle and the curb all
    right,
But where's the bloody horse?
On Some South African Novelists

We had no time for make-believe
So early each began
To wear his liver on his sleeve,
To snarl, and be an angry man.
Poets in Africa. Stanza 2

I love to see, when leaves depart,
The clear anatomy arrive,
Winter, the paragon of art,
That kills all forms of life and feeling
Save what is pure and will survive.
Autumn. Stanza 1

THOMAS EDMUND DEWEY
[1902–   ]

That's why it's time for a change.[1]
Campaign speech, San Francisco,
September 21, 1944

DANIEL WHITEHEAD HICKY
[1902–   ]

No friend like music when the last
    word's spoken
And every pleading is a plea in vain;
No friend like music when the heart is
    broken,
To mend its wings and give it flight
    again.
No Friend Like Music

LANGSTON HUGHES
[1902–   ]

De railroad bridge's
A sad song in de air.
Ever' time de trains pass
I wants to go somewhere.
Homesick Blues. Stanza 1

I swear to the Lord
I still can't see
Why Democracy means
Everybody but me.
The Black Man Speaks

[1] The phrase was used extensively in the campaigns of 1944, 1948, and 1952.

CHARLES AUGUSTUS LINDBERGH
[1902–]

We (that's my ship and I) took off rather suddenly. We had a report somewhere around 4 o'clock in the afternoon before that the weather would be fine, so we thought we would try it.

Lindbergh's Own Story, in The New York Times, May 23, 1927

I saw a fleet of fishing boats. . . . I flew down almost touching the craft and yelled at them, asking if I was on the right road to Ireland.

They just stared. Maybe they didn't hear me. Maybe I didn't hear them. Or maybe they thought I was just a crazy fool. An hour later I saw land.

Ibid.

OGDEN NASH
[1902–]

O money, money, money, I'm not necessarily one of those who think thee holy,
But I often stop to wonder how thou canst go out so fast when thou comest in so slowly.

Hymn to the Thing That Makes the Wolf Go [1]

There are two kinds of people who blow through life like a breeze,
And one kind is gossipers, and the other kind is gossipees.

I'm a Stranger Here Myself. I Have It on Good Authority

Another good thing about gossip is that it is within everybody's reach,
And it is much more interesting than any other form of speech.

Ibid.

Bankers Are Just Like Anybody Else, Except Richer

Ibid. Verse title

[1] From the *New York American*, January, 1934.

Dogs display reluctance and wrath
If you try to give them a bath.
They bury bones in hideaways
And half the time they trot sideaways.

I'm a Stranger Here Myself. An Introduction to Dogs, Stanza 4

City people always want the most faucets
And the comfortablest caucets.

Ibid. The City, Stanza 4

Barmaids Are Diviner Than Mermaids

Ibid. Verse title

There was a young belle of old Natchez
Whose garments were always in patchez.
When comment arose
On the state of her clothes,
She drawled, When Ah itchez, Ah scratchez!

Ibid. Requiem

There is only one way to achieve happiness on this terrestrial ball,
And that is to have either a clear conscience, or none at all.

Ibid. Inter-Office Memorandum

Sleep is perverse as human nature,
Sleep is perverse as a legislature,
Sleep is as forward as hives or goiters,
And where it is least desired, it loiters.

The Face Is Familiar. Read This Vibrant Exposé

Home is heaven and orgies are vile,
But I like an orgy, once in a while.

Ibid. Home, 99 44/100% Sweet Home

Women would rather be right than reasonable.

Good Intentions. Frailty, Thy Name Is a Misnomer

Candy
Is dandy
But liquor
Is quicker.

Many Long Years Ago. Reflections on Ice-Breaking

I think that I shall never see
A billboard lovely as a tree.
Indeed, unless the billboards fall
I'll never see a tree at all.

Ibid. Song of the Open Road

One would be in less danger
From the wiles of the stranger
If one's own kin and kith
Were more fun to be with.
Many Long Years Ago.
Family Court

The turtle lives 'twixt plated decks
Which practically conceal its sex.
I think it clever of the turtle
In such a fix to be so fertile.
Ibid. The Turtle

They have such refined and delicate
palates
That they can discover no one worthy
of their ballots,
And then when someone terrible gets
elected
They say, There, that's just what I expected!
Ibid. Election Day Is a Holiday

A bit of talcum
Is always walcum.
Ibid. Reflection on Babies

The old men know when an old man
dies.
Ibid. Old Men

There is something about a Martini,
A tingle remarkably pleasant;
A yellow, a mellow Martini;
I wish that I had one at present.
There is something about a Martini,
Ere the dining and dancing begin,
And to tell you the truth,
It is not the vermouth —
I think that perhaps it's the gin.
Ibid. A Drink with Something in It

They take a paper and they read the
headlines,
So they've heard of unemployment and
they've heard of breadlines,
And they philanthropically cure them
all
By getting up a costume charity ball.
Ibid. Pride Goeth Before a Raise

There are some people who are very re-
sourceful
At being remorseful,
And who apparently feel that the best
way to make friends
Is to do something terrible and then
make amends.
Ibid. Hearts of Gold

Women are ethereal beings, subsisting
entirely on chocolate marshmallow
nut sundaes and cantaloupe,
But they open up a package of cigarettes like a lioness opening up an
antelope.
Versus. Thoughts Thought
After a Bridge Party

Middle age is when you've met so many
people that every new person you
meet reminds you of someone else.
Ibid. Let's Not Climb the Wash-
ington Monument Tonight

A commuter is one who never knows
how a show comes out because he
has to leave early to catch a train
to get him back to the country in
time to catch a train to bring him
back to the city.
Ibid. The Banker's Special

I believe a little incompatibility is the
spice of life, particularly if he has
income and she is pattable.
Ibid. I Do, I Will, I Have

My garden will never make me famous,
I'm a horticultural ignoramus,
I can't tell a stringbean from a soybean,
Or even a girl bean from a boy bean.
Ibid. He Digs, He Dug, He Has Dug

When I remember bygone days
I think how evening follows morn;
So many I loved were not yet dead,
So many I love were not yet born.
Ibid. The Middle

He tells you when you've got on too
much lipstick,
And helps you with your girdle when
your hips stick.
Ibid. The Perfect Husband

A door is what a dog is perpetually on
the wrong side of.
The Private Dining Room. A
Dog's Best Friend Is His Il-
literacy

They are a higher form of life,
My dog, my daughter, and my wife,
Inhabitants of a fourth dimension
Too mystic for my comprehension.
Ibid. Father-in-Law of the Groom

THEODORE SPENCER
[1902–1949]

Eunuchs, abortive Platonists and
  priests
Speak always very wisely about love.
An Act of Life [1944]

JOHN ERNST STEINBECK
[1902–   ]

Man, unlike any other thing organic
or inorganic in the universe, grows beyond his work, walks up the stairs of
his concepts, emerges ahead of his accomplishments.
The Grapes of Wrath [1939].
Chap. 14
"Okie use' ta mean you was from
Oklahoma. Now it means you're scum.
Don't mean nothing itself, it's the way
they say it."
Ibid. Chap. 18
They had hoped to find a home, and
they found only hatred. Okies — the
owners hated them because the owners
knew they were soft and the Okies
strong, that they were fed and the
Okies hungry.
Ibid. Chap. 19

ERSKINE CALDWELL
[1903–   ]

Tobacco Road.
Title of novel [1] [1932]

CYRIL CONNOLLY
[1903–   ]

Spring is a call to action, hence to
disillusion, therefore April is called "the
cruellest month." [2]
The Unquiet Grave [1945]
There is no fury like a woman
searching for a new lover.
Ibid.
Obesity is a mental state, a disease
brought on by boredom and disappointment.
Ibid.

[1] The play [1933], adapted by JACK
KIRKLAND, had one of the longest runs in
American stage history.
[2] See T. S. Eliot, page 943b.

Melancholy and remorse form the
deep leaden keel which enables us to
sail into the wind of reality; we run
aground sooner than the flat-bottomed
pleasure-lovers, but we venture out in
weather that would sink them.
The Unquiet Grave

COUNTEE CULLEN
[1903–1946]

She thinks that even up in heaven
Her class lies late and snores,
While poor black cherubs rise at seven
To do celestial chores.
Epitaph: A Lady I Know
Though wet nor blow nor space I fear,
Yet fear I deeply, too,
Lest Death should meet and claim me
  ere
I keep Life's rendezvous.
I Have a Rendezvous with Life [1]

WILLIAM THOMAS CUMMINGS [2]
[1903–1944]

There are no atheists in the foxholes. [3]
Field Sermon on Bataan [1942]

MERRILL MOORE
[1903–1957]

Water has sunk more grievances than
  wine
And will continue to.
Hymn for Water. Stanza 2
The noise that Time makes.
M: 1000 Sonnets [1938]

GEORGE ORWELL
[1903–1950]

All animals are equal, but some animals are more equal than others.
Animal Farm [1945]. *Chap. 10*

[1] See Alan Seeger, page 947b.
[2] Father Cummings, of Maryknoll Mission,
was a member of the Chaplains Corps. He was
aboard an unmarked Japanese ship that was
transporting prisoners from the Philippines
to Japan when sunk by an American sub-
marine, December 15, 1944.
[3] Quoted by CARLOS P. ROMULO, *I Saw the
Fall of the Philippines* [1942], P. 263.

WILLIAM PLOMER
[1903–   ]

That was the Africa we knew,
Where, wandering alone,
We saw, heraldic in the heat,
A scorpion on a stone.
The Scorpion

PETER ARNO
[1904–   ]

I consider your conduct unethical
and lousy.
Caption for cartoon

CLIFTON FADIMAN
[1904–   ]

Ennui, felt on the proper occasions,
is a sign of intelligence.
Reading I've Liked [*1941*]

Man's painful desire to communicate
without coalescing.
Ibid.

MARGARET FISHBACK
[1904–   ]

The same old charitable lie
Repeated as the years scoot by
Perpetually makes a hit —
"You really haven't changed a bit!"
The Lie of the Land

CECIL DAY LEWIS
[1904–   ]

Tempt me no more; for I
Have known the lightning's hour,
The poet's inward pride,
The certainty of power.
Tempt Me No More. Stanza 1

And if our blood alone
Will melt this iron earth,
Take it. It is well spent
Easing a savior's birth.
Ibid. Stanza 7

I've heard them lilting at loom and
belting,
Lasses lilting before dawn of day:
But now they are silent, not gamesome
and gallant —

The flowers of the town are rotting
away.[1]
A Time to Dance

Come, live with me and be my love,
And we will all the pleasures prove [2]
Of peace and plenty, bed and board,
That chance employment may afford.
Ibid.

Rest from loving and be living.
Fallen is fallen past retrieving.
Rest from Loving

Slow drip the seconds, time is stalactite.
*As One Who Wanders into
Old Workings*

Make us a wind to shake the world!
The Magnetic Mountain. 31

Spring through death's iron guard
Her million blades shall thrust;
Love that was sleeping, not extinct,
Throw off the nightmare crust.
Ibid. 35

Sleep-walking on that silver wall, the
furious
Sick shapes and pregnant fancies of
your world.
Newsreel [*1941*]. *Stanza 3*

J. ROBERT OPPENHEIMER
[1904–   ]

In some sort of crude sense which no
vulgarity, no humor, no over-statement
can quite extinguish, the physicists have
known sin; and this is a knowledge
which they cannot lose.
*Physics in the Contemporary
World, lecture at Massachusetts
Institute of Technology, November 25, 1947*

EMERY REVES
[1904–   ]

The Golden Calf to which the most
devoted and mystic adoration of the
masses goes in our days is: Sovereignty.
No symbol carrying the pretension of a

[1] I've heard them lilting at our ewe-milking,
Lasses a-lilting before dawn o' day;
But now they are moaning on ilka green
loaning:
"The Flowers of the Forest are a' wede
away."
JANE ELLIOTT [1727–1805]:
A Lament for Flodden
[2] See Marlowe, page 123a.

deity caused so much misery, hatred, starvation and mass execution as the notion "Sovereignty of the Nation."
A Democratic Manifesto [*1942*].
Chap. 6

GRETA GARBO
[1905–   ]

I want to be alone.[1]
Attributed

PHYLLIS McGINLEY
[1905–   ]

We never sit down to our pottage,
We never go calm to our rest,
But lo! at the door of our cottage,
The knock of the Guest.
Elegy from a Country Dooryard.
Stanza 3

Meek-eyed parents hasten down the ramps
To greet their offspring, terrible from camps.
Ode to the End of Summer

HERBERT J. MULLER
[1905–   ]

Few have heard of Fra Luca Parioli, the inventor of double-entry bookkeeping; but he has probably had much more influence on human life than has Dante or Michelangelo.
The Uses of the Past [*1952*].
Chap. 8

ROBERT PENN WARREN
[1905–   ]

The annual sacrament of sea and sun,
Which browns the face and heals the heart . . .
But the mail lurks in the box at the house where you live.
End of Season. Stanzas 5 and 6

ALFRED BARRETT, S.J.
[1906–   ]

See how in God's design,
Layette to mound,

1 Garbo maintains that her most famous remark has always been misquoted. . . . "I only said, 'I want to be *let* alone!' " — JOHN BAINBRIDGE, in *Life* [January 24, 1955]

A lifetime of linen
Laps us round.
Linen

WYSTAN HUGH AUDEN
[1907–   ]

Cathedrals,
Luxury liners laden with souls,
Holding to the east their hulls of stone.
On This Island. XVII

Underneath the abject willow,
Lover, sulk no more;
Act from thought should quickly follow:
What is thinking for?
Ibid. XXII

Come to our bracing desert
Where eternity is eventful,
For the weather-glass
Is set at Alas,
The thermometer at Resentful.
For the Time Being. The Flight
into Egypt

Come to our well-run desert
Where anguish arrives by cable,
And the deadly sins
May be bought in tins
With instructions on the label.
Ibid.

In the nightmare of the dark
All the dogs of Europe bark,
And the living nations wait,
Each sequestered in its hate.
In Memory of W. B. Yeats [*1939*]

Intellectual disgrace
Stares from every human face,
And the seas of pity lie
Locked and frozen in each eye.
Ibid.

O stern proconsul of intractable provinces,
O poet of the difficult, dear addicted artist.
At the Grave of Henry James.
Stanza 5

Sob, heavy world
Sob as you spin,
Mantled in mist, remote from the happy.
The Age of Anxiety

CHRISTOPHER FRY
[1907–   ]

But life has such
Diversity, I sometimes remarkably lose
Eternity in the passing moment.
The Lady's Not for Burning
[*1950*]. *Act I*

Something compels us into
The terrible fallacy that man is desirable
And there's no escaping into truth.
Ibid. Act II

Campaigning
Love still pitches his tent of light
among
The suns and moons.
Ibid.

The best
Thing we can do is to make wherever
we're lost in
Look as much like home as we can.
Ibid. Act III

ANNE MORROW LINDBERGH
[1907–   ]

Rivers perhaps are the only physical features of the world that are at their best from the air. . . . Rivers stretch out serenely ahead as far as the eye can reach.
North to the Orient [*1935*].
Chap. 17

What did they call it in New England when they felt this same thing?
. . . "Journey-proud."
"Listen! the Wind" [1] [*1938*].
Chap. 18

One can never pay in gratitude; one can only pay "in kind" somewhere else in life.
Ibid. Chap. 19

The wave of the future is coming and there is no fighting it.
The Wave of the Future [*1940*]

Lost time was like a run in a stocking. It always got worse.
The Steep Ascent [*1944*]. *Chap. 3*

[1] See Humbert Wolfe, page 934a.

LOUIS MACNEICE
[1907–   ]

Holidays should be like this,
Free from over-emphasis,
Time for soul to stretch and spit
Before the world comes back on it.
Epilogue, for W. H. Auden [*1936*]

I have no liking to defer
To capitalist or bureaucrat;
As for your Social Register
You know what you can do with that!
Ballade in a Bad Temper [*1940*]

PAUL ENGLE
[1908–   ]

Wytham, Water Eaton, Wolvercote,
Old names worn water-smooth under
the tongue.
Corn [*1939*]

I came to that dark water-wandered
town,
Where, before proud stone was piled on
stone
To mark the frantic limits of the mind,
Oxen forded the mild, midland river.
Ibid. (Oxford)

The tense American nerve relaxed, I
lived
With a gray quietness that let the mind
Grow inward like a root.
Ibid.

I heard, down the long valley of my
bones,
The cry of home run like a calling
hound . . .
Belly and brain, I lived America.
Ibid.

HOWELL M. FORGY
[1908–   ]

Praise the Lord and pass the ammunition.[1]
*Said at Pearl Harbor,
December 7, 1941*

[1] Lieutenant Commander Forgy was serving as chaplain on a cruiser at the time of the Japanese attack, when he said these words to a chain of men handling ammunition. (Also title of a popular song by Frank Loesser [September, 1942].)

WILLIAM SAROYAN
[1908–   ]

The Time of Your Life.
Title of play [1] [*1939*]

What they do, boys, is creep up on you,
And I don't mean Indians.
I mean Americans, over the radio.
The Propagandists [*1940*]

If you listen to them, you will be listened to,
Saying what they said, and no longer the man you were.
Ibid.

If you give to a thief he cannot steal from you, and he is then no longer a thief.
The Human Comedy [*1943*].
Chap. 4

"How much does it cost to send a telegram to New Jersey?"
"Not nearly as much as it's worth."
Ibid. Chap. 17

STEPHEN SPENDER
[1909–   ]

I think continually of those who were truly great —
The names of those who in their lives fought for life,
Who wore at their hearts the fire's center.
I Think Continually of Those

Born of the sun they traveled a short while towards the sun,
And left the vivid air signed with their honour.
Ibid.

GEORGE CASPAR HOMANS
[1910–   ]

Liberty is a beloved discipline.
The Human Group [*1950*].
Chap. 12

W. R. RODGERS

Laugh at the skinny notice of your birth,
Or roar at your obese obituary.
Words

[1] Awarded the 1940 Pulitzer Prize, which Saroyan refused.

Your doubts are the private detectives
Employed by your dislike, to make a case
Against change or choice.
Words

GEORGE BARKER
[1913–   ]

What is all but a Woolworth welter of things?
Seven Munich Elegies. 5

Life is torpedoed and like a Titanic goes under
Threshing her ensigns
Against the dreadnought seas of blood and thunder
That flood our visions.
Ibid. 6

The chaos is come of the organized disorder,
The consistently inappropriate and the simple wrong.
First American Ode

NATHALIA CRANE
[1913–   ]

Oh, I'm in love with the janitor's boy,
And the janitor's boy loves me;
He's going to hunt for a desert isle
In our geography.
The Janitor's Boy [*1924*]. *Stanza 1*

I linger on the flathouse roof, the moonlight is divine.
But my heart is all a-flutter like the washing on the line.
The Flathouse Roof. Stanza 1

Once a pallid vestal
Doubted truth in blue;
Listed red as ruin,
Harried every hue.
The Vestal. Stanza 1

Every gaudy color
Is a bit of truth.
Ibid. Stanza 5

In the darkness, who would answer for the color of a rose,
Or the vestments of the May moth and the pilgrimage it goes?
The Blind Girl. Stanza 1

When the moon comes over Brooklyn

On time with the borough clock,
'Tis the same that saw Palmyra
And the walls of Antioch.
            The Moon of Brooklyn. Stanza 1
There is a glory
In a great mistake.

            Imperfection

DONALD FRANCIS MASON
[1913–   ]

Sighted sub, sank same.
            Radio message to U. S. Navy
            Base, January 28, 1942

MURIEL RUKEYSER
[1913–   ]

Women and poets see the truth arrive,
Then it is acted out,
The lives are lost, and all the newsboys
    shout.
            Beast in View [*1944*]. *Letter to*
                        the Front
The world of man's selection
May widen more and more.
Women in drudgery knew
They must be one of four:
Whores, artists, saints, and wives.
            Ibid. Wreath of Women

KARL JAY SHAPIRO
[1913–   ]

He cast his vote,
Distrusting all the elected but not the
    law.
            Elegy for a Dead Soldier
                        [*1944*]. *VII*
Above all else he loathed the homily,
The slogan and the ad. He paid his bill
But not for Congressmen at Bunker
    Hill.
Ideals were few and those there were
    not made
For conversation. He belonged to
    church
But never spoke of God. The Christmas
    tree,
The Easter egg, baptism, he observed,
Never denied the preacher on his perch,
And would not sign Resolved That or
    Whereas.
            Ibid. VIII

IRWIN SHAW
[1913–   ]

There are too many books I haven't
read, too many places I haven't seen,
too many memories I haven't kept long
enough.
            Bury the Dead [*1936*]
I got a religion that wants to take
heaven out of the clouds and plant it
right here on the earth where most of us
can get a slice of it.
            Ibid.

ROSS PARKER
[1914–   ]
AND
HUGHIE CHARLES
[1907–   ]

There'll always be an England
    While there's a busy street,
Wherever there's a turning wheel,
    A million marching feet.
            There'll Always Be an
                        England [*1939*]

DELMORE SCHWARTZ
[1914–   ]

In Dreams Begin Responsibilities.
            Title of book of poems [*1938*]
Save postage stamps or photographs,
But save your soul! Only the past is
    immortal.
            The Repetitive Heart

DYLAN THOMAS [1]
[1914–1953]

Light breaks where no sun shines;
Where no sea runs, the waters of the
    heart
Push in their tides.
            Light breaks where no sun shines
And death shall have no dominion.[2]
            Title and refrain of poem

[1] All these selections are from *Collected
Poems* [1953].
[2] See *Romans, VI, 9*, on page 1059b, and
Emily Brontë, page 592a.

After the first death there is no other.
A Refusal to Mourn the Death, by
Fire, of a Child in London
Forgotten mornings when he walked
with his mother
Through the parables
Of sun light
And the legend of the green chapels.
Poem in October
Do not go gentle into that good night,
Old age should burn and rave at close
of day;
Rage, rage against the dying of the
light.
Do not go gentle into
that good night
Now as I was young and easy under
the apple boughs
About the lilting house and happy as
the grass was green.
Fern Hill. Stanza 1
And the sabbath rang slowly
In the pebbles of the holy stream.
Ibid. Stanza 2
In the sun that is young once only,
Time let me play and be
Golden in the mercy of his means.
Ibid.
And honoured among foxes and pheas-
ants by the gay house
Under the new made clouds and happy
as the heart was long,
In the sun born over and over,
I ran my heedless ways.
Ibid. Stanza 5
Time held me green and dying
Though I sang in my chains like the
sea.
Ibid. Stanza 6

HAROLD ADAMSON

Comin' in on a Wing and a Prayer.
Title of popular song of World
War II [*1943*]

FLORENCE FRENCH DUNBAR
[1916–   ]

The Spring comes truly when, between
the rains,

The stiff new wasps ascend the window
panes.
Wasp Time

JOHN WALLER
[1917–   ]

Guns are left to do what words
Might have done earlier, properly used.
In Beirut
How frequently the last time
Comes and we do not know.
The Meaning of War

WILLIAM H. ("BILL") MAULDIN
[1921–   ]

I feel like a fugitive from th' law of
averages.
Up Front [*1944*]. *Caption*
for cartoon
Look at an infantryman's eyes and
you can tell how much war he has seen.
Ibid.
"He's right, Joe, when we ain't
fightin' we should ack like sojers."
Ibid.

QUEEN ELIZABETH II OF ENGLAND
[1926–   ]

My whole life, whether it be long or
short, shall be devoted to your service
and the service of our great imperial
family to which we all belong, but I
shall not have strength to carry out this
resolution alone unless you join in it
with me.
Radio broadcast from Capetown,
South Africa, to the British Com-
monwealth on her twenty-first
birthday [*April 21, 1947*]

CHARTER OF THE UNITED NATIONS

We, the peoples of the United Nations, determined to save succeeding
generations from the scourge of war,
which twice in our lifetime has brought
untold sorrow to mankind, and to re-
affirm faith in fundamental human

rights, in the dignity and worth of the human person, in the equal right of men and women and of nations large and small . . .

And for these ends to practice tolerance and live together in peace with one another as good neighbors . . .

Have resolved to combine our efforts to accomplish these aims.

Preamble [1] [*June, 1945*]

[1] The preamble was based on the draft written by JAN CHRISTIAN SMUTS [1870–1950].

ANONYMOUS

Sumer is icumen in,
 Lhude sing cuccu!
Groweth sed, and bloweth med,
And springth the wude nu —
 Sing cuccu!
Cuckoo Song [Circa 1250]

Castles in Spain.[1]
 Phrase from the French
 [13th century]

When Adam delved and Eve span
Who was then a gentleman?
 Text used by JOHN BALL *for*
 his speech at Blackheath to the
 men in Wat Tyler's Rebellion
 [1381]

Forgive and forget.
 Saying current since the
 14th century

I sing of a maiden
 That is makeless;
King of all kings
 To her son she ches.
 Carol. I Sing of a Maiden
 [15th century]

Western wind, when wilt thou blow?
The small rain down can rain, —
Christ, if my love were in my arms
And I in my bed again!
 Western Wind [Circa 1530]

Multiplication is vexation,
Division is as bad;
The rule of three doth puzzle me,
And practice drives me mad.
 Elizabethan MS. [1570]

There is a lady sweet and kind,
Was never face so pleased my mind;
I did but see her passing by,
And yet I love her till I die.
 Song [1570]

Greensleeves was all my joy,
 Greensleeves was my delight,

Greensleeves was my heart of gold,
 And who but my Lady Greensleeves?
 A Handful of Pleasant Delites
 [1584]. Greensleeves

Alas, my love, you do me wrong
 To cast me off discourteously,
When I have loved you so long,
 Delighting in your company.
 Ibid.

Shall I bid her go? What, and if I do?
Shall I bid her go, and spare not?
O no, no, no, I dare not.[1]
 Corydon's Farewell to Phillis.
 Stanza 2

Where griping griefs the heart would
 wound
And doleful dumps the mind oppress,
There music with her silver sound
With speed is wont to send redress.[2]
 A Song to the Lute in Musicke.
 Stanza 1

A fool and his money are soon parted.
 Saying current since the
 16th century

Turn again Whittington,
Lord Mayor of London.[3]
 Refrain of Bow Bells heard by
 Dick Whittington [Circa 1605]

Love not me for comely grace,
For my pleasing eye or face,
Nor for any outward part,
No, nor for a constant heart.
 In JOHN WILBYE, *Second Set of*
 Madrigals [1608]

 If wishes were horses, beggars might
ride.
 From JOHN RAY'S *English*
 Proverbs [1670]

[1] Paraphrased by Shakespeare in *Twelfth-
Night* [1598–1600], *Act II, Sc. 3.*
[2] Another version is used by Shakespeare
in *Romeo and Juliet* [1594–1595], *Act IV,
Sc. 5.*
[3] Richard Whittington, son of a London
mercer, rose to be mayor of London three
times before his death in 1423.

[1] Thou shalt make castels than in Spayne,
 And dreme of joye, al but in vayne.
 JEAN DE MEUN: *Romaunt of the Rose,*
 Fragment B, L. 2573 [circa 1277]

Begone, dull Care! I prithee begone
  from me!
Begone, dull Care! thou and I shall
  never agree.
In JOHN PLAYFORD, *Musical*
Companion [*1687*]

Though little, I'll work as hard as a
  Turk,
  If you'll give me employ,
To plow and sow, and reap and mow,
  And be a farmer's boy.
The Farmer's Boy [*before 1689*].
Stanza 2

Carriages without horses shall go,
And accidents fill the world with woe.
Prophecy Attributed to Mother
Shipton [1] [*17th century*]

Around the world thoughts shall fly
In the twinkling of an eye.
Ibid.

Under water men shall walk,
Shall ride, shall sleep, and talk;
In the air men shall be seen
In white, in black, and in green.
Ibid.

Iron in the water shall float
As easy as a wooden boat.
Ibid.

A swarm of bees in May
Is worth a load of hay;
A swarm of bees in June
Is worth a silver spoon;
A swarm of bees in July
Is not worth a fly.
Old English saying

  When poverty comes in at the door,
love flies out the window.
Saying current since the 17th
century

Please to remember the Fifth of November,
Gunpowder Treason and Plot.
Guy Fawkes's Rhyme, tradi-
tional in England since the
17th century

[1] Most of the prophecies attributed to
Mother Shipton — a witch and prophetess,
according to tradition, who lived in Yorkshire
in Tudor times — are fabrications of the seventeenth century and later.

THE NEW ENGLAND PRIMER [1]

In Adam's fall
We sinned all.

My Book and Heart
Must never part.

Young Obadias,
David, Josias, —
All were pious.

Peter denied
His Lord, and cryed.

Young Timothy
Learnt sin to fly.

Xerxes did die,
And so must I.

Zaccheus he
Did climb the tree
Our Lord to see.

Our days begin with trouble here,
  Our life is but a span,[2]
And cruel death is always near,
  So frail a thing is man.

Now I lay me down to take my sleep,[3]
I pray the Lord my soul to keep;
If I should die before I wake,
I pray the Lord my soul to take.

Sabina has a thousand charms
  To captivate my heart;
Her lovely eyes are Cupid's arms,
  And every look a dart:
But when the beauteous idiot speaks,
  She cures me of my pain;
Her tongue the servile fetters breaks
  And frees her slave again.
From Amphion Anglicus [*1700*]

[1] As early as 1691, Benjamin Harris of
Boston advertised the forthcoming second
impression of the the *New England Primer*.
The oldest known copy extant is dated 1737.
[2] See Bacon, page 121b.
[3] The first record of this prayer is found
in the *Enchiridion Leonis* [A. D. 1160]. The
early editions of the *Primer* give the prayer
as above. In the edition of 1784 the first line
is altered to read, "Now I lay me down to
sleep." In the edition of 1814 the second line
reads, "I pray thee, Lord, my soul to keep."

The Campbells are comin', oho, oho.
                    Song [*Circa 1715*]
The Girl I Left Behind Me.
                    Title of song [*1759*]
The United Voice of all His Majesty's free and loyal Subjects in America — Liberty and Property, and no Stamps.
          Motto of various American colonial newspapers [*1765–1766*]
Yankee Doodle came to town
Upon a little pony,
He stuck a feather in his hat
And called it macaroni.
                    Yankee Doodle [1]
Yankee Doodle, keep it up,
Yankee Doodle dandy,
Mind the music and the step,
And with the girls be handy.
                    Ibid. Chorus

It's all in the day's work.
          Saying current since the 18th century
Man may work from sun to sun,
But woman's work is never done.
                    Old saying

JUNIUS [2]

One precedent creates another. They soon accumulate and constitute law.

[1] This version was sufficiently popular in America in 1767 to be used in the ballad opera *The Disappointment, or, The Force of Credulity* [1767], by ANDREW BARTON.
          Father and I went up to camp,
          Along with Captain Goodwin;
          And there we saw the men and boys,
          As thick as hasty-pudding.
                    Yankee doodle do.
          Version used in The Contrast
                    [1790], *by* ROYALL TYLER
The origin of *Yankee Doodle* remains as mysterious as ever, unless it be deemed a positive result to have eliminated definitely every theory thus far advanced. — OSCAR GEORGE THEODORE SONNECK: *Report on The Star-Spangled Banner, Hail Columbia, America, Yankee Doodle* [1909]
[2] Pseudonym of the author of a series of letters that appeared in the *Public Advertiser* from 1769 to 1771, published in book form in 1772; they have been attributed, among others, to Sir Philip Francis, Lord Shelburne, Lord George Sackville, and Lord Temple.

What yesterday was fact, today is doctrine.
          The Letters of Junius [*1769–1771*]. *Dedication to the English Nation*

The liberty of the press is the Palladium of all the civil, political, and religious rights of an Englishman.
                    Ibid.

These are the gloomy companions of a disturbed imagination; the melancholy madness of poetry, without the inspiration.
          Ibid. VII, To Sir William Draper
                    [*March 3, 1769*]

There are some hereditary strokes of character by which a family may be as clearly distinguished as by the blackest features of the human face.
          Ibid. XII, To the Duke of Grafton [*May 30, 1769*]

I believe there is yet a spirit of resistance in this country, which will not submit to be oppressed; but I am sure there is a fund of good sense in this country, which cannot be deceived.
          Ibid. XVI, To the Printer of the Public Advertiser (H. S. Woodfall) [*July 19, 1769*]

We owe it to our ancestors to preserve entire those rights, which they have delivered to our care: we owe it to our posterity, not to suffer their dearest inheritance to be destroyed.
          Ibid. XX, To the Printer of the Public Advertiser [*August 8, 1769*]

When the constitution is openly invaded, when the first original right of the people, from which all laws derive their authority, is directly attacked, inferior grievances naturally lose their force, and are suffered to pass by without punishment or observation.
          Ibid. XXX, To the Printer of the Public Advertiser [*October 17, 1769*]

There is a moment of difficulty and danger at which flattery and falsehood can no longer deceive, and simplicity itself can no longer be misled.

> *The Letters of Junius. XXXV,*[1]
> *To the Printer of the Public Advertiser* [December 19, 1769]

They [the Americans] equally detest the pageantry of a King, and the supercilious hypocrisy of a bishop.[2]

> *Ibid.*

There is a holy mistaken zeal in politics as well as in religion. By persuading others, we convince ourselves.

> *Ibid.*

The least considerable man among us has an interest equal to the proudest nobleman, in the laws and constitution of his country, and is equally called upon to make a generous contribution in support of them; — whether it be the heart to conceive, the understanding to direct, or the hand to execute.[3]

> *Ibid. XXXVII, To the Printer of the Public Advertiser* [March 19, 1770]

We lament the mistakes of a good man, and do not begin to detest him until he affects to renounce his principles.

> *Ibid. XLI, To Lord Mansfield* [November 14, 1770]

The injustice done to an individual is sometimes of service to the public. Facts are apt to alarm us more than the most dangerous principles.

> *Ibid.*

An honest man, like the true religion, appeals to the understanding, or modestly confides in the internal evidence of his conscience. The impostor employs force instead of argument, imposes silence where he cannot convince, and propagates his character by the sword.

> *Ibid.*

[1] This letter is of great significance in the history of the freedom of the press. The publisher was prosecuted for seditious libel, and the jury brought in a verdict of "guilty of printing and publishing only." After a second trial, Woodfall was freed on payment of costs.
[2] See Rufus Choate, page 490a.
[3] See Gibbon, page 369a.

If individuals have no virtues, their vices may be of use to us.

> *The Letters of Junius. LIX, To the Printer of the Public Advertiser* [October 5, 1771]

The temple of fame is the shortest passage to riches and preferment.

> *Ibid.*

Rebellion to tyrants is obedience to God.[1]

> *Motto on Thomas Jefferson's Seal* [Circa 1776]

Lost is our old simplicity of times,
The world abounds with laws, and teems with crimes.

> *On the Proceedings Against America.*[2] *Stanza 1*

Our cargoes of meat, drink, and cloaths beat the Dutch.

> *Siege of Boston* [1775]

There is nothing new except what is forgotten.

> *Attributed to Mademoiselle Bertin, milliner to Marie Antoinette* [Circa 1785]

O Paddy dear, an' did ye hear the news that's goin' round?
The shamrock is by law forbid to grow on Irish ground!
No more St. Patrick's Day we'll keep, his colour can't be seen,
For there's a cruel law agin the wearin' o' the Green!

> *The Shan-von-Voght. Irish Song quoted in* TRENCH: *Realities of Irish Life*

For they're hangin' men an' women there for wearin' o' the Green.

> *Ibid.*

Christmas is coming, the geese are getting fat,
Please to put a penny in the old man's hat;
If you haven't got a penny, a ha'penny will do,

[1] The motto of one, I believe, of the regicides of Charles I. — *Letter from Jefferson to Edward Everett* [February 24, 1823]
Jefferson's reference probably is to John Bradshaw [1602-1659].
[2] In *The Pennsylvania Gazette*, February 8, 1775, "from a late London Magazine."

If you haven't got a ha'penny, God bless you!

Beggar's rhyme

From ghoulies and ghosties and long-leggety beasties
And things that go bump in the night,
Good Lord, deliver us!

Scottish prayer

The woods are full of them.

Quoted by ALEXANDER WILSON: *American Ornithology [1808]. Preface*

The cunning seldom gain their ends;
The wise are never without friends.

The Fox and the Hen, Moral [1]

A fox went out in a hungry plight
And he begged of the moon to give him light,
For he'd many miles to go that night
Before he could reach his den-O.

The Gray Goose. Stanza 1

One night when the wind it blew cold,
Blew bitter across the wild moor,
Young Mary she came with her child,
Wandering home to her own father's door.

Mary of the Wild Moor. [2]
Stanza 1

Oh, the praties they are small —
Over here, over here.
Oh, the praties they are small
When we dig 'em in the fall,
And we eat 'em, coats and all,
Full of fear, full of fear.

Irish Famine Song [1846–1847]

Oh, ye'll tak' the high road an' I'll tak' the low road,
An' I'll be in Scotland bafore ye;
But I and my true love will never meet again,
On the bonnie, bonnie banks o' Loch Lomond.

Scottish Song, Loch Lomond.
Refrain

So I said, "Old man, for whom digg'st thou this grave

[1] In JOHN PIERPONT's *Young Reader* [1843].
[2] Set to music by C. H. Keith and arranged for piano by Joseph W. Turner [1846].

In the heart of London town?"
And the deep-toned voice of the digger replied —
"We're laying a gas-pipe down!"

From the Sublime to the Ridiculous. [1] *Stanza 3*

Went out to milk and I didn't know how,
I milked the goat instead of the cow;
A monkey sittin' on a pile of straw
A-winkin' at his mother-in-law.
Turkey in the straw, turkey in the hay,
Roll 'em up and twist 'em up a high tuckahaw,
And hit 'em up a tune called Turkey in the Straw.

Turkey in the Straw. [2]
Stanza 1 and refrain

Sugar in the gourd and honey in the horn,
I never was so happy since the hour I was born.

Ibid. Stanza 6

You pays your money, and you takes your choice.

Caption to cartoon by JOHN LEECH *in Punch, January 3, 1846*

It's the 'ammer, 'ammer, 'ammer along the 'ard 'igh road.

Ibid. May 31, 1856 (A veterinary and a horseman discussing a horse's legs)

Women and children first.

The Birkenhead Drill [3] *[February 26, 1852]*

Frankie and Johnny were lovers, my gawd, how they could love,
Swore to be true to each other, true as the stars above;

[1] Included in *Course of Composition and Rhetoric* by GEORGE PAYN QUACKENBOS [1826–1881]
[2] The classical American rural tune . . . steps around like an apple-faced farmhand . . . as American as Andrew Jackson, Johnny Appleseed, and Corn on the Cob. — CARL SANDBURG: *The American Songbag* [1927]
[3] The women and children were the first to be removed from the sinking ship *Birkenhead*. See Kipling, page 818b.

He was her man, but he done her
wrong.
Frankie and Johnny.[1] *Stanza 1*

Och, Johnny, I hardly knew ye!
With drums and guns, and guns and
drums
The enemy nearly slew ye.
My darling dear, you look so queer,
Och, Johnny, I hardly knew ye.
Irish Folk Song. Stanza 1

Where are the legs with which you run,
When you went to carry a gun?
Indeed your dancing days are done —
Och, Johnny, I hardly knew ye.
Ibid. Stanza 3

Up and down the City Road,
In and out the Eagle,
That's the way the money goes —
Pop goes the weasel!
Popular song in London [2]
[Circa 1853]

All I want of you is a little see-vility,
and that of the commonest goddamned-
est kind.[3]
*"The New Bedford Classic," as
reported in* ZEPHANIAH W.
PEASE, *The History of New
Bedford* [*1918*]. *Supposed to
be said by the mate of a whaler
to his ill-humored captain*

You-all means a race or section,
Family, party, tribe, or clan;
You-all means the whole connection
Of the individual man.
*You-All (From The Richmond
Times-Dispatch)*

Some talk of Alexander, and some of
Hercules;
Of Hector, and Lysander, and such
great names as these;
But of all the world's brave heroes,
there's none that can compare

With a tow, row, row, row, row, row
for the British Grenadier.
The British Grenadiers

The holly and the ivy,
When they are both full grown,
Of all the trees that are in the wood,
The holly bears the crown:
The rising of the sun
And the running of the deer,
The playing of the merry organ,
Sweet singing in the choir.
Carol. The Holly and the Ivy

From the halls of Montezuma,
To the shores of Tripoli,
We fight our country's battles
On the land as on the sea.
U. S. Marines' Song. Stanza 1

If the Army and the Navy
Ever look on Heaven's scenes,
They will find the streets are guarded
by
The United States Marines.
Ibid. Stanza 4

There is a tavern in the town,
And there my true love sits him down,
And drinks his wine with laughter and
with glee,
And never, never thinks of me.
*There Is a Tavern in the Town.
Stanza 1*

Fare thee well for I must leave thee,
Do not let this parting grieve thee,
But remember that the best of friends
must part.
Ibid. Refrain

Adieu, adieu, kind friends, adieu, adieu.
adieu,
I can no longer stay with you.
I'll hang my harp on a weeping willow-
tree,[1]
And may the world go well with thee.
Ibid. Stanza 2

Mr. Finney had a turnip,
And it grew behind the barn,
And it grew, and it grew,
And the turnip did no harm.
Mr. Finney's Turnip. [2] *Stanza 1*

---

[1] Traditional ballad; there are innumerable
versions and verses.
[2] The weasel was a hatter's tool, and "pop"
was a term meaning to pawn or "hock." The
Eagle was a music hall in the City Road. The
song is attributed to W. R. MANDALE.
[3] Another traditional version, repudiated
by New Bedford authority, is that the skipper said: "All I want out of you is silence,
and damn little of that."

[1] See *Psalm CXXXVII, 2*, on page 1038a.
[2] Often attributed to Longfellow, who denied the authorship in a letter to George
Anderson, July 11, 1881.

Of all the funny things that live, in
   woodland, marsh, or bog,
That creep the ground or fly the air,
   the funniest thing's a frog.
> *The Scientific Frog [Circa*
> *1865]. Stanza 1*

I belong to that highly respectable
   tribe
Which is known as the Shabby Genteel . . .
Too proud to beg, too honest to steal.
> *The Shabby Genteel (Sung by*
> *Sol Smith Russell [1848–1901]*
> *in A Poor Relation)*

If any lift of mine may ease
   The burden of another,
God give me love and care and strength
   To help my ailing brother.
> *If Any Little Word of Mine*
> *[1880]. Stanza 2*

The sons of the prophet are brave men
   and bold,
And quite unaccustomed to fear,
But the bravest by far in the ranks of
   the Shah
Was Abdul the Bulbul Amir.
> *Abdul the Bulbul Amir. Stanza 1*

Now the heroes were plenty and well
   known to fame
In the troops that were led by the
   Czar,
And the bravest of these was a man by
   the name
Of Ivan Petruski Skavar.
> *Ibid. Stanza 3*

I'm Terence O'Reilly, I'm a man of renown . . .
If they'd let me be, I'd have Ireland
   free,
On the railroads you'd not pay any
   fare,
I'd have the United States under my
   thumb,
And I'd sleep in the President's chair.
> *Is That Mr. Reilly?* [1] *[1882].*
> *Stanza 1*

Is that Mr. Reilly, can anyone tell?
Is that Mr. Reilly that owns the hotel?

[1] Assumed to be the origin of the phrase
"leading the life of Riley," meaning to have
an easy time.

Well, if that's Mr. Reilly, they speak of
   so highly,
Upon me soul, Reilly, you're doin' quite
   well.
> *Is That Mr. Reilly? Chorus*

Sow a Thought, and you reap an Act;
Sow an Act, and you reap a Habit;
Sow a Habit, and you reap a Character;
Sow a Character, and you reap a Des-
   tiny.
> *Quoted by* SAMUEL SMILES
> *[1812–1904], in Life and La-*
> *bour [1887]*

Now is the time for all good men to
come to the aid of the party.
> *Practice sentence used in type-*
> *writing* [1]

As Maine goes, so goes the nation.[2]
> *American political maxim*
> *[Circa 1888]*

Sister Anne, do you see any one coming?
> *The anxious cry of Fatima, one*
> *of the wives of Bluebeard*

Slide, Kelly, Slide.
> *Title of song by* J. W. KELLY
> *[1889]*

Oh, Shenandoah, I long to hear you.
Away, you rolling river,
Oh Shenandoah, I long to hear you.
Away, I'm bound to go
'Cross the wide Missouri.
> *Song*

In the first person, simply *shall* foretells,
In *will* a threat or else a promise
   dwells;
Shall in the second and third does
   threat,

[1] Charles Weller, a court reporter, originated this expression in . . . 1867 to test the
efficiency of the first practical typewriter
which his friend Christopher Sholes had constructed. — *Life*, April 11, 1955
[2] As Maine goes, so goes Vermont. —
JAMES FARLEY: *Statement to press* [Novem-
ber 4, 1936] *after predicting that Roosevelt
would carry 46 states in the presidential election*

Will then simply foretells a future feat.
> *Grammar, Irish National Schools*

Try what you will, there's nothing like leather.
> *Nothing Like Leather*

The sweetest lives are those to duty wed,
Whose deeds, both great and small,
Are close-knit strands of an unbroken thread,
Where love ennobles all.
The world may sound no trumpet, ring no bells;
The book of life the shining record tells.
> *Attributed to Elizabeth Barrett Browning, but not found in her writings*

Ladling the butter from adjacent tubs,
Stubbs butters Freeman, Freeman butters Stubbs.
> *Variously quoted [Circa 1890], alluding to the mutual praise of two famous Oxford historians*

Lizzie Borden took an axe
And gave her mother forty whacks;
When she saw what she had done
She gave her father forty-one!
> *Rhyme popular after the murder trial of Lizzie Borden at Fall River, Massachusetts [June, 1893]*

The little cares that fretted me,
I lost them yesterday,
Among the fields above the sea,
Among the winds at play.
> *Out in the Fields, in St. Paul's Magazine, August 20, 1898*

Out in the fields with God!
> *Ibid.*

Remember the Maine! [1]
> *Slogan, Spanish-American War [1898]*

The halls of fame are open wide
And they are always full;
Some go in by the door called "push,"
And some by the door called "pull."
> *Quoted by Stanley Baldwin [1867–1947] in a speech in the House of Commons*

[1] On February 15, 1898, the American battleship *Maine* was blown up in Havana harbor, Cuba.

He who whispers down a well
About the goods he has to sell,
Will never reap the golden dollars
Like him who shows them round and hollers.
> *Quoted by the then Prince of Wales [1894–   ] (Duke of Windsor); thought to be of American origin*

The codfish lays ten thousand eggs,
  The homely hen lays one.
The codfish never cackles
  To tell you what she's done.
And so we scorn the codfish,
  While the humble hen we prize,
Which only goes to show you
  That it pays to advertise.
> *It Pays to Advertise*

Two ears and but a single tongue
By nature's laws to man belong;
The lesson she would teach is clear:
Repeat but half of what you hear.
> *Old jingle*

One white foot — try him,
Two white feet — buy him,
Three white feet — look well about him;
Four white feet — go without him. [1]
> *Rhyme for a horse-buyer*

An apple a day keeps the doctor away.
> *Current since the 19th century*

The great unwashed.
> *19th century expression*

The way to a man's heart is through his stomach.
> *Current since the 19th century*

All the world is queer save me and thee; and sometimes I think thee is a little queer.
> *Attributed to an unidentified Quaker, speaking to his wife*

Man is the only animal that eats when he is not hungry, drinks when he

[1] Three white feet and a white nose,
  Rip off his skin and throw him to the crows.
New Hampshire version of last two lines

is not thirsty, and makes love at all seasons.
> *Source unknown*

You can always tell a Harvard man, but you can't tell him much.
> *Attributed to* JAMES BARNES
> [*1866–1936*]

Keeping up with the Joneses.
> *Popular saying*

Paying through the nose.[1]
> *Popular phrase for excessive payment*

Rest and be thankful.
> *Inscription on stone seat in the Scottish Highlands, and title of one of Wordsworth's poems*

Wisdom of many and the wit of one.
> *Definition of a proverb* [2]

Doesn't amount to Hannah Cook.[3]
> *Saying common in Maine and on Cape Cod*

Drive a coach and six through an Act of Parliament.
> *Credited to Sir Stephen Rice* [*1637–1715*], *Chief Baron of the Exchequer, by* MACAULAY *in History of England* [*1849–1861*], *Chap. 12*

Free soil, free men, free speech, Frémont.
> *Rallying cry of the Republican Party in 1856, when John Charles Frémont* [*1813–1890*] *was the party's candidate for the presidency*

Dirty work at the crossroads.
> *Attributed* [1] *to* WALTER MELVILLE'S *melodrama The Girl Who Took the Wrong Turning, or, No Wedding Bells for Him*

The goose hangs high.[2]
> *Common saying for a favorable situation*

Hit's a lot worse to be soul-hungry than to be body-hungry.
> *A Kentucky mountain woman asking for her granddaughter to be admitted to Berea College high school* [*Circa 1900*]. *Quoted by* CARL R. WOODWARD.[3]

The Great White Way.
> *Title of novel* [*1901*] *by* ALBERT BIGELOW PAINE [*1861–1937*]

There ain't no such animal.
> *Comment of a New Jersey farmer looking at a dromedary at a circus: cartoon in Life, November 7, 1907, credited to Everybody's Magazine*

How old is Ann?
> *Popular saying in the early 20th century* [4]

The Pyramids first, which in Egypt were laid;
Next Babylon's Garden, for Amytis made;
Then Mausolos' Tomb of affection and guilt;
Fourth, the Temple of Dian in Ephesus built;
The Colossus of Rhodes, cast in brass, to the Sun;
Sixth, Jupiter's Statue, by Phidias done;

---

[1] Grimm says that Odin had a poll-tax which was called in Sweden a nose-tax; it was a penny per nose, or poll. — *Deutsche Rechts Alterthümer*

[2] Probably based on the definition of a proverb which Lord John Russell gave one morning at breakfast at Mardock's: "One man's wit, and all men's wisdom." — *Memoirs of Sir James Mackintosh* [*1765–1832*], *Vol. I, Page 473*

[3] Variously explained as a character who once lived on Campobello Island; a corruption of a phrase in Indian dialect; and a comparison with the worthlessness (for navigation) of a cook on board ship.

[1] In *Notes and Queries* (London).

[2] Originally, perhaps, "the goose *honks* high" — it cries and flies high. Wild geese fly higher when the weather is fine or promises to be fine. Hence, the prospects are bright; everything is favourable. — *Century Dictionary*

[3] In *The Wonderful World of Books*, edited by ALFRED STEFFERUD [*1953*].

[4] This question became well known when *The New York Press*, October 16, 1903, printed the problem: "Mary is 24 years old. She is twice as old as Ann was when Mary was as old as Ann is now. How old is Ann?" The answer is that Ann is 18.

The Pharos of Egypt comes last, we are
   told,
Or the Palace of Cyrus, cemented with
   gold.
                    *Seven Wonders of the
                     Ancient World*
Use it up, wear it out;
Make it do, or do without.
                    New England maxim
   Earned a precarious living by tak-
ing in one another's washing.
                    Origin unknown
Something old, something new,
Something borrowed, something blue,
And a lucky sixpence in her shoe.[1]
                    Wedding rhyme
   God looks after fools, drunkards, and
the United States.
                              Epigram
Oh, why don't you work
Like other men do?
How the hell can I work
When there's no work to do?
                    Hallelujah, I'm a Bum
                         [*Circa 1907*]
Every time I come to town
The boys keep kicking my dawg
   around;
Makes no difference if he is a hound,
They've got to quit kicking my dawg
   around.
                    Champ Clark campaign song
                              [*1912*]
Old soldiers never die;
They only fade away!
                    War song, British Army
                         [*1914–1918*]
She was poor but she was honest,
And her parents were the same,
Till she met a city feller,
And she lost her honest name.
                    War song [*1914–1918*]
   Fifty million Frenchmen can't be
wrong.[2]
                    *Saying popular with American
                     soldiers during World War I*
                     [*1917–1918*]

[1] There are variants for the less familiar
last line, such as "And a silver sixpence in
each shoe."
[2] Sometimes "forty" or "thirty" is heard
instead of "fifty." When Texas Guinan and

My aunt's charwoman's sister's son
Heard a policeman on his beat
Say to a nursemaid down our street
That he knew a man who had a friend
And he could tell when the war would
   end.
                    Jingle popular in 1917–1918
Don't sell America short.[1]
                    Popular American saying
                         [*1925–1929*]
Lord, through this hour
   Be Thou our Guide,
So by Thy power
   No foot shall slide.
                    Westminster Chimes
Climb high
Climb far
Your goal the sky
Your aim the star.
                    *Inscription on Hopkins Memo-
                     rial Steps, Williams College,
                     Williamstown, Massachusetts*
Mother, may I go out to swim?
Yes, my darling daughter:
Hang your clothes on a hickory limb
And don't go near the water.
                    Origin dubious
Lives of great men all remind us
   As their pages o'er we turn,
That we're apt to leave behind us
   Letters that we ought to burn.
                    Quoted by DR. A. S. W. ROSEN-
                    BACH *in A Book Hunter's Holi-
                    day* [*1936*]
See the happy moron,
   He doesn't give a damn.
I wish I were a moron —
   My God, perhaps I am!
                    *Incorrectly attributed to
                     Dorothy Parker*
You will eat, bye and bye,
In that glorious land above the sky;

her troupe were refused entry into France in
1931, she was quoted as saying: "It goes to
show that fifty million Frenchmen *can* be
wrong." She promptly renamed her show *Too
Hot for Paris*, and toured the United States
with it.
[1] The phrase may have stemmed from
"Never be a bear on the United States," attributed variously to JUNIUS S. MORGAN
[1813–1890] and J. P. MORGAN [1837–1913].

Work and pray, live on hay,
You'll get pie in the sky when you die.
The Preacher and the Slave [1]
The difficult we do immediately. The
impossible takes a little longer.
*Slogan of United States Army
Air Forces*

G. I. Joe.
*World War II term for
infantryman* [2]

Stay with me, God. The night is dark,
The night is cold: my little spark
Of courage dies. The night is long;
Be with me, God, and make me strong.
A Soldier — His Prayer. [3] *Stanza 1*

We sure liberated the hell out of this
place.
*American soldier in the ruins of
a French village, 1944; quoted
by* MAX MILLER *in The Far
Shore* [1945]

Spartan simplicity must be observed.
Nothing will be done merely because it
contributes to beauty, convenience,
comfort, or prestige.
*From the Office of the Chief
Signal Officer, U. S. Army,
May 29, 1945*

Soldiers who wish to be a hero
Are practically zero,
But those who wish to be civilians,
Jesus, they run into the millions.
*Army latrine inscription quoted
by* NORMAN ROSTEN *in The Big
Road* [1945]

Since wars begin in the minds of
men, it is in the minds of men that the
defences of peace must be constructed.
*Constitution of the United Na-
tions Educational, Scientific and
Cultural Organization* [1946]

---

[1] Attributed to Joe Hill in the 1927 edition
of *I.W.W. Songs.*
[2] This name, chosen for the soldier in
Lieutenant DAVE BREGER's comic strip for
Yank, the Army weekly, first appeared in
the issue of June 17, 1942. Writing in *Time*
[February 26, 1945], Lieutenant Breger said:
"I decided on 'G. I. Joe,' the 'G. I.' [Govern-
ment Issue] because of its prevalence in Army
talk, and the 'Joe' for the alliterative effect."
[3] This poem, found on a scrap of paper
in a slit trench in Tunisia during the battle
of El Agheila, was printed in *Poems from the*

We are not dealing simply with a
military or scientific problem but with
a problem in statecraft and the ways
of the human spirit.
*Report on the International
Control of Atomic Energy, published March 16, 1946* [1]

Relief from the terrible fear which
can do so much to engender the very
thing feared.
Ibid.

Anything constructive in relation to
atomic energy must inevitably be novel
and immensely difficult.
Ibid.

FOREIGN PROVERBS AND SAYINGS

LATIN

Actus non facit reum, nisi mens sit
rea.
The act is not criminal unless the
intent is criminal.
Legal maxim

Ad majorem Dei gloriam.
To the greater glory of God.
Motto of the Society of Jesus

Adeste, fideles,
Laeti triumphantes;
Venite, venite in Bethlehem.

O come, all ye faithful,
Joyful and triumphant,
O come ye, O come ye to Bethlehem.
Hymn, 18th Century

Ave Caesar, morituri te salutamus.
Hail Caesar, we who are about to
die salute you.
*Salutation of the Roman glad-
iators upon entering the arena*

Caveat emptor.
Let the buyer beware.
Proverb

Desert, by members of the British Eighth
Army [1944].
[1] Prepared for the Department of State by
a Board of Consultants: Chester I. Barnard,
J. Robert Oppenheimer, Charles A. Thomas,
Harry A. Winne, and David E. Lilienthal,
Chairman.

Cucullus non facit monachum.[1]
The cowl does not make a monk.
Medieval Latin proverb

De gustibus non disputandum.
There is no arguing about tastes.
Proverb

De minimis non curat lex.
The law is not concerned with trifles.
Legal maxim

Deus vult.
God wills it.
Motto of the Crusades [1095]

Divide et impera.
Divide and rule.
Ancient political maxim cited by MACHIAVELLI

E Pluribus Unum.
One out of many.
Motto on title page of the Gentleman's Journal [January, 1692], adopted as motto for seal of the United States, June 20, 1782

Et in Arcadia ego.
I too have lived in Arcadia.[2]
Inscription on a tomb in a painting by Guercino [Circa 1623]

Festina lente.
Make haste slowly.
Borrowed from the Greek

Mea culpa.
The fault is mine.
Latin phrase derived from the Mass

Non conscire sibi.
Conscious of no fault.
Latin saying

Omnis festinatio est a diabolo.
All haste is from the devil.
Medieval Latin proverb

---

[1] It takes more than a hood and sad eyes to make a monk. — *Albanian Proverb*
[2] This translation is now usually considered erroneous. The accepted translation is: I too am in Arcadia — that is, Even in Arcadia there am I [Death].
Also in a painting by Poussin [*circa* 1630]. E. PANOFSKY discusses the phrase in *Philosophy and History: Essays Presented to E. Cassirer* [1936].

Post hoc, ergo propter hoc.
After this, therefore because of this.
Definition of fallacy in logic

Pro bono publico.
For the public good.
Saying

Semper fidelis.
Ever faithful.
Motto of the U. S. Marine Corps

Si monumentum requiris, circumspice.
If you seek a monument, look about you.
Inscription on Sir Christopher Wren's tomb in St. Paul's Cathedral, London

Sic semper tyrannis.[1]
Thus ever to tyrants.
Motto of State of Virginia [Adopted 1779]

Sic transit gloria mundi.
Thus passes away the glory of this world.
Saying

FRENCH

Il ne faut pas être plus royaliste que le roi.
One must not be more royalist than the king.
Saying which originated under Louis XVI

Liberté! Egalité! Fraternité!
Liberty! Equality! Fraternity!
Phrase dating from before the French Revolution, officially adopted in 1793

Rien ne réussit comme le succès.
Nothing succeeds like success.
Proverb

Tout passe, tout casse, tout lasse.
Everything passes, everything perishes, everything palls.
Proverb

---

[1] The words of John Wilkes Booth as he shot Lincoln at Ford's Theater [April 14, 1865].

Ah, les bons vieux temps où nous
étions si malheureux!

Oh, the good old times when we
were so unhappy!
Saying

MISCELLANEOUS

Whatever kind of word thou speakest
the like shalt thou hear.
Greek Anthology. Book IX,
Epigram 382

When I am dead let fire destroy the
world; it matters not to me, for I am
safe.
Ibid. Fragment 430

Envy slays itself by its own arrows.
Ibid. Book X, Epigram 111

Give me today, and take tomorrow.
Quoted and condemned by
St. Chrysostom

One picture is worth more than ten
thousand words.
Chinese proverb

On the day of victory no one is tired.
Arab proverb

I came to the place of my birth, and
cried, "The friends of my youth, where
are they?" And echo answered, "Where
are they?"

Arab saying

BALLADS

For in my mind, of all mankind
I love but you alone.
The Nut-Brown Maid [15th
century]. Refrain

For I must to the green-wood go,
Alone, a banished man.
Ibid.

No burial this pretty pair
  Of any man receives,
Till Robin Red-breast piously
  Did cover them with leaves.
The Children in the Wood.
Stanza 16

The king sits in Dunfermline town
Drinking the blude-red wine.
Sir Patrick Spens.
Stanza 1

"To Noroway, to Noroway,
To Noroway o'er the faem;
The king's daughter o' Noroway,
'Tis thou must bring her hame."
Sir Patrick Spens.
Stanza 4

The first word that Sir Patrick read
So loud, loud laughed he;
The neist word that Sir Patrick read
The tear blinded his e'e.
Ibid. Stanza 5

"I saw the new moon late yestreen
Wi' the auld moon in her arm;
And if we gang to sea, master,
I fear we'll come to harm."
Ibid. Stanza 10

Half-owre, half-owre to Aberdour,
'Tis fifty fathoms deep;
And there lies gude Sir Patrick Spens,
Wi' the Scots lords at his feet!
Ibid. Stanza 19

The blinded boy that shoots so trim,[1]
From heaven down did hie.
King Cophetua and the
Beggar-maid. Stanza 2

It was a friar of orders gray [2]
Walked forth to tell his beads.
The Friar of Orders Gray.[3]
Stanza 1

Our joys as wingèd dreams do fly;
  Why then should sorrow last?
Since grief but aggravates thy loss,
  Grieve not for what is past.
Ibid. Stanza 13

King Stephen was a worthy peer,
His breeches cost him but a crown.
Take Thy Old Cloak About
Thee.[4] Stanza 7

It's pride that puts this country down;
Man, take thine old cloak about thee.
Ibid.

---

[1] Young Adam Cupid, he that shot so trim,
  When King Cophetua loved the beggar-
  maid!
SHAKESPEARE: *Romeo and Juliet*
  [1594–1595], *Act II, Sc. 1, L. 13*
[2] See Shakespeare, page 130b.
[3] THOMAS PERCY [1728–1811] composed
this ballad from various fragments of ancient
ballads found in Shakespeare's plays. It appeared in his *Reliques of Ancient English*
Poetry [1765].
[4] See Shakespeare, page 187b.

Fight on, my merry men all;
For why, my life is at an end.[1]
Chevy Chase

A fairer lady there never was seen
Than the blind beggar's daughter of
Bethnall Green.
The Beggar's Daughter of
Bethnall Green.[2] Stanza 33

When captains courageous,[3] whom
death could not daunt,
Did march to the siege of the city of
Gaunt,
They mustered their soldiers by two
and by three,
And the foremost in battle was Mary
Ambree.
Mary Ambree.[4] Stanza 1

Then let Jane Shore with sorrow sing,
That was belovèd of a king.
Jane Shore. Stanza 1

"I'll rest," said he, "but thou shalt
walk";
So doth this wandering Jew
From place to place, but cannot rest
For seeing countries new.
The Wandering Jew. Stanza 9

For thirty pence our Saviour was sold
Among the false Jews, as I have been
told;
And twenty-nine is the worth of thee,
For I think thou art one penny worser
than he.
King John and the Abbot of
Canterbury. Stanza 21

Glasgerion swore a full great oath,
By oak, and ash and thorn.[5]
Glasgerion. Stanza 19

[1] Says Johnnie, "Fight on, my merry men all,
I'm a little wounded, but I am not slain;
I will lay me down for to bleed a while,
Then I'll rise and fight with you again."
Johnnie Armstrong's Last Good-night,
St. 18 (DRYDEN's *Miscellanies* [1702])

[2] This very house was built by the blind
beggar of Bednall Green, so much talked of
and sung in ballads. — SAMUEL PEPYS: *Diary*
[June 26, 1663]

[3] Source of the title of RUDYARD KIPLING's
Captains Courageous.

[4] BEN JONSON calls any virago Mary Ambree, and JOHN FLETCHER alludes to Mary
Ambree in *The Scornful Lady* [1616].

[5] See Kipling, page 820b.

In Scarlet town, where I was born,
There was a fair maid dwellin',
Made every youth cry Well-a-way!
Her name was Barbara Allen.
Barbara Allen's Cruelty.
Stanza 1

All in the merry month of May,
When green buds they were swellin',
Young Jemmy Grove on his death-bed
lay,
For love of Barbara Allen.
Ibid. Stanza 2

So slowly, slowly rase she up,
And slowly she came nigh him,
And when she drew the curtain by —
"Young man, I think you're dyin'."
Ibid. Stanza 4

True Thomas lay on Huntlie Bank;
A ferlie he spied wi' his e'e;
And there he saw a lady bright
Come riding down by the Eildon Tree.
Thomas the Rhymer. Stanza 1

"A bed, a bed," Clerk Saunders said,
"A bed for you and me!"
"Fye na, fye na," said may Margaret,
"Till anes we married be!"
Clerk Saunders. Stanza 2

There were twa sisters sat in a bour;
   Binnorie, O Binnorie!
There came a knight to be their wooer,
   By the bonnie milldams o' Binnorie.
Binnorie. Stanza 1

There were three ravens sat on a tree,
They were as black as they might be.
The Three Ravens. Stanza 1

The one of them said to his make,
"Where shall we our breakfast take?"
Ibid. Stanza 2

Down there came a fallow doe
As great with young as she might go.
Ibid. Stanza 6

She buried him before the prime,
She was dead herself ere evensong
time.
Ibid. Stanza 9

God send every gentleman
Such hounds, such hawks, and such a
leman.
Ibid. Stanza 10

Ye Highlands and ye Lawlands,
O where hae ye been?

They hae slain the Earl of Murray,
And hae laid him on the green.
*The Bonny Earl of Murray.
Stanza 1*

O waly, waly, up the bank,
And waly, waly, doun the brae,
And waly, waly, yon burn-side,
Where I and my Love wont to gae!
Waly, Waly. Stanza 1

O waly, waly, gin love be bonnie,
A little time while it is new!
But when 'tis auld it waxeth cauld,
And fades awa' like morning dew.
Ibid. Stanza 2

But had I wist, before I kist,
That love had been sae ill to win,
I had lock'd my heart in a case o' gowd,
And pinn'd it wi' a siller pin.
Ibid. Stanza 5

"What gat ye to your dinner, Lord
Randal, my Son?
What gat ye to your dinner, my hand-
some young man?"
"I gat eels boil'd in broo'; mother,
make my bed soon,
For I'm weary wi' hunting, and fain
wald lie down."
Lord Randal

A ship I have got in the North Country
And she goes by the name of the
Golden Vanity,
O, I fear she will be taken by a Spanish
Gal-la-lee,
As she sails by the Low-lands low.
The Golden Vanity. Stanza 1

And when with envy Time, trans-
ported,
Shall think to rob us of our joys,
You'll in your girls again be courted,
And I'll go wooing in my boys.
Winifreda.[1] Stanza 8

But in vain she did conjure him
To depart her presence so;
Having a thousand tongues to allure
him,
And but one to bid him go.
Dulcina.[2] Stanza 2

[1] *Winifreda* appeared in Lewis's *Collection*
[1726].
[2] This song is mentioned by Izaak Walton
in *The Compleat Angler* [1653]. It has been
ascribed to Raleigh, on very doubtful authority.

Over the mountains,
And over the waves,
Under the fountains
And under the graves;
Under floods that are deepest,
Which Neptune obey,
Over rocks that are steepest,
Love will find out the way.
*Love Will Find Out the Way.
Stanza 1*

O what a plague is love
How shall I bear it?
She will inconstant prove,
I greatly fear it.
Phillida Flouts Me. Stanza 1

And let all women strive to be
As constant as Penelope.
Constant Penelope. Stanza 18

For without money, George,
A man is but a beast:
But bringing money, thou shalt be
Always my welcome guest.
*George Barnwell.[1] Part II,
Stanza 25*

EPITAPHS

A zealous Lock-Smith dyed of late,
And did arrive at heaven gate,
He stood without and would not
knocke,
Because he meant to picke the locke.
*Epitaph upon a Puritanicall
Lock-Smith; quoted by Wil-
liam Camden in Remaines
Concerning Britaine [1637]*

All the brothers were valiant, and
all the sisters virtuous.
*From the inscription on the
tomb of the Duchess of Newcastle in Westminster Abbey
[1673]*

A house she hath, 'tis made of such
good fashion,
The tenant ne'er shall pay for repara
tion,
Nor will the landlord ever raise her rent
Or turn her out of doors for non-pay-
ment;

[1] Inspired by George Lillo's play, *The
London Merchant, or, The History of George
Barnwell*, first acted in 1731.

From chimney-tax this cell is free,
To such a house who would not tenant
be?
    For Rebecca Bogess, Folkestone,
               August 22, 1688
It is so soon that I am done for,
I wonder what I was begun for.
    For a child aged three weeks,
        Cheltenham Churchyard
She tasted of life's bitter cup,
Refused to drink the potion up;
She turned her little head aside,
Disgusted with the task and died.
    For a child aged six months
Here lies John Knott:
His father was Knott before him,
He lived Knott, died Knott,
Yet underneath this stone doth lie
Knott christened, Knott begot,
And here he lies and still is Knott.
    Perthshire Churchyard
Here lie I, Martin Elginbrodde:
Ha'e mercy o' my soul, Lord God,
As I wad do, were I Lord God
And ye were Martin Elginbrodde.
    Aberdeen Churchyard (Quoted
    by GEORGE MACDONALD *in his*
    novel, David Elginbrod [1862],
    Chap. 13)
Beneath this stone, a lump of clay,
  Lies Arabella Young,
Who on the 24th of May
  Began to hold her tongue.
    British Museum Collection
Beneath this stone a lump of clay
  Lies Uncle Peter Daniels
Who too early in the month of May
  Took off his winter flannels.
    Medway, Massachusetts, 1746
Here sleeps in peace a Hampshire Grenadier,
Who caught his death by drinking cold
  small beer;
Soldiers, take heed from his untimely
  fall,
And when you're hot, drink strong, or
  not at all.
    Winchester Churchyard, 1764
A dying preacher I have been,
To dying hearers such as you.
Though dead, a preacher still I am
To such as come my grave to view.

Let this to you a warning be
That quickly you must follow me.
    Elder Samuel Waldo, South
    Dover (Wingdale) Cemetery,
    Dutchess County, New York,
    September 10, 1798
Immaturus obi: sed tu felicior annos
Vive meos, Bona Respublica! Vive
  tuos.
(I died young; but thou, O Good Republic,
Live out my years for me with better
  fortune.)
    Inscription, perhaps chosen by
    Thomas Jefferson, on the tomb
    of Meriwether Lewis [1774–
    1809], explorer of the Lewis
    and Clark expedition
Here lies Sir Jenkin Grout, who loved
his friend, and persuaded his enemy:
what his mouth ate, his hand paid for:
what his servants robbed, he restored:
if a woman gave him pleasure, he supported her in pain: he never forgot his
children: and whoso touched his finger,
drew after it his whole body.
    Quoted by RALPH WALDO EM-
    ERSON *in his essay, Manners*
    [1856]
This is the grave of Mike O'Day
Who died maintaining his right of way.
His right was clear, his will was strong,
But he's just as dead as if he'd been
  wrong.
    20th century

NURSERY RHYMES

Old Mother Goose,
When she wanted to wander,
Would ride through the air
On a very fine gander
    Old Mother Goose
Cock a doodle doo!
My dame has lost her shoe;
My master's lost his fiddling-stick,
And knows not what to do.
    Cock a Doodle Doo
Three blind mice, see how they run!
They all ran after the farmer's wife,
She cut off their tails with a carving-
  knife,

Did you ever see such a sight in your life,
    As three blind mice?
Three Blind Mice

A frog he would a-wooing go.
"Heigh-ho!" says Rowley.
A Frog He Would A-wooing Go

With a rowley powley gammon and spinach,
Heigh-ho! says Anthony Rowley.
Ibid. Chorus

Old King Cole
Was a merry old soul,
And a merry old soul was he,
He called for his pipe,
And he called for his bowl,
And he called for his fiddlers three.
Old King Cole

The King of France went up the hill,
With forty thousand men;
The King of France came down the hill,
And ne'er went up again.
The King of France

Jack Sprat could eat no fat,
His wife could eat no lean;
And so between them both, you see,
They licked the platter clean.
Jack Sprat

Rain, rain, go away,
Come again another day.
Rain, Rain

Pat-a-cake, pat-a-cake, baker's man,
Bake me a cake as fast as you can;
Pat it and prick it, and mark it with B,
Put it in the oven for baby and me.
Pat-a-cake

The lion and the unicorn
Were fighting for the crown;
The lion beat the unicorn
All round the town.
Some gave them white bread,
And some gave them brown;
Some gave them plum cake,
And sent them out of town.
The Lion and the Unicorn

Little Jack Horner sat in the corner,
Eating a Christmas pie:
He put in his thumb, and pulled out a plum,
And said, "What a good boy am I!"
Little Jack Horner

London Bridge is falling down,
My fair lady.
London Bridge

As I was going to St. Ives,
I met a man with seven wives,
Each wife had seven sacks,
Each sack had seven cats,
Each cat had seven kits:
Kits, cats, sacks, and wives,
How many were there going to St. Ives?
As I Was Going to St. Ives

The man in the wilderness asked of me
How many strawberries grew in the sea.
I answered him as I thought good,
"As many as red herrings grow in the wood."
The Man in the Wilderness

Lady-bug, lady-bug, fly away home,
Your house is on fire, and your children will burn.
Lady-bug, Lady-bug

Hickory, dickory dock,
The mouse ran up the clock,
The clock struck one,
The mouse ran down;
Hickory, dickory dock.
Hickory, Dickory Dock

Baa, baa, black sheep,
Have you any wool?
Yes, sir, yes, sir,
Three bags full:
One for my master,
And one for my dame,
And one for the little boy
Who lives down the lane.
Baa, Baa, Black Sheep

Mary, Mary, quite contrary,
How does your garden grow?
With silver bells, and cockle shells,
And pretty maids all in a row.
Mary, Mary, Quite Contrary

Oranges and lemons,
Say the bells of St. Clement's.
When will you pay me?
Say the bells of Old Bailey.
When I grow rich,
Say the bells of Shoreditch.
Oranges and Lemons

Here comes a candle to light you to bed,

Here comes a chopper to chop off your
head.
Oranges and Lemons

"Who killed Cock Robin?"
"I," said the sparrow,
"With my bow and arrow,
I killed Cock Robin." [1]
Who Killed Cock Robin?

"Who saw him die?"
"I," said the Fly,
"With my little eye,
I saw him die."
Ibid.

This little pig went to market;
This little pig stayed home;
This little pig had roast beef;
This little pig had none;
And this little pig cried, Wee, wee, wee!
All the way home.
This Little Pig

Little boy blue, come blow your horn,
The sheep's in the meadow, the cow's
in the corn;
But where is the boy who looks after
the sheep?
He's under the haystack fast asleep.
Will you wake him? No, not I,
For if I do, he'll be sure to cry.
Little Boy Blue

Simple Simon met a pieman
Going to the fair:
Says Simple Simon to the pieman,
"Let me taste your ware."
Simple Simon

Ding, dong, bell,
Pussy's in the well.
Who put her in?
Little Johnny Green.
Who pulled her out?
Big Jack Stout.
Ding, Dong, Bell

Little Tommy Tucker
Sings for his supper;
What shall we give him?
White bread and butter.
Little Tommy Tucker

[1] "Who killed John Keats?"
"I," said the Quarterly,
So savage and tartarly,
"'Twas one of my feats."
BYRON: *Letter to John Murray*
[July 30, 1821]

How shall he cut it
Without any knife?
How will he marry
Without any wife?
Little Tommy Tucker

Cross-patch,
Draw the latch,
Sit by the fire and spin:
Take a cup
And drink it up,
Then call your neighbors in.
Cross-patch

Hey diddle diddle
The cat and the fiddle,
The cow jumped over the moon;
The little dog laughed
To see such sport,
And the dish ran away with the spoon.
Hey Diddle Diddle

Three wise men of Gotham
Went to sea in a bowl:
If the bowl had been stronger,
My song would have been longer.
Three Wise Men of Gotham

Jack and Jill went up the hill
To fetch a pail of water;
Jack fell down and broke his crown,
And Jill came tumbling after.
Jack and Jill

See-saw, Margery Daw,
Jacky shall have a new master;
Jacky must have but a penny a day,
Because he can't work any faster.
See-saw, Margery Daw

Taffy was a Welshman, Taffy was a
thief;
Taffy came to my house and stole a
piece of beef.
Taffy Was a Welshman

The Queen of Hearts
She made some tarts,
All on a summer's day;
The Knave of Hearts
He stole the tarts,
And took them clean away.
The Queen of Hearts

Bye, baby bunting,
Daddy's gone a-hunting,
Gone to get a rabbit skin
To wrap the baby bunting in.
Bye, Baby Bunting

Come, let's to bed,
Says Sleepy-head;
Tarry a while, says Slow;
Put on the pot,
Says Greedy-gut,
We'll sup before we go.

Let's to Bed

Four and twenty tailors went to kill a
snail,
The best man among them durst not
touch her tail.
She put out her horns like a little
Kyloe cow,
Run, tailors, run, or she'll kill you all
e'en now.

Four and Twenty Tailors

Goosey goosey gander,
Whither shall I wander?
Upstairs and downstairs,
And in my lady's chamber;
There I met an old man who wouldn't
say his prayers;
I took him by the left leg,
And threw him down the stairs.

Goosey Goosey Gander

Sing a song of sixpence,
  A pocket full of rye,
Four and twenty blackbirds,
  Baked in a pie;
When the pie was opened,
  The birds began to sing;
Wasn't that a dainty dish
  To set before a king?

Sing a Song of Sixpence

The king was in his counting-house
  Counting out his money;
The queen was in the parlor
  Eating bread and honey;
The maid was in the garden
  Hanging out the clothes,
Along came a blackbird,
  And snipped off her nose.

Ibid.

There was an old woman who lived in
a shoe,
She had so many children she didn't
know what to do;
She gave them some broth without any
bread,
She whipped them all soundly and put
them to bed.

There Was an Old Woman

Ride a cock-horse to Banbury Cross,
To see a fine lady upon a white horse;
Rings on her fingers and bells on her
toes,
She shall have music wherever she goes.

Ride a Cock-Horse

Tom, Tom, the piper's son,
Stole a pig, and away he run;
The pig was eat, and Tom was beat,
And Tom went howling down the
street.

Tom, Tom, the Piper's Son

Tom, Tom, the piper's son,
He learned to play when he was young,
But all the tune that he could play,
Was "Over the hills and far away." [1]

Ibid.

"Where are you going to, my pretty
maid?"
"I'm going a-milking, sir," she said.

*Where Are You Going To, My
Pretty Maid?*

"My face is my fortune, sir," she said.

Ibid.

"Nobody asked you, sir," she said.

Ibid.

One a penny, two a penny, hot cross-
buns;
If you have no daughters, give them
to your sons.

Hot Cross-Buns

Pease-porridge hot, pease-porridge cold,
Pease-porridge in the pot, nine days
old.

Pease-porridge Hot

Curly-locks, Curly-locks,
Wilt thou be mine?
Thou shalt not wash dishes
Nor yet feed the swine.
But sit on a cushion
And sew a fine seam,
And feed upon strawberries,
Sugar and cream.

Curly-Locks

I had a little nut tree, nothing would it
bear
But a silver nutmeg and a golden pear;
The king of Spain's daughter came to
visit me,

[1] See D'Urfey, page 290b and Gay, page
308b.

And all for the sake of my little nut tree.
I Had a Little Nut Tree

Humpty Dumpty sat on a wall,
Humpty Dumpty had a great fall;
All the king's horses
And all the king's men
Couldn't put Humpty Dumpty together again.
Humpty Dumpty

Little Bo-Peep has lost her sheep,
And can't tell where to find them;
Leave them alone, and they'll come home,
Wagging their tails behind them.
Little Bo-Peep

Little Polly Flinders
Sat among the cinders,
Warming her pretty little toes.
Her mother came and caught her,
And whipped her little daughter
For spoiling her nice new clothes.
Little Polly Flinders

The north wind doth blow,
And we shall have snow,
And what will poor robin do then,
Poor thing?
He'll sit in a barn,
To keep himself warm,
And hide his head under his wing,
Poor thing!
The North Wind Doth Blow

Old Mother Hubbard
Went to the cupboard,
To fetch her poor dog a bone;
But when she got there
The cupboard was bare,
And so the poor dog had none.
Old Mother Hubbard

Pussy cat, pussy cat, where have you been?
I've been to London to look at the queen.
Pussy cat, pussy cat, what did you there?
I frightened a little mouse under the chair.
Pussy-Cat

Peter Piper picked a peck of pickled peppers;
A peck of pickled peppers Peter Piper picked.

If Peter Piper picked a peck of pickled peppers,
Where's the peck of pickled peppers Peter Piper picked?
Peter Piper

Monday's child is fair of face,
Tuesday's child is full of grace,
Wednesday's child is full of woe,
Thursday's child has far to go,
Friday's child is loving and giving,
Saturday's child has to work for its living,
But a child that's born on the Sabbath day
Is fair and wise and good and gay.
Rhyme

Solomon Grundy,
Born on a Monday,
Christened on Tuesday,
Married on Wednesday,
Took ill on Thursday,
Worse on Friday,
Died on Saturday,
Buried on Sunday:
This is the end
Of Solomon Grundy.
Solomon Grundy

What are little boys made of?
Snips and snails, and puppy-dogs' tails;
That's what little boys are made of.
What Are Little Boys Made Of?

What are little girls made of?
Sugar and spice, and everything nice;
That's what little girls are made of.
Ibid.

Hickety, pickety, my black hen,
She lays eggs for gentlemen;
Gentlemen come every day
To see what my black hen doth lay.
Hickety, Pickety

Little Miss Muffet
Sat on a tuffet,
Eating some curds and whey.
Along came a spider,
And sat down beside her,
And frightened Miss Muffet away.
Little Miss Muffet

Peter, Peter Pumpkin-eater,
Had a wife and couldn't keep her;
He put her in a pumpkin shell,
And there he kept her very well.
Peter, Peter Pumpkin-Eater

Jack, be nimble,
Jack, be quick,
Jack, jump over the candle-stick.
Jack Be Nimble

There was a crooked man, and he went
a crooked mile,
He found a crooked sixpence against a
crooked stile;
He bought a crooked cat, which caught
a crooked mouse,
And they all lived together in a little
crooked house.
There Was a Crooked Man

Diddle, diddle, dumpling, my son John,
He went to bed with his stockings on;
One shoe off, one shoe on;
Diddle, diddle, dumpling, my son John.
Diddle, Diddle, Dumpling

Rub-a-dub-dub,
Three men in a tub,
And who do you think they be?
The butcher, the baker,
The candlestick-maker;
Turn 'em out, knaves all three!
Rub-a-Dub-Dub

I saw three ships come sailing by,
Come sailing by, come sailing by,
I saw three ships come sailing by,
On New Year's Day in the morning.
I Saw Three Ships

In fir tar is,
In oak none is.
In mud eel is,
In clay none is.
Goats eat ivy.
Mares eat oats.
Rhyme

Lucy Locket lost her pocket,
Kitty Fisher found it;
There was not a penny in it,
But a ribbon round it.
Lucy Locket

There were three jolly huntsmen,
As I have heard them say,
And they would go a-hunting
Upon St. David's Day.
There Were Three Jolly Huntsmen

All day they hunted,
And nothing did they find,
But a ship a-sailing,
A-sailing with the wind.
Ibid.

O do you know the muffin man,
The muffin man, the muffin man,
O do you know the muffin man,
That lives in Drury Lane?
The Muffin Man

To market, to market to buy a fat pig,
Home again, home again, jiggety-jig.
To Market, To Market

Doctor Foster went to Gloucester
In a shower of rain;
He stepped in a puddle, up to his
middle,
And never went there again.
Doctor Foster

There was an old woman
Lived under a hill;
And if she's not gone,
She lives there still.
There Was an Old Woman

There was a little man, and he had a
little gun,
And his bullets were made of lead, lead,
lead;
He went to the brook, and saw a little
duck,
And shot it through the head, head,
head.
There Was a Little Man

Lavender's blue, dilly, dilly, lavender's
green;
When I am king, dilly, dilly, you shall
be queen.
Lavender's Blue

A dillar, a dollar,
A ten o'clock scholar,
What makes you come so soon?
You used to come at ten o'clock,
And now you come at noon.
A Dillar, a Dollar

I had a little pony,
His name was Dapple-Gray;
I lent him to a lady
To ride a mile away.
She whipped him, she slashed him,
She rode him through the mire;
I would not lend my pony now
For all the lady's hire.
I Had a Little Pony

Polly, put the kettle on,
Polly, put the kettle on,
Polly, put the kettle on,
We'll all have tea.

Sukey, take it off again,
Sukey, take it off again,
Sukey, take it off again,
They've all gone away.
Polly, Put the Kettle On

Little Tommy Tittlemouse
Lived in a little house;
He caught fishes
In other men's ditches.
Little Tommy Tittlemouse

The farmer in the dell, the farmer in
the dell,
Heigho! the derry oh, the farmer in the
dell.
The Farmer in the Dell

Hark! Hark! The dogs do bark,
The beggars are coming to town;
Some in rags, some in tags,
And some in velvet gowns.
Hark! Hark!

Ten little Indians standing in a line —
One went home, and then there were
nine.
Ten Little Indians

When good King Arthur ruled this
land,
He was a goodly king,
He bought three pecks of barley meal,
To make a bag pudding.
Good King Arthur

One misty, moisty morning,
When cloudy was the weather,
I chanced to meet an old man
Clothed all in leather;
He began to compliment,
And I began to grin —
"How do you do?" and "How do you
do?"
And "How do you do?" again!
One Misty, Moisty Morning

Bobby Shaftoe's gone to sea,
Silver buckles on his knee;

He'll come back and marry me,
Pretty Bobby Shaftoe.
Bobby Shaftoe

Bobby Shaftoe's fat and fair,
Combing down his yellow hair;
He's my love forevermore,
Pretty Bobby Shaftoe.
Ibid.

Fe, Fi, Fo, Fum!
I smell the blood of an Englishman;
Be he alive or be he dead,
I'll grind his bones to make my bread.
Fe, Fi, Fo, Fum

There was a man in our town,
And he was wondrous wise;
He jumped into a bramble bush
And scratched out both his eyes.
There Was a Man in Our Town

There were two blackbirds,
Sitting on a hill,
The one named Jack,
    The other named Jill;
Fly away, Jack! Fly Away, Jill!
Come again, Jack! Come again, Jill!
Two Blackbirds

This is the farmer sowing the corn,
That kept the cock that crowed in the
    morn,
That waked the priest all shaven and
    shorn,
That married the man all tattered and
    torn,
That kissed the maiden all forlorn,
That milked the cow with the crumpled
    horn,
That tossed the dog
That worried the cat
That killed the rat
That ate the malt
That lay in the house that Jack built.
The House that Jack Built

THE HOLY BIBLE

WYCLIFFE TRANSLATION
[1384]

This Bible is for the Government of the People, by the People, and for the People.

General Prologue

THE KING JAMES VERSION [1]
[1611]

OLD TESTAMENT

In the beginning God created the heaven and the earth.

Genesis. I, 1

And the earth was without form, and void; and darkness was upon the face of the deep. And the Spirit of God moved upon the face of the waters.

Ibid. 2

And God said, Let there be light; and there was light.

Ibid. 3

And the evening and the morning were the first day.

Ibid. 5

And God saw that it was good.

Ibid. 10

And God said, Let us make man in our image, after our likeness.

Ibid. 26

Male and female created he them.

Ibid. 27

Be fruitful, and multiply, and replenish the earth, and subdue it: and have dominion over the fish of the sea, and over the fowl of the air, and over

every living thing that moveth upon the earth.

Genesis. I, 28

And the Lord God formed man of the dust of the ground, and breathed into his nostrils the breath of life; and man became a living soul.

Ibid. II, 7

And the Lord God planted a garden eastward in Eden.

Ibid. 8

The tree of life also in the midst of the garden.

Ibid. 9

But of the tree of the knowledge of good and evil, thou shalt not eat of it: for in the day that thou eatest thereof thou shalt surely die.

Ibid. 17

It is not good that the man should be alone; I will make him an help meet for him.

Ibid. 18

And the Lord God caused a deep sleep to fall upon Adam, and he slept; and he took one of his ribs, and closed up the flesh instead thereof.

Ibid. 21

And the rib, which the Lord God had taken from man, made he a woman.

Ibid. 22

Bone of my bones, and flesh of my flesh.

Ibid. 23

Therefore shall a man leave his father and his mother, and shall cleave unto his wife: and they shall be one flesh.

Ibid. 24

Now the serpent was more subtile than any beast of the field.

Ibid. III, 1

Your eyes shall be opened, and ye shall be as gods, knowing good and evil.

Ibid. 5

[1] Among all our joys, there was no one that more filled our hearts, than the blessed continuance of the preaching of God's sacred Word among us; which is that inestimable treasure, which excelleth all the riches of the earth; because the fruit thereof extendeth itself, not only to the time spent in this transitory world, but directeth and disposeth men unto that eternal happiness which is above in heaven. — *The Translators' Dedication to James I*

And they sewed fig leaves together, and made themselves aprons.
Genesis. III, 7

And they heard the voice of the Lord God walking in the garden in the cool of the day.
Ibid. 8

The woman whom thou gavest to be with me, she gave me of the tree, and I did eat.
Ibid. 12

What is this that thou hast done? And the woman said, The serpent beguiled me, and I did eat.
Ibid. 13

In sorrow thou shalt bring forth children.
Ibid. 16

In the sweat of thy face shalt thou eat bread, till thou return unto the ground; for out of it wast thou taken: for dust thou art, and unto dust shalt thou return.
Ibid. 19

And Adam called his wife's name Eve; because she was the mother of all living.
Ibid. 20

So he drove out the man: and he placed at the east of the garden of Eden cherubims, and a flaming sword which turned every way, to keep the way of the tree of life.
Ibid. 24

And Abel was a keeper of sheep, but Cain was a tiller of the ground.
Ibid. IV, 2

Am I my brother's keeper?
Ibid. 9

The voice of thy brother's blood crieth unto me from the ground.
Ibid. 10

A fugitive and a vagabond shalt thou be in the earth.
Ibid. 12

My punishment is greater than I can bear.
Ibid. 13

And the Lord set a mark upon Cain.
Ibid. 15

And Cain went out from the presence of the Lord, and dwelt in the land of Nod.
Genesis. IV, 16

The father of such as dwell in tents.
Ibid. 20

Jubal: he was the father of all such as handle the harp and organ.
Ibid. 21

And Enoch walked with God.
Ibid. V, 24

And all the days of Methuselah were nine hundred sixty and nine years.
Ibid. 27

And Noah begat Shem, Ham, and Japheth.
Ibid. 32

There were giants in the earth in those days.
Ibid. VI, 4

Mighty men which were of old, men of renown.
Ibid.

Make thee an ark of gopher wood.
Ibid. 14

And of every living thing of all flesh, two of every sort shalt thou bring into the ark.
Ibid. 19

And the rain was upon the earth forty days and forty nights.
Ibid. VII, 12

But the dove found no rest for the sole of her foot.
Ibid. VIII, 9

And lo, in her mouth was an olive leaf plucked off.
Ibid. 11

For the imagination of man's heart is evil from his youth.
Ibid. 21

While the earth remaineth, seedtime and harvest, and cold and heat, and summer and winter, and day and night shall not cease.
Ibid. 22

I do set my bow in the cloud, and it shall be for a token of a covenant between me and the earth.
Ibid. IX, 13

Even as Nimrod the mighty hunter before the Lord.

Genesis. X, 9

Babel; because the Lord did there confound the language of all the earth.

Ibid. XI, 9

Let there be no strife, I pray thee, between me and thee . . . for we be brethren.

Ibid. XIII, 8

In a good old age.

Ibid. XV, 15

His [Ishmael's] hand will be against every man, and every man's hand against him.

Ibid. XVI, 12

Thy name shall be Abraham; for a father of many nations have I made thee.

Ibid. XVII, 5

My Lord, if now I have found favour in thy sight, pass not away, I pray thee, from thy servant.

Ibid. XVIII, 3

But his [Lot's] wife looked back from behind him, and she became a pillar of salt.

Ibid. XIX, 26

My son, God will provide himself a lamb for a burnt offering.

Ibid. XXII, 8

And he [Esau] sold his birthright unto Jacob.

Ibid. XXV, 33

The voice is Jacob's voice, but the hands are the hands of Esau.

Ibid. XXVII, 22

Thy brother came with subtilty, and hath taken away thy blessing.

Ibid. 35

He [Jacob] dreamed, and behold a ladder set up on the earth, and the top of it reached to heaven: and behold the angels of God ascending and descending on it.

Ibid. XXVIII, 12

Surely the Lord is in this place; and I knew it not.

Ibid. 16

This is none other but the house of God, and this is the gate of heaven.

Ibid. 17

Jacob served seven years for Rachel; and they seemed unto him but a few days, for the love he had to her.

Genesis. XXIX, 20

Mizpah; for he said, The Lord watch between me and thee, when we are absent one from another.

Ibid. XXXI, 49

I will not let thee go, except thou bless me.

Ibid. XXXII, 26

For I have seen God face to face, and my life is preserved.

Ibid. 30

Behold, this dreamer cometh.

Ibid. XXXVII, 19

They stript Joseph out of his coat, his coat of many colours.

Ibid. 23

And the lean and the ill-favoured kine did eat up the first seven fat kine.

Ibid. XLI, 20

There come seven years of great plenty throughout all the land of Egypt: And there shall arise after them seven years of famine.

Ibid. 29, 30

Ye shall bring down my gray hairs with sorrow to the grave.

Ibid. XLIV, 29

And ye shall eat the fat of the land.

Ibid. XLV, 18

Unstable as water, thou shalt not excel.

Ibid. XLIX, 4

Unto the utmost bound of the everlasting hills.

Ibid. 26

She took for him an ark of bulrushes, and daubed it with slime and with pitch.

Exodus. II, 3

I have been a stranger in a strange land.

Ibid. 22

Behold, the bush burned with fire, and the bush was not consumed.

Ibid. III, 2

Put off thy shoes from off thy feet, for the place whereon thou standest is holy ground.

Ibid. 5

A land flowing with milk and honey.[1]
Exodus. III, 8

And God said unto Moses, I AM THAT I AM.
Ibid. 14

I am slow of speech, and of a slow tongue.
Ibid. IV, 10

Ye shall no more give the people straw to make brick.
Ibid. V, 7

And he hardened Pharaoh's heart.
Ibid. VII, 13.

Let my people go.
Ibid. 16

Darkness which may be felt.
Ibid. X, 21

Your lamb shall be without blemish.
Ibid. XII, 5

And thus shall ye eat it; with your loins girded, your shoes on your feet, and your staff in your hand; and ye shall eat it in haste: it is the Lord's passover.
Ibid. 11

For I will pass through the land of Egypt this night, and will smite all the firstborn in the land of Egypt, both man and beast; and against all the gods of Egypt I will execute judgment: I am the Lord.
Ibid. 12

This day [Passover] shall be unto you for a memorial; and ye shall keep it a feast to the Lord throughout your generations.
Ibid. 14

Seven days shall ye eat unleavened bread.
Ibid. 15

There was a great cry in Egypt: for there was not a house where there was not one dead.
Ibid. 30

Remember this day, in which ye came out from Egypt, out of the house of bondage.
Ibid. XIII, 3

And the Lord went before them by day in a pillar of a cloud, to lead them

[1] Also in *XXXIII, 3, and Jeremiah, XI, 5.*

the way; and by night in a pillar of fire.
Exodus. XIII, 21

And Moses stretched out his hand over the sea; and the Lord caused the sea to go back by a strong east wind all that night, and made the sea dry land, and the waters were divided.
Ibid. XIV, 21

I will sing unto the Lord, for he hath triumphed gloriously: the horse and his rider hath he thrown into the sea.
Ibid. XV, 1

The Lord is my strength and song, and he is become my salvation.
Ibid. 2

The Lord is a man of war.
Ibid. 3

Thou sentest forth thy wrath, which consumed them as stubble.
Ibid. 7

Would to God we had died by the hand of the Lord in the land of Egypt, when we sat by the fleshpots, and when we did eat bread to the full.
Ibid. XVI, 3

It is manna.
Ibid. 15

Thou shalt have no other gods before me.
Ibid. XX, 2

Thou shalt not make unto thee any graven image.
Ibid. 4

For I the Lord thy God am a jealous God, visiting the iniquity of the fathers upon the children unto the third and fourth generation of them that hate me.
Ibid. 5

Thou shalt not take the name of the Lord thy God in vain.
Ibid. 7

Remember the sabbath day, to keep it holy.
Ibid. 8

Six days shalt thou labour, and do all thy work;
But the seventh day . . . thou shalt not do any work.
Ibid. 9, 10

Honour thy father and thy mother: that thy days may be long upon the land which the Lord thy God giveth thee.

Exodus. XX, 12

Thou shalt not kill
Thou shalt not commit adultery.
Thou shalt not steal.
Thou shalt not bear false witness against thy neighbour.
Thou shalt not covet thy neighbour's house, thou shalt not covet thy neighbour's wife, nor his manservant, nor his maidservant, nor his ox, nor his ass, nor any thing that is thy neighbour's.

Ibid. 13–17

But let not God speak with us, lest we die.

Ibid. 19

He that smiteth a man, so that he die, shall be surely put to death.

XXI. 12

Eye for eye, tooth for tooth,[1] hand for hand, foot for foot.

Ibid. 24

Behold, I send an Angel before thee, to keep thee in the way.

Ibid. XXIII, 20

Thou art a stiffnecked people.

Ibid. XXXIII, 3

Thou canst not see my face: for there shall no man see me, and live.

Ibid. 20

And he [Moses] was there with the Lord forty days and forty nights; he did neither eat bread, nor drink water. And he wrote upon the tables the words of the covenant, the ten commandments.

Ibid. XXXIV, 28

The swine . . . is unclean to you. Of their flesh shall ye not eat.

Leviticus. XI, 7, 8

Let him go for a scapegoat into the wilderness.

Ibid. XVI, 10

Thou shalt not go up and down as a talebearer among thy people.

Ibid. XIX, 16

Thou shalt love thy neighbour as thyself.[1]

Leviticus. XIX, 18

The Lord bless thee, and keep thee: The Lord make his face shine upon thee, and be gracious unto thee: The Lord lift up his countenance upon thee, and give thee peace.

Numbers. VI, 24, 25, 26

Sent to spy out the land.

Ibid. XIII, 16

And your children shall wander in the wilderness forty years.

Ibid. XIV, 33

The Lord opened the mouth of the ass, and she said unto Balaam, What have I done unto thee?

Ibid. XXII, 28

Let me die the death of the righteous, and let my last end be like his!

Ibid. XXIII, 10

God is not a man, that he should lie.

Ibid. 19

How goodly are thy tents, O Jacob, and thy tabernacles, O Israel!

Ibid. XXIV, 5

Be sure your sin will find you out.

Ibid. XXXII, 23

Thou shalt love the Lord thy God with all thine heart, and with all thy soul, and with all thy might.

Deuteronomy. VI, 5

The Lord thy God hath chosen thee to be a special people unto himself.

Ibid. VII, 6

Man doth not live by bread only,[2] but by every word that proceedeth out of the mouth of the Lord doth man live.

Ibid. VIII, 3

A dreamer of dreams.

Ibid. XIII, 1

The wife of thy bosom.

Ibid. 6

The poor shall never cease out of the land.

Ibid. XV, 11

[1] Also in *Matthew, V, 38.*

[1] Also in *Matthew, XIX, 19; XXII, 39; Mark, XII, 31, 33; Romans, XIII, 9; Galatians, V, 14; James, II, 8.*
[2] Also in *Matthew, IV, 4.*

And thou shalt become an astonishment, a proverb, and a byword, among all nations.

Deuteronomy. XXVIII, 37

In the morning thou shalt say, Would God it were even! and at even thou shalt say, Would God it were morning!

Ibid. 67

The secret things belong unto the Lord our God.

Ibid. XXIX, 29

He kept him as the apple of his eye.

Ibid. XXXII, 10

Jeshurun waxed fat, and kicked.

Ibid. 15

As thy days, so shall thy strength be.

Ibid. XXXIII, 25

The eternal God is thy refuge, and underneath are the everlasting arms.

Ibid. 27

No man knoweth of his [Moses's] sepulchre unto this day.

Ibid. XXXIV, 6

As I was with Moses, so I will be with thee: I will not fail thee, nor forsake thee.

Joshua. I, 5

Be strong and of a good courage;[1] be not afraid, neither be thou dismayed: for the Lord thy God is with thee whithersoever thou goest.

Ibid. 9

Mighty men of valour.

Ibid. VI, 2

And it came to pass, when the people heard the sound of the trumpet, and the people shouted with a great shout, that the wall fell down flat, so that the people went up into the city.

Ibid. 20

His fame was noised throughout all the country.

Ibid. 27

Hewers of wood and drawers of water.

Ibid. IX, 21

The sun stood still, and the moon stayed.

Ibid. X, 13

[1] Also in *Deuteronomy, XXI, 6, 7, 23.*

Old and stricken in years.

Joshua. XIII, 1

I am going the way of all the earth.

Ibid. XXIII, 14

They shall be as thorns in your sides.

Judges. II, 3

I arose a mother in Israel.

Ibid. V, 7

The stars in their courses fought against Sisera.

Ibid. 20

She brought forth butter in a lordly dish.

Ibid. 25

She [Jael] put her hand to the nail, and her right hand to the workmen's hammer; and with the hammer she smote Sisera, she smote off his head.

Ibid. 26

At her feet he bowed, he fell, he lay down: at her feet he bowed, he fell: where he bowed, there he fell down dead.

Ibid. 27

Why tarry the wheels of his chariots?

Ibid. 28

Is not the gleaning of the grapes of Ephraim better than the vintage of Abiezer?

Ibid. VIII, 2

Say now Shibboleth: and he said Sibboleth: for he could not frame to pronounce it right.

Ibid. XII, 6

There was a swarm of bees and honey in the carcase of the lion.

Ibid. XIV, 8

Out of the eater came forth meat, and out of the strong came forth sweetness.

Ibid. 14

If ye had not plowed with my heifer, ye had not found out my riddle.

Ibid. 18

He smote them hip and thigh.

Ibid. XV, 8

With the jawbone of an ass . . . have I slain a thousand men.

Ibid. 16

The Philistines be upon thee, Samson.

Ibid. XVI, 9

So the dead which he slew at his death were more than they which he slew in his life.

Judges. XVI, 30

From Dan even to Beer-sheba.

Ibid. XX, 1

All the people arose as one man.

Ibid. 8

In those days there was no king in Israel: every man did that which was right in his own eyes.

Ibid. XXI, 25

Whither thou goest, I will go; and where thou lodgest, I will lodge: thy people shall be my people, and thy God my God.

Ruth. I, 16

Let me glean and gather after the reapers among the sheaves.

Ibid. II, 7

Go not empty unto thy mother in law.

Ibid. III, 17

In the flower of their age.

1 Samuel. II, 33

The Lord called Samuel; and he answered, Here am I.

Ibid. III, 4

Speak, Lord; for thy servant heareth.

Ibid. 9

Be strong, and quit yourselves like men.

Ibid. IV, 9

The glory is departed from Israel: for the ark of God is taken.

Ibid. 22

Is Saul also among the prophets?

Ibid. X, 11

And all the people shouted, and said, God save the king.

Ibid. 24

A man after his own heart.

Ibid. XIII, 14

Every man's sword was against his fellow.

Ibid. XIV, 20

To obey is better than sacrifice, and to hearken than the fat of rams.

Ibid. XV, 22

For rebellion is as the sin of witchcraft, and stubbornness is as iniquity and idolatry.

1 Samuel. XV, 23

For the Lord seeth not as man seeth; for man looketh on the outward appearance, but the Lord looketh on the heart.

Ibid. XVI, 7

Let no man's heart fail because of him [Goliath].

Ibid. XVII, 32

And he [David] . . . chose him five smooth stones out of the brook.

Ibid. 40

So David prevailed over the Philistine with a sling and with a stone.

Ibid. 50

Saul hath slain his thousands, and David his ten thousands.

Ibid. XVIII, 7

And Jonathan . . . loved him [David] as he loved his own soul.

Ibid. XX, 17

I have played the fool.

Ibid. XXVI, 21

Tell it not in Gath, publish it not in the streets of Askelon.

2 Samuel. I, 20

Saul and Jonathan were lovely and pleasant in their lives, and in their death they were not divided: they were swifter than eagles, they were stronger than lions.

Ibid. 23

How are the mighty fallen in the midst of the battle!

Ibid. 25

Thy love to me was wonderful, passing the love of women.

Ibid. 26

How are the mighty fallen, and the weapons of war perished!

Ibid. 27

Abner . . . smote him under the fifth rib.

Ibid. II, 23

Know ye not that there is a prince and a great man fallen this day in Israel?

Ibid. III, 38

And David and all the house of Israel played before the Lord on all manner of instruments made of fir wood, even on harps, and on psalteries, and on timbrels, and on cornets, and on cymbals.

2 Samuel. VI, 5

And David danced before the Lord.

Ibid. 14

Tarry at Jericho until your beards be grown.[1]

Ibid. X, 5

Set ye Uriah in the forefront of the hottest battle.

Ibid. XI, 15

The poor man had nothing, save one little ewe lamb.

Ibid. XII, 3

Thou art the man.

Ibid. 7

Now he is dead, wherefore should I fast? Can I bring him back again? I shall go to him, but he shall not return to me.

Ibid. 23

For we must needs die, and are as water spilt on the ground, which cannot be gathered up again.

Ibid. XIV, 14

Would God I had died for thee, O Absalom, my son, my son!

Ibid. XVIII, 33

The Lord is my rock, and my fortress, and my deliverer.

Ibid. XXII, 2

David the son of Jesse . . . the sweet psalmist of Israel.

Ibid. XXIII, 1

A wise and an understanding heart.

1 Kings. III, 12

And the king said, Divide the living child in two, and give half to the one, and half to the other.

Ibid. 25

Then spake the woman whose the living child was unto the king, for her bowels yearned upon her son, and she said, O my lord, give her the living child, and in no wise slay it.

Ibid. 26

[1] Also in *1 Chronicles, XIX, 5.*

Then the king answered and said, Give her the living child.

1 Kings. III, 27

Many, as the sand which is by the sea in multitude.

Ibid. IV, 20

He [Solomon] spake three thousand proverbs: and his songs were a thousand and five.

Ibid. 32

So that there was neither hammer nor axe nor any tool of iron heard in the house, while it was in building.

Ibid. VI, 7

When the queen of Sheba heard of the fame of Solomon . . . she came to prove him with hard questions.

Ibid. X, 1

The half was not told me.

Ibid. 7

Once in three years came the navy of Tharshish, bringing gold, and silver, ivory, and apes, and peacocks.

Ibid. 22

King Solomon loved many strange women.

Ibid. XI, 1

And he had seven hundred wives, princesses, and three hundred concubines: and his wives turned away his heart.

Ibid. 3

My father hath chastised you with whips, but I will chastise you with scorpions.

Ibid. XII, 11

To your tents, O Israel.

Ibid. 16

He went and dwelt by the brook Cherith, that is before Jordan.

Ibid. XVII, 5

And the ravens brought him bread and flesh in the morning, and bread and flesh in the evening; and he drank of the brook.

Ibid. 6

I have commanded a widow woman there to sustain thee.

Ibid. 9

An handful of meal in a barrel, and a little oil in a cruse.

Ibid. 12

And the barrel of meal wasted not, neither did the cruse of oil fail.
1 Kings. XVII, 16

How long halt ye between two opinions?
Ibid. XVIII, 21

There ariseth a little cloud out of the sea, like a man's hand.
Ibid. 44

And he girded up his loins, and ran before Ahab.
Ibid. 46

But the Lord was not in the wind: and after the wind an earthquake; but the Lord was not in the earthquake:

And after the earthquake a fire; but the Lord was not in the fire: and after the fire a still small voice.
Ibid. XIX, 11, 12

Let not him that girdeth on his harness boast himself as he that putteth it off.
Ibid. XX, 11

Hast thou found me, O mine enemy?
Ibid. XXI, 20

The dogs shall eat Jezebel by the wall of Jezreel.
Ibid. 23

There appeared a chariot of fire, and horses of fire . . . and Elijah went up by a whirlwind into heaven.
2 Kings. II, 11

There is death in the pot.
Ibid. IV, 40

Are not Abana and Pharpar, rivers of Damascus, better than all the waters of Israel?
Ibid. V, 12

Is not the sound of his master's feet behind him?
Ibid. VI, 32

Is thy servant a dog, that he should do this great thing?
Ibid. VIII, 13

What hast thou to do with peace? turn thee behind me.
Ibid. IX, 18

The driving is like the driving of Jehu, the son of Nimshi; for he driveth furiously.
Ibid. 20

Jezebel heard of it; and she painted her face, and tired her head, and looked out at a window.
2 Kings. IX, 30

A land of corn and wine.
Ibid. XVIII, 32

Set thine house in order.
Ibid. XX, 1

I will wipe Jerusalem as a man wipeth a dish, wiping it, and turning it upside down.
Ibid. XXI, 13

His mercy endureth for ever.
1 Chronicles. XVI, 41

The Lord searcheth all hearts, and understandeth all the imaginations of the thoughts.
Ibid. XXVIII, 9

Our days on the earth are as a shadow.
Ibid. XXIX, 15

He [David] died in a good old age, full of days, riches, and honour.
Ibid. 28

The man whom the king delighteth to honour.
Esther. VI, 6

One that feared God, and eschewed evil.
Job. I, 1

Satan came also.
Ibid. 6

And the Lord said unto Satan, Whence comest thou? Then Satan answered the Lord, and said, From going to and fro in the earth, and from walking up and down in it.
Ibid. 7

Doth Job fear God for nought?
Ibid. 9

Naked came I out of my mother's womb, and naked shall I return thither: the Lord gave, and the Lord hath taken away; blessed be the name of the Lord.
Ibid. 21

Skin for skin, yea, all that a man hath, will he give for his life.
Ibid. II, 4

Curse God, and die.
Ibid. 9

Let the day perish wherein I was born, and the night in which it was said, there is a man child conceived.

Job. III, 3

There the wicked cease from troubling, and there the weary be at rest.

Ibid. 17

Who ever perished, being innocent? or where were the righteous cut off?

Ibid. IV, 7

Then a spirit passed before my face; the hair of my flesh stood up.

Ibid. 15

Shall mortal man be more just than God? shall a man be more pure than his maker?

Ibid. 17

Wrath killeth the foolish man, and envy slayeth the silly one.

Ibid. V, 2

Man is born unto trouble, as the sparks fly upward.

Ibid. 7

He taketh the wise in their own craftiness.

Ibid. 13

Thou shalt come to thy grave in a full age, like as a shock of corn cometh in his season.

Ibid. 26

How forcible are right words!

Ibid. VI, 25

My days are swifter than a weaver's shuttle, and are spent without hope.

Ibid. VII, 6

He shall return no more to his house, neither shall his place know him any more.[1]

Ibid. 10

I would not live alway: let me alone; for my days are vanity.

Ibid. 16

But how should man be just with God?

Ibid. IX, 2

[1] When a few years are come, then I shall go the way whence I shall not return. — *XVI, 22*
The place thereof shall know it no more. — *Psalm CIII, 16*

The land of darkness and the shadow of death.

Job. X, 21

Canst thou by searching find out God?

Ibid. XI, 7

And thine age shall be clearer than the noonday.

Ibid. 17

No doubt but ye are the people and wisdom shall die with you.

Ibid. XII, 2

The just upright man is laughed to scorn.

Ibid. 4

Speak to the earth, and it shall teach thee.

Ibid. 8

With the ancient is wisdom; and in length of days understanding.

Ibid. 12

He discovereth deep things out of darkness, and bringeth out to light the shadow of death.

Ibid. 22

Man that is born of a woman is of few days, and full of trouble.

Ibid. XIV, 1

He cometh forth like a flower, and is cut down: he fleeth also as a shadow, and continueth not.

Ibid. 2

But man dieth, and wasteth away: yea, man giveth up the ghost, and where is he?

Ibid. 10

If a man die, shall he live again?

Ibid. 14

Should a wise man utter vain knowledge, and fill his belly with the east wind?

Ibid. XV, 2

Miserable comforters are ye all.

Ibid. XVI, 2

My days are past.

Ibid. XVII, 11

I have said to corruption, Thou art my father: to the worm, Thou art my mother, and my sister.

Ibid. 14

The king of terrors.

Ibid. XVIII, 14

I am escaped with the skin of my teeth.

Job. XIX, 20

Oh that my words were now written! oh that they were printed in a book!

Ibid. 23

I know that my redeemer liveth, and that he shall stand at the latter day upon the earth.

Ibid. 25

And though after my skin worms destroy this body, yet in my flesh shall I see God.

Ibid. 26

Seeing the root of the matter is found in me.

Ibid. 28

Though wickedness be sweet in his mouth, though he hide it under his tongue.

Ibid. XX, 12

Shall any teach God knowledge?

Ibid. XXI, 22

Is it any pleasure to the Almighty, that thou art righteous?

Ibid. XXII, 3

They are of those that rebel against the light.

Ibid. XXIV, 13

The womb shall forget him; the worm shall feed sweetly on him; he shall be no more remembered.

Ibid. 20

Yea, the stars are not pure in his sight.

How much less man, that is a worm? and the son of man, which is a worm?

Ibid. XXV, 5–6

The land of the living.

Ibid. XXVIII, 13

The price of wisdom is above rubies.

Ibid. 18

And unto man he said, Behold, the fear of the Lord, that is wisdom; and to depart from evil is understanding.

Ibid. 28

When the ear heard me, then it blessed me; and when the eye saw me, it gave witness to me.

Ibid. XXIX, 11

I caused the widow's heart to sing for joy.

Job. XXIX, 13

I was eyes to the blind, and feet was I to the lame.

Ibid. 15

The house appointed for all living.

Ibid. XXX, 23

I am a brother to dragons, and a companion to owls.

Ibid. 29

My desire is, that the Almighty would answer me, and that mine adversary had written a book.

Ibid. XXXI, 35

Great men are not always wise.

Ibid. XXXII, 9

For I am full of matter, the spirit within me constraineth me.

Ibid. 18

One among a thousand.

Ibid. XXXIII, 23

Far be it from God, that he should do wickedness.

Ibid. XXXIV, 10

He multiplieth words without knowledge.

Ibid. XXXV, 16

Fair weather cometh out of the north.

Ibid. XXXVII, 22

Who is this that darkeneth counsel by words without knowledge?

Ibid. XXXVIII, 2

Gird up now thy loins like a man.

Ibid. 3

Where wast thou when I laid the foundations of the earth? declare, if thou hast understanding.

Ibid. 4

The morning stars sang together, and all the sons of God shouted for joy.

Ibid. 7

Hitherto shalt thou come, but no further: and here shall thy proud waves be stayed?

Ibid. 11

Hath the rain a father? or who hath begotten the drops of dew?

Ibid. 28

Canst thou bind the sweet influences of Pleiades, or loose the bands of Orion?

Job. XXXVIII, 31

Canst thou guide Arcturus with his sons?

Ibid. 32

He saith among the trumpets, Ha, ha; and he smelleth the battle afar off, the thunder of the captains, and the shouting.

Ibid. XXXIX, 25

Behold, I am vile; what shall I answer thee?

Ibid. XL, 4

Behold now behemoth, which I made with thee; he eateth grass as an ox.

Ibid. 15

Canst thou draw out leviathan with a hook?

Ibid. XLI, 1

Hard as a piece of the nether millstone.

Ibid. 24

He maketh the deep to boil like a pot.

Ibid. 31

He is a king over all the children of pride.

Ibid. 34

I have heard of thee by the hearing of the ear; but now mine eye seeth thee.

Ibid. XLII, 5

Blessed is the man that walketh not in the counsel of the ungodly, nor standeth in the way of sinners, nor sitteth in the seat of the scornful.

Psalms. I, 1

And he shall be like a tree planted by the rivers of water, that bringeth forth his fruit in his season; his leaf also shall not wither; and whatsoever he doeth shall prosper.

Ibid. 3

The ungodly are not so: but are like the chaff which the wind driveth away.

Ibid. 4

Serve the Lord with fear and rejoice with trembling.

Ibid. II, 11

Blessed are all they that put their trust in him.

Psalms. II, 12

Lord, lift thou up the light of thy countenance upon us.

Ibid. IV, 6

I will both lay me down in peace, and sleep.[1]

Ibid. 8

Out of the mouth of babes and sucklings hast thou ordained strength.

Ibid. VIII, 2

What is man, that thou art mindful of him? and the son of man, that thou visitest him?

Ibid. 4

Thou hast made him a little lower than the angels.

Ibid. 5

How excellent is thy name in all the earth.

Ibid. 9

Flee as a bird to your mountain.

Ibid. XI, 1

How long wilt thou forget me, O Lord?

Ibid. XIII, 1

The fool hath said in his heart, There is no God.

Ibid. XIV, 1; LIII, 1

He that sweareth to his own hurt, and changeth not.

Ibid. XV, 4

The lines are fallen unto me in pleasant places;[2] yea, I have a goodly heritage.

Ibid. XVI, 6

Keep me as the apple of the eye, hide me under the shadow of thy wings.

Ibid. XVII, 8

He rode upon a cherub, and did fly: yea, he did fly upon the wings of the wind.

Ibid. XVIII, 10

The heavens declare the glory of God; and the firmament showeth his handiwork.

Ibid. XIX, 1

---

[1] I will lay me down in peace, and take my rest. — *Book of Common Prayer, Psalm IV, 9*
[2] The lot is fallen unto me in a fair ground. — *Book of Common Prayer, Psalm XVI, 7*

Day unto day uttereth speech, and night unto night showeth knowledge.
Psalms. XIX, 2

As a bridegroom coming out of his chamber, and rejoiceth as a strong man to run a race.
Ibid. 5

And there is nothing hid from the heat thereof.
Ibid. 6

The judgments of the Lord are true and righteous altogether.
Ibid. 9

More to be desired are they than gold.
Ibid. 10

Sweeter also than honey and the honeycomb.
Ibid.

Cleanse thou me from secret faults.
Ibid. 12

Let the words of my mouth, and the meditation of my heart, be acceptable in thy sight.
Ibid. 14

My God, my God, why hast thou forsaken me? [1]
Ibid. XXII, 1

I may tell all my bones: they look and stare upon me.
Ibid. 17

The Lord is my shepherd; I shall not want.
Ibid. XXIII, 1

He maketh me to lie down in green pastures: he leadeth me beside the still waters.
Ibid. 2

He restoreth my soul: he leadeth me in the paths of righteousness for his name's sake.
Ibid. 3

Yea, though I walk through the valley of the shadow of death, I will fear no evil: for thou art with me; thy rod and thy staff they comfort me.
Ibid. 4

Thou preparest a table before me in the presence of mine enemies: thou

[1] See *Matthew, XXVII, 46,* on page 1055b.

anointest my head with oil; my cup runneth over.
Psalms. XXIII, 5

Surely goodness and mercy shall follow me all the days of my life: and I will dwell in the house of the Lord for ever.
Ibid. 6

The earth is the Lord's, and the fulness thereof; the world, and they that dwell therein.
Ibid. XXIV, 1

For he hath founded it upon the seas, and established it upon the floods.
Ibid. 2

Who shall ascend into the hill of the Lord? or who shall stand in his holy place?
Ibid. 3

He that hath clean hands, and a pure heart; who hath not lifted up his soul unto vanity, nor sworn deceitfully.
Ibid. 4

Who is this King of glory? The Lord of hosts, he is the King of glory.
Ibid. 10

The Lord is my light and my salvation; whom shall I fear? the Lord is the strength of my life; of whom shall I be afraid?
Ibid. XXVII, 1

The Lord is my strength and my shield.
Ibid. XXVIII, 7

Worship the Lord in the beauty of holiness.
Ibid. XXIX, 2

The voice of the Lord is upon the waters: the God of glory thundereth: the Lord is upon many waters.
Ibid. 3

Weeping may endure for a night, but joy cometh in the morning.
Ibid. XXX, 5

I am forgotten as a dead man out of mind: I am like a broken vessel.
Ibid. XXXI, 12

My times are in thy hand.
Ibid. 15

From the strife of tongues.
Ibid. 20

He fashioneth their hearts alike.
Psalms. XXXIII, 15

Keep thy tongue from evil, and thy lips from speaking guile.
Ibid. XXXIV, 13

Rescue my soul from their destructions, my darling from the lions.
Ibid. XXXV, 17

The meek shall inherit the earth.[1]
Ibid. XXXVII, 11

I have been young, and now am old; yet have I not seen the righteous forsaken, nor his seed begging bread.
Ibid. 25

I have seen the wicked in great power, and spreading[2] himself like a green bay tree.
Ibid. 35

Mark the perfect man, and behold the upright.
Ibid. 37

I said, I will take heed to my ways, that I sin not with my tongue.
Ibid. XXXIX, 1

My heart was hot within me, while I was musing the fire burned.
Ibid. 3

Lord, make me to know mine end, and the measure of my days, what it is; that I may know how frail I am.
Ibid. 4

Every man at his best state is altogether vanity.
Ibid. 5

He heapeth up riches, and knoweth not who shall gather them.
Ibid. 6

He brought me up also out of an horrible pit, out of the miry clay, and set my feet upon a rock, and established my goings.
Ibid. XL, 2

Blessed is he that considereth the poor; the Lord will deliver him in time of trouble.
Ibid. XLI, 1

As the hart panteth after the waterbrooks, so panteth my soul after thee.
Ibid. XLII, 1

Why art thou cast down, O my soul? and why art thou disquieted in me?
Psalms. XLII, 5, 11; XLIII, 5

Deep calleth unto deep.
Ibid. 7

My heart is inditing a good matter . . . my tongue is the pen of a ready writer.
Ibid. XLV, 1

God is our refuge and strength, a very present help in trouble.
Ibid. XLVI, 1

Therefore will we not fear, though the earth be removed, and though the mountains be carried into the midst of the sea.
Ibid. 2

Beautiful for situation, the joy of the whole earth, is Mount Zion . . . the city of the great King.
Ibid. XLVIII, 2

Man being in honour abideth not; he is like the beasts that perish.
Ibid. XLIX, 12

Every beast of the forest is mine, and the cattle upon a thousand hills.
Ibid. L, 10

I was shapen in iniquity; and in sin did my mother conceive me.
Ibid. LI, 5

Purge me with hyssop, and I shall be clean: wash me, and I shall be whiter than snow.
Ibid. 7

Create in me a clean heart, O God; and renew a right spirit within me.
Ibid. 10

Open thou my lips; and my mouth shall show forth thy praise.
Ibid. 15

A broken and a contrite heart.
Ibid. 17

Oh that I had wings like a dove!
Ibid. LV, 6

But it was thou, a man mine equal, my guide, and mine acquaintance.[1]
Ibid. 13

[1] See *Matthew, V, 5,* on page 1050b.
[2] Flourishing. — *Book of Common Prayer, Psalm XXXVII, 36*

[1] But it was even thou, my companion, my guide, and mine own familiar friend. — *Book of Common Prayer, Psalm LV, 14*
Mine own familiar friend. — *Psalm XLI, 9*

We took sweet counsel together.
Psalms. LV, 14

The words of his mouth were smoother than butter, but war was in his heart:[1] his words were softer than oil, yet were they drawn swords.
Ibid. 21

Put thou my tears into thy bottle: are they not in thy book?
Ibid. LVI, 8

They are like the deaf adder that stoppeth her ear;
Which will not hearken to the voice of charmers, charming never so wisely.[2]
Ibid. LVIII, 4, 5

Vain is the help of man.
Ibid. LX, 11; CVIII, 12

Lead me to the rock that is higher than I.
Ibid. LXI, 2

He only is my rock and my salvation; he is my defence; I shall not be moved.
Ibid. LXII, 6

Surely men of low degree are vanity, and men of high degree are a lie: to be laid in the balance, they are altogether lighter than vanity.
Ibid. 9

Thou renderest to every man according to his work.
Ibid. 12

My soul thirsteth for thee, my flesh longeth for thee in a dry and thirsty land, where no water is.
Ibid. LXIII, 1

Thou crownest the year with thy goodness.
Ibid. LXV, 11

The little hills rejoice on every side.
Ibid. 12

Make a joyful noise unto God, all ye lands.
Ibid. LXVI, 1

[1] The words of his mouth were softer than butter, having war in his heart. — *Book of Common Prayer, Psalm LV, 22*
[2] Like the deaf adder, that stoppeth her ears; which refuseth to hear the voice of the charmer, charm he never so wisely. — *The Book of Common Prayer, Psalm LVIII, 4, 5*

We went through fire and through water.
Psalms. LXVI, 12

God setteth the solitary in families
Ibid. LXVIII, 6

Cast me not off in the time of old age; forsake me not when my strength faileth.
Ibid. LXXI, 9

He shall come down like rain upon the mown grass.
Ibid. LXXII, 6

His enemies shall lick the dust.
Ibid. 9

His name shall endure for ever.
Ibid. 17

As a dream when one awaketh.
Ibid. LXXIII, 20

He putteth down one and setteth up another.
Ibid. LXXV, 7

A stubborn and rebellious generation.
Ibid. LXXVIII, 8

Man did eat angels' food.
Ibid. 25

How amiable are thy tabernacles, O Lord of hosts!
Ibid. LXXXIV, 1

They go from strength to strength.
Ibid. 7

A day in thy courts is better than a thousand. I had rather be a doorkeeper in the house of my God, than to dwell in the tents of wickedness.
Ibid. 10

Mercy and truth are met together: righteousness and peace have kissed each other.
Ibid. LXXXV, 10

A thousand years in thy sight are but as yesterday when it is past, and as a watch in the night.
Ibid. XC, 4

They are like grass which groweth up.
In the morning it flourisheth, and groweth up; in the evening it is cut down, and withereth.[1]
Ibid. 5, 6

[1] See *Isaiah, XL, 6, 8,* on page 1047a.

We spend our years as a tale that is told.[1]

Psalms. XC, 9

The days of our years are threescore years and ten; and if by reason of strength they be fourscore years, yet is their strength labour and sorrow; for it is soon cut off, and we fly away.[2]

Ibid. 10

So teach us to number our days, that we may apply our hearts unto wisdom.

Ibid. 12

Establish thou the work of our hands upon us; yea, the work of our hands establish thou it.

Ibid. 17

He that dwelleth in the secret place of the most High shall abide under the shadow of the Almighty.

Ibid. XCI, 1

I will say of the Lord, He is my refuge and my fortress: my God; in him will I trust.

Ibid. 2

Surely he shall deliver thee from the snare of the fowler, and from the noisome pestilence.

Ibid. 3

His truth shall be thy shield and buckler.

Ibid. 4

Thou shalt not be afraid for the terror by night; nor for the arrow that flieth by day.

Ibid. 5

Nor for the pestilence that walketh in darkness; nor for the destruction that wasteth at noonday.

Ibid. 6

A thousand shall fall at thy side, and ten thousand at thy right hand; but it shall not come nigh thee.

Ibid. 7

[1] We bring our years to an end, as it were a tale that is told. — *Book of Common Prayer, Psalm XL, 9*

[2] The days of our age are threescore and ten; and though men be so strong that they come to fourscore years, yet is their strength then but labour and sorrow; so soon passeth it away, and we are gone. — *Book of Common Prayer, Psalm XL, 10*

He shall give his angels charge over thee, to keep thee in all thy ways.

Psalms. XCI, 11

The righteous shall flourish like the palm tree: he shall grow like a cedar in Lebanon.

Ibid. XCII, 12

Mightier than the noise of many waters.

Ibid. XCIII, 4

In his hand are the deep places of the earth: the strength of the hills is his also.

Ibid. XCV, 4

The sea is his, and he made it: and his hands formed the dry land.

Ibid. 5

We are the people of his pasture, and the sheep of his land.

Ibid. 7

O sing unto the Lord a new song.

Ibid. XCVI, 1

The Lord reigneth; let the earth rejoice.

Ibid. XCVII, 1

Make a joyful noise unto the Lord, all ye lands.

Ibid. C, 1

As for man, his days are as grass: as a flower of the field, so he flourisheth.

Ibid. CIII, 15

The wind passeth over it, and it is gone; and the place thereof shall know it no more.

Ibid. 16

Wine that maketh glad the heart of man.

Ibid. CIV, 15

The trees of the Lord are full of sap; the cedars of Lebanon, which he hath planted.

Ibid. 16

Man goeth forth unto his work and to his labour until the evening.

Ibid. 23

Such as sit in darkness and in the shadow of death.

Ibid. CVII, 10

They that go down to the sea in ships, that do business in great waters.

Ibid. 23

They reel to and fro, and stagger like a drunken man, and are at their wits' end.

Psalms. CVII, 27

Thy people shall be willing in the day of thy power, in the beauties of holiness from the womb of the morning: thou hast the dew of thy youth.

Ibid. CX, 3

Thou art a priest for ever after the order of Melchizedek.

Ibid. 4

The fear of the Lord is the beginning of wisdom.

Ibid. CXI, 10

From the rising of the sun unto the going down of the same.

Ibid. CXIII, 3

The mountains skipped like rams, and the little hills like lambs.

Ibid. CXIV, 4

Eyes have they, but they see not. They have ears, but they hear not.[1]

Ibid. CXV, 6

I said in my haste, All men are liars.

Ibid. CXVI, 11

Precious in the sight of the Lord is the death of his saints.

Ibid. 15

The stone which the builders refused is become the head stone of the corner.[2]

Ibid. CXVIII, 22

This is the day which the Lord hath made.

Ibid. 24

Blessed be he that cometh in the name of the Lord.[3]

Ibid. 26

I have more understanding than all my teachers: for thy testimonies are my meditation.

Ibid. CXIX, 99

Thy word is a lamp unto my feet, and a light unto my path.

Ibid. 105

I will lift up mine eyes unto the hills, from whence cometh my help.

Ibid. CXXI, 1

[1] Also in *Psalm CXXXV, 16–17.*
[2] Also in *Matthew, XXI, 42.*
[3] Also in *Matthew, XXI, 9, XXIII, 39; Mark, XI, 9; Luke, XIII, 35.*

My help cometh from the Lord, which made heaven and earth.

Psalms. CXXI, 2

He will not suffer thy foot to be moved: he that keepeth thee will not slumber.

Ibid. 3

Behold, he that keepeth Israel shall neither slumber nor sleep.

Ibid. 4

The sun shall not smite thee by day, nor the moon by night.

Ibid. 6

The Lord shall preserve thy going out and thy coming in from this time forth, and even for evermore.

Ibid. 8

I was glad when they said unto me, Let us go into the house of the Lord.

Ibid. CXXII, 1

Peace be within thy walls, and prosperity within thy palaces.

Ibid. CXXII, 7

They that sow in tears shall reap in joy.

Ibid. CXXVI, 5

He that goeth forth and weepeth, bearing precious seed, shall doubtless come again with rejoicing, bringing his sheaves with him.

Ibid. 6

Except the Lord build the house, they labour in vain that build it.

Ibid. CXXVII, 1

He giveth his beloved sleep.

Ibid. 2

Happy is the man that hath his quiver full of them.

Ibid. 5

Out of the depths have I cried unto thee, O Lord.

Ibid. CXXX, 1

I will not give sleep to mine eyes, or slumber to mine eyelids.[1]

Ibid. CXXXII, 4

Behold, how good and how pleasant it is for brethren to dwell together in unity!

Ibid. CXXXIII, 1

[1] Also in *Proverbs, VI, 4.*

By the rivers of Babylon, there we sat down, yea, we wept, when we remembered Zion.[1]

Psalms. CXXXVII, 1

We hanged our harps upon the willows.

Ibid. 2

They that carried us away captive required of us a song; and they that wasted us required of us mirth, saying, sing us one of the songs of Zion.

Ibid. 3

How shall we sing the Lord's song in a strange land?

Ibid. 4

If I forget thee, O Jerusalem, let my right hand forget her cunning.

Ibid. 5

If I ascend up into heaven, thou art there: if I make my bed in hell, behold, thou art there.

Ibid. CXXXIX, 8

If I take the wings of the morning, and dwell in the uttermost parts of the sea.

Ibid. 9

I am fearfully and wonderfully made.

Ibid. 14

Teach me to do thy will.

Ibid. CXLIII, 10

That our sons may be as plants grown up in their youth; that our daughters may be as corner stones.

Ibid. CXLIV, 12

Put not your trust in princes.

Ibid. CXLVI, 3

Let every thing that hath breath praise the Lord.

Ibid. CL, 6

My son, if sinners entice thee, consent thou not.

Proverbs. I, 10

Wisdom crieth without; she uttereth her voice in the streets.

Ibid. 20

[1] By the waters of Babylon we sat down and wept: when we remembered thee, O Sion. — *Book of Common Prayer, Psalm CXXXVII, 1*

Length of days is in her right hand; and in her left hand riches and honour.

Proverbs. III, 16

Her ways are ways of pleasantness, and all her paths are peace.

Ibid. 17

Wisdom is the principal thing; therefore get wisdom; and with all thy getting get understanding.

Ibid. IV, 7

The path of the just is as the shining light, that shineth more and more unto the perfect day.

Ibid. 18

Keep thy heart with all diligence; for out of it are the issues of life.

Ibid. 23

For the lips of a strange woman drop as a honeycomb, and her mouth is smoother than oil:

But her end is bitter as wormwood, sharp as a two-edged sword.

Ibid. V, 3, 4

Go to the ant, thou sluggard; consider her ways, and be wise:

Which having no guide, overseer, or ruler,

Provideth her meat in the summer, and gathereth her food in the harvest.

Ibid. VI, 6–8

Yet a little sleep, a little slumber, a little folding of the hands to sleep.

Ibid. 10; XXIV, 33

Can a man take fire in his bosom, and his clothes not be burned?

Ibid. 27

Can one go upon hot coals, and his feet not be burned?

Ibid. 28

He goeth after her straightway, as an ox goeth to the slaughter.

Ibid. VII, 22

Wisdom is better than rubies.

Ibid. VIII, 11

I love them that love me; and those that seek me early shall find me.

Ibid. 17

Wisdom hath builded her house, she hath hewn out her seven pillars.

Ibid. IX, 1

Reprove not a scorner, lest he hate thee: rebuke a wise man, and he will love thee.
Proverbs. IX, 8

Stolen waters are sweet, and bread eaten in secret is pleasant.
Ibid. 17

A wise son maketh a glad father: but a foolish son is the heaviness of his mother.
Ibid. X, 1

The memory of the just is blessed: but the name of the wicked shall rot.
Ibid. 7

Hatred stirreth up strifes: but love covereth all sins.
Ibid. 12

In the multitude of counsellors there is safety.
Ibid. XI, 14; XXIV, 6

He that is surety for a stranger shall smart for it.
Ibid. 15

As a jewel of gold in a swine's snout, so is a fair woman which is without discretion.
Ibid. 22

He that trusteth in his riches shall fall.
Ibid. 28

A righteous man regardeth the life of his beast: but the tender mercies of the wicked are cruel.
Ibid. XII, 10

The way of a fool is right in his own eyes.
Ibid. 15

Hope deferred maketh the heart sick.
Ibid. XIII, 12

The way of transgressors is hard.
Ibid. 15

He that spareth his rod hateth his son: but he that loveth him chasteneth him betimes.
Ibid. 24

Fools make a mock at sin.
Ibid. XIV, 9

The heart knoweth his own bitterness; and a stranger doth not intermeddle with his joy.
Ibid. 10

Even in laughter the heart is sorrowful.
Proverbs. XIV, 13

The prudent man looketh well to his going.
Ibid. 15

The talk of the lips tendeth only to penury.
Ibid. 23

Righteousness exalteth a nation.
Ibid. 34

A soft answer turneth away wrath.
Ibid. XV, 1

A merry heart maketh a cheerful countenance.
Ibid. 13

He that is of a merry heart hath a continual feast.
Ibid. 15

Better is a dinner of herbs where love is, than a stalled ox and hatred therewith.
Ibid. 17

A word spoken in due season. how good is it!
Ibid. 23

Before honour is humility.
Ibid. 33; XVIII, 12

A man's heart deviseth his way; but the Lord directeth his steps.
Ibid. XVI, 9

Pride goeth before destruction, and an haughty spirit before a fall.
Ibid. 18

The hoary head is a crown of glory, if it be found in the way of righteousness.
Ibid. 31

He that is slow to anger is better than the mighty; and he that ruleth his spirit than he that taketh a city.
Ibid. 32

Whoso mocketh the poor reproacheth his Maker.
Ibid. XVII, 5

A gift is as a precious stone in the eyes of him that hath it.
Ibid. 8

He that repeateth a matter separateth very friends.
Ibid. 9

A merry heart doeth good like a medicine.
Proverbs. XVII, 22

Even a fool, when he holdeth his peace, is counted wise.
Ibid. 28

A fool's mouth is his destruction.
Ibid. XVIII, 7

A wounded spirit who can bear?
Ibid. 14

Whoso findeth a wife findeth a good thing.
Ibid. 22

A man that hath friends must show himself friendly: and there is a friend that sticketh closer than a brother.
Ibid. 24

Wealth maketh many friends.
Ibid. XIX, 4

He that hath pity upon the poor lendeth unto the Lord.
Ibid. 17

Wine is a mocker, strong drink is raging.
Ibid. XX, 1

It is an honour for a man to cease from strife: but every fool will be meddling.
Ibid. 3

The hearing ear and the seeing eye, the Lord hath made even both of them.
Ibid. 12

It is naught, it is naught, saith the buyer: but when he is gone his way, then he boasteth.
Ibid. 14

Bread of deceit is sweet to a man; but afterwards his mouth shall be filled with gravel.
Ibid. 17

Meddle not with him that flattereth with his lips.
Ibid. 19

The glory of young men is their strength: and the beauty of old men is the grey head.
Ibid. 29

It is better to dwell in a corner of the housetop, than with a brawling woman in a wide house.
Ibid. XXI, 9; XXV, 24

A good name is rather to be chosen than great riches.
Proverbs. XXII, 1

Train up a child in the way he should go: and when he is old he will not depart from it.
Ibid. 6

The borrower is servant to the lender.
Ibid. 7

Remove not the ancient landmark.
Ibid. 28

Seest thou a man diligent in his business? He shall stand before kings.
Ibid. 29

Put a knife to thy throat, if thou be a man given to appetite.
Ibid. XXIII, 2

Riches certainly make themselves wings.
Ibid. 5

As he thinketh in his heart, so is he.
Ibid. 7

The drunkard and the glutton shall come to poverty: and drowsiness shall clothe a man with rags.
Ibid. 21

Despise not thy mother when she is old.
Ibid. 22

Look not thou upon the wine when it is red, when it giveth his colour in the cup, when it moveth itself aright.
At the last it biteth like a serpent, and stingeth like an adder.
Ibid. 31, 32

A wise man is strong; yea, a man of knowledge increaseth strength.
Ibid. XXIV, 5

If thou faint in the day of adversity, thy strength is small.
Ibid. 10

Rejoice not when thine enemy falleth, and let not thine heart be glad when he stumbleth.
Ibid. 17

Fret not thyself because of evil men.
Ibid. 19

A word fitly spoken is like apples of gold in pictures of silver.
Ibid. XXV, 11

If thine enemy be hungry, give him bread to eat; and if he be thirsty, give him water to drink:

For thou shalt heap coals of fire upon his head.[1]

Proverbs. XXV, 21–22

As cold waters to a thirsty soul, so is good news from a far country.

Ibid. 25

For men to search their own glory is not glory.

Ibid. 27

Answer a fool according to his folly.

Ibid. XXVI, 5

As a dog returneth to his vomit, so a fool returneth to his folly.

Ibid. 11

Seest thou a man wise in his own conceit? There is more hope of a fool than of him.

Ibid. 12

The slothful man saith, There is a lion in the way; a lion is in the streets.

Ibid. 13

The sluggard is wiser in his own conceit than seven men that can render a reason.

Ibid. 16

Whoso diggeth a pit shall fall therein.

Ibid. 27

Boast not thyself of tomorrow; for thou knowest not what a day may bring forth.

Ibid. XXVII, 1

Let another man praise thee, and not thine own mouth.

Ibid. 2

Open rebuke is better than secret love.

Ibid. 5

Faithful are the wounds of a friend; but the kisses of an enemy are deceitful.

Ibid. 6

To the hungry soul every bitter thing is sweet.

Ibid. 7

Better is a neighbour that is near than a brother far off.

Ibid. 10

[1] See *Romans, XII, 20,* on page 1060a.

A continual dropping in a very rainy day and a contentious woman are alike.

Proverbs. XXVII, 15

Iron sharpeneth iron; so a man sharpeneth the countenance of his friend.

Ibid. 17

The wicked flee when no man pursueth; but the righteous are bold as a lion.

Ibid. XXVIII, 1

He that maketh haste to be rich shall not be innocent.

Ibid. 20

To have respect of persons is not good: for for a piece of bread that man will transgress.

Ibid. 21

He that trusteth in his own heart is a fool.

Ibid. 26

He that giveth unto the poor shall not lack.

Ibid. 27

A fool uttereth all his mind.

Ibid. XXIX, 11

Where there is no vision, the people perish.

Ibid. 18

A man's pride shall bring him low: but honour shall uphold the humble in spirit.

Ibid. 23

Accuse not a servant unto his master.

Ibid. XXX, 10

The horseleach hath two daughters, crying, Give, give.

Ibid. 15

The way of an eagle in the air; the way of a serpent upon a rock; the way of a ship in the midst of the sea; and the way of a man with a maid.

Ibid. 19

Give strong drink unto him that is ready to perish, and wine unto those that be of heavy hearts.

Ibid. XXXI, 6

Who can find a virtuous woman? for her price is far above rubies.

Ibid. 10

In her tongue is the law of kindness.

Ibid. 26

She looketh well to the ways of her household, and eateth not the bread of idleness.
Proverbs. XXXI, 27

Her children arise up, and call her blessed.
Ibid. 28

Many daughters have done virtuously, but thou excellest them all.
Ibid. 29

Vanity of vanities; all is vanity.
Ecclesiastes. I, 2; XII, 8

What profit hath a man of all his labour which he taketh under the sun?
Ibid. 3

One generation passeth away, and another generation cometh: but the earth abideth for ever.
Ibid. 4

All the rivers run into the sea; yet the sea is not full.
Ibid. 7

The eye is not satisfied with seeing, nor the ear filled with hearing.
Ibid. 8

There is no new thing under the sun.
Ibid. 9

Is there anything whereof it may be said, See, this is new? It hath been already of old time, which was before us.
Ibid. 10

I have seen all the works that are done under the sun; and, behold, all is vanity and vexation of spirit.
Ibid. 14

In much wisdom is much grief: and he that increaseth knowledge increaseth sorrow.
Ibid. 18

Wisdom excelleth folly, as far as light excelleth darkness.
Ibid. II, 13

The wise man's eyes are in his head; but the fool walketh in darkness.
Ibid. 14

One event happeneth to them all.
Ibid.

How dieth the wise man? as the fool.
Ibid. 16

To every thing there is a season, and a time to every purpose under the heaven.
Ecclesiastes. III, 1

A time to be born, and a time to die.
Ibid. 2

A time to weep, and a time to laugh; a time to mourn, and a time to dance.
Ibid. 4

A time to keep silence, and a time to speak.
Ibid. 7

Wherefore I praised the dead which are already dead, more than the living which are yet alive.
Ibid. IV, 2

Woe to him that is alone when he falleth.
Ibid. 10

A threefold cord is not quickly broken.
Ibid. 12

God is in heaven, and thou upon earth: therefore let thy words be few.
Ibid. V, 2

Better is it that thou shouldest not vow, than that thou shouldest vow and not pay.
Ibid. 5

The sleep of a labouring man is sweet.
Ibid. 12

But the abundance of the rich will not suffer him to sleep.
Ibid.

A good name is better than precious ointment; and the day of death than the day of one's birth.
Ibid. VII, 1

It is better to go to the house of mourning, than to go to the house of feasting.
Ibid. 2

Sorrow is better than laughter: for by the sadness of the countenance the heart is made better.
Ibid. 3

As the crackling of thorns under a pot, so is the laughter of the fool.
Ibid. 6

Better is the end of a thing than the beginning thereof.
Ibid. 8

In the day of prosperity be joyful, but in the day of adversity consider.
Ecclesiastes. VII, 14

Be not righteous over much.
Ibid. 16

There is not a just man upon earth, that doeth good, and sinneth not.
Ibid. 20

One man among a thousand have I found; but a woman among all those have I not found.
Ibid. 28

God hath made man upright; but they have sought out many inventions.
Ibid. 29

There is no discharge in that war.
Ibid. VIII, 8

A man hath no better thing under the sun, than to eat, and to drink, and to be merry.[1]
Ibid. 15

All things come alike to all: there is one event to the righteous, and to the wicked.
Ibid. IX, 2

A living dog is better than a dead lion.
Ibid. 4

The living know that they shall die: but the dead know not any thing, neither have they any more a reward; for the memory of them is forgotten.
Ibid. 5

Whatsover thy hand findeth to do, do it with thy might; for there is no work, nor device, nor knowledge, nor wisdom, in the grave, whither thou goest.
Ibid. 10

The race is not to the swift, nor the battle to the strong.
Ibid. 11

He that diggeth a pit shall fall into it; and whoso breaketh an hedge, a serpent shall bite him.
Ibid. X, 8

A feast is made for laughter, and wine maketh merry: but money answereth all things.
Ibid. 19

[1] Also in *Luke, XII, 19.*

A bird of the air shall carry the voice, and that which hath wings shall tell the matter.
Ecclesiastes. X, 20

Cast thy bread upon the waters: for thou shalt find it after many days.
Ibid. XI, 1

He that observeth the wind shall not sow; and he that regardeth the clouds shall not reap.
Ibid. 4

In the morning sow thy seed, and in the evening withhold not thine hand.
Ibid. 6

Rejoice, O young man, in thy youth.
Ibid. 9

Remember now thy Creator in the days of thy youth, while the evil days come not, nor the years draw nigh, when thou shalt say, I have no pleasure in them.
Ibid. XII, 1

While the sun, or the light, or the moon, or the stars, be not darkened, nor the clouds return after the rain.
Ibid. 2

In the day when the keepers of the house shall tremble, and the strong men shall bow themselves, and the grinders cease because they are few, and those that look out of the windows be darkened.
Ibid. 3

The doors shall be shut in the streets, when the sound of the grinding is low, and he shall rise up at the voice of the bird, and all the daughters of music shall be brought low.
Ibid. 4

The almond tree shall flourish, and the grasshopper shall be a burden, and desire shall fail; because man goeth to his long home, and the mourners go about the streets.
Ibid. 5

Or ever the silver cord be loosed, or the golden bowl be broken, or the pitcher be broken at the fountain, or the wheel broken at the cistern.
Ibid. 6

Then shall the dust return to the earth as it was: and the spirit shall return unto God who gave it.

Ecclesiastes. XII, 7

The words of the wise are as goads, and as nails fastened by the masters of assemblies.

Ibid. 11

Of making many books there is no end; and much study is a weariness of the flesh.

Ibid. 12

Let us hear the conclusion of the whole matter: Fear God, and keep his commandments; for this is the whole duty of man.

Ibid. 13

For God shall bring every work into judgment, with every secret thing, whether it be good, or whether it be evil.

Ibid. 14

The song of songs, which is Solomon's.

The Song of Solomon. I, 1

I am black, but comely, O ye daughters of Jerusalem, as the tents of Kedar, as the curtains of Solomon.

Ibid. 5

O thou fairest among women.

Ibid. 8

I am the rose of Sharon, and the lily of the valleys.

Ibid. II, 1

His banner over me was love.

Ibid. 4

Stay me with flagons, comfort me with apples: for I am sick of love.

Ibid. 5

Rise up, my love, my fair one, and come away.

For, lo! the winter is past, the rain is over and gone;

The flowers appear on the earth; the time of the singing of birds is come, and the voice of the turtle is heard in our land.

Ibid. 10–12

The little foxes, that spoil the vines.

Ibid. 15

Until the day break, and the shadows flee away.

The Song of Solomon. II, 17; IV, 6

By night on my bed I sought him whom my soul loveth: I sought him, but I found him not.

Ibid. III, 1

Thy two breasts are like two young roes that are twins, which feed among the lilies.

Ibid. IV, 5

Thou art all fair, my love; there is no spot in thee.

Ibid. 7

Awake, O north wind; and come, thou south; blow upon my garden, that the spices thereof may flow out. Let my beloved come into his garden, and eat his pleasant fruits.

Ibid. 16

My beloved put in his hand by the hole of the door, and my bowels were moved for him.

Ibid. V, 4

His mouth is most sweet: yea, he is altogether lovely. This is my beloved, and this is my friend, O daughters of Jerusalem.

Ibid. 16

Who is she that looketh forth as the morning, fair as the moon, clear as the sun, and terrible as an army with banners?

Ibid. VI, 10

Thy belly is like a heap of wheat set about with lilies.

Ibid. VII, 2

Thy neck is as a tower of ivory.

Ibid. 4

Like the best wine . . . that goeth down sweetly, causing the lips of those that are asleep to speak.

Ibid. 9

Set me as a seal upon thine heart, as a seal upon thine arm: for love is strong as death; jealousy is cruel as the grave.

Ibid. VIII, 6

Many waters cannot quench love, neither can the floods drown it.

Ibid. 7

We have a little sister, and she hath no breasts.

The Song of Solomon. VIII, 8

Make haste, my beloved, and be thou like to a roe or to a young hart upon the mountains of spices.

Ibid. 14

The ox knoweth his owner, and the ass his master's crib.

Isaiah. I, 3

The whole head is sick, and the whole heart faint.

Ibid. 5

As a lodge in a garden of cucumbers.

Ibid. 8

Bring no more vain oblations.

Ibid. 13

Come now, and let us reason together.

Ibid. 18

Though your sins be as scarlet, they shall be white as snow.

Ibid.

They shall beat their swords into plowshares, and their spears into pruning-hooks; nation shall not lift up sword against nation, neither shall they learn war any more.[1]

Ibid. II, 4

In that day a man shall cast his idols . . . to the moles and to the bats.

Ibid. 20

Cease ye from man, whose breath is in his nostrils.

Ibid. 22

The stay and the staff, the whole stay of bread, and the whole stay of water.

Ibid. III, 1

Grind the faces of the poor.

Ibid. 15

Walk with stretched forth necks and wanton eyes, walking and mincing as they go, and making a tinkling with their feet.

Ibid. 16

In that day seven women shall take hold of one man.

Ibid. IV, 1

[1] Also in *Joel, III, 10* and *Micah, IV, 3.*

Woe unto them that rise up early in the morning, that they may follow strong drink.

Isaiah. V, 11

Woe unto them that draw iniquity with cords of vanity, and sin as it were with a cart rope.

Ibid. 18

Woe unto them that call evil good, and good evil.

Ibid. 20

I saw also the Lord sitting upon a throne, high and lifted up, and his train filled the temple.

Ibid. VI, 1

Holy, holy, holy, is the Lord of hosts: the whole earth is full of his glory.

Ibid. 3

Then, said I, Lord, how long?

Ibid. 11

Behold, a virgin shall conceive, and bear a son, and shall call his name Immanuel.

Ibid. VII, 14

For a stone of stumbling and for a rock of offence.

Ibid. VIII, 14

The people that walked in darkness have seen a great light: they that dwell in the land of the shadow of death, upon them hath the light shined.

Ibid. IX, 2

For unto us a child is born, unto us a son is given: and the government shall be upon his shoulder: and his name shall be called Wonderful, Counsellor, The mighty God, The everlasting Father, The Prince of Peace.

Ibid. 6

The ancient and honourable.

Ibid. 15

And there shall come forth a rod out of the stem of Jesse, and a Branch shall grow out of his roots:

And the Spirit of the Lord shall rest upon him, the spirit of wisdom and understanding, the spirit of counsel and might, the spirit of knowledge and of the fear of the Lord.

Ibid. XI, 1, 2

The wolf also shall dwell with the lamb, and the leopard shall lie down with the kid.
Isaiah. XI, 6

How art thou fallen from heaven, O Lucifer, son of the morning!
Ibid. XIV, 12

Is this the man that made the earth to tremble, that did shake kingdoms?
Ibid. 16

Like the rushing of mighty waters.
Ibid. XVII, 12

Babylon is fallen, is fallen.
Ibid. XXI, 9

Watchman, what of the night?
Ibid. 11

Let us eat and drink; for tomorrow we shall die.
Ibid. XXII, 13

I will fasten him as a nail in a sure place.
Ibid. 23

Whose merchants are princes.
Ibid. XXIII, 8

A feast of fat things, a feast of wines on the lees.
Ibid. XXV, 6

He will swallow up death in victory; and the Lord God will wipe away tears from off all faces.
Ibid. 8

Thou wilt keep him in perfect peace, whose mind is stayed on thee.
Ibid. XXVI, 3

Hide thyself as it were for a little moment, until the indignation be overpast.
Ibid. 20

Leviathan, that crooked serpent . . . the dragon that is in the sea.
Ibid. XXVII, 1

For precept must be upon precept, precept upon precept; line upon line, line upon line; here a little, and there a little.
Ibid. XXVIII, 10

We have made a covenant with death, and with hell are we at agreement.
Ibid. 15

It shall be a vexation only to understand the report.
Isaiah. XXVIII, 19

They are drunken, but not with wine; they stagger, but not with strong drink.
Ibid. XXIX, 9

Their strength is to sit still.
Ibid. XXX, 7

Now go, write it before them in a table, and note it in a book, that it may be for the time to come for ever and ever.
Ibid. 8

The bread of adversity, and the water of affliction.
Ibid. 20

This is the way, walk ye in it.
Ibid. 21

And a man shall be as an hiding place from the wind, and a covert from the tempest; as rivers of water in a dry place, as the shadow of a great rock in a weary land.
Ibid. XXXII, 2

The desert shall rejoice, and blossom as the rose.
Ibid. XXXV, 1

Then the eyes of the blind shall be opened, and the ears of the deaf shall be unstopped.
Ibid. 5

Then shall the lame man leap as an hart, and the tongue of the dumb sing.
Ibid. 6

Sorrow and sighing shall flee away.
Ibid. 10

Thou trustest in the staff of this broken reed.
Ibid. XXXVI, 6

Set thine house in order.
Ibid. XXXVIII, 1

I shall go softly all my years in the bitterness of my soul.
Ibid. 15

Comfort ye my people.
Ibid. XL, 1

The voice of him that crieth in the wilderness, Prepare ye the way of the

Lord, make straight in the desert a highway for our God.[1]

Isaiah. XL, 3

Every valley shall be exalted, and every mountain and hill shall be made low: and the crooked shall be made straight, and the rough places plain.

Ibid. 4

All flesh is grass, and all the goodliness thereof is as the flower of the field.

Ibid. 6

The grass withereth, the flower fadeth:[2] but the word of our God shall stand for ever.

Ibid. 8

He shall feed his flock like a shepherd: he shall gather the lambs with his arm, and carry them in his bosom, and shall gently lead those that are with young.

Ibid. 11

The nations are as a drop of a bucket, and are counted as the small dust of the balance.

Ibid. 15

Have ye not known? have ye not heard? hath it not been told you from the beginning?

Ibid. 21

They that wait upon the Lord shall renew their strength; they shall mount up with wings as eagles; they shall run, and not be weary; and they shall walk, and not faint.

Ibid. 31

They helped every one his neighbour: and every one said to his brother, Be of good courage.

Ibid. XLI, 6

A bruised reed shall he not break, and the smoking flax shall he not quench.

Ibid. XLII, 3

There is no peace, saith the Lord, unto the wicked.

Ibid. XLVIII, 22

[1] See *Matthew, III, 3,* on page 1050a. Also in *Mark, I, 3; Luke, III, 4; John, I, 23.*
[2] See *Psalm XC, 5-6,* on page 1035b.

Can a woman forget her sucking child, that she should not have compassion on the son of her womb?

Isaiah. XLIX, 15

How beautiful upon the mountains are the feet of him that bringeth good tidings, that publisheth peace.

Ibid. LII, 7

They shall see eye to eye.

Ibid. 8

He is despised and rejected of men; a man of sorrows, and acquainted with grief.

Ibid. LIII, 3

All we like sheep have gone astray.

Ibid. 6

He is brought as a lamb to the slaughter.[1]

Ibid. 7

Ho, everyone that thirsteth, come ye to the waters.

Ibid. LV, 1

Let the wicked forsake his way, and the unrighteous man his thoughts.

Ibid. 7

For my thoughts are not your thoughts, neither are your ways my ways, saith the Lord.

Ibid. 8

A little one shall become a thousand, and a small one a strong nation.

Ibid. LX, 22

Give unto them beauty for ashes, the oil of joy for mourning, the garment of praise for the spirit of heaviness.

Ibid. LXI, 3

I have trodden the winepress alone.

Ibid. LXIII, 3

All our righteousnesses are as filthy rags; and we all do fade as a leaf.

Ibid. LXIV, 6

I am holier than thou.

Ibid. LXV, 5

As one whom his mother comforteth, so will I comfort you.

Ibid. LXVI, 13

Saying, Peace, peace; when there is no peace.

Jeremiah. VI, 14; VIII. 11

[1] Also in *Acts, VIII, 32.*

Stand ye in the ways, and see, and ask for the old paths, where is the good way, and walk therein.[1]

Jeremiah. VI, 16

Amend your ways and your doings.

Ibid. VII, 3; XXVI, 13

The harvest is past, the summer is ended, and we are not saved.

Ibid. VIII, 20

Is there no balm in Gilead? Is there no physician there?

Ibid. 22

Oh that I had in the wilderness a lodging place of wayfaring men!

Ibid. IX, 2

I will feed them . . . with wormwood, and give them water of gall to drink.

Ibid. 15; XXIII, 15

Can the Ethiopian change his skin, or the leopard his spots?

Ibid. XIII, 23

Her sun is gone down while it was yet day.

Ibid. XV, 9

A man of strife and a man of contention.

Ibid. 10

Written with a pen of iron, and with the point of a diamond.

Ibid. XVII, 1

He shall be as a tree planted by the waters, and that spreadeth out her roots by the river.

Ibid. 8

The heart is deceitful above all things, and desperately wicked: who can know it?

Ibid. 9

Thou art my hope in the day of evil.

Ibid. 17

He shall be buried with the burial of an ass.

Ibid. XXII, 19

O earth, earth, earth, hear the word of the Lord.

Ibid. 29

The fathers have eaten a sour grape,

[1] Stare super vias antiquas. — *The Vulgate.*

and the children's teeth are set on edge.[1]

Jeremiah. XXXI, 29

With my whole heart and with my whole soul.

Ibid. XXXII, 41

And seekest thou great things for thyself? seek them not.

Ibid. XLV, 5

Is it nothing to you, all ye that pass by? behold, and see if there be any sorrow like unto my sorrow.

Lamentations. I, 12

Their visage is blacker than a coal.[2]

Ibid. IV, 8

As it were a wheel in the middle of a wheel.

Ezekiel. I, 16

As is the mother, so is her daughter.

Ibid. XVI, 44

I will cause you to pass under the rod.

Ibid. XX, 37

The king of Babylon stood at the parting of the way.

Ibid. XXI, 21

Son of man, can these bones live? And I answered, O Lord God, thou knowest.

Ibid. XXXVII, 3

His legs of iron, his feet part of iron and part of clay.

Daniel. II, 33

Shadrach, Meshach, and Abed-nego, fell down bound into the midst of the burning fiery furnace.

Ibid. III, 23

Nebuchadnezzar . . . was driven from men, and did eat grass as oxen.

Ibid. IV, 33

Belshazzar the king made a great feast to a thousand of his lords.

Ibid. V, 1

And this is the writing that was written, MENE, MENE, TEKEL, UPHARSIN.

Ibid. 25

[1] Also in *Ezekiel, XVIII, 2.*
[2] The faces of them all are as the blackness of a kettle.—*Douay Bible* [1609], *Nahum, II,* 10. (The English version of the Roman Catholic Bible was first printed in Douay, France.)

MENE; God hath numbered thy kingdom and finished it.
Daniel. V, 26

TEKEL; Thou art weighed in the balances, and art found wanting.
Ibid. 27

PERES; Thy kingdom is divided, and given to the Medes and Persians.
Ibid. 28

His windows being open in his chamber toward Jerusalem.
Ibid. VI, 10

According to the law of the Medes and Persians, which altereth not.
Ibid. 12

They brought Daniel, and cast him into the den of lions.
Ibid. 16

So Daniel was taken up out of the den, and no manner of hurt was found upon him, because he believed in his God.
Ibid. 23

The Ancient of days.
Ibid. VII, 13

Many shall run to and fro, and knowledge shall be increased.
Ibid. XII, 4

Like people, like priest.
Hosea. IV, 9

They have sown the wind, and they shall reap the whirlwind.
Ibid. VIII, 7

I have multiplied visions, and used similitudes, by the ministry of the prophets.
Ibid. XII, 10

Your old men shall dream dreams, your young men shall see visions.
Joel. II, 28

Multitudes in the valley of decision.
Ibid. III, 14

They sold the righteous for silver, and the poor for a pair of shoes.
Amos. II, 6

Can two walk together, except they be agreed?
Ibid. III, 3

The houses of ivory shall perish.
Ibid. 15

And Jonah was in the belly of the fish three days and three nights.
Jonah. I, 17

They shall sit every man under his vine and under his fig-tree.[1]
Micah. IV, 4

What doth the Lord require of thee, but to do justly, and to love mercy, and to walk humbly with thy God?
Ibid. VI, 8

Write the vision, and make it plain upon tables, that he may run that readeth it.
Habakkuk. II, 2

The Lord is in his holy temple: let all the earth keep silence before him.
Ibid. 20

Ye have sown much, and bring in little.
Haggai. I, 6

He that earneth wages, earneth wages to put it into a bag with holes.
Ibid.

Your fathers, where are they? And the prophets, do they live forever?
Zechariah. I, 5

I have spread you abroad as the four winds of the heaven.
Ibid. II, 6

Not by might, nor by power, but by my spirit, saith the Lord of hosts.
Ibid. IV, 6

For who hath despised the day of small things?
Ibid. 10

They are the eyes of the Lord, which run to and fro through the whole earth.
Ibid.

Behold, thy King cometh unto thee . . . lowly, and riding upon an ass.
Ibid. IX, 9

Prisoners of hope.
Ibid. 12

I was wounded in the house of my friends.
Ibid. XIII, 6

Have we not all one father? hath not one God created us?
Malachi. II, 10

Behold, the day cometh.
Ibid. IV, 1

[1] See *1 Maccabees, XIV, 12,* on page 1067a.

But unto you that fear my name shall the Sun of righteousness arise with healing in his wings.

Malachi. IV, 2

He shall turn the heart of the fathers to the children, and the heart of the children to their fathers.

Ibid. 6

New Testament

And [Joseph] knew her not till she had brought forth her firstborn son: and he called his name Jesus.

Matthew. I, 25

Now when Jesus was born in Bethlehem of Judaea in the days of Herod the king, behold, there came wise men from the east to Jerusalem.

Ibid. II, 1

Where is he that is born King of the Jews? for we have seen his star in the east, and are come to worship him.

Ibid. 2

They saw the young child with Mary his mother, and fell down, and worshipped him; and . . . they presented unto him gifts; gold, and frankincense, and myrrh.

Ibid. 11

Rachel weeping for her children, and would not be comforted, because they are not.

Ibid. 18

Repent ye: for the kingdom of heaven is at hand.

Ibid. III, 2

The voice of one crying in the wilderness, Prepare ye the way of the Lord, make his paths straight.[1]

Ibid. 3

And his meat was locusts and wild honey.

Ibid. 4

O generation of vipers, who hath warned you to flee from the wrath to come?

Ibid. 7

This is my beloved Son, in whom I am well pleased.

Matthew. III, 17

Man shall not live by bread alone, but by every word that proceedeth out of the mouth of God.[1]

Ibid. IV, 4

Follow me, and I will make you fishers of men.

Ibid. 19

Blessed are the poor in spirit: for theirs is the kingdom of heaven.

Blessed are they that mourn: for they shall be comforted.

Blessed are the meek: for they shall inherit the earth.[2]

Blessed are they which do hunger and thirst after righteousness: for they shall be filled.

Blessed are the merciful: for they shall obtain mercy.

Blessed are the pure in heart: for they shall see God.

Blessed are the peacemakers: for they shall be called the children of God.

Ibid. V, 3–9

Ye are the salt of the earth: but if the salt have lost its savour, wherewith shall it be salted?

Ibid. 13

Ye are the light of the world. A city that is set on an hill cannot be hid.

Ibid. 14

Let your light so shine before men, that they may see your good works, and glorify your Father which is in heaven.

Ibid. 16

Think not that I am come to destroy the law, or the prophets: I am not come to destroy, but to fulfill.

Ibid. 17

Till heaven and earth pass, one jot or one tittle shall in no wise pass from the law, till all be fulfilled.

Ibid. 18

Whosoever looketh on a woman to lust after her hath committed adultery with her already in his heart.

Ibid. 28

[1] See *Isaiah, XL, 3*, on page 1046b–1047a. Also in *Mark, I, 3; Luke, III, 4; John, I, 23.*

[1] See *Deuteronomy, VIII, 3*, on page 1025b.
[2] See *Psalm XXXVII, 11*, on page 1034a.

If thy right eye offend thee, pluck it out, and cast it from thee: for it is profitable for thee that one of thy members should perish, and not that thy whole body should be cast into hell.

Matthew. V, 29

If thy right hand offend thee, cut it off.

Ibid. 30

Whosoever shall marry her that is divorced committeth adultery.

Ibid. 32

Swear not at all; neither by heaven; for it is God's throne:

Nor by the earth; for it is his footstool.

Ibid. 34, 35

Resist not evil.

Ibid. 39

Whosoever shall smite thee on thy right cheek, turn to him the other also.

Ibid.

Love your enemies, bless them that curse you, do good to them that hate you, and pray for them which despitefully use you, and persecute you.

Ibid. 44

He maketh his sun to rise on the evil and on the good, and sendeth rain on the just and on the unjust.

Ibid. 45

When thou doest alms, let not thy left hand know what thy right hand doeth.

Ibid. VI, 3

After this manner therefore pray ye: Our Father which art in heaven, Hallowed be thy name.

Thy kingdom come. Thy will be done in earth, as it is in heaven.

Give us this day our daily bread.

And forgive us our debts, as we forgive our debtors.

And lead us not into temptation, but deliver us from evil: For thine is the kingdom, and the power, and the glory, for ever. Amen.

Ibid. 9–13

Lay not up for yourselves treasures upon earth, where moth and rust doth corrupt, and where thieves break through and steal.

Matthew. VI, 19

Lay up for yourselves treasures in heaven.

Ibid. 20

For where your treasure is, there will your heart be also.

Ibid. 21

The light of the body is the eye.

Ibid. 22

No man can serve two masters.

Ibid. 24

Ye cannot serve God and mammon.

Ibid.

Behold the fowls of the air: for they sow not neither do they reap, nor gather into barns.

Ibid. 26

Which of you by taking thought can add one cubit unto his stature?

Ibid. 27

Consider the lilies of the field, how they grow; they toil not, neither do they spin.

Ibid. 28

Even Solomon in all his glory was not arrayed like one of these.

Ibid. 29

Take therefore no thought for the morrow: for the morrow shall take thought for the things of itself. Sufficient unto the day is the evil thereof.

Ibid. 34

Judge not, that ye be not judged.

Ibid. VII, 1

And why beholdest thou the mote that is in thy brother's eye, but considerest not the beam that is in thine own eye?

Ibid. 3

Neither cast ye your pearls before swine.

Ibid. 6

Ask, and it shall be given you; seek, and ye shall find; knock, and it shall be opened unto you.

Ibid. 7

Every one that asketh receiveth; and he that seeketh findeth.

Ibid. 8

Or what man is there of you, whom if his son ask bread, will he give him a stone?

Matthew. VII, 9

Therefore all things whatsoever ye would that men should do to you, do ye even so to them: for this is the law and the prophets.

Ibid. 12

Wide is the gate, and broad is the way, that leadeth to destruction.

Ibid. 13

Strait is the gate, and narrow is the way, which leadeth unto life, and few there be that find it.

Ibid. 14

Beware of false prophets, which come to you in sheep's clothing, but inwardly they are ravening wolves.

Ibid. 15

By their fruits ye shall know them.

Ibid. 20

It was founded upon a rock.

Ibid. 25

But the children of the kingdom shall be cast out into outer darkness: there shall be weeping and gnashing of teeth.

Ibid. VIII, 12

The foxes have holes, and the birds of the air have nests; but the Son of man hath not where to lay his head.

Ibid. 20

Let the dead bury their dead.

Ibid. 22

A man, named Matthew, sitting at the receipt of custom.

Ibid. IX, 9

They that be whole need not a physician, but they that are sick.

Ibid. 12

For I am not come to call the righteous, but sinners to repentance.

Ibid. 13

Neither do men put new wine into old bottles.

Ibid. 17

The harvest truly is plenteous, but the laborers are few.

Ibid. 37

Freely ye have received, freely give.

Ibid. X, 8

Be ye therefore wise as serpents, and harmless as doves.

Matthew. X, 16

The disciple is not above his master, nor the servant above his lord.

Ibid. 24

Are not two sparrows sold for a farthing? and one of them shall not fall on the ground without your Father.

Ibid. 29

But the very hairs of your head are all numbered.

Ibid. 30

I came not to send peace, but a sword.

Ibid. 34

He that findeth his life shall lose it: and he that loseth his life for my sake shall find it.

Ibid. 39

He that hath ears to hear, let him hear.

Ibid. XI, 15

A friend of publicans and sinners.

Ibid. XI, 19

Wisdom is justified of her children.[1]

Ibid.

Come unto me, all ye that labour and are heavy laden, and I will give you rest.

Take my yoke upon you, and learn of me; for I am meek and lowly in heart: and ye shall find rest unto your souls.

For my yoke is easy, and my burden is light.

Ibid. 28–30

He that is not with me is against me.

Ibid. XII, 30

The tree is known by his fruit.

Ibid. 33

Out of the abundance of the heart the mouth speaketh.

Ibid. 34

Because they had no root, they withered away.

Ibid. XIII, 6

But other fell into good ground, and brought forth fruit, some a hundredfold, some sixtyfold, some thirtyfold.

Ibid. 8

[1] Also in *Luke, VII, 35.*

The kingdom of heaven is like to a grain of mustard seed.
Matthew. XIII, 31

Pearl of great price.
Ibid. 46

Is not this the carpenter's son?
Ibid. 55

A prophet is not without honour, save in his own country.
Ibid. 57

The daughter of Herodias danced before them, and pleased Herod.
Ibid. XIV, 6

Give me here John Baptist's head in a charger.
Ibid. 8

We have here but five loaves, and two fishes.
Ibid. 17

And they did all eat, and were filled: and they took up of the fragments that remained twelve baskets full.
Ibid. 20

And in the fourth watch of the night Jesus went unto them, walking on the sea.
Ibid. 25

Be of good cheer; it is I; be not afraid.
Ibid. 27

O thou of little faith, wherefore didst thou doubt?
Ibid. 31

Of truth thou art the Son of God.
Ibid. 33

Not that which goeth into the mouth defileth a man; but that which cometh out of the mouth, this defileth a man.
Ibid. XV, 11

They be blind leaders of the blind. And if the blind lead the blind, both shall fall into the ditch.
Ibid. 14

The dogs eat of the crumbs which fall from their masters' table.
Ibid. 27

When it is evening, ye say, It will be fair weather: for the sky is red.
Ibid. XVI, 2

The signs of the times.
Ibid. 3

Thou art Peter, and upon this rock I will build my church.
Matthew. XVI, 18

I will give unto thee the keys of heaven.
Ibid. 19

Get thee behind me, Satan.[1]
Ibid. 23

What is a man profited, if he shall gain the whole world, and lose his own soul? [2]
Ibid. 26

Except ye be converted, and become as little children, ye shall not enter into the kingdom of heaven.
Ibid. XVIII, 3

The ninety and nine.
Ibid. 12, 13

Where two or three are gathered together in my name, there am I in the midst of them.
Ibid. 20

Until seventy times seven.
Ibid. 22

What therefore God hath joined together, let not man put asunder.[3]
Ibid. XIX, 6

If thou wilt be perfect, go and sell that thou hast, and give to the poor, and thou shalt have treasure in heaven.
Ibid. 21

It is easier for a camel to go through the eye of a needle, than for a rich man to enter into the kingdom of God.
Ibid. 24

But many that are first shall be last; and the last shall be first.
Ibid. 30

Borne the burden and heat of the day.
Ibid. XX, 12

Is it not lawful for me to do what I will with mine own?
Ibid. 15

Overthrew the tables of the money changers.
Ibid. XXI, 12

[1] Also in *Luke, IV, 8.*
[2] Also in *Mark, VIII, 36.*
[3] Those whom God hath joined together let no man put asunder.
Book of Common Prayer, Solemnization of Matrimony

My house shall be called the house of prayer; but ye have made it a den of thieves.

Matthew. XXI, 13

They made light of it.

Ibid. XXII, 5

For many are called, but few are chosen.

Ibid. 14

Render therefore unto Caesar the things which are Caesar's.[1]

Ibid. 21

Whosoever shall exalt himself shall be abased; and he that shall humble himself shall be exalted.

Ibid. XXIII, 12

Woe unto you . . for ye pay tithe of mint and anise and cummin.

Ibid. 23

Blind guides, which strain at a gnat, and swallow a camel.

Ibid. 24

Whited sepulchres, which indeed appear beautiful outward, but are within full of dead men's bones.

Ibid. 27

As a hen gathereth her chickens under her wings.

Ibid. 37

Wars and rumours of wars.[2]

Ibid. XXIV, 6

The end is not yet.

Ibid.

Abomination of desolation.[3]

Ibid. 15

False prophets.

Ibid. 24

Wheresoever the carcass is, there will the eagles be gathered together.

Ibid. 28

Heaven and earth shall pass away, but my words shall not pass away.

Ibid. 35

One shall be taken, and the other left.

Ibid. 40

Then shall the kingdom of heaven be likened unto ten virgins, which took

their lamps, and went forth to meet the bridegroom.

And five of them were wise, and five were foolish.

Matthew. XXV, 1, 2

Well done, thou good and faithful servant.

Ibid. 21

Unto every one that hath shall be given, and he shall have abundance; but from him that hath not shall be taken away even that which he hath.

Ibid. 29

And before him shall be gathered all nations: and he shall separate them one from another, as a shepherd divideth his sheep from the goats.

Ibid. 32

For I was an hungred, and ye gave me meat: I was thirsty, and ye gave me drink: I was a stranger, and ye took me in:

Naked, and ye clothed me: I was sick, and ye visited me: I was in prison, and ye came unto me.

Ibid. 35, 36

Inasmuch as ye have done it unto one of the least of these my brethren, ye have done it unto me.

Ibid. 40

An alabaster box of very precious ointment.

Ibid. XXVI, 7

To what purpose is this waste?

Ibid. 8

For ye have the poor always with you; but me ye have not always.

Ibid. 11

What will ye give me, and I will deliver him unto you? And they covenanted with him for thirty pieces of silver.

Ibid. 15

My time is at hand.

Ibid. 18

Verily I say unto you, that one of you shall betray me.

Ibid. 21

It had been good for that man if he had not been born.

Ibid. 24

---

[1] Also in *Mark, XII*, 17.
[2] Also in *Mark, XIII*, 7.
[3] Also in *Mark, XIII*, 14.

Jesus took bread, and blessed it, and brake it, and gave it to the disciples, and said, Take, eat; this is my body.

And he took the cup, and gave thanks, and gave it to them, saying, Drink ye all of it;

For this is my blood of the new testament, which is shed for many for the remission of sins.
Matthew. XXVI, 26–28

This night, before the cock crow, thou shalt deny me thrice.
Ibid. 34

O my Father, if it be possible, let this cup pass from me: nevertheless, not as I will, but as thou wilt.
Ibid. 39

Watch and pray, that ye enter not into temptation: the spirit indeed is willing, but the flesh is weak.
Ibid. 41

Hail, Master; and kissed him.
Ibid. 49

All they that take the sword shall perish with the sword.
Ibid. 52

Thy speech bewrayeth thee.
Ibid. 73

Then began he to curse and to swear, saying, I know not the man. And immediately the cock crew.
Ibid. 74

The potter's field, to bury strangers in.
Ibid. XXVII, 7

Have thou nothing to do with that just man.
Ibid. 19

Let him be crucified.
Ibid. 22

He took water, and washed his hands before the multitude, saying, I am innocent of the blood of this just person: see ye to it.
Ibid. 24

His blood be on us, and on our children.
Ibid. 25

A place called Golgotha, that is to say, a place of a skull.
Ibid. 33

This is Jesus the King of the Jews.
Matthew. XXVII, 37

He saved others; himself he cannot save.
Ibid. 42

Eli, Eli, lama sabachthani? that is to say, My God, my God, why hast thou forsaken me? [1]
Ibid. 46

And, behold, the veil of the temple was rent in twain from the top to the bottom; and the earth did quake, and the rocks rent.
Ibid. 51

His [the Angel of the Lord] countenance was like lightning, and his raiment white as snow.
Ibid. XXVIII, 3

Go ye therefore, and teach all nations.
Ibid. 19

Lo, I am with you alway, even unto the end of the world.
Ibid. 20

The latchet of whose shoes I am not worthy to stoop down and unloose.
Mark. I, 7

The sabbath was made for man, and not man for the sabbath.
Ibid. II, 27

If a house be divided against itself, that house cannot stand.
Ibid. III, 25

With what measure ye mete, it shall be measured to you.
Ibid. IV, 24

First the blade, then the ear, after that the full corn in the ear.
Ibid. 28

What manner of man is this?
Ibid. 41

My name is Legion: for we are many.
Ibid. V, 9

Clothed, and in his right mind.
Ibid. 15

My little daughter lieth at the point of death.
Ibid. 23

Knowing in himself that virtue had gone out of him.
Ibid. 30

[1] See *Psalm XXII, 1*, on page 1033a.

I see men as trees, walking.
Mark. VIII, 24

Lord, I believe; help thou mine unbelief.
Ibid. IX, 24

Suffer the little children to come unto me, and forbid them not; for such is the kingdom of God.[1]
Ibid. X, 14

Which devour widows' houses, and for a pretense make long prayers.
Ibid. XII, 40

And there came a certain poor widow, and she threw in two mites.
Ibid. 42

For many bare false witness against him.
Ibid. XIV, 56

Go ye into all the world, and preach the gospel to every creature.
Ibid. XVI, 15

Hail, thou that art highly favoured, the Lord is with thee; blessed art thou among women.
Luke. I, 28

And blessed is the fruit of thy womb.
Ibid. 42

My soul doth magnify the Lord.
Ibid. 46

For he hath regarded the low estate of his handmaiden: for, behold, from henceforth all generations shall call me blessed.
Ibid. 48

He hath put down the mighty from their seats, and exalted them of low degree.
Ibid. 52

He hath filled the hungry with good things; and the rich he hath sent empty away.
Ibid. 53

And she brought forth her firstborn son, and wrapped him in swaddling clothes, and laid him in a manger; because there was no room for them in the inn.
Ibid. II, 7

[1] Also in *Matthew, XIX, 14,* and *Luke, XVIII, 16.*

Shepherds abiding in the field, keeping watch over their flock by night.
Luke. II, 8

And, lo, the angel of the Lord came upon them, and the glory of the Lord shone round about them; and they were sore afraid.
Ibid. 9

Fear not: for, behold, I bring you good tidings of great joy, which shall be to all people.
Ibid. 10

Glory to God in the highest, and on earth peace, good will toward men.[1]
Ibid. 14

Lord, now lettest thou thy servant depart in peace.
Ibid. 29

A light to lighten the Gentiles.
Ibid. 32

Wist ye not that I must be about my Father's business?
Ibid. 49

His mother kept all these sayings in her heart.
Ibid. 51

The axe is laid unto the root of the trees.
Ibid. III, 9

Physician, heal thyself.
Ibid. IV, 23

Woe unto you, when all men shall speak well of you!
Ibid. VI, 26

Nothing is secret, that shall not be made manifest.
Ibid. VIII, 17

No man, having put his hand to the plough, and looking back, is fit for the kingdom of God.
Ibid. IX, 62

Peace be to this house.
Ibid. X, 5

The labourer is worthy of his hire.[2]
Ibid. 7

A certain man went down from Jerusalem to Jericho, and fell among thieves.
Ibid. 30

[1] The Douay Bible has "peace to men of good will."
[2] Also in *1 Timothy, V, 18.*

1056

He passed by on the other side.
Luke. X, 31

A certain Samaritan . . . had compassion on him.
Ibid. 33

Go, and do thou likewise.
Ibid. 37

But one thing is needful; and Mary hath chosen that good part which shall not be taken away from her.
Ibid. 42

Soul, thou hast much goods laid up for many years; take thine ease, eat, drink, and be merry.
Ibid. XII, 19

Thou fool, this night thy soul shall be required of thee.
Ibid. 20

Let your loins be girded about, and your lights burning.
Ibid. 35

The poor, and the maimed, and the halt, and the blind.
Ibid. XIV, 21

Which of you, intending to build a tower, sitteth not down first, and counteth the cost, whether he have sufficient to finish it?
Ibid. 28

Rejoice with me; for I have found my sheep which was lost.
Ibid. XV, 6

Wasted his substance with riotous living.
Ibid. 13

Bring hither the fatted calf, and kill it.
Ibid. 23

For this my son was dead, and is alive again; he was lost, and is found.
Ibid. 24

The children of this world are in their generation wiser than the children of light.
Ibid. XVI, 8

He that is faithful in that which is least is faithful also in much; and he that is unjust in the least is unjust also in much.
Ibid. 10

The beggar died, and was carried by the angels into Abraham's bosom.
Luke. XVI, 22

It were better for him that a millstone were hanged about his neck, and he cast into the sea.
Ibid. XVII, 2

Out of thine own mouth will I judge thee.
Ibid. XIX, 22

This do in remembrance of me.[1]
Ibid. XXII, 19

Father, forgive them; for they know not what they do.
Ibid. XXIII, 34

Father, into thy hands I commend my spirit.
Ibid. 46

He gave up the ghost.
Ibid.

He was a good man, and a just.
Ibid. 50

Did not our heart burn within us, while he talked with us?
Ibid. XXIV, 32

In the beginning was the Word, and the Word was with God, and the Word was God.
John. I, 1

And the light shineth in the darkness; and the darkness comprehended it not.
Ibid. 5

There was a man sent from God, whose name was John.
Ibid. 6

The true Light, which lighteth every man that cometh into the world.
Ibid. 9

The Word was made flesh, and dwelt among us.
Ibid. 14

Can there any good thing come out of Nazareth?
Ibid. 46

Woman, what have I to do with thee? mine hour is not yet come.
Ibid. II, 4

Make not my Father's house an house of merchandise.
Ibid. 16

[1] Also in *1 Corinthians, XI, 24.*

The wind bloweth where it listeth, and thou hearest the sound thereof, but canst not tell whence it cometh, and whither it goeth: so is every one that is born of the Spirit.

John. III, 8

For God so loved the world, that he gave his only begotten Son, that whosoever believeth in him should not perish, but have everlasting life.

Ibid. 16

Rise, take up thy bed, and walk.

Ibid. V, 8

He was a burning and a shining light.

Ibid. 35

What are they among so many?

Ibid. VI, 9

Gather up the fragments that remain, that nothing be lost.

Ibid. 12

I am the bread of life.

Ibid. 35

Judge not according to the appearance.

Ibid. VII, 24

He that is without sin among you, let him first cast a stone at her.

Ibid. VIII, 7

Neither do I condemn thee: go, and sin no more.

Ibid. 11

I am the light of the world: he that followeth me shall not walk in darkness, but shall have the light of life.

Ibid. 12

The truth shall make you free.

Ibid. 32

There is no truth in him.

Ibid. 44

The night cometh, when no man can work.

Ibid. IX, 4

Whether he be a sinner or no, I know not: one thing I know, that, whereas I was blind, now I see.

Ibid. 25

I am come that they might have life, and that they might have it more abundantly.

Ibid. X, 10

I am the resurrection and the life: he that believeth in me, though he were dead, yet shall he live:

And whosoever liveth and believeth in me shall never die.[1]

John. XI, 25, 26

Jesus wept.

Ibid. 35

Walk while ye have the light, lest darkness come upon you.

Ibid. XII, 35

That thou doest, do quickly.

Ibid. XIII, 27

A new commandment I give unto you, That ye love one another.

Ibid. 34

Let not your heart be troubled.

Ibid. XIV, 1

In my Father's house are many mansions: if it were not so, I would have told you. I go to prepare a place for you.

Ibid. 2

I will come again, and receive you unto myself; that where I am, there ye may be also.

Ibid. 3

I will not leave you comfortless.

Ibid. 18

Peace I leave with you.

Ibid. 27

Greater love hath no man than this, that a man lay down his life for his friends.

Ibid. XV, 13

Whither goest thou?

Ibid. XVI, 5

Ask, and ye shall receive, that your joy may be full.

Ibid. 24

Be of good cheer; I have overcome the world.

Ibid. 33

Now Barabbas was a robber.

Ibid. XVIII, 40

Behold the man!

Ibid. XIX, 5

It is finished.

Ibid. 30

[1] Also in *Book of Common Prayer, Burial of the Dead.*

And suddenly there came a sound from heaven as of a rushing mighty wind.

Acts. II, 2

And there appeared unto them cloven tongues like as of fire, and it sat upon each of them.

And they were all filled with the Holy Ghost, and began to speak with other tongues.

Ibid. 3, 4

Thy money perish with thee.

Ibid. VIII, 20

In the gall of bitterness, and in the bond of iniquity.

Ibid. 23

Saul, Saul, why persecutest thou me?

Ibid. IX, 4

It is hard for thee to kick against the pricks.

Ibid. 5

God is no respecter of persons.[1]

Ibid. X, 34

Come over into Macedonia, and help us.

Ibid. XVI, 9

Certain lewd fellows of the baser sort.

Ibid. XVII, 5

Men of Athens, I perceive that in all things ye are too superstitious.

Ibid. 22

For as I passed by, and beheld your devotions, I found an altar with this inscription, To the Unknown God.

Ibid. 23

For in him we live, and move, and have our being.

Ibid. 28

Mighty in the Scriptures.

Ibid. XVIII, 24

All with one voice about the space of two hours cried out, Great is Diana of the Ephesians.

Ibid. XIX, 34

It is more blessed to give than to receive.

Ibid. XX, 35

I am . . . a Jew of Tarsus, a city in Cilicia, a citizen of no mean city.

Ibid. XXI, 39

[1] See *Romans, II, 11*, on page 1059b.

Brought up in this city at the feet of Gamaliel.

Acts. XXII, 3

And the chief captain answered, With a great sum obtained I this freedom. And Paul said, But I was free born.

Ibid. 28

I am a Pharisee, the son of a Pharisee.

Ibid. XXIII, 6

When I have a convenient season, I will call for thee.

Ibid. XXIV, 25

I appeal unto Caesar.

Ibid. XXV, 11

Much learning doth make thee mad.

Ibid. XXVI, 24

Words of truth and soberness.

Ibid. 25

For this thing was not done in a corner.

Ibid. 26

Almost thou persuadest me to be a Christian.

Ibid. 28

Wherein thou judgest another, thou condemnest thyself.

Romans. II, 1

There is no respect of persons with God.

Ibid. 11

These, having not the law, are a law unto themselves.

Ibid. 14

God forbid.

Ibid. III, 31

Where no law is, there is no transgression.

Ibid. IV, 15

Who against hope believed in hope.

Ibid. 18

Where sin abounded, grace did much more abound.

Ibid. V, 20

Death hath no more dominion over him.

Ibid. VI, 9

Speak after the manner of men.

Ibid. 19

The wages of sin is death.

Ibid. 23

For the good that I would I do not; but the evil which I would not, that I do.

Romans. VII, 19

Heirs of God, and joint-heirs with Christ.

Ibid. VIII, 17

For we know that the whole creation groaneth and travaileth in pain together until now.

Ibid. 22

All things work together for good to them that love God.

Ibid. 28

If God be for us, who can be against us?

Ibid. 31

Neither death, nor life, nor angels, nor principalities, nor powers, nor things present, nor things to come,

Nor height, nor depth, nor any other creature, shall be able to separate us from the love of God, which is in Christ Jesus our Lord.

Ibid. 38, 39

Hath not the potter power over the clay, of the same lump to make one vessel unto honour, and another unto dishonour?

Ibid. IX, 21

Given to hospitality.

Ibid. XII, 13

Be not wise in your own conceits.

Ibid. 16

Recompense to no man evil for evil.

Ibid. 17

If it be possible, as much as lieth in you, live peaceably with all men.

Ibid. 18

Vengeance is mine; I will repay, saith the Lord.

Ibid. 19

If thine enemy hunger, feed him; if he thirst, give him drink: for in so doing thou shalt heap coals of fire on his head.[1]

Ibid. 20

Be not overcome of evil, but overcome evil with good.

Ibid. 21

[1] See *Proverbs, XXV, 21–22,* on page 1041a.

The powers that be are ordained of God.

Romans. XIII, 1

Render therefore to all their dues; tribute to whom tribute is due; custom to whom custom; fear to whom fear; honour to whom honour.

Ibid. 7

Owe no man anything, but to love one another.

Ibid. 8

Love is the fulfilling of the law.

Ibid. 10

Make not provision for the flesh, to fulfill the lusts thereof.

Ibid. 14

Doubtful disputations.

Ibid. XIV, 1

Let every man be fully persuaded in his own mind.

Ibid. 5

None of us liveth to himself.

Ibid. 7

Let us therefore follow after the things which make for peace.

Ibid. 19

God hath chosen the foolish things of the world to confound the wise; and God hath chosen the weak things of the world to confound the things which are mighty.

1 Corinthians. I, 27

As it is written,[1] eye hath not seen, nor ear heard.

Ibid. II, 9

I have planted, Apollos watered; but God gave the increase.

Ibid. III, 6

Every man's work shall be made manifest.

Ibid. 13

Not to think of men above that which is written.

Ibid. IV, 6

We are made a spectacle unto the world, and to angels, and to men.

Ibid. 9

Absent in body, but present in spirit.

Ibid. V, 3

[1] In *Isaiah, LXIV, 4.*

A little leaven leaveneth the whole lump.[1]

1 Corinthians. V, 6

It is better to marry than to burn.

Ibid. VII, 9

The fashion of this world passeth away.

Ibid. 31

Knowledge puffeth up, but charity edifieth.

Ibid. VIII, 1

I am made all things to all men.

Ibid. IX, 22

Let him that thinketh he standeth take heed lest he fall.

Ibid. X, 12

If a woman have long hair, it is a glory to her.

Ibid. XI, 15

Though I speak with the tongues of men and of angels, and have not charity, I am become as sounding brass, or a tinkling cymbal.

Ibid. XIII, 1

Though I have all faith, so that I could remove mountains, and have not charity, I am nothing.

Ibid. 2

And though I bestow all my goods to feed the poor, and though I give my body to be burned, and have not charity, it profiteth me nothing.

Ibid. 3

Charity suffereth long, and is kind; charity envieth not; charity vaunteth not itself, is not puffed up.

Ibid. 4

Beareth all things, believeth all things, hopeth all things, endureth all things.

Ibid. 7

Charity never faileth.

Ibid. 8

We know in part, and we prophesy in part.

Ibid. 9

When I was a child, I spake as a child, I understood as a child, I thought as a child: but when I became a man, I put away childish things.

Ibid. 11

[1] Also in *Galatians, V, 9.*

For now we see through a glass, darkly; but then face to face: now I know in part; but then shall I know even as also I am known.

1 Corinthians. XIII, 12

And now abideth faith, hope, charity, these three; but the greatest of these is charity.

Ibid. 13

If the trumpet give an uncertain sound, who shall prepare himself for battle?

Ibid. XIV, 8

Let all things be done decently and in order.

Ibid. 40

And last of all he was seen of me also, as of one born out of due time.

Ibid. XV, 8

But by the grace of God I am what I am.

Ibid. 10

But now is Christ risen from the dead, and become the firstfruits of them that slept.

For since by man came death, by man came also the resurrection of the dead.

For as in Adam all die, even so in Christ shall all be made alive.

Ibid. 20–22

The last enemy that shall be destroyed is death.

Ibid. 26

Evil communications corrupt good manners.

Ibid. 33

That which thou sowest is not quickened, except it die.

Ibid. 36

One star differeth from another star in glory.

Ibid. 41

It is sown in corruption, it is raised in incorruption.

Ibid. 42

The first man is of the earth, earthy.

Ibid. 47

Behold, I show you a mystery; We shall not all sleep, but shall all be changed,

In a moment, in the twinkling of an

eye, at the last trump: for the trumpet shall sound, and the dead shall be raised incorruptible, and we shall be changed.
1 Corinthians. XV, 51–52
Death is swallowed up in victory.
Ibid. 54
O death, where is thy sting? O grave, where is thy victory?
Ibid. 55
Watch ye, stand fast in the faith, quit you like men, be strong.
Ibid. XVI, 13
Not of the letter, but of the spirit; for the letter killeth, but the spirit giveth life.
2 Corinthians. III, 6
We have such hope, we use great plainness of speech.
Ibid. 12
The things which are seen are temporal; but the things which are not seen are eternal.
Ibid. IV, 18
We walk by faith, not by sight.
Ibid. V, 7
Now is the accepted time.
Ibid. VI, 2
By evil report and good report.
Ibid. 8
As having nothing, and yet possessing all things.
Ibid. 10
God loveth a cheerful giver.
Ibid. IX, 7
Though I be rude in speech.
Ibid. XI, 6
For ye suffer fools gladly, seeing ye yourselves are wise.
Ibid. 19
Forty stripes save one.
Ibid. 24
A thorn in the flesh.
Ibid. XII, 7
My strength is made perfect in weakness.
Ibid. 9
The grace of the Lord Jesus Christ, and the love of God, and the communion of the Holy Ghost, be with you all.
Ibid. XIII, 14

The right hands of fellowship.
Galatians. II, 9
Weak and beggarly elements.
Ibid. IV, 9
It is good to be zealously affected always in a good thing.
Ibid. 18
Ye are fallen from grace.
Ibid. V, 4
But the fruit of the Spirit is love, joy, peace, longsuffering, gentleness, goodness, faith,
Meekness, temperance.
Ibid. 22, 23
Every man shall bear his own burden.
Ibid. VI, 5
Whatsoever a man soweth, that shall he also reap.
Ibid. 7
Let us not be weary in well doing.
Ibid. 9
Carried about with every wind of doctrine.
Ephesians. IV, 14
Be ye angry, and sin not: let not the sun go down upon your wrath.
Ibid. 26
Put on the whole armour of God.
Ibid. VI, 11
For we wrestle not against flesh and blood, but against principalities, against powers, against the rulers of the darkness of this world, against spiritual wickedness in high places.
Ibid. 12
Wherefore take unto you the whole armour of God, that ye may be able to withstand in the evil day, and having done all, to stand.
Ibid. 13
To live is Christ, and to die is gain.
Philippians. I, 21
Work out your own salvation.
Ibid. II, 12
Whose God is their belly, and whose glory is in their shame.
Ibid. III, 19
The peace of God, which passeth all understanding.
Ibid. IV, 7

Whatsoever things are true, whatsoever things are honest, whatsoever things are just, whatsoever things are pure, whatsoever things are lovely, whatsoever things are of good report; if there be any virtue, and if there be any praise, think on these things.
Philippians. IV, 8

I have learned, in whatsoever state I am, therewith to be content.
Ibid. 11

Touch not; taste not; handle not.
Colossians. II, 21

Set your affections on things above, not on things on the earth.
Ibid. III, 2

Let your speech be alway with grace, seasoned with salt.
Ibid. IV, 6

Luke, the beloved physician.
Ibid. 14

Labour of love.
1 Thessalonians. I, 3

Study to be quiet, and to do your own business.
Ibid. IV, 11

Putting on the breastplate of faith and love; and for an helmet, the hope of salvation.
Ibid. V, 8

Prove all things; hold fast that which is good.
Ibid. 21

The law is good, if a man use it lawfully.
1 Timothy. I, 8

Not greedy of filthy lucre.
Ibid. III, 3

Drink no longer water, but use a little wine for thy stomach's sake.
Ibid. V, 23

We brought nothing into this world and it is certain we can carry nothing out.
Ibid. VI, 7

The love of money is the root of all evil.
Ibid. 10

Fight the good fight.
Ibid. 12

Rich in good works.
Ibid. 18

Science falsely so called.
1 Timothy. VI, 20

A workman that needeth not to be ashamed.
2 Timothy. II, 15

I have fought a good fight, I have finished my course, I have kept the faith.
Ibid. IV, 7

Alexander the coppersmith did me much evil: the Lord reward him according to his works.
Ibid. 14

Unto the pure all things are pure.
Titus. I, 15

Making mention of thee always in my prayers.
Philemon. I, 4

Such as have need of milk, and not of strong meat.
Hebrews. V, 12

Strong meat belongeth to them that are of full age.
Ibid. 14

Faith is the substance of things hoped for, the evidence of things not seen.
Ibid. XI, 1

We also are compassed about with so great a cloud of witnesses.
Ibid. XII, 1

The author and finisher of our faith.
Ibid. 2

Whom the Lord loveth he chasteneth.
Ibid. 6

The spirits of just men made perfect.
Ibid. 23

Be not forgetful to entertain strangers, for thereby some have entertained angels unawares.
Ibid. XIII, 2

Yesterday, and today, and forever.
Ibid. 8

For here we have no continuing city, but we seek one to come.
Ibid. 14

Let patience have her perfect work.
James. I, 4

Blessed is the man that endureth temptation; for when he is tried, he shall receive the crown of life.
James. I, 12

Every good gift and every perfect gift is from above.
Ibid. 17

No variableness, neither shadow of turning.
Ibid.

Be swift to hear, slow to speak, slow to wrath.
Ibid. 19

Unspotted from the world.
Ibid. 27

Faith without works is dead.
Ibid. II, 26

How great a matter a little fire kindleth!
Ibid. III, 5

The tongue can no man tame; it is an unruly evil.
Ibid. 8

This wisdom descendeth not from above, but is earthly, sensual, devilish.
Ibid. 15

Resist the Devil, and he will flee from you.
Ibid. IV, 7

Behold, we count them happy which endure. Ye have heard of the patience of Job, and have seen the end of the Lord.
Ibid. V, 11

The effectual fervent prayer of a righteous man availeth much.
Ibid. 16

Hope to the end.
1 Peter. I, 13

Abstain from fleshly lusts, which war against the soul.
Ibid. II, 11

Fear God. Honour the king.
Ibid. 17

Ornament of a meek and quiet spirit.
Ibid. III, 4

Giving honour unto the wife, as unto the weaker vessel.
Ibid. 7

Charity shall cover the multitude of sins.
Ibid. IV, 8

A crown of glory that fadeth not away.
1 Peter. V, 4

Be sober, be vigilant; because your adversary, the Devil, as a roaring lion, walketh about, seeking whom he may devour.
Ibid. 8

And the day star arise in your hearts.
2 Peter. I, 19

The dog is turned to his own vomit again.
Ibid. II, 22

Bowels of compassion.
1 John. III, 17

He that loveth not, knoweth not God; for God is love.
Ibid. IV, 8

There is no fear in love; but perfect love casteth out fear.
Ibid. 18

Be thou faithful unto death.
Revelation. II, 10

He shall rule them with a rod of iron.
Ibid. 27

Behold, I stand at the door and knock.
Ibid. III, 20

A pale horse: and his name that sat on him was Death.
Ibid. VI, 8

All nations, and kindreds, and people, and tongues.
Ibid. VII, 9

As the voice of many waters.[1]
Ibid. XIV, 2

They may rest from their labours; and their works do follow them.
Ibid. 13

And he gathered them together into a place called in the Hebrew tongue Armageddon.
Ibid. XVI, 16

Another book was opened, which is the book of life.
Ibid. XX, 12

I saw a new heaven and a new earth.
Ibid. XXI, 1

The holy city, new Jerusalem.
Ibid. 2

[1] The noise of many waters. — *Psalm XCIII, 4*

I am Alpha and Omega, the beginning and the end, the first and the last.
Revelation. XXI, 6

There shall be no night there.
Ibid. XXII, 5

Without are dogs.
Ibid. 15

THE APOCRYPHA [1]

How exceeding strong is wine! it causeth all men to err who drink it.
1 Esdras. III, 18

Ye must know that women have dominion over you: do ye not labour and toil, and give and bring all to the woman?
Ibid. IV, 22

Great is truth, and mighty above all things.[2]
Ibid. 41

Do right to the widow, judge for the fatherless, give to the poor, defend the orphan, clothe the naked.
2 Esdras. II, 20

What is past I know, but what is for to come I know not.
Ibid. IV, 46

Unto you is paradise opened.
Ibid. VIII, 52

Now therefore keep thy sorrow to thyself, and bear with a good courage that which hath befallen thee.
Ibid. X, 15

I shall light a candle of understanding in thine heart, which shall not be put out.
Ibid. XIV, 25

If thou hast abundance, give alms accordingly: if thou have but a little, be not afraid to give according to that little.
Tobit. IV, 8

[1] These books form part of the sacred literature of the Alexandrian Jews, and with the exception of *2 Esdras* are found interspersed with the Hebrew Scriptures in the ancient copies of the Septuagint, or Greek Version of the Old Testament. — *The Apocrypha According to the Authorized Version, Preface* (Oxford University Press)

[2] Magna est veritas et praevalet. — *The Vulgate, Book III* (uncanonical)

Honour thy father and thy mother in law, which are now thy parents.
Tobit. X, 12

Ye cannot find the depth of the heart of man, neither can ye perceive the things that he thinketh: then how can ye search out God, that hath made all these things, and know his mind, or comprehend his purpose?
Judith. VIII, 14

Put on her garments of gladness.
Ibid. X, 3

Our time is a very shadow that passeth away.
Wisdom of Solomon. II, 5

Let us crown ourselves with rosebuds before they be withered.
Ibid. 8

The souls of the righteous are in the hand of God, and there shall no torment touch them. In the sight of the unwise they seemed to die: and their departure is taken for misery, and their going from us to be utter destruction: but they are in peace.
Ibid. III, 1–3

They that put their trust in him shall understand the truth.
Ibid. 9

Wisdom is the gray hair unto men, and an unspotted life is old age.
Ibid. IV, 9

When I was born, I drew in the common air, and fell upon the earth, which is of like nature, and the first voice which I uttered was crying, as all others do.
Ibid. VII, 3

All men have one entrance into life, and the like going out.
Ibid. 6

Who can number the sand of the sea, and the drops of rain, and the days of eternity?
Ecclesiasticus. I, 2

If his understanding fail, have patience with him.
Ibid. 13

Observe the opportunity.
Ibid. IV, 20

Let not thine hand be stretched out to receive, and shut when thou shouldest repay.

Ecclesiasticus. IV, 31

A faithful friend is a strong defence: and he that hath found such an one hath found a treasure.

Ibid. VI, 14

Be not slow to visit the sick.

Ibid. VII, 35

Whatsoever thou takest in hand, remember the end, and thou shalt never do amiss.

Ibid. 36

Rejoice not over thy greatest enemy being dead, but remember that we die all.

Ibid. VIII, 7

Miss not the discourse of the elders.

Ibid. 9

Forsake not an old friend, for the new is not comparable to him. A new friend is as new wine: when it is old, thou shalt drink it with pleasure.

Ibid. IX, 10

In the day of prosperity there is a forgetfulness of affliction: and in the day of affliction there is no more remembrance of prosperity.

Ibid. XI, 25

He that toucheth pitch shall be defiled therewith.

Ibid. XIII, 1

A rich man beginning to fall is held up of his friends: but a poor man being down is thrust also away by his friends.

Ibid. 21

The heart of a man changeth his countenance, whether it be for good or evil: and a merry heart maketh a cheerful countenance.

Ibid. 25

Wine and women will make men of understanding to fall away.

Ibid. XIX, 2

Whether it be to friend or foe, talk not of other men's lives.

Ibid. 8

Gladness of the heart is the life of man, and the joyfulness of a man prolongeth his days.

Ibid. XXX, 22

Consider that I laboured not for myself only, but for all them that seek learning.

Ecclesiasticus. XXXIII, 17

Leave not a stain in thine honour.

Ibid. 22

Honour a physician with the honour due unto him.

Ibid. XXXVIII, 1

When the dead is at rest, let his remembrance rest; and be comforted for him, when his spirit is departed from him

Ibid. 23

How can he get wisdom . . . whose talk is of bullocks?

Ibid. 25

Look upon the rainbow, and praise him that made it.

Ibid. XLIII, 11

Let us now praise famous men, and our fathers that begat us.

Ibid. XLIV, 1

These were honoured in their generations, and were the glory of their times.

Ibid. 7

There be of them that have left a name behind them.

Ibid. 8

And some there be, which have no memorial.

Ibid. 9

Their bodies are buried in peace; but their name liveth for evermore.

Ibid. 14

His word burned like a lamp.

Ibid. XLVIII, 1

A scarecrow in a garden of cucumbers keepeth nothing.

Baruch. VI, 70

Was not Abraham found faithful in temptation, and it was imputed unto him for righteousness?

1 Maccabees. II, 52

With the God of heaven it is all one, to deliver with a great multitude, or a small company: For the victory of battle standeth not in the multitude of an host; but strength cometh from heaven.

Ibid. III, 18, 19

When he was at the last gasp.
1 Maccabees. VII, 9

The noble acts which he did, and his greatness, they are not written: for they were very many.
Ibid. IX, 22

Ask and learn.
Ibid. X, 72

Every man sat under his vine and his fig tree.[1]
Ibid. XIV, 12

We have been careful that they that will read may have delight, and that they that are desirous to commit to memory might have ease, and that all

[1] See *Micah, IV, 4,* on page 1049b.

into whose hands it comes might have profit.
2 Maccabees. II, 25

It is a foolish thing to make a long prologue, and to be short in the story itself.
Ibid. 32

Nicanor lay dead in his harness.
Ibid. XV, 28

If I have done well, and as is fitting, . . . it is that which I desired; but if slenderly and meanly, it is that which I could attain unto.
Ibid. 38

Speech finely framed delighteth the ears.
Ibid. 39

BOOK OF COMMON PRAYER [1]

The Scripture moveth us, in sundry places to acknowledge and confess our manifold sins and wickedness.

Morning Prayer. Minister's Opening Words

We have erred, and strayed from thy ways like lost sheep.

Ibid. General Confession

We have left undone those things which we ought to have done; and we have done those things which we ought not to have done.

Ibid.

The noble army of Martyrs.

Ibid. Te Deum

Make them to be numbered [2] with thy Saints, in glory everlasting.

Ibid.

I believe in God the Father Almighty, Maker of Heaven and earth: And in Jesus Christ his only Son our Lord: Who was conceived by the Holy Ghost, Born of the Virgin Mary; Suffered under Pontius Pilate, Was crucified, dead, and buried: He descended into hell; The third day he rose again from the dead: He ascended into heaven, And sitteth on the right hand of God the Father Almighty: From thence he shall come to judge the quick and the dead.

Ibid. The Apostles' Creed

Begotten of his Father before all worlds, God of God, Light of Light, Very God of very God; Begotten, not made; Being of one substance with the Father; By whom all things were made: Who for us men and for our salvation came down from heaven, And was incarnate by the Holy Ghost of the Virgin Mary, And was made man.

Ibid. The Nicene Creed

The author of peace and lover of concord, in knowledge of whom standeth our eternal life, whose service is perfect freedom.

Morning Prayer. A Collect for Peace

Afflicted, or distressed, in mind, body, or estate.

Ibid. A Prayer for All Conditions of Men

Lighten our darkness, we beseech thee, O Lord; and by thy great mercy defend us from all perils and dangers of this night.

Evening Prayer. Collect Against Perils for Aid

From envy, hatred, and malice, and all uncharitableness,

Good Lord, deliver us.

The Litany

The world, the flesh, and the devil.

Ibid.

From battle and murder, and from sudden death.

Ibid.

Give to all nations unity, peace, and concord.

Ibid

The kindly fruits of the earth.

Ibid.

Almighty God, unto whom all hearts are open, all desires known, and from whom no secrets are hid.

Holy Communion. Collect

Miserable sinners.[1]

Holy Communion. Exhortation

Read, mark, learn, and inwardly digest.

Collect for the Second Sunday in Advent

Renounce the devil and all his works, the vain pomp and glory of the world,

---

[1] American Revision [1928].

[2] In the Latin, this word is *munerari* (rewarded), and was mistaken, perhaps, by an early copyist, for *numerari* (numbered).

[1] The invocation, "Have mercy upon us, miserable sinners," was included in the Litany prior to the Revision of 1928. "Miserable offenders" appears in *Morning Prayer, A General Confession.*

with all covetous desires of the same, and the sinful desires of the flesh.

Holy Baptism. Of Children

The pomps and vanity of this wicked world and all the sinful lusts of the flesh.

Offices of Instruction (Catechism)

To keep my hands from picking and stealing.

Ibid. Answer 8

To do my duty in that state of life unto which it shall please God to call me.

Ibid. Answer 10

An outward and visible sign of an inward and spiritual grace.

Ibid. (On the Sacraments)

Forsaking all others, keep thee only unto her, so long as ye both shall live.

Solemnization of Matrimony

Let him now speak, or else hereafter for ever hold his peace.

Ibid.

To have and to hold from this day forward, for better for worse. for richer for poorer, in sickness and in health, to love and to cherish, till death us do part.

Ibid.

With this Ring I thee wed.

Ibid.

In the midst of life we are in death.[1]

Burial of the Dead. At the Grave

[1] This is derived from a Latin antiphon, said to have been composed by Notker, a monk of St. Gall, in 911, while watching some workmen building a bridge at Martinsbrücke, in peril of their lives. It forms the groundwork of Luther's antiphon *De Morte*.

Earth to earth, ashes to ashes, dust to dust; in sure and certain hope of the Resurrection unto eternal life.

Burial of the Dead. At the Grave

Show thy servant the light of thy countenance.

The Psalter. Psalms, XXXI, 18

God that maketh men to be of one mind in an house.

Ibid. LXVIII, 6

The iron entered into his soul.

Ibid. CV, 18

God, in whom we live and move and have our being.

Family Prayer. Morning

O Lord, support us all the day long, until the shadows lengthen and the evening comes, and the busy world is hushed, and the fever of life is over, and our work is done. Then in thy mercy grant us a safe lodging, and a holy rest, and peace at the last.[1]

Ibid. At Night

BOOK OF COMMON PRAYER, ENGLISH

Grant that the old Adam in these persons may be so buried, that the new man may be raised up in them.

Holy Baptism. Of Those of Riper Years

With all my worldly goods I thee endow.

Solemnization of Matrimony

[1] By Cardinal Newman.

THE KORAN

Translated [1734] by GEORGE SALE
[*1697–1736*]

Turn, therefore, thy face towards the holy temple of Mecca; and wherever ye be, turn your faces towards that place.
Chap. 2

Wherever ye be, God will bring you all back at the resurrection.
Ibid.

As for him who voluntarily performeth a good work, verily God is grateful and knowing.
Ibid.

Your God is one God; there is no God but He, the most merciful.
Ibid.

O true believers, take your necessary precautions against your enemies, and either go forth to war in separate parties, or go forth all together in a body.
Chap. 4

Fight for the religion of God.
Ibid.

O men, respect women who have borne you.
Ibid.

Wheresoever ye be, death will overtake you, although ye be in lofty towers.
Ibid.

Whosoever flieth from his country for the sake of God's true religion, shall find in the earth many forced to do the same, and plenty of provisions.
Ibid.

God loveth not the speaking ill of any one in public.
Chap. 4

Let not thy hand be tied up to thy neck; neither open it with an unbounded expansion, lest thou become worthy of reprehension, and be reduced to poverty.
Chap. 17

Of his mercy he hath made for you the night and the day, that ye may rest in the one, and may seek to obtain provision for yourself of his abundance, by your industry, in the other.
Chap. 28

If God should punish men according to what they deserve, he would not leave on the back of the earth so much as a beast.
Chap. 35

God obligeth no man to more than he hath given him ability to perform.
Chap. 65

Woe be unto those who pray, and who are negligent at their prayer: who play the hypocrites, and deny necessaries to the needy.
Chap. 107

O unbelievers, I will not worship that which ye worship; nor will ye worship that which I worship. . . . Ye have your religion, and I my religion.
Chap. 109

INDEX

INDEX

Entries are arranged alphabetically, with hyphenated words indexed as one word. Note the order for possessives and plurals of identical spelling.

Bird, another, sings better, 222a
or devil, 545a
Bird-cage, summer, 100a
Bird's, sweet, throat, 160a
Birds about a ruined place, 978a
were mad with glee, 673b
Birds' cries, 896a
Bird-song at morning, 752a

The letter *a* after the page number means that the entry is in the left column of the page cited; *b* indicates the right column.

Archaic, dialect, and other variant spellings in the text are retained in the index, with one exception: In the case of two standard modern variables of the same word, entries are combined under the preferred Webster spelling. For example, *bisy larke* appears under *bisy;* but references to *defence* and *defense* are combined under *defense.*

Action, materials of, are variable, 64a
  no noble, done, 305b
  nor utterance nor power of speech, 168b
  not thought but, 562b
  of the mind, 812a
  of tiger, 155a
  pious, 174a
  sharer of the, he describes, 628b
  single lovely, 603a
  sometime's by, dignified, 136a
  splendid and unselfish, 888a
  sportive or serious, 62a
  spring is a call to, 991a
  standard of every, 64a
  suit the, to the word, 175b
  thought is the child of, 511a
Actions, extreme, ascribed to vanity, 726a
  great and illustrious, 56a
  hostile, 54b
  image of, 69b
  increased by correspondent, 64b
  less conscious, 670b
  mean, to fear, 726a
  morality of, 344b
  most brilliant, 491a
  my, are my ministers, 289a
  not always, show the man, 314a
  of one side or other, in, 19b
  of the just, 237a
  ordinary, to habit, 726a
  performance of pleasant, 922b
  rectitude and sincerity of, 870a
  speaker of my living, 212a
  thousand, one purpose, 154b
  true recompense of gallant, 297b
  words are but shadow of, 57b
Active business, grown old in, 431a
  nothing so, is, 790b
  prey to the, 380a
  the vigilant the, the brave, 369a
Activity, art is a human, 643a
  manifestation of human, 722b
  mere change of, 594a
Activ'st part, 263b
Actor, condemn fault and not the, 184a
  language the, spoke, 339b
  rather than a critic, 868a
  stops and looks around, 563b
  well-graced, 140b
Actors are the usual three, 638b
  fill with, 161a
  too humble and obscure, 773b
  were all spirits, 210a
Actresses, white bosoms of your, 339a
Acts, angels are, 224b
  being seven ages, 161a
  bend, of government, 399a
  does well, nobly, 305b
  exemplary win good names, 117a
  first four, already past, 306b
  five, the just measure, 42a
  good, in memory, 119b
  illustrious, 242a
  like a king, 345a
  noble, and his greatness, 1067a
  of devotion to God, 367b
  of government, 426a
  of kindness and love, 403b
  our notable, 96oa
  reverence pervades our public, 20a
  such, fill a pen, 122b
  the best, 586a

Acts the brute, 272b
  the least, man who, 3b
Actual, dig deep into the, 720b
  man and romantic image, 969a
Actus non facit reum, 1009b
Acute enemy, written by an, 738a
  inquisitive dexterous, 360a
  manner, carp in, 281b
Acuteness of strength of mind, 435a
Ad infinitum, proceed, 296a
  majorem Dei gloriam, 1009b
  the homily the slogan the, 996a
Adad inundate his field, 3a
Adage, like the poor cat i' the, 93a, 196a
Adagios of islands, 982a
Adam, believe in, and Eve, 848a
  called his wife's name Eve, 1022a
  Cupid, young, 1011b
  debt of gratitude we owe, 677b
  deep sleep to fall upon, 1021b
  delved and Eve span, 999a
  gardener, and his wife, 547a
  goodliest man of men, 255b
  grant that the old, 1069b
  in, all die, 1061b
  so starved me, 573b
  was a gardener, 178a
  was but human, 677b
  whipped the offending, 154a
Adamant for drift, 868b
  frame of, 336a
Adamantine chains, 201a
Adam's ear, left voice in, 257b
  fall, 1000b
  profession, 178a
  sons born in sin, 223a
Adamses vote for Douglas, 793a
Adam-zad, no truce with, 816b
Adapt, Alcibiades could, himself, 54a
Adazzle dim, 724a
Add hue unto rainbow, 148a
  more to the abundance, 919b
  one cubit, 1051b
  what we can to life, 743b
Added insult to injury, 10a
  light, brings an, 630a
  little, to a little, 61a
  unto thee, 762b
Adder, deaf, 1035a
  stingeth like an, 1040b
Addict themselves to sack, 153b
Addicted, dear, artist, 993b
Adding fuel to the flame, 260b
  one to one, 570b
Addison, volumes of, 337b
Addition, agreeable, 41a
  of middle class turns scale, 26b
Addressing, Antony, a multitude, 57b
Adds a precious seeing, 133b
Adequate idea of true and false, 281b
Adeste fideles, 1009b
Adhere, time nor place did then, 196a
Adieu adieu kind friends, 1004b
  drop a tear and bid, 329a
  for evermore, 392a
  she cried, 308a
Adjectives, without any qualifying, 748b
Adjudged not by common judges, 336b

Adjunct, learning is, to ourself, 133b
Adjustment of all colonial claims, 771a
Administer'd, best, is best, 317b
Administered, well, States, 26b
Administration is in hands of the many, 20a
  said of my first, 919b
Admirable, express and, 173b
Admiral, Dewey was the, 713a
  kill one, 325a
  last of all an, came, 427b
Admiralty, if blood be the price of, 815a
Admiration, as great in, as herself, 212a
  from fastidious critics, 192b
  of the wisest, 508a
  of virtue, 250a
  restored to human, 449b
  right kind of money, 726a
  season your, 171a
  stands in the, 259a
  wealth or fame or, 761b
Admirations, teach, 778a
Admir'd, more, than by the negligent, 201a
Admire, do not like those whom we, 265b
  fools, men of sense approve, 311b
  for to, an' for the sea, 819a
  like those who, us, 43a, 265b
  most men, virtue, 259a
  that riches grow in hell, 253a
  where none, 343b
Admired by their domestics, 61b, 99b
Admirers, complaisance for their, 106a
Admires, meanly, mean things, 565a
Admiring bog, 646b
  in the gloomy shade, 242a
  nature's universal throne, 460b
Admission, just, of topics, 431b
  price to th' lake front, 835b
Admit absence, 216b
  impediments, 207a
  it frankly and try another, 918b
  me of thy crew, 245a
  of no defence, 283b
  the camel's nose, 464a
  them in your sight, 428a
Admits, genuine night, no ray, 278a
  life, not of delays, 341b
  no parallel, 48a
  not some exception, 222a
  of no modification, 44b
Admitted to that equal sky, 316a
Ado to interpret interpretations, 101a
A-doing nothing all day long, 881b
Adonais, soul of, 468b
  weep for, 467a
Adonis hath a sweete tooth, 112b
  in loveliness, 447b
Adopt new views, 539b
  that maturity of custom, 847b
Adoption, friends and their, tried, 171b
  land of their, or birth, 758a
Adorable, grace joined with wrinkles is, 498a
Adoration, breathless with, 407a
Adorations, desires and, 467b

Aim, most skillful archer miss his, 42a
no other, but war, 85b
of a true philosophy, 702b
our being's end and, 317b
rightly is wise man's task, 64a
rivalry of, 697a
two things to, at in life, 822b
your, the star, 1008b
Aimed at duck or plover, 380b
Aiming at a million, 570b
at the bless'd abodes, 120a, 316a
at what's far, 17a
Aims, above man's, 654a
movement with great, 951a
secret, of nature, 721a
Ain't heard nothin' yet, 936a
it awful Mabel, 914a
Air a chartered libertine, 154a
ache with, 159a
and a peculiar grace, 303b
and angels' purity, 216a
apple-blossoms fill the, 947b
Arabs of the, 795a
babbling gossip of the, 164a
baronial, or superiority, 973b
bird in the, 11a
bird of the, 1043b
bites shrewdly, 172a
breasts the keen, 354a
breathe the, again, 613a
breathe the vital, 6b
ceremonious, of gloom, 622b
Cervantes' serious, 321b
change of, a similar draught, 882a
common, 1065b
content to breathe his native, 309a
cutting the, 105b
dance upon the, 769b
drew in the common, 49b
earth and skies, 407a
eating, 153a
empire of the, 472b
enjoys the, it breathes, 403b
escape to outer, 37a
evening, is chilly in Cremona, 782b
excellent canopy the, 173b
fairer than evening, 123b
faith and philosophy are, 605a
feed on, 791a
flowers sweeter in the, 121b
flung my soul to the, 935a
fog and filthy, 194a
glory and blue, 519b
gods that wanton in the, 268a
growing strength in the, 869a
hang in, 151a
haunted, 948b
he flies through the, 700b
heedless, 613a
homeless, 690a
in sea or fire in earth or, 170a
in the, men shall be seen, 1000a
inebriate of, am I, 646a
instead of wasted upon, 613b
is calm and pleasant, 250a
is delicate, 195b
is delicious, 840b
is filled as she passes through, 686b
is full of sunlight, 757a
is wild with leaves, 934a
keel plows, 117b
liberal, 688a
littered with bits of gingham, 747b

Air, lived on, 880b
love free as, 313a
loves an inner, 986b
melted into thin, 210a
meteor to the troubled, 252b
mock the, with idle state, 349b
mocking the, 148b
morning, perfuming, 564a
nothing to breathe but, 775a
now, is hush'd, 351b
of Auld Lang Syne, 527b
of delightful studies, 250a
of great solemnity, 461a
of superiority, 594a
of the New World, 773a
oh, pride plume here buckle, 724b
passions fleet to, 145b
power in the, 757a
round ocean and the living, 404a
rules the, 930b
saw the, too much with hand, 175a
scent the morning, 172b
sewers annoy the, 258a
smiles and languish'd, 384b
splitting, with noise, 202b
sweet leaves to the, 134a
sweetly recommends itself, 195a
sweetness on the desert, 348b
thoughts shut up want, 306a
throw it up into the, 227b
to the countenance, 300b
tread in, 5a
trifles light as, 188b
use of, common to all, 97a
vivid, 995a
walking in an, of glory, 272a
warm the, in raw summers, 295b
was cooling and very still, 476b
waves in summer, 591b
where, might wash, 692a
wild spring, 911b
with barbarous dissonance, 248a
world-mothering, 724b
Air-drawn dagger, 197b
Airly, gut to git up, 600b
Airs, all, make one country, 222b
don't give yourself, 656b
martial, of England, 444b
melting, or martial, 365a
Naiad, brought me home, 543b
silence all the, 250b
soft Lydian, 245b
Airy, created in so, a fashion, 865a
ever so, a tread, 554a
footsteps of strange things, 513b
height, objects in an, 293b
masses and smooth, 432a
mountain, up the, 638a
navies, nations', 549a
nothing a local habitation, 142b
rings, skim the heath in, 309a
servitors, nimble and, 250a
shell, unseen within, 247a
thinness, 216b
tongues, 247a
Aisle, long-drawn, 348b
Aisles, monastic, 503a
of Christian Rome, 503a
of the woods, 803a
Ajax the great, 4a
Akin to pain, 522a
Akond of Swat, 581b

Alabama, I've come from, 636a
Alabaster box of precious ointment, 1054b
boxes, 643a
cities gleam, 781b
cut in, 143a
smooth as monumental, 190a
Alacrity in sinking, 180b
Aladdin's lamp, 602a
lamp, ready money is, 459b
Alamo, remember the, 517b
Alarm, ride and spread the, 524a
Alarming consequences, serious and, 366b
Alarms, all the world's, 827b
look of love, 386b
mortal, 278b
of struggle and flight, 622a
used to war's, 487b
Alas poor Yorick I knew him, 178b
weather-glass is set at, 993b
Albatross, fluttered round the lamp, 660a
I shot the, 421a
Alcestis, brought to me like, 251b
Alchemiz'd and free of space, 479a
Alchemy, courtesy is the true, 638b
happy, of mind, 326b
richest, 166b
Alcibiades had a handsome dog, 59a
with good men or bad, 54a
Alcides' equal, 48a
Alcohol and Christianity, 728a
Alcoran, Talmud and the, 120b
Aldebaran and Betelgueux, 704b
Alderman, fore-finger of an, 134b
Aldiborontiphoscophornio, 307b
Ale, all-powerful, 358a
British, 358b
cakes and, in fear, 9b
cakes and, no more, 164a
Christmas broach'd mightiest, 414b
drink your, 787a
English, 867b
God send thee good, 97a
large quart of myghty, 81a
London, 897a
man ale's the stuff, 786b
news much older than their, 356b
pined for cheerful, 358b
pot of, and safety, 155a
spicy nut-brown, 245b
turn out more, 668a
we drank and songs we sung, 668a
Aleak, world is all, 969a
Ale-house, honest, 236a
Ale's the stuff to drink, 786b
Alexander asked ambassadors, 32b
did not rejoice at Philip's success, 56a
I would be Diogenes were I not, 61a
noble dust of, 178b
some talk of, 1004a
the coppersmith, 1063b
unable to untie Gordian knot, 56b
wept that not one world yet conquered, 58a
Alexander's Ragtime Band, 94tb
Alexandrine, needless, ends the song, 311a
Algebra, tell what hour by, 238a
Algiers, lay dying in, 529b

Ashamed to own he has been in wrong, 321a
to sit upon his brow, 137a
with the noble shame, 599a
workman that needeth not be, 1063b
Ashbuds, more black than, 548a
Ashen flowers, agonized hopes and, 838b
skies they were, and sober, 545b
Ashes, beauty for, 1047b
cinders, dust, 480b
dead cold, 733b
follow blaze, 625a
from his, may be made, 179a, 551b
handful of, 895b
handful of grey, 627a
in fleeing the, 8a
inscribed over human, 451b
into, all my lust, 269a
aid old Troy in, 289b
lay my, at the roots, 886b
mocking to, 829a
new-create another heir, 212a
of his fathers, 493b
past is a bucket of, 898b
slumbers beneath the, 243b
splendid in, 241b
their wonted fires in our, 81a, 349a
to ashes, 1069b
to the taste, 453a
truth's sad, 605a
turns, or it prospers, 531b
was burnt to, 873b
Ashy the tall skull, 947a
Asia, people of, slaves to one man, 58a
Aside, daffed world, 151a
Asinorum, pons, 29a
A-sitting on a hill, 881b
Ask and it shall be given, 1051b
and learn, 1067a
and ye shall receive, 1058b
for information, 579a
for reward, 87b
for what you wish you had not got, 47b
I do not, for any crown, 654a
if like to pray with, 931b
if there is some mistake, 880b
me no more, 236b, 550b
me where they grow, 230a
never, never refuse, 332a
not a dinner to, a man to, 340a
nothing more of me sweet, 694b
of thee forgiveness, 193b
till ye receive, 412b
to know, 887a
we ask and, 619a
Askelon and Samarkand, 950a
streets of, 1027b
Asketh, every one that, receiveth, 1051b
Asking eye, explain the, 319b
God may be had for the, 600a
questions and writing them, 846b
too much, 401b
Asks no omen, 5a
Asleep by thy murmuring stream, 392b
devil is, 763b
each in world of his own, 58b
falls, with heartache, 879b

Asleep, hope they have not been, 652b
in lap of legends old, 480b
keep it quiet till it falls, 275a
lips of those that are, 1044b
man, 801a
never see ticket unless, 841b
the very houses seem, 407a
tide as moving seems, 557a
time has fallen, 650a
who knows not that he knows is, 754b
A-sparkle, morn set, 575a
Aspect and her eyes, 456a
commonplace, on life, 515a
discover a merciful, 726b
lend eye a terrible, 155a
more favourable, 208a
of the world changed, 272b
of this shore, 455a
sweet, of princes, 211a
with grave, he rose, 254a
remoter, of the law, 709a
Aspen tree, leaves of an, 912b
Aspens quiver willows whiten, 547b
Aspes leef, 78b
Aspics' tongues, 189a
Aspiration, prove an, 700a
Aspirations of men of good will, 954a
Aspire, rest bade, 568a
to highest place, 33a
to lay hands on golden key, 246b
Aspired no higher, 63b
what I, to be, 572a
Aspires to be a hero, 342a
towards condition of music, 702a
Aspiring soul, 526a
to be angels men rebel, 316a
to be gods, 120b
trees and men and grass, 605a
youth that fired the Ephesian dome, 241b
Asquith, affair between Margot, 967a
Ass, burial of an, 1048a
egregiously an, 187a
enamour'd of an, 142a
every, thinks he may kick, 378a
his master's crib, 1045a
jawbone of an, 1026b
law is a, a idiot, 576b
looked for his, 109a
nor his, 1025a
odd fantastic, Rousseau, 804b
opened the mouth of the, 1025b
prove an, 143a
riding upon an, 1049b
Robin thou'rt an, 491a
wild, stamps o'er his head, 531b
will carry his load, 109b
write me down an, 158b
Assaieth, naught, naught n'acheveth, 78b
Assail, scholar's life, 336a
troop and muster and, 963a
Assaille wyves pacience, 81b
Assails all he reads, 312a
Assassin, copperheads and the, 898b
Assassination could trammel up, 195b
tempered by, 398a
the extreme form of censorship, 766b

Assault and battery of the wind, 826b
of thoughts on unthinking, 925b
preparing his, 306a
Assay so hard, 78a
Assay'd, thrice he, 253a
Assays of bias, 173a
Assemble and to petition government, 376b
Assembled, souls of all, 242b
Assemblies, masters of, 1044a
tyranny of political, 515b
Assembly of good fellows, 336b
of portable plumbing, 957a
of reasonable men, 375b
posterity is a limited, 512b
Assent and you are sane, 646a
with civil leer, 319a
Assert eternal Providence, 252a
Assertion of private interests, 402a
Assertions, convince hearers of, 21a
Asses, bridge of, 29a
convenience of, 59a
mankind are the, 460a
too difficult for, 29a
Assets, grocer's, swell, 803a
most valuable, is a community, 743a
Asshen, fyr yreke in our, 81a
Assiduous wait upon her, 391a
Assigned, delusion, to him, 35a
hair's-breadth of time, 67b
Assignment, mighty, 986b
Assimilate, understand and, 982b
Assimilated, pure truth cannot be, 617b
Assisian, loved, 852b
Assist me up, 86b
reduced fellowman, 74b
Assistance, ask a just God's, 542a
child will turn for, 851b
give full, to all, 21b
of that Divine Being, 539a
which she administers, 400a
Assisted the sun in his rising, 589b
Associate, the good must, 359a
Association, general, of nations, 771a
of literary men, 494a
Associations, I detest all such, 494a
Ass's milk, white curd of, 319a
Assuage the anguish of bereavement, 541b
Assuaged by suspicion of a bad end, 857b
Assuages, time, sorrow, 32b
Assume a virtue, 177a
either sex, 252b
that we are alive, 817a
what I, you shall assume, 607a
Assumes some mark of virtue, 145b
the god, 280a
Assumption, gave without, 56a
Assurance, full, given by lookes, 114b
give world, of a man, 177a
make, double sure, 198b
of recorded history, 945a
praise not an, of survival, 844a
to the contrary, 229a
'twould be an, most dear, 629a
Assured, ignorant of what he's most, 184b
Assyrian came down like the wolf, 456a

Audacious head is lifted one inch, 661a
Audible laughter, ill-bred as, 356a
thawed and became, 61a
voice of the past, 475b
Audience, arrival of your, 434a
fit, find, 257a
for sake of a crowded, 22a
good play makes, interested, 865b
laugh at usual jokes, 22b
long the, sits before us, 432a
of beery wenches, 730a
sitting, looks, 304a
Audiences collected, 22b
equal interest to three, 563a
ever-renewed, 823a
there must be great, 611b
Auditor, weakness of his immediate, 925a
Aught of what he leaves, 179b
that I have done, 822a
Augment the old, a day to, 5a
Augments, one, its gaudy show, 415b
Augur misgovernment at a distance, 360a
Augurs, ill name of, 600a
mock their own presage, 206b
August abodes, 411a
not this, nor September, 983a
past surprises, 575b
Augustan age, the next, 493a
Augustine, Saint, 523b
Auld acquaintance be forgot, 392b
Lang Syne, 392b, 527b
moon in her arm, 1011b
nature swears, 391b
Robin Gray is kind, 380a
when 'tis, it waxeth cauld, 1013a
Auldest friends, nearest friends are, 751b
Aunt kept strict regard for truth, 849b
was off to the theatre, 849b
Auntie, did you feel no pain, 873b
Aunt's charwoman's sister's son, 1008b
Aunts, poverty, rivals, 784b
Aurora Borealis, 557a
daughter of the dawn, 6a
Leighs, no more, 533b
shows her brightening face, 329a
Aurore, Belle, 574a
Auspicious eye, 170a
Austere, beauty cold and, 962a
look, immaculate, 934b
man the most, 706a
most, of disciplines, 784a
serenity of Shangri-La, 985b
Austerlitz and Waterloo, 898a
weather, 358b
Austin, according to, 222a
Austria, Don John of, 867a
Austria-Hungary, peoples of, 771a
Austrian scientist with announcement, 949b
Authentic, most, creed, 662b
watch is shown, 261a
Author and finisher, 537a
and finisher of our faith, 1063b
any, in the world, 133b
brother, 431a
came out from bushes, 923b
choose, as you choose friend, 283b
cooperation of public with, 808b
first, of that thought, 508a

Author in each son, 287a
influence of an, 696b
master and, 75a
of confusion and lies, 224a
of liberty, 529b
of peace, 1068b
one work of some, 431a
publish even one line of an, 487a
relationship of, to his works, 772a
same steps as the, 478b
that's all author, 457a
the test of an, 627b
unsuccessful, turns critic, 424a
what I like in a good, 823a
what the, intended, 732b
who speaks about his books, 513a
worst thing you can do to, 342a
would his brother kill, 266b
Authority, age carries in it an, 301b
and place demonstrate tempers of men, 57a
and show of truth, 158b
and the laws, respect for, 20a
appoint to the exercise of, 361b
basis of moral, 617b
by whose, do you act, 446b
drest in a little brief, 184b
from others' books, 132b
of the state, 888a
old age has great, 34a
set in, 3a
those who submit to, 771a
tongue-tied by, 205b
young German's respect for, 882b
Author's explanations, 961a
literary reputation, 358a
prospects, gloomy as an, 513b
renown has been purchased, 446b
skill to give, 806a
soul, 969b
without the, knowing it, 804a
Authors and critics talk of the sublime, 371a
charged with debts to his, 508b
essayist atheist novelist, 556b
great old, 795b
have established a kind of rule, 300b
little band of, 778b
notion of gregarious, 494b
old, best to read, 119a
Plagiarè among good, 251a
praise of ancient, 229a
pretentious American, 908b
who please everyone, 844a
Authors' names, judge of, 311b
Autobiographies begin with chapter two, 861a
Autobiography, British, 782a
of Alice B. Toklas, 877b
saves a man or woman, 597a
Autocracy, double-headed eagle of the, 840b
ocean's deep, 887a
Autocrat must be a great barbarian, 773a
Autocratic sway of the west wind, 773a
Autograph, foolish, 431a
of God, 712a
Automatism criticism and wisdom, 976b
Automaton, mechanized, 464b

Autonomous development, opportunity of, 771a
Autumn dew, bright with, 471a
evening, sadly descends the, 623a
evenings, long dark, 569a
fruit, fell like, 276a
in the misty morn, 488a
no richer gift, has poured, 527a
nodding o'er yellow plain, 328a
poets sing, 647a
shone like warmth, 899b
some of us call it, 573b
that grew by reaping, 201b
trees, sing from the, 932b
winter and the spring, 230a
Autumnal face, 217a
leaves, thick as, 3b, 252b
tone, deep, 466a
Autumn-fields looking on the happy, 550b
Autumn's being, thou breath of, 466a
Avail, show the boy its little, 505a
Available as his birthright, 982b
Availeth, prayer, much, 1064a
struggle naught, 595b
Avarice ambition lust, 282b
deplorable piece of madness, 282b
dreams of, 342a
gratify, and luxury, 290a
hate is like death and, 490b
lust and rum, 796a
of which old men sicken, 214a
old-gentlemanly vice, 214a
Pride Envy, 75b
prudery a kind of, 447a
suspicion and asperity, 372b
Ave Caesar, 1009b
Avenge thy slaughter'd saints, 251b
Avenged 1440 times a day, 714a
satisfaction of knowing we are, 585b
Avengers, blind, 287a
Avenging day, great, 4a
sword unsheathe, 395a
Avenues of ill, 506b
Average, cold calculating, 687a
man goes to church six times, 844b
man, greater security for, 919a
man is curled, in the, 777a
person, insure the, 921a
Ph.D. thesis, 942b
Averages, fugitive from th' law of, 997b
Aversion, begin with a little, 380b
self-reliance is its, 501b
to labour, 290b
Avoid all extremes, 53b
as you would the plague, 73a
citations from poets, 22a
for fear of losing it, 286a
let men, us and we leap, 309b
perils which beset them, 282b
religion as a direct subject, 630a
seeking to, Charybdis, 145b
shame, 418b
surest way to, war, 290a
the reeking herd, 934a
what is to come, 177a
Avoidance, obvious, 784b
Avoided evils, 64b
Avoiding what they dislike, 283a
Avon, sweet Swan of, 219b
Avowed the erect the manly foe, 401b

Balm in Gilead, 1048a
  of hurt minds, 196b
  of the bruised heart, 122a
  off from anointed king, 139b
  the sceptre and the ball, 156a
  try tropic for your, 971a
Balmy sleep, 305a
  sweets, 120a
  warmth, spring brings, 35b
Baloney is flattery so thick, 973b
Balsam, bears no, for mistakes, 712b
Baltimore, Penn's town New York and, 506b
Bamboo-brier, sharp ez a, 738b
Ban, hurl the cynic's, 777b
  in every voice in every, 387b
  on it lays her, 717a
'Ban 'Ban Ca-Caliban, 209b
Banbury Cross, 1017b
Band, an elastic, 714a
  haven't got a, 892a
  heaven-born, 402b
  is playing somewhere, 808a
  little, of authors, 778b
  of brothers, 156b
  of exiles moored bark, 470a
  orange, of eve, 787b
  swell to beat the, 803a
  wearied, swoons to a waltz, 969b
  worries me to beat the, 914a
Bandersnatch, shun the frumious, 657b
Bands, cancels all, 151a
  coat and, and hymn-book, 517a
  dissolve the political, 373a
  of Orion, 1032a
  pursue culture in, 804a
Bane, deserve precious, 253a
  morality thou deadly, 390b
  no greater, to friendship, 33b
  of all genius, 464b
  of all good society, 370a
  precious, 915a
  to antidote, 705a
Baneful effects of spirit of party, 367a
Bang, not with a, 944a
Bangkok, in, at twelve o'clock, 982a
Bangor to the Rocky Range, 912a
Banish fear that lurks, 939a
  grief too great to, 486a
  pleasures, pain, 303a
  plump Jack, 150b
  they'd, us you know, 646a
  understanding, 18b
  with night we, sorrow, 227a
Banish'd yet true-born Englishman, 138b
Banished, fear can not be, 954a
  for my willful crime, 259a
  man, 1011a
  persons will be, 676b
  picturesque were, 718a
Banishment, bitter bread of, 139a
Banjo, wid my, on my knee, 636a
Bank and shoal of time, 195b
  broke the, at Monte Carlo, 748a
  first supernatural, 946b
  of violets, breathes upon, 163b
  sleeps upon this, 147a
  starved, of moss, 525a
  violet loves a sunny, 634b
  waly waly up the, 1013a
  whereon wild thyme blows, 141b
Bankers just like anybody else, 989a

Bank-note world, 463a
Bankrupt of life, 276b
  thief turns thief-taker, 424a
Banks, allegory on, of the Nile, 381a
  and braes o' bonie Doon, 392a
  and corporations, 444b
  bonnie, o' Lock Lomond, 1003a
  bonny, of Clyde, 850a
  green, of Shannon, 432b
  of the Seine the Thames, 493a
  trembled underneath her, 166a
  vast surplus in, 442a
Banned, that work had better be, 970a
Banner, blood-red, streams afar, 445a
  earth's green, shakes, 640a
  freedom's, 476b
  held his, high, 903b
  in the sky, 534b
  over me was love, 1044a
  pride carries, to the last, 652b
  royal, and all quality, 189a
  song for our, 499a
  star-spangled, 436a
  torn but flying, 454a
  with the strange device, 522a
Banners, all thy, wave, 433a
  army with, 1044b
  confusion on thy, wait, 349b
  flout the sky, 194a
  hang out our, 199b
  of thy dead, 803b
Banquet, behave in life as at a, 65a
  tables, hundred thousand, 661a
  when love sits down to the, 668a
Banqueter on worms, 772a
  sated, 34b
Banqueters, hundred thousand, 661a
Banquet-hall deserted, 440a
Banquets, first in, 4a
  of the gods, 40b
Banshee, mem'ry comes like a, 760a
  waters of, 790b
Baptism he observed, 996a
Baptist, clear-toned, bell, 635a
Baptist's, John, head, 1053a
Baptized in tears, 368a
Bar a single door, 767a
  and its moaning, 598a
  back of the, 877a
  birth's invidious, 552b
  crossed the, 557a
  doors in time of peace, 43a
  gold, of heaven, 640a
  harbor, be moaning, 598a
  hell should, the way, 909b
  neither is poverty a, 20a
  no moaning of the, 557a
  only, against it, 611b
  prisoner at the, 555b
  treat where any, is, 706a
  turn-pike, 485b
  when I went to the, 684a
Barabbas was a robber, 1058b
Barbara Allen, 1012b
Barbarian, autocrat must be a great, 773a
  weeping above his dead, 662a
Barbarians philistines and populace, 623a
Barbaric phase, growing mind at a, 832b
  showers on her kings, 253b
  yawp, 608b

Barbarism, destruction and, 926b
  fastnesses of ancient, 628a
  inflame and fix its, 832b
  theatre can flourish in, 720a
Barbarous dissonance, 248a
  frank, recklessness, 773a
  in beauty, 724b
  woman more, than man, 727a
Barber and collier fight, 332b
  Caesar's, 56b
  imprudently married the, 350b
  kept on shaving, 587a
  prating, 58b
Barber's shear, 565b
Barbers, haughty, 964b
Barber-shop, lights burn low in the, 964b
Barb'rous foes, 335b
  skill, adorning but a, 267a
Bard, from old or modern, 247a
  here dwelt, 328b
  lacked a sacred, 40a
  matchless, 358b
  more fat than, beseems, 328b
  voice of the, 386b
  who sang of Enchanter Indolence, 405a
  whom were none to praise, 405a
Bards in fealty to Apollo, 477a
  not made for, 425a
  of long ago, 854b
  of old enjoy'd in you, 384b
  of passion and of mirth, 482b
  of rhyme and metre free, 912a
  of the lyre, 38a
  Olympian, 503b
  Saints Heroes if we will, 619b
  sublime, 522a
Bare, back and side go, 97a
  bodkin, quietus make with, 174b
  earth, expos'd on the, 280a
  heads are just as, 955b
  imagination of a feast, 138b
  lay it, down to bone, 983b
  one, hour to live, 123b
  pate of a bald man, 10a
  ruin'd choirs, 206a
  to the buff, 752a
Bare-bosom'd night, 608a
Barefoot boy, 527a
  dance, on wedding day, 130a
  dervishes, 506b
  him that makes shoes go, 93a
Barefoote, goe long, 93b
Barefooted and bareheaded, 898b
Barère's Memoirs, 493b
Bargain and bid, 767b
  better, driven, 116a
  catch cold and starve, 203b
  way of, 151a
Barge like a burnish'd throne, 200b
Bark, bitter, and burning clove, 881a
  critic peep or cynic, 503b
  dogs delight to, and bite, 302b
  fancy runs her, ashore, 494b
  fatal and perfidious, 249a
  if my, sinks, 590b
  is on the sea, 456b
  is worse than his bite, 235a
  let no dog, 143a
  little, attendant sail, 318a
  moor your, 43b
  star to every wandering, 207
  trouble concerns not our, 51a
  watch-dog's honest, 457b
Barked at the Ox, 10b
Barkis is willin', 579a
Barks, Nicean, of yore, 543b

Battle, through the, through defeat, 609a
  to the strong, 757a, 1043a
  victory of, standeth not, 1066b
  was on once more, 625b
  went forth to, 937a
  who prepare himself for, 1061b
Battle-blood, all with the, gory, 637b
Battle-cry, freedom their, 626a
  of freedom, 613a
Battled for the true the just, 552b
Battlefield and patriot grave, 539b
  is holy ground, 459a
  of Italy, 964a
  we are met on a great, 540b
Battlefields which have their heroes, 497b
Battle-line, far-flung, 816a
Battlements, entrance under my, 195a
  frowning, 538a
  hid, of eternity, 790a
  towers and, 245a
Battle's lost and won, 194a
  sound, no war or, 244b
  van, 588a
  wreck, flame that lit the, 470a
Battles, fight our country's, 1004b
  fought all his, o'er again, 280a
  fought his, 274b
  in the midst of, 622a
  long ago, 407b
  morrow of his, 558b
  not a bit anxious about my, 940a
  rains fall after great, 55a
  sieges fortunes I have passed, 186a
  transacted by mechanism, 474b
  win our, by its aid, 584a
Batt'ning our flocks, 248b
Bauble, pleased with this, 317b
  shallow, boats, 181a
Baucis' busy care, 280b
Baudelaire and to Obermann, 751b
Baulking the end half-won, 815a
Bawd a bawd, call a, 28b
Bawl, Daddy heered him, 745a
Bawls for a physician, 747a
Bay, bowers are bare of, 786b
  come to self-same, 83b
  cyclone in the, 801b
  deep-mouth'd welcome, 457b
  green, tree, 1034a
  of Biscay O, 395b
  of Portugal, bottom like, 162b
  somebody bet on de, 636a
  the moon, 168b
Bay'd the whispering wind, 355b
Bayonet's contrition, 648b
Bayonets, by push of, 353a
Bays burn deep and chafe, 693a
  ling'ring, 335b
  to crown it, 233b
Be, better to, than not to be, 711a
  faithful unto death, 1064b
  no more, bear to, 413a
  not afraid ye waiting hearts, 633a
  not the first, 311a
  of good cheer, 1053a, 1058b
  of good courage, 1047a
  off or I'll kick you down-stairs, 656b
  or not to be, 174a
  poem should not mean but, 960b

Be strong, 1027a
  to, not to seem, 99b
  to, what we are, 749b
  upright, 66b
  were it not better not to, 546b
Beach, across the narrow, we flit, 674a
  briny, 658b
  fishermen that walk upon, 193a
  never shall break on the, 667a
  not the only pebble on the, 808a
  ocean on a western, 725b
  rolling, 637b
  rugged and without a, 287a
  shell from the strown, 529a
  stroll upon the, 588b
  walk upon the, 943a
Beaches, fight on the, 869a
Beacon of the wise, 181b
Beacons of hope ye appear, 623a
  of wise men, 633b
Bead on string of confusions, 878a
Beade of amber, flie within a, 52a
Beaded bubbles winking at the brim, 481b
Beadle to a humorous sigh, 133a
Beadroll, fames eternall, 113b
Beads and prayer-books, 317b
  few, are best, 231a
  heroes of finance are like, 641a
  pictures rosaries and pixes, 239b
  tell their, in drops of rain, 521a
  walked forth to tell his, 1011b
Beagle bit a kleagle, 864b
Beak, take in his, 904a
  take thy, from out my heart, 545a
  upon my face, 703a
Beaker full of the warm south, 481a
Be-all and the end-all here, 195b
Beam, full midday, 250b
  in thine own eye, 1051b
Beamish boy, 657b
Beams bemocked the sultry main, 422a
  candle throws its, 147a
  display, let my sun his, 39b
  from happy human eyes, 751b
  full-dazzling, 609b
  glide faster than sun's, 136a
  learn to bear, of love, 385a
  of wit on other souls, 277b
  orient, 256a
  scattered with all its, 443a
  sunny, did glide, 384b
  tricks his, 249b
  white moon, 952a
Bean, home of the, and the cod, 793a
  takes hair right off your, 975b
Bean-fed horse, 141a
Bean-rows, nine, will I have there, 824b
Beans, abstain from, 58a
  and brown bread, 760a
  better, and bacon in peace, 9b
  determined to know, 590b
  eat no, 221b
  full o', and benevolence, 510a
  no, in the almost perfect state, 894a
  on Saturday night, 805a
Bear a grudge, 29a
  a little more than I can, 934b
  a mother's tears, 37b
  a weight of woes, 6b

Bear all cheerfully, 557b
  another's misfortunes, 321a
  away the belle, 640b
  books, him up awhile, 289a
  burdens a man can, 113a
  bush supposed a, 142b
  cannot, levelling up, 340a
  courage up, 279b
  false witness, 1025a
  faults of man, 220b
  feel deep, fruit well, 620b
  fitted by nature to, 67b
  for which we, to live, 317b
  fruit then ripen, 64a
  gave pain to the, 494a
  his mild yoke, 251b
  his own burden, 1062b
  if I were a, 918a
  many, false witness, 1056a
  of all hard things to, and grin, 630b
  of very little brain, 918a
  patiently the results, 48b
  rugged Russian, 198a
  sing savageness out of a, 189b
  that walks like a man, 816a
  the bonds that gall, 693a
  the brunt, 572b
  the burden and the heat, 620a
  the latter, 331a
  the responsibility, 540b
  them breed and nurse, 380b
  them we can, 786b
  this yoke of must, 615b
  those ills we have, 174b
  to be no more, 413a
  up against them, 366b
  up and steer, 251b
  up beneath their unsuccess, 570a
  vapour sometime like a, 201a
  welcome in your eye, 195a
  we've fought the, before, 635a
  when you are an anvil, 234a
  which doth, him best, 124b
  whips and scorns of time, 174a
  wide and kick their owners, 380b
  with a good courage, 1065a
  with patience the injustice, 270a
  world doth but two nations, 269a
  yoke for others, 37b
Bear-baiting esteemed heathenish, 494a
  Puritan hated, 494a
Beard, built their nests in my, 580b
  Dutchman's, 165a
  grey, and glittering eye, 421a
  he that hath a, is more than a youth, 157a
  of formal cut, 161b
  old man with a, 580b
  on his face, 157a
  put aside my, 86b
  to shave man's, 105a
  the lion in his den, 414b
  tradition wears a snowy, 527b
  was grizzled, 171a
  white, 152b
  wrapped in his, and silence, 979b
Bearded grain, reaps the, 521a
  like the pard, 161a
  lips, sailors with, 523b
Beardless youth manages his taxed horse, 418a

Beards, until your, be grown, 1028a
  wag all, 96b
Beare, burdens a man can, 113a
Bearer's hands otherwise employed, 776a
Bearers from ordinary life, 946a
Bearest, live that thou, the strain, 840b
Beareth all things, 1061a
  name of Vanity Fair, 274a
Bearing boughs may live, 140a
  precious seed, 1037b
  with heroic resignation, 788b
Bearings glint, 982a
  near and remote, 628b
  of this observation, 578b
Bears a lovely face, 214b
  all its sons away, 303a
  and lions growl and fight, 302b
  better temper, 124a
  brave men, 28a
  bulls and the, 955b
  dancing dogs and, 854a
  greatest names, 260b
  his blushing honours, 211a
  his unforeseen disgrace, 303a
  in itself the causes, 344a
  instant proof, 936a
  lick their cubs, 99a
  name of life, 184b
  plagues a lover, 293a
  so patiently he, 430b
  thee dead, 152a
  when first born, 50a
Beast and the monk, 901b
  bring to a perfect, 50b
  chase had a, in view, 280b
  deem himself a God or, 316b
  every, of the forest, 1034b
  fit night for man or, 901a
  knows beast, 223b
  leave so much as a, 1070b
  life of his, 1039a
  little better than, 143b
  man and bird and, 422b
  man is but a, 1013b
  maw-crammed, 572a
  mongrel, 935a
  no, more savage, 57a
  owest the, no hide, 192a
  that wants discourse of reason, 170b
  very gentle, 142b
  watch the captured, 737b
  what rough, 826b
  when people call this, to mind, 848a
  wild, guards my way, 387b
Beastie, sleekit cowrin tim'rous, 390a
Beasties, long-leggety, 1003a
Beast's, life is cheap as, 191b
Beasts, ape the vilest of, 30b
  deserts full of wild, 53a
  fled to brutish, 168a
  insanity or ferocity in, 505b
  nature teaches, 202a
  of the field, 538a
  pair of very strange, 163a
  teaches, to know friends, 202a
  that have life and sense, 98b
  that perish, 1034b
  transform ourselves into, 188a
Beasts', not God's and not the, 572b
Beat, accurate rhythmic, 937b
  all your feathers, 214a
  an empty barrel, 903a

Beat, and I, on, 706b
  away blushes, 158b
  back the current, 699a
  double, of thundering drum, 278b
  forever the fens, 935a
  him when he sneezes, 656b
  his breast, 421a
  lark whose notes do, 137a
  me and hammer me, 899a
  one Englishman, three Frenchmen, 301a
  swords into ploughshares, 1044a
  the bush, 229a
  the drums, 291a
  the vaulty heaven, 137a
  two hearts that, as one, 5a
  upon my whorlèd ear, 724b
  voice above their, 790a
  waves of science, in vain, 614a
  with fist instead of stick, 238a
  worries me to, the band, 914a
  you, your pate, 315b
Beate the bush, 91a
Beaten gold my throne, 862b
  gold, poop was, 200b
  path, genius disdains a, 537a
  path to his door, 504b
  till they know what wood, 238b
  were they as the sand, 523b
  with his owne rod, 90b
Beatific, enjoy'd in vision, 253a
Beating canvas of a heavy foresail, 772a
  God does that, 604b
  hammer, 915b
  of his wings, 561b
  of my own heart, 543a
  of the pulse, 862a
  of the storm-waves, 808a
  up for recruits, 238a
Beats all the lies you can invent, 388a
  back envious siege, 139a
  golden bullet, it down, 212b
  heroic bosom, no more, 458a
  same heart, 620b
  the luckless collier, 332b
  upon high shore, 156a
Beau, Eb she called her, 852b
Beaumont, bid, lie little further, 219a
Beauteous bright creation, 74a
  death, dear, 272a
  evening calm and free, 407a
  eye of heaven, 148a
  files, commands the, 271b
  flower, may prove a, 135b
  idiot speaks, 1000b
  ladies' eyes, 116b
  not their, looks, 130b
Beauties, admire thy naked, 460b
  concealed, of a writer, 300b
  glory of honours, 216a
  hid from common sight, 630a
  in small proportions, 219b
  meaner, of the night, 213a
  modestly conceals her, 343b
  of holiness, 1037a
  pale unripened, 299b
  Quarles is sav'd by, 321b
  we have not seized again, 978b
Beautifier, no, of complexion, 505b
  rank is a great, 510a
Beautiful, all that's, drifts away, 825b
  all things bright and, 591b
  and free, 465b

Beautiful and ineffectual angel, 623b
  answer, 968b
  as roses, 502b
  as words, 866a
  be, and be sad, 619a
  being made, overmuch, 826b
  display of the grand and, 484a
  dreamer wake unto me, 636b
  Evelyn Hope is dead, 568a
  face a candid brow, 772b
  for situation, 1034b
  for spacious skies, 781a
  full, a faery's child, 480a
  in middle age, 958b
  incentive as a pang, 719a
  indisputably, 323b
  is love, 897a
  lady, here lies a most, 862b
  lovers of the, 20a
  made this world so, 810a
  manners, old men with, 933a
  mode of saying things, 621b
  more, than death, 607b
  old rime, 206b
  our sense of what is, 775b
  pea-green boat, 580b
  perfect whole, 655b
  quarto page, 381b
  question, 968b
  sacrifices, in her eyes, 851b
  scorn looks, 165a
  seems right, 519b
  sentiments weigh less, 603a
  singing Oh how, 821a
  smiling and, countryside, 782a
  snow, O the snow the, 632a
  so disappears the most, 379a
  soup, 657b
  stripped and swift, 980a
  taste for the, 471b
  the palace, 274a
  therefore to be wooed, 124b
  things are most useless, 605b
  things, walk about amidst, 807b
  to see, 760b
  to the best the most, 619a
  too, to live, 576b
  two most, words, 804b
  upon the mountains, 1047b
  venerable, or useful, 496a
  what may be approved as, 775b
  whatever is in any way, 67a
  wisdom, no joy in, 9a
  woman cooking dinner, 987b
  women of antiquity, 701b
  young and, being, 802b
Beautify, adorn and, our souls, 702b
Beauty a sufficient end, 826b
  a witty, is a power, 639b
  about a home life, 641a
  all is order and, 618b
  all that, gave, 348a
  always room for, 746b
  and decay, 467b
  and her chivalry, 452b
  and high degree, 946b
  and invulnerability, 852b
  and length of days, 691b
  and mystery of the ships, 523b
  and the stars were one, 854b
  and truth tho' never found, 708b
  and wisdom rarely conjoined, 51b
  as much, as could die, 218b
  as much, as they sing, 680b
  attractive, 105b

Beggars, deformity which, mimicked, 492a
do away with, 726b
might ride, 999b
mounted, 126a
must be no choosers, 228a
should be no choosers, 92b
when, die no comets seen, 167b
Beggary in the love reckon'd, 200a
Begged, living Homer, his bread, 227a
of the moon, 1003a
Begging bread, 1034a
them to taste brandy, 437b
Begin and cease and then begin, 622a
come back to it and, over, 879b
finish what I, 528a
get up and, again, 569a
in gladness, 406b
to smell a rat, 106b
with usual jokes, 22b
Beginning, from a bad, great friendships, 32a
and the end, 987a, 1065a
art of, 526a
at the, not the end, 986b
ay that's the old, 65b
bad, makes a bad ending, 17b
better the end than, 1042b
each venture is a new, 945a
end depends upon the, 62b
end of the, 871a
farther distance from the, 118b
for a friendship, 768a
grey, of years, 694b
half done who has made a, 41a
hard, maketh good ending, 91b
in my, is my end, 945a
in my end is my, 101b, 945a
in the, God created the heaven, 1021a
in the, was the word, 1057b
is most important part, 24a
long choosing and, late, 258a
love is the, of knowledge, 473a
never ending still, 280a
no great love in the, 180a
of a beginning, 831b
of a fray, 94b
of a new month or year, 882b
of fairies, 792a
of feast, 151b
of good, cometh good end, 92b
of journey, 21a
of life, 788a
of our end, 142b
of the cask, 7b
of the end, 384a
of things longer, 788b
of wisdom, 985b, 1037a
responsibility of, 642b
things best in their, 272a
told you from the, 1047a
Beginnings and endings are untidy, 838a
end to, of all wars, 922a
favorable to bold, 36b
return to our, 16a
small, 229b
Begins, charity, at home, 240b
life is closed life, 610b
life's year, and closes, 440a
nothing, and nothing ends, 789b
to be incredulous, 20a
with an M, 657a
Begone dull care, 1000a
Begot, how, how nourished, 145a

Begot in ventricle of memory, 133a
to whom related by whom, 313b
when they, me, 345b
Begotten by despair, 269a
flowers, 691b
of his Father, 1068a
Son, gave his only, 1058a
Begs pardon first, 162a
Beguil'd, be, by one, 189a
Beguile, light of light, 132a
strumpet's plague to, 189a
the thing I am, 187a
the time look like the time, 195a
you from grief, 541b
Beguiled the leisure of the crew, 681b
Beguiles, the pain of it, 345b
Beguiling, fortune, 343b
Begun for, wonder what I was, 1014a
not yet, to fight, 377b
things ended and things, 610b
Behave, how well I did, 785b
in a quarrel, 764b
in life as at a banquet, 65a
like a pig, 963a
like apes, 939a
mannerly at table, 750a
wish friends to, to us, 71b
Behaving as if you were in heaven, 766a
Behavior, complexion or form or, 505b
immediate check to loose, 301b
standard of, 849b
surfeit of our own, 191a
upon his good, 459a
which appears correct, 965a
Behemoth, behold now, 1032a
Behind, come no more, your scenes, 339a
falls down for those, 924a
get up, him, 345b
led his regiment from, 685b
never gets left, 807a
no longer forward nor, 527b
one must ride, 158a
the times, 830a
Behold a rainbow, 406a
a smile of God, 612a
and hear griefs, 15a
be what they, 312b
heaven and the earth, 83a
her judge for yourselves, 443b
I shall, your face, 660a
it very different from day, 351a
the man, 1058b
thy master, 326a
wandering moon, 246a
you again in dying, 752a
Beholder, heart of the, 984a
Beholders discover everybody's face, 294b
strike an awe into the, 295b
Beholding bright countenance, 250a
myself all rosy red, 842b
Behoving and unbehoving, 519a
Behynde, shame cometh, 15a
Be'ind, less than 'arf o' that, 818a
Being, applause of a single human, 342a
coming into, of composite things, 12a

Being darkly wise and rudely great, 316b
each young and beautiful, 802b
gives, to all things, 229b
is holiness harmony immortality, 616b
live move and have our, 1059a, 1069b
necessary, of Himself, 275a
one principle of, 68a
Penrod was merely a state of, 847a
pleasing anxious, 349a
this, of mine, 66a
Being's end and aim, 317b
Beings now latent in our thoughts, 831b
reasoning, were created, 66a
Belabored hound, cower like a, 583b
Beld, now your brow is, 392a
Beldame nigh to sit for us, 29b
Belfry, bats in the, 804a
clock in the, strikes one, 660b
Belgium's capital, 452b
Belgrave Square, hearts beat in, 683b
Belial, sons of, 252b
with words clothed, 254a
Belican, more than his, 904a
Belie all corners of world, 204a
Belief, believe in, 790b
England restores our, 956a
epoch of, 580a
history is, in falsehood, 622a
history is, in the senses, 622a
hope is, joy will come, 418b
in a beneficent power, 705a
in occurrence of improbable, 909a
in supernatural source of evil, 773a
live and die in this, 84a
my most ethereal, 804b
points of, 438b
prospect of, 194b
ripened into faith, 411a
Beliefs, lightly held, and prejudices, 831b
lost causes and forsaken, 621b
old dead ideas and old dead, 641b
swallow more, than he can digest, 784a
tremulous, agonized hopes, 838b
Believe a woman or an epitaph, 452a
all the fables in legends, 120b
any man than an artificer, 244a
easier to, than to deny, 688b
heard and do in part, 170a
her though I know she lies, 207b
I, in God, 400a
impossible things, 659a
in fairies, 792a
in God the Father, 1068a
in happiness, 889b
in heaven and hell, 774b
in love, 790b
in nothing, 594b
in one God and no more, 371a
in what I can't see, 703a
it or not, 967a
know what he ought to, 75a
make themselves, 98b
man makes us, oath, 13b
man's oath, 35b

Benefit written in water, 86b
Benefits, desire to receive greater, 265b
　disable, 162b
　in refusing, 282b
　liberty of the press ensures, 516a
　of a college education, 505a
　of scientific advances, 929b
　responsibilities and, 965b
　temperate diet will bring, 40b
Benevolence, calls trusting universal, 355a
　full o' beans and, 510a
Bengal, in, to move at all is seldom done, 982a
Benicia Boy, 573a
Benighted, pore, 'eathen, 818a
Benign is solitude, 404b
　nature so mild and, 306b
　sky, under that, 592a
Benignant information is his hobby, 854a
Benison fall on our meat, 231a
　of hot water, 938b
Bennet, Justice, of Derby, 273b
　Mrs., was stirring the fire, 428a
Bent, affection cannot hold the, 164b
　bow cannot always stand, 106b
　classic, 817a
　eyes idly, 140b
　find out the natural, 25a
　his bow, 3a
　just as the twig is, 314a
　mind is, to ill thy, 6b
　on doing evil, 44b
　on pleasure she was, 363b
　orthodox on carnage, 287a
　to make some port, 620b
　top of my, 176b
Benumbs all his faculties, 339a
　care's a canker that, 685b
Be'old this world so wide, 819a
Be-puffed be-painted too alas, 805a
Bequeath my soul to God, 121b
Bequeathed name of Washington, 455b
Bequest of wings was but a book, 646a
Bereavement, anguish of your, 541b
　pain, famine thirst, 654b
　speak comfort for great, 495a
Bereft of beauty, 130b
Berkeley, Bishop, 459b
Berkshire boulders, 960b
Bermoothes, still-vexed, 209a
Bermudas, remote, ride, 269a
Berries, harsh and crude, 248b
　two lovely, moulded, 142a
Berry, bright as a, 858b
　bush, poem hangs on the, 704b
　God could have made a better, 236a
Berry's cheek is plumper, 647b
Berth was of the wombe, 113a
Bertie displayed repugnance, 910a
Berye, broun as is a, 79b
Beseech you of your pardon, 188b
Beset, avoid perils which, them, 282b
Besotted myriads of people, 222b
Bespangling herb and tree, 231a
Bess, bold mare, 576b
　good Queen, 798a
　image of good Queen, 488b
　the landlord's daughter, 909b

Best, acts the, 586a
　administer'd is best, 317b
　advice, worst men give the, 586b
　age, in four things, 119a
　all is, 260b
　all was for, 571b
　all's for the, 561b
　almoner keeps back nothing, 73a
　and brightest come away, 469a
　and brightest leave us, 817b
　and happiest moments, 469a
　and the worst of this is, 694b
　at the greatest and the, 275a
　bear his mild yoke, 251b
　book we've had, 983a
　books haven't been written, 915b
　business you can go into, 562a
　butter, 656b
　cannot go quite true, 338b
　chosen language, 428b
　company when you read, 419a
　could would did, 118a
　days, afternoon of her, 128a
　dearest and the, 789a
　did it for the, 789b
　disguise, go naked is, 297b
　do the very, I know how, 542b
　doctors in the world, 296b
　dress, fair undress, 328a
　dressed in Sunday's, 427a
　fear not to touch the, 111a
　fools be a little wise, 215b
　foot forward, 148b
　forced to do your, 598b
　found her first and, 817a
　friends ever known, 791a
　garment, wears as his, 924b
　gave the people of his, 549b
　give to world the, you have, 723a
　gives his, 336a
　God knows, 841b
　good man with worst-natured muse, 289a
　have seen the, 806b
　he that comes last is, 221b
　his at last who says it, 508b
　hope for the, 418b
　I loved you, 289b
　ideas are common property, 47a
　in four things, 119a
　in kind, 523a
　in this kind but shadows, 142b
　is enemy of good, 325b
　is like the worst, 818b
　is never to be born, 486b
　is yet to be, 572a
　kind of victory, 109b
　lack all conviction, 826b
　laid schemes, 390a
　liar, 671a
　loveliest and the, 532a
　loves, that calls me Tom, 227a
　made the, of this, 394b
　make the, of mankind, 366b
　man among them, 1017a
　marry th', man on earth, 841a
　men, men of few words are, 155a
　men moulded out of faults, 185b
　moderation is, 53b
　never to have been born is, 16a
　not to seem but to be the, 13a
　nurse contemplation, 247b
　of all God's works, 258b

Best of all instructors, 44b
　of all possible worlds, 900a
　of all ways, 439a
　of dark and bright, 456a
　of friends must part, 1004b
　of me is diligence, 191a
　of men that e'er wore earth, 215a
　of now and here, 527b
　of our time, 190b
　of possible worlds, 324b
　of the cards at the table, 099a
　of things cloy, 5a
　of times, 580a
　old fashions please me, 130a
　old friends are, 119a
　opinion of the strongest is, 269b
　part of a picture, 507a
　part of valour, 152a
　past and to come seem, 153a
　policy, honesty is always, 108b
　political community, 26b
　portion of a good man's life, 403b
　possession, man's, 17b
　prayeth, who loveth best, 422b
　propagate the, that is known, 621b
　race hasn't been run, 915b
　schoolteachers in the world, 935b
　service for our country, 709b
　she can choose, 60b
　so much bad in the, of us, 711b
　sometimes forget, 187b
　stand and do the, 69a, 786b
　stolen sweets are, 298b
　stomachs not best thinkers, 325b
　subject they treat, 723b
　that has been known and said, 623b
　that is in one, 727a
　the kingdom provides, 839a
　thing between France and England, 509b
　thing, my speech the, 285b
　thing we can do, 994a
　things, in their beginning, 272a
　things upon earth, 653b
　those who love us, 754a
　though the, is bad, 786b
　to forget, 575a
　to live with, 757b
　to the, most beautiful, 619a
　trust that all is, 583a
　use of laws, 562b
　way of doing everything, 505a
　way out is through, 879b
　way to make friends, 990a
　we will do our, 870b
　what began, can't end worst, 573a
　what friend is, 96b
　when he is, 143b
　when people barely know him, 912b
　will come back to you, 723a
　wits greatest scholars, 223a
　women miss the, in life, 771b
　words in best order, 424a
　would heaven seem, 570a
　you get is an even break, 911b
　yuh ever poured, 978b
Best-humour'd man, 289a
Bestial, what remains is, 187b

Better to sink beneath the shock, 455b
to wear out, 283b
to weep at joy, 157a
use medicines at the outset, 46b
were it not, not to be, 546b
wisdom is, than rubies, 1038b
world for others, 763a
world than this, 159b
worse appear, reason, 253b
worst is, than none, 338b
you will not be, 672b
you'll be, soon, 536b
Bettered by the borrower, 251a
expectation, 156b
Bettering of my mind, 209a
Betters what is done, 208a
Between jest and earnest, 105b
the acting of a dreadful thing, 167a
the cradle and the grave, 327b
the cup and the lip, 223a
two hawks, 124a
two stools, 88a
Beulah peel me a grape, 968a
Bevy of fair women, 259a
Bewail the dead, 8a
Beware, all should cry beware, 420b
fury of a patient man, 277b
lest Heaven hate, 11a
lest you lose the substance, 9b
let the buyer, 1009b
my country, 816a
of entrance to a quarrel, 171b
of false prophets, 1052a
of judging people, 269b
of rashness, 540b
of the dog, 51a
of these stately gentlemen, 953b
opposed may, of thee, 171b
the ides of March, 166a
the Jabberwock my son, 657b
the Jubjub bird, 657b
the middle mind, 935a
Beweep my outcast state, 205a
Bewilder'd in the maze of schools, 310a
Bewildered as to which may be true, 514a
epoch, comfort that, 822b
Bewildering changes, 630a
Bewitch, prosperity doth, men, 225b
when art is too precise, 230b
Bewrayed, so well, as by manners, 114a
Bewrays more woe than words, 111a
style, us, 221b
Bias, assays of, 173a
strongest, rules, 310b
used to say, 70a
Biassed with compassion, 262a
Bible and a drum, 809a
command against stealing in, 675a
early familiarity with the, 783a
English, 492a
is for the government of the people, 1021a
is literature not dogma, 807a
nothin' truer in the, 735a
of the race is writ, 601b
read my, more, 708b
read the, day and night, 388b
studie litel on the, 79b

Bible, text of the, 782b
with my, by myself, 273a
Bibles, Gideon, 957b
laid open, 233a
Bibliophiles, Brooklyn for, 999a
Bibs, hold our, before our eyes, 861b
Bicam me weel, 81b
Bickering brattle, 390a
Bickerings to recount, 260b
Bicycle built for two, 828a
mechanics, 974a
Bid adieu, drop a tear and, 329a
all ill go by, 29b
come between and, us part, 328b
defiance to all force, 335a
for each poor blotted note, 767b
her go, 999b
me discourse, 131a
me good morning, 372b
me good-night and be kissed, 714b
me love, 230a
me to live, 230a
time return, 139b
world pass, 151a
you wake and rise to fight, 830b
Bidding, at his, speed, 251b
Master I've done thy, 877a
Bide by the buff and the blue, 394b
Bids remembrance rise, 353b
shepherd fold, 247a
Bier, murdered Lincoln's, 588b
Big battalions, God always for, 325b
book is a big nuisance, 29b
Bow-Wow strain, 428b
business, 779b
butter-and-egg man, 927b
city like a mother's knee, 801a
divide, great scramble and, 707b
game hunting, 950a
Jack Stout, 1016a
just as, for me, 798b
manly voice, 161b
round tear, 6a
round tears, 159b
shoulders, city of the, 898a
stealin' makes you emperor, 946b
stick, carry a, 779a
too, to cry, 540a
wars that make ambition virtue, 189a
window opening, 915a
with vengeance, 332b
Big-endians and small-endians, 295b
Bigger, no, than an agate-stone, 134a
not a, tent but command, 709b
seems no, than his head, 193a
than an elephant, 61a
than anything that can happen to me, 788b
than the belly, 235a
they come, 19b
Biggest dog has been a pup, 712a
fish I caught that got away, 746b
problem in the world, 912b
rascal on two legs, 65a
Bigile, waiteth to, 81a
Bigness as a star, 254b
which you see, 274a
Bigotry, honourable, 406a

Big-Sea-Water, 523a
Bile, sentences that stir my, 789b
B'iling water hit, whar de, 738b
Bill, as if God wrote the, 506b
as is young and tender, 564b
drawn on nature's reality, 474b
fellers call me, 747b
hold more than belican, 904a
larger, for a darker ill, 591a
of a mosquito, 801b
of Rights, landmarks in the, 976a
paid his, 996a
patience for his, 329b
tax relief, 921b
you were, and I was Joe, 535a
Billboard lovely as a tree, 989b
Billboards, unless the, fall, 989b
Billee, youngest he was little, 564b
Billet, bullet has its, 418a
Billiard, elliptical, balls, 685a
Billions of years, 945b
Billow of harmony, 809b
Billows, mitigate the, 46a
seas where, have rolled, 584b
smooth and bright, 658a
swelling and limitless, 422b
that never shall break, 667a
trusted to thy, 455a
where, never break, 292a
Billowy clouds of June, 890b
Bills, her, make known, 231b
Billy Bowling, 377a
heart to poke poor, 873b
in one of his nice new sashes, 873b
Billy-boil, waited for his, 809b
Billy-bong, camped by a, 809b
Bin of wine, 751a
sparkling from the, 74b
Bind another to its delight, 387a
fast, fast find, 91a
him to his native mountains, 354a
in body and in soul can, 413b
on thy sandals, 691a
safe, safe find, 96b
sweet influences of Pleiades, 1032a
the pow'r of pain, 617a
them heart and brow, 729b
up my wounds, 128b
up the nation's wounds, 542a
Binding, Hannah's at the window, shoes, 630b
nature fast in fate, 321a
steadfast in the broken, 962b
Binds its body in chains, 708b
mandamus, all alike, 381b
to himself a joy, 386b
together by passion, 406a
Binnorie O Binnorie, 1012b
Biographer, comes the, 725b
first thing to be done by a, 643b
Biographers, Boswell first of, 338b
Biographical sharpshooter, 661a
Biographies are but clothes of the man, 680a
essence of innumerable, 475b
geniuses have the shortest, 504a
Biography, America's history and, 611a
diminishes in interest, 597a
events which constitute a, 514b
good portrait is a kind of, 651a
heroic poem a, 474b
iv a hero, 834b
kept so far posted up, 585b
like big game hunting, 950a

Books obedient to my hand, 794b
 of all time, 605b
 of dried plants, 558a
 of honour razed quite, 205a
 of making, there is no end, 794b,
  912a, 1044a
 of the hour, 605b
 of universal appeal, 863b
 of which the backs and covers,
  576b
 old, are best, 780b
 old, old wine, old friends, 119a
 peace of great, 898b
 people die but, never, 921b
 popular American children's,
  804a
 put their names to their, 222b
 quit your, 403b
 read what, I please, 319a
 reading great, 942b
 reading my, in originals, 506a
 reading valueless, 605b
 real war never in the, 611a
 rural quiet friendship, 328a
 schoolboys from their, 135b
 show me the, he loves, 643b
 shut his, 800a
 shut out from reading good,
  933a
 small number of really good,
  782a
 some, are drenchèd sands, 650a
 some, are lies, 391b
 soul of past time in, 475b
 soul that feeds on, alone, 711b
 sweet serenity of, 525a
 tenets with, 314a
 that people give us, 847b
 that people talk about, 847b
 that we would like to read, 847b
 there are no, inside, 761a
 think for me, 430b
 three, on the soul, 571b
 thy toil o'er, 308a
 too many, I haven't read, 996b
 trees my, 161b
 university a collection of, 475b
 we think we ought to read, 847b
 were woman's looks, 439b
 which are no books, 430b
 which cannot be adequately reviewed, 700b
 which contain no lies, 723a
 with obsolete spelling, 776a
 you carry to the fire, 338b
Bookseller's, good price from the,
  358a
Book-store, so weak as in the,
  582b
Boon companions, offers made by,
  576a
 southern country, 622b
Boone the pioneer, 625b
Boot, appliances and means to,
  153b
 heels, bleatin' to your, 821a
 hey for, and horse, 598b
 saddle to horse, 567b
Booted and spurred to ride, 271a
Booth died blind, 902b
Bootless cries, 205a
Boots and shoes, 596a
 body, and britches, 959a
 boots boots boots, 819a
 died in my, 978b
 dying in my, 896b
 hauled on his, 587a
 long, hard boots, 899a
 look at his, 766a

Boots not to resist both wind and
  tide, 126b
 what, it with incessant care,
  248b
Booze, Georgia, is mighty fine,
  978b
Bo-Peep, little, 1018a
 played at, 231a
Borden, Lizzie, took an axe, 1006a
Border, blue bonnets over the,
  650b
 nor breed nor birth, 814a
 of Prussia, 485b
 through all the wide, 414b
Borders, death, upon our birth,
  220b
 no, time has, 949a
 of my realm, 97a
 on the ridiculous, 371a
Bore, all you pitied all you, 750a
 cleanliness a, 637a
 dead bodies, 149b
 every hero becomes a, 504a
 first lion thought last a, 420a
 life too short to, ourselves, 727a
 more contemptible than the,
  670a
 not only as sin but as a, 459a
 person who talks, 714a
 secret of being a, 326a
 their children, 766a
 to be in society, 769a
 to the man with the flute, 736a
 waking up the same person,
  822a
 we dread being alone with, 603b
 without abuse, 553a
Bored, man who lets himself be,
  670a
 mankind by thee would be less,
  798a
 talk to every man as if he, you,
  769a
 very much, if not there, 952b
Boredom did indeed cease, 728b
 disease brought on by, 991a
 gods struggle against, 394b
 inconstancy, anxiety, 272b
 pain and, 461b
Bores and bored, 459b
 augurs because they were, 600a
 through his castle wall, 139b
 you and then injects, 801b
Boring to live with, 931a
Born, all men are, free and equal,
  373a
 among gypsies or thieves, 959b
 an American, 445a
 anew, great order is, 36a
 as wasteful as tigers, 953b
 be, anywhere, 959a
 beauty, of murmuring sound,
  405b
 because of body's hunger, 930a
 before eyes, 939b
 begin to die as soon as, 62b
 below par, 839b
 better had they ne'er been, 417a
 better to be lowly, 210b
 blackest midnight, 245a
 bless'd who ne'er was, 294a
 but to die, 316b
 Christ the Lord is, 334b
 conceived and, in sin, 223a
 cross cause why we were, 133b
 cry for being, 122a
 day wherein I was, 1030a
 days, in my, 103b
 else wherefore, 554b

Born every minute, sucker, 557b
 every one, of the Spirit, 1058a
 for success, 506a
 for the universe, 357b
 friends are, not made, 696a
 genius must be, 280a
 glad I was not, before tea, 419b
 good if he had not been, 1054b
 good to be, on, 603a
 great, some are, 165a
 happiness was, a twin, 457b
 hour I was, 1003b
 house where I was, 487b
 I was being human, alone, 934b
 I was free, 1059b
 I was, get me, 946b
 I was, sneering, 684b
 immortal names not, to die,
  462b
 in a manger, 271b
 in bed, 263a
 in Bethlehem, 334b
 in Bethlehem of Judaea, 1050a
 in other's pain, 789b
 in silent darkness, 122a
 jealousy, with love, 266a
 king of the Jews, 1050a
 knew that before you were, 49a
 like eagles, to be free, 953b
 likenesses in brethren, 16b
 makes his own bed ere, 263b
 man is, free, 344a
 man is, unto trouble, 1030a
 Miniver Cheevy, too late, 846b
 naked, 49b
 never to be, at all, 486b
 never to have been, is best, 16a
 new, infant's tear, 387b
 no great man is, too soon, 840a
 no man is, an angler, 235b
 no man is, an artist, 235b
 nobly, is now a crime, 226b
 none of woman, shall harm,
  198b
 not, for death, 481b
 of a little sin, 963a
 of a woman, 1030b
 of the sun, 995a
 of the Virgin Mary, 1068a
 of thee, 798b
 of virgin mother, 244a
 on a Monday, 1018b
 one, out of due time, 1061b
 out of my due time, 666b
 over and over, 997a
 poet's made as well as, 219b
 powerless to be, 621b
 so many I love not yet, 990a
 some are, posthumously, 729a
 souls that were never, 986a
 sucker, every minute, 557b
 this I was, to do, 122a
 three distant ages, 279b
 thy light was, 617a
 time to be, 1042b
 to blush unseen, 348b
 to disastrous end, 114b
 to fly upward, 76b
 to freedom, 921a
 to inquire after truth, 100a
 to marshal his fellow-men, 663a
 to one possession, 679a
 to see it right, 173a
 to shame, 137a
 to sweet delight, 388a
 to the manner, 172a
 to the purple, 965b
 to wander, 953b
 to write converse, 318b

Cast, pale, of thought, 174b
  salt on a woman's tail, 239a
  set my life upon a, 128b
  thine eye on thine own fault, 635a
  thing we, to the ground, 639a
  this oil into the sea, 49a
  thy bread, 1043b
  why art thou, down, 1034b
  ye your pearls, 1051b
Castaway, go to his grave a, 821b
Caste, Brahmin, of New England, 536b
  of Vere de Vere, 547a
Castigation of offenders, 823b
Castilian, what best becomes a brave, 484b
Casting body's vest aside, 269a
  dim religious light, 246b
  his vote, 707a
  their golden crowns, 445b
Castle and fortress, 110b
  bores through, wall, 139b
  called Doubting Castle, 274b
  Garden, 906b
  gray, habitant of, 592a
  hath a pleasant seat, 195a
  in Spain, 587b
  man's house is his, 110b
  rich man in his, 591b
  strongest, tower and town, 212b
  walls and snowy summits, 550a
  whinstone house my, is, 476b
Castled crag of Drachenfels, 453a
Castle's strength will laugh, 199b
Castles in Spain, 999a
  in the clouds that pass, 328b
  went like lightnin', 967b
Casts sheep's eye at the wench, 107b
  single hair, shadow, 43b
Casual concourse of atoms, 292b
  good-bye, 968a
  tongues, restless hands and, 845b
Casuists, convocation of, 105a
Cat a dog and a pipe, 788a
  an indifferent mouser, 471b
  and a lie, 678a
  and the fiddle, 1016b
  bell the, 11a
  calico, replied mee-ow, 747b
  care killed a, 159a
  crooked, 1019a
  each, had seven kits, 1015b
  endow a college or a, 315a
  feet, fog comes on little, 898a
  had Tiberius been a, 623a
  harmless necessary, 145b
  has only nine lives, 678a
  he walked by himself, 820a
  I've got a little, 762a
  languishes loudly, 741a
  lion look no larger than the, 556b
  may looke on a King, 94a
  more ways of killing a, 598b
  nine lives like a, 28b, 93b
  on your hearthstone, 853b
  owest the, no perfume, 192a
  pensive, 853b
  play with my, 99a
  poor, i' the adage, 93a
  room to swing a, 579b
  that sits on hot stove-lid, 678b
  turning of the, 120b
  vanished quite slowly, 656b
  vice in a, 661a
  will mew, 179a

Cat, worried the, 1020b
  would eate fish, 93a
  would not wet feete, 93a
  would watch a mouse, 297a
Catalogue, dull, of common things, 480b
  in the, ye go for men, 197a
  no reading more delightful, 723a
  of human woes, 362a
  of things necessary, 286a
  unforgotten un-Homeric, 950b
  would sooner read a, 875b
Cataract, faint idea of a, 493b
  leaps in glory, 550a
  sounding, haunted me, 404a
Cataracts, silent, 423a
Catastrophe of the atomic bombs, 831b
  race between education and, 831b
  signal, or exaltation, 651a
  tickle, 153a
Catastrophes of race traceable, 605b
Catch a falling star, 215b
  an echo of the infinite, 709a
  and hold while I may, 91a
  another Antony, 202a
  arguments, proper time for, 540a
  as catch can, 350b
  cold and starve, 203b
  conscience of the king, 174a
  fit to, it, 341b
  hard to, and conquer, 639b
  him once upon the hip, 144a
  larks if heavens fall, 88b
  manners living as they rise, 315b
  nearest way, 195a
  nets to, the wind, 226a
  perdition, my soul, 188a
  physicians, diseases, 222b
  set a thief to, a thief, 58a
  small flies, 294b
  springes to, woodcocks, 172a
  the fragrant breeze, 961b
  up, you will never, 828b
  with his surcease success, 195b
Catch'd, swallow gudgeons ere, 11b
Catching, preserves one from, cold, 727b
Catch-words, lives by, 749b
Catechism ends, 151b
  engagement, 830a
Categorical, in order, 682b
Caterpillar, I don't see said the, 656a
Caterpillars of the commonwealth, 139a
Caters for the sparrow, 160a
Cathay, cycle of, 549a
  drink the poppies of, 528a
Cathedral, couldn't design a, 946b
  or a church, 805a
  so inspired as when it made a, 749a
  tunes, like weight of, 647b
Cathedrals luxury liners, 993b
Cather, in the spring the Willas, 977b
Catholic Church, 492b, 493a
  I was born a, 400a
  man who hath mightily won, 716a
Catholics, Negroes foreigners and, 537a
Cato asserted that wise men profited, 55a
  conquered's cause with, 51a
  give his little senate laws, 319a

Cato learned Greek at eighty, 525a
  on good acts, 119b
Cat's averse to fish, 347b
  eare, breed in the, 94a
  meat, mean as, 876a
Cats, all, be gray, 61a
  and monkeys, 718a
  do, eat bats, 656a
  each sack had seven, 1015b
  killed the, 570a
  rain, and dogs, 297a
  those who'll play with, 105a
Cattis eeris, 94a
Cattle beneath the British oak, 361a
  call the, home, 598a
  died as, 966a
  no hay for the, 59a
  shed, stood a lowly, 591b
  upon a thousand hills, 1034b
  women's rum, 737b
Catullus why not make haste to die, 35b
Caucasian mountaineers, 732b
Caucasus, thinking on frosty, 138b
Caucets, comfortablest, 989b
Caught, biggest fish I, 746b
  cold, well dressed woman never, 727b
  grievous to be, 40a
  his clear accents, 567b
  his death, 1014a
  my heav'nly jewel, 115b
  Scotchman, young, 341a
  sweete perfections, 114b
  trout, with tickling, 165a
Cauld, it waxeth, 1013a
Cauldron bubble, 198a
Cauliflower is nothing but cabbage, 678a
Cause, armor of a righteous, 793b
  avengers of religion's, 287a
  bad, will be supported, 370b
  Caledonia's, 394b
  comes to pass without, 329b
  died in virtue's, 129b
  every, produces more than one effect, 614b
  evolution not a, but a law, 700a
  fair face the, 123b
  for doubting one's own right, 951b
  found the spiritual, 616b
  hear me for my, 168a
  I'll try the whole, 656a
  idea of oneself as, 282a
  is in you, 76b
  it is just, 436a
  judge in his own, 45a
  kings can, or cure, 337b
  magnificent and awful, 364a
  may move dissension, 441b
  no, for despair, 38a
  no omen but his country's, 5a
  obstinacy in a bad, 240a
  of a long ten years' war, 289b
  of all men's misery, 112a
  of covetousness, 124a
  of disease quarrels, 290b
  of dullness in others, 343a
  of liberty, 366b
  of love, 784b
  of mankind, 438b
  of policy, 154a
  of this effect, 173b
  or the men of the Emerald Isle, 383b
  perseverance in a good, 345b

Child is father of the man, 406b
is little, 790b
Jesus Christ her little, 591b
keeps a secret so well as a, 497b
like a tired, 465a
little, I stand, 231a
look upon a little, 334a
Mary she came with her, 1003a
meet nurse for poetic, 414a
misses the unsaid good-night, 879b
Monday's, 1018b
naked new-born, 377b
never without an infant, 448b
of calamity, 676a
of grandmother Eve, 132b
of hope, 561a
of misery, 368a
of nature, a well-developed, 644a
of scorn, 846a
of the pure unclouded brow, 657b
old man is twice a, 174a
on a cloud I saw a, 385a
on the homeless street, 756a
painted, of dirt, 319a
ranked as a mere, 594a
Roland to the dark tower, 192a
saving a little, 699a
Shakespeare Fancy's, 245b
she was a, and I was a child, 546a
should always say what's true, 750a
should grow into the man, 525b
sick, in the basement, 760b
simplicity a, 278b
spare rod and spoil, 239a
spare th' rod an' spile th', 837a
spend their fury on a, 127a
spoil the, 84b
straying of a little, 800a
strike a, 765a
sung by any, of song, 732a
teach the, to doubt, 388a
tears of a, 853b
thankless, 191a
that's born on the Sabbath day, 1018b
thoughts of a, 660a
three years', 421a
trumpet of a, of Rome, 694b
unborn, 853a
unto us a, is born, 1045b
use of a new-born, 912b
what it is to be a, 790b
what will a, learn sooner, 320b
when I was a, 1061a
whom many fathers share, 308b
wise father knows own, 144b
with Mary his mother, 1050a
wretched, expires, 849a
you are like a flower, 486a
you'd say poor, 629b
Childes, no, pley, 81b
Childhood, days of, 428b
dwarfing of, 497a
eye of, fears, 196b
fleet, womanhood and, 522a
friends of our, 529a
make glad the heart of, 701b
manhood and decrepit age, 232a
noisy impertinence of, 603b
of the world, 743b
old age is second, 23a
scenes of my, 450a
second, 853a
shows the man, 259b

Childhood's cheek, tear down, 415b
hour, ever thus from, 441a
Childish ignorance, 488a
inconstant, proud, 477a
joy now lives in me, 913b
sweet, days, 406b
things, I put away, 1061a
toy, religion a, 123b
treble, 161b
Childishness, second, 161b
Childless and crownless, 454a
and bland, 686b
Children across the Atlantic, 566b
and fooles cannot lye, 93a
and fooles speake true, 93a
and fools want everything, 286a
are what the mothers are, 431b
as living arrows, 924a
become as little, 1053b
begin by loving parents, 768a
behold the chimpanzee, 805a
blood on us and on our, 1055a
breed of their, 288a
breeds contempt and, 680a
bright and agreeable, 64b
call her blessed, 1042a
called the, of God, 1050b
care of, 825a
come dear, let us away, 619b
comfort of thy, 128a
dear, wives and, 559a
devise to, yellow shores, 777a
drinkest tears of, 449a
fear to go in the dark, 119b
fits her, with something to do, 600b
follow'd with endearing wile, 356a
fonder of their, 27a
forget they have been, 631a
had so many, 1017a
he that hath wife and, 120a
hear the, weeping, 518b
heart of, to their fathers, 1050a
here my, have been born, 538b
holdeth, from play, 116a
human soul on the lips of, 498a
in sorrow thou shalt bring forth, 1022a
iniquity of fathers upon the, 1024b
inter parents, 16b
kind and natural, 154b
king over all, of pride, 1032a
know a lot about raising, 836b
laboring, 886b
laugh and play, 462b
learn to walk on frozen toes, 847a
learne to creepe, 93a
leave to, the dandelions, 776b
lips and hearts of little, 565a
little, of the wind, 762a
lost slain by arrows of frost, 634b
mother who talks about her, 513a
neither, nor gods, 815a
never forgot his, 1014b
never let angry passions rise, 302b
no longer any, 271a
of a larger growth, 323b
of an idle brain, 134b
of his own, till he had, 60b
of larger growth, 276a
of men, 620b
of one family fall out, 302b

Children of the brain, 294b
of the country, 783a
of the kingdom, 1052a
of the light, 621b
of this world, 1057a
of yesterday, 711a
other folks' dogs and, 843b
parents bore their, 766a
peacemakers called, of God, 125a
put our, on wheels, 891b
saying he would steal his, 677a
shall wander, 1025b
sins of the fathers upon, 18a
so act toward, 65a
somewhere, shout, 808a
spoke bad English, 804a
sports of, 354a
suffer the little, 1056a
talking to, in the dark, 976b
three eldest, of necessity, 672b
through survival of their, 702b
to those who are no longer, 777a
voices of, are heard, 385b
way to rear up, 519b
we and they are his, 571a
weeping for her, 1050a
who tumble barefooted, 898b
wife, and friends, 403a
will burn, 1015b
will not leave, 985b
will still have to toil, 739b
wisdom justified of her, 1052b
wiser than, of light, 1057a
with Hyacinth's temperament, 851b
women and, first, 1003b
women not used to bear, 54a
world in which, have existence, 580a
Children's children will have to toil, 739b
fate, for all our, 821b
gratitude, 827b
griefs are little, 790b
hour, 524a
popular American, books, 804a
teeth on edge, 1048b
Child's mistake fancies as lost, 790a
sob in the silence, 518b
strength, credulity the, 429b
tender years, 63a
Child-wife, it's only my, 579b
Chill companionship of waxen vines, 947b
courtesy grows, 703b
detraction stirs no sigh, 705b
icy and, 563b
in wintry age to feel no, 365b
November's sky, and drear, 414a
November's surly blast, 390a
penury repress'd their rage, 348b
the warmest heart, 630a
thy dreaming nights, 480a
whom age doth, 262a
wind is, 414b
you through and through, 747b
Chills, breathed its killing, 751b
of, and fever she died, 946b
the lap of May, 354a
Chillun, tun'nin' of de, in de bed, 859b
Chilly, feel, and grown old, 571a
man's fire, 598b
Chime, guide their, 269a
hours high heaven doth, 271b

Christian charity, rarity of, 489b
  charity, smile of, 808a
  darkness fell upon, 274b
  days, in these, 442b
  duty, views of, 597b
  endeavor hard on female pulchritude, 909a
  faithful man, 127b
  feels repentance on Sunday, 911a
  fled with a, 144b
  forgive them as a, 428a
  gentleman and a, 106a
  happy, child, 442b
  highest style of man, 306a
  ideal left untried, 852a
  ideal, still follow the, 618a
  in what peace a, can die, 301a
  love among the churches, 556b
  men be sure, 593a
  Mohammedan agnostic, 774b
  pearl of charity, 528a
  persuadest me to be a, 1059b
  Protestant or priest, 438b
  religion of late ages, 475a
  Rome, aisles of, 503a
  Science, 616b, 617a
  Scientists, 833b
  scratch the, 810a
  slave, you were a, 742a
  so good a, 752b
  Socialism, 593b
  soldiers, onward, 664a
  sorrow and mundane relish, 932b
  souls wrecked on shore, 668b
  true, every inch, 104a
  with four aces, 680b
  without hypocrisy, 660a
  world, richest monarch in, 394b
Christianity, alcohol and, 728a
  decline, because it is Jewish, 822a
  do not consider, a failure, 629b
  doctors had more, 833b
  local cult called, 705b
  most essential part of, 799a
  no fault of, 73a
  Post-office next to, the right arm, 472a
  takes a great deal of, 813b
  the one great curse, 728b
  those who have renounced, 618a
  was muscular, 513a
Christians, all denominations of, 339b
  good, good citizens, 442b
  have burnt each other, 457b
  love one another, 68b
  of best edition, 89b
  statesmen declare themselves, 728b
  want something for nothing, 766b
  were Christians, 902a
  what these, are, 144a
  whether papists or protestants, 339b
Christmas board, around the, 707a
  comes but once a year, 96a, 529a
  Day, before next, 911a
  Day, Jesus Christ born on, 635b
  Day may ever come again, 707a
  desire a rose at, 132b
  gambol oft could cheer, 414b
  goes to keep our, 758b
  happy, to all, 437a
  is coming, 1002b
  is here, 563b
  is over, 911b
  jest 'fore, 747b

Christmas, keep our, merry still, 414b
  keep, well, 578a
  make good cheer at, 96a
  may be called into question, 852a
  morn, blest, 617a
  night before, 437a
  pie, eating a, 1015a
  season of, spend, 737b
  tree the Easter egg, 996a
  won't be Christmas, 654a
Christmases, merry, 580b
Christmas-tide, I love the, 847b
Christom child, 154b
Christopher Robin goes hoppity, 917b, 918a
  Wren, Sir, 878b
Christ's blood streams, 123b
  heart, Lord, 507a
  in a sacred life, 543a
  progress, 271b
Christs that die upon the barricades, 767b
Christyan Scientists, 833b
Chronic anxiety about the weather, 688b
  hotel guests, 841b
  irritability, 697b
  melancholy, 705a
  wrongdoing or impotence, 779a
Chronicle of wasted time, 206b
  pride is his own, 181b
  small beer, 187a
  wars of kites, 260b
Chronicler, honest, as Griffith, 212a
Chronicles, brief, of the time, 174a
  love to read their, 586b
Chrononhotonthologos, 307b
Chuck 'im out the brute, 818a
Chuckle, little kind of low, 677a
  make one's fancy, 274b
Chums, temper of, 813a
Church and mart, 518b
  and Sabbath, 972b
  and science, 672a
  and state, 624a
  belonged to, 996a
  build my, 1053b
  built God a, 363b
  by daylight, 157a
  cathedral or a, 805a
  clock, stands the, 938a
  come all to, good people, 786a
  condemns state absolutism, 888a
  good old Dutch, bell, 635b
  husband not oftener to, 931b
  I like a, 503a
  inside of, 151a
  keep, and state separate, 624a
  keep Sabbath going to, 647a
  knoll'd to, 161a
  little, around the corner, 643b
  little grey, 619b
  miracles of the, 886a
  most folks don't go to, 677a
  near the, far from God, 92a
  neer to, further from God, 92a
  new hat carried into a, 448b
  prayers of, to preserve, 297a
  seed of the, 69a
  six times a year, 844b
  so to, went she, 786a
  some to, repair, 311a
  steeple, weathercock of, 369b
  supporting the, 707a
  to, and with my mourning, 285b
  to be of no, is dangerous, 337b

Church, warn't anybody at the, 677a
  way to parish, 160b
  wedding in the, 285a
  what no other, has understood, 493a
  where God built, 86b
  white, above thin trees, 875a
  who builds a, to God, 315a
  without a bishop, 490a
  world or, or state, 602a
Church-bell, where the, rings, 598b
Church-door, nor so wide as, 136b
Churches, bless all the, 541a
  chapels had been, 143b
  Christian love among the, 556b
  in flat countries, 411a
  peace of great, 898b
  scab of, 213b
Churchman, cowled, 503a
Churchyard, corner of a country, 361b
  Mellstock, 705a
  mould, 488b
  palsy-stricken, thing, 480b
Churchyards yawn, 176b
Churlish reply, 163a
Churn, magnet attract a silver, 683a
Chutes of gravitation, 985a
Chymist fiddler statesman, 277a
Cicada, wild, 957b
Cicero called Aristotle a river of gold, 57a
  Demosthenes or, 401 a
Cigar, fifty-cent, 911b
  give me a, 460b
  good five-cent, 759b
  good, is a smoke, 813a
  I smoked my last, 615b
  is a great comfort to a man, 510b
  post-prandial, 708b
Cigar-box lid, faces on a, 885b
Cigars, by the, they smoke, 837b
Cincinnatus of the west, 455b
  ploughing his land, 50a
Cinders ashes dust, 480b
  heaving, 902b
  sat among the, 1018a
C.I.O. veto power, 936b
Circle, all within this, move, 242a
  beyond our, of ideas, 740a
  deeds the, growing, 638b
  draw by own geometry the, 719a
  every man is center of a, 661b
  fools into, 160b
  glory like, in water, 124a
  grazes confines of space, 626a
  in which his claims are recognized, 513b
  life is a self-evolving, 512a
  live in as small a, 379a
  live too much in a, 512a
  of his own connections, 514b
  of the golden year, 548a
  of the upper ten, 640a
  small, of a wedding-ring, 298b
  swinging round the, 529a
  that shut me out, 756a
  vicious, 665a
  wheel is come full, 193b
  which can amuse itself with art, 702a
  within that, none durst walk, 275b
Circled orb, 135b
Circles, love that, home, 495b
  of blind ecstasy, 982a

Clad in blak or reed, 79b
  in complete steel, 247b
  in iron, 260a
  in sober livery, 255b
  morn in russet mantle, 170a
Claim, Bourbon or Nassau, higher,
    293b
  little, to virtue, 484b
  to originality among Irishmen,
    756b
Claiming for his own, 100b
Claims, adjustment of all colonial,
    771a
  are recognized, 513b
  honour, and reward, 41b
  of long descent, 547a
Clamb hill thegither, 392b
Clamor, loud, more or less insane,
    473a
  of the crowded street, 525b
  of waters, 690b
  persons who constantly, 444b
  without, for distinction, 617a
Clamoring hammering ring of it,
    926b
Clamorous, instant, eaves, 825a
  owl, 141b
  pauper feasteth, 561a
Clamors, Jove's dread, 189a
  of a venal press, 561b
  venom, 129b
Clam'rous lapwings, 309a
Clan, boasted race or, 888b
  sophist schools and learned,
    503a
Clang of hurrying feet, 582b
Clanging rookery, 548b
Clangour, trumpet's loud, 278b
Clap hands, Soul, 827a
  of thunder in a fair day, 275a
  your hands, 792a
  your padlock, 293b
Clapper, tongue is the, 158a
Claps her wings at heaven's gates,
    112b
Clap-trap, independent of all,
    669a
Claret and sherry, 262b
  bumper of, 449b
  is the liquor for boys, 342a
Clargy, sad fact to th', 837a
Clarifies, time, 883a
Clarion call, lark's is a. 741b
  sound the, 416b
Clarity, no heaven but, 988b
Clash forth life's common chord,
    574b
  ignorant armies, 622b
  may-bells, and chime, 704a
Clasp, reason why I, them, 627a
Clasped and clothed in the cloven
    clay, 692b
  hands, Niobe with, 634b
Clasps, gold, 134b
  the crag with crooked hands,
    553a
Class, citizens of the middle, 26b
  debtor, not dishonest, 689a
  ideas of its ruling, 593b
  is extinguished with him, 504a
  lies late and snores, 991b
  of modern capitalists, 593b
  one, of citizens, 325b
  revolutionary, 593a
  struggles, history of, 593a
  transfer from, to class, 974a
  while there is a lower, 761a
Classes, antagonism between, 593b
  books divisible into two, 605b

Classes face to face with the bour-
    geoisie, 593a
  hands of the higher, 376a
  masses against the, 534a
  men and, of men, 751a
  other, decay, 593a
  tempt the upper, 775b
  three, of intellects, 85b
  two, of poets, 508a
Classic a book which people praise,
    679a
  bent, 817a
  face thy Naiad airs, 543b
  ground, tread on, 298b
  in his own age, 492b
  literature is always modern, 511a
  produced by cooperation, 808b
  that the world has lost, 877b
  to make a cliché is to make a,
    858b
Classical quotation is the parole,
    342b
Classicism, instance of futile, 776b
Classics drowsily read, 505a
  have scarcely lost in absolute
    value, 776a
  more stimulating than, 959b
Clatter of arms drowns voice of
    law, 33b
  of Barrie's cans, 950b
  with his coach, 285b
Claw, painting a lion from the, 8a
  red in tooth and, 552b
Claw'd me in his clutch, 178b
Claws, how neatly spreads his,
    656a
  ragged, 942b
  skilful way you hide your, 842b
  that catch, 657b
Clay, all that was in, or stone,
    839b
  and wattles, 824b
  anneals the common, 977b
  blind his soul with, 551a
  cloven, 692b
  dead and turned to, 928a
  embrace of, 935a
  feet part of iron and part of,
    1048b
  hapless sons of, 529b
  has its own, 902b
  in, none is, 1019a
  inhabits common, 804b
  lies still, 785b
  life but breathing, 328a
  lump of, 1014a
  miry, 1034a
  nature had but little, 449b
  porcelain, of humankind, 279b
  power over the, 1060a
  precious porcelain of human,
    279b
  selfsame, 969a
  tenement of, 276b, 793a
  turf that wraps their, 351b
  turn'd to, 179a
  wetted, and left it, 61a
  wrought in common, 814a
  yes said Mr., 433b
Clay-shuttered doors, 790b
Clean and brave, 785b
  beds and wives, 937a
  brushed oiled and dainty, 897b
  forspent, 716b
  from my hand, 196b
  hands and a pure heart, 1033b
  heart, 1034b
  keep their teeth, 202a
  kind and, 966b

Clean, new broom sweepeth, 93b
  nice, dirt, 798a
  O Virgin, 84a
  obscene grave and light, 228b
  starved for a look, 206a
  strip language, 983b
  the pasture spring, 879a
  thing, art is the only, 739b
  towels not kept in bathroom,
    843a
Cleane through the minde, 112b
Cleaned the windows, 682a
Cleaner greener land, 818b
Clean-gleaming plates and cups,
    938b
Cleanin' up de whole mess, 954b
Cleanliest shift is to kiss, 162b
Cleanliness into godliness, 119a
  is a great virtue, 637a
  next to godliness, 118b
Cleanly live, 152a
  manger, cold and not too, 263b
  room, 236a
Cleanness of body, 118b
Cleans, one that, easy, 879a
Cleanse me from secret faults,
    1033a
  stuff'd bosom, 199b
Cleansed and anointed, 979a
Clean-shirt-day, on, he went
    abroad, 339a
Clean-winged hearth, 528a
Clear anatomy arrive, 988b
  and cool clear and cool, 598b
  and manifest as the nose, 90a
  as a whistle 323a
  as the sun, 1044b
  bells they sound so, 786a
  coast was, 122b
  conscience is a sure card, 112b
  conscience or none at all, 989b
  deep yet, 266b
  did he really seem quite, 569b
  ether, falls through the, 477a
  everything with Sidney, 936b
  eye, discern with this, 588b
  honour purchased, 145a
  in his great office, 195b
  legal principle, 437a
  myself of cants, 474b
  of all regret, 8b
  of all ties, 434a
  of permanent alliances, 367a
  one, call for me, 557a
  one rule to be, 447a
  read my title, 303a
  religion of heaven, 479a
  remembrance is free and, 165b
  sad thoughts doth, 272a
  shews, and true, 984a
  ship is, at last she leaps, 610b
  sky by bright waters, 583b
  spirit doth raise, 249a
  unchanged and universal light,
    310a
  unconquerable cry, 707b
  your mind of cant, 343a
Clearer eyes, view ourselves with,
    231b
  than is glass, 81a
  than the noonday, 1030b
Clear-eyed Athene, 5b
Clearing-house of the world, 681b
Clearly, seen, within myself, 802b
Clearness, celestial, 735a
  is a virtue of style, 823b
  of the intuitive powers, 559b
Clears, sail, top of the wave, 12a
Clear-toned Baptist bell, 635a

Cleave only unto the hairs, 708a
  the wood, 757a
  to heart of a true Englishman, 301a
  to her and worship her, 555a
  to sunnier side of doubt, 556b
  unto his wife, 1021b
Cleaves, one that, to me, 733b
Cleaving the darkness, 899b
Cleene, new brome swepth, 93b
Cleft devil's foot, 215b
  for me, 372a
  right through the core, 395a
Clemenceau had one illusion, 924b
Clemency, modesty, are species of nobility, 282a
Clennesse, ensample for to yive by, 171b
Cleopatra night drinks all, 717a
  put herself into coverlet, 56b
  the army the empire and, 502b
Cleopatra's nose, 272b
Clere conscience is a sure carde, 112b
Clerer than is glas, 81a
Clergy, die without benefit of, 857a
Clergyman close about the house, 671a
  no duty of a, 418b
  proud, 333b
  rarelier still the, 751a
  who is also man of business, 73a
Clergymen, men women and, 322b, 419a
Clergymen's households unhappy, 671a
Cleric before and lay behind, 238b
Clerical printless toe, 938a
Clerk foredoom'd, 318b
  of Oxenford, 79b
  Saunders, 1012b
  scarce less illustrious, 363b
  'twixt priest and, 230b
Clerkes, gretteste, noght wisest men, 81a
Clerks have missed the mark, 430a
Clever at envying a famous man, 8a
  good are so harsh to the, 708a
  if all good people were, 708a
  let who will be, 598a
  man, manage a, 814a
  of the turtle, 990a
  part which he means to be, 511a
  people were good, 708a
  pupil, encouraging a, 333b
  quality of stupid as of the, 461b
  reputation for being, 851b
  so rude to the good, 708a
  think oneself more, 265b
  versifier, 974b
  woman to manage a fool, 814a
  young hearts were not so, 786a
Cliché, to make a, 858b
Clicking clean brushed oiled, 897b
Clients, good counsellors lack no, 183b
Cliff, coign of the, 695b
  on the grass of the, 695b
  top of the, 701a
Cliffs, chalk, of Dover, 832b
  of fall frightful, 724b
  pillared, like sentries, 755b
  white, of Dover, 876a
Climate, achieve, 802a
  and soil, 406a
  change their, 41a
  climate within a, 886a
  coal is a portable, 505a

Climate, cold, or years, 258a
  fell upon an ungenial, 624a
  New England has a harsh, 748a
  scenery and invigorating, 859a
  state so blessed in, 880a
Climates councils governments, 548a
  preserving qualities in damp, 505b
Climax, verging toward some, 777b
Climb, fain would I, 111a
  high climb far, 1008b
  higher than sphery chime, 248b
  into the fold, 249a
  not if heart fails thee, 111a
  out beyond the limitations, 699b
  Sinais, 408b
  upward to what they were, 198b
Climbed, and step by step, 853a
  from sex to soul, 262b
  I, the hill, 854b
Climber-up of knees, 397b
Climber-upward turns his face, 167a
Climbing, men's hands are soiled in, 900a
  moon upon an empty sky, 825a
  sorrow, 191a
Climb'st the skies, 115b
Clime, from, to clime we speed, 885a
  happy fireside, 393a
  in every, adored, 320b
  in every age and, 7a
  in some brighter, 372b
  infernal, 534b
Climes, cloudless, and starry skies, 456a
  humours turn with, 314a
Cling for gold, 309b
  to faith beyond forms, 556b
Clings, desire of glory, longer, 63b
  fragrance such as never, 961b
  pain, cruelly to us, 479a
Clink of the ice in the pitcher, 747a
Clip an angel's wings, 480b
Clipper ship, 940b
Cliques which consist of one man, 766b
Cloak, camlet, 284a
  covers man like a, 109b
  martial, around him, 464a
  take thine old, about thee, 1011b
  'tis not alone my inky, 170b
  when you sleep in your, 616a
Cloaked, darkly, and standing, 742b
Cloathes, their own fine, 285b
Cloaths, meat drink and, 1002b
Clock, borough, 996a
  does strike by algebra, 238a
  early village, 128b
  forgot to wind up the, 345a
  in the belfry strikes one, 660b
  is always slow, 877b
  mouse ran up the, 1015b
  numbering, 140b
  old, ticks on, 955b
  Shrewsbury, 152a
  stands the church, 938a
  strikes two, 686b
  time runs, will strike, 123b
  turned into a sort of, 633b
  varnish'd, behind the door, 356b
  worn out with eating time, 276b
Clocks, make two, agree, 95a
  what need has he of, 840a
Clockwork joints of supple gold, 693b

Clod, cloud and, 922b
  in the soul and the, 571b
  kneaded, 185a
  of ailments and grievances, 765a
  of wayward marl, 157a
  plain man is the basic, 777a
  washed away by the sea, 218a
Clods, a man harrowing, 706b
Clog, generations atween clog and, 891b
  of his body, 243b
Cloister, close breath of the, 628a
Cloistered virtue, 250b
Clos'd in my true love's hand, 138a
Close connexion of bliss and bale, 719b
  designs and crooked counsels, 276b
  eye of day, 250a
  fifth shall, the drama, 306b
  friend to, his eyes, 280a
  grossly, it in, 147a
  I should, with the offer, 633b
  in dial's centre, 154b
  mouth catches no flies, 105b
  of life, our portion at, 16a
  on its wave, 609a
  open hand out of love, 726b
  scent survives their, 789b
  shorn sheep, 234b
  the shutters fast, 364b
  topsy-turvy, 638b
  up his eyes, 125b
  wall up, 155a
Close-button'd to the chin, 365b
Closed fr-ont dure, 833b
  in death th'attentive eyes, 338a
  life is, life begins, 610b
  lips hurt no one, 58a
  my life, twice, 646b
Close-knit strands, 1006a
Closeness and bettering of my mind, 209a
  gives melody to the voice, 40a
Closer, for secrecy no lady, 150a
  is He than breathing, 556a
  than a brother, 1040a
  than touch, 829a
Closes, death, a man's reputation, 301a
Closest correspondence, 359b
  human beings, 884a
Closet, do well in a, 323b
  in the world not in a, 323a
  of her mind, 876b
Closing, diapason, full in man, 278b
  innocence is, up his eyes, 122b
  rivets, 155b
  sweet, of an eye, 563a
  time, gentlemen it's, 929b
Clost, so, I could almost touch, 829b
Clot the bedded axle-tree, 944b
Cloth, cut cote after my, 92a
  meat drink and, 90a
  on a, untrue, 685a
Clothe a man with rags, 1040b
  my naked villany, 127b
  the naked, 1065a
Clothed and in his right mind, 1055b
  him not, 352b
  in reason's garb, 254a
  in suitable vesture, 22b
  in the cloven clay, 692b
  in white samite, 555b
  it with life, 444a
  naked and ye, me, 1054b

Come, passing or to, 827a
past and to, seem best, 153a
pensive nun, 246a
Romeo, forth, 137b
say I, no more, 830b
season when to, and to go, 320b
seeling night, 197b
suffer me to, to thee, 334b
that it should, to this, 170b
that they might have life, 1058a
they, they stay, 889b
things to, 274a, 1060a
thou'lt, no more, 194a
'tis not to, if it be now, 179b
to bury Caesar, 168a
to Carthage, 147a
to judgment, 146b
to me my dear Bozzy, 342b
to open purple testament, 139b
to pluck your berries, 248b
to see and be seen, 42b
unto me ye that labour, 1052b
up and see me sometime, 968a
upon the continents, 954b
Watson come, 782a
what is for to, I know not, 1065a
what is to, we know not, 741b
when it will come, 167b
when you call, 150b
when you're looked for, 584a
will ye no, back again, 398a
with bows bent, 691a
within a pint of wine, 301b
you back to Mandalay, 818a
Comedian can only last, 904b
country will need a, 904b
Comedies ended by a marriage, 458a
ridicule in his, 70b
Comedy, married philosopher belongs to, 727b
world is a, 350a
Comeliness, success that gives it, 303b
Comely, black but, 1044a
fashion to be glad, 612b
head, bowed his, 268b
let thy attyre bee, 112a
olde man, 112b
so pleasant so jolly, 377a
Comer, first, sped, 275b
grasps in the, 182a
Comers, welcomed to his house all, 777b
Comes blind fury, 249a
by gift of chance, 38a
by nature, 158a
conquering hero, 291a
here, the lady, 136b
hope never, 252a
if winter, 466a
once in a lifetime, 934a
safe home, 156b
thing, in his head, 127a
to pass without cause, 329b
too near that comes to be denied, 226b
unlook'd for, 310a
until the evening, 1069b
want for one who, not, 974b
Comest in so slowly, 989a
Comet shake out your locks, 894a
Cometh another generation, 1042a
forth like a flower, 1030b
in the name of the Lord, 1037a
late, 758a
shame, behynde, 15a
that which, out of mouth, 1053a

Comets amongst the stars, 333b
no, when beggars die, 167b
Comfort and violence, 941b
carry their, with them, 596b
cold, 229b
every sufferer, 664b
finds, in despair, 125a, 382a
for great bereavement, 495a
friends and foes, 354b
gives, in despair, 125a
giving them aid and, 376a
hope and, from above, 383a
in a face, 114b
like cold porridge, 209b
lust for, 924a
needn't be trying to, me, 732a
of the miserable, 46b
of thy children, 128a
so will I, you, 1047b
social, in a hospital, 520a
society in shipwreck is a, 43b
souls perplexed, 722b
tell you where your, lies, 670a
ten times more, 117a
that bewildered epoch, 822b
to my age, 160a
to one not sociable, 204b
to that grief, 158b
to the unhappy, 46b
two loves of, and despair, 207b
warn, and command, 409a
ye my people, 1046b
Comfortable advice, tea and, 479b
baith grand and, 791b
bird, 478b
career of prosperity, 565a
divine and, words, 554a
easy and, on a raft, 677a
feel in any member, 488b
people who're, 914a
Comfortablest caucets, 989b
Comfortably and thoroughly in debt, 564b
those who are, off, 966a
Comforted, folly of being, 825b
they shall be, 1050b
would not be, 1050a
Comforter, time is the only, 495a
Comforters, miserable, are ye all, 1030b
monitors also the, 625a
Comforteth like sunshine after rain, 131a
Comforting light of what you may do, 740b
piece of fiction, 908b
thought in time of trouble, 895a
Comfortless, leave you, 1058b
Comforts and hopes, 119b
creature, 292b
essential, of life, 484a
have increas'd, 384b
of life, 41a
of this weary pilgrimage, 342b
so-called, of life, 589b
us in our affliction, 29a
Comic, business of a, poet, 297b
perception of the, 508b
Comicality, broad and rich, 719b
Comin' in on a wing and a prayer, 997a
Coming, do you see anyone, 1005b
eye will mark our, 457b
far off his, shone, 257a
Father Abraham, 559a
glad of her, 285a
guest, welcome the, 6b, 319b
hold the fort I am, 613b
hour o'erflow with joy, 183a

Coming, I'm, my head is bending low, 636a
in, preserve thy, 1037b
into being of composite things, 12a
live for I'm, 37b
men, 761b
of the Lord, 597b
she is, my own my sweet, 554a
some are, some are going, 634a
sometimes, sometimes coy, 288a
when they seem, are going, 699a
Coming-in, simple, 144b
Comings and goings, 62b
Comings-in, what are thy, 156a
Comma on thy page of victories, 469b
Command, blind obedience to words of, 784a
brief, of Lee, 740a
Britain at heaven's, 328a
by his, these words are cut, 828a
correspondent to, 209a
him tasks, 189b
man to, 550b
more invitation than, 301b
move only in, 199a
my heart and me, 263a
not in mortals to, success, 299a
obedience, no power to, 26a
obedient to, of truth, 614a
of myself, 88b
patriarch to, of God, 614a
prize of a general is, 709b
sneer of cold, 465a
threaten and, 176b
warn comfort and, 409a
well-bred silence always at, 741a
when the strong, 803b
where I adore, 165a
you, your mother, 53b
Commanded and set up, 273a
God so, 258a
in affairs whereof they write, 98b
tears, 130a
the sun and the moon, 331b
to do without being, 71b
to turn people, 273a
Commander of the American armies, 331b
Commandeth her husband, 243b
Commanding of The Mantelpiece, 681b
Commandment, Eighth, 425a
new, I give unto you, 1058b
Commandments, keep his, 1044a
no Ten, 818b
set my ten, 125a
strong as the Ten, 645a
Ten, will not budge, 602b
two great, 492b
Commandress, great, of the world, 116b
Commands all light all influence, 224b
art necessary to one who, 85b
Fortune, men, 13a
the beauteous files, 271b
Commemorated by columns and inscriptions, 20b
Commend another's face, 343b
so great a poet, 280b
swains, her, 132a
Commendation of age, 119a
Commendations, good at sudden, 202a

Compounded of many simples, 162b
Comprehend his purpose, 1065b
to, is to forgive, 398a, 633a
Comprehends by itself, 85b
some bringer of that joy, 142b
Comprehension, too mystic for my, 990b
Comprehensive soul, largest and most, 275b
Compromise and barter, 360b
and things half done, 933b
between runnin' away, 836a
bourn of common sense, 953b
servile imitation, 559b
that's his idea of a, 625a
Compromises, what are facts but, 795b
Compromising documents, 773b
Compulsion, fools by heavenly, 191a
knowledge acquired under, 25a
reason on, 150a
sweet, 245a
upon writers to become sterile, 931b
Compulsive ardour gives the charge, 177a
course, icy current and, 189a
Compulsory, making education, on all, 603a
Compunctious visitings of nature, 195a
Computation backward from ourselves, 118b
material, 870b
Comrade, body's guest and, 65b
Comrades, cheer up, they will come, 613a
evangel-poem of, 607a
fiend with all his, 74a
friends and, 484b
hastens to join his, 463a
leave me here a little, 548b
love freedom, 897a
lovers friends, 630a
warriors Thracians, 583b
Comrades' eyes, drink in our, 627b
Comradeship behind a kiss, 876a
Con over this strain, 591b
Concatenation, bees in a, 357a
of circumstances, 444a
Concave, hell's, 253a
shores, 166a
Conceal bad news, 16a
half, the soul within, 551b
its own abuses, 433b
more he tries to, himself, 671a
no disguise can, love, 265a
skill to, one's skill, 265b
speech given to wise men to, 286b
speech to, our wants, 286b
speech to, their thoughts, 286b
speech to, thoughts, 325b
the mind, 286b
them like a vice, 753a
Concealed beauties of a writer, 300b
Concealing, art lies in, art, 668b
hazard of, 391a
how we think of ourselves, 680a
Concealment like a worm i' the bud, 164b
Concealments, soft, 770b
Conceals and shrouds him, 100a
modestly, her beauties, 343b
Conceit lies in his hamstring, 181a
pride and, the original sin, 297b

Conceit, what are they in their high, 503a
wiser in his own, 1041a
Conceited Frenchman Englishman Italian, 642a
man is satisfied, 858a
people, pity for, 596a
people, throw any away on, 596b
Conceits of the imagination, 543a
wise in your own, 1060a
Conceive a man, 969a
by this, the rest, 117b
heart to, 1002a
in sin did my mother, 1034b
nor name thee, 196b
tongue not able to, 142b
Conceived all and born in sin, 223a
by ingenious speculation, 84b
by the Holy Ghost, 1068a
in liberty, 540b
man child, 1030a
what heart, and dared, 570a
Conceives, confusedly, of a good, 76b
wit of man, 412b
Concentrate their energies, 763a
Concentrating it on a single enemy, 951a
Concentration camps, 905b
defeat brings prudence and, 783a
Concentred, wretch, all in self, 414a
Conception of the joyous prime, 113b
Conceptions of sovereignty, 977a
Concepts, stairs of his, 991a
Concern about happiness of peoples, 723a
conduct its largest, 623b
equal to those it does not, 497a
mankind's, is charity, 317b
themselves no further with me, 59a
Concerned, most, in my own interests, 31b
Concert of free peoples, 771a
Concessions of the weak, 359b
Conciliate with dignity, 343b
Conciliating, obsequious and, 446a
Conciliation of interests, 265a
of powers superior to man, 759a
Concision of Thucydides, 700a
Conclude as to both future and past, 55b
can man, anything, 696a
prayer, 279b
Concludendum, half gate to, 87a
Concludes with Cupid's curse, 116a
Conclusion, forty years to reach, 988a
impotent, 187a
of the whole matter, 1044a
this denoted a foregone, 189a
Conclusions, come to erroneous, 500b
from insufficient premises, 671b
Concord ice had bubbles in it, 935b
in pleasing, end, 260b
Lexington and Bunker Hill, 443b
lover of, 1068b
of sweet sounds, 147a
sweet milk of, 198b
travelled a good deal in, 589a

Concord, unity peace and, 1068b
what was created in, 865a
Concourse, casual, of atoms, 292b
Concrete cases, decide, 709b
fixed in, 861b
opportunity to act, 715a
Concubines, three hundred, 1028b
Concurrence, fortuitous, 355a
Concurrent, fortuitously, anyhow, 703a
Condemn an innocent one, 324b
as improbable fiction, 165b
censure of, another, 802b
fault and not the actor, 184a
people will, the one, 670b
you to death, 656a
Condemn'd alike to groan, 347b
to have an itching palm, 168b
Condemned cells of Newgate, 671a
into redemption, 158b
judge is, 44b
to perpetual exile, 690a
Condemnest thyself, 1059b
Condemns me for a villain, 128b
Condescend to take a bit, 295a
Condescension, triumphant, 973a
Condition, alter the, of a man, 202b
called war, 228b
decoyed into our, 285a
excited abnormal exhausting, 765b
good, in all respects, 285b
highest, takes rise in lowest, 46a
indolent but agreeable, 65b
inviolable, of life, 882b
no one content with his, 40a
of art, 772a
of estate, 285b
of feeling life, 718b
of his estate, 73b
of music, 702a
of social progress, 666a
unguarded, 264a
which confronts us, 512a, 689b
Conditions, meeting under certain, 336b
of our mental constitution, 534a
stars govern our, 192b
Condor's quill, 604a
Conduct, absurdity of, 336b
do not inspire, 266a
gives room for talk, 270a
is three-fourths of life, 623b
humane, is necessary, 618a
of chance, commit to, 100a
perilous to, 85a
rottenness begins in his, 374a
still right, 357b
unethical and lousy, 992a
Conducting the orchestral Strand, 810a, 854a
Conductor, passengers ask the, 898a
when you receive a fare, 645a
Cones, eat the, under his pines, 879b
Confabulate, if birds, or no, 366a
Confederacy, kept this, so long together, 539a
Confederate of tyrannies and shams, 679b
Confer, nothing to, 412a
Conference maketh a ready man, 121b
Conferred favour with a better grace, 56a
Confers benefit on any one, 98b
honour to him who, it, 302a

Damned, lie was dead and, 569b
may salute the eloquence, 980a
minutes tells he o'er, 188a
my books for me, 672b
not a, penny for tribute, 377b
of body and soul, 82ca
one, thing after another, 883b
perpetually, 123b
public be, 616a
see thee, first, 401a
spot, out, 199a
villain, smiling, 173a
Damnedest, politics the, 726a
Damning those they have no mind
to, 238b
Damocles, sword of, 670b
Damozel, blessed, leaned out, 640a
Damp and mould, 885b
dull and, without, 560a
grave too cold and, 437b
moist unpleasant body, 576b
my intended wing, 258a
nights are very, 660a
souls of housemaids, 943a
tonnage, 982a
Damsel lay deploring, 308a
of high lineage, 554b
with a dulcimer, 420b
Damsels of time, 506b
Dan Cupid regent of love-rhymes,
133a
even to Beer-sheba, 1027a
McGrew, 877a
to Beersheba, 346b
Danae, earth all, to the stars, 551a
Dance and drink and sing, 387a
and Provençal songs, 481a
and sing we are eternal, 774a
attendance, 212a
barefoot on wedding day, 130a
daisies that, on her way, 636b
delightful measure or, 138b
dresses to, in and flirt in, 632b
in the old dame yet, 894b
joke and rejoice, 262b
learns to skip, and kneel, 61a
like a wave of the sea, 825b
maids, in a ring, 212b
mehitabel dance, 894b
men must walk before they,
320a
merry love to, 825b
Pyrrhic, 458a
sing and eat and drink, 739b
sprightly, 409a
the antic hay, 123a
their wayward round, 405b
time to, 1042b
tipsy, and jollity, 247a
to violins, 769b
upon the air, 769b
who have learn'd to, 311a
will you won't you join the,
657a
with the pen, 728a
Danced along the dingy days, 646a
and then she, 499b
by the light of the moon, 581a
daughter of Herodias, 1053a
David, before the Lord, 1028a
death-fires, at night, 421b
his did, 969a
star, 157b
the moon on Monan's rill, 415a
till doomsday, 297b
to see that banner, 534b
Dancers, cymbals crash and, walk,
909b
dancing in tune, 554a

Dances, he, he has eyes of youth,
180b
in hamlets, on the green, 413b
in the wind, 278a
in what ethereal, 544a
she, such a way, 261b
train'd in sacred, 22b
Dancing, art of, 783b
broken of, 903a
emptier, in air, 140a
days are done, 135a, 1004a
days, past our, 135a
dogs and bears, 854a
flirting skimming along, 632a
if 'tis, you would be, 786b
in all its forms, 728a
in chequered shade, 245a
in the breeze, 409a
is wonderful training, 957a
jesting, drinking, 786a
merry, drinking time, 280b
more like wrestling than, 68a
most austere of disciplines, 784a
O heaven her, 499b
on a volcano, 472a
the loftiest of the arts, 783b
Dandelions, golden kisses called,
582b
leave to children the, 776b
Dandin, Georges, you wanted it so,
270b
Dandruff, toothpaste and the, ads,
982a
Dandy, candy is, 989b
Dandyism, cynicism is intellectual,
639a
Dane, more antique Roman than
a, 179a
never get rid of the, 820b
Danegeld, paid him the, 820b
Danger, above noise and, 271b
and long tempest, 566b
artist is in, of death, 982b
conquer without, 243a
delay always breeds, 106a
fear'd no, 278b
foretold, lurks within, 127a
gleams like sunshine, 17a
in loneliness is, 959a
is in discord, 523a
lurks within, 127a
moment of difficulty and, 1001b
nettle, 150a
never knew the, it incurred,
589a
of Popery, 301a
of violent death, 229a
on the deep, 485a
path that leadeth to, 131a
pleas'd with the, 276b
shape of, can dismay, 409b
sick, for the healthy, 727b
signal of, 463a
so much knowledge as to be out
of, 634a
spice of, 734b
wish the, intensified, 719a
Dangerous ages, forties are the,
960a
and bold attempts, 56b
art of giving presents, 953b
breakers of the Euxine, 459a
brow by night, 167a
Dan McGrew, 877a
delays are, in war, 124b
delays have, ends, 124b
demur you're straightway, 646a
edge of things, 571a
for good or evil, 925b

Dangerous, friends are much more,
748a
in me something, 179a
literature most, of professions,
700a
little knowledge is, 634a
mad bad and, to know, 449a
more, than discontinued labour,
497b
most, enterprise, 953b
most, of all spells, 510a
most, sea, 145b
most, situation, 967b
people who make no noise are,
269b
philanthropic enterprise, 953b
principles, 1002a
radical, 975a
realities are less, 861b
seas, trouble the, 36b
such men are, 166b
temptation, 212b
thing, little learning is a, 310b
thing, thirst is a, 788a
times, say nothing in, 227b
times, unprosperous and, 472a
to be of no church, 337b
to our peace and safety, 389b
turns to the, water and gazes,
75a
when they appear to retreat,
895a
world, into the, 387b
Danger's troubled night, 432b
Dangers and uncertain effects,
367b
compass'd round, 257a
enough to struggle with, 428b
greater, men environ, 597a
little, they may fear, 597a
loved me for, I had pass'd,
186b
no, fright, 336a
of the seas, 214a
of this earthly life, 665b
of this night, 1068b
thorns and, of world, 148b
thou canst make us scorn, 393b
Dangling that bright hard medal,
719b
Daniel cast into den of lions
1049a
come to judgment, 146b
second, 146b
taken out of the den, 1049a
Daniels, Uncle Peter, 1014a
Danish of Horrebow, 342a
Dank tarn of Auber, 545b
wild and, with foam, 598a
yellow drifts of leaves, 623a
Danny Deever, 817b
Dante, Keble or, or Job, 787b
of the dread Inferno, 571b
or Michelangelo, 993a
sleeps afar, 454a
Dappled, long, grass, 825a
things, glory to God for, 724a
turf at ease I sit, 407b
Dapple-dawn-drawn Falcon, 724a
Dapple-Gray, his name was, 1019
Darbies and Joans, 853a
Darby, always the same, my own
740b
saw the setting sun, 447b
Dare, and yet I may not, 111a
better than you, to think, 522
do all that may become a man
196a
do, what men, 158a

Dare eat breakfast, 155b
  for which we, to die, 317b
  its deadly terrors clasp, 387a
  love that and say so too, 215b
  mighty things, 778b
  much to, 926a
  never grudge the throe, 572a
  no no no I, not, 999b
  not cross the threshold, 335a
  not do an ill thing, 58a
  not wait upon I would, 93a, 196a
  speak truth as much as I, 99b
  the will to do the soul to, 415a
  to be true, 232b
  to call my soul my own, 519b
  to endure is greater than to, 566b
  to do our duty, 538b
  to live, 14b
  to love their country, 321a
  to say what others dare think, 638a
  to speak unreservedly, 671a
  what man, I dare, 198a
Dared, what heart conceived and, 570a
Dares, life that, send, 263b
  not put it to the touch, 262b
  not send his eye, 263a
  think one thing, 4b
  to call himself a man, 969a
  who, do more is none, 196a
Darien, silent upon a peak in, 477b
Darin' exploits iv a brave man, 834b
Daring, acting enduring and, 655b
  duds of, 795a
  in full dress, 460b
  loving are the, 634b
  nothing too high for mortal, 38a
  plot in extremity, 276b
  religion of well-doing and, 339b
  young man, 700b
Darius's horse, 491a
Dark, after that the, 557a
  age wherein he lived was, 266b
  all that led up is, to me, 398a, 633a
  amid the blaze of noon, 259b
  and bloody ground, 613a
  and lonely hiding-place, 422b
  and silver grave, 111b
  and the daylight, 524a
  as Erebus, 147a
  as good i' the, 230b
  as night, 207b
  as one's own heart, 514a
  as sages say, 586b
  as the world of man, 941a
  autumn evenings, 569a
  backward and abysm of time, 208b
  battlements, 397a
  blanket of the, 195a
  blonde or, 972b
  brightly for the, 956b
  brown is the river, 750a
  children fear to go in the, 119b
  cooling star, 872b
  days, these are not, 870b
  death or dreamful ease, 547b
  De Soto, 759b
  dominion, tired of his, 639a
  ever-during, surrounds me, 254b
  fear of the, 930a
  fiend, and wild, 933b
  fir-trees, and high, 488a
  go home in the, 802b

Dark, good many things in the, 973b
  gulf, stairway to a, 868b
  happiness, malicious have, 497a
  horse, 511a
  hour of adversity, 446a
  in the, and wet, 750a
  in the, like ourselves, 886a
  in thy, streets shineth, 669b
  irrecoverably, 259b
  light for us i' the, 573b
  names on earth are, 468b
  nightmare of the, 993b
  of the unfathomed center, 483b
  pile of human mockeries, 440b
  road whence no one returns, 35a
  Satanic mills, 388b
  sea, Egypt's, 440a
  secret love, 387a
  side, everyone has a, 679a
  sleep in the, 429b
  successive title long and, 277a
  sun to me is, 260a
  through the, cloud shining, 865a
  thy path be, as night, 582a
  water-wandered town, 994b
  we are for the, 201b
  what in me is, 252a
  what lieth, 686a
  what looks, in the distance, 688b
  with excessive bright, 254b
  with torment and with tears, 591b
  womb where I began, 896b
  world and wide, 251b, 804b
Dark-blue hunter, night the, 839b
Darken or grow bright, 471b
Darkened and desecrated country, 883b
  shut doors and, room, 63b
  sun light or moon be not, 1043b
Darkeneth counsel, 1031b
Darkens, night, the streets, 252b
Darker days, not speak of, 870b
  drink, angel of the, 532a
  grows the night, 353b
  grows the valley, 639b
  ill, larger bill for a, 591a
Darkest cavern, misery's, 338a
  clouds, sun breaks through, 130b
  day he believes in spring, 889b
  day will have pass'd, 365b
  heart, turn on gas in th', 836a
  hour is before dawn, 17a
  hour of ill, 17a
  night of the year, 685b
Darkies, time when, have to part, 636a
Darkling down the torrent, 336a
  I listen, 481b
  plain, here as on a, 622a
Darkly, seeth through a glass, 1061b
Darkly-brooding fear, 851a
Darkness again and a silence, 524b
  and with dangers, 257a
  and worms, 477b
  awful, and silence reign, 582a
  be over me, 515b
  brief, 524b
  cast into outer, 1052a
  cleaving the, 899b
  comprehended it not, 1057b
  crown of our life is, 692a
  dawn on our, 445a
  deep into that, peering, 545a

Darkness, deep things out of the, 1030b
  descending, of fear, 917a
  distinguishable as light from, 311a
  distrust, that may fall, 681a
  door of, 532b
  doubt and, 566b
  downward to, 906a
  embalmed, 481b
  enveloped American armada, 986a
  eternal, 75b
  falls from wings of night, 522a
  fool walketh in, 1042a
  gives light in, 125a
  go out into the, 881b
  great horror and, 274b
  horror of outer, 661b
  house is never still in, 791b
  how yields, to happy morn, 723b
  if there be sometimes a, 314a
  in silent, born, 122a
  in the, who would answer, 995b
  in, with a bundle of grief, 899a
  instruments of, 194b
  into the, they go, 962b
  is restful and agreeable, 51b
  jaws of, 141a
  land of, 1030b
  leaves the world to, 348a
  lest, come upon you, 1058b
  light excelleth, 1042a
  light from, 257a
  light shineth in the, 1057b
  lighten our, 1068b
  lost for eye in the, 610b
  man in the unsearchable, 722a
  night and storm and, 453b
  O in vain, 609a
  of her eyes, 854a
  of the damned, 538a
  of the land, 553a
  pain, and cold, 572b
  pestilence that walketh in, 1036a
  prince of, a gentleman, 192a
  raven down of, 247b
  rulers of, of world, 1062b
  scatters rear of, 245a
  school of, 733b
  season of, 580a
  shall cover us, 444a
  shares the, 961b
  sink beneath the wave of, 500a
  slope through, up to God, 552b
  such as sit in, 1036b
  the night, 257a
  through, struggling into view, 654b
  to peace and, and earth, 787b
  to the perfect day, 723b
  universal, buries all, 322b
  upon the face of the deep, 1021a
  walk in, 1058a
  walked in, 1045b
  which may be felt, 1024a
  wind was a torrent of, 909b
  year of now done, 725a
D.A.R., must be a, 805b
Dark-shining Pacific, 939b
Darksome hours, 378b
Darky's, old, heart, 758b
Darling buds of May, 204b
  Charlie is my, 402b
  dear you look so queer, 1004a
  from the lions, 1034a

Day for toil, 507a
foretells a pleasant, 586b
fragrant, is done, 831b
from once a, to once a week, 577a
gilded car of, 247a
go to bed by, 750a
goes by like a shadow, 635b
goeth, cometh night, 686a
grace of a, that is dead, 549b
great avenging, 4a
green garlands to the, 796b
happy soul hath summer's, 264a
hate the, 114b
hath but one eye, 755a
health and a, 501a
heat of the, 1053b
hope to make the, go through, 795a
hoping ever for the perfect, 560b
how troublesome is, 449b
I have lost a, 305b
I saved his life, 292a
idle singer of an empty, 666b
in its hotness, 620b
in thy courts, 1035b
infinite, excludes the night, 303a
is a perpetual morning, 590a
is always coming, 802b
is bursting with moments, 985a
is done, 522a
is dying in the west, 711a
is gone, 479b
is in the west, 970a
is like a year, 770a
is too near, 686a
it raineth every, 166a
I've lost a, 305b
jocund, 137a
join not in hot, 152b
of judgment by that name, 927b
kings upon their coronation, 279a
latter, upon the earth, 1031a
lengthens not a, 214b
let them have their, 826b
life is but a, 477b
life is but a, at most, 394a
light of fuller, 598b
light the, 257a
light was first named, 74a
little girl by, 889a
loads the, 251a
longer than wonder lasts, 126b
longest, is in June, 721a
lord it but a, 738a
lost one hundred years a, 777a
maddest merriest, 547a
made black, 429a
make the, a happy one, 419a
makes up the commonplace, 734a
maketh all things clear, 686a
man has but a, 888a
merry as, is long, 157a
morning shows the, 259b
most wasted, of all, 372a
mother of the, 526b
must follow as night the, 172a
must trot all, 331a
never so long, 94b
next, is never so good, 46a
night and, brother, 500b
night and, gates stand open, 37a

Day, night of time surpasseth, 241b
no, without a line, 50b
nor brought too long a, 487b
nor trust some later, 38b
now the, is over, 664a
now's the, now's the hour, 394a
O frabjous, 658a
of death than day of birth, 1042b
of deliverance, 367b
of empires has come, 681b
of judgment, 557a
of judgment, mercy on the, 774a
of my destiny's over, 456b
of one's birth, 1042b
of small nations, 681b
of small things, 1049b
of spirits, 271b
of victory, 1011a
oh doodah, 636a
one half in, 650a
one, in England, 814b
one, that is ours, 800b
our little systems have their, 551a
over the livelong, 740a
pleasures of the present, 329a
promise of your early, 445a
read five hours a, 340a
remember the sabbath, 1024b
returns not to me, 254b
runs through the roughest, 194b
St. Ursula's, 599a
see in a summer's, 141a
shall be unto you a memorial, 1024a
she put our heads together, 881a
shining hills of, 527b
shrouded, retreats, 721a
smite thee by, 1037b
so rare as a, in June, 600a
special happiness of each, 886a
star arise, 1064b
state and inclination of, 139b
style of the, of judgment, 750b
sufficient unto the, 1051b
sunbeam in a winter's, 327b
sweet Phosphor bring the, 231b
sweet, so cool, 232a
tender eye of pitiful, 197b
that Christ was crowned, 528b
the first, 1021a
they read no more, 448a
think that, lost, 305b
thirty-second, 777b
this bright, 591b
those who dream by, 544a
thou the, I the hour, 683b
to fire the brave, 5a
to search for God, 795b
Tuesday is to be the, 284b
uncertain glory of an April, 131b
unto day uttereth speech, 1033a
up so soon, 148b
varies every, 279a
vulgarize the, of judgment, 509a
warm precincts of the cheerful, 349a
we must part, 491b
weary, have end, 115a
welcome, 227a
well-spent, 84b
what a, may bring forth, 1041a
what hath this, deserv'd, 147b

Day, what thou hast done by, 233a
when heaven was falling, 787a
when I'll be going, 952b
which the Lord hath made, 1037a
without all hope of, 259b
work and thou wilt bless the, 583a
would God the, were dead, 693b
yield, to night, 124a
Daybreak everywhere, 526a
Daydreaming, need not be, 906b
Dayes, loose good, 114a
Day-labour, exact, 251b
Daylight, between the dark and the, 524a
burn, 134b
church by, 157a
found the common, sweet, 738a
keeps up, in the mind, 301a
mere, and the skies, 611a
must in death your, finish, 574b
never to drink by, 909b
night is but, sick, 147b
of prosperity, 446a
when, comes, 596a
Daylight's dauphin, 724a
past, 438a
Day's at the morn, 567a
business, know end of, 169a
disasters in his face, 356a
do the, work well, 744b
garish eye, 246b
good, work, 332a
life, death of each, 196b
long toil is past, 488a
march nearer home, 413a
occupations, pause in the, 524a
out and the labor done, 520a
wages, fair, 475b
work, all in a, 1001a
work, fair, 475b
work that earned it, 505a
Days, afternoon of her best, 128a
all my, are trances, 544a
alluvial march of, 982a
among the dead, 426b
ancient of, 1049a
and nights to Addison, 337b
are in the yellow leaf, 460b
are still and bright, 509b
are young and careless-hearted, 885a
as long as twenty, 406b
as thy, so thy strength, 1026a
be as a marriage day, 232a
beauty and length of, 691b
begin with trouble here, 1000b
better, that lie ahead, 939b
chequer-board of nights and, 533a
count on two, 15b
dancing, 135a
degenerate, 4a
depends on seasons and on, 889b
dividing lover and lover, 691b
ere half my, 251b
fall'n on evil, 257a
farewell for sober studious, 313a
find it after many, 1043b
fled him down the, 790a
flight of future, 253b
forty, and forty nights, 1022b, 1025a
friend of my better, 462b

Death, lead him to, 289a
leaden, 309a
left it almost fair, 733a
levels all ranks, 510a
lieth at point of, 1055b
life and, are equally jests, 544a
life and, like friendly chafferers, 741a
life and, upon one tether, 959b
life is ever lord of, 528a
life is perfected by, 518b
life more terrible than, 14b
life shadow of, 691b
life struck sharp on, 519b
life your, has bought, 907a
little room we take up in, 237a
living, 260a
long mysterious exodus of, 523b
long since, had majority, 241a
looked at steadily, 264b
looks gigantically down, 544a
love is posterior to, 647b
love is strong as, 1044b
love thee better after, 519b
love to woman is life or, 754a
lovely and soothing, 609b
loves a shining mark, 306a, 637a
low and delicious word, 609b
make, clear or life durable, 695b
makes equal high and low, 90b
makes his arrest, 897a
man at the point of, 290a
mature for, 258b
meet and claim me, 991b
men at point of, 138a
men fear, 119b
men of, that came against him, 274b
midst of life we are in, 1069a
Mrs. Browning's, 533b
more beautiful than, 607b
name that sat on him was, 699a, 1064b
nativity chance or, 180b
nature of his, 18b
nature wills, 68b
neither, nor life, 1060a
never gallop Pegasus to, 320a
no, and no life, 964a
no life except by, 631b
no one till his, be called unhappy, 520a
no such thing as, 584b
no work begun shall pause for, 573b
none ever died a natural, 880a
none hath joy of his, 693a
nor all of, to die, 413a
nor change, 466b
nor sorrow nor sad hope, 632b
not, but dying, 333b
not, but love, 519a
not, for who is he, 648a
not so much afraid of, 240b
nothing our own but, 139b
now I know is first breath, 655a
now to, devote, 258a
O eloquent just and mightie, 111b
O, where is thy sting, 1062a
Oates was walking to his, 842b
of dear friend, 143a
of each day's life, 196b
of friends, 890a

Death of friends, sorrow for the, 109b
of his saints, 1037a
of some of her, 896b
of the righteous, 1025b
old men's prayers for, 16b
on his pale horse, 258b
one in life and, 683b
or give me, 369a
outrage worse than, 423a
owe God a, 153b
pains and fears makes, 261a
pale, with impartial step, 38a
paleness of, 462a
pang preceding, 353b
paradise to what we fear of, 185a
plague us to, 325a
portal we call, 523a
possessed by, 943b
prepare for journey as for, 952b
privilege of putting him to, 418a
prize o', in battle, 601b
provides innocent amusement, 967b
quick and easy, 794a
re-creates an individual, 985b
reads the title clear, 574b
reaper whose name is, 521a
religious way to think of, 882b
remembered kisses after, 550b
rendezvous with, 947b
reports of my, are exaggerated, 679a
reptile struck with instant, 50a
resolved on victory or, 395a
restful, I cry, 205b
ribs of, 248a
ride not a free horse to, 109b
room for, 592a
ruling passion strong in, 314b
run their horse to, 126a
sad stories of, 139b
sane and sacred, 609b
save us from a, like this, 521b
sea of, and birth, 809b
secret of nature, 67a
seems but a covered way, 524b
sense of, in apprehension, 184b
sentence of Versailles, 951b
serenity of, 662a
shadow of, 1030b
shall be no more, 217b
shall have no dominion, 996b
sick unto, 288a
sickness sin and, 616b
silence deep as, 433a
silence when one spoke of, 558b
silent halls of, 470b
sisters, and night, 609b
sleep and, two twins, 5a
sleep before, 60a
sleep is a, 241a
sleep of, 174b
Sleep the brother of, 7a
sleep the sleep of, 389a
slew at his, 1027a
slue not him, 114b
smooth the bed of, 319b
so noble, 260b
sole equality on earth is, 586a
solemn note sounded by, 463a
someone's, a chorus-ending, 571a
stoop to, we must, 96b
strange that, should sing, 148b
stretch a hand in hour of, 857a

Death strikes down the innocent, 577a
stroke of, 202a
studied in his, 194b
succeeded life, 279b
suffered, rather than submit, 295b
sung a song of, 386b
surely put to, 1025a
swallow up, in victory, 1046a
swallowed up in victory, 1062a
sweats to, 150a
swoon to, 479b
talent which is, to hide, 251b
taste of, 3a
that makes life live, 574a
the healer, 13a
the lover of life, 741b
the sable smoke, 454b
there is no, 523a, 673b
there is no, in one sense, 890a
thing which makes men weep, 459b
this life this, 826a
thorns through which we walk to, 897a
thou shalt die, 217b
thou wast not born for, 481b
thousand doors lead to, 226a
till, us do part, 1069a
'tis, to us, 267a
tragedies are finished by, 458a
tramples it to fragments, 468b
treats us all alike, 680a
triumphant, his dart shook, 258b
true face of, 833b
twitching my ear, 37b
ugly sights of, 128a
unavoidable and imminent, 794a
unexpected, is best sort, 59b
unnoticed at birth and, 41b
vacancies by, 375a
valiant taste of, but once, 167b
valley of the shadow of, 1033a
vasty hall of, 621a
visit us with, daily, 229b
wages of sin is, 1059b
wait, nor be afraid, 572a
way to, 199b
ways of, are soothing, 741a
we fear, 184b
we live under shadow of, 670b
what men call life, 18a
what should it know of, 403a
where is thy sting, 775a, 1062a
who puts an end to pain, 555a
why fear, 607b
will have his day, 139b
will overtake you, 1070a
will seize doctor too, 214b
wish for, 15a
within a tavern, 74b
wits inherit after, 309b
world reconciles itself to, 514b
worse things waiting than, 692b
worst is, 139b
Death-bed, dreads a, like the meanest slave, 314a
Jemmy Grove on his, lay, 1012b
Scilurus on his, 58b
Death-fires danced at night, 421b
Deathless, dead, hour, 640b
is the royal race of hicks, 894a
lines, for all your, 912a
music, vibrations of, 845a
my renown, 4b
Death-moth be your mournful Psyche, 483a

Described nothing but what I
saw, 19b
Describing external things, 862a
Description, beggar'd all, 200b
full, of a happy state, 283b
of a tempest, 69b
would but make it less, 366b
Descriptions of fairest wights,
206b
Descry the happy dawning, 231a
Desecrated, darkened and, country,
883b
Desert air, waste sweetness on the,
348b
Arab in the, 339b
coast, threw upon a, 405a
come to our bracing, 993b
cool spot in the, 807a
dry, of a thousand lines, 320b
fly to the, 441b
gardens of the, 471a
in service, 182a
in the, a highway for God,
1047a
island, Zuleika on a, 857b
isle in our geography, 995b
leafless, of the mind, 455a
mice, building about to fall, 50a
Mr. Micawber, I never will,
579a
power to make world a, 987a
rats, a sinking ship, 50a
seafaring man on, of waters,
644a
seven domes across a, 972a
shall rejoice, 1046b
shores and, wildernesses, 247a
the tradition, 501a
they call peace, 63b
use every man after his, 174a
were my dwelling-place, 454b
where no life is found, 487b
you for creeds that refuse, 692a
you when storm descends, 43a
Deserted as a playwright, 876a
at his utmost need, 280a
Deserter, looked upon him as a,
324a
Desertion and death, 484b
Desert's awful frame, 602a
dusty face, 531b
Deserts are small, 262b
come by their, 566a
of barren sand, 475a
of sand, 803a
of vast eternity, 269a
power to make, bloom, 987a
sandy, full of wild beasts, 53a
the night, 260a
you at a pinch, 10b
Deserv'd, what hath this day, 147b
Deserve, according to what they,
1070b
better of mankind, 295b
hanging ten times, 100b
love can scarce, the name, 455b
neither liberty nor safety, 331a
no better than they get, 952a
precious bane, 253a, 915a
shipwreck, 290a
something you haven't to, 879b
you have what you, 270b
Deserved, no man, less, 624b
to have his merits allowed, 342b
which each person, 107b
Deserves, brave, the fair, 280a
love and thanks, 370a
no crown, 232a
not any fortune fair, 84a

Deserves, not every question, answer, 45b
one good turn, another, 51b
Deservest, serve Thee as Thou,
87b
Deserving, lost without, 187b
note, 230b
nothing, 476b
without honour, 116b
Desideratum of a volume, 430b
Design, couldn't, a cathedral, 946b
God's, 993a
men not result of, 100b
palpable, upon us, 478a
things difficult to, 337a
Design'd, masterpiece, 393a
Designed, God to ruin has, 18b
to make people stumble, 927b
us to live in society, 326a
Designing St. Paul's, 878b
Designs by Michael Angelo, 674b
citizens least given to evil, 50b
close, and crooked counsels,
276b
ladder to all high, 181a
of his bright imagination, 791a
weather getting up new, 675a
Desirability of a cocktail, 957a
Desirable, fallacy that man is,
994a
thing to be well descended, 57b
Desire a perpetual rack, 222a
and mystery, 529a
any worldly ease, 329b
arrows of, 388b
bloom of young, 349b
delight that consumes the, 692a
drink provokes the, 196b
end of every man's, 693b
face of his, 772a
flaming some old, 977b
from what I've tasted of, 880b
give me my inexpressible, 739b
gratified, 386b
gray spirit yearning in, 548a
hour that turns back, 76b
imp of blind, 817b
in his heart is a blind, 691b
is wish joy may come, 418b
kindle soft, 280b
know what he ought to, 75a
land of heart's, 825a
liveth not in fierce, 413b
love and, and hate, 833a
man's painful, to communicate,
992a
men believe that which they,
276a
mixing memory and, 943b
more love, 159b
more of it than they possess,
237a
nearer to the heart's, 533b
no more to, 107a
nothing so much, 45a
of fame, 555b
of glory clings longer, 63b
of knowledge, 345b, 722a
of life prolongs it, 457b
of power in excess, 120a
of the moth for a star, 468b
our, changes, 856a
outlive performance, 153a
peace, who would, 40b
rose at Christmas, 132b
sated, 812b
satisfied of your, 16a
second of, 525b
shall fail, 1043b

Desire, shining with, 9a
sick with, 827a
small beer, 125b
soul's sincere, 413a
strong, in play, 882b
that Almighty answer me, 1031b
that outruns the delight, 692a
the dead should be near us, 552a
to a bottle of hay, 142a
to appear natural, 266a
to get near to God, 732b
to get on in the world, 940b
to learn, 250b
to live again, 728b
to live beyond income, 671b
to move in harmony, 633a
to purchase, 165b
to receive greater benefits, 265b
to take medicine, 743b
to teach or give pleasure, 41b
to think well of oneself, 944a
transform into effective, 702b
two things the people, 63a
unspeakable, after knowledge,
620b
vision of fulfill'd, 533a
what you, is not mortal, 42b
whence this fond, 299b
which of us has his, 565a
with dead, doth not die, 413b
wonder and a wild, 573a
Desired, it is that which I, 1067b
more to be, than gold, 1033a
the sea, 815b
to fret a passage, 243b
where it is least, 989b
you are not one to be, 546b
Desires, all, known, 1068b
and adorations, 467b
and dreams and powers, 694a
before his eyes a true picture,
19b
covetous, 1069a
heart's, 159a
heaven is what each, 441a
huge army of world's, 132a
infinite in his, 463a
mastery of the, 727b
new year reviving old, 531a
submitting to, of mind, 118b
their mind, something, 35b
to live long, 295b
undaunted daughter of, 263b
vehemence of their, 516b
Desiring this man's art, 205a
Desirous, is there else on earth
308b
of honour and glory, 283a
to commit to memory, 1067a
Desist, ask leave to, 242b
Desk on which is a buzzer, 953a
student glued to his, 628b
to write upon, 239a
Desk's dead wood, 430a
Desks, stick close to your, 682b
Desolate creatures on the earth,
520a
no one so utterly, 521b
passions aching hours, 838b
sands, 584a
sector of the Somme, 960a
shores, whisperings around,
478a
wind-swept space, 680b
Desolating pestilence, 464b
the country, 714a
Desolation, abomination of, 1054a
and dim night, 544a
careless, 162a

Diogenes, I would be, were I not Alexander, 61a
lighted a candle, 72a
plucked a cock, 72a
praise those about to marry, 71b
struck the father, 224a
Dionysius of Halicarnassus, 303b
Dip their wings in tears, 552a
Diplomacy, ceremonial of, 512b
is to do and say, 939a
of such stuff is made, 907a
what, begun, 686a
Di-plomacy a philanthropic pur-soot, 835a
Diplomat, great, a Moby Dick, 907a
how do you know I am a, 842b
launch a heedless word, 774a
sits in silence, 974a
Diplomatic name for law of jungle, 958a
Diplomatist write an unpleasant truth, 761a
Diplomat's soul, in a, 907a
Diplomats women and crabs, 699a
Dipped his pen into the tears, 735a
Dipping oar, soft moves the, 395b
Dips, sun's rim, 421b
Dipt into the future, 548b
other, in night, 650a
Dirck galloped, 568a
Dire effects from civil discord, 300a
need, hour of, 715a
offence from amorous causes, 312a
revenge these redmen planned, 759b
Direct and control the course of nature, 759a
and divine relations, 866b
him where to look for it, 217a
lie, 163a
our lives to please, 283a
self-government, democracy is, 560b
to be, and honest, 189a
understanding to, 1002a
Directeth, the Lord, his steps, 83a, 1039b
Direction, all chance, thou canst not see, 316b
education starts a man, 24b
of his dreams, 590b
of public affairs, 641b
recoil in any, 12a
Directions, by indirections find, out, 173a
Directs the storm, 299a, 322a
Direful spring of woes, 3b
Direst cruelty, 195a
shapes of death, 628a
Dirge, by forms unseen their, is sung, 351b
for her the doubly dead, 544a
in marriage, 170a
Dirt, faithless leather met the, 305a
if, was trumps, 430b
loss of wealth is loss of, 90b
nice clean, 798a
painted child of, 319a
Dirty, all, and wet, 297a
British coaster, 896b
business, hand in such. 710a
'ide, for all 'is, 818a
linen, 399b

Dirty linen to wash, 324b
poor lot and, too, 879a
weed, tobacco is a, 975a
work at the crossroads, 1007b
work, creature's at his, 318b
work, to do his, 952a
Disable benefits of country, 162b
Disabused, by himself abused or, 317a
Disaffection, mark of, 860a
Disagree, fated always to, 833a
when doctors, 315a
Disagreeable man, I'm such a, 684b
more, to say than to do, 56b
truth, speak a, 372a
Disallow thee to be competent judge, 235a
Disappear, evil tends to, 609b
Disappoint myself, 108a
one cannot, a continent, 669a
that I may not, myself, 588b
Disappointed, for he shall never be, 315b
in the monkey, 680a
tide, 646b
unhousel'd, unaneled, 172b
woman, fury of a, 298a
Disappointing to the ear, 19b
Disappointment, brought on by boredom and, 991a
cold, and regret, 415b
feeling of, 430b
love's, endears, 575b
of manhood, 511a
we are to ourselves, 586b
Disappointments, too familiar with, 537a
Disappoints, God, 83a
Disapprobation, imagined approba-tion or, 530a
Disapprove of what you say, 326a
Disapproves that care, 251a
Disarm all hostility, 523b
Disarmament of such nations essential, 922b
Disarray, on, it lays its wing, 866a
Disaster and ill fortune, in times of, 56a
clouded the Union cause, 666a
meet with triumph and, 820b
occasions not causes of, 778b
proximity of, and ruin, 868a
sully their ecstacy with some, 32a
unmerciful, followed fast, 545a
Disasters in his morning face, 356a
make guilty of our, 191a
middle station had fewest, 292a
weary with, 197b
Disastrous chances, 186a
night, falling in, 560b
pledges, 935a
twilight, 253a
Disbanding hired armies, 473b
Disbelief in great men, 475a
willing suspension of, 424b
Discarded things excel those pur-sued, 41a
Discern with this clear eye, 588b
Discerning, gives genius better, 357a
Discharg'd, indebted and, 255a
Discharge, debt we must all of us, 231b
in the war, 819a
no, in that war, 1043a
produce debt instead of, 305a

Discharged through all eternity, 379a
with greater ease, 231b
Discharging less than tenth part, 182a
Disciple, he will have no, 490a
not above his master, 1052b
Disciples devout both gaze and adore, 654b
gave it to the, 1055a
Discipline, for the artist life is a, 784a
liberty is beloved, 995a
of shrews at home, 446a
war its organisation and, 85b
without pain, 784a
Disciplined inaction, 397b
Disciplines, most austere of, 784a
of wars, 155a
their lives, 516b
Disclose, think and ne'er, her mind, 187a
Discobolus standeth, 670a
Discomforts accompany my being blind, 286a
Disconnected accidents, 642b
Disconsolate, at gate of Eden stood, 441a
Discontent, discontented with di-vine, 599a
disorder disobedience, 359a
hang the head as, 220b
long nights in pensive, 114a
maintenance of candid, 702b
want and, 240a
winter of our, 127a
Discontented strife, stirs of, 220b
with divine discontent, 599a
Discontinued labour, 497b
Discord, age of, and strife, 124b
all, harmony not understood, 316b
danger is in, 523a
dire effects from civil, 300a
follows, 181a
music must investigate, 57b
so musical a, 142a
Discordant belligerent states, 443b
factious and, 446b
life, echo from our, 634a
powers, struggle of, 361a
sound, drum's, 362a
Discords and unpleasing sharps, 137a
Discourage love of study, 909a
Discouraged, Dewey feel, 713a
Discouraging word, seldom is heard a, 730b
Discourse and speeches, 154a
bid me, 131a
excellent dumb, 209b
fair, as sugar, 139a
good company and good, 236a
is ot death, 285a
man's, like Persian carpet, 53b
of reason, 170b
of the elders, 1066a
rather hear thy, 223b
showers of sweet, 263b
such large, 177b
sweet and voluble in, 133a
where two, 18a
Discourses, sweet, in our time, 137a
Discourteously, cast me off, 999b
Discover a deficiency, 402a
concealed beauties of a writer, 300b
everybody's face, 294b

Divorces, hats may make, 845a
Dixie, away down South in, 585a
Dixie lib an' die in, 585a
Dixit, ipse, 72b
Dizziness, love is like a, 402b
Dizzy turbulence eludes the eye, 408a
Dizzy way no wider than a hair, 892b
Do all we would, 595b
and say the nastiest thing, 939a
anything for oneself, 875b
as adversaries in law, 130a
as I say not as I do, 227b
as much for him, 99b
as they do at Rome, 109a
as they see done at Rome, 224a
as you would be done by, 323a
business of life to be and, 700a
doesn't so much matter what you, 719a
fact that he can, wrong, 679b
go thou and, likewise, 264a
good not enough, 700a
him little good, 340a
how not to it, 579b
in remembrance of me, 1057b
it please again, 873b
it with my might, 1043a
just as one pleases, 434a
justly and love mercy, 1049b
know what he ought to, 75a
let us, or die, 394a
make it, or do without, 1008a
more work in a day, 447b
much less what we, 586a
must not, too much of it, 605a
noble things, 598a
nobody else good, 222a
not want what we ought, 620b
nothing but comment, 101a
nothing but that, 208b
nothing's good, 595b
or die, let's meet and, 225a
other men, 577b
promise not to, a thing, 675a
right to the widow, 1065a
say and, everything, 67b
so little done so much to, 758a
so much in years to come, 791a
some said it might, good, 274a
something to, that day, 598b
the thing you have to do, 633b
the things I ought, 442b
theirs but to, and die, 553b
this or that, 282a
this will never, 410b
thou but thine, 257b
thou likewise, 1057a
to, a great right, 146a
two things at once, 43a
unto the other feller, 735a
well rang the Unitarian bell, 635a
were as easy as to know, 143a
what he thought he could not, 342a
what I, and what I dream, 519a
what is right, 633b
what man would, 571b
what men dare do, 158a
what then thou would'st, 260b
what, to be forever known, 267a
what you have to do, 65a
whate'er I, 595b
whate'er one likes, 567b
without being commanded, 71b
wrong to none, 182b
ye even so to them, 71b, 1052a

Doänt thou marry for munny, 556a
Dobie, sate upon her, 581b
Doch-an'-dorris, wee, 850a
Dock the tail of rhyme, 534b
Dock-yard fellow, 663a
Dockyards, nor canals and, 8a
Doctor and saint, 532a
apple a day keeps the, away, 1006b
birds should sing remarked the, 887a
death will seize, 204b
dismissing the, 396a
fee the, for nauseous draught, 280b
Fell, I do not love thee, 293a
Foster went to Gloucester, 1019b
his own, of divinity, 749a
silent, shook his head, 308a
three faces wears the, 747a
who knows her constitution, 596a
you never were my, 60b
Doctor's peaceful mission, 747a
pill, outliv'd the, 308b
rules, 527a
Doctors, best, in the world, 296b
cowardly dependence upon, 728a
diet prescribed by, 27b
give what they would take, 535a
had more Christianity, 833b
is all swabs, 750a
when, differ, 315a
when, disagree, 315a
Doctrine, accept no, 518a
every wind of, 343a, 1062b
from women's eyes this, 133b
heresy of, 527b
little difference in, 339b
not for the, but the music, 311a
of human depravity, 707b
of ignoble ease, 778b
of reward and punishment, 799a
of Shangri-La, 985b
of the strenuous life, 778b
point of, 68b
prove their, orthodox, 238b
so illogical and so dull, 925a
today is, 1001b
winds of, 250b
Doctrines of religion, 119a
plain and clear, 239b
Documents, compromising, 773b
historian wants more, 719b
Dodo never had a chance, 926b
Doe, down there came a fallow, 1012b
it in a high style, 273b
Doer and the thing done, 418b
it is for the, to suffer, 13a
Doer's deed, place dignified by, 183a
Doers, talkers are no good, 127b
Does, he who can, 765a
more than his captain can, 201a
neighbour says, thinks, 67a
'tis not what man, 571b
well acts nobly, 305b
works and, some poem, 476a
Doest every act as though thy last, 45b
that thou, do quickly, 1058b
Doeth good and sinneth not, 1043a
Doff it for shame, 148a
Doffed, lightly, his hat, 807b
Dog, Alcibiades had a handsome, 59a

Dog barked at the ox, 10b
be a, and bay the moon, 168b
beware of the, 51a
biggest, has been a pup, 712a
bites a man not news, 731a
boatswain a, 451b
broodin' over bein' a, 735a
cat a, and a pipe, 788a
circumcised, 190b
commends himself to our favour, 775b
cut-throat, 144a
dies like a, 528a
difference between a, and man, 678a
drunken, ragged head, 429a
empty house like a stray, 671b
every, his day, 104b, 598b
faithful, bear him company, 316a
Fala, 921b
fennel, 802a
fetch her poor, a bone, 1018a
gingham, went bow-wow-wow, 747b
give to, for new year's gift, 180b
give your heart to a, 819b
haire of, that bit us, 93b
Highness', at Kew, 321a
how many legs has a, 542b
if you pick up a starving, 678a
in life the firmest friend, 451b
in that town a, was found, 355a
in the manger, 222a
in the market-place a dead, 635a
inch of, 942a
is thy servant a, 1029a
it was that died, 355a
keep a, 73a
laughed to see such sport, 1016b
let no, bark, 143a
like a, he hunts in dreams, 548b
little toy, covered with dust, 747a
living, better than dead lion, 1043a
love me love my, 94b
man or a, 766a
mine enemy's, 193a
my daughter and my wife, 990b
my dear old, 655b
named Rover Towser Sport, 970b
next-door, 975b
not been the same, since, 921b
on the wrong side of door, 990b
returneth to his vomit, 1041a
something better than his, 548b
starv'd at master's gate, 388a
suspicious of some buried bone, 719b
Tam o' Shanter, 741a
therefore to this, 518b
third, one dog meets, 332b
throw at a, 159b
to be companion, 417b
tongue of, 198a
tossed the, 1020b
Tray, poor, 432b
truth's a, must to kennel, 191a
turned to own vomit, 1064b
walked out that day, 859a
whose, are you, 321a
why should a, have life, 194a
will have his day, 179a
young man's, with them, 859a
Dogerel, rym, 82b

Drew, quick-eyed love, nearer, 232b
 these tides of men, 946a
 with one long kiss, 123a
Dried plants, books of, 558a
 tubes are twisted and, 814b
Drift, adamant for, 868b
 along with current's flow, 910a
 beyond his love and care, 528a
 go with the, of things, 879a
 know your, 157b
 long years, 38b
 of pinions, 790b
 tell you my, 157b
 to and fro, 796b
 wait and obey, 822a
Drifted an hedonist, 933a
 hours that have, by, 717b
 white and, snow, 498b
Drifting down the big still river, 676b
 dust, Helen's lips are, 844b
Drifts away like the waters, 825b
 dank yellow, of leaves, 623a
Drift-wood bleached and dry, 674a
Drill, Birken'ead, 818b
 puts away the, 957a
 ye tarriers, 686b
Drink a cup to Scotland, 489b
 a little in, 301b
 ale's the stuff to, 786b
 and the devil, 750a
 angel of the darker, 532a
 as he brews so shall he, 218a
 as I, 326b
 by daylight, 909b
 can rise alone and, more, 449b
 come my lad, some beer, 338a
 dance and, and sing, 387a
 deep or taste not, 310b
 divine, 219a
 dogs, at the river Nile, 48b
 easy meat and, 817a
 eat and, as friends, 130a
 eat, and be merry, 1043a, 1057a
 every creature, but I, 267b
 every one that lives must, 690a
 felony to, small beer, 125b
 first the man takes a, 712b
 five reasons we should, 288b
 follow strong, 1045a
 for the thirsty, 109b
 for your lips to, 692b
 from the well, 635b
 gapes for, again, 267a
 give him water to, 1041a
 give me to, mandragora, 200a
 give strong, 1041b
 has been arranged, 957a
 health to the wonders, 856b
 hero must, brandy, 342a
 if he thirst give him, 1060a
 in our comrades' eyes, 627b
 into my eyes the shine, 961b
 it down, 686a
 it up, 1016b
 it with pleasure, 1066a
 let us, and be merry, 262b
 let us eat and, 1046a
 little more than enough to, 788a
 live that they may eat and, 60b
 man takes his first, 801a
 meat, and cloaths, 1002b
 meat, and cloth, 90a
 moderate pleasant food and, 282b
 more fine than mine host's, 482b

Drink, never refuse, after dark, 909b
 never taste who always, 219b
 no longer water, 1063a
 no more than a sponge, 88a
 no sperit, 601a
 nor any drop to, 421b
 not the third glass, 232b
 not to elevation, 332a
 oblivion of a day, 638b
 old wine best to, 119a
 one man's poison is another's, 34b
 one, of wine, 963b
 out of my own, 163a
 pawn intelligence to buy a, 968b
 pretty creature, 406a
 provokes the desire, 196b
 sit down and, with me, 688a
 stagger but not with strong, 1046b
 strong, is raging, 1040a
 strong or not at all, 1014a
 sweetest, be cup of sorrow, 857a
 taken to, 847a
 takes a drink, 712b
 takes the man, 712b
 taste any, once, 900a
 the poppies of Cathay, 528a
 thirsty and ye gave me, 1054b
 to her that each loves best, 433a
 to me only with thine eyes, 219a
 to the general joy, 197b
 to the lass, 382a
 today drown all sorrow, 225a
 victuals and, 23a
 water of gall to, 1048a
 what to, and wear, 492a
 what wine he liked to, 72a
 when and what he pleaseth, 92b
 while you live, 532a
 wild anarchy of, 219b
 will not, with you, 144a
 with him that wears a hood, 97a
 with me, 326b
 women, or snuff, 972b
 ye all of it, 1055a
 your ale, 787a
Drinke, cannot make him, 92b
Drinkest tears of children, 449a
Drinking a quart of milk, 948a
 and Sabbath-breaking, 449b
 cursed him in, 451b
 die, in an inn, 74b
 examined after, 18b
 fresh with constant, 267a
 gently, up the dew, 687b
 I'm for, honestly, 896b
 jesting dancing, 786a
 kept on, 846b
 largely sobers us again, 310b
 laughing quaffing time, 280b
 leaving, of wine, 284a
 mad with, 774a
 much, little thinking, 295a
 my griefs, 140a
 not the, but excess, 227a
 now's the time for, 38b
 poor and unhappy brains for, 187b
 rule for, 300b
 the blude-red wine, 1011a
 thirsteth still, 649b
 very merry dancing, 280b
 what's, 460b

Drinks and gapes for drink again, 267a
 his wine with laughter, 1004b
 long time between, 752b
 side so low she, water, 117b
 two, and you strut, 963b
 when he is not thirsty, 1006b
Drink-shops, strolling among the, 66a
Drip huge drops on your neck, 959a
 slow, the seconds, 992b
Dripping apple-trees, 961b
 came up, 923a
 their snow, 946b
 with coolness, 450a
Drips, heavenly love that, 745b
Drive a coach and six, 1007a
 enemy beyond the frontier, 399b
 me down the slopes of hell, 891a
 nature out, 972b
 nyght away, 77b
 one heat, out another, 117a
 out nature with a fork, 41a
 the hearts of men, 37a
Driven, better bargain, 116a
 by their weakness to noise, 59b
 snow, whiter than the, 347a
Drives, as dust that, 741b
 fat oxen, 343a
 her ploughshare o'er creation, 306a
 horses of the sun, 738a
 needs must when Devil, 89b
 night along with them, 531a
Driving gale, catch the, 317b
 of Jehu, 1029a
 sand, thick as, 3b
 woman is, at one thing, 766a
Driv'n by the spheres, 272a
Drizling drops that often redound, 34b
Drizzle, Nashville, 801b
Drizzly night, filthy Jersey on a, 967b
Droghte of March, 79a
Droll, difference is, 891a
 situations, appreciate the, 744a
Droning flight, beetle wheels his, 348a
Dronkenesse sepulture of mannes wit, 82a
Droop sick of its business, 404b
Droop'd in the western sky, 609b
Drooping eye, one auspicious and one, 170a
 repairs his, head, 249b
Drop a tear and bid adieu, 329a
 dimpled, 809a
 every, hinders needle, 489a
 gentle words, 7a
 half a, into Lake Superior, 536b
 I always, a quarter, 713a
 injects a stinging, 801b
 into thy mother's lap, 258b
 it if I tried, 819a
 lurks that bitter, 690a
 nations as a, of a bucket, 1047a
 nor any, to drink, 421b
 of allaying Tiber, 202a
 of blood, less than a, 76b
 of my country's blood, 561b
 of their essence, 855b
 one, would save my soul, 123b
 'ow quick we'd, 'er, 819a
 ruddy, of manly blood, 507a

Drop tears fast as Arabian trees, 190b
 which makes it run over, 372a
you'd, a tear, 268a
Drope, never, retourne may, 77b
Dropp'd from the zenith, 253b
 manna, 253b
Dropped from angel's wing, 411b
Droppes of rain perce hard marble, 34b
Droppeth as gentle rain, 146a
Dropping a rose-petal down the Grand Canyon, 895b
 continual, 1041b
 continual, wears away a stone, 34b
 down the ladder, 819a
 from the clouds, 327b
 from the veils of morning, 824b
Drops, drip their huge, 959a
 drizling, that often redound, 34b
 earliest to ground, 145b
 kindred, mingled into one, 364a
 little, of light, 242a
 little, of water, 626b
 of rain, 521a, 1065b
 of water poured into milk, 803a
 out of touch, 876a
 ruddy, that visit my heart, 167a
 sacred pity engender'd, 161a
 thousand pearly, 755a
 who hath begotten, of dew, 1031b
Dross, gods call, 601b
 show of, 144b
Drought or tempest, 731a
 rain snow hail and, 675b
Drove, face that, me mad, 717a
 out the man, 1022a
Drown, careless eye on men who, 339a
 corn my tears did, 233a
 drink today, all sorrow, 225a
 me in thy sister flood, 129a
 my book, 210a
 nor water, it, 496b
 on Lac St. Pierre, 758b
 tears shall, the wind, 195b
 the brim, 183a
 what pain it was to, 127b
Drown'd my glory in a shallow cup, 533a
Drownded, only, now and again, 857a
Drowned, ceremony of innocence is, 826b
 chance of being, 339b
 dreams somnambulisms, 604b
 honour, pluck up, 149b
 I think the water, 'em, 714b
 in its waters, 699a
 man not afraid of sea soon, 857a
Drowning mark, 208b
 'scape, thrice, 144b
 would be happiness, 576a
Drowns, clatter, voice of the law, 33b
 flowing limb in pleasure, 328a
 third draught, 163b
Drows'd with the fume of poppies, 482b
Drowsily, classics, read at home, 505a
Drowsiness clothe a man with rags, 1040b
Drowsy at that hour, 241b

Drowsy emperor, 827a
 head, pleasing land of, 328b
 man, dull ear of, 148a
 numbness pains my sense, 481a
 syrups of the world, 188b
 tinklings lull, 348a
 with harmony, 133b
Drudge sold to futurity, 981a
Drudgery at the desk's dead wood, 430a
 women in, 996a
Drug, humour is a, 685b
Drugs are quick, 138a
 better for you than any, 566a
Drum, Bible and a, 809a
 ecclesiastic, 238a
 jubilant, 976a
 made of his skin, 221b
 not a, was heard, 464a
 rumble of a distant, 531b
 spirit-stirring, 189a
 take my, to England, 803b
 them up the Channel, 803b
 thundering, cries hark, 278b
 war, throbbed no longer, 549a
Drum-beat, morning, 444b
Drumfires, walking into the, 898b
Drummer, hears a different, 590b
Drum's discordant sound, 362a
Drums and fifes, 732a
 and guns, 1004a
 and tramplings, 241b
 beat the, 291a
 muffled, 521a
 ruffle of, 804b
 rum-tumming everywhere, 892a
 when the, begin to roll, 613a
Drunk, all learned and all, 365a
 and lived in social intercourse, 340b
 delight of battle, 548a
 for ever, 787a
 from the same canteen, 643b
 gloriously, 365a
 hasten to be, 281a
 he hath not, ink, 133a
 hearts were, with a beauty, 839b
 is he who prostrate lies, 449b
 milk of Paradise, 420b
 once, and once sober, 19a
 pleasure to be, 332b
 queen shall be as, 332b
 stag at eve had, his fill, 415a
 though he never was, 396a
 whisky and smoked, 841b
 with sight of power, 816a
 your water and wine, 813a
Drunkard and the glutton, 1040b
 rolling English, 867b
 town, 985a
Drunkard's eye, 827b
Drunkards, fools, and the United States, 1008a
 notorious, 705a
Drunken but not with wine, 1046b
 dog ragged head, 429a
 man, stagger like a, 1037a
 man, whispering like a, 968b
 of things Lethean, 693a
 private of the Buffs, 558a
 sailor, lives like a, 128a
 scenes rattles, 429a
Drunkenness, babbling, 165b
 four degrees of, 497a
 identical with ruin, 72b
Dry all streams, 444b
 and thirsty land, 1035a
 as summer dust, 410b

Dry, books poky dull and, 847b
 death, fain die a, 208b
 desert of a thousand lines, 320b
 do so much in the, 105b
 drudgery, 430a
 fields burn, 716b
 good, oats, 142a
 good wine a friend or being, 288b
 hand a moist eye, 152b
 hot cold moist and, 102a, 254b
 I being, sit idly sipping, 664a
 keep your powder, 434a
 land, hands formed the, 1036b
 land, made the sea, 1024b
 light, perfect soul is a, 53a
 Martini, into a, 941a
 of blood, 480a
 one's eyes, 569a
 place, rivers in a, 1046b
 smooth-shaven green, 246a
 sun dry wind, 96b
 the starting tear, 681b
 them wither them, 222a
 time, your Mississippi in, 889b
 volumes of ethics, 373a
 weather will be, 803a
 well runs, 653b
 wine before sighs did, it, 233a
 wrung life, for your lips, 692b
Dryad, light-winged, of the trees, 481a
Dryden, copious, 320b
Drying up a single tear, 459a
Dub as gentlemen, 591a
Ducat, dead for a, 176b
Ducats, O my, 144b
Ducdame, name kind of, 160b
 what's that, 160b
Duchess, my last, 569b
 talking of axes said the, 656b
Duck, father carves the, 861b
 or plover, 380b
 saw a little, 1019b
Ducks and drakes with shillings, 116b
Duds of daring, 795a
Due, by, steps aspire, 246b
 give devil his, 104b
 give the credit, 309a
 more is thy, 194b
 season, word spoken in, 1039b
 that lifts it, 809a
 time, born out of my, 666b
 to gentle breeding, 14b
Dues of fellowship, 520a
Duke, every body praised the, 426b
 marquis, and a' that, 394a
 of Florence, 119b
 of Plaza Toro, 685b
 of Wellington's army, 345a
Dukedom, library was, large enough, 209a
 prize above my, 209a
Dulcimer, damsel with a, 420b
 on her, she played, 420b
Dull academic half-dozen, 883a
 age is, and mean, 527a
 and damp without, 560a
 and flowerless weed, 526b
 art, living nature not, 495b
 but eminent, 960a
 care, begone, 1000a
 care, challenge to, 435a
 catalogue of common things, 480b
 cold ear of death, 348b
 cold marble, 211b

Equal, death makes, high and low, 9ct
 division of unequal earnings, 441b
 ease unto my pain, 236b
 evils, when extreme, 243a
 eye, who sees with, 316a
 favor was, for both sides, 18b
 foot, with his eye, 126b
 hope, better or, 539a
 I am, and whole, 694b
 in the presence of death, 43a
 independence is, 891a
 inferiors revolt to be, 26b
 justice to all, 20a
 man mine, 1034b
 piece of justice, 240b
 portion, everyone take an, 60a
 power to maintain rights, 517b
 protection, 399a
 purpose, to the deed, 305b
 remember what he gets from an, 822a
 right of men and women, 998a
 scale, weighing in, 170a
 sky, admitted to that, 316a
 station, separate and, 373a
 syllables alone require, 311a
 thanks, 175b
 to a brother, 7b
 to all things, 357b
 to distance between fingers, 50a
 to those it does not concern, 497a
 velocity nothing human can, 19b
 which the tallest pine, 252b
Equality, believe in, of man, 371a
 justice and humanity, 842a
 liberty and, in democracy, 26b
 liberty, fraternity, 1010b
 of rights, 917b
 on earth is death, 586a
 permanent, of property, 515b
 shall not produce, 955b
 to equals and unequals, 25a
Equalizer, great, in the world, 743b
Equally balanced, opposite parties, 26b
 distributed, good sense is, 237a
Equals and unequals, equality to, 25a
 disinterested commerce between, 355a
 peace between, 770b
 revolt to be superior, 26b
Equanimity, cultivate such a measure of, 744a
 more supportable with, 670b
Equator, got as far as the, 564b
 speak disrespectfully of the, 418b
Equators, north poles and, 659b
Equilibrists lie here, 947a
Equilibrium, temporary, 905a
Equinox, who knows when was the, 241b
Equinoxes, precession of the, 557a
Equipment, shabby, deteriorating, 945a
Equitable of men, to the most, 45a
Equity a roguish thing, 227a
 according to conscience, 227a
 heir in, 878b
Equivocate, I will not, 517a
Equivocation will undo us, 178b
Era, dated a new, in his life, 50ca
 of wonderful nonsense, 970b
Eras when, die, 827b

Erasings of chords most fit, 716b
Ercles' vein, 141a
Ere, oon, it herde, 78b
Erebus, dark as, 147a
Erect and strong, 519b
 he can, himself, 122a
 the manly foe, 401b
Erected, least, spirit, 253a
 look, 278a
Erecting a grammar-school, 125b
Erection, cost of, 153a
Erects house of prayer, 291b
Eremite, nature's patient sleepless, 479b
Eres, wode hath, 80b
Erg and atom, 977b
Ermined and minked, 805a
 goosegirl, 981b
Ernulphus cursed, 346a
'Eroes, thin red, 817b
 thin red line of, 613a
Eros, mock not, 956b
Erotic emotion, 778a
Err, art may, 281a
 better to, with Pope, 452a
 causeth all men to, 1065a
 fifty times to one does, 289a
 from right path, 14b
 I prefer to, with Plato, 34a
 in opinion is human, 62a
 reas'ning but to, 316b
 to, is human, 311b
Errand, joyous, 533b
 sleveless, 91b
 Tom Fool's, 345b
Errand-boy in heaven, 604b
Erred, we have, 1068a
Erring, frail and, men, 952a
 judgment, blind man's, 310b
 men call chance, 248a
 reason's spite, 316b
 rod to check the, 409b
 sister's shame, 455a
 spirit, extravagant and, 170a
 thought not into evil, 689b
Erroneous conclusions, 500b
 soul of truth in things, 614b
Error chokes windows of the mind, 213b
 delay is preferable to, 374a
 force that welds men together, 642b
 give me a fruitful, 740a
 guilty of no, 435b
 has its martyrs, 324b
 human, is impatience, 927b
 ignorance is preferable to, 373b
 in narration, 74a
 in reas'ning pride our, lies, 316a
 is a hardy plant, 561a
 is immense, 303b
 men are liable to, 283a
 of opinion tolerated, 25 **a**, 374b
 of the moon, 190a
 of the would-be scholar, 510b
 old and gray-headed, 241a
 only, to be exposed, 908b
 pardon, 326a
 progress will destroy all, 617a
 redeem the human mind from, 522a
 reformers of, 375a
 show a man he is in, 283a
 sink of uncertainty and, 273a
 stronger than the hosts of, 793a
 troops of, 240a
 upon me prov'd, 207a
 wounded writhes in pain, 471b
Error's shore, wreck on, 673b

Errors are volitional, 917a
 committed many gross, 109a
 correct, shown to be errors, 539b
 ere, agonies and fears, 673b
 like straws, 276a
 more harmful than reasoned, 634a
 some female, fall, 312a
 stratagems which, seem, 310b
Errs in so considerable a passage, 109a
 man, while struggle lasts, 379b
Eruption, some strange, 169b
Eruptions, strange, 150b
Esau, hands of, 1023a
 swapped his copyright, 800b
Escape calumny, 175a
 every other danger, 27b
 from rope and gun, 308b
 let no guilty man, 623b
 make your, in time, 462a
 me never beloved, 569a
 never could, love, 73a
 poetry an, from emotion, 943b
 several quality nor worth, thee, 68a
 to outer air, 37a
 we cannot, history, 540a
Escaped from the deep sea, 75a
 with the skin of my teeth, 1031a
Escaping into truth, 994a
Escurial, thou art to me the, 234a
 Tuileries or the, 502b
Eskimo, little frosty, 750b
 Ootah the, 763b
Espied a feather of his own, 11b
 an old man, 264a
Espouse the everlasting sea, 407a
Espoused at the expense of life, 98b
 saint, my late, 251b
Essay a loose sally of mind, 336b
 in Atlantic Monthly, 908b
 make a short, 281a
Essayist atheist novelist realist, 556b
 typical, 793b
Essence and characteristic faculty, 722a
 fellowship with, 479a
 glassy, 184b
 impalpable drop of their, 855b
 is love, 472b
 look to the, of a thing, 68b
 love is God's, 672b
 of picture is the frame, 866b
 of inhumanity, 765a
Essences, two unbodied, 262b
Essential and unalienable rights, 373a
 articles, agree in, 339b
 comforts of life, 484a
 facts of life, 590a
 gaudiness of poetry, 906a
 liberty, give up, 331a
 poetry, 424a
 reality of creatures, 939b
 service to his country, 295b
 special and, product, 593b
 thing for happiness, 744b
 thing in form, 906a
 things more, 274a
 to see his good qualities, 472b
Essex Junction, who invented, 625b
Establish in the name of God, 903a
 school of the Lord's service, 73b
 the work of our hands, 1036a

Evils, greatest of, is poverty, 765b
 in government, 399a
 less grievous of two, 462a
 of all outward, 473a
 of idleness, 47a
 of two, the less, 27a
 old age accompanied with, 59b
 other, will mend, 491a
 past, and future evils, 264b
 present, triumph over it, 264b
 religion could urge mankind to, 34b
 three great, 325a
 two, monstrous, 946b
 two weak, 161a
 which never arrived, 507a
 with all its threatening, 611a
 working, for another, 7a
Ev'ning, grateful, mild, 256a
Evolution is not a force, 700a
 of things that wouldn't evolve, 777b
 some call it, 573b
Evolve, things that wouldn't, 777b
Ev'rywhere, sad and dreary, I roam, 636a
Ewe lamb, save one little, 1028a
Ewe-milking, lilting at our, 992b
Ex umbris and imaginibus, 496a
Exact day-labour, 251b
 justice to all men, 374b
 line was rigid and, 613a
 man, writing maketh an, 121b
Exacted through taxation, 689a
Exaction becomes ruthless extortion, 689a
Exactness and discrimination, 340b
 of beauty, 82a
 with, grinds he all, 522b
Exacts, life, for granting peace, 981b
Exaggerated, reports of my death are, 679a
Exaggeration, become crimes by, 496b
 chargeable with no, 435b
Exaltation from proximity of disaster, 868a
 of fortune or feeling, 651a
 of the defective, 776a
Exalted, every valley shall be, 1047a
 humble shall be, 1054a
 ideas of fancy, 22b
 Satan, sat, 253b
 them of low degree, 1056a
Exalts delights or adorns humanity, 449b
Examination, manners are always under, 505a
 minute, of facts, 897b
 of acts of government, 426a
Examine, I pause I, 101b
 laws of heat, 700a
 medicine has to, disease, 57b
Examined a second time, 18b
Example, annoyance of a good, 678b
 is the best precept, 10b
 more efficacious than precept, 10b
 of wit, 284b
 results of his own, 48b
 salutary influence of, 337b
 set us a good, 769a
 take an, from others, 33a
 terrible, 257a
 the school of mankind, 361b
 thy stream my great, 266b

Example you with thievery, 203b
Examples, good, of wise men, 55a
 philosophy teaching by, 304a
 provide bad, 265a
Exceed, flies worms and flowers, me, 302b
 never, your rights, 344a
Exceedin' accommodatin' character, 664b
Exceeding fair she was not, 116b
 poor man, 144a
 wise fair-spoken, 212a
Exceeds, half, the whole, 7a
 man's might, 182a
Excel, age, in pride of life, 620b
 arts in which the wise, 289b
 how much does one man, another, 31b
 in any profession, 435a
 in rituals and faith, 635a
 the bees for government, 102b
 those he pursues, 41a
 'tis useless to, 343b
Excellence, based on, of performance, 965a
 claim of, is recognized, 20a
 constant is a wondrous, 206b
 fair divided, 147b
 incredible standards of, 978b
 of what is in their hands, 15a
 to maturity, 46a
Excellencies, dwell upon, than imperfections, 300b
 of lively conversation, 372a
Excellent angler now with God, 236a
 beauty, 121a
 campaigning weather, 981a
 canopy the air, 173b
 dumb discourse, 209b
 everything that's, 683b
 fancy, 178b
 foppery of the world, 190b
 good, so so is very, 163a
 herb, 820a
 immodesty, 984a
 is thy name, 1032b
 lies before us, 398a
 marriage, 585b
 mastiffe, 284b
 mediocrity of ancient times, 101a
 no, soul is exempt, 48a
 old way, 825a
 original, just to an, 313b
 situation, 754b
 thing in woman, 193b
 things as difficult as rare, 283a
 things that are more, 781a
 to have a giant's strength, 184b
 to make a poet, 240a
 Watson cried, 782a
 wit, proverb old of, 524b
 works, largest number of, 325a
 wretch, 188a
Excellest, thou, them all, 1042a
Excelling nature, pattern of, 190a
Excels all other bliss, 101b
 at a plan or title-page, 353a
 good stomach, them all, 288a
 in something, 43a
 quirks of blazoning pens, 187a
Excelsior, strange device, 522a
Exception, admits not some, 222a
 painful to be an, 558b
Exceptional man deteriorated, 727a
Excepts, guilty man, 279a
Excess, give me, of it, 163b
 moderation even in, 511a

Excess, not the drinking but the, 227a
 nothing in, 31b, 69b
 of glory obscur'd, 253a
 of my responsive youth, 720a
 of severity, 700b
 of stupidity, 340a
 of wealth, 124a
 power in, 120a
 reform carried to an, 424a
 scant this, 145b
 surprise by a fine, 478a
 wasteful and ridiculous, 148a
Excessive, dark with, bright, 254b
 literary production, 596b
 politeness, treated me with, 909a
Exchange, credited to, 912a
 green, 936a
 of good offices, 265a
 of mutual protection, 26a
 one for the other given, 115b
 such wonders to, 949a
Exchanged hearts, 262a
Exchequer of the poor, 139a
 rob, 151a
Excise a hateful tax, 336b
 those to whom, is paid, 336b
Excite my amorous propensities, 339a
 us to love a woman, 105b
Excited abnormal exhausting condition, 765b
Excitement, hurried away by, 64b
 insane, at first, 697b
 of the heart, 545a
Excites envy, 290a
 the public odium, 433b
 us to arms, 278b
Exciting, found it less, 685b
Exclaim against second marriages, 333b
Excludes, infinite day, the night, 303a
 not till the sun, you, 610a
Exclusion, built colony on principle of, 629a
Exclusive predominance, 910b
 worms, 966b
Exclusiveness in our public life, 20a
Excrement, stolen from general, 203b
Excrescence superabundance, 981a
Excus'd his devilish deeds, 45a, 255b
Excuse, any, will serve a tyrant, 9b
 beauty is its own, 503b, 526b
 came prologue, 258b
 coy, 248b
 every man will plead, 227b
 fault worse by, 148b
 I will not, 517a
 in this delay, 136b
 lose without, 861b
 not a single, 816b
 prove an, for the glass, 382a
 thou make in this delay, 136b
Excuses, contests allow no, 12a
 himself, 97a
 ignorance, no man, 227b
 patch'd up your, 200b
Excusing, by, nothing pure love shows, 270a
 fault, 148b
Execrable shape, 254b
 scum of all villanies, 329b
Executant, no limit to attempt as an, 718b

Experienced angler, 788a
  industrious ambitious liar, 677b
  nothing real till it is, 478b
  too, a parent, 956b
Experiences, digests, like meats, 727b
  made by men and women, 770a
  of a great people, 770a
Experiencing, healed by, it to full, 856a
Experiment, frequency of, 338a
  great social and economic, 873b
  life is an, 710a
  man who makes the, 41b
  of dying, 243a
  on animals is justifiable, 530b
Experimental evidence, boundary of, 614a
  method of research, 530b
  youth is wholly, 753b
Experimentation, bold persistent, 918b
Experiments efforts discoveries successes, 718b
  fools', 530b
Expert knows more and more, 799a
  war, is a man ye niver heerd iv, 834b
Expired exultations, 809b
Expires in arms of an apothecary, 418a
  unawares morality, 322a
Expiring frog, 576a
Explain, spoil it by trying to, it, 381a
  the asking eye, 319b
  till all men doubt it, 322a
  time will, it all, 17b
Explanation, author's, 961a
  inaccuracy saves, 851b
  of a poem, 961a
Expletives their feeble aid do join, 311a
Explicitness not a necessary virtue, 823b
Explode a huge laugh, 804b
Exploits iv a brave man, 834b
  relating his own, 282a
Explorations, revel in long, 739a
Explore, learn'd is happy Nature to, 317a
  the horizon for a successor, 504a
  the thought, 319b
Explores His lowest hell, 704b
Exponent of breath, 647b
Expos'd on bare earth, 280a
Exposed him to evils of night, 264a
  intellect is improperly, 419a
  only error to be, 908b
Exposition of sleep, 142a
Express and admirable, 173b
  know but can't, 366b
  our wants, 286b
Express'd, but ne'er so well, 311a
  in fancy, 112a, 171b
Expressed, expression that cannot be, 606b
Expresses, how much it, 538b
Expressing itself beyond expression, 218b
Expression, brief in, 436b
  expressing itself beyond, 218b
  favourite, of Theophrastus, 71b
  freedom of speech and, 920b
  identical with ruin, 72b
  impassioned, 406a
  indescribable, 652b

Expression, modern manners of, 314a
  most perfect, of scorn, 766b
  natural, of villainy, 674b
  of this man's face, 610b
  poetry not, of personality, 943b
  that can not be expressed, 606b
  this, of ours, 65b
  thoughts which have not found, 822b
Expressive silence, come then, 328a
Exprest even such beauty, 206b
Expunge, fool enough to, 342a
Exquisite and strong, 291b
  joys too, to last, 412b
  music, ceasing of, 522b
  passions, 701b
  products of civilization, 932a
  song, nature sings her, 668b
  the bliss, 391b
  things, fail in attempting, 805b
  touch is denied me, 428b
Extempore, public, speech, 624b
Extend a simple maxim, 333a
  freedom to everyone, 964a
Extended wings, on, 906a
Extensive and honourable conquests, 360b
  observation observe, 335b
  scene of crowds, 369b
  view, observation with, 335b
Extensively observe mankind, 336a
Extent, learn, of our inheritance, 613b
  long, of life, 16b
  of its beauty and power, 492a
  pardon to the, that we love, 266a
Extenuate, for the brandy, nothing, 509b
  nothing, 190a
  the miseries of the past, 940b
Exterior, fair, is recommendation, 44a
  things, depends less on, 362b
External and visible evil and good, 630a
  fact, indifference to, 948a
  forms, differ widely in, 339b
  life, ideal or picture of, 761b
  ordinances, reimpressed by, 337b
  public grown superficial and, 795b
  things, care for, 701b
  things, describing, 867a
  trappings, 700a
Extinct, love that was sleeping not, 992b
  sole purpose of becoming, 926b
Extinction, course of ultimate, 537b
  endless, of unhappy hates, 621b
Extinguished, fire which seems, 243b
  his class is, with him, 504a
  his soul, 538a
  in the heart of man, 345a
  power guided not, 613b
Extinguisher, frown is no, 587b
Extinguishes natural candle, 288b
Extol, how shall we, thee, 798b
  the absent city, 40b
Extolling the past, 419b
Extortion, exaction becomes ruthless, 689a

Extortions cheerfully accepted, 951b
Extra bottle of Johannisberg, 381b
Extract from phenomena of nature, 916a
Extracted from many objects, 162b
Extracting sunbeams, 295b
Extraordinarily, sweat, 152b
Extraordinary rains fall, 55a
Extravagance, calls his generosity, 355a
  was clothes, 741a
Extravagant and erring spirit, 170a
  flaunting, quean, 381b
Extreme actions ascribed to vanity, 726a
  evils equal when they are, 243a
  had having and in quest to have, 207a
  law extreme injustice, 32b
  license, blossom into, 287b
  of wickedness or folly, 539a
  perplex'd in the, 190b
  remedies for extreme diseases, 22a
  savage, rude cruel, 207a
Extremes, avoid all, 53b
  bitter change of fierce, 254a
  fate of all, is such, 314a
  meet, 372a
  prevents, being dominant, 26b
  two, of passion, 193b
  utmost, 626b
Extremity, daring plot in, 276b
Exuberance of his own verbosity, 513a
  of miniature human beings, 985a
  sprouting out in wonderful, 537b
Exuberant spirits, 727b
Exudations of a man's brains, 346a
Exuding promises of Sunday mention, 973a
Exult, be secret and, 826a
  dare not suffer and cannot, 896a
  O shores, 610a
Exultation, a discoverer can experience, 940b
Exultations agonies and love, 407a
  expired, 809b
Eye, adorned in her husband's, 403a
  affection beaming in one, 577b
  and prospect of soul, 158b
  any, is an evil eye, 881b
  apple of his, 1026a
  apple of the, 1032b
  auspicious, 170a
  bear welcome in your, 195a
  beauteous, of heaven, 148a
  bend your, on vacancy, 177a
  careless, on men who drown, 339a
  cast a cold, on life, 828a
  cast a longing, 374a
  cast thine, on thine own fault, 635a
  casts a, 107b
  close, of day, 250a
  crack his glass, 886b
  day's garish, 246b
  defiance in their, 354a
  destroy the, of another, 3b
  discern with this clear, 588b
  distinguish by the, 47b

Fighting against valuation of Europe, 718a
  bellyful of, 204a
  cocks that will kill, 59a
  faiths, time has upset, 710a
  flocking and, 260b
  for the crown, 1015a
  in the streets, 332b
  lovely, along the whole line, 663a
  men abroad, 520b
  no talking until more, 974a
  races don't die out, 734b
  still and still destroying, 280a
  Téméraire, 803b
  the lost fight of virtue, 752b
  valour in feasting as in, 222a
  war consisteth not in, 229a
  what are we, for, 877b
  world worth, for, 983a
Fighting's, wherever, the game, 734b
Fights and runs away, 69a
  engage in bloody, 3b
  liquor love or, 787a
  quote the, historical, 682b
  strives and, and frets, 476b
  tea, 821b
Figs from thistles, 780b
  in the name of the prophet, 436b
  out of thistles, 555a
Figurative, life like the Scriptures, 480a
Figure, baby, of the giant mass, 181b, 832a
  fixed, for the time of scorn, 189b
  is handsome, 701a
  Lord Byron cuts a, 480a
  no, in company, 338a
  of its master's income, 913a
  of man at twice its size, 923b
  of the house, 153a
  seven is a good handy, 883a
  the thing we like, 494b
Figures and patterns, 53b
  facts and, 578a
  fallacious as facts except, 419b
  on a dial, 586a
  rude, of rough-hewn race, 814a
Filches from me my good name, 188a
File, marching single in endless, 506b
Files, burial in the, 817a
  commands the beauteous, 271b
  of time, 549a
Files-on-parade, 817b
Filial duty, lasting sense of, 373a
  reverence, act of, 795b
Filipinos, Norwegians or, 954b
Fill all the glasses there, 267b
  belly with the east wind, 1030b
  blown his, 246b
  come, up my cup, 417b
  ev'ry glass, 308b
  high the bowl, 458b
  his snuff-box, 293a
  hungry bellies, 229b
  many words won't, a bushel, 331a
  me from crown to toe, 195a
  sky with black clouds, 39b
  stag at eve had drunk his, 415a
  strike your, 234a
  the fife, 416b
  the life of man, 695a
  the stage with childhood, 232a

Fill the world with fools, 615a
  their lives with sweetness, 643a
  up a place, 159a
  up their proper places, 273a
Fill'd air with barbarous dissonance, 248a
  rosebuds, with snow, 221a
  sails, 260a
Filled, belly, with fair words, 55a
  body, and vacant mind, 156a
  by prevailing light, 100a
  hungry with good things, 1056a
  little barn well, 377b
  they shall be, 1050b
  wallet, with our vices, 35a
  with gravel, 1040a
  with noble risks, 418a
  with the Holy Ghost, 1059a
Filler for cross-word puzzle makers, 928a
Fillet, scorn under her solemn, 506b
Filleth all around about, 120a
Fillin' food, lithrachoor needs, 837a
Filling sky and earth below, 632a
  two buckets, one another, 140a
Fills, grief, room, 148a
  he, he bounds connects, 316b
Filly, foal in likeness of a, 141a
Filthy air, the fog and, 194a
  Jersey on a drizzly night, 967b
  lucre, 1063a
  rags, righteousnesses as, 1047b
  so, that nobody dared touch them, 494a
Fin, gold, in the porphyry font, 551a
Final hope is flat despair, 126a
  issue, judged in light of, 27b
  proof of greatness, 763a
  resting-place, 540b
  ruin fiercely drives, 306a
  sacrifice, 789a
  test of a leader, 952b
Finality, obstinate, 720a
Finance, heroes of, are like beads, 641a
Financial straits, serving one in, 21b
  throe volcanic, 777a
Find, criticism is the endeavor to, 733a
  fail to, you in, 830b
  faithful friends hard to, 220a
  fast bind fast, 91a
  fault, people talk and, 104a
  few there be that, it, 1052a
  fit instruments of ill, 312b
  happiness she does not, 336a
  himself left alone, 339a
  his mouth a rein, 693a
  Iris that shall, thee out, 125b
  it after many days, 1043b
  it among gross people, 338a
  know where we can, information, 341a
  me the men on earth, 652b
  means of evil, 252b
  mind's construction, 194b
  myself forty-three pounds worse, 284b
  myself much better, 284a
  not obliged to, understanding, 343a
  out cause of this effect, 173b
  out moonshine, 142a
  out the natural bent, 25a
  out where she has gone, 825a

Find quarrel in a straw, 177b
  rest from vain fancies, 66a
  safe bind safe, 96b
  seek and ye shall, 1051b
  seeking shall, him, 570b
  sure to, a use for it, 417b
  surprised to, it done, 340a
  the one just suited, 433a
  the other forth, 143b
  the virtue, 158b
  themselves, 754b
  things very much as always, 858b
  thy heart at home, 232a
  time to grow old, 306b
  to dream of not to, 967b
  to seek to, and not to yield, 548b
  turn to pleasure all they, 326b
  wealth ye, another keeps, 466a
  what I tell you is so, 608b
  what wisdom can you, 344b
Findeth, he that, his life, 1052b
  he that seeketh, 1051b
Finding smoother pebble, 288a
  withhold a single, 379b
Finds comfort in despair, 125a
  he who, himself, 620a
  Satan, some mischief, 302b
  young keeps young, 262a
Fine and independent living, 784a
  array, my silks and, 384b
  arts divorcing themselves from truth, 476a
  arts, music highest of, 614b
  by defect, 314b
  careless rapture, 569a
  coffin, out of white boards, 856b
  dress'd, as I will, 302b
  excess, surprise by a, 478a
  face of heaven so, 136b
  feathers make fine birds, 10a
  fellows, some are, 638b
  frenzy, 142b
  grave's a, and private place, 269a
  he may be just as, 975b
  how vast the, 309b
  issues, 183b
  less subtle and, 250a
  madness, 122b
  manners need support, 505b
  many, things to do, 891a
  nets and stratagems, 233a
  not for a, glossy surface, 354b
  passage you think, 341a
  rapture is over, 981b
  sense men call courtesy, 587a
  song for singing, 752a
  spun from a mind at peace, 42b
  thinking, worlds of, 449b
  too, a point, 579b
  work with so, a brush, 428b
Finer man, he had made a, 800a
Finery, modest woman in all her, 357a
Finest ambrosia, 810a
  edge is made, 112a
  hour, 869b
  spectacles in nature, 331a
  thing in London, 854a
  woman in nature, 301b
Finger ache, let our, 107a
  ambitious, 210a
  God's, touch'd him, 552b
  in every pie, 104b
  little, was in it, 104b
  more goodness in her little, 296b

Firm cloud before it fall, choose a, 314b
  ground of result and fact, 868a
  nerves shall never tremble, 198a
  of Grin and Barrett, 777a
  philosopher can scorn, 328a
  purpose, is equal to the deed, 305b
  reason, 409a
  stand like a, tower, 76a
  to this scoundrel maxim, 328b
  too tender or too, a heart, 313b
Firmament, absorb as, a flame, 648b
  base earth from, 139a
  blood streams in the, 123b
  brave o'erhanging, 173b
  curses of the, 281b
  glow'd with sapphires, 255b
  no fellow in the, 167b
  showeth his handiwork, 1032b
  spacious, on high, 299a
  state beneath the, 102b
Firmest flint doth weare, 34b
  friend, 451b
  in his shoes, 505a
  in the right, 542a
Firm-set, sure and, earth, 196a
Firs, great army of pointed, 742b
First, after last returns the, 573a
  among languages, 325a
  and second class citizens, 964a
  and the last, 1065a
  and wisest of them all, 259b
  and worst of all frauds, 586a
  author of that thought, 508a
  baby laughed, 792a
  begs pardon, 162a
  best country, 353b
  book was published, 792b
  breath our souls draw, 655a
  bringer of unwelcome news, 152a
  by whom the new are tried, 311a
  class laundry, 845a
  comer sped, 275b
  cunning tyrant, subjects of, 538a
  day, 1021a
  day even and morn, 257a
  day of spring, 757b
  days of distracting grief, 352b
  death, no other after the, 997a
  dream that comes, 736b
  drink, man takes his, 801a
  families in Virginia, 980a
  fault, clung to their, 567a
  fine careless rapture, 569a
  flower of their wilderness, 463b
  found her, and best, 817a
  garden made, 121a
  gentleman on earth, 853a
  glass for myself, 300b
  good die, 410b
  great benefactor, 678a
  guinea is more difficult, 344a
  highest compliment to the, 340b
  his, wife, 340b
  Homer, of heroic poets, 338b
  how, he met her, 564a
  human principle, 153b
  husband, detested her, 768a
  I had thee, 693b
  if not, in the first line, 358a
  in banquets, 4a
  in everything, one cannot be, 10a
  in war first in peace, 384a

First inclination an animal has, 72b
  is freedom of speech, 920b
  is law the last prerogative, 279a
  keep their, and have no second, 853a
  last everlasting day, 216a
  last was like the, 962a
  law of society, 960a
  lesson to be learned, 634a
  light was, named day, 74a
  magnitude, liar of the, 297b
  man among these fellows, 56b
  man of earth earthy, 1061b
  man's, disobedience, 251b
  morning shining and pure, 876a
  motion of a dreadful thing, 167a
  no last nor, 567b
  of my roaming, 762a
  of speech, 525b
  old civilization, 976b
  original right of the people, 1001b
  part of life, make use of, 288b
  passion, women in their, 266a
  person, in the, 1005b
  place is safe for no one, 46b
  planted a garden, 121a
  proud wish to be, 282b
  rank, battle of the, 497a
  rate, make the work, 709b
  rather be, in this town, 56b
  ripest fruit, falls, 139a
  say what you would be, 65a
  shall be last, 1053b
  sight, loved at, 123a
  sprightly running, 276a
  spring day, 757b
  step which counts, 327a
  Supernatural Bank, 946b
  sweet sleep of night, 466b
  tall silver poplar trees, 888b
  the infant, 161a
  time, does a thing for the, 651a
  to attack neighbours, 270a
  to be touch'd by thorns, 438a
  to fade away, 441a
  true gentleman, 215a
  voice I uttered, 49b, 1065b
  who was king, 324b
  wife, adored his, 768b
  woman's, love, 769a
  word that Sir Patrick read, 1011b
  words immigrant heard, 906b
  writers are first, 934a
  years of man, 337a
F.F.V.s, start counting, 980a
Firstborn, offspring of heav'n, 254b
  smite all the, 1024a
  son, brought forth her, 1050a, 1056a
First-class fightin' man, 818a
  men, training-school for, 611a
Firste vertu, 82b
Firstfruits of them that slept, 1061b
Firstling of the infant year, 237a
First-rate intelligence, 974b
  man is, 596b
Fir-trees dark and high, 488a
Fish, all is, that comth to net, 93a
  and guests, 774b
  belly of the, 1049b
  cat would eate, 93a
  cat's averse to, 347b
  crier, Jew, 898a
  dinners make man spring, 262b
  English literature a flying, 901b

Fish fiddle de-dee, 582a
  game, swims up stream, 778a
  I was a, 780a
  in troubled waters, 292b
  leap like little, 955a
  Martin Barton and, 920b
  never lost a little, 746b
  no more land say, 938a
  no, ye're buying, 416a
  nor flesh, 92a
  not with melancholy bait, 143a
  of the sea, 1021a
  other, to fry, 90a
  pleasant'st angling is to see, 157b
  poets like stinking, 425b
  pretty kettle of, 684a
  sensible, swims down, 778a
  sold for more than an ox, 59b
  swam over the syllabub sea, 581b
  terribly glad to be selling, 898a
  that hath fed of that worm, 177b
  that swim or swish, 887a
  the whale is not a table, 848a
  this, will bite, 157b
  we catched, and talked, 676b
  with the worm, 177b
Fishball, one, the waiter roars, 628a
Fish-balls on Sunday morning, 805a
Fisherman's boy, 549b
Fishermen that walk upon the beach, 193a
Fisher's chorus-note, 395b
Fishers of men, 1050b
  of song, 777b
Fishes, all the worse for the, 536b
  caught, in other men's ditches, 1020a
  five loaves and two, 1053a
  make little, talk, 358a
  marvel how, live in sea, 203b
  men lived like, 203b
  that tipple in the deep, 268a
  welcomes little, in, 656a
Fishified, how art thou, 136a
Fishing boats, fleet of, 989a
  never blow when he goes a, 235b
Fish-like, ancient and, smell, 209b
Fist instead of a stick, 238a
Fit and qualify men, 273a
  bed for this huge birth, 263b
  carcass, for hounds, 167a
  crooked counsels, 276b
  dish, for the gods, 167a
  for the kingdom of God, 1056b
  for treasons, 147a
  found, for the business, 293a
  in square hole, 679b
  instruments of ill, 312b
  instruments to make slaves, 334b
  must be, for it, 605a
  night for man or beast, 901a
  not, to compare men with gods, 35b
  of laughter, 24a
  only the, survive, 877a
  ordinary men are, 191a
  punishment, the crime, 685a
  request should be followed, 76a
  them to our brows, 979a
  to catch it, 341b
  to hold a candle, 323a
  to write upon it, 847b

Friends, family or, to aid you, 562a
few, and many books, 267a
flatterers from, 42a
for the sake of our, 33b
forgive our, 119b
forsake me, 469b
four, in the world, 272a
gifts to, 16b
go with anyone to death, 879b
golden, I had, 786a
good book the best of, 561a
hath he not always, 423b
have dropped off, 566b
have perished so, 668a
he who has a thousand, 73b
held up of his, 1066a
his foes as well as his, 772b
his truth proclaim, 277a
host of, while fortune smiles, 43a
house of my, 1049b
how to win, 942b
humblest, scorn not one, 412a
I have old and young, 668a
I write for money, 736b
if your, are sore, 320a
ignoring advice of, 616a
in peace, 373b
in the thirties we want, 975a
invalidated by marriage of his, 671b
joy has its, 970a
joy to, 6a
just, and brave enemies, 375a
keep a few, 752b
keep, with himself, 752b
kind hearts for, to fill, 751b
kindred comrades lovers, 630a
lapp'd in lead, 220a
laugh at your, 320a
laughter and the love of, 849a
lay down his life for his, 1058b
little, may prove great friends, 9b
live without, 653a
look upon my quiet face, 733a
look with as much love as his, 284a
make foes their, 510b
makes, without half trying, 862b
man that hath, 1040a
many many lady, 794b
misfortune of our best, 266a
more we love our, 270a
most constant of all, 655b
multitude of, 218a
nearest, are auldest friends, 751b
never-failing, 426b
new, leave the heart aglow, 830a
of a few fortunate readers, 778b
of my youth, 1011a
of our childhood, 529a
of the unlucky, 16b
old, are best, 119a
old, are most too home-like, 775a
old, best to trust, 119a
one or two, worth the name, 788a
one's, one can manage, 842a
opened a tavern for his, 840a
people people have for, 794a
perfidious, 119b
poor but honest, 183a
power in the hands of, 697b
quote one of my, 101a

Friends, remembering good, 139a
Romans countrymen, 168a
sacrifices of his, 954b
second glass for my, 300b
see what, I please, 319a
separateth very, 1039b
servant of parted, 666b
show me his, 643b
sing among their, 40a
soon be, again, 14b
spare to us our, 753b
sweet, farewell, 76b
teaches beasts to know, 202a
that I knew in my Maying, 762a
three firm, 423b
three good, 161b
thrice blessed are our, 889b
thrust away by his, 1066a
to behave to us, 71b
to congratulate friends, 278a
troops of, 199a
true, appear less mov'd, 42a
trust no, 12b
two bodies with one soul, 5a
warm with the, I make, 962b
we are not enemies but, 539b
we love so dear, 666b
we need new, 823a
wealth maketh many, 1040a
when, are dear, 372b
who come and gape and go, 622b
who frequent a house, 507b
who set forth at our side, 623a
wife children and, 403a
wise are never without, 1003a
women find few real, 343a
words make, 801b
write to amuse their, 840a
you and I were long, 331b
Friendship a disinterested commerce, 355a
an unstable anchorage, 14b
and conversation of companions, 300a
came but for, 440a
conciliation of interests, 265a
crown of love and, 479a
demands your, 431a
develop into a real, 769b
die away by negligence, 342b
distance endears, 485a
elegance of female, 337a
faded, 877b
fair, through thy, 507b
from wine what sudden, 308b
gift of, 744b
glad to be at, 286a
greatest ornament of, 33b
heart of, 499b
holy passion of, 678a
in, false, 276b
is a sheltering tree, 425a
is constant, 157a
is love without his wings, 451b
is the strongest, 726a
joys of, 886a
keep, in constant repair, 339b
like the holly-tree, 591b
lived on terms of, 33b
love and liberty, 425a
love, and marriage, 434a
love, charity, 182a
love like, steady, 440a
make, with me, 53b
messenger of, 666b
moment when, is formed, 371b
needs a parallelism, 697a

Friendship needs emotion to become love, 673a
needs no ceremony, 203a
not a bad beginning for, 768a
of the many, 668b
offices of, 98a
paltry, 544b
perfect, of two men, 771b
pious frauds of, 333b
rural quiet, books, 328a
sacrifices of, 851b
sounds too cold, 440b
swear an eternal, 270b
that like love is warm, 440a
two for, 590b
use him to have his, 96b
when love is in his heart, 761a
wing of, 577a
with all nations, 374b
with love and, stirred, 486b
Friendship's a little truer, 862b
name, speak to thee in, 440a
true, laws, 6b
Friendships allow no excuses, 12a
break and bend, 966b
each year to ancient, 602a
great, from bad beginning, 32a
man's, invalidated by marriage, 671b
Frietchie, Barbara, flag never waved, 956a
Frieth in her own grease, 81a
Frieze buttress nor coign, 195a
Friezes, wreathed, intertwine, 543b
Frigate, no, like a book, 647a
Fright, no dangers, him, 336a
perfect, 457a
wake in a, 451b
you out of seven senses, 90a
Frighted reign of chaos, 253a
Frightened a little mouse, 1018a
girl, crept like a, 767b
Miss Muffet away, 1018b
need to be thoroughly, 967b
rather, than hurt, 671a
to death, 510a
Frightens the Christ Child, 934b
Frightful fiend, 422a
mien, monster of so, 317a
more, than smoke, 498a
most, idea, 699b
sheer no-man-fathomed, 724b
Frightfulest of all masters, 475b
Frights isle from her propriety, 187b
Frigid tranquillity, 336b
Frind, Spain was our, 835b
Fringe, lunatic, 779b
upon her gown, 287a
Fringed curtains of thine eye, 209a
pool ferned grot, 645b
Fringing the dusty road, 600a
Fringy edges of the fight, 595b
Frisk away like schoolboys, 390b
'n the sun, 207b
Fritter my wig, 659a
Frittered away by detail, 590a
Frittering away his age, 419a
Fritters, dish of, 107a
Fritz the Great bullied, 474b
Frivolity, how rare how precious is, 901b
irresponsible, 513a
Frivolous work of polished idleness, 397b
Frocks and curls, 648b
Frog, expiring, 576a
funniest thing's a, 1005a

Frog he would a-wooing go, 1015a
  like a, to tell your name, 646a
  never bigger than a, 695a
  O to be a, 29b
  outjump any, 674a
  p'ints about that, 674b
  plaintive piping, 741a
  thus use your, 236a
  toe of, 198a
Frogs die in earnest, 62a
  throw stones at, 62a
Frolic architecture of the snow, 503b
  forward and, glee, 415a
  pay dear for their, 108b
  wine, outdid the, 231a
Frolics, gives o'er her, 853b
Fronded palms in air, 528a
Front, closed, dure, 833b
  deep on his, engraven, 254a
  head and, of my offending, 186a
  in, the sun climbs slow, 596a
  modest, of this small floor, 264a
  nor the back entrance, 513b
  of iron, 597a
  of Jove himself, 176b
  star of resplendent, 509b
  wrinkled, 127b
Frontier, drive enemy beyond the, 399b
  from Atlantic to Pacific, 868b
  Rhine is where our, lies, 832b
Frontier-grave is far away, 803b
Frost, arrows of early, 634b
  as actively doth burn, 177a
  death's untimely, 393a
  from purest snow, 202b
  is on the punkin, 746a
  killing, 211a
  six weeks to, 957b
  skirt the eternal, 423a
  was spectre-gray, 705b
  which binds so dear a head, 467a
Frosts are slain, 691b
Frosty but kindly, 160a
  fair, day, 275a
  kindly as well as, 603a
  little, Eskimo, 750b
  night, keen and, 471a
  pow, blessings on your, 392b
  thinking on, Caucasus, 138b
  wind made moan, 649b
Froth and bubble, life is mostly, 661b
  of falsehood, 695a
Frothy eloquence, 760a
  waves, hopping through the, 658b
Froward child, human life like a, 275a
  vindictive fellow, 58b
Frown and wrinkled lip, 465a
  beneath the foeman's, 558a
  how quickly she will, 118a
  is no extinguisher, 587b
  of hate, 388a
  trembled with fear at your, 597a
  yesterday's, 598a
Frowned, critic you have, 412a
Frowning battlements, 538a
  providence, behind a, 362b
  skies, forehead of the, 102b
Frowns are fairer far than smiles, 483b
  frown of, 388a
  o'er the winding Rhine, 453a

Frowst with a book by the fire, 820a
Frowsy couch in sorrow steep, 394b
Froze me to hear such talk, 677a
  or snew, 918a
  the genial current, 348b
Frozen as charity, 427b
  bosom bears, 185b
  by distance, 408a
  dynamite, cook the, 816a
  echo of the silent voice, 738b
  grass, trembling through, 480b
  infixed and, 254b
  locked and, in each eye, 993b
  milk comes, home in pail, 134a
  music, architecture is, 397b
  toes, walk on, 847a
  up in the horn, 369b
  up within, 622b
  zone, torrid or the, 236b
Frozen-hearted, he who was, 707b
Fructify, choice will not, 718b
Frugal, growing, of my gold, 587b
  is the chariot, 647a
  mind, 363b
  swain, 352b
  wise and, government, 374b
Frugality, cultivated industry and, 624a
Fruit and flower, renew both, 54a
  bear, then ripen, 64a
  bring down, unheard-of, 846a
  bringeth forth his, 1032a
  brought forth, 1052b
  cankers root and, alike, 972b
  capital is the, of labor, 539b
  drop like ripe, 258b
  evil, of a bad man, 7a
  fell like autumn, 276a
  flesh-coloured, 694b
  from such a seed, 454a
  gathers, from every tree, 780b
  known by his, 1052b
  live by, of their labor, 538a
  natural, of labor, 887b
  of all our long endeavor, 712b
  of great cultivation, 338a
  of loyal nature, 555a
  of sense is rarely found, 311a
  of that forbidden tree, 251b
  of the spirit, 1062b
  of thy womb, 1056a
  of war fruit of peace, 979b
  plucking the, of memory, 774a
  reaching to the, 258a
  renew both, and flower, 54a
  restore with cordial, 233a
  ripest, first falls, 139a
  that can fall without shaking, 322b
  thereof dust, 692a
  weakest kind of, 145b
  which I bore was the sun, 61b
  years mature into, 797a
Fruitage, flower and, is the world, 501b
Fruited plain, above the, 781a
Fruitful, be, and multiply, 1021a
  chaste fair and, 54b
  error, give me a, 740a
  field, sickle in the, 386b
  of golden deeds, 254b
  round jolly, face, 537b
Fruitfulness, mists and mellow, 482b
Fruition, hours crowned with, 65b
Fruitless, cold, moon, 140b

Fruitless must be any words of mine, 541b
  wishes, 290b
Fruits, by their, 1052a
  eat his pleasant, 1044b
  fairy, and flowers, 544a
  kindly, of the earth, 1068b
  no bees no, 488b
  of love, 461a
  of Rome, 947a
  of the earth, 12b
  plants, of life and beauty, 386b
  pleasant, do grow, 220b
Fruit-tree tops, 135b
Fruit-trees, fluttering about the, 681a
Frumious Bandersnatch, 657b
Frustrate ghost, 571a
  of his hope to write, 250a
Frustrated all their measures, 905b
Fry me or fritter my wig, 659a
  other fish to, 90a
Frye in his owene grece, 81a
Frying pan, out of the, 94a
Fuddled, too, to take care to observe, 301b
Fudge, call old notions, 602a
  two fifths sheer, 600b
Fudges and their historians, 493a
Führer is always right, 967a
Fuel, adding, to the flame, 260b
  of magnificence, 505a
  to maintain his fires, 237a
Fugitive and a vagabond, 1022t
  from the law of averages, 997b
  praise, and cloistered virtue, 250b
Fugues, like writing, 908a
Ful gret fool is he, 77b
Fulfill, I am come to, 1050b
  no mission to, 668b
Fulfill'd desire, vision of, 533a
Fulfilled, in heaven shall be, 630b
Fulfilling of the law, 1060b
Fulfillment, my prayer would, know, 615a
Fulfills great nature's plan, 390b
Full age, come to grave in a, 1030a
  and fair ones come and buy, 230a
  and fair, shining lance, 662a
  circle, wheel is come, 193b
  corn in the ear, 1055b
  fathom five, 209a
  fortune with both hands, 153b
  four seasons of the year, 962a
  grown, straight, 123b
  heart reveal presence, 425a
  it's as, of good-nature, 136b
  loaded, o' ruin, 731a
  man, reading maketh a, 121b
  many a glorious morning, 205a
  meal more than a blessing, 430a
  meridian of my glory, 211a
  midday beam, 250b
  o' beans and benevolence, 510a
  o' milk of human kindness, 195a
  of a sweet indifference, 708b
  of briers, 159b
  of days riches and honour, 1029b
  of direct cruelty, 195a
  of fear, 1003a
  of matter, 1031b
  of sound and fury, 199b
  of strange oaths, 161a

Gabriel give him a harp, 810a
Gadding vine, 248b
Gadire, isles of Javan or, 260a
Gaels of Ireland, 867b
Gage, hope's true, 111a
Gai, toujours, 894b
Gaieties, planned, 974b
Gaiety and the quiet mind, 753b
  gift of, 974b
Gain a victory, 54a
  are with, so fond, 131a
  at least some, 15b
  Corinth, 41b
  envy guile and lust of, 328b
  every way makes my, 190a
  for every thing you, 501b
  for the, of a few, 321a
  force upon plain of Marathon,
    337b
  fulsome love for, 309b
  great men, doubly, 510b
  hope of, allured, 681b
  ill-gotten good is nobody's, 84a
  is gain, 567a
  little patch of ground, 177b
  longs eagerly to, 35b
  new glories, a day to, 5a
  no, except by loss, 631b
  not base gains, 7b
  or lose it all, 262b
  serves and seeks for, 191a
  steady, of man, 527a
  the whole world, 1053b
  timely inn, 197b
  to die is, 20b, 1062b
  unbrib'd by, 436b
  unvex'd with all cares of, 308a
  who loses her shall, 725b
  who stood to, 33b
Gained a world, 712a
  by every sort of flattery, 324a
  done thought, or been, 475b
  for universe by success, 715b
  how little I have, 552b
  learning, most, 244a
  something for every thing
    missed, 501b
Gains, counts his sure, 412b
  draw their, 375b
  general kiss he, 383a
  how much time he, 67a
  light, make heavy purses, 116b
  wealthy gallant, the day, 84a
  without pains, 986b
Gaiters, gas and, 577a
Gal, nice young boy or, 890b
  swing dat yaller, 739a
  you loves better den yo' kin,
    859b
Galaxy, seen in the, 257b
Gale, catch the driving, 317b
  I bow to the threatening, 632a
  lightning and the, 534b
  no, that blew, 714b
  partake the, 318a
  passion is the, 317a
  simplest note that swells the,
    349b
  takes more than a, 821a
  wafted by the gentle, 396a
  yell for yell to a westerly, 772a
Galen, more killed than, cured,
  234a
Galilean lake, pilot of the, 249a
  pale, 693a
Galilee, rolls nightly on deep,
  456a
  Sea of, and the Dead Sea, 893a
Galileo, starry, 454a

Gall, bear the bonds that, 693a
  enough in thy ink, 165a
  honey or the, 810b
  of bitterness, 1059a
  water of, to drink, 1048a
Gal-la-lee, Spanish, 1013a
Gallant actions, true recompense
  of, 297b
  band, no soldier in that, 685b
  haughty, gay Lothario, 302a
  mast, bends the, 447b
  Ninetieth, aught of the, 612a
  not gamesome and, 992a
  old soldier of Tippecanoe, 499a
  oppose, breasts, 40b
  spirit, 520a
  steamer Ocean Queen, 663b
  trim, 350a
  wealthy, 84a
Gallantry, conscience and, 381b
  what men call, 457b
Gallants, deserted by the, 497b
Galled by reproachful words, 54b
  jade wince, 176a
Galleon, moon was a ghostly, 909b
Gallery critics, eyes of, 364a
  filled with works of art, 633a
  Grosvenor, 683b
  in that, 271a
  in which reporters sit, 473a
  which envenoms the play, 773b
Galley, Cervantes on his, 867a
  Turk's, 271a
  what was he doing in that, 271a
Galleys, over the sea our, went,
  567a
Galling crown, bowed with a, 846a
  load, life thou art a, 391a
  nothing so, to a people, 492a
Gallop and gallop about, 750a
  apace, 136b
  beggar ride a, 126a
  false, of verses, 162a
  Pegasus to death, 320a
  ride a, 126a
Galloped, I, Dirck galloped, 568a
  into midnight we, abreast, 568a
Gallops, time, 162a
Gallows and concentration camps,
  905b
  perfect, 208b
Gallows-foot and after, 819b
Gallows-tree, under the, 225a
Galls his kibe, 178b
  infants of the spring, 171a
Gallup Poll, 870b
Galoot's, till the last, ashore, 698b
Gals acts so or so, 518b
  and cotton bags, 450b
Galumphing, he went, back, 657b
Gamaliel, feet of, 1059b
Gambol, Christmas, oft could
  cheer, 414b
Gamboled, bunny, up, 853b
Gambols, where be your, 178b
Game, bade the, go on, 808a
  daughters of the, 182b
  doorbells are like a magic, 430a
  fashioned this quiet, 853a
  fighting's the, 734b
  fish swims up stream, 778a
  gunless, 777b
  how you played the, 910a
  is afoot, 782a
  is up, 204a
  life but a, at football, 416a
  little pleasure of the, 293b
  lost or won the, 494b
  love the, beyond the prize, 803a

Game of private theatricals, 715b
  of skill or chance, 776a
  of three, 831b
  one team in the, to win, 964b
  play the, 803b
  rigour of the, 429b
  royal, of goose, 356b
  rules of, are laws of nature,
    633b
  savage tribes pursue their, 382b
  solo, 877a
  that must be played, 846a
  war's a, 365a
  was empires, 460a
  whatever the, 587b
  within view of the law, 844b
  woman is his, 550b
Gamefish swims upstream, 778a
Game's afoot, 155a
Games, deceit or any sinful, 687a
  history better than, 842b
  rules the, 939b
Gamesome and gallant, 992a
Gamester, wise, 16b
Gammon and spinach, 579a, 1015a
Gander, very fine, 1014b
Gang a kennin' wrang, 311b, 391b
  aft a-gley, 390a
  at Forty-second Street, 892a
  grisly, 870b
  shoot the holl, 601a
  to sea, 1011b
Ganglion in nerves of society, 709a
Gangrene starting in a mildewed
  silo, 886b
Gang's, hail hail the, all here, 683a
Gangs, don't join too many, 881a
Gangway for de Lawd God Jehovah, 954a
Gaol, we who lie in, 770a
Gap in society, 435a
  in the side of mountains, 9b
  sleep out this, of time, 200a
Gapes for drink again, 267a
Garage, car out o', last evenin',
  841a
Garb, jester's motley, 893b
  reason's, 254a
Garbled speeches, 841a
Garcia, message to, 763a
Garden, Babylon's, 1007b
  blow upon my, 1044b
  come into the, Maud, 553b
  contain nothing but potatoes,
    560a
  cultivate our, 325a
  eastward in Eden, 1021b
  fairest, in her looks, 267b
  fairies at the bottom of our,
    889a
  ghost of a, 695b
  God first planted a, 121a
  God once loved a, 917a
  God planted a, 695b
  God the first, made, 121a
  half, and half house, 550a
  he who makes a, 889b
  how does your, grow, 1015b
  hyacinth, the wears, 531b
  in heaven, 760b
  in her face, 220b
  in my, goes a fiend, 933b
  is a lovesome thing, 645b
  look for us through this, 533b
  Lord God walking in the, 1022a
  maid was in the, 1017a
  my heart shall be thy, 736a
  o'ergrow the, 125a
  of cucumbers, 707a, 1045a

Garden of Eden, 1022a
  of Eden, Englishman into the, 594b
  of shut-eye town, 747a
  of sleep, 695b
  of song, 782b
  old Marm Hackett's, 587a
  our England is a, 821a
  paths, walk down the, 874b
  peopled, 378b
  playing in the, 853b
  rake, scratch my back with, 984a
  rosebud, of girls, 554a
  scarecrow in, of cucumbers, 1066b
  she went into the, 350b
  show me your, 108a
  small house and large, 267a
  this is the, 968b
  turn her out of the, 341a
  urn, 943a
  wall, set in a, 910b
  which does not look like open country, 379a
  who loves a, 364b, 490a
Garden-close, I know a little, 666b
Gardener Adam and his wife, 547a
  Adam was a, 178a
Gardener's, half a proper, work, 178a
Gardeners ditchers and grave-makers, 178a
  gardens were before, 121a
  our wills are, 186b
Gardening, liking for gardens and, 651a
Garden-plot to a deer-park, 718a
Garden's end, river at my, 320a
Gardens before gardeners, 121a
  bodies are our, 186b
  everywhere nightingales sing, 840b
  in trim, take his pleasure, 246a
  liking for, and gardening, 651a
  of the desert, 471a
  of the night, 721b
  salley, 824a
  seeing, in the spring, 917a
  such, not made by singing, 821a
  tell me how my, grows, 860b
Gardin, delightful, growes, 113b
Garfield sat on the other, 652a
Gargoyle often makes his perch, 805a
Garish, day's, eye, 246b
  sun, worship to the, 136b
Garland and singing robes, 250a
  of the war, 201b
  immortal, 250b
  sweetest, to sweetest maid, 307b
Garlands, green, to the day, 796b
  silken flanks with, 482b
  that fell forgot, 890b
  wither on your brow, 237b
  you may gather, there, 415b
Garleck onyons and lekes loved he, 80a
Garlic and sapphires, 944b
  eat no onions nor, 142b
Garment, hardship our, 869b
  new and eagerly expected, 580b
  of praise, 1047b
  wears as his best, 924b
Garmented in light, 466b
Garments, nothing chang'd but my, 192b
  of gladness, 1065b
  purses proud, poor, 130b

Garments, shining robes and, fair, 615a
  stuffs out vacant, 148a
  trailing, of the night, 520b
  were alwayes in patchez, 989b
Garnered lore, 712b
Garnish beauteous eye, 148a
Garnishing of nicotine, 973a
Garret, born in a, 350b
  four stories high, 89b
  in lonesome, 358b
  live in a, aloof, 680b
  living in a, 350b
Garrick, here lies David, 357b
Garrick's a salad, 357b
Garrulous to the very last, **610b**
Gars me greet, 393b
Garter on elastic band, 714a
  familiar as his, 154a
Garters amuse his riper stage, 317b
  tie her, fast, 330a
Garyulies and the Grand Panjandrum, 350b
Gas and gaiters, 577a
  lighting by, 534a
  smells awful, 966b
  turn on, in th' darkest heart, 836a
Gascoyne, Cadets of, 842a
Gaseous vertebrata, 909a
Gash is as painful to one, 791a
Gasp and stretch one's eyes, 849b
  at the last, 1067a
  fight till the last, 124a
  last, of love's breath, 122b
  Quintilian stare and, 251a
Gas-pipe, laying a, down, 1003b
Gate, after we pass the, 833a
  at one, make defence, 260a
  beggars at your, 547a
  Christ who holds the open, 896b
  don't bite at de front, 739a
  here at the, alone, 554a
  Hun is at the, 821b
  keeps the heavy, 770a
  knock once at every, 662a
  lark at heaven's, 204a
  leant upon a coppice, 705b
  love the double, 897a
  matters not how strait the, 741b
  near the sacred, 563b
  no latch ter de golden, 738b
  of breath, 692b
  of heaven, 1023a
  of the year, 881b
  passing through this, 937a
  past entered through another, 761b
  people wait at haven's, 862a
  poor man at his, 591b
  starv'd at his master's, 388a
  strait is the, 1052a
  wide is the, 1052a
  willow-cabin at your, 164a
  you come in the, 757b
Gate-post, 'twixt you me and the, 574b
Gates, area, 943a
  behind the, of Hercules, 712a
  claps her wings at heaven's, 112b
  ever-during, 257a
  lion on your old stone, 547a
  of Hell, detests him as the, 4b
  open ye everlasting, 257b
  shut the, of mercy, 349a
  stand open night and day, 37a
  storming heaven's, 980b
  to glorious and unknown, **901a**

Gates, unbarr'd the, of light, 25
  where wonder waits, 860b
Gateway shall be free unto a 737a
Gateways, gold, of the stars, 79
Gath, tell it not in, 1027b
Gather after the reapers, 1027a
  and squander, 623a
  birds of a feather, togeth 223b
  from the plain, 613a
  gear by every wile, 391a
  honey all the day, 302b
  ill habits, 280b
  nor, into barns, 1051b
  rose of love, 230b
  roses, never expect to, 29a
  tales, 42b
  the lambs, 1047a
  to the eyes, 550b
  up the fragments, 1058a
  what ancestors thrown awa 336b
  who shall, them, 1034a
  ye rosebuds, 230b
Gather'd enchanted herbs, 147a
Gathered all nations, 1054b
  cannot be, up again, 1028a
  not harshly plucked, 258b
  them together into Armageddc 1064b
  to thy heart, 736b
  together in my name, 1053b
Gatherer and disposer of me stuff, 101a
Gathering her brows, 393b
  rose without being pricked, 2
Gatherings, tidal, 939b
Gathers no moss, 45a
  samphire, 192b
Gat-toothed, I was, 81b
Gaudiness of poetry, 906a
Gaudy blabbing remorseful da 125b
  color, 995b
  day, 456a
  neat not, 429a
  night, let's have one other, 20
  rich not, 112a, 171b
  show, one augments its, 415b
Gaul, all, is divided, 34b
  to, to Greece, 363b
Gaunt, city of, 1012a
  thrush frail, and small, 705b
Gauntlet with a gift in 't, 519b
Gave, fortune never, enough, 11
  hand that, the blow, 277b
  me of the tree, 258b
  signs of woe, 258a
  up the ghost, 1057b
  us liberty at the same tim 373a
  what other women gave, 827
  without assumption, 56a
Gawain, 'twas not for every, 57
Gawd, bein', ain't a bed of rose 954b
  livin', that made you, 818a
Gay, bedeck'd ornate and, 260a
  castles in the clouds, 328b
  creation, boast amid its, 327
  delights, deck our girls for, 59
  face that's anything but, 563l
  gilded scenes, 298b
  great men be more, 491a
  haughty gallant, Lothario, 30
  her heart was warm and, 958
  house under new made cloud 997a

Gay, I would not if I could be, 396b
in such jocund company, 409a
life is over life was, 751a
mind is, but soul is melancholy, 725b
motes, 245b
nineties were not really, 890b
rhetoric, 248a
steer from grave to, 318a
Sunday, 615a
though, they run and leap, 736a
turn thy rapture move, 311a
Gayer than a greeting, 968a
Gayest of gay girls, 486b
Gayety of nations, 337b
Gaza, eyeless in, 259b
Gaz'd, and still they, 356b
Gaze at remote past, 856a
at the stars, 30b
disciples devout, and adore, 654b
knowledge hid from public, 498b
o' the time, 200a
on so fondly today, 438b
upon the Grail, 574a
Gazed but little thought, 409a
eyelids, 7a
themselves away, 404b
Gazelle, nurs'd a dear, 441a
Gazer see with mortal eyes, 655a
Gazes on the ground, 755b
Gazing rustics rang'd round, 356b
Gear, good wench for this, 144b
learning grace nor, 817a
Geese are getting fat, 1002b
are swans, 222b, 622b
like a snow cloud, 946b
thinks his own, swans, 222b
will gabble, 981b
Gehenna, down to, 819b
Gêlert, faithful, 403a
Gem, best, upon her zone, 503b
of purest ray serene, 348b
of the city's crown, 737b
of the old rock, 241a
song considered a perfect, 651b
that twinkling hangs, 366a
when others pick it up, 639a
Gemlike, hard, flame, 702a
Gems of heaven her starry train, 256a
rich and rare the, she wore, 438a
string of perfect, 348b
the starry girdle, 432a
General a disease, 229b
Alexander Smyth, 433b
aspects of the law, 709a
association of nations, 771a
built up in public opinion, 926b
caviare to the, 174a
ceremony, 156a
duty of humanity, 98b
joy of whole table, 197b
level, one inch above the, 661a
make him an ill, 100b
merit of a, 16a
mess of imprecision, 945a
no rule so, 222a
office and duties of a, 54b
prey of the rich on the poor, 374a
principle gives no help, 402a
prize of the, is command, 709b
propositions do not decide, 709b
Generalities, glittering, of natural right, 490b
Generality of men swayed by fear, 27a

Generality, vague, is a life-saver, 829a
Generalize opinions, 778a
Generals, I do not envy the, 608b
Ireland gives England her, 639b
or poets or statesmen, 675b
victories of mighty, 608b
Generation, from generation to, 300b
of men, lived with one, 55a
one, passeth away, 1042a
our, can produce glory, 956a
speak for the present, 433b
stubborn and rebellious, 1035b
Generations, countless, pass away, 902b
honoured in their, 1066b
minds of different, 932a
no hungry, tread thee down, 481b
of hard-working ancestry, 966a
pass like sand, 902b
people have been here many, 748b
shall call me blessed, 1056a
succeeding, will be idle, 739b
three, atween clog and clog, 891b
three, from shirtsleeves to wealth, 891b
Generator of future wars, 887b
Generosity, calls his extravagance, 355a
such as is possible, 751a
Generous, be just before you're, 382a
frank barbarous recklessness, 773a
more nearly, pleasanter, 977a
nature has been suffered, 359b
race, build not boast a, 327a
way is peaceful, just, 540b
Genevieve, sweet, 698b
Genial breezes, 670b
current of the soul, 348b
race, caryatids of a, 949a
sympathy, 528b
Geniality, prefer, to grammar, 784b
Genius, America not good place for, 672a
and the mortal instruments, 167a
appearance of a single great, 688a
capacity for taking trouble, 672a
disdains a beaten path, 537a
does what it must, 653b
doing impossible for talent is, 617b
for anti-climaxes, 969a
for painting, 505a
for splendid unselfish action, 888a
found respectable, 520a
gives, a better discerning, 357a
goes and folly stays, 506b
good sense body of poetic, 424b
guiding, of management, 874b
had to trust to native, 676b
hath electric power, 498b
he had a startling, 777b
homage which men of, have received, 492b
is a capacity, 334a
is a great aptitude, 334a
is an intuitive talent, 334a
is master of man, 653b

Genius is not immortal, 379a
is one per cent inspiration, 735b
is patience, 334a
legacies a great, leaves, 300b
literature an investment of, 688b
little vessel of my, 76a
makes no mistakes, 917a
man of absolute, 908a
man of, sees the world, 784a
man of, seldom ruined, 339b
man who does unique things, 841b
man's, is a deity, 12a
men of, do not excel, 435a
mint of, 650b
must be born, 280a
necessary ingredient of, 334a
never on well-worn paths, 48a
no question of Thoreau's, 718a
nursing mother of, 559b
obedience bane of all, 464b
of a good leader, 952b
of the constitution, 335a
of the place, implored the, 37b
of your independence, 538a
one science one, fit, 310a
parting, with sighing sent, 244b
perceiving in unhabitual way, 715b
raise the, 312b
roads of, 386a
sense and wit, 363a
spites do not harm true, 725b
step-mother ov, 595a
talk not of, baffled, 653b
taste is the feminine of, 533b
that in whose power man is, 603a
that power which dazzles, 776b
the capacity for taking trouble, 476a
thine own, gave final blow, 452a
three fifths of him, 600b
to be loved, 518b
to, the stern friend, 505a
true, kindles, 318b
we scarcely can praise, 357b
will live and thrive, 560a
without some madness, 48a
word-coining, 923a
wrought, 412b
your, is within, 63b
Geniuses have shortest biographies, 504a
Gen'rous birth, starves her, 348a
thought, never reach'd one, 314b
Genteel, shabby, 1005a
thing is the genteel thing, 357a
Gentian, God made a little, 647a
Gentil, he is, that dooth gentil dedis, 81b
knight, 79a
man, the grettest, 81b
Gentle, might of the, 456a
Gentiles, lighten the, 1056b
such boastings as the, use, 816a
Gentility, cottage of, 427a
Gentle and merciful and just, 471b
blood, signe to know the, 115a
breeding, due to, 14b
characteristics, healthy and, 514b
cousin of forest-green, 478b
decay, 275a
dullness loves a joke, 322a
ears of, and simple, 616a
earth lie lightly, 228b
fire, turn'd by a, 280b

Gettysburg or Waterloo, 809a
pile them high at, 898a
Ghastly dew, rain'd a, 548b
dreams, full of, 127b
fears, trembling cold in, 386a
pang, 421b
Ghost am I of winds that die, 733b
applaud the hollow, 622b
beck'ning, along moonlight
shade, 313b
comes up by them, 711a
frustrate, 571a
give up the, 105a
he gave up the, 1057b
make a, of him that lets me,
172b
man giveth up the, 1030b
of a garden, 695b
of shores, 712a
of sleigh-bells, 880a
old lover's, 216b
stubborn unlaid, 247b
vex not his, 194a
will walk in an English lane,
568b
wrought its, upon the floor,
544b
Ghosties and long-leggety beasties,
1003a
Ghostly, brain's old, house, 960b
galleon, moon was a, 909b
Ghosts created when first man
woke, 791b
creeping between the lines, 641b
from an enchanter fleeing, 466a
of defunct bodies, 238a
of robins and blue-birds, 681a
of youth and joy, 809b
suddenly, walked, 971b
they have depos'd, 139b
true love is like, 265a
Ghoul-haunted woodland of Weir,
545b
Ghoulies and ghosties, 1003a
G. I. Joe, 1009a
Giant branches tossed, 470a
column the shape of a mushroom, 945b
despair, owner was, 274b
dies, 326b
frame, man of, 471a
hit into a double, 911b
mass of things to come, 181b,
832a
pang great as when, dies, 185a
race before the flood, 279b
see farther than a, 221b
shoulders of a, 221b
tyrannous to use it like a, 184b
warrior, eats the, 634a
yet is that, very gentleness, 561a
Giant-dwarf Dan Cupid, 133a
Giant's robe upon a dwarfish thief,
199a
strength, 184b
unchained strength, 471a
wings prevent him walking, 618b
Giants, age of, 817b
in the earth, 1022b
strength of ancient, 6b
wage war like physical, 963b
Gibber, squeak and, in streets,
170a
Gibbets, cells and, for the man,
591a
keep lifted hand in awe, 305a
Gibbon is his prophet, 950a
Gibe, call it humor when they,
296a

Gibes, where be your, 178b
Giddy and unfirm, fancies are,
164b
fortune's wheel, 155b
habitation, and unsure, 153a
he that is, 130b
I am, 181b
maid, good-fortune is a, 486b
to ride backwards, 931a
wheel, turns the, 352b
Giddy-paced times, 164a
Gideon Bibles, 957b
Gift and not an acquisition, 772a
back of the, the giving, 667a
beauty is, of God, 71a
boy have not a woman's, 130a
cultivate, of taciturnity, 743b
feeling the East's, 570b
for a better and higher, 6a
for nought her priceless, 629b
gauntlet with a, 519b
gave a various, to each, 523a
good and perfect, 1064a
good sense is the, of Heaven,
315a
great love with little, 29b
great, of nature, 379a
great, of sleep, 742a
greatest, a soldier can acquire,
983b
greatest, God bestowed, 77a
heavenly, of poesy, 278b
heaven's last best, 256b
higher, of imagination, 784b
highest office in, iv people, 836b
is a portion of thyself, 502b
is as a precious stone, 1039b
New Year's, to the world, 631a
no richer, 527a
not so much to nature of, 749b
of chance, comes by, 38a
of fortune, 158a
of friendship, 744b
of gaiety, 974b
of Heaven, noblest, 17a
of imagination, 424b
of laughter, 884b
of martyrdom, 279a
of the gab, 469b
or grace surpassing this, 518a
rarest, to beauty common sense,
639a
spirit in which the, is rich, 829b
thanked their God for his, 980a
time with a, of tears, 691b
to know it, 160b
true love's the, 413b
without the giver, 600a
worth more than the, 243a
Gifted ones follow your calling,
500b
rarely, beings, 665b
small girl has explained, 839a
Gift-horse, look, in the mouth,
88a
Giftie, some power the, gie us,
391a
Gifts, adore my, instead of Me,
233b
always like the, I get, 847b
await no, from chance, 620a
cannot win with, honours, 273b
cluster of, 718b
distributed as, 689a
fairy, fading away, 438b
free, we scorn, 309b
goot, 180a
heaven's bounty lends, 496a
I fear Greeks bringing, 37a

Gifts, imprison his, 832a
lord's, 526b
misspent, 661b
more of his grace than, 213a
of a bad man, 17a
of God are strown, 445a
of the gods, 3b
of the wise ones, 829b
of thine, 627b
presented unto him, 1050a
range her little, 966b
rarer, than gold, 938b
rich, wax poor, 175a
that took all eyes, 506b
to friends, 16b
well timed, 288b
Gig, crew of the captain's, 682a
Gigantic hound, footprints of a,
782a
reservoir of good will, 964a
shadows futurity casts, 432b,
469a
shoe, shoemakers hang a, 445a
wilful young Chicago, 845b
Giggle gabble gobble git, 821b
mighty ha'd to, 859b
Gild refined gold, 148a
the vernal morn, 366a
Gilded and covered with velvet,
399b
and sticky, 935a
bricks, sold him, 894a
butterflies, 193b
cage, bird in a, 850a
car of day, 247a
eaves, fall upon her, 550b
fool, thinks better of a, 214b
gay, scenes, 298b
monuments of princes, 205b
show, slaves to their, 491a
small, fly, 193a
tomb of mediocre talent, 823a
vessel goes, 350a
wings, bug with, 319a
Gilds, love, the scene, 381a
Gilead, balm in, 1048a
Gills, draws in at his, 257a
Gilpin, long live he, 364a
Gilt, dust that is a little, 182a
highest peaks are, and rose, 840a
popinjays, 473a
Gimble, gyre and, in the wabe
657b
Gin, perhaps it's the, 990a
union of, and vermouth, 976b
Ginger hot i' the mouth, 164a
'ot sand an', 818a
sinament and, 232a
Gingerly, took up so, 131b
Gingham dog went bow-wow-wow,
747b
Gins, traps, and pitfalls, 564b
'Gins to pale his fire, 172b
Gird on thy sword, 721b
up thy loins like a man, 1031b
Girded, loins be, about, 1057a
up his loins, 1029a
Girdle, folds of a bright, furl'd,
622a
helps you with your, 990b
put, round earth, 141b
put, round world, 117a
starry, of the year, 432a
Girl arose that had red mournful
lips, 824b
bean from a boy bean, 990b
Burma, 818a
crept like a frightened, 767b
fair little, sat under a tree, 543a

Glorious epicurean paradox, 536a
  every thing honourable and, 366b
  eye shines on me still, 509b
  fault of angels, 313b
  gates to, and unknown, 901a
  gifts of the gods, 3b
  haven, 76a
  in a pipe, 460b
  in arms, 132b
  in thy just defence, 299a
  institution, 360b
  land above the sky, 1008b
  life, crowded hour of, 416b
  long and, past, 789b
  mirror, 455a
  more, the triumph, 370b
  morning, full many a, 205a
  pleasant thrilling, hours, 590b
  song of old, 560b
  summer by sun of York, 127b
  sunsets have birth in cities, 853a
  thing to be a pirate king, 682b
  to be an exception, 558b
  triumphs, win, 778b
  war, circumstance of, 189a
  works, these are thy, 256b
Gloriously drunk, 365a
  false, 39a
  succeeded, 987b
Glory, all things give him, 725a
  all-cloudless, 459a
  among men dies also, 8a
  and blue air, 519b
  and freshness of a dream, 408a
  and grief agree not well, 605a
  and shame of the universe, 273a
  and the dream, 408a
  belongs to our ancestors, 57b
  declare, of God, 1032b
  desire of, clings longer, 63b
  desirous of honour and, 283a
  doesn't mean a knock-down argument, 659a
  drown'd, in a shallow cup, 533a
  earth full of his, 1045b
  excess of, obscur'd, 253a
  folded, of his wings, 969b
  forgot was Britain's, 634b
  from his gray hairs gone, 527a
  from the earth, 408a
  full meridian of my, 211a
  glow, in thunder, 724b
  goin' ware, waits, 600b
  gown of, 111a
  greater, of God, 1009b
  guards with solemn round, 613a
  his food was, 494b
  height of her, 444a
  honor and undying fame, 956a
  impressed by spectacle of, 20a
  in a great mistake, 996a
  in hevin' nothin' o' the sort, 601a
  in his bosom, 597b
  in one day fill the stage, 232a
  in outstripping donkeys, 52b
  in the flower, 408b
  is all moonshine, 613b
  is departed from Israel, 1027a
  is that bright tragic thing, 648a
  is that of all adventurers, 953b
  is their shame, 1062b
  jest and riddle of the world, 317a
  land of hope and, 798b
  left him alone with his, 464a
  like a circle in water, 124a
  like a shooting star, 139a

Glory, long hair a, to her, 1061a
  love of, is most ardent, 301b
  made the sages smile, 458b
  majesty and might and, 809b
  name thee old, 501a
  no path of flowers leads to, 269b
  nothing so expensive as, 418b
  O the, of the winning, 639b
  of a representative, 359b
  of an April day, 131b
  of Him who moves everything, 77a
  of his country, 443a
  of honours beauties wits, 216a
  of my crown, 97b
  of rulers or of races, 900a
  of the coming of the Lord, 597b
  of the Creator, 118b
  of the Egdon waste, 704b
  of the Lord shone, 1056b
  of the universe, 530b
  of their times, 1066b
  of young men is strength, 1040a
  one, an' one shame, 600b
  or the grave, 432b
  passes away the, of this world, 1010b
  path of duty was way to, 553b
  paths of, 348b
  prayer gives God, 725a
  rainbow's, is shed, 469a
  search their own, 1041a
  shall not descend after him, 8b
  shows the way, 291a
  Solomon in all his, 1051b
  spread the morning's, 740a
  star differeth in, 1061b
  stars of, 476b
  sudden, 228b
  sun of thy, 500a
  sun question his, 647b
  survives, 20b
  that book doth share the, 134b
  that fadeth not away, 1064a
  that was Greece, 543b, 872b
  the colour the, the gold, 895b
  these in the robings of, 637b
  time's, is to calm, 131b
  to God in the highest, 1056b
  to the king of kings, 334b
  to the new-born king, 334b
  trailing clouds of, 408b
  triumph without, 243a
  true and honorable recompense, 297b
  vain pomp and, 211a, 1068b
  visions of, 350a
  waits thee, 438a
  walking in an air of, 272a
  who is this king of, 1033b
  who works for, 762b
  wild cataract leaps in, 550a
  wings lose all their, 441b
Glory's page, 437b
  small change, 496b
  thrill is o'er, 438a
Gloss of art, 357a
  on faint deeds, 203a
Glossary necessary to understand Chaucer, 933a
Glossy cherished anthracite, 956a
  cope is black as coal, 689b
  plumage dark and sleek, 395b
Gloucester, Doctor Foster went to, 1019b
Glove, iron hand in velvet, 95a
  upon that hand, 135a
Gloves on ere they touched meat, 979b

Gloves, through the fields in, 936a
  wear seemly, 534b
Glow, eyes, like sparks of fire, 231a
  neon, 941b
  of a kindly heart, 729b
Glow'd beyond nature warm, 320b
  the firmament with sapphires, 255b
Glowing axle, 247a
  embers through the room, 246a
  fire, before a, 864b
  hot, hammer iron when, 43b
  hours, chase the, 453a
  kiss had won, 488a
  life of its own times, 757b
Glow'red, as Tammie, 393b
Glows, in deep thicket's gloom, 378b
  in ev'ry heart, 305a
  while he reads, 310b
Glow-worm, eyes the, lend thee, 231a
  shows the matin to be near, 172b
Glow-worms, glories like, 226a
Glue and lime of love, 230a
Glued, pale student, to his desk, 628b
Glum, glance was, 685a
Glut sorrow on a morning rose, 483a
Gluts twice ten thousand caverns, 478a
Glutted market, 309b
Glutton, drunkard and the, 1040b
  idler and fool, 896a
Glynn, marshes of, 716b
Gnarling sorrow hath less power, 138b
Gnat, strain at a, 1054a
Gnats, small, mourn, 483a
Gnawing of a mouse, 962b
Gnaws my hat, 902b
Go about but cannot find, 978a
  and catch a falling star, 215b
  and do thou likewise, 1057a
  and find it, 815b
  and sin no more, 1058a
  and teach all nations, 1055b
  at once, 198a
  away, presently they, 889b
  beyond the mark, 266a
  bow thy head in gentle spite, 629a
  bump in the night, 1003a
  child in way he should, 1040b
  die and, we know not where, 185a
  don't ever try to, there, 967b
  find out and be damned, 815b
  forth and conquer a crown, 730a
  forth and seek, 897b
  forth in separate parties, 1070a
  forth with crowds, 959a
  from me, 519a
  gentle into that good night, 997a
  get thee to a nunnery, 175a
  his halves, 89a
  I shall, to him, 1028a
  I will not let thee, 330a
  in time let, 812b
  into the house of the Lord, 1037b
  like to, by myself, 434a
  litel bok, 79a
  little book, 751a
  lovely rose, 242a, 823a, 912a
  mark him well, 414a

God, Hannah, and me, 662b
 has a few of us, 572a
 has designed to ruin, 18b
 has given you one face, 175a
 has hung a sign, 445a
 has written all the books, 672a
 hath chosen foolish things, 1060b
 hath joined together, 1053b
 hath numbered thy kingdom, 1049a
 hath raised me high, 97b
 have mercy on the sinner, 947a
 have mercy on this sot, 74b
 have seen, face to face, 1023b
 have, thy friend, 96b
 he for, only, 255b
 he thinks that I am, 655b
 heirs of, 1060a
 help me Amen, 86b
 help our darkened country, 883b
 helps them that help themselves, 330b
 helps those, 13a
 himself can't kill them, 42a
 himself from, could not free, 503a
 himself scarce seemèd, 422a
 his father and his, 349b
 his life a breath of, 585b
 holy Lamb of, 388b
 homely verse to, is dear, 830b
 house of, 1023a
 how should man be just with, 1030a
 how they speak of, 890b
 I believe in, 400a
 I believe that, is overhead, 652a
 I b'lieve in, and the angels, 699a
 I never spoke with, 648a
 if, be for us, 1060a
 if, did not exist, 275a, 325b
 if this were enough, 752a
 in apprehension how like a, 173b
 in faces of men and women, 608b
 in his mercy lend her grace, 547b
 in his works and word, 304a
 in, is our trust, 436a
 in my flesh shall I see, 1031a
 in place of, to her child, 565a
 in Three Persons, 445b
 in whom we live, 1069b
 incomprehensibility of, 490b
 insult to, 567b
 is a verb not a noun, 972a
 is always there, 822a
 is an unutterable sight, 782b
 is and all is well, 528b
 is for big battalions, 325b
 is grateful and knowing, 1070a
 is here, 334a
 is in heaven, 1042b
 is living working still, 583a
 is love, 672a, 1064b
 is mightiest in power, 27b
 is not a man, 12b, 1025a
 is our refuge and strength, 1034b
 is seen God in the star, 571b
 is the only mind, 616b
 is their belly, 1062b
 is they are, 572b
 is thy refuge, 1026a
 is within, 63b
 jealous, 1024b
 Job fear, for nought, 1029b
 joy is grace we say to, 612b

God, joyful noise unto, 1035a
 just are the ways of, 260a
 justify ways of, 252a
 keeps thee from thy, 495b
 kindliest thing, ever made, 873a
 know what, and man is, 556a
 knows best, 841b
 knows it I am with them, 767b
 knows thou art a collop, 92b
 laid down His life, 737a
 laws of nature's, 373a
 laws of, the laws of man, 787a
 leap up to my, 123b
 leapt to life a, 463b
 learnt to fear, 500b
 lends aid to the worker, 13a
 lesser, had made the world, 555b
 let not, speak with us, 1025a
 let us be back'd with, 126b
 let us worship, he says, 390a
 lets them down, 952a
 lifetime of his, 604a
 Lion of, 73b
 live as if, beheld you, 47a
 looks after fools drunkards, 1008a
 looks up to nature's, 318a
 Lord, Almighty, 445b
 Lord, made them all, 591b
 loses faith in, and woman, 650a
 love and be wise, 43a
 loves an idle rainbow, 854b
 loves to help him who strives, 13a
 loveth a cheerful giver, 1062a
 loveth not knoweth not, 1064b
 loveth not speaking ill, 1070b
 lower law than, 655a
 made a heart of gold, 877b
 made a little gentian, 647a
 made all the creatures, 571a
 made him, 143b
 made it for this man, 558b
 made love, 804b
 made man, 804b
 made man upright, 1043a
 made men to enjoy felicity, 65a
 made the country, 121a, 364a
 made the vine, 805a
 made them high or lowly, 591b
 make our blunders wise, 903a
 make the will of, prevail, 623a
 makes all things good, 344a
 makes sech nights, 601a
 man in the bush with, may meet, 503a
 man is a fallen, 463a
 man sent from, 1057b
 man with, in majority, 95b
 man's word is, in man, 554a
 many are afraid of, 616a
 may be had for the asking, 600a
 may forgive sins, 507b
 men that, made mad, 867b
 Mencken Nathan and, 915b
 mighty fortress is our, 86b
 mills of, 522b
 ministers who spoke of, 590b
 mistake young man for Greek, 908b
 more just than, 1030a
 mother is the name for, 565a
 moves in a mysterious way, 362b
 must forever bless, 540b
 my, my Father and my Friend, 283b
 name of, upon his lips, 344b
 nature is the art of, 240a

God, near the Church far **from**, 92a
 nearer my, to thee, 515b
 necessary Being of Himself, 275a
 neglect, and his angels, 218a
 nest on the greatness of, 716b
 never made his work for man to mend, 280b
 never spoke of, 996a
 no, but God, 950a
 no, dare wrong a worm, 506b
 no, found stronger than death, 693a
 no respecter of persons, 1059a
 noblest work of, 224b, 318a, 390b
 not the, of nature, 233b
 not willing to do everything, 85b
 not worshipped by the herd, 897b
 nothing not, is greater, 608b
 nothynge more dyspleaseth, 84b
 now, alone knows, 688a
 obedience to, 1002b
 obligeth no man to more, 1070b
 o'erhead, 521a
 of Abraham, 264a
 of glory thundereth, 1033b
 of God, 1068a
 of heaven, worship the, 264a
 of music, 759b
 of my idolatry, 135b
 of nature placed in our power, 369a
 of our fathers, 816a, 260a
 of slep, 77b
 of storms, 534b
 of the Congo, 903a
 on our side, 427a
 on side of best digestion, 895a
 on whom each one depends, 655b
 once loved a garden, 917a
 one, and no more, 371a
 one, created us, 1049b
 one, in it all, 68a
 one nation under, 762b
 one, one law one element, 553a
 one towards, 619a
 only, can make a tree, 936b
 only who made us rich, 519b
 others call it, 573b
 our fathers, to thee, 529b
 our mind is, 28a
 out in the fields with, 1006a
 out of me, and man, 694b
 owe, a death, 153b
 pack and label men for, 790a
 Pan is dead, 61b
 peace of, 1062b
 peacemakers children of, 125a
 planted a garden, 695b
 plays upon this string first, 274b
 pleased, to visit us, 229b
 praise, sang Theocrite, 569b
 praises sing to, the King, 670a
 praising, with sweetest looks, 488a
 pray, keep me from being proud, 284a
 presume not, to scan, 316b
 prevail as sure as, reigns, 771b
 proportions the wind, 234b
 put another in for luck, 802b
 put your trust in, 434a
 reflect that, is just, 373b
 register of, 241b

God's peculiar light, 86a
plenty, 281a
poor who cannot wait, 525a
right hand and left, 586a
second mistake, 728b
side, one on, 562b
skirts, caught at, 569b
spies, 193b
the cure half-wrought, 747a
true princes, 604a
true religion, 1070a
ways is very quare, 969a
ways seem dark, 527b
ways to man, justify, 786b
we in, hand, 155b
will be done, 371b
will, sure they know, 979b
word, anvil of, 681b
works, best of all, 258b
Gods above, dwells with, 182a
all other, forsaking, 796b
angels would be, 120a, 316a
anger of the, falls, 18b
answer our prayers, 11a
approve the depth, 411b
are just, 193b
are monuments enough, 669b
are patient with the like, 68b
are we bards saints heroes, 619b
are well pleased, 223a
arrive when half-gods go, 504a
aspiring to be, if angels fell, 316a
by dozens, 99a
by the nine, he swore, 493b
call dross, 601b
call the, to witness, 203a
cannot strive, 70a
children nor, 815a
contend in vain, 394b
daughter of the, 547b
dish fit for the, 167a
do not know much about, 945a
doth diet, 246a
expedient that there be, 42b
fade but God abides, 707b
fashioned by men, 807b
fate or the, may give, 812b
fault of angels and of, 313b
favor of the, was equal, 18b
favour, whom the, 30a
forget the, are old, 738a
found favor with the, 51a
gifts of the, 3b
good, how he will talk, 291a
good the, provide, 280a
have made for you, 857b
help them that help themselves, 11a
hurled, out of their skies, 266b
kings it makes, 128b
labour of the, destroy, 312b
little tin, on wheels, 813a
live with the, 67b
made thee poetical, 162a
men compared with, 35b
moveth the might of, 17a
nearest to the, 70b
never old or die, 15b
nights and banquets of the, 40b
no other, before me, 1024b
of Egypt, 1024a
of the copybook maxims, 821a
of the market place, 821a
on the knees of the, 5b
opinion that there are no, 25b
pay for what the, had given, 858a
proud, and commodores, 603b

Gods, right idea of the, 25b
sent not corn, 202a
so many, so many creeds, 754a
strive for him equally, 17a
temples of his, 493b
thank whatever, may be, 741b
that wanton in the air, 268a
the country, 36b
themselves throw incense, 193b
they serve, 812b
to be young is to be one of immortal, 434b
utterance of the early, 483a
visit sins of fathers, 18a
voice of all the, 133b
ways of the, 66a
weapons of the, 19a
were good to you, 692b
what men or, are these, 482a
who haunt this place, 25b
woman is a dish for the, 201b
worship the, of the place, 224a
worship, with fruits, 12b
ye shall be as, 1021b
Gods' inferior, bear yourself as, 39a
thought was otherwise, 37a
Gods-Acre, calls the burial-ground, 522a
God-send a benefit received, 430a
good servant is a, 87a
Goe to bed with the lambe, 112b
Goes against my stomach, 161b
along the dark road, 35a
blows and, 885a
far beyond all panaceas, 223b
forth to war, 445b
proverb, 71a
time, by turns, 118a
Goeth a borrowing goeth a sorrowing, 96b
down sweetly, 1044b
forth and weepeth, 1037b
pride, before, 15a
Goethe has done his pilgrimage, 620a
Go-ethe, Shake Mulleary and, 761a
Goethe's sage mind, 620a
Going, all surely, somewhere, 610b
down of the sun, 843b, 1037a
down the wind, 284a
guest, speed the, 319b
looketh well to his, 1039b
men must endure their, 193b
not worth, to see, 342b
on before, 664a
out, preserve thy, 1037b
put off, and seeing, 65b
some are coming some are, 634a
stand not upon order of, 198a
the way of all flesh, 225b
the way of all the earth, 1026b
to and fro in the earth, 1029b
to keep us, 665b
to plays and carrying people, 286a
when they seem, they come, 699a
Goings, established my, 1034a
Goiters, forward as hives or, 989b
Gold, age of, fetch the, 244b
all that glisters is not, 77b
and amber shore, 787b
and pearl, robe of, 156a
and silks need not be new, 891a
and silver becks me, 148a
and silver ivory and apes, 1028b
and silver light, 825b

Gold and the lust, 973b
and treasure, 346b
angel writing in a book of, 448a
apples of, 1040b
bar of heaven, 640a
barrel of, 737a
base metal of humanity into, 743b
beaten, my throne, 862b
beneath his throat, 689b
better to me than, 708a
bow of burning, 388b
brass long loved as, 838b
bright, best read in, 480b
bright mane shine like, 385b
buttons, camlet cloak with, 284a
Caesar's, 885b
city of, 839a
clasps, 134b
clockwork joints of supple, 693b
cross of, 793a
crowned king, 928b
cursed lust for, 37a
curst be the, and silver, 351a
dust is, 257b
each wish a mint of, 398b
empowered with lands and, 923b
eyes of, and bramble-dew, 752a
fairy, 208a
female heart can, despise, 347b
fin in the porphyry font, 551a
fire is the test of, 47b
flow with tears of, 385b
forget the years of, 738a
frankincense and myrrh, 1050a
full tithe of, 591a
gateways of the stars, 790a
gild refined, 148a
give our, in princely sum, 791a
give your, no acid test, 877b
God made a heart of, 877b
gold gold gold, 488b
good as, 578a
great steamers white and, 819b
growing frugal of my, 587b
hairy, crown on 'er 'ead, 818a
hammered, 827a
harmless, 600a
harpes of, 560b
heart's worth, 153a
horse of, 968a
if, ruste, 80a
in phisik, 79b
jewel of, in a swine's snout, 1039a
kindest of all hosts, 9a
land of sand and ruin and, 692b
leaves of finest, 604a
like, to airy thinness beat, 216b
litel, in cofre, 79b
looking for, and silver, 591a
love the impotent for, 309b
lovede, in special, 79b
more to be desired than, 1033a
nails in temples, 600a
narrowing lust of, 553a
nightingale has a lyre of, 741b
none but temperate can carry, 25b
not al, that glareth, 77b
not woman's best adornment, 28a
old man's, 850a
orange glows, 378b
path of, 568a
patines of bright, 147a
plate sin with, 193a
poop was beaten, 200b
potable, 223b

Great Creator, 257b
  Creator drew his spirit, 281a
  creed, shadow of a, 959a
  cry but little wool, 83b
  cry in Egypt, 1024a
  cultivation, fruit of, 338a
  curtsy to, kings, 156b
  days, these are, 870b
  deal of knowledge, acquire, 340a
  deal of pains, 340a
  difficulties cannot be, 85b
  disguiser, death's a, 185b
  eater of beef, 163b
  elect from the, and wealthy, 566a
  end of life is action, 634a
  enterprises, impediments to, 120a
  events, march of, 812a
  example, thy stream my, 266b
  eyes, from those, 527a
  families of doubtful origin, 445a
  families of yesterday, 291b
  family, world appears like, 289a
  feast of languages, 133b
  flame follows tiny spark, 77a
  floods from simple sources, 183a
  fortitude of mind, 338b
  fortune is a great slavery, 48a
  friend to public amusements, 341a
  friends, little friends may prove, 9b
  friendships from bad beginning, 32a
  God, from thee we spring, 336a
  God our king, 530a
  god Pan is dead, 61b
  government of the United States, 770b
  gray ships come in, 862a
  grey-green greasy Limpopo, 819b
  guns, blew, 579b
  guns, winds blew, 377a
  head of things, 49a
  hearts true faith, 597b
  height of this, argument, 252a
  heir of fame, 244b
  hive the city, 267a
  horror and darkness, 274b
  ill can he rule, 113b
  Illusion, 865a
  imperial family, 997b
  impotently, 313a
  in life's small things, 602b
  in secret to be, 602a
  interpreter, 884b
  is Diana of the Ephesians, 1059a
  is truth, 496b
  is truth and mighty, 1065a
  is truth and shall prevail, 748b
  joy, good tidings of, 1056b
  know well I am not, 555a
  lakes of North America, 493a
  lever, mind is the, 443a
  liberty inspire our souls, 299a
  lie, fall victims to a, 951b
  light, have seen a, 1045b
  little fears grow, 176a
  love grows there, 176a
  love with a little gift, 29b
  man dies, 525a
  man does a thing for first time, 651a
  man fallen this day, 1027b
  man, great nose indicates, 842a
  man, nature removes a, 504a

Great man represents a ganglion, 709a
  man's curse, 310a
  man's memory, 176a
  many small make a, 82b
  men are truly obscene, 782b
  men as lunatics, 48a
  men be more gay than I, 491a
  men contending with adversity, 223a
  men, disbelief in, 475a
  men gain doubly, 510b
  men hallow a people, 419a
  men, heights reached by, 523b
  men, history the biography of, 475b
  men in, place, 120a
  men, level of its, 759b
  men, lives of, 521a, 1008b
  men not always wise, 1031b
  men not great scholars, 536a
  men owe their greatness, 772b
  men see that spiritual is stronger, 506a
  mind knows the power, 574a
  minds, fate of all, 462a
  minds, world must have, 586a
  moments are not turning points, 878a
  mountains and the sea, 986b
  music is a psychical storm, 809b
  nature's plan, 390b
  nature's second course, 196b
  Neptune's ocean, 196b
  no, man is born too soon, 840a
  no, thing created suddenly, 64a
  none hath the, unhappy, 302a
  none unhappy but the, 302a
  nose indicates a great man, 842a
  not like Caesar, 401a
  nothing, achieved without enthusiasm, 502b
  oaks, little strokes fell, 330b
  object, failure in a, 478b
  observer, he is a, 166b
  ocean, came over this, 229a
  ocean of truth, 288a
  old authors, 795b
  old times, 535b
  ones eat up little ones, 203b
  only know it shall be, 808b
  order of the ages is born, 36a
  our loss and grievous, 817b
  peaceful people, 770b
  people, experiences of a, 770a
  perhaps, 87b
  persons able to do great kindnesses, 108b
  pieces of good fortune, 332a
  pith and moment, 175a
  poetry should be, 478a
  poets can read them, only, 590a
  poets, to have, 611b
  price, pearl of, 1053a
  princess, saying of a, 345a
  purchase, alliance, 126b
  redemption from above, 244a
  release, in the peace of the, 742a
  right, to do a, 146a
  rightly to be, 177b
  rough diamond, 323b
  schools, flogging in our, 341b
  scorn of Hell, 76a
  seething surge of love, 665b
  sensibility, feels with, 339b
  sentiments, duration of, 727a
  share labours of the, 9b
  shout upon the hills, 756a
  show, foolery makes, 159a

Great show with little means, 565a
  some are born, 165a
  stage of fools, 193a
  star early droop'd, 609b
  states, responsibility of, 929a
  still keep their first, 853a
  sun in the firmament, 443a
  talk among people, 284b
  talkers, who know little are, 344b
  task remaining before us, 541a
  taskmaster's eye, 244b
  the little you give is, 630a
  there is no, and no small, 316b
  thing in prospect, 11a
  thing to pursue, 570a
  things both, and small, 422b
  things made of little things, 572b
  things of life, 897a
  things, seekest thou, 1048b
  things with small, compare, 36a
  those who were truly, 995a
  thoughts and good deeds, 585b
  thoughts come from heart, 115b
  thoughts, to think, 709a
  thoughts, who can mistake, 586a
  to be a, man and a saint, 619a
  to be, is to be misunderstood, 501b
  too, to be called after any name, 774b
  truly, who are truly good, 117b
  truth is, and shall prevail, 629b
  truths begin as blasphemies, 766a
  unwashed, 1006b
  voyage to the world unknown, 303b
  vulgar and the small, 267b
  weeds grow apace, 92b
  weight, entitled to, 433b
  welcome makes merry feast, 129a
  whatever was, seemed little, 492b
  white way, 1007b
  who is what he is from nature, 504a
  wide wonderful world, 626b
  willingness is, 85b
  winds let them be, 892a
  winds shorewards blow, 619b
  with child, 184a
  with young, 1012b
  wits jump, 109a
  wits near allied to madness, 276b
  work, life of Johnson a, 338b
Greater amount of room a people has, 951a
  are none beneath the sun, 820b
  bane to friendship, no, 330
  ease than hogs eat acorns, 238a
  felon loose, 713a
  force and better nature, 76b
  freedom greater security, 919a
  gives, feeling, 138b
  glory of God, 1009b
  he who is above temptation, 490a
  hulks draw deep, 181b
  inclination to hear you, 301b
  love hath no man, 1058b
  love, than his power, 673a
  man the greater courtesy, 555a
  monster or miracle, 100b

Hand, greater things produced by His, 229b
handle toward my, 196a
harp within my, 611b
hat in his, 338b
hath made our nation free, 535a
heart in his, 561a
heavier, than kings, 331a
heaving up my either, 231a
heav'n's, or will, 251b
here's my, 209b
hold fire in his, 138b
hold readily in your, 338b
holding out, for charity, 74b
hurts my, 189b
idle thunder in his lifted, 275b
immortal, or eye, 387a
imposition of a mightier, 492a
in hand with God, 889b
in hand with wand'ring steps, 259a
in its breeches pocket, 478a
industrious, from England, 641a
infection and the, of war, 138b
infinity in palm of your, 388a
iron, in velvet glove, 95a
keep the lifted, in awe, 305a
larger heart the kindlier, 553a
lays icy, on kings, 237b
leans cheek upon her, 135a
leaves thy, in mine, 519a
lend a, 624b
lets the curtain fall, 322b
licks the, just raised, 316a
lift up one, to heaven, 744a
like the dyer's, 207a
little thing in, 11a
living, warm and capable, 480a
man's, not able to taste, 142b
mortality's strong, 148b
muckrake in his, 274b
my time is at, 1054b
my times are in thy, 1033b
nature's sweet and cunning, 164a
Nelson's, 695b
not able to taste, 142b
not the, but the understanding, 107a
of God, 881b
of very healing, 873a
old nonchalance of the, 826b
on her bosom, 190a
one heart one, one nation, 535a
one iron, less, 735a
open, an easy shoe, 795a
our times are in his, 572a
over the lamp of life, 34b
paid for what his mouth ate, 1014b
papers in each, 318a
prompter's, is on his bell, 686b
raise a, against Rome, 887b
rash, in evil hour, 258a
red right, 253b
richest, showers, 253b
right, offend thee, 1051a
rosy, unbarr'd the gates, 256b
seen God's, through a lifetime, 571b
shake of the, 943b
so various, 260a
soft, and softer breast, 480a
stretch a, in hour of death, 857a
stretch out your, 65a
stretched out to receive, 1066a
strong as your, can make it, 888b
sweeten this little, 199a
sweeter in air than in, 121b

Hand, take a pen in his, 339a
tender inward of thy, 207a
that bore a nation, 663a
that hath made you fair, 185a
that held the dagger, 920b
that is honest and hearty, 412b
that kindles, 456a
that made us is divine, 299a
that ope'd the gate, 737a
that rocks the cradle, 606b
that rounded Peter's dome, 503a
things made entirely by, 886a
thoughtless, brush'd away, 387a
three lilies in her, 640b
threw a pearl away, 190b
time hath a taming, 495b
to execute, 369a, 1002a
to mouth, 102b
to one unfriended, 796a
to the plough, 1056b
touch of a vanish'd, 549b
tricks by sleight of, 298a
true love's, 138a
turn your, to, 106a
unbless'd thy, 6b
unearthly, presses the snib, 791b
unfriendly to tyrants, 271b
upon his head, 518b
upon my heart, 524b
upon thy mane, 455a
was on the oar, 23b
wash blood clean from my, 196b
waved her lily, 308a
we in God's, 155b
welcoming, 803a
whatsoever thou takest in, 269b
when he had not a pen in, 342b
whip in every honest, 189b
who hath seen her wave her, 547b
willow in her, 146b
win the, of woman, 514a
with his, the vessel made, 533a
work of our head and, 816b
Handclasp's a little stronger, 862b
Handel, care a farthing candle for, 430b
sings wisdom, 507b
Handel's, Mynheer, but a ninny, 232a
Handfasted, when we are, 417a
Handfasting, this we call, 417a
Hand-flung spears, 584b
Handful, fling us a, of stars, 933b
o' things I know, 698b
of ashes, 895b
of dust, 944a
of grey ashes, 627a
of meal in a barrel, 1028b
of sand, 977b
of silver, 567b
to the tribes that slumber, 470b
Handicap, poverty is a, 929b
Hand-in-glove, you and he were, 297a
Handiwork, firmament showeth his, 1032b
you give to God, 755b
Handkerchief of the Lord, 607b
Handle, lie the, which fits them, 536a
of a broom, 903a
of the big front door, 682a
one old jug without a, 581b
right and wrong, 65a, 370a
taste not, not, 1063a
toward my hand, 196a
Handled with a chain, 646a
Handler, nation's freight, 898a

Handles, everything has two, **65a**
everything hath two, 223a
Handmaid and nurse of enterprise, 925a
Handmaiden, low estate of his, 1056a
Hands, aching, and bleeding feet, 620a
acrost th' sea, 833b
administration in, of the many, 20a
all the rights in their, 517b
are blue, 581a
bearer's, otherwise employed, 776a
blesseth with two happy, 115a
business goes off a man's, 285b
by fairy, knell is rung, 351b
clap your, 792a
clasp, and weep a little, 486a
clasps the crag with crooked, 553a
clean, and a pure heart, 1033b
defended by all our, 557a
entergraft our, 216b
extended in straight line, 50a
failing, 860b
feed out of your tribe's, 821b
feel that I must wash my, 729a
fold my, and wait, 688b
foreign, clos'd thy dying eyes, 313b
formed the dry land, 1036b
from our, have power, 411b
from picking and stealing, 1069a
full, fortune with both, 153b
hammer away ye hostile, 754b
happiness in the, of others, 434a
hath not a Jew, 145a
hold much of heat, 946b
horny, of toil, 599b
if time be heavy on your, 547a
in your own, 817a
into thy, I commend, 1057b
join your, 127a
kiss her lips and take her, 825a
laid hold of by greedy, 537b
large and sinewy, 521b
lay thy soul full in her, 606b
laying violent, upon ship, 294b
lift up the, in prayer, 725a
little, make vain pretence, 656a
little, were never made, 302b
made before knives, 296b
many, make light worke, 94a
mischief for idle, 302b
mouths without, 281a
musket moulds in his, **747a**
my own fair, 295a
nearer than, and feet, 556a
new heraldry is, not hearts, **189a**
nobody has such small, 968b
not built with mortal, 279a
not without men's, 596a
now join your, 127a
of America, 888a
of Esau, 1023a
of mem'ry weave, 698b
of sisters death and night, 609b
of the higher classes, 376a
old, to young, 707a
on, and knees follow in it, 500b
on that golden key, 246b
oozing out at palms of my, 381a
pale, I loved, 812b
palms of your, will thicken, 793b
predatory human, 784b
reach out, amid the stars, **831b**

Harsh of cry, 981a
or burdensome, 73b
out of tune and, 175a
straining, discords, 137a
words of Mercury are, 134a
Harshness, no, gives offence, 311a
Hart, lame man leap as a, 1046b
panteth for water-brooks, 649a, 1034a
roe or young, 1045a
tyger's, in player's hide, 126a
ungalled play, 176a
willing, 91b
Harvard, Copeland of, 952b
fair, 463b
graduate of, 805a
man, can always tell a, 1007a
Square, floating over, 980b
whale ship my, 604a
Harvest, gathereth food in, 1038b
is past summer ended, 1048a
laughs with a, 509b
no, but a thorn, 233a
of a quiet eye, 405b
of old age is recollection, 34a
peaceful, days, 632a
seedtime and, 1022b
that I reap'd, 532a
thought not only of, 980a
truly is plenteous, 1052a
Harvest-home, stubble-land at, 149b
Harvests, ripening rich, 899b
wholesome, reaps, 490a
Harvest-time of love, 427b
Harwich, steamer from, 684a
Has, them that, gits, 735a
what a man, 109a
Haste, always in, 329b
in paying off obligation, 265b
is from the devil, 1010a
make, 148b
make, slowly, 1010a
maketh waste, 90b
married in, 130a
marry in, 900a
mounting in hot, 453a
now to my setting, 211a
one with moderate, 171a
thee nymph, 245a
this sweaty, 169b
to congratulate friends, 278a
weep to see you, away, 230b
wine that was spilt in, 890b
without rest without, 380a
wooed in, 130a
Hasten to be drunk, 281a
to their end, 205b
Hastening towards immortality, 600b
Hastens to join his comrades, 463a
Hastily and prudently, 45a
werke wel and, 82a
Hasty kiss snatch'd, 327b
marriage proveth well, 126b
marriage seldom proveth, 126b
need na start awa sae, 390a
orisons, patter out their, 966a
words which fly abroad, 474b
world, finished in this, 602a
Hasty-pudding, thick as, 1001a
Hat, cockle, and staff, 177b
dusty of, and shoe, 781b
fashion of his, 157a
forbade me to put off my, 273b
gnaws my, 902b
have a good, 534b
in his hand, 338b
is the ultimum moriens, 536a

Hat, lightly doffed his, 807b
little bird on Nellie's, 850a
new, carried into a church, 448b
not much worse for wear, 364a
off with your, 760b
old, stopping a chink, 680b
on account of his beaver, 581b
organ-grinder's, 713a
penny in the old man's, 1002b
put my, 338b
put off my, forbade me to, 273b
runcible, 580b
shocking, 535a
upon my head, 338b
wid my, caved in, 636a
Hatch'd, serpent's egg which, 167a
which, would grow mischievous, 167a
Hatched, count chickens before, 11b
silent when they, eggs, 244a
Hatchet, cut it with my, 395a
fergits where he buried a, 841a
Hate a dumpy woman, 457a
all miserable creatures, 461a
all women so, 216a
boughs of love and, 824a
cherish hearts that, thee, 211b
counsels not, 145a
each other so little, 778a
enough religion to make us, 295a
enough to hear prayers, 11a
envy dared not, 455b
foe without, 660a
for arts, 319a
found only on the stage, 458b
freedom for thought we, 710b
frown of, 388a
good to them that, you, 1051a
heats of, and lust, 785b
him mortally, 309b
him so as if to love him, 15a
I, and I love, 35b
I, war, 919b
I, inaccuracy, 672b
I, nobody, 296b
if hate be perfect, 554b
immortal, 252a
implacable in, 276b
is a fear, 972b
is the more enduring, 490b
keep, out, 933b
let them, provided they fear, 34a
love and, are emotions, 490b
love and desire and, 833a
man who builds his name, 308a
man you wronged, 63b
mankind, 203b
much to have, to forgive, 876a
naught I did in, 190a
no, lost between us, 108a
no sport in, 469a
nor love thy life nor, 52b, 258b
not fear not, 972b
of hate the scorn of scorn, 546a
of those below, 453a
one another and know it, 286a
owe no man, 161b
sequestered in its, 993b
smile to those who, 456b
sprung from my only, 135a
the day, 114b
the sin but love the sinner, 625b
the traitor, 53a
they would come to, 70a
think I know enough of, 880b
those hateful to us, not to, 14b
those I fight I do not, 826a

Hate to be unquiet at home, 286a
traitors and the treason love, 279a
twin of heathen, 556b
understand the folks they, 601a
whom they fear, 31a
whom they injured, 47b
woman learns how to, 727a
worst sin is not to, them, 764b
ye all, 267b
your neighbour, 492b
Hated, Caesar, the traitor, 53a
fat to be, 150b
how I should have, you, 672b
not for thy faults, 454a
past reason, 207a
the approximate, 884a
things I have, 959a
traitor, 279a
Hateful, self is, 273a
tax upon commodities, 336b
to us, 14b
woman once loved is most, 858a
Hater, very good, 338b
Haters, bless your, 556b
Hates and greeds of old Europe, 839a
endless extinction of unhappy, 621b
flatterers, 167a
loves more readily than it, 514a
loves or fears or, 412b
Hateth his son, 84b
Hath, unto everyone that, 1054b
Hating ill-natured gossip, 851a
no one love but only he, 454b
Hatred as well as love, 345a
battered by, 927a
comes from the heart, 461a
envy, and malice, 1068b
habitual, or fondness, 367a
healthy, of scoundrels, 476a
in a mind, 826b
intellectual, 827a
love nor, in the game, 727a
needs but to be seen, 317a
no rage like love to, turned, 298a
objects of, 858a
of entrenched greed, 919a
public odium and public, 433b
soul-destroying, 869b
stalled ox and, therewith, 1039b
stirreth up strifes, 1039a
Hats, babies in silk, 941a
may make divorces, 845a
off the flag is passing by, 804b
old trees, coats, 953a
seraphs swing their snowy, 646a
Hatter, the, 656b
Hatto, Bishop, 426a
Haud the wretch in order, 224a
Haughtiness, none possess such, 887a
of soul, 299b
Haughty barbers, 964b
dames in jewelled velvets, 604a
day fills his blue urn, 506a
gallant gay Lothario, 302a
old and, nation, 246b
one, cry, 914b
spirit before a fall, 1039b
vigilant blue-stocking, 493b
Haul down the American flag, 487a
Hauled on his boots, 587a
Haunch and the hump is obey, 816a
Haunt not the fringy edges, 595b
of every noxious reptile, 353a
of flies on summer eves, 481b

Haunt, public, 159b
 the rich man's door, 38b
 where they most breed and, 195b
 you yet, 890b
Haunted air, 948b
 by a demoniac throng, 731a
 by ghosts they have depos'd, 139b
 houses, 523b
 me like a passion, 404a
 spring and dale, 244b
 stream, 245b
 waning moon was, 420b
Haunts and obsesses my brain, 486a
 busy, of men, 470a
 love seldom, the breast, 309b
 me like a face half known, 780b
 me night and day, 928b
 suspicion, guilty mind, 127a
 the tempest, 618b
 thy days, 480a
Have, all we, and are, 821b
 more than thou showest, 191a
 not what we, 780b
 nought venter nought, 93a
 they lack I, 101b
 to, to hold, 812b, 1069a
 what we would have, 184b
Have-beens, no sense of, 706a
Have-much and Have-little, 108a
Haven, down to the, 556b
 glorious, 76a
 in sunny Palestine, 896b
 safe into the, glide, 334a
 under the hill, 549b
Haven's gate, people wait at, 862a
Havens dumb, green swell in the, 724b
 ports and happy, 138a
Having nothing nothing can he lose, 126b
 nothing yet possessing, 1062a
Having-been-in-danger, 884a
Having-gone-to-the-very-end, 884b
Havoc, cry, 168a
Hawk, know a, from a handsaw, 174a
 or a buzzard, 983a
 their wares, 949a
 wild, to the wind-swept sky, 815a
Hawk'd at and kill'd, 197a
Hawk-eyes and cheek of apple-blossom, 554b
Hawk's the darling of his fere, 29b
Hawks, between two, 124a
 such hounds such, 1012b
Hawthorn bush with seats, 355b
 hedge, 938a
 in the dale, 245a
 snow of the, 777a
Hawthorne to Montaigne to Baudelaire, 751b
Hay, bottle of, 142a
 cry was still more, 748a
 dance the antic, 123a
 farmers make, 803a
 for the cattle, 59a
 live on, 1009a
 make, when the sunne shineth, 91a
 needle in a bottle of, 107b
 turkey in the, 1003b
 world is a bundle of, 460a
 worth a load of, 1000a
Haycock, needle in the, 957b
Haydn, some cry up, 430b

Haystack, under the, fast asleep, 1016a
Hazard, art's long, 846b
 march to the unseen, 809a
 not the, but the play, 829b
 of concealing, 391a
 of new fortunes, 147b
 of the die, 128b
 runs a very great, 107a
 when a nation's life's at, 625a
Hazardous, definitions are, 336b
Haze, shimmering golden, 849b
 that side of the, 647a
Hazel, Glenartey's, shade, 415a
Hazel-switch for discovery of treasure, 823b
Hazlitt to Lamb to Wordsworth, 751b
He, faithful only, 256b
 for God only, 255b
 forget the, and she, 215b
 has given bees honey, 326a
 has invented history, 327a
 let's eat, 564b
 poorest, in England, 228b
 that is thy friend indeed, 220a
 that is without sin, 1058a
 think of yourself as, 844b
 who does not mind his belly, 340a
 who goes to bed sober, 225a
Head aches, when the, 107a
 and front of my offending, 186a
 and shoulders, bring in by, 100a
 and the hoof of the law, 815b
 anointest my, with oil, 1033b
 as full of quarrels, 136b
 at his, a grass-green turf, 177b
 audacious, is lifted, 661a
 binds so dear a, 467a
 bow thy, in gentle spite, 629a
 bowed his comely, 268b
 center the hub the king pin, 661a
 chills upon the, or heart, 751b
 chop off her, 656b
 chop off your, 1016a
 coals of fire upon his, 1041a
 complex problem of the, 811a
 concerned with outer weather, 881a
 contempt comes from the, 461a
 crack like that in her, 732a
 crotchets in thy, 180a
 crown in heart not, 126b
 crown of his, 158a, 451a
 crown of the, 50a
 crown old Winter's, 263b
 disorders of the, 19a
 dissever from the fair, 312b
 erect beneath the tragic years, 774a
 fame over his living, 468a
 gently falling on thy, 302b
 give him a blow on the, 72a
 good gray, 553a
 great, of things, 49a
 grown gray in vain, 468a
 guts in his, 181b
 hair of yon gray, 528a
 hair on my, stands up, 16a
 hairs of their owner's, 708a
 hand upon his, 518b
 hang the, as discontent, 220b
 hangs his, for shame, 627b
 hat upon my, 338b
 heaven upon earth to weary, 488b
 heels higher than my, 101a

Head, heels up to the, 750b
 hide his, under his wing, 1018a
 hit nail on the, 89a
 hoary, 529a
 hoary, is a crown of glory, 1039b
 horror's, 189a
 humour not more from the, 472b
 if she'd but turn her, 825b
 I'll eat my, 576b
* imperfections on my, 172b
 in my heart not on my, 126b
 in the heart or in the, 145a
 inside a wolf's mouth, 9b
 is bloody but unbowed, 741b
 keep good tongue in your, 209b
 kicked in the, by a mule, 828b
 King Charles's, 579a
 lay my, upon my grave, 241a
 lift my, till it strikes, 38a
 lock upon the shapely, 717b
 made up the lilac out of my, 934a
 man with the, 550b
 Medusa's, 960b
 my, is bending low, 636a
 no roof to shroud his, 227a
 not silver'd o'er, 364b
 not so long by the, 133b
 of the army, 400a
 of the table, 501a
 of this great widespread family, 812a
 off with her, 657a
 off with his, 128a
 old gray, 527b
 on her knee, 190a
 one small, 356b
 over, and heels, 35a
 plant thou no roses at my, 649b
 planted in the human, 461a
 pleasing land of drowsy, 328b
 ragged, seld-shaven, 429a
 repairs his drooping, 249b
 seems no bigger than his, 193a
 she bow'd, 246a
 shot it through the, 1019b
 silent doctor shook his, 308a
 silver'd o'er with age, 308a
 smote off his, 1026a
 some once lovely, 531b
 stand on your, 656a
 statuaries loved to copy, 492a
 stone of the corner, 1037a
 stroked down with a slipper, 32a
 stuff, with all such reading, 322a
 sweete tooth in his, 112b
 that wears a crown, 153b
 thing comes in his, 127a
 thoughts in our, 817a
 thoughts into a lover's, 405a
 tired her, 1029b
 to contrive, 369a
 trickled through my, 659a
 turned her little, aside, 1014a
 twenty years, of a household, 816a
 upon the lap of earth, 349a
 useful lesson to the, 365b
 very staid, 146a
 where to lay his, 1052a
 whole, is sick, 1043a
 wild ass stamps o'er his, 531b
 wires grow on her, 207b
 wise man's eyes in his, 1042a
 work of our, and hand, 816b
 worst fall on, 148b
 young body with old, 146a

Heart, absence absence in the, 946b
abundance of the, 1052b
ageless in your, 899b
alike conceived and dared, 570a
all thy, lies open unto me, 551a
and stomach of a king, 97a
and the soul and the senses, 571a
and voice oppressed, 593a
and voice would fail me, 645a
anniversaries of the, 526a
another heart divines, 524b
arrow for the, 460a
as a seal upon thine, 460a
as great as the world, 508a
as he thinketh in his, 1040b
as that of a little child, 566a
at rest within my breast, 385b
balm of the bruised, 122a
batter my, 217b
beating of my own, 543a
beats the, so kindly, 582b
because my, is pure, 549a
best, best brain, 662b
bitten me to the, 22a
blessed are pure in, 1050b
breast encloseth my poor, 127b
broken and contrite, 1034b
broken, lies here, 494a
bruis'd, was pierced, 186b
build on the human, 567a
burn within us, 413b
burning at the, of living, 977b
can push the sea, 961b
captain with the mighty, 756a
carries my, as stowaway, 876b
caused widow's, to sing, 1031b
change the, from red, 712b
changeth man's countenance, 1066a
chill the warmest, 630a
chills upon the head or, 751b
clean, 1034b
clean hands and a pure, 1033b
cold of his, 802a
command my, and me, 263a
committed adultery in his, 1050b
congenial to my, 357a
constant, 999b
consume my, away, 827a
courage of, or holiness, 849a
cracks a noble, 179b
crown is in my, 126b
cruelty has a human, 387b
cure thy, of love, 500a
cutting the, asunder, 923b
dark as one's own, 514a
darkies how my, grows weary, 636a
darling of my, 307b
deceitful and wicked, 1048a
depth of the, of man, 1065b
detests him, 4b
devils dwell in, of man, 240b
disease, housemaid's knee to, 862a
distress touching his, 371a
distrusting asks, 357a
do not devour thy, 72b
dry of blood, 480a
ease a, like a satin gown, 966a
ease thine, of love, 500a
eat not thy, 57b
eate thy, 114a
enrich not the, of another, 522b
everywhere he feels his, 3a
excitement of the, 545a
expends his whole, 379a

Heart fail because of Goliath, 1027b
faint, ne'er won fair lady, 107b
faint, never won fair lady, 684a
falsehood leads to the, 373b
felt along the, 403b
female, can gold despise, 347b
find thy, at home, 232a
find your, despair, 591a
fire that in the, resides, 620a
flaw'd, 193b
flowers of Thy, 441b
fond, till we meet, 329a
for any fate, 521a
for every fate, 456b
fountain of sweet tears, 406a
from itself kept, 689b
gathered to thy, 736b
give a loving, 230a
give me back my, 452b
give not your, away, 785b
give your, to a dog, 819b
gives his, and soul away, 785b
glad with all my, 122b
gladness of the, 1066a
glow of a kindly, 729b
glows in ev'ry, 305a
God made a, of gold, 877b
good, is better than all the heads, 510a
great thoughts come from, 115b
grieve his, 198b
grown cold, 468a
gushed from my, 422a
hand and, to this vote, 443a
happiest, that ever beat, 738a
happy as the, was long, 997a
happy the, that sighed, 122a
hard, of a child, 934b
hardened Pharaoh's, 1024a
has hidden treasures, 586b
has its love, 486a
has its reasons, 272b
hath but one eye, 755a
hath ne'er within him burned, 413b
hath 'scap'd this sorrow, 206a
hatred comes from the, 461a
have its say, 760b
healed the, that's broken, 558a
heals the, 993a
here in the country's, 800a
heresy of, 527b
hid in the, of love, 824b
high as my, 162a
his grave a nation's, 629a
hit a woman's, 509a
how dear to this, 450a
how goes it, 849a
how many a, must pass, 733b
humble and a contrite, 816a
humble human, in pain, 830b
hurt you to the, 679a
I am sick at, 169b
I told her all my, 386a
if every, were just frank, 270a
if, fails thee climb not, 111a
if guilt's in that, 439b
if one has no, 486b
imagination of man's, 1022b
in each, a little heaven, 294a
in every true woman's, 446a
in his hand, 561a
in the midst of crowds, 431a
in the, or in the head, 145a
in unison with all mankind, 741a
incense of the, 330a
infant, 431b

Heart, into her, too easy, 258a
is a lonely hunter, 762a
is all a-flutter, 995b
is getting softer, 606a
is Highland, 436a
is in a whirl, 829b
is inditing a good matter, 1034b
is like a singing bird, 649b
is made better, 1042b
is not here, 392b
is on the mountain still, 796b
is open wide tonight, 767a
is slow to learn, 962a
is sorrowful, 1039b
is there with thee, 797a
is turning home again, 757a
is wax moulded, 110a
is where the hills fling up, 796b
jot of, or hope, 251b
joys of our, 487b
keep thy, with diligence, 1038b
keep, when all have lost it, 566b
kep' goin' pity-pat, 601a
kept these sayings in her, 1056b
key to your, 519a
kind and gentle, 354b
knocked on my sullen, 751b
know truth by the, 272b
knoweth his own bitterness, 1039a
laid his hand upon my, 524b
language of the, 319b
languor is not in your, 623a
larger, the kindlier hand, 553a
larger was his, 277b
laughter of her, 958b
leaps up when I behold, 406a
leave the, aglow, 830a
let every, prepare Him room, 303a
let not thine, be glad, 1040b
let not your, be troubled, 1058b
level in her husband's, 164b
like bowl brimming over, 659b
little body with a mighty, 154b
live without, 653a
lock'd my, in a case o' gowd, 1013a
look in thy, 115b
look into any man's, 641a
looked into his father's, 987a
Lord looketh on the, 1027b
love lays hold on gentle, 75b
love that is in my, 486a
love-sick, dies, 961a
make glad the, of childhood, 701b
makes the, afraid, 488a
makes the, grow fonder, 485a
makes the, run over, 372a
maketh glad, the of man, 1036b
man after his own, 1027a
manly, 521b
man's, deviseth his way, 83a
man's, is small, 816b
may give a useful lesson, 365b
may go where it will, 43a
may heal or break, 558a
may she find all one, 624b
meditation of my, 1033a
meek and lowly in, 1052b
meet a mutual, 328b
memory plays tune on, 591a
mend the, 312b
merry, doeth good, 1040a
merry, goes all the day, 208a
merry, hath a continual feast, 1039b

Hollow winds begin to blow, 380a
Hollow-eyed sharp-looking wretch, 129b
Hollowness, machinations, treachery, 190b
Hollows, radiance fills their, 892a
  where those flowers grew, 712a
Holly and laurel wreaths entwine, 686b
  and the ivy, 1004b
  is dark, 592a
Holly-tree, friendship like the, 591b
Holmes, there goes Sherlock, 95b
Holy, all labor is noble and, 562a
  and enchanted, 420b
  and meek she cries, 386a
  angels guard thy bed, 302b
  anger and pious grief, 451a
  as severe, 185a
  birth, proclaim the, 670a
  book, Mohammed's truth in a, 543a
  city new Jerusalem, 1064b
  deadlock, 955a
  died to make men, 597b
  divine good amiable, 258b
  fair and wise is she, 132a
  faith that warmed our sires, 535a
  fields, 149a
  flag, nail to the mast her, 534b
  flame forever burneth, 427b
  function, 361b
  Ghost, communion of the, 1062a
  Ghost, conceived by the, 1068a
  Ghost, Father Son and, 287b
  Ghost, filled with the, 1059a
  Ghost, sin against the, 700b, 729a
  ground, 1023b
  ground, battle-field is, 459a
  ground, call it, 470a
  ground where there is sorrow, 770a
  hail, light, 254b
  health, 9a
  how, people look when seasick, 672b
  is the Lord of hosts, 1045b
  light, freedom's, 529b
  Lord God Almighty, 445b
  men could still be, 959b
  mistaken zeal in politics, 1002a
  nor Roman nor an empire, 324b
  not one who thinks thee, 989a
  passion of friendship, 678a
  place, candle in a, 912b
  place, stand in his, 1033b
  priest that to her speakes, 115a
  priests bless her, 200b
  profane clean obscene, 228b
  psalms, 116a
  rest, 1069b
  Roman Empire, 324b
  room, coming to that, 217b
  sabbath day to keep, 1024b
  sages once did sing, 244a
  spirit blessed soul, 547b
  stream, pebbles of the, 997a
  temple, Lord is in his, 1049b
  temple of Mecca, 1070a
  text of pike and gun, 238b
  thing, like some, 441a
  things, truth and rapture are, 896a
  time quiet as a nun, 407a
  towers of the silences, 959b
  tradition finally becomes, 726a

Holy water the priest consecrates, 593b
  white birds flying after, 896b
  word, ears have heard the, 386b
  writ, proofs of, 188b
  writ, stolen forth of, 127b
  writ, we learn in, 917a
Holystone the decks, 585a
Homage, from contemporaries full, 492b
  heaven and earth do her, 112a
  involuntary, of the low, 580a
  owes no, unto the sun, 241a
  to him your, bring, 754b
  vice pays to virtue, 265b
Home again and home again, 757a
  again jiggety-jig, 1019b
  and dined, 284b
  and dined upon cold meat, 285a
  any more at, like you, 941b
  at dusk they come, 801b
  at, with their own hearts, 514b
  be it ever so humble, 464b
  be it never so homely, 464b
  be thou thine own, 217a
  bring, wealth of the Indies, 342a
  came, for ever, 430a
  can't appreciate, 801a
  can't come, to dinner, 301b
  charity begins at, 240b
  come, tired with travel, 35a
  comes safe, 156b
  country friends all quitted, 428b
  cry of, 994b
  day's march nearer, 413a
  dear hut our, 330a
  do they miss me at, 629a
  draw near to their eternal, 242b
  dunce kept at, 363a
  each refinement found at, 389a
  far from the old folks at, 636a
  father dear father come, 660b
  find thy heart at, 232a
  footsteps hath turn'd, 413b
  free land in our beloved, 613a
  gives a child a, 896a
  go, and get a quiet sleep, 843b
  go, in the dark, 802b
  going far from, 962b
  going, two hours ago, 301b
  gone and ta'en thy wages, 204b
  hate to be unquiet at, 286a
  heart is turning, again, 757a
  hills of, 752a
  his only son myself at, 352b
  home at last, 488a
  homely, and simple pleasures, 788a
  homely features keep, 248a
  I am far from, 495b
  I am nearer, today, 630b
  I keep it staying at, 647a
  I'm going, 502b
  in the sea, 529a
  is bright with calm delight, 667b
  is heaven, 989b
  is on the deep, 432b
  is safest refuge, 110b
  is the place, 879b
  is the sailor, 751b
  iv opporchunity, 837a
  iv raypublican simplicity, 835b
  know when to rise and go, 699a
  liberty must begin at, 965a
  life is no more natural, 765b
  life, refuge from, 764b
  look as much like, 994a
  love has found its, 42a

Home, love of, 577a
  loved at, revered abroad, 390a
  man and wife have a, 6a
  man goeth to his long, 1043b
  man who thinks to found a, 840a
  men merriest when from, 154b
  my wife from Brampton, 285a
  native, deep imag'd, 6b
  no, in Europe save Paris, 729a
  no, like a raft, 677a
  no more delightful than, 34a
  no place like, 464b
  not wept so well at, 786b
  of fairest mould, 877b
  of lost causes, 621b
  of love, 206b
  of the bean and the cod, 793a
  of the brave, 436a
  of the sacred cod, 793a
  old England is our, 490b
  old Kentucky, good night, 636b
  on the rolling deep, 583b
  our eternal, 303a
  out of house and, 153a
  provided in the nineties, 891b
  rafters of the, 756a
  returned, the previous night, 866a
  returns, to find it, 756b
  safe in my sylvan, 503a
  seek further than at, 130a
  shall men come, 867a
  shortest way, 232a
  shoulder-high we bring you, 786a
  song of, and friends, 666b
  stay at, my heart, 525b
  stored for thee at, 790a
  strains to, and memory dear, 780a
  t' make it, 913b
  that our feet may leave, 535b
  there's no place like, 464b
  there's nobody at, 315b
  things foreign or things at, 274a
  think as though we had stayed, 901a
  till the cow comes, 228a
  to men's business, 119b
  true nature of, 606a
  turns again, 557a
  tyrants safely govern, 126b
  was better place, 160a
  we first knew, 529a
  wept so well at, 69a
  where the buffalo roam, 730b
  where we love is, 535b
  woman good for everything at 18a
  you'll be comin', again, 775b
Homebound fancy, 494b
Home-brought stuff from far seafaring, 795a
Home-keeping habits, 54b
  hearts, 525b
  youth have homely wits, 131b
Homeland, free in a living, 931a
Homeless air, 690a
  near a thousand homes, 403a
  street, child on the, 756a
Home-like, old friends are most too, 775a
Homely and innocent, 512b
  be it never so, 464b
  beauty of good old cause, 407c
  features keep home, 248a
  hen lays one, 1006b

Innocent thoughts, 458b
who ever perished being, 1030a
Innocently, live, 334a
Innocuous desuetude, 689a
Inns of molten blue, 646a
Innuendo, impropriety of his, 950a
Innumerable as the stars, 256b
bees, murmuring of, 551a
biographies, essence of, 475b
caravan, 470b
presumptions, in face of, 718b
race of men, 257a
Inoffensive untitled aristocracy, 536b
Inordinate fondness of a father, 333a
Inquire, shoot first and, afterwards, 965b
why things are as they are, 722a
Inquirer, modest not presumptuous, 304a
Inquiring, not too, critic, 969b
Inquiry about woman's pedigree, 105b
busy, made into meals, 62a
most careful and particular, 19b
unintimidated, 860a
Inquisition dogs, 556a
violates spirit of Constitution, 900b
Inquisitive, every man ought to be, 811a
study of law renders men, 360a
Insane and awful passion, 490a
excitement at first, 697b
loud clamor is more or less, 473a
love to speak of themselves, 688b
most, of passions, 765b
ordinarily he is, 487a
root, 194b
Insanity or ferocity in beasts, 505b
the logic of accurate mind, 536a
Insatiable and the unhappy, 823a
Inscription, altar with this, 1059a
Inscriptions, lapidary, 341b
Inscrutable colossal and alone, 730b
dumb, and grand, 622b
invisible, 132a
Insect, man is a mere, 701a
revenge the sting of a tiny, 10a
scraping on the surface, 690b
vile, 329b
Insects, both, and humans, 895a
coral, multitudinous, 612b
troublesome, of the hour, 361b
Insensibility, argues an, 430a
stark, 338b
Insensible, be earth, 258b
of the brevity of life, 290a
Inseparable, one and, 444a
perfect union one and, 842a
Inside he was impromptu, 801a
of church, 151a
out to show the lining, 879a
skinside is the, 855a
Inside-pocket of my mind, 958b
Insight, in hours of, will'd, 620a
Insignia, whatever its symbols its, 582b
Insignificancy and an earldom, 324a

Insignificant, man is, 861b
weak and, 19a
Insipid as the queen upon a card, 555b
dish, 723b
to a vulgar taste, 822b
Insipidly pleasing kind, 642b
Insist, like to pray with not, 931b
Insisture course proportion, 181a
Insolence and wine, 252b
of demagogues, 26b
of enormous animals, 19a
of office, 174b
strength without, 451b
Inspector of snow-storms, 589b
Inspiration, in proportion to the, 508a
no more, than in a plate of muffins, 765a
one per cent, 735b
purer sources of joyous, 559b
unapprehended, 432b, 468b
which gives to all work, 773a
Inspir'd, two bodies with one soul, 5a
Inspire, great liberty, our souls, 299a
meanest of your sons, 310b
they who, it most, 465b
we do not, conduct, 266a
Inspired mankind never so happily, 749a
sacred and, divinity, 118b
writer, endurable for, 672a
Inspires, fair fame, 318b
wine, us, 308b
Inspiring bold John Barleycorn, 393b
place can be, 975b
Inspirit, songs may, us, 567b
Installment, repays first, on his debt, 48a
Installments, demands to the vanquished in, 951b
Instances, modern, 161b
Instancy, majestic, 790a
Instant dole of praise, 815a
for an, means dominion, 648a
God's, men call years, 667a
quick of all time is the, 931a
rose both at, 152a
Instantly your forehead lowers, 343b
Instill a wanton sweetness, 328b
Instinct, healthy, for it, 672a
of looking around, 611b
of self-preservation, 775b
species of public, 472a
truth was felt by, 573b
volcanic political, 767a
women have a more subtle, 769a
Instincts, a few strong, 410b
heed no, but our own, 269b
high, 408b
malice basest of all, 680a
plant himself on his, 501a
satisfied in double, 697a
uncivilized Eastern, 813b
Institute and digest of anarchy, 361a
Institution is the lengthened shadow, 501b
let an, strain itself, 765b
life's a pleasant, 685b
pub a valuable, 955b
stand by the, he represents, 763a

Institution, such a glorious, 360b
such as are in the, 504b
Institutions alone create a nation, 512b
American, 444b
deprived of the liberal, 400a
endeavor to shape, 700a
established, 444b
liberal, 728a
man-made, 957b
neither for nor against, 608b
political, a superstructure, 850a
sought to destroy, 608b
supports, as venerable, 496a
this country with its, 539a
Instressed, his mystery must be, 725a
Instruct a wiser man, 49a
sorrows, 147b
Instruction about this and that, 763a
better the, 145a
evil by, 68b
in the laws of nature, 633a
makes men good, 27a
text of civil, 375a
Instructions, bloody, 195b
on the label, 993b
Instructors, practice is best of all, 44b
Instructs the reader, 287a
Instrument, critic a valuable, 719a
mind of man a musical, 613b
of trade and commerce, 666b
stringed, 53b
sweeter than sound of an, 240b
to know if moon shine, 239b
trying, to perform upon, 788a
tune the, here at door, 217b
Instruments, find fit, of ill, 312b
fit, to make slaves, 334b
genius and the mortal, 167a
made of fir wood, 1028a
mastery over musical, 785a
of darkness, 194b
thousand twangling, 209b
to plague us, 193b
Insubstantial pageant faded, 210a
Insufficient premises, conclusions from, 671b
Insular Tahiti, 604a
Insult added to injury, 10a
only cowards, dying majesty, 9b
sooner forgotten than an, 323a
to God, 567b
Insulted, allows himself to be, 243b
you as Lady Luck, 970b
Insulting foe, meet the, 383a
Insults of fortune, 333a
unavenged, 410b
Insupportable, repose is, 697b
which is unreasonable, 63b
Insured, they were heavily, 681b
Insurrection, inciters of servile, 666a
nature of an, 167a
Intangible world, we touch thee, 790b
Integrity, artist who retains his, 914a
blend of courage, 981b
clothed with, 270a
of nature, 344b
territorial, 771a
Intellect, an ant in his, 701a
by feelings and not by, 614b

Keerless man in his talk, 698b
Keg, fizz like wine in a, 894b
Kelly slide, slide, 1005b
Kellys, wherever there's, 734b
Kelmscott Press, 776a
Kelson, higher than the, is low, 603b
of the creation, 607b
Kelt, Slav Teuton, 556b
Ken, angels', 252a
years beyond our, 525a
Kennel, truth's a dog must to, 191a
Kent, from Northumberland to, 759a
Kentuckian rocks, carved deep in, 625b
Kentucky, boy in, who stubbed toe, 540a
boys are alligator-horses, 450b
in spite of old, 450b
moonlight is softest in, 725b
old, home good night, 636a
strain was in his voice, 730a
Kepe wel thy tonge, 82b
Kept awake as many nights, 961b
easier, than recovered, 371a
him as the apple of his eye, 1026a
his breath to cool pottage, 60b
it since by being dead, 275b
law by transgressing, 251a
my word, 862b
their blue eyes blue, 947a
these sayings in her heart, 1056b
thy truth so pure of old, 251b
upright, not be, 66b
we two, house, 706b
Kerke, narre to, farre from God, 92a
Kernels, corn is full of, 788b
Kerosene lamp, swallowed a lighted, 886b
Kerry, setters from, 858b
Kettle black, pot calls the, 109a
blackness of a, 1048b
Polly put the, on, 1019b
pretty, of fish, 684a
Kew, Highness' dog at, 321a
in lilac-time, 909b
Key, bondman's, 144a
door to which I found no, 532a
forever hold the, 737a
friend under own life's, 182b
golden, that opes palace, 246b
I have the, 788b
less a primer than a, 860b
to your heart, 519a
used, is always bright, 331a
with this same, 574b
with this, Shakespeare unlocked heart, 412a
Keys belonging to the locks, 754a
clutch the golden, 552b
fingers on these, 906a
of all the creeds, 551b
of heaven, 1053b
two massy, 249a
wandered over the noisy, 634a
Keystane, night's black arch the, 393b
Kibe, galls his, 178b
Kick against the pricks, 1059a
every ass thinks he may, 378a
in that part, 239a
me down stairs, 389a
their owners over, 380b

Kick them in the pants, 926a
wheel's, 895b
you down-stairs, 656b
Kick'd until they can feel, 239a
Kicked in the head by a mule, 828b
out of doors, 294b
waxed fat and, 1026a
Kicking my dawg around, 1008a
you seems the lot of curs, 533b
Kid, leopard lie down with the, 1046a
oh you, 936b
Kidney, man of my, 180b
Kildare, Cork and, 858b
Kilkinny, skies of ould, 859b
Kill a man as kill a good book, 250b
a woman who has injured you, 714a
all the lawyers, 125b
basilisk is sure to, 308b
bring fatted calf and, it, 1057a
bullet that will, me, 399b
cankers in musk-rose buds, 141b
cat, 159a
cocks that will, fighting, 59a
every author would his brother, 266b
him in the shell, 167a
I'll learn him or, him, 676a
in an artificial manner, 474b
kill kill, 193a
look as though he'd, his wife, 833b
mettle to, care, 159a
not yet canst thou, me, 217b
one admiral, 325a
one grasshopper, 902b
princes privileged to, 366b
surfeits sooner, than fasts, 261b
the bloom, 411b
them when they're said, 42a
thou shalt not, 1025a
time, how a man should, 89b
time without injuring eternity, 589b
to know to, to create, 619a
too apt before the, 267a
us for their sport, 192b
when you have to, a man, 872b
wife with kindness, 130b
you all e'en now, 1017a
you if you quote it, 829b
you must, him, 508b
Kill'd, hawk'd at and, 197a
Killed a calfe in high style, 273b
before he, the dragon, 867b
better be, than frightened, 510a
books cannot be, by fire, 921b
by overwork, 814a
by pin-pricks, 651a
care, a cat, 159a
effort very nearly, her, 849b
I'm, sire, 569b
more, than Galen cured, 234a
off by one critique, 694b, 695a
the goose and opened it, 11a
the rat that ate the malt, 1020b
while laughing at some jest, 817b
who, that cherry tree, 395a
Killeth the foolish man, 1030a
the letter, 1062a
Killing as the canker, 248b
chills, 751b

Killing frost, 211a
more ways of, a cat, 598b
the victim's sympathies, 696b
Kills a reasonable creature, 250b
all forms of life, 988b
reason itself, 250b
the thing he loves, 769b
who, a man, 250b
Kilmer tongue, 942a
Kiltartan Cross, my country is, 826a
Kin and kith, one's own, 990a
griefs of, 15a
little more than, 170a
makes whole world, 182a
stranger kith or, 767a
Kin' o' smily round the lips, 601a
Kind and clean, 966b
and gentle heart, 354b
art of being, 754a
as kings upon coronation day, 279a
be to her virtues very, 293b
best in this, but shadows, 142b
blund'ring, of melody, 277b
children, and natural, 154b
common dotages of human, 222b
cruel only to be, 177a
embrace of clay, 935a
enjoy her while she's, 278a
ferments of the worst, 306b
friend, time is a, 928b
had it been early had been, 339a
heart, for such a, 180b
hearts are more than coronets, 547a
hearts for friends to fill, 751b
her caressing, 343b
if you stop to be, 915a
is not therefore, 314a
kiss before we part, 329a
makes one wondrous, 977a
more nearly, and gentle, 977a
more than kin less than, 170a
new, of animal, 954b
newest, of ways, 154a
no best in, 523a
of alacrity in sinking, 180b
of borrowing, 251a
of man the country turns out, 507b
of posterity, 330a
of self-homicide, 286a
of wit, craves a, 165a
parent or merciless stepmother, 49a
pay in, 994a
plane tree's, 778b
plenty of the, 546b
relief, not seek for, 385b
shows herself more, 146b
the sex is to a soldier, 6b
to be honest to be, 752b
to my remains, 280a
tyrannies on human, 279a
umpire of miseries, 124b
weakest, of fruit, 145b
word to Christ, 573b
yet was he, 356b
you'd like to hold, 828a
Kinde, attractive, of grace, 114b
will creepe, 93a
Kinder laws to bring us back, 578b
let me be a little, 913b
than is necessary, 792a
Kindest of all hosts, 9a

Kindle a brighter than its own, 701a
cannot, when we will, 620a
fires to warm it, 630b
soft desire, 280b
Kindled by the master's spell, 396b
light here, 229b
love, by virtue, 76b
Kindles a wantonness, 230b
hand that, 456a
true genius, 318b
Kindleth little fire, 1064a
Kindlier hand, larger heart the, 553a
Kindliest thing God ever made, 873a
Kindliness of sheets, 938b
Kindling her undazzled eyes, 250b
Kindly as well as frosty, 603a
frosty but, 160a
fruits of the earth, 1068b
had we never lov'd sae, 392a
heart, glow of a, 729b
stars given a form so fair, 499a
use 'em, they rebel, 307a
wanderer loved and known, 654b
word or goodly act, 655a
Kindness and love, 403b
any, I can show, 300a
Christ took the, 573b
from the unkind, 924b
full of valour as of, 156a
have you had a, shown, 703a
in another's trouble, 661b
in women, 130b
kill wife with, 130b
large and plain, 979a
lavish, 445b
law of, 1041b
little deeds of, 626b
little word in, spoken, 557b
master-art of, 726b
mercy courage, mirth, 843b
milk of human, 195a, 950b
natural, 826b
no man show him any, 281b
not quite free from ridicule, 540b
road into his, 202b
save in the way of, 403a
tak a cup o', 392b
tempered every blow, 688a
to his majesty, 463a
treated with special, 932a
what wisdom greater than, 344b
who does a, not therefore kind, 314a
Kindnesses, for these, do me small mischief, 58b
great persons able to do great, 108b
proclaims, received, 109a
series of, 372a
which most leave undone, 599a
Kindred, brothers sons and, slain, 266b
comrades lovers friends, 630a
drops mingled into one, 364a
each age each, 601b
flower of her, 439a
gloom, 327b
medley of, 105a
only should behold, 15a
points of heaven, 412a
to the great God, 539b

Kindreds people and tongues, 1064b
Kine, lean and ill-favoured, 1023b
learn from the, ruminating, 726b
Pharaoh's lean, 150b
seven fat, 1023b
King a thing men have made, 228a
acts like a, 345a
and farewell, 139b
and shepherd even, 109b
Arthur ruled this land, 1020a
asked the queen, 917b
balm off from anointed, 139b
belovèd of a, 1012a
Belshazzar the, 1048b
best, of good fellows, 79b
by your own fireside, 103b
came not, 652b
cat may looke on a, 94a
catch conscience of the, 174a
Charles's head, 579a
chief defect of Henry, 849a
Christ, 969a
city of the great, 1034b
Cole, 1015a
Cophetua, 549b, 1011b
cotton is, 499b
dainty dish to set before the, 1017a
David and King Solomon, 794b
David wrote the psalms, 794b
discharge my duties as, 972a
divinity doth hedge a, 178a
earth receive her, 303a
easily as a, 166b
every inch a, 193a
fellow with the best, 79b
follow the, 554a
for our rightfu', 392a
fought my, 266b
George, dead soldiers of, 821a
glorious to be a pirate, 682b
glory to the new-born, 334b
glory to the, of kings, 334b
God save the, 307b, 1027a
gold crowned, 928b
Gorboduc, niece of, 166a
government without a, 490a
great as a, 377a
great God our, 530a
greater than the, 335a
grew vain, 280a
he is rightful, 754b
heart and stomach of a, 97a
heart of the, 759a
heaven's all gracious, 560b
Heav'n's eternal, 244a
honour the, 1064a
I am the Roman, 271a
I was a, in Babylon, 742a
idle, by this still hearth, 548a
in a carriage may ride, 533b
James call for old shoes, 119a
judge that no, can corrupt, 210b
lad that's born to be, 781b
Lear, by reading, 373a
long live our noble, 307b
long live the, 364a
man the, delighteth to honour, 1029b
mockery, of snow, 140b
more royalist than the, 1010b
mortal temples of a, 139b
never, dropped out of clouds, 227b
of all kings, 999a

King of artists, 669a
of Babylon, 1048b
of Boyville, 843a
of England cannot enter, 335a
of France went up the hill, 1015a
of hearts, 900a
of infinite space, 173b
of kings, 465a
of pain, 693a
of realms of endless joy, 936b
of shreds and patches, 177a
of Spain's daughter, 1017b
of terrors, 1030b
of the Jews, 1050a, 1055b
of the sea, 904a
old, dead, 154a
one's own sole, 703a
over children of pride, 1032a
pageantry of a, 1002a
Pandion is dead, 220a
pin the main spring, 661a
praises sing to God the, 670a
precedent a, of men, 696a
rank no, can give, 591a
reigns but does not govern, 101b
ruin seize thee ruthless, 349b
sad-eyed Hindu, 673a
sent me his dirty linen, 324b
serve my, and master, 211b
shake hands with a, 462b
show 'em who is, 894a
sits in Dunfermline town, 1011a
Solomon, King David and, 794b
Solomon loved many women, 1028b
Solomon wrote the proverbs, 794b
sovereign lord the, 288b
spider and, 591b
state without, or nobles, 490a
Stephen was a worthy peer, 187b, 1011b
still am I, of those, 140a
such a, Harry, 122b
sword of an angel, 388b
they were all looking for a, 631b
'tis so much to be a, 100a
title running 'fore the, 156a
was a fortunate soldier, 324b
was in his counting-house, 1017a
Wenceslas, 592b
when George the Third was, 39b
when I am, dilly dilly, 1019b
when you strike at a, 508b
who is law is, 117a
who is this, of glory, 1033b
who seeks to bestride the people, 538a
will not leave country, 985b
worm that hath eat of a, 177b
would change with me, 584b
year's pleasant, 212b
Kingdom, a little, I possess, 654a
almost in every, 223a
best the, provides, 839a
both crown and, 117b
by the foam, 947a
by the sea, 546a
children of the, 1052a
come, palaces in, 896a
enter, of God, 140b
enter, of heaven, 1053b
fit for the, of God, 1056b
for a horse, 128b

Kingdom for a little grave, 140a
for thine is the, 1051a
God hath numbered thy, 1049a
good mind possesses a, 48a
iv Hiven, 835a
like grain of mustard seed,
1053a
like to a little, 167a
my mind a, is, 101b
of daylight's dauphin, 724a
of God, enter, 140b
of God, fit for the, 1056b
of God, helping to establish,
643a
of God on earth, 914b
of God, such is the, 1056a
of heaven, enter, 1053b
of heaven is at hand, 1050a
of heaven likened, 1054a
of heaven, theirs is, 1050b
of perpetual night, 128a
peopled, 102b, 154b
rich man to enter, 1053b
snug little, 564a
such is the, of God, 1056a
theirs is, of heaven, 1050b
thy, come, 1051a
thy, is divided, 1049a
Kingdoms and empires of old,
584b
ant finds, 979b
are but cares, 83b
God had sifted three, 523b
goodly states and, 477a
kiss'd away, 201a
shake, 1046a
sifted three, 281b
Kingfishers catch fire, 724b
Kingly crown to gain, 445b
death, 467b
longest, line in Europe, 324b
state is, 251b
King's arm is very long, 19b
crown nor deputed sword, 184a
daughter o' Noroway, 1011b
English, abusing of, 180a
eye made horse fat, 57b
gate, on the, 652b
highway, quietly along, 345b
horses, all the, 1018a
men, all the, 1018a
name is tower of strength, 128b
own daughter, 885a
subject's duty is, 155b
Kings, a crown, seldom enjoy,
126b
all the rivers of the, 979a
and aces, 958a
and all their favorites, 216a
and idiots, 932a
and parliaments, 331a
and wealthy cities ruined, 35b
angels in the forms of, 374b
are like stars, 467a
as happy as, 750b
barrel-house, 902b
breath of, 390b
cabbages and, 658b
calm contending, 131b
can cause or cure, 337b
captains and the, depart, 816a
cashiering most, 473b
change my state with, 205a
crown seldom, enjoy, 126b
crown'd, saddest of all, 838b
curtsy to great, 156b
deaths of, 680b
divine right of, 538a
end of, 292a

Kings for such a tomb would die,
244b
foul guilt of eastern, 266b
game, would not play at, 365a
grammar knows how to con-
trol, 271a
he shall stand before, 1040b
hearts of, 146a
I know the, of England, 682b
it makes gods, 128a
king of, 465a
king of all, 999a
knocks at palaces of, 38a
lays his icy hand on, 237b
lords and Commons, 435b
lords or, of the earth, 606a
low ambition and pride of,
315b
may be blest, 393b
may love treason, 53a
must show their might, 520b
neglect heart's ease, 156a
no, though possess the crown,
292a
not, and lords but nations,
441b
of earth, 846a
of the sea, 619b
one of nature's little, 213b
plucker down of, 126a
republics and emperors, 99b
right divine of, 322a
royal throne of, 138b
showers on her, 253b
stories of the death of, 139b
surpasses the pride of, 676a
sword of justice lay down,
292a
teeming womb of royal, 139a
tired of, 506a
to run with me, 59a
tribe, of Samoa, 753a
twilight of the, 799b
tyrants from policy, 361a
upon their coronation day,
279a
vain the ambition of, 226a
walk with, 820b
were only, to fight, 520b
Kings' captives' births, 706b
Kinquering congs, 730a
Kinship with the stars, 638b
Kipling, Rudyards cease from,
789a
Kipling's If, 942a
Kirk, drop below the, 421a
is this the, 422a
ring it ye bells of the, 757a
Kiss, a little time to, and cling,
748b
ae fond, 392a
again with tears, 550a
and then away, 758a
cleanliest shift is to, 162b
comradeship behind a, 876a
coward does it with a, 769b
drew with one long, 123b
fades out from kiss to, 825b
flamed upon the, 947a
for to, his dear, 535b
general, he gains, 383a
give me a, 230b
her lips and take her hands,
825a
in Colin's eyes, 928b
kind, before we part, 329a
last lamenting, 216b
laughter's eager, 953a
leave a, but in the cup, 219a

Kiss, let us, and part, 122b
let's, afresh, 230b
long and fervent, 486b
make me immortal with a,
123b
many a glowing, 488a
me and be quiet, 322b
me Hardy, 390a
me sweet and twenty, 164a
me though you make believe,
612a
my eyelids when I lie cold,
687b
my hand to the stars, 724b
of blankets, 938b
of death, 864b
pant and, for gold, 309b
sigh too much or, too long,
631b
snatch'd hasty, 327b
Strephon's, 928b
tender inward of thy hand,
207a
that mortal's eyes, 760b
the fingers of the rain, 961b
the place to make it well, 442a
through a veil, 498a
till the cow comes home, 228a
to that, a score, 230b
two unbodied essences may,
262b
what is a, 230a
when we come together, 815a
which Jews might, 312a
with peace not slay, 887a
without a moustache, 810b
you take is better, 186b
Kiss'd again and chid and rail'd,
309b
away kingdoms, 201a
toy'd and, 308b
wild waves whist, 209a
Kissed, eight times you've, me,
485b
first we, beside the thorn, 721b
hail Master and, him, 1055a
hasn't been, in forty years,
958a
her on the spot, 517b
into smiles again, 686a
Jenny, me when we met, 448a
lips that I have, 178b
righteousness and peace have,
1035b
sad, mouth, 692b
the lovely grass, 938a
the maiden all forlorn, 1020b
them and put them there, 747a
Kisses, fill it with, 219a
from a female mouth, 457a
golden, 582b
if you have forgotten my, 694b
joy as it flies, 386b
many thousand, 201b
more than, 217a
my, bring again, 185b
of enemy are deceitful, 1041a
play'd at cards for, 112b
remembered, after death, 550b
stolen, much completer, 448a
what lies there are in, 486a
you quick and flies away, 486b
you quickly and is gone, 486b
Kissing don't last cookery do,
638b
fool that first invented, 296b
no more, after, 748b
to deceive, 612a
Kist, had I wist before I, 1013a

Learne to creepe, 93a
Learned, all, and all drunk, 365a
can never be, 424b
clan, sophist schools and, 503a
dust, 364b
first lesson to be, 634a
from others, 19b
having, to be, 949a
his great language, 567b
I from the shadow of a tree, 717b
in sorrow he, this truth, 688b
Jonson's, sock, 245b
judge, 146b
length and thundering sound, 356b
less is, there, 341b
let the, say what they can, 303b
love, in lady's eyes, 133b
lumber, loads of, 311b
make the, smile, 311a
man, grew within this, 123b
not, much by art, 226a
nothing and forgotten nothing, 384a
pedants must effect, 238a
root of Homer, 227a
seldom pretty fellows, 909a
silence from the talkative, 924b
some things not, quickly, 982b
soul that has not, to read, 711b
things I, from her, 907a
to aid the unfortunate, 37a
to know evil, 24a
to play when he was young, 1017b
unlearn what you have, 71b
women to be found, 325b
Learning an adjunct to ourself, 133b
and infused opinions, 154a
anecdote flock to their aid, 501a
branches of, 144a
breast where, lies, 309b
cast into the mire, 361a
dote on scraps of, 305a
doth make thee mad, 224a
earning and yearning, 978a
enflamed with study of, 250a
gained most, 244a
grace nor gear, 817a
great secretary of all, 236b
has its value, 269b
I desire, 390b
is nothing without manners, 932a
just enough of, to misquote, 452a
laws and, die, 592b
light liberty and, 513a
little, is dangerous thing, 310b
love he bore to, 356b
love of, 525a
much, doth make thee mad, 1059b
neglects, in youth, 18a
no man wiser for his, 227b
no royal road to, 29a
offence to, and to taste, 436b
out of much, become mad, 224a
pause from, to be wise, 336a
progeny of, 380b
put in evidence some, 776b
something new, 8a
time for you to be, now, 71a
wear your, like a watch, 323a
weight of, 553a
what, most necessary, 71b
whence is thy, 308a

Learning wiser grow without his books, 365b
wit, and sense, 262b
Learning's altar, 592b
triumph, 335b
Learns on de Pullman cars, 946b
to skip dance and kneel, 61a
Learnt, angling can never be fully, 235b
Lease, forty years', 566b
of my true love control, 206b
summer's, 204b
tampers with rent or, 573a
Least alone in solitude, 33b
and vilest things, 213b
considerable man, 1002a
erected spirit, 253a
faithful in that which is, 1057a
given when, said, 116b
happiest who suffers, 344b
important, what he says is, 700b
know, firmly believed what we, 98b
last not, in honour, 114b
man who acts the, 3b
miserable who enjoys, 344b
of all that goes, 928b
of evils choose, 27a
though last not, in love, 167b
unjust in the, 1057a
unto one of the, of these, 1054b
word said, done for the, 692b
Leather, brown as, 781b
clothed all in, 1020a
faithless, 305a
rest is but, or prunella, 317b
there's nothing like, 1006a
trod on shoe of, 104a
trod upon neat's, 166a
Leathern purse, silken or, 358b
wing, flits by on, 351b
wings, 141b
Leave a living name behind, 226a
all hope, 75a
and often took, 293b
ask, to desist, 242b
exempt from plunder, 809a
freedom or, to die, 626a
gave mushrumps, to grow, 118a
her to heaven, 172b
him to his pain, 378b
it unpicked, 153a
king will not, the country, 985b
lende me, to come, 115a
me here a little, 548b
me to repose, 350a
never takes his, 587b
never, till tomorrow, 330b
no stone unturned, 18a
not a stain, 1066b
not knowing when I may return, 538b
off the agony, 737a
on the back of the earth, 1070b
out the old one, 100a
peace I, with you, 1058b
purge and, sack, 152a
the lady Willy, 829a
the light of hope behind, 432a
the rest to heaven, 243a
the world no copy, 164a
their little lives in air, 309a
them laughing, 892a
them while you're looking good, 966a
this barren spot, 433a
this keen encounter, 127b
though thou, me, 693b

Leave to call me anything, 297a
to live by no man's leave, 816b
true of most we, behind, 595b
valiant bones in France, 156b
you comfortless, 1058b
your ankles freezing, 949a
Leaven leaveneth the whole lump, 1061a
lowly lives, 669a
of a lie, 459b
Leaves, air is wild with, 934a
and flowers do cover, 225b
are falling like its own, 466a
behind a sea so cruel, 76a
behind, name a person, 458b
cover them with, 1011a
dead are driven, 466a
ending on the rustling, 246b
falls as the, do, 225a
famous harmony of, 824b
getteth short of, 489a
green, whisp'ring overhead, 708a
grow on the tree, 824a
happier than those he behind, 630a
heart-shaped, 875a
his native shore, 443a
hold old, 936a
kitten playing with dead, 589a
lamentation of the, 825a
lisp of, 691a
long, cover me, 692a
naturally as, to a tree, 478a
no flowers no, 488b
no man has aught of what he, 179b
of an aspen tree, 912b
of life keep falling, 531a
of stone, 601b
of the Judgment Book unfold, 634b
on trees, like, 4b
our houses, 340a
paper, nor leaves of stone, 601b
passion, us weaker, 288b
poplars showed white of their, 680b
private conscience, 279a
rake the, away, 879a
see when, depart, 988b
shady, of destiny, 263b
shatter your, 248b
spread his sweet, 134a
swayed my, and flowers, 826a
sweetest, yet folded, 46oa
thick as autumnal, 3b, 252b
thou among the, hast never, known, 481b
though, are many, 826a
walk over the, 103a
were crispèd and sere, 545b
whispered behind the, 817a
words are like, 41b, 311a
yellow, do hang, 206a
yellow drifts of withered, 623a
Leave-takings are but wasted sadness, 788b
Leaving drinking of wine, 284a
his country for country's sake, 304b
me never alone, 706b
no footprint, 961b
nothing became him like the, 194b
Leavings, devil's, 321b
Lebanon, cedars of, 1036b
roots of the cedars of, 893a

Lecher in my sight, 193a
Lecheries, tinder to your, 947a
Lecture, curtain, 446a
  wish to hold a, 22a
Lectures, books from which, taken, 340b
  curtain, 309b
  do so much good as reading, 340b
  in her night-dress, 489a
  listen to scientific, 766b
  or a little charity, 608a
Led, all that, up is dark, 398a
  all the rest, 448a
  me towards the hills, 881b
  starry host, 255b
  the way to heaven, 307b
  weak minds, captive, 259a
Leda mother of Helen of Troy, 701b
Ledge, trod by rocky, 795b
Ledlow, Farmer, 705a
Lee, brief command of, 740a
Leedle, funny, poy, 713b
Leef, aspes, 78b
Leek, by this, I revenge, 156b
Leer, assent with civil, 319a
Lees, black, where lurks, 690a
  mere, is left, 197a
  wines on the, 1046a
Leetle Bateese, 759a
Leeward, soft shower to, 604b
Leewardings, such lovely, 604b
Left a name behind, 1066b
  behind, never gets, 807a
  half told, 246b
  hand, riches and honour in, 1038b
  leg, took him by the, 1017a
  my work but just begun, 652b
  no little things behind, 754a
  nor, a void, 338a
  one taken the other, 1054a
  only pleasure I have, 326a
  our country for our country's good, 304b
  the name, 336a
  thy, hand know, 1051a
  'tis better to be, 551b
  to be finished, 147b
  undone those things, 1068a
Leg, awkward of, 981a
  call a tail a, 542b
  caper and shake a, 894b
  decreasing, 152b
  honour set to, 151b
  is best part of the figure, 736b
  never breaks a, 807a
  one old timber, on him, 856b
  took him by the left, 1017a
  which, goes after which, 730b
Legacies, a great genius leaves, 300b
  left to strange police, 872b
Legacy, no, so rich as honesty, 183a
  thoughts of a good, 109b
Legal principle, 437a
Legalizer, time is a great, 908a
Legend, curious, still haunts me, 486a
  leaf-fring'd, 482a
  of the green chapels, 997a
Legends, believe all fables in the, 120b
  hear their, told, 586b
  mere, and myths, 987b
  old, asleep in lap of, 480b
Legible in the eie, 114b

Legion, my name is, 1055b
  of the lost ones, 818b
  soldier of the, 529b
  that never was 'listed, 815b
Legislate, judges do and must, 709b
Legislated into existence, 955a
Legislation, foundation of morals and, 324b
Legislative and executive, 368a
Legislators, unacknowledged, 469a
Legislature, perverse as a, 989b
  public opinion stronger than, 645a
Legitimate object of good government, 375a
  right to govern, 425b
Legs are staple articles, 730b
  biggest rascal on two, 65a
  break the, of time, 534b
  cannon-ball took off his, 487b
  crawl with, 421b
  dog's walking on hind, 340a
  English, 155b
  for necessity, 181b
  how many, has a dog, 542b
  never could have stood upon his, 578a
  of iron, 1048b
  of stone, 465a
  on his last, 214a
  petty men walk under his, 166a
  swept him off his little, 665b
  to go high use your, 726b
  were lost on him, 401b
  were such Diana shows, 231a
  with which you run, 1004a
  wooden, are not inherited, 857b
Leibniz, monads of, 932a
Leicester Square, farewell, 878a
Leisure, asked whether he was at, 58b
  beguiled the, of the crew, 681b
  conversation wants, 875b
  evidence of, 776a
  gentleman of, 775b
  hath no, who useth it not, 234b
  increased means and, 513a
  is the repose of passions, 434b
  never less at, 33b
  no blessed, 489a
  repeat at, 900a
  repent at, 130a
  retired, 246a
  so much, as to die, 60a
  strikes him as pleasure, 569b
  superfluous, 185a
  time, nine-tenths will be, 739b
  to be sick, 151a
  to make good, 129b
  true, one with true toil, 583a
  wed in, 130a
  what, to grow wise, 621b
Leisurely contemplation, 863b
Lekes, garleck onyons and eek, 80a
Leman, such hawks and such a, 1012b
Lemon, squeezing of a, 357a
  twelve miles from a, 419a
Lemonade, black eyes and, 439b
Lemons, oranges and, 1015b
Lemontrees, land where the, bloom, 378b
Lend a hand, 624b
  a kind of easiness, 177a
  eye terrible aspect, 155a
  eyes the glow-worm, 231a
  few that only, their ear, 122a

Lend, if not asked to, money, 678a
  I'll, you something, 165b
  less than thou owest, 191a
  me a heart replete, 124b
  me the stone strength, 939b
  me your ears, 168a
  men who, 429b
  neither ear nor glance, 464a
  us thine aid, 445a
  you the wings, 939b
Lende me leave to come, 115a
Lender, borrower is servant to, 1040b
  borrower nor a, 171b
Lendeth light, 114b
  unto the Lord, 1040a
Lending money confidentially, 341a
Lendings, off off you, 192a
Lends aid to the worker, 13a
  corruption lighter wings, 315a
  he that, gives, 234b
  Lord that, me life, 124b
  something to love He, us, 547b
  three things I never, 510a
  tongue vows, 172a
Length, drags its slow, along, 311a
  in, a span, 121b
  learned, and thundering sound, 356b
  of days in her right hand, 1038b
  of shambling limb, 588b
  of time, 338a
  stretch'd out chimney's, 245b
  twelvemonth's, 393a
  what it lacks in, 881b
Lengthen our days, 439a
  until the shadows, 1069b
  wishes, as sun declines, 306a
Lengthened sage advices, 393b
  shadow of one man, 501b
Lengthening chain, drags a, 353b
  shadows, as vapours rise, 277a
Lengthens not a day, 214b
Lenient arts, 319b
Lenity, too much, makes robbers bold, 126a
Lenore, sorrow for the lost, 544b
Lens, each age a, 649a
Lent, eagle who has, his plume, 11b
  him to a lady, 1019b
  is over and Easter won, 655b
  with, money evil is done, 606a
Lente currite noctis equi, 123b
Leonidas and Washington, 459a
  there is always a, 631a
Leopard change his spots, 1048a
  lie down with the kid, 1046a
Leopards, three white, 944b
Leprosy or thunder-stroke, 505b
  white as, 421b
Lerne, craft so long to, 78a
  gladly wolde he, 79b
Lesbia with her sparrow, 961b
Less, by hoping more they have, 131a
  conscious thoughts, 670b
  envy of, happier lands, 139a
  flogging in our schools, 341b
  he spoke, 876b
  is learned there, 341b
  little, what worlds away, 569a
  loved Caesar, 168a
  more and more about **less** and, 799a
  never, at leisure, 33b

Less, no, renown'd than war, 251a
of buying, 862b
of earth than heaven, 499a
party stick the, 120b
pious but not, a man, 270b
rather than be, 253b
than a drop of blood, 76b
than a man, 157a
than horrible imaginings, 194b
than meets the eye, 941a
than the dust, 812b
whatever you have spend, 342b
you mean you can't take, 657a
Lessen'd by another's anguish, 134b
her merit, yours, 343b
Lesser breeds without the law, 816a
god had made the world, 555b
restless minds, 586a
ruins, fame built on, 266b
than my name, 139b
Lesson, better, taught, 689b
first, to be learned, 634a
good, though often hard, 513b
grandest, 712a
jolly good, 816b
last, he learns thoroughly, 634a
most difficult, in the world, 60b
on grammar an impertinence, 627b
one, nature let me learn, 619a
still harder, 98a
this, seems to carry, 366a
time has taught us both a, 53b
useful, to the head, 365b
which takes men longest to learn, 771b
Lessons and tasks are all ended, 714a
from ancient dialecticians, 518a
grave these, on thy soul, 394b
have been represented, 333a
of paternalism, 689b
of two such, 458b
that I teach, 412b
three, I would write, 394b
time teaches many, 12b
Lest we forget, 816a
Let alone, all we ask is to be, 612a
alone thine enemy, 7b
dearly, or let alone, 231b
down the curtain, 87b
head to be, unfurnished, 89b
her alone she will court you, 218b
him give on, 277a
in the great Creator, 257b
it be forgotten, 928b
live, live and, 694a
love, love and, 694b
me alone, 1030a
me alone, song of, 612a
me be a little kinder, 913b
me not live, 223b
me to thy bosom fly, 334a
my people go, 1024a
no man's heart fail, 1027b
others enjoy the privilege, 326b
out, every reef may be safely, 12a
patience have her perfect work, 1063b
slip the dogs of war, 168a
the dead bury their dead, 1052a
thee go except thou bless, 330a
them eat cake, 345a

Let them into your life, 766a
there be light, 1021a
to live and, live, 617a
us alone time driveth, 547a
us do or die, 225a, 394a
us eat and drink, 1046a
us have peace, 623b
us live and love, 35a
us take it as it comes, 685b
us worship God he says, 390a
your mind alone, 971b
Lethe, go not to, 483a
river of oblivion, 254a
time is, 882a
wharf, 172b
Lethean, drunken of things, 693a
Lethe-wards had sunk, 481a
Let's look at the record, 864b
talk sense to American people, 986b
Lets in new light, 242b
Letter A, appeared the, 514a
better by speech than, 121b
better introduction than, 71a
charm in a, of yours, 681a
cover of a, 472a
from his wife, 659b
happy, tell him the page, 647b
my, to the world, 645b
not the, but the spirit, 1062a
of declination, 761a
of that after-life, 532b
pleasant to get a, from you, 681a
that would commit me, 565b
the, killeth, 1062a
till you write your, 215b
Lettered, lock'd, braw brass collar, 391a
Letters addressed to private persons, 487a
blessed be, 625a
Cadmus gave, 458b
foulest, 154a
four-and-twenty, 60a
golden, set, 148a
kept forever and unread, 681a
ladies when they write, 448b
lay aside, never to read, 379a
leave his, unopened, 504b
like writin' anonymous, 837a
lost his, watch and wallet, 687a
make your, safe, 565b
man of, must make up his mind, 690a
mingle souls, 217a
no arts no society, 229a
obscure industrious men of, 832a
physician and man of, 534b
racy as jabber of a saloon, 973a
republic of, 333a, 446b
search the fading, 962b
that we ought to burn, 1008b
they wrote over night, 840b
which Endymion wrote, 767a
Letter-writing, uncertain process of, 596a
Letting I dare not, 196a
Levee belongs to the state, 889b
water runs over the, 889b
Level at my abuses, 207a
down as far as themselves, 340a
hang, in balances of love, 673a
in her husband's heart, 164b
is the path, 7a

Level lines of woodwork, 794b
met upon the, 818b
of its great men, 759b
reduce human society to one, 558b
riding of the rolling, 724a
with their fount, 526a
Leveled, when fire has, everything, 948a
Levelers wish to level down, 340a
Leveling rancorous rational mind, 827b
up to themselves, 340a
Levell'd rule of streaming light, 247b
Levels all distinctions, 508b
of the eastern gate, 686a
Lever, mind is the great, 443a
Leviathan, draw out, 1032a
hugest of living creatures, 257a
that crooked serpent, 1046a
Levity, say it with the utmost, 764a
Lewd by night, 796a
certain, fellows, 1059a
the greedy the sinful and, 973b
Lexicography, lost in, 336b
Lexicon of youth, 510b
Lexington, Concord, and Bunker Hill, 443b
Lhude sing cuccu, 999a
Liable, men are, to error, 283a
statesmen, to give an account, 62a
Liar, answered little, 849b
doubt truth to be a, 173b
experienced industrious, 677b
indignant man such a, 727a
is lavish of oaths, 243a
of the first magnitude, 297b
old Time is a, 535a
or a madman, 344b
should have good memory, 52b
show me a, 234b
the best, 671a
will not be believed, 10b
Liars, all men are, 1037a
Cretans notorious as, 55b
ought to have good memories, 52b, 243b
Lib an' die in Dixie, 585a
Libellandum, I gat but, 87a
Libelous statements about my dog, 921b
Liberal air, 688a
and conservative parties, 920b
arts, study of, 43a
education, 105a
education, to love her was a, 301b
institutions, 400a, 728a
marshes of Glynn, 716b
obedience, infuses that, 360b
or a little conservative, 684a
party, remains a, 920a
starry-eyed, 948b
Liberalism is easiest thing in world, 641a
Liberality consists less in giving, 288b
Liberalize a man's mind, 637a
Liberate itself from social past, 874a
Liberated the hell out of this place, 1009a
Liberté egalité fraternité, 1010b
Libertie, enjoy delight with, 114b
Liberties, dramatist wants more, 719b

Line, slanting silver, 961b
   stretch to crack of doom, 198b
   upon line, 1046a
   upon line they reach the roof,
      725a
   ye grave for me, 910a
Lineage, damsel of high, 554b
   proud old, 927a
Lineaments, moulded the chang-
      ing, 702a
   of Gospell bookes, 114b
   of gratified desire, 386b
Lined himself with hope, 153a
   with good capon, 161b
Linen, dirty, to wash, 324b
   lifetime of, 993b
   old, wash whitest, 119a
   wash their dirty, 399b
   you're wearing out, 489a
Liner she's a lady, 814b
Liners, luxury, laden with souls,
      993b
Lines and life are free, 233a
   are fallen unto me, 1032b
   close in dial's centre, 154b
   dry desert of a thousand, 320b
   epigram of two, 52a
   for all your deathless, 912a
   ghosts creeping between the,
      641b
   hard stiff, of life, 528a
   in every angle greet, 269a
   level, of woodwork, 794b
   lord once own the happy, 311b
   these, made I, 37b
   town-crier spoke my, 175a
   washed my, away, 462a
Linger and labor there, 782b
   in our northern clime, 414b
   meadows where you, 749a
   on the flathouse roof, 995b
   out a purpos'd overthrow, 206a
   they do not live but, 222a
   to caress him, 584a
Lingered round them, 592a
Lingering dewdrop, protects the,
      412a
   sit, here, 272a
   spirit so, 858a
Lingers, borrowing, 152b
   into old age, 16a
   last rose, 38b
Lingo, outlandish, 389a
   unless you know the, 488a
Ling'ring bays, 335b
   flying, 312a
Lining, inside out to show the,
      879a
   there's a silver, 865b
   turn forth her silver, 247a
Link, each fresh, progress, 708b
   silver, the silken tie, 413b
   strength of one, in the cable,
      840b
Linkèd sweetness long drawn out,
      245b
Linnet, tear the, from the leaf,
      826b
Linnet's wings, 824b
Linnets, pipe but as the, sing,
      551b
Linsey-woolsey brother, 238b
   brothers, 322a
Lint, invisible strand of, 801b
Lintel low enough, 757b
Lion among ladies, 142a
   and the cock, 893a
   and the lizard, 531b
   and the unicorn, 1015a

Lion, beard the, in his den, 414b
   bearing, 464a
   bold as a, 1041b
   carcase of the, 1026b
   dead, 1043a
   devil as a roaring, 1064b
   fawns upon lamb, 127a
   from his lair, 417b
   hind mated by the, 183a
   in the chase, 403a
   is in the streets, 1041a
   is not so fierce, 234a
   lip of, 155b
   look no larger than the cat,
      556b
   not a, but a pard, 934b
   of God, 73b
   old, is dead, 378a
   on your old stone gates, 547a
   painting a, from the claw, 8a
   prince must be a, 55a
   roar like a, 963a
   roast, 589a
   rouse a, 149b
   vapour sometime like a, 201a
   wine, 497a
   woos his brides, 352b
   wrath of, is wisdom of God,
      386a
Lioness opening up an antelope,
      990b
Lionlike March, 690a
Lion's mane, dew-drop from the,
      182a
   Nemean, nerve, 172a
   ruddy eyes, 385b
   saw, shadow, 146b
   skin will not reach, 55a
   wear, hide, 148a
Lions, bears and, growl and fight,
      302b
   den of, 1049a
   my darling from the, 1034a
   stronger than, 1027b
   talks of roaring, 147b
Lip, between the cup and the, 223a
   contempt and anger of his, 165a
   coral, admires, 237a
   frown and wrinkled, 465a
   hair upon the upper, 950b
   is curved with pain, 686a
   keep a stiff upper, 630b
   language in her, 182b
   nectar on a, 381b
   not a, or eye we beauty call,
      310b
   reproof on her, 485a
   'twixt the cup and the, 223a
   vermeil-tinctur'd, 248a
Lippincut, Miss Fawn, 841a
Lips are dumb, 547a
   are now forbid to speak, 485a
   bearded, 523b
   but half regretful, 694a
   closed, hurt no one, 58a
   crimson in thy, and cheeks, 138a
   divine persuasion flows from, 4b
   drained by fevered, 483b
   drew my soul through my, 123b
   drop gentle words from his, 7a
   eternity was in our, 200a
   far from the, we love, 439a
   flattereth with his, 1040a
   for your, to drink, 692b
   forth to your, to quaff, 532b
   from speaking guile, 1034a
   Helen's, are drifting dust, 844b
   her, were red, 421b

Lips, her, were so near, 736a
   how came your, 854b
   Julia's, do smile, 230a
   kiss her, 825a
   let me put my, to it, 577b
   listen at its, 529a
   love at the, 880b
   mouldered the, 947a
   murmuring with its foamy, 625b
   name of God upon his, 344b
   of a strange woman, 1038b
   of children, 498a
   of dying men, 621b
   of inebriated virtue, 695a
   of those that are asleep, 1044b
   of truth, 440b
   once sanctified by hers, 533b
   ope my, 143a
   open thou my, 1034b
   part her, 230b
   persuasion hung upon his, 345b
   poverty to the very, 189b
   profound and fragile, 968b
   red mournful, 824a
   say God be pitiful, 518b
   smile on her, 414b
   smily round the, 601a
   suck forth my soul, 123b
   sweet, soft hand, 480a
   take cup to your, 219a
   take those, away, 185b
   talk of the, 1039b
   that are for others, 550b
   that I have kissed, 178b
   that love thy name, 803b
   that those, had language, 366a
   that touch, 948b
   that touch liquor, 828b
   that were dead, 953a
   to your attentive ear, 411a
   touch, and part with tears, 693b
   truth from his, 356a
   upon my, a song, 936a
   very good words for the, 580a
   weary, I close, 350a
   were red, 261b
   whispering with white, 453a
   words from his, 3b
   would keep from slips, 737a
Lips' red, 207b
   remark was oh you kid, 936b
Lipstick, when you've got too
      much, 990b
Liquefaction of her clothes, 231a
Liquescent and nebulous lustre,
      545b
Liquid, bitter, recommended, 978a
   dew of youth, 171b
   fire and distilled damnation,
      397a
   history, 776b
   lapse of murmuring streams,
      257b
   manure and guano, 954a
   notes, 250a
   surge, 203b
Liquidation of the British Em-
      pire, 871a
Liquor, brews livelier, than the
      muse, 786b
   bumper of good, 381b
   claret is the, for boys, 342a
   gives genius discerning, 357a
   is quicker, 989b
   lips that touch, 828b
   love or fights, 787a
   mint is in the, 806a
   swims enough good, 690a
   taste a, never brewed, 646a

Little, man wants but, 306a, 354b
  man what now, 965b
  man's affairs however, 339b
  means, great show with, 565a
  measure, shrunk to this, 167b
  men, for fear of, 638a
  men who know much say, 344b
  Miss Muffet, 1018b
  moment, what one knows of, 697a
  monstrous, voice, 141a
  more and how much it is, 569a
  more than kin, 170a
  more than little, 151a
  more tired at close of day, 740b
  nothing is, to him, 339b
  offering Germany too, 957b
  offering too, 401b
  old New York, 801b
  one become a thousand, 1047b
  one sleeps, while my, 550a
  ones gather around me, 714b
  ones, great ones eat up, 203b
  ones moan, 619b
  or nothing between them, 26b
  outcome much outcry, 9b
  people who know, 344b
  pin bores through castle wall, 139b
  pitchers have wide ears, 94a
  Polly Flinders, 1018a
  pot soon hot, 130b
  practise in, things, 64a
  pray love me, 230b
  rebellion is a good thing, 374a
  room, riches in a, 124a
  rule a little sway, 327b
  said is soon amended, 105b
  saw the, that is good, 609b
  set mankind, 376b
  share thy, with another, 796a
  ships of England, 950b
  sleep a little slumber, 1038b
  so, done, 552b, 758a
  sorrows sit and weep, 386a
  soul let us try try try, 440b
  soul scarce fledged, 695b
  sown much and bring in, 1049b
  star, twinkle twinkle, 442b
  stars, cut him out in, 136b
  stealin' gits you in jail, 946b
  strokes fell great oaks, 330b
  tasks make large return, 634b
  tent of blue, 769b
  thing in hand is worth more, 11a
  thing, life's a, 574a
  thing to do, 570a
  things affect little minds, 512a
  things go lessening, 572b
  things make likenesses, 16b
  things, release from, 981b
  think too, 277a
  this, world, 139a
  though, I'll work, 1000a
  time for laughter, 748b
  time to do so much, 921b
  tin gods on wheels, 813a
  tiny boy, 166a
  'tis, but 'tis all I have, 414a
  to be known, 338a
  Tommy Tittlemouse, 1020a
  Tommy Tucker, 1016a
  too, education, 272a
  too late or too, 957b
  too, to do, 820a
  town of Bethlehem, 669b
  toy dog covered with dust, 747a

Little trade, love the, 67a
  upon a little, 7b
  wanton boys, 211a
  we see in Nature, 410b
  western flower, 141b
  whatever was, seemed great, 492b
  wine for stomach's sake, 1063a
  wine into a wine-cooler, 69b
  wise the best fools be, 215b
  wonderful, our fathers knew, 820b
  word, lies in one, 138a
  words of love, 626b
  work a little play, 665b
  world, 885a
  worse than a man, 143b
  worth a sigh, 661b
  wren, hurt the, 388a
  wretched creature, 329b
  ye, stars, 255a
  you give is great, 630a
  you know about the age, 43a
Littleness, no sadder proof of, 475a
Littlenesses, thousand peering, 554a
Littlest doubts are fear, 176a
Liturgies, dull commercial, 845b
Liv'd a blessed time, 197a
  I have, today, 278a
Live a life half dead, 260a
  a thousand years, 412b
  according to convenience of asses, 59a
  afther fifty, 834b
  all that, must die, 170a
  all the days of your life, 297a
  all you can, 719a
  alone at peace, 922a
  alone in the bee-loud glade, 824b
  aloof from care, 29b
  always in best company, 419a
  among men as if God beheld you, 47a
  an American, 445a
  and die, I will to, 84a
  and die is all I have to do, 319a
  and labour till goal be won, 661b
  and laugh nor be dismayed, 846a
  and learn, 14a
  and let live, 694a
  and love, 35a
  and love in God's light, 86a
  and pray and sing, 193b
  as if you were eternal, 20b
  as men and not as ostriches, 922a
  at home at ease, 214a
  barren sister, 140b
  bearing boughs may, 140a
  better to, quietly, 596a
  beyond its income, 671b
  bid me to, 230a
  bravely to, on, 14b
  by bread alone, 1050b
  by bread only, 1025b
  by fruit of their labor, 538a
  by medicine, 333b
  by no man's leave, 816b
  by one man's will, 112a
  by sharping and robbing, 331b
  by thy light, 619b
  can these bones, 1048b
  cleanly, 152a

Live, come, with me, 123a
  completely happy, 9a
  completely in the present, 983b
  content, majority of men, 85b
  content with small means, 557b
  course on how to, 805b
  dare to, 14b
  dead shall, 278b
  designed us to, in society, 326a
  desires to, long, 295a
  dying we, 575a
  easy, and quiet die, 416b
  enough before thirty, 834b
  fear to, or die, 506b
  first with Julius, 900a
  for bread, 506b
  for I'm coming, 37b
  for others, 766a
  for what do we, 428a
  for which we bear to, 317b
  forever, do you want to, 898b
  forever, prophets do they, 1049b
  glad did I, 751a
  glad that I, am I, 764a
  hair that is shining, 938b
  how long we, 586a
  I, on hope, 721a
  I shall not, in vain, 645b
  I still, 445a
  I would not, alway, 1030a
  i' the sun, 16oa
  if we, so long, 817a
  in a crowd, 757b
  in all that we have lost, 606b
  in brass, 212a
  in clover, 27b
  in continual mortification, 329b
  in fragments no longer, 901b
  in hearts we leave behind, 433a
  in Little Broom Gardens, 883b
  in pleasure, 329a
  in state of ambitious poverty, 6b
  in the crowd of jollity, 337a
  in these degenerate days, 4a
  in wild anarchy of drink, 219b
  innocently, 334a
  just begins to, that day, 646b
  laborious days, 249a
  learn to live and, to learn, 634b
  let me, in my house, 777b
  let me not, 223b
  let me, unseen unknown, 309a
  lief not be as, 166a
  like a wretch, 222a
  like brutes, 76a
  like that stoic bird, 934a
  like the velvet mole, 934b
  long, our noble king, 307b
  longs in solitude to, 378b
  love that should help you to, 694b
  meanly they, within doors, 285b
  means whereby I, 146b
  mirth with thee I mean to, 245b
  move and have our being, 1059a, 1069b
  my own and die so too, 319a
  not how long you, 46a
  not in myself, 453b
  not the whole of life to, 413a
  not, to eat, 270b
  not while I, 694a
  o'er each scene, 312b
  on our knees, 921a
  one bare hour to, 123b
  one must eat to, 270b
  one's own sole king, 703a
  out my years for me, 1014b

Live out the lifetime of God, 604a
out thy life as the light, 694b
past years again, 276a
pattern to, and to die, 567b
peaceably with all men, 1060a
place not to, but to die in, 241a
proudly, 796a
pure speak true, 554a
rather than, in snuff, 111b
rationally, 67b
resolved to, a fool, 228a
rich than die rich, 342a
right way to, 720b
save means to, 209b
see so much nor, so long, 194a
shall he, again, 1030b
sink or swim, or die, 443a
so young never, long, 128a
soil is good to, on, 603a
speak them while I, 655a
sure to, well, 378a
taught you how to, 98a
teach him how to, 98a
teach me to, 287b
teach them to, 98a
teaching me the way to, 98a
that they may eat and drink, 60b
that thou bearest the strain, 840b
that when thy summons comes, 470b
the same life over, 661b
they do not, but linger, 222a
they pine I, 101b
things in their pride, 902b
those God loves do not, long, 30a
thou thy life, 721b
though dead yet shall he, 1058b
three good men, 150a
through all things, 654b
through all time, 537a
till married, 157b
to, and let live, 617a
to be further serviceable, 237b
to be the show and gaze, 200a
to desire to live again, 728b
to eat, 61a
to fight another day, 69a
to, in mankind, 902b
to, is Christ, 1062b
to, is like love, 672a
to, is to function, 710b
to lie awake, 796b
to please, 335b
to thee, 329a
together in peace, 998a
together with content, 54b
too beautiful to, 576b
too much in a circle, 512a
tried to, without him, 213a
true as I, 214a
twice enjoy one's past is to, 52a
unblemish'd let me, 310a
undaunted, 40b
upon vapour of a dungeon, 188b
we how we can, 127a
we, not as we wish, 27b
well on nothing a year, 565a
well, what thou liv'st, 52b, 259a
while ye may, 255b
while you, drink, 532a
while you live, 329a
wisdom to love to, 812b
wished to, deliberately, 590a
with a lame man, 57b

Live with her and live with thee, 245a
with honour, 796a
with me and be my love, 216a, 992b
with the gods, 67b
with thee and be thy love, 110b
with them is far less sweet, 439a
with you I should love to, 39a
with you or without you, 52b
with your inferiors, 566a
within our means, 665a
within the reach to, nobly, 47a
within the sense they quicken, 468b
without a common power, 228b
without books, 653a
without conscience, 653a
without cooks, 653a
without dining, 653b
without friends, 653a
without heart, 653a
without him, no life, 258a
without hope, 653a, 899a
without love, 653a
without playing the knave, 284a
without poetry music art, 653a
without Thee I cannot, 464a
you might as well, 966b
you still shall, 206a
your life well or ill, 25b
Lived amidst untrodden ways, 405a
and loved and closed the door, 752a
and loved and cursed, 720a
and loved another race, 464a
discover that I had not, 590a
happy, can say he has, 40a
here quarter of a century, 538b
I have, 39b
I have not, in vain, 300a
in social intercourse, 340b
in tide of times, 168a
in vain a painful thought, 424b
light in the spring, 620b
like a madman, 110a
longest, 66b
my day, I have, 39b
on air, 880b
on alms-basket of words, 133b
on silver screens, 977b
on terms of friendship, 33b
part of its contents, 933b
probable thou hast never, 673a
the great range of life, 845a
to eat, 60b
to flourish, 588b
under my woodside, 237b
unknown, 405b
way to know is to have, 720a
well laughed often, 905b
with one generation of men, 55a
without infamy or praise, 75a
Livelier, hope is, than despair, 722a
iris changes, 548b
joy, and more abiding, 722a
liquor than the muse, 786b
some, plaything, 317a
Liveliest effusions of wit, 428b
Livelihood, anxiety about means of, 875a
partner in my, 21b
slave for, 911b
Livelong day, over the, 740a
Lively and lasting sense, 373a
cock with, din, 245a

Lively, steer from, to severe, 318a
Liver turn to water, 802a
Liverpool Street, down inclines of, 901a
Livers, humble, 210b
Livery, clad in her sober, 255b
cunning, of hell, 185a
death's, 946a
shadow'd, 144a
Lives a woman true and fair, 215b
alone by book and creed, 711b
along the line, 102b
are faithful prayers, 552a
are lost, 996a
are marches to the grave, 521a
are strange dark interludes, 946b
as he ought to do, 225a
a-working for our, 578b
cat has only nine, 678a
competency, longer, 143b
contendedly, 38b
cuckold, in bliss, 188a
dedicate our, and fortunes, 771a
depend on snatching the carrion, 697b
dies in single blessedness, 140b
direct our, to please, 283a
disciplines their, 516b
do not pray for easy, 670a
elegantly on nothing a year, 564b
every one that, must drink it up, 690a
evil men do, after them, 168a
for meanest mortal known, 711b
for self alone, 711b
fortunes and, vote away, 638a
fortunes watcheth o'er our, 17a
gave their, and fondest hopes, 763a
he, in fame, 129b
he wakes, 468a
history in men's, 153b
ideal version of their, 823a
if two, join, 569a
in a state of war by nature, 296a
in bliss, 394b
in eternity's sun rise, 386b
in our alley, 307b
in purer, thy service find, 528b
in sweetest bud, 205a
in thy possession happy, 299a
industrious men's, 229b
knows not how other half, 235a
land in which he, 344b
leave their little, in air, 309a
leaven lowly, 669a
led merry merry, 794b
like a drunken sailor, 128a
lives more, than one, 770a
long, and true prosperities, 580b
long, who well lives, 103a
lovely and pleasant in their, 1027b
make barren our, 692a
make our, sublime, 521a
men who lead secret, 773b
men's, ye're buying, 416a
mistakes of their own, 698a
more lives than one, 770a
most, who thinks most, 586a
mould our, 670b
music in men's, 140b
never, who much receives, 350b
nine, like a cat, 28b, 93b
no life at all, 8a

Lords or kings of the earth, 606a

  princes and, may flourish, 355b

  Scots, at his feet, 1011b

  thousand of his, 1048b

  whose parents were Lord knows, 291b

  women who love their, 352b

Lordship, point out to your, 520b

Lordships, beseech, to be merciful, 119a

Lordships' pleasures, 212a

Lore and pride of man, 503a

  follow not her, 259a

  much, we leave you, 706a

  mystical, 432b

  no garnered, 712b

  of nicely-calculated less, 411b

  sum of a lasting, 966b

  volume of forgotten, 544b

Lorena, years creep slowly by, 632a

Lorn creetur, lone, 578b

  with-outen remedye, 82a

Lose, amaz'd and, way, 148b

  and neglect creeping hours, 161a

  arts, virtue, 939b

  connection with the masses, 951a

  encounter and, in the crowd, 653b

  findeth his life shall, it, 1052b

  gain or, it all, 262b

  get at one end, at other, 341b

  good we oft might win, 183b

  heart to fight and, 933b

  his own soul, 1053b

  his right, 329b

  if fate means you to, 914a

  if I should, 697a

  it in the moment you detect, 314a

  it that buy with much care, 143a

  my all, 313a

  myself in a mystery, 240a

  name of action, 175a

  neither past nor future, 66a

  never, heart in illness, 850b

  nobly save or meanly, 540b

  nothing can he, 126b

  one and the same thing, 66b

  one life to, for my country, 299b

  our grief, 670a

  our ventures, 169a

  play to win or toil to, 846b

  reasons for living, 63a

  some day you may, them all, 582a

  something for every thing you gain, 501b

  substance by grasping, 9b

  the common touch, 820b

  the touch of the one, 797a

  their dear delight, 206b

  their temperature, 956b

  this intellectual being, 253b

  thy love I lose my all, 313a

  thy self-respect, 66b

  time is most displeasing, 76a

  to-day win to-morrow, 103b

  tomorrow ground won today, 621a

  what he never had, 236a

  whatever you can, 43b

  wholly, its vitality, 701b

  win or, it all, 262b

  wings, all their glory, 441b

Lose without excuse, 861b

  your way, 202b

Loser, peace forced upon the, 770b

Loser's woe, enhance the, 415b

Losers, both should, be, 233b

  tell me if the lovers are, 899a

Loses both itself and friend, 171b

  democracy, its touch, 954a

  deservedly, his own, 48b

  faith in God and woman, 650a

  finds himself, his misery, 620a

  the past, 18a

  what one, one loses, 719a

  who, her shall gain, 725b

  who, who wins, 193b

  wise man never, anything, 98b

Loseth his life for my sake, 1052b

  other life than he liveth, 66a

Losing, avoid for fear of, it, 286a

  fight when he's sure of, 596b

  man who can fight when he's, 877b

  office, 152a

  rendered sager, 456b

Loss and possession are one, 848b

  better to incur, 30a

  great our, and grievous, 817b

  grief but aggravates thy, 1011b

  love's the ambassador of, 790a

  mocks my, of liberty, 384b

  most patient man in, 204a

  no gain except by, 631b

  of honest men's lives, 229b

  of sight, 259b

  of the sun, 324a

  of wealth is loss of dirt, 90b

  our hap is, 126a

  pleasure without, 110a

  promise to his, 290b

  so overwhelming, 541b

  thy so sore, 790b

  unknown is no loss, 43a

  woe for a lover's, 592b

Losses are restor'd, 205a

  base gains are same as, 7b

  fellow that had, 158b

  moral, of expediency, 964a

  troubles, anxieties, 702a

Lost a good captain, 100b

  all good to me is, 255a

  all is not, 252a

  all is, save honour, 87b

  all original brightness, 253a

  all was, 258a

  all was not, 400a

  and dead, 609b

  and waiting for you, 815b

  angel of ruined paradise, 467b

  associations and societies, 800b

  battle's, and won, 194a

  better to have fought and, 552a

  better to have loved and, 551b

  books by which printers, 244a

  breed of noble bloods, 166b

  but ane I've twa behin', 394a

  causes, home of, 621b

  combatants are, 332b

  content, land of, 786a

  even with the utterly, 544a

  every day to be, 343a

  every dream we thought, 630b

  fight of virtue, 752b

  for aye in darkness, 610b

  for want of nail shoe was, 330b

  France has, a battle, 954b

  friend in power is friend, 696b

  good notion is, 273b

  he was, and is found, 1057a

Lost heart stiffens, 944b

  her honest name, 1008a

  his letters watch and wallet, 687a

  his tail, 221b

  holding anchor, 127a

  how art thou, 258b

  I have, a day, 305b

  immortal part of myself, 187b

  in convent's solitary gloom, 313a

  in idle company, 284a

  in jest, 928b

  in lexicography, 336b

  in spiral of his conscience, 926b

  in the common mass of matter, 6a

  in the sweets, 308b

  in wand'ring mazes, 254a

  is our old simplicity, 1002b

  it forever, 572b

  just, when I was saved, 646b

  lack'd and, 158b

  last man on earth'll be, 737b

  little, pup, 853b

  live in all that we have, 606b

  love, poet should have a, 981b

  loved long since and, 495b

  lover in the husband, 343a

  many a year of strife well, 929a

  Mark Antony the world, 289b

  memory of the loved and, 541b

  men being once, 54a

  men, their reason, 168a

  Mule Flat, 979a

  my reputation, 187b

  never, a little fish, 746b

  no love, 108a

  not, but gone before, 47a

  nothing except a battle, 400b

  obscenes, like old idols, 866a

  one shaft, 143b

  ones, counting all our, 12b

  ones, legion of the, 818b

  or won the game, 494b

  people on whom nothing is, 718b

  praising what is, 183a

  race, 987b

  reformers and lawmakers, 800b

  reputation, comes not again, 430b

  restore what I have, 233a

  right and wrong reverends, 800b

  sea voices, 944b

  sheep, strayed like, 1068a

  sight of distant horizons, 840a

  sight of hidden away, 692b

  small, rafts, 893a

  so fallen so, 527a

  sooner, and worn, 164b

  state may be given up for, 344a

  sun is, 217a

  swallow'd up and, 253b

  than ever were, at sea, 668b

  think that day, 305b

  those who have, an infant, 448b

  time like a run, 994a

  time never found again, 331a

  to love and truth, 819a

  to sight to memory dear, 439b

  two golden hours, 484a

  upon the roundabouts, 859a

  virtue if, in a young man, 283b

  voice with hollaing, 152b

  what I forego is, forever, 412b

  what though the field be, 252a

  when honour is, 44a

  wherever we're, in, 994a

Love, dull sublunary lovers', 216b
each time we, 650a
earth's the right place for, 880a
ebb to humble, 189a
ectasy of, 173a
emphasis of passionate, 431b
end of a, or a season, 879a
ennobles all, 1006a
enough of woman's, 827b
every leaf, 618a
everything, 618a
everything that's old, 119a
exultations agonies and, 407a
fail out with those we, 550a
falleth from, 83b
failing in, at first sight, 813b
false or true, 824b
fans it, 781a
far from the lips we, 439a
fear to, thee sweet, 790a
feast of, is song, 668a
fickleness of the women I, 764b
fight for, 141b
finds comfort in despair, 125a
first learned in lady's eyes, 133b
fitter, for me, 216a
flies out the window, 1000a
flowers and fruits of, 461a
for a woman you respect, 761b
for Angela, 852b
for fellow-citizens, 367a
for ladies', unfit, 281a
for sake of being loved, 463a
for things afar, 13b
for this flag, 852b
for thy, I will not grieve, 693b
for timber, 962b
for your, to her, 130a
free as air, 313a
freedom comrades, 897a
freedom in my, 268b
friendship and marriage, 434a
friendship charity, 182a
friendship is, 451b
friendship needs emotion to become, 673a
from too much, of living, 694a
from whom the world begun,
721b
from whose eyelids dropped, 7a
fulfilling of the law, 1060b
fulsome, for gain, 309b
gather the rose of, 230b
gave them our, and fear, 571a
gilds the scene, 381a
gin, be bonnie, 1013a
give a little, to a child, 606a
give me a sign his, to prove,
611b
God from necessity is, 561a
God gave them, 884b
God gives us, 547b
God if You wish for our, 933b
God is, 672a, 1064b
God made, 804b
God the world and, 672b
goes toward love, 135b
good creditable acquaintance,
295a
good man's, 162b
good-night must thou go, 686a
great, with a little gift, 29b
greater, hath no man, 1058b
greater than his power, 673a
greatest, of life, 371b
greybeards call divine, 127a
grief bound up with our, 670a
grown faint and fretful, 694a
grows bitter with treason, 693a

Love had been sae ill to win,
1013a
hail wedded, 256a
half in, with easeful death, 481b
half makes, to you today, 781a
hang level in balances of, 673a
hardly seem worth thinking of,
825b
harvests that our, had sown,
899b
harvest-time of, 427b
has found its home, 42a
hate traitors and treason, 279a
have not found my thing to,
885a
he bore to learning, 356b
he had to her, 1023b
he was all for, 377a
heart that gives it, 872b
her till I die, 999a
her was a liberal education,
301b
he's my, forevermore, 1020b
hid in the heart of, 824b
him because he is good, 797a
him for enemies he has made,
636b
him so as if to hate him, 14b
hold, in, 933b
honesty and, doth mince, 187b
hope faith and, 394b
hope nor, nor a friend, 752a
hopeless, finds comfort, 382a
how do I, thee, 519b
how vast a memory has, 310a
human, thou spirit given, 543b
hunt down, together, 693a
I am sick of, 1044a
I and my, wont to gae, 1013a
I could not, thee dear so much,
268a
I hate and I, 35b
I told you, 386a
if ever thou shalt, 164a
if love be perfect, 554b
if, means affection, 953a
if music be the food of, 163b
if my, were in my arms, 999a
if she, me I will die, 229a
if there's delight in, 298a
if thou must, me, 519a
if, were what the rose is, 693a
if you speak, 157a
in a golden bowl, 384b
in a hut, 480b
in law or in, 587b
in my bosom, 116a
in search of a word, 716b
in, with the janitor's boy, 995b
innocence of, 164b
is a boy by poets styl'd, 239a
is a flame, 897a
is a greater law, 73b
is a mood to man, 754a
is a sickness, 122b
is anterior to life, 647b
is bitter, 948b
is blind, 144b
is blynd, 81b
is enough, 667a
is flower-like, 425a
is full of showers, 118a
is God's essence, 672b
is grown to ripeness, 547b
is heaven, 413b
is immortal, 707a
is in his heart, 761a
is indestructible, 427b
is left alone, 547b

Love is like a dizziness, 402b
is like a lovely rose, 649b
is like the wild rose-briar, 591b
is love, 892b
is more cruel than lust, 692a
is nature's second sun, 116b
is not all, 963a
is not love which alters, 207a
is of a birth as rare, 269a
is something so divine, 366b
is strong as death, 1044b
is sweet for a day, 693a
is swift sincere pious, 83b
is the coldest of critics, 631a
is the jewel, 885a
is the only priest, 662b
is then our duty, 308b
it I love it, 591a
its essence is, 472b
itself possess'd, 137b
itself shall slumber on, 468b
iz like the meazles, 594b
jealousy born together with,
266a
jot of former, 122b
joy and, triumphing, 254b
kelson of creation is, 607b
kept in, 893b
kindled by virtue, 76b
kindness shall win my, 130b
kisses tears and smiles, 409a
know her was to, her, 396b
knoweth no lawes, 92a
labour of, 1063a
land that I, 941b
laws of life truth and, 616b
lay thy phobias to rest, 928a
lays hold on gentle heart, 75b
learn to bear beams of, 385a
least that let men know, 131b
let him, tomorrow, 304b
let the warm, in, 482b
let those, now, 304b
let thy, be younger, 164b
let's contend no more, 568a
liberty to those who, it, 444a
light and calm thoughts, 423b
lightly turns to thoughts of, 548b
like death levels ranks, 510a
like everybody not in, 855b
like friendship steady, 440a
like, is warm, 440a
like ours can never die, 813a
like sunshine after rain, 131a
lime of, 230a
limited by limited strength, 490b
liquor, or fights, 787a
little, my love come to me, 892b
little words of, 626b
live and, 35a
live with me and be my, 123a,
992b
live with thee and be thy, 110b
live without, 653a
lodged in a woman's breast,
213a
look of, alarms, 386b
look with as much, as friends,
284a
looks not with eyes, 141a
Lord of, came down, 757a
lose the power to, 583b
lose thy, I lose my all, 313a
lost to, and truth, 819a
love alone can pore, 716b
love for the woman you, 761b
love, in others they, 266a
lovers who, truly, 723a
loves in higher, endure, 552a

Love, lyric, half angel, 573a
machine, 693b
made trouble, 804b
make me, him, 150a
make thee run into folly, 160a
make, what we choose, 897a
makes, at all seasons, 1007a
makes those young, 262a
man in, endures more, 728b
man in state of, 728b
man's, is a thing apart, 457b
man's peculiar duty to, 68a
marked my, by candle-light, 612b
marry the man they, 906a
marvellous mercies and infinite, 692b
may go to Jericho, 440a
May never month of, 118a
me litle love me long, 93b
me little, 230b
me long, 230b
me love my dog, 94b
men hope and, 378b
men, their martyrs, 618b
mercy and walk humbly, 1049b
mercy charity and, 577a
mercy pity peace and, 385b
might enter in, 767a
mighty pain to, 267b
ministers of, 423a
mischievous devil, 672a
mistress to the man I, 313a
moderately, 136b
more libertines than, 344b
more, or more disdain, 236b
more we, our friends, 270a
musick I, most, 285a
must have wings to fly, 846b
must kiss that mortal's eyes, 760b
my, and I did meet, 824a
my country's good, 202b
my, he purloined her away, 701a
my heart has its, 486a
my neighbor well, 438b
my own and only, of you, 595b
my, she is a kitten, 690b
my, soothes not me, 609a
never, a stranger, 959a
never believe her, is blind, 876b
never doubt I, 173b
never seek to tell thy, 386a
never seeking her own, 83b
never taint my, 189b
never, unless you bear with faults, 220b
never wholly could escape, 73a
no blessed leisure for, 489a
no cord hold so fast as, 223b
no disguise can conceal, 265a
no fear in, 1064b
no great, in the beginning, 180a
no, lost sir, 108a
no rage like, to hatred turned, 298a
noght oold as whan newe, 81b
none knew thee but to, thee, 462b
nor hatred in the game, 727a
not death but, 519a
not enough to make us, 295a
not for, but only gliding, 501a
not man the less, 454b
not me for comely grace, 999b
not my, to see, 114b
not the flower they pluck, 504a

Love not the wind, 133a
not ye hapless sons, 529b
nothing as a good fight, 918b
nothing in, 199a
nothing that we, over-much, 826b
now, is over, 823b
now, the more, 304b
O spirit of, 163b
obedience troops of friends, 199a
of a nine-year-old, 811b
of all that is and ever was, 665b
of beauty in the abstract, 479a
of bustle is not industry, 47a
of country, 577a
of every land, 950a
of flattery, 302a
of friends, laughter and the, 849a
of glory is most ardent, 301b
of God, 1062a
of her, become filled with, 20a
of herself she will not, 261a
of home, 577a
of justice, 265a
of learning, 525a
of liberty God has planted, 538a
of life increased, 371b
of love of life of death, 665b
of man, 21b
of money, 515b
of money as possession, 925a
of money is the root, 1063a
of my life came not, 760a
of nature, 470b
of other sights controls, 215a
of pleasure and love of sway, 314b
of praise howe'er concealed, 304b
of the British people, 360b
of the turtle, 455b
of the young for the young, 788a
of truth, 555b
of virtue, 344b
of war for itself, 490a
of wealth, 516b
of wealth or fame, 761b
of your wife, 813a
off with the old, 668a
old trees hats coats, 953a
once, 575b
one fairer than my, 134b
one leaf is for, 802b
one maiden only, 555a
one true light kindle to, 533a
only our, hath no decay, 216a
only, sprung from hate, 135a
orbit of the restless soul, 626a
our occupations, 578b
oyster may be crossed in, 382a
pain over, 898b
pains of, be sweeter far, 275b
pangs of dispriz'd, 174b
pardon to the extent we, 266a
passing that of dwellers, 748a
passing the, of woman, 1027b
paths lead to woman's, 225a
pent-up, of my heart, 736a
pest of, 479a
pity melts the mind to, 225a
pity's akin to, 225a
Platonic, 105b
play a dominant part, 810b
pleasure of, is in loving, 265b
poet without, 473a
poet's food is, and fame, 466a

Love, power and effect of, 223b
practice this thin, 262b
predilection and, 705a
priests speak wisely about, 991a
prince of, beheld, 384b
proof of, and power, 612a
prove likewise variable, 135b
pure, shows itself, 270a
purple light of, 349b
quick-ey'd, 232b
rather than, than money, 590b
regain, once possess'd, 260b
renders votaries credulous, 345a
renewal of, 31b
renews the strength of, 31b
respect or natural, 773a
rhymes so rare to, 725a
right to dissemble your, 389a
ruin'd, when built anew, 207a
rules the court, 413b
sang of, not of fame, 634b
seals of, but sealed in vain, 185b
season of, and laughter, 661b
secret, 1041a
seeketh only self to please, 387a
seething surge of, 665b
seldom haunts the breast, 309b
self-sacrificing, of a brute, 544b
separate us from, of God, 1060a
servant in, 82a
service of my, 789a
sets, a task like that, 448b
shackles of an old, 555a
shame with, at strife, 281a
she never told her, 164b
sick with, 961b
sidelong looks of, 355b
sigh to those who, me, 456b
sighed for the, of a ladye, 685a
silence in, bewrays woe, 111a
silent tongues of, 104a
sits down to the banquet, 668a
smile of, 387b
so, doth guide, 617a
so gentle in his view, 134b
so long as we, we serve, 752b
so many I, not yet born, 990b
so sweet, seemed, 721b
sole mortal thing, 629b
solitary places, 465b
some one to, 788a
something to, He lends us, 547b
sometimes called brotherly, 728a
sought is good, 165a
sovereynetee over hir, 81b
spare diet the cause, lasts, 261b
spirit compact of fire, 131a
spring of, gushed, 422a
spring of, resembleth, 131b
springs of, 585b
stand much in the cause of, 784b
stream of, 526b
strong son of God immortal, 551a
such a man, 323b
such I believe my, 86a
supreme value is, 799b
swears she is made of truth, 207b
sweet are words of, 673a
sweet as, 384a
sweet is true, 555a
sweet lovers, the spring, 163a
sweetest of all what, nor says, 673a
sweetest thing on earth, 737a

Lying, let me have no, 208b
  most things sleep, 233a
  nothing worth the, awake, 841b
  prayers for death are, 16b
  smallest amount of, 671a
  trade of, 52b
  vainness babbling drunkenness, 165b
  world given to, 152a
Lynn, stern-faced men set out from, 488a
Lyonnesse, set out for, 704b
Lyons looms, 597b
Lyre, bards of the, 38a
  forgot, 38b
  had been discovered, 602a
  half a silver, 968a
  make me thy, 466a
  minstrel's, 854b
  nightingale has a, of gold, 741b
  not from his, 567b
  'Omer smote 'is bloomin', 821a
  so long divine, 458a
  trembling I smite the, 974b
  waked the living, 348b
  within the sky, 543b
Lyres and flutes, 702a
Lyric love half angel, 573a
  minions, songs my, 486a
  most splendid ecclesiastical, 513a
Lyrical grave or satirical, 844b
Lysander, Hector and, 1004a

M, everything that begins with, 657a
Mab, Queen, hath been with you, 134b
Mabel, ain't it awful, 914a
MacArthur, General, speaking, 907b
Macassar, incomparable oil, 457a
Macaulay, cocksure as Tom, 436b
  like a book in breeches, 419b
  Lord, 622a
  Old Joe and so on, 483b
Macbeth does murder sleep, 196b
  none of woman born harm, 198b
  shall never vanquish'd be, 198b
  shall sleep no more, 196b
Macdonald, wherever, sits, 501a
Macedon, brought up like a rude, 28a
  river in, 156b
Macedonia, come over into, 1059a
  fly out of, 58b
MacGregor, my name is, 416b
Machiavel, every country hath its, 85a
  Nick, had ne'er a trick, 104a, 239b
Machinations hollowness treachery, 190b
Machine, a love, 693b
  beauty of a great, 938b
  called man, 578b
  crank, 75a
  ingenious, for turning, 930a
  justice is a, 837b
  politicians run behind the, 838a
  pulse of the, 409a
  typewriting, 897b
  you're not a man you're a, 764b
Machinery of the State, 435b
Machines, converting immature human beings into, 594a
  for making more machines, 866a
  slaves instead of masters, 783b
  we only hear, 977b

Mackerel, stinking, 150b
  stinks like rotten, 425b
Macro, unbraided, in no obscure terms, 56a
Mad as a March hare, 84b
  as Bedlam, 579a
  bad and dangerous to know, 449a
  birds were, with glee, 673b
  dog's tooth, 129b
  dogs and Englishmen, 981b
  drives men, 722b
  face that drove me, 717a
  fall, if they do not die, 476a
  fitter being sane than, 573a
  Fortune first makes, 18b
  idolatry, 181b
  if, I am not Sophocles, 16b
  in pursuit, 207a
  individually and nationally, 47b
  lads that drive me, 867b
  learning doth make thee, 224a
  makes men, 190a
  man is stark, 99a
  March days, 896b
  more or less, on one point, 813b
  much learning doth make thee, 1059b
  naked summer night, 608a
  north-north-west, 173a
  O fool I shall go, 191b
  out of too much learning, 224a
  pleasure sure in being, 277b
  practice drives me, 999a
  prose run, 318b
  provided a man is not, 344b
  pursuit, 482a
  sad and bad and, 572b
  saint run, 320b
  second draught makes him, 163b
  sense that the world was, 884b
  that he is, 'tis true, 173b
  undevout astronomer is, 306a
  we have all once been, 813b
  went, and bit the man, 355a
  wind's night-work, 503b
  with drinking, 774a
  world, 579a
  young futurists, 831b
Madam Blaize, lament for, 353a
  Sorrow scorns all this, 486b
Madame Bad Luck soberly comes, 486b
Madde March hare, 84b
Madden, made a mannikin merely to, 545b
  round the land, 318a
  to crime, 455b
Madder music and stronger wine, 833a
Maddest merriest day, 547a
Madding crowd's ignoble strife, 349a
Made and loveth all, 422b
  and preserves us a nation, 499a
  annihilating all that's, 269a
  as he is so was he, 722a
  begotten not, 1068a
  better, in that way than not made, 536a
  by whom all things were, 1068a
  'em pay dear, 108b
  fearfully and wonderfully, 1038a
  for use and benefit of men, 275a
  friends are born not, 696a
  inside of church, 151a
  light of it, 1054a
  mouths in a glass, 191b

Made no more bones, 103a
  nobody never, me, 563a
  nor, a pause, 338a
  of penetrable stuff, 176b
  poet's, as well as born, 219b
  Quintilian stare, 251a
  righteousness readable, 858b
  the best of this, 394b
  the sea dry land, 1024b
  thinking feel, 957a
  to mistress' eyebrow, 161a
  whole in faith, 84a
  you for a time out of marble, 36a
Madeleine, you shall see the lovely, 717b
Madeline's fair breast, 481a
Mademoiselle from Armenteers, 958a
Madison Square, Miss McFlimsey of, 632b
Madly, stars shot, 141b
Madman, liar or a, 344b
  lived like a, 110a
  whosoever shall call me, 35a
Madmen, pleasure none but, know, 277b
  worst of, 320b
Madness caused by thinking, 774a
  deplorable piece of, 282b
  despondency and, 406b
  devil's, war, 877b
  fine, 122b
  harmonious, 467a
  in the brain, 421a
  melancholy, of poetry, 1001b
  method in, 173b
  midsummer, 165b
  mixture of, 48a
  moon-struck, 258b
  much, is divinest sense, 646a
  much of, and more of sin, 544a
  much sense the starkest, 646a
  near allied to, 276b
  risen from hell, 691b
  species of, 282b
  strike with no, 972b
  that way, lies, 191b
  'tis, to defer, 222a
  to live like a wretch, 222a
  touch of, 48a
  you may call it, folly, 396b
Madonna, paint the Sistine, 955b
Madonnas, Rafael of the dear, 571b
Madrid, there was, 958b
Madrigal, woeful stuff this, 311b
Madrigals, birds sing, 123a
  that whisper softness, 250b
Maenad of Massachusetts, 695a
Maensac, Pierre de, 932b
Magazines, graves of little, 928a
  newspapers, and best-seller novel, 794b
  of myth, 893b
Maggie, when you and I were young, 699b
Magic and delicious power, 923b
  breaks his chains, 247b
  casements, 482a
  game, doorbells are like a, 430a
  in the distance, 909b
  mirror, reflected as in a, 708b
  numbers and persuasive sound, 298a
  of a cheerful face, 535a
  of a face, 237a
  of a name, 432a
  of the sea, 523b

Man, canst not be false to any, 172a
can't cudgel his own jackass, 708a
cast down every, his rod, 317a
catholic, 716a
cells and gibbets for the, 591a
certain of immortality, 773b
change in the dress of, 736b
charming characteristic of, 743b
child conceived, 1030a
child grow into the, 525b
child is father of the, 406b
childhood shows the, 259b
Christian faithful, 127b
city is the teacher of the, 9a
clothe a, with rags, 1040b
come forth thou fearful, 137a
comely olde, 112b
common-looking, 542b
conceive a, 969a
conference maketh a ready, 121b
consider how much he has, 301a
consists of body mind, 897b
contact with a religious, 729a
could ease a heart, 966a
covers, like a cloak, 109b
covetous, is ever in want, 41a
crime of being a young, 334b
crooked, 1019a
crucify the soul of, 222a
cursed alway by, 520b
dare do all that may become a, 196a
dares to call himself a, 969a
daring young, 700b
Darwinian, 684b
dead, cannot bite, 56a
dead, service or injury to the, 21a
decline to accept end of, 977a
defileth a, 1053a
degradation of, by poverty, 496b
delights not me, 174a
der shturdy oak, 713b
despise a tailless, 717a
destroy the eye of another, 3b
diapason closing full in, 278b
did eat angels' food, 1035b
dieth and wasteth away, 1030b
difference between a dog and, 678a
distinguishable from a gorilla, 564b
distinguishes, from animals, 743b
divide state of, 154b
divine as myself is dead, 609b
doth not live by bread only, 1025b
dream of a waking, 71a
dreams of possessing heart, 855b
drest in a little authority, 184b
drink takes the, 712b
drove out the, 1022a
dust was once the, 610a
dwells apart, 612b
dying, to dying men, 266b
each, winds up, 261a
ech, for himself, 80a
end try the, 153a
enough for a tear, 760b
envy is natural to, 19a
envying a, famous, 8a
errs while struggle lasts, 379b
escape every other danger, 27b
every, against every man, 229a
every, as Heaven made him, 107b

Man, every, can tame a shrew, 223b
every cry of every, 387b
every, good and bad angel, 221b
every, his greatest enemy, 240b
every, his own architect, 574b
every, is son of own works, 36a
every, mind own business, 105a
every, must play a part, 143a
every, persuades himself, 338a
every, was God or Devil, 277a
every, will be thy friend, 220a
evil fruit of a bad, 7a
excels another, how much one, 31b
exceptional, deteriorated, 727a
excess caused, to fall, 120a
fall of, 590b
fallacy that, is desirable, 994a
false man, 291a
feelings or views of such a, 428a
felt as a, 368a
figure of, at twice its size, 923b
figure of the reasonable, 955a
firin' at a target, 791b
first, among these fellows, 56b
first in war, 384a
first the, takes a drink, 712b
first years of, 337a
fit night for, or beast, 901a
foolish passionate, 827b
for the field, 550b
foremost, of all this world, 168b
foretells afar, 471b
forgotten, 707a, 918b
formed, of the dust, 1021b
frailty of a, 119b
free as nature first made, 275b
friend of, 777b
fury of a patient, 277b
gazing on the stars, 650b
get a new, 209b
gifts of a bad, 17a
give every, thy ear, 171b
give world assurance of a, 177a
given to appetite, 1040b
gives to, or woman, 785b
giveth up the ghost, 1030b
God is not a, 12b, 1025b
God made, 804b
God made it for this, 558b
God-intoxicated, 281b
God's a good, 158a
goes his own by-way, 291b
goes riding by, 750a
goeth forth unto his work, 1036b
going away with a handsomer, 731b
good great, inherits honor, 423b
good old, 158a, 498b
good or ill of, 64a
good, prolongs his life, 52a
goodliest, of men, 255b
gossamer fidelity of mere, 544b
great, dies, 525a
great, represents ganglion, 709a
greater, the greater courtesy, 555a
greatest fool is, 287a
grew within this learned, 123b
grows beyond his work, 991a
grows old may learn, 24b
half part of a blessed, 147b
happiness of common, 900a
happy a, as any in the world, 284b
happy, happy dole, 91a
happy is the, 23a
happy the, 326b

Man happy the citizen free, 497b
happy the, who can call today his own, 278a
hardly a, is now alive, 524a
harrowing clods, 706b
has left something undone, 68b
has no morrow, 15b
has shop to mind, 574b
has two irons in fire, 22b
has wrested from nature, 987a
hate, you have wronged, 63b
hath in life sins enough, 264a
hath penance done, 422a
he had made a finer, 800a
he was a, take him for all in all, 171a
he was, and a positivist, 637a
he was her, 1004a
heart of, 879a
heart of a, 815b
heart of a, is depress'd, 308b
heaven had made her such a, 186b
Heavenly Father invented, 680a
height of a, 50a
helpless, in ignorance, 336a
here lies a truly honest, 264a
highest style of, 306a
his own doctor of divinity, 749a
hold every, a debtor, 122a
honest and perfect, 224b
honest, appeals to understanding, 1002a
honest as any, 158a
honest exceeding poor, 144a
honest soul the perfect, 224b
honourable, yet write badly, 270a
how hard a, may labor, 771b
how poor a thing is, 122a
humour, according as he is, 33a
hungry man is not a free, 986b
I am a fatal, 565a
I know not the, 51b
I love and honour, 155b
I love not, the less, 454b
I loved in Rome, 962b
I shall know the, far better, 643b
if a, have an office, 953a
if a, look sharply, 121a
if, could only moult, 740b
if not the wedding-day, 333b
if you are a poor, 72a
if you are a rich, 72a
if you work for a, 763a
imagination of a, 478b
imagines he cannot do this, 282a
impossible for, 68b
in armor, 574a
in difficulties, 11b
in our town, 1020b
in the distant future, 530b
in the integrity of nature, 344b
in the wilderness, 1015b
in these days, is nobody, 585b
in unsearchable darkness, 722a
in wit a, 278b, 315b
instruct a wiser, 49a
interrupt a, 345b
intimates eternity to, 300a
is a fallen god, 463a
is a long time coming, 899a
is a marvellous vain subject, 97b
is a mere insect, 701a
is a military animal, 586b
is a noble animal, 241b
is a pliable animal, 617b
is a political animal, 26a

Man is a prisoner, 20b
is a reasoning animal, 47a
is a rope, 726b
is, an ape or an angel, 512b
is as old as he's feeling, 637a
is better than a book, 793b
is born free, 344a
is born into the world, 599b
is born unto trouble, 1030a
is but a beast, 1013b
is but a thinking reed, 272b
is by no means poor, 41a
is cause of the work, 857a
is dead, 527a
is equal iv ivry other man, 837b
is first-rate, 596b
is happy, 13b
is his own star, 224b
is like a phonograph, 765b
is like company he keeps, 18a
is little to be envied, 337b
is man and master of his fate, 35b, 554b
is most detestable, 680a
is neither angel nor brute, 272b
is, no more than this, 192a
is not the creature of circumstances, 511a
is not upon oath, 341b
is only animal that blushes, 679a
is so in the way in the house, 558a
is stark mad, 99a
is the dream of a shadow, 13b
is the hunter, 550b
is tired of London, 342a
is very apt to complain, 341b
it is so between, and man, 121a
it means a, 876a
Jesus was most scientific, 616b
joy in, in leaf in star, 780b
just upright, 1030b
justify God's ways to, 786b
kills the thing he loves, 769b
kind of, the country turns out, 507b
knew a, who had a friend, 1008b
know end of day's business, 169a
know myself a, 213b
know what God and, is, 556a
knows nothing without being taught, 49b
knows right from wrong, 679b
laborin', 600b
large-hearted, 518a
last, on earth'll be lost, 737b
last thing civilized by, 638b
law for, and law for thing, 503b
law not the, 484b
laws of God the laws of, 787a
lay down his life, 1058b
laying down his life, 984b
least considerable, 1002a
leave his father and mother, 1021b
let God and, decree, 787a
let no such, be trusted, 147a
let not, put asunder, 1053b
life of, less than a span, 121b
life of, solitary, 229a
little, what now, 965b
little worse than a, 143b
live by bread alone, 1050b
lives not upon bread alone, 749b
living-dead, 129b
look sad, 143a
looketh on outward appearance, 1027b
looking for a, 72a

Man looks small at a wedding, 978b
lopsided, runs fastest, 811b
Lord is a, of war, 1024b
lord of over his fellow, 774b
lose neither past nor future, 66a
loseth other life, 66a
lot of, but once to die, 232a
lot of, to suffer, 5b
love a, who is zealous, 342a
love is a mood to, 754a
love such a, 323b
love the, I marry, 906a
low, seeks a little thing, 570a
machine called, 578b
made him happy as a married, 340b
made the town, 121a, 364a
majority can never replace the, 951a
make a, spring, 262b
make a weak, your enemy, 594b
make, in our image, 1021a
make one worthy, my foe, 319a
makes no noise over good deed, 67b
makes the circumstances, 473b
makes us believe oath, 13b
manage a clever, 814a
manners makyth, 77a
man's inhumanity to, 390a
marks the earth with ruin, 454b
marries again, 768a
marry any sort of white, 562a
marry this, and woman together, 296a
matters not how, dies, 340b
may benefit his country, 20a
may escape from rope and gun, 308b
may redeem the past, 757b
may tak a neebor's part, 391a
may work from sun to sun, 1001a
meddles with them, 344a
memory of, 352a
middle-aged, concludes to build, 589a
mildest manner'd, 458a
military, in world, 155a
mind is the, 33a
mind of, a musical instrument, 613b
mind's the standard of the, 302b
mine equal, 1034b
misfortunes occasioned by, 49b
mistakes of a good, 1002a
moral, and man of honor, 909a
moral, was Werther, 564a
morality of vulgar, 727b
more sinn'd against, 191b
most married, I ever saw, 665a
most precious thing possessed by, 344b
must be a non-conformist, 501b
must eat peck of salt, 104a
must have his faults, 51b
must learn, 957a
must please himself, 616a
my, Friday, 292a
my mother's life made me a, 896b
nae, can tether time or tide, 91a
named Matthew, 1052a
natural, has two primal passions, 743a
need to see a woman, 953a
never extinguished in heart of, 345a

Man never falls so low, 560a
never is but always to be blest, 316a
never met a, I didn't like, 904b
never was harmed by truth, 68a
no beard less than a, 157a
no, became wicked all at once, 62b
no, but a blockhead, 341b
no, can feel himself alone, 791a
no, can serve two masters, 1051b
no, ever wetted clay and left it, 61a
no, is a hero to his valet, 61b
no, is an island, 218a
no, is happy, 45b
no, is happy without a hobby, 744b
no longer the, you were, 995a
no, loves life like him, 16a
no right to be a public, 577b
no, ruleth safely, 83a
no, so good, 100b
no, speak write to him, 281b
no such thing as an honest, 306b
no time for, to recover hair, 129a
no, truly knows another, 802b
no, was more foolish, 342b
no wedded, so hardy be, 81b
no, will supply thy want, 220a
no wise, quit a certainty, 337a
no, wiser for learning, 227b
no, worth having is true, 294a
no, written out of reputation, 292b
no young, believes he shall die, 434b
noblest work of, 662b
none more wonderful than, 14a
nor proudest of his works, 369a
not a, that lives, 404b
not afraid of the sea, 857a
not always actions show the, 314a
not good that, should be alone, 1021b
not trusted with government, 374b
nothing more fun than a, 967a
nothing out of artist not in, 909a
nothing yet contrived by, 341b
of absolute genius, 908a
of achievement, 478a
of action in state of thought, 838a
of all modern poets, 275b
of business, clergyman also a, 73a
of genius makes no mistakes, 917a
of genius sees the world, 784a
of genius seldom ruined, 339b
of giant frame, 471a
of God's own mould, 663a
of great estate, 42a
of knowledge increaseth strength, 118a
of letters must make up hi mind, 690a
of letters, physician and, 534a
of letters, skin of the, 651a
of mettle, 307a
of might, 584b
of my kidney, 180b
of peace, 891a
of profound feeling, 644a
of rank, 342b
of sorrows, 1047b
of sovereign parts, 132b

Marx explains unsocialized pairs, 960a
made same announcement, 955b
Marxian Socialism, 925a
Mary Ambree, 1012a
at thy window be, 393b
Bloody, 488b
child with his mother, 1050a
go and call the cattle, 598a
had a little lamb, 462b
hath chosen that good part, 1057a
helper of heartbreak, 911a
lovely still my, 365b
Mary quite contrary, 1015b
Morison, 393b
Saint Anne the mother of, 702a
she came with her child, 1003a
sweet Highland, 393a
was that mother mild, 591b
Mary-buds, winking, 204a
Maryland my Maryland, 702b
Mary's asleep by murmuring stream, 392b
Marys and Anns and Elizas, 535a
Masculine in its allurement, 904a
soul is a worker, 806b
Mask and antique pageantry, 245b
boldness is, for fear, 51a
Harlequin without his, 565b
like open truth, 297b
of care, 853a
shows as he removes the, 563b
Masked words abroad, 605b
Masks, bag of, 979a
Mason, a mere working, 416a
Masons, singing, 154b
Masquerade, street begins to, 704b
truth in, 459b
Masquerades, skim milk, as cream, 682b
Mass, blessed mutter of the, 570b
commodity, 985b
common, of matter, 6a
dead level of the, 604a
enormous, 4a
everyone has, of bad work, 671b
giant, of things to come, 181b, 832a
interests combined into one, 442a
jewelled, of millinery, 553b
man, problem of the, 915a
molten, 939a
obscure, of humanity, 514b
Paris worth a, 115b
response out of mass need, 985b
shapeless, a book of rules, 730b
sniffs round the, 719b
the, hardens, 939a
the mob the crowd the, 898a
yawning at the, 867a
Massachusetts, encomium upon, 443b
here's to old, 793a
Infantry, 666a
Maenad of, 695a
there she stands, 443b
Massacre, betray and lie and, 99b
not as sudden as a, 674b
Masses against the classes, 534a
airy, and smooth, 432a
bow ye, 683b
connection with the great, 951a
floundering, of ice, 563a
give me your huddled, 742b
long suits, 958a
mill and swarm, 963a
of people victims to lie, 951b

Masses, shapeless, of white flesh, 50a
superiority to the, 909a
write for the, 486b
Massive sandal set on stone, 962a
Massy, two, keys, 249a
Mast, bends the gallant, 447b
blown over-board, 127a
cut away the, 587a
drunken sailor on a, 128a
nail to the, her holy flag, 534b
nail'd her colors to the, 414a
of some great ammiral, 252b
Master, accuse not a servant to his, 1041b
and a task for life, 507b
and author, 75a
and make crouch, 573b
becomes a host then a, 924a
behold thy, 326a
both of science and of art, 731a
Ca-Caliban has a new, 209b
calls no man, 437a
creditor is worse than a, 497b
disciple not above his, 1052b
every card a, 958a
every man be, of his time, 197a
forces met their, 919b
genius is, of man, 653b
grief, 158a
hard for thee to, 68a
house without a, 502b
in that he knows her, 668b
in the presence of The, 566a
in your calling, 709a
into the woods my, went, 716a
I've done thy bidding, 877a
Jacky shall have a new, 1016b
man is, of his fate, 35b
mariner, 755b
melody, feels the, 914b
mendicants observe, 726b
mistress and two slaves, 714a
my despair, 507b
my whole life, 576a
need even more to be a, 717b
of all good workmen, 814b
of all whose language he speaks, 501a
of art as of life, 773b
of earth and sea, 823b
of himself, 39b, 226b
of his fate, 554b
of his time till seven, 197a
of my fate, 741b
of us all, 903a
one for my, 1015b
passion, 679b
passion in the breast, 317a
passive, lent his hand, 503b
prove so hard a, 721b
Ridley play the man, 87a
shuttles prepared by the, 711a
so I would not be a, 537b
speaker is the tear, 884b
spirits of this age, 167b
strong enough to be the, 344a
subtle, under heaven, 555a
such, such man, 96b
unwitting where their, dwells, 897a
which is to be, 659a
who's, who's man, 297a
Master-art of kindness, 726b
Mastered, Destiny waiteth for the, 13a
law in his private thoughts, 501a
Master-hand alone can reach, 310b

Mastering passion of his life, 748b
Masterly, wise and, inactivity, 397b
Masterpiece, appear as the flower, 668b
confusion made his, 197a
nature her, design'd, 393a
nature's chief, 289b
of nature, 502a
Masterpieces, heaven's, 966b
narrates adventures among, 723b
of the world, 976a
Master's crib, 1045a
feet, sound of his, 1029a
gate, starv'd at his, 388a
hand, jar in the best, 42a
income, 913a
lash, beneath his, 583b
lost his fiddling-stick, 1014b
spell, kindled by the, 396b
steps, 593a
words are forgotten, 822a
Masters, artist has the, in his eye, 515a
cannot all be, 185b
done away with, 727b
frightfulest of all, 475b
lords and rulers, 755b
no man can serve two, 1051b
noble and approv'd good, 186a
of assemblies, 1044a
of the things they write, 227b
of their fates, 166a
slaves instead of, 783b
spread yourselves, 141a
Masters' table, 1053a
Master-spirit, life-blood of a, 250b
Master-stroke is nature's part, 507a
Master-word looms large in meaning, 743b
Mastery, courage is, of fear, 678a
of a subject, 882b
of the desires, 727b
over a man, 722b
over musical instruments, 785a
propensity for, 776a
Mast-high ice, 421a
Mastiffe, excellent, 284b
Mastiffs of unmatchable courage, 155b
Mast'ry, strive here for, 254b
Masts, till, crack, 117a
Match it, fellow fault, 162a
for the devil, 980a
ne'er saw her, 134b
the mountains and the sea, 755b
Matched our buttons, 687b
us with His hour, 938b
Matches are made in heaven, 91a
Matchless bard, 358b
infantry, moved out that, 740a
swiftness, 5a
Mate, choose another, 417a
choose not alone a proper, 366a
for beauty, 510a
great artificer made my, 752a
in England, I've a, 582a
listen when his, talked, 930a
may choose another, 417a
of the Nancy brig, 681b
old bold, of Henry Morgan, 663a
took unto herself a, 407a
who be the maiden's, 413a
Mated, longing to be, 616b
Materia medica, 536b

Mind equal and beyond their fullness, 739b
equal to any undertaking, 578b
evangels of the, 915b
eyes in his, 141a
false volume of his single, 713b
farewell the tranquil, 188b
fool uttereth all his, 1041b
forever voyaging, 404b
frantic limits of the, 994b
gaiety and the quiet, 753b
gentle sensitive, 826b
gives to her, 343b
glance of the, 363b
glide by degrees out of, 337b
God is the only, 616b
Goethe's, 620a
golden, stoops not, 144b
good, possesses a kingdom, 48a
grateful, by owing owes not, 255a
great fortitude of, 338b
great, knows the power, 574a
greatest powers of the, 428b
grief develops powers of, 856a
grow inward like a root, 994b
growing, at a barbaric phase, 832b
grows old, 26a
grows torpid, 342a
happy alchemy of, 326b
has a, and knows it, 766b
has a thousand eyes, 755a
has mountains, 724b
has seldom had an equal, 981a
having a, of her own, 718a
heal the tortured, 471b
heart argues not the, 621b
heart to heart and mind to, 413b
her, was to be his, 718a
hinder the, 272a
his, a thought, 585b
his belly, 340a
his, or body to prefer, 316b
human, is ruined, 957a
humble and grateful, 64a
hunger for a well-stored, 741a
I do not, lying, 672b
idle, knows not what it wants, 31a
ignis fatuus of the, 289a
impressed on the, of a son, 373a
in his right, 1055b
in my, of all mankind, 1011a
inclineth man's, to atheism, 120b
infinite capacity of the human, 382a
ingratiate deeply with the, 298a
inside-pocket of my, 958b
interested the human, 701b
is bent to ill, 6b
is divided in telling, 13b
is gay but soul is melancholy, 725b
is its own place, 240b
is pitch'd, 365a
is proper judge of man, 48a
is the great lever, 443a
is the man himself, 33a
is troubled, 182a
is unsworn, 17b
it's all in the, 987b
keep your, even, 38b
kind of daylight in the, 301a
labyrinthine ways of my own, 790a
last best work the human, 393a
last infirmity of noble, 249a

Mind, laws without origin in the, 916a
lays by its burden, 35a
let the world, him, 570b
let thy dauntless, 126b
let your, alone, 971b
lets go a thousand things, 680b
levelling rancorous rational, 827b
liberalize a man's, 637a
loose sally of the, 336b
love looks with the, 141a
love's but a frailty of the, 298a
loyal nature and noble, 555a
lust of greedy, 35b
maimed, 244a
makes the body rich, 130b
man with a, 561b
man's unconquerable, 407a
march of the human, 360a
men to be of one, 1069b
minister to a, diseas'd, 199a
mostly in your, 967b
mould the secret, 695a
moult his, its errors, 740b
music breathing, 268a
my, a kingdom is, 101b
my business better, 284a
my compass, 326b
my, fixed on lofty ideal, 855b
my, forbids to crave, 101b
my, to me an empire is, 101b
narrow as neck of vinegar-cruet, 338a
narrow'd his, 357b
neither bushel nor barrel but, 743a
never be old man in, 34a
never brought to, 392b
never face so pleased my, 999a
no, is so well balanced, 697b
no malice in his, 498b
no, to be Florus, 66a
noble, disdains not to repent, 5a
nobler in the, to suffer, 174b
not acquainted with his, 51b
not changing one's, 875a
not in my perfect, 193b
not to be chang'd, 252b
o'erwrought, 705b
of man a musical instrument, 613b
of man, dwelling in the, 404a
of man, wont to show the, 8b
oppression of the, 288b
our, is God, 28a
out of sight is out of, 83a, 595b
own business, 105a
passion is a fever in the, 288a
peace of, 29b
peace to the, 664a
pen is the tongue of the, 108a
persecutes the, 279a
persuaded in his own, 1060b
perversion of the, 961a
physicians of a, diseased, 12b
pity arrests the, 916b
pity melts the, 225a
pleasant time with my, 654a
pleased to call his, 495a
plumb the Oriental, 813b
poison to his, 494b
poor the, without vanity, 726a
presence of, in danger, 282a
professional military, 831b
pulse in the eternal, 938b
quiet, is richer, 117b
quite vacant, 363b
raise and erect, 118b

Mind, reading is to the, 299a
reclothe us in our rightful, 528b
redeem the human, 522a
reign of, 440b
restive or sluggish, 739a
riddle of a woman's, 106a
rival him save with my, 969b
sane, in sound body, 63a
satisfy his, 588a
say this with presence of, 32a
seize upon the, 586a
serene for contemplation, 299b
serene of, 775a
she had a frugal, 363b
soon grows through them, 370b
sound, in a sound body, 283b
spoke the vacant, 356a
state of, once gone, 715a
state of, which creates revolutions, 26b
steady on its keel, 602b
strength of body and, 282a
Sumner's, 696b
suspicion haunts guilty, 127a
takes the, out of doors, 750a
tall policeman of my, 968b
that very fiery particle, 459b
their p's and q's, 671b
thing that teases the, 742b
things gone out of, 406a
things that feed the, 720a
this, must be understood, 616b
time out of, 103b, 962b
to ensure peace of, 828b
to laugh, 41a
to men a man is but a, 713b
touch my country's, 897b
tranquil, 66b
trouble enough in his own, 264a
troubled, be stranger, 232a
troubled sea of the, 479a
truth but in our, 465b
tumours of a troubl'd, 12b
twirls them in his, 704a
tyranny over the, of man, 374a
universal frame without, 120b
unsoundness of, 492a
untutor'd, sees God in clouds, 316a
villain's, 144a
vision of, supplements, 614b
waiting harp-strings of the, 617a
we can feed this, 403b
weakness of the human, 281b
what I am taught, 442b
what the swift, beholds, 962a
which renounces futile hope, 774b
wisdom calms the, 336a
wisest books in her, 267b
woman in the background of his, 771b
woman interested in a man's, 756b
worked her, to such a pitch, 730b
years bring philosophic, 408b
Mindanao, Zamboanga, 762b
Minde, cleane through the, 112b
gentle, by gentle deeds, 114a
never, did minde his grace, 114b
Minded their own business, 656b
what they were about, 345b
Mind-forg'd manacles, 387b
Mindful of the happy time, 73b
to rule with imperial sway, be, 37b
what it cost, 402b

Moon, begged of the, to give him light, 1003a
behold wandering, 246a
brilliant, and milky sky, 824b
build a bridge to the, 589a
by yonder blessed, 135b
climbing, upon empty sky, 825a
cold fruitless, 140b
come from the dying, 550a
comes over Brooklyn, 995b
commanded, to stand still, 331b
course of one revolving, 277a
cow jumped over the, 1016b
crimson, and azure eye, 395b
danced by the light of the, 581a
daughter of the, 523a
ebb and flow by the, 193b
error of the, 190a
everyone is a, 679a
fair as the, 1044b
follow changes of the, 188b
horned, 421b
hush with the setting, 554a
in a silver bag, 827b
inconstant, 135b
innocent, 789b
is like a flower, 385b
is my sister, 848b
kneaded by the, 705a
Lady, where are you roving, 543a
lies fair upon the straits, 622a
like to a silver bow, 140b
lucent as a rounded, 602b
made of green cheese, 88a
make guilty the, the stars, 191a
marsh beneath the, 935a
minions of the, 149a
more interested in earth, 756b
mortal, 206b
mortals call the, 466b
moving, went up the sky, 422a
nor the, by night, 1037b
ode to the, 854a
on Monan's rill, 415a
or stars be not darkened, 1043b
or sun or what you please, 130b
pale-faced, 149b
resolves into salt tears, 203b
revisit'st glimpses of the, 172a
rising in clouded majesty, 255b
said the wind to the, 631b
saw the new, late yestreen, 1011b
shine at full or no, 239b
shone bright on Mrs. Porter, 944a
shown the wintry, 481a
sigh for the, 665a
silent as the, 260a
silver apples of the, 825a
slowly silently now the, 862b
small, lightens more, 721a
sun and, should doubt, 388a
sun and stars brother, 500b
sun and, were sunk, 247b
sun stood still the, stayed, 1026a
swear not by the, 135b
sweet regent of the sky, 368b
takes up the wondrous tale, 299a
talk by a poet, 676b
that looks for us again, 533b
the stars the planets, 929a
thou climb'st skies, 115b
to the, complain, 348a
unmask her beauty to the, 171a
very wide awake the, and I, 684b
waning, was haunted, 420b
was a ghostly galleon, 909b
when the, shall rise, 213a

Moon, white, beams, 952a
will wax, 525b
Moon-calf, 209b
Moone, cast beyond the, 91b
Moonlecht necht, 850a
Moonlight and feeling are one, 469a
come to thee by, 909b
is divine, 995b
is softest in Kentucky, 725b
lulled by the, 636b
meet me by, 484b
not of the, 556b
ribbon of, 909b
rotten mackerel by, 425b
shade, beck'ning ghost along, 313b
sleeps upon this bank, 147a
unto sunlight, 549a
visit it by the pale, 413b
Moonlit cedar, from that, 621a
door, knocking on the, 862b
Moonrise, gradual as the, 616a
Moon's an arrant thief, 203b
unclouded grandeur, 464b
Moons, among the suns and, 994a
my old, and my new moons, 724a
reason has, 854b
while stars burn, increase, 547b
Moonshine, find out, 142a
its glory is all, 613b
Moon-struck madness, 258b
Moor, Hercules and Goth and, 703a
I never saw a, 648a
over the purple, 909b
wild, 1003a
your bark with two anchors, 43b
Moor'd, fleet was, in the Downs, 308a
Moore, Tom, a health to thee, 456b
Moorish fen, by lake or, 247b
Moorsfield London, 336b
Moping melancholy, 258b
mum, 685a
owl does complain, 348a
Mops, seven maids with seven, 658a
Moral and intellectual powers, 733a
and material welfare, 779b
artistic, personality, 611a
authority, basis of, 617b
character, bird of bad, 331b
conflict, van of every, 588a
courage with physical timidity, 705a
culture, highest stage in, 530a
effort, golf a form of, 844b
ends by settling the, 696a
Englishman thinks he is, 765a
enterprise, success of, 517b
everything's got a, 657a
evil and of good, 403b
free from, obligations, 420a
habits in men's lives, 55a
indifference is the malady, 617b
infection, 580a
inferiority, 679b
intellectual and, achievements, 637b
is what you feel good after, 982b
issues, 983b
losses of expediency, 964a
man and a man of honor, 909a
man was Werther, 564a
no one can be, till all are moral, 614b
obligation to be intelligent, 901a

Moral or an immoral book, 768a
persons attempting to find a, 676b
philosophy makes men grave, 121b
physical and, standard, 616b
point a, 336a
question for the heart, 811a
satire ever, ever new, 287a
sense of work of art, 719a
sense, women have, 696a
sensible well-bred man, 363a
sentiments, 472a
soil for aesthetic growth, 866a
spark out of stone easier than a, 689a
story with a, 801b
test, perception of beauty a, 589a
things, or things evangelical, 274a
world, intellectual and, 538b
Moralist set up the ignoble maxim, 783b
statesman cannot be a, 930b
Moralities, never mind about, 679a
Morality, blunderbuss against, 339a
enliven, with wit, 300a
foes of popular, 617b
in courage of making choice, 858b
is a private luxury, 697a
knows nothing of boundaries, 614b
middle class, 766a
needs emotion to become religion, 673a
no, where there is no free agency, 484a
of his actions, 344b
of vulgar man, 727b
periodical fits of, 492a
pernicious to general, 514b
sexless orgies of, 695a
temper wit with, 300a
thou deadly bane, 390b
treat politics and, apart, 700a
unawares, expires, 322a
veracity is heart of, 633b
wear his, 924b
which suits him, 778a
Moralize my song, 113a
Moralizing, philosopher's, 812b
Morals, about, 982b
and legislation, 324b
faith and, 407a
falsified by conventional, 861a
field of, 908a
make you dreary, 753a
of a money changer, 843a
of the market place, 849b
self-interest was bad, 919b
simply blind obedience, 784a
Morbid doubt, 753b
Morbidity, disgusting, 925b
Mordre wol out, 82a
More abundant life, 919a
and more about less and less, 799a
and more and more, 658b
and the few, 887b
blessed to give, 1059a
books upon books, 101a
brawn than brain, 36a
by hoping, they have less, 131a
easy to take, than nothing, 657a
elder than looks, 146b
giving thy sum of, 159b

Nutmeg-graters, rough as, **307a**
Nutmegs and cloves, 232a
Nutrition, draw, propagate and rot, 317a
Nutritive or suggestive truth, **719a**
Nuts, 981a
  are getting brown, 647b
  we's all poor, 946a
Nutshell, bounded in a, **173b**
Nygard, riche and, 77b
Nyght, rede and drive away the, 77b
Nymph, Eve Venus a, **514b**
  haste thee, 245a
  in thy orisons, 175a
  mountain, sweet liberty, 245a
  or grace of finer form, 415a
  sweet echo sweetest, 247a
Nympha pudica Deum vidit, 263a
Nymphs blush not he, 639b
  sisterhood of the, 36b

O cursed spite, 173a
  death where is thy sting, 1062a
  well for fisherman's boy, **549b**
  wild west wind, 466a
  wind if winter comes, 466a
Oafs, muddied, at the goals, 816b
Oak, adds a ring as to an, 602a
  and ash and thorn, 820b, 1012a
  as natural a growth as an, 562b
  bend a knotted, 298a
  fell the hardest-timber'd, 112b
  for angling-rod a sturdy, 242b
  greenest, 853a
  hardest-timbered, 126a
  heart of, are our ships, 347a
  hearts of, 90a
  hollow, our palace, 447b
  in, none is, 1019a
  man der schturdy, 713b
  raven on yon left-hand, 30a
  shadow of the British, 361a
  that grew thereby, 368b
  varnished, 959a
Oaken, old, bucket, 450a
Oaks are the true conservatives, 936a
  from little acorns grow, 401a
  little strokes fell great, 330b
  many strokes overthrow tallest, 112b
  of towering height, **336b**
Oar, no better companion than, 628b
  or jav'lin, never handled, **23b**
  put in her, 107b
  soft moves the dipping, 395b
  spread the thin, 317b
  wait the muffled, 528a
Oars, golden, 158a
  keep time, 269a, 438a
  trouble the seas with, 36b
  were silver, 200b
  with little skill are plied, 655b
Oat-cakes, Calvin, and sulphur, 418b
Oates walking to his death, 842b
Oath, break an, he never made, 239a
  Cophetua sware a royal, 549b
  corporal, 106b
  Glasgerion swore, 1012a
  hard-a-keeping, 132a
  he that imposes an, 239a
  Hippocratic, 21b
  honour more weight than, 69b
  man is not upon, 341b
  mouth-filling, **151a**

Oath, no woman believe man's, 35b
  not, that makes us believe, 13b
  trust a man on his, 203a
  whore's, 192b
Oaths are but words, **239a**
  false as dicer's, 176b
  lavish of, 243a
  strange, 161a
Oats a grain given to horses, **337a**
  definition of, 337a
  good dry, 142a
  mares eat, 1019a
  sow our spiritual wild, **671b**
  wild, will get sown, 830b
Obadias, David Josias, 1000b
Obdur'd breast, 254a
Obedience as aim or butt, **154b**
  bane of all genius, 464b
  blind, to words of command, 784a
  fear keeps men in, 224a
  honor love, 199a
  infuses that liberal, 360b
  into duty, 344a
  is best, 803b
  no power to command, **26a**
  to God, 1002b
  to government, 367a
Obedient, books, to my hand, 794b
  safe polite, and sterile, 931b
  servants, made them, 946a
  to their laws, 9a
Obelisk, strong and upright like an, 772b
Obermann, to Baudelaire and to, 751b
Oberon, jest to, 141a
Obese obituary, roar at your, 995a
Obesity is a mental state, 991a
Obey an old decree, 133b
  Anna whom three realms, 312b
  drift wait and, 822a
  haunch and the hump is, 816a
  its laws respect its flag, 842a
  monarchs must, 277b
  nature, necessity, 169a
  rogues, you well, **307a**
  that impulse, 830b
  the voice at eve, 506b
  to, is better than sacrifice, **1027a**
  woman to, 550b
Obeyed, and they, him, 331b
Obeying, constant, him, 243b
Obeys, humour most when she, 315a
  she, him, 523a
Obituary in the Boston Transcript, 805b
  notices them do part, 801b
  roar at your obese, 995a
Object be our country, 443a
  has he not another, 25a
  in possession, 65b
  legitimate, of good government, 375a
  most tremendous, of creation, 357a
  my, all sublime, 685a
  of government, 779b
  of government in peace and war, 900a
  of utility, 593b
  only of war, 370b
  paramount, in this struggle, 539b
  something valuable as its, 402a
  stampede to some new, 811a
  strange and high, 269a

Object, truth is the, of philosophy, 378a
Objections against another's oration, 61a
Objective is a more abundant life, 919a
Objects and knowledge curious, 610a
  earnest about these, 931b
  extracted from many, 162b
  in an airy height, 293b
  motives of travels, 65b
  of all thought, 404a
  of hatred, 858a
  out of their own power, 424a
  real, of their writing, 448b
  see their, always near, 435a
  spiritual significance to, 722a
  whoever tries for great, 55b
Oblations, vain, 1045a
Obligation, haste in paying off, 265b
  is reciprocal, 891a
  moral, to be intelligent, 901a
  of a novel, 718a
  opportunity implies an, 876b
  ow'd great, 294a
  possession without, **639a**
  sense of, 852b
  tie and, to posterity, 380b
  under least, to like, 719a
Obligations are yet with us, 444a
  free from moral, 420a
  of government, 689a
Obliged every one that I could, 398b
  not, to find understanding, 343a
  so obliging that he ne'er, 319a
  the other we are, to, 953a
  the wealthy, 4b
  to be thrifty or starve, 953b
  to make a cage of laws, 953b
Obligeth, no man to more, 1070b
Obliging, so, that he ne'er obliged, 319a
Oblique loves, 269a
Obliterate, no craft or custom shall, 847a
Oblivion, alms for, 182a
  and divine repose, 668a
  drink, of a day, 638b
  fame that comes after is, 66a
  formless ruin of, 182b
  gently replacing in, 648b
  iniquity of, 241b
  is not to be hired, 241b
  Lethe the river of, 254a
  mere, 161b
  moldered into, 446a
  my, is a very Antony, 200a
  razure of, 185b
  siftings on siftings in, 933a
  six months', 697a
  total neglect and, **431a**
Oblivion's sea, 893a
  silence seal, 412b
Oblivious antidote, 199a
Oblong into the triangular, 418b
Obnoxious laws, repeal of, 623b
Obscene, element of the, 782b
  grave and light, 228b
  great men are truly, 782b
  wings, sailing on, 422b
Obscenes, like old idols lost, 866~
Obscurantist, totalitarian and, 954b
Obscur'd, excess of glory, 253a
Obscure, actors too humble and, 773b

Palsied, eld, 184b
Palsy-stricken church-yard thing, 480b
Palter in a double sense, 199b
Paltry compensations, 544b
  decorum, 418a
  friendship, 544b
  how fleeting and, 67b
  thing, aged man but a, 827a
Paly flames, 155b
Pamby's, Namby, little rhymes, 307b
Pan and old Sylvanus, 36b
  babies like biscuits in a, 861a
  is dead, 61b
  out on the prophets, 698b
  turning of the cat in the, 120b
Panaceas, tobacco beyond all, 223b
Panama and its poverty, 484b
Pancakes, flat down as, 214a
Pandemonium city and proud seat of Lucifer, 258b
Panders, reason, will, 177a
Pandion is dead, 220a
Pandora, more lovely than, 256b
Panegyric, practitioner in, 382a
Pang as great as when giant dies, 185a
  beautiful incentive as a, 719a
  biting, while she sings, 352b
  each, imbues with a new colour, 454a
  ghastly, 421b
  is glad to fall away, 328b
  learn nor account the, 572a
  of all the partings gone, 789b
  preceding death, 353b
Pangs and fears, 211b
  keenest, the wretched find, 455a
  of dispriz'd love, 174b
  sweet, 164b
Panic, calm and without, 954a
  cowardice distinguished from, 983b
  never yet was any, 777a
Panic's in thy breastie, 390a
Panics have their uses, 370b
Panjandrum, Grand, himself, 350b
Pansies for thoughts, 178a
Pansy for lovers' thoughts, 116b
Pant and kiss for gold, 309b
  fond heart shall, 329a
Pantaloon, slipper'd, 161b
Panted, soul had, for years, 649a
Panteth after the waterbrooks, 1034a
  for the waterbrooks, 649a
Panting deer, 464a
  spirit free, lets the, 577a
  syllable, chase a, 363b
  time toil'd, 335b
  with, breath has escaped, 75a
Pants for twenty-one, 32oa
  he has neither vest nor, 670b
  kick them in the, 926a
Panza, Sancho, 912a
Papa potatoes poultry prunes, 580a
Paper, best loved, in Kansas, 843a
  blotted, 145b
  bullets of brain, 157b
  he hath not eat, 133a
  leaves nor leaves of stone, 601b
  money, comparable to, 784a
  put down rightly on, 742b
  tell your, 802a
  twelve ounces of, 956b

Paper you drop into the ballot-box, 589a
Paper-credit, blest, 315a
Paper-mill, built a, 126a
Papers, don't purtend to print, 601b
  evening, print what they do, 957a
  in each hand, 318a
  Sunday, 828b
  turns over your, 372b
  what I read in the, 904b
Papists or Protestants, 339b
Paps are centres of delight, 116a
Par, born below, 839b
Parables of sun light, 997a
Parade, glories in gunpowder and loves, 586b
  pomp and, 367b
  street, and uniforms, 892a
Parading round and round, 362a
Paradisal nature, 573a
Paradise, drunk the milk of, 420b
  England a, for women, 224a
  fool's, 110a
  from earth to, 892b
  has she cheapened, 629b
  heav'nly, that place, 220b
  in no mean, 700a
  is paradise, 110a
  Italy a, for horses, 224a
  itself were dim, 441a
  library which is your, 85a
  lighten earth from, 695b
  lost angel of a ruined, 467b
  man and woman may enter, 672b
  maturity is the gate of, 631a
  new-bathed in light of, 714b
  not only in my eyes, 77a
  O paradise, 584a
  of exiles, 465b
  of fools, 110a
  of individuality, 807a
  opening, 349b
  opens on the road to, 513b
  same old glimpse of, 788b
  sweet lies of, 439b
  the old road to, 911a
  thought destroy their, 347b
  to what we fear of death, 185a
  unto you is, opened, 1065a
  wilderness were, enow, 531b
Paradox, glorious epicurean, 536a
  mistaking a, for a discovery, 857a
Paragon, earthly, 204b
  winter the, of art, 988b
Paragraph, life's not a, 968b
Parallel, none can be his, 48a
  though infinite never meet, 269a
Parallelism of life, 697a
Parallels of latitude for a seine, 676a
Paralyzed in every function, 625b
Paramount object in this struggle, 539b
Paramour is thing of naught, 142b
Paraphrase, rash, can make amends, 314a
Parara in Asia Minor, 963b
Parasite of society, 728a
Parcel of their fortunes, 201a
  of vain strivings, 588b
Parcels of the dreadful past, 547a
Parching peelers, 856b
Parchment scribbled o'er, 125b

Pard, bearded like the, 161a
  not a lion but a, 934b
Pard-like spirit, 468a
Pardon error, 326a
  first begs, 162a
  for too much loving you, 188b
  I don't ax no, 691a
  me, thou bleeding piece of earth, 167b
  no word like, 140b
  one offence, 46a
  pity though not, 129a
  remorseful, slowly carried, 183b
  something to liberty, 360a
  they ne'er, who have done wrong, 47b
  to the extent that we love, 266a
  virtue of vice must, beg, 177a
Pardonable, to speak dishonourably is, 16a
Pardon'd all except her face, 459a
Pardons, never, those he injures, 47b
  offender never, 47b
  the ravens, 62b
Parent, duty a, owed to a child, 583a
  keep one, from the sky, 319b
  kind, or merciless stepmother, 49a
  knees, 377b
  of an art allied to invention, 24a
  of good, 256b
  of luxury is wealth, 24b
  of revolution and crime, 26a
  people's, 6a
  spark, fire outlives the, 468b
  too experienced a, 956b
Parental, mild, sway, 628b
Parenthesis, death is no, 968b
Parents are able to think calmly, 702b
  are apt to be foreigners, 631a
  bore their children, 766a
  children begin by loving, 768a
  children inter their, 16b
  do not know what they do, 429b
  girl needs good, 929b
  honor, 12b
  meek-eyed, 993a
  Philadelphia asks who were his, 679b
  teacher equal to my, 21b
  which are now thy, 1065b
  whose, the Lord knows, 291b
Parfit gentil knight, 79a
Paris counts an author, 287a
  go to, when they die, 768b
  is a woman's town, 757a
  last time I saw, 958b
  mighty, 827b
  no home in Europe save in, 729a
  no right speech out of, 84a
  perfumed, 525a
  Sir, a carpet-knight, 98a
  to Japan, 287a
  well worth a mass, 115b
Parish church, 160b
  look upon world as my, 329b
Park where peach-blossoms blew, 725a
Parks and palaces, 751b
  pairs in the, 960a
Parley, no truce or, 870b

People don't ask for facts, 973a
enlighten the, generally, 375b
envious were devoured, 71b
fear and distrust the, 376a
few fastidious, 822a
folly of the, 86a
food of the, 337a
fool some of the, all the time, 542b
foolish, without understanding, 292b
from the people and for the, 511a
gave the, of his best, 549b
God save the, 441b
God will be with His, 237b
good, all with one accord, 353a
good, in their wisdom, 537a
good of the, is chief law, 33b
governed by magistrates, 490a
government of all the, 560a
government of the, 541a, 842a
great peaceful, 770b
great talk among, 284b
hallow a whole, 419a
have some champion, 25a
health of the, 513a
his, are free, 440b
his, were his temple, 273a
how holy, look when sea-sick, 672b
I am the, the mob, 898a
I pity, 687b
identify themselves with the, 376a
in England would be better, 744b
in grief, 558a
in hotels strike no roots, 841b
in Scotland supports the, 337a
indictment against a whole, 360a
indomitable, 859a
influence, 942b
inurned, weep a, 493a
judge men by success, 265b
keep, from talking, 104a
keep, from vice, 341a
kindreds, and tongues, 1064b
know other, 27b
last, I should choose, 381a
let my, go, 1024a
like, like priest, 1049a
march, 899a
marry ancient, 244a
may eat grass, 474b
myriads of, 222b
narrow-souled, 321a
no doubt but ye are the, 1030b
not a book-reading, 794b
not characters, 982b
not include support of the, 689b
nothing is so galling to a, 492a
of customers, 352a
of his pasture, 1036b
of no great sense, 160b
of the Philippines, 907b
of the United States, 376a
officer of the, 425b
often grudge others, 10b
old, applaud it, 107a
on whom nothing is lost, 718b
opinion of the, 373b
opium of the, 593a
our soverign the, 443b
people have for friends, 794a
people marry, 794a
perish, 1041b

People, poor and rascally, 284a
power greater than the, 442a
protect interests of the, 920a
receiving from the, 333b
representative of the, 399b
representatives of the, 463b
right of the, to alter, 373a
right of the, to assemble, 376b
rule with primitive, 759a
see there is a, risen, 273b
sentiment of the, behind it, 698a
servants and agents of the, 689a
some, one loves best, 641b
special, 1025b
spontaneous cooperation of free, 771b
stiffnecked, 1025a
strong enough, 920a
sunless pleasures of weary, 701b
swarm into the streets, 86a
ten thousand, may lie in it, 304a
that walked in darkness, 1045b
the sunbeams, 245b
they were a, 961a
three millions of, 334b
thy, shall be my people, 1027a
thy, shall be willing, 1037a
to all the, you can, 330a
turn, to that inward light, 273a
two kinds of, on earth, 754a
ultimate justice of the, 539a
very nicest, 957a
voice of the, voice of God, 74a
wash their dirty linen, 399b
welfare of the, 779b
what gain is it to the, 737a
what is the city but the, 202b
what kind of, do they think we are, 871a
when wilt Thou save the, 441b
who do things, 885b
who have no weaknesses, 723a
who know little, 344b
who lift, 754a
who make no noise, 269a
who merely pray, 727a
who think they ought to be free, 359a
whom we most despise, 580b
who're comfortable, 914a
will fight for live for, 605b
will talk and find fault, 104a
will talk you know, 557b
wisdom and efficacy of the, 921a
with rivers as with, 757b
world that has such, in 't, 210a
world were not so full of, 894b
Peopled garden, 378b
kingdom, 102b, 154b
world must be, 157b
People's approval, secure other, 678b
government, 443b
hard necessities, 798b
hearts, high in the, 166b
hearts, Lord did dwell in, 273a
it's other, money, 631b
other, habits, 678a
parent, 6a
prayer glad diviner's theme, 277a
right maintain, 436b
sufferin', injye other, 836a
sustenance is exacted, 689a
will, broad-based upon her, 553a
Peoples and governments, 401b

Peoples, crime of slaughtering whole, 47b
do not know each other, 778a
great and small, 556b
life of, and of humanity, 642a
new-caught sullen, 817a
of Austria-Hungary, 771a
of the United Nations, 997b
rule the, with imperial sway, 37b
stronger, will pass us by, 779a
who have the courage, 925b
Peopling earth waters and sky, 287a
Peor and Baalim, 244b
Pepper his cabbage, 45b
Pepper-corn, I am a, 151a
Pepper'd the highest, 358a
Peppered, two of them, 150a
Peppers, peck of pickled, 1018a
Perce hard marble, 34b
Perceive, find little to, 412a
here a divided duty, 186b
things that he thinketh, 1065b
Perceived, so finely, and felt, 580b
Perceives things he has discarded, 41a
Perceiving how not to do it, 579b
in an unhabitual way, 715b
Percentage, small, will profit, 775a
Perceptible not in progress but result, 616a
Perception, adapt spiritual level to, 951a
of beauty, 589a
of the comic, 508b
quicken his, though dull, 787b
till our, end, 574b
universal, 757b
Perceptual anaesthesia, 908b
Perch and not their terror, 184a
eagles dare not, 127b
got down from his, 587a
on a cathedral or church, 805a
stand on the, 953b
Perchance to dream, 174b
Perched upon a bust of Pallas, 545a
Perches in the soul, 646b
Percolated, thought has, through, 803a
Percy and Douglas, song of, 116a
Perdition, bottomless, 252a
catch my soul, 188a
Père Lachaise, buried in, 497b
Peregrinations, men's labours and, 118b
Perennial pleasures plants, 490a
Perfect a thing as the clipper ship, 940b
accuracy in the newspaper, 842a
almost, state, 894a
creature, far more, 530b
day, darkness to the, 723b
day, end of a, 799a
day, hoping ever for the, 560b
day, shineth more unto the, 1038b
days, then if ever come, 600a
entire and whole and, 789a
forms, art's, 526b
freedom, whose service is, 1068b
friendship of two men, 771b
fright, 457a
gallows, 208b
good and, gift, 1064a
honest and, man, 224b
if love be, 554a
if thou wilt be, 1053b

Perpetual quarrel, 360b
  rack, 222a
  session, 927b
  steady and, serenity, 301a
  struggle for room and food, 530a
Perpetually damned, 123b
Perpetuate, repair and, it, 753a
Perplex and dash, 253b
Perplex'd in the extreme, 190b
Perplexed, souls, and distressed, 722b
  with error, 19b
Perplexes monarchs with fear, 253a
Persecute, pray for them which, you, 1051a
Persecutes the mind, 279a
Persecutest, why, thou me, 1059a
Persecution a bad and indirect way, 240b
  christened it, 596b
  first law of society, 960a
  will lead to strengthening, 951b
Persecutor, zealot may commence, 373b
Perseverance and soothing language, 374a
  in a good cause, 345b
  in disguise, 776b
  keeps honour bright, 182a
  more prevailing than violence, 55b
Persevere, strength to forbear and, 753b
Persia, past their first sleep in, 241b
  throne of, 491a
Persian carpet, 53b
  Gulf the Red Sea, 581b
  gulfs, pearls of thought in, 602b
  messengers, 19b
Persian-lambed, ermined and minked and, 805a
Persian's heaven, 439b
Persians, antique, 460a
  truth-loving, 972b
Persistent, more, more faithful, 855a
Person, age in a virtuous, 301b
  bore is, who talks, 714a
  easiest, to deceive, 510a
  esteemed, nod from a, 57a
  in the first, 1005b
  isolated naked, 917b
  master owns only your, 497b
  of respectable connections, 670b
  portrait of a, one knows, 379a
  really busy, 758a
  sacrificed to individual, 917b
  set thy, forth to sell, 212b
  there's no sich a, 578a
  to know what a, wants, 853b
  umble, 579a
  waking up always the same, 822a
  well-conducted, 564a
  which each, deserved, 71b
  who agrees with me, 513a
  who can't pay, 580a
  who disliked gravy, 270b
  wise, and a fool, 31b
Personage, less imposing, 435b
  play their, 103a
Personages, risk everything with great, 297b
Personal arrogance, 910b
  beauty a better introduction, 71a

Personal considerations, 623b
  experience should not be guide, 24b
  ideals, three, 744b
  immortality, endow myself with, 841b
  intercourse, correspondence and, 558a
  life as an individual, 882a
  likings, graves of his, 651a
  Northwest Passage, 933b
  opinions, rawness of his, 787b
  possessions, decline, 807b
  presence everywhere, 734b
  relationship, 988a
  ridicule is a shaft, 784b
  significance or insignificance, 540a
  slim and crooked but, 718a
Personalities, greater, than themselves, 895a
  trivial, decomposing, 923a
Personality, artistic moral, 611a
  creates outside of his own, 756b
  native, endows a man, 611a
  needs a good, 930a
  newspaper-man a double, 696b
  poetry an escape from, 943b
Personally defeated, 517a
  one to become, attach'd to, 610b
Persons, addressed to private, 487a
  attempting to find a motive, 676b
  deprived of judgment, 28b
  divers, 162a
  duty of all, to reflect, 32b
  eleven thousand, 295b
  first must be forgotten, 425b
  God in three, 445b
  great, able to do great kindnesses, 108b
  grown old in business, 431a
  living on annuities, 457b
  money rather than their, 344a
  more lives of obscure, 798b
  most knowing of, 47a
  no respect of, with God, 1059b
  no respect of place, nor time, 164a
  no respecter of, 1059a
  of good sense, 332a
  respect of, is not good, 1041b
  two distinct, 221b
  without education, 435a
Perspicuity of language, 74a
Perspicuous, enough if a work be, 425a
Perspiration, ninety-nine percent, 735b
Perspire, dig till you gently, 820a
Persuade, beauty doth of itself, 131a
  to woo to, prevail, 765a
  tongue to, 369a
Persuaded his enemy, 1014b
  in his own mind, 1060b
Persuades, every man, himself, 338a
  when speaking fails, 208a
Persuadest, almost, thou, me, 1059b
Persuading, by, others, 1002b
  fair-spoken, 212a
  revolting instead of, 375b
Persuasion and belief, 411a
  divine, flows from lips, 4b
  hung upon his lips, 345b

Persuasion shine all silver, 9a
  tries force because, fails, 574a
Persuasions, winged, 467b
Persuasive sound, magic numbers and, 298a
Pert as a schoolgirl, 684b
Perturbed spirit, 173b
Perturbs their minds, 516b
Peru, from China to, 335b
  Newton at, 493a
  with its riches, 484b
Pervades, spirit, public acts, 20b
Perverse as a legislature, 989b
  as human nature, 989b
  depravity of their nature, 290b
  imp of the, 545a
  opinion, men of, 15a
Perverseness one of primitive impulses, 544b
Perversion, enormous and innermost, 728b
  of the mind, 961a
Perverted by selfishness of man, 914b
  woman's cold, will, 469b
Pessimism as agreeable as optimism, 832b
  name men give to wisdom, 976b
Pessimist fears this is true, 900a
  not a, but a pejorist, 785a
  sees the hole, 891a
Pest of love, 479a
Pester'd with popinjay, 149b
Pestiferous superlatives, 808a
Pestilence, like a desolating, 464b
  noisome, 1036b
  that walketh in darkness, 1036a
Pestilence-stricken multitudes, 466a
Pestilent congregation of vapours, 173b
Petal, each finger nail a crimson, 973a
  root to crowning, 736a
  sleeps the crimson, 551a
  tip-tilted like the, 554b
Petals from blown roses, 547a
  on a wet black bough, 932b
Petar, hoist with his own, 177b
Peter, call him, 147b
  denied his Lord, 1000b
  Peter Pumpkin-eater, 1018b
  Piper, 1018a
  robbing, he paid Paul, 88b
  the thought that, spoke, 722b
  thou art, 1053b
  twenty times was, feared, 404a
  Uncle, Daniels, 1014a
Peterkin, quoth little, 426b
Peter's dome, hand that rounded, 503a
Petition government for a redress, 376b
Petrarch's wife, 458a
Petrified opinion, loyalty to, 680a
  truth, 674a
Petrifies the feeling, 391a
Petticoat, feet beneath her, 261a
  government, 446a
  tempestuous, 230b
Pettifogger, one produces the, 433b
Petty artery in this body, 172a
  causes, meanest motives and, 491a
  done the undone vast, 570a
  men walk under his legs, 166a
  minds, good fortune will elevate, 55b

Petty pace, creeps in this, 199b
repeated annoyances, 54b
suffering makes men, 875b
Pewter, no, and no pub, 947a
Phalanx, moved in perfect, 253a
Pyrrhic, 458a
Phantasma, interim is like a, 167a
Phantom days, 890b
of delight, 409a
of ourselves, 622b
of the hungry poor, 674a
pains of perished passion, 809b
Phantoms of hope, 337a
one by one the, go, 846a
Pharaoh's heart, 1024a
lean kine, 150b
Pharisee, I am a, 1059b
Pharos of Egypt comes last, 1008a
Pharpar, Abana and, 1029a
Phase in the life of the aged,
966a
new, in human history, 832a
Ph.D. thesis, 942b
Pheasants, honoured among foxes
and, 997a
Phenomena, laws from, of nature,
916a
of the universe, 633b
Phials hermetically sealed, 295b
Phidias, awful Jove young,
brought, 503a
carves wisdom, 507b
Philadelphia asks who were his
parents, 679b
most pecksniffian city, 908b
Philanthropic enterprises, of all,
953b
pursoot like shop-keepin', 835a
Philanthropically, cure them all,
990a
Philanthropist, delusion to the,
668b
Philanthropists in a time of famine, 509a
Philanthropy almost the only virtue, 590a
Philip betwixt two wicked persons, 59a
drunk to Philip sober, 19a
had success in his affairs, 56a
news of successes brought, 58b
Philippines, people of the, 907b
relief of the, 907b
Philistine, originally meant, 621b
prevailed over the, 1027b
what is called a, 461b
Philistines, apostle of the, 622a
barbarians, and populace, 623a
be upon thee Samson, 1026b
though the, may jostle, 683a
Philologists who chase a syllable,
363b
Philosopher, considered by, as
false, 369a
dies twice in Laertius, 69b
doesn't think in a vacuum, 798a
endure toothache, 159a
firm, can scorn, 328a
great memory does not make,
496a
greater, a man is, 735a
guide, and friend, 318a, 912a
married, belongs to comedy,
727b
muscular training of a, 64b
my definition, 654a
thinks like a, 345a
Philosopher's moralizing, 812b
stone, true, 743b

Philosopher's stones, 223b
Philosophers, all that, have
sought, 412b
exchange their ware for money,
702b
put their names to books, 222b
sayings of, 238b
sit in their sylvan hall, 654a
statesmen, and divines, 501b
wise, have judg'd, 239a
Philosophic mind, 408b
Philosophies of one age, 743a
Philosophize, ridicule philosophy
is to, 272b
Philosophre, al be that he was a,
79a
Philosophy, adversity's sweet milk,
137a
aim of a true, 702b
and wine are alike, 702b
any, in thee shepherd, 161b
ask not proud, 433a
attainment of the goal in, 784a
attainment of a true, 702b
axioms in, 478b
bladders of, 289a
calm lights of mild, 299a
charming is divine, 247b
conformable to truth, 722a
could find it out, 174a
divine, 552a
dreamt of in your, 173a
faith and, are air, 605a
genius for architecture or, 505a
hang up, 137a
inclineth mind to atheism, 120b
is nothing but discretion, 227b
mammalian, 949b
mere, is my faith, 240b
microscope of thought, 498a
natural, makes men deep, 121b
new, calls all in doubt, 217a
no stoicism and no, 605a
of sympathy and resemblance,
759a
one who studies, 64b
ridicule, 272b
teaching by examples, 304a
triumphs over past evils, 264b
truth is the object of, 738a
unless, can make a Juliet, 137a
whatever, may determine, 340b
will clip an angel's wings, 480b
Ph.D. thesis, 942b
Phisik, gold in, 79b
Phlegmatic emerged from indolence, 372b
Ph'lippines, sold us th', 835b
Phobias, lay thy, to rest, 928a
Phocaeans won, 19a
Phocion and Demosthenes, 57a
delivered an opinion, 59b
Phocion's oratory, 57a
Phoebus 'gins arise, 204a
Phoebus' lodging, 136b
wain, 247a
Phoenix builds her spicy nest,
236b
builds phoenix nest, 263b
knew a, in my youth, 826b
maiden, 212a
'Phone, why did you answer the,
971b
Phonograph with half-a-dozen rec-
ords, 765b
Phony war, this is a, 927a
Phosphor, sweet, bring the day,
231b
Photograph, carry it like a, 958b

Photographer, king of artists
would be, 669a
Photographs, save postage stamps
or, 996b
Photography, colourless, of a
printed record, 737b
portraiture is not, 948a
Phrase, ancient Saxon, 522a
caskets a vile modern, 515a
deal with pompous, 436b
fico for the, 180a
fill their mouths with hollow,
845b
measured, 406b
our names and a, or two, 893a
proverb'd with grandsire, 134b
soft, of peace, 186a
suitable vesture of, 22b
that with the public took, 376b
wings of a, and a flower, 823a
Phraseology, literary, 797b
Phrases, discourse in novel, 683a
goddamned, 894a
I detest, 789b
mint of, in his brain, 132b
of the soul, 915b
polite, and poses, 644a
retailer in, 298a
set of, learn't by rote, 295b
Phyllida my Phyllida, 703b
Phyllis is my only joy, 287b
Physic, best, to preserve health,
121a
professions of law and, 433b
take, pomp, 192a
to the dogs, 199b
wisdom beyond the rules of,
121a
Physical and metaphysical impossibility, 473a
and moral standard of mortals,
616b
and spiritual night, 497a
arguments and opinions, 101a
effect, as well as spiritual, 679b
giants, wage war like, 963b
life, give me fullness of, 739b
mental and, torture, 727b
pain, fear of, 930a
storms in the, world, 374a
three, facts, 661b
timidity, 705a
world, cultivation of the, 538b
Physically impossible, 382a
Physician, and man of letters,
534a
bawls for a, 747a
considers good of patient, 23b
deceive not thy, 233b
every grief to the, 234a
flower of our civilization, 751a
goodness of the, 22a
heal thyself, 1056b
honour a, 1066b
is no, there, 1048a
Luke the beloved, 1063b
observe the, 217b
of cureless ills, 13b
of the Iron Age, 620a
one, is confined, 19a
or lawyer, religion of my, 98a
regular-bred, 381b
rope-dancer, conjuror, 62b
swear by Apollo, 21b
who can do no good, 846b
whole need not a, 1052a
Physicians are grown cosmographers, 217b
best of all, 746b

Pleasure the chief good, 72b
  think with, or pain, 530a
  thy most pointed, 751b
  to be drunk, 332b
  to the Almighty, 1031a
  to the spectators, 494a
  trip up to the pole, 707a
  turn to, 326b
  ugliest trades have moments of, 509b
  walked a mile with, 907a
  well-spring of, 561a
  when, can be had, 341b
  when I play not, 1111a
  where is no, ta'en, 130a
  with pain for leaven, 691b
  without loss, 110a
  work thou for, 762b
  worldly ease or, 329b
  youth and, meet, 453a
  youth of, wasteful, 574b
Pleasure-dome, stately, decree, 420a
Pleasure-house, built my soul a, 546b
Pleasure-lovers, run aground sooner than flat-bottomed, 991b
Pleasures, all the, prove, 123a, 992b
  and palaces, 464b
  are like poppies, 393b
  banish pain, 303a
  being ill one of great, 671b
  calm, hover'd nigh, 328b
  daily cares, and needs, 594b
  doubling his, 396b
  every age has its, 286b
  homely home and simple, 788a
  lordships', 212a
  love and all his, 221a
  of heroic poesy, 243a
  of its, tired, 404b
  of the present day, 329a
  of youth, 34a
  perennial, plants, 490a
  preferable to all, of youth, 301b
  pretty, might one move, 110b
  purchases, of world cheap, 109b
  some new, prove, 216a
  sooth'd his soul to, 280a
  suck'd on country, 215a
  sunless, of weary people, 701b
  sweeter than other, 275b
  too refin'd to please, 314b
  unreproved, free, 245a
  whose, are the cheapest, 589a
  whose charms were broken, 586b
Pledge allegiance to the flag, 762b
  I will, with mine, 219a
  is still the same, 935a
  never signed no, 601a
  of the possible conformity, 806b
  to each other our lives, 373b
  to thee our love and toil, 820b
  you to a new deal, 918b
Pledged, to my, word am true, 948a
Pledges, disastrous, 935a
Pleiades, influences of, 1032a
Pleiads, rainy, wester, 787a
Plenteous, harvest truly is, 1052a
Plentiful as blackberries, 150a
  lack of wit, 173b
Plenty comes and goes, 663a
  ease and, 16b
  God's, 281a
  happy in the, giv'n, 317a
  however, silver dollars, 689a
  of provisions, 1070a

Plenty of the kind, 546b
  peace and, bed and board, 992b
  seven years of great, 1023b
Pley, no childes, 81b
Pliable animal, man is, 617b
  name of the other was, 274a
Pliant instrument of Executive will, 425b
Plight, hungry, 1003a
Pliny, is it, 344b
Plodders, continual, 132a
Plodding wins the race, 11a
Plods his weary way, 348a
Ploffskin Pluffskin Pelican jee, 582a
Plot, blessed, 139a
  daring, in extremity, 276b
  gunpowder treason and, 1000a
  hinges upon the scheme, 744a
  horror the soul of the, 544a
  invented new, 923b
  melodious, of beechen green, 481a
  new, in the cemetery, 873a
  passions spin the, 639a
  persons attempting to find a, 676b
  souls that cringe and, 600a
  survey the, 153a
  women guide the, 381a
Plots and conspiracies of history, 773b
  towns where the, hold more, 787b
Plow and sow and reap and mow, 1000a
  brother will follow the, 729b
  Christ the, 896b
  come friends who, the sea, 682b
  deep while sluggards sleep, 330b
  Farmer Ledlow late at, 705a
  following his, 406b
  for what avail the, 506b
  hand to the, 1056b
  I maun mind the, 447b
  quiet as a, laid by, 734b
  the sea, 46a
  the watery deep, 4a
Plowed with my heifer, 1026b
Plowing his four jugera of land, 50a
Plowman, heavy steps of the, 825a
  plods his weary way, 348a
Plows, keel, air, 117b
  leave our, and workshops, 559a
  the sand, 935a
Plowshare, drives her, o'er creation, 306a
  fashioned the first, 584b
  put not your, too deep, 417a
  stern ruin's, 391a
  too deep into new land, 417a
Plowshares, swords into, 1045a
Pluck a crow together, 129a
  allegiance, 150a
  berries harsh and crude, 248b
  blackberries, 520a
  bright honour, 149b
  down house, 242b
  drowned honour, 149b
  flower safety, 150a
  from memory a rooted sorrow, 199a
  hearts from them, 156a
  it out, 1051a
  out heart of my mystery, 176a
  out his flying feather, 693a
  out the hairpins, 894a
  sworn to weed and, 139a

Pluck takes us into difficulty, 616b
  the eyes of sentiment, 534b
  till time and times are done, 825a
  to fight, 596b
  you out of the crannies, 556a
Pluck'd feathers to wing the dart, 11b
  fruit she, 258a
  his gown, 356a
Plucked, Diogenes, a cock, 72a
  from my lapel, 801b
  gathered not harshly, 258b
  violets, 225a
Plucker down of kings, 126a
Plucking the fruit of memory, 774a
Plucks justice by the nose, 183b
Plum cake, some gave them, 1015a
  Mr. and Mrs. Lettie, 841a
  pulled out a, 1015a
Plumage, brightest, 981a
  decked in, new and fine, 641a
  glossy, dark and sleek, 395b
  pities the, 371a
Plumb the depths of emotion, 757b
  the Oriental mind, 813b
Plumbing, portable, 957a
Plume, air pride, here buckle, 724b
  blast-beruffled, 705b
  eagle who has lent his, 11b
  helmet and the, 547b
  white, 491b
  white, and a green lance, 976a
Plumed helmets gleamed, 628a
  knight, 662a
  troop, farewell the, 189a
  war-bonnet, 979a
Plumes, borrowed, 10a
  eagle's own, 11b
  her feathers, 247b
Plummet, deeper than did, sound, 210a
  sounds with a deeper, 800b
Plummet's, heavy, pace, 249b
Plump Jack, 150b
  why I'm so, 378a
Plumper, berry's cheek is, 647b
Plumpskin Ploshkin Pelican jill, 582a
Plumpy Bacchus with pink eyne, 201a
Plums, life's a pudding full of, 685b
Plunder, leave exempt from, 809a
  public, 442a
  slaughter steal, 63b
  system of, 594a
Plunged beneath material surface, 616b
  into sea of words, 923a
Pluribus, e, unum, 1010a
Plutarch, never such a man as, 58b
  three deaths in, 69b
Pluto, won the ear of, 245b
Plutocracy, government by a, 780a
Plutonian, dim, shore, 711b
  shore, night's, 545a
Pluto's cheek, 246a
Ply, learn to, the pen, 615b
  serve to, the sampler, 248a
Plymouth, pious ones of, 592b
  sand, only rock among the, 496b
Pneumatic bliss, 943b
  tire, wind in a, 754b
Po, wandering, 353b
Pobble who has no toes, 582a
Pocket, carried in my, 288a

Pocket full of rye, 1017a
  hand in its breeches, 478a
  into some wan's, 833b
  little in one's own, 107b
  Lucy Locket lost her, 1019a
  scruple to pick a, 291a
  touches the purse or, 573a
  very sling in my, 370a
  watch in a private, 323a
  wid a, full of tin, 636a
Pocketbook, full, often groans, 920b
Pocketed by most newspaper critics, 472b
Pocket-handkerchief before his streaming eyes, 658b
Pocket-knife, magic tool the, 450a
Pockets, changing contents of, 931b
  compensated out of their, 425b
Poe with his raven, 600b
Poem, discussing poet not, 933a
  explanation of, 961a
  fain would write a, 571b
  for one single good, 379a
  God wrote His loveliest, 888b
  hangs on the berry bush, 704b
  heroic, a biography, 474b
  I recall by its rhythm, 508b
  illuminated reader is the, 865a
  lonely as a tree, 936a
  make his life a heroic, 472b
  marred by superfluous verse, 526a
  music of, along with words, 857a
  not necessarily obscure, 425a
  of earth, 610b
  ought to be a true, 250a
  read a good, 378b
  round and perfect, 650a
  shot a, into the air, 912a
  should not mean but be, 960b
  to which we return, 424a
  United States the greatest, 607a
  works and does some, 476a
Poems are made by fools, 936b, 942a
  he who would write heroic, 472b
  Ibid's prose or, 855a
  in every volume of, 341b
  living, 524a
  more, produced, 880a
  no man reads, 52a
  seldom consist of poetry, 787b
  temporary, 336b
  Whitman's, 973a
Poesy, a drainless shower of light, 477b
  forgetting the great end of, 477b
  have participation of divineness, 118b
  heavenly gift of, 278b
  overwhelm myself in, 477b
  pleasures of heroic, 243a
Poet against poet, 7a
  and saint, 268a
  bad, is super-abundant, 923a
  bad, unconscious and conscious, 943b
  binds together, 406a
  bit by him that comes behind, 296a
  broad famous English, 214a
  buffoon and, 741b
  business of a comic, 297b
  cannot die, 549b
  can survive everything, 767b
  commend so great a, 280b

Poet could not but be gay, 409a
  creates outside of his own personality, 756b
  despised, 515a
  dies mute nature mourns, 413a
  discussing, not poem, 933a
  gathers fruit, 780b
  Goldsmith, naturalist, 337b
  he was a, 884a
  how does the, speak to men, 473a
  joyful let the, be, 592b
  liberty of a, 243a
  lies beneath this sod, 425b
  like the prince of the clouds, 618b
  limbs of the mangled, 40a
  lunatic lover and, 142b
  make a, excellent, 240a
  modest cough of a minor, 765b
  moon talk by a, 676b
  more confident than a bad, 52a
  more than the, expressed, 515a
  must be a chameleon, 791a
  no, and they died, 320b
  not a musician, 827a
  not the way of the great, 897b
  octogenarian, 823a
  of the difficult, 993b
  perhaps no person can be a, 492a
  pleasantest sort of a, 936b
  proof of a, 607a
  secure of a few copyists, 559b
  short-haired, 713a
  should always be hungry, 981b
  should avoid religion, 630a
  shuts the past against the, 516b
  soaring in high reason, 250a
  tadpole, 695a
  the priest the soldier the, 619a
  twirls them in his mind, 704a
  vision arose, 722a
  was ever, so trusted, 341a
  who's old and wise, 936b
  will follow the rainbow, 729b
  with so many felicities, 403a
  with the coward's tongue, 781a
  without love, 473a
  worthy of the name of, 476a
Poeta nascitur non fit, 424b
Poetess, maudlin, 318b
Poetic faith, which constitutes, 424b
  fields encompass me, 298b
  flights, 436b
  genius, good sense body of, 424b
  imagination, higher, 556b
  justice with lifted scale, 321b
  license, freer utterances of, 33a
  meet nurse for, child, 414a
  names, have given them less, 599a
  nook, 448a
  pains, pleasure in, 277b
  pearl, 604a
  wine-scented and, soul, 751b
Poetical, gods made thee, 162a
Poetics, never indulge in, 30b
Poeticule, tenth-rate, 695a
Poetry a criticism of life, 732b
  a medium for writing prose, 767b
  a mere mechanic art, 363a
  an escape from emotion, 943b
  architecture sculpture, 614b
  art, intrigue, 702a
  as well written as prose, 933a

Poetry, attainable in, 545b
  be a poet or enjoy, 492a
  beautiful mode of saying things, 621b
  breath and finer spirit, 406a
  brisker pipes than, 786b
  change in body of, 941a
  Chinese, 799a
  comes fine spun, 42b
  consist of, and nothing else, 787b
  cradled into, by wrong, 239b, 466a
  dawn of music, and art, 502a
  definition of pure, 756b
  definitions of prose and, 424a
  essential, 424a
  essential gaudiness of, 906a
  fettered, 388b
  fleshly school of, 708a
  forged slowly, 869a
  genius for painting, 505a
  gives pleasure, 702a
  good religious, 787b
  great things in, are song, 824a
  I know that is, 649b
  if, comes not naturally, 478a
  in the hearts of all men, 475b
  is comforting piece of fiction, 908b
  is difficult to read, 573b
  is man's rebellion, 900a
  is what Milton saw, 895b
  life's prose, 654a
  like a page of prancing, 647a
  line of, strays into my memory, 788a
  live without, music and art, 653a
  made subsequent, 250a
  melancholy madness of, 1001b
  music resembles, 310b
  never become popular art, 967a
  no lover of, can spare Chaucer, 508a
  nobody ought to read, 515a
  not a purpose but a passion, 544b
  not, but prose run mad, 318b
  not proper antithesis, 423b
  of earth, 477b
  of Lord Byron, 492b
  of speech, 454a
  of the commonplace, 744a
  of words, 546a
  old-fashioned, 236a
  over-poetical for, 567a
  painting and music, 388b
  prophecy and religion, 605a
  record of the best moments, 469a
  refreshment with a bit of, 637b
  Shakespeare wrote better, 798a
  she that with, is won, 239a
  should surprise, 478a
  silent, 62a
  speak as one who fed on, 510a
  speaking painting, 62a
  spontaneous overflow, 406a
  teaches the force of few words, 508a
  that has palpable design, 478a
  their universal pastime, 520b
  thinking in its higher forms is, 784a
  when, has a meaning, 787b
  where the Greeks had, 449b
  whining, 215b
  wit hope virtue, 501a

Poor might-have-beens, 742a
mortals make this earth bitter, 474b
my wife, wretch, 284a
naked wretches, 192a
nasty brutish and short, 229a
no disgrace t' be, 841a
none so, to do him reverence, 168a
nurture, land that gives, 28a
old astronomers, 846a
people putting on style, 737a
phantom of the hungry, 674a
pity upon the, 1040a
player that struts, 199b
prey of the rich on the, 374a
proud homes, 792b
purses proud garments, 130b
reliev'd the, 4b
rich and, are one, 16b
rich gifts wax, 175a
robin, 1018a
rogues talk of court news, 193b
scandals iv th', 834a
shall never cease, 1025b
simple flannels of the, 956b
so, he could not keep dog, 73a
sort of memory, 659a
soul sat sighing, 189b
spirits who neither enjoy much, 778b
splendid wings, 695a
sport not worth the candle, 234b
substitute, outside show is, 10a
succor the, my sisters, 763b
the mind without vanity, 726a
the wants that pinch the, 38b
they bid me gae by, 417a
they, I rich, 101b
though much they have, 101b
though the room be, indeed, 668a
Tom's a-cold, 192a
too, for a bribe, 350a
unsightly noisome things, 503a
was the loan at best, 860a
weak palsy-stricken thing, 480b
when, cried Caesar wept, 168a
when I am, 417a
wherefore the, complain, 427a
who are capable of joy, 823a
whoso mocketh the, 1039b
world what wilt thou do, 263b
wretch with a bottle, treat, 293a
ye who now do bless the, 593a
Poorer, for richer for, 1069a
Poorest he in England, 228b
man in his cottage, 335a
thing superfluous, 191b
Poorhouse, glorious hours in a, 590b
over the hill to the, 731b
Poorly clad, few friends and go, 680b
Pop goes the unerring rifle, 661a
goes the weasel, 1004a
Pope, better to err with, 452a
equal to that of, 309a
of Rome, 520b
Popery, in danger of, 301a
inclines a man to, 120b
Popinjay, buzzard or a, 983a
pester'd with, 149b
Popinjays or soot-smeared mumbo-jumbos, 473a
Poplar, edg'd with, pale, 244b
first tall silver, 888b
Poplar's gentle and tall, **778a**

Poplars showed white of their leaves, 680b
Popp'd in between election and hopes, 179a
Poppies blow between the crosses, 860b
drows'd with the fume of, 482b
of Cathay, 528a
pleasures are like, 393b
Poppy nor mandragora, 188b
or a lily in your hand, 683a
scattereth her, 241b
Pops and sighs out, 939a
Populace, barbarians philistines and, 623a
Roman, 525a
Popular American children's books, 804a
applause, ignominy of, 755a
applause, steered by, 57a
demand, heroes created by, 956a
favour bears her company, 44a
government, form of, 382b
marriage is, 765a
morality, foes of, 617b
not aim to be, 425a
over-great pleasure in being, 559b
prejudice in favour of two, 576b
propaganda has to be, 951a
truth not so, 460a
tunes, taste for, 862a
war will cease to be, 767b
Popularity is a crime, 286a
is glory's small change, 496b
Population able to read, 888a
agricultural, 50b
and wealth, 593b
human, of the world, 894a
hungry and squalid, 633b
Populi, vox, vox, Dei, 74a
Populous and smoky city, 466b
city pent, long in, 258a
rich and, a nation, 698b
Porcelain, precious, of human clay, 279b
Porches of mine ears, 172b
Pore benighted 'eathen, 818a
on thy dissolving score, 716b
ust to be so happy and so, 746a
Pores of the ocean, 466b
Pork, captain's biscuits and pickled, 564b
wheat and, though useful, 743a
Porpentine, fretful, 172b
Porphyry font, gold fin in the, 551a
Porpoise, there's a, close behind us, 656a
Porridge, cold, 209b
spare breath to cool, 60b
Porsena, Lars, of Clusium, 493b
Port after stormie seas, 113a
bent to make some, 620b
came to, last Sunday night, 722b
for men, 342a
is near the bells I hear, 610a
o' heaven, 803b
of men's labors, 118b
pride in their, 354a
Portable climate, coal is a, 505a
plumbing, 957a
Portal, fitful tracing of a, 906a
immortality's, 651b
opens to receive me, 397a
outermost, 692a
we call death, 523a

Portals are alternate night and day, 531b
errors, of discovery, 917a
Portentous clouds, gloomy and, 500a
phrase, 459b
sight, 422b
Porter, all, and skittles, 625a
of my father's lodge, 648a
Sweeney to Mrs., 944a
Portion at close of life, 16a
brief life is here our, 593a
everyone must take an equal, 60a
gift is a, of thyself, 502b
have no, in us, 833a
my, in this life, 250a
of a good man's life, 403b
of that around me, 453b
of the loveliness, 468a
wales a, 390a
Portions and parcels of dreadful past, 547a
of the soul of man, 599b
Portius, thy steady temper, 299a
Porto Bello, off to capture, 663a
Portrait a kind of biography, 651a
lifelike, drew, 339a
loth to sit for his, 858a
man's work a, of himself, 671a
of a person that one knows, 379a
painters of centuries ago, 610b
painting, 669a
painting, two styles of, 576b
Portraiture is not photography, 948a
Ports and happy havens, 138a
of slumber, 154a
thousands of miles apart, 524b
Portugal, bottom like Bay of, 162b
Poses, polite phrases and, 644a
Posies, thousand fragrant, 123a
Position, not certain of our own, 882a
of exclusive predominance, 910b
of unquestioned ascendancy, 594a
Positions, symmetry of their, 12a
Positive endeavors to preserve peace, 920a
moral sense, women have, 696a
nuisance and more trouble, 766b
promises, 956b
Positivist, he was man and a, 637a
Possess a poet's brain, 122b
and use virtue, 27a
belongs to greater power to, 100a
but one idea, 340b
in their bodies a poison, 50a
nothing, although I, 31b
one world, 215a
soul with patience, 279b
them not with fear, 156a
your souls in your patience, 279b
Possess'd, I die but first I have, 455b
love itself, 137b
regain love once, 260b
Possessed by a spirit of revolt, 641b
by death, 943b
by their money, 222a
most precious thing, 344b
no value the moment it is, **290b**

Poverty parent of revolution, 26a
parts good company, 417a
reduced to, 1070b
rising from affluence to, 677b
roundelay in praise of, 760b
shall come to, 1040b
state of ambitious, 62b
steep'd me in, 189b
the step-mother ov genius, 595a
unhappy, has no worse trait, 62b
worst of crimes is, 765b
Powder, food for, 151b
keep one in paint and, 932b
keep your, dry, 434a
leaden with paint and, 288b
Powder'd with stars, 257b
Powder's runnin' low, 803b
Power, Almighty, hurled, 252a
an easy thing O, Divine, 627b
and beauty of the minstrel's lyre, 854b
and command of myself, 88b
and effect of love, 223b
and its minions, 433b
answerable to his rage, 57a
apprehends truth by, 897b
balance of, 303b, 770b
beauty hath strange, 260b
because we had, 980a
behind the eye, 505b
belief in a beneficent, 705a
certainty of, 992a
cohesive, of public plunder, 442a
commitments and, in balance, 952b
common, to keep them in awe, 228b
community of, 770b
corrupts absolutely, 335a
desire of, in excess, 120a
divine shall wash, 425a
don't say in, 838a
drunk with sight of, 816a
earning and yearning, 978a
earthly, doth then show, 146a
effect of, and publicity, 696b
empire is, in trust, 277a
fame is the breath of, 774a
friend in, is friend lost, 696b
from the governed, 425b
genius hath electric, 498b
Germany a world, 951b
God is mightiest in, 27b
God's attribute, 672b
goodness armed with, 963b
has risen in government, 442a
how full of, 526b
hurtful, o'er virginity, 247b
I should like to see guided, 613b
in early days of his, 25a
in men to be silent, 281b
in the air, 757a
in the hands of friends, 697b
in whose, a man is, 603a
includes itself in, 181a
individualize infinite, 617a
infernal, to grow, 847a
international police, 779b
into will, 181a
is a trust, 511a
is apt to corrupt, 335a
is poison, 697b
judicial, distinct from legislative, 368a
knowledge is, 118a
lead life to sovereign, 546b
less confided, 502b

Power, less, to bite, 138b
life and, are scattered, 443a
like a pestilence, 464a
lose the, to will, 583b
love greater than his, 673a
love without, is destroyed, 963b
magic and delicious, 923b
make sure of, and influence, 341a
man's, of action, 282a
men call chance, 248a
mightiest, to soothe, 591b
moments of surplus, 914b
monuments of, 118a
nations possessing great, 900b
naught but misery brings, 484b
never yet was human, 457a
no man's, to live long, 47a
no, over the dead, 290a
no, shall dim or ravel, 962a
not by might nor by, 1049b
not exempted from her, 112a
not heaven upon past has, 278a
o' faith in gert to-morrows, 804a
of abstraction, 435a
of beauty, 281a
of gentleness, 574a
of giving pleasure, 702a
of grace, 432a
of impotence, 974a
of man shall harm Macbeth, 198b
of no calamity, 727a
of one fair face, 86a
of saying things too simple, 629b
of speech to stir men's blood, 168b
of surplus in banks, 442a
of the British Fleet, 862a
of the law, enfeebles the, 26a
of thought to get accepted, 710a
of versification, 309a
of words, 865a
oratory of, 728a
over the clay, 1060a
passing from the earth, 410b
placed in our, 369a
politically fer years, 841a
politics diplomatic name, 958a
politics obstruct paths, 922a
possess, without abusing it, 493b
pride of, 360a
prize for the powerful is, 709b
proof of love and, 612a
pure, politics, 958a
quietness not in one's, 495a
rapture of postponed, 709a
rather in, than use, 182b
reach and, of every man, 282b
relentless, 347b
rich have, 25a
seeds of godlike, 619b
sees what it has, of seeing, 725b
shadow of some unseen, 464b
situation of, and energy, 359a
speak to men with, 473a
stars whose, is never spent, 890b
struggle for, 587b
supreme of, 477b
sweetening and transfiguring, 728b
sword of, 471b
talent is in a man's, 603a
tends to corrupt, 335a, 663b
that fills the world with terror, 522a

Power that made and preserved us a nation, 499a
that waits and wins, 754b
there is no greater, 897b
titles, and pelf, 414a
to acquire that sense, 326a
to chain the fleeting fancy, 792b
to command obedience, 26a
to do me ill, 211b
to drink or rise, 449b
to guess unseen from seen, 718b
to harm without or within, 67a
to know all things, 213b
to live and act, 411b
to maintain their rights, 517b
to make world a desert, 987a
to recognize in your routine, 744a
to spurn, 648a
to suage tumours, 12b
to work remains, 710b
uttermost, 155b
vested in American courts, 515b
visitations of, to his heart, 502a
we give another to torment us, 510b
we here hold the, 540b
weird, in a spoken word, 772b
whence has come thy lasting, 699b
which dazzles mortal eyes, 776b
which has dotted the surface, 444a
who have most, have least liberty, 275a
wicked in great, 1034a
wielded by abnormal energy, 697b
witch hath, to charm, 170a
witty beauty is a, 639b
Powerful agent is the right word, 679b
and enduring an influence, 925a
as truth, 444a
barriers against tyranny, 515a
grace that lies in herbs, 136a
guns will make us, 977b
is the empire of habit, 44a
many, interests, 442a
mickle is the, grace, 136a
minorities, 799b
opiates for the conscience, 965a
potent more, 399a
prize for the, is power, 709b
rhyme, 205b
rich and, 399a
sets of vested interests, 672a
weapon of ignorance, 642b
Powerless to be born, 621b
trifling or, thing, 69b
Power's, in some unknown, employ, 621b
Powers, against, 1062b
as a state, 513a
clearness of intuitive, 559b
crown old Winter's head, 293b
daily exercised, 64b
divine and supreme, 224a
draw all, from them, 376a
frailty of our, 182b
greatest, of the mind, 428b
grief develops, of mind, 856a
heavenly, 521a
hindered by circumstances, 62b
ignorance of its latent, 614a
intellectual rights and, 437a
just, from the consent, 373a
knows you not ye heavenly 378b

Purple riot, 480b
testament of war, 139b
the sails, 200b
twilight, pilots of the, 548b
with love's wound, 141b
Purpled lawn with rosy lustre, 6a
Purple-robed and pauper-clad, 796a
Purple-stained mouth, 481b
Purport, whole, of literature, 978a
Purpos'd overthrow, 206a
Purpose a horse of that colour, 164a
being used for a, 765a
come to grips with half her, 897b
comprehend his, 1065b
constancy to, 512b
difference of, between Almighty, 542a
end in one, 154b
evil of that I, 17a
firm is equal to the deed, 305b
grant us the, 916a
infirm of, 196b
lie with, mos' profitable, 834a
nature's, 722a
not a slave to a, 981a
one increasing, 549a
passion ending doth, lose, 176a
plain and to, 157b
pushes his prudent, 305b
serves no industrial, 776a
shake my fell, 195a
speak it to no, 190b
spend it to no, 58a
time to every, 1042b
to a life beyond life, 250b
to regulate my room, 338a
unconquerable, 429b
what, is this waste, 1054b
Purposes, Almighty has his own, 542a
bend acts to selfish, 399a
life given for higher, 336b
of a society, 559a
of private enterprise, 965b
Purr myself to sleep with thunder, 676a
Purrs and never shows a tooth, 935a
like an epigram, 895a
Purse, agrees not with leanness of, 125a
consumption of, 152b
costly as thy, can buy, 171b
costly thy habit as thy, 112a
hide it in a, 73a
much in another man's, 107b
put money in thy, 186b
silk, out of sow's ear, 235a
silken or leathern, 358b
so little in his, 220a
sorrow's, is free, 634b
steal from the public, 987a
touches the, or pocket, 573a
Purses, light gains make heavy, 116b
shall be proud, 130b
Pursoot like shop-keepin', 835a
Pursuant, in, knowledge, 722a
Pursue as its shade, 311b
commanded other to, him, 58b
free to, truth, 919a
must not, a success, 875b
my reason to an O altitudo, 240a
nor any star, 959a

Pursue, not for nothing that we, life, 276a
provokes me always to, 629b
seem to fly it it will, 218b
the triumph, 318a
the worst, 42b
their own good, 280a
what is evil, 17a
with eagerness, 337a
Pursued it with forks and hope, 659b
small habits well, 376b
the panting deer, 464a
villain still, her, 737a
you the pursuer and she the, 765a
Pursuer, between her and her, 563a
you the, and she the pursued, 765a
Pursues, excel those he, 41a
sense of duty, 444a
Pursuing it from bed to bed, 966b
still achieving still, 521a
Pursuit of happiness, 373a, 921a
of knowledge, 435b
of sweetness and light, 623a
of unattainable perfection, 823a
same charm it had in, 65b
vain, of human glory, 236b
vain, of this and that, 532b
what mad, 482a
whole delight is in the, 321b
Pursy times, 177a
Push at the door, 491b
beyond her mark, 552a
door called, 1006a
of bayonets, 353a
on keep moving, 397a
Pushed, I can be, just so far, 839b
Pushes his prudent purpose, 305b
Puss-gentleman that's all perfume, 363a
Pussy cat, owl and the, 580b
cat where have you been, 1018a
my love, 580b
Pussy's in the well, 1016a
Put a tongue in every wound, 168b
antic disposition on, 173a
aside my beard, 86b
away childish things, 1061a
down the proud, 37b
enemies to flight, 221b
enemy in their mouths, 187b
fear out of your heart, 842a
forbade me to, off my hat, 273b
forward best foot, 148b
in every honest hand a whip, 189b
in her oar, 107b
money in thy purse, 186b
my hat, 338b
not trust in princes, 1038a
off going and seeing, 65b
off thy shoes, 1023b
off till tomorrow, 626b
off until tomorrow, 828b
on sour looks, 20a
on the pot, 1017a
on your fleece, 37b
out the light, 190a
plain tale, you down, 150a
same shoe on every foot, 45b
shoulder to the wheel, 223a
their names to their books, 222b
them to mending, 157b
this man and woman asunder, 296b
up with this, have had to, 32a

Put, up with which I will not, 872b
up your caravan, 854b
whole wit in a jest, 228a
you in this pickle, 103b
your armour on, 334b
your shoulder to the wheel, 11a
Putrid corpse of liberty, 926a
eggs of hope, 400b
Puts away the drill, 957a
it not unto the touch, 262b
on pretty looks, 148a
Putteth down one, 1035b
Putting herself into coverlet, 56b
it down in writing, 332a
love away, 648a
off the proof, 881a
off troublesome disguises, 256a
on breastplate of faith, 1063a
Putty brass an' paint, 819a
Puzzle a convocation of casuists, 105a
cross-word, makers, 928a
their brain, 357a
to the botanist, 668b
Puzzled and in the dark, 886a
Puzzles me more than Greek, 804b
the will, 174b
Pye, shine with, 452a
Pygmalion's images, 185a
Pyramid, bottom of economic, 918b
star-ypointing, 244b
Pyramids, first, 1007b
summit of yonder, 399a
Pyrenees, High, 849a
Pyrrhic dance, 458a
phalanx, 458a
Pyrrhus, should, overcome the Romans, 59a
Pythagoras, opinion with, 146a
said to his scholars, 221b
Pytheas scoffing at Demosthenes, 57a

Q. T., on the strict, 828a
Quack, other produces the, 433b
Quacks with pills political, 831a
Quadrangular, spots, of diamond form, 365a
Quadruped larger than a cat, 471b
Quaffed, jested, and swore, 558a
Quaffing, laughing, unthinking time, 280b
Quaint and curious volume, 544b
and curious war is, 706a
appetite in women reigns, 309b
enamell'd eyes, 249b
great figure, 903a
honour turn to dust, 269a
old Quaker town, 625a
orifice, 947a
spirits, 14a
Quake as an aspes leef, 78b
the earth did, 1055b
Quaker, quaint old, town, 625a
Quaker-maid, blue is the, 845a
Quakers, Justice Bennet called us, 273b
Quakings, achings and the, 535b
Qualifications, adverbs only, I respect, 720a
what are his, 638a
Qualified jury, appear before a, 766b
Qualify men to be ministers, 273a
Qualities as would wear well, 354b
essential to see his good, 473a
five, 797a

Rationed, so precious that it must be, 850b
Rations, have not your own, 821b
live upon our daily, 578b
Ratisbon, we French stormed, 569b
Rats and such small deer, 192a
desert a sinking ship, 50a
instinctively have quit it, 209a
they fought the dogs, 570a
Rattle his bones over the stones, 491b
pleased with a, 317a
stuttering rifles' rapid, 966a
the window-pane, 491b
Rattles, drunken scenes, 429a
Rattlesnake poised to strike, 921a
Rattling good history, 706a
o'er stony street, 453a
of a coach, 218a
of chains, 93rb
trumpet thunder, 587a
Ravage with impunity a rose, 567a
Ravaged plains, 362a
Ravages, irreparable, of time, 287b
Rav'd and grew more fierce, 233b
Rave no more 'gainst time or fate, 688b
old age should burn and, 997a
recite and madden, 318a
Ravel, dim or, 962a
Ravell'd sleave of care, 196b
Ravelled fleeces, 769b
Raven croaking on my left hand, 30a
ghastly grim and ancient, 545a
himself is hoarse, 195a
locks were like the, 392a
never flitting, 545a
Poe with his, 600b
quoth the, nevermore, 545a
ringlets, tied her, 660a
smoothing the, down, 247b
Ravening wolves, 1052a
Ravens brought him bread, 1028b
feed, 160a
pardons the, 62b
three, sat on a tree, 1012b
Raves, the wild wind, 674a
though the tempest, 720b
Raving rotting money-mad, 796a
Ravish'd ears, 280a
eyes, turn my, 298b
with whistling of a name, 267b, 318a
Ravished, younger hearings are, 133a
Raw, ate the fellow, 647a
in fields, 281a
inclement summers, 295b
material of opinion, 770a
nose looks red and, 134a
Rawness of his personal opinions, 787b
Ray, emits a brighter, 353b
every, of God's light, 618a
fancy's meteor, 390b
night admits no, 278a
of good hope, 700a
of hope is blown out, 538a
of sun and all the slope, 624a
on ray split the shroud, 575a
purest, serene, 348b
Rayformer, I don't like a, 836a
thinks he was ilicted, 835b
Rayless majesty, 305b
Raymimber, don't, his name, 834b
Rayn, huge, 78b
Raypublican, or anny other, 836a

Raypublican party broke ye, 834a
simplicity, 835b
Rays, diminished, 255a
young fancy's, 390b
Rayspictable f'r to be an athlete, 834a
Raze out written troubles, 199a
Razor ceases to act, 788a
polished, keen, 322b
Razors, keen intellects like, 446a
to my wounded heart, 129b
Razure of oblivion, 185b
Reach, all things above his, 226b
and power of every man, 282b
chance to, the land, 339a
man's, exceed his grasp, 570b
master-hand alone can, 310b
never, the shore, 729a
out of destruction's, 703a
out their hands amid stars, 831b
so tall to, the pole, 302b
the grapes, 10a
the small, 113b
where lion's skin will not, 55a
Reach'd, never, one gen'rous thought, 314b
Reached, when he has, ground, 339a
Reaches, beyond, of our souls, 172a
beyond their understanding, 266a
Reaching after fact and reason, 478a
out for reasons of interest, 720a
to the fruit, 258a
Reaction after marriage, 814a
against convention, 765b
attack is the, 341a
produces violent, 24a
watching his, to it, 984b
Reactions appearances memories, 720a
I still have, 720a
unpredictable, 821b
Reacts and reciprocates, 718b
Read a book only read by me, 406a
a good poem, 378b
a man's own writing, 596b
a time-table, 875b
and re-read and loved, 606a
and very few to, 405a
anything but a newspaper, 764a
as inclination leads, 339b
as much as other men, 273b
believed everything he, 828b
best company when you, 419a
blockhead ignorantly, 311b
careful that they that will, 1067a
deliberately and reservedly, 590a
fine things but never feel them, 478a
five hours a day, 340a
from sense of duty, 340a
he that runs may, 365b
his books were, 849b
his tombstone when dead, 655a
Homer once, 289b
if I have not, a book, 434b
in it no farther, 75b
in street-cars, 288a
learn to, slow, 273a
let himself be, 733a
manuals for making truce, 640a
many people, a song, 232b
mark learn, 1068b

Read me do not let me die, 962b
men may be, too much, 314a
my Bible more, 708b
my title clear, 303a
needed not books to, nature, 275b
nor write, 435a
not the poem we have, 424a
old authors best to, 119a
over your compositions, 341a
remember what I, 429a
resolved once more to, him, 284b
something sensational to, in the train, 769a
strange matters, 195a
teach the orphan-boy to, 547a
the book again, 569b
the chapters of mankind, 800a
their chronicles, 586b
their stoic backs, 947a
things particularly fine, 855a
to doubt or to scorn, 417a
to write and, comes by nature, 158a
vast population able to, 888a
was all he, of any book, 376b
what blockheads write, 323b
what books I please, 319a
what I, in the papers, 904b
what is twice, 337a
what to, and say, 492a
who, to doubt, 417a
why ladies, what they read, 725b
with joy then shut the book, 629b
without intention to, it, 341a
wits to, 219b
work I have, 435a
worthy to be, more than once, 40b
youngsters, it, 107a
Readable, righteousness, 858b
Reader, approbation of every, 107a
delights the, 287a
do some good to the, 787b
good, makes the good book, 508a
had you such stores, 403a
I married him, 586b
last, reads no more, 534b
look not at his picture, 219a
severe, makes allowances, 300b
who is illuminated, 865a
Readers, few judicious, 40b
friends of a few fortunate, 778b
give their, sleep, 321b
like my books, 117b
of the Boston Evening Transcript, 943b
partial and noisy, 502a
read by five hundred, 696b
Readers' minds may comprehend, 42a
Readeth, he may run that, it, 365b
Readiest, Rome's, champions, 129b
Readily, hold, in your hand, 338b
Readiness in an art, 882b
is all, 179b
to change from old to new laws, 26a
to stray far, 774a
Reading as was never read, 322a
book worth, 605b
books from which lectures taken, 340b

Reading, contemplation more than his, 273b
curst hard, 382b
decent, room and a library, 844b
distinguish what is worth, 888a
easy writing makes hard, 983b
employ themselves by, 290a
enthusiasms about, 910a
great books, 942b
greatest part of the night, 332a
he that I am, has most force, 99a
I prefer, 823a
is to the mind, 299a
King Lear, 373a
left off, 430b
maketh a full man, 121b
men of thought and, 632a
much, is an oppression, 288b
no, easier than a catalogue, 723a
of a book, 590a
peace is poor, 706a
shut out from, good books, 933a
soul of, 345b
tyrannical the habit of, 603b
valueless books, 605b
Reading-matter, sheer casual, 864a
Reads, all books he, 312a
as a task, 340a
but one book, 235a
glows while he, 310b
he, much, 166b
nothing but detective stories, 942a
poems no man, 52a
though running, 102a
Read'st black where I read white, 388b
Ready, Abra was, 294a
fire when, Gridley, 689b
for war, 290a
hands, true faith and, 597b
I wait until I am, 940a
in case of anything turning up, 579a
is heaven to stoop to him, 790b
man, conference maketh a, 121b
minds, becks our, 479a
money is Aladdin's lamp, 459b
money makes the man, 303b
money, sparing use of, 565a
necessity of being, 539b
to believe what is told him, 51a
to die with you, 39a
to ride, 524a
to smite once, 249b
to try fortunes, 153b
wait till that other is, 589b
way to virtue, 240b
when trouble came, 787a
with every nod to tumble, 128a
you'll find us, 578b
Ready-made opinions, 617b
Real and permanent grandeur, 607a
and safe progress, 304a
fight, if life be not a, 715b
friends, women find few, 343a
life is, 521a
life never was begun, 890b
nothing, till it is experienced, 478b
Simon Pure, 297a
spirit is the, and eternal, 616b
thing, 982a
thing, hiss the, 11b
utility in ships, 333b
war never in the books, 611a

Realist rhymester play your part, 556b
Realities are less dangerous, 861b
loves not, and creators, 501b
seeking only to face, 770b
sharpest of the, 719b
Reality, bill drawn on nature's, 474b
brings us joy of discovery, 856a
encounter, of experience, 916b
human kind cannot bear, 944b
idea and the, 944a
more than a small part of, 622a
of creatures, 939b
of distress, 371a
regulate imagination by, 338b
sail into the wind of, 991b
Realization of tomorrow, 922a
Realm, in any coin of any, 845b
moves to that mysterious, 470b
of France, ill unto, 84a
of silence, 596b
riding o'er the azure, 350a
we have never conquered, 931a
Realms, Anna whom three, obey, 312b
constancy lives in, above, 421a
of gold, 477a
whatever, to see, 353b
Reap an act, 1005b
as we have sown, 527a
as you sow ye are like to, 239a
blessings of freedom, 370b
by force, 105a
he that regardeth clouds shall not, 1043b
in joy, 1037b
neither do they, 1051b
our sowing, 666a
plow and sow and, and mow, 1000a
so shall he also, 29a
stranger came to, 930b
that shall he also, 1062b
the whirlwind, 1049a
Reap'd, chin new, 149b
harvest that I, 532a
Reaped the evil fruit, 7a
Reaper whose name is death, 521a
Reapers, gather after the, 1027a
Reaping, grew the more by, 201b
Reaps the bearded grain, 521a
Rear, remains forever in the, 855a
scatters, of darkness, 245a
shall march tomorrow, 638a
the tender thought, 328a
Rear'd the stage, 335b
Rearward of a conquer'd woe, 206a
Reas'ning but to err, 316b
pride our error lies, in, 316a
Reason a bird can sing, 889b
according to soundest, 67b
against it instinct for it, 672a
aim and, 379b
and conscience of men, 95a
and evaluation, 954a
and the will of God prevail, 623a
and welcome, 572a
art has as much, for being, 507b
astride on his, 294b
but from what we know, 316a
conscient, 722a
discourse of, 170b
easiest victory over, 950b
faith in supremacy of, 860a
feast of, 319b
fifty times to one does err, 289a
firm the temperate will, 409a

Reason for its own existence, 698b
for loving as well as working, 596b
godlike, 177b
has moons, 854b
high, of his fancies, 250a
human, needs only to will, 882b
humanity, and justice, 360a
ignis fatuus of the mind, 289a
I'll not listen to, 558a
irritable reaching after, 478a
is left free to combat it, 374b
is life of the law, 110a
is of no use to us, 366b
is our law, 258a
is the card, 317a
kills, itself, 250b
know the, why, 509a
know truth not only by, 272b
knows nothing of, 272b
let us, together, 1045a
lies between spur and bridle, 234b
men have lost their, 168a
never has failed men, 843a
no other but woman's, 131b
no sooner knew the, 163a
noble and most sovereign, 175a
noble in, 173b
nothing reasonable from pure, 866a
of so many senseless scholars, 288b
on compulsion, 150a
or any other, why, 288b
panders will, 177a
past, hunted, 207a
perfection of, 110b
psychological, 718b
pursue my, to an O altitudo, 240a
render a, 1041a
render a, for faith, 418b
rhyme nor, 115a
ruling passion conquers, 315a
sanctity of, 257a
scorn to give other, why, 462b
shapes and regulates, 64a
shared by thinking creatures, 68a
surprise the better, 977b
takes the, prisoner, 194b
theirs not to, why, 553b
to apprehend, 340a
to rule, 279a
under its own control, 68b
why I cannot tell, 293a
with a mule, 758b
with reasonable men, 517a
worse appear better, 253b
yield with a grace to, 879a
Reasonable, everything, may be supported, 63b
kills a, creature, 250b
man, the figure of the, 955a
men, assembly of, 375b
men, reason with, 517a
moderator death, 240b
nothing, from pure reason, 866a
number of fleas, 735a
the figure of the, 955a
women rather be right than, 989b
words, speak a few, 378b
wrong way seems the more, 756b
Reason'd high of providence, 254a
Reasoned errors, more harmful than, 634a

Red, cheeks were so, and so white, 599a
China, 964b
cloth, breast of her gown in, 514a
coat was, 427a
coats of, 863a
coral is far more, 207b
cravat, one in, 648a
ear, 383a
earth may run, 662a
earth the smack and tang, 756a
earth will be stained, 774b
for valor, 563b
give this cheek a little, 314a
glare, rockets', 436a
her lips were, 421b
herring, 92a
herrings, 1015b
Hoss Mountain, 746b
in tooth and claw, 552b
jolly, nose, 232a
life might stream again, 480a
lips were, 261b
listed, as ruin, 995b
making the green one, 196b
men scalped each other, 493a
morn betoken'd wrack, 131a
mournful lips, 824b
never blows so, the rose, 531b
nose, as a pink, 426a
nose looks, and raw, 134a
nose makes me ashamed, 285b
November's leaf, and sear, 414a
pale and hectic, 466a
red rose, my luve is like, 391b
red roses by the wall, 777a
right hand, 253b
rose is a falcon, 729b
rose proud rose, 824a
rose, thick with lily and, 666b
rose whispers of passion, 729b
roses, and violets blew, 113b
Sea and the Mediterranean, 581b
Sea place in your life, 799b
shone with a fiery, 704b
sky is, 1053a
slayer think he slays, 506b
spirits and gray, 214b
star in the corner, 985b
star sheds its ray, 395b
still and awful, 422a
tape, 579b
their, never dies, 703b
thin, 'eroes, 817b
toy soldier is, with rust, 747a
vintage, sea's, 717a
war's, techstone, 601b
wine of Shiraz, 930b
wine when it is, 1040b
with the blood of the dead, 831a
with wrong, 712b
wreath still as green and, 529a
Redbreast, robin, in a cage, 388a
Redcoats and Tories, 358b
Reddened all his breast, 528b
Reddening on the bough, 8b
Reddy to sacrifiss wife's brother, 664b
Rede and drive nyght away, 77b
recks not his own, 171b
you tent it, 393a
Redeem, man may, the past, 757b
the human mind, 522a
thy name, 327a
us from virtue, 692a
Redeemed humanity, 528b

Redeemer, know that my, liveth, 1031a
Redeeming love, triumph in, 383a
Redemption, everlasting, 158b
great, from above, 244a
Red-letter days, 429b
Red-line, thin, streak, 613a
Redmen, revenge these, planned, 759b
Redoubling your efforts, 806b
Redoubt, Troy's, 893b
Redound, drizling drops that often, 34b
Redress balance of the old, 401b
by mob law, 537a
of grievances, 376b
things past, 139a
wont to send, 999b
Reduce human society to one level, 558b
language to seven words, 924b
Reduced fellowman, assist, 74b
proud man, to want, 303a
to poverty, 1070b
Redundant summer, 575a
Reduplication, echo and, 515a
Reece, Captain, 681b
Reed bending to the force of the wind, 10b
bind our destinies to a, 510b
broken, 119a, 1046b
bruised, shall he not break, 1047a
love tunes the shepherd's, 413b
man is a thinking, 272b
man is but a, 272b
upon a, as upon a horse, 60b
Reeds at Runnymede, 821a
islets of, and osiers, 493a
Reef may be safely let out, 12a
of Norman's Woe, 521b
Reek of enlightenment, 913a
Reeking herd, 934a
into Cadiz Bay, 569a
up to heaven, 156b
Reel and rout, 421b
to and fro, 1037a
Reeled, sagged and, 902b
Reeling and writhing, 657a
from riot of religion, 695a
through endless summer days, 646a
Reels them off to every new visitor, 765b
Re-embark upon that unknown sea, 607b
Re-establishment of peace in Europe, 399b
Re-examined, solitary precedent never, 433b
Reference, full, to one consent, 154b
to some want, 402a
to the few intelligent persons, 515a
Refin'd, pleasures too, to please, 314b
Refine her sterling page, 287a
it ne'er so much, 218b
you cannot, it, 613b
Refined and chaste, a taste, 23a
and delicate palates, 990a
essay in Atlantic Monthly, 908b
gild, gold, 148a
point of felicity, 294b
Refinement, each, found at home, 389a
on principles of resistance, 360a
rather than fashion, 557b

Refines, how the style, 311b
Refining of sense of truthfulness, 885b
Reflect back her blushes, 439a
that God is just, 373b
that men acquired this empire, 20a
way to endure adversity, 32b
Reflected from surface of opinion, 23a
image in her eyes, 629a
see, lives of all men, 708b
Reflection, illustration and, 431b
intelligence, and judgment, 34a
remembrance and, how allied, 276b
Reflections, mortifying, 530b
on greatness of British Nation, 301a
Reflective memory stores, 412b
Reflects on want of breeding, 56b
Reflex of Cynthia's brow, 137a
Reform, attempting beneficial, 874a
carried to an excess, 424a
first step to, 698a
movements, lunatic fringe in, 779b
Reformation, age of revolution and, 374b
invention of printing and, 883a
of religion, 97b
Reformer, no fidget and no, 795a
Reformers, makes men martyrs and, 638a
of error, 375a
Reforming, melting and, 810a
other people's habits need, 678a
Reforms his plan, 305b
prayer that, the sinner, 616b
Refrain from eating as well as breathing, 351a
from evil, 27a
from peering, 13b
from setting yourself up as a judge, 25b
Refresh good acts with new, 118b
Refreshed with the blood of patriots, 374a
Refreshment, draught of cool, 483b
fill them full of, 522b
'mid the dust of strife, 663a
of your inner life, 637b
sought, from his thumb, 717a
Refrigerator, accursed bucket-shop of a, 821b
Refuge and my fortress, 1036a
and strength, 1034b
death's, for all, 680a
from confession, 444a
from home life, 764b
God is thy, 1026a
home is safest, 110b
in a secluded class, 932a
in adversity, 71b
last, of a scoundrel, 341a
of all old coquettes, 497b
of weak minds, 323b
Refusal of British peoples, 908a
to consider author's intention, 732b
Refuse a drink after dark, 909b
creeds that, and restrain, 692a
deference and applause, 370a
never, nor resign an office, 332a
thy name, 135a
till conversion of Jews, 268b
to learn its languages, 841b

Refuse, wretched, of your teeming shore, 742b
Refused a favor, 15b
  an interview, 802a
  stone the builders, 1037a
  to drink the potion up, 1014a
Refuses anything to necessity, 45a
Refusing all remedies, 122b
  in, benefits, 282b
Refutable, theory that is, 727a
Refute, no man tell how to, him, 227b
  who can, a sneer, 372b
Regain love once possess'd, 260b
  their respect and esteem, 542b
Regains confidence in himself, 463a
Regal solitude, 430b
  wealth can add nothing, 41a
Regard for truth, 849b
  to human affairs, 49a
  well-assured place in men's, 776a
Regardeth the clouds, 1043b
Regards, give my, to Broadway, 892a
  what is before his feet, 30b
Regeneration, earth smells, 639a
Regent, fair, of the night, 368b
  of love-rhymes, 133a
  sweet, of the sky, 368b
Regent's eyes, dewey were the, 713a
Regiment, led his, from behind, 685b
Region, calm, where no night, 231b
  of thick-ribbed ice, 185a
Regions, dwellers in more favored, 748a
  hitherto unexplored, 537a
  of the universal powers, 655b
Register of crimes and misfortunes, 369a
  of God, 241b
Reg'lar, everything's so awful, 675a
  pollytician, 835b
Reg'ment didn't need to send to find him, 819a
Regret can die, 552b
  cold disappointment and, 415b
  for ill we have done, 265b
  judge of my, 485a
  occasions I didn't embrace, 720a
  old age is a, 512a
  one asked of, 830a
  purchase, at such price, 27b
  remember and, 498b
  that I have but one life, 299b
  who may, what was, 913a
  wild with all, 550b
Regretful, lips but half, 694a
Regrets a discreditable act, 909a
  are the natural property, 577b
  come to resemble hopes, 594a
  past, and future fears, 532a
  series of congratulatory, 513a
  servants of, 949b
  wild, and bloody sweats, 769b
Regretted my speech, 46b
Regular and orderly composition, 336b
  icily, 553b
Regular-bred physician, 381b
Regulate imagination by reality, 338b
  my room, 338a
  our constitutions, 71a
  their pursuits of industry, 374b

Regulates, reason shapes and, 64a
Regulations, ignore the rules and, 828b
Regulus, Modestus said of, 65a
Rehearsal of the past, 454a
Rehearsals, improve sermon by many, 332a
Rehearse, tongues to be shall, 206a
Reign, fiercest agonies have short-est, 471b
  in hell, 252b
  long anxious labours of my, 812a
  o'er the herd would wish to, 415b
  of Antoninus, 369a
  of chaos, 253a
  of mind, 440b
  of the good Cynara, 833a
  of Saturn comes again, 36a
  pomp rule, but earth, 127a
  saints immortal, 303a
  secure their, 266b
  spurn her bounded, 335b
  the sceptred monarch, 6b
  what is pomp rule, 127a
Reigned with your loves, 97b
Reigns, at the risk of, of terror, 614b
  divisible into three, 950a
  king, but does not govern, 101b
  love of praise, more or less, 305a
  no crude surfeit, 247b
  order, in Warsaw, 420a
  quaint appetite in women, 309b
Reilly, Mr., 1005a
Reimpressed by external or-dinances, 337b
Rein, find his mouth a, 693a
  give dalliance too much, 209b
  hardly need the, 979b
  of a wimpling wing, 724a
  riband on my, 910b
Reinforce, we need not, ourselves, 505b
Reinforcement of forty thousand men, 400b
Reins, gae his bridle, a shake, 392a
Reissued fresh and new, 650b
Reiteration, men get opinions by, 520a
Reject, men, their prophets, 618b
  that which they, is wrong, 696a
Rejected of men, 1047b
  otherwise it is, 18b
Rejects, house, him, 318b
Rejoice, desert shall, 1046b
  hills, 1035a
  I hear thee and, 409a
  in thy youth, 1043b
  it's just as easy to, 745a
  learn to grieve and, 14b
  like grasshoppers, 4a
  not over thy enemy, 1066a
  not when thine enemy falleth, 1040b
  that America resisted, 334b
  we in ourselves, 423a
  why, at a birth, 678a
  with me, 1057a
  with trembling, 1032a
Rejoiced Sydney Smith, 651b
Rejoices in the lost lilac, 944b
Rejoiceth as a strong man, 1033a
Rejoicing, come again with, 1037b
  partake in her, 250b
Rejoicings, welcomes presents and, 578a

Rejoinder, report retort, repartee, 704a
Relate and embellish his adven-tures, 370a
  these unlucky deeds, 190a
Related, to whom, by whom begot, 313b
Relates to heaven and earth, 412b
Relating his own exploits, 282a
Relation and grade of society, 753a
  ennobling, 808b
  is mutual, 402a
  subtile, a secret harmony, 759a
  with criticised thing, 719b
Relations, able-bodid, 664b
  bundle of, 501b
  direct and even divine, 866b
  economical, of slavery, 499b
  educational, 758a
  my, troubled at me, 273a
  renewal of broken, 696b
  stop nowhere, 719a
  with a good joke, 866b
Relationship of an author to his works, 772a
  personal, 988a
  social as well as family, 783b
Relative, strong-willed, 514b
  way, set out one day in a, 866a
Relatives, fate makes our, 371a
  vagaries of unattached, 966a
Relativity, grief a matter of, 790b
Relaxation from one kind of labor, 723a
  mirth is, from gravity, 435a
Relaxes, memory as it grows fainter, 856a
Relearning what they once knew, 715b
Release, deadly forfeit, 244a
  ensured, 787b
  from little things, 981b
  peace of the great, 742a
  to the men behind the guns, 831a
Released, energy of atoms, 945b
Relentless power, 347b
  steel daily daggers of, 889b
Reliance against tyranny, 538a
  is in love of liberty, 538a
  open mind and a brave, 860a
Relics, cold and unhonour'd, 438a
  crosses, crucifixes, 239b
  hallow'd, 244b
Relief, for this, much thanks, 169b
  from serious work, 733a
  from the terrible fear, 1009b
  messenger of sure and swift, 746b
  not for the needy, 921b
  not seek for kind, 385b
  of man's estate, 118b
  of the Philippines, 907b
  queer sense of, and shame, 980b
  stand with bold, 436b
  to any laden life, 663a
  work brings its own, 713a
Relies, word no man, on, 288b
Reliev'd the poor, 4b
Relieve, a brother to, 391b
  our misfortunes, 243a
  the wretched his pride, 356a
Relieved, by desperate appliance, 177b
  divers, by exonerating, 223b
Religion a propitiation or con-ciliation, 759a
  and not atheism, 360a
  avoid, as a direct subject, 630a

Remembered, things to be, by, 959b
thy face, 810a
time, is grief forgotten, 691b
too late, 450a
we of this Congress will be, 540a
Zion, 1038a
Remembering happier things, 73b
soul, good friends, 139a
Remembers so many graves, 735b
Remember'st not slightest folly, 160a
Remembrance and reflection how allied, 276b
appear almost as a, 478a
bids, rise, 353b
breede continuall, 83a
burden our, 210a
do in, of me, 1057b
fallen from heaven, 691b
flash of unforeseen, 845b
free and clear, 165b
let his, rest, 1066b
makes, dear, 183a
of joys past, 418b
of my former misfortune, 105b
of prosperity, 1066a
of things past, 205a
rosemary for, 178a
spirits make us preserve, 34b
sweet, of the just, 237a, 290b
tokens of, 505b
writ in, 138b
Rememoring of a cursed past, 948a
Remind man of good turns, 27b
Reminding, keep, yourself of a thing, 956b
Reminds me very slightly of Oxford, 985b
never, us of others, 504a
Reminiscence, dramatic, 611a
Remission of sins, 1055a
Remnant of our Spartan dead, 458a
of their fires, 287a
of thy life, 66b
of uneasy light, 408a
sad, of decay, 584b
Remnants of remnants, 298a
of the good old time, 414b
Remold nearer the heart's desire, 533b
Remorse, access and passage to, 195a
farewell, 255a
for something yesterday, 722b
goes to sleep, 344b
melancholy and, 991b
the water-wagon for me, 829a
Remorseful, gaudy blabbing, day, 125b
mourners give to women's graves, 654b
pardon slowly carried, 183b
resourceful at being, 990a
Remote Bermudas ride, 269a
from cities liv'd a swain, 308a
from common use, 457a
from the happy, 993b
more, the more confused, 726a
past, gaze at, 856a
spot, do in that, 400a
unfriended melancholy slow, 353b
Remoter aspects of the law, 709a
charm, no need for a, 404a
world, gleams of a, 465a

Removable, definite and, causes, 799b
Remove mountains, 1061a
not ancient landmark, 1040b
the joint, 659a
to Dunsinane, 198b
Removed, though earth be, 1034b
Removes greatest ornament of friendship, 33b
three, as bad as fire, 330b
Remuneration the word for three farthings, 133a
Rend th' affrighted skies, 312b
timber which he strove to, 283b
Render back from out thy breast, 458a
deeds of mercy, 146a
honest and perfect man, 224b
life tolerable, 325a
other part wretched, 288b
therefore unto Caesar, 1054a
to all their dues, 1060b
Renderest to every man, 1035a
Renders a service to the state, 295b
its votaries credulous, 345a
life unsupportable, 290a
Rendezvous, not fail that, 948a
with death, 74b, 947b
with destiny, 919b
Rending of the heart called unhappiness, 856b
Renew a right spirit, 1034b
both fruit and flower, 54a
earth-born joy, 721b
old Aeson, 147a
their strength, 1047a
ties with the past, 906b
Renewal of broken relations, 696b
of love, 31b
watch the, of life, 664b
Renewed, forever, 939b
in a year in a day, 705a
Renewing of affection, 31b
Renews strength of love, 31b
Renneth, watir that doun, 77b
Renounce the devil, 1068b
them and try something else, 27b
when necessary, 752b
Renounces a futile hope, 774b
Renown and grace is dead, 197a
brighter in, than thy past, 500a
deathless my, 4b
has been purchased, 446b
highest of, 713a
leading to eminence and, 500b
left increased, behind, 800a
men of, 1022b
set the cause above, 803a
some for, 305a
'tis a marvel of great, 747a
unknown, 648a
worldly, 76b
Renown'd, no less, than war, 251a
Renowned, men of most, virtue, 251a
Rent by conflicting faiths, 287a
envious Casca made, 168a
is sorrow, 231b
man waiting for the, 963a
raise her, 1013b
sail when his canvas is, 47a
tampers with, or lease, 573a
veil was, in twain, 1055b
with civil feuds, 443b
Rents, what are thy, 156a
Reorganized upon the floor, 943b

Repaid, sacrifice was individually, 20b
Repair and perpetuate it, 753a
irreparable ravages, 287b
keep friendship in, 339b
keep it in, the rest of his days, 507b
some to church, 311a
Repaired, social fences have to be, 985a
Repairs his drooping head, 249b
Reparation for our rights, 335a
pay for, 1013b
Repartee, report retort rejoinder, 704a
Repay, disposition to, 109a
fear of having to, in kind, 282b
I will, saith the Lord, 1060a
shut when thou shouldest, 1066a
the wrongs of night, 231b
Repays first instalment on debt, 48a
Repeal of bad or obnoxious laws, 623b
Repeat a complete chapter, 342a
at leisure, 900a
but half of what you hear, 1006b
in vacant afternoon, 358b
Repeated and attributed to others, 396a
as the years scoot by, 992a
the four-and-twenty letters, 60a
Repeateth a matter, 1039b
Repeating it with air of solemnity, 461a
oft, they believe them, 294a
Repeats his words, 148a
history, itself, 55b
story of her birth, 299a
Repent at leisure, 130a
disdains not to, 5a
in vain, 28b
speak what they will, 220b
what's past, 177a
whichever you do you will, 70b
ye, 1050a
you will, by jingo, 488a
Repentance not regret for ill done, 265b
on a Sunday, 911a
sinners to, 1052a
tears of, 386b
to her lover, 355a
winter-garment of, 531a
Repented of three things, 55a
strove and much, 457b
that he arose sober, 264b
that he held his tongue, 46b
Repenting, after no, draws, 251a
Repents, world will not believe man, 554b
Repetition of the Cantilena, 437a
Repine because the laurel is not mine, 798a
Replacing, gently, in oblivion, 648b
Replenish the earth, 1021a
Replete, heart, with thankfulness, 124b
words, with guile, 258a
Replicandum, I gat ad, 87a
Replication of your sounds, 166a
Replied, hoary sage, 338a
my Lord, 233b
Replies, frame his fair, 5b
Reply, churlish, 163a
heavens and earth, 334a
I pause for a, 168a

Sabbath day child that's born on the, 1018b
day, remember the, 1024b
do not love the, 972b
keep, going to church, 647a
rang slowly, 997a
trouts bite best on the, 791b
was made for man, 1055b
Sabbath-breaking, drinking and, 449b
Sabbath-day, abhor and detest the, 677b
Sabidius, I do not love thee, 293a
Sabina has a thousand charms, 1000b
Sabine, crock two-eared of, make, 38a
St. John's and the, 557a
Sable beak and glossy plumage, 395b
cloud, 247a
goddess night, 305a
hearse, 230a
night, son of the, 122a
silver'd, 171a
smoke, 454b
Sables, suit of, 176a
Sabre, keep honor like your, 529b
Sabrina fair, 248a
Sacco's name, 948a
Sachem colors, 980a
Sack, addict themselves to, 153b
each, had seven cats, 1015b
empty, to stand upright, 331a
heaves his ponderous, 332b
if, and sugar be a fault, 150b
intolerable deal of, 150b
purge and leave, 152a
Sacked, Grecians, Troy, 123b
Sacks, each wife had seven, 1015b
Sacrament, annual, of sea and sun, 993a
of confirmation, 325a
spiritual virtue of, 72a
Sacred and inspired divinity, 118b
bard, lacked a, 40a
bronze button, 691a
charm within the letter, 472a
cod, home of the, 793a
custom, ancient, 287b
fires, veils her, 322a
flame, 803b
gate, near the, 563b
hair dissever, 312b
hold every moment, 883b
honor, fortunes and our, 373b
life, Christ's in a, 543a
literature, 973a
names, two most, 268a
pity, 161a
preacher cries, 329a
river Alph, 420b
sane and, death, 609b
source of sympathetic tears, 349b
things, or things profane, 274a
things, preserve as, 675b
time does not become, 688b
trust twice confided, 333b
ultimate and, thing, 866b
water, defile its, 737a
wine of dawn, 803b
Sacredly absurd, 820b
Sacrifice collectively made, 20b
compassion and, 977a
his repose, 359b
intolerable, 770b
love that makes the final, 789a
of the devil's leavings, 321b

Sacrifice, so costly a, 541b
still stands thine ancient, 816a
sweet, 210b
to obey is better than, 1027a
to the graces, 71a
to the Muses, 71a
turn delight into, 232b
unpitied, 359a
value of sentiment is, 837b
who are these coming to the, 482a
Sacrificed their lives and fortunes, 842a
Sacrifices It to your opinion, 359b
of friendship, 851b
of his friends, 954b
upon such, my Cordelia, 193b
woman can never forgive a man for, 875b
Sacrificing health strength and life, 933b
Sacrifiss my wife's brother, 664b
Sacrilege, recklessness and, 914b
Sacrilegious, most, murder, 197a
Sad, a little sunny and a little, 697b
all their songs are, 867b
and bad and mad, 572b
and happy days of yore, 750a
as angels, 346b
awfully, when it goes, 829a
be beautiful and be, 619a
but not bitter, 888a
by fits, 351b
cannot be, and lone, 706a
companion, 203b
enough without your woe, 753b
experience make me, 162b
eyes to make a monk, 1010a
fact to th' clargy, 837a
heart, drops that visit my, 167a
heart of Ruth, 482a
heart tires in a mile-a, 208a
heart, toil on, 587b
hemlocks, 662a
hope but, despair, 126a
hope, death nor sorrow nor, 632b
kissed mouth, 692b
lucidity of soul, 620a
man look, 143a
man's cordial, 598b
mechanic exercise, 551b
mine a, one, 143a
news bad news, 581b
offence to learning, 436b
old earth must borrow, 754a
or singing weather, 693a
remember and be, 649b
remnant of decay, 584b
rhyme of the men who clung, 567a
rose of all my days, 824a
sights, to see, 131b
song in de air, 988b
songs for me, sing no, 649b
soul take comfort, 674a
steps, with how, 115b
stories of death, 139b
stories of my mishaps, 129a
augurs mock own presage, 206b
sullen and, 327b
tale's best for winter, 208a
they say my verse is, 787a
thoughts and sunny weather, 605a
thoughts doth clear, 272a
thoughts to mind, 403b
time, weight of this, 194a

Sad, to see, sights, 131b
Turks becoming somewhat, 713a
uncertain rustling, 545a
ungathered rose, 534b
vicissitudes of things, 352b
votarist in palmer's weed, 247a
words of tongue or pen, 527b
world is, and dreary, 636a
world needs, all this, 754a
Sadder and a wiser man, 422b
than a sigh, 968a
than owl-songs, 459b
they are, even than I am, 664b
Saddest among kings of earth, 846a
I am, when I sing, 664b
jokes, one of Fate's, 11a
of all kings crown'd, 838b
of sights, 853b
sight when it's left alone, 936b
thing that can befall a soul, 650a
this sight to me, 928a
thought, tell of, 467a
when I sing, 485a
Saddle a horse, 105a
boot, to horse, 567b
come, your horses, 417b
no better place than the, 628b
short life in the, 795b
things are in the, 503b
your dreams, 915a
Saddled, ready, and bridled, 271a
Sad-eyed Hindu king, 673a
Sadly amused themselves, 435a
descends the autumn evening, 623a
I roam, 636a
so part we, 127a
why hear'st thou music, 204b
Sadness and longing, 522a
at this parting, 538b
diminishes man's power of action, 282a
diverter of, 235b
eternal note of, 622a
hour of, 712a
leave-takings are wasted, 788b
of her might, 483a
of the countenance, 1042b
of things, 665a
out of our, 810a
shade of, 527b
shady, of a vale, 483a
songs of, and of mirth, 523a
sweet though in, 466a
tale of more prevailing, 432b
this echo of pain, 486a
wraps in humorous, 162b
Saeva indignatio, 297a
Safe and sane Fourth, 830b
and smooth of heart, 968a
and sound your trust is, 307a
be silent and, 729b
bind safe find, 96b
brought, to land, 229b
comes, home, 156b
depository, 375b
distance, easy to be brave from, 9b
for democracy, 770b
from censure of tongues, 74a
from the many, 602a
I am, 1011a
in my sylvan home, 503a
in the hallowed quiets, 602a
into the haven glide, 334a
lodging and a holy rest, 1069b
make your letters, 565b

Sans teeth eyes taste everything, 161b

Santa Claus, many things besides, 873b

Claus, nobody shoots at, 864b

Claus, not believe in, 701a

Sap begins to stir, 795a

dried the, out of my veins, 825b

stirred not at a whisper, 700b

trees of the Lord full of, 1036b

Sapphire-blaze where angels tremble, 349b

Sapphires, garlic and, 944b

glow'd with living, 255b

Sappho, burning, loved and sung, 458a

the tenth, 8b

Sapping a solemn creed, 453b

S.A.R., must be a, 805b

Sarcasm the language of the devil, 473b

Sarcastic tongues, 74a

Sarcastikul, rote, 664b

Sartorial convention, 907a

Sash lowered when night comes, 881a

Sashes, one of his nice new, 873b

tying, fitting baby-shoes, 519b

Sat at good man's feast, 161a

back and smiled, 794a

like a cormorant, 255a

like patience on monument, 164b

on a hill retir'd, 254a

under his vine, 1067a

up in my room, 332a

Satan came also, 1029b

exalted sat, 253b

finds some mischief, 302b

get thee behind me, 1053b

interview with, 784b

limb of, 676a

now is wiser than of yore, 315a

the other towards, 619a

whence comest thou, 1029b

Satanic, dark, mills, 388b

school, 427a, 474a

Satchel and shining morning face, 161a

Sate, such on bard yet never, 23a

upon her dobie, 581b

Sated banqueter, 34b

desire, 812b

Sathan waiteth to bigile, 81a

Satiety of commendations, 203a

Satin gown, ease a heart like a, 966a

Satire be my song, 452a

ever moral ever new, 287a

for pointed, Buckhurst, 289a

is a sort of glass, 294b

like a polished razor keen, 322b

or sense, 319a

points at no defect, 296a

that includes the satirist, 811a

true, is not sneering, 811a

Satire's my weapon, 319b

Satirical Englishmen, 676a

musical miracle, 844b

Satirist, satire that includes the, 811a

Satisfaction, complacency and, 430a

is not lessened, 435a

of knowing we are avenged, 585b

of the intellect, 545a

of the tongue, 6a

secret, of thinking, 300a

Satisfaction, won a, and a triumph, 987b

Satisfactory, most, thing a man can do, 664b

Satisfied, come what will I am, 107a

conceited man is, 858a

greatest fools oft most, 287a

guest, 40b

lust of greedy mind is, 35b

no thought has, my soul, 739b

not, with seeing, 1042a

of your desire, 16a

well paid well, 146b

Satisfies no normal need, 975a

Satisfy his mind, 588a

myself mighty fair, 285b

none of these finally, 611a

poorly, our eyes, 213a

what will, the soul, 610a

Satisfy'd, illustrate them fully, 258b

Satisfying curiosity of young minds, 723b

God, 886b

Saturday, betwixt a, and Monday, 307b

died on, 1018b

does not always fall on, 574a

night, 398b

Review, Times and, 681b

what he did on, 911a

wife not looked for till, 285a

Saturday's child, 1018b

Saturdays, God does not pay, 574a

Saturn quiet as a stone, 483a

reign of, comes again, 36a

Satyr, Hyperion to a, 170b

stoic or a, 761b

Satyrs, men like, grazing, 123a

Sauce, cloyless, 200b

crier of green, 89a

no, like hunger, 107b

Sauced, dressed and, and seasoned, 92a

Saucepan, boiling, 69b

Saucy doubts and fears, 197b

knave, 401b

little bird on Nellie's hat, 850a

looks, deep-searched with, 132a

Saul also among the prophets, 1027a

and Jonathan were lovely, 1027b

hath slain his thousands, 1027b

why persecutest thou me, 1059a

Saunders, Clerk, 1012b

Saunter'd Europe round, 322a

Savage, be, again, 793b

breast, soothe the, 298a

by saint by, and by sage, 321a

contemplates his mother-in-law, 759a

extreme rude cruel, 207a

hordes, ruled, 628a

in man, 589a

indignation can no longer tear, 297a

men and uncouth manners, 359b

no beast more, 57a

noble, ran, 275b

pictures fill their gaps, 53a

place holy and enchanted, 420b

race, unequal laws unto a, 548a

the other of a, nature, 70a

tribes pursue their game, 382b

wilderness, 360b

woman, take some, 549a

Savage, young man who has not wept is a, 807b

Savageness, sing, out of a bear, 189b

Savages in an unknown island, 511b

of New York, 957a

Savage-wild, time and my intents are, 137b

Save, brother whom someone should, 755a

die but once to, our country, 299b

died to, us all, 591b

eternal Father strong to, 634b

God, the king, 307b, 1027a

God, the mark, 149b

God, the people, 441b

him can we, 379b

himself he cannot, 1055b

in forties they won't, us, 975a

in his own country, 1053a

know how to, the Union, 540a

me from the candid friend, 401b

my object is to, the Union, 539b

myriad men will, 775a

nobly, or meanly lose, 540b

nothing good, in the will, 65a

oh save, 620a

one drop would, my soul, 123a

or destroy slavery, 539b

our bacon, 89b

the old that's worth saving, 838a

the squadron, 574a

them by the barrel-load, 790a

to ruin to curse, 488b

when wilt Thou, the people, 441b

your soul, 996b

Saved, day I, his life, 292a

from itself, 783b

from outrage, 423a

just lost when I was, 646b

others, 1055b

penny, is a penny got, 328b

souls must be, 187b

them from the fearful fire, 663b

union of these states, 610a

we are not, 1048a

worth what you, 729b

Saves time, 658a

Saving a guilty person, 324b

a little child, 699a

in the middle, 7b

life by not swallowing pins, 839a

sin and the, 817a

virtue, tact is the, 743a

whiskey is the, of him, 676a

Savior's birth, easing a, 992a

Saviour, hide me O my, 334a

of 'is country, 818a

sold among false Jews, 1012a

Saviour's birth is celebrated, 170a

Savor fleeting delights, 463a

of content, 117b

of the mythical, 883a

salt have lost its, 1050b

seeming and, 208a

Savors of salt, 77a

Saw a new heaven and earth, 1064b

air too much with hand, 175a

and loved, 369b

came, and overcame, 153b

coughing drowns parson's, 134a

deeper into the beauty, 665a

I, and loved, 123a

Saw, I conquered, I came I, 59b
life steadily and whole, 619a
lion's shadow, 146b
my late espoused saint, 251b
myself or learned from others, 19b
tell what it, in a plain way, 605a
the manners in the face, 338a
the more he, 876b
three ships, 1019a
wedding in the church, 285a
with lifted eyes, 803b
Sawdust Caesar, 957b
Saws, wise, 161b
Saxon phrase, ancient, 522a
Saxpence under my thumb, 417a
Say and do everything, 67b
behind your back, 758a
can you see, 436a
defend your right to, it, 326a
disapprove of what you, 326a
do as I, not as I do, 227b
do not, things, 508a
don't, in power, 838a
each sufferer says his, 572a
first what you would be, 65a
having nothing to, 597a
heart have its, 760b
I had a thing to, 148a
in plain terms, 144a
it that should not say it, though I, 214b
it with flowers, 860b
it with music, 860b
Jack Robinson, 578a
laughed and said his, 563b
men will, or think, 262a
more than is necessary, 380b
more to, when I am dead, 39b
not of beauty she is good, 934b
not what you, but how, 650a
nothin' without compelled tu, 601b
nothing against a character, 341b
nothing but what hath been said, 221b
nothing to, 802a
quhat, thai, 112a
right thing to, 764a
thing to, 148a
things that make the greatest stir, 777b
this with presence of mind, 32a
very few, all they mean, 697b
what most I long to, 762a
what other people think, 638a
what others dare to think, 638a
what people, of us is true, 822b
what to, eat and drink, 492a
what you mean, 656b
when he has nothing to, 342b
when you've got a thing to, 739a
Sayin' nothin', 887a
Saying, beautiful mode of, things, 621b
common, among people, 273a
imported by Madame de Staël, 472b
is one thing, 99b
peace peace, 1047b
Plato, to Xenocrates, 71a
Queen Mary's, 568b
so in whining poetry, 215b
thoughtless, of a princess, 345a
veracity not in, 424b
way of, a thing, 908a

Saying, what it is it keeps on, 578b
what they said, 995a
wise for, nothing, 143a
Sayings, kept these, in her heart, 1056b
of philosophers, 238b
Says, a man, what he knows, 344b
a woman, what will please, 344b
neighbour, does thinks, 67a
never, a foolish thing, 289a
no one means all he, 697b
want to know what it, 578h
what he, outside his office, 593b
who is it that, most, 206a
who, it what he says, 700b
yet she, nothing, 135a
Say'st an undisputed thing, 534b
Scab of churches, 213b
Scabbard of the night, 794b
sword within its, sleeps, 891a
sword within the, keep, 280b
Scaffold high or battle's van, 588a
in the brothel or on the, 752b
truth forever on the, 599b
Scaffoldage, stretch'd footing and, 181b
Scalding grave, limp into the, 856b
Scale, geometric, 238a
middle class turns the, 26b
of opinion, 435a
of war and peace, 510b
on every golden, 656a
poetic justice with lifted, 321b
weighing in equal, 170a
Scallop-shell of quiet, 111a
Scalped, red men, each other, 493a
Scamp, wild young, 853a
Scampering as if Devil drove, 89b
Scan, presume not God to, 316b
your brother man, 311b, 391b
Scandal and the cry, 549b
greatest, waits on, 131b
or crit. of others, 931b
retired to their tea and, 297b
the doom of beauty, 42b
waits on greatest state, 131b
Scandalous, merry monarch, and poor, 289a
Scandals iv th' poor, 834a
Scanned the miracle, 964b
Scant, store of crowns be, 220a
this excess, 145b
Scanted men in hair, 129a
Scanter of your maiden presence, 172a
Scantiest materials, heroes from, 956a
Scanty, in longitude tho' sorely, 394a
vale of human life, 424b
'Scape drowning thrice, 144b
the tomb, 39b
Scapegoat, let him go for a, 1025a
'Scapes, hair-breadth, 186a
not calumnious strokes, 171a
Scar, man without one, 54b
mark us with a, 847a
oft a, if two lives join, 569a
Scarce, money not, 507b
seemèd there to be, 422a
Scarcity, owes its value to its, 336b
Scarecrow in garden of cucumbers, 1066b
of the law, 183b

Scarecrows of fools, 633b
Scared out of his seven senses, 90a
Scarf up tender eye of day, 197b
Scarfs garters gold, 317b
Scarlet coat, passion for a, 295b
creeper loves the elm, 634b
feather, flaunt a, 910b
leaf, sorrow and the, 605a
lily flamed, 795b
line was slender, 613a
of the maples, 795a
serge draped over stick, 983a
sins be as, 1045a
sins were, 849b
town where I was born, 1012b
Scars, jests at, 135a
marks and, I carry with me, 274b
Scat, w'en old Miss Rabbit say, 738b
Scatter and unloose it, 131a
her largesse, 973a
in its breeze, 440b
Scatter'd, bones lie, 251b
Scattered drift-wood, 674a
family, servant of the, 666b
life and power are, 443a
light-giving dawn, 8b
seeds, 930b
things are broken and, 855a
thou wert, to the wind, 546b
waters rave, 583b
Scattereth her poppy, 241b
Scattering, maniac, dust, 552a
Scatters rear of darkness thin, 245a
Scene, ask to see the distant, 495b
changes, 954a
each, a different dish, 304a
humanity a changing, 516a
last, of all, 161b
live o'er each, 312b
lofty, be acted o'er, 167b
love gilds the, 381a
memorable, 268b
mighty, of things, 434a
my dismal, 137b
no more than three in one, 42a
previous, or incident, 515a
world's a, of changes, 267a
Scenery and invigorating climate, 859a
too much, and fresh air, 802a
Scenes, admitted behind the, 651a
come no more behind your, 339a
gay gilded, 298b
of my childhood, 450a
Scent, amber, of odorous perfume, 260a
methinks I, morning air, 172b
of her hair, 960b
of pine, 172a
of the roses, 439b
rose's, is bitterness, 789b
survives their close, 789b
weed whose, the fair annoys, 363a
wich pays the best, 601a
Scents evening gale, 390a
sweet unmemoried, 721b
Scepter and the ball, 156a
from tyrants, 330b
shepherd's crook beside the, 510a
shows the force, 146a
stretches forth her leaden, 305b
Sceptred hermit, 462a
isle, 138b

Serene I fold my hands and wait, 688b
  peaceful state, 294b
  purest ray, 348b
  ways of death are, 741b
Serenely arriving, 609b
  full the epicure would say, 39b
Serenity of books, 525a
  of death, 662a
  of Shangri-La, 985b
  pure, of mind, 236a
  querulous, 428a
  steady and perpetual, 301a
Serfs, vassals and, at my side, 483b
Serge, old blue, 890a
  piece of scarlet, 983a
Sergeant at Belleau Woods, 898b
Series of congratulatory regrets, 513a
  of kindnesses, 372a
Serious air, Cervantes', 321b
  and alarming consequences, 366b
  and the smirk, 576b
  importance, no human thing is of, 25b
  in ridiculous matters, 59b
  nothing, in mortality, 197a
  occupation, 402a
  strenuous and, 952b
  takes himself, 904b
  writer and a solemn writer, 982b
Sermon, him who a, flies, 232b
  implies absence of everything agreeable, 418b
  improve delivery of a, 332a
  preach a better, 504b
  read a song not a, 232b
  see a, than hear one, 913b
  turn out a, 391a
Sermons and soda-water, 458a
  in stones, 159b
  no, in stones, 688b
  throw bricks and, 679b
  worth all, in the world, 446a
Serpent, Aaron's, 317a
  be the, under 't, 195a
  beguiled me, 1022a
  biteth like a, 1040b
  crooked, 1046a
  infernal, 252a
  more, than dove, 124a
  of old Nile, 200a
  shall bite him, 1043a
  sting twice, 145b
  strike at a, that hisses, 761a
  tempted me and I did eat, 573a
  trail of the, 441a
  upon a rock, 1041b
  was more subtile, 1021b
  wise as a, 829a
Serpent-detector, Bonaparte sent for a, 50a
Serpent's egg, think him as a, 167a
  tongue, woman with the, 781a
  tooth, sharper than a, 191a
Serpents, poison which acts upon, 50a
  remove two, seen in house, 50a
  strangled, 981a
  they become, 317a
  wise as, 124a, 1052b
Servant, accuse not a, to his master, 1041b
  accustom, to tell a lie, 340a
  borrower is, to lender, 1040b

Servant depart in peace, 1056b
  faithful and good, 87a
  girls in the kitchen, 856b
  good and faithful, 1054b
  in love, 82a
  is thy, a dog, 1029a
  judge public, by one act, 778b
  nor, above his lord, 1052b
  of God, well done, 256b
  of God's holiest charge, 352a
  of the scattered family, 666b
  pass not away from thy, 1023a
  show thy, the light, 1069b
  thy, heareth, 1027a
Servant's title, 526b
Servants, all sorts of, 577b
  and agents of the people, 689a
  as good as themselves, 108b
  fire is the best of, 475b
  made them obedient, 946a
  of light, 655a
  of regrets, 949b
  of sovereign or state, 120a
  of their human interests, 807b
  public, serve you right, 986b
  sons and, 83b
  usefulest of all, 475b
  what his, robbed, 1014a
Serv'd no private end, 315a
Serve a hitch in hell, 762b
  and not to dominate world, 929a
  any excuse will, a tyrant, 9b
  for sweet discourses, 137a
  God and mammon, 1051b
  his time to every trade, 452a
  in heaven, 252b
  my king and master, 211b
  on his knees, 116a
  other people, 642b
  so long as we love we, 752b
  state in choosing men to, 237b
  the future hour, 411b
  the Lord with fear, 1032a
  Thee as Thou deservest, 87b
  these woes shall, 137a
  they also, who only stand, 251b
  they, him best, 251b
  thy country and mankind, 666a
  time to, and to sin, 691b
  to ply the sampler, 248a
  two masters, 1051b
  us or cut us, 603a
  willing faithfully to, 237b
  with their money, 344a
Served God with half the zeal, 211b
  his kind by word and deed, 654b
  public must and will be, 288b
  you are, right, 270b
Serves a certain purpose, 697a
  and seeks for gain, 191a
  as paste and cover, 139b
  his country well, 324b
  it in the office of a wall, 139a
  literature, beyond all, 611a
  me most who serves his country best, 4b
  take current when it, 169a
Serveth not another's will, 213a
Service, ability for good, 361a
  as soon as public, ceases, 344a
  best, for our country, 709b
  beyond all recompense, 243b
  done the state some, 190a
  dyvyne, 79b

Service, essential, to his country, 295b
  greater than the god, 181b
  hard, must be done, 495b
  high and anthems clear, 246b
  is no heritage, 183a
  mutual, 794a
  of my love, 789a
  of our great imperial family, 997b
  of princes, 28b
  of the greatest, 21a
  offers of, so freely made, 576a
  pressed into, 879b
  ranks the same with God, 567b
  school of the Lord's, 73b
  shrink from, of his country, 370a
  small service is true, 412a
  strength of the ship is the, 840b
  strong for, still, 364b
  to others, 972a
  to the state, 295b
  want for, unforeseen, 442b
  weary and old with, 211a
  whose, is perfect freedom, 1068b
  yeoman, 179a
Serviceability, beauty or, 776a
Serviceable according to his folly, 773a
  to God and His people, 237b
Services, give, for nothing, 21b
  goods and, can be paid for, 864a
Servile fetters, 1000b
  imitation and complaisance, 559b
  insurrection, inciters of, 666a
  status and vicarious life, 776a
  to skyey influences, 184b
Serving, betrays instead of, 359b
  to die for her is, Thee, 535a
Serving-men, six honest, 819b
Servitors, nimble and airy, 250a
Servitude and license, 516a
  base laws of, 275b
  consequence of his crime, 380b
  freedom and not, 360a
Sesame, open, to every portal, 743b
  your open, 860b
Sesoun priketh every gentil herte, 80a
Sesquipedalianism is natural to Americans, 795b
Session, perpetual, 927b
Sessions of sweet silent thought, 205a
Sesun, somer, 78a
Set a beggar on horseback, 126a
  a thief to catch a thief, 58a
  among high tides, 148a
  candle in the sun, 223b
  faults, in note-book, 169a
  feet on firm earth, 229b
  foundation, on blood, 148b
  free half-regain'd Eurydice, 245b
  gloss on faint deeds, 203a
  gray life and apathetic end, 548a
  her on even keel, 14a
  his light little foot, 842a
  his seal, 177a
  honour, to leg, 151b
  in a garden wall, 910b

Set in authority, 3a
  it down that one may smile, 173a
  life at a pin's fee, 172a
  maimed and, at naught, 670a
  me as a seal, 1044b
  my life on any chance, 197b
  my life upon a cast, 128b
  my poor heart free, 185b
  of phrases learn't by rote, 295b
  out for Lyonnesse, 704b
  out one day in a relative way, 866a
  right to, where it wants to, 665a
  stars shine when sun is, 118a
  strive to, crooked straight, 667a
  table on a roar, 178b
  the cause above renown, 803a
  the example, 10b
  thine house in order, 1029b, 1046b
  thy person forth to sell, 212b
  wild the fettered hope, 912b
  you at your threshold down, 786a
  your affections, 1063a
Sets all the world in motion, 45b
  it light, 138b
  no hand to best policy, 14a
  soul in tune for himself, 274b
  two, of vested interests, 672a
  Venus, ere Mercury can rise, 309b
Sette world on six and sevene, 78b
Setter up and plucker down, 126a
Setters from Kerry, 858b
Setteth the solitary in families, 1035b
  up another, 1035b
Settin' up in heaven, 893b
Setting, had elsewhere its, 408a
  haste now to my, 211a
  in his western skies, 277a
  moon, hush with the, 554a
  sun and music at close, 138b
  sun, Darby saw the, 447b
  sun dropp'd, 253a
  sun, faces the, 796a
  sun, forsaking the, 56a
  sun, gather round the, 408b
  sun, Homer liken to, 72b
  sun, shut doors against, 203a
  sun, worshipped the, 56a
  suns, 404a
Settle a question rightly, 492a
  though there he, young, 629b
  virtue and riches seldom, 223a
Settled business, 121a
  gravity, 205b
  no question is ever, 754a
Settles, public opinion, everything, 680a
Seven ages, 161a
  and seventy divils, 856b
  apophthegms of, sages, 69b
  black cherubs rise at, 991b
  cities warred for Homer, 227a
  days shall ye eat, 1024a
  dials, lowly air of, 684a
  domes across a desert, 972a
  fat kine, 1023b
  fondly folded, 700b
  gout asthma and, maladies, 419a
  hours to law, 110b
  hundred pounds and possibilities, 180a

Seven hundred wives, 1028b
  is a good handy figure, 883a
  keep a thing, years, 417b
  maids with seven mops, 658a
  men that can render a reason, 1041a
  morning's at, 567a
  pillars, hewn out her, 1038b
  seasons back, 817a
  senses, out of, 90a
  sleepers' den, 215a
  stars and the solar year, 507a
  stars in her hair were, 640b
  states, cut up dadoes in, 935b
  to soothing slumber, 110b
  Tom's food for, long year, 192a
  wealthy towns contend, 227a
  wives, met a man with, 1015b
  women take hold of one man, 1045a
  words, group of, 778b
  years of great plenty, 1023b
Sevens, sixes and, 78b
Seventeen, blush that flies at, 813a
  he was, 911a
  trees from the zoo, 985a
Seventh day thou shalt not do work, 1024b
  Nones the, 96a
  on the, holystone the decks, 585a
Seventies, should have been done in the, 828b
Seventy, delight in men over, 769a
  springs, 785b
  times seven, 1053b
  years, keep up for, 923b
  years young, 537a
Seventy-five, eighteenth of April in, 524a
Sever for years, 451b
  how soon we must, 491b
  if once we, 430b
  my fond heart, 329a
  seek and, 960b
Several faces, put on two, 284a
  ways meet in one town, 154b
Severe critic on his own works, 479a
  eyes, 161b
  from pleasant to, 286b
  he was and stern to view, 356a
  holy as, 185a
  if, in aught, 356b
  sour-complexioned man, 235a
  steer from lively to, 318a
  who is merely just is, 324b
Severed from the heart, 328a
Severing rightly his from thine, 507a
Severity, excess of, 700b
Severn, out to strode, 867b
Sew, teach the orphan-girl to, 547a
  when women love to, 514b
Sewers annoy the air, 258a
Sewing as long as her eyes could see, 543a
  at once with double thread, 489a
  her long white seam, 612b
Sex, climbed from, to soul, 262b
  conceal its, 990a
  either, assume, 252b
  fair, 107b
  fair, is your department, 782a
  female of, 260a

Sex is, necessary, 971b
  no stronger than my, 167a
  occupied with the female, 923a
  omnipresent process of, 782b
  or complexion, 517a
  ornament of her, 577a
  our, is to be sold, 309b
  paragon of her gentle, 499a
  ruin of our, 352a
  started, 854a
  to a soldier kind, 6b
  to the last, 281a
  towers above her, 299b
  whose presence civilizes, 363a
Sexes, French say there are three, 419a
  look alike, 941b
Sexless orgies of morality, 695a
Sex's earliest latest care, 543a
Sextillions of infidels, 608a
Sexton tolled the bell, 487b
Sexually atrophied, 807a
Seyd, thing that is, is seyd, 82b
Shabby corner of God's allotment, 705a
  equipment deteriorating, 945a
  genteel, 1005a
  tigers, 854a
Shackles accidents, 201b
  of a historian, 243a
  of an old love, 555a
  their, fall, 364a
Shadder, heap o' sun an', 913a
Shade, as its, pursue, 311b
  boundless contiguity of, 364a
  by quivering aspen made, 414b
  chequered, 245a
  clutching the inviolable, 621a
  gentlemen of the, 149a
  ghost along the moonlight, 313b
  Glenartney's hazel, 415a
  green thought in a green, 269a
  half in, and half in sun, 440a
  him from the heat, 385a
  how small the, 830a
  kindliest thing God ever made, 873a
  measure by the, it casts, 567a
  no, no shine, 488b
  of a kulibar tree, 809b
  of brown, 959a
  of melancholy boughs, 161a
  of sadness, 527b
  of that which once was great, 407a
  of the old apple tree, 878a
  seats beneath the, 355b
  shade softening into, 328a
  sitting in a pleasant, 220a
  sitting in the, 821a
  sleep in the, 438a
  soft and luminous, 969b
  unperceiv'd, 328a
Shades are drawn with care, 964b
  evening, prevail, 299a
  millions of mixed, 604b
  of the prison-house, 408b
Shadie place, sunshine in the, 113a
Shadow and sun, 830a
  at morning, 944a
  by the, of death, 676a
  cloaked from head to foot, 551b
  day goes by like a, 635b
  days on earth are as a, 1029b
  dust and a, 40a
  falls the, 944a
  fleeth as a, 1030b

Star, to watch the evening, 581b
  troubling of a, 790a
  twinkle twinkle little, 442b
  we call the sun, 550a
  wind each ticking, 893b
  your aim the, 1008b
Starboard hand of every woe, 603b
Star-captains glow, 927a
Starch, soapsuds and the, 972b
Star-chamber matter of it, 180a
Star-cross'd lovers, 134a
Star-crowned heroes, 809a
Star-dials pointed to morn, 545b
Stare and sting forever, 960b
  do I stand and, 574b
  look and, upon me, 1033a
  make the public, 458a
  no time to stand and, 574b
  Quintilian, 251a
  stony British, 553b
  world might hear and, 751a
Stared, I, into the sky, 854b
Starers, stupid, and loud huzzas, 318a
Stark insensibility, 338b
  mad, man is, 99a
Starkest madness, much sense the, 646a
Starlight and dewdrop are waiting, 636b
  lit my lonesomeness, 704b
  lovely-asunder, 724b
  not of the, 556b
  on the sea, 762b
Star-like eyes, 237a
Starr'd face, night's, 479b
Starre, strives to touch the, 92a
Starred and stately nights, 604a
  on a, night Lucifer uprose, 639a
  silence and homeless air, 690a
Starry cope of heaven, 256b
  feet. walked with, 884b
  flag, beneath the, 613a
  floor the wat'ry shore, 386b
  folds, round of, 477a
  Galileo, 454a
  girdle of the year, 432a
  host, led the, 255b
  silence in the, sky, 410b
  skies, cloudless climes and, 456a
  stranger, 263b
  threshold of Jove's court, 246b
  train, 256a
  tree eternity, 708b
  wide and, sky, 751a
Starry-eyed idealists, 861b
  liberal or mystic, 948b
Stars above us govern, 192b
  across the sky in, 946a
  all Danaë to the, 551a
  and space above, 892b
  are in the quiet skies, 510a
  are in the right places, 976a
  are shining bright, 466b
  as many farewells as, 182b
  at heaven's border, 913a
  attired with, 249b
  beauty and the, were one, 854b
  beauty of a thousand, 123b
  blesses his, 299a
  breaking out the eternal, 609b
  broad stripes and bright, 436a
  burn the moons increase, 547b
  cold the, are, 688a
  comets amongst the, 333b

Stars, country far beyond the, 271b
  courses of the, 471b
  cut him out in little, 136b
  doubt the, are fire, 173b
  earth and all the, 607a
  fault is not in our, 166b
  flag is full of, 757a
  fleet of, is anchored, 927a
  fling us a handful of, 933b
  foretell the rising, 37b
  forget-me-nots of angels, 522b
  from them the, rise, 424b
  gave the first delight, 242a
  gaze at the, 30b
  gem the sky, 686a
  given a form so fair, 499a
  go down to rise, 673b
  gold gateways of the, 790a
  half quench'd in mists, 465b
  have influence upon me, 99a
  heaven feeds the, 37a
  heaven its, 486a
  hide diminish'd heads, 255a
  how doth the night bring, 723b
  ideals are like, 644a
  in her hair were seven, 640b
  in spite of nature and their, 238b
  in the purple dusk, 948b
  in their calm, 620b
  in their circling, 781a
  in their courses, 1026b
  innumerable as the, 256b
  invisible by day, 525a
  issued out to see the, 76a
  journey-work of the, 608a
  kings are like, 467a
  kinship with the, 638b
  kiss my hand to the, 724b
  like measles fade, 955b
  like, start from their spheres, 172b
  listen to, and birds, 557b
  little, will shine, 118a
  look for the, 412a
  look out upon the, 499b
  looking up at the, 677a
  love which moves sun and, 77a
  make guilty the, 191a
  man gazing on the, 650b
  men turn and see the, 725b
  million, were strewn, 721b
  moon and, are set, 750a
  moon or, be not darkened, 1043b
  moon the, the planets, 929a
  more in fault than they, 293b
  morning, together, 669b
  move still, 123b
  night and a shoal of, 831b
  night of the large few, 608a
  not pure in his sight, 1031a
  of glory, 476b
  of human race, 363a
  of midnight shall be dear, 405b
  of morning, 256b
  of the sky, 777a
  of the summer night, 522a
  of twilight fair, 409a
  on the sea, 456a
  owl looked up to the, 580b
  patient, 686a
  pavement, 257b
  powder'd with, 257b
  preserve the, from wrong, 409b
  put all, and candles out, 750b
  puts the, to flight, 531a

Stars, reach out their hands amid. 831b
  reckon time by, 810b
  rush out, 421b
  scatter'd into flight the, 531a
  seven, and solar year, 507a
  shining of the, 555b
  shooting, attend thee, 231a
  shot madly, 141b
  sight of the, 772b
  silence and the wakeful, 650a
  silent, go by, 669b
  some of us are looking at the, 768b
  steal to their sovran seats, 721a
  strikes the, 38a
  stripes, and colors, 563b
  sun moon and, brother, 500b
  that round her burn, 299a
  that sweep and turn and fly, 813a
  the brain of heaven, 639a
  threw down their spears, 387b
  till the, are old, 634b
  time and, below, 892b
  to thee appear, 257b
  train of, 742a
  true as the. above, 1003b
  two, keep not their motion. 152a
  untriangulated, 846a
  unutterably bright, 464b
  westward-going, 625b
  which night's blue arch adorn, 366a
  who build beneath the, 306a
  whose power is never spent, 890b
  with how splendid, 927b
  working till the, went out, 792b
  would have disappeared, 784a
  ye little, 255a
Star-scatter'd on the grass, 533b
Star-shine at night, 752a
Star-spangled banner, 436a
Start a hare, 149b
  and tremble under her feet, 554a
  counting F. F. V.s, 980a
  from her slumber, 619b
  from their spheres, 172b
  into her face, 158b
  straining upon, 155a
Started like a guilty thing, 170a
Starting, given it the, push, 837b
  tear, dry the, 681b
Startle, does not, or amaze, 478a
Startled heaven of my soul, 894a
Startles at destruction, 300a
Startling genius, he had a, 777b
  word, 451a
Starts, by, 'twas wild, 351b
  everything by, and nothing long, 277a
  think by fits and, 787a
Starvation, protect them from fear and, 920a
  ruin of woman by, 496b
Starv'd at his master's gate, 388a
  hackney sonneteer, 311b
Starve, catch cold and, 203b
  in ice, 254a
  nor stuff, 296a
  numerous train below, 289a
  though the body, 762b
  thrifty or, 953b
  upon the residue, 955b
  with nothing, 143b

Sterile truth, you can keep your, 740a
  with idleness, 186b
Sterilized, it wasn't, 853b
Sterling page, refine her, 287a
  worth, most of, 549a
Stern and distant shore, 808a
  and rock-bound coast, 470a
  and stubborn pride, 933b
  Caledonia, and wild, 414a
  daughter of the voice of God, 409b
  friend, to genius the, 505a
  joy, rule it with, 928a
  joy which warriors feel, 415b
  partisan, Hugo, 903b
  proconsul of intractable provinces, 993b
  resolve, 39a
  ruin's ploughshare, 391a
  severe and, to view, 356a
  true-born Englishman, 138b
Sterner days, speak rather of, 870b
  soldiers, 781b
  stuff, ambition made of, 168a
Sternest, nature's, painter, 452a
Stern-faced men, 488a
Stern'st good-night, 196a
Sterres, writen in the, 81a
Sterte. oon hole for to, 30a
  out of his sleep to, 80a
Sterves, seely steede, 93a
Stevenson was a roadmender, 753a
Stew is smokin' hot, 859b
  kept in a, 557b
  onions in the, 950a
Steward falls into the soup-tureen, 819b
Stewed prunes, longing for, 184a
Sthreet railrood comp'nies, 835a
Sthrong arm men iv th' Sinit, 835a
Stick, beat with fist instead of a, 238a
  carry a big, 779a
  close to your desks, 682a
  cobbler, to his last, 51a
  fell like a, 371a
  heap of, and stone, 706a
  man whose acquisitions, 715b
  more close than a brother, 819b
  on conversation's burs, 534b
  party, the less, 120b
  serge draped over a, 983a
  tattered coat upon a, 827a
  there I'll, 105a
  this old cove throwed, 612a
  to what you're at, 897a
Sticketh closer than a brother, 1040a
Sticking, aye, in a tree, 416b
Sticking-place, screw your courage to the, 196a
Stickle, perversely, at parts, 429a
Sticks in the heart's deep core, 388a
  nix hicks pix, 864b
  of sealing-wax, 578a
  to my own bones, 607b
  to the pot, 109a
Sticky, gilded and, 935a
Stiel, trewe as, 78b
Stiff in opinions, 277a
  lines of life, 528a
  new wasps, 997b
  'twill civilize thim, 834b
  twin compasses, 216b
  upper lip, keep a, 630b
  wrist grows, and old, 615b
Stiffen sinews, 155a

Stiffened worm, 640a
Stiffening of the vertebrae, 763a
Stiffens and rejoices, 944b
Stiffnecked people, 307a
Stiffness and the soul's arrest, 867a
Stifle, creed would, me, 891a
  opinion we are endeavoring to, 517b
Stifling snow, sleet or, 567a
Stigmatize, wallop and, 912a
Stile, before you come to, 104b
  crooked, 1019a
Still and awful red, 422a
  and lovely face, 863a
  and quiet conscience, 211b
  and serious thought, 405b
  commanded sun to stand, 331b
  days are, and bright, 509b
  evening and twilight gray, 255b
  falls the rain, 941a
  how, we see thee lie, 669b
  nights all white an', 601a
  nodding night, 608a
  not to sit, 820a
  question'd me the story, 186a
  quiet and, air, 250a
  raven, is sitting, 545a
  sad music of humanity, 404a
  small voice, 1029a
  small voice ot gratitude, 350a
  small voice spake unto me, 546b
  sowe eats up draffe, 92b
  spirit so, and quiet, 186a
  stand, you ever moving spheres, 123b
  stars move, 123b
  to be neat to be drest, 218b
  waters, 1033a
  waters, take heed of, 111a
  woman should be, 887a
Still-discordant wavering multitude, 152a
Stille, fol can not be, 78a
Stilled the rising tumult, 808a
Stiller town, townsman of a, 786a
Stillness, air a solemn, holds, 348a
  modest, and humility, 155a
  soft, and night, 147a
  world in solemn, lay, 560b
Still-remembered olden days, 849b
Still-soliciting eye, 190b
Still-vexed Bermoothes, 209a
Stilly, hum, sounds, 155b
  night, 439b
Stimulating, science, to imagination, 959b
Stimulus, we need some imaginative, 702b
Sting, a, a resentment, 770b
  bitter, is a little fault, 76a
  cold doth not, 213a
  O death where is thy, 775a, 1062a
  of a tiny insect, 10a
  of the rowelled steel, 813b
  serpent, twice, 145b
  stare and, forever, 960b
  that bids nor sit nor stand, 572a
  thorns to prick and, her, 172b
  with a little, 935a
Stinger, 'tis a, 214b
Stingeth like an adder, 1040b
Stinging drop, injects a, 801b
Stings, disturb it it, 307a
  endure, crowd and buzz, 267a
  hope that, 780b
  in the very flowers, 35a

Stings, stinks and, 319a
  wanton, and motions, 183b
  what, is justice, 908b
  you for your pains, 307a
Stingy with your blooming hair, 894a
Stink, stand by the fire and, 191a
  that thy name may not, 3a
Stinking fish, poets like, 425b
  mackerel, 150b
Stinks and stings, 319a
  like rotten mackerel, 425b
  stenches and several, 425a
Stipple, rose-moles all in, 724a
Stir a flower, 790a
  best not, the rice, 109a
  do not, fire with sword, 72b
  hell shall, for this, 156b
  make the greatest, 777b
  men's blood, 168b
  of echoes, 960b
  of the great Babel, 364b
  sap begins to, 795a
  see nor breathe nor, 896b
  smoke and, of this dim spot, 246b
  soft potential, 648a
  the fire, 364b
  the mixture well, 536b
  without great argument, 177b
Stirr'd, her face, with her dream, 458b
  like a fountain, 182a
  up with envy and revenge, 252a
Stirred with high hopes of living, 250a
Stirring, die when so much was, 60a
  living embers, 535b
  up some war, 252a
Stirrup, sprang to the, 568a
Stirs, affection, her spirit, 427b
  divinity that, within us, 300a
  of discontented strife, 220b
  this mortal frame, 423a
  to rouse a lion, 149b
Stitch, every, takes up its slack, 977b
  in time saves nine, 46b
  stitch stitch, 489a
Stitches, laugh yourselves into, 165a
Stithy, Vulcan's, 176a
Stock, common, of intellectual enjoyment, 791b
  dove whose echo resounds, 392b
  how his, went on, 427a
  ot harmless pleasure, 337b
  words once my, 280b
Stocking all the day, 353b, 356b
  draws a, up, 943b
Stockings, blue in, 520a
  coming out of her, 714a
  silk, and white bosoms, 339a
  went to bed with his, on, 1019a
  were hung by the chimney, 437a
  with long silk, 909b
  yellow, 165a
Stocks and stones, worship, 251b
Stoic backs, 947a
  bird, 934a
  of the woods, 433a
  or a satyr, 761b
Stoicism, no, and no philosophy, 605a
  Romans call it, 299b
Stoic's pride, 316b
Stoics, after manner of the, 119b
Stole a piece of beef, 1016b

Suck'd on country pleasures, 215a
Sucked the blood, 421b
  up out of sight, 519b
Sucker born every minute, 557b
  hello, 927b
Suckin', a li'l, 804a
Sucking child, forget her, 1047b
  dove, 141a
  the green from the ferns, 960b
Suckle fools and chronicle small
  beer, 187a
Suckled in a creed outworn, 410a
Sucklings, babes and, 1032b
Sucks eggs, 160a
  nurse asleep, 202a
  two souls, 216b
  where the bee, 210a
Sudden, all farewells should be,
  460a
  and quick in quarrel, 161b
  blackness, there in the, 960b
  blaze, burst out into, 249a
  commendations, 202a
  death, 1068b
  discovery, joy of, 908a
  fears, grown from, 456b
  from wine what, friendship,
  308b
  glory, 228b
  God answers sharp and, 519b
  if a thing comes, 127a
  storms are short, 138b
  sunlight on the sea, 929a
  surprised with, heat, 118a
  thought, splendour of a, 572b
  thought strikes me, 270b
  violent and, usurpations, 382b
  visitations daze the world, 494b
  wakin' a sudden weepin', 804a
  way of stealing on us, 887a
Suddin notion stops me, 886b
Sudetenland territorial claim, 950b
Sue, plead lament and, 414a
  pluck out the hairpins, 894a
Suez, east of, 818b
Suffer all alike, 201a
  better one, 277a
  dare not, and cannot exult, 896a
  detraction will not, it, 151b
  enjoy much nor, much, 778b
  fools gladly, 850a, 1062a
  for bad laws, 698a
  hell I, seems a heaven, 255a
  him to sleep, 1042b
  it is for the doer to, 13a
  lot of man to, 5b
  me to come to thee, 334b
  much to, 926a
  no ill and be unknown, 51b
  nobility to degenerate, 17b
  nobler in the mind to, 174b
  reveals truths by causing us to,
  856a
  rivalship of the wisest men,
  301a
  sea-change, 209a
  something, 55b
  the armed men, 980a
  the little children, 1056a
  the sea and the rains, 716a
  them no more, 506a
  them now and they'll o'ergrow,
  125a
  thy foot to be moved, 1037b
  who breathes must, 294a
  wrong no more, 493b
Sufferance, finds a pang in corporal, 184b
  is badge of our tribe, 144a

Suffered, being, rivers cannot
  quench, 127a
  corruption, 214b
  death rather than submit, 295b
  floundered enjoyed and, 720a
  him these hundred years, 264a
  little fire being, 127a
  mentioned as having, 51b
  nature ever, to crawl, 295b
  thou hast loved and, 632b
  under Pontius Pilate, 1068a
Sufferer, best of men was a, 215a
  comfort every, 664b
  says his say, 572a
Sufferin', injye other people's, 836a
Suffering, doing or, 252b
  enough to disarm, 523b
  fear of, injustice, 265a
  full extent of, 856a
  healed of a, 856a
  human race, he took the, 620a
  inconveniences, 107b
  knowledge by, entereth, 518b
  learn in, 239b, 466a
  makes men petty and vindictive,
  875b
  man ought to consume his
  smoke, 475b
  men, him who pitieth, 13a
  mental, undergone in streets,
  671a
  patient, of the minority, 588a
  sorrow misfortune and, 788b
  undergo severe, 51b
  will implant responsibility, 698a
  wisdom comes by, 12b
  years of change and, 592a
  yours has the, been, 526a
Sufferings, grave in human, 916b
  in my daily, 953a
  of right are graven deepest,
  667b
  poets by their, grow, 239b
Suffers by the heat of its defenders, 288a
  eagle, birds to sing, 130a
  happiest who, least, 344b
  his own hell, 37b
  nature of an insurrection, 167a
Suffer'st more of mortal griefs,
  156a
Suffice for those who belong, 609a
  let this, 117b
  to ensure your safety, 27b
Sufficiency, elegant, 328a
  virtue nor, 159a
Sufficient at one time, 238b
  conclusions, art of drawing,
  671b
  end, beauty a, 826b
  he is, 143b
  literary field, 717b
  of herself for happiness, 235b
  room, sea was not, 220a
  to demonstrate a providence,
  64a
  to finish, 153a
  to finish it, 1057a
  unto the day, 1051b
Suffrage, universal, 917b
Suff'rings, to each his, 347b
Suffusion of that light, 423b
Sugar and saltness agree, 357b
  and spice, 1018b
  be fault, 150b
  candy, made of, 871a
  fair discourse hath been as,
  139a
  feed on, and seed, 714b

Sugar in the gourd, 1003b
  mingled with the sand, 803a
  my hair, 657b
  o'er the devil himself, 174a
  without, in your tay, 686b
Sugar-Plum tree, 747a
Suggestion, yield to that, 194b
Suggestive, nutritive or, truth,
  719a
Suicide, die by, 537a
  is confession, 444a
  prevalence of, 784a
  thought of, consolation, 727a
Suicides, notorious drunkards,
  705a
Suin' sthreet railrood comp'nies,
  835a
Suing long to bide, 114a
Suit action to the word, 175b
  camlet cloak and a silk, 284a
  lightly won, 414a
  of ancient black, 903a
  of sables, 176a
  shall I be still in, 233a
  wear a courtly, 591a
Suitable preparation for war, 40b
  rewards, may bring, 37a
Suited, one just, to our mind,
  433a
Suitor, think that you are Ann's,
  765a
Suitors, see, following, 187a
Suits customary, of solemn black,
  170b
  masses long, 958a
  of woe, trappings and the, 170b
  out of, with fortune, 159b
  this, you very nicely, 270b
  wear strange, 162b
Sukey take it off again, 1020a
Sulk, lover, no more, 993b
Sulky sullen dame, 393b
Sullen and sad, 327b
  bell, 205b
  bell, sounds as a, 152a
  gloom, sunny light for, 489b
  heart, knocked on my, 751b
  horn, small but, 351b
  low with, roar, 246a
  new-caught, peoples, 817a
  shields, 937a
  sulky, dame, 393b
  untamed and intractable, 945a
  white surf, 604b
Sullenness against nature, 250b
Sully this ecstasy with disaster,
  32a
Sulphur, Calvin oat-cakes and,
  418b
Sultan after sultan, 531b
Sultan's turret, 531a
Sultans, poets are, 266b
Sultry, climate's, 457b
  horn, 248b
Sum, give our gold in a princely,
  791a
  giving thy, of more, 159b
  life is not doing a, 709b
  make up my, 179a
  of a lasting lore, 966b
  of all villanies, 329b
  of earthly bliss, 257b
  of good government, 374b
  of human happiness, 780b
  of human things, 376b
  of Shakespeare's wit, 506a
  trifles make the, of life, 579b
  two married people owe, 379a
  up at night, 233a

Surrender to luxurious revery, 809b
  unconditional and immediate, 623b
  we shall never, 869a
Surrendered every consonant they had, 713a
Surrenders, guard dies but never, 402b
Surreptitious peeps, 792b
Surrinder to such a flirt, 837b
Surrounding families, 428a
Surroundings, free from our, 882a
Surrounds, ever-during dark, me, 254b
Survey mankind, 335b
  monarch of all I, 363b
  plot, 153a
Survival of the fittest, 530a, 615a
  praise not an assurance of, 844a
  through, of their children, 702b
  without victory no, 869a
Survive in some typical American breast, 718a
  in wistful stone, 703b
  monuments of wit, 118a
  only the fit, 877a
  or perish, 443a
  their own reputation, 99a
  this nation will, 843a
Survived, not one, 3a
  pride of those who, 871b
Survives, glory, 20b
Survivor's affair, man's dying is the, 883a
Susan, Lady, 705a
Susanna don't you cry for me, 636a
Susceptible chancellor, 683b
Suspect everybody, 577a
  lest men, your tale, 308a
  thoughts of others, 144a
Suspected, new opinions are always, 283a
  to have committed errors, 109a
  wished wife to be not, 56b
Suspecting, ruminating without, it, 856a
Suspects, man, himself a fool, 305b
  yet soundly loves, 188a
Suspend your imagination, 983b
Suspenders, before invention of, 418a
  inclination of, to twist, 707b
  snap his, 886b
Suspense in news is torture, 260b
Suspension of disbelief, 424b
Suspicion, assuaged by, of bad end, 857b
  avarice, and asperity, 372b
  Caesar's wife above, 56b
  companion of mean souls, 370a
  full of eyes, 151b
  haunts guilty mind, 127a
  jealousy feeds upon, 265a
  object almost of, 701b
  pass from, to certainty, 265a
  spread a spirit of general, 860a
Suspicions, fresh, 188b
Suspicious friend, tim'rous foe and, 319a
  many religious people are, 813b
  of one another, 20a
  of some buried bone, 719b
Susquehanna's utmost springs, 382b
Sussex songs be sung, 848b

Sustain, prop that doth, my house, 146b
Sustained and soothed, 470b
Sustaining our sense of what is beautiful, 775b
Sustenance exacted through taxation, 689a
Svamp, valked by a dismal, 612a
Swabs, doctors is all, 750a
Swaddling clothes, 1056a
Swag, hungry clouds, on the deep, 385b
Swaggering underemphasis of New England, 942a
Swagman, jolly, 809b
Swain, frugal, 352b
  remote from cities liv'd a, 308a
Swains commend her, 132a
  ruined, 362a
Swaller our principles, 600b
Swallow a camel, 1054a
  all, prodigious ruin, 4a
  blow and, at same moment, 30b
  come before the, dares, 208a
  gudgeons, 11b
  more beliefs, 784a
  one, does not make a spring, 26b
  revenge, them up, 189a
  swallow flying south, 550b
  tough morsels to, 727b
  up death in victory, 1046a
Swallow'd bait, 207a
  sailors, in the flood, 127a
  up and lost, 253b
Swallowed a lighted kerosene lamp, 886b
  a ramrod, 64a
  easier, than a flap-dragon, 133b
  others to be, 121b
  up in death, 21a
  up in London, 792b
  up in victory, 1062a
Swallow-flights of song, 552a
Swallowing, saving life by not, pins, 839a
  wave, 268b
Swallow's wings, flies with, 128b
Swallows up the rest, 317a
Swam in a gondola, 162b
  priests, before my sight, 313b
Swamp, Lake of the Dismal, 437b
Swamp-elm club, strait-jacket or a, 760b
Swan, after many a summer dies the, 554a
  every goose a, 598b
  like a black, 63a
  of Avon, 219b
  on still St. Mary's lake, 488b
  pale faint, 148b
  shook slowly free, 969b
  swims on a lake, 488b
  think thy, a crow, 134b
  were I a, 64a
Swanee River, way down upon the, 636a
Swank, do not like his, 868a
Swanlike end fading in music, 21a, 145a
  let me sing and die, 458b
Swans are geese, 222b
  as much spirit of prophecy as, 21a
  geese are, 622b
  seem whiter, 102a
  ships sail like, asleep, 927a
  thinks his own geese, 222b

Swap horses while crossing the river, 541b
Swarm and troop and muster, 963a
  into the streets, 86a
  not good for the, 68a
  of bees and honey, 1026b
  of bees in May, 1000a
Swarms of minnows, 477a
  rude militia, 281a
Swart convict Bunyan, 604a
  crowes, 102a
  faery of the mine, 247b
Swarthy, ragged and weary and, 793b
Swashing and a martial outside, 159b
Swat, Ahkoond of, 581b
  Akond of, 581b
  what's the news from, 581b
Swath and all its twined flowers, 483a
Sway against a wall, 717b
  autocratic, of the west wind, 773a
  govern passions with absolute, 275a
  impious men bear, 299b
  in the wind, 943a
  little rule a little, 327b
  love of pleasure and love of, 314b
  mild parental, 628a
  mortall things doth, 114a
  prevail'd with double, 356a
  requir'd with gentle, 255b
  sceptred, 146a
  sweeping whirlwind's, 350a
Swayed by fear, 27a
Sways by submitting, 315a
  level in her husband's heart, 164b
  salt weed, in the stream, 619b
Swear, by yonder moon I, 135b
  do not, at all, 135b
  eat and eat I, 156b
  enough to make a deacon, 601a
  eternal friendship, 270b
  fear nothing to, 35b
  lovers, more performance, 181b
  no where lives a woman, 215b
  not at all, 1051a
  not by the moon, 135b
  rant and, 223b
  that beauty lives, 927a
  to the truth of a song, 293b
  when very angry, 678a
Sweareth to his own hurt, 1032b
Swearin', a little judicyous, 836a
Swears, auld nature, 391b
  he did her wrong, 131b
  she is made of truth, 207b
  with so much grace, 291a
Sweat and whine, 608a
  blood, and tear-wrung millions, 869a
  blood toil tears and, 869a
  brow is wet with honest, 521b
  but for promotion, 160a
  extraordinarily, 152b
  muck of, 354b
  of his brow, 589b
  of man's brow, 7b
  of man's brows, 346a
  of my brows, 103b
  of other men's faces, 542a
  of thy face, 1022a
  teares or, or blood, 869a
  under a weary life, 174b

Things, new, succeed, 231a
not always what they seem, 48b
not made for sake of words, 70a
not on, on the earth, 1063a
not seen are eternal, 1062a
not to do desperate, 589b
now are as they were, 68b
of little or no use, 54a
old unhappy far-off, 407b
ordinary commonplace, 428b
outward draw inward quality, 201a
part of the, that please, 341b
past or things to come, 274a
past redress, 139a
poor foolish, that live a day, 824a
possessing all, 213a, 422b
present nor things to come, 1060a
present worst, 153a
pretty state of, 684b
profane, things sacred or, 274a
proposed as things forgot, 311b
quick bright, 141a
rank and gross in nature, 170b
release from little, 981b
remembrance of, past, 205a
sacred or things profane, 274a
secret, belong unto God, 1026a
seen are temporal, 1062a
shadows of the, to be, 630b
shape of, to come, 832a
small, make base men, 125b
smell and taste of, 855a
so full of a number of, 750b
so many fine, to do, 891a
some, are of that nature, 274b
soul of goodness in, evil, 614b
soul of truth in, erroneous, 614b
standing thus unknown, 179b
strange, come out, 394b
such, to be, 552b
sum of human, 376b
surfeit of sweetest, 142a
sweet to taste, 138a
talk of, heavenly, 274a
thank Thee for the, I miss, 627b
that almost happen, 513b
that are more excellent, 781a
that didn't occur, 777b
that feed the mind, 720a
that go bump in the night, 1003a
that haven't been done before, 913b
that he thinketh, 1065b
that help with things that hurt, 719b
that mar or bless, 780b
that ne'er were, 261a
that stand, 888b
that trouble us now, 661b
that wouldn't divide, 731b
these, shall be, 707b
think on these, 1063a
thinking how, may be, 338b
those are the, to try, 913b
those who want the fewest, 70b
thoughts and, look older, 499b
three, for salvation of man, 75a
three, in a building, 379a
three silent, 892b
time for all, 108b
time for some, 108b
to be remembered by, 959b
to come, giant mass of, 181b
to come, things past or, 274a

Things, to talk of many, 658b
to their destruction draw, 216a
trophies and dead, 226a
two, at once, 43a
two, excite us to love, 105b
two noblest, sweetness and light, 294b
two, people desire, 63a
two, stand like stone, 661b
unattempted yet, 252a
uncomely and broken, 825a
under ground, 104b
unknown proposed, 311b
very much as always, 858b
vicissitudes in all, 31b
violently destroyed, 406a
voiceless, 911b
we have seen and have known, 721b
we live through all, 654b
we never do for our own sake, 33b
we see are shadows, 630b
wee unimportant, 987a
well said songs well sung, 930a
what mean the, unseen, 733b
what were the most necessary, 70b
whatsoever, are true, 1063a
which are Caesar's, 1054a
which elemented it, 216b
which I have seen, 408a
which they put in practice, 70b
who knows all, 722a
why and wherefore in all, 156b
why, are as they are, 722a
with more spirit chased, 144b
without all remedy, 197b
words are, 458b
worst, 974b
worth their observation, 301a
write well in laudable, 250a
ye lef' behind, 913b
Thing-um-a-jig, 659b
Think above that which is written, 1060b
always talk who never, 219b
and ne'er disclose her mind, 187a
another, talk one thing and, 44a
as though we stayed home, 901a
because I, him so, 131b
before thou speakest, 106a
beyond our circle of ideas, 740a
by fits and starts, 787a
clear feel deep, 620b
difficult to, nobly, 345a
do not try to, consciously, 822a
feel do as one pleases, 434a
fellows whom it hurts to, 786b
for yourselves, 326b
free to, and act, 669b
free to, speak and write, 376a
freedom to, 600b
great thoughts, 709a
greatly, or bravely die, 313b
he still has found, 341b
him as a serpent's egg, 167a
how much we, of ourselves, 680a
I, therefore I am, 237a
if one, it important, 715b
in the morning, 386a
in this batter'd caravanserai, 531b
is to be full of sorrow, 481b
it worth enjoying, 280a
know much and, for nothing, 220b
last opinion right, 311b

Think, later than you, 877b
men, all men mortal, 305b
men will say or, 262a
must not, of thee, 736b
no more, 786a
none, the great unhappy, 302a
not God at all, 260a
of your forefathers, 398b
of yourself as he, 844b
on these things, 1063a
only this of me, 938b
pleasant too to, on, 261b
quietly talk gently, 557b
say what other people, 638b
so then, 582a
sooner or later begins to, 846b
talk and never, 219b
talk for one who can, 605a
that day lost, 305b
their little set mankind, 376b
there is a God, 595b
they're thinking, 895b
those who, must govern, 354a
thousands perhaps millions, 458b
thy swan a crow, 134b
thy thought, 568a
too little, 277a
too little and talk too much, 219b
town that made feeling, 957a
upon dangers of the seas, 214a
we have enow, 220b
we have thoughts in our head, 817a
well of him, 763a
well of oneself, 944a
what is true, 633b
what others, of us, 530a
what thought can, 117b
what we, fits us for future, 586a
when I, I must speak, 162a
while we stop to, 43b
who dares, one thing, 4b
with the thoughts of the few, 699a
young, old men fools, 116b
Thinker, deep, or great ventriloquist, 822b
new, 811b
secret isolated joy of the, 709a
Thinkers, best stomachs not best, 325b
greatest, often amateurs, 784a
Thinketh, as he, in his heart, 1040b
he standeth, 1061a
perceive things that he, 1065b
Thinking, a mere pause from, 460b
curtsey while you're, 658a
effort of, 698a
fantastic summer's heat, 138b
future, must be world-wide, 964a
God does that, 604b
high, outcome of fine living, 784a
how things may be, 338b
I have not lived in vain, 300a
in another sense, 697a
in its lower grades, 784a
is but an idle waste, 436b
is coolness and calmness, 604b
is very rare, 956b
lays lads underground, 786a
made, feel, 957a
madness caused by, 774a
make people think they're, 895b
makes it so, 173b

Thinking, man, and working, 590a
man's, too highly of himself, 282a
much drinking little, 295a
none harmed through, 95b
on frosty Caucasus, 138b
plain living and high, 407a
prattle to be tedious, 140b
reed, man is but a, 272b
shifts we make to escape, 603b
things, impels all, 404a
thinks I this comes of not, 677a
too much of himself, 697b
too much, to have common thought, 314b
too precisely on th' event, 177b
weary of, 673a
what is, for, 993b
worlds of fine, 449b
Thinkings speak to me as to thy, 188a
Thinks a faultless piece to see, 261a, 310b
better of a gilded fool, 214b
he, too much, 166b
hearer, he can do as well, 20a
heart, tongue speaks, 158a
himself wise, 326a
in a marrow-bone, 827b
it luxury, 299a
know she, o' me, 818a
like a philosopher, 345a
most feels the noblest, 586a
never never, of me, 1004b
of war in time of peace, 223b
to get a living, 345a
too little or too much, 317a
what a man, of himself, 589b
what matters what anybody, 504b
what ne'er was nor is, 310b
who, must mourn, 294a
world turns round, 130b
Thinned, not one that would be, 984a
Thinner, gets, cracks wrinkles, 958b
Thinness, airy, 216b
Thinning of our ranks each year, 706a
Thins his jury, 279a
Thin-spun life, 249a
Third day he rose, 1068a
dog, one dog meets, 332b
draught drowns him, 163b
glass, drink not the, 232b
glass for good humour, 300b
in your bosom, 136a
is freedom from want, 920b
join'd former two to make a, 279b
most tolerable, party, 589a
of life is passed in sleep, 459b
of thought, 525b
place, no disgrace to stop at, 33a
shadowy, 569a
Third-class carriages, 766a
Third-rate, others are, 596b
Third's away two may keep counsel, 93b
Thirst after happiness, 345a
after righteousness, 1050b
bereavement pain, 654b
bread to one dying of, 761a
every, to the pot, 234a
fame is the, of youth, 453b
fell down for, 3a
for greatness, 942b

Thirst for more and more, 39b
if he, give him drink, 1060a
is a dangerous thing, 788a
man can raise a, 818b
of praise, 363a
of riches, 345b
that from the soul doth rise, 219a
wonderful as, 962a
would blister easier now, 648b
Thirsteth, drinking, still, 649b
ho everyone that, 1047b
soul, for thee, 1035a
Thirsting flowers, 466b
Thirsty and ye gave me drink, 1054b
busy curious, fly, 326b
drink for the, 109b
drinks when he is not, 1007a
dry and, land, 1035a
earth soaks up the rain, 267a
if he be, give him water, 1041a
soul, cold waters to a, 1041a
think what they say in Japan, 712a
Thirteen, maids of, 147b
Thirteenth month, 777b
Thirty cents, feel like, 829a
character set by age of, 715a
dayes, shapeless birth in, 50a
days hath September, 95b, 96a
for, pence my death devise, 233a
live enough before, 834b
live fully from, to sixty, 949b
man suspects himself a fool at, 305b
millyon newspapers a day, 835a
pence, for, 1012a
pieces of silver, 1054b
strong at, 234a
twenty-nine or, at the most, 768b
wrong side of, 296b
yards of board fence, 675a
years the life of most great treaties, 812a
years with that tongue, 810a
Thirtyfold, some, 1052b
Thirty-four, Lord Tomnoddy is, 638a
years old, 285b
Thirty-one, all the rest have, 96a
Thirty-second day, 777b
This above all, 171b
after, therefore because of this, 1010b
and a great deal more, 32a
is my own my native land, 413b
is old age, 258b
is the month, 244a
is the place, 496a
little pig went to market, 1016a
no tomorrow hath, 216a
pursuit of, and that, 532b
thing I was born to do, 122a
too shall pass away, 538b
too will pass away, 514b
was a man, 169b
will never do, 410b
Thisbe o'ertrip dew, 146b
Thistles, figs from, 780b
figs out of, 555a
Thomas, true, 1012b
Thombe of gold, 80a
Thongs, limp velum fitted with, 776a
Thoreau's talent, 718a

Thorn, bore away one bleeding, 528b
in the flesh, 1062a
kissed beside the, 721b
milk-white, 390a
no harvest but a, 233a
oak and ash and, 820b, 1012a
one, upon the ground, 528b
primrose peeps beneath the, 357a
rose without a, 383a
snail's on the, 567a
virgin, 140b
withering on the virgin, 410a
without, the rose, 255a
Thorn-curst world, 757a
Thornless growth, 649b
Thorns and briars become visible, 446b
and dangers of world, 148b
burrs and, of life, 477b
crackling of, 1042b
crown of, 476a, 793a
crowns of, endure, 667b
first to be touch'd by, 438a
grapes from, 780b
he that plants, 29a
in your sides, 1026b
no, go as deep as a rose's, 692a
pricked by, 28b
rose with all its, 649b
rosebud set with willful, 550a
roses have, 205a
that in her bosom lodge, 172b
through which we walk to death, 897a
which I have reap'd, 453b
Thorny green bed, 450a
hedge-hogs, 142a
life is, 421a
way to heaven, 171b
Thorough knowledge of human nature, 428b
Thoroughbreds the fleetest in Kentucky, 726a
Thoroughfare, fabled, 933b
Thoroughgoing silence intrigues, 850a
Thou and I are parted, 885a
art the man, 1028a
beside me singing, 531b
knowest Lord, 722b
not, 'tis we are deaf, 663b
wert not thine own reward, 798a
Thought above all and beyond all, 513b
absorbed in, 497b
act from, should follow, 993b
adds to the, much strength, 306b
and fancy faint, 615b
armour is his honest, 213a
as a child, 1061a
as a sage, 368a
beneath so slight a film, 646b
bound of human, 548a
brightest flashes in world of, 614a
can shatter us, 728b
chaos of, and passion, 317a
comforting, in time of trouble, 895a
confusion of, 518a
depends on the stomach, 325b
destroy their paradise, 347b
dinosaurs of, 874a
disruption of, 461b
do what he, he could not, 342a

Tree of diabolical knowledge, 380b
  of knowledge, 1021b
  of liberty must be refreshed, 374a
  of liberty only grows, 384a
  of life, 1021b, 1022a
  of life the middle tree, 255a
  only God can make a, 936b
  part of a living, 968a
  peach from the, 386a
  planted by rivers of water, 1032a
  planted by the waters, 1048a
  poem lovely as a, 936a
  rise to the top of the, 682a
  shadow of a, 717b
  shady cypress, 649b
  shake the, of life itself, 846a
  she gave me of the, 1022a
  singing in the amfalula, 747b
  slow deep, 968b
  spare that, 498b
  starry, eternity, 708b
  still our, is there, 622b
  thou the, and I the flower, 683b
  too happy happy, 478a
  'twas on a, they slew Him, 717a
  under the greenwood, 491a
  vine and fig, 1067a
  where is a common, 936a
  which did not know the love, 267b
  will be monument enough, 886b
Tree's inclined, as twig is bent, 314a
Trees, all the, are brown, 599a
  all the, are green, 598b
  among the gusty, 909b
  and fields tell me nothing, 316b
  and flowers and watercraft, 611b
  and men and grass, 605a
  and mountain-tops, 210b
  and plants, ties us to, 98b
  Arabian, 190b
  are brown, 988a
  beneath the, 409a
  green gits back in the, 745b
  grow and hills tower, 939b
  he plants, to benefit, 31a
  high in tufted, 245a
  in their blooming, 781a
  like leaves on, 4b
  loftiest, fall and perish, 19a
  lopped and cut grow again, 54a
  loveliest of, the cherry, 785a
  maddens me, 942a
  men as, walking, 1056a
  more, and larger blown down, 603a
  most shy and ladylike of, 600a
  my books, 161b
  New England, 979a
  ot the Lord full of sap, 1036b
  old, hats coats and things, 953a
  old, used to people, 979b
  on either hand, 750b
  quiet, 890b
  rest under shade of the, 979b
  root of the, 1056b
  seemed more resigned, 885b
  seventeen, from the zoo, 985a
  she can be silent as the, 841a
  tall ancestral, 469b
  that grow so fair, 820b
  that would march, 903b
  thin, in a city square, 875a
  tongues in, 159b

Trees uptorn darkness and worms, 477b
  walk'd among the ancient, 386b
  walking with the, 891a
  wonder about the, 880a
  you lover of, 568b
Tree-toad is a chef-d'oeuvre, 608a
  three-toed, 854a
Treetops, whispering, 796a
Trelawny, shall, die, 509a
Tremble, angels, while they gaze, 349b
  at the word of the Lord, 273b
  blood that does not, 76b
  for my country, 373b
  keepers of the house shall, 1043b
  let Sporus, 319a
  like a guilty thing, 408b
  made earth to, 1046a
  made Olympus, 6a
  my firm nerves shall never, 198a
  sail-yards, 117a
  to win the hand of woman, 514a
  under her feet, 554a
Trembled underneath her banks, 166a
  with fear at your frown, 597a
Trembler in the world's storm-troubled sphere, 592a
Tremblers, boding, learn'd to trace, 356a
Trembles as he writes, 310b
  in the breast, 413a
  to a lily, 703b
Trembling cold in ghastly fears, 386a
  from its birth, 649b
  hope, repose in, 349b
  hoping ling'ring, 312a
  I smite the lyre, 974b
  rejoice with, 1032a
  seized with a rosy, 842b
  tear stands, in her eye, 6a
Tremendous lie of sleep, 968b
  object of creation, 357a
  outsider, 953b
Tremulous beliefs agonized hopes, 838b
  cadence slow, 622a
Trenchant blade Toledo trusty, 238b
Trencher-friends, 203b
Trencher-man, valiant, 157a
Trenches, dig deep, 204b
Trespassers, downtrod by many, 12b
Trespasses against duty, 359a
  forgive us all our, 922b
Tresses, fair, ensnare, 312a
  like the morn, 248a
  long bright, 660b
  withered cheek and, gray, 413a
Trewe as stiel, 78b
Trial by juries, 374b
  democracy is on, 732a
  fiery, through which we pass, 540a
  for crimes against peace, 959b
  future great national, 541b
  of everything before arms, 32a
  truth is the, of itself, 218b
Trials of abounding wealth, 763b
  of life are nearly done, 699b
Triangles, encouraging, to break out, 866b
Triangular, oblong into the, 418a
  person in square hole, 418a
Tribal lays, 817a

Tribe, abhorr'd that senseless, 296a
  badge of our, 144a
  cynic, 888b
  highly respectable, 1005a
  may his, increase, 448a
  of fops, 190b
  richer than all his, 190b
  touchy, of poets, 41b
  were God Almighty's gentlemen, 277a
Tribe's hands, feed out of your, 821b
Tribes of Israel, 281b
  savage, pursue their game, 382b
  that slumber in its bosom, 470b
  two mighty, 459b
Tribune, Chicago responsible for Chicago, 941b
Tribute, bring my, to his grave, 414a
  laid all nature under, 396b
  not one cent for, 377b
  of a sigh, 773b
  passing, of a sigh, 349a
  to whom tribute is due, 1060b
  vain, of a smile, 413b
Tributes he pays to life, 976a
Trice, change in a, 692a
Trick, but get the, 677b
  confidence, still running, 953b
  little by little does the, 11a
  Nick Machiavel had ne'er a, 104a, 239b
  of English nation, 152b
  of singularity, 165b
  of truth, 892b
  when in doubt win the, 302a
  wins the, 704a
  worth two, 150a
Tricked by the British into war, 861b
Tricking and stopping, 946b
Trickled through my head, 659a
Trick's, when the long, over, 896a
Tricks by sleight of hand, 298a
  fantastic, before heaven, 184b
  fox has many, 7b
  hath strong imagination, 142b
  his beams, 249b
  in plain and simple faith, 168b
  that are vain, 686b
  ugly yahoo, 902b
  vanity plays lurid, 772b
  where be his tenures and, 178b
Trident and dolphins, 904a
  flatter Neptune for his, 202b
Tried a little failed much, 753a
  all the week to be good, 398b
  can't drop it if I, 819a
  Christian ideal not, 852a
  friend I have valued and, 438b
  hard to do the right, 689b
  to live without him, 213a
  to play Mozart, 955b
  we have never, it, 984a
  when he is, 1064a
  without consent been only, 226a
Tries for great objects, 55b
  no one knows till he, 46a
Trifle, at ev'ry, scorn to take offence, 311a
  bluer, skies are a, 862b
  careless, 194b
  love can, with itself, 132a
  of wives, 144b
  think naught a, 305a
Trifles, dispense with, 180a
  law is not concerned with, 1010a

Troubling, wicked cease from, 1030a
Troublous sights and sounds, 833b
  world, part in this, 127a
Trousers, bottoms of my, rolled, 943a
  never wear your best, 642a
  steam-engine in, 419a
  white flannel, 943a
Trout, build the, a crystal stair, 892b
  caught with tickling, 165a
  in the milk, 589a
  stipple upon, that swim, 724a
Trouthe is hyeste thyng, 82a
  thee shal delivere, 82b
Trouts bite best on the Sabbath, 791b
Trowel, laid on with a, 159a
Troy, another, for her to burn, 825b
  fir'd another, 280b
  Grecians sacked, 123b
  half, burnt, 152a
  heard, doubted, 459a
  imperial towers of, 312b
  laid old, in ashes, 289b
  ringing plains of windy, 548a
  tale of, divine, 246a
Troyan walls, 146b
Troy's proud glories, 4a
  redoubt, 893b
Truant disposition, 170b
  every, knew, 356a
  play, at his tales, 132b
Truce between virtue and vice, 590b
  or parley, 870b
  to navigation, 682b
  with Adam-zad, 816a
  with rosy frailties, 640a
Trudg'd along unknowing, 281a
Trudgin' my weary way, 731b
True, ah love let us be, 622a
  Amphitryon, 270b
  and false, idea of what is, 281b
  and honorable recompense, 297b
  and honorable wife, 167a
  and righteous altogether, 1033a
  apothecary, 138a
  as fate, 53a
  as flesh and blood, 133a
  as I live, 214a
  as taxes is, 579a
  as the dial to the sun, 239b
  as the needle to the pole, 239b
  as the stars above, 1003b
  as turnips is, 579a
  battled for the, the just, 552b
  be, while there yet is time, 890a
  beginning of our end, 142b
  best cannot go quite, 338b
  bewildered as to which may be, 514a
  birth, revolts from, 136a
  blue Presbyterian, 238a
  business precept, 577b
  child should always say what's, 750a
  children and fooles speake, 93a
  Christian every inch, 104a
  considered by people equally, 369a
  courage consists in fear, 290a
  critic dwell upon excellencies, 300b
  dare to be, 232b
  discoverers among them, 333b

True disputants like true sports-men, 321b
  distinguish, from false, 281b
  Douglas tender and, 635b
  dull minds, 446a
  ease in writing, 311a
  easy to be, 287b
  faith and ready hands, 597b
  friend that's, 390b
  friends, advanced, 620b
  friends appear less mov'd, 42a
  friendship needs none, 203a
  friendship's laws, 6b
  genius kindles, 318b
  genius, spites do not harm, 725b
  goddess in her walk, 36b
  good men and, 158a
  greatness to have frailty, 119b
  guid to be honest and, 394b
  hair divides the false and, 532b
  happiness is of retired nature, 300a
  hear your words and make them, 754a
  hearts lie wither'd, 439a
  hope is swift, 128b
  how, 803a
  I have married her, 186a
  I would be, 926a
  if we are, to plan, 647a
  illusory from the, 955b
  in and for itself, 402a
  industrious friend, 149a
  is not sure nor can be, 595b
  it is most, 221b
  joy in life, 765a
  judgments of the Lord are, 542a
  kept him falsely, 555a
  labourer, 161b
  last after the, be dead, 214b
  lords or kings of earth, 606a
  love is like ghosts, 265a
  love is never blind, 630a
  love know from another one, 177b
  love never did run smooth, 141a
  love sits him down, 1004b
  loved too, to keep a friend, 520a
  lovers admire naked beauties, 460b
  lovers are such as I am, 164b
  lovers, between, 984a
  lovers into strange capers, 160a
  love's hand, 138a
  love's the gift, 413b
  male never yet walked, 930a
  no man can be, to himself, 559b
  nobility exempt from fear, 125b
  nobility's, badge, 129b
  not too good to be, 293a
  nothing, but Heaven, 440a
  of a shopkeeper, 345a
  of most we leave behind, 595b
  one religion, as another, 224a
  original native of America, 331b
  pathos and sublime, 393a
  patriots all, 304b
  poem, ought to be a, 250a
  proves the substance, 311b
  revolts from, birth, 136a
  right praise and, perfection, 147a
  science and study of man, 316b
  security in social solidarity, 618a
  servant's title, 526b
  simple modest manly, 602a
  so thick it cannot be, 973b
  sons of mighty resolutions, 238b

True sorrow makes a silence, 970a
  soul so warm and, 437b
  speak, right wrong, 554a
  strange but, 46oa
  sure they are, 208b
  test of civilization, 340b
  that which was prov'd, 239b
  the blushful Hippocrene, 481a
  think what is, 633b
  Thomas lay on Huntlie Bank, 1012b
  'tis, 'tis pity he is mad, 173b
  to boasted race or clan, 888b
  to his Molly, 377a
  to his wife, 294a
  to kindred points, 412a
  to thine own self be, 171b
  trusty dusky vivid, 752a
  until my dreams all come, 952a
  use of speech, 286b
  virginity, power o'er, 247b
  way to be deceived, 265b
  well of, wit is truth, 639b
  what people say of us is, 822b
  whatsoever things are, 1063a
  when you met her, 215b
  wit is nature to advantage, 310b
  woman tells you, 309b
  wood of yew wood, 782a
  worship, every one's, 23b
  zeal and false, 324b
True-blue professor of literature, 932a
True-born, banish'd a, English-man, 138b
  stern, Englishman, 138b
True-fix'd and resting quality, 167b
True-hearted soldier, 499a
True-love hath my heart, 115b
Truer, faith is, than doubt, 685b
  friendship's a little, 862b
  than if they happened, 983b
Truest, man's, monument, 712a
  mirror, 403a
  nobility, 106b
  valour to dare to live, 14b
Truism, mill of a, 501a
Truly great, think continually of, 995a
  great who are truly good, 117b
  honest man, here lies a, 264a
Trump at the last, 1062a
  farewell the shrill, 189a
  tell the truth or, 677b
Trumpet, blow the, to arms, 370a
  give an uncertain sound, 1061b
  hear the rattling, thunder, 587a
  heard on high, 278b
  heart moved more than with, 116a
  of a child of Rome, 694b
  of the morn, 170a
  of time, 960b
  pride his own, 181b
  shall sound, 1062a
  shifted his, 358a
  sound of the, 1026a
  sound the, 291a
  sounds from hid battlements, 790a
  sounds signal of danger, 463a
  world may sound no, 1006a
Trumpet's loud clangour, 278b
Trumpets, angel, blow, 250a
  blow your, angels, 217b
  never a blare of, 809a
  noise of, 867a

Trumpets, snarling, 'gan to chide, 480b
  sounded for him, 274b
  thunderstorm or blare of, 882b
Trumpet-tongued angels, 195b
Trumps, if dirt was, 430b
Truncheon, marshal's, 184a
Trunk, hide it in your, 890a
  so large a, before, 848a
  spouts out a sea at his, 257a
Trunkless legs of stone, 465a
Trunks of men, 146a
Trust a friend who deserts you, 10b
  a little, that when we die, 666a
  all power is a, 511a
  at the end of Indian June, 813a
  becomes trustworthy as you, 449a
  built an absolute, 194b
  empire is power in, 277a
  faintly, the larger hope, 552b
  gentle Kate, 150a
  government is a, 433b
  in all things high, 551a
  in God, 418b
  in God and do the right, 582a
  in God is our, 436a
  in his cussedness, 698b
  love all, a few, 182b
  loyal to a, 763a
  man on his oath, 203a
  man to make him trustworthy, 839b
  nation's, 471b
  never, advice of man, 11b
  no agent, 157b
  no friends, 12b
  no future, 521a
  not a man's words, 500b
  not him with your secrets, 372b
  not one night's ice, 234a
  not the heart of that man, 474b
  not your daughters' minds, 186a
  office of more, 105a
  old friends best to, 119a
  on and think tomorrow will re-pay, 276a
  our happiness, 434a
  political magistracy is a, 361b
  public office is public, 293a
  put not your, in money, 536a
  put not your, in princes, 1038a
  put not your, in vinegar, 747b
  put your, in God, 434a
  sacred, twice confided, 333b
  safe and sound your, is, 307a
  some later day, 38b
  soothed by an unfaltering, 470b
  take you on, for beer, 760a
  that all is best, 583a
  that man in nothing, 346a
  they that put their, in him, 1032b, 1065b
  those who, me, 926a
  thou thy love, 606a
  to common fame, 504b
  to him armed with primer, 435b
  voter exercises a public, 689a
  who can, her, 863a
  Wordsworth's, 695b
Trusted a secret to a woman, 55a
  in one bottom, 143a
  let no such man be, 147a
  like fox, 151b
  should be, least, 8b
  to thy billows, 455a
  vanity of having been, 324a
  was ever poet so, 341a

Trustee held to something stricter, 849b
Trustees, officers of government are, 433b
Trustest in staff of broken reed, 119a, 1046b
Trusteth in his riches, 1039a
Trustful birds have built their nests, 721a
Trusting, calls, universal benevo-lence, 355a
  in Him who can go with me, 539a
  till faith move mountains, 573a
Trusts her, foolish the man who, 37a
  his ears, 18b
  in tameness of a wolf, 192b
  offices as public, 442a
  public, lodged in hands, 293a
Trustworthy, becomes, as you trust it, 449a
  no counsel is more, 84b
  noble, nor consistent, 832a
  none believe speeches, 35b
  way to make a man, 839b
Trusty drouthy cronie, 393b
  dusky vivid true, 752a
  in his deeds, 59a
Truth about her age, 851a
  all we shall know for, 826a
  all-conquering, 395a
  and his great soul, 573b
  and intellect, 76b
  and rapture of man, 896a
  and soberness, 1059b
  another way to, 897b
  be in the field, 251a
  beauty adventure art peace, 797a
  beauty, and love are one, 721b
  beauty and, tho' never found, 708b
  beauty is, 482b
  beauty must be, 478a
  being truth tell it, 89b
  between us two forevermore, 505b
  bitter barren, 606b
  born to inquire after, 100a
  bright countenance of, 250a
  bring, to light, 131b
  brings increase to her, 343b
  cannon-balls may aid the, 584a
  carp of, 173a
  cause of, 257a
  communicated by deeds of, 642b
  communication of, 423b
  crushed to earth, 471b
  deeds of, 642b
  depository of, 272b
  dignity of, 218b
  discovered in arts, 908b
  divorcing themselves from, 476a
  doubt, to be a liar, 173b
  doubted, in blue, 995b
  emblem of, overflowing, 450a
  enemies of, 240a
  entails ruin, 16a
  even when he speaks the, 10b
  every gaudy color a bit of, 995b
  evidence of, 433b
  fiction carries, in solution, 565b
  fiction lags after, 359b
  find effective and undeniable existence, 773b
  find out, by history, 54a
  fond of, 326a

Truth forever on the scaffold, 599b
  found, in all but one, 140a
  from his lips, 356a
  given me the, 928b
  good and, to borrow, 507a
  great is, 496b
  great is, and shall prevail, 748b
  great is the, and mighty, 1065a
  great ocean of, 288a
  harsh as, 517a
  has lasted a million years, 888b
  has most strength, 16b
  has not privilege, 101a
  has such a face, 278b
  has such a mien, 278b
  hath quiet breast, 138a
  his, proclaim, 277a
  honor and, and manhood, 888b
  I cannot tell how, may be, 413b
  I thought needed to be told, 542a
  ill-timed, 712b
  impossible to be soiled, 72b
  in every shepherd's tongue, 110b
  in groves of Academe, 41b
  in masquerade, 459b
  in sorrow he learned this, 688b
  in wine there is, 8b
  intention of communicating, 424b
  is always strange, 460a
  is found when men are free, 919a
  is great and shall prevail, 629b
  is marching on, 597b
  is on the march, 708a
  is one forever absolute, 562b
  is precious and divine, 239a
  is still the light, 560b
  is the best vindication, 541b
  is the nursing mother, 559b
  is the secret of eloquence, 617b
  is the trial of itself, 218b
  is truth, 185b, 892b
  itself decays, 605a
  justice is, in action, 512b
  keep abreast of, 600a
  keeps, from the people, 890a
  kept thy, so pure of old, 251b
  know, not only by reason, 272b
  laid waste with weapon of, 981a
  less remote from the, 373b
  let's tell them the, 986b
  lie which is half a, 556a
  lies within a little compass, 303b
  lips of, 440b
  lost to love and, 819a
  love, 326a
  love of, 555b
  love swears she is made of, 207b
  made one laugh by speaking the, 875b
  map of honour, loyalty, 125a
  Mark Twain told the, mainly, 676b
  mathematics possesses not only, 962a
  may bear all lights, 323b, 383b
  mercy and, are met, 1035b
  miscall'd simplicity, 205b
  Mohammed's, 543a
  most valuable thing we have, 678b
  mournful, 335b
  naked, 134a
  never hurts the teller, 574a

Walls, Troyan, 146b
  watches from his mountain, 553a
  well-builded, 8a
Walnuts and the wine, 546b
Walpole honorable gentleman, 334b
Wal'r my boy, 578b
Walrus and the carpenter, 658a
Walruses and whales, 604a
Walton, rodless, of the brooks, 777b
Waltz, swoons to a, 969b
Waltzes, congress does not run but it, 368h
Waly waly up the bank, 1013a
Wan, angels all pallid and, 544b
  so pale and, 261a
  with care, 149a
Wand, bright gold ring on her, 438a
  he walk'd with, 252b
  magician who has thrown aside, 862a
Wander, born to, 953b
  by the wind-beaten hill, 433a
  forth the sons of Belial, 252b
  hand in hand with love, 909b
  some inmate of the skies, 6b
  thoughts, through eternity, 253b
  where'er I, 138b
  whither shall I, 1017a
Wandered by the brookside, 543a
  east I've wandered west, 487a
  idly over the noisy keys, 634a
  lonely as a cloud, 409a
  through a valley steep, 863b
  today to the hill Maggie, 699b
Wanderer, kindly, loved and known, 654b
  merry, of night, 141a
  though like the, 515b
  weary wayworn, 543b
Wandering, all his wealth was, 874b
  bark, star to every, 207a
  behold, moon, 246a
  between two worlds, 621b
  by lone sea-breakers, 730a
  cloud that trailed, 769b
  Jew, 1012a
  minstrel I, 177a, 684b
  old with, 825a
  on a foreign strand, 414a
  Po, 353b
  so much do I love, 935a
  thought is tired of, 494b
  thought pollutes the day, 469a
  voice, or but a, 408a
  wind, voices of the, 655b
  with the train divine, 622b
Wanderings of the sky, 37b
Wanders further for pasture, 720a
  singing round the world, 950a
  whale that, round the pole, 848a
Wand'ring mazes, 254a
  steps and slow, 259a
Wane, moon will, 525b
Waning moon was haunted, 420b
Want and discontent, 240a
  chief, in life, 505b
  covetous man is ever in, 41a
  eternal, of pence, 88b
  for one who comes not, 974b
  freedom from, 920b
  get what you, 822b
  I shall not, 1033a
  it most like it least, 323a

Want, known and do not, it, 339a
  lonely, retir'd to die, 338a
  much I, which most would have, 101b
  nature did that, supply, 278b
  no man will supply thy, 220a
  not, waste not, 653b
  of a nail, 330b
  of decency is want of sense, 283b
  of nothing am I in, 31b
  of sense, charge me with, 659b
  of the creative spirit, 856a
  of thought, 488a
  of use, 342a
  of words or lack of breath, 260b
  pity their, of faith, 369b
  progress from, to want, 341b
  proud man reduced to, 303a
  reference to some, 402a
  thoughts shut up, air, 306a
  to be alone, 993a
  toil envy, 336a
  weariness and vice, 325a
  what I want when I want it, 829a
  woeful, 442b
Wanted, every man is, 502b
  lest it be missed or, 332a
  one immortal song, 277a
  you, it so Georges Dandin, 270b
Wanting is what, 575a
  soul is, there, 455a
  to commend so great a poet, 280b
  weighed and found, 1049a
  what is stolen, 188b
Wanton boys, as flies to, 192b
  boys that swim on bladders, 211a
  cranks and, wiles, 245a
  eyes, 1045a
  freak, 477a
  spirits look out, 182b
  stings and motions, 183b
  sweetness through breast, 328b
Wantoned with thy breakers, 455a
Wantonness in clothes, 230b
Wantons thro' the flowering thorn, 392a
Wantowne and a mery, 79b
Wants, devote to their daily, 25a
  express our, 286b
  how much he has more than he, 301a
  man, but little, 306a
  money means and content, 161b
  my, are few, 536a
  my, are many, 398b
  that pinch the poor, 38b
  tone your, and tastes down, 611a
  what a woman, 800a
War, aftermath of, 874a
  against the soul, 1064a
  amorous, 84a
  and arms I fly, 268a
  and deeds of carnage, 609b
  and its organisation, 85b
  and wine throve together, 640a
  anybody not against, 958b
  art statesmanship, 774a
  becoming impossible, 831b
  begun without money, 88b
  better than the most just, 331a
  between men and women, 971b
  betwixt princes, 99a

War, blast of, blows in ears, 155a
  brazen throat of, 259a
  breeds war again, 774a
  brings up human energy, 925b
  change the art of, 945b
  circumstance of glorious, 189a
  common man protection against, 926b
  condition called, 229a
  cursed, and racking tax, 416b
  dauntless in, 414b
  declaration of, against Holland, 275a
  delays are dangerous in, 124b
  despised race unproved in, 666a
  dogs of, 168a
  drum throbbed no longer, 549a
  enemies in, 373b
  even to the knife, 452b
  events of, 19b
  expert is a man ye niver heerd iv, 834b
  ez fer, I call it murder, 600b
  fatal to enter, 907b
  fever famine and, 743b
  first in, 384a
  fought with atomic bomb, 900b
  France has not lost the, 954b
  fruit of, fruit of peace, 979b
  gains nothing by successful, 783a
  given two cousins to the, 664b
  goes forth to, 445b
  good, or bad peace, 331a
  government in peace and, 905a
  great, and the petty peace, 832a
  great civil, 540b
  grim-visaged, 127b
  hath no fury like a non-combatant, 839a
  how much, he has seen, 997b
  hunger and, and weather, 781b
  I am tired and sick of, 613b
  I have seen, I hate war, 919b
  if a, should come, 814b
  if they mean to have a, 358b
  impious, 155a
  in his heart, 1035a
  infection and hand of, 138b
  involves in its progress, 371a
  is a contagion, 920a
  is a transfer of property, 974a
  is cruel, 613b
  is hell, 613b
  is inevitable, 900b
  is not inevitable, 799b
  is still the cry, 452b
  is toil and trouble, 280a
  its thousands slays, 366b
  just, since world began, 370b
  kept out, 893b
  lead this great peaceful people into, 770b
  levying, against them, 376a
  long tempest of the, 566b
  long ten years', 289b
  Lord is a man of, 1024b
  love and, are same thing, 108a
  love of, for itself, 490a
  loves to prey upon young, 16b
  lurking, leap out, 774a
  magnificent but it is not, 558b
  make, on the men, 979a
  makes good history, 706a
  marching as to, 664a
  mighty scourge of, 542a
  money the sinews of, 26a
  more than an end to, 922a

Waves of wretchedness, 487a
  on side of ablest navigators, 369b
  over the, 1013b
  proud, be stayed, 1031b
  reach their hands for it, 674a
  she will hear the, roar, 619b
  sleep in restless, 742b
  the bush, 416a
  the cypress, 551a
  tired, vainly breaking, 595b
  wave of all her, 815a
  what are the wild, saying, 582b
  which only he may walk, 969a
Waves', spent, riot, 693b
Waveth, beards, alle, 96b
Waving streamers, 260a
Wavy bodies 'gainst the streams, 477a
Wax and wane, 533b
  heart is, 110a
  moon will, 525b
  moulded as she pleases, 110a
  rich gifts, poor, 175a
  to receive, 110a
  virtue be as, 177a
  world, colder, 725b
Waxed fat and kicked, 1026a
Waxen minds, women have, 131b
  vines, 947b
Wax-works looked at for nothing, 658a
Way, all the, to heaven, 264a
  amaz'd and lose, 148b
  and ways and a way, 796b
  best, out is through, 879b
  cannot lose your, 202b
  creeping thing in sober, 592a
  death seems but a covered, 524b
  do bold things in a quiet, 597a
  down upon the Swanee River, 636a
  every one his own, 32b
  excellent old, 825a
  face like the milky, 261b
  followed still his crooked, 777a
  freed his soul the nearest, 338a
  gives people in grief their own, 558a
  glory shows the, 291a
  God moves in a mysterious, 362b
  great white, 1007b
  heav'n's pathless, 246a
  his soul shall go, 796b
  home's farthest, about, 232a
  I remember the, we parted, 694a
  I see my, as birds, 566b
  is all so very plain, 867b
  is long and steep, 7b
  is plain peaceful, 540b
  kept the humble, 738a
  less anxious to have our, 740b
  lies open onward, 655b
  life's weary, 810b
  long is the, and hard, 254a
  longest, round, 232a
  makes the, seem shorter, 235b
  mind my compass and my, 326b
  mony a weary, 487a
  musick and women I cannot but give, 285a
  my, of life, 199a
  nastieth thing in nicest, 939a
  no other, but through, 799b
  no, out no way back, 799b
  none trod before, 825a
  of a fool, 1039a

Way of a man with a maid, 815a
  of a serpent upon a rock, 1041b
  of all flesh, 225b
  of all the earth, 1026b
  of an eagle in the air, 1041b
  of bargain, 151a
  of peace, impose the, 37b
  of saying a thing, 908a
  of their own, 435a
  of transgressors, 1039a
  paid his, 345a
  path of duty was, to glory, 553b
  plods his weary, 348a
  prepare ye the, of the Lord, 1050a
  pretty Fanny's, 304b
  primrose, 751a
  return by the speediest, 16a
  safer than a known, 881b
  selfsame, 143b
  she may tyrannize, 231b
  shortest, home, 232a
  stood at parting of the, 1048b
  straight, was lost, 75a
  surest, to avoid war, 290a
  that I must tread alone, 470b
  that leadeth to destruction, 1052a
  they fight or love or sin, 812b
  this is the, 1046b
  to a man's heart, 1006b
  to be happy, 662b
  to be immortal, 240b
  to bliss, 232a
  to Corinth, 41b
  to dusty death, 199b
  to endure adversity, 32b
  to kill a wife, 130b
  to live, teaching me the, 98a
  to make sure of power, 341a
  to parish church, 160b
  to pay old debts, 227a
  to render life tolerable, 325a
  to spread a work, 341a
  took their solitary, 259a
  trod when men were men, 573a
  true, to be deceived, 265b
  was long the wind was cold, 413a
  went her unremembering, 789b
  whence I shall not return, 1030a
  wisdom finds a, 383b
Wayfaring men, 1048a
  men, lodging-place of, 364a, 454b
Ways, amend your, and doings, 1048a
  and a way, 796b
  are sweet on earth, 13a
  blood nipp'd and, foul, 134a
  careful, of duty, 528a
  cheerful, of men, 254b
  consider her, and be wise, 1038b
  dwelt among untrodden, 405a
  God's, seem dark, 527b
  in all the, you can, 329b
  in his, with men, 555b
  justify, of God, 252a
  labyrinthine, of my own mind, 790a
  let me count the, 519b
  neither your, my ways, 1047b
  newest kind of, 154a
  nine and sixty, 817a
  of contemporary criticism, 725b

Ways of death are soothing, 741b
  of God are just, 260a
  of hoar antiquity, 358b
  of pleasantness, 1038b
  of the gods, 66a
  perfect, of honour, 212a
  plan my, and rule my heart, 495b
  ran my heedless, 997a
  seem harsh and wild, 795a
  several, meet in one town, 154b
  so steep and strange, 800a
  stand ye in the, 1048a
  strayed from thy, 1068a
  take heed to my, 1034a
  thousand, it keeps the secret, 524b
  to lengthen our days, 439a
  vindicate the, of God to man 315b
Wayside inn of earth, 808b
Wayward boy, 133a
  dance their, round, 405b
  marl, 157a
  sisters depart in peace, 504b
  tetchy and, thy infancy, 128a
  thoughts, fond and, 405a
Wayworn, weary, wanderer, 534b
We are not amused, 606b
  happy few, 156b
  must eat we, 564b
  not thou 'tis, are deaf, 663b
  shall die alone, 272b
  the people in preamble, 865b
  took off rather suddenly, 989a
  two kept house, 706b
  us and ours, 820b
  who deceive ourselves, 344b
Weak and beggarly elements, 1062b
  and despised old man, 191b
  and feeble woman, 97a
  and insignificant, 19a
  and worthless imitators, 941a
  as a rained-on bee, 884b
  be his cause strong or, 600b
  become, if divided, 58b
  ceaseless devouring of the, 615a
  concessions of the, 359b
  fallen and the, 599b
  fine by defect and delicately, 314b
  flesh is, 1055a
  hand, cravens my, 204a
  hands though mighty heart, 468a
  head with strongest bias rules, 310b
  if any be but, 110a
  in courage, 386a
  in war a, defense, 281a
  list, confined within, 156b
  man your enemy, make a, 594b
  men as, and as strong, 541b
  men, like all, 875a
  minds, first defence of, 424a
  minds led captive, 259a
  minds, refuge of, 323b
  mortality's too, to bear them, 291b
  my spirit is too, 477b
  palsy-stricken thing, 480b
  pondered, and weary, 544b
  shall perish, 877a
  so, as in the book-store, 582b
  spirit quickens, 944b
  strength for the, 662b
  strong hands to, 707a

Wisdom never dwelt below, 286b
never lies, 5b
no human, can calculate, 371a
no joy even in beautiful, 9a
nor, in the grave, 1043a
nor much their, teaches, 549a
of a just content, 654a
of human contrivances, 360a
of its framers, 812a
of mankind creeps slowly, 509a
of many, 1007a
of our ancestors, 359a, 578a
of our sages, 374b
of tomorrow, 743a
or its fairest flower, 509a
part not dependent on, 772a
pessimism is name given to, 976b
pray for, and guidance, 625b
pray for, yet, 645a
prime, 257b
Raphael paints, 507b
that will never die, 669b
the mirrored shield, 468a
therefore get, 1638b
to be only wise, 806b
to be silent, 58a
to believe the heart, 806b
to love to live, 812b
too full of, 845a
unerring, never dwelt below, 286b
wealth of mankind is, 729b
what, can you find, 344b
where love and, dwell, 583a
whose lessons, 333a
will repudiate thee, 722a
wiser turn a larger, lends, 643b
with the ancient is, 1030b
world is governed with little, 227b
wrath of lion is, of God, 386a
Wisdom's aid, 351b
part, 330a
school, 214b
self seeks solitude, 247b
Wise, absolute strong and, 816b
all things, and wonderful, 591b
amazed temperate furious, 197a
among fools, 52b
among women, 692a
and frugal government, 374b
and good men, 471b
and good, must first be, 251a
and lovely, 962b
and masterly inactivity, 397b
and pious patience, 543a
and salutary neglect, 359b
and understanding heart, 1028a
and virtuous man, 57a
are never without friends, 1003a
arts in which the, excel, 289b
as a serpent, 829a
as serpents, 124a, 1052b
at fifty, 234a
be, soar not too high, 226b
be, today, 298a
be, with speed, 305a
beacon of the, 181b
become, from contemplation, 805b
bids fair to grow, 45b
bitter grave or over, 825a
book but a blast from the lungs, 949b
both true both, 267a
by nature, 226a
coffee makes the politician, 312b
confound the, 1060b

Wise, consider her ways and be, 1038b
country so virtuous and, 783a
crack that knows its father, 959b
darkly, and rudely great, 316b
days that make us happy make us, 896b
defer not till tomorrow to be, 298a
enough to keep own counsel, 106a
enough to play the fool, 165a
fair-spoken, 212a
father knows own child, 144b
five of them were, 1054b
folly to be, 347b
fool doth think he is, 163a
fool is counted, 1040a
for cure on exercise depend, 280b
gamester, 16b
God make our blunders, 903a
good to be merie and, 90b
government, 343b
great men not always, 1031b
guid to be merry and, 394b
he who thinks himself, 326a
healthy wealthy and, 330b
histories make men, 121b
I'm growing, 587b
in show, 251a
in the foreboding of evil, 12b
in the use of his pronouns, 699a
in their own craftiness, 1030a
in their own eyes, 351a
in your own conceits, 1060a
learn from foes, 23b
little, the best fools be, 215b
love and be, 43a
love that's, 846b
man, died like a, 110a
man does not try to hurry, 986b
man even, fool and, 109b
man have little influence, 19b
man, how dieth the, 1042a
man, hundred fools do not make, 951a
man is strong, 118a, 1040b
man knows himself a fool, 163a
man never loses anything, 98b
man never refuses, 45a
man, rebuke a, 1039a
man say, heard a, 785b
man to discover, 72b
man utter vain knowledge, 1030b
man who lets contest fall, 18a
man's eyes, 1042a
man's son, every, 164a
man's task, 64a
man's verdict, 571a
men as silly and as, 541b
men, beacons of, 633b
men from the east, 1050a
men have little foolery, 159a
men, not the part of, 62a
men, precedents established by, 433b
men profited by fools, 55a
men, prophecy of, 463a
men refrain to meddle, 86a
men say nothing, 227b
men, speech given to, 286b
men's counters, 228b
more, when he had a pen, 342b
never was so, a man, 524b
no, man quit a certainty, 337a
not, to let friendship die, 342b

Wise, not to the, the light, 757a
not wisdom to be only, 806b
old and, 936b
old and crafty and, 825a
old bird, 876b
old owl, 876b
one, nor ever does a, 289a
ones, gifts of the, 829b
passiveness, 403b
pause from learning to be, 336a
penny, pound foolish, 221b
person and a fool, 31b
philanthropists, 509a
reputed, 143a
safeguard known to the, 380a
saws, 161b
scepticism, 602b
seeing ye yourselves are, 850a
seem foolish among the, 52b
so young never live long, 128a
son maketh a glad father, 1039a
spirits of, 153a
stand to your work and be, 815a
statesmen foresee, 700a
strong, foolish, 777b
teach a monarch to be, 348a
the reverend head, 303a
though a man be, 14a
three, men of Gotham, 1016b
through time, 4a
thrush, that's the, 568b
to be, and love, 182a
to be swift is less than to be, 5b
to be the wealthy, 25b
to learn, 588a
to, man ports and happy havens, 138a
to resolve, 6a
too, to be a dogmatist, 496a
very coldly, 928b
what leisure to grow, 621b
who knows that he knows is, 754b
who soar, 412a
woman never yields, 447a
wondrous, 1020b
word to the, 109a, 331a
words of, are goads, 1044a
words taught in numbers, 114a
worldly, 231b
wretch, 314b
ye yourselves are, 1062a
you're sure to be, 440b
Wisely, act, on the thing apprehended, 797b
and slow, 136a
loved not, but too well, 190b
thrown away, 336b
who reasons, not therefore wise, 314a
worldly, 231b
Wiser being good than bad, 573a
cannot be, than the people, 987a
French, than they seem, 121a
grow, and better, 275a
in his own conceit, 1041a
in their generation, 1057a
left me none the, 907a
man, instruct a, 49a
man, sadder and a, 422b
no man, for learning, 227b
no, than a daw, 124b
Satan now is, 315a
second thoughts are, 17b
sorry you are, 945b

Woman, excellent thing in, 193b
excite us to love a, 105b
faded but still lovely, 974b
fat white, 936a
finest, should not detain me, 301b
for sweet understanding a, 132b
for the hearth, 550b
forget her sucking child, 1047b
fortune be a, 144b
fortune hath nature of a, 95a
frailty thy name is, 170b
fury like a, scorned, 298a
fury of a disappointed, 298a
gentle woman dare, 427b
gentler sister, 311b
give and bring all to the, 1065a
gives to man or, his heart, 785b
God created, 728b
God's second mistake, 728b
goes by the worse, 260a
good cry is a great comfort to a, 510b
good-natured, 429a
grieve, to be overmastered, 157a
hath nine lives, 28b, 93b
have I not found, 1043a
have long hair, 1061a
he that tastes, 308b
heart of, he loves, 855b
I am being, hard beset, 934b
I hate a dumpy, 457a
I love, 972a
if a, gave him pleasure, 1014b
in our hours of ease, 414b
in the background of his mind, 771b
in this humour wooed, 127b
inextinguishable passion of, 297b
infallibly to be gained, 324a
interest in a, 814a
is a dish for the gods, 201b
is a foreign land, 629b
is at heart a rake, 314b
is driving at one thing, 766a
is fickle and changeful, 37a
is his game, 550b
is only a woman, 813a
is so hard upon the woman, 550b
is the lesser man, 549a
is woman's ally, 17b
knew how to worship a, 690a
know I am a, 162a
known only through a man, 697a
laborin' man and laborin', 600b
large-brained, 518a
last thing civilized by man, 638b
lays his hand upon a, 403a
leader in the deed, 36b
learns how to hate, 727a
left too much alone, 846b
let us look for the, 496b
like a dewdrop, 569b
like that, 876a
lips of a strange, 1038b
listens without yawning, 814a
looketh on, to lust, 1050b
loses faith in God and, 650a
lost us Eden, 528a
love for a, you respect, 761b
love to, is life or death, 754a
lovely woman, 289b
loves her lover, 458a
man need to see a, 953a
man that is born of, 814b

Woman, man thinks, profound, 729a
marries again, 768a
marry this man and, together, 296a
mighty ills not done by, 289b
modest, in all her finery, 357a
more barbarous than man, 727a
more interested in a man's mind, 756a
moved like fountain troubled, 130b
much missed, 706b
nakedness of, 386a
necessarily an evil, 28a
never show a, that ye care, 821a
newly made, 185a
no, completely deceived, 773b
no, is an absolute fool, 773b
none of, born shall harm, 198b
not a, in world as precious, 856a
not a jealous, 955a
not even shallow, 729a
of her gentle sex, 499a
of her unborn child, 853a
of high thoughts, 514b
off with the old, 764a
often changes, 37a
oh woman, 6b
old, lived under a hill, 1019b
old, who lived in a shoe, 1017a
on the silver dollar, 898a
once embraced, 706a
once loved is most hateful, 858a
one hair of a, 223b
one that was a, 178b
one to show a, 571b
one would bury for nothing, 577b
oweth to her husband, 131a
passing the love of, 1027b
perfect, nobly planned, 409a
perfect woman, 225b
plain toilworn, 744a
play the, with mine eyes, 198b
poor lone, 153a
preaching, 340a
prime of life in, 24b
public is an old, 474b
put this man and, asunder, 296a
reckon it's just through a, 737b
roused, 576b
ruin of, by starvation, 496b
sat in unwomanly rags, 489a
says what will please, 344b
searching for a new lover, 991a
seeming paragon, 499a
seen not heard, 14b
sense of humour in the, 769a
shone one, 692b
should be good for everything, 17b
should be still, 887b
silliest, can manage a clever man, 814a
since creation of the world, 345b
still be a, to you, 304b
stoops to folly, 355a, 944a
style's the, 535b
sweeter, ne'er drew breath, 612b
take an elder, 164b
take some savage, 549a
takes her latest drink, 801a
talk to every, as if you loved her, 769a
tells you true, 309b
tempted me, 829b

Woman that deliberates is lost, 299b
that made a, cry, 631b
the mummer's part, 877a
the rib made he a, 1021b
the two combined in a, 932a
the world is curious about, 597a
therefore may be woo'd, 129b
therefore to be won, 124b
this the need of, 966b
thou gavest to be with me, 1022a
to obey, 550b
true and fair, 215b
trusted secret to a, 55a
universal act of, 801b
unto the man is, 523a
virtuous, 1041b
wailing for her demon-lover, 420b
want to be thin, 836b
wants what you're out of, 800a
wasteful, set her own price, 629b
what a, says to her lover, 35b
what have I to do with thee, 1057b
when I behold thee, 477a
who did not care, 816b
who has all the other riches, 745a
who has injured you, 714a
who knew she was well dressed, 727b
who takes a, must be undone, 308b
who understands, 857b
whose form is more dazzling, 739a
widow, to sustain thee, 1028b
wife was a penurious, 273b
will or won't, 307a
win the hand of, 514a
win, with his tongue, 132a
wise, never yields, 447a
with a slop-pail, 725a
with fair opportunities, 564b
with her man gone, 930b
with the heart, 550b
with the serpent's tongue, 781a
without discretion, 1039a
woman's body is the, 713b
won or the woman lost, 827a
would be more charming, 714a
would run through fire, 180b
yet think him an angel, 565b
you gave to eat, 756a
your wish is, to win, 565b
Woman-country wooed not wed, 569a
Womanhood and childhood fleet, 522a
heroic, 524a
specimen of indecorous, 514b
Womankind, faith in, 551a
Woman's advice, ask a, 440b
at best a contradiction, 315a
best adornment, 28a
body is the woman, 713b
breast, love lodged in a, 213a
cold perverted will, 469b
die because a, fair, 229a
ears are too lightly opened, 12b
eye, such beauty as a, 133b
eyes, light that lies in, 439b
feelings added to all this, 42b
first love, 769a
form, angel kneels in, 499a
gift, boy have not a, 130a

Wonder, miles around the, grew, 785b
my curiosity my, 809a
of our stage, 219a
publick, and mischief, 285a
still the, grew, 356b
struck with, 931a
ten days', 126b
waits, 860b
what I was begun for, 1014a
what you are, 442b
win that, of the world, 266b
Wondered much and sorrowed
more, 564b
Wonderful, all things wise and,
591b
bird is the pelican, 904a
grass upon your breast, 626b
his name shall be called, 1045b
is death, 464b
little our fathers knew, 820b
living side by side, 884a
most wonderful, 162a
none more, than man, 14a
nonsense, era of, 970b
nothing is more, than faith,
744b
seasoning of enjoyments, 270a
speeches, 931a
thy love to me was, 1027b
verses that swept the land, 816a
waters round you curled, 626b
white samite mystic, 555b
Wonderfully, fearfully and, made,
1038a
Wondering fearing doubting, 545a
Wonderland, summer's, 909b
Wonders, America is a land of,
516a
are many, 14a
carry with us the, 240a
hoots and, 141b
in one sight, 264a
of the western world, 856b
that I yet have heard, 167b
to exchange, 949a
to perform, 362b
world will not starve for, 866b
Wond'ring love, their watch of,
669b
Wondrous bloom, rooting to, 890b
cold, it grew, 421a
excellence, 206b
free, days have been, 304b
kind, fellow-feeling makes one,
221a
pitiful, 186b
plan, eye intent on, 393a
sweet and fair, 242a
tale, moon takes up the, 299a
wise, 1020b
Won't, a woman will or, 307a
when you will they, 32a
Wonted fires, live their, 349a
Woo her as the lion, 352b
men are April when they, 162b
slight me when I, 229a
that would, her, 186b
to persuade to prevail, 765a
were not made to, 141b
why having won her do I, 629b
with an unhairy chin, 673a
Woo'd and not unsought be won,
257b
long, and lately won, 415b
we should be, 141b
woman therefore may be, 129b
Wood and grass were only staples,
935b

Wood, bows down to, and stone,
445a
brown heath and shaggy, 414a
carrying timber into a, 40b
cleave the, 757a
desk's dead, 430a
great Birnam, 198b
heap on more, 414b
hewers of, 1026a
makes wing to the rooky, 197b
of English bows, 782a
old, best to burn, 119a
or boards or pigs, 504b
ten in the, 11a
they call the Rouge Bouquet,
936b
three long mountains and a,
961b
through the, 498b
vernal, 403b
what, a cudgel's of, 238b
wherever, can swim, 400a
Woodbine, luscious, 141b
Woodcocks, springs to catch, 172a
Wooded hills, river and the, 810b
Wooden boat, easy as a, 1000a
dialogue and sound, 181a
heads are inherited, 857b
leg, deef an' dumb an' has a,
834a
legs are not inherited, 857b
shoe, sailed off in a, 747a
throat was once a part, 968a
Wooden-shoes, round-heads and,
300a
Woodes have eares, 80b
Woodland, ghoul-haunted, of Weir,
545b
marsh or bog, 1005a
Woodlands, about the, I will go,
785b
leafless, 814b
Woodman spare that tree, 498b
spare the beechen tree, 433a
Wood-notes, warble native, wild,
245b
Wood-rose, loved the, 504a
Woods against a stormy sky, 470a
aisles of the, 803a
are full of them, 1003a
are lovely dark and deep, 880b
builds his house in the, 504b
enter these enchanted, 639b
fill up with snow, 880b
free from peril, 159b
fresh, and pastures new, 249b
have tongues, 80b
her wilds her waters her, 460b
I went to the, 590a
into the, my master went, 716b
light, go seaward, 447b
made for hunters of dreams,
777b
naked, and meadows brown,
471a
or steepy mountain yields, 123a
out of the, he came, 717a
pleasure in the pathless, 454b
shall answer, 115a
Shiloh's, 740b
stoic of the, 433a
streams and the, belong, 777b
untamed, 795b
walk in the, 502a
walking in the high, 848b
we'll to the, no more, 630a,
786b
wet wild, 820a
whose, these are, 880▸

Woods, wild in, the noble savage
ran, 275b
Woodshed, concludes to build a,
589a
Woodside, lived under my, 237b
Woodthrush singing, 944b
Woodwork, level lines of, 794b
Wood-world is one full peal of
praise, 554b
Wooed, beautiful therefore to be,
124b
in haste, 130a
not wed, 569a
too much, 95a
woman in this humour, 127b
Wooer, knight to be their, 1012b
who can flatter most, 640b
Woof, Iris', 247a
know her, her texture, 480b
weave the, 349b
Wooing, if I am not worth the
523b
in my boys, 1013a
the caress, 460b
Wool, great cry but little, 83b
have you any, 1015b
huswife's, 248a
of bat, 198a
white as, 712b
Wool-gathering, gone a, 109a
Woollen, lie in, 157a
Woolly fold, silent flock in, 480b
softest clothing, bright, 385a
Woolworth welter of things, 995b
Woos, man that, to win, 673a
your wife, 573a
Wop with a wiggle between, 819b
Word and a blow, 136b, 279b
and deed, both in, 20b
answer in one, 162a
at every, a reputation dies, 312b
at random spoken, 416a
break thy, 66b
bring in a new, 100a
burned like a lamp, 1066b
cannot speak a, 486b
chance, heard in an unexpected
quarter, 756b
cuckoo, of fear, 134a
cultured, 817a
deed and, would not revere, 74a
dies before thy uncreating, 322a
done for the least, said, 692b
doubled with an evil, 129a
ears have heard the holy, 386b
earth hear, of the Lord, 1048a
easier to speak not a, 83a
easy, for casual good-bye, 968a
eaten thee for a, 133b
every, stabs, 157b
every, that proceedeth, 1050b
first, Sir Patrick read, 1011b
fitly spoken, 1040b
flattering, 769b
flowering in a lonely, 556a
for word transcribed, 49a
forever 'tis a single, 651b
freedom is an indivisible, 964a
give and take back their, 785a
God in his works and, 304a
God the, that spake it, 97b
Greeks had a, for it, 935a
had no, to say, 769b
having but the, 898a
hears thy faintest, 263a
hob nob is his, 165b
honest man's, 108b
I shudder at the, 37a
in kindness spoken, 557b